MW00755814

Time-Saver Standards for Architectural Design Data

seventh edition

The Reference of Architectural Fundamentals

Time-Saver Standards for Architectural Design Data

seventh edition

The Reference of Architectural Fundamentals

Donald Watson, FAIA, editor-in-chief
Michael J. Crosbie, Ph.D., senior editor
John Hancock Callender *in memorium*

associate editors:
Donald Baerman, AIA
Walter Cooper
Martin Gehner, P.E.
William Hall
Bruce W. Hisley
Richard Rittelmann, FAIA
Timothy T. Taylor, AIA, ASTM

Library of Congress Cataloging-in-Publication Data

Time-saver standards for architectural design data / edited by
    Donald Watson, Michael J. Crosbie, John Hancock Callender—7th ed.
            p.   cm.
        Rev. ed. of: Time-saver standards for architectural design data.
    6th ed. c1982.
        Includes index.
        ISBN 0-07-068506-1
        1. Building—Handbooks, manuals, etc.   2. Building—Standards—
    Handbooks, manuals, etc.   3. Architectural design—Handbooks,
    manuals, etc.   I. Watson, Donald, 1937-   .   II. Crosbie, Michael
    J.   III. Callender, John Hancock.   IV. Title: Time-saver standards
    for architectural design data.
    TH151.T55   1997
    721—DC21   97-18390
                                                            CIP

Copyright © 1997, 1982, 1974, 1966, 1954, 1950, 1946 by McGraw-Hill, Inc. All rights reserved.
Printed in the United States of America. Except as permitted under the United States Copyright Act of
1976. No part of this publication may be reproduced or distributed in any form or by any means, or
stored in a data base or retrieval system, without the prior written permission of the publisher.

2345678 QPKQPK 9021098

The McGraw-Hill Professional Book Group editor is Wendy Lochner.

Printed and bound by

Book design: Sandra Olenik, Printworks, Ltd., Madison, CT, USA.
Computer graphics: Birch Bidwell
Assistant: Kathleen Beckert
www.Printworks-Ltd.com

Cover design: Sandra Olenik and Margaret Webster-Shapiro

Photography in this volume is by Donald Watson, FAIA, except as noted.

Disclaimer
The information in this book has been obtained from many sources, including government organizations, trade associations, manufacturers and
professionals in research and in practice. The publisher, editors and authors have made every reasonable effort to make this reference work
accurate and authoritative, but make no warranty, and assume no liability for the accuracy or completeness of the text, tables or illustrations or its
fitness for any particular purpose. The appearance of technical data or editorial material in this publication does not constitute endorsement,
warranty or guarantee by the publisher, editors or authors of any product, design, service, or process. It is the responsibility of users to apply their
professional knowledge in the use of information and recommendations contained in this book, to consult original sources for more detailed
information and to seek expert advice as required or as appropriate for the design and construction of buildings. Neither the authors, editors or
McGraw-Hill shall have any liability to any party for any damages resulting from the use, application or adaptation of information contained in
Time-Saver Standards, whether such damages be direct or indirect, or in the nature of lost profits or consequential damages. The Times-Saver
Standards is published with the understanding that McGraw-Hill is not engaged in providing architectural, engineering design or other profes-
sional services.

For more information about other McGraw-Hill materials, call 1-800-2-MCGRAW, in the United States. In other countries, call your
nearest McGraw-Hill office.

I.S.B.N. 0-07-068506-1

Contents

Contents

PART II DESIGN DATA

Contents

Contributors

Contributors to the 6th edition (represented in 7th edition revision)
Articles of the following authors are reprinted from the 6th edition of Time-Saver Standards (1982), acknowledging their legacy to professional knowledge represented in this volume:

William Blackwell, Architectual Consultant
Byron C. Bloomfield, AIA, Modular Building Standards Association
Ernest Irving Freese
Seymour Howard, Professor Emeritus of Architecture, Pratt Institute
Hans J. Milton, FRAIA, Center for Building Technology, National Bureau of Standards
Sterling M. Palm, AIA Architect
Philip P. Page, Jr., Consulting Engineer
Syska & Hennessy, Consulting Engineers
Howard P. Vermilya, AIA Architect

New contributions to the 7th edition

Authors:
The following authors have prepared articles for the Seventh Edition. Their contributions are gratefully acknowledged. Their professional addresses and contact information are indicated where appropriate.

AIA California Council. ADAPT Production Committee. 1303 J St., Sacramento, CA 95814. Gordon H. Chong, chair; Stephan Castellanos, Donald M. Comstock, Michael J. Bocchicchio, Sr., Dana Cuff, Ph.D., Betsey O. Dougherty, Joseph Ehrlich, Harry C. Hallenbeck, Lee Schwager, John G. Stafford, Bruce R. Starkweather, Arba H. Stinnett, Julie Thompson, Paul W. Welch, Jr.

Donald Baerman, AIA, 42 Wayland Street, North Haven, CT 06473. FAX (203) 288-7557.

Everett M. Barber, Jr., Sunsearch , Inc., P.O. Box 590, Guilford CT 06437. FAX (203) 458-9011.

Nancy Benner (1947-1997)

Charles C. Benton, Associate Professor, Department of Architecture, University of Califormia, Berkeley, CA 94720-1800.

William Bobenhausen, Steven Winter Associates, 50 Washington Street, Norwalk, CT 06854.

Elmer E. Botsai, FAIA, Professor Emeritus, School of Architecture, University of Hawaii at Manoa, Honolulu, HI 96822.

Brian Bowen, FRICS, Principal, Hanscomb, Inc., 1175 Peachtree Street, NE, Atlanta, GA 30309.

L. Reed Brantley and Ruth T. Brantley, 2908 Robert Place, Honolulu, HI 96816-1720.

John Bullough, Research Associate, Lighting Research Center, School of Architecture, Rensselaer Polytechnic Institute, Troy, NY 12180.

William Burke, Vital Signs Project, Department of Architecture, University of Califormia, 232 Wurster Hall #1500, Berkeley, CA 94720-1800.

John Carmody, College of Architecture and Landscape Architecture, University of Minnesota, 1425 University Avenue SE #220, Minneapolis, MN 55455.

Robert P. Charette, P.E., CVS, 138 Avenue Trenton, Montreal, Quebec H3P 1Z4.

Catherine Coombs, CIH, CSP, Steven Winter Associates, 50 Washington Street, Norwalk, CT 06854.

Walter Cooper, Flack + Kurtz, 475 Fifth Avenue, New York, NY 10017.

Michael J. Crosbie, Ph.D., 47 Grandview Terrace, Essex, CT 06426.

Dana Cuff, Ph.D., Professor, University of California, Los Angeles, School of Arts and Architecture, 405 Hilgard Avenue, Los Angeles, CA 90095-1427.

Arturo De La Vega, URS Greiner, 1120 Connecticut Ave., NW, Suite 1000, Washington, DC 20036.

Allan Daly, Department of Architecture, University of Califormia, 232 Wurster Hall #1500, Berkeley, CA 94720-1800.

Robert M. Darvas, Professor Emeritus, University of Michigan, College of Architecture and Urban Planning, 2000 Bonisteel Blvd., Ann Arbor, MI 48109-2069.

Carolyn Dasher, Portland Energy Conservation, Inc., 921 SW Washington, Suite 312, Portland, OR 97205.

Robert DeGrazio, Flack + Kurtz, 475 Fifth Avenue, New York, NY 10017.

John P. Eberhard, FAIA, 400 Madison Street, Apt. 702, Alexandria, VA 22314.

M. David Egan, P.E., PO Box 365, Anderson, SC 29622.

Benjamin Evans, FAIA (1926-1997)

Philip W. Fairey, Deputy Director, Florida Solar Energy Center, Clearlake Road, Cocoa, FL 32922-5703. http://www.fsec.ucf.edu

Martin D. Gehner, P.E., Professor of Architectural Engineering, School of Architecture, Yale University, New Haven, CT 06520.

Harry T. Gordon, FAIA, Burt Hill Kosar Rittelmann Associates, 1056 Thomas Jefferson Street, NW, Washington, DC 20007.

William Hall, MHTN Architects, 2 Exchange Place, Salt Lake City, UT 84111.

Steven Haas, Jaffe Holden Scarbrough Acoustics Inc., 114-A Washington Street, Norwalk, CT 06854.

Tudi Haasl, Portland Energy Conservation, Inc., 921 SW Washington,, Suite 312, Portland, OR 97205.

Volker Hartkopf, Ph.D., Professor and Director, Center for Building Performance and Diagnostics, Department of Architecture, Carnegie Mellon University, Pittsburgh, PA 15213-3890.

David S. Haviland, Hon. AIA, Professor, School of Architecture, Rensselaer Polytechnic Institute, 110 8th Street, Troy, NY 12180.

Bruce W. Hisley, 27 Northern Pike Trail, Fairfield, PA 17320

John Holton, P.E., Burt Hill Kosar Rittelmann, 400 Morgan Center, Butler, PA 16001.

Craig Huntington, S.E., Huntington Design Associates, Inc., 1736 Franklin Street Suite 500, Oakland, CA 94612.

Christopher Jaffe, Ph.D., Jaffe Holden Scarborough Acoustics, Inc., 144A Washington Street, Norwalk, CT 06854.

Jong-Jin Kim, Ph.D., Associate Professor, College of Architecture and Urban Planning, University of Michigan, Ann Arbor, MI 48109.

Hal Levin, Hal Levin & Associates, 2548 Empire Grade, Santa Cruz, CA 95060.

Vivian Loftness, AIA, Professor and Chair, Department of Architecture, Carnegie Mellon University, Pittsburgh, PA 15213-3890.

Joseph Lstiburek, P.Eng., Building Science Corporation, 70 Main Street, Westford, MA 01886. FAX (508) 589-5103.

Nadav Malin, Associate Editor, Environmental Building News, RR 1, Box 161, Brattleboro, VT 05301. FAX (802) 257-7304.

Fred M. Malven, Ph.D., Professor, Iowa State University, College of Design, Ames, IA 50011-3093.

Murray A. Milne, Professor Emeritus, School of the Arts and Architecture, UCLA, B-315 Perloff Hall, Los Angeles, CA 90095-1427. e-mail: milne@ucla.edu

James C. Myers, Simpson Gumpertz & Heger, 297 Broadway, Arlington, MA 02174

Jonathan Ochshorn, Associate Professor, Department of Architecture, Cornell University, Ithaca, NY 14853.

Elaine Ostroff, Adaptive Environments Center, Congress Street, Suite 301, Boston, MA 02210.

Donald Pearman, 2001 Hoover Avenue, Oakland, CA 94602

Wolfgang F. E. Preiser, Ph. D., University of Cincinnati, College of Design, Architecture, Art and Planning, Cincinnati, OH 45221-0016.

Richard Rittelmann, FAIA, Burt Hill Koser Rittelmann, 400 Morgan Center, Butler, PA 16001.

Stephen S. Ruggiero, Simpson Gumpertz & Heger, 297 Broadway, Arlington, MA 02174.

John P. S. Salmen, AIA , Universal Designers & Consultants, Inc. , 1700 Rockville Pike, Rockville, MD 20852. FAX (301) 770-4338.

Paul Scanlon, Burt Hill Koser Rittelmann, 400 Morgan Center, Butler, PA 16001.

Ulrich Schramm, Ph.D., Fakultat fur Architectur und Stadplanung, Universitat Stuttgart, Keplerstrasse 11, 70174 Stuttgart, Germany.

Stephen Selkowitz, Director, Windows and Daylighting Program. Lawrence Berkeley National Laboratory. One Cyclotron Road. Berkeley, CA 94720.

R. E. Shaeffer, P.E., Professor, Florida A&M University, School of Architecture, 1936 S. Martin Luther King Blvd., Tallahassee, FL 32307.

Peter R. Smith, Ph.D., FRAIA, Head, Department of Architectural Science, University of Sydney, Sydney, NSW 2006, Australia.

Karl Stum. P.E., Portland Energy Conservation, Inc., 921 SW Washington, Suite 312, Portland, OR 97205.

Russ Sullivan, P.E., Burt Hill Koser Rittelmann, 400 Morgan Center, Butler, PA 16001.

Steven V. Szokolay, P O Box 851, Kenmore, 4069, Queensland, Australia.

Timothy T. Taylor, AIA, URS Greiner, 1120 Connecticut Ave., NW, Suite 1000, Washington, DC 20036.

John Templer, 114 Verdier Road, Beauford, SC 29902.

Joel Ann Todd, The Scientific Consulting Group, Inc., 656 Quince Orchard Road, Suite 210, Gaithersburg, Maryland 20878-1409.

Francis Ventre, Ph.D., 4007 Rickover Road, Silver Spring, MD 20902.

Donald Watson, FAIA, 54 Larkspur Drive, Trumbull, CT 06611. lakesideDJ@aol.com

Alex Wilson, Editor, Environmental Building News, RR 1, Box 161, Brattleboro, VT 05301. FAX (802) 257-7304.

Additional contributors and reviewers
The special contributions and reviews of the following individuals are gratefuly acknowledged:

William A. Brenner, AIA, Executive Director, Construction Metrication Council, National Institute of Building Sciences, 1201 L Street, NW, Washington, DC 20005.

Jack Embersits, President, Facilities Resource Management Co., FRM Park, 135 New Road, Madison, CT 06443-2545.

Tom Fisher, Dean, College of Architecture and Landscape Architecture, University of Minneapolis, 1425 University Avenue, SE, Minneapolis MN 55455.

Rita M. Harrold, Director of Educational & Technical Development, Illuminating Engineering Society of North America, 120 Wall Street, New York, New York 10005-4001.

Steve Mawn, American Society for Testing and Materials, 100 Barr Harbor Drive, West Conshohocken, PA 19428.

Marietta Millet, Professor, Department of Architecture, University of Washington, 208 Gould Hall, Seattle, WA 98195.

Mark Rea, Director, Lighting Research Center, Rensselaer Polytechnic Institute, Troy, NY 12180.

Daniel L. Schodek, Professor, Harvard University Graduate School of Design, Cambridge, MA 02138.

Richard Solomon, P.E., Chief Building Fire Protection Engineer, National Fire Protection Association, One Batterymarch Park, Quincy, MA 02269-9101.

Fred Stitt, San Francisco Institute of Architecture, Box 749, Orinda, CA 94563.

Gordon Tully, AIA, Steven Winter Associates, 50 Washington Street, Norwalk, CT 06854.

Preface

With this the Seventh edition, a 60-year publishing tradition continues for Time-Saver Standards. Conceived in the mid-1930s as a compilation of reference articles, Time-Saver Standards features first appeared in *American Architect*, which subsequently merged with and continued the series in *Architectural Record*. The first hardbound edition of Time-Saver Standards was published in 1946, with the purpose then stated as [to assist in] "the greatest possible efficiency in drafting, design and specification writing."

In the Second Edition in 1950, the editorial intent was described as "[a volume of] carefully edited reference data in condensed graphic style." One contribution from this edition, authored by Sterling M. Palm, appears as a reprint in the present Volume's Appendix. In the Third Edition of 1954, the Preface offered the commentary, "the underlying formula of these pages was established in 1935. Since 1937, Architectural Record has been presenting each month, articles, graphs, tables and charts, with a minimum of verbiage...its compilation in Time-Saver Standards was a 'workbook' of material of this kind."

The Fourth edition of Time-Saver Standards, published in 1966, was the first edited by John Hancock Callender, who continued as Editor-in-Chief for the subsequent Fifth and Sixth editions. In his 1966 Preface, he wrote that the volume was "intended primarily to meet the needs of those who design buildings [and]—almost equally useful to draftsmen, contractors, superintendents, maintenance engineers, and students—to all in fact who design, construct and maintain buildings."

The Preface to each ensuing edition carried short statements by the Editor-in-Chief. In the Fifth edition (1974), perhaps in relief of many months of editing, John Hancock Calendar offered that,

> Now and again we hear it said that building has not changed significantly since the age of the pyramids. Anyone who subscribes to this view should be given the task of trying to keep Time-Saver Standards up to date. Society's needs and aspirations are constantly changing, making new demands on buildings; functional requirements change and new building types appear; building materials proliferate and new building techniques come into use, without displacing the old. The result is a constant increase in the amount of technical data needed by building designers.

In his Preface to Sixth edition (1982), John Hancock Callender used the occasion to comment upon the need to adopt metrication in the U. S. building industry. The present edition carries metric equivalents throughout the text wherever practical. The Appendix to the present Volume carries the most recent update of the ASTM standard on metrication, along with an introduction written for architects.

In preparing this the Seventh edition, the first revision in more than a dozen years, the editors were challenged in many respects. This is evident in the fact that the volume has been almost entirely rewritten, with new articles by over eighty authors. It is also evident in its new format and contents, expanded to include "Architectural Fundamentals."

Such dramatic changes respond to the substantial renewal of architectural knowledge and practice in the past decade. New materiasl and construction methods have replaced standard practices of even a dozen years ago. There is since then new information and recommended practices in architecture and new ways of communicating information throughout the architectural and building professions. Some of the topics in the present volume were not even identified much less considered as critical issues when the last edition of this volume was published.

Updated design data and product details are increasingly available in electronic form from manufacturers, assisted by yearly updates in McGraw-Hill's *Sweet's Catalog File*. At the same time, the design fundamentals and selection guidelines by which to locate and evaluate such data become all the more critical. All of the articles in the present edition are written to assist the architect in the general principles of understanding, selecting and evaluating the professional information and knowledge needed for practice. Each article lists key references within each topic.

Thus, at the beginning of its second half-century of publication, the purpose of the Seventh Edition of Time-Saver Standards can be summarized as a "knowledge guide"—a comprehensive overview of the fundamental knowledge and technology required for exemplary architectural practice.

"Knowledge building" itself is an act of creation. How one understands and thinks about architecture and its process of construction is part of the creative design process. Understanding the knowledge base of architecture is a process that itself can "be built" upon a solid framework, constructed of understandable parts and in a manner that reveals insights and connections. The editors and authors of Time-Saver Standards hope to inform, and also to inspire, the reader in pursuit of that endeavor.

Comments and submissions are welcomed

Because the knowledge base of architecture is changing constantly as building practices change in response to new materials, processes and project types, the succeeding volumes of Time-Saver Standards Series will build upon both electronic access and a regular revision print schedule. For this reason, reader responses to the contents of the present Volume and proposals for the Eighth Edition are solicited in the note below and the Reader Response Form found at the end of this Volume.

Any and all corrections, comments, critiques and suggestions regarding the contents and topics covered in this book are invited and will be gratefully received and acknowledged. A Reader Response Form is appended at the end of this volume, for your evaluation and comment. These and/or errors or omissions should be brought to the attention of the Editor-in-Chief.

Submissions of manuscripts or proposals for articles are invited on any topics related to the contents of *Time-Saver Standards for Architectural Design Data,* Eighth edition, now in preparation. Two print copies of proposed manuscripts and illustrations should be addressed to the Editor-in-Chief. Receipt of manuscripts will be acknowledged and, for those selected for consideration, author guidelines will be issued for final submission format.

> Donald Watson, FAIA, *Editor-in-Chief*
> Time-Saver Standards
> 54 Larkspur Drive
> Trumbull, CT 06611
> USA
> lakesideDJ@aol.com

Editors of the Seventh Edition

Donald Watson, FAIA is former Dean and currently Professor of Architecture at Rensselaer Polytechnic Institute, Troy, New York. He served as a U. S. Peace Corps Architect in Tunisia, North Africa from 1962-1965, becoming involved at the time in the research in indigenous architecture and its application to bioclimatic design. From 1970 to 1990, he was Visiting Professor at Yale School of Architecture and Chair of Yale's Master of Environmental Design Program. His architectural work has received design awards from AIA New England Region, Owens Corning Prize, U. S. DoE Energy Innovations, New England Governor's/Canadian Premiers, Energy Efficient Building Association, Compact House competition and Connecticut Society of Architects. He was founding principal and managing partner of ABODE, a design/build firm from 1982-1990. His major books include *Designing and Building a Solar House* (Garden Way) 1977, *Energy Conservation through Building Design* (McGraw-Hill) 1979, and *Climatic Building Design,* co-authored with Kenneth Labs, (McGraw-Hill) 1983, recipient of the 1984 Best Book in Architecture and Planning Award from the American Publishers Association.

Michael J. Crosbie, Ph.D., is active in architectural journalism, research, teaching, and practice. He received his doctorate in architecture from Catholic University. He has previously served as technical editor for *Architecture* and *Progressive Architecture,* magazines and is contributing editor to *Construction Specifier.* He is a senior architect at Steven Winter Associates, a building systems research and consulting firm in Norwalk, CT. Dr. Crosbie has won several journalism awards. He is the author of ten books on architectural subjects, and several hundred articles which have appeared in publications such as *Architectural Record, Architecture, Collier's Encyclopedia Yearbook, Construction Specifier, Fine Homebuilding, Historic Preservation, Landscape Architecture, Progressive Architecture,* and Wiley's *Encyclopedia of Architecture, Design, Engineering & Construction.* He has been a visiting lecturer/critic at University of Pennsylvania, Columbia University, University of California, Berkeley, University of Wisconsin/Milwaukee, Yale School of Architecture, and the Moscow Architectural Institute and is adjunct professor of architecture at the Roger Williams University School of Architecture.

In memorium

John Hancock Callender was responsible for the editorial direction of Time-Saver Standards from 1966 to 1984. The present edition carries the name of John Hancock Callender in recognition of his lifelong editorial contributions to the knowledge and practice of architecture.

John Hancock Callender, AIA (1908-1995) graduated from Yale College in 1928 and New York University School of Architecture 1939. He was researcher in low-cost housing materials at John B. Pierce Foundation from 1931 to 1943 and served with the Army Engineers 1943-45. He was consultant for the Revere Quality House Institute from 1948-1953, which became the Housing Research Foundation of Southwest Research Institute, San Antonio, Texas, pioneering in research in low cost housing innovations in the United States. He was a member of the faculties of Columbia University, Princeton University and Professor of Architecture at Pratt Institute, Brooklyn, New York, 1954 uÅ†1973. He authored *Before You Buy a House* (Crown Publishers) 1953. John Hancock Callender served as Editor-in-Chief of the Fourth, Fifth and Sixth editions of Time-Saver Standards and was founding editor of *Time-Saver Standards for Building Types.*

Exemplary professional and technical reference books
First juried selection. 1997.

Time Saver Standards Editors' Exemplary Book selections is a newly created award program to recognize outstanding professional and technical books in architecture and construction.

Professional and technical reference books for architecture are not easily composed. Information must be useful, authoritative and understandable, with a balance of visual representation and explanation for its integration in design. In the following selections, the jury lauds the accomplishments of the authors, editors and publishers of books that are technically relevant and also inspirational in promoting technical and professional excellence in architecture.

1997 Jury: Donald Baerman, Michael J. Crosbie, Martin Gehner, Richard Rittelmann, and Donald Watson.

Allen, Edward and Joseph Iano. 1995.
The Architect's Studio Companion: Rules of Thumb for Preliminary Design Second Edition
New York: John Wiley & Sons.
Design data organized for preliminary design, especially helpful for students of architecture and construction.

American Institute of Architects. 1996.
Architect's Handbook of Professional Practice Student Edition.
David Haviland, Hon. AIA, Editor. Washington, DC: AIA Press.
A comprehensive summary of information essential for professional practice. The student edition is in one volume and is especially helpful for both student and professional reference.

American Institute of Architects. 1994.
Architectural Graphic Standards.
Ninth Edition John Ray Hoke, FAIA, Editor-in-Chief
New York: John Wiley & Sons.
A digest of design data and details organized for easy reference, on all topics related to architecture and construction, with emphasis on graphic and visual information.

American Society of Heating, Refrigerating and Air-Conditioning Engineers. 1993.
ASHRAE Handbook of Fundamentals.
Atlanta: GA: American Society of Heating, Refrigerating and Air-Conditioning Engineers.
An essential reference for designers of mechanical systems for buildings, the standard professional reference for the HVAC and building design community.

Berger, Horst. 1996.
Light Structures Structures of Light: The Art and Engineering of Tensile Structures.
Basel-Boston-Berlin: Birkhauser Verlag.
A record of the author's career in development of inspired tensile structures integrating engineering and architecture.

Brantley, L. Reed and Ruth T. Brantley. 1996.
Building Materials Technology: Structural Performance and Environmental Impact.
New York: McGraw-Hill.
An authoritative review of building materials, explained in terms of their chemical and physical properties and the environmental implications of their use in buildings.

Canadian Wood Council. 1991.
Wood Reference Book.
Ottawa: Canadian Wood Council.
An excellent compilation of data for wood products, manufacturing processes, wood structural systems, connections and finishes, with excellent details and applications.

Elliott, Cecil D. 1991.
Technics and Architecture: The Development of Materials and Systems for Buildings.
Cambridge, MA: MIT Press.
An insightful and well documented history of the development of architectural and building technologies.

Givoni, Baruch. 1987.
Man, Climate and Architecture.
New York: Van Nostrand Reinhold. First Edition (1969) published by Applied Science Publishers, Ltd., London.
A classic work in the experimental tradition of building science, summarizing extensive monitoring and principles of building bioclimatology.

Illuminating Engineering Society of North America. 1993.
Lighting Handbook: Reference & Application. 8th edition
Mark S. Rea, Editor-in-Chief.
The authoritative and comprehensive reference for lighting applications in architecture.

Millet, Marietta S. 1996.
Light Revealing Architecture.
New York: Van Nostrand Reinhold.
Lighting for architecture, with an emphasis upon daylighting, presented as a design inspiration for architects as a way to understand technique, from historical and contemporary exemplars.

Orton, Andrew. 1988.
The Way We Build Now: form, scale and technique.
New York: Van Nostrand Reinhold.
An introduction to materials, structures, building physics and fire safety with excellent illustrations and examples.

Schodek, Daniel L. 1992.
Structures. Second Edition.
Englewood Cliffs: Prentice Hall.
A basic text on structures, clearly written for the architect student and professional reference, with comprehensive illustrations and metric equivalency.

Stein, Benjamin and John S. Reynolds. 1992.
Mechanical and Electrical Equipment for Buildings.
New York: John Wiley & Sons.
The long established classic reference on the topic, with complete technical description of building service systems for architects.

Tilley, Alvin R. and Henry Dreyfuss Associates. 1993
The Measure of Man and Woman: Human Factors in Design
New York: The Whitney Library of Design.
A documentation of human proportion and stature, including safety and accommodation for children and for differently abled. An essential reference for ergonomic design, by the founders of the field.

Templer, John. 1994.
The Staircase: History and Theory and Studies of Hazards, Falls and Safer Design.
Cambridge, MA: MIT Press.
A comprehensive treatment of precedents in stair design and contemporary design criteria, equally diligent in both its historical and technical analysis, including extensive research related to stair use and safety.

U. S. Department of Agriculture Forest Service. 1987.
Wood Handbook. Forest Products Laboratory Agricultural Handbook No. 72.
Springfield, VA: National Technical Information Service.
Comprehensive reference for use of wood in construction.

Introduction

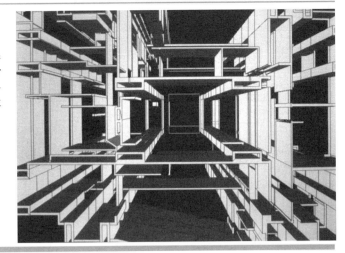

Summary: The Introduction provides an overview of the editorial organization of the Seventh Edition of Time-Saver Standards, including references to research on how architects utilize information, and a summary of its format and content.

I Knowledge of building

The technological knowledge base of architecture

"Information" is defined in communications theory as "that which resolves doubt." Information, in this view, is dependent upon the act of questioning and curiosity in the mind of the seeker. Data, in and of itself, does not "make sense." That depends upon a larger framework of knowledge, insight and reflection. In the profession of architecture, knowledge of building technique is an essential and motivating condition.

Technique, derived from the Greek *techne,* is the shared root of both "Architecture" and "Technology." Architecture is its root meaning is the "mastery of building." Technology, from *techne logos,* means "knowledge of technique." The term *techne* can be variously defined. It combines the sense of craft and knowledge learned through the act making, that is to say, through empirical experience. Craftspeople gain such knowledge in the skill of their hands and communicate it through the formal accomplishment of their art and craft.

Technological knowledge in architecture can thus be taken to mean knowledge gained in the making of buildings. The aspiration of the architect or master builder then, by definition, is to gain mastery of the knowledge of construction technology. This is a daunting aspiration, made continuously challenging by changes in construction technologies and in the values, economical, aesthetic and cultural, given to the task by architect and society.

Vitruvius gave the classic terms to the definition of architecture in setting forth the three "conditions of building well, *utilitas, firmitas and venustas,"* or as translated by Henry Wolton, "commodity, firmness and delight." Vitruvius's *de Architectura* is the first compendium of architectural knowledge, at least the oldest of known and extent texts. It includes in its scope all aspects of design and construction, from details of construction and building to city planning and climatic responses.

Geoffrey Scott, in *The Architecture of Humanism,* (1914), was not above offering pithy definitions of architecture, such as, "architecture is the art of organizing a mob of craftsmen." Scott's widely read treatise offers a view that emphasizes the importance of architectural style as a reflection of culture. Recalling Vitruvius, he defines architecture as "a humanized pattern of the world, a scheme of forms on which our life reflects its clarified image: this is its true aesthetic, and here should be sought the laws. . . of that third 'condition of well-building, its delight.'"

Kenneth Frampton in his history of architecture, *Studies in Tectonic Culture,* defines architecture as inseparable from construction technique and material culture. He cites Gottfried Semper's 1851 definition of architecture in terms of its construction components: (1) hearth, (2) earthwork, (3) framework/roof, and (4) enclosing membrane. This definition anticipates the classification of architectural elements used in Part II of this volume, classifying architectural data in terms of their place in the process of construction and assembly.

This, however, gets us only part way. Describing architecture in terms of its physical and technological elements does not convey the reasoning and the evaluation needed to guide the designer, the why and how by which particular materials and systems are selected. If the elements of construction are the "nouns," principles of design are still needed, "verbs" that give the connective logic. Also implicit in selecting one thing over another are qualifying "adjectives and adverbs," that is, the sense of value and evaluation which is ultimately represented by an ethical position: that buildings should stand up, that they should keep the rain out, that they should accommodate human habitation, comfort and productivity, that they should be equally accessible and enabling to all people of all ages, that they should not create negative environmental impact, and so forth. Some of these "design values" are required by law; others are not, but are dependent upon the values and ethical decisions of the designer, as described by Frances Ventre in his Part I article, "Architecture and Regulation."

How architects use information

D. W. MacKinnon (1962) provides a frequently referenced study of the ways that architects work, including how they process information, biased either by habit of mind or talent or by education and training. The study analyzed the personality and work habits of approximately 100 architects, selected to represent both "most creative" and a "representative cross-section" of architectural practitioners. The findings of the study determined that architects, particularly those considered "most creative," represent a set of personality traits and work habits that does distinguish the profession's ways of creative learning and practicing, which MacKinnon described as, "openness to new experience, aesthetic sensibility, cognitive flexibility, impatience with petty restraint and impoverishing inhibitions, independence of thought and action, unquestioning commitment to creative endeavor."

This study was referred to by Charles Burnette and Associates (1979) in a investigation of how architects use information, sponsored by the AIA Research Corporation and the National Engineering Laboratory

Author: Donald Watson, FAIA

Credits: The illustrations are from 1993 *Sweet's Catalog File* Selection Data, by permission of McGraw-Hill.

References: References are listed at the end of the first part of this article on the following page.

and published in two reports entitled, "Architects Access to Information" and "Making Information Useful to Architects." The reports also cite recommendations of Richard Kraus (1970) in formatting information for architects (Kraus's interest was computer-based information systems, but the recommendations apply broadly). Krause suggests that to respond to ways of thinking that are uniquely "architectural," an information system should:

(1) focus on geometric form, permitting visual assimilation;

(2) permit the designer to select the scale at which to operate, that is, in parts or wholes, or the broader context of the building;

(3) enable simultaneous consideration of a number of variables;

(4) help the designer to improve the creative insights during the design process.

These reports provide guidelines for an information system for architectural practice, that, although perhaps obvious, are noteworthy. Burnette recommends that an information system for architect should be:

(a) up-to-date,

(b) presented in a form to be readily used,

(c) appear consistently in the same format,

(d) be stated in performance terms, that is, be operationally useful,

(e) accurate and complete, with drawings precise and to scale,

(f) have an evaluation and feedback system.

Organization of Time Saver Standards

These references proved helpful to the editors of Time-Saver Standards in reformatting the present Edition. The feedback system provided by the Reader Response Form at the end of this Volume will be especially helpful in improving its publication.

The presentation of information in this edition of Time-Saver Standards is in two interrelated formats, first in Part I Architectural Fundamentals, which give the principles and cross-cutting discussion applicable to many topics and at many scales. In the terms suggested above, fundamentals provide the connecting verbs and qualifying adjectives and adverbs of the grammar of architectural knowledge. Part II Design Data are in these terms the "nouns," that is, the knowledge and information placed in the sequence of construction, as suggested by the Uniformat classification system.

The Uniformat system (the most recent version is called Uniformat II) is described in a Part I article by its authors, Robert Charette and Brian Bowen. It is a classification now widely adopted for building-related design data, first developed as an industry-wide standard for economic analysis of building components. It defines categories of the elements of building in terms of their place in the construction sequence. This classification has several advantages. Firstly, it follows the sequence of construction, from site preparation, foundation, and so forth through to enclosure and interior constructions and services. Secondly, it defines design and construction data by system assemblies, creating an easily understood locus of information by its place as a building element, which is most easily visualized and understandable to architects while designing.

The matrix of relationship between the Part I Architectural Fundamentals and the Part II Design Data, representing the Uniformat classification system, is indicated in Table 1.

Uniformat II is compatible with the MasterFormat, the established classification system used in construction specifications, described in Donald Baerman's Part I article, "Specifications." Historically, MasterFormat developed a listing of construction materials out of convenience to the builder in organizing construction, including quantity

takes-offs and purchase orders for materials from different suppliers. In short, MasterFormat is organized into distinct construction material categories as (they might be) ordered and delivered to a construction site *before* construction. Uniformat II organizes design, construction and materials data as components and assemblies *after* construction.

The matrix of relationship between Part II Design Data, representing the Uniformat classification, and MasterFormat Divisions is indicated in Table 2. These data are formatted throughout this volume with key images and graphic icons to provide an easily grasped visual reference to the design and construction thought process.▶

References

Bowen, Brian, Robert P. Charette and Harold E. Marshall. 1992. "UNIFORMAT II—A Recommended Classification for Building Elements and Related Sitework." Publication No. 841. Washington, DC: U. S. Department of Commerce National Institute of Standards and Technology.

Burnette, Charles and Associates. 1979. "The Architect's Access to Information." NTIS # PB 294855. and "Making Information Useful to Architects—An Analysis and Compendium of Practical Forms for the Delivery of Information." NTIS # PB 292782. Washington, DC: U. S. Department of Commerce National Technical Information Service.

Frampton, Kenneth. 1995. *Studies in Tectonic Culture: the Poetics of Construction in Nineteen and Twentieth Century Architecture.* Cambridge, MA: MIT Press. p. 85.

Kraus, R. and J. Myer. 1970. "Design: A Case History and Specification for a Computer System. in Moore, G., editor. *Emerging Methods in Environmental Design and Planning.* Cambridge, MA: MIT Press.

MacKinnon, D. W. 1962. "The Personality Correlates of Creativity: A Study of American Architects," *Proceedings of the 14th Congress on Applied Psychology,* Vol. 2. Munksgaard, pp. 11-39.

Scott, Geoffrey. 1914. *The Architecture of Humanism: A Study of the History of Taste.* London: Constable and Company, Ltd. Second Edition 1924. p. 41; p. 240.

Table 1. Matrix of Part I Architectural Fundamentals and Part II Design Data

Part II Design data (after Uniformat II classification)

Part I articles	A1	B1	B2	B3	C1	C2	C3	D1	D2	D3	D4	D5
1 Universal design			√		√	√	√	√	√	√	√	
2 Regulation		√			√	√	√	√		√	√	√
3 Bioclimatic design	√	√	√	√	√		√			√		
4 Solar control		√	√	√			√			√		√
5 Daylighting design		√	√	√	√	√						√
6 Natural ventilation	√	√	√	√		√				√		
7 Indoor air quality	√	√	√		√	√	√		√	√		
8 Acoustics		√	√		√	√	√	√	√	√		
9 History of technologies		√	√					√	√	√	√	√
10 Construction technology	√	√	√	√	√		√					
11 Intelligent buildings		√	√		√		√	√		√	√	√
12 Design of atriums		√	√	√	√	√	√	√		√	√	
13 Building economics	√	√	√		√		√			√		
14 Estimating	√	√	√	√	√		√			√		
15 Life cycle assessment		√	√		√		√		√	√		√
16 Construction waste	√				√		√					
17 Specifications	√	√	√	√	√		√	√	√	√		√
18 Design-Build	√	√								√		
19 Building commissioning:					√		√			√	√	√
20 Building performance					√	√	√	√		√		
21 Monitoring			√		√		√			√		√

LEGEND : Part II Design data

A	SUBSTRUCTURE
A1	Foundations and basement construction
B	SHELL
B1	Superstructure
B2	Exterior closure
B3	Roofing
C	INTERIORS
C1	Interior constructions
C2	Staircases
C3	Interior finishes
D	SERVICES
D1	Conveying Systems
D2	Plumbing
D3	HVAC
D4	Fire Protection
D5	Electrical

Table 2. Matrix of Part II Design Data and MasterFormat

MasterFormat Divisions	A1	B1	B2	B3	C1	C2	C3	D1	D2	D3	D4	D5
1 GENERAL CONDITIONS	√											
2 SITE CONSTRUCTION	√								√			√
3 CONCRETE	√	√	√									
4 MASONRY	√	√	√		√							
5 METAL	√	√	√		√							
6 WOOD & PLASTICS	√	√	√	√	√							
7 THERMAL/MOISTURE	√	√	√	√					√	√	√	
8 DOORS & WINDOWS			√	√	√	√						
9 FINISHES					√		√					
10 SPECIALTIES	√				√		√		√	√	√	
11 EQUIPMENT					√				√			√
12 FURNISHINGS					√		√			√		
13 SPECIAL CONSTRUCTION		√	√							√	√	√
14 CONVEYING SYSTEMS	√	√				√	√					√
15 MECHANICAL				√					√	√	√	√
16 ELECTRICAL						√	√			√	√	√

Column header spanning: **Part II Design data (after Uniformat II classification)**

LEGEND : Part II Design data

A	SUBSTRUCTURE
A1	Foundations and basement construction
B	SHELL
B1	Superstructure
B2	Exterior closure
B3	Roofing
C	INTERIORS
C1	Interior constructions
C2	Staircases
C3	Interior finishes
D	SERVICES
D1	Conveying Systems
D2	Plumbing
D3	HVAC
D4	Fire Protection
D5	Electrical

II Building of knowledge

Part II of this volume follows an outline suggested by Uniformat, representing the general sequence of construction as summarized in the prior section. This section provides a brief overview of its constituent elements as a framework for building a knowledge of design data related to its locus in the process of construction (Fig. 1).

A Substructure

Substructure, or below-ground construction, highlights critical structural considerations, including the capacity of soil to withstand the loads of a building, and diversion of water courses away from the building. For design of spaces below ground, including basements or fully habitable spaces, provisions for moisture control and for thermal insulation are critical. In some locales, for example southern United States, provisions of termite control are critical. In locales subject to earthquakes, the substructure and the details of construction at the earth's surface plate, are very critical. The point that demarks below-ground and above-ground construction is in almost all building a critical point of detail.

B Shell

The shell of building consists of the structure and the external enclosure or envelope that defines the internal environment and serves as barrier and/or selective filter to all environmental factors acting upon it. In general, the shell of a building is designed to last a long time, although components of the shell and enclosure assembly, such as roofing and sealants, require regular maintenance and cyclical replacement. The roof is the element of the shell most exposed to extreme climatic variation. Roofing systems protect the structure, but also may provide openings and access for daylighting, maintenance and fire protection. Walls are complex assemblies because they perform a wide range of often conflicting functions, including view, daylighting and sun tempering, protection of building systems, while presenting the predominant visible representation of the design within its natural and/or civic context.

C Interiors

Interiors includes elements for defining interior partitions, walls, ceilings, floor finishes and stairwells, and may or may not be separate from the superstructure or shell. Their purpose is to define, complete and make useable the interior spaces of the building. Some elements of the interior such as flooring and doors must sustain heavy use. Both ceilings and some flooring systems are frequently accessed to interstitial services spaces above and below. In general, interior constructions are intended to be regularly maintained and possibly frequently moved or replaced, especially to accommodate changing uses.

D Services

Services are distinct subsystems that complete the interior spaces, making them comfortable, safe and effective for habitation. They include conveying systems, plumbing, heating and cooling, fire protection, electrical and communication systems, each subject to frequent inspection, maintenance, upgrading and replacement.

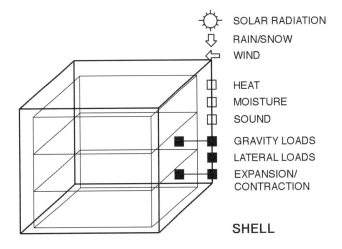

SOLAR RADIATION
RAIN/SNOW
WIND

HEAT
MOISTURE
SOUND

GRAVITY LOADS
LATERAL LOADS
EXPANSION/
CONTRACTION

SHELL

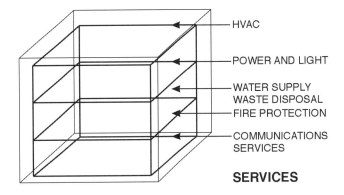

HVAC

POWER AND LIGHT

WATER SUPPLY
WASTE DISPOSAL
FIRE PROTECTION

COMMUNICATIONS
SERVICES

SERVICES

Fig. 1. Building elements

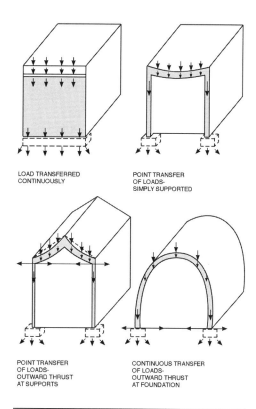

GRAVITY LOADS

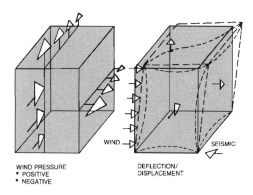

WIND / SEISMIC LOADS

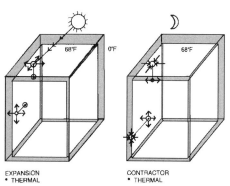

EXPANSION / CONTRACTION

Fig. 2. Structural forces

Structural and environmental forces

Building structures and shells are designed to withstand the structural loads and environmental forces generated from within and without, in regular use conditions, and also in the extremes of climate and of natural disaster (Figs. 2 and 3). To visualize the complex functioning of a building construction, its structure and systems, consider the loads and environmental forces imposed by:

- gravity loads
- wind/seismic loads
- expansion/contraction of materials
- heat and cold
- moisture and precipitation
- sound
- fire emergency

Gravity loads

The building shell and structure will always be subject to the gravity load of its own weight, referred to as dead load. A building shell will also have to sustain superimposed gravity and wind loads of varying magnitude and/or duration. These are referred to as live loads. All gravity loads are transferred through the envelope or components to the ground via rigid elements. The exception is in air-supported structures, where such loads are resisted through internal air pressure, with the ground then acting as counterweight to uplift.

Gravity loads will cause deformations in the envelope:

- in rigid envelopes due to dead loads only will be permanent but not necessarily unchanging: certain materials tend to continue to deform over time under sustained load even when there is no change in the magnitude of such load.

- deformations will also be amplified by superimposed live loads, generally reverting to their previous position after removal of the live loads, as long as stresses do not exceed the elastic limit of the material.

Wind/seismic loads

Wind forces—the flow of air against, around, and over a building shell or envelope—will affect the stability of the shell and structure:

- Vertical components facing the wind will be under positive pressure.

- Vertical components parallel to or facing away from the wind will be subject to negative air pressure, as will all horizontal or nearly horizontal surfaces.

- Lateral deflection or deformation of the vertical frame of an envelope is resisted by horizontal components of the enclosure, roof and floor assemblies, acting as diaphragms.

- The dead load of flat or nearly flat roof assemblies will counteract the negative wind pressure proportionately to the weight of each component: light horizontal envelopes may be deflected upwards.

- In locales subject to earthquakes, the effects of seismic loads require safety provisions to resist and minimize earthquake damage and to protect human life.

Expansion/contraction

Movement will occur in all components of the envelope due to variations in their internal temperature:

- Components of envelopes exposed to solar radiation gain heat and expand proportionately to their individual coefficients of expansion. Components adjacent to them but not thus exposed may remain at constant temperature and not expand at all: when such components are continuously attached to each other, they may fail due to differential movement.

- Components of an envelope may also swell and shrink due to changes in their internal moisture content.

- All components of an enclosure are in almost constant movement, interacting between each other based on their physical state and properties.

Heat and cold

Heat will flow through the envelope whenever a temperature differential exists between outside and inside surfaces. Such flow of heat must be controlled whenever the interior environment of an enclosure has to be maintained within limits of comfort:

- Flow of heat cannot be stopped entirely, but is impeded by insulation. Heat will also be gained by or lost by air leakage through the envelope whenever temperature and/or pressure differentials between interior and exterior environments exist.

- Air leakage can be minimized by making the envelope airtight. Completely preventing air leakage can seldom, if ever, be achieved.

Moisture

Air leaking through the envelope will transport water vapor. Water vapor condenses out of the air/vapor mixture when it drops below a specific temperature, called the dew point. Water vapor will also migrate from an area of higher vapor pressure to an area with lower vapor pressure, and will condense upon reaching the dew point. Condensation may occur within the envelope, which may lead to damage and possible failure of the envelope. Rain water may be drawn into or through an envelope by differences in air pressure across the skin.

Wind pressures against the exterior surfaces will be greater than interior air pressures, and such difference then becomes the driving force for water and air penetration into the interior.

Sound

Transmission of external sound through an envelope may have to be controlled for the comfort of the occupants. Transmission of sound through a barrier is inversely proportional to the mass of the barrier; light envelopes will be less effective than heavy ones. Any opening in the envelope will effectively destroy it usefulness as a barrier to sound transmission. Interior components of an enclosure, such as floor assemblies, partitions, ceilings may also be required to control sound:

- air borne sound within a space by absorbing it to reduce its intensity; reflecting and/or scattering it.

- air borne sound transmission from one space to adjacent ones.

- structure-borne sound by damping it, or by isolating its source.

Fire emergency

The envelope of a building shell or space enclosure and/or its components are required to resist the effects of fire for a specific minimum of time without a significant reduction of structural strength and/or stability to ensure the safety of the occupants. Generally, the interior structural assemblies of an enclosure are required by building codes to be fire-resistant rated for a specific time interval.

- walls to prevent the spread of interior fire, commonly referred to as fire walls, may be required to compartmentalize large spaces, or to separate different activities within a single enclosure.

- exterior walls may have to be fire-resistant rated when separation from adjacent enclosures is less than a specific minimum.

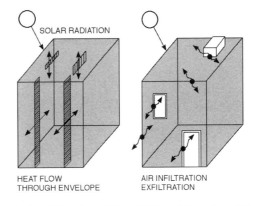

HEAT

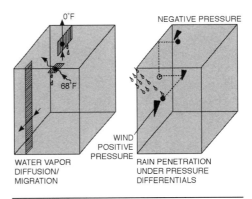

MOISTURE

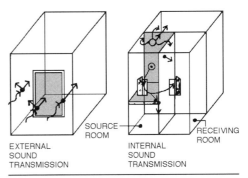

SOUND

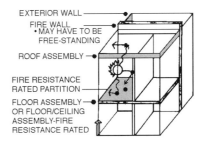

FIRE

Fig. 3. Environmental forces

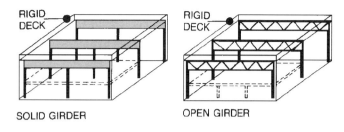

COLUMNS AND GIRDERS

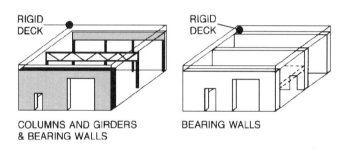

COLUMNS AND GIRDERS / BEARING WALLS

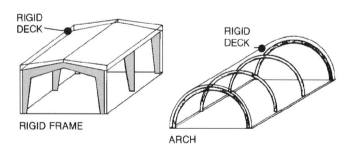

CURVED GIRDER

Fig. 4. Elements of structure

The Shell

B1 Elements of a building superstructure

The forces upon all building superstructures are defined by design loads, predicted from gravity and environmental forces described above. The most common structural materials are wood, steel, concrete and masonry, each described in separate articles in Part II, Chapter B1. Modern construction materials and applications include tensioned fabric structures, used for large span assembly spaces, and air-supported structures for temporary and partial occupancy applications (Fig. 4).

Columns and girders

Means of structural support for the envelope and/or interior elements of an enclosure may consist of:

- Horizontal elements to safely resist:

- gravity loads of a roof deck, or of floor deck or decks.

- gravity loads of walls when supported on such horizontal elements.

- lateral loads acting directly on such elements or transmitted through walls which they brace.

- Vertical elements to transmit gravity and lateral loads imposed upon them by horizontal elements and/or walls to the foundation/ground.

Columns and girders/bearing walls

Horizontal elements may be classified as:

- Primary: when the deck assembly or the decking component of such assembly bears directly on them.

- Secondary: when supporting the decking component of a deck assembly between widely spaced primary supports.

Primary horizontal elements are referred to as girders. Vertical elements which support them are columns. Secondary vertical elements are referred to as framing. A roof or floor assembly, whether alone or combined with framing to support it, is referred to as the deck or decking.

Girders

Girders may be:

- Solid web, also often referred to as beams of various materials, such as structural steel; solid or laminated wood; or reinforced concrete.

- Open web, commonly referred to as trusses of various materials, such as structural steel; or wood.

- Pitched or curved such as trusses with pitched or curved top chords supported on columns.

- Curved in different configurations, with the girder and columns being combined into one element; generally referred to as arches.

Primary horizontal supports may also be walls which combine girders and columns into one element called bearing walls, or portions of walls may function as columns commonly referred to as pilasters, to support point loads, such as by girders.

Curved decks (arches, vaults, domes)

Means of support for the envelope of an enclosure may consist of a curved monolithic deck only, commonly referred to as a structural shell which combines structural support and decking monolithically, usually capable of transmitting loads in more than two directions to foundation/ground. This type of structure, including arches, vaults and domes, are highly efficient for materials that have strength in compression, because it transmits gravity and lateral loads acting upon it essentially in compression, without bending or twisting. The curvature is principally influenced by requirements of load transfer; shapes may be barrel arches, domes, cones, hyperbolic paraboloids. Historical examples are of adobe and masonry. Reinforced concrete is most commonly used in modern building construction.

Tensioned fabric structures

Modern fabric materials and tensioned structures combine to offer a new technology for spanning and enclosing large volume spaces, with permanent, temporary and convertible variations. This class of structure, derivative of the traditional tent structure but utilizing the tensile strength of modern synthetic fabrics, has developed over the past thirty years and is made increasingly practical by improved analysis techniques and applications. Because they are lightweight, tensioned fabric structures are efficient in long span applications.

Air-supported structures

Air-supported structures are an alternative enclosure system, most commonly used for temporary or partial use. The means of support for an air-supported envelope consist of a flexible membrane, which generally functions as the complete enclosure, retained in position by a combination of anchored cable supports and/or air pressure only. There are two types, both of which have to be anchored to a foundation or directly to the ground against displacement by wind forces, and/or to resist uplift of pressurization:

- Air supported: when the interior is sufficiently pressurized to counteract the effects of gravity load of the membrane itself as well as all superimposed gravity and lateral loads. Interior is always under positive pressure and provisions to maintain such pressure are required at all penetrations through the membrane.

- Air inflated: when completely supported by pressurized air entrapped within the membrane. Interior of air inflated enclosure is at atmospheric pressure.

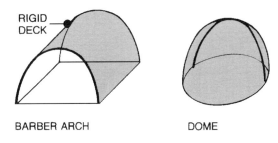

CURVED DECK

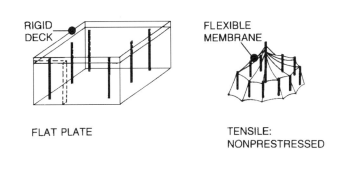

POINT SUPPORTERS

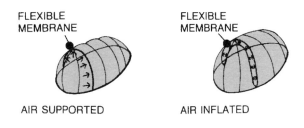

AIR PRESSURE

Fig. 4. (Continued) Elements of structure

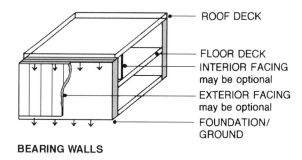

BEARING WALLS

ROOF DECK

FLOOR DECK
INTERIOR FACING
may be optional
EXTERIOR FACING
may be optional
FOUNDATION/
GROUND

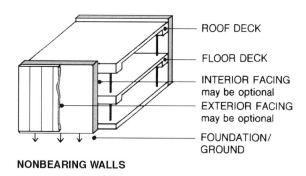

NONBEARING WALLS

ROOF DECK

FLOOR DECK

INTERIOR FACING
may be optional
EXTERIOR FACING
may be optional
FOUNDATION/
GROUND

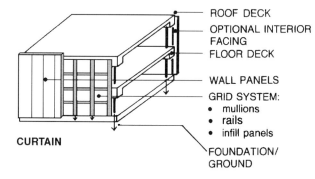

CURTAIN

ROOF DECK
OPTIONAL INTERIOR
FACING
FLOOR DECK

WALL PANELS

GRID SYSTEM:
• mullions
• rails
• infill panels
FOUNDATION/
GROUND

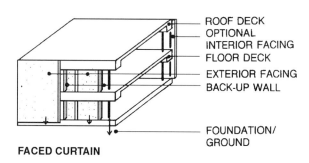

FACED CURTAIN

ROOF DECK
OPTIONAL
INTERIOR FACING
FLOOR DECK
EXTERIOR FACING
BACK-UP WALL

FOUNDATION/
GROUND

Fig. 5. Wall elements

B2 Exterior enclosure

The building enclosure is a continuous air and watertight barrier, maintained to separate the contained environment from that external to it. The barrier or envelope consists of a wall enclosure and roofing assembly covering the contained space (Figs. 5 and 6).

Walls and roofs may be separate distinct elements, or essentially one, without any clear differentiation between them. Design of building enclosures includes considerations of:

- thermal insulation,
- building movement,
- moisture control,
- corrosion of materials, especially metals.

Each of these design issues are discussed in detail in the Part II Chapter B2 on Exterior Closure. Complete exterior wall enclosures and assemblies include:

- wall systems.
- exterior doors and entries.
- windows.

The composition of a wall system and assembly commonly includes:

- Structural core: to resist gravity loads of the assembly itself, those that might be superimposed upon it, and lateral loads. The structural core may be a separate component such as framing or the core may function as the complete wall assembly.

- Exterior facing: to resist the effects of environmental factors. Exterior facing may be a separate component attached to and supported by the structural core, or it may be an integral part of such core.

- Interior facing, either as a required component to complete the wall assembly such as over framing or as an optional component added to satisfy functional and/or visual requirements.

- Together or separately, the elements of the exterior wall assembly must provide means of support against lateral forces, either wind or seismic, by columns or pilasters when span of wall is horizontal, by floor and roof assemblies when loads are transferred vertically.

Wall assemblies may be variously described and classified by one or several of the following characteristics:

- Bearing walls: carrying superimposed gravity loads in addition to their own weight.

- Nonbearing walls: not carrying superimposed gravity loads in addition to their own weight, whether capable of carrying such loads or not, and supported directly on foundations/ground.

- Curtain walls: nonbearing walls secured to and supported by the structural frame of an enclosure:

- Grid type walls: vertical and horizontal framing members supported by floor or roof assemblies and supporting between them various in-fill panels.

- Wall panels: prefabricated panels spanning between floor and roof or between floors and functioning as the complete wall assembly.

- Faced walls functioning as facing and/or continuous backup and support for various types of facings. Backup walls may be bearing, nonbearing, or curtain. Facings may be: off-site fabricated panels or units such as metal; or faced composite panels, or ceramic tile units assembled on site or made on-site, such as stucco.

- Masonry walls may be described as: composite (when consisting of two or more wythes of masonry where at least one wythe is dissimilar to other wythes) or; cavity (of two wythes of masonry built to provide an air space within the wall).

- Shear wall may be any of the above when the wall structure is designed to resist horizontal forces in the plane of the wall.

B3 Roofing

Roof assemblies, described in Part II Chapter B3, commonly include:

- roofing or roofing membrane to resist the effects of environmental factors, especially water proofing.

- substrate or decking for the roofing which not only carries the roofing but also resists the effects of all forces acting on the assembly.

- means of support for the deck: such as girders, bearing walls, columns.

- means of rainwater drainage, through gutter and downspout systems.
- openings, including skylights, hatchways, heat/smoke vents,
- accessories, including curbs, walkways, cupolas, relief vents, and snow guards (on sloped roofs).

Roof decks may be:

- decking or substrate, only when such decking is capable of spanning between widely spaced primary supports without the need for any secondary framing:

Long-span decking may be considered as combining decking and framing in one when its span exceeds an arbitrary maximum of eight feet.

- decking and widely spaced framing, eight feet or less on centers, with the framing spanning between widely spaced primary supports:

- decking and closely spaced framing, two feet or less on centers, with the framing spanning between primary supports.

- decking such as rigid panels or flexible membrane supported by a cable network.

Rigid roof assemblies may be flat, pitched, curved; or in any combination.

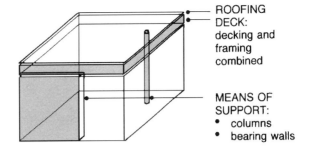

ROOFING
DECK:
decking and
framing
combined

MEANS OF
SUPPORT:
• columns
• bearing walls

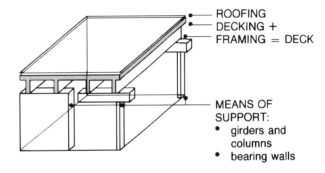

ROOFING
DECKING +
FRAMING = DECK

MEANS OF
SUPPORT:
• girders and
  columns
• bearing walls

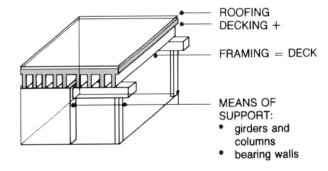

ROOFING
DECKING +

FRAMING = DECK

MEANS OF
SUPPORT:
• girders and
  columns
• bearing walls

Fig. 6. Roofing elements

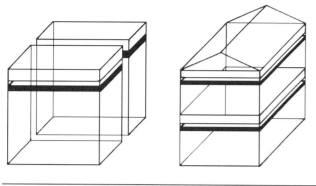

CEILINGS

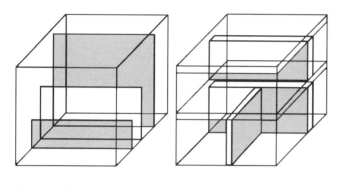

PARTITIONS

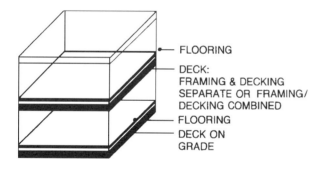

- FLOORING
- DECK:
  FRAMING & DECKING
  SEPARATE OR FRAMING/
  DECKING COMBINED
- FLOORING
- DECK ON
  GRADE

FLOORS

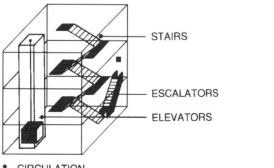

- STAIRS
- ESCALATORS
- ELEVATORS

- CIRCULATION
- CONVEYANCE

MEANS OF CIRCULATION

Fig. 7. Interior constructions. Note: Moving systems for circulation and conveyance are classified under Services

Interiors

C1 Interior construction

Interior constructions include ceiling, partition and interior door and wall panel and flooring systems (Fig. 7). Due to the need for changes in internal space arrangements, especially in modern office buildings, all elements of interior construction need to be accessible and flexible in rearrangement, replacement and upgrading, such as through dropped ceiling and raised flooring systems.

Ceilings systems

Ceiling systems are nonstructural components of an enclosure. Depending on their support on floor or roof assemblies. ceilings may be:

- visual screens and/or functional separation between an inhabited space and the underside of a floor or roof assembly above.

- integral components of floor or roof assemblies when such assemblies are required to be fire-resistant rated to protect the structural framing and/or decking from effects of fire.

Partitions

The space within an envelope may be fully or partly divided by partitions to:

- control movement through enclosed space.

- provide visual and/or speech privacy to the occupants.

- enclose different environments within a single envelope.

- separate or isolate different activities.

- prevent the spread of fire within the enclosed space.

Partitions may be:
- of different heights: below eye level, to above eye level, to ceiling, or to underside of floor or roof assembly above:

- fixed, relocatable, or operable; supported on, or suspended from floor or roof assemblies:

- when supported, they are capable of carrying their own weight, but generally not superimposed loads.

Floors

Floors are flat, commonly horizontal surfaces within the envelope of an enclosure. Flooring finishes and their substrates may be subject to heavy use. Floor assemblies include:

- flooring: to resist the effects of traffic over the surface of the floor deck.

- deck: to support all loads imposed on the floor assembly.

- means of support for the deck.

C2 Staircases

Staircases are provided for convenience of access and communication between levels of a building, and are determined to meet standards of emergency egress and refuge areas, universal design and accessibility. Stairs are critical elements of a building, because of their heavy use and the resulting need for safety, given special emphasis in the Part II Chapter C2, "Stairwells." Means of circulation between two or more floors or levels may include:

- stairs for foot traffic.

- ramps for foot traffic, universal design accessibility, and vehicular traffic.

- ladders for limited access.

Services

D1 Conveying systems

Design criteria for design of escalators and elevators are described in the Part II Chapter D1, "Conveying systems." Means of conveyance/circulation between floors or levels may include:

- escalators for continuous movement of large number of persons.
- elevators for intermittent movement of persons or goods.
- dumbwaiters for continuous or intermittent movement of goods.
- moving sidewalks.

D2 Plumbing

All buildings housing human activity must be provided with portable water in quantities sufficient to meet the needs of the occupants and related activities. Plumbing system design is best conceived as part of a water conservation plan: fresh water is a critical health and environmental issue and can be aided by use of water conserving plumbing within buildings and design of landscaping features that retain and filter water in its path to the local aquifer.

- Water supply systems distribute water to fixtures or devices which serve as the terminals of such system.
- Waste water systems removes used and polluted water, based on the anticipated quantities of water flow through all fixtures.

D3 Heating and air conditioning (HVAC)

HVAC design consists of mechanically assisted systems to control of temperature, humidity and the quality of air within an enclosure, at comfort levels acceptable to the occupants. HVAC systems generally include:

- Heating plant to supply sufficient heat to replace that transmitted and lost to the exterior through the envelope.
- Equipment to cool and dehumidify the air: chiller, condenser, fans, pumps.
- Humidifier to maintain the air at desired level of relative humidity.
- Distribution system: supply and return, and filters.
- Fresh air supply.
- Exhaust systems to rid the interior of polluted air.

D4 Fire protection

Fire safety in buildings is a principal consideration and is greatly aided by proper design of building spaces, access and egress ways, materials and protection systems, described in the Part II Chapter D4, "Fire Protection." Modern fire protection systems greatly improve fire safety through fire detection and suppression systems, including:

- sprinkler systems.
- standpipe systems.
- fire extinguishers and cabinets strategically placed throughout a building.
- fire alarm systems.

D5 Electrical systems

Electrical systems include electric power, telephone and communications, and electrical specialties, such as audio-visual and security systems. These systems have experienced rapid improvement and development, indicated in the articles in Part II Electrical systems.

Design of lighting provides an opportunity for energy conservation and improved human comfort, productivity and amenity, especially when carefully integrated with daylighting.

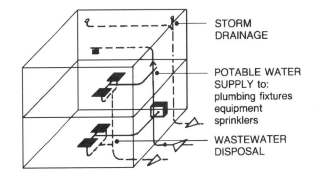

STORM DRAINAGE

POTABLE WATER SUPPLY to:
plumbing fixtures
equipment
sprinklers

WASTEWATER DISPOSAL

PLUMBING SYSTEMS

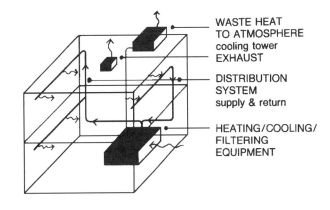

WASTE HEAT TO ATMOSPHERE
cooling tower EXHAUST

DISTRIBUTION SYSTEM
supply & return

HEATING/COOLING/FILTERING EQUIPMENT

HVAC

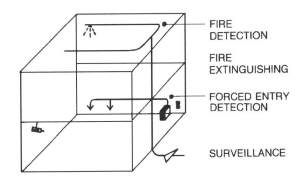

FIRE DETECTION

FIRE EXTINGUISHING

FORCED ENTRY DETECTION

SURVEILLANCE

FIRE PROTECTION

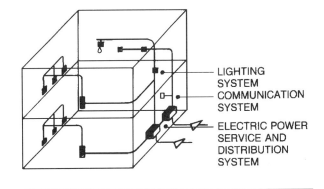

LIGHTING SYSTEM

COMMUNICATION SYSTEM

ELECTRIC POWER SERVICE AND DISTRIBUTION SYSTEM

ELECTRICAL SYSTEMS

Fig. 8. Services

ARCHITECTURAL FUNDAMENTALS 1

1
Universal design and accessible design

John P. S. Salmen
Elaine Ostroff

Summary: Universal design is an approach to architectural design that considers the entire range of capacities and potentials of people and how they use buildings and products throughout their lives. The approach goes beyond technical standards that provide only minimal accessibility in compliance with regulations and extends design to increase the capacities of men, women and children of all ages and abilities.

Key words: accessibility, Americans with Disabilities Act, disability, ergonomics, human factors, universal design.

Fig. 1. Creating places for people. Public rest seats with differentiated heights. Davis, CA. Brian Donnelly Design.

What is universal design?

The goal of universal design could be said is create buildings, places and details that provide a supportive environment to the largest number of individuals throughout life's variety of changing circumstances. All people experience changes in mobility, agility, and perceptual acuity throughout their life spans, from childhood to adulthood. At any time in our lives, we may experience temporary or permanent physical or psychological impairments which may be disabling and which may increase our dependence upon certain aspects of the physical environment. In addition, people are diverse in size, preferences and abilities. Universal design responds to these conditions and potentials and seeks to extend the human capacity by accommodation supported by the designed environment.

Universal design is an evolving design discipline that builds upon and attempts to go beyond the minimum standards for "accessible design," to create designs that are sensitive to the needs and thus useable by the largest possible number of users. Unlike accessible design, there are no regulations which define or enforce universal design. Instead, architects and landscape architects sensitive to the issues of universal design recognize that everyone at some time in their life is likely to experience a disabling condition, thus requiring increased accommodation by design. Universal design involves both a design sensitivity and sensibility that seek to understand and support the full range of human capacities. Ergonomics and human factor analysis, an applied anthropometric approach to design pioneered beginning in the 1930s by Henry Dreyfuss and Alvin R. Tilley (Henry Dreyfuss Associates 1993) are part of the inherited discipline and ethic of universal design. Universal design goes beyond any static conception and seeks to enable and enhance the changing abilities of humans throughout their life span, and the changing demographics of our society as we move into the 21st Century.

Universal design makes designer, user and building owner more sensitive to what can be done to improve the long-term quality of what we build. Design and long-term building quality is improved by designing for easier access, reduced accidents, easier wayfinding and transit of people and goods, and design details for people of all ages, sizes, and capacities.

Universal design also recognizes that within the long life span of a building-properly conceived as a fifty- to one hundred-year life cycle or longer, the average and standard norms of human dimensions and capacities are changing. In the U. S., for example, the height (and weight) of the average individual is increasing with each generation (see Appendix page *AP-3*). This suggests anticipation of changing dimensional and safety standards to respond to the demographics of our society. What passed as minimal height requirements fifty years ago accommodates a decreasing portion of the population. Accommodation to an older population requires increased design sensitivity to sensory and mobility impairments.

Demographics

The need and demand for universally designed spaces and products is much larger than the current population of 49 million people with disabilities in the U. S. Everyone over their lifetime will experience some temporary or permanent disability. The market includes children, people who must move around with luggage or other encumbrances, people with temporary disabilities and especially older people. The aging baby-boom generation is undoubtedly the true beneficiary of universal design for three reasons.

- The 21st century is going to see a tremendous growth in the numbers of people over the age of 65 (Fig. 2).

- More than half the people over 65 have a physical disability.

- By 2025, the average life span is expected to reach 100 years of age for people in developed countries (primarily due to advances in medical technology).

Mistaken myths of universal design

- *Myth*: Costs for universal design are higher.

  Fact: It costs no more to universally design a space or product. It does take more thinking and attention to the users. Such steps normally pay for themselves many times over in reduced design failure and reduced costs of changing environments after they are built. Through thinking through all uses, the long term durability and usefulness of a design is increased.

Authors: John P. S. Salmen, AIA and Elaine Ostroff

Credits: Photographs are from Universal Designers and Consultants (1996).

References: Barrier Free Environments. 1996. *Fair Housing Design Manual.* Publication B181. Washington, DC: HUD. Fair Housing Clearing House. (800) 343 2442.

Henry Dreyfuss Associates. 1993. *The Measure of Man and Woman: Human Factors in Design.* New York: Whitney Library of Design.

U. S. Department of Justice. 1994 revised. *ADA Standards for Accessible Design.* 28 CFR Part 36, Appendix A. Washington, DC: U. S. Department of Justice.

Additional references and resources are listed at the end of this article.

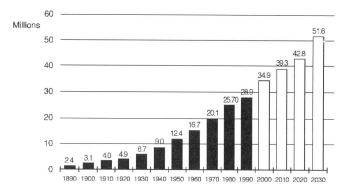

Fig. 2. Population Age 65 and older
(Sources: U. S. Bureau of the Census: Historical Statistics of the United States, Colonial Times to 1970, Series B107-115; Current Population Reports, Series P-23, No. 59; and Statistical Abstract of the United States. 1991 (111th edition), Tables No. 13, 18, 22, and 41; and James Pirkl 1994, Transgenerational Design. New York: Van Nostrand Reinhold)

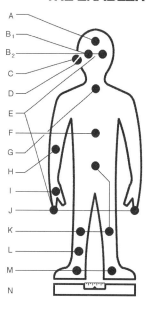

THE ENABLER

DIFFICULTY INTERPRETING INFORMATION — A
SEVERE LOSS OF SIGHT — B₁
COMPLETE LOSS OF SIGHT — B₂
SEVERE LOSS OF HEARING — C
PREVALENCE OF POOR BALANCE — D
INCOORDINATION — E
LIMITATIONS OF STAMINA — F
DIFFICULTY MOVING HEAD — G
DIFFICULTY REACHING WITH ARMS — H
DIFFICULTY IN HANDLING AND FINGERING — I
LOSS OF UPPER EXTREMITY SKILLS — J
DIFFICULTY BENDING, KNEELING, ETC. — K
RELIANCE ON WALKING AIDS — L
INABILITY TO USE LOWER EXTREMITIES — M
EXTREMES OF SIZE AND WEIGHT — N

Fig. 3. The "Enabler Model" (Steinfeld, et al. 1979)

- *Myth:* Few people need universal design.

  Fact: The number of people who benefit from universal design is very great. All individuals have special conditions and requirements at different times of life. Universal design considers those needs and abilities recognizing people with disabilities, as well as young and aging individuals, plus those who associate with and assist them. Universal design addresses the users over their entire life span for the building or product over its entire life span.

- *Myth:* One size fits all.

  Fact: Universal design seeks to accommodate difference and variation, not minimally acceptable averages. Strategies may include adjustable or interchangeable elements, designing spaces so that they can be easily customized, and allowing flexibility of use, although sometimes a single solution may fit all.

Guidelines for universal design

The following principles describe guidelines for universal design developed by the Center for Universal Design (1995), whose web page listed in the additional references illustrates applications. The guidelines offer criteria to use in design, or in evaluating designs:

- *Simple and intuitive use:* Use of the design is easy to understand, regardless of the user's experience, knowledge, language skills, or current concentration level.

- *Equitable use:* The design does not disadvantage or stigmatize any group of users.

- *Perceptible information:* The design communicates necessary information effectively to the user, regardless of ambient conditions or the user's sensory abilities.

- *Tolerance for error:* The design minimizes hazards and the adverse consequences of accidental or unintended fatigue.

- *Flexibility in use:* The design accommodates a wide range of individual preferences and abilities.

- *Low physical effort:* The design can be used efficiently and comfortably and with a minimum of fatigue.

- *Size and space for approach and use:* Appropriate size and space is provided for approach, reach, manipulation, and use, regardless of the user's body size, posture, or mobility. Henry Dreyfuss Associates (1993) provides a number of templates for ergonomic analysis of hand and body for design of furniture and environmental settings.

What is accessible design?

Accessible design is design that meets standards that allow people with disabilities to enjoy a minimum level of access to environments and products. Since 1988 with the passage of the Fair Housing Amendments Act, and in 1990 with the passage of the Americans with Disabilities Act (ADA), accessibility standards now cover much of what is newly constructed or renovated.

Unlike earlier federal requirements that were restricted to facilities built with federal support, these far reaching new regulations cover privately owned as well as government supported facilities, programs and services. Accessibility criteria are found in building codes and accessibility criteria such as the Americans with Disabilities Act Standards for Accessible Design, the Fair Housing Amendment Act Accessibility Guidelines or the American National Standard Accessible and Usable Buildings and Facilities CABO/ANSI A117.1 These prescribe a compliance approach to design, where the designer meets the minimum criteria to allow a specific class of people—those with disabilities—to use the environment without much difficulty. Accessible design is a more positive term for what was previously called "barrier free" or "handicap design," both being examples of unfortunate terminology which focuses on the negative process of eliminating barriers that confront people with disabilities. These minimum requirements provide a baseline that universal designers can build upon.

People are so diverse and adaptable that design standards to quantify how people use objects and spaces must be general. In the late 1970's Rolf Faste and Edward Steinfeld cataloged the major functional abilities that could be limited by disability. Their "Enabler Model" summarizes the environmental implications of limitations in the 17 major functional areas found in people with disabilities, often in combinations (Fig. 3).

Accessibility standards have simplified this overwhelming diversity down to three main groups of conditions shown below with the related component of the environment. By understanding the physical implications of these broad groups of disabling conditions designers can understand the criteria in the building codes and standards.

- *Sensory impairments: Design of information systems.*

This includes vision, hearing and speech impairments including total and partial loss of function and leads us to the design recommendation for redundancy of communication media to insure that everyone can receive information and express themselves over communication systems. For example, reinforcing both lighting and circulation cues, wayfinding can be enhanced. Or by providing both audible and visual alarms, everyone will be able to know when an emergency occurs.

- *Dexterity impairments: Design of operating controls and hardware.*

This includes people with limitations in the use of their hands and fingers and suggests the "closed fist rule," testing selection of equipment controls and hardware by operating it with a closed fist. In addition, this addresses the location of equipment and controls so that they are within the range of reach of people who use wheelchairs and those who are of short stature.

- *Mobility impairments: Space and circulation systems.*

This includes people who use walkers, crutches, canes and wheelchairs plus those who have difficulty climbing stairs or going long distances. The T-turn and 5 ft. (1.52 m) diameter turning area provide key plan evaluation criteria here. These concepts and the accessible route of travel insure that all people have accessible and safe passage from the perimeter of a site to and through all areas of a facility.

Conflicting Criteria

Accessibility has overlapping regulations and civil rights implications as established by U. S. law. Designers face the challenge of sorting out the specific accessibility regulations that apply to their work as well as of understanding the purpose and the technical requirements. In addition to overarching federal standards required by the ADA, each state has its own access regulations. There is a concerted national effort to adopt more uniform, harmonious regulations, but designers must be aware that if elements of the state regulation are more stringent, they supersede the federal standard.

In addition, the civil rights aspect of both the Fair Housing Amendments Act and the ADA establish requirements that go beyond the technical requirements. For example, the new requirement in the ADA to attempt barrier removal in existing buildings (even when no renovations are planned) is not detailed in the Standards but is discussed in the full ADA regulation (Department of Justice 1994). The professional responsibilities and liability of the designer are being redefined through these regulations. Applications of these regulations as defined by ADA language are interpreted by evolving legal case law and in resulting guidelines, such as those of U. S. HUD which establish public housing standards and of the Equal Employment Opportunity Commission which establish U. S. workplace standards.

The universal design process

The issues raised by accessibility regulations are best addressed and combined in a commitment to universal design. The more one knows

Fig. 4. Renovated entry landscape with sloping walkway and outdoor seating platform to Hunnewell Visitors Center at the Arnold Arboretum. Jamaica Plain, MA. Carol R. Johnson Associates, Landscape Architects.

Fig. 5. Entry terrace modifications, including ramp and handrails, blending with historic design. Hopedale Town Hall, Hopedale, MA. Nichols Design Associates, Architects.

Fig. 6. Multisensory signage, combining "full spatial" tactile and visual text and maps and infrared talking signs. The Lighthouse, New York, NY. Roger Whitehouse & Company, Graphics.

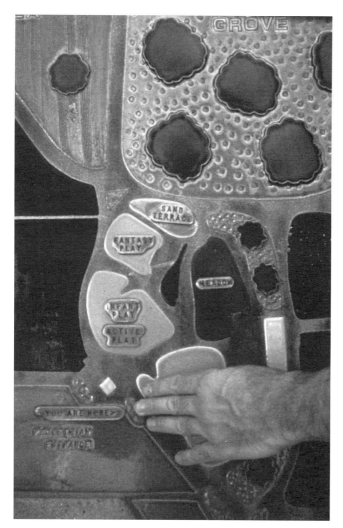

Fig. 7. Signage with raised tactile and visual guide, including textures of water and trees as map to public park, which also includes wind chimes for aural orientation. Flood Park, San Mateo County, CA. Moore Iacofano Goltsman, Landscape Architects.

Fig. 8. Public toilet accommodating all users including families. Automatic sensor controls of plumbing. Visual and tactile operating instructions in various languages. San Francisco, CA. J. C. Decaux International with Ron Mace and Barry Atwood.

as a designer, the better the resulting design. But universal design considerations are as complex and in a sense as unpredictable as the variety of human experience and capacities. No one knows it all. This simple fact demands that the approach to universal design involve many people representing a range of insights from the beginning of the programming and design process. Designers cannot get such information from books, databases or design criteria alone. Designers must involve the future users, the customers of the design, through universal design reviews.

Universal design reviews undertaken at critical early and evolving phases of the design process are opportunities to improve any design, eliminate errors, improve its user friendliness and at the same time involve and thus satisfy the special needs of owners and occupants of the resulting building. Because no one person can anticipate all possible perceptions and needs, a design should be given broad discussion and review, with input from many points of view. Designers must listen to and hear from perceptive spokespeople who can articulate the needs and responses of:

- People of all stages of life, from the point of view of the youngster whose eye level is half that of adults to elders and others who have difficulty with mobility, lighting distractions and disorientation at transition points in a building.

- Wheel-chair users and people with other physical differences, which can be a common as left- and right-handedness.

- People with visual and aural impairments.

- Persons who maintain and service our buildings, carrying heavy loads or other potential impediments to safe travel.

- All people under conditions of emergency.

This requires that the process of universal design be broadly representative, user responsive and participatory. Because many lay persons cannot visualize actual conditions from plans or drawings, universal designing reviews may require alternative media including three-dimensional models, virtual reality simulations, and, in some cases, full scale mock up prototypes, whereby all can experience, critically evaluate and offer ways to improve a design in process. The more diverse the group, the better. It is only in this way that designers can keep up with and come to understand how our changing culture will be using our environments and products in the 21st century.

Examples of universal design

In 1996, the National Endowment for the Arts and the National Building Museum sponsored a search for examples of universal design in the fields of architecture, interior design, landscape architecture, graphic design and industrial design. This juried selection features the work of designers who are reaching "beyond compliance" with the Americans with Disabilities Act to create products and environments that are useable by people with the broadest possible range of abilities throughout their life (Figs. 1 and 4-15).

The more that designers learns from the diverse users of the environment, the more sensitive and sophisticated our universal designs become. Some the best examples of special design are almost invisible to see because they blend in so well with their environmental context. Design inspirations such as those revealed in photographs that accompany this article are the best way to convey both the simplicity and complexity of universal design. They exemplify the principal message of universal design, to extend our design ethic and sensibilities in order to enhance the abilities of all people who will occupy our designs.

Additional references and resources

U. S. Access Board. *ADA Accessibility Guidelines.* www.access-board.gov. (800) USA-ABLE.

ADA Regional Disability and Business Technical Assistance Centers. (800) 949 4 ADA.

Barrier Free Environments. 1996. *ADA Highlights Slide Show on the Americans with Disabilities Act Standards for Accessible Design.* Raleigh, NC: Barrier Free Environments.

CABO/ANSI. 1997. *American National Standard for Accessible and Usable Buildings and Facilities.* CABO/ANSI A117.1. Falls Church, VA: Council of American Building Officials. www.cabo.org/a117.htm.

Center for Universal Design. 1995. *Principles of Universal Design.* Raleigh, NC: North Carolina State University. (800) 647-6777. www.ncsu.edu/ncsu/design/cud/

Mueller, James P. 1992. *Workplace Workbook 2.0: An Illustrated Guide to Workplace Accommodation and Technology.* Amherst, MA: Human Resource Development Press.

Pirkl, James. 1994. *Transgenerational Design.* New York: Van Nostrand Reinhold. *(continued)*

Fig. 9. Talking sign system, providing a directionally-sensitive voice message, including bus schedule, transmitted by infrared light to a hand-held receiver. San Francisco, CA. Smith-Kettlewell/Talking Signs, Inc.

Fig. 10. Meandering Brook designed for active water play for children of all capacities. Children's Museum, Boston, MA. Carol R. Johnson Associates, Landscape Architects.

Fig. 11. Dual height viewports for children of all ages in doors, part of wayfinding system at the Lighthouse, New York City, NY. Steven M. Goldberg, FAIA and Jan Keane, FAIA, Mitchell/Giurgola Architects.

Steinfeld, Edward, Steven Schroeder, James Duncan, Rolfe Faste, Deborah Chollet, Marylin Bishop, Peter Wirth and Paul Cardell. 1979, 1986. *Access to the Built Environment: a review of literature.* Prepared for U. S. HUD, Office of Policy Development and Research. Publication #660. Rockville, MD: HUD User.

U. S. Department of Agriculture (USDA) Forest Service, et al. 1993. *Universal Access to Outdoor Recreation: A Design Guide.* Berkeley, CA: MIG Communications.

U. S. Department of Justice. 1994 revised. *ADA Standards for Accessible Design.* 28 CFR Part 36, App. A. Washington, DC: U. S. Department of Justice.

Universal Designers and Consultants. 1996. *Images of Excellence in Universal Design.* Rockville, MD: Universal Designers & Consultants, Inc.

Universal Design Newsletter. Rockville, MD: Universal Designers & Consultants, Inc.

Welch, Polly. 1995. *Strategies for Teaching Universal Design.* Boston, MA: Adaptive Environments.

Fig. 12. Full length entry sidelight at doorways. Center for Universal Design, Raleigh, NC. Ronald Mace.

Fig. 14. Swing Clear Hinge, allowing a door to be fully opened for wider access. Gilreath and Associates, Interior Designers.

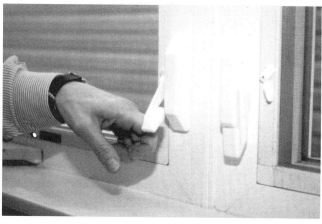

Fig. 13. G. E. Real Life Design Kitchen including adjustable height appliances and counters, natural light and high contract trim for users with low vision. Mary Jo Peterson, Interior Design.

Fig. 15. Window Lock/Latch, accommodating dexterity limitations and "aging in place." Owens Residence, Chicago, IL. Design One, Industrial Design.

Architecture and regulation: a realization of social ethics

Francis T. Ventre

Summary: Citing Alvar Aalto's ethical stance that architecture should "do no harm," professional ethics are reviewed alongside developments in architectural theory, codes of conduct and building regulation.

Key words: code of professional conduct, design theory, professional ethics, regulation.

Tuberculosis Sanatorium. Paimio, Finland. Alvar Aalto, Architect. 1928-33.

Ethics and design are so densely intertwined, so intimately interactive, that ethical issues in architectural pedagogy are almost always arise in the context of a specific design situation. There is, of course, the obligatory acknowledgment of "professional ethics" in the equally obligatory "professional practice" course late in the undergraduate's career. Thus sequestered, however, professional ethics is exposed to not nearly as much scrutiny as is the moral dimension of design work. Moral development, in other words, is—or should be—an important subsidiary outcome of an architectural education. Nor is this emergency of ethics out of design discourse surprising, when one considers that the first comprehensive theory of design (and most succinct and intellectually coherent) issued from Aristotle's *Nicomachean Ethics.*[1]

Ethics and design share more than a common intellectual ancestor, for what I would like to call the "design attitude" appears in the works of the principal ethicists throughout the development of western philosophy. By design attitude I mean, following Aristotle and C. S. Pierce and scores of moral philosophers between them, the proposing, effectuating, and evaluating of any action in terms of its consequences.[2] In other words, design is the forethought of purposive, intentional action, and the consequences of that action are evaluated against the purposes and intentions that precipitated the action in the first place.

Not all design theorists subscribe to this definition of design. Nor, for that matter, are all ethicists consequentialists, believing that ethical matters are utterly contingent upon outcomes or results.[3] Consequestialism entails a position on social values analogous to the secular economic theories of the eighteenth century. Utilitarians and the more obscure seventeenth century Christian pacifists who proposed, in the words of Ralph Cutworth, that "the greatest benevolence of every rational agent towards all constitutes the happiest state of all, and therefore the common good of all is the supreme law."[4]

While the teleologically disposed ethicists claim that things are right or moral if they have good consequences, ethicists of the obligationist or deontic persuasion take the view that there are absolutes in ethics, that some motives or attitudes—honesty, promise-keeping, respect for persons, and (an example from medical practice and research) "informed consent"—are in themselves morally right, and transcendently so, making of ethics an unflinching duty rather than an exercise of discriminating judgments about anticipated outcomes. The distinction, though, may be only momentary. For, as Dewey argues, when it is recognized that 'motive' is but an abbreviated name for the attitude and predisposition towards ends embodied in disposition, all ground for making a sharp separation between motive and intention falls away."[5]

With these "metaethical" categories in mind, a rereading of the design-theoretical literature, both the abundant prescriptive exportations and explanatory treatises and the infrequent descriptive accounts, might be instructive. Such a review exceeds the scope of the present article. However, a consideration of the deliberations of one notable designer allows us to examine the stability of these metaethical categories for architecture.

Alvar Aalto articulated his own design ethics in a 1940 article published in America, one that deserves more attention from Aalto's acolytes the architectural academy. (Perhaps it was because Aalto's completed works are so sensually gratifying, so compellingly beautiful, that we all slight him by not attending to what he wrote and said.) Aalto believed that the "only way to humanize architecture" was to use methods which always are a combination of technical, physical, and psychological phenomena, never any one of them alone."[6] Moreover, continued Aalto, "technical functionalism is correct only if enlarged to cover even the psychophysical field." Aalto illustrated his

---

Author: Francis T. Ventre, Ph.D.

Credits: First published in *Via 10,* Graduate School of Fine Arts, University of Pennsylvania, Philadelphia, PA. 1990, and reproduced by permission of the publisher. The author thanks Professors Norman Grover, religion, and Scott Poole, architecture, both of Virginia Polytechnic Institute; and Ed Robbins, architecture, of Massachusetts Institute of Technology, who commended on an earlier draft of this essay. Photos, except as noted: Archives of the Society of Finnish Architects (SAFA).

References and notes:

[1] Aristotle. *Nichomachean Ethics.* trans. M. Ostwald. 1962. Indianapolis: Bobbs-Merrill.

[2] C. S. Pierce. 1905. "What Pragmatism Is." *The Monist* 15:161-181. This article is reproduced in many of the anthologies on pragmatism. One is H. S. Thayer, ed. 1970. *Pragmatism: The Classic Writings.* New York: New American Library.

[3] These metaethical categories are distinguished, often with slightly different terminology, in virtually every reference or text on ethics. A recent exposition close to the subject of this paper is T. L. Beauchamp and T. P. Pinkard, eds. 1983. *Ethics and Public Policy: An Introduction to Ethics.* Englewood Cliffs, NJ: Prentice-IIall.

[4] E. Flower. "Ethics of Peace," in *Dictionary of the History of Ideas.* ed. Philip P. Wiener. 1973. Vol. III. New York: Charles Scribners Sons.

[5] J. Dewey. 1960. *Theory of the Moral Life.* New York: Holt, Rinehart and Winston.

Fig. 1. Municipal Library. Viipuri, Finland.
Alvar Aalto, Architect. 1927-35.

Fig. 2. Modulated ceiling to direct sound to rear of
auditorium. Viipuri Municipal Library.

(Notes continued)

[6]
Alvar Aalto. "The Humanizing of Architecture." Technology Review 43, no. 1 (1940). All Aalto quotes are from his article. Aalto scholar Richard Peters of the University of California, Berkeley, told me, while discussing the *Technology Review* article, that Aalto had expressed himself much more vividly on these distinctions in several unpublished writings.

[7]
Internationale Kongresse fur Neues Bauen. 1930. *Die Wobuung fur dos Existenzminimum.* Frankfurt. This document provides comparative analyses of typical plans as well as articles and is reproduced with plan annotations in English, in O. M. Ungers and I. Ungers, eds. 1979. *Documents of Modern Architecture.* Nendeln Liechtenstein Kraus.

[8]
Alvar Aalto. "Rationalism and Man." lecture to the Annual meeting of the Swedish Craft Society, 9 May 1935. Condensed in W. C. Miller. 1984. *Alvar Aalto: An Annotated Bibliography.* New York: Garland Press.

[9]
Pierce's later, more mature articulation of his consequentialism as it relates specifically to ethics takes this view. See Charles Hartschorne and Paul Weiss, eds. 1960-66. C. S. Pierce *Collected Papers.* Cambridge, MA: Belknap Press of Harvard University Press. 5:411-437.

argument with recollections, design sketches and photographs of the Paimio Tuberculosis Sanatorium (1929-33) and the Viipuri Municipal Library (1930- 35). With modesty emboldened by ethical belief, Aalto argued that the responsible designer must inflict no harm on building users, nor even provide environments unsuitable for their use. His specific example was the library's "indirect daylighting" using conical concrete skylights. Aalto was drawn to this design to preempt an ethically unacceptable alternative: To provide [an unmodulated] natural or an artificial light which destroys the human eye or is unsuitable for its use means reactionary architecture even if the building should otherwise be of high constructive value." Here Aalto appears, in ethical terms, to be a consequentialist.

Aalto exercised himself over the total effects of the library's lighting scheme and the sanitorium's patient rooms, and not on their visual appearance alone. Aalto acknowledged that "The examples mentioned here are very tiny problems. But they are very close to the human being and hence become more important than problems of much larger scope." Coming "very close to the human being" signifies Aalto's defection from the abstract utilitarianism promulgated by CIAM and which he had himself earlier proselytized among his fellow Finns. Aalto participated in the 1929 CIAM Conference on the Minimum Dwelling held in Frankfurt.[7] Even the title of the conference suggests a utilitarian maximizing of total benefits (or goods) and minimizing of disbenefits (or harms), all at the level of total social aggregates. There was, moreover, in CIAM (and in *die Neue Sachlichkeit* —the "New Objectivity"—ideology of the time) the obligationist focus on a method that would override all other considerations, such as the evaluation of results. Returning from Frankfurt, Aalto conveyed these ideas in lectures, articles, and newspaper interviews as part of his early efforts to spur Finnish society toward its rendezvous with the modern sensibility.

Within ten years, however, Aalto would shift his attention (and allegiance) from CIAM's abstract statistical aggregates to specific users, seemingly one at a time.[8] Is this moving from one extreme to the other simply apostasy? The latter would be an axiological counterpart to the eclecticism of Aalto's architectural style, his coming to terms with the sense of place and tradition that the then-ascendant International Style aesthetic denied. I believe it is the latter because, as he did stylistically, Aalto in this case fused opposite tendencies into one. In metaethical terms, he adopted the consequentialist approach that renders evaluative choice or judgment according to results. Going beyond that, he appears to have said that even the least harm to the user should override any other consideration—for instance, "high constructive value," as he put it—and rule out the design action entirely. That seems to be an absolute obligational ethic—a designer's general duty, if you will—that overrides any specific consequentialist consideration.[9]

What concerned Aalto was the extent to which designers, whose professional acts bring consequences to others, should be accountable to those others (at Paimio, the patients and their technical agents, the acousticians; at Viipuri, the readers and their technical agents, the visual psychophysicists). This concern prescribed both a universalized obligation and a critical sense of consequences relevant to a specific situational context. Aalto's ethical stance, however, runs counter to some strongly held and long-standing beliefs of practicing or aspiring design professionals. Designers become designers, in part, because it is a professional role that provides a vehicle for personal fulfillment in a time when the organization of economic life threatens to relegate individual self-actualization to the nighttime and weekend fringes of a world that Wordsworth complains is "too much with us."

If I read Aalto correctly, that fulfillment cannot come at the cost of harm to others. The proposition that the gifted and talented are exempt from such rules of proper conduct would have dismayed Aalto as much as it energized Nietzsche and his present-day epigones. But professional designers do submit to such rules; it is part of what distinguishes professionals from amateurs.

Professional ethics

Universally accepted definitions of "the professions" all refer to the professional's concern with the welfare of the wider society in which the professional operates. Personal, individual advantage—even in the sublimated forms of aesthetic gratification or technical mastery—is not to be gained at the expense of the welfare of the larger social unit. Aalto went farther: for him, no single user should suffer.

These sentiments are what distinguish the professional practice of design from, say, the amateur's pursuits in sculpture or woodworking (arts and crafts that have manifest similarities to the concerns of architectural designers). This might have been on Aalto's mind in the passages cited earlier. Most systems of ethics propose or at least address the normative criteria for dealing with moral problems such as the one just suggested: to what extent does the moral person maximize his or her own good and to what extent does she or he maximize the good accruing to others, whether to Aalto's users one at a time, or to the greatest number? Here, indeed, is a contrast with a healthy egoism, an issue we take up again at the close of this discussion.[10]

Most discussions of professional ethics, whether in the classroom or in the professional society, address what William F. May terms "quandaries of practice." The utilitarian calculus may be applied toward the resolution of these quandaries. Its scope, however, would be much narrower than the "all towards all" referred to by Cudworth. It would be counting only the short- and long-term benefits or disbenefits to the professional transaction's immediate participants. Moreover, May points out, "much [professional] behavior is far from exemplary, it is merely customary; ethics is not ethos; morals is [sic] not reducible to mores."[11]

Codes of professional ethics offer guidance to the practitioner seeking to resolve the quandaries encountered in everyday work (for instance, candor in scheduling and cost-estimating or tersgiversating to accommodate client preferences) reducing the backsliding that Professor May warns against. A code of professional ethics renders at this microscale the same kind of inspiration, guidance, and blessing to the commercially advantageous marriage-of-convenience of professional and client that an ecclesiastical ceremony might bring to a marriage. And peccadilloes transpire in ethical firms even as they do in sanctified marriages.

To be sure, these codes of practice are revised from time to time, but not because ethical principles have changed. Rather, expanding technology and evolving social expectations present new dilemmas to the conscientious professional in design and construction.[12] And, it must be reported, many professional societies had changes in codes of ethics thrust upon them in the 1970s by a United States Department of Justice that had read into such codes a "subornation of collusion in restraint of trade" among the subscribing professionals. The American Institute of Architects' code, for instance, was ruled to be in violation of the Sherman Act by a U. S. court in a 1979 civil antitrust suit brought by a member it had suspended for a year.[13] In consequence, the AIA adopted in 1986 and promulgated to its members in 1987 a revised *Code of Ethics and Professional Conduct*. But within a year of its reissuance, the AIA president—no doubt feeling harassed—wrote a "Dear Colleague" letter advising that "the AIA is at present subject of an inquiry by the Antitrust Division of the Department of Justice."[14] Legislating a collective morality is, under the U. S. Constitution, a daunting challenge.

These new situations are familiar to attentive readers of the professional and trade press that regularly offer continuing commentaries by lawyers and jurists in addition to the regular reporting of pivotal

(Notes continued)

[10]
W. F. May. "Professional Ethics: Setting, Terrain, and Teacher." in D. Callahan and S. Bok, eds. 1980. *Ethics Teaching in Higher Education*. New York: Plenum.

[11]
W. F. May. *op. cit*. p. 238

[12]
The February 1988 *Progressive Architecture* "Reader Poll Report" lists 25 specific actions that 1,300 respondents ranked from "unethical actions" to "normal practices" in architecture. An interesting outcome of this poll of readers was the listing of "several situations perceived as either unethical or as normal business practices by substantial portions of the respondents." P/A termed these six actions "split decisions." This reveals the ambiguity of moral issues and underscores the need for continued ethical vigilance. For a discussion of the emergence of novel issues in ethics, see G. Winter. 1966. *Elements for a Social Ethic: Scientific and Ethical Perspectives on Social Process*. New York: Macmillan.

[13]
"Ethics Code Walks Fine Line." ENR (formerly *Engineering News-Record*), 19 June 1986, p. 27.

[14]
The cited version of the code is described in "Convention Approves 'Code of Professional Responsibility.'" *Architecture*. July 1986, pp. 11-12. The letter appears in AIA Memo, 2 September 1987. The most recent revision of the Code of Ethics & Professional Conduct appears in AIArchitect, May 1997, the Institute's monthly newsletter. Washington, DC: American Institute of Architects.

Fig. 3. Town Hall. Saynatsalo, Finland. Alvar Aalto, Architect. 1949-52.

Fig. 4. Expression of structural truss. Saynatsalo Town Hall.

(Notes continued)

[15]
M. Wachs. 1985. *Ethics in Planning*. New Brunswick, NJ: Center for Urban Policy Research, Rutgers University; A. E. Stamps. 1986. "Teaching Design Ethics." *Architectural Technology*. May/June 1986; H. D. Robertson. 1987. "Developing Ethics Education in the Construction Education Program." *Proceedings of the 23rd Annual Conference of the Associated Schools of Construction*. West Lafayette, IN: Purdue University.

[16]
W. F. May. *op. cit.* p. 238.

court cases or arbitration decisions affecting professionals at work. Teachers of professional ethics courses in schools of planing, design, and construction or, more typically, teachers of the professional practice courses incorporating ethics education, make use of this case material also.[15]

The cases typically encountered in professional ethics discussions tend to focus on the private (in the sense of individual) success of morally responsible professionals. I believe there is a much stronger argument for moving ethical discussion away from the particularities of the individual resolving a moral dilemma. I would propose to move the discussion—and the search for May's "inspiration of exemplary performance"—away from the isolated conscientious designer as an individual and toward the institutions within which all professionals—both the morally aware and the ethically obtuse—must operate.[16]

This institutional approach would direct attention to the ethical values and power relations reflected in the very rule structures and modes of professional discourse within which individual decisions of conscience must work themselves out. All such cases occur and are resolved in a social reference larger and wider than even the most elaborate quandary that the private practitioner experiences. I propose that the morality of *social* as contrasted with *individual* ethics confronts the architectural designer (and indeed the entire building community) most vividly in the formation and execution of the public policies that frame and create the conditions for design and construction.

Regulation: social ethics reified and objectified
Societies, usually acting through governments, preempt entire classes of design decisions, restricting and sometimes totally removing areas of design freedom, reserving those decisions to society as a whole, acting through regulatory institutions.[17] This is now done routinely, in all the world's advanced economies. Less developed societies also regulate design and construction, but they tend to employ more diffuse, culture-wide mechanisms rather than special-purpose regulatory agencies.

Regulations, broadly considered, are the means by which societies, using the coercive powers of government, mediate the private actions of individuals. Of course, private actions know other limitations as well. Commercial transactions between informed individuals, for example, are limited by the mutualy-agreed-upon contract. And it is usually these latter quotidian transactions that are grist for the professional practice course's "ethics case study" mill. But contrast those commercial transactions with regulation: the reach of public policy is broad where commercial law is limited; public regulations are coercive where commercial contracts are subject to mutual consent.

Because they are intended to be universally and uniformly applied and coercively enforced, regulations must be carefully circumscribed either by stature, legal precedent, or (more significant for innovative designers) by technical knowledge. Design and construction are, in short, regulated industries. Building regulations reflect, however imperfectly, a society-wide understanding of what that society expects of its buildings and their environs. Only when that expectation is shared consensually does it become, at least in democratic states, a moral imperative enforced upon all.

The operative term here is consensus, meaning more than a majority but less than unanimity. And here, exactly, is where postmodernism is most instructively contrasted with modernism. To a modernist (for example, the CIAM-era Aalto) a social ethic must be objectified. That is, it must "[attain] a reality that confronts its original producers as a facticity external to and other than themselves."[18] This modernist objectification renders ethical beliefs universal and accessible to rational method. Otherwise, the modernist argument continues, ethics would be merely a state of individual and subjective (and possibly solipsistic) consciousness.

Table 1. An approximate chronology of the widening of the building regulatory purview in the United States.

Date	Objective	Method	Initiating Advocates
1880	Curtail typhoid and noisome nuisance	Protected water supply; sewage treatment	Sanitary engineers, public health physicians
1890	Improve housing and health	Indoor plumbing	Housing reformers, plumbers
1900	Prevent conflagration	Sprinkler protection of individual structures and fire service to multi-building districts	Fire insurance underwriters
1920	Continue fire to building of origin	Fire endurance concept	Fire researchers, fire services, fire underwriters
1965	Continue fire to room and floor of origin	Fire zonation	Fire researchers, fire services, fire underwriters
1975	Energy conservation	Energy-use targets for overall building and/or components	Resource conservation groups
1978	Historic preservation	Alternative regulatory devices	Local and architectural history buffs (and professionals)
1980	Accessibility for handicapped	Performance requirements or perspecitve geometrics	Architects (led voluntary efforts in 1950s), paralyzed veterans, disabled citizens, gerontologists
1990	Indoor air quality	Air management, real-time monitoring	Office worker unions, health organizations

Constructionists in philosophy and deconstructionists in literary studies, both of whom (but especially the latter) have influenced recent academic architectural discourse, have only recently separated fact from value and are dubious about separating knowledge from action.[19] Aalto, in his mature years, adopted what we now recognize to be this postmodernist program. He seems to have abandoned the search for universal solutions and sought situationally or contextually relevant standards for his own work. In so doing, Aalto anticipated Michel Foucault's arguments in *The Birth of the Clinic*.[20] Instead of evaluating behavior (or, one could say, candidate designs) relative to idealized, universalistic norms, Foucault proposes that situationally relevant standards be employed.

But what keeps situationally relevant standards from degenerating into solipsism? A partial response (to be amplified later in this essay) is that designers do not work in isolation and are enjoined from self-indulgence by governmental fiat, by economic imperatives (referring both to tighter building budgets and more knowledgeable clients), by constituent and adjacent technologies, and by social sanction.

But who historically has assumed the task of inventing or interpreting what buildings and environments should do and be? Once that vision is articulated, who negotiates it through the wider public discourse that legitimizes emergent community values or public policies in democracies with representative governments? Table I shows a cursory chronology of nearly a century of community interventions into design and construction practice in the United States, providing some perspective.

Regulations have evolved (primarily) to meet newly sanctioned social needs and (secondarily) to take advantage of new technological opportunities. From the initial retributory penalties of the Code of Hammurabi (1955–1912 BC) that exacted a sentence of death from any builder whose building's failure resulted in the owner's death[21] through the Assizes of 1189 that proscribed the use of thatch in the densely populated portions of London,[22] the regulatory climate changed slowly. But the explosive growth of cities in the nineteenth century forced both a broadening of societal ends and an institutionalization of regulatory means from the 1880s to the present.

Table 1 reveals that the regulatory purview widened to embrace expanding notions of public health, safety, and welfare. These amplifications of the police powers of the state are traceable to both a deeper understanding of phenomena linking environmental stressors of various kinds to health effects and to the effective publicizing employed by public interest advocates near the turn of the twentieth century.

Although J. Archea and B. R. Connell have shown that the specific technical rationales for some of these Progressive-era reforms are erroneous in the light of current knowledge, the regulations promulgated at the time remain largely intact.[23] Some continue to be enforced. What might account for this persistence in the absence of supporting evidence? Is it sheer bureaucratic inertia? I nominate instead the potency of the initial images used by the Progressive-era pamphleteers.

Let me illustrate: at the same session of the Environmental Design Research Association's 17th Annual Meeting that was addressed by Archea and Connell, David Hattis displayed Jacob Riis's images, including "Bandits' Roost" at 59 1/2 Mulberry Street, taken on February 12, 1888, that bestowed on these dwellings their notoriety! The effect on the EDRA audience of mature researchers was striking. After 90 years and more, those photographs still retained their shock value. So much so that it may be unlikely that the regulations the helped promulgate will soon be repealed. It is not bureaucratic inertia but persistence in the public that keeps these regulations intact.

Are regulations reversible? In principle, they are; legislatures can formally repeal regulatory statutes and administrative agencies can

---

(Notes contiued)

[17]
This section's arguments, only outlined here, are amplified in F. T. Ventre. "The Policy Environment for Environment and Behavior Research." in E. H. Zube and G. T. Moore. eds. 1989. *Advances in Environment, Behavior, and Design.* New York: Plenum Press.

[18]
P. L. Berger. 1969. *The Sacred Canopy: Elements of a Sociological Theory of Religion.* New York: Doubleday-Anchor.

[19]
J. Lave. 1988. *Cognition in Practice.* Cambridge, England: Cambridge University Press; J. Coulter. 1979. *The Social Construction of Mind.* London: Macmillan; A. R. Louch. 1966. *Explanation and Human Action.* Berkeley, CA: University of California Press.

[20]
Michel Foucault 1973. *The Birth of the Clinic: An Archaeology of Medical Perception.* New York: Pantheon.

achieve the same effect by selective enforcement.[24] But in practice, regulations are all but irreversible. Allen Bloom's reading of the history of liberal political through from Hobbes and Locke to John Stuard Mill and John Dewey concludes that:

> It was possible to expand the space exempt from legitimate social and political regulation only by contracting the claims to moral and political knowledge. . . . In the end it begins to appear that full freedom [to live as one pleases] can be attained only when there is no such knowledge at all.[25]

Regulation: professional values collectivized

So it is the state of knowledge—moral and political knowledge according to Bloom; and practical knowledge, too, which according to Dewey has a moral force of its own—that drives regulation's juggernaut. But whose knowledge? The regulatory expansion after the 1920s seems to owe more to a public will rallied and given form by the cultural preferences and superior technical knowledge of articulate minorities who could link that preference and knowledge to wide social concerns.

Histories of the professions tell of their addressing the widely shared needs of the societies they have served.[26] Shared needs often began as latent, unexpressed, perhaps even unconscious tendencies or longings that were given form, reinforcement, and articulation by the profession with cognizance over the particular domain of ideas.[27] Rendering this service to society helps to reinforce the profession's status by evoking a social warrant for its existence on terms highly favorable to the profession. This drawing out of a latent societal mandate is a realization of the sociopolitical realm of (Jean Baptiste) Say's law that "supply creates its own demand," originally formulated to explain the dynamics of economic markets.

Modern-day occupations and professions express their specific concerns not only to their employers or clients but also to the social organizations or governmental agencies, usually regulatory agencies, that have cognizance over the activity in question. Working through the cognizant organization enables the prescribing profession to address all of society and not just those entities (either organizational or individual) with whom they are joined in a specific, contractually defined commercial relation. And the subject that each of the prescribing professions addresses is a core value of the initiating professional (for physicians, wellness; for accountants, fidelity and accuracy; for airline pilots, safety of passenger and crew). That core is then shown to be widely shared in the society at large. This enables the initiating profession to establish its hegemony over that aspect of social life: the entire society then becomes a collective client for the services of the collective profession.

However, the tactic of gaining wider public support for architectural values through congenial regulation is not likely to work today for three reasons: the first having to do with the public's skepticism of government; the second with the core values of the architectural culture; and the third, the widening gap between architecture and its public. A discussion of the first two reasons follows; the third recurs at the conclusion of this paper.

Regarding the public's skepticism of government: twenty years of Naderite public interest litigation has instructed consumers and even political liberals to an attitude once associated mainly with political conservatives: be more skeptical of regulatory agencies and, especially, the extent to which they may be "captured" by the very groups they were initially intended to regulate.[28]

The second reason that architects are unlikely to make strategic use of regulatory policies, even to advance their livelihoods, requires some elaboration. Architects are unlikely to employ this method is not because it is manipulative or that they are insufficiently cynical. Rather, a positive regulatory strategy to institutionalize the profession's core

_____(Notes continued)_____

[21]
Code of Hammurabi. trans. R. F. Harper. 1903. Chicago: University of Chicago Press.

[22]
R. S. Ferguson. 1974. The Development of a Knowledge-Based Code. Ottawa: National Research Council Canada, Division of Building Research. 426:2, citing Corporation of London Records Office Liber de Antiquis Legibus, folios 45–58.

[23]
J. Archea and B. R. Connell. "Architecture as an Instrument of Public Health: Mandating Practice Prior to the Conduct of Systematic Inquiry." in Proceedings of EDRA 17. Atlanta, GA, April, 1986. Oklahoma City, OK: Environmental Design Research Association.

[24]
D. J. Galligan. 1986. Discretionary Powers: A Legal Study of Official Discretion. New York: Oxford University Press. How regulations operate in Chicago is described in B. D. Jones. 1985. Governing Buildings and Building Government: A New Perspective on the Old Party. University, AL: University of Alabama Press.

[25]
Alan Bloom. 1987. The Closing of the American Mind. New York: Simon and Schuster. p. 28.

[26]
Sociologies of the professions convey this message. A review of the field is T. J. Johnson. 1972. Professions and Power. London: Macmillan. A sociological analysis emphasizing the primacy of autonomy in the architectural case is M. S. Larson. 1979. The Rise of Professionalism. Berkeley, CA: University of California Press.

[27]
G. Gurvitch. 1971. The Social Frameworks of Knowledge. New York: Harper and Row; K. Mannheim. 1936. Ideology and Utopia. New York. Harcourt Brace; D. Bloor. 1976. Knowledge and Social Imagery. London: Routledge and Kegan Paul; W. J. Goode pointed out that no social mandate will be forthcoming if the profession's values are too far removed from the community's value consensus in "Community Within a Community: The Professions." American Sociological Review 22 (1957): p. 197.

[28]
F. Sabatier. "Social Movements and Regulatory Agencies: Towards a More Adequate—and Less Pessimistic—Theory of Client Capture." Policy Sciences 6 (1975): pp. 301–342.

values would not be adopted because the furtherance of such an aggressive regulatory scheme (even it were to materially benefit the architectural profession) is in fundamental opposition to a devoutly held aspiration of the professional designer: to realize one's own creative vision.

Architecture is singular among the professions in its pursuit of this aspiration. This could explain why transactions over which the designers nominally preside, and from which they earn their livelihood, are regulated by agencies largely responsive to others, principally the special interest advocates of the building products vendors and of the building owning, -insuring, or -using groups in society.[29] It is these non-designers who have established and now maintain the rule structures and modes of discourse within which design is done.[30]

Ironically, this situation, the circumscription of design freedom, has come about because of the higher value that designers place on the liberty to operate with less hindrance from socially imposed restraints, whether those restraints are in the form of codified knowledge of the world around us—which explains both the perennial deprecation of technical studies and its consequent, the only recent emergence of research activities in architecture schools—or the more obvious hindrance visited upon them by regulatory institutions. This reluctance to discipline talent or, if you like, creative expression, is an inherited trait, a part of the profession's intellectual endowment, so to speak, and further conditioned by academic preparation and later professional socialization. Consider, for a start, the family tree. Architects are, in spite of themselves, siblings of Gadamerian aestheticism, children of Heideggerian existentialism, nieces and nephews of Nietzsche (an antiformal, anticlassicizing opponent of codified moral theories), and grandchildren of Schillerian Romanticism that sought through creative expression alone both truth itself and rescue from alienation. Little of our recent intellectual heritage is culturally conservative, and regulation is nothing if not culturally conservative.

Given this heritage, it is little wonder that designers have ceded so utilitarian and rationalistic a thing as the building regulatory system to others, principally the agents of building products manufacturers and suppliers. Regulatory reform is a slow-moving, painstaking, co-operative endeavor performed anonymously and, consequently, is unlikely to attract the participation of those whose important secondary reference is to personal expression. Architects—who like to consider themselves artists but do not want to be paid like them—only reluctantly concede that they operate as a regulated industry within highly codified institutional structures and modes of discourse.

In the architectural academy, the feeling is even stronger. There regulation is anathema, to be cursed, reviled, and shunned (except for that obligatory lecture in that same obligatory course in professional practice referred to in the first paragraph of this essay). This reluctance breeds alienation and withdrawal and designers, refraining from controlling the system, are instead controlled by it. There are exceptions. The late Fazlur Khan, a gifted structural designer at Skidmore Owings and Merrill in Chicago, was acutely perceptive about regulation and applied himself to regulatory reform efforts in that city.[31] But our Romantic heritage brings us, at worst, into obdurate opposition to or, at best, ambivalence toward the aspect of regulation that is, ethically speaking, its sinister side: paternalism, the "imposing [of] constraints on an individual's liberty for the purpose of promoting his or her own good."[32]

Regulations are in every way paternalistic and not the least deferential: the verb forms they employ are in the imperative mood, leaving no doubt about who defers to whom. With an appropriate preamble prevening, building and development regulations really do tell one and all what is permitted in the built environment and, more emphatically, what is not. Moreover, these pronouncements are enforceable with the coercive power of the state. But because architects tend to

(Notes continued)

[29]
F. T. Ventre. 1973. "Social Control of Technological Innovation: The Regulation of Building Construction." Ph.D. dissertation, Massachusetts Institute of Technology.

[30]
A. D. King, ed. 1980. *Buildings and Society: Essays on the Social Development of the Built Environment.* London: Routledge and Kegan Paul; P. L. Knox. "The Social Production of the Built Environment." *Ekistics* 295 (July/August 1982): pp. 291–297. Also see P. L. Knox, ed. 1988. *The Design Professions and the Built Environment.* London: Croom Helm.

[31]
From personal communications during the years that Dr. Khan served on the National Academies of Science/Engineering-administered Technical Evaluation Panels that "peer reviewed" the programs of the National Bureau of Standards/Center for Building Technology.

[32]
D. F. Thompson. "Paternalism in Medicine, Law, and Public Policy" in D. Callahan and S. Bok, eds. 1980. *Ethics Teaching in Higher Education.* New York: Plenum.

Fig. 5. Technical University, Otaniemi, Finland. Alvar Aalto, Architect. 1964. Photo: Marja Palmqvist Watson

follow the egoist-libertarian rather than the utilitarian-collectivist conception of social ethics (remember Aalto's warning), they are ambivalent about taking up anything like fundamental reform of an essentially imperative instrument. This means that regulatory matters—social ethics in action—are largely in the hands of others.

It was not always this way. The chronology of Table 1 reveals that designers have brought important issues into the public consciousness and then helped organize society-wide support for public policies of sound moral principle. Earnest instruction on architecture, its pleasures and its effects, was successfully imparted to large publics in America several times in this century. Where these matters bore on public safety, health, and welfare, the technically informed discussion was energized with an unmistakable moral fervor. And the regulatory powers of the state were subsequently guided by a specific moral vision that had first been articulated by designers and other building professionals and later endorsed by a much wider public. Consider California and how Sym van der Ryn and Barry Wasserman, in their successive tenures (during the administration of Governor Jerry Brown) made the Office of the State Architect a "bully pulpit" for climate- and user-responsive design policies and regulations not only for California but for the nation.

The obscuring of a profession's core values

Other professions have successfully proselytized their core values to the wider society. These engagements of the public have provided strong, if perhaps transient, boosts to each profession's welfare. Why then has the public embraced so few architectural values as a basis for public policy? Martin Filler, reflecting on the one-hundred-year effort to enlist a public constituency for architectural values through criticism in the public as well as the professional press, could identify only three recent successes: "historic preservation, ecology, and zoning."[33] What accounts for this lapse and, more important, how can it be remedied? Filler says:

> One essential approach is to attempt to break down the wall of professional hocus-pocus that surrounds both the profession of architecture and much of the writing about it. To a greater extent than pertains in media that produce works that can be kept behind closed doors but still be enjoyed by people, architecture virtually demands the kind of consensus that can emerge only if the public is constantly instructed in the concepts and concerns that ought to inform architectural initiative and decision making.[34]

But the chief articulators and expositors of American architecture's "concepts and concerns" seem to be withdrawing from the concerns of public life. This is indeed ironic for just when the principal professional society, the AIA, actively sought wider public participation by creating both a new category of membership and a publication to serve it, architecture's wider conversation—as articulated by the profession's academic wing and then promulgated by the writers and critics who retail that message to the nation's cultural elite—has veered sharply away from the comprehensible ordering of the tangible, palpable, physical environment as its main topic and has turned instead into the forest of exotic conceits and arcana from such fields as literary criticism and, somewhat earlier, semiotics.[35] Highbrow architectural criticism was, until just yesterday, an exegesis on "deconstructionist" critics, notably Jacques Derrida and Michel Foucault.[36] Deconstructionism, by the way, does not mean tearing down or never erecting a building; it is a literary theory whose main message seems to be that literature can carry no message because the meaning of language is itself ultimately undecidable. Deconstructionism teaches that a:

> "secondary" or "supplemental" text is already implicit within a "primary" or "host" text, such that it becomes difficult to establish clear boundaries between the two texts so related.[37]

(Notes continued)

[33]
M. Filler. "American Architecture and Its Criticism: Reflections on the State of the Arts." in T. A. Marder, ed. 1985. *The Critical Edge: Controversy in Recent American Architecture.* Cambridge, MA: MIT Press. p. 31.

[34] *ibid.*

[35]
For a sample of architecture interpreted in the manner of the literary art, see *VIA 8. Architecture and Literature*, published for the University of Pennsylvania's Graduate School of Fine Arts by Rizzoli, New York, 1986. For an early view of architecture interpreted in the manner of semiotics, see G. Broadbent et al., eds. 1980. *Meaning and Behavior in the Built Environment.* New York: Wiley.

[36]
J. Derrida 1983. *Margins of Philosophy.* Chicago: University of Chicago Press. In this work, Derrida says it is a "mistake to believe" that a text may be deciphered without a "prerequisite and highly complex elaboration." For an elaboration on Derrida and his relation to antecedents and his contemporary Michel Foucault, see A. Megill. 1985. *Prophets of Extremity: Nietzsche, Heidegger, Foucault, Derrida.* Berkeley, CA: University of California Press. How Foucault's structures and discourses play out in planning and design is discussed in S. T. Rowels, "Knowledge-Power and Professional Practice." in P. L. Knox, ed. 1988. *The Design Professions and the Built Environment.* London: Croom Helm. pp. 175–207. I have found Foucault to be more provocative in his interviews. A good sampling of his ideas that illuminate regulation and regulatory institutions are interviews edited by Colin Gordon. 1980. *Power/Knowledge.* New York: Pantheon.

[37]
D. H. Fisher. "Dealing with Derrida." *Journal of Aesthetics and Art Criticism* 45 (Spring 1987): p. 298.

Under deconstructionism's method, texts, and by extension, buildings and their environs, are to be assayed by eliminating any metaphysical or ethnocentric assumptions through an active role of defining meaning, sometimes by reliance on new word construction, etymology, puns and other word play.[38]

The deconstructionist critical movement curtails the centuries-long (at lease since Alberti) suzerainty of the creator, be it author or designer. Hermeneutics, the art and science of interpretation, of which deconstructionism is but a part, is now the locus of creative endeavor. Indeed, the "interpreter's creative activity is more important than the text," laments Allen Bloom in his thoroughly dyspeptic best-selling 1987 critique of American higher education, "there is no text, only interpretation."[39]

James Marston Fitch, in an *Architectural Record* article, several years ago decried this flight from immediately-sensed environmental data among architectural writers and thinkers at its incipience. Michael Benedikt has recently argued for a "High Realism" that celebrates materiality over abstraction.[40] Jacques Barzun has attacked increasingly opaque literary analysis that is as far removed from the cognitive experience of the reader as hermeneutics is from the perceptions of people living and working in the environments that the architectural intelligensia has so recently deconstructed.[41]

So arcane and remote from palpable experience have architectural theory, criticism, and method become that the once-salutary dissimilarity between architecture (the discipline) in the world of the academy and architecture (the profession) in the world of practice is widening to the point of total discordance.[42] A signed editorial in *Architecture*, made this point vividly, citing a "wide diversity between schools and practitioners in the very ways they look at architecture. They differ in their perspectives, their agendas, their points of emphasis." [43] Given the dynamic of university faculty recruitment, promotion, and retention and the search for academic and scholarly respectability on the one hand and the imperatives of commercial survival based on technical reliability, fiscal accountability, and clear-headed probity all wrapped in attractive packaging on the other, the divergence is likely to be greater in the future.[44] This bifurcation is likely to induce an early cynicism among students, a truly regrettable outcome against which all teachers and practitioners must strive.

Not only is architectural discourse growing remote from the general public's experience of buildings and their environs. The turn toward the arcane has won neither adherents nor recognition from among those whom E. D. Hirsch, Jr. has called the "culturally literate."[45] John Morris Dixon analyzed Hirsch's sixty-four-page list of terms that culturally competent Americans should know and was annoyed to find only three (none of them esoteric) from architecture's vocabulary.[46] Thomas Hines assayed over seventy articles in journals of opinion reacting either "positively" or "negatively" toward Tom Wolfe's attack on the prevailing values of America's architectural culture.[47] Hines found the controversy salutary and himself right in the middle, chiding Wolfe for "thin research and . . . reckless writing" and scolding the architectural intelligentsia for "self-defeating arrogance . . . toward the public or publics they are committed to serve."[48] So the architectural profession may find itself thrice alienated: from the world of commerce, from its academic wing, and from its primary patrons, the core (and corps) of reflective, cultured Americans.[49]

If the core values of the profession are to inform, instruct, and thereby insinuate themselves as the core values of the society—the path taken by other expansionist professions stoutly assisted by their academic wings—then some important changes need to be made. Needed, that is, if architecture is to take the offensive, enlarging its constituency by realizing Hine's hoped-for outcome of the *From Bauhaus to Our House* controversy; namely, a "greater public knowledge and aware-

Fig. 6. Skylighting of main auditorium. Otaniemi Technical University. Photo: Marja Palmqvist Watson

(Notes continued)

[38]
Random House Dictionary of the English Language. 2d Ed., unabridged. New York: Random House (1987): p. 519.

[39]
Bloom, Alan. *op. cit.* [Note 25] p. 379.

[40]
J. M. Fitch. "Physical and Metaphysical in Architectural Criticism." *Architectural Record,* July 1982, pp. 114–119; M. Benedikt. 1987. *For an Architecture of Reality.* New York: Lumen Books.

[41]
J. Barzun. "A Little Matter of Sense." *New York Times Book Review.* 21 June 1987.

[42]
Stanford Anderson elaborated the distinction between the profession and the discipline in "On Criticism." *Places* 4, no. 1, (187): 7–8.

[43]
Donald Canty. *Architecture.* August 1987, p. 29.

[44]
Robert Gutman. "Educating Architects: Pedagogy and the Pendulum." *The Public Interest* 80 (Summer 1985), pp. 67–91; L. Nesmith. "Economist Choate and Others Explore Economy and Market." *Architecture.* August 1987.

[45]
E. D. Hirsch, Jr. 1987. *Cultural Literacy: What Every American Needs to Know.* Boston: Houghton Mifflin. "The list" runs from p. 152 to p. 215.

[46]
J. M. Dixon. signed editorial. *Progressive Architecture.* July 1987. p. 7.

[47]
T. Hines. "Conversing with the Compound." *Design Book Review.* Fall 1987, pp. 13–19.

[48]
ibid, p. 19.

[49]
L. Nesmith, op. cit. [note 44] p. 14, describes the current symptoms. Underlying causes are suggested in F. T. Ventre. "Building in Eclipse, Architecture in Secession" in *Progressive Architecture,* December 1982, pp. 58–61.

ness of architectural issues and a greater professional sense of responsibility to that public."[50]

Is this a realistic expectation? Yes and no: the public is not so apathetic as before. But an apathetic public may be preferred to one aroused to hostility and cynicism; witness the reaction, both public and professional, to Prince Charles's philippics on postwar architecture, urban design, and planning in Great Britain.[51]

If the prospects for a positive strategy of professional proselytizing are, at best, mixed, then what is the prognosis for a defensive strategy, for defending the profession's values, status and, ultimately, markets from encroachment by others? Take the last issue: encroachment. Architects sense that the interior designers, facilities managers, and other technical specialists are intent on poaching on the profession's

territory.[52] A unified profession, of course, could muster a stouter defense. And, as the guilds of old assured themselves a monopoly of certain trades by presenting to the medieval burghers the promise of a guaranteed minimum level of competence, so do modern professions seek the same assurance by restricting (through licensing) access to the market for building design and consulting services. So, we are back now to regulation, the subject of this essay.

A course of action

We confront the issue of social ethics: how should a society, and specifically its governments, be organized and what specific policies should those organizations pursue in the matter of the design and construction of the built and induced environment? And which of those design and construction concerns are central enough to that society's core beliefs and aspirations to be recast as moral imperatives and enforced upon all? Of course, the principal organizations representing the design and construction industries do address themselves to legislative bodies developing broad policies with respect to social practice of all kinds. To the point for the present discussion, however, is the extent to which designers and the organizations and the professional peers that speak for them will tackle policies that bear more directly on the central concerns and core values of the design community.

What are today's architectural core values, and what structures mediate the sustained relation between the profession and the laity? As for values, a new beginning may be at hand: in 1987 the AIA launched "The Search for Shelter . . . to confront the plight of America's homeless and dispossessed."[53] But where may the mediating structures be found?

I submit that they are among the institutions that regulate all the parties affected by architecture, not only those involved in it professionally or self-consciously. Economic relations of the latter type are generally regulated by the commercial law enforced by the threat of criminal prosecution and civil litigation and by the conventions of business practice enforced by custom; these relations apply to the specific architectural professional—whether an individual or a firm—and a specific, fee-paying client that has engaged that professional. But what I am addressing here is something larger: a "meta-narrative" within which the entire society acts as a collective client for the services of the collective profession.

More extensive relations of this type have been successfully initiated and then managed by other occupations in the past but much less successfully by the profession of architecture today for the reasons already specified plus one more: the postmodern sensibility that dominates academic architectural discourse today manifests an "incredulity toward meta-narratives."[54] This incredulity may lie at the base of the public's current skepticism—given voice by Prince Charles toward architecture and planning.[55]

The rules for tomorrow's design and construction are yet to be written. But these rules most certainly *will* be written, whether by enlightened and sensitive designers intent on the creation of environments that enhance human potential for knowing a good life or by others who do not share that aspiration.

Ought not the core values of architecture then serve as a basis for a social ethic for the built and induced environment? The true test of our commitment to those values is in our readiness to share them widely. How to turn a universalistic, largely negative and coercive authority—the regulatory system—into a positive stimulus for achieving highly differentiated environments that inform and liberate is no easy task. Nor is it ever completed. But it will be difficult for society to get what it needs and wants from its architecture and just as difficult for architects to provide what is needed and wanted without undertaking these enabling actions.

_____*(Notes continued)*_____

[50]
T. Hines, *op. cit.* p. 13.

[51]
H. Raines. "Defying Tradition: Prince Charles Recasts His Role," *The New York Times Magazine*. 21 February 1988, 23ff; P. Goldberger ("Architecture View" column), "Should the Prince Send Modernism to the Tower?" *The New York Times*. March 13, 1988, p. H33.

[52]
"P/A Reader Poll: Fees and Encroachment." *Progressive Architecture*. November 1987, 15–19. Analyses fees and fears of U. S. architectural firms facing increasing competition from other providers of design services. The profession's response is documented in "Licensing Interior Designers: tutorial on AIA position." *F. W. Dodge Construction News*. July 1987. p. 35.

[53]
D. J. Hackl. "President's Annual Report." *AIA Memo*. January 1988.

[54]
J. F. Lyotard. 1984. *The Postmodern Condition: A Report on Knowledge*. Minneapolis: University of Minnesota Press.

[55]
"Prince Charles Criticizes City Planning 'Disasters.'" *Christian Science Monitor*. 7 March 1988, p. 2. Said he, "Although there is no one who appreciates or values experts more than I do . . . it is important not to be intimidated by them."

3
Bioclimatic design

Donald Watson
Murray Milne

Summary: Bioclimatic design is based on analysis of the climate and ambient energy represented by sun, wind, temperature and humidity. Bioclimatic design that is responsive to specific regions and microclimates thus provides an enduring inspiration for architecture.

Lamasery. Himalayan Kingdom of Bhutan. Wind-protected, sun exposed courtyard creates a moderated microclimate.

Key words: bioclimatic design, Building Bioclimatic Chart, meteorological data, psychrometric chart.

1 Introduction

Timeless lessons of climate-responsive design are evident in indigenous and traditional architecture throughout the world. Bioclimatic design has developed out of a sensitivity to ecological and regional contexts and the need to conserve energy and environmental resources. Bioclimatic approaches to architecture offer a way to design for long-term and sustainable use of environmental and material resources.

Bioclimatic design was promoted in a series of publications in the 1950s (Fitch and Siple 1952 and Olgyay and Olgyay 1957). In using the term "bioclimatic," architectural design is linked to the biological, physiological and psychological need for health and comfort. Bioclimatic approaches to architecture attempt to create comfort conditions in buildings by understanding the microclimate and resulting design strategies that include natural ventilation, daylighting, and passive heating and cooling.

The architecture of early modern architects—Walter Gropius, Marcel Breuer, Le Corbusier, and Antonin Raymond, among others—recognized the design inspiration offered by site-specific climatic variables and indigenous exemplars. When air-conditioning systems became widely available at the end of the 1950s, interest in bioclimatic design suddenly became less evident in professional and popular literature. The topic reemerged in response to energy shortages of the 1970s—when "passive solar design" became the popular term to described the approach, at first emphasizing solar heating but broadened to include passive cooling and daylighting. With the emergence of global environmental concerns of the 1990s—recognizing that reduced fossil fuel consumption has "cascading" effects in reducing pollution and global warming—bioclimatic design was enlarged to include landscape, water, and waste nutrient recovery. In these approaches, architecture and environmental systems are conceived as an integral part of sustaining the health and ecology of building, site and region.

Some bioclimatic design techniques—earth-sheltering is an example—can contribute to comfort and reduce both heating and cooling loads year-round. Other techniques are useful only part of the year. The effectiveness of passive solar heating, for example, is very specific to the need for heating and otherwise needs to be tempered by sunshading

and thermal mass. Natural ventilation can provide comfort in all seasons, especially in summer when it can reduce or eliminate the need for air conditioning in some climates. Costly mechanical (refrigerant) cooling is often required simply because a building's unprotected window orientation or uninsulated roofs turn it into a "solar oven," collecting more heat than is needed or tolerable. The effect is evident inside most any west-facing glass window-wall. Even when temperatures and local breezes create comfort conditions outside, design that ignores its climatic context will result in a building that is both uncomfortable and wastes energy.

All buildings experience interruptions of conventional energy availability, often coincident with weather extremes and disasters. A prudent approach to design of all buildings would provide bioclimatic means to insure at least subsistence levels of heating, cooling, and daylighting for comfort, health and safety. For the long-term, in which conventional energy shortages and emergencies are unpredictable but perhaps inevitable, buildings without natural heating, cooling and lighting impose serious liabilities on occupants and owners. In July 1995, the city of Chicago experienced 700 heat-related deaths during five days of dangerously high temperatures and humidity and low wind speeds. A disproportionate number of these fatalities occurred among older, infirm and inner city residents on the top floors of apartments without mechanical or ventilative cooling (Center for Building Science 1996). The single-most available strategy to mitigate excessive overheating in such cases is ventilation, to prevent buildings from acting like solar ovens. Related bioclimatic techniques in roof design and surfacing could also greatly reduce such liabilities.

2 Characterization of regional climates

Characterization of different climatic zones are typically reported, for example, to indicate critical zones for landscape planting, agriculture and horticulture, based on the species-specific climatic requirements for germination and growth. It is possible to posit an equivalent characterization of "building bioclimatic regions," based on the appropriateness and comparative effectiveness for various bioclimatic design techniques.

Authors: Donald Watson, FAIA and Murray Milne

Credits: Baruch Givoni and Kenneth Labs contributed immeasurably to the development of the authors' work described in this article. Figs. 1, 2, 3, 6 and 7a are reproduced by permission of *Architectural Graphic Standards*. Eighth Edition. John Ray Hoke, Jr. editor. New York: John Wiley & Sons.

References: Milne, Murray. 1997. *Energy Design Tools.* Web Page, Department of Architecture and Urban Design. University of California Los Angeles (UCLA). http://www.aud.ucla.edu/energy-design-tools (If this web address changes, e-mail: webmaster@aud.ucla.edu).

Watson, Donald and Kenneth Labs. 1983, revised 1993. *Climatic Building Design.* New York: McGraw-Hill.

Additional references follow at the end of this article.

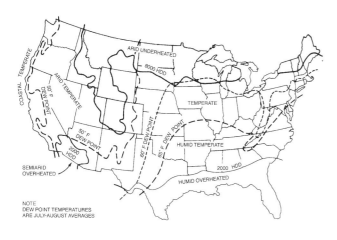

Fig. 1. U. S. regions based on bioclimatic design conditions.

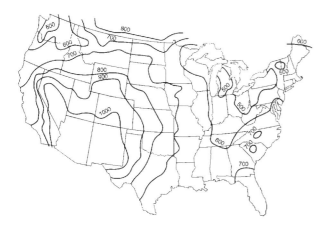

Fig. 2. Passive solar heating potential of south-facing windows (Btu/SF/day). Source: Dr. Douglas Balcomb, National Renewable Energy Laboratory.

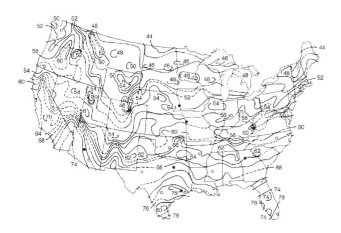

Fig. 3. Deep ground temperature (F) Source: National Well Water Association.

Fig. 1 indicates an approximate characterization of United States regions, within which similar bioclimatic design principles and practices predominate. While computer analysis and on-site monitoring now gives the designer the capacity to analyze each locale and microclimate, the regional characterization offers a way to understand macroclimatic factors, including continental and regional geography, proximity to mountain ranges and water bodies.

Indicated in Fig. 1, regions exceeding 8,000 annual heating degree days (HDD) are defined as predominately "underheated," that is, case the need for heating predominates, such as through direct solar gain and energy conservation. The large temperate area between 2,000-8,000 HDD has both heating and cooling requirements that must be balanced to assure that design techniques favored for one condition are compatible with all others. Sun-tempering (that is, modest but careful use of south-facing windows) may provide a substantial portion of winter heating, but must also be dimensioned to provide summer shading. Regions with less than 2,000 HDD require little heating in comparison to cooling and are thus defined as "overheated."

The relative effectiveness of passive cooling strategies follows in part the climatic characterization from "arid" to "humid." That is, the suitability of ventilation and evaporative cooling as cooling strategies are related to atmospheric humidity during summer (overheated) months. Those with dew points averaging less than 50F may be considered "arid." Regions having a combined July and August average dew point temperature greater than 65F (18.3°C) may be considered "humid." The entire southeast quadrant of the U. S. has mean daily humidity readings exceeding comfort limits under still air conditions. The main bioclimatic strategy of this region is thus to use shading and ventilation, to minimize if not to replace mechanical dehumidification and air conditioning, which may be required as a function of building type and climate.

The 50F (10°C) dewpoint temperature is an arbitrary way of defining the upper limit of arid conditions, but is convenient since it produces an outdoor daily temperature range of roughly 30F (17°C) dry-bulb. Arid and semiarid conditions favor evaporative and radiative cooling and generally discourage summer daytime ventilation, since the air is both hot and dry. Thermal mass is especially effective in arid regions with extremely high daily maxima with nighttime lows that fall within the comfort range.

3 Principles of bioclimatic design

Bioclimatic design strategies are effective for "envelope-dominated" structures, to provide a large portion if not all of the energy required to maintain comfort conditions. "Internal load dominated" buildings—such as hospitals, offices, commercial kitchens, windowless stores—experience high internal gains imposed by the heat of occupancy, lights, and equipment. In such cases, the external climatic conditions may have a more complex influence on achieving comfort and low energy utilization. However, as internal loads are reduced through energy-efficient design—that is, low-wattage equipment and lighting, occupancy scheduling and zoning—the effects of climate become more obvious and immediate. All buildings can benefit from available daylighting, so that its related heating and cooling impacts and means of control are essential for all buildings.

The "resources" of bioclimatic design are the natural flows of energy in and around a building—created by the interaction of sun, wind, precipitation, vegetation, temperature and humidity in the air and in the ground. In some instances, this "ambient energy" is useful immediately or stored for later use, and in other cases, it is best rejected or minimized. There is a limited number of "pathways" by which heat is gained or lost between the interior and the external climate (Fig. 4). These can be understood in terms of the classic definitions of heating energy transfer mechanics, and from these, the resulting bioclimatic design strategies can be defined (Fig. 5).

- *Conduction*—from hotter object to cooler object by direct contact.

- *Convection*—from the air film next to a hotter object by exposure to cooler air currents.

- Radiation—from hotter object to cooler object within the direct view of each other regardless of the temperature of air between.

- *Evaporation*—the change of phase from liquid to gaseous state: The sensible heat (dry-bulb temperature) in the air is lowered by the latent heat absorbed from air when moisture is evaporated.

- *Thermal storage*—from heat charge and discharge both diurnally and seasonally, a function of its specific heat, weight, and conductivity. Although not usually listed alongside the four classic means of heat transport, this role of thermal storage is helpful in understanding the heat transfer physics of building climatology.

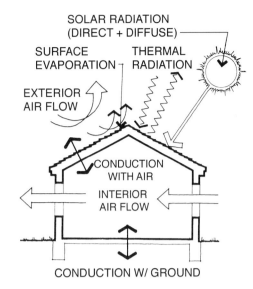

Fig. 4. Paths of energy exchange at the building microclimate (Watson and Labs 1993)

Fig. 5. Strategies of bioclimatic design

Bioclimatic design strategy	Predominant season [1]	Process of heat transfer			
		Conduction	Convection	Radiation	Evaporation
Minimize conductive heat flow.	winter and summer [2]				
Delay periodic heat flow	winter and summer				
Minimize infiltration	winter and summer [2]				
Provide thermal storage [3]	winter and summer				
Promote solar gain	winter				
Minimize external air flow	winter				
Promote ventilation	summer				
Minimize solar gain	summer				
Promote radiant cooling	summer				
Promote evaporative cooling	summer				

NOTES:
[1] Properly described as "underheated and overheated."
[2] In overheated periods where air-conditioning is required.
[3] Thermal storage may in very unusual cases utilize "phase change" materials and the latent heat capacities of chemicals such as eutectic salts.

4 Bioclimatic design strategies

In winter (or underheated periods), the objectives of bioclimatic design are to resist loss of heat from the building envelope and to promote gain of solar heat. In summer (or overheated periods), these objectives are the reverse, to resist solar gain and to promote loss of heat from the building interior. The strategies can be set forth as:

- *Minimize conductive heat flow.* This strategy is achieved by using insulation. It is effective when the outdoor temperature is significantly different either lower or higher than the interior comfort range. In summer, this strategy should be considered whenever ambient temperatures are within or above the comfort range and where natural cooling strategies cannot be relied upon to achieve comfort (that is, mechanical air conditioning is necessary).

- *Delay periodic heat flow.* While the insulation value of building materials is well understood, it is not as widely appreciated that building envelope materials also can delay heat flows that can be used to improve comfort and to lower energy costs. Time-lag through masonry walls, for example, can delay the day's thermal impact until evening and is a particularly valuable technique in hot arid climates with wide day-night temperature variations. Techniques of earth-sheltering and berming also exploit the long-term heat flow effect of subsurface construction.

- *Minimize infiltration.* "Infiltration" refers to uncontrolled air leakage through joints, cracks, and faulty seals in construction and around doors and windows. Infiltration (and the resulting "exfiltration" of heated or cooled air) is considered the largest and potentially the most intractable source of energy loss in a building, once other practical insulation measures have been taken.

- *Provide thermal storage.* Thermal mass inside of the insulated envelope is critical to dampening the swings in air temperature and in storing heat in winter and "coolth" in summer. (The term "coolth," coined by John Yellott, describes the heat storage capacity of a cooled thermal mass, that is, its capacity to serve as a heat sink for cooling).

- *Promote solar gain.* The sun can provide a substantial portion of winter heating energy through elements such as equatorial-facing windows and greenhouses, and other passive solar techniques which utilize spaces to collect, store, and transfer solar heat.

- *Minimize external air flow.* Winter winds increase the rate of heat loss from a building by "washing away" heat and thus accelerating the cooling of the exterior envelope and also by increasing infiltration (or more properly, exfiltration) losses. Siting and shaping a building to minimize wind exposure or providing wind-breaks can reduce the impact of such winds.

- *Promote ventilation.* Cooling by air flow through an interior may be propelled by two natural processes, cross-ventilation (wind driven) and stack-effect ventilation (driven by the buoyancy of heated air even in the absence of external wind pressure). A fan can be used to augment natural ventilation cooling in the absence of sufficient wind or stack-pressure differential.

- *Minimize solar gain.* The best means for ensuring comfort from the heat of summer is to minimize the effects of the direct sun, the primary source of overheating, by shading windows from the sun, or otherwise minimizing the building surfaces exposed to summer sun, by use of radiant barriers, and by insulation.

- *Promote radiant cooling.* A building can lose heat effectively if the mean radiant temperature of the materials at its outer surface is greater than that of its surroundings, principally the night sky. The mean radiant temperature of the building surface is determined by the intensity of solar irradiation, the material surface (film coefficient) and by the emissivity of its exterior surface (its ability to "emit" or re-radiate heat). This contributes little, however, if the building envelope is well insulated.

- *Promote evaporative cooling.* Sensible cooling of a building interior can be achieved by evaporating moisture into the incoming air stream (or, if an existing roof has little insulation, by evaporatively cooling the exterior envelope, such as by a roof spray.) These are simple and traditional techniques and most useful in hot-dry climates if water is available for controlled usage. Modern evaporative cooling is achieved with an economizer-cycle evaporative cooling system, instead of, or in conjunction with, refrigerant air conditioning.

5 Bioclimatic analysis

Analysis of climatic data is a first step in any bioclimatic design. While it is a simple matter to obtain local climatic data, some vigilance is required in applying it. Preliminary design direction and rules of thumb can be determined by graphing bioclimatic data. While the method can be done by hand, computer-assisted methods allow this approach to be increasingly accurate. This article describes this approach for preliminary analysis of local climate and for identifying effective design strategies.

Humans are comfortable within a relatively small range of temperature and humidity conditions, roughly between 68-80F (20-26.7°C) and 20-80% relative humidity (RH), referred to on psychrometric charts as the "comfort zone." These provide a partial description of conditions required for comfort. Other variables include environmental indices—radiant temperature and rate of air flow—as well as clothing and activity (metabolic rate). While such criteria describe relatively universal requirements in which all humans are "comfortable," there are significant differences in and varying tolerance for discomfort and the conditions in which stress is felt, depending upon age, sex, state of health, cultural conditioning and expectations.

Givoni (1976) and Milne and Givoni (1979) have proposed a design method using the Building Bioclimatic Chart (Fig. 6). It is based upon the psychometric format, overlaying it with zones defining parameters for the appropriate bioclimatic design techniques to create human comfort in a building interior. If local outdoor temperatures and humidity fall within specified zones, the designer is alerted to opportunities to use bioclimatic design strategies to create effective interior comfort.

Example of pre-design bioclimatic analysis

The method, appropriate as pre-design analysis, can be illustrated using Kansas City data (Figs. 7a and 7c). By charting annual weather data for Kansas City, bioclimatic design strategies and priorities are identified according to the percent of hours falling into the various "Building Bioclimatic Chart" zones. Fig. 7a plots seven months of the year in Kansas City with monthly maxima and minima. Fig. 7b indicates the "zones" of the Building Bioclimatic Chart in terms of their climatic parameters, and also a numbering system, used for convenience in tabulation. Fig. 7c displays a tabulated summary for Kansas City, indicating percent hours per year that weather data falls within the various "zones" delineated in the Building Bioclimatic Chart (also indicated in Table 1).

The data tabulated in Fig. 7c and Table 1 tell a story of the annual bioclimatic conditions for Kansas City:

- 14% of annual hours fall within the comfort zone (line 1 in Table 1), in which one is comfortable under a shade tree.

- Heating is required for 64% of the year (line 2).

- Of the 64% hours that heating is required, one half (32%) are

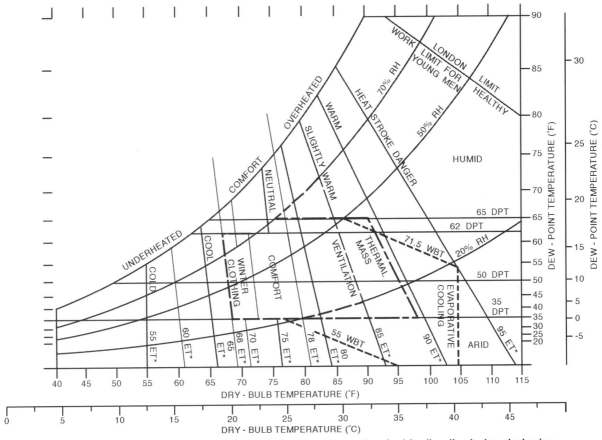

Fig. 6. Building Bioclimatic Chart, indicating parameters for bioclimatic design strategies.
Based on Givoni (1976) and Arens (1986).

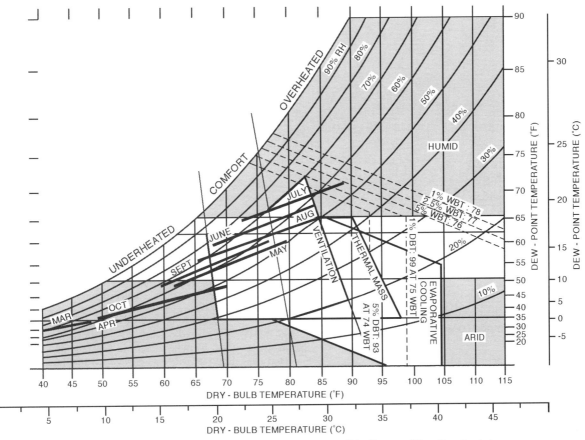

Fig. 7a. Building Bioclimatic Chart with monthly Kansas City climate data.

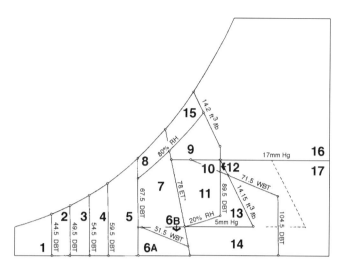

Fig. 7b. Building Bioclimatic Chart indicated parameters of the "zones" used for tabulation (Watson and Labs 1993).

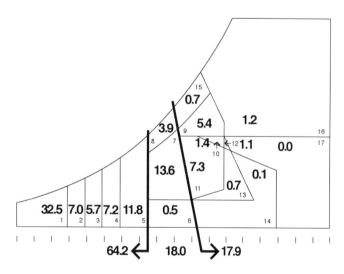

Fig. 7c. Building Bioclimatic Chart summary for Kansas City (Watson and Labs 1993).

between 45F and 68F, indicating the potential for sun-tempering (that is to say, well placed south-facing windows can reduce the mechanical heating requirement by one-half.) To limit the design to sun-tempering underestimates the solar potential, but its great value is as an easily accomplished strategy in any and all cases. Reference to Fig. 2 indicates the relative passive solar heating potential.

- 18% of annual hours require some form of cooling (line 3 in Table 1). However, by inspection of line 10, two-thirds of these cooling hours are within the effectiveness of passive cooling strategies.

- Ventilation is effective for creating cooling for 14% of the year (line 7).

- Evaporative cooling is effective for 8% of annual hours (line 8).

- Utilization of thermal mass for "coolth," is effective for 11% of hours (line 9). It is effective beyond this percent for both thermal heating storage (winter) and damping temperature fluctuations (year-round).

While the last three passive cooling percentages are not additive (that is, their hours of effectiveness overlap), the last two lines of Table 1 indicate that:

- 6% of the annual hours in Kansas City are beyond passive cooling strategies (line 10).

- However about two-thirds of this time, or 4% annual hours (line 11), require dehumidification alone, not cooling. Typically, dehumidification is provided by mechanical (refrigerant) cooling as a means of lowering humidity by cooling and condensate removal. The potential for more energy-efficient mechanical dehumidication is apparent by comparing the last two lines of Table 1.

The pre-design guidelines of bioclimatic design for Kansas City are therefore to:

- Provide a well-insulated structure with solar heating capacity (helpful for 64% of the year).

- Capitalize upon sun-tempering (effective more than 32% of the year).

- Provide shading of windows in the overheated period (needed 36% of the year).

- Design for controlled ventilation for cooling (14% of the year).

- A minor portion of the year (6%) is beyond passive cooling effectiveness, but dehumidfication alone can possibly reduce this energy demand by two-thirds.

When climatic data indicated in Table 1 are read for representative climatic locations across the U. S., other conclusions become evident. The wide variation in climatic conditions require region and site-specific study of the relative effectiveness of bioclimatic strategies. Such data summaries and bioclimatic design guidelines for U. S. locations are provided for "long-hand" calculation in Watson and Labs (1993) and for computer simulation in Milne (1997), including calculation of internal gains and nighttime ventilation of thermal mass, both of which extend the effectiveness of specific strategies.

In regions of the world where extensive climatic data are not available and where, for example, data is limited only to monthly averages of temperature and humidity, available data may not be coincident and must be interpreted with caution and only for "rough-cut" analysis. However, as is increasingly available throughout the world as in the United States, coincident climatic data are compiled from long-term readings and available on computer files, so that designers can obtain quite complete reference data. (See "Computer-aided bioclimate analysis" below.)

Table 1. Bioclimatic design data for representative U. S. locations. Percentages indicate the yearly average that outside climatic conditions suggest specific design strategies (Watson and Labs 1993).

	Seattle	Los Angeles	Phoenix	Salt Lake	Kansas City	Minneapolis	Atlanta	Hartford	Miami
	Coastal Temperate [2]	Arid Temperate	Semiarid Overheated	Arid Underheated	Temperate	Arid Underheated	Humid Temerate	Temperate	Humid Overheated

% Hours/Year bioclimatic conditions are:

	Seattle	Los Angeles	Phoenix	Salt Lake	Kansas City	Minneapolis	Atlanta	Hartford	Miami
1 Within comfort zone 7 (68F-78ET*, 5mm Hg-80% RH) [1]	6	15	13	11	14	11	13	9	18
2 Heating is required (< 68F) zones 1-5	93	80	45	76	64	79	59	80	16
3 Cooling is required (> 78ET*) zones 9-17	1	2	36	10	18	7	17	7	50
4 Promote solar heating zones 1-5	93	80	45	76	64	79	59	80	16
5 Sun-tempering is very effective zones 2-5	59	79	37	34	32	32	41	36	15
6 Restrict solar gain (shading) zones 6-17	7	20	56	21	36	21	41	21	84
7 Promote ventilation zones 8, 9,10	1	2	14	5	14	6	14	5	35
8 Promote evaporative cooling zones 11, 13-14, and 6B	1	2	30	12	8	4	7	4	7
9 Utilize thermal mass for "coolth" zones 10, 11, 12, 13	1	2	28	8	11	5	9	4	9
10 Beyond passive cooling effectiveness zones 8, 15, 16, 17	0	1	3	0	6	3	13	6	31
11 Dehumification alone [3] will provide cooling zone 8	0	1	1	0	4	3	2	5	16

NOTES:

[1] The area or "zone" of the psychrometric chart indicated by numerical designation in Fig. 7b.

[2] Approximate climatic characterization indicated in the U. S. Regional map Fig. 1.

[3] High percentage compare to "Beyond passive cooling effectiveness" indicates potential of demumidification without refrigerant cooling.

6   Bioclimatic design techniques

Just as there are differences in the climatic conditions, so do their application in design. Each locale has its own bioclimatic profile, sometimes evident in indigenous and long-established building practices. Bioclimatic design techniques can be set forth as a set of design opportunities (as elaborated in Watson and Labs 1993):

- *Wind breaks* (winter): Two design techniques serve the function of minimizing winter wind exposure:

  - Use neighboring land forms, structures, or vegetation for winter wind protection.

  - Shape and orient the building shell to minimize winter wind turbulence.

- *Thermal envelope* (winter): Isolating the interior space from the hot summer and cold winter climate, such as:

  - Minimize the outside wall and roof areas (ratio of exterior surface to enclosed volume).

  - Use attic space as buffer zone between interior and outside climate.

  - Use basement or crawl space as buffer zone between interior and grounds.

  - Centralize heat sources within building interior.

  - Use vestibule or exterior "wind-shield" at entryways.

  - Locate low-use spaces, storage, utility and garage areas to provide climatic buffers.

  - Subdivide interior to create separate heating and cooling zones.

  - Select insulating materials for resistance to heat flow through building envelope.

  - Apply vapor barriers to warm side to control moisture migration.

  - Develop construction details to minimize air infiltration and exfiltration.

  - Select high-capacitance materials to dampen heat flow through the building envelope.

  - Provide insulating controls at glazing.

  - Minimize window and door openings on north, east, and/or west walls.

  - Detail window and door construction to prevent undesired air infiltration.

  - Provide ventilation openings for air low to and from specific spaces and appliances.

  - Use heat reflective (or radiant barriers) on (or below) surfaces oriented to summer sun.

- *Solar windows and walls* (winter): Using the winter sun for heating a building through solar-oriented windows and walls is provided by a number of techniques:

  - Maximize reflectivity of ground and building surfaces outside windows facing the winter sun.

  - Shape and orient the building shell to maximize exposure to winter sun.

  - Use high-capacitance thermal mass materials in the interior to store solar heat gain.

  - Use solar wall and roof collectors on equatorial-oriented surfaces.

  - Optimize the area of equatorial-facing glazing.

  - Use clerestory skylights for winter solar gain and natural illumination.

- *Indoor/outdoor rooms* (winter and summer): Courtyards, covered patios, seasonal screened and glassed-in porches, greenhouses, atriums and sun spaces can be located in the building plan for summer cooling and winter heating benefits, as in these three techniques:

  - Provide outdoor semi-protected areas for year-round climate moderation.

  - Provide solar-oriented interior zone for maximum solar heat gain.

  - Plan specific rooms or functions to coincide with solar orientation.

- *Earth-sheltering* (winter and summer): Techniques such as covering earth against the walls of a building or on the roof, or building a concrete floor on the ground, have a number of climatic advantages for thermal storage and damping temperature fluctuations (daily and seasonally), providing wind protection and reducing envelope heat loss (winter and summer). These techniques are often referred to as earth-contact or earth-sheltering design:

  - Recess structure below grade or raise existing grade for earth-sheltering.

  - Use slab-on-grade construction for ground temperature heat exchange.

  - Use earth-covered or sod roofs.

- *Thermally massive construction* (summer and winter): Particularly effective in hot arid zones, or in more temperate zones with cold clear winters. Thermally massive construction provides a "thermal fly wheel." absorbing heat during the day from solar radiation and convection from indoor air which can create comfort if it is cooled at night, if necessary through nighttime ventilative cooling (if air temperatures fall within the comfort zone).

  - Use high mass construction with outside insulation and nighttime ventilation techniques in summers.

- *Sun shading* (summer): Because the sun angles are different in summer than in winter, it is possible to shade windows from the sun during the overheated summer period while allowing it to reach the window surfaces and spaces in winter. Thus the concept to provide sun shading does not need to conflict with winter solar design concepts.

  - Minimize reflectivity of ground and building surfaces outside windows facing the summer sun.

  - Use neighboring land forms, structures, or vegetation for summer sun.

  - Shape and orient the building shell to minimize exposure to summer sun.

  - Provide seasonally operable shading, including deciduous trees.

- *Natural ventilation* (summer and seasonal): Natural ventilation is a simple concept by which to cool a building.

  - Use neighboring land forms, structures, or vegetation to increase exposure to summer breezes.

  - Shape and orient the building shell to maximize exposure to summer breezes.

  - Use "open plan" interior to promote air flow.

  - Provide vertical air shafts to promote "thermal chimney" or stack-effect air flow.

  - Use double roof construction for ventilation within the building shell.

  - Orient door and window openings to facilitate natural ventilation from prevailing summer breezes.

  - Use wingwalls, overhangs, and louvers to direct summer wind flow into interior.

- Use louvered wall for maximum ventilation control.

- Use roof monitors for "stack effect" ventilation.

• *Plants and water* (summer): Several techniques provide cooling by the use of plants and water near building surfaces for shading and evaporative cooling.

- Use ground cover and planting for site cooling.

- Maximize on-site evaporative cooling.
- Use planting next to building skin.

- Use roof spray or roof ponds for evaporative cooling.

7 Computer-aided bioclimate analysis

Recently developed energy design tools make it possible to utilize hourly weather data to accurately analyze climate. This enables the designer to apply sophisticated bioclimatic analysis to any location in the United States, thus providing a systematic basis to guide design judgment. Designers with access to an IBM-compatible micro-computer can apply the bioclimatic analysis and design approach presented in this article, using microcomputer design tools.

Climate Consultant: This software that plots weather data, including temperatures, wind velocity, sky cover, percent sunshine, beam and horizontal irradiation. It uses these data to create psychometric charts, timetables of bioclimatic needs, sun charts and sun dials showing times of solar needs and shading requirements. It also displays 3-D plots of temperature, wind speed, and related climatic data and is cross-referenced to bioclimatic design practices presented in Watson and Labs (1993). It can be down-loaded at no cost from the World Wide Web (Milne 1997). Fig. 20 indicates a typical bioclimatic chart generated by Climate Consultant, indicating an annual summary for Minneapolis and in the upper left, the percent that bioclimatic strategies are effective, similar to data in Table 1.

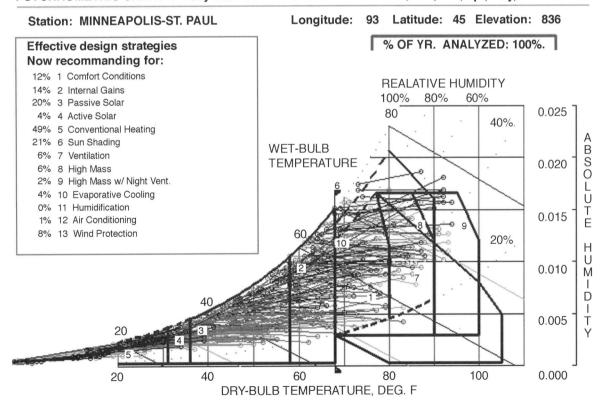

PSYCHROMETRIC CHART : Daily Max. & Min. Points Plotted for Jan, Feb, Mar, Apr, May,

Station: MINNEAPOLIS-ST. PAUL   **Longitude: 93 Latitude: 45 Elevation: 836**

Effective design strategies
Now recommanding for:

12% 1 Comfort Conditions
14% 2 Internal Gains
20% 3 Passive Solar
 4% 4 Active Solar
49% 5 Conventional Heating
21% 6 Sun Shading
 6% 7 Ventilation
 6% 8 High Mass
 2% 9 High Mass w/ Night Vent.
 4% 10 Evaporative Cooling
 0% 11 Humidification
 1% 12 Air Conditioning
 8% 13 Wind Protection

% OF YR. ANALYZED: 100%.

Fig. 20. Computer display (in numerous colors) of the Building Bioclimatic Chart for Minneapolis, MN. Tabulation on left of screen is similar to data in Table 1 above. (Milne and Li 1997).

Fig. 8. Sea Ranch, CA. Windbreaks in site planning and building elements created wind-protected courtyards. Esherick, Homsey, Dodge and Davis, Architects and Planners.

Fig. 9. Green Pre-Fab Homes, Rockford, IL. 1944. The first to be called "solar houses,"
Architects George and William Keck's home designs, beginning in the mid-1930s, combined south-facing glass, sun shading and internal thermal mass.

Fig. 10. Elementary School. Athens, VT.
Translucent water columns placed in the south window absorbs solar heat while also transmitting daylight. An insulating curtain closes the units at night. John Rogers and George Heller, Architects.

The Typical Meteorological Year (TMY) contains simultaneous climatic data for all 8,760 hours in a "typical" year. Available for 250 cities (airport data) locations, mostly in the United States, each file contains one complete year of hourly data, including direct (beam) solar radiation, total horizontal solar radiation, dry-bulb temperature, dew-point humidity, wind speed and cloud cover. Electronic files of climatic data for most U. S. locations (major airports) are available through various sources on the World-Wide Web, NREL (1996) and Rutgers University (1994).

Bioclimatic design combines insight and knowledge by establishing climatic design data at the beginning of design and monitoring performance results. The designer can thereby gain an understanding of bioclimatic design strategies and techniques that are most effective in specific regions and microclimates as an enduring inspiration of architecture. (See examples in Figures 8-19)

Definitions of temperature and humidity

Temperature is defined as the thermal state of matter with reference to its tendency to communicate heat to matter in contact with it. Temperature is an index of the thermal energy content of materials, disregarding energies stored in chemical bonds and in the atomic structure of matter.

- *Fahrenheit temperature* (F) refers to temperature measured on a scale devised by G. D. Fahrenheit, the inventor of the alcohol and mercury thermometers, in the early 18th century. On the Fahrenheit scale, the freezing point of water is 32F and its boiling point is 212F at normal atmospheric pressure. It is said that Fahrenheit chose the gradations he used because it divides into 100 units the range of temperatures most commonly found in nature. The Fahrenheit scale, therefore, has a more humanistic basis than other temperature scales.
- *Celsius temperature* (°C) refers to temperatures measured on a scale devised in 1742 by Anders Celsius, a Swedish astronomer. The Celsius scale is graduated into 100 units between the freezing temperature of water (0°C) and its boiling point at normal atmospheric pressure (100°C) and is, consequently, commonly referred to as the *Centigrade scale.*
- *Dry-bulb temperature* (DBT) is the temperature measured by an ordinary (dry-bulb) thermometer, and is independent of the moisture content of the air. It is also called "sensible temperature."
- *Wet-bulb temperature* (WBT) is an indicator of the total heat content (or enthalpy) of the air, that is, of its combined sensible and latent heats. It is the temperature measured by a thermometer having a wetted sleeve over the bulb from which water can evaporate freely.
- *Dew point temperature* (DPT) is the temperature of a surface upon which moisture contained in the air will condense. Stated differently, it is the temperature at which a given quantity of air will become saturated (reach 100% relative humidity) if chilled at constant pressure. It is thus another indicator of the moisture content of the air. Dew point temperature is not easily measured directly; it is conveniently found on a psychrometric chart if dry-bulb and wet-bulb temperatures are known.

Humidity is a general term referring to the water vapor contained in the air. Like the word "temperature," however, the type of "humidity" must be defined.

- *Absolute humidity* is defined as the weight of water vapor contained in a unit volume of air; typical units are pounds of water per pound of dry air or grains of water per cubic foot. Absolute humidity is also known as the water vapor density (D_v).
- *Relative humidity* (RH) is defined as the (dimensionless) ratio of

the amount of moisture contained in the air under specified conditions to the amount of moisture contained in the air at saturation at the same (dry bulb) temperature. Relative humidity can be computed as the ratio of existing vapor pressure to vapor pressure at saturation, or the ratio of absolute humidity to absolute humidity at saturation existing at the same temperature and barometric pressure.

- *Water vapor pressure* (P_v) is that part of the atmospheric pressure ("partial pressure") which is exerted due to the amount of water vapor present in the air It is expressed in terms of absolute pressure as inches of mercury (in. Hg) or pounds per square inch (psi).

Additional references

Arens, E., R. Gonzales, and L. Berglund. 1986. "Thermal Comfort Under an Extended Range of Environmental Conditions." *ASHRAE Transactions.* Vol. 92. Part 1. Atlanta: ASHRAE Publications.

Center for Building Science. 1996. "Urban Heat Catastrophes: The Summer 1995 Chicago Heat Wave." *Center for Building Science News.* Fall 1996. Berkeley, CA: Lawrence Berkeley National Laboratory.

Fitch, James Marston and Paul Siple, editors. 1952. *AIA/House Beautiful Regional Climate Study.* Originally published in *AIA Bulletin* 1949-1952. Ann Arbor, MI: University Microfiche.

Givoni, Baruch. 1976. *Man, Climate and Architecture.* London: Applied Science Publishers. 2nd Edition.

Milne, Murray and Baruch Givoni. 1979. "Architectural Design Based on Climate" in Donald Watson, editor. *Energy Conservation Through Building Design.* New York: ARB/McGraw Hill Book Company. [out of print: archival copies available from the editor].

Milne, Murray and Yung-Hsin Li. 1994. "Climate Consultant 2.0: A New Design Tool for Visualizing Climate." *Proceedings of the 1994 ACSA Architectural Technology Conference.* Washington, DC; Association of Collegiate Schools of Architecture Publications.

NREL. 1996. "TMY-2 Typical Meteorological Year Climate Data Files." National Renewable Energy Laboratory. http://rredc.nrel.gov:80/solar/old_data/nsrdb/tmy2/ (If this web address changes, e-mail: webmaster@nrel.gov).

Olgyay, Aladar and Victor Olgyay. 1957. *Design with Climate.* Princeton: Princeton University Press.

Rutgers University. 1994. Department of Engineering. "TMY Typical Meteorological Year Climate Data Files." http://oipea-www.rutgers.edu/html_docs/TMY/tmy.html (If this web address changes, e-mail: webmaster@rutgers.edu).

Fig. 12. Adobe home. Papago Indian Nation, Arizona. A centuries-old building tradition evident in informal house construction provides thermal time delay in hot-arid climate. Overhangs provide shading and protect the adobe

Fig. 13. Adobe home. Al Hudaydah, Yemen. Located in a hot humid area on the Red Sea, most summer hours are above the comfort zone. The sleeping cot in the courtyard provides some relief and radiant/ventilative cooling comfort at nighttime.

Fig. 11. Skytherm House. Atascadero, CA. 1973.
Developed by Harold Hay

The Skytherm System includes a plastic enclosed roof pond thermally linked to the interior and covered on the outside by movable insulating panels. Alternate positioning of the panels either to cover or to expose the roof pond allows the system to operate in four modes: (1) winter day: to absorb winter daytime solar heat (panels open), (2) winter night: to radiate heat gain to the interior at night (panels closed). (3) summer day: to serve as heat sink for internal gain (panels closed) and (4) summer night: to radiate heat gain to the night sky (open).

Fig. 14. Earth-covered Home. New Canaan, CT. Earth-sheltering and solar design. Donald Watson, FAIA, Architect and Builder.

Fig. 15. Scantion Student Housing near Aarhus, Denmark. Earth-sheltering and solar design. K. Friis and E. Moltke, Architects.

Fig. 16. Taliesin West. Scottsdale, AZ. Movable shading and subgrade thermally massive construction create a cooling microclimate. Frank Lloyd Wright, Architect.

Fig. 17. "San Francisco" a restored manor near New Orleans. Shading and ventilative cooling provided by porches, cross-ventilation, and double-roof "thermal chimney" construction. Photo: Robert Perron.

Fig. 18. Palace of the Alhambra, Granada, Spain. 14th Century. Combination of shading, thermal mass and evaporative cooling create a comfortable microclimate. Photo: Cesar Pelli.

Fig. 19. Paley Park. New York City. A shaded and cooled microclimate. Waterfall creates evaporative cooling and sets up local breezes, also creating acoustic masking of street traffic.

4

Solar control

Steven V. Szokolay

Summary: Solar control utilizes beneficial sunshine for passive heating and for daylighting and minimizes liabilities of overheating through sunshading, orientation and related fenestration designs. The earth-sun geometrical relationship is descirbed, both in heliocentric and lococentric terms. Calculation methods for solar angles and graphic methods and applications of the equidistant solar charts are described, with emphasis on design of shading devices. A review is presented of various "sun-machines" or simulators used for model studies.

Key words: altitude, azimuth, heliodons, overshadowing, shading devices, shadow angles, solar angles, sun penetration.

Solar and Astronomical Observatory. Jaipur, India. circa 1710.
(photo: Alec Purves).

Fundamentals

In most industrialized countries, buildings are responsible for 40—45% of the national total energy consumption. Much of this energy (up to 2/3) is used for thermal controls: heating and air conditioning (HVAC). The amount of energy needed for HVAC depends very much on the design of the building, its thermal performance, its climatic suitability. An additional portion is required for lighting. Much of this energy demand can be reduced by proper fenestration design, including solar control and shading devices.

The two most important climatic factors that influence the thermal behavior of a building are air temperature and solar radiation (although winds and humidity also have an effect). Solar radiation can cause severe overheating in summer (in some cases even in winter), or it can increase the air conditioning load, whilst it can be beneficial in winter, reducing the heating requirement or perhaps even eliminate the need for heating by using conventional forms of energy. One of the first tasks of a designer is to determine when solar heat input is desirable and when solar radiation is to be excluded. The next step will then be to provide the appropriate solar control. A prerequisite of designing the solar control is to know the sun's position at any time of the year and then to relate it to the building.

There may be a number of non-geometrical controls available: for solid elements the color (reflectance/absorptance) of the surfaces or for windows the use of heat absorbing or heat rejecting glasses. These however rarely provide the desired control: always reducing the daylighting of the interior spaces (daylighting is one of the most effective ways of energy conservation) and always reducing the solar heat input, even when it would be desirable. There is no seasonal selectivity and no responsiveness.

Some recently developed photochromatic or thermochromatic glasses may be responsive but not selective: when, in response to light or a thermal effect, they become dark, they will reduce daylight as well as solar heat transmission. The most efficacious method of solar control is the use of some form of external shading device, which provides a barrier to solar radiation before it would reach the window glass when solar gain is not desirable. It is easy to design a device which would block out all sun penetration. Such a device would unduly restrict daylighting. The task is to avoid overdesigning the device. Such shading devices can be designed, tailor-made for any situation, provided that the designer fully understands solar geometry.

The earth-sun relationship

Heliocentric view: The earth is almost spherical in shape, some 7,900 miles (12,700 km) in diameter and it revolves around the sun in a slightly elliptical (almost circular) orbit (Fig. 1). The full revolution takes 365.26 days and as the calendar year is 365 days, some adjustments are necessary: one extra day every four years (the leap-year). This takes care of 0.25 days per year. The remaining 0.01 day per year is compensated by a one day adjustment at the turn of each century. The earth—sun distance is approximately 93 million miles (150 million km), varying between:

95 million miles (152 million km) at aphelion, on July 1 and
92 million miles (147 million km) at perihelion, on January 1

The plane of the earth's revolution is referred to as the ecliptic. The earth's axis of rotation is tilted 23.45° from the normal to the plane of the ecliptic. The angle between the earth's equator and the ecliptic (or the earth - sun line) is the declination (DEC) and it varies between +23.45° on June 22 (northern solstice) and -23.45° on December 22 (southern solstice), as shown in Fig. 2. (For practical purposes using ±23.5° gives an acceptable precision). On equinox days (approximately March 22 and September 22) the earth—sun line is within the plane of the equator, thus DEC = 0°. The variation of this declination is shown by a sinusoidal curve in Fig. 3. (Note that some sources nominate the equinox and solstice dates differently, e.g. as March 21, or June 21, or Sept. 23, etc.—this depends on the year within the leap-year cycle and the exact time of day when the event occurs.)

Geographical latitude of a point on the earth's surface is the angle subtended at the center of the earth between the plane of the equator and the line connecting the center with the surface point considered (the "vertical" line) as Fig. 4 indicates. Points having the same latitude form a latitude circle. The north pole is +90°, the south pole -90°, whilst the equator is 0° latitude. The extreme latitudes where the sun reaches the zenith at mid-summer are the tropics (Fig. 5):

LAT = +23.45° is the tropic of Cancer and
LAT = -23.45° is the tropic of Capricorn.

The arctic circles (at LAT = ±66.55°) mark the extreme positions where at mid-summer the sun is above the horizon all day and at mid-winter the sun does not rise at all.

Author: Steven V. Szokolay

References: Szokolay, S. V. 1980. *Environmental Science Handbook for Architects*. London: Longman (Construction Press) and New York: Wiley/Halsted Press.

Szokolay, S. V. 1996. *Solar Geometry*. PLEA Note 1. Brisbane, Australia: PLEA/University of Queensland.

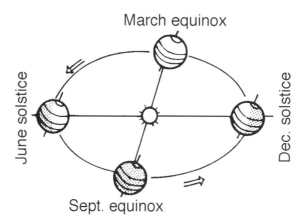

Fig. 1. The earth's orbit

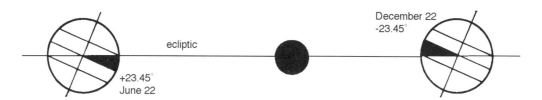

Fig. 2. Section of the earth's orbit

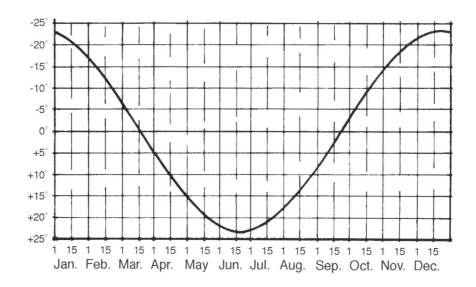

Fig. 3. Annual variation of declination (mean of the leap-year cycle)

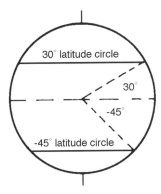

Fig. 4. Definition of geographical latitude

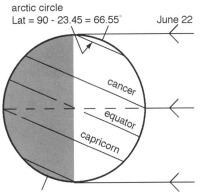

Fig. 5. Definition of the tropics

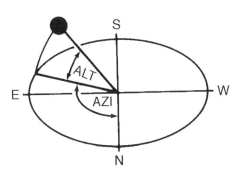

Fig. 6. Definition of solar position angles

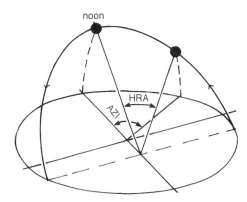

Fig. 7. Definition of hour angle (HRA)

Lococentric view: In most practical work we go back to the view before the time of Copernicus (1543 AD) and consider our point of location (hence: loco-centric) as the center of the "celestial dome." The ground is assumed to be flat and limited by the horizon circle. The sun's apparent position on this celestial dome is defined by two angles (Fig. 6):

- altitude (ALT)—measured in the vertical plane, between the sun's direction and the horizon plane; in some texts this is referred to as "elevation."

- azimuth (AZI)—the direction of the sun measured in the horizontal plane from north in a clockwise direction (thus east = 90°, south = 180°, west = 270°, whilst north can be 0° or 360°) also referred to by some as "bearing." Many authors (in the northern hemisphere) use 0° for south and have -90° for east and +90° for west, north being ±180°. Some in the southern hemisphere use the converse: north = 0°, going through east (+90°) to +180° for south and through west (-90°)to -180°. The 0—360 convention here adopted is the only one valid for any location.

The zenith angle (ZEN) is measured between the sun's direction and the vertical and it is the supplementary angle of the altitude:

$$ZEN = 90° - ALT$$

The hour angle (HRA) expresses the time of day with respect to the solar noon: it is the angular distance, measured within the plane of the sun's apparent path (Fig. 7) between the sun's position and its position at noon, i. e. the solar meridian (the plane of the local longitude which contains the zenith and the sun's noon position). As the hourly rotation of the earth is 360°/24h = 15°/h, HRA is 15° for each hour from solar noon:

$$HRA = 15 * (h - 12)$$

where h = the hour considered (24-hour clock) so HRA is negative for the morning and positive for the afternoon hours

e.g: for 9 am: HRA = 15 * (9 - 12) = -45°
but: for 2 pm: HRA = 15 * (14 - 12) = +30°

Solar time is measured from solar noon, i.e. noon is taken to be when the sun appears to cross the local meridian. This will be the same as the local (clock-) time only at the reference longitude of the local time zone. The time adjustment is normally one hour for each 15° of longitude from Greenwich, but the boundaries of the local time zone are subject to social convention (or official definitions). In most applications it makes no difference which time system is used: the duration of exposure is the same. All calculations and most graphs use solar time. Converting to local time is necessary only when time of day is critical.

For example: Australian eastern time is based on the 150° longitude, i.e. Greenwich + 10 hours. However Queensland extends from 138° to 153° longitude, so in Brisbane (153°) solar noon will be earlier than clock noon. As 1 hour = 60 minutes, the sun's apparent movement is 60/15 = 4 minutes of time per degree of longitude, in Brisbane the sun will cross the local meridian 4 * (150 - 153) = -12, i.e. .12 minutes before noon, at 11:48 local clock time. At the western boundary of the state solar noon will occur 4 * (150 - 138) = 48 minutes after solar noon, i.e. at 12:48 local clock time.

Due to the variation of the earth's speed in its revolution around the sun (faster at perihelion but slowing down at aphelion) and minor irregularities in its rotation, the time from noon-to-noon is not always exactly 24 hours. Clocks are set to the average length of the day, which

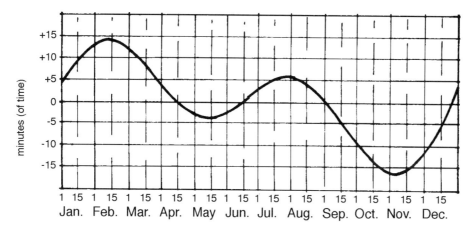

Fig. 8. Annual variation of the 'equation of time' (EQT)

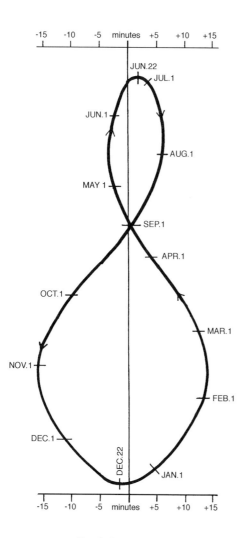

Fig. 9. The analemma

gives the mean time. The mean time at Greenwich is referred to as GMT, but recently also as UT (universal time). On any reference longitude, the local mean time deviates from solar time by up to -16 minutes in November and +14 minutes in February. The function expressing this variation is the equation of time (Fig. 8) and its graphic representation is the analemma (Fig. 9). Then solar time + EQT = local mean time Some texts show the same curve as Fig. 8 but with opposite signs. The values read from those would be used as local mean time + EQT = solar time.

Calculation methods

If the calendar date is expressed as the number of day of the year (NDY), i.e. starting with January 1, March 22 would be NDY = 31 + 28 + 22 = 81 and December 31: NDY = 365, then the declination can be estimated from the following simple expression. To synchronize the sine curve with the calendar, the distance from the March equinox to the end of year (284 days) is added to the NDY. As the year (365 days) corresponds to the full circle (360°), the ratio 360/365 = 0.986 must be applied as a multiplier, thus:

$$DEC = 23.45 * \sin[0.986 * (284 + NDY)]$$

If the DEC is known and the time of day is expressed by the hour angle, HRA, then altitude angle will be:

$$ALT = \arcsin(\sin DEC * \sin LAT + \cos DEC * \cos LAT * \cos HRA)$$

Two expressions are available for the azimuth:

$$AZI = \arccos[(\cos LAT * \sin DEC - \cos DEC * \sin LAT * \cos HRA) / \cos ALT]$$

or

$$AZI = \arcsin[(\cos DEC * \sin HRA) / \cos ALT]$$

The results will be between 0 and 180°, i.e. for a.m. only; for afternoon hours, take

$$AZI = 360 - AZI.$$ The sunrise hour angle is:

$$SRH = \arccos(-\tan DEC * \tan LAT)$$

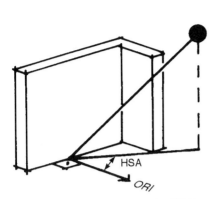

Fig.10. Horizontal shadow angle (HSA)

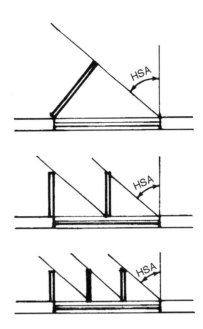

Fig.11. Some vertical shading devices giving the same HSA

and the sunrise time is:

SRT = 12 - [arccos(-tanDEC*tanLAT)/15]

The azimuth angle at sunrise will be:

SRA=arccos(cosLAT*sinDEC+tanLAT*tanDEC*sinLAT*cosDEC)

Derivations of these equations are given in Szokolay (1996). The performance of vertical shading devices is measured by the horizontal shadow angle: HSA (Fig. 10). This is defined as the difference between the azimuth angle of the sun and the orientation azimuth (ORI) of the building face (sometimes referred to as the azimuth difference):

HSA = AZI - ORI

This will be positive if the sun is clockwise from the orientation, but negative when the sun is anticlockwise. For machine calculation the following checks must be included:

if 90°< |HSA| < 270° then the sun is behind the facade, the elevation is in shade.
If HSA > 270° then HSA = HSA - 360°
if HSA < -270° then HSA = HSA + 360°

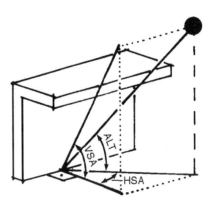

Fig.12. Vertical shadow angle (VSA)

Fig. 11 indicates that many different devices may have the same HSA. The performance of horizontal shading devices is measured by the vertical shadow angle (VSA), sometimes referred to as "profile angle." Fig. 12 defines the VSA, which is measured as the sun's position projected parallel with the building face onto a vertical plane normal to that building face, and it can be found from the expression:

VSA = arctan(tanALT/cosHSA)

Another definition of VSA is as the angle between two planes meeting along a horizontal line on the building face which contains the point considered, one being the horizontal plane and the other a tilted plane which contains the sun (Fig. 13). Both HSA and VSA can be used either to quantify the performance of a given shading device or to specify the required shading performance for a device yet to be

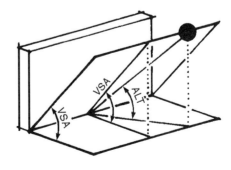

Fig.13. Relationship of VSA and ALT

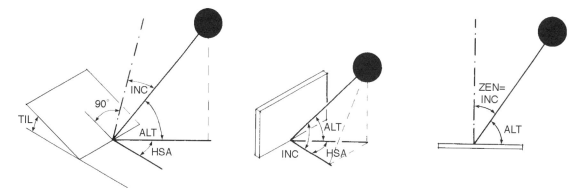

Fig.14. Angle of incidence

designed, to be effective at given times. If the angle of incidence (INC) is to be found, the following expressions can be useful. Referring to Fig. 14, first the general case:

INC = arccos(sinALT*cosTIL+cosALT*sinTIL*cosHSA)
where TIL = tilt angle of the receiving plane from the horizontal

For a vertical surface, as TIL = 90°, cosTIL = 0, thus the first term becomes zero and sinTIL = 1, so it drops out and we are left with:

INC = arccos(cosALT*cosHSA)

and for a horizontal plane:

INC = ZEN = 90° - ALT

Graphic methods

Fig. 15 shows the celestial domes for LAT = 28° north and south locations, as well as the north-south vertical sections of both (looking

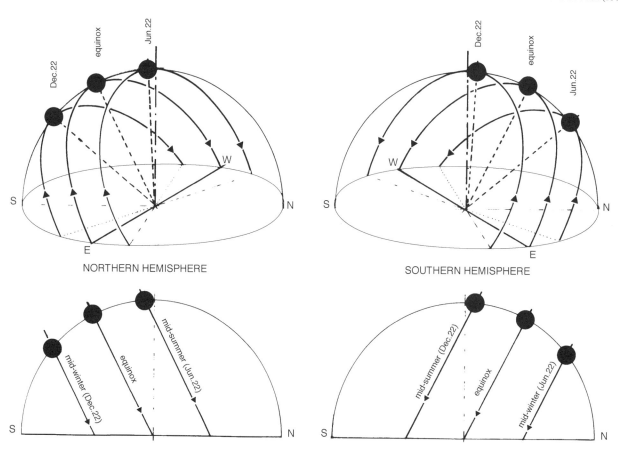

Fig.15. The celestial dome or sky vault and its section looking west

towards the west). In each case three sun-path lines are indicated: for the summer and winter solstices and the middle one for the equinoxes. All graphic methods employ some 2-D representation of the 3-D celestial dome. The sun's paths for various dates can then be plotted on such a 2-D diagram.

Fig. 16 explains three methods of constructing a 2-D diagram: all three giving horizontal circles. Altitudes (in these examples) are indicated on the section at 15° intervals. On the plan these are represented by concentric circles.

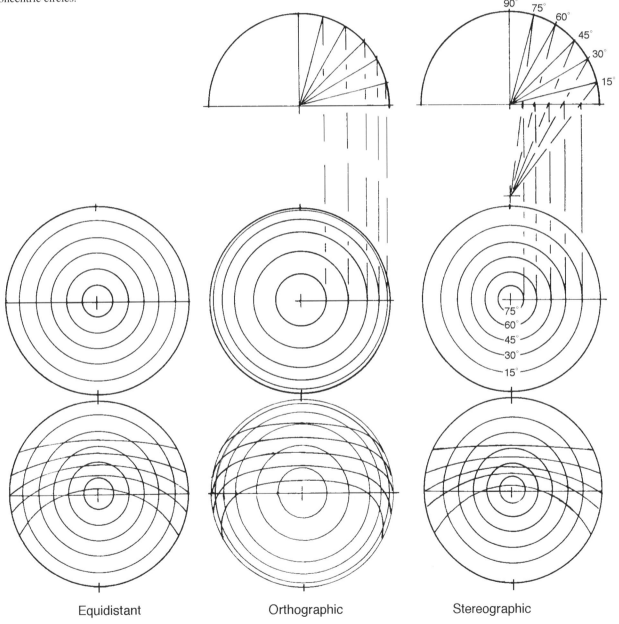

| Equidistant | Orthographic | Stereographic |

Fig.16. Construction of horizontal sunpath diagrams

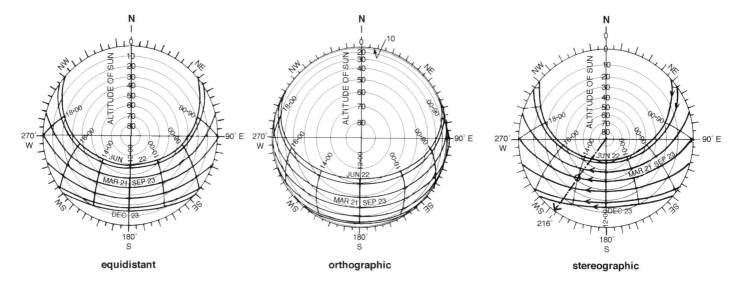

Fig.17. Three types of sun-path diagram, LAT = 38°

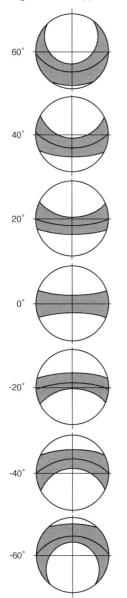

Fig.18. The pattern of changing sun-paths from the equator towards the poles

The orthographic (or parallel) projection can be likened to the spherical Chinese rice-paper lamp-shade with its wire rings. When laid flat on a table, it is the 2-D diagram; when the center is lifted until the largest ring remains on the table, it becomes the 3-D sky-vault, the wire rings being the various altitude circles. In this projection the altitude circles are at a very close spacing near the horizon, leading to loss of accuracy. It is sometimes used at low latitudes (tropical areas), but it is not acceptable at higher latitudes, low sun-angles.

The stereographic (or radial) projection, originally developed by Phillips (1948), overcomes this problem. It uses the theoretical nadir point as the center for radial projection lines. An advantage of this projection is that all sun-path lines are circular arcs and can be constructed by a very simple method. This became the most widely used projection world-wide and is adopted in ISO/DIS 6399-1.

The equidistant representation is the most widely used one in the U.S., as such charts are available from LOF (Libby-Owens-Ford). This is not a projection but a calculated construct, where the altitude circles are equally spaced and the calculated sun-path lines are plotted .

Three sun-path lines are always shown for the four cardinal dates: summer and winter solstices and one line for the two equinoxes. Sun-paths for several intermediate dates can be shown, but their spacing varies with the particular publication. Short hour lines cross the sun-paths. These normally refer to mean solar time, thus noon is a short straight line at the center. Note that in all three forms of representation, the equinox sun-path starts exactly at east (sunrise) and terminates at west (sunset) at exactly 06:00 and 18:00 h respectively.

Fig. 17 shows three charts for LAT = 38°. On the stereographic chart the way of reading the sun's position is indicated. Find the sun position angle for March 21 at 14:00 h: locate the 14:00 h point along the equinox sun-path line (marked by a small circle) and project this point from the center to the perimeter, where the azimuth can be read as AZI = 216°. The altitude is found by interpolating the time-point between the adjacent altitude circles: in this case just above the 30° circle, approximately ALT = 32°.

Fig. 18 presents the pattern of shifting sun-path lines from the equator (LAT = 0°), where the paths are symmetrical, towards the poles, up to 60°. At the poles, the sun-paths would be concentric circles, or rather a spiral, up to 23.45° above the horizon for mid-summer, following the horizon circle at the equinoxes and not visible (below the horizon) for the winter half-year. The difference between equidistant and stereographic charts is not much, the methods of use are the same, but care must be taken not to use a stereographic protractor with an equidistant chart, or vice-verse, as this could lead to serious errors.

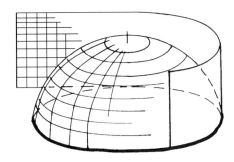

Vertical diagrams

A cylindrical projection is shown in Fig. 19: the hemisphere is radially (horizontally) projected onto the inside surface of a circumscribed cylinder. It is similar to the Mercator map-projection. The altitude circles are compressed towards the zenith and the horizontal dimensions, correct at the horizon, are stretched increasingly with the altitude: the zenith point becomes a line of the same length as the horizon circle. A version of this cylindrical projection is the Waldram diagram (Fig. 20), which uses the 45° altitude as the center-line, so both the very low and very high latitude lines are compressed. Fig. 21 gives an example of such a Waldram sun-path diagram. This compression is avoided by the projection method shown in Fig. 22, where the spacing of latitude lines is still decreasing, but not as drastically as above. Some authors go a step further and use an equidistant vertical chart, which is not a projection, but a calculated construct. An example of this is given in Fig. 23 for the same latitude as Fig. 21. This method has been adopted (amongst others) by Mazria (1979).

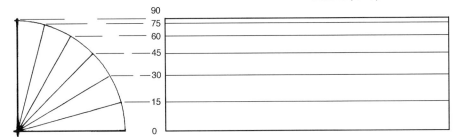

Fig.19. Cylindrical projection

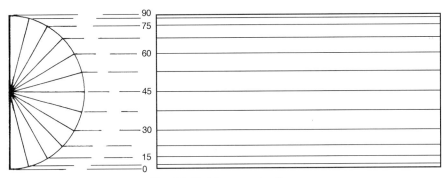

Fig. 20. Waldram projection

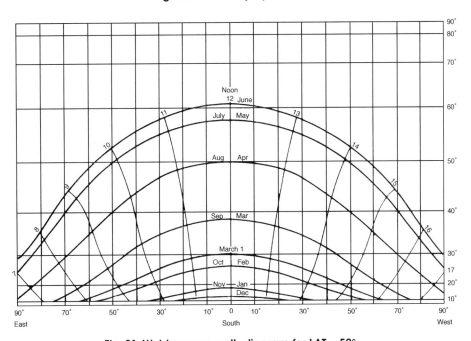

Fig. 21. Waldram sun-path diagram for LAT = 52°

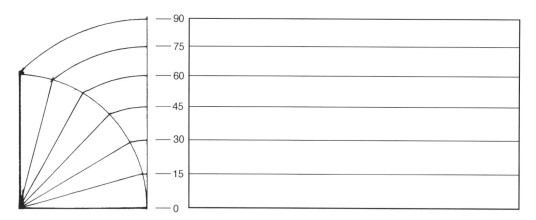

Fig. 22. An improved projection of altitudes

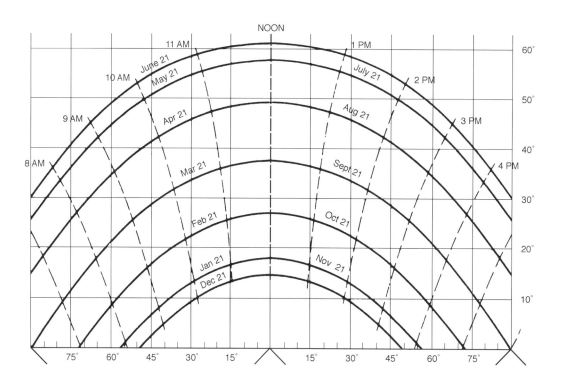

Fig. 23. An equidistant vertical sun-path diagram, LAT = 52°

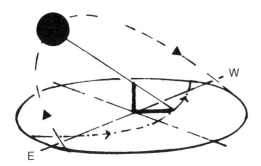

Fig. 24. Horizontal sun-dial

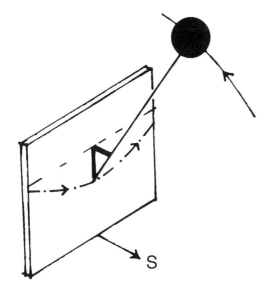

Fig. 25. Vertical sun-dial

Gnomonic projections

Sun-clocks or sun-dials have been used for millennia. There are two basic types: horizontal and vertical (there are also numerous tilted varieties). With a horizontal sun-dial, the direction of the shadow cast by the gnomonic (a rod or pin) indicates the time of day. Conversely, if the direction of this shadow for a particular hour is known, then the direction of the sun (its AZI angle) can be predicted.

If the length of the gnomonic is known, then the length of the shadow cast will indicate the solar altitude (ALT) angle. During the day the tip of the shadow will describe a curved line, which can be adopted as the sun-path line for that day (Fig. 24). This way a set of sun-path lines can be constructed for various dates and thus a gnomonic horizontal sun-path diagram created. The principles of a vertical sundial are similar, except that the gnomonic is protruding horizontally from a vertical plane onto which the shadow is cast (Fig. 25).

Fig. 26 presents a horizontal gnomonic (or perspective) sun-path diagram for an equatorial location and Fig. 27 for LAT = 32°. Vertical sun-path perspectives can be used for shading design, but for every latitude a different diagram would be required for every orientation. However, one set of horizontal diagrams is only necessary, as for any vertical plane there is a parallel plane somewhere on the earth's surface. Fig. 28 explains this relationship for a north- (or south-) facing surface and Fig. 29 extends this for vertical surfaces of any orientation. A parallel horizontal surface is found along a great circle which lies in the direction of orientation of that vertical surface.

The selected horizontal sun-path diagram can then be used vertically. Its equinox line will be horizontal for a north or south facing elevation, but will be tilted for other elevations. A full set of such horizontal gnomonic sun-path diagrams is presented in the supplement of *Windows and environment*, by W. Burt *et al.*(1969), where a method of selecting the appropriate horizontal chart, as well as tiling and calibrating it is given (also in Lynes 1968). The method is fully described and a reduced set of charts (8° latitude intervals) is presented in Szokolay (1980).

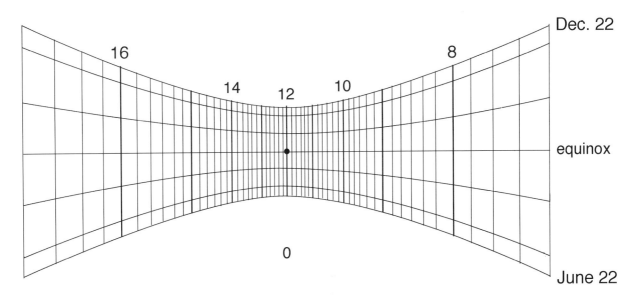

Fig. 26. Gnomonic sun-path diagram for LAT = 0°

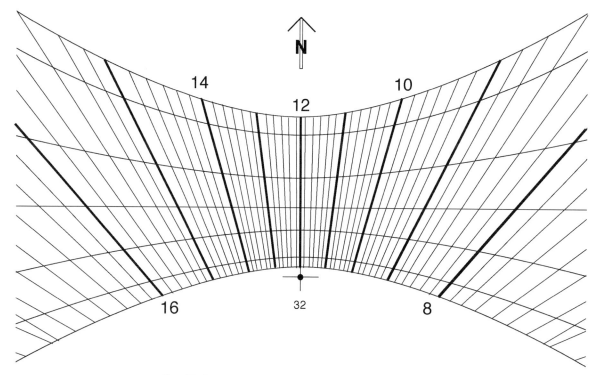

Fig. 27. Gnomonic sun-path diagram for LAT = 32°

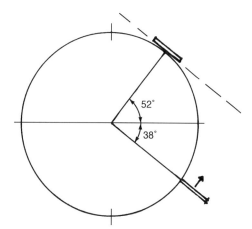

Fig. 28. A north-facing vertical surface parallel
with a horizontal

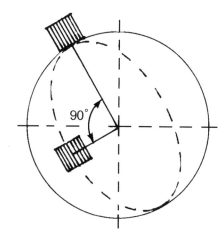

Fig. 29. A S/E facing vertical surface parallel with a
horizontal, along a great circle

Shadow cast

These sun-path diagrams are practically the same as in Givoni (1969) the "flagpole shadow paths." The "flagpole method" can be useful in constructing the shadow cast by a complex object at a specified time. The method is introduced by a simple example. Fig. 30 shows the plan and elevation of a small office block, located at LAT = 30°. Construct the shadow cast on November 3, at 08:00 h. The solar position angles have been read from the sun-path diagram: AZI = 140° and ALT = 40°. Imagine a flagpole located at each of points 1 and 2. Draw the direction of shadow cast at both points by the sun at 140° (towards 140 + 180 = 320°). Draw a line perpendicular to this direction at both flagpole points, to a length corresponding to the "flagpole" heights (6 m and 18 m respectively). From the tip of these draw a line to the ALT angle, and where this intersects the direction-line, it will mark the length of shadow. Given the two corners of the shadow cast, its outline can be completed by drawing parallel lines.

APPLICATION

Sketch design thinking

Solar radiation falling on a window consists of three components: beam (direct) radiation, diffuse (sky) radiation and reflected radiation (from ground, other buildings, *etc.*). External shading devices can eliminate the beam component, which is normally the largest and also serve to reduce the diffuse component. As the sun's (apparent) movement is unchangeable, solar orientation of the building is very important. This is paramount: whilst many other decisions in design are negotiable, orientation cannot be compromised. This is especially so if at some part of the year solar heat input is desirable. This period of desirable passive solar heating should be determined. Then the overheated period should also be determined, i. e. the dates when solar radiation should be excluded. At the sketch design stage this can be taken as the time when the mean temperature is higher than the lower comfort limit, as indicated by Fig. 31. The daily temperature profile can be considered at a later stage to ascertain the hours when shading is necessary. Keep in mind that an equatorial orientation (directly facing the equator) is the only one where a fixed horizontal shading device can give an automatic seasonal adjustment: exclude the summer

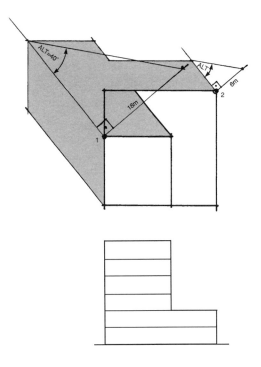

Fig. 30. The flagpole method used for shadow casting

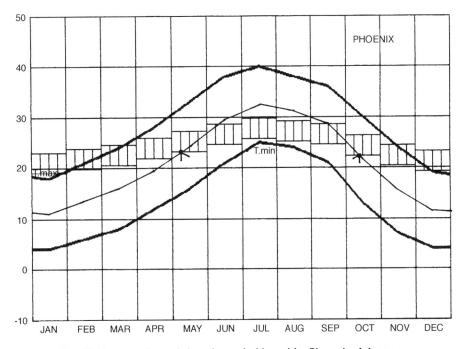

Fig. 31. Temperature plot and comfort band for Phoenix, Arizona

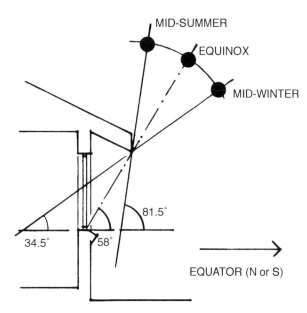

Fig. 32. Automatic seasonal adjustment: equator-facing window

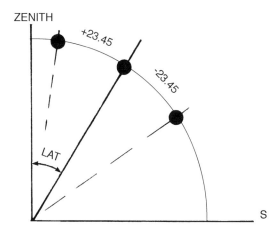

Fig. 33. Equinox sun position

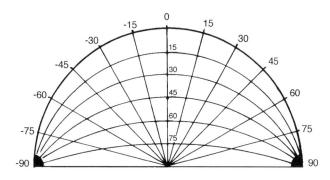

Fig. 34. The shadow angle protractor

(high angle) sun, but allow sun penetration in winter, when the sun is at a low angle (Fig. 32). Another general principle is that for an equator-facing (or near equator facing) window a horizontal device would give a better performance, but for a window of east or west (or near east or west) orientation a vertical device may be more effective.

A useful rule-of-thumb is that the solar altitude at equinox is 90°-LAT, i.e. the latitude of the location (Fig. 33). From this the sun moves 23.5° up at mid-summer and 23.5° down at mid-winter. Comparing this with Fig. 15 shows that at equinox the noon altitude line coincides with the sectional view of the sun-path, indicating that the VSA (for an equator-facing window) will be constant for the whole day. If this is adopted initially as the VSA, then the sun would be fully excluded for the summer half-year and it would penetrate to an increasing extent after the autumn equinox, reaching its maximum at the winter solstice. It can be adjusted later when the design is being refined.

A working method
The performance of shading devices is indicated by their shading masks. These can be constructed with the aid of the shadow angle protractor (Fig. 34). This is a semicircular transparent sheet, of the same diameter as the sun-path diagram. It has a set of radial lines, marked from 0 at the center to -90° anticlockwise and +90° clockwise. This is the HSA scale. It also has a set of arc lines, converging to the left and right corners and spaced at the centerline the same as the corresponding altitude circles of the sun-path diagram. These indicate the VSA (both scales here are at 15° spacing).

A vertical shading device will give a sectoral shaped shading mask. The pair of vertical fins shown in Fig. 35 will produce the shading mask shown in Fig. 36. Dotted lines drawn to the center point of the window indicate 50% shading, represented by the dotted lines drawn parallel with these on the shading mask. This shading mask can then be superimposed on the sun-path diagram, with its centerline corresponding to the orientation of the window, which will be shaded at the times covered by the shading mask Fig. 37). The base line of the protractor represents the line of building elevation examined. At any times below that, the sun would be behind the building, the elevation would be in shade.

- Note that the sun-path lines (calendar dates) and the hour lines form a date x hour coordinate system, representing the year. The only unusual feature is that the lines are not straight, but curved.

The canopy above a window (one kind of horizontal shading device) shown in Fig. 38 gives a vertical shadow angle (VSA) of 60°. The shading mask of this will be segmental in shape, bounded by the 60° arc, as indicated by Fig. 39. The dotted line drawn to the mid-height point of the window and the corresponding dotted arc of the shading mask indicate 50% shading. Fig. 40 shows this shading mask superimposed on the sun-path diagram.

The design process is best illustrated by an example. The overheated period has been defined (for Phoenix, Arizona) by Fig. 31: it extends over five months, from early May to mid-October. These dates are then marked on the sun-path diagram. From mid-October a gradually increasing amount of solar input is desirable to elevate the indoor mean: adequate building mass could ensure that (in winter) the daily maximum does not exceed the upper comfort limit.

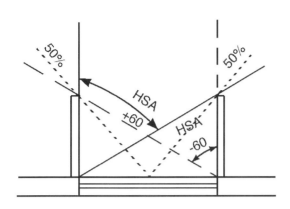

Fig. 35. HSA of a pair of vertical fins

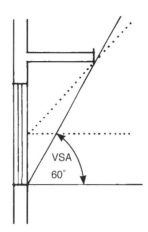

Fig. 38. VSA of a horizontal shading device: a canopy

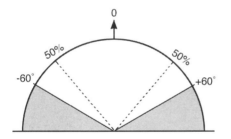

Fig. 36. Shading mask of the fins shown in Fig.35

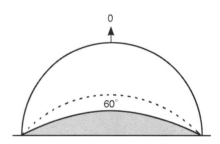

Fig.39. Shading mask of the canopy shown in Fig.38

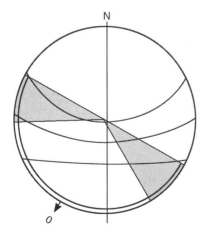

Fig. 37. Shading mask superimposed on the sun-path diagram for ORI = 210°

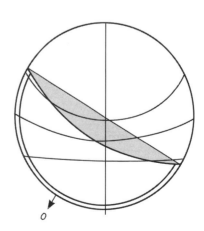

Fig. 40. Shading mask superimposed on the sunpath diagram

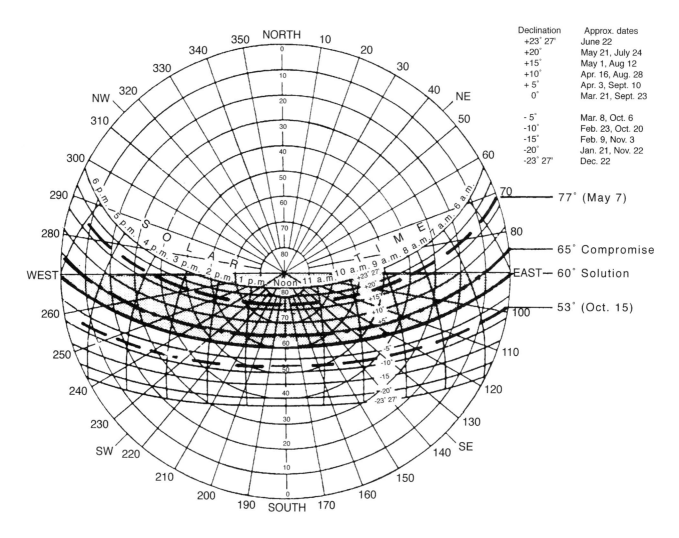

Declination	Approx. dates
+23° 27'	June 22
+20°	May 21, July 24
+15°	May 1, Aug 12
+10°	Apr. 16, Aug. 28
+ 5°	Apr. 3, Sept. 10
0°	Mar. 21, Sept. 23
- 5°	Mar. 8, Oct. 6
-10°	Feb. 23, Oct. 20
-15°	Feb. 9, Nov. 3
-20°	Jan. 21, Nov. 22
-23° 27'	Dec. 22

77° (May 7)
65° Compromise
60° Solution
53° (Oct. 15)

Fig. 41. Working with the sun-path diagram

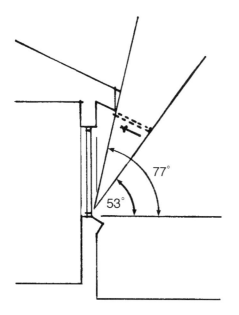

Fig. 42. Combined fixed and retractable device

The (LAT = 30°) sun-path diagram (Fig. 41) shows that the early May sun-path line (interpolated between May 1 and 21) is quite different from the mid-October line (interpolated between October 6 and 20). This is an indication of the general phenomenon that changes of microclimatic temperature lag behind the sun's movement by about a month. The latter is symmetrical about the solstices (June 22 and Dec. 22), whilst the peak temperature occurs at late July and the minimum in late January.

The following requirements can be read for a south-facing window:

May 7:	VSA = 77°
Oct. 15:	VSA = 53°

The compromise of VSA = 65° would give cut-off dates of about Apr. 3 and Sept. 10. If overheating is less tolerable than a slight underheating (which is generally the case) the compromise can be biased in the direction of more shading: say VSA = .60°. This would give cut-offs at the equinox dates.

- Note that for equinox cut-off the VSA curve exactly matches the sun-path line, so there is no need to use the protractor: For the whole day VSA = HSA at noon.

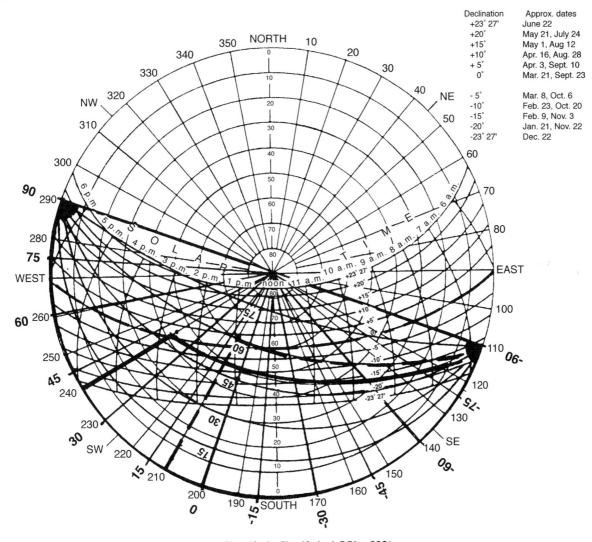

Declination	Approx. dates
+23° 27'	June 22
+20°	May 21, July 24
+15°	May 1, Aug 12
+10°	Apr. 16, Aug. 28
+ 5°	Apr. 3, Sept. 10
0°	Mar. 21, Sept. 23
- 5°	Mar. 8, Oct. 6
-10°	Feb. 23, Oct. 20
-15°	Feb. 9, Nov. 3
-20°	Jan. 21, Nov. 22
-23° 27'	Dec. 22

Fig. 43. As Fig.41, but ORI = 200°

For an exact solution, to avoid the above compromise, a fixed device could be provided for the higher VSA (77°), with a retractable extension down to the lower VSA (53°), as shown in Fig. 42.

If the orientation of the window were other than due south, say 200° (west of south), then the protractor must be used. Fig. 43 shows that a horizontal device is ineffective for the late afternoon sun. A vertical device, e.g., a baffle at the western side of the window, should be used to assist. For full cut-off at the equinox dates, several combinations are possible, such as:

(1) VSA = 50° with HSA = 40 - 90°
(2) VSA = 60° with HSA = 10 - 90°

If the first solution were adopted, the projection of the eaves (or some similar device) at the window head level would need to be:
    x = 1.2 / tan50 = 1.0 m
with solution (2), this would be only: x = 1.2 / tan60 = 0.7 m

The latter may impose a need for a very obstructive vertical device (HSA = 10°) and as solution (1) is not excessive, it is adopted, producing the shading mask shown in Fig. 44. The final step is to translate this "performance specification" into an actual device.

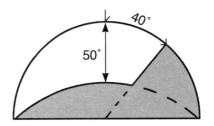

Fig. 44. The resulting shading mask

Fig. 45 shows the section and plan of the window. The west side baffle should project:

$$y = 1.5 / \tan 40 = 1.78 \text{ m}$$

which is rather large, so perhaps two baffles of half the size (0.89 m) can be adopted to give the same HSA, shown in Fig. 45.

Use of the protractor with the sun-path diagram allows viewing the overall pattern of shading effects and thus the making of informed decisions. The accuracy of the method is limited by the size of the diagram and even the eye-sight of the user. When a design has been adopted, it is fairly easy to do a few calculations (using the expressions given in the calculations above) to verify the graphic results and determine the final dimensions. It is essential that the intuitive and imaginative design of shading devices be based on such an analysis. Equally important, graphic and numerical results should be mitigated by intelligence and qualitative judgment.

Shading devices

There are three basic types of external shading devices: horizontal, vertical and egg-crate. A horizontal device will always give a segmental shaped shading mask, as shown in Figs. 38-39 and its performance is measured by the VSA. Some sub-types are:

* eaves overhang
* canopy at window head or higher
* a light-shelf designed to act also as a shade
* horizontal louvers (or brise-soleil = sun-breaks) with straight or tilted blades
* jalousie shutters
* awnings (canvas, plastic, etc.)
* combinations, *e.g.*, a canopy with slats suspended at its edge

The last three may also be adjustable.

A vertical device will always give a sectoral shaped shading mask, as shown in Fig. 35-36 and its performance is measured by the HSA. Some sub-types are:

* vertical fins or baffles
* vertical louvers, fixed.
* vertical louvers, adjustable.

Egg-crate (or combination) devices give a shading mask which is a composite of the above two. Some sub-types are:

* grille blocks, rectangular
* grille blocks, polygonal
* fins, both horizontal and vertical (equal or unequal)
* vertical fixed fins with horizontal (adjustable) louvers.

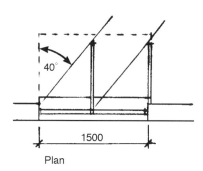

Section

Plan

Fig. 45. Section and plan of window with the device

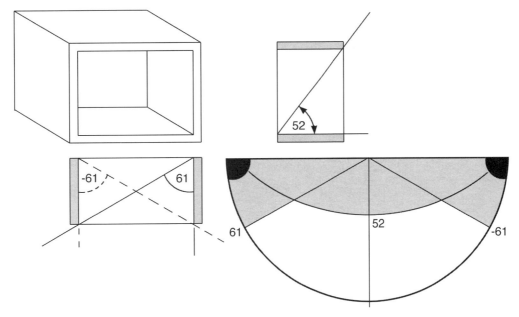

Fig. 46. Mask of a rectangular grille block

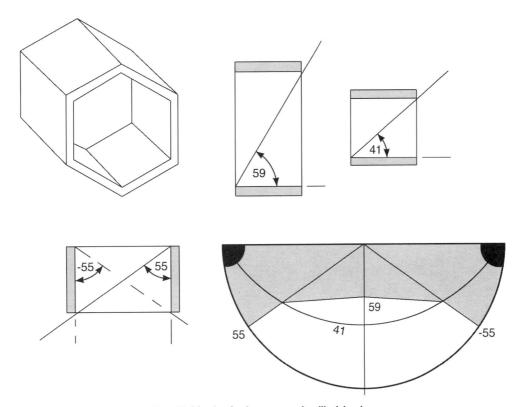

Fig. 47. Mask of a hexagonal grille block

The shading mask of these must be constructed from its components, as shown in Fig. 46 for a rectangular grille block and in Fig. 47 for a hexagonal one. Shade cloths, timber lattices, the Arab mashrabyya (carved wooden screens), or the Persian and Indian perforated stone screens, are not considered to be "shading devices." They are beautiful, allow ventilation whilst ensuring privacy, but they have no selectivity in time or in kind of radiation. They simply block out a certain percentage of all incoming radiation at all times of the year, including daylight.

Several books, such as Olgyay and Olgyay (1957), give a systematic review of shading devices and present a wide range of examples.

Sun penetration

The system of sun-path diagrams and protractor can be used to determine sun penetration through an opening at a given time or a sequence of time points. The method is best demonstrated through an example:

Consider a 1 meter square window, with a sill height of 0.9 meters, facing 165° (S/SE). The location is LAT = 30° (say Houston, Texas).

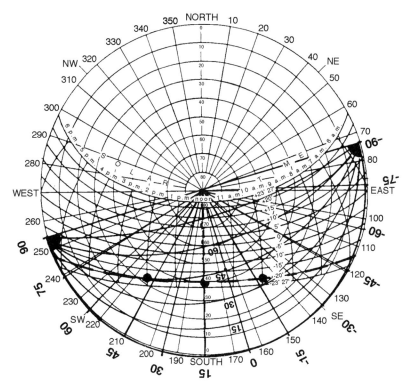

Fig. 48. Sunpath diagram, with protractor overlaid

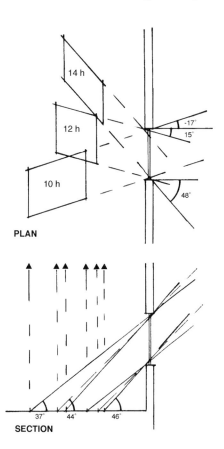

Fig. 49. Construction of sunlit patch

Determine the sun penetration on January 21, at 10, 12 and 14 h. Take the 30° sun-path diagram and mark the three time-points on the Jan. 21 sun-path line. Superimpose the protractor with the appropriate orientation (Fig. 48). For HSA values use the radial lines to the perimeter and for VSA interpolate between the arc lines. The readings can be tabulated as follows:

hour	HSA	VSA
10	-17	37
12	15	44
14	48	46

Draw a plan and section of the window. Plot the HSAs on the plan: draw two parallel lines for each time-point, tangential to the window jambs (Fig. 49). These will determine the direction of sun penetration. The VSA is actually the projection of the solar altitude angle onto a vertical plane normal to the window considered, which is the plane of our section. Therefore plot the VSAs on this section and draw two parallel lines for each-time point, touching the inside edge of the window sill and the outside edge of the head. These will mark on the floor the depth of sun penetration. Project these points up to the plan to define the edges parallel to the window of the rhomboid-shaped sun-patches.

Sideways extent of canopy

Fig. 50a is the plan and 50b the elevation of a 1 meter square, south-facing window, located at 30° latitude, with a canopy designed to give full shading at equinox dates. The required VSA has been established as 55°. To satisfy this, the projection of the canopy should be x = 1 / tan55 = 0.7 m.

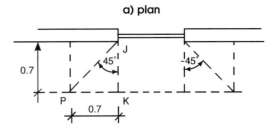

a) plan

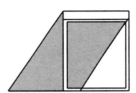

b) elevation, original

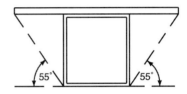

c) elevation, canopy extended

Fig. 50. Sideways extension of canopy:

This, with the same width as the window gives full shading at noon, when the sun is directly opposite the window, but not earlier and later. Assume that we want full shading between 10 and 14 h. With the protractor the required HSAs can be read: At 10 h: -45° and at 14 h: +45°. There are two simple ways to determine how far the canopy should extend sideways beyond the window jambs.

(1) On the plan of the window, indicate the edge of the canopy over with a dashed line. ; draw the HSA (-45 and +45°) outwards from the window edges. Point P, where this line intersects the edge-of-canopy line will mark the necessary sideways extent of the canopy. This can also be confirmed by calculation: from the JPK triangle: x = tan 45 ₊ 0.7 = 0. 7

(2) The construction can be performed on the elevation itself: we use the protractor to project the 10 and 14 h solar altitude points onto the plane of the wall, overlaying it on the sun-path diagram so that its centerline coincides with the wall (turning it 90° from the normally used position); placing the centerline to point towards the east (Fig. 51) we can read the VSA for 10 h as 55°. Reading for 14h would be the same, with the protractor pointing west.

Fig. 50b shows the shadow cast at 10 h by the original (1 m wide) canopy and Fig. 50c shows in elevation, to what extent the canopy should be lengthened to give full shading at the required times.

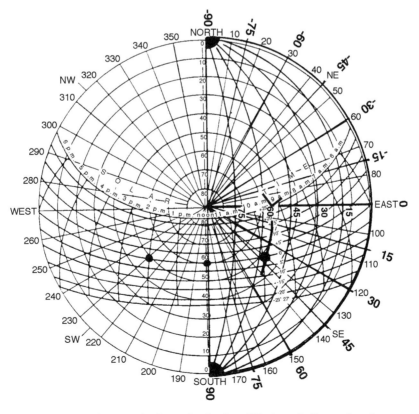

Fig. 51. Use of protractor to project solar altitude onto the wall surface

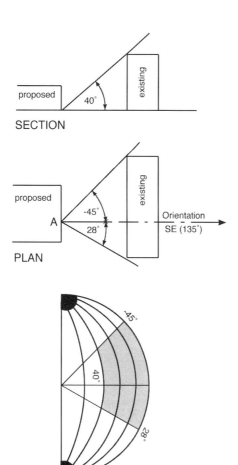

Fig. 52. Oversahdowing by a building:
construction of shading mask

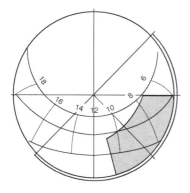

Fig. 53. Shading mask laid over sunpath diagram

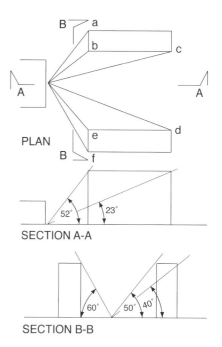

Fig. 54. Overshadowing by two buildings

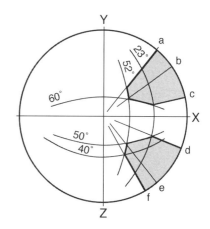

Fig. 55. Construction of shading mask

Overshadowing

The concept of shading masks can be extended to evaluate the overshadowing effect of adjacent buildings or other obstructions. The technique is best explained by an example:

• Question: For what period is point A of a proposed building overshadowed by the neighboring existing building?

Assume that the building is located at LAT = 42° and it is facing 135° (S/E). Take a tracing of the shadow angle protractor and transfer onto it the angles subtended by the obstruction at point A, both in plan and in section, as shown on Fig. 52. This gives the shading mask of that building for the point considered. This can be placed over the appropriate sun-path diagram with the correct orientation (Fig. 53) and the period of overshadowing can be read. In this instance, look at the three cardinal dates:

June 22:   no overshadowing
Equinoxes: shade from sunrise to 10:00 a.m.
December 22: shade from sunrise to about 10:45 a.m.

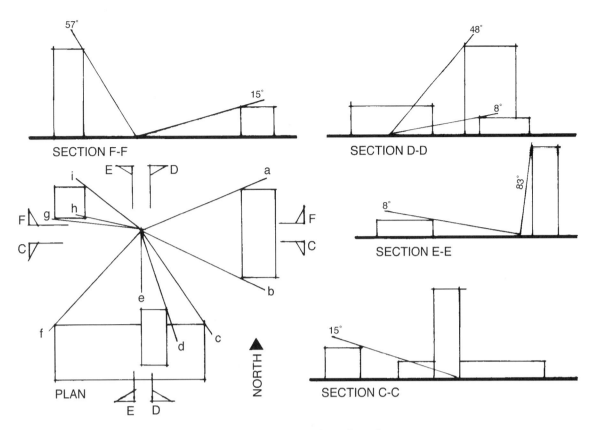

Fig. 56. Site survey: relevant angles

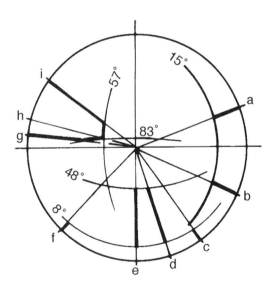

Fig. 57. Construction of shading mask

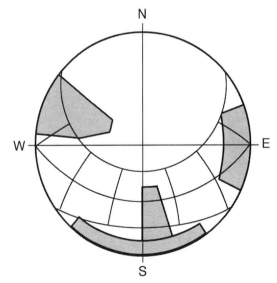

Fig. 58. Shading mask over sun-paths

Fig. 54 shows a more complex situation, where two existing buildings can cast a shadow over the point considered. To construct a shading mask: for horizontal angles draw radial lines parallel to those drawn on plan to the edges of the building. The altitudes measured from section are taken as the VSAs: use the shadow angle protractor so that its centerline is in the plane of the section, e.g.: direction X for section A-A (mark the 52° and 23° VSA arcs), for section BB: direction Y for the upper block and direction Z for the lower one. Fig. 55 shows the construction of the shading mask.

The technique can also be used for a site survey: to plot all obstructing objects that may overshadow a selected point of the site. Fig. 56 shows plan and sections of the site with the existing buildings and Fig. 57 explains the construction of the shading mask. This mask can then be laid over the appropriate sun-path diagram and the period of overshadowing can be read, as indicated by Fig. 58. If a full-field camera with a 180° fish-eye lens were to be placed at point A, pointing vertically upwards, the photo produced would be similar to this shading mask. A set of sun-path diagrams may be adapted for use as overlays to such photos.

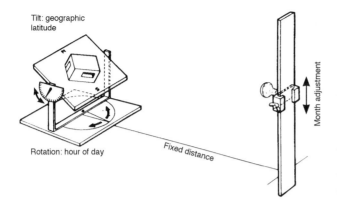

Fig. 59. The heliodon (UK)

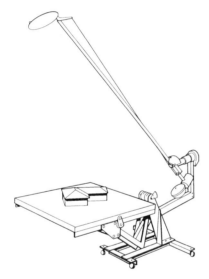

Fig. 60. The Australian solarscope

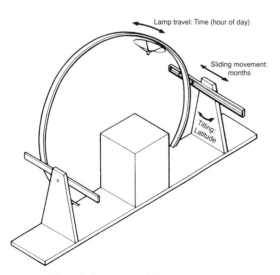

Fig. 61. A very realistic solarscope

SUN-SIMULATORS FOR MODEL STUDIES

Many devices have been developed to simulate the solar geometry and allow the study of shading with the use of physical models. These devices are very useful teaching tools, but their value in design is limited. They are useful to check the behavior of a design hypothesis, to assist visualization and the examination of shading of buildings with complex geometries, to demonstrate the shading performance on a model, possibly by photographs of the model with shadows cast on different dates and times. Such photos can be useful in some controversial building permit applications, for presentation to clients or even in some court cases.

All these devices employ a lamp to simulate the sun. A small light source gives a divergent beam at the model, resulting in shadows of parallel edges becoming divergent. This effect can be reduced by increasing the lamp-to-model distance or by using a large diameter light source. The device must allow three sets of adjustments:

1. for geographical latitude
2. for the calendar date
3. for the time of day.

The oldest such device is the heliodon (Building Research Station UK 1932). The model must be fixed to a table, which tilts to simulate the latitude (horizontal for the poles, vertical for the equator), and rotates to give the time of day (Fig. 59). The sun-lamp is attached to a slider on a vertical rail at a known distance: the topmost position for summer solstice and the lowest position for mid-winter. The lamp level with the model simulates the equinoxes.

The solarscope, developed by the Commonwealth Experimental Building Station in Sydney (1946) is shown in Fig. 60. A spotlight is aimed at a mirror at the end of a long arm, which reflects the light down onto the model table (thus doubling the effective distance). This arm swings around a horizontal axis to represent the hour of day and tilts forward or up to give the calendar dates. The table can be lowered, which lifts the fulcrum of the arm and tips the mirror forward for high latitudes, or the table is lifted, lowering the fulcrum and raising the mirror for equatorial latitudes.

The solarscope developed at the (then) Polytechnic of Central London in 1968 is perhaps the most convincing educational tool: the arc (3/4 circle) rail describes the sun's path for the given day (Fig. 61). A motorized carriage travels on this rail from sunrise to sunset, on which a 26-inch (650 mm) diameter mirror is mounted, with a small high intensity lamp at its focal point. This gives a parallel beam for models up to 26 inches (650 mm) diameter. The rail itself slides sideways on two cross-bars, giving the calendar adjustment and these cross-bars tilt to provide the latitude adjustment. A rather similar device was constructed at the University of Southern California at about the same time (Fig. 62). The sun-lamp is mounted on a cross-bar, which allows the calendar adjustment and this bar travels along the arc rail to give the time of day. The tilting of the rail provides the latitude adjustment.

A simplified version of this operates at the University of Buenos Aires (Fig. 63). This consists of three semi-circular arcs (corresponding to the equinox and two solstice sun-paths), fixed to two tiling cross-bars, which give the latitude adjustment. A total of 39 small lamps are mounted on the rails (3 x 13) at 15° intervals, corresponding to the hours of the day. If this device is used only for one given location, then the tilting bars can be eliminated and the three arcs can be fixed to the table at the appropriate tilt.

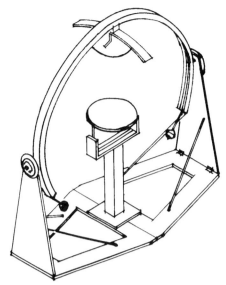

Fig. 62. A Californian heliodon

The SUNLIGHT heliodon (Fig. 64) is lightweight and manually operated. It is designed to simulate the illumination received on earth from the sun for latitudes 0-70 degrees, at any day of the year and any hour of the day. It is astronomically correct in demonstrating the motion of the sun in a physically realistic way. This heliodon is in use in the Architecture Schools of Yale University and Rensselaer Polytechnic Institute. SUNLIGHT, Madison, CT USA. (http://www. Printworks-Ltd.com/heliodon)

The simplest method for shading studies is the use of some form of sun-dial, in conjunction with a model. This is to be fixed to the base of the model to be examined, with the north-points matching. The model is then tilted and turned, until the tip of the gnomon's shadow points at the time point (date and hour) or interest. Fig. 65 is the 'universal' or 'polar' sun-dial. This is to be tilted from the model's horizontal according to the location's latitude, as indicated by the quandrant scales.

Additional references

Burt, W. *et al.* 1969. *Windows and environment* (+ supplement) Newton-le-Willows, England: Pilkington Environmental Advisory Service / McCorquodale & Co., Ltd.

Givoni, B. 1969. *Man, Climate and Architecture*. London: Applied Science Publishers.

Libby-Owens-Ford (LOF) Glass Company. Sun angle calculator. 811 Madison Ave. Toledo, OH. 43695.

Lynes, J. 1968. "Sunlight: Direct and diffused." Section 2 of *A J Handbook: Building Environment*. 16 Oct. - 20 Nov. 1968. London: The Architects Journal.

Mazria, E. 1979. *The Passive Solar Energy Book*. Emmaus, PA: Rodale Press.

Olgyay, A. and Olgyay, V. 1957. *Solar Control and Shading Devices*. Princeton: Princeton University Press.

Phillips, R. O. 1948. *Sunshine and shade in Australasia. Technical Study No. 23*. Sydney: Commonwealth Experimental Building Station.

Smithsonian Institute. (undated) *Smithsonian Meteorological Tables: Sun-path diagrams*. Washington, DC: Smithsonian Institute.

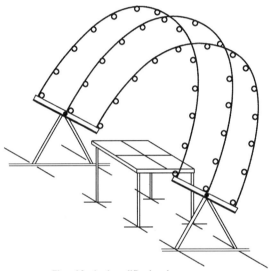

Fig. 63. A simplified solarscope

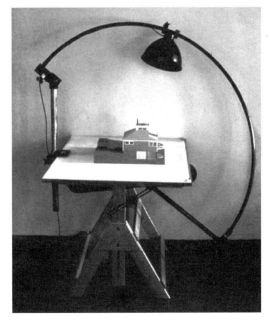

Fig. 64. SUNLIGHT heliodon

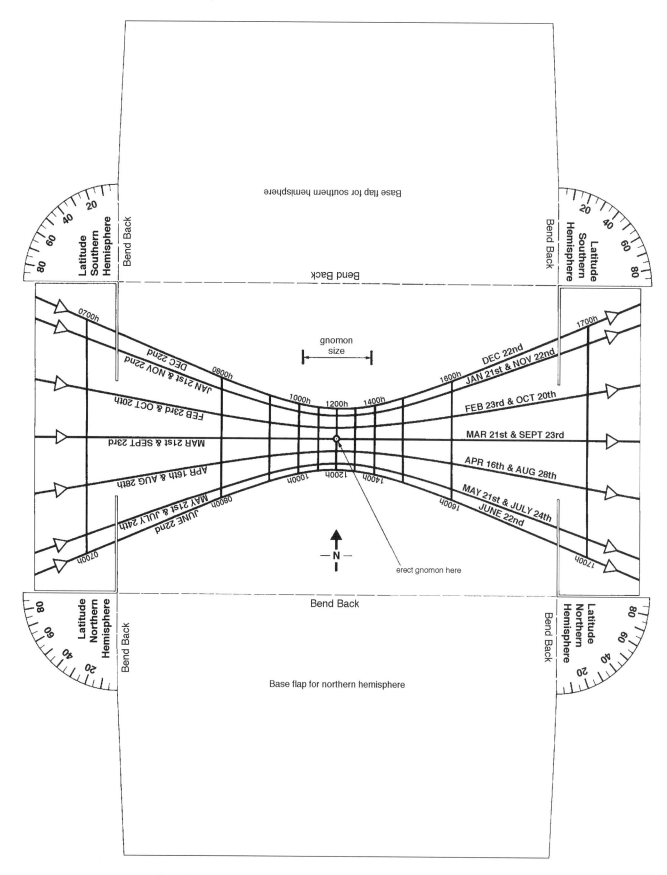

Fig. 65. Universal Sundial (by permission of Pilkington Industries)

5
Daylighting design

Benjamin Evans

Fig. 1. Woodland color and sunlighting

Summary: Principles of daylighting design combine aesthetic and psychological qualities of light, building orientation, cross-section, interior finishes, window design, and integration with electric lighting. Daylight is part of architecture, in both its historical, theoretical, and technical conception, with a unique capacity to inspire people and to illuminate the elements of its design.

Key words: contrast, daylighting, glare, lighting, light shelves, sky brightness, skylights, sunlighting, veiling reflections.

People like daylight. We like interior spaces to have plenty of daylight. The variety and range of light and color that we experience in a forest grove engages all of our senses (Fig. 1). Daylighting design could aspire to the same inspirational effect. If people like something, it stands to reason they will consider it valuable and that when they have it they will be more satisfied and productive than when they don't have it. This is all the justification architects need to introduce daylighting into building design.

While daylighting can be employed to conserve energy and can enhance visibility, the principal values of daylighting are more intangible. Many factors are involved with the use of daylight in buildings:

- aesthetics: the play of light from windows on surfaces and textures casting interesting shadows; the endless variety of mood and appearances due to the movement of the sun;

- psychological response: the sense of well-being associated with daylight and the sense of orientation that comes with being "connected" with the exterior;

- health: improved resistance to infections, skin disorders, and cardiovascular impairment;

- energy/cost: reduction in electric use and related air conditioning load from electric lighting.

Physiological benefits of daylighting
A number of physiological benefits derive from lighting to humans, animals, and plants. Some types of growth, orientation, sexual stimulation, migration patterns, egg production, and other attributes are dependent on light content, duration, and intensity.

- *Full-spectrum lighting.* A trend in recent years has been to stimulate the use of so-called "full spectrum" electric lamps in buildings on the assumption that humans evolved in the natural environment and that, therefore, the sunlight's total spectrum must be useful and valuable. It is a simple matter to accord with this assumption by using daylight whenever possible.

Ultraviolet radiation, for instance, is essential to human health. It prevents rickets, helps keep the skin in a healthy condition, is responsible for the production of vitamin D in the body (thus reducing the incidence of broken bones in the elderly), and it destroys germs. Ultraviolet dilates the capillaries of the skin, reduces blood pressure, quickens the pulse rate and appetite, stimulates energetic activity, produces a feeling of well-being, reduces fatigue, and may even increase work output. There are dangers from overexposure to ultraviolet such as skin cancer, wrinkles, and possible eye damage, but most of the benefits and none of the liabilities have been directly associated with the use of daylight in buildings.

- *Stimulus.* The human organism is not adapted to unrelieved or steady stimuli or to the complete lack of stimuli. Uniformity in the environment produces monotony when humans are exposed to it for long periods. The constantly changing nature of daylight automatically and naturally responds to the need of the body and mind for a change of stimuli.

Although the body responds to steady-state conditions by changing itself, if the monotony is long continued, the body's ability to respond to stimuli will gradually deteriorate. People require reasonable stimuli to remain sensitive and alert. On the other hand, overstimulation from lighting (such as direct bright light in the eye) can lead to emotional as well as physical fatigue. The goal in lighting design is to avoid excessive stimulation from direct light sources while providing some visual flexibility and stimuli. The proper introduction of daylight into the interior environment is the most effective way to provide such variation.

Author: Benjamin Evans, FAIA

Credits: Portions of this article appeared in *Architecture Magazine*, February 1987 and are reproduced by permission of the publisher.

References: Evans, Benjamin. 1987. "Basics of Daylight Design: Treating natural light as an architectural element." February, 1987. *Architecture*. Washington, DC: Architecture Magazine.

IESNA. 1993. *The Lighting Handbook.* Mark S. Rea, editor. New York: Illuminating Engineering Society of North American.

Lam, William M. C. 1986. *Sunlighting: Formgiver for Architecture.* New York: Van Nostrand Reinhold.

Millet, Marietta S. 1996. *Light Revealing Architecture.* New York: Van Nostrand Reinhold.

Robbins, Claude L. and Kerri C. Hunter. 1982. "Daylight Availability Data for Selected Cities in the United States." Golden, CO: Solar Energy Research Institute (SERI).

Romm, Joseph J. 1994. *Lean and Clean Management.* New York: Kodansha America, Inc.

Watson, Donald. 1996. *Daylight model testing as a research/design assignment.* Vital Signs Curriculum Materials Project. Troy, NY: Rensselaer Polytechnic Institute School of Architecture. <<http://www.ced.berkeley.edu/cedr/vs/index.html>>

- *Orientation.* The human need for a recognizable relation to the outside environment is well known. Aviators who lose contact with the horizon are subject to vertigo. Passengers on a ship or airplane are more likely to experience seasickness if they are below decks with no visual contact with the horizon. People inside buildings who lose contact with the exterior may feel insecure about possible escape from fire. People are frustrated and distracted (perhaps subconsciously) when not able to sense what the weather is outside and to have some sense of nature's time.

Psychological benefits of daylighting

There are psychological benefits as well, not readily quantified, but evident in qualitative human responses:

- *Sunshine.* The presence of direct sunshine in the interior environment is one of the strongest psychological benefits. The evidence of a desire by most people for some direct sun is strong. Although direct sun on a visual task may produce excessive brightness differences, some direct sun in proper location and quantity is stimulating and desirable. Daylighting design can often include direct sun without destroying visual acuity.

- *View.* A view to the exterior is another psychological benefit to building occupants. While techniques for admitting daylight are not necessarily directly related to a window with a view, they most often are related. Windows, daylight, and a view go together. Numerous studies have established that people consider a view to be very important. Any leasing agent of building space will confirm the fact that tenants usually are willing to pay more for office space with windows than for windowless spaces.

What constitutes a valuable view is generally related to the information content in the view and the distance between occupant and window. The best views (and the most information content) are those that include some sky, horizon, and foreground. More important however, is a view containing a balance of synthetic and natural things with some element of movement, change, and surprise involved. The closer the occupant is to the window (and, hence, a total view) the more the satisfaction will be. Broad horizontal windows are more satisfying than narrow vertical windows, an optimal size being about 20 to 30 percent of the exterior (window) wall.

- *Brightness gradients and color constancy.* Daylight generally produces a gradation and color of light on surfaces and objects that biologically is "natural" for humans. Daylight is the "standard" against which the human mind measures all things seen, probably because of a lifetime association with daylight. A gradation of daylight on a wall surface from a window will seem natural, and the wall will look smooth. Uneven lighting from electric sources will likely make the walls appear uneven. Colors seen with daylight will appear real and appropriate through something called "color constancy," even though the color produced by daylight will vary from dawn to noon to dusk, as well as by color reflection from adjacent surfaces. A shopper purchasing new clothing often knows to check the apparent color of the material next to the window where daylight is available.

Criteria for lighting design

There are several ways to consider lighting. Some are essentially aesthetic. Satisfaction with the results of any aesthetically-based lighting design will depend on the skills of the designer and the perception of the viewer. Another way to consider lighting is in terms of how well it allows people to see what they want to see. This kind of lighting quality is easy to define, if not so easy to apply.

Studies of industrial worksites have established that daylighting provides multidirectional lighting and directly contributes to error reduction (Romm 1994). When the ability to see and perceive fine detail in a surface or object is considered necessary or highly desirable (especially where not seeing the detail will cause undesirable results, such as accounting errors), then the object must be well lighted and the quality of the lighting can be judged through two primary characteristics: contrast and glare.

Contrast is necessary for good visual perception, the result of luminous (or brightness) differences that, in turn, are dependent upon the illuminance falling on the task and the reflectivity (ability to reflect light) of the task. The printed words on an illuminated newspaper are of low reflectance, and hence, low luminance, while the white paper itself is of high luminance (or brightness). The contrast between the two is what allows them to be perceived by the human eye. There must first be sufficient light to invoke a visual response. Hence, the need for a certain quantity of illuminance (light).

With a given quantity of lighting, there can be different contrast ratios in a task that produce different visual conditions. For this reason, illuminance levels are not a sufficient criteria for judging or specifying the quality of the lighting environment. Luminance differences are more important.

On the other hand, it is possible to produce excessive contrast: contrast that impedes good visual response. A bright light in the field of view will detract from one's ability to see other surrounding objects. An oncoming auto headlight in the dark of night will prevent a view of the dark roadway. A ceiling-mounted luminaire will detract from a person's ability to see a nearby task when both are in the field of view. For this reason, luminaires need some type of shielding device to prevent a direct view of the lamps. Bright clouds seen through a window will also prevent or detract from the ability to see tasks in the same field of view, such as the interior of an outside wall or a book between clouds and the viewer.

Glare is usually associated with brightness differences (too much light in the field of view) or with reflected light. Light reflecting off a task or its visual surround, even one with a low reflectance (for example, printing on a page), can reduce or eliminate our ability to see the task. This kind of glare is called a "veiling reflection," so named because it "veils" (reduces or eliminates) our ability to see the task by reducing the contrast. Such glare is the result of a bright light shining off a task at the "mirror angle" (as a light on the ceiling might be reflected in a mirror placed on the task). It is for this reason that the ceiling is generally a poor place for locating luminaires (unless properly located and/or shielded with respect to the occupant's task) and that windows, generally located to the viewer's side, produce good quality task light without veiling reflections.

Veiling reflections cause loss of contrast. It takes 10 to 15 percent more illumination to make up for each one percent loss in contrast due to veiling reflections. Most tasks thus require two to three times as much illumination from overhead sources as from sidewall lighting. Good quality lighting for visual tasks, then, is a matter of bringing in sufficient light of the direction and quality to produce clarity without excessive contrast or glare.

Programming for daylight

The decision to include strategies and elements of daylighting in a design is generally left to the architect. Clients are not usually aware that this issue requires special attention. Making extensive use of daylight often calls for significant trade-offs, as well as decisions of design and building operation—lighting controls and switches that will be used—so it is important that the client and facilities manager be made aware of the choices.

In early programming, objectives should be set for the visual environment and the types of lighting to be employed. Daylighting is not an afterthought or a simple matter of applying some shading controls to the windows any more than one can just "stick" luminaires in the ceiling (as often the apparent case). The quality of illumination, how well people wish to see inside a building is a key factor in the design, occupant productivity and satisfaction, operation, energy consumption, and long-term costs. Use of a building under emergency conditions (that is, with temporary loss of power) may also suggest daylighting approaches in areas related to life safety such as exitways.

In the context of energy, building energy performance standards adopted by states and municipalities provide targeted building energy use for specific types of buildings and site conditions, in which case lighting quantities may be proscribed. These must be evaluated in terms of the resulting lighting quality.

Specific goals related to daylighting of buildings may be stated in simple terms:

- Design to achieve daylight in all feasible areas in significant, useful quantities,

- Distribute daylight reasonably uniformly, with no significant dark spots, (although variation within the visible range is acceptable and can provide desirable relief).

- Avoid allowing direct sunshine into the building interior in such a way that it may cause visual discomfort (excessive brightness differences) or visual disability (glare). Assess the design for all possible sun penetration angles.

- Provide daylight sensitive controls for the electric lighting so that it will be dimmed or turned off when not needed.

Each of these goals must be evaluated against prevailing standards. Recommended light levels for various visual tasks as well as criteria for judging other goals related to good visual acuity and quality lighting are given in IESNA (1993).

The visual process includes too many other variables to permit illumination quantity levels to be the ultimate criteria. Brightness patterns and sunlight and shadow need to be thoughtfully considered under all of the changing conditions that might prevail throughout the year. Climate and building type (occupancy) will be a factor for the amount of glass that can be optimally used for thermal as well as daylighting control.

The sculpturing process
The design of architecture for daylighting begins with consideration of site, climate, and the neighborhood and extends to building geometry, surface materials and finish treatments, apertures and glazing.

During the principal hours of daylight, there is almost always enough light available from the sun and sky to provide illumination for most human visual tasks. Consider that on an average clear day there is typically 5,000-8,000 (or more) footcandles (fc) outside and that reading legibility is provided by illumination 50 to 80 fc, one can roughly generalize that there is 100 times the level of daylight illumination available than is needed. Design for daylighting involves the art of making such daylight-source illumination both tolerable and useable by reflection, diffusion and redirection. This is much like the design of a lighting fixture or luminaire, only in the case of a daylit building, the (solar) light source changes in location and intensity throughout the day and year.

It is not necessary that daylighting conditions be precisely predictable. The designer can establish a set of goals to be achieved within a reasonable range of expected exterior daylight conditions and then set forth to make the most of available daylight, while providing a supplemental or alternative electric lighting system to contribute additional light when conditions require.

Sky conditions
There are three types of sky conditions generally considered in daylighting design:

- *Clear sky*, which provides a relatively steady source of low-intensity light with direct sun of high intensity. For buildings designed for climates with prevailing clear skies, solar control (sun-shading) is generally required and can be reliably dimensioned, depending on the requisites of underheated versus overheated conditions. In hot arid climates (such as a desert location), window apertures can be very small and utilize reflected light to protect the interior against direct sun and glare, and yet provide high levels of illumination.

- *Overcast sky*, which may be a very dark under dark clouds, or which may be very bright and "hazy," low level lighting, but diffusely cast from the entire sky dome (that is, nearly omnidirectional). An overcast sky can be excessively bright when viewed from inside the building, or it may be quite dark. In climates with prevailing cloudy skies, fixed exterior sun control is generally not advisable since it increases darkness and shading under overcast conditions. Interior shades for glare control from all directions may be needed.

- *Partly cloudy sky* can be considered a third type of sky from the standpoint of daylighting design, characterized by partial or intermittent clouds and by a blue background with bright, white clouds (oftentimes passing and changing rapidly), with direct sunshine penetrating off and on. Intensities on the ground can change rapidly. Passing clouds viewed from the interior can be exceedingly bright, causing glare and visual discomfort. In climates with such intermittent conditions, a combination of fixed and movable sun and light controls is recommended.

Data are available based on calculations of anticipated daylight at particular locations based on the month, day, time of day, and building orientation (Robbins and Hunter 1982). Calculated data are reasonably accurate and empirically quantified. However, these do not include allowances for cloud cover conditions and, therefore, must be modified by data on localized cloud cover, represented in typical airport data.

Site and building orientation
Selection of the building site or of the building location within a site might be influenced by daylighting considerations. While none need prohibit the use of daylight, several site features to be considered include:

- Location of the building on the site so that daylight can reach the apertures without significant interference from nearby obstacles (such as tall buildings, mountains, or trees).

- Highly reflective surfaces near the site, such as glass-covered buildings that could cause excessive glare.

- Trees and shrubs on the site that might give shade and reduce sky glare from the interior.

- Bright ground surfaces that can be used to reflect daylight into the interior (as much as 40 percent of interior daylight can come reflected from ground surfaces). Glare from reflecting ground or window sill surfaces needs to be avoided.

Most any building orientation can effectively make use of daylighting, although the amount and type of daylight available will vary with each wall surface. The essential difference in the quantity and quality of daylight received from different orientations has to do with the location of the direct sun. Direct sun may have to be shaded and the intensity of the daylight will vary in the northern hemisphere from south ("equatorial facing", east-west, and north ("polar orientation"). In the southern hemisphere, of course the equatorial and polar orientations are the obverse. There is some difference in the brightness and color of the sky in different quadrants, but this is of only minor importance to the designer.

Fig. 2. Carpenter Center for the Visual Arts. Harvard University, Cambridge, MA. Architect: Le Corbusier.

Fig. 3. Lighting model. Tennessee Valley Authority Headquarters (TVA). Chattanooga, TN. Architects Collaborative and CRS, in joint venture. Van der Ryn/Calthorpe, Partners and William Lam, consultants. Photo: courtesy of Sarah Harkness, FAIA.

Fig. 4. Light reflectors along the interior of TVA Headquarters atrium

Openings to the polar orientation will probably require larger glass areas than other orientations to achieve similar results. There can be certain advantages to the polar orientation (that is, little or no sun control is necessary and illumination tends to be soft and diffuse), but sky glare control may still be necessary.

East and west fenestration must deal with the early morning and late afternoon low-altitude sun, which tends to move up and across the sky in relatively rapid fashion causing excessive brightness and potential overheating. Some type of vertical shielding is generally most effective (such as vertical louvers or zig-zag walls) on east and west facades, with the nagging problem that each orientation experiences extreme conditions of sun for one-half of the daylight hours and complete shade for the other half. Fixed louvers tend to interface with a view out but can be quite effective in letting daylight in and in reflecting and diffusing its effect.

The equatorial-facing facade provides the best opportunity for daylighting and utilization of the "solar resource." This orientation receives direct sun throughout the day and is most easily controlled by short horizontal sun shades and light shelves (horizontally placed light reflectors), keeping the high sun out in the summer but allowing winter low-altitude sun penetration if desirable. Sky brightness will still be a factor to be dealt with.

Shape guides daylight

Perhaps the most significant design determinant in the use of daylight is the geometry of the building—walls, ceilings, floors, windows, and how they relate to each other. Architecture has always been shaped by considerations for sunlight and daylight—ancient Greek and Roman villas and baths, Gothic cathedrals of the 13th and 14th centuries, nineteenth century industrial buildings, masterworks of Frank Lloyd Wright, Alvar Aalto, and Louis Kahn, and school buildings of the 1950s by William Caudill, among others.

- *Building configuration.* Daylighting of multistory buildings will be most effective if long and narrow so that daylight can penetrate from both sides. A rule-of-thumb is that with reasonably sized fenestration, daylighting can be quite easily achieved to a depth of about 15 ft. (4.5 m) inward from the aperture; with windows open to a high ceiling, about 20 ft. (6 m) inward from the aperture. These values can be increased with designs that extend the illumination by reflection (from light-shelves) and by light-colored surfaces, in documented examples from 30 to 40 ft. (9 to 12 m) (Lam 1986). In single-story buildings, skylights or clerestories can be used, thus permitting the building to assume a more square shape.

Often the footprint (or floor plan) of the building can be sculptured to achieve shading from the direct sun and/or to control the view from the interior. Carpenter Center at Harvard (Fig. 2) is an example of breaking up the exterior wall surface to prevent direct sun penetration while still allowing daylight reflection and view. Atria, light wells, and courtyards can be used to effectively admit daylight, not only into the well openings, but into adjacent interior spaces as well, as in the TVA Headquarters Building, Chattanooga, TN (Figs. 3 and 4).

In reviewing geometric and design options, it is useful for the designer to understand some of the quantitative relationships that go with various geometric forms. A review of measured illumination levels for various types of building designs can be helpful as can simple calculations, but experience is also a good teacher. Designers should manipulate the forms and measure the results before they can understand the quantitative relationships. Such experience can be acquired through model studies, as indicated in the accompanying illustrations.

- *Window Height.* The window size and height above the workplane are among the most important geometric factors in daylighting design. The higher the space, the farther will be the daylight penetration. Naturally, bigger windows admit more daylight. But the height of the windows is the more significant factor in getting the daylight deep into the interior. The height of the ceiling above the floor has little effect on the daylight if windows are not placed high in the exterior wall.

- *Room Depth.* Tests by the author have shown that as the depth of the room becomes greater, everything else remaining the same, the level of daylight intensity throughout becomes less—a simple matter of spreading the same quantity of incoming light over a larger area. A 28-ft. (8.5 m) deep room has 18 percent less light at a point near the back wall than at the same relative position in a 24 ft. (7.3 m) room; a 32 ft. (9.8 m) room, 28 percent less.

The traditional rule-of-thumb (in some cases a state code stipulation) that recommends that the depth of the room should not be more than two and one-half times the height of the window is somewhat applicable, but it assumes that the window is continuous from one side wall to the other.

- *Surface Reflectance.* The effects of various wall surfaces can be seen from the following example: Consider a simple rectangular room with windows on one end, with all interior surfaces painted white. Consider that the measured illumination on a fixed desk is assumed to be 100 percent, as a base reference (all white room). When the back wall (away from the window) is painted flat black, the illumination on the desk is reduced to 50 percent of the original intensity; with the side walls only painted black the intensity is reduced to 62 percent; with the floor only painted black the illumination is reduced to 68 percent; and with the ceiling painted black, to 39 percent.

Such figures, the results of tests by the author, show the *ceiling* to be the most important surface in reflecting daylight coming into the room and reaching the task. Next in importance is the *back wall*, then the *side walls*, and finally, the *floor*. This indicates at least two design guidelines: keep the ceiling as light in color as possible and use the floor surface for deep colors. Dark colors on the floor will have the least negative effect on the daylighting of tasks.

- *Overhangs.* Building overhangs can be very useful for sun and rain control. Although they do reduce the quantity of daylight within the building, particularly next to the window wall, they are especially effective in reflecting light from outside ground planes back into the interior of the building. The result is a more even distribution of light in the space. Test results indicate a 39 percent drop in illumination near the window of a unilaterally lighted room with the addition of a six-foot overhang, but only a 22 percent drop near the interior wall. Overhangs are also helpful in reducing the area of bright sky that can be seen from within the interior, although the effect is usually minimal.

Apertures are critical

The amount of daylight that enters any opening (aperture) is proportional to the size of the opening, the transmissivity of the glazing, and, of course, the daylight available to enter. The amount of daylight that reaches any point in the interior is related to the area and brightness of both the exterior sources of daylight and interior daylit surfaces that are "seen" from that particular point. Thus, a point close to the aperture "sees" a larger portion of the sky and has a higher illumination level than a point farther away from the aperture. Interior surfaces also contribute daylight to the task and are influenced by light reflected from other surfaces.

- *Light shelves.* A light shelf is a horizontal plane placed below the top of a window, usually just above door height allowing light to be reflected from its upper surface to the ceiling level. The light shelf can be placed entirely outside, or in combination of outside-inside.

When the top surface of the light shelf is exposed to direct sun, it reflects daylight to the interior ceiling and thus extends light farther into the room. When compared to a fenestration of the same dimension without the light shelf, the interior illumination with a light shelf will be less, because the light shelf blocks out some of the light, most noticeably near the window plane. (Sometimes window sills may be extended as with a thick wall section or with a bay-window configuration to act as a light shelf, in which case it does increase the amount of illumination that is reflected to the interior, although this may be a source of undesirable glare if it is within the vision cone of the occupant.)

While the contribution of light shelves and light reflecting surfaces within the window may no add to the quantity of interior daylighting, the quality of the result is improved. Its effect is to distribute light more evenly and more deeply into the interior. The light shelf may be white or highly reflective (as with polished metal) to increase the daylight reflectance. As with any lighting scheme that uses the ceiling as a reflective surface, ceiling finishes and materials have to be carefully selected and installed, since any flaws and/or joints are revealed and made sharper by horizontal or grazing light.

Light shelves are ineffective when exposed to diffuse skylight only, since they are designed to reflect "beam" radiation. Thus their use anywhere but on equatorial-facing fenestration will not be productive.

- *Skylights.* The illumination falling on the horizontal plane of the roof may be many times that which strikes the vertical plane of a window even under an overcast sky. To allow the eye to adjust to the bright skylighting source, some shadowing and reflecting surfaces are needed (Fig. 5).

Fig. 5. Corcoran Gallery, Washington, skylight modeled after the dome of the Pantheon. Shadowing provided by the coffers allows the eye to adjust to its lighting intensity.

Fig. 6. Baker House Student Lounge, Massachusetts Institute of Technology, Cambridge, MA. Alvar Aalto. 1947. Splayed conical skylights provide substantial daylighting.

In environments where visual acuity is critical, such as classrooms, libraries and offices, the diffuse skylight, directly viewable from below, may produce excessive brightness and to cause disabling veiling reflections on tasks below, just as electric luminaires can. However, daylight from skylights can be controlled through the use of splayed wells and louvers, to minimize veiling reflections. Diffuse plastic or opaque glass in skylights tend to diminish the biological benefits of daylight by modifying visual contact with the weather. There seems little logic in using diffuse glazing.

Skylights reduce energy consumption by reducing the need for electric lighting, and they admit heat from the sun in winter, reducing the need for other internal heating, which can be significant. However, skylights lose some interior heat and electric light to the cooler outside air and admit heat from the outside during the air-conditioning season. The determination of whether or not skylights will be economically viable in a particular situation must include a year-round analysis of both positive and negative aspects based on local climatic conditions. A properly designed skylight system with daylight and heat transfer controls for both day and night operation will prove viable on a year-round basis in almost all localities. Much like a lighting fixture, the conical skylights familiar in work by Alvar Aalto spread daylighting from small apertures (Fig. 6).

- *Clerestories.* Clerestories have many of the attributes of skylights except that they occur in the vertical rather than the horizontal plane and, therefore, are exposed to less quantity of direct daylight than are skylights. They can however gain illumination by reflection from adjacent roof surfaces and can be oriented to prevent penetration of direct sun. When built in combination with an interior reflector or light shelf, a clerestory can bounce great quantities of direct sun against the ceiling providing significant levels of illumination on the tasks below, and at the same time blocking the view from below of the bright sky (Fig. 7). The penetration of direct sun through clerestories can be eliminated with proper orientation or with the addition of overhangs and/or horizontal louvers, on the interior or exterior. Light colored roof surfaces adjacent to the clerestories can increase the reflection of daylight to the interior.

Documented examples, such as Johnson Controls Office Building in Salt Lake (Fig. 8), have demonstrated that an equatorial-facing clerestory can provide sufficient illumination to eliminate the use of electric light under year-round daylight conditions (Lam 1986).

Fig. 7. South-facing clerestories with louvers. Public Library, Mt. Airy, NC. Mazria/Schiff, Architects. 1982. Louver baffles provide shading and light diffusion.

Fig. 8. South-facing clerestory. Johnson Controls Office Building. Salt Lake City, UT. Douglas Drake, Architect, Donald Watson, FAIA and William Lam, consultants. 1982.

Devices that control daylight

A variety of daylight controlling devices may be helpful in getting the daylight to where it is needed and for eliminating excessively bright areas from view. Some of these controls are dynamic (they can be moved) and some are static (they remain in place permanently). Dynamic controls have the advantage of allowing for change in response to changing sky conditions, thereby improving the efficiency of the design, but have the disadvantage of requiring either an operator (usually the occupants, an unreliable source in general) or an expensive automatic device, which can be difficult to maintain. Static controls are less troublesome but also less responsive and efficient.

- *Louvers.* There are a variety of types of louvers for daylight control. They may be small, movable, and on the interior (such as venetian blinds), or they may be large and fixed on the exterior as were commonly found on buildings of the 1940s. Regardless of type, they perform basically the same way. One of the most effective is the venetian blind. Venetian blinds can be adjusted to exclude direct sun but reflect its light to the ceiling where it will bounce into the interior areas, while still allowing a view to the exterior, or they can be tilted to the closed position to block light and view. They can be adjusted to all lighting conditions and thus have great versatility, if actually used! Light colored blinds are far more effective for lighting and also more conducive to thermal comfort: under direct sun and in the closed position, dark venetian blinds will heat up more readily than light colored, and radiate that heat to the interior.

Horizontal louvers and overhangs are most effective for high altitude sun such as on the south fenestration. Vertical louvers are most effective for low altitude sun such as on the east and west facades. For situations where both high and low sun must be considered (southwest facade), "egg crate" louvers are often the most effective control.

- *Glazing.* The most popular types of glazing materials include clear glass, tinted glass, and other glasses referred to as "selectively transmitting" glasses. All glazing materials are somewhat selectively transmitting, that is, they permit the passage of some parts of the radiant energy spectrum (light), while reflecting or absorbing other parts (heat producing). For instance, 1/4-inch (6.4 mm) clean, clear glass transmits about 90 percent of the visible energy which strikes it, while allowing only about 79 percent of the infrared (heat producing) radiant energy to pass through.

The tinted, transparent glasses (and plastics) have been popular because of their ability to reduce the apparent brightness of exterior surfaces when seen from the interior. These glasses are produced principally in gray or bronze, or variations thereof. The use of tinted glasses that change the color of the daylight should be avoided because of the color distortion which results. Transmissivity values of these tinted materials range from the very dark (10-15 percent), to the very light (70-80 percent) and their transmittance of the infrared spectrum (heat) is only slightly more restricted—usually 10-15 percent below that of the visible transmittance.

While tinted glazing can be a useful tool in creating a lighting environment, its use in a building to be daylighted is self defeating since it prevents the penetration of the useful daylight. Tinted glazing is recommended for use only when the primary source of interior light is from other locations (that is, skylights or electric lights) and the tinted glazing is used only for viewing out.

If the transmissivity of tinted glass is around 60 percent or above, most occupants of a building will not be aware of the situation when they are inside, unless they can also see to the exterior through some clear glass or an opening at the same time. Once people become aware of the tinted glass, they tend to find it a little frustrating because of its unnaturalness. Tinted glass below about 50 percent transmissivity may be noticeable and invoke a feeling of impending rain.

Manufacturers of glass are developing glasses that are more selective in transmitting beneficial light. Some glazing materials, for instance, reflect (rather than transmit or absorb) a higher percent of the sun's heat-producing energy while allowing a greater percent of visible light transmission. Such glasses offer some advantage in the light-heat tradeoff process, but manufacturer literature can sometimes be misleading through the use of claims not substantiated by their own technical data. Caution should be exercised in the selection of the most cost effective glazing materials.

Special systems

With lighting as both an aesthetic and technical impetus, there are numerous developments that extend daylight applications. With a "light pipe," using variations of fiber optics, or even a water-filled plastic tube, it is possible to configure the pipe so that sunlight is transported through the tube and around bends and corners with very little absorption and loss of light. This is done via various devices such as mirrors, heliostats, lenses, light pipes, and other light reflecting and transporting devices. One approach, referred to as active solar optics, includes powered heliostats which track the sun and reflect direct sunlight into a building. The success of transporting direct sunlight effectively and economically is still dependent on refinement and/or development of more efficient and cheaper heliostats, mirrors, lenses, and other equipment.

Related systems include methods of reflecting sunlight into buildings via mirrors and light wells, sometimes with lenses, as well as methods which employ reflective louvers or light shelves in the fenestration. For Morgan Hall, Harvard Business School, William Lam designed a large horizontal reflector that moves to follow the monthly solar altitude and to reflect sunlight down a relatively narrow fourstoried lightwell. The University of Michigan Law Library skylight incorporate mirrored surfaces mounted vertically within its mullion structure that reflect and diffuse daylight down a multi-storied underground atrium (Figs. 9 and 10).

The dramatic effect of sunlight reflection and refraction is captured within the skylights of the Chapel at Harvard Business School (Fig. 11). Transparent and translucent building materials are being developed that increase the effect of daylighting. Glass balconies, walkways and stairways at Hartford Atheneum diffuse and transmit sunlight within its remodeled entry gallery (Fig. 12).

Energy and cost issues

In the school buildings of the 1950s, daylighting was justified because of its contributions to good visual conditions. In buildings of the 1970s, the justification was based primarily upon the energy savings possible with daylighting. For energy conservation to be justified from the standpoint of using daylighting, there must be a reduction from the norm in energy use for electric lighting and/or for cooling/ heating. Thus, energy conservation is related not only to the introduction of daylight but to the proper use and control of electric lighting.

The design of daylighting and electric lighting are best undertaken collaboratively and sensitively from the earliest design schematic. The Ritz Hotel Tea Room, London, provides an example of integrating daylight and electric light (Fig. 13). Its low-level electric lighting is augmented by highly reflective surfaces. Located on the west side, afternoon sunlight enters late afternoon, when tea is served. Other nineteenth century examples, configured when daylight was the primary source of lighting, illustrate the point. The Boston Public Library Reading Room by McKim, Mead and White is illuminated by the combination of table lamps (task lighting) and high windows (Fig. 14).

Cost-effective use of daylighting is linked to the reduction in energy use for electric lighting and for air conditioning. If the consumption of energy from electric lights can be reduced, the energy needed for

Fig. 9. Lightwell of Michigan Law Library. Gunnar Birkerts, Architect. 1974.

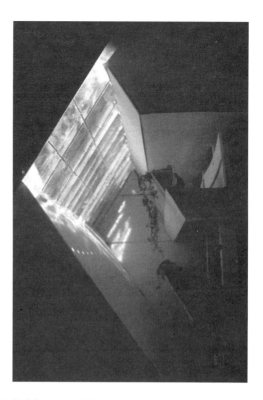

Fig. 10. Lightmodel of Michigan Law Library. Daylight model study by Genevieve Black and Kirsten Youngren. Equinox 12 noon. Daylight factor = 5%. (Watson 1996)

Fig. 11. Skylights of the Chapel at Harvard Business School, Cambridge, MA. Architect: Moshe Safdie; Sculptor: Charles Ross; Prism steering design and installation: Thomas Hopper. 1990. Oil-filled prisms are computer-controlled to track the sun and create a continuously refracted sunbeam.

Fig. 12. Atheneum Museum, Hartford, CT. Remodeling of Entryway. 1996. Glass walkways (seen above at right of photo) diffuse daylight throughout the entry gallery. Ta-Soo Kim, Architect.

dumping the heat from those lights to the outside can also be reduced. These savings must be balanced against the heat gains and losses associated with the daylighting system through windows and skylights.

The assumption is often made that good daylighting design will increase the capital cost in a building. If the design concept is confined to a rectangular space with windows on one wall, there is little that can be done to make daylighting effective without adding to the building's first cost. However, if daylighting is a prime consideration in the total design—allowed to influence spatial relationships, form, and detail from the very beginning of the design process—the first-cost investments attributable to daylight may be small or nonexistent.

Daylighting is part of the total building cost-benefit and should not be treated as an "add-on." The cost benefit of design for daylighting must be considered in conjunction with other lighting costs and benefits, with solar heat gains and losses, with energy uses and saving and so forth. There is no simple conclusion about the cost of daylighting that can be applied to all building designs. Presently available daylighting analysis methods range from the use of simple graphic tools to sophisticated mainframe computers and physical scale-model studies.

Daylighting analysis
All analysis methods, whether graphic, mathematical, or physical, are attempts to simulate a full-scale condition. The difference in the various analytical tools available is in the parameters that can be included

Fig. 13. Ritz Hotel Tea Room, London. Skylighting admits afternoon sunlight around tea time. Example suggested by King Lui Wu.

Fig. 14. Boston Public Library Reading Room, illuminated by combination of reading lights and high windows.

Fig. 15. Riola Church, Bologna, Italy. Alvar Aalto, Architect. 1966. Daylight model study by Jay Adams and Jon Vandervelde. Summer solstice 9 am. Daylight factor = 12%

Fig. 16. Church of the Light. Osaka Prefecture. Japan. Tadao Ando, Architect. 1989. Daylight model study Hiro Ogino and Peter Sprouse. Winter solstice 9 am. Daylight factor = 2%

and the accuracy the results. A simple graphic overlay can be used to size a window under overcast sky conditions, but the result will be far from a reproduction of reality. A small programmable calculator can provide comparison of two design alternatives under certain limited conditions. Personal computer programs allow more complex analysis, but a still limited to parameters that must be understood for useful results. A mainframe computer analysis can provide fairly accurate results within certain important limits, but it can also couple daylighting concerns with the thermal, energy, and cost concerns involved.

A physical scale model can produce quite accurate results if constructed and tested under appropriate conditions. In the design of Shell Oil Headquarters, a series of lighting models from small-scale to full-scale provided for its systematic development, modeled under actual sky conditions at the site (Figs. 17a-17d).

Perhaps because of its visually apparent results and the fact that scale modeling is part of the architect's stock in trade, the most useful daylighting analysis for the designer can come from the use of scale models. Scale models can provide an indication of approximate illu-

mination to be expected under various types of skies and allow comparison of various design alternatives. They also allow an architect and lighting designer to accurate simulate the year-round lighting conditions that are obtained by the building design, with its range of results shown in accompanying illustrations (Watson 1996).

Daylight has been around for a long time, but is often talked about as if it were mysterious, to be handled by experts only. Daylight is part of architecture, in both its historical, theoretical, and technical conception, with a unique capacity to inspire people and to illuminate the elements of its design.

NOTE: Figs. 10, 15 and 16 are examples of daylighting models by students of architecture at the University of Oregon and at Rensselaer Polytechnic Institute (Watson 1996). Date and time indicates the daylighting at the hour simulated in the photo. The daylight factors equals exterior illumination divided by interior illumination and are measured at the center of the space under standardized "universal sky" conditions (1000 fc). These indicate the percentage of daylight illumination against a universal measure.

Fig. 17. Shell Oil Headquarters Building. Houston, TX. CRS Architects. Lighting consultant: Benjamin Evans, 1983.

(a) Initial lighting model of office module; (b) mock-ups of small-scale and full-scale models, movable to various orientations; (c) Inside the full scale mock-up; (d) Built office, featuring light reflectors and diffusers, with ceiling used as light reflector for daylight and for electric light. (Photos courtesy of CRS).

a

c

b

d

Natural ventilation

Benjamin Evans

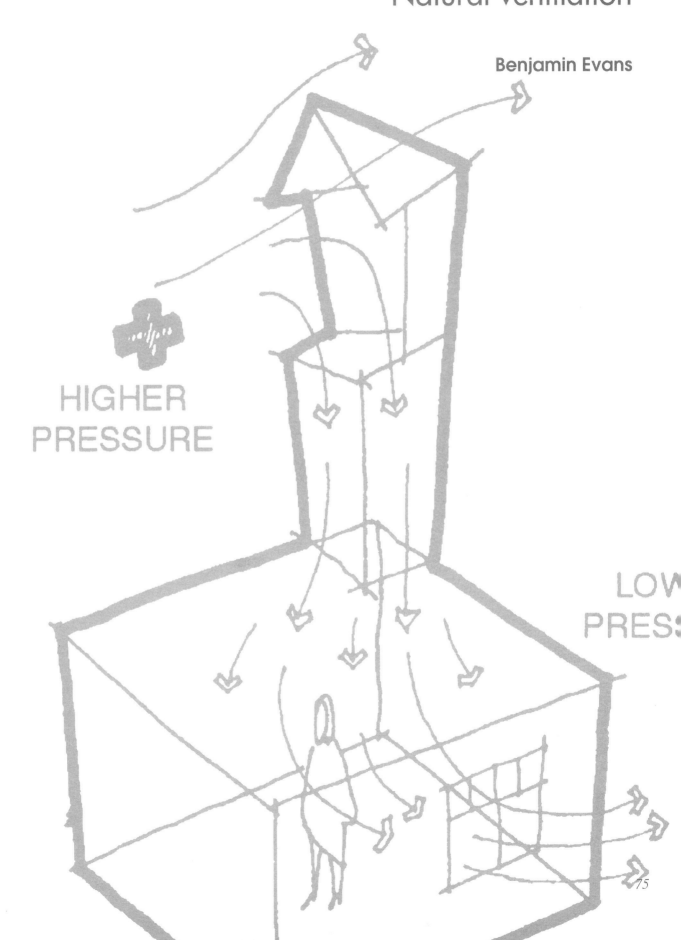

HIGHER
PRESSURE

LOW
PRESS

Natural ventilation with porches, extended wings, adjustable louvers and shutters, attic ventilators (under eaves) and roof monitors.

Summary: "Ventilation," deriving from the Latin *ventus* and meaning the movement of air, is used to define air change in buildings from fan-driven mechanical systems or from natural air flow through ventilating openings. This article discusses natural (wind-pressure driven) air flow principles and design techniques for ventilation to satisfy human comfort.

Key words: air flow, bioclimatic design, natural venitilation, stack effect, turbulence, Venturi effect, wind shadow.

Natural ventilation in buildings is intended to cool the body directly by convection across the skin and body, and absorption of perspiration. The air flow must be directed towards the "living" or occupied zones of a building. Air exchange may be done with some air velocity, but generally, low-velocity mechanical system designs have little direct effect on the human physiological cooling system to transpperspiration). Openings in a building can be manipulated to increase or decrease the speed of the air movement.

Often considered part of "bioclimatic design," natural ventilation is effective for cooling buildings that are properly shaded and otherwise designed to suit local climatic conditions, such as air- and earth temperatures, relative humidity, daily and seasonal wind and breeze direction. In many locations and building types, these climatic design elements can provide the principal source of cooling comfort in buildings (Watson and Labs 1993).

Going into a non-air conditioned building during hot weather is like going from the frying pan into the oven, where the air is hot and stagnant. This is a waste because, at a surprising number of places and times, the interior would be a lot more comfortable if a breeze could get inside. Our buildings tend to hold heat when we least want it. Buildings are too often designed so that the outside air can't get inside to cool the occupants or the building.

It doesn't have to be that way. Before mechanical air conditioning systems became widely available in the late 1950s and throughout the history of architecture, all sorts of techniques used to take advantage of natural air currents. Ancient Greeks and Romans provided *porticos* around their temples for shade and breeze. Ancient Egyptians and other desert peoples put scoops on their roofs to funnel air through their homes, cooled by evaporating water jars. The frontier Americans built dog-trots plans (breezeways across the building core) and porches so they could sit in their rocking chairs and enjoy the cool breeze.

Such techniques are not lost to us. Air conditioning and mechanical cooling has to us seemed easier than paying attention to design with climate. There are of course times and places when natural airflow isn't appropriate or won't help much. If your nose is stuffy from an allergy and the air outside is hot and humid, you'll want cool, filtered air instead of an outdoor breeze. In instances of extremely hot and humid air, natural ventilation only increases moisture laden perspiration. Still, almost everywhere, there are times of the day and year when a natural breeze in the shade is more than sufficient for comfort.

The physics of natural ventilation

Breezes act according to the laws of nature. The designer must understand certain scientific principles before deciding with accuracy how to control air movement. For thousands of years, people managed to capitalize on air movement in building design based largely on intuition alone. It wasn't until the middle of the 18th century that scientists began to experiment with air and to try to explain what it is and how it works.

An early theory was that air pressure had something to do with electricity (which people didn't understand either). Some thought that the clouds were held up by electricity and that electricity caused smoke to rise. In 1783, a French couple tried to catch smoke (and electricity) in a paper bag and accidentally invented the hot-air balloon. Around the turn of the century, a French physicist substituted helium for hot air in a balloon and discovered the principle of air pressure, which is fundamental to understanding air movement: a body of higher-pressure air will move (expand) toward a body of lower-pressure air. Put simply, as the pressure of air (or gas) increases, it expands and becomes lighter, thereby tending to rise, or move, until it finds a place in the atmosphere where the surrounding pressure is the same (Fig. 1).

Global air pressure differences are caused principally by the sun warming some parts of the earth, with the earth, in turn, warming the air, while other parts of the earth and air are not warmed as much, such as polar ice caps and   forests (Fig. 2). The result is that the warmed air (higher pressure) tries to move toward the cooler air (lower pressure).

The rotating motion of the earth also has an influence on geographic air movements. As the earth spins, it pulls the air around with it, but the air doesn't entirely keep up. There is slippage. At about this point, those studying air mechanics realized that air has mass and therefore is affected by gravity and follows the law of inertia—mass once set in motion tends to continue straight until its direction and speed are changed by some outside force.

Author: Benjamin Evans, FAIA

Credits: An earlier version of this article appeared as "Letting Fresh Air Back into Buildings: The evolving state of natural ventilation," in *Architecture.* March, 1989 and is reproduced by permission of the publisher. Illustrations are by the author.

References: Evans, Benjamin. 1957. *Natural Air Flow In and Around Buildings.* College Station, TX: Texas Engineering Research Station.

Chandra, Subrato, Philip W. Fairey and Robert S. Spain. 1982. *Handbook for Designing Naturally Ventilated Buildings.* Publication FSEC-CR-60-82. Cocoa, FL: Florida Solar Energy Center.

Watson, Donald and Kenneth Labs. 1983. Revised 1993. *Climatic Building Design.* New York: McGraw-Hill.

Fig. 1. The buoyancy of heated air rising to equal pressure

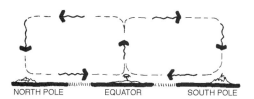

NORTH POLE   EQUATOR   SOUTH POLE

Fig. 2. The stratospheric wind machine

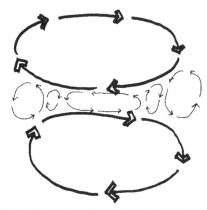

Fig. 3. The microdynamics of wind eddies

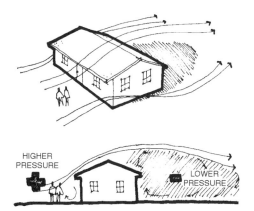

HIGHER PRESSURE   LOWER PRESSURE

Fig. 4. Wind shadows on the leeward side of a building or object

At the global scale, some of the outside forces are mountains, forests, land masses ice caps, and geographic formations. Geographic features affect the origins and movement of the wind because the wind moving over the ground and other objects causes friction, slowing some parts of the air.

All three phenomena—pressure difference, inertia, and friction—produce turbulence, so that air doesn't often move smoothly along a straight path. It takes short darts here and there, speeds up, and slows down. When two currents of air are traveling in opposite directions, they always will be separated by a series of eddies because adjacent particles of air always move in the same direction. Laboratory studies have shown that these eddies range from the very large through a series of adjacent eddies to the microscopic, which cannot be seen with the naked eye (Fig. 3). But at the scale of a single building, for purposes of preliminary understanding and calculation in building design, we presume that air moves in fairly well-defined paths.

This assumption that air behaves roughly as a laminar (layered) air flow in well-defined paths is sufficient for an initial understanding of how air may move around and through a building. Such assumptions must be further refined to anticipate the effects of the turbulence that is a result of real wind conditions. This second level or advance analysis often requires careful wind-tunnel or full scale air flow model testing.

An important set of air movement phenomena is explained by the Bernoulli theorem of fluid behavior (which considers air to be a fluid). Defined by the 18th-century Swiss mathematician, the Bernoulli theorem includes the observation that fluid pressure decreases as the rate of fluid movement increases. For example, an airfoil, which is what allows aircraft to fly, is flat on the bottom and humped on the top. The hump makes air flow faster over the top of the wing, which means—as we know from Bernoulli—air pressure over the wings goes down and the airplane goes up.

Another fluid property of air is that, when flow is temporarily constricted, as when the air enters an hourglass-shaped funnel, its speed increases inside the constriction (accompanied by pressure decrease). The phenomenon was observed and recorded by Giovanni Venturi, the 19th-century Italian physicist for whom the effect is named. To see how the Venturi effect occurs at building scale, envision the windward (high-pressure) wall as a flat funnel and a windward inlet, such as an open window or door, as the constriction. As long as an outlet is sufficiently sized, air flowing through the inlet will move faster than the outside breeze.

Assume that a gentle breeze is blowing along the earth's surface, coming from a high-pressure air mass over in the next county to a lower-pressure air mass somewhere down the road. On striking a solid object—a simple cube-shaped building, for instance—air movement is interrupted. As air piles up in front (upwind) of the object, its pressure increases until forced over and around the solid object, creating a lower-pressure area behind the object (downwind). Air in this lower-pressure area on the downwind side is eddying and moving slowly back upwind toward the solid object. This protected area is called the "wind shadow" (Fig. 4).

Designing for natural ventilation

The greatest pressure differential around a building occurs when the wind strikes it perpendicularly. This creates the largest wind shadow and, thus, the lowest downwind pressure. If we could move the building around until its smallest dimension faced into the wind, we would see that this would produce the smallest wind shadow and least pressure downwind. If we put a number of buildings together on a site, we will get a variety of wind shadows and patterns, and each building will get hit by less wind than if it were all by itself. Each building affects the others. Often, the designer will be looking for patterns that will allow the maximum amount of wind to hit each building.

Since air moves from higher pressure to lower pressure, it makes sense to put a building's breeze inlets adjacent to the higher-pressure areas and breeze outlets adjacent to the lower-pressure areas. To determine the best places for inlets and outlets, therefore, the designer needs to have some idea of where high and low pressures will occur on the building surfaces. On a simple cube shape, the windward face of the cube is under positive pressure, relative to ambient air pressure. The top, back, and sides are under negative pressure. An inlet on the windward face and an outlet on any of the other surfaces will produce cross ventilation.

If the wind approaches the cube from a 45-degree angle, there is a variety of pressures on the surfaces. Pressure areas are less distinct, making it more difficult for us to find the best high-pressure area for the inlet (Fig. 5).

Fig. 6 shows relative air speeds above a simple block-shaped building. The contour line marked 1.0 represents wind movement at the prevailing wind speed, or 100 percent. The .4 line represents the area of speed that is 40 percent of that of the prevailing breeze. Looking at these wind pressures in terms of the building structure, once can see that the roof and the downwind walls are all in negative pressure areas and tend to he pulled away by the wind.

Everyone knows that hot air rises. This is not a contradiction to the statement that air is moved by pressure differences. As the temperature of a body of air rises, the air pressure differences cause it to flow toward a lower- pressure area, usually higher up. These "stack effect" currents are useful in exhausting unwanted air from a building, such as the air that might collect under a skylight or next to the ceiling, but they are of little benefit in directly cooling people through evaporation, simply because the currents are not moving fast enough and usually do not pass through the living zone (the areas where people are). The stack effect, however, creates air exchange in the absence of outside wind pressure, familiar in a "tee-pee" design where the opening at the top allows heated air to escape and cooler replacement air enters under the bottom flaps or lower openings. In low-rise buildings, stack-effect currents are particularly effective at night when the cooler night air can be brought in to carry to the outside the heat that has been absorbed by building materials during the day.

What isn't commonly recognized is that prevailing breezes may almost always overcome or offset the effects of upward air movement driven by thermal differences. In the worst case, an opening at the top of a space intended to exhaust air by stack effect might be result a "short circuit" in which case outside breezes push the warm air back down into the occupied zone of the interior. This can be addressed by offering choices in manipulating the upper level exhaust. The "roof monitor" placed at the top of a stair well in traditional 19th century houses provides an example. If the opening to leeward is opened large and with a small crack to windward, mild cross ventilation will overcome the stack effect and carry the heat out via the breeze. A stack effect can work in conjunction with cross ventilation. Like a sailboat, ventilation controls often have to be set for prevailing breeze conditions.

In some Middle East countries, "windscoops" have been used for hundreds of years to induce natural interior ventilation (Fig. 7). These windscoops rise above the roofs of houses to create pressure areas that pull the air into downstairs rooms, either down the scoop when the wind blows from one direction, or into windows and out of the windscoop when the prevailing wind is from the opposite direction. Windscoops do not push or force the air down the tower. Acting as Bernoulli's theorem describes, air movement into the interior is created by pressure differences that result from wind blowing over the windscoops and the building.

A similar construction also used in the Middle East to induce natural airflow is the "venting tower" (Fig. 8). Here, the tower rises above the

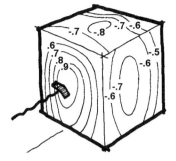

SURFACE PRESSURE

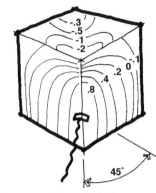

Fig. 6. Cross-section of wind pressure effects

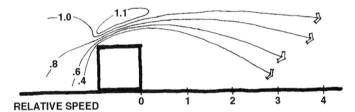

RELATIVE SPEED

Fig. 5. Differential pressures as a function of geometry and wind exposure

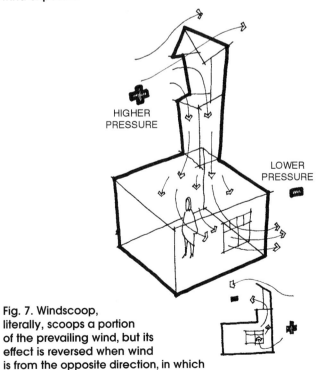

HIGHER PRESSURE

LOWER PRESSURE

Fig. 7. Windscoop, literally, scoops a portion of the prevailing wind, but its effect is reversed when wind is from the opposite direction, in which case it operates like a venting tower (small-scale section)

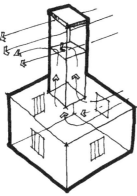

Fig. 8. A venting tower, with its upper portion designed for exhaust by wind-induced suction

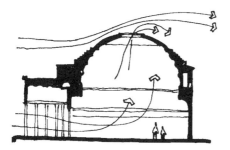

Fig. 9. The Pantheon's *oculus* (open to outdoor air) also functions as an exhaust vent, due to the glancing effect of wind currents

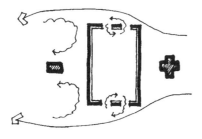

Fig. 10. A plan with little cross ventilation, given no openings to provide for cross-ventilation of prevailing breezes

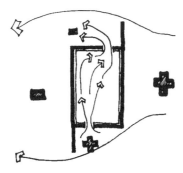

Fig. 11. A modest correction of the Fig. 10 plan, created by extending a wall to capture some breeze

building roof to interrupt the wind and create a low-pressure area, regardless of the direction of the prevailing winds. The low pressure over this venting tower pulls air into the building from higher pressures below. This system may require opening of the lower windows toward a high-pressure area.

The principle is evident in the Pantheon of Rome (Fig. 9). The round opening at the crown of the dome allows the low pressure created above the dome by prevailing breezes, regardless of direction, to draw or suck fresh air out of the top, forcing replacement air to enter the interior through the lower exterior doors.

However achieved, cross ventilation is not a matter of "filling a building with air," as much as moving air through the building. For cross ventilation, air needs a way in and a way out. The designer must provide for judicious use of outlets as well as inlets.

A simple way to conceive of a building designed for natural ventilation is to view it in silhouette from the direction of the prevailing breeze, just as the wind "sees it." The building surfaces, the combination of solids and voids (ventilating openings) are in a sense an "air blockage" (in no air passes through the building) or an "air filter and funnel" (in which case, air is slowed in some instances, speeded up in others by perturbations and the Venturi effect). The effectiveness of the ventilation design can be considered by how well the building acts as filter and funnel, directing air flow to where people might be occupying the building and made comfortable by the cooling breeze.

If we punch a hole through the building from the windward side to the downwind side, it is easy to see that some of the air would move through from the high pressure upwind to the lower pressure downwind rather than going all the way around the building. This is commonly called "cross ventilation." It is the fundamental process by which air is moved through the inside of a building.

The principle that air flows from high pressure to low pressure helps us analyze airflow patterns. Fig. 10 depicts a building oriented so that the wind approaches from a side with no windward inlets. Obviously, there will not be much air movement inside the building even when the windows on the ends of the building are wide open. There will be high pressure on the upwind side, low pressure on the downwind side, and low-pressure areas at both ends.

To get the air to move through the windows from one end of the building to the other, we need to create a new high-pressure area on one end (the inlet) and a lower-pressure area on the other end (the outlet). The solution is to attach a windbreak (Fig. 11) that will create a high-pressure area immediately in front of the windbreak (at one end of the building). Another windbreak on the opposite end of the building toward the downwind side will tend to further reduce the low-pressure area there and so draw the air from one end of the building to the other, or crossways to the prevailing breeze. This solution will probably not create an ideal interior environment, but it will be better than before.

"Windscreens" designed as permeable screens to let some wind leak through work better than "windbreaks" designed as non-permeable barriers, although this at first may seem a counterintuitive result. A solid fence doesn't provide as much protection to its lee as a screen or fence that has some holes in it (Fig. 12). Wind speed in the wind shadow is slower behind a screen with the perforations than behind a solid fence. (In Fig. 12, the air flow effect is expressed as a percent reduction of uninterrupted wind speed.)

Trees and shrubs also can be used as windscreens, and they are full of 'holes,' but they can also be used to direct the air so that people can take advantage of the cool breeze in otherwise protected areas. The designer has to consider whether the intent is to channel breezes for cooling or whether to provide a windbreak protection and be careful to plant trees accordingly (Fig. 13).

What happens to the breeze once it gets into the building? As mentioned, air has mass and inertia. Like a ball, once it starts rolling, it will keep rolling until it hits something or eventually slows down and stops due to friction with the ground. At those times when increased air speed contributes to cooling comfort, one will be more comfortable inside such a constricting opening than outside it. The Venturi effect will increase the wind speed to our convenience.

Once directed by the inlet into the building, the breeze will tend to keep going straight until it hits something. It's easy to see how walls and doors will force the air in one direction and then another. Also note that a breeze does not move directly from the inlet to the outlet, except in special cases. The pattern of an incoming breeze is not affected by the location of the outlet.

The size of the outlet does have an effect, though. As was mentioned in the discussion of the Venturi effect, in a simple building, if the inlet-to-outlet ratio is exaggerated, the result will be a very fast movement of air through the inlet (the speed of the air at the inlet may exceed the exterior air speed considerably). The effect also occurs around buildings, such as where the bulk of a building is raised above the lower level (open plaza) or where two buildings are placed close together.

Air speed is important in cooling people. The faster the air moves, the more moisture and heat it will take away from our bodies by evaporation. We can get maximum air speed just inside an inlet by having a small inlet and a very large opposite outlet (Fig. 14). The common and intuitive idea of placing windows to face the breeze doesn't work best. The ratio of the inlet to outlet determines the speed of the airflow. If we have a small inlet opening, say 1 sq. ft. (.09 sq. m) and a large outlet, say l2 ft. sq. (1.1 sq. m), we could generate a pretty fast breeze. And if we put our rocking chair up next to the smaller hole, we would get a good cooling breeze right on our nose. Of course, back in the rear of the building near the outlet, the breeze would be pretty slow and we wouldn't want to put our rocking chair there. The best compromise for good air speed throughout the interior is to have the outlet about 10 percent larger than the size of the inlet.

Air speed may also be important in cooling the building itself when the outside air is cooler than the inside surfaces of the building. By convection, the moving air picks up the heat from the walls, floors, ceilings, furniture, *etc.*, and carries it on to the outside (Fig. 15). If we let the cool night air into our usually hot buildings, the cool air will reduce the heat stored in the building materials and leave that space with a "heat sink" to help provide a cooling effect for the next day. (In this case, nighttime ventilation cools the thermal mass of the building. The effect is most noticeable in hot dry climates with large day to night temperature swings).

While air speed is important, the quantity of air moved through the interior (air change) is the most important factor, and that is accomplished with inlets and outlets about the same size. We shouldn't confuse air speed for cooling people with air changes for cooling buildings. Obviously, for cooling people, we must get the breeze to them. If a breeze doesn't blow through the occupied living zone, then it can't be very helpful in cooling by evaporation. Likewise, if the moving air doesn't get to all the building surfaces, it won't cool them either.

In a school in Oklahoma, an architect designed big windows and openings over the corridor for a through breeze (Fig. 16). Early studies in the Texas Engineering Experiment Station wind tunnel showed a shadow in the leeward classroom, so the architect added louvers in the plenum over the corridor. The louvers not only direct the breeze

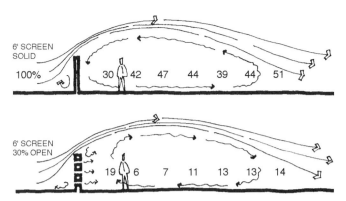

Fig. 12. Comparison of a solid windbreak and a windscreen

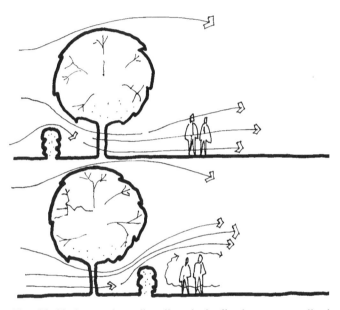

Fig. 13. Various microclimatic wind effects as a result of landscape plantings

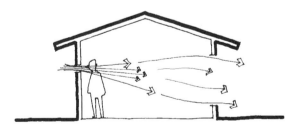

Fig. 14. A ventilation diagram intended to cool people, by direct exposure to increased air flow, created by the Venturi effect

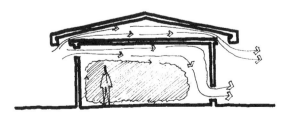

Fig. 15. A ventilation diagram intended to cool building surfaces

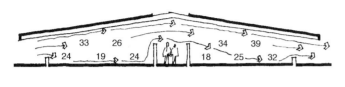

MIAMI, OKLAHOMA

Fig. 16. Comparison of air flow across a classroom building created by modifications of ceiling geometry

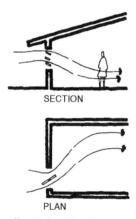

SECTION

PLAN

Fig. 17. The effect of a direction vane at the window opening

down into the occupied zone of the classroom but also shield the brightness of the skylights from direct view below.

Another factor that may be used to control the path that breezes takes when moving through a building is the location of the inlet in the face of the building surface (windward face). In a rectangular building with the inlet in the center of the windward fenestration, the air will tend to move straight through the opening. If the inlet is off-center, the breeze will tend to enter the opening and move off to one side. This happens because the air pressure on the exterior fenestration will be greater over the larger wall surface and smaller over the smaller wall surface, relative to the location of the opening.

The pressure differences on exterior fenestration cause "surface vectors," or currents that move along the surface of the building, seeking a way around or through. Projections on the fenestration—overhangs, louvers, and columns—can alter these pressure differences further and change the way the breeze is forced into the inlet. As the breeze starts to flow into the inlet, the way the inlet is designed will also affect the pattern the air takes.

Most conventional windows provide some control of breeze. This is the simple opening that lets air come in but doesn't give it direction. With a simple opening, the direction of the incoming breeze is determined by the location of the inlet (window) in the windward fenestration. With a horizontal vane window, the air will follow the direction of the window vane—up or down. The sideways direction of the breeze is still a function of the location of the inlet in the windward wall. With a vertical vane window, the air can be directed right or left. Again, the up or down pattern will be determined by the location of the inlet in the windward wall. To allow the occupant to direct the incoming breeze, the designer should provide for the appropriate choices in the aperture type (Fig. 17).

Examples

The following case studies of air patterns around typical groups of buildings illustrate the application of air-movement principles to ventilation problems.

Window selection and placement.

In the design for a bedroom in Texas (Fig. 18), the casement windows (a) direct the incoming breeze into the room near the ceiling. Venetian blinds (b) direct the breeze down into the living zone of the room. Locating the casement windows nearer the floor (c) would also allow the breeze to flow through the living zone. But, if awning windows (d) had been used instead of the casements, they would have thrown the air up to the ceiling and over the living zone. Selecting the proper location for the window, as well as the proper window type, is important to produce the desired airflow.

A sunshade.

In a classroom design (Fig. 19), the breeze comes in downward and through the occupied zone where it can cool the students (a). But, when the sunshade was added to the windows, it caused the windward surface, pressure patterns to change and the breeze coming in through the windows to be directed upward, above the occupied zone. The unintended effect was solved via wind modeling studies by a simple slot in the sunshade (b) which allowed the surface pressure difference to return to normal and the breeze to be directed down into the occupied zone again.

Controlling the flow.

In this case (Fig. 20), the flow patterns and speeds for a double-loaded corridor building are manipulated, offering ways to get the breeze into the occupied zone and indicating some relative air speeds while the inlets and outlets remain constant in size. In the top diagram (a), the windows are simple openings and the corridor walls are pierced with large openings near the floor. The scheme provides a flow of air

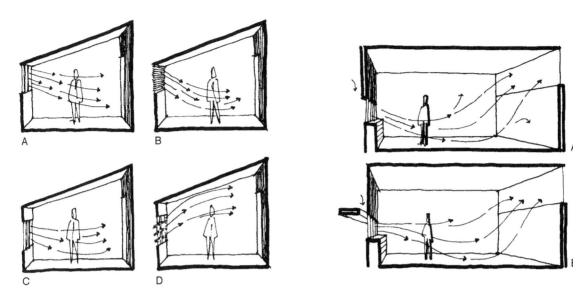

Fig. 18. Ventilating a single room

Fig. 19. Sunshading windows

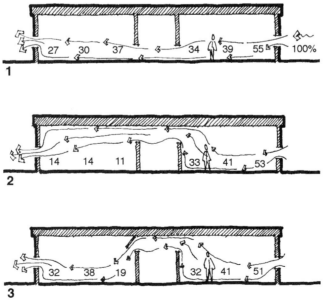

Fig. 20. Various cross-section manipulations of a double-loaded corridor classroom building. (Interior air speeds are given as a percent of the outdoor uninterrupted wind speed.)

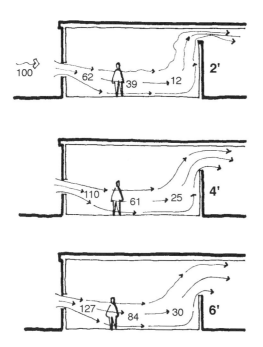

Fig. 21. Varying the height of a corridor wall significantly alters the wind cooling effect

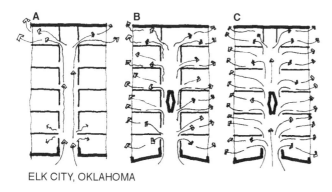

ELK CITY, OKLAHOMA

Fig. 22. Plan studies of a classroom wing, with ventilation provided longitudinally

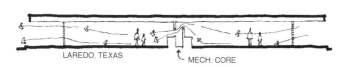

LAREDO, TEXAS   MECH. CORE

Fig. 23. Longitudinal cross-section of an air flow design through a classroom building core

throughout the living zone of the cross section. In the second diagram (b), high corridor openings provide little breeze in the downwind living zone. The third diagram (c) suggests one way to redirect the downwind breeze. A low opening in the downwind corridor wall is another way. Note in Fig. 21 that, with a two-foot inlet and four- or six-foot high corridor opening, created by varying the wall height, the incoming breeze is made faster than the prevailing outside wind, by the familiar Venturi effect.

Interior windbreak.
The site for this school in Elk City, OK by CRS Architects (Fig. 22) and its programming requirements, dictated that the long dimension of the building be parallel to prevailing breezes. As a result, there wasn't much opportunity to get breezes into the building except through the narrow end and into the wide corridor, which was to double as a gathering place or "commons." Since the school was designed in the days before air-conditioned schools were widespread, natural airflow was considered an essential design issue.

(a) The first wind tunnel tests at the Texas Engineering Experiment Station showed that breezes that came into the building were funneled down the corridor and out the windows of the furthermost classrooms.

(b) A little creative study in the wind tunnel indicated that, if some sort of solid object were placed in the corridor, or commons, and if its location were judiciously selected, it would cause the incoming air to build up pressure and flow more or less uniformly out the windows of all classrooms. The need for extra space suggested that this "solid object" could be a small office.

(c) In the first schemes, open classroom doors provided the principal inlets for the breeze, but finally the designers opted to put "slot ventilators" along the corridor walls and provide opportunity for the incoming breeze to spread throughout the classroom areas.

Cooling through the core.
A school in Laredo, TX designed by CRS (Fig. 23), also was built before air-conditioned schools became common. Although summers in Laredo are quite hot and dry, for most of the school year the weather is moderately warm.

The basic concept of the school envisioned a central core between the back-to-back classrooms, to provide some mechanical, electrical, and plumbing services to the classroom areas and also to encourage cross-ventilation. The breeze moves into the upwind classroom and is directed into the living zone. It then moves into the central core chamber and hence down into the downwind classroom through a grill in the wall, and finally out the downwind windows. Wind tunnel tests in Texas Engineering Research Station showed that the scheme was feasible. The building is oriented to catch the prevailing breeze, when there is one, and the school certainly more comfortable than most of the non-air conditioned buildings in that climate.

The architect designing a naturally ventilated building can be guided by the principles outlined here. When complex building forms are developed, the resulting pressure differences and air flow patterns will be difficult if not impossible to predict. The best approach is to test the proposed design with a scale model, introduced into a steady wind stream and analyzed with smoke tracers or other tell-tales. Best modeling results are achieved in a boundary-layer steady-flow wind tunnel as may be available at research laboratories and universities . Research citations and design application guidelines can be found in the references.

7
Indoor air quality

Hal Levin

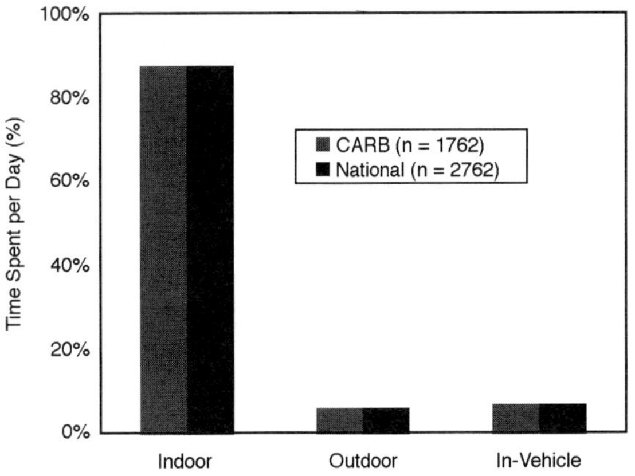

Fig. 1. Time spent indoors, outdoors and in-vehicles

Summary: Indoor air quality (IAQ) has become an increasingly important building design consideration due to growth in occupant health and comfort problems attributed to poor IAQ. Designers can greatly improve indoor air quality by considering it throughout the design process.

Key words: air quality, contaminants, indoor pollution, occupant health, pollutant sources, ventilation.

What is Indoor Air Quality (IAQ)?

Indoor air pollution is not new. As long as 30,000 years ago, when cave people took fire into caves, they became polluters as well as victims of indoor air pollution. This remained the case for those living in dwellings heated by wood-burning, still evident in indigenous traditions today. As land-based, agricultural communities evolved into urban, industrial societies, pollution both indoors and out increased significantly, in the latter case produced by industrial sources.

Awareness of indoor pollution is also not new. Benjamin Franklin in his development of wood stove designs and his contemporary Count Rumford who developed the smoke shelf sought to mitigate the indoor air pollution created by wood-burning devices. But significant attention to indoor pollution only began in the early 1970s in northern Europe and Japan. In the late 1970s, awareness of high formaldehyde concentrations in mobile homes and manufactured housing brought about increased awareness in North America. Problems related to asbestos, radon, lead, Legionnaires' Disease, solvents, pesticides, and many other contaminants have brought about far greater awareness of indoor air quality. Much of what we know today about indoor pollution is the result of research done in the last twenty five years.

Indoor air quality can defined by the presence or absence of pollutants—unwanted odorous, irritating, and toxic gases, particles, and microbes. Good indoor air quality is achieved, therefore, by providing air that is reasonably free of contaminants that are odorous, toxic, or irritating. Uncontaminated air is almost 80 percent nitrogen and 20% oxygen, with other components being present only at trace concentrations.

Air (indoors or outdoors) typically contains scores or even hundreds of contaminants at trace concentrations. Fortunately, this air does not generally have noticeable deleterious effects on materials, people, or other living things. But some contaminants at concentrations even as low as one part per billion (ppb) or less can cause adverse reactions. A few, extremely toxic gases (dioxins, for example) are thought harmful at parts per trillion (ppt) concentrations.

Table 2 shows the concentrations of the most common gases in typical indoor and outdoor air and of a few other constituents of interest for IAQ. As can be seen in the table, concentrations of many gases are one or two orders of magnitude (ten or a hundred times) higher indoors than outdoors. This is the result of the presence and strength of sources of these gases indoors, the limited mixing volume in enclosed spaces, and the low ventilation rate (air change rate) of outdoor air to dilute and replace the contaminated air. Of course, for most contaminants, indoor air cannot be much cleaner than outdoor air.

It can be seen in Table 2 that the composition of relatively pure air is dominated by the common gases Nitrogen and Oxygen, with only trace concentrations of other components. The moisture content of air is highly variable, ranging from almost no moisture in the desert or high mountains to saturated air (100% relative humidity) in very humid climates or during rainstorms. Note that contaminant levels indoors are generally higher than outdoors, sometimes by a factor of 10 or even 100. This is one reason IAQ is so important.

There are two fundamental reasons IAQ is so important:

- Contaminant concentrations are generally higher than outdoors

- Most people spend most of their time indoors.

Table 2 indicates that contaminant levels measured indoors are generally higher than outdoors, sometimes by a factor of 10 or even 100. This is one reason IAQ is so important. The other reason is because the majority of people in industrialized countries spend more than 90% of their time indoors. Fig. 1 indicates comparable results from both California (CARB) and national studies. So, exposure to air pollution (defined as concentration times time spent) appears to be far more significant indoors than outdoors.

1 Determinants of Indoor Air Quality

IAQ is constantly changing within and between spaces in a building. The overall quality of the air can be determined by a mass-balance model accounting for all sources and sinks. This relationship is presented by the oversimplified equation:

$$\text{Concentration} = \text{sources} - \text{sinks}$$

Thus, the steady state concentration of contaminants is the sum of all the source generation rates minus the sum of all the contaminant removal process rates. There are a multitude of sources and sinks, as described below. Each of these is subject to large variation over time, often on the order of a factor of two, ten, or even one hundred. Thus, the composition of indoor air is dynamic; it is constantly changing. Usually, the characteristics of a few dominant sources and the ventilation rate will be adequate to estimate (to a first order approximation) the concentrations of concern.

Author: Hal Levin

References: ASHRAE. 1989. Standard 62-1989 "Ventilation for Acceptable Indoor Air Quality." Atlanta, GA: American Society of Heating, Refrigerating, and Air-Conditioning Engineers.

Additional references are listed at the end of this article.

Table 1. Evolution in awareness of building environmental problems

1960s
- Commercial buildings more isolated from outdoor environment - sealed windows, deeper profiles, widespread reliance on mechanical systems for ventilation and increasing use of air-conditioning.
- Built and filled increasingly with synthetic materials.

1970s
- Energy conservation drove ventilation rates down
- Indoor air quality and climate problems proliferated.
- 1976 - Legionnaire's Disease outbreak at Philadelphia hotel, 171 people affected, 29 died.
- Formaldehyde levels high, especially in mobile homes and manufactured housing using pressed wood products made with formaldehyde-based binders.

1980s
- Awareness of Sick Building Syndrome (SBS) and Building Related Illness (BRI) grows.
- Problem buildings taught the we must integrate approaches to thermal comfort, indoor air quality, and energy management.
- Law suits and workers compensation cases for SBS problems proliferate, increase building owner, occupant, and designer awareness and concern.

1990s
- Indoor air quality science advances.
- Increased attention to water intrusion, microbial problems in buildings
- Tobacco smoking banned on airline flights and in many public access buildings throughout the United States.
- Scientists confirm appearance of ozone hole over Antarctic,
- It is even more evident that, as ecologists have said for years, 'everything is connected to everything.'

Table 2. Typical concentrations and ranges of selected components of indoor and outdoor air.
(ranges shown in parentheses) *

Outdoor air concentrations	Constituent name	Indoor air concentrations
780,840 ppm (78%)	Nitrogen	na
209,460 ppm (20.9%)	Oxygen	na
332 ppm (275-450 ppm)	Carbon dioxide	325 ppm (300-2500 ppm)
7 ppb (5-30 ppb)	Formaldehyde	30 ppb (15-300 ppb)
50 $\mu g/m^3$ (10 - 250 $\mu g/m^3$)	VOCs	200 $\mu g/m^3$ (75 - 20,000 $\mu g/m^3$)
~15 ppb (5-250 ppb)	Ozone (O_3)	15 ppb (3-80 ppb)
15 $\mu g/m^3$ (10 - 100 $\mu g/m^3$)	Particles < 10 μm dia	25 $\mu g/m^3$ (10 - 200 $\mu g/m^3$)
10 - 100 cfu/m³	Fungi	30 cfu/m3 (10-5000 cfu/m³)

*ppm - parts per million
ppb = parts per billion
$\mu g/m^3$ = microgram per cubic meter of air
cfu/m³ = colony forming units per cubic meter of air

Table 3. Determinants of Indoor Air Quality (IAQ)

POLLUTANT SOURCES
- Outdoor Air, Soil, Water
- Building Envelope
- Building Equipment
- Finishes and Furnishings
- Machines and Appliances
- Occupants
- Occupant Activities
- Maintenance and Cleaning

POLLUTANT REMOVAL MECHANISMS and SINKS)
- Sinks (Deposition and Sorption)
- Ventilation
- Air Cleaning and Filtration
- Chemical Transformation

Virtually all of the terms of the equation are dynamic, so that while the steady state concept may be useful for analysis, steady state conditions do not actually occur in normal buildings.

Air pollution sources

The most effective way to control indoor air quality is to eliminate or control the sources. Where they cannot be controlled, they should be addressed by design. There are so many sources of indoor air pollutants, that it is impossible to control them all; however, by identifying them early in the design process, they can be controlled.

The designer has a great deal of control over some important sources of indoor air pollutants, particularly the chemicals emitted from building materials and furnishings. Furthermore, the chemicals required to clean, maintain, refurnish, and replace finish materials should be known when selecting and specifying the materials. Early in their product lives, building materials generally tend to be fairly strong emitters of pollutants, particularly of volatile organic chemicals. After they have been exposed to the environment, their emissions decay considerably.

As a general rule, contaminant concentrations due to emissions from many new "dry" materials decrease by about a factor of two to five in the first week and by another factor of two to five in the next one to three months. Thus, in general, there is a decrease in source strength of a factor of ten in the first few months after construction.

An important exception applies to wet products (such as adhesives, paints, caulks, and sealants) whose emissions decay much more rapidly as a result of the drying or curing process. The reduction in emissions from these products is a matter of hours and days rather than weeks and months. Of course any covering (such as wall-covering, carpet, paneling, and so forth) applied over a wet-applied product will affect (inhibit) emissions once installed, extending considerably the time required for emissions to reach very low rates.

Another important type of exception includes solid products (such as composite wood products) that generally have fairly stable, long term emissions. Formaldehyde emissions from particle board tend to be almost as strong a year or two after installation as they are when the products are new.

For all materials, cleaning, maintenance, refinishing, and replacement materials and products can involve introduction of new, strong sources of contaminants over the life of the product. Additional chemicals may be required to remove old products, and emissions may be increased by disturbing many products. Therefore, the total life cycle of materials should be considered when selecting and specifying for good IAQ.

Fig. 2 shows the sum of the measured concentrations of selected volatile organic compounds—known as SumVOC—measured in ten buildings as early as one week after construction until almost three years after construction. As might be expected, the highest concentrations clearly occur in newly-constructed buildings, and the aged buildings generally have low concentrations. (Cleaning and maintenance as well as occupant activities and equipment can confuse the analysis of the concentration patterns in buildings that are in use.) The pattern of concentrations in Fig. 2 indicates that emissions are strong from building materials, and, also, that emissions decay significantly in the early life of a building. Even the concentrations measured at one week are considerably below those that would have been found just a few days earlier.

Fig. 3 presents VOC measurements from three buildings clearly illustrating the rapid decay pattern in VOC concentrations early in the lives of newly-constructed buildings. The general pattern shown by the three buildings is that concentrations fall rather rapidly after the completion of construction. The reduced concentrations may result in

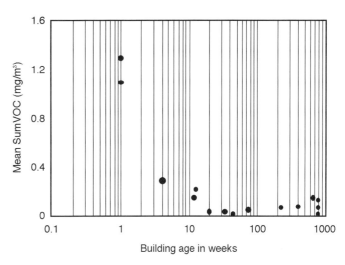

Fig. 2. SumVOC Concentrations from the EPA Public Buildings Study
(Note: x-axis, building age in weeks, is shown in logarithmic scale).

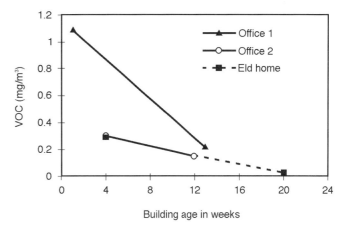

Fig. 3. VOC concentrations as a function of building age in three new buildings

significant part from the start-up and regular operation of the ventilation system. Thus, it is important to ensure that materials have cured and aged sufficiently and that ventilation systems are properly operating before occupancy of newly-constructed or renovated buildings. Construction in a portion of an occupied building should be well contained and isolated from occupied areas to prevent occupant exposure to elevated contaminant concentrations.

In general, emission rates decay exponentially after reaching an initial peak. (The exception is materials that are created to be sources of emissions such as air fresheners—actually, odor-masking devices— or "pest strips.") Emission rates decay exponentially whether emissions are high or low, and whether emissions decay rapidly, as in wet products, or slowly, as in most sheet materials, textiles, and other "solid" dry products. That is, the decay will be sharp at first and steadily decline until the slope of the decay curve is almost parallel to the x (time) axis. For wet products (tested without a material applied over them as is the case for adhesives), the decay will typically be on the order of a factor of ten in about ten hours. For a dry product, such as carpets, it may take 100 hours or more for this large a reduction in emissions.

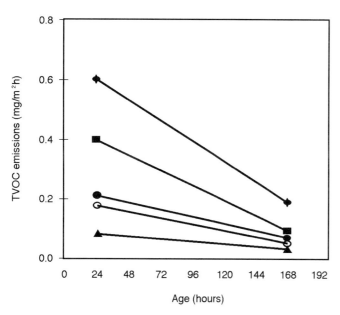

Fig. 4. TVOC emission factor decays over one week from various carpet assemblies (Source: Hodgson et al. 1992)

Fig. 4. shows emission rates during one week from each of five carpet assemblies. While each of these is at a different original and final source strength, they all show significant decreases in emission rates from hour 24 to hour 168. In these tests, material and product samples are normally collected at the manufacturing site immediately after they are produced and they are packaged in air tight containers. The samples are kept in the containers during transport to the laboratory and until the time of the test, at which time the samples are removed from the containers just before being placed in the test chamber.

Emission decay rates following the pattern shown in Fig. 4 are typical of many types of building materials. Wet-applied products (paints, adhesives, caulks) have even more rapid decays, but, of course, they tend to have very much stronger initial emissions - sometimes by a factor of 100 higher than carpet emissions. Fig. 4 also shows that there are significant differences both at 24 hours and at 168 hours among the five products. This illustrates the importance of carefully selecting products based on emissions data. Tests following standard procedures established by ASTM are now available for many products of interest for indoor air quality, and more industries are testing their products all the time. In general, lower emissions can be assumed to be better. However, the exact chemical composition of the emissions is important since chemicals different greatly in their toxicity and irritation potency. Designers should require emissions data for all major finish materials and the should require chemical composition data on all wet-applied products. these data can usefully inform product selection choices.

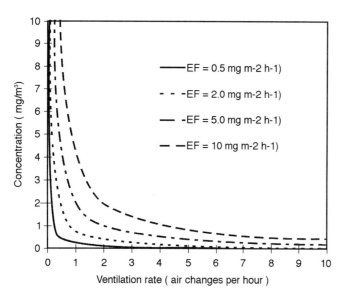

Fig. 5. Contaminant concentration as a function of source strength and air exchange rate.

(Note: EF = emission factor typically reported in milligrams per square meter per hour - mg/m^3 - h)

Fig. 4 shows tests of five different carpets samples from four different types of carpet. Clearly the various types of carpets have very different initial and final emissions. Tests of most materials conducted for longer periods of time show that emissions decay very rapidly at first and then slow to much lower, almost steady, long-term rates. The magnitude of these long-term emissions also varies greatly from product to product and should be assessed before selecting products.

The most fundamental relationship in indoor air quality is that between contaminant sources, removal mechanisms, and concentrations. Fig. 5 shows that the emission rate (source strength) is an extremely important determinant of contaminant concentrations. This relationship holds for virtually any type of contaminant. By reducing source strengths, less ventilation will be required to maintain the same air quality. Note that below 0.5 air changes per hour (ach), concentrations tend to climb rather steeply. Above 2 ach, concentrations decrease rather slowly. Thus, in the critical zone where most buildings operate most of the time, it is extremely important to minimize source strengths by design. This will reduce the capacity of the ventilation system required and the cost to operate and maintain it.

Fig. 5 shows this relationship for various source strengths and air exchange rates. Most public access buildings have air exchange rates between 0.5 and 5 ach most of the time. Typical office buildings that meet the ASHRAE Standard 62 minimum ventilation rate of 15 cubic feet per minute per person (cfm/p) will have a minimum design ventilation rate of about 0.9 ach. Research shows that their actual ventilation rates tend to be between 0.5 ach and 1.5 ach most of the time. Very tight houses or very poorly ventilated offices or retail spaces might have ventilation rates of 0.4 or 0.5 ach. Air leakage through a typical office building's exterior envelope will usually be between 0.2 and 0.4 ach, depending on indoor/ outdoor temperature differences and on outdoor wind velocity. Schools, at typical occupant densities and meeting the ASHRAE ventilation standard requirement of 15 cfm/p, will have about 3 ach.

Emission rates vary greatly from one product to another and over time for a given product. Even small differences in the production process can significantly impact emissions. Thus, it is important for designers to carefully select and specify the building materials and products for which they are responsible.

An example of emissions variation among products and within products over time is carpet. While most carpets emit 0.3 mg/m²·hr (or less) total volatile organic chemicals (TVOC) when new and less than 0.020 mg/m²·hr TVOC when a week old, some types of carpets can emit 1 mg/m²·hr or more when new. Carpet cushions can be much stronger emitters than carpets, and carpet adhesive can be even stronger sources still.

Carpets and carpet cushions will tend to emit weakly but over a very long period of time while adhesives will have very strong initial emissions and then rapidly decrease to much lower rates. The nature of the material covering the adhesive will have an important impact on how rapidly the emissions from the adhesive can reach the air. A dense backing on a carpet can suppress emissions from an adhesive and result in low level emissions for years after installation. Paints, caulks, sealants, and adhesives can emit several or even tens of mg/m²·hr when first applied, but then decay rapidly to hundreds or even only tens of μg/m²·h. All of these sources continue to emit for a very long time, often for years after they are initially installed.

Pollution sinks

Deposition and sorption
Gases and vapors can adsorb, and particles can deposit, on surfaces. These gases and vapors are in constant flux, moving from the surfaces to the air and back again.

Some of the larger particles (> 1 μm diameter) can also be dislodged from surfaces and redeposit elsewhere, while smaller particles (< 1 μm diameter) tend to remain on surfaces until dislodged by deliberate cleaning. Particles (that are heavy enough) can fall to horizontal surfaces due to gravity, or stick to both vertical and horizontal surfaces due to implication or (in the case of lighter particles) diffusion, electrostatic forces, and thermophoresis. (When a temperature gradient is established in a gas, the aerosol particles in that gas experience a force in the direction of decreasing temperature. The motion of the aerosol particle that results from this force is called thermophoresis. This is why there often are dark stains on ceilings and walls above light bulbs and other concentrated heat sources.)

Gases attach to surfaces by a process known as sorption and they re-enter the air from the surfaces by desorption. They can be removed from the indoor environment either by dilution ventilation or filtration while they are airborne or by cleaning while they are on surfaces. Gases can also adsorb onto particles in the air. Particles (that are heavy enough) can fall out to the floor by gravity or stick to surfaces (including both horizontal and vertical surfaces) by deposition.

Dust on floors or wall surfaces can be re-suspended in the air when the surface is disturbed by people walking on or near it, by the vibration caused by many ordinary human activities, or even by cleaning and vacuuming activities. Nearly everyone is familiar with the smell of dust in the air after vacuuming with ordinary household vacuum cleaners. Studies have shown that airborne dust levels are actually higher after vacuuming with most typical equipment.

The rate of removal of dust from the air by gravity and by deposition on surfaces is dependent on the size of the particles involved. A particle's size determines whether it can be inhaled by humans and how far into the respiratory tract it will lodge. The most important characteristics of aerosols are "mean diameter" and the distribution of particle diameters. The "aerodynamic diameter" is the product of the physical diameter multiplied by the square root of the density. Deposition of particles in the respiratory tract is a function of the aerodynamic diameter. Typically in indoor air, the majority of the mass is in coarse particles but the largest number of particles is in the fine fraction.

Large (coarse) particles settle out of the air by gravity. But most particles are small (fine), and tend to stay in suspension until the collide with another particle and the two particles stick together or until they collide with a surface and stick to the surface. Fine particles attach equally to vertical and to horizontal surfaces. This is important for cleaning, since substantial amounts of dust accumulate on vertical surfaces which are infrequently cleaned. Yet, when people walk past dusty surfaces, the air turbulence can result in re-suspension of the dust particles. Vibration of surfaces can also cause deposited dust to be re-suspended in the air.

Contaminants clearly can be re-emitted from surfaces where they have adsorbed or deposited. These surfaces then are considered "secondary" sources. There is an on-going exchange of gases and particles between surfaces and the air. There is also the possibility that occupants will be exposed to contaminants that are on surfaces, even if only temporarily. (See routes of exposure below.)

Ventilation
Ventilation is an important removal mechanism (or sink) for contaminants. By replacing the air in a space periodically, the contaminants generated in the space are kept to lower concentrations. One air exchange - the supply of a volume of air equal to the volume of the space - will generally result in the removal of about two-thirds of the concentrations of the air contaminants. Thus, more than a single air exchange is needed to reduce concentrations to near zero. Therefore, whenever contaminants are generated at a point source, such as an appliance or an activity of an occupant, it is most effective to apply exhaust ventilation at that point. This prevents the contaminant from mixing in the air generally in the space.

Filtration and air cleaning
An important method of controlled pollutant removal is filtration and air cleaning. Air cleaning refers to the removal of both particulate matter and gaseous contaminants. Filtration generally refers to the use of media filters, although electrostatic precipitation is also used to remove particulate matter. Various media including charcoal and potassium permanganate are used to remove gaseous contaminants. These media for gaseous removal are not widely used in non-industrial or specialized settings, although their use is becoming more common as the quality of air gains more importance in the public mind.

Filters remove particulate matter from the air by various means including interception, impaction, and electrostatic deposition. The choice of filters depends largely on the size and type of particles that must be removed as well as the velocity of the air stream through the filter medium. Various media are available with glass fibers being the most commonly used. Typical residential "throwaway" filters are extremely inefficient, removing only very large objects. They do not effectively remove particles of concern for health or comfort. Modern media and filter design can produce highly efficient filters without creating significant pressure drop across the filter.

Removal of fine particles, particles less than 2.5 μm diameter, requires efficient filters. These are the particles of greatest concern for health, since they penetrate into the respiratory tract. Effective removal of particles less than 1 μm diameter requires filters even more efficient—usually referred to as HEPA, high efficiency particle arrestance. Such filters specifically are 99.97% efficient at removing particles in the 0.3 μm diameter range, the size that penetrates deepest into the respiratory tract and ends up on the lung surfaces. The HEPA filters are rather expensive and they cause a fairly large drop in static pressure (large resistance to air moving through). Thus, they require more powerful fans and the use of more energy for the same flow rate of air to be moved across a given cross-sectional area of filter. The general solution for HEPA and other high performance filters is to increase the cross-sectional area of the filter exposed to the air stream, thus allowing a lower velocity and less pressure drop.

Chemical transformation

Recent research shows that chemical transformation occurs commonly in indoor air. The reaction products may be more irritating compounds than the chemicals creating the reaction. For example, ozone (from outdoors, or generated by appliances such as photocopiers and laser printers) reacts with chemicals released from SBR latex-backed carpets to create highly irritating aldehydes. So, when a new carpet is installed in an office with lots of office machines, and people complain of eye, skin, or respiratory tract irritation, the cause may be the result of this chemical reaction. There are numerous, almost limitless other such chemical reactions possible in indoor air.

2 Pollutants of concern

Because indoor air contains numerous constituents, it is impossible to consider all of them thoroughly. Therefore, it is important to identify the most important contaminants in any situation. This is usually done on the basis of the sources that are known or expected to appear.

- Chemicals:
- Organic chemicals (solvents, binders, pesticides, fire retardants) e.g., Formaldehyde
- Inorganic chemicals: (combustion by-products such as NO_x, SO_x, CO, CO_2)
- Particulate matter (respirable, coarse vs. fine).
- Microbial contaminants: fungi, bacteria, and viruses.

Concern in non-residential buildings is toward organic gases, microbes, and, occasionally, particulate matter. Many organic gases, perhaps as many as two or three hundred, could be found in the air of a typical building, although mostly at extremely low concentrations. These gases have many sources, but the most common are occupants and their clothing, building materials, building housekeeping and maintenance products, building equipment, consumer products, and appliances. Solvents commonly used in various products are ubiquitous. Chlorinated compounds found in cleaning, sanitizing, and pest control products are also common.

In non-residential environments, exposure to combustion by-products is limited, usually coming either from tobacco smoking or from intrusion of motor vehicle exhaust gases. Attached garages are often implicated in elevated concentrations of carbon monoxide or nitrogen oxides both in residential and non-residential buildings. Poor location of building air intakes results in entrainment of motor vehicle exhausts from adjacent roadways, driveways, and loading docks.

Inadequate separation of air intakes from combustion device exhausts can also be the source of combustion gases and particles found indoors.

In residences, combustion by-products from gas-fired appliances, especially cooking and water heating, can be a concern. Wood burning stoves and fireplaces can also be sources of both gaseous and particulate matter contaminants, some of which are very toxic. In both residential and non-residential buildings, environmental tobacco smoke (ETS) is a concern.

The preferred method of reducing the concentration of many indoor contaminants is through control of strong sources. Dwelling units require ventilation to exhaust local sources of moisture and odors as well as distributed sources of moisture, bioeffluents (CO_2, pathogens, odors), and VOCs. However, indoor air quality can be enhanced through an awareness of source management on the part of the designer, the builder, the owner and the occupants. The role of mite allergens is of particular interest to residential indoor air quality. Allergy and asthma may result from exposure to mite fecal material which is commonly found in residential environments due to the availability of habitat (carpet, bedding and upholstery) as well as an ample food supply - human skin flakes. A relative humidity of 70 to 90% is optimal for mite growth, but mites can survive when the relative humidity is as low as 45 to 50%. Reducing the relative humidity to levels at which they do not grow is the primary engineering means of controlling the growth and reproduction of mites.

Although not itself a pollutant, water (or water vapor) can cause indoor air to deteriorate by its effects on materials and its contribution to microbial growth. Water intrusion, accidental spills, leaks, condensation on cool surfaces, and indoor water sources (including human respiration) can lead to IAQ problems. When humidities are high, microbial growth is more likely and more vigorous. When carbon-containing materials get wet, they can support mold growth. Dust mites thrive in moist environments. Dust mite feces cause allergic reactions and are believed responsible for a recent and rapid increase in asthma cases both in the U. S. and in northern Europe. As a result, water intrusion, spills, and high humidities are all of concern.

Microbial growth requires nutrients and moisture. Viruses require moisture to survive. Since fungi and bacteria are ubiquitous, it is the presence or absence of conditions for growth that determines whether their numbers reach hazardous levels. Human exposure occurs when microbes accumulate and there is a mechanism for dissemination of the microbes, usually by disturbance of the substrate or matrix where they are growing. Bacteria such as Legionella pneumophila, the organism that causes Legionnaires' Disease, grows in water and is usually aerosolized, either by spas, water features, therapeutic water baths, or cooling towers. Once airborne, these organisms must be inhaled for them to colonize the human respiratory tract and cause disease. Even non-viable organisms (dead spores, bacteria parts) are important because they can cause allergic or asthmatic reactions.

3 Health effects

Exposure and human daily intake

Adults breath about 10 cubic meters or more of air (equivalent to the air volume in a small bathroom or kitchen) each day. The air volume actually inspired depends on body size, activity level, and other factors. The air is taken into the lung where the oxygen is transferred to the bloodstream. The expired air contains much less oxygen, and much more carbon dioxide (roughly 40,000 ppm).

Even if a gas is present in air at a concentration as high as 1 mg/m³, it only results in an intake between 10 to 20 milligrams (or 1 to 2 percent of a gram, or 0.035 to 0.07 ounces per day). In fact as seen above, most individual contaminants are present only at concentration of 0.01

mg/m³, 0.001 mg/m³, or even less. And the total intake amount is not absorbed by the body. This later quantity is defined as the delivered dose.

Routes of exposure for air contaminants

There are three major routes of exposure, ways by which contaminants in the air (or on surfaces) can enter the body. These routes are through:

- lungs (inhalation).

- skin (absorption).

- inadvertent ingestion (ingestion).

Contaminants reach the lungs not only by inhalation but also by skin absorption or by inadvertent ingestion. The later routes of exposure are generally much larger for children than for adults based on normal behavior, clothing habits, and tendency to put their hands in their mouths often. Since air contaminants may also be found on surfaces, the hands of children become important means of increasing exposure to air pollutants.

For example, children living in homes contaminated with Pentachlorophenol (a formerly widely-used wood preservative, now with severely restricted indoor use) were reported to have 5 to 7 times the body burdens (blood serum and urine PCP metabolite concentrations) that adults living in the same homes had. Pentachlorophenol is not very volatile, so much of it stays on surfaces rather than getting into the air, resulting in exposure for decades after its initial application.

Comparing intake of air, water and food

A comparison of daily intakes of water, food, and air shows the importance of air relative to other media (food and water) in terms of contaminant exposures. Adult females and males inhale about 7.7 and 10 kg respectively of air daily (average adult lifetime). Children inhale from about 3.6 to 10 kg of air daily (depending on age or size and activity). In contrast, adults drink only about 2.1 kg/day and children drink about 1.1 kg/day of liquids. So, our exposure is far greater to air than to water (and other liquids). Measurements have shown that exposure to chlorine from showering is greater than from drinking and eating foods prepared with water. Chlorine in water evaporates more rapidly when it is heated, accounting for elevated concentrations in shower air during showering. Chlorine exposure in the shower is through both inhalation and skin absorption.

Exposure to inhaled indoor air pollutants

The fate of inhaled contaminants is important both in terms of the health effects and in terms of the need and means to control them. Gases or vapors that are water soluble or highly reactive will deposit predominately in the upper respiratory tract. While these can cause irritation, they are less likely to cause significant health harm. Exceptions might be gases like formaldehyde which is highly water soluble and is a carcinogen. Less water soluble or reactive gases and volatile organic compounds (VOCs) continue down the respiratory tract. The uptake of these gases and VOCs into the blood depends upon the blood/air partition coefficient. Peak uptake of inhaled contaminants is around 80% of the inhaled mass and lowest uptake is only a few percent. Metabolism of a VOC increases its uptake.

The deposition of particles in the respiratory tract is size dependent. The smallest particles - from 0.05 μm median diameter deposit by diffusion primarily in the pulmonary region (50% - 65%) and also in the tracheo-bronchial region (25%-40%). As particle sizes increase above 0.3 μm, a growing fraction of deposition occurs in the nasopharynx region by sedimentation up to about 5 μm diameter and then by impaction up to 100 μm diameter. Typical building air filters do not effectively remove particles smaller than 1 μm diameter, and the smaller the particle, the less effectively common filters perform.

Health effects of concern

There are numerous health effects attributed to exposure to indoor air pollutants. They include a broad range from minor to life-threatening and from rare to common. Of greatest interest, perhaps, are common respiratory illnesses. Absence from work and impaired performance related to acute respiratory infections cost as much as $60 billion annually in the United States in lost productivity. Since many respiratory ailments begin with the growth of a micro-organism in the respiratory tract, the organism must be inhaled. Thus, it must be airborne, or, in most cases is thought to be airborne. Infectious agents include viruses and bacteria. The most common are the rhinovirus and the adenovirus, believed responsible for the vast majority of such illnesses. Fungi can also cause acute illness including pneumonia. Two important diseases that have received much attention lately are Legionnaires' Disease and Tuberculosis.

Building Related Illness (BRI)

An illness or disease known to be caused by exposures in buildings is classified as a building-related illness. Generally, avoidance of further exposure is recommended or prescribed. Some well-known building-related illnesses include the following:

- Legionnaire's Disease

- Pontiac Fever

- Hypersensitivity pneumonititis

- Humidifier fever

- Lung cancer from radon or environmental tobacco smoke (ETS) exposure.

While tuberculosis, influenza, or even a common-cold that occurs as a result of exposure in a building are classified as BRI, it may not be possible to know exactly where such exposures occur in individual cases.

Sick Building Syndrome (SBS)

Office, school, and other building occupants generally report one or more of several common health and comfort problems when investigators conduct surveys. Usually occupants are asked whether they had experienced any of a number of specific symptoms during the past week or month, how frequently, and whether the symptoms abate when the occupants leave the building. Surveys show that between 15 - 45% of building occupants typically say they experienced one or more of the several symptoms considered part of the sick building syndrome (SBS).

Table 4. Health effects of indoor pollutants

- Infectious disease: flu, cold, pneumonia (Legionnaires' Disease, Pontiac fever)

- Cancer, other genetic toxicity, teratogenicity - (Ecotoxicity)

- Asthma and allergy

- CNS, skin, GI, respiratory, circulatory, musculoskeletal, and other systemic effects

- SBS (Sick Building Syndrome)

- Irritation

- Comfort

Sick building syndrome is not a disease itself. Like the flu, it refers to certain types of symptoms or sets of symptoms. Elevated prevalence of the symptoms in a building is considered evidence that the building is causing the problems. Researchers usually consider only symptoms that abate when occupants leave the building to be SBS symptoms. SBS symptoms include the following:

- General symptoms including fatigue, headache, nausea, dizziness, and difficulties in concentrating.

- Mucous membrane symptoms such as itching, burning, or irritation of the eyes; irritated, stuffy, or runny nose, hoarse or dry throat; and cough.

- Skin symptoms such as dryness, itching, burning, tightness, or stinging of facial skin, erythema (reddening of the skin); scaling, itching scalp or ears; or, dryness or itching of the hands.

Studies are done to determine what building, environmental, and personal factors are associated with elevated rates of SBS symptoms. The studies do not determine whether the symptoms are, in fact, caused by the building, or whether they are simply present in the general population. Prudence suggests that where strong associations exist between risk factors and SBS symptom prevalence, these factors should be addressed. Problems frequently associated with elevated SBS prevalence include the following:

Table 5. Types of predominant environmental stressors for Indoor Air Quality problems

Type of Environmental Stressor	Frequency (%)
Chemical and Particulate Contaminants	75
with odor discomfort	70
Thermal discomfort	55
Microbiological contaminants	45
Nonthermal humidity problems	30

(with eye irritation and mold growth from low- and high relative humidities respectively

Building factors

- Low ventilation rates (< 20 cfm/p)

- Ventilation operations (<10 hours / day)

- Insufficient materials control

- Fleecy (high surface area) materials

- Carpets

- Air-conditioning

Building environmental factors

- High temperature

- High humidity

- Low relative humidity

- Volatile hydrocarbons

- Microbial Volatile Organic Compounds

- Dust

Building use / occupancy factors

- High occupant density

- VDT use

- Photocopiers present

Occupant factors

- Perception of "dry air"

These factors represent "risk factors" for SBS. The "cause" of SBS symptoms is multi-factorial. That is, it appears that various factors contribute to the occurrence of SBS symptoms, although one or a few factors may dominate in any particular problem building or portion of a building. In general, it seems logical that addressing or controlling these factors will reduce the incidence of SBS symptoms in a building and also reduce the risk of BRI.

Table 6. HVAC system causes of IAQ problems in buildings

Problem Category	Physical cause		Frequency (%)
Design			
	System problems		
		Inadequate outdoor air	75
		Inadequate supply air distribution to occupied spaces	65
		Inadequate return/exhaust air	75
	Equipment problems		
		Inadequate filtration of supply air	65
		Inadequate drain lines and drain pans	60
		Contaminated ductwork or duct linings	45
		Malfunctioning humidifiers	
		Inadequte access panels to equipment	60
Operations			
		Inapproprite control strategies	90
		Inadequate maintenance	75
		Thermal and contaminant load changes	60

James E. Woods, P. E., a pioneer of IAQ research, has extensively investigated many severe problem buildings. He stated that he never found a building with BRI that didn't also have SBS. On the basis of his investigations, he reported the "predominant stressors" and the percent of problem buildings in which they were found as shown in Table 5. Table 6 lists HVAC system deficiencies and their frequency of occurrence in problem buildings investigated by Woods.

Productivity and IAQ

An indirect effect of exposure to indoor air pollutants is lost productivity. Since the common cold and many types of flu are believed transmitted through the air, respiratory illnesses that affect most people once or twice a year, or more, can be considered at least partly a result of poor indoor air quality. While it is difficult to measure the relationship between indoor air quality and productivity (office work, school, and retail), it is clear that there is a strong connection.

It is difficult to directly establish the linkages between productivity and the quality of the indoor environment. However, much indirect evidence exists. Such evidence is available from various measures including those listed in Table 7.

Table 7. Indoor environment - productivity linkages

- death
- job injury, HP, ASTHMA
- doctor visits
- days absent
- task performance
- attention span

4 Building ecology

General: meso, meta, micro

For convenience, the environment can be divided into three scales: "meso, meta, and micro." From an indoor air quality perspective, the "meso environment" is the environment in which the building is located. It includes the soil, groundwater, air, and neighboring structures and natural features. The "meta environment" is the building itself. It includes the building shell or envelope, the structure, equipment, services, finishes, and furnishings. While the meta- and meso-environments are important for IAQ, the "micro-environment" (also referred to as the occupant's personal environment) is the most important. This is the immediate space around an occupant, and it contains the air to which the occupant is exposed and from which he or she will inhale.

Occupant activities are the most important determinants of exposure to indoor air pollutants. Contaminants disperse after they are released into the air from the source. If they are of similar temperature and buoyancy as the air into which they are released, they generally disperse by molecular diffusion in a spherical pattern, that is, in all directions from the source. When the contaminant is at a much higher or lower temperature than the environment, thermal forces dominant the plume dispersal until the contaminant temperature is closer to the air temperature. When air movement (convection) is sufficient, contaminants are carried away from the source by air currents.

Thus, removing contaminants close to the source, as with toilet or kitchen exhausts, is an effective approach to controlling contaminant exposure. Appliances that are known sources or activities that are known to generate contaminants should be conducted with ventilation that prevents dispersal of the contaminants into the general environment where it will be harder to remove. Similarly, supplying clean air to the occupants' breathing zone is also an effective way to minimize exposure to contaminants.

Humans respond to the total environment

The body integrates all of the stresses to which it is exposed. These stresses can be physical, chemical, or biological. Table 8 lists these factors. Personal factors (listed in Table 9) can modify the human physiological response to environmental stressors. The social and institutional environment can also be a source of stress that affects the body's response due to physiological changes mediated by the endocrine system. A common example of this is the fear response—an adrenaline "rush" enables humans to defend themselves against threats to their life or well-being. Of course, caffeine, tobacco, drugs and alcohol affect the way humans respond to environmental stressors. Research on humans and animal subjects has clearly shown responses to environmental stress are strongly affected by psychological state. Table 8 shows the broad range of environmental factors to which the body is exposed.

Table 8. Environmental factors to which the body responds

CHEMICAL
  Organic gases and vapors
    Solvents
    Plastics
    Pesticides
    Fire retardants
    Human and other animal metabolites
  Inorganic gases and vapors
    Combustion products
    Soil particles
    Atmospheric constituents
PHYSICAL
  Thermal factors:
    Temperature, Air velocity, Radiant asymmetry
  Moisture
  Electromagnetic energy
    Visible light
    Ultraviolet light
    Infrared radiation
    Cosmic radiation
    Extremely low frequency
    Ionizing radiation
  Electrostatic fields
  Mechanical energy
    Noise
    Vibration
BIOLOGICAL
  Types of organisms
    Virus, Bacteria, Fungi
  Status
    Viable or Non-viable
  Effects
    Infectious agents, Allergens, Odorants, Asthmagenics

Table 9. Personal factors that modify human response to environmental factors

Age - gender
Genetics
Race
Nationality
Blood type, etc.
Psyche
Attitude
Emotional depth (anxiety, fear, anger)
Intelligence (perceived vs. Real hazard; perception of the environment itself)
Personality
Interests
Value
Physical condition
Sensory proceses: vision (blind/visually impaired); audition (deaf); pressure and pain; temperature; kinesthesis (handicapped); taste and small.
Health status: hospitalized, handicapped.
Past experience

Building environment: air, light, thermal, acoustic

Ventilation

Ventilation can be mechanical or "natural" (either passive or active). The purpose of ventilation is to remove heat, moisture, and contaminants or to reduce the concentrations of contaminants.

Pressure differences drive ventilation in buildings. Infiltration rates (ventilation through openings in the building envelope) are heavily dependent on pressure differences resulting from indoor-outdoor temperature differences or wind induced positive and negative pressurization of different sides of a building. Stack effect results in relatively higher (positive) pressure at the top and lower (negative) pressure at the bottom of a building. So, air leaks out of the top and in at the bottom. Overall, the flows in and out through all pathways and by all means must be balanced.

Within a building, pressure differences cause for air (and, therefore, airborne contaminant) movement from one location to another. This is extremely important for the designer. Knowing where pollutants will be generated or where they will occur naturally and keeping such areas negatively pressurized relative to the adjacent areas is important to avoid unwanted distribution of the contaminants from one location to another. Locations of activities or equipment that will be strong sources of contaminants should be provided with exhaust ventilation or surrounded by spaces that are positively pressurized relative to the source location. Sensitive areas should always be isolated by pressure and fixed barriers where feasible.

Ventilation standards

The most important ventilation standard is published by ASHRAE, the American Society of Heating, Refrigerating, and Air-conditioning Engineers. ASHRAE has led in developing an understanding of IAQ in the United States since the early 1980s when the Society made a commitment to make IAQ an important issue. Its ventilation standard, ASHRAE Standard 62-1989, "Ventilation for Acceptable Indoor Air Quality," is the basis for most building code ventilation requirements and is probably the most important and valuable single document a building design professional can consult. It is currently under revision; and the revised standard is considerably more comprehensive and more detailed than the Standard 62-1989. The public Review Draft of the revised standard (62-1989R), dated July 1996, is available on the World Wide Web (see "Additional References").

In general, many important aspects of the standard have been ignored while the minimum requirements for outdoor air ventilation rates have been considered. Buildings codes often incorporate all or part of ASHRAE Standard 62-1989 by reference or by actual adopted language. In some cases, they simply adopt the ventilation rates from the standard.

Minimum rates in Standard 62-1989 include 15 cfm/p in many typical spaces such as offices, schools, and public assembly spaces. Open office areas, educational laboratories, and commercial dining rooms require 20 cfm/p. The draft proposed revision provides a minimum ventilation rate per occupant plus a minimum ventilation rate per square foot based on the type of building use. In general, the total ventilation required by draft revision is similar to that required by Standard 62-89, although certain spaces including school classrooms require less. In any case, the ASHRAE standard and the code should be consulted and the actual or anticipated loads should be clearly identified as the basis for design ventilation rates.

Other important aspects of Standard 62 address systems, contaminant sources, design and HVAC systems documentation, control of moisture, cleaning of contaminated outdoor air, and many other factors critical for good IAQ. Regrettably, many HVAC system design engineers use no more than the Standard's minimum ventilation rates. In order to reduce equipment size and costs and to minimize energy consumption, they use the minimum values as maximum values. While energy conservation is an important goal, and cost is always an important factor, indoor pollution loads, like other loads, vary greatly vary from building to building and from space to space within buildings. Knowing the right amount of ventilation is difficult, but the rates established in the ASHRAE standard should be regarded only as a starting place, not as the final authority. Specific identification of contaminant sources and estimation of the loads should be done as part of the ventilation system design process.

Ventilation systems can be sources of contaminants. Particular concern is warranted for the quality of filters and the frequency of their replacement, the cleanliness of heat exchange coils and drip pans, and the moistening and deterioration of duct liners. Thermal liners should always be on the outside of ductwork, Acoustic insulation should be kept to the minimum, and it should be protected from dirt and moisture which, when they accumulate, can lead to a deterioration in the liner material, erosion, and microbial growth.

Thermal comfort and air quality

Many cases of IAQ complaints have been resolved by better controlling the thermal environment. There are two important factors that would support this. First, people tend to be more sensitive to odors as temperatures rise, and, therefore, they find air quality less acceptable. Research results shown in Fig. 6 indicate that as air temperature and humidity increase, people find air less fresh and more stale. The data in Fig. 6 are from a laboratory study where the quality of the air was held constant while the temperature and humidity were varied. The same decreased assessment of air quality was true at various activity levels and for various indicators of air quality.

Secondly, as temperature rises, the emissions (off-gassing) of chemicals increases. This is because emissions are controlled by vapor pressure, and vapor pressure increases as temperature increases.

Just as warm water evaporates more rapidly than cold water, so all organic chemicals evaporate from solid materials more rapidly as the temperature increases. A large part of the short term effect is dominated by evaporation of chemicals at or near the surface of materials. The longer term effects are controlled by the diffusion of chemicals through the solid materials in which they occur. The chemicals deep within a material like plywood or particleboard must not only evaporate, but they must also migrate through the dense matrix of the material. Thus, the emissions of formaldehyde from pressed wood products using formaldehyde resin-based binders continue for a very long time—typically several years are required to achieve significant reductions in emissions from these products.

Guidelines for thermal comfort are embodied in ASHRAE Standard 55-1996, "Thermal Environmental Conditions for Human Occupancy." This standard involves a complex formula derived from scores of research projects, almost entirely conducted under controlled laboratory conditions. It establishes a comfort envelope including temperature, humidity, radiant temperature, and air movement as the key variables. The ASHRAE thermal comfort envelope does not consider air quality. However, research has shown that perceived air quality decreases as temperatures rise in the upper end of the envelope. The personal factors that affect thermal comfort are metabolism and clothing. Of course the designer has no control over these but should anticipate them based on planned building use.

Since most building thermal control systems rely only on dry bulb temperature or, in some cases, also on humidity, it can be expected that not all occupants will necessarily be thermally comfortable. Furthermore, in the careful laboratory studies, even at the optimum temperature—defined as that temperature where an equal number of people find it too hot and too cold—somewhere around 6 to 12 percent of the subjects will be dissatisfied with the thermal conditions. Research in actual field settings has found an even larger number of dissatisfied occupants. As temperature increases above the optimum, the number of people becoming too warm will increase more rapidly than the number of people who were too cold will become comfortable. As temperatures drop below the optimum, similarly the number becoming too cold increases more rapidly than formerly too warm people become comfortable.

When indoor environments are controlled to certain general conditions, significant numbers of occupants will prefer either warmer or cooler temperatures. Individual control over the thermal environment has been proposed as one solution to this problem. Similar preferences for noise levels, light levels, privacy, and so forth mean that there will always be some people who would prefer different conditions. Individual control over other environmental parameters can also increase occupant satisfaction with the environment. Occupants with a sense of well-being are presumably more productive and healthy.

Noise and lighting

Recent research has shown that increasing the noise level can reduce tolerance of poor indoor air quality. The precise relationships are not well-understood, and research is fairly sparse on the subject. Nevertheless, it is important to remember that the body integrates all the stresses in the environment to which it is exposed, and there is a limit to the amount of stress it can tolerate. Thus, glare or inadequate illumination can also cause stress that reduce tolerance for the indoor air quality.

5 Designing for good Indoor Air Quality

There are innumerable things that designers can (and should) do to achieve good indoor air quality. Although designers are not in control of all of them, they control many and can influence or contribute to many others. The most important thing is to focus on the impacts of design on sources, ventilation, and building operation and maintenance.

Source control is the most effective way to ensure good indoor air quality. Following are the various source control options:

- Source elimination by removal or substitution.

- Source reduction by careful materials selection and specification, by minimizing use of strong sources.

- Source isolation by location, barriers, pressure management.

- Minimize sinks (secondary sources) by reducing fleecy surfaces exposed to the circulating air.

Ventilation is the next most important indoor air quality control strategy, after source control is accomplished. The major components of the ventilation strategy are as follow:

- Ensure adequate air exchange rate.

- Local exhaust to control point sources.

- Air distribution to avoid dead zones.

- Air cleaning and filtration to remove gaseous contaminants from outdoor air and recirculated air.

- Lower Temperature, Humidity to reduce emissions and improve occupant responses to contaminants.

- Air movement to ensure comfort, circulation.

- Minimize use of porous materials exposed inside air supply and distribution systems.

Life cycle design for good IAQ

Designers can impact indoor air quality in every stage of the building process, throughout the life cycle. The phases when IAQ should be considered are

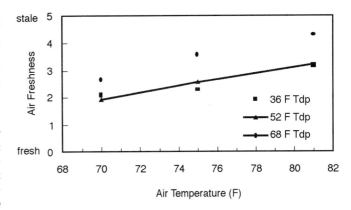

Fig. 6. Perception of air freshness as a function of air temperature and humidity (Tdp = dew point temperature. The three curves represent approximately 35, 50 and 65% relative humidity).

- Programming and planning
- Site analysis and design
- Overall building configuration
- Building environmental control scheme
- Selecting and specifying building materials and furnishings
- Construction procedures
- Building commissioning
- Building operation and maintenance
- Building renovation and adaptive re-use

Following is a brief listing of important details and a discussion for each of these life cycle phases.

Programming and planning

Good IAQ starts in the planning stages of a building's life. Following are the important aspects of an effective design approach to the planning phase:

- Establish IAQ objectives and criteria.
- Evaluate overall project environs - air, water, soil.
- Identify pollutant-generating activities / equipment.
- Identify pollutant-sensitive activities / occupants.
- Plan control of major pollutant sources.
- Plan protection of sensitive individuals / activities.
- Plan construction schedule to allow IAQ assurance.

Anticipating the needs to deal with IAQ issues throughout the life cycle is invaluable. Establishing IAQ objectives and criteria begins the process and allows everything that follows to be assessed and evaluated within an explicit framework. One of the most important elements is scheduling to allow for complete commissioning and a thorough building flush out before occupancy.

Site analysis and design

Site selection, analysis, and design are all important to achieving good building air quality. Following are some of the key points of an effective approach to this phase of design:

- Evaluate air, water, soil for contaminants.
- Evaluate surrounding and historical uses.
- Determinate impact of climate, wind.
- Locate buildings, site features to minimize negative impacts.
- Specify filtration and air cleaning requirements based on the assessment of the surrounding environment.

Overall building configuration

The basic building configuration can strongly influence indoor air quality. The following key factors should be considered:

- Locate openings away from pollutant sources.
- Use thermal mass to temper temperature swings.
- Minimize reliance on mechanical ventilation and air cleaning by use of source control measures such as selection of low-emitting materials.
- Control air movement by design to avoid positive pressure in spaces with strong sources.
- Isolate pollutant generating activities.

Building environmental control scheme

The conceptual design of building environmental control is one of the most important determines of IAQ over the life of the building. This includes the general approach that will be used to establish and main-

tain healthy, comfortable, and supportive indoor environmental conditions. It includes the mechanisms and their control to maintain atmospheric (air quality, thermal, and moisture), light, and acoustic conditions. The environmental control scheme should be conceived simultaneously and jointly with the overall building configuration and the selection of the major structural and finish materials. Key elements of the environmental control scheme are:

- Program thermal and pollutant control approach rather than just thermal loads.
- Identify loads for each space, zone, at various times and use conditions.
- Design flexible system to adapt to changing needs over time.
- Plan redundancy in critical components where feasible, to allow preventive maintenance or repair without system down-time.
- Specify backward compatible components and inter-operability.
- Describe system components thoroughly in documentation.
- Describe system operation in simple terms, sequences, and controls.
- Design for easy inspection and maintenance of all components.

Specifying building materials and furnishings

Just as thermal loads are controlled by minimizing heat gains and losses through the building envelope, indoor air quality loads can be limited by the selection and specification of building materials and furnishings. A great deal of information on the content of building materials and, for some products, on their chemical emissions. Requiring this information in the pre-bid phase (design development, construction documents) allows designers to use the information to compare products.

Many building products and materials evidence strong emissions early in their product-lives. For others, emissions can last over a large portion of the product's useful life. Since the variations among products available to serve the same function, it is important to carefully select building materials. The major steps in IAQ-oriented materials selection and specification process are discussed in this section.

An extremely important consideration in selecting materials is the life cycle emissions. If they require periodic application of chemicals for maintenance of appearance or wear resistance, then these chemical emissions should be considered when the materials are selected. The durability of the materials will also determine its expected service life, and periodic replacement should be evaluated in terms of the emissions associated with removal and replacement materials.

Following are the key points to consider for selecting and specifying materials:

- Identify most important materials, components, and products.
- Require pre-qualification submittals.
- Identify manufacturer responsibility for suitability of products to achieve good IAQ.
- Screen candidate materials.
- Require manufacturers to submit information.
- Contact reliable, cooperative manufacturers to identify most suitable products.
- Evaluate submitted data.
- Require additional data if necessary.
- Consider maintenance requirements, useful life.
- Select most suitable products.

Emissions data

It is important to obtain emissions data whenever available to evaluate potential sources of emissions and compare candidate products. But interpretation of emissions test data is not trivial, and requires care in obtaining data from comparable tests. An excellent source of information on VOC sources is available from the California Department of Health Services. (See references for more detail.)

Emissions data are generally reported in mg/m³ or µg/m³. Composite wood product formaldehyde emission tests are still often reported in PPM, or parts per million. However, PPM is not an emission rate, it is a concentration. The wood products industry has reported emissions this way for some time - back into the early 80s at least. This sort of reporting simply does not provide emissions rates. One must know the loading factor—in the case of composite wood products, the area of the emission source per volume of the test chamber—and the ventilation rate to be able to calculate an emission factor or emission rate.

An emission rate must be stated in mass units per unit of time. For sheet materials such as composite wood panels, a unit of area should also be given. This might be called an area specific emission rate, or a normalized emission rate. So, the formaldehyde emission rate from composite wood products would be stated in micrograms or milligrams of formaldehyde per square meter per hour - µg/m² • h.

For details of emissions testing and the reporting and meaning of results, consult ASTM Standard D5116-90. At this writing, it is under revision. The original standard is the most authoritative guide to emissions testing available (ASTM 1990).

For the computationally inclined designer, the equation for emission factor is:

$$EF = C(Q)/A$$

where

EF = emission factor, mg m^{-2} h^{-1},
C = equilibrium changer concentration, mg/m³,
Q = flow through chamber, m³/h, and
A = sample area, m².

An equivalent expression is also used:

$$EF = C(N/L)$$

where

N = chamber air exchange rate, h^{-1}
L = chamber loading, m²/m³.

Note that N = Q/V, where V = chamber volume, m^3.

An emission rate would involve multiplying the area of source material times the emission factor, and would be stated in units of mass per unit time.

Construction procedures

Many preventive measures can be employed during construction to avoid the generation, spread, and accumulation of VOCs in buildings under construction or renovation. The most important is the use of adequate ventilation during installation of strong emission sources. The most important steps are:

- Require thermal, moisture control, protection for installation of all sensitive materials.

- Require HVAC operational (or temporary) when building is closed-in.

- Operate HVAC on maximum outside air during installation of wet products, finishes, and furnishings.

- Temporary filters during dusty operations.

- Clean and flush building thoroughly prior to initial occupancy.

- Fully commission HVAC system including full and part loads in all major modes of operation.

Building commissioning

Building commissioning is so environmentally and economically beneficial that it is difficult to ignore its potential. Energy savings are said to pay back the costs within 6 to 18 months. IAQ improvements are so dramatic that the costs can also be considered paid back two or three fold by the avoided employee illness, lost productivity, and problem resolution. Commissioning is an effective way to minimize the potential for IAQ problems, especially in buildings with mechanical ventilation systems.

Among other things, HVAC system commissioning according to ASHRAE Guideline 1, requires the preparation and assembly of complete documentation of design assumptions. The process of assembling the information and the use of the information can improve communication and eliminate problems by making explicit and available the basis of design and its expected performance. Verification of the design assumptions by the client will reduce designer liability and improve the likelihood that the building will meet the occupants' needs. The availability of HVAC system documentation can improve the ability of building operators to achieve good IAQ. Research has shown that the closer building performance is to the design assumptions, the lower the SBS symptom prevalence. This may be attributable to the fact that there has been effective communication from design through construction to operation - an ideal condition.

A recent survey documented the benefits given in Table 10. These include energy, IAQ, and thermal performance.

Table 10. Benefits of commissioning. (Source: PECI. 1997)

Benefits of Commissioning	*Percentage reporting the benefits*
Energy Savings*	82%
Thermal comfort	46%
Indoor air quality	25%
Improved operation and maintenance	42%
Improved occupant morale	8%
Timely project completion	7%
Liability avoidance	6%
Reduced change orders	8%

* >70%documented energy savings by metering or monitoring

Some keys to effective commissioning include:

- Specify full HVAC commissioning process.

- Assemble all requisite documentation.

- Demonstrate performance in all critical modes under full and part loads.

- Specify warranty protection period commencing after completed commissioning.

- Ensure that building operational personnel receive adequate training.

- Provide completed documentation including design assumptions for each major air handler, zone, and space.

Building operation and maintenance

While designers cannot be responsible for effective building operation and maintenance, they can enable and facilitate it by considering it thoroughly during design. Involvement of building operational personnel during design can further improve the ability of designers to anticipate actually building use requirements. The following are key design considerations related to operation and maintenance:

- Design must consider maintenance and operational requirements of all specified materials and equipment.

- All equipment must be fully accessible for inspection, maintenance, replacement.

- Tie warranties to proper maintenance fully specified by manufacturers, installers, or other appropriate parties.

- Review manufacturer's maintenance requirements prior to specifying any product.

- Consider IAQ impacts of all maintenance, re-finishing, and re-placement procedures.

Building renovation and adaptive re-use

Since most buildings are constantly being changed and remodelling during occupancy can pose significant compromises of IAQ and related problems, it is important for designers to anticipate the changes likely to occur. This is difficult since the initial use is always most easily defined, but the future use is not. Built-in flexibility based on an assumption of multiple changes over a building's life will enhance the ability of the building to respond to the actual demands placed on it. Following are some key considerations related to building renovation and adaptive re-use with significant indoor air implications:

- Obtain design assumptions regarding thermal and contaminant loads for HVAC systems in-place.

- Consider contamination control during construction with partial occupancy.

- Isolate occupied areas from construction fumes and dusts.

- Provide temporary ventilation, if necessary, to construction zone.

- Provide for full HVAC testing, adjusting, and balancing after all changes.

- Provide for full re-commissioning.

Good indoor air quality is not an accident. It occurs by design. Considering IAQ throughout a building's entire life is an important element of achieving good IAQ. Designers have enormous influence over IAQ even though they cannot control all the important factors. By taking advantage of the enormous increase in understanding of the factors that determine IAQ, designers can create healthy, productive buildings.

Additional references

Alevantis, Leon. 1996. "Reducing occupant exposure to volatile organic compounds (VOCs) from office building construction materials: non-binding guidelines." Berkeley: California Department of Health Services. Available at no cost: Indoor Air Quality Section, Dept. of Health Services, 2151 Berkeley Way, Berkeley, CA 94704-1011. (510) 540 2132. Email: <hw1.lalevant@hw1.cahwnet.gov>.

ASHRAE. 1996. Guideline 1-96. "Guideline for Commissioning of HVAC Systems" Atlanta, GA: American Society of Heating, Refrigerating, and Air-Conditioning Engineers.

ASHRAE. 1996. Standard 55-1996. "Thermal Environmental Conditions for Human Occupancy" Atlanta, GA: American Society of Heating, Refrigerating, and Air-Conditioning Engineers.

ASHRAE. 1996. Standard 62-1989R "Public Review Draft, Ventilation for Acceptable Indoor Air Quality." July 1996. Atlanta, GA: American Society of Heating, Refrigerating, and Air-Conditioning Engineers. URL: www.ashrae.org (then enter "Standards")

ASTM. 1990. Standard D5116-90. Standard Guide for Small-Scale Environmental Chamber Determinations of Organic Emissions from Indoor Materials/Products" in *Annual Book of ASTM Standards, Volume 11.03, Atmospheric Analysis; Occupational Health and Safety; Protective Clothing*. West Conshocken, PA: American Society for Testing and Materials. pp. 467-478.

Banham, Reyner. 1984. *The Architecture of the Well-Tempered Environment*. Second Edition. Chicago: University of Chicago Press.

Berglund, Birgitta, and Thomas Lindvall. 1990. "Sensory Criteria for Healthy Buildings" in *Proceedings of the Fifth International Conference on Indoor Air Quality and Climate, Indoor Air '90*. 5: 65-79.

Berglund, L. G. and W. S. Cain, 1989. "Perceived air quality and the thermal environment" in *IAQ 89, The Human Equation: Health and Comfort*. Atlanta, GA: American Society for Heating, Refrigerating and Air-Conditioning Engineers and the Society for Occupational and Environmental Health. pp. 93-99.

Cone, J., and M. Hodgson, editors. *Problem Buildings: Building Associated Illness and the Sick Building Syndrome*. Philadelphia, PA: Hanley & Belfus. (215) 546-7293.

EPA. 1991. "Indoor Air Quality: A Guide for Building Owners and Facility Managers." EPA/400/1-91/033. December 1991. U. S. EPA Indoor Air Division. Washington, DC: Superintendent of Documents.

EPA and the National Environmental Health Association. 1991. *Introduction to Indoor Air Quality: A Self-Paced Learning Module*. (EPA/400/3-91/002) and *Introduction to Indoor Air Quality: A Reference Manual*. (EPA/400/3-91/003) July 1991. Available from the National Environmental Health Association, 720 South Colorado Boulevard, South Tower, Suite 970, Denver, CO 80222. (303) 756-9090.

Godish, Thad. 1989. *Indoor Air Pollution Control*. Chelsea, MI: Lewis Publishers.

Hinkle, L. E. and W. C. Loring. 1977. *The Effect of the Man-Made Environment on Health and Behavior*. (DHEW Publication no. CDC 77-8318). Atlanta, GA: U. S. Public Health Service Center for Disease Control.

Hodgson, A. T., J. D. Wooley, and J. M Daisey. 1992. "Volatile Organic Chemical Emissions from Carpets." Final Report April 1992. (LBL-31916, UC 600). Washington, DC: Directorate of Health Sciences. U. S. Consumer Products Safety Commission.

Levin H. 1989. "Building materials and indoor air quality." in J. E. Cone and M. J. Hodgson, editors. *Occupational Medicine: State of the Art Reviews*. Vol. 4, No. 4, Oct.-Dec, 1989. Philadelphia, PA: Hanley & Belfus. pp. 667-694.

Levin, H. 1991. "Critical Building Design Factors for Indoor Air Quality and Climate: Current Status and Predicted Trends." *Indoor Air*, Vol. 1, no. 1. Copenhagen: Munksgaard.

Levin, H. 1991. "Controlling Sources of Indoor Air Pollution." *Indoor Air Bulletin*, Vol. 1, no. 6. Santa Cruz, CA: Indoor Air Information Service. (408) 426-6624).

Levin, H. 1995. "Emissions Testing and Indoor Air Quality," in *Proceedings of Indoor Air Quality, Ventilation, and Energy Conservation in Buildings*." Montreal, Canada, May 9-12, 1995. Montreal: Concordia University.

Levin, H. and Hodgson, A. T. 1996. "Screening and Selecting Building Materials and Products Based on Their Emissions of VOCs" in B. Tichenor, editor. *Methods for Characterizing Indoor Sources and Sinks* (STP 1287). West Conshocken, PA: American Society for Testing and Materials.

PECI. 1997. *Proceedings of the 5th National building Commissioning Conference*. Portland, OR: Portland Energy Conservation, Inc.

Acoustics: theory and applications

M. David Egan
Steven Hass
Christopher Jaffe

Summary: Part I presents a brief summary of key acoustical definitions and concepts. Part II presents application and examples for specific types of spaces, including performance halls, offices and lecture halls.

Key words: acoustics, ambient noise, decibel, frequency, masking, noise exposure limits, reverberation, vibration.

Greek amphitheatre at Epidaurus circa 350 BC.

Part I Acoustics: theory and definitions

Sound and vibrations

Sound is a vibration in an elastic medium such as air, water, most building materials, and the earth. (Noise can be defined as unwanted sound, that is, annoying sound made by others or very loud sound which may cause hearing loss.)

An elastic medium returns to its normal state after a force is removed. Pressure is a force per unit area. Sound energy progresses rapidly, producing extremely small changes in atmospheric pressure, and can travel great distances. However, each vibrating particle moves only an infinitesimal amount to either side of its normal position. It "bumps" adjacent particles and imparts most of its motion and energy to them. A full circuit by a displaced particle is called a cycle. The time required for one complete cycle is called the period and the number of complete cycles per second is the frequency of vibration. Consequently, the reciprocal of frequency is the period. Frequency is measured in cycles per second, the unit for which is called the hertz (abbreviated Hz).

A pure tone is vibration produced at a single frequency. Fig. 1 depicts the variation in pressure caused by striking a tuning fork, which produces an almost pure tone by vibrating adjacent air molecules. Symphonic music consists of numerous tones at different frequencies and pressures (that is, a tone is composed of a fundamental frequency with multiples of the fundamental, called harmonics). In Fig. 1, the prongs of the tuning fork alternately compress and rarefy adjacent air particles. This cyclical motion causes a chain reaction between adjacent air particles so that the waves (but not the air particles) propagate away from the tuning fork.

Frequency of sound

Frequency is the rate of repetition of a periodic event. Sound in air consists of a series of compressions and rarefactions due to air particles set into motion by a vibrating source. The frequency of a sound wave is determined by the number of times per second a given molecule of air vibrates about its neutral position. The greater the number of complete vibrations (called cycles), the higher the frequency. The unit of frequency is the hertz (Hz). Pitch is the subjective response of human hearing to frequency. Low frequencies generally are considered "boomy," and high frequencies "screechy" or "hissy."

Most sound sources, except for pure tones, contain energy over a wide range of frequencies. For measurement, analysis, and specification of sound, the frequency range is divided into sections (called bands). One common standard division is into 10 octave bands identified by their center frequencies: 31.5, 63, 125, 250, 500, 1000, 2000, 4000, 8000, and 16,000 Hz.

Sound level meters can measure energy within octave bands by using electronic filters to eliminate the energy in the frequency regions outside the band of interest. The sound level covering the entire frequency range of octave bands is referred to as the overall level.

Wavelength

As sound passes through air, the to-and-fro motion of the particles alternately pushes together and draws apart adjacent air particles, forming regions of rarefaction and compression. Wavelength is the distance a sound wave travels during one cycle of vibration. It also is the distance between adjacent regions where identical conditions of particle displacement occur, as shown below by the wire spring (called a "slinky" toy). When shaken at one end, the wave moves along the slinky, but the particles only move back and forth about their normal positions.

Sound waves in air also are analogous to the ripples (or waves) caused by a stone dropped into still water. The concentric ripples vividly show patterns of molecules transferring energy to adjacent molecules along the surface of the water. In air, however, sound spreads in all directions.

Velocity of sound

Sound travels at a velocity that depends primarily on the elasticity and density of the medium. In air, at normal temperature and atmospheric pressure, the velocity of sound is approximately 1,130 feet per second (ft/s), or almost 800 mi./h. This is extremely slow when compared to the velocity of light, which is about 186,000 mi./s, but much faster than even hurricane winds.

In building air distribution systems, the air velocity at registers, diffusers, and in ducts is so much slower than the velocity of sound that its effect can be neglected. For example, an extremely high air velocity of 2000 ft/min (about 33 ft/s) in a duct is less than 3 percent of the velocity of sound in air. Consequently, airborne sound travels with equal ease upstream and downstream within most air ducts!

Authors: Part I: M. David Egan, P. E.; Part II: Steven Haas and Christopher Jaffe, Ph.D.

References for Part I: ASHRAE. 1993. *ASHRAE Handbook Fundamentals.* Chapter 7 "Sound and Vibration." Atlanta, GA: American Society of Heating, Refrigerating and Air-Conditioning Engineers.

Egan, M. David. 1988. *Architectural Acoustics.* New York: McGraw-Hill.

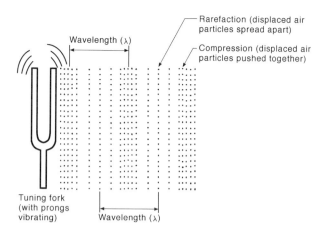

Fig. 1. Wavelength in air from a vibrating tuning fork. (Egan 1988)

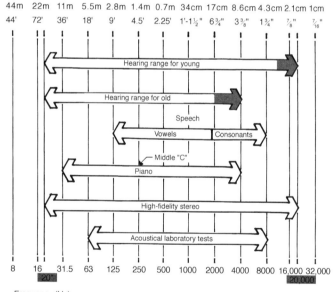

Frequency (Hz)

*Vibrations below 20 Hz are not audible, but can be felt.

Fig. 2. Wavelength scales. Vibrations below 20 Hz. are not audible by humans, but can be felt. (Egan 1988)

However, sound may travel at a very fast 16,000 ft/s along steel pipes and duct walls. It is therefore important to block or isolate paths where sound energy can travel through building materials (called structure-bome sound) to sensitive areas great distances away where it may be regenerated as airborne sound.

In buildings, the effect of temperature on sound also is negligible. For example, a 20F rise or drop in room air temperature is significant in temperature range, but would cause only a 2 percent change in the velocity of sound in air.

Frequency ranges of audible sounds

Hearing ranges for both young and older persons (> 20 years old) are shown in Fig. 2. A healthy young person is capable of hearing sound energy from about 20 to 20,000 Hz. Hearing sensitivity, especially the upper frequency limit, diminishes with increasing age even without adverse effects from diseases and noise—a condition called "presbycusis."

Long-term and repeated exposure to intense sounds and noises of everyday living can cause permanent hearing damage (called "sociocusis"), and short-term exposure can cause temporary loss. Consequently, the extent of the hearing sensitivity for an individual depends on many factors, including age, sex, ethnicity, previous exposure to high noise levels from the workplace, gunfire, power tools, or loud music. All other hearing losses (that is, caused by mumps, drugs, accidents) are called "nosocusis." An audiologist should be consulted if a "ringing" sensation occurs in ears after exposure to moderately loud noise or if sounds seem muffled or dull.

Also indicated in Fig. 2 are frequency ranges for human speech (divided into consonants, which contain most of the information for articulation, and vowels!, piano music, stereo sounds, and acoustical laboratory tests (that is, tests used to determine absorption and isolation properties of building materials). Human speech contains energy from about 125 to 8000 Hz. Women's vocal cords are generally thinner and shorter than men's, so the wavelengths produced are smaller. This is the reason the female frequency of vibration for speech is normally higher. Wavelengths in S.I. and English units are indicated by the scales at the top of the graph above the corresponding frequency.

Sensitivity of hearing

The graph in Fig. 3 shows the tremendous range of sound levels in decibels (abbreviated dB). and frequency in hertz over which healthy young persons can hear. Also shown on the graph is the frequency range for "conversational" speech, which occurs in the region where the ear is most sensitive. For comparison, the region where symphonic music occurs is indicated on the graph by the large shaded area extending at mid-frequencies from below 25 dB to over 100 dB (called dynamic range). The dynamic range for individual instruments can vary from 30 dB (woodwinds) to 50 dB (strings). The lowest level of musical sound energy that can be detected by the audience largely depends on the background noise in the music hall, and the upper level depends on the acoustical characteristics of the hall. Electronically amplified rock music in arenas and coliseums far exceeds the maximum sound levels for a large symphonic orchestra. Rock music, purposefully amplified to be at the threshold of feeling ("tingling" in the ear), is considered to be a significant cause of sociocusis.

Inverse-square law

Sound waves from a point source outdoors with no obstructions (called free-field conditions) are virtually spherical and expand outward from the source as shown in Fig. 4. A point source has physical dimensions of size that are far less than the distance an observer is away from the source.

Power is a basic quantity of energy flow. Although both acoustical and electric energies are measured in Watts, they are different forms of energy and cause different responses. For instance, 10 Watts (abbreviated W) of electric energy at an incandescent lamp produces a very dim light, whereas 10 W of acoustical energy at a loudspeaker can produce an extremely loud sound. Peak power for musical instruments can range from 0.05 W for a clarinet to 25 W for a bass drum.

Decibels

Ernst Weber and Gustav Fechner (nineteenth-century German scientists) discovered that nearly all human sensations are proportional to the logarithm of the intensity of the stimulus. In acoustics, the bel unit (named in honor of Alexander Graham Bell) was first used to relate the intensity of sound to an intensity level corresponding to the human hearing sensation.

Some common, easily recognized sounds are listed below in order of increasing sound levels in decibels. The sound levels shown for occupied rooms are only representative activity levels and do not represent criteria for design. Note also that thresholds vary among individuals. The human hearing range from the threshold of audibility at 0 dB to the threshold of pain at 130 dB represents a tremendous intensity ratio of 1 to 10 trillion (10,000,000,000,000). This is such a wide range of hearing sensitivity that it may be hard to imagine at first. For example, if a bathroom scale had a sensitivity range comparable to that of the human ear, it would have to be sensitive enough to weigh both a human hair and a 30-story building! Logarithms allow the huge range of human hearing sensitivity to be conveniently represented by smaller numbers.

It is difficult to measure sound intensity directly. However, sound intensity is proportional to the square of sound pressure, which can more easily be measured by sound level meters. In air under normal atmospheric conditions, sound intensity level and sound pressure level are nearly identical.

Noise exposure limits

In 1971, the U. S. Department of Labor established the Occupational Safety and Health Administration (OSHA) and adopted regulations to protect against hearing loss caused by exposure to noise in the workplace. The permissible daily upper limit of noise exposure in A-weighted decibels (abbreviated dBA) for continuous noise is shown on in the graph of Fig. 6 for 1983 rules and regulations. Single-number decibels in dBA units are measured by sound level meters with internal electronic networks that tend to discriminate with frequency like the human ear does at low sound levels. Amplified rock music at 120 dBA and higher would exceed even the shortest permissible noise exposure. Exposure to impulsive noise such as gunfire or impact noise from heavy machinery should not exceed 140 dBA peak sound level.

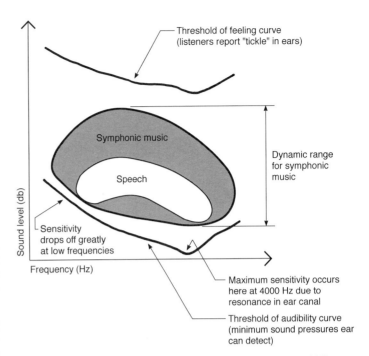

Fig. 3. Human audible sound level and frequency (Egan 1988)

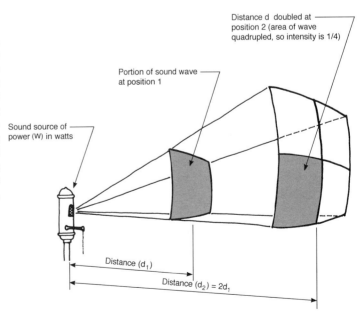

Fig. 4. Inverse-square law (Egan 1988)

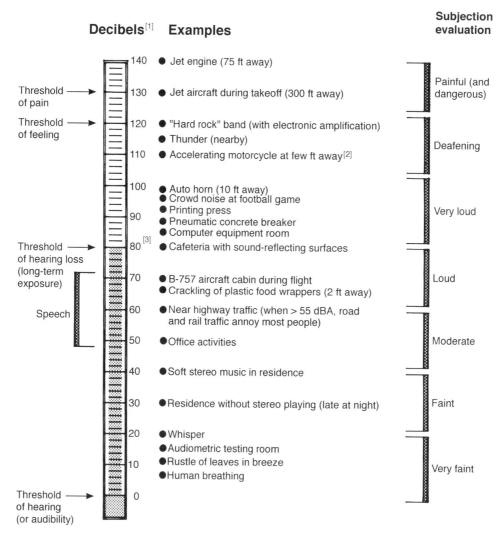

Fig. 5. Common sounds in decibels (Egan 1988)

[1] Decibels (dBA) are weighted values measured by a sound level meter.
[2] 150 ft. from a motorcycle can equal the noise level at less than 2000 ft. from a jet aircraft.
[3] Continuous exposure to sound energy above 80 dBA can be hazardous to health and can cause hearing loss for some persons.

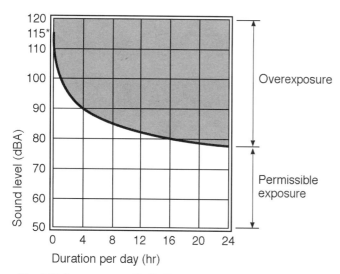

Although exposure limits are given in dBA, only octave-band (or narrower) analysis of noise will give a more complete picture of how severe the problems are at specific frequencies. This kind of detailed information (called frequency analysis) is also needed to determine the corrective measures because solutions for high-frequency noise problems may differ considerably from those for low- frequency. Corrective measures can involve reducing noise levels at the source (that is, by redesign of noisy equipment or industrial processes), interrupting the path, protecting the receiver (by using individual hearing protection devices), or combinations of all these measures.

Fig. 6. Noise exposure limits. Upper limit (not design value) for exposure to continuous noise in the workplace without hearing testing program or use of hearing-protection devices. (Egan 1988).

Part II Applications

Part II provides an overview of acoustic issues encountered in building design with emphasis upon practical application of acoustic concepts. Acoustical terms are defined and common misconceptions about acoustics in building design are discussed in terms of acoustical materials, sound attenuation techniques, and special requirements for performance spaces, office spaces, and educational facilities.

2 The discipline of architectural acoustics involves primarily three areas:

- Room acoustics.
- Sound isolation.
- Building services noise and vibration control.

Room acoustics design begins with establishing basic size, shape and finish materials of a given space to achieve a certain room sound. These criteria are based largely upon the intended function and occupancy of the room.

Specific criteria to be determined include:

- Cubic volume and reverberation time. RT60 is a recommended standard and indicates a time (RT) in a room that a sound takes to decay 60 decibels from its original level when abruptly terminated.

- Room dimensional proportions (length-to-width and height-to-width ratios) and shaping.

- Type, location, orientation, and shaping of sound reflecting, absorbing and diffusing surfaces.

Sound isolation involves the prevention of airborne and structure-borne noise and vibration generated in one space from entering an adjacent space and having an adverse affect on the occupants or the function of the room (Fig. 1).

Specific criteria to be established include:

- Identification and quantification of all potential noise sources—interior and exterior—that would influence the function of an occupied space within a building.

- Sound attenuation required for all boundary surfaces—*i.e.*, walls, floors, ceilings, doors, and windows—at all frequencies of interest.

- Calculation and selection, based on laboratory and field sound isolation test results, of partition constructions that will meet the necessary acoustic attenuation.

- Requirements for structural decoupling techniques through the use of resilient or "floating" connections between acoustical partitions and building structure.

- Identification and treatment of potential sound leaks at intersections and penetrations of sound-critical partitions.

Building services noise and vibration control ensures that mechanical, electrical, plumbing, and transportation equipment contained within the building do not contribute to an excessive amount of noise and vibration in any occupied space. Sources of noise and vibration include:

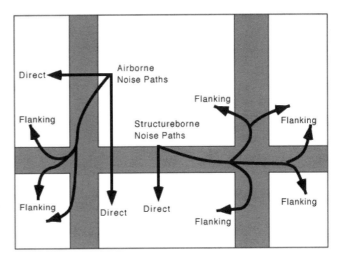

Fig. 1. Possible direct and flanking paths for sound transmission

- HVAC systems:
  - Air-handling units
  - Variable-air volume and fan-powered terminal units Ductwork
  - Diffusers, registers, and grilles
- Plumbing systems:
  - Chillers
  - Cooling towers
  - Boilers
  - Pumps
  - Piping & valves
  - Restroom, laundry, and other fixtures
- Electrical Systems:
  - Transformers
  - Generators
  - Dimmers
  - Lighting fixtures

Common acoustical terminology

Absorption coefficient: Integer number between 0.00 and 1.00 representing the total percentage of sound energy absorbed by a material at a specific frequency. A sound absorption coefficient of 0.00 indicates complete reflection of sound; a sound absorption coefficient of 1.00

References for Part II: Acoustical Society of America, Woodbury, NY (800-344-6901).

Beranek, L. 1996. *Concert and Opera Halls: How They Sound.* New York: Acoustical Society of America.

Burris-Meyer, H. and L. S. Goodfriend. 1957. *Acoustics for the Architect.* New York: Reinhold Publishing Corporation.

Egan, M. David. 1988. *Architectural Acoustics.* New York: McGraw-Hill.

Harris, C. M. 1994. *Noise Control in Buildings: A Guide for Architects and Engineers.* New York: McGraw-Hill.

Knudsen, V. O. and C. M. Harris. 1978. *Acoustical Designing in Architecture.* New York: Acoustical Society of America.

National Council of Acoustical Consultants, Springfield, NJ (201-564-5859).

indicates complete absorption of sound. Concrete and painted masonry, having absorption coefficients between 0.01 and 0.02 at most frequencies, are considered to be very sound-reflective materials. Materials exhibiting a high degree of sound absorption with coefficients above 0.90 include thick—4 in. (10 cm) or greater—fiberglass insulation panels and certain suspended acoustical ceiling tiles. Data published for some acoustical materials may show absorption coefficients greater than 1.00 at one or more frequencies. This is because the effective absorbing surface area in a thick or shaped material is greater than the material's face area used to determine the absorption coefficient.

Ambient noise: Average level of sound energy occurring within an architectural environment at a specified time due to various noise sources in and around the space. Also referred to as "background noise," the ambient sound level in most cases is determined by the output of the mechanical system serving the room along with any other equipment (copy machines, computers, etc.) that might be in operation. See also NC Curves below.

Break-in/break-out noise: Transfer of acoustic energy between the interior of a duct or pipe and the surrounding space.

Dead room: Room containing a large amount of sound-absorbing material.

Diffuse sound field: Room in which sound waves travel equally in all directions and the sound energy level is approximately constant throughout the entire room volume – except close to the boundaries of the room. In such a room, it is difficult to identify the direction from which a sound originates unless one is very close to the source.

Diffusive material: Material in a room that causes sound waves hitting its surface to be scattered in multiple directions. Examples of diffusive shapes include convex or splayed walls and ceilings, coffers, columns, pilasters, and very ornate architectural surfaces. Hard furniture and sound-absorbing panels spaced at intervals along a reflective boundary surface will also add diffusion to a room.

Flanking path: Path between adjacent spaces other than through a common partition through which sound or vibration is transferred (See Fig. 1 on previous page).

Flutter echo: Rapid series of reflections usually created when a sound is played between two hard and parallel room surfaces. Flutter echo is often perceived as a "buzzing" or "ringing" sound and can be detrimental to the clarity or intelligibility of a sound. Simple solutions for eliminating this occurrence include: creating an offsetting angle of at least 5° between the two surfaces, adding sound absorptive materials to one or both surfaces, or adding diffusive shaping to the surfaces.

Live room: Room containing very little sound absorbing materials.

Masking: Acoustic condition in which the energy level of one sound source is sufficiently greater than another and impairs one's ability to hear the lower level sound. Masking noise is often related to the ambient noise level from the HVAC systems or other continuously operating equipment in the space. The presence of audible masking noise can be a positive attribute, such as in an open-plan office where the noise might improve speech privacy by preventing nearby conversations from being intelligibly heard. Where mechanical and other existing systems are too quiet to provide sound privacy, distributed loudspeaker systems may be integrated into the ceilings of the spaces to artificially generate the necessary noise to create "positive masking." Masking noise, however, can also create a negative condition in a symphony concert hall where low-level instrumental or vocal passages might not be clearly heard over the ambient noise of the hall. For this reason, acoustic designers of performance spaces strive to achieve very low (inaudible) ambient sound levels for performance and other sound-critical spaces.

Reverberation time: Amount of time at a specific frequency that a sound in an enclosed space takes to decrease 60 decibels in level after the source sound has stopped. The reverberation time gives a listener the sense of the size, liveness and warmth of a room. Reverberation time increases proportionally with the cubic volume of the room and decreases proportionally with the quantity of sound-absorbing surfaces in the room.

Sound-critical: Term used to describe a room in which the programmed usage requires specific attention to room acoustic, sound isolation or building systems noise control design. Architects, engineers and acoustical consultants should define with the owners and occupants of a building the list of sound-critical—sometimes referred to as "sound-sensitive" or "acoustically-critical"—spaces very early in the design process.

Source and receiving room: Terms used in sound and vibration isolation analysis to designate the room containing the sound or vibration producing source (source room) and an adjacent (receiving) room requiring that the source noise be attenuated by the intervening partitions to a specified noise level.

Space layout considerations
When designing a plan based on a programmed number and type of spaces, consider the relationship between noise-producing spaces and sound-critical spaces sensitive to intruding sound. Two spaces—one noisy and one quiet—located immediately adjacent to each other will require thick, massive, and costly intervening partitions, upgraded sound absorbing treatments, and special noise control measures with the HVAC system. These requirements can be reduced by separating the two spaces with acoustical buffer spaces. These include:

- buffer spaces
- corridors
- lobbies
- storage rooms
- stairwells
- electrical/janitorial closets
- offices not requiring sound privacy

This listing includes some of the most commonly used acoustical buffer zones in buildings. Depending on individual circumstances, any one of the above listed spaces may contain activity or equipment that generates enough noise to no longer allow the space to be effectively used as a buffer zone. An authority in the acoustic layout of building spaces should be consulted for all projects containing sound-sensitive spaces.

Fig. 2 illustrates the effect of locating a mechanical equipment room adjacent to several private offices and the positive benefits of rearranging the spaces to include a buffer zone between the offices and equipment room.

Acoustical materials
Architectural surfaces need to be designed to either reflect sound, absorb sound, or diffuse sound. Each type of surface has its own specific criteria and applications for being incorporated into a space.

- Reflective surfaces are considered to be essentially flat or slightly shaped planes of hard building materials including gypsum board, wood, plywood, plaster, heavy metal, glass, masonry, and concrete.

- Should be of sufficient mass, thickness, and stiffness to avoid becoming absorbers of low-frequency sound energy where this is not desired (see discussion of Absorptive Surfaces below).

- Should be of sufficient dimension to reflect all frequencies of interest. An 8-foot (2.4-m) surface width will reflect energy above

500 Hz, which is sufficient for most speech and music applications since frequencies below 500 Hz are more omnidirectional in nature and not easily directed towards a specific location.

- Can create problems by being located and oriented such that sound generated a certain distance away can reflect back to its point of origin delayed in time and thus cause a discernible and troublesome echo.

- *Absorptive surfaces are primarily used for the following applications:*
- Reverberation Control: reduction of reverberant sound energy to improve speech intelligibility and source localization.

- Sound Level Control: reduction of sound or noise buildup in a room to maintain appropriate listening levels and improve sound isolation to nearby spaces.

- Echo and Reflection Control: elimination of perceived single echoes, multiple flutter echoes, or unwanted sound reflections from room surfaces.

- Diffusion Enhancement: mixing of sound in a room by alternating sound absorptive and sound reflective materials.

Absorptive surfaces be any of three basic types of materials:
- Porous materials include fibrous materials, foam, carpet, acoustic ceiling tile, and draperies that convert sound energy into heat by friction. Example: fabric-covered 1 in. (2.5 cm) thick fiberglass insulation panels mounted on a wall or ceiling.

- Vibrating panels thin sound-reflective materials rigidly or resiliently mounted over an airspace that dissipate sound energy by converting it first to vibrational energy. Example: a 1/4 in. (6 mm) plywood sheet over an airspace (with or without fibrous materials in the airspace).

- Volume resonators - materials containing openings leading to a hollow cavity in which sound energy is dissipated. Example: slotted concrete blocks (with or without fibrous materials in the cores).

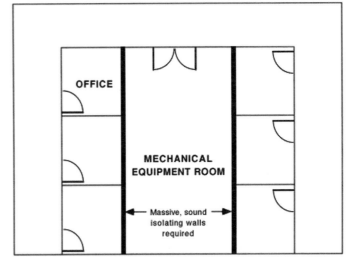

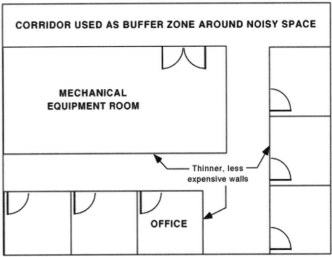

Fig. 2. Using buffer zones for acoustic isolation.

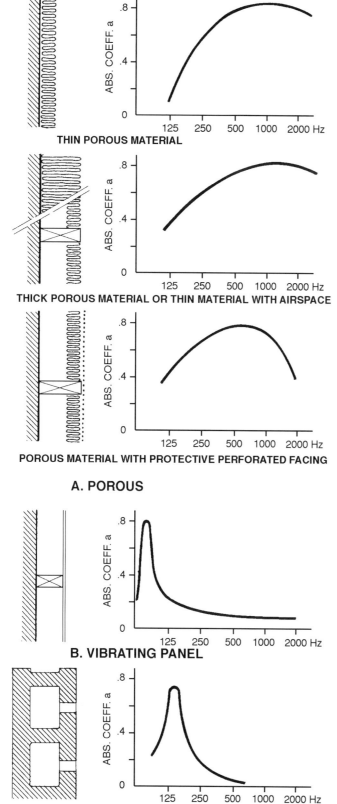

THIN POROUS MATERIAL

THICK POROUS MATERIAL OR THIN MATERIAL WITH AIRSPACE

POROUS MATERIAL WITH PROTECTIVE PERFORATED FACING

A. POROUS

B. VIBRATING PANEL

C. VOLUME RESONATOR

Fig. 3. Basic types and relative efficiencies of sound-absorbing materials.

Fig. 3 shows a graphical representation of the above types of sound absorbing materials along with typical levels of absorption versus frequency.

Absorbtive surfaces exhibit improved low-frequency absorption with increasing airspace behind the materials. They are most efficient when applied in smaller panels distributed evenly on a room's boundary surfaces versus large panel areas concentrated on one or two surfaces.

Diffusive Surfaces are materials having a non-planer shaping or random articulation that result in the redirection and redistribution of sound energy impacting their surfaces.

- Promote diffusion, or even distribution, of sound in a room which creates in a listener the sense of being enveloped in a sound generated within the room.

- Are typically sound-reflective surfaces formed into convex, splayed or randomly articulated shapes.

- Are not concave surfaces which can cause uneven focusing of sound energy.

See Fig. 4 for the most common diffusive surface shapes.

General issues related to mechanical noise and vibration control

Mechanical rooms, especially those containing large high pressure fans, chillers, boilers, pumps, etc., should be located remotely from important listening spaces. The closer the mechanical equipment to the sound-critical spaces, the more massive and complex the required intervening construction. In some cases, double wall constructions, grade location of the equipment, and structural joints around the mechanical room may be necessary.

Mechanical rooms containing only small to medium horsepower, low-pressure fans and perhaps a few small pumps also are best located remotely from sound-critical spaces. If this cannot be done, the mechanical room should be located on grade or on an upper floor with a dense concrete slab at least 6-in. (15-cm) thick with a 4-in, (10-cm) housekeeping pad under the equipment. The slabs should be supported by stiff structural members spanning no more than 30 feet (9 m). The worst possible situation is to locate mechanical equipment on the sound-critical space's roof. Too much noise is almost assured in this case. Avoid locating major mechanical equipment directly above or beside the sound-critical space.

Buffer zones such as corridors, storage areas, etc., should be located between a mechanical room and the sound-critical space. If this can not be done, a full acoustic separation joint with double column structure will be required between the mechanical room and the critical spaces. A lightweight roof deck should not span continuously between a mechanical room and a sound-critical space. Sound or vibration will travel along the lightweight construction (flank the intervening wall or slab) and radiate into the space.

Additional design checklist items include:

• Mechanical room doors should lead to non-critical building areas only. These doors may require acoustical seals or, in very critical cases, sound-rated acoustical doors. Similarly, fresh-air intake and exhaust-air discharge openings should not lead to critical outdoor areas or to locations where noise can re-enter the building through windows, doors, or vents.

- Shafts leaving mechanical rooms and passing by sound-critical spaces should be sealed to the ductwork so that no direct openings exist to the mechanical rooms.

- Shaft walls adjacent to quiet areas generally should be of medium to heavy weight masonry.

- On its way to the sound-critical space, a duct often passes different spaces which may or may not be sound critical. The sound transmission loss properties of rectangular duct is low and noise can break in or break out.

- Close to the fan, noise levels in ductwork are usually high. A duct that enters sound-critical spaces immediately after leaving the mechanical room should be avoided. After the duct noise has been attenuated, the duct should not re-enter noisy areas.

- If situations described above cannot be avoided, using double-wall insulated round or multiple round ductwork is the best solution. Wrapping or enclosing rectangular ducts with sound isolation materials will be necessary if round duct cannot be used.

- Only ducts serving sound-critical spaces should be run over the ceilings of these spaces.

- Locate floor-mounted major equipment on grade, or position it near supporting columns or major beams. Mid-span locations are least desirable. Locate suspended equipment so it can be supported from beams, joists, or other relatively heavy structural members. Avoid direct support from lightweight slabs or roof decks wherever possible. Frame between major beams for support, if necessary.

- Keep machinery room spans to a minimum and make supporting structure as stiff as possible, since structural deflections will have to be compensated for by increased equipment spring isolator static deflections, which is not always possible or practical.

- Sound-critical space air delivery and return systems must be low velocity in order to avoid producing turbulent air noise that would enter the space. Since ductwork in critical systems is lined internally with glass fiber sound-absorbing material, noise will be attenuated along the duct. Therefore, the lowest

velocities must exist at supply and return openings. Air velocities may gradually increase along the duct back towards the supply or return fan.

Generally:

Trunk duct velocity:	1000 FPM or less
Main ducts from sound-critical spaces:	700 FPM or less
Ducts approaching diffusers, grilles:	400 FPM or less

Applications to specific types of spaces

Acoustics of performance spaces

Room acoustic issues: The cubic volume of the performance space needs to be appropriate to the designated program in order to provide for the proper loudness level and amount of reverberation for each program type. Volume is usually determined as a ratio of the number of seats in the hall including performers on stage if the stage and house volumes are coupled with each other.

Hall Program	*Range of acoustical volume*
Theatrical and amplified events only	200-300 ft³/seat
Unamplified music (excluding pipe organ)	300-450 ft³/seat
Organ music	450-600 ft³/seat

- A balance of sound reflecting, absorbing, and diffusing sounds must be designed to achieve reflection patterns and reverberation time appropriate to the given program in the space (speech, music, amplified events, etc.).

- Different programs have different acoustic requirements: Speech, drama and amplified music require shorter reverberation times typically less than 1.2 seconds. Symphonic, opera and organ music all require longer reverberation times typically greater than 1.6 seconds.

• To achieve an acoustic variation in a performance hall that must accommodate a wide range of programs, one or a combination of both of the following devices are used:

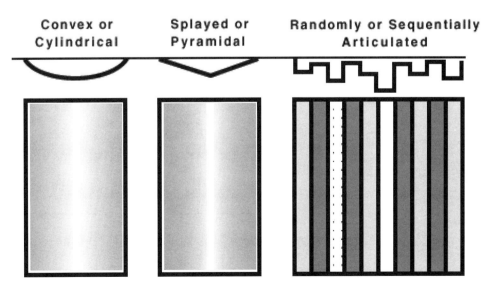

Fig. 4. Common shapes that promote sound diffusion.

- Modulation of effective room acoustic volume through the use of hard, reflective "chambers" in the upper stage or audience seating areas.

- Increasing/decreasing the amount of sound absorbing materials through the use of draperies, banners, panels that can be either fully exposed, partially exposed, or concealed depending on the requirements of the event.

• For optimal intelligibility of music and speech, ensure that wall and ceiling surfaces in the stage or "sending" end of the room are sound-reflective and somewhat diffusive to both project sound out to an audience and to enhance performers' abilities to hear themselves and blend with one another.

• Room shape is very important for providing the necessary side wall reflections that contribute to an accurate sense of spaciousness and fullness of sound in the space. Rooms based on the rectangular form (with added wall shaping) often provide the strongest coverage of side wall, or lateral, reflections. Wide fan shapes and semicircular floor plans focus sound very unevenly causing "hot spots" and "dead zones" of sound.

• In addition to lateral reflections, sound reflections arriving from the ceiling and stage area (orchestra shell or other acoustical enclosures) shortly after the arrival of the direct sound contribute to presence, spaciousness and intelligibility. Fig. 5 depicts the most common paths of early sound reflections to a listener.

• The width of a performance hall should be as narrow as possible to avoid delayed reflections from the side walls being perceived as echoes, especially to those in the center seating sections.

• To accommodate the maximum number of audience seats while avoiding delayed reflections and poor sightlines, it is often necessary for the width of the side walls to be very narrow (not much wider than the proscenium opening or stage platform width) in the front of the room and gradually increase to a wider rectangular form one-third to one-half of the distance toward the rear of the audience seating area.

• Balcony fascia and under-balcony ceilings need to be shaped like a sound diffuser or treated with limited amounts of sound absorption to avoid long, delayed reflections and echoes.

• Balcony depth for halls with unamplified music and speech should be a maximum of 1.5 times and preferably equal to the height of the opening at the front of the balcony to assure good overhead reflection coverage to all seats under the balcony.

Sound and vibration isolation issues. Sound and vibration isolation requirements are primarily dependent on:

- Desired ambient noise level in the room

- Level of noise and vibration sources in adjacent or nearby spaces

- Level of exterior sound and vibration from traffic, aircraft, or other noise sources outside the exposed envelope of the space

It is critical during the early design phases of a project that the design team come to an agreement with the client and owner on the degree of sound isolation required from intermittent noise events. For example, the requirement to completely isolate the sound of a fire engine or ambulance that may pass by the performance hall once or twice a week would have a major impact on the performance space's con-

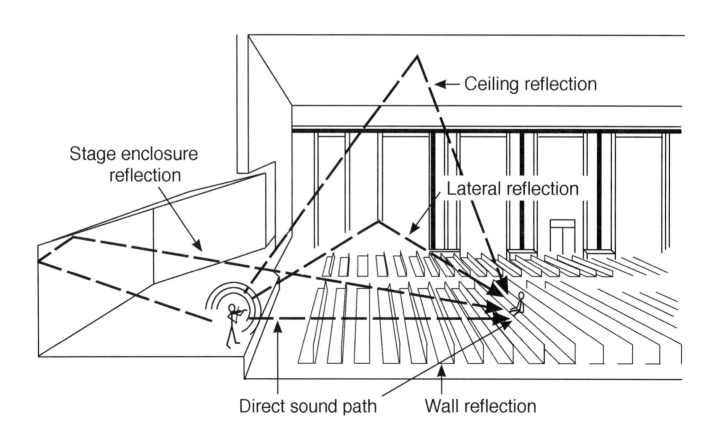

Fig. 5. Possible paths for early sound reflection.

struction complexity and cost, and may result in programmatic cutbacks in other areas of the building. Figure 6 illustrates the relationship between increased sound isolation requirements and budget costs.

- The walls of a performance space must be a minimum of one course of masonry or a multi-layer/multi-stud drywall construction depending on surrounding conditions. This construction may or may not incorporate the interior finish materials and wall shaping required for appropriate room acoustics.

- It is rarely the case where a performance space is located completely remote from other noise and vibration producing rooms such as mechanical equipment rooms, loading and receiving areas, public lobbies, and other performance and rehearsal spaces. For this reason, it is often advisable to structurally separate the performance space from these other areas through the use of an acoustical isolation joint.

Acoustical Isolation Joint (AIJ). The purpose of an AIJ is to create a complete structural break between two or more parts of a building with vibration producing equipment housed on one side only.

- An AIJ is formed by double lines of offset columns separated by a minimum of a 2 in. (5 cm) airspace extending all the way from the footings through the roof with nothing rigid bridging the two structures. The double set of columns may also be separated by a corridor with the corridor slab on each level cantilevered from one of the column lines.

- In general, an AIJ must begin and end at an exterior wall so that structure-borne vibration can not flank around the AIJ at an interior partition.

- Ductwork, piping, and other services crossing the AIJ must not make rigid contact with either structure by the use of neoprene compression seals at the point of penetration.

- Steel reinforcement must not cross the AIJ.

- Under certain specified conditions, it is possible for the AIJ to also serve as a building expansion joint.

- It is advisable to use the services of an experienced acoustical consultant to develop the details of the AIJ with the architect and structural engineer.

- Roofs of performance spaces must be concrete slabs or concrete on decking even if outside noise conditions are relatively quiet. The reasons are:

- Rain, hail, and sleet hitting a lightweight metal roof, even with a built-up insulated roofing system, will transmit significant noise into the performance space and be quite distracting, if not unbearable, for listeners and performers alike.

- A lightweight roof acts as a vibrating panel absorber (see Fig. 3) and absorbs excessive low-frequency energy causing the space to severely lack low-end room response, or warmth, for music.

- Sound and light locks should be used for all entrances into a performance hall, including onto stage. These are basically two doors or two sets of doors in tandem separated by a vestibule containing sound absorbing materials (carpeted floor, acoustic ceiling tile, absorptive wall panels, etc.). Each door should either be a standard solid-core wood or hollow metal door with specially chosen acoustic seals applied around its perimeter, or a factory manufactured acoustical door guaranteed by laboratory testing to meet a certain sound-isolation rating. These doors are usually designated by their single number STC rating. When determining the sound isolation rating of an acoustic door, however, the one-third octave band transmission loss values should be provided by the door manufacturer for a direct comparison of performance.

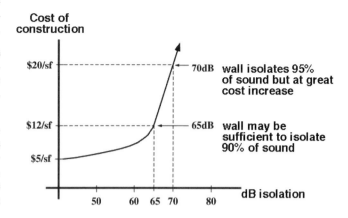

Fig. 6. Relationship between construction cost and level of sound isolation.

Mechanical system noise control issues. The following issues are specific to performance spaces and supplement the earlier section on mechanical systems noise and vibration control:

- Performance spaces are usually rated with a noise criterion around NC (or PNC) 15-20. Under special circumstances, the noise criterion rating will be higher or lower than this range. Under no conditions should the noise rating be designed to higher than NC 25, for this will significantly degrade the intelligibility and dynamic range of the hall.

- Supply and return ductwork serving a performance space must be kept at low velocities and, therefore, will be quite large if the quantity of airflow (cfm) is substantial. As an example, the maximum velocity in a main supply duct located over a performance space should be about 700 fpm. With an airflow of 20,000 cfm, the equivalent duct diameter would be 6 feet (1.8 m)! Coordination of these large ducts with structure, catwalks, lighting, and acoustical reflecting surfaces should occur throughout the entire design period.

- Spiral-round ductwork is recommended within the ceiling volume of a performance hall because large, rectangular ductwork acts as a low-frequency sound absorbing material.

- The most effective method of air distribution in a performance hall combines a low-velocity overhead supply "dump" and a distributed return air system under the audience seating (or on the lower side walls for a smaller room). Because of the low velocities required, diffusers on supply openings do not function effectively and are best omitted, relying on the return air system to pull the supply air over the audience.

Acoustics of office buildings
The basic acoustical and speech-privacy requirements of enclosed and open-plan offices are:

- To talk without having conversations understood by neighboring workers.

- To not be distracted from nearby conversations and other intruding noises.

- To allow face-to-face 6 feet (1.8 m) apart conversations to be clearly heard and comprehended.

- Sound absorbing surfaces in each office and throughout the open-plan areas reduces the ability for sound to travel long distances. Carpeted floors and acoustic ceiling tile with an NRC rating of 0.70 and higher are the most effective means of providing sound absorption in an office.

- A noise criterion rating of NC 35 - 40 will provide enough noise to help mask the transfer of conversational sounds, yet will not be so noisy that the intelligibility of local conversations will be impaired. A rating of NC 30 - 35 is also acceptable for private offices with higher quality construction and good physical distance between employees.

- In enclosed offices where a high degree of speech privacy is required, standard construction (including single-layer drywall partitions that do or do not extend up to the deck) and unsealed hollow doors typically do not provide enough sound isolation.

- To improve sound isolation and speech privacy in enclosed offices:

  - Add an extra layer of gypsum board on one or both sides of the separating walls.

  - Extend walls up to the deck and seal around the top and bottom of the walls with a non-hardening airtight acoustical caulking.

  - Ensure that the office door is at least solid-core wood or hollow metal construction and add specialized acoustic seals around the perimeter of the door.

  - Ensure that ductwork does not pass directly between adjacent offices, which will allow conversational sound to cross between two or more rooms through the duct. This is known as crosstalk noise.

  - Run main supply and return ductwork in corridors and branch into each office separately. Add internal acoustic duct lining to some or all of the ductwork for an even greater crosstalk noise reduction.

  - Refer to comments above for sound absorptive treatments and establishment of ambient noise levels.

- To improve sound isolation and speech privacy in open-plan office areas:

  - Maximize distance between noise sources and listeners (*i.e.*, between adjacent employees and between noisy office equipment and the nearest employee). Where practical, offset workstations so that employees do not have a direct line of sight (or sound) to one another.

  - Construct partial-height free-standing walls between employee stations having solid-core construction with applied sound absorbing panels on both sides. The walls should be at least 5 feet (1.5 m) high and 10 feet (3 m) wide (centered in plan on the worker location). These will serve as both sound isolation barriers and reducers of sound reflections.

  - Refer to comments above for other sound absorptive treatments and establishment of ambient noise levels.

Acoustics of educational facilities

Proper control of sound in a learning and teaching facility is of critical importance for allowing good aural communication between teachers and students. The following guidelines should be used:

Room acoustic issues. When selecting finishes for teaching spaces, a proper balance between sound-absorptive and sound-reflective materials is necessary to produce an environment that is not overly reverberant (reducing intelligibility of speech) nor excessively "dry" (results in an unnatural, uncomfortable feeling for most occupants).

- Typical classrooms and meeting rooms should have a lay-in acoustic tile ceiling with the specified tile having a minimum Noise Reduction Coefficient (NRC) rating of 0.65.

- Carpet on floors will absorb some sound, but should mainly be considered for control of footfall noise.

- Walls typically should be a hard, sound-reflective material, such as gypsum board or masonry, Shaping and diffusion on walls in larger rooms should be considered to improve speech reflection patterns and eliminate flutter echoes.

- Corridors should have the same requirements for the ceiling tile. Carpet is a very effective means of reducing footfall noise in the corridors, and should be considered when possible. High-traffic corridors built completely with hard materials (*e.g.*, gypsum walls and ceilings, VCT floor) will almost certainly result in a build up of sound that could be intrusive on adjacent critical rooms.

- Acoustically-sensitive spaces such as auditoriums, music rooms, and lecture halls will require special consideration for room finishes and shaping of walls and ceilings in order to achieve good projection and balance of sound energy. A specialist in acoustics should be advised for these areas whenever possible.

Sound isolation issues. Walls separating classrooms, laboratories, and meeting rooms should be a minimum construction of two layers of 5/8 in. (1.6 cm) gypsum board on one side of a metal stud and one layer of 5/8 in. (1.6 cm) gypsum board on the other. Batt insulation should be placed in the stud cavities. Joints on the two layer side should be staggered, and the perimeter of the walls at the top and bottom should be caulked on both sides with a non-hardening acoustical sealant. These walls should also extend all the way up to the underside of the slab or deck of the floor above.

- For improved sound isolation between rooms that produce sound louder than average speech levels, the above construction should be supplemented with an additional layer of 5/8 in. (1.6 cm) gypsum board on the single layer side, and changing the metal studs from a single to a double staggered or separated configuration.

- Corridor walls from classrooms, laboratories, and meeting rooms should be a minimum of a single layer of 5/8 in. (1.6 cm) gypsum board on each side of a metal stud, with batt insulation placed in the stud cavities. The comments listed above for the walls between adjacent rooms also apply for these walls. For further improvements in sound isolation (*e.g.*, for rooms located off of high-traffic corridors), the construction listed for walls separating adjacent classrooms may be used.

- Doors should typically not be located between two classrooms or other sound-critical spaces. Also avoid facing two doors directly across from each other in a corridor. Where noise from a corridor is a concern, doors should be a minimum construction of solid-core wood or hollow metal with applied acoustical door seals and sweeps to control sound leakage around the perimeter of the doors. Ideally, the seals and sweeps should be manufactured specifically for control of sound.

- Where exterior noise exists outside of a classroom or other sound-critical space, the windows should be specified as an insulating assembly with different pane thicknesses, *e.g.*: 1/4 in. pane–1/2 in. airspace–3/8 in. pane. (0.64 cm–1.3 cm–.95 cm). Laminated glass may be used for either or both panes to further improve sound isolation.

- Again, acoustically sensitive spaces for speech and music require specialized partition constructions and selection of doors and windows.

Mechanical noise control issues. Achieving the proper level of ambient noise in an academic space is critical. If the level is too high, communication between teachers and students will be partially or fully masked. If too low, the slightest noises (pencils dropping, rustling of papers, etc..) will appear to be intensified in their level of disturbance. Below is a table of ambient noise criteria based on the single number "RC" (Room Criteria) curves. The values and ranges are based on judgment and experience, not on quantitative evaluations of human reactions. They represent general limits of acceptability for typical building occupancies. Higher or lower values may be appropriate and should be based on a careful analysis of economics, space usage, and user needs. They are not intended to serve by themselves as a basis for a contractual requirement.

Table 1. Common acoustical acronyms and their definitions

Acronym	Term	Definition	Acoustical Category
NC	Noise Criteria	The NC level of a room is a rating of the noise level of an interior space. The NC number is associated with a series of sound energy level-versus-frequency curves known as Noise Criterion curves. For new construction, an NC level is established based on the room type and its intended function, and is used as a goal in the design of sound isolation construction and the attenuation of mechanical systems noise. To determine the NC rating of an existing space, octave-band noise level measurements are taken and plotted against the series of NC curve spectra. The NC value is set by the lowest curve that lies completely above the measured spectrum values.	Ambient Noise
RC	Room Criteria	Alternate rating system to the Noise Criteria system preferred by many because it designates the tonal quality of a spectrum as well as its level. Terms such as Neutral (N), Rumbly(R), Hissy(H) and Perceptible Vibration (RV) are added to the single RC number to rate an existing space. For a full description of the method of achieving an RC rating, refer to the references at the end of this chapter.	Ambient Noise
STC	Sound Transmission Class	A single number method of rating the sound isolation performance of a partition, door or window. The STC number is associated with a series of sound attenuation-versus-frequency curves. The higher the STC number, the better a partition isolates sound overall. A partition is assigned an STC rating in an acoustical test laboratory by placing the test partition between two rooms, generating a loud noise source on one side and measuring the difference in level between the two rooms. This difference, along with the total absorption of the receiving room and the common area of the partition, are used to calculate a series of one-third octave band decibel reductions known as Transmission Loss values. STC numbers should be used only as a broad comparison between two or more partitions. For a thorough sound isolation design, the Transmission Loss values should be evaluated based on the frequency content of the source noise and the specific NC level required in an adjacent space.	Sound Isolation
TL	Transmission Loss	See description of STC above.	Sound Isolation
NIC	Noise Isolation Class	Similar to an STC rating, but is a result of a field measurement of an existing partition. The NIC value does not include the receiving room absorption and the area of the common partition in its calculation.	Sound Isolation
IIC	Impact Insulation Class	Like the STC value, the IIC is a single number rating of a composite floor and ceiling construction's effectiveness in reducing the level of sound created by an object impacting on its surface above. To measure IIC, an impacting source is activated in an upper room and the resulting sound levels are measured in the room below. These levels are then compared to a series of IIC curves to establish the actual rating of the assembly.	Sound Isolation
NRC	Noise Reduction Coefficient	The NRC value is a single number method of rating the sound absorbing effectiveness of an acoustical material. It is defined as the arithmetic average of the material's measured sound absorption coefficients at the 250Hz, 500Hz, 1000Hz and 2000Hz octave bands. These frequency bands represent the range of sound most associated with speech. If the material is required to absorb very low or high frequencies of sound, the individual sound absorption coefficients should be used for comparison, rather than the NRC value.	Sound Absorption

Table 2. Top Ten Acoustical Myths/Misconceptions

Myth/Misconception	Reality
10. Fiberglass or foam placed on a wall will prevent sound from going through the wall.	These materials only absorb sound and do not provide a barrier to it. Heavier building materials and resilient attachments to structure are the best methods for isolating sound.
9. Carpet on a floor will reduce sound transmission to a room below.	Carpet is a sound absorbing material mainly at high frequencies, and has very little airborne sound isolation properties. Carpet does, however, reduce the amount of impact sound from footfall or things dropped transmitting to the space below.
8. Carpet on a floor will reduce the amount of street noise coming through a window.	Once again, because carpet absorbs mainly high frequency sounds, it has negligible effect at the mid-and low-frequencies which constitute the vast majority of exterior sounds.
7. Paint on the walls affects the acoustics of a room.	Paint has no effect on the acoustics of a room, except, perhaps, a psycho-acoustical effect (*e.g.*, a brightly-colored room often makes people perceive the room as more acoustically live).
6. Egg cartons on the wall improve the sound of the space.	While egg cartons do have some sound-absorbing and diffusing properties, they are concentrated in a relatively narrow frequency band and do not effect the quality of speech or music to any significant degree. They also have negligible sound isolation properties.
5. Adding insulation to a sheetrock wall will keep all sound from going through it.	Insulation between stud cavities in a sheetrock partition does improve the sound isolation value of a partition and should be used whenever possible. The improvement, however, is too small to bring about an appreciable difference in the degree of isolation, and the insulation should only be thought of as a partial solution to upgrading the isolation of a partition.
4. A sound attenuator in an air duct will eliminate all noise from the HVAC system.	Sound attenuators (also known as "duct silencers" or "sound-traps") are one of a number of tools used for noise reduction in an HVAC system. Depending on the distance of the air-handling unit to the diffuser or grille in the occupied space, the ductwork distribution and the sound levels produced by the equipment, additional noise control measures, including internal duct lining and acoustic plenums, may be required.
3. The colors in a room (walls, furniture, *etc.*) affect the acoustics of the space.	Once again, the only effect a color in a room may have is a psycho-acoustical perceived difference in the sound quality.
2. Wood is good.	Wood is often considered the best material to use in a music performance space. This is only true depending on the application of the wood. It must be of enough thickness to not absorb low-frequency sound where this is not desirable. It must also be appropriately oriented and shaped to provide reflection and diffusion to the right locations and to not create late-arriving echoes back to the stage and front-of-house areas. See the discussion on Acoustics of Performance Spaces later in this Section for more information.
1. Soundproofing	This word is the catch-all phrase used by many for improving anything that has to do with acoustics. "Soundproofing" implies building a room that will keep all possible sounds outside the space from transferring in, and all sounds generated in the space from transferring out. Building construction can be designed to attenuate a fixed degree of sound, but cannot theoretically prevent all possible sounds from passing through the boundaries of the room, except in extremely rare (and expensive) situations. Better terminology to use when describing a client's acoustical needs may perhaps be "Noise Reduction" (for sound isolation) and "Sound Enhancement" (for room acoustics).

Table 3. Design Guidelines for HVAC System Noise in Educational Spaces

Space	RC Level
Classrooms	30-35 (max)
Lecture Halls/Large Classrooms for more than 50 (unamplified speech)	30-35 (max)
Lecture Halls/Large Classrooms for more than 50 (amplified speech)	35-40 (max)
Libraries	30-40
Gymnasiums/Natatoriums	40-50
Laboratories (minimal speech communication)	45-55
Laboratories (extensive telephone use, speech communication)	40-50
Laboratories (group teaching)	35-45

History of building and urban technologies

John P. Eberhard

Bradbury Building, Los Angeles, CA. 1890

Summary: Seven inventions, all developed in the closing decades of the 19th century, transformed the nature of building technologies and in turn the design of cities and regional landscapes: steel structures, elevators, electric lighting, central heating, indoor plumbing, the telephone and the automobile. They still define the nature of building and urban technologies today. These systems are being brought into question by their environmental impacts, possibly setting the stage for another equally inventive era of technological innovation.

Key words: automobile, building technology, elevators, heating, lighting, plumbing, steel structural systems, telephone

Architects who practice at the end of the 20th century face a proliferation of new materials and substantial changes in their methods of practice introduced by electronics. However, those who practiced at the beginning of the 20th century faced even larger challenges. The Columbian Exposition of 1893 was the last major architectural design effort to be based on systems of building which had changed little "since the age of the pyramids." The basic systems of buildings and the urban context into which buildings were inserted were changing dramatically as the result of inventions introduced in the last 25 years of the 19th century. These inventions not only changed what a building could be, but altered in a fundamental way how the architecture of cities could be imagined (Fig. 1).

A remarkable set of seven inventions were developed towards the end of the 19th century to change the design and operation of cities. Each of these inventions were to have a profound impact on the design of buildings and cities. Each still forms the technological basis for cities at the end of the 20th century. These inventions were:

- steel structural systems
- elevators
- the electric light
- central heating
- indoor plumbing
- telephones
- automobiles.

With the possible exception of the telephone, no major invention introduced into the fabric of 19th century cities was without its antecedents. And no invention, including the telephone, was capable of being utilized in urban areas without the support of a large array of public and private investments in the infrastructure of the city. For example, the electric light (a primary invention) was of no use without the generating stations for electricity, distribution systems for electrical power, wiring systems within buildings, and fixtures to receive the bulbs.

The organization of architectural specifications, building codes, reference works for architects and engineers tend to have chapters devoted to each of the supporting systems for these seven inventions. The structure of local city and county government regulatory bodies and national licensing examinations are dictated by these seven systems. Even university education tends to be organized around structural engineering, electrical engineering, mechanical engineering, communications engineering, transportation engineering, etc. to prepare each new generation to deal with the development, design and maintenance of these systems.

Structural framing systems

From before the era of pyramid construction, masonry was used to construct buildings. From small bricks to the giant stones of the pyramids, architects created buildings whose configuration was limited by how high masonry could be stacked and how far apart supporting masonry units could be spaced. If the enclosure at the top of a structure was of flat masonry (Greek and Roman temples), their supports could not be very far apart. If timber was used for the roof, then the distance between supports could be greater. With the development of the arch and the dome, the span became greater and grander. With the introduction of iron and steel structural systems in the 19th century, all of these limitations changed.

There is no fixed time in history, or any single building, that can be said to represent the first use of a structural steel, although the Home Insurance Building in Chicago is generally given that credit. Architect William Le Baron Jenny could not have designed the Home Insurance Building if Bessemer had not first invented a process of making steel, if Andrew Carnegie and others had not invested in the great steel mills of Pittsburgh, and if earlier uses of cast iron and wrought iron had not lead the way. By the end of the century architects would be indebted to an engineer, Charles Louis Strobel, who designed the wide-flange steel beam which became the structural system of choice from 1895 onward. Even with the introduction of reinforced concrete structures during the 20th century, many tall building designers still prefer to use structural steel (Fig. 2).

Vertical movement (conveying) systems

There is a chicken-and-egg question associated with the elevator: It would not have been practical to design buildings more than five or six floors in height if people were going to be required to use stairs, the historical method of vertical movement in building. Although Otis is credited with the invention of the elevator and was the founder of the company that still carries his name, his revolutionary invention was the safety latch which made the modern passenger elevator practical. None of the buildings in the 1893 Chicago Exposition had elevators, even though it was becoming common to design them into the office buildings that filled the voids left in the Chicago landscape by the great fire of 1871 (Fig. 3).

The components of an elevator system are more than the cab, which is all that most people see in their daily rides. The most common

Author: John P. Eberhard, FAIA

References: Elliott, Cecil D. 1991. *Technics and Architecture: The Development of Materials and Systems for Buildings.* Cambridge, MA: MIT Press.

Table 1. Historical overview

Historical examples of Urban Systems	Discovery or Primary Invention	Precursors to 2nd Generation	Second Generation of Urban Systems
masonry walls timber roofs arches & domes	smelting iron ore Bessemer Process for steel	cast iron (1813) wrought iron (1855) Eiffel Tower (1889)	**STEEL STRUCTURES** for buildings (1883) Home Insurance Bldg.
stairways ramps & pulleys	Safety latch for elevators/hoist (1853)	mechanical lifts hydraulic lifts Elisha Graves Otis	**ELEVATOR** Equitable Bldg. (1870)
daylight candles oil lamps	light bulb (1880) Thomas Edison electrical power	gas lights with piping from central station (1882)	**ELECTRIC LIGHTS** generators, transmission wiring and fixtures source
fire in the hearth fireplaces shady places	oil-burner (1868) gas burner (1902) air-conditioner (1932)	steam engine coal furnace ventilating fans	**CENTRAL HEATING** burners/ducts/controls refrigerants/condensers
privies and night soil scavengers slop jars	flushing valve and water closet (1778 to 1878)	water piping (1872) storm sewers (1875)	**INDOOR PLUMBING** toilet/water/sewer
messengers town crier mail	telephonics Alexander G. Bell basic patent (1876)	telegraph (1850) (Morse Code)	**TELEPHONE** switching centers phones and wires
oxen horseback horse & carriage	internal combustion Gottlieb Daimler patented (1885)	steam buggy (1865) electric car oil wells	**AUTOMOBILE** Benz (1893) Ford (1896)

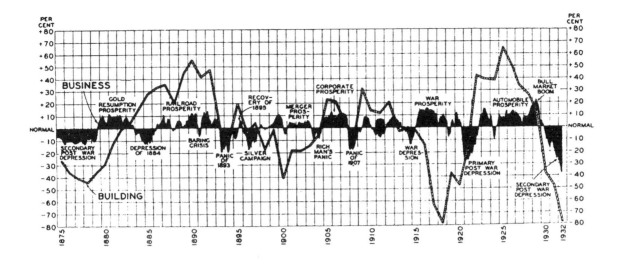

Fig. 1. Building activity in the United States 1875-1932. (Journal, American Statistical Association. Elliott, 1991)

elevator installations of today are not much changed from the original Otis installations. Today there more sophisticated electronic controls are used, especially in very tall buildings, to provide more effective scheduling and maintenance information. Escalators (introduced in 1900) are used for moving large volumes of passengers up and down in the major entrances to large buildings. New concepts of vertical movement combined with horizontal movement will likely emerge in the 21st century, requiring architects to rethink the integration of vertical/horizontal movement systems into high-rise buildings.

Fig. 2. Steel skeleton separated from building skin in 1881

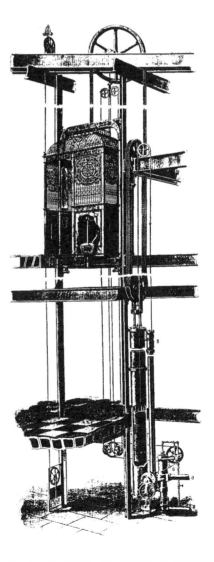

Fig. 3. Hydrolic elevator (Scientific American, 1899. Elliott. 1991)

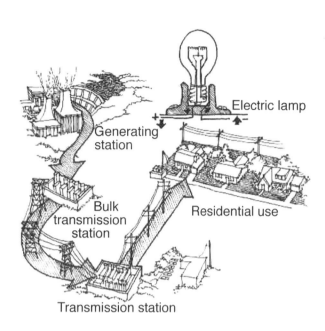

Fig.4. Electric lights

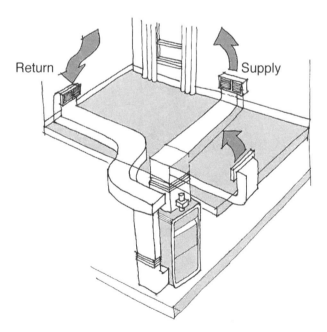

Fig. 5. Central heating system

Lighting systems

Daylight has always been the fundamental source of light for interior use in buildings, especially after glass for windows became common in the 17th century. ("Artificial lighting" or alternatives to daylighting techniques for seeing is technically known as a lamp). The earliest lamps were burning sticks or glowing coals held in braziers. Candles made of beeswax were used by the Romans. Candles made from animal fat have been used in Europe since the Middle Ages. By the 4th century BC in Greece, oil lamps were in general use. These were usually simple vessels made of stone, clay, bone, or shell in which a wick of flax or cotton was set. In the 18th century a Swiss chemist, Aime Argand, invented a lamp that used a tubular wick enclosed between two cylinders of metal (later replaced with a glass cylinder). As early as colonial times in America, wick lamps were fitted with screws for adjusting the flame.

With the introduction of illuminating gas early in the 19th century, a method of distribution of the gas within cities as well as a gas lamp became the dominant lighting system. With a feverish burst of inventions, including many electric light bulbs, the last years of the 19th century saw Edison's lighting devices come to dominate how buildings would be lighted for all of the 20th century (Fig 4). The design of buildings with dense floor plans deemed practical for human activities—but which thus minimized or prohibited any use of natural daylight— began to emerge. The combination of steel structures, elevators, and electrical power linked to electrical lighting made tall buildings a possibility. Only towards the end of the 20th century have questions been widely recognized about depriving office workers of natural daylight (and ventilation), forcing a reconsideration of the dense office blocks of earlier years. Once introduced into the building, electrical systems made a range of other devices possible, including the late 20th century set of inventions utilizing electronics.

Heating and cooling systems

Perhaps the first form of shelter for humans was a cave with an open fire in the center for protection against the cold and from wild animals. One of the earliest devices for heating houses was the fireplace and/or a stove in which wood or coal could be burned. Many modern houses still have fireplaces valued for their psychological and esthetic satisfaction more than for their heating capacity. In warm climates, or at those times of the years when the weather is warm, buildings have historically been cooled with natural ventilation and various shading devices. During the 1970's, when a major concern with energy conservation was in evidence, architects turned to historical models for natural ways of ventilation and shading to help avoid the large use of energy associated with modern cooling systems.

Towards the latter part of the 20th century as oil and gas motors became replacements for earlier steam engines, these energy sources and their associated technologies began to find their way into heating systems for buildings. At the turn of the century, because it was plentiful and cheap and because air pollution was not yet a concern of urban dwellers, coal was the primary source of heat for central furnaces for warm air heating and boilers for hot water or steam distribution (Fig. 5). The logistics of mining and distributing coal has by the end of the 20th century largely been replaced by gas, oil and electrical sources of energy. The rise in electrical heating systems occurred at a time when natural gas was in short supply and when cooling systems seemed more easily designed around electrical methods.

Plumbing systems

Obtaining fresh water for drinking purposes is as old as human existence. Evidence of urban water supply systems can still be seen in ancient Knossos, Petra and Hydrabad. In Roman times an aqueduct, named El Puente, carried water from Spain's Frio River to the city of Segovia. Built in the 1st century AD, the aqueduct runs both above and below ground and stretches for a total of 10 miles (16 km). These two tiers of arches reach a height of 93.5 feet (28.5 m).

It was not until near the end of the 19th century that water for use in disposing of human wastes was seriously developed (Fig 6). As with other urban systems, there was no one invention nor a single event in history when the total system came into existence. The key invention was a flushing valve for the water closet (toilet) which worked well enough to allow city water authorities to allow them to be attached to water systems. Once this gap was bridged, the introduction of "indoor plumbing" into the house and commercial buildings spread at a reasonable rate. As late as 1940, however, cities the size of St. Louis, Missouri still had less than 50% of the housing units equipped with indoor toilets. A primary reason for this relatively slow utilization rate is the larger urban system of water supply and waste disposal associated with providing indoor plumbing. One hundred years after development of the water-flush toilet, concerns about water consumption, water body and aquifer pollution suggests the need for new technologies for water conservation and waste nutrient recovery.

Communication systems

The early telephones (shown in Fig. 7 with original Bell phone in the center) were derived from the basic patent Alexander Graham Bell obtained in 1876. While working on sound transmission for the deaf, he discovered that steady electric current can be altered to resemble the vibrations made by the human voice. Once the instrument was invented, an urban system of telephone switching centers, wires (originally strung along poles), relays, etc. had to be put in place. International calls became possible once a cable was laid along the ocean floor (about 1912). It can be argued that the modern office building was made possible by the telephone, connecting thousands of workers at their desks directly to other workers in all parts of the building, city, the country, and the world

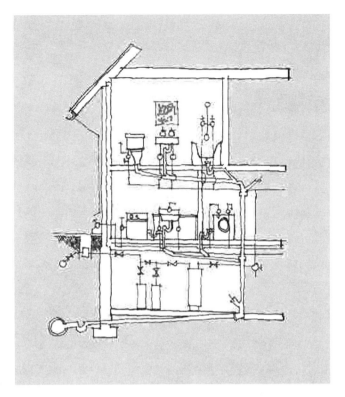

Fig. 6. Indoor plumbing system

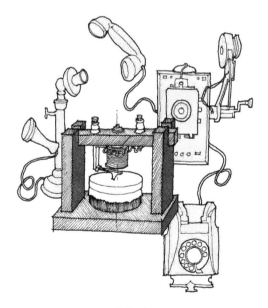

Fig. 7. Telephone

With the advent of the electronic era towards the end of the 20th century, a greatly expanded communications network was introduced by linking computer-based systems to phone systems and satellite transmission. While these advanced systems have done little to change the architectural shape of the city (in Western society), they have created new challenges for the design of office buildings and other facilities tied to electronic networks. Local area networks (LANS) have become so much in demand by modern organizations that buildings which cannot provide for them, either by access, clearances, increases in power capacity and similar opportunities for upgrading, are doomed to be abandoned or replaced.

Personal transportation systems

The internal combustion engine by Daimler is the primary invention leading to the automobile. Ford and Benz applied Daimler's invention to a horseless carriage, and then went on to organize automobile production companies. They relied on others to find oil wells, develop petroleum products and distribute them as fuel and lubricants for the automobile.

Designing and building roads (Fig 8) along which to operate the automobiles was also an important step in creating a personal means of transportation. In large cities the network of roads, parking spaces, service stations, and repair garages become complex systems. This single invention could be said to have for better or worse transformed the landscape of cities, regions and, in the case of the United States, an entire continent with the development of Interstate Highway system beginning in the late 1940s. The architectural design issues of large scale cities and the buildings which are central to their commercial and institutional facilities, are dependent on effective interfacing with the car and related personal transportation networks, as well as with the public transportation systems.

Fig. 8. Freeway in the city

10
Construction materials technology

L. Reed Brantley
Ruth T. Brantley

Summary: The principle materials of building technology are reviewed, with emphasis upon their chemical and physical properties and contemporary applications in modern construction. Definitions are provided along with important considerations of environmental health and safety.

Key words: building construction, concrete, glass, masonry, metals, plastics, polymers, sealants, wood.

1   Cement and concrete (See examples of materials in Figs 1-13)
Concrete, used extensively in buildings, is one of the most complicated chemical and physical materials of construction, combining cement, water, and aggregates. A substance that forms a plastic paste when mixed with water, bonds to aggregates, and sets to form a solid material is known as a cementitious material. Common examples are slaked lime and portland cement, from which concrete is made.

Portland cement
A patent for making portland cement from limestone was issued in 1824. It received its name from its resemblance to a building stone found on a small island off the coast of England. In preparation of portland cement, raw materials are crushed, mixed, and ground to prepare the desired proportion of lime, silica, alumina, and iron.

There are four main chemical components of cement which are combined in different proportions to make up the five main types of portland cement. Normal portland cement, or type I. is still the standard cement in use. More specialized portland cements include type II, characterized by a more moderate heat of hydration during setting; type III, a high early-strength cement; type IV, low heat of hydration during setting; and type V, a sulfate-resisting cement for use in areas where high sulfate concentrations occur in soil or water. Specifications for these five portland cements are given by the American Society for Testing and Materials in standard ASTM C 150.

Hydration, setting, and hardening: The action of water on cement can be better understood by starting with the action of water on plaster of paris, and on slaked lime as used in mortar and in whitewash.

- *Setting of gypsum plaster:* Setting of partially dehydrated calcium sulfate (plaster of paris) illustrates the setting and hardening by recrystallization.

- *Setting of lime:* Lime is a general term used in industry to indicate either quicklime (calcium oxide) or slaked (hydrated) lime (calcium hydroxide). Slaked lime is used in stucco, mortar, and whitewash.

Setting and hardening of portland cement: The setting and hardening of portland cement is much more complicated, due to the different proportions of the four main cementitious compounds in the various kinds of portland cement. When the cement particles are mixed with water, a series of changes occur.

- Water reacts with the surface of the cement particle, and the product forms a supersaturated solution from which a gel-like mass of fibrous crystals precipitates. This gelatinous coating around the particle acts like a barrier to seal off the particle from further reaction. However, "free" water slowly diffuses into the gel by osmosis (spontaneous dilution of the gel solution). This water reaches the unreacted surface of the particle and forms more hydrates. The gel swells as this process continues. Finally, the swollen gel ruptures and fills in the spaces between cement particles and aggregates to form a semisolid gel. This network of tiny crystals produces the initial set. The process takes about an hour for standard cement.

- The crystals slowly interact and recrystalize into larger fibers to form a strong network that characterizes the hardened cement. This "final set" marking the beginning of the hardening process, usually starts about 10 hours after mixing with water.

- The rate of hydration of cement is dependent upon the fineness of the clinker. The finer the cement particles, the more surface area there is for reaction with water. Therefore, the finer the cement is ground, the quicker the setting and stiffening occur. In practice, the hydration of the cement particle only penetrates about a fraction of the way into the surface. Experiments have shown that hardened concrete can be reground and used in place of fresh concrete a second time, and even a third time before the interior of the cement particle becomes completely hydrated. Could reusing old concrete be a solution to the enormous amounts destined for our overflowing municipal dumps?

Concrete
Concrete consists of cement, water, sand, rock, and sand aggregates and admixtures. Admixtures are added during the mixing of the concrete to produce special properties. They can alter the setting, hardening, strength, and durability of the concrete. Some of the common admixtures provide water reduction and air entrainment.

Authors: L. Reed Brantley and Ruth T. Brantley

Credits: This article is excerpted from Brantley and Brantley (1996) by permission of the publisher. The authors are indebted to the encouragement and guidance of Elmer E. Botsai, Professor and former Dean of the School of Architecture, University of Hawaii at Manoa.

References: American Society for Testing and Materials, 1916 Race Street, Philadelphia, PA 19103.

Brantley, L. Reed and Ruth T. Brantley. 1996. *Building Materials Technology: Structural Performance & Environmental Impact.* New York: McGraw-Hill.

Fig. 1. Brick wall construction with terra cotta tilework. Troy, NY.

Fig. 2. Adobe block and brick construction. Spanish Mission, Capistrano, CA.

Curing the freshly placed concrete is an important factor in its strength and durability. Setting, hydration, and crystal-growth sequence should not be interrupted, particularly during the first 48 hours for type III early-setting portland cement. This is twice as long as required for general-purpose type I. The surface of the cement should never be allowed to dry, for this indicates a scarcity of water for the hydration process. If the surface becomes dry, water for the hydration process is insufficient and a serious decrease in the quality of the concrete will result. Frequent sprinkling may be needed. In hot, dry weather it may be necessary to leave the forms in place and cover exposed surfaces with a sheet of polyethylene or other suitable material.

The smaller the water/cement ratio (increased cement) the higher the compressive strength of the concrete. Impurities in water can affect the strength of the concrete and its setting time, cause sulfate deterioration and efflorescence, and promote corrosion of reinforcing steel. A simple rule is that if the water is potable (drinkable), it is suitable for concrete.

Porosity of concrete leads to both physical and chemical deterioration. Some porosity can be expected. Aggregates can be a major source of porosity if their size distribution is not uniform. If the aggregates are not distributed uniformly in size, the spaces between them leave voids that will fill with water and air. This will require excess cement paste to fill the voids in order to cement the particles together and maintain the strength of the concrete. For a better fit and optimum concrete strength, the ideal shape of the aggregates is cubical, flat, or elongated with a rough surface for good adhesion. They should not be rounded or smooth.

Aggregates make up about 75 percent of concrete. Although thought of as an inexpensive filler, aggregates provide strength to the concrete since they are usually stronger than the cement holding them together. For best results, particles should be graded in size so the aggregates can fit closely together to form a strong, tightly packed structure.

Admixtures are chemicals added to concrete to modify the physical properties. An admixture often affects more than one property, so side effects must be considered if they are used. For example, water-reducing agents increase workability and can act as set retarders. Water reducers can also increase the early strength of concrete.

High-range superplasticizer water reducers: The superplasticizer admixtures are also known as superfluidizers, super water reducers, and high-range water reducers. Their action is that of a surface-tension reducing agent (surfactant) that breaks up cement aggregates into smaller groups of suspended cement particles to make the cement mixture more fluid. This class of admixtures has been called superplasticizers because they increase the plasticity and workability of concrete mixes.

Accelerators: In cold weather, accelerating admixtures help to restore more normal setting and early strength times. Accelerators compensate for the reduction in ambient temperature and the resulting slower rate of reaction. Early strength and set development do not ensure greater final strength. Other desirable properties may be reduced.

A set retarder is an admixture that extends the workability and setting period of concrete. When working in hot climates, set retarders can compensate for the rapid setting due to the increase in temperature, but they are effective only during the first week of setting. Accelerators provide early strength for concrete. Water reducers and retarders contain similar ingredients and produce similar results.

Air-entrainment agents: Entrainment agents, such as the surfactants, act as emulsifiers and foaming agents to improve the plasticity and workability of the water paste. They also reduce bleeding by stabilizing the gelatinous mixture.

Reinforced concrete

Concrete can be reinforced with steel bars (re-bars) and with steel cables in prestressed concrete. Re-bars have lugs (deformations) at regular intervals to increase mechanical adhesion. It was once believed that concrete could protect steel from corrosion by keeping out moisture and oxygen. Instead, corrosion is retarded by the passivity of steel due to the alkalinity of the concrete.

Prestressing concrete is a way to compensate for concrete's low tensile strength. A beam is prestressed by stretching a high-tensile-strength cable down the length of a concrete form. Then the cable is put under tension and stretched by using jacks at either end. High-strength concrete is poured into the form around the cable. The concrete bonds to the cable as it hardens. When the jacks are removed, both the cable and the concrete beam remain under the amount of tension desired.

Another method of forming prestressed concrete is to post-tension the cable. This requires the cable to be encased in a thin steel or paper tube (within the form) and anchored at the ends before the concrete fills the form. After the concrete has hardened, the cable can be more easily put under tension with jacks at the ends of the beam or structure. This can be done after the beam is in place on the work site. Finally the tube is filled with grout to complete the prestressed concrete beam.

Polymer concrete

Polymer concrete (portland cement replaced by a polymer) has a lower rate of water absorption, higher resistance to cycles of freezing and thawing, better resistance to chemicals, greater strength, and excellent adhesion qualities compared to most other building materials. The most commonly used resins (polyesters and acrylics) are mixed with the aggregate as a monomer with a cross-linking agent (a hardener) and a catalyst to reach full polymerization. Polymer concrete is usually reinforced with metal fibers, glass fibers, or mats of glass fiber. The use of polymer fibers (such as polypropylene) as a replacement for asbestos in cement has received much attention.

Concrete: common problems and corrections

Some of the common building problems related to concrete as listed here with their causes and suggestions for correction.

- Sulfate deterioration of concrete is caused by moisture and sulfate salts in the soil that is in contact with concrete foundations, floor slabs, and walls. Type V sulfate-resisting cement is made for this purpose. To correct the problem (if the soil cannot be kept away from the concrete), better drainage might keep the soil dry and the salts in solid, not solution, form.

- Efflorescence is the appearance of an unsightly fluffy white crust on the surface of walls. It is caused by salts in solution (in the concrete, the stone, or the bricks) moving to the surface of an interior or exterior wall. As the water evaporates from the salt solution in dry weather, a loose mass of white, powdery salts remains. Some relief from efflorescence can be gained by treating the surface of the wall with a water repellent and sealing all cracks and joints to keep out rain.

- Freeze-thaw cracks (forming in concrete in subfreezing weather) can be caused by concrete with a water/cement ratio that is too large. This can produce tiny crevices and voids around the aggregates, allowing penet≤ation of water into the concrete by wind-driven rain. Tremendous forces, produced by the expansion of water as it freezes to form ice, cause spalls (flakes or chips) and cracks in the concrete. Correction requires waterproofing the surface of the concrete with a polymer-modified cement-based surface coating. Further protection could be gained by applying a protective coat of paint.

Fig. 3. Serpentine brick wall. University of Virginia, Charlottesville, VA. Thomas Jefferson, Architect.

Fig. 4. Split oak rail fence. Smoky Mountains, TN.

- Corrosion of steel re-bars can cause cracks and rust stains to appear in the concrete.

- Leaks in concrete roofs or parking decks are due to water penetrating the surface. A waterproof coating alone rarely works because the cracks continue to grow. A solution is to use epoxy in the clean cracks and to fill them with a flexible sealant material.

2 Masonry

Historic cathedrals, stone bridges, and walls testify to the early development of stone masonry. The Romans are credited with perfecting the design of the large cathedral arches and domes. Wattle and daub walls of homes in Britain have been standing for centuries. Walls are constructed of interwoven willow wands filled with dung and mud and packed between timbers. Brick, also developed and used centuries ago, is one of our oldest human-made building materials.

Modern masonry units may be defined as any type of small, solid, or hollow units of building material that are held together with mortar. These units usually include stone, cast stone, cement brick and concrete block, clay brick and tile, and glass blocks. Vital to the successful performance of each of these masonry unit systems is the selection of the proper mortar to hold the units together and keep out the weather. Since no machine has yet been invented to assemble the masonry units in place, the performance of the masonry structure depends on the quality of the mortar, the skill of the mason, and exposure to the environment. Severe environmental conditions, such as torrential rains and intense sunshine, require more careful design and higher-quality ingredients than do the more protected environments. This is especially true if these masonry structures are to withstand earthquakes or hurricanes.

Masonry mortar

Less than 1 percent of the weight of masonry structures consists of the mortar holding them together. Cement, hydrated lime, aggregates, and water are the necessary ingredients that make this feat possible.

Four ingredients are essential to the satisfactory performance of mortar. Cement provides mortar with the necessary strength; hydrated lime provides the elasticity and water retention so necessary for workability; sand provides durability and strength in addition to acting as a filler; and an optimum amount of water is necessary for good bonding, plasticity, and workability. Selecting the correct ingredients is important for the optimum performance of the mortar.

Physical properties of mortar: In some ways the properties of mortar are more critical than those for concrete. Compressive strength is one of the main assets of cured concrete. In addition to compressive strength, mortar must have adequate bond strength, shear strength, and durability. Successful performance depends on its workability and its skillful application. Workability, one of the most essential properties of mortar, determines the success of its application. Mortar must have a strong bonding strength, which requires that the mortar be able to flow into crevices and small voids.

Thickness for optimum bond strength: A general rule for an adhesive is: the thinner the layer of the bonding mixture, the stronger the bond. It is best to use only enough mortar to fill the irregularities in the surface of the materials being held together. Most adhesive failures are due to flaws or imperfections in the adhesive layer itself.

Grout masonry: After a masonry structure is completed, grout is used to fill in the remaining crevices and joints. Grout differs from masonry mortar in its fluidity since it is poured and not spread into place with a trowel. Masonry grout is essentially composed of portland or blended cement, fine or coarse sand, water, and a small amount (if any) of calcium hydroxide.

Structural masonry

Structural masonry is divided into load-bearing, non-load-bearing, and decorative veneers used on walls of buildings. Concrete masonry includes the assembly of walls of solid or hollow units. They may be reinforced or nonreinforced and interior or exterior walls. The walls may contain clay, tile, or glass units.

- *Masonry units:* Masonry units are composed of stone, cement, clay, or glass and are made in hollow or solid blocks. Clay bricks can be either load-bearing or non-load-bearing.

- *Concrete blocks:* Concrete blocks can be solid or hollow, but the hollow 8- by 8- by 16- in. (20- by 20- by 40-cm) blocks are the most common. They can be load-bearing or non-load-bearing. The three types of blocks are classified as being of normal weight, medium weight, and lightweight, depending on the weight of the aggregate contained.

Clay masonry units

Some of the most durable building materials are made of clay: bricks, ceramic tile, and terra cotta. In contrast to the concrete masonry units, which depend on the ingredients reacting with water, clay masonry units are heated until the clay melts and flows over the surface of the aggregates. This bonds the aggregates together and forms an impervious, vitreous ceramic material with good compressive strength.

- *Clay bricks:* The type of clay selected and its processing determine the structure and characteristics of clay units in building structures. Most bricks and structural tiles are made by the stiff-mud process with 12 to 15 percent moisture content providing the needed plasticity. Clay bricks must be laid in place with care to obtain a secure bond with the mortar. These bricks, unlike concrete masonry units, are not delivered at the job site conditioned to the humidity of the surroundings. They absorb water from the mortar by capillary attraction and, thus, dehydrate the mortar. To avoid this problem, the bricks are soaked with water and left to dry to the ambient humidity conditions.

- *Clay tile:* Clay tiles are often used as facing that is anchored to the structural steel framing of the building. Although its popularity has diminished, the use of clay tile for restoration purposes continues. In addition to its use for load-bearing and non-load-bearing wall structures, it is used for floors and interior walls.

- *Terra cotta tile:* The term *terra cotta* stands for "fired earth." Although terra cotta tile has been used for centuries, dating back to the days of the Romans, it is no longer popular and is used mainly in restorations.

Stone masonry

Stones that qualify as building materials can be classified as granite, limestone, coral, sandstone, slate, marble, and lava. These can vary greatly in compressive strength—between varieties of stones and between stones from the same source. This is due to the complexity of their compositions and wide variations in the percentage of mineral components.

- *Granite,* used as a building material since the beginning of civilization, is a visibly crystalline igneous rock with granular texture and composed of quartz, feldspar, mica, and hornblende.

- *Limestone,* a sedimentary rock composed mainly of calcium carbonate or magnesium carbonate, is durable, workable, and distributed throughout the earth's crust. Fossilized remains of animals (fish, shells, coral) and plants are evident in most limestone.

- *Travertine,* a form of limestone found in deposits at the mouth of a hot spring, can be polished and often resembles marble.

- *Coral limestone,* composed of reef-forming coral often of great extent, consists chiefly of calcareous skeletons of corals, coral sands, and the solid limestone resulting from their compaction. This coral limestone forms on the ocean floor bordering the shores of islands and lagoons. Plentiful, inexpensive, and used often in the eighteenth and nineteenth centuries in the Hawaiian Islands, coral is now quarried very carefully due to ecological concerns and has become expensive.

- *Sandstone,* a sedimentary rock composed of individual sand or quartz grains held together by cementitious material, contains a high degree of iron oxide which gives it a red or brown color.

- *Slate,* a group name for various fine-grained rocks derived from mudstone, siltstone, and high-silica clays and shale sedimentary deposits, is characterized by planes which easily split into thin sheets and lines. Slate roofing tiles are used extensively in Europe.

- *Marble,* a metamorphic crystalline limestone composed of calcite or dolomite, is highly polished for commercial uses. Marble has been used for structural purposes throughout the centuries. In modern practice, marble is used as a beautiful interior and exterior veneer over a structural framework.

- *Lava* is a crystalline or glassy igneous rock formed by the cooling of molten rock from volcanic vents and fissures. This rock can be very dense and heavy, or light in weight and bubbly.

Glass blocks

Produced in a variety of sizes, colors, and surface textures, glass blocks may be solid or hollow. In addition to their aesthetic appearance, their high transition of light somewhat reduces the need for interior illumination during daylight hours. The strength of glass blocks is much lower than that of most masonry units. Glass blocks are not intended to be used as load-bearing units. Hollow glass blocks can be used as thermal and sound barriers.

Plaster

Applied by hand or by machinery, plaster refers to the finished cementitious coating used on the exterior and interior walls of buildings to provide a smooth, finished appearance. Composed of cement and a plaster-grade aggregate—and, as an option, slaked lime—plaster should have a consistency appropriate to its method of application, have good durability, and withstand most kinds of weather. As in mortar, the slaked lime provides plasticity and the needed workability.

An external cement plaster, called stucco, is much used in mild climates. Plaster is as strong and durable as concrete and can be considered a modified form of concrete mortar. To avoid the need for papering or painting, the plaster may contain a mineral pigment or have a textured surface.

Masonry: common problems and their prevention

Structural failure does not always mean that the cement must have greater strength; more often failure occurs in the mortar. Failures occur when stresses converging on a weak point in the structure exceed the strength of the material in a flawed region. In other words, structural failures usually occur at a much lower stress than the ultimate strength of the material. Thus correction would require that the excess mortar be reduced. This principle applies to all types of cementitious adhesives.

Environmental hazards: Although stone, baked clay products, and cement are some of the most durable building materials, even they can deteriorate in contact with the chemicals in the soil or desert sand and moisture. The oxides of nitrogen from automobile exhaust, smog, and "vog" (volcanic emissions) and the industrial smokestack emissions of oxides of sulfur carried on the smoke particulates all become acids. In the presence of moisture in the clouds, acid rain results. This acid rain not only kills trees, it also reacts with and slowly destroys the surfaces of our buildings.

3 Metals

It is not surprising that metals are widely used in all types of construction. Aluminum, the most abundant metallic element, makes up an estimated 8 percent of the earth's crust. Iron is in second place with about 5 percent. Metallic iron, alloyed with a small amount of nickel, is found in meteorites that strike the earth. This natural source of iron, when fashioned into tools and weapons, influenced the development of early civilizations. Iron continues to play a vital part in our lives.

Metals can be divided into two types: *ferrous* and *nonferrous.* Iron and its many steel alloys are ferrous metals; aluminum, copper, and zinc are some of the common nonferrous metals. Metals are typically so malleable that they can be hammered into thin sheets and are so ductile that they can be drawn into thin wires.

Iron and its alloys

The two carbon steels *austenite* and *ferrite* have quite different physical properties, such as ductility, strength, and corrosion resistance.

- *Austenite formation temperature:* Austenite, an alloy of carbon in iron, is a solid solution of carbon in gamma iron face-centered cubic crystals (fcc). The maximum solubility of carbon in this fcc iron structure is 2 percent. Austenite, ductile enough to be cold-worked to increase its hardness, is nonmagnetic and has a larger electrical resistance and thermal expansion coefficient than ferrite.

- *Ferrite formation temperature:* Ferrite is a solid solution of carbon in the bcc (body-centered cubic crystal) structure of alpha iron. Ferrite is more ductile than austenite and is easily cold-worked. Chromium, molybdenum, tungsten, and silicon, by substitution, form alloys that are much used in the building industry.

Stainless-steel alloys

There are three main classes of stainless steels: austenite, ferrite, and *martensite.* The stainless-steel alloys differ in composition, metallurgical structure, workability, magnetic nature, and corrosion resistance. Austenitic stainless steels of the 18-8 type are most often used when highly corrosion-resistant decorative and nonmagnetic properties are required. They are the most ductile of the stainless steels and are used to form tubes and sheets. Ferritic stainless steels contain chromium but no nickel. Their excellent corrosion resistance explains their use in chemical plants. Martensitic stainless steels are formed by the addition of chromium and can have up to 1 percent carbon.

Common nonferrous alloys

- *Aluminum metal* does not occur in nature. It is made by the electrolysis of a molten mixture of bauxite (aluminum oxide ore) and cryolite (sodium aluminum fluoride). In addition to its light weight, it has moderate resistance to corrosion due to the rapid formation of a thin, transparent, tightly adherent aluminum oxide coating. Thicker oxide coatings are produced by an electrolytic process known as anodizing. The large amount of electric energy required for the production of aluminum makes it a prime candidate for recycling.

- *Copper and its alloys:* Copper is used extensively in the pure state and in alloys. In its purest form it is used as a conductor of electricity in the electric wiring of homes and buildings. As an alloy, copper is often used for roof gutters and water pipes because of its excellent resistance to corrosion. Copper is very ductile and can be drawn into wires and extruded into tubing. It can be cold-worked to increase its strength. However, as in the practice with aluminum, it is usually alloyed with numerous other elements if more strength is needed.

- *Copper alloys:* Copper-zinc alloys are known as brasses. Copper-tin, or true bronzes, are another well-known class of copper alloys. The presence of tin contributes more corrosion resistance,

Fig. 5. Taliesen West. Scottsdale, AZ. Masonry construction. Frank Lloyd Wright, Architect.

Fig. 6. Hartford Seminary. Ironwork and enamel panel construction. West Hartford, CT. Richard Meier, Architect.

hardness, and abrasion (wear) resistance than the softer brass alloys of copper-zinc. There are a variety of copper-nickel alloys that include Monel, a highly corrosion-resistant alloy.

- *High-performance metal composites:* Additional strength can be obtained in an alloy by forming a high-performance fiber-reinforced composite. Fibers such as graphite, silicon carbide, silicon nitride, boron nitride, and alumina are common. The need of the aerospace industry to find lighter and stronger metallic systems has spurred research and produced exciting results in advanced materials engineering for potential building applications.

Metals: building problems and amelioration

Metallic corrosion can be kept to a minimum by using certain precautions. Cavities, crevices, surface irregularities, and contact between dissimilar metals are to be avoided in the design of exposed surfaces. Metallic surfaces must be accessible for inspection and treatment. To make full use of corrosion technology, preventive measures should be incorporated at the design stage. This is vitally important if there is exposure to a marine environment, high humidity, or corrosive chemical emissions.

When using corrosion-resistant materials, allowance should be made for the synergistic effects of unusual metal stress, flexure, and fatigue on corrosion. Avoiding the expense of specialty materials by designing to the maximum stress level is a dangerous temptation. Adequate drainage is essential in the design of flat roofs, around metal joints, or in other areas that can collect water and dirt which will cause early corrosion or related failure. Poor welding practices can destroy the corrosion resistance of specialty alloys.

Methods of corrosion protection can be grouped under chemical treatment, electrochemical prevention, and environmental protection. The choice of method must be made on an individual basis, depending on the situations encountered. (See Brantley and Brantley 1996 for a complete discussion of corrosion and its mitigation and "Corrosion of Metals" in Chapter B3 of this Volume).

4   Wood

Wood is one of the oldest building materials. In dry climates it is extremely durable. However, in humid environments wood is attacked by bacteria, fungi, and insects as part of nature's essential recycling process.

Wood for industrial use, including building applications, falls into two classes: *softwoods* and *hardwoods*. Softwoods are from coniferous trees, namely, pine, spruce, fir, hemlock, cedar, redwood, and cypress. Hardwoods are dense, close-grained, and from deciduous trees, such as oak, walnut, cherry, maple, teak, and mahogany. Hardwoods have many slender elongated cells and grain irregularities that make them harder to work or split. The difference between softwood and hardwood is not so much in the hardness as in the degree of difficulty of working. (See Brantley and Brantley 1996 for a discussion of causes and prevention measures of wood destruction and deterioration due to moisture and insects damage and "Termite Control" in Chapter B1 of this Volume.)

The chemical composition of wood is complex, but the most important ingredients are cellulose, pentosan, and lignin. Cellulose, obtained from wood and cotton, is a high-molecular-weight carbohydrate. Pentosan, a complex carbohydrate by-product of wood, is used as an animal food. It is a natural polymer of pentose, which is a five-carbon atom sugar. Lignin makes up about one-fourth of the composition of wood. A by-product of the papermaking industry, it is a phenylpropane polymer and serves as a binder to hold the cellulose fibers together.

Structural panel composites

In an effort to conserve and use the limited supply of timber more efficiently, plywood, hardboard, and particleboard panels have become well established in their use in the building industry. Plywood fills a need for thin wood panels with more structural strength and less warping than a solid sheet of lumber of similar thickness. Hardboard and particleboard panels are scrap lumber, shavings, and fibers recycled into composite panels.

- *Plywood:* When hardwood is soaked with water or steamed, it can be cut into thin sheets called veneer facing. After drying and pressing flat, the sheets of hardwood veneer can be glued to enclose sheets of softwood cores. Hardwood veneer plywood is suitable for use as paneling and as furniture. Softwood, cut into thin veneer sheets and glued together as three or more sheets make an economical plywood with improved dimensional stability, stiffness, and strength. The strength of the composite, with the grain of each ply alternating at right angles to the ply above and below, makes high-grade plywood superior to most metals in strength-to-weight ratio. Some of the advantages of plywood, compared to the wood it came from, are that it has a lower expansion coefficient and less tendency to warp, is stiffer and stronger, and does not split easily.

- *Particleboard:* The properties and performance of particleboard depend on the orientation of the particles, their nature, the kind of resin, and the amount of adhesive used to bond the particles together. Particleboard is known by many other names, such as composition board, chipboard, flakeboard, waferboard, and oriented standard board (OSB). This economical product, made by sealing a core of shredded wood chips, fibers, or particles between veneer facings, uses waste wood and small scraps of low-grade lumber. Some of the names more accurately describe the composition of the board.

5 Polymers and plastics

Polymers

Polymers with different structures and properties exist even though they share the same chemical elements in the same proportions by weight. Rubber occurs as a natural polymer. Cellulose nitrate (celluloid), one of the first synthetic plastics, was made by treating cellulose fibers (from cotton or wood) with nitric acid. Polymers are of interest in construction materials technology because of the unique chemical and physical properties.

Physical properties of polymers: Polymers can be made easily to have unique physical properties. These properties include a characteristic glass-transition temperature, plasticity when warmed, a large thermal expansion compared to metals, visoelasticity, and high permeability to some vapors and gases. These properties provide special roles for polymers for filling and joining building materials, such as structural dampers.

Coefficient of expansion: Organic polymers have larger thermal expansion coefficients than metals or other building materials. The thermal expansion coefficients of linear polymers are about twice those of cross-linked polymers, which in turn are about twice those of aluminum or glass. To better match the expansion of polymers as they warm, inorganic fillers are used. Most common fillers are powdered silica, aluminum, and aluminum oxide. Besides providing a better match of expansion coefficients, fillers can provide corrosion resistance, shear and tensile strength, and reduction in gas and vapor permeability.

Plastics

Some selected monomer combinations produce polymers with the physical properties needed for elastomers, fibers, or plastics more easily than others. Such properties can be built into almost any polymer.

Plastics are organic compounds that, in some stage of formation, can be shaped by flow and can be molded. Their structure and high molecular weight give them unusual properties. Plastics need to have a

compromise of fibrous and elastomeric properties. To be flexible instead of brittle like glass, the polymer must be used above its glass-transition temperature. This temperature is more dependent on chain structure, freedom of chain movement, stiffness, and interchain bonding than it is on molecular weight. For example, polystyrene, polymethylmethacrylate, and poly (vinyl chloride) are brittle and have a low impact strength at ambient temperatures.

Plastics are an important part of our lives, replacing metals, glass, ceramics, and other common building materials. Indeed, the volume used notably exceeds that of metals (Table 1). Sheet plastic is an important illustration of the replacement of glass where a nearly unbreakable, shatterproof, transparent light-weight material is needed. Such uses include glazing of windows and skylights with optional features of solar and glare control. Exterior uses include enclosures of elevated walkways between buildings. Interior uses include display windows, curtain walls, and space dividers.

Sheets of acrylic or polycarbonate plastic are made by cell casting or by a continuous process. Tinted, mirrorized, and hollow-core acrylic sheets are also made in limited sizes and thicknesses. Continuous cast-sheet plastic is made by pouring a catalyzed liquid monomer onto a continuously moving stainless-steel sheet belt and polymerizing the plastic as it passes through an oven. This continuous sheet is rolled up around a reel.

Acrylics and polycarbonates are unique building materials because of their long-term resistance to weather without a significant deterioration in appearance or properties. Polycarbonate has phenomenal impact resistance, which remains higher than that of many other transparent plastics such as poly (vinyl chloride), cellulose acetate butyrate, and polystyrene.

Table 1. Plastic as a building material

Type of plastic	*Applications*
Acrylic	Glazing, lighting fixtures
Acrylonitrile	Window frames
Polybutylene terephthalate	Countertops, sinks
Polycarbonate	Flat sheets, windows, skylights
Polyethylene	Piping
Polyphenylene oxide	Roofing panels
Polystyrene	Insulation, sheathing
Polyurethane	Insulation, roofing systems
Poly (vinyl chloride)	Molding, siding, window frames
Urea formaldehyde	Countertops

Table 2. Material Safety Data Sheets (MSDS)

Chemical manufacturers and distributors are required to provide material safety data sheets (MSDS) to consumers and to put warning labels on their products. The MSDS on a product should provide information on the chemical and physical hazards of the material. However, many MSDSs are incomplete and lack accurate information. Trace amounts of chemicals are not required to be reported. The MSDS should be used as a guide only, and if more detailed information is needed, the manufacturer can be contacted directly. Compare several products before making a decision.

Sections of the MSDS and the information they should provide include:

1.   Chemical identity and manufacture information
2.   Hazardous ingredients and identity information
3.   Physical and chemical characteristics
4.   Fire and explosion hazard data
5.   Reactivity data
6.   Health hazard and medical treatment information
7.   Precautions for safe handling and use
8.   Control measures to avoid overexposure

Table 3. Plastic recycling information

Number/Symbol	Name	Common use
1 PET	Polyethylene teraphthalate	Soft-drink bottles, microwave food-bags and trays, packing film.
2 HDPE	High-density polyethylene	Trash bags, milk cartons, soap and bleach bottles, pipes and molded fittings.
3 V	Poly (vinyl chloride)	Plastic wrap for meats, cookingoil bottles, conduits, plumbing pipes, siding, gutters.
4 LDPE	Low-density polyethylene	Grocery store vegetable and food-wrap. Wire and cable coatings, insulation.
5 PP	Polypropylene	Packaging film, housewares, auto parts, air filters.
6 PS	Polystyrene	Foamed packaging and insulation, refrigerator doors, air-conditioner cases, radio / TV cabinets.

Natural and synthetic rubber

Natural and synthetic rubbers are examples of elastomeric substances that recover fully when stretched to twice their length. Examples are butyl, neoprene, nitrile, and polysulfide rubbers. They are used to modify thermosetting polymers, improving their resistance to peel and fatigue. Natural rubber is a linear polymer of isoprene obtained as latex from the rubber tree. Synthetic rubbers include polybutadiene, made from the monomer butadiene, and a chlorinated derivative of butadiene, called chloroprene, which is used to make neoprene rubber.

Adhesives

The development of synthetic resins with superior properties has resulted in the increased use of adhesives in the construction industry. Adhesives have an advantage over rivets and bolt fasteners by distributing stress over larger areas of a joint. The important physical properties of adhesives are cohesive strength, adherence, fluidity, and wettability of the substrate.

Health hazards

Before using any product, ask for the Material Safety Data Sheet (MSDS) and read it (Table 2). You should know the chemicals you are using and what precautions to take to prevent health and environmental problems connected with the product.

- *Sulfuryl fluoride,* used in termite fumigation, is toxic by inhalation with a very low threshold limit value (TLV).

- Most *polymers* are made from toxic monomers. When polymers are heated, especially linear polymers, they decompose to release their toxic monomers. If polymeric materials are disposed of by incineration, the noxious gases are lung and eye irritants and are toxic if inhaled over extended periods of time.

- *Polyurethane foam* burns readily to produce hydrogen cyanide (a toxic gas) along with a dense, black smoke. Some polymers, such as phenol formaldehyde resins used in wallboards and carpets, are suspected of releasing formaldehyde by slow decomposition at room temperature. Over an extended period of time, formaldehyde can be a serious health hazard. When considering toxic substances, the length of time exposed as well as the concentration of the gas are both of vital importance.

- *Urea, melamine,* and *phenol formaldehyde* resins are much used in industrial adhesives. Their slow decomposition at ambient temperature releases formaldehyde gas into the air. Formaldehyde, toxic by inhalation with a 1-part-per-million threshold limit value, is an irritant and a carcinogen. Epoxy resins are much used in the building industry because of their outstanding bond strength and durability. Epoxy adhesives have such a short shelf life (must be used a few minutes after mixing the ingredients) that most of them are marketed in two parts and are mixed just before using. Vapors in the uncured state are a strong irritant and cause severe dermatitis.

- Most *solvents* are highly flammable and have a low flash point (ignition temperature). Long-time exposure to low concentrations of toxic vapors and carcinogens is of increasing concern to the public.

- A good rule to remember: if you can smell a chemical, you should avoid exposure to it.

Recycling of plastics

A commendable step in the sorting of plastics has been the general acceptance of a code for plastics manufacturers. The code is embossed on each plastic article sold. Two groups that have pioneered this system of labeling plastics are the Society of Plastics Industry and the American Society for Testing and Materials (ASTM D 1971). Table 3 provides a summary of the common types of plastics, their identification numbers, and their symbols.

6 Sealants

Adhesives and sealants are usually discussed together, but there are differences. Adhesives are intended to hold surfaces together; sealants are intended to exclude or contain substances. In surface preparation, formulation, and application, adhesives and sealants have much in common with one another and with paints.

Sealants must have low viscosity so that they can be extruded or poured, yet they must harden to form a bond with the substrate, not flow under stress, and not crack or leak. The purpose of a sealant is to prevent the passage of air, water, and heat through the joints and seams on the exterior of buildings.

The movement capability of a sealant in a joint is one of the most important properties to evaluate when determining expected performance. This capability is the maximum extension or compression (compared to its original dimension when installed) that a sealant can make without experiencing bond failure. The movement capability is a unique parameter of the sealant that involves many of its physical properties. Movement capability is rated as + - 5 percent, + - 12.5 percent, + - 25 percent, or + - 50 percent. The plus indicates the maximum extension; the maximum compression is indicated by the minus sign.

Sealant types

Introduced as the first elastomeric sealant for use in modern curtain-wall construction, polysulfides easily replaced oil-based caulks and were an immediate success. However, with the discovery of even higher-performance sealants, the popularity and use of polysulfides has declined.

- *Oil-based caulks:* Oil-based caulking compounds are prepared from a variety of natural oils, such as linseed oil. They may contain fillers, catalysts, solvents, and plasticizers.

- *Polysulfide sealants:* Polysulfide sealants, based on a form of rubber, are prepared by pouring dichloroethylformal into sodium polysulfide (a solution of sulfur in sodium sulfide) in the presence of an emulsifying agent. They are purchased in two parts and cure when mixed because of the lead-dioxide catalyst in one of the separate containers.

- *Butyl sealants:* Because of their movement capability, butyl sealants rapidly replaced the polysulfide sealants when butyl rubber became available in the 1950s. Low-cost butyl sealants have good stability and are resistant to water and organic solvents. One of the properties of butyl sealants that makes them superior to the polysulfides and competitive with the acrylic sealants is their + 12.5 percent movement capability. These butyl sealants have good water resistance and good adhesion formulation. Their stickiness, until they skin over, causes them to pick up dust from the air. They become stiff in cold weather and soft in hot weather.

- *Acrylic sealants:* The acrylics are water emulsions of a formulated acrylic in a small amount of water with detergent and an emulsifying agent. Acrylics have good bonding ability and adhere to a wide variety of surfaces. The maximum movement capability of acrylic sealants is + 12.5 percent of the joint width. However, loss of water over a period of time causes these sealants to harden and lose some of their moderate movement capability. They are somewhat flexible, but have poor elastic recovery.

- *Urethane sealants:* Urethane sealants rank second among the sealants used in industry. A chief component is a polyurethane. Two-component urethane sealants require the thorough mixing of two packages.

- *Silicone sealants:* Silicone sealants rank first among the sealants used in industry and are most used in high-rise buildings. Their high performance, resistance to low temperatures, high ozone re-

Fig. 7. Free University of Berlin. Demountable concrete and steel panel construction. Shadrach Woods of Candilis, Josic, Woods, Architects.

Fig. 8. House. Amazon rain forest tradition (reconstructed at Fairchild Gardens, Coral Gables, FL). Demountable hardwood, bamboo, and reed construction.

Fig. 9. Crystal Palace. Demountable glass, wood and cast iron structure.

Fig. 10. Interior detailing of concrete form joints. Salk Institute, La Jolla, CA. Office of Jonas Salk. Louis Kahn, Architect.

Fig. 11. Interior detailing of wood joinery. Hiroshi Ohi, Architect.

sistance, good adhesion to surfaces, and very high movement capability continue to make them the favorite product, regardless of high cost. Silicone sealants cure by reacting on contact with the moisture in the air to form acetic acid, which provides their characteristic odor.

The usual formulations of silicone sealants provide long service in exposure to harsh environments, good stability, high peel and tear resistance, and low shrinkage and weight loss. Silicones have a natural resistance to weathering due to the stability of the silicone polymer. They have set another record with the maximum movement capability increased to + 100 percent extension and - 50 percent compression.

Health hazards of sealants

The solvents used in sealants may include chlorinated hydrocarbons (toxic to the liver) and aromatic solvents (such as benzene and toluene) that are carcinogenic. The amines used as curing agents for the epoxies may cause dermatitis of the hands and face and, if inhaled, serious respiratory problems.

Most polymers are made from toxic monomers. When polymers are heated in a fire, especially linear polymers, they decompose to release their monomers. Polyurethane foam burns readily to produce hydrogen cyanide (a toxic gas) along with a dense, black smoke. Some polymers such as phenol formaldehyde, which is used in wallboard and carpets, are suspected of releasing formaldehyde by slowly decomposing at room temperature. Over an extended period, formaldehyde may be a serious health hazard.

If polymeric materials are disposed of by incineration, the noxious gases are respiratory irritants and are toxic if inhaled over extended periods. Because burning materials often emit caustic and deadly gases, more deaths from fires are caused by smoke inhalation than by burns.

7 Glass

One of the oldest building materials, glass dates back 5000 years to our earliest recorded history. The first known producers of glass were the Egyptians; then production moved to Venice. The invention of the glass blower's pipe in the first century BC allowed glass to be heated to a higher temperature and then blown and shaped.

Glass formation

The conventional method of making glass is to cool a molten mixture of silicates so rapidly that it does not have time to crystallize. This method of formation is the reason why glass is known as an undercooled liquid. By using modern techniques, glass can be formed by a wide variety of methods, such as vapor condensation, precipitation from solution, cooling molten mixtures under high pressure, and high-energy radiation of crystals. Consequently, the definition of a glass has been modified by some scientists to describe its characteristic properties rather than its method of formation. In addition to the usual properties of solids, such as rigidity, hardness, and brittleness, these properties include transparency, high viscosity, and lack of an ordered large-scale crystalline structure.

Thus, the ASTM definition of glass is, "An inorganic mixture that has been melted and cooled to a rigid condition without crystallizing." Sheet glass is prepared by molten glass passing between water-cooled rollers as it cools. The surface roughness can be removed by grinding and polishing to make plate glass. However, this process has largely been replaced by the float glass process, in which the molten glass flows from the furnace so that it floats along the surface of molten tin.

Kinds of glass

The most common commercial use of glass is the manufacture of glass containers. Next in importance is glass used in windows for buildings and automobiles.

The two main types of industrial glass in common use are soda-lime (soft) glass and borosilicate glass. These are clear, hard, brittle amorphous solids. Soda-lime glass, the most common, consists of a basic mixture of sand, soda ash, and lime. The addition of small amounts of magnesium oxide reduces its tendency to crystallize, whereas a small amount of alumina increases its durability.

- *Plate glass:* Plate glass has the same composition as window glass (soda-lime silica) and differs from it only in the method of manufacture. The differences are first, the longer time of annealing (3 or 4 days), which eliminates the distortion and strain effects of rapid cooling, and second, the intensive grinding and polishing, which remove local imperfections and produce a bright, highly reflective finish.

- *Photosensitive glass:* By incorporating tiny crystals of chlorides of copper, silver, or gold into a molten glass, brief exposure to sunlight produces a temporarily darkened glass as the chloride is decomposed to form the metal and chlorine. However, unlike the latent image formed by light on silver halides suspended in gelatin in a photographic film, the chlorine atom has nothing to combine with chemically inside the glass. Therefore, the metal and the chlorine reform as a colorless halide when the glass is no longer exposed to light, making it suitable for indoor-outdoor dark glasses.

- *Safety glass:* When broken, glass has a tendency to form long cracks and large fragments with razor like edges, even when annealed (heat-treated to remove internal strains). Specially manufactured to avoid flying fragments, safety glass is made by introducing a wire or plastic composite or by tempering, thereby greatly reducing the size of the glass fragments.

- *Wired glass:* Wired glass is a type of safety glass with a wire framework designed to reduce the danger of flying glass. Although this glass is no stronger than the same glass without a wire mesh, the wire not only retards the extension of cracks but holds the fragments together to keep them from flying into long, jagged slivers.

- *Tempered glass:* Glass is tempered (toughened) by reheating it in its finished shape at 1202F (650°C) until it becomes soft. By cooling rapidly both sides of the glass at the same time with jets of air or by immersion (quenching) in a bath of oil, both sides of the glass are given a permanent compressive stress without stressing the still fluid interior of the glass. Tempered glass is reported to shatter spontaneously, but this is rare. Extensive research has provided only speculation as to the cause. Some of the more plausible reasons are the presence of impurities such as nickel sulfide "stones," faulty tempering, faulty glazing installations, accumulation of scratches, and excessive solar radiation stress. The safety features of tempered glass easily outweigh any problems. Since a mass of tempered glass chips falling from a height could be dangerous, precautions should be considered. For example, if used above ground level in double-glazed (insulating glass) windows, tempered glass might be limited to use as the inside panel. Or the windows could be recessed to provide a ledge to catch any falling glass. Or the ground directly below could be a landscaped area rather than a busy passageway.

- *Laminated glass:* Laminated glass is a type of safety glass. It consists of a thin sheet of plastic between two sheets of thin glass. The sheet of plastic needs to be a clear and tear-resistant film, such as polyvinyl butyral, which is then heat-sealed under pressure between the glass sheets to form a unit.

- *Insulated glass:* An insulated-glass window assembly consists of two sheets of glass separated by an air space and sealed together into a unit. The air between the two is confined in place by a sealant. The purpose of this air space is to reduce the flow of heat energy entering or leaving the building through the glass. By insulating the inner sheet of glass, this glass is kept from being chilled below the dew point of the air inside the building, thus preventing it from fogging over.

Fig. 12. Coral limestone steps, Viscaya, Miami.

Fig. 13. Marble wall, Vietnam Memorial, Washington, DC.
Maya Lin, Architect.

- *Solar-control glass:* Solar radiation passes through glass easily. Coming through windows, it overheats the interiors of buildings during the hot season of the year, causing an energy load on an air-conditioning system. During its multiple reflections around the interior of the building, this radiant energy is converted into thermal (heat) energy. This process is the familiar greenhouse effect. These are several methods being used to prevent this heat buildup and glare.

- *Tinted glass:* Tinting window glass is another way to insulate the interior of a building from solar radiation and glare. Glass can be body-tinted or surface-tinted. Gray and bronze body-tinted glass 1/4 in. (6 mm) thick lets through about half the incident solar energy, including the same fraction of the visible light. By contrast, the same thickness of body-tinted green glass lets through only about half the solar energy and about three-fourths of the visible light. There is little difference in the absorption of solar energy. The amount of visible light absorbed depends on the color.

- *Coated glass:* Another way to keep solar radiation from passing through the glass into the building is to use glass that is coated on one side with a film of indium tin oxide (ITO). The coatings are available as films deposited directly on the glass or as a plastic film which can be laminated to glass.

- *Structural glazing:* The concept of using adhesives in structural glazing originated when accelerated weatherometer tests of silicone sealants exposed to water and ultraviolet light predicted their long-term performance. These results encouraged some leading engineers and architects to look on silicone sealants as glazing adhesives that could tolerate full exposure to the environment. After using silicone adhesives successfully to cement glass store fronts and first-floor windows in place, its use was expanded to windows in high-rise buildings.

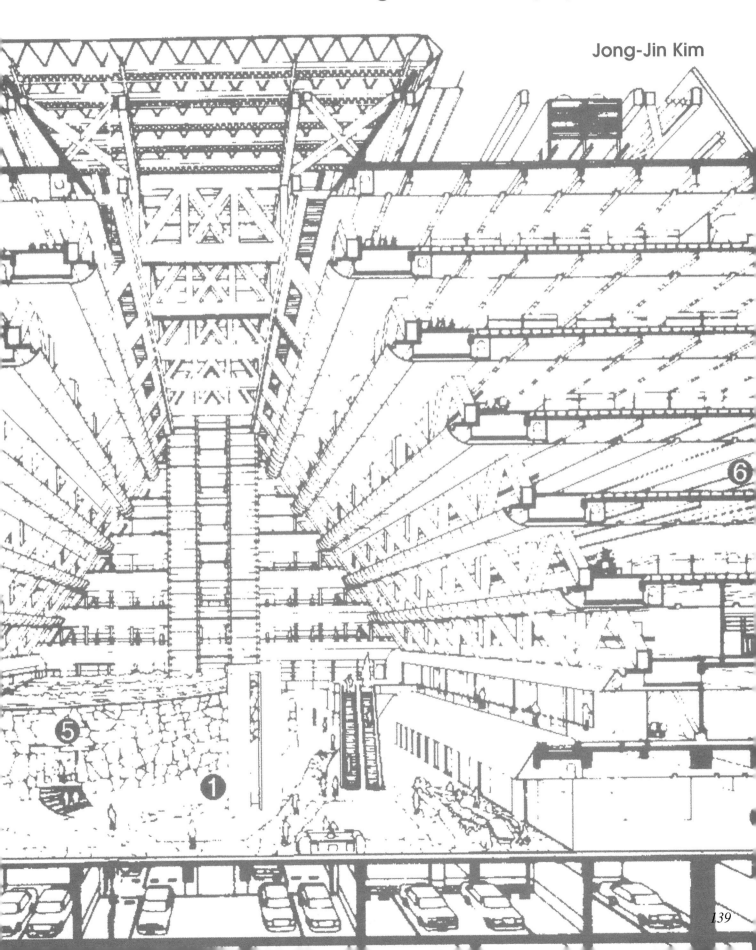

Jong-Jin Kim

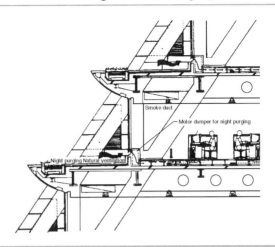

Summary: Intelligent building systems define an approach to building design emphasizing integration of electronic innovations and related technologies, including structure, systems, services and management. Design considerations include building infrastructure to accommodate telecommunication, daylighting, lighting, HVAC systems, conveying systems, and numerous options for security, fire safety, operations controls and monitoring.

Key words: Intelligent building, lighting, office automation, telecommunication infrastructure, workstation.

The concept of intelligent buildings has emerged from the increasing utilization of electronic technologies in building systems controls and operations. Advancing computer and electronic technologies have opened the way for innovations in a variety of building systems. A number of building products with automatic features have been developed. Electronic building systems and automated building components have been installed in recently constructed buildings. All buildings constructed today are likely to be equipped with some degree of advanced technologies that were not available in the past.

The spread of electronic telecommunication and office technologies has changed work-patterns in buildings. Modern work environments require diverse information services and accommodate emerging office technologies, including access to telecommunication networks and electronic office equipment, necessitating a new design approach that integrates electronic controls and capabilities and also provides flexibility in accommodating future expansion and office equipment.

Although technology is a primary agent for these changes, the capacity for automation and intelligence system responses in buildings cannot be achieved solely by the application of technologies. Technology in the end is only as useful as the choices it provides for people, either to be free of mundane operational tasks or to offer options to adapt the built environment to changing needs. Other factors that play key roles including futures-oriented programming, options in functional space organization, and the integration of building and environmental control technologies that can either be automated and/or, equally important, controlled by occupants. Designers need to rethink the way buildings are programmed and designed with a clearly defined options for the long-term adaptations, changes in technology, and changes in use patterns that will result. Technological improvements thus complement attention to ergonomic workstations, and individual control of thermal, luminous and acoustic qualities.

According to the definition proposed by the former Intelligent Building Institute, an "intelligent building" is:

• one that provides a productive and cost-effective environment through optimization of its four basic elements—structure, systems, services and management—and the interrelationships between them. Intelligent buildings help business owners, property managers and occupants realize their goals in the areas of cost, comfort, convenience, safety, long-term flexibility and marketability.

This performance-based definition does not specify or characterize the technical and design features that qualify buildings as intelligent buildings. No threshold between 'intelligent buildings' and 'conventional buildings' is defined. This article is based on the premise that intelligence in buildings is achieved through the rational design of both a building and its constituent systems to meet its life cycle missions. An intelligent building is designed to be compatible with its particular cultural, climatic, and technological contexts. Building users in different regions or cultures will require different work environments. Design solutions suitable in one region may not be directly applicable to other regions or countries.

While designing for future expansion and flexibility is important, the over-design of the building infrastructure or systems for all conceivable options is in most cases not economically feasible. Sophisticated and technically complex building systems are not necessarily effective in increasing occupant productivity or well-being, per se. Overly complex systems not fully tried and tested are more likely to experience system breakdowns and maintenance concerns. In addition, highly automated systems may be inconvenient for building users and operators not familiar with these systems. For these reasons, automation and the application of electronic technologies do not necessarily equate to intelligence in buildings. The principal goals of intelligent building systems are to:

• Increase occupant well-being and productivity.
• Achieve cost-efficiency by optimizing initial construction costs and long-term operation and maintenance costs.
• Provide flexibility for accommodating future technological changes.

To achieve these goals, the design of intelligent buildings systems requires a high degree of coordination between project team members from the early stages of the design process. The building owner, the architect, and the technical experts should have a common understanding of the building's immediate and long-term missions (National Research Council 1988). Technical expertise include structure, HVAC, lighting, interior design, controls engineering, office automa-

Author: Jong-Jin Kim, Ph.D.

References: BICSI. 1995. *Telecommunications Distribution Methods Manual*, Vols. 1 and 2. Tampa, FL: Building Industry Consulting Services International.

Electronic Industries Association. 1990. *EIA/TIA Standard-569: Commercial Building Standard for Telecommunications Pathways and Spaces.* Washington, DC: Electronic Industry Association.

National Research Council. 1988. *Electronically Enhanced Office Buildings. Publication PB98107320.* Washington DC: National Technical Information Service, U.S. Department of Commerce.

tion, building commissioning and telecommunication specialists. In particular, telecommunication system experts play a central role in architectural and system design decision making processes. Technical team integration at the early stages of the design process is thus essential to coordinate whole system design, construction and building management approaches that meet the needs of owners, operators and occupants during the building's life cycle. In addition to the generic human, physical, and external factors that encompass all building design, intelligent systems design requires consideration of the following aspects:

- future-oriented telecommunication infrastructure
- office automation
- intelligent card systems
- energy efficient thermal systems
- facilities to improve occupant amenity
- building commissioning, operation and management systems

Telecommunication systems

Prior to the emergence of electronic communication technologies, the primary means of communication was through telephones. Because wiring required to transmit voice signals was relatively simple, building facilities and communication infrastructure necessary to accommodate communication equipment and cables were relatively insignificant in terms of building design and construction. As inter- and intra-building communications have become significant activities for all building types, but especially in offices, schools, and even residential buildings, the volume and the types of communication signals have increased. In addition to voice signals, telecommunication systems now transmit a variety of digital data and building control signals. Computers are replacing telephones as the primary mode of communication. With the expanding use of multimedia technologies and the Internet, data communications containing digital texts and images are becoming the dominant component of information communications.

Telecommunication networks are the neurological system of intelligent buildings. They serve as channels for transporting voice and data, as well as for controlling environmental, security, audio-visual, sensing, alarms, and paging systems. These functions can be easily expanded to monitor and detect air-quality, structural and related building failure indices. Transmitting a large volume of multimedia digital data or signals necessitates a high transmission speed, protection from external signal noises, and security in telecommunication systems. From the design standpoint, flexibility for future expansion and spatial arrangements, fire safety, water protection, and signal noise reduction are important factors in the design of the building telecommunication infrastructure.

Flexibility for Future Expansion: As the use of telecommunication systems expands, the number of cables, the volume of equipment, and the pathway spaces necessary to accommodate these systems will increase. Providing additional spaces at the initial design stages to install future wiring or equipment will reduce the time and cost of expanding the telecommunication infrastructure in the future. When frequent changes in space use and workstation layouts are expected, it is economical in terms of life cycle costs to provide horizontal pathways that allow flexible access to telecommunication networks. Although the functional necessity and the economic feasibility of access floors are still in debate, several alternative methods for providing universal telecommunication access are available. Judicious decisions should be made with respect to the telecommunication pathways at the early stages of building design, taking into account short-term and long-term space use and occupancy patterns, initial building budgets, and durability and maintenance of telecommunication cables.

Fire Safety: It is important to consider prevention, detection, suppression, and containment strategies in the design of fire protection for telecommunication systems. Telecommunication cables coated with fire protective chemical materials have a high flash point temperature. However, once ignited, they produce extremely toxic gases. Therefore, telecommunication equipment rooms must be equipped with fire protection systems. When telecommunication pathways penetrate the fire-zone perimeter, the integrity of a fire-rated barrier is disrupted. Any holes created by penetrations of telecommunication pathways through fire barriers must be sealed by fire-stops. A variety of fire-stop materials are available, such as putty, caulk, fiber wool, and fire-stop pillows to seal irregular openings. For standard modular openings, pre-manufactured elastomeric components shaped to fit around standard cables, conduits, and tubes are also available. Elastomeric fire-stops are more durable than irregular fire-stops. They provide reliable pressure and environmental sealing, resistance to shock and vibration, and flexibility for reconfiguration.

Water Protection: In order to prevent damage to network connections, telecommunication cables and equipment should be protected from water. To ensure adequate protection, several factors should be considered with respect to the water-proofing of telecommunication spaces and pathways. Cables and other connection devices in horizontal pathways should be raised above the floor surface using cable trays or shelves. The doors to telecommunication equipment rooms and closets should have sills to prevent the possible infiltration of water from adjacent floors. The fire-stops or other materials for fixing cable to floors should be splayed so that they do not collect water.

Signal Noise Reduction: A major contributors of noise in telecommunication wiring systems is electromagnetic interference from electrical power lines. To reduce this interference, it is necessary to separate telecommunication cables and equipment from electrical power lines. The minimum separation distance depends on the type of cable shielding and the voltage of electrical power lines. The dimensions of electrical equipment and pathways should conform to the separation distances recommended by the telecommunication industry (Electronic Industry Association 1990).

Telecommunication spaces and pathways

The spaces and pathways for housing telecommunication equipment and cables constitute the telecommunication infrastructure. This infrastructure encompasses a number of components required for networking telecommunication cables between buildings, floors, and telecommunication closets and work areas, and generally consists of the following facilities (BICSI 1995):

- entrance facilities
- equipment rooms
- telecommunication closets
- backbone pathways
- horizontal pathways

Entrance Facilities: The entrance facilities refer to the link between building interior and exterior telecommunication networks that occurs through the exterior building envelope, and continues to the entrance room or space. Telecommunication signals typically enter a building through the wall below grade from an underground tunnel. However, airborne signals enter the building through antennae installed on top of the building. In positioning these antennae, line-of-sight and signal interference should be taken into account.

Equipment Room: The equipment room provides a space for the termination of the telecommunication network entrance from a building exterior to interior, cross-connections between inter-building and intra-building backbone cables, and private board exchange (PBX) equipment. The dimensions and the minimum space requirements for the equipment room are generally proportional to the gross floor area of the building. The recommended equipment room floor area is shown in Table 1.

Table 1. Equipment room floor area

Workstations	Area ft²	(m²)
Up to 100	150	(13.9)
101 – 400	400	(37.1)
401 – 800	800	(79.2)
801 – 1200	1200	(111.3)

Telecommunication Closets: Telecommunication closets are located on each floor, providing cross-connections between vertical and horizontal distribution pathways. A minimum of one closet is required for every 10,000 square feet (929 sq. meters) of floor area. The maximum length of the horizontal distribution pathways, the distance between the closet and a workstation, should not exceed 300 feet (91.4 meters). This facilitates higher communication speeds and reduces cable maintenance concerns. For a building with a large floor area, it is advantageous to distribute the closets in several zones, with a closet being located centrally within the zone it serves. To shorten the vertical distance between the closets, it is preferable to stack the closets one above another. The recommended closet size is shown in Table 2.

Table 2. Telecommunication closet size

Serving Area ft² m²	Closet Dimensions ft	(m)
10,000	10 x 11	(3.04 x 3.35)
8,000	10 x 9	(3.04 x 2.74)
5,000	10 x 7	(3.04 x 2.13)

Backbone Pathways: Backbone pathways provide the main telecommunication links between buildings (inter-building pathways) or within buildings (intra-building pathways), and the connections between telecommunication closets. When telecommunication closets are stacked one above another, the intra-building backbone pathways are vertical. However, in most buildings, some portions of the backbone pathway are horizontal, especially those between the telecommunication equipment room and closets. Vertical backbone pathways pass through floor openings within the telecommunication closets. These openings are generally rectangular or circular, and are surrounded by slot or sleeve walls. After the cables are installed, the floor openings must be sealed with fire-stops. When 4 inch (10.2 cm.) conduits are used, one sleeve or conduit for every 50,000 square feet (4,645 square meters) of usable floor area is recommended. In addition, two spares should be provided for a minimum total of three sleeves or conduits. For a building where a high level of telecommunication is expected, additional sleeves or slots are necessary. Backbone pathway slots and sleeves are inexpensive to install, and providing additional ones during the initial construction phase will avoid costly installations in the future.

Horizontal Pathways: Horizontal pathways refer to the pathways that house the cables between telecommunication closets and work area outlets. Because of their close relationships to the building structure and space organization, the design of horizontal pathways are the single most important aspect of telecommunication infrastructure design. The type of horizontal pathways selected has a significant impact on the floor-to-floor height of the building. The layout of the horizontal pathways determines user accessibility to the telecommunication networks, which in turn affects the workstation layout. Horizontal pathways should be designed considering the following factors:

- workstation layouts
- floor-to-floor heights
- floor and ceiling structural systems
- HVAC air-supply systems
- construction and maintenance costs

In conventional buildings, horizontal pathways have been typically provided in the ceiling plenums, and the final cable links to the workstations occur through walls. Locating telecommunication outlets on walls surfaces limits their accessibility and the options for workstation layouts. In large open floor plans, utility columns or partitions can provide pathways from the ceiling to the workstations. Although economical, the ceiling-based horizontal pathways have limitations in meeting the needs of flexible telecommunication access. In addition, utility columns are often visually undesirable in large open office plans. The recent trend is to provide horizontal pathways under the floor. In selecting a horizontal pathway system, a variety of factors should be considered, including initial cost, maintenance, floor structure, work patterns, and aesthetic compatibility. Several methods of installing under-floor horizontal pathways are available.

- conduits
- poke-throughs
- under-carpet units
- under-floor ducts
- cellular floors
- access floors

Access floors

Access floors are the most costly but allow most flexibility. They also provide a space in which various building services can be placed, including electrical wiring, LANs, and air supply (Fig. 1). The height

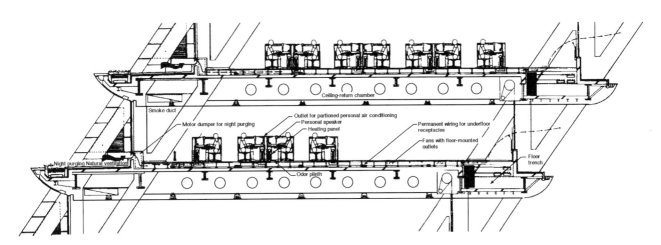

Fig. 1. Access floors in the Panasonic Building. Tokyo. 1992. Nikken Sekkei.

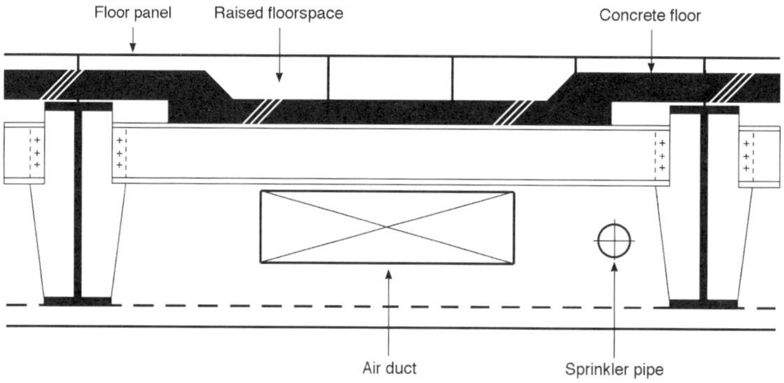

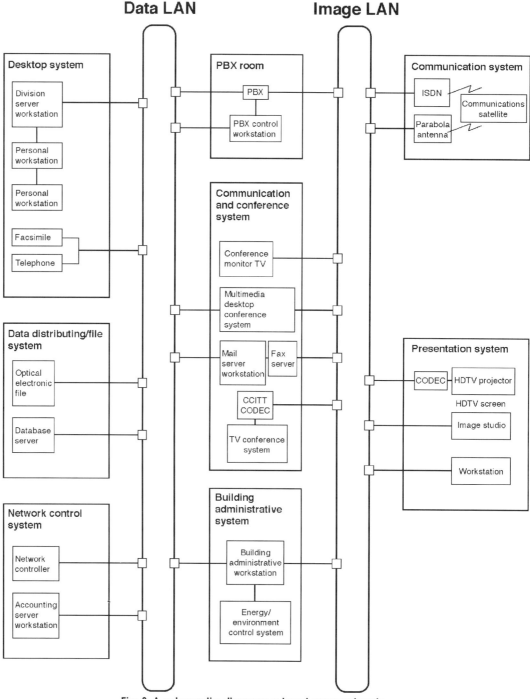

Fig. 2. Structural details of an access floor

Fig. 3. A schematic diagram a local area network

of access floors varies from 2 to 24 inches (5.1 cm to 61 cm) depending on the functions they serve. When they are designed mainly for housing electrical wires, telephone lines, and local area networks, a minimal height of 2 inches is required. When conditioned air is supplied through an access floor, a height of up to 12 inches (30.5 cm) or more is necessary to reduce friction between air and floor surfaces. The height of an access floor can vary within its span. This can occur when the concrete slab between major structural beams (girders) is lowered to create a higher space for the access floor (Fig. 2). This type of structural design reduces the building height and thus construction costs. Access floors are typically laid out in a grid of 18 inch (47.7 cm) square floor panels, four of which compose a 3 foot (91.4 cm) service module. This module (in customary U.S. units) is common in intelligent buildings, and contains a floor-mounted air supply unit, an under-floor receptacle for electrical wiring, and local area networks.

Local area networks

Local Area Networks (LANs) based on fiber-optic cables are the backbone of intelligent buildings. These networks allow for the transfer of electronic signals/data between a variety of building subsystems, including computer, telecommunication, environmental control, accounting, disaster prevention, and security systems (Fig. 3). More than one local area network is installed in a building, each dedicated to a particular type of signal.

Audiovisual systems

Large screen television and audiovisual systems are common features in the lecture halls, large conference rooms, and meeting rooms of intelligent buildings. To receive radio and TV signals from outside, office buildings are frequently equipped with rooftop aerial antennae and satellite communication equipment. When a building is under the electronic shadow of adjacent obstructions, devices for relaying electronic signals are installed. Teleconferencing systems are not yet widely used in office buildings. However, with cost reductions and mass pro-duction, their installation will increase exponentially in the near future. The rapid advance of technologies that support teleconferencing (audio conferencing) systems will further increase the use of these systems. Teleconferencing systems typically consist of several individual speakers for participants, pencil pad digitizers, two video cameras, and TV monitors. The cameras move automatically, and are directed to a person who speaks by voice recognition technology. One TV monitor displays a speaker and the other displays input signals written or drawn on a key pad, allowing the participants to communicate graphically.

Intelligent cards

Intelligent cards (ICs) carried by each individual visiting and/or occupying a building play a major role in building security systems. With intelligent cards, all occupant movements within a building can be traced from the initial entry to the building in the morning to the final exit in the evening. In addition to the security function, these cards serve multiple purposes, such as access keys, environmental control devices, cash and credit cards, banking cards, and employee identification cards. Intelligent cards of various types are being used in many office buildings, and their use for all purposes will obviously be extended to multiple applications in the future. As a function of building design and operation, intelligent cards are integrated with other building subsystems, such as vertical transportation, lighting, environmental control and computing systems. Thus, when an employee enters a main entrance lobby using an intelligent card, the central building administration system sends an elevator to the lobby. In times or building areas of low occupancy, the intelligent card sends instructions to turn on the lights and the air distribution unit. In the evening, intelligent cards help to determine whether a space is occupied, and if it is unoccupied, the environmental systems are turned off automatically. In addition, intelligent cards are used in cash-free buildings for purchases within the building's shops and cafeterias, deposits and withdrawals of money, and automatic payroll deposits.

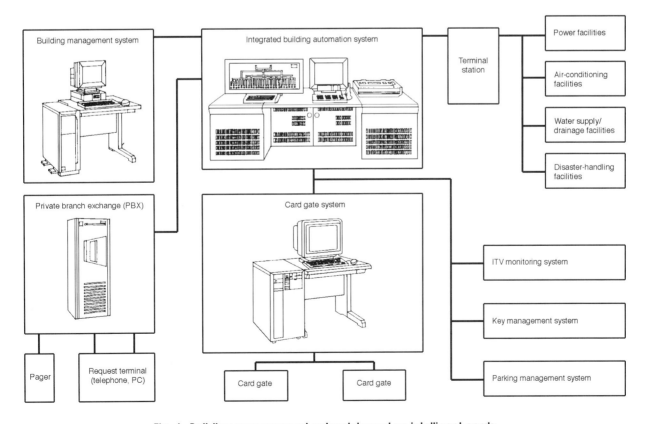

Fig. 4. Building management network based on intelligent cards

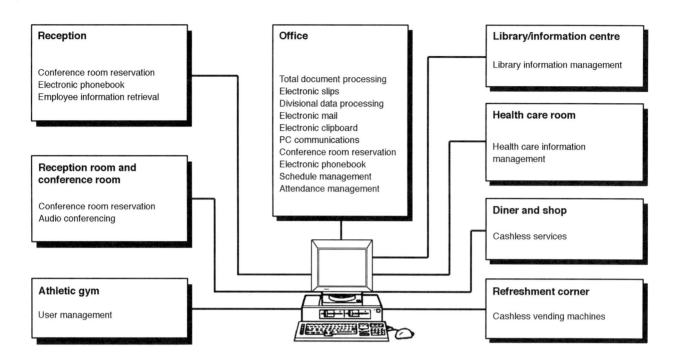

Fig. 5. Office automation network

Office automation

Office automation is geared towards improving operational efficiency and employee productivity by utilizing LANs and computers in information processing, databases, and communications. Office automation systems can be categorized into two groups: general office automation systems designed for the typical business operations of office buildings, and applied office automation systems customized for the specific demands of any trade or business building, such as schools, shops, hotels, and government buildings. Key features of office automation systems include:

- Communications: electronic mail, electronic bulletin boards, electronic newspapers, audiovisual conferencing;

- Databases: telephone directories, information libraries;

- Office Administration: room reservation, schedule management, attendance management, healthcare information management, employee information retrieval, divisional data processing, cashless systems;

- Office Production: document processing and transfer, personnel file cabinets, appointments.

Physical integration of office automation systems is accomplished via local area networks. The types and features of office automation systems depend on the intended use of the building. Owner-occupied buildings require highly customized office automation systems that meet current and future office requirements. For tenant office buildings, providing an infrastructure that can meet basic needs is a first priority. Office automation systems should be designed considering the spatial and temporal office use patterns. When a workstation is shared by many persons, automation systems allow for the secure and private access of a particular user's personal electronic documents and computing environment.

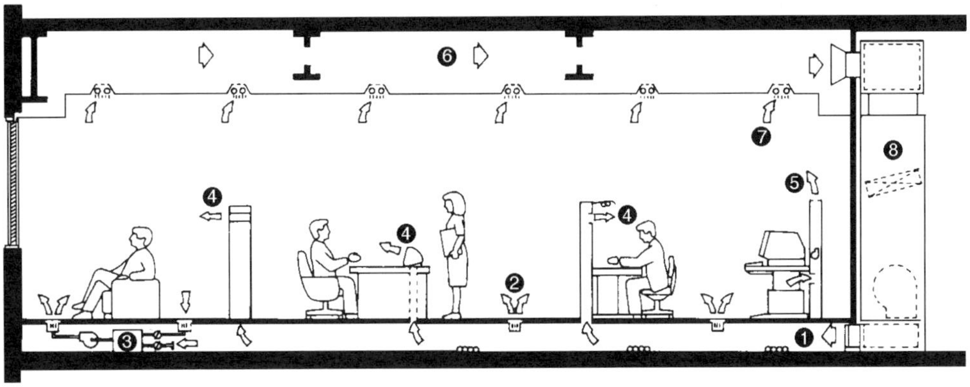

① Air supply through raised floor **②** Floor air supply fan **③** Underfloor fan coil unit
④ Individual environmental control modules **⑤** Exhaust fan for protecting internal heat gain diffusion
⑥ Return air plenum **⑦** Air return through lighting fixture **⑧** Low-noise air-handling unit

Fig. 6. Floor supply and ceiling return supply system

Thermal comfort systems
Intelligent office buildings generally are more energy intensive than
office buildings constructed in the past, the primary reason being that
they are equipped with more electronic appliances, including computers, fax machines, televisions, and other building automation facilities. Electrical equipment for office automation not only consumes
electric energy, but also increases the cooling load on HVAC equipment, although improvements in technology improve on this with
successive models. In any case, the energy intensiveness of intelligent buildings presents a challenge to building designers. Existing
buildings that are upgraded with highly intensive modern telecommunications may also require increased mechanical system and cooling capacity. The energy implications of various components of intelligent buildings must thus be critically reviewed to find design and
technological solutions that make them more energy efficient. Intelligent HVAC controls, able to anticipate and rapidly respond to changes
in occupancy and weather conditions, provide the means to reduce
the energy requirements while increasing the electronic capacity of
the modern workplace.

Floor-Mounted Air Supply Units: Air supply through access floors is
typically accomplished without ducts. In such cases, the entire access
floor chamber functions as the supply ducts of a conventional HVAC
system. Pressurizing the entire access floor requires a great deal of
fan power, and therefore significantly increases energy consumption.
In order to make supply air flow efficiently without pressurizing the
entire access floor chamber, floor-mounted air supply units are installed beneath the floor surfaces. A floor-mounted air supply unit is
basically a variable speed fan housed in a can. The top cover of the
unit is the air diffuser grill. The direction and volume of supply air
can be varied by either changing the fan speed or adjusting the grill
opening size (Fig. 6).

Floor Supply and Ceiling Return Systems: Floor air supply systems have advantages over the ceiling air supply systems of conventional HVAC distribution systems for both heating and cooling modes. For the winter heating mode, warm air can be directly supplied to human bodies before being exhausted to return ducts in the ceiling. This avoids the short-circuiting of warm supply air directly to return ducts that occurs in many conventional air distribution systems. It has the further advantage of supplying fresh air at the occupant zone rather than at the ceiling where likelihood of accumulated dust and pollutants is higher. For the summer cooling mode, cool heavier air stays in the lower portion of an interior space, creating a cool air zone near occupants while pushing warm air upward toward the ceiling. This again avoids the short-circuiting of supply air. A disadvantage of floor air supply systems is the increased possibility of exposing occupants to temperatures that are cooler in summer or warmer in the winter (depending on set-point temperatures of the delivery air supply). Occupants are also subject to higher speeds of air movement creating potential draught concerns. Therefore, it is important to locate the floor-mounted air supply units at a sufficient distance away from occupants. Allowing occupants to modify the speed and the direction of supply air is beneficial in increasing individual thermal comfort.

Decentralized Environmental Control Systems: A general trend is the decentralization of environmental systems, with many smaller equipment units dispersed in strategic locations throughout the building. Decentralized environmental systems have many advantages over centralized systems. In case of a breakdown, decentralized systems affect only a small area of the building. Because breakdowns affect smaller areas and equipment, the replacement cost is less. By distributing mechanical equipment in many locations, the length of horizontal services (e.g. ducts and electrical wiring) can be shortened and duct sizes reduced, thus saving required clearance dimensions. Decentralized systems allow for greater flexibility of response to varying loads during the course of a day and a year. In order to fully utilize a decentralized control system, the control zone should be further individualized so that one occupant can feel free to adjust air temperature, lighting levels, and volume of ventilation without being concerned about affecting other occupants' thermal well-being.

Furniture-Integrated Control Systems: Furniture-integrated environmental control systems allow for highly individualized environmental control. They provide occupants with full control of the ventilation, air temperature and lighting level within their individual task areas. The supply air is typically brought up through access floors and supplied to two outlets on the partition wall, one under the desk and the other above. The volume of the air supply can be adjusted by an electronic controller to a particular setting. Thermostats can be integrated with a telephone on a user's desk. These thermostats measure air temperature within each workstation. The conditioned air supply to each workstation can be controlled by the telephone. In addition, the speed of ventilation from the supply outlets in furniture-integrated systems can be made variable to mimic natural wind cycles.

Building Energy Management: In addition to local control systems, a centralized energy and building management system is typically installed in large modern buildings. A computerized building management system monitors and controls security, fire safety, lighting, HVAC systems, room temperatures, vertical transportation, and other building operations. A centralized energy management system plays a major role in monitoring energy consumption patterns and provides various data useful to facility managers in making operational decisions. Because office buildings are subject to peak load charges in determining their electricity rates, building owners must carefully control

and manipulation electric energy consumption. This is required so that the peak load permissible by the contract with the utility company is not exceeded and penalty charges avoided. Typical strategies for controlling electricity consumption include switching the cooling equipment from electric chillers to gas-powered absorption ones, turning off non-essential operations (that is, lighting and air distributions), and changing thermostat set points.

Thermal Storages: As a way of reducing peak loads, more buildings are being equipped with thermal storage for both heating and cooling efficiency. Many new office buildings utilize ice-source thermal storage, refrigerated during off-peak and typically evening hours and available for cooling in the following days. Ice storage systems have the advantage of being able to store more energy per unit of volume than water-source storage systems, utilizing the energy represented in the latent heat of fusion (heat represented in the change of phase of water to ice). While storage systems are most often located in below ground containers due to weight, by locating the thermal storage on the mechanical floor at the top of the building, the natural circulation of refrigerants to space air-conditioning systems can be utilized. The thermal storage tanks can also function as counter weights in the earthquake resistance system. In this case, the flexible connections supporting the storage tanks dampen the sway of the building when horizontal forces are applied during earthquakes.

Lighting systems
Innovations in lighting systems is moving towards the use of variable lighting level and occupancy zone options with individual controls adjustable to the specific needs of a work environment. conventional buildings, small individual offices typically have an individual control switch. Lighting systems of large open offices shared by many employees are controlled by a centralized switch that covers a large floor area, with the capability to adjust to variations in daylighting and occupancy.

Automatic Control: The control hardware of lighting systems is increasingly automated. Magnetic ballasts are being replaced by electronic ballasts, which allow for fluorescent lamps to be dimmed. Remote light controllers are being developed to take the place of manual switches. In these cases, each lighting zone of a large office building has a sensor mounted on the ceiling, and by using a remote controller, a lighting system can be turned on and off. The automatic control of lighting systems is also being accomplished by infrared human occupancy sensors, and by door locks that function as switches for lighting systems. Door lock switches are presently used in airplane restrooms. The incorporation of intelligent cards allows for the automatic control of the lighting system of a space or a group of spaces.

Lighting System Design: In many cases, the electric lighting systems of office buildings consist of florescent lamps arranged in a 5 foot (1.5 meter) square grid module. Within this module, other building services, such as supply air diffusers, return air inlets, sprinklers, smoke detectors, and other ceiling-mounted sensors are integrated. In addition, the use of electronically controlled lighting systems is increasing. Many buildings have ceiling-mounted sensors that control lighting systems. In these systems, each lighting zone has a sensor that detects control signals from a remote control. Uniform lighting systems are commonly used in office buildings, and the importance of non-uniform lighting design is not widely recognized. Along with the trend of individualized partitioned offices and increased design for low-reflective CRT environments, low-level ambient indirect lighting systems augmented by task lighting are increasingly applied in office buildings.

Daylighting systems

Along with the development of electronic ballasts, the daylighting has been explored to reduce electric energy consumption. Advances have been made in control sensors, automatic shading devices, and glazing materials for windows and skylights. Building typological studies have been conducted to find building forms and elements that most effectively bring daylight into building interiors. Some of these elements include atria, courtyards, light-shelves, and light-pipes. In the Panasonic Building, the entire building volume is organized on two sides around a large atrium at the center (Fig. 7).

In many buildings, automated interior shading devices (venetian blinds) controlled by outdoor sensors or interior remote controllers are being installed. Some buildings have automated shading devices, with or without daylight sensors, installed only in special rooms. The automatic adjustment of shading positions can be provided in two directions: vertical (up and down) movement, and rotation of blind angles. Although the shading device movements of some buildings are programmed to respond to outdoor climatic conditions using daylight sensors, the method for controlling shading devices needs to take into account window locations, window orientation, outdoor temperature, and solar radiation levels.

Fiber-Optic Application in Daylighting: The daylighting of the perimeter zones of office buildings can be achieved with windows. However, without special reflecting devices, such as venetian blinds and light shelves, only a limited depth of the perimeter zones can be illuminated by daylight which may also be considered excessive without light contöol options. New technologies are being developed, including fiber-optic techniques. Light pipes finished with highly reflective surfaces are also being explored.

Occupant amenity

Increasing occupant well-being and productivity is the most important objective of intelligent buildings. In buildings that incorporate occupant amenity as a design concept, all aspects of the building design and operation are affected, and may range from outdoor landscaping to building environmental systems to interior furniture design. Resulting spaces and facilities for increasing occupant comfort include outdoor gardens, employee lounges, refreshment rooms, guest rooms, sporting rooms and facilities, hygienic restrooms and ergonomic furniture systems. Air quality enhancements are being researched. Low levels of aroma are believed to enhance occupants sense of well being and worker productivity. Most critical in the increasing

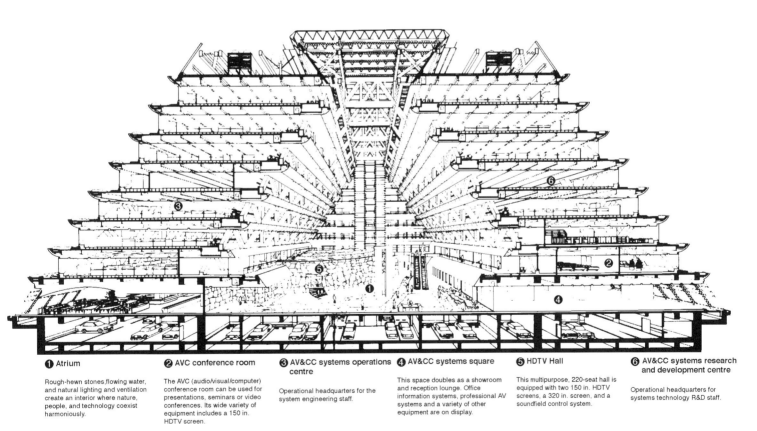

❶ Atrium

Rough-hewn stones,flowing water, and natural lighting and ventilation create an interior where nature, people, and technology coexist harmoniously.

❷ AVC conference room

The AVC (audio/visual/computer) conference room can be used for presentations, seminars or video conferences. Its wide variety of equipment includes a 150 in. HDTV screen.

❸ AV&CC systems operations centre

Operational headquarters for the system engineering staff.

❹ AV&CC systems square

This space doubles as a showroom and reception lounge. Office information systems, professional AV systems and a variety of other equipment are on display.

❺ HDTV Hall

This multipurpose, 220-seat hall is equipped with two 150 in. HDTV screens, a 320 in. screen, and a soundfield control system.

❻ AV&CC systems research and development centre

Operational headquarters for systems technology R&D staff.

Fig. 7. A cross-section of the Panasonic Building. Tokyo. 1992. Nikken Sekkei.

technologically driven environment are individual choices and options that can be made available to affect the conditions in which occupants feel most comfortable and in effective control of their environmental conditions.

Environmental conservation

A variety of environmental conservation strategies are being implemented in new buildings that include water conservation through the recycling of domestic gray water, the collection of rainwater, the integration of smaller toilet tanks with a sink, and the utilization of infrared sensing devices in plumbing fixtures. In many buildings, these systems are made part of "indoor wetlands" or nearby bioswales that incorporate water cleaning in outdoor gardens that serve as community facilities for residents and as sanctuaries for wildlife. The creation of natural settings within the building through elements such as atria increases the psychological well-being of occupants, the luminous quality of interior spaces, and the energy efficiency of the building. In addition to vegetation, other elements used to create natural indoor settings in public buildings include water fountains, creeks, natural stone finishes, and small aquariums, typically illuminated by daylight to enhance their natural features and aesthetic quality. Recycling systems are incorporated into buildings to make it easy and obvious for building occupants to recycle waste products, including source separation on each floor of a building, vertical collection chutes and a clear and functional process of waste reduction and recovery. Recycled building materials are used in both residential and commercial buildings. Such features can be made obvious as part of environmental education.

End note

Since the early 1980s, significant technological advances have been made in intelligent buildings rapidly being developed and implemented in building design and construction. The increased sophistication of electronic controls offers new opportunities by which buildings can perform better. At the same time, the increasing technological complexity requires greater integration in design and greater vigilance in building commissioning and monitoring to assure that buildings are actually performing and maintained as designed. Issues pertaining to intelligent building technologies need continued research and development. These include studies of the relationship between occupant choice and well-being, air-quality provided by natural ventilation and mechanical systems, and the interaction between the technological workplace environment and the physical environment. New office planning prototypes need to be developed so as to reflect changing office technologies, work patterns, and work environments expected in the future. In recent years, the demand for new office buildings has shrunk in the U.S. and other advanced countries. Under these circumstances, there is increasing pressure to make intelligent buildings more economically viable. In addition, the impact of the environmental movement is evident in the entire building sector. An increasingly important attribute of intelligent building systems design will thus be environmental conservation.◗

Organizations involved with Intelligent Building Systems

Building Industry Consulting Services International
10500 University Center Drive, Suite 100
Tampa, FL 33612-6415

Telecommunications Industry Association
2500 Wilson Boulevard
Arlington, VA 22201

Standards Processing Coordinators
Federal Information Processing Standards
National Institute of Standards and Technology
Gaithersburg, MD 20899

Institute of Electrical and Electronic Engineers
345 East 47th Street
New York, NY 10017

National Research Council
2102 Constitution Avenue, NW
Washington, DC 20418

Smart House
400 Prince George's Boulevard
Upper Marlboro, MD 20772-8731

12
Design of atriums for people and plants

Donald Watson

Summary: Atriums offer many energy design opportunities, depending upon climatic resources, to provide natural heating, cooling, lighting and plants. It is necessary to establish a clear design goals, outlined in this article by an overview of solar heating, natural cooling and daylighting choices. Provisions for healthy planting and indoor gardens can also be combined with atrium design to benefit both plants and people.

Key words: atrium, daylighting, designing for plants, horticulture, microclimate, natural cooling, solar heating.

New Canaan Nature Center Solar Wintergarden, New Canaan, CT
Buchanan/Watson Architects 1984

The atrium concept of climate-control has been used throughout the history of architecture and in indigenous building in all climates of the globe. Suggested by its Latin meaning as "heart" or an open courtyard of a Roman house, the term atrium as used today is a protected courtyard or glazed wintergarden placed within a building. Modern atrium design incorporates many architectural elements—wall enclosures, sun-oriented openings, shading and ventilation devices, and subtle means of modifying temperature and humidity—suggested by examples that derive from the courtyard designs of Roman, early Christian, and Islamic building and 19th-Century greenhouses and glass-covered arcades of Great Britain and France.

Atriums offer many energy design opportunities: first, comfort is achieved by gradual transition from outside climate to building interior; second, designed properly, protected spaces and buffer zones create natural and free flowing energy by reducing or by eliminating the need to otherwise heat, cool, or light building interiors. Depending on climatic resources and building use, the emphasis in atrium design has to be balanced between occupancy and comfort criteria and the relative need for heating, cooling, and/or lighting.

How the atrium can work as an energy-efficient modifier of climate is best seen by examining separately its potential for natural heating, cooling, and lighting. The first and most important step is to establish a clear set of energy design goals appropriate to the specific atrium design. The resulting solution will depend upon its program (whether for circulation only or for longer term and sedentary human comfort and/or for plant propagation and horticultural display) and the resulting environmental control requirements.

Solar heating
If heating efficiency alone is the primary energy design goal of the atrium, the following design principles should be paramount:

H1. To maximize winter solar heat gain, orient the atrium aperture (openings and glazing) to the equator. If possible, the glazing should be vertical or sloped not lower than a tilt angle equal to the local latitude.

H2. For heat storage and radiant distribution, place interior masonry directly in the path of the winter sun. This is most useful if the heated wall or floor surface will in turn directly radiate to building occupants.

H3. To prevent excessive nighttime heat loss, consider an insulating system for the glazing, such as insulating curtains or high performance multi-layered window systems.

H4. To recover the heat that rises by natural convection to the top of the atrium, place a return air duct high in the space, possibly augmenting its temperature by placing it directly in the sun. Heat recovery can be accomplished if the warm air is redistributed either to the lower area of the atrium (a ceiling fan) or redirected (and cleaned) to the mechanical system, or through a heat exchanger if the air must be exhausted for health and air-quality reasons.

Because a large air volume must be heated, an atrium is not an efficient solar collector per se. But the high volume helps to make an overheated space acceptable, especially if the warmest air rises to the top. If the atrium is surrounded by building on all sides, direct winter sun is difficult if not impossible to capture except at the top of the skylight enclosure. However, by facing a large skylight and/or window opening towards the equator, direct winter solar heating becomes entirely feasible.

In cool climates, an atrium used as a solar heat collector would require as much winter sunlight as possible. In overbright conditions, dark finishes on surfaces where the sun strikes will help reduce glare and also to store heat. On surfaces not in direct sun, light finishes may be best to reflect light, especially welcomed under cloudy conditions. In most locations and uses, glass should be completely shaded from the summer sun. Although not practical for large atriums, in some applications greenhouse-type movable insulation might be considered to reduce nighttime heat loss.

Natural cooling
Several guidelines related to the use of an atrium design as an intermediary or buffer zone apply to both heating and cooling. If an unconditioned atrium is located in a building interior, the heat loss is from the warmer surrounding spaces into the atrium. In buildings with large internal gains due to occupants, lighting, and machines, the atrium may require cooling throughout the year. If one were to design exclusively for cooling, the following principles would predominate:

C1. To minimize solar gain, provide shade for the summer sun. According to the particular building-use, the local climate and the resulting balance point (the outside temperature below which heating is required), the "overheated" season when sun shading is needed may extend well into the autumn months. While fixed shading devices suffice for much of the summer period, movable shading is the only exact means by which to match the seasonal shading requirements at all times. In buildings in warm climates, sunshading may be needed throughout the year.

Author: Donald Watson, FAIA

References: Architectural Graphic Standards (Ninth edition) "Atriums."

Watson, Donald 1982. "The Energy Within the Space Within." *Progressive Architecture,* July 1982. [out of print].

C2. Use the atrium as an air plenum in the mechanical system of the building. The great advantage is one of economy, but heat recovery options (discussed above) and ventilation become most effective when the natural air flow in the atrium is in the same direction and integrated with the mechanical system.

C3. To facilitate natural ventilation, create a vertical "chimney" effect by placing ventilating outlets high (preferably in the free-flow air stream well above the roof) and by providing cool "replacement air" inlets at the atrium bottom, with attention that the airstream is clean, that is, free of car exhaust or other pollutants.

The inlet air steam can be cooled naturally, such as accessed from a shaded area. In hot, dry climates, passing the inlet air over water such as an aerated fountain or landscape area is particularly effective to create evaporative cooling. Allowing the atrium to cool by ventilation at night is effective in climates where summer nighttime temperatures are lower than daytime (greater than 15F difference), in which case the cooling effect can be carried into the next day by materials such as masonry (although, as a rule, if the average daily temperature is above 78F (25.5°C), thermally massive materials are disadvantageous in non-air-conditioned spaces because they do not cool as rapidly as a thermally light structure). The microclimatic dynamic no different than that evident in the Indian teepee—when stack ventilation is possible through a roof aperture, the space will ventilate naturally even in the absence of outside breezes, by the driving force of heated air. If air-conditioning of the atrium is needed but can be restricted to the lower area of the space, it can be done reasonably; cold air, being heavier, will pool at the bottom.

While there is apparent conflict between the heating design principle to maximize solar gain and the cooling design principle to minimize it, the sun does cooperate by its change in its apparent solar position with respect to the building. There are, however, design choices to be balanced between the requirements for sunshading and those for daylighting. The ideal location for a sunshading screen is on the outside of the glazing, where it can be wind-cooled. When the outside air ranges about 80F (26.7°C), glass areas even if shaded admits undesired heat gain by conduction. In truly warm climates, a minimum of glazed aperture should be used to prevent undesired heat gain, in which case the small amount of glazing should be placed where it is most effective for daylighting. Heat-absorbent or heat-reflective glass, the common solution to reduce solar heat gain, also reduces the illumination level and, if facing the equator, it also reduces desirable winter heat gain.

In temperate-to-cool climates, heat gain through a skylight can be tolerated if the space is high, so that heat builds up well above the occupancy zone and there is good ventilation. In hot climates, an atrium will perform better as an unconditioned space if it is a shaded but otherwise open courtyard.

Daylighting

In all climates, an atrium can be used for daylighting. Electric lighting cost savings can be achieved, but only if the daylighting system works; that is, if it replaces the use of artificial lighting. (Many daylit buildings end up with the electric lights in full use regardless of lighting levels needed.) Atriums serve a particularly useful function in daylighting design for an entire building by balancing light levels—thus reducing brightness ratios—across the interior floors of a building. If, for example, an open office floor has a window wall on only one side, typically more electric lighting is required than would be required without natural lighting to reduce the brightness ratio. An atrium light court at the building interior could provide such balanced "two source" lighting. An atrium designed as a "lighting fixture" that reflects, directs, or diffuses sunlight, can be one of the most pleasing means of controlling light.

The following principles apply to atrium design for daylighting:

L1. To maximize daylight, an atrium cross-section should be stepped open to the entire sky dome in predominantly cloudy areas. In predominantly sunny sites, atrium geometry can by based upon heating and/or cooling solar orientation principles.

L2. To maximize light, window or skylight apertures should be designed for the predominant sky condition. If the predominant sky condition is cloudy and maximum daylight is required (as in a northern climate wintergarden), consider clear glazing oriented to the entire sky dome, with movable sun controls for sunny conditions. If the predominant sky condition is sunny, orient the glazing according to heating and/or cooling design requirements.

L3. Provide sun-and-glare control by geometry of aperture, surface treatment, color, and adjustable shades or curtains. Designing for daylighting involves compromise to meet widely varying sky conditions. What works in bright sun conditions will not be adequate for cloudy conditions. An opaque overhang or louver, for example, may create particularly somber shadowing on a cloudy day. Light is already made diffuse by a cloudy sky, falling nearly equally from all directions; the sides of the atrium thus cast gray shadows on all sides. For predominantly cloudy conditions, a clear skylight is the right choice. Bright haze will nonetheless cause intolerable glare at least to a view upwards. Under sunny conditions, the same skylight is the least satisfactory choice because of overlighting and overheating. The designer's choice is to compromise. Unless the local climate is truly cloudy and the atrium requires high levels of illumination, partial skylighting can achieve a balance of natural lighting, heating, and cooling. Partial skylighting (that is, a skylight design that occupies only a portion of the roof surface) offers the further advantage of controlling glare and sunlight by providing reflecting and shading surfaces to the view, such as by the coffers of the skylights. Because it is reduced in light intensity and contrast, a surface illuminated by reflected light is far more acceptable to the human eye than a direct view of a bright window area. Movable shades for glare and sun control provide a further, surprisingly simple means of balancing for the variety of conditions. This can be provided simply by operable canvas or fiberglass shades.

The relative importance of these design principles for heating, cooling, and daylighting can be weighted according to building type and the local climate. In the northern United States and in Canada, particularly for residential units or apartments that might be grouped around an atrium, the solar heating potential predominates, while the natural cooling potential predominates in the southern United States. In commercial and institutional structures, natural cooling and daylighting are both important. In this case, the local climate would determine the relative importance of openness achieved with large and clear skylighting (most appropriate for cloudy temperate-to-cool regions) or of closed and shaded skylighting (most appropriate for sunny warm regions). While no one set of recommendations fits any one climate, the relative importance of each of the design principles is indicated by climatic region in Table 1.

Garden atriums

Plants have an important role in buffer zones. If the requirements of plants are understood, healthy greenery can be incorporated into atrium design and contribute to human comfort, amenity and energy conservation. Plants, however when uncomfortable, cannot move. Major planting losses have been reported in gardened atriums because the bioclimatic requirements were not achieved. A greenhouse for year-round crop or plant production is intended to create spring-summer or the growing-period climate throughout the year. A wintergarden replicates spring-summer conditions for plant growth in wintertime by

Table 1. Relative Importance of Design Principles in Various Climates

	COLD/CLOUDY Seattle Chicago Minneapolis	COOL/SUNNY Denver St. Louis Boston	WARM/DRY LosAngeles Phoenix Midland TX	HOT/WET Houston New Orleans Miami
HEATING				
H1 To maximize winter solar heat gain, orient the atrium aperture to the south.	●	□	▼	
H2 For radiant heat storage and distribution, place interior masonry directly in the path of the winter sun.	▼	□	●	
H3 To prevent excessive nighttime heat loss, consider an insulating system for the glazing.	●	□		
H4 To recover heat, place a return air duct high in the space, directly in the sun	□	●	▼	
COOLING				
C1 To minimize solar gain, provide shade from the summer sun.		□	□	●
C2 Use the atrium as an air plenum in the mechanical system of the building.	□	□	□	□
C3 To facilitate natural ventilation, create a vertical "chimney" effect with high outlets and low inlets.	□	□	□	●
LIGHTING				
L1 To maximize daylight, use a stepped section (in predominantly cloudy areas).	□	▼		
L2 To maximize daylight, select skylight glazing for predominant sky condition (clear and horizontal in predominantly cloudy areas).	□	□	□	□
L3 Provide sun- and glare-control	□	□	●	□

Key: ● = Very important; □ = positive benefit; ▼ = discretionary

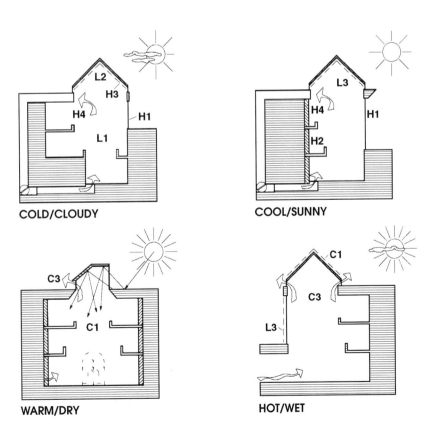

COLD/CLOUDY COOL/SUNNY WARM/DRY HOT/WET

Fig. 1. Atrium designs for solar daylighting, heating, gardens, and natural cooling.

maximizing winter daylight exposure and by solar heating. Plants need ample light but not excessive heat. Although it varies according to plant species, as a general rule planting areas require full overhead skylighting (essentially to simulate their indigenous growing condition). Most plants are overheated if their roots range above 65F (18.3°C). Their growth slows when the root temperature drops below 45F (7.2°C). As a result, a greenhouse has the general problem of overheating (as well as overlighting) during any sunny day and of underlighting (in intensity and duration) during any cloudy winter day.

Fig. 2. Isabella Stuart Gardner Museum. Boston, MA. E. H. Sears, Architect. 1902.

Fig. 3. Ford Foundation Headquarters. New York. Roche Dinkerloo, Architects. Dan Kiley, Landscape Architect. 1955.

If the function of the atrium includes plant propagation or horticultural exhibit (replicating the indigenous climate in which the display plants flower), then clear-glass skylighting is needed for the cloudy days and adjustable shading and overheating controls are needed for sunny days. If the plant beds are heated directly, by water piping for example, then root temperatures can be maintained in the optimum range without heating the air. As a result, the air temperature in the atrium can be cool for people, that is in the 50F (10°C) range, with the resulting advantage of providing a defense against superheating the space. People can be comfortable in lower air temperatures if exposed to the radiant warmth of the sun and/or if the radiant temperature of surrounding surfaces is correspondingly higher, that is, ranging above 80F (26.7°C). Lower atrium temperature offers a further advantage to plants and energy-efficient space operation because evaporation from plants is slowed, saving water and energy (1000 Btu are removed from the sensible heat of the space with each pound of water that evaporates). Plant growth is aided by air movement, if gentle and pervasive. Air circulation reduces excessive moisture build-up at the plant leaf and circulates CO_2, needed during the daytime growth cycle. The requirements for healthy planting and indoor gardening can thus be combined with energy-efficient atrium design for benefit of both plants and people.

Atrium design can be integral to a bioclimatic approach to heating, cooling and lighting buildings, while adding the restorative benefit of planting. The Gardner Museum in Boston provides a turn-of-the-century U.S. precedent. wherin a Venetian Renaissance garden forms the central organizing space (Fig. 2). The Ford Foundation in New York City 1955 incorporates a landscaped atrium within an office building (Fig.3). The TVA Headquarters design in Chatanooga derives from an atrium cross-section for daylighting and for planting (Fig. 4). These examples demonstrate the amenity offered by atrium design adapted to the opportunities of their particular building type and climate.

Fig. 4. TVA Office Building Chattanooga, TN. The Architects Collaborative (TAC). 1984.

13
Building economics

David S. Haviland

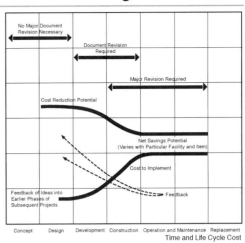

Summary: Building economics is the art and science of making economic decisions—the best ways to allocate scarce ownership and operating dollars—at every step in the building process, from project definition through design and construction to commissioning and operation. This article provides a brief overview of building economics and life-cycle cost analysis, which accounts for all costs of building ownership over the life of the building investment.

Key words: budgeting, engineering economics, financial investment, life cycle cost analysis and operating cost.

Buildings require resources to design, construct and operate. At $80 per square foot, a new 2,000 square foot residence costs $160,000 to build; this is four times the median income of American families. A university constructing a 100,000 square foot science facility at $150/square foot plus another 25% in project development costs finds itself raising or borrowing more than $18 million to bring the facility to the day the ribbon is cut.

This is only the beginning. Once a new or renovated project is occupied and in use, it requires continuing investment. Data from many sources indicate that ownership and operating costs (those designated "project-in-use-costs" in Table 1) total from $8 to $30 per square foot each year, with an average annual cost of perhaps $15 per square foot. For our university science building, this may represent another $1.5 million per year in building ownership costs.

Most building projects are financed. Their owners borrow funds or raise them in the bond market, adding annual interest costs that may range from 6% to 12%. A full 20-year, 8% mortgage on the residence above will cost its owner $16,230 each year. For the university science building, the debt service—repayment of principal and interest—on $18 million in 6%, 30-year bonds is more than $1.3 million each year.

Scope of Building Economics

Given the large numbers involved, it is not surprising that costs and economy are fundamentally important to building owners. Owners typically want to know:

- How much the project will cost—often owners want this information long before the design is detailed enough to produce a careful estimate.
- How the planning, design, and construction decisions being made at each step influence project cost.
- How the benefits to be produced compare to the costs of constructing and operating the project.

Building economics includes making economic decisions—the best way to allocate scarce resources—at every step in the building process. Project definition, design, construction, commissioning, and operation involve thousands of decisions affecting the allocation of the owner's ownership and operating dollars (Table 1).

Investment Thinking

Taken together, the three questions asked above require those who own, finance, and design new and renovated facilities to view buildings as investments. Most building owners seek financing. Even if they have the resources, owners are not always willing to invest them in a project with low liquidity—that is, if they need the funds for something else, they may not be able to sell the building at the price they seek when they seek it. People and institutions who supply money charge *interest* for its use, and this is a substantial additional project cost.

Even if an owner incurs no interest charges by using its own funds, it foregoes the opportunity to use the money for some other investment. Thus, there is an *opportunity cost* for using one's own funds for a building project.

Finally, those who have money to lend or invest have other possibilities for economic return. Spending the money on a building project competes with these alternatives. Some owners insist any discretionary expenditure on the building project earn a *minimum attractive rate of return.*

Investment thinking raises these questions:

- How productive will an investment be (in the project or in an alternative design concept, system, or detail)?
- Will the benefits outweigh the costs?
- If there is more than one choice, which is the most productive?
- Is there a better way of using my money than investing it in this way?

Author: David S. Haviland, Hon. AIA

References: Bowen, Brian. 1994. "Construction Cost Management." in David Haviland, ed. *The Architect's Handbook of Professional Practice.* Washington, DC: The American Institute of Architects.

Haviland, David. 1977, 1978. *Life Cycle Cost Analysis: A Guide for Architects* and *Life Cycle Cost Analysis: Using it in Practice.* Washington, DC: The American Institute of Architects.

Johnson, Robert E. 1990. *The Economics of Building: A Practical Guide for the Design Professional.* New York: John Wiley & Sons.

Kirk, Stephen J., and Alphonse J. Dell'Isola. 1995. *Life Cycle Costing for Design Professionals.* New York: McGraw Hill.

Means Building Construction Cost Data. 1997. Kingston, RI: R. S. Means Company, updated and published annually. Means publishes cost data for use in all phases of project budgeting and estimating.

Ruegg, Rosalie T. and Marshall, Harold E. 1990. *Building Economics: Theory and Practice.* New York: Van Nostrand Reinhold.

Table 1. Typical project cost and budget elements

Budget element	Some design decisions influencing cost of this element
Site Costs	
1. Acquisition Cost of purchasing or leasing the site; includes costs of options, legal and brokerage fees, site financing 2. Improvement Cost of bringing the site to the point where one can build on it: access, remediation, clearing and grading, drainage, retaining structures, utilities, landscaping, application and approvals, permit and impact fees 3. Holding costs Costs of holding the land, including real estate taxes, utilities, insurance, security, maintenance	• Program evaluation and site "fit" • Siting decisions: requirements for access roads, utility connections • Siting decisions: requirements for clearing, grading, cuts and fills, detention/retention ponds • Siting decisions: need for accommodation to neighbor and sensitivity to neighborhood and community context and issues • Need for regulatory reviews, variances, and other administrative or judicial relief
Project Development Costs	
1. Design Costs of predesign facility surveys, marketing, feasibility, programming, and financing studies; site development including selection, utility, and environmental studies; design and documentation; bidding or negotiation; and construction contract administration services. 2. Interim financing Construction loan costs including interest, fees, insurance, origination charges 3. Other fees Surveying, geotechnical, market and feasibility, legal, accounting, costs related to sale or rental of space or units, settlement costs including title, insurance, tax reserves, etc. 4. Owner project management Owner costs of managing consultants and contractors, organizing internal "clients," seeking approvals, etc.	• Range of services needed • Number of schemes and other iterations required • Services pricing and compensation • Total construction cost (amount to be financed) • Construction period (time before funds are repaid)
Construction Costs	
1. Materials Selection and integration of construction materials and subsystems to be used 2. On-site labor Building trade and labor required to install materials and subsystems 3. Contractor overhead Contractors' site management costs (field personnel and facilities, tools, equipment, temporary construction and utilities, staging and scaffolding, safety, cleaning, protection, permits, insurances, bonds) as well as main office and profit requirements 4. Design and construction contingency Reservation of funds to address uncertainties in construction: owner changes, design errors or omissions. unexpected field conditions	• Use of standard vs. custom products • Product shortages, lead times to purchase • Repetition, economies of scale • Constructability and waste • Number, variety, availability of trades required • Trade work rules and jurisdiction • Crew size and composition • Special equipment needed to install products and systems • Building siting: effects on work conditions, materials handling and storage, protection of adjacent property, *etc.* • "General conditions" contract requirements for insurances, bonds, safety, security, temporary construction, *etc.* • Speed and thoroughness in addressing shop drawings and submittals, design changes, and claims during construction
Project-in-Use Costs	
1. Commissioning Project start-up including move in, fit out, systems shake-out, maintenance training, record drawing, warranty services 2. Permanent financing Debt service (repayment of principal and interest) as well as mortgage origination fees and charges 3. Operation and maintenance Facility operating personnel, security, cleaning, mechanical systems maintenance, trash removal, lawn and grounds maintenance, snow removal, energy and energy systems costs, property and liability insurance, taxes, water and sewer, property management 4. Major maintenance, repair, and replacements Major maintenance, repair, and period replacement of facility components, assemblies, and subsystems 5. Cyclical renewal Periodic upgrading of design or systems in response to functional, organizational, tecnhnological, or market requirements	• Total construction cost (amount to be financed) • Finishes (cleaning, replacement) • Energy-conscious design (U-values, windows, active and passive systems, etc.) • Layout (*e.g.*, snow plowing, surveillance of public spaces) • Selection of interior and exterior finishes, windows and doors, roofing, elevators, lighting, mechanical and electrical systems, ground cover and paving • Anticipation of in-use changes in the initial design, *e.g.*, new interior or exterior treatments, recabling, lighting retrofits, possibilities for adding to the facility, etc.

Table 2. Investment decisions

Project definition and scope	• Build, lease, or reorganize (personnel, technology, or process solutions that do not require new or better facilities) • Build new or renovate • Probable "economic life" of processes in the building (how long before they are obsolete or require complete upgrading or replacement?) • Approaches to expansion, flexibility, adaptability • Major program elements and performance requirements • Site selection
Programming and design concepts	• Functional analyses • Building configuration, footprint, and massing • Basic layout and compartmentation approaches • Siting and orientation • Envelope and fenestration concepts • Underground construction • Interstitial space (floors, utility corridors, *etc.*) • Pre-engineered or coordinated systems
Design development: Structure	• Subsystems selection, modules, bay sizes • Integration of mechanical systems • Exposed vs. covered
Design development: Envelope	• Energy conservation features • Daylighting and shading elements • Cleaning devices and equipment
Design development: Interior construction	• Demountability and flexibility • Built-in furnishings • Finishes
Design development: Mechanical and electrical systems	• Individual units *vs.* distributed systems • Zoning and layout concepts • Lighting and daylighting • Active and passive solar systems • Energy management systems • Heat/waste recovery systems • Efficiency decisions
Sitework	• Paving and ground cover decisions • Parking alternatives • Lighting
Bidding and Construction	• Redesign as part of construction contract negotiation • Analysis of contractor-proposed substitutions • Design changes during construction
Commissioning and Start-up	• Testing and turnover of building systems • Maintenance programming and training • Tenant-related design decisions
Project in use	• Decisions on building repairs, replacements, upgrades • Space reallocation and reorganization • Refurbishing and renovation

Investment-related decisions are made at every step, from the earliest judgment to build or not to build, and continue as the project is designed, constructed, and commissioned. Sometimes these decisions are based on formal financial feasibility studies, such as those done to seek financing for commercial and institutional projects.

Once the building is in operation, the cycle begins each time the owner considers whether and how to invest in reconfiguration, new technology, major maintenance, systems upgrades, or complete renovation of the building to meet new needs (Table 2).

Baseline Cost
Most new construction projects have a built-in cost that establishes a kind of investment baseline. While the variety of conditions under

which projects are conceived, constructed, and operated make this baseline number hard to isolate, there are some fundamental forces at work creating project cost:

• The fundamental characteristics of the product. Buildings are large and provide high levels of performance. Inherently costly, they must be durable and last a long time, requiring continuos maintenance and adding to their expense.
• Building code requirements. Codes set structural, habitation, fire safety, accessibility, energy, and environmental requirements that must be met. Perhaps 80 percent or more of a project's standards and costs are established by such regulations and cannot be reduced.

Table 3. Discount factors and their formulas

Key: P   *single present sum*   D   *discount rate*
          F   *single future sum*   N   *number of time periods*
          A   *recurring annual sum*   ^   *raise to power*

Factor Formula (for tables) Formula (spreadsheet format)	Description	Example situation
Single Compound Amount (SCA) $F=P*SCA$ $F=P*((1+D)^n)$	The future value (F) of a present sum (P)	What is the future sum of a single amount saved today?
Single Present Worth (SPW) $P=F*SPW$ $P=F*(1/((1+D)^n))$	The present value (P) of a future sum (F)	What is the present value of a future replacement?
Uniform Compound Amount (UCA) $F=A*UCA$ $F=A*((((1+D)^n)-1)/D)$	The future value (F) of a series of annual payments (A)	What future sum will be achieved if a sum is added each year to a replacement reserve?
Uniform Sinking Fund (USF) $A=F*USF$ $A=F*(D/(((1+D)^N)-1))$	The annual payment (A) required to achieve a future sum (F)	What is the annual amount needed to achieve a future replacement cost?
Uniform Present Worth (UPW) $P=A*UPW$ $P=A*((((1+D)^N)-1)/(D*(1+D)^N))$	The present worth (P) of a sum of annual payments (A)	What is the present value of annual energy costs?
Uniform Capital Recovery (UCR) $A=P*UCR$ $A=P*((D*(1+D)^N)/(((1+D)^N)-1))$	The annual payment (A) required to achieve a present sum (P)	What is the annual payment required to pay off a mortgage?

- Program requirements. The owner's scope, quality, and time requirements establish a "value profile" that may well exceed code and regulatory requirements.
- Site and location. The site offers its own access, topographic, and geotechnical challenges; it also situates the project within a specific—and often demanding—set of planning, zoning, and environmental regulations.

While it is difficult to isolate a specific project's baseline cost, it is not so hard to identify this cost for a large class of similar buildings. For example, a scan of building construction cost data such as data published by R. S. Means provides a useful overview of the range of costs as a function of building type.

Design Decisions and Life Cycle Cost Analysis

Even with a baseline cost, owners and designers make many choices influencing construction and operating costs.

While building codes place restrictions, they offer choices of construction materials and systems, requiring that buildings be made of noncombustible elements if they are to be larger or taller. While codes may limit heat loss to conserve energy, they do not stop owners and designers from going further, adding conservation features that, among other benefits, reduce energy costs over the life of the building. Finally, a building's value profile—levels of quality and amenity above the baseline—may vary substantially from one project to the next.

At every step, designers have choices to make, and many of these have economic consequences for the building or for those using it. Some of these design decisions involve costs and/or benefits spread over time. Design alternatives may have different initial construction costs as well as different patterns of continuing costs or savings. To assess the economic consequences of selecting one option or another, it is necessary to summarize and relate these costs and savings over time.

Life cycle cost analysis (engineering economics) is an economic decision process that assists in deciding among alternative building investments by comparing the significant differential costs of ownership over a given time period and in equivalent dollars.

The key lies in "equivalent dollars." Money has time value; a dollar spent today has different value from a dollar required five years from now. As a simple example, consider two options, one of which costs $1,000 today and another costing $700 today and requiring another $300 five years from now. Selecting the first requires $1,000 now. The second requires $700 and a $235 deposit in a savings account that earns 5% annual interest. Interest earned on the $235 brings the account to $300 in five years. As a result, the second option requires only $935 in today's dollars.

Here is another view of money's time value. An efficient energy system costs an extra $10,000 to purchase and install, and it will save an estimated $1,000 a year in energy costs. A simple calculation suggests the extra cost is paid back in ten years. The owner, however, will have to add the $10,000 to the construction budget—and then finance it. With a 20-year, 10% mortgage, the extra $10,000 requires an annual debt service of $1,175—a cost that exceeds the $1,000 savings!

Accounting for the time value of money—"discounting"—involves the use of the formulas in Table 3. These formulas can be used to convert a single future value into present dollars (e.g., the $300 required five years from now in the first example above becomes $235 in today's dollars given a 5% interest rate) or to convert a present sum (the extra $10,000 required in the second example) into an annual cost (the $1,175 in the same example) given a time period and an

Table 4. Discount tables (excerpts)

Single Present Worth
SPW

Find: P (a nonrecurring present amount)
Knowing: F (a nonrecurring future amount)

n	4%	6%	8%	10%	12%	15%	20%	25%
1	0.962	0.943	0.926	0.909	0.893	0.870	0.833	0.800
2	0.925	0.890	0.857	0.826	0.797	0.756	0.694	0.640
3	0.889	0.840	0.794	0.751	0.712	0.658	0.579	0.512
4	0.855	0.792	0.735	0.683	0.636	0.572	0.482	0.410
5	0.822	0.747	0.681	0.621	0.567	0.497	0.402	0.328
6	0.790	0.705	0.630	0.564	0.507	0.432	0.335	0.262
7	0.760	0.665	0.583	0.513	0.452	0.376	0.279	0.210
8	0.731	0.627	0.540	0.467	0.404	0.327	0.233	0.168
9	0.703	0.592	0.500	0.424	0.361	0.284	0.194	0.134
10	0.676	0.558	0.463	0.386	0.322	0.247	0.162	0.107
11	0.650	0.527	0.429	0.350	0.287	0.215	0.135	0.086
12	0.625	0.497	0.397	0.319	0.257	0.187	0.112	0.069
13	0.601	0.469	0.368	0.290	0.229	0.163	0.093	0.055
14	0.577	0.442	0.340	0.263	0.205	0.141	0.078	0.044
15	0.555	0.417	0.315	0.239	0.183	0.123	0.065	0.035
16	0.534	0.394	0.292	0.218	0.163	0.107	0.054	0.028
17	0.513	0.371	0.270	0.198	0.146	0.093	0.045	0.023
18	0.494	0.350	0.250	0.180	0.130	0.081	0.038	0.018
19	0.475	0.331	0.232	0.164	0.116	0.070	0.031	0.014
20	0.456	0.312	0.215	0.149	0.104	0.061	0.026	0.012

Uniform Present Worth
UPW

Find: P (a nonrecurring present amount)
Knowing: A (a recurring annual amount)

n	4%	6%	8%	10%	12%	15%	20%	25%
1	0.962	0.943	0.926	0.909	0.893	0.870	0.833	0.800
2	1.886	1.833	1.783	1.736	1.690	1.626	1.528	1.440
3	2.775	2.673	2.577	2.487	2.402	2.283	2.106	1.952
4	3.630	3.465	3.312	3.170	3.037	2.855	2.589	2.362
5	4.452	4.212	3.993	3.791	3.605	3.352	2.991	2.689
6	5.242	4.917	4.623	4.355	4.111	3.784	3.326	2.951
7	6.002	5.582	5.206	4.868	4.564	4.160	3.605	3.161
8	6.733	6.210	5.747	5.335	4.968	4.487	3.837	3.329
9	7.435	6.802	6.247	5.759	5.328	4.772	4.031	3.463
10	8.111	7.360	6.710	6.145	5.650	5.019	4.192	3.571
11	8.760	7.887	7.139	6.495	5.938	5.234	4.327	3.656
12	9.385	8.384	7.536	6.814	6.194	5.421	4.439	3.725
13	9.986	8.853	7.904	7.103	6.424	5.583	4.533	3.780
14	10.563	9.295	8.244	7.367	6.628	5.724	4.611	3.824
15	11.118	9.712	8.559	7.606	6.811	5.847	4.675	3.859
16	11.652	10.106	8.851	7.824	6.974	5.954	4.730	3.887
17	12.166	10.477	9.122	8.022	7.120	6.047	4.775	3.910
18	12.659	10.828	9.372	8.201	7.250	6.128	4.812	3.928
19	13.134	11.158	9.604	8.365	7.366	6.198	4.843	3.942
20	13.590	11.470	9.818	8.514	7.469	6.259	4.870	3.954

Uniform Capital Recovery
UCR

Find: A (a recurring annual amount)
Knowing: P (a nonrecurring present amount)
Also known as the mortgage constant (k)

n	4%	6%	8%	10%	12%	15%	20%	25%
1	1.040	1.060	1.080	1.100	1.120	1.150	1.200	1.250
2	0.530	0.545	0.561	0.576	0.592	0.615	0.655	0.694
3	0.360	0.374	0.388	0.402	0.416	0.438	0.475	0.512
4	0.275	0.289	0.302	0.315	0.329	0.350	0.386	0.423
5	0.225	0.237	0.250	0.264	0.277	0.298	0.334	0.372
6	0.191	0.203	0.216	0.230	0.243	0.264	0.301	0.339
7	0.167	0.179	0.192	0.205	0.219	0.240	0.277	0.316
8	0.149	0.161	0.174	0.187	0.201	0.223	0.261	0.300
9	0.134	0.147	0.160	0.174	0.188	0.210	0.248	0.289
10	0.123	0.136	0.149	0.163	0.177	0.199	0.239	0.280
11	0.114	0.127	0.140	0.154	0.168	0.191	0.231	0.273
12	0.107	0.119	0.133	0.147	0.161	0.184	0.225	0.268
13	0.100	0.113	0.127	0.141	0.156	0.179	0.221	0.265
14	0.095	0.108	0.121	0.136	0.151	0.175	0.217	0.262
15	0.090	0.103	0.117	0.131	0.147	0.171	0.214	0.259
16	0.086	0.099	0.113	0.128	0.143	0.168	0.211	0.257
17	0.082	0.095	0.110	0.125	0.140	0.165	0.209	0.256
18	0.079	0.092	0.107	0.122	0.138	0.163	0.208	0.255
19	0.076	0.090	0.104	0.120	0.136	0.161	0.206	0.254
20	0.074	0.087	0.102	0.117	0.134	0.160	0.205	0.253

Table 5. Life Cycle Cost Analysis in Eight Steps

Step	Issues and Guidance
Step 1 Establish design options	Focus on important design decisions where: • Substantial dollars are involved • There are clear design alternatives and choices • Continuing costs and/or benefits differ among choices • Initial and continuing costs and benefits can be estimated and translated to dollars
Step 2 Establish owner's timeframe	When is the present (year 0) and how long into the future should costs and/or benefits be considered? • Year 0 is usually the project development period • Disregard already-incurred ("sunk") costs prior to year 0 • Tie the analysis timeframe to the owner's investment objectives; often this is 5 to 20 years rather than 50 to 100 years • May want to consider multiple timeframes to isolate a future "breakeven" point where the decision changes from one choice to another
Step 3 Establish owner's investment goals	Establish the discount rate for the analysis; may be • Cost of borrowing funds (interest rate) • Opportunity cost • Minimum attractive rate of return • Specified by a government agency Establish owner's approach to handling: • Inflation and escalation • Rates of return (before-tax, after-tax, etc.)
Step 4: Decide which costs (savings) to include	Present single nonrecurring costs (P) • Purchase and installation • Associated design costs
Step 5 Diagram costs and savings Usual conventions: Costs are down arrows; savings are up (see diagram at right)	Future single nonrecurring costs (F) • Repairs and replacements (what years?) • Salvage value Annual recurring costs or savings (A) • Energy • Maintenance • Other operating costs Include only costs or savings that differ among the alternatives being considered
Step 6 Establish the measure of total life cycle cost	Bring all costs and savings to their present worth costs • Present sums stated at their full value • Future and annual recurring sums brought to P OR bring all costs and savings to a uniform annual cost • Annual recurring costs stated at their full value • Present and future single sums brought to A
Step 7 Do the analysis Use these factors (see Table 4)	
Step 8 Reflect upon, interpret, and present the results	Take time to answer these important questions: • Are the right alternatives and costs being considered? • Are the investment assumptions appropriate? • Do the results appear to be logical? • How sensitive are the results to changes in future costs or savings? inflation and escalation? variations in timeframe and discount rate? • How best to formulate and present the results? • What are the important noneconomic issues and how might they influence the decision?

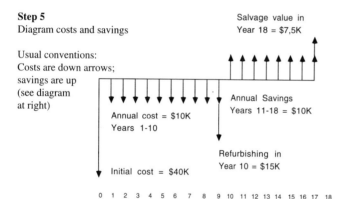

Salvage value in
Year 18 = $7,5K

Annual Savings
Years 11-18 = $10K

Annual cost = $10K
Years 1-10

Refurbishing in
Year 10 = $15K

Initial cost = $40K

0 1 2 3 4 5 6 7 8 9 10 11 12 13 14 15 16 17 18

Find	Given	Use	
P	F	SPW	Single Present Worth
P	A	UPW	Uniform Present Worth
A	P	UCR	Uniform Capital Recovery
A	F	USF	Uniform Sinking Fund
F	P	SCA	Single Compound Amount
F	A	UCA	Uniform Compound Amount

Table. 6. Example life cycle cost analysis

The designer is considering two alternative energy systems. Alternative A costs $12,000 to purchase and install; annual energy costs are expected to be $2,000 a year, and the system requires $6,000 in replacements ten years from now. Alternative B costs $20,000 to purchase and install, requires no significant replacement, and incurs energy costs of $500 a year. Which is the more economical choice? Key assumptions:

• The owner expects to borrow all funds (including the extra purchase costs of Alternative B) at 10%, and asks you to use this discount rate.
• The owner expects to own the facility for at least 15 years and asks you to use this analysis timeframe.
• Other relevant costs e.g., routine maintenance) are equal for the two alternatives.
• Energy costs will not escalate.

Life Cycle Cost Analysis, bringing all costs to present terms (P):

ALTERNATIVE A

					Present Worth :
Purchase (P)	$12,000	=	already stated as a present sum		$ 12,000
Replacement (F)	6,000	x	0.386 (SPW,10%,10 yrs)	=	2,316
Annual energy (A)	2,000	x	7.606 (UPW,10%,15 yrs)	=	15,212
			Total Present Worth Cost		$ 29,528

ALTERNATIVE B

Purchase (P)	$20,000	=	already stated as a present sum		$ 20,000
Annual energy (A)	500	x	7.616 (UPW,10%,15 yrs)	=	3,803
			Total Present Worth Cost		$ 23,803

COMPARISON: Alternative B has the lowest life cycle cost by: $ 5,725

Note: To consider annual escalation (e.g., for the annual energy cost), it is possible to use a Uniform Present Worth Modified (UPWM) factor, which includes an escalation rate. In this example, this step is not really necessary because any annual escalation in energy cost will add more total present worth cost to Alternative A than to B, making A even less economical.

interest—or "discount"—rate. Because the discount formulas raise very small numbers to large powers, it is common to use computers or tables such as excerpted in Table 4.

Doing life cycle cost analyses requires the eight steps outlined in Table 5. Diagramming (Step 5) is, of course, optional but it helps the analyst sort out recurring and nonrecurring costs and savings over time in more complex analyses.

Life cycle cost analysis has many uses and applications. The example in Table 6 translates all costs, including nonrecurring future costs (F) as well as recurring annual costs (A) into present (P) dollars. The alternative with the lowest total present value—or total present worth cost—is the most economical choice. This can be used to make the selection, or it can be used to measure the cost of making a less economical but overall better design choice. The technique can also be used as part of internal rate of return (at what discount rate do two alternatives have equal economic value?) and breakeven (at what point in the future do two alternatives have equal economic value?)

Representative impacts for life cycle cost elements are summarized in Figs. 1 and 2 on the succeeding pages (after Kirk and Dell'Isola, 1995).

Table 7. Budgeting and estimating approaches

Project stage	General approaches	Sources of information, techniques, systerms
Project budgeting Budget evaluation Program evaluation Early conceptual design	Units of program Area (square foot) Volume (cubic foot)	Owner experience Published averages, medians Architect, builder experience
	Order-of-magnitude (area modified for size, location)	Means order-of-magnitude estimate
	Economic value models	Financial feasibility analysis
	Simple parametric models	Comparables and appraisal techniques, *e.g.*, Boeckh, Dodge, Marshall & Swift
Later conceptual design Early schematic design	Complex parametric models based on initial subsystems analysis and selection	Systems-based estimates, *e.g.*, Means Square Foot Costs Dodge systems estimating
Later schematic design Design development	Subsystems evaluation and estimating	Assemblies-based systems, e.g., Means Assemblies Cost Data Dodge Systems Costs VNR Design Cost File
Construction and bidding documents	Unit-in-place estimates for key detail design decisions	Contractor or CM cost files
	Detailed construction cost estimate	Unit-in-place systems, *e.g.*, Means Construction Cost Data Dodge Pricing & Scheduling Manual
	Pre-bid estimate	VNR Building Cost File Lee Saylor Construction Costs
Bidding, award and construction	Detailed estimates for proposed substitutions, change orders, special field problems, and claims	Contractor or CM cost files

Construction Budgets and Estimates

At various points in a project's evolution, and certainly as part of any life cycle cost analysis, it is necessary to forecast the cost of the project or one or more of its aspects.

Budgeting begins by understanding what costs will likely be incurred, when they will arise, and who is responsible for managing them. Construction cost—the cost of the materials, on-site labor, equipment, and contractor's overhead and profit—is only part of the total project budget. As suggested in Table 1, the total budget may include costs of site acquisition, development, and holding as well as a variety of project development costs which may, themselves, represent a 25 percent addition to construction cost.

Project budgets are, in fact, the earliest cost estimates for a project. As more is known about the design of the project, cost estimating can become more informed and complete. Table 7 summarizes some of the methods available at various points in a project's evolution.

Fig. 1. Relative values of (a) first cost, (b) maintenance, (c) energy cost, and (d) replacement cost.

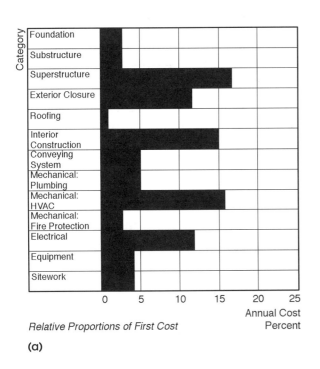

Relative Proportions of First Cost

(a)

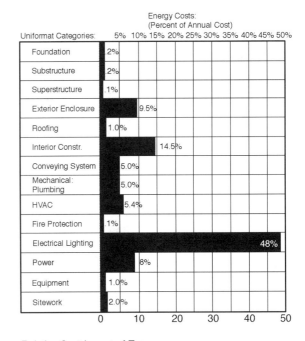

Relative Cost Impact of Energy

(c)

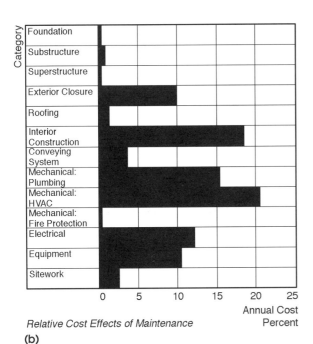

Relative Cost Effects of Maintenance

(b)

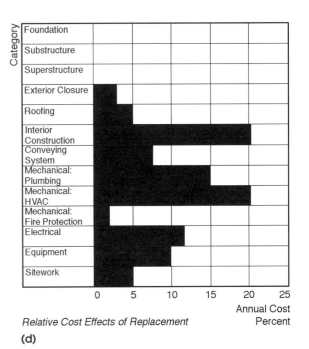

Relative Cost Effects of Replacement

(d)

Fig. 2. Life cycle cost distribution—typical office building (Kirk and Dell'Isola, 1995).

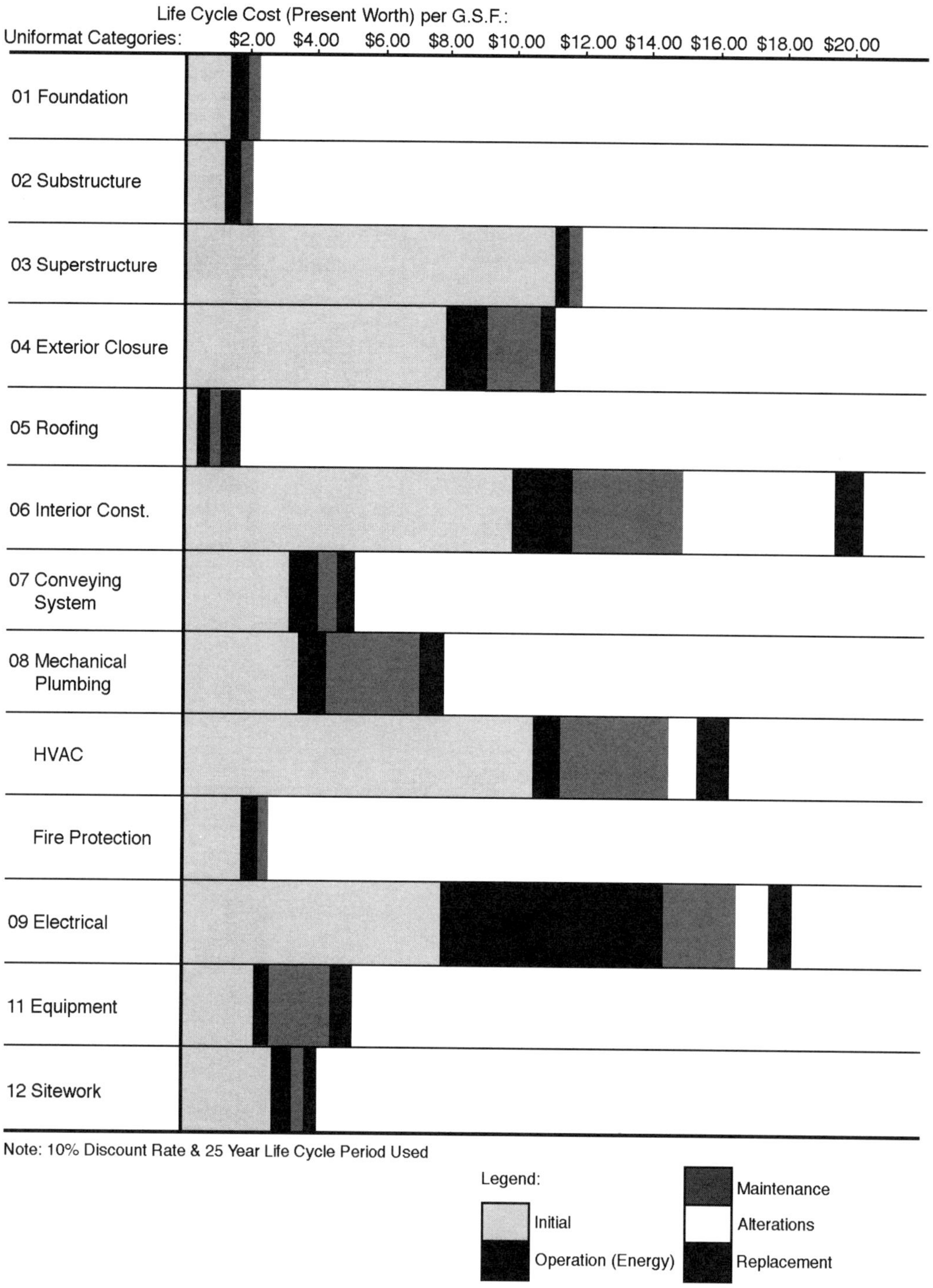

Life Cycle Cost (Present Worth) per G.S.F.:

Uniformat Categories:	$2.00	$4.00	$6.00	$8.00	$10.00	$12.00	$14.00	$16.00	$18.00	$20.00

01 Foundation

02 Substructure

03 Superstructure

04 Exterior Closure

05 Roofing

06 Interior Const.

07 Conveying System

08 Mechanical Plumbing

HVAC

Fire Protection

09 Electrical

11 Equipment

12 Sitework

Note: 10% Discount Rate & 25 Year Life Cycle Period Used

Legend:

Initial

Operation (Energy)

Maintenance

Alterations

Replacement

14
Estimating and design cost analysis

Robert P. Charette
Brian Bowen

	Basement Construction		A1010	Stan
B10			A1020	Spec
	Superstructure		A1030	Slab
B20			A2010	Baser
	Exterior Closure		A2020	Basen
			B1010	Floor
B30			B1020	Roof C
	Roofing		B2010	Exterio
C10			B2020	Exterio
	Interior Construction		B2030	Exterior
			B3010	Roof Co
20			B3020	Roof Ope
	Staircases		C1010	Partitions
30			C1020	Interior D
	Interior Finishes		C1030	Specialties
			C2010	Stair Const
			C2020	Stair Finish
	Conveying Systen		C3010	Wall F
			C3020	

Summary: UNIFORMAT II provides a classification and systematic approach for estimating and design cost analysis. The classification is outlined, including a comparison of design vs. construction estimate objectives, building and sitework elements, sources of cost data, and a worked example of design cost analysis.

Key words: assemblies, building elements classification, cost estimates, preliminary design, systems, UNIFORMAT II.

1   Introduction

Need for a classification of building elements

The building industry needs a format or classification framework to serve as a consistent reference for the description, analysis, evaluation, monitoring, and management of facilities during their life cycle, from the planning, feasibility and design stages through to construction, occupancy and disposal. A classification of building elements such as UNIFORMAT II provides an approach to meeting these objectives.

Building elements are traditionally defined as major components, common to most buildings, that perform a given function, regardless of the design specification, construction method, or materials used. In practice, an element may be any part of a logical work breakdown structure whose purpose is to control project scope, cost, time and quality.

The development of the first elemental classification is attributed to the British Ministry of Education following the post World War II school-expansion program. The methodology was adapted to construction programs in other British Commonwealth countries, such as Canada, and then to the United States in the early 1970s. In 1973, the American Institute of Architects undertook to develop an elemental estimating format called MASTERCOST. In conjunction with the General Services Administration, a consensus format named UNIFORMAT was produced. Though not an official national standard, it has since formed the basis for any elemental format called for in the United States. In 1989, the American Society of Testing Materials (ASTM) Sub-Committee E06.81 on Building Economics appointed a task group to develop a UNIFORMAT standard. In 1992, the National Institute of Standards and Technology (NIST) issued a special publication (Bowen, Charette, and Marshall 1992), in which the name UNIFORMAT II was selected to emphasize that it is an elemental classification similar to the original UNIFORMAT. Improvements based on experience since its first inception made it more comprehensive, particularly with respect to mechanical systems and sitework.

In 1992, the Construction Specifications Institute (CSI) issued an interim edition of UNIFORMAT based on the work in progress of ASTM. CSI also published a practice entitled "FF/180 - Preliminary Project Descriptions and Outline Specifications" which recommended the use of an elemental project description (specification) based on UNIFORMAT at the schematic design phase. The objective of the classification format was to improve communications and coordination among all parties involved in a project, particularly between the design team and the client. The ASTM standard was approved in 1993 and designated E 1557-93 "Standard Classification for Building Elements and Related Sitework - UNIFORMAT II." In 1996, revisions were made (ASTM 1996), providing a distinctive alpha-numeric designation for the elements similar to that incorporated by CSI (1992). Designated as E-1557-96, the newly revised ASTM classification of elements is listed in Table 1.

The objective for establishing UNIFORMAT as a national and international standard was to provide a degree of consistency in cost planning, cost control, and estimating during the programming and design phases of a project. The Construction Specifications Institute (CSI) recommends UNIFORMAT II for schematic phase preliminary project descriptions. Numerous applications demonstrate that the classification system can provide a link between all phases of facilities programming and design and for all phases of the life cycle of a project, including construction and operations.

Element selection criteria

The following criteria are the basis for deciding what items to include as elements in the classification and in which parts of the classification to assign or list them.

- The UNIFORMAT II classification is applicable to any building type, while allowing for details appropriate for specialized buildings or cases. The classification of building elements is separate from the classification of building-related sitework. The classification is hierarchical to allow different levels of cost analysis, aggregation and summarization. It is easily related and/or referenced to other elemental classifications such as the original UNIFORMAT and the classification of the Canadian Institute of Quantity Surveyors (CIQS).

- Items to be included in the classification are determined as any element that has bearing on project cost, significant either in magnitude or quantity and which help in understanding constructability and cost. Elemental categories provide a framework for cost control and other applications such as early design specifications. The

Authors: Robert P. Charette, P. E., CVS and Brian Bowen, FRICS

Credits: Roger J. Grant of R. S. Means Company provided the office building data for the worked example estimates in this article.

References: ASTM 1996. *Standard Classification for Building Elements and Related Sitework - UNIFORMAT II.* ASTM Designation E1557-96. West Conshohocken, PA: American Society for Testing and Materials.

Additional references appear at the end of this article.

Table 1. UNIFORMAT II Classification

Level 1 Major Group Elements	Level 2 Group Elements		Level 3 Individual Elements	
A SUBSTRUCTURE	A10	Foundations	A1010 A1020 A1030	Standard Foundations Special Foundations Slab on Grade
	A20	Basement Construction	A2010 A2020	Basement Excavation Basement Walls
B SHELL	B10	Superstructure	B1010 B1020	Floor Construction Roof Construction
	B20	Exterior Closure	B2010 B2020 B2030	Exterior Walls Exterior Windows Exterior Doors
	B30	Roofing	B3010 B3020	Roof Coverings Roof Openings
C INTERIORS	C10	Interior Construction	C1010 C1020 C1030	Partitions Interior Doors Specialties
	C20	Staircases	C2010 C2020	Stair Construction Stair Finishes
	C30	Interior Finishes	C3010 C3020 C3030	Wall Finishes Floor Finishes Ceiling Finishes
D SERVICES	D10	Conveying Systems	D1010 D1020 D1030	Elevators Escalators & Moving Walks Material Handling Systems
	D20	Plumbing	D2010 D2020 D2030 D2040 D2050	Plumbing Fixtures Domestic Water Distribution Sanitary Waste Rain Water Drainage Special Plumbing Systems
	D30	HVAC	D3010 D3020 D3030 D3040 D3050 D3060 D3070 D3080	Energy Supply Heat Generating Systems Cooling Generating Systems Distribution Systems Terminal & Package Units Controls and Instrumentation Special HVAC Systems & Equipment Systems Testing & Balancing
	D40	Fire Protection	D4010 D4020 D4030 D4040	Fire Protection Sprinkler Systems Stand-Pipe and Hose Systems Fire Protection Specialties Special Fire Protection Systems
	D50	Electrical	D5010 D5020 D5030 D5040	Electrical Service & Distribution Lighting & Branch Wiring Communication & Security Systems Special Electrical Systems
E EQUIPMENT & FURNISHINGS	E10	Equipment	E1010 E1020 E1030 E1040	Commercial Equipment Institutional Equipment Vehicular Equipment Other Equipment
	E20	Furnishings	E2010 E2020	Fixed Furnishings Movable Furnishings
F SPECIAL CONSTRUCTION & DEMOLITION	F10	Special Construction	F1010 F1020 F1030 F1040 F1050	Special Structures Integrated Construction Special Construction Systems Special Facilities Special Controls and Instrumentation
	F20	Selective Building Demolition	F2010 F2020	Building Elements Demolition Hazardous Components Abatement

Level 1 Major Group Elements	Level 2 Group Elements		Level 3 Individual Elements	
G BUILDING SITEWORK	G10	Site Preparation	G1010 G1020 G1030 G1040	Site Clearing Site Demolition and Relocations Site Earthwork Hazardous Waste Remediation
	G20	Site Improvements	G2010 G2020 G2030 G2040 G2050	Roadways Parking Lots Pedestrian Paving Site Development Landscaping
	G30	Site Civil/Mechanical Utilities	G3010 G3020 G3030 G3040 G3050 G3060 G3070	Water Supply & Distribution Systems Sanitary Sewer Systems Storm Sewer Systems Heating Distribution Cooling Distribution Fuel Distribution Other Civil/Mechanical Utilities
	G40	Site Electrical Utilities	G4010 G4020 G4030 G4040	Electrical Distribution Exterior Lighting Exterior Communications & Security Other Electrical Utilities
	G50	Other Site Construction	G5010 G5020	Service Tunnels Other Site Systems & Equipment

decision as to where, to include specific items among various categories or classification elements is based on professional judgment. If it is not obvious based on where a particular item may logically be placed in the building system, a simple guideline is to choose that classification category or element where design and building professionals in current practice normally look for such items.

- UNIFORMAT II is not intended to classify elements of major civil works other than buildings. It is obviously based upon the definition of elements in the construction of buildings. The UNIFORMAT II classification of building-related sitework has been developed to provide a compatible system for guidance so that planners of the larger infrastructure related to buildings do not have to resort to multiple elemental classifications for one project.

Description of UNIFORMAT II elements

Tables B-1 and B-2 (See Appendix B-10) present the UNIFORMAT II classification, as building and building-related sitework, respectively and given as three hierarchical levels:

- Level 1 for major group elements.
- Level 2 for group elements.
- Level 3 for individual elements.

A full description or index of specific items included and excluded at Level 3 is provided in ASTM (1996). Listings of inclusions and exclusions are not intended to be exhaustive. Rather, they provide a general outline of what to expect in that element consistent with the selection criteria outlined above. Exclusions are listed to help readers find items quickly. An example of inclusions and exclusions presented in the standard is shown in Table 2 for A10 *Foundations*.

Table 2. Description of UNIFORMAT II
Elements for A10 - *Foundations* (after ASTM Standard E1557-96).

A 1010 - Standard Foundations

Includes

- wall and column foundations
- foundation walls up to level of top of slab on grade
- anchor plates
- pile caps
- foundation excavation backfill and compaction
- footings and bases
- perimeter insulation
- perimeter drainage

Excludes

- general excavation to reduce levels (see G1030 -Site Earthwork)
- excavation for basements (see A2010-Basement Excavation)
- basement walls (see A2020 - Basement Walls)
- under-slab drainage and insulation (see A1030-Slab on Grade)

A 1020 - Special Foundations

Includes

- piling
- caissons
- underpinning
- dewatering
- raft foundations
- any other special foundation conditions

Excludes

- pile caps (see A1010 - Standard Foundations)
- rock excavation unless associated with Special Foundations (see A1010-Standard Foundations and A2010 - Basement Excavation)

A 1030 - Slab on Grade

Includes

- structural
- inclined slabs on grade
- trenches and pits
- bases
- under-slab drainage
- under-slab insulation

Excludes

- standard applied floor finishes (see C3020 - *Floor Finishes*)
- hardeners and sealers to the slab (see C3020 - *Floor Finishes*)

2 Design versus construction estimates

Overview

Building design and construction estimates in North America are based either on a *product classification*, in which case costs are listed by materials quantities independent of their place in the construction assembly or an *elemental classification* (also referred to as an "assemblies" or" systems" classification) in which case costs are directly attributable to component and assembly quantities.

Construction estimates based on product classification most commonly reference the CSI/CSC MASTERFORMAT Divisions 1-16, whose primary application is for construction documents-phase specifications. This classification system, widely adopted in the building trades, derives from contractor practices for convenience of price quotations from traditional construction materials/product sources, that is the specifications are used as the key reference in contractor estimates and bid proposals. Many trades incorporate products from more than one CSI/CSC Division. Therefore, MASTERFORMAT is not to be considered a non-redundant "trade classification." MASTERFORMAT may also be used for design estimates because specifications are based on MASTERFORMAT.

Given the emphasis now being placed on limited project budgets defined in design phases if not before, and the need for designers to clearly understand costs related to their early planning and design decisions, the UNIFORMAT classification is more suitable for design cost analysis and budget control. UNIFORMAT II estimates are structured to facilitate design cost analysis and monitoring from the programming phase through to completion of working drawings. Costing based on components, assemblies and systems permit a designer to understand costs based on design decisions directly at hand. Furthermore, early design specifications based on UNIFORMAT II can be directly linked to the specification. A caution, however, is that due to the differences noted, such estimates are not recommended for preparing trade estimates and are not a substitute for MASTERFORMAT.

Elemental estimate objectives

Using UNIFORMAT II to structure elemental estimates during the programming and design phases of a project will assist in:

- Breaking down construction tasks into a simple, logical, hierarchical Work Breakdown Structure (WBS) of elements / systems / assemblies, that follows the construction sequence. Having a suitable WBS established early and consistently developed throughout the project is one of the basic principles of effective project management.

- Preparing relatively simple but overall accurate estimates during programming and early design, which find their validity in the accuracy and currency of the element cost figures. Readily assessing the costs of major changes at any phase of programming and design, evidenced by the record of design drawings.

- Indicating the anticipated quality level of a building and its elements, by reference to both design specification and cost impact reflected in the element unit rates and providing effective design cost analysis based on the parameters and ratios generated in the system summaries.

- Setting Design-to-Cost (DTC) targets for each discipline based on the facilities program estimate and establishing effective monitoring of costs element by element from the facilities programming phase through completion of final design (the audit trail).

- Identifying cost overruns and clarifying design and specification alternatives at the earliest possible so that corrective action may be initiated without delay.

- Reutilizing, verifying and updating cost data from previous projects to develop data base of accurate, realistic, elemental budgets for future projects (*cf.* Parker and Dell'Isola 1991).

Element cost data sources

Element costs are obtained from published cost manuals, historical cost data, or built up from assembly and component costs.

- *Published elemental cost data.* The annual R. S. Means "Assemblies Cost Data" manual provides element and assemblies costs. Although currently structured according to the original UNIFORMAT, the data can readily be used for UNIFORMAT II estimates as in the example presented below.

- The annual R. S. Means "Square Foot Cost Data" manual also includes an *assemblies section* based on the original UNIFORMAT, as do other annual cost manuals, including R. S. Means Mechanical and Electrical cost manuals. For example, Fig. 1 illustrates a brick face and concrete block insulated wall (Element B2010) priced at $20.40 per square foot. Fig. 2 illustrates a slab-on-grade (Element A1010) priced at $2.73 per square foot. (Note that unit costs include all sub-contractor mark-ups, but not the General Contractor percentage for general conditions, overhead and profit.)

- *Historical elemental cost data.* Historical costs from similar projects adjusted for inflation are a valuable source of data input for elemental estimates. Such data will be most easily used if structured in the same format as UNIFORMAT II. Percentages for allowances, contingencies, escalation, and overhead and profit should be formatted in a consistent manner. Given the criticality of cost assumptions, unit costs assumptions might be reviewed with experienced builders and construction managers and, in critical cases verified by site observation of total time and materials utilization for similar elements and assemblies.

- *Built-up elemental cost data.* Elemental costs can be built up from component and assemblies costs. Figs. 1 and 2 illustrate how costs are built up from component costs for B2010 - Exterior Walls and A1010 - Slab on Grade. In the case of B1020 - Floor Construction, the element cost would be built-up from assembly costs for the floor structure and the columns.

3 Elemental estimate example

Office building example

A simple office building described in Fig. 3 illustrates the application of the UNIFORMAT II classification for estimating, The building has eight floor levels above ground level, one basement parking level, and a total gross floor area of 54,000 sq. ft. A brief description or outline specification based on the UNIFORMAT II classification is presented in the caption, which links the estimate directly to the specification, thereby improving project team communications and coordination.

The estimate summaries are presented in four distinct tables to facilitate design cost analysis.

- Table 3 illustrates an example element cost calculation for *floor finishes*, with rates based on U. S. averages costs.

- Table 4 is an example *building elemental cost summary*. This is a stand alone estimate that provides the total estimated cost of the building (including all contingencies, escalation, overhead and profit) as well as analytic parameters and ratios for design cost analysis, *i.e.*, the total estimated cost for the building only is readily identified, *i.e.*, $4,781,072 ($88.54 per sq. ft. of gross ft. area.

- Table 5 indicates an example *sitework elemental cost summary.* This is also a stand alone estimate that allows total estimated sitework costs to be treated as a distinct separate entity from the building costs, *i.e.*, $208,012.

- Table 6 is an example *total construction cost summary.*, with a breakdown of costs and percentages to analyze the total construction cost of $4,989,084.

With design estimates formatted in a consistent manner from programming phase through to final design and from project to project, communications and coordination among team members is improved. The elemental cost summaries shown in the example tabulations incorporate the features that facilitate this result, *e.g.*:

- Element units of measurement are consistent, allowing unit costs to be readily analyzed.

- Client and owner representatives can submit comments earlier because their quality expectations are described in the outline specifications and are reflected in the element unit rates presented to them.

- Numerous parameters and ratios are generated to allow effective design cost analysis.

Element units of measurement
For most elements, appropriate units of measurement can be selected to allow elemental unit rates to be developed for cost analysis. For example:

A1010 - *Standard Foundations* are measured in terms of footprint area (FPA). The cost of A1010 in the example is $30,433 and based on an element quantity of 6,000 SF FPA. The unit rate is $5.07 / SF per unit FPA, a meaningful number for cost analysis.

B3010 - *Roof Coverings* are measured in terms of roof area (SF). The cost in the example is $17,506 and based on an element quantity of 6,000 SF of roof area the unit rate is $2.92 / SF roof area.

C1010 - *Partitions* are measured in terms of the area of partitions (SF). The cost in the example is $160,846 and based on an element quantity of 28,979 SF. The unit rate is $5.55 per SF (note that in the summary, the rate is the average unit cost of partitions).

D3030 - *Cooling Generation* is measured in terms of tons refrigeration (TR). The cost in the example is $137,200, and based on a 150-ton chiller plant. The unit rate is $915 per TR.

Table 3. Element Costs for C3020 - *Floor Finishes.*

Code [1]	Description	Qty (SF)	Rate ($)	Cost ($)
C3020	Floor Finishes	37,350	3.74 [2]	139,791.00
6.6-100-0060	Office Carpeting	33,075	3.31	109,478.25
6.6-100-1100	Terrazzo for lobby, corridor and toilet rooms	2,175	7.41	16,116.75
6.6-100-1720	Ceramic tiles for washrooms	2,100	6.76	14,196.00

Notes:
[1] The Code designations for line items are from 1997 R. S. Means "Assemblies Cost Data" manual.
[2] The resulting rate of $3.74 / SF of finished floor area shown for element C3020-*Floor Finishes*, is an average rate for the element based on the total quantity and total cost of floor finishes.

TABLE 4: UNIFORMAT II BUILDING ELEMENTAL COST SUMMARY

LEVEL 2 GROUP ELEMENTS / Level 3 Elements	Ratio Qty/GFA	ELEMENT Quantity	Unit	Rate	Amount	Cost per Unit GFA	% Trade Cost
A10 FOUNDATIONS					**48,733**	**0.90**	**1.2%**
A1010 Standard Foundations	0.11	6,000.	FPA	5.07	30,433	0.56	
A1020 Special Foundations							
A1030 Slab on Grade	0.11	6,000.	SF	3.05	18,300	0.34	
A20 BASEMENT CONSTRUCTION					**75,492**	**1.40**	**1.9%**
A2010 Basement Excavation	0.05	2,667.	CY	10.18	27,162	0.50	
A2020 Basement Walls	0.07	3,840.	SF	12.59	48,330	0.90	
B10 SUPERSTRUCTURE					**620,264**	**11.49**	**15.4%**
B1010 Floor Construction	0.89	48,000.	SF	12.08	580,032	10.74	
B1020 Roof Construction	0.11	6,000.	SF	6.71	40,231	0.75	
B20 EXTERIOR CLOSURE					**662,477**	**12.08**	**16.2%**
B2010 Exterior Walls	0.47	25,500.	SF	15.45	393,869	7.29	
B2020 Exterior Windows	0.12	6,500.	SF	38.76	251,923	4.67	
B2030 Exterior Doors	0.00	4.	LVS	1,671.25	6,685	0.12	
B30 ROOFING					**18,255**	**0.34**	**0.5%**
B3010 Roof Coverings	0.11	6,000.	SF	2.92	17,506	0.32	
B3020 Roof Openings	0.00	1.	EA	749.00	749	0.01	
C10 INTERIOR CONSTRUCTION					**208,314**	**3.86**	**5.2%**
C1010 Partitions	0.54	28,979.	SF	5.55	160,846	2.98	
C1020 Interior Doors	0.00	66.	EA	530.00	34,980	0.65	
C1030 Specialties	0.00	1.	Lot	12,487.85	12,488	0.23	
C20 STAIRCASES					**103,500**	**1.92**	**2.6%**
C2010 Stair Construction	0.00	18.	FLT	5,750.00	103,500	1.92	
C2020 Stair Finishes							
C30 INTERIOR FINISHES					**335,828**	**6.22**	**8.4%**
C3010 Wall Finishes	0.81	43,484.	SF	2.59	112,837	2.09	
C3020 Floor Finishes	0.69	37,350.	SF	3.74	139,791	2.59	
C3030 Ceiling Finishes	0.77	41,600.	SF	2.00	83,200	1.54	
D10 CONVEYING SYSTEMS					**249,360**	**4.62**	**6.2%**
D1010 Elevators	0.00	18.	STS	13,853.33	249,360	4.62	
D1020 Escalators & Moving Walks							
D1030 Material Handling Systems							
D20 PLUMBING					**124,059**	**2.30**	**3.1%**
D2010 Plumbing Fixtures	0.00	78.	FIX	1,019.94	79,555	1.47	
D2020 Domestic Water Distribution	0.00	39.	FIX	507.36	19,787	0.37	
D2030 Sanitary Waste	0.00	39.	FIX	476.41	18,580	0.34	
D2040 Rain Water Drainage	0.11	6,000.	SF	1.02	6,137	0.11	
D2050 Special Plumbing Systems							
D30 HVAC					**767,885**	**14.03**	**18.9%**
D3010 Energy Supply							
D3020 Heat Generating Systems	0.01	765.	MBH	30.03	22,975	0.43	
D3030 Cooling Generating Systems	0.00	150.	TR	914.67	137,200	2.54	
D3040 Distribution Systems	0.89	48,000.	SF	10.19	488,960	9.05	
D3050 Terminal & Package Units	0.11	6,000.	SF	1.48	8,850	0.16	
D3060 Controls and Instrumentation	1.00	54,000.	SF	1.60	86,400	1.60	
D3070 Special HVAC Systems & Equipment							
D3080 Systems Testing & Balancing	1.00	54,000.	SF	0.25	13,500	0.25	
D40 FIRE PROTECTION					**110,340**	**2.04**	**2.7%**
D4010 Fire Protection and Sprinkler Systems	0.01	270.	HDS	320.22	86,460	1.60	
D4020 Stand-pipe and Hose Systems	0.00	9.	CAB	2,653.33	23,880	0.44	
D4030 Fire Protection Specialties							
D4040 Special Fire Protection Systems							
D50 ELECTRICAL					**639,576**	**11.84**	**15.9%**
D5010 Electrical Service & Distribution	0.01	360.	kW	203.68	73,326	1.36	
D5020 Lighting & Branch Wiring	0.01	360.	kW	1,205.92	434,130	8.04	
D5030 Communication and Security Systems	1.00	54,000.	SF	2.14	115,725	2.14	
D5040 Special Electrical Systems	1.00	54,000.	SF	0.30	16,395	0.30	
E10 EQUIPMENT					**16,595**	**0.31**	**0.4%**
E1010 Commercial Equipment							
E1020 Institutional Equipment							
E1030 Vehicular Equipment	0.00	1.	Lot	9,960.00	9,960	0.18	
E1040 Other Equipment	0.00	1.	Lot	6,635.00	6,635	0.12	
E20 FURNISHINGS					**58,212**	**1.08**	**1.4%**
E2010 Fixed Furnishings	0.00	1.	Lot	58,212.00	58,212	1.08	
E2020 Movable Furnishings							
F10 SPECIAL CONSTRUCTION							
F1010 Special Structures							
F1020 Integrated Construction							
F1030 Special Construction Systems							
F1040 Special Facilities							
F1050 Special Controls and Instrumentation							
F20 SELECTIVE BUILDING DEMOLITION							
F2010 Building Elements Demolition							
F2020 Hazardous Components Abatement							
Building Trade Cost without Design Allowance:					**$4,018,890**	**$74.42**	**100.0%**
Z10 DESIGN ALLOWANCE				5.00%	200,944	3.72	
Building Trade Cost (BTC):					**$4,219,834**	**$78.15**	**105.0%**
Z20 OVERHEAD & PROFIT					**421,983**	**7.81**	**10.5%**
Z2010 Overhead				7.00%	295,388	5.47	
Z2020 Profit				3.00%	126,595	2.34	
Building Construction Cost without Inflation:					**$4,641,818**	**$85.96**	**115.5%**
Z30 INFLATION ALLOWANCE				3.00%	139,255	2.58	
Building Construction Cost (BCC):					**$4,781,072**	**$88.54**	**119.0%**

LEVEL 1 MAJOR GROUP ELEMENTS

A Substructure	124.2
B Shell	1,291.0
C Interiors	647.6
D Services	1,881.2
E Furnishings & Equip.	74.8
F Special Constr. & Dem.	
G Sitework	174.9
Z Allowances and OH&P	795.3
Project Total ($,000):	**4,989.1**

PARAMETERS

Location:	Washington D.C
Facility Type:	Office Building
Cost Index:	1
Estimate Type:	Schematic
Reference:	TRB-2
Revision Date:	25-Mar-97
Estimate Date:	01-Jan-97
Start Date:	15-Sep-97
Finish Date:	15-Jun-98
Design GFA:	54,000 SF
Program GFA:	52,000 SF
Difference:	2,000 SF
TSA:	43,560 SF
FPA:	6,000 SF
NSA:	37,560 SF

ABBREVIATIONS

TSA: Total Site Area
FPA: Foot Print Area
GFA: Gross Floor Area
NSA: Net Site Area

BTC: Building Trade Cost
BCC: Building Construction Cost

STC: Sitework Trade Cost
SCC: Sitework Construction Cost
TCC: Total Construction Cost

NOTES

1. The classification conforms to ASTM Designation E1557-96 "Standard Classification of Building Elements and Related Sitework - UNIFORMAT II".

2. The "Building Trade Cost without Design Allowance" is designated as the 100% value; this figure is the Design-to-Cost (DTC) objective for designers based on trade level costing.

3. Construction contingencies (part of the project costs) and taxes are not included in the summaries.

TABLE 2: UNIFORMAT II SITEWORK ELEMENTAL COST SUMMARY

LEVEL 2 GROUP ELEMENTS / Level 3 Elements		Ratio Qty/NSA	ELEMENT Quantity	Unit	Rate	Amount	Cost per Unit NSA	% Trade Cost
G10	**SITE PREPARATION**					**19,673**	**0.52**	**11.3%**
G1010	Site Cleaning	0.23	8,501.3	CY	0.31	2,663	0.07	
G1020	Site Demolition & Relocation							
G1030	Site Earthworks	1.16	43,650.	SF	0.39	17,010	0.45	
G1040	Hazardous Waste Remediation							
G20	**SITE IMPROVEMENTS**					**47,103**	**1.25**	**26.9%**
G2010	Roadways	0.06	2,400.	SF	3.53	8,460	0.23	
G2020	Parking Lots	0.50	18,600.	SF	1.45	26,970	0.72	
G2030	Pedestrian Paving	0.01	300.	SF	4.03	1,208	0.03	
G2040	Site Development							
G2050	Landscaping	0.43	16,260.	SF	0.64	10,466	0.28	
G30	**SITE CIVIL/MECH. UTILITIES**					**91,800**	**2.44**	**52.5%**
G3010	Water Supply & Distribution	0.00	80.	LF	20.24	1,619	0.04	
G3020	Sanitary Sewer Systems	0.00	120.	LF	6.07	728	0.02	
G3030	Storm Sewer Systems	1.00	37,650.	SF	2.04	76,795	2.04	
G3040	Heating Distribution							
G3050	Cooling Distribution							
G3060	Fuel Distribution	0.00	135.	LF	21.49	2,901	0.08	
G3070	Other Civil / Mech. Utilities	0.43	16,260.	SF	0.60	9,756	0.26	
G40	**SITE ELECTRICAL UTILITIES**					**16,276**	**0.43**	**9.3%**
G4010	Electrical Distribution	0.00	160.	LF	23.05	3,688	0.10	
G4020	Exterior Lighting	0.50	18,600.	SF	0.65	12,084	0.32	
G4030	Exterior Communication & Security Syst.	0.00	150.	LF	3.36	504	0.01	
G4040	Other Electrical Utility Systems							
G50	**OTHER SITE CONSTRUCTION**							
G5010	Service Tunnels							
G5020	Other Site Systems & Equipments							
	Sitework Trade Cost without Design Allowance:					$174,852	$4.66	100.0%
Z50	**DESIGN ALLOWANCE**				5.00%	8,743	0.23	
	Sitework Trade Cost (STC):					$183,594	$4.89	105.0%
Z60	**OVERHEAD & PROFIT**					**18,359**	**0.49**	**10.5%**
Z6010	Overhead				7.00%	12,852	0.34	
Z6020	Profit				3.00%	5,508	0.15	
	Sitework Construction Cost without Inflation:					$201,954	$5.38	115.5%
Z70	**INFLATION ALLOWANCE**				3.00%	6,059	0.16	
	Sitework Construction Cost (SCC):					$208,012	$5.54	119.0%

LEVEL 1 MAJOR GROUP ELEMENTS

A	Substructure	124.2
B	Shell	1,291.0
C	Interiors	647.6
D	Services	1,881.2
E	Furnishings & Equip.	74.8
F	Special Constr. & Dem.	
G	Sitework	174.9
Z	Allowances and OH&P	795.3
	Project Total ($,000):	4,989.1

PARAMETERS

Location:	Washington D.C
Facility Type:	Office Building
Cost Index:	1
Estimate Type:	Schematic
Reference:	TRB-2
Revision Date:	25-Mar-97
Estimate Date:	01-Jan-97
Start Date:	15-Sep-97
Finish Date:	15-Jun-98
Design GFA:	54,000 SF
Program GFA:	52,000 SF
Difference:	2,000 SF
TSA:	43,560 SF
FPA:	6,000 SF
NSA:	37,560 SF

TABLE 3: TOTAL CONSTRUCTION COST SUMMARY (TCC)

COSTS	Building Amount	%	Sitework Amount	%	Total Amount	%	Cumulative Amount	%
Trade Cost without Design Allowance	4,018,890	80.6%	174,852	3.5%	4,193,741	84.1%	4,193,741	84.1%
Design Allowance	200,944	4.0%	8,743	0.2%	209,687	4.2%	4,403,428	88.3%
Overhead & Profit	421,983	8.5%	18,359	0.4%	440,343	8.8%	4,843,771	97.1%
Inflation Allowance	139,255	2.8%	6,059	0.1%	145,313	2.9%	4,989,084	100.0%
Total Construction Cost (TCC):	4,781,072	95.8%	208,012	4.2%	4,989,084	100.0%		

ABBREVIATIONS

TSA: Total Site Area
FPA: Foot Print Area
GFA: Gross Floor Area
NSA: Net Site Area

BTC: Building Trade Cost
BCC: Building Construction Cost

STC: Sitework Trade Cost
SCC: Sitework Construction Cost
TCC: Total Construction Cost

NOTES

1. The classification conforms to ASTM Designation E1557-96 "Standard Classification of Building Elements and Related Sitework - UNIFORMAT II".

2. The "Building Trade Cost without Design Allowance" is designated as the 100% value; this figure is the Design-to-Cost (DTC) objective for designers based on trade level costing.

3. Construction contingencies (part of the project costs) and taxes are not included in the summaries.

EXTERIOR CLOSURE	A4.1-272	Brick Face Composite Wall

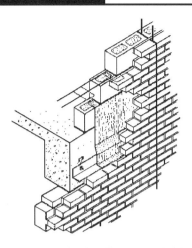

Exterior brick face composite walls are defined in the following terms: type of face brick and backup masonry, thickness of backup masonry and insulation. A special section is included on triple wythe construction at the back. Seven types of face brick are shown with various thicknesses of seven types of backup. All systems include a brick shelf, ties to the backup and necessary dampproofing, flashing, and control joints every 20'.

System Components	QUANTITY	UNIT	COST PER S.F.		
			MAT.	INST.	TOTAL
SYSTEM 4.1-272-1120					
COMPOSITE WALL, STANDARD BRICK FACE, 6" C.M.U. BACKUP, PERLITE FILL					
Face brick veneer, standard, running bond	1.000	S.F.	4.76	6.80	11.56
Wash brick	1.000	S.F.	.22	.59	.81
Concrete block backup, 6" thick	1.000	S.F.	.96	3.73	4.69
Wall ties	.300	Ea.	.04	.09	.13
Perlite insulation, poured	1.000	S.F.	.26	.19	.45
Flashing, aluminum	.100	S.F.	.09	.26	.35
Shelf angle	1.000	Lb.	.63	.66	1.29
Control joint	.050	L.F.	.09	.03	.12
Backer rod and sealant	.100	L.F.	.02	.25	.27
Collar joint	1.000	S.F.	.40	.33	.73
TOTAL			7.47	12.93	20.40

Fig. 1. Element B2010 - Exterior wall components
Source: Means (1997).

SUBSTRUCTURES	A2.1-200	Plain & Reinforced Slab-on-Grade

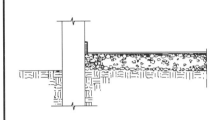

There are four types of Slab on Grade Systems listed: Non-industrial, Light industrial, Industrial and Heavy industrial. Each type is listed two ways: reinforced and non-reinforced. A Slab on Grade system includes three passes with a grader; 6" of compacted gravel fill; polyethylene vapor barrier; 3500 p.s.i. concrete placed by chute; bituminous fibre expansion joint; all necessary edge forms (4 uses); steel trowel finish; and sprayed-on membrane curing compound.

The Expanded System Listing shows costs on a per square foot basis. Thicknesses of the slabs range from 4" to 8". Non-industrial applications are for foot traffic only with negligible abrasion. Light industrial applications are for pneumatic wheels and light abrasion. Industrial applications are for solid rubber wheels and moderate abrasion. Heavy Industrial applications are for steel wheels and severe abrasion. All slabs are either shown unreinforced or reinforced with welded wire fabric.

System Components	QUANTITY	UNIT	COST PER S.F.		
			MAT.	INST.	TOTAL
SYSTEM 2.1-200-2220 SLAB ON GRADE, 4" THICK, NON INDUSTRIAL, NON REINFORCED					
Fine grade, 3 passes with grader and roller	.110	S.Y.		.32	.32
Gravel under floor slab, 6" deep, compacted	1.000	S.F.	.12	.18	.30
Polyethylene vapor barrier, standard, .006" thick	1.000	S.F.	.03	.09	.12
Concrete ready mix, regular weight, 3500 psi	.012	C.Y.	.72		.72
Place and vibrate concrete for slab on grade, 4" thick, direct chute	.012	C.Y.		.19	.19
Expansion joint, premolded bituminous fiber, 1/2" x 6"	.100	L.F.	.13	.19	.32
Edge forms in place for slab on grade to 6" high, 4 uses	.030	L.F.	.01	.06	.07
Cure with sprayed membrane curing compound	1.000	S.F.	.02	.05	.07
Finishing floor, monolithic steel trowel	1.000	S.F.		.62	.62
TOTAL			1.03	1.70	2.73

Fig. 2. Element A1010 - Slab-on-grade components
Source: Means (1997).

Fig. 3. Example - office building plans and elevation (source: R. S. Means 1997).

Front Elevation

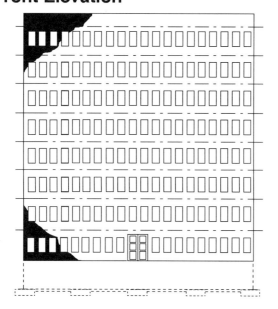

Basement Plan

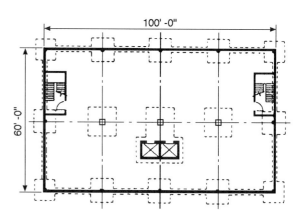

Ground Floor Plan

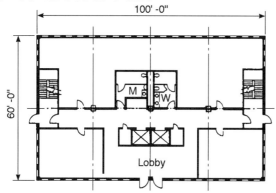

Typical Floor Plan

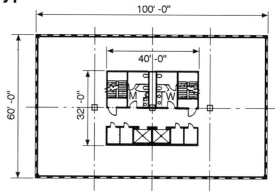

Example office building and sitework description.

GENERAL: Building size - 60' x 100', 8 floors, 12' floor-to-floor height, 4' high parapet, full basement with 11'-8" floor to floor, bay size 25' x 30', ceiling heights - 9' in office area and 8' in core area. One acre site.

A10 FOUNDATIONS - Concrete spread and strip footings, 4" concrete slab on grade.

A20 BASEMENT CONSTRUCTION - 12' high, 12" thick waterproofed basement walls, normal soil conditions for excavation.

B10 SUPERSTRUCTURE - Steel columns, wide flange; 3 hr. fire rated; floors, composite steel frame and deck with concrete slab; roof, steel beams, open web joists and deck.

B20 EXTERIOR CLOSURE - Walls; North, East and West, brick and lightweight concrete block with 2" cavity insulation, 25% window; South, 8" lightweight concrete block insulated, 10% window. Doors, aluminum and glass at 1st floor level, insulated automatic basement garage door. Windows, aluminum, 3'-0" x 5'-4" insulating glass.

B30 ROOFING - Tar and gravel, 4 ply, 2" rigid insulation, R12.5; one roof access hatch.

C10 INTERIOR CONSTRUCTION - Core - 6" lightweight concrete block partitions, full height. Corridors - 1st and 2nd floor - 3 5/8" steel studs with fire rated gypsum board, full height. Toilet partitions. Doors - hollow metal; Specialties - toilet accessories, directory board.

C20 STAIRCASES - Steel with concrete fill.

C30 INTERIOR FINISHES - Wall Finishes - lobby, mahogany paneling on furring, remainder plaster finish to ceiling height (partition and wall surfaces), paint. Floor Finishes - 1st floor lobby, corridors and toilet rooms, terrazzo, remainder, concrete, tenant developed 2nd thru 8th, toilet rooms, ceramic tiles, office and corridor, carpet. Ceiling Finishes - 24" x 48" fiberglass board on Tee grid.

D10 CONVEYING SYSTEMS - Two 2500 lb capacity, 200 F.P.M., geared elevators, 9 stops.

D20 PLUMBING - Wall hung lavatories and water closets; service sinks. Gas-fired domestic hot water heater and reservoir; copper distribution piping throughout. Cast iron sanitary waste piping; drains in each washroom floor and parking level. 4" CI roof drains and PVC piping.

D30 HVAC - Fire tube gas-fired water boiler and 150 ton water-cooled chiller installed in penthouse. Perimeter hot water finned tube radiation with wall to wall enclosures. 48,000 CFM built-up air handling unit for office floors. Low velocity air supply and return air distribution. 5500 CFM direct gas-fired parking garage air handling ventilation unit with air supply distribution and exhaust system. Pneumatic control system with central control.

D40 FIRE PROTECTION - Standard sprinkler system in office area; dry sprinklers in basement parking area; 4" standpipe, 9 hose cabinets.

D60 ELECTRICAL - Service, panel board and feeder, 2000 amps. Lighting, 1st thru 8th, 15 fluorescent fixtures / 1000 SF, 3 watts/SF. Basement 10 fluorescent fixtures / 1000 SF, 2 Watts/ SF. Receptacles 1st thru 8th, 16.5 / 1000 SF, 2 Watts/SF. Basement, 10 receptacles / 1000 SF, 1.2 Watts/SF. Air conditioning, 4 Watts/SF; miscellaneous connections 1.2 Watts/SF; Elevator power, two 10-HP 230 volt motors; wall switches, 2/1000 SF. Fire detection system, pull stations, signals, smoke and heat detectors. Emergency lighting generator, 30 KW.

E10 EQUIPMENT - Automatic parking garage access gate, dock leveler, waste handling compactor.

E20 FURNISHINGS - Vertical venetian blinds for all exterior windows. Washroom vanities.

G SITEWORK - The one acre site (43,560 SF) must be cleared and excavated in part to obtain required elevations; paved parking stalls with barriers and painted lines; shrubs, trees and hydraulic seeding for landscaping; water supply, sanitary and storm sewers; gas service piping; underground electrical power and cabling in conduit, exterior lighting, duct bank for telephone cabling; lawn sprinkler system.

Element rates and quality levels

Element rates are indicative of the their quality level; as a result, using cost modeling techniques, relatively accurate estimates can be prepared at the programming and schematic phases without detailed drawings. For example, based on a quality level scale of one to four developed by the General Services Administration (GSA), the costs attributed to B2010 - *Exterior Walls* could be selected from Table 7.

Analytic parameters and ratios

The following analytic parameters and ratios can be automatically generated in elemental estimate summaries:

- Cost of the element per unit gross floor area (Column "Cost Per Unit GFA") *e.g.*, from the example for D4010 - *Sprinkler Systems*, $1.60 per SF GFA.

- The average rate for an element based on the quantity, *e.g.*, from the example, for C3020 - *Floor Finishes*, the average cost / SF based on the actual quantity of 37,350 SF is $3.74.

- Quantity of the element per unit gross floor area (ratio "Qty/GFA") *e.g.*, from the example for C1010 - *Partitions*, 0.54 SF per SF GFA.

- Percentage trade cost of Level 2 Group Elements (Column "% Trade Cost") *e.g.*, from the example the cost of D50 - *Electrical* is 18.9% of the total building cost.

An understanding of parameters and ratios, that can be developed from documentation and experience, will facilitate the preparation of elemental budget estimates and the rapid analysis of detailed elemental estimate summaries.

Allowances, contingencies, overhead and profit

Allowances, contingencies and overhead and profit must be presented in a consistent manner for all estimates. A standardized presentation format for these costs will facilitate the reconciliation of estimates from different sources, a task that is usually most difficult and time consuming because they are usually calculated in any number of ways. These mark-ups could be formatted as shown in Tables B1 and B2; the format is based on a logic that facilitates cost analysis.

Note that construction contingencies, though part of project costs, are not included in the estimate summaries when represent the anticipated General Contractor's bid.

4   Design cost analysis

UNIFORMAT II elemental estimate cost summaries as shown in Tables 4 to 6 provide analytic data that would be difficult if not impossible to extract from trade or MASTERFORMAT Divisions 1-16 estimates. Some of the questions that could be asked in analyzing the office building estimate example, and the answers, follow:

Q: For the Superstructure B10, what is the unit cost and percentage of total building construction cost?

A: The unit cost $11.49 / SF and the superstructure represents 16.4% of the total building construction costs.

Q: What is the unit cost of quality level of exterior walls (B2010)?

A: The unit cost is $15.45 / SF, a commercial quality level (Level 3).

Q: What is the ratio of partition area to GFA and how is the partition (C1010) unit elemental rate interpreted?

A: The ratio is 0.54, *i.e.* for every square foot of floor area, there is 0.54 SF of partition; the average unit rate for partitions is $5.55 / SF, which indicates better quality than standard metal stud and gypsum partitions.

Q: What is the cost per ton of the chilled water plant (D3030 - *Cooling Generation Systems*) and the area per ton of refrigeration?

A: The cost per ton is $915, what may be expected for a water-cooled chiller system of this capacity; the area per ton is 320 SF, an average figure.

Q: What is the total estimated building construction cost exclusive of taxes and unit rate per GFA?

A: The total building construction cost is $4,781,000 and the cost / SF $88.54, within the range of acceptable costs for this type of building.

Q: What is the parking lot surface percentage of total net site area?

A: The parking lot G2020 has 18,600 SF, which is 50% of the net site area of 36,750 SF (Ratio QTY/NSA).

Q: What amounts have been included in the total construction cost of $4,989,000 for design and inflation allowances, and what percentage of the total do they represent?

A: From Table B3, $209,687 has been included for a design allowance and $145,313 for inflation; these numbers represent 4.2% and 2.9% of total construction costs respectively, *i.e.* a total of 7.1%.

Q: Does the building design GFA conform to space program requirements?

A: Table B1 parameters indicate that the current design at 54,000 SF exceeds the program area of 52,000 SF by 2,000 SF or 3.7%; this is one of the first items to address in reducing the cost of the building.

As seen from the above, effective design cost analysis can be performed rapidly if the data generated is suitably structured. Elements whose cost exceeds the norm can be identified early on in a project, and corrective action taken to contain costs within the allocated budget, thus avoiding time consuming and costly redesigns at a later date.

Table 7. Quality Levels and Costs for B2010 *Exterior Walls.*

Quality Level	Element Description	Cost ($/SF)
1. Monumental	Granite	$65.00
2. Federal	Curtain Wall	$38.00
3. Corporate	Sandwich Wall	$18.00
4. Commercial	Metal Cladding	$12.00

Other applications

Additional applications have emerged since the publication@of UNIFORMAT II as an ASTM standard in 1993. The range of applications extends from the planning phase of a facility to all phases of its construction and life cycle maintenance and covers:

- *Facilities planning and programming.* For performance specifications and design criteria, space program requirements schedules, budgeting and program estimates.

- *Facilities design.* For schematic and design development phase specifications, design estimates and cost control, functional area estimates, scheduling, risk analysis (Monte Carlo simulation), filing product literature, CAD layering, code conformity analysis, and classifying construction graphic standards.

- *Building construction.* For progress reports, deficiency reports, mortgage monitoring, commissioning.

- *Facilities and assets management.* For maintenance planning and budgeting, building condition assessment, long term capital replacement budgeting, reserve funds, capital cost evaluation.

- *Other applications* include structuring element / assemblies cost data manuals, maintenance and repair cost data manuals, life cycle costing data, and directing value engineering sessions.

Additional references

Bowen, Brian, Robert Charette, and Harold Marshall. 1992. *UNIFORMAT II - A Recommended Classification for Building Elements and Related Sitework.* NIST Special Publication 841. Gaithersburg, VA: National Institute of Standards and Technology,

Bowen, Brian. 1994. "Construction Cost Management." *The Architect's Handbook of Professional Practice.* American Institute of Architects. David Haviland, editor. Washington D. C. AIA Press.

Charette, Robert and Anik Shooner. 1995. "Using UNIFORMAT II in Preliminary Design and Planning." Chapter 25. *Means Square Foot Estimating.* Second Edition. Kingston, MA: R. S. Means Company.

R. S. Means. 1997. *Means Assemblies Cost Data Manual.* Kingston, MA: R. S. Means Company.

Parker, Donald E. and Dell'Isola, Alphonse J. 1991. *Project Budgeting for Buildings.* New York: Van Nostrand Reinhold.

CSI. 1992. "FF/180: Preliminary Project Descriptions and Outline Specifications." *CSI Manual of Practice.* Alexandria, VA: The Construction Specifications Institute.

Environmental life cycle assessment

Joel Ann Todd
Nadav Malin
Alex Wilson

Summary: Part I provides an overview of Life Cycle Assessment as part of environmentally responsible design, defining a framework for gathering, analyzing, and organizing information so that design alternatives can be compared from an environmental perspective. Part II describes information sources and a simplified approach for environmental life cycle assessment of building materials and products.

Key words: environmental impact, materials, life cycle assessment, products, resource recovery, specifications.

Roman stones reused in a Tuscany village

Part I: Environmental Life Cycle Assessment

Many characteristics are currently used to define "environmental" approaches to building design, such as energy efficiency, use of materials with recycled content, and use of lower-emitting products. By focusing only on a single criterion, however, other perhaps more important environmental considerations are ignored. Further, in many cases, these approaches only consider the building in operation or the product at its point of manufacture or use; the remainder of the life cycle is often excluded. Environmental life cycle assessment (LCA) provides a way of addressing these shortcomings by looking at environmental consequences from cradle-to-grave, that is, from the extraction of raw materials used in manufacture to final disposal or reuse/recycling. Some prefer to think of LCA as "cradle-to-cradle" to emphasize the importance of re-use and recycling at the end of life. LCA also includes all types of environmental effects. This comprehensive approach distinguishes LCA from other approaches for assessing environmental preferability. LCA provides a framework for identifying all of the environmental factors and provides information that assists in assessing which designs or products are preferable overall.

LCA is not a new concept. First applied to environmental and energy issues in the 1960s, it has received increasing attention in recent years. Efforts in several countries to implement environmental labeling programs have renewed the interest in LCA as a method for acquiring and analyzing data to support these programs. Further, there has been an increasing recognition that many environmental programs of the past have succeeded only in transferring pollution from one medium to another—from water to air, from air to solid waste, etc. More holistic approaches to solving environmental problems are needed. Recent emphases on pollution prevention have led those in industry and government to look beyond their own boundaries for the causes of pollution both upstream and downstream from the production process—during the entire life cycle of products and their constituents. Life cycle assessments are increasingly being used to document claims of environmental "friendliness" or to imply superiority of one product or material over another.

What is life cycle thinking?

Life cycle thinking is a way of approaching a decision. It considers environmental factors both upstream and downstream from the standpoint or purview of the decision maker—the architect, designer, builder, or building owner. It broadens the decision maker's perspective and helps to answer important questions about the environmental outcomes and preferability of design alternatives.

Life cycle thinking can be applied to many decisions that the architect faces. One obvious application is in the specification of materials—it provides information that helps in determining environmental preferability of material alternatives. For example, is it better from an environmental perspective to specify a locally-made product even if it is less energy efficient or one that must be transported further to the site? Life cycle thinking can help in answering such questions and can also be applied to other decisions. Other examples include:

• In siting a project, what environmental burdens are associated with new infrastructure requirements for potential sites? Can a project be considered "environmentally responsible" if it is located far from its users and is not served by public transportation?

• Is it better from an environmental perspective to demolish and rebuild an existing building or to renovate the existing structure? What are the trade-offs among factors such as reducing the solid waste from demolition and avoiding the life cycle impacts of new structural materials vs. potential compromises in energy efficiency?

Anyone can and should engage in life cycle thinking. It does not require overly sophisticated methods or detailed databases. It simply requires the broadening perspective of life cycle thinking.

What is Life Cycle Assessment?

Life Cycle Assessment (LCA) is a method for gathering and analyzing information to assist in answering questions such as those posed above. LCA identifies the processes, materials, and energy required during the life cycle along with the environmental burdens that occur as a result. These environmental burdens can be the result of energy production and consumption, waste generation and disposal, or natural resource use and depletion. Each process, such as mining of ore or manufacturing of a product, is examined using the template illustrated in Fig. 1. Raw or processed materials, energy, and water flow into the process, while the product (such as ore from a mining process or final product from a manufacturing process), as well as wastes, flow out of the process.

LCA explores the life cycle stages defined on the next page (Fig. 2).

• Material Acquisition and Preparation. This stage includes all activities that occur prior to acquisition of "feedstock" materials and pri-

Authors: Part I: Joel Ann Todd; Part II: Nadav Malin and Alex Wilson

Credits: James B. White and the U.S. Environmental Protection Agency have contributed to the development of this article's approach to environmental life cycle assessment and its application to buildings and materials.

References: American Institute of Architects. 1996. *Environmental Resource Guide.* New York: John Wiley & Sons. Additional references are contained in the body of the text and accompanying tables.

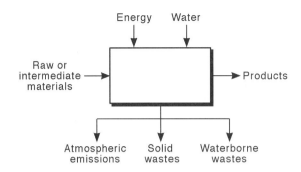

Fig. 1. Life cycle assessment template

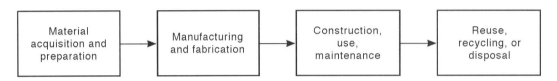

Fig. 2. Life cycle framework (after American Institute of Architects 1996)

mary resources by the manufacturer of the product or material that is the subject of study. It includes mining of ores, minerals, and rocks; extraction of petroleum and natural gas; harvesting of trees; growing and harvesting of agricultural products; and raising and slaughter or shearing of animals. It includes processing of these raw materials into the products needed by the manufacturer. This can include crushing, grinding, and calcinining of minerals and rocks; beneficiation of ores; refining of petroleum; production of chemicals; manufacture of intermediate products; and other activities. This stage also includes transportation of the materials and the acquisition of recovered and recycled materials. The major environmental issues at this stage are natural resource use and depletion, energy consumption, water consumption, and waste generation and their impacts on health and the environment.

- *Manufacture and Fabrication.* This stage includes all of the processes that convert feedstock materials into the final product to be ready for distribution and use. It includes packaging of the product. The major environmental issues at this stage are energy consumption, water consumption, and waste generation (including that used for packaging).

- *Construction, Use, and Maintenance.* This stage includes transportation of the product to the jobsite; the installation of the material in the building; maintenance requirements; and durability and anticipated life of the material. A major health and environmental issue at this stage is indoor air quality. Another important issue is the effect of the material on building energy performance (thermal, lighting, etc.) Construction waste is an issue of concern, best made into a resource recovery program.

- *Reuse, Recycling, and Disposal.* This stage includes the handling of building materials upon remodeling, renovation, or demolition of the building. Building materials constitute an enormous quantity of solid waste. In most parts of the U.S., the infrastructure for recovery and reuse or recycling of renovation and demolition waste is only now being established. Materials that are recyclable may be incorporated into components or assemblies, making their re-

covery difficult. Some building materials contain hazardous materials and must receive special treatment for disposal.

Methods have been developed for conducting LCA studies by the U.S. Environmental Protection Agency (Vigon *et al.* 1993), the Society for Environmental Toxicology and Chemistry (Consoli *et al.* 1993 and Fava *et al.* 1991), and individual researchers (Curran 1996). LCA practitioners have defined four components of a complete LCA:

- A scoping and goal setting process, during which study objectives are defined and study boundaries established

- An inventory, which identifies inputs of energy and materials as well as outputs consisting of air emissions, waterborne wastes, and solid waste at each stage of the life cycle

- An impact assessment, which characterizes and assesses the ecological and human health impacts of inputs and outputs identified in the inventory

- An interpretation or improvement assessment, which evaluates opportunities for prevention or reduction of environmental burdens.

These components are not conducted in a sequential, linear fashion. The impacts of interest should be considered to assist in shaping the inventory and then revisited as the inventory data are gathered and analyzed. Improvements can be identified at any point during the study. And the study scope can be narrowed or broadened in response to the information gathered.

What can an LCA tell us?

The LCA inventory will provide information on the total amounts of various pollutants produced during the life cycle. For example, it will enable the decision maker to compare two alternative products in terms of total greenhouse gases produced during the life cycle of each. While this can be useful, it can also be frustrating, since one product will appear to be superior in terms of one set of pollutants and a second product will appear to be superior in terms of another set of pollut-

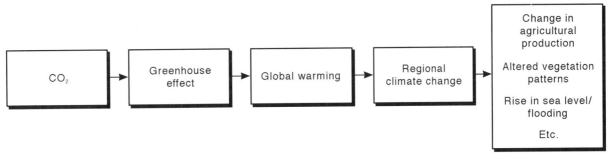

Fig. 3. Sample impact chain

ants. Users of LCAs should be cautious, however, in relying on studies that aggregate all of the inventory information into one or a few final rating numbers. Although such reports may be attractive in their ease of use, they oversimplify the information and the user cannot understand what the ratings really mean. Furthermore, it might not be clear what the effects of those pollutants are—could they potentially cause cancer in an exposed population or is their effect limited to skin irritation? The LCA impact assessment is intended to provide answers to this and other similar questions.

The impact assessment identifies the potential impacts that could result from the activities included in the inventory. It includes ecological impacts as well as impacts on human health that could result from environmental changes. Assessment of impact can be quite complex. The releases of wastes and consumption of resources can often lead to more than one impact, and each impact can also lead to additional impacts.

Impacts from the processes in the life cycle can include effects on the atmosphere and air quality, surface and groundwater quality and availability, and land or soil quality and availability. Depletion of resources and effects on habitats and biodiversity are also included. Specifically, we must consider:

- *Atmosphere and air quality.* Potential impacts include stratospheric ozone depletion, contribution to the greenhouse effect and global warming, degradation of visibility, addition of toxic and hazardous substances, contribution to ground-level ozone or smog, acidification, and odors. The first two impacts are global in nature; the others are more localized. These impacts could also affect the health of plant and animal species, including humans. They could also have effects on the built environment and the social and economic structure of communities.

- *Quality and availability of surface water and groundwater.* Potential impacts include acidification, eutrophication (or increase in nutrients, often with oxygen deficiency), nitrification, thermal changes, increases in turbidity, contamination with toxic or hazardous substances, chemical alteration, and depletion. These impacts could result in further impacts on aquatic communities, including changes in productivity, reduced reproduction, disease, and death, and on human health and welfare, including changes in morbidity and mortality, as well as loss of economic and recreational resources. Most water quality impacts occur on a regional or local scale and are dependent on regional or local characteristics of receiving waters.

- *Quality and availability of land and soil.* Potential impacts include acidification, erosion and changes in geomorphology, soil compaction, and alteration of soil chemistry (including chemical transformations and depletion of nutrients). It also includes removal of land from available stock, for use as a landfill or other

storage area for solid wastes and sludges, or alteration of land so that its productivity or habitability is changed.

- *Use or depletion of resources.* Since most of the resources that are used during the life cycles of building materials are finite, it is important to note the depletion of resources and the effects of acquiring these resources for building material manufacture on future worldwide resource availability. Examination of impacts on resource availability focuses on non-renewable resources, defined as those that are not being replaced or are being replaced over such a long time frame that it is not relevant to human beings. An important component of this definition is that the resource is not merely able to be replaced but that it is being replaced.

- *Habitat alteration or loss.* Alteration or loss of habitat and subsequent effects on biodiversity and individual species relates changes in the water, air, or land to potential effects on animal and/or plant communities, with particular emphasis on those that are rare or endangered. This category of impact is receiving more emphasis as people become more aware and concerned about the importance and value of maintaining biodiversity and preventing the extinction of species as well as minimizing the disruption of ecosystems whenever possible.

These environmental impacts can also affect human health. LCA can identify effects on human health in three areas:

- *Potential impacts on workers and installers.* Effects can result from exposure to chemicals, dust, and other potential health hazards.

- *Potential impacts on building occupants or users.* This area focuses on indoor air quality and its effects on building users (occupants, tenants, visitors, and maintenance workers), a topic of considerable concern to architects and designers.

- *Potential impacts on the community or general population.* In many cases, the information available on possible human health effects of the chemicals or other materials released during the life cycle of the building material is more generic. This information is based on laboratory testing and other studies, and generally relates the effects to dosage or exposure levels.

The LCA cannot tell the decision maker what the "correct" decision is. LCA can only contribute information to assist in the decision. The key is to begin to incorporate life cycle thinking into the design process. Then, the architect can seek out sources that present this information in the most useful ways. The Environmental Resource Guide (American Institute of Architects 1996) presents a streamlined approach to LCA and has made an effort to present LCA information on materials in understandable applications reports. Efforts continue to develop high quality life cycle data and to present this information in formats that can be applied to design.

Table 1. Estimated embodied energy of several insulation materials

Material	Embodied Energy in Btu/lb. (MJ/kg)	Mass per insulating unit[1] in lbs. (kg)	Embodied Energy per insulating unit in Btu (MJ)
Cellulose[2]	750 (1.8)	0.90 (0.41)	676 (0.7)
Fiberglass[3]	12,000 (28)	0.38 (0.17)	4,550 (5)
Mineral wool[4]	6,500 (15)	0.76 (0.34)	4,950 (5)
EPS[5]	32,000 (75)	0.39 (0.18)	12,700 (13)
Polyiso[6]	30,000 (70)	0.48 (0.22)	14,300 (15)

1. "Insulating unit" refers to the mass of insulation required for R-20 for one ft^2 at standard density.
2. Cellulose embodied energy data from personal communication with manufacturers. Assumes density of 2.0 lb/ft^3, R-value of 3.7/inch.
3. Fiberglass embodied energy data from the final report: "Comparative Energy Evaluation of Plastic Products and Their Alternatives for the Building and Construction and Transportation Industries," 1991, Franklin Associates, Ltd., prepared for The Society of the Plastics Industry, Inc. Assumes density of 0.75 lb/ft^3, R-value of 3.3/inch.
4. Mineral wool embodied energy data from Roxul, Inc. Assumes density of 1.66 lb/ft^3, R-value of 3.6/inch.
5. EPS embodied energy data from the German report, *Lebenswegbilanz von EPS-Dämmstoff*, Interdisziplinäre Forschungsgemeinschaft (InFo), Kunstoff e.V. Includes caloric Btu value of EPS. Assumes density of .94 lb/ft^3, R-value of 4.0/inch.
6. Polyisocyanurate embodied energy data from the final report: "Comparative Energy Evaluation of Plastic Products and Their Alternatives for the Building and Construction and Transportation Industries," 1991, Franklin Associates, Ltd., prepared for The Society of the Plastics Industry, Inc. Includes caloric Btu value of polyisocyanurate. Assumes density of 2.0 lb/ft^3, R-value of 7.0/inch.
Compiled by *Environmental Building News*, 3/21/95.

LCA and life cycle thinking allow the architect to go beyond the simplistic approaches that are based only on one or two elements, such as energy efficiency or recycling. There is no cookbook for environmentally responsible design, but LCA and life cycle thinking provide critical questions and useful tools to better inform the design process.

Part I: references

Consoli, F., D. Allen, I. Boustead, *et al.* 1993. *Guidelines for Life-Cycle Assessment: A "Code of Practice."* Pensacola, FL: Society of Environmental Toxicology and Chemistry.

Curran, M.A. 1996. *Environmental Life Cycle Assessment.* New York: McGraw-Hill.

Fava, J.A., R. Denison, B. Jones, et al. 1991. *A Technical Framework for Life-Cycle Assessments.* Pensacola, FL: Society of Environmental Toxicology and Chemistry.

Vigon, B.W., D.A. Tolle, B.W. Cornaby, *et al.* 1993. *Life-Cycle Assessment: Inventory Guidelines and Principles.* EPA/600/R-92/245. Washington, DC: U.S. Environmental Protection Agency.

Part II: Environmental Materials Selection

Choosing the right materials, products and components for a building is not an easy task under any circumstances. Environmental criteria can provide information to best practices and the need for durable, safe, easily maintained and replaced materials, all of which directly improve design and building quality and ultimately the ecological systems that are thus sustained. Environmental awareness does not bring "automatic" design methods or data to provide ready-made answers. Making the right decision requires judgment continuously informed by new information as more manufacturers and contractors develop better products and practices.

Ultimately the designer or specifier must use available information to make "best practice" decisions, and even these may change during the process of construction. A capacity to verify material selections, alternates and substitutions is also necessary. These design responsibilities are assisted by a number of data sources. The questions that the designer poses about environmental impacts are critical. A set of questions outlined below provides a guide to assist in the materials decision-making process.

Product life cycle

Most Life Cycle Assessments (LCAs) are based on an inventory of inputs and outputs. The attempt is made to identify all raw materials

and energy consumed in the production, use, and disposal of the product, as well as contingent pollutants and byproducts. Depending upon available data, the inventory may be detailed and quantitative or it may be cursory, in an attempt to highlight the most significant energy and environmental inputs and outputs. A subset of this inventory is the energy required to extract, transport, and process a material. Called the embodied energy of the material production process, this is often a good indicator of larger environmental impacts because of the pollution associated with energy generation in the manufacturing process. Embodied energy data for common insulation materials is compared in Table 1.

LCA examines the environmental impacts of each of these material and energy flows. This involves as much art as science due to the nearly impossible task of tracking ecological impacts as they ripple through the world's natural systems. LCAs done for specific products may include a final step—identifying areas for improvement. Given the complexity of analyzing the life cycle of a specific product, LCAs are usually undertaken only by relatively large manufacturers committed to reducing the environmental impacts of their processes. Fully detailed information is rarely fully available but significant findings are reported in professional and research literature.

Strategies for compiling environmental materials information

Designers who specify environmental materials (that is, materials selected to improve environmental quality and reduce negative impacts) may rely on a range of sources for their information. Professional associations, local and state agencies and recycling councils and environmental organizations offer some information resources. An array of published materials is becoming available. Software tools are being developed that may offer more flexibility in how the information can be searched and formatted.

Architects and designers may begin to learn about the environmental impacts of materials by querying manufacturers and suppliers directly. If sales representatives are knowledgeable about environmental issues, that is a fair indication that a company takes such issues seriously. Such queries often reach technical support personnel or those working in development to find out where the raw materials come from and how they are processed. As most manufacturers are inclined to share only positive information about their products, it helps to seek out competitive sources to understand the full range of environmental impacts of a product manufacture and use.

Table 2. Material selection guides

Publication info	# materials compared	Background info	Type of ranking	Source of the data	Comments
Environmental Building News, RR 1, Box 161 Brattleboro, VT 05301 802/257-7300, 802/257-7304 (fax), info@ebuild.com (e-mail)	16 detailed material articles as of 1/97, addressing about 50 different materials	Moderate to Extensive	None	Published literature, communication with experts and manufacturers	Recommendations often provide guidance on how best to use each material; specific products are mentioned by name.
Environmental Resource Guide Joseph Demkin, editor, The American Institute of Architects; John Wiley & Sons	26 detailed Material Reports; 8 Application Reports comparing a total of 55 materials (1997 edition)	Very extensive— detailed reports and tables explaining all ratings	White-gray-black in 14 environmental categories, plus split rankings where design can affect performance	Published literature, communication with experts and manufacturers	Recommendations also provide guidance on how best to use each material.
Handbook of Sustainable Building James & James Science Publishers (U.K.), PO Box 605, Herndon, VA 22070; 703/435-7064, 703/689-0660 (fax)	80 sections. each comparing 3-7 materials (April 1996 edition)	Moderate: little detail with rankings, but some background material in a later section	1st, 2nd, and 3rd choices, and "not recommended" for most materials. Also a "basic selection" considering cost availability	Proprietary LCA database	British translation of Dutch text. Good introductory overview on sustainable construction. Ratings are in two parts, one for new construction and one for renovation.
Green Spec Siegel & Strain Architects 1295 59th Street Emeryville, CA 94608	None	Extensive considerations by CSI category for Sections 1-9	None	Published literature, communication with experts and manufacturers.	Written in formal specification format, describes environmental considertions for materials in each section.
Building material Ecological Sustainability Index Partridge Partners, 23 Ben Boyd Road, Neutral Bay, NSW 2089, Australia; +61 2 9923 1788, +61 2 9929 7096 (fax) ecostruc@zeta.org.au	29 materials and 23 building components (assemblies) (December 1995 edition)	Limited: brief comments within the table, good introduction on the methodology	1 to 5 in 16 categories, combined into total scores for 3 major categories, and further calculated for complete assemblies	Authors' research, published data	Sophisticated weighting system for environmental categores—each area of concern is given a weighting factor that becomes part of the scoring formula. Use phase is excluded from the analysis.

Architectural firms known for their environmental specialization often develop their "office" materials data base through such active information searches. Some firms distribute questionnaires to suppliers, asking for extensive information on the composition and environmental performance of their products. A firm can improve response if it indicates that companies providing such information will be preferred suppliers. In increasing instances, environmental impact information is available in the form of a certification or evaluation from an independent agency. There are two common types of certification: those that establish the overall environmental performance of a product based on a predetermined set of criteria, and those that simply verify a specific claim made by the manufacturer, such as specified level of recycled content. In the U.S., the first type of certification is performed by the Washington, D.C.-based nonprofit organization Green Seal, and the second by a for-profit company in Oakland, California, Scientific Certification Systems, Inc.

Material Safety Data Sheets (MSDS) are available from manufacturers for almost all products. Obtaining an MSDS for a product is a relatively easy way to find out what it consists of, although some specifics may be left vague if considered proprietary. These data sheets also list potential health impacts of the ingredients in each product, so are particularly useful in assessing possible health impacts to construction workers and building occupants. Additionally, a client may have the resources to assist with environmental assessment of products. In some agencies, organizations and institutions, such as scientific, governmental or educational institutions, in-house staff may have the capacity to help to make such assessments.

Generic LCA studies

Simplified summaries or streamlined LCAs for building materials assist designers who may not have the time or resources for first-hand research. Such assessments are for generic materials rather than specific products, so they are usually generalized in LCA terms. They analyze the flows of materials and energy considered typical for the particular industry and the environmental impacts that commonly stem from those flows. While not as accurate as a detailed LCA, the streamlined summaries provide a good starting point for comparing materials. Several such assessments are listed in Table 2.

Most publications that provide guidelines to building material selection do so in the form of ratings or rankings of the alternatives for a particular application.

These approaches may try to synthesize all the considerations into one overall ranking hierarchy in a single summation or they may break out various environmental aspects and rank each material separately for each aspect, thus providing more information for the user.

Product directories

The other type of information source is the listing of environmentally preferable products. Directories are available in many different formats in print or electronic media. Some are specific to a particular category of products, such as those containing recycled-content. Others are more general, including products that are considered to have environmental advantages over the alternatives. See Table 3 for some specific references. Software tools are being developed—not yet available in commercial release—to provide assistance with building material selection by processing large amounts of data and presenting the user with relatively simple summaries.

Table 3. Product directories

Publication info	# of listings	Amount of detail on each	Categories of materials included	Publication format	Comments
Guide to Resource Efficient Building Elements Center for Resourceful Building Technology PO Box 100 Missoula, MT 59806 406/549-7678 406/549-4100 (fax) crbt@montana.com (e-mail)	425 manufacturers	Descriptions of applications and comments on each products, plus overview articles on each section.	Any that utilize materials efficiently, including recycled-content	Perfect-bound book, updated annually	One of the first, and most reliable sources.
The Harris Directory 522 Acequia Madre Santa Fe, NM 87501 505/995-0337, 505/995-1180 (fax) bjharris@igc.apc.org (e-mail)	1,000 products	Listing includes amount of recycled content, appropriate uses	Recycled-content materials	Computer diskette for PC or Mac, updated semiannually	Very thorough and up-to-date
REDI Guide Communications, Inc. PO Box 5920 Eugene, OR 97405-0911 541/484-9353, 541/484-1645 (fax) iris@oikos.com (e-mail) http://oikos.com	1,700 companies, including green design and building professionals	Almost none	Energy efficient, recycled, low-toxic, resource efficient	Spiral-bound booklet, free Internet access to listings only.	Access to Iris database on Internet is valuable, listings provide no information about the products.
Sustainable Landscapes and Gardens: the resource guide. Environmental Resources Inc. 2041 E. Hollywood Ave. Salt Lake City, UT 84108 801/485-0280	2,100 listings from 1,300 companies and organiations	Comments and descriptions of varying length	Products and materials used in landscaping	Perfect-bound text on recycled newsprint	Very comprehensive listings within the landscape area
The Sustainable Design Resource Guide for Colorado and theWestern Mountain Region. AIA Denver Chapter 1526 15th St. Denver, CO 80202 303/446-2266 303/446-0066(fax)	700 listings	Descriptions of each product, plus overview articles on each section.	Energy efficient, recycled, low-toxic, resource efficient	3-ring binder, diskette for IBM-PC or Macintosh	Good overall directory, with regional suppliers, and articles.

A simplified approach

Outlined below it is a simplified approach methodology for environmental selection of materials. The approach is characterized by a set of questions not normally posed in selecting building materials. The results of this process are only as good as the resulting search and knowledge-base that may result. The steps set up by the twelve questions described below cannot take the place of a thorough understanding of the life-cycles of the materials and their environmental impacts. They are intended to offer a checklist of sorts to seek out and apply that knowledge.

The twelve questions cover the life cycle of the materials, but not in the usual order. While the LCAs of many consumer products focus on the production and disposal issues, in the case of many building materials, the use phase of the product is most significant because of the relatively long lifetime over which building materials are in use. Building materials have a use-dominated life cycle. The use phase may not be the most important stage for every material one might consider, but in most cases this is where the most significant environmental benefits or liabilities can be found.

The manufacturing or production stage is usually the second-most critical, especially for highly processed or manufactured materials that are becoming increasingly common. Many of these materials contain hazardous or toxic components, or they generate toxic intermediaries in the production process. Some materials, such as aluminum, require a great deal of energy for processing. Generating that energy typically results in pollution and other negative environmental impacts that should also be considered.

Raw materials extraction and preparation phase is typically next in descending importance. Finally, the disposal stage can be important due to the shear volume of material that buildings embody. It falls at the end of this list, however, because of the long useful life of most building materials and the recyclability of many of them. Additionally, much of a building's mass can be utilized as clean fill, so the potential impact on solid waste landfills could be mitigated by construction demolition and waste reduction and recovery.

This listing should not be taken to mean that all materials will have their environmental burdens ranked in this order. For materials used in a natural or minimally processed state, such as wood or stone, the raw material extraction phase may be more significant than the first two, while the most significant impacts of many synthetic materials may be found in the manufacturing stage. A few products, such as preservative-treated wood, may be most problematic in the fourth stage, disposal.

- **Steps 1 thru 3: the use phase.**
  Two of the most significant sources of environmental impact from building materials are energy use in the building and possible impacts on occupant health. Considerations of impacts in the use phase depend not only on the material in question, but also on the application for that material.

- **Step 1.** *Energy use:* Will the material in question (in the relevant application) have a measurable impact on building energy use? If yes (as for materials such as glazing, insulation, mechanical systems), avoid options that do not significantly contribute to reducing energy consumption. For materials that result in an energy-efficiency only with the addition of other components, then also include the impact of the additional components. Examples include glazing systems that require exterior shading systems for efficiency, and light-gauge steel framing that requires foam sheathing to prevent thermal bridging, and so forth.

- **Step 2.** *Occupant health:* Might products in this application affect the health of building occupants? If yes (interior furnishings, interior finishes, mechanical systems), avoid materials that are

likely to adversely affect occupant health, and design systems to minimize possible adverse effects when sources of indoor pollution cannot be avoided.

- **Step 3.** *Durability and maintenance:* Are products in this application likely to need replacement, special treatment, or repair multiple times during the life of the structure? If yes (roofing, coatings, sealants), avoid products with short expected lifespans (unless made from low-impact, renewable materials and easily recycled), or products that require frequent, high impact maintenance procedures. Also, design the structure for flexibility so that those materials that may become obsolete before they wear out (such as wiring) can be replaced with minimal disruption and cost.

- **Steps 4 thru 6: Manufacturing.**
  The remaining steps or questions pertain less to the application (how a material or product is used) and more to the material itself. They require knowledge of the raw materials that go into each product.

- **Step 4.** *Hazardous by-products:* Are significant toxic or hazardous intermediaries or by-products created during manufacture, and if so, how significant is the risk of their release to the environment or risk of hazard to worker health? Where toxic by-products are either generated in large quantities or in small but uncontrolled quantities (smelting of zinc, production of petrochemicals), the building material in question should be avoided if possible, or sourced from a company with high environmental standards and verification procedures.

- **Step 5.** *Energy use:* How energy-intensive is the manufacturing process? If a building material and/or component is relatively energy-intensive in its manufacture (aluminum, plastics) compared to the alternatives, its use should be minimized. It is not the energy use itself that is of concern, however, but the pollution from its generation and use; industries using clean-burning or renewable energy sources have lower burdens than those relying on coal or petroleum. Results will vary depending upon changing manufacturing processes.

- **Step 6.** *Waste from manufacturing:* How much solid waste is generated in the manufacturing process? If significant amounts of solid waste are generated that are not readily usable for other purposes (tailings from mining of copper and other metals), seek alternative materials, or materials from companies with progressive recycling programs.

- **Steps 7 thru 9: Raw Materials.**
  Step 7. *Resource limitations:* Are any of the component materials from rare or endangered environments or resources? If yes (threatened tree species, old-growth timber), avoid these products, unless they can be sourced from recycled material.

- **Step 8.** *Impacts of resource extraction:* Are there significant ecological impacts from the process of mining or harvesting the raw materials? If yes (damage to rain forests from bauxite mining for aluminum, or timber harvesting on steep slopes with unstable soils), seek suppliers of material from recycled stock, or those with credible third-party verification of environmentally sound harvesting methods.

- **Step 9.** *Transportation:* Are the primary raw materials located a great distance from your site? If yes, seek appropriate alternative materials from more local sources.
- Final steps: Disposal or Reuse.

- **Step 10.** *Demolition waste:* Can the material be easily separated out for reuse or recycling after its useful life in the structure is over? While most materials that are used in large quantities in

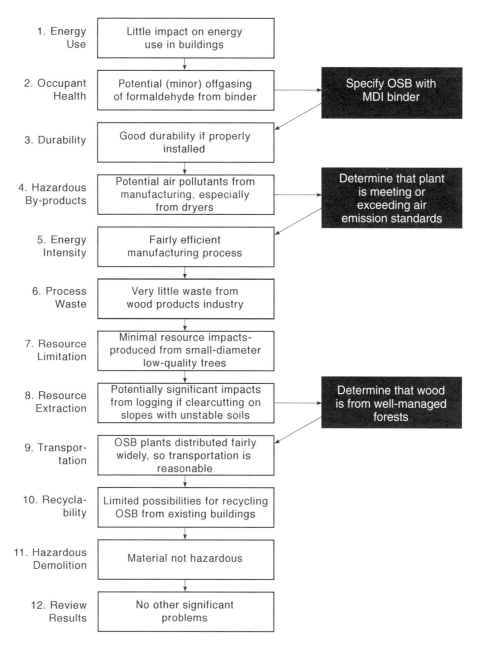

1. Energy Use	Little impact on energy use in buildings	
2. Occupant Health	Potential (minor) offgasing of formaldehyde from binder	Specify OSB with MDI binder
3. Durability	Good durability if properly installed	
4. Hazardous By-products	Potential air pollutants from manufacturing, especially from dryers	Determine that plant is meeting or exceeding air emission standards
5. Energy Intensity	Fairly efficient manufacturing process	
6. Process Waste	Very little waste from wood products industry	
7. Resource Limitation	Minimal resource impacts- produced from small-diameter low-quality trees	
8. Resource Extraction	Potentially significant impacts from logging if clearcutting on slopes with unstable soils	Determine that wood is from well-managed forests
9. Transportation	OSB plants distributed fairly widely, so transportation is reasonable	
10. Recyclability	Limited possibilities for recycling OSB from existing buildings	
11. Hazardous Demolition	Material not hazardous	
12. Review Results	No other significant problems	

Fig. 4. Example: the simplified methodology applied to oriented-strand board sheathing

building construction (steel, concrete) can be at least partially recycled, others are less recyclable and may become a disposal problem in the future. Examples include products that combine different materials (such as fiberglass composites) or undergo a fundamental chemical change during manufacture (polyurethane foams). Consider the future recyclability of products chosen.

- **Step 11.** *Hazardous materials from demolition:* Might the material become a toxic or hazardous waste problem after the end of its useful life? If yes, (preservative-treated wood), seek alternative products or construction systems that require less of the material in question.

- **Step 12.** *Review the results:* Go over any concerns that have been raised about the products under cossideration and look for other life-cycle and environmental impacts that might be specific to a particular material. For example, with drywall and spray-in open-

cell polyurethane foam insulation, waste generated at the job site is a potential problem.

Building material selection is an area where designers and specifiers make an enormous difference in the overall environmental impact of a building for relatively little cost. Further, by specifying materials and processes that reduce waste and improve resource conservation, a contribution is made to the local community and economy well beyond the building project. It is also an area where building designers can encourage manufacturing industries to improve their processes of production and the life-cycle quality of their products.

Ongoing developments and changing production processes continually offer new options to designers and specifiers. The best environmental approach is that brought by the architect, engineer and builder in undertaking architectural practices with an insistent set of environmental concerns and questions.▶

16
Construction and demolition waste management

Harry T. Gordon

Summary: Construction and demolition (C&D) activities generate large quantities of waste. Most of this material is disposed of in landfills. C&D materials are estimated to be 20-30% of the volume of landfills. There is an increasing effort to reuse or recycle construction materials. Roles of the architect include designing a comprehensive materials flow plan for building constructors and users, specifying recycled content materials and products and assisting the owner and contractor in a C&D Management Plan.

Key words: Construction waste, deconstruction, demolition, landfill, modular coordination, recycling, renovation, reuse.

On-site separation of wood scraps for recycling. photo: NAHB/RC

Construction material waste, generated during construction and re-modeling or demolition, is normally disposed of in landfills. The practice is costly in terms of both economic and environmental loss. Used construction materials and entire buildings normally destroyed and buried in landfill or incinerated, represent a resource stream that, in a sense, can be "mined." Many architects, builders, and owners wish to reduce the volume of construction and demolition (C&D) waste materials that are disposed of in landfills. In some parts of the country, a recycling program for C&D waste is mandated by law. In some cases, the costs of disposing of the C&D materials in a landfill are high enough to encourage recovery and recycling of major portions of the waste stream. The economic advantages of establishing a recycling program are appreciably greater when there is a local infrastructure of businesses that accept C&D waste materials for reuse or recycling.

There are important differences between "construction waste" generated by the packaging, residue and excess of new construction materials produced during construction, and "demolition waste" or debris from remodeling and/or on-site destruction of an existing building structure. Demolition waste is inherently more contaminated and often mixed in with or "commingled" with all other waste from the start, making it more difficult to include a wider range of materials in a waste recovery program (Malin 1995).

Although statistics are limited, studies of the quantities and composition of C&D waste have been undertaken by determining the percentage (volume and weight) of construction-related debris in the waste stream. The National Association of Home Builders Research Center (NAHB/RC) estimates that new residential construction generates three to five pounds of waste material per square foot of building floor area and that roughly 80% of a home building waste stream is recyclable (Yost & Lund 1997). NAHB/RC further estimates that 100,000 residential buildings are demolished each year in the U.S., accounting for more than 8 million tons of wood, plaster, drywall, metals, masonry, and other building materials, potentially reusable but for the most part ending up in local landfills (Fig. 1).

A study by Gershon, Brickner & Bratton (1993) of the composition of C&D waste from eight residential and eight commercial building projects shows significant differences in C&D materials waste by type and quality, depending upon the type of construction (or reconstruction), illustrated in Table 1. The opportunities and priorities for recycling are thus quite different for new vs. renovation, and residential vs. commercial projects. Most small-scale building or residential C&D

waste is disposed of in municipal solid waste landfills. In some states, most construction waste goes into specialized Construction & Demolition (C&D) waste landfills, which frequently have less restrictive environmental standards, since much of the material is inert. However, this has lead to illegal dumping of more hazardous waste in these landfills that originate from demolition debris (Wilson 1992). EPA regulations, set to take effect in 1998, will require states to implement the monitoring of these hazardous materials at C&D landfills (Yost & Lund 1997). Some states and localities may also have separately designated sites for Land Clearing and Inert Debris (LCID) that accept concrete, masonry and similar bulk fill.

Reduce—Reuse—Recycle

C&D material conservation can be achieved by variations upon the familiar theme of "Reduce, Reuse, Recycle," the so-called three "Rs" which provide a mnemonic of the consecutive steps in resource conservation and recovery. Attention to design and construction can substantially reduce the quantities of waste generated in the first place. A recent study shows that in-line framing, increased joist spacing, modular coordination and layout, and similar techniques, reduced the rate of wood waste generation of a single family detached house by two-thirds, from 1.5 pounds per square foot for conventional construction to 0.5 pounds per square foot (Yost & Lund 1997).

Items being replaced in a renovation but which still have value, can be recovered for reuse. This is best accomplished by using "deconstruction" techniques, defined as careful and selective removal of building materials for reuse, in contrast to brute force destruction and demolition at building sites which adds to air and possibly soil and water pollution. Wood is a common example of a material that is salvaged from older buildings and reused directly or processed to produce other construction materials such as flooring. Brick, glass, casework, porcelain fixtures, tiles and other products can also be reused. Because of coatings on architectural glass and windows, it is difficult to recycle these products if reuse is not an option.

Recycling of C&D materials is accomplished through source separation, either on the construction site or at an off-site handling facility. High value C&D materials such as metals are routinely recycled for economic benefit; the resulting recycled content products may be used in construction or other industries. Packaging materials such as corrugated cardboard and plastics also have a high recycling value and should be separated from the C&D waste stream.

Author: Harry T. Gordon, FAIA

References: Wilson, Alex and Nadav Malin, editors. *Environmental Building News.* Brattleboro, VT. 05301. This bimonthly newsletter publishes articles and current references on environmental approaches to design and construction, construction and demolition waste and related topics. Other references listed at the end of this article.

Another form of recycling occurs when medium value materials, such as wood or drywall scrap, are used to make new construction products. Some manufacturers have developed policies to take back their products at the end of their useful life. For example, nylon carpet (the most commonly used type), can be shredded (or fiberized) to create reinforcements for plastics and asphalt materials. Some fiberized carpet is also used as a component of carpet cushion. Several manufacturers now take responsibility for carpet replacement and thus, of "cradle to cradle" resource recovery.

Wood and site clearing materials can be mulched or composted. Unpainted gypsum board waste can be pulverized and used as a soil additive. Combustible materials can also be incinerated to generate electricity, although this alternative is not usually considered to be recycling and contributes to the pollution caused by incineration.

Waste recycling approaches

The commonly used methods of construction recycling defined in Malin (1995) are:

- Source separation on-site
- Time-based separation by the hauler
- Commingled delivery to off-site separation

Source separation on-site usually involves multiple bins or disposal areas in the site, for each type of material. Construction workers are trained to place materials into the proper bins or areas. Each material type is then transported to a facility that can make the best economic use of it, sometimes by reuse within the same construction site. Some high value materials such as metals may be sold. Other materials may cost the contractor less to dispose of at a recycling facility than at a landfill. This margin or difference between recycling cost *vs.* landfill

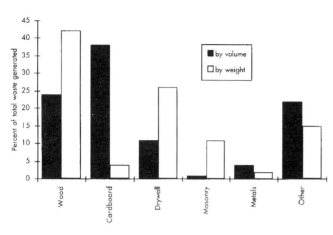

Fig. 1. Various construction materials by percent of total generated construction waste, based on NAHB/RC studies (after Yost and Lund 1997).

Table 1. Composition of primary C&D materials for each building sector (by percent of total weight for each sector).

	Wood	Gypsum	Concrete	Masonry	Roof Board	Pressboard	Metals Units	Misc. Materials
Resid Renov	31%	12%	<1%	4%	11%	2%	2%	27%
Resid New	15%	14%	8%	2%	1%	6%	1%	36%
Resid Demo	24%	1%	15%	20%	1%	<1%	2%	34%
Comm Renov	13%	4%	22%	19%	13%	1%	5%	18%
Comm Demo	17%	<1%	2%	0	0	12%	8%	55%

Wood includes dimensioned wood and plywood, but not treated wood.
Gypsum board includes painted and unpainted.
Concrete excludes rebar reinforcement.
Masonry Units includes concrete block and brick.
Roof Materials includes felts and shingles.
Pressboard also includes chipboard.
Metals includes ferrous and nonferrous.
Miscellaneous Fines are mixed materials of <1/2 in (1.27 cm) diameter.
Remaining quantities for each sector are generally less than 2% total weight for that sector. New construction projects often have corrugated cardboard packaging that can be recycled. Some projects also have vegetation from land clearing.

Source: Gershman et al. (1993).

cost varies widely throughout the U.S., and is the most significant factor in achieving high rates of waste recovery and diverting C&D materials from landfills.

Time-based separation by the hauler relies on the fact that different types of C&D materials are generated at different phases of the construction or demolition process. The C&D hauler makes frequent trips to the site, transporting the materials, and then separating and recycling the materials as appropriate. This approach minimizes the need for multiple material containers, which is an advantage on restricted construction sites.

Commingled delivery essentially the "one dumpster" approach for removal and delivery to off-site separation facilities is increasingly used where sophisticated C&D recovery facilities exist. These facilities use a combination of manual separation and sophisticated mechanical processors, including crushers, shakers, screens, and magnets to separate C&D materials, achieving a high rate of diversion from landfills. While this approach does not take advantage of on-site materials recovery and re-use, it simplifies materials handling and does not require much of a change of construction waste removal practices.

The economic variables of site, transport, tipping fees, and local markets for recycled content products constitute the most significant factor in the effectiveness of C&D recycling. The cost of landfilling C&D waste materials varies widely throughout the U.S., typically falling in the range of $20/ton to $80/ton (1997 cost range). Since any method of separating recyclable materials involves some labor cost, the highest rates of diversion occur when the landfill tipping fees are highest. Another important consideration is the transportation distances (and costs) between construction and recycling or landfill sites.

Effective C&D recycling also depends on an infrastructure of private businesses that accept source separated materials and then reuse or recycle them. In some locations, not-for-profit organizations have been set up to receive donated, reusable C&D materials, which are then used for charitable purposes such as repair of low income housing. In some such cases, builders are offered a "tax donation" for material so provided. In many metropolitan regions, local government agencies have created a directory of recycling markets, organized by material type. This can be very useful in developing a C&D waste management plan where "market demand" for recycled content can have the effect of "pulling" the materials out of the waste stream.

C&D waste management plan

Prior to the initiation of construction or demolition, the contractor should prepare a C&D Waste Management Plan. Many contractors have found that establishing a comprehensive plan enables them to be cost competitive, offering lower bids because of lower wastage costs and potential income from materials recovery and reuse. To assist in such planning, when construction documents are prepared by an architect or engineer, the specifications should require the preparation of a plan with the following elements:

- Identification of primary construction materials: These will vary depending on the building systems that are used and whether the project is new construction, renovation, or demolition.

- Estimate of material quantities: For demolition work this can be readily calculated. For new construction and renovation, the waste quantities will require some experienced judgment (see Tables 2 and 3).

- Identification of potentially recyclable materials: The types of materials that can be effectively recycled depends largely on available recycling outlets. An alternative is on-site recycling, such as mulching or pulverizing untreated wood or unpainted drywall.

- Estimate of cost impacts of recycling: This estimate should compare the labor, hauling, and tipping costs of recycling and disposal alternatives.

- Identification of on-site storage and separation requirements: The number, type, and location of containers for recyclable materials separation should be identified. Each container should be clearly labeled to identify the type of material that may be placed there. In some areas, multi-lingual labeling is valuable. A training program for the employees of the contractor and subcontractors should also be developed to avoid contamination with inappropriate materials or landfilling of recyclable materials. The general construction contract and each subcontract should contain provisions requiring compliance with the waste management plan.

- Description of transportation methods: The plan should identify the hauler to be used for each material type.

- Description of destinations: The plan should identify the recycling company or disposal site for each material type.

- Reporting: The plan should require records of the types and quantities of materials that are recycled and the quantities of material that is landfilled.

Table 2. Estimated Residential Waste Generation Rates. Quantities are per square foot (lb./SF) of floor area.

Wood (1)	1.3—2.1	lb./SF
Gypsum board	1.0—1.2	lb./SF
Cardboard (2)	0.1—0.5	lb./SF
Metals	0.02—0.13	lb./SF
Other Waste	0.5—1.3	lb./SF
Total Waste Generation	3.0—5.2	lb./SF

NOTES:
(1) Range for wood waste depends on material used for wall sheathing, siding, trim, and roofing.
(2) Range for cardboard depends on type of siding and whether windows, doors, and cabinetry are locally manufactured.

Source: Yost & Lund (1997).

Table 3. Volume-Weight Conversions in pounds per cubic yard (lb./CY) and cubic yard per ton (CY/ton).

Wood	300	lb./CY	=	6.7	CY/ton
Cardboard	30-100	lb./CY	=	20-50	CY/ton
Drywall	400	lb./CY	=	5	CY/ton
Mixed Waste	350	lb./CY	=	5.7	CY/ton

Source: Yost & Lund (1997).

Related topics

The approach to reducing the waste normally lost in the process of construction and building occupancy is best undertaken comprehensively, defined as a design goal from initial programming discussions, and carried through design and construction to occupancy maintenance procedures. A significant role of the architect can be expressed in the following ways:

Designing a comprehensive materials flow plan for building users. Recycling waste materials produced during the life of the building requires careful consideration of the types and volumes of materials that will be generated. The building program should include:

-   A protocol, adopted by the building owner, operations manager and staff and occupants, on the type of material separation that is appropriate during occupancy and use of the building, with incentives for waste reduction and recovery operations procedures. In many cases, these steps can realize cost reductions in procurement and operations efficiencies.

-   Methods and routes of moving materials throughout a building, from delivery and unpacking, to storage and use, such as sorting and separation bins and chutes, for example, chutes for source separation at each floor. This is best coordinated with the operations of building cleaning and maintenance and can add to improved appearance, cleanliness, and ease of maintenance.

-   Recycling storage requirements in working areas and at loading docks.

-   If appropriate (as in food preparation and dining areas), means to remove vegetable waste for on-site composting. This demonstrates the value of "nutrient" recovery and soil enrichment for on-site landscaping.

Specifying recycled content materials and products. In addition to reducing, reusing, and recycling construction waste, the architect and builder can specify and utilize recycled content building materials. Using materials with a high content of post-consumer waste materials is an especially effective means of reducing landfilling. There are a number of publications to assist the architectural specifications writer in specifying waste management requirements. National Recycling Coalition (1995) lists examples that illustrate the potential for recycled products in construction, the choices for which are increasing as more construction products are introduced with recycled content. WasteSpec (Triangle J Council of Governments 1995) provides model specification language addressing waste reduction techniques during construction, reuse of constuction waste material on the constrtuction site, salvage of C&D waste material and related topics.

Assisting the contractor in a C&D Management Plan. It is the contractors right and responsibility to manage all materials and methods of construction within the construction site, including means of delivery and disposal, defined by contractual law and applicable regulations. Recycling waste materials produced during the operation of the building requires careful consideration of the types and volumes of materials that will be generated. This is an important topic of "pre-bidding" discussion with builders, so that the designers understand the contractor's needs and requirements for materials handling within the construction site. The architect is able to facilitate the C&D Management Plan by seeking shared understandings of the needs and opportunities for improved waste management and resource recovery in the construction process.

References

AIA/AGC. 1997. AIA/AGC *Statement on Voluntary Measures to Reduce, Recover, and Reuse Building Construction Site Waste.* Washington, DC: American Institute of Architects.

Gershman, Brickner & Bratton. 1993. "What's in a Building?" *Demolition Age,* 9/93. Doylestown, PA: National Assocaition of Demolition Contractors.

Malin, Nadav. 1995. "What is New in Construction Waste Management?" *EBN* 4(6), Nov./Dec. 1995. Brattleboro, VT: *Environmental Building News.*

National Association of Home Builders. [Undated]. *Construction Site Recycling,* Washington, DC: National Association of Home Builders.

National Recycling Coalition. 1995. *Building for Tomorrow: Buy Recycled Guidebook for the Commercial Construction Industry.* Alexandria, VA: National Recycling Coalition. (703) 683-9025.

Triangle J Council of Governments. 1995. *WasteSpec.* July 1995. Research Triangle Park: NC: Triangle J Council of Governments.

Wilson, Alex. 1992. "Dealing with Construction Waste: Innovative Solutions for a Tough Problem." *EBN* 1(3), Nov./Dec. 1992. Brattleboro, VT: *Environmental Building News.*

Woods, Randy. 1996. "C&D Recycling Blooms in the City of Roses." *Waste Age.* Oct. 1996. Washington, DC: Environmental Industry Associations.

Yost, Peter & Eric Lund. 1997. *Residential Construction Waste Management - A Builder's Field Guide.* Upper Marlboro, MD: National Association of Home Builders Research Center.

17
Construction specifications

Donald Baerman

Summary: The Specifications are an integral part of the Contract Documents for any construction project. They determine the materials and systems used on the project and the quality for the workmanship. This article reviews exemplary practices of specification writing.

Key words: MASTERFORMAT, project manual, specifications, specification writing style, UNIFORMAT classification system.

FACILITIES and Spaces
Facilities and Spaces
SYSTEMS AND ASSEMBLIES
Systems and Assemblies
CONSTRUCTION PRODUCTS AND ACTIVITIES
DIVISION 1 GENERAL REQUIREMENTS
01100   Summary
01200   Price and Payment Procedures
01300   Administrative Requirements
01400   Quality Requirements
01500   Temporary Facilities and Controls
01600   Product Requirements
01700   Execution Requirements
01800   Facility Operation
01900   Facility Decommissioning
SITE CONSTRUCTION
Materials and Methods

Contract documents

Documentation for every construction project includes among the Contract Documents an agreement, a project manual, specifications, drawings, addenda and change orders.

- *Agreement* (part of the Contract Documents).

- *Project Manual*

- *Title Page* and *Table of Contents* (not part of the Contract Documents).

- *Bidding Requirements* (not part of the Contract Documents under AIA General Conditions, but may be part of the Contract Documents under engineers', municipal, and some other General Conditions).

- *Conditions of the Contract* (part of the Contract Documents). Include General Conditions and Supplementary Conditions.

- *Specifications* (part of the Contract Documents).

- *Drawings* (part of the Contract Documents).

- *Addenda* (part of the Contract Documents). May contain both Drawings and written material. Often bound into Project Manual. If they exceed about 5% of the original Contract Documents, they become pudenda (in Latin, "those things of which one should be ashamed").

- *Change orders* and other modifications (part of the Contract Documents).

Information best represented in the Specifications

- The Contract Documents are complementary, that is, what is required by a part of them is required for all. Communicate each bit of information once; don't try to communicate the information in more than one place. For clarity and coordination, make reference in other parts of the Documents to the place where the information is located.

- In general, draw what is best drawn and write what is best written. Minimize written information on Drawings, and minimize drawings in the Specifications.

- The Specifications include qualitative requirements for products, materials, and workmanship. They should stipulate product and workmanship quality standards, installation, guarantees, handling, environmental conditions, and similar requirements.

- The Drawings are a pictorial representation of the project, showing shapes, sizes, locations, and relationship of parts one to the others. They may also contain schematic diagrams and schedules.

- The organization of Drawings is spacial, representing three spacial dimensions on a two-dimensional medium. The organization of Specifications is more abstract, according to the CSI MASTERFORMAT. It is a one-dimensional text stream. It is confusing to try to show each type of information in the other's format.

- Consider how to make the information clear to those who use the Contract Documents. For example, don't specify products in inappropriate parts.

- Many parties use the Contract Documents. The Specifications should be so clear, understandable, and correct that all parties who use them will understand what is required. The major parties who will use the Specifications include:

- The design team, composed of the prime design professional and consultants, professional construction managers, and cost estimating consultants.

Author: Donald Baerman

Credits: This article is based on practices established by the Construction Specifications Institute. Examples for types of specifications provided by Michael Timchula while a student. Walter Damuck contributed to the section on writing new specifications.

References: American Institute of Architects. 1994. *Architect's Handbook of Professional Practice.* David Haviland, Editor. Washington, DC: AIA Press.

ASTM. 1996. *Standard Classification for Building Elements and Related Sitework—UNIFORMAT II.* ASTM designation E1557-96. West Conshohocken, PA: American Society for Testing and Materials.

CSI. 1997. *CSI Manual of Practice.* Alexandria, VA: Construction Specifications Institute.

CSI. 1995. *CSI MASTERFORMAT.* Alexandria, VA: Construction Specifications Institute.

Rosenfeld, Walter. 1985. *The Practical Specifier, a Manual of Construction Documentation for Architects.* New York: McGraw-Hill.

- Owner, the Owner's lawyer, insurance agent, bank, etc.

- Bidders, Contractor, Subcontractors, suppliers, foremen, and workers.

- Product manufacturers and distributors.

- Building officials, state education department staff, public health officials, environmental protection officials, and other regulatory agencies. Code compliance should be demonstrated where the officials expect to find it.

- Lawyers for both sides in a dispute. The language and content should be well-considered and not open to differing interpretations.

- People who will use the documents in the future, such as future architects and engineers designing additions and alterations and future building managers.

Representative problems

Following are examples (from actual cases) which could have been avoided by proper Specifications:

- *Foundations:* Failure to excavate down to good bearing material in a western library.

- *Substructure:* Leakage because of an inadequate waterproofing and subsurface drainage system.

- *Superstructure:* Specifying modern welding techniques and materials to connect to old structural steel, leading to hydrogen embrittlement and cracking of the old steel.

- *Exterior closure:* Leakage because of lack of proper underlayment and flashings under vertical board siding.

- *Roofing:* Leaking of cedar shingles because of lining up of first and third course joints.

- *Interior construction:* Inadequate provision of finishes to resist soiling.

- *Conveying systems:* Lack of coordination between elevators.

- *Mechanical and electrical systems:* Lack of proper balancing.

- *Site work:* Inadequate soil compaction.

Integration vs. fragmentation of the Construction Documents

- Specifications and products selection are parts of the same process. The specifier often selects the products and systems, and in any case normally evaluates them.

- Perhaps ideally one person or one integrated team should develop the Project from its inception through the beginning of its operation, producing all documents. On the other hand, it helps to have a more objective person or team look at the Project closely, and one way to do this is through a specifier, whether in-house or not.

Some examples of improper organization of information

- Avoid instructions about spacial information in Specifications, for example [Genesis 6:14-16/KJV]:

  "Make thee an ark of gopher wood; rooms shalt thou make in the ark, and shalt pitch it within and without with pitch. And this is the fashion which thou shalt make it of: The length of the ark shall be three hundred cubits, the breadth of it fifty cubits, and the height of it thirty cubits. A window shalt thou make to the ark, and in a cubit shalt thou finish it above; and the door of the

  ark shalt thou set in the side thereof; with lower, second, and third stories shalt thou make it."

- Avoid instructions about Specifications on Drawings:

  "(arrow) Four-ply built-up 20-year-warranted roof membrane with gravel aggregate and coal tar bitumen."

Types of Specifications

Each method of specifying has its own advantages and disadvantages.

- Unspecified: Use this for temporary products, or not at all.

  Example: "Provide indigestion relief."

- Allowance: Use allowances when vital facts required for product selection are unavailable, or when the Owner hasn't made a sufficient decision. Allowances are sometimes used (for shame) when the designer hasn't had time to select a product or (for double shame) to subvert competition. The discrepancy between the allowed cost and the actual cost is adjusted by Change Order.

  Example: "Allow $2 for purchase of a package of indigestion relief medicine."

- Proprietary specifications: This method gives the greatest control and the greatest responsibility. If the product is unfit, the specifier may be held responsible. Costs may rise because of lack of competition.

  Example: "Alka-Seltzer™"

- Performance specifications: The performance required of the product or system is specified, but the method of achieving it is left to the supplier. Evaluation of the product, especially over time, may be difficult. This method of specifying is often accompanied by a list of standard tests to which the product will be subjected. For large projects, this method encourages innovative product development and thus may be competitive and economical.

  Example: "Relief shall be just a swallow away."

- Descriptive specifications: Every known aspect of the product is described, but the manufacturer and trade mark are not stipulated. Properly used, this method of specifying is competitive and economical. It is not in the spirit of free competition to describe a product that only one manufacturer can supply.

  Example: "Indigestion relief: mixture of sodium bicarbonate, aspirin, and citric acid compressed into a tablet, 1/8" x 1-1/4", and packed in a glass or plastic bottle, not openable by small children but easily openable by adults, with a wad of cotton inside the cap."

- Reference specifications: Standards have been established by such organizations as American Society for Testing and Materials, Architectural Woodwork Institute, and American Architectural Manufacturers Association. These standards are non-proprietary, and thus competitive and economical. Sometimes they are descriptive, sometimes they are performance-based, and sometimes they contain elements of each. Where reference specifications are available, they offer known quality at a competitive price. But the specifier should know the standards, some of which allow different grades.

  Example: "Indigestion relief: Federal Specification I-HAVE-A-HEADACHE; Hangover Grade."

- "Or equal," "or equivalent," *etc.* The use of such terms is potentially confusing unless the basis of determination and the person or agency who will determine equivalency are clearly stated. When the intent is to allow competition, it is better specifications practice to use performance, descriptive, and reference specifications.

Sources of Specification information

- Standard printed information resources:

  - Sweet's Catalog File.

  - CSI Spec Data Sheets.

  - Spec Data II and other microfilm and microfiche systems. Spec Data II is published by Information Handling Services, (800) 241-7824.

  - Computer data banks.

  - Trade association literature.

  - Manufacturers' literature.

  - Construction and professional magazines and technical books, especially proceedings of ASTM symposia. An excellent way to stay current is to purchase ASTM symposia proceedings, read the abstracts which precede each article, and read those articles most relevant to your practice.

  - Publications of U.S. National Institute of Standards and Technology and National Research Council, Canada.

  - General association standards such as ASTM.

  - Text books and books of standards such as this volume.

  - Master specifications, both in-house and prepared by associations and publishers.

Person to person resources

- *Seminars.* Note especially:

  - National Institute of Technology and Standards (formerly National Bureau of Standards).

  - National Roofing Contractors Association, Western Wood Products, *etc.*

  - University of Wisconsin Division of Continuing Education, Madison, WI.

  - National Research Council Canada, Ottawa, Canada, K1A OR6.

  - CSI, Association for Preservation Technology, local AIA chapter seminars, and professional and trade association convention seminars.

- *Sales and industry association representatives:*

  - Some questions to ask: What's wrong with the product? What are its limitations? How long will it last, and how do you know? What support will the manufacturer give if the product fails? What technical support, in the office and in the field, can the manufacturer provide? Where can I see an old installation? (check this) What are the names of some of the older users? What's it made of? What general or industry reference specifications does the product conform to, if any? Will you back up your statements in writing? Why are you crying?

  - Should you let the salesperson write your Specifications? Answer: never! Should you let the salesperson review them? Answer: yes, they may well find errors and tell you of them.

- *Experience:*

  - Learn from work. Ask questions. Follow up the process whereby Construction Documents become constructed buildings, and modify your specifications to avoid problems you see.

  - During travel, watch what's being done. Take photos of what works and what doesn't work. Ask construction people and other architects about their work.

  - Determine what characteristics are critical to performance and which aren't.

Some cautions

- The name may be the same, but the product may change.

- If in doubt, try a sample installation or in-the-field test. For example, if the Specifications call for mortar mixing water to be drinkable, ask the Superintendent or foreman to drink some. If the product is supposed to resist stress, impose that stress. If the product is supposed to be waterproof, soak it in water. If it's supposed to resist severe abuse, throw it down stairs.

- Use previous office Specifications with great caution. Recent example: "Boiler breeching insulation: asbestos."

CSI MASTERFORMAT

The paleo-specificene era is characterized by project documents with indefinite location of subject matter in pre-CSI specifications. Each office and each project had its own organization, and finding where a product was specified was difficult. Characteristics of the CSI MASTERFORMAT include:

- There are 16 Divisions, with non-varying numerical designations to describe content areas.

- Sections, under the divisions, are used as appropriate.

- Broad-scope and narrow-scope sections are included. The choice depends on the size and complexity of the project. Excessively long broad-scope sections may be hard to use, and an excessive number of short, narrow-scope divisions waste words and paper.

- Each of the three parts of the CSI Section Format conveys a different type of information (See Table 1).

- *Part 1 General:* This part includes specific requirements related to procedures and administration of the particular section.

- *Part 2:* Products: This part includes information about systems, materials, manufactured units, equipment, components, and accessories, includes mixes, fabrication, and finishing prior to installation or incorporation into the project. This part may also include products furnished for incorporation under other sections.

- *Part 3 Execution:* This part involves basic on-site labor and should include provisions for incorporating products into the project. The products incorporated may be specified in Part 2, or may be furnished under other sections.

- *Scope paragraphs:* Some specifiers list exactly what is specified in each section. This is helpful to those who use the specifications, but the specifier must be totally inclusive; what's left out is not specified to be part of the Work.

- Some specifiers use a paragraph such as "The portion of the Work specified in this section includes all labor, material, services, and other items and performance required to achieve the successful completion of the Project." In the writer's opinion, this is an attempt to require a level of performance which is already stipulated in the General Conditions; it is redundant and unnecessary.

- The writer uses the following paragraph, suitably amended if the Conditions of the Contract are not AIA A201: "The AIA General Conditions, Article 1.2.3, states that the Contract Documents are complementary." The scope of the section is what is specified in the section.

- Related sections: As defined by CSI (1995),

Statements drawing the reader's attention to other specification sections dealing with work directly related to this section. This should be used sparingly to avoid assuming the contractor's responsibility for coordinating work. Listing should be limited to other sections with specific requirements pertaining to this work. If related work is specified to be performed "by others" or "not in contract," it is considered to be "by owner."

UNIFORMAT, II standard classification system
The UNIFORMAT II (ASTM 1996) provides a classification system for elemental design estimates and preliminary project descriptions. Because the CSI MASTERFORMAT is the standard for Construction Documents, including Specifications, UNIFORMAT doesn't usually appear in construction documents. It's advantages are for preliminary design and cost-estimating. UNIFORMAT defines elements of buildings as components of assemblies and systems, according to the place in the building construction (convenient for design and preliminary estimates), rather than as separate materials sections (convenient to construction specializations, trades and suppliers). It is independent of the CSI MASTERFORMAT (see "Introduction" for a comparison). As defined in ASTM (1996),"The classification serves as a consistent reference for analysis, evaluation, and monitoring during the feasibility, planning, and design stages of buildings" and to ensure "continuity in the economic evaluation of building projects over time and from project to project."

Specification language
Wording of past and present specifications:

- *Ben John Small abbreviated language*. This method allows for fewer words. Its contemporary contribution to specifications writing is exemplified as follows: "Steel: ASTM A36." Other parts of the system have mostly gone out of use.

- *Thou shalt:* "The Contractor (or This Contractor, or The General Contractor, etc.) shall build the partition." This usage is obsolete, and it uses too many words. Note that "The Contractor" is defined in the General Conditions, while "This Contractor" and "the Plumbing Contractor" are not so defined and are not parties to the Contract.

- *Infinitive form:* "The partition to be built." While economical of words, this usage is awkward and obsolete.

- *Punitive language:* "The Contractor will be punished if he doesn't build the partition, and he shall do so at no additional cost to the Owner." The words are excessive, and the form is insulting to one of the major parties in the execution of the Work.

- *Passive voice:* "The partition shall be built." This form was originally intended to be silent as to which party performs each portion of the Work. Is uses excessive words, and it is awkward and obsolete.

- *Contemporary usage:* imperative and indicative moods, active voice: "Build the partition," "The woodwork for transparent finish shall be mahogany."

Specification writing style
- Keep a dictionary, grammar guide, and usage guide within reach of your desk.

- If you remember, from secondary school, how to diagram sentences, do so when the meaning is not fully clear. In any case, decide what are the essential parts of each sentence. Strip the sentence of adjectives and adverbs, and see if it is still a proper sen-

tence of adjectives and adverbs, and see if it is still a proper sentence; then add only the useful adjectives and adverbs.

- The predicate should agree with the subject. Bad example: "Paint is one of those coatings which is used to finish interior surfaces." The phrase "which is used" modifies the noun "coatings." Since "coatings" is plural, the verb in the modifier should be plural also. The sentence should be: "Paint is one of those coatings which <u>are</u> used to finish interior surfaces." Or you can say, more simply, "Paint is used as an interior finish material."

- Use parallel construction. Bad example: "Sand the woodwork, paint it, and the paint shall be nontoxic." One of several proper sentences would be: "Sand the woodwork, and paint it with nontoxic paint."

- Capitalization: In addition to normal good grammar (Sam, Arkansas, Thursday, etc.) capitalize the parts of the Contract Documents and the parties identified in the Contract. If in doubt see the AIA General Conditions (American Institute of Architects 1994).

- Punctuation. There are some discrepancies between American English and British English. Since American legal usage mostly follows British usage, the General Conditions mostly follow British usage. The writer recommends consistent usage and prefers the usage recommended by CSI, which is American usage.

- Word and sentence length. Shorter is better. Words not commonly understood by all parties using the Documents should be avoided, and made-up words should be strictly avoided by specifiers. If it isn't in the dictionary, don't use it. Example: "parget" is in the dictionary, while "parge" isn't.

- Pronoun use. It is better to use nouns than pronouns. If you use pronouns, their meaning must not be ambiguous.

- Unnecessary words waste paper and time.

- "All" is implied. "Drive the nails" is better than "Drive all the nails."

Some rules peculiar to specifications writing
- The "method of the residual legatee" avoids omissions. Example: "Use float glass in windows, and use tempered safety glass for all other glazing." Thus no type of glass was left out.

- Scope by inclusion *vs.* exclusion. Exclusive usage avoids omissions. "Provide new tempered safety glass for windows in existing building except the existing stained glass window in the Guru's office."

If people tell you that they don't understand your specifications, make them clearer.

- Vocabulary, from CSI Manual of Practice:

- "Amount" refers to money. "Quantity" refers to everything else.
- "Any." Better not to use it.
- "As per" is redundant; both words mean the same thing, the second word being Latin.
- "Balance," not "remainder."
- "Either," not "both."
- "Flammable," not "inflammable."
- "Install," "furnish," "provide," "furnish and install." The following, making use of the "method of the residual legatee," are the writer's recommended definitions. Paragraph references apply to the AIA General Conditions Document A201 (American Institute of Architects 1994).

1.2.5.1. When applied to materials and equipment, the words "furnish," "install," and "provide" shall mean the following:

The word "provide" shall mean to furnish, pay for, deliver, install, adjust, clean, and otherwise make materials and equipment fit for their intended use, as specified in Paragraph 3.4.1 of the General Conditions.

The word "furnish" shall mean to secure, pay for, deliver to site, unload, uncrate, and store materials.

The word "install" shall mean to place in position, incorporate in the work, adjust, clean, make fit for use, and perform all services specified in General Conditions Paragraph 3.4.1 except those included under the definition of the word "furnish" above.

The phrase "furnish and install" shall be equivalent to the word "provide."

- "Insure," "assure," "ensure." These words refer to services provided by insurance companies, not architects and engineers.

- "Observe," not "supervise" or "inspect." Read the General Conditions. Perform the services which are delegated to the design professional, no more and no fewer. Refer to such services in the same language used in the General Conditions. Remember that an architect supervises only his/her own staff; the contractor supervises the Work.

- "Replace," not "provide new." If one specifies that broken glass be replaced with new glass, he/she has not specified what to do where the old glass has been broken out completely.

- "Shall" *vs.* "will." Specifications usage follows general usage. In general, the Contractor shall and the Owner and Architect will.

• Abbreviations.

- It's best to use only the abbreviations which are defined in the Documents.

- Don't use "*etc.*" in Specifications. Actual wording seen in a set of Specifications: "Provide all labor and materials required for a complete library except for the security system, furniture, *etc.*" In other words, don't provide anything.

• Symbols, money, and numbers.

- Use only common and clear symbols.

- Refer to money in words and numbers, "One Million Dollars ($1,000,000). It is not necessary to state numbers other than currency amounts in words and numbers; numbers alone are adequate.

- Metric system: See the Appendix (ASTM 1993). The convention used as in this volume is to use the more common units, followed by the less common units in parentheses. This will change as the International System becomes more widely used in the American construction industry.

Techniques of producing specifications

• Manuscript and cut-and-paste. This was a common method decades ago, consisting of paragraphs cut from old specifications interspersed with hand-written text. It is time-consuming, and it encourages errors and omissions.

• Hard copy master specifications were a progressive method decades ago. It was similar to "cut and paste," except that it was based on a master specification instead of old specifications. This method is too time-consuming for contemporary use. The proof reading time alone makes it uneconomical.

• Electronic editing and printing is the preferred, economical method of producing specifications today. The document to be edited may be previously-used specifications (risky), master specifications prepared in the office, or one of several master specifications systems

available from professional associations and firms. The systems listed below are available in hard copy and various electronic media.

- "Masterspec" is the most widely used and comprehensive master guide specification system for the architectural, engineering, interior design, and landscape architecture professions and the construction industry. It includes master text, evaluation recommendations, lists of standards, reference materials, and manufacturers. It also includes checklists for coordination between drawings and other specifications sections. "Masterspec" is available in several systems, including standard Masterspec, Masterspec Small Project, and Masterspec Outline. References are kept up-to-date by AIA Masterspec, Washington, DC.

- "Masterworks," produced by Masterspec and McGraw-Hill Information Systems, is a system which presents a series of questions to the specifier. Once the questions have been answered, the system produces the draft specifications sections for further review and editing.

- CSI "Spectext," created and owned by Construction Sciences Research Foundation and maintained and published by National Institute of Building Sciences, Washington, DC. It is available in several versions, including "Spectext Outline." Its contents and characteristics are similar to those of Masterspec.

How to write a new specification section

This procedure applies to sections not available as part of a master specifications system. One may also use this procedure to create ones own master specifications system.

• First, know about the performance expected of the components being specified.

• Figure out how the products will be used, how they will interrelate with other construction components, and when their installation will occur in the construction process. In former days, the writer specified that windows be in place before plaster was applied, and that the plaster be dry before the windows were installed. The reality of construction notwithstanding, both requirements made sense by themselves.

• First write the INSTALLATION portion of the specifications section, part of PART 3 first.

• List and specify the materials and equipment needed to provide the product, PART 2.

• Specify the preparations needed for the product and the cleaning, adjusting, and similar services needed to put it into use, remainder of PART 3.

• Specify the submittals (shop drawings, product data, certifications, warranties, maintenance manuals, replacement parts lists) and other general requirements, PART 1.

• Play the devil's advocate. Try to find out what could happen to cause trouble in spite of your specifications. For example, if you specify a roof system which requires pumping hot bitumen to the top of a limestone building, consider the possibility of spills, and do something about it. You could use a different system, or you could require a heat-resistant, impermeable protective system on the building at the point of pumping.

• Show the section to salespeople, friends, other architects, manufacturers, lawyers, etc. Compare it to the major prefabricated master systems, if available. Refine it over time.

• After the product has generally been specified store the section as your master. Then make it specific for the particular project on which you are working.

Table 1. LEVEL TWO NUMBERS AND TITLES of CSI Format
(by permission of Construction Specifications Institute)

INTRODUCTORY INFORMATION
00001	Project Title Page
00005	Certifications Page
00007	Seals Page
00010	Table of Contents
00015	List of Drawings
00020	List of Schedules

BIDDING REQUIREMENTS
00100	Bid Solicitation
00200	Instructions to Bidders
00300	Information Available to Bidders
00400	Bid Forms and Supplements
00490	Bidding Addenda

CONTRACTING REQUIREMENTS
00500	Agreement
00600	Bonds and Certificates
00700	General Conditions
00800	Supplementary Conditions
00900	Addenda and Modifications

FACILITIES AND SPACES
Facilities and Spaces

SYSTEMS AND ASSEMBLIES
Systems and Assemblies

CONSTRUCTION PRODUCTS AND ACTIVITIES

DIVISION 1 GENERAL REQUIREMENTS
01100	Summary
01200	Price and Payment Procedures
01300	Administrative Requirements
01400	Quality Requirements
01500	Temporary Facilities and Controls
01600	Product Requirements
01700	Execution Requirements
01800	Facility Operation
01900	Facility Decommissioning

DIVISION 2 SITE CONSTRUCTION
02050	Basic Site Materials and Methods
02100	Site Remediation
02200	Site Preparation
02300	Earthwork
02400	Tunneling, Boring, and Jacking
02450	Foundation and Load-Bearing Elements
02500	Utility Services
02600	Drainage and Containment
02700	Bases, Ballasts, Pavements, and Appurtenances
02800	Site Improvements and Amenities
02900	Planting
02950	Site Restoration and Rehabilitation

DIVISION 3 CONCRETE
03050	Basic Concrete Materials and Methods
03100	Concrete Forms and Accessories
03200	Concrete Reinforcement
03300	Cast-in-Place Concrete
03400	Precast Concrete
03500	Cementitious Decks and Underlayment
03600	Grouts
03700	Mass Concrete
03900	Concrete Restoration and Cleaning

DIVISION 4 MASONRY
04050	Basic Masonry Materials and Methods
04200	Masonry Units
04400	Stone
04500	Refractories
04700	Corrosion-Resistant Masonry
04800	Masonry Assemblies
04900	Masonry Restoration and Cleaning

DIVISION 5 METAL
05050	Basic Metal Materials and Methods
05100	Structural Metal Framing
05200	Metal Joists
05300	Metal Deck
05400	Cold-Formed Metal Framing
05500	Metal Fabrications
05600	Hydraulic Fabrications
05650	Railroad Track and Accessories
05700	Ornamental Metal
05800	Expansion Control
05900	Metal Restoration and Cleaning

DIVISION 6 WOOD AND PLASTICS
06050	Basic Wood and Plastic Materials and Methods
06100	Rough Carpentry
06200	Finish Carpentry
06400	Architectural Woodwork
06500	Structural Plastics
06600	Plastic Fabrication
06900	Wood and Plastic Restoration and Cleaning

DIVISION 7 THERMAL AND MOISTURE PROTECTION
07050	Basic Thermal and Moisture Protection Materials and Methods
07100	Dampproofing and Waterproofing
07200	Thermal Protection
07300	Shingles, Roof Tiles, and Roof Coverings
07400	Roofing and Siding Panels
07500	Membrane Roofing
07600	Flashing and Sheet Metal
07700	Roof Specialties and Accessories
07800	Fire and Smoke Protection
07900	Joint Sealers

DIVISION 8 DOORS AND WINDOWS
08050	Basic Door and Window Materials and Methods
08100	Metal Doors and Frames
08200	Wood and Plastic Doors
08300	Specialty Doors
08400	Entrances and Storefronts
08500	Windows
08600	Skylights
08700	Hardware
08800	Glazing
08900	Glazed Curtain Wall

DIVISION 9 FINISHES
09050	Basic Finish Materials and Methods
09100	Metal Support Assemblies
09200	Plaster and Gypsum Board
09300	Tile
09400	Terrazzo
09500	Ceilings
09600	Flooring
09700	Wall Finishes
09800	Acoustical Treatment
09900	Paints and Coatings

DIVISION 10 SPECIALTIES
10100	Visual Display Boards
10150	Compartments and Cubicles
10200	Louvers and Vents
10240	Grilles and Screens
10250	Service Walls
10260	Wall and Corner Guards
10270	Access Flooring
10290	Pest Control
10300	Fireplaces and Stoves
10340	Manufactured Exterior Specialties
10350	Flagpoles
10400	Identification Devices
10500	Lockers

Table 1. LEVEL TWO NUMBERS AND TITLES of CSI Format (continued)

10520 Fire Protection Specialties
10530 Protective Covers
10550 Postal Specialties
10600 Partitions
10670 Storage Shelving
10700 Exterior Protection
10750 Telephone Specialties
10800 Toilet, Bath, and Laundry Accessories
10880 Scales
10900 Wardrobes and Closet Specialties

DIVISION 11 EQUIPMENT
11010 Maintenance Equipment
11020 Security and Vault Equipment
11030 Teller and Service Equipment
11040 Ecclesiastical Equipment
11050 Library Equipment
11060 Theater and Stage Equipment
11070 Instrumental Equipment
11080 Registration Equipment
11090 Checkroom Equipment
11100 Mercantile Equipment
11110 Commercial Laundry and Dry Cleaning Equipment
11120 Vending Equipment
11130 Audio-Visual Equipment
11140 Vehicle Service Equipment
11150 Parking Control Equipment
11160 Loading Dock Equipment
11170 Solid Waste Handling Equipment
11190 Detention Equipment
11200 Water Supply and Treatment Equipment
11280 Hydraulic Gates and Valves
11300 Fluid Waste Treatment and Disposal Equipment
11400 Food Service Equipment
11450 Residential Equipment
11460 Unit Kitchens
11470 Darkroom Equipment
11480 Athletic, Recreational, and Therapeutic Equipment
11500 Industrial and Process Equipment
11600 Laboratory Equipment
11650 Planetarium Equipment
11660 Observatory Equipment
11680 Office Equipment
11700 Medical Equipment
11780 Mortuary Equipment
11850 Navigation Equipment
11870 Agricultural Equipment
11900 Exhibit Equipment

DIVISION 12 FURNISHINGS
12050 Fabrics
12100 Art
12300 Manufactured Casework
12400 Furnishings and Accessories
12500 Furniture
12600 Multiple Seating
12700 Systems Furniture
12800 Interior Plants and Planters
12900 Furnishings Restoration and Repair

DIVISION 13 SPECIAL CONSTRUCTION
13010 Air-Supported Structures
13020 Building Modules
13030 Special Purpose Rooms
13080 Sound, Vibration, and Seismic Control
13090 Radiation Protection
13100 Lightning Protection
13110 Cathodic Protection
13120 Pre-Engineered Structures
13150 Swimming Pools
13160 Aquariums
13165 Aquatic Park Facilities

13170 Tubs and Pools
13175 Ice Rinks
13185 Kennels and Animal Shelters
13190 Site-Constructed Incinerators
13200 Storage Tanks
13220 Filter Underdrains and Media
13230 Digester Covers and Appurtenances
13240 Oxygenation Systems
13260 Sludge Conditioning Systems
13280 Hazardous Material Remediation
13400 Measurement and Control Instrumentation
13500 Recording Instrumentation
13550 Transportation Control Instrumentation
13600 Solar and Wind Energy Equipment
13700 Security Access and Surveillance
13800 Building Automation and Control
13850 Detection and Alarm
13900 Fire Suppression

DIVISION 14 CONVEYING SYSTEMS
14100 Dumbwaiters
14200 Elevators
14300 Escalators and Moving Walks
14400 Lifts
14500 Material Handling
14600 Hoists and Cranes
14700 Turntables
14800 Scaffolding
14900 Transportation

DIVISION 15 MECHANICAL
15050 Basic Mechanical Materials and Methods
15100 Building Services Piping
15200 Process Piping
15300 Fire Protection Piping
15400 Plumbing Fixtures and Equipment
15500 Heat-Generation Equipment
15600 Refrigeration Equipment
15700 Heating, Ventilating, and Air Conditioning Equipment
15800 Air Distribution
15900 HVAC Instrumentation and Controls
15950 Testing, Adjusting, and Balancing

DIVISION 16 ELECTRICAL
16050 Basic Electrical Materials and Methods
16100 Wiring Methods
16200 Electrical Power
16300 Transmission and Distribution
16400 Low-Voltage Distribution
16500 Lighting
16700 Communications
16800 Sound and Video

Design-Build delivery system

Dana Cuff

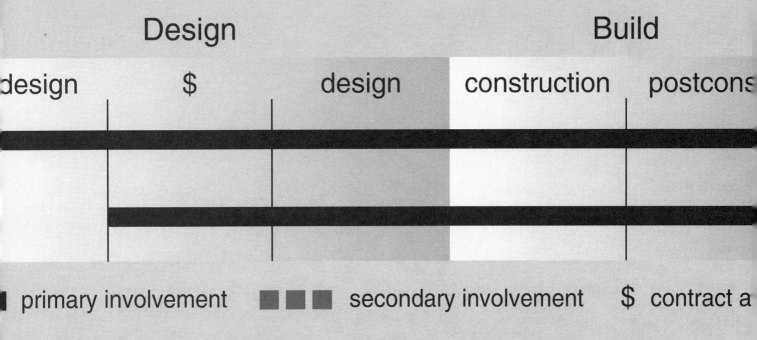

Summary: Design-build is a delivery method that offers the owner the ability to contract with a single entity to provide both design and construction services. While design-build can be used with any project, it is most prevalent in private-sector work but is growing in acceptance for public-sector work. Its effectiveness is more likely to be realized by experienced owners for projects where cost or time is the prime concern.

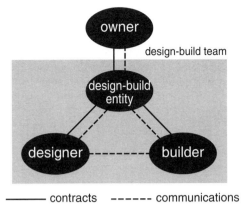

Fig. 1. Design-Build relationship diagram

Key words: contract relationship, delivery method, design-build, joint venture, project delivery, project management.

Characteristics of Design-Build

In design-build, the services of the architect and the contractor are combined into a single design-build entity. It is characterized by its single contract with the owner and by the overlapping of design and construction services. There are two phases in the design-build method: the design and the construction of the building, both provided continuously by a single source. The two primary parties to the contract are the owner and the design-build entity.

Phases

Selecting the design-builder can be complex process, particularly for public-sector projects. The selection of private-sector design-build teams can be much less formal. The formal procurement of design-build services will have three phases:

- *Phase 1:* The owner defines the project and the scope of work and prepares conceptual, preliminary design documents so that a design-builder can be chosen and a price bid or negotiated. The degree of specificity of the documents varies but can include materials lists, site information, descriptions of level of quality expected, performance criteria, structural systems to be used, budget parameters, and project schedule. Many owners will seek the services of an architect for predesign expertise.

- *Phase 2:* When design documents are roughly between 5% and 30% complete (in early schematic design) information is distributed to potential design-build contenders. Design-build entities respond to the owner's request with preliminary designs and cost estimates. Private-sector owners may chose a more straightforward and informal method of hiring the design-builder, particularly if they have worked with the team previously. In either case, by low bid, design competition, qualifications, or a combination of these, a design-build team is selected. A price is fixed at this point.

- *Phase 3:* The design-builder completes the design documents with the contractor's input and construction follows.

Contract Relationships

The main parties in this process are the owner and the design-build entity. Each may be an individual or any legally constituted entity; the owner may be public or private. The owner contracts directly with the design-builder for both the design and the construction services. There is no contractual relationship between the owner and the architect or the owner and the contractor.

The design-build team is normally structured in one of three ways:

- *In-house:* The design-build entity has design and construction professionals on staff. Architect and contractor are employees in this option.

- *Contract:* The design-build entity does not have permanent staff to carry out the design or the construction aspects of the project and so hires the needed expertise. An architecture firm, an architecture/engineering firm, or a construction firm may serve as the design-builder, which in turn contracts with either an architect or a contractor as needed to complete the design-build team. Alternatively, the design-builder may be a business entity that contracts with both architect and contractor as independent subcontractors.

- *Joint venture:* The architect and contractor form a team, legally structured as a partnership, corporation, or joint venture, to   complete a specific project. Licensure regulations may prohibit certain types of partnerships between architects and nonprofessionals.

Appropriate Use

Any type of project may be appropriate, private or public (where permitted by law), large or small, with sophisticated owners or those with little experience. The design-build option may be preferable when:

- The owner needs an early cost commitment.

- The owner considers controlling risk a high priority.

Authors: Dana Cuff and AIA California Council

Credits: This article is adapted from *Handbook on Project Delivery*, AIA California Council ADAPT Production Committee (see Contributors section of this volume for full listing).

AIA California Council. 1996. *Handbook on Project Delivery*. Sacramento, CA: AIA California Council.

References: Denning, James. "Design-Build Goes Public." *Civil Engineering*, Vol. 62, No. 7, July 1992, pp. 76-79.

Design-Build Institute of America. 1010 Massachusetts Avenue, NW. Washington, DC 20001. Publications list available.

Haviland, David. 1994. "Delivery Options" in *The Architect's Handbook of Professional Practice*. Washington, DC: American Institute of Architects.

Twomey, Timothy R. 1989. *Understanding the Legal Aspects of Design-Build*. Kingston, MA: R. S. Means Co.

- The project is complex, requiring close coordination of design and construction expertise or an extreme amount of coordination as when multiple prime consultants are involved.

- The project is clearly defined at an early stage and the owner is able to specify all requirements. Some private-sector design-build teams are selected on a request for qualifications (RFQ) and the team develops project requirements.

- The project is process oriented.

- The owner wishes to fast track the project, to keep design and construction developing simultaneously, and to save time.

Responsibilities of Design-Build parties

Ownership (Fig. 2). The owner is responsible for :

- Determining the goals and requirements for the project, sometimes to a high degree of specificity.

- Acquiring a usable site for the project.

- Financing the project.

- Preparing the materials for the design-build entity's selection.

- Directing the design-build team.

Management: Since there is no separate management entity, the owner is responsible for the overall project management. In some cases the owner may choose to have some project management functions added to the responsibilities of the design-builder. The owner's most important management duties are:

- Managing the predesign process of gathering information and setting standards.

- Managing the bidding or negotiation process for the design- build contract.

- Administering the contract.

Design: The design-build team is responsible for design activities such as:

- Developing the design for the project within budgetary commitments.

- Processing entitlements related to design responsibilities, such as planning approvals and zoning variances.

- Ensuring regulatory and code compliance.

- Preparing estimates of the probable construction costs.

- Preparing construction documents.

Construction: The design-build team is also responsible for construction activities such as:

- Guaranteeing the actual cost of construction.

- Obtaining entitlements related to construction, such as building and encroachment permits.

- Maintaining the construction schedule.

- Preparing shop drawings and other documents necessary to accomplish the work.

- Coordinating the bids and work of subcontractors and prime trades.
- Job-site safety.

- Providing methods and means of construction.

- Fulfilling the requirements of the construction documents.

- Guaranteeing the quality of the construction.

- Correcting any deficiencies covered by the guarantee.

Ensuring Quality

Design-build is most often chosen as a project delivery method because of the simplicity of the single contract for both design and build, and for its emphasis on speed and economy. Quality is often not the highest priority for projects utilizing this delivery method but can be if made a priority in the procurement methodology.

Owner's Perspective

- With design-build, the owner has little quality control over details because such decisions rest with the design-builder. It is more important in design-build than in other methods for the owner to specify the expected quality and technical requirements in the precontractual documents.

- The ongoing collaboration of architect and contractor within the design-build entity may result in inventive design solutions and problem solving during the length of the project schedule. Overall design quality may improve through the team effort.

- Some owners dealing with highly changeable constraints, be they programmatic or financial, believe they receive a higher quality building in terms of function when the design and construction phases are collapsed.

- Some owners use the design competition as a means to generate design alternatives and to be able to predict the level of quality that the design-builder can achieve for a fixed price. Design competitions can result in a high-quality product for the owner's budget.

- Since the final cost is bid on early schematic design, there may be misunderstandings about the level of quality implied by the drawings. Particularly for those owners who maintain their buildings for many years, quality standards must be carefully set so that low construction cost does not lead to high maintenance and life-cycle costs.

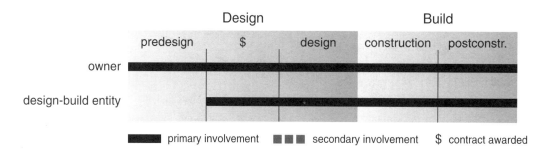

Fig. 2. Design-Build project phasing

Architect's Perspective

- Some architects contend that design-build compromises quality because an independent architect is not fully responsible during the design phase. Architects have less control over quality in design-build than in those methods where they contract directly with the owner. unless they are the leader of the design-build team.

- Design decisions regarding quality can be affected by the availability and cost of products and systems that meet the owner's design criteria.

- The architect may have a better chance to control cost decisions that affect quality during the later stages of the project, since decisions regarding changes may be made by the whole design-build team, rather than by the architect or the contractor separately. The architect must have sufficient status as a leader or member of the design-build entity for this influence to be effective. When the architect contracts with the builder, there are insufficient checks and balances on quality. Particularly when the contractor has the incentive of keeping all or a portion of any savings under the bid price, quality tends to deteriorate.

Contractor's Perspective

- The conflict between delivering a high-quality project at a fixed price may contribute to compromises in quality.

- Early construction input during design increases the building's quality and constructability.

- If the constructor is selected by qualifications rather than low bid, there is a built-in incentive to deliver a quality product in order to obtain repeat work with the owner.

Schedule and cost

The design-build method has grown in popularity because it can have certain advantages over the traditional method in terms of controlling time and cost.

Schedule

Whether the design-build method is faster than other methods depends upon the point at which the clock starts running. From the point that design and construction contracts are signed, design-build is the fastest method of project delivery. But if delivery options are compared from the point of defining the project's scope and requirements, then the differences in time begin to diminish.

Factors that lengthen the project schedule
- The owner incurs more time developing the project requirements, preparing submittal requests, and evaluating submittals, particularly with public-sector projects.

- Since the project time line is rapid with this method, owners can delay the process by taking time to make decisions or select materials.

Factors that shorten project schedule
- The owner participates primarily at the beginning of the process and typically "signs off" on the project at the point when the design-build entity is hired. The owner's limited participation can make the design process more efficient. For public-sector projects, the time line may be shorter because there is one procurement rather than two.

- The design-builder is motivated to move quickly on the project in order to reduce costs and to meet the schedule specified in the contract.

- The structure of the design-build entity makes it easy to fast track the project.

- Since designers and contractors work within a single entity, communication can be streamlined and decisions accelerated. Based on past collaboration, the contractor on the design-build team may be able to work with less fully developed construction documents.

Cost

Predictability of final costs is most reliable with this project delivery system since the design-builder is responsible for all cost estimating and commits to the cost of construction early in the design phase. The cost commitment from a design-builder is usually in a price guarantee, which avoids the cost overruns associated with traditional project delivery methods.

Ownership

- The owner should maintain a reasonable contingency allowance for the project prior to bid. The cost of preparing extensive materials for obtaining bids, particularly for public-sector projects, must be budgeted.

- The potential for change orders is substantially reduced in this method since the design-builder is responsible for all design and construction, reducing the claims for extras. Owner-initiated scope changes or discovery of unknown site conditions would constitute legitimate bases for change orders.

Management

Since the owner is responsible for management, no additional costs are involved. However, if the owner contracts some or all of this function to the design-builder, additional costs will result.

Design-Builder

The design-builder is usually compensated relative to the scope of the services provided. The fee is usually based upon either cost-plus with a guaranteed maximum price or lump sum. In some cases a separate fee is paid for the schematic design, and the construction cost commitment is made at a later stage in the design process.

Design
- The architect is paid according to the contractual relationship with the design-builder. For example, the architect can be a joint-venture partner sharing risk and profit, a subcontractor receiving standard architectural fees, or an employee receiving a salary.

- Since design-builders typically provide free schematic design services as part of the bid or qualifications package, they do so at risk. Stipends are sometimes provided for this phase.

- Since the design-builder is often cost driven, low fees must be offset by expeditious working methods.

Construction
As with the architect, the contractor is paid according to the contractual relationship with the design-builder.

Selection processes

Three basic methods are appropriate for selecting a design-build team: qualifications, price, negotiations, or a combination of these methods. In addition, a design competition is sometimes added as part of the selection process, particularly with large projects. All of the selection processes begin with the owner's description of the scope and budget for the project. It is essential that the owner's description be as complete as possible before the selection process begins.

Qualifications-based selection (QBS)
Often, the design-build team is asked to identify a fee for its services as part of the qualifications information. This is acceptable and reasonable only when the owner has fully defined the project scope and standard of quality, thereby providing sufficient information for determining the fee.

- Public agencies as owners: Federal law requires that design professionals such as architects must be selected based on qualifications; most states and local jurisdictions have similar statutes. However, federal QBS law does not apply to design-build entities, complicating the selection process by public agencies unless special statutes apply. The principles of QBS can be applied to design-build selections by creating a two-phase selection process whereby the first step is to shortlist based on qualifications.

- Private owners: Although qualifications-based selection is not required of private owners, most recognize its benefits for selecting the design-build team. Selection methods used by private owners vary, but are rarely as complex as the public process.

Low-bid selection method
The design-build team can be selected solely on the basis of lowest bid, but most owners prefer to add considerations of qualifications to price. This can be accomplished by conducting a prequalifications screen, which narrows the list of potential bidders to a predetermined number. This selected group is then invited to bid on the project. The open-bid requirement for public owners can be a potential problem since there is no regulatory licensure of design-builders. If the design-builder has underbid the cost of the project, the results may be less than satisfactory construction.

Negotiation method
The design-build team can be selected on the basis of negotiation. This method is somewhat less formal than QBS or low bid but can be effective, especially when the owner is experienced with the process. Design-builders are invited to respond to an announcement of the scope and requirements for the project. Interested entities are interviewed, and the selected team negotiates a contract with the owner, including all necessary costs. This method works best when quality is the primary criteria.

Design competitions
Including a design competition as part of the selection process allows the owner to evaluate the design and cost inputs of several design-build teams before choosing one. Design competitions for design-build contracts are the subject of great debate, for the following two reasons:

- Competitions limit the design process, which inherently requires more input from the owner, thoughtful development from the designer, and interaction between the two parties. The interaction between the architect and the owner may be restricted or uneven.

- Competitions are very costly for the competing design-build teams. To make the up-front risk worthwhile to competing design-build entities, owners must prepare requirements carefully. Some owners compensate teams that are not awarded the project with a fee or stipend for their effort. Owners must be sensitive to up-front costs and are encouraged to limit the preselection products that will be accepted.

Special concerns about Design-Build

Conflict of interest
The actions of architects and contractors are guided by ethical standards set by the national organizations to which they belong. The design-build method inherently gives rise to some unusual ethical issues since there is a direct contractual relationship between the design-build entity, the architect and/or the contractor. The responsibilities of the various parties are not always clear and there is a potential for conflict of interest.

In order to minimize the potential for conflict of interest, the issue should be addressed in the contract between the owner and the design-build entity.

Ownership of documents
In traditional project delivery processes, the architect retains owner-ship of the documents and copyright capabilities. In this method, ownership rights and copyright may pass to the design-build entity through their subcontract with the architect. Special contractual provisions can be created if the owner requires ownership of certain documents, as is the case for some public agencies.

Insurance
The management of risk is a critical part of any construction project. Some risks can be transferred through the purchase of insurance. Even when a risk is insurable, determining the coverages needed and putting the insurance in place is a complex and demanding task, particularly with design-build. Many insurance providers are seeking to assist design professionals and other consultants to work effectively in these areas. Each party is encouraged to seek the advice of an agent or broker who is knowledgeable about providing coverage for design-build specifically.

- The owner may require certificates of insurance or other evidence that the design professionals and contractors carry insurance in an amount appropriate to their respective roles and the size of the project.

- This would include, at a minimum, professional liability, general liability, worker's compensation, automobile liability, real and personal property, and perhaps builders risk and surety.

- Depending on the nature of the project, the owner may require pollution and/or environmental impairment coverage be carried by the design-build entity. The design-build entity in turn may require appropriate insurances from their sub-consultants and subcontractors.

- For larger projects, owners may want to consider both a wrap-up policy for the contractor, which combines general liability and worker's compensation, and an architect/engineer project policy, which provides professional liability coverage on a project-specific basis and normally covers all the design professionals on the project.

Liability and indemnity
The liability of the parties in design-build depends upon the role of each party and the responsibilities assumed by their contract. This may range from the assumption of all the responsibility and liability for both design and construction to about the same liability as under a traditional delivery method to less liability than traditionally exists.

- In some cases, the owner requires contractual hold harmless clauses in favor of the owner and, in turn, the design-build entity may require architects and contractors to include hold harmless clauses in its favor. Such special contractual provisions need to be negotiated between all parties relating to indemnity. The advice of legal counsel is recommended.

- Some insurance carriers are reporting statistically fewer claims with design-build than other delivery methods.

Dispute resolution
This method generally reduces the number of disputes since disagreements are internalized within the design-build entity. The adversarial relationships between architects and contractors in the traditional project delivery system no longer directly affect the owner, since both professionals are working in the interests of the design-builder. Good methods for internal resolution of disagreements within the design-build team ultimately contribute to a greater chance for successful project delivery.

- The standard systems of dispute resolution, mediation, and arbitration can be invoked to settle most disputes; however, their use is not well established for this project delivery method. Dispute resolution should be carefully addressed in the contract between the owner and the design-build entity.

Building commissioning: a guide for architects

Carolyn Dasher
Nancy Benner
Tudi Haasl
Karl Stum

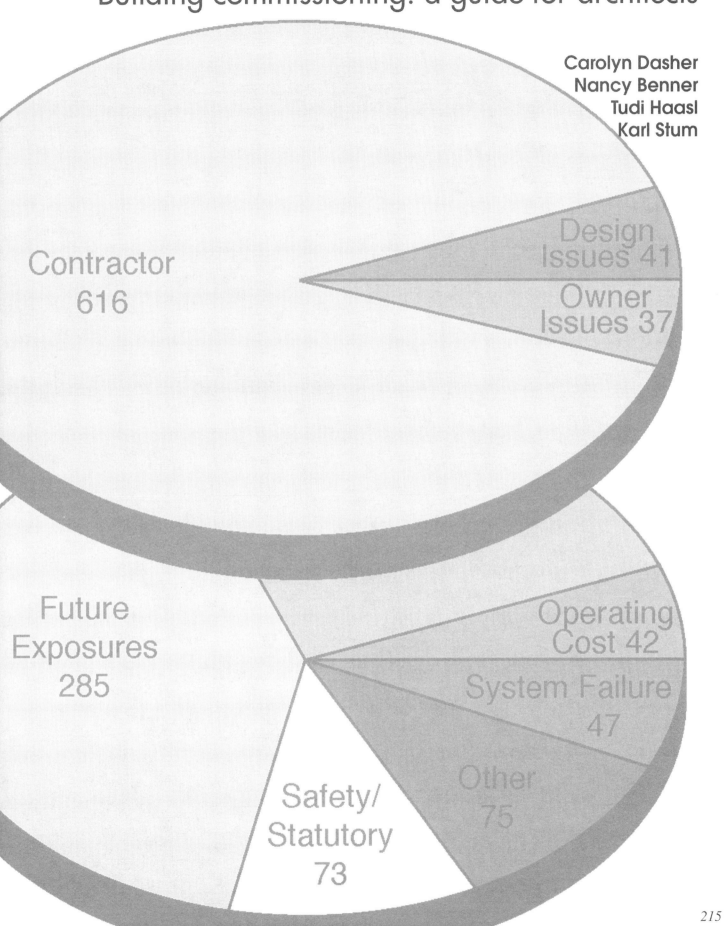

Summary: Building commissioning ensures that buildings and systems are designed, installed, tested, and able to perform to conform with the design intent. Commissioning initiated during design provides quality assurance for focused areas of the design and sets up a systematic process for the commissioning during the construction phase.

Key words: building commissioning, HVAC, performance measures, quality control, testing, verification.

Blower door testing to check insulation and air-exchange provisions

1 Introduction

Building commissioning is defined in ASHRAE (1995) as "the process for achieving, verifying, and documenting the performance of a building to meet [its] operational needs within the capabilities of the design and to meet the design documentation and the owner's functional criteria, including preparation of operator personnel." Building commissioning protocols begin with client program definition and includes design, construction, start-up, and training, and provides evaluation and maintenance procedures to be applied throughout the life of the building.

Commissioning is occasionally confused with systems testing, adjusting and balancing (TAB). Testing, adjusting and balancing measures building air and water flows. Commissioning encompasses a much broader scope of work. Commissioning involves functional testing to determine how well building envelope, mechanical and electrical systems work together. Functional tests of equipment and systems also help determine whether the equipment meets operational goals or whether it needs to be adjusted to increase efficiency and effectiveness. Commissioning results in fewer call-backs, long-term tenant satisfaction, lower energy bills, avoided equipment replacement costs, and an improved profit margin for building owners.

When architects incorporate commissioning into their projects, they provide a value-added service that checks equipment, processes, and system integration through each phase of construction, ensuring the delivery of a building that satisfies everyone. The objectives of commissioning during the design phase are to ensure that the design meets the owner's needs, to document design intent, and to ensure that specifications are adequate. In doing so, an architect should consider:

* Communicating the benefits as part of initial program definition,

* Help owners select a commissioning agent or retain a commissioning agent on their firms' staff,

* Ensure that specifications meet commissioning criteria, and include the role of a commissioning agent in all phases of design and construction.

Significant components of commissioning during the design phase are developing the commissioning plan, performing design review, documenting design intent, and developing commissioning specifi-

cations. These tasks define the scope of the commissioning effort. Documenting design intent clarifies the decisions that need to be made during the design process, assists new operators in understanding the building, and provides a basis for repairs and planning build-outs and renovations.

To become involved in the building commissioning process, architects should study the entire process of testing, verification and monitoring building systems, gain expertise in mechanical and control systems (the main targets of commissioning), document the intent of their designs, and help owners understand the benefits of commissioning.

Design deficiencies will invariably be identified during commissioning. Architects must be prepared for this and have methods for dealing with these deficiencies. Typically, items stemming from architect design responsibilities as well as client decisions are identified. Most deficiencies, however, revealed in the commissioning process are construction adminstration and/or contractor responsibilities (Fig. 1).

Benefits of building commissioning

Until recently, the most frequently mentioned benefit of commissioning was its energy-related value. The energy savings and improved performance expected from facility upgrades are ensured by building commissioning. While this benefit is significant, it is far outweighed by the non-energy-related benefits of commissioning. These include:

* Fewer system deficiencies at building construction "close-out."

* Improved indoor air quality, occupant comfort, and productivity.

* Decreased potential for liability related to indoor air quality.

* Reduced operation and maintenance and equipment replacement costs.

Fewer deficiencies at construction "close-out"

Building owners often accept buildings at the end of construction whose systems may ostensibly "work," but do not work optimally or as intended. During the rush to complete essential building elements prior to occupancy, owners may overlook incomplete or deficient systems. Many owners have neither the time nor the resources to deal with the burden of remedying deficiencies perceived as "less important." Some system deficiencies are not noticed during close-out, be-

Authors: Carolyn Dasher, Nancy Benner, Tudi Haasl, and Karl Stum, P. E

References: ASHRAE. 1995. "Building Commissioning." Chapter 39. *1995 ASHRAE Handbook Heating, Ventilation and Air-Conditioning Applications.* Atlanta, GA: American Society of Heating, Refrigerating and Air-Conditioning Engineers.

Dasher, Carolyn, Nancy Benner, Tudi Haasl, and Karl Stum. 1996. *Commissioning for Better Buildings.* Portland, OR: Portland Energy Conservation, Inc.

Additional references are listed at the end of this article.

Responsibility

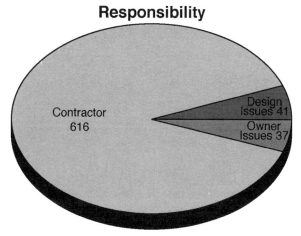

	Deficiencies	% Total
Contractor		
Craftsmanship	252	36%
Non-Compliance	289	42%
Incomplete	75	11%
Subtotal	616	89%
Design Issues	41	6%
Owner Issue		
Non Contract Item	18	3%
Future Design Item	19	2%
Subtotal	37	5%
TOTAL	694	100%

Program Impact

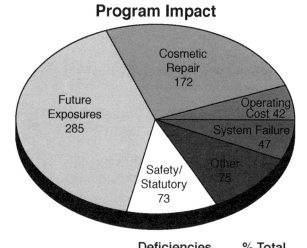

	Deficiencies	% Total
Cosmetic Repair	172	25%
Future Exposure	285	41%
Operating Cost	42	6%
Safety/Statutory	73	11%
System Failure	47	7%
Other	75	10%
TOTAL	694	100%

Fig. 1. Summary of construction deficiencies identified in a building commissioning process. (Source: Facilities Resource Management Company, Madison, CT).

cause inspections and punch lists focus primarily on items that are critical to obtaining regulatory occupancy permits and opening the building.

Once the building is turned over to the owner, overlooked deficiencies must be addressed. Getting contractors to return to the job after substantial completion and occupancy can be difficult with the result that "less important" deficiencies are never fully addressed. Deficiencies not identified before occupancy may come to the attention of facility staff only by tenant complaints or through routine operations. Facility staff often spend their own time correcting items that should fall under the responsibility of the contractor. Other deficiencies may be significant enough that the facility staff attempts the difficult process of asking the contractor to return and make the corrections. Still other deficiencies go permanently undetected, to the detriment of building control, energy use, equipment reliability and tenant comfort.

The primary goal of commissioning is to prevent or mitigate all of these problems. The commissioning agent's task is to identify system deficiencies as early in the project as possible and to track their status until they are corrected. By identifying deficiencies early and by using a systematic process for making corrections, the commissioning agent assists the construction team in providing building systems, prior to occupancy, with significantly fewer defects.

Indoor air quality, comfort and productivity

Surveys indicate that comfort problems are common in many U. S. commercial buildings. A recent Occupational Safety and Health Administration (OSHA) report noted that in 20-30% of commercial buildings some form of indoor air quality problems are reported. Building occupants complain of symptoms ranging from headaches and fatigue to severe allergic reactions. In severe cases, occupants have developed Legionnaire's disease, a potentially fatal bacterial illness. The National Institute of Occupational Safety and Health surveyed 350 buildings with deficient indoor air quality and found that more than half of the complaints stemmed from HVAC systems that were not maintained properly. Although little research has been completed to document the link between comfort and productivity, common sense tells us that comfortable employees are more productive than uncomfortable employees.

Commissioning also improves the productivity of processes, especially in industrial facilities. By ensuring that equipment performs optimally and efficiently, commissioning can help reduce equipment downtime and improve production rates. Building commissioning is a due diligence approach to avoid the expenses and productivity losses associated with poor indoor air quality and employee discomfort. In existing buildings, commissioning detects current and potential indoor air quality/comfort problems and helps identify solutions.

Reduced liability related to indoor air quality

The commissioning process should include testing of outside-air flow rates, a primary factor affecting indoor air quality. If an existing building has deficiencies, the commissioning agent also records the repairs made. Commissioning should be repeated throughout the life of a building, and performance documentation should be updated regularly. This documentation provides owners with a record of building performance that can be used as evidence in the event of a lawsuit.

Commissioning also helps prevent many indoor air quality problems through its focus on training building operators in the proper maintenance of building systems. Properly run and maintained HVAC systems, with clean coils and air intakes and regularly-changed filters, are less likely to contribute to indoor air quality problems. In addition, trained operators can spot potential air quality and ventilation problems before they develop.

Reduced O&M and equipment replacement costs

Operation and maintenance (O&M) and equipment replacement costs will always take up a portion of building budgets. However, vigilant O&M protocols help to minimize life cycle costs by diagnostic maintenance, rather than failure correction. The commissioning process establishes sound operation and maintenance building practices and trains operators in carrying out these practices.

Commissioning also allows building owners to avoid premature equipment replacement costs. Commissioning verifies that equipment is installed and operating properly. Equipment that operates as intended lasts longer, works more reliably and needs fewer repairs during its lifetime. By promoting equipment reliability, commissioning reduces service, energy and maintenance costs.

2   The commissioning process

This section provides an introductory overview of the commissioning process and the roles of various parties in the process, in which the owner, owner representative or architect may:

- Engage a commissioning agent (through the architect or independently).

- Hire design professionals amenable to commissioning. Include commissioning and/or coordination with commissioning services.

- Include commissioning in the design phase.

- Include clear commissioning specifications in the construction documents.

- Monitor the commissioning work, read the commissioning reports, and act on recommendations for fixing deficiencies.

Selecting a commissioning agent

Owners (or architects acting as owner representatives) can use a competitive request for proposal (RFP) process to make the selection. In the RFP, require evidence of methodology, previous, relevant commissioning experience, including the depth of commissioning experience (what some call commissioning is no more than traditional testing and balancing). Recommended commissioning agent qualifications are discussed in more detail in the following pages.

Owners have several parties to choose from when selecting a commissioning agent. They include:

- Independent third party.

- Design professional.

- General contractor

- Mechanical contractor

Each option has advantages and disadvantages. The final choice may depend on the complexity and the specific needs of the particular project. Owners should understand that costs for commissioning services are not included in standard contracts for these parties.

- *Independent third party.* An independent commissioning agent, under contract to the owner (or to the owner's construction or project manager) rather than the design professional or general contractor, can play a clearly defined objective role and ensure that the owner will truly get the building performance expected. The independent third party option offers owners the most objectivity, but also entails more coordination and management of an additional contract, which may result in higher first costs than some of the other options. For large and/or complex projects, especially in buildings with highly integrated, sophisticated systems, these higher first costs are outweighed by future savings from commissioning.

Independent commissioning agents, who are often design engineers or architects, should have qualifications suggested below under "Commissioning agent qualifications." Hands-on experience with building systems is especially critical. It is important to involve the indepen-

dent agent as early in the design phase as possible. This allows the agent the opportunity to document the design intent for the project, begin scheduling commissioning activities, and begin writing commissioning specifications into bid documents for other contractors. For existing buildings, the commissioning agent will need to try to determine from building documentation what the original design intent was, what the current use of the building requires of its systems, and how it relates to any planned renovations or upgrades.

- *Design professional.* For projects ranging up to 100,000 square feet, using the design professional as the commissioning agent is often a good option, provided that the project specifications detail the commissioning requirements. The advantage of using the design professional as the commissioning agent is that he or she is already familiar with the design intent of the project. This familiarity somewhat reduces first costs and provides for single contract responsibility (through that design professional's contract). Most design professionals have the ability to write specifications and oversee the commissioning process. However, they may not have adequate experience in day-to-day construction processes and troubleshooting systems. Owners considering this option should bear in mind that commissioning is not included in most design professional fees. Commissioning provisions must be written into the design professional's contract, so that firms can include these services in their work scope, deliverables and fees.

- *General contractor.* General contractors, provided they have experience with projects of similar size and complexity, have the scheduling and construction background necessary to supervise a commissioning agent. However, they typically need to hire a commissioning agent to directly supervise tests performed by installing contractors. It has been argued that it is not in the owner's best interest to have the commissioning agent work for the general contractor because of the obvious conflict of interest. On the other hand, because they want to meet project deadlines, general contractors have more of an incentive to cooperate in scheduling and completing the commissioning work. Commissioning often reduces the number of call-backs on a project, and thus improves the general contractor's profit margin. If the commissioning agent will be under contract to the general contractor, it is recommended that the agent be hired as an independent contractor without affiliation to any firm on the design or construction team and that the agent report to the owner's representative (usually the construction or project manager).

- *Mechanical contractor.* It was once standard practice for many mechanical contracting firms to conduct performance tests and systematic check-out procedures for equipment they installed. (This is often the prevailing practice for small construction projects, such as residences). As construction budgets became tighter, this standard service was dropped from most projects. Mechanical contractors may have the knowledge and capability to test mechanical equipment. Some would contend that it is difficult for mechanical contractors to objectively test and assess their own work, especially since repairing deficiencies found through commissioning may increase their costs. But many owners have good relationships with their contractors, and it may be appropriate to use them as commissioning agents in cases, most appropriate where:

- The project size and level of complexity is limited.

– One mechanical contractor performs all of the mechanical work on a project.

– Project specifications clearly detail the commissioning requirements.

Commissioning agent qualifications

Currently, there is no standard certification or licensing process for commissioning agents. It is therefore up to each owner or architect to determine commissioning agent qualifications appropriate for a given project. Below are representative guidelines for selecting a qualified commissioning agent.

In general, for complex projects, a commissioning agent who will personally develop the commissioning test plans and directly supervise the commissioning work should meet these qualifications:

- Experience in design, specification, or installation of commercial building mechanical control systems. This experience may also be related to general HVAC systems.

- Record of prior projects involving successful troubleshooting and/or performance verification of buildings of at least similar size as the current project. Experience with new and/or existing buildings, depending on the current project.

- Meet owner's liability requirements.

- Experience working with project teams and conducting scoping meetings; good communication skills.

- Demonstrated capacity to write commissioning specifications for bid documents.

- Prior projects involving commissioning of HVAC, mechanical controls, and lighting control systems in buildings of similar size to the current project. This experience includes the writing of functional performance test plans.

- Experience in design installation and/or troubleshooting of direct digital controls and energy management systems, if applicable.

- Demonstrated familiarity with testing instrumentation.

- Knowledge and familiarity with air/water testing and balancing.

- Experience in planning and delivering O&M training.

3   Responsibilities of project team members

Members of a design-construction project team, like components of integrated building systems, need to interact in order to perform their tasks successfully. Commissioning actually facilitates this interaction, because it sets clear performance expectations and requires communication among all team members.

The construction project should begin with a commissioning scoping meeting, which all team members attend. At this meeting, the roles of each team member are outlined and the commissioning process and schedule are described. The project team most often includes the building owner or developer, general contractor, commissioning agent, design professionals, contractors, subcontractors and manufacturer's representatives. The team may also include the facility manager and/or building operator, and possibly testing specialists and utility representatives. Ideally, each of these parties contributes to the commissioning process.

Of course, few situations are ideal. Budget considerations and special project characteristics may expand or minimize the commissioning roles and responsibilities described below. Owners should consult with their commissioning agents about potentially combining some of the following roles. The commissioning agent can review the scope of commissioning and advise the owner on how best to consolidate roles and tasks.

Role of building owner/developer

The building owner's most significant responsibility is to clearly communicate expectations about the project outcome. Often the owner is represented by a construction manager or project manager, who is given the authority over project budgets and goals. The owner's expectations are used by the designer to establish the design intent of the project and by the commissioning agent to evaluate whether this intent is met. Other responsibilities of the building owner or owner's representative include:

- Hiring the commissioning agent and other members of the project team, preferably using a competitive request for proposal process.

- Determining the project's budget, schedule, and operating requirements.

- Working with the commissioning agent to determine commissioning goals.

- Facilitating communication between the commissioning agent and other project team members.

- Approving start-up and functional test completion (or delegating this task to a construction or project manager).

- Attending building training sessions when appropriate.

Role of the general contractor/construction manager

The general contractor and/or construction manager assists with the development and implementation of functional performance testing for all systems. This involves assisting in gathering information (for existing buildings these may include shop drawings, operations and maintenance manuals, and as-built documents) for review by the project team. The general contractor or construction manager facilitates the commissioning schedule by coordinating activities with owner representatives and subcontractors.

Role of the commissioning agent

The commissioning agent's primary tasks include:

- Ensuring the completion of adequate design intent documentation.

- Providing input on design features that facilitate commissioning and future operation and maintenance.

- Assisting in developing commissioning specifications for the bid documents.

- Developing the commissioning plan.

- Writing prefunctional and functional performance tests.

- Ensuring that team members understand their specified commissioning responsibilities and fulfill them on schedule.

- Submitting regular reports to the building owner or project manager.

- Directing all functional performance testing and approving contractor start-up tests, air and water testing and balancing, and duct pressure testing. The commissioning agent may also perform some functional performance tests.

- Writing a final commissioning report documenting the final evaluation of the systems' capabilities to meet design intent and owner needs.

- Reviewing and commenting on technical considerations from design through construction, in order to facilitate sound operation and maintenance of the building.

- Reviewing contractor and manufacturer training plans prior to delivery to operators and facility managers.

- Reviewing operation and maintenance manuals and design intent documentation for completeness.

Role of design professionals

The primary commissioning responsibilities of design professionals are to document the design intent for all systems and controls and to make sure that commissioning is included in the bid specifications. The designer should also monitor construction activities and review and approve project documentation (shop drawings, operation and maintenance manuals, as-built drawings). For very complex projects, the commissioning agent may ask the designer to review commissioning plans and functional performance tests. The commissioning agent may also ask the designer to visit the site during construction or renovation (beyond the designer's typical construction observation responsibilities) to ensure that work is performed according to plans.

If this is the case, the design professional's bid should include funds to cover these visits. As mentioned, the design firm may be responsible for hiring and overseeing the commissioning agent.

Role of contractors/subcontractors

Contractors and subcontractors are responsible for performing commissioning functions described in their bid specifications. These may include assisting with developing the commissioning schedule, conducting performance tests (under the supervision of the commissioning agent) of the systems they install, adjusting systems where appropriate, and documenting system startup. Contractors and subcontractors are also responsible for training building operators in the proper operation and maintenance of systems and providing operation and maintenance manuals on the equipment they install.

Role of manufacturer's representatives

Manufacturers' representatives provide the commissioning agent with manufacturer specifications for the equipment installed. They may also assist contractors with operation and maintenance training and with functional performance testing, especially in situations where warranties may be affected by test results or procedures.

Role of facility manager/building operator

The building operator should assist with (or at least be present for) as much of the functional testing as possible. This improves operator understanding of equipment and control strategies. The operator should also attend training sessions provided by manufacturer's representatives and contractors.

Role of testing specialists

If special testing is needed due to the complexity of the project, the specialists performing these tests should also be involved in commissioning. Test results and recommendations from these specialists should be submitted to the commissioning agent for review. They may also be required to review documentation relating to the systems they test and to train operators on the proper use of this equipment.

Role of utility representative

Some utilities offer services that can compliment the commissioning process. The local utility should be contacted to find out what services they can provide.

4   Steps in the commissioning process

Because commissioning all building systems is rarely practical or even necessary, owners need to determine what level of commissioning is best and most cost effective for their project. Many factors affect this decision, including:

- Complexity of the building systems.

- Building type and size.

- Whether the project is new construction, or the renovation or tune-up of an existing building.

- How much the owner is willing to spend and capacity to undertake life-cycle costing and O&M protocols.

- Building tenant or occupant demographics, especially related to O&M protocols.

The level of commissioning detail is usually dictated by the complexity of the systems and controls installed. The more complex the project, the higher the risk of systems not performing as intended. As a general rule, all projects that include controls, energy management control systems, pneumatic equipment, integrated systems, HVAC-related plant equipment and air distribution systems ought to be commissioned. Systems that are considered "complex" have:

- Sophisticated controls and control strategies.

- Complicated sequences of operation.

- High degree of interaction with other systems and building equipment.

Experts commonly place the following energy conservation measures on their "must commission" lists:

- Electric lighting and daylighting controls.

- Energy management systems and control strategies.

- Variable speed drives.

- Ventilation air control, including fume hoods.

- Building pressurization control.

- Any specialized equipment.

Level 1 commissioning

Level 1 commissioning is a less formal process and requires the involvement of fewer players. Commissioning agents performing this less rigorous form of commissioning may find a "boilerplate" commissioning plan is sufficient, and thus less time and money are spent developing the commissioning plan. During the design phase, the commissioning agent reviews design documents and ensures that commissioning is incorporated into the project specifications. For existing buildings, the commissioning agent may interview building operation staff about maintenance practices, building usage and their concerns. Steps in Level 1 commissioning include:

- Site inspection of the installation, including verifying that the specified equipment was properly installed.

- Calibration checks for most sensors and thermostats and checks for proper setpoints.

- Simple functional performance tests, often using "boilerplate" forms.

- Verification of occupancy schedules to ensure proper settings.

- Verification that the owner and the persons required to operate the equipment have had proper training.

- Preparation of a final report detailing the commissioning findings.

Level 2 commissioning

Level 2 commissioning is a more rigorous process that involves more players. The commissioning agent performing this level of commissioning generally develops a customized commissioning plan and conducts a project scoping meeting to review the plan with other players. With complex projects, there are two approaches to Level 2 commissioning of HVAC and controls systems:

- Point-by-point verification.

- Specialized testing to assure performance without the expense of point-by-point testing.

Specialized testing may follow a proprietary approach that varies depending on the commissioning agent. When using specialized instead of point-by-point testing, the owner must rely on the commissioning agent to ensure that testing meets the desired degree of rigor and thoroughness.

As with Level 1, the commissioning agent reviews design documentation, interviews building operators, and ensures that commissioning requirements are clearly spelled out in the project specifications. Steps in Level 2 commissioning include:

- Commissioning agent review of design documentation that clearly describes design intent and includes such details as equipment specifications, sequence of operation, equipment submittals, setpoint schedules, occupancy schedules, and manufacturers' performance data.

- Development and execution of prefunctional performance tests and checklists for each piece of equipment or system, or documentation of completed start-up tests.

- Completion of rigorous functional performance tests (to test and verify such performance indicators as capacity, efficiency, sequence of operation, proper flows, and how other equipment influences equipment performance).

- Verification that O&M manuals are complete, available and accessible on site.

- Verification that operating staff have been trained to properly operate and maintain the equipment or system and that they have been instructed on how the equipment or system is integrated with the rest of the building's systems.

- Development or verification of a preventive maintenance plan or service contract. (Service contracts should have a preventive maintenance component that goes beyond merely responding to trouble calls and needed repairs.)

- Preparation of a final report detailing the commissioning findings.

The commissioning process is integrated with the phases of the design, construction, renovation, and retrofit processes. These include:

- Predesign phase.

- Design phase.

- Construction/installation phase.

- Acceptance (project close-out) phase

- Post acceptance/occupancy phase

Table 1 shows how these phases correspond to construction and renovation project phase designations.

Table 1. Commissioning tasks corresponding to project phases.

Commissioning Phase	Project Phase
Predesign	**Planning Phase**
■ commissioning agent hired	■ design team chosen
Design	**Design Phase**
■ develop commissioning plan ■ hold commissioning scoping meeting ■ submit design intent documentation ■ develop commissioning specifications ■ review of design by commissioning agent	■ building designed ■ bid documents prepared ■ job awarded to General Contractor
Construction/Installation	**Construction Phase**
■ submitted documentation reviewed ■ develop and execute prefunctional ■ checklists ■ develop functional test plans	■ construction of facility ■ startup of equipment
Acceptance	**Acceptance Phase**
■ execute functional tests ■ verify operator training ■ approve O&M manuals	■ training completed ■ documentation completed ■ building accepted by owner
Post-acceptance/Occupancy	**Occupancy Phase**
■ perform deferred tests (if any)	■ ongoing O&M

The following discussion briefly describes the commissioning activities associated with each phase of a project, emphasizing the role of the commissioning agent. Given the importance of the architect's understanding and administrative of the design and building process, the critical commissioning steps to be coordinated during design are further detailed in the ensuing section, "The commissioning process during design."

Commissioning tasks during predesign phase

The predesign phase is the ideal time for the owner to select a commissioning agent. Early selection allows the commissioning agent to play an advisory role during the conceptual process. It can also increase buy-in for commissioning from other team members because the agent is involved from the beginning. Otherwise, the team may view the commissioning agent as an outsider who does not really understand the project.

Commissioning during the design phase

The goal of commissioning during the design phase is to ensure that the efficiency and operational concepts for building systems that were developed during programming are included in the final design. The main commissioning tasks during this phase are compiling and reviewing design intent documents, incorporating commissioning into bid specifications, and reviewing bid documents.

The bid specifications developed during the design phase define the design intent of each system and include commissioning requirements for the mechanical, electrical and controls contractors. Specifications should include any special equipment or instrumentation that must be installed for obtaining measurements during performance testing. They should also describe the responsibility that contractors will have for preparing operation and maintenance manuals for equipment installed. The commissioning agent reviews these bid documents and all other design intent and contract documents.

During this phase, the commissioning agent can serve a significant role in developing a building's operation and maintenance program or suggesting improvements for a program already in place. The agent interviews the facility manager to determine operating staff ability and availability to operate and maintain building equipment and systems. The commissioning agent also reviews the design documents and drawings to ensure that equipment is accessible for maintenance.

Commissioning tasks during construction

During this phase, the commissioning agent reviews contractor submittals and operation and maintenance manuals and may write test plans for each system and piece of equipment to be commissioned. The agent also visits the construction site and notes any conditions that might affect system performance or operation.

Prefunctional testing, which ensures that equipment is properly installed and ready for functional performance testing, occurs during the construction phase. The commissioning agent approves and may oversee start-up and prefunctional testing and makes sure that any deficiencies are remedied before functional testing begins.

The commissioning agent should involve the building operation staff in the prefunctional and functional testing as much as possible. Doing so improves operator understanding of the proper operation of equipment and systems. It also provides operators with valuable hands-on training in running and troubleshooting the equipment they will manage. The commissioning agent may write various reports during construction that document testing progress as well as deficiencies that may affect future building performance.

Commissioning tasks during project close-out

The functional performance tests written during the construction phase are modified, if necessary, during the acceptance phase to reflect any changes in installations. The commissioning agent then uses the tests to document and verify the proper operation of equipment and systems according to the contract documents. Most often, the commissioning agent directs the tests, but actual equipment operation during the tests is performed by subcontractors, particularly the controls contractor. If corrective measures are required, the commissioning agent makes sure that they meet the owner's criteria and the design intent. Acceptable performance is reached when equipment or systems meet specified design parameters under full-load and part-load conditions during all modes of operation, as outlined in the commissioning test plan.

The acceptance phase is complete when the facility has moved from the static construction state to operation free of deficiencies. Control of the building may have been transferred from the design/construction team to the owner and building operators prior to the completion of the acceptance phase. Part of this transfer involves training building operators in the operation and maintenance of equipment and systems. Preferably this training begins during the construction/installation phase. If training was not included in the construction/installation phase, it should begin before the end of the acceptance phase.

In addition, the commissioning agent may oversee training sessions as specified in the bid documents that installing contractors, designers and manufacturers' representatives will conduct. The agent also verifies that operation and maintenance manuals are complete and available for use during the training sessions. Finally, if any modifications to operation and maintenance practices are made based on the training, the agent makes sure that the manuals are updated to reflect these changes. All building staff responsible for operating and maintaining complex building equipment, especially energy management systems, should be required to participate in the training.

Commissioning tasks during occupancy phase

Even though the project is considered complete, some commissioning tasks are properly continued throughout the life of the building. These tasks include ensuring that equipment and systems continue to function properly and documenting changes in equipment and building usage. It may be appropriate to continue working with the commissioning agent at the beginning of this phase, so the agent can review and recommend methods for carrying out these functions.

When performing testing during post-occupancy, the commissioning agent or test engineer must be careful not to void any equipment warranties. The building owner should require that contractors provide the commissioning agent with a full set of warranty conditions for each piece of equipment to be commissioned.

If any testing was delayed because of site or equipment conditions or inclement weather, this testing should be completed during this phase. Any necessary seasonal testing should also be performed during post-acceptance. Although some testing of heating and cooling systems can be performed under simulated conditions during the off-season, natural conditions usually provide more reliable results. Simulation can be more expensive than testing under natural conditions. If the building is already occupied, (especially if it is occupied 24 hours a day), simulation may be impossible. Owners should consider recommissioning their facilities periodically under all seasonally conditions to ensure that performance levels continue to meet design intent.

Additionally, commissioning of systems considered as "whole building assemblies" may be appropriate, including HVAC, lighting, controls and contingent architectural elements (such as windows, furniture and/or operable shading), in that the combination of system elements may impose special conditions not anticipated when components are considered individually.

5 The commissioning process during design

Survey reports of owners and professionals who have participated in commissioning projects consistently report that all respondents felt commissioning should begin earlier—in the design phase. This remainder of this article details the process and procedures for commissioning during design, and the responsibilities of the architect, design engineers, owner and commissioning agent.

The design team needs clear objectives for performing commissioning-focused quality assurance procedures on its design and for developing drawings and specifications that facilitate commissioning during the construction phase, including clear and complete commissioning specifications. This process requires that a commissioning agent perform additional design reviews focusing on specific areas that are critical to the success of the commissioning process and areas where problems are frequently found.

Objectives of commissioning during design

Commissioning during design is intended to achieve the following objectives:

- Provide commissioning-focused design review.

- Ensure that the design and operational intent are clearly documented and followed.

- Ensure that commissioning for the construction phase is adequately reflected in the bid documents.

- Commissioning during design facilitates the construction-phase commissioning and provides some additional design review in areas of special concern to the owner. (Commissioning during design, as described here, is not intended to provide quality assurance for the entire design process, although if rigorous design review options were chosen it could approach that).

Commissioning responsibilities during design

The commissioning process during design is illustrated in Fig. 2 and enumerated in Table 2. The following tasks comprise the commissioning work during design:

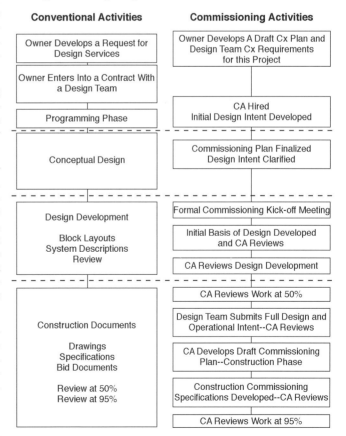

Fig. 2. Commission activities during design.

Table 2. Commissioning roles and responsibilities during design.

Task	Design Phase Commissioning Responsibilities and Tasks		Parties Involved					
			Commissioning Agent	Architect	Mechanical Designer	Electrical Designer	Owner's Design Representative	Owner's Const. Representative
1	**Coordinate the Cx work during Design**	Lead-->	X or	X or			X	
	a. Plan and schedule meetings		X	X			X	
	b. See that all tasks are carried out		X	X			X	
	c.							
2	**Finalize the Cx plan for Design Phase**	Lead-->	X					
	a. Edit the original Cx Plan as necessary		X					
	b. Review and comment on Cx plan			X			X	
	c.							
3	**Perform design development review [1]**	Lead-->	X					
	a. After completion of Design Development, review design concepts of the areas		X	–	–	–	–	
4	**Develop design documentation**	Lead-->	X or	X				
	a. Provide design documentation format and assistance		X					
	b. Write design documentation for systems checked under Task 4			X	X	X	X	
	c. Review and approve design documentation for clarity and completeness		X				X	
5	**Develop draft Cx plan for Construction Phase**	Lead-->	X					
	a. Develop drafts of the commissioning plan-construction phase		X					
	b. Review Cx plan						X	X
6	**Develop Cx specifications for construction**	Lead-->	X					
	a. Assist in, review & approve all sections		X					X
	b. Adapt Cx guide specs & include in Division 1		X	X				
	c. Adapt Cx guide specs & include in Division 15 (mechanical)				X			
	d. Adapt Cx guide specs & include in Division 16 (electrical)					X		
	e. Adapt Cx guide specs in special Cx Division		X					
	f. Adapt Cx guide specs & include in Division							
7	**Review final drawings and specifications [1]**	Lead-->	X					
	a. Review drawings & specifications at ~50% & ~95% complete		X	–	–	–	–	–

- Coordinate the commissioning activities.
- Finalize the design phase commissioning plan.
- Perform a review of design development.
- Develop clear and comprehensive design documentation.
- Develop the draft commissioning plan for the construction phase
- Develop commissioning specifications for the construction bid documents.
- Perform a final review of the drawings and specifications

In Table 2, each of these tasks is listed with associated subtasks. The table indicates which design team members are responsible for each task and indicates the member typically assigned to lead the task.

Task 1. Coordinate the commissioning during design.
The commissioning agent, a member of the A/E team or one of the owner's staff, handles overall coordination of the commissioning during design. The agent begins by coordinating the effort to document the initial design intent and finalizing the design phase commissioning plan. The commissioning agent holds a kick-off meeting with the design team as soon as the mechanical and electrical designers are selected and after the Commissioning Plan has been finalized (Task 2).

At this meeting, the commissioning agent outlines the roles and responsibilities of the project team members and reviews the commissioning plan outline and schedule. Team members provide comment on the plan and schedule, and the commissioning agent uses these suggestions to complete the final commissioning plan. The commissioning agent attends selected design team meetings to review the design and note potential system performance problems. The commissioning agent recommends changes to improve energy efficiency, operation and maintenance, and equipment reliability. Making these changes during the design phase, rather than after construction begins, saves money in the long run.

Task 2. Finalize the design phase commissioning plan.
The commissioning coordinator for the design phase makes clarifications and changes to the original design phase Commissioning Plan (provided by the owner during the request for proposal stage) and submits it to the architect, the commissioning agent and the owner's design representative for approval. This final plan guides the commissioning work during design. The plan contains:

- Description of the objectives of the design-phase commissioning.
- list of players, roles and task responsibilities.
- Outline of the management structure.
- Description of how the plan will be implemented.
- Schedule timeline.
- Specific details about design reviews.
- List of systems and components being commissioned.
- Design documentation and reporting formats.
- Methods for the development of a draft construction phase commissioning plan and for the final construction phase commissioning specifications.

Task 3. Perform a design development review.
At the end of design development, the commissioning agent reviews the design along with the other design team members. The commissioning agent compares the design with the interests and needs of the owner as identified in the programming report or the design intent document of the programming and conceptual design phases. The commissioning agent may also compare the proposed design against any company design guides or standards of the owner for specified areas. Owners should not assume that the commissioning agent is an expert in all areas. The commissioning agent or owner may sub-contract to specialized experts for review in areas where the owner wants review, but where the commissioning agent is not qualified. Some topic areas that are suggested for consideration in the design review at this stage are:

- Commissioning facilitation. Input regarding making the building easier to commission. (see details below).
- Energy efficiency. General efficiency of building shell, building layout, HVAC system types, and lighting system type.
- Operations and Maintenance (O&M). How building O&M can be made easier (accessibility and system control).
- Indoor Environmental Quality (IEQ). How thermal, visual, acoustical comfort or air quality can be improved.
- Functionality. How the design can be changed to improve functionality for occupants/tenants.
- Environmental Sustainability. How the building materials and systems and landscaping, construction and maintenance practices can impose less of an impact on the environment.
- Life Cycle Costs. Life cycle assessment of options relative to energy efficiency, O&M, IEQ or functionality.

Although the commissioning agent may review items as listed above, they are not responsible for design concept, design criteria or compliance with codes. These responsibilities ultimately reside with the A/E. The results of the commissioning facilitation review are documented and submitted to the design phase commissioning coordinator and forwarded to the design team members who issue a written response.

Commissioning facilitation
One of the primary tasks for the commissioning agent is reviewing the design documents to facilitate commissioning during construction. The construction-phase commissioning process can be made easier and more effective if certain features are included in the design. The added up-front costs for most of these features can be justified because they reduce the cost of commissioning, allow for a better commissioning job and reduce the O&M costs for the building. Below is a list of some of these features. Not all are addressed in detail in the design development review. However, they should be brought to the attention of the A/E at this time, so that they can be incorporated during the construction documents phase.

- Clear and rigorous design documentation, including detailed and complete sequences of operation.
- An HVAC fire and emergency power response matrix that lists all equipment and components (air handlers, dampers, valves) with their status and action during a fire alarm and under emergency power.
- Access for reading gages, entering doors and panels, observing and replacing filters, coils, etc.
- Required isolation valves, dampers, interlocks, and piping to allow for manual overrides, simulating failures, seasons and other testing conditions.
- Sufficient monitoring points in the building automation system (BAS) , even beyond that necessary to control the systems, to facilitate performance verification and O&M.
- Adequate trending and reporting features in the BAS.
- Pressure and temperature (P/T) plugs close to controlling sensors for verifying their calibration.
- Pressure gages, thermometers and flow meters in strategic areas for verifying system performance and ongoing O&M.

- Pressure and temperature (P/T) plugs at less critical areas or on smaller equipment where gages and thermometers would be over-kill.

- Specification of the location and criteria for the VAV duct static pressure sensor and chilled water differential pressure sensor.

- Adequate balancing valves, flow metering and control stations and control system functions to facilitate and verify reliable test and balance.

- Clear and complete commissioning specifications for the construction phase.

- Complete O&M documentation requirements in the specifications.

- Complete training requirements in the specifications.

- Review entire document and building information management plan from design through construction and turnover to ensure adequacy and compliance with the owner's program.

Task 4. Develop design documentation.
Specifically identifying and developing the design intent and basis of design provides each party involved, at each respective stage, an understanding of the building systems. This allows team members to perform their respective responsibilities regarding the design, construction or operation of the building.

The design documentation differs from traditional specifications in that it provides a more narrative description of the system or issue and "frames" the issue or building component with clear and useful background information. However, design documentation often includes parts of specifications. In general, specifications detail what is to be done on a component level, while design documentation explains why something is done and, in general terms, how design and operating objectives will be accomplished. Sections of the design documentation can look like specifications, especially where tasks depart from conventional practice, for example, energy efficient design and construction.

For the purposes of building commissioning, design documentation includes the salient information from the programming report, the conceptual design phase and from the design and construction process necessary to guide the design, verify compliance during construction and aid building operations. Design documentation consists of two dynamic components: design intent and the basis of design.

Design intent
The design intent is a dynamic document that provides the explanation of the ideas, concepts and criteria that are considered to be very important to the owner. It is initially the outcome of the programming and conceptual design phases. The design intent document should cover the following, for each system, major component, facility and area:

- Objectives and functional use of the system, equipment or facility.

- General quality of materials and construction.

- Occupancy requirements.

- Indoor environmental quality, IEQ (space temperature, relative humidity, indoor air quality (IAQ), noise level, illumination level).

- Performance criteria (general efficiency, energy and tolerances of the IEQ objectives).

- Budget considerations and limitations.

- Restrictions and limitations of system or facility.

- Very general system description.

- Internal loads assumptions.

- Zoning descriptions.

- Ventilation requirements.

- Envelope requirements.

- Equipment sizing calculations and criteria.

- All sequences of operation.

- Energy efficiency control strategies.

- Design intent for all efficiency measures.

- Reference to pertinent local or state compliance documents.

Basis of design
The basis of design is the documentation of the primary thought processes and assumptions behind design decisions that were made to meet the design intent. The basis of design describes the systems, components, conditions and methods chosen to meet the intent. Some reiterating of the design intent may be included. The following should be included in the basis of design:

Specific description of systems, components and methods for achieving the design intent objectives. (For example, for a rooftop air conditioning unit include: why this system was chosen above others, details of size, efficiencies, areas served, capacity control details, compressors, coils, dampers, setpoints, filters, economizers, minimum ventilation control, control type, noise and vibration criteria, tie-in to other systems, sequences of operation under all modes of operation, and control strategies).

- Equipment maintainability.

- Fire, life, safety: criteria, general strategy narrative and detailed sequences.

- Emergency power control and function.

- Energy performance.

- Ventilation strategies and methods.

- Complete sequences of operation, including setpoints and control parameters.

- Schedules.

- Codes and standards applicable.

- Primary load and design assumptions.

- Diversity a used in sizing.

- Occupant density and function.

- Indoor conditions (space temperature, relative humidity, lighting power density, ventilation and infiltration rates).

- Outdoor conditions.

- Glazing fraction, U-value and shading coefficient.

Information of secondary importance to the commissioning and operation of the building should be documented by the design team, but is not normally included in the design documentation described here or included in the O&M manuals (such as wall R-values, thermal mass, and other energy performance assumptions). These values may be of interest in computer simulation of energy analysis, which may be compared to future monitored performance.

The detail of both the design intent and basis of design increase as the design process progresses, as described in Table 3. In the beginning, the design documentation required is primarily a narrative of the building system descriptions, the purpose of the systems, how the systems will meet those objectives and why this system or method was chosen above others. As the design process progresses, the design documentation includes the basis of design, a specific description of the system and components, its function, how it relates to other systems, sequences of operation, and operating control parameters.

Table 3. Progress of design documentation.

Stage	Issues Addressed	Responsible Parties
Programming	The owner's and tenant's needs are identified in detail. The applicable parts of the programming report become the initial design intent.	Owner Architect
Conceptual Design and Design Dev.	Design intent clarified. Basis of design begun: overall system descriptions, objectives of systems, general methods of achieving objectives, etc.	Owner Architect
Construction Documents and Specification Development	Above, but in more detail, including complete basis of design: complete system & component description, specific methods of achieving system objectives, design & load assumptions, applicable codes and standards, complete sequences of operation and control strategies	Architect Design Engineers
As-Built Documentation	Above, plus Adjusted sequences with final control parameters	Design Engineers Installing Contractors Building Operator Architect

The initial design intent from the programming phase is developed by the architect with review by the entire design team and commissioning agent. The architect, or other assigned party, acts as the design documentation task leader and coordinates the creation of the full design documentation by the design team. Each member of the team provides the written basis of design and detailed sequences of operation for the areas of design that are their responsibility. They submit the documentation in parts to the task lead at the pre-determined phases of design. The architect, task leader and commissioning agent review, comment on and approve the submissions. U. S. Department of Energy (1996) contains an example of a format for combining the design intent and basis of design into one document. It also discusses the timeline for developing various parts of the documentation.

The following parts of the design intent and basis of design should be selected from the project documentation and included as an integral part of the bid specifications:

- A design narrative describing the system in general.

- The objectives of each system and its functional use.

- The full sequence of operations under all modes and conditions.

- The setpoints and operating parameters.

- Performance criteria and applicable codes and standards.

- Design team members prepare a final as-built copy to be included in the O&M manuals at the end of construction. At minimum, this documentation should cover the systems going to be commissioned.

Task 5. Develop draft commissioning plan for construction.
When the drawings, specifications (not including commissioning specifications) and design documentation are sufficiently complete (say, 50% to 75%), the commissioning agent develops the draft commissioning plan for the project. The plan contains a list of the systems and specific equipment and components to be commissioned and the general modes to be tested with the probable testing method. In addition, sections of standard language regarding process, responsibilities, O&M documentation, training and scheduling are included.

When completed, this first draft of the commissioning plan provides the general scope for the development of the construction commis-

sioning specifications (Task 7). After all drawings and specifications are complete, the commissioning agent updates the construction-phase commissioning plan. This draft of the commissioning plan should be included as part of the construction bid documents. The owner's representatives review both drafts of the plan and the commissioning agent makes recommended changes. Refer to the additional references listed below for further details and examples of commissioning plans.

Task 6. Develop commissioning specifications
Commissioning specification bid documents are developed by members of the design team as part of the commissioning process during design. The specifications provide information that allows those bidding on the project to understand clearly how the commissioning process works and specifically what role they have in the process. They provide the requirements and process for properly executing the commissioning work with sufficient detail and clarity to facilitate enforcement.

The commissioning specifications provide the bidders with a clear description of the extent of the verification testing required. They detail testing requirements including what to test, under which conditions to test, acceptance criteria and acceptable test methods. The documentation, reporting, general scheduling requirements should also be included. The specifications should name the party responsible for writing, executing, witnessing and signing-off tests. The specifications should also outline the relationship between start-up, prefunctional checklists, manual functional performance tests, control system trend logs and stand-alone data logging. The inclusion of example tests and checklists is recommended. The specifications should also detail the operator training and the O&M documentation and O&M plan requirements. Detailed specific functional test procedures are not necessarily required prior to bidding. They may be developed during the construction phase, if the other testing details previously listed are included in the specifications.

The responsibilities for developing the individual sections of the commissioning specifications are listed above in Table 2. The commissioning agent coordinates the commissioning specification effort and provides assistance as needed to all team members. Each team member submits the complete specification of any division with references to commissioning to the commissioning agent and to the owner's construction representative for review. Each page should contain the file name and date of the document. Areas where the commissioning specifications deviate significantly from any guide specifications should be recorded. The commissioning agent reviews the specifications and provides written comments to each designer who edits and resubmits the specifications.

Task 7. Perform a review of drawings and specifications.
The commissioning agent reviews the full set of Construction Documents and specifications when approximately 50% and 95% complete, along with the traditional design team members. The parts of this review that deal with commissioning specifications will have been completed in Task 6.

The commissioning agent compares the design with the interests and needs of the owner as identified in the programming report and the design intent document. The commissioning agent also compares the proposed design against any company standards or guides for areas specified by the owner. The commissioning agent may also identify any improvements in areas not specifically mentioned in the company standards.

The commissioning agent is not responsible for design concept, design criteria or compliance with codes. The commissioning agent does not verify the designers' calculations or proof schematics or layouts in detail nor perform the constructibility review unless specifically assigned. For example, the commissioning agent does not verify appropriate pipe or duct sizing, but may provide comments on unusually tight or restrictive duct layouts and bends or a poor location of a static pressure sensor. As in the design development review, commissioning agents should only review design in areas where they have expertise. The commissioning agent or owner may sub-contract to specialized experts for review in areas where the owner wants review that the commissioning agent is not qualified to conduct.

This review is documented in writing and submitted to the design phase commissioning coordinator and forwarded to the design team members who issue a written response. The commissioning specification review is detailed in Task 6.

Highest priority items for review at this stage are:

-   Commissioning specifications. Verify that bid documents adequately specify building commissioning and that there are adequate monitoring and control points specified to facilitate commissioning and O&M.

-   Commissioning facilitation. The commissioning agent should provide input regarding making the building easier to commission. (see details in the Commissioning Facilitation section above).

-   Control system & control strategies. Review HVAC, lighting, fire control, security control system, strategies and sequences of operation for adequacy and efficiency.

-   O&M documentation. Verify that building O&M plan and documentation requirements specified are adequate.

-   Training Requirements. Verify that operator training requirements specified are adequate.

Other items recommended for review include:

-   Component energy efficiency. Review for adequacy of the efficiency of building shell components, HVAC systems and lighting systems.

-   Operations and maintenance. Review for effects of specified systems and layout toward facilitating O&M (equipment accessibility, system control).

-   Indoor environmental quality. Review to ensure that systems relating to thermal, visual, acoustical, air quality comfort and air distribution are in accordance with design intent.

-   Environmental sustainability. Review to ensure that the building materials, landscaping, use of water resources and waste management are in accordance with the design intent.

-   Functionality for tenants. Review to ensure that the design meets the functionality needs of the tenants.

-   Review of engineering assumptions. Review the engineering assumptions relating to equipment sizing, energy efficiency decisions and HVAC cost-benefit calculations.

-   Life cycle costs. Perform a life cycle assessment of the primary competing systems relative to energy efficiency, O&M, IEQ and functionality.

Design to facilitate operation and maintenance

The owner, facility manager, and commissioning agent can help to establish provisions in the building design to ensure that the benefits gained from commissioning persist over time. Some of these practices include:

-   Establishing and implementing a preventive maintenance program for all building equipment and systems.

-   Reviewing monthly utility bills for unexpected changes in building energy use.

-   Using energy accounting software to track building energy use.

-   Tracking all maintenance, scheduled or unscheduled, for each piece of equipment. Periodic reviews of these documents will often indicate whether certain pieces of equipment require tuning up.

-   Updating building documentation to reflect current building usage and any equipment change-outs.

-   Establishing an indoor air quality program for the building.

-   Assessing operator training needs annually.

To provide for successful operation and maintenance begins in the design phase of a project. Building owners and architects have begun to recognize the importance of soliciting input from operation and maintenance staff during the early stages of building design. Building operation and maintenance staff can make design recommendations that facilitate good operation and maintenance practices. The more convenient it is for staff to perform regular checks and maintenance on building systems, the better building performance needs can be met and costly maintenance can be avoided.

Examples of design recommendations by which an architect's design can help simplify operation and maintenance are:

-   Provide clear access to service and maintain all critical points of a buildings systems.

-   Provide ground floor access to the chiller room through a connected loading dock.

-   Provide one or more roll-up doors of sufficient size to permit removal and replacement of separate elements without having to disassemble adjacent equipment.

-   Provide sufficient clearance and illumination on all sides of the equipment to perform all maintenance, including regular cleaning.

-   Install hoist or crane equipment over banks of heavy equipment, such as chillers.

-   Install sufficient valves to permit the isolation of an individual system elements without having to shut down the entire system.

-   Install walkways around elevated equipment.

-   Provide roof access with adequate openings via stairs, not ladders.

- Provide clearly accessible and easily used monitoring, for example, to evaluate the performance of individual system elements.

6 Summary

A joint effort by the architect, mechanical and electrical designers, owner representatives and the commissioning agent is required for building commissioning, a process that is ideally begun during design (See Fig. 3 on following page).

Commissioning during the design phase includes design reviews by the commissioning agent. These reviews focus principally on facilitating commissioning during the construction phase but are also essential to evaluate areas of special concern to the owner and the design team. Through a team effort, commissioning specifications for the construction phase are developed to provide the construction contractors with information necessary to bid the commissioning tasks and to execute them properly. This process will improve the quality of the installation of the building systems and ensure that the design intent and owner's operational needs are met.

Additional references

ASHRAE. 1996. "The HVAC Commissioning Process." *ASHRAE Guidelines 1-1989R Public Review Draft.* Atlanta, GA: American Society of Heating, Refrigerating and Air-Conditioning Engineers.

Elovitz, Kenneth M. 1994. "Design for Commissioning." *ASHRAE Journal.* October 1994. Atlanta, GA: American Society of Heating, Refrigerating and Air-Conditioning Engineers.

Heinz, John and Rick Casault. 1996. *The Building Commissioning Handbook.* Alexandria, Virginia: Association of Higher Education Facilities Officers.

Herzog, Peter. 1997. *Energy-Efficient Operation of Commercial Buildings: Redefining the Energy Manager's Job.* New York: McGraw-Hill.

NEEB. 1993. *Procedural Standards for Building Systems Commissioning.* First Edition. Rockville, Maryland: National Environmental Balancing Bureau.

PECI. 1992. *Building Commissioning Guidelines.* Second Edition. Prepared for Bonneville Power Administration. Portland, Oregon: Portland Energy Conservation, Inc.

PECI. 1993-1996. *Proceedings* (annual) National Conferences on Building Commissioning. Portland, Oregon: Portland Energy Conservation, Inc.

Tseng, Paul C. 1994. "Design Quality Control: The Real Challenge for Commissioning for Designers," *Proceedings Fourth National Conference on Building Commissioning.* Portland, OR: Portland Energy Conservation, Inc.

U. S. Army Corps of Engineers. 1995. *Engineering and Design Systems Commissioning Procedures.* Publication ER1110-345-723. Washington, DC: U. S. Army Corps of Engineers.

U. S. Department of Energy. 1996. *Model Commissioning Plan and Guide Specifications.* Prepared by Portland Energy Conservation, Inc. for U. S. DoE Region 10. To order an electronic version, call NIST 1-800-553-6847.

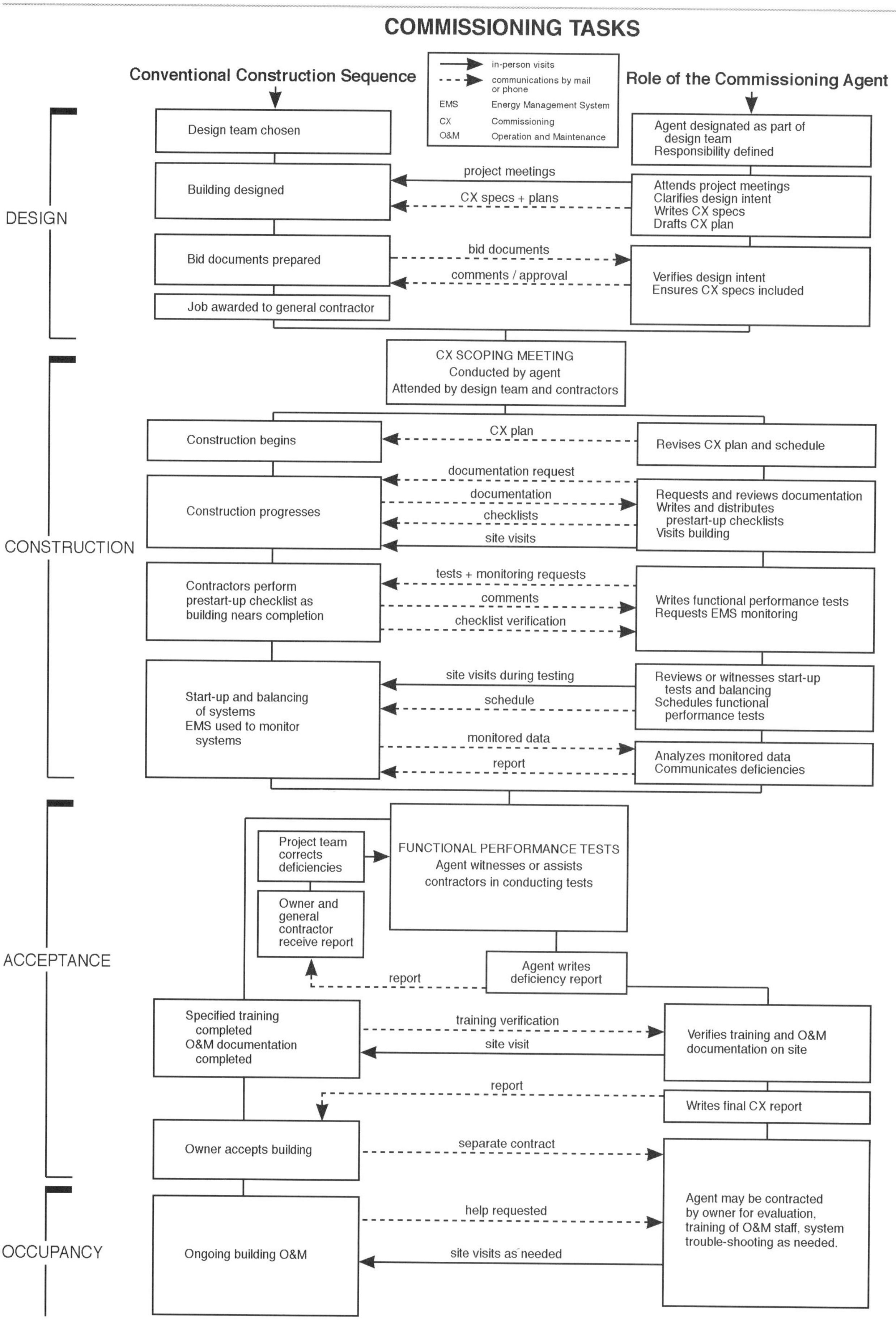

COMMISSIONING TASKS

Conventional Construction Sequence

→	in-person visits
- - →	communications by mail or phone
EMS	Energy Management System
CX	Commissioning
O&M	Operation and Maintenance

Role of the Commissioning Agent

DESIGN

Design team chosen

Agent designated as part of design team
Responsibility defined

Building designed
— project meetings —
— CX specs + plans —

Attends project meetings
Clarifies design intent
Writes CX specs
Drafts CX plan

Bid documents prepared
— bid documents —
— comments / approval —

Verifies design intent
Ensures CX specs included

Job awarded to general contractor

CX SCOPING MEETING
Conducted by agent
Attended by design team and contractors

CONSTRUCTION

Construction begins
— CX plan —

Revises CX plan and schedule

Construction progresses
— documentation request —
— documentation —
— checklists —
— site visits —

Requests and reviews documentation
Writes and distributes prestart-up checklists
Visits building

Contractors perform prestart-up checklist as building nears completion
— tests + monitoring requests —
— comments —
— checklist verification —

Writes functional performance tests
Requests EMS monitoring

Start-up and balancing of systems
EMS used to monitor systems
— site visits during testing —
— schedule —
— monitored data —
— report —

Reviews or witnesses start-up tests and balancing
Schedules functional performance tests

Analyzes monitored data
Communicates deficiencies

ACCEPTANCE

Project team corrects deficiencies

FUNCTIONAL PERFORMANCE TESTS
Agent witnesses or assists contractors in conducting tests

Owner and general contractor receive report

Agent writes deficiency report
— report —

Specified training completed
O&M documentation completed
— training verification —
— site visit —

Verifies training and O&M documentation on site

— report —

Writes final CX report

Owner accepts building
— separate contract —

OCCUPANCY

Ongoing building O&M
— help requested —
— site visits as needed —

Agent may be contracted by owner for evaluation, training of O&M staff, system trouble-shooting as needed.

Fig. 3. Commissioning tasks (after ASHRAE 1995)

Building performance evaluation

Wolfgang F. E. Preiser
Ulrich Schramm

Summary: The Building Performance Evaluation (BPE) process encompasses design and technical performance of buildings alongside human performance criteria. BPEs offer feedback on design and contribute to architectural knowledge. This article outlines a comprehensive approach to building performance evaluation applicable to all architectural projects.

Photo: Donald Baerman, AIA

Key words: building performance, environment/behavior studies, post-occupancy evaluation, occupant surveys.

The role architecture plays becomes ever more important in the context of globalization of business and institutions. On one hand, this trend implies standardization of floor plans and building types, for example, hotels tend to conform to worldwide institutional standards of room sizes, floor plans, and amenities. On the other hand, social and cultural differences and varied building traditions require differentiation in design adapted to its locale, even for identical building types. Office building interiors, for example, reflect wide differences in socio-cultural expectations, organizational and management styles, space allocation standards, communication methods and work processes.

For a given building type, location and cultural context, the expected performance of the building needs to be defined and communicated to those who design and ultimately use the facility. The physical and technical performance of buildings is directly linked to its qualities as perceived by the building occupants, that is to say, attitudes of occupants are as significant in how a building is evaluated as its qualities defined by independent measures. Further, a design has to be evaluated by how it is used, not how it appears to the designer. For example, staircases with poorly differentiated colors and materials for risers and treads, or that are poorly lit, or even with a distracting view, are frequently cited for accidental slips and falls for people, whether or not they have vision or mobility problems. In this case, evaluation of the design requires an understanding of both physical aspects of the design and how it is perceived by users. The example demonstrates how the physical, technical and behavioral performance of buildings—involving quantitative and qualitative measures—are inextricably linked to evaluation of performance.

The elements and levels of Building Performance Evaluation (BPE) are described below as categories for specifying the expected quantitative and qualitative performance scales and types of built environments: types and numbers of expected users; use patterns; health, safety and security criteria; functional criteria; social, psychological and cultural criteria; ambient environment criteria; spatial relationships; equipment criteria; code criteria; special requirements; and, last but not least, an estimate of needed space (Preiser, Rabinowitz, and White 1988). BPE constitutes an important step in validating performance standards that may exist, or, that may have to be developed for a given building type. BPE helps to audit facilities in an effort to ascertain whether they work for their clients, providers and users. Six phases of the building life cycle are discussed below: planning, programming, design, construction, occupancy, and recycling. By using performance language, building performance can be specified in facility programs, translated into designs, and then realized in construction. Subsequently, the occupied facility can be evaluated in terms of the expected performance as compared to the actual performance measures that can be obtained from the facility and its users.

An Integrative Framework for BPE

The proposed integrative framework attempts to respect the complex nature of performance evaluation in the building delivery cycle, as well as the life cycle of buildings. This framework defines the building delivery cycle from an architect's perspective, showing its cyclic evolution and refinement toward a moving target, achieving better building performance overall and better quality as perceived by the building occupants (Fig. 1).

At the center of the model is actual building performance, both measured quantitatively and experienced qualitatively. It represents the outcome of the building delivery cycle as well as building performance during its life cycle. It also shows the respective six sub-phases: strategic planning, programming, construction, design, occupancy, and, recycling. Each of these phases has internal reviews and feedback loops. Each phase is thus connected with its respective state-of-the-art knowledge contained in building type specific databases, as well as global knowledge and the literature in general. The phases and feedback loops of the framework can be described as follows:

Authors: Wolfgang F.E. Preiser, Ph.D. and Ulrich Schramm, Ph.D.

References: Baird, G., J. Gray, N. Isaacs, D. Kernohan, and G. McIndoe, editors. 1996. *Building Evaluation Techniques.* New York: McGraw-Hill Book Company.

National Research Council, Building Research Board. 1987. Post-Occupancy *Evaluation Practices in the Building Process: Opportunities for Improvement.* Washington, DC: National Academy Press.

Preiser, Wolfgang F.E., Harvey Z. Rabinowitz, and Edward T. White. 1988. *Post-Occupancy Evaluation.* New York: Van Nostrand Reinhold. [out of print: contact author regarding availability of remaining copies].

Preiser, Wolfgang F.E. 1996. "Applying the Performance Concept to Post-Occupancy Evaluation." *Proceedings* CIB-ASTM-ISO-RILEM 3rd International Symposium. Tel Aviv, Israel. [c/o APCIB Secretariat, National Building Research Institute. Technion. Haifa 32000, Israel].

Preiser, Wolfgang F.E. editor. 1989. *Building Evaluation.* New York: Plenum.

Schramm, U. 1996. "Post-Occupancy Evaluation in the Cross-Cultural Context: A Field Study on the Performance of Health Care Facilities in Egypt and other Countries." *Proceedings* CIB-ASTM-ISO-RILEM 3rd International Symposium. Tel Aviv, Israel. [op. cit.]

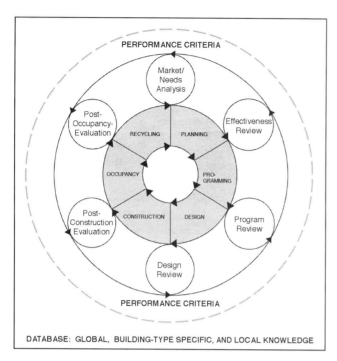

Fig. 1. An Integrative Framework for Building Performance Evaluation

Phase 1 - Planning: The beginning point of the building delivery cycle is the strategic plan which establishes medium and long-term needs of an organization through market/needs analysis which, in turn, is based on mission and goals, as well as facility audits. Audits match needed items (including space) with existing resources in order to establish actual demand.

Loop 1 - Effectiveness Review: Outcomes of strategic planning are reviewed in relation to big issue categories such as corporate symbolism and image, visibility in the context surrounding the site, innovative technology, flexibility and adaptive re-use, initial capital cost, operating and maintenance cost, and costs of replacement and recycling at the end of the useful life of a building.

Phase 2 - Programming: Once effectiveness review, cost estimating and budgeting has occurred, a project has become a reality and programming can begin.

Loop 2 - Program Review: The end of this phase is marked by program review involving the client, the programmer, and representatives of the actual occupant groups.

Phase 3 - Design: This phase contains the steps of schematic design, design development and working drawings/construction documents.

Loop 3 - Design Review: The design phase has evaluative loops in the form of design review or troubleshooting involving the architect, the programmer, and representatives of the client organization. The development of knowledge-based and computer-aided design (CAD) techniques makes it possible to apply evaluations during the earliest design phases. This allows designers to consider the effects of design decisions from various perspectives, while it is still not too late to make modifications in the design.

Phase 4 - Construction: In this phase construction managers and architects share in construction administration and quality control to assure contractual compliance.

Loop 4 - Post-Construction Evaluation: The end of the construction phase is marked by post-construction evaluation, an inspection which results in "punch lists," that is, items that need to be completed prior to commissioning and acceptance of the building by the client.

Phase 5 - Occupancy: During this phase, move-in and start-up of the facility occur, as well as fine-tuning by adjusting the facility and its occupants to achieve optimal functioning.

Loop 5 - POE: BPE during this phase occurs in the form of POEs carried out six to twelve months after occupancy, thereby providing feedback on what works in the facility and what doesn't. POEs will assist in testing hypotheses made in prototype programs and designs for new building types, for which no precedents exist. Alternatively, they can be used to identify issues and problems in the performance of occupied buildings, and further suggest ways to solve these. Further, POEs are ideally carried out in regular intervals, that is, in two- to five-year cycles, especially in organizations with recurring building programs.

Phase 6 - Recycling: On the one hand, recycling of buildings to similar or different uses has become quite common: Lofts have been converted to artist studios and apartments; railway stations have been transformed into museums of various kinds; office buildings have been turned into hotels; and, factory space has been remodeled into offices or educational facilities. On the other hand, this phase constitutes the end of the useful life of a building when the building is decommissioned and removed from the site. In cases where construction and demolition waste reduction practices are in place, building materials with potential of re-use will be sorted and recycled into new products. At this point, hazardous materials such as chemicals and radioactive waste are removed in order to reconstitute the site for new purposes.

Loop 6 - Market/Needs Analysis: This loop involves evaluation of the market of the building type in question in general, and the client organization's needs in particular. It can involve the assessment of the rehabilitation potential of an abandoned or stripped-down building shell, or the potential of a prospective site in terms of anticipated project needs. The end point of this evolutionary cycle is also the beginning point of the next building delivery cycle.

The Performance Concept

Underlying the evaluation framework is the "Performance Concept." Historically, building performance was evaluated in an informal manner. The lessons learned were applied in the next building cycle of a similar facility type. Because of relatively slow change in the evolution of building types in the past, knowledge about their performance was passed on from generation to generation of building specialists. These were often craftspeople with multiple skills—artists/designers/draftsmen/builders, in one and the same person—who had almost total control over the building delivery process. They also had a thorough knowledge of the context in which the client operated.

This situation has totally changed with increasing specialization, not only in the construction industry, but also in the demands clients place on facilities. The situation is made more difficult due to the fact that no one person or group seems to be in control of the building delivery process. Rather, major building decisions tend to be made by committees, all the while that an increasing number of technical and regulatory requirements are placed upon facilities, such as handicapped accessibility, energy conservation, hazardous waste disposal, fire safety, occupational health and safety requirements, and so on. As a result, the performance of facilities needs to be well articulated and documented, usually in the form of the facility program (Preiser 1996).

Fig. 3 illustrates the performance concept in the context of POE, as well as the basic outcomes of POEs from a short, medium and long-term perspective, as described below. The concept is shown as part of a systematic process which compares explicitly stated performance criteria with the actual, measured performance of the building. This comparison, the core of the evaluation process, implies that the expected performance can be expressed clearly in performance language in the form of criteria. Whereas facility programming is the process of systematically collecting, documenting, and communicating the criteria for the expected performance of a facility, POE is the inverse in that it compares the actual performance with the expected criteria and performance.

Client goals and objectives are initially translated into performance criteria by the client representative or facility programmer, and then used by the architect to design the facility. They are subject to change over time, and thus, they introduce biases at each point: the evaluator's expertise and values introduce a certain bias. Users of a facility with their perceptions and changing requirements introduce yet another bias and source of subjectivity. The performance concept is thus the basis for conducting a "reality check" by developing and auditing performance criteria in assessing building performance within the local parameters.

BPE thus serves a pivotal role in design decisions of programmers, designers, and facility managers. Building performance criteria are an expression and translation of client/provider and occupant goals and objectives, functions and activities, and environmental conditions that are required. Performance expectations need to be specified for each category of spaces and the facility overall. They are commonly documented in the form of a functional program (or brief) and communicated to all parties involved in the building delivery cycle. In addition, the design program and criteria should be part of a permanent record or case history accessible to those responsible for the building throughout its life cycle.

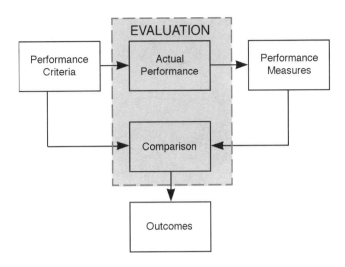

Fig. 2. The performance concept

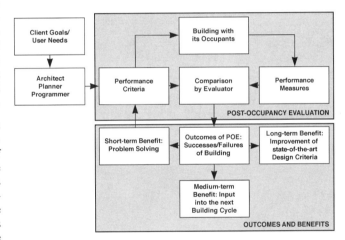

Fig. 3. The performance concept and the basic POE-outcomes

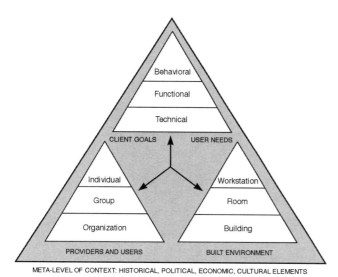

Fig. 4. Elements and Levels of Building Performance Evaluation

Elements and Levels of BPE

The elements and levels of BPE describe the interrelationships that exist between the built environment, providers and users, and client goals/user needs (Fig. 4). Each of the categories are presented:

- Built environment: Workstations, rooms, buildings, and entire complexes of buildings or facilities

- Providers and users: Individuals, groups, and organizations

- Client goals and user needs: This hierarchy of performance levels includes technical (health, safety, security), functional (functionality, efficiency, work flow), behavioral (social, psychological, cultural) and aesthetic

- Contextual elements: The above, well-established categories are embedded in a fourth, overarching category at the global or "meta" level of context related performance elements. They are process driven, that is, they deal with overall vision as well as historical, political, economic, cultural and other significant elements.

Performance Criteria

For BPE to be objective, actual performance of buildings is measured against established performance criteria. There are several sources for such criteria:

- Published literature: Published literature can provide explicit or implicit evaluation criteria. Explicit criteria are contained in reference works and publications. Implicit criteria can be derived from research journals or conference proceedings which contain the findings and recommendations of research linking the built environment and people. Implicit criteria require interpretation and validation by the evaluator as data need to be assessed for appropriateness to a given context.

- Analogs and precedents: In cases where a new building type is being designed, performance criteria need to be compiled for spaces and buildings for which no precedents exist. In these cases, the most expedient method for obtaining performance criteria is to use so-called analogs, that is, to "borrow" criteria from similar, but not identical, space types, and to use educated guesses to adapt them to the situation at hand. For example, in designing new centers for non-intrusive cancer treatments in the 1980s, the question had to be asked: Should it be a free-standing facility or should it be integrated into a major hospital? Should the scale be non-institutional and the ambiance be home-like, as opposed to a cold institutional atmosphere? These questions led to designs intended to create a "deinstituionalized" and humane environment of modest scale and with an empathetic ambiance which would help reduce the stress cancer patients and families. As an example along similar lines, when the residential and day-care facilities for Alzheimer's patients were first designed, little knowledge existed as to which performance criteria would be appropriate for patients at different stages of the development of the disease. Through design research, a number of hypotheses about patients' needs and abilities—such as wayfinding, socializing and other daily activities—were tested and have subsequently found their way into the design guidelines.

- POEs: The third source of criteria development is performance evaluation and feedback through POEs. Key design concepts, building typology, and the actual operations of facilities are evaluated. Feedback can be generated by specialist consultants in POE, for example, or by facilities managers who monitor certain performance aspects of buildings on a daily basis. Evaluation includes the performance of materials and finishes, their maintainability and durability, cost of replacement, and, frequency of repair. This pertains also to the performance of hardware, such as window systems, locking systems, as well as heating and air-conditioning systems. POE feedback thus adds information on the local context to what is considered state-of-the-art knowledge in a given building type.

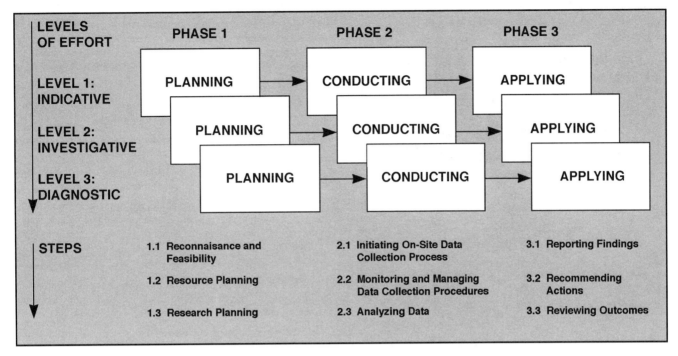

Fig. 5. Post-Occupancy Evaluation Process Model

• Resident experts: A fourth source for performance criteria are knowledgeable people or "resident experts," that is, people familiar with the operation of the facility in question. People who are experienced running programs in a given facility type, are likely to represent such informed judgment and experience. To help elicit such expertise, focus sessions can be used to discuss advantages or disadvantages of certain performance aspects of the facility type in question. Furthermore, representative user group and consensus discussion can be used to generate performance criteria that are appropriate for the tasks at hand.

Evaluation Methods

Major contributions to the field of building evaluation are identified by Preiser, Rabinowitz, and White (1988) and by Baird et al. (1996) which also offers several state-of-the-art methods for monitoring and understanding building performance used worldwide. These methods explore the side of "demand," that is, the occupant requirements, as well as the "supply" side, that is, the buildings' capabilities to meet these requirements. Although there are some similarities among methods in terms of providing systematic means of measuring the quality of buildings, they differ in their target audiences, their scope, and systems of measurement.

Several observations can be made about the evolution of evaluation methods over the last 30 years:

• Evaluation efforts started with fairly modest and typically singular case studies. Over the years, the level of sophistication has increased and greater validity of data has been witnessed.

• Standardization is beginning to be employed in evaluation methodology in the quest for making evaluations replicable and more generalizable.

POE as a Major Sub-Process of BPE

BPE constitutes a comprehensive approach to evaluating buildings. Over the past 30 years, the most sustained of these efforts turned out to be the process called *Post-Occupancy Evaluation*. Based on the cumulative experience of a number of researchers and practitioners, a model was developed which outlines in three phases and nine steps the process a typical POE goes through (Preiser, Rabinowitz, and White 1988). It features three levels of effort at which POEs can be undertaken: indicative, investigative, and diagnostic (see Fig. 5):

• *Indicative POEs* are quick, walk-through evaluations, involving structured interviews with key personnel, group meetings with end-users, as well as inspections in which both positive and negative aspects of building performance are documented photographically and/or in notes.

• *Investigative POEs* are more in-depth and they utilize interviews and survey questionnaires, in addition to photographic/video recordings, and physical measurements. They typically involve a number of buildings of the same type.

• *Diagnostic POEs* are focused, longitudinal and cross-sectional evaluation studies of such performance aspects as stair safety, orientation and wayfinding, privacy, overcrowding, and so forth.

The most common is the indicative POE which can be carried out within a few hours of on-site data gathering. Typically, an executive summary results with prioritized issues and recommendations for action. Results are usually available within a matter of days after the site visit. Investigative POEs can take anywhere from a week to several months, depending on the depth of investigation and the amount of personnel involved on the part of the client organization whose building(s) are to be evaluated. Diagnostic POEs resemble traditional

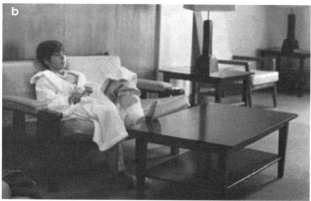

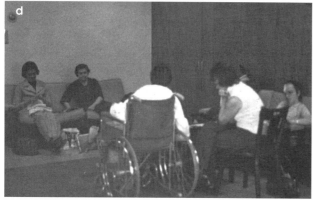

in-depth research in a very focused topic area. It can take from months to years and requires highly sophisticated data gathering and analysis techniques.

At each level of effort, the four categories of BPE elements need to be taken into consideration. The fourth category of contextual elements can be accommodated in the POE process model depicted in Step 1 (reconnaissance and feasibility) of the planning phase, and in Step 3 (data analysis) of the conducting phase.

POE Outcomes: The outcomes of building performance evaluations can have short, medium and long term implications:

- *Short term Outcomes:* These include user feedback on problems in buildings and identification of appropriate solutions.

- *Medium term Outcomes:* These include applying the positive and negative lessons learned to inform the next building delivery cycle.

- *Long term Outcomes:* These are aimed at the creation of databases, clearinghouses and the generation of planning and design criteria for specific building types. Database development as identified below assumes a critical role in linking post-occupancy evaluation with facility programming.

Evaluations help complex organizations with communication about building performance (See Fig 6). Thus, feedback from occupants combined with state-of-the-art knowledge:

- Improves building performance (quality) in terms of health, safety and security, functionality and psychological/cultural satisfaction.

- Adds to the state-of-the-art knowledge, local experience and contextual factors.

- Saves cost of maintaining and operating facilities over the life cycle.

- Improves morale of occupants and staff.

- Helps to create databases.

- Generates benchmarks/successful concepts.

- Helps to generate guidelines.

In summary, building performance evaluation (BPE) identifies both successes and failures in building performance, with an emphasis on human factors and the interaction with the design of physical setting and building systems. Benefits are by no means limited to the outcomes of POEs of facilities. BPEs made part of standard practice help to establish a performance-based approach to design, an evaluative stance that helps improve outcomes throughout the design and building delivery cycle, extending through the life cycle of the building. The benefits are several: better quality of the built environment; greater occupant comfort and a more satisfactory experience in visiting, using, or working in a facility; improved staff morale; improved productivity; and, significant cost savings. Most important of all, building performance evaluation contributes to the state-of-the-art knowledge of environmental design research and thus make significant contributions towards improving the profession of architecture.

Fig. 6. Observing behavior patterns

Documentation of four different and potentially conflicting activities and uses within one waiting lounge (in an Adolescent Care Unit of a University Hospital). Observed activities include: (a) Contemplation and search for relief and quiet, including looking out the window and creating privacy with a newspaper, (b) Watching TV, (c) Physical therapy activity, (d) Socializing during visiting hours. (Donald Watson, FAIA).

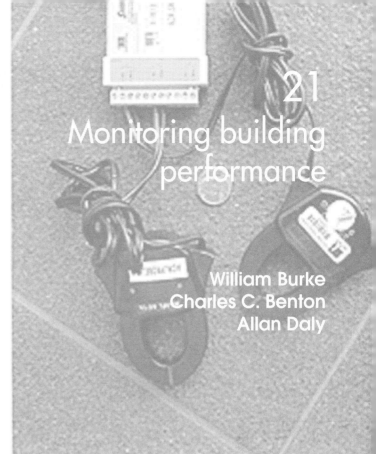

21
Monitoring building performance

William Burke
Charles C. Benton
Allan Daly

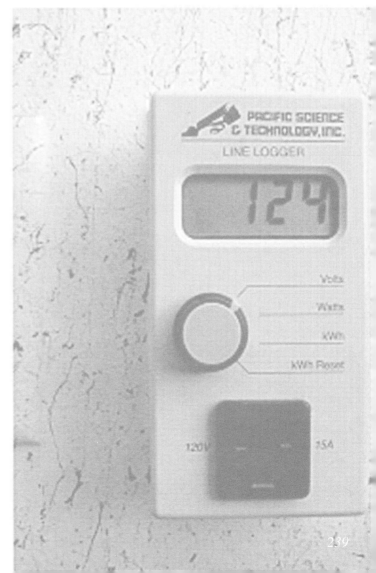

Fig. 1. Hand-held illuminance meter

Summary: A process for monitoring buildings is presented, along with suggestions to assist individuals conducting such an evaluation, including instruments used to measure the performance of buildings and building systems. The practicing of building performance measurement as part of the design process can lead to a record of systematic lessons learned and improved levels of design and building performance.

Key words: building performance, comfort, control systems, energy efficiency, indoor environment, post-occupancy evaluation.

Architects and designers need to understand the impact of design decisions upon complex building systems and to the effects of their choices upon indoor air quality, occupant health and comfort, and energy consumption. Without this knowledge, an architect will encounter difficulties in integrating site decisions, design elements and technical systems in a way that can effectively meet the needs of building owners and occupants. Many design professionals and their clients know too little about the way buildings perform following occupancy. Owners and managers may have more information as a result of their ongoing involvement with building operations. Yet there is relatively little documented information on occupant use patterns or the performance of building systems. Post-occupancy evaluation can increase the knowledge base, both individual and collective, of how buildings actually perform.

Effective documentation of building performance requires on-site measurement of environmental conditions. Previously, gathering data from buildings was a complicated and daunting task. However, recent development of microprocessor-based measurement devices have greatly simplified the process. Available instrumentation makes it much easier for building professionals to learn how theirs designs actually perform and operate.

This article focuses on methods for on-site exploration and measurement of building performance through relatively simple means available to students and professionals in architecture and others in the building industry. The discussion is addressed primarily to those interested in improving their monitoring and measurement skills to better understand how buildings actually operate. The design process should not be considered complete until results are evaluated. Monitored data is also essential to those interested in achieving greater energy efficiency in buildings or in making preliminary diagnoses of the causes and possible correction of building performance problems. ASHRAE provides two excellent sources appropriate for more in-depth examinations of building performance (ASHRAE 1991 and ASHRAE 1993).

Broadly speaking, building performance investigations fall into two categories: energy resource efficiency or occupant health and comfort. Each of these categories cover a number of key areas, including occupant-related environmental conditions, such as thermal comfort, qualities of the visual environment, and indoor air quality; occupant behavior and use patterns; the performance of building control systems; the performance of component parts of building systems; and the energy performance of the overall building and its major systems. A number of these topics are addressed below.

A basic model for field measurement

A successful building evaluation involving on-site measurement typically has five elements, derived from questions one might ask in following standard scientific methodology:

1   Identification of the objective of the study: What is the question you are trying to answer?

2   Establishment of methods: What are the best, or most practical, means of answering the questions posed?

3   The field work itself: What steps are taken in execution of the methods?

4   Analysis of the data: What is the best way to organize and summarize collected data?

5   Framing conclusions: Did you answer your original question? Does the data suggest additional questions or investigations? What lessons are to be learned for future applications?

Studies of the physical environment vary widely in the accuracy of the measurement technology, in spatial detail, and in the frequency at which data are collected. A research study might collect data with highly accurate instruments at frequent time intervals (once per minute) over a large spatial area (hundreds of instrument locations). However, an architect can learn a great deal from relatively simple monitoring methods, using modest equipment to take a small number of measurements.

The following discussion emphasizes accessible methods of investigation, that in many instances provide a first level understanding prior to more in-depth and specialized research. For example, Fig. 1 above illustrates a very simple measurement tool and approach by which illuminance levels are monitored using a hand held metering device. Spot measurements enable designers to obtain an experiential understanding of how lighting from both daylighting and electric lighting sources combine in creating both qualitative and quantitative effects, as well as to calibrate results of lighting and architectural design against performance standards and code requirements.

Authors: William Burke, Charles C. Benton, and Allan Daly

References: References: *Vital Signs Curriculum Materials Project.* http://www.ced.berkeley.edu/cedr/vs/index.html. This site primarily serves architecture school faculty and students. It includes a list of building measurement equipment and manufacturers. It also offers a number of case studies as models for building investigations.

Additional references are listed at the end of this article.

Applying the model
The five-part investigative model enumerated above can be applied to either a site or a building.

Site studies are usually conducted prior to the start of design or renovation with the intent to gain place-specific microclimate information. The study identifies how a site's microclimate differs from the regional climate, or how given locations vary from the rest of the area. The findings can be used to develop a design that responds to climate features, improving energy efficiency and occupant comfort.

When applied to existing structures, the investigative model provides insight and understanding of how building systems actually perform and how a building is really used by its occupants. This information has both short- and long-term uses. In the short term, the data collected may suggest changes, upgrades or renovations that lead to greater efficiency and occupant comfort. Evaluative studies may identify whether the performance of building systems has declined over time, reveal opportunities for financial savings from energy conservation, and/or play an important role in diagnosing the causes of occupant discomfort or poor indoor air quality. As part of the building commissioning process, measured evaluations can indicate whether building systems achieve the standards to which they were designed and provide the basis for system adjustments.

In the longer term, studies based on the investigative model enable designers to evaluate whether the intent of particular design approaches has been achieved. Lessons learned from collected data can influence future work. An architect who understands how the impact of external thermal loads leads to occupant discomfort and poor energy performance is less likely to site a future building in a way that exacerbates these loads. A designer who has experienced and then monitored the causes of glare and visual discomfort is more likely to place a high priority on providing balanced light with adequate daylight and user controls. Information about the past operation of building control systems and individual systems or components can inform the specification and detailing of high performance systems and components. Observation and documentation of occupant use patterns or their responses to design features in past projects can result in constructive improvements and occupant-sensitive design.

Measured studies also provide the investigator with a direct, experiential understanding of standards related to building systems. For example, many building professionals lack the training to differentiate between 20 and 50 foot-candles by sense alone. As a result, they may unthinkingly specify greater illumination levels than are needed by building users for either comfort or task requirements. An awareness of what measurements and standards mean in practice lessens the likelihood that inefficiency will be designed into a building in this way.

Methods
Beginning a field investigation is a simple and a somewhat intuitive process. One learns to shape an investigation to fit the amount of time available. A one day investigation will be less complex than a four week study, but it can still uncover meaningful information.

The single most important step in a building investigation is to identify the questions one seeks to answer. The mental discipline here is to frame a question in the form of a hypothesis that can be proved or disproved. One may do this by making a hunch about the answer to the question posed and about what the implications or meaning of that answer would be. Then begin with a brief exploratory visit to the building. Do this even if you have framed a very specific question. The purpose of this visit is to assure that you understand the context for your question and the range of factors that might influence it. During this visit, write down thoughts, observations and other questions about the building that come to mind. At the end of this exploratory visit rethink your initial hypothesis and revise it if necessary. Ask yourself what you expect to learn by testing the hypothesis to see

if it's true or false. Finally, list some of the ways you could go about testing your hypothesis. These three pieces, the hypothesis, what it might mean, and how you will test it, define the scope of your study.

Common topics for investigation
As mentioned, building performance investigations generally fall into two broad categories: resource efficiency or occupant health and comfort, each embracing a range of possible topics. This breadth is illustrated by the following examples.

Thermal comfort
A study of the thermal conditions in different areas of a building is an example of one type of investigation within the category of occupant health and comfort. If occupants at the perimeter of a building complain of thermal discomfort, radiant heat transfer could be the cause. In a building with single pane windows under cold climate conditions, occupants radiate body heat to the cold glass. As a result they feel chilled. Conversely, in a building with heat absorbing glass, occupants at the perimeter gain radiant energy from the glazing. Thermal discomfort due to overheating follows. Sometimes both conditions can occur in the same day. Identifying temperatures at the interior surface of the glass and comparing them to interior air temperatures can identify glazing patterns that contribute to occupant discomfort. (Fig. 2)

Extensive perimeter glazing systems have implications for building energy use as well. As a result of user complaints regarding thermal conditions, greater amounts of heating and cooling will be required to reduce occupant discomfort. Identifying the cause of the complaints and taking remedial action to eliminate or lessen thermal discomfort can also lead to a decrease in building energy consumption.

Visual comfort
Assessments of visual comfort are another common occupant related study. Measurement of the luminance levels of surfaces within the visual field of occupants, together with brief surveys or interviews, could identify patterns of good visual environments or diagnose the causes of poor ones. Glare-prone conditions are identified by a high ratio for two adjacent luminance values, particularly when these surfaces are encountered in the normal field of view.

Ventilation rate
The measurement of carbon dioxide (CO_2) levels in indoor air represents a third example of a study of occupant related environmental conditions. Carbon dioxide levels can serve as proxy measurements for air ventilation rates with higher concentrations associated with sensations of stuffiness. A simple study measuring CO_2 levels over a period of a week or two can provide an indication of whether ventilation rates in a given space are adequate to maintain occupant comfort.

Occupant use patterns
Investigations of use patterns reveal how occupants use a building and its features. For example, is a space designed as a college classroom used just during scheduled class hours or does it serve additional purposes? How should lighting in such a room be controlled? This type of study might involve a survey of building occupants to determine whether and how they use the space. It could also involve the use of time-lapse video photography to identify patterns of use. A time history of the room's occupancy compared against data indicating when light fixtures draw power can be very useful. This technique identifies the potential for energy and financial savings from implementation of a lighting control system that includes occupancy sensors. The required information could easily be collected by recording data over time from an occupancy sensor and light meter.

Control systems
Post-occupancy studies of building control systems provide a check on the design of the original system and determine whether it is op-

erating in the patterns anticipated. This kind of study can serve as the basis for adjustments to the existing system and refinements to the design of future control systems.

In a control system study conducted in Minnesota, the consulting firm Herzog/Wheeler and Associates employed a technique useful in almost all quick performance investigations. The building studied included heating elements at the roof used to prevent the buildup of snow. The consultants began by asking building operators to describe or "declare" how the control system regulating the heating elements should behave. The operators drew a graph representing power use over time, showing heating elements starting up in response to the presence of snow. They believed there was a sensor on the roof that recognized snowfall.

The investigators then collected data characterizing the actual performance of the heating elements and compared this information to the expectations of the operators. The data showed that the heating elements were in fact controlled by a timer, turning on every day for several hours regardless of weather conditions. Side by side comparison of the expected result and the actual condition presented a strong argument for improvements to the control system. The juxtaposition of data from just a few days using this "declare and compare" method can be very informative (Fig 3).

Documented information on the performance of control systems can also enable architects to make more fully informed design decisions. For example, do computer-controlled shading devices provide enough of an increase in energy performance over mechanically operated shades to offset their greater initial cost? Informal, point-in-time studies of both types of systems will provide the information to begin to answer this question. While the determination of exact savings at the system and building scale requires more elaborate protocols, a simple study can provide an indication of whether computer control is a strategy worth pursuing.

Measurement devices

Prior to describing some of the measurement devices currently in use, we offer a word about sources for these instruments. If you do not have access to measurement equipment, you may be able to borrow some of these tools. Many gas or electric power utilities will lend equipment to individuals within the company's service territory for use in measuring a building's performance. A number of power companies now operate energy resource centers or technical assistance programs that include support for studies of building performance. One utility, PG&E in California, operates a tool lending library for its customers at the PG&E Energy Center in San Francisco. Academic institutions are another possible source of instrument loans. Inquire with faculty members at university departments of architecture, mechanical and electrical engineering, and public health. You may also be able to borrow instruments from manufacturers and vendors of building components, such as local lighting equipment firms.

The technology of measurement has changed rapidly in recent years. In particular, microprocessors, digital displays, and new sensing methods have combined to make instruments capable, inexpensive, and easy to use. Instruments commonly used for building measurement fall into four broad classes: hand-held instruments, microprocessor-based data recorders, data acquisition systems, and sensors. These devices provide two types of readings, spot measurements and time series data. A spot measurement provides a "snapshot" reading of a physical parameter such as temperature, displaying the temperature at the time the reading is taken. A device capable of collecting time series data provides a series of readings over time. The interval between each reading and the overall length of time during which readings are taken can usually be set by the user. Typically, time series data are downloaded from the measurement device to a computer, where it can be read, formatted, and graphed using a spreadsheet program (Fig.4).

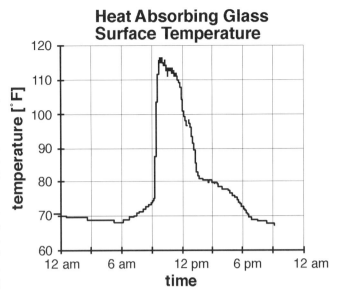

Heat Absorbing Glass Surface Temperature

Fig. 2. Southeast facing, heat absorbing glass plot radiates warmth to occupants at a building exterior for several hours before and immediately following noon.

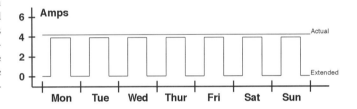

Fig. 3. "Declare and Compare."
In a commercial kitchen, staff manually operate the makeup air unit and exhaust hood. Building management expected that use would   reflect periods of kitchen use, with the unit operating when the room is occupied and shut down during unoccupied hours. When monitored, actual use indicated continuous operation during occupied and unoccupied hours. This considerable variance indicates a potential for energy savings.

Hand-held instruments are portable devices designed primarily around the task of collecting "snapshot" sample readings. Hand-held instruments are available for measuring air temperature, surface temperature, relative humidity, air velocity, pressure, illuminance, luminance, electric current, electric power, voltage, electric and magnetic fields (EMF), and carbon dioxide (CO_2) among other variables. Most hand-held instruments now include microprocessors for the acquisition, scaling, and display of measurements. This approach allows for the recording of minima, maxima, and means over longer periods. In addition, many hand-held instruments provide a DC voltage output signal that varies proportionally to the instrument's reading of the moment (Fig 5). This allows the recording of time-series readings with the addition of a data acquisition system (see description below).

Micro-data recorders combine a sensor, and inexpensive analog-to-digital converter, non-volatile memory, and a computer interface. The resulting device, sometimes as small as a matchbox, records a single variable such as temperature, humidity, illuminance, pressure, or voltage at regular intervals (such as five minutes) for periods of weeks. Once programmed through a simple computer interface, the micro data recorders are autonomous and can easily be placed in survey locations.

The price of these devices is low enough that they have displaced the paper chart recorders once common for these tasks. It is worth noting that micro data recorders often have 8-bit analog to digital converters. This means that they can only read 256 different levels of a signal. As a result, their graphic output has limitations. Curves in graphs drawn from data collected with these recorders often have a jagged or stepped quality.

Data acquisition systems are multi-channel data recording devices that offer more programmability and greater precision than micro data recorders. These devices allow the packaging of data collection software into a pre-scripted process. Contemporary data acquisition systems are much like a Swiss Army knife. They collect a versatile set of tools in a compact, battery-powered package that can be used with a modest amount of training.

Sensors provide input options for the data acquisition systems. Examples include devices for the measurement of illuminance, radiation, fluid flow, pressure, temperature, and occupancy (Fig 6).

It is beyond the scope of this article to describe the tools appropriate to studies of every performance topic. To indicate some of the possible choices, Table 1 lists tools useful for examining several variables related to the thermal and visual environments. In the table we describe instruments appropriate for several generic categories of measurement:

(1) low-cost instruments for projects on a limited budget,

(2) "snapshot" devices to capture accurate measurements at a specific point in time,

(3) time series devices to record a variable at fixed time intervals, and

(4) high accuracy devices to provide research-grade data.

As might be expected the selection of an instrument involves compromise between cost, accuracy, and capabilities For more information on the uses of specific measurement devices, see Table 1 and the references at the conclusion of this article.

The on-site investigation
The on-site process varies depending upon the nature of the study at hand. Evaluating the efficiency of an HVAC component will be substantially different from a study of occupant perception of indoor air quality. The first might involve the instrumented measurement of electric current while the second could involve occupant surveys, measurement of air change rates, and laboratory analyses of air samples.

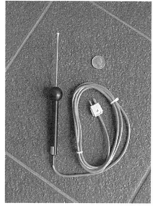

Fig. 4. Sensors and transducers.
From the upper left clockwise: a simple globe thermometer made with type T thermocouple and a 38-mm ping-pong ball sphere, a split-coil current transformer for AC current measurements, a miniature illuminance sensor and mounting plate, and a thermocouple-based surface temperature probe. A U. S. quarter is shown for scale.

Similarly, a one day visit with hand-held instruments will differ from an investigation involving the collection of time series data over several days or weeks.

No matter the topic or method of investigation, three key issues must be understood and balanced: time, space and detail. Deciding how best to manage them is key to successfully testing your hypothesis and answering your question.

Time

In considering time, the most important questions are what are the time intervals and timespan appropriate to the collection of data to answer your question. The aim in considering time interval is to establish a complete picture of the variable being measured without collecting an overwhelming amount of information. To establish the pattern of temperature swings over a one week period, a collection interval of twelve hours is too long to create an accurate picture, while one of thirty seconds produces more information than necessary. Readings taken every fifteen minutes would offer reasonable accuracy and a manageable database.

Similarly timespan, or the period between the first and last times you collect data, must be appropriate to your question. An investigation comparing electric lighting use and occupancy patterns in a school or office could produce useful information over a timespan of a few days or a week. An in-depth study of the response of thermal mass to outdoor temperature conditions would require a timespan of a season or longer. Collecting data over a few hours would not provide meaningful information.

Space

In considering space, you must identify the locations in a building that are representative. If using instruments and dataloggers, you must establish where to place the sensors. In a study of air stratification, for example, you would collect data from a range of heights within a room.

Detail

Detail requires that you consider the resolution of data you need to collect in order to answer your research question. In studying occupant comfort, collecting data accurate to 0.1F would be finer than is necessary. Conversely, data collected at a sensitivity of 5F would be too coarse.

Theoretically, one could collect finely detailed data at very short time intervals over a long time period at a great many points throughout a building. In practice, though, resources are limited, be they person hours, times of building access, or equipment. It may be possible to study a small location within a much larger space at frequent time intervals and with great detail. However, for some hypotheses it may be preferable to study more locations at less frequent time intervals and with less detail. A successful study balances the coverage of time, scale and detail for a given investigation against available resources.

A bit of practical advice

Be sure to obtain permission from the building owner or facility manager prior to beginning your investigation. Where possible, within the requirements of your investigation, place sensors where they will be easily accessible yet will not interfere with the activities of building occupants. If you place equipment in exterior locations, protect the device from the elements. If you leave measurement devices in place to collect data over time, attach a business card to the instrument and a brief note explaining that you are gathering information on building performance.

Speak to the occupants of the building or space. Given an understanding of what you are doing, occupants will usually be helpful, interested, and good sources of contextual information.

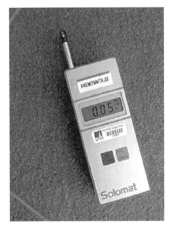

Fig. 5. Hand-held instruments.
From the upper left clockwise: An electronic temperature and humidity meter; a vane-based directional anemometer with current, maximum, and average modes; an extended range (up to 100,000 lux) illuminance meter; a current meter with integrated split-coil current transformer and recording capabilities; a hot-wire directional anemometer; and an illuminance sensor with matched electronic display module. A quarter is shown for scale.

Table 1. Examples of measurement devices used in investigations of thermal and visual conditions in existing buildings

Variable	Units	Example Measurement Devices			
		low cost	"snapshop"	time series	high accuracy
air °C temperature (dry bulb)		stem thermometer ($30)	hand-held elecronic thermometer ($250)	single-channel datalogger ($150)	Packaged Indoor Climate
humidity relative humidity, dew point temp., wet bulb)	RH%	sling psychrometer ($95)	hand-held electronic humidity meter ($450)	single-channel datalogger ($150)	(a single recording device that gathers reading from several sensors)
air velocity	m/s	smoke puffer ($10)	directional hot wire anemometer ($500)	directional hot wire anemometer & single-channel voltage recorder (+$1150)	($13,000)
radiant temperature (mean radiant temp., globe temp.)	°C	self-assembled globe & stem thermometer $30)	self-assembled globe & electronic thermometer ($250)	self-assembled globe & single-channel temperature datalogger ($150)	
radiant asymmetry	°C	n/a	n/a	n/a	
illuminance	lux (lumens /m²)	analog illuminance meter ($150)	digital illuminance meter ($750)	illuminance transducer & DAS ($1200)	NIST-traceable electronic illuminance meter ($1500)
luminance	cd/m²	optical comparator		digital luminance meter & DAS ($3500)	digital luminance meter ($2500)

Graphical analysis of data

A general purpose tool for the analysis phase of your investigation is a computer spreadsheet. These programs manage the quantities of data typical of a building study. More importantly, they are useful in transforming numerical information into a graphical format. Graphs are a useful way to visualize the data you gather, making it possible to identify the patterns or anomalies that reveal how a building performs. For further information, see Tufte (1983) and Tukey (1977).

Use the "Declare and Compare" method previously mentioned to examine data in a way that compares expected versus measured conditions. Before graphing your data with a spreadsheet, draw a freehand sketch showing how you expect the graphic data to appear. When comparing this sketch to the actual data, look for variations between the two. These points of variation make excellent starting points for further consideration and often point toward your conclusions. Tukey comments, "The greatest value of a picture is when it forces us to notice what we never expected to see."

Conclusions from the investigation

In drawing a conclusion from your investigation, gather together the findings from your investigation. Restate your hypothesis and consider how your data and analysis support or disprove it. If the analysis of your data produced results different than expected, think about possible explanations for the difference or differences. Also consider the degree of validity of the data. Were there unusual circumstances during the investigation that could explain the results? How long and thorough was the investigation? With these in mind, choose the best possible explanation or explanations that prove or disprove the hypothesis you tested. On occasions this involves the collection of additional data.

Examples of building measurement

Two examples of the field evaluation of existing buildings follow. In the first, investigators measured lighting conditions and lighting system performance in a large office building. The building design sought to maximize daylighting and minimize the need for electric lighting. Investigators compared their findings against expected conditions and proposed changes leading to improved operation of the system. In the second example, building management undertook an investigation in response to occupant complaints. By measuring CO_2 concentrations within a university lecture hall over the course of several weeks, the managers established whether ventilation rates were adequate to patterns and densities of use.

Lockheed Building 157, located in Sunnyvale, California, incorporates a coordinated set of lighting features designed to reduce electrical energy consumption for ambient lighting. Completed in 1983, the scheme was often published in the architectural press as an innovative example of daylighting. To provide significant daylight without glare, the architects designed a system that combines architectural features for the admission and distribution of daylight, a dimmable electric lighting system, and a control system to operate the electric lights in response to available daylight. The building configuration was driven by daylighting criteria from the early conceptual design phase. In 1985, representatives from Pacific Gas & Electric, the local utility for Building 157, and Lawrence Berkeley National Laboratory conducted an investigation to evaluate the energy-efficient design (Figs. 7 and 8).

Building measurement

In an initial exploratory visit, hand-held illuminance meters were used to gauge how effectively daylight penetrated deep into the office space. These meters were also used to get a feel for how light levels varied perpendicular to and parallel with the glazed facades, and how the light levels varied from floor to floor. Investigators confirmed that useful daylight was reaching 40 ft. (12 m) and more into the office space and that significant variation in horizontal plane illuminance

Fig. 6. Diminutive dataloggers.

From the upper left clockwise: a single-channel temperature recorder with capacity for 8,000 measurements; a three-channel current logger (shown with two current transformers attached); a single channel voltage recorder shown connected to a passive infrared occupancy detector; and a current, voltage and power meter that accumulates energy use as well for items plugged into a duplex outlet.

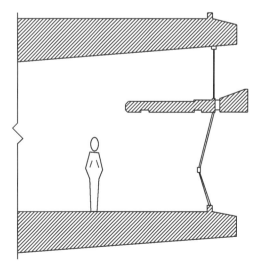

Fig. 7. At north and south exterior walls of Lockheed Building 157 large lightshelves are located just inside the glazing.

Located 7.5 ft. (2.3 m) above the floor and extending 12.3 ft. (3.8 m) into the building, these serve as light reflectors and glare control baffles. The south side of the building has an additional exterior lightshelf that shades the window below. For glare and solar control, low transmittance glass was installed below the lightshelf and clear glazing above the lightshelf.

Fig. 8. The daylight-admitting atrium of Lockheed Building 157.

occurred only perpendicular to the windows. Also, they discovered that light levels varied little by floor.

During the first inspection of the building, investigators noticed that something was amiss in the operation of the electric lighting system. The electric lighting system appeared to be operating at near full power in areas where daylight far exceeded target illuminance levels. This observation helped shape the planning of the rest of the study.

The measurement program for the main study employed battery-operated data acquisition systems connected to illuminance sensors, temperature sensors, and watt transducers placed in representative daylight zones. Data were collected as 15–minute averages of measurements at 10–second intervals. Readings were made for 4–week periods in each of three seasons for three separate daylight zones. Lighting power demand for individual circuits was monitored using watt transducers installed in local electrical closets. An additional set of sensors measured air and surface temperatures.

Findings

The architectural features of the building work well in providing interior daylight for ambient lighting. Interior illuminance levels exceeded 35 foot-candles (the ambient target) for major portions of a typical day in most portions of the building throughout the year. Investigators discovered interesting light level variations that were related to the 20° west-of-south orientation and the higher angle of the sun in summer.

Under manual control, a test of the electric light dimming system worked properly. Each circuit operated well through its entire dimming range. Curves of illuminance versus power demand were created for each dimmer and the data matched the pattern published by the manufacturer with one important exception. Investigators discovered that the actual maximum dimming levels occurred at 22 to 29 percent as compared to the manufacturer's claims of 15 percent for the units.

The investigators' hunch based on the exploratory visit was correct in regards to the lighting control system. Data comparing interior illuminance and electric power revealed widespread variation in the performance of the electric light control systems. A majority of the control circuits failed to dim properly, thus causing excess use of electric power. In several cases, circuits were dimming to only 90 percent of full power during periods when interior illuminance levels exceeded target levels by a factor of four.

Conclusions from the investigation

Monitored data from this investigation indicated that the architectural daylighting features of the Lockheed Building 157 perform admirably and contribute significant daylight to most areas of the building. The field tests also established that, under manual control, the electric light dimming hardware is capable of dimming to, on average, 27 percent of full power. Operational savings, however, were limited by inappropriate performance of the control system in most of the building's lighting circuits (Fig 9).

With this information in hand, the same team of investigators returned to Building 157 in 1988 to modify the lighting control system to capture the potential savings. Using similar data collection and analysis techniques, the team was able to demonstrate low cost changes to the system that substantially increased efficiency of the lighting system. The changes were implemented in 1991.

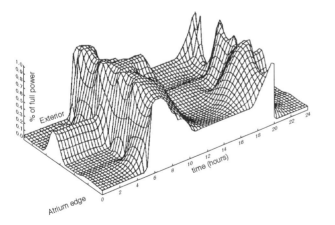

Fig. 9. Dimming patterns for the south wing of Lockheed Building 157 on a clear August day after the controls retrofit.
This plot shows lighting power demand as height of surface vs. location in building and time-of-day. The lighting circuits are turned on around 6 am and ramp to full power. Significant dimming occurs by 9:30 am as the sun reaches the slightly west of south facing facade. Dimming is achieved across the entire 90 ft. (27 m) depth of the wing until approximately 6 pm.

Evaluating ventilation rates by measuring CO_2 concentrations

Auditorium users on the campus of a public university complained of hot, stuffy conditions during evening lectures. They believed that the HVAC system was not supplying the room with adequate amounts of fresh air.

To test their theory that the HVAC system was the cause of occupant complaints, building management monitored CO_2 levels in the auditorium. CO_2 levels can serve as a proxy indicator for whether room air change rate is adequate. Ambient levels of CO_2 in fresh outdoor air are approximately 400 parts per million (PPM). If ample fresh air is delivered to a space, then CO_2 levels should remain close to this level. The accepted upper limit for CO_2 levels in an indoor space is 1000 PPM according to ASHRAE Standard 62–89.

With limited equipment and resources available, the investigators placed a borrowed CO_2 monitor in the room. They took advantage of the monitor's analog voltage output by connecting the monitor to an inexpensive, single-channel voltage logger. This setup recorded CO_2 levels over time. The investigators set the logger to record voltage readings representing CO_2 concentrations at five minute intervals. The monitor and logger then ran for a period of three weeks. At the end of the measurement period, the building managers downloaded the voltage data from the logger to a laptop computer, storing the data in a computer spreadsheet file.

Since the intent of the investigation was to examine CO_2 levels in the room over the course of the testing period, the investigators decided to look at all the data in a single graph. Voltage data were converted to CO_2 readings (1 VDC = 1,000 PPM CO_2). To create the graph, 5-minute-average data were combined into 1-hour averages. Investigators then plotted the data on a 3D surface graph (Fig. 10).

The graph shows that CO_2 levels varied in response to occupancy at the first measured location – high in the room near the return air intake. The levels remained near ambient early in the morning (the foreground of the graph) before the first class and late at night after the last class. On the weekends, the CO_2 concentrations were also low as can be seen in the repeating valleys running from the front to the back of the graph. During the occupied school hours of the day, CO_2 levels rose and fell with changing occupancy.

At two times during early phases in the monitoring period the concentrations rose just above the 1000 PPM level. Twice later in the monitored period the concentrations rose again, almost to the 1800 PPM level. These peaks are most likely associated with dense occupancy or a special use event. The first 1800 PPM level peak occurred on a Saturday when the lecture hall is not normally in use. Except for these four 1-hour periods, during the 3 weeks of monitoring the CO_2 levels were consistently below the 1000 PPM recommended upper limit.

In reviewing the data, the investigators decided that readings from a second location would be useful. The sensor had originally been placed high in the space, close to both a supply vent and the return vent. It was possible that fresh air from the supply vent was "short circuiting" directly into the return vent. In this case the sensor would have accurately measured CO_2 concentrations that were lower than the conditions experienced by occupants in the lecture hall.

To test whether CO_2 levels high in the room were different from those in the occupied zone, investigators moved the sensor to a lower position and recorded another four weeks worth of data. These data were handled in the same fashion as the previous set and converted into a 3D surface plot. That graph is shown in Fig. 11 below.

The data from this second measurement period show that CO_2 levels in the occupied zone seem to match closely those near the return air duct. The CO_2 concentration pattern recorded in the first week of the second monitoring period closely resembles the pattern from the first week of the earlier monitoring period. If it is assumed that both of these weeks held typical occupancies, then the CO_2 measurements high in the room prove to be a good indicator of CO_2 levels in the occupied zone.

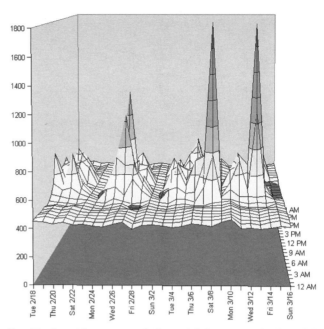

Fig. 10. Graphic representation of CO_2 concentration data collected in a lecture hall at a large university.
The graph shows that CO_2 levels varied in response to occupancy. The levels remained near ambient levels early in the morning (the foreground of the graph) and late at night. On the weekends, the CO_2 concentrations were also low as can be seen in the repeating valleys running from the front to the back of the graph. During daytime school hours, CO_2 levels rose and fell with changing occupancy.

KEY TO FIGS. 10 & 11

- 1600-1800
- 1400-1600
- 1200-1400
- 1000-1200
- 800-1000
- 600-800
- 400-600
- 200-400
- 0-200

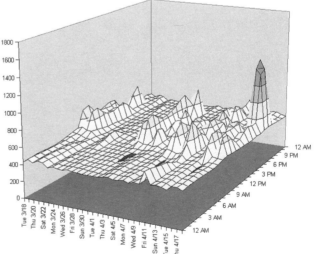

Fig. 11.
Data from the second measurement period show that CO_2 levels in the occupied zone closely matched those near the return air duct. CO_2 concentration patterns recorded in the first week of the second monitoring period closely resembles the pattern from the first week of the earlier monitoring period.

Another feature of the data worth noting in the second monitoring period are the consistent readings of approximately 400 PPM during the second week. The University closed for spring break during this time interval and the lecture hall was not used. As a result of this investigation, building managers concluded that the HVAC system serving this auditorium functioned adequately at most times. During especially dense occupancies the system had trouble providing adequate fresh air to the space. With this information, the managers set out to make special arrangements for those occasional periods of time.

Conclusion

A simple investigation can reveal many things about how a building actually operates. With the new measurement devices now available, undertaking a building evaluation is more straightforward than ever before. An improved understanding of building performance can inform the design decision making of architects and engineers. It can also result in improved conditions for occupants, and savings for building owners and operators. In addition, improvements to energy efficiency are a proven means of reducing the impact of buildings upon the global environment.

Changes in building measurement approaches and technology continue to occur at a fast pace. To keep abreast of new developments, there are several resources. The Vital Signs Project is an architectural education program that encourages and assists students undertaking measured evaluations of existing buildings. The project's internet site offers information on building evaluation and measurement devices that should be of interest to practicing professionals. Energy Crossroads is an internet site established by Lawrence Berkeley National Laboratory. It organizes a wide array of pointers to energy-efficiency resources on the World Wide Web. Sensors Magazine contains news on building measurement equipment and equipment manufacturers. For more information on these resources, see the references below.

Additional references

ASHRAE 1991. *Handbook. Heating, Ventilating, and Air Conditioning Applications.* Chapter 37, "Building Energy Monitoring." Atlanta, GA: American Society of Heating, Refrigerating and Air-Conditioning Engineers.

ASHRAE. 1993. *Handbook of Fundamentals.* Chapter 13, "Measurement and Instruments." Atlanta, GA: American Society of Heating, Refrigerating and Air-Conditioning Engineers.

Energy Crossroads. http://eande.lbl.gov/CBS/eXroads/ This internet site, established by Lawrence Berkeley National Laboratory, organizes a wide array of pointers to energy-efficiency resources on the World Wide Web.

PG&E Energy Center, 851 Howard St., San Francisco, CA 94103 http://www.pge.com/pec/ This internet site offers a description of the services available to building professionals, owners, and managers through a utility operated energy center.

Tufte, Edward R. 1983. *The Visual Display of Quantitative Information.* Cheshire, CT, Graphics Press.

Tukey, John W. 1977. *Exploratory Data Analysis.* Menlo Park, CA: Addison-Wesley Publishing.

Sensors Magazine. Peterborough, NH: Helmers Publishing, Inc. Fax 603-924-7408.

DESIGN DATA   II

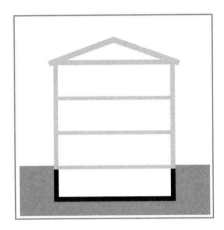

A SUBSTRUCTURE

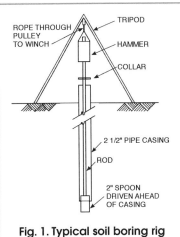

Fig. 1. Typical soil boring rig

Labels in figure:
ROPE THROUGH PULLEY TO WINCH — TRIPOD — HAMMER — COLLAR — 2 1/2" PIPE CASING — ROD — 2" SPOON DRIVEN AHEAD OF CASING

Soils and foundation types

Summary: This article provides an overview of soils and foundation types. Soil bearing capacity and soil tests are reviewed along with substructure foundations, including piers, piles, caissons and footing design.

Key words: borings, caissons, piers, piles, soil bearing capacity, spread footings, wall footings.

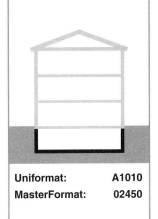

Uniformat:	A1010
MasterFormat:	02450

1 Evaluating the bearing capacity of soil

The first step in evaluating the bearing capacity of the soil is site reconnaissance, noting existing buildings, rock outcroppings, streams, and bodies of water. A topographical survey locating these items plus important trees should follow. In areas of substantial previous construction, reference to old maps may indicate features long removed from the landscape.

Subsurface investigation is most often done by borings, but test pits are also used. A typical boring rig (Fig. 1), consists of a tripod or frame with a pulley and a small winch.

A hammer is raised by the winch and allowed to fall free, driving a pipe casing into the ground. The casing is cleaned out by a water jet. At stated intervals, normally every 5 ft. (1.5 m), a piece of split pipe (called a spoon) is guided through the casing and driven ahead of the lead end to obtain a sample. The spoon is then withdrawn and opened so that the samples may be identified and placed in a sample jar.

The number of blows necessary to drive the spoon 1 ft. gives important information as to the compactness of the soil. Generally a 300-lb. hammer falling 18 in. is used for advancing the casing and a 140-lb. hammer falling 30 in. is used to drive the spoon. When rock is reached, a rotary power takeoff on the hoist drives a core bit uncased into the rock. Rock core samples are recovered, identified, and placed in sample boxes. The soil boring contractor then furnishes a drawing giving the location and ground elevation of the holes, a scale section of each hole showing materials encountered, and a log of the casing and spoon blows.

Many codes as well as good engineering practice dictate boring locations about 50 ft. (15 m) on center within the building outline. Soils or geotechnical engineers may typically designate critical points with respect to either site configuration and/or the proposed building footprint. Abnormal ground conditions may require closer spacing. Depth of borings are typically 15 to 20 ft. (4.5 to 6 m) below foundation level, with one or more borings deeper to look for weak lower levels.

Test pits give a more immediate idea of the soil conditions but are limited to a depth of about 10 ft. (3 m). Dug with a backhoe, they give a method for economical and visually evident evaluation. Where rock is near the surface, a possible picture of the rock profile is obtained.

Once the type and degree of compactness of soil has been established, its supporting ability must be evaluated. Table 1 shows representative values for presumptive bearing capacities as listed in two national codes. Local codes may have different values.

When a soil load test is required, a 2-ft. (60 cm) square plate is loaded to the proposed design load and held until no settlement is observed in 24 hr. The load is then increased 50 percent and held until no settlement is observed in 24 hr. If the settlement does not exceed 3/4 in. (20 mm) under the design load and if under the overload it does not exceed 60 per cent of that observed under the design load, the test is satisfactory.

2 Selecting a foundation type

One of the most important decisions in designing and constructing any building is determination of its connection to the earth which supports the structure. The earth's substrata is investigated and tested to help define the soil conditions beneath a site of a proposed foundation. Yet even the most thorough investigation encounters only a small portion of the soils and a foundation design relies heavily on interpretation of the data from soil tests.

The most common types of footings are the spread footings and wall footings. These are used where the soil bearing capacity is adequate for the applied loads. The applied loads accumulate from either column loads or bearing wall loads. Variations of spread footings include eccentric footings, where center of the superimposed load does not line up with the resultant center of the soil bearing pressure, combined footings, where two or more columns must share one footing, and matt footings, where the required superimposed loads require most of the building's footprint to transfer the accumulated loads to relatively weak soil bearing capacity. Pile foundations are required where poor surface and near surface soils are weak and column like shafts must be used to penetrate the weak soil and reach acceptable supporting stratum and greater depths below grade. Piles are tied together with pile caps upon which the building's columns or walls are supported. When large column loads exist, caissons are used as extensions to columns. Caissons typically are larger in diameter and longer. They rely on end bearing directly on earth with very high bearing capacity.

Retaining walls are used where a grade change occurs and the upper levels must be stabilized behind a wall. The wall portion of the foundation extends vertically cantilevered from a substantial and carefully designed footing.

When good bearing material occurs directly under the building excavation, spread footings are designed for uniform bearing on the soil. The most common footing for square and round columns are square footings. Table 2 illustrates some sizes of square column footings

Authors: Philip P. Page, Jr.; edited for 7th edition by Martin D. Gehner, P. E.

Table 1. Presumptive soil bearing values.

Class of Material	Allowable values: pounds per sq. ft.	
	BOCA[1]	UBC[2]
1. Crystalline Bedrock	12,000	12,000
2. Sedimentary Rock	6,000	6,000
3. Sandy Gravel and Gravel	5,000	6,000
4. Sand, Silty Sand, Clayey Sand, Silty Gravel and Clayey Gravel	3,000	4,500
5. Clay, Sandy Clay, Silty Clay and Clayey Silt	2,000	3,000

[1] The BOCA National Building Code/1993. Building Officials and Code Administrators International, Inc.

[2] The Uniform Building Code, 1997. International Conference of Building Officials, 1997.
These values are taken for a footing 3' - 0" below grade. Refer to the Code for other widths and shallower depths of footings.

Table 2. Square column footings - soil bearing value: 3000 psf.

Note: Table 2 has been prepared according to ACI 318-89. Strength design: $f'_c = 3,000$; $f_y = 60,000$. Tabulated column loads are actual not unfactored.

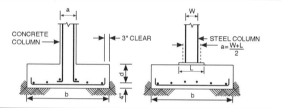

Column load, kips	b, ft	d, in.	a, in. (minimum)	Reinforcement each way
45	4' -0"	12	12	6- #4
57	4' -6"	12	12	6- #4
70	5' -0"	12	12	7- #4
85	5' -6"	12	12	5- #5
101	6' -0"	12	12	6- #5
118	6' -6"	12	12	7- #5
136	7' -0"	14	12	8- #5
156	7' -6"	14	12	7- #6
176	8' -0"	16	12	7- #6
199	8' -6"	16	12	9- #6
221	9' -0"	18	13	9- #6
246	9' -6"	18	13	8- #7
270	10' -0"	20	14	8- #7
298	10' -6"	20	14	10- #7
324	11' -0"	22	14	10- #7
354	11' -6"	22	14	9- #8
382	12' -0"	24	15	9- #8
443	13' -0"	26	15	11- #8
509	14' -0"	28	16	10- #9
580	15' -0"	30	17	11- #9
653	16' -0"	32	18	13- #9

reinforced with steel bars of grade $F_y = 60$ ksi [kips per square inch. A kip is equal to 1000 lb.].

The concentrated load of the steel column requires a steel bearing plate to distribute and transfer the load to an acceptable stress on the concrete footing, which in turn distributes the load to the soil at the allowable soil pressures. This condition is generally detailed as shown in Fig. 2. Sometimes the load must be distributed over a large area to lower-strength material by an I-beam grillage as schematically shown in Fig. 3. A reinforced concrete column often bears directly on the footing and the stress in the column reinforcing is transferred to the footing by steel dowels as indicated in Fig. 4.

Bearing walls have continuous footings under them as shown in Fig. 5. When the footing projection beyond the face of the wall equals D/2 or less, the footing requires no tensile reinforcement. When the projection is greater than D/2, reinforcement across the footing is required to carry the tensile stresses. As a rule, a footing that is twice as deep as its projection will require no reinforcing. Longitudinal reinforcement is desirable to help distribute more uniform pressures on the soil.

Where a lot line or interference from another footing precludes the use of square footings, a combined footing may serve two or more columns. Fig. 6 shows examples of popular types of combined footings. Note that the centers of gravity of the plan area of the footing and the load from the column must coincide.

Wall footings often intersect column footings or column piers. Fig. 7 illustrates such a condition. Footing and wall reinforcement is required to develop continuity through the intersection unless specific expansion joints are properly installed.

Piers supporting grade beams extend to footings placed on bearing strata substantially below the general excavation. The grade beams, designed as flexural members, carry wall and floor loads to the piers as diagrammed in Fig. 8. If the grade beam is shallower than the frost penetration depth, frost bevels may be placed on the beam soffits to prevent frost heave. Unreinforced concrete piers are limited to a height-to-thickness ratio of six. A more slender pier must be designed as a reinforced column.

Dowels develop the strength of the column reinforcing into the pier. Small dowels between the pier and the footing prevent pier displacement during backfilling. In areas of varying and unpredictable bearing elevations, field adjustments may easily be made to the height of the pier.

For even deeper bearing strata, piles are used. Concrete pile caps then support the columns and grade beams. The choice between walls and footings, piers and grade beams, or piles and grade beams is determined by soil conditions, by the requirements of the building's structural system, and cost. The requirement of many codes—that a pile be at least 10 ft. (3 m) long in order to provide adequate lateral stability—often determines the change-over depth between piers and short piles.

Mats can distribute loads to large areas, permitting light soil bearing loads on weak material. Hydraulic mats resist upward water pressure. Because of the various possible arrangements and loads, each mat becomes a specialized custom design.

Eccentric footings

When the center of a footing's upward pressure cannot be placed directly under the column or wall, methods must be employed to distribute the resulting eccentric footing loading without the uneven pressure exceeding the allowable bearing pressure. Building codes generally limit the projection into the street to 1 ft. beyond the property line. Thus footings under columns located on the property lines are

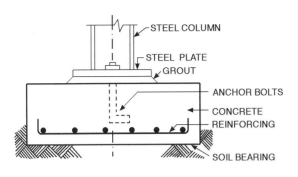

Fig. 2. Steel column on spread footing

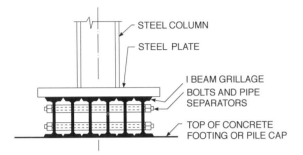

Fig. 3. Steel grillage

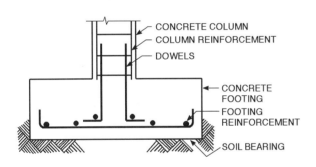

Fig. 4. Concrete column on spread footing

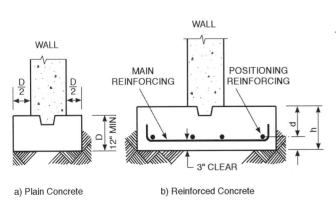

a) Plain Concrete   b) Reinforced Concrete

Fig. 5. Typical wall footings

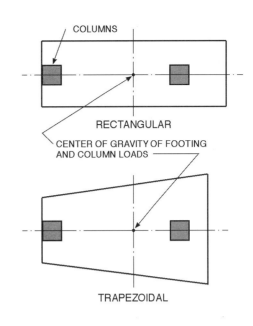

Fig. 6. Plan views of combined footings

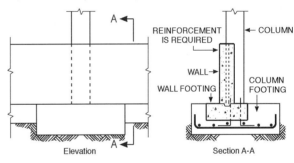

Fig. 7. Typical foundation wall and column footings

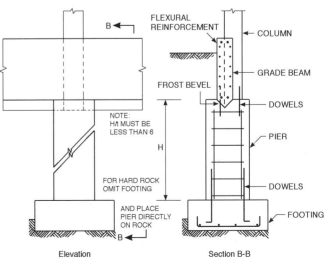

Fig. 8. Typical grade beam and pier

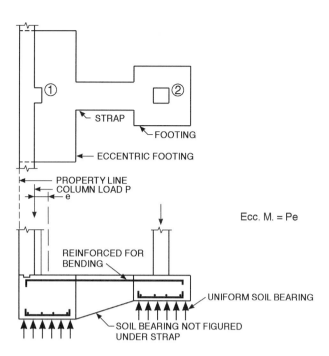

Fig. 9. Pumphandle footing. Note: footing cannot be concentric with column 1 because it would cross the property line. Therefore the eccentricity is balanced by the use of the strap and hold-down load of column 2.

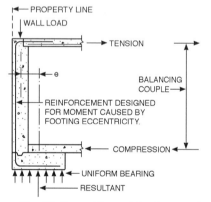

Fig. 10. Eccentric wall footing section

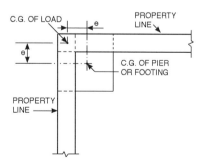

Fig. 11. Eccentric corner footing plan. Note: eccentricities are removed by walls acting as pumphandles. Each wall removes the eccentricity normal to it.

eccentric to the columns as illustrated in Figure 9. Straps, reinforced concrete beams, are carried back to an adjacent column for a hold-down load to counterbalance the eccentric moment. The footings are proportioned so that the pressures are uniform and similar under both footings. The strap is reinforced to resist the bending caused by the eccentricity and is not considered as furnishing bearing support. The bending caused by the eccentric loading may be resisted vertically rather than horizontally by a couple composed of tension in the first floor and compression in the basement as seen in Fig. 10. The wall reinforcing required may be substantial. At corners, walls or grade beams permit the employment of special footing as seen in the example of Fig. 11.

Foundations to rock

Rock, having the highest bearing capacity, is often the only acceptable foundation available for heavy loads. Piers carry the loads directly to rock. On hard rock, piers require no footing, as the capacity of the rock is almost that of concrete. Typical column and grade beam construction is employed.

Where rock occurs more than 10 to 15 ft. (3 to 4.5 m) below the grade beam soffits, piers become too costly. Clusters of piles driven to rock and encased in a pile cap can support substantial loads. For heavier loads, caissons are used. Caissons are big holes drilled through the weak soil strata down to rock. The drilled voids are then filled with concrete. Piles or caissons may vary in length from 15 to over 100 ft. (4.5 to over 30 m).

Piles

Piles carry loads to strata below the ground surface either by end bearing, which are called bearing piles, or by surface friction along their sides which are called friction piles. The soft material through which the pile is driven provides lateral stability, but for structures over water the piles must be designed as columns.

Pile capacity is generally established by test load or driving resistance. Load tests are used to establish capacity. Driving resistance measurements are used to ensure that all piles are driven as hard as the test piles. Piles are generally grouped in clusters connected by pile caps.

Borings are essential for proper pile evaluation. Individual piles may test to a capacity greater than their contribution to the capacity of a cluster. A soft stratum underlying a hard one may not be able to support the total load delivered from the hard stratum even though the resistance of the hard stratum may indicate satisfactory pile support as indicated in Fig. 12. Different piles shown in Fig. 13 have evolved with certain characteristics, briefly described as follows:

- Types I and II are cast-in-place concrete piles. A light-gage steel shell, driven on a mandrel which is then withdrawn, is inspected and filled with concrete. Care must be taken to avoid collapsing of the shell when an adjacent pile is driven.

- Type III is similar to Types I and II except that the shell gage is heavier and no mandrel is required.

- Type IV is an open-end steel pipe. It is excavated, often by air jet, as it is advanced, and then filled with concrete after refusal has been reached. In lieu of reaching refusal, driving may stop while a concrete plug is placed and then redriving will seat it. The advantage is less disturbance to adjacent structures.

- Type V is a closed-end pile. After driving, it is filled with concrete. Often it is used inside buildings with low head room. Shorter lengths are simply spliced with steel collars.

- Type VI is a precast concrete pile. It is good in marine structures but requires heavy handling equipment and accurate estimation of tip elevation as it is difficult to cut off in the field.

- Type VII is a wood pile-the least expensive. Where the pile is partially exposed permanently above water level, it must be treated with a wood preservative.

- Type VIII, a composite wood and concrete pile, is seldom used. The timber is kept below groundwater and a greater over-all length is achieved. A closed-end pipe pile may be used in place of the timber section.

- Type IX is a rolled steel H section. It is the cheapest of the higher-capacity piles. Protection must be provided when driving through cinder fill or other rust-producing material.

- Type X is a drilled-in caisson. A 24-in. (60 cm) round pipe is driven to rock and cleaned out. A rock socket is drilled and cleaned, a steel H-section core is set, and the shell is filled with concrete. This is good for very heavy loads.

Piles almost always are installed in groups of three or more. Table 3 is included to represent a few simple examples of pile cap sizes and shapes along with representative capacities of the cap and the column being supported. For heavier column loads the reader is referred to a structural engineer for analysis of specific foundation requirements of the building(s) under consideration.

Piles are located with a low degree of precision. They can easily be 6 in. (15cm.) or more from their desired location. If building columns, which are located with much greater precision, were to be located on single piles, the centerlines would rarely coincide. The resulting eccentric loads in both the column and the pile would generate unwanted moments in both members. A similar condition could exist around one axis for a column supported by a two pile foundation. Groupings of three or more piles provide a degree of safety and redundancy should one pile be driven slightly out of alignment. Lateral stability of the group increases with three piles as compared to fewer piles.

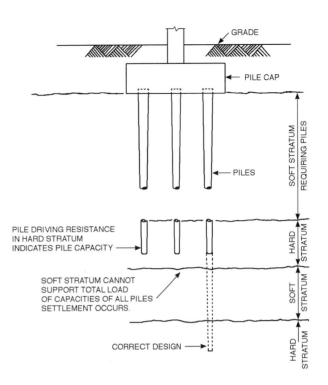

Fig. 12. Piles incorrectly seated in hard statum above soft stratum.

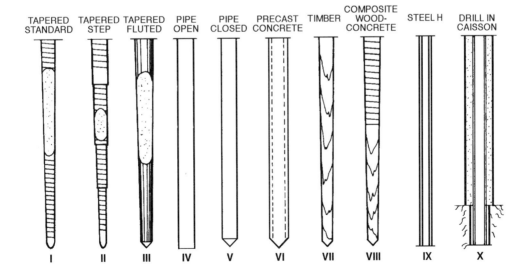

Fig. 13. Types of piles

Table 3. Standard pile caps

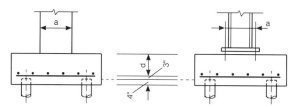

No. of piles	Plan	All caps				Fy = 60 KSI reinforcement	
		Pile value, kips	Column load, kips	d, in.	a, min.	Long way	Short way
3		20	56	15	7	3 bands of 4- #4	
		30	86	15	9	3 bands of 4- #4	
		40	116	17	9	3 bands of 3- #5	
		50	145	18	10	3 bands of 3- #5	
		60	175	19	10	3 bands of 4- #5	
		80	235	20	11	3 bands of 4- #5	
		100	295	21	12	3 bands of 4- #5	
		120	355	21	14	3 bands of 4- #5	
4		20	73	14	8	5- #5	5- #5
		30	113	15	9	6- #5	6- #5
		40	152	16	10	6- #5	6- #5
		50	192	17	11	6- #5	6- #5
		60	232	18	12	5- #6	5- #6
		80	312	18	14	5- #6	5- #6
		100	392	19	15	6- #6	6- #6
		120	472	20	15	5- #7	5- #7

Retaining walls

Summary: This section provides an overview of the structural requirements of basement and retaining walls with illustrative examples, including free standing cantilevered designs.

Key words: retaining walls, basement walls, lateral pressure, Rankine theory, weep holes.

Uniformat:	A1010
	G2040
MasterFormat:	02450

Retaining walls hold back or retain earth between disparate grade level. Typically, the wall is cantilevered from a footing extending up beyond the grade on one side and retaining a higher level grade on the opposite side. Basement walls may also be considered retaining walls, However, they are supported at the lowest end by the basement floor slab and at the top by the floor framing system. Both types of walls must resist the lateral pressures generated by loose soils or, in some cases, by water pressures. The soil being retained should be well drained in order to minimize the forces of water and ice.

A basement wall must be designed to resist lateral pressures from adjacent earth. Typically the wall spans from the basement floor to the first floor, depicted in Fig. 1(a), and acts as the structural element between those two points. Fig. 1(b) illustrates typical forces on a basement wall. The first-floor structural plane must act as a diaphragm able to transfer the reaction from the top of wall to the end walls, or to intermediate cross walls. The diaphragm plane must be secured to the top of the end walls which in turn act as shear walls transmitting the forces down to the footings. To offer an insight to wall thickness and the reinforcement required relative to wall height, Table 1 lists several cases which have been analyzed for the lateral loads shown.

Free standing cantilevered retaining walls rely on the weight of the wall plus the weight of earth over the footing for stability. In addition, the friction between the earth and the footing is essential to resist sliding of the footing. The characteristic elements of a retaining wall design are shown in Fig. 2(a). The Rankine theory of earth thrust, represented in Fig. 2(b). assumes that the thrust is zero at the top and a maximum at the base, giving a triangular loading. The thrust is produced by the sliding of the wedge of soil between the earth below the angle of repose and the ground surface. The thrust for earth backfilled against the wall is commonly computed as 28.6 psf per foot of height of grade above the footing. If groundwater saturates the soil throughout this height the design lateral force against the wall increases to 62.5 psf per foot of height of grade above the footing.

The importance of effective water drainage and release of any hydrostatic pressure behind the wall can not be overemphasized. Weep holes through the vertical wall along with footing drains used in conjunction with gravel or crushed stone backfill allow water to drain away from the wall.

A wide variety of site conditions and retaining wall requirements influence the design of retaining walls. The determination of the specific's site variant conditions along with the applicable wall design criteria require consideration by an engineer experienced with soil mechanics.

To illustrate the design of one simple type of cantilevered retaining wall, the example of Table 2 takes one set of assumptions and varies the wall height. This freestanding retaining wall is designed so that the resultant of the force of the soil pressure and the gravity loads passes through the middle third of the footing, preventing uplift. The advantage of this approach is to easily proportion the footing and wall based on the limit of the peak allowable soil bearing pressure. Where the soil is particularly compressible, the resultant should pass near the center of the footing to give uniform soil loading. With the resultant at the edge of the middle third, compressible soils may give differential settlement, causing the wall to tilt. Such rotation is very detrimental to a retaining wall.

Retaining wall may also be built with masonry. Stone masonry, concrete masonry or brick masonry may be used. The latter two materials may also be reinforced. When using a built-up modular unit for a retaining wall always means that the wall must be thicker and massive. For walls of shorter height, these materials can be interesting and successful. Because they are more vulnerable for cracking and breaking, these materials are often used creatively using undulating or zig-zag plan forms. The masonry TEK (NCMA 1996) notes should be referenced for further structural design and detailing opportunities.

Author: Martin D. Gehner, P. E.

References: ACI. 1989. *Building Code Requirements for Reinforced Concrete.* ACI 318-89. Detroit, MI: American Concrete Institute.

CRSI. 1996. *CRSI Handbook.* Schaumburg, IL: Concrete Reinforcing Steel Institute.

NCMA. 1996. *TEK Manual for Concrete Masonry Design and Construction.* Herndon, VI: National Concrete Masonry Association.

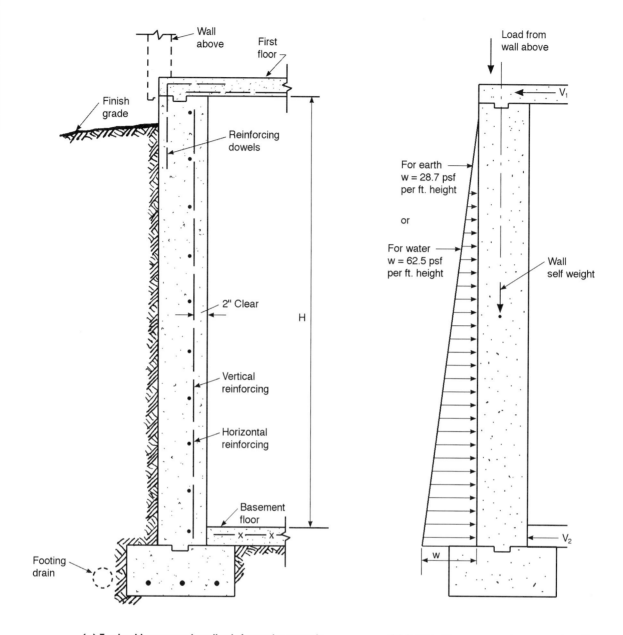

(a) Typical basement wall reinforced concrete

(b) Typical forces on a basement wall

Fig. 1. Basement foundation wall

Table 1. Basement wall resisting lateral pressure (ASI 318-89. Strength design: f'_c = 3,000 psi; F_y = 40,000 psi.)

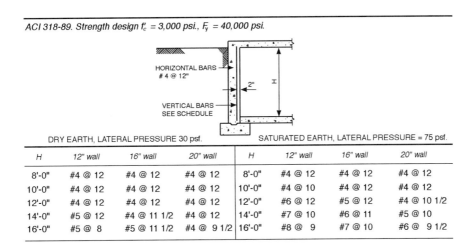

ACI 318-89. Strength design f'_c = 3,000 psi., F_y = 40,000 psi.

DRY EARTH, LATERAL PRESSURE 30 psf.				SATURATED EARTH, LATERAL PRESSURE = 75 psf.			
H	12" wall	16" wall	20" wall	H	12" wall	16" wall	20" wall
8'-0"	#4 @ 12	#4 @ 12	#4 @ 12	8'-0"	#4 @ 12	#4 @ 12	#4 @ 12
10'-0"	#4 @ 12	#4 @ 12	#4 @ 12	10'-0"	#4 @ 10	#4 @ 12	#4 @ 12
12'-0"	#4 @ 12	#4 @ 12	#4 @ 12	12'-0"	#6 @ 12	#5 @ 12	#4 @ 10 1/2
14'-0"	#5 @ 12	#4 @ 11 1/2	#4 @ 12	14'-0"	#7 @ 10	#6 @ 11	#5 @ 10
16'-0"	#5 @ 8	#5 @ 11 1/2	#4 @ 9 1/2	16'-0"	#8 @ 9	#7 @ 10	#6 @ 9 1/2

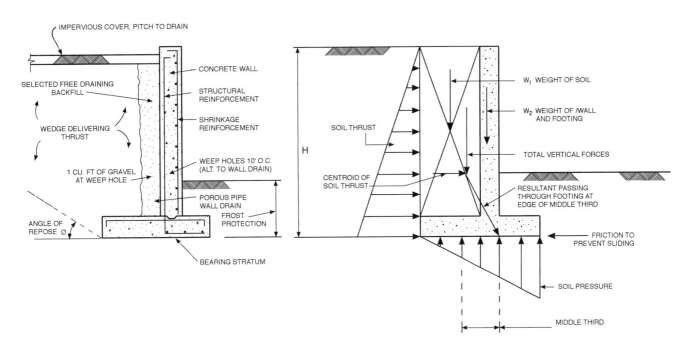

(a) Essential elements of a retaining wall   (b) Essential forces for a retaining wall

Fig. 2. Retaining wall

Table 2. Cantilever retaining walls (ACI 318-89). Strength design: f'_c = 3,000 psi; F_y = 60,000 psi.

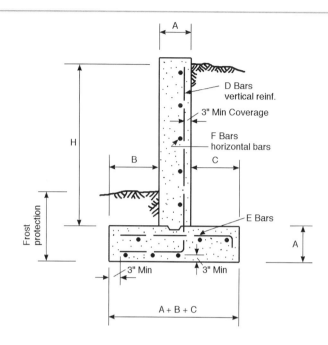

Height H	A	B	C	Toe pressure psf	D Bars	E Bars	F Bars
4'-0"	1'-0"	1'-2"	6"	872	#4 @ 12"c/c	—	#4 @ 8" c/c
5'-0"	1'-0"	1'-5"	8"	924	#4 @ 12"	—	#4 @ 8"
6'-0"	1'-0"	1'-8"	10"	1000	#4 @ 12"	—	#4 @ 8"
7'-0"	1'-0"	1'-11"	11"	1079	#4 @ 12"	—	#4 @ 8"
8'-0"	1'-0"	2'-2"	1'-0"	1207	#4 @ 12"	#4 @ 12" c/c	#4 @ 8"
9'-0"	1'-0"	2'-5"	1'-2"	1352	#4 @ 10"	#4 @ 12"	#5 @ 12"
10'-0"	1'-0"	2'-8"	1'-5"	1452	#5 @ 12"	#4 @ 12"	#5 @ 12"
12'-0"	1'-0"	3'-2"	1'-11"	1649	#5 @ 11"	#4 @ 12"	#5 @ 12"
14'-0"	1'-2"	3'-8"	2'-3"	1873	#6 @ 12"	#4 @ 12"	#5 @ 11"
16'-0"	1'-4"	4'-2"	2'-6"	2128	#6 @ 10"	#4 @ 10"	#5 @ 10"

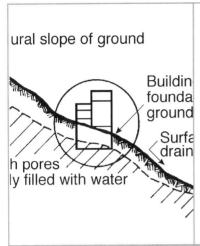

Subsurface moisture protection

Summary: Controlling water entry into the subsurface parts of a building is critical, in that the uses and contents of such spaces may be harmed by water and dampness. Moisture protection strategies discussed in this article include dampproofing, waterproofing, and subsurface drainage systems.

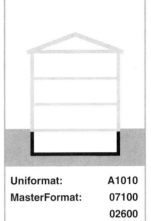

Key words: dampproofing, footing drains, groundwater, perimeter drainage, subsurface drainage, vapor retarders.

Uniformat:	A1010
MasterFormat:	07100
	02600

Since waterproofing of the subsurface portions of a building is difficult to remedy, the reliability of the waterproofing and moisture control strategies is critical. Methods of moisture control of substructures, discussed in this article, include:

1 Dampproofing, which retards the passage of water in the absence of hydrostatic pressure.

2 Waterproofing, which prevents the passage of water, under hydrostatic pressure, through subsurface foundation walls, slabs, or both.

3 Subsurface drainage, which removes water from proximity to the foundations and subsurface slabs.

Groundwater

In most regions, there is some dampness in the soil under and around buildings from both surface and underground water conditions (Fig. 1). The dampness usually comes from rain water or local ground water near the surface, but in some desert regions the moisture movement is up from deep earth. Under the most severe conditions, there is standing water under hydrostatic pressure above or near the bottom of the foundations, either all the time or some of the time. More commonly, there is water in the ground during and after rain, and there is dampness which can penetrate the walls and slabs-on-grade by capillary action and through small cracks and voids.

(1) Groundwater level tends to follow ground contour—deeper on hills, shallower in valleys.

(2) Rainfall percolates through ground to recharge groundwater. Groundwater level varies with amount of rainfall.

(3) Springs occur where local ground depressions place ground level below groundwater level.

Sources of information on the soil and water conditions which prevail in the locality and at specific building sites include all-season measuring of ground water in a test boring, consultation with a geotechnical engineer, and consultation with local building officials. Long-term flooding records, as well as recent storm patterns (which in many localities are exceeding long-term records), provide equally critical reference data.

Conditions requiring subsurface moisture protection
In some cases, the subsurface spaces of a building are not critical; valuable goods are not stored there, and the spaces are not used for critical operations. In these instances, occasional leaking may be tolerated, and neither dampproofing nor waterproofing may be needed.

Dampproofing is generally adequate to retard passage of water into a basement, and subsurface drainage is provided by natural ground absorption and/or evaporation, under the following combination of conditions:

- If a building is built on very porous soil,

- If the standing ground water level is always well below the basement, and

- If moisture from ground runoff, roof drainage, and similar sources is directed away from the building (by swales, underground drainage pipes, and similar means).

Waterproofing which is intended to exclude all water from a building under all foreseeable conditions in the safe choice if any combination of these factors exists:

- If the standing ground water is near or above the basement floor level,

- If water from other sources is not directed away from the building,

- If building contents and activities in the belowground spaces are valuable and critical.

- If discharge of water from a subsurface drainage system is not practical.

Subsurface drainage is an excellent method of avoiding water entry into the basement:

- If a building site has standing ground water which is sometimes above the basement floor, or

- If the soil is not sufficiently porous to act as a natural drainage bed.

Author: Donald Baerman, AIA

References: American Concrete Institute. *Design of Slabs on Grade.* ACI 360R-92. Detroit, MI: American Concrete Institute.

Labs, Kenneth *et al.* 1988. *Building Construction Design Handbook.* Minneapolis, MN: University of Minnesota Underground Space Center. [Out of print]

Massari, Giovanni and Ippolito. 1985. "Damp Buildings Old and New." *Association for Preservation Technology Bulletin.* XVII-1-85. Williamsburg, VA: Association for Preservation Technology. (540) 373-1621.

National Roofing Contractors Association. 1990. *The NRCA Roofing and Waterproofing Manual.* Rosemont, IL: National Roofing Contractors Association.

A redundant combination of surface drainage, subsurface drainage, and dampproofing or waterproofing is a prudent design choice.

If the cost of achieving total protection from substructural leaking under all conditions is very high, the building owner/manager may choose to tolerate the cost of replacing equipment periodically. An example is the decision to save the cost of fully waterproofing a basement balanced against the cost of replacing the heating system if a 100-year storm should occur. This decision should be made explicitly and accurately recorded as part of the design record.

Caution: If a basement is exposed to high standing ground water, its substructure must be able sustain the maximum possible pressure (62.4 pounds per foot of depth per square foot). One way to achieve such protection is to design the basement floor slab to be heavier than the water displaced and the walls to resist the water load, and another way is to design the entire substructure to resist the load of the displaced water, in the manner of a boat. The writer has seen a floor slab which was broken and forced by underground water pressure up into the first floor. If basement flooding under extreme conditions is tolerable, the substructure can be designed with "burst-in" panels to relieve the stress by allowing the basement to fill with water. In any case, design of a basement to resist a significant hydrostatic head of water should be performed by a structural engineer.

In critical or questionable situations, a good design decision might be to eliminate subsurface spaces or to make them noncritical:

- If there is no reliable outfall for subsurface drainage,

- If analysis shows that there may be troublesome ground water, and

- If the construction and maintenance budget won't permit waterproofing,

With any system of subsurface moisture protection, it is highly desirable to keep surface water away from the building. Slope the grade down away from the building, incorporating swales and area drains as needed. Do not discharge rain water, parking lot drainage, and other surface water to areas near the foundations. Keep basement windows and hatches well above grade or in drained areaways.

If subsurface drainage is used to remove significant volumes of water, a civil engineer should be consulted to determine the size and slope of the pipe and the outfall. Many urban and suburban localities require that on-site storm water retainage tanks and/or on-site swales for percolation of surface runoff be provided. In most localities, surface runoff to adjacent properties is disallowed. Some surface runoff may contain harmful chemicals or pollutants. Discharging large volumes of water may also require approval by the Environmental Protection Agency, city engineer, and other officials.

Permeability of concrete and masonry foundations

If concrete is designed, formulated, and placed with sufficient care, it can be made waterproof. Formulation and mixing of waterproof concrete are specified in ACI 301, paragraph 3.4.2. Water stops are specified in ACI 301, paragraph 6.3. Full-time observation of the placement by a structural engineer is recommended.

Unless very special controls are applied to concrete foundation construction, and at masonry foundations, it is prudent to assume that there will be voids and cracks in the foundation materials which will admit water. Water may wick through the foundation walls, and the ground may be temporarily saturated outside the walls during heavy rainfall.

In addition to water entry through basement slabs and foundation walls, water may "wick" slowly by capillary action upward in foundation walls which are in contact with damp ground. This process is known as "rising damp". In new buildings the inclusion of a waterproof flashing course at the base of foundation walls is a good method of avoiding rising damp. For recommendations regarding remedial work on existing buildings, see Massari, Giovanni and Ippolito (1985).

1   Dampproofing

Under those conditions listed above, when dampproofing is judged to be adequate, a brush or trowel coat of waterproofing material applied to the outside of the foundations is an inexpensive way to bridge over minute imperfections and cracks and to retard capillary infiltration. The surface should be cleaned and repaired first. A thick 1/8 in. (3.6 mm) coating with a non-asbestos fibrated trowel mastic will be more effective at filling voids and bridging small cracks than a thinner coating.

Waterproofing materials, as described below, may be used as dampproofing. They are generally more effective, and more expensive, than dampproof brush and trowel coatings.

Subslab vapor retarders
Subslab vapor retarders serve to retard the passage of water vapor from the earth up through the slab on grade and to retard the wicking of moisture from the earth into the slab. Subslab vapor retarders are not waterproofing; they are not intended to stop water under hydrostatic pressure. Granular fill under slabs on grade is more reliable than a vapor retarder in resisting capillary action. Factors determining whether or not to use a subslab vapor retarder include:

- Based on an analysis of vapor flow, is the net vapor flow up from the earth or down to the earth? Under many conditions, a subslab vapor retarder will make the basement slab damper.

- Will a subslab vapor retarder slow the initial drying of the concrete? The answer is often yes.

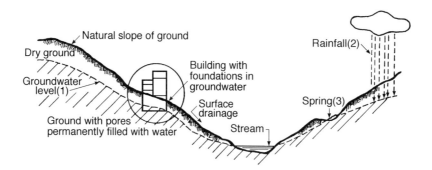

Fig 1. Basic Factors affecting groundwater level,

- Do the requirements of manufacturers' associations and manu-facturers require a vapor retarder? Example: The Resilient Floor Covering Institute.

See ACI 360R-92, *Design of Slabs on Grade*, paragraph 9.8, which recommends not using vapor retarders in direct contact with slabs on grade. The recommendation is to place the vapor retarder, if there is one, under the porous fill and to "choke off" the top of the porous fill with sand. Excess bleed water can then pass out the bottom of the slab, allowing faster finishing.

A major cause of basement dampness is condensation of humid air on cool surfaces. A vapor retarder, waterproofing, and dampproofing will have little effect on this process. In general, condensation can be re-duced by keeping the partial vapor pressure in the basement low (dry air) and keeping the surfaces in the basement warm. Expanded, ex-truded polystyrene insulation or foamed glass insulation under the slab and outside the walls helps keep the basement surfaces warm. Designing the mechanical system to keep the basement warm in win-ter and dry in summer, or providing dehumidifiers, helps keep the partial vapor pressure low.

2 Waterproofing

First, and most important, determine the nature of the surface and subsurface water. This may require consultation with a geotechnical engineer and people familiar with the site. The writer has seen a shal-low river completely surround a house, filling the basement, during spring melting, while the site was dry in other seasons. Determine whether there will be water under hydrostatic pressure under the base-ment slabs on grade.

Make sure that the structure is designed to resist the full displacement force of the water under all conditions.

Methods, materials, and details for waterproofing are included in NRCA 90. The following is a summary. In all cases the substrate should be clean, repaired, dry, and at the temperature recommended by the manufacturer.

- Hot asphalt or coal tar bitumen built-up membranes (applied to earth side). These are similar to built-up roofing. The number of plies is recommended in NRCA 90.
- Modified bitumen membranes, either hot-applied or self-adhesive (applied to earth side). Hot-applied modified bitumen membranes are similar to modified bitumen roofing. Self-adhesive rubber-ized asphalt membranes are placed over patched, primed surfaces.
- Butyl and EPDM rubber membranes (applied to earth side).
- PVC membranes (applied to earth side).
- Rubber and PVC membranes should be installed with water cut-offs dividing the waterproofed area into sections, since water which penetrates may travel between the foundation and the membrane.
- Fluid-applied elastomeric membranes (applied to earth side). These materials achieve intimate bond to the surfaces, and thus water travel between the membrane and the wall is resisted.
- Hot rubberized asphalt materials (applied to earth side). These are similar to fluid-applied elastomeric membranes.
- Bentonite clay waterproofing (applied to earth side). This mate-rial swells greatly upon contact with water, and the gel thus pro-duced waterproofs the surface. These materials can migrate and "heal" small voids and cracks, and they achieve intimate contact with the surface. They must be applied directly to the slab or wall. They are not suitable for above-ground use.
- Metallic waterproofing (applied to earth side or interior side).
- Cementitious waterproofing (applied to earth side or interior side).

- Crystalline waterproofing (applied to earth side or interior side).
- Metallic, cementitious, and crystalline waterproofing are rigid. Movement in the substrate may crack them. However, the sub-structure of a building is usually stable.
- Other miscellaneous materials are listed in the NRCA Manual.

Waterproofing systems applied to the earth side have the advantage of being compressed between the foundations and the water. Systems applied to the interior side have the advantage of being applied after some or all of the foundation shrinkage and settlement has occurred, and they may be inspected, maintained, and repaired while the build-ing is in use, without disruptive, expensive excavation. It is good de-sign to allow access to the basement surfaces which are waterproofed by this method.

Application of a membrane waterproofing system under slabs on grade may require the placement of a subslab over which the waterproof membrane is installed. Protection board is then applied over the wa-terproofing, and the wearing slab is installed over that.

In all cases, the waterproofing must be protected against construction damage. If insulation is installed over the waterproofing, it may serve as protection. Otherwise, a special protection board is recommended. Full-time observation during backfilling is prudent.

Quality control of subsurface waterproofing

Subsurface waterproofing is not a forgiving system, since even a small imperfection in the system may allow an intolerable amount of water to enter. Whereas a roof can be inspected and repaired, many subsur-face waterproofing systems cannot be so inspected and repaired, and they must perform without fail for the life of the building. Some meth-ods of special quality control include:

- Special observation of the work, especially the joints such as that between the slab waterproofing and the wall waterproofing. Spe-cial observation may be performed by the manufacturer's repre-sentative as well as the architect or engineer.
- Redundancy, such as membrane plus bentonite, membrane plus subsurface drainage, and bentonite on the outside and cementitious, metallic, or crystalline waterproofing on the inside.
- Automatic sump pumps with a perimeter drainage trench and with an emergency generator. Sump pumps have the added advantage of taking care of water from burst pipes, severe roof leaks, and similar water which finds its way to the basement.
- Sumps with power and through-wall sleeves for emergency use of a sump pump.
- Special attention to penetrations through the slabs and walls.

3 Subsurface drainage

Requirements of subsurface drainage

Subsurface drainage should, at best, drain to a fully reliable outfall such as a lower part of the site, a storm drain, or a drywell of adequate capacity. Although subsurface drainage can be directed to a sump pump, the same storm which causes the heavy rain may cause a power failure. If subsurface drainage is critical, and if it depends on a sump pump, the pump and its power source should be highly reliable, for example, more than one pump and an emergency generator backup. If the outfall is a storm or combination sewer, there must be provi-sions against backflow during deluge conditions.

If the outfall is to grade or a natural waterway, there should be durable screening to keep animals out, and there should be rip-rap (fist-sized broken face rock) to prevent soil erosion. The proper functioning of subsurface drainage system may be critical, so there should be in-

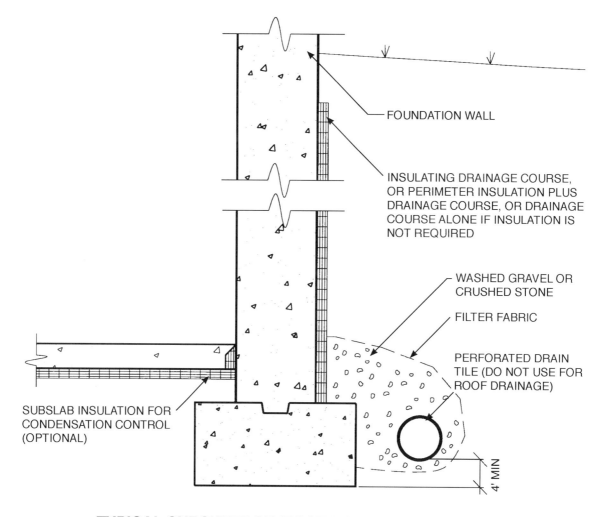

FOUNDATION WALL

INSULATING DRAINAGE COURSE,
OR PERIMETER INSULATION PLUS
DRAINAGE COURSE, OR DRAINAGE
COURSE ALONE IF INSULATION IS
NOT REQUIRED

WASHED GRAVEL OR
CRUSHED STONE

FILTER FABRIC

PERFORATED DRAIN
TILE (DO NOT USE FOR
ROOF DRAINAGE)

SUBSLAB INSULATION FOR
CONDENSATION CONTROL
(OPTIONAL)

4' MIN

TYPICAL SUBSURFACE (FOOTING) DRAIN

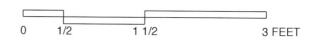

0   1/2   1 1/2   3 FEET

Fig. 2. Typical subsurface (footing) drain

A1.3 Subsurface moisture protection · A1 Foundations and basement construction

SUBSTRUCTURE A1

tense observation of its installation and backfill. There are documented cases where such systems which were crushed and made inoperable by boulders in the backfill.

To check and maintain subsurface drain lines, there should be one or more cleanouts extended to grade. Upon completion of the system, the system must be tested by discharging water into the cleanouts to verify free and positive drainage.

If grade discharge, a storm sewer, or a reliable drywell system are not available, the storm water may drain to a sump pump. However, the sump pump and its power should be highly reliable and redundant.

Footing drainage systems

Elements of a subsurface drainage system (Fig. 2):

- There must be a reliable outfall. The pipe from the collection pipe to the outfall should not be perforated.

- The foundation wall should, under most conditions, be dampproofed or waterproofed.

- The collection pipe should always be separate from other storm drainage such as rain water leader discharge, out to a point well below the footing elevation.

- The collection pipe is normally about 4 in. (10 cm) above the level of the adjacent footing bottom.

- The collection pipe can be perforated plastic or porous concrete. 6-in. (15.2-cm) diameter is a reasonable minimum size. The perforated collection pipe should be sloped a minimum of 1% (about 1/8 in. per foot) toward the outfall.

- Around the collection pipe, there should be a porous bed of washed gravel or crushed stone without fines, large enough not to pass through the perforations in the pipe. Around the crushed stone there should be a wrapper of filter fabric.

- There should be a porous drainage course or bed immediately outside the foundations, from grade down to the footings, embedded in the gravel or crushed stone which surrounds the collection pipe.

- Gravel and crushed stone have been used as a drainage course. They should be separated from the soil with filter fabric, and they should be continuous full height. The filter fabric, gravel or crushed stone, and backfill must be placed together. The difficulty in achieving a good gravel or crushed stone drainage course explains the wide use of proprietary products instead.

- A number of commercial products function as drainage courses. They include deformed plastic sheet with filter fabric overlay, deformed plastic filament with filter fabric overlay, and porous polystyrene beads. There are also several commercial products which combine a drainage course with perimeter insulation. They include scored expanded, extruded polystyrene foam with filter fabric overlay and porous polystyrene beads. In addition to   serving as perimeter insulation, such products keep the foundations warm and thus reduce condensation of humid air on the basement surfaces.

- A proper drainage course outside the foundations has another function besides drainage: it reduces the capillary movement of soil moisture into the foundations.

It is good practice to keep surface water away from the foundations, even if there is a subsurface drainage system. Grades should slope down away from the building. Rain water leaders and area drains should discharge into drain pipes separate from the subsurface drainage. If rainwater drips directly from the roof eaves, provide a wide porous drip bed with its own perforated drainage system.

Other types of subsurface drainage

If there is persistent or occasional water under hydrostatic pressure under the basement floor slab, especially if there is no effective waterproofing under the slab, an overall system of underfloor drainage

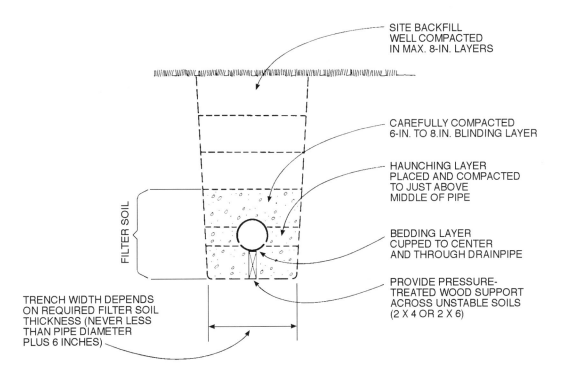

SITE BACKFILL
WELL COMPACTED
IN MAX. 8-IN. LAYERS

CAREFULLY COMPACTED
6-IN. TO 8.IN. BLINDING LAYER

HAUNCHING LAYER
PLACED AND COMPACTED
TO JUST ABOVE
MIDDLE OF PIPE

BEDDING LAYER
CUPPED TO CENTER
AND THROUGH DRAINPIPE

PROVIDE PRESSURE-
TREATED WOOD SUPPORT
ACROSS UNSTABLE SOILS
(2 X 4 OR 2 X 6)

FILTER SOIL

TRENCH WIDTH DEPENDS
ON REQUIRED FILTER SOIL
THICKNESS (NEVER LESS
THAN PIPE DIAMETER
PLUS 6 INCHES)

Fig. 3. Drain line using soil filter (Labs *et. al.* 1988)

may be used. Over filter fabric a bed of washed gravel or crushed stone is placed, at least 8 in. (20.3 cm) deep, with perforated drain pipe distributed throughout. The perforated drain pipe should be sloped at least 1% (about 1/8 in. per foot) toward the outfall. There should be openings in the footings through which the drain pipes pass. On top of the gravel or crushed stone, place an additional sheet of filter fabric, and then a bed of sand to permit the slab to shrink as it cures and dries.

If there is persistent or occasional water under hydrostatic pressure outside the foundations or under the slab, waterproofing may be more appropriate than subsurface drainage, or it may be used in addition to subsurface drainage. For moisture prone sites and/or critical subsurface construction on sites sloping towards the building, the additional provision of swales, intercepting drains or curtain drains placed on the uphill sides offers a further prudent "first line" defense of water diversion and moisture control. (Figs. 3 - 5).

If the volume of water is great, its disposal may be a problem, and it may affect other parts of the project and neighboring sites. Also, sub-

surface drainage, like a well, tends to run more freely with time, as the silt clears from the soil.

Areaways sometimes become clogged with leaves and other debris and with silt, and they may cease functioning. Since areaways are seldom seen, they may not be maintained. During heavy rain, the areaways may overflow through doors or windows into the building. Some ways to avoid problems include:

- The areaway gratings should be as large as practicable. Small, flat gratings can be clogged easily.

- For small areaways, a bed of washed gravel or crushed stone makes a good bottom.

- If the areaway does not need to be open, a cover will keep rain and debris out.

- If the areaway does need to be open for ventilation, a mesh cover with screening small enough to keep leaves out is desirable. The cover should be removable for cleaning.▶

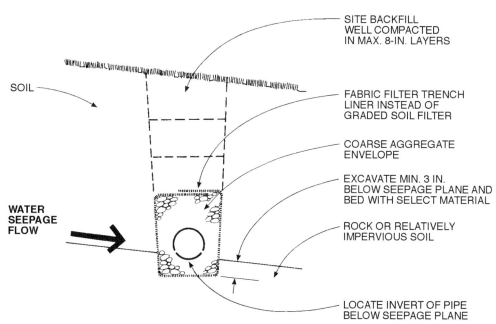

SITE BACKFILL WELL COMPACTED IN MAX. 8-IN. LAYERS

SOIL

FABRIC FILTER TRENCH LINER INSTEAD OF GRADED SOIL FILTER

COARSE AGGREGATE ENVELOPE

EXCAVATE MIN. 3 IN. BELOW SEEPAGE PLANE AND BED WITH SELECT MATERIAL

WATER SEEPAGE FLOW

ROCK OR RELATIVELY IMPERVIOUS SOIL

LOCATE INVERT OF PIPE BELOW SEEPAGE PLANE

Fig. 4. Intercepting drain using fabric filter (Labs _et. al._ 1988)

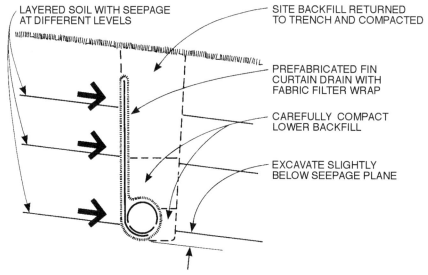

LAYERED SOIL WITH SEEPAGE AT DIFFERENT LEVELS

SITE BACKFILL RETURNED TO TRENCH AND COMPACTED

PREFABRICATED FIN CURTAIN DRAIN WITH FABRIC FILTER WRAP

CAREFULLY COMPACT LOWER BACKFILL

EXCAVATE SLIGHTLY BELOW SEEPAGE PLANE

Fig. 5. Curtain drain (Labs _et. al._ 1988)

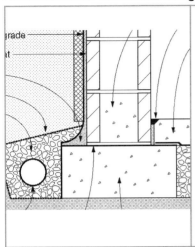

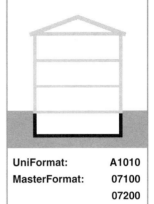

Residential foundation design

Summary: Good practices of foundation design and construction mean not only insulating to save energy, but also providing effective structural design as well as moisture, termite, radon and soil gas control where appropriate. This article provides recommendations for foundation design for residential basements, crawl spaces and slabs-on-grade.

Key words: basement, crawl space, foundation, residential, insulation, moisture control.

UniFormat:	A1010
MasterFormat:	07100
	07200

The foundation of a residential or small commercial structure is a somewhat invisible and sometimes ignored component of the building. It is increasingly evident, however, that attention to good foundation design and construction has significant benefits and can avoid some serious future problems.

Insulating any type of foundation is likely to result in warmer floors during winter in above-grade spaces, thus improving comfort as well as reducing energy use. Insulating basement foundations creates more comfortable conditions in below-grade space as well, making it more usable for a variety of purposes at relatively low cost. Raising basement temperatures by using insulation can also reduce condensation, thus minimizing problems with mold and mildew.

In addition to energy conservation and thermal comfort, good foundation design must be structurally sound, prevent water and moisture problems, and control termites and radon where appropriate. The importance of these issues increases with an energy-efficient design because some potential problems are caused by incorrect insulating practices. Under certain circumstances, the structural integrity of a foundation can be negatively affected by insulation when water control is not adequate. Without properly installing vapor diffusion retarders and adequate air sealing, moisture can degrade foundation insulation and other moisture problems can be created. Improperly installed foundation insulation may also provide entry paths for termites. Insulating and sealing a foundation to save energy results in a tighter building with less infiltration. If radon is present, it can accumulate and reach higher levels in the building than if greater outside air exchange was occurring. All of these potential side effects can be avoided if recommended practices are followed.

The three basic types of foundations—full basement, crawl space, and slab-on-grade—are shown in Fig. 1. The most common foundation materials are cast-in-place concrete and concrete block foundation walls with a concrete floor slab. Other systems include pressure-preservative-treated wood foundations, precast concrete foundation walls, masonry or concrete piers, cast-in-place concrete sandwich panels, and various masonry systems. A slab-on-grade construction with an integral concrete grade beam at the slab edge is common in climates with a shallow frost depth. In colder climates, deeper cast-

in-place concrete walls and concrete block walls are more common, although a shallower footing can sometimes be used depending on soil type, groundwater conditions, and insulation placement.

Most of the foundation types and construction systems described above can be designed to meet necessary structural, thermal, radon, soil gas, termite and moisture or water control requirements. Factors affecting the choice of foundation type and construction system include site conditions, overall building design, the climate, and local market preferences as well as construction costs.

1 Basements

Précis: This section summarizes suggested practices related to basements. Recommended optimal levels of insulation are presented. Recommendations are given for two distinct basement conditions: (1) a fully conditioned (heated and cooled) deep basement, and (2) an unconditioned deep basement. A brief summary of basement design practices is given, covering structural design, location of insulation, and moisture control.

The term "deep basement" refers to a 7- to 10-foot-high (2.1 to 3.0 m) basement wall with no more than the upper 25 percent exposed above grade. "Fully conditioned" means that the basement is heated and cooled to set thermostat levels similar to above-grade spaces: typically at least 70F (21C) during the heating season, and no higher than 78F (26C) during the cooling season. The "unconditioned deep basement" is identical to the conditioned deep basement except that the space is not directly heated or cooled to maintain a temperature in the 70F to 78F (21C to 26C) comfort range. Instead, it is assumed that the basement temperature fluctuates during the year based on heat transfer between the basement and various other heat sources and sinks including the above-grade space, the surrounding soil, and the furnace and ducts within the basement. Generally, the temperature of the unconditioned space ranges between 55F (13C) and 70F (21C) most of the year in most U. S. climates.

Insulation configurations

Tables 1 and 2 include illustrations and descriptions of a variety of basement insulation configurations. Two basic construction systems are shown—a concrete (or masonry) basement wall and a pressure-

Authors: John Carmody and Joseph Lstiburek, P.Eng.

References: Carmody, John, Jeff Christian, and Kenneth Labs. 1991. *Builder's Foundation Handbook.* Oak Ridge National Laboratory Report No. ORNL/CON-295. Springfield, VA: U. S. Department of Commerce National Technical Information Service.

Labs, Kenneth, John Carmody, Ray Sterling, Lester Shen, Yu Joe Huang, and Danny Parker. 1988. *Building Foundation Design Handbook.* Minneapolis, MN: University of Minnesota [out of print].

Lstiburek, Joseph, and John Carmody. 1993. *Moisture Control Handbook.* New York: Van Nostrand Reinhold Company. (Note: Figures from this source have been revised for this article, as indicated by the notation "revised 1997")

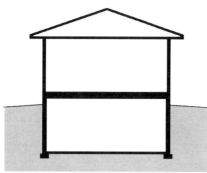

A: Deep basement

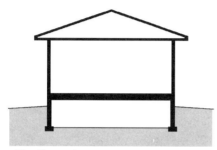

B: Crawl space

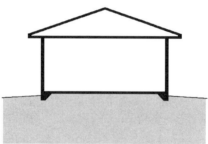

C: Slab-on-grade

Fig.1. Basic foundation types

preservative-treated wood basement wall. For conditioned basements, shown in Table 1, there are three general approaches to insulating the concrete/masonry wall:

- On the exterior covering the upper half of the wall.
- On the exterior covering the entire wall.
- On the interior covering the entire wall.

With pressure-preservative-treated wood construction, mineral wool batt insulation is placed in the cavities between the wood studs.

Table 2, which addresses unconditioned basements, includes the same set of configurations used in Table 1, as well as three additional cases where insulation is placed between the floor joists in the ceiling above the unconditioned basement. This approach thermally separates the basement from the above-grade space, resulting in lower basement temperatures in winter and usually necessitating insulation of exposed ducts and pipes in the basement. Basement ceiling insulation can be applied with either construction system—concrete/masonry or wood basement walls—but is most commonly used with concrete/masonry foundations.

Recommended insulation levels

In order to identify the most economical amount of insulation for the basement configurations shown in Tables 1 and 2, a life cycle cost analysis was undertaken that takes into account a number of economic variables including installation costs, mortgage rates, HVAC efficiencies, and fuel escalation rates. The case with the lowest 30-year life cycle cost was determined for five U. S. cities at three different fuel cost levels. The economic methodology and assumptions used to determine the optimal insulation levels in these figures is briefly summarized at the end of this article and explained in more detail in Labs *et al.* (1988).

Economically optimal configurations are shown by the darkened circles in Tables 1 and 2 in the following categories:

- Concrete/masonry wall with exterior insulation.
- Concrete/masonry wall with interior insulation without including the cost for interior finish material.
- Concrete/masonry wall with interior insulation which includes the cost for "sheetrock" (gypsum board).
- Pressure-preservative-treated wood wall insulation.
- Ceiling insulation (shown only in Table 2).

Configurations are recommended for a range of climates and fuel prices in each of these categories, but the different categories of cases are not directly compared with each other. In other words, there is an optimal amount of exterior insulation recommended for a given climate and fuel price, and there is a different optimal amount of insulation for interior insulation with sheetrock. Where there is no darkened circle in a particular category, insulation is not economically justified under the assumptions used.

Fully conditioned basements

For fully conditioned basements with concrete/masonry walls, exterior insulation is justified at three fuel price levels in all climate zones except the warmest one, which includes cities such as Los Angeles and Miami. In most locations, R-10 insulation or greater covering the entire wall on the exterior is justified with a fully conditioned basement. For interior insulation even higher levels of insulation are generally recommended ranging from R-11 to R-19 in most cases. The variable of whether or not sheetrock is included in the cost of installation appears to have relatively little impact on the recommendations. For pressure-preservative-treated wood walls, R-19 insulation is justified in almost all locations at all fuel price levels. This is due to the low initial cost of installing insulation within the available stud cavity of the wood foundation.

Table 1. Insulation recommendations for fully conditioned deep basements. Source: Carmody *et al.* (1991).

A: Concrete or Masonry Foundation Walls with Exterior Insulation

CONFIGURATION	DESCRIPTION	RECOMMENDED CONFIGURATIONS AT THREE FUEL PRICE LEVELS														
		0-2000 HDD (LOS ANG)			2-4000 HDD (FT WORTH)			4-6000 HDD (KAN CITY)			6-8000 HDD (CHICAGO)			8-10000 HDD (MPLS)		
		L	M	H	L	M	H	L	M	H	L	M	H	L	M	H
EXTERIOR: HALF WALL	NO INSULATION	●	●	○	○	○	○	○	○	○	○	○	○	○	○	○
	4 FT: R-5 RIGID	○	○	●	●	○	○	○	○	○	○	○	○	○	○	○
	4 FT: R-10 RIGID	○	○	○	○	○	○	○	○	○	○	○	○	○	○	○
EXTERIOR: FULL WALL	8 FT: R-5 RIGID	○	○	○	○	○	○	○	○	○	○	○	○	○	○	○
	8 FT: R-10 RIGID	○	○	○	○	●	●	●	●	○	●	●	○	●	○	○
	8 FT: R-15 RIGID	○	○	○	○	○	○	○	○	●	○	○	●	○	●	●
	8 FT: R-20 RIGID	○	○	○	○	○	○	○	○	○	○	○	○	○	○	○

B: Concrete or Masonry Foundation Walls with Interior Insulation (Costs do not include interior finish material)

INTERIOR: FULL WALL	DESCRIPTION	L	M	H	L	M	H	L	M	H	L	M	H	L	M	H
	NO INSULATION	○	○	○	○	○	○	○	○	○	○	○	○	○	○	○
	8 FT: R-6 RIGID	●	○	○	○	○	○	○	○	○	○	○	○	○	○	○
	8 FT: R-8 RIGID	○	○	○	○	○	○	○	○	○	○	○	○	○	○	○
	8 FT: R-11 BATT	○	●	●	●	●	●	●	○	○	●	○	○	○	○	○
	8 FT: R-19 BATT	○	○	○	○	○	○	○	●	●	○	●	●	●	●	●

C: Concrete or Masonry Foundation Walls with Interior Insulation (Costs include sheetrock on interior wall)

INTERIOR: FULL WALL	DESCRIPTION	L	M	H	L	M	H	L	M	H	L	M	H	L	M	H
	NO INSULATION	●	●	○	○	○	○	○	○	○	○	○	○	○	○	○
	8 FT: R-6 RIGID	○	○	○	○	○	○	○	○	○	○	○	○	○	○	○
	8 FT: R-8 RIGID	○	○	○	○	○	○	○	○	○	○	○	○	○	○	○
	8 FT: R-11 BATT	○	○	●	●	●	●	●	●	○	●	○	○	●	○	○
	8 FT: R-19 BATT	○	○	○	○	○	○	○	○	●	○	●	●	○	●	●

D: Pressure-Treated Wood Foundation Walls

WOOD: FULL WALL	DESCRIPTION	L	M	H	L	M	H	L	M	H	L	M	H	L	M	H
	NO INSULATION	●	●	○	○	○	○	○	○	○	○	○	○	○	○	○
	8 FT: R-11 BATT	○	○	●	●	○	○	○	○	○	○	○	○	○	○	○
	8 FT: R-19 BATT	○	○	○	○	●	●	●	●	●	●	●	●	●	●	●
	8 FT: R-30 BATT	○	○	○	○	○	○	○	○	○	○	○	○	○	○	○

Notes: These recommendations are based on assumptions that are summarized at the end of this section. The darkened circle represents the recommended level of insulation in each column for each of the basic insulation configurations.
L, H, and M refer to the low, medium, and high fuel cost levels indicated in Table 5.

Table 2. Insulation recommendations for unconditioned deep basements. Source: Carmody *et al.* (1991).

A: Concrete or Masonry Foundation Walls with Exterior Insulation

| CONFIGURATION | DESCRIPTION | RECOMMENDED CONFIGURATIONS AT THREE FUEL PRICE LEVELS | | | | | | | | | | | | | | |
| | | 0-2000 HDD (LOS ANG) | | | 2-4000 HDD (FT WORTH) | | | 4-6000 HDD (KAN CITY) | | | 6-8000 HDD (CHICAGO) | | | 8-10000 HDD (MPLS) | | |
		L	M	H	L	M	H	L	M	H	L	M	H	L	M	H
EXTERIOR: HALF WALL	NO INSULATION	●	●	●	●	●	●	●	●	○	●	○	○	○	○	○
	4 FT: R-5 RIGID	○	○	○	○	○	○	○	○	●	○	●	●	●	●	○
	4 FT: R-10 RIGID	○	○	○	○	○	○	○	○	○	○	○	○	○	○	○
EXTERIOR: FULL WALL	8 FT: R-5 RIGID	○	○	○	○	○	○	○	○	○	○	○	○	○	○	○
	8 FT: R-10 RIGID	○	○	○	○	○	○	○	○	○	○	○	○	○	○	●
	8 FT: R-15 RIGID	○	○	○	○	○	○	○	○	○	○	○	○	○	○	○
	8 FT: R-20 RIGID	○	○	○	○	○	○	○	○	○	○	○	○	○	○	○

B: Concrete or Masonry Foundation Walls with Interior Insulation (Costs do not include interior finish material)

CONFIGURATION	DESCRIPTION	L	M	H	L	M	H	L	M	H	L	M	H	L	M	H
INTERIOR: FULL WALL	NO INSULATION	●	●	●	●	●	●	●	○	○	○	○	○	○	○	○
	8 FT: R-6 RIGID	○	○	○	○	○	○	○	○	○	○	○	○	○	○	○
	8 FT: R-8 RIGID	○	○	○	○	○	○	○	○	○	○	○	○	○	○	○
	8 FT: R-11 BATT	○	○	○	○	○	○	○	●	●	●	●	●	●	●	●
	8 FT: R-19 BATT	○	○	○	○	○	○	○	○	○	○	○	○	○	○	○

C: Concrete or Masonry Foundation Walls with Interior Insulation (Costs include sheetrock on interior wall)

CONFIGURATION	DESCRIPTION	L	M	H	L	M	H	L	M	H	L	M	H	L	M	H
INTERIOR: FULL WALL	NO INSULATION	●	●	●	●	●	●	●	●	●	●	●	○	●	○	○
	8 FT: R-6 RIGID	○	○	○	○	○	○	○	○	○	○	○	○	○	○	○
	8 FT: R-8 RIGID	○	○	○	○	○	○	○	○	○	○	○	○	○	○	○
	8 FT: R-11 BATT	○	○	○	○	○	○	○	○	○	○	○	●	○	●	●
	8 FT: R-19 BATT	○	○	○	○	○	○	○	○	○	○	○	○	○	○	○

D: Pressure-Treated Wood Foundation Walls

CONFIGURATION	DESCRIPTION	L	M	H	L	M	H	L	M	H	L	M	H	L	M	H
WOOD: FULL WALL	NO INSULATION	●	●	●	●	●	●	●	○	○	○	○	○	○	○	○
	8 FT: R-11 BATT	○	○	○	○	○	○	○	●	●	●	●	●	●	○	○
	8 FT: R-19 BATT	○	○	○	○	○	○	○	○	○	○	○	○	○	●	●
	8 FT: R-30 BATT	○	○	○	○	○	○	○	○	○	○	○	○	○	○	○

E: Concrete or Masonry Foundation Walls with Ceiling Insulation

CONFIGURATION	DESCRIPTION	L	M	H	L	M	H	L	M	H	L	M	H	L	M	H
CEILING	NO INSULATION	●	●	●	●	●	●	○	○	○	○	○	○	○	○	○
	R-11 BATT	○	○	○	○	○	○	●	●	○	○	○	○	○	○	○
	R-19 BATT	○	○	○	○	○	○	○	○	○	○	○	○	○	○	○
	R-30 BATT	○	○	○	○	○	○	○	○	●	●	●	●	●	●	●

Notes: These recommendations are based on assumptions that are summarized at the end of this section. The darkened circle represents the recommended level of insulation in each column for each of the basic insulation configurations. L, H, and M refer to the low, medium, and high fuel cost levels indicated in Table 5.

Unconditioned basements

Compared with recommended insulation levels for fully conditioned basements, lower levels are economically justified in unconditioned basements in most locations due to generally lower basement temperatures. For concrete/masonry walls with exterior insulation, R-5 insulation on the upper wall is justified only in the colder climates at low (L) and medium (M) fuel prices. At the high fuel price level (H), R-5 insulation on the upper wall is justified in moderate climates, while R-10 insulation on the entire wall is recommended in the coldest cities. For interior insulation without sheetrock, R-11 is recommended in moderate to cold climates at all fuel price levels. Including the cost of sheetrock, however, reduces the number of cases where interior insulation is economically justified. For basements with pressure-preservative-treated wood walls, R-11 to R-19 insulation is justified in moderate to cold climates. When ceiling insulation is placed over an unconditioned basement, R-30 insulation is justified in colder cities and some insulation is justified in most cities.

Comparison of insulation systems

Generally, insulating pressure-preservative-treated wood walls is more cost-effective than insulating concrete/masonry walls to an equivalent level. This is because the cavity exists between studs in a wood wall system and the incremental cost of installing batt insulation in these cavities is relatively low. Thus, a higher R-value is economically justified for wood wall systems.

On concrete/masonry basement walls, interior insulation is generally more cost-effective than an equivalent amount of exterior insulation. This is because the labor and material costs for rigid insulation with protective covering required for an exterior installation typically exceed the cost of interior insulation. Even though the cost of studs and sheetrock may be included in an interior installation, the incremental cost of batt installation is relatively little. If rigid insulation is used in an interior application, the installation cost is less than placing it on the exterior. Because it does not have to withstand exposure to water and soil pressure below grade as it does on the exterior, a less expensive material can be used. Costs are further reduced since interior insulation does not require a protective flashing or coating to prevent degradation from ultraviolet light as well as mechanical deterioration.

Insulating the ceiling of an unconditioned basement is generally more cost-effective than insulating the walls of an unconditioned basement to an equivalent level. This is because placing batt insulation into the existing spaces between floor joists represents a much smaller incremental cost than placing insulation on the walls. Thus higher levels of ceiling insulation can be economically justified when compared to wall insulation.

In spite of the apparent energy efficiency of wood versus concrete/masonry basement walls, this is only one of many cost and performance issues to be considered. Likewise, on a concrete/masonry foundation wall, the economic benefit of interior versus exterior insulation may be offset by other practical, performance, and aesthetic considerations discussed elsewhere in this book. Although ceiling insulation in an unconditioned basement appears more cost-effective than wall insulation, this approach may be undesirable in colder climates since pipes and ducts may be exposed to freezing temperatures and the space will be unusable for many purposes. In all cases the choice of foundation type and insulation system must be based on many factors in addition to energy cost-effectiveness.

Exterior insulation placement

The concrete masonry basement wall assembly shown in Fig. 2 illustrates rigid insulation board on the exterior. In this case, rigid insulation covers the exterior of the rim joist, and cavity insulation (with a vapor diffusion retarder) is placed between joists on the rim joist interior. Rigid insulation placed on the exterior surface of a concrete or masonry basement wall has some of the following advantages over interior placement:

- Provides continuous insulation with no thermal bridges.

- Protects and maintains the waterproofing and structural wall at moderate temperatures.

- Minimizes moisture condensation problems.

- Does not reduce interior basement floor area.

Exterior insulation at the rim joist leaves joists and sill plates open to inspection from the interior for termites and decay. On the other hand, exterior insulation on the wall can provide a path for termites if not treated adequately and can prevent inspection of the wall from the exterior.

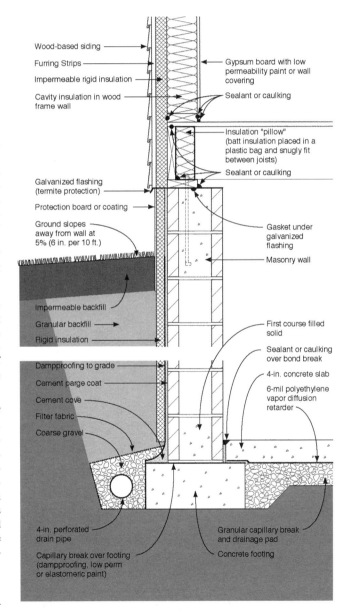

Fig. 2. Concrete masonry basement with exterior insulation

Note: This detail is suitable for an underheated (cool) or mixed (temperate) climate. Source: Lstiburek and Carmody (1993)—revised 1997.

Interior insulation placement

The concrete basement wall assembly shown in Fig. 3 illustrates cavity insulation in a wood frame wall on the interior of the foundation wall. Cavity insulation is placed between joists on the rim joist interior, and rigid insulation covers the rim joist on the exterior as well. A layer of rigid insulation is also shown beneath the concrete floor slab.

Interior insulation is an effective alternative to exterior insulation. Interior insulation placement is generally less expensive than exterior placement if the cost of the interior finish materials is not included. However, this does not leave the wall with a finished, durable surface. Energy savings may be reduced with some systems and details due to thermal bridges. For example, partial interior wall insulation is not recommended because of the possible circumventing of the insulation through the wall construction. Insulation can be placed on the inside of the rim joist but with greater risk of condensation problems and less access to wood joists and sills for termite inspection from the interior.

With a wood foundation system, insulation is placed in the stud cavities similarly to insulation in an above-grade wood frame wall. A 2-in. (5 cm) air space should be provided between the end of the insulation and the bottom plate of the foundation wall. This approach has a relatively low cost and provides sufficient space for considerable insulation thickness.

Insulation placement in the basement ceiling of an unconditioned basement is another acceptable alternative. This approach is relatively low in cost and provides significant energy savings. However, ceiling insulation should be used with caution in colder climates where pipes may freeze and structural damage may result from lowering the frost depth.

Other insulation approaches

In addition to more conventional interior or exterior placement, there are several systems that incorporate insulation into the construction of the concrete or masonry walls. These include:

- Rigid foam plastic insulation cast within a concrete wall.

- Polystyrene beads or granular insulation materials poured into the cavities of conventional masonry walls.

- Systems of concrete blocks with insulating foam inserts.

- Formed, interlocking rigid foam units that serve as a permanent, insulating form for cast-in-place concrete.

- Masonry blocks made with polystyrene beads instead of aggregate in the concrete mixture, resulting in significantly higher R-values. However, the effectiveness of systems that insulate only a portion of the wall area should be evaluated closely because thermal bridges through the insulation can impact the total performance significantly.

Structural design of residential basement walls

The major structural components of a basement are the wall, the footing, and the floor (see Figs. 2 and 3 above). Basement walls are typically constructed of cast-in-place concrete, concrete masonry units, or pressure-preservative-treated wood. Basement walls must be designed to resist lateral loads from the soil and vertical loads from the structure above. The lateral loads on the wall depend on the height of the fill, the soil type, soil moisture content, and whether the building is located in an area of low or high seismic activity. Requirements for wall thickness, concrete strength, and reinforcing are given in building codes. Where simple limits are exceeded, a structural engineer should be consulted.

Concrete spread footings provide support beneath basement concrete and masonry walls and columns. Footings must be designed with adequate size to distribute the load to the soil. Unless founded on bed-

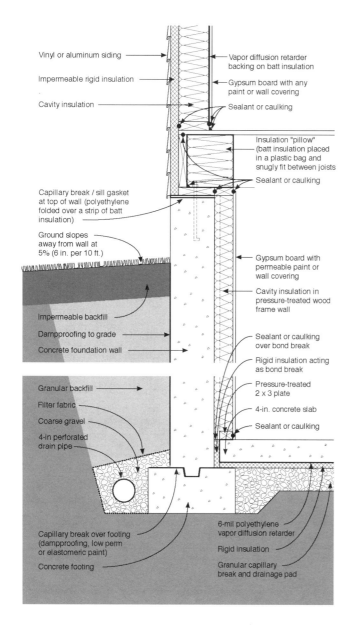

Vinyl or aluminum siding

Impermeable rigid insulation

Cavity insulation

Capillary break / sill gasket at top of wall (polyethylene folded over a strip of batt insulation)

Ground slopes away from wall at 5% (6 in. per 10 ft.)

Impermeable backfill

Dampproofing to grade

Concrete foundation wall

Granular backfill

Filter fabric

Coarse gravel

4-in perforated drain pipe

Capillary break over footing (dampproofing, low perm or elastomeric paint)

Concrete footing

Vapor diffusion retarder backing on batt insulation

Gypsum board with any paint or wall covering

Sealant or caulking

Insulation "pillow" (batt insulation placed in a plastic bag and snugly fit between joists

Sealant or caulking

Gypsum board with permeable paint or wall covering

Cavity insulation in pressure-treated wood frame wall

Sealant or caulking over bond break

Rigid insulation acting as bond break

Pressure-treated 2 x 3 plate

4-in. concrete slab

Sealant or caulking

6-mil polyethylene vapor diffusion retarder

Rigid insulation

Granular capillary break and drainage pad

Fig. 3. Cast-in-place concrete basement with interior insulation.
Note: This detail is suitable for an underheated (cool) climate.
Source: Lstiburek and Carmody (1993)—revised 1997.

rock or proven non-frost-susceptible soils, footings must be placed beneath the maximum frost penetration depth or be insulated to prevent frost penetration. A compacted gravel bed serves as the footing under a wood foundation wall when designed in accordance with the National Forest Products Association's wood foundations design specifications.

Concrete slab-on-grade floors are generally designed to have sufficient strength to support floor loads without reinforcing when poured on undisturbed or compacted soil. The use of welded wire fabric and concrete with a low water/cement ratio can reduce shrinkage cracking, which is an important concern for appearance and for reducing potential radon infiltration.

Where expansive soils are present or in areas of high seismic activity, special foundation construction techniques may be necessary. In these cases, consultation with local building officials and a structural engineer is recommended.

Moisture control in basements
Keeping water out of basements is a major concern in many regions. The source of water is primarily from rainfall, snow melt, and sometimes irrigation on the surface. In some cases, the groundwater table is near or above the basement floor level at times during the year. The moisture enters the basement through four mechanisms: liquid flow, capillary suction, air movement, and vapor diffusion. Not all basement moisture problems originate from outside the structure. Concrete and masonry walls contain a significant amount of moisture from construction that is released in the months after construction. Internal moisture sources can also contribute, and ventilation of the basement with warm, moist air can result in condensation on colder surfaces.

Generally, there are three basic lines of defense against water problems in basements:

- Surface drainage.
- Subsurface drainage.
- Dampproofing or waterproofing on the wall surface.

The goal of surface drainage is to keep water from surface sources away from the foundation by sloping the ground surface and using gutters and downspouts for roof drainage. The goal of subsurface drainage is to intercept, collect, and carry away any water in the ground surrounding the basement. Components of a subsurface system can include porous backfill, drainage mat materials or insulated drainage boards, and perforated drainpipes in a gravel bed along the footing or beneath the slab that drain to a sump or to daylight.

The final line of defense—waterproofing—is intended to keep out water that finds its way to the wall of the structure. First, it is important to distinguish between the need for dampproofing versus waterproofing. In most cases a dampproof coating is recommended to reduce vapor and capillary draw transmission from the soil through the basement wall. A dampproof coating, however, is not effective in preventing water from entering through the wall.

Waterproofing is recommended:

- On sites with anticipated water problems or poor drainage.
- When finished basement space is planned, or
- On any foundation built where intermittent hydrostatic pressure occurs against the basement wall due to rainfall, irrigation, or snow melt. On sites where the basement floor could be below the water table, a crawl space or slab-on-grade foundation is recommended.

The key strategies for basement moisture control shown in Figs. 2 and 3 are:

- Rainwater is controlled by gutters and downspouts, impermeable soil cap over backfill, and grade sloping away from the building.

- Groundwater is controlled by free-draining backfill and a drain pipe at the footing. A drainage mat can be used in place of the free-draining backfill.

- Capillary suction is controlled by a dampproof coating on the exterior wall, a break over the footing, a break over the top of the concrete wall, and a layer of gravel under the slab.

- In Fig. 2 (masonry wall with exterior insulation), air movement into the space is controlled by sealing the concrete slab to the concrete foundation wall with caulking, filling the first course of masonry with mortar, sealing the sill/rim joist area, and placing a polyethylene air retarder under the floor slab that extends over the footing. In Fig. 3 (masonry wall with exterior insulation), air movement is controlled by sealing the sill/rim joist area, and sealing the polyethylene air retarder under the floor slab to the gypsum board on the basement wall.

- Vapor diffusion from the surrounding soil is controlled by the dampproof coating on the wall exterior and the polyethylene sheet beneath the floor slab.

- Insulation on the outside of the basement wall and the rim joist raises the wall temperature and limits potential condensation (Fig. 2).

- With exterior insulation (Fig. 3), the exposed concrete masonry wall can dry toward the interior. With interior insulation (Fig. 2), it is important to place no vapor diffusion retarder on the interior in order to allow drying toward the interior. This prevents moisture from the construction or from outside the wall from being trapped in the assembly. Vapor permeable or semi-vapor permeable interior surface finishes must be used on walls to prevent drying.

2 Crawl spaces

Précis: This section summarizes suggested practices related to crawl spaces. Recommended optimal levels of insulation are presented for vented and unvented crawl spaces. A brief summary of crawl space design practices is given, including location of insulation, structural design, and moisture control.

To provide energy use information for buildings with crawl space foundations, heating and cooling loads were simulated for a variety of insulation placements and thicknesses in representative U. S. climates (Labs *et al.* 1988). Two types of crawl spaces were analyzed for energy purpose—vented and unvented. Generally most major building codes require vents near each corner. These vents may have operable louvers. The vented crawl space is assumed to have venting area openings of 1 sq. ft. (0.30 sq. m) per 1500 sq. ft. (460 sq. m) of floor area. The temperature of the vented crawl space varies between the interior house temperature and the exterior temperature. The unvented crawl space is assumed to have vents fully closed, leaving only gaps in construction that could allow infiltration. Unvented crawl spaces insulated at the perimeter are similar to unheated basements, with temperatures that fluctuate between 50-70F (10-21C) most of the year, depending on climate and insulation placement.

Crawl spaces can vary in height and relationship to exterior grade. It is assumed in the cases shown here that crawl space walls are 2 ft. high (0.6 m) with only the upper 8 in. (20 cm) of the foundation wall exposed above grade on the exterior side.

Insulation configurations
Table 3 includes illustrations and descriptions of a variety of crawl space insulation configurations. Two basic construction systems are shown for unvented crawl spaces a concrete (or masonry) foundation wall and a pressure-preservative-treated wood foundation wall. For vented crawl spaces, concrete (or masonry) walls are shown.

Table 3. Insulation recommendations for crawl spaces. Source: Carmody *et al.* (1991)

A: Unvented Crawl Space - Concrete or Masonry Foundation Walls with Exterior Insulation

CONFIGURATION	DESCRIPTION	0-2000 HDD (LOS ANG)			2-4000 HDD (FT WORTH)			4-6000 HDD (KAN CITY)			6-8000 HDD (CHICAGO)			8-10000 HDD (MPLS)		
		L	M	H	L	M	H	L	M	H	L	M	H	L	M	H
EXTERIOR VERTICAL	NO INSULATION	●	●	●	●	○	○	○	○	○	○	○	○	○	○	○
	2 FT: R-5 RIGID	○	○	○	○	●	●	●	○	○	●	○	○	○	○	○
	2 FT: R-10 RIGID	○	○	○	○	○	○	○	●	●	○	●	●	●	●	●

B: Unvented Crawl Space - Concrete or Masonry Foundation Walls with Interior Insulation

CONFIGURATION	DESCRIPTION	L	M	H	L	M	H	L	M	H	L	M	H	L	M	H
INTERIOR VERTICAL	NO INSULATION	●	●	●	○	○	○	○	○	○	○	○	○	○	○	○
	2 FT: R-5 RIGID	○	○	○	●	●	●	●	●	●	●	○	○	○	○	○
	2 FT: R-10 RIGID	○	○	○	○	○	○	○	○	○	○	○	○	○	○	○
INTERIOR VERTICAL AND HORIZONTAL	2 FT/2 FT: R-5 RIGID	○	○	○	○	○	○	○	○	○	○	●	●	●	●	○
	2 FT/4 FT: R-5 RIGID	○	○	○	○	○	○	○	○	○	○	○	○	○	○	○
	2 FT/2 FT: R-10 RIGID	○	○	○	○	○	○	○	○	○	○	○	○	○	○	●
	2 FT/4 FT: R-10 RIGID	○	○	○	○	○	○	○	○	○	○	○	○	○	○	○

C: Unvented Crawl Space - Pressure-Treated Wood Foundation Walls

CONFIGURATION	DESCRIPTION	L	M	H	L	M	H	L	M	H	L	M	H	L	M	H
WITHIN WOOD WALL	NO INSULATION	●	●	●	●	●	○	○	○	○	○	○	○	○	○	○
	2 FT: R-11 BATT	○	○	○	○	○	●	●	●	○	○	○	○	○	○	○
	2 FT: R-19 BATT	○	○	○	○	○	○	○	○	●	●	●	●	●	●	●

D: Vented Crawl Space - Concrete or Masonry Foundation Walls with Ceiling Insulation

CONFIGURATION	DESCRIPTION	L	M	H	L	M	H	L	M	H	L	M	H	L	M	H
CEILING	NO INSULATION	○	○	○	○	○	○	○	○	○	○	○	○	○	○	○
	R-11 BATT	●	●	●	●	●	○	○	○	○	○	○	○	○	○	○
	R-19 BATT	○	○	○	○	○	●	●	●	●	●	●	○	●	○	○
	R-30 BATT	○	○	○	○	○	○	○	○	○	○	○	●	○	●	●

Notes: These recommendations are based on assumptions that are summarized at the end of this section. The darkened circle represents the recommended level of insulation in each column for each of the basic insulation configurations. L, H, and M refer to the low, medium, and high fuel cost levels indicated in Table 5.

In a vented crawl space, insulation is placed between the floor joists in the crawl space ceiling. In an unvented crawl space, the two most common approaches to insulating concrete/masonry walls are:

- Covering the entire wall on the exterior, and

- Covering the entire wall on the interior.

In addition to these conventional approaches, insulation can be placed on the interior wall and horizontally on the perimeter of the crawl space floor extending either 2 or 4 feet (0.6 or 1.2 m) into the space. With pressure-preservative-treated wood construction, batt insulation is placed in the cavities between the wood studs.

Recommended insulation levels

In order to identify the most economical amount of insulation for the crawl space configurations shown in Table 3, a life cycle cost analysis was undertaken that takes into account a number of economic variables including installation costs, mortgage rates, HVAC efficiencies, and fuel escalation rates. The case with the lowest 30-year life cycle cost was determined for five U. S. cities at three different fuel cost levels. The economic methodology and assumptions used to determine the optimal insulation levels in these figures is briefly summarized at the end of this article and explained in more detail in Labs *et al.* (1988).

Economically optimal configurations are shown by the darkened circles in Table 3 in the following categories:

- Unvented crawl spaces with concrete/masonry walls and exterior insulation.

- Unvented crawl spaces with concrete/masonry walls and interior insulation.

- Unvented crawl spaces with wood walls.

- Vented crawl spaces with concrete walls.

Configurations are recommended for a range of climates and fuel prices in each of these categories, but the different categories of cases are not directly compared with each other. In other words, there is an optimal amount of exterior insulation recommended for a given climate and fuel price, and there is a different optimal amount of insulation for interior insulation. Where there is no darkened circle in a particular category, insulation is not economically justified under the assumptions used.

For unvented crawl spaces with concrete/masonry walls, exterior insulation ranging from R-5 to R-10 is justified at all fuel price levels (shown in Table 3) in all climate zones except the warmest one. Similar levels of interior insulation are recommended. However in colder climates, placing insulation horizontally on the crawl space floor in addition to the wall is frequently the optimal configuration. If the crawl space wall is higher than 2 ft. (0.6 m), as it often must be to reach frost depth in a colder climate, it is advisable to extend the vertical insulation to the footing. Although simulation results for crawl spaces with higher walls and deeper footings are not shown here, the need for insulation placed deeper than 2 ft. (0.6 m) in cold climates is obvious and is reflected by the economic benefits of placing insulation on the floor of a shallower crawl space.

For unvented crawl spaces with pressure-preservative-treated wood walls, insulation ranging from R-11 to R-19 is justified in moderate and colder climates. In vented crawl spaces, ceiling insulation ranging from R-11 to R-30 is recommended in all climates at all fuel price levels.

Comparison of insulation systems for crawl spaces

Insulating the ceiling of a vented crawl space is generally more cost-effective than insulating the walls of an unvented crawl space to an equivalent level. This is because placing mineral wool batt insulation into the existing spaces between floor joists represents a much smaller incremental cost than placing rigid insulation on the walls. Thus higher levels of insulation are recommended in the floor above a vented crawl space than for the walls of an unvented space.

When exterior and interior insulation are compared for an unvented crawl space with concrete/masonry walls, thermal results are very similar for equivalent amounts of insulation. Since it is assumed that exterior insulation costs more to install, however, interior placement is always economically optimal in comparison. This increased cost for an exterior insulation is attributed to the need for protective covering and a higher quality rigid insulation that can withstand exposure to water and soil pressure.

Generally, insulating pressure-preservative-treated wood walls is more cost-effective than insulating concrete/masonry walls to an equivalent level. This is because the cavity exists between studs in a wood wall system and the incremental cost of installing batt insulation in these cavities is relatively low. Thus, a higher R-value is economically justified for wood wall systems.

In spite of the apparent energy efficiency of wood versus concrete/masonry basement walls, this is only one of many cost and performance issues to be considered. Likewise, on a concrete/masonry foundation wall, the economic benefit of interior versus exterior insulation may be offset by other practical, performance, and aesthetic considerations discussed elsewhere in this book. Although ceiling insulation in a vented crawl space appears more cost-effective than wall insulation in an unvented space, a vented crawl space may be undesirable in colder climates since pipes and ducts may be exposed to freezing temperatures. In all cases the choice of foundation type and insulation system must be based on many factors in addition to energy cost-effectiveness.

Vented crawl space

The vented crawl space shown in Fig. 4 utilizes a concrete foundation wall. Faced batt insulation (with the faced side down) is placed between the floor joists above the crawl space. This batt insulation partially covers the rim joist on the interior. A continuous vapor diffusion retarder is placed on the floor of the crawl space.

The principal perceived advantage of a vented crawl space over an unvented one is that venting can minimize radon and moisture-related decay hazards by diluting the crawl space air. Venting can complement other moisture and radon control measures such as ground cover and proper drainage. However, although increased air flow in the crawl space may offer some dilution potential for ground source moisture and radon, it will not necessarily solve a serious moisture or radon problem.

The principal disadvantages of a vented crawl space over an unvented one are that:

- Pipes and ducts must be insulated against heat loss and freezing.

- A larger area usually must be insulated, which may increase the cost.

- In some climates warm humid air circulated into the cool crawl space can actually cause excessive moisture levels in wood.

If a vented crawl space is insulated (Fig. 4), the insulation is always located in the ceiling. Most commonly, batt insulation is placed between the floor joists. The depth of these joist spaces accommodates high insulation levels at a relatively low incremental cost. This placement usually leaves sill plates open to inspection for termites or decay.

Unvented crawl space with exterior insulation

The unvented crawl space shown in Fig. 5 illustrates a concrete foundation wall with rigid insulation board on the interior. Cavity insulation (with a vapor diffusion retarder) is placed between joists on the rim joist interior. A continuous vapor diffusion retarder is placed on the floor of the crawl space, extends up the interior face of the insulation board, and over the top of the foundation wall.

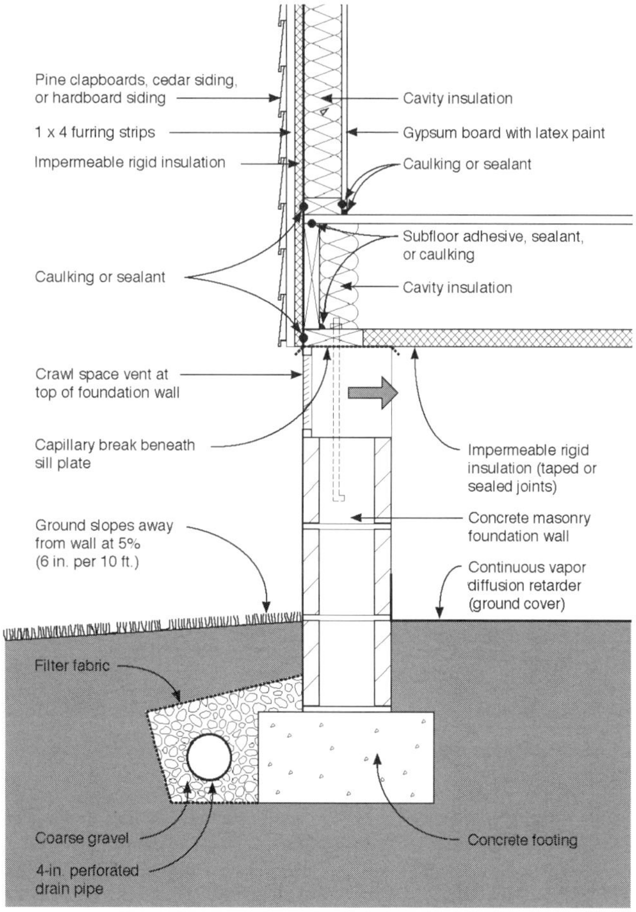

Rigid insulation placed on the exterior surface of a concrete or masonry wall has some advantages over interior placement: It can provide continuous insulation with no thermal bridges, protect structural walls at moderate temperatures, and minimize moisture condensation problems. Exterior insulation at the rim joist leaves joists and sill plates open to inspection from the interior for termites and decay. On the other hand, exterior insulation on the wall can be a path for termites and can prevent inspection of the wall from the exterior. If needed, a termite screen should be installed through the insulation where the sill plate rests on the foundation wall. Vertical exterior insulation on a crawl space wall can extend as deep as the top of the footing and, if desired, be supplemented by extending the insulation horizontally from the face of the foundation wall.

Unvented crawl space with interior insulation
The unvented crawl space shown in Fig. 6 illustrates a concrete masonry foundation wall with faced batt insulation covering the interior wall and extending over the floor perimeter. Rigid insulation covers the exterior of the rim joist, and cavity insulation (with a vapor diffusion retarder) is placed between joists on the rim joist interior. A continuous vapor diffusion retarder is placed on the floor of the crawl space and extends over the interior face and top of the foundation wall.

Interior crawl space wall insulation is more common than exterior, primarily because it is less expensive since no protective covering is required. On the other hand, interior wall insulation may be considered less desirable than exterior insulation for the following reasons:

- Increases the exposure of the wall to thermal stress and freezing.

- It may increase the likelihood of condensation on sill plates, band joists, and joist ends.

- It often results in some thermal bridges through framing members.

- It may require installation of a flame spread resistant cover.

Rigid board insulation is easier to apply to the interior wall than batt insulation since it requires no framing for support, is continuous, can be installed prior to backfilling against the foundation wall or installing the floor, and may require no additional vapor retarder. Insulation placed around the crawl space floor perimeter can provide additional thermal protection; however, it may also create additional paths for termite entry. Batt insulation is commonly placed inside the rim joist. This rim-joist insulation should be covered on the inside face with a polyethylene vapor retarder or a rigid foam insulation, sealed around the edges, to act as a vapor retarder. In place of batts, simply using tight-fitting rigid foam pieces in the spaces between the floor joists is an effective solution.

Less expensive batts are an alternative to rigid foam insulation on the interior crawl space wall. It is possible to install them in a crawl space similar to a basement installation. One way is to provide a furred-out stud wall and a vapor retarder on the studs. This is a more expensive and less common approach than simply using rigid foam with no furring. A common, low-cost approach to insulating crawl space walls is simply draping batts with a vapor retarder facing over the inside of the wall. In most states, codes require the batt vapor retarder cover be approved with respect to flame spread. These can be laid loosely on the ground at the perimeter to reduce heat loss through the footing. With this approach, it is difficult to maintain the continuity of the vapor retarder around the joist ends and to seal the termination of the vapor retarder. Good installations are difficult because of cramped

Pine clapboards, cedar siding, or hardboard siding

1 x 4 furring strips

Impermeable rigid insulation

Cavity insulation

Gypsum board with latex paint

Caulking or sealant

Subfloor adhesive, sealant, or caulking

Caulking or sealant

Cavity insulation

Crawl space vent at top of foundation wall

Capillary break beneath sill plate

Impermeable rigid insulation (taped or sealed joints)

Concrete masonry foundation wall

Ground slopes away from wall at 5% (6 in. per 10 ft.)

Continuous vapor diffusion retarder (ground cover)

Filter fabric

Coarse gravel

4-in. perforated drain pipe

Concrete footing

Fig. 4. Vented crawl space. Note: This detail is suitable for a mixed (temperate) climate. Source: Lstiburek and Carmody (1993)—revised 1997.

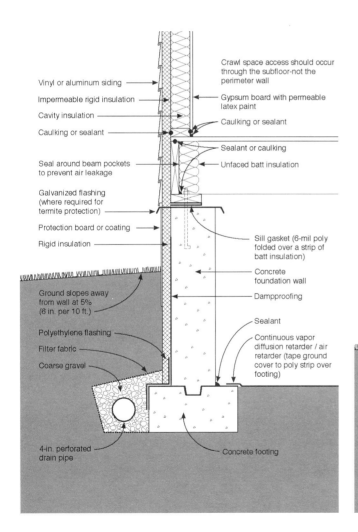

Vinyl or aluminum siding

Impermeable rigid insulation

Cavity insulation

Caulking or sealant

Crawl space access should occur through the subfloor-not the perimeter wall

Gypsum board with permeable latex paint

Caulking or sealant

Sealant or caulking

Unfaced batt insulation

Seal around beam pockets to prevent air leakage

Galvanized flashing (where required for termite protection)

Protection board or coating

Rigid insulation

Sill gasket (6-mil poly folded over a strip of batt insulation)

Concrete foundation wall

Dampproofing

Ground slopes away from wall at 5% (6 in. per 10 ft.)

Polyethylene flashing

Filter fabric

Coarse gravel

Sealant

Continuous vapor diffusion retarder / air retarder (tape ground cover to poly strip over footing)

4-in. perforated drain pipe

Concrete footing

Fig. 5. Unvented crawl space with exterior insulation. Note: This detail is suitable for a mixed (temperate) or overheated (warm) climate. Source: Lstiburek and Carmody (1993)—revised 1997.

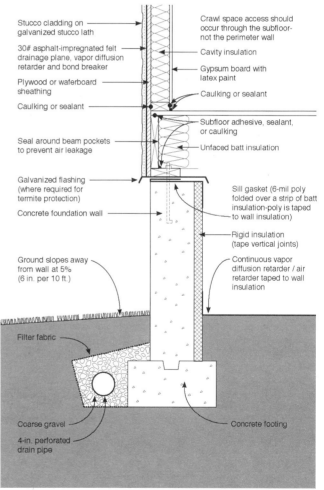

Stucco cladding on galvanized stucco lath

30# asphalt-impregnated felt drainage plane, vapor diffusion retarder and bond breaker

Plywood or waferboard sheathing

Caulking or sealant

Crawl space access should occur through the subfloor-not the perimeter wall

Cavity insulation

Gypsum board with latex paint

Caulking or sealant

Subfloor adhesive, sealant, or caulking

Unfaced batt insulation

Seal around beam pockets to prevent air leakage

Galvanized flashing (where required for termite protection)

Concrete foundation wall

Sill gasket (6-mil poly folded over a strip of batt insulation-poly is taped to wall insulation)

Rigid insulation (tape vertical joints)

Ground slopes away from wall at 5% (6 in. per 10 ft.)

Continuous vapor diffusion retarder / air retarder taped to wall insulation

Filter fabric

Coarse gravel

4-in. perforated drain pipe

Concrete footing

Fig. 6. Unvented crawl space with interior insulation. Note: This detail is suitable for a mixed (temperate) or overheated (warm) climate. Source: Lstiburek and Carmody (1993)—revised 1997.

working conditions, and a vapor-proof installation will prevent easy inspection for termites.

With a pressure-preservative-treated wood foundation system, insulation is placed in the stud cavities similar to above-grade insulation in a wood frame wall. This approach has a relatively low cost and provides sufficient space for considerable insulation thickness. In addition to more conventional interior or exterior placement, there are several systems that incorporate insulation into the construction of the concrete or masonry walls. These are described in the previous section on basements.

Structural design of crawl spaces

The major structural components of a crawl space are the wall and the footing (see above Figs. 4, 5 and 6). Crawl space walls are typically constructed of cast-in-place concrete, concrete masonry units, or pressure-treated wood. Crawl space walls must resist any lateral loads from the soil and vertical loads from the structure above. The lateral loads on the wall depend on the height of the fill, the soil type and moisture content, and whether the building is located in an area of low or high seismic activity. In place of a structural foundation wall and continuous spread footing, the structure can be supported on piers or piles with beams in between. These beams between piers support the structure above and transfer the load back to the piers.

Concrete spread footings provide support beneath concrete and masonry crawl space walls and/or columns. Footings must be designed with adequate size to distribute the load to the soil and be placed beneath the maximum frost penetration depth unless founded on bedrock or proven non-frost-susceptible soil or insulated to prevent frost penetration. A compacted gravel bed serves as the footing under a wood foundation wall when designed in accordance with the National Forest Products Association's wood foundation specification. Since the interior temperature of a vented crawl space may be below freezing in very cold climates, footings must be below the frost depth with respect to both interior and exterior grade unless otherwise protected.

Where expansive soils are present or in areas of high seismic activity, special foundation construction techniques may be necessary. In these cases, consultation with local building officials and a structural engineer is recommended.

Moisture control in crawl spaces

Although a crawl space foundation is not as deep as a full basement, it is highly desirable to keep it dry. Good surface drainage is always recommended and, in many cases, subsurface drainage systems may be desirable. The goal of surface drainage is to keep water away from the foundation by sloping the ground surface and using gutters and downspouts for roof drainage. On sites with a high water table or poorly draining soil, one recommended solution is to keep the crawl space floor above or at the same level as exterior grade (Figs. 4 and 6). On sites with porous soil and no water table near the surface, placing the crawl space floor below the surface is acceptable with no requirement for a subdrainage system.

Where it is necessary or desirable to place the crawl space floor beneath the existing grade and the soil is nonporous, a subsurface perimeter drainage system similar to that used for a basement is recommended (see Fig. 5). In some cases a sump pump may be necessary. On a sloping site, subdrainage may be required on the uphill side if the soil is nonporous. Generally no waterproofing or dampproofing on the exterior foundation walls of crawl spaces is considered necessary, assuming drainage is adequate.

The key strategies for crawl space moisture control shown in Figs. 4, 5 and 6 are:

* Rainwater is controlled by gutters and downspouts, as well as grade sloping away from the building.

* Groundwater is controlled by a drain pipe at the footing.

* Ventilation through open vents in the crawl space walls removes moisture from the crawl space interior.

* In a vented crawl space (Fig. 4), capillary suction is controlled by a break on top of the foundation wall. In an unvented crawl space (Fig. 5), capillary suction is controlled by a dampproof coating on the exterior wall, a break over the footing, and a break over the top of the foundation wall.

* In a vented crawl space (Fig. 4), air movement is controlled by pressurizing the above-grade conditioned space, limiting or sealing all penetrations between the crawl space and the conditioned space, and sealing the sill/rim joist area. If sealed properly, the subfloor forms an air retarder. In an unvented crawl space (Figs. 5 and 6), air movement into the space is controlled by pressurizing the crawl space, limiting or sealing all penetrations, sealing the sill/rim joist area, and placing a polyethylene sheet over the crawl space floor. All joints of the polyethylene ground cover are sealed and it is taped to the polyethylene or rigid insulation on the wall to form an air retarder.

* Vapor diffusion from the surrounding soil is controlled by the dampproof coating on the wall exterior and the polyethylene ground cover (Fig. 5).

* In a vented crawl space (Fig. 4), vapor diffusion from the crawl space is prevented from entering the above-grade space by the impermeable subfloor material. A vapor diffusion retarder backing protects the batt insulation between the joists from crawl space moisture.

* In the case of insulation on the outside of the foundation wall and the rim joist, the wall temperature is raised which limits potential condensation.

* In a vented crawl space, drying toward the interior or exterior of the floor joist assembly is limited, however, the crawl space itself can dry since it is vented. With exterior insulation, the exposed concrete wall can dry toward the interior.

3 Slab-on-grade foundations

Précis: This section summarizes suggested practices related to slab-on-grade foundations. First, recommended optimal levels of insulation are presented. A brief summary of slab-on-grade foundation design practices is given covering structural design, location of insulation, and moisture control.

To provide energy use information for buildings with slab-on-grade foundations, heating and cooling loads were simulated for different insulation placements and thicknesses in a variety of U. S. climates (Labs *et al.* 1988). Key assumptions are that the interior space above the slab is heated to a temperature of 70F (21C) and cooled to a temperature of 78F (26C) when required.

Insulation configurations

Table 4 includes illustrations and descriptions of a variety of slab-on-grade insulation configurations. The construction system in all cases is a concrete (or masonry) foundation wall extending either 2 or 4 feet (0.6 or 1.2 m) deep with the upper 8 inches (20 cm) of the foundation wall exposed on the exterior.

The three most common approaches to insulating slab-on-grade foundations with concrete/masonry walls are:

* Placing insulation vertically on the entire exterior surface of the foundation wall 2 or 4 ft. (0.6 or 1.2 m) deep.

* Placing insulation vertically on the entire interior surface of the foundation wall 2 or 4 ft. (0.6 or 1.2 m) deep.

* Placing insulation horizontally under the slab perimeter extending 2 or 4 ft. (0.6 or 1.2 m).

When insulation is placed either vertically or horizontally on the interior, it is important to place insulation in the joint between the slab edge and foundation wall. It is not necessary to place more than R-5 insulation in this joint. For example, even when R-15 insulation is recommended for the foundation wall, only R-5 insulation in the joint proves to be cost-effective.

In addition to these conventional approaches, some cases were simulated where insulation is placed horizontally on the building exterior (extending either 2 or 4 feet (0.6 or 1.2 m) into the surrounding soil). In some regions it is common practice to have a shallower footing than 2 ft. (0.6 m) or have no foundation wall at all—just a thickened slab edge. In these cases, a full 2 ft.(0.6 m) of vertical insulation is not an option; however, additional horizontal insulation placement on the exterior is possible.

Recommended insulation levels

In order to identify the most economical amount of insulation for the slab-on-grade configurations shown in Table 4, a life cycle cost analysis was undertaken that takes into account a number of economic variables including installation costs, mortgage rates, HVAC efficiencies, and fuel escalation rates. The case with the lowest 30-year life cycle cost was determined for five U. S. cities at three different fuel cost levels. The economic methodology and assumptions used to determine the optimal insulation levels in these figures is briefly summarized at the end of this article and explained in more detail in Labs *et al.* (1988).

Economically optimal configurations are shown by the darkened circles in Table 4 in the following categories:

- Exterior insulation placed vertically on the foundation wall.

- Interior insulation placed vertically on the foundation wall.

- Interior insulation placed horizontally beneath the slab perimeter.

- Exterior insulation extending outward horizontally from the foundation wall.

Configurations are recommended for a range of climates and fuel prices in each of these categories, but the different categories of cases are not directly compared with each other. In other words, there is an optimal amount of exterior vertical insulation recommended for a given climate and fuel price, and there is a different optimal amount of interior insulation placed vertically. Where there is no darkened circle in a particular category, insulation is not economically justified under the assumptions used.

Exterior vertical insulation ranging from R-5 to R-10 is justified in all climate zones except the warmest one. As the climate becomes colder and fuel prices increase, the recommended R-value and depth of insulation increase as well. Similar levels of interior insulation are recommended for both vertical and horizontal placement. For exterior insulation extending outward horizontally, a 2-ft. (0.6 m) wide section of R-5 insulation is recommended at all fuel price levels and in all climate zones except the warmest one.

It should be noted that for all cases with interior vertical or horizontal insulation, it is assumed that R-5 insulation is placed in the gap between the slab edge and the foundation wall. A simulation with no insulation in the gap indicates that energy savings are reduced by approximately 40 percent, compared with a similar configuration with the R-5 slab edge insulation in place.

Comparison of insulation approaches

When exterior and interior vertical insulation are compared, thermal results are very similar for equivalent amounts of insulation. Since it is assumed that exterior insulation costs more to install, however, interior placement is always economically optimal in comparison. This increased cost for an exterior insulation is attributed to the need for protective covering.

Interior insulation placed horizontally beneath the slab perimeter performs almost identically to interior vertical insulation in terms of energy savings. However, interior vertical insulation is slightly more cost-effective than placement beneath the slab perimeter because the installation cost of the horizontal approach is slightly higher (although not as high as exterior vertical insulation).

Exterior horizontal insulation actually saves more energy for an equivalent amount of insulation compared with the other alternatives; however, it is the least cost-effective approach. In fact, exterior horizontal insulation is not directly comparable to the other cases since it actually requires an extra foot of vertical insulation before it extends horizontally. Thus, costs are higher due to the protective cover as well as the additional amount of material.

In spite of the apparent cost-effectiveness of interior vertical insulation compared with the other approaches, this is only one of many cost and performance issues to be considered. The economic benefit of interior vertical insulation may be offset by other practical, performance, and aesthetic considerations.

Exterior insulation at the slab edge

The slab-on-grade foundation assembly shown in Fig. 7 illustrates the use of a concrete masonry foundation wall. Rigid insulation covers the exterior vertical face of the wall. A polyethylene vapor diffusion retarder is placed beneath the floor slab and continues through the wall/slab joint and over the top of the foundation wall.

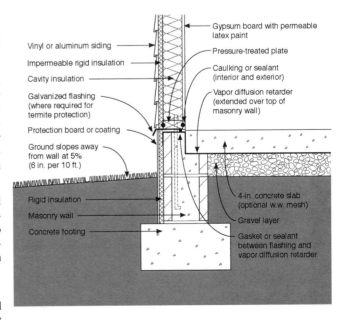

Fig. 7. Slab-on-grade foundation with exterior insulation. Note: This detail is suitable for a mixed (temperate) or overheated (warm) climate. Source: Lstiburek and Carmody (1993)—revised 1997.

SUBSTRUCTURE — A1

Table 4. Insulation recommendations for slab-on-grade foundations. Source: Carmody et al. (1991).

A: Concrete or Masonry Foundation Wall with Exterior Insulation Placed Vertically

CONFIGURATION	DESCRIPTION	0-2000 HDD (LOS ANG)			2-4000 HDD (FT WORTH)			4-6000 HDD (KAN CITY)			6-8000 HDD (CHICAGO)			8-10000 HDD (MPLS)		
		L	M	H	L	M	H	L	M	H	L	M	H	L	M	H
EXTERIOR VERTICAL	NO INSULATION	●	●	●	●	○	○	○	○	○	○	○	○	○	○	○
	2 FT DEEP: R-5	○	○	○	○	●	●	●	●	○	●	○	○	●	○	○
	2 FT DEEP: R-10	○	○	○	○	○	○	○	○	○	○	○	○	○	○	○
	4 FT DEEP: R-5	○	○	○	○	○	○	○	○	○	○	●	○	○	●	○
	4 FT DEEP: R-10	○	○	○	○	○	○	○	○	●	○	○	●	○	○	●
	4 FT DEEP: R-15	○	○	○	○	○	○	○	○	○	○	○	○	○	○	○
	4 FT DEEP: R-20	○	○	○	○	○	○	○	○	○	○	○	○	○	○	○

B: Concrete or Masonry Foundation Walls with Interior Insulation Placed Vertically

CONFIGURATION	DESCRIPTION	L	M	H	L	M	H	L	M	H	L	M	H	L	M	H
INTERIOR VERTICAL	NO INSULATION	●	●	●	○	○	○	○	○	○	○	○	○	○	○	○
	2 FT DEEP: R-5	○	○	○	●	●	●	●	●	○	●	○	○	●	○	○
	2 FT DEEP: R-10	○	○	○	○	○	○	○	○	○	○	○	○	○	○	○
	4 FT DEEP: R-5	○	○	○	○	○	○	○	○	●	○	●	○	○	●	○
	4 FT DEEP: R-10	○	○	○	○	○	○	○	○	○	○	○	●	○	○	●
	4 FT DEEP: R-15	○	○	○	○	○	○	○	○	○	○	○	○	○	○	○
	4 FT DEEP: R-20	○	○	○	○	○	○	○	○	○	○	○	○	○	○	○

C: Concrete or Masonry Foundation Walls with Interior Insulation Placed Horizontally Under Slab Perimeter

CONFIGURATION	DESCRIPTION	L	M	H	L	M	H	L	M	H	L	M	H	L	M	H
INTERIOR HORIZONTAL	NO INSULATION	●	●	●	●	○	○	○	○	○	○	○	○	○	○	○
	2 FT WIDE: R-5	○	○	○	○	●	●	●	●	○	●	○	○	○	○	○
	2 FT WIDE: R-10	○	○	○	○	○	○	○	○	○	○	○	○	○	○	○
	4 FT WIDE: R-5	○	○	○	○	○	○	○	○	●	○	●	○	●	●	○
	4 FT WIDE: R-10	○	○	○	○	○	○	○	○	○	○	○	●	○	○	●

D: Concrete or Masonry Foundation Walls with Exterior Insulation Extending Outward Horizontally

CONFIGURATION	DESCRIPTION	L	M	H	L	M	H	L	M	H	L	M	H	L	M	H
EXTERIOR HORIZONTAL	NO INSULATION	●	●	●	○	○	○	○	○	○	○	○	○	○	○	○
	2 FT WIDE: R-5	○	○	○	●	●	●	●	●	●	●	●	●	●	●	●
	2 FT WIDE: R-10	○	○	○	○	○	○	○	○	○	○	○	○	○	○	○
	4 FT WIDE: R-5	○	○	○	○	○	○	○	○	○	○	○	○	○	○	○
	4 FT WIDE: R-10	○	○	○	○	○	○	○	○	○	○	○	○	○	○	○

Notes: These recommendations are based on assumptions that are summarized at the end of this section. The darkened circle represents the recommended level of insulation in each column for each of the basic insulation configurations. L, H, and M refer to the low, medium, and high fuel cost levels indicated in Table 5.

Placing insulation vertically outside the foundation wall or grade beam effectively insulates the exposed slab edge above grade and extends down to reduce heat flow from the floor slab to the ground surface outside the building. Vertical exterior insulation is the only method of reducing heat loss at the edge of an integral grade beam and slab foundation. A major advantage of exterior insulation is that the interior joint between the slab and foundation wall need not be insulated, which simplifies construction. Several drawbacks, however, are that rigid insulation should be covered above grade with a protective board, coating, or flashing material, and with brick facings, a thermal short can be created that bypasses both the foundation and above-grade insulation. A limitation is that the depth of the exterior insulation is controlled by the footing depth. Additional exterior insulation can be provided by extending insulation horizontally from the foundation wall. Since this approach can control frost penetration near the footing, it can be used to reduce footing depth requirements under certain circumstances. This can substantially reduce the initial foundation construction cost.

Interior insulation at the slab perimeter

The slab-on-grade foundation assembly shown in Fig. 8 illustrates the use of a concrete foundation wall supporting a wood frame above-grade wall assembly with brick veneer. Rigid insulation is laid horizontally beneath the perimeter of the concrete floor slab and in the wall/slab joint. A polyethylene vapor diffusion retarder is placed beneath the floor slab and continues through the wall/slab joint and over the top of the foundation wall.

Insulation also can be placed vertically on the interior of the foundation wall or horizontally under the slab. In both cases, heat loss from the floor is reduced and the difficulty of placing and protecting exterior insulation is avoided. Interior vertical insulation is limited to the depth of the footing but underslab insulation is not limited in this respect. Usually the outer 2 to 4 ft. (0.6 or 1.2 m) of the slab perimeter is insulated but the entire floor may be insulated if desired.

It is essential to insulate the joint between the slab and the foundation wall whenever insulation is placed inside the foundation wall or under the slab. Otherwise, a significant amount of heat transfer occurs through the thermal bridge at the slab edge. In Fig. 8 the notched wall section permits 1 in. (2.54 cm) of rigid insulation to be placed in the joint.

Another option for insulating a slab-on-grade foundation is to place insulation above the floor slab. A wood floor deck can be placed on sleepers, leaving cavities that can be filled with rigid board or batt insulation, or a wood floor deck can be placed directly on rigid insulation above the slab. This approach avoids some of the construction detail problems inherent in the more conventional approaches discussed above, but may lead to greater frost depth in the vicinity of the slab edge.

Structural design of slab-on-grade foundations

The major structural components of a slab-on-grade foundation are the floor slab itself and either grade beams or foundation walls with footings at the perimeter of the slab (see Figs. 7 and 8). In some cases additional footings (often a thickened slab) are necessary under bearing walls or columns in the center of the slab. Concrete slab-on-grade floors are generally designed to have sufficient strength to support floor loads without reinforcing when poured on undisturbed or compacted soil. The proper use of welded wire fabric and concrete with a low water/cement ratio can reduce shrinkage cracking, which is an important concern for appearance and for reducing potential radon infiltration.

Foundation walls are typically constructed of cast-in-place concrete or concrete masonry units. Foundation walls must be designed to resist vertical loads from the structure above and transfer these loads to

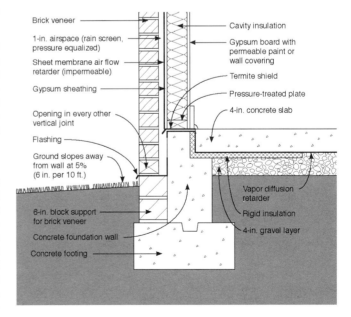

Brick veneer

1-in. airspace (rain screen, pressure equalized)

Sheet membrane air flow retarder (impermeable)

Gypsum sheathing

Opening in every other vertical joint

Flashing

Ground slopes away from wall at 5% (6 in. per 10 ft.)

6-in. block support for brick veneer

Concrete foundation wall

Concrete footing

Cavity insulation

Gypsum board with permeable paint or wall covering

Termite shield

Pressure-treated plate

4-in. concrete slab

Vapor diffusion retarder

Rigid insulation

4-in. gravel layer

Fig. 8. Slab-on-grade foundation with interior insulation. Note: This detail is suitable for a mixed (temperate) or overheated (warm) climate. Source: Lstiburek and Carmody (1993)—revised 1997.

the footing. Concrete spread footings must provide support beneath foundation walls and columns. Similarly, grade beams at the edge of the foundation support the superstructure above. Footings must be designed with adequate bearing area to distribute the load to the soil and be placed beneath the maximum frost penetration depth or be insulated to prevent frost penetration.

Where expansive soils are present or in areas of high seismic activity, special foundation construction techniques may be necessary. In these cases, consultation with local building officials and a structural engineer is recommended.

Moisture control in slab-on-grade construction

Good surface drainage techniques are always recommended for slab-on-grade foundations. The goal of surface drainage is to keep water away from the foundation by sloping the ground surface and using gutters and downspouts for roof drainage. Because a slab-on-grade floor is above the surrounding exterior grade, no subsurface drainage system or waterproofing is required. On sites with a high water table, the floor should be raised above existing grade as much as possible and a layer of gravel can be placed beneath the slab to ensure that drainage occurs and moisture problems are avoided.

The key strategies for slab-on-grade moisture control shown in Figs. 7 and 8 are:

- Rainwater is controlled by gutters and downspouts, and grade sloping away from the building.

- Air movement into the space from the ground is controlled by a polyethylene sheet placed beneath the floor slab.

- Vapor diffusion from the surrounding soil is also controlled by the polyethylene sheet placed beneath the floor slab.

- Avoid ductwork beneath the slab and minimize other slab penetrations to control air movement and vapor diffusion.

- Capillary suction is controlled by a layer of gravel under the slab, and the polyethylene sheet which extends over the top of the foundation wall.

Assumptions used in the energy analysis

The insulation recommendations are based on a set of underlying assumptions. Fuel price assumptions used in this analysis are shown in Table 5. The total heating system efficiency is 68 percent and the cooling System Energy Efficiency Rating (SEER) is 9.2 with 10 percent duct losses. Energy price inflation and mortgage conditions are selected to allow maximum simple payback of 18 years with average paybacks of about 13 years. The total installed costs for all insulation systems considered in this analysis are given in Carmody, Christian and Labs (1991). Installation costs used in this analysis are based on average U. S. costs in 1987. For the exterior cases, costs include labor and materials for extruded polystyrene insulation and the required protective covering and flashing above grade. For the interior cases, costs include labor and materials for expanded polystyrene. All costs include a 30 percent builder markup and a 30 percent subcontractor markup for overhead and profit.

Table 5. Fuel price assumptions used in analysis. Source: Carmody *et al.* (1991)

Season	Fuel Type	Low (L) Fuel Price Level	Medium (M) Fuel Price Level	High (H) Fuel Price Level
Heating	Natural Gas	$0.37 per therm	$0.56 per therm	$0.84 per therm
	Fuel Oil	$0.53 per gallon	$0.79 per gallon	$1.19 per gallon
	Propane	$0.34 per gallon	$0.52 per gallon	$0.76 per gallon
Cooling	Electricity	$0.51 per kWh	$0.76 per kWh	$0.11 per kWh

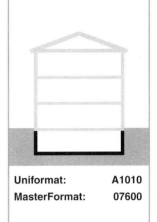

Termite control

Antenna not "elbowed"

Stubs left when wing detaches

Middle part of body not narrow

Wings similiar in shape, size, and pattern

Winged termite identification

Summary: Termite damage can affect the physical stability of a building structure. It can be eliminated or minimized by proper termite shield design and preventive maintenance precautions. Protection of the building construction and interior against termites is mandatory in susceptible locations. Methods of protection are physical and chemical barriers, although such barriers are not impenetrable. Termite shields provide a permanent physical barrier and are installed at all susceptible points of entry.

Key words: termite protection, physical barriers, chemical barriers, termite shield, under-building ventilation.

Uniformat:	A1010
MasterFormat:	07600

Termite Protection

Termite damage in wood structures can be substantial and, if allowed to persist, can affect the physical stability of a building structure. The likelihood of such infestation can be minimized by proper termite shield design, in addition to related installation and preventive maintenance precautions.

There are four types of termites:

- Subterranean termites are the most common, and most often follow the primary stages of decay;
- Drywood termites are the next most common, and fly into attics and basements to infest the framing material;
- Dampwood termites are the least common nationally, and are normally found in small quantities in extremely wet locations;
- Formosan termites are found in small numbers in such places as Florida and Hawaii.

Termites require damp, rotting wood, and will carry in moisture and fungi to rot sound wood so they can feed on it. These conditions require a constant source of moisture, usually obtained from the soil. Termite access to unprotected structures is gained through cracks in concrete or masonry foundations or walls, or through the wood portion of the house frame. Termites also build tunnellike structures called shelter tubes over foundation posts and walls to gain access.

Protection of the building construction and interior against termites is mandatory in susceptible locations (see Fig. 1 on following page). Methods of protection are of two types, physical and chemical barriers. Physical barriers are recommended in order to reduce or preclude chemical treatment, which must be periodically renewed. With the exception of treated lumber, barriers are marginally effective only for subterranean termites. Such barriers are not effective with dampwood, drywood, or Formosan termites, and additional precautions must be taken.

The map on the following page indicates the hazard from termites in different parts of the United States, although it is important to remember that decay is a hearty invitation to termites. Proper waterproofing will reduce decay problems. Local distribution of termites may be spotty, and a given site may be more or less hazardous than indicated by the map. Protection is required in all cases in Region I and, in most cases, in Region II. Protection is usually not required in Region III and rarely if ever in Region IV.

Physical barriers

Acceptable physical barriers include:

- Concrete foundations, free of cracks and porous areas, for basement and crawl space types of construction except where masonry or masonry veneer walls extend below top of foundation wall and are less than 8" above finish grade.

- Monolithic framed concrete slab, reinforced to minimize cracking with at least 6X6 10/10 wwf in areas where winter design temperature exceeds +15F (-10°C), extending wall-to-wall without openings or joints. Piping, ductwork, and other penetration of slab must be thoroughly sealed. Interior and exterior sill plates in contact with the concrete slab should be treated wood.

- Foundations caps of cast-in-place concrete, not less than 4" thick, reinforced with two No. 3 bars. Cap shall be placed continuously on top of all unit masonry foundations and piers and shall be the full width of wall, extending through voids in masonry veneer or faced masonry walls.

- Proper waterproofing of doors, windows, and the extension of roofs over exterior walls. Buildings detailed with proper waterproofing will prevent decay, reducing the threat of subterranean termites.

- Attic vents should be screened to prevent the infestation of drywood termites.

Chemical barriers

Chemical barriers consist of soil poisoning and pressure-treated lumber.

Soil poisoning: application of chemicals must conform to standards established by the U.S. Environmental Protection Agency. Chemical soil treatment should not be used where there is a possibility of contamination of a water source or edible food supply. Application of chemical barriers in most states is permitted by a licensed pest control operator, not by tradespeople or homeowners.

Author: Don Pearman; Copper Development Association.

References: HUD Minimum Property Standards 1975. U.S. Department of Housing and Urban Development.

Labs, Kenneth *et al.* 1988. *Building Foundation Design Handbook.* Minneapolis, MN: Underground Space Center. [out of print]

Moore, H.B. 1979. *Wood-Inhibiting Insects in Houses: Their Identification, Biology, Prevention, and Control.* Washington, D.C.: U.S. Government Printing Office.

Don Pearman. 1988. *The Termite Report.* Oakland, CA: Pear Press.

A1 SUBSTRUCTURE

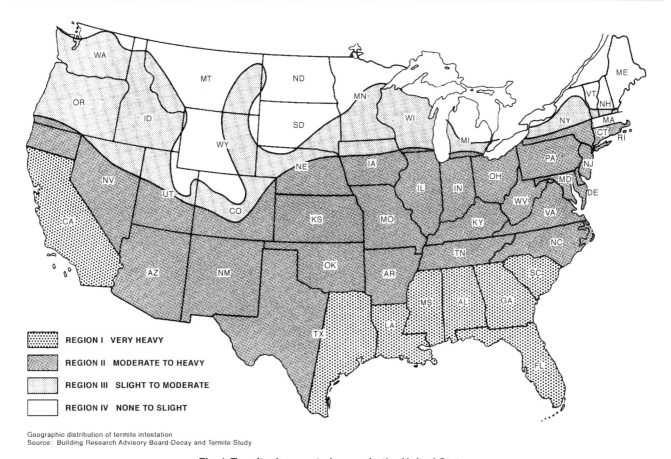

REGION I   VERY HEAVY

REGION II   MODERATE TO HEAVY

REGION III   SLIGHT TO MODERATE

REGION IV   NONE TO SLIGHT

Geographic distribution of termite infestation
Source: Building Research Advisory Board-Decay and Termite Study

Fig. 1. Termite damage to homes in the United States.

Pressure treated lumber: lumber or plywood treated for the prevention of decay protects against termite infestation and must be labeled with a permanent mark, indicating the applicable standard. When pressure treated lumber is cut, the cut area should be treated with an appropriate fungicide in order to maintain the continuity of thechemical barrier. When treated lumber is used, the members to be treated are:

• Frame construction: basement or crawl space sill plates.

• Frame construction: slab-on-ground other than monolithic: sole plates.

• Masonry veneer construction: sole plates.

• Masonry wall construction: sole plates.

• Masonry wall construction, slab-on-ground: sole plates.

In addition to protective measures, periodic inspection is necessary. For example, with exterior insulation, provide a visible horizontal strip of at least 8 in. (20 cm) cut out of exterior insulation 12 in. (30.5 cm) above grade to permit inspection for the presence of termite tunnels.

Protective measures assume compliance with the following standards of construction, which have as their purpose proper waterproofing of the building and the reduction of moisture in the soil and in the building, which will result in the reduction of rotting conditions that furnish food for termites.

• Adequate drainage for the site and building.

• Minimum clearance (8") between ground and wood.

• Adequate ventilation of structural spaces.

• Proper flashing, including termite shields.

• Installation of vapor barriers and sheathing papers where required.

• Removal of stumps, roots, wood scraps, and other likely termite locations from the immediate building perimeter and, as appropriate, from the building site.

Termite shield design
Termite shields are intended to provide a permanent physical barrier to termite entry into the building construction or interior and are installed at all susceptible points of entry. Shields may be shop- or field-formed metal, such as copper or other corrosion resistant metals. Properly installed shields may prevent termites from invading the wooden portion of the structure and also act as a moisture barrier, although some experts believe that they are marginally effective for termites.

There are two types of shields: barrier shields, which are recommended in most cases, and deflector shields, which are appropriate only when vigilant inspection is provided. Regular inspection is required in order to discover the presence of telltale "tubes" built by tube-building termites. Termites building a shelter tube from the ground moisture to building woodwork are forced to move out around the shield as indicated at the "point of detection" (Fig. 2). The shelter tube, exposed at this point, can be easily broken off so that any termites that may have gained access to the building are cut off from their essential moisture. This procedure, repeated several times, apparently discourages tube-building termites.

Barrier Shield

Barrier shield design is required where inspection of the shield is difficult or impossible. It is designed so that termites building up over the stone or concrete foundations are blocked from entry into the woodwork of the house above by the projection of the shield. Two basic barrier type shields are shown in Fig. 2 details. These vary as to edge detail, and all requiring lapped or locked-formed seals at the joints (tightly malleted into position). Sharp edge metal rather than rolled edges is recommended to further discourage tube-building termites. Any loose joints provide access to termites.

Deflector shield

This shield, shown in Fig. 3, does not in itself provide an impossible barrier to the termites. It is employed only in areas accessible for periodic inspections, such as the interior wall of a basement room or on the outside of a brick porch.

Under building ventilation

Termites in or around a building isolated by shields generally make an effort to restore contact with ground moisture. If a shallow unexcavated area is available, termites may connect by means of a shelter tube. Adequate ventilation of under-building areas should defeat such attempts (*e.g.*, undersides of porches, decks, and other superstructure extended beyond foundations). Under moist conditions, lengthy shelter tubes can be formed, but under dry conditions the tubes have the appearance of sand and the consistency of lightweight cellulose, and tend to crumble and collapse. Under building ventilation is also critical to reduce moisture that helps encourage fungi, which attracts subterranean termites (see Fig. 5).

Termite damage is shown in Fig. 4. Figs. 6 and 7 shown on the next page provide additional information on termite control measures for crawl space foundation, and common points of termite entry.

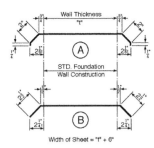

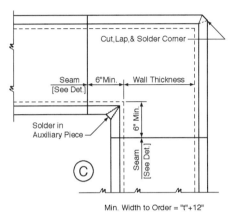

Fig. 2. Barrier shield

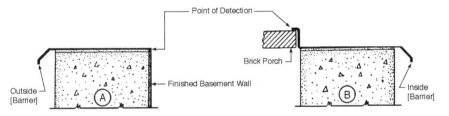

Fig. 3. Deflector shield

Fig. 4. Termite damage

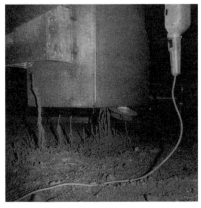

Fig. 5. Termite tubes

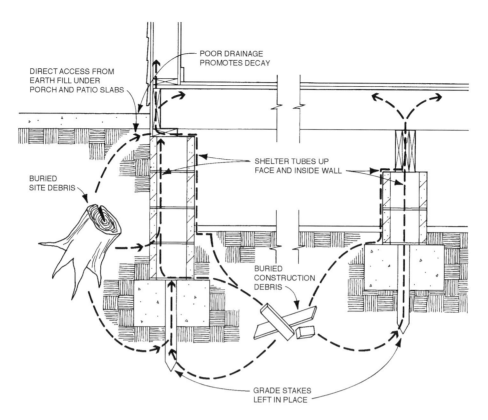

Fig. 6. Common points of termite entry (Labs *et al.* 1988)

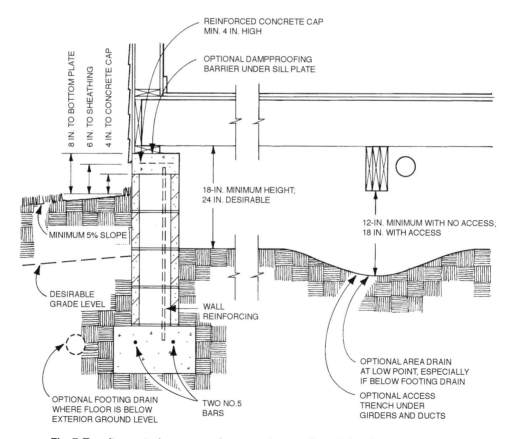

Fig. 7. Termite control measures for a crawl space foundation (Labs *et al.* 1988)

B   SHELL

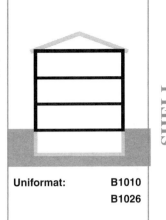

Fig. 1. Structural frame

ROOF/FLOOR DECK

VERTICAL SUPPORTS

An overview of structures

Summary: This article is an outline of basic structural approaches with emphasis upon conventional systems and constructability. It provides an introduction to subsequent articles in this chapter and a guide for preliminary architectural design.

Key words: concrete, deformation, frame, slabs, steel, trusses, wood.

Uniformat: B1010
               B1026

SHELL   B1

Frame

The structural frame of a building (Fig. 1) should be selected to provide the most economical means of support for all loads and resistance to all forces that may be reasonably expected to be imposed upon the enclosure during its intended in-service life:

- without creating any hazard to its occupants or users.

- without excessive deformations and sideways and/or annoying.

- with proper provisions for possible or anticipated abnormal in-service conditions, such as fire, explosions, inadvertent overloading.

The structural frame generally consists of:

- Roof deck: either horizontal, pitched, or curved assemblies.

- Floor decks: commonly flat horizontal assemblies:

- suspended above grade.

- supported above grade by piles driven into the ground.

- supported on the ground and independent of the structural frame.

- Vertical supports or primary framing: to hold roof/floor decks in place and to carry all loads to the foundations.

- Foundations: to transfer all loads to the ground.

Vertical support: types

Roof and floor decks (Fig. 2) may be supported by various means:

- Bearing walls: which provide continuous support for the decks:

- bearing walls may be wood framed, of masonry, or of cast-in-place or precast concrete.

- Pilasters: load bearing segments of nonbearing walls supporting girders, the horizontal component of a vertical support assembly, which in turn carry the roof/floor decks:

- pilasters are commonly tied into the nonbearing wall either of masonry or of concrete of which they are a part; when incorporated into a framed nonbearing wall, they are also referred to as "posts."

- Column and girder assemblies: of wood, steel, or of reinforced concrete, either cast-in-place or precast:

- reinforced masonry columns are also used.

- Columns only: which provide point support for decks, usually of monolithic reinforced concrete.

- columns are either of structural steel or of reinforced concrete.

Roof/floor deck: types

Roof/floor decks (Fig. 3) carry all loads and resist all forces they are subjected to and transmit them to the vertical support assemblies between which they span.

The principal components of roof/floor deck assemblies are:

- Decking: the structural top surface component of the deck.

- Framing: structural components which support the decking. Framing and decking may be separate and distinct components or they may form a single element without any differentiation between them.

The assembly of framing and decking—the deck—may consist of:

- Monolithic framing/decking: such as in cast-in-place reinforced concrete decks.

- Fabricated components: which combined framing and decking into a single unit, such as precast concrete shapes, long span metal decks, stressed skin panels.

- Framing and decking assembled at the site to function as roof/floor decks:

- framing may be prefabricated off-site to simplify site assembly, such as in pre-engineered space frames.

Framing/decking: cast-in-place

Decks: cast-in-place reinforced concrete combining framing and decking into single element (Figs. 4):

- Two-way slabs: generally of uniform thickness, may be thickened at columns to increase resistance to shear thus increasing load carrying capacity:

- minimum of three continuous spans in each direction required for direct design of flat decks.

- generally limited to square or rectangular bays with ratios of width to length of less than two.

- relatively shallow depth of construction but extensive formwork generally required.

- when of uniform thickness throughout, slabs may be cast on the ground stacked, thus requiring minimal formwork, and then lifted into their final position.

- two-way slabs generally not recommended when numerous larger openings through decks are required: larger openings require special framing.

Credits: The section adapted from 1993 SWEETS Catalogs File Selection Data, Mc-Graw Hill, by permission of the publisher.

References: Schodek, Daniel L. 1992. *Structures.* Second Edition. Englewood Cliffs, NJ: Prentice Hall

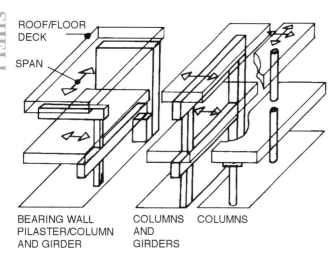

Fig. 2. Vertical support types

BEARING WALL PILASTER/COLUMN AND GIRDER

COLUMNS AND GIRDERS

COLUMNS

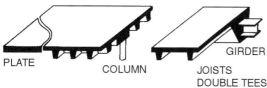

PLATE

COLUMN

GIRDER

JOISTS DOUBLE TEES

FRAMING/DECKING: CAST-IN-PLACE/PRECAST

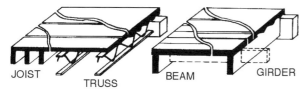

JOIST

TRUSS

BEAM

GIRDER

FRAMIING AND DECKING: SITE ASSEMBLED

Fig. 3. Roof/floor deck types

- conduits for electrical and communications wiring may be embedded in decks, but the size of conduits is generally limited.

- effects of deflection in decks and of cold flow, or creep, in concrete columns of multistory structures must be considered during selection and detailing of exterior walls, partitions, and nonresilient flooring.

• One-way Slabs: thin sections functioning as decking cast-in-place monolithically with framing of uniformly spaced ribs of various depths:

- when closely spaced, the ribs are generally referred to as "joists," when spaced further apart, as "beams."

- the ribs are supported by girders spanning in one direction between columns.

- uniform depth construction may be attained by casting joists integrally with wide concrete girders of the same depth.

Supports are generally concrete columns except for lift slabs where structural steel pipe columns are used:

- point support of columns only for two-way flat and waffle slabs.

- columns and girders for two-way framed and one-way slabs.

• Assemblies with concrete girders and, or columns may have fire resistance rating without the need for additional fireproofing.

Framing/decking: separately fabricated units
Decks of precast reinforced concrete components of essentially uniform overall depth, which combine decking and framing into a single unit and are capable of spanning between vertical supports (Fig. 5):

- generally used for light to moderate loading conditions only.

- larger openings through decks require supplementary means of support.

- acceptable extent of deflection rather than strength of components may be the governing consideration during selection.

- when used for floor decks, addition of concrete topping is required to level the surface; topping may be required, and is often recommended, for roof decks.

- joints between units require grouting during installation.

- wiring may be run through cores of hollow-core plank.

- decks may have fire resistance rating without need for additional fireproofing.

Supports may be any combination of: bearing walls, either masonry or concrete, columns and girders of structural steel or concrete.

- spacing of supports: from about 12 up to 40 feet for hollowcore plank; 12 to 24 feet for solid slabs.

Framing/decking: monolithically fabricated units

Monolithic decks: assemblies of precast reinforced concrete components in which framing and decking are cast monolithically (Fig. 6):

- essentially precast sections of one-way slabs.

- generally used with widely spaced supports.

- smaller openings in decks may be made by cutting out decking between framing ribs; large openings require supplementary supports.

- acceptable extent of deflection rather than strength may govern selection, especially for upper ranges of allowable spans, camber usually provided.

- concrete topping required for floor decks, may be required for roof decks to provide level substrate for roofing.

- conduits for electrical/communications wiring may be embedded in topping, but size of conduit is quite limited, may otherwise cause cracking in topping.

- decks may have fire resistance rating without need for additional fireproofing.

Supports may be any combination of: bearing walls of reinforced masonry or concrete, columns and girders of reinforced concrete or structural steel.

- spacing of supports from 40 to about 120 feet.

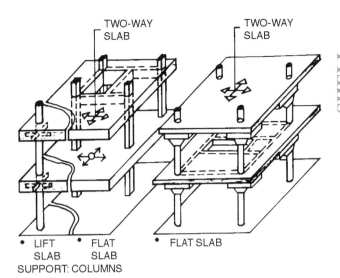

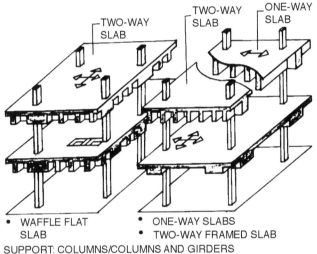

Fig. 4. Framing/decking: cast-in-place

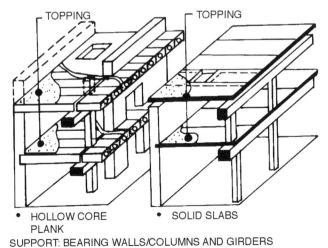

Fig. 5. Framing/decking: fabricated units

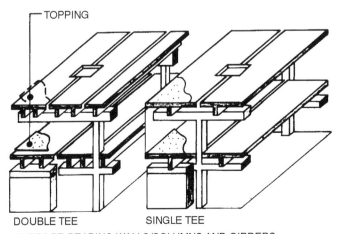

Fig. 6. Framing/decking: fabricated and monolithic units

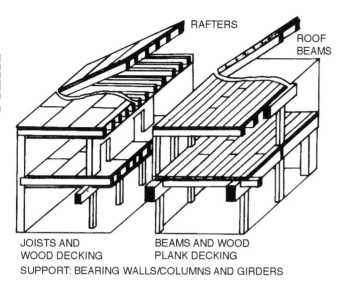

JOISTS AND
WOOD DECKING

BEAMS AND WOOD
PLANK DECKING

SUPPORT: BEARING WALLS/COLUMNS AND GIRDERS

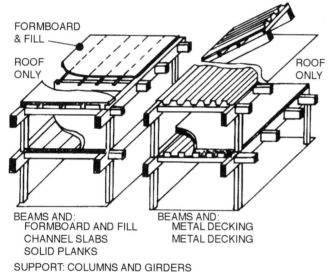

BEAMS AND:
    FORMBOARD AND FILL
    CHANNEL SLABS
    SOLID PLANKS

BEAMS AND:
    METAL DECKING
    METAL DECKING

SUPPORT: COLUMNS AND GIRDERS

Fig. 7. Solid frame and decking: site assembled

Solid framing and decking: site assembled

Decks: framing and decking as separate components assembled on site in their final location (Fig. 7).

- Solid framing is commonly referred to as:

- joists: when horizontal and spaced 12 to 24 inches on centers, rafters or roof joists: when pitched and part of a roof deck.

- beams: when spaced 4 to about 8 feet on centers and spanning between girders or bearing wails; also referred to as "purlins" when horizontal and spanning between pitched roof framing girders.

- Spacing of framing is principally determined by properties of decking used:

- load carrying capacity of decking.

- extent of deflection allowable or acceptable.

- size of decking when joints between individual pieces have to extend over framing members for proper support.

- spacing may be reduced below the maximum allowable for specific type of decking in order to provide increased load-carrying capacity or to span between supports of a section of a roof/floor-deck while maintaining the same overall depth of construction throughout.

- Size of framing is generally controlled by allowable stresses in bending and/or shear for short spans, allowable deflection for long spans: especially when inelastic components of an enclosure are also supported by such framing, such as ceiling membranes of plaster or gypsum board, or inelastic flooring.

- Framing may be of solid wood, laminated wood, light-gauge steel, structural steel:

- precast reinforced concrete beams may also be used with some types of decking, but such usage is not common.

- Decking generally spans one-way between framing members and may be: solid wood; laminated wood; wood composites; precast gypsum, or precast concrete of various densities; formed lightgauge steel with or without cementitious fill; composite of formboards, steel subpurlins, and cementitious fill.

Supports may be any combination of: framed, masonry or concrete bearing walls; columns and girders of solid wood, laminated wood, structural steel:

- reinforced concrete girders may also be used with some decks but such usage is not common.

Open framing and decking: site assembled

Decks: framing and decking as separate components assembled on site in their final location (Fig. 8). Open framing may be:

- Light trusses of solid wood or wood and steel bar composites: generally spaced 24 inches on centers and supporting solid or composite wood decking.

- Short-span and long-span steel bar joists: commonly 24 or more inches on centers for floor decks, 4 to 6 feet or more on centers for roof decks, depending on properties of deck used:

- decking commonly used: formed light-gauge steel with or without cementitious fill; formboard, steel subpurlins and cementitious fill; precast cementitious slabs or planks; cementitious fill on metal lath; wood composites when nailing strips are attached to top flanges of steel bar joists.

- proprietary system of steel bar joists and cast-in-place concrete decking providing composite action under load in the deck assembly is available.

- steel bar joists may be used as rafters in pitched roof decks but such usage is not common.

- objectionable vibrations may occur in floor decks framed with short-span steel bar joist when their spans are in the upper range of those allowable.

- deflections in steel bar joists used in dead level roof-decks may result in ponding of rainwater unless drains are provided in all such low spots.

- Purlins/beams in pitched roof-decks should be braced against rotation under eccentric load and lateral sag due to their own weight.

Open framing allows running electrical/communications wiring, small diameter piping, and small size ductwork within the depth of the deck assembly:

- more easily accomplished when deck assembly is supported on girders of open cross section.

Supports may be:

- For light wood trusses: bearing walls of wood frame, masonry, concrete; columns and girders of wood, structural steel, less often of concrete.

- For steel bar joists: bearing walls of light-gauge steel frame, masonry, concrete; columns and girders of structural steel, less often of concrete.

Open framing and decking: pre-engineered

Decks: framing and decking as separate components, site assembled (Fig. 9).

- Framing:

- two-way interlocking braced truss system, in triangular, diagonal, hexagonal, or rectangular grid of structural steel or aluminum.

- horizontal or curved, used to roof over large open spaces.

- supported by columns, which may be randomly located, may be supported on bearing walls. System permits two-way overhangs.

- to simplify construction, the size of members is either the same throughout, or a limited number of sizes is used: the majority of members must be oversized so that the most heavily loaded would not be overstressed.

- may be assembled on the ground and lifted into place.

- ductwork, piping, conduits for electrical and telephone wiring may be run within space frame.

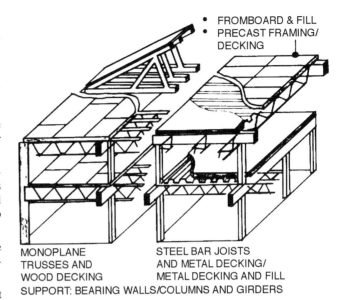

- FROMBOARD & FILL
- PRECAST FRAMING/ DECKING

MONOPLANE
TRUSSES AND
WOOD DECKING

STEEL BAR JOISTS
AND METAL DECKING/
METAL DECKING AND FILL

SUPPORT: BEARING WALLS/COLUMNS AND GIRDERS

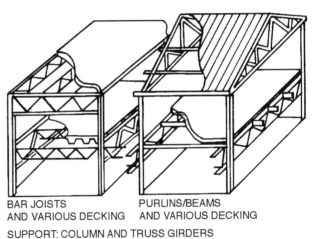

BAR JOISTS
AND VARIOUS DECKING

PURLINS/BEAMS
AND VARIOUS DECKING

SUPPORT: COLUMN AND TRUSS GIRDERS

Fig. 8. Open framing and decking: site assembled

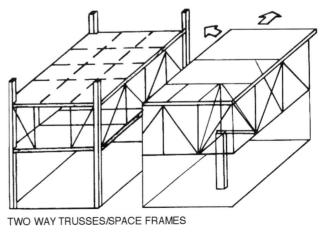

TWO WAY TRUSSES/SPACE FRAMES
SUPPORT: COLUMNS

Fig. 9. Open framing and decking: pre-engineered

B1

SHELL

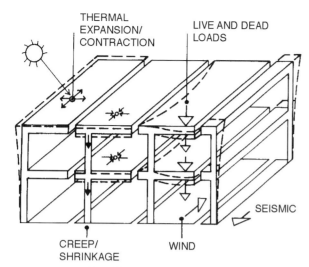

THERMAL EXPANSION/ CONTRACTION

LIVE AND DEAD LOADS

SEISMIC

CREEP/ SHRINKAGE

WIND

Fig. 10. Deformations defined

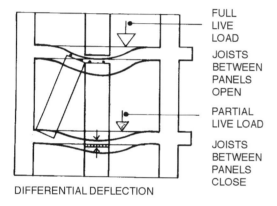

FULL LIVE LOAD

JOISTS BETWEEN PANELS OPEN

PARTIAL LIVE LOAD

JOISTS BETWEEN PANELS CLOSE

DIFFERENTIAL DEFLECTION

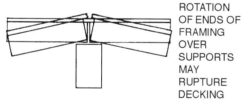

ROTATION OF ENDS OF FRAMING OVER SUPPORTS MAY RUPTURE DECKING

SIMPLY SUPPORTED DECK AT SUPPORTS

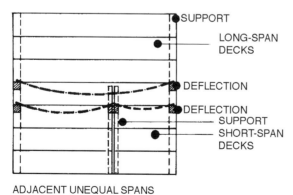

SUPPORT

LONG-SPAN DECKS

DEFLECTION

DEFLECTION

SUPPORT

SHORT-SPAN DECKS

ADJACENT UNEQUAL SPANS

Fig. 11. Structural deformation in decks and girders

- Decking may be: transparent or translucent, such as plastics, glass; formed light gauge metal; cementitious; wood or wood composites where permitted by building codes.
- Most commonly used for roofs, but can be designed for floor loading also; full story-height space frames have been built to serve as mechanical equipment floors.

Deformation in structural frames

All structural frames are subject to deformations (Fig. 10):

- *Deflection:* the differential change in length between two opposite faces of a horizontal or vertical assembly or component of a structural frame. Deflection may result from:

- bending loads: when one face shortens under compression while the other elongates under tension.

- temperature differential: when one face remains stable or contracts while the other expands.

- moisture differential: when one face remains stable or shrinks while the other swells.

- *Plastic flow:* shortening of vertical components, such as columns, or deflection in horizontal assemblies and/or components, such as monolithic concrete decks, under long-term sustained loading; also commonly referred to as "creep:"

- concrete in particular and wood are subject to creep, while its effect on structural steel is insignificant.

- *Shrinkage:* the overall volumetric change due to changes in moisture content.

- *Lateral displacement,* also often referred to as "sway" or "drift," of frames due to wind or seismic forces.

Deformation in decks and girders

Components of horizontal frames such as framing, decking, girders are always subject to deflection due to bending and to varying extent the effects of lateral displacement (Fig. 11):

- they may also be subject to: deflection due to temperature differential especially in roof decks, moisture differential when of materials thus affected.

- plastic flow and shrinkage may further aggravate the effects of deflection.

Deformations to be expected in specific materials and their effects should be considered during preliminary selection of a structural frame:

- *Steel* is essentially elastic within allowable stresses, is not affected by moisture, and does not creep to any significant amount:

- deflection due to live load is the principal consideration, differential thermal expansion/contraction generally being a less significant factor.

- camber may be provided in girders to compensate for deflection generally for that due to dead load only which will also add to the cost of fabrication.

- *Concrete* is subject to deflection under load, creep, shrinkage, thermal expansion/contraction:

- deflection under permanent load continues to increase for several years due to shrinkage and creep: the total deflection to be provided for in design is the sum of creep deflection from permanent or sustained long-term loads (largely irreversible deflection due to live loads), plus the deflection effects of temperature and moisture differentials.

- creep, which may amount to as much as 2.5 to 3 times the load-induced deflection, will result in loss of prestress, but will also relieve stress concentrations which otherwise might developed.

- *Wood* is affected by changes in overall moisture content, moisture and temperature gradients across a given section, deflection due to loads, and creep:

  - wood is subject to continuous volumetric changes of about 3 percent across the grain due to changes in its moisture content under normal in-service conditions.

  - creep will occur in wood when under sustained load, with the amount to be expected varying with different species.

Deformation in columns and walls

Vertical elements of a structural frame such as columns, bearing walls are always subject to deflection due to lateral loads, lateral displacement, and to varying extent effects of bending due to vertical loads (Fig. 12):

- axial loads are seldom truly that, and any eccentricity will cause bending stresses to develop.

- lateral displacement or sway in tall structures may be well within safe limits structurally, but may be far in excess of maximum allowable values for a particular curtain wall system to function properly.

- columns and bearing walls may also be subject to deflection due to temperature or moisture differential through their section and to plastic flow, depending on the properties of their constituent materials.

- *Steel*: is generally affected by lateral forces, bending due to eccentric loading, and differential thermal expansion/contraction.

- *Concrete*: is subject to creep and shrinkage in addition to bending, thermal and moisture differentials.

- shrinkage and creep in concrete during and after construction will result in shortening of the structural frame, which may amount to as little as 0.10 inch or more than 0.60 inch for a sixty foot high structure, depending on: at which stage of construction the frame is fully loaded, size of columns, reinforcing provided, differences in ambient relative humidity.

- reinforcing of concrete will tend to minimize creep but will not prevent it.

- when connections between a structural frame of concrete and a rigid wall assembly supported by it do not allow for creep related shortening of the frame, shearing action between the frame and the wall may develop, and may lead to damage or failure of the wall.

- *Wood* columns will be affected by moisture and temperature differential across their section and bending:

  - shrinkage along the grain is considerably less than across the grain and generally is not a significant factor.

  - when vertical components of a multistory wood framed structure bear on horizontal framing at intermediate levels, the shrinkage and creep across the grain in such framing will result in shortening of the frame, with the extent varying constantly with changes in ambient relative humidity.

Deformation effects on partitions

Deformations in the structural frame will also affect interior elements of enclosures (Fig. 13). Movement and subsequent cracking of partitions may be caused by:

- deflection in floor deck and/or girders which support the partition and/or foundation settlement, with either resulting in vertical cracking, commonly the full height of the partition.

- lateral displacement or distortion of the frame, with the resulting racking action often leading to corner cracking in partitions.

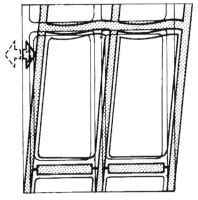

FRAME WILL DEFORM UNDER WIND OR SEISMIC FORCE AND MAY AFFECT EXTERIOR WALLS AND/OR FACINGS IN ADDITION TO POSITIVE OR NEGATIVE WIND PRESSURES ACTING ON SUCH WALLS

LATERAL DISPLACEMENT

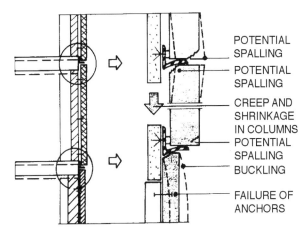

POTENTIAL SPALLING

POTENTIAL SPALLING

CREEP AND SHRINKAGE IN COLUMNS

POTENTIAL SPALLING

BUCKLING

FAILURE OF ANCHORS

SHORTENING OF FRAME

Fig. 12. Structural deformation in columns and walls

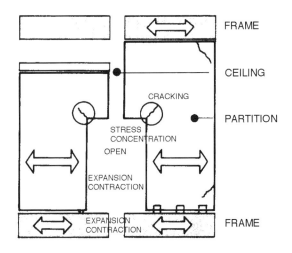

FRAME

CEILING

CRACKING

PARTITION

STRESS CONCENTRATION

OPEN

EXPANSION CONTRACTION

EXPANSION CONTRACTION

FRAME

Fig. 13. Deformation effects on partitions

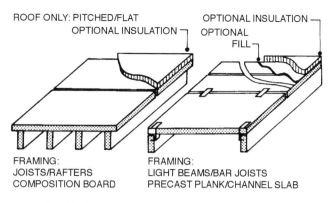

Fig. 14. Framing and decking: site assembled

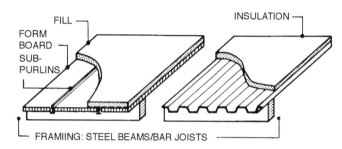

Fig. 15. Roof only: flat

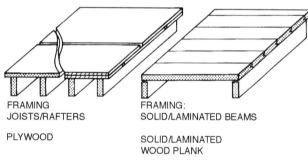

Fig. 16. Roof: flat or pitched/floor

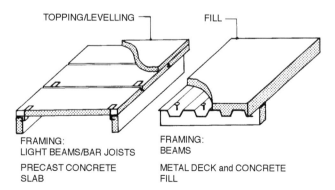

Fig. 17. Roof/floor: flat

- thermal expansion/contraction in the frame, when at different rate than the corresponding movement in the partition.

- shrinkage or moisture-induced volumetric changes in the frame and/or partition.

Cracking in partitions may also be caused by factors not directly related to deformations in the structural frame:

- expansion/contraction in the partition itself.

- stress concentrations in abrupt changes in cross-sectional area, such as at openings.

Roof and floor decks: typical assemblies

Decking component of site assembled roof/floor decks may be:

- Composition or wood particle board: generally used in framed structures as roof sheathing only:

- usually 4 feet wide, 8 to 12 feet long.

- strength in bending and dimensional stability under varying moisture conditions are primary considerations.

- Plywood: for roof sheathing and floor decking in wood or metal framed structures:

- thickness varies from 3/8 inch for roof sheathing up to 1-1/4 inches with tongue and groove edges for floor decking.

- 4 feet wide, 8 to 12 feet long, with 8 feet being the most readily available length.

- Wood plank: either solid or laminated:

- solid wood boards of one inch or 1 1/4 inch nominal thickness may be used as roof sheathing or subfloordecking, but such usage is no longer common.

- solid wood decking of 2 to 4 inch nominal thickness is available, but has largely been replaced by laminated decking. Laminated decking is available either 3-ply or 5-ply with thickness ranging from 3 to 5 inches, in lengths of 6 feet or longer, in increments of 1 foot.

- spans for planks range from 5 to about 16 feet; lay-up generally random over 2 or more supports.

- Planks of precast concrete or cement bound wood fiber; also precast concrete channel slabs:

- generally 2 to 4 inches thick, 16 to 48 inches wide, spanning 8 to 10 feet, plank generally tongue and groove, metal edged tongue and groove available.

- commonly secured to steel framing by metal clips; some may also be nailed.

- common usage is as roof decking only; has been used for lightly loaded floors.

- Precast concrete slabs are similar to precast plank except that they are thicker, generally 4 to 8 inches, and used principally for floor decking:

- concrete topping of about 2 inches in thickness required for floors.

- spans range from 12 to 24 feet, may function as framing/decking combined.

- Formboards of cement bound organic or mineral fibers, supported by steel subpurlins between framing, with site placed usually lightweight concrete fill:

- subpurlin spacing 24 to 33 inches: spans 6 to 10 feet.

- Metal deck: usually of formed light-gauge steel either coated or galvanized; generally 28 to 20 gauge for depths of 1/2 to 1 1/2 inches, 22 to 16 gauge for depths of 1 1/2 to 3 inches commonly, but available up to 6 inches of various configurations.

- 1/2 inch to 1-1/2 inch deep often used as centering or permanent formwork for cast-in-place concrete floordecks over steel bar joist or light steel beam framing, spaced 2 to 8 feet on centers.

- metal decking for roofs may be used with site placed lightweight concrete or gypsum fill or more commonly with insulation only; types incorporating sound absorbing materials in ribs are available; spans for 1-1/2 inch depth 4 to 8 feet, for 3 inch depth 8 to 12 feet.

Framing and decking: site assembled

• Metal decking for floors: generally 22 to 16 gauge, 1-1/2 to 3 inches deep (Fig. 18):

- spans range from 6 to 14 feet depending on gauge and depth of deck, and thickness of concrete fill.

- available with closed cells, also referred to as cellular deck, to provide space for electrical/communications wiring.

- always filled with site placed normal weight or lightweight concrete, usually reinforced.

- decking may be formed to interlock with concrete fill for composite action; in addition metal studs may be welded through decking to top flanges of framing for their composite action with fill thus reducing their size.

• Grating: of metal or glass fiber reinforced plastic.

Framing/decking combined: fabricated

• Single or double tee's: precast of reinforced commonly prestressed concrete combining framing and decking into a single unit (Fig. 19):

- double tee: generally 12 to 32 inches deep and 8 to 10 feet wide; normally spanning 20 to 80 feet, potentially up to 95 feet.

- single tee: Usually 24 to 48 inches deep and 8 to 10 feet wide; normally spanning 50 to 110 feet, potentially up to 120 feet.

- camber generally provided to minimize apparent deflection under load.

• Hollow-core plank: precast of reinforced commonly prestressed concrete combining framing and decking into a single unit:

- depth varies from 4 to 12 inches; width, from 16 inches to 8 feet.

- spans generally from 12 to about 50 feet; potentially up to 55 feet.

Framing/decking combined: cast-in-place

Reinforced in directions monolithically placed concrete decks combining framing and decking (Fig. 20):

- spans for light loading to about 30 feet; 20 to 25 feet for heavy loads.

• Flat plate: a two-way slab of uniform thickness throughout.

• Flat slab: generally thickened over columns by drop panels to increase resistance to shear; tops of column may also be flared out for the same purpose.

• Waffle flat slab: thin decking and a grid of joists cast-in-place monolithically:

- joists are omitted over columns to form solid panels which may also be deeper than the joists to increase resistance to shear.

• Two-way slab: solid relatively thin decking supported by girders along column center lines.

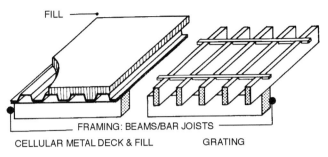

FILL

FRAMING: BEAMS/BAR JOISTS
CELLULAR METAL DECK & FILL   GRATING

Fig. 18. Metal framing and decking: site assembled

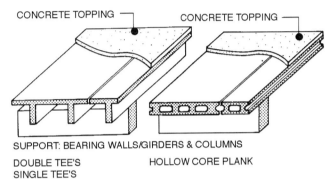

CONCRETE TOPPING   CONCRETE TOPPING

SUPPORT: BEARING WALLS/GIRDERS & COLUMNS
DOUBLE TEE'S   HOLLOW CORE PLANK
SINGLE TEE'S

Fig. 19. Precast framing/decking: fabricated

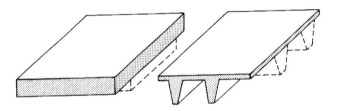

SUPPORT: COLUMNS/COLUMNS AND GIRDERS
FLAT PLATE/SLAB   ONE-WAY JOISTS
ONE- TWO-WAY SLAB   TWO-WAY JOISTS

Fig. 20. Framing/decking: monolithic concrete

SHELL

B1

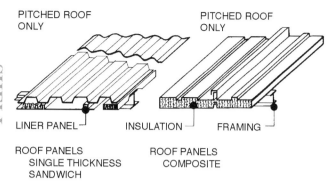

LINER PANEL — INSULATION — FRAMING —

ROOF PANELS
SINGLE THICKNESS
SANDWICH

ROOF PANELS
COMPOSITE

Fig. 21. Framing/decking: metal panels

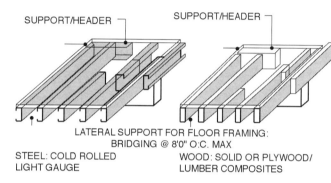

SUPPORT/HEADER —   SUPPORT/HEADER —

LATERAL SUPPORT FOR FLOOR FRAMING:
BRIDGING @ 8'0" O.C. MAX

STEEL: COLD ROLLED
LIGHT GAUGE

WOOD: SOLID OR PLYWOOD/
LUMBER COMPOSITES

Fig. 22. Joists/rafters

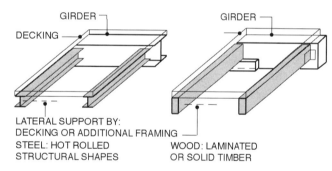

GIRDER —   GIRDER —

DECKING —

LATERAL SUPPORT BY:
DECKING OR ADDITIONAL FRAMING —

STEEL: HOT ROLLED
STRUCTURAL SHAPES

WOOD: LAMINATED
OR SOLID TIMBER

Fig. 23. Beams

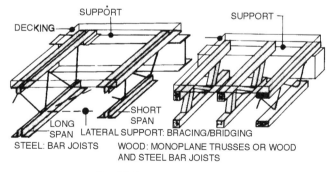

SUPPORT —   SUPPORT —

DECKING —

LONG SPAN   SHORT SPAN   LATERAL SUPPORT: BRACING/BRIDGING

STEEL: BAR JOISTS   WOOD: MONOPLANE TRUSSES OR WOOD
AND STEEL BAR JOISTS

Fig. 24. Trusses: flat top chord

Decking/roofing combined

Formed metal panels which function as combined roof decking and roofing (Fig. 21):

- available in: galvanized steel, either plain or prefinished, aluminum coated steel, aluminum, either plain or prefinished.

- may be single thickness or a built-up sandwich consisting of: exterior face panel, subgirts, insulation, and interior face panel.

- composite: with a rigid insulating core sandwiched between two face panels.

- spans generally 6 to 12 feet.

- supported by purlins which span between roof girders spaced about 20 to 30 feet on centers.

Roof/floor decks: typical framing

Joists/rafters

- Cold rolled light-gauge shapes used as roof/floor framing:

- gauge varies from 20 to 12; depth, from 6 to 12 inches.

- connections are made by welding and/or by self-drilling, self-tapping screws.

- allowable stresses and design in accordance with Specification for the Design of Cold-Formed Steel Structural Members, American Iron and Steel Institute (AISI).

- Dimensional lumber, 2 to 4 inches thick and 6 inches or more in width, used as roof/floor framing:

- moisture content should not exceed 19 percent.

- allowable stresses and design generally in accordance with National Design Specification for Wood Construction, National Forest and Paper Association (NFPA).

Beams

- Hot-rolled structural shapes:

- spacing usually 6 to 14 feet when used as framing supported on girders.

- connections welded and/or bolted.

- rolling mill tolerances have been established under ASTM Standard Specification for Rolled Steel Plates, Shapes, Sheet Piling, and Bars for Structural Use.

- decking usually used include: formed metal; precast concrete slabs, plank, channel slabs; cement bound organic fiber plank and boards.

- Laminated dimensional lumber or solid timber:

- spacing depends on decking selected: up to 4 feet for plywood, 6 to 8 feet for 2 inch nominal plank, 9 to 16 for 3 inch plank, up to 20 feet for 5 inch plank.

- available treated for resistance to decay.

Trusses: flat top chord

- Steel bar joists available as short-span and long-span framing:

- short-span bar joists usually 8 to 30 inches deep with spans from about 10 to 60 feet.

- long-span: 18 to 72 inches deep with spans from about 30 to 140 feet.

- connections to supports generally used: welding to steel girders or to steel bearing plates anchored in concrete or masonry; anchors to masonry.

- may be doubled, or tripled, to carry localized concentrated loads.

Trusses/beams: pitched/curved

- Monoplane trusses of dimensional lumber, or of top and bottom chords of wood with steel bar webs:

- spacing generally between 12 to 24 inches on centers.

- depth varies from 12 to 48 inches; spans for light loading, from 20 to 60 feet.

- Monoplane trusses of dimensional lumber:

- spacing generally 2 feet on centers using 3/8 inch thick plywood decking.

- spans up to 60 feet based on allowable tension value in bottom chord.

- slope usually from 2 inches per foot to 6 inches per foot, allowable spans increase with increase in slope.

- monoplane trusses, either with pitched or flat top chord, available of fire-retardant treated wood.

- Curved beams and arches of laminated surfaced dimensional lumber in various shapes:

- nominal width commonly from 3 to 10 inches for beams, up to 16 inches for arches.

- available treated for resistance to decay, but not fireretardant treated.

- commonly used with solid or laminated wood plank decking.

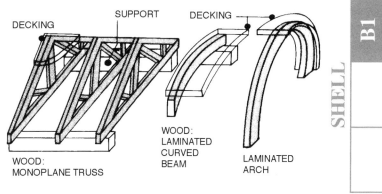

Fig. 25. Trusses/beams: pitched/curved

Summary of preliminary structural considerations

Structural frame

The structural frame is an integral part of any site assembled enclosure. Often a clear distinction cannot be made between what might be termed as a purely structural or a purely architectural component of such enclosure:

- Decking and framing of roof/floor decks may function:

- structurally: by carrying all superimposed gravity loads between vertical supports, and commonly by transferring lateral loads to vertical supports or other elements of the structural frame.

- architecturally: by serving as the substrate for roofing or flooring, or as substrate and flooring combined.

- Bearing walls are both a structural support for roof/floor decks and the vertical component of the envelope of such enclosure.

- Movement and/or deformations in the structural frame will affect most or all architectural components; conversely, movement or deformation in such components may affect the structural frame.

Preliminary considerations of a structural frame should primarily include roof/floor-decks which shelter and support the activities for which an enclosure is being provided:

Framing/decking combined:

Three basic types within the group are:

- Flat plate: which has a completely flat underside.

- Flat slab: with dropped panels at columns, columns generally round, with flared tops.

- Waffle slab: with solid panels of the same depth as slab at columns, and the rest of slab waffled to reduce the dead load of construction.

- Flat plates and flat slabs present few, or no obstructions to horizontal distribution of mechanical/electrical systems, but the vertical distribution must be carefully considered as openings in these assemblies are limited as to location and size.

Standard reusable forms available to be used in forming flat and waffle slabs include:

- forms for waffle slabs.
- steel forms for round columns with flared capitals, generally used for flat slab construction; and fiber tubes for forming round columns, often used with waffle slabs.

Two-way slabs are:

- generally economical for moderate spans and heavy loads.
- when minimum depth of construction is needed, edge beams may be made shallow and wide, in which case the columns need not line up as long as they fall within the width of the shallow beam.
- Two-way slabs with shallow beams may be used in multistory apartment construction when the underside of the slab can remain exposed.
- Ceilings are generally not used with two-way slab assemblies, nor are they required for a fire rated assembly.

Fabricated framing/decking:

- Precast concrete units used for flooring usually require a concrete topping:
- to even out all irregularities between individual units.
- to improve the load carrying ability of the units.
- to improve fire resistance of the assembly.
- Concrete toppings may also be required for roofs:
- to provide a smooth surface for the roofing.
- to improve the thermal resistance of the assembly when insulating concrete fill is used.

Framing and decking - site assembled:

- Joist framing utilizes light, closely spaced members. A variety of materials, sizes, and shapes is available. Joist framing is:
- versatile, economical system for residential, commercial, and light industrial construction where: spans are short to moderate, loads are light.
- prefabricated stressed skin panels consisting of plywood faces and wood joist ribs are available, widely used in prefabricated housing.
- Beam framing is the most versatile type with a wide choice of materials, sizes, and shapes. Beam framing is:
- most economical for moderate spans and moderate loads,
- can also be adapted to carry heavy loads, with a corresponding increase in unit cost.
- not suitable for long spans.
- when beams frame into girders, the depth of girder usually determines the overall depth of construction.
- Framed assemblies, with the exception of steel bar joists, will not permit ductwork, piping, and conduits to be run within the depth of the framing members, thus requiring additional depth between floors to accommodate such services.

Decking component selection will be influenced by the framing components:

- Wood planking or plywood may be used over metal framing:
- should be secured using self-tapping metal screws or
- a wood nailer should be attached to the top flange of the member first.

- Roll-formed metal decking, when in light gauges, is difficult to weld to supporting steel framing; the use of welding washers is recommended:
- decking spanning between widely spaced framing may require temporary shoring during placement of concrete fill.
- Precast planks, whether of concrete, or fiberboard:
- are generally secured to metal framing using special clips supplied by plank manufacturer.
- diaphragm action is not provided in a roof assembly by precast planks attached in this manner.
- Wood planking, either solid or laminated, is best suited for:
- post-and-beam or heavy timber framing.
- to span between laminated arches or rigid frames where it generally also serves as the finished interior surface.

Spans

Allowable spans of any structural systems are determined by combined dead and live loads and the relative capacities of the various materials and systems. Structural and construction considerations include:

- Stress capacity of components of a given structural system.
- Allowable or acceptable deflection limits, which may vary:
- allowable deflection is often given as a ratio of 1/360 of clear span, without regard to properties of the frame and/or components affected by it, and may not be sufficient to prevent deformations developing: inelastic materials may crack considerably before the limit of 1/360 of span is reached.
- Camber is normally provided in steel, glue-lam, and precast concrete members to compensate for live and dead load deflections. In roof framing such camber may be increased to facilitate storm drainage.

Bracing between framing members is required in many structural systems as the forces on the beams, trusses or joists may cause lateral buckling.

- Diaphragm action to resist lateral wind and seismic forces can be achieved in a number of ways to reduce isolated stresses and transmit them through the entire system:
- in wood framing assemblies, usually by diagonal planking or plywood used for decking.
- in steel framed assemblies, by diagonal bracing, or by roll-formed metal decking.
- in concrete assemblies by combined stress capacities of steel reinforcement and concrete coverage.
- To qualify as a diaphragm, a floor and/or roof assembly must be capable of transmitting lateral forces to vertical components of the structural frame, such as shear walls, without deflecting to where such deflection could cause damage to a vertical component.
- the effects of lateral loads on the exposed components of roof and floor assemblies
- the roofing membrane and flooring
- should be investigated: structural frames adequate to resist all vertical and lateral loads may still deform too excessively for some types of flooring and/or roofing.

Other considerations may include:

- A column, once installed, can, in most instances, no longer be removed.

- Each type of floor and roof assembly has a certain range over which it is most economical.

- The longer the span, the greater the overall depth of the assembly and the greater the cost per unit of area covered.

Trusses as primary supports

Heavy trusses are used as girders, the primary supports, to carry roof/ floor-decks:

- Typical configurations for trusses are: crescent, also known as bowstring, with straight or curved bottom chord; double-pitched with straight bottom chord; double-pitched with straight bottom chord; double-pitched with pitched bottom chord, also known as scissors truss; single-pitch with straight bottom chord, referred to as sawtooth:

- lateral bracing for top chords must be provided; secondary framing selected will influence spacing of trusses.

- thermal expansion of long-span trusses must be considered in the details of supports.

- concentrated loads to be supported at panel points only.

- long-span, flat top chord trusses are not economical in wood.

- pitched top chord trusses in wood are not economical for spans over 60 feet; in long span trusses, wood is best suited for bow-string types.

- ceilings, light fixtures, or equipment may be suspended from the bottom chords of trusses.

- long-span trusses generally fabricated off-site. Shape and size of individual panels will be influenced by available transportation facilities, clearances at underpasses, and limitations imposed by applicable state laws.

- Floor to floor height trusses, incorporated in partitions, have been used:

- in residential construction.

- in industrial buildings where mechanical equipment and services to the floor above could be located within the trusses.

- such trusses have also been used in multistory construction to carry suspended lower floors.

Arches

Arches are curved frames combining girders and columns into a single unit. The configurations may be:

- radial, parabolic, tudor, gothic, A-frame, rigid frames.

- rigid frames are arches with straight rather than curved or sloping vertical components.

- arches may be two-hinged at supports, or three-hinged at supports and crown.

- waterproofing of hinged joint at crown may present a problem.

- outward thrust at supports must be resisted by foundations, buttresses or horizontal ties.

- Site assembled arches functioning as girders may be:

- structural steel shapes, about 20 feet on centers.

- reinforced concrete, about 20 feet on centers.

Arches, domes and vaults, consisting of curved monolithic decks, which combine means of support and envelope into one:

- of cast-in-place reinforced concrete.

- of essentially constant cross section throughout, or of heavier

sections such as ribs, curved girders connected with thin diaphragms.

- extensive formwork generally required:

- small domes may be cast over flexible membranes inflated to resist the weight of fresh concrete.

Barrel vaults generally used in multiples, with adjacent shells bracing each other:

- half-shells, with an opening at the crown to admit light and/or air are also used.

A comparison of wood, steel and concrete systems is indicated in Figs. 26, 27 and 28 from Schodek (1992), which provides a thorough discussion of the various system options. In Figs. 26, note that in order that typical sizes of different timber members can be relatively compared, the diagrams are scaled to represent typical span lengths for each of the respective elements. The span lengths that are actually possible for each element are noted by the "minimum" and "maximum" span marks.

Articles follow in this chapter that explore each of these structural options. The above discussion does not include tensioned fabric structures, which are considered in a separate article in this chapter.

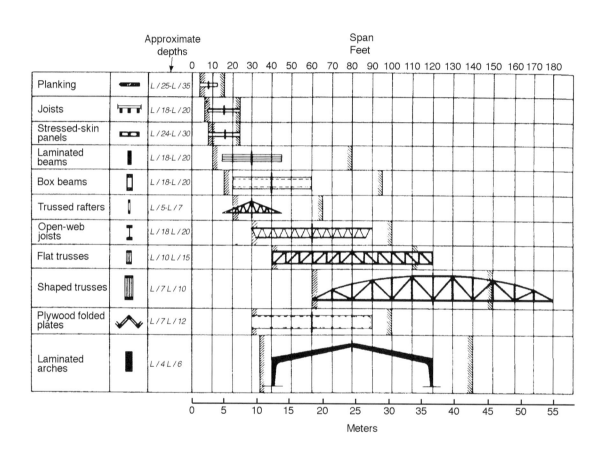

Fig. 26. Approximate span ranges for timber systems. Source: Schodek (1992). Reproduced by permission of Prentice Hall.

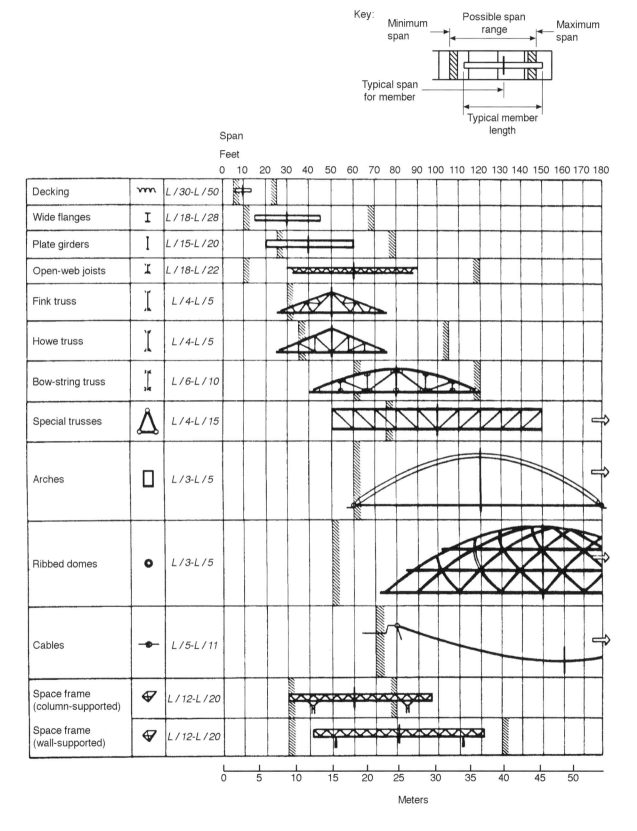

Fig. 27. Aproximate span ranges for steel systems. Source: Schodek (1992). Reproduced by permission of Prentice Hall.

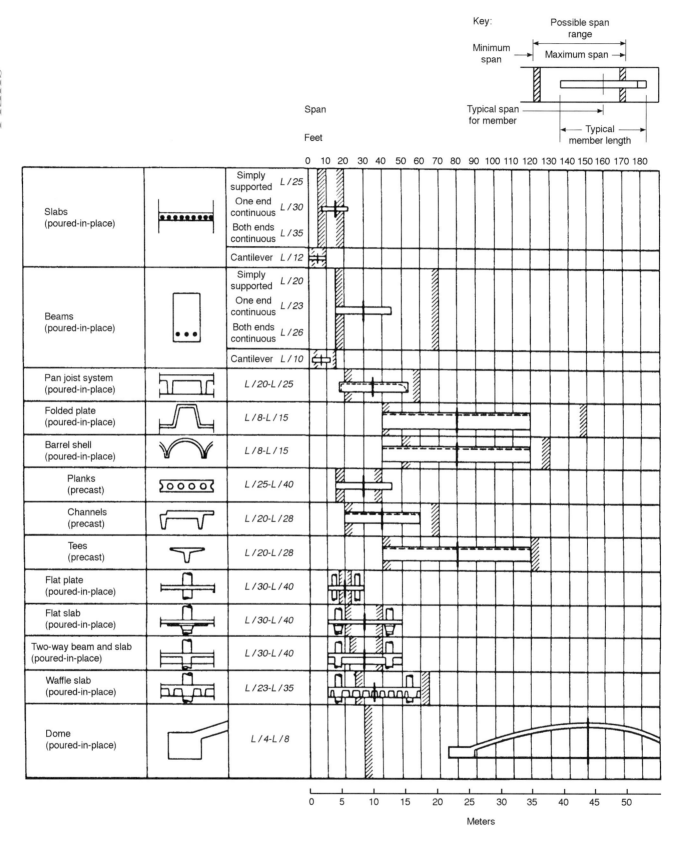

Fig. 28. approximate span for reinforced concrete systems.
Source: Schodek (1992). Reproduced by permission of Prentice Hall.

Design loads

Summary: The various loads imposed on a building's structure are defined as design loads, and include "dead loads," the permanent forces in and on a building, and "live loads" generated by variable conditions internally and externally. Internal live loads are created by occupants, movable equipment and thermal or vibratory conditions caused from internal operations. External live loads are imposed by wind, water, snow, earthquakes, thermal changes and soil pressures.

Key words: earthquake, live loads, dead loads, occupancy loads, snow, wind.

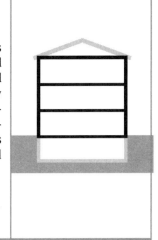

Overview of design loads

Assessing the varied forces imposed on a building during its lifetime requires a thorough understanding of the building, including:

- how it will be used,

- where it is located,

- the geologic soil conditions of the site,

- applicable code requirements,

- the characteristics and interactions of materials used, and

- the methods employed to construct it.

Classification of all such forces are commonly translated into the type of design loads, as follows:

- Dead Loads: Dead loads consist of all forces which are permanent forces in and on a building. These include:

- Gravitational forces accumulated from the materials used to construct the frame, the enclosures, the finishes and the fixed operating systems.

- Loads from equipment which is installed permanently in identified locations within the building.

- Live Loads: Live loads consist of all forces generated by variable conditions internally and externally.

- Internal live loads are created by occupants, movable furniture, temporary storage items, movable equipment and thermal or vibratory conditions caused from internal operations.

- External live loads are imposed by wind, water, snow, earthquakes, thermal changes and soil pressures.

- Impact loads from any source may add to live load considerations.

1 Dead loads

The source of dead loads is primarily generated by the accumulation of weights from all permanently fixed parts of the constructed building. Typical examples of common dead loads are:

- All the structural elements, enclosing walls, floors, roofs, ceilings, interior walls, built-in furniture, and

- Fixed-in-place equipment like heating/cooling equipment, plumbing, light fixtures, fans and ducts.

For these types of loads, the recommended minimum loads have been established in order to maintain some consistency in basic values for materials and construction systems. Table 1 lists the weights of common building materials and constructions. Table 2 contains volumetric weights of materials. The actual dead loads must always be figured on the basis of the actual amount of material used at the location being analyzed. Both tables are useful resources for known quantities of materials contributing to the dead load portion of total load on a structure.

Dead loads are often approximated as uniformly distributed loads for known structural systems such as floor framing systems including all finishes. The following is an example of the dead load summary of a common structural floor system:

Item	Uniform dead load (pounds per sq. ft.)
Vinyl tile finish flooring	1.4
3 in. concrete deck over	37.5
steel deck form	1.2
Steel floor joists (estimated)	5.1
Suspended ceiling w/ metal lath and plaster	10.0
Light fixture allowance	.8
Total uniform dead load =	56.0 psf

Concentrated loads are large loads applied at a point or over a very small area. The typical illustration of a concentrated dead load is where one end of a secondary beam is supported at a designated location by a primary beam. For instance, a structural floor slab is supported by secondary beams spaced at 8'-0" center to center (c/c). These secondary beams are in turn supported by another more primary beam. The first causes a concentrated load on the primary beam at the points of connection, occurring at 8'-0" c/c.

Another example: consider that a piece of equipment has a fixed location and weighs 2800 pounds. It has four legs, each attached to the supporting floor structural system. Each leg transmits 700 pounds on the floor at an identifiable point of application. That unique point of application will determine the requirements of the supporting structural element. The size of the concentrated load and its location will

Author: Martin D. Gehner, P.E.

References: AASHTO. 1992. *Standard Specification for Highway Bridges.* HB-15-92. Washington, DC: American Association of State Highway and Transportation Officials.

ASCE. 1996. *Minimum Design Loads for Buildings and Other Structures.* ANSI/ASCE 7-95. New York: American Society of Civil Engineers.

BOCA. 1993. *National Building Code.* Twelfth edition. Country Club Hills, IL: Building Officials & Code Administrators International.

B1

SHELL

Table 1. Dead Loads - weights of building materials and construction [1]

Weights of masonry include mortar but not plaster coatings. For coatings add the weight appropriate for the type of coating material. Average values of weights are given. In some cases there is considerable range of weight for the same construction due to different manufacturers of similar products.

	Load, psf		Load, psf		Load, psf
Walls:		**Walls** (continued)		**Floors:** (continued)	
Clay brick:		Wood: (continued):		Wood joists:	
4 in. high absorption	34	2x4 studs plastered one side	12	2x8 @ 16 in. o.c.	2.3
4 in. medium absorption	39	2x4 studs plastered two sides	22	2x10 @ 16 in. o.c.	2.9
4 in., low absorption	46	2x6 studs plastered one side	13	2x12 @ 16 in. o.c.	3.5
8 in., high absorption	69	2x6 studs plastered two sides	23	1 3/4x12 Trus Joist @ 16 in.	2.1
8 in., medium absorption	79			1 3/4x14 Trus Joist @ 16 in.	2.3
8 in., low absorption	89	**Floors:**		1 3/4x16 Trus Joist @ 16 in.	2.6
Sand-lime brick:		Cement finish, per inch thick	12	Waterproofing, 5 ply membrane	3
4 in.	38	Concrete slab: per inch thick			
8 in.	74	Plain, stone aggregate	12	**Ceilings:**	
Concrete brick:		Plain, lightweight aggregate	8.5	Acoustic fiber tile	1
4 in., heavy aggregate	46	Reinforced, stone aggregate	12.5	Plaster on tile or concrete	5
4 in., lightweight aggregate	33	Reinforced, lightweight	9.5	Plaster on metal lath	10
8 in., heavy aggregate	89	One way ribbed 20 in. forms		Suspended metal lath and plaster	15
8 in., lightweight aggregate	68	with 5 in. wide by 10 in.		Solid i in. T.&G. wood	2.5
Concrete block:		high rib and 2.5 in. topping	60		
4 in., heavy aggregate	30	One-way ribbed 30 in. forms		**Roofs:**	
4 in., lightweight aggregate	20	with 5 in. wide by 10 in.		Asphalt shingles	2
6 in., heavy aggregate	42	high rib and 2.5 in. topping	52	Cement tile:	
6 in., lightweight aggregate	28	Two-way ribbed slab19 in.		2 in. book tile	12
8 in., heavy aggregate	55	forms with 5 in. wide by		3 in. book tile	20
8 in., lightweight aggregate	37	10 in. high ribs and 3 in.		Roman tile	12
12 in., heavy aggregate	85	topping	71.3	Spanish tile	19
12 in., lightwt. aggregate	55	Two-way ribbed slab 30 in.		Composition built-up:	
Clay tile, 4 in.	23	forms with 6 in. wide by		Three-ply ready roofing	1.5
Facing tile, 4 in.	25	10 in. high ribs and 3 in.		Three-ply felt and gravel	5.5
Glass block, 4 in.	18	topping	79.8	Five-ply felt and gravel	6.5
Gypsum block, 4 in.	12.5	Precast hollow core slab		Copper or tin	1.4
Plaster:		6 in. with 2 in. topping	70	Corrugated metal:	
Solid plaster, 1 in.	10	Precast hollow core slab		20 gauge steel	1.7
Solid plaster, 2 in.	20	8 in. with 2 in. topping	82	24 gauge steel	1.2
Hollow plaster, 4 in	22	Cork tile	0.5	28 gauge steel	0.8
Gypsum, 1 in. on metal lath	8	Gypsum slab, per in. thick	5	Decking: per in. of thickness	
Cement, 1 in. on metal lath	10	Hardwood, per in. thick	4	Concrete plank	12.5
Stucco, 7/8 in.	10	Linoleum or vinyl tile	1.4	Poured gypsum	6.5
Terra-cotta tile	25	Plywood, per in. thick	3	Vermiculite concrete	2.6
Windows, glass, frame and sash	8	Terrazzo, 1 in. on 2 in. concrete		Wood plank or plywood	3.4
Wood:		base	32	Insulation: per in. of thickness	
2x4 studs @ 12 in. o.c.	1.8	Timber decking:		Fiberglass, bat	0.5
2x4 studs @ 16 in. o.c.	1.4	2 in. nominal thickness	4.1	Fiberglass, rigid	1.5
2x6 studs @ 12 in. o.c.	2.9	3 in. nominal thickness	6.8	Loose fill	0.5
2x6 studs @ 16 in. o.c.	2.2	4 in. nominal thickness	9.6	Polystyrene board	0.2
				Skylight, frame and lexan	8
				Slate, 1/4 in. thick	10
				Wood Shingles	3

[1] Data is adapted from American National Standard Building Code Requirements For Minimum Design Loads in Buildings and Other Structures (ANSI A58.1-192)

Table 2. Volummetric Weights of Materials for Design Loads

Values are representative of materials only and may vary slightly.

	lb/ft^3		lb/ft^3		lb/ft^3
Concrete and Masonry:		**Liquids:**		**Minerals:**	
Concrete, Plain:		Alcohol	49	Asbestos	143
Lightweight aggregate	108	Acids:		Bauxite	159
Stone aggregate	144	Muriatic	75	Borax	109
Concrete, reinforced:		Nitric	94	Chalk	137
Lightweight aggregate	111	Sulfuric	112	Dolomite	181
Stone aggregate	150	Gasoline	42	Feldspar	159
Masonry:		Petroleum, crude	55	Gypsum, alabaster	159
Brick, Soft	100	Oils:		Lime, hydrated	45
Brick, Medium	115	Vegetable	75	Magnesite	187
Brick, Hard	130	Mineral and lubricants	57	Pumice	40
Granite	153	Water:		Quartz, flint	165
Limestone	147	Fresh	62.4	Sandstone, bluestone	147
Marble	156	Ice	57	Shale, slate	172
Sandstone	137	Sea water	64		
Terra cotta	120	Snow, fresh fallen	8	**Plastics:**	
				Acrylics	74
Earth excavated:		**Metals and Alloys:**		Cellulosics	80
Clay:		Aluminum, cast or rolled	165	Fluorocarbons	137
Dry	63	Antimony	416	Melamine	94
Damp and plastic	110	Brass, cast or rolled	526	Phenolics	119
Mixed with gravel, dry	100	Bronze	552	Polyethylene	56
Coal:		Chromium	443	Polystyrene	66
Anthracite	58	Copper, cast or rolled	556	Polyurethane	81
Coke	32	Gold, cast or hammered	1205	Reinforced polyesters	131
Earth:		Iron, cast	450	Silicones	117
Dry	95	Wrought	480	Vinyls	104
Moist	96	Steel	490		
Mud	115	Stainless	500	**Other Solids:**	
Peat, turf	32	Lead	710	Asphaltum	81
Riprap:		Magnesium	109	Glass:	
Sandstone	90	Manganese	456	Common	156
Shale	105	Nickel	545	Plate or crown	161
Sand and gravel:		Monel metal	556	Grains:	
Dry and loose	105	Platinum	1330	Barley	39
Packed	115	Silver, cast or hammered	590	Corn, rye, wheat	48
Wet	120	Tin, cast or hammered	459	Oats	32
		Tungsten	1180	Pitch	69
		Vanadium	372	Tar, bituminous	75
		Zinc, cast or rolled	449		

Table 3. Minimum uniformly distributed live loads

Occupancy or use	Live load, psf[1]	Occupancy or use	Live load, psf[1]
Office buildings:		Offices	50
Apartments (see Residential)		Lobbies	100
Armories and drill rooms	150	Corridors above first floor	80
Assembly halls and other places of		File and computer rooms require	
assembly		heavier loads based upon	
Fixed seats	60	anticipated occupancy	
Movable seats	100	Penal institutions:	
Platforms (assembly)	100	Cell blocks	40
Balcony (exterior)	100	Corridors	100
On one- and two- family residences only		Residential:	
and not exceeding 100 sq.ft.	60	Multifamily houses:	
Bowling alleys, poolrooms, and		Private apartments	40
similar recreational areas	75	Public rooms	100
Corridors:		Corridors	80
First floor	100	Dwellings:	
Other floors same as occupancy		First floor	40
served except as indicated		Second floor and habitable attics	20
Dance halls and ballrooms	100	Uninhabitable attics	20
Dining rooms and restraurants	100	Hotels:	
Dwellings (see Residential)		Guest rooms	40
Fire escapes	100	Public rooms	100
On multi- or single-family residential		Corridors serving public rooms	100
buildings only	40	Corridors	80
Garages (passenger cars only)	50	Reviewing stands and bleachers	100
For trucks and buses use AASHTO HB-15*		Schools:	
lane loads		Classrooms	40
		Corridors	80
Grandstands (see Reviewing stands)		Sidewalks, vehicular driveways, and yards	
Gymnasiums, main floors and balconies	100	subject to trucking	250
Hospitals:		Skating rinks	100
Operating rooms, laboratories	60	Stairs and exitways	100
Private rooms	40	Storage warehouse, light	125
Wards	40	Storage warehouse, heavy	250
Corridors above the first floor	80	Stores:	
Hotels (see Residential)		Retail:	
Libraries:		First-floor, rooms	100
Reading rooms	60	Upper floors	75
Stack rooms (books and shelving at		Wholesale	125
65 pcf) but not less than	150	Theaters:	
Corridors above first floor	80	Aisles, corridors, and lobbies	100
Manufacturing:		Orchestra floors	60
Light	125	Balconies	60
Heavy	250	Stage floors	150
Marquees	75	Yards and terraces, pedestrians	100

*American Association of State Highway and Transportation Officials
[1] 1 psf = 4.88 kg/m^2

significantly influence the required size, shape, and bracing of the supporting structural element, along with the detailed connection securing the leg to the structure.

2 Live loads

All variable loads imposed on a building are live loads by definition. Live loads are always additive to dead loads to determine the structural requirements of the building. For reasons of analytical clarity and to understand the structural requirements under different combinations of live and dead loads, gravitational live loads are investigated separately from lateral or angular-applied live loads imposed from winds and earthquakes.

Occupancy loads

Occupancy loads are the typical gravitational loads which a structure must safely support. Occupancy loads include forces not only from people movements but also from reasonable allowances for movable furniture within a space. Table 3 lists the minimum uniformly distributed live loads established by U. S. Codes for the design of building structures. A prudent designer will always assess the adequacy of these minimum values in order to match the design requirement with the real conditions associated with the building's functions.

Concentrated live loads

In addition to the uniform occupancy loads, in cases where live loads generate concentrations, the concentrated loads of Table 4 must be included. Unless otherwise specified, the indicated concentration of load is assumed to occupy an area of 2'-6" square, and located so as to produce the maximum stress conditions in the supporting structural member.

Machinery and elevators

For structural safety, the weight of machinery and moving loads shall be increased as follows to allow for impact conditions:

- For elevator machinery, the loads to be increased 100 percent;

- For lightweight machinery driven by motor or shaft, the loads to be increased by 20 percent;

- For power driven reciprocating machinery, the load to be increased by 50 percent;

- For hangers of floors and balconies, the loads to be increased by 33 percent. The increases for all machinery should be verified by the manufacturer's recommendations.

Cranes moving on fixed tracks

All craneways shall have their design loads increased for impact as follows:

- A vertical force equal to 25 percent of the maximum wheel load;

- A lateral force equal to 20 percent of the trolley weight plus the lifted load applied one-half at the top of each rail;

- A longitudinal force equal to 10 percent of the maximum wheel loads of the crane applied at the top rail.

Reduction in live loads

Design live loads on a structure may be reduced under certain limitations as specified by the governing code. Generally, as stated in ANSI (1996), the minimum design live load for members having an influence area of 400 square feet or more is permitted to be reduced in accordance with the following equation:

$$L = L_o \left(0.25 + \frac{15}{A_i} \right)$$

where:
L = the reduced live load in pounds per square foot
L_o = the unreduced live load in pounds per square foot
A_i = Influence area in square feet, taken as four times the tributary area for a column, two times the tributary area for a beam, and the panel area for a two-way slab.

Table 4. Concetrated loads

Location	Load lb
Elevator machine room grating (an area of 4 sq in.)	300
Finish light floor plate construction (an area of 1 sq in)	200
Garages	*
Office floors	2,000
Scuttles, skylight ribs, and accessible ceilings	200
Sidewalks	8,000
Stair treads (on center of tread)	300

Floors in garages or portions of buildings used for storage of motor vehicles shall be designed for the uniformly distributed live loads of Table 3 or the following concentrated loads:

For passenger care accommodating not more than nine passengers. 2,000 lb. acting on an area of 20 sq. in.

Mechanical parking structure without slab or deck, passenger cars only. 1500 lb per wheel.

For trucks or buses, maximum axle load on an area of 20 sq in.

B1

SHELL

Table 5. Minimum roof live loads

in pounds per square foot of horizontal projection

	Tributary loaded area in square feet for any structural member		
Roof slope	0 to 200	201 to 600	Over 600
Flat or rise less than 4 in. per ft Arch or dome with rise less than 1/8 of span	20	16	12
Rise 4 in. per ft to less than 12 in. per ft Arch or dome with rise 1/8 of span to less than 3/8 of span	16	14	12
Rise 12 in. per ft and greater Arch or dome with rise 3/8 of span or greater	12	12	12

The limitations of this reduction shall not be less than:

- 50 percent of the unreduced live load for members supporting one floor, and

- not less than 40 percent of the unreduced live load for members supporting more than one floor.

For live loads of 100 psf or less, no reduction may be made for occupied areas of public assembly, for garages, for one-way slabs or for roofs. For live loads greater than 100 psf, the design live load have some limitations which must be determined by the code authority having jurisdiction for the building. For live loads greater than 100 psf, no reduction shall be made for design live loads except for the design live loads on columns which may be reduced 20 percent.

Minimum roof loads and snow loads
Ordinary roofs shall be designed for minimum design live loads as stated in Table 5 or as snow loads as specified for the specific building location, whichever is greater. Each roof must be carefully considered for proper water drainage. If deflections of members might cause ponding of water or snow, then additional associated loads should be added to the design live load.

When roofs are used for incidental promenade purposes, they shall be designed for a minimum live load of 60 psf. If the roof is used for assembly purposes or for roof-gardens, then the minimum design live load shall be 100 psf. Design live loads for other special roof uses should be directed and approved by the building official of the code authority having jurisdiction.

Snow live loads to be used for the design of buildings or other structures are given on a map such as the illustrative reference of Fig. 1. Basic ground snow loads are given in pounds per square foot for a 50-year recurrence interval.

For buildings which present a high degree of hazard to life and property, a design snow load for a 100-year recurrence interval or equivalent value shall be used. For regions where unusually high snow fall accumulation occurs, such as in mountain regions, the design snow load should be determined by the local requirements. For buildings with no human occupants, the snow load may be taken for a 25-year recurrence interval.

Snow loads on roofs vary according to the multiple complications of roof forms, wind patterns and exposure. All codes have provisions which must be met according to the specific roof conditions. These must be assessed carefully in order to determine the possible increased loads due to drifting or accumulations. Some highly pitched roofs over heated areas may create slides to accumulate on adjacent roofs or roof segments over unheated portions. The variables are numerous and worst cases must be understood in determining the governing condition for maximum stress on supporting members.

Soil and hydrostatic pressures
For vertical structures below grade provision must be made to determine the superimposed pressures from soils, from high water tables, or from surcharges on the soils from fixed or moving loads. Lateral pressures from adjacent soils place an increasing uniform load on the wall from grade down to the height of the wall. If the wall restrains water, the full hydrostatic pressure on the wall must be included as a design load.

In the design of basement floors and similar horizontal construction below grade, the upward pressure of water, if any, shall be taken as the full hydrostatic pressure over the entire floor area.

Wind loads
Assessing the magnitude of wind loads on buildings requires extensive investigation of basic velocity wind pressures prevailing at the

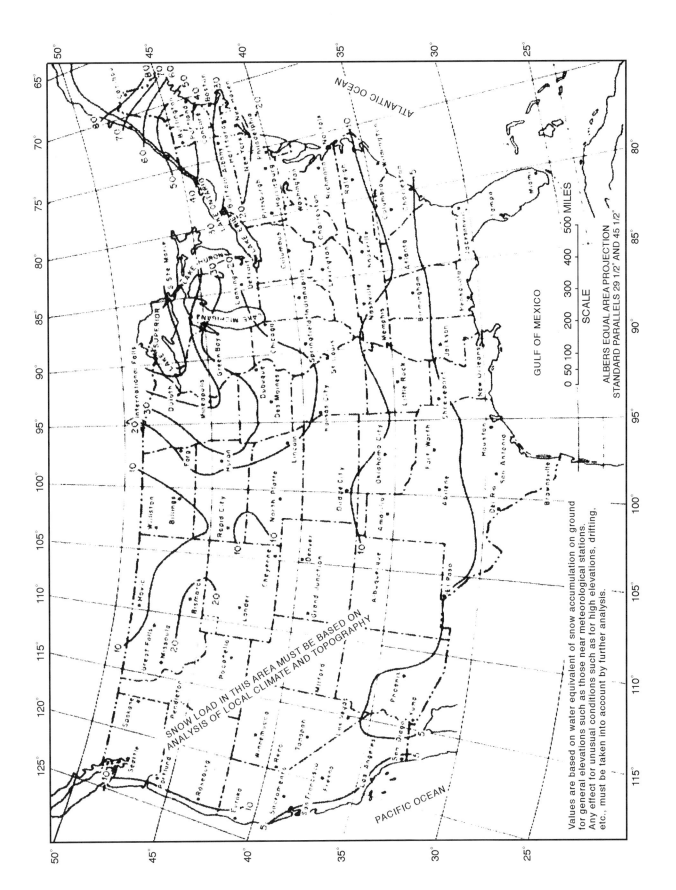

Fig. 1. Basic ground snow loads

building site, the building's form(s), its structural system(s), its foundations and soil conditions, and its surrounding urban or open terrain. Sustained pressures on the whole structure must be considered from each potential face of incidence. Further consideration must be given to forces from wind gusts and to limits of lateral movement. Building elements, such as individual windows, doors, wall panels, roof eaves and similar building parts, must be investigated for the higher pressures from larger local wind forces dislodging these elements from their secured locations.

For guidance in the assessment of wind loads on buildings and other structures the reader is referred to the applicable code having jurisdiction or to the standard outlined in Section 6, Wind Loads (ASCE 1996).

Earthquake loads

Every building and every portion thereof are designed and constructed to resist the stresses produced by lateral forces. Such forces are assumed to come from any horizontal direction. The source of lateral forces may be either from winds or from earthquakes and the engineer may assume that the loads therefrom will not occur simultaneously. Recent research and study of the effects of earthquakes on buildings and structures has permitted extensive development of the analysis and design of earthquake resistant buildings.

For guidance in the assessment of earthquake loads on buildings and other structures the reader is referred to the applicable code having jurisdiction or to the standard described in detail in Section 9, Earthquake Loads (ANSI 1996).

Combining loads

Except when applicable codes make other provisions, all the loads listed herein shall be considered to act in the following combinations, whichever produce the greatest resistant requirements in the building, foundation, or structural member concerned. The most demanding strength requirement may occur when one or more of the following general combinations of loading:

1. D	where: D = dead load
2. D + L	L = live load
3. D + (W or E)	W = wind load
4. D + T	E = earthquake load
5. D + L + (W or E)	T = load due to contraction
6. D + L + T	or expansion resulting
7. D + (W or E) + T	from temperature changes
8. D + L + (W or E) + T	or other causes

When using the analysis method Allowable Stress Design, the total of the combined load effects may be multiplied by the following applicable probability factors:

- 1.0 for combinations 1 through 4

- 0.75 for combinations 5 through 7

- 0.66 for combination 8

When using the analysis method Strength Design, the service loads are multiplied by safety factors identified as load factors. Common load factors are 1.4 for dead loads and 1.7 for live loads. When combined, the total design loads are then referred to as ultimate loads. Load factors for wind and earthquake loads are described in ANSI (1996).

Structural design-wood

Summary: This section provides an overview of common applications of wood as a structural material. Topics covered include light wood framing and trusses, timber and stressed-skin panel construction.

Humpback Bridge near Covington, Virginia. 1857. Courtesy: Eric DeLony, National Park Service.

Key words: engineered wood, joists, laminated wood, plywood, rafters, stressed skin panels, timber, trusses, wood.

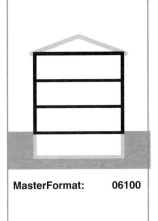

MasterFormat: 06100

SHELL

B1

One of the oldest construction materials throughout history, every building tradition has discovered ways to design and craft wood materials at hand into unique applications, including substantial bridge and architectural structures. The wide variety of wood species offer distinct properties for unique and beautiful interpretations for design and construction. The following information provides guidance for common structural applications. As a renewable resource, many species of wood are excellent sustainable yield materials which are of importance to the designer and builder. Due to increasing demand, new engineered wood products are being produced. Many of these new products decrease the waste of wood fragments while increasing the predictability of performance of structural wood members.

Classifications and grading processes of wood material respond directly to the identification of specific properties and applications. The variables of grain, density, knots, shakes and moisture content present a material which in its natural state must be used with sensitive insight to properly design for its unique characteristics and properties. The material is very strong by nature. Natural variations can be controlled by selective cutting and bonding. The newer structural wood products are produced by cutting out the weak and variable portions of the natural material and then reforming it into products which enhance the natural material's properties. Such processes reduce the negative influence of knots, splits and shakes in the manufactured product.

This section presents wood products which are important to structural applications in buildings. The products included are lumber, timber, wood decking, plywood, laminated members, trus-joists, and proprietary engineered wood formulations. Fig. 1 shows typical wood sections.

Lumber

Structural lumber is rough-sawn from logs and then planed and surfaced to a standard net size. A full-cut piece is referred to as the nominal size; however the rough-cut piece is cut smaller and then finished to the actual size, sometimes referred to as the dressed size, of the piece. A complete listing of all sizes, with associated section properties, can be found in the National Design Specification (AFPA 1992) and in most wood reference manuals. Representative examples are shown in Table 1.

Sawn lumber is cut into lengths with rectangular and square cross sections. The narrow dimension is always referred to as the thickness and the larger dimension referred to as the width. Normal identifying reference is by nominal size, such a 2x8 or 2x12, whereas actual detailing and construction must use the actual piece size. Lumber of rectangular cross section, 2 to 4 inches in thickness and 4 inches or more in width are typically used for structural framing purposes like floor joists, roof rafters and similar structural elements. These types of members are loaded on the narrow face. Wood studs, commonly 2x4s or 2x6s spaced 12 inches to 16 inches on center, are installed as wall framing to carry gravitational loads primarily with additional capacity for lateral wind loads.

Timber

Timber beams have cross sections 3 inches or more in thickness and 8 inches or more in width and graded according to its strength in bending when loaded on the narrow face. Lumber of square, or nearly square sections, 5"x5" or larger are graded for the primary use as columns and posts carrying longitudinal loads. They are suitable for uses in which strength in bending is possible but not the primary stress.

Author: Martin D. Gehner, P.E.

Credits: Illustrations are developed from National Forest Products Association (now American Forest and Paper Association) publications. The section on stressed skin panels, adapted from Time Saver Standards 6th edition, was originally authored by William J. LeMessurier and Albert G. H. Dietz.

References: AFPA. 1992. *ANSI/NFoPA NDS-1991 National Design Specification for Wood Construction.* Revised 1991 edition. Washington, DC: American Forest & Paper Association.

AFPA. 1992. *ANSI/NFoPA NDS-1991 National Design Specification Supplement, Design Values for Wood Construction.* Revised edition. Washington, DC: American Forest & Paper Association.

American Institute of Timber Construction (AITC). 1994. *Timber Construction Manual.* Fourth edition. New York: John Wiley & Sons.

American Plywood Association (APA) - The Engineered Wood Association. *Grades and Specifications.* Tacoma, WA: American Plywood Association.

Canadian Wood Council. (CWC). 1991. *Wood Reference Handbook.* Ottawa: Canadian Wood Council.

Western Wood Products Association (WWPA) 1996. *Western Woods Use Book, Structural Data and Design Tables.* Fourth edition. Portland, OR: Western Wood Products Association.

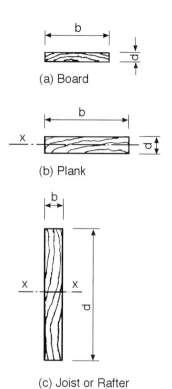

(a) Board

(b) Plank

(c) Joist or Rafter

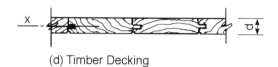

(d) Timber Decking

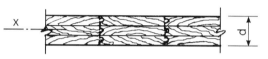

(e) Laminated Wood Decking

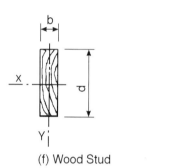

(f) Wood Stud

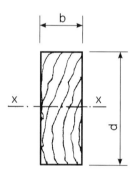

(g) Timber Beam

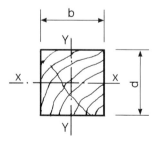

(h) Timber Post or Column

Table 1. Examples of section sizes of standard sawn lumber.

Nominal Size b x d	Standard Dressed Size, b x d inches
1 x 4	3/4" x 3-1/2"
1 x 6	3/4" x 5-1/2"
1 x 8	3/4" x 7-1/4"
2 x 6	1-1/2" x 5-1/2"
2 x 8	1-1/2" x 7-1/4"
2 x 10	1-1/2" x 9-1/4"
2 x 12	1-1/2" x 11-1/4"
3 x 12	2-1/2" x 11-1/4"
4 x 4	3-1/2" x 3-1/2"
4 x 6	3-1/2" x 5-1/2"
4 x 8	3-1/2" x 7-1/4"
4 x 10	3-1/2" x 9-1/4"

Fig. 1. Typical wood sections. (note: TJI™, Microlam™ and Parallam™ are registered trademarks of Trus Joist MacMillan, Boise, Idaho.)

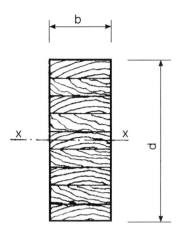

(i) Laminated Beam

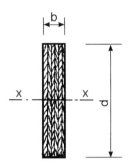

(j) Microlam Beam

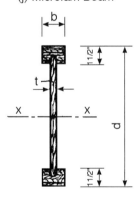

(k) Trus Joint

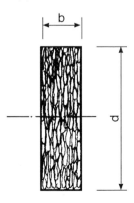

(l) Paralam Beam

Wood decking

When a piece of lumber is placed in a position where it is loaded on the wide face of the member, it is referred to as a plank. Plank boards are frequently milled so that edges are shaped with tongues and grooves so that when installed against another they form a deck. Decking may be used in residential or industrial buildings for floors or roofs. In residential construction where loads are light, deflection and bending usually govern the structural design while appearance will govern the quality of grade specified. The most common nominal depths of timber deck is 2, 3 and 4 inches. Typical spans for tongue and grooved deck systems range from 3'-0" to 12'-0". In light frame floor and roof framing systems where joists and rafters are spaced 16 inches on center, the deck is called a sub-floor. The most popular sub-flooring material used is plywood with thickness of 5/8 to 1 inch depending on the joist spacing.

Although 6 to 10 inch depths of timber deck are possible for spans up to 20'-0", these depths of deck will likely be laminated from smaller boards. When decking is used for longer spans, or for heavy industrial loads, deeper sections are required. For those types of applications boards or planks are glue laminated to standard depths and then milled with tongues and grooves. Wood lamination may also be accomplished using mechanical fasteners like nails. Obviously, nailed lamination requires the piece to be used with the narrow face positioned upright in the same position as a joist or rafter. A large amount of material is required for this type of wood deck construction. Therefore such a structural system needs careful assessment as to its proper use compared to alternate more efficient structural systems.

Laminated wood

Laminated wood members are sections larger and longer than most natural timbers. They are made from smaller select wood boards which are glued and pressure clamped. Knots and other natural defects are removed from the wood pieces and then rejoined with fingered type lap joints. When the glue has dried, the sections are planed and sanded to a finished size. The individual pieces to be laminated are either 3/4 inch or 1-1/2 inch thick boards. For straight rectangular beams or columns 1-1/2 inch thick plank are stacked and glued together. For curved members, such as arches, 3/4 inch thick boards are stacked, bent and glued together. All bent wood has a limited radius of curvature permitted based on the thickness of the individual ply. Laminated wood members range in size for 2-1/2 to 8-3/4 inch thick by 6 to 48 inches deep. Spans for laminated beams range from 10'-0" up to 50'-0".

Some unpredictable wood variables are removed in laminated members thereby allowing higher strengths to be achieved. For instance, knots are removed from all fibers which will be subjected to tension stress. Allowable stresses in bending and shear increase significantly. Both add valued predictability to the strength of the material in the composite section. With relatively modest increases in modulus of elasticity the deflection of a bending member may govern the size and proportion of the member.

A second form of glued laminated wood members are sections which are built-up from wood veneers. In the most common form, plywood

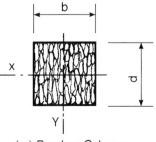

(m) Paralam Column

Fig. 1. Typical wood selections (continued)

Table 2. Common nails and schedule for light framing

RECOMMENDED NAILING SCHEDULE USING COMMON NAILS

Joist to sill or girder, toe nail	**3-8d**
Bridging to joist, toe nail each end	**2-8d**
Ledger strip	**3-16d**
	at each joist
1" x 6" subfloor or less to each joist, face nail	**2-8d**
Over 1" x 6" subfloor to each joist, face nail	**3-8d**
2" subfloor to joist or girder, blind and face nail	**2-16d**
Sole plate to joist or blocking, face nail	**16d @ 16" oc**
Top plate to stud, end nail	**2-16d**
Stud to sole plate, toe nail	**4-8d**
Doubled studs, face nail	**16d @ 24" oc**
Doubled top plates, face nail	**16d @ 16" oc**
Top plates, laps and intersections, face nail	**2-16d**
Continuous header, two pieces	**16d @ 16" oc**
	along each edge
Ceiling joists to plate, toe nail	**3-8d**
Continuous header to stud, toe nail	**4-8d**
Ceiling joists, laps over partitions, face nail	**3-16d**
Ceiling joists to parallel rafters, face nail	**3-16d**
Rafter to plate, toe nail	**3-8d**
1-inch brace to each stud and plate, face nail	**2-8d**
1" x 8" sheathing or less to each bearing, face nail	**2-8d**
Over 1' x 8" sheathing to each bearing, face nail	**3-8d**
Built-up corner studs	**16d @ 24" oc**
Built-up girders and beams	**20d @ 32" oc**
	along each edge

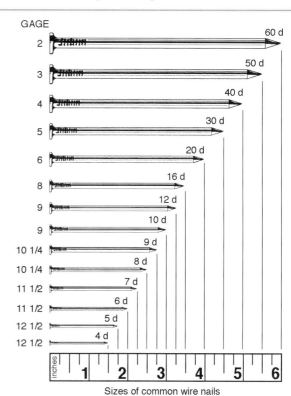

Sizes of common wire nails

is manufactured with veneers, about 0.1 inch thick, layered with grain alternated at 90 degrees glued together. The typical 4 feet by 8 feet sheet comes in thicknesses from 1/4 inch to 1-1/8 inch. Plywood is designated by two basic types according to exposure and durability. Exterior type is manufactured with a waterproof glue and the higher grade of veneers. Interior plywood sheets are manufactured with the inclusion of lower grade veneers and may use a glue less resistant to moisture. Plywood can be manufactured from over 70 species of wood. The numerous variations can accommodate rough framing construction or the best of furniture and finished cabinetry. When selecting and specifying plywood for specific applications, refer to plywood performance standards in publications from the American Plywood Association.

Thin wood veneers can be glued with the natural grain running in one direction. Products manufactured from it have strength properties significantly more predicable due to the control over conservative safety allowances for stress reductions due to moisture, knots, splits, shakes and other features of natural wood. These laminated members are referred to as "Microlam" sections produced as Microlam™. Available sections are 1-3/4 inches and 3-1/2 inches thick by depths of 5-1/2 inches to 18 inches. Lengths may be cut to meet the specific applications. These sections provide higher strength for wood beams and framing headers.

A product which combines the strength advantages of the Microlam with the strength of plywood in shear through the thickness is the Trus Joist manufactured as TJI™, a registered trademark of Trus Joist MacMillan and are for joists and rafters. The top and bottom chords are made from laminated wood veneers with parallel grain and the member's web is plywood. The members are available with several choices of chord width along with several choices of overall depth from 9-1/2 inches to 16 inches. This I shaped section is a very efficient use of material. The higher flexural and shear strengths can achieve longer spans in typical residential floor and roof construction. Accordingly the designer must assess the deflection criteria with equal

importance. Equally important are the ways this product is detailed for anchorage, lateral bracing, blocking and bridging of each member.

Bonded parallel strands of wood are bonded together to form a rectangular section called Parallam™. This product has strength properties similar to the Microlam. Its dimensional stability is very useful for applications as wood columns. Rectangular sections are manufactured with selected thicknesses ranging from 1-3/4 inches to 7 inches and depths ranging from 9-1/2 inches to 18 inches. Column sections may be selected from 3-1/2 inches square up to 7 inches square. Connection details must be carefully considered. The product is very hard and does not receive nails like natural wood lumber. Bolts, metal plates and pins are mechanical fasteners of choice for securing these members.

Light Wood Framing

For many small scaled buildings, including residential types, light wood framing systems are used for economy of structure. As world wide demands increase for building materials, the use of wood as a renewable resource gains importance for building. The craft of working with wood continues to attract individuals not only for general framing construction but also for the highly skilled levels of crafting furniture and cabinetry.

After the trees are cut into boards, veneers, lumber and timbers, the pieces are processed to meet the standards of moisture, strength and grading appropriate for designated applications. In light framing construction a variety of lumber sizes are nailed together to form a whole building. Walls are typically 2x4 or 2x6 studs spaced at 16 inches on center. Floors and roofs are made with 2x8s, 2x10s, or 2x12s spaced 12 or 16 inches on center. In residential construction one common framing system is the platform frame construction as shown in Figs. 2a and 2b. These figures identify the terminology and location for each wood piece. Table 2 lists recommended nail fasteners for connecting the parts together.

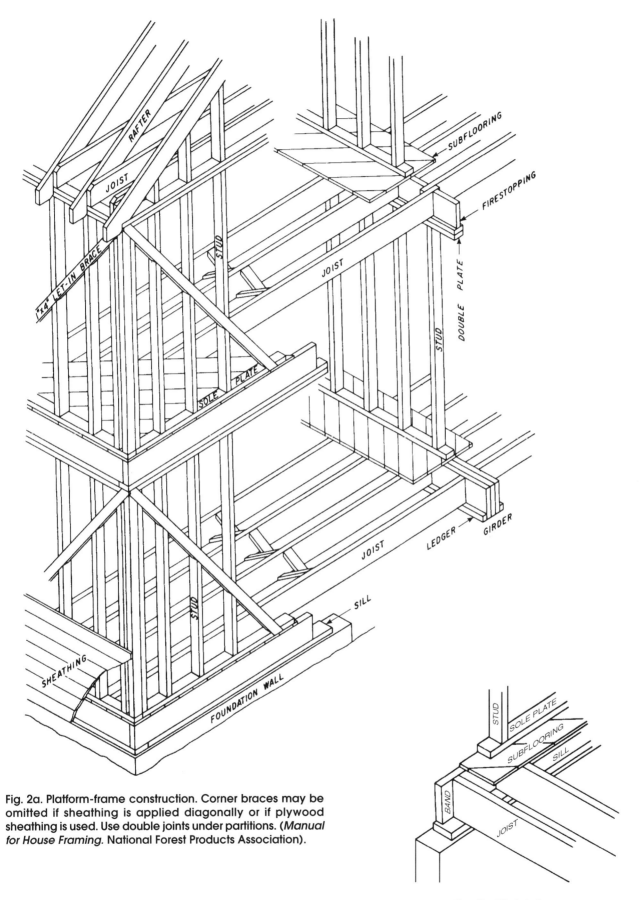

Fig. 2a. Platform-frame construction. Corner braces may be omitted if sheathing is applied diagonally or if plywood sheathing is used. Use double joints under partitions. (*Manual for House Framing*. National Forest Products Association).

Fig. 2b. Sill detail

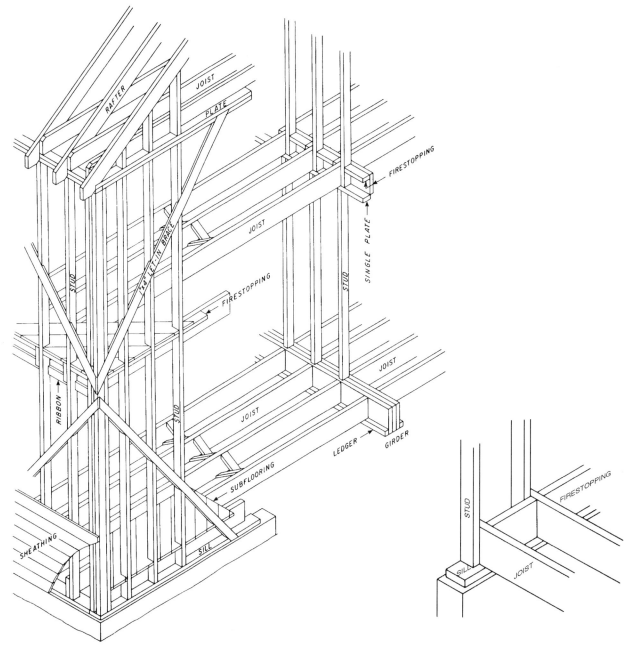

Fig. 3a. Balloon-frame construction (included for historical reference). Corner bracing omitted if sheathing applied diagonally or if plywood sheathing is used.

Fig. 3b. Sill detail - balloon-frame construction.

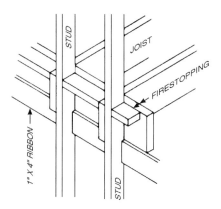

Fig. 3c. Second-floor framing of exterior wall - balloon-frame construction.

The advantage of platform frame construction is that when each floor system is completed it becomes an excellent working platform for constructing the next story or the roof of the building. Fig. 2b shows a detail of the position of each piece of lumber relative to the supporting foundation wall, to the first floor framing and to the exterior wall of the next story. (The sill must be anchored to the foundation wall by anchor bolts shown in Fig. 9, below). Remembering that wood shrinks more across the grain than in the direction parallel to the grain, this sill detail will have measurable shrinkage across the combination of sole plate, joists and sill plate. The designer is challenged with need to maintain the same amount of shrinkage throughout any single horizontal floor plane.

Balloon frame construction is an historic system of light frame construction. As shown in Fig. 3a, the primary advantage of this system is the continuity of the vertical exterior wall studs. Longer studs are harder to install and align. Less vertical shrinkage occurs in two stories of height because the vertical studs pass through the second floor. A comparison of the sill detail, Fig. 3b, with the sill detail of platform frame construction, Fig. 2b, reveals fewer pieces of lumber shrinking under the bearing wall structural studs.

The second floor detail of Fig. 3c illustrates the use of a ledger support under the floor joists. In this system of construction each floor joist is secured directly to a stud and to the ledger.

The Figs. 4 through 19 show a variety of ordinary details inherent with light frame construction. In Fig. 4, the important issue is to keep the wood framing at least 8 inches above the finish grade and to slope the grade away from the building so the water drains away from the building. One example of a foundation wall with footing is illustrated in Fig. 5. On the interior of a building wood columns are often supported by footings just below a concrete floor slab. For this type of

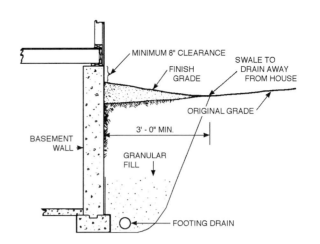

Fig. 4. Foundation plate

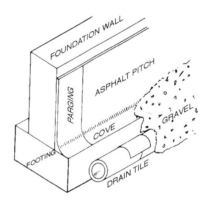

Fig. 5. Foundation and footing

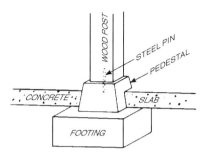

Fig. 6. Footing for basement column

column, Fig. 6 shows two important requirements. First, the column should be raised above the finished floor in order to minimize the moisture contacting the end grain of the wood. A fastener is required to secure the column end in position.

All corners and wall intersections of light frame construction must serve a structural requirement to carry axial load but also must accommodate the attachment of wall finishes. The corner column shown in Fig. 8 is a typical example of how multiple studs are positioned and joined to serve both of these requirements.

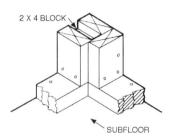

Fig. 8. Standard corner detail

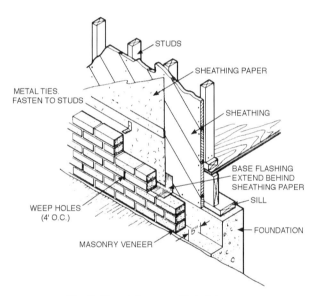

Fig. 7. Wood-frame with brick veneer

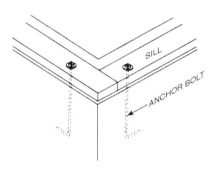

Fig. 9. Anchorage of sill to foundation wall. Anchor bolts, 1/2 in. In diameter, should be spaced not more than 4 ft. Apart and embedded at least 8 inches in concrete or 15 inches in masonry.

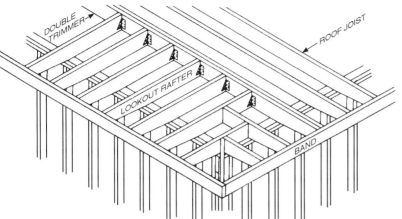

Fig. 10. Corner detail of flat roof, with overhang of less than 3 ft.

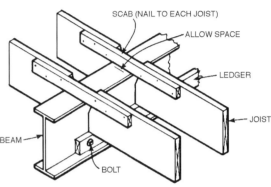

Fig. 13. Steel girder with ledger and wood scab ties

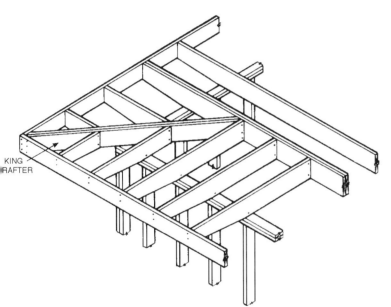

Fig. 11. Corner detail of flat roof with overhang of more than 3 ft.

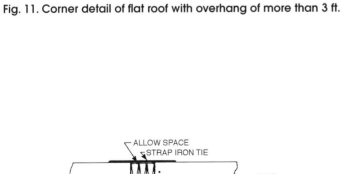

Fig. 12. Wood girder with ledger and metal ties

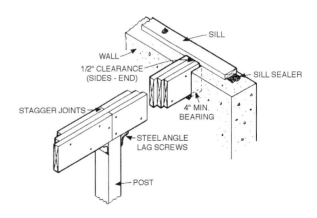

Fig. 14. Built-up wood girder on wood column and foundation pocket

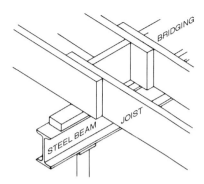

Fig. 15. Joists on steel girder

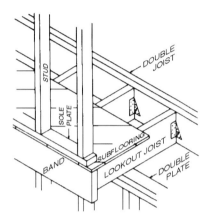

Fig. 16. Overhanging second floor with joists parallel to wall below

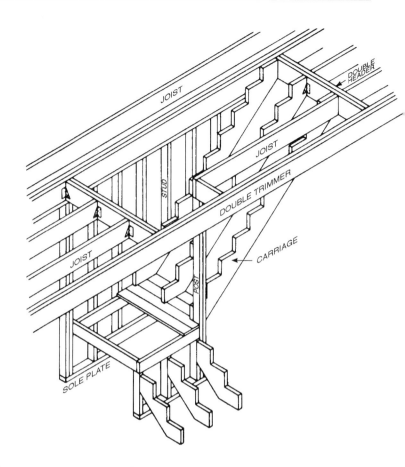

Fig. 18. Framing for stairway with landing

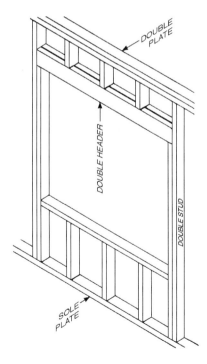

Fig. 17. Framing around exterior wall opening. For openings over 6 ft. Wide, use triple studs, with the header bearing on two studs at each side.

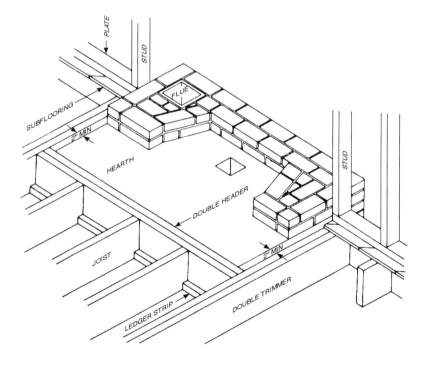

Fig. 19. Floor framing around fireplace. Wood framing must be kept 2 in. Clear of all fireplace and chimney masonry.

Example 1. Comparative floor joists

A wood joist floor framing system having a constant load is investigated to show the limits of the spans which may be used based on a specified species of wood and on using the wortking stress method of analysis.

Live load = 40 psf   Dead loads: 3/4" hardwood flooring   = 4.0 psf   Material:

Dead load = 21 psf

w = plf

span, ft.

3/8" plywood underlayment	= 1.2
5/8" plywood subfloor	= 1.8
estimated joist self-weight	= 3.0
plaster ceiling	= 10.0
misc. equipment allowance	= 1.0
	21.0 psf

Material:
Douglas Fir-Larch , No.1 & Btr.
F_b = 1150 psi
F_v = 95 psi
E = 1,800,000 psi

joists spaced @ 16" o.c.; w = 61 psf x 1.33 ft. = 81.1 plf; $V_{maximum} = \dfrac{wL}{2}$; $M_{maximum} = \dfrac{wL^2}{8}$;   maximum $= \dfrac{L}{360}$

allowable stresses: F_b = 1150 x C_r (1.15) = 1322 psi C_r is the repetitive member factor
                   F_v = 95 x C_h (1.33) = 126 psi C_h is the shear stress factor for limiting splits on the wide face

Span ft.	V_{max} lbs.	$A_{required}$ "2	M_{max} ft. lbs.	$S_{required}$ "3	Δ max "	$I_{required}$ "4	Joist size
6'-0"	243	2.9	365	3.3*	0.20	6.5	2 x 6
8"-0"	324	3.9	649	5.9*	0.27	15.4	2 x 6
10'-0"	406	4.8	1014	9.2*	0.33	30.8	2 x 8
12'-0"	487	5.8	1460	13.3*	0.40	52.5	2 x 10
14'-0"	568	6.8	1987	18.0*	0.47	82.8	2 x 10
16'-0"	649	7.7	2595	23.6	0.53	141.0*	2 x 12
18'-0"	730	8.7	3285	29.8	0.60	178.0*	2 x 12
20'-0"	811	9.7	4055	36.8	0.67	242.0*	2 x 14

* indicates the governing condition

Wood joists and rafters are installed at a spacing of 12, 16 or 24 inches on center. The module of 16 inches on center is the most frequently used. This repetitive use of the same sized member results in a distribution of live load over more than one member. In cases of floor joists, either diagonal cross bridging or solid block bridging is recommended at intervals of five to eight feet. Bridging helps to distribute concentrated loads onto multiple adjacent joists. Bridging also has the added advantage of laterally bracing the top and bottom edges of the joists thereby restraining them from buckling. A floor or roof deck which is well secured to the repetitive members will continually brace it.

Many tables exist in the referenced publications to aid in the selection of members for specific loads, spans, and specified grades of material. When designing a member for strength, the critical basic requirements are shear, bending and deflection. Each requirement has a direct relation to the size and proportion of a section. The design of a joist for shear requires adequate area for the cross section. To meet the maximum bending moment requirement a section modulus relative to a designated axis of bending must be provided. Restraint of the bent member from vertical movement is achieved by providing sufficient stmoment of inertia in a section relative to the bent axis. For shorter spans with heavy loads shear stress tends to be the condition determining the member size. With light loads and long spans either the

flexural condition or the deflection of the member will generally govern the sizing and proportioning requirements of the member.

Most wood data source references are filled with specific information to design wood members. These references are valuable resources in the design and comparison of wood structural systems. The National Design Specification (AFPA 1992) establishes many adjustment factors to modify the allowable stress design values for structural members. There are fourteen such factors listed in AFPA (1992). Ten of these effect the allowable bending stress, F_b. Three adjustment factors apply to the allowable shear stress, F_v, and two adjustment factors apply to the modulus of elasticity, E. When designing wood members, the engineer must assess which factors apply to a specific building and the importance of each applicable factor. A process of preliminary design of members may be appropriate to establish workable architectural dimensions and then refine the analysis to assure that each applicable factor has been considered.

In order to gain insight into common and efficient uses of specific wood members, the following illustrations are presented to compare applications.

Example 1 provides some insight into these strength requirements. With a constant load imposed on simply supported floor framing sys-

Example 2. Comparative floor beams

A wood floor framing system with a uniformly distributed load has joists supported by wood beams.
The beams carry a tributary width of 8 feet. Three different wood beam products are compared for
the sampling of spans shown. The comparative choices of beam types have different allowable stresses.

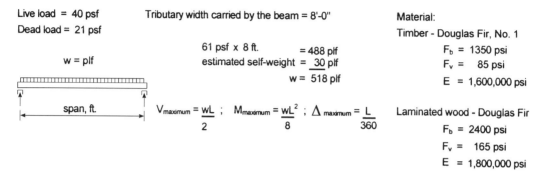

Live load = 40 psf
Dead load = 21 psf

Tributary width carried by the beam = 8'-0"

w = plf

61 psf x 8 ft. = 488 plf
estimated self-weight = 30 plf
w = 518 plf

span, ft.

$V_{maximum} = \dfrac{wL}{2}$; $M_{maximum} = \dfrac{wL^2}{8}$; $\Delta_{maximum} = \dfrac{L}{360}$

Material:
Timber - Douglas Fir, No. 1
F_b = 1350 psi
F_v = 85 psi
E = 1,600,000 psi

Laminated wood - Douglas Fir
F_b = 2400 psi
F_v = 165 psi
E = 1,800,000 psi

Laminated Microlam
F_b = 2925 psi
F_v = 285 psi
E = 2,000,000 psi

				Comparative required wood sections		
Span, ft.	V_{max} lbs.	M_{max} ft.lbs.	Δ_{max} in.	Timber Nominal size, in.	Laminated size, in.	Microlam size, in.
12'-0"	3,108	9,324	0.40	6 x 10	3-1/8 x 12	1-3/4 x 14
16'-0"	4,144	16,576	0.53	6 x 14	3-1/8 x 15	3-1/2 x 14
20'-0"	5,180	25,900	0.67	6 x 18	5-1/8 x 16-1/2	3-1/2 x 18
24'-0"	6,216	37,296	0.80	6 x 20	5-1/8 x 19-1/2	5-1/4 x 18
28'-0"	7,252	50,764	0.93	6 x 24	5-1/8 x 25-1/2	n.r.[1]

[1]. Not recommended, design requirement exceeds standard product sizes.

tem shown, the shorter spans between 6 to 14 feet have bending stresses determining the minimum size joist which must be used. The longer spans above 16 feet will have both the flexural and the deflection requirement governing the minimum size of member to be selected. Variables such as joist spacing and grade of material are viable considerations in the selection of an appropriate section. Once a basic section size is determined, then the wood adjustment factors must be considered in order to meet the additional requirements of the National Design Specification. These adjustment factors include adjustments for duration of load, moisture exposure, size and others noted in the specification.

Spans up to 20 feet are shown in this example only because they fall in the range of stock lumber. For spans greater than 20 feet, wood products such as the Trus joist or a truss type member are efficient alternatives. The longer the span, the more careful one must be to the vertical deflection and the lateral stability criteria. Long thin members may require precautions for handling and installation.

Timber beams are used less today than historically. Not only are large timber members scarce they require lower allowable stresses associated with natural wood. The result is that bigger section are required as compared to laminated members. Example 2 illustrates such a comparison. As spans increase the deflection requirements control the selection criteria. When deflection controls the design, the laminated wood member has the advantage over other beam types because it can be built with a camber. The camber frequently used is 1.5 times the dead load deflection.

Light-frame trusses

Wood trusses are often used in the roof framing system of residential and light commercial buildings. They are very efficient structural members easily manufactured from stock lumber of 2x4s, 2x6s, 2x8s and 2x10s. Typical spans range from 20 feet up to 50 feet at a common spacing of 16 or 24 inches on center. A 3/4 inch thick plywood deck is secured to the top chord and internal bracing must be used to maintain alignment and hold the entire array vertical. Repetitive units

Example No. 3 Light-frame truss

A roof framing system has wood trusses built from stock lumber and spaced at 16 inches on center. The spans are varied to illustrate the range of efficient applications using a minimum quantity of material. The top chord has a plywood deck which is nailed and continuously supports the chord laterally. The bottom chord supports a plastered ceiling and 10 inches of batt insulation. The chart shows the results of member sizes for respective spans. All members have been designed for combined axial and bending stress along with applicable adjustment factors for the lumber selected.

Roof live load   = 35 psf (horizontal projection)
Roof dead load   = 10 psf (horizontal projection)
Ceiling dead load = 17 psf
Truss spacing = 16 " c/c
w_1 = 45 psf x 1.33 ft. = 60 plf
w_2 = 17 psf x 1.33 ft. = 23 plf

Material: Southern Pine No. 1
F_b = 1,850 psi
F_t = 1,050 psi
F_c = 1,850 psi
F_c = 565 psi
F_v = 100 psi
E = 1,700,000 psi

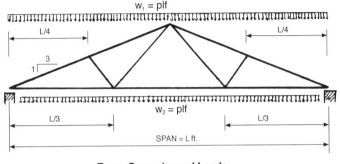

Truss Geometry and Loads

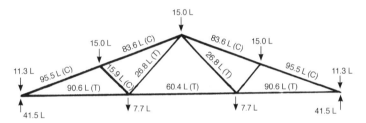

External and Internal Forces (lbs.)
in Terms of Truss Span L (ft.)

Truss	Member sizes for spans		
Span L	Top	Bottom	All diagonal
ft.	chords	chords	webs
20'-0"	2 x 4	2 x 4	2 x 4
30'-0"	2 x 6	2 x 6	2 x 4
40'-0"	2 x 8	2 x 6	2 x 4
50'-0"	2 x 8	2 x 8	2 x 4

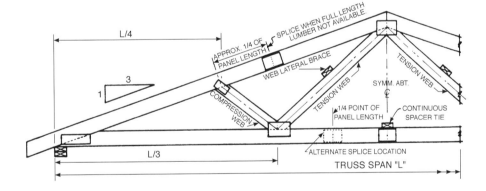

are produced in quantities at fabricating plants and then the units are bundled and shipped via truck to the building site.

The chords and web members are connected with 18 or 20 gauge galvanized steel gusset plates. These plates have 1/2 inch prongs punched and twisted. They are pressed and nailed into each member at a joint on both faces of the truss. Gusset plates are offset 1/4 inch with respect to each other on each face of the joint. Camber of 1.5 times the dead load deflection is recommended for the bottom chord and is to be introduced during fabrication. Data on different truss types, member sizes, plate sizes and designs for other roof pitches are available from local wood truss manufacturers and from companies mar-

keting the metal connectors. Example 3 is intended to illustrate one light-frame truss type with a typical roof and ceiling load. The four spans in the example begin to show the incremental increases in member size as the span increases while keeping basic unit loads constant.

Trusses are efficient structural members for a roof framing system. By comparison, a space with a cathedral ceiling open for the 50'-0" span would require rafters supported by the side walls and by a ridge beam at the center. The rafters at 16 inches on center could be either 3 x 14s custom ordered lumber for a 25'-0" span or a Trus Joist 2-1/4" wide by 16" deep. Either of these choices require more material for the framing system as compared to the light-frame truss.

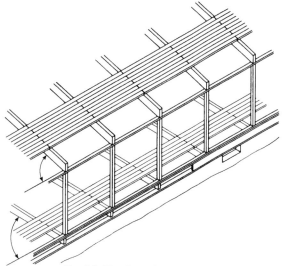

Fig. 20. Plank and beam framing

Timber construction

Historic industrial buildings frequently used large solid wood beams supported by masonry walls and square interior wood columns. The floor deck consisted of tongue and grooved wood plank. As tools and machinery developed so did the fabricating processes for preparing wood products for construction. The larger wood sections previously identified as heavy timber construction converted to the manufacture of laminated timber sections. Connections of heavy timber construction express some very basic principles for detailing larger wood members where the transfer of heavy loads are concentrated.

Fig. 20 illustrates a schematic structural system of plank and beam. Depending on the spacing between beams, the tongue and grooved plank extended as a continuous wood deck over multiple spans. Often the plank ends are tongue and grooved in order to allow end joints to occur in a selective random, but staggered, pattern. The intent is to develop continuity of the wood deck and therein have the opportunity to control deflections, reduce maximum bending stresses or increase the deck span. The diagram highlights the basic system without showing the additional requirement of stability of the whole building.

Fig. 21 illustrates alternate ways to detail a connection of wood beams into a supporting masonry wall. The angular end cut on the beam represents a *fire cut*. The idea is that if a beam fails because of fire, it will collapse without damaging the masonry wall and pocket of support. Fig. 26 is a similar detail located at a party wall.

Figs. 24 through 28 depict a variety of connections where secondary beams are supported by primary beams in floor framing systems. Metal hangers provide strong connections which are easy to install. However if wood to wood connections are desired the designer must carefully size each member based on net sections at notches and cuts into the wood members. Such notches and cuts often require increased section size due to the reduced section at the cut. Crafted wood to wood connections may be developed through the study of traditional crafts including the pinned mortise and tendon joint.

Beam to column connections are shown in Figs. 23, 29 and 30. Classic heavy timber beam to column joints, as detailed in Fig. 23 and shown for historical reference, have been simplified to common metal connectors used in today's construction, especially for glued laminated members.

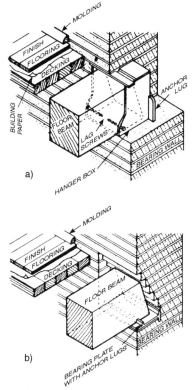

Fig. 21. Floor framing at exterior wall

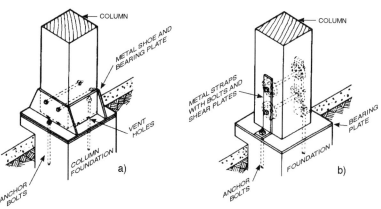

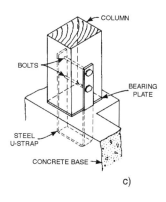

Fig. 22. Column anchorage

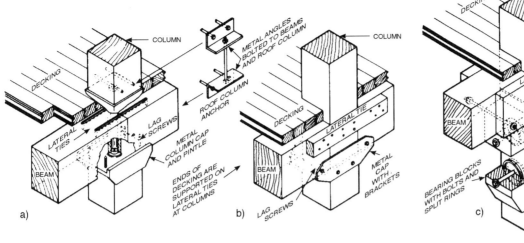

Fig. 23. Floor, beam and column timber framing

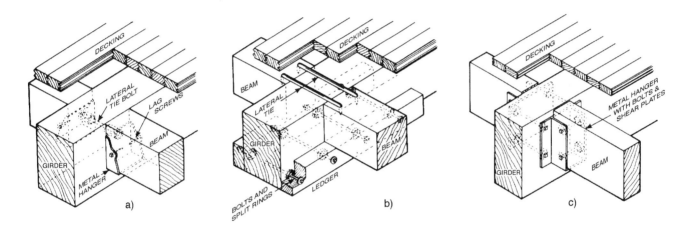

Fig. 24. Beam and girder heavy timber framing

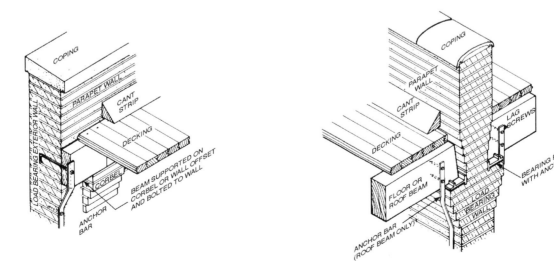

Fig. 25. Roof framing at exterior wall

Fig. 26. Roof framing at fire or party wall

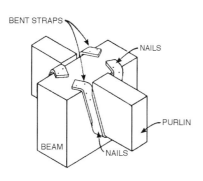

Fig. 27. Bent strap purlin hanger

Glued laminated timber sections can have greater depth and greater length than are attainable in natural solid timber. Sections may be laminated with varied widths, depths, curvatures and tapers to create numerous choices of beams and arches. In a section where bending stresses dominate , outer plies can be selected for high strength, or appearance, with lower grade wood relegated for the inner plies. Each piece of wood can be inspected before fabrication to avoid hidden defects as may occur in solid timber. All pieces to be laminated can be seasoned uniformly before fabrication thereby reducing chances of shakes and checks as found in solid timbers. Inspection and seasoning before fabrication permit the use of higher design stresses as compared to solid timber. The *Timber Construction Manual* (AITC 1994) contains extensive data on laminated beams, arches, columns, decks, diaphragms and fasteners.

For preliminary design purposes, Table 3 shows common structural wood members and the range of applicability within common structural system types.

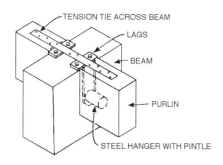

Fig. 28. Concealed purlin hanger

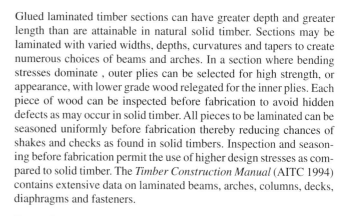

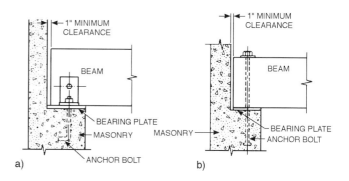

Fig. 29. Beam anchorage

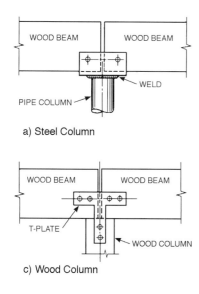

a) Steel Column

c) Wood Column

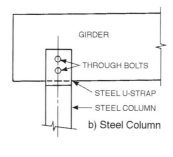

b) Steel Column

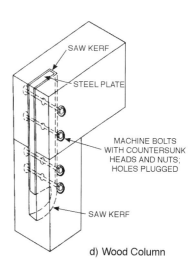

d) Wood Column

Fig. 30. Beam to column connections

Table 3. Common Structural Wood Member Sizes and Range of Applicability

Type of Structural Unit	Section Size Range		Spacing center to center	Span Range, ft.
	b, inches	d, inches		
Plank deck	continuous	2", 3" & 4"	n/a	4 ft. to 16 ft.
Laminated deck	continuous	3" & 4"	n/a	4 ft. to 20 ft.
Lumber rafters	2"[1]	4" to 12"	12", 16" or 24"	6 ft. to 20 ft.
Trus-joist rafters	1-1/2" to 3-1/2"	9-1/2" to 16"	12", 16" or 24"	6 ft. to 30 ft.
Lumber joists	2"[1]	4" to 12"	12" or 16"	6 ft. to 20 ft.
Trus-joist joists	1-1/2" to 3-1/2"	9-1/2" to 16"	12" or 16"	6 ft. to 24 ft.
Solid timber beams	3" to 12"[1]	8" to 24"	4 ft. to 16 ft.	8 ft. to 26 ft.
Laminated beams	2-1/2" to 10-3/4"	6" to 60"[3]	4 ft. to 20 ft.	8 ft. to 60 ft.
Microlam beams	1-3/4" & 3-1/2"	5-1/2" to 18"	[2]	6 ft. to 30 ft.
Paralam beams	1-3/4" to 7"	9-1/4" to 18"	[2]	6 ft. to 30 ft.
Light frame wood trusses	2"[1]	varies	16" or 24"	20 ft. to 50 ft.
Wood trusses	varies	varies	8 ft. to 16 ft.	30 ft. to 60 ft.
Arch rafter (laminated)	varies	varies	16" or 24"	20 ft. to 50 ft.
Three hinged arch	varies	varies	8 ft. to 16 ft.	40 ft. to 100 ft.
Lamella arch (rise/span = 1/8 to 1/4)	continuous	8" to 16"	n/a	40 ft. to 120 ft.

[1] Nominal lumber dimension

[2] Member best used as a single beam in light frame construction

[3] Deeper sections up to 81" are possible

B1

Stressed skin panels

Stresses-skin panel construction provides a means to extend the strength of separate wood materials by their composite action. In stressed-skin panels, plywood is firmly fastened to one or both edges of ribs (joists, rafters, or studs) to make the skins, which act integrally with the ribs and provide enhanced resistance to bending or buckling. Fig. 31 illustrates these principles and present cross-sections of stressed-skin plywood panels for floors and roofs of houses. All panels use standard 4-ft wide plywood with the face grain parallel to the joists. The lengths of the panels vary, the maximum safe length in each case being a function of loading, joist grade, size, spacing, and plywood thickness and grade. References include *Design of Plywood Stressed-Skin Panels* and *Fabrication of Plywood Stressed-Skin Panels* (American Plywood Association).

The structural action of a stressed-skin panel is similar to a wide-flange steel beam. The top skin carries compressive stress and the bottom carries tension. Because the skins tend to slip horizontally in relation to one another, important shearing stresses exist between the plywood and the ribs and also within the ribs. The only practical way to transmit this shear is by a rigidly glued joint between the plywood and the ribs.

The top face of the panel has additional stresses since it must carry loads between joists. When the top face serves as a floor with only an asphalt tile, linoleum, or carpet covering, it must be 36 in. minimum if joists are 16 in. On center. For roof construction not intended for use as a deck, a 1/2 inch-thick top cover is usually satisfactory.

To obtain satisfactory glued joints, pressure must be applied along the glue line. The best technique, obtainable only in a shop, is to use presses to apply a pressure of at least 150 lb. per square inch of contact area uniformly along the entire glue line. In place of mechanical pressure methods, nail-gluing may be used.

Nails shall be at least 4d for plywood up to 3/8 in. thick, 6d for 1/2 to 7/8 in. plywood, and 8d for 1 to 1-1/8 in. plywood. They shall be spaced not to exceed 3 in. along the framing members for plywood through 3/8 in., or 4 in. for plywood 1/2 in. and thicker, using one line for lumber 2 in. thick or less, and two lines for lumber more than 2 in. and up to 4 in. thick.

The glue employed is extremely important. For panels which are not exposed to weather or high relative humidities, casein and urea resin glues will provide satisfactory bonds. For panels exposed to moisture, a highly moisture-resistant adhesive such as resorcinol formaldehyde or, with heated presses, phenol formaldehyde resins and melamine formaldehyde resins may be used.

Typical connections are shown in Fig. 32. For panels longer than 8 ft, the plywood faces must be spliced, since plywood is usually not readily obtainable in longer sheets. These splices can be located anywhere within the span, but it is best to locate the splices as near the ends as possible. The splice may be made with a strip of plywood of the same thickness as the plywood joined, and glued under pressure.

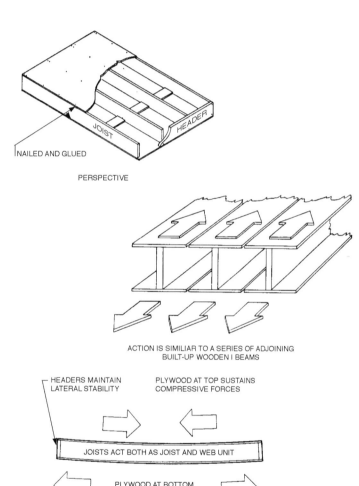

NAILED AND GLUED

PERSPECTIVE

ACTION IS SIMILIAR TO A SERIES OF ADJOINING
BUILT-UP WOODEN I BEAMS

HEADERS MAINTAIN
LATERAL STABILITY

PLYWOOD AT TOP SUSTAINS
COMPRESSIVE FORCES

JOISTS ACT BOTH AS JOIST AND WEB UNIT

PLYWOOD AT BOTTOM
TAKES TENSILE STRESSES

Fig. 31. Stressed skin panel concept

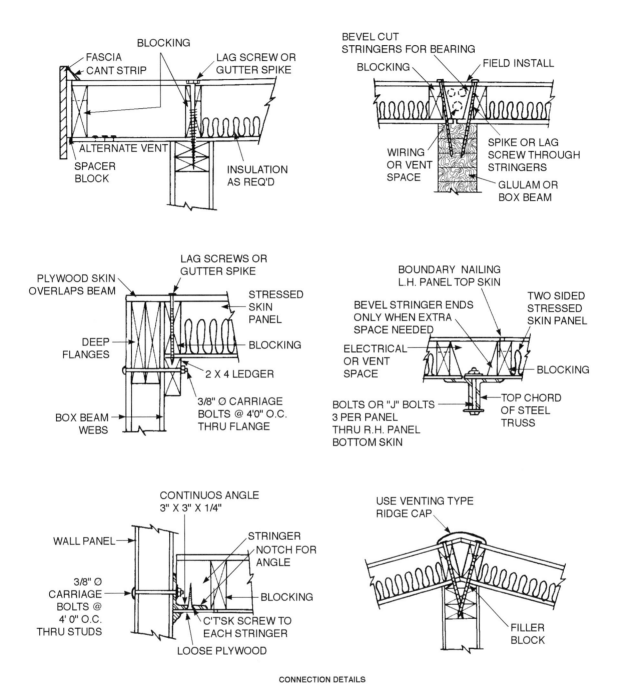

FASCIA
CANT STRIP
BLOCKING
LAG SCREW OR
GUTTER SPIKE
ALTERNATE VENT
SPACER
BLOCK
INSULATION
AS REQ'D

BEVEL CUT
STRINGERS FOR BEARING
BLOCKING
FIELD INSTALL
WIRING
OR VENT
SPACE
SPIKE OR LAG
SCREW THROUGH
STRINGERS
GLULAM OR
BOX BEAM

PLYWOOD SKIN
OVERLAPS BEAM
LAG SCREWS OR
GUTTER SPIKE
STRESSED
SKIN
PANEL
DEEP
FLANGES
BLOCKING
2 X 4 LEDGER
BOX BEAM
WEBS
3/8" Ø CARRIAGE
BOLTS @ 4'0" O.C.
THRU FLANGE

BOUNDARY NAILING
L.H. PANEL TOP SKIN
BEVEL STRINGER ENDS
ONLY WHEN EXTRA
SPACE NEEDED
TWO SIDED
STRESSED
SKIN PANEL
ELECTRICAL
OR VENT
SPACE
BLOCKING
BOLTS OR "J" BOLTS
3 PER PANEL
THRU R.H. PANEL
BOTTOM SKIN
TOP CHORD
OF STEEL
TRUSS

WALL PANEL
CONTINUOS ANGLE
3" X 3" X 1/4"
STRINGER
NOTCH FOR
ANGLE
3/8" Ø
CARRIAGE
BOLTS @
4' 0" O.C.
THRU STUDS
BLOCKING
C'T'SK SCREW TO
EACH STRINGER
LOOSE PLYWOOD

USE VENTING TYPE
RIDGE CAP
FILLER
BLOCK

CONNECTION DETAILS

Fig. 32. Stressed skin panel details

Structural design–steel

Summary: This section describes the material properties of structural steel; related steel products and systems with structural applications; preliminary structural design methods for steel columns, beams and tension elements; connections for structural steel elements; and steel systems for floor framing, trusses and building frames.

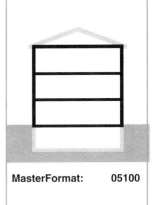

MasterFormat: 05100

Deere Company Headquarters, Moline, IL. Eero Saarinen, Architect.

Key words: beams, bolts, columns, frames, girders, steel, structure, tension, trusses, welds.

SHELL   B1

Overview of material properties

Only certain material properties of steel are discussed here—specifically, those that have bearing on the structural behavior of steel members. The most obvious, and important, structural properties are those relating force to deformation, or stress to strain. Knowing how a material sample contracts or elongates as it is stressed up to failure provides a crucial model for its performance in an actual structure. Not only is its ultimate stress (or strength) indicated, but also a measure of its resistance to strain (modulus of elasticity), its linear (and presumably elastic) and/or non-linear (plastic) behavior, and its ability to absorb energy without fracturing (ductility).

Ductility is important in a structural member because it allows concentrations of high stress to be absorbed and redistributed without causing sudden, catastrophic failure. Ductile failures are preferred to brittle failures, since the large strains possible with ductile materials give warning of collapse in advance of the actual failure.

A linear relationship between stress and strain is an indicator of elastic behavior—the return of a material to its original shape after being stressed and then unstressed. Structures are expected to behave elastically under normal "service" loads; but plastic behavior, characterized by permanent deformations, needs to be considered when ultimate, or failure, loads are being computed.

Typical stress-strain curves for steel are shown in Fig. 1 and Fig. 2. The most striking aspects of these stress-strain curves are the incredibly high strength (both yield and ultimate strength), modulus of elasticity (indicated by the slope of the curve), and ductility (related to the area under the stress-strain curve) of steel relative to other commonly-used structural materials such as concrete and wood.

As shown in Fig. 1 and Fig. 2, steel has a distinct elastic region in which stresses are proportional to strains (up to point "A"), and a plastic region that begins with the yielding of the material and continues until a so-called "strain-hardening" region is reached (from point "A" to point "C"). The yield stress defines the limit of elastic behavior, and can be taken as 36 ksi [kips per square inch. One kip = 1000 pounds] for the most commonly used structural steel (designated ASTM A36).

Within the plastic range, yielded material strains considerably under constant stress (the yield stress), but does not rupture. In fact, rupture only occurs at the end of the strain-hardening region, at an ultimate or failure stress (strength) much higher than the yield stress (point "D"). Bending cold-formed steel (see below) to create structural shapes out of flat sheets or plates of steel stretches the material at the outer edges of these bends beyond both the elastic and plastic regions, and into the strain-hardening region. This actually increases the strength of these structural elements, even though the direction of stretching is perpendicular to the longitudinal axis of the element.

High-strength steels (with yield stresses up to 65 ksi or higher) are available, but their utility is limited in the following two ways: First, the modulus of elasticity of steel does not increase as strength increases, but is virtually the same for all steel (29,000 - 30,000 ksi). Reducing the size of structural elements because they are stronger makes it more likely that problems with serviceability (that is, deflections and vibrations) will surface since these effects are related, not to strength, but to the modulus of elasticity.

Second, increased strength is correlated with decreased ductility, and a greater susceptibility to fatigue failure. Therefore, where dynamic and cyclic loading is expected, high-strength steel is not recommended; where dead load dominates, and the load history of the structural element is expected to be relatively stable, high-strength steel may be appropriate, as long as the first criteria relating to stiffness (modulus of elasticity) is met. The most commonly used steels, along with their minimum yield and ultimate stresses, are listed in Tables 1 and 2, as well as in the Manual of Steel Construction (AISC 1989).

Aside from this stress-strain data, material properties can also be effected by environmental conditions, manufacturing processes, or the way in which loads are applied. Steel is subject to corrosion if not protected, and loss of strength and stiffness at high temperatures if not fireproofed. While these are extremely important material properties, the structural design of steel elements presupposes that these issues have been addressed within the architectural design process. Specifically, steel is typically fireproofed by being encased in a fire-resistive material such as gypsum board, plaster, or concrete; or by

Author: Jonathan Ochshorn

References: AISC. 1989. *Manual of Steel Construction.* Allowable Stress Design. 9th ed. Chicago, IL: American Institute of Steel Construction

AISC. 1986. *Manual of Steel Construction.* Load & Resistance Factor Design. 1st ed. Chicago, IL: American Institute of Steel Construction

ASCE. 1994. *Minimum Design Loads for Buildings and Other Structures.* New York: American Society of Civil Engineers

Sweet's General Building & Renovation Catalog File. 1996. New York: McGraw-Hill.

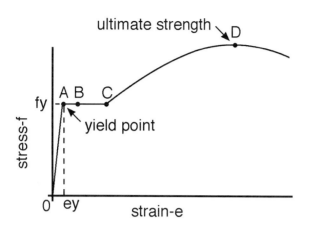

Fig. 1. Stress-strain curve for steel

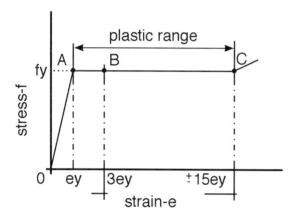

Fig. 2. Detail of plastic range of stress-strain curve

Table 1. Types of structural steel for use in building construction

ASTM designation	Primary use in construction
	Carbon steel
A36	All-purpose carbon-grade steel used for construction of buildings and bridges
	High-strength low alloy steel
A242	For exceptionally high corrsion resistance: more expensive; suitable for use in uncoated conditions.
A441	Welded structures where weight saving is important; excellent impact resistance; corrosion resistance twice that of carbon stell.
A572	Excellent formability and weldability; economical where strength and light weight are vital design objectives; the range of yield strengths offers designers a selection of steel to closely match their varried requirements.
A588	The atmospheric corrosion resistance of this steel is 4-6 times that of carbon steel; if unpainted, a tightly adhering oxide coating forms on surface to prevent progressive oxidation; for use where weight reduction, weldability, and maintenance costs are considerations.

Table 2. Minimum yield and ultimate stresses for structural steel

ASTM designation	Thickness, in	F_y Minimum yield stress, ksi	F_u Minimum tensile stress, ksi
A36	To 8" incl.	36.0	58.0
A242	To 3/4" incl.	50.0	70.0
	3/4" to 1-1/2" incl.	46.0	67.0
	1-1/2" to 4" incl.	42.0	63.0
A441	To 3/4" incl.	50.0	70.0
	3/4" to 1-1/2" incl.	46.0	67.0
	1-12" to 4" incl.	42.0	63.0
	4" to 8 incl.	40.0	60.0
A572 grade 42	To 4" incl.	42.0	60.0
A572 grade 50	To 1-1/2" incl.	50.0	65.0
A572 grade 60	To 1" incl.	60.0	75.0
A572 grade 65	To 1/2" incl.	65.0	80.0
A588	To 4" incl.	50.0	70.0
	4" to 5" incl.	46.0	67.0
	5" to 8" incl.	42.0	63.0

the application of a sprayed-on thin film intumescent (expanding when heated) paint; or, most commonly, by the application of a sprayed-on or troweled-on cementitious coating (Fig. 3). Steel can be protected from corrosion by being encased within various fire-proofing materials, or by being painted.

Hot-rolled steel shapes contain residual stresses even before they are loaded. These are caused by the uneven cooling of the shapes after they are rolled at temperatures of about 2000F. The exposed flanges and webs cool and contract sooner than the web-flange intersections; the contraction of these junction points is then inhibited by the adjacent areas which have already cooled, so they are forced into tension as they simultaneously compress the areas that cooled first. Residual stresses have an impact on the inelastic buckling of steel columns, since partial yielding of the cross-section occurs at a lower compressive stress than would be the case if the residual compressive stresses "locked" into the column were not present.

The behavior of structural elements is conditioned by the particular shapes into which these materials are formed, and the particular material qualities selected. Steel structures can be fabricated from elements having an enormous range of strengths, sizes and geometric configurations, subject only to the constraints imposed by manufacturing technologies, transportation and handling, and the requirements of safety and serviceability. In practice, though, the usual range is smaller, limited to standard shapes and sizes endorsed by industry associations.

Wide-flange shapes are commonly used for both beams and columns within steel-framed structures. They are designated by a capital W, followed by the cross-section's nominal depth and weight per linear foot. For example, a W14x38 has a nominal depth of 14 inches and weighs 38 pounds per linear foot. While any wide-flange shape may be used as either a column or beam, in practice beam sections tend to be more elongated (with much greater resistance to bending about their strong axes), while column sections tend to have more square proportions (in order to lessen the disparity between radii of gyration about the two potential axes of buckling). Unlike "I-beam" sections, whose flange surfaces are not parallel (the inner surface slopes about 16% relative to the outer surface), wide-flange sections have parallel flange surfaces, making it somewhat easier to make connections to other structural elements. Wide-flange sections are manufactured in groups with a common set of inner rollers. Within each of these groups, the dimensions and properties are varied by increasing the overall depth of the section (thereby increasing the flange thickness) and letting the web thickness increase as well. For this reason, actual depths may differ considerably from the nominal depths given to each group of shapes.

Dimensions and section properties of commonly available W shapes are tabulated in the "Dimensions and Properties" section of the Manual of Steel Construction (AISC 1989). Other shapes, such as channels (C or MC), angles (L), standard "I-beams" (S), and various hollow structural shapes (HSS) such as pipes and tubing also have many structural applications. Standard dimensions and properties for these shapes are also tabulated (AISC 1989). The designation for channels (C and MC) follows that for wide-flange sections, with the nominal depth in inches followed by the weight in pounds per linear foot. For angles, three numbers are given after the symbol, L: the first two are the overall lengths of the two legs; the third is the leg thickness (always the same for both legs).

Related products

Aside from standard rolled structural shapes, several other structural applications of steel should be noted:

- Cold-formed steel is made by bending steel sheet (typically with 90-degree bends) into various cross-sectional shapes, used prima-

rily as studs (closely-spaced vertical compression elements), joists (closely-spaced beams), corrugated decks, or elements comprising light-weight trusses. Corrugated steel decks constitute the floor and roof system for almost all steel-framed buildings. For floor systems, they are often designed compositely with concrete fill, effectively creating a reinforced concrete floor system in which the reinforcement (and formwork) consists of the steel deck itself. Manufacturers of these cold-formed products provide tables containing section properties and allowable loads, or stresses.

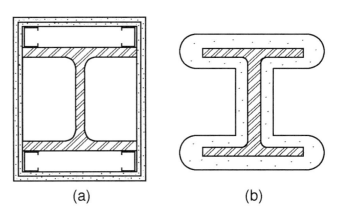

(a)   (b)

Fig. 3. Fireproofing of steel members with (a) gypsum board and (b) sprayed-on cementitious fireproofing

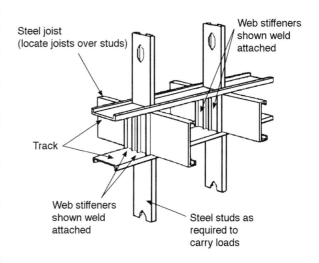

Steel joist (locate joists over studs)

Web stiffeners shown weld attached

Track

Web stiffeners shown weld attached

Steel studs as required to carry loads

Fig. 4. Cold-formed steel studs and joists

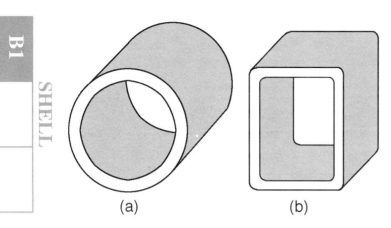

Fig. 5. Hollow structural shapes: (a) pipes and (b) square and rectangular tubes

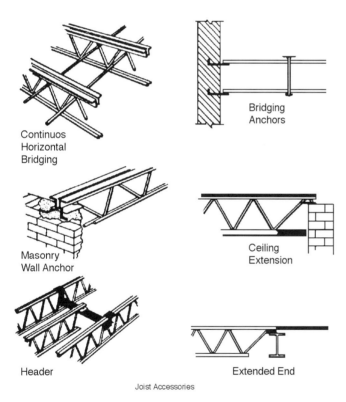

Continuos Horizontal Bridging

Masonry Wall Anchor

Header

Bridging Anchors

Ceiling Extension

Extended End

Joist Accessories

Fig. 6. Open web steel joists

- Hollow structural shapes can be formed from flat sheets or plates bent and then welded under pressure; these can be formed into circular shaped pipes, or square and rectangular structural tubing.

- Open-web steel joists are lightweight prefabricated trusses made from steel angles and rods. Spans of up to 144 feet are possible with "deep longspan" or DLH-series joists; regular "longspan" (LH-series) joists span up to 96 feet, while ordinary H-series joists span up to 60 feet. These products are relatively flexible, subject to vibration, and are most often used to support roof structures in large 1-story commercial or industrial buildings.

- Space-frame (actually "space-truss") systems consisting of linear elements and connecting nodes are manufactured by numerous companies.

- Cables and rods can be used as structural elements where the only expected stresses are tension, or where the element is pre-stressed into tension: the flexibility of these elements prevents them from sustaining any compressive or bending stresses. Applications include elements within trusses, bridges, and membrane structures.

Manufacturer's data and specifications for many of these steel products, including corrugated metal decks, open-web steel joists, light gauge steel framing, and space frame systems can be found in Division 5 of Sweet's Data Files (1996).

Design methods

Allowable stress design

Uncertainties abound in structural engineering. These include not only the nature of loads and the strength and stiffness of structural materials in resisting these loads; but also the appropriateness of mathematical models used in design and analysis, and the degree to which actual built structures conform to the plans and specifications produced by their designers. Structural design approaches can be characterized by the extent to which these uncertainties are made explicit. The simplest approach to designing steel structures uses a single factor of safety to define an allowable stress for a given type of structural behavior, that is, bending. If actual (that is, calculated) stresses do not exceed these allowable stresses, the structure is considered to be safe.

In steel Allowable Stress Design [ASD], the factor of safety is made explicit, and is most often multiplied by the yield stress to obtain the allowable stress. In practice, the factor of safety ranges from 2/3 for adequately braced and proportioned beams to 12/23 or lower for slender steel columns.

In allowable stress design, dead and live loads are simply added together, in spite of the fact that dead loads can be predicted with a higher degree of certainty than live loads. Thus, if two structures carry the same total load, but one structure has a higher percentage of dead load, the structures will have different degrees of safety when designed using the allowable stress method. That is, the structure with more dead load will be statistically safer, since the actual dead load acting on the structure is more likely to correspond to the calculated dead load than is the case with live load.

Allowable stress design is sometimes called working stress design, since the loads used in the method ("service loads") represent those expected to actually occur during the life of the structure.

Load and resistance factor design

A more recent approach to the design of steel structures explicitly considers the probabilistic nature of loads and the resistance of structural materials to those loads. Instead of regulating the design of structural elements by defining an upper limit to their "working stresses," Load and Resistance Factor Design [LRFD] is based upon the highest stress that the steel can withstand before failing or otherwise becoming structurally useless—this "limit state" is most often taken as the onset of buckling for columns, or the complete yielding of a cross-section for beams (that is, the creation of a so-called "plastic hinge").

Using this method, the required strength of a structural element, calculated using loads multiplied by load factors (that correspond to their respective uncertainties), must not exceed the design strength of that element, calculated by multiplying the strength, or "failure" stress, of the material by resistance factors (that account for the variability of those stresses, and the consequences of failure). In the discussion that follows for steel elements, we use allowable stress design.

Tension elements
Elements subjected to tension provide the simplest mathematical model relating internal force and stress: axial stress = force / cross-sectional area.

This equation is simple and straight-forward because it corresponds to the simplest pattern of strain that can develop within the cross-section of a structural element, assumed to be uniformly distributed across the entire cross-section. For this reason, it can be defined as force per unit area. Classical "strength of materials" texts use the symbol, σ, for axial stress, so that we get $\sigma = P / A$, where P is the internal force at a cross-section with area, A. By axial stress, we mean stress "acting" parallel to the longitudinal axis of the structural element, or stress causing the element to strain in the direction of its longitudinal axis. Tension is an axial stress causing elongation; compression is an axial stress causing shortening or contraction.

In considering particular structural materials, including steel, stresses are often represented by the letter F rather than σ, and capitalized when referring to allowable, yield or ultimate stresses. For example, F_y refers to the yield stress of steel; F_u refers to the ultimate stress of steel (the highest stress, or "strength," of steel reached within the strain-hardening region); while F_t (not to be confused with the "top-story force" F_t used in seismic calculations) symbolizes allowable tensile stress and F_a refers to allowable axial compressive stress. Lower-case f, with appropriate subscripts, is often used to refer to the actual stress being computed. An exception to this convention occurs in reinforced concrete strength design, where the yield stress of reinforcing steel (F_y in steel design) is given a lower-case designation, f_y. In any case, for axial tension in steel, allowable stress design requires that $f_t \le F_t$.

Unlike tension elements designed in timber, two modes of "failure" are considered when designing bolted steel tension members. First, the element might become functionally useless if yielding occurs across its gross area, at the yield stress, F_y. Since internal tensile forces are generally uniform throughout the entire length of the element, yielding would result in extremely large deformations. On the other hand, if yielding commenced on the net area (where bolt holes reduce the gross area), the part of the element subjected to yield strains would be limited to the local area around the bolts, and excessive deformations would not occur. However, a second mode of failure might occur at these bolt holes: rupture of the element could occur if, after yielding, the stresses across the net area reached the ultimate stress, F_u.

Another difference in the design of wood and steel tension elements occurs because non-rectangular cross-sections are often used in steel. If connections are made through only certain parts of the cross-section, as illustrated in Fig. 7, the net area in the vicinity of the connection will be effectively reduced, depending on the geometry of the elements being joined, and the number of bolts being used. This reduced effective net area, A_e, is obtained by multiplying the net area, A_n, by a reduction coefficient, U, ranging from 0.9 to 0.75 as described in Table 3.

Where all parts (that, flanges and webs) of a cross-section are connected, and the so-called shear-lag effect described above cannot occur, the coefficient U is taken as 1.0, and the effective net area equals the net area. For short connection fittings like splice plates and gusset plates, U is also taken as 1.0, but $A_e = A_n$ cannot exceed 0.85 times the gross area. Finally, the lengths of tension members, other than rods and cables, are limited to a slenderness ratio (defined as the ratio of

Table 3. Shear lag coefficient, bolted steel connections in tension

Condition	U
• W,M,S and tees	0.90
• connection to flange	
• 3 bolts per line, minimum	
• flange width at least 2/3 beam depth	
• 3 bolts per line, minimum	0.85
• any other condition	
• 2 bolts per line, minimum	0.75

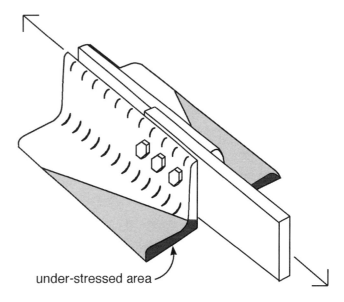

under-stressed area

Fig. 7. Shear lag in bolted tension connection

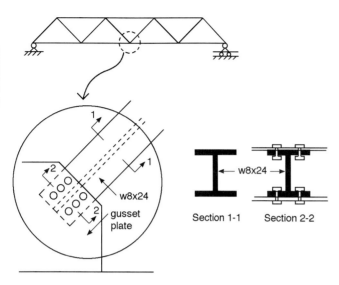

Fig. 8. Truss member stressed in tension

length to least radius of gyration) of 300, to prevent excessive vibrations and protect against damage during transportation and erection.

From the above discussion, it can be seen that two values for the allowable stress in tension need to be determined: one for yielding of the gross area; and one for failure (rupture) of the effective net area. These two values are $F_t^{gross} = 0.6 F_y$ and $F_t^{net} = 0.5 F_u$ where F_t^{gross} and F_t^{net} are the allowable tensile stresses for steel corresponding to the two modes of "failure;" F_y is the yield stress; and F_u is the ultimate stress for steel .

The following example illustrates the application of these principles to a steel tension problem. Note that different procedures are used for cables, eyebars, and threaded rods.

Example 1: Steel tension element analysis
Find the maximum tension load, P, that can be applied to a W8x24 element connected to gusset plates within a truss with 3/4" diameter bolts, as shown in Fig. 8. Assume A36 steel. Note that bolt hole diameter can be taken as bolt diameter plus 1/8", or 7/8".

- *Solution overview*: Find cross-sectional dimensions and material properties; find gross area capacity; find effective net area capacity; governing capacity is the lower of the two values.

- *Problem solution*: The cross-sectional dimensions of a W8x24 are found from "Dimensions and Properties" tables of the Manual (AISC 1989):

- $A_g = 7.08$ in^2;

- $d = 7.93$ in.;

- $b_f = 6.495$ in.;

- $t_f = 0.400$ in.

The yield and ultimate stresses of A36 steel are $F_y = 36$ ksi; and $F_u = 58$ ksi (AISC 1989).
To find the capacity, P, based on yielding of the gross area:

- $F_t^{gross} = 0.6 F_y = 0.6(36) = 22$ ksi.

- $P = F_t^{gross} \times A_g = 22(7.08) = 156$ k.

To find the capacity, P, based on rupturing of the effective net area:

- U = 0.90 (Table 3) since the following criteria are met: W-shape? yes; connection to flange? yes; b_f at least 2/3 d? yes; 3 bolts per line, minimum? yes.

- $A_n = A_g$ - (no. of holes) (hole diameter x t_f) = 7.08 - 4(7/8 x 0.400) = 5.68 in^2.

- $A_e = U \times A_n = 0.9(5.68) = 5.11$ in^2.

- $F_t^{net} = 0.5 F_u = 0.5(58) = 29$ ksi.

- $P = F_t^{net} \times A_e = 29(5.11) = 148$ k.

Conclusion: failure on effective net area governs since 148 k. < 156 k. The capacity (allowable load) is 148 k.

Solution for steel threaded rods: Since the size of tension elements is not constrained by the consideration of buckling, relatively small-diameter steel rods are often used, threaded at the ends to facilitate their connection to adjacent elements. Threaded rods are designed using an allowable tensile stress, $F_t = 0.33 F_u$, which is assumed to be resisted by the gross area of the unthreaded part of the rod. While there are no limits on slenderness, diameters are normally at least 1/500 of the length; and the minimum diameter rod permitted in structural applications is 5/8 inch.

Columns
Columns are vertical elements subjected to compressive stress; nothing, however, prevents us from applying the same design and analysis methods to any compressive element, whether vertical, horizontal or

inclined. Compression is similar to tension, since both types of structural actions result in a uniform distribution of axial stresses over a cross-section taken through the element. But allowable stress in compression is often limited by the phenomenon of buckling, in which the element suddenly deforms out of its axial alignment at a stress that may be significantly lower than the stress causing compressive crushing.

Leonard Euler calculated in the 18th century that deflections perpendicular to the member's axis increase rapidly in the vicinity of a particular ("critical") load, at which point the column fails; and that the value of this load is independent of any initial eccentricity. In other words, even with the smallest imaginable deviation from axiality, a column will buckle at some critical load. Since no perfectly axial columns (or loads) can exist, all columns behaving elastically will buckle at the critical buckling stress derived by Euler:

$$\sigma_{cr} = p^2 E / (KL / r)^2$$

In this well-known equation,

-   E is the modulus of elasticity;

-   K is a coefficient that depends on the column's end constraints;

-   L is the unbraced length of the column; and

-   r (sometimes given the symbol, r) is the radius of gyration with respect to the unbraced length, equal to the square root of the quantity I / A.

Where the unbraced length is the same for both axes of the column, r (or I) is taken as the smaller of the two possible values, that is, r_{min} (or I_{min}). The term L/r, or KL/r is called the column's slenderness ratio. Values for K can be found in Table C-C2.1 in AISC (1989).

The strength of a steel column is limited in two ways: either it will crush at its compressive stress, or buckle at some critical stress that is different from, and independent of, its strength in compression. Euler's equation for critical buckling stress works well for slender columns, but gives increasingly inaccurate results as the slenderness of columns decreases and the effects of crushing begin to interact with the idealized conditions from which Euler's equation was derived.

Slender steel columns are designed using the Euler buckling equation, while "non-slender" columns, which buckle inelastically, or crush without buckling, are designed according to equations formulated to fit empirical data. Residual compressive stresses within hot-rolled steel sections precipitate this inelastic buckling, as they cause local yielding to occur sooner than might otherwise be expected. Unlike timber column design, the design equations corresponding to elastic and inelastic buckling have not been integrated into a single unified formula, so the underlying rationale remains more apparent. The slenderness ratio dividing elastic from inelastic buckling is set, somewhat arbitrarily, at the point where the Euler critical buckling stress equals one half of the yield stress. Additionally, the maximum slenderness ratio should not exceed 200 for steel axial compression elements.

Rather than directly applying the equations for elastic and inelastic buckling to the solution of axial compression problems in steel, allowable stress tables (for analysis, Tables C-36 and C-50) or allowable axial load tables (for design, Allowable Concentric Loads on Columns) are more often used (AISC 1989).

Example 2: Steel column design
Select the lightest (most economical) wide-flange section for the 1st-floor column illustrated in Fig. 9. Assume office occupancy (with live load = 50 psf); a roof (construction/maintenance) live load = 20 psf; a typical steel floor system and an allowance for steel stud partitions resulting in a dead load of 55 psf on each floor. Assume pin-ended (simple) connections. Use A36 steel.

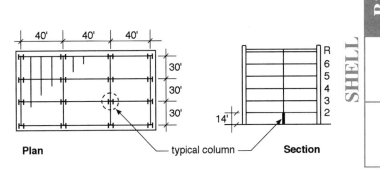

Fig. 9. Typical column in steel framed building

- Solution overview: Find total load on column; find effective length; select lightest section from table (AISC 1989).

- Problem solution: Find total column load:

• "Unreduced" Live load (LL) = 50 psf;

• Live load reduction: The maximum live load is unlikely to occur simultaneously on all floors of the office building; according to procedures outlined in Minimum Design Loads for Buildings and Other Structures (ASCE 1994), the maximum live load reduction coefficient of 0.4 may be used in this case, so that the reduced live load = 50(0.4) = 20 psf. Dead load (DL) = 55 psf; Roof live load (CL) = 20 psf;

• Find total column load:
  LL = 5 floors x (25' x 40') x (20 psf) = 100,000#;
  DL = 6 floors x (25' x 40') x (55 psf) = 330,000#;
  CL = 1 floor x (25' x 40') x (20 psf) = 20,000#
  Total column load = 450,000# = 450 k.

Find the unbraced effective length: Kl = (1.0) (14) = 14 feet
Select the most economical section:

• Using the "Allowable axial loads in kips" column tables (AISC 1989), pick the lightest acceptable section from each "nominal depth" group (that is, one W10, one W12, one W14), to assemble a group of "likely candidates;" that is:
  W10x100 can support 503 k;
  W12x87 can support 459 k;
  W14x90 can support 497 k.

• Choose lightest section: W12x87 is the most economical since its weight per linear foot (87 pounds) is smallest.

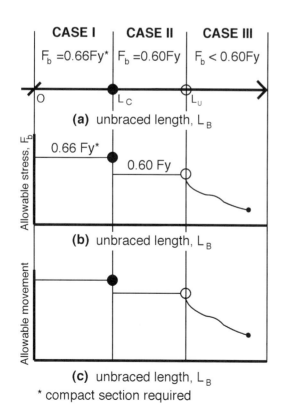

CASE I   **CASE II**   **CASE III**

$F_b = 0.66 Fy*$ $F_b = 0.60 Fy$ $F_b < 0.60 Fy$

(a) unbraced length, L_B

$0.66 Fy*$

$0.60 Fy$

(b) unbraced length, L_B

Allowable stress, F_b

Allowable movement

(c) unbraced length, L_B

* compact section required

Fig. 10. Unbraced length of beams: relationship to (a) L_c and L_u; (b) allowable stress; and (c) allowable moment

Beams

Like all structural elements, beams are both stressed and subject to deformations when loaded. Both of these considerations must be accounted for in the design of steel beams.

Beams are stressed when they bend because the action of bending causes an elongation on one side, resulting in tension; and a shortening on the other side, resulting in compression. From this geometry, the basic bending stress relationship can be derived:

$f_{b\,max} = M / S$, where:

$f_{b\,max}$ is the maximum bending stress at a given cross-section;

M is the bending moment at that section; and

S is the section modulus.

To design a beam using the allowable stress method, find the required section modulus by dividing the maximum bending moment by the allowable bending stress, that is:

$S_{required} = M_{max} / F_{b\,allowable}$

Then, using tabulated design aids (AISC 1989), select a cross-section whose section modulus is at least as large as the required value. It should be emphasized that this selection is provisional, and must be checked for both deflection and shear.

Laterally-unsupported beams

When the compression flange of a beam is not continuously braced, lateral-torsional buckling can reduce the allowable bending stress. How much this stress is reduced depends on whether the beam buckles before or after the cross-section begins to yield. Three different cases are possible:

• *Case I*: If a beam can develop a "plastic hinge" without buckling, the maximum allowable bending stress of $0.66F_y$ is used. In addition to lateral-torsional buckling, various types of local flange and web buckling must also be prevented from occurring before this so-called plastic moment is reached. Local buckling is prevented by limiting the ratio of flange width to flange thickness, as well as web width to web thickness. Sections proportioned so that local buckling will not occur are called compact sections; these sections must be used to qualify for the allowable stress of $0.66F_y$. As it turns out, all the wide-flange shapes listed in the Manual of Steel Construction (AISC 1989) are compact sections when made from A36 steel. For 50 ksi steel, all but three (W8x10, W10x12 and W40x192) are compact.

• *Case II*: A smaller nominal allowable bending stress of $0.6F_y$ is given to beams that can sustain an elastic moment without buckling, but not a plastic moment.

• *Case III*: When lateral-torsional buckling occurs before the elastic moment is reached, the allowable bending stress is reduced below $0.6F_y$, based on the explicit calculation of the critical buckling stress.

For a given "compact" cross-sectional shape, it is the unbraced length between lateral supports, L_b, that determines which of the cases described above applies. As L_b approaches zero, that is, as the compressive flange of the beam becomes more or less continuously braced, Case I governs. At the other extreme, for large unbraced lengths, Case III governs. For a given cross-section, the critical lengths separating Case I from Case II, and Case II from Case III, can be computed.

These critical lengths, L_c and L_u, are shown in relationship to the cases described above in Fig. 10(a). For a given cross-sectional shape, L_c is the largest unbraced length that can sustain a plastic moment; while L_u is the largest unbraced length that can sustain an elastic moment. Fig. 10(b) shows schematically how the allowable bending stress, F_b, changes as the unbraced length increases. Alternatively, the unbraced length can be plotted against allowable moment by multiplying the allowable bending stress by the section modulus, as shown in Fig. 10(c). It is this latter form that serves as a design aid for steel beams whose compression flanges are not continuously braced. For any bending moment (in foot-kips) and unbraced length (in feet), the "Allowable Moments in Beams" graphs in the Manual of Steel Construction (AISC 1989) can be used to locate the lightest acceptable wide-flange cross-section, using 36 ksi or 50 ksi steel.

Laterally-braced beams
Where the compression flange is laterally braced against buckling, the required section modulus (in³) can be found directly from:

required $S_x = M_{max} / F_b$, where:

- M_{max} = the maximum bending moment (in-k); and
- F_b = the allowable bending stress = $0.66F_y$ for compact sections (ksi).

Choosing the lightest (that is, most economical) section is facilitated by the use of the "Allowable Stress Design Selection Tables" (AISC 1989) in which steel cross-sections are ranked, first in terms of section modulus, and then by least weight (indicated by bold-faced entries).

Internal forces perpendicular to the longitudinal axis of beams may also exist along with bending moments at any cross-section, consistent with the requirements of equilibrium. These shear forces are distributed over the cross-sectional surface according to the general shear stress equation derived in strength of materials texts. For steel wide-flange shapes, simplified procedures can be used, based on the average stress on the cross-section, neglecting the overhanging flange areas; that is, the actual maximum shear stress in a beam can be taken as:

$f_v = V / (d\, t_w)$, where

- f_v = the maximum shear stress within the cross-section;
- V = the total shear force at the cross-section;
- d = the cross-sectional depth; and t_w = the web thickness. This value for the actual shear stress can then be compared with the allowable shear stress for steel—taken as $F_v = 0.4\, F_y$ (or 14.5 ksi for A36 steel)—in order to check whether a beam designed for bending stress is acceptable for shear.

While the elongation or contraction of axially-loaded members along their longitudinal axes is usually of little consequence, beams may experience excessive deflection perpendicular to their longitudinal axes, making them unserviceable. Limits on deflection are based on several considerations, including minimizing vibrations, thereby improving occupant comfort; preventing cracking of ceiling materials, partitions, or cladding supported by the beams; and promoting positive drainage (for roof beams) in order to avoid ponding of water at mid-span. These limits are generally expressed as a fraction of the span, L (Table 4). Additional values for the recommended minimum depth of spanning elements are also tabulated (Table 5). Formulas for the calculation of mid-span deflections are given in the Manual of Steel Construction (AISC 1989).

Example 3: Steel beam design
Using A36 steel, design the typical beam and girder for the library stack area shown in Fig. 11. Assume a dead load of 47 psf and a live load of 150 psf. Assume that the beams are continuously braced by the floor deck, and that the girders are braced only by the beams framing into them.

- *Solution overview*: Find loads; compute maximum bending moment and shear force; use appropriate tables to select beams for bending; then check for shear and deflection.

- *Problem solution, beam design*:

Table 5. Recommended minimum depths for deflection control

floor beams	roof beams
[1]L/800Fy)or [2]L/20	[1]L/(1000/Fy)

[1]Fy is in ksi units, *eg.*, 36 ksi for A36 steel: L is the span.
[2]Use L/20 for vibration control over large partition-free floor areas.

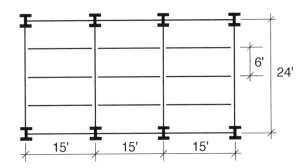
Fig. 11. Framing plan

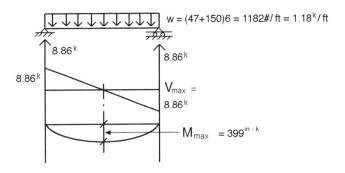
Fig. 12. Load, shear and moment diagrams

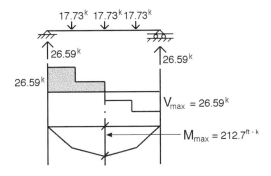
Fig. 13. Load, shear and moment diagrams

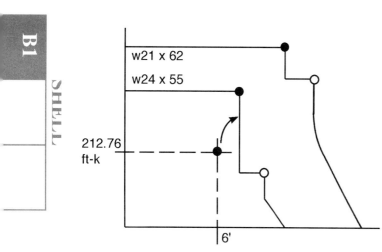

Fig. 14. Use of "Allowable Moment" design graphs

- Create load, shear and moment diagrams (Fig. 12) to determine critical (that is, maximum) shear force and bending moment. The total distributed load, w = (150+47)6 = 1182 #/ft = 1.18 k/ft.

- Find allowable bending stress: Since beam is laterally braced by floor deck and section is compact; $F_b = 0.66F_y = 0.66(36) = 24$ ksi;

- Compute required $S_x = M_{max}/F_b = 399/24 = 16.62$ in³.

- Select W12x16 with actual $S_x = 17.1$ in³ from "Allowable Stress Design Section Table" (AISC 1989).

- Check shear: Allowable shear stress, $F_v = 0.4F_y = 0.4(36) = 14.5$ ksi; actual shear stress, $f_v = V / (d\, t_w) = 8.86 / (11.99 \times 0.22) = 3.36$ ksi < allowable shear stress, so beam is OK for shear.

- Check deflection: The allowable live load deflection for a floor beam = span/360 = L/360 = 15(12)/360 = 0.5 in. (Table 4); the actual deflection, from "Beam Diagrams and Formulas" (AISC 1989), is equal to $5wL^4/(384EI_x) = 0.34"$.

In this equation, the modulus of elasticity of steel, E, can be taken as 29,000 ksi, the moment of inertia, I_x (in.⁴) can be found in "Dimensions and Properties" tables (AISC 1989), and the distributed load, w, is calculated for live loads only. Note that where the distributed load is measured in units of kips/ft. and the span, L, is measured in units of feet, the deflection equation must be multiplied by 12³ to reconcile the incompatible units. Since the actual deflection of 0.34" < allowable deflection = 0.5 in., the beam is OK for deflection.

- **Problem solution, girder design:**

- Create load, shear and moment diagrams (Fig. 13) to determine critical (that is, maximum) shear force and bending moment. Each concentrated load is twice the typical beam reaction, or 17.73 k. [Alternatively, compute using tributary areas; that is, P = (150+47)(15x6) = 17730 # = 17.73 k.]

- Since allowable bending stress cannot be determined directly (girder is not continually braced), use "Allowable Moment" design graphs (AISC 1989) to select beam directly for M = 212.76 ft-k and L_b = 6 ft. Select W24x55 (Fig. 14).

- Check shear: Allowable shear stress, $F_v = 0.4F_y = 0.4(36) = 14.5$ ksi; actual shear stress, $f_v = V / (d\, t_w) = 26.595 / (23.57 \times 0.395) = 2.86$ ksi < allowable shear stress, so beam is OK for shear.

- Check deflection: The allowable live load deflection for a floor beam = span/360 = L/360 = 24(12)/360 = 0.8 in.; the actual deflection, from "Beam Diagrams and Formulas, Table of Concentrated Load Equivalents" (AISC 1989), is equal to: $ePl^3/(EI)$; where:

- e = 0.0495 for three equally spaced concentrated loads on a simply-supported span, and

- l = span in inches = 24(12) = 288 in.

As before, the modulus of elasticity of steel, E, can be taken as 29,000 ksi; the moment of inertia, I_x = 1350 in⁴, can be found in "Dimensions and Properties" tables (AISC 1989); and the concentrated load, P = 13.5 kips, is calculated for live loads only. Substituting these values into the equation, we get an actual live load deflection = 0.4 in. Since this value is less than the allowable deflection of 0.5 in., the beam is OK for deflection.

Typical construction details

Steel building frames typically consist of beams, girders and columns which are fastened together using high-strength bolts or welds. Welded connections are often used to create rigid ("Type 1") joints, while bolts are commonly used for simple shear ("Type 2") connections, although bolts or welds can be used in either case. In fact, welds and bolts can be used within the same connection, even in cases where a simple connection is desired. This occurs, for example, where clip angles, welded to one structural element in the shop, are bolted to another structural element in the field. Semi-rigid ("Type 3") connections fall somewhere between the first two types. In general, connections are detailed so that welding, where necessary, occurs as much as possible in the shop, while connections that must be made in the field are designed to be bolted. Examples of typical simple and rigid connections (beam to girder, and girder to column) are illustrated in Fig. 15.

Aside from the intersection of beams, girders and columns, two other connection conditions should noted: column to column; and column to foundation. In the first case, column joints are typically placed somewhat above the floor elevation, so as not to interfere with the connection of beams and girders to the column (Fig. 16). Additionally, the columns are often fabricated in lengths of two stories to reduce the number of field connections. The connection of columns to the concrete foundation is most often mediated by a steel baseplate, welded to the column in the shop, that can be precisely aligned using leveling nuts or shims and then grouted as shown in Fig. 17.

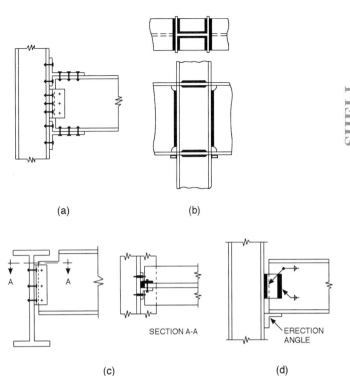

(a)   (b)

(c)   (d)

Fig. 15. Typical steel connections: (a) Type 1 bolted; (b) Type 1 welded (with stiffener plates); (c) Type 2 bolted; and (d) Type 2 welded

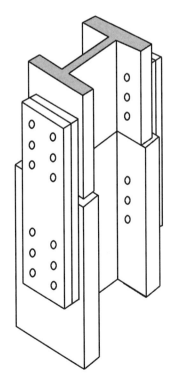

Fig. 16. Bolted column to column splice

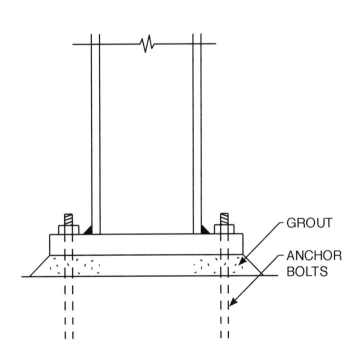

Fig. 17. Typical column baseplate

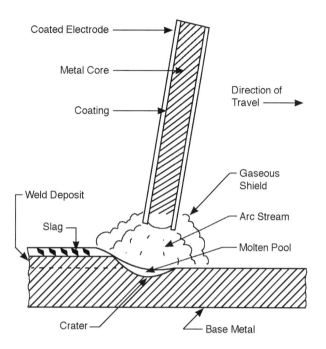

Fig. 18. Shielded metal arc welding

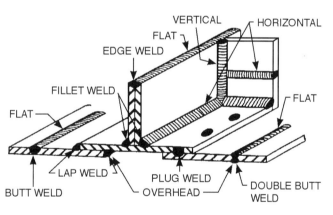

Fig. 19. Types of welds

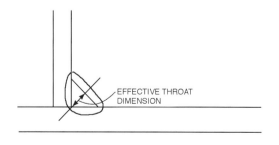

Fig. 20. Section through convex fillet weld

Welded connections

Structural elements can be monolithically connected when the surfaces to be joined are heated sufficiently and then allowed to cool. In practice, the surfaces to be joined are not fused directly; instead, metal from an separate electrode is fused with the base metal of the two steel surfaces to be joined. In Shielded Metal Arc Welding [SMAW], a 6500F electric arc forms in the gap between the electrode and steel as the electrode is moved along the weld line (Fig. 18), melting the electrode into the base metal to form a continuous metal connection. A coating on the electrode containing flux forms a gaseous shield that protects the molten weld from reacting chemically with oxygen and nitrogen in the atmosphere, and facilitates the removal of oxides in the weld metal. Flux can be supplied separately from the electrode in submerged arc welding, an automated process associated more with shop-welding than with field-welding.

Various shapes of welds can be created, the most common being the triangular fillet weld. The position of the weld is also of interest: flat and horizontal welds are easiest to create, while vertical and overhead welds are more difficult, and therefore more expensive (Fig. 19).

The design of SMAW fillet welds is governed by their strength in shear, so that the capacity of a particular weld can be found by multiplying the allowable shear stress of the weld material (taken as 0.3 x the ultimate strength of the electrode used; that is, 0.3 x 70 ksi for an E70 electrode) by the area of the anticipated failure plane in shear. The area of this failure plane is simply the length of the weld multiplied by the effective throat dimension, as shown in Fig. 20.

Standard welding symbols and examples of their use are illustrated in Fig. 21 and Fig. 22.

Bolted connections

Allowable loads for ordinary and high-strength bolts used in shear are given in Table I-D of the Manual of Steel Construction (AISC 1989). There are several parameters appearing in this table that influence bolt capacity:

- Bolt strength: the two commonly-used high-strength bolt types are designated A325 and A490, the latter being significantly stronger. For secondary structural members, ordinary A307 bolts (also known as machine bolts, or common bolts) can be used.

- Connection type: although all high-strength bolts are tightened to the point where some friction develops between the metal pieces being joined, bolted connections can be designed either on this basis (slip critical, SC connections) or by using the bearing strength of the bolt and "plate" material as a criteria (bearing N or X connections). "N"-type bearing connections occur where bolt threads appear in the shear plane; "X"-type bearing connections are designed so that the bolt threads are excluded from the shear plane. Note that SC connections must also be designed to resist bearing stresses.

- Hole type: various types of bolt holes can be used, including standard round holes (STD) and long-slotted holes (LSL), allowing some flexibility in detailing.

- Loading: values for both single and double shear are given (double shear refers to a condition where three plates rather than two engage the bolt in shear, so that the total shear force is divided into two shearing planes, effectively cutting the stress in half).

For both slip critical and bearing connections, the bearing capacity of the steel plate material to be joined must also be considered. Table I-E (AISC 1989) lists allowable loads for various thicknesses of steel plate, various commonly-used bolt sizes (3/4", 7/8" and 1" diameter), and various steel strengths (ranging from $F_u = 58$ ksi to $F_u = 100$ ksi).

For bolts subjected to tension, Table I-A (AISC 1989) gives allowable loads for bolt sizes ranging from 5/7" to 1-1/2". Where both tension and shear act simultaneously on a bearing connection, the allowable shear and tension stresses are limited to values listed in Tables J3.2 and J3.3 (AISC 1989).

Steel floor and roof framing systems
The flat floor surfaces characteristic of steel-framed buildings are most often designed using corrugated steel deck with concrete fill spanning between evenly-spaced steel beams which are in turn supported by steel girders framing into a grid of steel columns. The framing module is thus determined by the spanning capacity of the steel deck. This, in turn, depends on the deck's gauge (the thickness of the steel plate from which it is formed), the depth of its corrugations, the total depth of the slab (including the concrete fill), and the live and dead floor loads. Typical spans ranging from 8' to 12' can be achieved using 2" steel decks with a total slab depth of about 4". A schematic detail section showing the relationship between beam, girder and deck for a steel-framed building is illustrated in Fig. 23.

Precast concrete slab panels can also be used in place of corrugated steel decks and steel beams, spanning directly between steel girders. Cast-in-place concrete slabs over steel beams are much less commonly encountered since they introduce the additional cost of concrete formwork without eliminating the cost of structural steel elements.

Roof framing systems are similar to floor framing systems except for two important differences. First, concrete fill is often eliminated, and the steel deck alone is designed to span between beams. The roofing membrane is then placed over a substrate which has been fastened to the steel deck. For conventional roofs, the substrate is often rigid insulation, as shown in Fig. 24.

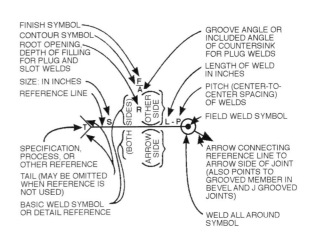

Fig. 21. Standard welding symbols

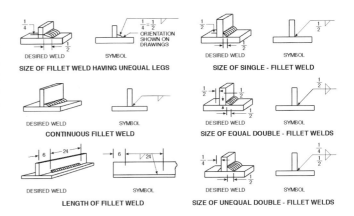

Fig. 22. Use of welding symbols

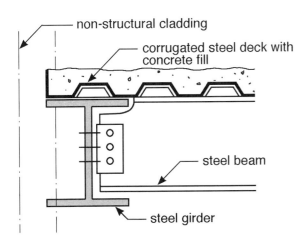

Fig. 23. Typical steel floor framing

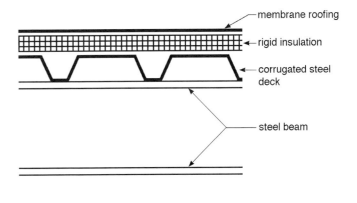

Fig. 24. Typical steel roof deck

The second important difference between roof and floor framing systems is that roof framing elements are often sloped towards roof drains. While this doesn't ordinarily have much of an effect on the framing plan, the minimum slope requirements for low-sloped roofs can have a major impact on the building section. For example, where a 100'-wide roof is designed to slope up 1/4" for each foot measured horizontally from a centrally-placed roof drain, the height added to the building elevation due to the slope of the roof would be (50 feet) x (1/4" per foot) = 12-1/2 inches. As an alternative to sloping the structural steel roof-framing elements to accommodate the need for roof drainage, it is possible to design a flat roof deck and create a sloping surface with either light-weight concrete fill, or tapered roof insulation.

Steel trusses

Steel trusses range in size from the relatively lightweight standardized open-web steel joists described earlier, to wind and seismic bracing systems spanning from the foundation to the roof of multi-story buildings. The design of each truss element starts with the calculation of the axial force to be resisted. For trusses acting as simply-supported spanning members, elements comprising the top chord are generally in compression and those in the bottom chord are generally in tension — echoing the pattern of internal forces that emerges in a conventional beam, similarly loaded. Once the axial force has been computed, the design of a particular truss bar is no different in principle than the design of either a steel column (where the axial force is compression) or a steel tension element.

In practice, the bars of the top and bottom chords are often made continuous, and the connection of these chords to the vertical and diagonal bars becomes the major detailing issue. Gusset plates are commonly used as a mediating device between the various intersecting steel members in bolted construction; whereas in welded tubular steel trusses, the individual truss members are brought directly into contact with each other. Fig. 25 shows typical connection details for bolted and welded steel trusses.

Steel building frames

The structural design of a steel building frame must account for both vertical loads (typically live, dead and snow loads) as well as horizontal loads (typically wind and seismic loads). Strategies for resisting the vertical loads have already been suggested in the section on floor and roof framing, and are essentially the same for all steel buildings: loads originating at any point are transferred by the structural deck to the supporting beams and girders, at which point they are picked up by the building columns and transferred ultimately to the foundation system. What distinguishes one framing system from another is really the way in which lateral loads are resisted. Two general strategies are available for resisting these horizontal forces: either the joints between columns and girders are made rigid (creating a moment-resisting frame), or diagonal bracing elements are placed within the rectilinear frame (creating a truss).

Where trusses are used, they are most often hidden within the building core or behind opaque cladding material at the outside wall (so that the programming of building functions is not compromised by the appearance of truss diagonals); less frequently, they are expressed as part of the building's external form. Where moment-resisting frames are used, they are most commonly located at the outside faces of the building. Schematic examples of these bracing strategies are illustrated in Fig. 26.

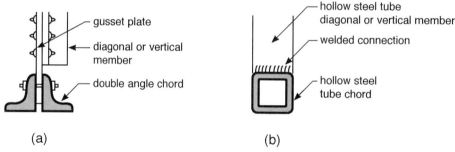

(a)   (b)

Fig. 25. Typical connection details for (a) bolted and (b) welded steel trusses

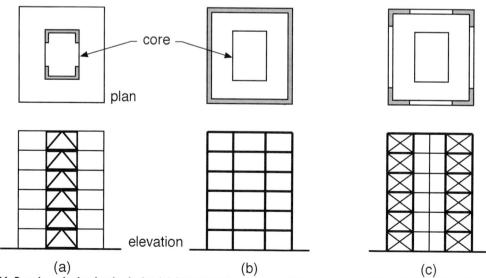

(a)   (b)   (c)

Fig. 26. Bracing strategies include: (a) truss bracing in core; (b) moment-resisting frame at exterior face; and (c) truss bracing at exterior face

Railway Station Lyon-Satolas, France. Santiago Calatrava, Architect and Engineer. 1989-94. Photo: Alexander Tzonis

Structural design–concrete

Summary: This article presents the basic design concepts of reinforced concrete structures, including beams, columns and floor/roof deck systems. It is intended to be helpful to architects in formulating a framing concept, and in the selection of a perliminary design

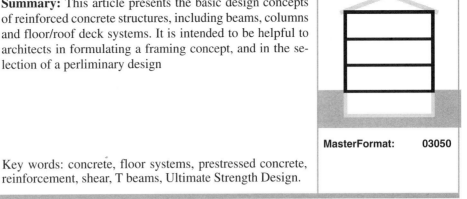

MasterFormat: 03050

Key words: concrete, floor systems, prestressed concrete, reinforcement, shear, T beams, Ultimate Strength Design.

SHELL B1

Introduction

The chapter following is intended to enable the reader to understand the basic ideas underlying the design of reinforced concrete structures. It should be helpful in formulating a framing concept, and in the selection of a preliminary design. Reinforced concrete structures are inherently indeterminate structures, the analysis of the internal forces (moments, shears and axial forces) cannot be performed by statically determinate models. Furthermore, in the analysis of indeterminate structures the length of the members and their relative sizes all influence the resulting shears and moments in the members. Thus this chapter should be used by the architectural designer to understand the ramifications of a selected framing system, and to arrive at some reasonable preliminary estimates of layout and member sizes. Final design of members, reinforcing quantities and details should be left to the consulting structural engineer.

Concrete materials

Concrete is a mixture composed of a filler material (aggregate) bound together by a hardened paste. The hardened paste is the result of a chemical reaction, called hydration, between cement and water. In addition admixtures - various chemicals, usually in liquid form - are often used to impart desirable qualities to the freshly mixed and/or to the hardened concrete. The paste fills the voids between the aggregate particles, gravel or crushed stone and sand, and binds them together. The aggregate size distribution is carefully controlled in order to minimize the resulting voids that must be filled with the paste. Minimizing the amount of paste helps to minimize the amount of cement, which is the most expensive ingredient of the mixture, for it requires a large amount of energy in its manufacture. The proportions of the aggregate in normal weight concrete is about 65 to 75 per cent by volume, while the paste makes up about 33 to 23 per cent. The remaining volume is air.

The quality of the concrete depends upon the binding agent, *i.e.* the quality of the paste. The hydration process requires the presence of moisture. Since the cement can utilize only so much moisture, excess water will evaporate through capillaries, leaving voids behind, that reduces practically all the desirable qualities of the hardened concrete. Thus it is important to keep the amount of water in the mix to the absolute minimum, that still permits the concrete to be workable and moldable. Concrete made with just enough water for the hydration process will not be sufficiently workable, furthermore during handling and placement there will be inevitably some water loss due to evaporation and absorption by the form work, leaving insufficient moisture behind for the hydration process.

Practically all of the physical and mechanical properties of the hardened concrete are related to the ratio of water to the cement by weight. Thus for example a water/cement ratio of 0.45 means that in the mix 45 lb. of water is used for every 100 lb. of cement.

Keeping the water/cement ratio as small as practicable helps, among other attributes: to increase the compressive and flexural strength; to reduce the permeability; to reduce shrinkage and the formation of shrinkage cracks; to increase durability and resistance to wear. The adjacent diagram (Fig.1) clearly shows the relationship between the compressive strength and the water/cement ratio in concretes made with equal amounts of cement per cubic yard.

As mentioned above, admixtures are often used to enhance the properties of the freshly mixed or hardened concrete. Admixtures are most commonly used to:

- accelerate or retard the setting time and the hardening;
- reduce the amount of water in the mix, while maintaining good workability;
- increase water tightness;
- intentionally entrain air for increased freeze/thaw resistance.

Properties of hardened concrete
Compressive strength
In architectural structures the most commonly required strengths are between 3,000 psi to 6,000 psi, measured on 6" diameter, 12" high cylinders at 28 days of age. Stronger concretes are sometimes used

Author: Robert M. Darvas

References: American Concrete Institute, 1996. *ACI Manual of Concrete Practice, Parts 1-5,* Detroit, MI: American Concrete Institute. A collection of the Institute's Standards offers state of the art reports on any aspect of concrete materials, manufacturing, design and construction standards and methods.

Concrete Reinforcing Steel Institute, 1996. *CRSI Handbook,* Schaumburg, IL: Concrete Reinforcing Steel Institute. A large collection of design tables for sizing concrete structural elements, including columns, beams, joists, slabs, one and two way systems, including size and reinforcing required for given loading.

Precast / Pretstressed Concrete Institute, 1992. *PCI Design Handbook. Chicago, IL: Prestressed Concrete Institute.* Product suformation and design selection tables of standard precast and prestressed products (hollow core slabs, single and double T sections, beams, *etc.*). Problems of Architectural Precast Concrete, connections between precast elements are also discussed in great detail.

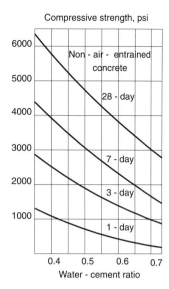

Compressive strength, psi

Non - air - entrained concrete

28 - day

7 - day

3 - day

1 - day

Water - cement ratio

Fig. 1. Concrete compressive strength (psi) (From the Portland Cement Association: Design and Control of Concrete Mixtures).

in columns of high-rise buildings. The cylinder strength is symbolized as f'_c.

Tensile strength
Concrete has rather limited tensile strength. The ultimate flexural tensile strength (also known as the Modulus of Rupture) shows a great variability, but it may be assumed to be $f_r = 7.5\sqrt{f'_c}$ (f'_c must be entered in psi unit)

Modulus of Elasticity
$E_c = 33w^{1.5}\sqrt{f'_c}$; where w is the weight of the concrete in pcf unit.

Weight
Normal weight concrete (made with gravel or crushed stone as coarse aggregate) weighs about 145 pcf. Reinforced concrete is usually taken as 150 pcf to account for the higher unit weight of the steel reinforcing.

Lightweight structural concretes are also produced, using rotary kiln expanded clays, shales and clays, or expanded slags. These concretes weigh significantly less, in the range of 110 to 120 pcf, thus their use may be warranted, when the benefit of the reduction in self weight exceeds the added cost for the more expensive aggregate.

Thermal expansion coefficient
6×10^{-6} in/in/degF, very close to that of steel, thus the two materials may expand or contract without significant stresses resulting.

Durability
This is usually used to refer to the freeze/thaw resistance of the concrete, although some times the reference is to resistance to other environmental factors. Chemicals that attack concrete are many. Chlorides (road salts) attack concrete as well, although the major problem is the corrosion of the reinforcing in the presence of chlorides.

Air entrainment
During the mixing of the fresh concrete, chemicals form tiny air bubbles (about 300 billion per cubic yard) uniformly distributed in the mixture. When concrete saturated with water in its capillary voids is subject to freezing, the expanding ice produces hydraulic pressures in the yet unfrozen liquid. These pressures result in tensile stresses in the concrete that can lead to rupture. The entrained air voids are thought to act as reservoirs into which the excess fluid volume can be pushed. 5% to 7% of entrained air volume is practical for this purpose, and its use does not lead to significant strength loss. Air entrainment also helps the workability, thus the amount of water can be reduced.

Volumetric changes in concrete structures
Volumetric changes, *i.e.* deformations, are caused chiefly by four different effects.

Elastic deformations (or instantaneous deformations) occur in all structural elements when loaded. They may be calculated using methods established by elastic theory. However, since reinforced concrete is a composite material, the calculation becomes more complicated (and the resulting accuracy less certain) than with more homogenous materials, like steel. A further difficulty presents itself with the fact, that beams and slabs in monolithic structures crack in the tensile region even if the cracks are largely invisible at normal service loads. At the location of the cracks, the Moment of Inertia of the section is drastically reduced, that in turn leads to larger deflections, than calculated values obtained by using gross section properties throughout.

Control of deflections is a primary design objective. Deflections, both instantaneous and long term (see below), if excessive, may seriously compromise the structure and may jeopardize the performance of the attached "non-structural" elements of the building. Roofs may not drain properly; partitions supported by the structure may crack; doors and windows may distort if excessive deflections take place. The most important action in this respect is the selection of appropriately deep structural elements. In the paragraph discussing typical floor systems, values of minimum overall structural depth are given. Experience shows that the use of such minimum depths lead to good serviceability, *i.e.* adequate control of deflections.

Shrinkage occurs when the fresh concrete sets (setting shrinkage), then during the hardening process (drying shrinkage). The amount of shrinkage varies with many factors. Low water/cement ratio of the concrete mix, limiting the length of a concrete pour and careful curing process helps to minimize shrinkage. While it is difficult to predict, an average contraction of 0.0002 to 0.0003 inch per inch may be used to estimate the length change in reinforced concrete structures. If the resulting length change could freely take place without restraint, no stresses would result. However most concrete structures are restrained against free change of length by either their physical ties to an already constructed portion, or restrained by friction forces on the formwork or the subgrade. These restraints result in tensile stresses in the concrete structure. Concrete, especially at the early stages of strength development, has very limited tensile strength, and when the shrinkage caused stresses exceed the then available tensile strength, cracking will result.

Thermal movements occur due to the change of temperature. Expansion or contraction takes place at the rate of 0.000 006 (six millionth) inch per inch per degree of Fahrenheit. While it seems to be a small number, a 50 degrees change will cause 3/8" change in every 100 ft length. Just as in the case of shrinkage, unrestrained length change will not cause stresses in the structure, however if the movement is restrained, tensile or compressive stresses will result. Even more problematic, when a structural element is subject to differential temperature changes. For example, exterior building panels may bend or warp, when there is a differential temperature between their faces. In columns that are partially exposed, additional bending moments develop due to the differential temperature between their inside and outside face. In tall buildings, an exposed exterior column will change its length with respect to the interior columns, forcing the floor structure to bend in order to follow the differential length change.

Creep is a phenomenon identified with long term deformations due to sustained stresses. Columns will shorten, flexural members (beams, slabs *etc.*) will show increased deflections with age. Creep deformations add 100% to 200% to the instantaneous deformations. Creep begins as soon as a concrete element starts to carry loads, and continues at a diminishing rate for as long as the concrete carries load. Most creep deformation, however takes place in the first two years. Among many different factors, the most important one is the age of the concrete when it is first loaded, *i.e.* the further along in its strength development, the less creep deformation will result.

The design concept

Design of concrete structures (or any other structure, for that matter), that begins with the selection of a structural system, may be viewed as satisfying several concurrent goals.

- satisfying functional layout
- adequate strength;
- good serviceability; (usually means control of deflections)
- economy;
- aesthetic requirements (architectural appearance);

Most monolithic reinforced concrete structures will require extensive mechanical and electrical services, that are usually delivered within the space between the concrete floor structure and the suspended ceiling below it. Thus very often the availability of maximum structural depth and economy, *i.e.* the overall cost governs the selection of the structural system.

Ultimate strength design (USD)

In the present context *design* means the finding of appropriately sized members (together with the required reinforcing) that may be deemed of having adequate strength. *Adequate strength* means to design a section that has a certain amount of reserve capacity, over and beyond the strength that is called upon in the everyday service life of the structure.

Structural elements are subject to service load effects (moments, shears, axial forces) acting on a particular section of a member. The service effect comes from two parts. One comes from loads that are *permanently* present, inherent within or attached to the structure: these are referred to as *dead loads*. The other part comes from loads, whose nature is transitory, some times they are present, other times they are not, like people, furnishings, wind, seismic loads, etc. These are referred to as *live loads*. The two together form the expected true loads our structure may encounter during its lifetime.

The nature of the dead and live loads are such that the former ones are more predictable and easier to estimate their magnitude. Live loads on the other hand are more difficult to predict, their nature may be such that either the magnitude cannot be defined with any reasonable certainty, or their action is far from being static in nature, they more resemble quick dynamic impulses. Since dynamic impulses create an, albeit temporary, overstress on our structural elements, live loads need a more careful handling to insure that temporary excess live loads will not result in the failure of the structure or element.

Load factors

In order to have a *safe design*, or adequate strength, we need strength so that the structure is not going to fail if either we underestimated somewhat the actually occurring loads, or for whatever reasons there is a certain amount of excess load placed on our structure. Hence we employ load factors, *i.e.* we arbitrarily magnify the actual loads (or the moments therefrom) and thus create the demand on the strength. The demand states for example that the structure (or more precisely: the section under investigation) must have an ultimate strength (*i.e.* before it may fail) not less than

$$U = 1.4 \times D + 1.7 \times L$$
$$\text{or} \quad U = 0.75 \times (1.4 \times D + 1.7 \times L + 1.7 \times W)$$
$$\text{or} \quad U = 0.9 \times D + 1.3 \times W$$

(when seismic loads are considered, substitute 1.1 x E for W)
where

    U = Required (Ultimate) Strength
    D = Effect from dead loads
    L = Effect from prescribed live loads
    W = Effect from wind loads
    E = Effect from seismic loads

The multipliers applied to the effects in the various load combinations are the *load factors*. These are intended to guard against accidental over-loading of the structure, they also recognize our incomplete knowledge in establishing loads more precisely.

Design (ultimate) strength

Ultimate strength of the section comes from the sizes, materials employed, and the amount of reinforcing furnished. This is the *supply, i.e.* the strength furnished by the design. For example, in flexural design this will be designated as M_n or "nominal moment strength." Nominal strength is an assumed strength, provided everything goes according to plans. To allow things to go slightly wrong during construction we take this nominal strength and employ a *strength reduction factor* (Ø-factor) to define the *useful (or useable) strength.*

Hence the problem of ultimate strength design may be stated by the following:

- **Demand   Supply**
- (required strength   design strength)

For example, for a beam subject to gravity loads only:

$$M_u \quad \text{Ø}M_n \quad \text{or} \quad 1.4 \times M_D + 1.7 \times M_L \quad \text{Ø}M_n$$

Different Ø factors are used for different effects.
    Flexure   Ø = 0.90
    Shear   Ø = 0.85
    Axial compression (tied columns)   Ø = 0.70

On the left hand side of the above *inequality* is the demand. The demand as was noted above depends only on the span, type of beam (*i.e.* simply supported, cantilevered *etc.*) and the loads. All information comes from static analysis.

On the right hand side however, we have the supplied strength of the section, that depends upon the size (shape) of the cross section, the quality of the materials employed (f'_c and f_y), and the amount of reinforcing furnished. Thus one may see, that while the left hand side is unique, the right hand side is undefined, *i.e.* there are infinite different sizes, shapes, reinforcing combinations that may satisfy a given problem. Economy, among other considerations, dictates that we should not *over-design* too much.

Assumptions for ultimate strength design.

(The Code Requirements and Commentary following below are extracted from ACI 318-92 Building Code Requirements for Reinforced Concrete)*

Code requirements

10.2.1 - Strength design of members for flexure and axial loads shall be based on assumptions given in Sections 10.2.2 through 10.2.7 and on satisfaction of applicable conditions of equilibrium and compatibility of strains.

10.2.2.- Strain in reinforcement and concrete shall be assumed directly proportional to the distance from the neutral axis

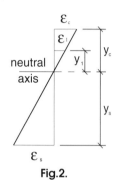

Fig.2.

10.2.3 - Maximum usable strain at extreme concrete compression fiber shall be assumed equal to 0.003

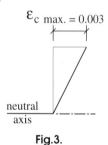

Fig.3.

10.2.4 - Stress in reinforcement below specified yield strength f_y for grade of reinforcement used shall be taken as E_s times steel strain. For strains greater than that corresponding to f_y stress in reinforcement shall be considered independent of strain and equal to f_y

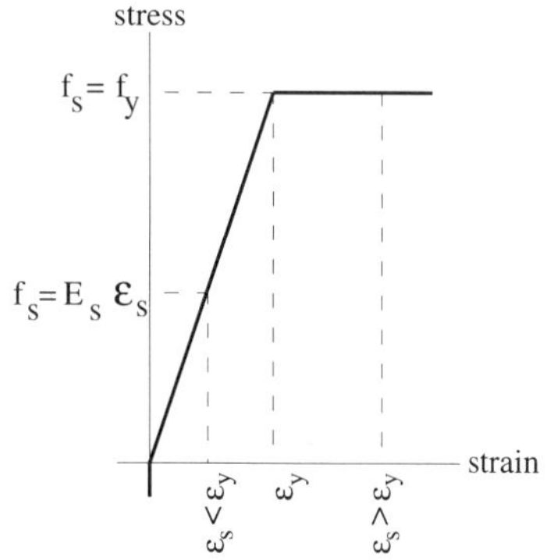

stress

$f_s = f_y$

$f_s = E_s \, \varepsilon_s$

strain

$\varepsilon_s < \varepsilon_y$ ε_y $\varepsilon_s > \varepsilon_y$

for $f_y = 40$ ksi, $\varepsilon_y = 0.00138$
for $f_y = 60$ ksi, $\varepsilon_y = 0.00207$

Fig.4.

Commentary

The strength of the member computed by the strength design method of the Code requires that two basic conditions be satisfied: (1) static equilibrium and (2) compatibility of strain. Equilibrium between the compressive and tensile forces acting on the cross section at nominal strength must be satisfied. Compatibility between the stress and strain for the concrete and the reinforcement at nominal strength conditions must also be established within the design assumptions allowed by Section 10.2.

Many tests have confirmed that the distribution of strain is essentially linear across the reinforced concrete section, even near ultimate strength.

Both the strain in reinforcement and in concrete are assumed to be proportional to the distance from the neutral axis.

$$\frac{\varepsilon_1}{y_1} = \frac{\varepsilon_c}{y_c} = \frac{\varepsilon_s}{y_s}$$

The maximum concrete compressive strain at crushing of the concrete has been observed in tests of various kinds to vary from 0.003 to higher than 0.008 under special conditions. However, the strain at which ultimate moments are developed is usually about 0.003 to 0.004 for members of normal proportions and materials.

For the reinforcement it is reasonably accurate to assume that the stress in the reinforcement is proportional to strain below the yield strength f_y. The increase in strength due to strain hardening after yielding is neglected. The assumptions are:

when $\varepsilon_s < \varepsilon_y$ (yield strain)
then $A_s f_s = A_s E_s \varepsilon_s$

when $\varepsilon_s >= \varepsilon_y$
then $A_s f_s = A_s f_y$

The modulus of elasticity of steel reinforcement E_s may be taken as 29,000,000 psi.

*American Concrete Institute, 1992. *Building Code Requirements of Reinforced Concrete* (ACI 318-89) and Commentary (ACI 318R-89), Detroit, MI.

Assumptions for ultimate strength design* (continued)

Code requirements

10.2.5 - Tensile strength of concrete shall be neglected in axial and flexural calculations of reinforced concrete.

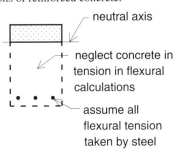

Fig.5.

10.2.6 - Relationship between concrete compressive stress distribution and concrete strain may be assumed to be rectangular, trapezoidal, parabolic, or any other shape that results in prediction of strength in substantial agreement with results of comprehensive tests.

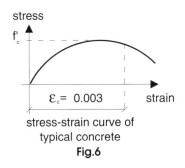

Fig.6

10.2.7 - Requirements of 10.2.6 are satisfied by an equivalent rectangular concrete stress distribution defined by the following:

10.2.7.1 - Concrete stress of 85f $'_c$ shall be assumed uniformly distributed over an equivalent compression zone bounded by edges of the cross section and a straight line parallel to the neutral axis at a distance a = β_1c from the fiber of maximum compressive strain.

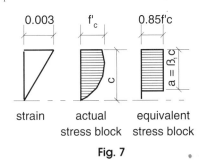

Fig. 7

10.2.7.2 - Distance c from fiber of maximum strain to the neutral axis shall be measured in a direction perpendicular to that axis.

10.2.7.3 - Factor β shall be taken as 0.85 for concrete strengths f $'_c$ up to and including 4000 psi. For strengths above 4000 psi, β_1 shall be reduced continuously at a rate of 0.05 for each 1000 psi of strength in excess of 4000 psi, but β_1 shall not be taken less than 0.65.

Commentary

The tensile strength of concrete in flexure (modulus of rupture) is a more variable property than the compressive strength and is about 10-15 percent of the compressive strength. Tensile strength of concrete is neglected in strength design. For members with normal percentages of reinforcement, this assumption is in good agreement with tests.

The strength of concrete in tension, however, is important in cracking and deflection considerations at service loads.

This assumption recognizes the inelastic stress distribution of concrete at high stress. As maximum stress is approached, the stress strain relationship of concrete is not a straight line but some form of a curve (stress is not proportional to strain). The general shape of a stress strain curve is primarily a function of concrete strength and consists of a rising curve from zero to a maximum at a compressive strain between 0.0015 and 0.002, followed by a descending curve to an ultimate strain (crushing of the concrete) from 0.003 to higher than 0.008. As indicated under 10.2.3, the Code sets the maximum usable strain at 0.003 for design.

For practical design the Code allows the use of a rectangular compressive stress distribution (stress block) to replace the more exact concrete stress distributions. In the equivalent rectangular stress block, an average stress of 0.85f'$_c$ is used with a rectangle of depth a = β_1c. The β_1 of 0.85 for concrete with f'$_c$ <= 4,000 psi and 0.05 less for each 1,000 psi of f'$_c$ in excess of 4,000 psi was determined experimentally.

*American Concrete Institute, 1992. *Building Code Requirements of Reinforced Concrete* (ACI 318-89) and Commentary (ACI 318R-89), Detroit, MI.

Flexure (Bending) of rectangular concrete beams

In the following we shall establish the value of the expected nominal strength as a function of the size of the beam, the amount of reinforcement, the quality of the materials used, *i.e.* the strength of the concrete and that of the steel.

Notation: (Fig.8)

a = depth of equivalent stress block (in.)

A_s = area of tensile reinforcement (sq.in.)

b = width of compression face of member (in.)

d = distance from the extreme compression fiber to centroid of tensile reinforcement ("effective depth") (in.)

h = overall depth of member (in.)

ρ = ratio of tension reinforcement = A_s/bd

Ø = strength reduction factor (Ø = 0.9 for flexure)

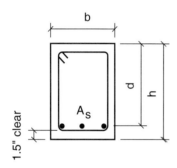

Fig. 8. Typical rectangular reinforced concrete beam

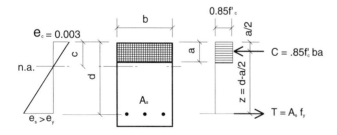

Fig. 9. Strain and stress on reinforced concrete beam

The adjacent diagram (Fig.9) shows the strain distribution over the cross section at failure and the assumed (for calculation purposes) stress distribution. The internal couple forming the resisting moment is shown. C is the sum of the compressive stresses, while T is the tension in the reinforcement.

From equilibrium: T = C, *i.e.* $A_s f_y = 0.85 f'_c ba$

From here "a" (the depth of the equivalent stress block) may be expressed as:

$$a = \frac{A_s f y}{0.85 f'_c b}$$

The nominal flexural strength of the section then may be calculated from the value of the internal couple.

$$M_n = Cz = 0.85 f'_c ba\ (d-a/2)$$
$$\text{or } M_n = Tz = A_s f_y\ (d-a/2)$$

(Note that the same concrete cross section may have different flexural strength with different amounts of reinforcing in it.)

The usable moment capacity is then : $Ø\ M_n$

The above equations are then adequate to calculate the flexural strength of a section, when everything is known about the section. (Problem of *investigation*, *i.e.* we try to verify that a section has adequate strength to satisfy the demanded ultimate strength.)

Example:

Given: h = 20" b = 12" f'_c = 3 ksi f_y = 60 ksi
A_s = 3-#7 bars = 1.80 in²

Solution: The working depth, d = h - concrete cover - stirrup diameter - 1/2 of reinf. bar diameter
d = 20.0 - 1.5 - 0.375 - 0.875/2 = 17.69"
a = (1.80) 60 / 0.85 (3)12 = 3.53"
$Ø M_n$ = 0.9 (1.80) 60 [17.69 - 3.53/2] = 1,548 k-10

the problem of *design*, however, *i.e.* the search for a section with a certain amount of reinforcement to satisfy a demanded ultimate strength, is a somewhat more involved procedure. We may notice that in the expression(s) defining the nominal strength, there are five different items (f'_c, f_y, b, d and A_s). Unfortunately we have only one equation that expresses the fact that

$$M_u <= Ø M_n$$

The normal design procedure is to select four of the unknowns and calculate the fifth from the above equation. Usually, we decide on the strength of the concrete (f'_c) and the quality of steel (f_y) for the whole project. Then we select an estimated concrete section (b and h). This leaves only the required amount of reinforcing to be calculated.

$$M_u = Ø A_s f_y\ (d-a/2) \text{ substituting } a = \frac{A_s f_y}{0.85 f'_c\ b}$$

and reorganizing we may obtain

$$\left(\frac{0.5294\ fy^2}{f'_c\ b} \right) A_s{}^2 - \left(0.9\ f_y\ d \right) A_s + M_u = 0$$

$$\text{let } K_1 = \left(\frac{0.5294\ fy^2}{f'_c\ b} \right) \text{ and } K_2 = 0.9\ f_y d \quad \text{then}$$

$$A_s = \frac{K_2 - \sqrt{K_2{}^2 - 4\ K_1\ M_u}}{2\ K_1}$$

All units must be consistent!

Example: Given: $M_u = 210$ k-ft $= 2,520$ k-in
              Select: $h = 24"$ $b = 14"$ $f'_c = 4$ ksi $f_y = 60$ ksi

(since we do not yet know the size of the reinforcing, we can only estimate the value of d; a good and practical estimate is d = h - 2.5") then: $d_{est} = 21.5"$ then

$$[0.5294 \ (\frac{60^2}{4 \times 14})] \ A_s^2 - [0.9 \ (60) \ 21.5] \ A_s + 2,520 = 0$$

$A_s = 2.33$ in^2 select: 3-#8 bars; $A_s = 2.37$ in^2

There are other methods and design aids, that help with the solution. By introducing a parameter called "steel ratio,"

$$p = \frac{As}{b \ d} \ , \ \text{and letting} \ \ R = \phi \ p \ f_y \ \left[1 - \frac{p \ f_y}{1.7 \ f_c} \right],$$

the design equation can be brought to :

$$M_u \ R \ b \ d^2 \ \text{or} \ R \ M_u \ / \ (b \ d^2)$$

There are design tables that list R as a function of p, f'$_c$ and f$_y$, thus p can be selected to correspond to a required R value, after which A$_s$ can be found.

T beams

In a monolithic floor construction we rarely have isolated rectangular beams. Instead we have beams that are continuous over several spans with slabs spanning between them. The adjacent slabs in the positive moment regions help to carry the compressive stresses. The stress block at ultimate strength becomes wider and shallower, increasing the (d-a/2) moment arm, and thus helps to reduce the amount of required reinforcing.

The adjacent sketch(Fig.10) illustrates the point. On the cantilevers (or more precisely in the zone of negative moments) tension is on the top and compression is on the bottom. There the beam is like a rectangular section, the adjacent slabs are in the tension zone, and only the web of the beam is available to carry compression.

On the other hand in the positive moment region compression is on the top and the slab, that forms part of the beam due to monolithic action, helps the beam to carry the compressions.

The ACI Code provides instructions about the width of slab that may be used in the design of T beams.

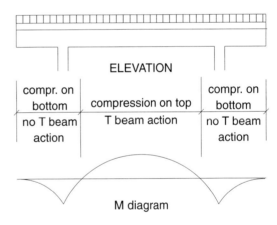

Fig 10. T beam

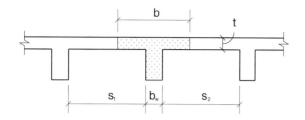

Fig. 11. T beam effective flange

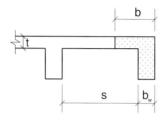

Fig 12. Effective flange on one side only

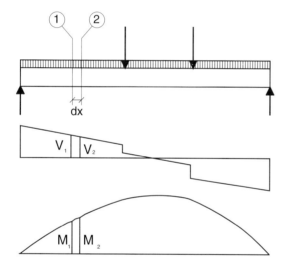

Fig 13. Shear and moment diagram

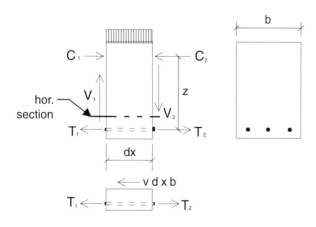

Fig. 14. Beam detail

Width of the slab effective as a T beam flange shall not exceed one quarter of the span length of the beam, and the effective overhanging flange width on each side of the web shall not exceed (Fig.11):

(a) eight times the slab thickness, and

(b) one half the clear distance to the next web.

In other words:

b is the least of   span/4

           or $16t + b_w$

           or $b_w + s_1/2 + s_2/2$

For beams that have a slab on one side only, the formulae modify as follows (Fig. 12):

b is the least of: $b_w + span/12$

           or $b_w + 6t$

           or $b_w + s/2$

Shear in reinforced concrete beams

The adjacent sketch (Fig.13) shows a reinforced concrete beam, its shear and moment diagrams due to some kind of load as indicated. On the beam we selected a small length of the beam, bounded by sections 1 and 2. The small length is designated as dx. As we may observe there are differences in the shear and the moment at the two respective sections, *i.e.* $V_1 > V_2$ and $M_1 < M_2$.

As the reader may recall, the change in the moment equals to the area under the shear diagram and the rate of change in the moment equals to the magnitude of the shear. Mathematically this was expressed as:

$$\frac{dM}{dx} = V \qquad or \qquad \frac{M_2 - M_1}{dx} = V$$

If we substitute the moments with the internal couples, *i.e.* $M_1 = T_1 z = C_1 z$ and $M_2 = T_2 z = C_2 z$, then we may observe that $T_1 < T_2$ since $M_1 < M_2$

When we further isolate a small part of the beam that is below the "horizontal section" indicated on the adjacent diagram,(Fig.14) then we find that for equilibrium purposes we have to have a horizontal force acting on that horizontal section that helps to restore the equilib⁻ium on that small part. The area of that "horizontal section" is "b dx and if the stress (*i.e.* the force per unit area) is designated by "v" then we can derive the following relationship:

$$T_2 - T_1 = \frac{M_2}{z} - \frac{M_1}{z} = \frac{dM}{z}$$

from equilibrium: $T_2 - T_1 = v \; b \; dx$

hence: $\frac{dM}{z} = v \; b \; dx$

rearranging the terms we may write : $V = \frac{dM}{dx} = v \; b \; z$

On the adjacent sketch (Fig.15) an isolated part of the beam is shown in elevation. Within this portion of the beam (somewhere inside) a small 1"x1"x1" cube is selected. On the elevation of this cube the shear stresses are also indicated. Previously we showed what causes the horizontal shears. Notice that the horizontal shears form a couple (on the sketch it is a counter clockwise couple). Since a couple can be kept in equilibrium by another couple, we conclude that a clockwise couple is needed on this cube. This clockwise couple is furnished by equal magnitude shears on the vertical side of the cube. The appearance of shears both on the horizontal sections and on the vertical sections of a beam is known as the "duality of shears", meaning that shears are always present on both the horizontal surface and on the vertical surface of a little elementary cube inside of the beam and they are equal in magnitude.

Shears do not cause the problem for concrete, as a matter of fact concrete is quite strong in shear. However when we isolate the unit cube and continue our "detective" work, we find that if we form the resultant of two of the shears on the top and the left, and also from the bottom and the right respectively. These are trying to tear our cube apart perpendicular to the diagonal shown. When we separate the cube into two triangular wedges, we note that for equilibrium purposes we need stresses perpendicular to that diagonal cut. The sum total of these tensile stresses must be equal to v √2. Since the area of the diagonal cut is 1 √2, we may conclude that the stresses acting on that diagonal cut equal to "v" psi (or ksi), *i.e.* the magnitude of the *diagonal tensile stresses* equal to that of the shear stresses (Figs. 16, 17, 18).

Concrete is weak in tension, therefore there is a potential that the diagonal tensions may tear the beam apart. There are many such potential cracks. The horizontal component of the diagonal tension can be resisted by the horizontal reinforcing. The vertical component requires a special reinforcing called stirrups. Stirrups are usually small diameter bars (#3 or #4).

Since we may have a potential crack at any place where the shears are large, we usually need stirrups along a good portion of the beam at both ends where the shears are large (Fig.19).

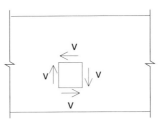

Fig. 15. Isolated beam detail

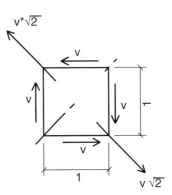

Fig. 16. Shear forces on isolated concrete cube

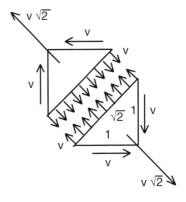

Fig. 17. Cracking potential in beam

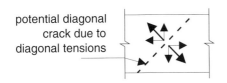

potential diagonal crack due to diagonal tensions

Fig. 18. Diagonal tension

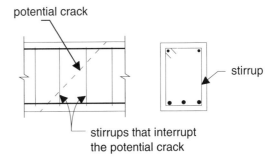

potential crack

stirrup

stirrups that interrupt the potential crack

Fig 19. Stirrup reinforcing

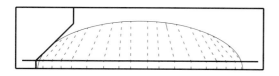

Fig. 20. Simple model of beam stresses

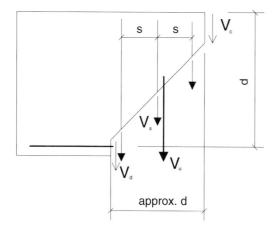

Fig. 21. Shear forces

While the explanation above created the impression that the cracks are exactly "diagonal" *i.e.* 45 degrees to the axis of the beam, the truth is more complicated than that, for the longitudinal stresses (compression above the neutral axis and tension below) modify the direction of these tensions, but for design purposes a simple model can be created as shown here (Fig.20).

Accordingly we assume that there is a potential crack which is crossed by a number of stirrups (n), that are at "s" spacing apart. The action of V_u is resisted by "friction" created in the compression zone (V_c), the sum of the tensions created in the stirrups' legs (V_s), and a so called dowel action from the vertical shear resistance of the horizontal reinforcing (V_d). This latter one is neglected by the Code. The remaining two, *i.e.* V_c plus V_s then form the resistance, *i.e.* the so called shear strength (Fig.21). (Please remember that the shear is used as a measure of the diagonal tension.)

The design equation is then:

$$V_u \leq \emptyset\, V_n = \emptyset\,(\,V_c + V_s\,)$$

V_c is the assumed nominal shear strength contributed by the concrete and it can be calculated in beams as:

$$V_c = 2\sqrt{f_c}\, b\, d \qquad (f_c \text{ must be entered in psi units})$$

V_s is the nominal shear strength provided by the stirrups:

$$V_s = A_v\, f_y\, d/s$$

Notation:

> A_v = sum of the cross section area of stirrup legs
> s = spacing of stirrups
> b_w = width of the web of concrete beams
> d = distance from extreme compression fiber to centroid of tensile reinforcement
> $\emptyset$ = strength reduction factor (0.85 for shear)

(Derivation of V_s: $V_s = n\,(A_v\, f_y)$, assuming that "n" stirrups cross the potential 45 deg. crack.

> since $n\, s \quad d$, thus $n = d/s$
> hence: $V_s = A_v\, f_y\, d/s$

Design procedure for shear in concrete beams:

1. Find V_u at section under investigation;

2. Calculate $V_c = 2\sqrt{f_c}\, b\, d$

3. Calculate $V_s = (V_u/\emptyset) - V_c$

4. Select stirrup size (usually #3 or #4)

5. Calculate the spacing required at the section under investigation as

$$s = \frac{A_v\, f_y\, d}{V_s}$$

(Since a single stirrup has 2 legs, they will both work as part of V_s, thus A_v equals to twice the cross-sectional area of a stirrup.)

Notes:

a. The maximum permitted spacing is *the least* of the following:

    1. the spacing calculated above

or   2. $s_{max} = d/2$ when $V_s <= 4 \sqrt{f'_c}\, b_w\, d$

or $s = \dfrac{d}{4}$ when $4\sqrt{f'_c}\, b_w\, d < V_s < 8\sqrt{f'_c}\, b_w\, d$

or   3. $s_{max} = A_v\, f_y\, / (50\, b_w)$

b. A minimum area of shear reinforcement must be provided where

    $V_u > \emptyset\, V_c\, / 2$ except in slabs and footings;
                              or in concrete joist construction;

c. Sections located less than distance "d" from the face of the support may be designed for the same V_u as that computed at a distance "d" from the face of the support.

Reinforced concrete columns

Fig. 22 shows part of a concrete frame. The deformation shown is that of a simply supported beam. Simply supported beams are characterized by free rotations at the ends. Free rotation means lack of restraints, or with other words: lack of end moments. However, in a monolithically built reinforced concrete structure the ends of the beams cannot rotate freely, since at the joints beams and columns must rotate an identical amount. The columns are trying to resist the rotation of the beam, the beam "drags" them along to some equilibrium position as shown on Fig. 23.

For the equilibrium of the joint, M = 0, the beam moment(s) are kept in equilibrium by the column moments, as shown on Fig. 24.

When one examines a system of beams and columns as shown here on Fig. 25, it is easy to follow the transfer of shears and moments from beams to columns and vice versa. Shears at the ends of the beams become axial loads on the columns. In addition, the moments from the floor above and below the column tend to bend the column into a "double curve". This is much more pronounced at exterior columns, than at interior columns, where loads on the neighboring beams try to rotate the common node in opposite directions, thus the bending on the columns is not as great, at least not from gravity loads.

As it may be seen, at any section of the column we may find an axial force (P_u) and a moment (M_u). These were calculated from factored loads and represent the demand on the section under consideration. The design equations now are much more complex, since the strength must satisfy two (or three, when in the truly general situation the column is bent around two axes!!) items simultaneously.

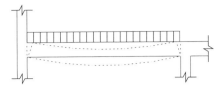

Fig. 22. Simply supported concrete frme

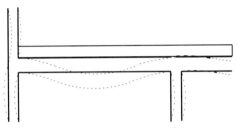

Fig. 23. Monolithic concrete frame

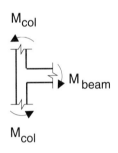

Fig. 24. Equilibrium of the joint

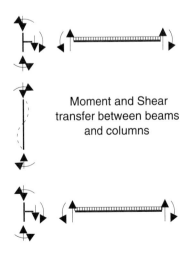

Moment and Shear
transfer between beams
and columns

Fig. 25. Transfer of shears and moments

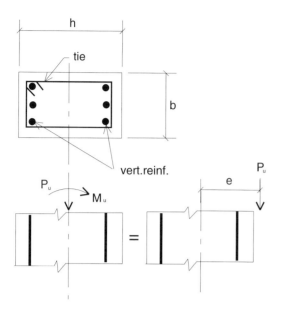

Fig 26. The effect of axial forces

If we examine a column section (or a short length of a column) on which a given P_u and M_u act, as shown, (Fig.26), we see that the axial force creates compression throughout the section (both concrete and vertical steel are in compression), while the bending moment creates compression on the right hand side and tension on the left hand side. On the right hand side the compressive effects of the axial force and the moment add up. On the left side we cannot be sure what will happen. There the tension from the moment and the compression from the axial force work against each other. If the tension from the moment is small, then the compression will "win" and the whole section will be in compression with the maximum occurring on the right side. On the other hand, if the moment is large, the tension on the left side will "overwhelm" the compression from the axial force and a net amount of tension will result. Since the concrete is assumed to take no tension, only the amount of the reinforcing steel on the tension side will be available to resist it.

Note: A system consisting an axial force and a moment may also be represented by a statically equivalent system of a force at an eccentricity. For the two systems to be equivalent we must have

$$P_u e = M_u \ \ or \ \ e = \frac{M_u}{P_u}$$

In flexure a given section with a given amount of reinforcing has an easily calculable ultimate moment. In columns, however, a given column section with a given amount of reinforcing *may fail either due to excessive compression* under the combined effects of the axial load and the moment, *or it might fail in tension.* Either failure mode is possible depending on the relative magnitudes of P_u and M_u. There are an infinite number of axial force and moment combinations that represent failure condition for a given column (*i.e.* a column with known materials, cross section and reinforcing). These ultimate axial force and moment combinations can be represented in a graph called *interaction diagram.*

 The different possibilities of failures may be shown in the following five diagrams, each of which represents a particular "failure mode." The interpretation of the P_u force is such that it is just large enough to create the conditions shown on the *strain diagrams* (Fig. 27).

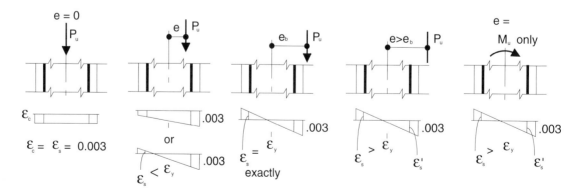

Fig. 27. Failure modes

The diagram on the right (Fig. 28) is a so-called interaction diagram. For every imaginable column section with a given amount of reinforcing one can construct an interaction diagram. Any pair of force and moment can be represented in the coordinate system as a point, and the force and moment pair will not cause failure in the given column as long as the point falls within the curve. Any point on the curve or outside of the curve represent the combined action of a force and a moment that will cause failure in the column section. The "safe zone" on the diagram simply means the scaling of the failure curve by a factor Ø. The Code selects this as Ø=0.7 for tied columns.

Ties are used to enable the reinforcing bars that are long and slender compression elements to develop their full yield strength without buckling. In order to achieve that goal we select the following as the maximum allowable spacing of the ties:

spacing<= 16 D (where D = diameter of the longitudinal bars)
       <= 48 tie diameters
       <= b (where b is the *shorter* cross sectional dimension of the column)
Ties are at least #3 up to and including #10 longitudinal bars
              #4 for longitudinal bars #11 and larger

Typical floor systems

Flat plate (Fig. 29) structures are often used for moderate spans and loads. The forming cost is the least of all possible systems, it provides for the least structural depth and thus for the least floor to floor height. The span/depth ratios most commonly used are between 28 and 32, the lower value should be used when the exterior or corner panels are unstiffened by the incorporation of an edge beam. It is also the most economical, when the spans are about 26 ft or less. Beyond 26 ft, the slab becomes too thick, with corresponding increase of its self weight. If larger spans are desired, the Architect either has to select a different structural system, or a pre-stressed (post tensioned) version must be used.

Fig.30 shows the schematic deformation diagram of a flat plate under load. While the largest deflections are in the center of the bay, the most highly stressed zones occur in the vicinity of the supports. Since all the loads must travel toward the columns, the available zone (see Fig. 31) through which shears must travel becomes smaller and smaller, thus the unit shear increases, and reaches a maximum at or near the interface of the column and the slab. The large shears are also indicative of sharp change in the moments that occur in the vicinity of the columns. Shears cause diagonal tensions (see later) in structures subject to flexure. Since concrete is quite weak in resisting tension, failure can result. The failure surface may be envisioned as a truncated pyramid. (See Fig.32). This phenomenon is known as punching shear, *i.e.* the column "punches" through the slab, or more precisely the slab fails and falls down around the column.

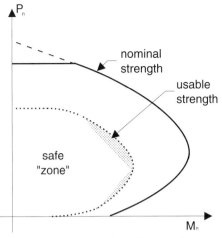

Fig. 28. "Interaction diagram"

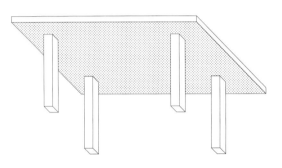

Fig. 29. Flat plate

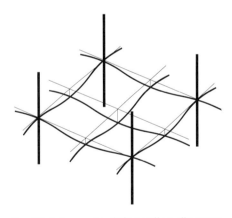

Fig. 30. Schematic deformation diagram

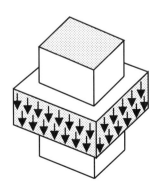

Fig. 31. Failure surface at shear zone

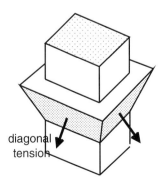

Fig. 32. Failure surface at shear zone

B1

SHELL

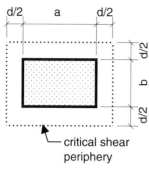

Fig. 33. Plan of column

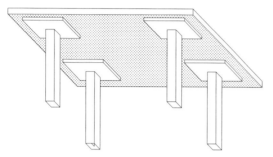

Fig. 34. Flat slab with drop panels

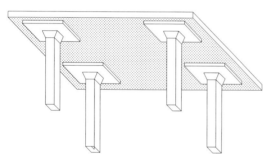

Fig. 35. Flat slab with drop panels and column capitals

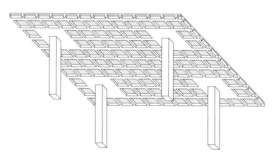

Fig. 36. Waffle slab

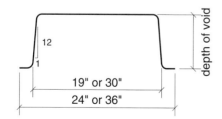

Standard depth:
6", 8", 10", 12" for 19" wide voids
8", 10", 12", 14", 16", 20" for 30" wide voids

Fig. 37. Standard void dimensions of waffle systems

The ACI Code deals with this rather complex problem by offering a simple model for design, that has been shown by tests to offer an appropriate safety against failure. Instead of working with the tension on a slanted surface, it assumes to have a *critical shear periphery* located at d/2 distance from the face of the column in every direction. (d = the working depth of the slab, and maybe assumed approximately as [h - 1.25"] for preliminary design purposes.

$$V_u \leq \phi V_n = \phi V_c \quad where \quad V_c = (2 + \frac{4}{\beta_c})\sqrt{f_c'}\,b_o d$$

$$but \quad V_c \leq 4\sqrt{f_c'}\,b_o d$$

b_o = length of the shear periphery = $(2a+2b+4d)$

β_c = the aspect ratio of the longer face to the shorter face of the column. It does not become significant unless it is larger than 2.

It is important to notice, that the size of the critical shear surface, upon which the available shear strength depends, is governed by the thickness of the slab on the one hand, and the dimensions of the column section on the other. Furthermore, openings through the slab near the column create discontinuity in the shear surface and seriously weaken the available strength. Thus, in the planning of the building layout, vertical chases should not be located in the immediate vicinity of columns. Special reinforcing made up of either reinforcing bars, or of wide flange steel sections are sometimes used to increase the shear strength of the critical zone.

Flat plate and flat slab structures need not necessarily be laid out in a regular fashion. Columns may be offset from a regular pattern so long as the slab span/depth ratios between the columns do not increase beyond the values given above in either direction. Moderate length cantilevers are actually beneficial, for they provide increased shear surface at exterior columns and also help to reduce the deflections of the slab in exterior or corner bays.

Flat Slab structures (Fig. 34 and 35) are actually plates that are reinforced by either drop panels, or column capitals, or both. Its use is warranted for moderate spans (up to 30 to 32 ft) and high superimposed loads. The increased forming cost may be justified, for the system provides maximum ceiling space between the drop panels, and even in the area of drop panels, the loss of depth is quite minimal. The column capitals help to enlarge the column/slab interface periphery, thus helping with the critical shear transfer from the slab to the column. The drop panels help in many ways. The increased slab thickness provide for the potential of greater flexural strength, it increases the size (and therefore the strength) of the critical shear periphery. Furthermore, the greater thickness also represents greater stiffness, *i.e.* resistance to deformation, thus helps to reduce the deflections in the middle of the bay. Drop panels, if used, must extend to a distance at least one-sixth of the span in each direction, and its depth below the slab must be at least one-quarter of the thickness of the slab. The thickness of the slab for good serviceability should be selected between span/32 to span/36.

Waffle Slab structures (Fig. 36) are thick flat plate structures, with the concrete removed in zones where not required by strength considerations. They are economical structures for spans up to 60 ft, square, or nearly so, bays, loaded with light and moderate loads. The voids are formed by steel (or fiberglass) "domes", that are reusable, thus very economical. These domes are available in standardized sizes (see Fig. 37), although wider or odd shaped domes are also used to satisfy some design objective. The domes are tapered, usually 1 in 12, that permits easy removal after the concrete has sufficiently cured. When carefully done, and finished after the removal of the forms, the two way joists provide for a pleasing appearance as well.

While the lips on the domes, when laid out side by side, form 5" wide joists for the 19" voids and 6" wide joists for the 30" wide voids, it is not a requirement that forces the designer to work with 24" or 36" planning modules. Since the domes are always laid out on a flat plywood deck, the spacing between the domes can be adjusted, so by making the joists wider than standard at the base, virtually any column spacing can be accommodated, while maintaining a uniform appearance. By leaving out the domes around the columns, a shear head is automatically formed to provide for increased shear strength. The slab over the domes is typically 3" thick, unless large concentrated loads or increased fire rating requirements warrant the use of a thicker slab. The slab is reinforced with a light welded wire fabric that helps with control of potential shrinkage and temperature cracks.

Another popular form of structure is shown on Fig. 38. Wide beams form a two-way grid of beams between columns, the depth is equal to the depth of the two-way joist system. This arrangement provides for somewhat easier layout of reinforcing in the negative moment regions around the columns.

One-way joists spanning between beams are essentially closely spaced beam elements (Fig. 39). In order to qualify for the joist designation by the ACI Code, the space between them must not exceed 30". The forms used are made of various materials. Steel, fiberglass, fiber board, corrugated card board forms are readily available, made with or without the edge lip (Fig. 40). However, forms without the edge lip tend to bulge sideways during construction under the lateral pressure of the freshly poured concrete, and the resulting joist widths are going to be uneven. Forms are also available with square or tapered ends. The tapered ends provide for increased shear capacity as well as increased moment capacity at the negative moment regions (Fig. 41).

The one way joist system is often used when the bays are elongated, *i.e.* in one direction the column spacing exceeds the spacing in the other direction by about 40% or more. At such span ratios, the advantage of two way behavior is greatly reduced, and it is more economical to use one way systems, *i.e.* beams spanning between columns, and joists spanning between the beams. It is most economical to span the beams in the shorter spans and the joists in the longer span. For ease of forming, the depth of the beams are often selected to be equal to the depth of the joists. In order to provide for the necessary shear and moment capacity, the beams are made considerably wider than the columns' faces into which they frame. Beams deeper than the joists occupy additional ceiling space, and require additional forming cost (Fig. 42, a and b).

The slab over the voids is typically 3" thick, unless large concentrated loads or increased fire rating requirements warrant the use of a thicker slab. The slab is reinforced with a light welded wire fabric that helps with control of potential shrinkage and temperature cracks. The overall depth of the joist (including the slab's thickness) should be selected in accordance with Table 1 taken from the ACI Code. (See next page). The ratios listed therein give satisfactory performance for most structural elements. However, the designer should be aware, that these are minimum depth values, and as the fine print in the Code warns the user, should be used for "Members not supporting or attached to partitions or other construction likely to be damaged by large deflections." Thus special attention should be given to the attachment of walls to the underside of concrete structural elements, so that due to creep caused long term deflections, such elements do not start to use such walls as supports. Furthermore, for crack free performance masonry walls require, that the deflection of the supporting beams should not exceed span/600. Careful attention is recommended to such details.

From note b) it is clear, that if the depth must be minimized beyond the values listed in the table, the designer has the choice of using

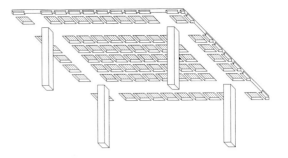

Fig. 38. Waffle slab with two-way beams

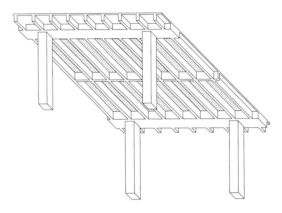

Fig. 39. One-way joists and beams

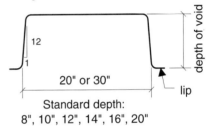

12
1
20" or 30"
depth of void
lip
Standard depth:
8", 10", 12", 14", 16", 20"

Fig. 40. Standard steel form dimensions of one-way systems

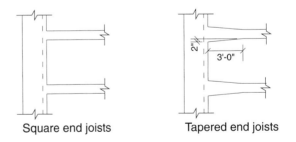

2"   3'-0"

Square end joists   Tapered end joists

Fig. 41. Ends of concrete joists

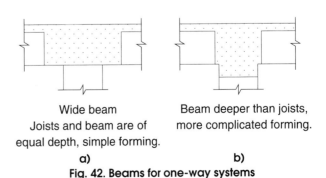

Wide beam   Beam deeper than joists,
Joists and beam are of   more complicated forming.
equal depth, simple forming.
a)   b)

Fig. 42. Beams for one-way systems

B1

SHELL

Table 1. Minimum thickness of non-prestressed beams or one-way slabs, unless deflections are computed.*

Member	Simply supported	One end continuous	Both ends continuous	Cantilever
Solid one-way slabs	span/20	span/24	span/28	span/10
Beams or joists	span/16	span/18.5	span/21	span/8

Values given shall be used directly for members with normal weight concrete and Grade 60 reinforcement. For other conditions the values shall be modified as follows:

a) For structural lightweight concrete having unit weight in the range of 90-120 pcf, the values shall be multiplied by $(1.65 - 0.005w_c)$ but not less than 1.09, where w_c is the unit weight in pcf.

b) For f_y other than 60,000 psi, the values shall be multiplied by $(0.4 + f_y/100,000)$.

*ACI 318-89, Building Code Requirements for Reinforced Concrete, American Concrete Institute, Detroit, MI.

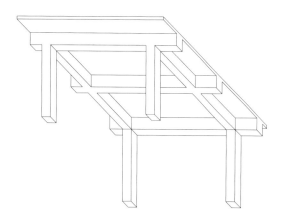

Fig 43. Slabs and beams system

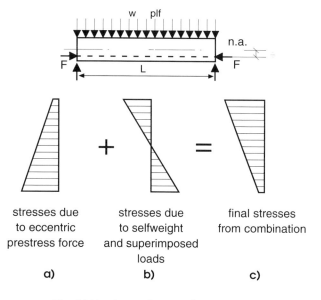

stresses due to eccentric prestress force	stresses due to selfweight and superimposed loads	final stresses from combination
a)	b)	c)

Fig. 44. Prestressed concrete principles

Grade 40 ($f_y = 40,000$ psi) reinforcing. This will result in about 50% more reinforcing in the member, that in turn reduces the strain in the reinforcing steel at service load condition. Reduced strain in the reinforcing provides for reduced deflection in a member. Since it is not a wise thing to use a different grade reinforcing for a few selected members on a project, it is permissible to use Grade 60 steel equal in cross sectional area as the calculated amount of steel that would be necessary with the use of Grade 40 steel.

Slabs and Beams system (Fig. 43) is an economical choice, when the bays are elongated, and the superimposed loads are large, especially when the structure is subject to large line loads. Large through the slab openings can be easily accommodated virtually anywhere in the floor. It results in larger structural depth, than the other systems described above, the forming cost is also usually higher. These seeming disadvantages are balanced by the economical concrete and reinforcing usage in the system. The system also provides for a clear and unambiguous transfer of moments between beams and columns, that is a real advantage in high wind and/or seismic zones, when the structural frame is called upon in the resisting of large lateral loads on the building.

Prestressed concrete

The concept of prestressing means the introduction of stresses into the concrete structural element, that when combined with other stresses created by selfweight and superimposed loads, a desirable state of stresses will result in the element. Since, as it was mentioned before, the tensile strength of concrete is rather limited (and not very reliable), it is discounted in design.

Fig. 44 illustrates the principle involved. An F prestressing force creates a stress distribution shown in Fig. 44, a. Depending on the eccentricity (e), the stress at the top may be compression as shown, or tension. The uniformly distributed loads create tension at the bottom and compression at the top. (Fig. 44, b) When the two are combined, the stress distribution shown in Fig.44, c, is obtained. Again, depending on the magnitude and the eccentricity of the F force, the section will have compression throughout as shown, or a small amount of tension may result in the bottom.

Prestressing has two different approaches, *i.e.* pre-tensioniong and post-tensioning. In the former, the prestressing wires or strands are tensioned by stretching and fixing against a bulkhead, then the concrete is poured around them in the desirable shape and form. After the concrete has gained sufficient strength, the strands are released and the force in them is transferred into the concrete element by the bond established between the strands and the cured concrete. This method is applicable for precast and prestressed elements produced in manufacturing plants. The production techniques often involve the casting of elements in long (up to 600 ft) casting beds, that permits the simultaneous fabrication of many elements with a single tensioning of the strands. Accelerated curing techniques permit the release of the strands in only 8 to 12 hours after the placement of the concrete, thus a 24 hour manufacturing cycle can be maintained. The production is highly mechanized and great quality control can be obtained.

In post-tensioning, as the name aptly indicates, the concrete structure is poured in situ with conduits containing the prestressing strands pre-placed into the form work. After the concrete has gained sufficient strength with one end of the strand fixed into position, a hydraulic prestressing jack is applied to the other end. Using the cured concrete as the bulkhead, the strand is tensioned by stretching. After the stressing, the end is anchored, thus preventing its snapping back to its original length. The space around the strand within the conduit may be grouted (grouted tendons), or left free (ungrouted tendons), in which case only the end anchorages provide for the maintenance of the prestressing force. There are many proprietary prestressing (post-tensioning) systems on the market, using different anchorage designs.

Structural design - masonry

Summary: A review of structural masonry construction is provided with guidelines for structural design of masonry, including details for brick and concrete masonry units and construction considerations.

Key words: brick, concrete masonry, masonry, engineered masonry.

Uniformat:	2010
MasterFormat:	04050

SHELL

B1

Introduction

Masonry is construction which uses brick, block, stone or glass manufactured or cut in easily handled units and bonded together through mortar, grout, reinforcing and metal ties. Throughout history masonry has been a construction material where its strength in compression is paramount. As recent research has developed for this material and method of construction reinforced masonry has developed with significant advantages in performance especially when subjected to earthquake loads.

Masonry codes historically were product driven. A brick code, a concrete masonry code, a clay tile code all had similar standards but each was different according to industry standards combined with the industry's empirical methods. The 1995 *Building Code Requirements for Masonry Structures and Specifications for Masonry Structures* (ACI 530.1-95/ASCE 6-95/TMS 602-95) results from years of research and coordinated efforts to establish one comprehensive masonry code which includes the many different masonry materials. Nearly all forms of masonry are covered including clay and shale brick, concrete block, stone, unreinforced, reinforced, empirical, glass unit masonry, and anchored veneer masonry along with mortar, grout and metal accessories.

The analysis and design for masonry structures is based on the allowable stress design (ASD) methodology. Allowable stresses have been used in masonry design for many years and reflects the extensive research and experience documented over the last century. The allowable stress design provisions are based on the following assumptions:

1   Masonry materials are linearly elastic under service loads;

2   Stress is directly proportional to strain under service loads;

3   Masonry materials behave homogeneously; and

4   Sections plane before bending remain plane after bending. Service loads are used as the basis of design and the masonry unit of brick or block, together with the mortar and grout, essentially act a one unit rather than separately.

Allowable stresses are based on failure stresses with a factor of safety in the range of 2 to 5. The 1995 code also has a provision, not included in previous masonry standards, which requires the effects of restraint of movement due to prestressing, vibrations, impact, shrinkage, expansion, temperature changes, creep, unequal settlement of supports and differential movements be considered in the design. The code states design coefficients for thermal expansion, moisture expansion, shrinkage and creep for masonry.

For strength, the specified compressive strength of masonry, f'_m, must be determined by the designer and verified by the contractor. The modulus of elasticity, E_m, may be determined by the secant method from prism tests. Deflection limits are imposed for masonry beams and lintels which support unreinforced masonry. The deflection should not exceed L/600 nor 0.3 inch where L is the span of the member.

In unreinforced masonry, the small tensile stresses are taken into consideration in the design of members. Allowable flexural stresses reflect a factor of safety of 2.5 to 3.5. Any reinforcement placed in unreinforced masonry, by definition, is for shrinkage or for other reasons. Allowable shear stresses are based upon a parabolic shear stress

Author: Martin D. Gehner, P. E.

Credits: Brick Institute of America

References: American Concrete Institute (ACI), American Society of Civil Engineers (ASCE), and The Masonry Society (TMS). 1995. *Building Code Requirements for Masonry Structures* (ACI 530-95/ASCE 5-95/TMS 602-95); and *Specification for Masonry Structures* (ACI 530.1-95/ASCE 6-95/TMS 602-95). Detroit, MI: American Concrete Institute.

Beall, Christine. 1994. *Masonry Design and Detailing for Architects, Engineers and Builders.* Englewood Cliffs, NJ: Prentice-Hall.

Brick Institute of America (BIA). 1996. *Technical Notes on Brick Construction.* Reston, VA: Brick Institute of America.

International Masonry Institute. 1991. *Masonry Bibliography: 1830-1982; Masonry Bibliography, Volume II: 1983-1987; Masonry Bibliography, Volume III: 1987-1990.* Washington, DC: International Masonry Institute.

National Concrete Masonry Association (NCMA). 1996. *TEK Manual for Concrete Masonry Design and Construction.* Herndon, VA: National Concrete Masonry Institute.

Orton, Andrew. 1992. *Structural Design of Masonry.* New York: John Wiley & Sons.

Portland Cement Association (PCA) 1991. *The Concrete Masonry Handbook for Architects, Engineers and Builders.* Skokie, IL: Portland Cement Association.

distribution rather than on an average shear stress as in previous codes. For axial compressive stresses, the slenderness ratio for unreinforced masonry is a function of the radius of gyration of the member's cross section. The factor of safety is 4 for unreinforced masonry. Previous codes imposed limits on slenderness as they defined relative to thickness of wall. The 1995 code the slenderness reduction factor becomes very small as the structural element gets more slender.

In reinforced masonry, steel reinforcement carries all tensile forces in a bending member. Reinforcement may also provide resistance to shear forces. Minimum amounts of reinforcement are determined by design except for seismic provisions. The allowable flexural compressive stress is the same as for unreinforced masonry.

Masonry materials

Stone

As a natural inorganic substance stone is identified by its geologic origin. *Igneous rock* is formed by solidifying and cooling of molten material lying deep within the earth and thrust to its surface by volcanic action. Granite is the only building stone of this origin. *Sedimentary rock* is formed by waterborne deposits of minerals produced by the weathering and destruction of igneous rock. Sandstone, shale and limestone are building stone from this source. *Metamorphic rock* is either igneous or sedimentary material whose structure has been changed by extreme heat and pressure. Marble, slate and quartzite are building stone in this category. Good building stone contains silica and calcareous materials.

Stone masonry is not only a structural material very good in compression but also a durable finish material. All stone used in stone masonry must satisfy requirements of strength, hardness, workability, durability and appearance. Table 1 shows properties of common building stones.

Brick

Clay and shale as raw materials ceramic characteristics. When a ground mixture is shaped and subjected to a controlled firing temperature in a kiln, the silicates melt to fuse the particles to a specified level of vitrification (crystallization from heat fusion). The resulting strength and weathering characteristics of the brick unit make it one of the most durable building materials.

Bricks are manufactured in many different types, shapes and sizes. Building brick is used as a structural material where strength, dura-

bility and appearance must be specified according to the building application and location. Durability and weather resistance is governed by the American Society of Testing Materials (ASTM) *Standard Specification for Building Brick, C62*. Grades are SW (severe weathering), MW (moderate weathering) and NW (negligible weathering). Most reference sources include a map of the United States which shows the zones where SW, MW and NW grades are permitted. Brick of grade SW are used where a high resistance to frost action and exposure conditions where the masonry is exposed to water and freezing temperatures. In addition grade SW brick is used for below grade structures and for all horizontal surfaces under all weathering conditions. Brick of grade MW is used in regions subject to freezing when the brick is not exposed to water permeation. It is used for vertical walls and piers above grade in regions with moderate weathering conditions. NW brick is used in interior installations and in vertical application in regions where there will be little weathering exposure. Most manufacturers make brick to meet the SW weathering grades so that their product may be shipped all regions of the country. Some brick manufacturers may select to produce only MW grades.

The manufacturers can furnish certification of the grade of brick furnished. Further standards for appearance, dimensional tolerances and moisture absorption are elaborated on in the published information of the referenced documents.

Brick sizes and shapes are varied and custom orders are always possible. Fig. 1 shows common brick sizes with nominal dimensions. Actual dimensions vary according to the thickness of the mortar joint. In general, higher quality brick construction will have mortar joints 3/8 inch in thickness. For best coordination with other construction dimensions, actual dimensions of bricks and mortar joints in courses and stretchers must be detailed and specified. Normally brick is listed by the dimensions of thickness x height x length.

Brick are classified as solid or hollow. A solid brick is one whose net cross-sectional area in every plane to the bearing surface is 75% or more of its gross section measured in the same plane. Simplified, a solid brick has a maximum coring of 25% of the gross area. A hollow brick is one whose net cross-sectional area in every plane parallel to the bearing surface is less than 75% of its gross section area measured in the same plane. Holes in brick permit more even drying and firing of the units, reduce the amount of fuel to fire the units, and reduce the weight for shipping costs. Frogs in bricks are depressions located on the bed surface of the unit and are useful for the same purposes as core voids. Cores and frogs increase the mechanical bonding of indi-

Table 1. Properties of common building stones
Source: National Bureau of Standards Reports

Rock type	Origin	Principle ingredient	Weight lb./cu. ft.	Specific gravity	Compressive strength, psi
Granite	Igneous	Silica	170	2.61-2.70	7,000-60,000
Marble	Metamorphic	Calcium carbonate	165	2.64-2.72	8,000-50,000
Slate	Metamorphic	Calcium carbonate	170	2.74-2.82	10,000-15,000
Limestone	Sedimentary	Calcium carbonate	165	2.10-2.75	2,600-28,000
Sandstone	Sedimentary	Calcium carbonate	155	2.14-2.66	5,000-20,000

vidual brick units and improve the structural performance of walls. They also improve the ease of handling each unit for masons when constructing a wall.

The brick pattern on the wall surface reflects the method for constructing the wall as well as the bonding of wythes together. Figs. 2 through 6 represent five very common patterns. The running bond consists entirely of stretchers. Since no header brick connecting two wythes, metal ties must be used for structural connection. Common bond has header brick every sixth course. Flemish bond consists of alternate stretcher and header brick in every course and English bond has alternate courses of stretchers and headers. For more elaborate illustration of variations of bonds, refer to the referenced documents.

Type of joint
The mortar joints which bond the masonry units together is of great importance for durability of masonry as well as vital to the aesthetic appearance. Four types are show in Fig. 7 and other variations are possible. These four are:

1. Weathered
2. Flush
3. Vee
4. Concave

A mason has a separate tool to create each type. Although all four are considered to be weather resistant, types 3 and 4 have the best resis-

tance to weather. The tool which is used to create the finish also presses and spreads the mortar tightly in the joint after it has been partially set. For appearance decisions, sample walls are readily built on the job site so as to compare the color, the joint, the joint color, and the quality of craft to review and establish the standard for masons to achieve on that project.

Concrete masonry units
Concrete masonry units (CMUs) are made from cement and aggregate materials which are hardened by chemical reactions rather than by ceramic fusion as in the manufacture of clay brick. Concrete masonry units include concrete brick, concrete block, cast stone and cellular concrete block. Concrete masonry units are produced from a mixture of Portland cement and aggregates in sizes and colors. Aggregates may be gravel, crushed stone, cinders, burned clay, blast furnace slag and sand. Combinations permit normal concrete weight units or light-weight units. Raw materials are proportioned with water and the controlled mixed is pressed into preformed casting dyes. The pressure formed units are removed from the dyes, stacked and cured in high-pressure autoclaves.

Unit sizes and shapes, including core size, vary according to the type of unit manufactured. Fig. 8 shows typical shapes of concrete masonry units. The dimensions are modular based on a nominal 8 inches high by 16 inches long. The widths are commonly 4, 6, 8, 10, 12, and 16 inches. With mortar joints of 3/8 inch the actual sizes are the nominal dimensions less 3/8 inch in all directions. The number and size of

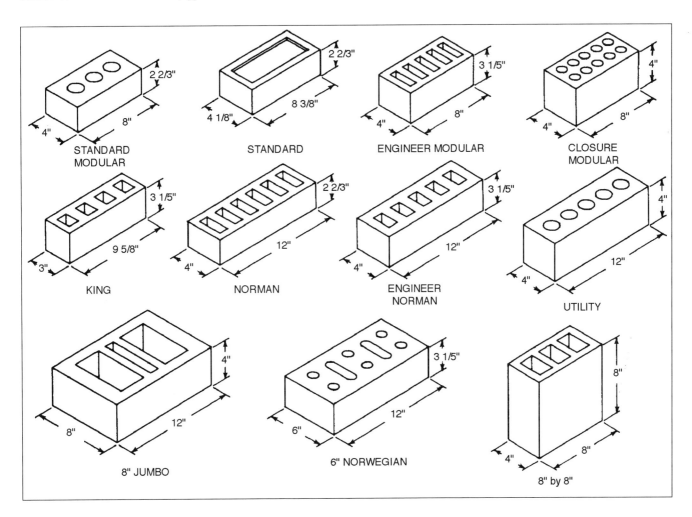

Fig. 1. Brick sizes (nominal dimensions)
Source: Brick Institute of America. Technical Notes on Brick Construction 9B, December 1995.

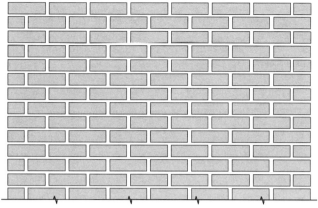

Fig. 2. Running bond

Fig. 3. Common bond with headers every sixth course

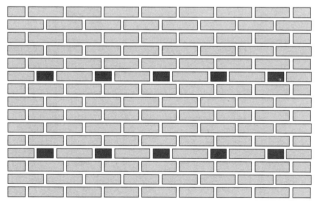

Fig. 4. Common bond with Flemish headers every sixth course

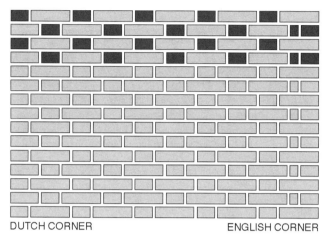

DUTCH CORNER   ENGLISH CORNER

Fig. 5. Flemish bond

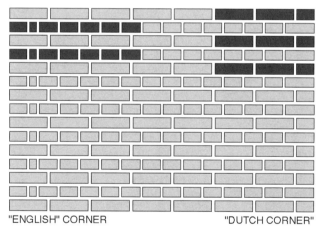

"ENGLISH" CORNER   "DUTCH CORNER"

Fig. 6. English bond

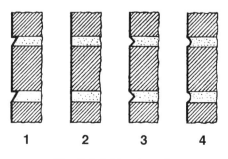

1   2   3   4

Fig. 7. Joint treatments

cores vary according to manufacturer and application. Solid units and hollow units are defined the same as for brick. A solid unit has void cores up to 25% of the gross area in cross section. Hollow units will have up to 75% void cores. Standard specifications are controlled by criteria established by The American Society for Testing and Materials (ASTM). *The Concrete Masonry Handbook for Architects, Engineers and Builders* (1991) provides an excellent reference for design, detailing, and specification data on masonry construction.

Cast stone is widely used in masonry construction in products such as lintels, sills, copings and veneer units. Selected aggregates of granite or marble may be used for color. The faces may be ground and polished as desired for the application.

Mortar

Mortar is the bonding medium for masonry. It must function to bond the masonry units together as well as to seal the construction against air and moisture penetration. Also, it must bond with steel reinforcing which strengthens the masonry and with metal ties and anchor bolts which join the building components together. For structural components of a building mortar strength, performance, durability are equally as important as the masonry unit. The quality of craft and installation not only control the mortar but also the integrity of the whole of masonry elements being constructed.

The ingredients of mortar and grout are cement, lime, sand, and water. Cement gives the mortar strength and durability. Lime adds workability and elasticity. Sand acts as a filler and gives the mix strength and economy. Water gives the mix plasticity. Together these ingredients must be proportioned to achieve the highest quality of this cement based bonding agent. Five types of mortar are available, of which only four are appropriate for structural masonry. Table 2 lists the types along with their respective prism test requirements of strength.

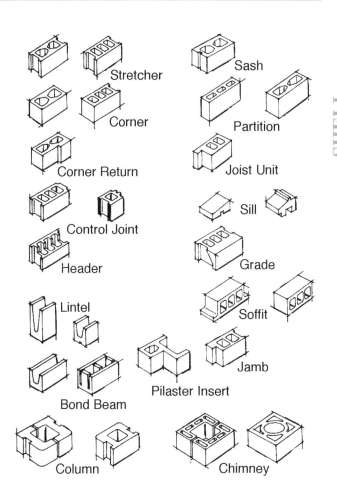

Fig. 8. Typical shapes of concrete masonry units

Table 2. Mortar types (ASTM C270-73)

Mortar type	Minimum average compressive strength of three 2 in. cubes at 28 days, psi	Parts by volume			
		Portland cement	Msonry cement	Hydrated lime or lime putty	Aggregate measured in damp, loose condition
M	2,500	1	1 (Type II)		Not less than 2 1/2 and not more than 3 times the sum of the volumes of the cements and lime used.
		1		1/4	
S	1,800	1/2	1 Type II)		
		1		Over 1/4 to 1/2	
N	750		1 (Type II)		
		1		Over 1/2 to 1 1/4	
O	350		1 (Type I or II)		
		1		Over 1 1/4 to 2 1/2	

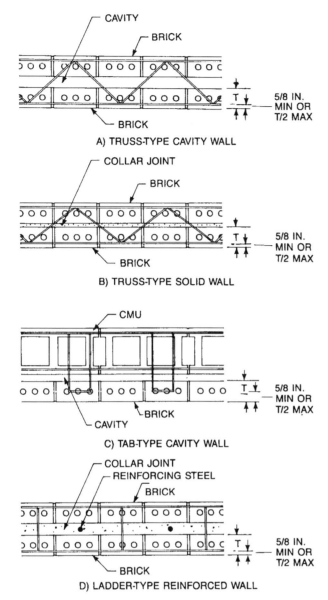

Fig. 9. Joint reinforcement details (Source: Brick Institute of America).

Selection of mortar type is a function of the requirements for the finished structural element. Where high lateral strength is required on walls or piers, a mortar with high tensile bond strength is desired. For load bearing walls, high compressive strength or shear strength may govern the design. Consideration of durability or color may be a primary determinant for the mortar. Not all mortar types have the same qualities so recommended uses are illustrated in Table 3.

Type M mortar has high compressive strength and greater durability than other mortar types. It is recommended for reinforced and unreinforced masonry which is subject to high compressive loads, severe frost action or high lateral forces. Because of its durability, it is specifically recommended for unreinforced masonry below grade and for masonry in contact with the earth such as foundation walls, retaining walls, walks, sewers, and manholes.

Type S mortar has reasonably high compressive strength. Tests indicate that the tensile bond strength with brick approaches the maximum attainable with cement-lime mortars. It is recommended for use in reinforced masonry, for unreinforced masonry where maximum flexural strength is required, and for use where mortar adhesion is the sole bonding agent between facing and backing as with ceramic veneers.

Type N mortar is a medium strength mortar suitable for general use in exposed masonry above grade. It is highly recommended for parapet walls, chimneys, and exterior walls subjected to severe exposure.

Type O mortar is a low strength mortar suitable for general interior use in non-load bearing masonry. It is never recommended in masonry potentially subject to freezing. Because of its high lime content it has excellent workability and therefore is the favorite among masons. *Type K* mortar is not recommended for use in any structural application.

Masonry accessories

Accessory items are an integral part of masonry construction. Horizontal joint reinforcement, metal anchors, metal ties, anchor bolts, flashing materials and control or expansion joint materials all are part of good masonry construction. Steel is most frequently used and it must be galvanized or coated in order to protect it from corrosion. Caused by oxidation corrosion requires careful consideration for all accessories used in masonry construction.

Horizontal joint reinforcement is used primarily to control shrinkage cracks in the masonry. It is also used to tie multiple wythes of masonry together and to anchor masonry veneer. Horizontal joint reinforcement consists of two or more longitudinal wires, 9 gauge or slightly larger, with 12 gauge cross wires welded to the longitudinal wires. Two basic types are produced; namely, a ladder type and a trussed type. The ladder type has the cross wires welded at 90 degrees to the longitudinal wires and spaced at about 16 inches. The trussed type has cross wires bent like webs of a truss with the bend welded to the longitudinal wires. Both basic types have several variations. The longitudinal wires are laid in the mortar joint along the faces of the masonry. The cross wires should also be embedded in mortar over the webs of the masonry. Fig. 9 shows plan view of typical joint reinforcement and Fig. 10 shows a plan view of adjustable joint reinforcement. Joint reinforcement needs to turn corners (Fig. 30 below shows one illustration of that condition).

Masonry anchors secure the masonry wall to its structural support such as a beams, columns or another wall. Examples are shown in the construction details in Figs. 11 through 14. Masonry ties connect masonry wythes together or connect a veneer to a backup wall of some other material, such as a stud wall. Several unit tie details are illustrated in Fig. 15. Adjustable unit tie details are referenced in Fig. 16. Masonry fasteners are used to attach other building elements to the masonry such as the case where wood furring strips are secured to a masonry wall.

Table 3. Types of mortar required for various kinds of masonry

Foundations:
Footings	M or S
Walls of solid units	M, S, or N
Walls of hollow units	M or S
Hollow walls	M or S

Masonry other than foundation masonry:
Piers of solid masonry	M, S, or N
Piers of hollow units	M or S
Walls of solid masonry	M, S, N, or O

Walls of solid masonry, other than parapet walls or rubble stone walls, not less than 12 in. thick nor more than 35 ft. in height, supported laterally at intervals not exceeding 12 times the wall thickness	M, S, N, or O,
Walls of hollow units; loadbearing or exterior, and hollow walls 12 in. or more in thickness	M, S, or N
Hollow walls, less than 12 in. in thickness where assumed design wind pressure:*	
(a) exceeds 20 psf	M, or S
(b) does not exceed 20 psf	M, S, or N

Glass-block masonry	M,S, or N
Nonbearing partitions or fireproofing composed of structural clay tile or concrete masonry units	M, S, N, O, or gypsum
Gypsum partition tile or block	Gypsum
Fire brick	Refractory air setting mortar

Linings of existing masonry, either above or below gradde	M or S
Masonry other than above	M, S, or N

For design wind pressures, see section on Design Loads

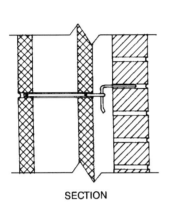

SECTION

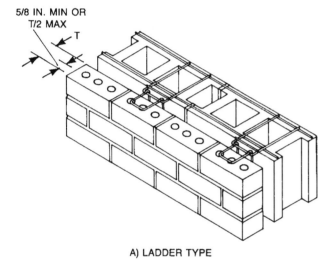

5/8 IN. MIN OR
T/2 MAX
T

A) LADDER TYPE

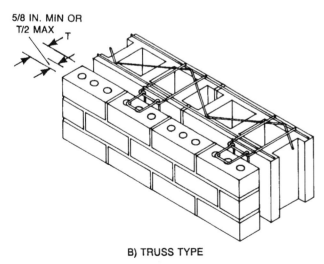

5/8 IN. MIN OR
T/2 MAX
T

B) TRUSS TYPE

**Fig. 10. Adjustable assembly details
(Source: Brick Institute of America)**

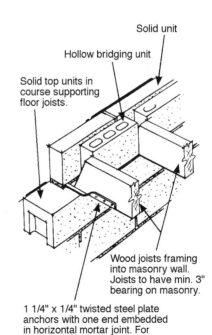

Solid unit

Hollow bridging unit

Solid top units in
course supporting
floor joists.

Wood joists framing
into masonry wall.
Joists to have min. 3"
bearing on masonry.

1 1/4" x 1/4" twisted steel plate
anchors with one end embedded
in horizontal mortar joint. For
required anchor spacing. see text.

Fig. 11. Anchoring wood joists to masonry wall

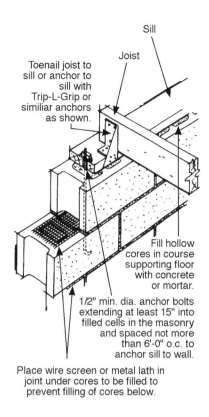

Toenail joist to sill or anchor to sill with Trip-L-Grip or similiar anchors as shown.

Sill

Joist

Fill hollow cores in course supporting floor with concrete or mortar.

1/2" min. dia. anchor bolts extending at least 15" into filled cells in the masonry and spaced not more than 6'-0" o.c. to anchor sill to wall.

Place wire screen or metal lath in joint under cores to be filled to prevent filling of cores below.

Fig. 12. Anchoring wood sill to foundation

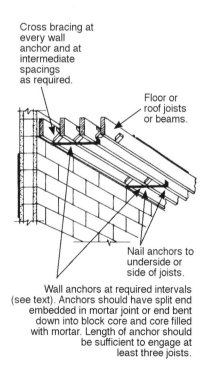

Cross bracing at every wall anchor and at intermediate spacings as required.

Floor or roof joists or beams.

Nail anchors to underside or side of joists.

Wall anchors at required intervals (see text). Anchors should have split end embedded in mortar joint or end bent down into block core and core filled with mortar. Length of anchor should be sufficient to engage at least three joists.

Fig. 13. Anchoring parallel joists to masonry wall

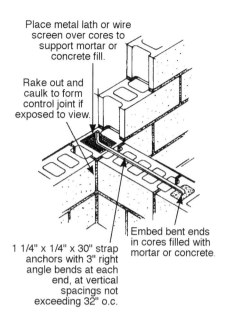

Place metal lath or wire screen over cores to support mortar or concrete fill.

Rake out and caulk to form control joint if exposed to view.

1 1/4" x 1/4" x 30" strap anchors with 3" right angle bends at each end, at vertical spacings not exceeding 32" o.c.

Embed bent ends in cores filled with mortar or concrete.

Fig. 14. Anchorage of intersecting bearing walls

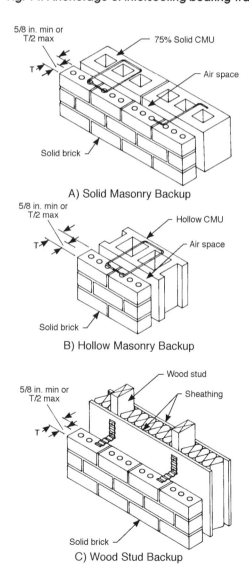

5/8 in. min or T/2 max

75% Solid CMU

Air space

T

Solid brick

A) Solid Masonry Backup

5/8 in. min or T/2 max

Hollow CMU

Air space

T

Solid brick

B) Hollow Masonry Backup

Wood stud

Sheathing

5/8 in. min or T/2 max

T

Solid brick

C) Wood Stud Backup

Fig. 15. Unit tie details (Source: Brick Institute of America)

All metal accessories must be galvanized and spaced at intervals which are recommended by industry standards. In masonry veneers attached to a reinforced concrete frame building, steel shelf angles will support the masonry vertically at one floor level and at the next level the masonry connection should be one which supports lateral loads only. Above the lateral connection, a soft masonry joint is necessary to accommodate any differential movements within the veneer and the supporting structure. A variety of construction details are included in Figs. 17 through 29 to depict different applications of masonry being used as panel walls connected to other structural frames or as bearing walls in relation to foundations, floors and roofs.

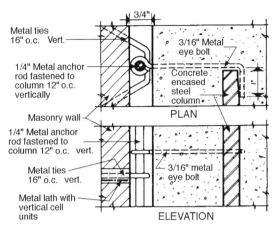

Fig. 18. Wall anchorage details

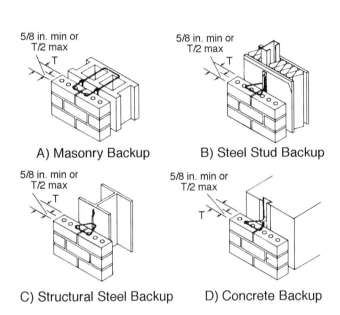

A) Masonry Backup **B) Steel Stud Backup**

C) Structural Steel Backup **D) Concrete Backup**

**Fig. 16. Adjustable unit tie details
(Source: Brick Institute of America)**

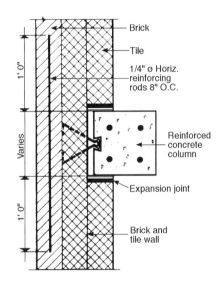

Fig. 19. Column partially enclosed in masonry

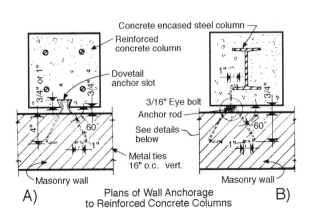

**Fig. 17. Plans of wall anchorage to reinforced
concrete columns**

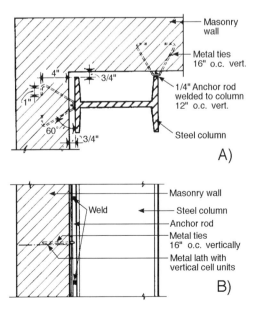

**Fig. 20. Wall anchorage to steel column in plan (a)
and elevation (b)**

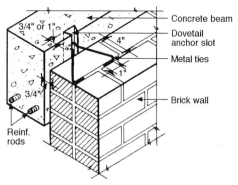

a) Wall Anchorage to Concrete Beam

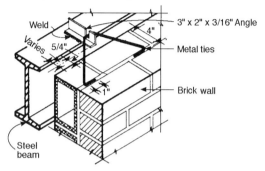

b) Wall Anchorage to Steel Beam

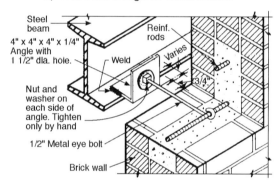

c) Alternate Wall Anchorage to Steel Beam

Fig. 21. Typical beam-wall anchorage

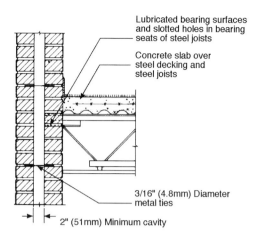

Fig. 22. Anchorage of steel floor joists

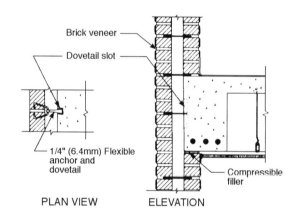

PLAN VIEW   ELEVATION

Fig. 23. Flexible anchorage to concrete frame

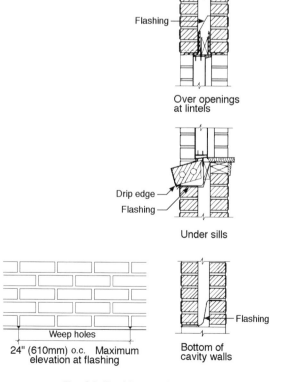

Fig. 24. Flashing and week holes

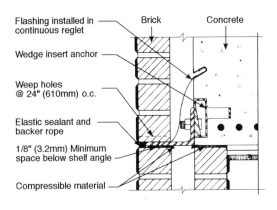

Fig. 25. Steel shelf angles

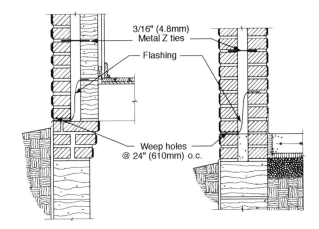

Fig. 26. Foundation details

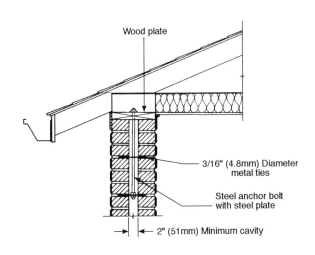

Fig. 27. Anchorage of wood roof framing

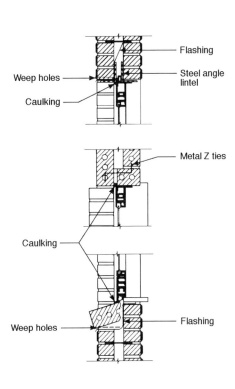

Fig. 28. Commercial metal window

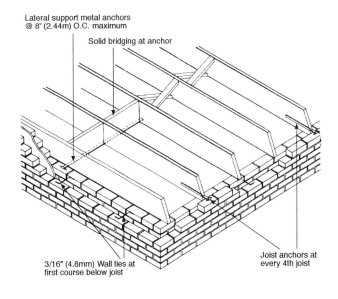

Fig. 29. Anchorage of wood floor framing

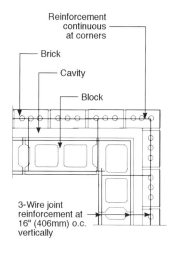

Fig. 30. Horizontal wall reinforcement at corner

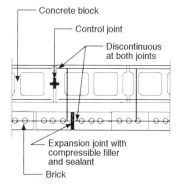

Fig. 31. Masonry control joint detail

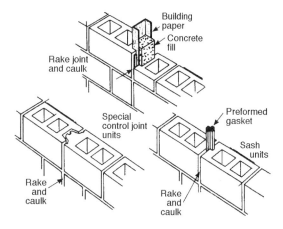

Fig. 32. Typical control joint details

Figs. 30 - 32 suggest versions of control joints in masonry walls. A control joint is used in masonry to create a plane of weakness which controls the location of cracks due to shrinkage and creep. Control joints are located so that the structural integrity of the masonry is not impaired.

Structural design of masonry

Masonry is construction which provides excellent compressive strength. Its usual mass and weight creates an opportunity for its compressive strength to be emphasized in forms and structures dependent on that property. Even though it is a brittle construction element, masonry does have a small tensile strength but not enough to rely on as a principle stress. Whether brick, concrete block, stone or glass, the basic unit is stronger in compression than the composite structural element as units are bonded together with mortar joints. The skill required to construct a well crafted masonry wall is very important to the structural integrity of a building.

Codes distinguish methods of structural analysis as engineered masonry design and empirical design. The latter format allows traditional approaches based on historical experience. Although experience is an asset in the design of any structure, empirical design of masonry structures uses conservative allowable stresses which underestimate the real strength of quality material and construction methods.

Engineered masonry is further distinguished for unreinforced masonry and reinforced masonry. Obviously the major distinction is whether tensile reinforcement is required to maintain the integrity of the structural elements. By current codes, the design and analysis of structural elements and systems rely on the *allowable stress design* (ASD) method. Accordingly, structures and their component members are designed by elastic analysis using service loads and allowable stresses.

Together with the allowable stress design method the actual working section of masonry which is carrying load must be distinguished from the gross section which has voids as the products are manufactured. Furthermore not all webs have mortar between units. Details and specifications must be clear about gross section and the net section which is actually providing the strength and transmitting load. Figs. 33 and 34 convey the idea about determining the net section for various types of walls, some grouted, some solid and some hollow.

General Criteria: General criteria for clay masonry and concrete masonry includes considerations regarding loads and materials. Load combinations which must be considered to determine the governing conditions of design are as follows:

1. D   where: D = dead load or related internal moments and forces

2. D + L   L = live load or related internal moments and forces

3. D + L + (W or E)[1]   W = wind load or related internal moments and forces

4. D + W[1]   E = load effects of earthquake or related internal moments and forces

5. 0.9D + E[1]   H = lateral pressure of soil or related internal moments and forces

6. D + L + (H or F)   F = lateral pressure of liquids or related internal moments and forces

7. D + (H or F)

8. D + L + T

9. D + T

NOTE 1: Allowable stresses may be increased by 1/3 when considering this load combination.

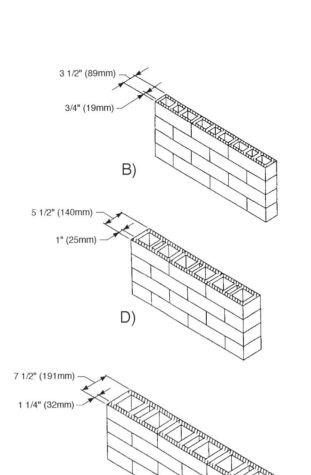

Fig. 33. Net section for axial load - ungrouted walls

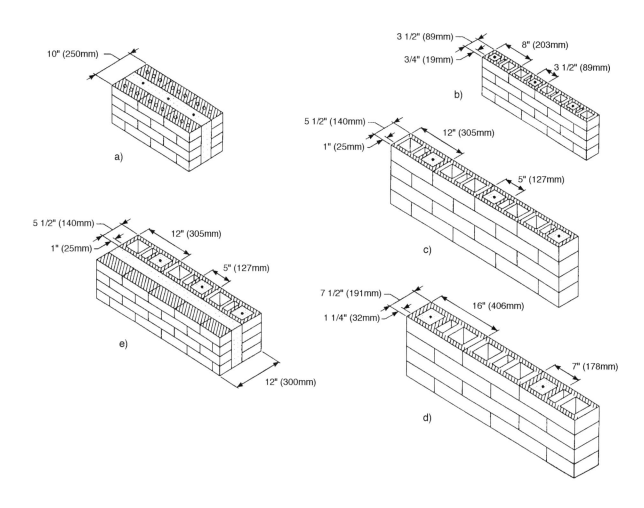

Fig. 34. Net section for axial load - grouted walls

Material Properties: General material properties which must be considered to determine the applicable specified materials are as indicated in Tables 4 and 5:

Engineered design of unreinforced masonry - Allowable stress criteria

Axial compression and flexure:

$$f_a \quad F_a$$
$$f_b \quad F_b$$
$$P \quad 0.25 P_e$$
$$F_a = 0.25 f'_m [1 - (h/140r)^2] \text{ for } h/r \quad 99$$
$$F_a = 0.25 f'_m (70 r/h)^2 \text{ for } h/r \quad 99$$
$$F_b = 0.33 f'_m$$
$$P_e = (\pi^2 E_m I/h^2)(1 - 0.577 e/r)^3$$
$$(f_a/F_a) + (f_b/F_b) \quad 1$$

where: e = eccentricity of axial load, in.
  f_a = calculated axial compressive stress, psi
  F_a = allowable axial compressive stress, psi
  f_b = calculated flexure compressive stress, psi
  F_b = allowable flexure compressive stress, psi
  f'_m = specified compressive stress of masonry, psi
  h = effective height of a column or wall, in.
  I = moment of inertia, masonry net section, in.^{4}
  P = design axial load, lbs.
  P_e = Euler buckling load, lbs
  r = radius of gyration, in.

Shear: in-plane shear shall not exceed any of:

$$F_v \quad v + 0.45 N_v/A_n$$
$$F_v \quad 1.5\sqrt{f'_m}$$
$$F_v \quad 120 \text{ psi}$$

where: A_n = net cross section area of masonry, in.^{2}
  F_v = allowable shear stress in masonry, psi
  N_v = force acting normal to shear stress, lbs.
  v = shear stress of masonry in running bond, psi
  37 psi for partially grouted masonry
  60 psi for solid grouted masonry

Allowable flexural tension (Table 6)

Engineered design of reinforced masonry - Allowable stress criteria

Reinforced masonry construction requires special consideration of the placement of the unit masonry, the placement of the steel reinforcing rods both vertically and horizontally, and the grout which fills and bonds all the pieces together to create an effective structural wall. Vertical reinforcement is placed in aligned cores which must have potential for grout to surround the steel rod and yet bond with the masonry units. The running mortar joints are limited in size thereby creating the need to detail the horizontal reinforcing in appropriately fashioned longitudinal joints which must be filled with grout. Figs. 35 through 40 identify a few examples of reinforced masonry construction. More complete information is available in the references noted.

Table 4. Clay Masonry

Net area compressive strength of units, psi	Moduli of Elasticity, E_m, psi $\times 10^6$		
	Type N mortar	Type S mortar	Type M mortar
12,000 and up	2.8	3.0	3.0
10,000	2.4	2.9	3.0
8,000	2.0	2.4	2.8
6,000	1.6	1.9	2.2
4,000	1.2	1.4	1.6
2,000	0.8	0.9	1.0

Table 5. Concrete Masonry

Net area compressive strength of units, psi	Moduli of Elasticity, E_m, psi $\times 10^6$	
	Type N mortar	Type M mortar
6,000 and up	-	3.5
5,000	2.8	3.2
4,000	2.6	2.9
3,000	2.3	2.5
2,500	2.2	2.4
2,000	1.8	2.2
1,500	1.5	1.6

Table 6. Allowable flexural tension, F_b, psi

Masonry type	Portland cement/lime mortar		Masonry cement mortar	
	M or S	N	M or S	N
Normal to bed joints				
Solid units	40	30	24	15
Hollow units[1]				
Ungrouted	25	19	15	9
Fully grouted	68	58	41	26
Parallel to bed joints in running bond				
Solid units	80	60	48	30
Hollow units				
Ungrouted	50	38	30	19
Partially grouted	50	38	30	19
Fully grouted	80	60	48	30

[1]. For partially grouted masonry, allowable stresses shall be determined on the basis of linear interpolation between hollow units that are fully grouted or ungrouted and hollow units based on amount of grouting.

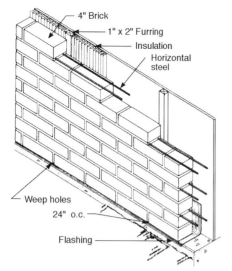

Fig. 35. Isometric of 4-in. reinforced brick curtain wall with furring, insulation and interior finish.

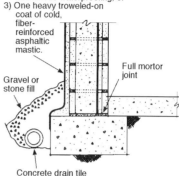

RECOMMENDED PROTECTIVE COATING FOR WATERPROOFING EXTERIOR FACE OF WALLS:

1) Two 1/4 inch coats of portland cement plaster, or
2) One 1/4 inch coat of portland cement plaster plus two brush coats of bituminous waterproofing, or
3) One heavy troweled-on coat of cold, fiber-reinforced asphaltic mastic.

Fig. 38. Typical footing detail

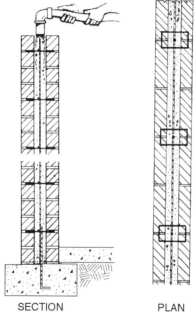

SECTION   PLAN

Fig. 36. "High-lift" grouted reinforced masonry wall

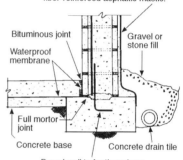

RECOMMENDED PROTECTIVE COATINGS FOR WATERPROOFING EXTERIOR FACE OF WALLS:

1) Two 1/4 inch thick coats of portland cement plaster plus two brush coats of bituminous waterproofing, or.
2) One 1/4 inch thick coat of portland cement plaster plus one heavy troweled-on coat of cold, fiber-reinforced asphaltic mastic.

Dowel wall to footing where floor cannot be assumed to support wall laterally; as where bituminous joint is used between floor and wall.

Fig. 39. Footing detail for very wet soil

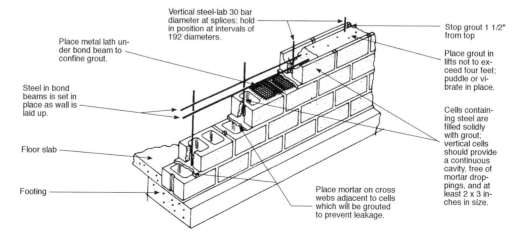

Fig. 37. Typical reinforced concrete masonry construction

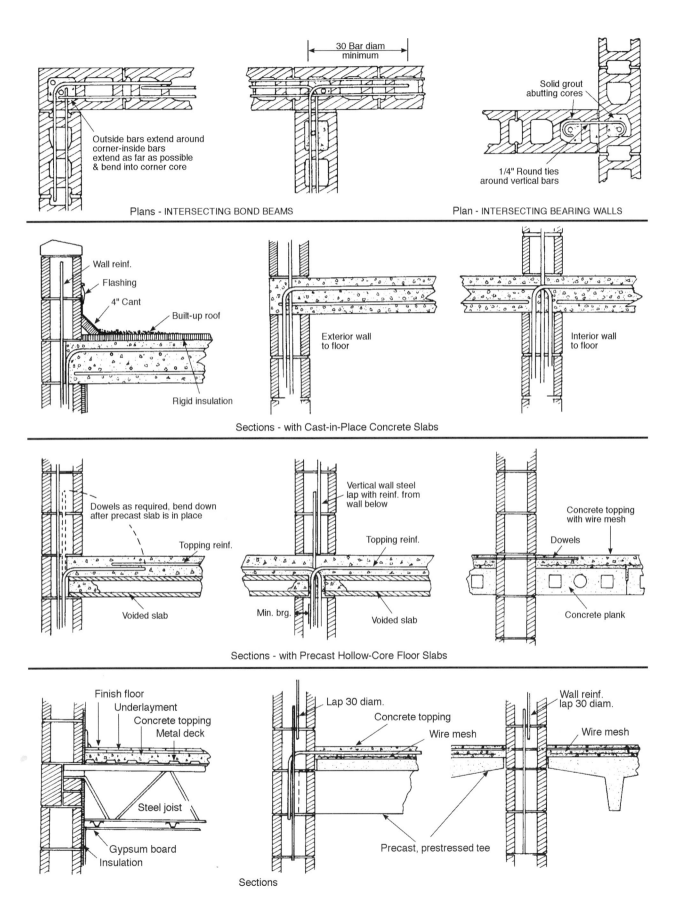

Plans - INTERSECTING BOND BEAMS

Plan - INTERSECTING BEARING WALLS

Sections - with Cast-in-Place Concrete Slabs

Sections - with Precast Hollow-Core Floor Slabs

Sections

Fig. 40. Construction details, reinforced concrete masonry

B1

SHELL

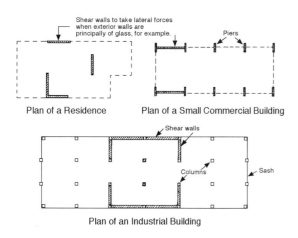

Fig. 41. Reinforced masonry shear walls

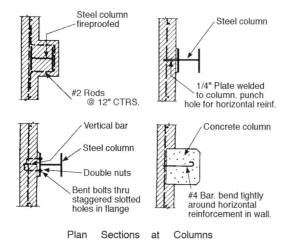

Plan   Sections   at   Columns

Fig. 42. Attachment of reinforced masonry shear walls to structural column

Axial compression and flexure:

$$P_a = (0.25 \, f'_m A_n + 0.65 \, A_{st} F_s)\,[1 - (h/140r)^2] \text{ for } h/r \text{ w } 99$$

$$P_a = (0.25 \, f'_m A_n + 0.65 \, A_{st} F_s)\,(70 \, r/h)^2 \text{ for } h/r \text{ y } 99$$

$$F_b = 0.33 \, f'm$$

where: A_{st} = total area of longitudinal reinforcing steel, in.^{2}
$\quad$ d = distance from extreme compression fiber to centroid of tensile reinforcement, in.
$\quad F_s$ = allowable tensile or compressive stress in reinforcing steel, psi
$\quad$ M = maximum moment at point of shear design, in. lbs.
$\quad P_a$ = maximum allowable compressive force in reinforced masonry due to axial force, lbs
$\quad$ V = design shear force, lbs

Shear:

Flexural member $\qquad F_v \quad f'_m$, with 50 psi max.

Shear wall (M/Vd v 1) $\quad F_v \quad 0.33\,[4 - (M/Vd)] \quad f'_m$, with 80 - 45 (V/Md) max.

Shear wall (M/Vd y 1) $\quad F_v \quad f'_m$, with 35 psi max.

Tension in reinforcement:

Grade 40 or 50 $\qquad F_s = 20,000$ psi

Grade 60 $\qquad F_s = 24,000$ psi

Joint reinforcement $F_s = 30,000$ psi

All of these criteria must be translated into actual structural members which have strength, proportion and stability. The basic requirements of axial stress, bending stress, shear and deflection are fundamental to the design of structural components. The building's structural system must function as a whole structure which has strength and stability yet compatibility with the architectural requirements. The references contain charts and guides which help to gain insight to size and proportion of members. This information is useful for preliminary evaluations about the relationship of structural strength and form to architectural design development.

When reinforced masonry walls have the potential to resist lateral forces on a building. These walls are referred to as shear walls. Schematic plans are suggested in Fig. 41. Such walls must be tied to the structural frame so that forces may be transmitted through the frame and applied to the shear walls. Fig. 42 show typical connections to columns. Similar connections to beams in the system may be required.

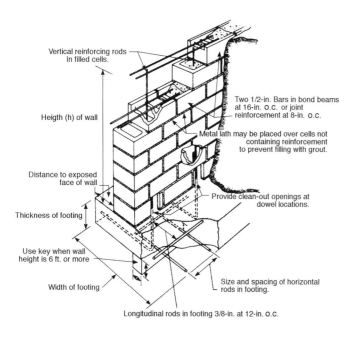

Fig. 43. Reinforced concrete masonry retailing wall

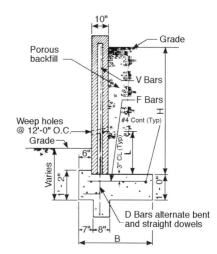

Fig. 44. Section through typical low, reinforced brick masonry retaining wall

Retaining walls

Reinforced masonry may be used for retaining walls. The masonry unit may be concrete block with filled cores, as shown in Fig. 43, or brick with a grouted cavity as shown in Fig. 44. The brick with grouted cavity type is recommended for low retaining walls. A 10 inch thick reinforced brick wall with grouted cavity has capacity to retain earth up to a height of six feet. By comparison, a 12 in.-thick reinforced concrete masonry retaining wall, with reinforcement in grouted cores, may be designed for a height of about eight feet. Beyond these heights for retaining earth, reinforced concrete is more efficient structurally and it may be built with a masonry veneer. All walls must be properly capped to prevent the entry of water into any voids of the masonry.

Provision should be made to prevent accumulation of water behind a retaining wall. Four inch diameter weep holes located at 5 to 10 ft. spacing are recommended. The backfill behind the retaining wall should be gravel and granular material so that water may drain away from the wall. Waterproofing the back face of the retaining wall is recommended in locations of severe frost and heavy rainfall. During construction of a reinforced masonry retaining wall, backfill should be accomplished until at least seven days after grouting. Heavy surcharges of force should be avoided.

Lintels

A lintel is a horizontal beam placed over a wall opening to carry the load in the wall above it. Lintels may be structural steel, reinforced masonry or reinforced concrete. Historically, arches, including flat arches, were alternative options. Structural steel lintels are common lintels for masonry walls. Steel angles are the simplest shapes to accommodate the masonry and still provide strength to carry moderate loads. For heavier loads, I beams or channels together with steel plates may be selected options. Refer to Fig. 46. The outstanding leg of the angle or plate should be 3-1/2 in. to support a nominal 4 in. masonry wythe.

The determination of the load to be carried by the lintel is illustrated in Fig. 45. The weight of the masonry above the lintel is assumed as the weight of a triangular section whose height is one-half the clear span of the opening. To the dead load of the wall must be added the uniform dead and live loads of floors and roofs that frame into the wall above the opening and below the apex of a 45 degree triangle. Assessment of this load may be completed by simply comparing the dimensions D and $L/2$ in Fig. 45. Concentrated loads from beams framing into the wall above may be distributed over the wall from the edge of the beam's bearing on the wall projected at a 60 degree angle.

The lintel's bearing area must be determined in accordance with the allowable masonry stresses permitted for compressive axial load. Deflection of the lintel must be limited to $L/600$ where L is the span of the lintel in inches. Refer to Fig. 47 for one sample detail of a reinforced masonry lintel. In order to reduce the potential for cracks occurring at the corners of openings, reinforcement is often installed as

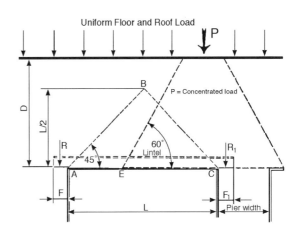

Fig. 45. Computing loads on a lintel

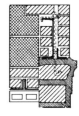

Fig. 46. Reinforced brick lintel in cavity wall

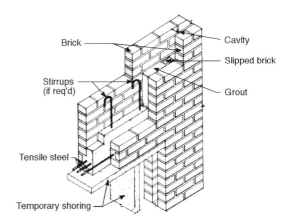

Fig. 47. Reinforced brick lintel in cavity wall

B1

SHELL

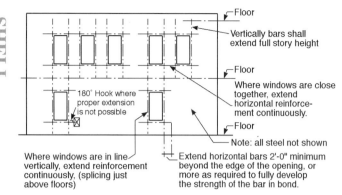

Wall Elevation Showing Reinforcement Around Openings

Sections at Edge of Openings

Fig. 48. Typical reinforcement around wall openings

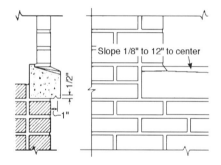

Fig. 49. Sill detail to prevent wash

shown in the elevation of Fig. 48. This reinforcement is best accomplished with the installation of reinforced masonry structural lintels and in conjunction with reinforced masonry walls. Further data for common lintel sizes and capacities is available in the industry's resources.

Brick masonry surface treatments

The formation of efflorescence is from water soluble salts migrating to the surface of the masonry. As water evaporates the salts show up as whit deposits. The way to eliminate efflorescence is to reduce all contributing factors to a minimum. The following procedures are recommended as a means to that end.

1   Reduce the amount of soluble salts in the masonry materials by:

-   Specifying that all wall facing and trim materials pass a "wick test" for efflorescence.

-   Testing mortar for efflorescence.

2   Prevent contact between facing and backup by use of cavity-wall construction or flashing.

3   Keep moisture out of wall by use of:

-   Hard-burned brick or tile facing.

-   Cavity-wall or solid metal-tied wall construction.

-   Good workmanship (all joints thoroughly filled).

-   Protection of the tops of walls during construction.

-   Projecting sills and copings, with drip slots underneath (Fig. 49).

-   Flashing, especially at all intersections of wall and roof, under all horizontal elements such as copings and sills, and just above finished grade, to prevent rise of moisture by capillarity from the foundation.

-   Caulking, carefully applied, around all door and window frames.

-   Vapor barrier and ventilation to prevent condensation within walls.

Cleaning

Many new buildings are irreparably damaged by improper cleaning. The most common causes of such damage are:

1   Failure to saturate masonry before application of cleaning agent.

2   Use of too strong acid solution;

3   Failure to protect windows and trim.

It is recommended that any cleaning agent be tried first on a sample wall, using a minimum area of 20 sq. ft., and left for at least a week.

To clean unglazed masonry surfaces, remove large particles with a wood paddle and saturate the surface with water. Apply a 10 percent solution of muriatic acid, not more than 1 part acid to 9 parts water, to an area of not more than 15 to 20 sq. ft. Then wash the surface with clear water.

To cut labor costs, high-pressure water is sometimes used; nozzle pressures range between 400 and 700 psi at a flow rate of 3 to 8 gal/min. Two hoses may be used, one with cleaning solution, the other with plain water. Dry sandblasting is also sometimes used.

To clean glazed surfaces, scrub with soap and water only. Use no acid and no metal scrapers on glazed surfaces.

Efflorescence can usually be removed with soap and water and a stiff scrubbing brush. If necessary, use dilute muriatic acid, as described above. A type of efflorescence known as "green stain" may be caused by the action of muriatic acid on some types of masonry. Since this type cannot be foreseen it is important to make a preliminary test on a sample wall. Green stain is difficult to remove: try oxalic acid, 2 lb. per 5 gal of water, brushed or sprayed on and washed off after several hours. If necessary follow with sodium hydroxide, such as one 12-oz. can of "Drano" per qt. of water, applied liberally with paint brush and hosed off after three days.

Methods for cleaning old buildings are listed in order of frequency of use as follows:

1   High-pressure steam-best for relatively impervious facing materials.

2   Sand blasting-used mostly on porous materials such as limestone, sandstone, and unglazed brick; cannot be used on glazed or polished surfaces.

3   Hand washing-expensive; used only on small buildings.

4   High-pressure cold water-good if there is ample water supply and suitable method of disposing of waste.

5   Chemical and steam-used for removing coatings such as paint.

Before deciding to clean an old building, consider carefully whether it is advisable. The "dirt" may be simply weathered masonry, not accumulated deposits, and the cleaning process may remove the actual surface of the masonry.

Stain removal

The removal of stains, such as those caused by rust, smoke, copper, oil, and the like, requires special treatment appropriate to the type of stain and the type of masonry. See Technical Notes on Brick Construction No. 20 Revised, published by the Brick Institute of America.

Painting

Paints are applied to masonry walls for decorative effect and as a barrier to rain penetration. They must not, however, prevent the wall from "breathing," that is, prevent moisture within the wall from escaping by evaporation from the surface. Cement-based paints and water-thinned emulsion paints are highly permeable to water vapor and are recommended for exterior use. New masonry walls intended to be painted should not be cleaned with acid.

Cement-based paint should be applied to a wall only after it has cured for at least a month and has been dampened thoroughly by spraying. Apply heavy coats with a stiff brush, allowing at least 24 hours between coats. During this time and for several days after the final coat keep the wall damp by periodic spraying. Water-thinned emulsion paints, commonly called latex paints, can be applied to damp uncured

walls; since they are quick-drying, additional coats can be applied without waiting. Polyvinyl acetate and acrylic emulsions are generally the most satisfactory of the water-thinned paints.

Solvent-thinned paints should be applied only to completely dry, clean surfaces. Oil-based and alkyd paints are nonpermeable and are not recommended for exterior masonry. Oil-based paints are highly susceptible to alkalides and new masonry must be thoroughly neutralized before being painted; zinc chloride or zinc sulfate solution, 2 to 3 1/2 lb. per gallon of water, is often used for this purpose. Several days of drying is usually required between coats. Synthetic rubber and chlorinated rubber paints can be applied to damp, alkaline surfaces, and can be used on exterior masonry.

Waterproofing

Silicones are widely used for waterproofing, or more correctly dampproofing, masonry walls. Without actually sealing openings, silicones retard water absorption by creating a negative capillarity which repels water. Silicones may be water-based or solvent-based and may be applied by brush or spray. Normally, silicones cause no perceptible color change, but they sometimes bleach artificially colored mortar. They penetrate the masonry to a depth of 1/8 to 1/4 in. and their effective life is from 5 to 10 years. Foundation walls below grade should be waterproofed with one or preferably two coats of Portland cement mortar (1 : 1-1/2); after curing, apply hot bituminous coating or a cold asphalt emulsion coating.

Coatings for concrete masonry

Fill coats

Fill coats or primer-sealers are used to fill the voids in porous concrete masonry and on coarse-textured masonry before the application of finish coats. Fill coats contain regular Portland cement as a binder and finely graded siliceous sand filler. An alternate product is acrylic latex or polyvinyl acetate latex combined with the Portland cement binder. Fill coats are applied by brushing the material into the voids of the surface. Skilled workmanship is necessary for successful results. Those fill coats which do not contain latex require application to a moist surface and moist curing for hydration of the Portland cement constituent. The fillers containing latex do not require moist curing because the latex retards evaporation of moisture, thereby making it available for hydration of the cement binder.

Portland cement paints

These paints are sold in powdered form in a variety of colors and are mixed with water just before use. They are produced in standard and heavy-duty types. The standard type contains a minimum of 65 per cent Portland cement by weight and is suitable for general use. The heavy-duty type contains 80 per cent Portland cement and is used where there is excessive and continuous contact with moisture, such as in swimming pools. Each type is available with a siliceous sand additive for use as a filler on porous surfaces. Portland cement paints set by hydration of the cement which bonds to the masonry surface. The paints are applied to moist surfaces by stiff brush. The surface is dampened by fine water spray for 48 to 72 hours until the cement cures. Portland cement paints contain little organic material and are not subject to attack from alkali found in new concrete. They have a history of success in waterproofing masonry when properly applied and cured.

Latex paints

Latex paints, inherently resistant to alkali, are made of water emulsions of resinous materials. They dry throughout as soon as the water of emulsion has evaporated, usually within 1 to 2 hours. Styrene-butadiene is one of the original synthetic chemical coatings and is still in use. Other latex coatings such as polyvinyl acetate and acrylic resin are presently in greater demand and are also available as clear coat-

B1

SHELL

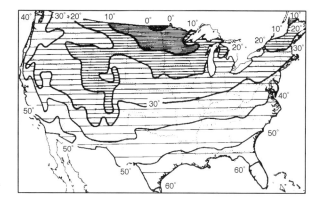

Fig. 50. Average daily mean temperature (degrees Farenheit) in January

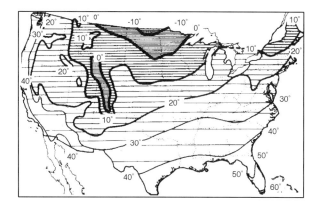

Fig. 51. Average daily minimum temperature (degrees Farenheit) in January

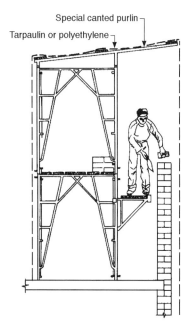

Fig. 52. Scafford-type enclosure

ings for colorless applications. All latex paints are available as opaque coatings. Latex paints may be applied to damp or dry surfaces and require no curing. Although acrylic latex is somewhat higher in cost than the other latex waterproofing materials, it has demonstrated superior resistance to penetration by rain and shown greater overall durability.

Oil-base paints

Oil-base paints are manufactured from natural oil resins or synthetic alkyd resins. Similar to conventional house paints, the oil-base paints designed for use on masonry are usually reinforced by certain resins to improve their resistance to alkali. They may be applied by brush, roller, or spray. A dry masonry surface is required at the time of application and the effective alkalinity of the surface must be reduced through aging the masonry or application of surface pretreatment. Oil-base paints which are subjected to dampness from within the masonry may fail from blistering and peeling.

Epoxy coatings

These coatings are based on epoxy or urethane resins to which a catalyst is added just before application. The epoxies are highly resistant to alkali and form an impervious film. Outdoor exposure of epoxy paints results in chalking, which must be removed by washing with soap and water to restore the original appearance. The high cost of the material and difficulty experienced in application have limited the use of epoxies to specialized requirements. They are not recommended for general use on concrete masonry.

Silicone-based coatings

Silicone is a colorless resinous material produced by a synthetic process from silicon dioxide. When applied to masonry surfaces, silicone-based coatings do not cause a change in color or texture. Without actually sealing openings, silicones retard water absorption by changing the contact angle between water and the walls of capillary pores in the masonry. Silicones do not bridge large openings; therefore, fill coats are desirable on coarse-textured masonry. Application of silicone-based coatings is commonly accomplished by flooding the surface with a low-pressure spray head.

Bituminous coatings

These coatings are produced from coal tar or asphalt and are furnished in solid form to be melted for hot application. They are also available in liquid form, either diluted in solvent or emulsified with water, for application at normal temperature. Hot application of bituminous coatings may be made alone or in combination with felt or other reinforcing fabric to form a built-up membrane. Where considerable hydrostatic pressure is exerted upon the coating, the built-up membrane has the distinct advantage of maintaining continuity of waterproofing over possible imperfections in the wall. The low cost and excellent resistance to penetration of water favor the use of bituminous coatings where appearance is not important, such as below-grade portions of basement walls.

Cold weather construction

Cold weather construction, long familiar in northern Europe and Russia, is necessary in this country. The advantages of early occupancy and the reduction of construction time, with its heavy carrying charges, more than compensate for the additional cost. According to a Canadian study, cold weather construction costs average between 0.75 and 1.5 % of the total construction cost.

The maps, Figs. 50 and 51 show the part of the lower states United States where cold weather construction is a problem. In general, it is that area lying north of the 30F line in Fig. 50 or the 20F line in Fig. 51. It should be noted that the recommendations below call for supplementary heat only when the daily mean temperature is 20F (-7°C) or lower,

A clear distinction should be made between cold weather concreting and masonry construction. Generally concrete is placed in forms which absorb little water from the concrete and prevent evaporation into the atmosphere. On the other hand, in masonry construction thin layers of mortar are placed between thicker absorbent units which absorb water from the mortar and stiffen it. The degree of saturation of the mortar is therefore lowered and the water-cement ratio is reduced. Hence little water is actually left to freeze in the mortar and cause damage by expansion.

After extensive research, the International Masonry Industry All-Weather Council issued in 1970 Guide Specifications for Cold Weather Masonry Construction, the principal provisions of which are summarized here: All materials must be delivered dry and kept fully covered at all times. Brick units should be more absorbent than those used in normal construction. Absorbent brick should be sprinkled before laying with heated water, above 70F if the units (that is, ambient conditions) are above 32F, and above 130F when ambient conditions are below 32F.

Type S or Type M mortar is recommended, or the use of mortar made with Type III Portland cement, high early strength. Sand, if frozen, must be heated before mixing. Ideal mortar temperature is 70 + 10F; the mixing temperature selected should be maintained within 10%. Admixtures in general, and antifreezes in particular, are not recommended. Accelerators, such as calcium chloride, may be used up to a maximum of 2 percent of the Portland cement by weight provided that the masonry does not contain metal, which is severely corroded by the salt. Coloring pigments should be limited to 10 percent (carbon black to 2 percent) of the cement content by weight; they may retard the setting of the mortar, which is an undesirable effect in cold weather construction.

Masonry must not be laid on a frozen or snow or ice-covered bed. Such a bed must be heated until it is dry to the touch. Masonry damaged by freezing must be removed before continuing construction.

Construction enclosures may be of many types. Small buildings are often completely enclosed in a tent or inflated structure. A simple type of scaffold enclosure is shown in Fig. 52. A roof enclosure suitable for multistory buildings is shown in Fig. 53. A summary of recommendations for cold-weather construction is listed in Table 7.▶

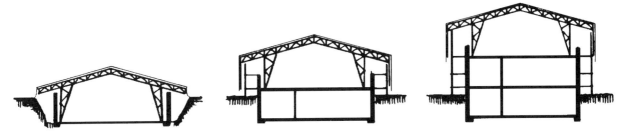

Fig. 53. Roof-type enclosures for multistory construction site.

Table 7. Summary of recommendations for cold weather construction

Temperature* °F	Construction	Protection
40-32	Heat sand or mixing water to produce mortar temperatures between 40 and 120°	Protect top of masonry from rain or snow by waterproof membrane extending down sides a minimum of 2 ft for 24 hr.
32-24	Heat sand and water to produce mortar temperatures between 40 and 120° F. Maintain temperatures of	Cover masonry completely with waterproof membrane for 24 hr.
25-20	Heat sand and water to pruduce mortar temperatures between 40 and 120° F. Maintain mortar temperatures on boards above freezing. Provide supplementary heat on both sides of walls. Provide windbreaks when wind is over 15 mph (Table 76).	Cover masonry completely with insulating blankets for 24 hr.
20 and below	Heat sand and water to provide mortar temperatures between 40 and 120° F. Provide enclosure and supplementary heat to maintain air temperature above 32° F. Temperature of units when laid shall be not less than 20° F.	Maintain masonry temperatures above 32° for 24 hr. by enclosure and supplementary heat supplied by electric blankets, infrared lamps, or other methods.

*Air temperature at time of construction, and mean daily air temperature during period of protection.

Earthquake resistant design

Summary: Earthquake damage to architectural components is not a trivial issue in either economic or social terms. The architect holds the responsibility for design decisions for each building in a particular area, whether or not such considerations are required by code, client or any other influence. The purpose of this "primer" is to make these responsibilities clear.

Key words: earthquake resistant design, geologic faults, life safety, Mercalli Intensity Scale, Richter Scale, seismic forces.

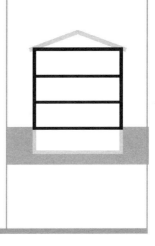

SHELL   B1

Given the potential magnitude of seismic forces and general level of construction practices, it is not surprising that when an earthquake occurs, people are often safer in an open field than they are in buildings that are supposed to shelter them. Earthquakes rarely kill people directly, but buildings do—unless specific precautions are taken. If the architect ignores seismic activity, a primary duty is neglected by not responding to specific environmental site conditions. Particularly during the planning stages, the architect's decisions about earthquake protection have critical implications for life safety.

Failures of service systems and emergency facilities can precipitate secondary disasters (most of the 1906 San Francisco loss was caused by fire resulting from damage due to ground shaking which severed the water supply system). Even in the absence of such consequences, there still can be serious consequential losses such as business interruption, displacement of families, the possibility of looting, rioting, and other social disasters. Further, where major interruptions occur in critical facilities such as hospitals, utilities and communication centers, the ability of the community to recover from the primary disaster may be drastically reduced.

If architects are to effectively communicate with the engineering profession and the public, it is necessary to understand the basic language of earthquake resistant design. A glossary of terms concludes this section. Terms are phrased in nontechnical language wherever possible; however, technical terms are used wherever appropriate.

1 Earthquakes—causes and effects

General theory of earth movement: plate tectonics

The theory of plate tectonics asserts that the crust and upper mantle of the earth are made up of six major and six or more minor internally rigid plates (or segments of the lithosphere) which slowly, continuously and independently slide over the interior of the earth. The plates meet in "convergence zones" and separate in "divergence zones." Plate motion is thought to create earthquakes, volcanoes and other geologic phenomena as internally rigid plates slowly, continuously and independently slide over the interior of the earth.

At *zones of divergence* molten rock from beneath the crust surges up to fill in the resulting rift and forms a ridge. This has occurred at mid-ocean locations as exemplified by the Mid-Atlantic Ridge and East Pacific Rise. The Red Sea is an example of a young spreading ridge.

At *zones of convergence,* subduction occurs—one plate slides under the other forming a trench, and returns material from the leading edge of the lower plate to the earth's interior. The Aleutian Trench is an example of a subduction zone. The subcontinent of India colliding with the Asian continent, thrusting under the Himalayas, and the Nazca plate in the Pacific Ocean underthrusting the Andes Mountains on the South American plate, exemplify mountain building in a subduction zone where the resisting force of the overlying plate forces the folding and piling up of the subducting plate edge.

Plates also can slide past each other laterally as well as rotate, since one or both plates move relative to the other. For example, the Pacific plate, which borders the West Coast of the United States, is moving northwesterly past the North American plate along the San Andreas Fault in California at the rate of 2.5 inches (6.4 centimeters) per year. Ninety percent of all earthquakes occur in the vicinity of plate boundaries. The other ten percent occur at faults located within plates. These are far less well understood than the interaction of different plates.

Fault types/resulting land forms

The geological fault represents the vertical plane intersection along which earth movement takes place and is the source of the ground shaking characteristic of an earthquake. Several fault types exist in the earth's crust, some of which are related to plate boundary action. Not all fault planes break through the surface of the crust to be visible to the eye. Fault planes occur to varying depths, and hypocenters (foci of earthquakes) may occur at any depth along these planes (Fig. 1a).

Author: Elmer E. Botsai, FAIA

Credits: This article is updated and adapted from Elmer E. Botsai *et al.* 1977. AIA Research Corporation. John P. Eberhard, President. Duncan Wilson, Project Co-Director. Illustrations by Thomas V. Vonier.

References: Arnold, Christopher, Richard Eisner, and Eric Elsesser. 1994. *Buildings at Risk: Seismic Design Basics for Practicing Architects.* DC: AIA/ACSA Council on Architectural Research.

Botsai, Elmer E., Alfred Goldberg, John Fisher, Henry Lagorio and Thomas D. Wosser. 1977. *Architects and Earthquakes.* National Science Foundation Report—AIA Research Corporation. Publication Stock No. 038-000-00331-3. Washington, DC: Superintendent of Documents, U. S. Government Printing Office.

Culver, Charles G. *et al.* 1975. *Natural Hazards Evaluation of Existing Buildings.* Building Science Series 61. Washington, DC: U. S. Department of Commerce, National Bureau of Standards.

B1

SHELL

Fig. 1a. Quiescent fault

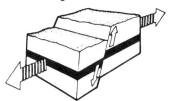

Fig. 1b. Normal fault

Fig. 1c. Thrust or reverse fault

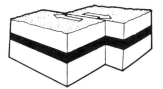

Fig. 1d. Lateral slip, strike slip or transform fault

Fig. 1e. Normal and slip fault combination

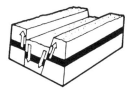

Fig. 1f. Graben

Fig. 1g. Horst

In normal faults (Fig. 1b), rocks on either side of the fault zone tend to pull apart creating tension at the fault. When the tension is sufficient to cause rupture, the overlying block moves down the fault line. Some normal faults occur along plate boundaries as plates pull apart.

In thrust or reverse faults (Fig. 1c), the rocks on either side of the fault zone tend to push together creating compression at the fault. When the compression is great enough to cause rupture, the overlying block moves up the slope ("dip") of the fault plane. Some thrust faults occur along plate boundaries as plates collide, as in the Alps.

In lateral slip (strike slip or transform faults) (Fig. 1d), movement is sideways along a nearly vertical fault plane. In some lateral slip faults two plates are sliding past each other, as in the San Andreas Fault.

Combinations of normal and slip or reverse end slip faults occur when movement is diagonal to the principal forces (Fig. 1e). When one or more normal faults run parallel to each other, earth movement can create a *graben* or a *horst* (Figs. 1f, 1g). A graben is a long, narrow trough caused by tensional crustal forces, thus causing fault blocks to drop between parallel faults. A horst is a ridge or plateau caused by fault blocks which are elevated in relation to parallel, outward-dipping normal faults.

Effects of earthquakes
The physical effects of earthquakes depend upon many parameters, including magnitude of earthquake, geologic conditions, location and depth of focus, intensity and duration of ground shaking, and the design and construction of buildings and other man-made structures. Sociologic effects are dependent upon factors such as density of population, time of day of the earthquake and community preparedness for the possibility of such an event.

Four basic causes of earthquake-induced damage are: ground rupture in fault zones, ground failure, tsunamis, and ground shaking.

1. Ground rupture in fault zones
An earthquake may or may not produce ground rupture along the fault zone. If a rupture does occur, it may be very limited or may extend over hundreds of miles, as in the 1906 San Francisco earthquake. Ground displacement along the fault can be horizontal, vertical or both, and may be measured in inches or several feet as previously mentioned. It can occur along a sharp line or can be distributed across a fault zone. Obviously, a structure directly astride such a break will be severely damaged. However, "proximity" to a fault does not necessarily carry a higher risk than location at some distance from the fault, the point being that damage from ground rupture is certain to occur only when the structure is astride the fault break.

2. Ground failure
Earthquake induced ground failure has been observed in the form of landslides, settlement and liquefaction. Ground failures can be the result of vibration induced densification of cohesionless soils or loose back fills, flow slides of earth masses due to liquefaction of underlying material, landslides in clay soils, sloping fills and liquefaction of saturated sands.

The phenomenon of liquefaction can occur in sands of relatively uniform size when saturated with water. When this material is subjected to vibration, the resulting upward flow of water can turn the material into a composition similar to "quicksand" with accompanying loss of foundation support. The most dramatic example of liquefaction occurred in Niigata, Japan during the earthquake of 1964. Several apartment buildings tipped completely on their back while remaining otherwise intact.

Ground failures are particularly damaging to support systems such as water lines, sewers, gas mains, communication lines, and transportation facilities. Loss of these systems after an earthquake has serious effects on both health and life safety, causing fires and reducing the ability to fight them and spreading disease.

3. Tsunamis

A tsunami or seismic seawave is produced by abrupt movement of land masses on the ocean floor. Tsunamis are very high velocity waves with long periods of oscillation. Their low wave height gives little evidence of their existence in the open sea. However, as the waves approach land, their velocity decreases and their height increases. Inundation heights of 20 to 30 feet (6 to 9 meters) are typically observed during tsunamis. The tsunami accompanying the 1964 Prince William Sound, Alaska earthquake reached 220 feet (67 m).

4. Ground Shaking

The effect of ground shaking on structures is a principal area of consideration in the design of earthquake resistant buildings. As the earth vibrates, all elements on the ground surface, whether natural or man-made, will respond to that vibration in varying degrees. Induced vibrations and displacements can destroy a structure unless it has been designed and constructed to be earthquake resistant. Whereas static vertical loads (dead and live) can be reasonably and accurately determined, the violent and random nature of dynamic conditions due to earthquakes makes the determination of seismic design loads extremely difficult. However, experience has shown that reasonable and prudent practices can mitigate life safety hazards under earthquake conditions.

Ground shaking factors

Earthquake location and depth of focus are significant factors in ground shaking. The depth of focus affects the amount of energy that reaches the surface, and hence the severity of shaking. Most damaging earthquakes are associated with a relatively shallow depth of focus less than 20 miles (32 km) deep. The energy released from a shallow earthquake may be expended over a relatively small area. Depending on the soils involved, much of the energy is often dissipated. In contrast, seismic energy from deep-seated shocks travels greater distances. Clearly, this will affect the resultant ground shaking.

The length of a fault break will also significantly affect ground shaking since it is a major determinant in creating the duration and "magnitude" of the earthquake.

While total earthquake energy may dissipate with distance from the epicenter, it is misleading to believe that this results in less risk to life or property. Short-period ground motions tend to die out more rapidly with distance than do longer period motions. Long-period vibrations tend to coincide with the longer natural periods of vibration of tall structures, causing resonance (Fig. 2). Low-rise buildings have shorter natural periods of oscillation, tall buildings have longer natural periods of oscillation. Therefore, the resonance effect is very significant among the damaging effects on buildings. For example, during the 1964 Prince William Sound, Alaska earthquake, tall buildings in Anchorage—80 miles (130 km) away from the epicenter—suffered significant damage.

Local soil conditions also have a significant effect on ground shaking. Basic rock motion has certain characteristics of frequency, acceleration, velocity and amplitude. These characteristics are affected by local geologic and soil conditions. Rock motion is modified by the depth of soil overburden, which increases the amplitude of motion and emphasizes longer dominant periods of vibration. The total effect depends upon the type of material in each stratum of the ground, the depth of each type, and the total depth to bed rock.

Experience from the 1906 San Francisco earthquake and the 1967 Caracas, Venezuela earthquake suggests that small, rigid, well-designed buildings may perform better on soft ground, whereas taller, flexible buildings on the same ground that are more "in tune" with the lower frequency ground vibrations may experience greater movement. Conversely, on rock or firm ground, the more rigid buildings may respond to the higher frequency vibrations, while the taller buildings may not be so severely affected. Current opinion leans toward the inclusion of a site-structure resonance factor in the formula for the determination of earthquake forces. This factor relates the fundamental period of the structure to the characteristic period of the site.

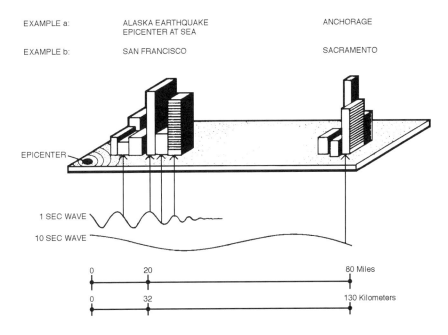

Fig. 2. Relative wave motion effects

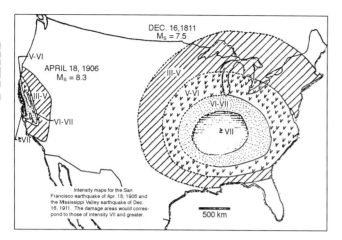

Fig. 3. Intensity VII areas in the U. S.

Map comparing intensities VII—areas which could expect damage—for the 1906 San Francisco and 1971 San Fernando earthquakes on the West Coast with the 1811 New Madrid and 1886 Charleston earthquakes in the East.

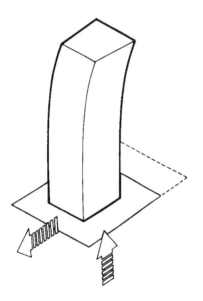

Fig. 4. The building should be able to undergo extended periods of ground shaking without failure.

Measuring and mapping earthquakes

"Richter magnitude," named after its developer, Charles F. Richter, is the most commonly used term in describing the size of an earthquake The Richter scale is based on the motion of a standard seismograph located 62 miles (100 kilometers) from the epicenter. Adjustments are made for seismographs of other types or when a seismograph is located other than 62 miles from the epicenter. The amplitude of the largest wave recorded by the standard seismograph at the standard distance is measured in terms of microns. The logarithm (base 10) of that number is defined as the Richter magnitude. Because the scale is logarithmic, the increase of recorded motion from one whole number to the next is tenfold. Thus, a "Richter 6" records ten times the amplitude of a "Richter 5," a "Richter 7" 100 times as much as a "Richter 5," and so forth.

Approximate correlations have been developed between an earthquake's total energy and Richter magnitude, with a one unit increase in magnitude approximating a 30-fold increase in energy release. The Prince William Sound, Alaska, earthquake of 1964 had a magnitude of 8.4, while San Francisco in 1906 experienced an 8.3 magnitude The New Madrid, Missouri, earthquakes of 1811-12 have been assigned magnitudes of greater than 8, based upon observed effects The damaging California earthquakes in San Fernando (1971), Long Beach (1933) and Santa Barbara (1925) had Richter magnitudes of 6.6, 6.3 and 6.3 respectively. Significant damage to earthquake-resistant buildings may be generally slight for earthquakes with a magnitude less than 5.5 to 6.

While the Richter magnitude gives a reasonable guide for estimating the total energy released in an earthquake, it is not sufficient—in fact is often misleading—as it fails to deal with displacement or acceleration for describing the local effects of an earthquake. A number of intensity scales have been devised to describe effects of ground motion at a given location.

The generally accepted intensity scale in the United States is the Modified Mercalli Intensity Scale (*cf.* Table 2 at end of chapter). Although the scale of intensity is determined and assigned by a trained observer, the rating is still very dependent upon subjective reactions and personal descriptions gathered from residents of the locale. Intensity scales of one type or another have been used throughout history; but relating these recorded intensities to today's occurrences is difficult because of changes in construction techniques, building design, and people's perceptions.

Following an earthquake, an *isoseismal* map can be prepared. These maps note intensities in various areas around the earthquake. Drawing a line which connects points of equal intensity produces an isoseismal map. The maps show that intensity decreases with increasing distance from the epicenter, a result of the attenuation of earthquake energy with distance (Fig. 3).

Attempts have been made to relate earthquake intensity with postulated earthquakes of varying Richter magnitudes along particular faults in an attempt to devise a seismic risk map. The assumptions necessary for such a projection are necessarily rather gross and lead to results that are at best subjective and approximate. Current efforts are being made to establish earthquake design levels based on recorded history and probabilities. The term "return period" has been coined. It is a probabilistic term which is not meant to imply that earthquakes of any given size will return in accordance with any set pattern. Since recorded seismic history is extremely short, random occurrence must be expected. No one can say, with the present state-of-the-art, when the 1812 New Madrid earthquake might recur.

2 Effects of earthquakes on structures

Earthquake forces in structures result from the erratic omnidirectional motion of the ground. The vertical aspects of these motions, up until recently, were neglected in building design because they were engineered to resist the forces of gravity. Recently, with the understanding that vertical acceleration of quakes can exceed 1 g., the vertical motion effects and design implications are being actively researched.

Response of buildings to ground motion
Ground motions are normally described in terms of acceleration velocity and displacement of the ground at a particular location. These all vary with time as the ground vibrates. The longer the time involved, the more cycles of displacement the structure will have to experience and the greater the need for absorption of the energies involved. Earthquakes vary from only a few seconds of ground shaking to several minutes. Therefore, the building should be able to undergo these extended periods of ground shaking without failure (Fig. 4).

Strong motion earthquake instruments (seismographs) have been developed to record actual earthquake vibrations in terms of ground acceleration. Although many records were obtained during the 1971 San Fernando earthquake, prior to that time very few instruments were located near the sites of significant earthquakes. The record of the 1940 El Centro, California, earthquake was used for many years as the "model" for studies since it was the best record available. Most recently, the Northridge, CA earthquake of 1994 has been used due to its extensive documentation.

Structures that are fixed to the ground in a more or less rigid manner respond to the ground motions. As the base of the structure moves, the upper portions tend to lag behind due to inertia. The resultant force is represented by the force F (in Fig. 4). The force F is equal to M (mass) times A (acceleration); hence, the higher the acceleration, the greater the resultant force on the structure.

Imagine that the ground, having accelerated in one direction and having moved out from under the structure, suddenly stops. The structure, being somewhat flexible, will spring back to the vertical or upright position, providing the initial shock has not exceeded the strength of the structure and resulted in collapse. The process of bending back and forth produces swaying in taller structures and continues until the earthquake induced energy is dissipated. The building acts as a pendulum with respect to the ground, with the rate and frequency of the swing (*i.e.*, the swaying) a function of building height, mass, cross-section area and related factors (Fig. 5).

Relation of wave motion to structural behavior
The rate of oscillation, or "natural period" of a structure, is an extremely important factor because earthquakes do not result in ground movement in only one direction, as assumed in the example above. In fact, the ground oscillates back and forth, in all directions. Consider what would happen if, at the same time that the upper part of the structure begins to move to catch up with the initial displacement, the ground motion reverses itself. Complex deflections may result as the building vibrates in all its modes of vibration in response to ground motion (Fig. 6). The ground motion may coincide with the natural period of the building, resulting in resonance.

It is therefore extremely important in basic seismic design that the probable frequency of ground motion as well as the natural period of the structure be considered. In early design theory, design was based on the concept of simple harmonic motion in earthquakes, *i.e.*, wave motions of uniform frequency and intensity. Clearly, predictions about failures in design would depend upon the assumptions of the frequency of motion, as well as building form. However, experience shows that earthquakes are dominated by more or less random motions of varying frequencies. As a result, M. A. Biot proposed m 1933 that a "spectrum" of frequencies be used for evaluation of earthquake designs that would more adequately evaluate the response of different structures to various kinds of ground motion.

Table 1. Energies of some major earthquakes

Location	Date	Richter Magnitude
Anchorage, Alaska	1964	8.5
San Francisco, California	1906	8.2
Kern County, California	1952	7.7
El Cenuo, California	1940	7.1
Northridge, California	1994	6.8
Long Beach, California	1913	6.3
San Francisco, California	1957	5.3

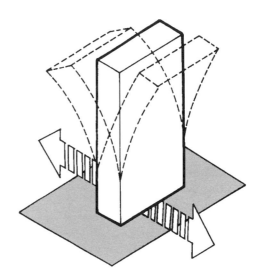

Fig. 5. Pendulum action

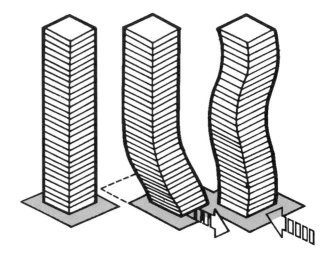

Fig. 6. Effects of cyclic reversals on ground acceleration. At the same time that the upper part of the structure begins to move to catch up with the initial displacement, the ground motion reverses itself.

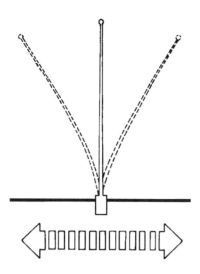

Fig. 7A. Flexibility illustrated by a thin flagpole that can sway considerably without fracture or permanent displacement.

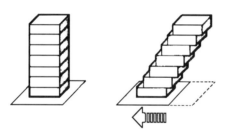

Fig. 7b. The opposite situation is represented by a stack of unreinforced bricks whose movement results in permanent displacement of each brick when a horizontal force is applied.

However, a building is not a simple pendulum. It is generally conceived as a series of masses at each floor level that will respond with several modes of vibration. The theoretical response of the structure will depend on the input motion, the periods of vibration of the various modes, the masses at the various floor levels, and damping.

Methods of dealing with the earthquake forces

The way the structure absorbs or transfers the energy released by an earthquake will determine the success or failure of the building's seismic resistant design and construction. The energy transfer and energy dissipation mechanisms involved should be such that no damage would occur. The desired flexibility is illustrated by a thin flagpole that can sway considerably without fracture or permanent displacement (Fig. 7a). The opposite situation is represented by a stack of unreinforced bricks whose movements result in permanent displacement of each brick when a horizontal force is applied. The stack is quickly toppled. If the bricks were cemented together with epoxy, or heavily reinforced and tied to the base so as to act as a single mass of bricks rather than as single bricks, then the stack would be very rigid and would resist displacement forces until the mass fractured (Fig. 7b).

The principle of Basic Isolation is to reduce the lateral accelerations and velocities that a building's structural system will experience by lengthening the period (of the building) and allowing for increased displacements. These systems have been used effectively in retrofitting older (and stiffer) structures in seismic upgrading programs. Although consideration must be given to increased displacement during an earthquake, the reduced accelerations allow for less intrusive lateral systems to be used during an upgrade.

Tuned Mass Dampeners attempt to reduce the lateral displacement of a building moving in its first mode of vibration. This system has been used primarily to increase human comfort in tall buildings subjected to wind loads.

The recent development of Base Isolation and Tuned Mass Dampeners can only have a beneficial effect in mitigating damage and improving safety and comfort. However, authoritative judgment does not concur that these new innovations will necessarily solve all serious problems.

Impact of architectural form on stiffness and flexibility

Nearly all buildings combine some elements that are "flexible" with other elements that are fundamentally "stiff." The improper combinations of such elements may create problems in building performance under earthquake loading. These combinations can result in designs that not only have highly variable behavior in earthquakes, but also can aggravate the effects of earthquakes on the building. A classic example of this condition is the use of masonry wall infill between moment resisting frame members when the wall is not designed as a component of the frame. Since most of these problems derive from basic architectural decisions as to the plan and form of the building, it is extremely important for the architect to understand them.

Effect of building shape on response to seismic forces

One of the most critical decisions regarding the ability of buildings to withstand earthquakes is the choice of basic plan shape and configuration. Given that earthquake forces at a site can come from any and all directions, and act upon all elements of the building virtually simultaneously, the obvious "best choice" is a building which is symmetrical in plan and elevation, and therefore equally capable of withstanding forces imposed from any direction.

However, given other constraints such as shape of site and functional requirements, rarely can the architect satisfy this demand. Therefore, an understanding of how variations in plan and elevation symmetry can affect performance is important.

Consider a building with an irregular plan shape, such as an "L" or "T" configuration. The wings might experience different movements depending upon their orientation relative to the direction of earthquake force (Fig. 8). For example, in a N-S directed earthquake, the N-S wing of an L- or T- shaped building will be relatively stiffer since its long axis is parallel to the earthquake motion; it would not move significantly. On the other hand, the E-W wing is shallow in the direction of the earthquake motion. Unless designed to have adequate capacity to absorb and dissipate the forces it can suffer greater damage, particularly at the point where the wings connect.

Since the structure is a unit, torsion movements are created by the earthquake. Torsion is the result of rotation of an eccentric or a less rigid mass about the basic or the more rigid mass of the building. Under earthquake motion, it can cause rotation of the mass of an E-W wing relative to the mass of a N-S wing (Fig. 9).

Torsion can also occur in regular-shaped buildings whenever the relative stiffness of one part of the structure is different from another. For example, in a rectangular building with a very stiff off- center core area, and the remainder of the structure flexible, torsion will develop in the flexible portion around the stiffer core (right-hand plan in Fig. 9). Regular-shaped buildings with balanced stiffness elements therefore avoid the secondary effects of torsion and differential movement.

It also should be noted that irregular shapes that can experience torsion effects are not solely limited to irregularities in the plan or section of the building. Differences occurring in building shapes such as where upper stories of a tall structure have greater floor area than

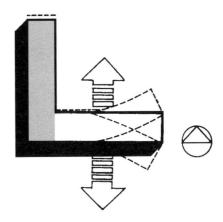

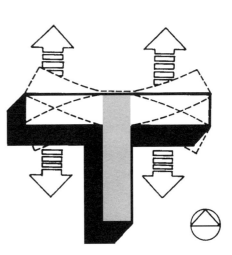

Fig. 8. Stiffness of structure related to building plan

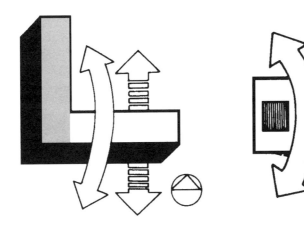

Fig. 9. Torsion effects on building plan.

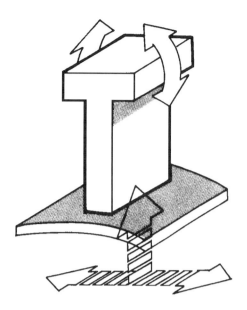

Fig. 10. Oblique view of vertical torsion effect

those below, can result in similar torsion problems because of vertical accelerations (Fig. 10). There will also be an increase in the differential displacements between the tower and the extended portion of the building due to greater stiffness provided by the increased floor size.

Effect of seismic forces on building systems

Ideally, a building should be designed either with infinite stiffness or with all its elements capable of absorbing deflections; in other words, an infinitely flexible but stable system. Since buildings rarely fit either ideal system, the designer must fully understand the seismic performance of the system employed.

Most buildings are designed with a mixture of stiff and flexible concepts. Some of these combinations when used unwisely may cause serious damage and collapse of structures. The "open first floor" concept commonly used today—placement of a rigid upper structure on a flexible column system—exemplifies this problem. The flexible columns are expected to resist exaggerated and concentrated forces, yet may not be designed to take these loads.

A similar problem is created when the designer inadvertently weakens a stiff wall (shear wall) with many openings. For instance, even if the openings are rather narrow, flanked by wall segments, the result may no longer be a truly stiff wall, but rather a series of thin, wide columns. If these wall segments are not then designed as columns, they may well fail under seismic forces.

Materials

Different materials react differently with respect to inelastic behavior. Ductile materials, such as steel, have an extended inelastic range in which they can undergo permanent deformation without rupture. On the other hand, brittle materials such as brick display almost no inelastic behavior under loading, and experience sudden failure at or near the elastic limit. The same is true, relatively speaking, of glass, unreinforced concrete and a variety of other common building materials.

Ductility, an important characteristic of materials, refers to the ability of a material to absorb energy while undergoing inelastic deformation without failure, particularly when the direction of the forces involved changes several times. In brittle materials cracking may have occurred, and therefore, more and more displacement occurs with continued applied force, so the strength deteriorates. On the other hand, ductile materials can undergo many cycles of loading with the same large energy absorbing capability. Without proper reinforcement, concrete and other brittle materials have low ductility values.

Ductile building systems include steel frames, ductile concrete frames and wood diaphragm construction. Where the connections of the system used are ductile and numerous, the overall performance is improved considerably. Ductility can be thought of as providing a quality of toughness which, to a large extent, determines a building's survival under seismic conditions.

Architectural design concept and its effect on building seismic performance

As has been stated before, the shape chosen by the designer for the structure will determine its response to seismic forces, including the development of torsion effects as well as differential movements of parts of the building. The extent of glazing, the number of glazed facades, the size of spandrel elements, and the location of the exterior column line are among the architectural design factors which directly affect a building's seismic performance.

Both architect and engineer have to recognize and understand how design decisions may create serious seismic effects on a structure. For example, the architect who desires to design an open first story must take into account the problem raised by placing a rigid structure over the open story. Similarly, if a shear wall structure is proposed,

Fig. 11. Statue of Louis Agassiz dislodged during 1906 San Francisco earthquake. Stanford University campus.

the architect must understand that numerous openings will affect the seismic performance of such a wall.

Cantilevered balconies, cornices, parapets, railings, sunshades, statues, signs and planters must be structurally designed with sufficient capability to resist seismic forces. Also the weight of materials chosen can increase or decrease the required design loads. Fig 11 demonstrates how statues must be properly anchored to resist seismic forces. Louis Agassiz fell from his perch on Stanford University campus. 1906 San Francisco earthquake.

Relationship to adjoining buildings
The architect must consider how a building is sited relative to other structures. Adequate separations must be provided to avoid "banging" since individual structures do not have identical modes of response. During an earthquake, each building will attempt to swing like a complex pendulum with its fundamental period of response. The amount of horizontal movement of a building from its original vertical position is called drift. If the clearance between two buildings of different periods is not at least equal to the sum of the calculated *drift* values of each structure, the buildings, acting as two pendulums will bang together causing considerable damage.

Critical need to tie structural system together
Since seismic forces affect all parts of a building, the building must act as a unit to resist these forces. If the structure is not tied together to respond as a unit, the separate elements or components of the building will respond individually and failure can occur beginning at the weakest element or component. The result would be a shift in load carrying or resisting ability of other elements which then also can fail due to overloading.

The nature and completeness of the connections will determine the ability of the structural system to perform. Typical connection conditions which can fail include the use of brittle rather than ductile connections, or the spacing of fasteners at too close intervals so that connecting members fail. In addition, reinforcement bars may not be adequately anchored or spliced to develop the full strength of the connection. For example, the beam-column intersection in ductile concrete construction may not be fully developed to carry the seismic loads through the necessary reversals it may undergo.

In masonry construction, if the floor systems are not properly tied to the walls, under seismic forces the walls may move independent of the floors causing either the walls to fail or the floors to drop. This is also true wherever the design requires that the building components bear specific relationships, one to the other, in order to perform. Only by assuring adequate ties, proper detailing and careful construction can the design assumptions be carried out.

Dissimilarity of wind and earthquake loads
For many years, most building codes have referred to designing for wind or for earthquakes in similar terms, and, for many years, architects and engineers have failed to recognize the important differences between these forces. There is fundamental difference in the way in which lateral loads are transmitted to a building from earthquake and wind. In the case of earthquake, the load is transmitted to the building from its base. Thus, the entire building as well as the building contents will experience the force. In general, the magnitude of this force which individual members experience is proportional to their mass. On the other hand, in the case of wind, the load is transmitted to the building through its envelope. Thus the cladding and its supporting members experience the initial effects of the wind load. Except for the structural members, the interior of the building including its contents will not experience the wind loads directly as long as the envelope remains intact (Culver *et al.* 1975).

Furthermore, excluding tornado effects, wind forces quantified by the code are usually conservative and generally all that is required is adequate stiffness in tall buildings to prevent excessive swaying.

However, earthquake resistant design is another matter entirely. Despite recent advancements in recording of earthquakes, dynamic analyses, computer applications, etc., it still is impossible to "define" a maximum design earthquake force with absolute confidence. It is important to recognize that our evaluation of earthquake design forces is just a good working approximation. But it does give the architect and engineer a basis for design which should be adequate if the nature of earthquakes and earthquake resistant design is understood.

In designing for wind forces, it is expected that buildings will resist the design wind loads without damage of any kind. The building is expected to perform entirely within the elastic limit of its materials. However, in earthquake resistant design due to the far greater magnitude of the forces and displacements involved, it is expected that some components of the structure may exceed the elastic limit in responding to significant earthquakes and therefore some damage may occur under these conditions. Further, in designing for wind forces, a building's base is assumed to be stationary. In earthquakes, both the base and the superstructure move.

This difference in design concept must be recognized. Whereas many buildings with brittle materials and brittle connections have survived wind loads for many years, they would not stand a chance in a significant earthquake. Earthquake resistant buildings must be "tied together" in all respects and contain the ductility and toughness which are necessary properties if they are to survive the omnidirectional violent actions of an earthquake.

Clearly, in tall buildings, wind governs lateral force loads. However, it would be a serious mistake to assume that a building properly designed for hurricane force lateral loads would provide proper protection from seismic forces. The actions of wind and earthquake are entirely dissimilar. In addition to the vertical action of earthquakes, seismic forces normally affect all components, structural as well as nonstructural, of the entire building as opposed to wind, which generally affects only the exterior shell and perhaps the basic frame.

3 Interaction of building components
Nonstructural components must be properly integrated with or effectively isolated from the basic structural frame to excessive damage to the building and the incumbent threat to life under earthquake induced movements.

The interaction between nonstructural components and structural systems can be divided into two basic relationships. These relationships are: the effect of the nonstructural components on the structural system; and, the structural system's effect on components.

- The effect of most nonstructural components on the performance of the structure is in most cases neutral, and generally does not cause undue problems when this interaction is overlooked. However, in certain cases significant modifications to the building's structural response can occur under seismic loading as a result of nonstructural-structural interaction. These modifications of response generally occur when the nonstructural component has some degree of rigidity and/or mass that causes an unexpected stiffening effect on portions of the structure. Classic examples of this are non- bearing masonry walls and firewalls, spandrels, and stair framing and other vertical shaftways, particularly when intermediate landings are tied to columns. These cause a stiffening of the structure, a consideration which must be included in the basic design considerations.

- The second action is the effect of the basic structure's movement on the nonstructural components. The following section addresses these effects.

Building drift
The horizontal displacement of basic building elements is usually most critical to nonstructural components. All floors do not drift at the same

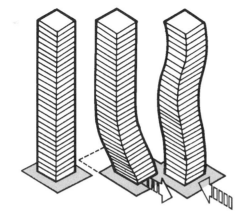

Fig. 12a. Some floors of the building tend to move in one direction while floors above or below these tend to move in the opposite direction in a relatively tall building.

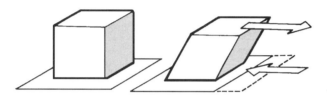

Fig. 12b. Drift diagram showing lateral displacement and resulting foreshortening.

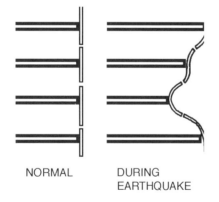

NORMAL   DURING
                EARTHQUAKE

SIMPLE SPAN CURTAIN WALL

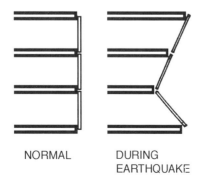

NORMAL   DURING
                EARTHQUAKE

Fig. 13. Effect of cantilevered exterior walls *vs.* simple span. The exterior curtain wall that is anchored at each floor slab and is cantilevered both up and down can be severely affected.

rate or time, and this action causes a horizontal displacement between floors. This action, while usually cumulative, does rapidly change direction due to the earthquake forces acting at the base of the structure, and in a relatively tall building, can result in some floors of the building tending to move in one direction while floors above or below these are tending to move in the opposite direction (Figs. 12a and 12b). This differential movement between floors can and does affect all full-floor height elements of a building.

The accumulation of drift affects only those nonstructural components that are continuous over more than one floor. Even here the effect is dependent upon the detailing of the component. For example, an exterior curtain wall that spans floor-to-floor in a simple span is seldom affected by cumulative action (Fig. 13). However, the exterior curtain wall that is anchored at each floor slab and is cantilevered both up and down can be severely affected. Unless properly designed, the imposed racking of the elements can result in major failures of the wall system.

Simple shearing or racking action due to drift can be imposed on all floor-to-floor and some floor-to-ceiling components by the differential lateral movement between adjacent floor systems. In some cases bending occurs because the movement is perpendicular to the component.

Problems also develop for components fitted tightly against columns due to the deflection action of the column. Under severe drift conditions, the resulting foreshortening of the relative floor-to-floor height can cause crushing. The design team should always expect that these forces will not run exactly parallel to the component and therefore, the actual movement will produce combined effects of shear, bending and, possibly if the elements are restrained, crushing.

Building torsion
This action, usually brought about by the eccentric lateral resistance or mass of the basic structure, causes the building to twist vertically. It should be noted that torsion in a building sometimes results from the stiffness of rigid or massive nonstructural components such as in-fill walls. The basic effects of torsion on components are quite similar to drift and will result in the same problems as those produced by drift.

Displacement of cantilevered members
Due to their unique nature, cantilevers tend to exaggerate the joint rotation of the structural frame (Fig. 14). Under seismic loading cantilevers must receive special consideration. The unrestrained end condition can result in vertical displacement of a considerable magnitude. It is quite realistic to expect this vertical displacement to be in opposite directions on adjacent floors. Since a high percentage of cantilever construction involves exterior walls, these conditions can create a significant hazard to life safety because of glass breakage and falling wall elements.

Other factors
An additional factor should be considered: seismic forces are a time process in addition to a force process. As such, the various components of a building will not necessarily move as a unit even within a single floor. Therefore, the designer can expect maximum movements to occur at various components at various times and must act accordingly. All of the above actions may take place simultaneously and produce movements between the nonstructural and structural components that are quite complex.

Essentially, it is the deformation of the structural elements that controls the magnitude of relative movements between the basic structure and the nonstructural components. As has been repeatedly stressed, structure is but one factor in determining how the building responds to seismic forces. The magnitude of relative movements is determined by the complex interaction of overall building form, plan, structural systems, mass, materials, details and subsystems design. As such, the overall design of the building will control the magnitude of movement involved. The more monolithic and rigid the building, the less relative movement. On the other hand, in many cases flexibility is a desirable feature from a structural point of view; therefore, these alternate approaches must be coordinated in the final design.

Design strategies for components

Two design concepts can be utilized in the approach to nonstructural component design: the deformation approach, and the detached approach.

- The *deformation approach* is most useful when the structure is rigid, and expected movements are small. The designer may choose to rely on the ability of materials to respond to stress through their inherent elastic response. In a rigid basic structure this is usually not too difficult to achieve. Most nonstructural component materials will equal or exceed the basic structural material in allowable deformation. However, consideration must be given to component shapes and connection details. The architect must also take into account those materials or components that do not readily deform, such as glass; these brittle materials must be isolated properly to protect them.

In the *detached approach*, the designer relies on detailing of the nonstructural components to keep them relatively free from the movement of the basic structure and thus avoid direct stresses. This method of design utilizes the extensive use of hinges, slip joints and resilient edge conditions. In the utilization of these tools, the architect must remember to consider rotation and three-directional movement in order to avoid any binding action that will negate the effective action of these details.

The architect should also give consideration to combining the above approaches in the more flexible buildings. It is not unreasonable to design systems that will allow for usual seismic deflections in the detached approach and then expect that under excessive seismic movement the inherent flexibility of the component material will provide the additional resiliency needed to avoid damage to the component.

Another facet of proper seismic design that may be overlooked by the architect is the interworkings of one nonstructural component with another. In addition to being able to effectively respond to the basic structural movement, the components must be able to respond to each other. This can become somewhat tricky at intersections, and when a composite approach is being used. Classic examples of failure in this area are:

- Rigidly fastened duct work or sprinklers penetrating a nonlaterally braced suspended ceiling may move, tearing off sprinkler heads, ductwork, and/or ceiling parts.

- Suspended ceilings that rely on partitions for their lateral resistance, or partitions relying on the ceiling for their lateral resistance, may "all fall down."

Most nonstructural components are, in effect, small scale structures and, as such, have mass, shape and different materials just as buildings do. Each of these components is subject not only to external forces but to its own internal reactions to seismic forces. Therefore, these nonstructural components must have their own integrity if they are to survive severe earthquakes. In many cases for nonstructural components such as plaster walls, ductwork and conduits, their normal integrity is usually adequate to resist seismic forces, provided they are properly connected to the building.

Certain nonstructural components are, however, extremely vulnerable to damage. These components usually fall into the category of having thin sections accompanied by heavy mass. Typical examples are:

- Non-bearing masonry walls.

- Parapets.

- Lightweight metal curtain walls with thick or insulating glass.

Importance of connections and fastenings

The importance of proper connection design cannot be overemphasized. Careful attention to this phase of design often can make the difference between success and failure under seismic loading. Com-

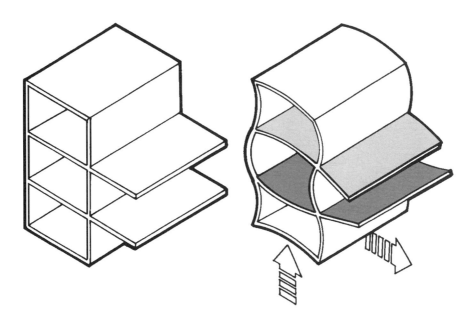

Fig. 14. Cantilevers tend to exaggerate the joint rotation of the structural frame. Vertical displacement can be in opposite directions on adjacent floors.

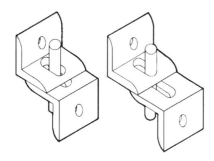

Fig. 15. Connection of double-clip angles. The extended position is the critical condition when subject to stresses.

monly, connections are the weakest links in seismic design. This is true both in the fastening of nonstructural components to the structure, and in the basic structural system. A careful review of nonstructural component failures has shown that many occur at points of connection. At these points stresses tend to concentrate or change direction and thus often exceed the limits of the design. Some considerations of causes of these excessive stresses in nonstructural components are discussed below.

- Inadequate tolerances for seismic movement will transmit impact loads to adjacent parts. Tolerances for movement must be provided in addition to normal construction tolerances.

- Too often the designer fails to take into account the limitations of bearing pressures on fastenings. This is particularly true in threaded fastenings where the threads cause a sizable reduction in cross-section as well as bearing area of members.

- Another critical area is in light gauge material, particularly aluminum. Excessive bearing pressure will cause yield in hole size and then "pull out." One such area of concern is the use of screws in extruded slots. These connections are extremely weak and should be avoided in critical elements.

Some connections for the attachment of components use various adjustable connections such as the double clip angle. In usual practice these are drawn in their normal position with construction tolerances not indicated (Fig. 15). Often the connection is considered in its normal position and not in its extended position which is the critical condition when subjected to stresses.

Welding is used frequently in contemporary construction. In cases of on-site field welding, residual stresses remain in the material welded requiring careful consideration of how the connection is detailed. Three areas of concern are:

- Welding builds up local internal stresses, particularly at end points. These residual stresses can increase the chance of failure when the connection is further stressed due to seismic action.

- Light gauge welding often results in burn through, particularly when light gauge material is connected to heavy structural shapes. A further concern in light gauge welding is with regard to galvanized material. The action of the zinc coating in the welding process causes gas pockets in the weld bead and can reduce the effective value of the weld. Both of these conditions seriously reduce the ability to resist seismic forces.

Welded steel moment frames have been a common lateral bracing system for medium and high-rise construction throughout the United States and the world. Prior to the Northridge Earthquake, it had been considered one of the most seismic-resistant structural systems. The widespread damage of these systems during the 1994 Northridge earthquake promoted intense research into the reasons for these unexpected failures. Although research is ongoing, some conclusions are:

- After the Northridge Earthquake, the governing codes changed to delete the prequalified connections option and substituted a requirement that connections (for a welded steel movement frame) be demonstrated by tests or calculations as being capable of developing the required inelastic demands (during an earthquake) considering variations in material yield strength and strain hardening.

- Certain welding electrodes are suspected of having insufficient "fracture toughness" to perform well during dynamic loading.

At the present time, many of the details and connections in buildings may be dictated by local custom and practice in the construction industry, and not by consideration of seismic loading conditions. The need for basic research and professional education is perhaps as great in this area as in any related to seismic design.

4 Earthquake considerations in architectural design

To this point, the discussion has covered how earthquakes generate forces and some design considerations relating how basic architectural concepts—such as cantilevers, open first stories and irregular plan shapes—withstand such forces. Unfortunately, this leaves the impression that the major problem is structural design, which is not the case. Certainly, the structural design is critical, for if the structure fails, little else is of consequence. Table 3 provides a summary of structural system alternatives with commentary regarding earthquake suitability. The remainder of this discussion shows why the scope of earthquake design should be extended beyond structure to architectural design considerations.

As discussed above, motion in the structure is transmitted to the nonstructural components in a variety of ways. Lateral motion of the building due to ground acceleration was given as the predominant factor. Ground motion causes the building to move, with relative story drift occurring, which in turn creates stresses and forces on nonstructural components. The movement of one floor relative to another creates shear forces on the walls that are tightly fitted between them. If the deflection is large, a reduction in vertical height will occur, causing crushing of the wall.

Both shearing and crushing forces can be transmitted internally through one component into another; the racking wall stresses the window frame which crushes the glass. Connections also can fail. When the structure starts moving, anything that is attached to that structure, directly or indirectly, is subject to damage or destruction unless properly designed. Every part of the building and everything within the building requires design and construction attention.

Damage and destruction are important because they have profound effects on our lives. This rather obvious deduction is the basis for a meaningful life safety approach to earthquake design from the architect's point of view. Earthquake damage to buildings is critical because it disrupts vital functions; it represents economic losses for families and businesses; and, most importantly, it threatens injury and death to building occupants and people in the vicinity of buildings. Therefore, criteria for earthquake design should center around mitigating these consequences, not simply ensuring the survival of the structural frame. In short, architects can begin to set meaningful priorities in earthquake design by first stating the design goals that we wish to accomplish, which one can posit as a strategy for responsible earthquake resistant design:

*   Design and build to the expected standards of performance of the building as it affects life safety and property damage.

*   Establish basic planning and design parameters (form, shape) that will best meet the performance criteria.

*   Integrate the various building components within the basic planning and design parameters, giving attention to appropriate life safety criteria.

To apply this strategy, consider the following requirements as criteria for earthquake resistant design:

*   *Requirement 1: Protection of building occupants and the public adjacent to a building during an earthquake.*

During an earthquake, the greatest immediate hazard to persons in or near a building is the danger of being hit by falling objects. During the ground shaking, occupants are safest finding shelter under a desk, table or counter.

Assuming that the basic structure does not collapse, the dangers to which occupants still are exposed during a severe earthquake include toppling of free standing furniture, equipment and storage systems such as filing cabinets and bookshelves. Wall mounted objects such as clocks and artwork are shaken loose and flung around the room. Suspended ceiling components may pop out, throwing snapped-off lighting fixtures, mechanical diffusers sprinkler heads and other components down with them. Hazards from flooding and live wires may then be present. Door frames may be bent by racking partitions, and may jam the doors shut. Partitions may be crushed or may collapse. If the partitions contain utility lines these may be broken, creating secondary hazards such as electric shock and fire. Racking walls bend window frames, causing glass to shatter and sending dangerous shards into the room or to the outside. Sashes may shear from their fastenings and may fall into or cascade outside the building.

Design consideration has to be extended to a building exterior. Persons outside a building can be hit by falling parapets, facade panels or elements, glass or other debris.

In order to protect persons from such hazards, building components and systems must be designed with the potential dangers in mind. Population densities of buildings also are included in these critical design considerations.

Requirement 2: Disaster control and emergency subsystems must remain operable after an earthquake.

Designers must consider the prospect that there will be casualties within buildings and that people will be unable to escape. These people and the building itself will be subjected to secondary hazards caused by earthquake damage. Among the most critical are:

*   *Fire:* Fires can begin at a variety of locations during an earthquake, such as in mechanical rooms, kitchens, laboratories; that is, wherever fuel or electric lines rupture.

*   *Electrical hazards:* Collapse of ceilings or partitions or dislocation of electrical appliances may leave wiring exposed which creates danger of shock, or results in sparking which can lead to fire or explosion.

*   *Flooding:* Broken water pipes or sanitary lines may lead to flooding of various parts of the building.

As noted, fire protection devices can be damaged or destroyed when sprinkler heads are snapped off by collapsing ceilings. Flooding from the fire pipe system is an immediate consequence. Hoses can be torn off and fire extinguishers may be damaged when ripped off their mountings or crushed in wall encasements. They may be inaccessible or blocked by debris. Alarm systems are subject to both mechanical and electrical failures. Water supplies for fire fighting may be cut off by broken standpipes and mains inside or outside the building. Fire escapes may be blocked by debris or may have sheared completely off the building.

In order to prevent such secondary disasters, control and emergency systems such as the fire protection system should be designed to remain intact after the earthquake.

Requirement 3: Occupants must be able to evacuate a building quickly and safely after an earthquake when it is safe to do so.

While it may be an instinctive reaction for occupants to attempt to evacuate a building during an earthquake, this is the most dangerous action to take due to falling objects. Once ground shaking ceases, evacuation can begin. Quick and orderly evacuation should be accomplished because of the possibility of potentially hazardous secondary disasters such as explosions and fires, or aftershocks.

Considerable hazards can be encountered during evacuation. In an exit corridor or on a stairway, the occupant may encounter debris from ceilings, partitions and fixtures, making walking hazardous or impossible. If the lighting system fails and the occupants cannot see the way out, they may fall over obstacles. The danger is especially acute in interior stairways, where darkness makes it impossible to see missing stairs and railings, debris and other hazards. For this and other reasons, stairwells should be provided with at least a level of daylighting for directional wayfinding.

Experience indicates that elevators have been extremely vulnerable to damage in earthquakes. As the building shakes, counterweights and other equipment may be torn from their connections and tossed around; striking the elevator cabs and causing guide rails and other systems to fail. Entire elevator shafts and stairwells which are attached to the building exterior, when improperly designed, may experience shearing forces that cause them to break away completely from the building.

Upon reaching the exit, the occupant may find the doorway blocked by collapsed upper story walls, fallen parapets, balconies, cornices or pieces of roofing. Broken glass hinders safe passage. The door itself may not open if the frame has been bent out of alignment. Once outside, the evacuee also risks being struck by loosened debris falling from the building's exterior.

These potential hazards to life safety should be mitigated through careful consideration by the design team.

Requirement 4: Rescue and emergency workers must be able to enter the building immediately after an earthquake, encountering minimum interference and danger.

After an earthquake, access to and passage within a building can be blocked to rescue and emergency workers for the same reasons that movement within and egress from the building are hindered for occupants. Review the hazards listed in Requirement 3, above.

Rescue and emergency personnel need clear passageways to remove casualties. They need to find control and emergency subsystems operable in order to cope with fire and flooding.

Requirement 5: The building must be returned to useful service as quickly as possible.

The total "cost" of any earthquake is measured in at least two parts: the direct consequences of bodily injury or death and property damage, and the costs of social disruption and economic losses related to the inability of a city to function at full capacity after an earthquake. The latter costs—due to interruption of social and economic processes—have two components as well. The more obvious one is the loss of business activity and revenues. The less obvious one is the cost of having to divert many resources to repair and restore services and buildings. Clearly, it is desirable to minimize these costs by minimizing damage and disruption.

This minimization is perhaps the most difficult task for the architect to undertake since virtually every component in a building is subject to earthquake damage and loss. Since it is not practical to prevent damage to all components, it must be decided which of the subsystems are the most critical to continued functioning in the building after an earthquake, and concentrate upon preventive design for these subsystems. Among the most important are:

• *Sewage disposal and potable water supply:* These subsystems are important in larger buildings and especially in critical facilities such as hospitals. Vertical piping systems are particularly subject to damage due to horizontal forces and overstressing of connections and joints.

• *Electric power:* Many important functions in all types of buildings are critically dependent upon the availability of electrical power, in-

cluding lighting, communications, heating/cooling, vertical transportation, etc.

• *Mechanical systems* should be sufficiently operational to provide at least minimum environmental control, particularly in critical use facilities.

The relative importance of subsystems depends a great deal on factors such as building occupancy, size, location, and climate. For example, maintenance of a communications system is more critical in a hospital or police station than in a residential building.

Requirement 6: The building and personal property within the building should remain as secure as possible after the earthquake.

One of the unpleasant facts to contemplate is that during or after any civil or natural disaster, the danger of looting and vandalism is imminent. Looting deters the quick restoration of social order. The components contributing to the security of the building should remain as intact as possible after an earthquake.

Maintaining the integrity of the exterior shell of the building may be the most difficult aspect of maintaining security. As noted in several places, glass breakage is a severe problem in any earthquake. Broken windows and doors are an obvious disruption of building security. The collapse of any part of the lower facade creates a similar problem. Therefore, reduction of property damage in general can alleviate security problems.

After the establishment of appropriate priorities and performance criteria, architects can then efficiently utilize their own and their consultants' broad range of knowledge and expertise to design appropriate earthquake-resistant buildings within set parameters. Due diligence in earthquake-resistant design and provisions for life safety in the event of such disasters is a primary responsibility of the architect. To consider such factors early and thoroughly throughout the design and construction process is the single-most effective measure to mitigate the disastrous effects of earthquakes.

Glossary of terms

Acceleration—rate of change of velocity with time.

Accelerogram—the record from an accelerograph showing acceleration as a function of time.

Accelerograph—a strong-motion earthquake instrument recording ground (or base) acceleration.

Aftershock—an earthquake, usually a member of an aftershock series often within the span of several months following the occurrence of a large earthquake (main shock). The magnitude of an aftershock is usually smaller than the main shock.

Amplification—an increase in earthquake motion as a result of resonance of the natural period of vibration with that of the forcing vibration.

Amplitude—maximum deviation from mean or center line of a wave.

Aseismic region—one that is relatively free of earthquakes.

Attenuation—reduction of amplitude or change in wave due to energy dissipation over distance with time.

Axial load—force coincident with primary axis of a member.

Base isolation—a method whereby a building superstructure is separated from its foundation with various shock-absorbing materials intended to mitigate the characteristics of earthquake forces transmitted to the building.

Base shear—total shear force acting at the base of a structure.

Bilinear—representation by two straight lines of the stress versus strain properties of a material, one straight line to the yield point and the second line beyond.

Brittle failure—Failure in material which generally has a very limited plastic range; material subject to sudden failure without warning.

Compression and dilatation—(rarefacation)—Used in connection with longitudinal waves, as in acoustics. They refer to the nature of the motion at a given point, usually a recording station. When the ray emerges to the surface, displacement upward and away from the hypocenter corresponds to compression, the opposite to dilatation.

Convergence zone—A band along which moving tectonic plates collide and land area is lost either by shortening and crustal thickening or by subduction and destruction of crust.

Core—The central part of the earth below a depth of 2,900 kilometers. It is thought to be composed of iron and nickel and to be molten on the outside with a central solid inner core.

Creep (along a fault)—Very slow periodic or episodic movement along a fault trace unaccompanied by earthquakes.

Crust—The lithosphere, the outer 80 kilometers of the earth's surface made up of crustal rocks, sediment and basalt. General composition is silicon-aluminum-iron.

Damping—A rate at which natural vibration decays as a result of absorption of energy.

Deflection—Displacement of a member due to application of external force.

Depths of foci—Earthquakes are commonly classed by the depth of the focus or hypocenter beneath the earth's surface: shallow (0-70 kilometers), intermediate (70-300 kilometers), and deep (300-700 kilometers).

Diaphragm—Generally a horizontal girder composed of a web (such as a floor or roof slab) with adequate flanges, which distributes lateral forces to the vertical resisting elements.

Divergence zone—A belt along which tectonic plates move apart and new crust is created.

Drift—In buildings, the horizontal displacement of basic building elements due to lateral earthquake forces.

Ductility—Ability to withstand inelastic strain without fracturing.

Elasticity—The ability of a material to return to its original form or condition after a displacing force is removed.

Elastoplastic—Total range of stress, including expansion beyond elastic limit into the plastic range.

Energy absorption—Energy is absorbed as a structure distorts inelastically.

Energy dissipation—Reduction in intensity of earthquake shock waves with time and distance, or by transmission through discontinuous materials with different absorption capabilities.

Epicenter—The point on the earth's surface vertically above the focus or hypocenter of an earthquake.

Failure mode—The manner in which a structure fails (column buckling, overturning of structure, etc.).

Fault—Planar or gently curved fracture in the earth's crust across which relative displacement has occurred.

Normal fault—A fault under tension where the overlying block moves down the dip or slope of the fault plane.

Strike-slip fault (or lateral slip)—A fault whose relative displacement is purely horizontal.

Thrust (reverse) fault—A fault under compression where the overlying block moves up the dip of the fault plane.

Oblique-slip fault—A combination of normal and slip or thrust and slip faults whose movement is diagonal along the dip of the fault plane.

Faulting—The movement which produces relative displacement of adjacent rock masses along a fracture.

Fault zones—Instead of being a single clear fracture, the zone is hundreds or thousands of feet wide; the fault zone consists of numerous interlacing small faults.

Flexible system—A system that will sustain relatively large displacements without failure.

Felt area—Total extent of area where an earthquake is felt.

Focal depth—Depth of the earthquake focus (or hypocenter) below the ground surface.

Focus (of an earthquake)—The point at which the rupture occurs; synonymous with hypocenter. (It marks the origin of the elastic waves of an earthquake.)

Frames:

Moment frame—One which is capable of resisting bending movements in the joints, enabling it to resist lateral forces or unsymmetrical vertical loads through overall bending action of the frame. Stability is achieved through bending action rather than bracing.

Braced frame—One which is dependent upon diagonal braces for stability and capacity to resist lateral forces.

Frequency—Referring to vibrations; the number of wave peaks which pass through a point in a unit of time, usually measured in cycles per second.

Fundamental period—The longest period (duration in time of one full cycle of oscillatory motion) for which a structure or soil column shows a response peak, commonly the period of maximum response.

Graben (rift valley)—Long, narrow trough bounded by one or more parallel normal faults. These down-dropped fault blocks are caused by tensional crustal forces.

Ground failure—A situation in which the ground does not hold together such as landsliding, mud flows and liquefaction.

Ground movement—A general term; includes all aspects of motion (acceleration, particle velocity, displacement).

Ground acceleration—Acceleration of the ground due to earthquake forces.

Ground velocity—Velocity of the ground during an earthquake.

SHELL

B1

Ground displacement—The distance which ground moves from its original position during an earthquake.

Hypocenter—The point below the epicenter at which an earthquake actually begins; the focus.

Inelastic behavior—Behavior of an element beyond its elastic limit.

Intensity—A subjective measure of the force of an earthquake at a particular place as determined by its effects on persons structures and earth materials. Intensity is a measure of effects as contrasted with magnitude which is a measure of energy. The principal scale used in the United States today is the Modified Mercalli, 1956 version (Table 2).

Isoseismals—Map contours drawn to define limits of estimated intensity of shaking for a given earthquake.

Lateral force coefficients—Factors applied to the weight of a structure or its parts to determine lateral force for aseismic structural design.

Liquefaction—Transformation of a granular material (soil) from a solid state into a liquefied state as a consequence of increased pore-water pressure induced by vibrations.

Macrozones—Large zones of earthquake activity such as zones designated by the Uniform Building Code map.

Magnification factor—An increase in lateral forces at a specific site for a specific factor.

Magnitude—A measure of earthquake size which describes the amount of energy released.

Mantle—The main bulk of the earth between the crust and core varying in depth from 40 to 3,480 kilometers.

Modal analysis—Determination of design earthquake forces based upon the theoretical response of a structure in its several modes of vibration to excitation.

Mud flow—Mass movement of material finer than sand, lubricated with large amounts of water.

Natural frequency—The constant frequency of a vibrating system in the state of natural oscillation.

Higher modes of vibration—Structures and elements have a number of natural modes of vibration.

Mode—The shape of the vibration curve.

Period—The time for a wave crest to traverse a distance equal to one wave length or the time for two successive wave crests to pass a fixed point; the inverse of frequency.

Nonstructural components—Those building components which are not intended primarily for the structural support and bracing of the building.

Out of phase—The state where a structure in motion is not at the same frequency as the ground motion; or where equipment in a building is at a different frequency from the structure.

Period—See Natural frequency.

Plate tectonics—The theory and study of plate formation, movement, interaction, and destruction; the theory which explains seismicity, volcanism, mountain building and paleomagnetic evidence in terms of plate motions.

Resonance—Induced oscillations of maximum amplitude produced in a physical spectrum when an applied oscillatory motion and the natural oscillatory frequency of the system are the same.

Response—Effect produced on a structure by earthquake ground motion.

Return period of earthquakes—The time period (years) in which the probability is 63 percent that an earthquake of a certain magnitude will recur.

Richter Magnitude Scale—A measure of earthquake size which describes the amount of energy released. The measure is determined by taking the common logarithm (base 10) of the largest ground motion observed during the arrival of a P-wave or seismic surface wave and applying a standard correction for distance to the epicenter.

Rift—A fault trough formed in a divergence zone or in other areas in tension. (See Graben).

Rigidity—Relative stiffness of a structure or element. In numerical terms, equal to the reciprocal of displacement caused by a unit force.

Sag pond—A pond occupying a depression along a fault. The depression is due to uneven settling of the ground or other causes.

Scarp—A cliff, escarpment, or steep slope of some extent formed by a fault or a cliff or steep slope along the margin of a plateau, mesa or terrace.

Seiche—A standing wave on the surface of water in an enclosed or semi-enclosed basin (lake, bay or harbor).

Seismicity—The world-wide or local distribution of earthquakes in space and time; a general term for the number of earthquakes in a unit of time, or for relative earthquake activity.

Seismograph—An instrument which writes or tapes a permanent continuous record of earth motion, a seismogram.

Seismoscope—A device which indicates the occurrence of an earthquake but does not write or tape a record.

Shear distribution—Distribution of lateral forces along the height or width of a building.

Shear wall—A wall designed to resist lateral forces parallel to the wall. A shear wall is normally vertical, although not necessarily so.

Simple harmonic motion—Oscillatory motion of a wave, single frequency. Essentially a vibratory displacement such as that described by a weight which is attached to one end of a spring and allowed to vibrate freely.

Spectra—A plot indicating maximum earthquake response with respect to natural period or frequency of the structure or element. Response can show acceleration, velocity, displacement, shear or other properties of response.

Stability—Resistance to displacement or overturning.

Stiffness—Rigidity, or the reciprocal of flexibility.

Strain release—Movement along a fault plane; can be gradual or abrupt.

Subduction—The sinking of a plate under an overriding plate in a convergence zone.

Time dependent response analysis—Study of the behavior of a structure as it responds to a specific ground motion.

Trench—A long and narrow deep trough in the sea floor; interpreted as marking the line along which a plate bends down into a subduction zone.

Tsunami—A sea wave produced by large areal displacements of the ocean bottom, the result of earthquakes or volcanic activity.

Vibration—A periodic motion which repeats itself after a definite interval of time.

Wave:

Longitudinal wave—Pure compressional wave with volume changes.

Love wave—Transverse vibration of seismic surface wave.

Rayleigh wave—Forward and vertical vibration of seismic surface waves.

P-wave—The primary or fastest waves traveling away from a seismic event through the earth's crust, and consisting of a train of compressions and dilatations of the material.

S-wave—Shear wave, produced essentially by the shearing or tearing motions of earthquakes at right angles to the direction of wave propagation.

Seismic surface wave—A seismic wave that follows the earth's surface only, with a speed less than that of S- waves.

Wave length—The distance between successive similar points on two wave cycles.

Table 2. The Mercalli Intensity Scale

The generally accepted intensity scale in the United States. (*Original Mercalli Scale description shown in italics*. Further detail as modified by Charles F. Richter in 1956). Source: Mineral Information Service, May 1969, p. 77.

Masonry A: Good workmanship and mortar. Reinforced, designed to resist lateral forces.

Masonry B: Good workmanship and mortar, reinforced.

Masonry C: Good workmanship and mortar, unreinforced.

Masonry D: Poor workmanship and mortar; weak materials, such as adobe.

Intensity classification   *if most of these effects are observed*

I - Just detectable by experienced observers. Microseisms.

Earthquake shaking not felt. But people may observe marginal effects of large distant earthquakes without identifying these effects as earthquake-caused. Among them: trees, structures, liquids, bodies of water sway slowly, or doors swing slowly.

II - Felt by few. Delicately poised objects may sway.

Effect on people: Shaking felt by those at rest, especially if they are indoors, and by those on upper floors.

III - Vibration but still unrecognized by many. Feeble.

Effect on people: Felt by most people indoors. Some can estimate duration of shaking. But many may not recognize shaking of building as caused by the passing of light trucks.

IV - Felt by many indoors but by few outdoors. Moderate.

Other effects: Hanging objects swing.
Structural effects: Windows or doors rattle. Wooden walls and frames creak.

V - Felt by almost all. Many awakened. Unstable objects moved.

Effect on people: Felt by everyone indoors. Many estimate duration of shaking. But they still may not recognize it as caused by an earthquake. The shaking is like that caused by the passing of heavy trucks, though sometimes, instead, people may feel the sensation of a jolt, as if a heavy ball had struck the walls.
Other effects: Hanging objects swing. Standing autos rock. Crockery clashes, dishes rattle or glasses clink.
Structural effects: Doors close, open or swing. Windows rattle.

VI - Felt by all. Heavy objects moved. Alarm. Strong.

Effect on people: Felt by everyone indoors and by most people outdoors. Many now estimate not only the duration of shaking but also its direction and have no doubt as to its cause. Sleepers wakened.
Other effects: Hanging objects swing. Shutters or pictures move. Pendulum clocks stop, start or change rate. Standing autos rock. Crockery clashes, dishes rattle or glasses clink. Liquids disturbed, some spilled. Small unstable objects displaced or upset.
Structural effects: Weak plaster and Masonry D crack. Windows break. Doors close, open or swing

VII - General alarm. Weak buildings considerably damaged. Very strong.

Effect on people: Felt by everyone. Many are frightened and run outdoors. People walk unsteadily.

Other effects: Small church or school bells ring. Pictures thrown off walls, knickknacks and books off shelves. Dishes or glasses broken. Furniture moved or overturned. Trees, bushes shaken visibly, or heard to rustle.
Structural effects: Masonry D damaged; some cracks in Masonry C. Weak chimneys break at roof line. Plaster, loose bricks, stones, tiles, cornices, unbraced parapets and architectural ornaments fall. Concrete irrigation ditches damaged.

VII - Damage general except in proofed buildings. Heavy objects overturned.

Effect on people: Difficult to stand. Shaking noticed by auto drivers.
Other effects: Waves on ponds; water turbid with mud. Small slides and caving in along sand or gravel banks. Large bells ring. Furniture broken. Hanging objects quiver.
Structural effects: Masonry D heavily damaged; Masonry C damaged, partially collapses in some cases; some damage to Masonry B; none to Masonry A. Stucco and some masonry walls fall. Chimneys, factory stacks, monuments, towers, elevated tanks twist or fall. Frame houses moved on foundations if not bolted down; loose panel walls thrown out. Decayed piling broken off.

IX - Buildings shifted from foundations, collapse, ground cracks. Heavily destructive.

Effect on people: General fright. People thrown to ground.
Other effects: Changes in flow or temperature of springs and wells. Cracks in wet ground and on steep slopes. Steering of autos affected. Branches broken from trees.
Structural effects: Masonry D destroyed; Masonry C heavily damaged, sometimes with complete collapse; Masonry B is seriously damaged. General damage to foundations. Frame structures, if not bolted, shifted off foundations. Frames racked. Reservoirs seriously damaged. Underground pipes broken.

X - Masonry buildings destroyed, rails bent, serious ground fissures. Devastating.

Effect on people: General panic.
Other effects: Conspicuous cracks in ground. In areas of soft ground, sand is ejected through holes and piles up into a small crater, and, in muddy areas, water fountains are formed.
Structural effects: Most masonry and frame structures destroyed along with their foundations. Some well-built wooden structures and bridges destroyed. Serious damage to dams, dikes and embankments. Railroads bent slightly.

XI - Few if any structures left standing. Bridges down. Rails twisted. Catastrophic.

Effect on people: General panic.
Other effects: Large landslides. Water thrown on banks of canals, rivers, and lakes. Sand and mud shifted horizontally on beaches and flat land.
Structural effects: General destruction of buildings. Underground pipelines completely out of service. Railroads bent greatly.

XII - Damage total. Vibrations distort vision. Objects thrown into air. Major catastrophe.

Effect on people: General panic.
Other effects: Same as for Intensity XI.
Structural effects: Damage nearly total, the ultimate catastrophe.
Other effects: Large rock masses displaced. Lines of sight and level distorted. Objects thrown into air.

Table 3. Summary of seismic performance of structural systems (after Arnold 1994).

Summary of Seismic Performance of Structural Systems				
Structural System	EQ Performance	Test Data	Specific Bldg. Perf. & Energy Absorption	General Comments
Wood Frame	SF 1906, etc. ALA 1964 Variable to *Good*	1950's DFPA etc.	-SF Bldgs. performed reasonably well even though not detailed. -Energy Absorption is excellent.	-Connection details are critical. -Configuration is significant.
Unreinforced Masonry Wall	SF 1906 SB 1925 LB 1933 Variable to *Poor*	? Recent SEADSC	-Unreinf. masonry has performed poorly when <u>not</u> tied together. -Energy absorption is good if system integrity is maintained.	-Continuity and ties between walls and diaphragm is essential.
Steel Frame w/Mas Infill	SF 1906 Variable to *Good*	?	-SF Bldgs. performed very well. -Energy absorption is excellent.	-Bldg. form must be uniform, relatively small bay sizes.
R/C Wall	SF 1957 ALA 1964 JAPAN 1966 Variable to *Poor*	?	-Bldgs. in Alaska, SF and Japan performed poorly w/spandrel and pier failure -Brittle system.	-Proportion of spandrel and piers is critical, detail for ductility and shear.
Steel Brace	SF 1906 TAFT 1952 Variable to *Good*	Univ. of Mich. Japan UCB	-Major braced systems performed well. -Minor bracing and tension braces performed poorly.	-Details and proportions are critical.
Steel Moment Frame	LA 1971 JAPAN 1978 ? *Good*	Lehigh UCB	LA and Japanese Bldgs. performed well. -Energy absorption is excellent	-Both conventional and D.F. have performed well if designed for drift.
Concrete S.W.	CARAC 1965 ALA 1964 LA 1971 ALG. 1980 *Variable*	PCA U. of Ill. UCB	-Poor performance w/ discontinuous walls. •San Francisco, Alaska, Algeria, Caracas. -Uneven energy absorp.	-*Configuration* is *critical*, soft story or L-shape w/torsion have produced failures.
P/C Concrete	ALA 1964 BULGARIA 1978 SF 1980 Variable to *Poor*	Japan ?	-Poor performance in 1964, 1978, 1980 -Brittle Failure	-Details for continuity are critical. -*Ductility* must be achieved.
R/C DMF	LA 1971 ? *Good*	PCA Texas Toronto UCB	-Good perf. in 1971, LA. -System will crack. -Energy absorption is good.	-Details *critical*

Tension fabric structures

Caterpillar tents.

Summary: Tension fabric structures provide an efficient means of spanning large spaces. This article and its references introduce the basic principles, materials, and fabrication and erection procedures utilized with tensioned fabric structures, including a brief overview of historical and contemporary precedents and fundamentals of design.

Key words: cable domes, cable nets, fabrics structures, large-spans, tension fabrics.

| UniFormat: | B1020 |
| MasterFormat: | 13120 |

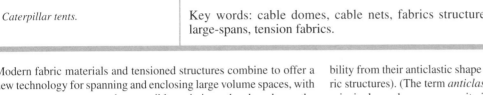

Modern fabric materials and tensioned structures combine to offer a new technology for spanning and enclosing large volume spaces, with permanent, temporary and convertible variations, developed over the past thirty years and made increasingly practical by improved analysis techniques and applications. State-of-the-art materials—typically PTFE (Teflon)-coated fiberglass, silicone-coated fiberglass, and vinyl-coated polyesters—are inherently waterproof and require very little maintenance. Because these materials are lightweight, tensioned fabric structures are extremely efficient in long span applications and are easily constructed, sometimes with substantial savings in the foundation and supporting structure costs.

Conventional structures rely on internal rigidity (stiffness) to achieve stability and to carry loads. Fabric structures, constructed of elements that have little or no bending or shear stiffness (cables and membrane), rely on their form and internal prestress alone to perform the same functions. What makes these structures more complicated to design than their conventional counterparts is that they tend to be highly nonlinear in their behavior. This is a desirable quality, since if properly designed, tensioned fabric structures will increase their capacity to carry load as they deform.

The design of a tensioned fabric structure can be separated into two distinct phases: *shape determination* or form finding and *analysis under load.*

- *Shape determination* involves the "design" of a structure whose form is not known in advance; changes in internal prestress will change the shape of the overall structure.

- *Analysis* of the system requires the solution of equations for the deformed configuration, a shape that is also unknown in advance.

If the stresses in the elements are too high or if the deformations are greater than acceptable, the designer is free to change the shape of the structure by revising the prestress or by modifying the boundary conditions. Once designed, the remaining steps to completion of the structure are fabrication and erection.

Cable nets

The forerunners of contemporary tensioned fabric structures were cable net structures utilizing steel cables in tension and deriving their sta-

bility from their anticlastic shape (as do contemporary tensioned fabric structures). (The term *anticlastic* describes a surface in which the principal members are opposite in sine, *i.e.,* saddled-shaped. Its opposite is *synclastic.*) Among the most influential is the first one constructed in North America, the Dorton Arena in Raleigh, North Carolina, 1951, designed by architect Matthew Nowicki and engineer Fred Severud. Other early cable roofs include Eero Saarinen's Yale University Hockey Rink, 1957, also engineered by Severud, and the Sydney Myer Music Bowl in Australia, 1958, designed by architect Robin Boyd and engineer Bill Irwin.

Tensioned fabric structures

Applications of fabric structures to provide shade and shelter have ancient precedents in tent and sail technology. An example is depicted in mosaics at Pompeii, interpreted by scholars to depict a shade fabric structure for the Roman Coliseum (See Figure 1 on following page). Familiar indigenous examples are found in the vernacular building traditions throughout the world, such as the *kibitka* (conical shape), the *yurts,* and the *black tent* structures typical of desert nomadic tribes, which include examples of both single and double fabrics, in the latter case with ventilation between.

The era of modern tensioned fabric structures began with a small bandstand designed and built by Frei Otto for the Federal Garden Exhibition in Cassel, Germany in 1955 (IL Publications). Because the available fabric lacked sufficient strength, these canopies were limited in span to around 80 feet (26 meters) or less. Among Frei Otto's best known works are two large cable nets. With architect Rudolph Gotbrod, he designed the German Pavilion for EXPO '67 in Montreal, Canada and with architect Behnisch and Partners, the Olympic Stadium for the 1972 Munich Olympics. From 1968 to 1983, Horst Berger and David Geiger were partners in projects that explored different approaches to tensioned fabric structures. Geiger worked mostly with air-supported structures and Berger with tensioned fabric membranes. In 1976 Horst Berger, working with the architectural firm of H2L2, designed two fabric structures for the Bicentennial celebration in Philadelphia, the first of many Berger designs using a ridge-and-valley geometry.

The largest fabric roof to date is the Haj Terminal Building at Jeddah, Saudi Arabia, 1985, which receives many thousand pilgrims who make

Authors: R. E. Shaeffer, P.E. and Craig Huntington, S.E.

Credits: This article is adapted from Chapters 1 and 2 of Shaeffer (1996) by permission of the American Society of Civil Engineers.

References: Berger, Horst. 1996. *Light Structures Structures of Light: The Art and Engineering of Tensile Architecture.* Basel, Switzerland: Birkhauser—Verlag.

Shaeffer, R. E., editor. 1996. *Tensioned Fabric Structures: A Practical Introduction.* New York: American Society of Civil Engineers.

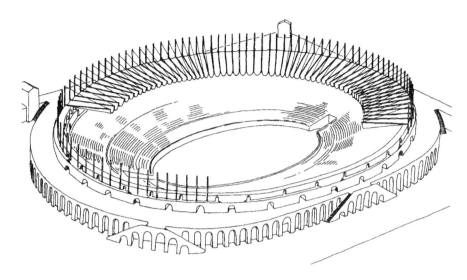

Fig. 1. Hypothetical reconstruction of Roman shade structures, called *vela.* Courtesy of Rainer Graefe (Berger 1996). Also see NOVA (1996).

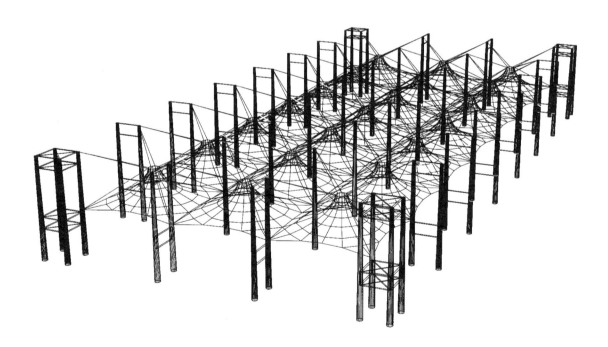

Fig. 2. Computer generated perspective of Haj Terminal, Jeddah, Saudi Arabia (Berger 1996).

the journey to Mecca each year (Fig. 2). It was designed by the architect-engineer firm of Skidmore-Owings-Merrill with Horst Berger as a consultant. In 1989, Berger designed a canopy for the roof deck of Arthur Erikson's San Diego Convention Center. Spanning almost 330 feet (100 meters), it provides shade and rain protection for exhibits, concerts and banquets. It consists of five ridge-and-valley modules each having a pair of flying struts, i.e., vertical masts which do not deliver their loads to the base level, but are suspended in the air by cables. In 1992, the Pier Six Concert Pavilion in Baltimore Inner Harbor was designed by Todd Dalland of FTL Associates, providing seating for 3400 concert goers. At the stage end, the fabric attaches to a curved concrete beam and makes a unique transition to the metal roof of a masonry building.

At the end of 1993, the Great Hall of the Denver Airport was completed (Figs. 3–5). The fabric roof covers approximately 35 acres (14 hectares) including the enclosed landside terminal, with plan dimensions of 990 feet (300 meters) by 230 feet (70 meters). C. W. Fentress and J. H. Bradburn, Architects with Horst Berger and Ed DePaola of Severud Associates, Engineers, created the roof structure. Its membrane consists of two layers of PTFE-coated fiberglass several inches (600 mm) apart. The inner layer provides thermal insulation and acoustic absorbency. The intermediary airspace is "closed," that is, does not allow air change in order to minimize dust laden air entrainment. The fabric roof is otherwise not insulated, as energy analysis determined that the contribution of natural lighting and passive solar heating due to its high transmissivity outweighed any incremental improvement that would be gained by increasing insulation values.

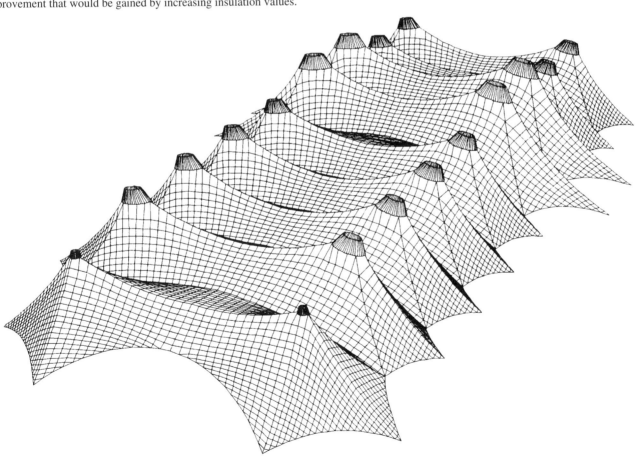

Fig. 3. Geodesic net analysis of the Denver Airport Terminal Building (Berger 1996).

B1

SHELL

Fig. 4. Denver International Airport Terminal. W.C. Fentress and J. H. Bradburn, Architects. 1993

Fig. 5. South wall of Denver International Airport Terminal.

The south wall enclosure of the Terminal consists of a glass curtain wall (Fig. 5) cantilevered from the main floor by a system of cables and struts, in some cases as much as 59 feet (18 meters). The closure system between the glass walls (having limited deformation capability) and the fabric roof (needing to sustain large deformations under wind and snow loading) utilizes a continuous inflated tube, more than 3 feet-4 inches (1 meter) in diameter. Many see the Denver Airport as a test case for large tensioned fabric structures. Located in an area of significant snowfall and other adverse weather conditions, its success could mean the development of many large fabric enclosure schemes.

Cable domes

The latest technology for long-span roofs is the fabric-covered cable dome, a structural system based upon R. Buckminster Fuller's transegrity domes of the late 1950s. The basic scheme is circular in plan using radial trusses made of cables except for vertical compression struts. Circular hoops provide the bottom chord forces (Fig. 6). The first successful cable domes were constructed in Seoul, Korea for the 1986 Asian Games, later used for the 1988 Olympics. The first cable dome in the United States is the Geiger-designed Redbird Arena on the campus of Illinois State University. It is elliptical, 300 by 250 feet (90 by 77 meters) in plan, heavily insulated between the outer structural fabric and inner fabric. It has only one tension hoop between the inner tension ring and the perimeter compression ring. This visually emphasizes the peaks created by the vertical struts and gives the roof a more crown-like appearance. The largest cable dome to date is the Georgia Dome in Atlanta, 1992, with the roof structure design by Matthys Levy of Weidlinger Associates. Designed for football, it is an oval, 770 feet by 610 feet (235 by 186 meters) in plan with a 185-foot (56-meter) truss running down the middle.

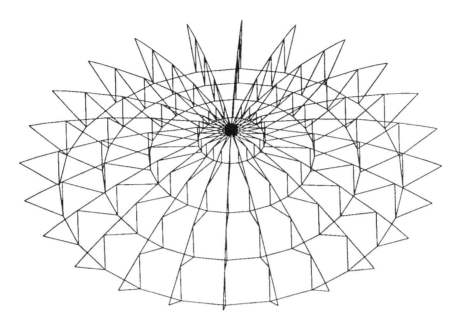

Fig. 6. Cable dome schematic (R. E. Shaeffer 1996).

The design and construction process

Design and construction team for tensioned fabric structures

The means by which a fabric roof stands up and the way that it looks are inseparable. Supporting masts typically are left exposed and steel cables pass through space or lay against the fabric so that they remain visible from either above or below the roof. Even the layout of the seaming of the fabric, selected to minimize material waste and reflect predominant stress patterns, becomes a strong visual element of the design. The seams help the observer to appreciate the shape of the roof. Depending on their orientation, seams may serve to visually emphasize radial, circumferential, linear, or other aspects of its geometry. Due to their slenderness, fabrics typically have negligible resistance to either bending or compression. Because of these limitations in load carrying ability, the fabric must be shaped in a very precise manner that allows it to carry all applied loads purely in tension. The determination of these shapes is less commonplace and more complex than determination of the layout of a conventional concrete or steel frame. The design typically requires the services of a structural engineer specializing in tensioned fabric structures for assistance in determining the form of the roof, along with close coordination with the tensile fabric supplier. It is thus imperative that the engineering designer or consultant with detailed knowledge of fabric structure behavior be involved at the inception of the project, so that a shape is developed which responds to fabric and cable curvature requirements and provides appropriate behavior under load.

Building department interface

Lack of widespread knowledge of tensioned fabric structures and the limited recognition of this construction type in building codes pose special problems in interfacing with building officials. Use of tensile fabric technologies may require a high degree of technical validation from the engineer in order to fulfill their obligation to assure public safety and adherence to building codes. Extensive documentation

may be required, much of it unique to tensioned fabric structures. This includes:

* A general description of the characteristics of the structure, including large deflection behavior and anisotropic material properties.

* Information required to understand the methodology of shape finding and analysis computer programs.

* Reports on relevant fire testing.

* Shape finding and analysis computer runs.

* Calculations for cables and steel or other supporting members.

* Drawings showing the layout of fabric panels, typical fabric seams, interfaces of fabric with the supporting structure, typical cable details, fabric tensioning details, *etc.*

Tensioned fabric roof structures may be commissioned either by the design/build approach or by an engineering consultant with specialized knowledge of the technology who is retained by the architect or owner. The consultant may completely design the roof (appropriate for new applications) or may be retained only to provide general parameters and review of the roof contractor's detailed engineering (more modest and repetitive applications). The design/build approach offers several obvious advantages due to the need for close coordination throughout design, engineering, detailing, construction and longer term performance evaluation.

Performance considerations

While contemporary tensioned fabric structures have been designed for a wide range of loadings and for climatic conditions found throughout the globe, the nature of membrane construction and the commonly used fabric materials lead to certain generalizations about appropriate design loads and climatic applications. The load bearing characteristics of tensioned fabric structures are governed by the high deformability of membranes under load, and may be generalized as follows:

- Dead load from the membrane is generally less than 1 lb/SF (50 N/m²) and hence negligible.

- Roof live loads are generally intended to account for construction phase loads such as roofing materials that are not relevant to fabric construction. Lacking code provisions specifically tailored for membrane construction, however, fabric roofs are design for the (larger) normal loads required by codes.

- Seismic loads are generally not a factor in design, because of the low mass of the fabric.

- Wind is often the predominant loading on the fabric roof. The membrane must have adequate curvature and pretensioning to resist wind loads without excessive flutter. The curving forms of the roofs often make adoption of building code formulas for wind loading problematic. Larger or more complex structures, particularly those in highly variable terrain, often require wind tunnel testing for accurate prediction of wind loads.

- Moderate snowfall can successfully be resisted in structures that have prestress sufficient to prevent large deflections that will lead to ponding, additional deflection, and eventual overload of the roof. Relatively high roof slopes are useful in helping the slippery surface shed snow, and also aid in preventing ponding. Snow melting equipment, usually in the form of a furnace producing forced hot air blowing under the membrane, is a useful and perhaps necessary fail-safe provision in regions subject to heavy snow load.

- Point loads such as heavy lights, signs, or scoreboards present special design problems due to the high deformability of membranes. Heavy loads must generally be supported from rigid mast or arch supports or at angle changes in cabling.

The characteristics of most contemporary fabrics—translucency, high reflectivity of light, and low insulating value—are readily adapted to use in temperate or hot climates with ample sunshine. In climates that combine warmth and high humidity, caution must be taken against the growth of mold or algae caused either by condensation or standing water on the outside of the fabric. While tensioned fabric structures have traditionally provided less favorable energy use in cold climates, the use of liner membranes with dead air space and, more recently, insulated fabrics have improved their performance dramatically. In such climates, measures should be considered to prevent excessive condensation, particularly for applications such as swimming pools, zoos, or botanical gardens. There are dual reasons: first, to prevent dripping on areas below, but also to minimize the visual damage due to accumulated dirt or staining. In susceptible locations, consideration should be given to venting inside air, installing condensate gutters, or providing an air circulation system.

Spatial considerations

Because of the curvature requirements of the membrane, tensioned fabric structures typically have fairly tall profiles in elevation, and cannot easily be adapted to the flat roof profile characteristic of conventional construction. An attractive feature of tensioned fabric structures is their enormous range of spanning capability. Membranes have been used in a number of applications as an alternative to translucent glazing, using pretensioned fabric without curvature over spans up to about 13 feet (4 meters). Tensioned fabric supported on arches or other shaping elements is common in skylight applications with spans of up to 50 feet (15.2 meters) or more. Fabric has been applied just as effectively in stadiums and other assembly structures with spans of up to 820 feet (250 meters). In these applications, the fabric is typi-

cally restrained or supported by steel cabling in conjunction with air pressure or rigid steel elements, so that the unsupported span of the fabric itself is seldom greater than 50 feet (15.2 meters). While air-supported and cable dome roofs have been sheathed in materials other than fabric, the fabric provides a significant portion of the strength and stiffness of these roofs, and is integral to their global behavior. Because of their membrane behavior, the forms of fabric roofs can be manipulated only within limited bounds determined by the engineer. The exposure of structural connections in the finished structure, furthermore, makes the detailing of connections by the engineer an important part of the structure's appearance.

Fire safety

Contemporary tensioned fabric structures have the ability to provide fire safety far better than that of traditional non-synthetic tending materials. In general, contemporary fiberglass fabrics are able to achieve non-combustible ratings.

Energy use and lighting

Fabrics in common use are characterized by low insulating ability, low thermal mass, high reflectivity of light, and low-to-moderate translucency. These characteristics have made them readily applicable to use in temperate or hot climates with high solar radiation. Daylighting through the white fabrics that are commonly used for permanent architectural applications is characteristically bright and diffused. These features are favorable to applications such as sports facilities, exhibit halls, and landscaped atriums or other skylight type applications. The magnitude of daylighting is often altered by varying the translucency of the fabric or adding a liner membrane or insulation. Fiberglass fabrics coated with either PTFE or silicone are available with translucencies in excess of 20%, adequate to support a wide range of plant growth. A summary of the characteristics of various conventional and fabric roofing assemblies is given in Table 1.

Acoustic performance

The acoustical performance of structural fabrics is characterized by high reflectivity of sound vibrations, particularly in the frequency range of 500 to 2000 Hertz. This reflectivity can result in poor sound for musical performances and difficulty in understanding speech. The focused reflection of sound due to the geometrical shape of certain roofs can also hamper acoustic performance, particularly in air-supported structures or arch supported roofs that have a generally concave roof profile from the interior. Sound transmission loss through fabric is another important consideration in airports or other structures where it is required to shield building occupants from outside noise. Sound reflectivity can be decreased and transmission loss increased by the installation of lightweight, porous liner fabrics. Fiberglass insulation between the two fabric layers can further increase transmission loss. The effects of such measures on daylighting, insulation, and fire safety must be considered in their selection, however. Vertical banners can also be suspended at intervals under the fabric in order to increase sound absorption and break up the geometry of the curved fabric.

Maintenance, durability, and inspection

The durability of tensioned fabric structures and their maintenance requirements represent the combined result of design, materials, construction, and environment. Design factors that influence durability and maintenance include:

- Determination of appropriate loads and accurate stress analysis as required to prevent tears or other damage.

- Where structures are located in an unsafe area or on an unsecured site, structures should be configured to knife cuts or other vandalism.

Table 1. Comparison of performance values of various tensioned fabric assemblies, compared to conventional roofing, shown as Assembly 1.

Properties / Assembly No.		Assembly 1	Assembly 2	Assembly 3	Assembly 4	Assembly 5	Assembly 6
Solar	Reflectance	10-50%	30-75%	65-75%	60-65%	60-70%	60-70%
	Absorption	50-90%	13-68%	13-19%	12-20%	28-43%	28-35%
	Transmission	0	2-12%	6-22%	15-28%	4-6%	2-5%
U-value	Summer (12 km/h)	Varies	0.75	0.81	0.81	0.45	0.08-0.14
	Winter (24 km/h Wind)	Varies	1.15	1.20	1.20	0.54	0.08.14

Assembly 1: Conventional roofing
Assembly 2: PVC fabric
Assembly 3: PTFE glass fabric
Assembly 4: Silicone/glass fabric
Assembly 5: PTFE glass w/liner & 250 mm air space
Assembly 6: PTFE glass w/translucent insulation

- Cables, arches, mast peaks, and other discontinuities in the fabric provide potential locations of stress concentration or abrasion.

Exposure to ultraviolet radiation from direct sunlight is the primary environmental factor in fabric durability. Polyester based fabrics are generally more susceptible to UV damage than fiberglass-based fabrics, although coatings of Tedlar and other materials have improved their durability. At certain sites, consideration must also be given to soiling effects from air pollution, engine exhaust, or other sources, and to potential abrasion damage from wind-driven sand or other matter.

Glossary

Anisotropic: The feature of fabric wherein the physical properties and behavior are not the same in all directions.

Anticlastic: A surface with positive (Gaussian) curvature in one principal direction and negative (Gaussian) curvature in the other. A saddle shaped surface.

Butt seam: Seam created when the two pieces being joined are butted together and joined with a strip twice the width of the seam.

Cable cuff: Edge treatment in which the fabric is folded over on itself to form a pocket in which a catenary cable can be installed.

Catenary: The curve theoretically formed by a perfectly flexible, uniformly dense, inextensible "cable" suspended from each of two end points. In fabric structures experience, this shape is probably not ever truly developed, but is commonly used to describe the shape developed at the boundary of a uniformly stressed fabric structure attached to a cable which is restrained only at its end points.

Connection: Joint, usually mechanical, between two separate components. for example, a wended seam, a cable fitting connected to a weldment, or fabric clamped to a perimeter member.

Connection flexibility: A characteristic of a connection which allows for motion between components, such as translation (sliding) or rotation.

Equilibrium shape: The configuration that a tensioned fabric surface assumes when boundary conditions, prestress level, and prestress distribution are defined.

Form finding (form generation): The process of determining the equilibrium shape of a fabric structure.

Geodesic: Of, or pertaining to circles of a sphere, or of arcs of such circles, hence a pattern created by the intersections of great-circle lines of arcs, or their chords.

Geodesic dome. Term given by R. Buckminster Fuller in U. S. Patent 2,682,235 (1954) to describe spherical structures made up of a grid of polygons, typically of short lightweight bars or struts forming triangles, diamonds or hexagons.

Lap Seam: Seam created when the two pieces being joined are overlapped by the width of the seam.

Light reflectivity: A measure of the portion of light striking a fabric surface that rebounds from the surface without being absorbed or transmitted.

Light transmission: A measure of the portion of light striking a fabric surface that passes through the fabric and into the space to provide daylighting.

Modulus of elasticity: The ratio of the change in stress to the change in strain. Usually defined as a force per unit width of a membrane material. (This is not identical to the definition of modulus of elasticity as given for traditional structural materials.)

Non-developable: A characteristic of a surface that cannot be formed using a single flat sheet of material, *e.g.*, a doubly curved surface such as a sphere or a saddle-shape.

Prestress: The stress state that exists in a fabric structure when it is not acted upon by service loads; usually induced by the boundary conditions of the fabric

Sleeve: A tube of fabric which loosely contains a structural element such as a cable, rod, arch, *etc.*

Sound reflectivity: A measure of the portion that rebounds from the surface without being absorbed or transmitted. Sound reflectivity frequency range.

Sound transmission: A measure of the portion of sound striking a fabric surface that passes through it.

Topping: An additional coating sometimes used on fabric for greater protection against ultraviolet (UV) degradation purposes.

Transegrity. A term given by R. Buckminster Fuller in U. S. Patent 2,063,521 (1962) to describe various tension-cable and compression-strut truss shapes held in equilibrium by "discontinuous compression and continuous tension," such that its structural integrity is completed by tension.

Turnbuckle: Threaded device used with cables or rods to allow adjustment.

Ultraviolet (UV) degradation: The deterioration of a fabric under long-term exposure to sunlight.

Warp yarn: The long straight yarns in the long direction of a piece of fabric.

Weft yarn: The shorter yarns of a fabric which usually run at right angles to the warp yarns. Also called the fill yarns.

Weldment: Connection component, usually steel, for the attachment of cables and/or fabric. It may be free of connected to other fabrics.

Additional references

ASCE. 1994. *Spatial Lattice and Tension Structures.* Proceedings of the IASS/ASCE Structures Symposium. John F. Abel, John W. Leonard and Celina U. Fenalba, editors. New York: American Society of Civil Engineers. (also available from IFAI).

Drew, Philip. 1979. *Tensile Architecture.* Boulder, CO: Westview Press.

Ishii, K. 1995. *Membrane Structures in Japan.* Tokyo: SFS Publishing Company. (also available from IFAI).

IFAI. Industrial Fabrics Association International. *Fabrics & Architecture.* Bi-monthly trade journal. St. Paul, MN: Industrial Fabrics Association International. (1-800-225-4324).

IL Publications. The work of Frei Otto and colleagues at the Insititut für Leichte Flächentragwerke (Institute for Lightweight Structures). Stuttgart, Germany: Universität Stuttgart. FAX 49/711 685 3789.

NOVA. 1996. *Secrets of Lost Empires: Colosseum.* Video that documents the archeological reconstruction of various Roman *vela*, demonstrating competing hypotheses of early Roman tent and sail technology. South Burlington, VT: NOVA Videos. (1-800-255-9424).

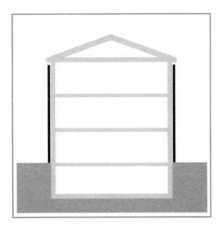

B   SHELL

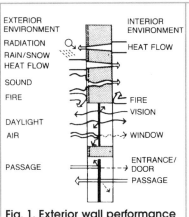

Fig. 1. Exterior wall performance factors

Exterior wall systems: an overview

Summary: An overview is provided of expeterioir wall assemblies, including performamance and preliminary design selection criteria, system types and schematic deatils.

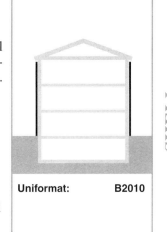

Uniformat: B2010

Key words: bearing walls, curtain walls, framed walls, panel systems, wall facings, wind pressure.

SHELL

B2

1   Exterior walls: an overview

Exterior walls and assemblies separate the external environment and function as a barrier and/or selective filter (Fig. 1). Their multiple functions may be included into one assembly, or separated into distinct components. Their combined performance criteria include:

- Aesthetic:

- provide views, controlled visibility and awareness of the external environment.

- present the architectural design intentions within a cultural and environmental context.

- provide for life-long maintenance, repair, replacement and disassembly.

- Structural and safety:

- carry vertical loads or protect the building structure that does so.

- resist lateral wind forces and may also be subject to seismic loads.

- minimize the effects of external or internal fire hazard.

- provide basic security.

- Environmental control:

- control of heat flow between the two environments, utilizing bioclimatic advantages of sun, light, breeze and fresh air.

- controlling water vapor migration from one environment to another, including minimizing damaging condensation on or within the wall construction.

- admit daylight to the interior environment or control its transmittance.

- allow controlled movement of air from one environment to another, while minimizing uncontrolled air infiltration/exfiltration through the envelope.

- minimize the transmission of sound.

- screen and protect the structure and interior from penetration of rain, snow and ice.

Structural loads and forces

The structural role of walls includes providing stability under all environmental conditions, while allowing for movement (Figs. 2 and Fig. 3):

Walls which do not carry superimposed loads of the structural frame must only resist wind loads between horizontal and/or vertical supports, and transmit such loads to the supporting frame. On medium- to high-rise buildings, and buildings within the wind flow around adjacent buildings, wind pressures are complex and varied within the aerodynamic microclimate. Provisions for resistance to extreme wind are somewhat similar to but are nonetheless distinct from earthquake resistance design. Provisions for one set of conditions may or may not address the other. Each requires separate analysis.

Wind pressure may be:

- positive, pushing the wall against the supporting horizontal frame and causing it to deform or deflect inward.

- negative, pulling the wall away from supporting frame and causing outward deflection.

- parallel to wall, which may result in shearing stresses in the wall due to interaction between it and the supporting horizontal frame.

Walls which carry superimposed loads of the structural frame may also be subject to eccentric loading which will result in further deflection in them, either adding to that induced by lateral loads or counteracting it.

Walls will be affected by thermal expansion/contraction within them as well as in the structural frame to which they are connected:

- Solar radiation striking a wall or parts thereof will cause expansion, and such expansion may be differential. The juncture of walls with different exposures to solar radiation should provide for differential movement between the walls joined.

- Long walls may require control joints to limit extent of cumulative movement thus magnitude of resultant stresses; expansion joints, when the structural frame itself is divided into sections to limit expansion/contraction.

- Differential movement may occur between walls and horizontal assemblies: flat roof assembly may be expanding while walls which are continuously connected to it or are supporting it may be expanding at different rates, or may be contracting depending on their exposure.

- Monolithic walls of concrete and walls of masonry units may also be subject to shrinkage induced stresses in addition to thermal stresses, and may require control joints to minimize the possibility off cracking.

Credits: This article is excerpted from 1993 *Sweets Catalog* File Selection Data, by permission of McGraw-Hill.

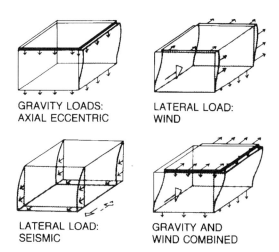

Fig. 2. Structural forces and exterior wall stability

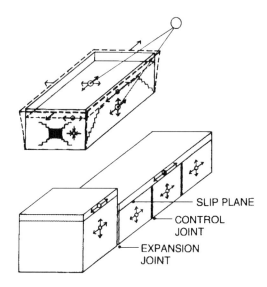

SLIP PLANE

CONTROL JOINT

EXPANSION JOINT

Fig. 3. Structural forces and exterior wall movement

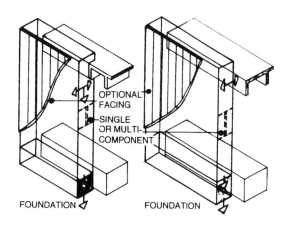

OPTIONAL FACING

SINGLE OR MULTI-COMPONENT

FOUNDATION

FOUNDATION

Fig. 4. Bearing/nonbearing stacked and monolithic wall types

2 Exterior wall types

Bearing/nonbearing: stacked and monolithic walls

Stacked or monolithic assemblies normally use compatible structural frame: steel, concrete, light-gauge metal or wood framed. Careful consideration must be given to location and spacing of joints to control temperature/moisture induced expansion and contraction. Bearing and nonbearing wall assemblies are constructed of both stacked units, generally at the job site often manually, and monolithic units, assembled with lift equipment.

Stacked types, typically assembled as shown in Fig. 4, include:

- Single or double wythe of concrete block, generally with reinforcing in horizontal joints to control shrinkage induced cracking; bearing or nonbearing. Outer wythe may be left exposed, may receive applied coating, or may be faced.

- Single wythe of reinforced brick masonry, generally nonbearing; or outer wythe of brick bonded to an inner wythe of concrete block or structural tile, bearing or nonbearing.

- Cavity: two wythes separated by an airspace. Outer wythe usually of brick, inner wythe either brick or concrete block, bonded with metal ties.

Monolithic units, also indicated in Fig. 4, include:

- Concrete, poured-in-place, reinforced as a minimum to control shrinkage stresses when nonbearing.

- Concrete, site precast large panels, reinforced to control erection and shrinkage and/or superimposed load induced stresses.

Bearing/nonbearing framed walls

Typically constructed of closely spaced light-gauge metal or wood studs, with exterior faces secured against lateral displacement in the plane of the wall by structural sheathing connected to them, or by diagonal braces when sheathing that is used is nonstructural (Fig. 5).These wall types are generally used with framed floor/roof assemblies only and are generally capable of supporting superimposed loads, whether thus used or not.:

- posts of support concentrated loads of the structural frame may be incorporated into the framing.

- studs may be faced both sides with structural sheathing, generally plywood glued or glued and nailed to studs, to function as stressed skin panels.

- exterior generally faced over sheathing; some facings may act as combined facing and/or structural sheathing.

- interior generally faced, with the facing often also functioning as secondary bracing to the framing.

- insulation generally placed between studs, wiring and small diameter piping may be run through studs.

- moisture control through site-built assemblies must be careful designed and installed.

Curtain walls: grid type

Curtain wall grid-type assemblies and systems (Fig. 6) include:

- mullions spanning between floor, or floor and roof framing, supported and laterally braced by such framing.

- rails connected to, supported by, and laterally braced by mullions.

- infill panels, also referred to as glazing panels, generally with edges of the same thickness whether transparent or opaque, held in place by mullions and rails. Windows and/or doors may be used in lieu of panels.

Infill panels may be:

- monolithic of single thickness; glazing of tinted, patterned, opaque glass; panels of cement bound mineral fiber, patterned, pigmented, coated.

- monolithic, spaced: glazing of two or more lights of glass or of plastic, or combinations thereof, assembled into units with air spaces between them to reduce flow of heat through them.

- composite, laminated: glazing of glass and plastic, panels of prefinished metal faces with cores of rigid insulation or rigid boards.

- formed: panels of metal faces with formed edges, generally with insulation between them.

3 Curtain wall panels

Curtain wall panels are generally intended to function as the entire wall assembly spanning between floor/roof assemblies; supported and laterally braced by such assemblies (Fig. 7):

- intermediate supports between the floor/roof assemblies may be used to reduce the span of thin panels for more economical installation.

- length of panels may be limited by manufacturing processes and/or shipping constraints.

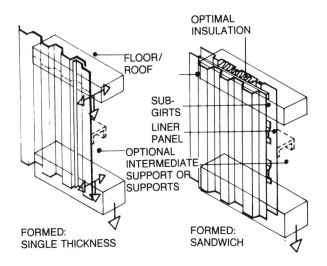

FORMED: SINGLE THICKNESS

FORMED: SANDWICH

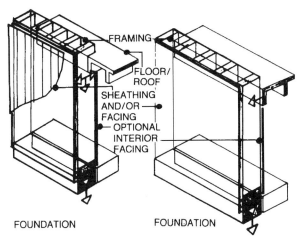

Fig. 5. Bearing/nonbearing framed wall types

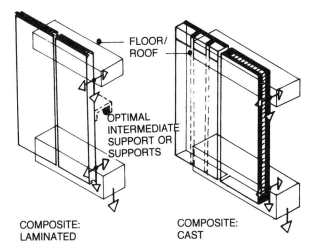

COMPOSITE: LAMINATED

COMPOSITE: CAST

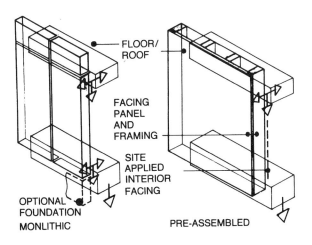

Fig. 6. Curtain walls: grid type

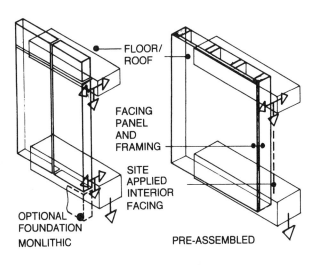

Fig. 7. Curtain wall panel types

SHELL

B2

- *Formed panels*

- Single thickness panels: of metal, either nonferrous or anticorrosion treated ferrous, formed in various configurations to impart rigidity to the section; of plastic in various configurations; of cement-bound mineral fiber, generally corrugated.

- Sandwich panels: single thickness metal panel outer face, connected to and supported through subgirts by a formed metal inner face, generally with insulation between the two faces. The inner face is attached to and supported by continuous structural steel framing. The outer face is connected to subgirts using exposed fasteners or concealed clips.

- Sandwich panels are available as fire-resistant rated assemblies.

- Metal panels may be unfinished when nonferrous, surface treated or coated.

- Compatible structural frame: steel. May be installed on concrete frame if structural steel supports are added.

- *Composite panels*
  There two generic types of composite panels are laminated and cast.

  Composite, laminated: Outer face of: metal either flat, formed, or stamped, generally with applied coating; flat cement-bound mineral fiber, either textured or coated.

- panel interior cores of rigid boards, rigid insulation, fiber or metal honeycomb.

- interior face may be exposed core or similar to outer face.

- panels secured to steel supports with concealed fasteners or formed metal clips.

- compatible structural frame: steel. May be used with concrete frame if steel supports are added.

  Composite, cast: of polymer or regular concrete with insulation between the outer and inner faces.

- outer face may be lightly to heavily textured or of exposed aggregate inner face generally smooth.

- secured to framing with structural steel clips.

- intermediate supports not commonly used.

- compatible structural frame: steel, concrete.

- *Monolithic panels*
  Solid or monolithic masonry panels are generally of regular concrete, with either normal or lightweight aggregate:

- outer face either flat, textured, or molded/sculptured.

- inner face generally smooth.

- secured to framing with structural steel clips.

- intermediate support are seldom used when one or two stories in height may be supported directly on foundation and laterally braced by the structural frame.

- compatible structural frame: steel, concrete.

- *Preassembled panel systems*

  Total envelope and structural systems are available with prefinished facing panels, attached to preassembled framing and shipped to the site as ready-to-be-installed units. Compatible structural frame includes steel or concrete.

4 Wall facing types

All walls, whether exterior or interior, consist of at least two elements: the outer faces and the core or body between them. The wall may be single component, such as the fabric of a tent, or it may be an assembly of multiple layers of different components, but the two basic elements will still be present.

The outer surfaces of a solid stone or brick wall may be finished for appearance or durability, but that will not constitute a facing. But when stone is combined with a concrete wall to protect and enhance it, it becomes a facing, whether dependent on the concrete for stability or not. A sheet of metal such as aluminum will always constitute a facing, whether single thickness or laminated to a backing, formed or flat, when used as the outer surface of a solid core wall assembly or attached to open framing. Generic exterior wall facing types indicated in Fig. 8 include:

- *Facing panels*
  Facing panels are applied over a back-up wall and secured to the wall and/or structural frame:

- back-up may be of stacked units, generally concrete block, or framed.

- facing panels may require subframing to be installed over the back-up wall for proper attachment and/or alignment;

- light, thin panels may be attached to solid plumb surfaces using adhesives, such as high modulus silicone, but such methods of attachment is not common.

- *Unit assemblies*

  Assemblies of units, such as shingles, stone, tile or brick masonry; and strips such as vertical or horizontal siding; applied over a back-up wall:

- back-up generally framed with nailable sheathing, may also be stacked units, such as concrete block, but nailable furring strips have to be then installed over the wall.

- horizontal siding, when sufficiently rigid, may be attached directly to the studs of a framed wall, and sheathing omitted when the structural frame provides the required rigidity.

- *Surfacing*

  Surfacing includes factory-applied or site applications such as stucco, select aggregate, bonded to a back-up wall:

- back-up may be: stacked units, generally concrete block, monolithic concrete, either cast-in-place or precast, sheathed framing, or rigid insulation secured to back-up wall.

- stucco applied over framed back-up wall may be over sheathing, or the sheathing may be omitted.

5 Exterior walls: selection considerations

Principal design considerations during selection of an exterior wall assembly include:

- Function of the building and requirements it imposes. Extensive areas of glazing required and their distribution over the plane of the walls may narrow the choice of wall type, or preclude the efficient use of a bearing walls.

- Form of the building, whether low- or high-rise, may influence the choice of a particular type. Bearing walls are generally only economical up to about ten stories in height.

- Structural frame, whether short or long span, and the spacing of horizontal framing members may affect the choice. Short spans and closely spaced horizontal framing members would allow for efficient use of bearing walls, as would uniform compartmentalization of interior space.

- Ground conditions may impose limitations on the entire building. Soils with poor bearing capacity may require that all components be as light as practicable. Differential settlement to be expected may preclude the use of rigid wall assemblies.

- Structural stability and integrity under all loads. Walls interact with the structural frame to contribute to its strength or rigidity, or the structural frame may impose loads on walls they were not intended to resist through dimensional changes in the frame.

- Durability under all environmental factors, or service life as a measure of the time until some loss of function occurs. It is critical that all wall components be selected to endure and/or to be replaced in an accessible and non-disruptive maintenance and repair process. The environment at any plane of the wall assembly is determined by the arrangement and properties of its components, and durability is reflected in the ultimate cost of maintaining all the required functions of the wall assembly over its intended service life.

- Economy in initial and maintenance costs. Initial cost may be reduced by selecting lower quality components, but generally only at the expense of increased maintenance cost or reduced service life.

- Aesthetic quality. Form, overall pattern of components, color, texture may be varied over a wide range without affecting other considerations, but inadequacies in design which allow problems such as cracks or runoff staining to develop may severely affect the aesthetic quality of a building.

6   Curtain walls

Typical curtain wall system types are indicated in Fig. 9. Mullion types are indicated in Fig. 10.

- *Grid curtain walls:*

  Grid systems are pressure equalized system of vertical and horizontal framing members attached to the structural frame and supporting transparent, translucent, or opaque infill panels. The grid curtain wall is generally can be further characterized, depending on method of delivery and assembly:

- Stick system: with the vertical members, or mullions, and horizontal members, or rails, assembled at the site using sleeves to connect mullions and splines to connect the rails. Movements in the wall assembly and/or the structural frame are generally accommodated at splices of framing members and in the glazing pockets of rails.

- Unitized stick system: with prefabricated vertical mullions and two-piece interlocking rails, which are connected to mullions with splines. Movements in wall and/or the structural frame are taken at joints in mullions and in the interlocking rails. This system is generally more expensive than the stick system, but is able to better accommodate thermal expansion and contraction.

- Unit system: with shop prefabricated interlocking mullions and rails, often preglazed and shipped to the site as units. Movements in the wall assembly and/or structural frame are accommodated in the interlocking mullions and rails. This system has the advantage of closer tolerances and greater capacity for accommodating movement. The disadvantages are increased material and fabrication costs, and necessity of maintaining closer tolerances in the structural frame.

Additional considerations applicable to all grid systems are:

- amount of adjustment available within the system to accommodate field conditions, such as misalignments in the structural frame.

- maintaining the structural integrity of the system under in-service conditions, such as horizontal displacement, or sway, in the structural frame under lateral loads.

- window washing equipment is required for high-rise buildings with fixed glazing, and the additional load imposed thereby on mullions becomes a factor.

PANELS

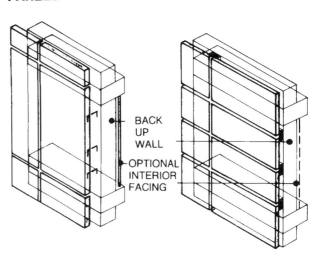

UNITS/STRIPS: ATTACHED

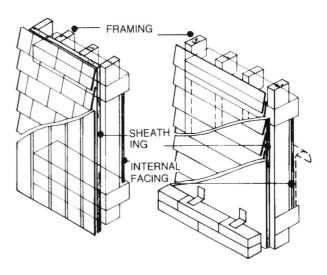

UNITS/SURFACING: BONDED

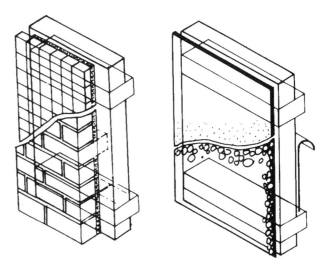

Fig. 8. Wall facing types

STICK

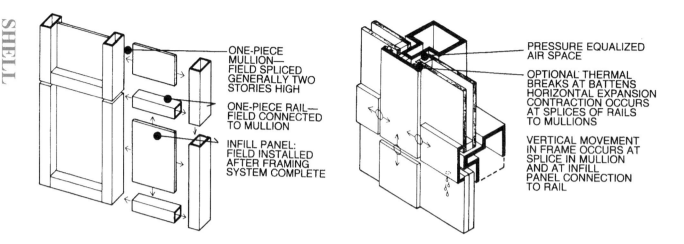

ONE-PIECE
MULLION—
FIELD SPLICED
GENERALLY TWO
STORIES HIGH

ONE-PIECE RAIL—
FIELD CONNECTED
TO MULLION

INFILL PANEL:
FIELD INSTALLED
AFTER FRAMING
SYSTEM COMPLETE

PRESSURE EQUALIZED
AIR SPACE

OPTIONAL THERMAL
BREAKS AT BATTENS
HORIZONTAL EXPANSION
CONTRACTION OCCURS
AT SPLICES OF RAILS
TO MULLIONS

VERTICAL MOVEMENT
IN FRAME OCCURS AT
SPLICE IN MULLION
AND AT INFILL
PANEL CONNECTION
TO RAIL

UNITIZED STICK

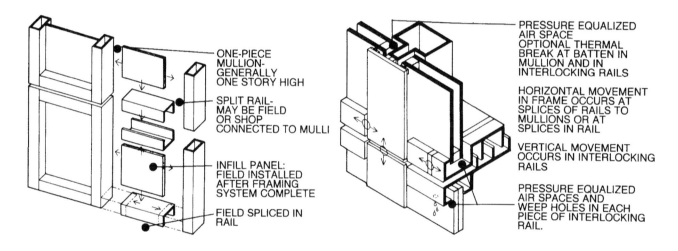

ONE-PIECE
MULLION-
GENERALLY
ONE STORY HIGH

SPLIT RAIL-
MAY BE FIELD
OR SHOP
CONNECTED TO MULLI

INFILL PANEL:
FIELD INSTALLED
AFTER FRAMING
SYSTEM COMPLETE

FIELD SPLICED IN
RAIL

PRESSURE EQUALIZED
AIR SPACE
OPTIONAL THERMAL
BREAK AT BATTEN IN
MULLION AND IN
INTERLOCKING RAILS

HORIZONTAL MOVEMENT
IN FRAME OCCURS AT
SPLICES OF RAILS TO
MULLIONS OR AT
SPLICES IN RAIL

VERTICAL MOVEMENT
OCCURS IN INTERLOCKING
RAILS

PRESSURE EQUALIZED
AIR SPACES AND
WEEP HOLES IN EACH
PIECE OF INTERLOCKING
RAIL.

UNITIZED

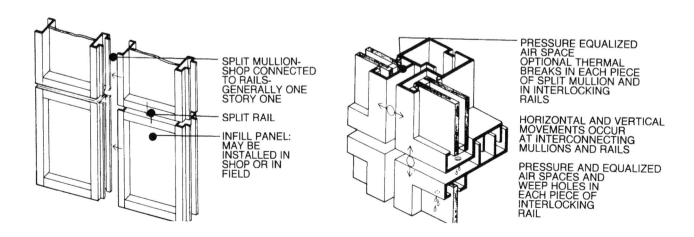

SPLIT MULLION-
SHOP CONNECTED
TO RAILS-
GENERALLY ONE
STORY ONE

SPLIT RAIL

INFILL PANEL:
MAY BE
INSTALLED IN
SHOP OR IN
FIELD

PRESSURE EQUALIZED
AIR SPACE
OPTIONAL THERMAL
BREAKS IN EACH PIECE
OF SPLIT MULLION AND
IN INTERLOCKING
RAILS

HORIZONTAL AND VERTICAL
MOVEMENTS OCCUR
AT INTERCONNECTING
MULLIONS AND RAILS

PRESSURE AND EQUALIZED
AIR SPACES AND
WEEP HOLES IN
EACH PIECE OF
INTERLOCKING
RAIL

Fig. 9. Grid type curtain walls

SHELL · B2

BATTEN GLAZING

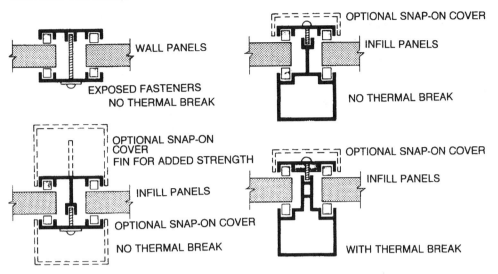

WALL PANELS
EXPOSED FASTENERS
NO THERMAL BREAK

OPTIONAL SNAP-ON COVER
INFILL PANELS
NO THERMAL BREAK

OPTIONAL SNAP-ON COVER
FIN FOR ADDED STRENGTH
INFILL PANELS
OPTIONAL SNAP-ON COVER
NO THERMAL BREAK

OPTIONAL SNAP-ON COVER
INFILL PANELS
WITH THERMAL BREAK

STOP GLAZING

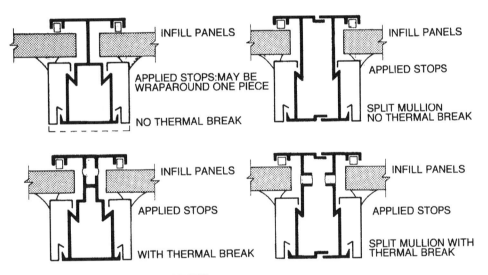

INFILL PANELS
APPLIED STOPS:MAY BE WRAPAROUND ONE PIECE
NO THERMAL BREAK

INFILL PANELS
APPLIED STOPS
SPLIT MULLION NO THERMAL BREAK

INFILL PANELS
APPLIED STOPS
WITH THERMAL BREAK

INFILL PANELS
APPLIED STOPS
SPLIT MULLION WITH THERMAL BREAK

GASKET AND BUTT GLAZING

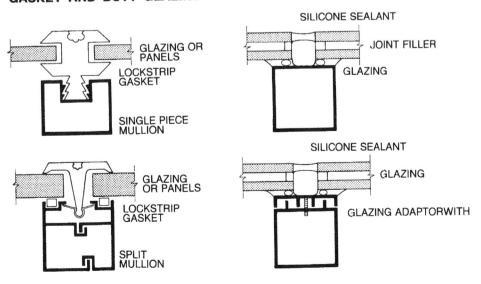

GLAZING OR PANELS
LOCKSTRIP GASKET
SINGLE PIECE MULLION

SILICONE SEALANT
JOINT FILLER
GLAZING

GLAZING OR PANELS
LOCKSTRIP GASKET
SPLIT MULLION

SILICONE SEALANT
GLAZING
GLAZING ADAPTORWITH

Fig. 10. Curtain wall mullion types.

- *Wall panel systems:*

  Wall panel systems include an array of panels assemblies capable of functioning as a complete wall assembly. Preliminary considerations of the wall panel system may be influenced by:

  - Functional considerations: when occupancy activities require either a virtually opaque wall, or when a limited amount only of openings, such as windows and/or doors is required.

  - Openings in most wall panels require secondary framing to support the frame of the opening and the free edges of adjacent panels.

  - Erection considerations: wall panels are always erected from the outside, and connections to the structural frame are generally also made from the outside, except for some types which may be backfastened.

  - Weight: ranges from very light, such as single thickness of formed metal, to very heavy, such as sculptured of precast concrete.

- *Deformation in curtain walls:*

  Negative air pressure on a given wall of a tall building, especially at corners, may significantly exceed positive air pressures that the same wall could be subjected to if direction of wind reverses. Negative air pressure may also be augmented when buildings are maintained under positive pressure:

- Air pressure, either negative or positive, acting on a grid curtain wall, will cause bending in the framing members and infill panels held by them, with each component then deflecting proportionately to its relative rigidity.

- Mullions as the principal framing members are relatively rigid and can easily be reinforced, thus bending stresses and resulting deflections can be kept within safe limits.

- Rails are generally short members and relatively rigid.

- Infill panels, especially transparent ones, may deform when subjected to the same air pressures , and as a result may fail in tension, or be pulled out of the framing members.

- In grid curtain walls, excessive deformation or deflection of the framing members under lateral loads may affect the infill panels or their connections to framing member, or may be visually unacceptable.

- Generally deflections should not exceed 1/180 of the span or a 3/4 in. (19 mm) maximum deviation from a straight line between supports.

- Deflections in panels of curtain wall panel systems may generally be as high as 1/120 of span if not visually objectionable; alternatively, allowable stresses in bending will determine maximum spans.

- *Pressure equalization provisions in curtain walls*

  Pressure equalization in curtain wall assemblies provides one means of, or line of defense for, undesired water penetration. In such approaches, confined air spaces, or air pressure equalization chambers, are incorporated into mullions and rails, with openings to the outside generally located in soffit areas of rails to protect them from heavy wetting. Air pressure equalization chambers are compartmentalized to prevent differential air pressures in developing within each chamber. Double seals are provided at connections of infill panels to mullions and rails: the outer seal acts as a deferent seal to water penetration but is not relied upon to completely prevent it; the inner seal acts as an air seal to substantially reduce air from the interior to the air chamber. Pressures in air chambers will not be effectively equalized unless the aggregate area of all openings to the outside is considerably larger than the

total area of all openings to the inside. The ratio of ten to one is considered minimal by the Architectural Aluminum Manufacturers Association.

7 Bearing walls

Bearing walls act simultaneously as structure and enclosure to support superimposed loads from floor, roof and other wall assemblies and transfer the resultant forces downward to the foundations. Bearing walls withstand the flexural moment and shears caused by lateral and vertical loads and serve as bracing to other parts of the structure. Bearing walls below grade withstand lateral soil and sometimes also hydrostatic pressure and resist seismic tremors in some areas. (See Chapter B1 in this Volume for articles on masonry wall structures and on earthquake design).

Bearing walls may be identical to a curtain wall in construction and a nonbearing wall, or a partition when one story or less in height; or may become a curtain wall without any change if its bearing capacity is not utilized; or may be bearing for a certain portion of it and nonbearing, or curtain wall, for remaining portions.

When numerous large openings have to be provided, even with uniformly applied floor/roof framing loads, the wall will become a series of piers or posts; the loading on the footing will be uneven and the wall assembly will no longer function as a true bearing wall. Under such conditions, a portion or the entire wall may have to be replaced with a structural frame.

Bearing walls can be generally classified as:

- *Stacked unit walls:*
  Made up of relatively small units stacked upon each other:

  - in various patterns or bonds in one or more wythes, contiguous or separate.

  - in various forms: brick, block, ashlar, rubble.

  - of various materials: stone, burned clay, concrete.

  - bonded by mortar of various types or laid dry.

  - reinforced or unreinforced.

- *Monolithic reinforced concrete:*
  There are three major types: cast-in place, tilt-up and precast:

  - Cast-in-place thin concrete walls are usually integrally connected to the floor and roof slabs and to each other, thus forming a crate-like form with excellent lateral stiffness. Buildings of 16 stories and more have been erected by this method.

  - An often more convenient method is the so-called "tilt-up," where walls are cast flat on the ground or on a platform next to their final position, then picked up by a crane and tilted into place. Connecting pours to surrounding structure are then generally made.

  - Precast concrete bearing walls are generally ribbed panels, single or double tees. Connections are usually made by preformed fasteners with/without additional concrete placed.

- *Framed construction:*
  Made of small, closely spaced vertical members, connected to plates top and bottom and covered by a skin.

  - wood framed walls of which balloon and platform frames are best known.

  - metal framed walls, where metal studs replace wood.

- *Deformations in bearing and nonbearing walls:*
  Lateral stability of walls is always a consideration:

  - for bearing and nonbearing walls, the allowable stresses in bending under lateral load, or under combined lateral and gravity loads will determine maximum unsupported height or length.

- empirically established ratios of unbraced height/length to thickness of wall, or slenderness ratio, may be used for some types in lieu of calculating actual stresses.

Concentrically loaded, single component wall assembly will be in compression throughout its thickness:

- horizontal loads will cause bending in the assembly and change the magnitude of compressive stresses; in slender wall assemblies tension may occur under heavy wind loads.

- effect on facings is seldom if ever significant.

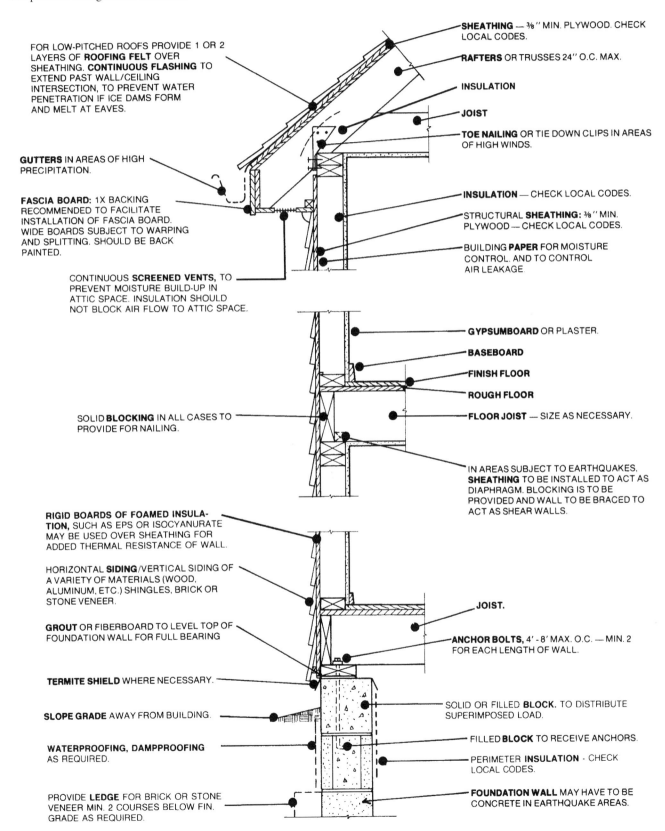

Fig. 11. Bearing walls: wood framed anchorage and connections

Eccentrically loaded wall assemblies may develop tensile stresses due to bending depending on the magnitude and/or eccentricity of the load. Facings may be affected when eccentric loading, horizontal forces and thermal expansion combine to increase bending stresses in the wall assembly.

Multi-component bearing wall assemblies, such as a bearing cavity wall, may not develop bending stresses even when carrying an eccentric load, provided the load is distributed between the two wythes:

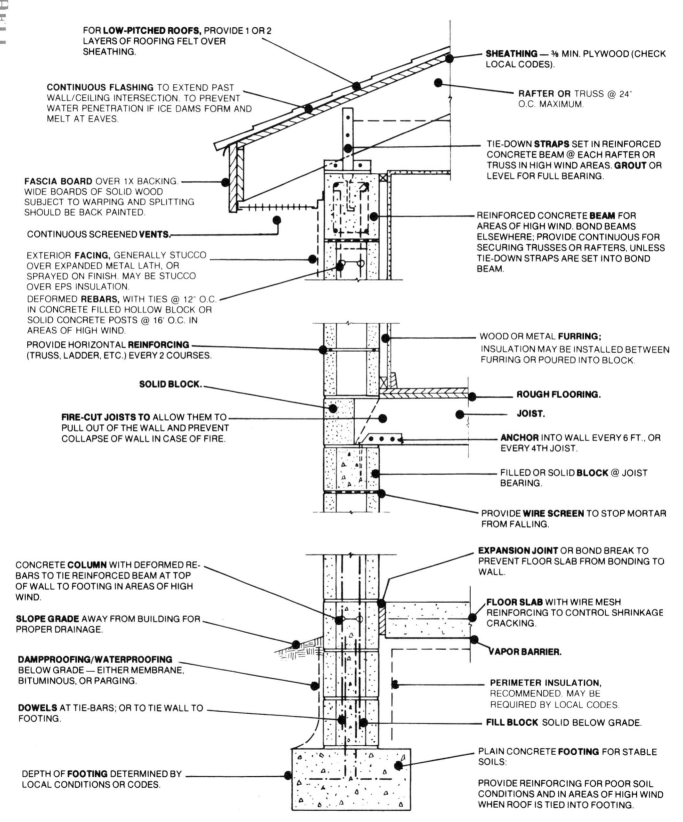

FOR **LOW-PITCHED ROOFS,** PROVIDE 1 OR 2 LAYERS OF ROOFING FELT OVER SHEATHING.

CONTINUOUS FLASHING TO EXTEND PAST WALL/CEILING INTERSECTION. TO PREVENT WATER PENETRATION IF ICE DAMS FORM AND MELT AT EAVES.

FASCIA BOARD OVER 1X BACKING. WIDE BOARDS OF SOLID WOOD SUBJECT TO WARPING AND SPLITTING SHOULD BE BACK PAINTED.

CONTINUOUS SCREENED **VENTS.**

EXTERIOR **FACING,** GENERALLY STUCCO OVER EXPANDED METAL LATH, OR SPRAYED ON FINISH. MAY BE STUCCO OVER EPS INSULATION.

DEFORMED **REBARS,** WITH TIES @ 12" O.C. IN CONCRETE FILLED HOLLOW BLOCK OR SOLID CONCRETE POSTS @ 16' O.C. IN AREAS OF HIGH WIND.

PROVIDE HORIZONTAL **REINFORCING** (TRUSS, LADDER, ETC.) EVERY 2 COURSES.

SOLID BLOCK.

FIRE-CUT JOISTS TO ALLOW THEM TO PULL OUT OF THE WALL AND PREVENT COLLAPSE OF WALL IN CASE OF FIRE.

CONCRETE **COLUMN** WITH DEFORMED RE-BARS TO TIE REINFORCED BEAM AT TOP OF WALL TO FOOTING IN AREAS OF HIGH WIND.

SLOPE GRADE AWAY FROM BUILDING FOR PROPER DRAINAGE.

DAMPPROOFING/WATERPROOFING BELOW GRADE — EITHER MEMBRANE, BITUMINOUS, OR PARGING.

DOWELS AT TIE-BARS; OR TO TIE WALL TO FOOTING.

DEPTH OF **FOOTING** DETERMINED BY LOCAL CONDITIONS OR CODES.

SHEATHING — ⅜ MIN. PLYWOOD (CHECK LOCAL CODES).

RAFTER OR TRUSS @ 24" O.C. MAXIMUM.

TIE-DOWN **STRAPS** SET IN REINFORCED CONCRETE BEAM @ EACH RAFTER OR TRUSS IN HIGH WIND AREAS. **GROUT** OR LEVEL FOR FULL BEARING.

REINFORCED CONCRETE **BEAM** FOR AREAS OF HIGH WIND. BOND BEAMS ELSEWHERE; PROVIDE CONTINUOUS FOR SECURING TRUSSES OR RAFTERS, UNLESS TIE-DOWN STRAPS ARE SET INTO BOND BEAM.

WOOD OR METAL **FURRING;** INSULATION MAY BE INSTALLED BETWEEN FURRING OR POURED INTO BLOCK.

ROUGH FLOORING.

JOIST.

ANCHOR INTO WALL EVERY 6 FT., OR EVERY 4TH JOIST.

FILLED OR SOLID **BLOCK** @ JOIST BEARING.

PROVIDE **WIRE SCREEN** TO STOP MORTAR FROM FALLING.

EXPANSION JOINT OR BOND BREAK TO PREVENT FLOOR SLAB FROM BONDING TO WALL.

FLOOR SLAB WITH WIRE MESH REINFORCING TO CONTROL SHRINKAGE CRACKING.

VAPOR BARRIER.

PERIMETER INSULATION, RECOMMENDED. MAY BE REQUIRED BY LOCAL CODES.

FILL BLOCK SOLID BELOW GRADE.

PLAIN CONCRETE **FOOTING** FOR STABLE SOILS:

PROVIDE REINFORCING FOR POOR SOIL CONDITIONS AND IN AREAS OF HIGH WIND WHEN ROOF IS TIED INTO FOOTING.

Fig. 12. Bearing walls: masonry single wythe

- bending may develop in slender exterior facing wythes under extreme horizontal load and the influence of thermal expansion/contraction.

- thermal and moisture induced movements rather than horizontal loads will generally be the more important considerations.

- vertical loads will affect wall assembly only when safe working stresses in component materials are exceeded.

When walls are faced to enhance their resistance to detrimental effects of external environment, or because of aesthetic considerations, the physical properties of such facings may dictate the structural requirements of the wall:

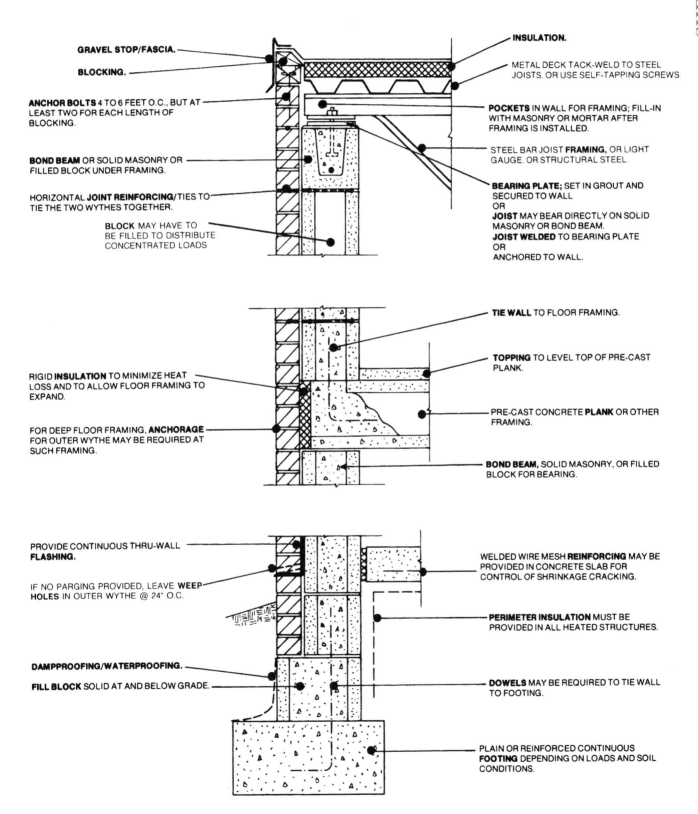

GRAVEL STOP/FASCIA.

BLOCKING.

ANCHOR BOLTS 4 TO 6 FEET O.C., BUT AT LEAST TWO FOR EACH LENGTH OF BLOCKING.

BOND BEAM OR SOLID MASONRY OR FILLED BLOCK UNDER FRAMING.

HORIZONTAL **JOINT REINFORCING**/TIES TO TIE THE TWO WYTHES TOGETHER.

BLOCK MAY HAVE TO BE FILLED TO DISTRIBUTE CONCENTRATED LOADS

INSULATION.

METAL DECK TACK-WELD TO STEEL JOISTS. OR USE SELF-TAPPING SCREWS.

POCKETS IN WALL FOR FRAMING; FILL-IN WITH MASONRY OR MORTAR AFTER FRAMING IS INSTALLED.

STEEL BAR JOIST **FRAMING,** OR LIGHT GAUGE. OR STRUCTURAL STEEL.

BEARING PLATE; SET IN GROUT AND SECURED TO WALL
OR
JOIST MAY BEAR DIRECTLY ON SOLID MASONRY OR BOND BEAM.
JOIST WELDED TO BEARING PLATE
OR
ANCHORED TO WALL.

RIGID **INSULATION** TO MINIMIZE HEAT LOSS AND TO ALLOW FLOOR FRAMING TO EXPAND.

FOR DEEP FLOOR FRAMING, **ANCHORAGE** FOR OUTER WYTHE MAY BE REQUIRED AT SUCH FRAMING.

TIE WALL TO FLOOR FRAMING.

TOPPING TO LEVEL TOP OF PRE-CAST PLANK.

PRE-CAST CONCRETE **PLANK** OR OTHER FRAMING.

BOND BEAM, SOLID MASONRY, OR FILLED BLOCK FOR BEARING.

PROVIDE CONTINUOUS THRU-WALL **FLASHING.**

IF NO PARGING PROVIDED, LEAVE **WEEP HOLES** IN OUTER WYTHE @ 24" O.C.

DAMPPROOFING/WATERPROOFING.

FILL BLOCK SOLID AT AND BELOW GRADE.

WELDED WIRE MESH **REINFORCING** MAY BE PROVIDED IN CONCRETE SLAB FOR CONTROL OF SHRINKAGE CRACKING.

PERIMETER INSULATION MUST BE PROVIDED IN ALL HEATED STRUCTURES.

DOWELS MAY BE REQUIRED TO TIE WALL TO FOOTING.

PLAIN OR REINFORCED CONTINUOUS **FOOTING** DEPENDING ON LOADS AND SOIL CONDITIONS.

Fig. 13. Bearing walls: masonry anchorage and connections

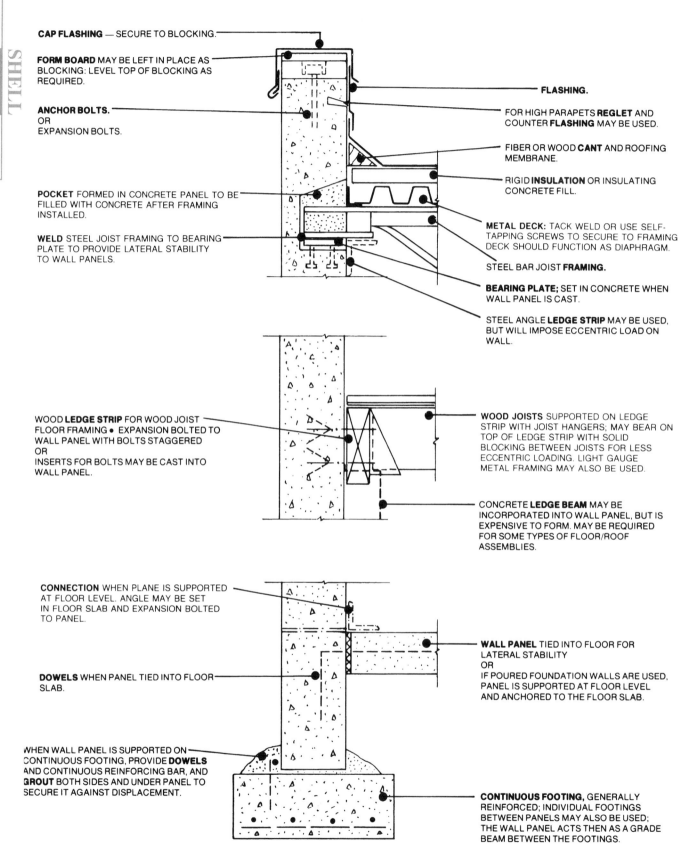

CAP FLASHING — SECURE TO BLOCKING.

FORM BOARD MAY BE LEFT IN PLACE AS BLOCKING; LEVEL TOP OF BLOCKING AS REQUIRED.

ANCHOR BOLTS.
OR
EXPANSION BOLTS.

POCKET FORMED IN CONCRETE PANEL TO BE FILLED WITH CONCRETE AFTER FRAMING INSTALLED.

WELD STEEL JOIST FRAMING TO BEARING PLATE TO PROVIDE LATERAL STABILITY TO WALL PANELS.

FLASHING.

FOR HIGH PARAPETS **REGLET** AND COUNTER **FLASHING** MAY BE USED.

FIBER OR WOOD **CANT** AND ROOFING MEMBRANE.

RIGID **INSULATION** OR INSULATING CONCRETE FILL.

METAL DECK: TACK WELD OR USE SELF-TAPPING SCREWS TO SECURE TO FRAMING DECK SHOULD FUNCTION AS DIAPHRAGM.

STEEL BAR JOIST **FRAMING.**

BEARING PLATE; SET IN CONCRETE WHEN WALL PANEL IS CAST.

STEEL ANGLE **LEDGE STRIP** MAY BE USED, BUT WILL IMPOSE ECCENTRIC LOAD ON WALL.

WOOD **LEDGE STRIP** FOR WOOD JOIST FLOOR FRAMING • EXPANSION BOLTED TO WALL PANEL WITH BOLTS STAGGERED
OR
INSERTS FOR BOLTS MAY BE CAST INTO WALL PANEL.

WOOD JOISTS SUPPORTED ON LEDGE STRIP WITH JOIST HANGERS; MAY BEAR ON TOP OF LEDGE STRIP WITH SOLID BLOCKING BETWEEN JOISTS FOR LESS ECCENTRIC LOADING. LIGHT GAUGE METAL FRAMING MAY ALSO BE USED.

CONCRETE **LEDGE BEAM** MAY BE INCORPORATED INTO WALL PANEL, BUT IS EXPENSIVE TO FORM. MAY BE REQUIRED FOR SOME TYPES OF FLOOR/ROOF ASSEMBLIES.

CONNECTION WHEN PLANE IS SUPPORTED AT FLOOR LEVEL. ANGLE MAY BE SET IN FLOOR SLAB AND EXPANSION BOLTED TO PANEL.

DOWELS WHEN PANEL TIED INTO FLOOR SLAB.

WALL PANEL TIED INTO FLOOR FOR LATERAL STABILITY
OR
IF POURED FOUNDATION WALLS ARE USED, PANEL IS SUPPORTED AT FLOOR LEVEL AND ANCHORED TO THE FLOOR SLAB.

WHEN WALL PANEL IS SUPPORTED ON CONTINUOUS FOOTING, PROVIDE **DOWELS** AND CONTINUOUS REINFORCING BAR, AND **GROUT** BOTH SIDES AND UNDER PANEL TO SECURE IT AGAINST DISPLACEMENT.

CONTINUOUS FOOTING, GENERALLY REINFORCED; INDIVIDUAL FOOTINGS BETWEEN PANELS MAY ALSO BE USED; THE WALL PANEL ACTS THEN AS A GRADE BEAM BETWEEN THE FOOTINGS.

Fig. 14. Bearing walls: concrete pre-cast and tilt-up

FRAMED:

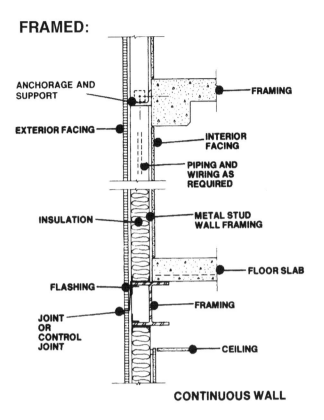

CONTINUOUS WALL

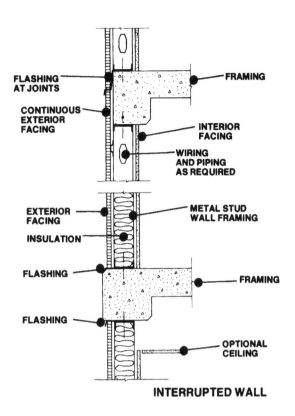

INTERRUPTED WALL

STACKED:

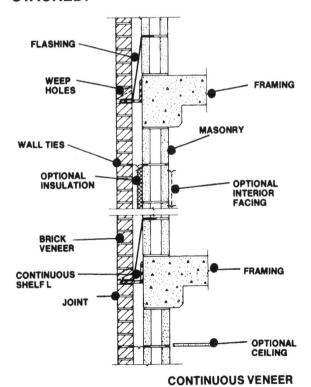

CONTINUOUS VENEER

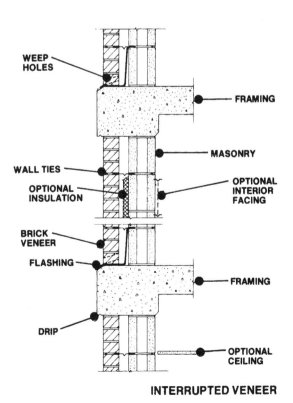

INTERRUPTED VENEER

Fig. 15. Bearing walls: used as curtain walls

SHELL

B2

- deflection in walls faced with stucco, plaster, or other inelastic materials my be limited to minimize the possibility of cracks developing in such facings.

Walls when supported by or connected to the structural frame will generally be affected by deformations in the frame. The entire envelope must therefore be considered during the selection of its constituent parts.

The preceeding pages (Figs. 11 - 15) give schematic and representative details of bearing wall assemblies. Critical considerations of insulation, moisture control, weathertightness and related design details are discussed in subsequent articles in this Chapter.

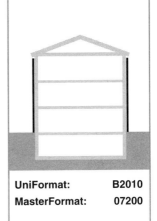

Thermal insulation

Summary: Thermal insulation helps improve comfort, conserves energy, and protects structures from thermal and freezing damage. Reviewed here are principles of heat flow through the building envelope and design guidelines for placement of insulation.

Key words: condensation, heat gain, heat loss, thermal insulation, thermal resistance, U value.

UniFormat:	B2010
MasterFormat:	07200

SHELL

B2

Introduction

Insulation may be defined as materials or features of construction provided to minimize the flow of heat between the spaces separated. By reducing heat flow, insulation will:

- to conserve energy used for heating and cooling.

- reduce temperature fluctuations and increase comfort within the enclosed space.

- to protect buildings and other structures from thermal damage, freezing damage, frost heaving, and damage from condensation of water vapor.

In addition to reducing heat flow between spaces, insulation may be used to:

- control surface temperatures of building components (such as piping, ductwork, and equipment) for economy in operation, comfort of occupants, or safety.

- prevent water vapor condensation on cold surfaces.

- reduce water vapor transmission, properly seen as the separate but related topic of moisture control.

- a significant contribution of most types of insulation is also in reducing levels of airborne sound transmitted through walls, partitions, floors, and ceilings.

In this article, the theoretical principles of heat flow are presented in Part 1. Insulation types and applications are discussed in Part 2. In the concluding section, Part 3, summary comments are offered for designing insulation as one factor in optimized building envelope and HVAC system design.

1 Theory of heat flow dynamics

This section reviews the thermodynamic principles of heat flow with respect to the building envelope in order to provide a theoretical background to the role of thermal insulation in designing buildings.

1.1 Human thermal comfort

There are six major variables in human thermal comfort (Fanger 1970):

- Air temperature

- Ambient radiant temperature

- Humidity

- Dress (a 1940's business suit is given the thermal insulation value of 1 "clo".)

- Air velocity

- Metabolic rate, or activity level.

Variables which do not appear to vary in reporting the parameters of human thermal comfort (in which experimental subjects report that they feel comfortable) include sex, age, place of origin and residence, skin color, and body form and weight. The perceived "discomfort" and physiological ability to tolerate discomfort and thermal stress may vary according to these and other variables. In other words, the human "comfort" zone is relatively universal independent of age, health, sex. (However, reports of "discomfort" and actual stress appear to vary as a function of many variables, such as acculturation.)

Of the variables listed, architects and engineers have some control of air temperature, ambient radiant temperature, humidity, and air velocity. Thermal insulation affects mainly air temperature and ambient radiant temperature, and those variables are very important to thermal comfort inside most buildings.

Body comfort in an enclosed space largely depends on the balance between heat produced internally in the body and the temperature and humidity of the surrounding air and the surface (radiant) temperatures of the surrounding envelope. Any changes in the ambient or surrounding surface temperature, when the factor of humidity is disregarded, will change the comfort level. The dynamics of heat flow within and through a building envelope at low exterior temperatures is depicted in Fig. 1.

1.1 Forms of heat transfer

How heat passes through materials is described by the classical principles of heat dynamics and combinations of them, restated here as an

Author: Donald Bearman, AIA

Credits: The portions of this article on heat flow definitions and illustrations are excerpted from *1993 SWEET'S Catalog File Selection Data*, by permission of McGraw-Hill. The author is indebted for contributions to this discussion by Larry Berglund, Ph.D., John B. Pierce Foundation, Yale University.

References: ASHRAE Fundamentals. Atlanta, GA: American Society of Heating, Refrigerating and Air Conditioning Engineers. 1993 (or latest edition).

Additional references are listed at the end of this article.

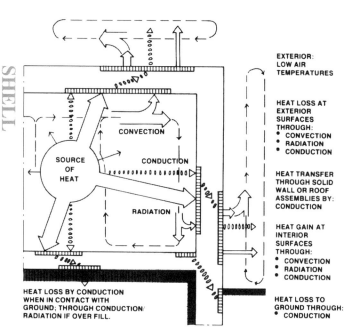

EXTERIOR:
LOW AIR
TEMPERATURES

HEAT LOSS AT
EXTERIOR
SURFACES
THROUGH:
• CONVECTION
• RADIATION
• CONDUCTION

HEAT TRANSFER
THROUGH SOLID
WALL OR ROOF
ASSEMBLIES BY:
CONDUCTION

HEAT GAIN AT
INTERIOR
SURFACES
THROUGH:
• CONVECTION
• RADIATION
• CONDUCTION

HEAT LOSS TO
GROUND THROUGH:
• CONDUCTION

CONVECTION

CONDUCTION

SOURCE
OF
HEAT

RADIATION

HEAT LOSS BY CONDUCTION
WHEN IN CONTACT WITH
GROUND; THROUGH CONDUCTION/
RADIATION IF OVER FILL.

Fig. 1. Heat flow in and around the building envelope.

introduction to understanding the design principles and applications of insulation.

• Conduction, the transfer of heat by direct contact between two parts of a stationary system, caused by a temperature difference between those two parts. An example of conductive heat loss is warming your feet in bed by pressing them to your spouse's back, and an example of insulation from conductive heat loss is wearing socks while doing so.

• Convection, the transfer of heat from one material to another by the circulation or movement of an intermediary fluid, such as a liquid or gas. Diffusion can be considered a form of convection for the purposes of this definition. An example of convection is warming your hands by blowing on them, and an example of convective insulation is stepping behind a wind shelter.

• Radiation, the transfer of heat by electromagnetic waves, irrespective of the temperature of the intervening medium such as air. An example of radiation is warming yourself by standing in sunlight, and an example of radiative insulation (radiant barrier) is placing a reflective surface inside a car window.

• Evaporation is also a form of heat transfer by phase change, not directly relevant to insulating properties of materials but part of thermal heat loss, such as water cooling a roof surface when it evaporates, absorbing "latent heat" in order to drive the evaporation process. Similarly, when ice melts on a roof surface, it gives "back: the latent heat originally required to freeze water into ice. In well insulated roofs, neither of these effects is significant.

• A related process in heat transfer dynamics is the heat storage effect or thermal time lag of heat in materials with high thermal mass or capacitance, such as adobe or masonry. Heat moves into and out of such materials very slowly, and for this reason, we say it is "stored" in the material's mass. Time lag effects explain some effects related to insulating buildings.

An example of a complex heat and mass transfer that occurs in buildings and involving all of these mechanisms is as follows (an actual case):

- Water enters an insulated steep roof system through a leak.

- The interior finish is warmed by a combination of convective and radiant heat from the room below.

- The heat passes by conduction from the interior through the finish and vapor retarder.

- The water is warmed by conduction, and it undergoes a phase change, becoming water vapor.

- The water vapor diffuses through the insulation in all directions and passes by diffusion and convection to the underside of the roof sheathing.

- At the roof sheathing. the water vapor condenses, transferring phase change heat to the sheathing.

- The heat passes through the roof sheathing and covering by conduction, and it leaves the system by a combination of radiation to the sky, convection to the air, and convection to the rain water running down the roof.

- After building up droplets on the underside of the roof sheathing, the water drips down through the insulation to the vapor retarder, and the process continues.

- After a while the entire system is sopping wet, and it is difficult to find the source of the moisture. The architect is called to explain the matter.

1.1.1   Radiation and reflectivity

Radiation is the phenomenon of heat transfer by radiant energy through space (without the need of a medium of transfer) from a body or material at a higher temperature to bodies or materials at lower temperatures which are in its line of sight (Fig. 2).

- Heat transfer by radiation increases significantly as the temperature of the emitting surface rises.

- Solar energy striking a surface will be partially reflected and partially absorbed, with the fractions primarily dependent on the selectivity or reflectance of the surface:

- A dark (selective) surface may absorb about 90 percent, while a white (reflective) one will absorb from 20 to 40 percent, reflecting the balance.

- The difference between maximum temperatures of reflective and selective surfaces exposed to solar irradiation may be as much as 60F as a result of their surface reflectance.

- Even though reflectance of two light surfaces may be similar, their emissivity may differ, resulting in significantly higher temperatures in those with lower emissivity under the same exposure.

1.1.2   Radiation and emissivity

Temperature and emissivity of the surface will determine how heat gained is reradiated (Fig. 3).

- Painted surfaces have a higher coefficient of emissivity: most of the heat absorbed will be reradiated faster.

- The color of a painted surface has little effect on emissivity: black and white lacquers at 100 to 200F both have an emissivity range of 0.80 to 0.95.

Metallic surfaces, especially when polished, have much lower coefficients of emissivity. Unpainted Metallic surfaces therefore will reradiate more slowly than painted surfaces and remain hotter.

- bright aluminum foil is 0.04 to 0.05

- commercial grade polished copper is 0.03, but 0.78 when heavily oxidized.

- aluminum coated roofing 0.1 to 0.2.

1.1.3   Convection and surface conductance

Heat will flow through a solid body when there is a temperature differential between air on opposite sides (Fig. 4).

- Heat gain and heat loss by and from the body will be by convection: air in contact with the surfaces will either give up heat to the body, or pick up heat from it:

- Natural convection will take place when the motion of air is due entirely to differences in density.

- Forced convection occurs when the air motion is augmented by external forces.

The transfer of heat from or to air is affected by the layer of air adjacent to the surfaces of a body, or the surface film:

- Surface film is a layer of stagnant air which clings to the surface of any object and offers resistance to the flow of heat.

- The heat flow through a surface film, the convective surface conductance, in general use is the design value for interior surfaces: still air generally assumed at .65 Btu/hr. sq. ft. per degree F. Since this varies somewhat depending on surface material, relative position of surface, direction of heat flow and temperature, other design values are sometimes used. The design value for exterior surface, whether vertical or horizontal, with 15 MPH wind is 6 Btu/hr. sq. ft. per degree F. These design values are incorporated into the temperature gradient calculations offered below.

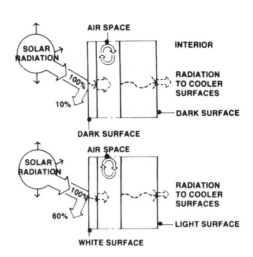

Fig. 2. Radiation: reflectivity

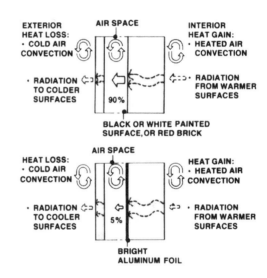

Fig. 3. Radiation: emissivity

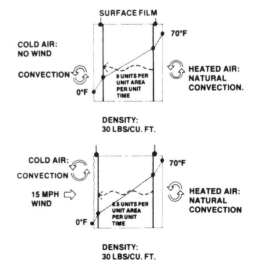

Fig. 4. Convection: surface conductance

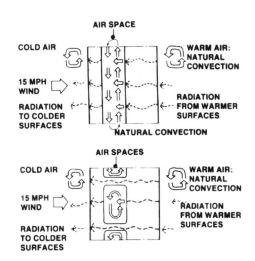

Fig. 5. Convection and radiation: vertical air space

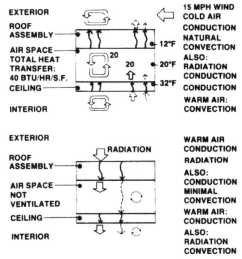

Fig. 6. Convection and radiation: horizontal air space

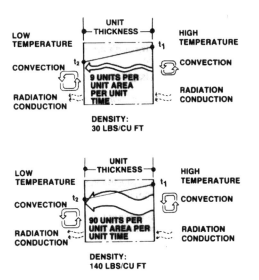

Fig. 7. Conduction

1.1.4 Convection and radiation: vertical air space

Heat transfer through an air space incorporated into a vertical assembly will be by natural convection within the air space: temperature differences between the surfaces of components facing the air space will set up convective currents within the air space (Fig. 5). The amount of heat transferred will:

- increase with increase in temperature differences of the two surfaces.

- will not be significantly affected by the temperature level.

Radiation will occur through the air space from the warm surface to the cold one. The amount of heat transferred by radiation will vary:

- with the temperature difference.

- also with temperature level, increasing rapidly with increase in surface temperature levels.

At low temperature levels, convection will be the controlling factor: at very high temperatures, the controlling factor is radiation. When vertical air space is broken up into a number of horizontal cells:

- heat transfer by convection is reduced by minimizing convective currents.

- transfer by radiation will remain unchanged.

- the horizontal divisions will allow some heat transfer through them by conduction.

1.1.5 Convection and radiation: horizontal air space

Heat transfer through horizontal air spaces will differ depending on the direction of heat flow (Fig. 6). Upward heat flow through an air space will be by convection and radiation, similar to that for vertical air space. When the flow of heat is downward, the air in contact with the upper warmer component will also be warmer and less dense than air in contact with the lower colder component:

- heat transfer will be by radiation.

- convection will be at a minimum.

- a small amount will be transferred by conduction.

The transfer by radiation is the same through vertical and horizontal air spaces. Assuming that at normal temperatures, the emitting surface has a coefficient of 0.9—such as for painted surfaces or red brick—the heat transfer by radiation might be about 50 percent of the total heat transferred. If a bright metallic surface is substituted, heat transfer by radiation may be reduced to about 5 percent of the total.

1.1.6 Conduction

Conduction is the transfer of heat from one part of the body to another part, or from one body to another which is in physical contact with it, without any appreciable displacement of the particles of the body or bodies (Fig. 7). Heat continues to flow as long as a temperature difference exists within the body, or between bodies in contact with one another.

The rate of heat flow depends upon the conductivity of the body. Conductivity of materials varies with differences in their densities: low density materials have voids in them, which contain air or other gaseous substances and which impede the transfer of heat by increasing the cross sectional area or length of travel:

- Regular weight concrete with a density of 140 lb./cu. ft. has a coefficient of conductivity of $k = 9.09$.

- Cellular concrete with a density of 30 lb./cu. ft. has a coefficient of $k = .90$. In this case, the transfer of heat will be 10 times less per unit area per unit time for the less dense material under the same difference in surface temperatures.

1.2 Temperature variations and units of measure

1.2.1 Equivalent temperature

Heat gain and heat loss in assemblies is normally calculated at the time of greatest heat flow which implies that such conditions remain the same at all times. This approach is referred to as the steady state of heat flow. It assumes that:

- the rate of heat flow through the assembly will not vary with time.

- temperature differentials within the assembly, and outside of it, will remain constant.

Actual conditions do change almost constantly, especially when an assembly is exposed to variable solar radiation, resulting in an unsteady state of heat flow. An assembly may be exposed to instantaneous heat gain through solar radiation, which will first be absorbed by the surface layer. The temperature of this layer will rise above the temperature of the remainder of the assembly, and also above the temperature of outdoor air:

- heat flow will occur into both regions of lower temperatures

- the amount of heat flowing in either direction will depend on the resistance of the assembly and the surface film coefficient.

The unsteady flow of heat or dynamic response generally is accounted for by using the equivalent temperature difference (Fig. 8):

- The temperature difference which reflects the total heat flow through an assembly caused by variable solar radiation and outdoor temperature.

- The solar irradiation required to establish its amount at a given location can be found in ASHRAE *HVAC Applications* (ASHRAE 1991 or latest edition).

- Design temperature differentials for a given location are available from the local U. S. Weather Bureau.

1.2.2 Varying outdoor temperatures

The equivalent temperature difference must take into account the duration of the exposure during various times of the day (Fig. 9). Outside temperatures vary with a resultant immediate effect on the flow of heat. For examples, if outdoor temperature suddenly drops from 95 to 85F (from 35°C to 29.5°C):

- heat continues to flow from the interior surface of the assembly into an interior space at 80F (26.6°F).

- there is also heat flow from the outer surface of the assembly to now cooler outside air.

- therefore the amount of heat stored within the assembly is reduced.

If the outside temperature rises again to 95F (35°C) after several hours and the outer surface of the assembly begins to gain heat, the flow of heat from the inner surface of the assembly into the interior space does not immediately rise to its previous level:

- the inner surface remains slightly above the temperature of the interior air due to negligible heat flow when outdoor temperature was at 85°F (29.5°C).

- heat flow into the interior increases gradually returning to the previous level only after the temperature of the entire assembly has risen to a point where the steady state condition is re-established.

1.2.3 Time lag

The interval between the change In outdoor temperature and the temperature of the inner surface is known as the time lag (Fig. 10). It is due mostly to the heat required to raise the temperature of the assembly itself. Time lag is the time required to establish steady state condition through an assembly: for heat to travel through an assembly from the warm surface to the colder one:

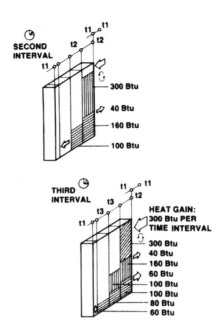

Fig. 8. Equivalent temperature

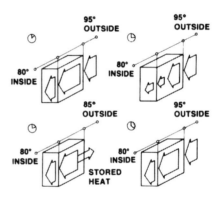

Fig. 9. Varying outdoor temperatures

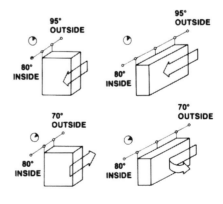

Fig. 10. Time lag

SHELL

B2

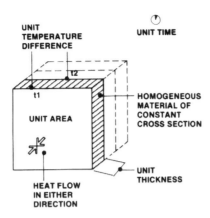

Fig. 11. Conductivity

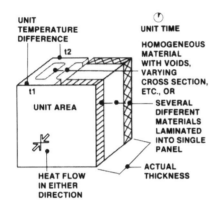

Fig. 12. Conductance

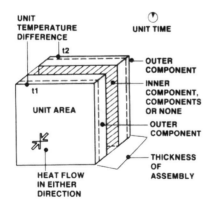

Fig. 13. Transmittance

Thin lightweight assemblies have little mass and do not require large amounts of heat to raise their temperature:

- The steady state temperature distribution is reached soon after the temperature of their outer surface rises.

- Since little heat is stored in such assemblies, the temperature of the inner surface drops quickly after a drop in outside temperatures: the time lag is short.

Dense, thick assemblies have a large heat storage capacity:

- A considerable amount of time may be required for the heat being absorbed at the outer surface to reach the inner surface.

- Should the temperature at the outer surface drop before the heat reaches the inner surface, the flow will reverse and heat will flow back to the outer surface; and from there to the cooler outside air.

- Heat will be stored in the assembly, some of it being released when outdoor temperature falls below the temperature of the assembly, then replenished as outdoor temperature rises.

- The thermal capacity of an assembly is determined by the volume x the density of the materials incorporated into the assembly x the specific heat of the material.

1.2.4 Conductivity

Thermal conductivity designated k, is a property of homogeneous material (Fig. 11):

- It is measured by the quantity of units of heat passing through a unit thickness, per unit area, in unit time, when a unit temperature difference is maintained between the outer surfaces of the material. Coefficients of conductivity are not additive.

Generally used units are:

- units of heat given by British Thermal Unit, or Btu, which is the amount of heat required to raise the temperature of one pound of water from 63F to 64F.

- unit thickness: one inch.

- unit area: one square foot.

- unit time: one hour.

- unit temperature difference: one degree F.

Resistivity, designated by r or 1/k, is the reciprocal of conductivity:

- it is measured by the temperature difference in degrees F between smooth parallel outer surfaces of one inch thick material that are required to cause one Btu to flow through one square foot per hour, or: r = temperature difference in degrees F per inch per one square foot per hour, divided by Btu. Coefficients of resistivity are additive.

1.2.5 Conductance

Thermal Conductance designated C, measures the rate of heat flow through the actual thickness of homogeneous, nonhomogeneous, or composite materials (Fig. 12):

- Composite materials are those where the cross sectional area is not identical throughout, such s as in hollow core concrete block, or where a product consists of several layers of similar or different material, such as plywood or built-up roofing.

- Conductance is defined as the heat flow in Btu per hour through one square foot area of given thickness for one degree F difference in temperature between the outer surfaces.

- Coefficients of conductance should not be added.

Thermal Resistance, designated R or 1/C, is the reciprocal of conductance:

- It is a unit for the resistance to heat flow through a given thickness of a homogeneous, nonhomogeneous, or composite material.

- It is measured by the temperature difference in degrees F between the outer surfaces required to cause one Btu to flow through one square foot per hour: R = temperature difference in degrees F divided by Btu per one square foot per hour.

- Resistance (R) values may be added.

1.2.6   U value

Thermal Transmittance, designated as U-value, is the measure of heat flow through a component of the building, whether vertical or horizontal, when a difference between air temperatures on either side of such component exists (Fig. 13):

- The effect of air spaces 3/4 in. and wider, incorporated into the assemblies, and that of surface air films is included in the coefficient of thermal transmittance.

- Thermal transmittance is measured by Btu per hour through one square foot, when the temperature difference is one degree F between the air at the two surfaces of the assembly.

- The U-value is the reciprocal of the sum of all thermal resistances of the components, or the total resistance to heat flow through a complete assembly: Sum. R = R of surface film + R of outer component or components + R of air space or spaces + R of inner component or components + R of surface film.

- U-values are not additive: when modifications of an assembly are investigated, thermal resistances (R values) should be used.

1.3   Calculating heat flow: a short-form method

ASHRAE Fundamentals, Chapter 20 "Thermal Insulation and Vapor Retarders—Fundamentals" gives the standard procedure for calculating heat flow. For those who are comfortable with engineering calculations, the writer suggests going directly to that document. The following is a short-form method, intended as a very brief summary, illustrating the above stated definitions.

- Heat passes from the warm side of materials and systems to the cold side. If the temperature at the two sides is the same, heat does not pass. Coldness is not considered a quality; it is simply a lower heat.

- Materials pass through different materials at different rates. Gold, aluminum, and other metals conduct heat at very high rates, while plastic foams and other insulating materials, that is, those with devious paths, conduct heat poorly. The time rate of heat conduction through gold is approximately a thousand times as great as the rate through polyisocyanurate foam. Also, foam is less expensive.

- The time rate of thermal conductivity of materials is represented by the symbols "C" and "k," and the time rate of the total heat flow from the fluid on the warm side of the construction to the fluid on the cool side is represented by "U" or "U-factor."

- "C" conductance, is the time rate of heat flow through the unit area of a body per unit of temperature difference.

- "k" conductivity, is the time rate of heat flow through the unit area of a homogeneous material per unit of thickness.

- "Btu" British thermal units, is a measure of heat energy required to raise the temperature of one pound of water one degree Fahrenheit (F). Calorie and calorie are the comparable measures used in the SI (metric) system.

- The resistance to heat flow is the reciprocal of thermal conductance, and is represented by "R." The reciprocal of conductivity is resistivity, represented by "r." (Although it is convenient to assume that these factors and rates are constant for any material, this is not the case. Many materials vary in their insulating value according to such factors as temperature and dampness.)

Heat flow can be calculated by knowing the temperatures on both sides of construction and the thermal resistance, or insulating value, of the construction. Thermal resistance values can be added to give the total thermal resistance of the construction system.

Table 1. Thermal resistance of common building materials.

Material R-value	Thickness	
Air film, exterior, 15 mph wind		0.17
Air film, interior		0.52
Aluminum	per inch	0.008
Asphalt shingles	normal	0.44
Brick, common		
80 lb.	cubic ft./inch	0.45-0.31
100 lb.	cubic ft./inch	0.30-0.23
120 lb.	cubic ft./inch	0.23-0.16
Built-up roofing	3/8"	0.33
Carpet and fibrous pad	normal	2.08
Cellular glass	per inch	2.86
Cellulosic insulation (milled paper or wood pulp)	per inch	3.70-3.13
Cellular polyisocyanurate (gas-impermeable facers)	per inch	7.20
Cellular polyurethane/ polyisocyanurate (unfaced)	per inch	6.25-5.56
Concrete, normal weight	per inch	0.08
Concrete masonry units, lightweight	8 inch	3.2-1.90
Same with perlite filled cores		5.3-3.9
Concrete masonry units, normal weight	8 inch	1.11-0.97
Same with perlite filled cores		2.0
Douglas Fir-Larch	per inch	1.06-0.99
Expanded perlite, organic bonded	per inch	2.78
Expanded polystyrene, extruded (smooth skin surface)	per inch	5.00
Expanded polystyrene beadboard	per inch	4.00
Cellular glass	per inch	2.7
Foil-faced polyethylene foam, heat flow down	1/4"	10.74
Glass fiber, organic bonded	per inch	4.00
Gypsum or plaster board	0.5 inches	0.45
Gypsum plaster: sand aggregate	per inch	0.18
Mineral fiber batts processed from rock, slag, or glass	nom. 6 inch	22
Oak	per inch	0.89-0.80
Particleboard		
low density	per inch	1.41
medium density	per inch	1.06
high density	per inch	0.85
Plywood (Douglas Fir)	per inch	1.25
Shingles, wood, 16 inches, 7-1/2" exposure		0.87
Siding, wood	0.5 thick	0.81
Stucco	per inch	0.20
Western redcedar	per inch	1.48-1.11
Wood, hardwood finish	0.75 inches	0.68

Consider the wall of a wood frame house. The composition of the wall, from outside to inside, is follows. The values in this example are given in inch-pound units as degrees Fahrenheit (F), Btu, and inches. Comparable units can be transposed for the SI (metric) system.

• *Given that:*

-   The air film on the outside of the wall. At 15 miles per hour the thermal resistance of that air film is assumed to be 0.17.

-   1/2" wood siding. The thermal resistance is approximately 0.81.

-   Underlayment or air infiltration retarder. The thermal resistance is so low as to be negligible.

-   1/2" plywood sheathing. The thermal resistance is approximately 0.63.

-   Nominal 2" x 6" studs 24" o.c. The thermal resistance is approximately 5.5. The portion of the wall with studs is 1.5 / 24 = 0.06

-   Between the studs: Nominal 6" fiberglass batt insulation. The thermal resistance is approximately 19. The portion of the wall between the studs is 0.94.

-   Vapor retarder. The thermal resistance is so low as to be negligible.

-   1/2" gypsum wallboard. The thermal resistance is 0.45.

-   Inside air film. The thermal resistance is approximately 0.61. Note: one of the reasons why blowing air against the inside of a window clears condensation is that it lowers the thermal resistance of the inside air film and thus warms the glass.

• *Solution:*

-   The total thermal resistance between the studs is the sum of the appropriate figures above, 21.67.

-   The total thermal resistance at the studs is the sum of the appropriate figures above, 8.17.

-   Multiplying the thermal resistance between the studs x 0.94, and multiplying the thermal resistance at the studs x 0.06: the average thermal resistance for the wall, combining studs and insulated spaces between the studs, is 20.86.

-   The heat loss through this wall will be the reciprocal of the total thermal resistance. 1 / 20.86 = 0.048. This is the U-factor, meaning that 0.048 Btu of heat will pass through the wall per hour per square foot of wall per degree F temperature difference.

-   The U-factor and Resistance are the reciprocal of one another, and a graph showing their relationship is hyperbolic. The curve is asymptotic (approaching but never reaching zero). No matter how much insulation is used, the heat loss will always be above zero, and no matter how little insulation is used, the heat loss will be finite. The heat loss advantage of using a little insulation is great, but adding the same amount again has less advantage.

There is a point of little return, where adding more insulation has virtually no advantage. For example:

-   Adding 1" of extruded, expanded polystyrene to a thin sheet of aluminum increases the R value and resistance to heat flow from .79 to 5.79, or more than seven-fold. It decreases the U-factor from 1.26 to .17, which is a difference of 1.09.

-   Adding an additional inch of extruded, expanded polystyrene to the previous system changes the R value from 5.79 to 10.79. It decreases the U-factor from .17 to .09, which is a difference of .08, much lower than the previous figure.

-   Adding an additional inch of extruded, expanded polystyrene to the previous system changes the R value from 10.79 to 15.79. It decreases the U-factor from .09 to .06, a difference of .03.

-   Adding an additional inch of extruded, expanded polystyrene to the previous system changes the R value from 15.79 to 20.79, or less than 1-1/3 times the previous value. It decreases the U-factor from .06 to .05, a difference of .01.

The U-value is (approximately) proportional to the money spent on fuel. If the money value per Btu per year is $2.00, the savings per square foot in going from no insulation to 1" of insulation, as calculated above, is 1.09 x $2.00 = $2.18 (example in Southern New England). Under the same conditions, adding 3" of additional insulation will save $.24.

As the calculation shows, it makes more sense to add insulation to parts of a building which have little or no insulation, while adding more insulation to a well-insulated building may not pay for itself.

Table 1 indicates common thermal resistance factors, compiled from various sources, principally from *ASHRAE Fundamentals.* A complete tabulation along with the thermal properties of common building materials and assemblies can be found in the Appendix: Insulation.

There are also doors and windows in walls, form which thermal resistance figures are available from manufacturers (often given only for the center of the units, but properly calculated for the entire assembly, including perimeter losses). A typical 1-3/4" solid core wood flush door would have a thermal resistance of about 3.0. A typical clad double-hung wood window with insulating glass might have a thermal resistance of about 3.0.

For fixed glazing and other glazing not listed in manufacturers' literature, the following figures are typical. Note, however, that the thermal resistance figures for glass include the insulating values for interior and exterior air films, not the glass alone.

-   One sheet of 3/32" monolithic glass: 0.89.

-   One sheet of 1/4" float glass: 0.92. Note that the thickness of the glass has little effect on the thermal resistance; glass by itself is a very poor insulator.

-   Insulating glass composed of two sheets of 1/4" float glass and 1/2" dry air space: 2.08.

-   Insulating glass, as above, with low-emissivity coating, which reflects radiant heat back inside: 3.0.

-   Insulating glass, as above, with low-emissivity coating and also argon-filled space: 3.57.

For skylights, manufacturers' data is available. Most skylights have deep metal rafters, so that the metal area exposed to the inside air is large. The relative areas of glass and frame are important in estimating heat loss. The primary route of heat transfer from the outer rafter covers to the inner rafters is probably the metal fasteners. This suggests a good use of reinforced polymer fasteners, which have much lower thermal conductivity.

2   Insulation types

The practical ideal insulation is a vacuum or air when kept completely motionless in a space separating two solid components. Air, however, cannot be kept motionless even in a narrow vertical cavity (as in a wall assembly).

-   Convective currents develop, which transfer heat from the warm side of the cavity to the colder one.

-   Radiation from the warm side to the colder one takes place whether the air moves or is still.

-   In an air space broken up horizontally into tiny compartments convective currents can be effectively minimized, and the excellent insulating properties of still air utilized.

Mass type insulation reduces the flow of heat by preventing convection in entrapped air and also by forming a barrier to radiation. Some types (such as foamed plastics, or cellular glass) trap small quantities of air or other gaseous substances in closed cells. The heat flow through the cells is greatly reduced because convection currents are virtually eliminated in small cells. Size of the cells is critical:

- if they are too large, convective heat flow within them may become significant.

- if they are too small, or there are too few of them, conduction through the solid material surrounding the cells increases, offsetting the insulating value of the cells.

- granular materials (such as perlite, vermiculite, granulated foam) trap air in relatively large voids and consequently may have poorer insulating properties than materials with numerous small cells.

- fibrous materials (such as glass fibers or cellulose) depend for performance on the air's characteristic to cling to all exposed surfaces in thin films, thus reducing the heat flow.

Fibrous materials will perform best at a specified optimum density:

- if compressed to higher than optimum density, heat flow will increase since fiber will touch fiber and some of the surface air film will be lost.

- if fluffed up too much, more heat may be transmitted by convection or radiation through the large voids.

Reflective insulation—properly called radiant barriers—reduce the transfer of heat through air spaces by minimizing radiation of energy from the warmer, or emitting, surface of one of the components which enclose an air space to a colder, or receiving, surface of the other component:

- Emissivities of various building materials at the same surface temperature vary: radiation across an air space between two polished aluminum surfaces will be only about 3 percent of that between two black surfaces.

- Reflective materials act as insulation because of their low surface emissivity by reflecting incident radiant energy: in a cavity wall up to 60 percent of heat transfer is estimated to be by radiation. (See "Radiant Barrier Systems" in Chapter B3 Roofing).

Of all of these, the principal way in which thermal insulation works is the capacity of that material to resist heat flow by forming a tortuous path through the material, around voids. The more efficient insulation types are also made from materials with poor thermal conductance. Low emissivity materials and coatings reflect radiant heat.

Inorganic fibers, including fiber glass, mineral wool, spun basalt, asbestos, ceramic fibers, and others. These may be in the form of loose fibers, batts, and semi-rigid boards.

Asbestos was used in the past for thermal insulation. It has been found to cause cancer, and its use is restricted today. Other fibers are being used where asbestos used to be used. The following caution is the final paragraph in Skinner (1988): "After a thousand years of use, asbestos is being replaced by other, often fibrous, materials. It remains to be seen whether the substitutes will be as successful, commercially and financially, or more or less hazardous. We are certainly not going to do without fibrous inorganic materials nor expunge them from our environment."

Representative insulation materials include:

- Organic fibers, including cellulose fibers, bagasse, thatch, and wood fibers.

- Inorganic foams, including foamed glass, cellular concrete, hollow glass bead concrete, perlite, and vermiculite. Expanded poly-

styrene bead concrete can also be considered in this category, since the main function of the beads is to create voids in the concrete.

- Organic foams, including expanded polystyrene, polyurethane foam, and polyisocyanurate foam. Cork is a natural form of void-filled organic material.

- Metal foils and metal foil laminated on other materials. One form combines shiny aluminum foil with flexible polyethylene foam, and its manufacturer reports very favorable insulation values, especially where radiant heat is the predominant mode of heat transfer.

- Composite materials combining several of the materials listed above.

- Natural materials of low thermal resistance which, nevertheless, act as thermal insulators and also provide thermal storage include earth, masonry, and turf.

2.1 Perimeter and foundation insulation

Perimeter and other foundation insulation reduces heat loss through the foundation walls. It may be installed outside the foundations, inside the foundations, integral with the foundations, under slabs on grade, or in a combination of these locations. Common perimeter insulation types include expanded polystyrene board and fibrous glass board. There is some evidence that insects can attack polystyrene insulation, and cellular glass and fibrous glass insulation may be a good alternative material. (See "Residential Foundation Design" in Chapter A1 of this Volume).

2.2 Wall insulation

Selection of the type of insulation to be used should also include consideration of the method of its installation within the wall assembly. Wall assemblies may be insulated by:

- Batt insulation, between studs, available unfaced or with reflective foil of paper face.

- Foamed-in-place insulation between studs.

- Rigid-board insulation sheathing, placed on outside, within or on the inside face. Each location has an impact on constructability and attachment details.

- Foamed-in-place insulation may be placed within masonry cavities.

- Concrete Masonry Units (CMUs) available with rigid insulation inserts cast-in during fabrication.

- Rigid board insulation, laminated or clip attached, to inside face of masonry walls. Furring strips may have to be provided between the boards to facilitate attachment of interior facing materials.

- Loose insulation fill within masonry cavities.

- Monolithic in-place concrete assemblies may be insulated with rigid board insulation laminated or clip attached to interior face. Precast and tilt-up concrete assemblies may be Insulated by:

- Rigid board insulation between interior and exterior courses of a sandwich panel.

Water vapor migration is either by diffusion, or by air leakage; and is generally controlled by providing a vapor retarder on the warm side of the wall. Vapor retarders consist of materials that resist the diffusion of vapor through them under the action of a difference in pressure, such as plastic film metallic foil, coated paper, and, to a certain extent, applied coatings. (See "Moisture Control" in this Chapter).

Walls in existing buildings may be insulated with blown-in or foamed-in insulation, however, consideration should be given to:

- ensuring that all voids in wall assembly are completely filled.

- possible settlement of blown-in insulation.

- water vapor migrating by diffusion or by air leakage into the wall assembly, condensing within the wall and causing rapid deterioration of exterior facing or even the wall assembly itself.

2.2.1 Masonry wall insulation

- Expanded polystyrene board and some other materials can be installed in the cavities of masonry cavity walls and veneer walls. It can be made with an integral drainage course to keep the cavity drainage from being clogged with mortar.

- Fibrous glass and other inorganic fiber insulation boards may also be used in wall cavities.

Workmanship is especially important for masonry wall insulation. Once the walls are built, inspection is impossible. Unless the insulation is secured tightly to one of the wythes, cold air can circulate around and behind the insulation, greatly reducing its effect. Unsecured cavity insulation acts like a warm coat unbuttoned.

- Expanded polystyrene inserts are available for concrete masonry units, installed in the factory or field.

- Foam-in-place polyurethane and polyisocyanurate can be placed in wall cavities, where they expand and fill the space. An early example is the CBS building in Manhattan, Eero Saarinen, Architect.

- Various types of insulation can be installed on the inside of masonry walls, and special furring systems with little or no thermal bridging are available.

- An innovative system used for fruit storage and other uses incorporates a thick extruded, expanded polystyrene core and concrete faces, held together through the insulation with permanent reinforced polymer form ties.

- Exterior insulation and finish systems (EIFS) can be applied to the masonry exterior. The insulation may be extruded expanded polystyrene board or expanded polystyrene bead board. This system may be applied over other types of structure.

2.2.2 Frame wall insulation

- The most common type of insulation is fibrous glass batts. Other types of insulation for stud spaces include foam-in-place polyurethane, polyisocyanurate, and other plastic foams, other inorganic fiber batts, blown-in fibrous glass, blown in cellulose fibers, and reflective foil systems.

- If there are plumbing lines in exterior walls (not a good idea, but sometimes necessary), the insulation should be installed outside the pipes and, just as important, not inside the pipes. If the separation is small, use a highly efficient insulation.

- Various types of board insulation can be installed inside or outside the frame. They have the advantages of potentially high insulation value per unit thickness and not being penetrated by the framing members. The siding or interior finish is installed over them. If they are used instead of plywood sheathing, other forms of bracing are required to replace the shear value of the plywood.

- Integral wall materials and insulation.

- Wood fiber Portland cement roof panels have been used as wall panels with integral insulating qualities.

- Cellular concrete panels have been used as bearing and non-load bearing walls with integral insulation. Expanded polystyrene bead concrete has been used in the same way.

- Log houses have thick wooden walls, with fair insulating properties.

2.2.3 Roof and attic insulation

- Roof insulation may be installed above the roof structure. It has the advantage of being an unbroken layer. Available materials include organic foam board, organic and inorganic fiber board, cellular concrete, and cellular glass board. Protected membrane roof systems have the insulation above the membrane, and the insulation is extruded, expanded polystyrene board. The insulation above the membrane must be protected from sunlight, and it must be ballasted to prevent its blowing off. (See Chapter B3 Roofing in this Volume). *ASHRAE Fundamentals* recommends that roof insulation be placed above the structure of low-slope roofs. One important advantage is that the roof structure is protected from thermal changes and potential resulting damage.

- Roof insulation may be integral with the roof structure. Thick wood plank roof decks have enough insulating quality for mild climates. Another form of integral roof deck is Portland cement-wood fiber planks. Reinforced cellular concrete planks have been used as roof decking.

- Roof insulation may be installed under the roof. This is the normal method for steep roofs, and it is also used for low-slope roofs. The insulation may be between the attic floor joists, between the rafters, or in between. Common materials include fibrous glass batts, blown-in fibrous glass, and blown-in cellulose fibers. Other materials can also be used. It is difficult to avoid multiple penetrations of the insulation, and, in the writer's experience, it is common for there to be voids in the insulation.

- There are several other cautions regarding the use of roof and ceiling insulation between framing members. Unless the insulation is secured at the eaves, the insulation may impede proper insulation above it. Also, and probably more important, the insulation may lift and the eaves, and cold winter air may pass under the insulation. Attic insulation is sometimes be omitted over walls containing plumbing lines, thus chilling the occupants and freezing the pipes. It is prudent for the architect to inspect the attic insulation carefully before substantial completion of the construction. It is worth the expense to have thermographic studies made of buildings during their first winter, to verify proper placement of insulation.

- One of the most important functions of roof and attic insulation is to limit summer heat gain. The sun's heat is delivered as radiant heat. Light, heat-reflective roof coverings are available at little or no additional cost, and they are very effective. Radiant barrier systems, with the reflective surfaces facing air spaces, are also effective.

Soffit insulation has the same characteristics as ceiling insulation. If there are plumbing lines between the framing members, they should be above the insulation, and there should be no insulation above the pipes.

2.2.4 Basement insulation

- Basement ceiling insulation may be used in place of perimeter insulation and interior basement wall insulation. Depending on the use of the basement and the relative areas of the basement ceiling and walls, the choice may be the one or the other. The writer favors insulating the basement walls in most cases, but most houses with basements in the writer's area have insulated basement ceilings. The most common fault with basement ceiling insulation is that it tends to be incomplete. Even if just a few voids in the insulation exist per joist space, cold air from the basement will circulate above and below the insulation. This is the unbuttoned coat syndrome again. The writer recommends careful, void-free installation and application of a gypsum board ceiling or poultry netting retainer. Plumbing pipes are best kept above the insulation, and all mechanical equipment and pipes in the cold base-ment must be insulated.

- There may be a problem with insulated water pipes in very cold areas. If the water doesn't flow often, the insulation will only slow the water's freezing, not stop it. A heat source is needed to stop freezing.

3   Summary: Insulative envelope design

Design, calculation and installation details of insulation is often speci-fied by rote reference to prevailing codes and standards, but this ap-proach, however expeditious, fails to benefit from the interactive role of thermal insulation, moisture control and protection of building materials. There are substantial economies to be realized through op-timally insulated envelopes that account for the role that thermal mass and solar and other time lag factors might serve in balancing reducing HVAC equipment sizing and operating costs.

3.1   Thermal storage capacity

The thermal mass of masonry and concrete walls can be used in heat loss calculations to show lowered heat loss. The method is described in Brick Institute of America and National Concrete Masonry Asso-ciation publications. Heat storage capacity of walls can be used to significant advantage:

- to reduce peak heat gain and thereby reduce cooling loads on mechanical equipment (when the masonry surface is exposed to interior air).

- to reduce heat losses through timelag (when there is partial to significant heat flow through the envelope).

- to store heat absorbed through solar energy and release it when needed (as in glass-covered masonry walls or in interior masonry exposed to solar irradiation).

To analyze time lag and heat storage capacity of a design, a "dynamic analysis" of heat gain/ loss is required that takes into account the hourly changes in weather conditions as well as the thermal storage capacity of the structure, and closely predicts the peak loads required to deter-mine the size of equipment needed to control the interior environ-ment of a structure.

3.2   Water vapor condensation

The dew point method of calculating whether or not water vapor con-densation will occur is made determinate by the existence of one va-por retarder. However, recent research has shown that vapor move-ment in buildings is much more complex than was thought. Air al-most always contains a certain amount of water vapor. The maximum amount of vapor that can be contained at constant pressure is directly proportional to the temperature of the air/ vapor mixture:

- When air at a given temperature, saturated with water vapor, is cooled, or comes into contact with a colder surface, water vapor will continuously condense as long as the temperature of the air/ vapor mixture drops.

- Insulation incorporated into assemblies of an enclosure changes the temperature gradients through them, thereby increasing the likelihood of condensation within the assemblies:

- Condensation may occur within the insulation, if it is permeable, and increase its density, thereby lowering its thermal resistance.

The analysis of water vapor transport and moisture control is described in the ensuing article "Moisture Control" in this Chapter. Here, a brief comment is needed in order to emphasize that insulation and mois-ture control issues must be considered together in designing the build-ing envelope and assembly.

In its simplest form, water vapor condensation requires low tempera-tures and high partial vapor pressure. "Partial vapor pressure" is the

absolute (not relative) humidity, or the part of the air pressure which is exerted by the water vapor in the air. Under normal temperatures fit for human life, water vapor makes up a relatively small part of the total air pressure:

- at 0F(-18°C), partial vapor pressure at saturation is approximately 1/10th of 1% of the air pressure.

- at 32F (0°C), partial vapor pressure is 6/10 of 1%.

- at 70F (21°C), partial vapor pressure is 2-1/2%.

- at 100F (38°C), partial vapor pressure is 6%.

Condensation will not occur unless the partial vapor pressure is high enough and the temperature is low enough. To predict whether water vapor condensation will occur, the conditions must be quantified, and fairly complex calculations are required. Most building construction is affected by water vapor condensation, and the effect is mostly harm-ful. Examples are wet insulation, rotting wood structure, and damp, spalling masonry.

3.3   Insulation, envelope and HVAC systems

Determining how much insulation to use should involve the follow-ing minimum considerations:

- Conforming to code requirements. This step alone may come close to being a proper level or amount of insulation, but this judgment has to be considered in terms of site and building specific factors. Higher insulation values may permit lower mechanical system installation sizing and usage.

- Making a best guess as to the likelihood of future energy costs and cost escalation compared to general inflation. Unless one has special information, assume that energy inflation will approxi-mate general inflation.

- Drawing a graph, or making a series of calculations, of dollar sav-ings vs. the cost of additional insulation. After a certain increase in insulation thickness, the added provision of insulation may re-quire higher costs for the envelope. For complex buildings, utili-zation of computer simulation programs is required for more ac-curate thermal dynamic analysis.

- Adding factors having to do with the durability of the building and its possible vulnerability to condensation, as affected by insu-lation.

- Adding the time-value of money.

- Note that too much insulation may be wasteful of irreplaceable resources and money.

- Adding ethical factors regarding non-cash values of reducing fuel use and using resources to increase the insulation.

The role and effectiveness of thermal resistance of the building enve-lope is dependent on these dynamic variables:

- the daily and seasonal temperatures imposed by weather, as a func-tion of average and extreme climate norms.

- the daily flux of internal heat gain, as a function of occupancy, building type, electric lighting and equipment loads.

- the amount and placement of windows and skylights, especially the respective benefit or liability of solar heat gain during underheated or overheated periods.

- the HVAC system type, thermal controls and response time of the HVAC system.

- occupancy profile of the building, for example, limited to day-time use compared to 24 hour occupancy.

For example:
- a well insulated exterior wall (including high R windows), may preclude the need for perimeter heating, or may permit downsized heating and cooling plant capacity, thus saving in HVAC installation and operating costs.

- thermal mass exposed to the building interior and insulated on the outside will serve as a "heat sink" for typically overheated hours and occupancy conditions, thus reducing cooling plant sizes and operating costs.

- poorly insluated masonry structures will require longer "start up" of heating time to reach comfortable indoor air and radiant surface temperatures.

- the interior temperature of a well insulated structure that is used only during the day may "float," that is, remain relatively stable with the HVAC system turned down or off, requiring less energy and less "start up" time at the beginning of the following day.

- well insulated structures, on the other hand, require careful provision of fresh-air ventilation supplied to all portions of the space, but especially those subject to temperature flux (such as near window areas).

- an improperly insulated building envelope (wall or roof) may create moisture control and condensation, potentially damaging to both the building envelope and to objects within (such as in museums).

For all of these reasons, the determination of insulation values for major building components (ceilings/roofs, walls and windows) needs to be analyzed alongside thermal mass, building occupancy and equipment loads, lighting and mechanical system design and sizing.

The relative effectiveness of insulation, thermal mass for heat storage, and solar irradiation through windows requires complex calculations, now possible through widely available computer simulation programs. Such analysis is needed to "optimize" the building envelope design and often demonstrates that reduced mechanical system sizing and cycling are possible with increases of thermal insulation and thermal mass, creating design guidelines for cost-justified improvements in the building envelope.▶

Additional references

Fanger, P. O. 1970. *Thermal Comfort, Analysis and Applications in Environmental Engineering.* New York: McGraw-Hill.

Sixth Canadian Masonry Symposium. 1992. *Proceedings of the Sixth Canadian Masonry Symposium.* Saskatoon, Canada: Civil Engineering Department, University of Saskatchewan.

Skinner, H. Catherine, *et al.* 1988, *Asbestos and Other Fibrous Materials.* New York, Oxford University Press.

Trechsel, Heinz R., editor, *Moisture Control in Buildings*, 1994. Philadelphia, PA: American Society for Testing and Materials (ASTM) .

U. S. HUD. 1994. *Design Guide for Frost-protected Shallow Footings.* Washington, DC: Department of Housing and Urban Development, Office of Policy Development and Research.

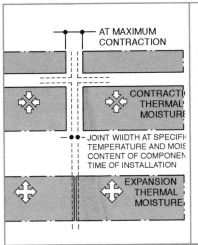

AT MAXIMUM CONTRACTION

CONTRACTI[ON] THERMA[L] MOISTURE

JOINT WIIDTH AT SPECIFI[C] TEMPERATURE AND MOIS[TURE] CONTENT OF COMPONEN[TS] TIME OF INSTALLATION

EXPANSION THERMAL MOISTURE

Building movement

Summary: Causes for building movement include changes in thermal, moisture and humidity conditions, structural failure and imposed stresses, including expansive clay movement under foundations. This article discusses how an architect can design details to accommodate such dimensional movement.

Key words: expansion coefficient, frost expansion, joint sealants, movement joints, thermal expansion.

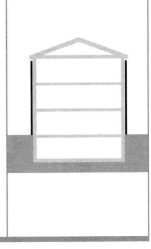

SHELL B2

All materials expand or contract when heated or cooled and/or when taking on moisture or drying. While much of this movement may occur at the time of construction, the process of movement of materials and components in buildings is continuous., often referred to colloquially as the process of "breathing." For design analysis, three types of movement in buildings can be characterized as linear, differential and transverse.

- *Linear movement* (Fig. 1), or dimensional change within building components, is a continual process due to variations:

  - in internal temperature of the components regardless of material used.

  - in exterior temperatures.

- *Differential movement* (Fig. 2), differential dimensional changes between components:

  - different coefficients of expansion and contraction of the components. For example, a 10 ft. sq. panel of aluminum will contract .155 in. For a temperature drop of 100F; an adjacent masonry panel of the same size will only contract .037 inches, or only 20% as much, under the same conditions.

  - different rates of shrinkage and swelling due to changes in internal moisture content between components, or within the component. Dimensional changes in wood during loss or gain of moisture vary depending on whether expansion is tangential in the direction of growth rings, or radial across growth rings. A piece of green Douglas fir will shrink about 1.5% tangentially and about 2.5% radially when dried to 20% moisture content, the volumetric change being about 3.7%.

  - differential movement may also result from movements in the supporting frame acting simultaneously with thermal and/or moisture movements.

- *Transverse movement* (Fig. 3) or movement perpendicular to the plane of components, may result from differences in the magnitude of lateral loads action on adjacent components or from bending stresses:

  - differences in pressures on vertical components, such as wall panels.

  - moving loads over horizontal components, when the edge of one is free to deflect.

- deflection due to thermal or moisture movement in a component with two edges restrained which is adjacent to an unrestrained component.

- deflection due to horizontal loads on a free edge of a component next to an attached edge of another component.

- differences in deflection between a relatively stiff component next to a flexible one.

- deflection in two components with rigid, spaced connections between them, when they are restrained at their edges or when under lateral load.

- deformation in components due to differentials in temperature between opposite faces of one component, or differences in moisture gain/loss, such a warping in wood.

The thermal movement behavior of common building materials is indicated in Table A. Coefficients of expansion are listed in unit-per-degree temperature difference. Coefficients of expansion are without linear dimension, being feet/feet, meter/meter, and cubit/cubit. The values differ according to which temperature scale one uses. Coefficients of expansion for other materials are listed in the "Miscellaneous" section of the *A.I.S.C. Steel Construction Manual*, where the coefficients listed are per 100F, while those listed below are per degree, as in Brick Institute of America (1991) and in other references.

But reader beware: values for coefficients of thermal expansion vary, sometimes greatly, according to source and exact material. Example: While single values for concrete are listed in various references, other references indicate a 100% difference in coefficient of expansion depending on the aggregate used. Also, the coefficient of expansion is not truly uniform throughout the full range of temperatures. Prudent practice is to assume a little more movement than tabulated values and resulting calculations indicate.

For coal-tar bitumen, the coefficient listed in Table A is higher than that shown for built-up roofing, organic felt, and asphalt. At higher temperatures, the coefficient is less. This is why some roofs split in very cold weather. Fiberglass felts, with greater strength than organic felts, are more resistant to splitting. Organic felts are weaker in the transverse direction; fiberglass felts are approximately equal in strength in all directions. Membrane roofing materials generally become flexible when warm, so thermal expansion of the roof membrane is not a

---

Author: Donald Baerman, AIA

Credits: Figs. 1 thru 3 are from *Sweets Catalog File*. Other drawings created by Wynne Mun.

References: Gordon, J. E. 1988. *The Science of Structures and Materials.* New York: Scientific American Library.

Additional references are included at the end of this article.

B2 SHELL

LINEAR

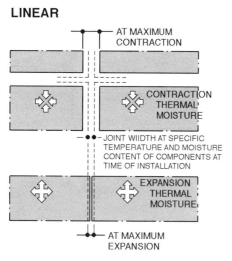

Fig. 1 Linear movement

DIFFERENTIAL

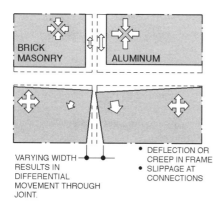

Fig. 2 Differential movement

TRANSVERSE

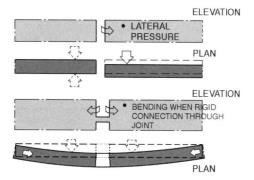

Fig. 3. Transverse movement

Table A. Coefficients of expansion of common building materials.

Material	Coefficient of expansion per Degree F.	Coefficient of expansion per Degree C.	Movement per 100F per 100'
Aluminum	.0000128	.0000230	1.54"
Milled Steel:	.0000065	.0000117	0.78"
Granite; limestone similar:	.0000047	.0000085	0.56"
Brick masonry:	.0000036	.0000065	0.43"
Fire clay brick masonry:	.0000025	.0000045	0.30"
CMU, normal aggregate:	.0000052	.0000094	0.62"
CMU, lightweight aggregate:	.0000031 to .0000046	.0000056 to .0000083	0.37" to 0.55"
Concrete, limestone aggregate:	.0000033	.0000060	0.40"
Concrete, traprock aggregate.	.0000039	.0000070	0.47"
Concrete, granite aggregate:	.0000044	.0000080	0.53"
Concrete, certain l.w. agg.:	.0000050	.0000090	0.60"
Concrete, quartzite aggregate:	.0000067	.0000120	0.80"
Fir, parallel to the grain:	.0000021	.0000038	0.25" [1]
Fir perpendicular to the grain:	.000032.	.000058	6.91"
Glass:	.000008.	.000014	0.96"
"Pyrex" glass:	.0000018	.0000032	0.22" [2]
Polycarbonate glazing sheet:	.000037	.000067	4.44" [3]
Built-up roofing, felt and asphalt, range 0F—30F:	.000037	.000067	4.4"
Reinforced plastics:	.000035	.000063	4.2"
Aramid fibers:	.000001	.0000018	0.12" [4]
Polyethylene:	.000195	.000351	23.4"

Notes:
[1] This is a very low value (but not zero).
[2] Source: Corning Glass Works.
[3] This value is almost 5 times as great as that of glass; glazing details may have to be modified to accommodate this movement.
[4] Note that this is an extremely low value. Source: Akzo Fibers Division.

problem. These materials become more rigid when cold, so shrinkage may cause damage if the membrane is not adequately anchored.

Possible causes of thermal movement

- Daily or seasonal air temperature changes.

- Diurnal movement of the sun and its heating effects, including reflection from adjacent surfaces, cooling winds, snow, ice and rain.

- Thin materials exposed to the environment and coupled to massive materials, even if the coefficients of expansion of the two materials are similar, will change temperature more rapidly.

- Loss of initial heat from hydration of massive concrete.

- Cooling by operation of building environmental control equipment, such as air conditioning and cold storage systems.

- Heating by operation of fuel-burning equipment and chimneys.

- Fire. This is normally the most severe thermal change which can affect buildings. Even components which are not destroyed by fire can be severely damaged by thermal movement, and the damage may not be immediately evident.

- Low temperatures before occupancy of building and during abandonment. Some of the greatest "normal" stresses may be imposed during construction.

- Differential movement occurs when different parts of a system are exposed to different temperatures. For example, a highly insulated building with closely controlled interior temperatures experiences little temperature change and therefore little thermally induced movement on the inside of the walls. The outer portion of the walls may vary greatly in temperature, from below 0F (-17.8°C) up to 140F (60°C) or more for dark surfaces in the sun. Roofs, oriented nearly perpendicular to the noonday sun in summer, may get even hotter. The exterior of well-insulated buildings experience greater thermal movement than those of poorly-insulated buildings.

- Building components intended not to change temperature may be exposed to temperature changes as a result of insulation failure. If, for example, the roof insulation becomes saturated with water, then the structural roof deck may get hotter in summer and cooler in winter than was anticipated by the design.

Examples of thermal movement problems

- Masonry walls expand in summer due to seasonal warming. In winter, due to seasonal cooling and having little tensile strength, they may crack rather than returning to their initial size. Brick arches and lintels, especially soldier and rowlock-coursed lintels, having more mortar joints than the adjoining masonry, are highly resistant to thermal cracking. Heavy, solid masonry buildings with heated interiors do not generally suffer damage from thermal movement as much as insulated buildings, but elements exposed on both sides to the exterior, such as parapets, do suffer damage.

- Damage from thermal expansion and shrinkage does not necessarily occur within the first year. Such damage may take many years to become visible.

- Tinted glass which is partly exposed to the sun and partly in shade may shatter.

- Massive concrete structures may become hot during hydration of the cement, and may shrink and crack when this internal heat has passed out of them.

- In winter the outside of chimneys become cold while the flue becomes hot. If the two are rigidly connected, the outside is exposed to tensile stresses and possibly to cracking.

- Concrete lintels in brick walls often show cracks at the end mortar joints. There are several causes:

  - Concrete shrinks with age, while brick expands with age.

  - There are multiple mortar joints in the brick, while the lintel has joints at the ends only. Mortar joints are, or should be, more flexible than the masonry units.

  - Concrete has a higher coefficient of thermal expansion than brick.

- Rigid building elements may expand to the extreme during fires, thus destroying or lessening the structural integrity of the building.

- A building interior designed to undergo slight change of temperature during its service life may be exposed to very low or high temperatures during construction.

Calculating movement

It is possible to calculate the probable maximum movement of building components, using the coefficients listed in Table A. The length of the element multiplied by the thermal difference multiplied by the coefficient of expansion gives the movement length.

- *Example 1:* A dark masonry wall 100 ft. long in New England. Assume that it was built at 50F average temperature.

  - In summer assume that the wall is heated by sunlight to 130F. The temperature difference from built condition to service condition is 80F. Therefore, 80F X 100' X .0000034 = .0271 ft. = .33 in.

  - In winter assume that the wall occasionally chills to 0F. The temperature difference is 50F. Therefore, 50F X 100' X .0000034 = .2 in.

Since the summer condition causes the greater movement, design for that figure. If the wall were built in hotter or colder weather, the expansion or contraction from the "as built" size would be greater. In this case the extremes are unlikely, since it would be improper to build the wall below 40F or above 90F.

It is not always evident why a wall develops one large crack rather than several smaller cracks. To some extent this can be predicted empirically, by observing similar construction. For example, it appears that a long, narrow panel is more likely to crack more often than a similar panel which is broader, and cracks usually occur where walls are weakened by doors and windows. "Fracture mechanics" relates to such phenomena; see Gordon (1988) for an elementary discussion of fracture mechanics.

There are numerous examples of uninsulated solid masonry buildings which do not undergo cracking from thermal movement. The probable reason is that the interior is always at a stable temperature and the exterior is structurally bonded to it. The stress is accommodated by elastic behavior in the masonry. It is common, however, for parapets of such buildings to crack.

Design of flexible movement joints

Flexible movement joints may extend through the building, dividing the building into parts which may expand and contract independently of one another. It is important that the flexible movement joints in the various components be located in line or close together. Traditionally such joints are called "expansion joints."

Flexible movement joints may simply extend through walls and other parts of the exterior closure. They allow differential movement of the components in which they occur. Such joints are sometimes called "control joints," but that term is not in accord with current usage. Sources of movement joint details for some different types of construction. For brick masonry, see Brick Institute of America (1991). For concrete masonry, see NCMA (1973). Fig. 4 shows one type of movement joint.

SHELL

B2

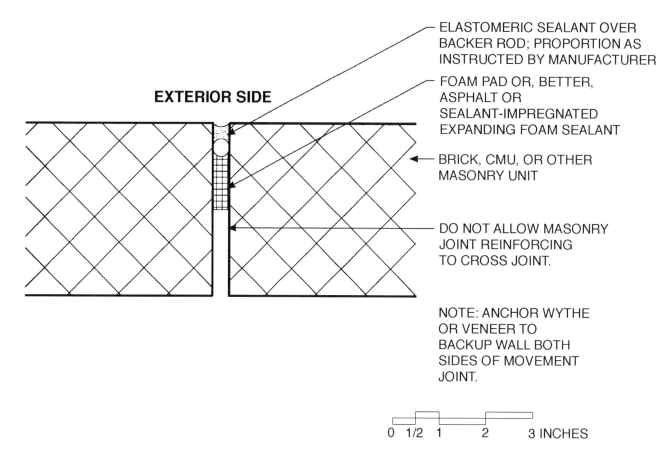

EXTERIOR SIDE

ELASTOMERIC SEALANT OVER
BACKER ROD; PROPORTION AS
INSTRUCTED BY MANUFACTURER

FOAM PAD OR, BETTER,
ASPHALT OR
SEALANT-IMPREGNATED
EXPANDING FOAM SEALANT

BRICK, CMU, OR OTHER
MASONRY UNIT

DO NOT ALLOW MASONRY
JOINT REINFORCING
TO CROSS JOINT.

NOTE: ANCHOR WYTHE
OR VENEER TO
BACKUP WALL BOTH
SIDES OF MOVEMENT
JOINT.

0   1/2   1   2   3 INCHES

Fig. 4. Flexible movement joint

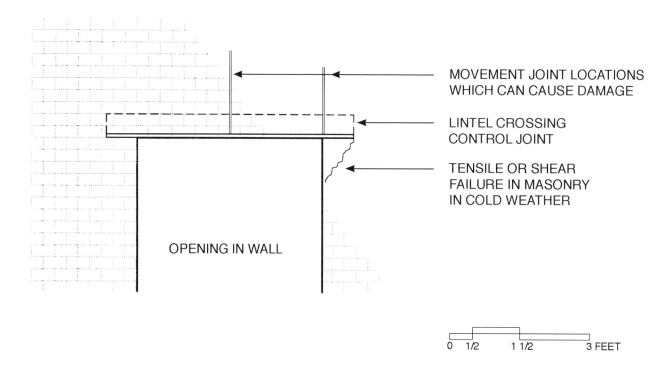

MOVEMENT JOINT LOCATIONS
WHICH CAN CAUSE DAMAGE

LINTEL CROSSING
CONTROL JOINT

TENSILE OR SHEAR
FAILURE IN MASONRY
IN COLD WEATHER

OPENING IN WALL

0   1/2   1 1/2   3 FEET

Fig. 5. Masonry damage from lintel crossing movement joint

Rules of thumb for placement of flexible movement joints for different types of construction in temperate climates include:

- Solid brick wall, heated and not insulated: joints placement every 250 ft. (76 m) is the industry recommendation; this author recommends 80 ft. (24 m).

- Insulated brick cavity or veneer wall with window and door openings, outer wythe: placement every 100 ft. (30.5 m) is industry recommendation; this author recommends 40 ft. (12 m). This guideline is also recommended for parapets and unheated buildings. The brick recommendations do not mention the ratio of height to length. If the height is small, the writer recommends spacing the joints closer to one another.

- For concrete masonry ("block") walls, insulated and heated and with masonry joint reinforcement placed 16 in. (40.6 cm.) o.c., the industry recommendation is that the "panel length" (a "panel" being defined as the section isolated by movement joint) should be no more than three times as long as it is high and no more than 50 ft. (15 m) in length between joints. This author recommends 30 ft. (9 m) between joints. If the wall is longer than three times as long as it is high, or if it is unheated, this author recommends 20 ft. (6 m).

The above guidelines assume a temperate climate similar to that of the middle part of the United States, which experiences an average temperature range of from -10 to +90F (-23 to +32°C). In climates with a smaller temperature range, the spacing for movement joints may be increased. In climates with larger temperature range, they should be decreased. For example, Saskatoon, Canada has a temperature range from -40 to 104F (-40 to +40°C), and thus the temperature range differential is 144F (80°C)!

Also recommended is the use of grouted, reinforced bond beams and grouted, reinforced intermittent cores in masonry. This practice permits longer panels between joints. Post-tensioned bond beams permit yet longer panels between joints.

Openings and abrupt changes in shape create stress concentrations and may require strategically located movement joints even if the spacing is not great. Movement joints should not intersect lintels over openings (Fig. 5).

To design the movement joints

- Calculate the temperature differential. The extent of movement will vary with the temperature during construction and in service. Since the designer may not be able to predict this, assume the worst. For example, if a wall will vary in temperature from -10F to 130F (23°C to 55°C) , and if the specifications permit work to take place between 40F to 90F (4°C to 32°C), the possible extremes are:

- Wall built at 40F. In service it may get 50F colder and 90F warmer. Use 90F. as the temperature differential.

- Wall built at 90F. In services it may get 100F colder and 40F warmer. Use 100F. as the temperature differential.

- The larger temperature differential is 100F.

- *Example 2a:* Assume, for an example, insulated brick masonry with movement joints 40 ft. apart. The 40 ft. panel length X 100F temperature differential X coefficient of thermal expansion of .0000034 = .014 ft. = .16 in. If the sealant to be used in the joint permits 25% movement, the joint must be at least 4 times the movement, or 0.67 in. With more extensible and compressible sealants, the joint width can be less wide. The author recommends never designing movement joints less than about 3/8" wide.

- *Example 2b:* If, as a second example, assume you wish to follow industry recommendations instead of the author's more conserva-

tive ones. Suppose that the panels are 100 ft. long and that the other parameters do not change. The movement will then be .034 ft. = .41 in. If the sealant permits 25% movement (such as acrylic polymeric sealant), the joint should be 1.63 in. wide. If the sealant permits 50% extension or compression, the joint could theoretically be .81 in. wide. However, buildings don't always perform as intended. We cannot reasonably assume that the center of each panel will remain fixed and that the ends will move equally. Sometimes the fixed portion of the panel is at one end or near it. Suppose the two adjacent panels, as described in this example, "stick fast" near their far ends. The common joint will then move more than 3/4 in., and a 3/4 in. wide joint may extend to 1-1/2 in. Recommendation: be conservative; few architects can reasonably regret having called for too many and too wide movement joints. Careful and clever design can make movement joints nearly invisible.

One should consider the penetrations which may resist the intended movement. A solidly grouted pipe passing through a wall may be subjected to stress when the wall moves. A metal roof may impose stresses on flashed vents and skylights which penetrate it. Windows anchored to the inside and the outside of a wall may be stressed by movement of the outer wythe.

Components with differing thermal expansion characteristics, such as a steel frame and a masonry wall, should be isolated from one another enough to allow differential movement. Anchorage should be flexible. Although steel and masonry have similar coefficients of expansion, they are often exposed to different temperatures.

A masonry wall composed of brick, with a lower coefficient of expansion on the outside, and Concrete Masonry Units (CMU), with a higher coefficient of expansion on the inside, is somewhat self-compensating. The outer wythe is exposed to greater temperature changes and has a lower coefficient of thermal expansion. Thus the joints on the inside may be reasonably placed far apart.

Moisture expansion and shrinkage

Wood

Wood, as cut, contains several kinds of moisture. Free moisture filling the cells does not affect shrinkage. Chemically combined water (the "hydrate" of carbohydrate) is not lost unless the wood burns, rots, and is digested by insects. The water, and the loss of water, which causes shrinkage, is absorbed and adsorbed on the cell walls.

When wood is dried below 25-30% moisture content, the water on the cell walls is lost, and the wood experiences shrinkage. The point at which shrinkage starts is called the "fiber saturation point." Throughout the normal range of service conditions, the wood expands during periods of high humidity and shrinks during periods of low humidity. The expansion of wood varies approximately (but only approximately) with the relative humidity. A table giving moisture content at various temperatures and relative humidities is found in Forest Products Laboratory (1987). By combining the results of this table with tables giving the expansion by moisture content in the same reference, one can calculate the relationship of humidity and moisture expansion as a function of grain or cut (Fig. 6).

- The expansion and shrinkage is least in the direction of the grain, almost (but not quite) nil.

- The expansion and shrinkage is moderately high perpendicular to the growth rings. For Douglas fir the difference, from fiber-saturated to oven dry, is about 4.1%.

- The expansion and shrinkage is highest tangential to the growth rings. For Douglas fir the difference from fiber-saturated to oven dry is about 7.6%.

B2 SHELL

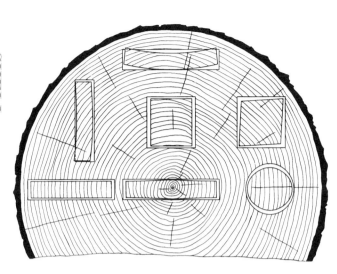

Fig. 6. Variations in wood cuts and grains. Source: Forest Products Laboratory (1987).

- The in-service range of moisture content of wood is not always as great as is shown above. However, the shrinkage from "S-GRN" to the dryness experienced in an unhumidified building in winter in cold climates may approximate that range.

- Shrinkage is approximately proportional; for a given change in moisture from fiber-saturation point to oven dry, the same proportional change occurs in shrinkage.

Normally, for rough framing of buildings, the moisture content should be below 19% by weight, and for critical applications, it is available dried to 15% moisture content. If the lumber is first dried, then surfaced (planed to a standard size), the grade stamp will show "S-DRY" or "MC-15" (15% moisture content). Since all lumber is not identical, the lumber is more uniform in size if it is surfaced after drying. If uniformity is not important, lumber which is labeled "S-GRN" (surfaced "green" before drying) may be used if it is tested for moisture content before use. Or if shrinkage doesn't matter at all, the wood may be used at whatever moisture content it happens to have upon delivery.

Relatively inexpensive moisture meters are available for testing wood on the job. A number of such instruments are sold by PRG and by Delmhorst (see Additional References below). To measure the inner parts of framing lumber, order hammer-driven electrodes.

Finish woodwork is normally milled at about 12% moisture content and allowed to reach equilibrium moisture content in its place of installation. There is an incorrect belief that it makes no difference whether the wood is dry or not, since, after the first rain, it's saturated with water anyway. That isn't usually true.

To avoid problems with movement of wood

- Avoid wood framing with a lot of horizontal-grain wood framing in conjunction with a material which does not have the same ex-

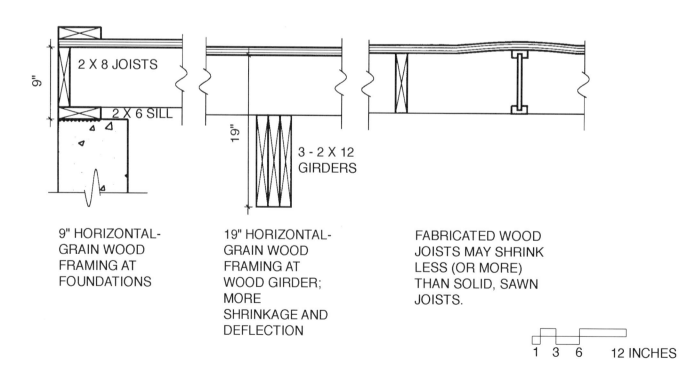

9" HORIZONTAL-GRAIN WOOD FRAMING AT FOUNDATIONS

19" HORIZONTAL-GRAIN WOOD FRAMING AT WOOD GIRDER; MORE SHRINKAGE AND DEFLECTION

FABRICATED WOOD JOISTS MAY SHRINK LESS (OR MORE) THAN SOLID, SAWN JOISTS.

Fig. 7. Differential wood framing shrinkage

pansion characteristics. For example, if you intend to apply conventional stucco or brick veneer to a wood frame building, use balloon framing instead of platform framing. If you must apply stucco or brick veneer to a building with platform framing, consider continuous vertical furring or horizontal expansion joints at the floor framing.

- The depth of horizontal wood framing should be the same throughout the structure. If you design the framing above foundations with 12 in. of horizontal framing lumber, there should be 12 in. of horizontal framing lumber at the girders also. This can be accomplished by using steel girders or by framing the joists nearly flush with wood girders, using multi-nailed joist hangers, not straps (Fig. 7).

- Be careful about using sawn lumber and fabricated structural wood products together; if one shrinks more than the other the floors and ceilings may be uneven.

- Avoid massive wooden members over which gypsum wallboard or plaster is to be applied. Such a detail will almost certainly crack. If you must have massive wooden members covered with wallboard, detail resilient furring between the two, or separate the support for the finish from the structural members (Fig. 8).

- When applying wood siding, do not nail each course with multiple nails too far apart. For board-and-batten siding, nail boards midway between battens, and nail battens through the joint between the boards. Nail wide clapboards just above the top of the course below. Don't allow T&G or board siding to be installed too tight; allow for expansion. Leave gaps between wooden shingles.

- Leave gaps of at least 1/8 in. between the sides and ends of plywood panels. If the plywood is for ceramic tile installation, follow Tile Council of America recommendations (1/8 in. gaps).

SHELL   **B2**

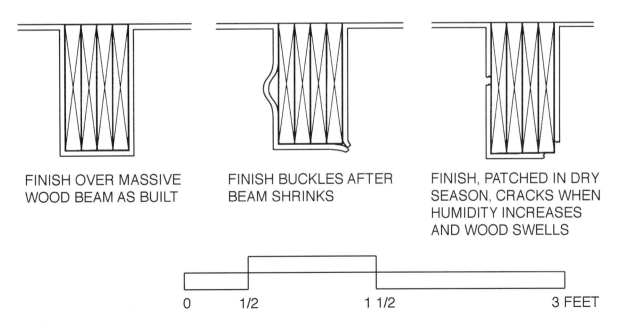

FINISH OVER MASSIVE
WOOD BEAM AS BUILT

FINISH BUCKLES AFTER
BEAM SHRINKS

FINISH, PATCHED IN DRY
SEASON, CRACKS WHEN
HUMIDITY INCREASES
AND WOOD SWELLS

0   1/2   1 1/2   3 FEET

Fig. 8. Rigid finish over massive wooden members

SHELL

B2

- Detail woodwork not to show shrinkage cracks.

- Real stile and rail paneling must have expansion space around the panels, and the panels should not be rigidly mounted.

- Do not install wood shingles tight to one another.

- If possible, allow woodwork and wood floors to reach equilibrium moisture before installing them. Use a moisture meter to verify this. If at all possible, the humidity in the space while the woodwork is being installed should be close to that which will prevail during occupancy.

- Wooden flooring is prone to moisture expansion problems, and "floating" wooden flooring is especially prone to such problems.

- For "floating" wooden flooring, the subfloor should be in two layers, and the layers should be thoroughly adhered and fastened to one another to act as a continuous diaphragm. As the floor shrinks in times of low humidity, it must have the strength to retain its integrity.

- There should be an expansion space around the entire perimeter. This can be hidden by the wall base (Fig. 9).

- If the humidity conditions are expected to vary greatly between installation and service, or during service, make allowances during installation. If the floor is installed during very dry conditions (cold weather, heated interior, and no humidification), the flooring should not be installed tight; leave a little space between the strips. If the floor is installed during very humid conditions, drive the strips tight to one another.

- For extreme variation in humidity, as in a vacation house left unoccupied in winter, treat the wood with a preservative water-repellent solution before installation. Sanding will remove the treated top wood, but the finish will serve the same purpose. And don't expect a smooth-as-glass finish and total absence of gaps in such buildings.

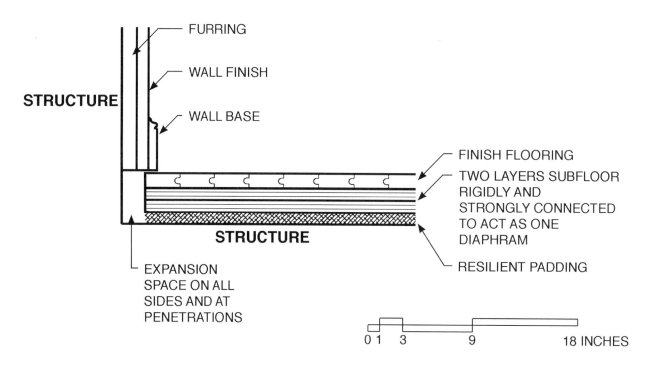

Fig. 9. Floating wood floor

For demanding applications, wood should be aged long enough not only for drying but to relax its internal stresses and become stable with prevailing site conditions. In the writer's opinion, the frequent splitting and disntegrating of exterior wood columns is mainly due to the wood's not being aged and selected as it once was. To offer an extreme but illustrative case of the level of care taken in woodcraft, one major concert piano manufacturer selects its wood, ages it outdoors under cover for a year, then discards 90%, kiln-dries the remainder and further rejects half of that, culling only 5% of the original for use in manufacture of the final instrument.

Concrete and concrete masonry
Concrete shrinks as the water adsorbed on the surfaces of the calcium silicate hydrate crystals in the hydrated cement paste dries, and it shrinks as the water in the small capillaries dries. In general the shrinkage of concrete is minimized if the water/cement ratio is kept as low as practicable.

- Concrete masonry is subject to expansion and shrinkage as is concrete. Lightweight masonry units are more likely to exhibit this characteristic than normal weight units.

- Moisture-controlled masonry units are more stable than uncontrolled ones.

- The partially-completed and completed masonry should be protected against rain and snow by covering the work.

Tile and other thin finishes
The backer board should have low expansion and shrinkage from moisture and temperature, similar to those of the tile. Glass-reinforced mortar board and glass-reinforced and faced gypsum sheathing are appropriate; products containing wood fiber are not.

- The backer board edges should be spaced apart as recommended by its manufacturer. Joints in the tile should correspond to joints in the backer board.

- Ceramic tile will expand as it ages. Sealant in the joints, or an elastic latex mortar, or both will help absorb the movement harmlessly (Fig. 10).

Expansive clays
Certain clays, such as bentonite, absorb many times their volume in water and expand accordingly. This expansion in and around building foundation soils reportedly represents one of the largest natural building destroyers in the U. S., contending in numbers with building losses from earthquakes, floods, and windstorms. The usual mechanism is that the placement of the building on the expansive clay soil interrupts normal evaporation and causes the clays to become wetter and to expand. Other types of moisture change, such as discharge of roof and paving drainage near a building, have similar effects. The expansive force is probably most destructive on large, lightly loaded members such as slabs on grade. These members are displaced upward.

If your proposed site has expansive clay soils, or if there is any substantial probability of its having them, the safe course if to retain a geotechnical engineer familiar with the local conditions and to design accordingly. The local building department should be consulted as to the prevalence of expansive clays in the area.

One effective method of avoiding damage from expansive clay soil is called "void forming." A compressible material such as thick corrugated cardboard is used to form slabs on grade, which slabs must be reinforced as supported slabs. The void forms serve only as the base on which the concrete is placed. When the clay expands, it crushes the cardboard. Another method is to form the slabs above the soil. Void forming and other construction methods to avoid damage from expansive clay soils should be designed by geotechnical engineers familiar with the problem.

Freezing, frost heaving, and salt crystallization
Freezing of water in absorbent building materials may cause the materials to burst. For example, water-saturated masonry and concrete can disintegrate after freezing.

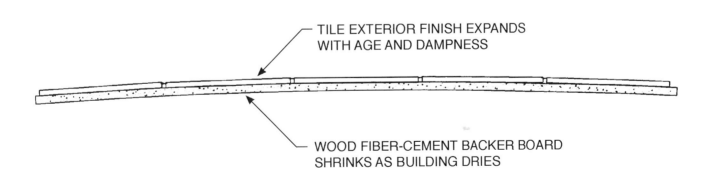

Fig. 10. Bowing from coupled materials with different expansion characteristics and exposures

TILE EXTERIOR FINISH EXPANDS WITH AGE AND DAMPNESS

WOOD FIBER-CEMENT BACKER BOARD SHRINKS AS BUILDING DRIES

Frost heaving can move and damage buildings. Water-laden soil can expand upon freezing and cause enough upward pressure to damage the building or component.

Keep water away from the footings by providing porous fill and drainage. Prevent freezing of the soil under the footings by using adequate soil cover or, under special conditions, by using insulation below grade. Use of insulation to allow the footings to be closer to grade may require convincing the building official that the system is valid (see U. S. HUD 1994).

The insulation method of frost protection is especially useful in building alterations. Remember that frost heaving could damage slabs-on-grade before the building is enclosed and heated.

In some cold climates, with lightly-loaded foundations, freezing soil to the sides of the foundation can lift the foundations up above the footings. An inch of polystyrene insulation on the cold side(s) will help avoid this problem (Fig. 11).

Movement of salt-laden moisture within porous building materials can cause salts to crystallize near the surfaces where the water evaporates. The salts exert great expansive forces (9,000 psi; 1,305 MPa for halite) which can cause surface spalling. If the moisture movement is upward in the walls, it is called "rising damp." For a discussion of "rising damp" and methods to remedy it, see Massari, Giovanni and Ippolito (1985). Other *Association for Preservation Technology* publications describe ways of desalinating salt-saturated masonry.

Building movement from failure, degradation, or change of its components

Some examples of such materials failure-induced movement include:

- Expansion of concrete from alkali-silica and sulfate reactions.

- Expansion of corroding steel lintels and reinforcing; expansion and spalling of concrete reinforcing; corrosion of other iron and steel products. See accompanying article on Corrosion of Metals.

• Decay and insect damage in wooden structures.

• Excessive and differential foundation settlement.

• Shrinkage (and embrittlement) of some organic materials, such as plasticized polymers.

Additional references

Brick Institute of America. 1991. *"Movement; Design and Detailing of Movement Joints."* Technical Notes, Number 18A. Reston, VA: Brick Institute of America.

Forest Products Laboratory. 1987. *Wood Handbook: Wood as an Engineering Material.* Madison, WI: Forest Service, U. S. Department of Agriculture.

Gordon, J. E. 1978. *Structures, or Why Things Don't Fall Down.* New York: Da Capo Press.

Hoadley, R. Bruce. 1980. *Understanding Wood.* Newtown, CT: The Taunton Press.

Massari, Giovanni and Ippolito. 1985. "Damp Buildings Old and New." *Association for Preservation Technology Bulletin.* XVII-1-85. Williamsburg, VA: Association for Preservation Technology.

NCMA. 1973. "Design of Concrete Masonry for Crack Control." NCMA-TEK 53. Herndon, VA: National Concrete Masonry Association.

U. S. HUD. 1994. Office of Policy Development and Research. *Design Guide for Frost-protected Shallow Footings.* Washington, DC: U. S. Department of Housing and Urban Development.

Sources of moisture meters for testing wood:

Delmhorst Instrument Company, 51 Indian Lane East, Towaco, NJ 07082. (800) 222-0638

PRG, Inc., P. O. Box 1768, Rockville, MD 20849-1768. (301) 309-2222

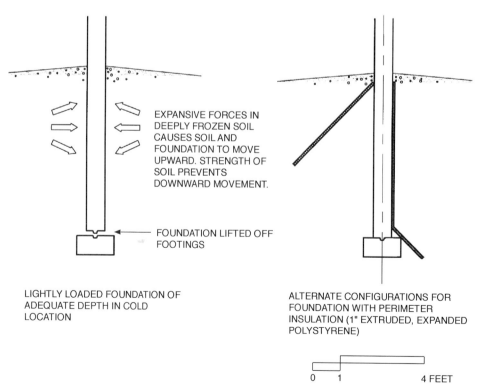

EXPANSIVE FORCES IN DEEPLY FROZEN SOIL CAUSES SOIL AND FOUNDATION TO MOVE UPWARD. STRENGTH OF SOIL PREVENTS DOWNWARD MOVEMENT.

FOUNDATION LIFTED OFF FOOTINGS

LIGHTLY LOADED FOUNDATION OF ADEQUATE DEPTH IN COLD LOCATION

ALTERNATE CONFIGURATIONS FOR FOUNDATION WITH PERIMETER INSULATION (1" EXTRUDED, EXPANDED POLYSTYRENE)

0   1   4 FEET

Fig. 11. Thermal protection of foundations in cold climates.

Corrosion of metals

SHELL B2

Summary: Corrosion of metals affects nearly all parts of buildings and their environment, evidenced in still extant but corroding iron masonry dowels used by the ancient Greeks in the Parthenon to vastly more critical corrosion of contemporary parking garages and highway structures. Design guidelines are offered to mitigate and control corrosion conditions in buildings.

Corroded steel beam, with web totally destroyed as removed from under a masonry bearing wall.

Key words: Anodic protection, cathodic protection, corrosion, paint, rust, rust-resistant treatments and coatings.

Uniformat:	B2010
MasterFormat:	05050

Corrosion in general

Current opinion is that all metal corrosion reactions are electrochemical, and that these reactions are best understood by application of thermodynamic principles. The following summary is, however, in terms of "classic" corrosion theory. For a discussion of modern thermodynamic corrosion theory, see Fontana (1986). For more information on corrosion of different iron and steel structures, see Steel Structures Painting Council (1993).

Even if only one metal is involved, small differences in electric potential cause electrons to flow in the metal. If adjoining metals are different, and especially if they are far apart on the galvanic series, the reaction will be more rapid. In a fresh water environment, the following galvanic series, from "more noble" to "less noble" applies (in a wet environment, metals toward the bottom of the series will corrode in contact with those toward the top).

Monel
Copper
Stainless steel
Lead
Tin on steel
Galvanized iron or steel
Zinc
Aluminum
Magnesium

One of the most common examples of galvanic corrosion with dissimilar metals is the corrosion of steel domestic water pipe coupled to copper pipe. The galvanic series is different in sea water and other aqueous solutions (Fontana 1986).

"Biological corrosion" is corrosion in which living organisms affect the corrosion. Examples are destruction of protective coatings and changing the pH of the environment. One actual case example is the rusting of a microwave tower, in which shrouding of the tower was required by a local architectural review board.

- The shrouding protected the interior from rain and high winds. The shelter allowed pigeons to nest within and also prevented the droppings from being washed away by the rain. The droppings produced ammonia-rich conditions against the protective paint on the steel which then saponified and peeled off. After the ammonia passed off, the droppings fermented, producing acidic conditions at the steel, retaining water from dew and other sources. The steel then corroded. After cleaning, the diagnostic remedy was relatively simple, to close the small openings through which pigeons gained access and to maintain the tight closure.

Iron and steel corrosion

The corrosion of iron and steel is among the most harmful natural environmental forces acting on buildings. Iron can corrode under a number of different conditions in damp environments. The following are some of the more common modes:

- Iron in oxygen-free acid environment.

$Fe + 2(HCl) -> FeCl_2 + H_2$

Cathodic reaction: $2H^+ + 2e -> H_2$
(Hydrogen ions in solution combine with electrons at the cathode to form hydrogen.)

Anodic reaction: $Fe -> Fe^{+2} + 2e$
(Iron gives off electrons which pass through the metal to the cathode; ferric ions go into solution.)

See Fig. 1 on next page.

- Iron in aerated environment, neutral or basic.

$O_2 + 2H_2O + 2Fe -> 4OH^- + 2Fe^{+2} -> 2 FeOH_2$

Cathodic reaction: $O_2 + 2H_2O + 4e -> 4OH^-$
(Oxygen in solution and water combine with electrons at the cathode and form hydroxyl ions in solution.)

Anodic reaction: $Fe -> Fe^{+2} + 2e$
(Iron gives off electrons which pass through the metal to the cathode; ferric ions go into solution.)

Then: $Fe^{+2} + 2(OH)^- -> Fe(OH)_2$
(Ferric ions and hydroxyl ions combine to form ferric hydroxide.)

Then: $2Fe(OH)_2 + O_2 -> Fe_2O_3 + H_2O$
(Ferric hydroxide and oxygen combine to form hematite ((brown rust)) and water.)

And this product can be further oxidized to FeO (ferric oxide•
Iron in aerated acid water. See Fig. 2 on next page.

Author: Donald Baerman, AIA

References: Brantley, L. Reed and Ruth T. Brantley. 1995. *Building Materials Technology: Structural Performance and Environmental Impact.* New York: McGraw-Hill.

Fontana, Mars G, and Norbert D. Greene. 1986. *Corrosion Engineering.* New York: McGraw-Hill.

Steel Structures Painting Council. 1993. *Steel Structures Painting Manual.* Pittsburgh: Steel Structures Painting Council.

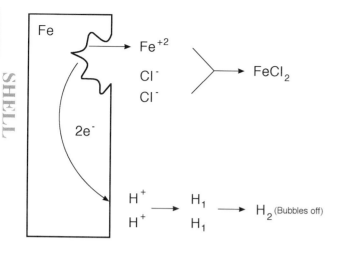

Fig. 1. Iron in oxygen-free acid environment (solution)

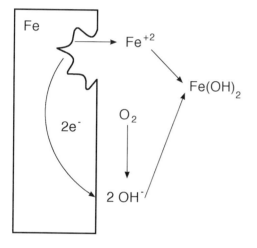

Fig. 2. Iron in aerated environment, netural or basic

- Iron in aerated acid water.

  $$2Fe + O_2 + 4H^+ -> 2H_2O + 2Fe^2$$

  Cathodic reaction: $0_2 + 4H^+ + 4e -> 2H_2O$
  (Oxygen and hydrogen ions in solution combine with electrons at the cathode to form water.)

  Anodic reaction: $Fe -> Fe^{+2} + 2e$
  (Iron gives off electrons which pass through the metal to the cathode; ferric ions go into solution.) See Fig. 3.

- Iron and copper, or other "noble" metal, coupled.

  The reactions are similar to those described above, but the coupled metals may create a greater differential in potentials between the anode and cathode, and the reaction is more rapid. See Fig. 4. In aerated water, it is as follows:

The primary harm from steel corrosion is the weakening of the structural steel itself.

Some of the products of corrosion reactions, in addition to destruction of the steel itself, can be harmful to the building.

- Hydroxyl ions can attack the paint. Atomic hydrogen, produced in some corrosion reactions, can embrittle certain steels, especially high strength steels, and it can form "blisters" where there are voids within the metal. Note the unfortunate coincidence: parking garages are often built with prestressed concrete, which contains reinforcing strands of high-strength steel under stress. Parking garages in cold regions have salt tracked into them. The cover of precast, prestressed concrete over reinforcing is generally less than 1-1/2", because the flanges are thin.

- The iron oxides and hydroxide are hydrates; they contain bonded water. They are roughly about 10 times as voluminous as the iron. Their expansive force is mighty; they can burst concrete and masonry, and they can break fasteners. Rust expansion is a major destroyer of the built environment. See Fig. 5.

Other types of corrosion of concern to architects

In building locations subject to acid deposition (acid rain), a residue of acid may remain on roofs after the rain dries and acid aerosols may settle there. When the acid rain dries on chemically inert surfaces, and when additional acid aerosols settle, the acids become concentrated. Rain will dilute the acid and wash it off, but mist and dew on the roof may dissolve the acid residue without diluting it much, and the resulting acid may attack copper, lead-coated copper, and some other roofing metals, removing the protective patina. Without a coating of protective patina, copper's durability is reduced. If the copper is designed not to accept runoff from other surfaces, or if it is protected by zinc sacrificial anodes, it is very durable. See Fig. 6.

- Intergranular corrosion (corrosion of one alloy component) may occur in alloys. One type is dezincification of brass, commonly called "crystallization."

- Lead may leach out of domestic water lines, solder, and fixtures, and make the domestic water toxic.

- Stainless steel in an environment with halide ions suffers "autocatalytic corrosion;" the corrosion occurs in small pits and may cause premature failure. Thus, stainless steel ceiling hangers over chlorinated swimming pools are not a wise design choice.

- Aluminum will corrode in the presence of hydroxyl ions. Hydroxyl ions are found in concrete and masonry mortar. This is a rapid reaction. If aluminum is embedded in fresh concrete, an area of hydrogen bubbles can sometimes be seen at the surface above it. Since concrete is rich in hydroxyl ions, wetting of the concrete-aluminum boundary may continue to cause corrosion in the completed building.

Some methods of corrosion prevention

In general, subvert any part of the corrosion reaction. The following are some of the strategies for doing so:

- Since the reactions listed above are aqueous reactions, prevent the metals from getting wet. This protection must be highly reliable. The writer has seen unpainted, uncorroded steel in the attics of buildings nearly a century old and an unrusted twenty year old tobacco can in the Nevada desert. However, if a leak occurs and the steel gets wet, corrosion will proceed.

- Select proper materials. For severe service, consider high-silica cast iron, certain types of wrought iron (if available), stainless steel, bronze, or other noncorroding metals. Where materials vulnerable to corrosion are used in a damp environment, protect them by one of the methods listed below.

- Provide anodic protection. This is based on a property of iron and some other metals to "passivate" at an intermediate level of oxidizing power. Paint coatings such as zinc chromate and red lead protect by this mechanism.

- Provide cathodic protection. This is similar to the galvanic corrosion noted above, but the protective metal is less noble than the material being protected. The protected base metal becomes the cathode, and the less noble metal, such as zinc or aluminum, becomes the sacrificial anode. This is the basis for protection by the zinc coating on galvanized steel. However, since the protective anodic metal is sacrificed, there is a time limit to this protection. In some cases the sacrificial anode may be replaced, but galvanized steel inside construction cannot easily be replaced.

Cathodic protection can be provided by blocks of sacrificial anodic metal. Cathodic and anodic protection can also be provided by applying a direct current to the metal and its environment. Protection using these methods should be designed by a corrosion engineer. A commonly seen use of cathodic protection is the zinc blocks coupled to underground steel fuel tanks.

Maintaining a high pH (hydroxyl-rich) environment will protect steel unless there are halide ions present. ("pH" is a measure of the acidity and alkalinity of a solution. "7" is neutral, below 7 is acid, and above 7 is alkaline. The numbers are on a logarithmic scale; each unit above 7 is 10 times the previous unit, and every unit below 7 is 1/10 the previous unit.) Thus steel framing and reinforcing steel encased in concrete and masonry are generally not subject to corrosion. However:

- The embedment must be great enough to avoid neutralizing the alkaline environment by acid deposition. Special quality control is needed to maintain the proper separation of embedded steel from exterior surfaces. Using "chairs" between the reinforcing and the side and bottom forms is one method of maintaining proper separation. Vigilant inspection with a mirror or flashlight is another.

- The concrete or masonry must be sound and relatively uncracked.

- There must be no penetration by chloride and other halide ions. Chlorides and other halides "depassivate" the surface of the metal. The chemical mechanism by which they do this is apparently not known with certainty, but appears to concern complex reactions with the passivation layer. Therefore some methods which protect steel in an salt-free environment don't work in an environment rich in chlorides and other halides.

- Corrosion-inhibiting admixtures for concrete are available. Also, highly impermeable concrete and concrete with durable coatings will resist the penetration of halide ions.

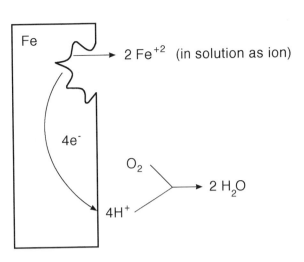

Fig. 3. Iron in aerated acid water

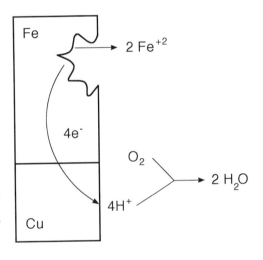

Fig. 4. Galvanic couple (similar to example in Fig. 3)

SHELL

B2

Fig. 5. Brick masonry cracked by expansion of carroding

Fig. 6. Pitting and corrosion of copper flashing as a result of runoff from membrane roof.

- Apply coatings. This is the predominant method of corrosion protection, but has its problems. Most paints of most types are somewhat porous, and many paints do not contain corrosion-inhibitive pigments. Corrosion-protective coatings for each specific environment should be selected through consultation with a technical representative of the selected paint manufacturer or, for critical applications, a corrosion engineer. The Steel Structures Painting Manual (1993) contains recommendations for preparing, priming, and painting steel structures under numerous service conditions. Preparation, priming, and painting may be specified by reference to SSPC standard specifications.

- A few coatings, including coal tar enamel, are totally non-porous, but it is prudent to assume that paint coatings are somewhat porous.

- Most organic corrosion-resistant coatings (paints), such as red lead and zinc chromate, protect by creating an oxidizing polarized layer at the metal surface. See "anodic protection" above. They are not recommended for total or frequent immersion, however.

- A few organic corrosion-resistant coatings (paints), such as zinc dust primer, protect by becoming sacrificial anodes and thus making the steel the cathode. The zinc must be tightly packed and within a few angstrom units of the surface of the metal (the zinc-rich primer must be applied almost immediately after abrasive blasting). These paints are called "zinc rich primers and paints."

- Epoxy coatings are commonly applied to concrete reinforcing bars in critical environments. Epoxy coatings are not harmed by an alkaline environment, while most alkyd and oleoresinous paints are saponified and loosened in that environment.

- Applying most finish paints directly to the metal does not give good protection; they need a proper primer. The preparation must also be proper.

- There is a synergistic effect with the use of coatings and catalytic protection. There is an advantage to using zinc dust polymer coatings over abrasive-blasted steel, in that both cathodic protection and an impermeable layer are employed. Applying a proper protective coating over galvanized steel protects the zinc coating and thus prolongs the life of the coating and its protection

Good design practice

While specialized corrosion protection may require the services of a corrosion engineer, the following good design practices can be implemented by the architect, and can be highly effective.

- Protect corrosion-vulnerable components from water. Design all details to be free-draining.

- Maintain a proper environment near corrodible metals. For example, don't locate lead-acid batteries near structural steel. Don't locate steel structures in a place formerly or presently used to store salt. Low temperatures retard corrosion. Hot, steamy environments hasten corrosion.

- Protecting steel from corrosion in a halide-rich environment is difficult and often unreliable. Parking garage decks in areas where melting salts are used in winter, especially the floors which are not exposed to rain washing, are highly vulnerable to corrosion. Cathodic and anodic protection is currently being used for bridge structures, and such protection can be used for parking structures as well. The design of such protection is performed by corrosion engineers, but it is the architect's role to request consultation with the corrosion engineer when appropriate. One beneficial maintenance operation is to wash the lower floors of parking garages with clear water in the spring, but the designer can't be sure that this maintenance will be performed.

- Increase wall thicknesses to allow some corrosion without affecting required strength. Example: cast iron roof drains corrode, but their thickness, together with the slow corrosion rate of cast iron, allows them to function for the life of the roof.

- Avoid open joints. Welded joints and rolled sections resist internal corrosion, while riveted and bolted connections are more prone to such corrosion. Where it is appropriate to use riveted or bolted connections exposed to a corrosive environment, provide special protection. (See Fig. 7)

- Design to facilitate cleaning, maintenance, and replacement. Design inspection panels at critical joints.

- Avoid corrosive conditions at stress concentrations (or, avoid stress concentrations in corrosive environments). Stress concentrations cause differences in potential and thus galvanic corrosion.

- Avoid electrical circuits in metal in corrosive environments. Electrical circuits cause differences in potential and thus galvanic corrosion.

- Avoid heterogeneity of metals, especially metals far apart in the galvanic series.

- Observe and learn from experience in the locale where you practice. What works in Houston won't necessarily work in Montpelier. When practicing outside of your familiar area, confer with architects and engineers familiar with the environmental factors specific to the locale of the building project.

- Insulate galvanic couples. For example, isolate steel from copper pipe in water supply lines.

- Keep the exposed area of the cathode small, and keep the exposed area of the anode large. A copper nail in a steel sheet is not very harmful, but a steel nail in a copper sheet is harmed. If you can only protect half the system, protect the cathodic part.

- Note that "weathering steel" ("Corten" and "Miari-R") resists corrosion except in salt atmospheres and where exposed to standing water. Follow the manufacturer's precautions.

- In metals imbedded in concrete:

- Maintain adequate cover, following the recommendations of the American Concrete Institute and increasing the cover where practicable. Exercise tight quality control regarding this. Inspect the formwork, using a good flashlight on dark days and a mirror on bright days. Do not permit the concrete to be placed until certain that there is no metal near the outside forms. This applies to tie wires as well as reinforcing. Specify "chairs" between the reinforcing and the outside forms.

- Maintain a high pH. Note that acid deposition can neutralize the concrete, especially if the concrete cover is thin. To some extent, coating old concrete with lime wash (calcium hydroxide plus binders and other admixtures) may stop neutralizing by acid deposition.

- Concrete should be of high quality and nonporous. Avoid excess water in the mix. Use water-reducing admixture or other means to lower the water content. Consider silica fume precipitate. Remember that nonstructural concrete must be treated with the same care as structural concrete.

- Avoid chlorides. Don't add them, and don't allow use of aggregates and water containing chlorides (salt sand; salt used to melt ice in the mixer, *etc.*). Note that some proprietary products may contain chlorides without saying so. Consider having plastic concrete tested for chlorides. The chloride content allowed under codes may not be safe; consider using a lower limit. A desirable limit, but hard to attain, is 0.1%. by weight of cement. ACI permits 2%, with less for prestressed work.

Fig. 7. Corrosion between bolted steel plates.

SHELL

B2

- If the concrete will be exposed to chlorides (near ocean, in parking garage, in swimming pool, etc.), the integral or applied protection to exclude chlorides must be in place before exposure. Such methods do not work after the chlorides have already penetrated the concrete. Methods of sealing the concrete include coatings, penetrating water repellents, and very nonporous concrete. Some success has been reported regarding removal of chlorides by setting up an electrical current. A positive charge is imposed on the top of the concrete, drawing the chloride anions to the top where they can be washed off.

- Avoid cracking. Discuss methods with the structural engineer. Remember that nonstructural concrete must be protected from cracking as well as structural concrete. Cracking is especially likely at areas of tension and thermal movement concentration.

- Galvanize reinforcing, or use epoxy-coated reinforcing, or use stainless steel, or use nonmetallic reinforcing such as alkali-resistant fiberglass and aramid fiber. These methods should be used in conjunction with good design; they may not be adequate by themselves.

- Patches in concrete at reinforcing can create a galvanic cell which makes other parts of the reinforcing anodic. For this reason the steel should be coated with an electrically insulating coating before the concrete is patched.

- Salt splash zones in concrete and masonry are vulnerable to corrosion. Salt splash zones which are covered and not washed by rain are especially vulnerable.

- Don't necessarily trust older concrete; the problem of chloride was not adequately recognized until the mid-1960's. Older buildings may be in the process of corroding. Many of the buildings on Alcatraz Island were allegedly built of concrete mixed with sea water, and they are in ruin.

- Apply phosphate or other pretreatment of steel surfaces. This offers corrosion protection, and it aids in paint adhesion.

- On every project consider possible corrosion problems, and seek professional advice when in doubt. For example:

- Parking garages in climates where melting salt is used.

- Swimming pools.

- Structures near highways where melting salt is used.

- Structures near salt water.

- Structures with strong underground electrical currents.

- Structures in contaminated soil.

- Structures with critical metal components which cannot be inspected and repaired in the future.

Other sources of information

- MIT Corrosion Laboratory, Cambridge, MA and other university-affiliated corrosion laboratories.

- Members of National Association of Corrosion Engineers (NACE), 1440 South Creek Drive, Houston, TX 77084-4906.

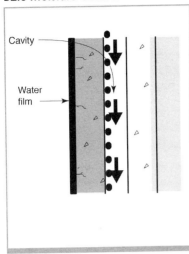

Cavity

Water film

Moisture control

Summary: The building science of controlling moisture migration through the exterior envelope is presented, based upon the physics of rain, water drainage, condensation and moisture transport and choices of wall materials and detailing. Appropriate design and detailing strategies are discussed as appropriate to specific climate, rainfall and temperature characteristics.

Key words: air flow retarders, condensation, moisture vapor control, perm, rain control, vapor diffusion.

Uniformat:	B2010
MasterFormat:	07100

SHELL B2

Moisture mitigation can be neatly summarized as rain, ground water and moisture vapor control. If, as a designer or builder, you can keep rain out of a building, keep ground water out of a building, keep moisture vapor out of a building, and let moisture vapor out of a building if it gets in, you will not have moisture problems. Rain control and moisture vapor control will be discussed in this section. Control of ground water is described elsewhere in this volume and will not be discussed here.

1 Rain control

Rain is the single most important factor to control in order to construct a durable structure. Although controlling rain has preoccupied builders for thousands of years, significant insight into the physics of rain and its control was not developed until the middle of this century by building scientists in Norway and Canada. Both countries are blessed with miserable climates which no doubt made the issue pressing.

Experience from tradition based practices combined with the physics of rain has provided an understanding of effective design and construction strategies to control rain entry. The strategies are varied based on the frequency and severity of rain.

The amount of annual rainfall determines the amount of rain control needed. No rain, no rain control needed. Little rain, little rain control needed. Lots of rain, lots of rain control needed. Although obvious, this is often overlooked by codes, designers, and builders. Strategies which work in Las Vegas do not necessarily work in Seattle. In simple terms, the amount of rainfall deposited on a building surface determines the type of approach necessary to control rain.

Wind strength, wind direction, and rainfall intensity determine in a general way the amount of wind-driven rain deposited. These are factors governed by climate, not by design and construction. The actual distribution of rain on a building is determined by the pattern of wind flow around buildings. This, to a limited extent, can be influenced by design and construction.

Once deposited on a building surface, rainwater flow over the building surface will be determined by gravity, wind flow across the surface, and wall-surface features such as overhangs, flashings, sills, copings, and mullions. Gravity cannot be influenced by design and construction, and wind flow over building surfaces can only be influenced marginally. However, wall-surface features are completely within the control of the designer and builder. Tradition-based practice has a legacy of developing architectural detailing features that have been used to direct water along particular paths or to cause it to drip free of the wall. Overhangs were developed for a reason. Flashings with rigid drip edges protruding from building faces were specified for a reason. Extended window sills were installed for a reason.

Rain penetration into and through building surfaces is governed by capillary, momentum, surface tension, gravity, and wind (air pressure) forces. Capillary forces draw rain water into pores and tiny cracks, while the remaining forces direct rain water into larger openings.

In practice, capillarity can be controlled by capillary breaks, capillary resistant materials or by providing a receptor for capillary moisture (Fig. 1). Momentum can be controlled by eliminating openings that go straight through the wall assembly (Fig. 2). Rain entry by surface tension can be controlled by the use of drip edges and kerfs (Fig. 3). Using flashings, and layering the wall assembly elements to drain water to the exterior (providing a "drainage plane") can be used to control rain water from entering by gravity flow (Fig. 4), along with simultaneously satisfying the requirements for control of momentum and surface tension forces. Sufficiently overlapping the wall assembly elements or layers comprising the drainage plane can also control entry of rain water by air pressure differences. Finally, locating a pressure equalized air space immediately behind the exterior cladding can be used to control entry of rain water by air pressure differences by reducing those air pressure differences (Fig. 5).

Coupling a pressure equalized air space with a capillary resistant drainage plane represents the state-of-the-art for Norwegian and Canadian rain control practices. This approach addresses all of the driving forces responsible for rain penetration into and through building surfaces under the severest exposures.

This understanding of the physics of rain leads to the following general approach to rain control:

- Reduce the amount of rainwater deposited and flowing on building surfaces.

- Control rainwater deposited and flowing on building surfaces.

Author: Joseph Lstiburek, P.Eng.

References: Hutcheon, Neil B. And Gustav O. P. Handegord. 1989. *Building Science for a Cold Climate.* New Brunswick, Canada: Construction Technology Centre.

Lstiburek, Joseph. 1997. *Builder's Guide: Cold Climates.* Westford, MA: Building Science Corporation.

Lstiburek, Joseph. Joseph and John Carmody. 1994. *Moisture Control Handook.* New York: Van Nostrand Reinhold.

SHELL

B2

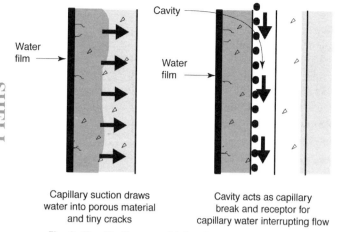

Capillary suction draws water into porous material and tiny cracks

Cavity acts as capillary break and receptor for capillary water interrupting flow

Fig. 1. Capillarity as a driving force for rain entry
- Capillary suction draws water into porous material and tiny cracks.
- Cavity acts as capillary break and receptor for capillary water interrupting flow.

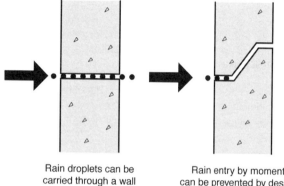

Rain droplets can be carried through a wall by their own momentum

Rain entry by momentum can be prevented by designing wall systems with no straight through openings

Fig. 2. Momentum as a driving force for rain entry
- Rain droplets can be carried through a wall by their own momentum.
- Rain entry by momentum can be prevented by designing wall systems with no straight through openings.

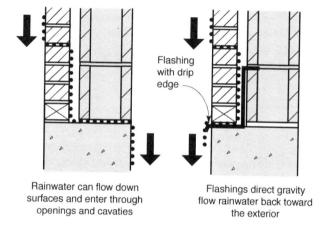

Rainwater can flow down surfaces and enter through openings and cavaties

Flashings direct gravity flow rainwater back toward the exterior

Fig. 4. Gravity as a driving force for rain entry
- Rainwater can flow down surfaces and enter through openings and cavities.
- Flashings direct gravity flow rainwater back toward the exterior.

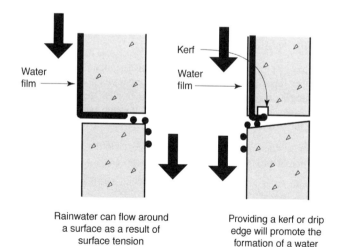

Rainwater can flow around a surface as a result of surface tension

Providing a kerf or drip edge will promote the formation of a water droplet and interrupt flow

Fig. 3. Surface tension as a driving force for rain entry
- Rainwater can flow around a surface as a result of surface tension.
- Providing a kerf or drip edge will promote the formation of a water droplet and interrupt flow.

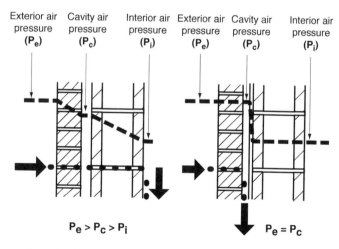

$P_e > P_c > P_i$

$P_e = P_c$

Driven by air pressure differences, rain droplets are drawn through wall openings from the exterior to the interior

By creating pressure equalization between the exterior and cavity air, air pressure is diminished as a driving force for rain entry.

Fig. 5. Air Pressure Difference as a Driving Force for Rain Entry
- Driven by air pressure differences, rain droplets are drawn through wall openings from the exterior to the interior.
- By creating pressure equalization between the exterior and cavity air, air pressure is diminished as a driving force for rain entry.

The first part of the general approach to rain control involves locating buildings so that they are sheltered from prevailing winds, providing roof overhangs and massing features to shelter exterior walls and reduce wind flow over building surfaces, and finally, providing architectural detailing to shed rainwater from building faces.

The second part of the general approach to rain control involves dealing with capillary, momentum, surface tension, gravity and air pressure forces acting on rainwater deposited on building surfaces.

The second part of the general approach to rain control employs two general design principles:

- Face-sealed/barrier approaches:
- Storage/reservoir systems (Fig. 6), appropriate for all rain exposures.
- Non-storage/non-reservoir systems (Fig. 7), appropriate for locations with less than 30 inches average annual precipitation.

- Water-managed approaches:
- Drain-screen systems (Fig. 8), appropriate for locations with less than 50 inches average annual precipitation.
- Rain-screen systems (Fig. 9), appropriate for locations with less than 60 inches average annual precipitation.
- Pressure equalized rain-screen (PER) systems (Fig. 10), appropriate for all rain exposures.

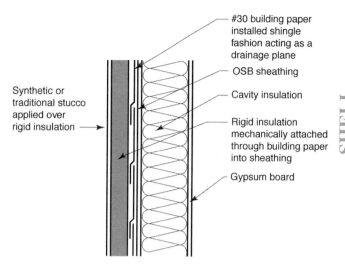

Fig. 8. Water managed wall drain-screen system (drainage plane)
- Should not be used in regions where the average annual precipitation exceeds 50 inches.
- Should not be used in regions where the average annual precipitation exceeds 30 inches.

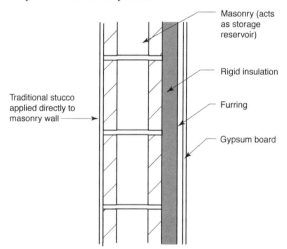

Fig. 6. Face-sealed barrier wall storage reservoir system
- Some rain entry past exterior face permitted.
- Penetrating rain stored in mass of wall until drying occurs to interior or exterior.

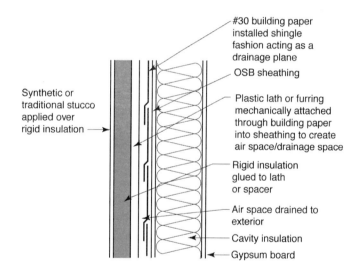

Fig. 9. Water managed wall rain-screen system (drainage plane with srainage space)
- Should not be used in regions where the average annual precipitation exceeds 60 inches.

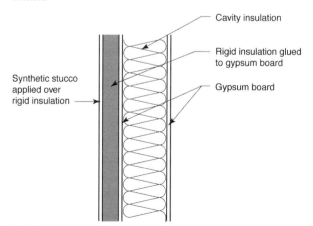

Fig. 7. Face-sealed barrier wall non-storage non-reservoir system
- No rain entry past exterior face permitted.

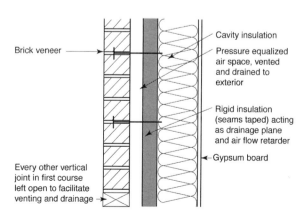

Fig. 10. Water managed wall pressure equalized rain-screen system (drainage plane with pressure equalized drainage space)
- Should be used in regions where the average annual precipitation exceeds 60 inches.

Pressure Equalized Rain Screen	▓	Over 60"
Rain Screen	▓	50" - 60"
Drainage Plane	▓	30" - 50"
Face Seal	▓	Under 30"

Fig. 11. Annual rainfall map

Rain is permitted to enter through the cladding skin in the three systems listed above as the water-managed approach: drain-screen, rainscreen or pressure equalized rain-screen (PER) systems. "Drain the rain" is the cornerstone of water managed systems. In the three water managed systems, drainage of water is provided by a capillary resistant drainage plane or a capillary resistant drainage plane coupled with an air space behind the cladding. If the air space has sufficient venting to the exterior to equalize the pressure difference between the exterior and the cavity, the system is classified as a PER design.

In the face-sealed barrier approach, the exterior face is the only means to control rain entry. In storage/reservoir systems, some rain is permitted to enter and is stored in the mass of the wall assembly until drying occurs to either the exterior or interior. In non-storage/non-reservoir systems, no rain can be permitted to enter.

The performance of a specific system is determined by frequency of rain, severity of rain, system design, selection of materials, workmanship, and maintenance. In general, water-managed systems outperform face-sealed/barrier systems due to their more forgiving nature. However, face-sealed/barrier systems constructed from water resistant materials that employ significant storage have a long historical track-record of exemplary performance even in the most severe rain exposures. These "massive" wall assemblies constructed out of masonry, limestone, granite and concrete, many of which are 18 in. (46 cm.) or more thick, were typically used in public buildings such as courthouses, libraries, schools and hospitals.

The least forgiving and least water resistant assembly is a face-sealed/barrier wall constructed from water sensitive materials that does not have storage capacity. Most external insulation finish systems (EIFS) are of this type and, from the point of view of moisture control, should be considered as best limited to climate zones which see little rain, less than 30 in. (76 cm.) average annual precipitation.

The most forgiving and most water resistant assembly is a pressure equalized rain screen wall constructed from water resistant materials. These types of assembles perform well in the most severe rain exposures (more than 60 in. (152 cm.) average annual precipitation).

Water managed strategies should be used in climate regions where average annual rainfall exceeds 30 in. (76 cm.) (Fig. 11). Drain-screen systems (drainage planes without drainage spaces) should be limited to regions where average annual rainfall is less than 50 in. (127 cm.) and rain-screen systems (drainage planes with drainage spaces) should be limited to regions where average annual rainfall is less than 60 in. (152 cm.). Pressure equalized rain-screen systems (drainage planes with pressure equalized drainage spaces) should be used wherever average annual rainfall is greater than 60 in. (152 cm.).

Face-sealed/barrier strategies should be carefully considered. Non-storage/non-reservoir systems constructed out of water sensitive materials should be limited to regions where average annual rainfall is less than 30 in. (76 cm.). Storage/reservoir systems constructed with water resistant materials can be built anywhere. However, their performance is design, workmanship, and materials dependent. In general, these systems should be limited to regions or to designs with high drying potentials to the exterior, interior or, better still, to both.

Drainage plane continuity

The most common approach to rain control is the use of a drainage plane. This drainage plane is typically a "tar paper" or building paper. More recently, the term "housewrap" has been introduced to describe building papers that are not asphalt impregnated felts ("tar papers"). Drainage planes can also be created by sealing or layering water resistant sheathings such as a rigid insulation or a foil covered structural sheathing. In order to effectively "drain the rain," the drainage plane must provide drainage plane continuity especially at "punched openings" such as windows and doors. Other critical areas for drainage plane continuity are where roofs and decks intersect walls.

2   Moisture vapor control

Two seemingly innocuous requirements for building envelope assemblies bedevil builders and designers almost endlessly:

*   Keep moisture vapor out.
*   Let the moisture vapor out, if it gets in.

It gets complicated because, sometimes the best strategies to keep moisture vapor out also trap moisture vapor in. This can be a problem if the assemblies start out wet because of rain and the use of wet materials (wet framing, concrete, masonry or damp spray cellulose, fiberglass or rock wool cavity insulation).

It gets more complicated because of climate. In general moisture vapor moves from the warm side of building assemblies to the cold side of building assemblies. This means different strategies are needed for different climates. The designer also has to take into account differences between summer and winter.

Water vapor moves in two ways, by vapor diffusion and by air transport. If the designer understands the two ways, and knows the climate zone, the problem can be addressed and solved. However, techniques that are effective at controlling vapor diffusion can be ineffective at controlling air transported moisture, and vice versa.

Building assemblies, regardless of climate zone, need to control the migration of moisture as a result of both vapor diffusion and air transport. Techniques which are effective in controlling vapor diffusion can be very different from those which control air transported moisture.

Vapor diffusion and air transport of vapor

Vapor diffusion is the movement of moisture in the vapor state through a material as a result of a vapor pressure difference (concentration gradient) or a temperature difference (thermal gradient). It is often confused with the movement of moisture in the vapor state into building assemblies as a result of air movement. Vapor diffusion moves moisture from an area of higher vapor pressure to an area of lower vapor pressure, as well as from the warm side of an assembly to the cold side. Air transport of moisture will move moisture from an area of higher air pressure to an area of lower air pressure if moisture is contained in the moving air (Fig. 12).

Vapor pressure is a term used to describe the concentration of moisture at a specific location. It refers to the density of water molecules in air. For example, a cubic foot of air containing 2 trillion molecules of water in the vapor state has a higher vapor pressure (or higher water vapor density) than a cubic foot of air containing 1 trillion molecules of water in the vapor state. Moisture will migrate by diffusion from where there is more moisture to where there is less. Hence, moisture in the vapor state migrates by diffusion from areas of higher vapor pressure to areas of lower vapor pressure.

Moisture in the vapor state also moves from the warm side of an assembly to the cold side of an assembly. This type of moisture transport is called "thermally driven diffusion." Moisture vapor condenses on cold surfaces. These cold surfaces act as "dehumidifiers" pulling more moisture towards them.

Vapor diffusion and air transport of water vapor act independently of one another. Vapor diffusion will transport moisture through materials and assemblies in the absence of an air pressure difference if a vapor pressure or temperature difference exists. Furthermore, vapor diffusion will transport moisture in the opposite direction of small air-pressure differences, if an opposing vapor pressure or temperature difference exists. For example, in a hot, humid climate, the exterior is typically at a high vapor pressure and high temperature during the

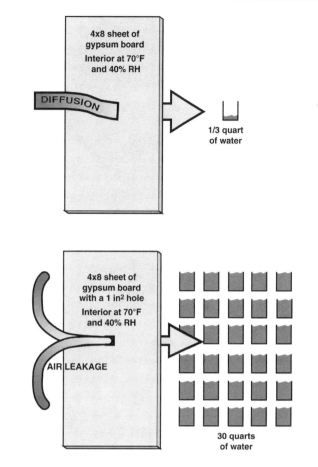

Diffusion vs air leakage

In most cold climates, 1/3 of a quart of water can be collected by diffusion through gypsum board without a vapor diffusion retarder; 30 quarts of water can be collected through air leakage.

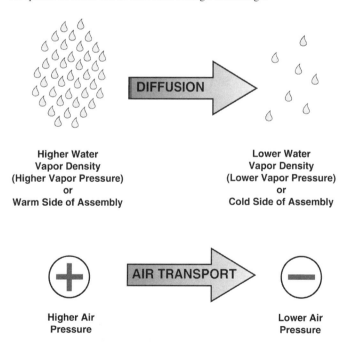

Fig. 12. Water Vapor Movement

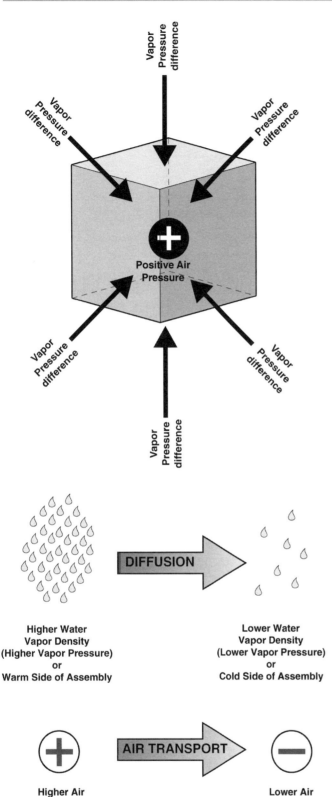

Fig. 13. Opposing Air and Vapor Pressure Differences

- Cube is under higher air pressure but lower vapor pressure relative to surroundings.
- Vapor pressure acts inward in this example.
- Air pressure acts outward in this example.

summer. In addition, the interior air-conditioned space is maintained at a cold temperature and at a low vapor pressure through the dehumidification characteristics of the air conditioning system. This causes vapor diffusion to move water vapor from the exterior towards the interior. This will occur even if the interior conditioned space is maintained at a higher air pressure (a pressurized enclosure) relative to the exterior (Fig. 13).

Vapor diffusion retarders

The function of a vapor diffusion retarder is to control the entry of water vapor into building assemblies by the mechanism of vapor diffusion. The vapor diffusion retarder may be required to control the diffusion entry of water vapor into building assemblies from the interior of a building, from the exterior of a building or from both the interior and exterior.

Vapor diffusion retarders should not be confused with air flow retarders whose function is to control the movement of air through building assemblies. In some instances, air flow retarder systems may also have specific material properties which also allow them to perform as vapor diffusion retarders. For example, a rubber membrane on the exterior of a masonry wall installed in a continuous manner is a very effective air flow retarder. The physical properties of rubber also give it the characteristics of a vapor diffusion retarder. Similarly, a continuous, sealed polyethylene ground cover installed in an unvented, conditioned crawl space acts as both an air flow retarder and a vapor diffusion retarder. The opposite situation is also common. For example, a building paper or a house wrap installed in a continuous manner can be a very effective air flow retarder. However, the physical properties of most building papers and house wraps (they are vapor permeable - they "breathe") do not allow them to act as effective vapor diffusion retarders.

Water vapor permeability

The key physical property which distinguishes vapor diffusion retarders from other materials, is permeability to water vapor. Materials which retard water vapor flow are said to be impermeable. Materials which allow water vapor to pass through them are said to be permeable. However, there are degrees of impermeablity and permeability and the classification of materials typically is quite arbitrary. Furthermore, under changing conditions, some materials which initially are "impermeable," can become "permeable." For example, plywood sheathing under typical conditions is relatively impermeable. However, once plywood becomes wet, it also can become relatively permeable. As a result we tend to refer to plywood as a semipermeable material.

The unit of measurement typically used in characterizing permeability is a "perm." Many building codes define a vapor diffusion retarder as a material which has a permeability of one perm or less.

Materials which are generally classed as impermeable to water vapor are: rubber membranes, polyethylene film, glass, aluminum foil, sheet metal, oil based paints, bitumen impregnated kraft paper, almost all wall coverings and their adhesives, foil faced insulating and non-insulating sheathings.

Materials which are generally classed as semi-permeable to water vapor are: plywood, OSB, expanded polystyrene (EPS), extruded polystyrene (XPS), fiber-faced insocyanurate, heavy asphalt impregnated building papers (30# building paper) and most latex-based paints. Depending on the specific assembly design, construction and climate, all of these materials may or may not be considered to act as vapor diffusion retarders. Typically, these materials are considered to be more vapor permeable than vapor impermeable. Again, the classifications tend to be quite arbitrary.

Materials which are generally classed as permeable to water vapor are: unpainted gypsum board and plaster, fiberglass insulation, cellulose insulation, dimensional lumber and board lumber, unpainted stucco, some latex-based paints, masonry, brick, lightweight asphalt-impregnated building papers (15# building paper), asphalt-impregnated fiberboard sheathings, and "house wraps."

3   Air flow retarders

The key physical properties which distinguish air flow retarders from other materials are continuity and the ability to resist air pressure differences. Continuity refers to absence of holes, openings and penetrations. Large quantities of moisture can be transported through relatively small openings by air transport if the moving air contains moisture and if an air pressure differential also exists. For this reason, air flow retarders must be installed in such a manner that even small holes, openings and penetrations are eliminated.

Air flow retarders must also resist the air pressure differences which can act across them. These air pressure differences occur as a combination of wind, stack and mechanical system effects. Rigid materials such as interior gypsum board, exterior sheathing and rigid draft stopping materials are effective air retarders due to their ability to resist air pressure differences.

Magnitude of vapor diffusion and air transport of vapor

The differences in the significance and magnitude of vapor diffusion and air transported moisture are typically misunderstood. Air movement as a moisture transport mechanism is typically far more important than vapor diffusion in many (not all) conditions. The movement of water vapor through a 3/4" (19 mm) square hole as a result of a 10 Pascal air pressure differential is 100 times greater than the movement of water vapor as a result of vapor diffusion through 32 sq. foot (2.9 sq. meter) sheet of gypsum board under normal heating or cooling conditions (see Fig. 14).

In most climates, if the movement of moisture laden air into a wall or building assembly is eliminated, movement of moisture by vapor diffusion is not likely to be significant. The notable exceptions are hot, humid climates or rain wetted walls experiencing solar heating. Furthermore, the amount of vapor which diffuses through a building component is a direct function of area. That is, if 90 percent of the building envelope area is covered with a vapor diffusion retarder, then that vapor diffusion retarder is 90 percent effective. In other words, continuity of the vapor diffusion retarder is not as significant as the continuity of the air flow retarder. For instance, polyethylene film which may have tears and numerous punctures present will act as an effective vapor diffusion retarder, whereas at the same time it is a poor air flow retarder. Similarly, the kraft facing on fiberglass batts installed in exterior walls acts as an effective vapor diffusion retarder, in spite of the numerous gaps and joints in the kraft facing.

It is possible and often practical to use one material as the air flow retarder and a different material as the vapor diffusion retarder. However, the air flow retarder must be continuous and free from holes, whereas the vapor diffusion retarder need not be.

In practice, it is not possible to eliminate all holes and install a "perfect" air flow retarder. Most strategies to control air transported moisture depend on the combination of an air flow retarder, air pressure differential control and interior/exterior moisture condition control in order to be effective. Air flow retarders are often utilized to eliminate the major openings in building envelopes in order to allow the practical control of air pressure differentials. It is easier to pressurize or depressurize a building envelope made tight through the installation of an air flow retarder than a leaky building envelope. The interior moisture levels in a tight building envelope are also much easier to control by ventilation and dehumidification than those in a leaky building envelope.

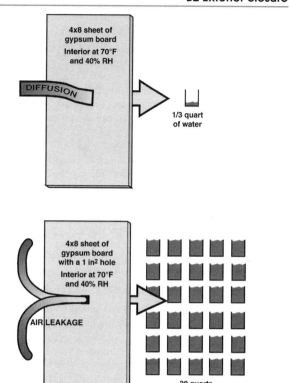

Diffusion vs air leakage

In most cold climates, 1/3 of a quart of water can be collected by diffusion through gypsum board without a vapor diffusion retarder; 30 quarts of water can be collected through air leakage.

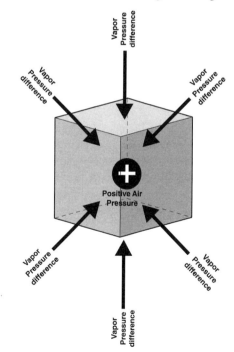

Opposing Air and Vapor Pressure Differences

- Cube is under higher air pressure but lower vapor pressure relative to surroundings.
- Vapor pressure acts inward in this example.
- Air pressure acts outward in this example.

Fig. 14. Diffusion Vs. Air Leakage

In most cold climates, 1/2 of a quart of water can be collected by diffusion through gypsum board without a vapor diffusion retarder; 30 quarts of water can be collected through air leakage.

Combining approaches

In most building assemblies, various combinations of materials and approaches are often incorporated to provide for both vapor diffusion control and air transported moisture control. For example, controlling air transported moisture can be accomplished by controlling the air pressure acting across a building assembly. The air pressure control is facilitated by installing an air flow retarder such as glued (or gasketed) interior gypsum board in conjunction with draft stopping. For example, in cold climates during heating periods, maintaining a slight negative air pressure within the conditioned space will control the exfiltration of interior moisture-laden air. However, this control of air-transported moisture will not control the migration of water vapor as a result of vapor diffusion. Accordingly, installing a vapor diffusion retarder towards the interior of the building assembly, such as the kraft paper backing on fiberglass batts is also typically necessary. Alternatives to the kraft paper backing are low permeability paint on the interior gypsum board surfaces, the foil backing on foil-backed gypsum board, sheet polyethylene installed between the interior gypsum board and the wall framing, or almost any interior wall covering.

In the above example, control of both vapor diffusion and air transported moisture in cold climates during heating periods can be enhanced by maintaining the interior conditioned space at relatively low moisture levels through the use of controlled ventilation and source control. Also, in the above example, control of air transported moisture during cooling periods (when moisture flow is typically from the exterior towards the interior) can be facilitated by maintaining a slight positive air pressure across the building envelope, thereby preventing the infiltration of exterior, hot, humid air.

4 Overall strategy

Building assemblies need to be protected from wetting that may result from air transport and vapor diffusion. The typical strategies used involve vapor diffusion retarders, air flow retarders, air pressure control, and control of interior moisture levels through ventilation and dehumidification via air conditioning. The location of air flow retarders and vapor diffusion retarders, pressurization versus depressurization, and ventilation versus dehumidification depend on climate location and season.

The overall strategy is to keep building assemblies from getting wet from the interior, from getting wet from the exterior, and allowing them to dry to either the interior or exterior should they get wet or start out wet as a result of the construction process or through the use of wet materials.

In general, moisture moves from warm to cold. In cold climates, moisture from the interior conditioned spaces attempts to get to the exterior by passing through the building envelope. In hot climates, moisture from the exterior attempts to get to the cooled interior by passing through the building envelope.

Cold climates

In cold climates and during heating periods, building assemblies need to be protected from getting wet from the interior. As such, vapor diffusion retarders and air flow retarders are installed towards the interior warm surfaces. Furthermore, conditioned spaces should be maintained at relatively low moisture levels through the use of controlled ventilation (dilution) and source control.

In cold climates, the goal is to make it as difficult as possible for the building assemblies to get wet from the interior. The first line of defense is the control of moisture entry from the interior by installing interior vapor diffusion retarders, interior air flow retarders along with ventilation (dilution with exterior air) and source control to limit interior moisture levels. Since it is likely that building assemblies will get wet, a degree of forgiveness should also be designed into building

assemblies, allowing them to dry should they get wet. In cold climates and during heating periods, building assemblies dry towards the exterior. Therefore, permeable ("breathable") materials are often specified as exterior sheathings.

Therefore, in general, in cold climates, air flow retarders and vapor diffusion retarders are installed on the interior of building assemblies, and building assemblies are allowed to dry to the exterior by installing permeable sheathings towards the exterior. A "classic" cold climate wall assembly is presented in Fig. 15.

Hot climates

In hot climates and during cooling periods the opposite is true. Building assemblies need to be protected from getting wet from the exterior, and allowed to dry towards the interior. Accordingly, air flow retarders and vapor diffusion retarders are installed on the exterior of building assemblies, and building assemblies are allowed to dry towards the interior by using permeable interior wall finishes, installing cavity insulations without vapor diffusion retarders (unbacked fiberglass batts) and avoiding interior wall coverings such as vinyl wallpaper. Furthermore, conditioned spaces are maintained at a slight positive air pressure with conditioned (dehumidified) air in order to limit the infiltration of exterior, warm, humid air. A "classic" hot climate wall assembly is presented in Fig. 16.

Mixed climates

In mixed climates, the situation becomes more complicated. Building assemblies need to be protected from getting wet from both the interior and exterior, and be allowed to dry to either the exterior or interior. Three general strategies are typically employed:

- Selecting either a classic heating climate assembly or classic cooling climate assembly, using air pressure control (typically only pressurization during cooling), using interior moisture control (ventilation/air change during heating, dehumidification/air conditioning during cooling) and relying on the forgiveness of the classic approaches to dry the accumulated moisture (from opposite season exposure) to either the interior of exterior. In other words, the moisture accumulated in a cold climate wall assembly exposed to hot climate conditions is anticipated to dry towards the exterior when the cold climate assembly finally sees heating conditions, and vice versa for hot climate building assemblies;

- Adopting a "flow-through" approach by using permeable building materials on both the interior and exterior surfaces of building assemblies to allow water vapor by diffusion to "flow-through" the building assembly without accumulating. Flow would be from the interior to exterior during heating periods, and from the exterior towards the interior during cooling periods. In this approach, air pressure control and using interior moisture control would also occur. The location of the air flow retarder can be towards the interior (sealed interior gypsum board), or towards the exterior (sealed exterior sheathing). A "classic" flow-through wall assembly is presented in Fig. 17; or

- Installing the vapor diffusion retarder roughly in the middle of the assembly from a thermal perspective. This is typically accomplished by installing impermeable or semi-permeable insulating sheathing on the exterior of a frame cavity wall. For example, installing 1.5 in. (3.8 cm.) of foil-faced insulating sheathing (approximately R 10) on the exterior of a 2x6 in. (5 x15 cm.) frame cavity wall insulated with unfaced fiberglass batt insulation (approximately R 19). The vapor diffusion retarder is the interior face of the exterior impermeable insulating sheathing (Fig. 18). If the wall assembly total thermal resistance is R 29 (R 19 plus R 10), the location of the vapor diffusion retarder is 65 percent of the way (thermally) towards the exterior (19/29 = .65). In this approach air pressure control and utilizing interior moisture control

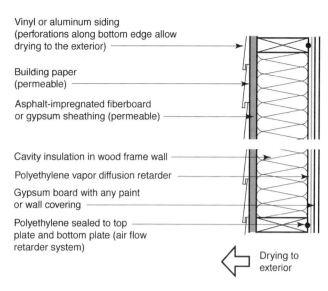

Vinyl or aluminum siding
(perforations along bottom edge allow
drying to the exterior)

Building paper
(permeable)

Asphalt-impregnated fiberboard
or gypsum sheathing (permeable)

Cavity insulation in wood frame wall

Polyethylene vapor diffusion retarder

Gypsum board with any paint
or wall covering

Polyethylene sealed to top
plate and bottom plate (air flow
retarder system)

⇐ Drying to exterior

Fig. 15. Classic cold climate wall assembly
- Vapor diffusion retarder to the interior
- Air flow retarder to the interior
- Permeable exterior sheathing
- Ventilation provides air change (dilution) and also limits the interior moisture levels.

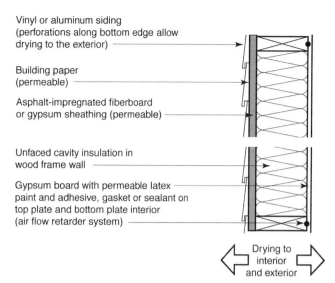

Vinyl or aluminum siding
(perforations along bottom edge allow
drying to the exterior)

Building paper
(permeable)

Asphalt-impregnated fiberboard
or gypsum sheathing (permeable)

Unfaced cavity insulation in
wood frame wall

Gypsum board with permeable latex
paint and adhesive, gasket or sealant on
top plate and bottom plate interior
(air flow retarder system)

⇐ Drying to interior and exterior ⇒

Fig. 17. Classic flow-through wall assembly
- Permeable interior surface and finish and permeable exterior sheathing
- Interior conditioned space is maintained at a slight positive air pressure with respect to the exterior to limit the infiltration of exterior moisture-laden air during cooling.
- Ventilation provides air change (dilution) and also limits the interior moisture levels during heating.
- Air conditioning/dehumidification limits the interior moisture levels during cooling.
- Air conditioning also provides dehumidification (moisture removal) from interior.

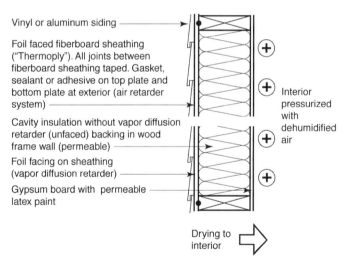

Vinyl or aluminum siding

Foil faced fiberboard sheathing
("Thermoply"). All joints between
fiberboard sheathing taped. Gasket,
sealant or adhesive on top plate and
bottom plate at exterior (air retarder
system)

Cavity insulation without vapor diffusion
retarder (unfaced) backing in wood
frame wall (permeable)

Foil facing on sheathing
(vapor diffusion retarder)

Gypsum board with permeable
latex paint

(+) (+) (+) (+) Interior pressurized with dehumidified air

Drying to interior ⇒

Air pressure acts to the exterior
Vapor pressure acts to the interior

Fig. 16. Classic hot climate wall assembly
- Vapor diffusion retarder to the exterior
- Air flow retarder to the exterior
- Pressurization of conditioned space
- Impermeable exterior sheathing
- Permeable interior wall finish
- Interior conditioned space is maintained at a slight positive air pressure with respect to the exterior to limit the infiltration of exterior, hot, humid air.

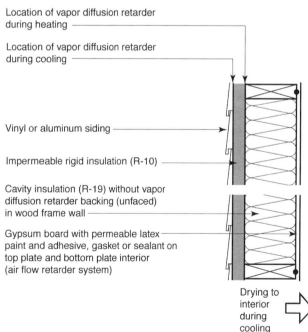

Location of vapor diffusion retarder
during heating

Location of vapor diffusion retarder
during cooling

Vinyl or aluminum siding

Impermeable rigid insulation (R-10)

Cavity insulation (R-19) without vapor
diffusion retarder backing (unfaced)
in wood frame wall

Gypsum board with permeable latex
paint and adhesive, gasket or sealant on
top plate and bottom plate interior
(air flow retarder system)

Drying to interior during cooling ⇒

Fig. 18. Vapor diffusion retarder in the middle of the wall
- Air flow retarder to the interior
- Permeable interior wall finish
- Interior conditioned space is maintained at a slight positive air pressure with respect to the exterior to limit the infiltration of exterior moisture-laden air during cooling.
- Ventilation provides air change (dilution) and also limits the interior moisture levels during heating.
- Air conditioning/dehumidification limits the interior moisture levels during cooling.

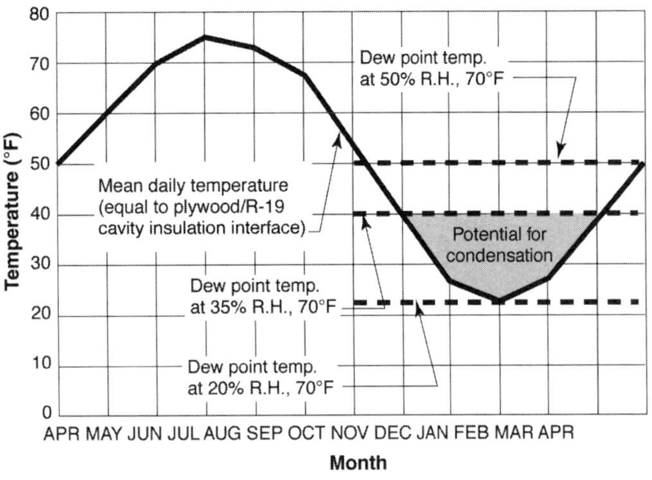

SHELL

B2

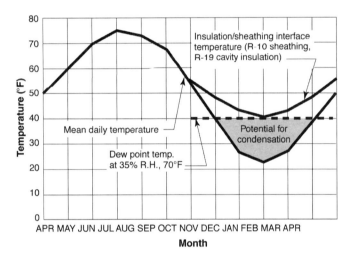

Fig. 19. Potential for condensation in a wood frame wall cavity in Chicago, IL

- By reducing interior moisture levels, the potential condensation is reduced or eliminated.

Fig. 20. Potential for condensation in a wood frame wall cavity without an interior vapor diffusion retarder in Chicago, IL

- The R-10 insulating sheathing raises the dew point temperature at the first condensing surface so that no condensation will occur when interior

would also occur. The location of the air flow retarder can be towards the interior or exterior.

The advantage of the wall assembly described in Fig. 18 is that an interior vapor diffusion retarder is not necessary. In fact, locating an interior vapor diffusion retarder at this location would be detrimental, as it would not allow the wall assembly to dry towards the interior during cooling periods. The wall assembly is more forgiving without the interior vapor diffusion retarder than if one were installed. If an interior vapor diffusion retarder were installed, this would result in a vapor diffusion retarder on both sides of the assembly significantly impairing durability.

Note that this discussion relates to a wall located in a mixed climate with an exterior impermeable or semi-permeable insulating sheathing. Could a similar argument be made for a heating climate wall assembly? Could one construct a wall in a heating climate without an interior vapor diffusion retarder? How about a wall in a heating climate with an exterior vapor diffusion retarder and no interior vapor diffusion retarder? The answer is "yes" to both questions, but with caveats.

5   Control of condensing surface temperatures

The performance of a wall assembly in a cold climate without an interior vapor diffusion retarder (such as the wall described in Fig. 18) can be more easily understood in terms of condensation potentials and the control of condensing surface temperatures.

Fig. 19 illustrates the performance of a 2x6 in. (5 x15 cm.) wall with semi-permeable plywood sheathing (perm rating of about 0.5 perms, dry cup; 3.0 perms, wet cup) covered with building paper and painted wood siding located in Chicago. The wood siding is installed directly over the building paper without an airspace or provision for drainage. The interior conditioned space is maintained at a relative humidity of 35 percent at 70F (21°C). For purposes of this example, it is assumed that no interior vapor diffusion retarder is installed (unpainted drywall as an interior finish over unfaced fiberglass!). This illustrates a case we would never want to construct in a cold climate, a wall with a vapor diffusion retarder on the exterior (semi-permeable plywood sheathing and painted wood siding without an airspace) and no vapor diffusion retarder on the interior.

The mean daily ambient temperature over a one-year period is plotted. The temperature of the insulation/plywood sheathing interface (back side of the plywood sheathing) is approximately equivalent to the mean daily ambient temperature, since the thermal resistance values of the siding, building paper and the plywood sheathing are small compared to the thermal resistance of the insulation in the wall cavity. The dew point temperature of the interior air/water vapor mix is approximately 40F (4.4°C). This can be found from examining a psychrometric chart. In other words, whenever the back side of the plywood sheathing drops below 40F (4.4°C), the potential for condensation exists at that interface should moisture migrate from the interior conditioned space via vapor diffusion or air movement.

From the plot it is clear that the mean daily temperature of the back side of the plywood sheathing drops below the dew point temperature of the interior air at the beginning of November and does not go above the dew point temperature until early March. The shaded area under the dew point line is the potential for condensation, or wetting potential for this assembly should moisture from the interior reach the back side of the plywood sheathing. With no interior vapor diffusion retarder, moisture from the interior will reach the back side of the plywood sheathing.

Fig. 20 illustrates the performance of the wall assembly described in Fig. 18, a 2x6 in. (5 x15 cm.) wall insulated on the exterior with 1.5 in. (3.8 cm.) of rigid foil-faced impermeable insulating sheathing (approximately R 10, perm rating of about 0.5 perms, wet cup and dry cup), located in Chicago. The wall cavity is insulated with unfaced fiberglass batt insulation (approximately R 19). Unpainted drywall is again the interior finish (no interior vapor diffusion retarder). Now this wall assembly also has a vapor diffusion retarder on the exterior, but with a huge difference. This exterior vapor diffusion retarder has a significant insulating value since it is a rigid insulation. The temperature of the first condensing surface within the wall assembly, namely the cavity insulation/rigid insulation interface (the back side of the rigid insulation), is raised above the interior dew point temperature because of the insulating value of the rigid insulation. This illustrates a case we could construct in a cold climate, a wall with a "warm" vapor diffusion retarder on the exterior and no vapor diffusion retarder on the interior.

The temperature of the condensing surface (back side of the rigid insulation) is calculated in the following manner. Divide the thermal resistance to the exterior of the condensing surface by the total thermal resistance of the wall. Then multiply this ratio by the temperature difference between the interior and exterior. Finally, add this to the outside base temperature.

- $T \text{(interface)} = R\text{(exterior)}/R\text{(total)} \times (T_{in} - T_{out}) + T_{out}$, where:

  - $T \text{(interface)}$ = the temperature at the sheathing/insulation interface or the temperature of the first condensing surface
  - $R \text{(exterior)}$ = the R-value of the exterior sheathing
  - $R \text{(total)}$ = the total R-value of the entire wall assembly
  - T_{in} = the interior temperature
  - T_{out} = the exterior temperature

The R 10 insulating sheathing raises the dew point temperature at the first condensing surface so that no condensation will occur with interior conditions of 35 percent relative humidity at 70F (21°C). In other words, no interior vapor diffusion retarder of any kind is necessary with this wall assembly if the interior relative humidity is kept below 35 percent. This is a "caveat" for this wall assembly. Now remember, this wall is located in Chicago. This is another "caveat" for this wall assembly.

What happens if we move this wall to Minneapolis? Big change. Minneapolis is a miserable place in the winter. The interior relative humidity would have to be kept below 25 percent to prevent condensation at the first condensing surface. What happens if we move the wall back to Chicago, and install a modest interior vapor diffusion retarder, such as one coat of a standard interior latex paint (perm rating of about 2 perms) over the previously unpainted drywall (perm rating of 20)? If we control air leakage, interior relative humidity can be raised above 50 percent before condensation occurs.

What happens if we move this wall to Raleigh, NC and reduce the thickness of the rigid insulation? Another big change. Raleigh, NC has a moderate winter. Fig. 21 illustrates the performance of a 2x6 in. (5 x15 cm.) wall insulated on the exterior with 1.0 in. (2.54 cm.) of rigid foil-faced impermeable insulating sheathing (approximately R-7.5, perm rating of about 0.5 perms, wet cup and dry cup), located in Raleigh, NC.

In Raleigh, NC, with no interior vapor diffusion retarder of any kind, condensation will not occur in this wall assembly until interior moisture levels are raised above 45 percent, 70F (21°C) during the coldest part of the heating season. Since these interior conditions are not likely (or desirable), the potential for condensation in this wall assembly is small.

Table 1. Cold climate wall assembly characteristics (All wall asemblies compatible with dry applied cavity insulations)

Permeable	Non-insulating Fiberboard	Asphalt Impregnated	Building Paper Required	Damp Spray Cellulose
	Gypsum Board	Building Paper Required	Damp Spray Cellulose	
	Insulating	Rigid Fiberglass	Can Come with Building	Damp Spray Cellulose
Semi-Permeable	Non-Insulating	Plywood	Building Paper Required	Damp Spray Cellulose only with Airspace Between Cladding and Building Paper
		O.S.B.	Building Paper Required	Damp Spray Cellulose only with Airspace Between Cladding and Building Paper
	Insulating	Expanded Polysyrene	Building Paper Not Required	Damp Spray Cellulose Not Recommended
		Extruding Polystyrene	Building Paper Not Required	Damp Spray Cellulose Not Recommended
		Fiberfaced	Building Paper Not Required	Damp Spray Cellulose Not Recommended
Impermeable	Non-Insulating	Thermoply	Building Paper Not Required	Damp Spray Cellulose Not Recommended
	Insulating	Foil Faced Isocyanurate	Building Paper Not Required	Damp Spray Cellulose Not Recommended

SHELL

B2

6   Sheathings and cavity insulation

Exterior sheathings can be permeable, semi-permeable, impermeable, insulating and non-insulating. Mixing and matching sheathings, building papers and cavity insulation can be challenging. The following guidelines are offered:

- Impermeable non-insulating sheathings are not recommended in cold climates (drying not possible to interior due requirement for interior vapor diffusion retarder, condensing surface temperature not controlled due to non-insulating sheathing).

- Impermeable and semi-permeable sheathings (except plywood or OSB due to their higher permeability) are not recommended for use with damp spray cellulose cavity insulation in cold climates (drying not possible to interior due to interior vapor diffusion retarder).

- Impermeable insulating sheathings should be of sufficient thermal resistance to control condensation at cavity insulation/sheathing interfaces.

- Permeable sheathings are not recommended for use with brick veneers and stuccos due to moisture flow reversal from solar radiation (sun heats wet brick driving moisture into wall assembly through permeable sheathing), unless a polyethylene interior vapor diffusion retarder is installed to protect the interior gypsum board from the exterior moisture.

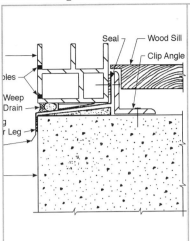

Watertight exterior walls

Summary: This article reviews principals of design for two categories of wall waterproofing systems, barrier walls and cavity walls, and examines applications to various types of wall systems, including single-wythe masonry veneers, precast concrete wall panels, glass/metal curtain walls, and exterior insulation and finish systems (EIFS). Features for reliable and durable waterproofing are reviewed, in view of problems found in field investigations and remedial options for leaking walls.

Key words: barrier walls, cavity walls, curtain walls, EIFS, flashings, masonry veneers, precast panels, sealants.

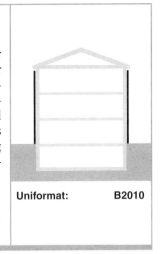

Uniformat: B2010

SHELL

B2

Exterior building walls generally consist of an exterior veneer or cladding that provides the weathering surface of the building, a backup that provides structural support for the veneer, and an interior finish applied to the backup. Buildings from the early 1900's have relatively massive exterior walls with multiple layers of thick absorptive materials separating the exterior surface from the interior finishes. The articulation of the exterior facade promoted drainage away from wall openings; these designs typically incorporated secondary waterproofing barriers or built-in flashings for long-term performance.

Current trends in exterior wall design have led to increasingly thin, lightweight veneers with little separation between exterior surfaces and interior finishes. In many cases, secondary barriers and through-wall flashings are absent from the design, and surface water flows freely over exposed joints and wall openings. As a result, the occurrence of exterior wall leakage problems has increased, including consequential degradation from such leakage, such as deterioration or corrosion of hidden wall components and damage to interior finishes, within the first few years of service. Other related issues of moisture migration and condensation within the building envelope are discussed in a separate article on "Moisture Control."

In this article, two fundamental approaches to waterproofing exterior walls are considered:

- "barrier wall" construction: use the exterior surfacing as the sole waterproofing barrier.

- "cavity wall" construction - provide a waterproof barrier behind the exterior surfacing to collect and drain water that penetrates the veneer back to the exterior.

Rainwater on exterior walls

A sound approach to aid in the waterproofing of exterior walls is to shield them from rain, such as by using cornices, overhangs, belt courses or similar features. Unfortunately, the effectiveness of this approach is limited to low-rise construction. As building height increases, rain accompanied by even slight wind tends to wet the wall surfaces despite such shielding features. The following examines two categories of exposure to the elements: rainwater flow over the wall surface with and without the driving pressure of wind.

Gravity-induced water flow

Water that flows down exterior walls soaks into absorbent surfacing materials and flows Into cracks or other openings in or between the various wall components. Gravity, surface tension, and capillary action allow water to penetrate the openings even when wind and its driving pressure are absent. Experience in evaluating and testing various wall systems is that much of the leakage can be replicated by allowing water to flow over the wall system without application of a differential pressure across the wall, i.e., wind pressure. While wind is a key element in the waterproofing design of wall systems, the designer should reduce the exposure of the wall components and joinery from water flow due to gravity.

Providing slight outward slopes to horizontal surfaces avoids ponding of water and directs water away from the wall and joinery. Shingling or overlapping materials at joints in the direction of water flow reduces the severity of joint exposure to water.

Critical areas of the wall should be shielded from the flow of water down the wall. Setting windows back from the face of the wall is an example of this approach. Providing an exposed drip edge on metal extrusions or flashings above horizontal joints reduces the exposure of the joints to rain water. Projecting subsills that extend beyond window lambs and continuous ledges or belt courses shed water away from vulnerable joints, and break up concentrated water flows and spread them more evenly over the wall surface.

These approaches use physical building features to provide permanent protection of the vulnerable areas with little maintenance requirements. However, such features do not insure watertight wall construction; the design must account for the effects of wind-driven rain.

Authors: Stephen S. Ruggiero and James C. Myers

Credits: This article is excerpted from Ruggiero and Myers (1991) by permission of the American Society for Testing and Materials (ASTM). The authors thank the principals and associates of Simpson Gumpertz & Heger Inc. for support in writing this article.

References: AAMA. 1985. *Design Windloads For Buildings And Boundary Layer Wind Tunnel Testing. AAMA Aluminum Curtain Wall Series No. 11.* Des Plaines, IL: American Architectural Manufacturers Association.

Brick Institute of America. 1985. "Water Resistance of Brick Masonry, Construction and Workmanship." *Technical Notes on Brick Construction Revised.* Reston, VA: Brick Institute of America.

Myers, J. C. 1990. "Window Sill Flashings: The Why and How." *Progressive Architecture.* June, 1990.

Ruggiero, S. S., and Myers, J. C. 1991. "Design and Construction of Watertight Exterior Building Walls." *Water in Exterior Building Walls: Problems and Solutions.* ASTM STP 1107. Thomas A. Schwartz, editor. Philadelphia: American Society for Testing and Materials.

SHELL

B2

Wind-driven rain

Wind creates two types of driving forces on rainwater: the momentum of the raindrops (splashing) and differential pressure across the exterior wall. The momentum of wind-driven raindrops allows them to penetrate openings approximately 1/4 in. (6 mm) or wider. Narrower openings cause the raindrop to shatter with less penetration into the opening. Wind pressures can counteract the effects of gravity and cause water to "flow uphill." But most importantly, wind creates a pressure differential across the wall that forces water through cracks and openings in the wall cladding. Water held within the cladding due to capillary forces will flow readily toward the interior under small differential pressures. Designers need to consider these forces that act on wall systems, particularly on taller buildings and those in windy locations, such as shorelines of lakes and oceans. AAMA (1985) contains details on calculations of wind pressures on buildings.

Conceptually, wall waterproofing systems fall into two categories, depending upon the means by which they control rainwater and the driving forces discussed above. *Barrier walls* rely on the exterior cladding and surface seals at joints to prevent water penetration to the interior. *Cavity walls* rely, in part, on the cladding to shed rainwater, but include a backup waterproofing system to collect water that penetrates the cladding surface and drain It back outside. These two categories provide a convenient basis for examining the waterproofing fundamentals discussed below, However, many wall systems consist of combinations or variations of these two types. In a subsequent section of this paper, we discuss the application of these fundamentals to commonly used wall systems.

Barrier walls

Barrier wall designs require that the exterior wall materials and joinery block passage of all water at the exterior face of the wall. These systems typically have no waterproofing redundancy and little tolerance for construction variations and defects. Key factors in the performance of barrier walls are discussed below.

The basic cladding element must be relatively impermeable and cannot develop through cracks in the course of weathering and reacting to thermal or moisture cycles. Some materials contain more redundancy than others and reduce the chances of leakage. For example, multi-wythe brick masonry can tolerate some deficiencies in construction of one of the wythes without creating through-cracks. Some materials absorb and contain limited moisture without significant material deterioration or leakage to the interior. Design considerations include:

- Joints in the wall system at openings or between cladding elements must be sealed with materials that do not split or debond from the cladding.

- The cladding must be continuous and uncracked along the sealant bond line. Typically, cladding joints are sealed during construction (in the field) with liquid-applied sealants. It is unreasonable to expect the application of these materials to be perfect.

- Substrate surfaces must be sound and uncracked and then cleaned and prepared for sealing. Joint backup materials need to be positioned properly, and sealant materials must be mixed in some cases and then applied.

- The sealant materials must withstand joint movement and weathering without deterioration.

Given all of these variables, some deficiencies in the joint seals are likely to occur both upon initial installation and as the sealant ages. Under the best circumstances, the number of deficiencies are small and leakage is not widespread, but maintenance of the seals is necessary to avoid increased leakage. In field surveys and testing, significant leakage problems have been found in buildings with single joint seals that contain defects along as little as 1% of their length. This

does not provide much allowance for variability in construction of such joints. A common method to improve the watertightness of sealant joints is to provide two seals in one joint. This is discussed further below.

Incorporating shielding elements within the cladding to protect the joints can improve barrier wall performance significantly. Overlapping the wall elements at joints, recessing the seals and windows from the face of the wall, and providing overhangs and drip edges are examples of such features. Unfortunately, recent trends in wall design eliminate such features and, instead, set the glazing and joint seals flush with the exterior surface, providing little or no shielding from rainwater and from the deteriorating effects of ultraviolet (UV) radiation on organic sealants.

Elements within wall openings, such as windows, must be watertight and cannot leak from frame corners or face joints. Windows typically contain joints between the horizontal and vertical framing members that are sealed with gaskets or liquid-applied sealants. For reasons discussed above, corner seals that are constructed with liquid-applied sealants are not likely to be watertight. In addition, handling and installation of the window frame can disturb or break these seals. For these and other reasons, it is prudent to install a flashing, such as a sheet metal pan, along the bottom of the window to collect leakage through the window glazing or frame joints and direct it back to the outside (Fig. 1). Myers (1990) provides more detailed information on window sill flashings.

Many barrier walls do not incorporate such a flashing in keeping with the concept that the surface seal is the only defense needed against water penetration. In many cases, this results in water leakage into the building.

Wall openings interrupt the cladding. Some barrier walls, such as multi-wythe brick masonry, may absorb and contain some water within the cladding. As this water seeps down within these materials, it can leak to the inside at the top of the wall openings, unless a flashing is installed in this location to collect water and drain it to the exterior.

Field experience is that barrier walls generally are problematic because the combination of imperfect average workmanship and degradation of materials by weathering result in deficiencies in the barrier that allow some water leakage. The extent and nature of leakage problems that develop depend on the types of materials used, the quality of workmanship, and the frequency of maintenance.

Cavity walls

The cavity wall concept differs fundamentally from the barrier wall concept, in that the exterior surfacing screens the rain from the waterproofing layer that is placed behind it, rather than acting as the sole barrier to water entry. This concept acknowledges, and accounts for the inevitable penetration of some water through the exterior veneer and joinery. As such, it avoids some of the primary drawbacks of the barrier wall approach and can possess a high degree of reliability and durability. The details of cavity wall construction can take different forms depending upon the veneer type and backup construction. Its fundamental design elements include the following:

- The exterior veneer provides the initial barrier to water penetration. While the veneer is not expected to prohibit all water entry, it should not contain significant cracks, openings, or unsealed joints. Differential air pressure acts across this veneer and drives water through it.

- An airspace isolates the inner, or backup wall, from the exterior veneer. Water that penetrates the veneer flows downward in this cavity, minimizing any contact with the backup wall construction. The width of the airspace varies depending upon the veneer materials and the likelihood of creating obstructions during construction of the veneer, but generally ranges from 1 to 2 in. (2.5 to 5 cm).

- A continuous waterproofing layer should cover the backup wall to shed any small amounts of water that inevitably cross the air space by splashing or by direct flow at cavity obstructions or at veneer anchor ties that span the cavity. Asphalt-saturated felts, shingled with the flow of water, are commonly placed on the exterior face of the backup wall. Because the veneer and cavity control much of the water and the veneer shields the cavity from wind-driven rain, the requirements for this waterproofing layer are much less severe than if it were exposed on the face of a building. The combination of a protective screen and a waterproofing layer provide significant redundancy in these systems with resultant long-term reliability.

- Horizontal runs of through-wall flashings must be located at regular vertical intervals to collect the water that flows downward within the veneer and cavity space. The inboard end of the flashing should turn upward at the backup wall and the wall waterproofing layer should shingle over it. The flashing should extend from the backup wall, across the cavity, through the veneer, and terminate with an exposed drip edge at the front of the veneer to prevent water from running back underneath the flashing (Fig. 2). Providing slight outward slope to the horizontal part of the flashing to promote drainage and avoid ponding on the flashing enhances reliability and durability. Sloped quick-set mortar beds or closely-spaced tapered shims beneath the flashing can provide such slope.

- Along the length of the wall, the flashing needs to be continuous and seamed watertight at joints and corners. Expansion joints should be incorporated in continuous flashings that are made with rigid materials, such as sheet metal, to accommodate thermally-induced movement of the flashing and cladding. At terminations, the flashing should turn up and the corner should be sealed watertight to prevent water from draining off the end of the flashing and into the building. Weep openings are needed in the veneer at the flashing level to permit drainage of water from the flashing to the exterior. Size and spacing of these weep holes varies with the veneer materials.

Pressure-equalized design concept

An approach that is related to the cavity wall concept is pressure-equalized design, which provides an air barrier inboard of the veneer, instead of, or in addition to, a waterproofing layer. By preventing air penetration through the backup wall and by sufficiently venting the cavity (air chamber) to the outside air, the pressure differential across the exterior veneer is reduced, or eliminated, during wind-driven rains, thus removing a primary driving force for water penetration. Essential elements for pressure-equalized systems include the following:

- The air barrier must be continuous and properly sealed to all wall openings such as windows and doors. The air chamber is not simply a ventilated space. Because wind pressures vary considerably over the face of the wall, the air chamber should be compartmentalized to avoid air flow, and accompanying water flow, from high pressure to low pressure regions.

- The air barrier and its supporting wall, typically the backup wall, must have adequate strength to resist wind loads on the building.

- The exterior veneer serves as the primary rain screen or barrier to water penetration. However, the joints between veneer elements are left open to some degree to allow efficient pressurization of the air chamber behind the veneer. Wind-driven rain inevitably penetrates the open joint areas due to momentum of the raindrops.

- Backup waterproofing layers are needed at the joints or the joints should be configured to control this form of penetration, e.g., ship-lap geometry.

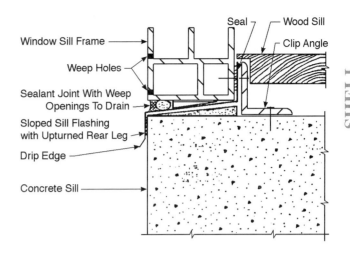

Fig. 1. Schematic cross-section of window sill flashing. The flashing collects water that penetrates the window, such as at corners, and drains it back to the exterior through weep holes. Window frame also has drainage ability.

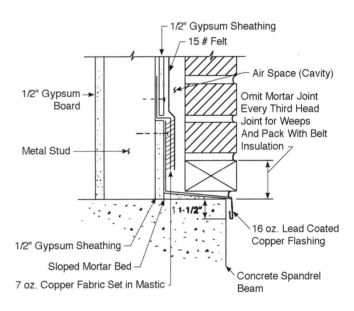

Fig. 2. Through-wall flashing of brick veneer/steel stud wall.

- Internal drainage devices, such as through-wall flashings, are required at regular vertical Intervals to collect water that penetrates the cladding and direct it back to the exterior.

The balance of this article describes the composition of some common exterior wall systems, the application of the design principals discussed above, and key features to incorporate in the design and construction of these systems, with the emphasis of the discussion on control of water penetration, along with common problems with these systems, and remedial options for leaking systems.

Cavity wall masonry veneers

A typical masonry veneer wall consists of nominal 4 in. (10 cm) thick brick veneer with a 2 in. (5 cm) wide air space (cavity) that separates it from the backup wall. Wire ties embedded in the veneer bridge the cavity and are attached to a backup wall to stabilize the veneer against wind loads. A layer of felt waterproofing covers the backup wall, *i.e.*, concrete masonry units or gypsum sheathing board/steel stud wall. Mastics have been used to waterproof concrete masonry unit backup walls, but these mastics can crack as the backup moves in response to changes in thermal, moisture, and loading conditions.

Single-wythe masonry veneers must be designed as a cavity wall to properly control water penetration through the veneer. These walls contain many mortar joints and some inevitable brick-to-mortar separations due to normal material and construction variations that allow water penetration. In addition, some moisture may soak through these somewhat absorptive materials. Proper selection of masonry materials and complete filling of mortar joints can minimize, but not eliminate, water penetration through the veneer. The cavity wall approach is necessary to accommodate this inevitable water penetration.

An important aspect in the construction of these systems is maintaining a clear cavity and avoiding accumulations of mortar droppings on the through-wall flashings. Care in placing the mortar and setting the brick units can reduce the amount of mortar oozing out from the cavity-side of the mortar joint and falling into the cavity. *Cf.* Brick Institute of America (1985) for further details. A cavity width of 2 in. (5 cm) makes it easier to control the mortar and reduce droppings into the cavity than with narrower cavities. However, there is documentation of successful construction with narrower cavities.

Through-wall flashing is the most essential element to successful waterproofing of single-wythe veneers. Steel relieving angles that support the veneer are typically located at each floor level, and the flashings should be located on each angle to limit the accumulation of water within the wall cavity, as well as to limit the distance it travels, before being weeped to the exterior. In some cases, exposed concrete spandrel beams support the brick veneer. Through-wall flashing is necessary at these areas, particularly since the spandrel beam tends to funnel any water leakage directly to the interior floor.

Through-wall flashings are also required to protect the heads and sills of wall openings against water penetration, such as at windows. Flashings at the head of the window are absolutely essential for cavity wall construction to collect the water draining down the wall cavity above the window head. Many windows are placed directly below the veneer relieving angles, and the flashing that covers the angle serves to protect the window head as well. Avoid penetrating the flashing with fasteners used to anchor the window head.

If the windows are placed into separate, "punched" openings in the wall, a loose steel lintel typically supports the brick veneer above the opening. A head flashing should cover the angle and integrate with the backup wall waterproofing. The flashing should extend beyond the sides of the opening and the ends of the flashing must turn up with watertight corners, *i.e.*, bulk head or end-dam, to prevent water from flowing off the ends of the flashing and into the wall

assembly. Aligning bulk heads with a head joint in the veneer allows the bulk head to extend outward to the face of the veneer.

Sill flashings are generally necessary to waterproofing window openings. When the interior face of the window frame aligns with the interior face of the veneer, then any leakage through the sill-to-jamb frame corner or around the window frame may flow into and be weeped out of the cavity reducing the importance of a sill flashing. Recommended practice is to use sill flashings regardless of frame position, to protect against inadvertent transmission of water to the backup at wood blocking or other "rough opening" materials and sill anchors.

Sill flashings can be created that direct the water into the cavity, rather than extending the flashing through the veneer, to avoid the aesthetic impact of an exposed flashing and drip edge. Such an approach requires careful consideration of the path of water flow within the cavity, the impact of additional water in the cavity, and the construction details. Avoid penetrating the horizontal portions of sill flashing with window anchors, and use fasteners with seals through the vertical legs of the flashing to reduce the severity of exposure of these penetrations to water (as above in Fig. 1).

The sides or jambs of the opening also require some protection as the waterproofing layer terminates at this location and, therefore, provides an avenue for penetration of water that flows in the cavity. This area is particularly vulnerable when the brick veneer forms a ninety-degree corner at the jambs, since the return edge of the brick may reduce the width of the cavity. Mortar tends to accumulate in such areas and directs water against the window lambs. Many jamb flashing details are available, depending upon the type of window framing. Consider the use of sheet metals or copper fabric flashing. These flashings need to integrate with head and sill flashings and shingle properly over the sill flashing.

Flashings must be constructed from durable materials that can withstand abuse during construction of the brick veneer. Sixteen ounce lead-coated copper and 26-gauge stainless steel have superior strength, corrosion and staining resistance, and can be bent and soldered to form durable watertight geometries. The seams between sections of flashing can be soldered or strip flashed with uncured rubber sheet to provide continuity of the waterproofing. Also, these metals can protrude beyond the face of the veneer to form drip edges that protect vulnerable sealant joints at "soft joints" below relieving angles and at the heads of windows.

To facilitate the installation of through-wall flashing—particularly its integration with the gypsum sheathing or concrete block at the backup wall—a two-piece flashing assembly consisting of copper fabric and lead-coated copper or stainless steel is convenient. The 7-oz. copper fabric can be shingled into the gypsum sheathing or concrete block slightly above the flashing level and protrude from the sheathing. When the through-wall flashing is placed at a later time, the copper fabric is then lapped over the rear upturned leg of the flashing (as above in Fig. 2).

The design of the through-wall flashing should provide adjustment capability to move the flashing in or out to maintain a uniform exposure of the drip edge over the masonry. Turning up the rear leg less than ninety degrees allows such flexibility.

Common Problems

Some flashing materials, such as lightweight copper fabric (less than 5 oz.) and thin unreinforced polyvinyl chloride (PVC) roll flashing (less than 1 mm, 10 to 30 mils) are readily punctured and torn during construction of the brick veneer, including after they are mounted on the backup wall when the wind slaps them against the building. These materials are not stiff enough to maintain formed shapes and are damaged by UV exposure. Therefore, they cannot be formed to provide an exposed drip edge. The final positioning and seaming is commonly done by the mason, not a waterproofing contractor. Forensic examination of building failures frequently find that joints are lapped and unsealed, or not lapped at all, particularly at corners. Lack of coordination of the various trades and failure to integrate the wall components is a common problem with this system.

Documented investigations a number of walls with leakage problems include cases in which PVC roll flashings have become brittle and developed cracks and splits. PVC is a rigid plastic, which is made flexible during manufacturing by the addition of oils and "plasticizers." Embrittlement due to plasticizer migration is common to all PVC materials and is a significant problem with the relatively thin PVC roll flashings. Such PVC can be embrittled within two years of service, particularly where the flashing is under mechanical stress (e.g., where the flashing spans over an offset or where mortar has accumulated on the flashing).

Aggravating any flashing deficiencies is the common problem of mortar accumulation in the wall cavity and on the flashing, and use of small, widely spaced weep holes. Keeping the cavity clear requires close attention by the mason. For weepholes, we suggest providing open head joints filled with glass fiber batt insulation to maximize drainage from the flashing and prevent insect entry.

A common weakness in some flashing designs is to terminate the flashing behind the face of the veneer, concealing it from view. This practice can allow the water to run back underneath the flashing as it tries to drain from the cavity. This water then can either be conducted inside directly, such as with exposed concrete spandrel beams, or it can collect on steel support angles. The water on the steel angles can corrode the angles, and it tends to run along the angle and leak into the backup wall at joints in the angle or at the ends of the angle.

Extending the flashing through the wall and providing an exposed drip edge avoids this problem. An alternative is to fully adhere the flashing to prevent water from running underneath it. This alternative is not as reliable as the drip-edge approach, since it relies on the quality and durability of the adhesive installation and it requires a joint-free substrate for continuous adhesion.

Other forensic examinations include building projects where head or sill flashings are not included and leakage results. Also, a number of leakage problems result from poor flashing design, e.g., missing end-pans, unsealed joints and corners, penetrations by fasteners that anchor the window head or sill, etc. Flexible flashings should be folded to form a watertight corner, and should not be cut at the corner.

Remedial options

Remediation for leaking masonry veneers fall into three general categories:

- surface coatings,

- flashing replacement, or

- replacement of the wall.

Attempts to eliminate leakage through use of surface sealers and water repellents, such as siloxanes, are not generally successful. They are tried frequently because they are low-cost and low-disruption options compared to flashing or wall replacement. However, this approach does not treat the root cause of the leakage problems, which is usually traceable to defects in the flashing. Instead, the sealer attempts to reduce the volume of water penetrating the veneer and reaching the flashing, in a sense, reverting to barrier wall construction.

Sealers can reduce the surface absorption and capillary draw of masonry walls and, thereby, reduce the amount of water penetrating the veneer via these paths and reaching the flashings. Generally, however, the sealers do not seal the separations or cracks between the

mortar and the masonry units and water will continue to penetrate the veneer through these paths. In many masonry veneers, these separations are the predominant source of water entry, and leakage will continue despite sealer application. Frequent reapplication is necessary over the life of the building to maintain the effectiveness, if any, of the sealer.

A common repair is to replace defective flashings. This requires removing several courses of masonry at the flashing level in "leg and leg" fashion. Three- to six-foot (one- to two-meter) sections of masonry are removed, while adjacent sections are left in place between these areas or shoring is installed to temporarily support the veneer above. The flashing is repaired or replaced in the areas of removed masonry. The masonry is replaced and the process repeated until all flashing is repaired or replaced. At the same time, the base of the cavity can be cleared of any mortar obstructions, and proper weep holes incorporated.

Generally, the decision to replace the entire wall is due to other deficiencies beyond leakage problems, such as Inadequate veneer ties, defects in the masonry materials, or deterioration of the backup wall components from the on-going leakage.

Precast concrete

These wall systems typically contain large prefabricated wall panels that are attached to the structure at a few discrete points to resist gravity and wind loads. There are horizontal and vertical joints between the panels. Strip windows, i.e., a continuous horizontal band of windows, are common with this system. Typically, a steel stud wall behind the panel supports the interior finishes, or metal furring, is attached to the interior face of the panel to receive interior finishes.

Precast concrete panel systems can be barrier walls or cavity walls, including pressure-equalized designs. Barrier wall construction results from sequencing the wall erection such that the panels enclose the structural frame quickly and in advance of interior wall construction. Consequently, access to the exterior face of the interior walls cannot be achieved for installation of a waterproofing layer or air barrier.

To properly implement cavity wall construction, the backup wall must be installed before the panels, and, therefore, must be capable of resisting wind loads during construction. Installation of the waterproofing layer, particularly the seal around panel attachment anchors, and the continuous through-wall flashings with associated seams and transitions typically requires access from the exterior and coordination with panel erection so that these operations can be completed as each panel is erected. Prefabrication and mounting of the flashing before erection can help reduce coordination problems. All of these factors increase the cost of the project and can reduce overall floor space. Consequently, the majority of precast panel wall systems are designed as barrier walls.

Architectural precast concrete wall panels can develop full-depth cracks, commonly at the reentrant corners in the panels. Cracking is more common in sandwich panels—i.e., those with insulation placed within the panel during casting,—than in solid concrete panels, due to greater thermal gradients across the panel depth. Proper quality control in manufacturing and handling during erection can reduce full-depth cracks in the field of these panels. Using panels with simple geometries, i.e., rectangular without "punched" openings, and simple anchorage arrangements that avoid restraint of thermally-induced bowing further reduces the likelihood of cracking.

Accordingly, solid precast concrete panels can provide a fairly effective, but not always perfect, barrier against water penetration. Unlike some other wall systems that rely on light-gauge steel framing and gypsum sheathing for attachment, precast concrete panel systems rely on relatively thick steel angles and similar substantial materials for structural support and the system can tolerate some water entry without rapid structural deterioration.

SHELL

B2

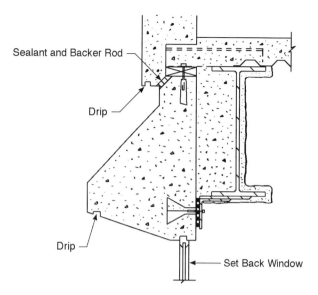

Fig. 3. Vertical section showing horizontal joinery in precast concrete panels. Note ship-lap geometry and recessed sealant to shield the joint from the weather.

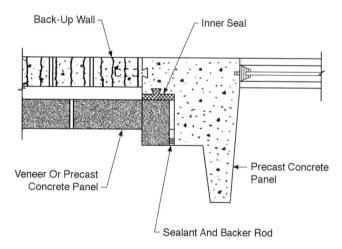

Fig. 4. Plan section showing vertical joinery in precast concrete panels. Note that panel geometry shields vertical joint from weather. Water that penetrates outer seal does not have a direct path to the interior.

The joints between panels can be significant sources of water penetration. Several options for waterproofing the joints are available. The simplest form of protection at the joinery consists of a single line of sealant material, typically a liquid-applied sealant, placed in a butt joint at the face of the panels. This approach is not as reliable as other methods because some water inevitably penetrates these single sealant joints and the butt joint configuration allows direct transmission to the interior. Half-lapped or ship-lapped joints can improve single joint seal performance, particularly when the sealant is recessed within the joint. (Fig. 3). Further, some panel edge geometries can protect the recessed sealant by including preformed drip edges at horizontal joints and raised shoulders along vertical joints to reduce sideways flow of wind-driven water over the sealant (Fig. 4).

Diagnostics examinations indicate that polyurethane or polysulfide sealants shielded from prolonged UV exposure are in much better condition, i.e., less surface crazing, splitting, debonding and hardening, that sealants placed on the face of the building under direct UV exposure.

Joint reliability can be improved further by installing two seals in each joint, one near the face of the panel and the other set some distance behind the outer joint. This two-stage approach provides redundancy in the system and protects the inner seal from the elements. This approach requires the installation of weep openings in the exterior seal to allow water contained by the inner seal to exit the cavity between joint seals. At vertical joints, the inner seal must turn out to the plane of the exterior seal at regular intervals to force water out of the joint (Fig. 5).

This termination requires care in detailing and construction. Some outward slope or offset joinery should be incorporated in the horizontal panel joints to promote drainage. Failure to provide these weep openings results in water trapped within the wall and ponding against both seals. This accelerates deterioration of the sealant material and its bond to the substrate.

A more reliable approach is to incorporate a horizontal flashing at the base of the vertical joints. This avoids the problem-prone weep hole detail in the two-stage approach and reduces reliance on the horizontal sealants. Flashings can be incorporated easily with strip window systems, because continuous window sill and head flashings can be installed after the panels are erected. Metal flashings to drain water from the system are thus recommended.

Panel openings, such as at "punched" windows, require sill flashings. The panel edges can be configured to shield the perimeter joints, direct the flow of water away from the opening, and restrict the transmission of water to the interior, such as with steps or jogs in the panel edge inboard of the sealant joint. Head flashings generally cannot be installed, because the ends of the flashing cannot turn up into the solid concrete panel.

A common approach, instead of using a head flashing, is to install a two-stage sealant joint along the head and jambs of the windows and direct the water between the seals into the sill flashing for drainage. A proper seal of the top edge of the upturned end of the sill flashing to the concrete jamb is critical to prevent the water that flows down between the jamb seals from bypassing the sill flashing. A practical detail here is the use of sheet rubber sill flashings adhered to the concrete and separate pieces of sheet metal, i.e., counterflashing, set into a sealant-filled reglet to cover the top edge of the upturned end of the flashing.

Common problems
Exposed aggregate finishes on the panels present an irregular surface for sealant adhesion. It is nearly impossible to tool the sealant into the surface irregularities, resulting in pinholes and leakage. A better ap-

proach is to use panels where the sides and perimeter of the face of the panel is finished smooth, thus confining the exposed aggregate to the central portion of the panel.

Panels commonly develop hairline shrinkage cracks, particularly at the perimeter edges and at corners of punched openings, despite controlled curing procedures. These cracks create avenues for water to bypass shallow joint sealants, even when they have good adhesion to the panels.

Remedial options

Cracks through the panel can be epoxy-injected to prevent water penetration, provided the crack arose from overstress during improper handling and overstresses will not reoccur, such as with thermal bowing conditions. Access to both faces of the panel is required to construct a dam to retain the epoxy on one face and to inject the epoxy on the opposite face. The repair may blend well with the concrete when dry, but can stand out when the panel is wetted, due to the differences in porosity between the epoxy and the surrounding concrete.

Cracks in areas of ongoing movement require less rigid repair materials to maintain a seal and allow movement. The crack can be routed to form a shallow, narrow groove on the face of the panel, at least 3/8 x 3/8 in. (9 x 9 cm) release tape applied to the base of the groove, and liquid-applied sealant installed. The release tape is needed to distribute the crack movement over an unbonded area of the sealant and avoid strain concentrations in the sealant. This type of repair may not match the appearance of the surrounding concrete.

Generally, joint repairs involve upgrading single-stage sealant joints to two-stage seals that are drained with weep holes through the exterior seal. This can be difficult when existing joints are narrow, since access is needed through the joint near the back of the panel to construct the inner seal. Cutting the joint wider for some partial depth of the panel can resolve this problem, but may be costly.

Depending upon the configuration of the panels and their layout, it may be possible to install flashings along the base of the panels. With certain panel layouts, one may be able to slide a flashing into a horizontal joint between panels, although this is tedious and many obstructions such as anchors and shims arise. This type of repair is not commonly used.

Where flashings have been omitted from window sills, it is possible to install such flashings. In some cases, flashings can be installed without removing the existing windows, but often window removal is necessary and less costly. If windows are not removed, any existing sill anchors need to be cut and shims have to be removed. This approach also requires substantial clearance between the frame and the supporting structure, and is not feasible when narrow sill perimeter sealant joints exist. In some cases, it is possible to remove wood blocking below the window to increase the clearance. Flexible flashing materials, such as sheet rubber, are useful, since they can be slid through narrow openings and turned up on the inside of the frame.

Glass/metal curtain walls

Curtain walls are metal-framed walls with various infill materials, glass being the most common. Most frames are assembled from individual horizontal and vertical members, *i.e.*, stick systems. Metal-to-metal framing intersections and glazing-to-framing joints are sealed commonly with foam or dense rubber gaskets, or liquid-applied sealants. At some corners, rubber plugs or pieces of metal are incorporated with the sealant to fill gaps in the framing.

These systems use a variety of cavity wall and pressure-equalized design principles for waterproofing. Manufacturers of these systems generally recognize that some water will penetrate the joints in the system, including the glazing and framing joint seals. Therefore, curtain walls generally are designed to drain the water that penetrates

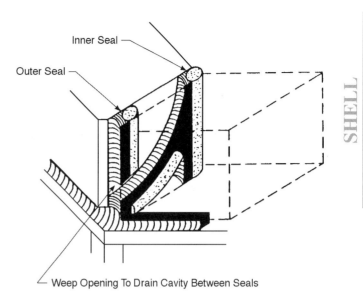

Inner Seal

Outer Seal

Weep Opening To Drain Cavity Between Seals

Fig. 5. A two-stage remedial vertical seal with weep openings at the base of the joint.

SHELL

B2

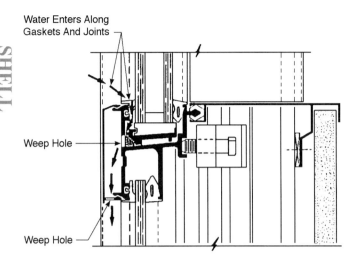

Water Enters Along
Gaskets And Joints

Weep Hole

Weep Hole

Fig. 6. Cross-section of a curtain wall. Note secondary drainage capability of the pocket below glass. Base of the pocket is sloped outward to promote drainage through weep holes.

these joints down to each sill (horizontal framing member) where it is weeped back to the outside (Fig. 6).

The sill member generally acts as a trough or gutter and, as such, it must have corners and intersections sealed permanently watertight. Weep holes in the sill should be protected by covers or shielded to avoid direct inward flow of water. In many systems, the inboard side of the sill gutter is sealed airtight, resembling to some degree a pressure-equalized design.

Traditionally, curtain walls do not incorporate through-wall flashings, except at the base of the wall, relying instead on the sill gutters and their corner seals at vertical members to collect and contain penetrating water at frequent vertical intervals until it weeps out of the sill gutter. This approach lacks the reliability that a separate flashing provides, in that the corner seals are formed from liquid-applied sealants which are not as reliable or durable as the soldered corners in sheet metal flashings for example.

Unfortunately, the service life of these sealants is much shorter than that expected for the wall system. While the system may perform well for many years, there typically is not a reliable means for replacing the seals in the future when they deteriorate. While this is a weakness, the systems generally perform better than barrier wall systems because they provide some secondary drainage capability and do not rely solely on a single exterior seal for waterproofing.

The critical requirement for these systems is providing a durable seal for the corner joinery where the horizontal member abuts the continuous vertical member. The most common means for creating this seal is to install preformed gaskets and/or liquid-applied sealant over the joined metal extrusions. The better designs incorporate the following features:

- A slight outward slope along the bottom of the horizontal member directs water outward and reduces the magnitude and duration of water contact with these critical joint seals. Prompt drainage limits leakage volume at any seal defects and improves the durability of the sealant which degrades when immersed in water.

- Frame extrusions without complex geometries and differing materials, such as screw bosses, offsets and thermal breaks, increase the chances of creating a continuous seal at corner intersections.

- Systems that permit construction of the corner seals in the factory, as opposed to on-site, generally have a greater chance of success due to better control on surface preparation and cleaning and better supervision of the sealing process.

Expansion joints in vertical members are a particularly difficult area in the framing to maintain a watertight seal. Generally, the joint incorporates a backup plate behind gapped ends of the members, and the plate is bedded in a non-curing butyl-based sealant. One of the edges in such a joint faces against the flow of water, inviting water entry. Incorporating a backup plate that fits behind the upper member and laps over the lower member is one approach to avoid this weakness, but it is not commonly used. With either approach, the movement of the vertical members concentrates at one point along the glazing seal and inevitably creates an unsealed opening at this point.

Another alternative is to create a butt sealant joint at the expansion joint to avoid impeding the water flow and distribute the movement of the ends of the vertical members. This requires providing solid watertight end caps on the members, and is not commonly done. Typically, the systems accept these weaknesses and attempt to collect water that penetrates the expansion joints in the drained sills.

Common problems

The most prevalent problems are defects in the corner joinery seals, including omission of the seals altogether due to fabrication and erection oversights in some cases. Other defects include:

- Pinholes or discontinuities in the internal corner seals due to the complexity of the intersecting members and difficulty in accessing certain spots along the joint,

- Poor adhesion of sealants due to improper cleaning and surface preparation, incompatibility with various materials particularly at plastic and rubber components such as thermal breaks, and deterioration of the sealant material with age and exposure to ponding water.

Frequently, other defects are found in the external seals that allow significant water entry into the system, which tends to exacerbate leakage at any corner seal defects. Glazing seals are the most common source of water entry to the framing system. Gasket shrinkage or improper installation cause gaskets to pull away from the frame at the glazing corners. Gaskets require proper installation methods to avoid stretching and the resulting "shrinkage" over time as the gasket relieves this built-in stretch. Some gaskets also shrink due to material behavior, *i.e.*, weathering and loss of plasticizers. Nonuniform compression on the gaskets, due to accumulated fabrication tolerances or variable tightening of pressure bar glazing bead fasteners, can allow water penetration.

Recommended practice suggests constructing external glazing seals with liquid-applied sealants, *i.e.*, wet seals, as opposed to preformed dry gaskets. The wet seals avoid gasket joinery and compression pressure problems, since they are continuous and adhered to the substrate. Wet seals are subject to some defects due to installation tolerances, but experience is that they prevent more water penetration than dry gasketed systems. They require outside access for glass installation and replacement, and sometimes are not used for this reason.

In some cases, such as at the base of a curtain wall or at windows, the sill frames are anchored to the structure with fasteners that penetrate the sill gutter and any underlying flashing. Fastener holes provide an avenue for water penetration. Sealant materials, if any, used to cover the fastener heads only provide short-term protection as they often loose bond when subject to "ponding" water. Fig. 1 above shows a detail for fastening the sill frame with a clip angle and fastener into the rear of the frame to avoid penetrating the horizontal portion of the sill flashing. Penetrations through the upturned rear leg have a very minor exposure to water, compared to those in the horizontal part of the flashing.

Remedial options

Remedies for leaking glass/metal curtain walls include two approaches using sealant materials; flashing installation generally is not feasible with these systems.

- One option is to wet seal all external joints in the system, *i.e.*, seal them with liquid-applied sealants. This option typically is tried because of it imposes relatively low cost and low disruption. This approach however does not treat the common fundamental defects that exist in the waterproofing system, *i.e.*, leaking internal seals, but instead attempts to make a barrier system out of the curtain wall and prevent water from reaching the corner seals. As such, it contains the drawbacks of any barrier system, and some degree of on-going leakage is likely with the extent depending on the quality, durability, and maintenance of the wet seals.

- Another option is to reconstruct the corner seals. This approach has included various schemes ranging from drilling portholes and blindly pumping sealant into the hidden corner areas, to partial disassembly of the curtain wall, including removal of glass lites, pressure bars, or frame members to repair the corner seals. The

former approach is never found to be effective due to the inability to clean, prepare and inspect the joint, while the latter approach can be successful, provided reasonable access to the joint for cleaning and remedial sealant application and tooling can be obtained. Wet sealing the system after corner seal repairs is prudent to reduce reliance upon the internal remedial seals.

Exterior Insulation And Finish (EIFS) systems

Exterior Insulation and Finish Systems (EIFS) typically consist of polystyrene insulation boards, which are covered by a polymer modified cementitious coating (synthetic stucco) that is reinforced with glass fiber mesh. Generally, the coating consists of two layers, a base coat and a finish coat, which is called the *lamina*. The insulation boards are usually adhered to exterior gypsum sheathing on a steel stud backup wall. In some systems, the insulation boards are fastened mechanically to the steel studs. Most EIFS installations have been field constructed, as opposed to panelized, and have been adhered, rather than mechanically-attached, to the backup wall.

EIFS systems use barrier wall principles and lack any cavity or waterproofed backup. Traditional cement plaster stucco wall systems can incorporate a drainage layer through the use of asphalt-impregnated felt behind the metal lath. While this is not a clear drainage cavity, the field experience is that the felt can control water that may penetrate at cracks or joints in the stucco wall, if it directs this water onto a through-wall flashing. However, this places the metal lath and fasteners in a moist environment and invites corrosion problems.

With the EIFS composite of materials, such a waterproofing layer cannot be incorporated, because it would interrupt the adhesive attachment of the insulation or plaster coats. It may be possible to incorporate a waterproofing layer if the system is mechanically attached, but such an approach has not been documented in practice. Like traditional stucco, the fasteners with mechanically-attached EIFS systems are in a corrosive environment and subject to premature failure.

EIFS systems rely solely on the polymer modified stucco coating and joint sealants to resist water leakage. Rain penetration through EIFS clad walls typically occurs at cracks in the lamina, at defects in the joint seals, and through unflashed window frame corners and joinery. Gypsum sheathing, if used, may degrade readily when exposed to water. Structural deterioration of the gypsum sheathing, fasteners and steel studs, and loss of attachment, become a greater concern than just discomfort of the building occupants and damage to interior finishes due to water leakage.

Control of cracking is important in these systems, particularly the control of cracks that occur over the joints between insulation boards. Hairline cracks that do not penetrate through the lamina have no leakage-related consequence. However, if cracks occur through the lamina especially over joints in the insulation boards, water has a ready path to the water-sensitive exterior gypsum sheathing board, particularly under differential air pressures across the wall. Causes of cracking are discussed further in the section below.

Methods of waterproofing the joints between panels and the need for sill flashings at windows and other wall penetrations are similar to that discussed previously for precast concrete panels.

Common Problems

Problems with EIFS systems can result from cracking of the lamina, which must remain unbroken for watertightness. The authors have seen buildings where vertical or horizontal control joints are omitted and this has produced significant cracking, particularly on elevations with strong solar exposures. Some manufacturers of adhered systems have asserted that the system is "soft" and can "float" in response to thermal cycles. Consequently, these systems sometimes are designed without vertical control joints to subdivide building elevations into discrete panels. The polystyrene insulation has a relatively high coefficient of thermal movement. The lamina and the composite EIFS system have a lower coefficient, based on our testing of laboratory samples and measurement of movements on actual building walls, but the coefficient is sizable and requires due consideration in design.

We recommend that wall elevations be subdivided by control joints. Until designers can agree on a minimum joint spacing, we recommend spacing the control joints spaced approximately each 20 to 30 ft. (7 to 10 m), since this generally is consistent with spacings used with other cladding materials. These control joints are in addition to those normally required by the manufacturer, such as at intersections of dissimilar materials or where structural movement may occur, *i.e.*, vertical joints at intersecting walls and horizontal joints at floor levels with flexible edge beams or slabs.

Cracks typically develop at the reentrant corners formed by window openings. In many cases, the insulation board joints align with the window corner, creating a plane of weakness in the EIFS substrate aligned with a point of high stress caused by the window opening penetrating through the face of the panel. These cracks can allow direct water entry or water can bypass the window perimeter sealant where the crack and sealant intersect. Corner cracking can be reduced by cutting a single insulation board to fit each window corner such that board joints do not align with the window corners and by following manufacturers' recommendations to install extra layers of diagonally oriented reinforcing at all opening corners.

Prolonged exposure to moisture softens some EIFS finish coats. At sealed panel joints, the softening can permit cohesive failure within the lamina when the joints move and the sealant pulls on the finish coat. Using low modulus urethane or silicone sealants helps reduce the stresses on the finish coat, but there is not yet an extensive track-record of use in these systems.

During field investigations and water tests, the authors have found that leakage from sill-to-jamb window frame corners penetrates behind the lamina and insulation when sill flashings are omitted from the window opening. As a result, the exterior gypsum sheathing often has significant hidden deterioration in the vicinity of such window sill corners, horizontal sliding windows, which are commonly used in residential complexes, are particularly prone to frame corner leakage.

The weather-stripping seals on the sliding joints tend to allow more water entry into the window system, especially as the weather-stripping deteriorates from use, than do seals on other styles of windows. In addition, the sill acts like a gutter as it does in a curtain wall, increasing the exposure of the corner joinery seals to water compared to other styles of windows where water does not collect in the sill.

In many leakage investigations, it has been established that these system problems are exacerbated by the flush-glazed, flat surface profile of the facade that does not shield the vulnerable surface seals.

Remedial options

Since EIFS is a barrier system with components readily damaged by water, the system requires frequent inspection and maintenance to limit water entry and consequential damages. Further, if significant leakage is occurring, a critical evaluation of the concealed conditions is needed to determine the scope of repairs.

Repair of cracks in the lamina vary with the cause of the crack. If cracks result from movements within the system that apply concentrated stresses to the lamina, remedial control joints should be installed to accommodate the movements. This requires removing the EIFS to form a joint and grinding the adjacent finish coat back to the existing base coat, wrapping the joint edges with reinforcing mesh and base coat that extends onto the back of the insulation (back-wrapping), and sealing the joint. Remediation steps are to patch non-moving cracks, grind the finish coat back to the base coat and rout the crack; fill the routed area with new insulation and rasp flush; and install new mesh reinforcing in new base coat, and a new finish coat.

With these systems, even simply cutting out the old sealant to repair defects can be a significant undertaking. Grinding to remove all traces of the old sealant, which is generally good practice when resealing, may damage the lamina. Bonding the new sealant to the remnants of the old failed sealant is not generally good practice, depending upon the materials involved. Upgrading single-stage sealant joints to two-stage joints is more difficult than with other wall systems, since the insulation and properly-applied coating may not extend deep enough to permit proper installation of dual seals. Significant cutting and patching would be needed to install a remedial flashing to drain the joints in this system.

Summary

Exterior wall systems that incorporate cavity-wall waterproofing principles are the most reliable in preventing water leakage to the building interior. The key component for these systems is the through-wall flashing which should be durable and have an expected service life equivalent to that of the entire wall system. Proper attention to the detailing and installation of these flashings is crucial to the success of a cavity wall system. Lower durability flashings with limited track records should be avoided due to the high cost of future replacement of failed flashings.

Barrier wall systems with modifications to incorporate some degree of secondary drainage capability, particularly at vulnerable joints, can provide levels of watertightness acceptable to some building owners, if sound, durable materials are used to form the barrier. Barrier walls that rely solely on surface seals and which use components that deteriorate readily from water that penetrates flaws in those seals do not provide a level of waterproofing reliability acceptable to most building owners.

All wall systems, and in particular barrier walls, can benefit from shielding provided by proper articulation of the wall surface to promote water drainage away from vulnerable joints.

Ultimately, the building owner and architects should make an informed decision when selecting the wall system, based on analysis of waterproofing reliability and the contractor's estimate of costs, *i.e.*, affordability. An established maintenance protocol is necessary for all buildings. Given the expected level of maintenance, design and construction detailing should provide for reliability over the life of the building. Critical to the owner's evaluation is a clear understanding of the likelihood of leakage, the consequential damages from leakage, and life cycle costs and disruption associated with repairs, maintenance and replacement of the various cladding systems.

ENTRANCE

Exterior doors and hardware

Summary: This article provides an overview of exterior doors and entrances, both for pedestrian and vehicular traffic, with criteria for their selection and specification. Included are swinging doors, sliding doors, revolving doors, fire doors and other special constructions and hardware.

Key words: building type, entrances, environmental influences, door hardware, door types.

Uniformat:	B2030
MasterFormat:	08400
	08700

SHELL

B2

1 Exterior doors: overview

1.1 Design and selection criteria

Exterior door assemblies separate exterior from interior environments while controlling passage, isolating and resisting the effects of external/internal factors such as differential wind pressures, sound, light, air infiltration/exfiltration, water penetration, fire, explosion, forced entry, building frame deformations, and pests. Entrance doors are movable segments of the envelope of a space made to open and close quickly and easily whenever passage to and from an enclosed space through its envelope is required (Fig. 1).

To function properly, doors must:

- move freely when passage is required;
- be held securely within the opening when passage is to be prevented;
- seal the opening completely, when environments have to be separated, or internal/external factors isolated.

Pedestrian access may consist of a series of doors, of one or more functional types:

- fixed panels - transparent, translucent, or opaque - on one or both sides of the door, or above the door;
- the entrance doors may be separated with an air lock, or a vestibule, which may also include fixed panels on the sides or above the doors;
- canopies or awnings to provide shelter from the weather may also become a component of the entrance assembly;
- a continuous stream of air or an air curtain, to keep out insects and dust, or to prevent cold or hot outside air from mixing with interior air, may also be a major component of such an assembly.

For vehicular/service entrances, a range of components and accessories may be included which are designed to help the convenient and sheltered loading and unloading of goods, including:

- canopies; loading docks, with movable platforms, bumpers and guards; loading-dock shelters.

1.1.1 Occupancy and use

Building type and occupancy will be the most important design deter-

minant. Total capacity, or the number of exit units needed, will be determined by the applicable building codes. The configuration will be determined by:

- the circulation pattern of the building occupants coming and leaving.
- maximum number of people entering/leaving the building at peak load time.
- number of people entering/leaving at other times of the day.
- number of hours in twenty-four when building remains open.
- minimum distance or separation between sets of doors in vestibules, based on the need to create an airlock separation between outdoor and indoor climate. Many people wait for rides inside entry vestibules, which might be best accommodated by seating.
- capacity as a means of egress to satisfy code requirement.
- when considered as an emergency egress or exitway, the direction of swing must be in direction of flow of traffic to a place of refuge.

For both average and for peak load conditions, consider:

- number, distribution, and type by operation of the entrance doors, including consideration of universal design goals to assist persons with limited physical capacities, those carrying packages and so forth.
- number and distribution of the fixed dividing components - sidelights and transoms, principally as a function of the need for visibility and of security.
- design and location of sheltering components: awnings, canopies, vestibules, air curtains.
- design and structure of the assembly encompassing frame. The frame system can also develop into a curtain-wall system.
- all possible and conceivable uses as might be presented by people with open umbrellas, baby carriages, service deliveries, or bicycles must be considered to avoid conflicting and possibly unsafe patterns of use.
- vision panels for safety and security; size and location, to be coordinated with the location and type of lighting.

Author: Timothy T. Taylor

Credits: This article is based upon definitions and illustrations originally appearing in 1993 *Sweets Catalog File* Selection Data, reproduced by permission, with updates on specifications provided by Timothy T. Taylor. Tables courtesy of the American Architectural Manufacturers Association, the National Association of Architectural Metal Manufacturers, and the National Wood Window and Door Association.

References: References and resources are listed at the end of this article.

B2 SHELL

OPENING

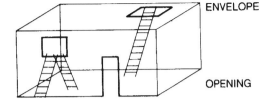

ENVELOPE

OPENING

ENVELOPE

OPENING

DOOR

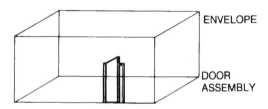

ENVELOPE

DOOR ASSEMBLY

ENVELOPE

DOOR ASSEMBLIES

ENTRANCE

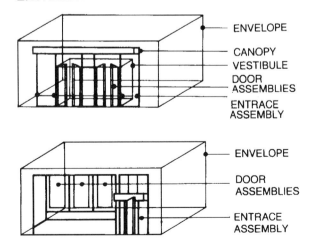

ENVELOPE
CANOPY
VESTIBULE
DOOR ASSEMBLIES
ENTRACE ASSEMBLY

ENVELOPE
DOOR ASSEMBLIES
ENTRACE ASSEMBLY

Fig. 1. Exterior door system components

1.1.2 Security

Security requirements of the building envelope at the entrance should be considered:

- What security requirements are created by the design program?

- Is vandalism a concern?

- Is visual surveillance and recognition through the entrance required?

- How can security improved by lighting to allow recognition and identification?

1.1.3 Universal design and accessibility

Entrance selection for universal design must be concerned from the point of view of access, movement and dimensional limitations of all individuals of varying stature, strength, mobility and encumbrances, such as packages or baby carriages. Power-activated doors, even if not required, should be considered for universal design accommodation, for safety and convenience. For doors whose operation is impaired by air pressure, consider balanced pivots or power actuators. Related items for the design consideration are:

- including space for common courtesy, that is, to hold doors for others and for inside waiting:

- minimum door width/clear opening.

- maximum force to open door.

- level changes at entrance.

- hardware requirements and location.

1.1.4 Safety considerations

- Codes generally require safety glazing to reduce accidents due to broken glass.

- Door swings, location of stops and other applied hardware must be considered to avoid interference with traffic flow through door.

- The arc of a door swing should exceed 90 degrees to allow the full width of the door opening to be unobstructed.

- Hinge jambs should be at least 6 in. (15 cm) from a wall perpendicular to a building face to prevent the user's hands from being pinched between the door and the wall. If hinged jambs for two door have to be adjacent, there should be enough distance between them to permit the doors to swing through an arc of 110 degrees.

- If doors hung on center pivots are hung in pairs, they should be hinged at the side jamb and not at the center mullion. Doors hinged off a common mullion may create problems: hardware to prevent one door from swinging into the path of the other could subject the door to excessive forces with resulting severe damage.

- All-glass doors and sidelights should be clearly identified to prevent the possibility of people walking into them accidentally. Insufficient lighting, or excessive lighting, veiling reflections and glare can create complicating vision and visibility problems.

- Swinging doors should be located to clear passing pedestrian traffic without interference.

1.1.5 Environmental influences

Climatic conditions which have a direct influence on the design of the entrance assembly include:

- temperature range and extremes.

- prevailing winds, or microclimatic effects at the entry, which may significantly impair ease and safety of operation.

- precipitation, particularly ice and snow conditions, and resulting imposition on entrance materials of sand, salt and chemicals used for ice melting.

- atmospheric conditions: humidity, presence of salt spray, corrosive agents.

Aspects of entrance design most influenced by the climatic considerations above should include:

- incorporation of sun and rain protecting devices and wind screens. Visibility of stairs, railings, and the entry doors themselves should not be impaired by sun angle and glare.

- use of vestibules and of revolving doors may minimize drafts and provide better separation of outside and inside environments.

- concern for sufficient structural strength of entrance frame. In this case, long-term durability is important, along with ease of use, which is related to door weight.

- selection of types of door operation and of hardware for efficient opening in all weather conditions and for adequate durability.

- selection of component construction, glazing and weather-stripping to minimize air and water infiltration and heat loss.

1.1.6 Weathertightness

Exterior doors are subjected to all the effects of natural forces: solar heat, rain, and wind. For ordinary installations, closed doors cannot be expected to exclude water or stop air movement completely under all conditions. One explanation for this is that space clearances must be provided around each door to permit ease of operation, thermal expansion, and construction tolerances.

In mechanically ventilated buildings, there is likely to be a difference in air pressure between the inside and outside at entrances. In the case of entryways located near heavily trafficked areas or loading zones, noxious fumes can enter the building from outside. Where it is a critical concern and where doorways or service areas cannot otherwise be relocated, this air leakage can be controlled in several ways:

- entrance vestibules.

- revolving door entrances.

- weather-stripping.

Entrances may need to isolate the interior from the exterior acoustically: Weather-stripping is effective in sound isolation. When selecting weather-stripping, consider:

- weather sealing components: do they comply with energy code restrictions?

- tighter fit due to seals means that more effort and strength is needed to operate the doors.

1.2 Exterior door types

- *Pedestrian doors:* The closure panel, or door, is generally classified by the method used to allow its opening and closing. There are three major types of pedestrian entrance doors:

- swinging, where the door panel is anchored to a supporting frame by hinges or is pivoted top and bottom.

- sliding, where the door panel slides to one side either top hung from a supporting frame or bottom supported; with either bottom or top guides.

- revolving, where door panels are attached to a center rotating post; operating within a self-supporting enclosure.

In general, exterior door type is selected on the basis of desired operation:

- *Swinging doors,* either single-action or double-action:

- provide versatility in permitting large or small passage capacity.

- permit manual or power actuation, but:

- may require considerable strength to open in certain weather conditions.

- do not provide the best protection against drafts and heat loss.

- *Sliding doors* are:

- safest, especially where people carrying large objects, packages, baggage, as in air terminals, shopping centers, and active delivery ways.

- present least obstruction inside and outside and will act in any weather.

- must be power-actuated when serving as entrances of any size.

- permit exchange outside air to or from the building interior unless a vestibule design is used.

- *Revolving doors* are most effective for:

- sealing the outside environment from the interior without use of a vestibule.

- handling an orderly trickle of pedestrians in and out of buildings,

- have limited capacity and cannot handle peak loads.

- are difficult for people with large objects and do not meet universal access requirements.

- *Vehicular doors:* Vehicular doors should be so located that exhaust fumes from vehicles do not enter the building. The major functional types of vehicular/service entrance doors are:

- swinging

- sliding - to one or both sides - in large or small segments

- vertical rise - in large or small segments

1.3 Components of entrance door assembly (Fig. 2)

- *Jamb/header:* vertical and horizontal frame members forming the sides of an entrance or door assembly. In a door assembly, the hinge jamb is the frame member at which the hinges or pivots are mounted.

- *Mullion:* vertical framing member holding and supporting fixed glazing or opaque infill panels. May be single piece or split; with or without thermal breaks.

- *Transom bar:* horizontal framing member which separates the door opening from the transom above. Transom bars may contain operating hardware for doors, such as closers or automatic operators.

- *Transom bracket:* a bracket to support all-glass transom over an all-glass door when no transom bar is used.

- *Sidelight:* fixed light or lights of glass located adjacent to a door opening. Wet or dry glazed, with dry glazing more commonly used. Sidelight base: may be a single piece, built up of several framing members, or a masonry or concrete curb may be used for support of the bottom frame. In either case, provisions to seal the gap between the bottom of the entrance assembly and supporting construction should be incorporated in the design of the assembly.

1.3.1 Design components

- Expansion/contraction: in the assembly must not be restricted within the opening and proper clearances in the opening and at connections must be incorporated in the design. Movement within the assembly may be accommodated by providing for slippage at joints or in split mullions.

- Door frames, especially in large assemblies, should be independent of other framing to minimize effects of thermal movement.

- Deflection in horizontal members may impose loads on glass and may cause breakage and/or prevent proper operation of doors. When staggered concentrated loads have to be carried by a hori-

COMPONENTS OF ASSEMBLY

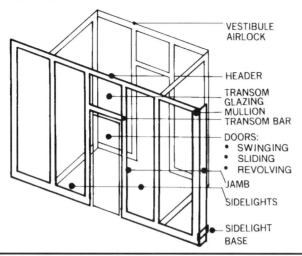

VESTIBULE AIRLOCK
HEADER
TRANSOM GLAZING
MULLION
TRANSOM BAR
DOORS:
• SWINGING
• SLIDING
• REVOLVING
JAMB
SIDELIGHTS
SIDELIGHT BASE

DESIGN COMPONENTS

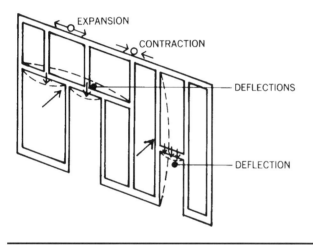

EXPANSION
CONTRACTION
DEFLECTIONS
DEFLECTION

FRAMING MEMBERS

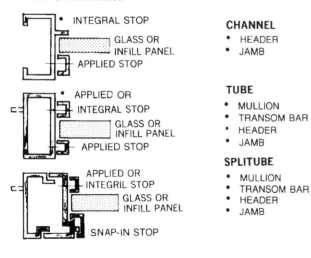

• INTEGRAL STOP
GLASS OR INFILL PANEL
• APPLIED STOP

• APPLIED OR INTEGRAL STOP
GLASS OR INFILL PANEL
• APPLIED STOP

APPLIED OR INTEGRIL STOP
GLASS OR INFILL PANEL
SNAP-IN STOP

CHANNEL
• HEADER
• JAMB

TUBE
• MULLION
• TRANSOM BAR
• HEADER
• JAMB

SPLITUBE
• MULLION
• TRANSOM BAR
• HEADER
• JAMB

Fig. 2. Entrance assemblies

zontal framing member, such member may have to be reinforced to limit deflection, or the assembly should be redesigned. Lateral loads may result in excessive deflection in long horizontal members and reinforcing may be required.

- Deflection in vertical members may affect operation of doors, and may have to be less than the acceptable maximum of approximately 1/180 of span for other framing members.

- Split mullions supporting doors hung from them may require reinforcement since they generally are not stiff enough to hold doors securely and in proper alignment.

1.3.2 Framing members

Door framing members are commonly available as stock items, however, custom frames are also available. They must be selected to compliment the function of the door opening. Building use and environmental factors are prime considerations. Door frame types include:

- built-up frames

- brake or roll formed

- extruded, formed, or tubular

Framing members for entrance assemblies, commonly used and available as stock items, are of extruded aluminum, generally clear or color anodized. Baked-on finishes, such as fluorocarbons and siliconized polymers, are also available.

- Channels are generally used as perimeter framing when the assembly is to be installed in a masonry or framed wall. Options available in stock shapes are: integral stop, recess for flush glazing. Modified shapes available with thermal breaks, and for lockstrip gasket glazing.

- Tubes are used as perimeter framing, vertical and horizontal framing members and as covers for structural steel channel or tub reinforcement. Options available in stock shapes are: integral stop, recesses for flush glazing. Modified shapes incorporating thermal breaks and/or provisions for lockstrip gasket glazing are available.

- Split tubes may be used for perimeter framing and as vertical/ horizontal framing. Integral stops and recesses for flush glazing available in stock shapes. Modified shapes with thermal breaks and/or for lockstrip glazing available.

• *Built-up frames*

- assembled frames with prehung door are available.

- two-piece adjustable frames are available.

- when wood frames are used in masonry walls a subframe is recommended.

- structural shape or bent plate frames are generally limited to industrial type construction; hinges are generally surface mounted, recess for latch is drilled in the field.

- drip cap at head recommended.

- closers cannot be concealed in frame; they may be surface mounted on frame or on door.

- wood and structural shape frames are generally prepared to receive hardware in the field.

- wood frames and trim for sliding doors are available clad in aluminum or PVC.

• *Brake or roll formed frames*

- usually available bonderized and prime painted; galvanized metal is available when specified.

- various sizes and shapes are available; wrap-around shapes are generally used for drywall construction.

- when installed in masonry walls, jambs, and head are typically filled solid with mortar.

- prefabricated shapes are available in standard lengths.

- drip cap is recommended when the face of the frame is flush with the outside face of the wall.

- frames should be factory prepped to receive hardware.

• Extruded frames, *formed,* or *tubular*

- aluminum extrusions are available in clear and color anodized as well as painted.

- various shapes and sizes are available.

- extruded sections with curved glass or metal fixed panels are used for revolving door enclosures.

- drip caps, either attached to frame or installed in the wall at the head of the frame, are recommended when the face of frame is flush with the outside face of the wall.

- frames should be factory prepared to receive hardware.

2 Design criteria and selection checklists

2.1 Checklist for pedestrian traffic doors

• General considerations include:

- Provide vision panels for all swinging doors unless locked at all times to prevent the leaf from swinging in the face of a person approaching the entrance from the opposite side.

- All-glass doors should be marked for easy identification within standard vision to prevent injury to persons from walking into the glass.

- Package-type entrance should be reviewed for the number of cycles the assembly can be used without deterioration in function.

• Resistance to corrosion may be an important factor in the selection of entrances. When corrosion resistance is reviewed, it should concern both the base materials and finishes of the components. Consider the building microclimate:

- humidity and salt spray will affect certain finishes.

- sunlight may degrade certain materials.

- environmental pollution will affect certain materials and finishes.

- materials which are vulnerable to corrosion can be upgraded by applied coatings or finishes.

- aluminum alloys are highly reactive with some metal types.

- cement products react with aluminum alloys. Provide coatings or physical separation.

- water runoff over metal surfaces can produce ion flow which causes staining or corrosion. Review all materials used in the construction of the building envelope.

• Sound transmission (applies to exterior and interior doors) through the door and along its perimeter should fit the STC (sound transmission class) of the entire assembly; accordingly, doors selected may be:

- hollow doors with sound deadening insulation.

- solid core doors.

- solid core doors faced with sound absorbing material.

- doors in partitions with high STC requirements have to be completely sealed around the entire perimeter:

- even a small gap will result in sound leakage enough to drastically lower the STC of the entire assembly.

• When pressure differentials exist between the two sides of the door, air/gas leakage under pressure should be prevented:

- compressible or mechanically inflatable seals along the entire perimeter are required.

- seals will also effectively prevent light passage; simple weatherstripping may be adequate when resistance to light leakage only is required.

- in certain continuous traffic locations, flexible doors may be selected which minimize leakage of air - conditioned, polluted, and so forth - when opened.

• Doors located where they are subject to the impact of constant traffic:

- solid-core metal-clad wood doors are good in resisting frequent impact but high in cost.

- hollow-core wood doors are easily broken and hollow metal doors are easily dented.

- doors may be reinforced to minimize damage when accidentally hit.

• In doors used for cooler or freezer assemblies: resistance to heat flow around the entire assembly is critical:

- freezer doors are generally provided with perimeter heating cables to prevent freeze-ups due to water vapor condensation and freezing.

• Doors may be located in radiation resistant assemblies. The range of requirements is:

- from a low level such as of an X-ray machine in a physician's office to that of an atomic reactor.

- for low-level radiation protection, lead-lined doors and frames are available.

- most other applications require special design.

• Resistance to impact:

- solid core doors have high impact resistance. Under severe conditions, metal-clad or solid-corewood doors are recommended. Flush glass doors and hollow-core wood or hollow-core metal doors are least resistant.

- flush doors are generally stronger than stile and rail doors.

- face width, and thickness of the stile-and-rail frame members will affect overall strength.

- hollow-core wood doors are not recommended for exterior exposure.

• Oversized doors and lead-lined doors, because of their weight:

- require more rugged hinges, frames and closers.

- power actuators may be needed if operating effort becomes excessive.

- due to the stresses incurred by oversized doors, the choice of hardware may be limited.

• Vision panels, louvers required; and any special configurations, such as clutch doors.

• Fire-resistance rating requirements: Not all door panels can be fire rated.

• Standards used in the construction of door panels are in general as follows:

- for wood panels - NWMA and AWI.

- for metal and glass doors - NAAMA and AAMA.

- for all-glass doors - FGMA and SIGMA, but safety standard ANSI as enforced by the Consumer Product Safety Commission must be followed.

SHELL

B2

- In selecting panel materials, note:

- wood components are available in a wide variety of wood species and finish grades:

- flush doors come in architectural, premium, custom and standard grades.

- stile and rail doors are fabricated from solid wood sections, either hardwood or softwood, and in various grades.

- wood components will normally not withstand exterior exposure without some type of protective coating.

2.2 Checklist for service and vehicular entrances and doors

2.2.1 Anticipated traffic

General considerations include anticipated traffic, which may suggest:

- For power-operated materials-handling equipment, such as fork lift trucks: consider biparting sliding, multipanel vertical sliding, sectional, roll-up, and telescoping types.

- For vehicular traffic, such as automobiles and trucks:

- Consider multipanel vertical sliding, sectional, roll-up and telescoping types.

- For low frequency use, where available clearances between entrances must be kept to a minimum, consider swinging bi-folding, or four-folding types.

- For large equipment, such as aircraft:

- openings up to 30 ft. (9 m) high x 130 ft. (40 m) wide: single-panel canopy type.

- openings up to 50 ft. (15 m) high x 130 ft. (40 m) wide: bi-folding canopy type.

- higher and wider openings: multipanel sliding. Multipanel types require room for stacking panels beyond the clear opening provided.

2.2.2 Frequency of use

High frequency use may preclude selection of certain types of entrances and require power operators, special controls, or other options.

- In all instances the need for power operators should be investigated; power operators add to cost of the installation an maintenance requirements.

- Ease of operation under adverse conditions, such as high winds, especially for large doors, may limit selection to horizontal sliding, vertical sliding, sectional, and roll-up types.

- Time required to open and close the door panels may also be a factor, especially for high frequency use entrances.

- Insulation within the door panel and possibility of efficient weatherstripping may be a consideration for low frequency use entrances.

- Isolation or separation of service traffic, especially standing vehicles, in ways that allow the exhaust fumes to inadvertently enter the building, such as through stairwells and/or fresh air intakes.

2.2.3 Environmental factors

- wind loads, especially for large entrances, affect the choice of entrance type to avoid damage to entrance, and to allow operation under high wind conditions.

- type of core material or frame construction: to resist horizontal wind forces without excessive deflection.

- canopy-type doors will, in addition, be subject to vertical wind force or uplift when in open position.

- thermal movement should be considered for very high or very wide door panels.

- impact resistance may be a consideration for high frequency use vehicular entrances.

- in general, sectional and roll-up types are easily damaged, but also are simpler to repair.

2.2.4 Clearances for service and vehicular entrances and doors

Clearance required for proper operation should be considered.

- *Swinging type entrances*

- width of panels generally limited by allowable loads on hinges and frames.

- width and height limited for panels requiring fire-resistance ratings.

- select surface mounted hinges when appearance is not a consideration.

- use mortise or unit locks/latches for durability and/o, security.

- power operation should be considered for high frequency use entrances or oversized door panels and when opening speed is important.

- *Sliding entrances*

- width and height of panels generally not limited except for panels requiring fire-resistance ratings.

- top track limited to smaller sizes of single panel and bi-parting types.

- inclined top track with fusible link catch available for normally open entrances required to be selfclosing in case of fire.

- counterweights may be added:

- for ease in opening and closing.

- to make door with horizontal track self-closing in case of fire.

- clear space should be provided near door for counterweights.

- multipanel type are generally power operated using endless chain, or motor-driven bottom rollers.

- for multipanel type in wide openings, excessive deflection of framing, which supports the top guides, will prevent opening or closing of door.

- side-coiling type may also be used with curving tracks. Only top track with bottom guides can be used for this type.

- *Vertical rise entrances*

- width and height of panels generally not limited except for panels requiring fire-resistance ratings.

- multipanel vertical slide and canopy types generally used for special conditions, and are individually designed for each application.

- sectional and roll-up types most widely used; standard sizes are available.

- roll-up types are limited in width by structural properties of slats, which have to transmit wind forces to jamb guides.

- multipanel vertical sliding type may also be used with curving tracks.

3 Specification of exterior door systems

3.1 Specification of glazed doors

This section includes selection data relevant to interior swinging stile and rail glazed doors. Types of glazed doors are discussed, along with selection criteria and glass light sizes.

- *Selection criteria include:*
- grade
- model
- door thickness
- outer face material and thickness
- veneer matching
- internal construction
- light openings
- *Grade (model)*
- steel doors: extra heavy duty
- wood doors: custom or premium (stile and rail)
- aluminum doors: custom (stile and rail)
- *Door thickness*
- steel doors: 1-3/4 in. (4.5 cm)
- wood doors: 2-1/4 in., 1-3/4 in., 1-3/8 in. (5.7 cm, 4.5 cm, 3.5 cm)
- aluminum doors: 1-3/4 in. (4.5 cm)
- *Outer face material and thickness*
- steel doors: hot or cold rolled steel sheet, galvanized steel sheet, stainless steel, bronze, or brass; 16 gage thickness.
- wood doors: dimensional lumber stock for transparent (plain, rift, or quarter sawn) finishing or opaque finishing, or standard thickness hardwood face veneers overlaid with medium density overlay veneer, natural hardwood veneer, or plastic laminate directly applied to core construction; composed of one ply.
- *Veneer matching*
- matching between individual pieces of veneer: book, slip, or random match
- assembly of spliced veneer on a face: sequence matching from opening to opening must be specified; examples include balanced, center balanced, and running matching
- *Internal construction*
- steel doors: tubular steel
- wood doors: dimensional lumber stock for transparent or opaque finishing or veneering
- aluminum doors: tubular aluminum
- *Light openings*
- steel doors: fully tempered or laminated safety glass; minimum bottom rail, stiles, top and intermediate rail heights of 3-1/2 in. (8.9 cm).
- wood doors: fully tempered or laminated safety glass; minimum recommended bottom rail height of 10 in. (25 cm), minimum stiles, top and intermediate rail heights of 4-1/2 in. (11 cm).
- aluminum doors: fully tempered or laminated safety glass; typical bottom rail, stiles, top and intermediate rail heights of 2-3/16 in. (5.5 cm), 4 in. (10 cm), and 5 in. (12.7 cm).

3.2 Specification of sliding doors

Horizontal sliding doors are advantageous for:

- unusually wide openings.
- where clearances do not permit use of swinging doors.
- operation of sliding doors is not hindered by windy conditions or differences in air pressure between indoors and outdoors.

For certain usage, horizontal sliding doors:

- may have to be motorized to increase traffic flow through the entrance.
- panic exit features may need to be incorporated to let people move through the door panels without injury during emergency egress.

Sliding entrances are manufactured as assemblies. Since a single manufacturer provides all components, the selections to be made will deal more with the style, materials, finishes, and accessories available than with the range of components and combinations available. Sliding entrances are normally selected for view and illumination as well as ingress/egress. Unless the doors are power-operated, sliding entrances are normally used for infrequent or low traffic entrances.

Sliding doors consist of one or more panels of framed, or unframed, glass, metal or wood which, in turn, are contained in an overall frame designed so that one or more panels are moveable in a horizontal direction. Each panel may be moveable, or some panels may be moveable with others fixed in a single opening. Panels may lock, or interlock with each other or may contact a jamb member where the panel is capable of being securely locked. Sliding doors can be fabricated principally with either aluminum or wood materials.

3.2.1 Aluminum sliding doors

- *Performance*
- Aluminum sliding doors are available in four performance grade designations as indicated in Table 1. The performance grade standards represented here are from American Architectural Manufacturers Association (AAMA) 101-93 *Voluntary Specifications for Aluminum and PolyVinyl Chloride (PVC) Prime Windows and Glass Doors.*
- Performance is designated by a number that follows the type and grade designation. For instance, a residential sliding glass door may be designated SGD-R15. The number establishes the design pressure, in this example being 15 pounds per sq. ft. (psf). The structural test pressure for all doors is 50% higher than the design pressure which, in the example, would be 22.5 psf.
- A maximum limit to deflection of 1/175 under the structural load test applies only to the Architectural door designation. However, it is good practice to research and specify sliding glass doors that are designed to meet this criteria to avoid the problems arising from excessive flexing of a sliding door and frame assembly.
- Air and water performance values shown are the minimum required to meet the designation grades indicated.
- Use of products exceeding the performance levels in Table 1 may be necessary where severe wind conditions, wind loading, special

Table 1. Sliding glass aluminum door designations

Designation	Type	Structural Design	Water Resistance	Air Infiltration	Force to Open
SGD-R15	Residential	15	2.86 psf	0.37 cfm @ 1.57 psf	30 lbf
SDG-C20	Commercial	20	3.00 psf	0.37 cfm @ 1.57 psf	30 lbf
SDG-HC40	Heavy Comm.	40	6.00 psf	0.37 cfm @ 6.24 psf	40 lbf
SDG-AW40	Architectural	40	8.00 psf	0.30 cfm @ 6,24 psf	40 lbf

SHELL

B2

Table 2. Architectural coating designations

Architectural Classification	Thickness (mils)	Weight (Mg/sq.in.)	Application
Architectural Class I	0.7 min.	27 min.	Interior architectural items subject to normal wear, and for exterior items that receive a minimal amount of cleaning and maitenance. Higher performing "hardcoat" Class I coatings may be achieved by increasing coating thickness to between 1 and 3 mils.
Architectural Class II	0.4 to 0.7	17 to 27	Interior items not subject to excessive wear or abrasion.

condensation and heat transmission criteria, or type of building project are encountered.

- *Materials*

- Aluminum is lightweight, non-rusting, nearly maintenance free, decorative, and non-rotting material. It can be formed by extrusion, bent from sheet, cast, and joined by heliarc welding into many shapes, sizes, and forms.

- Aluminum has a high coefficient of thermal expansion (0.000013 per inch per degree F) and its thermal resistance factor is almost zero. Lower thermal resistance factors increase the tendency of interior water vapor to condense on, or in, window framing members in cold weather.

- Aluminum sliding glass doors that incorporate higher-priced thermal break construction increase thermal resistance factors. Use of insulating glass units, dual lines of high performance gaskets and weather-stripping, and careful, proper, and competent installation procedures offset the low thermal resistance factors inherent in aluminum by reducing air infiltration.

- *Finishes*

- Clear lacquer or naturally developed aluminum oxide coatings are the minimal forms of coating protection to aluminum during construction where subsequent field applied coatings are intended.

- Aluminum components of aluminum sliding glass doors normally are factory finished with some form of a protective, decorative anodized or organic coating.

- Anodic coatings are composed of aluminum oxide and are a part of the aluminum substrate. By carefully controlling the thickness, density, and hardness of the anodized coating, a substantial performance and durability improvement over lacquered and naturally developed oxide coatings can be achieved. Anodized coatings have limited color availability.

- Organic coatings are either baked on or air dried and are available in a great array of performance and durability levels as well as color selection. Factory applied and baked on, organic coatings typically outperform air dried types. Some baked on, fluropolymer based, organic coatings outperform anodized coatings for color retention, chalk, and humidity resistance.

- Most organic coatings that are used for aluminum components of sliding doors should meet or exceed the requirements of AAMA 603.8 Pigmented Organic Coatings on Extruded Aluminum or AAMA 605.2 High Performance Organic Coatings on Architectural Extrusions and Panels. AAMA 605.2 is more stringent than AAMA 603.8. The two standard classification levels of architectural anodized coatings promulgated by the Aluminum Association (AA) and the National Association of Architectural Metal Manufacturers (NAAMM) are indicated in Table 2.

3.2.2   Wood sliding doors

- *Performance*

- Wood sliding doors are available in three performance grade designations as indicated in Table 3. The performance grade standards represented in this text are from National Wood Window and Door Association (NWWDA) Standard I.S.3 Wood Sliding Patio Doors.

- Performance is designated by a number that follows grade designation. The number establishes the design pressure, in this example being 20 pounds per sq. ft. (psf). The structural test pressure for all doors is 50% higher than the design pressure which, in our example would be 30 psf.

- A maximum limit to deflection of 0.1% of the span at the positive and negative grade designated test pressure applies to each grade.

- Air and water performance values shown are the minimum required to meet the designation grades indicated.

- Use of products exceeding the performance levels in Table 3 may be necessary where severe wind conditions, wind loadings, special condensation and heat transmission criteria, more stringent deflection criteria, or type of building project are encountered.

- *Materials*

- Wood is lightweight, non-rusting, and decorative material. It can be formed by machining into many shapes, sizes, and forms.

- Wood has a lower coefficient of thermal expansion than aluminum, however, if the moisture content of the wood is affected by ambient humidity fluctuations then shrinking and swelling may occur and result in door component dimensional change.

- The thermal resistance factor of wood is higher than aluminum. Higher thermal resistance factors reduce the tendency of interior water vapor to condense on or within window framing members in cold weather.

- Use of insulating glass units, dual lines of high performance gaskets and weather-stripping, and careful, proper, and competent installation procedures aid in increasing the high thermal resistance factors inherent in wood by reducing air infiltration.

3.3 Specification of swinging entrances

Since all components which comprise swinging entrances can be manufactured independently, the selection of the proper components for a specific application is as important as the selection of the basic entrance type.

In selecting a swinging door, consider:

- single-action doors can swing 90° or more in one direction only.

- double-action doors can swing 90° or more in each direction.

- far more styles, types, materials, and accessories are available for swinging entrances than for any other type.

As indicated in Fig. 3, doors may be mounted either on butt hinges or on pivots. Hinges provide maximum free opening width, but impose strain on jamb. Commonly three hinges for standard height door. Pivots may be center, offset. or swinging. Center pivots required for double-acting doors, and generally required for automatically operated doors. Pivots preferred to hinges for heavy doors or for unusually severe service. Closers may be mounted concealed in the top rail of the frame, exposed on the top rail, or surface mounted on the door. Floor closers are recessed in the floor construction.

The following points should be considered for each swinging door assembly:

- *Size and configuration*

- Swinging doors are generally available in sizes up to 4 ft. (1.2 m) wide and 10 ft. (3 m) high.

- Width: The wider a door leaf the greater its weight, the higher the stresses on the hinging hardware and frames, and the more difficult it will be to open.

- Height: The taller a door leaf the greater its weight, and the higher the occurrence of door leaf deformations and excessive flexibility. Selecting wider door stiles, greater door thickness, and additional hinging hardware components can offset the effects of greater door height.

- *Building type and anticipated building use*

- building egress: when considered as an exit, direction of swing must be in direction of flow of traffic to area of refuge.

- balanced and center-pivoted doors reduce clear openings of swinging doors.

Table 3. Sliding glass wood door designations

Designation	Structural Design	Water Resistance	Air Infiltration	Force to Open
Grade 20	20	2.86 psf 1.57 psf	0.34 cfm @	25 lbf
Grade 40	40	4.43 psf 1.57 psf	0.25 cfm @	30 lbf
Grade 60	60	6.24 psf 1.57 psf	0.10 cfm @	35 lbf

COMPONENTS OF DOOR ASSEMBLY

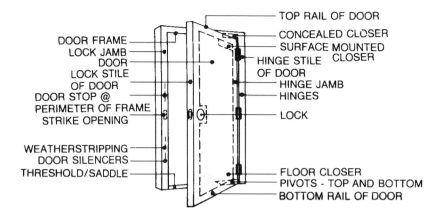

FLUSH DOORS

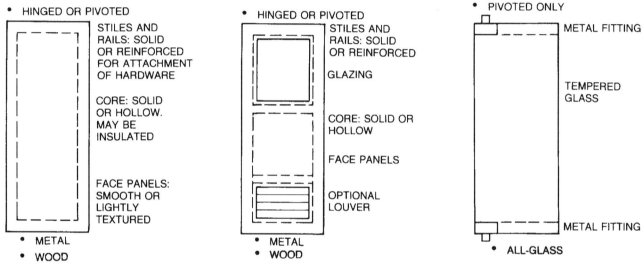

STILE AND RAIL DOORS

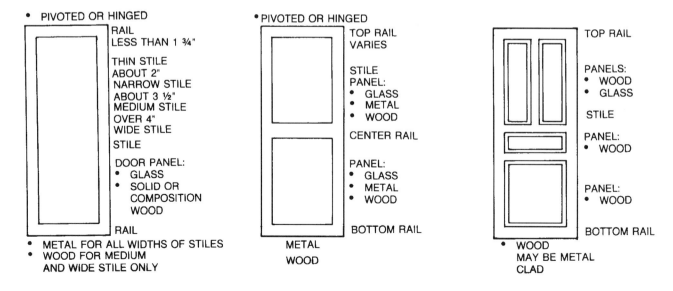

Fig. 3. Door assemblies: swinging door types

- the dynamics of building population use: a single pair of swinging doors can handle a small building population effectively.

- security requirements: swinging doors can be custom fabricated to incorporate card readers or coded number access devices coupled with magnetic locks and metal detectors.

- accessibility for the disabled: large swinging doors may be difficult to operate for disabled people especially in instances where excessive wind and stack pressures are encountered. In order to address this concern swinging doors can be provided with automatic door operators with opening and closing speed controls.

- weather-tightness: swinging doors can be fabricated, or provided with, a positive continuous seal around each door leaf. Double-acting doors cannot be made as weather tight as single-acting doors.

- *Environmental influences and climatic conditions*

- temperature range: project specific ambient and surface temperatures should be considered in the selection of materials for swinging doors.

- prevailing winds: swinging door assemblies should be designed to resist positive and negative wind loads as determined from local code requirements, by analytical methods, or from data obtained through wind tunnel analyses.

- precipitation: the presence of de-icing salts may cause corrosion of unprotected swinging door components.

- atmospheric conditions: project-specific humidity, salt spray, and air pollution should be considered in the selection of materials for swinging doors.

- UV Exposure: project-specific sun exposure should be considered in the selection of organic and inorganic coatings on exposed components of swinging doors.

- *Other factors influencing swinging door entrance design*

- stack pressure: the greater the stack pressure, the greater the potential for energy loss. The entrance area suction, or pressure, increases as both the difference between the inside and outside air temperatures widens and as the building gets taller.

- suitable structural support for the swinging door opening frame should always be provided.

- door hardware: tall buildings, and buildings in areas with tall buildings, can create large downdrafts affecting swinging door performance. Hydraulic, electric, or pneumatic door operators and balanced door pivots, are sometimes incorporated into swinging door assemblies to offset downdrafts as well as the effects of excessive stack pressures and door weight. Operators are normally set for an adjustable time to open of between one to five seconds.

- glazing and weather-stripping selected to minimize air infiltration/exfiltration and water penetration.

- codes normally require safety glazing to reduce accidents due to broken glass.

3.4   Specification of revolving doors

Revolving doors are a form of exterior door assembly that is typically selected for entries which carry a continuous flow of traffic without very high peaks and where air infiltration/exfiltration must be kept to an absolute minimum. Revolving door entrances are manufactured as assemblies. The manufacturer will provide all components required for installation. When selecting revolving doors, consider that they are generally selected for:

- entries which carry a continuous flow of traffic without very high peaks.

- they keep interchange of inside and outside air to a relatively small amount compared to other types of doors.

- they are usually used in combination with swinging doors because of revolving doors' inability to handle large volumes of people in short periods of time.

- building codes prohibit the use of revolving doors for some types of occupancy because of the limited traffic flow in emergencies:

- where permitted as exits, they have limitations imposed by local building codes.

- may not, in some instances, provide more than 50 percent of the required exit capacity at any location. The remaining capacity must be supplied by swinging doors within close proximity.

Revolving doors may be power assisted to facilitate traffic through them. Revolving-door entrances normally provide a panic-releasing device which automatically releases a door panel in case of:

- entrapment of the user.

- accidental jamming or impact on the door leaves.

- revolving doors are provided with speed governors to limit the maximum speed at which the door leaves will travel.

The following points should be considered for each revolving door assembly:

- *Size and configuration*

- Revolving doors are only available as a complete package. Diameters vary from 6 to 8 ft. (1.8 m to 2.4 m) as standard with 7 ft. (2.1 m) being the standard height. Wider doors are generally recommended for easier traffic flow, especially in buildings where hand carried luggage is a factor.

- Three-wing and four-wing doors are available as standard from many manufacturers. Four-wing types are generally more energy efficient while three-wing types provide more space for people in wheelchairs.

- *Building type and anticipated building use*

- building egress: some building codes restrict the use of revolving doors to provide full exit capacity for certain building occupancies because of their limitations to traffic flow in emergencies. In such situations, exit capacity is made up by the provision of adjacent swinging entrance doors. Revolving doors should be equipped with an emergency release mechanism to book-fold wings, and a manual or power-assisted speed controller.

- dynamics of building population use: a single revolving door can handle a small building population effectively. The larger the building the greater the quantity of revolving doors required to accommodate peak building population entrance/exit times.

- security requirements: revolving doors can be custom fabricated to incorporate card readers or coded number access devices coupled with magnetic locks and metal detectors.

- accessibility: standard-size revolving doors are difficult to operate by those with limited physical capacities and by those transporting large objects. To address these concerns, custom revolving doors can be manufactured that incorporate wider wings and door speed controls.

- weather-tightness: revolving doors are fabricated to incorporate a positive, continuous seal around the door assembly perimeter and completely around each door wing. In addition, with power-assisted operators revolving doors stop automatically with their wings in quarter-point position, providing an air lock within the enclosure that reduces air infiltration/exfiltration.

- *Environmental influences and climatic conditions*

- temperature range: project-specific ambient and surface temperatures should be considered in the selection of materials for revolving doors.

- prevailing winds: revolving door assemblies should be designed to resist positive and negative wind loads as determined from local code requirements, by analytical methods, or from data obtained through wind tunnel analyses.

- precipitation: in geographic locations that receive heavy snowfall, foot grilles are sometimes incorporated into revolving door installations to prevent the accumulation of snow within the enclosure. The presence of de-icing salts may cause corrosion of unprotected revolving door components.

- atmospheric conditions: project-specific humidity, salt spray, and air pollution should be considered in the selection of materials for revolving doors.

- UV exposure: project-specific sun exposure should be considered in the selection of organic and inorganic coatings on exposed components of revolving doors.

- *Other factors influencing revolving door entrance design*

- energy efficiency: revolving doors are much more energy efficient than swinging doors. A single bank of revolving doors is more energy efficient than double bank of swinging doors.

- stack pressure: the greater the stack pressure, the greater the potential for energy loss. The entrance area suction, or pressure, increases as both the difference between the inside and outside air temperatures widens and as the building gets taller.

- suitable structural support for the revolving door opening frame should be provided.

- door hardware: tall buildings, and buildings in areas with tall buildings, can create large downdrafts affecting revolving door performance. Manual or power-assisted speed controllers, often sized to comply with code-mandated speeds, are used to prevent rapid acceleration and spinning of revolving doors caused by downdrafts.

- glazing and weather-stripping should be selected to minimize air infiltration/exfiltration and water penetration.

- codes normally require safety glazing to reduce accidents due to broken glass.

3.5   Specification of fire doors

This section includes selection data relevant to interior fire rated, standard steel, and wood doors. Types of fire doors are discussed, along with selection criteria and limitations on glass light sizes.

- *Types of doors include:*
- swinging steel doors
- swinging wood doors
- sliding steel doors
- *Selection criteria include:*
- grade
- model
- door thickness
- fire resistance ratings and sizes
- outer face material and thickness
- veneer matching
- internal construction
- louver types
- light openings
- fabrication tolerances
- *Grade (model):*

- steel doors: standard, heavy, and extra heavy duty (full flush or seamless design

- wood doors: economy, custom, and premium (seam-free only)

- sliding steel doors: custom (full flush or seamless design)

- *Door thickness*

- steel doors: 1-3/4 in. (4.5 cm)

- wood doors: 1-3/4 in., 1-3/8 in. (4.5 cm, 3.5 cm)

- sliding steel doors: 1-3/4 to 4-1/8 in. (4.5 to 10.5 cm)

- *Fire resistance ratings and sizes:*

- swinging steel doors: 20 minutes through 120 minutes

- wood doors: 1-3/4 in. (4.5 cm), 1-3/8 in. (3.5 cm) thick: 20 minutes; 1-3/4 in. (4.5 cm) thick: 45, 60, and 90 minutes

- sliding steel doors: 45 minutes to 240 minutes

- temperature rise ratings: Available in both steel and wood to 250F maximum temperature rise after 30 minutes.

- *Face sizes*

- steel doors: 4 ft. x 10 ft. (1.2 m x 3 m) singles; 8 ft. x 10 ft. (2.4 m x 3 m) pairs.

- wood doors: 4 ft. x 9 ft. (1.2 m x 2.7 m) singles; 8 ft. x 9 ft. (2.4 m x 2.7 m) parallel pairs; 8 ft. x 8 ft. (2.4 m x 2.4 m) double egress 45 and 60 minutes; 4 ft. x 10 ft. (1.2 m x 3 m) singles; 8 ft. x 8 ft. (2.4 m x 2.4 m) parallel pairs; 8 ft. x 8 ft. (2.4 m x 2.4 m) double egress 90 minutes; 4 ft. x 10 ft. (1.2 m x 3 m) singles; 8 ft. x 8 ft. (2.4 m x 2.4 m) parallel pairs.

- sliding steel doors: refer to Table 1

- *Outer face material and thickness*

- steel doors: hot or cold rolled steel sheet, galvanized steel sheet, electro-zinc coated steel sheet, stainless steel, bronze, or brass; 20, 18, 16, 14 gage thicknesses; embossed patterns available.

- wood doors: standard thickness hardwood face veneers overlaid with medium density overlay veneer, natural hardwood veneer, plastic laminate, or hardboard directly applied to core construction; composed of two, three, or four plies having an overall approximate thickness of 1/16 in.(1.5 mm); one ply of 1/8 in. (3 mm) for hardboard faces.

- sliding steel doors: hot or cold rolled steel sheet, galvanized steel sheet, stainless steel.

- *Veneer matching*

- matching between individual pieces of veneer: book, slip, or random match.

- assembly of spliced veneer on a face: sequence matching from opening to opening must be specified; examples include balanced, center balanced, and running matching.

- *Internal construction*

- steel doors: unitized steel grid, vertical steel stiffeners, mineral fiberboard.

- wood doors:

  20-minute doors: particleboard and glued block core, asbestos-free incombustible mineral.

- 45-, 60-, 90-minute doors: asbestos-free incombustible mineral.

- sliding steel doors: rectangular steel framing with intermediate steel tube members, fiberglass filler.

- *Louver types*

- may not be used on a door opening in a means of egress. Some manufacturers are permitted to use on doors fire rated up to 90 minutes; most are limited in area to 576 sq. in. (3700 sq. cm) with maximum 24 in. (60 cm) length or width.

- steel doors: some manufacturers are not permitted to mix fusible link louvers on doors having light openings, panic devices, or doors exceeding 12 ft. (3.7 m) high.

- wood doors: some manufacturers are not permitted to mix fusible link louvers on doors having light openings, panic devices, hardboard faces, or doors exceeding 9 ft. (2.7 m) high.

• *Light openings in steel fire doors:*

- 20, 30, and 45 minutes: maximum single light 1296 sq. in. (8360 sq. cm) with no dimension exceeding 54 in. (1.4 m).

- 60, and 90 minutes: maximum single light 100 sq. in. (645 sq. cm).

- 120 minutes: no light permitted

• *Light openings in steel fire doors:* Same criteria is permitted for steel doors, however the following is known to be available:

- 20 and 30 minutes: maximum single light 1296 sq. in. (8360 sq. cm) with no dimension exceeding 54 in. (1.4 m).

- 45 minutes: maximum 1296 sq. in. (8360 sq. cm) singles; maximum 100 sq. in. (645 sq. cm) parallel pairs and double egress.

- 60 and 90 minutes: maximum 100 sq. in. (645 sq. cm) singles and parallel pairs.

- sliding steel doors: lights available in doors rated to 240 minutes

3.6 Specification of overhead doors

Overhead doors are a form of exterior door assembly that is usually selected to control door openings such as can be found at loading docks, garage entrances, and airplane hangers. Selection criteria and issues regarding door function, size, and operation are discussed. The following points should be considered for each overhead door assembly:

• Size and configuration

- Width and height of panels making up overhead doors are generally available in the sizes indicated in Table 5. Larger, custom sizes are available. Fire-rated models have limited size availability.

- Overhead doors are limited in width by structural properties of slats, which must transmit wind forces to jamb guides.

• Building type and anticipated building use

- building egress: overhead doors are not intended as a means of egress.

- the dynamics of building population use: estimated cycles per day varies with building type and use. Standard and High Cycle spring sets are selected where lifetime door cycling is not anticipated to exceed less than 50,000 cycles or 100,000 cycles, respectively. High cycle springs are also selected where high use or corrosive environments are anticipated.

- operation options: manual, crank, and gear; motorized operations are typically available for all overhead doors.

- security requirements: overhead doors can be custom fabricated to incorporate card readers or coded number access devices coupled with door controllers and operators.

- accessibility for the universal design criteria: manually operated overhead doors are difficult to operate. To address this concern, overhead doors with motorized operators can be manufactured.

- weather-tightness: overhead doors are fabricated to incorporate positive seals around the door assembly perimeter that resist air infiltration/exfiltration. These seals cannot exclude water or stop

Table 4. Sliding fire door sizes (single, centerparting and 2 panel tele types)

Core	Skin Gage	Labeled Size (Max)	Oversize Label	Temperature Rise
Composite (fiberglas)	14 to 18	12'-0" x 12'-0"	40'-0" x 40'-0"	450 F
Hollow metal	14 to 20	12'-0" x 12'-0"	34'-0"x 20'-0"	not available
Composite (mineral fiberboard)	14 to 20	12'-0" x 12'-0"	34'-0" 20"-0'	not available

Table 5: Average available maximum sizes of overhead doors

Type	Width x Height (Feet)
Sectional	36 x 20
Roll up	30 x 30
Rolling grille	Varies
Telescoping	20 x 20
Canopy	60 x 30

AUTOMATIC DOOR OPERATORS

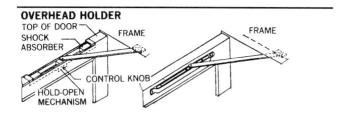

ULTRASONIC DEVICE
OPERATOR-OPTIONAL
LOCATIONS.

CONTACT SWITCH

PHOTOELECTRONIC
CELL
DEMOTE SWITCH

FLOOR MAT

POWER UNIT

PANIC EXIT DEVICES

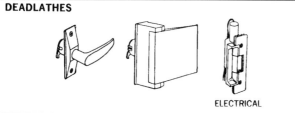

LATCH FOR
CONCEALED ROD
TYPE-LATCHES
TOP AND BOTTOM

LATCH FOR CENTER
RIM LATCH-BOLT TYPE

OVERHEAD HOLDER

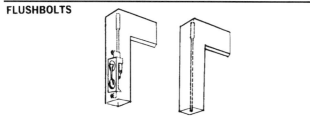

TOP OF DOOR
SHOCK
ABSORBER
FRAME
FRAME
CONTROL KNOB
HOLD-OPEN
MECHANISM

DEADLATHES

ELECTRICAL

FLUSHBOLTS

Fig. 4. Doorframe hardware

air movement completely. Door curtains of perforated slat, slotted slats, or bar grille design would not be weather-tight.

- Environmental influences and climatic conditions

- temperature range: project-specific ambient and surface temperatures should be considered in the selection of materials for overhead doors.

- prevailing winds: overhead door assemblies should be designed to resist positive and negative wind loads as determined from local code requirements, by analytical methods, or from data obtained through wind tunnel analyses.

- precipitation: The presence of de-icing salts may cause corrosion of unprotected overhead door components.

- atmospheric conditions: project-specific humidity, salt spray, and air pollution should be considered in the selection of materials for overhead doors.

- UV exposure: project specific sun exposure should be considered in the selection of organic and inorganic coatings on exposed components of overhead doors.

Other factors influencing on overhead door design:

- Energy efficiency: overhead doors are normally made to be energy efficient by the incorporation of neoprene, silicone, EPDM, or PVC and nylon brush-type seals at the head, jamb, and bottom bar components of the door assembly to control air infiltration/exfiltration. Curtain slats can be fabricated with foamed in place, or rigid block, type insulation to increase thermal performance. Curtain slats can be fabricated from PVC.

- Suitable structural support for the overhead door opening frame and hangers should be provided.

- Door hardware with a capacity and durability should be selected to provide adequate performance of the door assembly. Torsion springs are generally used and counterweights are usually required when door is in a fire-rated opening. Counterweights hold the door in the open position and are released by fusible link, smoke detectors, or loss of power from initiation of a fire alarm system.

- Sheltering components may be provided to aid in the convenient and sheltered loading and unloading of goods such as canopies, opening seals, bumpers, guards, and loading dock shelters and air curtains.

4 Door frames and hardware selection checklist

Elements of entrance door frames and hardware are shown in Fig. 4. This section describes general selection criteria, in terms of:

- frames
- closers
- hinges and pivots
- locks and latches

SHELL

B2

4.1 Frames

The entrance frame can be a simple frame surrounding a door panel, or a series of members holding fixed panels as well as the door panels.

- The frame and the trim may be integral or made of separate pieces. Entrance frame must be strong enough to resist wind load without excessive deflection, to avoid the possibility of deformation of the frame with resultant:

  - cracking of fixed glass panels.

  - binding of door panels.

  - opening of joints in frame.

- Door frames in wood construction require:
  - rough-in bucks secured to the structural frame for secure attachment and operation.

  - can receive complete "pre-hung" door assemblies or be site fabricated.

  - joints between frame and wall are covered by trim.

  - finished wood frames are generally field fitted to exact conditions.

- Door frames in metal construction:
  - are often set in before the wall is filled in and serve as framing members.

  - frames and doors may be pre-hung and pre-assembled and come as a package. Protection of metal frames and prehung doors during installation and remainder of construction often requires considerable care.

- Metal entrance frames may be of:
  - built-up rolled sections.

  - brake formed metal sections.

  - roll formed metal sections.

  - extrusions.

4.2 Closers

The next major entrance component to be considered are closers, manual and powered.

- Closers for doors are either overhead or floor-type and either fully concealed, semi-concealed, or surface mounted. All manually operated closers require a certain amount of force to open the door panel. Therefore, depending on the type of entrance desired, power-actuation may be required:

- Oversize doors may become too heavy to be opened manually.

- All entrance types are generally available with power-actuation.

- When selecting power-actuation, consider safety. People must be protected from inadvertent operation of power-actuated door leaves. Review the type of sensors to be used.

- Swinging doors normally require guard rails or other architectural barriers to protect people from their swing.

- Sliding doors need a pocket or other barrier to prevent contact with people during operation.

- Revolving doors must have a speed control to limit number of revolutions.

- Some definitions of door hardware:

  - Automatic closing device: causes the door to close when activated by detector through rate of temperature rise, smoke, or other products of combustion.

  - Automatic closing door is normally in open position, and is closed by an automatic closing device in case of fire.

  - Center latch: is used to hold two leaves of bi-parting doors together.

  - Self-closing door: will return to the closed position after having been opened and released.

4.3 Hinges and pivots

The other entrance components to be considered simultaneously with the selection of closers are hinges, or devices on which doors turn or swing, to open and close:

- Hinges may be concealed or exposed.

- Butts are the most common type of hinge used today. They are usually mortised into the edge of the door.

  - are generally mounted on a door 5 in. (13 cm) from the head and 10 in. (25 cm) from the floor.

  - when a third butt is required to minimize warping of door, it is mounted equidistant between top and bottom hinges.

- Pivots are stronger and more durable than hinges and are better able to withstand the racking stresses to which doors are subjected.

 Their use is generally recommended for

- oversize doors, heavy doors.

- entrance doors of high frequency use.

4.4 Locks and latches

Locks and latches are used to hold doors in the closed position:

- A deadbolt is often used in conjunction with a latch, in which case the unit is known as a lock.

  - for doors which need not be latched or locked during the normal work day, Push Pull plates are normally used in lieu of latch sets or locks.

  - doors with push pull plates may be provided with a dead bolt if there is a need to secure them at certain times.

  - hardware is a factor in determining the ultimate security of the entrance:

- Mortise locks are the most secure type of lock. Deadbolts provide superior protection to latch bolts.

- The proper location of door silencers on swinging entrances can prevent latch lock tampering.

- Special armor plates are available for protecting lock cylinders.

- Electronic latches, hinges, card readers, and other devices are available for specific security requirements.

- Panic devices for mass exit in emergencies are installed on exterior doors which serve as legal exits from a building.

- Entrance, exit and door hardware is a very diverse and highly intricate subject. Architects rarely specify such hardware without the benefit of the expertise of a hardware consultant. Installation of some entrance types and component types create special requirements:

  - one piece hollow metal frames are normally installed before-the wall construction is complete.

  - recessed floor closures need openings in floor slabs and adequate slab depth.

  - revolving door entrances require special care in the installation of the floor within the enclosure for smoothness and flatness.

  - hardware should be reviewed to determine its operating life.

References and resources

American Architectural Manufacturers Association, 1827 Walden Office Square, Suite 104, Schaumburg, IL 60173-4268; 847-303-5664 (phone).

Door and Hardware Institute, 14170 New Brook Drive, Chantilly, VA 22021-2223; 703-222-2010 (phone).

National Association of Architectural Metal Manufacturers, 8 S. Michigan Ave., Suite 1000, Chicago, IL 60603-3305; 312-456-5590 (phone).

National Fire Protection Association, One Batterymarch Park, Quincy, MA 02269-9101, 800-344-3555 (phone).

National Wood Window and Door Association, 1400 E. Touhy Avenue, Suite G-54, Des Plaines, IL 60018; 800-223-2301 (phone).

Steel Door Institute, 30200 Detroit Road, Cleveland, OH 44145-1967; 216-899-0010 (phone).

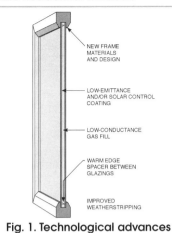

Fig. 1. Technological advances in windows

Residential windows

Summary: Window units are one of the most important components affecting energy performance and comfort in residential buildings. New window technologies provide improved performance and an array of design options. This article provides an introduction to the energy-related aspects of windows and provides guidelines for window selection in different U. S. climates.

Key words: energy efficiency, residential windows.

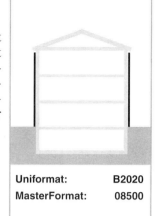

| Uniformat: | B2020 |
| MasterFormat: | 08500 |

In recent years, windows have undergone a technological revolution. They are no longer the weak link in energy-efficient home design. In the winter, high performance windows reduce heat loss considerably, provide greater thermal comfort, and reduce the risk of condensation. In summer, it is now possible to have expansive views and daylight while significantly reducing solar heat gain. These changes create many new options for architects, builders, and homeowners, making window selection a more complex process. Choosing a window involves many considerations related to aesthetics, function, energy performance, and cost. This article focuses primarily on the energy performance considerations in comparing windows. First, recent technological advances are identified, followed by descriptions of the energy-related properties of windows, condensation potential, and window rating systems. Then, window selection based on energy performance is discussed in more detail for different U. S. climate zones.

Technological improvements

Some technological innovations appearing in today's window products are described briefly below.

- *Glazing unit structure*

Multiple layers of glass or plastic films improve thermal resistance and reduce the heat loss attributed to convection between window layers. Additional layers also provide more surfaces for low-E or solar control coatings.

- *Low-emittance coatings*

Low-emittance or low-E coatings are highly transparent and virtually invisible, but have a high reflectance (low emittance) to long-wavelength infrared radiation. This reduces long-wavelength radiative heat transfer between glazing layers by a factor of 5 to 10, thereby reducing total heat transfer between two glazing layers. Low-emittance coatings may be applied directly to glass surfaces, or to thin sheets of plastic (films) which are suspended in the air cavity between the interior and exterior glazing layers. In effect, a window with a low-E coating can transmit a significant amount of daylight as well as passive solar heat gain, while significantly reducing heat loss.

- *Low-conductance gas fills*

With the use of a low-emittance coating, heat transfer across a gap is dominated by conduction and natural convection. While air is a relatively good insulator, there are other gases (such as argon, krypton, and carbon dioxide) with lower thermal conductivity. Using one of these nontoxic gases in an insulating glass unit can reduce heat transfer between the glazing layers.

- *Solar control glazing and coatings*

To reduce cooling loads, new types of tinted glass and new coatings can be specified that reduce the impact of the sun's heat without sacrificing view. Spectrally selective glazing and coatings absorb and reflect the infrared portion of sunlight while transmitting visible daylight, thus reducing solar heat gain coefficients and the resulting cooling loads. These solar control coatings can also have low-emittance characteristics. In effect, a window with a spectrally selective coating or tint can significantly reduce solar heat gain while providing more daylight than traditional reflective or tinted glazing.

- *Warm edge spacers*

Heat transfer through the metal spacers that are used to separate glazing layers can increase heat loss and cause condensation to form at the edge of the window. "Warm edge" spacers use new materials and better design to reduce this effect.

- *Thermally improved sash and frame*

Traditional sash and frame designs contribute to heat loss and can represent a large fraction of the total loss when high-performance glass is used. New materials and improved designs can reduce this loss.

- *Improved weather-stripping*

Better weather-strips are now available to reduce air leakage, and most are of more durable materials that will provide improved performance over a longer time period.

Energy-related properties on windows

Heat flows through a window assembly in three ways: conduction, convection, and radiation. When these basic mechanisms of heat transfer are applied to the performance of windows, they interact in complex ways. Three energy performance characteristics of windows are used to portray how energy is transferred and a fourth indicates the amount of daylight transmitted (Table 1).

- *Heat flow*

When there is a temperature difference between inside and outside, heat is transferred through the window frame and glazing by the combined effects of conduction, convection, and radiation. This is indicated in terms of the U-factor of a window assembly. It is expressed in units of Btu/hr-sq. ft-F (W/sq. m-°C). The U-factor may be expressed for the glass alone or the entire window, which includes the effect of the frame and the spacer materials. The lower the U-factor, the greater a window's resistance to heat flow. A window's insulating value is indicated in terms of its R-value, which is the reciprocal of U-value.

Authors: John Carmody and Stephen Selkowitz

References: Carmody, John, Stephen Selkowitz, and Lisa Heschong. 1996. *Residential Windows: New Technologies and Energy Performance.* New York: W.W. Norton & Company.

Table 1. Properties of Some Typical Windows. (Source: Carmody, Selkowitz and Heschong, Residential Windows, 1996)

window description	Total window unit U-value SHGC VT			Center of glass only U-value SHGC VT		
Single-glazed Clear glass Aluminum frame*	1.30	0.79	0.69	1.11	0,86	0.90
Double-glazed Clear glass Aluminum frame**	0.64	0.65	0.62	0.49	0.76	0.81
Double-glazed Bronze tinted glass Aluminum frame**	0.64	0.55	0.47	0.49	0.62	0.61
Double glased Clear glass Wood or vinyl frame	0.49	0.58	0.57	0.49	0.76	0.81
Double-glazed Low-E (high solar gain) Argon gas fill Wood or vinyl frame	0.33	0.55	0.52	0.32	0.74	0.74
Double-glaze Low-E (medium solar gain) Argon gas fill Wood or vinyl frame	0.30	0.44	0.56	0.26	0.58	0.78
Double-glazed Specrally selective low-E (low solar gain) Argon gas fill Wood or vinyl frame	0.29	0.31	0.51	0.24	0.41	0.72
Triple-glazed Clear glass Wood or vinyl frame	0.34	0.52	0.53	0.31	0.69	0.75
Triple-glazed Two low-E coatings Krypton gas fill Wood or vinyl frame	0.15	0.37	0.48	0.11	0.49	0.68

*   No thermal break in frame.
**   Thermal break in frame.
   All values for total windows are based on a 2-foot by 4-foot casement window.
   Units for all U-values are Btu/hr-sq ft-°F.
   SHGC = solar heat gain coefficient.
   VT = visible transmittance.

- *Heat gain from solar radiation*

Regardless of outside temperature, heat can be gained through windows by direct or indirect solar radiation. The ability to control this heat gain through windows is indicated in terms of the solar heat gain coefficient (SHGC). The SHGC is the fraction of incident solar radiation admitted through a window, both directly transmitted, and absorbed and subsequently released inward. The solar heat gain coefficient has replaced the shading coefficient as the standard indicator of a window's shading ability. It is expressed as a number between 0 and 1. The lower a window's solar heat gain coefficient, the less solar heat it transmits, and the greater its shading ability.

- *Infiltration*

Heat loss and gain also occur by infiltration through cracks in the window assembly. This effect is measured in terms of the amount of air (cubic feet or meters per minute) that passes through a unit area of window (square foot or meter) or window perimeter length (foot or meter) under given pressure conditions. It is indicated by an air leakage rating (AL). In reality, infiltration varies with wind-driven and temperature-driven pressure changes. Infiltration also contributes to summer cooling loads in some climates by raising the interior humidity level.

- *Visible transmittance*

Visible transmittance (VT) is an optical property that indicates the amount of visible light transmitted through the glass. Although VT does not directly affect heating and cooling energy use, it is used in the evaluation of energy-efficient windows. For example, two windows may have similar solar heat gain control properties, however one may transmit more daylight as indicated by the visible transmittance. The visible transmittance may then be the basis for choosing one window over another. Specifically, VT is the percentage or fraction of the visible spectrum (380 to 720 nanometers) weighted by the sensitivity of the eye, that is transmitted through the glazing. The higher the VT, the more daylight is transmitted.

- *Condensation potential*

Reducing the risk of condensation on windows is an important aspect of selecting a window. Fig. 2 shows condensation potential on glazing (center of glass) at various outdoor temperature and indoor relative humidity conditions. Condensation can occur at any points that fall on or above the curves. (Note: All air spaces are 1/2 inch; all coatings are e = 0.10).

- *Example 1:*

At 20F (-7°C) outside temperature, condensation will form on the inner surface of double glazing any time the indoor relative humidity is 52 percent or higher. It will form at an indoor relative humidity of 70 percent or higher if a double-pane window with low-E and argon is used.

- *Example 2:*

In a cold climate where winter night temperatures drop to -10F (-23°C), we want to maintain 65% humidity without condensation. A double-glazed window with low-E and argon will show condensation at 57% relative humidity, so the triple glazing with two low-E coatings and argon is needed to prevent condensation.

Window rating systems

The National Fenestration Rating Council (NFRC) was established in 1989 to develop a fair, accurate, and credible rating system for fenestration products. This was in response to the technological advances and increasing complexity of these products, which manufacturers wanted to take credit for but which cannot be easily visually verified. NFRC has developed a window energy rating system based on whole product performance. This accurately accounts for the energy-related effects of all the products' component parts, and prevents information about a single component from being compared in a misleading way to other whole product properties. At this time, NFRC labels on window units give ratings for U-value, solar heat gain coefficient, and visible light transmittance. Soon labels will include air infiltration rates and an annual heating and cooling rating. NFRC procedures started to be incorporated in state energy codes in 1992. The 1992 National Energy Policy Act provided for the development of a national rating system. The U. S. Department of Energy has selected the NFRC program and certified it as the national rating system. In addition, the NFRC procedures are now referenced in and being incorporated into the Model Energy Code and ASHRAE Standards 90.1 and 90.2.

Selecting and energy efficient window

One important practical reason to select energy efficient windows is to reduce the annual cost of heating and cooling your home. This makes good economic sense for most building owners and it also contributes to national and global efforts to reduce the environmental impacts of non-renewable energy use. It can be a relatively painless and even profitable way for every family to help improve the environment in which we live. In order to select a window which will lower heating and cooling costs, you first need to estimate how much energy the furnace and air conditioner will consume. This is influ-

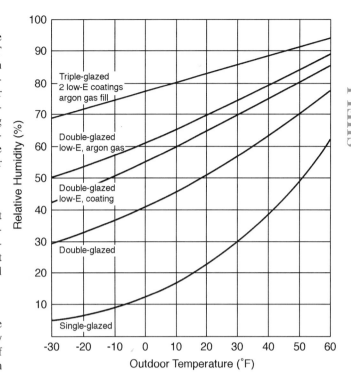

Fig. 2. Condensation Potential on Windows. Source: Carmody, Selkowitz and Heschong (1996)

enced not only by the window properties as you would expect, but by a series of other factors including the house location and microclimate, house characteristics, occupant use patterns, and cost of energy.

Getting an accurate estimate of the annual energy consumption can take a little analysis. As explained below, this can best be done today with some simplified computer tools. But it is not always important to get an accurate quantitative analysis of energy and cost savings—frequently a comparative analysis or ranking is sufficient to guide your choice. For example, the designer may already have narrowed the decision to two or three window options and just want to pick the one with lower heating energy use. In this case, a more simplified set of guidelines may suffice and the new heating and cooling energy ratings being developed by NFRC will be most appropriate.

To evaluate windows with respect to energy performance, various types of information and tools are available:

- Evaluate the window based on its energy-related properties applied to your climate.

- Use an annual energy performance rating system to evaluate heating and cooling energy use.

- Use a computer program to compare energy use and utility costs.

Each of these approaches is described in more detail in the remainder of this section. Selecting a window based on energy performance may involve two additional considerations—the impact on peak heating and cooling loads, and the long-term ability of the window unit to maintain its energy performance characteristics. These additional energy issues are discussed at the end of this section along with the role of codes and standards in improving window energy efficiency.

In addition to quantitative issues such as the actual cost of heating fuel or electricity for cooling, energy performance characteristics are linked to other less measurable issues such as thermal comfort and condensation resistance, as noted earlier in the chapter. Choosing a better-performing window to save on fuel costs will also improve comfort and performance in these other areas.

Using the basic energy-related properties

The three key properties are U-factor, solar heat gain coefficient (SHGC), and air leakage rating. Visible transmittance (VT) is another property used in comparing windows. These are the first properties to appear on NFRC window labels (U-factor was introduced first, followed by SHGC and VT; air leakage ratings will be added soon). Fig. 3 indicates guidelines for using the basic energy properties in choosing a window. Note that these guidelines are different for distinct climate regions. Until there is a reliable annual performance rating in place or unless one is using a computer program, these properties are the main basis for making energy performance decisions.

Using an annual energy performance rating

Even though there are code minimums, guidelines, and recommended levels for the basic properties found on the NFRC label, they do not, in themselves, give the consumer a clear indication of the actual impact on energy costs. To accurately determine annual energy performance and cost, they must be calculated using a sophisticated computer program that takes into account the properties of the windows being compared, and a detailed description of the house design, the climate, and the way in which the house is to be operated. Unfortunately, computerized tools are not always accessible to designers, builders, and homeowners to use in making a window purchasing decision, or they may be too time consuming to use.

To overcome the limitations of requiring detailed computer simulations for each situation, the window industry is developing a simplified annual energy rating system for windows as well as a companion computer-based approach. This annual energy rating, currently being refined by the U. S. Department of Energy and window industry researchers in cooperation with the National Fenestration Rating Council, will be adopted as part of the official rating system of the NFRC. The winter savings indicator is referred to as the Heating Rating (HR) and the summer savings indicator is the Cooling Rating (CR). The final format of the HR and CR rating system is under development. Once this process is complete, HR and CR values promise to be better indicators of relative energy use than the basic window properties such as U-factor. However, they will still be a comparative performance indicator similar to miles-per-gallon ratings for automobiles. The use of computer tools, such as RESFEN described below, is required for more accurate calculation of specific annual energy use or cost savings, described below.

Using a simplified computer program (RESFEN)

Rating systems such as HR and CR are based on computer calculations of energy performance, but they have limitations because simplified assumptions are built into the calculations. With the use of computer programs, it is possible to remove most of the limitations of the HR/CR rating system and generate energy savings values for any set of windows in a specific house. In this case, the user defines the house with a series of selections from a menu: location, heating and cooling system type and efficiency, utility rates, floor area, window area, window orientation, and interior/exterior shading. A specific window or set of windows for each orientation is selected and specified by their U-factor, SHGC, and air leakage rate. The program then calculates the annual energy use and cost in a matter of seconds.

As with all simulation programs, there are still assumptions and approximations that must be understood, and there is a short learning period associated with using the program. It is anticipated that the RESFEN program will be approved by NFRC for those who are willing to invest a little more time and effort in the window selection process. RESFEN has also been used in an electronic kiosk form at a window store. The rapidly evolving interest nationwide in delivering information electronically is making selection tools like RESFEN which is available to homeowners and design professionals over the World Wide Web (URL is listed below under "Resources").

- *Example 1: Window selection in an underheated climate*

Using a computer simulation program, four possible window choices are compared for a typical house in Madison, Wisconsin. In addition, the energy use for the same house with poor windows is shown in the first bar of Fig. 4 to provide a comparison to an older, existing structure with single-glazed windows. Window A in Fig. 4 is a typical clear, double-glazed unit—the most common cold-climate window installed in the U. S. during the period from 1970 to about 1985. Window B has a high-transmission low-E coating, while Window C has a spectrally selective low-E coating. Window B is designed to reduce winter heat loss (low U-factor) and provide winter solar heat gain (high SHGC). Window C also reduces winter heat loss (low U-factor) but it reduces solar heat gain as well (low SHGC). Window D, with triple glazing and two low-E coatings, is representative of the most efficient window on the market today with respect to winter heat loss (very low U-factor).

Fig. 4 illustrates that there are significant savings in annual heating costs by using windows with low U-values (Windows B and C) instead of double-glazed, clear units (Window A) or the single-glazed case. The high-transmission low-E unit (Window B) is slightly better than the spectrally selective low-E unit (Window C) in heating season performance, but Window C is clearly better during the cooling season. The triple-glazed unit (Window D), with its very low U-value, results in even greater heating season savings.

To make a window selection based on this energy performance data, it is necessary to factor in the other issues discussed throughout this chapter. Improvements in energy performance must be weighed against both initial and life-cycle costs. In addition, there are benefits of greater comfort with reduced risk of condensation. The benefit of reducing cooling costs in this climate must be examined in terms of whether air conditioning is installed in the house; however, the increased comfort of a window with a low SHGC is a factor to be considered whether or not the homeowner is paying for cooling.

In applying these typical results to your particular situation, remember that our example is a relatively small house (1500 sq. ft) with an average amount of window area (231 sq. ft). The fuel and electricity rates shown on the figures are national averages. Instead of drawing conclusions from average conditions such as these, the best way to compare different windows is by using a computer tool such as RESFEN where you can base decisions on your own house design and fuel costs for your area.

- *Example 2: Window selection in an overheated climate*

Similar to the heating climate example above, a computer simulation program is used to compare four possible window choices for a typical house in Phoenix, Arizona. Again, the energy use for the same house with poor windows is shown in the first bar of Fig. 5 to provide a comparison to an older, existing structure with single-glazed windows. Window A in Fig. 5 is a typical clear, double-glazed unit. Window B, with bronze-tinted glass, represents a traditional approach to reducing solar heat gain (note the somewhat reduced SHGC accompanied by a significant reduction in daylight—lower VT). Window C represents the relatively new technology of using a spectrally selective low-E coating (a low SHGC combined with a relatively high VT). Window D, which combines a spectrally selective low-E coating with tinted glass, represents further reduction in summer heat gain (very low SHGC), but at the cost of losing daylight as well (low VT).

Fig. 5 illustrates that there are significant savings in annual cooling costs by using windows with low solar heat gain coefficients (Windows C and D) instead of double-glazed, clear units or traditional bronze-tinted glass (Windows A and B). Savings are even greater when compared to the single-glazed case which is common in many existing homes of warmer regions. Windows C and D, with their low U-

	Description	Heating Climate	Mixed Climate	Cooling Climate
Heat Flow (U-value) 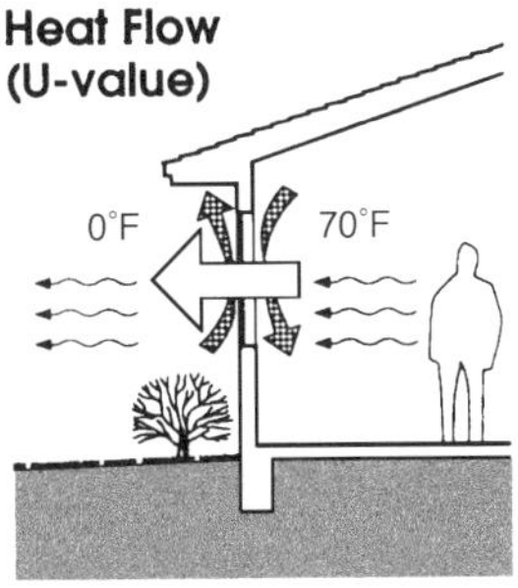	The rate of heat transfer is indicated in terms of the U-value (U-factor) of a window assembly. The insulating value is indicated by the R-value, which is the inverse of the U-value. The lower the U-value, the greater a window's resistance to heat flow and the better its insulating value.	PRIMARY FACTOR: A low U-value is the most important window property in cold climates.	PRIMARY FACTOR: A low U-value is one important window property in mixed climates.	A low U-value is helpful during hot days or whenever heating is needed, but it is less important than SHGC in warm climates.
Solar Heat Gain (SHGC) 	The SHGC is the fraction of incident solar radiation admitted through a window, both directly transmitted, and absorbed and subsequently released inward. SHGC is expressed as a number between 0 and 1. The lower a window's SHGC, the less solar heat it transmits.	A high SHGC increases passive solar gain for heating, but reduces cooling season performance. A low SHGC improves cooling season performance, but reduces passive solar heating.	PRIMARY FACTOR: A low SHGC is one important window property in mixed climates.	PRIMARY FACTOR: A low SHGC is the most important window property in warm climates.
Infiltration (AL) 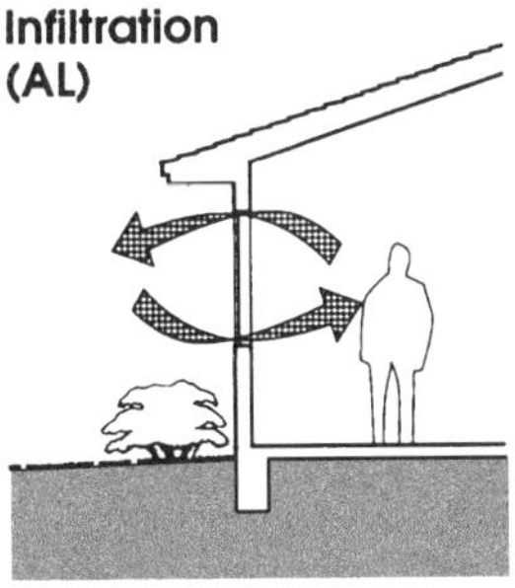	Heat loss and gain occur by infiltration through leaks in the window assembly. The air leakage rating (AL) is expressed as cubic feet of air passing through an equivalent square foot of window area. The lower the AL, the less air will pass through leaks in the window assembly.	The air leakage rating (AL) is an important window property in cold climates. Air leakage should not exceed 0.56 cfm/sq ft.	The air leakage rating (AL) is an important window property in mixed climates. Air leakage should not exceed 0.56 cfm/sq ft.	The air leakage rating (AL) is generally less important in warm climates. However, infiltration can contribute to excessive summer cooling loads by introducing humid outdoor air.
Daylight (VT) 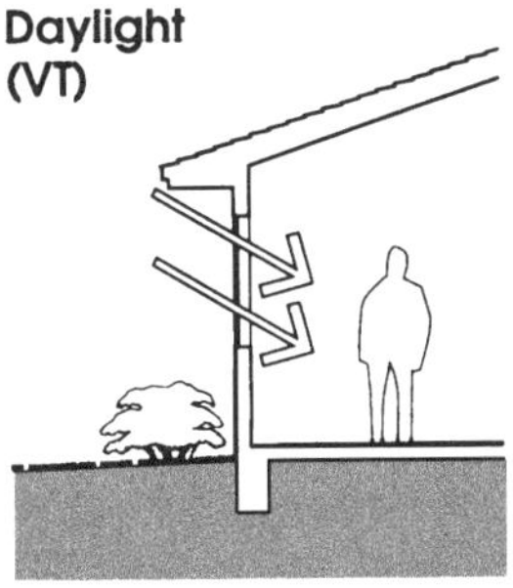	The visible transmittance (VT) is an optical property that indicates the amount of visible light transmitted through the glass. VT is expressed as a number between 0 and 1. The higher the VT, the more daylight is transmitted.	A high VT is desirable to maximize daylight and view.	A high VT is desirable to maximize daylight and view.	A high VT is desirable to maximize daylight and view, but this must be balanced against the need to control solar gain and glare in hot climates.

Fig. 3. Energy-related properties of windows. Source: Carmody, Selkowitz and Heschong (1996)

values, also reduce heating costs in a warm climate where there is some heating required.

Just as with the underheated climate example, making a window selection in an overheated climate based on this energy performance data must include the other issues. Improvements in energy performance must be weighed against both initial and life-cycle costs. In addition, there are benefits of greater comfort in both summer and winter. The conclusion from this might be that Windows C and D are almost equal in terms of energy performance. A critical factor then becomes the amount of daylight they allow. If maximizing light and

view is your goal, then Window C is the obvious choice. Window D might be selected if glare control is an overriding concern.

As noted for the overheated climate example, consider that this is for a relatively small house (1500 sq. ft) with an average amount of window area (231 sq. ft). The fuel and electricity rates shown on the figures are national averages.

- *Example 3: Window selection in a mixed climate*

The previous two examples have focused on the regions of more extreme climate in the United States. In terms of analyzing energy per-

U.S. Cooling Climate Zone.
(Boundaries of the climate zones are approximate.)

A. Clear double glazing

- Double glazing
- Wood or vinyl frame

B. High-transmission low-E coating

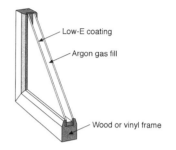

- Low-E coating
- Argon gas fill
- Wood or vinyl frame

C. Spectrally selective low-E coating

- Spectrally selective low-E coating
- Argon gas fill
- Wood or vinyl frame

D. Triple glazing with low-E coating

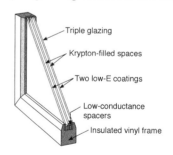

- Triple glazing
- Krypton-filled spaces
- Two low-E coatings
- Low-conductance spacers
- Insulated vinyl frame

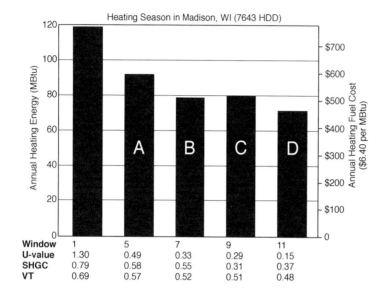

Heating Season in Madison, WI (7643 HDD)

Window	1	5	7	9	11
U-value	1.30	0.49	0.33	0.29	0.15
SHGC	0.79	0.58	0.55	0.31	0.37
VT	0.69	0.57	0.52	0.51	0.48

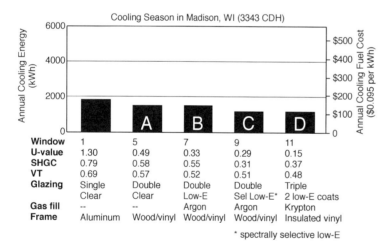

Cooling Season in Madison, WI (3343 CDH)

Window	1	5	7	9	11
U-value	1.30	0.49	0.33	0.29	0.15
SHGC	0.79	0.58	0.55	0.31	0.37
VT	0.69	0.57	0.52	0.51	0.48
Glazing	Single Clear	Double Clear	Double Low-E	Double Sel Low-E*	Triple 2 low-E coats
Gas fill	--	--	Argon	Argon	Krypton
Frame	Aluminum	Wood/vinyl	Wood/vinyl	Wood/vinyl	Insulated vinyl

* spectrally selective low-E

Note: The annual energy performance figures shown here are for a
typical 1540 sq ft house with 231 sq ft of window area (15% of floor area).
The windows are equally distributed on all four sides of the house and are
unshaded. U-factor, SHGC, and VT are for the total window including
frames. HDD=heating degree days. CDH=cooling degree hours.
**kWh-kilowatt hours. Mbtu=millions of Btu. The fuel and electricity prices
represent national averages.**

Fig. 4. Comparing windows in an underheated climate. Source: Carmody, Selkowitz and Heschong (1996)

SHELL B2

U.S. Cooling Climate Zone.
(Boundaries of the climate zones are approximate.)

A. Clear double glazing

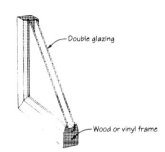

Double glazing

Wood or vinyl frame

B. Double glazing with bronze tint

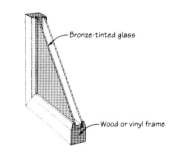

Bronze-tinted glass

Wood or vinyl frame

C. Spectrally selective low-E coating

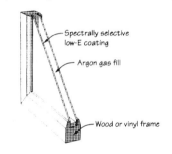

Spectrally selective low-E coating

Argon gas fill

Wood or vinyl frame

D. Spectrally selective low-E coating with tinted glass

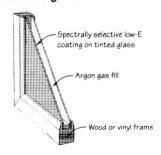

Spectrally selective low-E coating on tinted glass

Argon gas fill

Wood or vinyl frame

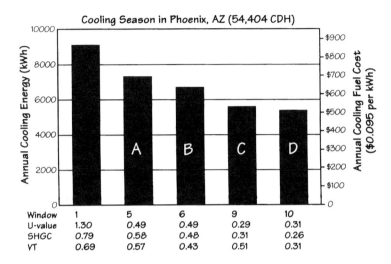

Cooling Season in Phoenix, AZ (54,404 CDH)

Window	1	5	6	9	10
U-value	1.30	0.49	0.49	0.29	0.31
SHGC	0.79	0.58	0.48	0.31	0.26
VT	0.69	0.57	0.43	0.51	0.31

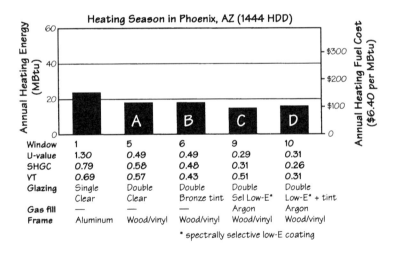

Heating Season in Phoenix, AZ (1444 HDD)

Window	1	5	6	9	10
U-value	1.30	0.49	0.49	0.29	0.31
SHGC	0.79	0.58	0.48	0.31	0.26
VT	0.69	0.57	0.43	0.51	0.31
Glazing	Single Clear	Double Clear	Double Bronze tint	Double Sel Low-E*	Double Low-E* + tint
Gas fill	—	—	—	Argon	Argon
Frame	Aluminum	Wood/vinyl	Wood/vinyl	Wood/vinyl	Wood/vinyl

* spectrally selective low-E coating

Note: The annual energy performance figures shown here are for a typical 1540 sq ft house with 231 sq ft of window area (15% of floor area). The windows are equally distributed on all four sides of the house and are unshaded. U-factor, SHGC, and VT are for the total window including frames. HDD=heating degree days. CDH=cooling degree hours. kWh=kilowatt hours. Mbtu=millions of Btu. The fuel and electricity prices represent national averages.

Fig. 5. Comparing windows in an overheated climate. Source: Carmody, Selkowitz and Heschong (1996)

formance, these climates are easier to address because one season clearly predominates, so decisions are clearly weighted in favor of winter heating in the north and summer cooling in the south. The great area in between is often referred to as a mixed heating and cooling or temperate climate zone. In these cases, the relative importance of the heating and cooling season performance will vary with location, and utility costs.

The comments for the previous heating and cooling climate examples all apply to some degree in a mixed climate. Because heating and cooling costs must be balanced in mixed climates and then combined with all of the other selection factors, it is important to use a reliable computer tool such as RESFEN where you can base decisions on your own house design and fuel costs for your area.

Definitions

ABSORPTANCE. The ratio of radiant energy absorbed to total incident radiant energy in a glazing system.

EMITTANCE. The ratio of the radiant flux emitted by a specimen to that emitted by a blackbody at the same temperature and under the same conditions.

AIR LEAKAGE RATING. A measure of the rate of infiltration around a window or skylight in the presence of a specific pressure difference. It is expressed in units of cubic feet per minute per square foot of window area (cfm/sq. ft) or cubic feet per minute per foot of window perimeter length (cfm/ft). The lower a window's air leakage rating, the better its airtightness.

COMPOSITE FRAME: A frame consisting of two or more materials—for example, an interior wood element with an exterior fiberglass element.

DOUBLE GLAZING. In general, two thicknesses of glass separated by an air space within an opening to improve insulation against heat transfer and/or sound transmission. In factory-made double glazing units, the air between the glass sheets is thoroughly dried and the space is sealed airtight, eliminating possible condensation and providing superior insulating properties.

GAS FILL. A gas other than air, usually argon or krypton, placed between window or skylight glazing panes to reduce the U-factor by suppressing conduction and convection.

LIGHT-TO-SOLAR-GAIN-RATIO. A measure of the ability of a glazing to provide light without excessive solar heat gain. It is the ratio between the visible transmittance of a glazing and its solar heat gain coefficient. Abbreviated LSG.

LOW CONDUCTANCE SPACERS. An assembly of materials designed to reduce heat transfer at the edge of an insulating window. Spacers are placed between the panes of glass in a double- or triple-glazed window.

LOW-EMITTANCE (LOW-E) COATING. Microscopically thin, virtually invisible, metal or metallic oxide layers deposited on a window or skylight glazing surface primarily to reduce the U-factor by suppressing radiative heat flow. A typical type of low-E coating is transparent to the solar spectrum (visible light and short-wave infrared radiation) and reflective of long-wave infrared radiation.

R-VALUE. A measure of the resistance of a glazing material or fenestration assembly to heat flow. It is the inverse of the U-factor (R = 1/U) and is expressed in units of hr-sq ft-F/Btu. A high-R-value window has a greater resistance to heat flow and a higher insulating value than one with a low R-value.

REFLECTANCE. The ratio of reflected radiant energy to incident radiant energy.

SHADING COEFFICIENT (SC). A measure of the ability of a window or skylight to transmit solar heat, relative to that ability for 1/8-inch clear, double- strength, single glass. It is being phased out in favor of the solar heat gain coefficient, and is approximately equal to the SHGC multiplied by 1.15. It is expressed as a number without units between 0 and 1. The lower a window's solar heat gain coefficient or shading coefficient, the less solar heat it transmits, and the greater is its shading ability.

SOLAR HEAT GAIN COEFFICIENT (SHGC). The fraction of incident solar radiation admitted through a window or skylight, both directly transmitted, and absorbed and subsequently released inward. The solar heat gain coefficient has replaced the shading coefficient as the standard indicator of a window's shading ability. It is expressed as a number between 0 and 1. The lower a window's solar heat gain coefficient, the less solar heat it transmits, and the greater its shading ability. SHGC can be expressed in terms of the glass alone or can refer to the entire window assembly.

SPECTRALLY SELECTIVE GLAZING. A coated or tinted glazing with optical properties that are transparent to some wavelengths of energy and reflective to others. Typical spectrally selective coatings are transparent to visible light and reflect short-wave and long-wave infrared radiation. Usually the term spectrally selective is applied to glazing that reduce heat gain while providing substantial daylight.

SUPERWINDOW. A window with a very low U-factor, typically less than 0.15, achieved through the use of multiple glazing, low-E coatings, and gas fills.

TRANSMITTANCE. The percentage of radiation that can pass through glazing. Transmittance can be defined for different types of light or energy, that is, visible light transmittance, UV transmittance, or total solar energy transmittance.

U-FACTOR (U-VALUE). A measure of the rate of non-solar heat loss or gain through a material or assembly. It is expressed in units of Btu/hr-sq ft-F (W/sq m-°C). Values are normally given for NFRC/ASHRAE winter conditions of 0F (18° C) outdoor temperature, 70F (21° C) indoor temperature, 15 mph wind, and no solar load. The U-factor may be expressed for the glass alone or the entire window, which includes the effect of the frame and the spacer materials. The lower the U-factor, the greater a window's resistance to heat flow and the better its insulating value.

VISIBLE TRANSMITTANCE (VT). The percentage or fraction of the visible spectrum (380 to 720 nanometers) weighted by the sensitivity of the eye, that is transmitted through the glazing.

Resources

National Fenestration Rating Council (NFRC)
1300 Spring Street, Suite 120
Silver Spring, MD USA 20910
Phone: (301) 589-NFRC

RESFEN is a computer program for calculating the annual heating and cooling energy use and costs due to fenestration systems. RESFEN also calculates their contribution to peak heating and cooling loads. It is available from the NFRC at the address above.
RESFEN can be downloaded at:
http://eande.lbl.gov/BTP/BTP.html
In the future, an interactive version of RESFEN will be directly accessible at this web site.

B SHELL

Roofing systems

Summary: Roofing must withstand the extremes of climate but also the subtle nature of moisture, materials and movement of a building over time. This chapter provides an introduction to roofing and technical references for design of roofing systems.

Roofs of Burmuda

Key words: built-up roofing, flashing, membrane roofing, metal roofing, protected membrane, single-ply roofing.

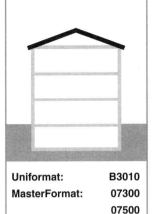

Uniformat:	B3010
MasterFormat:	07300
	07500

SHELL

B3

1 Introduction to roofing design practices

Roofing as an element of architecture and construction presents a challenging topic. The design of roofs is a significant part of the architectural vocabulary, in many cases, taken to by synonymous with the idea of shelter. Additionally, a continuous challenge of architects and builders had been, in plain terms, "to keep the rain out." To these challenges, always present in the history of architecture, are dramatic new technological developments in materials and systems that have made possible a revolution in the past few decades in the way roofs are designed and built. Technological developments and improvements continue, as does the experience from the field, represented by professional and industry-based research and publications. At the same time, architects and builders are increasingly involved with remodeling of older roofing systems, in which case repair or replacement has to conform to existing conditions and be informed and improved by recent developments.

These factors presents an intriguing set of challenges for the architect. If the architect does not understand the physics and technology of roof design, this will likely be revealed in important design details or their absence, and possibly flaws and eventual roof failure. On the other hand, the information and research on good roofing design and construction practice is, perhaps as much as any other element of a building, changing and improving from year to year. Simply keeping informed and up-to-date requires time and attention. What was good practice ten years ago, may be deemed improper, or at least not best practice, today.

This chapter adopts the language and introduces technical references being developed by the roofing industry, which provide recommendations of good practices for roofing systems, many of which are proprietary and all requiring close adherence to recommended detailing.

The knowledgeable practitioner of good roofing design and practice must therefore understand current roofing technologies and be guided by principles and practices, outlined in this article, referenced to current industry developments and recommendations.

1.1 Performance requirements for roofs

All roofing systems perform essentially the same weather protective functions, irrespective of building type and climate. In many instances, the roofing is a strong visual element, so that its aesthetic character is critical.

Of all elements of a building, roofing is exposed to the greatest climatic stress. In equatorial climates, the roofing assembly is the singlemost critical building element for protection against sun, which may include reflective surfaces and/or radiant barriers. In such climates, roofing is also exposed to extremes of torrential downpours and winds. In cold to temperate climates, the roof endures daily and seasonal cycle of freeze-thaw action and provides protection for thermal insulation.

The performance requirements for roofing can thus be enumerated as:

* To protect the building interior from water and snow entry during all weather conditions which prevail at the site.

* To maintain waterproofing for a period of several decades, at least, with normal maintenance.

* To protect occupants and contents from thermal discomfort, and to conserve energy (accomplished by insulation and by roof reflection and/or radiant barriers, sometimes as part of the roofing assembly, and in all cases, protected by the roofing.)

* To control vapor transmission and condensation, both to protect building materials and components and to provide environmental control of interior conditions, sometimes as part of the roofing assembly, and in all cases, protected by the roofing.

* To be safely and easily accessible for inspection and maintenance, and removable with a minimum of problems when replacement is required.

* To protect occupants and the public from harm caused by falling and blowing materials from the roof surfaces, including accumulated snow and ice slides.

Author: Donald Baerman, AIA

Credits: This chapter summarizes recommended roofing practices and details shown more completely in publications of The National Roofing Contractors Association, whose assistance is gratefully acknowledged.

References: Asphalt Roofing Manufacturers Association. 1996. *Residential Asphalt Roofing Manual*. Rockville, MD: Asphalt Roofing Manufacturers Association.

NRCA. 1996. *NRCA Roofing and Waterproofing Manual - Fourth Edition*. Rosemont, IL: National Roofing Contractors Association.

SMACNA. 1993. *Architectural Sheet Metal Manual - Fifth Edition*. 4201 Lafayette Center Drive, Chantilly, VA: Sheet Metal and Air Conditioning Contractors' Association.

- In some uses, to withstand pedestrian, equipment maintenance, and other traffic without harm to occupants or to roofing materials.

- To be safe, that is, physiologically benign, during construction and use. The fumes of some roofing materials are harmful to workers and the public and they are often unpleasant.

1.2 Types of roofing systems

The major types of available roof systems are generically defined as steep-slope or low-slope systems, based upon their slope which in turn determines or explains the principles and physical mechanics behind their design, fabrication and assembly.

- Steep-slope systems are generally designed to shed water quickly, by gravity and are not necessarily water-tight.

- Low-slope systems, while also designed to shed water, are designed as essentially water impermeable systems.

1.2.1 Steep roof systems

The primary mechanism in most steep roof systems for keeping water out is gravity and water flow: the shingle units lap in such a way that water would have to run uphill to penetrate the system. Counteracting forces acting to allow water into the building through the roofing assembly include capillary action, air pressure differential, and the (lateral) kinetic force of driven rain. Steep roofs keep the rain out if the force of gravity is greater than the other forces acting on the roof.

The principal steep-roof systems are:

- shingle roofing

- sheet metal roofs

- roll roofing and membrane roofing

- other systems not in widespread use, such as thatch roofs.

1.2.2 Low-slope roof systems

The primary mechanism in low-sloped systems for keeping water out is to form an impenetrable membrane without significant openings through which water could pass. There are currently considered to be six generic types of low-slope systems, with a seventh,"protected membrane" systems being defined by its positioning of elements, not its generic materials. This last type also describes the waterproofing strategy of earth-covered roof terraces.

- Built-up roof membrane

- Modified bitumen roofing

- Thermoplastic and thermoset single-ply roof systems

- Liquid-applied roof coating systems

- Protected membrane roof systems

- Sprayed polyurethane roofs

- Soldered flat-lock seam metal roofs

1.3 Recommended slopes

A determining initial decision in roofing system selection is the desired roof slope, from which many other decisions derive. Table 1 provides is a general guide to proper slopes, assuming proper fastening of the system. For specific information on manufacturers' systems approved for certain slopes, consult the manufacturers' manuals.

Roof systems which drain fully and quickly are least likely to leak, or to leak badly. Roofs which are very steep are difficult to repair and maintain. Therefore, all other factors being equal, the "ideal" low-slope roof system would slope about 8% (1 in. per foot), and the ideal" steep roof system would slope about 30-33% (4 in. per foot). In practice, many other criteria determine the slope.

1.4 Other factors for selection of roof systems

- Appearance. A great variety of colors and textures are available,

and a roof can be a major opportunity for aesthetic expression. Determination of roof slope and roof type also lead to other important aesthetic criteria. Low-slope configurations will require a positive drainage system for quick removal of roof rainwater, which determines design decisions for scuppers, drainpipes, length of slope to outfall and roof curb heights. These are too often underestimated out of an aesthetic intention to minimize roof appearance or curb height. Steep-slope configurations may also require gutters and downspouts, affecting the projected distance of the roof eave. If gutters are not used (to create free falling rain, ice and snow run-off), the eave projection and spaces and building elements below become critical. The resulting appearance of lines and shadows at the top edge of building elevations have great bearing upon the building appearance. If a building is seen from above, its "roofscape" becomes, in a sense, the "fifth facade" of the aesthetic of the building design.

- Economy. Under most conditions, the lowest first cost and life cycle cost for steep roofs is an unlaminated asphalt shingle roof system (in the writer's opinion). The cost of the various types of low-slope roof systems varies, with no system being plainly the most economical in the short run or for the life of the installation.

- Energy conservation: Roofs and their assemblies are a significant element in the overall building energy system. The roofing surface is the largest outside surface for single-storied or low-rise building. They are, of all the building components, generally the easiest to insulate well. Probably the greatest detrimental heat exchange occurs by absorption of solar heat in summer. To conserve energy, the roof should:

- Reflect a large part of summer solar heat gain. Light-colored roofs reflect more heat than darker ones.

- Resist conductive heat gain and loss.

- Resist air infiltration and exfiltration to and from the spaces inside the insulation barrier.

- Ventilation of the attic, rafter space, or joist space, above the insulation, has beneficial effects on moisture removal, but it has only limited effect in removing summer solar heat; the greater part of the solar heat transfer is by radiation. Thus a heat-reflective roof surface, one or more reflective heat barriers in the insulation system, or a combination of these methods is more effective than excessive venting.

- Method of attachment (fasteners). While virtually any system can be installed over wooden sheathing, adhered or ballasted systems are better for use over concrete slabs, to eliminate the need for any penetration of the slab. While some systems permit a variety of fasteners, others require special fasteners. For example: It is expensive to use mechanical fasteners to adhere a roof system to structural concrete; adhesion with hot asphalt or other adhesives is the normal method of attachment. Cement-wood fiber panels and gypsum panels require special fasteners made for this purpose. The usual way to fasten a roof to steel deck is self-tapping screws, but they penetrate the steel deck and look unsightly where the deck is exposed below. One (expensive) way to fasten invisibly to a steel deck is to fasten plywood over the steel deck with screws from below.

- Resistance to damage from use and abuse. Protected membrane roof systems have the vulnerable membrane protected under ballast and insulation. Built-up roof systems have considerable resistance to damage, except that they may crack when cold. Sprayed polyurethane roof systems are highly vulnerable to damage from use and abuse. Some sprayed polyurethane roofs are vulnerable to damage from birds.

- Slip resistance. Thermoplastic and thermoset systems, smooth-surface modified bitumen systems, and most metal roof systems

Table 1. Recommended roof slopes

Roof type	Minimum slope	Maximum slope
Built-up membrane roofs		
- asphalt roof systems:	2%	
- asphalt-fiberglass membrane roofs:		50%
- aggregate-surface asphalt-fiberglass membrane		33%
- coal tar membrane roofs	2% [1]	
Modified bitumen and composite membrane	2%	
- aggregate-surface modified bitumen		33%
- mineral-surface and smooth-surface modified bitumen		50%
Single-ply thermoplastic and thermoset membrane	2%	
- ballasted systems		17%
- mechanically-attached smooth-surface systems		no limitation
Protected membrane roof systems	2%	8%
Sprayed polyurethane foam systems	2%	no limitation [2]
Asphalt shingle roofs		
- with normal underlayment	33%	no limitation
- with special underlayment installation.	25%	no limitation
Asphalt roll roofing	17%[3]	no limitation
Slate roofs	33%[4]	no limitation
Tile roofs	33%	no limitation
Wood shakes and shingles	33%	no limitation
Metal roofing	note [5]	
- flat-locked and soldered seam systems	2%	
- for limited areas	dead level.	
- metal steep roof systems	25%	no limitation

NOTES

[1] This limit is to retard the tendency of coal tar bitumen to flow.

[2] No general industry slope recommendations published for these systems; good practice guideline is shown.

[3] This material has been used on "dead level" roofs and roofs with a slope less than 2 in 12 or 17%, but such use is not recommended; use low-slope systems for such low slopes.

[4] Slates can be set essentially level as a paving over low-slope membrane roof systems and waterproofing systems.

[5] Since metal roofing varies greatly, no general slope recommendations can be given. Some metal roof systems are recommended by their manufacturers for slopes similar to that of low-slope membrane roof systems (2%).

are slippery when wet. Therefore, especially if the edges are not guarded, a person could slip and fall over the edges. It would be prudent to call for warning signs.

- Long-term maintenance. Durability under longer or life-cycle conditions can be extended with regular inspection and preventative maintenance protocols. Like all assemblies, the weakest link in the attachment and/or substrate components may account for premature failure of the entire assembly.

- Weight of the roofing system. Compared to required live loads that may be expected from snow, ice and water, the weight of different roofing choices may not be a determining factor. But systems do vary in their "dead load" weight:

Roofing	Weight (lb./100 sq. ft.)
Clay tile	800 - 2000
Slate	600 - 1600
Felt and gravel	550 - 650
Asphalt shingles	130 - 325
Wood shingles	200 - 300
Corrugated metal	100 - 175
Copper (16 oz.)	116 - 145

his article reviews basic system definitions and selected design guidelines with selected illustrative details for low-slope and for steep-slope roofing systems. In this discussion, reference and use is made of definitions and guidelines of roofing industry publications, especially NRCA (1996) Chapter One, "Handbook of Accepted Roofing Knowledge." This is done for several purposes, first to use the technical terms and definitions adopted through consensus agreement in the roofing industry, and second, to introduce and make easier the access to more complete technical data thus referenced.

In the following discussion, every attempt is made to properly reference the source of recommendations. Where not otherwise cited, the recommendations are those of the writer, based upon over thirty years of roofing specification and forensic experience. This has lead the writer to recommend some practices that may exceed industry recommendations: the adage that "if something can go wrong, it will go wrong" applies as much or more so to roofing details as any other building component, warranted all the more because roof inspection and maintenance is often made difficult by circumstances of weather and/or inaccessibility.

This article concludes with summary guidelines for responsible roofing design practices, along with additional references and resources necessary for design detailing and specification of selected roofing systems.

2   Low-slope roof systems

The following discussion of roofing system elements follows the definitions and recommendations as offered by National Roofing Contractors Association "Handbook of Accepted Roofing Knowledge," the first chapter of the NRCA Roofing and Waterproofing Manual (NRCA 1996).

Low slope roofing systems and assemblies consist of the following elements:

1   the structural deck or substrate.
2   slope and drainage system.
3   moisture control and vapor retarders.
4   insulation.
5   expansion joints and area dividers.
6   roof coverings and membranes.
7   cants, curbs, nailers and flashing.
8   aggregates and/or other surfacing
9   mechanical curbs and penetrations.

2.1   Structural deck

Good roof systems depend upon the structural integrity of the substrate or roof deck. To ensure the construction of a quality roof deck, provisions for the following items should be included in the design of the roof deck:

- live loads, including moving installation equipment, workers, material stored on the roof, wind, snow, ice and rain.

- dead loads, such as mechanical equipment, ducting, piping, or conduit the deck itself, any sheathing overlayment, roof membrane, insulation and ballast, and any future re-covering of the roof system. Rolling rooftop construction loads can exceed 600 pounds (272 kg) in quite small areas (such as dollies used to transport roofing materials).

- deck strength.

- deflection.

- drainage.

- placement of expansion joints and area dividers.

- curb and penetration members and detailing.

Common structural deck ("substrate") types include:

- Cement-wood fiber deck panels

- Lightweight Insulating concrete decks

- Poured gypsum concrete deck

- Precast gypsum panel roof decks

- Steel decks

- Structural concrete roof decks

- Thermosetting insulating fills (typically perlite aggregate and hot asphalt binder)

- Wood plank and wood panel (plywood or approved OSB) roof decks

The structural deck supports the roofing and all dead and live loads on it. It resists snow drift loading, impounded rain loading, equipment loading, wind loading, and wind uplift. Under the greatest loading, the roof should not deflect beyond the point at which full drainage occurs.

- If there are parapets or other structures containing water, include the weight of all water which can be impounded as part of the live load, or (more reasonably) provide overflow scuppers or other redundant drainage.

- Give special attention to deflection under concentrated roof loads, such as rooftop mechanical equipment. One way to limit such deflection is to provide separate structural support, independent of the main roof structural system, under heavy equipment. Another way is to make the whole roof very stiff. Do not allow local deflection to create a pond around mechanical equipment.

2.2   Slope and drainage system

NRCA recommends, as does accepted good practice, that all roofs be designed and built to ensure positive drainage, essentially considering the entire path of water removal from the roof and away from the building. Ponding water can be detrimental to roof systems and can result in:

- deterioration of the roof surface and membrane.

- debris accumulation, vegetation and fungal growth, and resulting membrane damage.

- deck deflections sometimes resulting in structural and other complications.

- ice formation and resulting membrane degradation of damage.

- tensile splitting of water-weakened organic or asbestos felts.

- difficulties in repair should leaks occur.

- water entry into the building if the roof membrane is punctured or fails in a ponding area.

- voiding of manufacturers' warrantees.

Because every roof has its own specific set of drainage conditions, the architect must design for proper drainage for the entire roof and all related areas. The designer should not simply specify a standard slope without analysis and provision of how it is accomplished. NRCA recommends as an industry standard the design and installation criterion that there be no ponding of water 48 hours after rainfall, under ambient drying conditions. Tapered insulation systems can be used to achieve thorough drainage. Tapered saddles should be designed between drains, and crickets should be designed on the upslope side of mechanical, skylight and other curbs to promote drainage of these areas.

All low slope roof systems must be designed to drain easily, without ponding and/or complicating connections to areas susceptible to water, ice and freeze/thaw damage. (See "Gutters and Downspouts" in this Chapter.) Provision of adequate crickets and saddles may be included in the slope of the substrate or added by built up sections (Fig. 1).

2.3   Moisture control and vapor retarders
The term "vapor retarders" refers to a broad range of materials that are used to control the flow of moisture vapor from the interior of the building into the roof system.

Vapor retarders for use in low-slope roof assemblies generally fall into two classes:

-   bituminous vapor retarders utilize a continuous film of bitumen to serve as the vapor resistant element. A typical two-ply reinforced installation can provide a vapor retarder that is rated less than .005 perms, which for most roof construction purposes is considered so near zero permeance that it can be a very effective vapor retarder.

-   non-bituminous vapor retarders are typically composed of a sheet material that serves as the vapor retarder and an adhesive tape or heat- or solvent-welding process is used to seal the laps. These include PVC films, Kraft paper, and aluminum-foil laminates, which may provide vapor retarders having permeability ratings ranging from .1 to .5 perms.

Special consideration is required for design and application of vapor retarders and the entire roof assembly for specialty facilities, including buildings with high interior relative humidity (such as swimming pools) and facilities with very low relative humidity (such as cold storage and freezer facilities).

A rule-of-thumb method is offered in NRCA (1996) that the designer may consider as a preliminary guide to use of vapor retarders in low-sloped roof assemblies: The need for a vapor retarder should be considered when the two following conditions are anticipated:

1   The outside average January temperature is below 40F (4°C).

2   The expected interior winter humidity is 45% or greater.

For information on moisture control in roof assemblies, guidelines on dewpoint calculations and additional information on vapor diffusion and retarders, see NRCA Energy Manual and NRCA Roofing and Waterproofing Manual (1996).

2.4   Insulation
In most climates, insulation is included in the roof system to improve comfort and to minimize energy use. In addition, roof insulation may decrease the range of thermal expansion of the structure. For low-slope roof systems, the best location is usually above the structural deck. For conventional membrane roof systems, the insulation is under the membrane. For protected membrane roof systems, the insulation is above the membrane. (See "Thermal insulation" in Chapter B2 of this Volume).

Except in protected membrane roof systems, rigid roof insulation usually provides in low-slope systems both the insulation for the building and a substrate to which the roofing membrane is applied. Therefore roof insulation must be compatible with, and provide adequate support for, the membrane and other rooftop materials and permit limited rooftop traffic, such as for roof inspection and maintenance.

For protected membrane roof systems, the only approved insulation is extruded, expanded polystyrene. It is resistant to water penetration, but it is vulnerable to attack from high heat and ultraviolet radiation. For roofing areas without adequate strength to support ballast, a proprietary system is available, composed of tongue-and-groove expanded, extruded polystyrene panels with a thin latex mortar cap, to protect against sunlight.

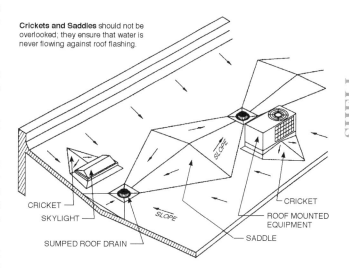

Crickets and Saddles should not be overlooked; they ensure that water is never flowing against roof flashing.

CRICKET
SKYLIGHT
SUMPED ROOF DRAIN
SLOPE
SLOPE
CRICKET
ROOF MOUNTED EQUIPMENT
SADDLE

Fig. 1. Cricket and saddles are part of low-slope roof design, ensuring that water is never flowing against roof flashings. (Source: *Roofing Specifier*, January 1997)

SHELL

B3

For conventional membrane roof systems, the following types of rigid insulation can be used:

- cellular glass
- glass fiber
- mineral fiber
- perlite
- phenolic foam
- polyisocyanurate board
- polystyrene foam (expanded or extruded)
- polyurethane foam
- wood fiberboard
- vegetable fiberboard
- composite board

Of these, polyisocyanurate has the highest insulating value per unit of thickness. It is also resistant to the temperatures which occur during roof system installation. Most manufacturers require that a thin layer of vegetable fiber, perlite board, or other vapor-porous insulation be used between polyisocyanurate insulation and the roof membrane. The reason is to allow water vapor, which may form in great volume when heat is applied during roof construction, to dissipate harmlessly.

2.5 Expansion joints and area dividers

Roof expansion joints are used to minimize the effects of stresses and movements of a building's components and to prevent these stresses from splitting, buckling/bridging or damaging the roof system. Expansion joints in the roof assembly (here considered as combined roof membrane, insulation and roof deck) should be placed in the same location as the building's structural expansion joints (although they may also be required in other locations). Each of a buildings components has varying coefficients of expansion, and each is subject to varying temperature changes, and resultant thermal movement.

NRCA recommends that roof expansion joints should be provided:

- where expansion or contraction joints are provided in the structural assembly.
- where steel framing, structural steel, or decking change direction.
- where separate wings of L, U and T or similar configurations exist n the building roof plan.
- where the type of decking changes, for example, where a precast concrete deck and a steel deck abut.
- wherever additions are connected to existing buildings.
- at junctions where interior heating conditions change.
- wherever differential movement might occur between vertical walls and the roof deck.

Area dividers: Where expansion joints are not provided, or where the distance between expansion joints is excessive, area dividers may help control thermal stresses in a roof system (here defined as independent of the movement of the structural deck). Area dividers minimize the transmission of stress from one area of the roof to another by dividing the roof into smaller sections. NRCA recommendations indicate that these sections be of rectangular shape and uniformly spaced where possible.

2.6 Roof coverings and membranes.

Low-slope systems generally use roof membranes intended to serve as water impermeable coverings designed to protect the structure from water entry. The roof covering resists infiltration of water. It also resists attack by UV radiation, atmospheric pollution, roof traffic, thermal movement, hot and cold temperatures, and animals. Low slope

system types include the following types:

- built-up roof membrane
- modified bitumen roofing
- thermoplastic and thermoset single-ply roof systems
- liquid-applied roof coating systems
- protected membrane roof systems
- sprayed polyurethane roofs
- soldered flat-lock seam metal roofs

2.6.1 Built-up roof membrane

The built-up roof (BUR) membrane is composed of moppings or layers of bitumen (asphalt or cold tar) which are the waterproof components of the membrane. Plies of reinforcement fabric are installed between each layer of bitumen. Traditionally, bituminous membranes have been installed in multiply-ply configurations, with three to six layers of bitumen applied between layers (plies) of reinforcing fabric to compose the "built-up" membrane. Built-up roofs are highly dependent on the skill and integrity of the workers who construct them.

2.6.2 Modified bitumen roofing

Modified bitumen roofing (MBR) is composed of a fiber mat, which may contain glass fibers, polyester fibers, or both, and a mixture of asphalt and plastic which impregnates and coats the mat. The surface may be plain, coated with mineral granules, or laminated with aluminum, copper, or stainless steel foil. The back is surfaced with thin polyethylene film, which melts during application. The rolls are approximately 36 in. (92 cm) in width. One common type of modified bitumen roof consists of a fiberglass-modified bitumen base sheet and a mineral granule-coated modified bitumen cap sheet. The sheets are unrolled and lapped at the joints. Some systems are installed with hot asphalt, some are installed by torch-fusion, and some are a combination.

2.6.3 Thermoplastic and thermoset single-ply systems

"Thermoplastic" materials form because of heat of fusion without a change in chemical composition and are thus distinguished from thermosets (see below) in that there is no chemical cross-linking. Because of their nature, some thermoplastic membranes may be seamed by either heat (hot air) or solvent welding. Thermoplastic membranes are single-ply flexible sheet materials that are divided into the following categories:

- Polyvinyl Chloride (PVC)
- PVC Alloys or compounded thermoplastics
- Polyisobutylene (PIB)
- Thermoplastic resin (TPC)

"Thermoset" membranes are those whose principal polymers are chemically cross-linked. This chemical cross-linkage is commonly referred to as "vulcanization" (increase of strength and elasticity of rubber due to combination of sulfur compounds with high heat) or "curing." They are strong and flexible, making them ideal for certain types of roofing applications (Fig. 3). The common classes of thermoset roof membranes are:

- Neoprene (CR)
- Chlorosulfonated polyethylene - Hypalon (CSPE)
- Epichlorophydrin (ECH)
- Ethylene Propylene Diene Monomer or Terpolymer (EPDM)

Thermoplastic single-ply roof systems are joined at the seams with solvent or heat. Thermoset single-ply roof systems are joined with special cement, double-sided tape, or, for some systems, with heat. Heat-joined thermoset materials are shipped to the job uncured, in which state they can be softened and joined by heat. They cure in place, after which they do not soften when heated. Some are available in white, advantageous where sunlight reflectivity is desired, such as to reduce cooling loads or to reflect light to clerestories. They can be installed in the following ways:

- loose-laid with ballast.

- fully-adhered to the insulation below, the insulation being mechanically attached to the structural deck.

- mechanically-attached. The attachments are either covered by the adjacent sheets or are sealed watertight.

2.6.4 Liquid-applied roof coating systems

Liquid-applied roof coating systems are relatively new. They are seamless, and so flashings are simplified. The manufacturers recommend use on top of most other systems and materials. These systems are not described in the NRCA Manual.

2.6.5 Protected membrane roof systems

"Protected membrane roofing" describes an approach to low-slope roofing in which the waterproofing membrane is protected from extreme weather conditions and mechanical damage by covering with insulating panels and ballast. The materials for protected membrane roof systems vary. The special characteristic of protected membrane roof systems is that the insulation is installed above the membrane.

Protected membrane roof systems (membranes protected by polystyrene board, also functioning as thermal insulation placed on the outside of the membrane) can incorporate any of the membrane systems listed above. Extruded, expanded polystyrene board insulation is placed over the membrane, and a sheet of water-permeable polymer fabric is laid over the insulation. Stone ballast, pavers, or a combination of them is then used to hold the insulation in place and to protect the insulation from sunlight. Since the membrane serves as a vapor retarder, and since it is under and inside the insulation, this system excels in avoiding condensation. It is the system of choice in art museums, swimming pools, and other occupancies with high humidity.

Since the membrane is protected from harm coming from above, it is also the system of choice for rooftop terraces and similar uses. If the membrane is adhered water-tight to the substrate, migration of water from leaks, under the membrane, is limited. One problem with this type of roof is that it is difficult to locate leaks from above.

- Ballasts or pavers: Some roof systems contain ballasts or pavers to hold the remainder of the roof system down. The roof edges must be raised a minimum 4 in. (10 cm) or more, to prevent the ballast's blowing off.

- Earth-covered roof terraces: Earth-covered roofs follow similar principles, since the roofing is essentially characterized as a protected membrane roofing system. Because of the difficulty of post-construction inspection and repair, earth-covered systems require double, if not triple, redundancy in design of site water coursing, drainage, and waterproofing of the entire structure as a complete system. NRCA manual does not include earth-covered construction.

2.6.7 Sprayed polyurethane roofs

Sprayed polyurethane roofs are formed in place by spraying liquid polymer onto the substrate. The liquid then foams and expands, after which it becomes rigid. Flashings, slopes, and other forms can be made integral with the rest of the system. The foam has limited resistance to moisture penetration and poor resistance to ultra-violet radiation, so it is coated with various types of liquid-applied protective coating. Some types of coating require aggregate to be bonded into the coating to discourage eating of the foam by birds. Traffic walkways are necessary for sprayed polyurethane roofs.

Fig. 2. Pouring asphalt over built-up roof felts, and embedding gravel aggregate.

Fig. 3. Thermoset membrane roof, Ingalls Ice Skating Rink, Yale University, New Haven, CT. Eero Saarinen, Architect; F. J. Dahill Co., Roofing Contractor. The membrane roof protects surfaces that vary from very steep to low slope and accommodates flexing of the structure. 1957.

SHELL

B3

Fig. 4. Improperly-soldered flat lock sheet metal joint. Solder does not penetrate joint. Also note corrosion from acid deposition and from western redcedar shingle runoff.

2.6.8 Soldered flat-lock seam metal roofs

Soldered flat-lock seam metal roofs are assembled in place. With proper workmanship, they can be reliable and durable. The design must take account of thermal expansion, since the metal is rigid and has only limited ability to deform when heated and cooled. This roof type can only be applied by highly-skilled sheet metal workers who know how to solder the seams (Fig. 4). The seams are first coated with solder ("pretinned"), unless the metal is already coated. The metal is then heated, and the solder is touched to the outside of the seam. If the procedure is proper, the solder will draw into the seam, filling it. The writer suggests requiring a demonstration of soldering before the work is performed. Cut open the sample seam to make sure that the solder has penetrated fully.

Proprietary low-slope metal roof systems require complete and careful attention to the manufacturer's recommendations. The writer suggests having the initial work performed in the presence, and under the supervision, of the manufacturer's trained and authorized representative.

2.7 Cants, curbs, nailers and flashing

Quite often, the part of any roof system most vulnerable to water entry is that point at which the horizontal roof deck intersects with a vertical surface or penetration. Designers should carefully consider the design of all flashing details.

- Cants. The bending radius of bituminous roofing materials is generally limited to 45 degrees. To allow for this limited bending radius, cant strips must be provided at any 90 degree angle change such as created by roof-to-wall, roof-to-curb or other roof-to-vertical surface intersection.

- Units curbs. Mechanical units using curbs that have built-in metal base flashing flanges can be difficult to seal for the long term and, therefore, are not recommended for use with bituminous roof membranes. Some single-ply roof membranes may utilize prefabricated curbs with metal "self-flashing" flanges to be embedded in the roof membrane.

- Nailers. It is recommended that well-secured, decay resistant (that is, preservative treated) wood blocking be carefully designed and provided at all roof perimeters and penetrations for fastening membrane flashing and sheet metal components. Wood nailers should be provided on all prefabricated curbs and hatches for attachment of membrane base flashing.

- Flashing. There are two types of flashing: membrane flashing and sheet metal flashing. Membrane base flashing is generally composed of strips of compatible membrane materials used to close-in or flash roof-to-vertical surface intersections or transitions. On metal units and other raised-curb equipment, metal flashing (counterflashing and cap flashing) should be installed to cover the top edge and overlap the upper portion of membrane base flashing. Plumbing vent stacks and all other pipe projections through the membrane require metal flashing collars or membrane pipe flashing "boots." Metal flanges should be stripped in with membrane flashing plies or strips.

2.8 Aggregates and/or other surfacing

Some roof membranes may require certain types of surfacing to provide fire resistance, weathering protection, reflectivity, and/or a wearing surface for traffic. Rounded river-washed or water-worn gravel, crushed stone, slag, or marble-chips are used for aggregate-surfaced and some ballasted roofs. Gravel or aggregate surfacing for built-up roof membranes is usually set in hot bitumen, which is applied either by a bitumen spreader or by hand. Gravel is placed by machine or by hand with a scoop shovel.

2.9 Mechanical curbs and penetrations

To avoid deck deflections from damaging the roof, the structural design of the roof deck should always allow for the concentrated loading of mechanical equipment. Vibrations from roof-mounted or joins mounted mechanical equipment should be isolated from the roof membrane and flashing. Some poorly designed or poorly installed equipment may allow moisture to enter the building either from the exterior or from condensation within.

NRCA recommends clearance criteria between mechanical equipment and adjacent perimeters, curbs and walls to facilitate proper installation of roofing materials. A minimum of 12 in. (25 cm) is recom-

mended and 24 in. (50 cm.) for larger units. Projections through the roof not be located in valleys or drainage areas. Condensate from roof-mounted mechanical equipment should be directed to a positive drainage or outflow.

2.10 Roofing details for low-slope systems

NRCA (1996) contains recommended details for most roof systems. It is available in printed form and on CD ROM. The following are several details from that reference (Figs. 5 - 10).

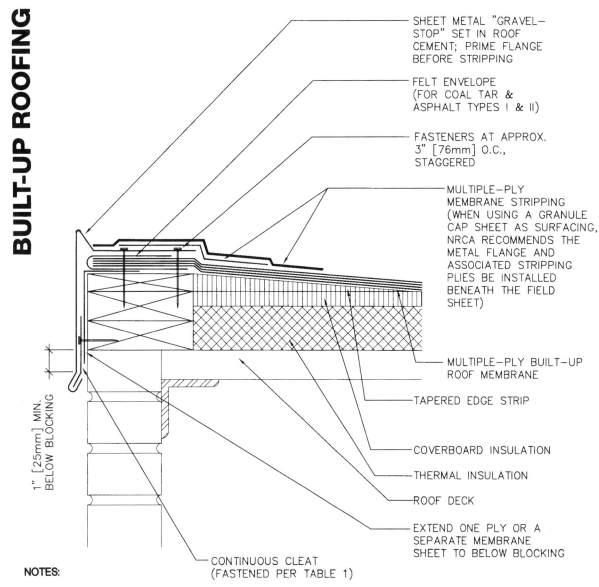

BUILT-UP ROOFING

SHEET METAL "GRAVEL-STOP" SET IN ROOF CEMENT; PRIME FLANGE BEFORE STRIPPING

FELT ENVELOPE (FOR COAL TAR & ASPHALT TYPES I & II)

FASTENERS AT APPROX. 3" [76mm] O.C., STAGGERED

MULTIPLE-PLY MEMBRANE STRIPPING (WHEN USING A GRANULE CAP SHEET AS SURFACING, NRCA RECOMMENDS THE METAL FLANGE AND ASSOCIATED STRIPPING PLIES BE INSTALLED BENEATH THE FIELD SHEET)

MULTIPLE-PLY BUILT-UP ROOF MEMBRANE

TAPERED EDGE STRIP

COVERBOARD INSULATION

THERMAL INSULATION

ROOF DECK

EXTEND ONE PLY OR A SEPARATE MEMBRANE SHEET TO BELOW BLOCKING

1" [25mm] MIN. BELOW BLOCKING

CONTINUOUS CLEAT (FASTENED PER TABLE 1)

NOTES:

1. NRCA SUGGESTS AVOIDING (WHERE POSSIBLE) FLASHING DETAILS THAT REQUIRE RIGID METAL FLANGES TO BE EMBEDDED OR SANDWICHED INTO THE ROOF MEMBRANE. (SEE BUR-1 FOR THE PREFERRED PERIMETER CONSTRUCTION.)
2. THIS DETAIL SHOULD BE USED ONLY WHERE THE DECK IS SUPPORTED BY THE OUTSIDE WALL.
3. ATTACH NAILER TO WALL WITH SUITABLE FASTENERS.
4. WOOD BLOCKING MAY BE SLOTTED FOR VENTING OF WET-FILL DECKS OR OTHER CONSTRUCTIONS WHERE APPLICABLE.
5. FREQUENT NAILING OF SHEET METAL FLANGE IS NECESSARY TO MINIMIZE THERMAL MOVEMENT.
6. REFER TO BUR/MB TABLE 1 FOR METAL THICKNESS AND CLEAT REQUIREMENT.
7. NRCA SUGGESTS THAT THE TOP STRIPPING PLY BE A HEAVY-WEIGHT REINFORCED POLYMER MODIFIED BITUMEN SHEET TO HELP STRIPPING PLIES ACCOMMODATE THERMAL MOVEMENT OF METAL.

Fig. 5. Embedded edge metal flashing (gravel stop). (NRCA BUR-3S): This is a typical low roof edge for a built-up roof. Note that the first ply of roofing felt is folded back to form an envelope, which contains the bitumen. If the envelope is omitted, or if it breaks, coal tar will drip down the wall.

SHELL

B3

MODIFIED BITUMEN ROOFING

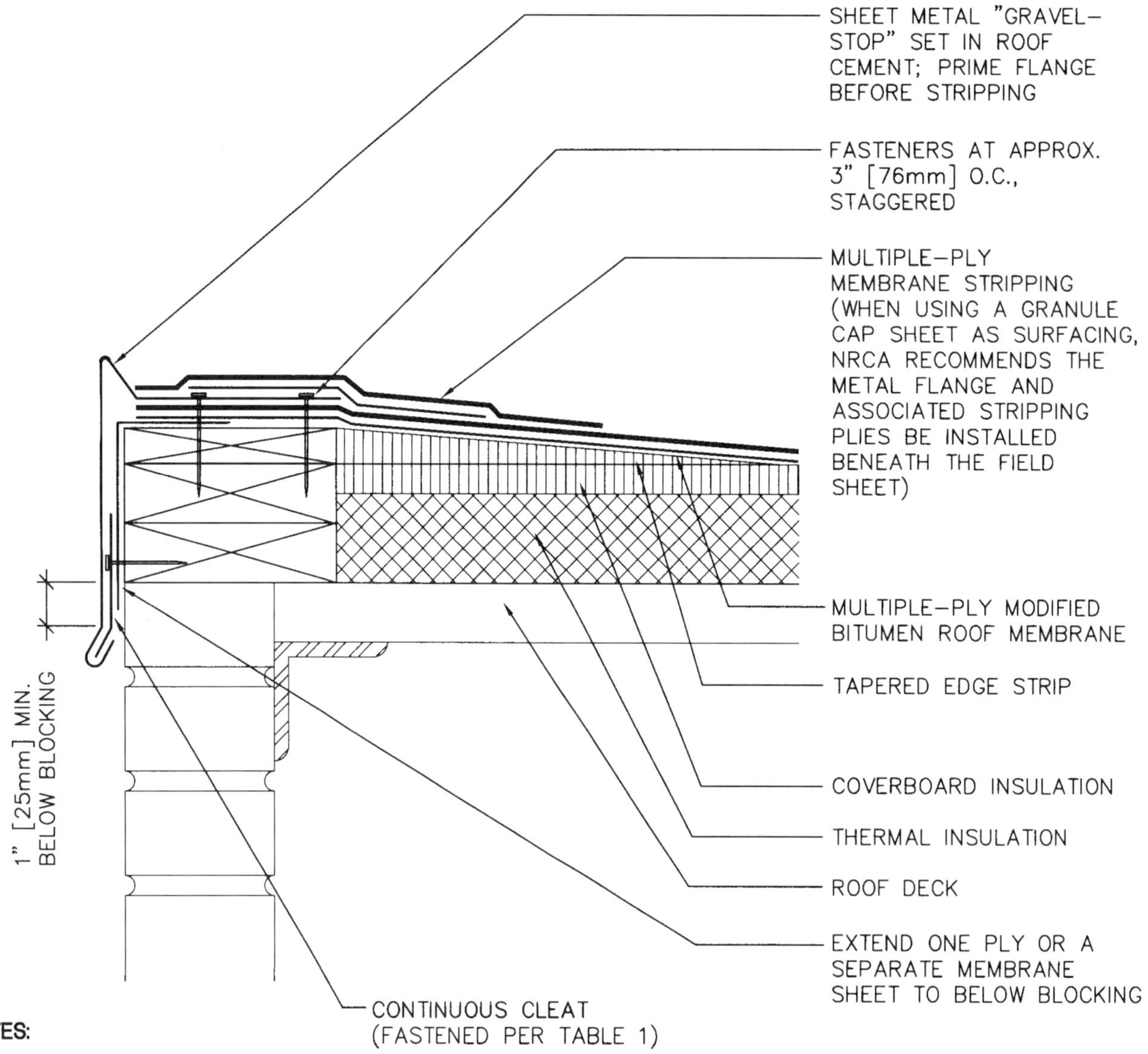

SHEET METAL "GRAVEL-STOP" SET IN ROOF CEMENT; PRIME FLANGE BEFORE STRIPPING

FASTENERS AT APPROX. 3" [76mm] O.C., STAGGERED

MULTIPLE-PLY MEMBRANE STRIPPING (WHEN USING A GRANULE CAP SHEET AS SURFACING, NRCA RECOMMENDS THE METAL FLANGE AND ASSOCIATED STRIPPING PLIES BE INSTALLED BENEATH THE FIELD SHEET)

MULTIPLE-PLY MODIFIED BITUMEN ROOF MEMBRANE

TAPERED EDGE STRIP

COVERBOARD INSULATION

THERMAL INSULATION

ROOF DECK

EXTEND ONE PLY OR A SEPARATE MEMBRANE SHEET TO BELOW BLOCKING

1" [25mm] MIN. BELOW BLOCKING

CONTINUOUS CLEAT (FASTENED PER TABLE 1)

NOTES:

1. NRCA SUGGESTS AVOIDING (WHERE POSSIBLE) FLASHING DETAILS THAT REQUIRE RIGID METAL FLANGES TO BE EMBEDDED OR SANDWICHED INTO THE ROOF MEMBRANE. (SEE MB-1 FOR THE PREFERRED PERIMETER CONSTRUCTION.)
2. THIS DETAIL SHOULD BE USED ONLY WHERE THE DECK IS SUPPORTED BY THE OUTSIDE WALL.
3. ATTACH NAILER TO WALL WITH SUITABLE FASTENERS.
4. WOOD BLOCKING MAY BE SLOTTED FOR VENTING OF WET-FILL DECKS OR OTHER CONSTRUCTIONS WHERE APPLICABLE.
5. FREQUENT NAILING OF SHEET METAL FLANGE IS NECESSARY TO MINIMIZE THERMAL MOVEMENT.
6. REFER TO BUR/MB TABLE 1 FOR METAL THICKNESS AND CLEAT REQUIREMENT.
7. NRCA SUGGESTS THAT THE TOP STRIPPING PLY BE A HEAVY-WEIGHT REINFORCED POLYMER MODIFIED BITUMEN SHEET TO HELP STRIPPING PLIES ACCOMMODATE THERMAL MOVEMENT OF METAL.

Fig. 6. Embedded edge metal flashing (gravel stop). (NRCA detail MB-3S): This detail is similar to Fig. 5, but there is one major difference and advantage: The base sheet extends over the edge, behind the metal fascia. This detail will tolerate some leaking at the edge joint, since water which penetrates through the junctions of different materials will be above the base sheet and thus kept out of the building. Some manufacturers permit modified bitumen edge details with built-up roofs, and the writer recommends that practice.

BUILT-UP ROOFING

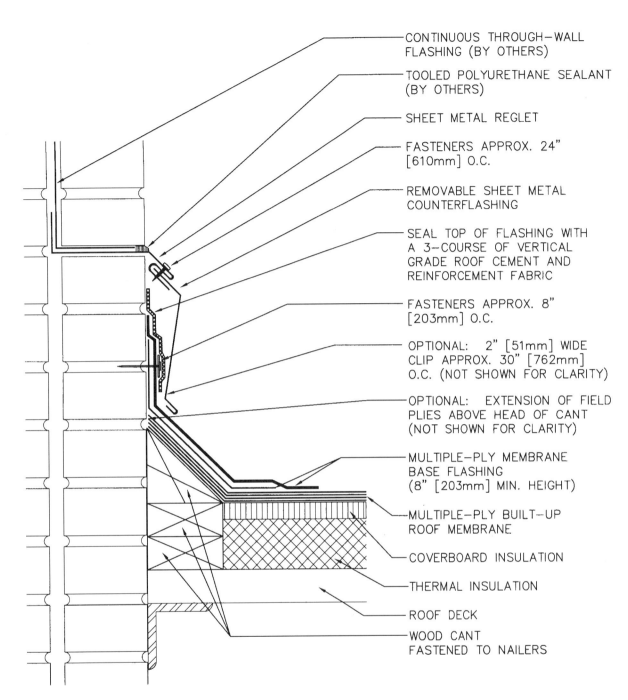

CONTINUOUS THROUGH—WALL FLASHING (BY OTHERS)

TOOLED POLYURETHANE SEALANT (BY OTHERS)

SHEET METAL REGLET

FASTENERS APPROX. 24" [610mm] O.C.

REMOVABLE SHEET METAL COUNTERFLASHING

SEAL TOP OF FLASHING WITH A 3—COURSE OF VERTICAL GRADE ROOF CEMENT AND REINFORCEMENT FABRIC

FASTENERS APPROX. 8" [203mm] O.C.

OPTIONAL: 2" [51mm] WIDE CLIP APPROX. 30" [762mm] O.C. (NOT SHOWN FOR CLARITY)

OPTIONAL: EXTENSION OF FIELD PLIES ABOVE HEAD OF CANT (NOT SHOWN FOR CLARITY)

MULTIPLE—PLY MEMBRANE BASE FLASHING (8" [203mm] MIN. HEIGHT)

MULTIPLE—PLY BUILT—UP ROOF MEMBRANE

COVERBOARD INSULATION

THERMAL INSULATION

ROOF DECK

WOOD CANT FASTENED TO NAILERS

NOTES:

1. THIS DETAIL SHOULD BE USED ONLY WHERE THE DECK IS SUPPORTED BY THE WALL.
2. THE JOINTS IN THE SHEET METAL COUNTERFLASHING SHOULD NOT BE SOLDERED.
3. OPTION: IF WOOD NAILERS ARE NOT USED, A FIBER CANT STRIP SET IN BITUMEN OR ADHESIVE MAY BE USED.
4. SEE TABLE 2 FOR ALTERNATE SHEET METAL COUNTERFLASHING TERMINATIONS.

Fig. 7. Base flashing for wall-supported deck. (NRCA detail BUR-5S): This is a detail for the intersection of a roof and a masonry wall, the roof being supported by the wall. Note that the metal counterflashing is made in two pieces, so that it can be taken off for installation of the base flashing. Note also that the counterflashing is joined to through-wall flashing in the masonry wall. The writer also recommends weep tubes where the counterflashing meets the masonry wall, to let out water which may find its way into the cavity. If the wall and roof move differentially, a different detail, for expansion joints, should be used.

THERMOPLASTIC ROOFING

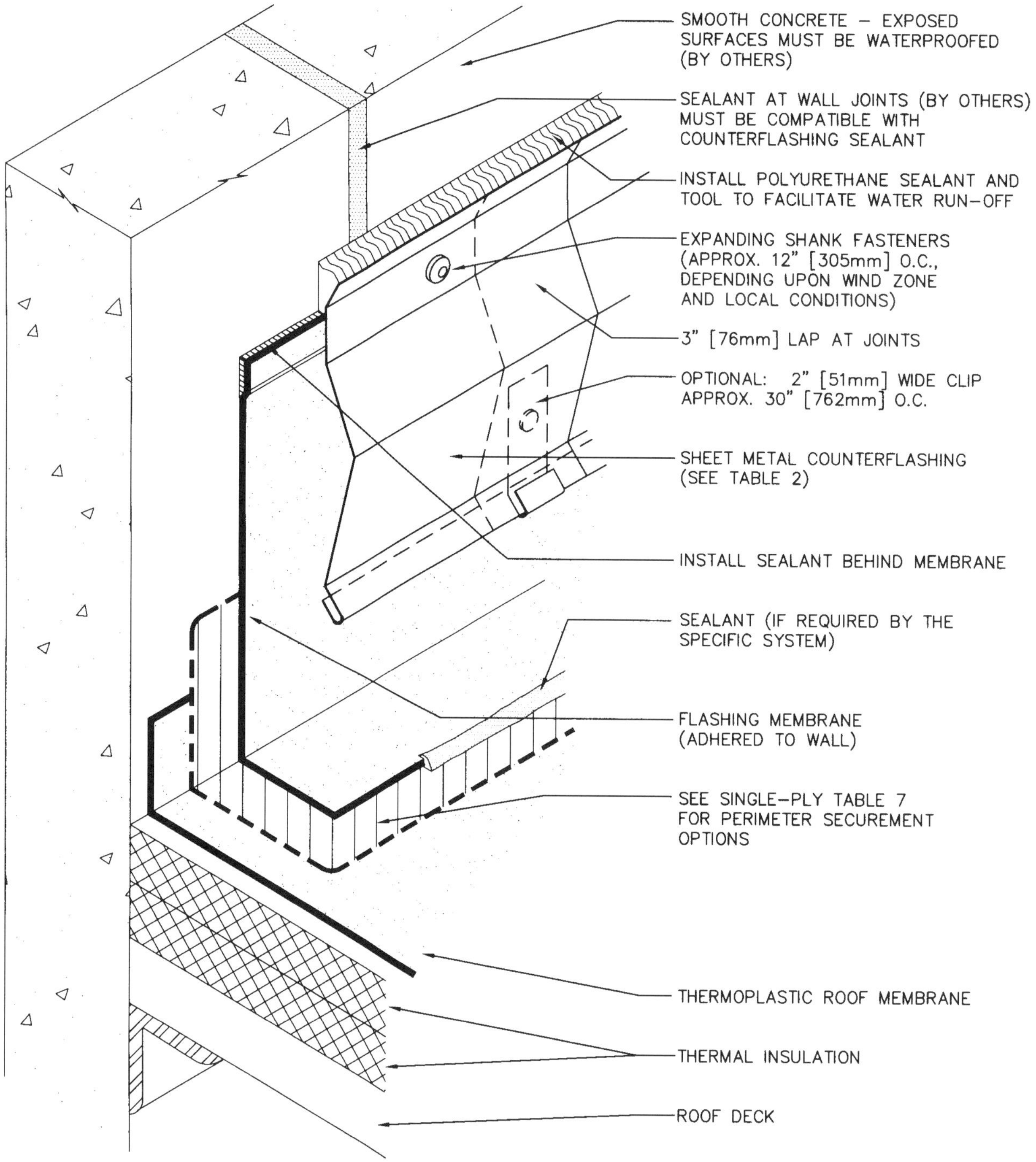

SMOOTH CONCRETE — EXPOSED
SURFACES MUST BE WATERPROOFED
(BY OTHERS)

SEALANT AT WALL JOINTS (BY OTHERS)
MUST BE COMPATIBLE WITH
COUNTERFLASHING SEALANT

INSTALL POLYURETHANE SEALANT AND
TOOL TO FACILITATE WATER RUN—OFF

EXPANDING SHANK FASTENERS
(APPROX. 12" [305mm] O.C.,
DEPENDING UPON WIND ZONE
AND LOCAL CONDITIONS)

3" [76mm] LAP AT JOINTS

OPTIONAL: 2" [51mm] WIDE CLIP
APPROX. 30" [762mm] O.C.

SHEET METAL COUNTERFLASHING
(SEE TABLE 2)

INSTALL SEALANT BEHIND MEMBRANE

SEALANT (IF REQUIRED BY THE
SPECIFIC SYSTEM)

FLASHING MEMBRANE
(ADHERED TO WALL)

SEE SINGLE—PLY TABLE 7
FOR PERIMETER SECUREMENT
OPTIONS

THERMOPLASTIC ROOF MEMBRANE

THERMAL INSULATION

ROOF DECK

NOTES:

1. THIS DETAIL SHOULD BE USED ONLY WHERE THE DECK IS SUPPORTED BY THE WALL.
2. TOP LAYER OF INSULATION CAN BE EITHER THERMAL INSULATION OR COVERBOARD INSULATION.
3. SLIP SHEET MAY BE REQUIRED BELOW MEMBRANE WHEN OVERLAYING SOME INSULATIONS OR SUBSTRATES.

Fig. 8. Thermosplastic roofing. (NRCA detail TP-6): This is a detail for the intersection of a concrete wall and a roof, the roof being supported on the wall. Note that the counterflashing is applied to the face of the concrete and sealed. In the writer's experience, surface-applied counterflashings are more reliable than flashing inserted into cast or sawn reglets in the wall.

THERMOSET ROOFING

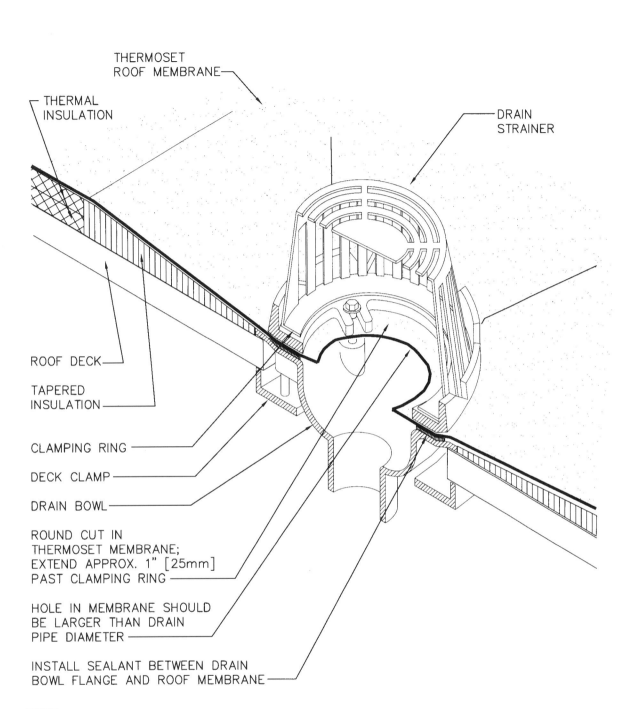

THERMOSET
ROOF MEMBRANE

THERMAL
INSULATION

DRAIN
STRAINER

ROOF DECK

TAPERED
INSULATION

CLAMPING RING

DECK CLAMP

DRAIN BOWL

ROUND CUT IN
THERMOSET MEMBRANE;
EXTEND APPROX. 1" [25mm]
PAST CLAMPING RING

HOLE IN MEMBRANE SHOULD
BE LARGER THAN DRAIN
PIPE DIAMETER

INSTALL SEALANT BETWEEN DRAIN
BOWL FLANGE AND ROOF MEMBRANE

NOTE:

1. THE USE OF A METAL DECK SUMP PAN IS NOT RECOMMENDED. HOWEVER, DRAIN RECEIVER/BEARING PLATES ARE APPLICABLE WITH SOME PROJECTS.

Fig. 9. Roof drain. (NRCA detail TS-22): The drain is shown recessed in a wide sump, to ensure that water is not impounded. The roof membrane is installed over the drain bowl flange, and then a clamping ring is installed on top of the membrane. When the bolts are tightened, the clamping ring "pinches" the membrane, creating a water-tight joint. The drain strainer keeps objects out of the drain.

BUILT-UP ROOFING

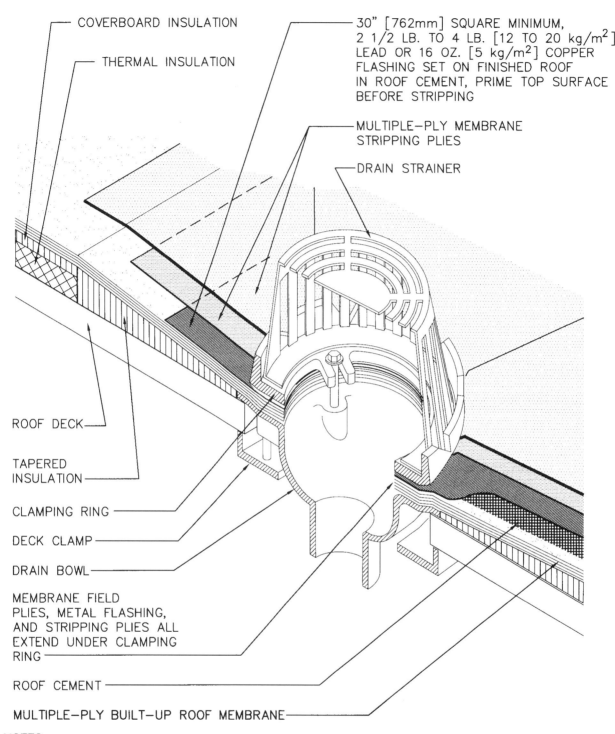

COVERBOARD INSULATION

THERMAL INSULATION

30" [762mm] SQUARE MINIMUM, 2 1/2 LB. TO 4 LB. [12 TO 20 kg/m^2] LEAD OR 16 OZ. [5 kg/m^2] COPPER FLASHING SET ON FINISHED ROOF IN ROOF CEMENT, PRIME TOP SURFACE BEFORE STRIPPING

MULTIPLE−PLY MEMBRANE STRIPPING PLIES

DRAIN STRAINER

ROOF DECK

TAPERED INSULATION

CLAMPING RING

DECK CLAMP

DRAIN BOWL

MEMBRANE FIELD PLIES, METAL FLASHING, AND STRIPPING PLIES ALL EXTEND UNDER CLAMPING RING

ROOF CEMENT

MULTIPLE−PLY BUILT−UP ROOF MEMBRANE

NOTES:

1. THE USE OF A METAL DECK SUMP PAN IS NOT RECOMMENDED.   HOWEVER, DRAIN RECEIVER/BEARING PLATES ARE APPLICABLE WITH SOME PROJECTS.
2. DO NOT APPLY COAL TAR OR DEAD LEVEL ASPHALT INTO DRAIN SUMP.

Fig. 10. Roof drain. (NRCA detail BUR-23): Roof drains for built-up roofs require more plies of roofing and flashing than drains for other systems. Unless the drain is placed in a wide and deep sump, the buildup of plies will create a dam around the drain, impounding water. Another advantage of the sump is that the insulation is thin there, and internal warmth from the building will tend to melt ice and snow from the drains and their immediate perimeter.

3 Steep slope roof systems

While similar principles may apply, the components of steep slope roofing systems are somewhat more simplified compared to low-slope systems; many of the various roofing system functions are provided by fewer elements:

1 the structural deck or substrate

2 roofing, meaning the roof coverings

3 flashing

Slope and drainage, and expansion joints and/or area dividers are accommodated by the nature of the steep slope systems., although flashing is as critical in the water drainage design. Mechanical attachments and penetrations deserve similar vigilance as low-slope systems. Moisture control and insulation functions are often separated from the roofing assembly and accommodated in the ceiling, well below the roofing assembly. Nonetheless, ventilation of, and inspection access to, roof-ceiling interstitial spaces and/or attic spaces remain critical design issues.

3.1   Structural deck or substrate

- Substrate: The substrate or structural deck supports the roof and all dead and live loads on it. It resists snow drift loading, equipment loading, wind loading, and wind uplift. Positive and negative wind loading may be a major force acting on a steep roof system.

- Underlayment. In virtually all climates, there should be underlayment over the whole roof, and it should be made waterproof at penetrations (this is common sense, but perhaps one in a thousand roofs has properly installed underlayment). It should extend fully to the rakes and eaves. General industry recommendations favor use of fiberglass-reinforced asphalt-saturated and, sometimes, asphalt-saturated and coated underlayment. For expensive and long-lived steep roof systems, the writer recommends modified bitumen-saturated and coated fiberglass base sheet as an underlayment.

3.2   Roofing

Steep slope roofing types include:

- Shingle roofing

- Sheet metal roofs

- Roll roofing and membrane roofing

- Other systems

- Shingle roofing

Shingle roofing systems of wood, metal, asphalt, clay tile, slate, synthetic tile and slate, concrete, and various others.

- Sheet metal roofs

Sheet metal roofs, both factory-fabricated systems and custom systems fabricated in the shop or field and assembled in the field. Sometimes designated "architectural metal panel roofing systems," these are typically designed to be used on steep enough slopes that will shed water rapidly from the metal panel surface, so typically the seams are not watertight. Solid roof sheathing is required for architectural metal panel roof systems and underlayment is recommended.

- Roll roofing and membrane roofing

Mineral-surface roll roofing and some membrane roof materials, such as single-ply and modified bitumen, may be used for steep roofs. Other than slope considerations, their application in construction follow low-slope roofing practices.

- Other systems

Thatch roofing, while relatively esoteric in modern construction application, is also properly defined as a steep roofed system. It is used in indigenous applications throughout the world and has been restored as a building craft tradition.

Steep-slope roofs use watershedding roof coverings, intended to shed water from upslope courses down over neighboring courses and off the roof or to a water drainage and gutter system. The shingles, slates, tiles, or other steep roof system is then applied, following the manufacturer's and industry recommendations. The architect should take, read, and keep on file the manufacturer's instructions printed on the shingle wrappers.

3.2.1   Shingle roofing

Shingle roofing systems of wood, metal, asphalt, clay tile, slate, synthetic tile and slate, concrete, and various others.

3.2.2   Asphalt shingles

Asphalt shingles are well understood in the industry, and their installation doesn't require great skill. (Steep slope asphalt materials are referred to as "prepared asphalt roofing products" in American Society of Testing Material Standards.)

Common problems are the use of smooth nails (as against annular-groove nails and other deformed shank nails), failure to leave 1/8 in. (3.18 mm) gaps between plywood panels, improper anchorage of the first courses at the eaves, improper edge conditions, and failure to install both eave flashing and underlayment. Normal warranties do not apply when wind velocity exceeds 54 miles per hour, but there are manufacturers' and industry recommendations for greater wind resistance.

The asphalt shingles are installed with at least four deformed-shank galvanized steel nails per strip. The writer recommends six nails where high wind occurs. The first course of shingles is trimmed, removing the tabs, and then firmly nailed. The self-seal strips in the trimmed, concealed bottom course will adhere to the bottom exposed course and make the eave shingles tight and wind-resistant. In addition, shingles at the rakes may require cementing in high wind areas.

Table 2. Typical asphalt shingles. (NRCA 1996)

PRODUCT	1 ASTM DESIGNATION	2 CONFIGURATION	3 PER SQUARE		4 APPROX. SIZE		5 TYPICAL EXPOSURE	6 UNDERWRITERS LISTING
			SHINGLES	BUNDLES	WIDTH	LENGTH		
STRIP SHINGLE MORE THAN ONE THICKNESS PER STRIP LAMINATED	FIBERGLASS D 3462 ORGANIC D 225	VARIOUS EDGE, SURFACE TEXTURE AND APPLICATION TREATMENTS	64 TO 90	3 TO 5	11-1/2" (292mm) TO 1'-3" (381mm)	3' (914mm) TO 3'-4" (1016mm)	4" (102mm) TO 8" (203mm)	A OR C
STRIP SHINGLE SINGLE THICKNESS PER STRIP	FIBERGLASS D 3462 ORGANIC D 225	VARIOUS EDGE, SURFACE TEXTURE AND APPLICATION TREATMENTS	65 TO 80	3 OR 4	1' (305mm) TO 1'-5" (432mm)	3' (914MM) OR 3'-4" (1016MM)	4" (102mm) TO 7 1/2" (191mm)	A OR C
SELF-SEALING STRIP SHINGLE "3 -TAB"	FIBERGLASS D 3462 ORGANIC D 225	CONVENTIONAL 3 TAB	65 TO 80	3 TYP.	1' (305mm) TO 1'-1 1/4" (337mm)	3' (914mm) TO 3'-4" (1016mm)	5 5/8" (143mm) OR 5" (127mm)	A OR C
		2 OR MORE TAB	65 TO 80	3 OR 4				
SELF-SEALING STRIP SHINGLE NO CUT OUT	FIBERGLASS D 3462 ORGANIC D 225	VARIOUS EDGE AND TEXTURE TREATMENTS	65 TO 81	3 OR 4	1' (305mm) OR 1'-1 1/4" (337mm)	3' (914mm) TO 3'-4" (1016mm)	5" (127mm) OR 5 5/8" (143mm)	A OR C
INDIVIDUAL LOCK DOWN BASIC "T"-LOCK DESIGN	ORGANIC	SEVERAL DESIGN VARIATIONS	72 TO 120	3 OR 4	1'-6" (457mm) TO 1'-10 1/4" (565mm)	1'-8" (508mm) TO 1'-10 1/2" (572mm)	-	A OR C

NOTE - ALL WEIGHTS AND DIMENSIONS ARE APPROXIMATE

OTHER TYPES AVAILABLE FROM SOME MANUFACTURERS IN CERTAIN AREAS OF THE COUNTRY

The felt of which the shingles are manufactured may be fiberglass or organic felt. A variety of sizes and shapes is available. Virtually all asphalt shingles are manufactured with self-seal tabs. It is prudent to make sure that the self-seal tabs soften and adhere properly; if they don't, require sealing with roof cement, a hot air gun, or other means (Table 2).

3.2.3 Wood shingles and shakes

Most wood shingles are made from western redcedar, but they are also made from Atlantic white cedar, eastern white pine, and other species. They can be installed over spaced nailers or solid roof sheathing (Fig. 11). The minimum shingle length for normal application is three times the exposure plus one inch or more. Wood shakes are similar to shingles, but they are thicker and more irregular. They are installed with #30 felt or equivalent material between all courses.

The industry associations require that the joints in adjoining courses be offset substantially and that the joints in every three courses not line up exactly, as a precaution against future splitting and water entry locations. (Fig. 12). The writer recommends that joints in every three courses be offset at least 2 in. (5 cm). As with all roof systems, the manufacturer's and industry recommendations should be followed carefully. Eave flashings are recommended.

3.2.4 Slates and tiles

Slates, tiles, and synthetic slates and tiles are selected for architectural style and appearance, and may also be a system of choice in areas prone to air-borne fire hazard, such as forest fires. These systems are installed over eave flashing and underlayment, best considered as a continuous and complete moisture protection system itself.

Slate roofing is a durable, dense and sound rock. It is a time-tested, weather and fire-resistant material, available in thickness from 3/16 in. to 2 in. Zinc coated, copper weld or copper nails are used for fastening through machine-punched holes in the slate. Nail penetrations should be protected with sealant as wall as by overlapping of slate.

Clay tile is available either molded into several shapes or flat. Vitrified clay tile has water absorption of 3 percent or less, which facilitated rapid water run-off and can withstand freeze-thaw cycling. Copper flashing is used for valleys, fastened with cleats and not soldered. Care must be taken during installation to ensure proper blending of colors and matching width and length dimensions. Corrosion of copper gutters and other valley materials should be considered where conditions of acid rain deposition prevail.

Concrete tile is available either as roll or flat shapes, similar to clay tile. Exposed surfaces are generally finished with synthetic oxide pigmented cementitious material. Moisture absorbtion should be investigated; if tiles absorb moisture, roofing problems may ensue.

Installation of slate and tile systems require more skill than that of asphalt shingles. Manufacturers and industry groups publish installation instructions.

3.2.5 Sheet metal roofing

Sheet metal roofs include both factory-fabricated systems and custom systems fabricated in the shop or field and assembled in the field. Sometimes designated "architectural metal panel roofing systems," these are typically designed to be used on steep enough slopes that will shed water rapidly from the metal panel surface, so typically the seams are not watertight. Solid roof sheathing is required for architectural metal panel roof systems and underlayment is recommended. Available metals include:

• *Copper and lead-coated copper*

These materials have a long history of successful use on roofs. They are easy to form and solder. They are highly ductile, and so they tend to yield harmlessly when stressed. (See "Corrosion of Metals" in Chapter B2 of this Volume regarding corrosion of copper and lead-coated copper). In building locations subject to air-borne acid deposition (acid rain residue and directly-deposited acid aerosol), dew and mist may dissolve acid deposits on roofs and wash the concentrated acid onto sheet metal. In the writer's experience, roofs made entirely from copper are not harmed, but copper and lead-coated copper roofs which receive drainage from other, nonreactive materials are corroded (Fig. 13). Some protective methods include:

- Detail the roof so that no water flows from nonreactive materials onto copper and lead-coated copper. A roof made entirely from copper is one way to accomplish this.

- Use sheet metal not subject to acid corrosion, such as aluminum, stainless steel, and Terne-coated stainless steel, where a flow of acid from above will occur.

- Install sacrificial zinc anodes at the point where the acid runs onto the copper. The writer has found this method to be successful, but he hasn't yet determined how much zinc is needed nor how long it will last.

• *Aluminum*

Aluminum is vulnerable to attack by hydroxyl ions, but most roofs are not exposed to alkali conditions. Aluminum is not vulnerable to attack from the concentrations of acid which occur on roofs. Although very thin aluminum is used on residences, the writer recommends following the SMACNA Manual recommendations for proper minimum gauge. Aluminum is available with highly durable finishes, including fluorocarbon polymer coatings. Contrary to conventional wisdom, the writer has found that proper aluminum alloys with proper finish are not subject to corrosion from salt spray.

Fig. 11. Western redcedar shingle roof on First Presbyterian Church, New Haven, CT. John Dinkeloo, Architect. 1966.

Fig. 12. Split shingles: the first and third course joints lined up in many places. When the intermediate shingles split, there was a clear path through the shingles for rain water.)

Fig. 13. Copper roof with well-developed light green patina. Below the glass and aluminum skylight, the patina has been removed by acid runoff.

Fig. 14. Ice dam at eaves of steep roof. Thick deposit of ice causes melt water to back up and run through laps and joints in shingle roof. Eave flashing is intended to tolerate ice damming and prevent melting water from entering building.

- *Steel*

Plain galvanized steel, aluminized steel, and aluminum-zinc alloy coated steel are not satisfactory for roofing sheet metal exposed to acid runoff in those parts of the country with heavy rainfall and acid deposition. The protective coating is eroded rapidly. They have been used successfully in other parts of the country, however. They have the advantages of economy, strength, and low coefficient of thermal expansion. Durable finishes are available.

- *Terne*

Terne (trade name of Follansbee Steel Corp.), a steel that is coated with an alloy of tin and lead, has a long history of use as a roof covering. It must be painted and kept painted for durability.

- *Stainless steel*

Stainless steel and Terne-coated stainless steel are highly durable metals. Terne-coated stainless steel is glossy upon first exposure, but it turns matte gray with exposure. Stainless steel is subject to stress-hardening, and thus it is harder to work than copper, and it may rip rather than yield when exposed to great stress. Terne-coated stainless steel can be soldered well. In parts of the country exposed to acid deposition, where the metal must be soldered and where the metal will receive acid residue, Terne-coated stainless steel is the sheet metal of choice in the writer's opinion.

- *Lead*

Lead has a long history of successful use. The writer observed a lead roofing pan on Salisbury Cathedral dated 1814, and Sir Bernard M. Feilden states that the lead roof on the Pantheon in Rome was installed in 1601. It is widely used on monumental buildings in Britain. Lead can be formed to nearly any shape, including curved, nonplanar shapes. It is highly durable. Runoff from lead and lead-coated copper roofs is toxic, and the destination of the water which washes from lead should be considered. Since lead fuel additives and lead paint pigment are no longer used, lead leached from roofing may be one of the major contemporary sources of lead pollution. Unfortunately, there aren't satisfactory substitute products in all cases.

- *Zinc*

Zinc and zinc alloys have many of the same characteristics as copper. They are durable and easy to form and to solder. Although the writer hasn't seen acid damage to zinc alloys, it probably occurs. One use of zinc and zinc alloy is for metal roof shingles.

- *Monel*

Monel is a very highly durable metal occasionally used for roofing, a trademark material named after Alfred Monel, its developer and manufacturer. It is a composite allow of nickel, copper, iron, manganese, silicon and carbon that is very resistant to corrosion.

- *Porcelain-enameled steel*

Porcelain-enameled steel roof tiles, long associated with "your host of the highways," are very durable. Its most fragile or susceptible points are nicks that may occur in handling, installation or maintenance.

Thicknesses for typical roof components are recommended in the SNACNA Handbook.

3.3 Flashing

- Eave flashing. In climates which may be subject to freezing temperatures, there should be eave flashing to prevent water from ice dams from entering the building (Fig. 14). Code requirements vary. In areas governed by the BOCA National Building Code, the eave flashing must extend 2 ft. (60 cm) up from the intersecting plane of the interior wall surface. The writer recommends 4 ft. (1.2 m) or more.

SHELL

B3

- There should be metal or other valley liners, eave drips, and rake drips. Certain metals, in certain regions of the country, are subject to acid deposit corrosion. If metal valleys are used, the writer recommends using a rubber or modified bitumen redundant valley under the metal. Modified bitumen and rubber may also be used as a valley liner without metal.

- Where people may pass below the eaves, consider requiring snow guards. The writer recommends snow guards throughout the roof, up to the ridge, to avoid damage to the snow guards from an avalanche of snow. Also, where people may pass below the eaves, consider the danger of icicles. One way to avoid icicle danger is to plant shrubs under the eaves, and another way is to include ice melting cable in the gutters and downspouts. See "Roof Accessories" in this Chapter.

Some aphorisms for use of sheet metal flashing:

- Sheet metals, being rigid, will not accommodate excessive expansion and contraction. Therefore the sheet metal roofing components must be detailed to accommodate movement (Fig. 15). Where moving components join stable components, strict adherence to SMACNA details is especially important. In addition, the joints which are not detailed to move must be fastened firmly. Solder alone may not be adequate; rivets may be necessary.

- Some sheet metals and their fasteners are subject to galvanic corrosion. If dissimilar metals can't be kept apart, the cathode should be small and the anode should be large. Steel nails used to fasten copper, lead-coated copper, stainless steel, and Monel will corrode to destruction very rapidly.

- In most cases a redundant underlayment is desirable, especially at eaves and valleys. In climates subject to ice damming, valleys and underlayment should be wider than normal. Underlayment should be lapped over eave flashing throughout, sealed to penetrations. (See "Gutters and Downspouts" in this Chapter)

- Where the steep roofs adjoin walls above, turn the underlayment up. Install metal or modified bitumen step flashing lapped between the shingles. Install metal stepped counterflashings above. The metal step counterflashings should be joined to through-wall flashing at masonry walls and should be extended up behind the underlayment and siding for wood-sided walls.

- Joints made by simply lapping adjacent sheets are not waterproof. Applying sealant over the open end of a lap is not waterproof for long.

- One way to make joints in metal flashing waterproof is to bed the lap in nonhardening butyl sealant (a product offered by only a few producers). It must be in the joint, not on the outside of the joint.

- Another way to make metal flashing joints waterproof is to form flat lock seams. This is an excellent method, but it requires much skill and is not often used today.

- In the writer's experience the way to make sheet metal joints waterproof with the greatest assurance of success is to apply a continuous flexible flashing under the sheet metal.

4   Summary

4.1   Guidelines for designing a roof system

- Be a knowledgeable designer: First, become familiar with the NRCA "Handbook of Accepted Roofing Knowledge." If you haven't read it, don't design roofs.

- Seek out local expertise and experience. Select one or more general systems appropriate to the project and the prevailing and extreme conditions of the locale. If you are not experienced in roof-

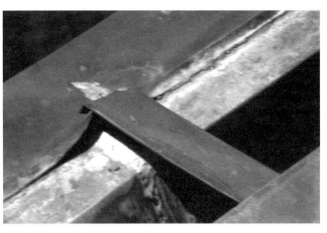

Fig. 15. Expansion joint not properly constructed; moving elements join fixed elements rigidly, and the joint has twisted and broken.

ing design, discuss your selections with another architect, a respected roofing contractor, or both. If several systems are appropriate and equivalent, consider allowing the contractor to use whichever one he/she wishes, assigning clear lines of responsibility for contract and subcontract administration and for corrections of subsequent problems.

- Incorporate manufacturer recommendations: Incorporate the appropriate National Roofing Contractors Association and Sheet Metal and Air Conditioning Contractors Association specifications and details into your design.

- Design proper vapor retarders: Determine whether a vapor retarder is to be used. The writer recommends against having more than one vapor retarder, since such practice may entrap moisture. Where there is a likelihood of vapor condensation, the protected membrane roof system is usually the system of choice. In making the decision on whether to include a vapor retarder, consult the ASHRAE Handbook of Fundamentals as well as the NRCA Roofing and Waterproofing Manual. In climates where condensation only occurs under unusual conditions, and where the roof system has the ability to absorb the moisture which may condense under those conditions, a vapor retarder is probably neither necessary nor desirable.

- Apply and/or exceed existing codes: Find out what codes and regulations, such as insurance requirements for wind uplift and code requirements for fire resistance, apply, and select systems which conform to those codes and regulations.

- Create positive drainage: Determine the drainage from the SMACNA Handbook, the BOCA National Plumbing Code, or other code which applies. The SMACNA Handbook recommendations are reproduced in the "Gutters and Downspouts" in this Chapter. Provide redundant drainage in case the primary drainage becomes clogged. The roof must drain freely and completely under all conditions of live load and dead load deflection. Roofing distributors may be willing to help you lay out the roof slopes; they have computers programmed to perform such layouts. If practicable, keep drains in areas of maximum deflection, and keep them away from walls and parapets which may cause leaves to pile up and/or snow/ice damage.

- Anticipate and design for extreme conditions: Perform calculations to determine the required wind load, wind uplift load, and snow load, or have your structural engineering consultant do so. Design the structure and roof system accordingly.

- Be the devil in the details: After the design is mostly finished, play the devil's advocate. Try to find the ways that water can enter your system, and then correct the design to exclude water. Better yet, have this critical review conducted by a knowledgeable person, in your office or from another office, who is not part of the design team for the project.

- Design penetrations carefully: When designing roof penetrations, keep them well apart from one another and from parapets and walls. When designing supports for roof accessories, leave enough room under them for the roofers to work.

- For repair and replacement of roofing, inspect and remove unsatisfactory conditions: If there is an existing roof, determine whether it must be removed before application of the new roof. This writer recommends removing the old roof in almost all cases, one reason being that you can then inspect the structure for possible decay and damage. If the existing roof is to be removed, partially or fully, have it tested for possible asbestos content, and require conformity with environmental protection, public health, and OSHA regulations.

- Help define a roof maintenance program: Determine how the roof will be maintained, repaired, and removed at the end of its useful life. When replacement occurs, two-piece counterflashings make the work easier and better. For a very steep roof, consider anchors built into the system for attachment of equipment and safety lines. Access hatches and ladder guards high on the steep roof and at all levels of low-slope roofs will make it possible to perform maintenance and repairs properly. They will also allow the architect to observe and inspect the work safely.

- Use manufacturer's technical resources: Require that the roof system manufacturer's representative be on the job as the work starts and at its completion. Discuss all details, and learn from the representative.

- Follow-up: Go back a year later, and document what changes have occurred. Issue appropriate maintenance and/or follow-up recommendations to building owner/operator. Incorporate lessons learned from documented experience into office practices.

4.2 Accessing available information

The materials technology of modern roofing materials is constantly evolving, at times dramatically based on new materials and also upon on-going field testing and experience. At the same time, technical information is also being constantly updated. The prudent designer and specifier of roof systems must therefore constantly refer to most recent technical literature, much of it developed by the roofing industry. There are differences in recommendations among the industry groups. For example, SMACNA recommends metal base flashings for low-slope roofs, and NRCA doesn't. Most roof system manufacturers have catalogs and manuals showing the proper use of their products. The following commentary provides a guide to these sources.

- For a person not familiar with roofing technology, the best single source is the National Roofing Contractors Association (NRCA) "Handbook of Accepted Roofing Knowledge," the first chapter of the *NRCA Roofing and Waterproofing Manual.*

- The NRCA publishes yearly guides to major roof types, listing manufacturers, data, and available warranties under the titles "Commercial Low-slope Roofing Materials Guide" and "Residential Steep-slope Roofing Materials Guide." The Association also publishes a monthly magazine, *Professional Roofing*, with articles on low-slope and steep roofing. This is an especially current reference on problems in roofing technology applications and what is being done to solve them.

- The U. S. National Institute of Standards and Technology (NIST), together with NRCA and other professional and industry associations, sponsors international symposia on roofing every few years. The proceedings of these symposia are published and report on the very latest research information on roofs, and probable future trends.

- The sheet metal industry has published a thorough manual for the use of its products: Sheet Metal and Air Conditioning Contractors' Association (SMACNA) *Architectural Sheet Metal Manual.* Details are available on CAD.

- The Asphalt Roofing Manufacturers Association publishes the Residential Asphalt Roofing Manual.

- The Cedar Shake and Shingle Bureau *Design and Application Manual* applies to this association's products.

- The Vermont Structural Slate Co., Fair Haven, VT, distributes *Slate Roofs*, which is a reprinting of a 1926 manual on slate roof construction.

- *The Roofing Specifier* (TRS) is a monthly trade journal with technical features and briefings available without charge to qualified professionals. 131 West 1st Street, Duluth, MN 55802-2065. Tel. (218) 723-9200.

Gutters and downspouts

Summary: The most common method of rain water removal from steep roofs is by gutters and downspouts. Other methods include direct discharge from the eaves (particularly common in cold regions), water diverters, and gutters discharging into internal leaders. Some low-slope roofs discharge through scuppers into leader heads and downspouts.

Key words: downspouts, leaders, roof drainage, roof gutters.

Water spout, Wells Cathedral, Wells, UK

Uniformat:	D2040
MasterFormat:	07600

SHELL

B3

Overview of roof drainage options

In many locales, it is common to allow water to drain directly off the edges of steep roofs. Except in very dry areas, direct drainage should be used in conjunction with wide overhangs and, where there is a basement, a drip bed at the ground and subsurface drainage. Direct drainage is especially common is regions subject to severe cold weather, where ice and snow may remain on roofs for long periods and where gutters and downspouts don't function in winter. Water diverters may be used to avoid discharge of water over doorways and other pedestrian walkways.

The most common type of roof drainage for steep roofs is a combination of gutters and downspouts (the words "leader" and "downspout" both refer to pipes conducting water down from a roof). The gutters should be designed to accept all normal roof runoff, and the downspouts should be able to discharge all water which flows to them quickly.

Water diverters are sometimes used in place of gutters. Instead of being mounted under the eaves, water diverters are mounted above the roof plane. While diverters do not extend to the edge of the eaves, and thus allow they do some dripping, they are not prone to clogging.

Waterspouts or gargoyles may lead the water out from the wall and allow it to drip into a pool or drip bed below. Chains, in a detail familiar in traditional Japanese architecture, are sometimes used to lead the water to the ground.

Although the predominant method of draining low-slope roofs is by internal drains, gutters and downspouts are sometimes used instead. Some low-slope roofs are drained through scuppers at the perimeter into leader heads and then into downspouts. Some other low-slope roofs are drained from low edges into gutters, which in turn drain into downspouts, or directly to the ground from the roof edges. Still other low-slope roofs discharge from projected water spouts directly to the ground.

All roof drain systems in cold regions may form icicles, except internal leaders in heated buildings. Therefore one should not design sidewalks under the eaves. It may be prudent to design landscaping beds or rock drip beds to keep people from passing under the eaves. Alternatively, a good quality electric snow melting system in the gutters and downspouts will, when it functions, avoid icicles.

Material used for gutters and downspouts

- *Copper and lead-coated copper*
  These materials have a long history of successful use on roofs.

They are easy to form and solder. They are highly ductile, and so they tend to yield harmlessly when stressed. See "Corrosion of Metals" in Chapter B2 regarding corrosion of copper and lead-coated copper from acid deposition. In those parts of the country subject to acid deposition (acid rain residue and directly-deposited acid aerosol), dew and mist may dissolve acid deposits on roofs and wash the concentrated acid onto sheet metal. In the writer's experience, roofs made entirely from copper are not harmed, but copper and lead-coated copper roofs which receive drainage from other, nonreactive or acid-producing materials are corroded. Gutters and downspouts, being at the bottom of the system, are especially vulnerable to acid corrosion. Some protective methods include:

- Detail the roof so that no water flows from other, nonreactive materials onto copper and lead-coated copper. A roof made entirely from copper is one way to accomplish this.

- Use thicker copper, such as 20-ounce, and plan for replacement within 15-20 years.

- Use sheet metal not subject to acid corrosion, such as aluminum, stainless steel, and Terne-coated stainless steel for gutters and downspouts ("Terne" is a trade name for a product of Follansbee Steel Corp.).

- Install sacrificial zinc anodes at the eaves, where the acid runs into the gutters.

- *Aluminum*
  Aluminum is vulnerable to attack by hydroxyl ions, but concentrated hydroxyl ions are rare on roofs. Aluminum is not vulnerable to attack from the concentrations of acid which occur on roofs. Although very thin aluminum is used on residences, the SMACNA Manual recommends the proper minimum gauge for architectural use. Aluminum is available with highly durable finishes, including fluorocarbon polymer coatings. Contrary to conventional wisdom, the writer has found that proper aluminum alloys with proper finish are not subject to corrosion from salt spray. In the writer's opinion, aluminum is the material of choice for gutters and downspouts which don't require soldering.

- *Galvanized steel*
  Plain galvanized steel, aluminized steel, and aluminum-zinc alloy coated steel may not be satisfactory for gutters, downspouts, valleys, and other roofing sheet metal exposed to concentrated runoff in those parts of the country with frequent rainfall and acid

---

Author: Donald Baerman, AIA

References: SMACNA. 1993. *Architectural Sheet Metal Manual - Fifth Edition.* Sheet Metal and Air Conditioning Contractors' Association, 4201 Lafayette Center Drive, Chantilly, VA 20151.

Fig. 1. Built-in gutter. Yale University Hall of Graduate Studies. 1932. James Gamble Rogers, Architect.

deposition. The protective coating may be eroded rapidly. They have been used successfully in other parts of the country, however, and if properly maintained and periodically painted, they give good service. They have the advantages of economy, strength, and low coefficient of thermal expansion. Durable finishes are available.

- *Stainless steel and Terne*
  Stainless steel and Terne-coated stainless steel are highly durable metals. Terne-coated stainless steel is glossy upon first exposure, but it turns matte gray with exposure. Stainless steel is subject to stress-hardening, and thus it is harder to work than copper, and it may rip rather than yield when exposed to great stress. Terne-coated stainless steel can be soldered well. In parts of the country exposed to acid deposition, where the metal must be soldered, Terne-coated stainless steel is the sheet metal of choice in the writer's opinion.

- *Zinc and zinc alloys*
  Zinc and zinc alloys have many of the same characteristics as copper. They are durable and easy to form and solder. Although the writer hasn't seen acid damage to zinc alloys, it probably occurs.

Monel is a very highly durable metal occasionally used for gutters and downspouts.

Metal thicknesses for gutters and downspouts are recommended in the SNACNA Handbook.

- *Wood*
  Gutters may be made from decay-resistant woods, and they have given decades of satisfactory use. They are of course best detailed as easily removable to provide for replacement. They are used for historic preservation and replication details. Modern single-ply roofing materials, both thermoplastic and thermoset, are not subject to the problems of thermal expansion and corrosion which affect metal gutters. Wooden or other gutters, lined with single-ply roof membrane material, give durable and beneficial service.

Types of gutters and water diverters

The simplest type of gutter, and generally the least troublesome, is a sheet metal hanging gutter installed under the eaves. These gutters may be half-round, rectangular, or other shapes. A great diversity of products to support such gutters are available, some of which are shown in the SMACNA Architectural Sheet Metal Manual and one of which is shown below.

Built-in gutters have been common, especially on monumental buildings with steep roofs (Fig. 1). Built-in gutters allow little room for error; such gutters must be fabricated and installed by highly-skilled workers following the recommendations of the SMACNA Architectural Sheet Metal Manual. The Architect should require proof of skill and experience on the part of the workers who will fabricate and install such systems; the writer has seen many built-in gutters which looked superficially like proper designs but which were not properly made. The Architect should understand how to solder the seams. The seams are first coated with solder ("pretinned"), unless the metal is already coated. The metal is then heated, and the solder is touched to the outside of the seam. If the procedure is proper, the solder will draw into the seam, filling it. The writer suggests requiring a demonstration of soldering before the work is performed. Cut open the sample seam to make sure that the solder has penetrated fully.

Because of the location of built-in gutters, where a leak could often result in considerable damage to the building, the writer recommends a redundant flexible gutter liner under and behind the metal gutter. The flexible liner should have its own drains, preferably in such a location that drainage will be seen and reported.

Metal built-in gutters, being stiff, require provisions for thermal expansion and shrinkage. Expansion joints should be designed between the drains, and the seams should be very firmly fastened, as with rivets as well as solder. (Details are provided in SMACNA 1993).

Gutter expansion joints are quite complex, and they should be fabricated and installed only by highly-skilled sheet metal workers. While SMACNA details do not show a redundant, flexible liner under the gutter, the writer recommends such protection. The flexible liner should be covered with a sheet of lubricating building paper to allow movement.

Many of the problems of sheet metal built-in gutters can be avoided by using flexible materials. These materials don't require expansion joints, and they are not subject to corrosion. They are relatively easy to repair and replace.

Wide, shallow gutters do not usually become clogged with leaves and other debris; the wind helps clear them. Most gutters, however, do become clogged, and cleaning of the gutters may be expensive and difficult. Light-duty gutters on multistory buildings with steep roofs are particularly difficult to clean, especially without damaging the gutters with the ladders (ladders equipped with standoffs should be used).

One way to avoid the need for frequent cleaning is to mount a screen over the gutter. A simple screen installation is shown in Fig. 3. The screened gutter detail allows leaves and other debris to wash off, while

Fig. 2. Rubber-lined gutter

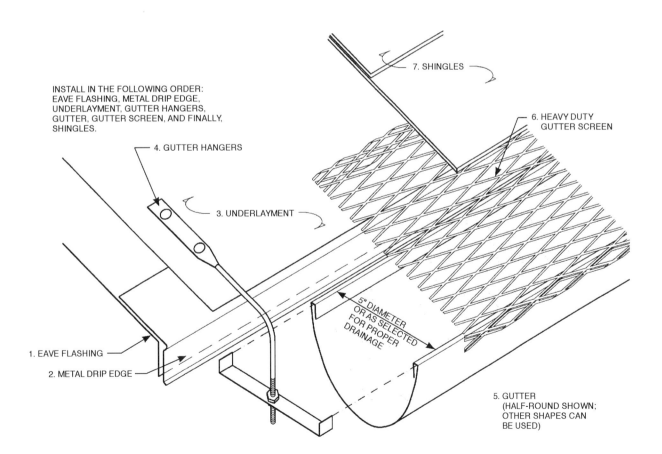

INSTALL IN THE FOLLOWING ORDER:
EAVE FLASHING, METAL DRIP EDGE,
UNDERLAYMENT, GUTTER HANGERS,
GUTTER, GUTTER SCREEN, AND FINALLY,
SHINGLES.

7. SHINGLES

6. HEAVY DUTY GUTTER SCREEN

4. GUTTER HANGERS

3. UNDERLAYMENT

5" DIAMETER OR AS SELECTED FOR PROPER DRAINAGE

1. EAVE FLASHING

2. METAL DRIP EDGE

5. GUTTER
(HALF-ROUND SHOWN;
OTHER SHAPES CAN
BE USED)

HANGING ADJUSTABLE GUTTER AND SCREEN

SCALE: 6" = 1'-0"   DWC: DETAILS\GUTTER

Fig. 3. Hanging adjustable gutter and screen (SMACNA 1993)

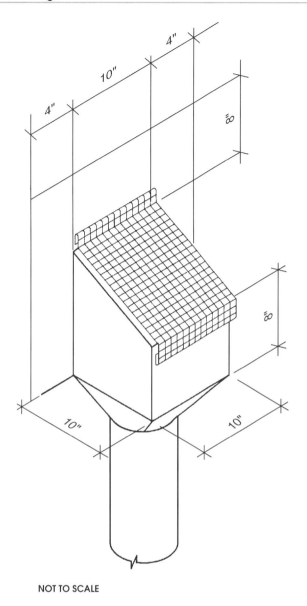

NOT TO SCALE

Fig. 4. Isometric of simple basic leader head with screen

Fig. 5. Scupper and leader head, City of York, UK.

the water flows through the screen. The screen should be in the plane of the roof, and it should pass over the gutter; it should not be mounted flat on top of the gutter. If gutter hangers are fastened to the roof sheathing, they should be installed before the shingles, to be concealed. Adjustable gutter hangers allow adjustment after installation, so that the gutters will drain thoroughly.

Gutters can make ice dams more troublesome. Eave flashing should extend behind hung gutters and, for built-in gutters, under the gutters.

Another type of drainage is a scupper, leader head or "conductor head," and downspout. To avoid stopping up of the gutters and upper downspouts, design an air gap between the scupper and the top of the leader head. Provide a sloped screen on top of the leader head (Fig. 4). Leader heads are an opportunity for innovative design; they may be very simple or decorative (Figs. 5-7).

In place of gutters, water diverters may be used. They are less likely than gutters to become clogged with leaves, and they are easier to keep clear. The eave flashing should extend at least 2 ft. above the diverters. There will necessarily be some dripping from the eaves below the diverter, but most of the water will be directed to the downspout (Fig. 8).

Corrugated round and rectangular downspouts may expand a little from ice without being damaged. Electrical resistance heaters in the downspouts, as well as the gutters, will melt ice and help clear the downspouts. Such equipment uses energy, and it is expended only when required by freezing conditions.

For cold climates, open front downspouts are recommended by SMACNA. Except during deluge conditions, the water flow will remain in contact with the three sides of the downspout. At the transition from gutter to downspout, the back of the open-front downspout should gently curve forward and then backward to receive the flow of water from all sides of the gutter outlet. The writer has timed the flow at about 3 miles per hour. At very high water volume, the water stream may "break away" from the downspout, but under those conditions some free-falling water will probably be tolerable. The writer's experience is that the drainage recommended by SMACNA (Table 2), will work for open-front downspouts as well as for closed downspouts. Thus, if 4 in. wide x 3 in. deep closed downspout is adequate, a 4 in. wide open downspout will also be adequate. Open front downspouts will develop icicles in cold weather. The icicles will, however, melt faster than the ice inside closed downspouts (Figs. 9 and 10).

Downspouts should not discharge directly on the ground near foundations of buildings with basements or crawl spaces. Proper methods of discharge include:

- Boots connected to subsurface drain lines. Do not discharge rain water into perforated footing drains; the two should be separate. Drain boots serving open-front leaders should have sloped screens above the boots, to prevent leaves from clogging the underground drain lines.

- Drained drip beds, trenches, surface gutters, swales, French drains, and other surface and shallow drains.

Fig. 6. Newly-cast lead leader head, Calke Abbey, Derbyshire, UK.

Fig. 7. Scupper and leader head, First Church of Christ, Scientist, Berkeley, CA. Bernard Maybeck, Architect.

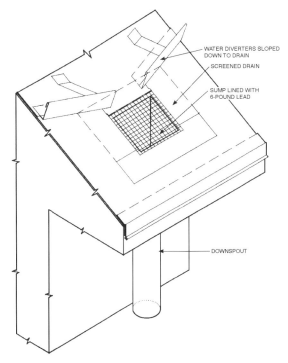

WATER DIVERTERS SLOPED DOWN TO DRAIN

SCREENED DRAIN

SUMP LINED WITH 6-POUND LEAD

DOWNSPOUT

ISOMETRIC DETAIL OF DRAIN @ SLOPED EAVES
NOT TO SCALE

Fig. 8. Water diverter and drain.

Fig. 9. Stylized acanthus leaf on open-front leader. Donald Baerman, AIA Architect.

Fig. 10. Stylized lily head on open-front leader. Donald Baerman, AIA Architect.

Downspout straps and their fasteners should be heavy duty and resistant to corrosion; in cold climates they may have to support a column of ice. The writer recommends a minimum of 0.04 in. for light-duty residential downspouts and twice that for architectural downspouts. There should be downspout straps at the top and bottom of the downspout, above and below offsets, and (in the writer's opinion) no further than 12 ft. apart elsewhere.

Where valleys discharge into gutters, consider adding water diverters to prevent the full flow from the valleys from overshooting the gutters.

Sometimes gutters discharge into internal leaders or into leader heads which discharge into internal leaders. As long as the internal leaders do not leak, and as long as the building is heated, this is an excellent method of drainage. The internal leaders will not become clogged with ice. As with all plumbing systems, the internal leaders should be accessible for inspection, maintenance, and replacement, and they should have cleanouts.

Water spouts, or gargoyles, are a way of carrying water away from the building walls and foundations. The water may then fall onto a gravel or sculptural drip bed or into a pool.

Estimating rainfall and drainage capacity

The BOCA National Plumbing Code and other codes stipulate the required drainage capacity. The Sheet Metal and Air Conditioning Contractors' Association, Architectural Sheet Metal Manual has recommended sizes for leaders and downspouts (Tables 1 and 2). This latter reference is not mandatory, but it is prudent to follow its recommendations. Recommended drainage capacity figures are given for five year, ten year, and maximum storms. One of the factors in determining drainage capacity is the effect of delayed drainage. If the effect of delayed drainage would be catastrophic, the values for "100 Year Storms," plus a safety margin, should be used. If there is no detrimental effect from delayed drainage, a lower value, but not less than that which is code-mandated, may be used.▶

Table 1. Dimensions of standard downspouts. A = area of 1/4 in. (6.4 mm) undersized inlet. (SMACNA 1993).

TYPE	AREA		"A" Size		Nominal Size		Actual	
Plain Round	sq.in.	sq.mm.	sq.in	sq.mm.	in. mm.		in.	mm.
	7.07	4560	5.94	3831	3 76		3	76
	12.57	810	11.04	7120	4 102		4	102
	19.63	12661	17.71	11422	5 127		5	127
	28.27	18234	25.95	16737	6 152		6	152
	50.24	32404	47.15	30411	8 203		8	203
Corrugated Round	5.94	3831			3 76		3	76
	11.04	7120			4 102		4	102
	17.72	11429			5 127		5	127
	25.97	16750			6 152		6	152
Plain Rectangular	3.94	2541	3.00	1935	2 51		1.75x2.25	44x57
	6.00	3870	4.80	3096	3 76		2x3	51x76
	12.00	7740	10.31	6649	4 102		3x4	76x102
	20.00	12900	15.75	10158	5 127		3.75x4.75	95x121
	24.00	15480	21.56	13906	6 152		4x6	102x152
Rectangular Corrugated	3.80	2451	3.00	1935	2 51		1.75x2.25	44x57
	7.73	4985	6.38	4155	3 76		2.37x3.25	60x83
	11.70	7621	10.00	6513	4 102		2.75x4.25	70x108
	18.75	12213	16.63	10832	5 127		3.75x5	95x127

"A" = area of 1/4 in.(6.4 mm) undersized inlet.

Table 2. Rainfall data and drainage factors for major U. S. Locations. Intensities are based on records and statistical projections. The may occasionally be exceeded either in the general location or within microclimatic local areas. (SMACNA 1993)

	A STORMS WHICH SHOULD BE EXCEEDED ONLY ONCE IN 10 YEARS				B STORMS WHICH SHOULD BE EXCEEDED ONLY ONCE IN 100 YEARS			
	Intensity lasting 5 minutes		Calculated roof area drained per downspout area		Intensity lasting 5 minutes		Calculated roof area drained per downspout area	
	in/hr	mm/hr	sq ft/ sq in	sq mn/ 100 sq mm	in/hr	mm/hr	sq ft/ sq in	sq m/ 100 sq mm
ALABAMA: Birmingham	7.5	191	160	2.30	10.1	256	120	1.7
Mobile	8.2	208	150	2.10	10.8	274	110	1.6
ALASKA: Fairbanks	2.1	53	570	8.30	3.8	97	310	4.5
Juneau	1.7	43	700	10.10	2.3	57	530	7.60
ARIZONA: Phoenix	5.6	141	220	3.10	8.8	224	140	2.00
Tucson	6.1	155	200	2.80	9.1	232	130	1.90
ARKANSAS: Bentonville	7.4	187	160	2.30	10.2	259	120	1.70
Little Rock	7.4	187	160	2.30	10.0	253	120	1.70
CALIFORNIA: Los Angeles	4.9	124	250	3.50	6.7	170	180	2.60
Sacramento	2.5	64	480	6.90	3.9	100	310	4.40
San Francisco	2.7	68	450	6.4	3.7	93	330	4.70
San Diego	2.2	57	540	7.80	3.1	78	390	5.60
COLORADO: Denver	5.7	146	210	3.00	9.1	232	130	1.90
Boulder	6.4	164	190	2.70	9.4	238	130	1.80
CONNECTICUT: Hartford	6.2	158	190	2.8	8.7	221	140	2.00
DISTRICT OF COLUMBIA	7.1	180	170	2.4	9.7	247	120	1.80
FLORIDA: Jacksonville	7.9	200	150	2.20	10.1	256	120	1.70
Miami	7.7	195	160	2.20	9.8	250	120	1.80
Tampa	8.3	212	140	2.10	10.8	274	110	1.60
GEORGIA: Atlanta	7.3	186	160	2.4	9.9	251	120	1.70
HAWAII: Honolulu	8.7	221	140	2.00	12.0	305	100	1.40
Kahului	7.0	177	170	2.50	12.0	305	100	1.40
Hilo	17.4	442	70	1.00	19.2	488	60	0.90
Lihue	10.4	265	110	1.70	14.4	366	80	1.20
IDAHO: Boise	1.8	46	660	9.50	3.3	84	360	5.20
ILLINOIS: Chicago	6.8	172	180	2.60	9.3	236	130	1.90
INDIANA: Indianapolis	6.8	173	180	2.50	9.4	239	130	1.80
IOWA: Des Moines	7.3	186	160	2.40	10.3	262	120	1.70
KANSAS: Wichita	7.5	191	160	2.30	10.5	267	110	1.60
KENTUCKY: Louisville	6.9	175	170	2.50	9.4	238	130	1.80
LOUISIANA: New Orleans	8.3	211	140	2.10	10.9	277	110	1.60
MAINE: Portland	5.4	136	220	3.20	7.6	192	160	2.30
MARYLAND: Baltimore	7.1	181	170	2.40	9.7	247	120	1.80
MASSACHUSETTS: Boston	5.3	134	230	3.3	7.2	183	170	2.40
MICHIGAN: Detroit	6.4	162	190	2.70	8.9	226	140	1.90
MINNESOTA: Minneapolis	7.0	178	170	2.50	10.0	253	120	1.70

Continued on next page

Table 2. Rainfall data and drainage factors for major U. S. Locations. *continued*

	A STORMS WHICH SHOULD BE EXCEEDED ONLY ONCE IN 10 YEARS				B STORMS WHICH SHOULD BE EXCEEDED ONLY ONCE IN 100 YEARS			
	Intensity lasting 5 minutes		Calculated roof area drained per downspout area		Intensity lasting 5 minutes		Calculated roof area drained per downspout area	
	in/hr	mm/hr	sq ft/ sq in	sq mn/ 100 sq mm	in/hr	mm/hr	sq ft/ sq in	sq m/ 100 sq mm
MISSOURI: Kansas City	7.4	187	160	2.30	10.4	265	110	1.70
Saint Louis	7.1	181	170	2.40	9.9	251	120	1.70
MONTANA: Helena	1.8	46	660	9.50	3.1	77	390	5.70
Missoula	1.8	46	660	9.50	2.4	61	500	7.20
NEBRASKA: Omaha	7.4	188	160	2.30	10.5	267	110	1.60
NEVADA: Reno	2.3	57	530	7.60	4.5	114	270	3.90
Las Vegas	2.1	53	570	8.3	5.2	133	230	3.30
NEW JERSEY: Trenton	6.7	170	180	2.60	9.3	236	130	1.90
NEW MEXICO: Albuquerque	4.0	102	300	4.30	6.7	171	180	2.60
Santa Fe	4.5	115	270	3.80	6.4	169	180	2.60
NEW YORK: Albany	6.5	165	190	2.70	9.1	232	130	1.90
Buffalo	6.0	152	200	2.90	8.4	213	140	2.10
New York City	6.7	169	180	2.60	9.2	235	130	1.90
NORTH CAROLINA: Raleigh	7.3	185	160	2.40	9.8	250	120	1.80
NORTH DAKOTA: Bismark	6.6	167	180	2.60	9.8	250	120	1.80
OHIO: Cincinnati	6.8	172	180	2.50	9.3	236	130	1.90
Cleveland	6.3	160	190	2.70	8.8	223	140	2.00
OKLAHOMA: Oklahoma City	7.6	193	160	2.30	10.5	267	110	1.60
OREGON: Baker	2.2	56	550	7.90	3.8	97	310	4.50
Portland	2.1	53	570	8.30	3.0	76	400	5.80
PENNSYLVANIA: Philadelphia	6.8	172	180	2.60	9.4	238	130	1.80
Pittsburgh	6.4	163	190	2.70	8.8	224	140	2.00
RHODE ISLAND: Providence	5.6	143	210	3.10	7.8	198	150	2.20
SOUTH CAROLINA: Charleston	7.2	184	170	2.40	9.4	238	130	1.80
TENNESSEE: Memphis	7.4	187	160	2.30	10.0	253	120	1.70
Knoxville	6.7	169	180	2.60	9.0	229	130	1.90
TEXAS: Fort Worth	7.6	193	193	160	10.5	267	110	1.60
Dallas	7.6	194	160	2.30	10.5	267	110	1.60
Houston	8.2	208	150	2.10	10.8	274	110	1.60
San Antonio	7.6	193	160	2.30	10.5	267	110	1.60
UTAH: Provo	3.0	75	410	5.80	5.2	131	230	3.30
Salt Lake City	2.8	71	430	6.20	4.3	108	280	4.10
VIRGINIA: Norfolk	7.1	181	170	2.40	9.5	242	130	1.80
WASHINGTON: Seattle	2.1	53	570	8.30	3.3	84	360	5.20
Spokane	2.1	53	570	8.30	3.5	90	340	4.90
WEST VIRGINIA: Parkersburg	6.6	168	180	2.60	9.1	230	130	1.90
WISCONSIN: Madison	6.8	172	180	2.50	9.5	241	130	1.80
Milwaukee	6.6	168	180	2.60	9.1	232	130	1.90
WYOMING: Cheyenne	5.7	146	210	3.00	9.9	252	120	1.70

These intensities are based on records and statistical projections. They may occasionally be exceeded either in the general area or at small areas within the designated city.

Alvar Aalto. Rautatalo Jurhuset.
Helsinki. 1951.

Roof openings and accessories

Summary: Openings and accessories are integral parts of a roofing assembly and include skylights, hatches and smoke/heat vents, facilitating safety and maintenance. Additional roof accessories discussed briefly in this article include ridge and relief vents, roof walkways, and snow guards.

Key words: heat/smoke venting, hatches, relief vents, ridge vents, skylights, snow guards.

Uniformat:	B3020
MasterFormat:	07700
	07800

Introduction

Roof openings include skylights, hatches and heat/smoke venting. While their purposes are different (see Part I articles "Daylighting" and "Natural ventilation" and Chapter D4 "Fire protection"), the design and installation of roof openings share common features. Together with water/moisture protection and rainwater drainage system discussed in prior articles in this chapter, provision of roof openings and accessories are an essential part of design and construction of a complete roofing system.

Generics forms and functions of roofing openings, depicted in Fig. 1, include:

- Skylights for daylighting and (if operable) for ventilation. Skylights provide a simple means of admitting daylighting for spaces directly below. Hinge-type skylights (for sloped roof installations) are also referred to as roof windows. Multiple glazing (double- and triple-glazed units) are available for improved resistance to heat flow. Some skylight units have integral vents, to relieve built-up overheated air temperatures within the skylight assembly, and also integral shading devices that can be used to preclude solar heat gain and glare.

- Hatches provide access to the roof for maintenance personnel, combined with access ladders or stairs. These may also provide for emergency escape (not classified as an exitway), access for firefighters, and access for large equipment. Operable skylights may serve the same functions.

- Smoke/heat vents function to reduce interior heat build-up during a fire by opening automatically in case of fire.

Skylights, hatches and heat/smoke vents are available as preassembled units or framed assemblies of stock components. All skylight, hatchway, and vent units must be securely attached to the roof assembly: structural or miscellaneous steel frames may be required at openings in deck. Provisions for attaching a light gauge metal flashing flange of the unit to the roof substrate/decking may be required, such as wood blocking.

1 Skylights

Traditional skylights were and are fabricated from metal or wood frames and sheets of glass. A wood-framed glass skylight assembly supported by a cast-iron structure formed the roof of the Crystal Palace, built in 1851. Most skylights are now fabricated from aluminum, plastic, or a combination of aluminum, plastic, and wood and available as preassembled units shipped to the site ready to be installed, or as assemblies of units, or framed assemblies of stock components, prefabricated off site and then site assembled. Skylights and assemblies of skylights must be designed for safety and protection against environmental forces:

- to prevent accidental breakage from falling or wind-blown objects and accidental falls from the roof deck.

- to withstand wind pressures, both positive and negative, rain penetration, live loads of snow and ice.

- to provide for drainage of condensate water and/or water that penetrates under severe conditions.

- to provide for cleaning of both interior and exterior surfaces.

Basic skylight units are available as:

- Self-flashing, without curb:

- for installation directly into roofing.

- with flashing flange integral with glazing or with added flat flashing flange.

- generally used on pitched roofs only without a curb since flashing to prevent water penetration is difficult if not impossible to achieve on flat roofs.

- Self-flashing with curb:

- shipped to site preassembled with a prefabricated curb,

- curbs generally 4 in. to 12 in. (10 cm to 30 cm) high.

- curbs commonly insulated; with flashing and counterflashing flanges.

Author: Donald Baerman, AIA

Credits: The section on heat/smoke venting was reviewed by Bruce W. Hisley, Chair of the Fire Protection Technical Program, National Fire Academy and by Robert Solomon, NFPA, where contributions are gratefully acknowledged.

References: NFPA. 1996. *NFPA Fire Protection Handbook.* 18th Edition. Quincy, MA: National Fire Protection Association. 1-800-344-3555.

NFPA. 1997. *Guide for Smoke and Heat Venting.* Quincy, MA: National Fire Protection Association.

NRCA. 1996. *NRCA Roofing and Waterproofing Manual - Fourth Edition.* National Roofing Contractors Association. 10255 West Higgins Road, Suite 600, Rosemont, IL 60018-5607

SMCNA. 1993. *Architectural Sheet Metal Manual - Fifth Edition.* Sheet Metal and Air Conditioning Contractors' Association. 4201 Lafayette Center Drive, Chantilly, VA 20151

DAYLIGHTING, VENTILATION

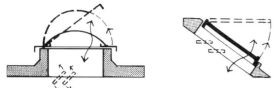

ACCESS TO ROOF

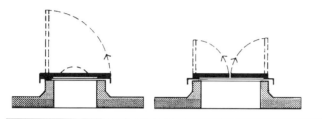

FIRE/EXPLOSION VENTING

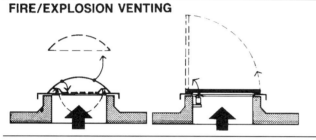

SAFETY

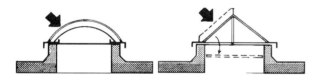

EXTERNAL FACTORS

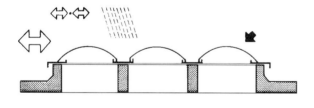

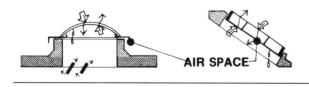

AIR SPACE

Fig. 1. Functions of roof openings. (Source: 1993 *Sweets Catalog File* Selection Data)

- when counterflashing flanges are short, additional counterflashing may be required to prevent water penetration.

- where deck is field cut for skylight, trim pieces may be required to finish the exposed edges of decking.

• Framed assembly with or without curb:

- mounted on built-up curb with frame and counterflashing for mounting on built-up curb. Recommended minimum height for curb is 8 in. (20 cm) above roofing.

- prefabricated curbs for use in lieu of site built curbs are available without or with insulation.

All framed skylights are custom designed by manufacturers to meet necessary roof and/or wind loads.

- Mullion spacing for framed skylights is generally limited to standard glass widths.

- Dimensional limitations on a skylight assembly will further be imposed by requirements for adequate drainage of rain/storm water from roof. Additionally, condensate gutters are required in the body of the skylight assembly as well as around its perimeter (see below).

Standard plastic skylights and roof windows are available from a number of manufacturers.
Metal-framed and combination wood and metal-framed skylights with pre-engineered, prefabricated components are available from many manufacturers. Large custom skylights, specially engineered for their application and often combining the skylights with the roof structure, are made by a few firms. One or more manufacturers also make glass prism-concrete skylights.

In addition to the industry association publications listed in the references, detailed recommendations and details are available from skylight manufacturers

Skylight drainage and condensate control
The basic condensation control measures include:

- Condensation will occur on cool or cold surfaces exposed to the interior (moist) air. Double- or triple-glazing and thermal breaks incorporated around the framing and assembly (within it if available) will help reduce condensation.

- Usually a separation is made where the glazing member is bolted into the framing member by use of a glazing gasket.

- All good skylights should have condensation gutters and they should drain to the exterior or to a leader.

- Mechanical (warm air system) design may properly include blanketing the skylight with warm air to reduce condensation.

• Most skylights combine glazing gaskets with a system of drain channels formed integrally on the frame members. The head and purlin channels lead to rafter drains, which in turn discharge to sill flashing drained to the exterior. Moisture from interior air will condense on the coldest surface, often the skylight assembly. In very moist environments, such as pools and greenhouses, the resulting condensation and water formation can be considerable. The drains, properly designed and installed, serve to intercept both rainwater leaks and condensed water and direct it harmlessly to the outside.

• Many plastic dome, pyramid, and cylindrical skylights have perimeter drains to discharge leaks and condensation. Although building maintenance workers frequently apply sealant at the perimeter, the units are designed to function without such sealant. In restraining thermal movement, sealants so applied may also harm the skylight.

- Some framed skylights depend on a perfect seal at the glazing, without drain channels. Others have partial drain channels, eliminating the head channels. Skylight detailing and installation is thus critical in such cases to assure that channels are properly assembled and installed so as to allow the water out. In detailing the skylight assemblies and in reviewing shop drawings, the architect should check that every glass-frame joint has drain channels and that the drain channels drain continuously from top to bottom.

- In very cold climates, it would be prudent to heat the bottom drain troughs and weep holes, to avoid freezing of the drainage system. Since the bottoms of skylights often have heaters to counteract drafts of cold air, the source of the heat may easily be available.

- Purlin framing should be designed to prevent water from impounding above, because such water and the dirt and algae which deposit there are unsightly.

- Small wooden and composite sky windows do not usually incorporate drainage channels. They depend on the lapping of an upper, glazed unit over a base unit. For the most part, they give good service. If such skylights are "ganged" together, submit the joint details for review by the manufacturer.

- Although some skylight manufacturers do not include drainage channels and, instead, depend on the absolute seal of wet or gasket glazing, the writer's experience with them has not been good. It is likely that some of them function properly some of the time, but designer and specifier beware.

Glass manufacturers list their thermal resistance in their catalogs. A typical insulating glass system composed of two layers of 1/4 in. glass with low-emissivity coating on the #3 surface and with argon gas in the sealed space, has a U-factor of .28 at night in winter, the thermal resistance (R value) thus being 3.6 (in English units). Skylight frames usually have a larger area exposed on the inside than on the outside, and thus the relationship between heat transfer and interior temperature is not a simple calculation. The interior surfaces, exposed to the warm interior air, will be substantially warmer than would be the case if there were equivalent areas inside and outside, and that warmth will retard condensation. If the system has been tested for thermal conductivity, ask the manufacturer for the assumed or test values of interior surface temperature of the rafters and purlins.

Some skylight manufacturers list the Condensation Resistance Factor, or CRF. The American Architectural Manufacturers Association Standard 1503.1-88, "Voluntary Test Method for Thermal Transmittance and Condensation Resistance of Windows, Doors and Glazed Wall Sections," sets the procedure for testing. ANAI/AAMA 101-93, "Voluntary Specifications for Aluminum and Poly (Vinyl Chloride) (PVC) Prime Windows and Glass Doors," establishes industry recommended maximum humidity levels. The Specification also lists the minimum recommended CRF (higher is better) for various outside air temperatures and inside relative humidity, up to 40%.

These recommendations do not include in their humidity range the conditions normally found in swimming pools and other spaces with higher humidity and higher temperatures. Therefore the architect designing and specifying skylights for high humidity applications should consult the skylight manufacturer and observe similar skylights operating under similar conditions of exterior and interior temperature and relative humidity.

Structural strength of skylight glazing
Structural considerations include:

- Skylight units should be adequately designed to resist forces of winds at roof level, both positive and negative. Positive pressures prevail for steep sloping surfaces; negative for flat or low pitch.

- Required resistance to live loads is generally equal to that of roof.

Forces which must be resisted by skylights include dead load, snow load, positive wind load, negative wind load, and, in some regions, seismic loads. The building code which applies to the location gives the method of calculating the combined load. The architect should stipulate and check that the skylight manufacturer submits structural calculations, performed by a structural engineer registered in the state where the project is located, showing adequate strength.

There are three ways to calculate the required glass strength. Building codes list one method, which the writer has found generally to be the least conservative. Most glass manufacturers provide load charts for calculating glass strength. The most conservative method, in most cases, is described in ASTM E1300-84, "Standard Practice for Determining the Minimum Thickness and Type of Glass Required to Resist a Specified Load." Thickness calculations are different from most structural calculations in that standard practice is to select glass with a probable failure of approximately eight lites per thousand. Glass is very strong, but it fails at a very small load compared to its theoretical load. The writer recommends selecting glass by use of all three standards, meeting or exceeding the requirements of the most stringent standard.

Building codes have specific requirements for skylight glazing. In some cases, protective screens below the glass are required. In all cases, a prudent design choice, even if not required by code, for spaces where people will be under the skylights is to design and specify a glazing material which will stay in place when broken.

The possibility of a person's accidental falling through a skylight should be considered, and suitable protection designed. Reported examples of such falls include a roofer's falling through a plastic dome skylight when the roof ripping machine was inadvertently put into reverse gear, an adolescent's falling through a cylindrical skylight while walking on it, and a campus policeman's falling through a skylight while trying to chase students off. In addition, skylights may be a way to breach the building's security.

Light and temperature control
Skylights can be a source of excessive solar heat gain and glare, and they can thus lead to discomfort and high air conditioning costs. The use of shades and reflective glass are two ways to limit such conditions, but the location, orientation, and size of the skylights are the first practical means of control against solar overheating.

Most skylights have lower thermal resistance than most wall and roof systems, and they must be integrated into a whole-building energy conservation plan. Properly configured, skylights can be part of a passive solar heating and/or lighting system design.

Many types of glazing will admit ultra-violet radiation and visible light in the violet end of the spectrum (wave lengths below 400 nanometers are most harmful). The UV radiation may fade materials. One effective way to screen UV radiation (partially) is by use of laminated safety glass with a UV-screening interlayer.

Summary: skylight selection checklist
In determining the desired form and size of the skylight unit/ assembly, consider:

- *Daylight and environmental control:*

- orientation and the resulting solar penetration angles, winter and summer, in the given geographic location.

- prevailing winds direction and force.

- precipitation quantity and patterns.

- *Views into and out of the building through clear skylights:*

- overhanging trees.

- adjacent buildings.

SHELL

B3

SHELL

B3

-   nearby streetlights.

-   other parts of same building.

-   views into building from adjacent higher areas.

-   *Profile*

The more a formed plastic dome is raised, the greater its ability to refract light of the low early morning and late afternoon sun, which:

-   maximizes the use of natural light; but

-   increases the solar heat gain.

-   *Related criteria*

-   security and roof safety.

-   maintainability and cleanabililty.

-   susceptibility of adjoining interior materials to staining.

-   insect screening and cleaning, if skylight is operable.

-   *Skylight glazing*

The following glazing materials are listed in an approximate descending order of approximate cost:

-   formed acrylic with mar resistant finish.

-   formed acrylic.

-   polycarbonates.

-   flat acrylic.

-   laminated glass.

-   tempered glass.

-   clear polished wire glass.

-   textured, obscure wire glass.

-   *Proper glazing methods:*

-   exposed gasketing of some types may be subject to material breakdown due to ultraviolet rays of sun. EPDM gasketing does not appear to be vulnerable to such damage.

-   small valleys created at bottom of sloped glazing and horizontal glazing cap will hold water.

-   sloped glazing or domed acrylic glazing is almost self-cleaning as the sloped shapes facilitate rain washing the surface.

-   normal skylight glazing is not designed to support persons. Special thicknesses and provisions are necessary if maintenance personnel is to walk on glazed surfaces.

-   *Safety and security measures may include:*

Plain glass skylights should be protected by a screen to protect occupants below in the event of breakage. Codes often permit laminated glass, tempered glass, wire glass, acrylic, polycarbonates and fiberglass, all subject to their individual characters for resistance to impact and breaking. Consult the provisions of local codes. Subject to security level required, which in high security areas may require security alarm devices, precautions against forced entry through a framed skylight should preclude:

-   possibility of disassembly of framing.

-   ease of removing snap-on cover.

-   low melting point of glazing: acrylics materials are easily burned through with a torch.

2   Hatches

Roof hatches (also referred to as "scuttles," derived from nautical terminology) are available as preassembled units, shipped to the site ready to be installed. Non-stock sizes may be available for hatches on special order.

Roof hatches are intended to provide safe and easy access to the roof, and they have provisions for locking. Opening sizes, as well as access ways to a hatchway, should be generous, rather than minimal, to accommodate large equipment and furniture, and service and maintenance personnel and/or firefighters (with equipment). Manufactured units are generally safer, more convenient, and more durable than site-built hatches. Having never ever seen a steel roof hatch painted as directed on the label, the writer recommends utilizing particularly vigilant verification or specifying all-aluminum construction. Some manufactured roof hatches include safety posts which can be raised above the open hatch. For hatches on steep roofs, the writer recommends safety rings securely fastened either inside or outside the hatches, for attaching safety ropes.

Roof hatches are commonly available with integral curbs including flashing and counterflashing flanges, without or with insulation: cover generally solid, but may incorporate glazing. usually spring assisted opening; may also be motor operated, especially for large units.

Hatchway selection considerations

-   Operable root hatches and skylights must open automatically if used for smoke/fire venting (see below).

-   Hatches must be able to open with a maximum snow load on them.

-   In evaluating the quality of a hatchway unit, consider how often the unit will be used; this will help determine:

-   type of access: ladder, ship stair, regular stair. size of opening.

-   type of operation: manual, powered, force required to open unit.

-   durability of operating mechanism components, such as: compression spring operators, shock absorbers, spring latches, hold-open devices, and weather-stripping.

-   Fire-resistive features required may include a "label" requirement, having passed fire resistance or operating tests performed by an acceptable laboratory, such as Underwriters Laboratories (UL) or Factory Mutual (FM) fire underwriters approval.

-   Safety features include:

-   telescoping cylinder cover on the compression spring to prevent injuries from pinching or catching clothes in the spring coils.

-   counterbalancing by spring operators to automatically lock the cover in an open position, preventing it from slamming shut on a person.

-   Consider the possibility of utilizing glazed covers for daylighting.

3   Heat/smoke vents

Heat/smoke vents are roof openings designed to open upon exposure to heat. Operation usually occurs from activation of a fusible link mechanism. In some cases, operation may also be initiated by operation of a fire alarm system or by some manual mechanism. Such vents are often times required for use in certain occupancies with large quantities of combustible contents such as manufacturing facilities and warehouses. Automatic venting of heat and smoke through the use of heat/smoke vents can work to reduce the loss of property and minimize damage in single story buildings used for manufacturing. The vents should be accessible for periodic inspection, testing and maintenance, and for replacing the fusible link or other type of actuating device.

UL Listed FM Approved heat/smoke vents are only available as preassembled units and are shipped to the site ready to be installed. Heat/smoke vents are commonly available with integral curbs provided with flashing and counterflashing flanges. There are two types of vents, both of which are designed for manual override operation from the floor of the building or from the exterior by means of a wire or cable pull release. These include:

-   melt-down plastic glazing which softens and drops out of the frame when exposed to high temperature; a bar to prevent the plastic from dropping to the floor is generally incorporated into the unit, which has to be replaced once exposed to fire.

- automatic opening: solid or glazed cover with springs held closed by a fusible link, which melts when the temperature rises to a predetermined point and releases the springs for automatic opening of the cover. This type may be reused after a fire, if not damaged, by replacing fusible link.

Explosion relief vents are similar to smoke/heat vents in construction:

- plastic glazed units deform under rise in pressure and are released from frame:

- may be replaced in frame if not damaged.

- solid or glazed cover units are also rise-in-pressure activated releasing springs which automatically open the cover:

- may be reused if not damaged.

Design and selection considerations

Fires occurring in large undivided floor areas present an extremely difficult environment for fire fighters, especially when the fires occur well into the interior of the building. If fire fighters are unable to enter the structure and move to the seat of the fire due to the accumulation of smoke and heat at the floor level. Their efforts may be reduced to the inefficient application of fire fighting water during manual suppression operations. Heat and smoke vents can open automatically when the heat generated by the fire rises to the ceiling during the fire. This in turn will:

- permit hot gases and smoke to escape.

- stop the descent of the smoke layer from the ceiling.

- lower the gas temperatures at the ceiling.

When heat from a fire contacts the fusible link on the vent or vents closest to the source of the fire, they will open when the temperature of the link reaches its predetermined operating point. The result is:

- heated gas and smoke is removed from the building.

- spread of heated gas and smoke at the ceiling is reduced.

- firefighters are able to better identify the source of the fire, thereby enabling them to more efficiently direct their hose streams to the source of the fire.

The requirements for when heat and smoke venting are to be installed in a building can usually be found in the model building codes and fire prevention codes. For example, vents are usually mandated for large area, large volume, single story structures such as those used for storage or manufacturing. A sufficient number of vents must be distributed over the entire roof area to assure reasonable early venting of a fire regardless of its location. In warehouse occupancies, the size and spacing of the vents can be determined for each building depending upon hazard classification related to the type of storage commodity (contents), Class I-Class IV, as determined by NFPA, *Standard for General Storage.*

Smoke/heat vent area requirements, based upon the hazard classification of the building contents, are represented by the following range of values:

- ratio of roof smoke/heat vent area to floor area: 1/30 to 1/100

- vent spacing: 75 ft. to 120 ft. (22 m to 36 m) on center.

In addition, methods and techniques are now becoming available to the designer which will permit the use of engineered or performance based designed for these systems.

In addition to these applications, heat/smoke vents are also sometimes required for the following areas:

- stairwells.

- elevator hoistways.

- areas behind the proscenium in theaters.

When determining the number of vents needed to satisfy the total required vent area, it should be recognized that the venting can be accomplished more effectively through the use of several small units rather than with a few large units. The size of the vent required is based on its open area (approximately equal to its frame size). Also consider the spacing of vents in relation to interior spaces and their uses, and their possible use to also serve as skylights.

An unresolved issue: heat/smoke venting in sprinklered buildings

There are various views on the controversial and as yet unresolved issue surrounding the use of automatic venting in fully sprinklered buildings. Research and testing are being conducted before definitely establishing the benefits, if any, and detriments which can be recognized from installing automatically operating vents in sprinklered buildings. If automatic vents are used in sprinklered buildings, vents should not be positioned directly above any of the ceiling level sprinklers.

4 Other roof accessories

Other roof accessories, as listed in the CSI MasterFormat, briefly mentioned below, include manufactured curbs, relief vents, ridge vents, roof walk boards and walkways, and snow guards. Additional roof accessories, included in Sweet's Catalog, are cupolas, weather vanes, and ornamental dormers.

- *Manufactured curbs*
  In many cases curbs can be built of rough carpentry materials, sometimes treated for fire resistance and sometimes treated to resist decay. An alternative is manufactured curbs, which are produced as part of some single-ply roofing systems and also by independent manufacturers. Each manufacturer has its own design and requirements. The writer cautions the architect to require product information and shop drawings showing how all junctions and other conditions are to be built.

- *Relief vents (for roof and/or attic ventilation)*
  Relief vents and gravity vents allow movement of air in and out of the attic or other space under the roof. Generic vents are described and detailed in the SMACNA Manual. A guide to sizing relief vents is offered by the BOCA Code, which requires the ventilation aperture to be 1/150 times the horizontal attic area or, with good vapor retarders or with balanced ventilation (with inlets and outlets), 1/300 times the horizontal attic area.

- *Ridge vents (for roof and/or ventilation)*
  Ridge vents can be part of an attic or framing ventilation system. A number of manufactured products are available and represented in Sweet's Catalog File. Generic vents are shown in the SMACNA Manual. Most vents are adjustable for roof slope, and many contain filter material to exclude wind-driven rain and snow. To allow ridge vents to facilitate continuous (exhaust) venting, an equal area of inlet vents should be located within the roof area, such as eave vent openings.

The most common fastening method recommended by manufacturers is simply to nail the ridge shingles through the vent material. Having seen ridges installed in this manner which have blown off, the writer suggests a more reliable method:

- Make sure that there is an opening in the roof sheathing to allow air to pass through.

- Install the ridge vent.

- Install a strip of smooth-surface modified bitumen roof membrane over the ridge vent, and fasten it with corrosion-resistant screws

A. SHINGLES FASTENED IN PLACE WITH SCREWS THROUGH RIDGE VENT AND WOODEN DECKING

B. MODIFIED BITUMEN

C. RIDGE VENT

D. SHINGLES

E. UNDERLAYMENT

F. WOODEN DECKING

G. WOOD FRAMING

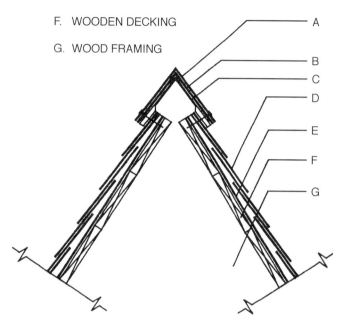

Fig. 2. Ridge with vent.

Fig. 3. Installation of snow guards. courtesy: M. J. Mullane Co., Hudson, MA.

and disks. Then heat the modified bitumen until it is tacky, and embed the ridge shingles in it, using roof cement between the shingles.

- Or, install a strip of mineral-surface modified bitumen roof membrane over the ridge vent, fastening it as recommended above (Fig. 2).

• *Roof walk boards and walkways*
One method of allowing traffic to cross roofs without injuring the membrane is to call for walk boards. They may be manufactured or made on the job, in either case being made from durable materials. Safe access to all parts of a roof system will encourage proper maintenance and inspection. Roof walk boards should be held in place by mechanical fastenings or by gravity. Each panel should be small enough to be lifted for maintenance, and the sleepers should be padded so as not to harm the roof.

Another method of protecting roofs from traffic is walkways, which are normally adhered to the membrane. Types include asphalt-saturated felts, rubber, and padded pavers. Some have been found to injure roofs; follow the roof system manufacturer's recommendations. Roof walkways should not impede drainage.

• *Snow guards*
Ice and snow can build up on steep roofs and then slide off in considerable quantity. The falling material can damage the building and its components, and it can injure people. Snow guards are intended to retard such occurrences. The writer has seen the built-in gutter and cornice ripped off a major public building by sliding ice. Snow guards vary from simple, utilitarian designs to highly decorative ones (Fig. 3). Generic designs are included in the SMACNA Manual.

Except for locales in which experience has shown galvanized or painted steel to be durable (and in which areas the snow usually doesn't fall), snow guards should be made from highly durable materials such as copper, bronze, aluminum, and stainless steel.

Manufacturers will assist architects in determining the spacing of the snow guards. To avoid damaging the snow guards from the force of sliding snow and ice, snow guards should be installed throughout the roof, not just at the eaves. A typical installation would be 16 guards per square of roofing (one snow guard per six square feet).

If the snow guards are distributed evenly throughout the roof, the force they must resist is no greater than the force imposed on the same area by friction. The manufacturer can recommend the required fasteners, which should be of the same material as the guards.

Radiant barrier systems

Summary: Radiant barrier systems provides an alternative and supplement to insulation in roof systems as a means to reduce the cooling load imposed by solar radiation, particularly critical in overheated climates and in existing buildings that require improved cooling load reduction. This article provides a briefing on radiant barrier system design and installation.

Key words: emissivity, insulation, solar spectrum, radiation, radiant barrier.

① Top side of truss under sheathing
② Below bottom chord
③ Over ceiling insulation

Uniformat:	B1020
MasterFormat:	07200

SHELL

B3

In warm climates, a number of strategies are depended on to keep heat out of buildings. Mostly, these affect heat gains by conduction or convection. In the average building, insulating walls and ceilings primarily restricts conduction. Double-glazed windows restrict both conductive and convective heat gain. However, radiation—the third means of heat transfer—except is largely ignored in using window treatments and coatings that reflect, absorb or shade from solar energy. Research points to potential for reducing heat gain in buildings by controlling radiation through the use of radiant barrier systems (RBS).

To understand why RBS are important, a short discussion of radiation potentials is helpful (Fig. 1). Radiation travels only in a strait line. On earth, regions of different temperatures that "see" each other exchange energy via far infrared radiation in the 4 to 40 micron wavelength band. (A micron is a millionth of a meter.) Sunlight, on the other hand, consists of much shorter wavelengths in the 0.2 to 2.6 microns band. Unlike the visible portion of the solar spectrum (0.4 to 0.7 microns), the "near infrared" portion of the solar spectrum (0.7 to 2.6 microns) is invisible. "Far-infrared" radiation is also invisible. Near infrared radiation is generated by the sun and far infrared radiation is generated by all bodies on earth. Far infrared radiation is sometimes called "thermal" or "long-wave" radiation. The effect of both is heat and, in air conditioned buildings, this heat is unwanted. Radiant barrier systems are a method of stopping far-infrared radiation from getting to building interiors and increasing air conditioning loads.

Radiant barrier systems

A radiant barrier system is defined by the American Society for Testing and Materials (ASTM 1990) in Standard C 1158-90 as "a building construction consisting of a low emittance (normally 0.1 or less) surface (usually aluminum foil) bounded by an open air space." The definition given by this Standard goes on to stipulate that, "a RBS is used for the sole purpose of limiting heat transfer by radiation . . ."

Given this definition, work on the topic can be cited to more than fifty years ago. In 1940, G. B. Wilkes published a paper in ASHVE (American Society of Heating and Ventilating Engineers the predecessor of ASHRAE) entitled "Thermal Test Coefficients of Aluminum Insulation for Buildings," where he provided results of experiments and tests, along with commentary of materials property issues like degradation. Experimental applications also appear in House Beautiful's series of articles on climate design in the 1949-51 era.

Radiant barrier systems comprise an air space with one or more of its boundaries functioning as a radiant barrier. Radiant barriers are materials that restrict the transfer of far-infrared radiation across an air space. They do this by not emitting radiant energy. A material with this capability is said to have a very *low emissivity*. The lower the emissivity, the better the radiant barrier.

Emissivity values range from 0 to 1. The laws of optics stipulate that for any given wavelength, a material's emissivity plus its transmissivity plus its reflectivity must equal one. Opaque materials have a transmissivity of zero, so their emissivity plus their reflectivity must equal one. It follows, therefore, that their emissivity must equal one minus their reflectivity.

Materials that radiate very well have high emissivities and those that radiate very poorly have low emissivities. Most common building materials, including glass and paints of all colors, have high emissivities of 0.9 or greater. Such materials are capable of transferring far infrared radiation at 90% or more of their temperature potential. These materials are ineffective barriers to radiant energy transfer. On the other hand, aluminum foil is an excellent radiant barrier. It has a low emissivity (0.05), therefore, it eliminates 95% of the far infrared radiation energy transfer potential.

Aluminum foil, however, is a very good thermal conductor. Consequently, it has an extremely low R-value. However, if it is placed between materials that are attempting to transfer energy by radiation (rather than conduction) and if it is separated from these materials by an open air space, the foil effectively eliminates the normal radiant energy exchange across the air space. (If the air space is evacuated, the result is a Dewar's flask, or "thermos bottle"—one of the most effective heat transfer reduction systems known.)

This is the operating principle of a radiant barrier system, and it often can be used to significantly reduce the flow of heat through building components and systems.

Sunlight and heat

A material's response to far-infrared radiation can be quite different from its response to sunlight. Since a large percentage of sunlight is in the visible range, we characterize materials by color and clarity. White paint reflects far more solar radiation than does black paint. But in the far-infrared band, white paint absorbs slightly more radiation than does black paint. This surprising fact indicates that a material's far-infrared properties cannot be judged by sight. Fig. 2 compares the solar and far infrared characteristics of some common opaque building materials.

Author: Philip Fairey

References: ASTM. 1990. Standard C 1158-90, "Standard Practice for Use and Installation of Radiant Barrier Systems in Building Construction." Philadelphia, PA: American Society for Testing and Materials.

Additional references are listed at the end of this article.

SHELL

B3

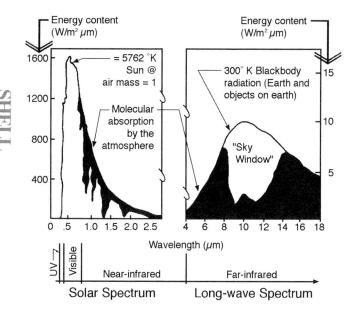

Fig. 1. Solar (short-wave) and thermal (long-wave) spectrum

Fig. 2 shows only opaque materials. Transparent materials also respond differently to solar and far-infrared radiation. Common window glass, for example, transmits more than 85% of incident sunlight but absorbs more than 85% of the far-infrared radiation that strikes it. The "solar greenhouse effect" results in part from this phenomenon. Solar energy readily passes through the glass and is absorbed by the opaque surfaces within the space. When these heated surfaces begin to radiate to cooler surfaces, the glass absorbs most of this far-infrared radiation, trapping much of the original solar gains inside the space as heat.

Roof systems

A house attic offers excellent potential for use of radiant barrier systems: first, because the roof is the surface most exposed to solar radiation, and second, because most of the solar gain absorbed by the roof is transmitted down to the attic floor by far infrared radiation. Since the attic airspace separates the hot roof surface from the ceiling, no heat will move down by conduction, and the heat will not convect down from the hot roof to the ceiling because heated air rises.

If one places a radiant barrier (layer of foil) in the airspace between the hot roof deck and the cooler attic floor (insulation), almost all radiant heat transfer can be eliminated. Studies at the Florida Solar Energy Center (FSEC) indicate that, under peak day conditions, total

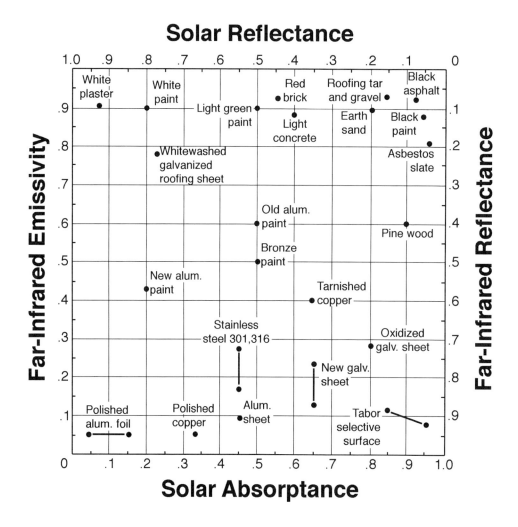

Fig. 2. Emissivity values of common roofing and radiant barrier materials

heat transfer down through ceilings can be reduced by more than 40% in this way. Fig. 3 shows measured ceiling heat gains for side-by-side attic spaces monitored at FSEC. These results occur because the radiant barrier significantly reduces the top surface temperature of the ceiling insulation.

Heat transferred upward through attics (winter heat loss) won't be affected as much because a greater part of total upward heat transfer occurs by convection (heated air rising). That is why radiant barriers in roof systems are a more effective *cooling* rather than heating strategy and why they may be of great benefit to southern homeowners. In a typical southern home, an attic radiant barrier could cut annual cooling costs by 6–12% and peak cooling loads by 15%. An important component of an effective attic radiant barrier system is effective attic ventilation, which can normally be achieved by continuous soffit and ridge vents.

Most roof types already contain some kind of attic or airspace that can accommodate an effective radiant barrier system. In new construction it should be easy to install radiant barrier systems regardless of roof pitch. Fig. 4 shows three possible generic locations for radiant barriers in attics. When first installed, there will be no significant difference in the effectiveness of these locations. But in time, location 3 will suffer because of dust accumulation, which decreases performance. Dust can't collect on the underside of the radiant barriers at locations 1 or 2.

Location 2 is often considered best because it offers the potential for separately ventilating the space between the radiant barrier and hot roof deck and the attic space itself. This results in an attic air temperature somewhat closer to the conditioned space temperature in both winter and summer. As with location 3, dust may collect on the top of location 2, but a radiant barrier surface facing downward will perform as well as one facing upward. Therefore, for reasons of dust accumulation, use location 1 or 2 and depend on the down side for radiation control.

In new construction, another alternative may offer the advantages of location 2 and the construction ease of location 1. This construction places the radiant barrier on top of the roof rafters (or trusses) before the roof decking is applied. It is installed so that it droops approximately 2 in. (5 cm) below the upper surface of the roof structure. When the roof decking is applied, an airspace separates it from the radiant barrier in a way similar to that of location 2. This airspace also can be vented separately from the attic. As with location 2 the most reflective radiant barrier surface should face downward toward the attic airspace.

Multiple layers
Economics bode against more than one radiant barrier in attics. The first barrier surface eliminates about 95% of the radiant heat transfer across the attic. Adding more layers can affect only 95% of the remaining 5%. (This is not necessarily true in wall systems, where heat transfer by air convection can account for a greater percentage of total heat transfer).

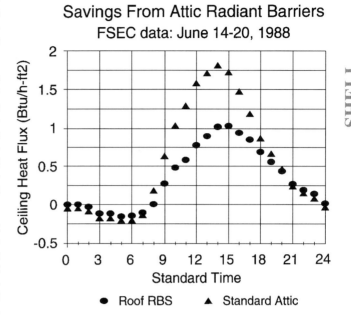

Fig. 3. Savings from attic radiant barriers (data: FSEC June 14-20, 1988)

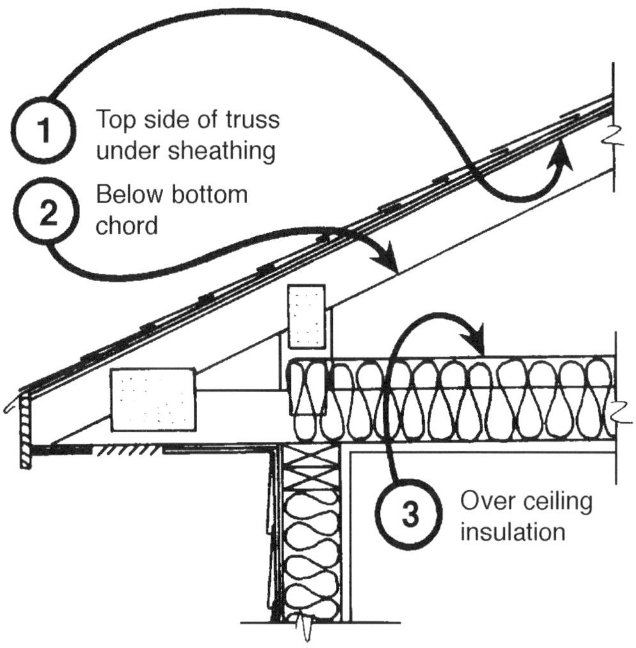

SHELL

B3

① Top side of truss under sheathing

② Below bottom chord

③ Over ceiling insulation

Fig. 4. Alternatives for radiant barrier placement

Tightness

It is not necessary to form airtight seals with radiant barriers; radiant energy travels in a straight line through the air but not in the air. In fact, if you choose location 3 (Fig. 4), you should use a perforated foil product that will allow the free passage of vapor out of the insulation during winter. This may also apply to location 1 in some cases, because the barrier is in contact with the roof decking. Location 2 should not have moisture condensation problems because it has an airspace on both sides of the radiant barrier.

Frequently asked questions

Q: What are the benefits of radiant barriers in attics?

In hot climates, benefits of attic radiant barriers include both dollar savings and increased comfort. Without a radiant barrier, a roof radiates solar-generated heat to the insulation below it. The insulation absorbs the heat and gradually transfers it to the material it touches—principally, the ceiling. This heat transfer makes the air conditioner run longer and consume more electricity. An aluminum foil radiant barrier blocks 95 percent of the heat radiated down by the roof so it can't reach the insulation.

In summer, when a roof gets very hot, a radiant barrier cuts air-conditioning costs by blocking a sizable portion of the downward heat gain into the building.

In the warm spring and fall, radiant barriers may save even more energy and cooling dollars by increasing our personal comfort. During these milder seasons, outdoor air temperatures are comfortable much of the time. Yet solar energy still heats up the roof, insulation, attic air and ceiling to temperatures that can create uncomfortably warm conditions on the interior. An attic radiant barrier stops almost all of this downward heat transfer so that occupants can stay comfortable without air conditioning during mild weather.

Radiant barriers can expand the use of space. For instance, uninsulated, unconditioned spaces such as garages, porches and workrooms can be more comfortable with radiant barriers. And because radiant barriers keep attics cooler, the space is more usable for storage.

An additional benefit: a cooler attic transfers less heat into air-conditioner ducts, so the cooling system operates more efficiently.

Q: How do radiant barriers "block" heat transfer?

Aluminum foil—the operative material in attic radiant barriers—has two physical properties of interest here. First, it reflects thermal radiation very well. Second, it emits (gives off) very little heat. In other words, aluminum is a good heat reflector and a bad heat radiator.

Your grandmother probably made use of these properties through "kitchen physics." She covered the Thanksgiving turkey with a loose "tent" of aluminum foil before she put it in the oven. The foil reflected the oven's thermal radiation, so the meat cooked as evenly on top as on the bottom. She removed the foil briefly to let the skin brown, but when she took the bird from the oven, she "tented" it with foil again. Since aluminum doesn't emit much heat, the turkey stayed hot until the rest of the meal was ready.

Cooking a turkey is a simple analogy, but the same principles of physics apply to an attic radiant barrier. Aluminum foil across the attic air-space reflects heat radiated by the roof. Even if the radiant barrier material has only one aluminum foil side and that side faces down, it still stops downward heat transfer because the foil will not emit—it will not radiate the roof's heat to the insulation below it.

Q: Are claims of greater savings untrue?

As in most cases, claims for radiant barriers that sound too good to be true are too good to be true. If your roof accounts for less than 20 percent of your cooling load, then an attic radiant barrier can't possibly save more than 20 percent on your bills.

Claims of greater savings may simply be the results of misunderstanding. For instance, FSEC has measured and reported that radiant barriers can reduce heat gain through R-19 insulated ceilings by over 40 percent. If the ceiling portion of the total cooling load is 20 percent, that's a reduction of 40 percent of 20 percent, which amounts to 8 percent savings on the total cooling load. An attic radiant barrier can save about 8–12 percent on air-conditioning costs in the U. S. Southeast.

Q: What kinds of radiant barrier materials are available?

There are many types of radiant barrier materials on the market, and more are being developed as radiant barriers become more widely used. Five generic types are most common:

- Single-sided foil (one foil side) with another material backing such as Kraft paper or polypropylene. Some products are further strengthened by fiber webbing sandwiched between foil and backing. The strength of the backing materials is important since unreinforced foil tears very easily.

- Double-sided foil with reinforcement between the foil layers. Reinforcement may be cardboard, Kraft paper, mylar or fiber webbing.

- Foil-faced insulation. The insulating material may be polyisocyanurate, polyethylene "air-bubble" packing or other materials that impede heat conduction.

- Multi-layered foil systems. When fully extended and installed so that the foil layers do not touch, these products also form insulating airspaces.

Some of these products have R-values, which may be properly claimed as a representation only if the product was tested according to Federal Trade Commission regulations for insulation.

Although it is not by definition a radiant barrier, there is a low-emissivity paint available that can be applied directly to the underside of the roof decking.

Q: Which material is best?

A few common-sense characteristics of radiant barriers provide a guideline to material selection and include:

- Emissivity (the lower the better)
- Fire rating (as required by building codes)
- Ease of handling
- Strength of reinforcement
- Width appropriate for installation
- Low cost.

Q: The RBS material has only one foil side; should the foil face the roof?

No. In attics, single-sided radiant barrier material should be installed with the foil side facing down. This may run counter to our intuitive feel for "how things work" but it does work, and work well.

To understand how it works remember the two properties of aluminum foil from the Thanksgiving turkey analogy: foil reflects radiant energy very well but does not radiate heat well. It does not emit heat to the cooler surfaces around it.

If installed as a single-sided radiant barrier with the foil side facing up, the aluminum will (for a time) reflect the thermal energy radiated by the hot roof.

If installed as a single-sided radiant barrier with the foil side facing down, the aluminum simply will not radiate the heat it gains from the roof to the cooler insulation it faces.

At first, a single-sided radiant barrier will work equally well with the foil facing up or down. But over time, dust will reduce the radiant barrier effect by allowing the foil to absorb rather than reflect thermal radiation. However, a radiant barrier with the foil side facing down will not collect dust on the foil and will continue to stop radiant heat transfer from the hot roof to the insulation over the life of the insulation.

Even if a double-sided radiant barrier material is used, it is best to install it at the rafter level so that the bottom side faces the attic airspace and will not collect dust.

Q: Can't I just roll the material out on top of the insulation?

It's not recommended to place the material directly on top of insulation. In this type of installation, dust will accumulate on the foil surface facing the roof. In time, the dust will negate the radiant barrier effect. In addition, problems could develop with moisture condensation.

Q: Will heat build up in the roof and damage my shingles?

It's extremely unlikely. The Florida Solar Energy Center has measured the temperatures of roof shingles above attic radiant barriers on hot, sunny summer days. Depending on the color of the shingles, their peak temperatures are only 2–5F higher than the temperature of shingles under the same conditions with a radiant barrier.

Roofing materials are manufactured to withstand the high temperatures to which they are frequently exposed. A 2–5F increase in peak temperatures that normally reach 160–190F should have no adverse affect.

Q: What about the shingle warranty?

Shingle warranties should not be subject to cancellation by the manufacturer on the basis of radiant barrier nstallation. However, it may be wise to review the warranty to be sure that work of this nature will not void it. Inquire directly of the manufacturer. Any changes in warranty should be substantiated in writing.

Additional references

Fairey, P. 1990. "Seasonal Prediction of Roof-Mounted Attic Radiant Barrier System Performance from Measured Test Data." Proceedings of *ACEEE 1990 Summer Study on Energy in Buildings*. Vol. 1. Washington, DC: American Council for an Energy-Efficient Economy.

Fairey, P., 1984. "Radiant Energy Transfer and Radiant Barrier Systems in Buildings." FSEC-DN-6. Cocoa, FL: Florida Solar Energy Center.

Fairey, P. 1984. "Designing and Installing Radiant Barrier Systems." FSEC-DN-7. Cocoa, FL: Florida Solar Energy Center.

Fairey, P. 1982. "Effects of Infrared Radiation Barriers on the Effective Thermal Resistance of Building Envelopes." *Proceedings of ASHRAE/DOE Conference on Thermal Performance of the Exterior Envelopes of Buildings II*, Las Vegas, NV.

Fairey, P. and M. Swami. 1992. "Attic Radiant Barrier Systems: A Sensitivity Analysis of Performance Parameters." *International Journal of Energy Research*, Vol. 16, pp 1-12. New York: John Wiley & Sons, Ltd.

continued

SHELL

B3

Fairey, P., M. Swami, and D. Beal. 1988. "RBS Technology – Task 3 Report." Contract Report, FSEC-CR-211-88. Florida Solar Energy Center, Cocoa, FL.

Fairey, P., et al. 1983. The Thermal Performance of Selected Building Envelope Components in Warm Humid Climates." *Proceedings of the 1983 ASME Solar Division Conference*, Orlando, FL.

FSEC. 1986. *Radiant Barriers: How They Work and How to Install Them.* videotape. Cocoa, FL: Florida Solar Energy Center.

Joy, F. A. "Improving Attic Space Insulating Values." *ASHRAE Transactions*, Vol. 64, 1958.

Levins, W. P., and M. A. Karnitz, 1986. "Cooling-Energy Measurements of Unoccupied Single-Family Houses with Attics Containing Radiant Barriers." Oak Ridge National Laboratory, Contract Report, DE-ACO5-84OR21400.

Parker, D., P. Fairey and L. Gu. 1991. "A Stratified Air Model for Simulation of Attic Thermal Performance." *Insulation Materials: Testing and Applications*. Volume 2, ASTM STP 1116, R. S. Graves and D. C. Wysocki, editors. Philadelphia, PA: American Society of Testing and Materials.

Van Straaten, J. F. 1967. *Thermal Performance of Buildings*. pp. 142-160. New York: Elsevier Publishing.

Wilkes, G. B. July 1939. "Reflective Insulation." *Journal of Industrial and Engineering Chemistry*, 31D:832.

C   INTERIORS

INTERIORS   C1

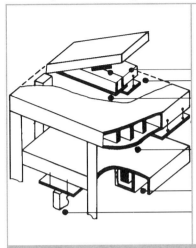

Suspended ceiling systems

Summary: This article provides an overview of the most common suspended ceiling substrate and finish options, including metal ceiling and acoustical ceilings, including material options, performance characteristics, specification information, and installation procedures.

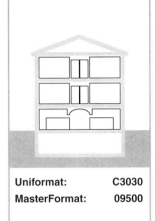

Uniformat:	C3030
MasterFormat:	09500

Key words: acoustical tiles, linear metal ceilings, open cell metal panels, suspension systems.

INTERIORS C1

Ceiling systems are nonstructural components supported by the structural frame above and provide:

- visual screen or visual/maintenance separation between the inhabited space and the underside of the structural frame.

- sound absorbing screen.

- integral component of a fire-resistant rated roof or floor assembly, when the structural frame is not fire-resistive itself.

Ceiling membranes and substrates may be attached directly to the structural frame, or suspended from them (Fig. 1). This section describes the second of these approaches. See the following article, "Wall and ceiling finishes," in Chapter C3 for discussion of the most common direct attachment systems.

In selecting a ceiling system, the following requirements of an entire system assembly should be considered (Fig. 2):

- *Sound control*
  Sound can be controlled by minimizing sound transmission pathways through ceiling joints, penetrations and plenums connecting adjacent spaces.

- *Fire resistant rating*
  Fire resistive ratings are most commonly applied as part of the structural system. Ratings are established for entire roof/ceiling and/or floor assemblies, not for the ceiling components alone.

- *Heat flow and air/water vapor control*
  Heat flow and moisture flow will occur through joints and penetrations in ceiling systems. Significant undesired heat gain can occur from overheated spaces below uninsulated roofs, requiring that the ceiling system provide uninterrupted and unbreeched insulation, which in practice is not easily achieved when the ceiling plenum also contains lighting fixtures and other mechanical equipment and access. Also, water vapor may be transported into spaces below the roofing and above ceiling systems by air movement and/or by condensation on cold surfaces, such as penetrating attachments (nails, metal hangers, and other materials that are good heat conductors). Such condensation may damage the building materials and assembly and cause staining of ceiling finishes.

The basic design considerations in selecting a ceiling assembly are:

- type of construction and the sequence of construction.

- type and extent of mechanical and electrical service (requiring close coordination of all engineering specialties).

- performance requirements (listed above) and life-cycle maintenance.

The requirements of HVAC, lighting, acoustics, structure and related infrastructure services the dimensional requirements and sequence of construction and maintenance require coordination during preliminary design and dimensioning. Too little space between ceiling system and the roof/floor above creates conflicts between various services. Too much space adds to building height and cost. Various choices of integration of services in open framing and closed framing are diagrammed in Fig. 3.

Along with the above criteria and system types, ceiling systems are selected based on aesthetic appearance, which may suggest concealed grid or exposed grid alternatives, as well as various shaped units (Fig. 4). Systems reviewed below include:

- Metal ceiling systems, including linear, open-cell, baffle type, and metal pan systems.

- Acoustical ceilings, including acoustical tile and panels systems.

1 Metal ceiling systems

Metal ceilings are a specialty ceiling used where appearance is important or where a metal surface for durability or moisture resistance is desirable. They provide more difficult access to equipment than other ceilings. Within the framework of the linear design, they can handle a wide variety of shapes and colors.

Metal ceilings are composed of ceiling panel and the support system. The metal ceiling types, each discussed in turn below, are:

- Linear metal ceiling systems.

- Metallic pan ceilings systems.

Linear metal ceilings systems

- *Ceiling panels*

- Panels are formed from aluminum sheets into a variety of shapes.

Author: William Hall

Credits: Illustrations are from 1993. *Sweet's Catalog File Selection Data* by permission of McGraw-Hill.

References: ASTM 1993. ASTM E1374. Standard Guide for Open Office Acoustics and Applicable ASTM Standards. West Conshohocken, PA: American Society for Testing and Materials.

CISCA. 1994. *Acoustical Ceilings: Use and Practice.* St. Charles, IL: Ceiling and Interior Systems Construction Association.

CEILINGS

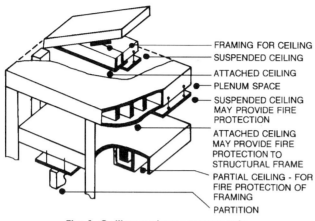

FRAMING FOR CEILING
SUSPENDED CEILING
ATTACHED CEILING
PLENUM SPACE
SUSPENDED CEILING MAY PROVIDE FIRE PROTECTION
ATTACHED CEILING MAY PROVIDE FIRE PROTECTION TO STRUCTURAL FRAME
PARTIAL CEILING - FOR FIRE PROTECTION OF FRAMING
PARTITION

Fig. 1. Ceiling system components

SOUND

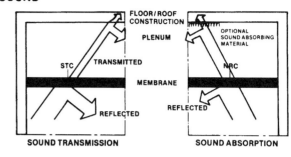

SOUND TRANSMISSION   SOUND ABSORPTION

FIRE

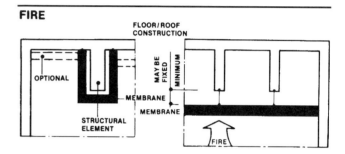

HEAT FLOW

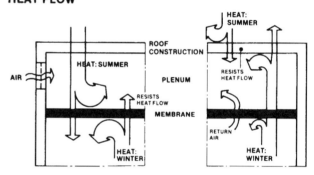

AIR/WATER VAPOR LEAKAGE

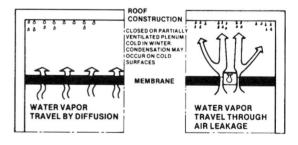

Fig. 2. Performance criteria of ceilings as part of roof/floor assemblies

Type and extent of mechanical/electrical services to be provided will influence the selection of the entire assembly:

■ **Space must be provided** within the plenum for feeder lines serving the enclosed space or a group of enclosed spaces; feeder lines may need to run above the ceiling membrane of one space to serve adjacent space(s).

■ **The usual arrangement** and order of installation of mechanical/electrical service lines is:
• wiring/piping first;
• ductwork, next
• lights, diffusers, return grilles, public address systems, etc., last.

■ Of all services, **only the automatic sprinkler system** must be located in a rigid prescribed pattern; all other systems allow for varying degrees of flexibility.

■ **Depth of plenum space** above a level membrane will be determined primarily:
• at points where service lines cross
• where service lines clear the deepest member of floor/roof framing.

OPEN FRAMING

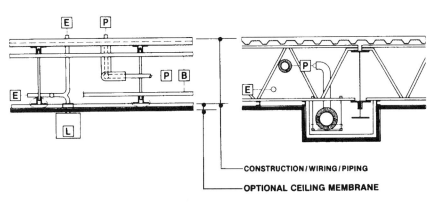

— CONSTRUCTION/WIRING/PIPING
— OPTIONAL CEILING MEMBRANE

■ **Framing:** open web steel bar joists and rolled steel or open web joist girders; short span wood trusses; generally 2' o.c. for floors.

■ **Wiring and piping:** may be run between or through joists and through joist girders, if provided:
• **web members** of joists should be lined up during installation.
• **clearance** between web members should be carefully checked, especially when flanged piping is used.
• **installation of piping** through joists is generally more costly since shorter lengths of pipe may have to be used and more labor is usually required.
• **running rigid ductwork** through open web joists is not practical; generally only flexible small-diameter circular ducts can be used.

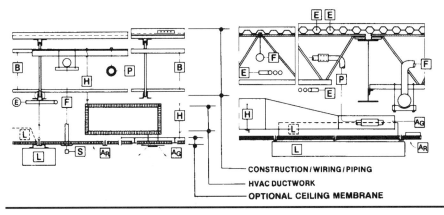

— CONSTRUCTION/WIRING/PIPING
— HVAC DUCTWORK
— OPTIONAL CEILING MEMBRANE

■ **Framing:** open web steel bar joists and rolled steel or open web joist girders; steel or wood trusses.

■ **Wiring and ductwork:** may generally be suspended from metal deck, heavier piping should be supported from framing at panel points.
• **metal deck** with tabs for connecting hangers is available.
• **ducts** may be flattened to clear girders or where two ducts or duct and piping cross; flattening ducts will increase resistance to air flow.
• layout of **fire protection piping** should allow for draining entire system.
• **light fixtures** may be recessed, surface mounted, or suspended.

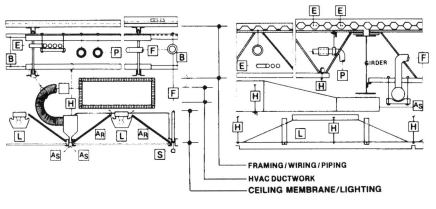

— FRAMING/WIRING/PIPING
— HVAC DUCTWORK
— CEILING MEMBRANE/LIGHTING

■ **Framing:** open web bar joists and rolled steel or open web joist girders; or trusses.

■ **Wiring, piping and ductwork** location and supports similar to those for penetrated membranes:
• **modular components,** such as diffusers, air return grilles, and lighting fixtures to fit the suspension grid, are used;
• **pre-assembled modules** with mechanical/electrical/sound control components incorporated may be installed into a suspension grid.
• **clearances** must be provided for tilting tile, fixtures, or modules into place.
• larger diameter piping is difficult to install through joists.

Fig. 3. Integration of services above ceiling assemblies.

■ **The symbols used are:**
[As] Conditioned air supply ductwork and outlets.
[AR] Inlets for plenum or ducted air return to heating/cooling system.
[P] Plumbing and/or heating/cooling piping: such as domestic hot/cold water, steam, hot/chilled water for heating/cooling, roof drain leaders.

[S] Sprinkler heads.
[F] Fire protection piping: main feeders, branches.
[E] Electrical power and lighting wiring: communication systems wiring.
[L] Lighting fixtures.
[H] Hangers: either wire or strap.
[B] Bracing for framing members.

■ For information on structural frame and ceiling membranes, refer to respective sections.

SOLID FRAMING

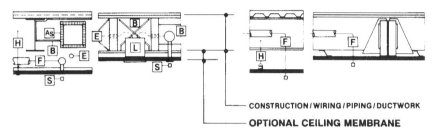

CONSTRUCTION/WIRING/PIPING/DUCTWORK
OPTIONAL CEILING MEMBRANE

■ **Framing:** rolled steel beams and girders; wood or metal joists with flush or dropped girders.

■ **Wiring and/or small diameter piping** may be run through field-drilled holes in wood joists, or through pre-punched holes in metal joists:
• installing **long straight runs** of piping through wood or metal joists is impractical; flexible tubing only can be installed.
• **steel beams/girders** can be drilled to allow wiring or small diameter piping, but drilling is costly and larger holes may require reinforcing the web.
• **ductwork** may be run parallel to rolled steel framing, but clearing lateral bracing between framing and girders may present a problem.
• **ductwork between** wood or metal joists would have to clear bracing: sizes are limited.

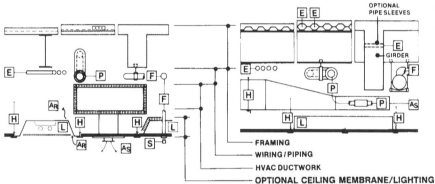

FRAMING
WIRING/PIPING
HVAC DUCTWORK
OPTIONAL CEILING MEMBRANE/LIGHTING

■ **Framing:** rolled steel beams and girders; reinforced concrete joists and beams; reinforced concrete beams and girders.

■ **Wiring and piping:** may be run between framing members, but has to clear lateral bracing members in steel framing; it is generally dropped to clear girders.
• **pipe sleeves** for wiring and small diameter piping may be cast into reinforced concrete girders.
• for fire-resistance rated assemblies, recessed **lighting fixtures are boxed-in** above the ceiling membrane to maintain its continuity.
• **in exposed grid** suspension systems, clearance for tilting tile, fixtures or panels into place must be provided.

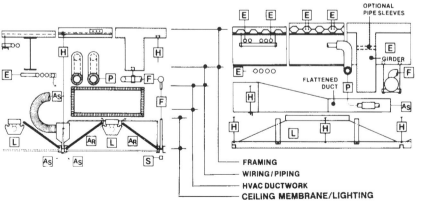

FRAMING
WIRING/PIPING
HVAC DUCTWORK
CEILING MEMBRANE/LIGHTING

■ **Framing:** rolled steel beams and girders; reinforced concrete beams and girders.

■ **Wiring, piping and ductwork:** location and supports similar to those for penetrated membranes:
• **modular components** to fit the suspension grid are generally used;
• **preassembled modules** with mechanical/electrical/sound control components may be installed into a suspended grid.
• **piping** may be run between beams, but is generally dropped to clear girders.
• **pipe sleeves** may be cast into reinforced concrete girders, but diameter is limited.
• **steel girders** may be cut to allow service lines to pass, but openings generally have to be reinforced.

Fig. 3. Integration of services above ceiling assemblies *(continued)*

CONCEALED GRID, SHAPED UNITS

METAL PAN TILE

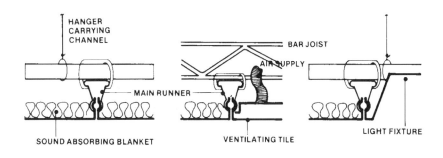

LINEAR PANELS

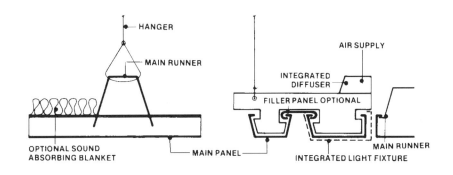

BAFFLES

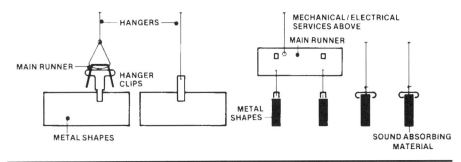

CONCEALED GRID, FLAT UNITS

KERFED EDGE

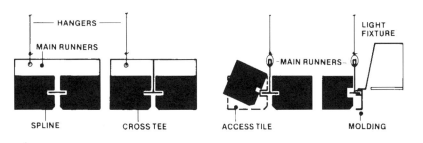

Fig. 4. Suspended ceiling types

EXPOSED GRID: FLAT UNITS

SQUARE EDGE

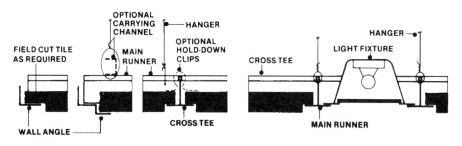

RECESSED EDGE

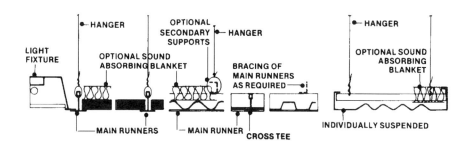

EXPOSED GRID: SHAPED UNITS

INLAY PANELS, CORRUGATED, RIBBED

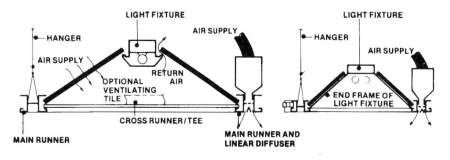

PRE-ASSEMBLED MODULES

Fig. 4. Suspended ceiling types (continued)

C1

INTERIORS

- Typical metal thickness is .025 in. (0.6 mm) and .032 in. (0.8 mm).

- Panels can range between 4 ft. (1,220 mm) and 20 ft. (6,096 mm).

- Panels are shaped into strips that come in 2 in., 4 in., 6 in., and 8 in. (51 mm, 102 mm, 152 mm, and 203 mm) in width.

- Panel edges are either square or radiused.

- Panels are designed to snap into specially designed carriers that hold them in place.

- Panels are designed to be linear in design and are installed with approximately 1/2 in. (13 mm) between panels. This reveal is open to the plenum above.

- Panels also come in a design that is formed with an extension that encloses the space between the panels.

• *Panel finishes*

- Standard finish is a special, baked on polyester paint available in a variety of colors.

- Metallic colors are available for additional cost.

- Special colors are available for additional cost.

• Support system

The support system is composed of the following elements, each described in turn below:

- carriers.

- support wires.

- cross channels.

- struts

• *Carriers*

- Comprised of a cold formed metal piece in a trapezoid shape with shaped bottom elements to which the panels are attached.

- Carriers come in 12 ft. (3,658 mm) lengths.

- Carriers are typically installed at 4 ft. (1,220 mm) on centers.

- The bottom elements are designed to allow easy, snap-on installation of the panels as well as correct alignment and spacing.

- Carriers come in straight lengths as well as radiused sections for shaped installations.

• *Support wires*

- Installed in a manner and spacing typical of a standard T- bar suspension system.

- In some situations, stabilizers are installed between carriers every 4 ft.-0 in. (1,220 mm) to increase rigidity.

• *Cross channels*

- 1-1/2 in. x 3/4 in. (38 mm x 19 mm) 20 ga. channels wired crosswise to the carriers adding stability to the system.

- Where additional support is required, cross channels are installed before the support wires, and wires are attached to the channels.

• *Struts*

- These are fastened to the channels close to the support wires and attached to the structure above as specific conditions require.

- Struts resist the up and down motion of a ceiling as a result of wind or seismic forces.

Open cell metal ceiling systems

This system incorporates the ceiling support system with the ceiling design element itself, and is composed of the following elements:

- 8 ft. (2,438 mm) long hanger runners.

- 4 ft. (1,220 mm) long cross runners that attach perpendicular to the hanger runners at any cell location. These create a 4 ft. x 4 ft. (1,220 mm x 1,220 mm) grid.

- 2 ft. (610 mm) long intermediate cross runners that attach to the other elements breaking down the grid to 2 ft. x 4 ft. (610 mm x 1,220 mm) or 2 ft. x 2 ft. (610 mm x 610 mm).

- Ancillary grids that break down the grid into cell sizes varying from 3 in. to 8 in. (76 mm to 203 mm) square.

- These elements are .20 gauge aluminum and are 3/8 in. (10 mm) and 2 in. (51 mm) wide by 1.2 in. (30 mm), 1.6 in. (41 mm), and 2 in. (51 mm) high.

- Suspension wires are used to attach to the hanger runners every 4 ft.-0 in. (1,220 mm).

• The variety and sizes of elements available allows the creation of an open cell ceiling system in many configurations in order creating a custom ceiling design.

• Building elements normally hidden from view are exposed through the cells of the ceiling; since the ceiling system is suspended below these elements, they are not as noticeable.

- In many cases, everything above the grid location is painted out in a dark color to make it less noticeable.

- Installing the light fixtures at the same height as the grid accomplishes much the same thing.

Baffle type metal ceiling systems

This type of ceiling system is similar to the open cell systems but has a much more linear look. Baffle ceilings are composed of two parts: carriers and metal baffles.

• *Carriers*

- Carriers support the baffles.

- There are two different carriers for this type of ceiling: cold formed metal shaped similar to those used with linear ceilings where baffles are attached in the same manner; and standard 15/16 in. (24 mm) T-bar suspension element similar to those used in standard acoustic suspension systems. Baffles are attached to the bottom of the T-bar with a baffle suspension clip and are installed perpendicular to the T-bar.

- Carriers are suspended from above by support wires at 4 ft. (1,220 mm) o.c.

- Carriers are normally installed horizontally but can be installed at an angle.

• *Metal baffles* come in two configurations:

- A formed, .025 in. (0.6 mm) aluminum shape with a "kinked" shape at the bottom and a flange at the top for mounting. Comes in 4 in., 6 in., and 8 in. (102 mm, 152 mm, and 203 mm) deep sizes with the two deeper sizes having an additional "kink" in the middle for additional stability.

- A formed, .032 in. (0.8 mm) aluminum shape with a mounting flange on top and a 3/4 in. (19 mm) radiused element at the bottom. Comes in 8 in. and 12 in. (203 mm and 305 mm) depths but also can be special ordered in 6 in., 7 in., 9 in. 10 in. and 11 in. (152 mm, 178 mm, 229 mm, 254 mm, and 280 mm) depths and in 12 ft. (3,658 mm) lengths.

- Metal baffles come in finishes similar to those provided for the linear systems.

Metal pan ceiling systems

Metal pan ceilings are the most common type of metal ceiling, which can be configured as a decorative element or to handle a specific utilitarian function. Composed of two parts: metal pan; panel support system.

- *Metal pan*

- Panels are manufactured in .040 in. (1 mm) thick aluminum as well as hot dipped, galvanized steel.

- Panels are formed up 1 in. (25 mm) at the sides forming a pan. These flanges take a variety of configurations:

- Some panels have a square edge designed to fit down onto the support system in the same manner as a standard lay-in acoustic panel. These have a specially designed angled edge that is designed to snap under the bulb at the top edge of the suspension tee, creating a tight locked connection and enabling the panels to stay in place. This locking panel is ideal for installations that need frequent washing with high pressure hoses or limited impact abuse.

- Another panel style is installed with special clips that attach to the T-bar, allowing the panel to hang below the grid so that the panel edges adjoin each other. A reveal joint between panels of this style is also available.

- Common size is 2 ft. x 2 ft. (610 mm x 610 mm), which is normally used in the more decorative installations. 2 ft. x 4 ft. (610 mm x 1,220 mm) panels are also available.

- Panels are designed to fit into or attach to a standard T- bar suspension.

- *Panel finishes and properties*

- Panels are available in a wide variety of standard baked on paint colors.

- Metallic colors are available.

- Custom colors are available for an additional cost as well as a minimum square footage requirement. Check with the manufacturer for specific requirements.

- Metal pans do not have any acoustic value in their standard configuration. Panels are available in a perforated design with .080 in. (2 mm) diameter holes staggered at 45 degrees at approximately 1/4 in. (6 mm) separation. This helps dissipate the sound.

- Acoustical batt insulation may be laid on top of the pans to further increase their sound dissipation. Consult with an acoustical engineer for the appropriate thickness required for a specific installation.

- *Panel support system*

- In most cases, the support system is identical with the standard T-bar suspensions system discussed elsewhere.

- The grid is available in 2 ft. x 2 ft. (610 mm x 610 mm) as well as 2 ft. x 4 ft. (610 mm x 1,220 mm).

- Hanger wires and seismic restraint wires are identical to the standard T-bar system.

- *Metal pan ceiling accessories*
  Each type of ceiling has its own variety of specially designed accessories to handle special conditions, such as:

- Edge conditions where ceilings meet walls or where a ceiling stops and an edge cap is required.

- Trims designed to go around standard or specially designed light fixtures or HVAC grills.

- Special conditions where it is desirable to modify the spacing, angle, or location of installation.

- Radiused locations.

- For any application where special conditions require a variation from the standard configuration or installation, consult with the manufacturer to determine available accessories.

2 Acoustical ceilings

Acoustical ceilings are composed of two parts: the acoustical tile or panel and the support structure. They are a inexpensive method of creating a flat ceiling surface with relatively easy accessibility to plenum space above the ceiling. Design issues include tile patterns, colors, textures, and edge detailing. For related installations of acoustical wall panel systems, see the following article in this Chapter, "Interior partitions and panels."

- *Acoustical ceiling properties*

- A measure of each ceiling's sound capabilities is usually published by each manufacturer and indicated by the NRC rating.

- A ceiling's rating is only a part of the acoustics of the entire space. Therefore, unless consulting with an acoustic engineer, use the relative ratings between different panels to help choose the appropriate ceiling.

- Most acoustical ceilings are painted white to enhance light reflectance. A reflectance value of .75 is common. Light Reflectance (LR) ratings are expressed as a percentage of light reflected; .80 is the upper limit.

- Most manufacturers make ceiling systems with fire ratings, which are given to the entire ceiling assembly and not just a particular ceiling tile or panel.

- *Special conditions:*

Most manufacturers make panels systems that address the following special conditions:

- High humidity: foil-faced and metal-faced products help the ceiling panel resist humidity.

- Chemical and corrosive fumes: The most common is chlorine such as that present in indoor swimming pools. This is commonly resisted by using stainless steel components or, better yet, nickel-copper alloy fasteners and hangers.

- Most manufacturers make abuse-resistant panels that incorporate properties such indention resistance, friability, and sag resistance.

Acoustical panel materials

Acoustical ceilings are manufactured of two different materials:

- Cellulose- or wood-fiber-based products.

- Mineral wood-based products.

- *Cellulose-based acoustical ceilings* are:

- Manufactured from wood chips that have been washed, soaked, and densified into a thick, pulp mixture that is pressed into this sheets that are cut into a variety of sizes.

- The back is sanded to a flat surface while the front is embossed into a variety of patterns or textures and painted. Some patterns are even embossed with small holes.

- Quite light in weight and more economical when compared with mineral wool.

- *Mineral wool-based acoustical ceilings* are:

- Manufactured in a manner similar to that described above.

- Made from a mixture of mineral wool and a binder made from starch, craft paper, and clay.

- Mixture is dispensed evenly onto a moving belt or conveyor that runs under a forming wire. The stiffness of the mixture as it runs under the wire determine its texture.

- If other textures are desired, the material can be formed accordingly.

- Mineral wool ceilings are heavier and more brittle than the cellulose base product, but they yield a heavier texture and are more costly.

- Fiberglass acoustical ceilings are:

- Manufactured from a densified, resin-impregnated fiberglass material that is reasonably hard, stiff, will not sag in the middle of the panel, and will hold its shape after cutting into specific sizes at the factory.

- Usually used in high-performance acoustical products.

- Fiberglass panels are usually wrapped in a textured plastic membrane or with a rough textured cloth.

- Panels are made in thicknesses of from 3/4 in. to 2 in. (19 mm to 51 mm).

- Panels may or may not be foil backed.

- *Special acoustical ceilings:*

- Most manufacturers make panels that are covered or wrapped in other materials to alter their performance characteristics or appearance.

- Panels can be coated with a dense ceramic material for high moisture applications. Adds strength to the tile as well as increases its resistance to dirt and grease.

- Panels can be coated with a polymeric finish which performs similarly.

- Panels can be clad with a vinyl faced aluminum that is extremely resistant to chlorine fumes, grease, and dirt.

- Mylar-clad panels are suitable where an extra degree of cleanliness is desired such as computer clean rooms or hospital environments.

- To increase durability, panels can be made with an epoxy- like binder additive, or covered with metal. These are desirable in detention facilities or schools.

- Where appearance is a primary concern, panels can be wrapped in fabric, which is available in a variety of textures and colors. This type of ceiling panel is difficult to clean.

- With the variety of wood species available, wood veneer on plywood cut to the 2 ft. x 2 ft. or 2 ft. x 4 ft. (610 mm x 610 mm or 610 mm x 1220 mm) can be used to upgrade ceiling appearance.

- Wood veneer panels are heavier than most; mounting structure should be given careful consideration.

Types of acoustical ceilings

There are two basic types of acoustical ceilings, each discussed in turn:

- Acoustical tile ceilings have a concealed or semi-exposed ceiling suspension system.

- Acoustical panel ceilings have an exposed ceiling suspension system.

Acoustical tile ceilings

Tile ceilings are normally made in smaller sizes, most usually in 12 in. (305 mm) square. Tiles have the following edges or joints:

- Kerfed or splined edges.

- Rabbeted edges.

- Flanged edges.

- Tongue-and-groove edges.

- Consult with manufacturer to determine the specific edge condition for each product.

- Tile ceilings do not allow access to elements and equipment above the ceiling as easily as with panel ceilings.

- Access to the ceiling plenum is provided in a number of ways:

- With an access door installed into the tile, which is visible if the door is flush with the tile; a tile installed onto the door surface can hide the door somewhat.

- Concealed systems installed with Z-clips may be accessed with a special tool or moving access clips within the grid.

Acoustical panels

Acoustical panel ceilings are most commonly made in 2 ft. x 2 ft. and 2 ft. x 4 ft. (610 mm x 610 mm and 610 mm x 1220 mm) sizes. Acoustical panels are installed into a suspended T-bar grid system.

- The most common edges are:

- Square: edges of the panels are finished with a simple perpendicular edge. The panel sits flush with the bottom of the suspension grid.

- Tegular: edges are routed, enabling the tile to sit down farther into the suspension grid, for a more formal and finished look.

- Modifications of the tegular edge: these come in many forms, such as a radiused edge or stepped edge.

- Panels come in a variety of colors, depending on the style. Not all colors are available in all styles.

- Panels are available in other styles not concerning the panel texture. In most cases, they are part of the regular edged styles. Some of these styles are as follows:

- The 2 ft. x 4 ft. (610 mm x 1220 mm) panel has a routed groove across the tile dividing it in half, enabling it look like a 2 ft. x 2 ft. (610 mm x 610 mm) panel.

- Panels can be designed with a multitude of routed grooves, dividing the tile into 12 in., 6 in., and 4 in. (305 mm, 152 mm, and 102 mm) squares. Each manufacturer has tiles that are similar to one another, and unique styles.

- Other variations add grooves in a linear manner for a distinctive appearance.

- Some of the newest designs have routed grooves in straight or radiused patterns to form a distinctive appearance when all the tiles are installed. The pattern spans many tiles. The grooves have square, radiused, or stepped edges.

- Since a particular panel style by a certain manufacturer may not have a counterpart in another manufacturer's line, familiarity with each manufacturer's designs is essential.

Ceiling support system

- Acoustical tiles are normally attached in three ways:

- direct hung system.

- indirect hung system.

- furring bar system.

- Acoustical tile systems may use:

- direct hung systems, where the main runners of the system are hung directly from the structure.

- indirect hung systems, where the main runners are attached to channels that are hung from the structure.

- furring bar systems, where the ceiling tile is attached to wood furring strips attached to the structure above.

- *Suspended T-bar system*

- The standard system for all acoustic panel ceilings.

- A pre-manufactured system composed of a system of "T-bars" suspended at a specified height above the floor by suspension wires.

- The system is composed of the following elements:

- Main runners: T-bars that are normally supplied in 20 ft. (6100 mm) pieces; installed first to form the back bone of the system.

- Intermediate runners: also T-bars but are only 4 ft. or 2 ft. (1220 mm and 610 mm). The 4 ft. (1220 mm) members are installed between the main runners at 4 ft. (1220 mm) increments creating a square grid. Additional 4 ft. (1220 mm) intermediate runners are installed perpendicular to the previously installed intermediates forming a 2 ft. x 4 ft. (610 mm x 1220 mm) grid. This is the system for a standard 2x4 lay-in system. The 2 ft. (610 mm) runners are installed between the 4 ft. (1220 mm) runners creating a 2 ft. (610 mm) grid.

- T-bars are normally painted a flat, off white color although custom colors are available.

- T-bar runners are available in a few different configurations. The most common T-bar is 15/16 in. (24 mm) wide. A popular thin line or narrow line T-bar size is 9/16 in. (14 mm) wide.

- T-bar designs with a small slot in the bottom of the T forming a small reveal add a sophisticated look to the ceiling.

- *Suspension wires*

- Suspension wires were fastened to the T-bar at one end and to the structure above at the other.

- Wires are attached to the T-bar at 4 ft.-0 in. (1220 mm) centers providing overall support for the entire ceiling system.

- *Seismic considerations*

- Some building codes in seismic regions now require additional support for suspended ceilings.

- During a seismic event, a suspended ceiling will move vertically. Codes require a rigid strut installed between the grid and the structure above at 4 ft.-0 in. (1220 mm) centers resisting this upward movement.

- Codes require four angled wires installed on 12 ft. (3658 mm) centers at 90 degrees to adjacent wires. This configuration resist seismic forces that tended to buckle T-bars.

- Codes also require a wire attached to each of the four corners of 2 ft. x 4 ft. (610 mm x 1220 mm) lights installed into the grid to keep them from dropping out of the ceiling during a seismic event.

Installation

- Installation of a suspended acoustic lay-in panel ceiling is relatively simple.

- A rotating laser beam device is placed in the center of the room or space at the intended height of the ceiling. The laser displays the exact height on the wall where the ceiling is to be installed.

- Hanger wires are then installed by shooting or otherwise attaching a connector into the bottom of the floor above, to which the hanger wires are attached. These wires must not be attached to the structure, but to the floor surface above.

- Edge angles are attached to the wall at the appropriate height indicated by the laser.

- T-bars are attached to the hanger wires. The bottom of the T-bars is trued up by aligning it with the laser beam.

- Lights and HVAC grills are installed into the grid. Most of the work above the grid, at this point, has been completed.

- Ceiling panels are installed last, laid into the grid at the appropriate locations.

- Installers must take care to carefully cut around any element that exists within each of the grid elements, such as recessed down lights, sprinkler heads, and ceiling mounted speakers.

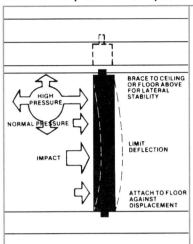

Interior partitions and panels

Summary: This articles provides an overview of interior wall partitions, fixed, movable and demountable systems, bathroom partitions and acoustical wall panel systems, including performance characteristics, sizes and selection guidelines.

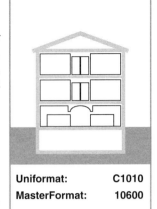

Key words: accordion partitions, acoustical wall panels, demountable partitions, fixed partitions, panel systems.

Uniformat:	C1010
MasterFormat:	10600

INTERIORS   C1

Interior wall and partition systems are a means for vertical division of interior spaces to provide (Fig 1):

- permanent (or semi-permanent) physical, visual or acoustical separation.

- permanent (or semi-permanent) separation of spaces for fire control and safety.

- selective and changeable partitioning to accommodate variable (in some cases unspecified) programmatic uses and/or environmental conditions.

This article reviews issues of design and selection of interior partitions to accommodate varying conditions and/or flexible uses. Structural, acoustical and fire safety considerations of permanent building elements are discussed elsewhere in this Volume. While fixed partitions may be constructed of any standard building materials, operable partitions are available only as site-assembled assembled manufactured components.

Preliminary selection of interior partitions generally includes performance requirements of vision, control of movement or passage, sound, and desire for flexibility (Fig. 2 and 3).

Design considerations of interior partitions include:

- Stability to resist:

- normal design air pressure experienced in pressurized interiors, generally five pounds per sq. ft. (exceeded in special rooms conditions, such as testing rooms).

- suspended loads, such as equipment, shelves and cabinets.

- concentrated horizontal loads, such as accidental impacts.

- Structural and acoustical characteristics of the adjoining floors, ceilings and walls:

- sound may outflank the partition through the ceiling/roof/ or floor construction.

- sound may also outflank adjoining spaces through closely located exterior windows or interior doors.

- Air leakage and heat flow may occur:

- around lighting fixtures recessed in the ceiling.

- between acoustical tiles and their suspension system.

- under and/or over the partition if not completely sealed.

- at electrical, plumbing or duct penetrations through the partition or adjoining construction.

Types of interior partition and panel assemblies reviewed in this article include:

1 Fixed partitions

2 Operable partitions, panel or accordion type

3 Demountable partitions

4 Toilet partitions

5 Acoustical wall panels

1 Fixed partitions

Fixed partitions offer the widest choice of materials and types of assembly. Fixed partitions are designed to be permanently installed and may provide specific fire ratings as well as sound or acoustical properties. They are generally nonload-bearing. The types of fixed partitions include:

- simple fixed partitions, used mainly to divide space.

- fire-rated fixed partitions for required fire ratings around rooms and corridors.

- acoustically rated fixed partitions to create an acoustic isolation between spaces.

Composition of partitions

- *Gypsum board and metal studs*

- This type is by far the most common.

- Metal studs of varying dimensions are installed into a C-shaped top and bottom track.

- Tracks are installed onto the floor substrate; onto the ceiling above; suspended from diagonal support studs some specified distance above the ceiling; onto the bottom of the floor deck above.

Authors: William Hall

Credits: Illustrations are from 1993 *Sweets Catalog File Selection Data*, by permission of McGraw-Hill.

References: ATBCB. 1991. *Americans with Disabilities Act Accessibility Guidelines for Buildings and Facilities (ADAAG).* Washington, DC: U. S. Architectural & Transportation Barriers Compliance Board.

NSSEA. 1987. Operable Walls Manufacturers Section. *Sound Control Performance of Operable Walls.* Silver Spring, MD: National School Supply and Equipment Association.

OSHA 1996. *Sanitation.* CFR 29, Section 1. Washington, DC: Occupational Safety and Health Administration, U. S. Department of Labor.

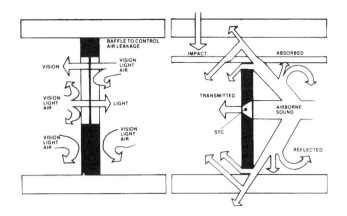

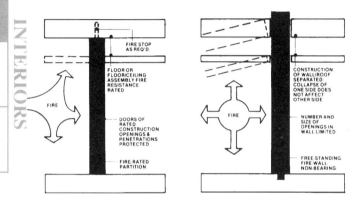

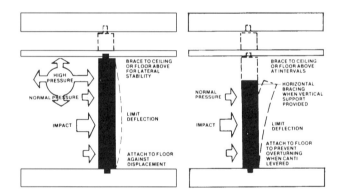

Fig. 1. Performance characteristics of interior walls

- Gypsum board is installed onto both sides of the studs.

• *Gypsum board and wood studs*

- Not common in commercial use because of obvious fire-rating limitations.

- Wood studs of varying dimensions are installed between top and bottom plates.

- Plates can be installed in a manner similar to the metal stud tracks.

• *Plaster partitions*

- Not as common as they were 20 years ago, but still an economical method of dividing space.

- Standard metal studs or specially designed plaster supports are installed with lath being applied to one or both sides.

- Plaster is then applied to the lath as directed by the manufacturer.

• *Glass blocks*

- Translucent masonry style blocks or "bricks" installed in courses in a manner to bricks.

- Available in a variety of patterns and translucency.

- Not designed to be load-bearing.

• *Masonry*

- Not commonly used as a partition material except for appearance reasons.

- When used as veneer, construction is masonry over another system.

• *Size and/or gauge*

Size and/or gauge generally depend on the height of the wall.

- 2x4 in. wood studs are sufficient for walls up to approximately 8 ft. to 10 ft. (2438 mm to 3050 mm) in height.

- 22 gauge metals studs of 3-5/8 in. (92 mm) width is sufficient for the same height.

- For higher walls, consult the manufacturers' or suppliers' published data.

• *Spacing of framing members*

Spacing of structural elements is dependent upon the type and thickness of the surfacing material.

- 1/2 in. (13 mm) gypsum surface material normally requires 16 in. (406 mm) maximum spacing.

- 5/8 in. (16 mm) gypsum board normally requires 24" (610 mm) maximum spacing.

• *Surface material*

- gypsum board (the most prevalent).

- plaster.

- where privacy, security, acoustics or a fire rating are not important, there are many other materials that can divide the space, and may include but are not limited to wood strips in a variety of configurations, screens or louvers, metal panels and glass.

- function of these materials may range from utilitarian to decorative uses.

- appearance may be an important factor.

Rated partitions

• *Fire resistance*

Fire resistance indicates the ability of a particular wall assembly to contain a fire or the heat generated from a fire. A partition's fire rating is indicated by the amount of time it will prevent the spread of fire.

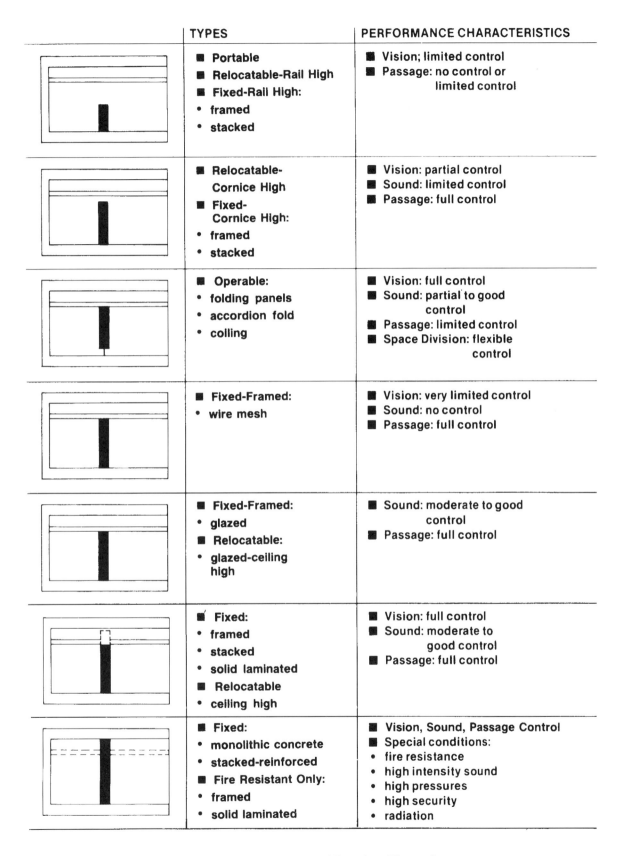

	TYPES	PERFORMANCE CHARACTERISTICS
	■ Portable ■ Relocatable-Rail High ■ Fixed-Rail High: • framed • stacked	■ Vision; limited control ■ Passage: no control or 　　　　　limited control
	■ Relocatable- 　Cornice High ■ Fixed- 　Cornice High: • framed • stacked	■ Vision: partial control ■ Sound: limited control ■ Passage: full control
	■ Operable: • folding panels • accordion fold • colling	■ Vision: full control ■ Sound: partial to good 　　　　　control ■ Passage: limited control ■ Space Division: flexible 　　　　　control
	■ Fixed-Framed: • wire mesh	■ Vision: very limited control ■ Sound: no control ■ Passage: full control
	■ Fixed-Framed: • glazed ■ Relocatable: • glazed-ceiling 　high	■ Sound: moderate to good 　　　　　control ■ Passage: full control
	■ Fixed: • framed • stacked • solid laminated ■ Relocatable • ceiling high	■ Vision: full control ■ Sound: moderate to 　　　　　good control ■ Passage: full control
	■ Fixed: • monolithic concrete • stacked-reinforced ■ Fire Resistant Only: • framed • solid laminated	■ Vision, Sound, Passage Control ■ Special conditions: • fire resistance • high intensity sound • high pressures • high security • radiation

Fig. 2. Performance characteristics of partition systems

● denotes common usage
○ denotes possible usage

C1 INTERIORS

TYPE	MAXIMUM UNBRACED HEIGHT range in feet	MAXIMUM UNBRACED LENGTH, range in feet	USE/CONTROL SEPARATION				ISOLATION					
			VISION ONLY	SOUND ONLY	VISION AND SOUND	PASSAGE	FIRE	HEAT FLOW	HIGH INTENSITY SOUND	HIGH PRESSURE	RADIATION	FORCED ENTRY
FRAMED	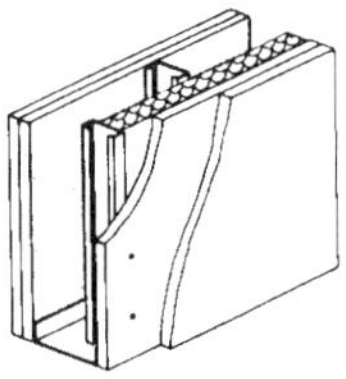 16 to 18	10 to 12	●	●	●	●	●	●	●		○	
SOLID-LAMINATED	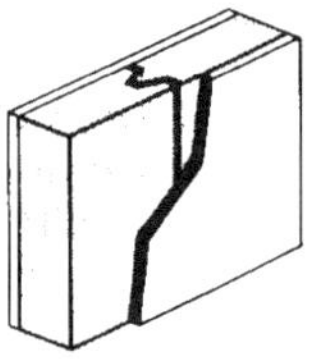 8 to 9	8 to 10	●		●	●	●					
RELOCATABLE	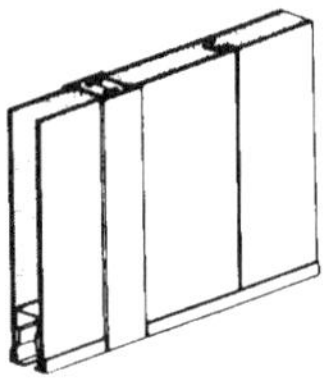 8 to 12	8 to 15	●	●	●	○	○					
OPERABLE PORTABLE	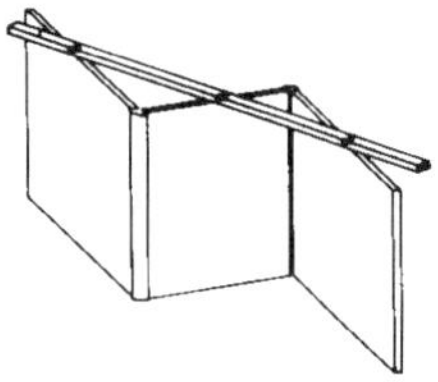 no limit for top-hung	no limit / 6 to 8	●		●	●	○					
STACKED	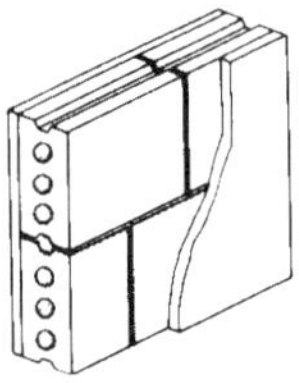 12 to 16 for 4" thick	12 to 16 for 4" thick			●	●	●		○	○	○	●
MONOLITHIC	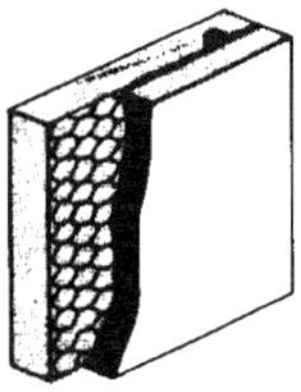 20 to 40	varies			●	●	●		●	●	●	●

Fig. 3. Partition types and uses

- For instance, a 1-hour wall will prevent the spread of a fire across the partition for at least 1 hour.

- For a partition to obtain a specific fire rating, it must be constructed of specific materials and in a specific manner or configuration.

- Requirements for these materials and configurations are designated in *ASTM Standard E119, Fire Tests of Building Construction and Materials.*

- Fire rating requirements for partitions are set by local building code officials.

• *Fire resistive standards*

Standards for fire resistive construction are published by Underwriters Laboratories (UL). Most manufacturers of fire resistive materials, such as plaster or gypsum board, publish "quick selector" lists to aid in selecting the best design for the desired fire rating. Manufacturer will normally cross reference these designs with the UL numbers and other pertinent information. Designs will specifically indicate:

- materials (studs and gypsum board) that may be used.

- exact placement or parameters to aid in the proper placement of these materials.

- specific information regarding the type, quantity, and placement of required fasteners.

- other pertinent information needed for its proper construction.

• *Acoustical standards*

A partition's acoustical properties depend upon a wide variety of factors and is not an exact science. Criteria for these properties are based on those aspects that can be attained by reasonably simple methods. Isolating the partition from other elements (such as one side from the other, or the partition from ceiling or floors) inhibits sound from spreading into adjacent rooms. Installing a sound absorbing material also inhibits sound transmission. Sealing all joints, penetrations, and holes with appropriate sealants or fillers will increase the function of the partitions. Most manufacturers' "quick selector" lists of fire-rated designs also included acoustical properties. They comply with the above criteria by:

- filling the space between the studs with a sound absorbing material such as batt insulation.

- the two partition surfaces are isolated from one another by staggering the studs or separating them by building two one-sided walls a distance apart.

- filling all joints and holes with a special acoustical sealant.

2 Operable partitions

Operable partitions are semi-permanent walls used to divide spaces. Their size and applications range from small prefabricated units similar to a multi-fold door to entire walls which open to join several spaces into one. They are common in large conference rooms, hotel meeting rooms, schools, and other places where there is need for flexibility in the size and division of spaces. They come in flat panel as well as folding configurations, and may be fire rated or have acoustical properties. Types of operable partitions are:

- panel type

- accordion type

Panel partitions

This type of operable partition is characterized by numerous, flat panels that, when fit together, form a temporary wall.

• *Panels*

- Wood frame panels range from 1-3/4 in. to 3 in. (44 mm to 76 mm) thick.

- Steel reinforced aluminum frame panels have face sheets of gypsum board or particle board, in panel thicknesses between 3 in. to 4 in. (76 mm to 102 mm).

- Steel frame panels range from 2-3/4 in. to 4 in. (70 mm to 102 mm) thick.

• *Support structure*

Depending on the type of rollers or carriers, panels are supported by a continuous, steel track mounted into the ceiling. Consult with each manufacturer regarding specific requirements for each type of track.

- Rollers or carriers, available with various types of mechanisms, move the panels within the track. The type of carrier or roller depends greatly on the weight of the panel.

- Carriers are composed of a steel rod attached to the panel with a plastic, Teflon, or other synthetic disk designed to move easily within the track, and are primarily used with panels that don't weigh much.

- Rollers are composed of a steel rod attached to the panel at one end, attached to ball bearing rollers, and are designed for heavier panels.

• *Support elements*

- The track needs to be supported from the structure above. Each manufacturer provides their own details suggesting recommended methods for this support.

- The most common method uses double threaded steel rods at 24 in. (610 mm) o.c., one on each side of the track. These rods attach to the track at the bottom side and to steel angles that are attached to the structure above.

- Since the manufacturer supplies some of these parts, and sub contractors supply others, the drawings and specifications need to be clear about who supplies what. Consult each manufacturer about what is supplied with their product.

• *Panel arrangement*

Depending on the length of the opening, the weight of the panels, and the manufacturer, the panels may be arranged in three ways:

- Individual panels are separate elements that are moved individually into their storage area one by one. There are two carriers per panel, and travel is restricted to a straight line.

Maximum panel height is approximately 20 ft. (6100 mm) and are typically moved manually.

- Paired panels are hinged together so that the panels are folded together and moved as one element into their storage area. There is one carrier per panel, which can travel in straight or curved lines, with tracks intersecting. Maximum panel height is approximately 40 ft. (12.2 m) and may be stored in a remote location.

- Continuously hinged panels hinged together into a long string. Panel travel is restricted to a straight line, and large panels that are part of high and/or long partitions may need to be motorized. Maximum panel height is approximately 26 ft. (7.9 m).

• *Panel weight*

- determined by the size of the panel.

- construction of the panel.

- STC (Sound Transmission Class) rating of the panel.

- accessories that might be on the panel.

- weight of the combined panels should be considered since the structure of the building must be used to hold support it.

- panels exert an evenly distributed load over the entire length of the track when they are closed. Panels exert a concentrated load in the stack area when the panels are stored. The structural engineer should plan for these varying loads.

- because of the tolerances between the door bottom and the floor, excessive deflection cannot be tolerated.

- panels range from 8 to 14 lb./sq. ft. (300 to 525kg/sq. m).

• *Fire-rated panels*

- Configuration is available only in the steel frame type.

- Most manufacturers offer a fire-rated style. Consult with manufacturer for specific characteristics.

• *Other panel characteristics*

- Panels that are electrically operated must be continuously hinged and center stacked.

- Panels are secured in place normally by a retractable element in the bottom of the door that is extended against the floor, holding it in place.

- Panels are joined edge to edge by a type of tongue and groove edge with resilient material within to create a sound seal.

Accordion partitions

Accordion type partitions, used for easily moved visual screening and flexible space dividers, are composed of the track, partition components, following components:

• *The track:*

- made of extruded aluminum or steel.

- installed onto or into the ceiling.

- is attached to a wood header or to threaded steel rods attached to the structure above in a manner similar to that described with panel type partitions.

- has one or several large slots lengthwise for the wheels attached to the folding partition to glide in.

• *Partition components*

- Top is composed of steel members to which small wheels are attached that fit into the slot(s) in the track in the ceiling.

- The steel members can be hinged or pantograph type members that enable the partition to fold up like an accordion and still provide support the entire partition.

- Attached or anchored post or edge is a vertical member attached securely to the wall at one end.

- Partition folds away or toward this end when being opened or closed.

- Latch or moveable end is a vertical steel or aluminum element that fits into a grooved track attached to the wall. It also encompasses the latch and locking mechanism that hooks or latches to this attached element keeping it in a closed or locked position.

- The accordion panel is composed of numerous metal, plastic, or wood pieces that are connected with a metal hinge or flexible plastic attachment strip.

- The bottom seal is a linear plastic strip attached to the folding element and functions like a sweep to help block light and/or sound.

• *Accordion partition sizes*

- Commonly come in heights up to 20 ft. (6100 mm); larger sizes are available by special order.

- Commonly available in lengths up to 40 ft. (12.2 m); special order.

• *Accordion partition configuration*

Accordion partitions come in two basic configurations:

- bi-parting, in which the partition is attached at opposing walls and meets and latches in the center.

single panel, which is one piece that attaches to the wall. It stacks where it attaches and closes and latches at the opposite wall.

• *Stack space*

- Each type and model of operable partition requires different amounts of space to stack properly.

- Whether a model stacks remotely or directly, at one side of the wall or both, stack space for the partition when it is open must be planned for.

- Stack space will depend on the thickness of the panel and the amount of material within the panel.

• *Weight*

- Weight of panel is a concern because it affects the loads on the structure.

- Weight of the panel will depend on the size and height of the partition, and the construction and thickness of the partition.

3 Demountable partitions

Demountable partitions are wall systems designed to be placed in semi-permanent fixed positions, but attached so that they can be moved easily and frequently, in some types without special tools or construction equipment. Such systems are usually modular on 24 in. (610 mm) centers and can include windows, doors, and other elements. Demountable partitions are installed directly over the floor finish material and fasten to the bottom of the ceiling, thus allowing for relocation.

• *Advantages of demountable partitions systems*

- designed to be easily relocatable as space needs change.

- have the appearance of standard gypsum board walls.

- designed to fit together without joint treatments or painting.

- can be installed directly over carpet, making it easy to relocate walls quickly.

- approximately 40% less costly than standard gypsum board walls.

- one-hour fire rating can be easily achieved.

- acoustical properties similar to a standard gypsum board walls are easily attained with the addition of acoustical batt installed between the studs.

- If desired, panels are available in unfinished gypsum board that may be taped and finished to blend with permanent walls.

- may have tax code advantages in U. S. business tax interpretations, in that they may be classified as furniture or equipment, depreciated over a 7-year period, as opposed to approximately 30 years for permanent construction.

• *Disadvantages*

- Because of gypsum board component, walls are subject to damage in the same manner.

- Because some demountable partitions contain doors, side lights, windows, and similar elements, a certain portion of the relocated wall is not reusable unless configured in the same manner.

Demountable partitions are composed of four major elements, a runner, track, studs or support frames, and panels:

• *Steel floor runner*

- made of galvanized steel.

- commonly 1-7/8 in. (48 mm) wide by 1-1/8 in. (29 mm) high.

- attached to the floor substrate either directly or through the floor finish material.

• *Ceiling track*

- made of steel or aluminum

- painted or bronze anodized (aluminum only) finish.
- commonly 3-5/8 in. (92 mm) wide by 1-1/4 in. (32 mm) high.
- fastened to the bottom of the ceiling.
- *Studs or support frames*
- rolled, galvanized steel, or extruded aluminum.
- available in either "H" or "T" configuration.
- designed to be fit between the floor and ceiling tracks at 24 in. (610 mm) o.c.
- *Panels*
- most common material is gypsum board.
- tackable "Micor" panel also used.
- commonly 3/4 in. (19 mm) thick by 24 in. (610 mm) wide.
- panels have a beveled edge to facilitate alignment of panel joints.
- panel edges are kerfed to provide a slot for the alignment clips.
- panels are wrapped in vinyl wallcovering.
- panels also available in metal surfacing as well as a tackable fabric covering.
- panels are attached to studs with alignment clips.

Demountable partition trims and clips

Most partition assemblies also include trim and clip attachments, typically:

- *Base trim*
- painted or anodized aluminum.
- painted steel.
- prefinished wood.
- resilient rubber or vinyl.
- *Ceiling trim*
- aluminum
- steel
- wood
- *Attachment clips*

Most typically galvanized steel, clips are attach to the studs and fit into the kerfed slot in the gypsum board during installation. Miscellaneous other clips are used in a variety of other situations depending on the manufacturer or need.

Finishes

Partition systems are commonly available with durable and decorative finishes. Standard finishes include:

- vinyl wallcovering patterns and colors.
- fabric wallcovering patterns and colors.
- baked enamel colors for metal panels.

Many manufacturers will allow wallcoverings and fabrics that are other than the standard ones they provide to be installed on the panels. Consult with the manufacturer to determine possible finishes. Many manufacturers have non-standard finishes for their metal panels. These include:

- stainless steel.
- baked enamel colors that are non-standard.
- powder-coated paint colors.
- porcelain enamel chalk board finishes.
- plastic laminate colors and patterns.

4 Toilet partitions

Toilet partitions divide individual toilet stalls to provide privacy. There are several different types of panels that may be installed in a variety of configurations. Each panel type is available in a variety of colors. Hardware is normally provided in a variety of durable types and styles.

Partition components include panels, pilasters (vertical supports), doors and/or screens, and hardware:

- *Panels*
- Typically these are the panels that form the elements between or and the ends of toilet stalls.
- *Pilasters*
- elements that form the jambs for the doors.
- serve as connector elements between the panels and the doors.
- can be anywhere from a few inches wide to a few feet wide, depending on the toilet stall configuration.
- *Doors*

Toilet stall doors are normally 2 ft. (610 mm) wide and swing in.

- Doors to ADA accessible stalls are a minimum of 32 in. (813 mm) wide and swing out.
- *Brackets, hinges, and latches*
- made from extruded aluminum, stainless steel, or chrome plated brass.
- used to fasten the entire partition system to the surrounding materials and to each other.

Types of toilet partition panels

- *Baked enamel steel*
- Panels are normally 1 in. (305 mm) thick and composed of two sheets of 20 ga. bonderized, galvanized steel laminated to a honeycomb core.
- Edges are similar steel sheets formed to a radius-edge molding.
- Different manufacturers have their proprietary methods to obtain generally the same look.
- Finish is typically a baked enamel finish with a variety of colors offered by each manufacturer.
- Powder-coated paints are also available from some manufacturers for added durability.
- This is the most common type of panel, providing the most durability for the cost.
- *Stainless steel*
- Panels are normally 1 in. (25 mm) thick, and composed of two sheets of 20 gauge type 304 stainless steel laminated to a honeycomb core.
- Edges are similar steel sheets formed to a radius-edge molding.
- Different manufacturers have their proprietary methods to obtain generally the same look.
- Finish is commonly a brushed stainless steel.
- Typical used in installations where rust might be a problem.
- Stainless steel panels are more costly than baked enamel.
- *Plastic laminate*
- Panels are normally about 7/8 in. (22 mm) thick and are composed of two .050 in. (1.3 mm) thick pressure plastic sheets laminated over a three ply, resin impregnated, 45-pound density particleboard core.

- Finish colors are available from standard colors provided by the manufacturer.

• *Solid phenolic*

- Panels are normally 1/2 in. (13 mm) thick, with doors 3/4 in. (19 mm) thick.

- Class B fire rating.

- Material and color is solid throughout thickness, with no core material.

- Colors are chosen from those available from the manufacturer. Many manufacturers provide phenolic colors that are the same as the plastic laminate colors.

- Phenolic partitions are suitable in areas of extremely high humidity and where frequent, direct water contact is common.

- Graffiti resistant (paint is easily removed) and extremely scratch resistant.

• *Stone*

- Panels are normally 1 in. (25 mm) thick.

- Panels and pilasters are typically stone. Doors are wood, metal, or plastic laminate.

- Granite and marble are the most common stones used with color availability subject to the manufacturer.

- Stone is durable and suitable in high water and humidity situations.

• *Wood*

- Not a common choice but an attractive one in appearance.

- Pilasters are solid, dimensioned wood; panels and doors are commonly stile and rail construction.

- Consult with the manufacturer for availability of wood species and stain colors.

Toilet stall and partition sizes

Dimensions for toilet stalls are determined by the architect. Common sizes are as follows:

- Width of stalls is typically 3 ft. (914 mm).

- ADA accessible stalls are between 42 in. and 5 ft. (1067 mm and 1524 mm) depending on the specific ADA requirements and local code requirements.

- Depth of stalls is typically 5 ft. (1524 mm).

- Height of panels and doors are is typically 58 in. (1473 mm); typical pilasters dimensions include: 70 in. (1778 mm) high with the floor mounted system, and 80 in. (2032 mm) high when used with a 2-1/2" in. (64 mm) high horizontal top railing in the overhead braced system.

Configurations

Toilet partitions are typically available from manufacturers in the following configurations:

• *Overhead braced*

- Pilasters in this style are attached to the floor at the base with expansion bolts hidden within the base.

- Panels are attached between the walls and the pilasters with brackets.

- The tops of the pilasters are fastened to each other with a horizontal top railing that attaches to each pilaster and to the adjacent wall surface.

- This type of configuration forms an extremely stable partition.

• *Floor mounted*

- Pilasters in this style are attached to a horizontal 3/8 in. (10 mm) steel bar with special bolts that fasten both to the bar and a cylindrical anchor. This is attached to the floor with heavy gauge expansion bolts.

- Since this forms the major support for the partition system, this is an extremely strong connection.

- Panels and doors are fastened to the pilasters and walls with typical brackets.

- No horizontal support rail is needed.

- An extremely clean and simple looking partition system.

• *Ceiling mounted*

- Similar to floor-mounted systems, except that the system is attached at the ceiling and not the floor.

- Pilasters are fastened to the ceiling by a support system similar to the floor mounted system, except the expansion bolts are replaced with 3/8 in. (10mm) threaded rod and bolts that fasten to the ceiling and a support structure above the ceiling.

- Common technique where no connection to the floor is desired, or where ease of mopping is important.

Other design considerations

The following items should be considered when specifying and designing a toilet partition system:

- wall construction.

- floor finishes.

- ceiling structure.

- use of building (public office building, school, correctional facility).

- age of users.

- maintenance requirements.

- vandal-resistance.

- moisture-resistance.

5 Acoustical wall systems

Acoustical wall systems have specially made or installed panels, panel applications or materials that are wrapped in fabric and attached to the wall. These panels have acoustical properties and can add refinement to the overall design of a space.

System types

Acoustical wall systems come in two basic configurations:

- Rigid fiberglass is the most common type of acoustical panel. It is factory made and installed on site.

- Soft fiberglass batt with separate, rigid frame is a more recent type of system.

• Types of panels are:

- Standard panels have medium density fiberglass, with reasonable stability for panels to retain their shape after installation. They have good noise absorption and a class "A" fire resistant rating.

- Tackable panels have a standard panel at the core, and an additional layer of 1/8 in. (3 mm) high density fiberglass bonded to the face side of the core panel. This panel is highly tackable, has reasonable impact resistance, the same acoustical properties as the standard panel. Fabrics are not stretchable.

- Impact resistant panels have a standard panel at the core, with a woven fiberglass fabric bonded to it. This panel has high resistance to impact damage and is suitable for stretchable fabrics.

- • Specialized panels have a standard panel at the core, with a felted fiberglass mesh bonded to it under tension and pressure. This panel is suitable for fine fabrics and/or installation on surfaces that have reasonable irregularities that might "telegraph" or show through the panel.

- • Reflective panels are made from 1/2 in. (13 mm) gypsum board with 20 gauge steel edge angles. Battens are installed behind the gypsum board to make up the desired panel thickness. This panel is used where an acoustical reflective surface is desired, and are designed to look identical to the acoustically rated panels that may or may not be adjacent to them.

Special performance panels

- • High absorption panels are two-panels-thick at the perimeter and one-panel-thick at the center, with the void filled with low density acoustical batting, which increases its absorption.

- • Low frequency absorptive panels are wrapped in a special non-perforated vinyl fabric. These panels are ideal where absorption of low frequency sounds is necessary, as most high and middle frequency sounds are not absorbed. Panels are useful in recording studios or concert halls.

- • Double density panels are also designed to absorb low frequency sounds. They are formed from two panels: the outside panel has a higher density than the interior one and they are separated by a 30 mil vinyl septum. This design also limits sound transmission through the panel.

- • Absorptive transmission loss panels are formed with a standard panel attached to gypsum board. These panels are designed to absorb sound within a room while keeping out other sounds.

- • Other designs are available that help to control reverberation time, double wrapped panels to help control sound within a space, and diffuser panels of varying thickness to help diffuse sound.

Typical panel edges

Panel edges are subject to a lot of wear and tear. They also contribute significantly to the overall appearance of the installation, and thus are an important design consideration.

- • *Types of edge configurations*

- - square edge: perpendicular to the face.

- - bullnose edge: has a large radius approximately 1/2 in. to 3/4 in. (13 mm to 19 mm) depending on the thickness of the panel.

- - chamfered edge: has a 45-degree chamfer starting at approximately half the panel thickness.

- - radiused edge: similar to a bullnose edge but can vary from what is called a pencil radius edge to a radius equal to the thickness of the panel.

- - mitered edge: at 45-degrees to the face and starts at the back edge of the panel.

- - metal and plastic edges are available in configurations designed to meet a variety of structural or installation criteria.

- • *Panel finishes*

- - Panels are completely upholstered.

- - Most manufacturers have a wide variety of fabrics made from polyester, wool, flannels, etc. as well as some vinyl fabrics. All are available in a variety of colors and patterns.

- - Panels may be upholstered with the client's own material to achieve the desired color or design intent.

- - Almost any fabric may be used as long as it is reasonably stable. Most manufacturers will evaluate sample fabrics for appropriateness.

- - When standard fabrics are used, flame spread ratings of 25 or less can be achieved. Check with manufacturer's publish data on flame spread.

- • *Panel mounting methods*

Panels are mounted to the wall by a variety of methods:

- - Mechanical "Z" clips: Specially shaped clips are installed both to the wall and to the back of the panel in two or more locations. They are designed so that the panel is pressed onto the wall and slid downward so that the clips engage each other.

- - Velcro fasteners: Strips of Velcro are attached to both the wall and the panel in appropriate quantity and locations based on the size of the panel. The panel is then pressed into place.

- - Adhesives: Panels may be attached with the use of adhesives. This is a more or less permanent method because the panels cannot be easily removed for cleaning or repair.

- - Magnets: A more recent innovation for installation. Magnets are installed at specified locations on the panel and the panel is pressed into place.

- • *Specialized uses or configurations*

- - Most manufacturers do custom sized or shaped panels.

- - Some specialized configurations may not be possible. Consult with the manufacturer to determine capabilities and cost.

- - Special edge configurations are possible. Submit design to manufacturer for their approval.

- - Ceiling installations are also available.

- • *Rigid fiberglass panel design variations*

- - Similar in construction to the standard design.

- - Difference in that the hardened edge is replaced with a separate plastic edge that is attached during the manufacturing process.

- - Fabric is wrapped around the entire panel, including the attached edges.

- - This design offers increased resistance to impact damage at the edges as well as increased torsional stability.

Site fabricated acoustical panels

- • *Composition*

- - A rigid, vinyl frame that is stapled to wall surface with specially designed staples at 2 in. (51 mm) o.c.

- - A sub-surface installed within the vinyl frame work. This sub-surface consists of one of the following:

  1/2 in. (13 mm) thick compressible, acoustical, fire-resistant polyester batt.

  3/8 in. (10 mm) thick, tackable, fire-retardant panel.

  3/8 in. (10 mm) thick, fire-retardant, plywood panel suitable for nailing or mounting heavy objects such as pictures, artwork, or signage.

- - Fabric is stretched tightly over the framework and tucked into slots in the sides of the framework with a special tool.

- • *Edge profiles*

Profiles of edges of panels are formed by the shape of the vinyl frame.

- - Radius edge: has an approximate 3/8 in. (10 mm) radius.

- - Square edge: perpendicular to surface of the wall and requires a 1/2 in. (13 mm) reveal or space between panels.

- - Beveled edge: has a 60-degree angle with the edge of the panel.

- - Monolithic edge: used in place of sewn seams that show stitching

INTERIORS   C1

and press marks. It creates a clean, finished looking joint. It also facilitates easier changing of fabrics.

- *Panel thickness*
- Dependent upon the thickness of the vinyl framework.
- Standard thickness is 3/8 in. (10 mm).
- Alternate thickness is 1 in. (25 mm) framework typical of special, high-efficiency acoustic panel design.

- *Special considerations*
- Special techniques are available to handle inside, outside edges, wrapped corners, and special reveals.
- Designs are available to cover doors frames and other elements.
- Tackable, acoustical, and nailable surfaces can be mixed under the same piece of fabric.

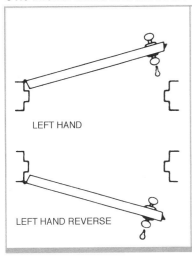

LEFT HAND

LEFT HAND REVERSE

Interior doors and hardware

Summary: This section includes design criteria and selection data relevant to interior doors, including standard doors and special doors, door finishes and hardware.

Key words: aluminum doors, door finishes, door stops, finishes, hinges, latchsets, locksets, steel doors, wood doors.

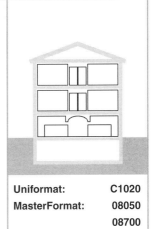

Uniformat:	C1020
MasterFormat:	08050
	08700

INTERIORS   C1

Interior doors provide separation between spaces, for a variety of purposes including: traffic control, visual privacy, acoustical separation, fire separation, control of environmental conditions, and service and maintenance access. Doors and door hardware may subject to special requirements of heavy usage, accommodation for persons wheeled carts, persons carrying packages or equipment, and other universal design and accessibility considerations. General design considerations include:

- Vision panels to minimize accidental opening into opposing traffic, especially for swinging doors.

- All glass doors should be marked to prevent accidental use.

- Sound transmission through the door, its perimeter and assembly, where acoustical privacy is required.

- Doors, frame and hardware in fire-rated enclosures have to meet the specified classification.

- Air/gas leakage under pressure should be prevented.

- Provision for resistance to impact against the door and the door or door hardware against adjacent surfaces.

Special door considerations include:

- Freezer doors are generally provided with perimeter heating cables to prevent freeze-ups due to water vapor and freezing.

- Doors located in radiation-resistant assemblies require special construction and assembly.

This article reviews the types and related specification of interior standard doors, special doors, door finishes and door hardware. Also see, as appropriate, "Exterior doors and hardware" in Chapter B2 of this Volume.

1 Standard interior doors

- Standard door assemblies consist of three principal elements:
- door leaves
- frame
- hardware
- Types of interior doors include:
- steel doors
- wood doors
- aluminum doors

- polymer doors
- Selection criteria include:
- grade
- model
- door thickness
- standard sizes
- outer face material and thickness
- veneer matching
- internal construction
- louver types
- Grade:
- steel doors (standard, heavy, and extra heavy duty: refer to Table 1)
- wood doors (economy, custom, and premium; refer to Table 2)
- aluminum doors (custom)
- polymer doors (custom)
- Model:
- steel doors (full flush or seamless design)
- wood doors (seam-free only)
- aluminum doors (full flush only)
- polymer doors (full flush only)
- Standard widths range from 2 ft. - 4 ft, with various increments per standard thickness. Standard door thickness:
- steel doors: 1-3/4 in. (4.5 cm), 1-3/8 in. (3.5 cm)
- wood doors: 2-1/4 in. (5.7 cm), 1-3/4 in. (4.5 cm), 1-3/8 in. (3.5 cm)
- aluminum doors: 1-3/4 in. (4.5 cm)
- polymer doors: 1-3/4 in. (4.5 cm)
- Outer face material and thickness:
- Steel doors: hot or cold rolled steel sheet, galvanized steel sheet, electro-zinc coated steel sheet, stainless steel, bronze or brass; 20, 18, 16, 14 gage thickness; embossed patterns available.
- Wood doors: standard thickness hardwood face veneers overlaid with medium density overlay veneer, natural hardwood veneer, plastic laminate, or hardboard directly applied to core construction; composed of two, three, or four plies having an overall ap-

Author: Timothy T. Taylor

Credits: Table 1 courtesy of Steel Door Institute. Illustrations are from *Sweets Catalog File* Section Data 1993, by permission of McGraw-Hill, unless otherwise noted.

References: References are listed at the end of this article.

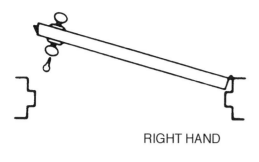

RIGHT HAND

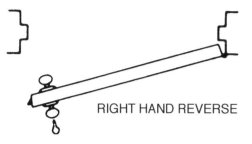

RIGHT HAND REVERSE

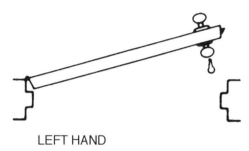

LEFT HAND

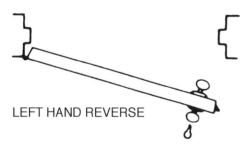

LEFT HAND REVERSE

Fig. 1. Standard nomenclature for doors (courtesy Door and Hardware Institute).

proximate thickness of 1/16 in. (1.5 mm); one ply of 1/8 in. (3 mm) for hardboard faces.

- Aluminum doors: 1/8 in. (3 mm) thick tempered hardboard overlaid with ribbed or smooth 0.040 in. (1 mm), 0.062 in. (1.6 mm), or 0.090 in. (2.3 mm) thick aluminum sheet face.

- Polymer doors: fiber glass (FRP) or thermoplastic (ABS) colored polymers; .120 in. (3 mm) thickness; embossed patterns available.

• Veneer matching:

- Matching between individual pieces of veneer: book, slip or random match.

- Assembly of spliced veneer on a face: sequence matching from opening to opening must be specified, examples include balanced, center balanced, and running matching.

• Internal construction:

- Steel doors: Kraft honeycomb, rigid plastic, unitized steel grid, vertical steel stiffeners.

- Wood doors: particleboard, glued block core, paper honeycomb, or wood fiber hollow core; cores may be specified as bonded (for highest performance) or nonbonded to veneers.

- Aluminum doors: paper honeycomb or rigid insulation core framed with aluminum tubes.

- Polymer doors: rigid plastic and aluminum tubes.

• Louver types:

- Sight proof

- Light proof

• Handing of doors:

- Strictly speaking, the door itself is either right or left hand; the locks and latches may be reverse bevel. Handing is normally determined in accordance with the conventions indicated in Fig. 1.

- Hardware can be handed in three main ways: universal, reversible, and handed. Universal can be used in any position such as a door stop. Reversible can have the hand changed by revolving from left to right, by turning upside down, or by reversing some part of the mechanism such as can be found on certain mortised and bored locks and latchsets. Handed (not reversible) can be used only on doors of the hand for which that hardware is designed, such as can be found with beveled or rabbeted lock fronts.

- For most doors the hand is determined from the outside. The outside is the side from which security is necessary. In a series of connecting rooms, such as in a hotel suite, the outside will be the side of each successive door as you come to it proceeding from the entrance in. For two rooms of equal importance with a passage in between, the outside is the passage side. The specifier should be alert to prevent any confusion over which side is the outside, particularly when split finishes are desired.

2 Special doors

This section includes selection data relevant to interior swinging, acoustical, and X-ray doors, available in wood and steel, depending on application.

• Special door assemblies consist of three principal elements:

- door leaves

- frame

- hardware

• Selection criteria include:

- grade

- model

- door thickness

C1

INTERIORS

Table 1. Steel door grades. (Source: Steel Door Institute, SDI 108-90, Table II)

BUILDING TYPES	STANDARD STEEL DOOR GRADES			DOOR THICKNESS		DOOR DESIGN NOMENCLATURE					
	GRADE I STANDARD DUTY 1¾" or 1⅜"	GRADE II HEAVY DUTY (1¾" ONLY)	GRADE III EXTRA HEAVY DUTY (1¾" ONLY)	1¾"	1¾" or 1⅜"	F	G	V	FG	N	L
APARTMENT											
MAIN ENTRANCE			•	•			•		•	•	
UNIT ENTRANCE	•	•		•		•					
BEDROOM	•				•	•					
BATHROOM	•				•	•					
CLOSET	•				•	•					•
STAIRWELL		•	•	•					•		
DORMITORY											
MAIN ENTRANCE			•	•			•		•	•	
UNIT ENTRANCE	•	•		•		•					
BEDROOM	•			•		•					
BATHROOM	•			•		•					
CLOSET	•				•	•					•
STAIRWELL		•	•	•					•		
HOTEL - MOTEL											
UNIT ENTRANCE	•	•		•		•					
BATHROOM	•				•	•					
CLOSET	•				•	•					•
STAIRWELL		•	•	•					•		
STORAGE & UTILITY	•	•		•		•					•
HOSPITAL - NURSING HOME											
MAIN ENTRANCE			•	•			•		•	•	
PATIENT ROOM		•		•		•					
STAIRWELL		•	•	•					•		
OPERATING & EXAM.		•	•	•		•					
BATHROOM	•			•		•					
CLOSET	•				•	•					•
RECREATION		•		•		•			•		
KITCHEN		•	•	•					•		
INDUSTRIAL											
ENTRANCE & EXIT			•	•			•		•	•	
OFFICE	•	•		•		•	•				
PRODUCTION		•		•		•					
TOILET		•	•	•		•					•
TOOL		•		•		•					
TRUCKING		•		•					•		
MONORAIL		•		•					•		
OFFICE											
ENTRANCE			•	•			•		•	•	
INDIVIDUAL OFFICE	•				•	•	•				
CLOSET	•				•	•					•
TOILET		•	•	•		•					
STAIRWELL		•	•	•					•		
EQUIPMENT		•	•	•		•					
BOILER		•	•	•		•					•
SCHOOL											
ENTRANCE & EXIT			•	•			•		•	•	
CLASSROOM		•		•			•			•	
TOILET		•	•	•		•					
GYMNASIUM		•	•	•		•		•			
CAFETERIA		•	•	•				•			
STAIRWELL		•	•	•					•		
CLOSET	•			•		•					•

Basic Door Designs

FLUSH (F)

HALF GLASS (G)

NARROW LITE (NL)

VISION LITE (V)

BOTTOM LOUVER (L)

DUTCH DOOR (D)

FULL GLASS (FG)

FULL LOUVER (FL)

INTERIORS

C1

Table 2. Wood door grades. (Source: Architectural Wood-work Quality Standards, 6th Ed. Version 1.1 1994)

Grade	Description
Economy:	This grade defines the minimum expectation of quality, workmanship, materials and installation of wood doors.
Custom:	This grade is specified for most conventional wood door fabrication. It provides a well defined degree of control over the quality of workmanship, materials and installation of wood doors.
Premium:	This grade is specified when the highest degree of control over the quality of workmanship, materials and installation of wood doors. It is usually reserved for doors in special projects, feature areas within a project, and high end commercial and monumental projects.

- face sizes
- fire resistance ratings
- sound (acoustical) ratings
- X-ray door lead thickness
- outer face material and thickness
- veneer matching
- internal construction
- light openings

• Grade (model)
- steel doors: standard, heavy and extra heavy duty (full flush or seamless design).
- wood doors: custom and premium (seam-free only).

• Door thickness:
- acoustical doors: 1-3/4 to 3 in. (4.5 to 7.5 cm).
- X-ray doors: 1-3/4 to 2-1/2 in. (4.5 to 6.4 cm).

• Face sizes:
- acoustical doors: maximum 4 ft. x 10 ft. (1.2 m x 3 m) singles.
- X-ray doors: maximum 4 ft. x 8 ft. (1.2 m x 2.4 m) singles, 8 ft. x 8 ft. (2.4 m x 2.4 m) pairs.

• Fire resistance ratings:
- Acoustical doors: varies from 20 minutes to 45 minutes (wood) and to 90 minutes (steel)
- X-ray doors: 20 minutes (wood) and up to 90 minutes (steel)

• Sound Transmission Class (STC) range available varies with door and frame construction and detailing
- Steel doors: 1-3/4 in. (up to 52), above 1-3/4 in. to 3 in. (52 to 55).
- Wood doors: 1-3/4 in. (37 to 45), 2-1/4 in. (47 to 51).

• X-ray door lead thickness
- Steel doors: 1/32 to 5/32 in. (0.8 to 4 mm).
- Wood doors; 1/32 to 1/2 in. (0.8 to 12.5 mm) when located at door center or from 1/32 to 1/8 in. (0.8 to 3 mm) when located immediately beneath outer face material on both sides of door.

• Outer face material and thickness
- Steel doors: hot or cold rolled steel sheet, galvanized steel sheet, stainless steel, bronze, or brass; 16-gage thickness.
- Wood doors: standard thickness hardwood face veneers overlaid with medium density overlay veneer, natural hardwood veneer, or plastic laminate directly applied to core construction, composed of two, three, or four plies having an overall approximate thickness of 1/16 in. (1.5 mm).

• Veneer matching
- Matching between individual pieces of veneer: book, slip, or random match.
- Assembly of spliced veneer on a face: sequence matching from opening to opening must be specified; examples include balanced, center balanced, and running matching.

• Internal construction
- Steel doors: unitized steel grid, vertical steel stiffeners, supplemented with acoustical damping materials.
- Wood doors: high density particleboard core at x-ray doors; combination of high density particleboard and acoustical damping materials at acoustical doors.

• Light openings

- Steel doors: STC ratings of up to 51 available for maximum single light size of 300 sq. in. (1935 sq. cm) in an 1-3/4 in. (4.5 cm) thick door.

- Wood doors: Typically light size not to exceed 40% of door area for both acoustical and X-ray doors.

3 Door finishing

This section includes selection data relevant to interior door finishing. Selection criteria for wood and carbon steel doors are discussed, as are substrate preparation, and the various grades and qualities of metal finishes.

Selection criteria

- Properties to be considered for wood and carbon steel door finishes include:

- Flow: the ease with which a coating can be applied. Too much flow will cause the coating to run, low flow may cause brush or roller marks.

- Leveling: the ability of a coating to smooth out after application.

- Film thickness: directly related to the degree of protection a coating will provide.

- Drying time: the period of time the coating may be subject to surface contamination.

- Permeability: the degree to which water vapor may migrate through the coating to an area of lower vapor pressure.

- Wetting: the maximum distance or penetration the vehicle is capable of delivering the coating on a specific surface. The lower the wetting ability the more thorough the surface preparation must be to ensure adequate adhesion.

- Type and degree of exposure to environmental factors such as:

- solar radiation

- humidity extremes

- temperature extremes

- polluted atmospheres

- chemicals

- Degree to which substrate is likely to deteriorate if coating fails.
- In service conditions changing over time.

- Cost considerations include:

- substrate preparation

- finish system application

Substrate preparation

- Unless the surface is in proper condition coatings will not:

- adhere well

- provide required protection

- have desired appearance

- Purpose of primers:

- to improve adhesion of the finish coating to the substrate

- Substrate condition:

- Surface contaminants and defects reduce adhesion of coating and may cause blistering, peeling, and flaking.

- Rusting nail holes, dents, and crevices need to be patched or filled.

- All particles clinging to the surface must be removed.

- Wood surfaces:

- Refer to selection criteria on Table 3 for finishes. The following issues should be considered:

- Fillers for open grain natural hardwood veneers, such as oak, are recommended to smooth out surface and to minimize absorption of topcoat; stain may be added to filler.

- Edges of doors should be sealed to prevent absorption of moisture.

Table 3. Wood door and frame interior finishes

Surface	Coating System	Topcoat: Type and Base	Principal Binder	Sheen (G,S,or F)	Substrate Condition (1,2,3,4)
MDO veneer and hardboard: 1st alternate	opaque; water or solvent	topcoat[2] primer	alkyd alkyd	G, S	3 1,3
MDO veneer and hardboard: 2nd alternate	opaque; water or solvent	topcoat[2] primer	acrylid (W) alkyd (S)	S	4 1,3
Natural hardboard veneer: 1st alternate	clear; solvent	topcoat[1]	alkyd conversion	G, S, F	1,3
Natural hardboard veneer: varnish (S) 2nd alternate	clear; solvent	topcoat[1]	urethane	G, S	1,3
Natural hardboard veneer: varnish (S) 3rd alternate	clear; water	topcoat[1]	conversion	G, S, F	1,3

Principal Binder: (W) Water; (S) Solvent
Sheen: (G) Glass; (S) Semi-gloss; (F) Flat
Substrate Surface Condition: (1) Average preparation; (2) Excellent preparation; (3) Dry only; (4) May be damp
[1]Two topcoats over compatible sealer over stain and filler (if desired)
[2]Two topcoats

- Wood may exhibit different degrees of absorption.

- Wood may contain water soluble dyes that may be released by moisture penetration.

- Wood must be dry before coating is applied.

- Wood should be sanded smooth, knots and resin streaks should be sealed with shellac.

• Veneer matching

- Matching between individual pieces of veneer: book, slip, or random match.

- Assembly of spliced veneer on a face: sequence matching from opening to opening must be specified; examples include balanced, center balanced, and running matching.

• Metal surfaces

- Refer to selection criteria on Tables 4-7 for finishes.

- The degree of surface preparation required and the methods used vary for different primers and top coats and may range from simple manual wire brushing to remove loose rust or mill scale, to extensive chemical treatments, grinding or blast cleaning.

- Cleaning methods for ferrous metals include mechanical and chemical methods:

- Mechanical methods include: hand cleaning; power tool cleaning; blast cleaning.

- Chemical methods include: solvent wiping and degreasing; alkali cleaning; steam cleaning; acid cleaning.

- Pretreatment methods for ferrous metals include: hot phosphate treatment; cold phosphate treatment; wash primers; zinc coating (primer required over wipe coat type galvanizing).

4   Door hardware

Door hardware finishes

• *General*

- Except for a comparatively few instances where plastics, woods, and ceramics are used, door hardware is made from metal.

- The finish of the metal must be carefully distinguished from the base metal.

- Some finishes can be obtained by electroplating on a dissimilar metal; for some finishes (such as chromium) this is the only method.

- A magnet can be used to detect iron or steel base metal beneath the plating.

• *Durability*

- The durability of the finish is greater on unplated metals, when the finishing process is applied directly to the base metal.

- Non-ferrous base metals and stainless steels finished in natural color are the most durable.

- Improvements in chromium plating make this a long lasting finish.

• *Base metal*

- Hardware base metal may be either cast, extruded, forged, or wrought (fabricated) from thin sheet material.

- Cast metals can be machined, etched, or carved to yield a great variety of designs.

- Extruded metals produce designs having linear characteristics.
- Forged metal is hammered, pressed, or rolled into shapes that are smooth and dense and whose serviceability is directly related to its thickness.

Table 4. Metal door and frame interior finishes

Surface	Coating System	Topcoat: Type and Base	Principal Binder	Sheen (G,S,or F)	Substrate Condition (1,2,3,4)
Primed carbon steel, hot or cold rolled: 1st alternate	opaque; solvent	topcoat	alkyd	G, S	4
Primed carbon steel, hot or cold rolled: 2nd alternate	opaque; water	topcoat	acrylic (W)	G	1, 3
Unprimed carbon steel, hot or cold rolled: 1st alternate	opaque; solvent	topcoat primer	alkyd	G, S, F	G, S, F 3 1, 3
Unprimed carbon steel, hot or cold rolled: 2nd alternate	opaque; water	topcoat primer	acrylic (W) alkyd	S, F	4 1,3
Carbon steel, galvanized and electro-zinc coated: 1st alternate	opaque; solvent	topcoat primer	alkyd zinc dust, zinc chromate	G, S, F	3
Carbon steel, galvanized and electro-zinc coated: 2nd alternate	opaque; solvent	topcoat	zinc dust, zinc chromate	F	3

Principal Binder: (W) Water; (S) Solvent
Sheen: (G) Glass; (S) Semi-gloss; (F) Flat
Substrate Surface Condition: (1) Average preparation; (2) Excellent preparation; (3) Dry only; (4) May be damp

Table 5. Aluminum door and frame interior finishes[1]

Classification	Thickness	Weight (Mils)	Application (Mg/sq. in.)
Architectural Class I	0.7 min.	27 min.	Interior architectural items subject to normal wear, and for exterior items that receive a minimal amount of cleaning and maintenance. Higher performing "hardcoat" Class I coatings may be achieved by increasing coating thickness to between 1 and 3 mils.
Architectural Class II	0.4 to 0.7	17 to 27	Interior items not subject to excessive wear or abrasion.

[1]Aluminum door and frame components are typically factory finished with some form of a protective, decorative, anodized, or organic coating. Anodic coatings are composed of aluminum oxide and are a part of the aluminum substrate. By carefully controlling the thickness, density, and hardness of the anodized coating, a substantial performance and durability improvement over lacquered and naturally developed oxide coatings can be achieved. Anodized coatings have limited color availability. Organic coatings are either baked on or air dried and are available in a great array of performance and durability levels as well as color selection. Factory applied and baked on organic coatings typically outperform air dried types. Some baked on, fluropolymer based, organic coatings outperform anodized coatings for color retention, chalk, and humidity resistance. Most organic coatings that are used for aluminum door and frame components should meet or exceed the requirements of AAMA 603.8 Pigmented Organic Coatings on Extruded Aluminum or AAMA 605.2 High Performance Organic Coatings on Architectural Extrusions and Panels. AAMA 605.2 is more stringent than AAMA 603.8. The two standard classification levels of architectural anodized coatings promulgated by the Aluminum Association (AA) and the National Association of Architectural Metal Manufacturers (NAAMM).

Table 6. Standard stainless steel door and frame finishes[1]

Designation	Description
No.1	Unpolished, rough dull surface produced by hot rolling followed by annealing and descaling.
No 2D	Unpolished, dull cold rolled finish produced by cold rolling followed by annealing and descaling.
No 2B	Unpolished, dull cold rolled finish produced by cold rolling followed by annealing and descaling.
No.3	Polish obtained by finishing with an approximately 100 grit abrasive.
No. 4	Bright polish finish obtained by finishing with an approximately 120 to 150 grit mesh abrasive yielding a distinctive grit lines (directional satin graining). Most commonly selected stainless steel finish.
No. 6	Soft satin polish finish obtained by Tampico brushing a No. 4 finish using medium abrasive.
No. 7	Highly reflective polish finish produced by buffing a surface that has first been finely ground but grit lines are not removed.
No. 8	Most commonly found, highest reflective, mirror polished finish produced by polishing with successively finer abrasives then buffing with a fine buffing compound. The final finish is essentially free of grit lines.

[1]Stainless steel door and frame components are typically selected where cleanliness, corrosion resistance or aesthetics are a primary concern. Type 304 is the most commonly used alloy for most applications, except where corrosion resistance is of major concern, in which case Type 316 is normally chosen. Satin polished finishes are typically chosen mainly due to its ease of maintenance, however, reflective polishes are often selected at monumental door entrances. The two standard finish designations are promulgated by the Architectural Metal Products Division of the National Association of Architectural Metal Manufacturers (NAAMM).

Table 7: Most common bronze and brass door and frame finishes[1]

Finish	Designation	Description and Method of Finishing
Buffed	M21-C12-06x	Mechanically buffed to mirror reflectivity by cutting with oxide or silicone carbide compounds followed by buffing with aluminum oxide buffing compounds, a chemical cleaning, and one or more coats of air dried, clear, organic lacquer for resistance of the finish to oxidation (tarnishing).
Directional	M31-C12-06x	Wheel or belt polished with aluminum oxide or silicone carbide abrasives of 180 to 240 grit followed by a chemical cleaning, and one or more coats of air dried, clear, organic lacquer for resistance of the finish to oxidation (tarnishing).

[1]Bronze or brass door and frame components are typically selected where aesthetics are a primary concern. Alloy 385 (yellow brassy cast) and 220 (red cast) are the most commonly used copper alloys. Directional textured (satin) finish is typically chosen mainly due to its ease of maintenance, however, buffed (mirror polished) finishes are often selected at monumental door entrances. Standard finish designations are promulgated by the Architectural Metal Products Division of the National Association of Architectural Metal Manufacturers (NAAMM).

INTERIORS

C1

- Wrought metal is rolled into flat sheets or strips and cut, punched, and bent into a desired form.

- Practically all metals used are alloys of two or more elements, and each manufacturer may vary the chemical composition of its alloys.

- Brass is essentially an alloy of copper and zinc.

- Technically, bronze is a copper-tin alloy; commercially, however, the term includes not only copper-tin alloys but also certain copper-zinc alloys having a typical bronze color. White bronze refers to a large number of copper-nickel-zinc alloys in which the copper predominates.

- Monel metal, a nickel copper alloy in which the nickel is 67%, is well known for its great durability and corrosion resistance.

- Aluminum is widely used as a hardware metal, with various alloys being employed to produce cast, wrought, extruded or forged members. Exposed surfaces are usually given an anodic treatment which produces a surface film that preserves the original color.

- Stainless steel is increasingly employed despite its relatively high cost. No surface treatment other than polishing or scouring is needed, nor is maintenance required to preserve this finish. Hardware fabricated from this metal is usually produced from sheets or extrusions, although some casting has been achieved. Its strength, durability, and resistance to corrosion make it highly desirable for heavy-duty use.

• *Standard finishes*

The Builder's Hardware Manufacturers Association (BHMA) standard A156.18-1993 lists 122 finishes. The BHMA code assigns separate numbers to finishes applied to each separate base material except when brass or bronze can be used without affecting the final finish. Comparative finishes should match when viewed approximately 2 ft. (60 cm) apart and 3 ft. (90 cm) away on the same plane and under the same lighting conditions. BHMA categories are defined as follows:

- Category A: Those finishes that match BHMA match plates when viewed according to the formula described above.

- Category B: Those finishes that are unstable and vary when applied to different alloys and forms of base material. These finishes are compatible with the BHMA match plates, but these finishes cannot and do not match from one alloy or form of material to the next and from one manufacturer to the next.

- Category C: Includes ornamental finishes found on all forms of material. The material is blackened or oxidized then relieved or highlighted, usually by hand. Aesthetically, it is not desirable that they match but they shall be compatible.

- Category D: Functional protective finishes where appearance is not a factor.

- Category E: Those finishes which are equivalent in appearance only when compared with the corresponding Category A BHMA match plate and viewed under the formula described above.

• *Handing of hardware*

- Doors are either right or left hand; the locks and latches may be reverse bevel. Handing is normally determined in accordance with the conventions indicated above in Fig. 1.

- Hardware can be handed in three main ways, universal, reversible, and handed: Universal can be used in any position such as a door stop. Reversible can have the hand changed by revolving from left to right, by turning upside down, or by reversing some part of the mechanism such as can be found on certain mortised and bored locks and latchsets. Handed (not reversible) can be used only on doors of the hand for which that hardware is designed such as can be found with beveled or rabbeted lock fronts.

- For most doors the hand is determined from the outside. The outside is the side from which security is necessary. In a series of connecting rooms, such as in a hotel suite, the outside will be the side of each successive door as you come to it proceeding from the entrance in. For two rooms of equal importance with a passage in between, the outside is the passage side.

• *Hinge types*

There are four basic types of hinges (Fig. 2):

- full mortise

- half mortise

- full surface

- half surface

- Within each type there is a variety of styles, each designed for a particular use. In addition there are other design types, such as olive knuckle, pivot, concealed, and paumelle.

- A butt hinge is a hinge which is designed to be mortised into the butt edge of a door and into the rabbet of a door frame.

- Hinges are available in wrought steel, brass, bronze, stainless steel, and aluminum; non-ferrous hinges should be equipped with stainless steel pins.

- Hinge pins may be ordered with button, hospital, ball, steeple, or other decorator tips.

- Bearings may be plain, ball, oil-impregnated, or nylon anti-friction; plain bearings should not be used for heavy doors or those equipped with door closing devices.

• *Hinge quantity*

The number of hinges per door varies with the height of the door; generally a minimum of three per door is recommended but two may suffice for doors up to 5 ft.-0 in.(1.5 m) high. Three are recommended for doors between 5 ft.-0 in.(1.5 m) and 7 ft.-6 in.(2.25 m) high; and one additional hinge for each additional 30 in.(75 cm) of height. Size of hinges depends on the weight of the door, width of the door, and the frequency of use, refer to Table 8 for hinge size recommendations.

• *Locks*

Locks are one of the more important categories of door hardware (Fig. 3). The names used for locks originally were selected to identify either the type of construction or installation. Considering the great variety of functions, types, sizes, weights, security and convenience features of locks, considerable experience is required to fully understand how to select the proper lock for a particular application. The locks most commonly used in all types of construction are discussed below.

- Bored: These types of locks are installed in a door having two round holes at right angles to one another, one through the face of the door to hold the lock body, and the other in the edge of the door to receive the latch mechanism. Bored type locks have the keyway and/or locking device, such as push or turn buttons, in the knobs or levers. They are made in three service grades: 1 (heavy), 2 (medium), and 3 (light) duty. Regular backsets for this lock type can vary from 2-3/8 in.(6 cm) to 42 in.(1 m).

- Preassembled: The preassembled type lock is installed in a rectangular notch cut into the door edge. This lock has all the parts assembled as a unit at the factory, and when installed little or no disassembly is required. Like bored locks, preassembled locks have the keyway in the knob or lever. Locking devices are in the knob or inner case. They are made in one service grade (Grade 1 heavy) and have a standard backset of 2-3/4 in.(7 cm).

- Mortised: A mortise lock is installed in a prepared recess (mortise) in a door. The working mechanism is contained in a rectan-

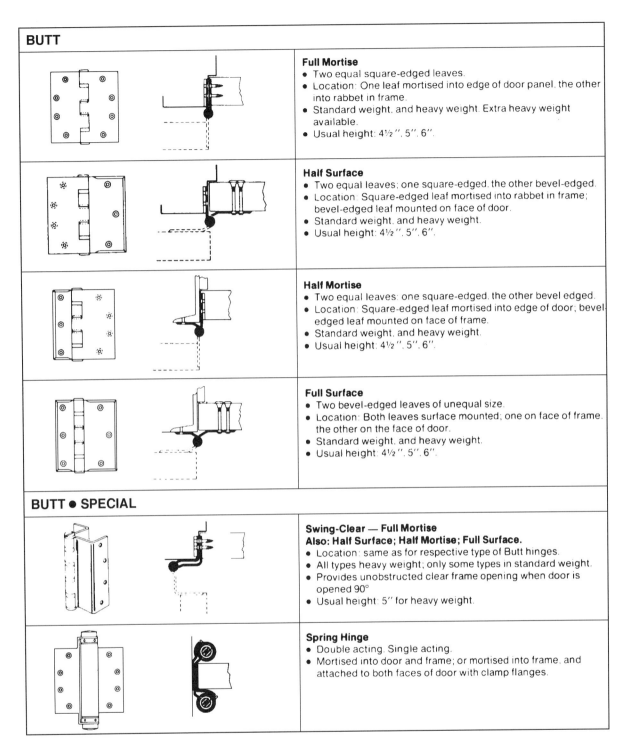

BUTT

Full Mortise
- Two equal square-edged leaves.
- Location: One leaf mortised into edge of door panel, the other into rabbet in frame.
- Standard weight, and heavy weight. Extra heavy weight available.
- Usual height: 4½″, 5″, 6″.

Half Surface
- Two equal leaves; one square-edged, the other bevel-edged.
- Location: Square-edged leaf mortised into rabbet in frame; bevel-edged leaf mounted on face of door.
- Standard weight, and heavy weight.
- Usual height: 4½″, 5″, 6″.

Half Mortise
- Two equal leaves; one square-edged, the other bevel edged.
- Location: Square-edged leaf mortised into edge of door; bevel-edged leaf mounted on face of frame.
- Standard weight, and heavy weight.
- Usual height: 4½″, 5″, 6″.

Full Surface
- Two bevel-edged leaves of unequal size.
- Location: Both leaves surface mounted; one on face of frame, the other on the face of door.
- Standard weight, and heavy weight.
- Usual height: 4½″, 5″, 6″.

BUTT • SPECIAL

Swing-Clear — Full Mortise
Also: Half Surface; Half Mortise; Full Surface.
- Location: same as for respective type of Butt hinges.
- All types heavy weight; only some types in standard weight.
- Provides unobstructed clear frame opening when door is opened 90°
- Usual height: 5″ for heavy weight.

Spring Hinge
- Double acting. Single acting.
- Mortised into door and frame; or mortised into frame, and attached to both faces of door with clamp flanges.

Fig. 2. Door hinge types (Source: *Sweet's Catalog File Selection Data* 1993 by permission of McGraw-Hill)

INTERIORS   C1

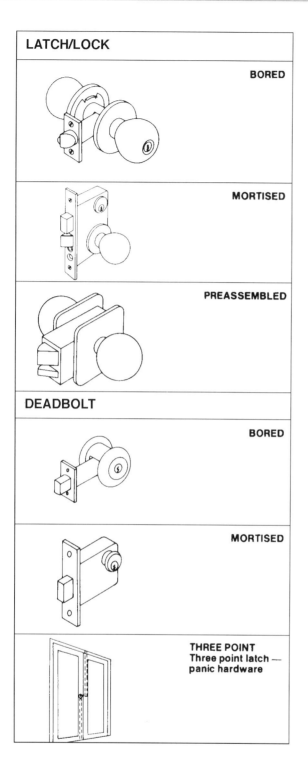

Fig. 3. Door lock types and uses (Source: *Sweet's Catalog File Selection Data* **1993 by permission of McGraw-Hill)**

gular shaped case with appropriate holes into which the required components, cylinder, knob or lever, and turn piece spindles are inserted to complete the working assembly. They are typically only available in one service grade (Grade 1 heavy) and have a standard backset of 2-3/4 in.(7 cm).

- *Exit devices*

- An exit device is a locking or latching device that may always be released by depressing a cross or touch bar. It is sometimes called a panic bolt, exit bolt, panic device, or panic exit hardware; however exit device is the preferred term.

- Doors in public buildings that are used for egress purposes, such as exterior doors from a corridor, usually are required by the governing building code to be equipped with exit devices.

- There are four types of exit devices: rim, mortise, surface vertical rod, and concealed vertical rod.

- Since all functions are not available in each type, individual exit device manufacturers should be contacted for availability.

- *Door plates*

- The purpose of push, mop, kick, armor, and stretcher plates is to protect the surface finish of the door from the impact of items such as carts, finger rings, shoes or cleaning mops.

- Plates should be fabricated from corrosion resistant material and have beveled edges.

- Plates should be a minimum of 0.050 in. (1.25 mm) thick. Mop plates are typically 4 in.(10 cm) high, kick plates 8 in.(20 cm) to 16 in. (40 cm) high, armor plates to 42 in. (1 m) high, and stretcher plates 6 in. (15 cm) to 12 in. (30 cm) high. Push plates should be 8 in. (20 cm) wide x 16 in. (40 cm) high.

- *Door bolts*

- Nearly all bolts fall into one of two categories, flush or surface.

- The lever operated extension flush bolt is used widely for fastening the inactive leaf of a pair of doors.

- Surface bolts are simpler to install as they require no mortising but they typically provide less security.

- Many variations of bolts are produced and designed for specific purposes.

- *Door closers*

- A door closer, when properly installed and adjusted, should control the door throughout the opening and closing wings (Fig. 4).

- It combines three basic components: (1) a power source to close the door; (2) a checking source to control the rate at which the door closes; and (3) a connecting component (arm) that transmits the closing force from the door to the frame.

Table 8. Hinge size recommendations

Door Thickness (inches)	Door Width	Minimum Hinge Height (inches)
7/8" or 1"	any	2-1/2" std. wgt.
1-1/8"	to 36"	3" std. wgt.
1-3/8"	to 36"	3-1/2" std. wgt.
1-3/8"	over 36"	4" std. wgt.
1-3/4"	to 41"	4-1/2" std. wgt.
1-3/4"	over 41"	4-1/2" heavy wgt.
1-3/4"to 2-1/4"	any	5" heavy wgt.*

* to be used for heavy doors of high frequency or unusual stress

- In all modern closers, the source of power is a spring, while the checking action is achieved by a hydraulic mechanism. The spring and checking mechanism are connected to a common shaft, and arms attached to this shaft act as linkage to communicate movement between the door and mechanism.

- In addition to serving as linkage, the arms (through leverage) can amplify the power of the spring, providing maximum power at the latch point.

- The closing speed is controlled by an adjustable valve or valves which regulate the flow of hydraulic fluid.

- Additional features for safety and convenience also are available in many types of closers. These include backcheck, delayed action, adjustable spring power, and a variety of hold-open functions.

- Door closers may be surface mounted or concealed in the door, frame, or floor. Surface mounted and concealed in the door are used exclusively for single acting doors, while floor closers and frame concealed closers may be used either for single or double acting doors.

- Floor closers and frame-concealed closers for single-acting doors may be either offset or center hung. For double-acting doors these closers are always center hung.

- Doors utilizing center hung closers, whether single- or double-acting, must be installed with pivots that are provided as a component of the closer assembly.

- For single-acting offset installations pivots may be a component part of the mechanism or the door may be independently hung on hinges or pivots.

- Electromagnetic and pneumatic door closers that are capable of holding open fire and smoke doors have virtually eliminated fusible link door closers, which most jurisdictions no longer accept in areas of human occupancy. These fail-safe, UL listed devices provide a means for holding open the door in any position, allowing it to be released manually as well as by a smoke detector.

- *Hospital door hardware*

Hardware for hospitals and other health-related institutions includes items that might not be found in any other type of building. This is because this building type is utilized by people who are aged, infirm, sick, or disabled, all of which may have a need to operate hardware with the least amount of effort.

- Hinges: Modifications of hinges may include hospital tips for added safety and ease of sanitation, special length and shape of leaves to swing doors clear of an opening, and hinges of special sizes and gages to carry the weight of lead-lined doors. Pivot hinges, pivot sets, and floor closers are furnished of special construction to swing doors with lead lining, which are often extremely heavy.

- Lead-lined door hardware: Lead lining of complete areas, including doors and frames, prevents exposure to harmful rays. If lead is removed when hardware preparations are made, then lead shielding must be applied to the hardware. Surface-mounted hardware may be put into place with lead washers or plugs under the screw heads. Mortise locksets or deadlocks may be furnished with a lead wrapped case. Bored type locks may have the latch unit lead wrapped. In all cases the trim involved may be lead lined or lead filled.

- Hospital pulls: Designed to be mounted with the open end down to allow the door to be operated by the wrist, arm, or forearm when the hands are occupied. On non-self-closing doors these pulls are sometimes mounted back-to-back with a push plate behind the pull for door protection. Sometimes the push plate will have

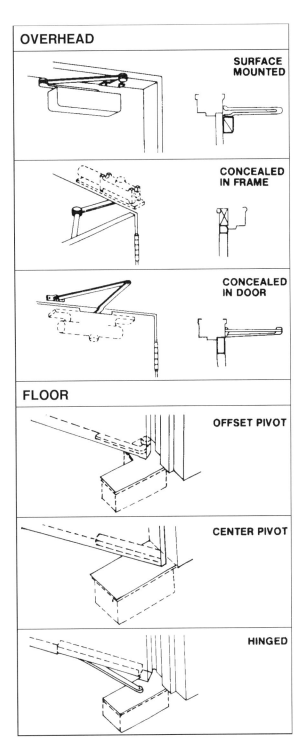

Fig. 4. Door closures types and uses (Source: *Sweet's Catalog File Selection Data* 1993 by permission of McGraw-Hill)

INTERIORS C1

an offset at the bottom of the plate so that it may be used as a combination push and pull.

- Door protection: Door protection in hospitals is essential. In addition to normal usage, hospital doors are subject to abuse from wheelchairs, rolling beds, stretchers, and all types of carts. Hand operated and mechanized cleaning machinery may cause damage. In several areas of a hospital it is not unusual to have several protective plates, such as mop, kick, armor, or stretcher, as well as edgings, on particular doors.

• *Key control systems*

- A key control system is by definition an organization of keys within a unit of cabinets in order to regulate the use of and assign responsibility for each individual key in the system.

- The system itself consists of a choice of small, medium, or large capacity cabinets or drawers that include key hooks, key markers, receipt holders, and cross indexed file cards for identification purposes.

- The management of the system requires the appointment of responsible people to issue, record, receive, and maintain the keys filed. It is desirable to furnish such systems complete with keys affixed to hooks and all cards properly organized.

• *Door holders and stops*

- A door should be controlled at the desired limit of its opening cycle in order to prevent damage to an adjacent wall, column, equipment, the door, or its hardware. This control is achieved by stops and holders, which may located at the floor, wall, or overhead.

• *Electro-magnetic holders and smoke detectors*

- Magnetic door holders may be used legally to hold open fire doors and smoke barrier doors, whereas holders discussed above under section "Door holders and stops" may not.

- Magnetic holders are occasionally used on security doors, which may or may not be fire rated or smoke doors.

- Magnetic holders are available with varying projections between the wall and the door at the hold-open position to accommodate various construction conditions. Floor models are also available for single doors or two doors, back to back, but these should be considered only when the construction details preclude the use of floor models.

- Magnetic door holders must be connected to the fire alarm system or smoke detectors or both when they are used on an opening that is fire rated or is a smoke door assembly.

- The rules concerning the location and the specifics of the interfacing connection will vary somewhat depending on the local authority having jurisdiction. There also must be an approved device for closing smoke barrier doors and in the case of fire-rated doors, for latching them.

• *Miscellaneous hardware*

- There are many items of hardware, not necessarily related to doors, which usually are required on most building projects.

- These are items that are included to avoid incomplete installation with the consequent necessity for additional work involving added expense and inconvenience.

- These items typically include: padlocks and hasps, coat hooks, thresholds, cylinders for rolling garage doors, stair gate closers, gasketing, alarm devices, chain locks, slide bolts, door knockers, and silencers.

• *Sliding door hardware*

- Sliding doors cover a wide range, from the tiny closet or cabinet door moved by the light touch of a finger, to enormous installations of a ton or more, motor driven, and put in place only with the assistance of a factory trained mechanic.

- There is a variety of architectural hardware used in connection with these doors including not only track and hanger assemblies but appurtenant hardware such as stops, pulls, guides, and latches or locks.

- Heavy industrial doors are usually of the bi-parting variety; they meet in the center of the opening and are hung to lap the opening.

- Residential and institutional sliding doors may be bypassing, bi-parting, bi-folding, pocket or overhead types. The selection is based on the use intended and/or the space available.

- The critical points to consider in selecting hardware for these doors are load-bearing capacity of the track and hanger assembly, the anti-friction feature of the hanger wheels, wall and ceiling construction, and attachment.

- Quieter operation is likely if hanger wheels are of nylon composition and have ball, roller, or oil-impregnated bearings.

References

American Architectural Manufacturers Association, 1827 Walden Office Square, Suite 104, Schaumburg, IL 60173-4268; 847-303-5664 (phone); 847-303-5774 (fax).

Architectural Woodwork Institute, 13924 Braddock Road, Suite 100, Centerville, VA; 703-222-1100 (phone); 703-222-2499 (fax).

Builder's Hardware Manufacturers Association, 355 Lexington Avenue, 17th Floor, New York, NY 10017-6603; 212-661-4261 (phone)

Door and Hardware Institute, 14170 New Brook Drive, Chantilly, VA 22021-2223; 703-222-2010 (phone); 703-222-2410 (fax).

National Association of Architectural Metal Manufacturers, 8 S. Michigan Ave., Suite 1000, Chicago, IL 60603-3305; 312-456-5590 (phone); 312-580-0165 (fax).

National Fire Protection Association, One Batterymarch Park, Quincy, MA 02269-9101, 800-344-3555 (phone); 617-984-7057 (fax).

National Wood Window and Door Association, 1400 E. Touhy Avenue, Suite G-54, Des Plaines, IL 60018; 800-223-2301 (phone).

Steel Door Institute, 30200 Detroit Road, Cleveland, OH 44145-1967; 216-899-0010 (phone); 216-892-1404 (fax).

Johnson Controls Office, Salt Lake City. Douglas Drake, AIA and Donald Watson, FAIA. 1984.

Flexible office infrastructure

Summary: Flexible infrastructures improve workplace productivity, environmental quality and energy efficiency and facilitate reconfiguration of space and technology in contemporary buildings, including user choices for fresh air, temperature control, daylight and view, light control, work group choices with privacy options, network access and ergonomic furniture.

Key words: energy efficiency, environmental quality, ergonomics, flexible grid, infrastructure, productivity.

Uniformat:	C1010
	C1030
MasterFormat:	10150

The state of the art in advanced workplaces

To address issues of long-term productivity and organizational effectiveness, it is time to move beyond definitions of code compliant buildings and even "high tech" buildings, to the creation of truly "motivational" buildings. Motivational buildings provide environmental performance at a level that consistently and reliably ensures health, comfort, security and financial effectiveness, while supporting high levels of productivity with continuing organizational and technological change. In contrast to present practice, motivational buildings rely on guarantees that every building occupant, at their individual workstation, will be supplied with critical infrastructural services:

- Basic infrastructures every occupant/workstation needs individually:
- fresh air.
- temperature control.
- lighting control.
- daylight and view, reduced isolation from outdoors.
- privacy and working quiet.
- network access, multiple data, power, voice connections.
- ergonomic furniture.
- environmentally appropriate finishes.

Johnson Controls coined the term "Quality Built Environments" to describe the necessity for productive environments that attract the best workforce, offer personalized infrastructure and control, and support continuous change in organizational and technological configurations through infrastructure flexibility. What is actually supplied at the workstation in old and new buildings, however, does not mirror this obvious list of environmental and technical needs for today's workers. Since the 1950's, we have been investing the minimum amount possible in our hidden building infrastructures, from least-cost thermal zoning to minimum lighting control to jerry-rigged network connections.

- What every occupant/workstation actually gets collectively:
- variable air supply, dependent on thermal demand.
- blanket supply of cooling, large zones for 15 people average.
- uniform, high-level lighting.

- rare daylight and view, isolation from outdoors.
- rare working quiet and privacy control.
- one data connection, non relocatable.
- 2-power connections, non relocatable.
- one-voice connection, non relocatable.
- pre-computers furniture, non ergonomic.
- unmeasured indoor pollutant sources, including increasing electromagnetic radiation (EMR).

Two conditions in present facilities combine to make the inadequacies of "least-cost" building infrastructure even worse today. First, there is a rapid increase in desktop technology, each requiring multiple connections to data, power and voice networks and increased cooling. Second, there is a rapid exploration of new space planning concepts to reflect new organizational structures and "teaming" work approaches, which radically redistributes the density of workstations, equipment and space enclosures (Fig. 1).

The least-cost, "blanket" conditioning and networking offered in present day buildings emphatically cannot accommodate these organizational changes. Indeed, new technologies and new space planning concepts are introduced into buildings often without any modification of the building's base systems—cooling, ventilation, lighting, networking, or ceiling/acoustics—with disastrous results. In corporate eagerness to try new organizational concepts, there is little corresponding discussion of the need for each workstation to sustain key independent services, with serious concerns and failures occurring with each spatial renovation.

- New technologies and new space planning concepts: potential stresses in existing subsystem and service infrastructures:
- Cooling and thermal quality: capacitance, diffuser grid density and location, control.
- Ventilation and air quality: zoning, diffuser grid density and location, control.
- Lighting and visual quality: grid density and location, control.

Authors: Vivian Loftness, AIA and Volker Hartkopf, Ph.D.

Credits: This article is adapted from "Flexible Infrastructure for Environmental Quality, Productivity, and Energy Effectiveness in the Office of the Future" by Vivian Loftness, AIA, Volker Hartkopf, Ph.D., Ardeshir Mahdavi, Ph.D., Jayakrishna Shankavaram, and Stephen Lee, AIA. Center for Building Performance and Diagnostics (CBPD), Department of Architecture, Carnegie Mellon University. The study was funded by USA CERL and the Advanced Building Systems Integration Consortium (ABSIC) and CBPD.

References: ABSIC. 1988-1997. *Field Studies of Advanced Technology and Intelligent Buildings: Research Report Series.* Advanced Building Systems Integration Consortium (ABSIC) Pittsburgh, PA: Carnegie Mellon University, Center for Building Performance and Diagnostics.

Additional references are listed at the end of this article.

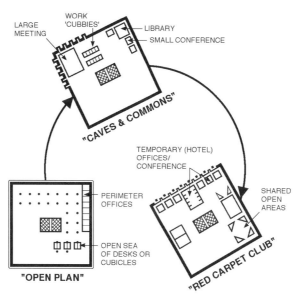

Fig. 1. Dynamic organizations need the ability to continuously reconfigure workplace types over time and space.

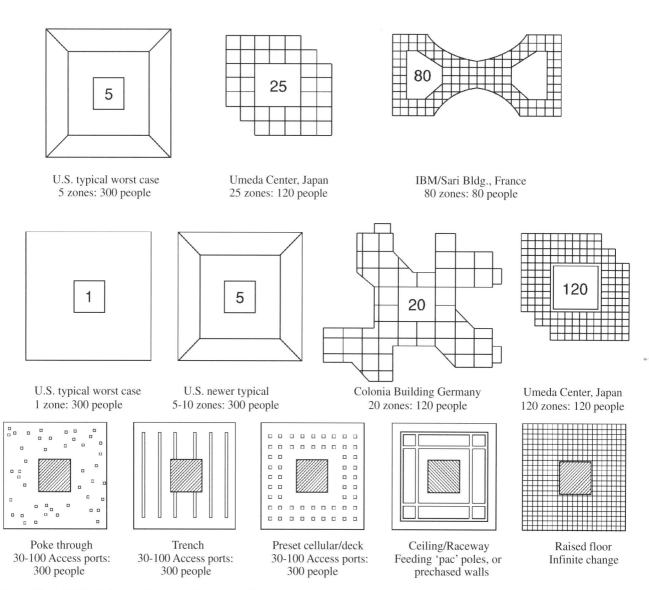

Fig. 2. Most U.S. buildings suffer from large undifferentiated zones for "blanket" heating, ventilation and cooling, "blanket" lighting, and "blanket" networking, with serious system and performance failures occurring with each spatial renovation (ABSIC International Studies 1988-1993).

- Access to window, building enclosure control.

- Rank, territoriality and personalization.

- Voice connectivity.

- Data connectivity.

- Power connectivity.

- Wall systems, spatial modification and material reuse.

- Ceiling systems and closure, acoustics and light.

- Work storage and access.

If fixed, open plan concepts such as "universal" or box/cubicle workstations are adequately serviced for each occupant at the outset (not a given), the potential stresses in relation to existing systems and services will be low. However, if dynamic workplace concepts are being considered, if an organization is intended to evolve in size, mission and structure, or if workspaces are being planned for changing tenant

users and equipment densities, then major shifts in the selection of HVAC, lighting, enclosure, and networking subsystems and service must be pursued (Fig. 2).

Design approaches to absorb change and avoid obsolescence
User-based infrastructures are modular, reconfigurable, and expandable for all key services: ventilation air, thermal conditioning, lighting, data/voice and power networks. The dynamic reconfigurations of space and technology typical in buildings today cannot be accommodated through the existing service infrastructure, neither the "blanket systems" for uniform open-plan configurations or the idiosyncratic systems for unique configurations. Instead what is needed are flexible infrastructures capable of changing location and density of service. Flexible Grid - Flexible Density - Flexible Closure Systems are a constellation of building subsystems that permit each individual (or workstation) to set the location and density of HVAC, lighting, telecommunications, and furniture, and the level of workspace enclosure (ABSIC/CERL 1993).

Table 1. Choices in zoning and individual control in flexible infrastructures.

Heating, Cooling and Ventilation Systems

Selection of Mechanical System Type
Zone Size, Density and Location of Diffusers
   Micro-Zoning, a zone per Workstation
   Floor/Furniture Based Air Supply Systems, or
   Flexible-Grid, Flexible-Density Ceiling HVAC
   Increase Supply and Return Air Densities, relocatable

Separating the Ventilation from Thermal Conditioning
   Task-Driven Ventilation or Constant-Volume Ventilation
   Water-Based Thermal Conditioning & Air Based Ventilation
   Displacement Ventilation
   Radiant Heating and Cooling
   Thermal Load Balancing

Controls
   Air Speed, Volume , and Temperature Controls
   Density and Location of Diffuser Control
   Outside Air Content and Filtration Controls; Purge Cycles

Lighting and Daylighting Systems

Fixture Efficiency/Efficacy

High Level, Ceiling-Based, Task-Ambient Lighting
   Uniform and Non-Uniform Task-Ambient
   Density and Location of Task-Ambient Fixtures
   Direct and Indirect Lighting
   Lighting Zones: Density of On-Off or Dimming Controllers
Relocatable and Individually Controllable Systems

Low-Level Ambient Lighting with Controllable Task Lights at the Workstation
   Design of Ambient Lighting and Contrast Glare
   Density & Location of Task Lights Directional & Occupancy Controls

Effective Daylight Utilization
   Light Shelves, Diffusers, Reflectors and Lenses
   Building Surface/Volume and Orientation
   Room Configuration
   Effective Electric Lighting Interfaces & Controls

Enclosure Systems

Environmental Contact for the Individual
   Increased Building Periphery, Windows & Views
   Access to Open Air Landscaped Areas for Work and R&R

Sunlight and Daylight - the Layered Facade
   High Visible Transmission Glass with Light Redirection Devices
   Sunshading: Exterior, Interior and Integral Devices
   Lighting System Interfaces and Controls

Thermal Balancing Facades
   Reduced MRT Differentials, Infiltration and Conductive Losses
   High Performance Facades- High R, Low S.C.
   Air Flow Windows and Water Flow Mullions
   Photovoltaic and Thermal Storage Facades
   Double Envelope Facades

Natural Ventilation and the Open Window

Electrical & Telecommunication Systems

The Merging of Data, Voice, Video,
and Environmental Sensors & Controls into Networking Systems

Network Neighborhoods and Satellite Closets
Homerun, Star Horizontal Network Configurations
Increased Horizontal Plenums: Floor, Ceiling, Furniture, Wireless
Power Quantity, Quality, Reduced Interference, Reconfigurable,
   Relocatable, Expandable Outlet Boxes for
   Data, Power, Voice, Video and more.
Changing Workstation Peripherals/Desktop Hardware
Shared Equipment & Social Centers
Teaming/Conferencing Networks and Spaces
Individual Controls and Energy Management
Recyclability and Resource Management

EXISTING SERVICE/UTILITY

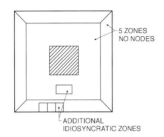

CONCEPT OF GRID & NODES

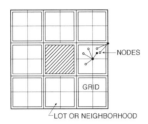

Fig. 3. The dynamics of technology, workstation density and teaming concepts make large zones less capable of delivering adequate environmental quality than do neighborhood and individual zones.

These services could be split ambient and task systems where users set task requirement and the central system responds with the appropriate ambient conditions, or they can be fully relocatable task systems such as those we enjoy in our home or car. The Advanced Buildings Systems Integration Consortium, a university-industry-government effort to improve building performance, has begun to identify a range of existing and innovative building subsystem configurations that will support long term environmental, technical and physical quality in each individual workstation in the face of rapid change (Table 1).

We need to move beyond embedded technologies in buildings to end user technologies. Both the next generation of new buildings and the re-valuing of existing buildings must explore the attributes of micro-zoning and user modifiable systems - through neighborhood service grids and individual user responsive nodes. The manufacturers of building components and subsystems will have to develop products that are compatible in open architectural systems, user modifiable, expandable and relocatable through modularity, and support multiple vendor plug-in capability.

The concept of grids and nodes: ensuring seven basic needs of each individual.

Flexible user-based infrastructures ensure that each occupant in a building will have access to all the basic needs for a healthy, productive workplace: air quality, temperature control, daylight and view, electric light control, privacy and working quiet, network access and ergonometric furniture. This access can only be provided by a shift away from centrally controlled infrastructures to the concept of grids and nodes (Fig. 3 and Table 2).

Table 2. Individual workstation-based provisions for ventilation, cooling, heating, lighting, data, power, voice would ensure that each worker has environmental and technical service regardless of organizational and workplace dynamics.

Services Needed at Workgroup	Services Needed at Workstation
HORIZONTAL	
Grids	**Nodes**
Data	Data Outlets (1-4 per person)
Voice	Voice Outlets (1-2)
Video	Video Outlets (1)
Power	Power Outlets (1-10)
Structural Columns	Structural Beams
Furniture	Worksurface: Horizontal + Vertical
Ceiling Grid	Ceiling Tiles
Ambient Lighting	Lighting Fixtures (1-6)
Floor Grid	Floor Tiles
Thermal Service	Diffusers/Radiators (1-6)
Plumbing	Kitchenettes
Security	Doors
Fire	Sprinklers
Environmental Control/Zones	Sensor/Controllers (1-4)
Acoustic/Sound System	Speakers, Acoustic Materials
Windows	Viewing Cone
Core to Shell Distance	Wayfinding, Access to Vert. Service
VERTICAL	
Floor to Floor Height	Horizontal Plenum Size and Access
Horiz. Plenum: Ceiling, Floor, Furniture	Size and Access to Services
Floor to Ceiling Height	Light & Air Distrib., Service Access
Panel/Wall Height	Light & Air Distrib., Service Access

The grids establish the overall capacity available to support the working group or neighborhood (fresh air, cooling, power and network capacitance, given maximum occupant densities). The nodes must be flexible in terms of location, density, and type of service offered. These grids and nodes should not be dealt with in isolation but as compatible assemblies and in some cases integrated systems. "Plug and play" technologies developed in non-building markets assume distributed capability, user differences in customization, and the ability for end users to help themselves if systems are not meeting requirements.

1 Fresh air for each individual.

Three approaches are described by which to provide individualized fresh air supply.

- Split thermal and ventilation systems.
- User control of fresh air quantities; purge cycles.
- Operable windows with thermal balancing facades.

Split thermal and ventilation systems: There are advantages to separating thermal conditioning from ventilation/breathing air supply, in both central and task-air systems. With a constant volume of 100% outside air for ventilation needs only (potentially conditioned to appropriate temperatures and humilities), much smaller ducts can be utilized with a guarantee of adequate amounts of outside air regardless of season and internal thermal loads. Since air is an inefficient thermal transport media, the constant volume ventilation system can be coupled with a wider range of energy-efficient thermal conditioning options (beyond the traditional air-based systems), such as water based heat pumps, fan-coils, radiant heating and radiant cooling systems, and load balancing facades (which use waste heat to eliminate perimeter heating loads.) In the Intelligent Workplace Laboratory at Carnegie Mellon University (Loftness et al. 1995b), a constant volume ventilation system and operable windows is combined with a variety of water-based thermal conditioning systems (water flow mullions, radiant ceilings, and water cooled equipment systems) for thermal comfort and air quality, as well as energy efficiency, through load balancing and user control (Fig. 4). Pursuing an all-air approach, the Hines Development Interests have introduced dual duct systems splitting ventilation and cooling in a Texas tenant office building to guarantee long term air quality, system reliability, and improved energy efficiencies. They consider that the modest increased costs of these split thermal and ventilation systems contribute significantly to their 97% occupancy rates in a competitive real estate market.

Operable windows: The separation of ventilation air from thermal conditioning also enables operable windows to be re-introduced in buildings (Fig. 5). While a dedicated constant volume ventilation system guarantees the needed levels of outside air at the desk, the separate thermal conditioning system can be shut off to avoid unnecessary heating and cooling. In the Ministry of Finance and Budget in Paris, a constant volume supply of 100% outside air (unconditioned) ensures ventilation requirements regardless of the outdoor wind conditions. When occupants open windows to cope with local overheating and indoor air stagnation, or to enjoy the outdoors, the perimeter fan coil units (for thermal conditioning only) will shut off to avoid energy waste while the constant volume ventilation air supply continues. A split system offers significant gains for ensuring thermal comfort and air quality, increasing energy efficiency through zoning and load matching, as well as reopening the opportunities for operable windows in the workplace - critical to both perceived and actual comfort and air quality.

Local control of ventilation rates and purge cycles: User control of fresh air quantities will allow local response to high pollutant loads, high occupancies, smokers, and individual user demands, without reducing the effectiveness of the overall system. In the IBM Headquar-

Fig. 4. Excess heat from equipment and lights can be pumped piped through internal water-flow mullions by Gartner Industries, eliminating the need for perimeter heating. (Intelligent Workplace).

Fig. 5. In the Ministry of Finance, Paris, operable windows provide fresh air, but reduce energy waste by shutting off the perimeter heating/ cooling unit when the nearby window is open. (ABSIC).

Fig. 6. Introduction of one fan-coil per person, providing a highly modularized HVAC system. IBM/Sari-France, Ministry of Finance, France. (ABSIC).

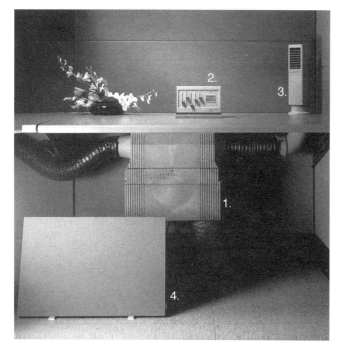

Fig. 7. Personalized Environmental Module (PEM™), developed by Johnson Controls, permits individual control of task air temperature, air speed and air direction. Key: (1) mixing box, (2) control panel, (3) desktop diffuser, (4) radiant panel.

ters in Paris, the facility manager can independently set the outside air content for each workstation, as a result of the provision of a fan-coil unit per workstation (bundled into four mechanical rooms per floor) fed by significant quantities of outside air. In addition, the system has allowed IBM to install a 5-minute "purge" button for each workstation, so that individuals can call for 100% outside air for a five-minute period to clear the air as needed after intense working (or cleaning) sessions.

2   *Temperature control for each individual.*

• Decreased zone size to one zone per person.

• User control of air temperature, air direction, air speed.

• User control of radiant temperature.

• Split ambient and task temperature control.

Decreased zone size: A majority of thermal failures in occupied buildings are the result of oversized thermal and ventilation zones, with only "blanket' or large zone control. While justified by budget restrictions, the consequence can be much higher operational costs, high levels of dissatisfaction, and increasing instances of building related illnesses. The most valuable step towards providing increased comfort is to a higher level of zoning ensuring environmental conditions for work groups no greater than 4-6 people, with capability for some level of individual control.

User control of air temperature: The most prevalent example of individual control over supply air temperature is found in perimeter conditioning systems such as fan-coil units, heat pumps and induction units (Fig. 6) In each of these systems, the user can set supply air temperature, either through water flow control or air mixing control. The introduction of these temperature control alternatives, with a maximum band of +/- 2°C has eliminated calls to facilities management about overheating and drafts. Whenever large numbers of individuals are calling for maximum heating or cooling, the central system can respond with modified supply air or supply water temperatures. The combination of workstation-based thermal conditioning systems (driven by occupancy presence) with ambient thermal systems, set to much broader standards of comfort, can yield maximum energy savings to accompany the gains in individual comfort.

User control of air speed and volume: Unlike ceiling distribution systems, many of the floor and furniture based air supply systems do provide user control of air speed and volume. Examples include Tate's Task Air Module™, Hiross's Flexible Space System™, Johnson Controls Inc. PEM™ (Fig. 7). An increase in ceiling air diffusers beyond that typically required by codes (to a minimum of one diffuser per occupant) could permit control over air speed and direction for improved thermal comfort for each individual with occupancy sensors and variable speed fans in the central system to ensure maximum energy efficiency.

User control of air direction: Control over the direction of the air supply could provide the least costly alternative to control over air speed and volume as a thermal comfort strategy. The recognition that air distribution patterns from ceiling diffusers may be heavily affected by furniture layout, as well as occupancy and equipment density and location, would suggest the benefits of control over air flow direction to maintain the necessary air volume without direct drafts or furniture blockage. The comfort differences between cold air and warm air distribution patterns from the same diffuser would also suggest individual or automatic control over air flow direction. The introduction of operable vanes in overhead diffusers to allow the redirection of air in different directions (without shut down), would provide significant improvement for matching air flow direction to needs in the highly changeable workplace.

Almost all of the floor and desktop air supply systems offer directional control for the user. In a number of floor-based systems, adjustable grills are provided for each supply air diffuser, capable of being oriented to the occupant for cooling, or set in a jet pattern for ambient conditioning. The various floor-based air distribution systems have been designed with the assumption of a minimum of one diffuser per person, and an optimum of six diffusers per person.

3   Access to daylight and view for each individual.

Individual access to daylight and view is achievable through:

- Improved access to windows, 23 ft. (7 m) maximum distance.

- Increased visible transmission of glass to 50% minimum, with shading and brightness contrast control.

- Light redirection and control devices for effective delighting.

- Increase access to outdoor workplaces.

Access to daylight and view: In the increasingly computer-bound workplace, we should commit ourselves to increasing building periphery so that each workstation is guaranteed a view. This view of the outdoors should have content—views of pedestrians, trees and community life—to maintain our sense of time and season. The view should not be obscured by highly reflective glazing, which reduces visibility below 35%, demands electric lighting in spite of daylight availability and is more likely to reflect interior lights as glare. Equally valuable is a commitment to increase individual and group access to open air work spaces (Fig. 8). This suggests a shift away from megaplexes and high rise buildings, towards open air campus and village planning, as well as a commitment to operable windows and distributed doors, terraces and landscaping.

Sunshading and high visible transmission glass: New developments in glazing offer high visual transmittance with controlled solar transmittance. For effective daylighting and maximum views, visible transmittance should be above 50%, rather than the 15-20% common in office buildings. It is possible to achieve light and view transmittances over 50% while maintaining shading coefficients under 45% to keep the solar cooling loads as low as possible for the internally load dominated office buildings. External shading devices and light redirection devices are far more effective measures to minimizing overall energy loads with maximum environmental contact in the workplace. A study from Lawrence Berkeley Laboratories demonstrates that exterior operable shading devices, and even interior shading devices, were more cost effective and energy/resource effective than tinted glass in all regions of the U. S. (Winkelmann & Lokmanhekim 1981).

Daylighting and light redirection: Since electric lighting loads and cooling from solar gains and lights are the two largest components of peak demand in commercial buildings, the use of daylight without solar heat gain is a key strategy to long term environmental quality and energy effectiveness. The most cost effective demand-side management solutions are those that directly eliminate these loads (Sullivan et. al., 1992), and studies have shown a correlation between daylight and human health benefits (Küller & Wetterberg 1992) as well as energy benefits (Mahdavi et. al. 1995a). In the Lockheed building in Sunnyvale, California, the daylighting design uses deep light shelves, sloped ceilings, and a top-lit central atrium to provide 70% of the required ambient illumination throughout the year in a deep open plan office space, with a 15% reduction in absenteeism (Romm 1994).

Although guidelines for effective daylighting in offices have long been established—relating percent of aperture, ceiling height, room depth and color, and sunlight redirection devices at the window—a key design change required is the commitment to a layered facade. The Intelligent Workplace Laboratory introduces a layered facade that enables seasonally and daily dynamic control of the light, heat, and ven-

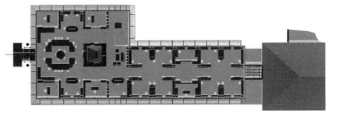

Fig. 8. Plan of the Intelligent Workplace Laboratory at Carnegie Mellon University ensures access to windows and views.

tilation energies of the natural environment. By displacing mechanical and electrical loads, these facades provide near term savings, sustainability, and long term environmental satisfaction.

4   Lighting control.

Recent development and innovations in lighting design and applications include:

- Relocatable task-ambient lighting.

- Smaller zone size, with sensors and individual controls.

- Split task and ambient lighting.

- Daylight interface.

Relocatable task-ambient lighting: In conventional office design, changing the density or location of ceiling-based task-ambient fixtures is a costly procedure. Multiple unions must be brought in and must disrupt workstations, remove ceilings, walls and light troffers, rewiring fixtures and switches into new settings. As a result, neither the density nor the location of fixtures change in most office reconfiguration projects, unless a total renovation is underway. Consequently, the fixture grid must be overdesigned initially to ensure adequate working light levels in a wide range of reconfigurations. To eliminate this energy and material waste, one alternative is reconfigurable ceiling lights where density and location can be changed by the occupant or in-house staff. Austrian lighting designer, Dr. Bartenbach, has designed such a system for Colonia Insurance Headquarters in Cologne, Germany and for the Lloyds of London Headquarters building. In Colonia (Fig. 9), octagonal acoustic ceiling tiles are interchangeable with light-weight "salad bowl" light fixtures to enable the simple relocation of fixtures along with each desk or room reconfiguration. The density of fixtures can also be simply modified, since the pigtail connections (male-female plugs) allow fixtures to be added or subtracted from any circuit and its corresponding light switch.

Fig. 9. Modular reconfigurable ceiling with plug-in capability to add or subtract fixtures with various workstation layouts. Colonia Headquarters, Cologne, Germany (ABSIC).

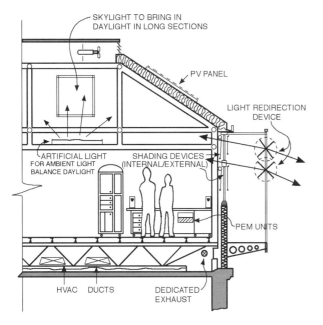

Fig. 10. Lighting diagram of the Intelligent Workplace at Carnegie Mellon University makes includes light redirection devces, skylights and shading for effective daylighting.

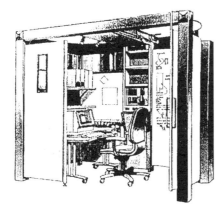

Fig. 11. Personal Harbor™ Steelcase is representative of modules that allow variable levels of closure and privacy.

Minimum zone size and increased on-off controls: As electronic and solid state ballasts increase in sophistication and decrease in price, the payback of individual fixture controls over traditional "blanket" on-off controls is typically less than two years in energy savings alone. Supplying advanced electronic ballasts for each fixture will support a variety of control options from manual on/off, to timers, to occupancy sensors, to daylight/photocell readers, to lamp depreciation controllers, to peak load shedding strategies. As a result, individual tenant/users and facility managers can vary or assemble combinations of these six control strategies, sending "intelligence" to low-voltage data network controllers such as Siemens Instabus™ to help optimize energy performance and user satisfaction.

Split task and ambient lighting with user controls: An excellent alternative for achieving proper light levels at each individual workstation is the shift to low-level ambient lighting with task lights at each workstation. The introduction of an ambient lighting system (typically indirect) in conjunction with task lights can cut office energy use by 30% or more, with light levels better matched to workstation use, while less total light is used. Additional savings comes from the reduced load on the air conditioning system. Selection of task lights specifications is critical to visual performance and energy conservation. Each workstation should have at a minimum of one or two task lights; they should be relocatable by the user to match worksurface configuration and use; they should have adjustable arm/directional control; and there should be occupancy sensors for automatic shutdown when the workstation is unoccupied. In short, split task and ambient systems should have daylight response for the ambient lighting, and user control of task light location, density, and on/off switching.

Effective daylight utilization with controllable electric lighting interface. Effective daylight utilization with controllable electric lighting interfaces offer significant savings in lighting power demand and cooling costs (Fig. 10). These savings can offset the first costs of lighting control systems, in some cases by 50%, and even offset the additional costs of more sophisticated shading and glazing systems (Selkowitz 1989). The corporate campus of Blue Cross/Blue Shield, New Haven, CT receives 30% of interior illumination requirements from the daylighting, saving substantially in lighting and cooling costs and contributing to higher employee morale (Dubbs 1991).

5   Workplaces for teaming as well as for privacy and working quiet.

The seemingly conflicting requirements for collaborative working as well as visual and acoustical privacy for individuals is accomplished by variable space closure and furniture reconfigurability.

- Closeable spaces for sustained individual concentration on tasks.
- Project rooms for sustained group work without creating disturbances.
- Relocatable kit of parts for organizational change.

Variable space closure and furniture reconfigurability. Corporations around the world are discovering that organizations need stronger collective work processes and more productive individual/concentrated work settings (cf. Table C). To achieve both of these goals, interior space plans are shifting to combinations of closed and open spaces, micro-workstations, mobile workstations, and project rooms. Among other furniture manufacturers, Steelcase has been developing Personal Harbors™ (Fig. 11) and Coves™ which support the configuration of small partially closable individual offices; mobile furniture pieces that can be taken to alternate work locations; and a growing array of shared work area furniture for conferences, relaxing, concentrating, teaming, laying out or presenting work, and accessing multi–media.

6   Network access: data, voice, and power.

Flexible network connections are critical to the dynamic office, suggesting the following innovations:

- Modular, reconfigurable, addable ports/outlets.

- Raised floor based, integrated power, data, voice, video and cabling harnesses.

- Service pubs for shared equipment.

Modular outlet boxes and homeruns to distributed satellite network centers: At the desk, each individual today requires multiple data, voice, and power outlets, with significant variations in density and functionality over time and over space, task, and equipment changes. Modular floor or furniture boxes are needed, with interchangeable outlets for multiple data, phone, power, and environmental controls, to fully support today's constant layout and activity changes, providing reconfigurable infrastructures without waste (Fig. 12). When modular outlet boxes are connected directly, in home-run configurations, to distributed satellite closets for working neighborhoods of 35-50 people, then all changes in hardware density and functionality can occur at the two ends—by clip-connects on the vertical patch panel and clip connects at the boxes (Fig. 13).

Raised floors and open cable tray horizontal distribution: The present interest in universal, box, or single size workstations is driven in part by the desire to reduce overall space demands and the furniture kit of parts, as well as by the desire to facilitate one-time prewiring with least-cost poke-throughs. However, this solution may fall short in supporting new concepts in workstyle and communication that require more major changes in furniture layout as well as hardware and networking. The demands of dynamic, workplaces may be best served by accessible, spacious plenum designs through raised floors to modular floor boxes to open cable trays in the furniture, or through open ceiling cable trays to spacious panel wall channels to modular panel boxes. Given the quantity of existing office area, ceiling distributed systems of HVAC and telecommunications will always maintain a significant market. The effective use of ceilings as horizontal distribution plenums is dependent, however, on the development of integrated ceiling/cable trays and pre-chased modular wall and furniture systems to bring the network capability down to the desk. Meanwhile, internationally, there is growing emphasis on raised floor technologies for the horizontal distribution of cables and of conditioned air. The raised floor distribution provides ease of network access, growth, and change (of both cabling and HVAC), as well as the improved performance of floor air-supply systems in relation to many ceiling "down-draft systems."

Service pubs and multi-media conference hubs: Two additions in office planning today are distributed multi-media conference spaces or project rooms, and shared service spaces. In defining the flexible infrastructures needed in buildings, it is important to anticipate the major increase in teaming and conference spaces—distributed through-

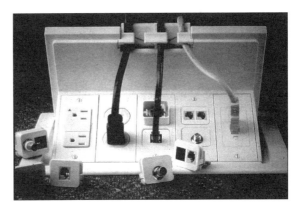

Fig. 12. AMP Floor Box provides multiple and interchangeable access to power, data and voice networks.

Fig. 13. Distributed satellite closet serving 10,000 sq. ft. (930 sp. meters) offer greater control, reliability and flexibility to meet individual needs (POWERFLOR™).

INTERIORS   C1

Table 3. Dynamic, multidisciplinary teams demand reconfigurable workspaces on a project by project basis, similar to the "skunk works" of successful industrial innovation. (Demarco & Lister 1987).

How do softward developers spend their time?

Work mode	Percent of time
Working alone	30%
Working with one other person	50%
Working with two or more people	20%

out the workplace—and corresponding needs for ventilation, thermal conditioning, and networks to support computer presentation, video presentation, and teleconferencing. At the same time, shared equipment centers are in increased use throughout the workplace, to provide shared access to the latest copiers, fax machines, laser printers, new hardware, as well as to provide a social, information exchange center for the workplace. (Fig. 14).

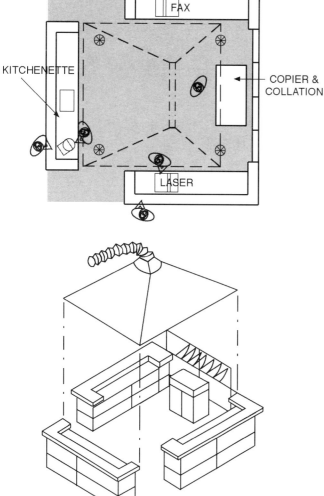

7 Ergonomic Furniture

Ergonomic design is based upon a detailed analysis of human anatomy, posture and motion studies, and has lead to a number of advantages in interior systems, including: ergonomic chairs, adjustable supports for keyboard screens and copy stands, variable height work surfaces, task lighting, and integrated cable management. To ensure a uniformly high quality of interiors and furniture specification, purchase and layout planning, performance guidelines should include:

- Anthropometric work surfaces.
- Adequate worksurface, reconfigurable, with adjustable height.
- Adequate storage, storage walls.
- Adjustable height/ position keyboard, screen and document support.
- Ergonomic chairs.
- Adjustable seat height, with locking mechanism.
- Swivel on five to six castor base.
- Adjustable back height/lumbar support position.
- Adjustable height armrests.
- Relocatable infrastructures.
- Floor based worksurfaces, modular, L or U configurations.
- Modular, stackable wall systems, variable enclosure with glass.
- Significantly increased storage with the workstation and workgroup.
- Dedicated lights, adjustable levels, relocatable.
- Dedicated air.
- Dedicated thermal control.
- Dedicated networks: data, voice, power, video, environmental control.
- Environmentally benign materials and finishes.

With the redistribution of work responsibilities and related telecommunications equipment, there is a need to shift away from the traditional allocation of office space size and furniture by rank to allocations by task or function. Although secretaries traditionally are assigned less workspace than their managers, secretary's workspace must often accommodate computers, modems, typewriters, printers, fax machines, phones and file servers to support management activity. Although a salesperson may function effectively with a phone and a 5 foot (1.52 m) worksurface with files maintained in a central file bank or even a car, a researcher relies on extensive files and books and computer networking to complete their tasks. Consequently, the office of the future must consider the range of tasks and effective workstyles in the determination of workplace size and furniture options.

Justifying the investment in motivational buildings

There are a number of justifications can be considered to support the case why owners or lessors would want to invest in high performance, quality built environments:

- Reduced property management costs, reliable assembly and maintenance.
- Reconfigurability, response time/costs, outsourcing costs.
- Reduced life cycle costs.

Fig. 14. Flexible service pubs accomodate replacements and advances in computers and equipment, allow for separate air circulation and create places for social and professional interaction.

- Reduced obsolescence of materials, assemblies and buildings.

- Reduced liability costs, risk avoidance.

- Increased profit in ownership, leveraged buying power.

- Reduced organizational and technological upgrading of "churn" costs.

- Reduced costs for health/safety/absenteeism and compensation.

- Reduced training/retention costs.

- Reduced fatigue, lost productivity costs.

- Reduced shut down costs for remodeling.

Table 4 and Figs. 15 through 21 illustrate a range of these factors, including productivity, health, energy, environment, and technological change. However, it is important to realize that corporate and federal investment in work environments often is not built on comparative cost/effectiveness studies but on strong beliefs in and commitments to workplaces and workers. For example, investment in "office automation" has reached over $1 trillion in the U. S. for desktop hardware over the past 10 years, invested on the perception of massive improvement in white collar productivity. However, the breakthrough in overall office productivity that has been anticipated as a result of new office technology in and of itself has not materialized. Investments in office and factory technology between 1973-1993 (computer and advanced telecommunication) has not realized more than a few percentages of increase in productivity (*New York Times* 1996). On the other hand, studies indicate that a combination or "complementarity" of technology and environmental improvements can increase productivity with substantial increments reportedly ranging from 2% to 20%, ascribable to the combined results of technology, workstation design and environmental quality improvements (Romm 1994).

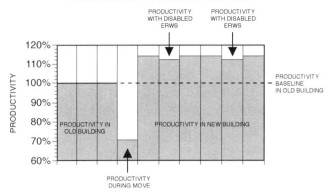

PRODUCTIVITY CHANGE OVER TIME

Fig. 15. Computer programmers in larger workspaces with less acoustic and visual disruption, performed on average 2.6 times better (the top quartile) than those in smaller spaces without acoustic and visual control (the bottom quartile). (DeMarco and Lister 1987).

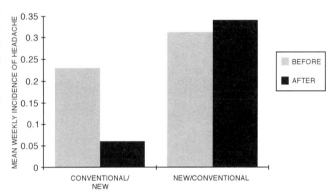

Fig. 16a. Average weekly incidence of episodes of headaches was lower among subjects exposed to new high performance ballasts compared to conventional ballasts (Wilkins et al. 1989).

Table 4. Environments of the Best and Worst Performers in the Coding War Games

Environmental Factor	Those Who Performed in 1st Quartile	Those Who Performed in 4th Quartile
1. How much dedicated workspace do you have?	78 sq. ft.	46 sq. ft
2. Is it acceptably quiet?	57% yes	29% yes
3. Is it acceptably private?	62% yes	19% yes
4. Can you silence your phone?	52% yes	10% yes
5. Can you divert your calls?	76% yes	19% yes
6. Do people often interrupt you needlessly?	38% yes	76% yes

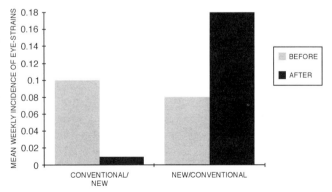

Fig. 16b. Average weekly incidence of episodes of eyestrain was lower among subjects exposed to new was lower among subjects exposed to new high performance ballasts compared to conventional ballasts (Wilkins et al. 1989).

C1

INTERIORS

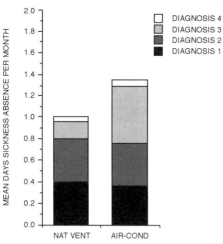

Fig. 17a. Case 1: A shift from a naturally ventilated building in a sealed building resulted in increase absenteeism and sick building symptoms.

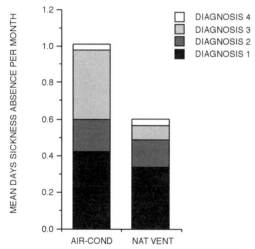

Fig. 17b. Case 2: A shift from a sealed building to a naturally ventilated building resulted in decrease sick building symptoms. (Robertson et al. 1990).

Conclusion

The advantage of distributed systems, micro-zoning and user-controlled services is that individuals can configure and reconfigure their own environmental and technical conditions. Calling a facilities manager each time there is a need to turn on or off the heat or lights, to plug in a new piece of hardware, or to relocate zones, diffusers and switches, is an antiquated concept defying the potential of intelligent buildings. At the same time, further "automating" already inadequate blanket and idiosyncratic services also defies the concept of intelligence.

Indeed, the dynamics in space planning and technology in today's work environment cannot be accommodated through the existing service infrastructure—neither the "blanket systems" for uniform open plan configurations nor the idiosyncratic systems for unique configurations. What is needed are flexible grid flexible density flexible closure systems—a constellation of building systems that permit each individual (workstation) to set the location and density of: ventilation and thermal conditioning; lighting; telecommunications; and furniture, including the level of workspace enclosure. The move to relocatable, user based infrastructures also ensures a major increase in the use of natural resources—daylight, natural ventilation, passive and active solar energy—for environmental conditioning. The effective use of natural conditioning strategies will significantly improve worker health and long term productivity, as well as providing exportable, advanced building solutions that can be sustainable for the rapidly developing nations.

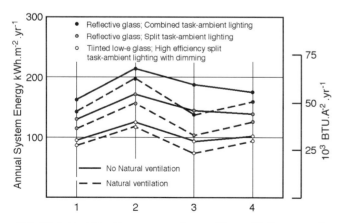

Fig. 18. Annual system energy drops with ventilation even for large zone buildings (Mahdavi *et. al* 1996).

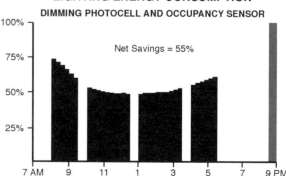

Fig. 19. A combination of dimming photocells with occupancy sensors allows for a total net energy savings of 55 percent. (Ranieri 1991).

Additional references

ABSIC/CERL 1995. *Process Methodology for Flexible Density Building Design*. U. S. Corps of Engineers Research Laboratory Research Report, 1993-95, Phase II. Pittsburgh, PA: Center for Building Performance and Diagnostics, Carnegie Mellon University.

DeMarco, T. and T. Lister. 1987. *Peopleware: Productive Projects and Teams*. New York: Dorset House Publishing.

DOE. 1994. *The Intelligent Workplace Retrofit Initiative, Field Studies of the Major Issues Facing Existing Office Building Owners, Managers & Users,*. DOE Building Studies. Pittsburgh, PA: Carnegie Mellon University, Center for Building Performance and Diagnostics.

Dubbs, Dana. 1991. "Blue Cross Cuts Cost with Daylighting." *Facilities Design & Management*. pg. 25, October 1991.

Forrester Research. 1993. "Computing Strategy." The Forrester Report. Vol. 12, No. 3, 1995.

Hartkopf, V., V. Loftness, P. Drake, F. Dubin, P. Mill, G. Ziga. 1988. *Designing the Office of the Future: The Japanese Approach to Tomorrow's Workplace*. New York: John Wiley & Sons.

Kroner, W., J. A. Stark-Martin, T. Willemain. 1992. *Using Advanced Office Technology to Increase Productivity: The Impact of Environmentally Responsive Workstations (ERWs) on Productivity and Worker Attitude, The West Bend Mutual Study*. Troy, NY: School of Architecture. Rensselaer Polytechnic Institute.

Küller, R. and Wetterberg, L. 1992. "Melatonin, Cortisol, EEG, ECG and Subjective Comfort in Healthy Humans: Impact of Two Fluorescent lamp Types at Two Light Intensities." *International Journal of Lighting Research and Technology*. Vol. 25(2), pg. 71-81. 1993.

Loftness, V., V. Hartkopf, A. Mahdavi, S. Lee, J. Shankavaram and K. J. Tu. 1995(a). "The Relationship of Environmental Quality in Buildings to Productivity, Energy Effectiveness, Comfort and Health: How Much Proof Do We Need?" *World Workplace '95. Proceedings of the 1995 International Facility Management Association Conference*. Pg. 115-130. Houston, TX: International Facility Management Association.

Loftness, V., V. Hartkopf, S. Lee, J. Shankavaram and P. Mathew. 1995(b). "User-based Control Choices in Relation to Thermal Comfort, Air Quality and Energy Effectiveness." *Proceedings of Second International Conference on IAQ, Ventilation and Energy Conservation in Buildings*. Montreal: Concordia University Center for Building Studies.

Mahdavi, A., P. Mathew, S. Kumar, V. Hartkopf, V. Loftness. 1995(a). "Effects of Lighting, Zoning, and Control Strategies on Energy Use in Commercial Buildings." *Journal of the Illuminating Engineering Society*. Vol. 24, No. 1, Winter 1995. pp. 25-35.

Mahdavi, A., V. Hartkopf, P. Mathew. 1995(b). "The Potential for Improving the Energy Performance of HVAC, Lighting, and Enclosure Systems in Commercial Buildings." *Proceedings of Tsinghua-HVAC-'95: International Symposium on Heating, Ventilation, and Air Conditioning*. Beijing: Tsinghua University.

New York Times. 1996. "We're Meaner, Leaner, and Going Nowhere Fast." *New York Times Week In Review*. Sunday, May 4, 1996.

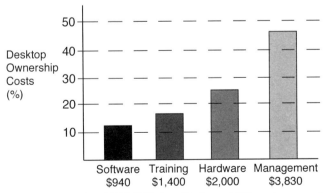

Model based on 5000 PC's in a Fortune 1,000 environment

Fig. 20. Annual costs for keeping desk-top technology current far exceed one-time costs for environmental quality in the individual workspace.

Ranieri, David. 1991. "Effective Light Control for the Modern Office." *Architectural Lighting*, pg. 36, April 1991.

Robertson, A., S., K. T. Roberts, P. S. Burge, G. Raw. 1990. "The Effect of Change in Building Ventilation Category on Sickness Absence Rates and the Prevalence of Sick Building Syndrome." *Proceedings Indoor Air, 90: The Fifth International Conference on Indoor Air Quality and Climate*. p. 237-242. New York: Pergamon Press.

Romm, Joseph J. 1994. *Lean and Clean Management: How to Boost Profits and Productivity by Reducing Pollution*. New York: Kodansha America.

Selkowitz, S. 1989. "Evaluation of Advanced Glazing Technologies." *Building Design and Human Performance*; Nancy Ruck, editor. New York: Van Nostrand Reinhold.

Sullivan, R., E. S. Lee, S. Selkowitz. 1992. *A Method of Optimizing Solar Control and Daylighting Performance in Commercial Office Buildings*. Report No. LBL-32931/BS-291. Berkeley, CA: Lawrence Berkeley Laboratory.

Winkelmann, F. & M. Lokmanhekim. 1981. *Cycle Cost and Energy-Use Analysis of Sun-Control and Daylighting Options in a High-Rise Office Building*, Report No. LBL-12298. Berkeley, CA: Lawrence Berkeley Laboratory.

Wilkins, A. J., I. Nimmo-Smith, A. I. Slater, L. Bedocs. 1989. "Fluorescent Lighting, Headaches and Eyestrain." *Lighting Research and Technology*. Vol. 21(1), pp. 11-18.

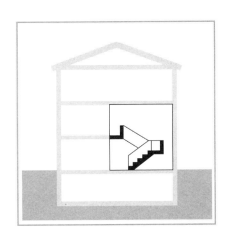

C INTERIORS

Viscaya, Coral Gables, FL

Stair design checklist

Summary: A recommended design sequence and checklist of information is presented for design of stairs. A history and theoretical background of stair design and a complete discussion of design criteria and recommendations is found in Templer (1994), from which this section is reproduced. A glossary of terms is appended.

Key words: floor patterns, guardrails, handrails, headroom clearance, landings, nosings, ramps, riser-tread dimensions.

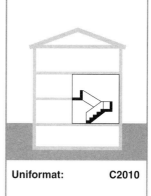

Uniformat:	C2010

INTERIORS

C2

Establish preliminary stair configuration

Preliminary selection of stair configuration depends on the floor space available, the floor-to-floor height, pedestrian movement volumes and patterns, and the groups of people who will use the stair.

Stair user group

The potential users may be able-bodied adults, specific handicapped groups, children, the elderly, or all of these groups. The potential use of the stair may be as a means of access and egress; in a public or monumental location, with a large volume of pedestrians; or in a private location. There are special design considerations for some groups:

- Disabled: Provide an alternative access way so those who cannot use stairs are not denied entry.

- Elderly and disabled: For the elderly and some handicapped people, designs that depend only on stair access and egress should be avoided.

- People carrying food, drinks, and supplies: Avoid placing stairs where people will routinely carry food and drink that may spill on the treads. Avoid stair designs where workers must carry bulky or heavy objects, or anything else that may limit their view of the treads or affect their balance.

- Children: Stairs for use by children need an additional, lower handrail. The minimum distance between balustrading must be less than a 3 1/2-inch (8.89 cm) sphere to prevent the passage of a small child. For control of toddlers, the stair may be closed by a gate.

Factors that affect location

- Where large crowds of people will use the stairs (theaters, stadia, fire egress for large buildings), the stair should be located so that it does not cause a hazardous bottleneck by making a sudden change of direction, such as a dog-leg stair. The stair should be located to encourage continuous direct flow.

- Avoid pedestrian movement directional conflicts at the top and bottom of the stair. Fig. 1 shows a stair leading directly to and across a passage with heavy traffic.

- Avoid direction, view, and illumination changes. Fig. 2 illustrates several potentially hazardous layout conditions—the bottom of a stair where sunlight may blind users or a fascinating view that may distract attention.

- Avoid entry-or exitway hazards. Fig. 3 shows a door opening directly onto a landing.

- Avoid a configuration that violates the "keep-right" principle (the convention in the United States.) Helical flights that ascend by spiraling up to the right, and dog-leg and other layouts that ascend to the right, enable those ascending to keep to the right with little effort. This reduces the likelihood of conflicts with those descending (Fig. 4).

- Avoid fire escape stairs that continue past the ground-floor egress point down into a basement. These may mislead people during an emergency, drawing them down to a dead end.

- The existing environment may limit the amount of space available for a stair. If this constraint exists, establish the size of area that is available.

Stair types and performance

- Direction and flow: The direction of travel that people will take to and from the top and bottom of the stair will be affected by the stair layout, and vice versa.

- Stair shape, area, and performance: The amount of floor space a staircase occupies is related to its shape. Some layouts use less space than others, and some are more effective than others for moving stretchers, furniture, crowds of people, and so on.

Determine Dimensional Restraints

Stair design in buildings may be governed by several codes and standards. Refer to the applicable building code, fire code, handicapped code, occupational safety and health regulations, Department of Housing and Urban Development Standards, ANSI Specifications, and other applicable codes. The recommendations here are based on research findings, not code requirements.

Author: John Templer

References: Fruin, John J. 1987. *Pedestrian Planning and Design*. Mobile, AL.: Elevator World.

Pushkarev, Boris S., and Jeffrey M. Zupan. 1975. *Urban Space for Pedestrians*. Cambridge, Mass: MIT Press.

Templer, John, Craig Zimring, and Jean Wineman. 1980. *The Feasibility of Accommodating Physically Handicapped Individuals on Pedestrian Over- and Undercrossing Structures*. Washington, DC: Federal Highway Administration.

Templer, John. 1994. *The Staircase: History and Theories and Studies of Hazards, Falls, and Safer Design*. Cambridge, MA: MIT Press.

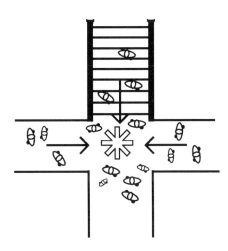

Fig. 1. Avoid conflicting pedestrian movement directions
at the top or bottom of the stair

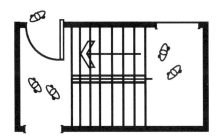

Fig. 3. Avoid entering or exit hazards

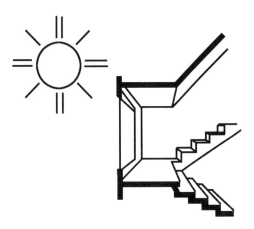

Fig. 2. Avoid direction, view, and illumination changes

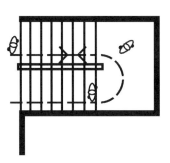

Fig. 4. Avoid keep-right conflicts

Width

Stair width should be a function of comfort, capacity, and reach (handrail availability). The minimum design width of stairs for single-file use should be 29 inches (74 cm) for a public place. For comfort, about 38 inches (97 cm) is necessary. Side-by-side walking clearance dictates a width between walls of at least 56 inches (1.42 m), a module of 28 inches (71.12 cm). A more comfortable module of 34.5 inches (87.63 cm) dictates a minimum width of 69 inches (1.75 m).

The stair must be wide enough for the expected volume of traffic. The capacity of the stair is expressed in people per minute per foot (or per meter) width. To plan for the expected flow per minute, one must consider the occupancy of the space to be served. The total occupant load per building floor can be found by dividing the floor area by the occupant density, using square feet per person (m²/person). Estimates of occupant density per building type are given in Table 1. Dividing the anticipated total occupant load of the floor (for example) by the average evacuation time of the people yields the number of people per minute who will pass a point on the stair. For a walkway leading to a stair, Table 2 provides a level of service. Generally only levels 4 to 8 are acceptable. Level 3 may be acceptable for bulk arrival (platoon) situations. However, this should be carefully considered. For the stair itself, Table 3 recommends the use of no levels higher than E.

However, to avoid or minimize the likelihood of queues forming, level E should be avoided also and level D used in discretion. Using level E, 13-17 persons per 12-inch (30.1 cm) width of stair per minute, we might use 15 persons per foot width of stair per minute to establish the required width of the stair. This would give the effective width. To allow for handrails, adjoining walls, and so on, another 14 inches (35.6 cm) may be necessary. A stair to evacuate 200 people, who take an average of 2 minutes to reach the stair, must be able to carry 100 people per minute. At a maximum flow of 15 people per foot width per minute, an effective stair width of 6.67 feet (2.03 m) will be required. Based on a module of 28 inches (71 cm), 7 feet (2.13 m) will be a better effective width. Allowing for adjoining walls and handrails, a total of about 8.17 feet (2.49 m) will thus be necessary.

Table 1. Estimate of occupant numbers for various types of building

Occupancy	Occupant Load		Maximum Travel Distance	
	Square feet per person	Square meters per person	Feet	Meters
Residential	200	18.6	100	30.5
Educational			150	45.7
classrooms	20	1.9	100	30.5
shops	50	4.7		
Institutional				
sleeping areas	120	11.2	100	30.5
treatment areas	240	22.3		
Assembly	15	1.4		
without fixed seats	6	0.6	100	30.5
standing areas	3	0.3		
Business	100	9.3	100	30.5
Mercantile			150	45.7
first floor	30	2.8		
other floors	60	5.6		
storage and shipping	100	9.3		
Industrial	100	9.3	100	30.5
Storage	300	27.9	100	30.5
Hazardous	100	9.3	75	22.9

Table 2. Levels of pedestrian density in movement on the level

Average Area per Person, sq. ft. (m²)	Characteristics	Average Area per Person, sq. ft. (m²)	Characteristics
Level 1: 2 to 5 (0.2—0.5)	Flow: erratic, on verge of complete stoppage. Average speed: shuffling only, 0-30 m/min.) Choice of speed: none, movement only with the crowd. Crossing or reverse movement: impossible. Conflicts: physical contact unavoidable. Passing: impossible	*Level 5:* 15 to 18 (1.4—1.7)	Flow: 12-15 PPM/ft. (39-49 PPM/m), 56-70 percent of maximum capacity. Average speed: about 80 percent of free flow, 240-270 ft./min. (73-82 m/min.) Choice of speed: restricted except for slow walkers. Crossing or reverse movement: restricted, with conflicts. Conflicts: probably high. Passing: rarely possible without touching
Level 2: 5 to 7 (0.5-0.7)	Flow: 23-25 PPM/ft. (75-82 PPM/m), a maximum in traffic stream under pressure[a]. Average speed: mostly shuffling, 100-180 ft./min. (30±-55 m/min.) Choice of speed: none, movement only with the crowd. Crossing or reverse movement: most difficult. Conflicts: physical contact probable, conflicts unavoidable. Passing: impossible	*Level 6:* 18 to 25 (1.7—2.3)	Flow: 10-12 PPM/ft. (33-39 PPM/m), roughly 50 percent of maximum capacity. Average speed: more than 80 percent of free flow, 270-290 ft./min. (82-88 m/min.) Choice of speed: unless stream similar, restricted by bunching. Crossing or reverse movement: possible, with conflicts. Conflicts: probably high. Passing: difficult without abrupt maneuvers
Level 3: 7 to 11 (0.7-1.0)	Flow: 19-23 PPM/ft. (62-75 PPM/m), attains a maximum in relaxed traffic streams. Average speed: about 70 percent of free flow, 180-200 ft./min. (55-61 m/min.) Choice of speed: practically none. Crossing or reverse movement: severely restricted, with conflicts. Conflicts: physical contact probable, conflicts unavoidable. Passing: impossible	Level 7: 25 to 40 (2.3-3.7)	Flow: 7-10 PPM/ft. (20-33 PPM/m), roughly one-third of maximum capacity. Average speed: nearly free flow, 290-310 ft./min. (88-94 m/min.) Choice of speed: occasionally impeded. Crossing or reverse movement: possible with occasional conflicts. Conflicts: about 50 percent probability. Passing: possible, but with interference
Level 4: 15 to 18 (1.0-1.4)	Flow: 15-19 PPM/ft. (49-62 PPM/m), 65-80 percent of maximum capacity. Average speed: about 75 percent of free flow, 200-240 ft./min. (61-73 m/min.) Choice of speed: restricted, constant adjustments of gait needed. Crossing or reverse movement: severely restricted, with conflicts. Conflicts: unavoidable. Passing: rarely possible without touching	Level 8 Over 40 (over 3.7)	Flow: one-fifth maximum capacity or less. Average speed: virtually as chosen. Choice of speed: virtually unrestricted. Crossing or reverse movement: free. Conflicts: maneuvering needed to avoid conflicts. Passing: free, with some maneuvering

[a]PPM/ft.: pedestrians per minute per foot width of walkway; PPM/m: pedestrians per minute per meter width of walkway.

Source: Pushkarev and Zupan (1975). Flow and speed figures derived from Fruin (1987)

INTERIORS

C2

Table 3. Levels of pedestrian density in movement on stairs

Average Area per Person, sq. ft. (m²)   *Characteristics*

Level F: Flow: up to 20 PPM/ft. (66 PPM/m), flow attains a maximum, but is Less than 4 (0.37) erratic with frequent stoppages and verges on complete breakdown[a]
          Average horizontal speed: shuffling, 0—70 ft./min (0—21 m/min)
          Choice of speed: none
          Passing: impossible
          Queuing at stair entrance: yes

Level E: Flow: 13—17 PPM/ft. (43—56 PPM/m), intermittent stoppages
4 to 7   Average horizontal speed: 70—90 ft./min (21—27 m/min)
(0.37—0.65)   Choice of speed: none
          Passing: impossible
          Queuing at stair entrance: yes

Level D: Flow: 10—13 PPM/ft. (33—43 PPM/m)
7 to 10   Average horizontal speed: 90—95 ft./min (27—29 m/min)
(0.65—0.93)   Choice of speed: restricted
          Passing: impossible
          Queuing at stair entrance: some at higher flow level

Level C: Flow: 7—10 PPM/ft. (23—33 PPM/m)
10 to 15   Average horizontal speed: 95—100 ft./min. (29—30m/min)
(0.93—1.4)   Choice of speed: restricted
          Passing: impossible
          Queuing at stair entrance: none

Level B: Flow: 5—7 PPM/ft. (16—23 PPM/m)
15 to 20   Average horizontal speed: 100 ft./min. (30 m/min)
(1.4—1.9)   Choice of speed: freely selected
          Passing: restricted
          Queuing at stair entrance: none

Level A: Flow: 5 or less PPM/ft. (16 PPM/m or less)
More than 20   Average horizontal speed: 100 ft./min. (30 m/min)
(1.9)   Choice of speed: freely selected
          Passing: at will
          Queuing at stair entrance: none

[a]*PPM/ft.: pedestrians per minute per foot width of walkway; PPM/m: pedestrians per minute per meter width of walkway*

Source: Fruin (1987).

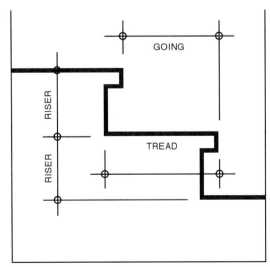

Fig. 5. Riser, tread, and going

Riser-tread dimensions

Table 4 gives acceptable rise and going (the horizontal distance between two nosings) relationships based on energy expenditures and potential for safer gait. Riser heights that are more than 7.33 inches (18.6 cm) and goings less than 11 inches (27.9 cm) are not recommended. Going dimensions greater than 14 inches (36.6 cm) may also be acceptable, but no research is available to confirm or deny this. In the table, dimensional increments between entries are also acceptable. Applicable codes and standards may differ from these recommendations.

The riser height (Fig. 5) is the vertical height of a single step. The going is the horizontal distance, in plan, from the nosing edge of a step to the nosing edge of the next adjoining step. The tread depth is the horizontal distance, in plan, of a tread. Some codes require a nosing overhang if the treads are small. Dimensions of adjoining risers and treads must be constructed to be constant and regular.

Landings

Landings of stairs that have no change of direction are called intermediate landings. A change in direction of 90 degrees results in a quarter-landing (wide L), and a change in direction of 180 degrees produces a half-landing (narrow U). Landings on long flights of stairs are necessary to provide a resting place for stair users, to form turning zones, and, in the event of a fall, to break the force of the fall. The minimum width of the landing must be equal to that of the widest flight of steps that reaches it. The minimum clear depth must equal the widest stair run or 48 inches (1.21 m), whichever is larger.

Headroom

Headroom is measured vertically from the front edge of the nosing of a step to the finished ceiling. It should never be less than 6 feet, 7 inches (2 m).

Length of Run

A stair flight should always consist of three or more risers. The flight should not have too many steps without a landing. In many codes the maximum number of risers permitted in a flight is eighteen.

Develop Configuration Layout

Layout techniques vary in implementation with the configuration chosen, but in all cases, an acceptable and consistent riser and tread relationship should be adhered to in order to provide a layout requiring minimum energy expenditure as well as maximum potential for safety. This section suggests techniques for laying out several types of stair.

Table 4. Range of rise and going relationships for comfort and safety

Rise	Goings						
INCHES							
7.2	11						
7	11						
6.5	11	11.5	12	12.5			
6	11	11.5	12	12.5	13	13.5	14
5.5	11	11.5	12	12.5	13		
5	11	11.5	12				
4.6	11						
CENTIMETERS							
18.3	27.9						
17.8	27.9						
16.5	27.9	29.2	30.5	31.8			
15.2	27.9	29.2	30.5	31.8	33.0	34.3	35.6
14.0	27.9	29.2	30.5	31.8	33.0		
12.7	27.9	29.2	30.5				
11.7	27.9						

The following symbols and abbreviations are used in the discussion below:

Stair			Ramp	
H	=	Floor-to-floor height	=	Elevation change
L	=	Length of run between first from and last riser nosing	=	Length of run bottom to top
n	=	Number of risers		
p	=	Number of treads		
R	=	Riser height		
G	=	Going depth		

Straight Flight Stairs

- Determine floor-to-floor height (H). Select acceptable riser (R) and going (G) dimensions. If space is limited, choose maximum riser (R) and minimum going (G).

- Determine the number of risers (n):

$$n = \frac{H}{R}$$

Set n equal to the nearest whole number, and adjust the riser dimension accordingly.

- The number of treads is equal to the number of risers minus 1:

$$p = n - 1$$

- The length of run equals the going dimension times the number of treads:

$$L = G \times p$$

Table 5. Dimensions for Spiral Stairs: Going Depth at Walking Line[a]

Inches

Exterior Diameter of Stair	54	60	66	72	78	84	90	96	102			
Diameter of Walking Line	32.7	38.7	44.7	50.7	56.7	62.7	68.7		80.7			

Number of treads in circle — Going depth at walking line[b]

Number of treads in circle									
11	9.22	10.90	12.60						
12		10.01	11.57	13.13					
13		9.26	10.70	12.14	13.58				
14			9.96	11.29	12.63	13.96			
15			9.30	10.55	11.80	13.04			
16				9.90	11.07	12.24	13.41		
17				9.32	10.43	11.53	12.63	13.73	
18					9.85	10.89	11.94	12.98	
19					9.34	10.33	11.31	12.30	13.29
20						9.81	10.75	11.69	12.63

Centimeters

Exterior Diameter of Stair	140	150	160	170	180	190	200	210	220	230	240	250
Diameter of Walk Line	86	96	106	116	126	136	146	156	166	176	186	196

Number of treads in circle — Going depth at walking line[c]

Number of treads in circle												
11	24.2	27.0	29.9	32.7	35.5							
12		24.8	27.4	30.0	32.6	35.2						
13			25.4	27.8	30.2	32.5						
14			23.6	25.8	28.0	30.3	32.5	34.7				
15				24.1	26.2	28.3	30.4	32.4	34.5			
16					24.6	26.5	28.5	30.4	32.4	34.1		
17					23.2	25.0	26.8	28.7	30.5	32.3	34.2	
18						23.6	25.4	27.1	28.8	30.6	32.3	34.0
19							24.0	25.7	27.3	29.0	30.6	32.3
20							22.8	24.4	26.0	27.5	29.1	30.7

[a]Exterior diameter and exterior radius are measured from the inside of the outer handrail of the stair; walking line is estimated as 10.63 inches (27 cm) from the inside of the handrail.

[b]Going at walking line is calculated from $2 \sin\alpha/2(r_{ex}—10.73)$, where r_{ex} is the exterior radius of the stair and a is the angle between the front and back lines of a tread. Values to the right of the stepped line are acceptable.

[c]Going at walking line is calculated from $\sin\alpha/2(r_{ex}—27)$, where r_{ex} is the exterior radius of the stair and a is the angle between the front and back lines of a tread. Values to the right of the stepped line are acceptable.

Flights with winders and splayed steps

By definition, a winder is a wedge-shaped step of varying tread width. To obtain treads of about equal widths, the steps preceding and following the turn may be splayed.

- The narrow portion of the tread should be at least 4 inches (10.2 cm) at a distance of 6 inches (15.2 cm) from the end of the tread or inside of the stringer. At the walking line, 10.6 inches (27.0 cm) from the newel or outside handrail the going must be at least 11 inches (27.9 cm).

- Do not run a step edge into a corner.

- Splayed steps and winders should rise in a clockwise direction where possible. This puts the wide portions of the treads to the right-hand side when going downstairs.

Spiral Stairs

- From 12 to 20 steps can be accommodated in a full circle. The tread angle can range from 30 to 18 degrees.

- Typically, the line of the nosings does not radiate out from the geometrical center of the stair but "dances" to some extent.

- The greater the number of steps there are in the circle, the greater is the available headroom clearance but the smaller is the effective going.

- Headroom clearance should not be less than 6 feet, 7 inches (2 m).

- A stair that one ascends in a clockwise fashion has the advantage that, in descent, the handrail is on the right-hand side.

- The walking line is taken as 10.6 inches (27.0 cm) from the outside of the newel or the inside of the outer handrail.

- At a distance of 6 inches (15 cm) from the newel or inside stringer, the tread must have a depth that is greater than 4 inches (10.2 cm). At the walking line, the going should not be less than 11 inches (27.9 cm).

- To develop a dimensionally acceptable layout, proceed as follows:

(1) Establish the diameter of the stair and the positions of the first and last risers.

(2) Determine the number of risers:

$$n = \frac{H}{R}$$

(3) Determine the number of steps and the going dimension at the walking line by using Table 5, which shows the going dimension where the stair diameter and the number of treads in the plan circle are known.

(4) Check the headroom clearance at the most unfavorable point. If the headroom is inadequate, change the number of steps.

Helical Stairs with an Open Well

- A clockwise ascent layout is preferable.

- The actual walking line rise-going dimensions should not exceed acceptable limits. Table 6 shows the going dimension (in the direction of the run) at 1-foot (30-cm) intervals from the center of the circle for seven different tread angles. A minimum going dimension of 11 inches (28 cm) should be chosen for the walking line 10.6 inches (27 cm) from the inside or outside handrail.

Table 6. Going dimensions for helical stairs with an open well

Number of Treads in Circle	22.5	25.7	30	36	45	60	90
Tread Angle (degrees)	16	14	12	10	8	6	4
Distance from center of circle (feet)	Going dimension (inches)						
3	10.0						
4	13.4	11.7					
5	16.7	14.6	12.5	10.5			
6	20.0	17.5	15.1	12.6	10.0		
7		20.5	17.6	14.6	11.7		
8			20.1	16.7	13.4	10.0	
9				18.8	15.1	11.3	
10					16.7	12.6	
11						13.8	
12						15.1	10.1
13						16.3	10.9
14						17.6	11.7
15							12.6
Distance from center of circle (meters)	Going dimension (centimeters)						
0.91	25.3						
1.22	33.9	29.7	25.5				
1.52	42.3	37.0	31.8	26.5			
1.83	50.9	44.6	38.3	31.9	25.5		
2.13			44.5	37.1	29.7		
2.44				42.5	34.0	25.5	
2.74					38.2	28.7	
3.05						31.9	21.3
3.35						35.1	23.4
3.66						38.3	25.5
3.96							27.6

Ramps

By definition, a ramp is any part of a constructed pedestrian circulation way with a slope greater than 5 percent. Acceptable gradients for ramps depend on the length of ramp to be used and the location of landings.

- To determine if a ramp will be an acceptable solution for an existing site condition the designer must determine elevation change (H) and the length of run (L). This length is the horizontal distance over which the elevation change takes place, minus the length of any landings.

- If H/L is less than the maximum gradient given in Table 7 for ramps of this length, then a ramp may be used. If H/L is greater than the maximum gradient shorten the length (L) by adding an intermediate landing and check the table again.

- To establish the maximum length of the ramp between landings, consult Table 8.

Refine and detail

Step Shape

- Nosings: Abrupt nosing overhangs (cf. Fig. 6) and any overhang that is greater than 3/4 inch (1.9 cm) should not be constructed. Where a nosing is needed, provide backward-sloping nosing overhangs (less than 3/4 inch) where this is possible.

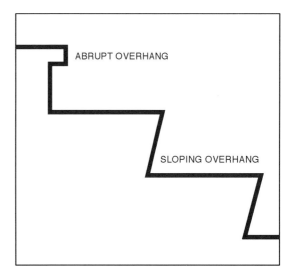

Fig. 6. Nosing overhangs

Table 7. Acceptable Ramp Gradients, Maximum Rise and Length

Gradient	Maximum Rise in Single Run		Total Length, Excluding Landings		
1:8—1:10	3 inches	(7.6 cm)	24—30	inches	(61—76 cm)
1:10.1—1.11	9 feet	(2.74 m)	91—99	inches	(28—30 m)
1:11.1—1:13	14 feet	(4.27 m)	155—182	inches	(47—55 m)
1:13.1—1:15	16 feet	(4.88 m)	210—240	inches	(64—73 m)
1:15.1—1:16	20 feet	(6.10 m)	302—320	inches	(92—98 m)

Note: building, fire, and handicapped codes may require different gradients.
Source: Templer *et al.* (1980)

Table 8. Maximum length between landings on ramps

Maximum Ramp Length	Gradient 1:15.9	1:14.3	1:13.7	1:12.7	1:11.6	1:10
IN FEET						
Between bottom and landing 1	95 (5.9)	85 (6.0)	80 (5.8)	75 (5.9)	65 (5.6)	45 (4.5)
Between landing 1 and 2	75 (10.7)	70 (10.9)	65 (10.6)	55 (10.3)	55 (10.3)	45 (9.0)
Between landing 2 and 3	45 (13.5)	45 (14.0)	45 (13.9)	45 (13.8)	45 (14.2)	
Between landing 3 and 4	30 (15.4)	30 (16.1)	30 (16.1)			
Between landing 4 and 5	30 (17.3)					
Between landing 5 and 6	30 (19.2)					
IN METERS						
Between bottom and landing 1	29 (1.8)	30 (1.8)	24 (1.8)	23 (1.8)	20 (1.7)	14 (1.4)
Between landing 1 and 2	23 (3.3)	21 (3.3)	20 (3.2)	17 (3.1)	17 (3.1)	14 (2.7)
Between landing 2 and 3	14 (4.1)	14 (4.3)	14 (4.2)	14 (4.2)	14 (4.3)	
Between landing 3 and 4	9 (4.7)	9 (4.9)	9 (4.9)			
Between landing 4 and 5	9 (5.3)					
Between landing 5 and 6	9 (5.9)					

Note: figures in parentheses show total height ascended.

- Wash: A wash is needed to throw water off external steps. It should not exceed about a 1:60 slope.

- Dimensional regularity: Risers, treads, and nosing projections must be constructed with a high degree of dimensional consistency, and in fact most building codes wisely insist on this. The differences in dimension between the largest and smallest in a flight and between those in adjoining steps should not exceed 3/16 inch (0.48 cm). This is by no means too exacting a standard for contemporary building practices.

Materials

The appropriate choice of material for stair treads is likely to influenced by several factors: structural considerations, the type and volume of traffic, appearance, resistance to wear and sometimes chemicals and the climate, ease of maintenance and cleaning, cost, slip resistance, and how comfortable it is to walk on. Avoid soft woods and stone that may erode easily.

- Floor patterns: Avoid the use of textures or patterns or nosing strips that make it difficult to discern the edge of the nosings. Use colors to emphasize the edge.

- Carpet fixing: Avoid step and, particularly, nosing designs that will prevent carpeting from being fixed firmly.

- Slip resistance: Coefficients of Friction (COF) greater than 0.3 may be adequate to prevent slips on level, dry, step surfaces in internal stairs at normal rates of climb, but coefficients of 0.5 are considered preferable and safer. The most critical area for slips is at the nosing, but it is better to ensure that the whole tread has an adequate COF rather than to add abrasive nosing strips that may be visually confusing and may cause trips. Ramps require careful consideration to prevent slips. For a chosen COF for level surfaces, Table 9 shows the equivalent COF that will be required to obviate slips at various ramp gradients. The left-hand column shows a range of coefficients of friction such as might be chosen for a level walkway. The remaining columns show the coefficients necessary to provide equal slip resistance for various ramp gradients (for a person who does not change pace on the ramp).

- Tread surface: The surface of stair treads should be smooth, free from projecting joints stable under the loads with no tendency to shift underfoot, and with nothing to catch the shoe.

- Injurious materials: The stair as well as the handrails and balustrading should be free from projecting elements, sharp edges and corners, and any rough surfaces, bars, rods, and other elements that have a small section. Instead, as with the interior of the car, smooth, flat, impact-attenuating surfaces and gentle curves should be used.

Handrails

- Location: A stair that is 35 inches (88.9 cm) wide between the walls and with a rail on one side has the maximum feasible width if the rail must fall within the reach of adult users. A 47-inch (1.19 cm) wide stair with handrails on both sides is the maximum width for both rails to be always available to adult users. Current codes permit a single rail for stairs up to 44 inches (.12 m) and two rails for stairs up to 88 inches (2.24 m).

- Height: From the forward edge of the nosing to the top of the handrail should be 36 to 40 inches (0.91—1.02 m), but codes usually require 30 to 34 inches (76.2—86.4 cm). For children, an intermediate rail that is 21.8 to 28.7 inches (55.4—72.9 cm) should be provided.

- Extent: Handrails should extend horizontally a minimum of 12 inches (30.5 cm) beyond the top of the stair and beyond the bottom riser for a distance equal to the tread width and then continue horizontally for 12 inches (30.5 cm). The handrails should not project into walkways; the ends should return to the floor or adjoining walls. Handrails should continue along at least one side of a landing.

- Size and shape: A circular handrail 1-1/2 inch (3.8 cm) diameter is most effective for gripping.

- Spacing distance from walls: The clearance between a handrail and an adjoining wall, assuming a circular handrail with 1-1/2 inch (3.8 cm) diameter, should not be less than 3.65 inches (9.3 cm).

Table 9. Static Coefficient of Friction for Level Surfaces and for Various Gradients

Level	1:20	1.18	1:16	1:14	1:12	1:10	1:8	1:6	1:4
.80	.89	.90	.91	.92	.95	.98	1.03	1.12	1.31
.75	.83	.84	.85	.87	.89	.92	.97	1.05	1.23
.70	.78	.79	.80	.81	.83	.86	.90	.98	1.15
.65	.72	.73	.74	.76	.78	.80	.84	.92	1.07
.60	.67	.68	.69	.70	.72	.74	.78	.85	1.00
.55	.62	.62	.63	.65	.66	.69	.72	.79	.93
.50	.56	.57	.58	.59	.61	.63	.67	.73	.86
.45	.51	.52	.53	.54	.55	.58	.61	.67	.79
.40	.46	.47	.47	.49	.50	.52	.53	.61	.72
.35	.41	.41	.42	.43	.45	.47	.50	.55	.66
.30	.36	.36	.37	.38	.39	.41	.44	.49	.59

- Materials: Handrails should not be too slippery or too rough. Rails that are lightly padded like auto steering wheels can provide the correct range of friction characteristics, may enable better grip forces to occur, and are less likely to cause trauma if they are hit in a fall. Handrail materials should not conduct or retail heat to the degree that they become untouchable. Handrails must not be permitted to deteriorate so their surfaces become splintered or pitted with rust. Finally, the color of handrails should be carefully chosen so they are always highly visible.

Guardrails

- Height: Guardrails should not be less than 42 inches (1.07 m) high unless the width is greater than 6 inches (15.2 cm). In that case, the minimum height of the guardrail should not be less than 48 inches (1.22 m) minus B, where B is the minimum width of the top surface of the guardrail. Thus, if the width of the top surface of the guardrail is 20 inches (25.4 cm), the height may be 38 inches (0.97 m)—48 inches less 10 inches. The rail height should never be less than 30 inches (76.2 cm). The design should discourage people from climbing onto a rail from which they may overbalance and fall.

- Structural loading: Most codes require the system to be able to withstand a test load without much deflection. A typical test requires the system to withstand a 200-pound (90.7 kg) vertical load at the midspan of the rail, with a deflection that does not exceed the length of the rail divided by 96. For a horizontal load test, the system may be required to withstand 200 pounds (90.7 kg), measured at the top of the rail at its midspan, with a deflection that does not exceed the sum of the rail height divided by 24 plus the rail length between vertical supports divided by 96. When the load is applied at a vertical support, the deflection may not exceed the rail height divided by 12. In public buildings, there is a greater danger of extreme loading, so a higher standard of structural strength is required. The test load is increased by 50 percent (or 65 percent in some circumstances such as balconies). For one- and two-story residential buildings, the test load may be reduced by 50 percent.

- Baluster spacing: As a check of spacing, it should not be possible to pass a sphere of 3 1/2-inch (8.9 cm) diameter through the balustrading.

Illumination

Proper illumination of a stairway is essential for both comfort and safety. Adequate lighting must be provided under both electric lighting and daylighting conditions, with attention to daylighting and solar glare and reflections that may occur only at specific times of the year. The following guidelines address accident prevention and safety recommendations that are restated in the following section on designing stairs to reduce and eliminate accidents.

- Adequate illumination, either natural or electric, must be provided. The IES recommendation of 5 to 20 foot-candles (54—215 lux) for most applications seems to be much more realistic for stair safety than those minimum levels permitted by most building codes. A minimum of 8 foot-candles (86 lux) may be adequate.

- The illumination should be reasonably constant over the whole stair.

- Window and artificial light sources should not be placed where the stair user must include them and the steps in the same direct field of vision, and shadows on the steps should be avoided.

- For reflectance, the IES recommends 21 to 31 percent for floors.

- If the stair is located where there is any risk that someone might stumble into it unexpectedly, permanent supplementary artificial illumination should be provided.

- The switches that control the stair lights should be placed sufficiently far from the stair so there is no risk of a person's falling while reaching for the switch. Three-way switches should be used at the top and bottom of the stairs.

Glossary of common terms used in stair design

Balustrade: the entire infilling from handrail down to floor level at the edge of a stair.

Banister: a baluster (corruption of baluster).

Carriage (or carriage piece, rough string, bearer, stair horse): an inclined timber placed between the two strings against the underside of wide stairs to support them in the middle.

Circular stair: a helical stair.

Close string (or closed string): a string that extends above the edges of the risers and treads, covering them on the outside.

Commode step: a riser curved in plan, generally at the foot of a stair.

Dextral stair: a stair that turns to the right during ascent.

Dog-legged stair (or dog-leg): a stair with two flights separated by a half-landing, and having no stairwell, so that the upper flight returns parallel to the lower flight.

Ergonomics: the interaction between work and people, particularly, the design of machines, chairs, tables, etc. to suit the body and to permit work with the least fatigue.

Flight: a series of steps between landings.

Going: the horizontal distance between two successive nosings. (In a helical stair the going varies.) The sum of the goings of a straight flight stair is the going of the flight.

Gradient of a stair: the ratio between going and riser; the angle of inclination.

Guardrail: a protective railing designed to prevent people or objects from falling into open well, stairwell, or similar space.

Handrail: a rail forming the top of a balustrade.

Handrail scroll: a spiral ending to a handrail.

Helical stair: the correct but not the usual name for a spiral stair.

Landing: a platform at the top, bottom, or between flights of a staircase.

Monkey tail: a downward scroll at the end of a handrail.

Newel (or newel post): the post around which wind the steps of a circular stair. Also applied to the post into which the handrail is framed.

Nosing: the front and usually rounded edge to a stair tread. It frequently projects over the riser below it.

Nosing overhand: the distance that the nosing edge of a step projects beyond the back of the tread below.

Open stair: a stair that is open on one or both sides.

Piano nobile: the principal floor of a house, raised one floor above ground level.

Ramp: an inclined plane for passage of traffic.

Riser: the upright face of a step.

INTERIORS

C2

Riser height (or rise): the vertical distance from the top of a step at the nosing to the top of an adjoining step at the nosing.

Sinistral stair: a stair that turns to the left in ascent.

Spiral stair (or helical stair): a circular stair in which all the treads are winders.

Stair: (1) a series of steps with or without landings, giving access from level to level; (2) one step, consisting of a tread and a riser.

Stairwell: see Well.

Step: one unit of a stair, consisting of a riser and a tread. It may be a flier or a winder.

String (or stringer): a sloping board at each end of the treads that carries the treads and risers of a stair.

Tread: the (usually) horizontal surface of a step; also the length (from front to back) of such a surface.

Wash (or kilt): a slight sloping of treads to throw off rainwater.

Well: an open space through one or more floors.

Winding stair: a spiral stair; a circular or elliptical geometrical stair.

Special attention to top of stairs

Stair design to reduce injuries

Summary: An overview of significant design issues and recommendations is provided to increase stair safety by design. Experience and research related to accidents are summarized related to stair location, layouts, views, lighting and use conditions. These provide guidelines for stair design to reduce accidents by diligent design and permanent construction and maintenance.

Key words: handrails, nosings, risers, safety, stair design, treads, wash.

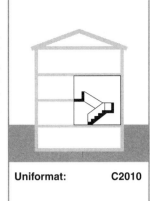

Uniformat: C2010

INTERIORS C2

What causes falls?

People have incidents on stairs when certain conditions are present. There are credible explanations why these conditions are dangerous. Defects can be reduced and eliminated by appropriate design, responsible construction, and vigilant maintenance. The following commentary provides an overview of conditions to be avoided. Design recommendations are highlighted as bulleted items. A detailed discussion is provided in Templer (1992).

Inappropriateness of stairs: Because stairs are inherently more dangerous than level walkways or ramps, there are some circumstances in which they should not be used, no matter how well designed and constructed.

- When feasible, stairs should not be the sole means of access or egress, particularly for elderly and physically limited people and in places where alcohol is served.

- If changes of level are inevitable, alternative means of access and egress, such as ramps and elevators, should be provided.

An inappropriate connector: Stairs are sometimes located where they will be significantly more dangerous.

- If people traveling between two adjacent areas are likely to be carrying bulky or heavy articles, the areas should not be linked by means of steps. The change of level should be avoided, or the areas linked in some other way.

- If there is a likelihood that potentially slippery materials such as food or drinks may be accidentally spilled on the stairs, the stairs should be isolated from the source and traffic pattern of handling the lubricant.

Hidden flights and dangerous locations: Steps are sometimes located where they may not be noticed. People may fall down stairs because they are unaware of the stair.

- For the safety of the severely visually impaired, stairs should be located out of direct pedestrian ways so that pedestrians must make an intentional (if minor) detour to use them.

- Doors by a landing should not open directly onto a flight of stairs.

- Steps and stairs should be located where they may be easily seen before they are encountered. This may mean that night lights and similar permanent illumination must be provided, or it may mean that in daylight the steps must be made to contrast visually with their surroundings.

- Single steps should not be built except at thresholds, curbs, and other places where they are customarily found Even in some of these places, if there is any doubt whether they will be noticed, the best solution is usually to eliminate them.

- Where it is considered likely that some severely visually impaired people or small children may fall into the stair, the stair may have to be closed off by means of a self-closing gate or some equally effective device.

More and less dangerous stair layouts: Many building codes and conventional wisdom suggest that helical stairs, long straight flights, and stairs with winders are dangerous and should be avoided or prohibited for many uses. Despite some attention paid to the hypotheses in the most significant stair studies, these conclusions are still not entirely established or substantiated.

- Long straight flight stairs without landings are usually prohibited by building codes and should not be built.

- Dog-leg and similar layouts with short flights are safer than straight flight stairs.

- Dog-leg, helical, and complex layouts should ascend in a clockwise direction to avoid the generation of conflicting streams of traffic.

- For stadia, auditoriums, and other locations with substantial traffic volumes, to avoid the risk of people being crushed in the event of panic, stair layouts with abrupt turns should not be constructed.

- The stair must be large enough for the anticipated volume of pedestrians.

Too long or too short flights: Most construction codes impose limits to the number of steps permitted in one flight. Before concluding that long flights are safer, one must examine where most accidents occur. Templer (1992) cites research reports where one-third of stair incidents occurred on either the first or last step; an additional 25 percent occurred on the second or next-to-last step; and another 12 percent on the third or third-from-the-last step. That is, 70 percent of accidents occurred on the top three or bottom three steps.

- Special attention must be paid to the design and construction of the top three and bottom three steps in any flight.

The issue of (dangerous) views from stairs: some research: If views from stairwells distract us from attending to the stairs, a misstep be-

Author: John Templer

Reference: Templer, John. 1992. *The Staircase: Studies of Hazards, Falls, and Safer Design.* Cambridge, MA: MIT Press.

comes more likely. Findings from some studies would suggest that interesting views from stairs are inherently dangerous and only un-adorned, enclosed stair tunnels are safe from danger of distracting views. The findings are not conclusive, however: The problem may be caused not simply as a function of views per se but by whether they distract our attention to the complete exclusion of alternative interesting scenes.

The problem seems to be related to sudden changes in view as one passes from step to step. A stair that is open to an architecturally stimulating space and even enclosed by it is not necessarily hazardous unless the view is completely absorbing or, more particularly, is presented only at certain points on the stair in combination with other environmental distractions.

- As a generality, anything that induces stair users to focus attention on the stair rather than the surroundings increases safety. Where this is not possible, the views should be wide open at all points on the stair, not suddenly revealed at certain places and certainly not only at the top three or bottom three steps by the landings where most accidents occur.

Where is the tread edge? Precise information is needed about the exact location of the front edge of the tread of each step. In ascent, finding the nosing edge is not usually difficult because it is close to the eyes and because both risers and treads are visible. In descent, the tread edge may be inadvertently camouflaged, even for those with perfect vision, as a result of the step design,

- Avoid the use of flooring and carpet patterns and abrasive strips that may be visually confused with the edge of the nosing.

- Increase the visual contrast between adjoining treads. This may be achieved by a modest change of tone.

Stairs in poor lighting conditions: Our ability to walk safely on stairs is contingent upon sufficient illumination to permit us to see the stair clearly.

- Adequate illumination, either natural or electric, must be provided. The Illuminating Engineers Society (IES) recommendation of 20 foot-candles (215 lux) for most applications seems to be much more realistic standard for stair safety than those permitted by many building codes.

- The illumination should be reasonably constant over the whole stair. Shadows on the steps should be avoided, which in effect are equivalent to absence of illumination.

- Window and electric light sources should not be placed where the stair user must include them, and the steps, in the same direct field of vision.

- In terms of reflectance, the IES recommends 21 to 31 percent for floors.

- If the stair is located where there is any risk that someone might stumble into it unexpectedly, then permanent supplementary electric lighting should be provided.

- The switches that control the stair lights should be placed sufficiently far from the stair so that there is no risk of a person's falling while reaching for the switch. Similarly, three-way switches should be conveniently placed at the top and bottom landings of the stairs.

- Stairways placed near windows and doors may experience blinding sun rays or glare for selective periods of the year and thus be poorly illuminated for certain periods due to absence of light and sun control.

Risers and treads: The dimensions of risers and treads control our gait, our agility and comfort, and the probability of accidents.

- The upper limit for riser height, the lower limit for tread depth, and the best combination of dimension for risers and treads for the most usual circumstances in buildings have been established (see Table 4 of preceding article C2-1), providing quite explicit design criteria and norms.

Projecting nosings: A nosing projection that is no more than about 11/16 inch (1.75 cm) adds a modicum of safety compared to a flight with no nosings or a flight with larger nosings. Where the nosing overhang is formed by simply sloping the riser back from the nosing edge, this seems to cause no difficulties, and these are generally permitted. Fixing carpeting around steps that have abrupt nosing overhangs is difficult to install and are easily loosened. Carpets are often left to bulge out around the projection without adequate fixing. The looseness of the carpet and the lack of definition of the edge of the nosing then become a new hazard.

- Abrupt nosing overhangs, and any overhand greater than 11/16 inch (1.75 cm), should not be constructed.

- Nosings of 11/16 inch (1.75 cm) or less seem to make steps safer.

- Backward-sloping nosing overhangs should be used rather than abrupt nosings.

Tread surfaces and materials: The appropriate choice of a material for stair treads will be influenced by structural considerations, the type and volume of traffic, appearance, resistance to wear, and, sometimes, chemicals and the climate, ease of maintenance and cleaning, cost, slip resistance, and walking comfort. No materials seem to be significantly safer or less safe than any others if they are properly maintained.

- The surface of stair treads and nosings should be smooth and even. It should be free from projecting joints or nosing strips and stable under the loads, with no tendency to shift underfoot.

- The surface should have unacceptable coefficient of friction. (Recommended values for slip-resistance coefficient are presented in the prior section.)

The wash: The wash is the slope of the tread from riser to nosing edge. A wash is provided to throw water off the stair or to make the risers less high and therefore easier to climb.

- The slope of the wash should not exceed about 1:60.

Handrails, guardrails, and balustrades: Handrails, guardrails, and balustrades are each needed for quite different purposes. The purpose of guardrails and balustrades is to protect people from falling over the edge of a platform, landing, balcony, stair, and so on. Handrails serve to prevent a loss of balance, to help one regain balance, to help pull oneself up a stair, and for directional guidance and stability. See Section C2001 for recommended dimensions.

The way the stair is built: Some of the greatest accident reductions can be realized simply by insisting that stairs be constructed according to the original design and that a reasonable level of precision be present in the finished product.

- Risers, treads, and nosing projections must be constructed with a high degree of dimensional consistency (most building codes wisely insist on this). The differences in dimension between the largest and smallest in a flight and between those in adjoining steps should not exceed 3/16 inch (0.48 cm). This is by no means too exacting a standard for contemporary building practices.

The way the stair is maintained: Levels of deterioration and damage that might be acceptable for level walkway surfaces cannot be tolerated on stairs; the risk of a serious injury is too great. The greatest danger comes from any structural weakness that may cause any part of the stair to break during use. Nearly as bad is the condition where the treads on the surface material are chipped, torn, splintered, loose, or excessively worn. Of as much concern are handrails and balusters that are broken, missing, or loose. Ease of stair maintenance can be helped by design that allows easy cleaning and inspection.

• Stairs should never be used as a location for storing objects.

• Stairs must be kept clean and free from precipitation, dust, dirt, and anything else that might act to trigger slips and trips.

• The surface finish of treads (and carpets especially) must not be allowed to deteriorate noticeably.

• Handrails and balustrades must be kept in good repair, firmly fixed, and structurally sound.

• Electric illumination sources must be kept in good operating condition.

Reducing injuries from stair accidents: Stair accidents can be reduced by intelligent design, construction, maintenance, and use, but this is not enough. Toward this end, the idea of the soft stair is proposed. Using our experience with safer automobile experiences and by a careful choice of materials and details, stairs can be designed to obviate certain types of injuries resulting from falls, and to greatly reduce the severity of others.

• Most injuries from stair falls are caused by collision with the steps and landings, so the greatest rewards in injury reduction will be derived from softening these—rounding the nosings and reducing the hardness of the surfaces. These measures must be undertaken with due discretion. The rounding of the nosing must not substantially reduce the size of the tread, and the walking surfaces must not be made so soft as to interfere with a normal gait.

• In addition to the steps and landings, impact energy-attenuating materials should be applied to all the surfaces that a victim may fall against. Walls at the side of the stair or at the end of the landing should be padded, as should any balustrading. Even the handrails should be treated like the steering wheel of many modern cars with a firm but compressible material that provides a good grip but can still reduce the impact of a blow.

• Most cuts will come from bumping up against edges and corners such as those sometimes found on nosings or aluminum nosing inserts. Balustrades and handrails frequently are made from rectangular or square bars or wood sections, and stringers are formed from timber or plates. Frequently, these sections are left with sharp-edged corners.

INTERIORS

C2

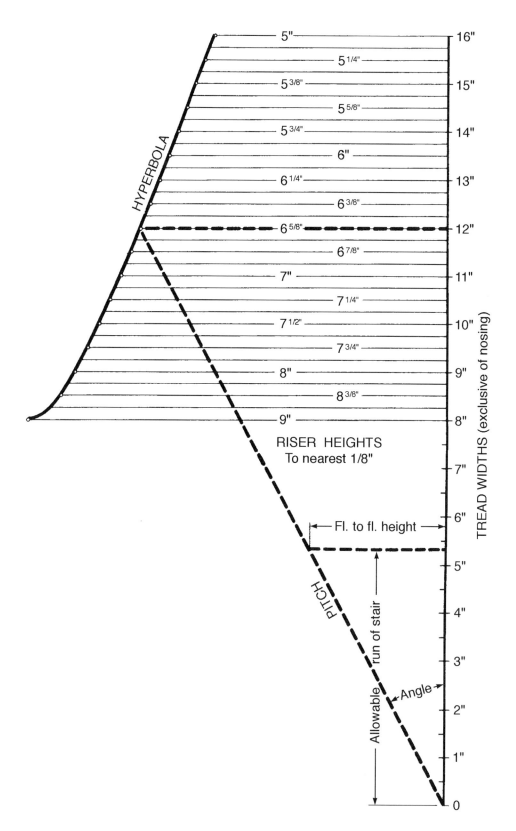

Fig 1. Proportional tread and riser nomograph
All dimensions are 1/2 full size
Metric conversion factor: 1 inch = 25.4 mm = 2.54 cm

Boston Public Library, Boston, MA McKim, Mead and White, 1888.

Stair dimensioning

Summary: A graphic means for preliminary design check for stair dimensions is provided by a riser/tread nomograph and references to standard stair designs including provision for exitway refuge areas.

Key words: refuge areas, riser, stair run, stair dimensions, tread.

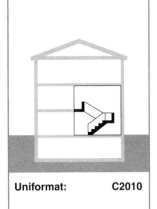

Uniformat:	C2010

INTERIORS

C2

These pages provide stair dimensional data for preliminary reference only. Dimensions for stair design in most building types are covered in explicit terms by local building codes. A complete discussion with reference to building codes prevalent in North America is provided in Allen and Iano (1995).

Tread and riser nomograph

The nomograph (Fig. 1) provides a quick reference check of proportional dimensions for stair layouts. Data include proportional tread width and riser height and tabular material giving handrail heights, headroom, and stair gradients for stairs with risers from 5 to 9 inches (12.7 to 22.86 cm). Note: a riser of 8-1/4" (21.95 cm) is the maximum height proscribed in common building codes for residential stairs.

- Dimensions of stair treads and risers are proportional and can be plotted on a hyperbola, reproduced here in the form of a working chart. Dimensions are accurate to the nearest 1/8 in. (3.18 mm).

- In all cases the width of tread is exclusive of a nosing.

- The average height of risers shown, 7 in. (17.8 cm) , is proportional to a tread of 11 in. (27.9 cm), a combination that produces a stair which is comfortable and generally economical. At the lower extreme, a riser of 5 in. (12.7 cm) produces a tread of 16 in. (40.6 cm) which approximates the proportions of a brick step with a tread equal to two stretchers and a rise equal to two courses.

Using the nomograph

Dimensions are accurate to half-full-size. Thus, readings can be made directly and proportionally without need for calculation.

- To find proper riser for a given tread: Read tread line to given width and select riser at intersection

- To find proper tread for a given riser: Select riser to nearest 1/8 in. (3.18 mm) and read tread width to nearest 1/2 in. (1.27 cm) or nearest 1/4 in. (.635 cm) by interpolation at intersection with tread line.

- To find tread and riser for given height and run of stair: Scale the length of run of stair on tread line. Draw floor to floor height at same scale. Draw pitch of stair. Where pitch intersects hyperbola, measure riser (at half-full-size) to tread line. Read tread width directly or measure at half-full-size.

- To find run of stair for given height, tread and riser: Select riser height. Connect intersection at hyperbola with 0 on tread line, establishing pitch. Draw floor-to-floor height to scale, intersecting pitch and perpendicular to tread line. Length of stair run is found at same scale as height on tread line from 0 to intersection of floor-to-floor height.

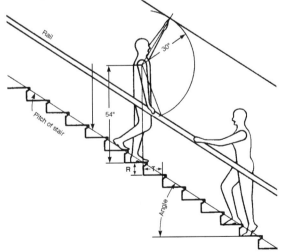

Author: Ernest Irving Freese

References: Allen, Edward and Joseph Iano. *The Architect's Studio Companion: Rules of Thumb for Preliminary Design.* 2nd edition. 1995. New York: John Wiley & Sons.

Henry Dreyfuss Associates. 1993. *The Measure of Man and Woman.* New York: Whitney Library of Design.

Ramsey/Sleeper. 1994. *Architectural Graphic Standards.* Ninth Edition. "Egress Planning" pp. 23-28. New York: John Wiley & Sons.

INTERIORS

C2

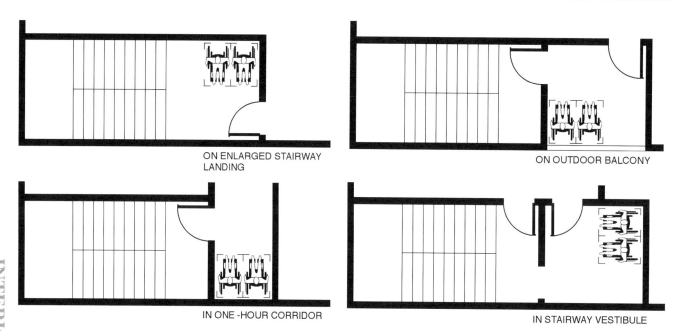

Fig. 2. Provision of refuge areas (after Allen and Iano 1995).

Stair layout to provide areas of refuge

The American with Disabilities Act along with universal design practices provide for means of safe egress and refuge within smoke-protected areas and exitways, properly considered along with stairwell design. Areas of refuge are fire-protected zones for people unable to use stairs to await assistance in an emergency. A wheelchair space

30 in. by 48 in. (76.2 cm by 122 cm) free and clear of the exit pathway must typically be provided for every 200 occupants or portion thereof per floor, with a minimum of two places per area of refuge. Fig. 2 indicates provision of refuge areas for individuals in wheelchairs (after Allen and Iano 1995). Fig. 3 indicates overall dimensioning guidelines.

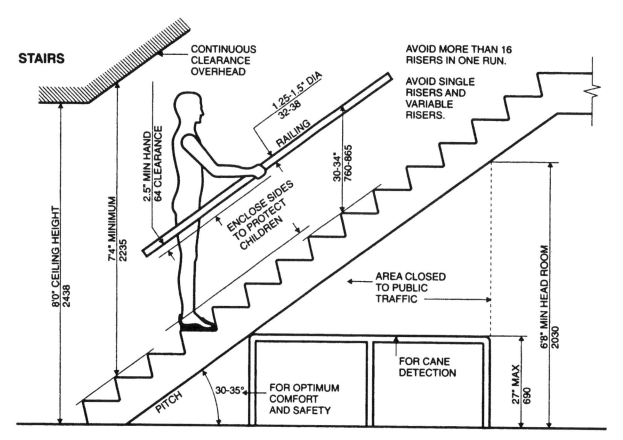

Fig. 3. Stairway dimensioning. Reproduced by permission. Henry Dreyfuss Associates. 1993. *The Measure of Man and Woman.* **New York: Whitney Library of Design.**

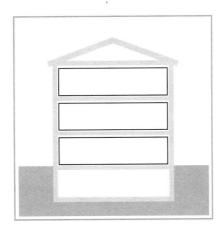

C INTERIORS

*Tiled ceiling. Blue Mosque. Isfahan.
Photo: Stanley Hallet, FAIA*

Wall and ceiling finishes

Summary: This article provides an overview of wall and ceiling substrates and finishes, including gypsum board, plaster, wood paneling, stone panels, paints and stains, and wallcoverings. Discussed are material options, suitable substrates, performance characteristics, typical sizes, and specification notes.

Key words: gypsum board, paint, plaster, solvent, veneers.

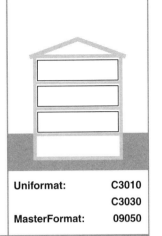

Uniformat:	C3010
	C3030
MasterFormat:	09050

INTERIORS

C3

This article reviews common interior wall substrates and finish options, some also applicable as ceiling finish systems. Each material and construction method is the subject of extensive detail and development, represented in the references and in manufacturer data, summarized in Sweets Catalog Files. The following summary describes these substrates and finishes in terms of their generic properties and performance characteristics as an overview for consideration in preliminary design and specification:

1 Gypsum Board

2 Plaster

3 Wood paneling

4 Stone wall panels and tiles

5 Paints and stains

6 Wallcoverings

1 Gypsum board

Gypsum board is the most common wall and ceiling surfacing material currently in use. It is composed of a gypsum core with a paper backing on two sides to help stabilize the panels and to provide a suitable surface for paint or other finishes. It comes in a several thicknesses, sizes, and utility grades. Types include:

- *Standard gypsum board*
- composed of standard thicknesses of gypsum with paper surfacing.
- manufactured in standard sizes and thicknesses.
- provides an extremely flat surface.
- must be installed upon a suitable support system.
- inherently fire resistant.
- *Type "X" gypsum board*
- greater fire resistance than standard gypsum board.
- fire resistance gained from adding fiberglass and fire- resistive additives to the gypsum mixture.

- heavier and stronger than standard gypsum board.
- *Foil backed panels*
- incorporates a foil backing on rear of panel.
- can be used as a vapor retarder installed on exterior walls.
- must be installed where moisture will not be trapped within the wall; coordinate with specific manufacturer's data.
- *Water-resistant gypsum board*
- also known as green or blue board because of the color of the facing paper.
- core and facing papers are treated to increase water resistance.
- specifically designed to be used as a substrate for impervious ceramic tile and similar materials.
- suitable for showers and tub surrounds with surfaces exposed to, but not submerged in, water.
- not for use in applications that are subject to standing water or steam.
- *Glass-mat, water-resistant gypsum backing board*
- proprietary name is Dens-Shield Tile Backer.
- similar to water resistant gypsum board but of better quality.
- coated fiberglass matt surfaces provide water resistance.
- suitable for soffits and other exterior areas exposed to the weather.
- *Cementitious backer board*
- has Portland cement core.
- faced with two fiberglass mesh mats.
- specifically designed for most tile finishes.
- water resistant but not a waterproof barrier.
- *Exterior gypsum board or gypsum sheathing*
- Designed for soffits, base layers for exterior insulation finish systems (EIFS), and other exterior uses not directly exposed to the weather.

Author: William Hall

References: Gere, Alex S. 1995. *Recommended Practices for the Use of Natural Stone in Construction.* Purdys, NY: Building Stone Institute.

National Gypsum Co. *Gypsum Construction Guide.* Charlotte, NC: National Gypsum Co.

PDCA. *Architectural Specification Manual, Painting, Repainting, Wallcovering and Gypsum Board Finishing.* Kent, WA: Painting and Decorating Contractors of America.

TCA. 1992. *Handbook for Ceramic Tile Installation.* Clemson, SC: Tile Council of America.

Weismantel, Guy E., editor. 1981. *Paint Handbook.* New York: McGraw-Hill.

- Faced with brown paper not suitable for painting.

Basic gypsum board configurations

• *Width and lengths*

- Standard width is 4 ft. (1,220 mm).

- Lengths available are: 8, 9, 10, 12 and 14 ft. (2,438 mm, 2,743 mm, 3,048 mm, 3,658 mm, and 4,267 mm).

• *Thickness*

- 5/8 in. (16 mm) is most common for commercial uses.

- 1/2 in. (13 mm) typical for residential uses.

- 1/4 in. and 3/8 in. (6 mm and 10 mm) panels used for special applications such as curved walls or as an overlay onto other surfaces.

- 1 in. (25 mm) for utility panels.

• *Edges*

- square edges typical for applications where thick finish materials will be installed over it and flat, hidden joints are not a consideration.

- tapered edges are typical where joints are taped and mudded so they will be hidden when the wall is painted, or other relatively thin finish materials are used.

- tongue-and-groove joints are used to ensure that panel edges remain aligned.

- other edge configurations include rounded and beveled.

• *Joint treatments*

If a joint between two sheets of gypsum board is to be hidden behind another material, the appearance of the joint is not critical. However, most interior walls need smooth, hidden joints. This process is as follows:

- Joint is first spread with a thin layer of mud (powdered gypsum and water).

- Paper tape 2 in. to 3 in. (51 mm to 76 mm) wide is pressed into the mud over the joint, left to dry, and then sanded.

- A second coat of mud is spread about 6 in. (152 mm) wide over the tape, left to dry, and then sanded.

- A third coat of topping compound is spread about 9 in. to 12 in. (229 mm to 305 mm) wide. Topping compound is much finer, dries faster, is left to dry, and then sanded to the finished surface.

- The entire joint will now blend with the surrounding surface and be hidden after painting or other finishes are applied.

- Inside corners are treated similarly, except that the paper tape is bent to fit into the corner before it is installed.

- Outside corners are treated similar except that, instead of tape, a metal corner bead is used. This is a thin metal angle with perforated flanges (pressed into the mud) and a rounded corner.

Gypsum board systems

All gypsum board must be installed on its own support system. Most installations will take one of the following forms:

• *Light gauge steel stud framing*

- The most common support for gypsum board.

- Normally, 3-5/8 in. and 6 in. (86 mm and 152 mm) wide studs are the most common.

- Other widths are 1-5/8 in. and 2-1/2 in. (41 mm and 64 mm) among other sizes.

- Metal studs are 20 or 22 gauge for lengths less than 10' (3,048 mm).

- Studs are installed into metal "C" shaped tracks attached to the floor and ceiling.

- Spacing is 16 in. (406 mm) o.c. maximum for 1/2 in. (13 mm) gypsum board; 24 in. (610 mm) o.c. maximum for 5/8 in. (16 mm) gypsum board.

- Gypsum board is screwed to the studs.

- Spacing of fasteners is to be as specified by gypsum board manufacturer.

• *Furring or clips*

When gypsum board is to be installed over masonry, around steel, or in circumstances where a flat substrate is not available, then a furring system is used. Furring is a one-sided wall in front of or around another element, that usually provides little structural support, and rely on the assembly (clips and gypsum board) attached to the substrate to provide stability. Furring materials include:

- 7/8 in. (22 mm) metal furring channels or "hat" channels.

- 1-5/8 in. (41 mm) metal studs.

- Standard metal studs 2-1/2 in. or 3-5/8 in. (64 mm or 92 mm) widths.

- "Z" Clips: metal clips or strips bent into a "Z" shape with one side attached to the substrate and the other used to attach the gypsum board. This assembly is often installed with rigid insulation between the clips.

• *Wood stud system*
- Similar to metal stud systems.

- More common in small commercial and residential construction.

- Certain building types do not allow wood studs for fire code classification reasons.

• *U.L. systems*

Because of its inherent fire resistive properties, gypsum board is a fundamental element in a wide variety of fire-rated systems. Underwriters Laboratories (U.L.) has tested specific construction configurations and, as a result, has assigned a unique number to that system.

- If the system is constructed according to the prescriptive design, building officials have agreed to approve that system as having that specific fire rating.

- Specific requirements are given regarding its construction.

- All specific requirements are published in the *Fire Resistive Standards Handbook* by Underwriters Laboratories.

- Most gypsum board manufacturers publish these system designs with their associated fire rating and U.L. numbers.

• *"Shaft wall" systems*

- A special system of studs and gypsum board designed for installation around stairs or elevator shafts.

- Composed of "C-H" metal studs, 1 in. (25 mm) gypsum board liner panels, and a combination multiple layers of 1/2 in. or 5/8 in. (13 mm or 16 mm) gypsum board. The number of layers depends on the fire rating.

- Fire ratings vary from 1 to 4 hours.

- The 1 in. (25 mm) panels fit into the "H" portion of the studs and the gypsum board panels are attached to the face of the "C" portion.

- Depth of the wall depends on the varying depth of the "C" portion of the studs.

• *"Vent Shaft" systems*

INTERIORS

C3

- A special system composed entirely of gypsum board panels.

- 1 in. (25 mm) gypsum board liner panels as a core.

- Layer of 1/2 in. (13 mm) or 5/8 in. (16 mm) gypsum board on each side of the liner panels.

- Fire rating depends on the thickness of the gypsum board.

- Core panel is offset from the outside panels a couple of inches creating a tongue and groove situation that enables one set of panels to tightly fit into the adjacent set.

- Panels are attached to top and bottom metal tracks that are attached to the floor and ceiling.

Gypsum board ceiling systems

Many of the systems for walls can be adapted for use on ceilings. Types include:

- *Direct applied system*

- Gypsum board is installed and attached directly to the bottom of the structural elements.

- This is typical where the structure is metal or wood joists.

- Joists are no farther apart an required by the thickness of the gypsum board; normally between 16 in. and 24 in. (406 mm and 610 mm).

- Also typical where other building systems are run between the joists.

- *Furred system*

Gypsum board is installed on furring strips that are attached to the bottom of the structural system. Typical furring systems include:

- Furring strips: 7/8 in. (22 mm) metal furring strips, known as "hat channels" because of their shape.

- 1x2 in. (2.5x5 cm) wood strips.

- Steel studs: used where the structural elements are farther apart than the gypsum board will tolerate. Furring strips are screwed to the bottom of wood joists or wired to the bottom of steel joists or other structure.

- *Suspended systems*

- Suspends an attachment system from hanger wires installed in a manner similar to that used for suspended acoustic ceilings.

2   Plaster

One of the oldest types of wall surfacing materials, plaster is composed of a lath or base material installed over a support system or substrate, and between two and three coats of plaster. An extremely flat and hard surface, it has no joints or nail holes to patch, and resists abrasion. Plaster application components include:

- sub-structure

- lath

- base coat

- brown coat

- finish coat

Types of lath

- *Gypsum lath*

- Made similar to gypsum board except the paper covering is more rough to help create a bond between the lath and the plaster.

- Available in a panels 16 in. x 48 in. (406 mm x 1,220 mm) and in 3/8 in. (10 mm) and 1/2 in. (13 mm) widths.

- Fire-rated panels are available in the same size but only in 3/8 in. (10 mm) thickness.

- *Metal lath*

- Made of both galvanized or painted steel.

- Lath is made in a mesh with diamond shaped holes of approximately 5/16 in. (8 mm) width.

- Available in panels 27 in. x 96 in. (686 mm x 2,438 mm).

- Self furring mesh has dimples pressed into it allowing the mesh to be accurately spaced away from the substrate.

- Other variations known as rib lath are offered in several configurations for added strength and rigidity to increase plaster strength and to help reduce cracking.

- Combination lath is a combination of metal lath and a sub-structure of CR channel studs, with a top and bottom L-runner. It occupies less than half of the space of conventional studs and lath and costs less because the channels, runners, and lath are installed at the same time.

- *Lath accessories*

- A variety of galvanized metal shapes that are used in certain situations, and include corner beads; square edge casings or stops; expansion joints; miscellaneous other shapes to handle more specialized problem areas.

- Accessories are normally made from galvanized steel but all zinc shapes are also available on a special order basis.

- Accessories are installed at the same time as the lath before plaster installation begins.

Plaster surfaces

Plaster coatings are applied in a two- or three-step process, depending on the thickness of the plaster surface desired. Different mixes of plaster are used for each.

- *Base coat*

- Also known as the scratch coat.

- Composed of neat plaster and an aggregate such as sand, vermiculite, perlite, hair, sisal, or glass fibers. Water is normally added at the job site.

- This coat is designed to be a base for the application of the finish coat of plaster. For greater strength or thickness, the addition of another coat, known as the brown coat, is required.

- Base coat plasters are available premixed from the factory with a perlite or vermiculite aggregate, with the plaster requiring only the addition of water at the job site. Its advantages are: uniformity because of its factory mixing; light weight because of the aggregate; higher insulating value due to the aggregate.

Finish plaster coat

Finish plasters are designed to be applied with a trowel to a thickness of not more than 1/16 in. (2 mm). Most manufacturers also make premixed plasters that require only the addition of water. Finish plasters come in several types:

- *Gauging plasters*

- designed to be mixed with water and lime at the job site.

- available in either quick or slow set types, depending on amount of lime.

- proper proportions in mixing is essential for appropriate strength and hardness.

- most common mixture for interior surfaces is two parts of lime to one part of plaster by weight.

- *Molding plasters*

- very finely ground mixes designed for ornamental uses.

INTERIORS

C3

- normally cast or molded into a variety of ornamental shapes.

- when running shapes are required, such as cornices or other molding, this mixture plaster type is mixed 2 to 1 with lime.

- *Acoustical plasters*

- factory-mixed products with acoustical properties gained from acoustical aggregates.

- *Keene's cement*

- made for high-density plasters. Lime is typically added to increase workability.

- *Lime additive*

- used in many types of finish plasters to provide early strength and help counteract shrinkage.

- Type N (normal) lime requires soaking for 12 or more hours until it is workable.

- Type S (hydrated) lime can be used almost immediately after mixing with water.

- *Veneer plaster*

- has characteristics that are a combination of lath, plaster, and gypsum board.

- similar to gypsum board with a highly absorptive paper.

- composed of a thin coat or two of a special designed plaster.

- quicker to install than conventional plaster.

- less costly than standard lath and plaster.

- has a higher resistance to cracking.

- plaster base and finish coat plasters pre-mixed at the factory.

- *Plaster installation*

- installed onto the substrate.

- base coat is applied by trowel to the lath.

- may be scratched to varying degrees to enhance the bite of the top coat of plaster.

- if needed, a second or brown coat of plaster is troweled on and leveled to approximately the thickness desired.

- a thin final or finish coat is applied and smoothed in preparation for other applied finishes.

3   Wood paneling

Wood paneling has been used for centuries as a method of covering a wall surface. Paneling may be made with either solid or veneered wood from a wide variety of wood species. Design considerations include grain patterns, wood species, edge detailing, stain or finish colors, and size of panels.

Wood terminology

- *Sawn wood*

- boards: pieces with the smallest dimension of 1 in. (25 mm) or less.

- lumber: pieces the smallest dimension of between 1 in. and 2 in. (25 mm and 51 mm).

- timber: pieces of wood with the smallest dimension greater than 2 in. (51 mm).

- *Flat-sawn*

- the board is cut from the log with its larger dimension parallel to the direction of the rings or grain.

- grain lines are farther apart and more open.

- wearability is decreased.

- *Quarter sawn*

- The board is cut from the log with its larger dimension perpendicular to the grain.

- Grain lines are much closer together.

- Wood piece is more dense and wearability is increased.

- *Types of wood paneling*

- Solid wood: Paneling made from multiple pieces of one thickness of solid wood joined together at the edges.

- Wood veneered plywood: Paneling pieces made of multiple layers of thinly sliced wood veneers glued together to form a thick panel.

Wood veneer

Veneer is cut into slices by two methods:

- *Peeling method:*

  Veneer is cut off a log by spinning it about its center and peeling off one long, thin layer.

- *Slicing method:*

  Veneer is cut off a log by attaching a half or quarter of a log to a steel block, holding it while a blade is moved vertically, or the log is rotated against a blade, slicing off thin strips of wood known as flitches. The orientation of the slices determines the grain pattern. Cutting with the grain creates an open grained pattern; cutting across the grain creates a tight, straight pattern.

- *Types of cuts*

- Rotary cut veneer: Cut by the peeling process, veneer is quite open and wild. This type of veneer is the most economical, and is often used for plywood.

- Flat sliced veneer: Sliced with the grain at the outside of the log in straight slices. Grain pattern is somewhat closer and tighter, with cathedrals in the grain meeting.

- Quarter cut veneer: Cut perpendicular to the grain in straight slices; grain pattern is straight and loose.

- Rift cut veneer: Cut perpendicular to the grain in rotary slices; grain pattern is very straight and tight.

- Re-manufactured veneers: a new method of making appearance grade veneers. Made by cutting numerous, somewhat thick veneers from 1/8 in. to 1/4 in. (3 mm to 6 mm), gluing them together in a large stack, and re-slicing them perpendicular to the original direction. Makes the graining pattern quite similar to a straight or rift cut because it is composed of numerous, very narrow bands of wood set side by side. Allows beautiful veneers to be cut from nonendangered species, as the grain is simulated by the narrow strips veneer and colors of stain are designed to be similar to those of endangered species.

Plywood

Plywood is most common element of wood paneling. It is used for wood paneling in two ways:

- Exterior or outside veneer on one side is specifically ordered in available species from the factory.

- Flitches from vendors specializing in veneers are custom applied in a custom millwork shop.

- *Advantages*
- Extremely stable and flat.

- Allows the use of woods that normally would not work well for paneling such as burls or re-manufactured veneers.

- Does not warp like solid wood.

- *Plywood sizes*

- Most common thicknesses are 1/4 in., 3/8 in., 1/2 in., 5/8 in., and 3/4 in. (6 mm, 10 mm, 13 mm, 16 mm, and 19 mm).

- Non standard thicknesses range from 3/32 in. to 2-1/4 in. (2 mm to 57 mm).

- Most common sheet size is 4 ft. x 8 ft. (1,220 mm x 2,438 mm).

- Other lengths are available such as 10 ft. and 12 ft. (3,048 mm and 3,658 mm).

- *Plywood grades and types*
  Plywood is available in utility, structural, and appearance grades; the latter being the most appropriate for paneling.

- Standard: Made of multiple layers of veneers glued together; number of layers depends on thickness. Exterior veneers determine its appearance. Interior layers are laid up crosswise to the adjacent layer and, with the glue and resins used in the process, add strength and stability to the sheet.

- Specialty grades: Similar to standard plywood in most respects. Number and thicknesses of veneers can vary controlling the density, strength, and stability of the finish product.

- Lumber core plywood: A hybrid material, composed of an exterior veneer on the outside of both sides, a cross veneer beneath, and a core of numerous, small strips of solid lumber glued side by side. It is used primarily for strength and rigidity in furniture, casework, and other applications where torsional strength is not necessary.

- Particle board core plywood: Similar to lumber core plywood except that the lumber core is replaced by a dense particle board core. Typical in applications needing a more economical material.

Veneer patterns

Because most veneers having desirable appearance qualities are sliced off a log in narrow strips or "flitches" approximately 9 in. to 15 in. (229 mm to 381 mm) wide, they must be joined edge to edge to make panels of any appreciable width. There is a variety of patterns:

- *Slip matched veneers*
  Veneers are laid up just as they are sliced off the log. Almost identical flitches are placed side by side creating a linear pattern.

- *Book matched veneers*
  Veneers are laid up in a similar manner but alternately exposing the back of one flitch and the face of the next creating a pattern similar to the pages of a book creating a symmetrical pattern.

- *Diamond reverse patterns*
  Veneers are laid up similar to the book match but flitches are mirrored in a horizontal as well as vertical direction creating the diamond like pattern.

- *Other patterns*
  Flitches can be laid up in almost any pattern desirable. Patterns are dependent on the species and the size and configuration of the paneling.

Paneling configurations

Wood paneling may be configured in a wide variety of configurations with their only limitations based on the physical limitations of the material. Configuration types include:

- *Traditional*
  A combination of panels and moldings. Common moldings include base, wainscot or chair rail, and crown mold. These may be used for their shape only, or to help fasten the panels to the wall.

- *Contemporary*
  Much simpler than traditional, using the beauty of the wood as its main feature. A base is still common but chair rail and crown mold

may not be present. The panels are joined one to another with several joints: butt joint, rabbet joint, tongue and groove joint. The edges are handled in several ways:

- Edges are butt together with a minimal, hairline joint.

- Edges are chamfered to enhance the joint and make alignment not as important.

- The edge of each panel may have a small, narrow, solid wood band covering the edge of the panel. This band may be exposed on the face of the panel or hidden behind the surface veneer.

- The edges may be separated by 1 in. (25 mm) or more, creating a reveal with a painted or metal surface on the substrate behind to enhance the joint.

Mounting methods

Panels are attached to the substrate by numerous methods:

- *Z-clips*
  Metal clips bent in a "Z" shape. One clip is mounted to the substrate and another to the panel. Several pairs of clips are evenly spaced across the panel. During installation, the panel is pushed against the wall and slid down onto the adjacent clip securing it to the wall.

- *Mechanical attachment*
  Screws or bolts are fastened through the panel to the substrate behind. The fastener heads may be exposed or recessed and filled with putty or plugged with wood plugs.

- *Adhesive*
  An adhesive is spread evenly or placed in large "dots" on the back of the panel and pressed in place on the substrate.

- *Moldings*
  Panels are held in place with a perimeter molding that is nailed or screwed to the substrate.

4 Stone wall panels and tiles

Many of the characteristics and properties of stone used in flooring apply to stone wall panels. All types of stone and textures may be used for installation on a wall as well as a floor surface. However, there are a few differences, discussed below.

- *Panel weight and sizes*

- The major consideration when using stone wall panels is the weight and size that must be supported by the attachment of the material to the wall.

- The overall weight of the panel should not exceed the capacity of its method of attachment.

- The overall size of each panel should be within the capacity of workers, with or without lifts, to reasonably handle. If a panel is too heavy or too large to be comfortably handled by two workers, it might be too large. Either make special arrangements for winches, lifts, etc. or use a smaller panel. Keep in mind that some heavy equipment may be difficult to get inside a building.

- Overall size should not exceed 8 ft. x 5 ft. (2,438 mm x 1,524 mm).

- The most common thickness is 3/4 in. (19 mm), but 1-1/4 in. (29 mm) is available.

- The hardness of the stone will affect size. The larger the length to width ratio, the more a stone panel tends to bend and flex. Consult with the supplier to determine the best dimensional ratio of the stone type to be used.

- Size may also be limited by the individual characteristics of each piece of stone. Veins or checks that are some of the prized appearance features of marble, for example, may be a weakness limiting the overall size of the panel. Consult with the supplier.

- Tiles are a popular and less costly way to achieve a stone wall finish. Tiles are normally cut in 12 in. (305 mm) squares and are approximately 1/2 in. (13 mm) thick.

• *Stone appearance*

- Each variety of stone has its own characteristics, colors, and grain patterns. These should be taken into consideration when designing the placement of the panels.

- Stone types that have the more prominent patterns can be matched in much the same manner as is wood. Book match patterns are an excellent way to enhance or highlight the stone.

- Prominent features the stone can be a factor in the size and dimension of the panels.

- Because panels are to be installed on the wall, wearability is not a factor. Polished surfaces are a very popular finish for stone because it makes colors deeper and natural features more prominent.

Installation of stone panels

Since stone panels are normally quite narrow with respect to their other dimensions, standard mortar and grout installation methods are inappropriate. Installation methods for stone wall panels require careful attention to the type and quality of the substrate. There are several basic methods of installing stone onto a wall surface.

• Types of substrates

- Because stone is a heavy wall finish material, the attachment must transfer this weight through the wall to the floor or other structural elements. This means that the substrate must be strong and substantial.

- Masonry or concrete are the most obvious choice for substrate material. The mass of these materials gives them sufficient strength to support the stone.

- Studs and sheathing are a common support for stone. The studs should be a heavier gauge than for partitions; 18 gauge or stronger.

- Sheathing may be used to which to fasten the stone, or as a backing for stability. In this latter case, holes or openings of 3 in. to 4 in. (76 mm to 102 mm) diameter are cut into the substrate exposing the studs. The attachment system tied directly to them.

- Plywood sheathing is strong enough to handle both methods discussed above.

- Gypsum board is also a good sheathing or backing material. But, with stone panels of any reasonable size, attachment to the studs behind the board is important.

• *Adhesive*

- This method is typical for stone tiles and small panels.

- Especially strong adhesive is used to hold the tiles to the wall and securely in place, from the first placement through the curing process.

- The adhesive is spread with a notched trowel and the tiles are pressed into the adhesive.

- Tiles must be spaced evenly depending on the desired joints.

• *Wire ties*

- This is the most common method of installing stone wall tiles.

- Wires are attached to the back of the stone panel and either to an attachment angle mounted to the substrate or through a hole in the sheathing to the studs behind.

- As this method is somewhat like hanging a loop on a hook on the wall, plaster spots are placed at approximately 12 in. to 18 in. (305 mm to 457 mm) on center in both directions on the panels. These spots are placed between the substrate and the panel back and are intended to keep the panel stable and the distance between the panel and substrate consistent.

• *Mechanical anchors*

- Anchors consist of stainless steel clips that fasten into dovetail grooves cut into the backside of the stone. The clips fasten to the substrate with stainless steel screws.

- In installations where walls are higher than usual, or the stone is thicker than usual, horizontal angles mounted to the substrate are installed for additional support.

• *Joints*

- Minimal or "marble" joints are 1/8 in. (3 mm) or less, to minimize their appearance. Joints are filled with an unsanded grout or left open.

- Standard joints are 1/8 in. to 3/16 in. (3 mm to 5 mm), grouted or filled with a backer rod and caulking. The caulked joint is the more common joint today because it allows movement of individual panels without cracking the joint.

- Reveal joints are 1/2 in. (13 mm) or larger, not grouted or caulked. They are left open with the exposed surface painted or covered with a metal strip or a laminate. Reveal joints can be used as an accent. The panel must be installed with its back as close to the substrate as possible to minimize this distance.

5 Paints and stains

Paint is a combination of liquid and solid materials that can be brushed, rolled, or sprayed onto a surface. As it dries, paint forms a hard, dense coating. It is the most common of interior finish materials and inexpensive. Paint is composed of four basic elements, each one of which is important and adds specific properties to the paint:

- vehicle
- pigment
- body
- additives

Vehicle

This is the liquid portion of the paint. It gives the paint its consistency or body and its ability to stick to whatever surface it is applied to. It is composed of two parts: a binder and a solvent.

• *Binders*

- Binders are the transparent part of the vehicle that holds the pigment particles together forming the surface film as it cures. It also determines the quality and durability of the paint. Types of binders include:

- Oil binders: Most commonly linseed oil, although other oils can be used; also the most common and durable of binders until more recently, as they have been replaced with latex and alkyd paints. Oil binders are reasonably durable, but they have a strong odor and do not tolerate moisture well.

- Alkyd binders: These are oil modified resins and cure by means of oxidation. The resins improve hardness and resistance to moisture. They can be mixed in a wide range of colors. Mixing with linseed oil quickens drying time and helps to prevent fading. This is one of the more popular binders in use today.

- Latex binders: These are water-soluble and can be mixed, thinned, and cleaned with water. This type of paint dries by means of evaporation and leaves a tough, insoluble finish. There is little odor, it is not flammable, and resists fading. The finished surface is not as hard as other binder types but research is improving this property.

- Oleoresin binders: A mixture of drying oils and hard resins, they are typical of varnish. A disadvantage is that they yellow with age.

- Phenolic binders: Composed of synthetic resins and oils, similar to varnish, and available in pigmented as well as clear products. A disadvantage is that they tend to darken when used outside.

- Rubber-based binders: Resins are based on synthetic rubber, are highly water resistant, and suitable for used in areas that are subject to high moisture conditions. Dries quickly.

- Urethane binders: A recent evolution from the urethane finishes that were substituted for varnish, these are extremely durable, available in combinations with and without oil-based products.

- Other binders: There are other products with specialized properties based on other binders. These are excellent products but the manufacturer's data should be consulted before specifying. They include vinyl, silicone, and acrylics.

- *Solvents*

- Solvents are the part of the vehicle that mixes with the binder and holds it and the pigments in suspension until they cure or dry.

- Solvents act as a thinning agent allowing each coat to be uniformly and evenly applied.

- They control the oxidation or evaporation of the coating, ensuring appropriate drying times for each coat.

- Types of solvents include hydrocarbon (oil based solvent); oxygenated (water based solvent); terpene solvent.

Pigment

Composed of evenly sized particles that are suspended in the vehicle. Classified as organic or inorganic.

- Properties of pigments

- Pigment is the part of paint that gives it color.

- Pigment helps to determine a paint's opacity or "hiding" qualities or its ability to cover the substrate without having it show through. The addition of a "shading" agent such as lamp black increases paint opacity and reduces the need for costly materials in the body.

- Gloss, a reference to the amount of light the finished surface reflects, is a function of the size of the pigment particles and the amount of vehicle surrounding it. Larger pigment particles create a more rough surface that diffuses the light making it appear flat. Smaller particles allow them to be more completely surrounded by the vehicle creating a flatter surface that reflects more light. Typical finishes include high gloss, semigloss, low luster, eggshell, and flat.

Body

The body contains the majority of what constitutes paint. It is composed mainly of white metallic salts. Lead carbonate was commonly used many years ago but was replaced for health reasons.

- *Common materials*

- Zinc oxide: common for lower quality paints, inexpensive and safe.

- Titanium dioxide: excellent hiding capabilities, but is more costly.

- *Extenders*

- These allow the manufacturer to use the less of the more costly fillers while still retaining the desired opacity.

- Common extenders are calcium carbonate and talc.

- Use of extenders does not cheapen the quality of the paint, but provides a way to maintain the desired hiding characteristics, when used in reasonable amounts, without adding unnecessary cost.

Additives

Additives are components that are added to the paint mixture that change or modify its characteristics in specific ways to accomplish specific qualities.

- *Drier*
  Additives that shorten the drying or curing time.

- *Coalescing agents*
  Used with latex paints to encourage uniformity of the latex elements as they group together during the drying process.

- *Anti-skinning agents*
  Retard the formation of a skin in fast drying paints, especially when used from a can, so that it can be properly applied.

- *Wetting agents*
  Aid the binders in completely and evenly coating the pigment particles. This helps guarantee the even distribution of color as well as film formation.

- *Suspension agents*
  Help keep the pigment particles in suspension so they do not settle to the bottom of the container.

- *Preservatives*
  Prevent the growth of bacteria within the paint.

- *Viscosity control agents*
  Aid in controlling a paint's thickness to ensure proper flow and consistency during application.

Varnish

This is a group of transparent products that also include urethane coatings.

- *Composition*

- resins: help to reduce drying time while increasing hardness.

- drying oils: add an element of flexibility as well as durability.

- solvents

- dryers

- *Characteristics*

- Varnishes are classified by their oil length. This is a measure of the ratio of the amount of oil to resin contained within the product.

- Long oil products: have a greater amount of oil than resin; a more flexible finish; drying time is longer; typically used in exterior applications.

- Short oil products: have more resin than oil; quick drying; have a harder finish.

- Medium oil products: have properties that are a blend of long oil and short oil products.

- Varnish is available in gloss and satin finishes.

Stain

Stain is a transparent coating that penetrates wood.

- *Composition*

- Mixture of solvents, pigments, and additives.

- Solvents are a primary ingredient, making it quite thin when compared to paints.

- *Characteristics*

- Stain is able to penetrate into the pores of wood because of its low viscosity, depositing pigment and oils. Residual pigments and oils are then wiped off.

- Stains have the ability to color and treat wood while leaving the beauty of its grain exposed.

- Available in both oil and water based products.

- Available in solid or reasonably opaque versions as well as the standard transparent type.

Lacquer

• *Composition*

- Main ingredient is a solvent with higher volatility than either stain or varnish. This allows it to dry very quickly allowing the application of many coats.

• *Characteristics*

- Lacquers must be applied under controlled conditions because of their ability to dry fast.

- They have a high gloss finish.

- They dry to an extremely hard finish.

- Lacquers are made in both transparent versions as well as pigmented or paint versions.

Preparatory coatings

• *Primers*

- Intended to be applied directly on the substrate.

- Designed to increase adhesion between the paint and the surface to which it is to be applied.

- Proper substrate preparation such as cleaning and light sanding should also be done in addition to the application of a primer.

• *Sealers*

- Products designed to seal porous surfaces such as wood.

- Help paints and primers to remain on the surface and not be absorbed into the surfaces pores.

- Seals in some natural dyes and chemicals that might stain or harm the intended coating to be applied.

- Help to prepare the substrate in preparation for other finishes.

• *Fillers*

- Designed to fill in the small cracks and pores of wood or concrete block.

- Common practice is to apply a wood filler when a high gloss finish is to be used.

• *Surface preparation*

- One of the most important parts of applying a coating.

- Remove all dust, dirt, wax, moisture or anything that might impede the adhesion of the coating being applied.

- Follow manufacturer's recommendations in the preparation of all surfaces.

6   Wallcoverings

After paint, wallcovering are the more popular wall finish materials. Consisting of rolls of paper or vinyl, they are a relatively economical finishing technique. Commercial wallcovering is manufactured in several widths as well as thickness designed to provide service for a variety of locations. Other types are made from paper, woven grasses, or other fibers, as well as paper backed fabrics. Wallcovering types include:

- vinyl wallcovering

- paper wallcovering

- special wallcovering

Vinyl wallcovering

All vinyl wallcoverings are composed of three elements: backing material; vinyl material; an applied finish material.

• *Backing*
  All vinyl wallcoverings must have a backing fabric of some kind. They are normally classed into three types:

• *Scrim*

- A light gauge, loosely woven fabric.

- Specifically designed for light weight wallcoverings.

- Also available in a non-woven variety.

• *Osnaburg*

- A more tightly woven fabric made with a heavier gauge thread.

- Designed for medium weight wallcoverings.

- Also available in a non-woven product.

• *Drill*

- For heavy duty wallcoverings.

- Made with a tough, tightly woven, heavy gauge yarn.

- Imparts specific desirable properties to the wallcovering such as: added strength; resistance to abrasion; stability for textured patterns.

Vinyl material

• *Composition*

- PVC (polyvinyl chloride) resins, which add strength and abrasion resistance.

- Plasticizers, which add pliability and help facilitate processing. Specific plasticizers can also add fire resistance, stain resistance, and aging resistance.

- Stabilizers helps the PVC to retain their colors during processing.

- Pigments are responsible for the color within the product; they are the most expensive part of a wallcovering.

- Fillers such as calcium carbonate (the most common) are used to partially replace other elements to lower the cost or to change the look.

- Fungicides or fire retardants are common additives.

• *Applied finish material*
  Polyvinylfloride coating applied to the surface of the wallcovering.

- Added as a protection for the wallcovering.

- Provides added protection for paints, pens, markers, and other damage that might be hard to remove otherwise.

- An optional finish that is applied on many wallcoverings.

• *The manufacturing process*

Vinyl wallcoverings are made by two manufacturing processes:

- Calendaring: This process pours liquid vinyl onto hot rollers that squeeze it into very thin sheets. It is then either laminated with an adhesive to the fabric backing at that time or stored for later use.

- Plastisol: In this process, the liquid PVC is poured and spread evenly over the fabric as it moves by on a conveyor and is fused to it at high temperature.

• *Sizes*

- Most typically manufactured in wide widths of 48 in. to 54 in. (1,220 mm to 1,372 mm).

- Also available in 27 in. (686 mm) widths.

- Wide widths are available in rolls of 50 to 75 linear yards (46 m to 69 m).

- The 27 in. (686 mm) width is available in double rolls of 30 to 35 sq. yd. (9.3 sq. m to 11 sq. m) per roll.

- *Classification*
  Commercial vinyl wallcoverings are classified into three types:

- Type I: Classified as a light duty wallcovering, it is made on a scrim or non-woven backing. It is the least costly grade, with a total weight of between 7 and 13 ounces per sq. yd. (166 and 308 kg per sq. m).

- Type II: Classified as a medium duty wallcovering, it is made on an Osnaburg, Drill, or nonwoven backing. It has a total weight of between 13 and 22 ounces per sq. yd. (308 and 521 kg per sq. m.) and is more durable than Type I, suitable for use in corridors, class-rooms, etc.

- Type III: Classified as a heavy duty wallcovering, it is made on a Drill fabric backing. It has a total weight of more than 22 ounces per sq. yd. (521 kg per sq. m). It is suitable for use in high traffic situations such as hospital corridors, and lobbies.

- *Commercial wallcovering characteristics*
  For every wallcovering made, there is a list published by the manufacturer that identifies how it performs in a variety of circumstances:

- Minimum coating weight: Indicates the amount of vinyl in the wallcovering, not including the backing.

- Breaking strength: When pulled evenly across a width of wallcovering, this is the force required to pull it apart.

- Tearing strength: When pulled from one point, this is the force required to tear it.

- Adhesion: A measure of how well the wallcovering will adhere to the wall surface.

- Lightfastness: An indication of how well the wallcovering resists facing when exposed to the sun for a time. Ideally, no change should be observable.

- Abrasion resistance: A measure of the wallcovering's ability to resist wearing when subjected to repetitive wear in one place.

- Shrinkage: Indicates the maximum percentage the wallcovering will shrink after installation on the wall.

- Flame spread: A measure of how quickly a wallcovering will be completely engulfed by flames.

- Smoke development: A measure of the amount of smoke a wallcovering will develop and the speed with which it develops when it begins to burn.

- Cold crack and heat aging: Indicates how a wallcovering will perform when it gets very hot or cold.

Custom wallcoverings

Many manufacturers will run custom wallcoverings. Most manufacturers require a minimum order of between 300 to 500 yd. (274 m to 457 m) although there is a trend toward reduced or no minimum amounts on certain patterns. The most common custom characteristics are:

- special colors.

- special patterns or textures.

- special wallcoverings with enhanced characteristics not restricted to the group above.

Paper wallcoverings

Wallcoverings made primarily of paper are primarily intended for the residential market; although they may be commercially used in light duty locations. Paper wallcoverings (or "wallpaper") are primarily made from:

- A reasonably heavy gauge paper with the pattern printed or impressed onto the face of the paper.

- A light vinyl coating to protect the paper and improve wearability.

- Mainly available in 27 in. (686 mm) wide double rolls of 30 to 35 sq. yd. (27 to 32 sq. m) per roll. Check with the manufacturer to determine roll coverage.

Special wallcoverings

Such wallcoverings are different enough from standard wallcoverings that they are grouped in a special category:

- *Lincrusta and Anaglypta*

- Similar to a light gauge linoleum in content and construction.

- Anaglypta is made from materials based in either vinyl or wood fibers.

- Both are a very heavy gauge material manufactured in rolls, borders, or cut-length panels.

- Installed with a specially manufactured adhesive of a very thick consistency suitable to adhere the wallcovering securely to the wall.

- *Wall cloth*

- A thick, pellon like wallcovering manufactured of fibers and a binder.

- Designed for installation on walls with unwanted textures, joints or non-moving cracks.

- Not an "cure all" for wall problems but it will hide cracks that would show through other wallcoverings.

Installation of wallcoverings

Wallcoverings come prepared for installation by two methods:

- *Pre-pasted wallcovering*

- Comes with adhesive or "paste" factory applied to the back of the wallcovering.

- Wallcovering is cut to length and then submerged in a water box for a short period of time, wetting the paste. The piece is then "booked," that is, the pasted sides of the wallcovering are folded against each other to allow all the adhesive to moisten.

- Wallcovering is then unfolded and pressed onto the wall surface, smoothed out, and the edges rolled flat.

- Some wallcovering needs to have the edges trimmed but most these days come pre-trimmed from the factory.

- *Unpasted wallcovering*

- This type of wallcovering is typical of most of the commercial wallcoverings available today.

- Pre-mixed adhesive is spread on the backside of the wallcovering and it is then pressed onto the wall surface, smoothed out, and the edges rolled.

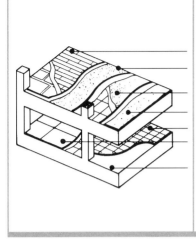

Flooring

Summary: An overview of the characteristics of various flooring systems, including brick, stone, wood, terrazzo, resilient flooring, carpeting, ceramic tile, and access flooring. Discussed are material options, substrates, performance characteristics, sizes and specification data.

Key words: access flooring, brick, carpeting, resilient flooring, stone, terrazzo, tile, wood flooring.

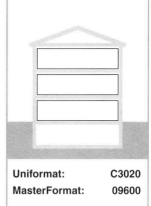

Uniformat:	C3020
MasterFormat:	09600

Flooring selection is an important design decision, aesthetically and technically. People will look down at the floor and to where it may lead the eye for a sense of sure-footedness, direction and mobility. Flooring is the singlemost exposed element of a building interior because of constant and often heavy use. Flooring must therefore provide:

- durability and endurance given the type of foot (and wheel) traffic and intensity of use.

- resistance to abrasion from use and abuse of dirt or sand particles and spills of chemicals and other liquids.

- resistance or permeability to moisture intrusion (from the substrate if on or below grade) or other moisture vapor migration.

- resistance to impact generated damage, including change of dimension of substrate and other construction elements.

- ability to be cleaned, maintained and replaced in whole or part.

- resistance to insect infestation.

As a result, the performance criteria for flooring selection can be listed as the following:

- durable to resist abrasion, indentation, compression, accidental impacts, and dust and dirt.

- chemically inert to resist cleaning compounds, disinfectants, solvents, lubricants and other substances that may be spilled.

- comfortable to reduce fatigue of walking, standing and/or running.

- safe, non-slippery, non-tripping, non flammable and also non-conductive or non-static.

The floor finishing surfaces, and their areas that may first reveal wear and tear, will also "mirror" any unevenness, cracks, joints or other imperfections in the flooring substrate, so that the entire flooring system must be designed and installed with equal care (Fig. 1) The following flooring types, summarized with selection guidelines in Table 1 (See end of article), are reviewed in this article:

1 brick flooring

2 stone flooring

3 wood flooring

4 terrazzo flooring

5 resilient flooring

7 ceramic tile flooring

8 access flooring

1 Brick flooring

One of the oldest floor materials. It is durable, available in an array of colors, textures, and can be installed in a variety of patterns. It is a hard surface flooring material with excellent wearing characteristics. Of all the many sizes and shapes of bricks that are made and can be installed, the most common are:

- brick pavers: 2-1/4 in. thick x 4 in. wide x 8 in. long (57 mm x 102 mm x 204 mm).

- split pavers: 1-1/8 in. thick x 4 in. wide x 8 in. long (29 mm x 102 mm x 204 mm).

Criteria for pavers and split pavers include:

- *Weather classes*

- SX: Water can saturate the brick and it can be exposed to freezing conditions.

- MX: An exterior brick that should not be exposed to freezing conditions.

- NX: An interior brick that should not be subjected to freezing when wet.

- Although interiors are not normally subjected to freezing and thawing, the SX and MX bricks are more durable.

- *Traffic types*

Author: William Hall

References: Brick Institute of America. 1992. *Brick Floors and Pavements: Part I.* Technical Notes 14 Revised. Reston, VA: Brick Institute of America

Carpet and Rug Institute. 1994. *The Carpet Specifier's , CA: Handbook.* 5th edition. Dalton, GA: Carpet and Rug Institute.

Ceramic Tile Institute. 1991. *Tile Manual.* Los Angeles: Ceramic Tile Institute.

"Hardwood Flooring." *The WoodBook '90.* P.O. Box 5613, Montgomery, AL 36103-5613.

National Terrazzo and Mosaic Association. *Terrazzo Technical Information.* Des Plains, IL: National Terrazzo and Mosaic Association. (800) 323-9736.

RFCI. 1993. *Recommended Installation Specifications for Vinyl Composition, Solid Vinyl and Asphalt Tile Floorings.* RFCI-IS2. Rockville, MD: Resilient Floor Covering Institute.

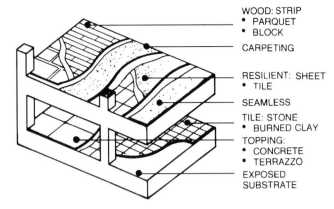

WOOD: STRIP
 • PARQUET
 • BLOCK
CARPETING
RESILIENT: SHEET
 • TILE
SEAMLESS
TILE: STONE
 • BURNED CLAY
TOPPING:
 • CONCRETE
 • TERRAZZO
EXPOSED
SUBSTRATE

Fig. 1. Floor assembly systems

- Type I: used on driveways and in building entrances normally exposed to a high degree of abrasion.

- Type II: used on exterior walkways and floors that may be subjected to a medium amount of abrasion.

- Type III: used on floors and patios exposed to a low amount of abrasion, typical of most residential situations.

Brick material characteristics by category

- *PS: a general category*

- Applies to bricks that are installed with mortar and grout in any pattern or without mortar and grout in patterns that do not require close dimensional tolerances.

- Dimensional tolerances:
  1/8 in. up to 3 in. in length (3 mm up to 76 mm).
  3/16 in. from 3 in. to 5 in. in length (5 mm from 76 mm to 127 mm).
  1/4 in. from 5 in. to 8 in. in length (6 mm from 127 mm to 204 mm).

- Warpage limits:
  3/32 in. (2 mm) in units with dimensions up to 8 in. (204 mm).
  1/8 in. (3 mm) in units with dimensions from 8 in. to 12 in. (204 mm to 305 mm).
  5/32 in. (4 mm) in units with dimensions from 12 in. to 16 in. (305 mm to 406 mm).

- Chipage limits:
  5/16 in. (8 mm) at edges and 1/2 in. (13 mm) at corners.
  No single unit allowed to have a total length of chips of more than 10% of the exposed perimeter.

- *PX: category superior to the PS grade*

- Appropriate where special patterns or other conditions require units manufactured with a high degree of uniformity.

- Dimensional tolerances:
  Half of what is allowed with PS.

- Warpage limits:
  1/16 in. (2 mm) up to 8 in. (204 mm).
  3/32 in. (2 mm) from 8 in. to 12 in. (204 mm to 305 mm).
  1/8 in. (3 mm) from 12 in. to 16 in. (305 mm to 406 mm).

- Chipage limits:
  1/4 in. (6 mm) at edges.
  3/8 in. (10 mm) at corners.

- **PA: category for specially selected units**.
- Intended for units with specific characteristics related to color, texture, and size.

- Other specific requirements and/or exceptions regarding durability within the weather classifications and traffic performance must be evaluated with respect to the individual needs of the particular job. Coordinate these with the specifications writer and brick manufacturer/supplier.

Installation
There are three methods of installing brick flooring:

- *Loose lay*

- This method entails laying the brick into place with no mortar or grout. The weight of the brick and the adjacent units hold the brick flooring in place.

- Most common in exterior applications but can be used for interiors.

- Joints must be sealed to keep out dirt and moisture.

- *Thick-set installation*

There are two common methods:

- Brick is wet set into a wet or soft mortar bed similar to methods used by masons.

INTERIORS

C3

- Brick is set onto a dry or cured mortar bed similar to methods used by tile setters.

- Mortar can be mixed as per all designs discussed in the ceramic tile section.

- Brick may be installed by "buttering" the unit with mortar on all sides and bottom and then pushing it into the mortar bed.

- Brick may be installed like tile, with the units set into a wet mortar bed with spaced joints. After curing, the joints are grouted.

- Thick-set advantages: provides a method to handle an uneven or rough subfloor; provides the only way to install a cleavage membrane to allow installation to deal with sub-floors that will deflect to some degree.

- Thick-set disadvantages: overall thickness of the brick flooring system is greater than with other systems; overall weight is higher; must coordinate greater system thickness with adjacent materials.

- *Thin-set installation*

- similar to thin-set ceramic tile installations.

- requires greater tolerances in brick sizing.

2   Stone flooring

Stone flooring is a very durable floor finish material consisting of slabs of stone installed onto a cementitious setting bed. Stone is chosen for its durability, the variety of colors, textures, and patterns. Design considerations include, tile or slab size, joint size, thicknesses. There are many types of stone available, which come in a wide variety of colors, thicknesses, textures, and finishes.

- *Granite*

One of the more popular stones. Its composition is a mixture of quartz, mica, feldspar and hornblende, granite has as a granular appearance from fine to coarse. Grain patterns are normally uniform, but irregularities can form veins or other shapes. Common colors are pink, beige, white, brown, black, green, and red. Its characteristics include:

- high compressive strength.

- low water absorption rate.

- good resistance to abrasion.

- surface can take polished, honed, and flamed finishes.

- Because of its hardness, granite can retain a polished finish even under a moderate amount of wear and abrasion.

- *Marble*

One of the most beautiful and colorful of all stone materials. Its composition is a mixture of limestone that has been heated up and cooled forming a metamorphic stone. Marble's characteristic veining is formed by minerals that were not mixed completely during the stone's. Marble's colors are function of the content of the minerals in the stone:

- Red, pink, yellow, and brown are caused by iron oxide.

- Green is from mica, chlorites, and silicates.

- Grey, black, and blue are from oil based materials.

- Veins can be a weak point: consult with the stone supplier to determine if a particular stone has had problems.

Classification of marbles:

- Class A: Best grade; very uniform in color and consistency; veins of different colors are similar in color and texture to surrounding material; quite strong.

- Class B, C, and D: progressively more veining and normally small voids between the veins and the surrounding material; voids are filled with wax or other methods of helping to retain the strength of the stone across the width of the piece.

- Classifications mainly deal with the number and severity of faults or veins and have nothing to do with other criteria such as color, and hardness.

- *Slate*

Slate is a metamorphic stone made from sedimentary shale that has been folded and compacted by metamorphosis. These layers allow it to be split into thin layers with "cleft" surfaces.

- Slate normally "cleaves" or splits in one direction.

- Comes in a wide variety of colors and textures.

- Common colors are black, dark blue, and grey and caused by carbon based elements.

- Purple, red, yellow, brown, and green are due to iron materials.

- *Limestone*

Limestone is sedimentary stone made from calcium carbonate that has not gone through the metamorphic process.

- Often, hard limestones that are able to be polished are classified as marble.

- Densities range from 110 psf (5 kPa) which is quite soft, to 160 psf (7 kPa).

- Typical limestones are also known under the names travertine, oolite, dolomite, calccarenite, crystalline and coquina.

- Because it is sedimentary in composition, limestone may contain spots, shells, and pit holes.

- Less costly than marble or granite.

- *Other stone*

With the large variety of stone available from many different quarries, the color, content, and other characteristics can vary widely. There are groups of stone types that fall into this category whose characteristics will vary with the quarry and part of the world. What may be suitable for flooring in one location may not be suitable in another. Sandstone and quartzite are common types. Contact the local supplier, inspect available stone, and determine typical characteristics before making a final selection.

Stone flooring characteristics

- *Panel size*

- Size of stone panels is largely determined by how it is cut from the quarry. This differs by the type of stone, its hardness, quality of veining, and other characteristics.

- Main consideration is stability after it is cut. For instance, if a cut panel tends to break, then it is probably too wide or thin. Most quarries know the optimal sizes for each type of stone that they quarry.

- Typical thicknesses are 3/4 in. (19 mm) and 1-1/4 in. (32 mm) but other thicknesses may be available.

- Stone can typically be cut in widths up to 4 ft. (1,220 mm) and in lengths up to 10 ft. and 12 ft. (3,048 mm and 3,658 mm). The main limitation is material weight. Large panels are very heavy and will require special handling to install. Plan the size and placement of the installation to determine its feasibility.

- Stone tiles are common, cut in 12 in. (305 mm) square sizes and are between 1/4 in. (6 mm) and 1/2 in. (13 mm) thick.

- *Hardness and abrasion resistance*

- These characteristics affect a stone's ability to retain a polish. All stone will wear, but a harder stone will appear as intended for a much longer time.

- Soft stones will tend to wear in areas of greatest traffic.

- Hardness and abrasion resistance affect a stone's ability to resist water absorption or staining.

- Soft stone is more porous and will tend to retain dirt more readily than hard stone.

- *Slip resistance*

Slip resistance is related to the texture of the surface; the smoother or more polished the surface, the more "slippery" it is. The Americans with Disabilities Act (ADA) recommends a minimum coefficient of friction of 0.6 for most floors; ramps should have a rating of 0.8 (these are only recommendations). There are three tests for determining the coefficient of fiction or the slip resistance of stone flooring. All of these tests provide reasonable results but do have their limitations. Results should be used as a guide in choosing stone slip resistance. The best guide is common sense: more texture provides more slip resistance. The tests are:

- The James Machine

- The NBS - Brungraber Tester

- The PTI Drag Sled Tester

Installation

Stone flooring may be installed on a steel or wood structure as long as the floor is stiff enough to keep the deflection to less than 1/720 of the span. Methods of installation are similar to that required by ceramic tile and brick. Installation has two main parts: setting or mortar bed; grout.

- *Setting or mortar bed*

Because of the size and weight of stone panels, the thick- set method of installation is most common. There are two typical ways to do this:

- The stone is wet set into a wet or soft mortar bed similar to methods used by masons.

- The stone is set onto a dry or cured mortar bed similar to methods used by tile setters. This assumes that the stone panels are quite flat on the back side.

- Mortar can be mixed as per the recommendations in the ceramic tile section.

- In the masonry method, the stone is installed by "buttering" the panels back and sides with mortar and it is then pushed into the mortar bed.

- In the tile setting method, the stone is set into a wet mortar bed with spaced joints. After curing, the joints are grouted.

- Stone tiles are set by either the thick-set or thin-set method for ceramic tile.

- The tile-setting method allows for an uneven or rough subfloor, and is also the only way to install a cleavage membrane to allow the installation to accommodate sub-floors that deflect to some degree.

- As with brick, the overall thickness of the installation is greater than with ceramic tile.

- *Grout*

- The same standards for ceramic tile are used.

- Normally, unsanded grout is used for joints less than 1/8 in. (3 mm) and sanded grouts for all those larger than 1/8 in. (3 mm).

- If polished stone is used, unsanded grouts are recommended to protect polished surfaces from scratching as the grout is applied and wiped off.

3   Wood flooring

Wood flooring is a popular finish material made of pieces or strips of wood attached or bonded to a substrate. With the availability of a wide variety of designs, colors, and grain patterns, it can be used in most applications. Wood flooring may be installed over a variety of substrates by several methods. Types of wood flooring include:

- *Plank flooring*

- Individual planks of wood are 4 in. to 12 in. (102 mm to 305 mm) wide.

- Requires both nailing and screwing for installation.

- *Strip flooring*

- Individual strips of wood are 2 in. to 4 in. (51 mm to 102 mm) wide.

- Strips are nailed to substrate through a tongue at the edge of each strip.

- *Parquet flooring*

Parquet is composed of a variety of small strips or pieces of wood arranged in a variety of configurations or patterns. Most commonly made of 3/4 in. x 6 in. (19 mm x 152 mm) strips of oak that form 6 in. (152 mm) squares arranged in a basket weave pattern. The configurations of wood strips are:

- Edges are tongue and groove or square.

- Patterns vary per manufacturer or the desired effect.

- Some manufacturers will pre-assemble different wood species and patterns together into larger sizes forming 12 in. or 18 in. (305 mm or 457 mm) squares onto a sub-surface such as plywood. This simplifies installation and can improve stability.

- *Grades of wood*

- Grading varies according to manufacturer as well as between wood species. Each manufacturer grades the product as well as the different cuts of wood.

- With the exception of the less restrictive grades, the qualities are similar and, for the most part, relate to the visual aspects.

- Grading is different between unfinished and pre-finished flooring.

- Hardness of wood has a direct relation to its serviceability.

- *Configuration of wood strips*

Wood strips are cut mainly in two ways:

- Quarter sawn or vertical grained, cut so that the edge of the grain is perpendicular to the face of the wood strip. This is more durable, shrinks or swells less across the width of the strip and finishes better than plain sawn.

- Plain sawn or flat grained, cut with the grain parallel to the face of the wood strip, more economical, bur less durable than quarter-sawn because of the open grain.

Laminated wood

The manufacturer laminates the strip(s) of wood onto a stable backing such as a high density plywood with a special adhesive.

- Actual wood surface is thinner than normal.

- More stable because of the combination of wood veneer and plywood backing.

- Strength can be engineered.

- Enables wood species, cuts, and appearance to be used that would be inappropriate with solid lumber such as burls or crotches, etc.

Joints

Because all wood flooring is composed of many individual pieces, the joints between these pieces is very important.

- *Types of joints*

- Butt joints: Individual pieces of wood have square edges. Each piece of wood is face nailed to the substrate with the nail heads set into the wood and the holes filled.

INTERIORS

C3

- Doweled joints: Edges are joined by a series of dowels that are inserted into holes drilled perpendicular to the face of the board. The dowels are glued into one board. The adjacent board has identical holes that fit over the dowels. Tapping the adjacent board toward the other achieves a tight joint.

- Spline joints: A groove is cut lengthwise in the opposite edges of the board. During installation, a small-sized strip known as a spline is inserted into the groove on one board and the adjacent board is tightly fitted onto this assembly, forming a tight joint.

- Tongue and groove joints: This is the most common method of joining wood strips on a wood floor. A groove is cut into one edge of the board. An integral spline or tongue is routed onto the opposite edge. During installation, the tongue of one board is fitted into the groove of the adjacent board. The board is blind nailed to the substrate by nailing it at an angle through the tongue into the substrate. The next board hides the nails. Blind nailing is only needed at the edges close to the walls.

Installation

There are two types of wood floor installation:

- nailable: where the flooring can be nailed to the substrate.

- non-nailable: where flooring is attached to the substrate in a manner other than using nails, such as adhesive.

• *Nailable floor installations*

- typical of strip and plank flooring.

- installed to a wood subfloor that has been glued to a core floor or nailed to wood joists or installed on "sleepers" on top of a concrete floor.

- sleepers are random length, treated 2x4s, 18 in. to 48 in. (457 mm to 1,220 mm) long, installed perpendicular to the desired direction of the wood flooring.

- sleepers are set into hot asphalt that acts as an adhesive.

- flooring is nailed to the sleepers.

- If moisture is present, a layer of polyethylene should be laid over the sleepers.

- design must allow for the greater thickness of sleepers and flooring, which requires more coordination and can be more expensive.

• *Non-nailable floor installations*

- typical of most parquet floors and wood tiles.

- assumes the substrate is dry and level.

- installed over a mastic or adhesive spread with a notched trowel as per manufacturer's recommendations.

- tile is installed from centerpoint out and trimmed at walls.

- tiles are trimmed to within 1/4 in. to 3/4 in. (6 mm to 19 mm) of wall to allow for movement.

• *Variations of typical wood floors*

- beveled or v-shaped joints.

- hand distressing gives the appearance of an old floor.

- unfinished: typical of sports floors; requires sanding and an applied finish after installation.

- pre-sealed: sanded and sealed at the factory; requires only a final applied finish.

- pre-finished: sanded, sealed, and finished at the factory; requires only installation.

Specialty wood floors

• *Laminated wood flooring*

- composed of multiple layers of wood veneers similar to plywood.

- yields a more stable unit.

• *Acrylic impregnated wood flooring*

- acrylic resin is applied, under pressure, to the wood surface.

- enhances durability substantially.

- enhances characteristics of the wood such as density, compressive strength, flame spread, and color.

• *Foam underlaid wood flooring*

- Wood has a dense layer of foam rubber laminated to its backside.

- increases resiliency.

Preparation of wood flooring for finishing

With unfinished flooring, the preparation of the floor for the application of the finish is an important step toward a complete wood floor installation. Each step is important, and are as follows:

• *Sanding*

- Levels out the minute differences between adjacent boards and differences within each board.

• *Filling and cleaning*

- Cracks in the wood surface (nail holes, small open knots) are filled.

- Some species need an application of liquid filler that minimizes the absorption of the finish into the wood pores.

- Dust is removed by vacuuming and a final wipe with a tack cloth.

Types of wood flooring finishes

• *Polyurethane*

- most durable of all the finishes.

- resists damage by moisture.

- composed of synthetic resins with high wear capabilities.

- resists yellowing.

- all polyurethanes are not equal. The essential ingredient in a well-wearing polyurethane finish is a high solids content.

• *Varnish*

- traditional floor finish until the past few years.

- dries to a glossy finish.

- durable

- darkens with age. It is difficult to blend repairs with adjacent material.

• *Shellac*

- not as common as other finishes.

- dries to a high-gloss finish.

- dries quickly.

- easy to apply.

- does not yellow or darken.

- easily chipped.

- easily damaged by moisture.

• *Lacquer*

- no longer commonly used.

- similar to varnish.

- repairs blend in because the new material dissolves the old material where they overlap.

- dries extremely fast making application much more difficult.

INTERIORS

C3

• *Penetrating finishes*

- penetrate into the wood and then harden to seal it.

- not as long lasting as surface finishes.

- must be re-applied on a regular basis.

- buffing provides a temporary luster.

- wax may be applied to provide a high gloss.

4 Terrazzo Flooring

Terrazzo is a mixture of stone chips mixed with a cementitious or resinous matrix, poured onto a floor surface and ground smooth. Terrazzo can be made in a variety of colors and patterns that depend on the stone used. This type of floor surfacing is very durable, handsome and finished into an extremely flat surface. Terrazzo is composed of:

- marble, glass, or granite chips (other aggregates may be used).

- A matrix of Portland cement, modified Portland cement, or a resinous slurry.

Terrazzo materials

• *Chips*

- The most common stone used in the chips is marble.

- Other less popular stones are granite, onyx, travertine, quartz.

- Other materials are glass, pea gravel, and river stone.

- Stone such as gravel or quartz provide a more rustic look.

- The main criteria is that the chips are hard enough to allow them to be polished.

- Chips are classified by their size. Sizes vary from #0 which measures 1/16 in. to 1/8 in. (2 mm to 3 mm), up to #8 which measures 1 in. to 1-1/8 in. (25 mm to 29 mm).

- Even though the stone/matrix mixture is ground smooth, the size of the chip will vary the pattern or overall look of the finished product.

• *Color of terrazzo is varied by:*

- different colors or varieties of stone.

- mixing a color additive to the matrix.

• *Patterns can be created by:*

- varying the color of the chips and/or matrix within a specific area that is separated from other areas by thin steel divider or control strips.

- size of the chips can be varied in much the same way as specified above.

- the divider strips can form patterns, shapes, and other forms that divide up the flooring surface. The width of these strips can vary also.

• *Terrazzo matrices (binders)*

- Portland cement, composed of Portland cement, pigments, and water.

- modified Portland cement, composed of Portland cement, a variety of additives, pigments, and water.

- resinous matrices, composed of polyacrylate modified cement, epoxy or polyester materials. This matrix is normally used in thin-set applications.

Terrazzo types

Resinous terrazzo

Used primarily in thin-set applications, where the desire is to limit the overall thickness of the installation or where specific characteristics are needed.

• *Polyacrylate based:*

- a modified cement product where the polyacrylate material is an additive to a cementitious matrix.

- has a high bond strength.

- resistant to water, snow melting, and salts.

- free from objectionable odors during installation and curing.

- moisture permeable for areas where moisture is a problem.

- has a limited color range.

• *Epoxy based:*

- high bond strength.

- resistant to mild acids and stains.

- resists impact loads and weight indentations.

- suitable for exterior use.

- light colors tend to yellow in sunlight.

- has the ability to bridge some substrate cracking when installed for a flexible isolation membrane.

• polyester resin based:

- high compressive strength.

- high resistance to abrasion and indentations.

- non-yellowing.

- exceptional resistance to weathering and chemicals.

- during application, gives of an extreme odor requiring respirators or other precautions.

- used mainly where the above characteristics are required.

Conductive terrazzo

- conducts static charges away from floor surfaces.

- conductive material is carbon black and is mixed with the matrix (matrix is black in color).

- suitable in computer rooms and other areas where static electric build up can damage equipment.

Terrazzo installation

A terrazzo installation is only as good as the substrate onto which it is constructed. Specifications for terrazzo should relate to the substrate.

• *Cementitious installation on a sand cushion.*

- 1/2 in. to 3/4 in. (13 mm to 19 mm) thick terrazzo topping.

- 2-1/2 in. (64 mm) reinforced mortar bed.

- isolation membrane.

- thin bed of sand.

- divider strips at 48 in. (1,220 mm) o.c. maximum.

• *Bonded installation.*

- 1/2 in. to 3/4 in. (13 mm to 19 mm) thick terrazzo topping.

- 1-1/4 in. (32 mm) mortar bed.

- mortar bed bonded to a concrete slab.

- divider strips at 96 in. (2,438 mm) o.c. maximum.

• *Monolithic installation.*

- 1/2 in. to 3/4 in. (13 mm to 19 mm) thick terrazzo topping.

- installation directly over concrete slab.

- divider strips at 20 ft. (6,100 mm) o.c. maximum.

• *Installation on metal deck.*

- 1/2 in. to 3/4 in. (13 mm to 19 mm) thick terrazzo topping.

- 2-1/2 in. (64 mm) thick reinforced concrete slab measured from the top of the deck.
- divider strips at 36 in. (914 mm) o.c. maximum.
- *Structural installation.*
- 1/2 in. to 3/4 in. (13 mm to 19 mm) thick terrazzo topping.
- 4-1/2 in. (114 mm) thick reinforced concrete slab over a vapor barrier.
- divider strips at 96 in. (2,438 mm) o.c. maximum.
- *Rustic installation.*
- similar to above installations except chips or gravel are carefully installed but not ground.
- used where slip resistance or a texture is desired.

5 Resilient Flooring

One of the most economical of flooring materials, it comes in a variety of colors, textures, patterns, and resilience. They are easy to install and require minimal floor preparation beyond a flat, clean surface. Most common types of resilient flooring are:

- VCT
- vinyl tile
- sheet vinyl
- rubber
- cork and other (less common) materials

VCT tile

VCT (Vinyl Composition Tile) is the most common of all the resilient flooring.

- composition: fillers (80%), vinyl resin (10%), plasticizers (5%), stabilizers (3%).
- normally 1/8 in. (3 mm) thick.
- 12-inches-square (305 mm-square) is the most common size.
- has a wide variety of variegated colors and patterns.
- can simulate other materials.
- approximately 75 psi (518 kPa) load limit.
- accent strips in solid colors.
- *Vinyl Tile*

Vinyl tile is a grade superior to VCT.

- composition: fillers (65%), vinyl resins (25%), plasticizers(10%), stabilizers (3%).
- approximately 75% more compressive strength than VCT: 125 psi (863 kPa) load limit.
- higher resistance to abrasion.
- more costly than VCT.
- *Sheet vinyl*

Sheet vinyl is available in rolls in a variety of configurations and made in two formats: filled sheet vinyl and solid sheet vinyl. Filled sheet vinyl:

- made in three layers.
- wear layer is made from vinyl and is .05 in. to .08 in. (1 mm to 2 mm) thick.
- composed of vinyl tile chips set in a matrix of pure vinyl.
- backing is composed of a felt material adhered to the wear layer, which acts as a stabilizer and increases flexibility.

Solid sheet vinyl is:

- made with no backing.

- wear layer is the entire thickness of the material.
- designed for heavy duty use.
- contains more plasticizers and less fillers.
- has excellent resilience and resistance to abrasion, chemicals, and wear.
- higher cost.
- because it lacks a backing, a good substrate is critical.
- made most commonly in 6 ft. (1,829 mm) widths.
- most common thickness is .08 in. (2 mm).
- *Cushioned sheet vinyl*

Cushioned sheet vinyl is a modification of the standard filled sheet vinyl, composed of four layers: felt backing.

- cushion composed of plasticizers; vinyl chip or solid vinyl layer (the pattern).
- wear layer usually made of clear vinyl from .010 in. to .020 in. (0.25 mm to 0.5 mm) thick.
- common in residential or light commercial uses.
- common width is 12 ft. (3,658 mm).
- superb resilience.
- reduced impact noise in spaces below.
- because of cushion, this material can be easily punctured or torn.
- *Rubber flooring*
- manufactured in tile or sheet format.
- tiles are most commonly available 9 in. (229 mm) and 12 in. (305 mm) square sizes.
- available 1/16 in. (2 mm) and 1/8 in. (3 mm) thick
- embossed with raised pattern (most common are dots or squares).
- most common colors are solid, although variegated colors are available.
- excellent resistance to abrasion and to cigarette burns.
- vegetable oils stain quite easily.
- colors tend to be dark.
- *Less common flooring materials*
- contemporary versions of linoleum.
- cork.
- troweled on or fluid applied flooring materials.

Installation procedures

All resilient flooring, because of its thickness, depends upon a good substrate and the proper adhesive for a good installation.

- *Substrate preparation*
- Must be clean of all dirt and debris that might inhibit adhesion or show through tile.
- Cracks or holes must be filled or repaired.
- *Adhesives*
- Applied with a notched trowel. This assures that the appropriate amount is troweled onto the floor.
- Tiles should be installed from the center out, and edge tiles should be trimmed.
- The finished installation should be rolled with a heavy roller to assure a flat, level surface and eliminate air bubbles.
- Sheet goods need to have the seams rolled to assure that they are flat.

6   Carpet Flooring

Carpeting consists mainly of yarns or fibers combined together to form a heavy fabric that is installed on a floor surface. It is one of the most popular flooring materials, available in a number of different fibers, and a very wide variety of colors and patterns. Carpeting is made from many fibers that are twisted or spun together forming yarns. There are many types of fibers, but can be classified into two categories:

- natural fibers

- man-made fibers

• *Natural fibers*

- Wool: the most popular natural fiber, also the highest in cost.

- Cotton: used mainly in residential applications.

- Flax: not commonly used.

- Silk: used alone or mixed with wool; common in oriental rugs.

• *Man-made fibers*

- Nylon: the most common man-made fiber.

- Olefin: made from polyproplene; based on ethylene, or propylene; strong, light, and extremely resistant to chemicals; usually solution dyed; popular with indoor-outdoor carpeting; tends to crush, although methods such as tighter spinning or increasing carpet density have helped.

- Polyester: made in staple form; fibers designed to help hide soil; has a soft feel and a bulky look; crushes but this problem has been overcome by heat setting its shape as well as those mentioned above with olefin.

- Acrylics: similar to the look and touch of wool; lightweight; resists deterioration by chemicals; resists fading; usually solution dyed.

• *Yarn types*

- Staple: composed of numerous short fibers spun together into a single yarn strand, typical of natural fibers.

- Continuous filament: several long fibers twisted together to form a single yarn strand.

Types of carpeting

- woven

- tufted

- fusion bonded

- knitted

• *Woven carpeting*

- as the name implies, this carpet is woven with warp, weft, and pile yarns.

- longer wearing.

- dimensional stable.

- more costly than most other types.

- slower to make.

- patterns are easy to incorporate.

- types of woven carpeting include velvet, Wilton, and Axminster

• *Tufted carpeting*

- Yarns are punched with many needles through a primary backing material made of jute or a woven synthetic material.

- Normally comes 12 ft. (3,658 mm) wide although can be made 6 ft. (1,830 mm) wide or 15 ft. (4,572 mm) wide.

- Secondary backing material is glued to the tufted primary backing with a latex glue to secure tufts and to make it more dimensionally stable.

- Accounts for about 95% of all broadloom carpeting made in the U. S.

- Types of tufted carpeting include:

Loop pile: tufted with continuous loops or stitches of yarn in a variety of spacing and heights creating a wide variety of patterns with colors, pile heights, etc.

Cut pile: Made the same as loop pile carpeting then loops are sheared off exposing the ends of the yarn.

Combination: Sometimes known as a "velva-loop" carpet, this combines both cut and loop in a variety of patterns.

• *Fusion bonded carpeting*

- Most common method of making carpet tiles.

- Yarn is sandwiched between two backing materials covered with an adhesive, then fused to the backing with heat. A knife is run between the two backing materials creating two, cut-pile carpets

The dyeing process

Most yarn is colored or dyed at some time during the manufacturing process to allow the finished carpet to achieve its intended look or design. There are several methods of dying yarn: solution dyeing, stock dyeing, yarn dyeing, piece dyeing, and printed carpet.

• *Solution dyeing*

Dye is mixed with the molten fiber before being extruded into its final shape.

- Advantages: constant color throughout the fiber; high colorfast and color retention properties; resistant to damage or bleaching by strong chemicals; resists fading from sunlight.

- Disadvantages: higher cost; somewhat limited color selection

• *Stock dyeing*

Fibers are dyed before they are spun into yarn.

- Advantages: color consistency

- Disadvantages: larger amounts of colored fibers must be stocked to ensure that all possible color combinations of carpets orders can be filled.

• *Yarn dyeing*

Fibers are dyed after they are spun into yarn.

- Advantages: carpet manufacturer buys undyed yarn in bulk and then dyes the colors as they are needed.

- Disadvantages: less color fast; less resistant to fading from sunlight

• *Piece dyeing*

Carpet is tufted with undyed yarn, then the carpet ends are joined and the loop is run through the dye to color the yarns.

- Advantages: manufacturer can store large amounts of undyed carpet and dye only what is needed.

- Disadvantages: since this process can only dye approx. 1,000 yd. (914 m) of carpet per vat of dye, the size of the dye lot is limited.

• *Printed carpet*

Specific patterns can be printed onto either undyed or dyed carpet yielding a wide variety of patterns, colors, or combinations of the two.

• *Carpet characteristics*

- Pile height: Length or height of the tufted yarns measured from the backing to the top.

- Gauge: Distance between tufting needles across the width of the carpet.

- Stitches per inch: the carpet density; refers to the needles per inch times stitches per inch.

INTERIORS

C3

- Face weight: Number of ounces of yarn in the carpet pile.

- Primary backing: The carpet yarns are tufted into this fabric, made from jute or polypropelyne.

- Secondary backing: Glued with a latex adhesive to the primary backing.

• *Methods of installation*

- installation over pad with perimeter tackstrips holding down edges.

- direct glue down.

- carpet glued to pad and pad glued to floor.

• *Types of padding*

- felt or hair pads

- rubber padding of two types: flat rubber padding graded by thickness (1/16 in. to 5/16 in.) (2 mm to 8 mm); waffle pad shaped in a waffle pattern and graded by the ounce (40 to 120 oz.) (1 kg to 3 kg).

- urethane foam pad: solid prime urethane foam graded by thickness; bonded or rebonded pad made from pieces or chunks of foam pad bonded together, graded by density and thickness.

7 Ceramic tile flooring

Ceramic tile is a blend of clay, shale, and other natural materials that are pressed or extruded into a variety of shapes. These are then fired under high temperatures for specific periods of time creating the finished product. A very durable floor finish, suitable for a wide variety of installations including high moisture environments. Most common types of ceramic tile:

- glazed tile

- unglazed tile

- quarry tile

Glazed tile

Glazed tile is composed of two parts:

• *The body or "bisque"*

- has a water absorption rate of 18% or less.

- made from different clays such red or "cottoforte" clay; white clay; yellow or "majolica" clay.

- these clays form a stable base to which the glazes are applied.

- relatively soft when compared with other ceramic tiles.

• *The glaze*

- creates an impervious finish when applied.

- after firing, the glaze creates a glass like surface.

- increases the durability of the tiles surface.

- lowers the slip resistance of the surface of the tile unless a texture or abrasive additive is applied.

- normally applied in two coats; one for opacity and color and one for gloss.

- glazed tiles are between 1/4 in. and 5/16 in. (6 mm and 8 mm) thick.

• *Unglazed tile*

- made from clays that, when fired, produce a tile that is much harder and more dense.

- clays are made into tiles by the either the dust-pressed method or the plastic method.

- tile is consistent in color and content through its entire thickness.

- classified as either impervious or vitreous.

- has a water absorption rate of 0.5% to 3%.

- classifications yield a tile that has outstanding wearability.

- unglazed tiles are normally less than 1/4 in. (6 mm) thick.

• *Quarry tile*

- very durable tile made from materials and by methods similar to brick.

- about 1/2 in. to 3/4 in. (13 mm to 19 mm) thick.

- may be either glazed or unglazed.

- most common size is 6 in. x 6 in. (152 mm x 152 mm), although other sizes are available.

- water absorption is less than 5%.

- most prevalent color is red, but browns, yellows, and greys are available.

- stain resistant but not stain proof. Resistant to oils, moisture, and most chemicals.

- commonly installed in high traffic or high use areas such as kitchens.

- made in a variety of hardnesses and textures. Hardness depends on type of clay and length of firing.

- available with smooth finishes or embossed textures such as raised elements similar to that on diamond plate steel.

- special mixtures of different colored clay yield a visual "grain" like pattern when fired.

- abrasive aggregate is mixed with clays on the surface creating a slip resistant surface.

- specialty glazes may be applied to the surface.

- normally installed with standard masonry mortar and with 3/8 in. (10 mm) joints.

• *Ceramic tile terminology*

- pavers: tiles larger than 6 sq. in. (3,870 sq. mm).

- mosaic: tiles that are smaller than 6 sq. in. (3,870 sq. mm).

- porcelain tiles: pavers that are most commonly unglazed and very dense in composition.

Standards and specifications

• *Tile size*

- will vary with the type of tile and manufacturer.

- sizes are normally nominal sizes, not exact dimensions.

- overall size is related to tile thickness. If a tile is thin, then its size must be such that it will not bend or break under load.

• *Tile shapes*

- ceramic tiles are most commonly made in square or rectangular shapes.

- hexagonal and octagonal shapes are also available from some manufacturers.

- special shapes are available. The following represents the most common shapes: beads, bull noses, counter trims, curbs, nosing, inside and outside corners, caps

• *Porosity*

Since all tiles absorb some water, porosity is a function of its durability and strength. Porosity classifications:

- impervious: absorption rate of less than 0.5%.

- vitreous: absorption rate of between 0.5% and 3%.

- semivitreous: absorption rate of between 3% to 7%.

- nonvitreous: absorption rate of between 7% to 18%.

INTERIORS

C3

INTERIORS

C3

- *Hardness*
- This characteristic is a function of the type of clay used and its firing time as well as the hardness and thickness of the glaze, if any.
- Hardness also depends on the type of tile. For example, a 4-1/4 in. (108 mm) square glazed wall tile is made in virtually the same manner with the same materials by most manufacturers. It is not dependent on any published industry standards.

- *Grades*
- Standard grade characteristics: Material free from any visible defects at a distance of 3 ft. (1 m); color and texture are consistent throughout; no structural defects.
- Seconds grade characteristics: Same as above except visible defects cannot be seen from 10 ft. (3 m) away.
- Specialty grade characteristics: Specifically designed for any special tile; this category conforms to the specifications of each particular specialty tile.

- *Slip resistance*
- Primarily a consideration when ceramic tile is installed on a floor surface.
- Many factors can affect the slip resistance of tile, such as: whether the tile is wet or dry; the composition of the shoe soles that come in contact with it.
- Methods of obtaining resistance to slipping:
- Abrasive particles added to the clay mixture or the surface of the formed tile before firing.
- Embossed or shaped designs on the surface of the tile.
- Specially designed glazing formulated to increase the coefficient of friction.
- Manufacturers usually do not make specific recommendations regarding slip resistance because of many variables.
- Slip resistance should be evaluated for each situation, considering all factors that might affect floor use.

Installation

A ceramic tile installation has two main parts: mortar or setting bed; grout.

- *Mortar or setting bed*
- Holds the tile to the substrate.
- Mortar creates a setting bet upon which the tile is installed.
- Setting bed should be a flat, stable surface to resist any movement that might break the bond between the tile and the mortar.

- *The setting bed configurations*
- Thick-set: The most common method until recently; commonly 1-1/4 in. (32 mm) thick for floors and 3/4 in. (19 mm) for walls to create the required stable surface over the substrate; allows the installer to level or smooth small irregularities in the substrate; allows the installer to slope the tile surface towards a drain without sloping the substrate; provides space enough to reinforce the setting bed if needed.
- Thin-set: Now the most common method; setting bed is between 3/32 in. (2 mm) and 1/8 in. (3 mm) thick; more of an adhesive than a mortar; thin-set mortars have additives that help them develop the required strength without the depth; develop a stronger bond with the material to resist tile popping loose when subjected to moderate loads; thickness of the installation is negligible.

- *Types of mortar*
- Portland cement mortar: Normally used in thick-set installations;

similar to masonry mortar in composition; composed of between six to seven parts sand, one part Portland cement, and one part water.

- Dry-set mortar: similar to above but with special additives that help in the retention of water during the installation and curing process, as well as increasing bond strength to the tile; can be used primarily as an adhesive when installing over an existing setting bed, as well as directly over the substrate; normally used in thin-set applications.
- Latex Portland cement mortar: similar to dry-set mortar with the addition of a latex type additive that gives the installed mortar a degree of flexibility to resist cracking during any anticipated minimal movement; must be allowed to dry completely before tile installation, which can be up to 48 hours in some cases.
- Epoxy mortar: composed of epoxy resins and hardeners; when cured forms an extremely hard base; has a high bond strength with the tile and the substrate and high impact resistance; has excellent resistance to chemicals.
- Modified epoxy mortar: similar to above, with the addition of Portland cement and sand, which yields a mortar base that gives a high bond strength and is economical, with minimal shrinkage.
- Furan mortar: a chemical resistant mortar; formulated to be installed over, wood, concrete, steel plate, plywood, and ceramic tile.

- *Types of adhesives*
- Organic: made from organic materials and "glues" the tile to the substrate; cannot be used outside.
- Epoxy based: main ingredients are epoxy resins and hardeners used to increase bond strength.

- *Grout*
- applied between the joints of the tile.
- bonds the edges of the tile together and resists lateral movement.
- fills the space between the tiles to keep out dirt and debris.
- similar to mortar but much finer and more smooth.

- *Types of grout*
- Portland cement grout: made primarily from Portland cement and other elements; forms a water resistant grout; primarily used on floors.
- Sand Portland cement grout: most commonly used grout for both walls and floors; a mixture of sand, Portland cement and water.
- Dry set grout: similar properties to dry set mortar.
- Latex Portland cement grout: a combination of any of the above and latex additives; leaves a film on the tile that is difficult to remove unless it is wiped off immediately after installation.
- Mastic grout: similar to adhesive mortars; not suitable for high used installations.
- Silicone rubber grout: a silicone based grout with an almost instantaneous bond to the tile; resists shrinking, staining, moisture damage, and cracking.

- *Important installation considerations*
- Substrate preparation: A tile installation is only as good as the substrate onto which it is installed. Therefore, a flat, stable substrate is essential: repair any large cracks; fill any small cracks; clean entire substrate surface.
- Setting bed: If there is any doubt regarding the stability of the substrate, consider a thick-set installation with or without reinforcement, or a special, epoxy thin-set installation.

8 Access flooring

Access flooring is a system composed of removable flooring panels and a structural grid to support the panels, creating a space below the floor for air movement and/or a variety of electrical and communications wiring. This type of flooring is suitable where frequent access and/or high VAC loads make this type of system desirable. Components include:

- flooring panels: usually manufactured in 24 in. x 24 in. (610 mm x 610 mm) squares.

- understructure: the elements that actually support the floor panels such as pedestals and, if required, stringers

- substrate

System parameters

- *Structural characteristics*

A variety of tests rate access flooring capacity in the following areas:

- maximum deflection

- permanent set

- ultimate load

- durability or deformation under loads due to castor or rolling traffic.

- axial load capacity of pedestals

- *Fire characteristics*

- flame spread rating of less than 25.

- all materials to be non-combustible.

- a wood core is acceptable when is completely enclosed within a metal pan or panel.

- *Acoustical characteristics*

- solid panels help to reduce sound transmission and therefore tend to be quieter.

- heavier help reduce sound transmission.

- carpet helps to reduce reflected sound.

- *Thermal or insulating characteristics*

- If the space below the floor is being used to condition the space above, the ability of the floor to transmit temperature could be a factor.

- Formed steel panels and cast aluminum panels transmit temperature changes quickly through thermal bridging.

- Steel encased wood core panels and cementitious-filled steel panels transmit temperature changes less efficiently.

- *Electrical characteristics*

Access flooring may either help or hinder the electrical characteristics in an office space.

- static electricity: controlled by humidity and low static carpet.

- electric shock protection: understructure of the flooring should be grounded.

- elimination of electrical interference: requires protection of wiring below the floor from interference from radio waves, and electromagnetic radiation.

Types of panels

- steel covered wood core panels

- unfilled formed steel panels

- filled formed steel panels

- die cast aluminum panels

- lightweight concrete filled steel pan panels

- bolted reinforced concrete panels

Steel covered wood-core panels

- *Uses:*

- general offices and computer rooms.

- panels are not interchangeable with other accessible flooring systems.

- *Panel weight:*

- 7 to 8 lb./sf (263 to 300 kg/sm) without stringers.

- 8 to 9.5 lb./sf (300 to 356 kg/sm) with stringers.

- *Structural characteristics:*

- 1,000 to 1,200 lb./sf (37,500 to 45,000 kg/sm) for medium concentrated loads.

- 500 to 800 lb./sf (18,750 to 30,000 kg/sm) for medium to light rolling loads.

- may be improved with stronger understructures.

- normally stringers are below the panel instead of between panels, limiting underfloor clearance.

- *Other:*

- Fire characteristics: Flamespread is 25 or less per ASTM E84.

- Thermal: wood core provides good thermal properties.

- Acoustical: wood helps to absorb traffic and machine noise. Wood also provides a solid feeling.

Unfilled formed steel panels

- *Uses:*

- computer equipment and clean rooms.

- panels are interchangeable with cement filled formed steel panels.

- *Panel weight:*

- 6.4 to 8.4 lb./sf (375 to 315 kg/sm) without stringers.

- 7.1 to 9.1 lb./sf (266 to 341 kg/sm) with stringers.

- *Structural characteristics:*

- 1,000 to 1,500 lb./sf (37,500 to 56,250 kg/sm) for concentrated loads.

- Rolling loads limited to wheel #2 loads (per CISCA A/F standards).

- *Other:*

- Fire characteristics: non-combustible.

- Thermal: poor; highly conductive.

- Acoustical: hollow panel construction can resonate impact loads such as foot traffic.

Filled formed steel panels

- *Uses:*

- general offices, computer rooms and light manufacturing.

- panels are interchangeable with formed steel panels.

- *Panel weight:*

- 8.9 to 11 lb./sf (334 to 413 kg/sm) without stringers.

- 10.1 to 12.6 lb./sf (380 to 473 kg/sm) with stringers.

- *Structural characteristics:*

- 1,000 to 3,000 lb./sf (37,500 to 112,500 kg/sm) for concentrated loads.

INTERIORS

C3

- 600 to 3,000 lb./sf (22,500 to 112,500 kg/sm) for rolling loads.
- *Other:*
  - Fire characteristics: non combustible.
- Thermal: fair to good, depending on thickness.
- Acoustical: traffic noise deadened by use of the cementitious fill material. Panels have a solid feel.

Die-cast aluminum panels

- *Uses:*
  - clean rooms, computer rooms, labs, and facilities that might require a panel with non-ferrous composition.
  - panels are not interchangeable.
- *Panel weight:*

4.5 lb./sf (170 kg/sm).

- *Structural characteristics:*

1,000 lb./sf (37,500 kg/sm) for concentrated and rolling loads.

- *Other:*
  - Fire characteristics: non-combustible.
  - Thermal: poor, highly conductive
  - Acoustical: sound reduced to some degree by the fit between panels and the pedestals.

Lightweight concrete filled steel pan

- *Uses:*
  - general office.
  - stingers, when used, support from under the panel reducing under-floor clearance.
- *Panel weight:*

11.5 to 13.5 lb./sf (431 to 506 kg/sm).

- *Structural characteristics:*

1,000 to 2,000 lb./sf (37,500 to 75,000 kg/sm).

- *Other:*
  - Fire characteristics: non-combustible.
  - Thermal: performs better than filled formed steel panels due to the consistent thickness of the panels.
  - Acoustical: sound absorption is enhanced because of the concrete core. Panels have a solid feel.

Types of understructures

The understructure is a necessary part of all access floor systems. This system provides both support for vertical or gravity loads as well as lateral loads. The support system is composed of the pedestals and, when required, stringers. There are two types of understructure systems:

- stringerless systems or those support systems that are designed to be installed without the use of stringers.
- stringer systems or those that require the installation of stringers for complete systems.
- *Pedestals*

Pedestal components and characteristics:

- head: provides a method of attachment of the panel and stringers, if required.
- base: either adhered, bolted, or otherwise attached to the substrate.
- threaded rod: telescopes into both the base and head.
- pedestal assembly provides the means of adjusting the height of the floor.
- attachment of the base to the floor adds lateral stability to the floor system.
- *Stringers*

Stringer components and characteristics:

- If panel edges are supported, it can help increase the capacity of the gravity load support.
- Provide additional lateral support that may be required according to panel used.
- Systems that require frequent access normally require stringers.
- *Snap-on stringers*
  - designed to be installed by interlocking edges with pedestals heads.
  - make removal much easier and quicker.
  - stringers are normally one bay long or 2 ft. (610 mm).
- *Bolted stringers*
  - bolted to pedestals.
  - provide greater lateral than snap on systems.
  - stringers are two to three bays long or 4 ft. to 6 ft. (1,220 mm to 1,830 mm).
  - cross stringers are one bay long or 2 ft. (610 mm).
  - takes more times and effort to gain access to underfloor cavity.
- *Stringerless systems*
  - systems that, because of design requirements, do not need stringers.
  - depend on the cantilever action and the attachment of the base to the floor for main support.
  - typical pedestal supports four panels at the corners.
  - stringerless systems provide maximum access to floor cavity.
  - stringerless systems are not as strong as stringer systems.
- *Gravity held panels*
  - panels are held in place by nesting specially designed edges.
  - finish floor heights are less than with bolted connections.
- *Bolted down panels*
  - panels held down by bolting corners to pedestal heads.
  - stronger than gravity held panels.
  - requires either carpet tiles or a resilient tile surface to allow access to fasteners.
  - requires greater time and effort to gain access to the underfloor cavity.

Table 1. Guide to selection of flooring system type

Suitable flooring when appearance is important	Typical in service conditions	When appearance is secondary
brick stone	light traffic dry conditions	monolithic concrete
wood terrazzo resilient flooring carpeting	occasional use of mild cleaning solvents	
brick stone terrazzo resilient flooring	light traffic frequently wet conditions frequent use of mild cleaning solvents	monolithic concrete w/ non-slip topping
brick resilient flooring	light to moderate traffic wet conditions frequent use of strong cleaning solvents subject to chemically active spills	acid resistant coatings utility resilient flooring
brick some wood (end-grain block and/or treated) terrazzo some resilient flooring some carpeting	heavy traffic occasionally wet conditions occasional use of mild cleaning solvents	concrete topping utility-grade wood (solid)
brick stone terrazzo wood (acrylic treated) some resilient flooring	heavy traffic dry conditions tracked-in moisture and dirt occasional use of mild cleaning solvents	concrete topping utility resilient flooring
brick stone terrazzo some resilient flooring	heavy traffic frequently wet freezing temperatures	concrete topping
brick paving stone (granite) paving	heavy wheeled traffic dry to moderate wet conditions	utility grade wood
none applicable	heavy metal wheeled traffic dry to wet conditions	metal floor plate concrete filled steel grating

INTERIORS

C3

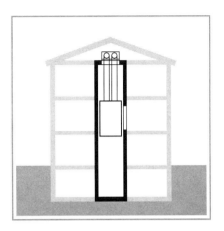

D SERVICES

D1

SERVICES

*Hyatt Regency atrium. Atlanta, GA.
John Portman, FAIA, Architect*

Escalators and elevators

Summary: Design principles and criteria are reviewed for planning, sizing, selection and layout of escalator and elevators, along with mechanical and dimensional details.

Key words: elevators, escalators, moving walkways.

Uniformat:	D1010
MasterFormat:	14200
	14300

Escalators and moving walkways

An escalator or moving walk is a conveyor-belt for people. If the rate of arrival is not excessive, each passenger can step on immediately without waiting, be transported to the other end, and step off immediately. Only when the rate of arrival exceeds the transporting capacity is there any need to queue. This advantage of instant service is achieved at a considerable cost in other capabilities. In the usual types of escalators and walkways, these limitations are as follows:

- Since the equipment does not stop, the passenger must accelerate to full speed in the action of stepping on, that is in the length of one step. This effectively limits the speed of the machine to walking pace.

- Movement is linear, with passengers exiting in the order they entered. This means that each machine can only operate between two fixed points, unlike an elevator, which can have many intermediate stops.

- The angle of incline is limited. Therefore any significant vertical rise is accompanied by a far greater horizontal movement, whether this is desired or not. A moving walk (that is, with a surface that does not form steps during its travel), can be built at any angle from horizontal to 15°. For escalators (which do form steps) the angle is normally 30°, and deviations from this are rare.

- Riding on an escalator requires a certain degree of agility and locomotor skill. It is not suitable for a wheelchair. A baby carriage or a small baggage trolley can be carried, with some inconvenience. It presents difficulty for the visually impaired, since it is necessary to observe the arrival of the treads. These disadvantages occur to a lesser degree with a moving walkway.

Each machine operates in only one direction at a time, so that two-way traffic requires two separate escalators or walkways. However, in peak times one can be reversed, so that both operate in the major direction of travel.

Escalators are widely used to transport large numbers of people over a relatively short vertical distance. A single escalator has the same capacity as a large bank of elevators. There is little need for direction signs, since it is obvious where the escalator is going, and the passengers have the benefit of an uninterrupted view during their travel. By contrast, an elevator disappears behind closed doors and the passengers do not see the arrival floor until the doors open.

Escalators are also useful in the planning of a building with a large pedestrian traffic flow, in directing that flow in the desired direction. This principle is used to advantage in the airport terminal building at Charles de Gaulle Airport in Paris. Incoming and outgoing passengers are transported from one side to the other of the donut-shaped building, and also from one floor to another, by a number of escalators that criss-cross the hole in the donut. This is not only quicker but also more foolproof than directing people to go "halfway around and two floors down."

Horizontal moving walks are less common, mainly because people are more willing to walk horizontally than they are to walk up or down stairs. If the speed of the moving walk is the same as walking pace, there is no great time advantage in using it. There is the disadvantage that, once on the walk, one is not able to stop and browse until the next exit is reached.

The use of moving walks in buildings is limited to very large horizontal buildings, such as transportation terminals, where the advantages include the following:

- Long travel distances, so that walking is tiring for many people.

- Many passengers are carrying baggage and may be fatigued from a long journey.

- There are definite entry and exit points (such as the terminal lounges at an airport), and little need to stop between them.

- Passengers in a hurry can walk on the moving walkway, thereby doubling their speed.

Urban people-movers

The horizontal movement of people is receiving more interest in the field of urban design than in buildings. Railways, subways and bus lines carry most of the commuter traffic in large cities, while automobiles provide a more personalized service at the expense of large areas of land devoted to freeways and parking lots, and a higher fuel consumption than mass-transit systems.

Most short-distance transportation downtown is done on foot, which limits the practical distance between stops in the transit systems, or the distance between car parking and the destination of the user. The transit systems could operate faster, and perhaps with fewer lines, if there was another scale of transport between them and the pedestrian, and the car parking could be further from the center of downtown.

Author: Peter R. Smith, Ph.D., FRAIA

Credits: Portions are excerpted from a longer article by the author in Cowan (1991) and is reprinted by permission of the publisher.

References: Smith, Peter R. "The Movement of People and Goods." In Henry J. Cowan, editor. 1991. *Handbook of Architectural Technology.* New York: Van Nostrand Reinhold.

Dadras, Aly S. 1995. *Electric Systems for Architects.* New York: McGraw-Hill

SERVICES

D1

The conventional moving walkway, operating at pedestrian speed does not offer enough advantage over walking. Experimental designs have been developed for accelerating moving walks, where the passenger enters at walking pace and is accelerated to four to five times that speed for most of the journey, and gently decelerated again before leaving. Other people-mover designs involve the use of vehicles, so that passengers have the opportunity to sit. Options include stopping to allow entry and exit; or slowing to allow stepping on or off; or a combination of slowing and a short moving walk that matches the speed of the slowed vehicle.

The treads of a moving walkway travel as an endless belt, returning to the original point by a path immediately under the walkway. Thus they can be installed in sidewalks or other public places with relatively little disruption to other traffic. Each one can be the length of a city block, so that the passengers can cross the road on foot, and the installation has minimal conflict with other traffic. In any system involving the use of vehicles, the vehicles must complete a round trip, thus interfering with roads and other pedestrian routes. These systems therefore usually have to operate either above or below grade. Escalators are used to take the passengers from ground level to the transport system level.

Mechanical details
A moving walkway requires a firm, flat surface to stand on; close mechanical tolerances at the edges and exit point to prevent injury; and moving handrails to provide a means of maintaining balance. It is acceptable to stand on a flat surface that slopes up or down as much as 15° from the horizontal (1 in 3.7), since it is not necessary to walk, and there is a handrail to hold. By way of comparison, ramps within buildings are limited by building codes to a much flatter slope, usually 1 in 10 or 1 in 12.

The surface is formed from individual panels, usually of cast aluminum, hinged together as an endless chain. Outside the U. S., some moving walks are built using reinforced-rubber conveyor belting running on closely spaced rollers. The ride is slightly uncomfortable, since the rollers can be felt as one's feet pass over them. There is also some danger of the passengers' feet or clothing being caught against the edges, or at the point of exit.

Escalators can be built steeper than moving walks because they form themselves into discrete horizontal steps. The industry standard is 30° from the horizontal (1 in 1.7), although in Europe some escalators are built at 35° inclination. The steps are about 14 in. (340 mm) deep (front to back) and 8 in. (200 mm) high. This is convenient for standing on, but much larger than a normal stairway. When an escalator is stopped, it forms a rather inconvenient stairway.

An escalator has the same requirements as a moving walk, and in addition the risers between the treads must be able to appear and dis-

appear during the travel without trapping clothing or feet. The key to safety at the risers and the exits is the comb system. Both treads and risers have a grooved surface. A comb on the back of the tread engages the grooves in the riser, and a comb on the edge of the floor opening engages the grooves in the tread, so that any loose clothing or footwear is prevented from becoming caught.

In early escalators, the grooves and combs were about 2 in. (50 mm) wide, which along with a considerable mechanical clearance caused some difficulty with small heels, umbrella tips, and children's toes. Modern treads are made of cast aluminum, with small and accurate grooves 4 in. (100 mm) wide and minimum clearances.

Escalator treads run on wheels fore and aft, each pair of wheels following a different track. The geometry of the two tracks enables the treads to move either horizontally or along the slope, while maintaining a horizontal surface. They return underneath, thus requiring a considerable depth through the escalator enclosure. Moving walk treads are similar except they simply follow the slope of the walk, without forming risers.

Physical sizes
Since the speed of escalators is fairly standard, their carrying capacity depends on the width. In the U. S. and Canada the width is given between the balustrades, while in Europe the tread width is used. The balustrade width is 8 in. (200 mm) greater than the tread width, since people are widest at the hips, and there is no point in making the expensive treads and mechanical components wider than necessary.

The common widths are:

- 48 in. (1200 mm) between balustrades which fits two people per tread.

- 32 in. (800 mm) between balustrades which takes one person comfortably per tread, and occasionally two.

Speeds and capacities
The "standard" speed for escalators is 90 feet per minute (fpm) (0.45 m/s), measured in the direction of travel. Few people have difficulty in getting on at this speed. In public transport applications, the speed may be increased to 120 fpm (0.6 m/s) in peak hours. Experienced commuters who are in a hurry find this satisfactory. After peak hours the speed is reduced, because irregular users and the infirm may otherwise hesitate too long before getting on, thus negating any benefit of the higher speed. Moving walkways can run faster than escalators, mainly because it is easier to step onto a continuous flat surface than to have to identify a tread. Walkway speeds are commonly 180 fpm (0.9 m/s) if horizontal, reducing to 140 fpm (0.7 m/s) or less for a slope of 15°.

The capacity of an escalator or walkway depends on its speed and the degree of filling of the treads. It has been observed that passengers commonly fill escalators to about half their theoretical maximum ca-

Table 1. Typical carrying capacities of escalators and walkways. (Smith 1993)

	Width between Balustrades, in.	Tread Width, mm	Speed, fpm	Speed, m/s	Max. Capacity, Persons/ 5 min.	Nominal Capacity, Persons/ 5 min.
Escalator	32	600	90	0.45	425	170
			120	0.6	560	225
Escalator	48	1000	90	0.45	680	340
			120	0.6	900	450
Walkway	48	1000	180	0.9	1200	600
			140	0.7	900	450

fpm = feet per minute

pacity, although in some public transport applications the degree of filling is greater. Sometimes (for example, in the London underground) passengers are disciplined to stand on one side of the 48 in. escalators so that those in a greater hurry can walk past them on the other side. In this case it is possible to achieve a carrying capacity greater than 100% of the theoretical maximum.

Unlike elevators, where the length of travel reduces the performance, the capacity of an escalator (Table 1) is independent of its length. (The longer escalator, of course, has more treads and is therefore a "bigger" escalator.)

Elevators

Although the escalator is the logical result of mechanizing a stairway, the elevator was actually invented earlier, because it evolved from earlier machines for elevating merchandise by mechanical or animal power. In the early 19th century, elevators were used for freight movement and driven by steam power, first developed in England *circa* 1835 where it was called the *teagle*. In 1845 Sir William Thompson invented the first hydraulic elevator. In 1852, Elisha Graves Otis invented the safety brake for elevators, exhibited in New York City in 1854, inaugurating the era of vertical transportation in buildings, which in turn contributed to make the 20th century skyscraper feasible. In 1878, Otis installed the first hydraulic passenger elevator in a 111-foot building in New York City. By 1903, the first gearless traction elevators were installed in the 182-foot Beaver Building in New York, operating at a speed of 500 foot per minute. The first "autotronic" elevators, operated without attendants, were installed in the Atlantic Refining Building in Dallas in 1950. In 1979, the first fully integrated microcomputer system was incorporated, called "Elevonic 101," designed and developed by the Otis Elevator Company to control the entire elevator operation (Dadras 1995).

The elevator is the "batch process" of transporting people in buildings. In this respect its traffic pattern has much in common with a bus, which has a fixed route but only stops when there are passengers to get on or off.

One advantage that a modern elevator installation has over most other transport systems is that all the landing and car calls are processed by a central computer, which can assess the demands and dispatch the most appropriate car to answer each call. This results in a few calls not being answered in turn, with priority being given to handling the bulk of the traffic more expeditiously.

As noted above, a single escalator does not provide a full service because it only operates in one direction. A single elevator can provide two-way service to a number of floors, but there are reasons why it is unlikely to provide a satisfactory service in most cases. The principal objections to a single elevator are the need for routine servicing, and the possibility of breakdown, either of which leave the building with no service at all. Of course it is possible for two elevators to be out of service simultaneously, but the probability of this happening is much lower than with one.

Criteria for design of an elevator installation

Elevators are called on to serve different functions according to the size and nature of the building and their location in it. The most familiar are the passenger elevators which provide the principal passenger transport between levels in a multistory building, but may have a secondary role for carrying furniture or emergency personnel from time to time. Some elevators are used only occasionally to carry incapacitated people or goods in a low-rise building, or goods or vehicles or hospital patients or hotel guests with baggage. The criteria will therefore depend on the purpose.

An important requirement in providing an elevator service for a building is the location of the elevators (in one or more groups, depending on the size of the building) in relation to access from the entrances

and also in relation to the layout of the upper floors. Since elevator shafts are normally vertical, their location on plan imposes a major constraint on every floor of the building. If the building is not of uniform height, at least one elevator group must be located in the tallest portion.

The main criteria for the design of an elevator group can be summarized under a few headings:

- Capacity to handle the passengers as they arrive, with minimum queuing, expressed as a percentage of the total building population that can be handled in the peak 5-minute period.

- Frequency to provide an available car for arriving passengers without excessive waiting, expressed as the average time interval between cars.

- Car size to handle the largest items required to be carried, for example, an occasional item of furniture, or a hospital bed with attendant, or a group of hotel guests with their baggage.

- Speed of total trip, so that passengers do not perceive the total service as excessively slow

In addition there are many details that should be considered for the comfort and convenience of the users:

- A means of finding the elevator lobby that serves the user's destination floor. If there is only one zone of elevators, then a simple direction sign will suffice, but it is even better if at least one elevator door is visible from the entrance of the building. If there are multiple zones, then some signing is necessary in addition.

- Call buttons that are easy to find, and unambiguous for "up" and "down" calls. The location of the call buttons should encourage passengers to stand in a favorable position to watch all the cars in the group, and to move quickly to whichever comes first. The buttons should indicate that a call has been registered. People will become impatient more quickly if there is no indication that they are being served. If there are several buttons that all serve the same purpose, they must all light up to register a call, otherwise users will be uncertain whether they should press one or all the buttons.

- Lights or indicators, and an audible indication as well, to indicate which car is arriving and in which direction it will travel. The indicators should be above head level to be visible above a crowd. When there is a computerized control system, the indicator can be illuminated as soon as the system has decided which car will arrive next. Early indication allows waiting passengers to move in the right direction, and can save a few seconds of loading time each time a car is loaded.

- Enough first-floor lobby space for the crowding that is expected at the up peak. Fig. 1 shows the usual recommendations.

- One set of buttons on the landing, and floor buttons in the car, should be at a level that can be reached by a person in a wheelchair, or a small child.

Layout of elevator groups

As mentioned, one elevator seldom provides a reliable service. In most cases, a group of three or more is needed to ensure that the waiting interval between them is not too great. To function as a group, the cars must all be close enough that an intending user can take whichever one arrives first. A moderately fast walking speed is 3 ft. per second (0.9 m/s). If the landing doors are to remain open for 4 seconds, then an unobstructed person can walk briskly a distance of 12 ft. (3.6 m) before they begin to close again. Obviously, all the landing doors should be closer than this to all the waiting passengers, so that none feels anxious that the doors will close prematurely.

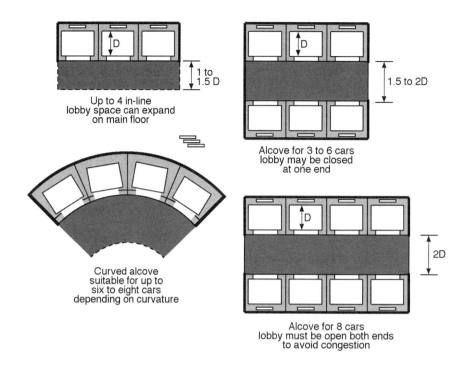

Fig. 1. Recommended lobby dimensions for various layouts of elevator groups. (Smith 1993)

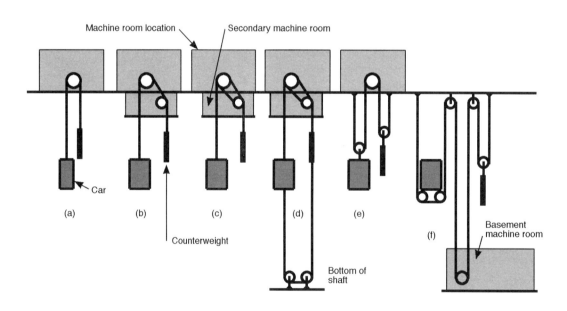

Fig. 2. Various ways of arranging the roping for traction-type elevators. (Smith 1993)

Two or three cars can conveniently be located side by side. There is no need to look over one's shoulder, and they are all close by. Four in a row or two opposite two are both acceptable for a group of four. Five in a row is beginning to be too long a distance to walk. There are some installations of six in a row where the door-open time has had to be increased because of the extended walking distances mentioned above. Increasing the time spent at each landing reduces the performance of the group. Five, six, seven, or eight cars are best located opposite each other.

There are very few installations with more than eight cars in a group. With larger numbers of cars, one is not filled before the next arrives, and this causes confusion. The number of people waiting in the lobby becomes excessive. Zoning is likely to provide a better service.

Figs. 2 and 3 illustrate related elevator design criteria. Fig. 2 illustrates elevator traction-type elevators, characterized by arrangements of the roping:

(a) Single wrap using only the traction sheave. This is only possible for small cars because the distance between can and counterweight centers is limited.

(b) Single wrap with divertor sheave. Allows more freedom in locating the counterweight.

(c) Double-wrap. The same as (b), except that an extra wrap of the ropes gives more reliable traction.

(d) Compensator ropes are added in tall buildings. The lower ropes are merely moving ballast to compensate for the weight of the moving hoist ropes.

(e) 2:1 roping. The ropes move twice as fast as the car. This allows a gearless machine to be used on a slower car than would otherwise be feasible.

(f) Underslung car. The machine room can be located in the basement, to reduce the height needed at the top of the building.

Fig. 3 illustrates the hydraulic elevator alternatives are:

(a) With a one-piece or telescopic ram beneath the car. The ram itself provides the overspeed and overtravel protection.

(b) With the ram in the shaft, using a machine chain or rope to operate the car itself. Normal safety devices are needed as with any rope-operated elevator.

Tables 2 and 3 offers planning criteria for elevator design and selection based upon building type and capacity. The remaining pages in this chapter offer various details to guide design dimensioning. See Figs. 4–12.

Fig. 3. Hydraulic elevators. (Smith 1993)

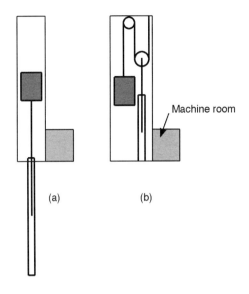

(a)　　　　(b)

Machine room

Table 3. Design parameters for elevator selection.

$$P = F - F\left(1 - \frac{1}{F}\right)^{C}$$

where 　P = probable number of stops
　　　　F = number of floors served above ground
　　　　C = capacity of car on average trip (taken as no more than 80 percent of the maximum number of passengers)

Table 2. Approximate sizes and ratings of elevator cars. (Smith 1993)

Capacity		Passengers		Inside, W x D		Shaft, W x D	
		Max.	Average	in.	mm	in.	mm
2000	900	12	10	68 x 51	1700 x 1300	89 x 83	2200 x 2100
2500	1150	16	13	82 x 51	2100 x 1300	102 x 83	2550 x 2100
3000	1350	20	16	82 x 55	2100 x 1400	102 x 88	2550 x 2200
3500	1600	24	19	82 x 66	2100 x 1650	102 x 96	2550 x 2400
4000	1800	28	22	92 x 66	2300 x 1650	114 x 96	2850 x 2400

D1

SERVICES

Electric traction elevator
Passenger service
Gearless machine
Capacity: 2,500 to 4,000 lbs
Speed: 700 to 1,200 fpm

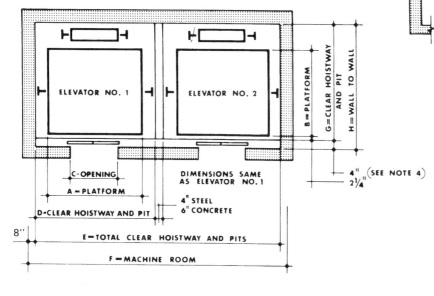

Notes:

1. *American National Safety Code for Elevators* and local codes govern elevator installation.

2. When total cab height exceeds 9', add excess to J.

3. When there is occupied space below elevator pit, increase G and H by 3" to allow for counterweight safeties.

4. When flush transoms are desired, increase 4" to 5½"; increase H by 1½".

5. When 6" divider beam is used, add 2" to E. Where seismic protection is required, allow 8" or more.

6. Alternate platform dimensions.

7. Provide machine room with access and ventilation as required by code.

8. For poured concrete structures, additional clearances are recommended.

Capacity, lb	Speed, fpm	Dimensions										
		A	B	C	D	E	F	G	H	J	K	L
2,500	700	7'-0"	5'-0"	3'-6"	8'-6"	17'-6"	22'-6"	6'-5½"	6'-9½"	26'-6"	12'-6"	
	800									29'-0"	14'-0"	23'-0"
3,000	700	7'-0"	5'-6"	3'-6"	8'-6"	17'-6"	22'-6"	6'-11½"	7'-3½"	26'-6"	12'-6"	
	800									29'-0"	14'-0"	23'-0"
	1,000									30'-9"	18'-0"	
3,500 (Note 6)	800	7'-0"	6'-2"	3'-6"	8'-6"	17'-6"	22'-6"	7'-7½"	7'-11½"	29'-0"	14'-0"	
	1,000									30'-9"	18'-0"	24'-0"
	1,200									31'-6"	19'-6"	
3,500	800	8'-0"	5'-6"	4'-0"	9'-6"	19'-6"	24'-0"	6'-11½"	7'-3½"	29'-0"	14'-0"	
	1,000									30'-9"	18'-0"	24'-0"
	1,200									31'-6"	19'-6"	
4,000	800	8'-0"	6'-2"	4'-0"	9'-6"	19'-6"	24'-0"	7'-7½"	7'-11½"	29'-0"	14'-0"	
	1,000									30'-9"	18'-0"	24'-0"
	1,200									31'-6"	19'-6"	

Fig. 4

SERVICES

D1

Electric traction elevator
Hospital service
Geared and gearless machines
Capacity: 4,000 to 5,000 lbs
Speed: 200 to 800 fpm

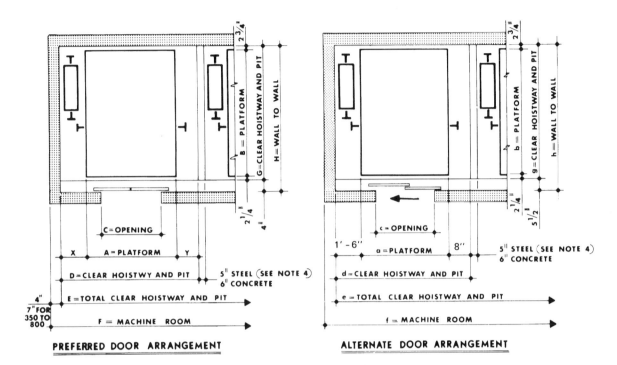

PREFERRED DOOR ARRANGEMENT   **ALTERNATE DOOR ARRANGEMENT**

Notes:

1. *American National Safety Code for Elevators* and local codes govern elevator installation.

2. For vertical dimensions, see sectional view of passenger elevators of the same speed.

3. When total cab height exceeds 9′, add excess to J.

4. When 6″ divider beam is used, add 1″ to E. Where seismic protection is required, allow 8″ or more.

5. Provide machine room with access and ventilation as required by code.

6. For poured concrete structures, additional clearances are recommended.

Capacity, lb	Speed fpm	Dimensions																						
		Preferred arrangement												Alternate arrangement									
		A	B	C	D	E	F	G	H	J	K	L	X	Y	a	b	c	d	e	f	g	h	i	k	l
4,000	200									16′-9″	5′-0″	13′-6″											16′-9″	5′-0″	13′-6″
	300									17′-6″	6′-9″	13′-6″											17′-6″	6′-9″	13′-6″
	350	5′-8″	8′-8″	4′-0″	18′-10″	18′-2″	25′-9″	9′-1″	9′-5″	18′-0″	7′-8″	14′-0″	1′-7″	1′-7″	5′-8″	8′-8″	4′-0″	7′-10″	16′-2″	23′-9″	9′-1″	9′-6½″	18′-0″	7′-8″	14′-0″
	500									25′-0″	10′-0″												25′-0″	10′-0″	
	800									29′-0″													29′-0″		
4,500	200									16′-9″	5′-0″	13′-6″											16′-9″	5′-0″	13′-6″
	300									17′-6″	6′-9″	13′-6″											17′-6″	6′-9″	13′-6″
	350	6′-0″	8′-11″	4′-0″	18′-10″	18′-2″	25′-9″	9′-4″	9′-8″	18′-0″	7′-8″	14′-0″	1′-5″	1′-5″	6′-0″	9′-0″	4′-3″	8′-2″	16′-10″	23′-9″	9′-5″	9′-10½″	18′-0″	7′-8″	14′-0″
	500									25′-0″	10′-0″												25′-0″	10′-0″	
	800									29′-0″													29′-0″		
5,000	200									16′-9″	5′-2″	13′-6″											16′-9″	5′-2″	13′-6″
	300									18′-0″	6′-9″	13′-6″											18′-0″	6′-9″	13′-6″
	350	6′-0″	9′-6″	4′-0″	18′-10″	18′-2″	25′-9″	9′-11″	10′-3″	18′-6″	7′-8″	14′-0″	1′-5″	1′-5″	6′-0″	9′-7″	4′-8″	8′-2″	16′-10″	23′-9″	10′-0″	10′-5½″	18′-6″	7′-6″	14′-0″
	500									25′-6″	10′-3″												25′-6″	10′-3″	
	800									29′-6″													29′-6″		

Fig. 5

Electric traction elevator
Freight service
Geared machine
Capacity: 4,000 to 10,000 lbs
Speed: 75 to 200 fpm

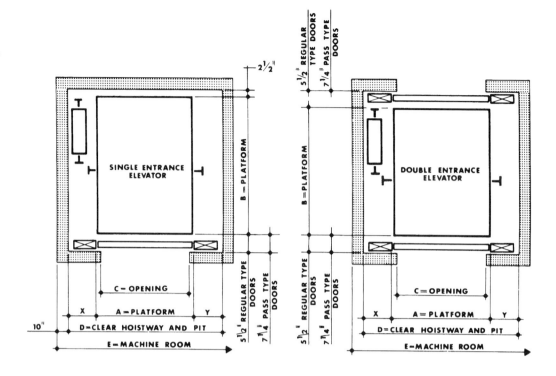

Notes:

1. *American National Safety Code for Elevators* and local codes govern elevator installation.

2. Dimensions provided are based on class A loading. For power truck loading and/or other special loadings, (classes B, C1, C2, C3) see code requirements.

3. Provide machine room with access and ventilation as required by code.

4. See door detail sheet for vertical biparting door requirements.

5. When door height exceeds 8', add excess to G.

6. For poured concrete structures, additional clearances are recommended.

Capacity, lb	Speed, fpm	Dimensions										
		A	B		C	D	E	F	G	H	X	Y
			Single entrance	Double entrance								
4,000	75	6'-4"	7'-6"	7'-7"	6'-0"	8'-7"	11'-6"	5'-0"	16'-6"	13'-9"	1'-4"	11"
	100						12'-8"	5'-0"	16'-6"	13'-9"		
	200						14'-0"	5'-6"	17'-6"	15'-4"		
5,000	75	7'-4"	8'-0"	8'-1"	7'-0"	9'-7"	11'-6"	5'-0"	16'-6"	13'-9"	1'-4"	11"
	100						12'-8"	5'-0"	16'-6"	13'-9"		
	200						14'-0"	5'-6"	17'-6"	15'-4"		
6,000	75	8'-4"	8'-0"	8'-1"	8'-0"	10'-9"	11'-6"	5'-0"	16'-6"	13'-9"	1'-6"	11"
	100						12'-8"	5'-0"	16'-6"	13'-9"		
	200						14'-0"	5'-6"	17'-6"	15'-4"		
8,000	75	8'-4"	10'-6"	10'-7"	8'-0"	10'-11"	12'-0"	5'-6"	17'-0"	13'-9"	1'-8"	11"
	100						13'-0"	5'-6"	17'-0"	13'-9"		
	200						14'-6"	5'-6"	18'-0"	15'-4"		
10,000	75	8'-4"	12'-6"	12'-7"	8'-0"	10'-11"	12'-0"	5'-6"	17'-0"	15'-4"	1'-8"	11"
	100						13'-0"	5'-6"	17'-0"	15'-4"		
	200						14'-6"	6'-0"	18'-0"	15'-10"		

Fig. 6

Hydraulic elevator
Passenger and hospital service
Capacity: 2,000 to 4,000 lbs (passenger)
            4,000 to 5,000 lbs (hospital)
Speed: 50 to 150 fpm

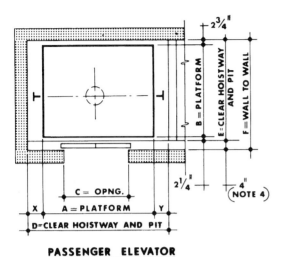

PASSENGER ELEVATOR

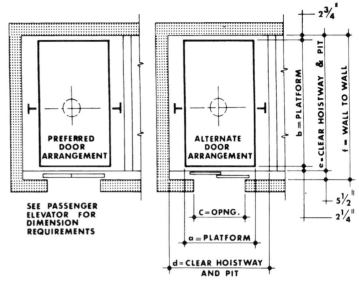

HOSPITAL TYPE ELEVATOR

Notes:

1. *American National Safety Code for Elevators* and local codes govern elevator installation.

2. For vertical dimensions, see sectional view of hydraulic freight service elevator, sheet 7.

3. When total cab height exceeds 9', add excess to H.

4. When flush transoms are desired, increase 4" to 5½"; increase F by 1½".

5. Alternate platform dimensions.

6. Provide machine room with access and ventilation as required by code.

7. Where seismic protection is required, allow 8" or more for divider beam.

Passenger elevator dimensions

Capacity, lb	A	B	C	D	E	F	X	Y	G	H	J
2,000	6'-4"	4'-5"	3'-0"	7'-8"	4'-10"	5'-2"					
2,500	7'-0"	5'-0"	3'-6"	8'-4"	5'-5"	5'-9"					
3,000	7'-0"	5'-6"	3'-6"	8'-4"	5'-11"	6'-3"	8"	8"	7'-0"	13'-0"	4'-6"
3,500 Note 5	7'-0"	6'-2"	3'-6"	8'-4"	6'-7"	6'-11"					
3,500	8'-0"	5'-6"	4'-0"	9'-4"	5'-11"	6'-3"					
4,000	8'-0"	6'-2"	4'-0"	9'-4"	6'-7"	6'-11"					

Hospital type elevator dimensions, preferred door arrangement

Capacity lb	A	B	C	D	E	F	X	Y	G	H	J
4,000	5'-8"	8'-8"	4'-0"	8'-10"	9'-1"	9'-5"	1'-7"	1'-7"			4'-6"
4,500	6'-0"	9'-0"	4'-0"	8'-10"	9'-5"	9'-9"	1'-5"	1'-5"	7'-0"	13'-0"	4'-6"
5,000	6'-0"	9'-6"	4'-0"	8'-10"	9'-5"	9'-9"	1'-2"	1'-2"			5'-0"

Hospital type elevator dimensions, alternate door arrangement

Capacity lb	a	b	c	d	e	f	x	y	g	h	i
4,000	5'-8"	8'-8"	4'-0"	7'-7"	9'-1"	9'-6½"	1'-3"				4'-6"
4,500	6'-0"	9'-0"	4'-0"	7'-4"	9'-5"	9'-10½"	8"	8"	7'-0"	13'-0"	4'-6"
5,000	6'-0"	9'-6"	4'-3"	7'-10"	9'-5"	10'-4½"	8"				5'-0"

Fig. 7

SERVICES

D1

Electric traction elevator
Freight service
Geared machine
Capacity: 4,000 to 10,000 lbs
Speed: 75 to 200 fpm

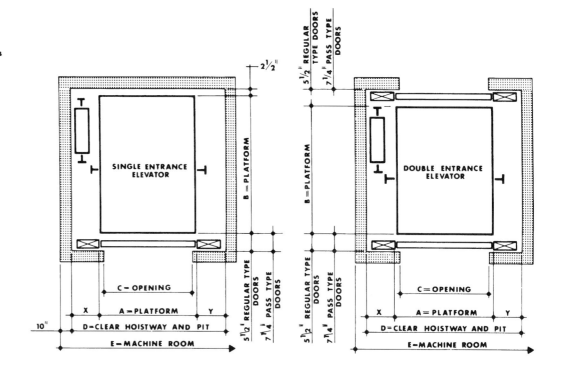

Notes:

1. *American National Safety Code for Elevators* and local codes govern elevator installation.

2. Dimensions provided are based on class A loading. For power truck loading and/or other special loadings, (classes B, C1, C2, C3) see code requirements.

3. Provide machine room with access and ventilation as required by code.

4. See door detail sheet for vertical biparting door requirements.

5. When door height exceeds 8', add excess to G.

6. For poured concrete structures, additional clearances are recommended.

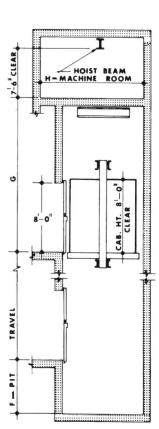

Capacity, lb	Speed, fpm	A	B		C	D	E	F	G	H	X	Y
			Single entrance	Double entrance								
4,000	75	6'-4"	7'-6"	7'-7"	6'-0"	8'-7"	11'-6"	5'-0"	16'-6"	13'-9"	1'-4"	11"
	100						12'-8"	5'-0"	16'-6"	13'-9"		
	200						14'-0"	5'-6"	17'-6"	15'-4"		
5,000	75	7'-4"	8'-0"	8'-1"	7'-0"	9'-7"	11'-6"	5'-0"	16'-6"	13'-9"	1'-4"	11"
	100						12'-8"	5'-0"	16'-6"	13'-9"		
	200						14'-0"	5'-6"	17'-6"	15'-4"		
6,000	75	8'-4"	8'-0"	8'-1"	8'-0"	10'-9"	11'-6"	5'-0"	16'-6"	13'-9"	1'-6"	11"
	100						12'-8"	5'-0"	16'-6"	13'-9"		
	200						14'-0"	5'-6"	17'-6"	15'-4"		
8,000	75	8'-4"	10'-6"	10'-7"	8'-0"	10'-11"	12'-0"	5'-6"	17'-0"	13'-9"	1'-8"	11"
	100						13'-0"	5'-6"	17'-0"	13'-9"		
	200						14'-6"	5'-6"	18'-0"	15'-4"		
10,000	75	8'-4"	12'-6"	12'-7"	8'-0"	10'-11"	12'-0"	5'-6"	17'-0"	15'-4"	1'-8"	11"
	100						13'-0"	5'-6"	17'-0"	15'-4"		
	200						14'-6"	6'-0"	18'-0"	15'-10"		

Fig. 8

Hydraulic elevator
Passenger and hospital service
Capacity: 2,000 to 4,000 lbs (passenger)
          4,000 to 5,000 lbs (hospital)
Speed: 50 to 150 fpm

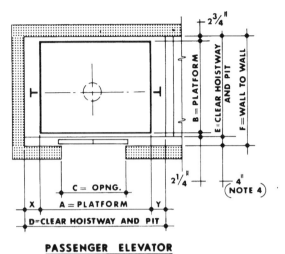

PASSENGER ELEVATOR

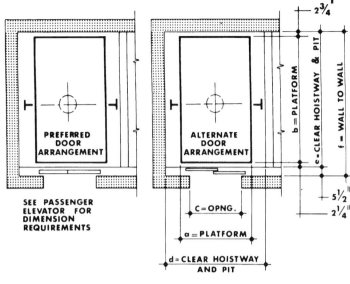

SEE PASSENGER
ELEVATOR FOR
DIMENSION
REQUIREMENTS

HOSPITAL TYPE ELEVATOR

Notes:

1. *American National Safety Code for Elevators* and local codes govern elevator installation.

2. For vertical dimensions, see sectional view of hydraulic freight service elevator, sheet 7.

3. When total cab height exceeds 9', add excess to H.

4. When flush transoms are desired, increase 4" to 5½"; increase F by 1½".

5. Alternate platform dimensions.

6. Provide machine room with access and ventilation as required by code.

7. Where seismic protection is required, allow 8" or more for divider beam.

Passenger elevator dimensions

Capacity, lb	A	B	C	D	E	F	X	Y	G	H	J
2,000	6'-4"	4'-5"	3'-0"	7'-8"	4'-10"	5'-2"					
2,500	7'-0"	5'-0"	3'-6"	8'-4"	5'-5"	5'-9"					
3,000	7'-0"	5'-6"	3'-6"	8'-4"	5'-11"	6'-3"	8"	8"	7'-0"	13'-0"	4'-6"
3,500											
Note 5	7'-0"	6'-2"	3'-6"	8'-4"	6'-7"	6'-11"					
3,500	8'-0"	5'-6"	4'-0"	9'-4"	5'-11"	6'-3"					
4,000	8'-0"	6'-2"	4'-0"	9'-4"	6'-7"	6'-11"					

Hospital type elevator dimensions, preferred door arrangement

Capacity lb	A	B	C	D	E	F	X	Y	G	H	J
4,000	5'-8"	8'-8"	4'-0"	8'-10"	9'-1"	9'-5"	1'-7"	1'-7"			4'-6"
4,500	6'-0"	9'-0"	4'-0"	8'-10"	9'-5"	9'-9"	1'-5"	1'-5"	7'-0"	13'-0"	4'-6"
5,000	6'-0"	9'-6"	4'-0"	8'-10"	9'-5"	9'-9"	1'-2"	1'-2"			5'-0"

Hospital type elevator dimensions, alternate door arrangement

Capacity lb	a	b	c	d	e	f	x	y	g	h	j
4,000	5'-8"	8'-8"	4'-0"	7'-7"	9'-1"	9'-6½"	1'-3"				4'-6"
4,500	6'-0"	9'-0"	4'-0"	7'-4"	9'-5"	9'-10½"	8"	8"	7'-0"	13'-0"	4'-6"
5,000	6'-0"	9'-6"	4'-3"	7'-10"	9'-5"	10'-4½"	8"				5'-0"

Fig. 9

Hydraulic elevator
Freight service
Capacity: 2,000 to 10,000 lbs
Speed: 50 to 150 fpm

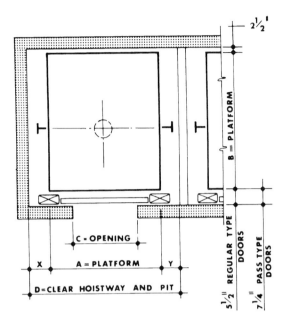

FREIGHT ELEVATOR

Notes:

1. *American National Safety Code for Elevators and* local codes govern elevator installation.

2. Dimensions provided are based on class A loading for power truck loading and/or other special loadings (Classes B, C-1, C-2, C-3) see code requirements.

3. Provide a machine room of approx. 9 x 11 x 7 ft high for a single elevator. Larger area is required when two or more power units are used or for two (2) elevators with a common machine room. Machine room can be located remote from shaft, preferably on the lowest level served. Provide machine room with access and ventilation as required by code.

4. When door height exceeds 8 ft, add excess to H.

5. See door detail sheet for vertical biparting door requirements.

6. A waterproof outer casing is recommended. It is required when water condition is known to exist.

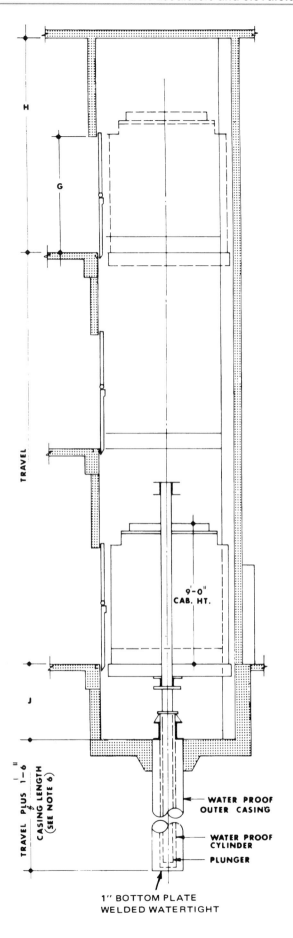

Capacity, lb	Dimensions								
	A	B	C	D	X	Y	G	H	J
2,000	4'-4"	5'-6"	4'-0"	6'-2"					
3,000	5'-4"	6'-6"	5'-0"	7'-2"					4'-6"
4,000	6'-4"	7'-6"	6'-0"	8'-2"					
5,000	7'-4"	8'-0"	7'-0"	9'-2"	11"	11"	8'-0"	15'-0"	
6,000	8'-4"	8'-0"	8'-0"	10'-2"					5'-0"
8,000	8'-4"	10'-6"	8'-0"	10'-2"					
10,000	8'-4"	12'-6"	8'-0"	10'-2"					5'-6"

Fig. 10

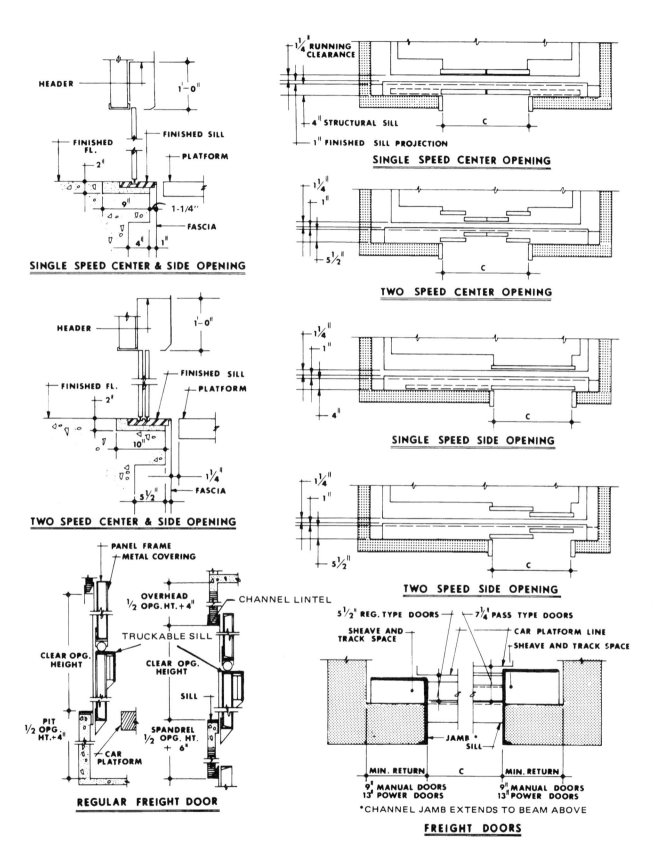

SINGLE SPEED CENTER & SIDE OPENING

TWO SPEED CENTER & SIDE OPENING

REGULAR FREIGHT DOOR

SINGLE SPEED CENTER OPENING

TWO SPEED CENTER OPENING

SINGLE SPEED SIDE OPENING

TWO SPEED SIDE OPENING

FREIGHT DOORS

*CHANNEL JAMB EXTENDS TO BEAM ABOVE

NOTE: FRONT WALLS SHOULD BE LEFT OUT UNTIL ENTRANCES ARE SET IN PLACE, OR MINIMUM ROUGH OPENING PROVIDED 12' WIDER AND 6" HIGHER THAN DOORWAY SIZE.

Fig. 11

By SYSKA AND HENNESSY, INC., *Consulting Engineers*

See American National Safety Code for Elevators, Dumbwaiters, Escalators, Moving Walks, ANSI A17.1-1978.

Electric stairway
Angle of incline: 30 deg
Speed: 90 or 120 fpm
Width: 32 or 48 in.

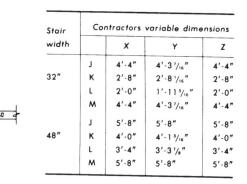

Stair width		Contractors variable dimensions		
		X	Y	Z
32"	J	4'-4"	4'-3 7/16"	4'-4"
	K	2'-8"	2'-8 1/16"	2'-8"
	L	2'-0"	1'-11 5/16"	2'-0"
	M	4'-4"	4'-3 7/16"	4'-4"
48"	J	5'-8"	5'-8"	5'-8"
	K	4'-0"	4'-1 3/16"	4'-0"
	L	3'-4"	3'-3 7/8"	3'-4"
	M	5'-8"	5'-8"	5'-8"

	Contractors variable dimensions		
	X	Y	Z
A	5'-8"	4'-9"	6'-6"
B	9'-2"	10'-1"	8'-4"
C	4'-7 7/8"	3'-8 15/16"	5'-2 9/16"
D	5'-5 1/8"	6'-7"	5'-4 1/16"
E	3'-4 3/4"	3'-6 3/8"	3'-2 7/16"
F	3'-4 1/2"	3'-7"	3'-8 1/2"
G	3'-11"	3'-11"	4'-2"
H	Moving stair rise		
I	12'-10"	12'-4"	13'-3"

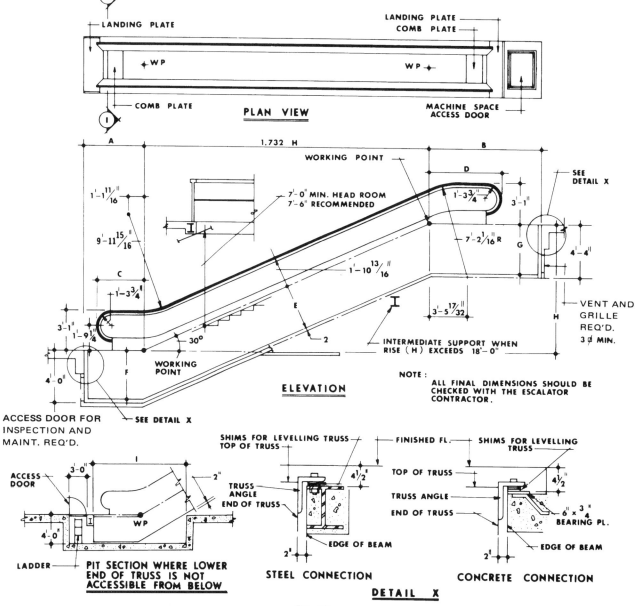

Fig. 12

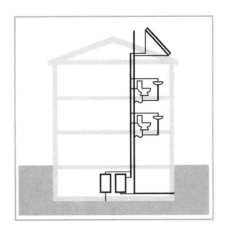

D SERVICES

D2

SERVICES

D2

SERVICES

Plumbing systems

Summary: Water distribution and plumbing systems are sized according to codes and occupancy, related to fixture unit count or water system demand. System design includes hot and cold water lines, domestic hot water systems, pressure and flow, and tank capacities. Fixtures choices include a variety of dimensional, accessibility, finishes, and energy (water) conservation options.

Key words: cold and hot water lines, pipe layouts, plumbing fixtures, pressure and flow, tank capacity, valves.

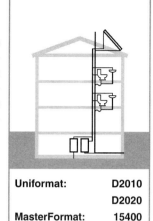

Uniformat:	D2010
	D2020
MasterFormat:	15400

1 Water distribution systems

Water distribution layouts

Pipes for hot and cold water are sized for permanently clean interior bores, taht is, free of obstruction. It is assumed that the supply water will be relatively soft (low calcium carbonate), so that no precipitated coating will form within pipe walls, which would reduce inside pipe diameters and prevent free flow of water. In localities where the water contains a concentration of hardness (higher levels of calcium carbonate) sufficient to cause even a slight precipitation in cold water lines, or if the water quality exceeds the health authority requirements or taste standards for human tolerance, the main line feeding the building must be filtered through a water softener.

For design purposes, an architect should understand the principles of water distribution and piping system layout, in order to adaquately providenecessary clearances and accessible spaces for horizontal and vertical runs of piping, to provide for insulation to prevent condensation (and resulting dripping and staining), to design proper hanging and attachment, and provide for plubing servicing and maintenance. Like any system design, the best approach is to provide chases and runs for adaquate water distribution, that is direct and free of unnecessary turns which may unecessarily reduces flow and create locations for blockage.

The diagramatic layouts in Fig. 1 shows typical good practice in the design of hot and cold water distribution systems for small buildings, most typical of residences. The layouts are based on the essentials of distribution under various sets of practical conditions, but should not be interpreted as a complete solution to any specific problem. Related vents required from each fixture are not shown. The pipe sizes and arrangements are typical for dwellings that contain two bathrooms in addition to a first floor lavatory, toilet, kitchen sink, and clothes washer.

The values given in Tables 1, 2, and 3 are for water consumption evaluation and fixture unit count for water supply systems.

Cold water lines

- Taps

- Taps from the street water main are usually 3/4 in. (20 cm) for single-family residences containing a total amount of fixtures equivalent to those commonly found in three bathrooms, a kitchen, and laundry.

- Pipe may vary in size depending on the fixture unit count or de-mand, usually represented by Gallons Per Minute (GPM) or litres/second (l/s).

- Codes

- Most regional plumbing codes in the U. S. require pressure reducing valves where street main pressure exceeds 80 psi (550 kPa).

- An approved pressure reducing valve should be installed in the water service pipe near the entrance of the water service pipe into the structure, except where the water feeds a water pressure booster.

- The pressure at any fixture normally should not exceed 80 psi (550 kPa) under no-flow conditions.

- Drain valves. A drain valve should be installed in the lowest branch of the basement so that the entire system can be completely drained.

- Main shut-off valve: A main shut-off valve should be provided in each water supply pipe at each of the following locations:

- On the street side near the curb.

- At the entrance into the structure.

- On the discharge side of the water meter.

- On the base of every riser.

- At the supply of any equipment.

- At the connection to any fixture.

- Water hammer arresters

- Water hammer arresters or shock absorbers will prevent water hammering throughout the piping system. They are typically located after the first fixture of a group of fixtures.

- Arrestor devices are also recommended where quick-closing valves are utilized.

- Water softeners

- Water softeners are available in various sizes and types, all of which require a salt tank for regeneration.

- Regeneration can be accomplished manually or automatically; automatic regeneration is usually controlled by a meter on the softened water line, a floor drain for waste water is essential if a water softening equipment is provided.

- Pipe insulation

Author: Arturo De La Vega

References: BOCA. 1990. *BOCA National Plumbing Code.* Country Club Hills, IL: Building Officials and Code Administration.

Additonal references are listed at the end of this article.

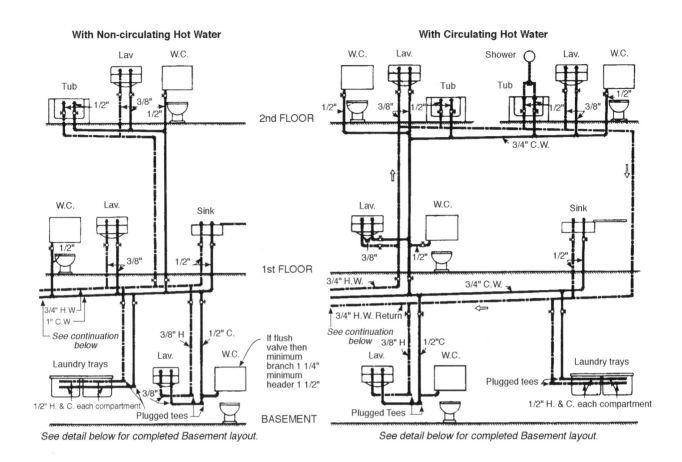

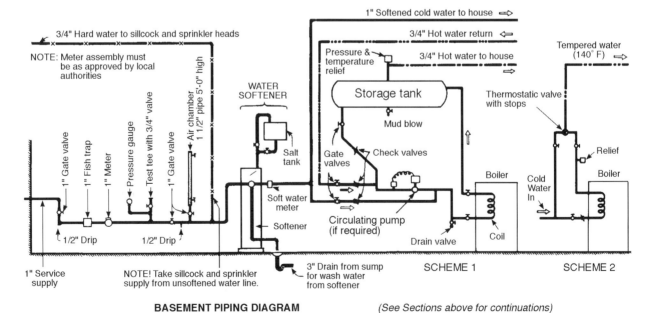

BASEMENT PIPING DIAGRAM   *(See Sections above for continuations)*

Fig. 1. Residential piping system diagrams.

Table 1. Design criteria for daily water requirements based on building occupancy. Source: Building Officials and Code Administration (1990).

Type of occupancy	Minimum quantity of water per person per day in gallons (or as indicated)
Small dwelling and cottages with seasonal occupancy	50
Single family dwellings	75
Multiple family dwellings (apartments)	60
Rooming houses	40
Boarding houses	50
Additional kitchen usage for nonresident boarders	10
Hotels without private baths	50
Hotels with private baths (2 persons per room)	60
Restaurants (toilet and kitchen usage per patron)	7 to 10
Restaurants (kitchen usage per meal served)	2 1/2 to 3
Additional for bars and cocktail lounges	2
Tourist camps or trailer parks with central bathhouse	35
Tourist camps or mobile home parks with individual bath units	50
Resort camps (night and day) with limited plumbing	50
Luxury camps	100 to 150
Work or construction camps (semipermanent)	50
Camp (with complete plumbing)	45 (Ind.w.s.)
Camp (with flush toilets, no showers)	25 (Ind.w.s.)
Day camp (no meals served)	15
Day schools, without cafeteria, gymnasiums, or showers	15
Day schools with cafeterias, but no gymnasiums or showers	20
Day schools with cafeterias, gymnasiums and showers	25
Boarding schools	75 to 100
Day workers at schools and offices (per shift)	15
Hospitals (per bed)	150-250
Institutions other than hospitals (per bed)	75 to 125
Factories (gallons per person per shift, exclusive of industrial wastes)	15 to 35
Picnic parks [toilet usage only (gallons per picnicker)]	5
Picnic parks with bathhouses, showers and flush toilets	10
Swimming pools and bathhouses	10
Luxury residences and estates	100 to 150
Country clubs (per resident member)	100
Country clubs (per nonresident member)	25
Motel (per bed space)	40
Motels with bath, toilet, and kitchen range	50
Drive-in theaters (per car space)	5
Movie theaters (per auditorium seat)	5
Airports (per passenger)	3 to 5
Self-service laundries (gallons per wash, i.e., per customer)	50
Stores (per toilet room)	400
Service stations (per vehicle serviced)	10

Table 2. Supply fixture unit values for various plumbing fixtures. Source: Building Officials and Code Administration (1990).

Fixture or group[a]	Type of supply control	Supply fixture unit values		
		Hot	Cold	Total[b]
Bathroom group	Flush tank	3	4.5	6
Bathroom group	Flush valve	3	6	8
Bathtub	Faucet	1.5	1.5	2
Bidet	Faucet	1.5	1.5	2
Combination fixture	Faucet	2	2	3
Kitchen sink	Faucet	1.5	1.5	2
Laundry tray	Faucet	2	2	3
Lavatory	Faucet	1.5	1.5	2
Pedestal urinal	Flush valve		10	10
Restaurant sink	Faucet	3	3	4
Service sink	Faucet	1.5	1.5	2
Shower head	Mixing valve	3	3	4
Stall or wall urinal	Flush tank		3	3
Stall or wall urinal	Flush valve		5	5
Water closet	Flush tank		5	5
Water closet	Flush valve		10	10

Note a. For fixtures not listed, factors may be assumed by comparing the fixture to a listed one using water in similar quantities and at similar rates. Note b. For fixtures with both hot and cold water supplies, the weights for maximum separate demands may be taken as three fourths of the total supply fixture unit value.

Table 3. Water distribution system design criteria required capacities at fixture supply pipe outlets. Source: Building Officials and Code Administration (1990).

Fixture supply outlet serving	Flow rate[b] (gpm)	Flow pressure[b] (psi)
Bathtub	4	8
Bidet	2	4
Combination fixture	4	8
Dishwasher, residential	2.75	8
Drinking fountain	0.75	8
Laundry tray	4	8
Lavatory	2	8
Shower	3	8
Shower, temperature controlled	3	20
Sillcock, hose bibb	5	8
Sink, residential	2.5	8
Sink, service	3	8
Urinal, valve	15	15
Water closet, blow out, flushometer valve	35	25
Water closet, flushometer tank	1.6	8
Water closet, tank, close coupled	3	8
Water closet, tank, one piece	6	20
Water closet, siphonic, flushometer valve	25	15

Note b. 1 pound per square inch = 6.894 kPa: 1 gallon per minute = 3.785

- Insulation of water lines is necessary to prevent undesirable condensation from cold water lines.

Hot water lines

A simple form of circulation can be accomplished by connecting the hot water pipe supply after the last fixture connected to a recirculating line as a simple loop below the floor of the highest level.

Circulation serves to prevent waste of water and provides the added benefit of instantaneous hot water availability. The type of circulating hot water distribution shown is adaptable to large residences. A more elaborate type would require individual supply and return risers to serve superimposed fixtures or bathrooms.

Hot water lines should also be insulated to avoid waste of energy due the heat loss, and for this purpose typically 1/2 in. to 1 in. (1.25 cm to 2.5 cm) fiber glass insulation is used. Shut-off valves are also required in the same fashion as indicated for cold water lines. The water heater detail diagram shown will guide the designer, where to locate check valves, recirculating pump, and relief valve.

Hot water system size

The variety of uses for domestic hot water and lifestyles make it difficult to determine system requirements and sizing. The designer should refer to the *ASHRAE Handbook,* the *ASPE Fundamentals of Plumbing Design*, and manufacturers catalogs.

Besides the sizing of the system, it is important to select the most efficient and economical energy source. Fuel choice will depending on local energy costs and availability. The most common sources include:

- gas fired.

- oil fired.

- electric.

- steam generated.

- solar water heaters.

Other factors to be consdiered at the beginning of the design include:

- storage tank requirements.

- space availability.

- peak instantaneous demand.

- water temperature requirements.

- water treatment.

Table 4 provides a guide for hot water demand requirements based on the hourly hot water consumption per fixture. Special consideration should be given to the following types of facilities that have high hot-water demand, such as motels, hospitals, nursing homes, laboratories, and food service establishments.

The probable maximum demand is the result of the hourly hot water demand times the demand factor (line l9 in Table 4). The storage tank capacity is the result of probable maximum demand times the storage capacity factor (line 20 in Table 4).

An efficiency factor is an important consideration. For example, gas water heaters can be expected to have an efficiency factor of 75% to 90%. Verification from manufacturers data and equipment performance results reported in current literature is necessary.

Example: Hospital Facility

	Qty.		GPH		Subtotal
Showers	20	x	75	=	1500
Lavatories	10	x	6	=	60
Laundry Tubs	10	x	28	=	280
Washers	18	x	28	=	504

Possible maximum demand = 2344 GPH
Probable maximum demand = 2344 x 0.25 = 586 GPH
Heater or coil capacity 586 GPH recovery
Storage tank capacity 586 x 0.60 = 352 gallons

Table 4. Hot water demand per fixture for various types of buildings. Gallons of water per hour per fixture, calculated at a final temperature of 140F (60°C). Source: *ASHRAE Systems and Equipment Handbook.* 1995.

	Apartment House	Club	Gym- nasium	Hospital	Industrial Hotel	Office Plant	Private Building	Residence	School	YMCA
1. Basins, private lavatory	2 (7.6)	2 (7.6)	2 (7.6)	2 (7.6)	2 (7.6)	2 (7.6)	2 (7.6)	2 (7.6)	2 (7.6)	2 (7.6)
2. Basins, public lavatory	4 (15.2)	6 (22.7)	8 (30.3)	6 (22.7)	8 (30.3)	12 (45.5)	6 (22.7)	—	15 (56.8)	8 (30.3)
3. Bathtubs	20 (75.8)	20 (75.8)	30 (113.7)	20 (75.8)	20 (75.8)	—	—	20 (75.8)	—	30 (113.7)
4. Dishwashers[a]	15 (56.8)	50-150 (189.5-568.5)	—	50-150 (189.5-568.5)	50-200 (189.5-758)	20-100 (75.8-379)	—	15 (56.8)	20-100 (75.8-379)	20-100 (75.8-379)
5. Foot basins	3 (11.4)	3 (11.4)	12 (45.5)	3 (11.4)	3 (11.4)	12 (45.5)	—	3 (11.4)	3 (11.4)	12 (45.5)
6. Kitchen sink	10 (37.9)	20 (75.8)	—	30 (113.7)	20 (75.8)	20 (75.8)	10 (37.9)	20 (75.8)	20 (75.8)	
7. Laundry, stationary tubs	20 (75.8)	28 (106.1)	—	28 (106.1)	28 (106.1)	—	—	20 (75.8)	—	28 (106.1)
8. Pantry sink	5 (18.9)	10 (37.9)	—	10 (37.9)	10 (37.9)	—	10 (37.9)	5 (18.9)	10 (37.9)	10 (37.9)
9. Showers	30 (113.7)	150 (568.5)	225 (852.7)	30 (113.7)	30 (113.7)	225 (852.7)	225 (852.7)			
10. Service sink	20 (75.8)	20 (75.8)	—	20 (75.8)	30 (113.7)	20 (75.8)	20 (75.8)	15 (56.8)	20 (75.8)	20 (75.8)
11. Hydrotherapeutic showers				400 (1516.0)						
12. Hubbard baths				600 (2274.0)						
13. Leg baths				100 (379.0)						
14. Arm baths				35 (132.6)						
15. Sitz baths				30 (113.7)						
16. Continuous-flow baths				165 (625.4)						
17. Circular wash sinks				20 (75.8)	20 (75.8)	30 (113.7)	20 (75.8)		30 (113.7)	
18. Semicircular wash sinks				10 (37.9)	10 (37.9)	15 (56.8)	10 (37.9)		15 (56.8)	
19. DEMAND FACTOR	0.30	0.30	0.40	0.25	0.25	0.40	0.30	0.40	0.40	
20. STORAGE CAPACITY FACTOR[b]	1.25	0.90	1.00	0.60	0.80	1.00	2.00	0.70	1.00	1.00

[a] Dishwasher requirements should be taken from this table or from manufacturer's data for the model to be used, if this is known.
[b] Ratio of storage tank capacity to probable maximum demand/h. Storage capacity may be reduced where an unlimited supply of steam is available from a central street steam system or large boiler plant.

Recovery of the unit and storage tank can be interpolated to balance or increase either the capacity of the unit, based on space availability and minimum code requirements

Pressure and flow

- Plumbing fixtures require certain pressure and flow to function properly. Street pressure is normally enough to satisfy the requirements of residences and two- to five-story buildings.

- An engineer should verify the existing pressure and flow characteristics from city authorities. For structures in excess of five stories the engineer should select any of the following means to provide adequate pressure and flow to the plumbing fixtures within the structure:

• Booster pumps can be a duplex system or several duplex systems supplying different zones. A structure taller than five stories should be divided in zones of not more than 12 stories. Booster systems can be complimented with storage tanks at the highest level of each zone.

• Another alternative for pressuring the system is to provide a pneumatic booster system with the following components: booster pump, compressor, pneumatic tank, valves, and controllers.

• Tanks used in booster systems have also been used for the dual purpose of water supply and as a reserve for fire protection.

Tank capacity

The required capacity of a tank varies with the capacity and running time of the structure or fill pumps. A half-hour supply of domestic water is generally sufficient if pump capacity is equal to the hourly load. Table 5 gives water consumption figures that can be used to determine tank and pump capacities.

For example, assume that a commercial office building has an occupancy of 4,500 persons:

4,500 times 3.8 gallons per hour per person = 17,100 gal. per hour
Tank should have a half-hour supply = 8,550 gal.
Pump should have one-hour supply = 17,100 gal. per hour
The pump capacity will be 285 GPM (18 l/s).

It is normal practice to design a system with a standby pump to provide water service in the event of a system shutdown; and if additional requirements for make-up water are necessitated by air conditioning systems.

Piping materials

Available water service piping materials include the following:
- Acrylonitrile butadiene (ABS plastic pipe).

- Brass pipe.

- Copper or Copper-alloy pipe.

- Copper or Copper-alloy tubing (Type K, WK, L, WL, M, or WM).

- Chlorinated polyvinyl Chloride (CPVC plastic pipe).

- Ductile iron water pipe.

- Galvanized steel pipe.

- Polybutylene (PE plastic pipe and tubing).

- Polyethylene (PE plastic pipe or tubing).

- Polyvinyl chloride (PVC plastic pipe).

Available water distribution piping materials include the following:

- Brass pipe

- Chlorinated polyvinyl chloride (CPVC plastic pipe and tubing)

- Copper or copper alloy pipe

- Copper or copper alloy tubing (Type K, L, or M)

Table 5. Water consumption in office buildings

Building type	Gal. per hour/person
Commercial no air-conditioning	3.8
Commercial with air-conditioning	7.2 – 9

SERVICES   D2

- Galvanized steel pipe

- Polybutylene (PB plastic pipe and tubing)

2 Plumbing fixtures

Selection Criteria

Before specifying plumbing fixtures the designer should become familiar with plumbing fixture manufacturer's catalog information and associated components as fitting, faucets, toilet seats, flash valves, and supports. Each plumbing fixture must include a receptor drain or strainer, trap, cold water supply or hot and cold water supply, trim, accessories, appliances, appurtenances, equipment, and supports. Selection criteria for plumbing fixtures include the following:

- Fitting body types: Cast brass, brass, or copper underbody with chrome-plated escutcheon, plastic underbody with chrome-plated escutcheon, plastic.

- Finishes: Polished chrome plated, polished brass, polished gold plated, and colored plastic finishes.

- Handle types: Dual handle, ornamental metal, and porcelain lever, dual three- and four-arm, dual metal or crystal knob, single lever, dual lever 4 in. (10 cm) and 6 in. (15 cm) wrist blade, push button, self closing.

- Fixture clearances: Proper clearances between fixtures, and between fixtures and walls must be used in the layout of washrooms and bathrooms to ensure ease of installation, ease of use, and maintenance (Figs. 2 and 3).

- Accessibility for the disabled: The layout of plumbing fixtures should be guided by considerations of universaal design and accessibility, which is governed by the Americans with Disabilities Act (ADA). Accessible plumbing fixtures must be provided in public buildings and where required by code and authorities having jurisdiction providing handicapped accessibility to lavatories, sinks, water closets, and water coolers.

- Water closets: Two types of water closets are commonly used in new construction. Wall-hanging type fixtures, with a flush valve, are the preference in public buildings to allow toe space for wheelchair foot rest, to facilitate approach to the seat, and to allow access for cleaning below the fixture. The other type of water closet is the tank type, typically used in residential buildings. In either case, the bowl should be elongated to provide handicapped accessibility.

- Lavatories: The most common types of lavatories used in new construction include: wall hung, counter top, and pedestal types. Lavatories come in a variety of shapes and styles. Some common styles include back splashes, self rim, one-piece bowls, and undercounter mounted. Lavatories for handicapped access must be provided with a clear dimension of 30 in. (75 cm) under each lavatory and have insulated supply and drain lines to prevent injury and burns.

- Showers: Prefabricated showers and shower compartments are manufactured in several configurations. A shower compartment should have a minimum of 900 sq. in. (5,800 sq. cm) of interior

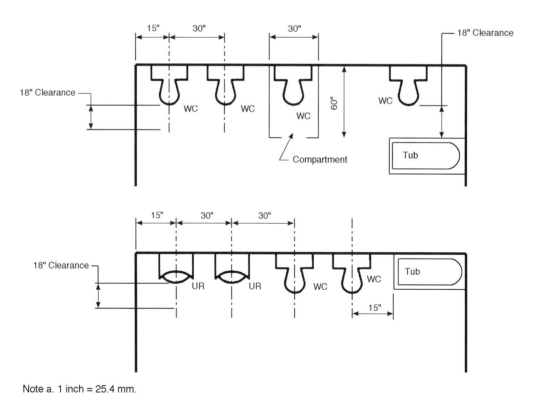

Note a. 1 inch = 25.4 mm.

Fig. 2. Plumbing fixture clearances.

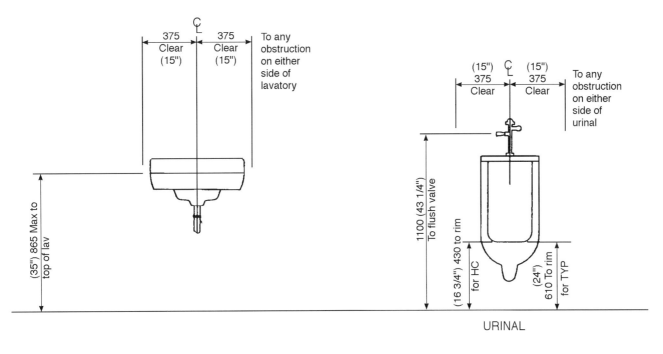

URINAL

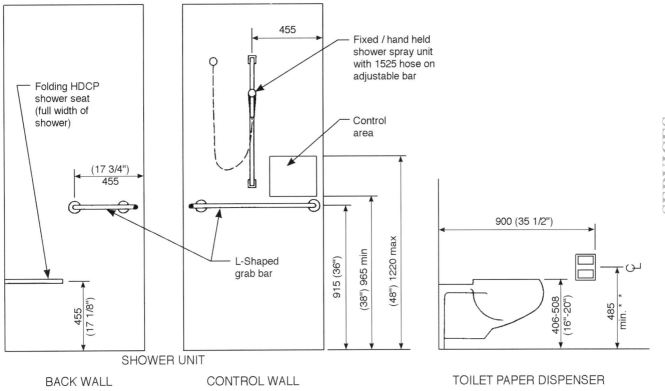

SHOWER UNIT

BACK WALL   CONTROL WALL   TOILET PAPER DISPENSER

Fig. 3. Plumbing fixture typical dimensions.

cross sectional area and have not less than 3 in. (75 cm) minimum dimension measured from its finished interior dimension, exclusive of fixture valves, shower heads, soap dishes, and safety grab bars. The minimum required area and dimension is measured from the finished interior dimension at a height equal to the top of the threshold and at a point tangent to its center line.

- Urinals: Urinals are typically selected for use in mens toilet rooms intended for use by the public. They should have a visible water trap seal without strainer to permit maintenance. For the purposes of water conservation, urinals should be selected that incorporate a maximum of 1.5 gallons (5.7 l) of water per flushing cycle.

- Sinks: Sinks are typically selected for use in kitchens and laboratories. They can be provided with many different types of faucets and finishes. The most common sink finish is stainless steel because of its durability and resistance to foreign materials. Residential kitchen sinks often are provided with a grinder, hose spray, and faucet. Dishwashers used in residential kitchens often are designed to share the supply and drain lines used for the sink.

- Water coolers and drinking fountains: Because of the different applications to a variety types of spaces and locations, the choice of style is wide, and the designer has the freedom to select shapes and colors to improve the aesthetic appearance of the units, as long as handicapped accessibility clearances are provided.

- Service sinks: These fixtures are required in janitor closets or maintenance areas. The most common styles are: floor mounted, wall hung, and mop sinks. Another variety of this fixture is the laundry sink that may be used with support legs. Service sinks must be provided with hose connection and vacuum breakers.

Water conservation

The U. S. Energy Policy Act of 1992 requires that plumbing fixtures manufactured for use in the U. S. after January 1, 1994 have the following maximum flow rates and consumption in gallons per minute (gpm) and litre/sec (l/s), gallons (gal.) and litres (l):

- Lavatory and sink faucet: 2.5 gpm (0.16 l/s).

- Shower head: 2.5 gpm (0.16 l/s)

- Water closet: Types as follows:

- Flushometer valve: 1.6 gal. (6 l) per flushing cycle

- Flushometer tank type: 1.6 gal. (6 l) per flushing cycle

- Commercial, tank with flush valve 3.5 gal. (13.2 l) per flushing cycle

- Residential, tank with flush valve 1.6 gal. (6 l) per flushing cycle

- Urinals: 1 gal. (3.8 l) per flushing cycle.

Additional references

American National Standards Institute, 11 West 42nd St., New York, NY 10036.

American Society of Heating, Refrigeration, and Air-Conditioning Engineers, 1791 Tullie Circle, NE, Atlanta, GA 30329.

American Society of Mechanical Engineers, 345 East 47th St., New York, NY 10017.

American Society of Plumbing Engineers, 3617 Thousand Oaks Blvd., Suite 210, Westlake, CA 91362.

American Society of Sanitary Engineering, PO Box 40362, Bay Village, OH 44140.

American Society for Testing and Materials, 100 Barr Harbor Dr., West Conshohocken, PA 19428-2959.

Council of American Building Officials, 5203 Leesburg Pike, Suite 201, Falls Church, VA 22041.

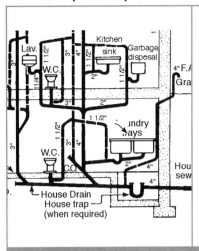

Sanitary waste systems

Summary: This section includes guidelines for sizing sanitary waste drainage piping in the forms of waste stacks and branches, building drains and sewers, drainage fixture unit values, slope of horizontal drainage, and horizontal building storm drains.

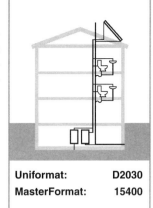

Key words: fixture unit ratings, floor drains, pipe diameter, piping, sanitary drains, stacks, vents.

Uniformat:	D2030
MasterFormat:	15400

Waste system sizing

- Sanitary drainage systems are designed to carry wastes from plumbing fixtures and floor drains to public sanitary sewers or septic tanks.

- To apply proper sizing and slope to drainage and vent pipes, the engineer should use applicable model building codes and regulations, and consult the authority having jurisdiction.

- The discharge ratings for the most commonly used plumbing fixtures are given in Table 1; capacities of horizontal branches and stacks are given in Table 2; the size and maximum lengths of vents in relation to safe carrying capacities of soil and waste pipes are found in Table 3; size of vent stacks and stack vents on Table 4. Data on the capacities of building sewers are also shown on Table 5.

- All tables have been extracted from the *BOCA National Plumbing Code*. Caution is advised that the values in the tables do not always agree with all current model, and local, building codes. Where differences exist, local requirements govern. However, the data can be used to establish limiting requirements for drainage system design.

Fixture unit ratings

- The capacities of drainage pipes are listed in fixture units, and the loads are added as they are collected in the drainage piping. To facilitate the understanding of the floor plans, and to facilitate adequate space allowance for the piping system, the designer should develop diagrams that sequentially show the system and coordinate with other engineering disciplines such as civil, structural, mechanical, electrical, communication, and fire protection.

- The designer should also consider other sources of continuous or semicontinuous flow into the drainage system, such as from pumps, sump ejectors, and air conditioning equipment. These loads are commonly computed as one fixture unit equaling 7.5 gallons per minute (28.35 l/m).

- With these parameters the designer will be able to determine the pipe sizes, slopes and location of stacks in the safest and most economic way.

Stack capacities

- Waste stacks are the vertical pipes collecting all the horizontal drainage branches from each floor (Figs. 1 and 2). They are commonly known as "intervals." A stack can take two branches from

the same level with a 45 Y fitting or sanitary T, and that also will be an interval, in other words, the collection of pipe branches in each level is an interval.

Vent requirements

- The size and length of vent pipes are directly dependent upon the volume of discharge for which the soil and waste pipe are designed.

- Unless adequate venting is provided, the flow of fixture discharges through soil or waste stacks can produce pressure variations in branches that may damage the seals of fixture traps by blowing them from positive or back pressure in lower parts of the system, or syphoning them because of negative pressure in upper sections.

- Tables list permissible sizes and lengths for the vent stack and branch vents necessary to ensure the proper functioning of a drainage system.

Sanitary building drains

- Building drains are typically placed at the lowest piping invert elevation in a drainage system. Building drains receive wastes from soil, waste, and other drainage pipes inside a structure and convey them into the building sewer. The required size of the building drain for a given drainage load can be read directly from Table 5. Typical rules of thumb for sizing building drains are as follows:

Rule 1: Determine the total drainage requirements in fixture units from Table 1.

Rule 2: Establish pitch of drain or slope from Table 7, particularly in small installations a lesser pitch would increase the possibility of fouling, generally a 1/4 in. per foot pitch is preferred.

Rule 3. Select the required pipe diameter from Table 5. The proper sizes for branches and stacks can be taken from Table 2.

- Tables 5 and 2 are based on gravity flow of one-half full drain, and at the same time full flow capacity is reached at approximately that point because of trapped air.

- Drainage pipe going from a horizontal to a vertical line uses short turn fittings; but in going from a vertical flow to a horizontal flow, a long turn fitting is used (sweep elbow).

- The waste effluent is calculated in sequence starting from the furthest and highest fixture, or branch, and ending at the lowest fixture, or branch, to properly size the stack.

Author: Arturo De La Vega

References: BOCA. 1990. *BOCA National Plumbing Code.* Country Club Hills, IL: Building Officials and Code Administration.

Additonal references are listed at the end of this article.

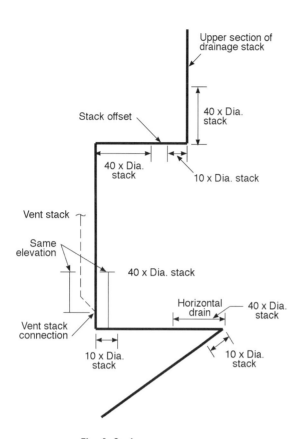

Fig. 1. Suds pressure zones

Critical limitations to consider in any drainage system

- No branch or fixture should be connected within 10 pipe diameters downstream from the base of the soil or waste stack.

- Indirect waste should to discharge through an air gap into a trapped fixture.

- Combination waste and vent should only be used for floor drains, standpipes, sinks and lavatories, which should discharge to a vented drainage pipe.

- Chemical waste should be completely separated from the sanitary drainage system.

- The minimum size for underground drain pipe should be 2 in. (5 cm).

- The size of the drain pipe should not be reduced in size in the direction of the flow.

- Drainage for future fixtures should be terminated with an approved cap or plug.

- Dead ends are prohibited in the installation or removal of any part of a drainage system. The application of code requirements should be accurate in this and other related matters.

- A fixture should not be connected to horizontal piping from the base of the stack within 40 pipe diameters from the stack to prevent backup of fixtures on the lower floor caused by a hydraulic jump at the base of the stack. Suds pressure zones exist in the piping as shown in Fig. 1 and fixture connections in this areas should be avoided.

- Suds pressure zones should be considered to exist at the indicated locations in sanitary drainage and vent systems when the piping serves fixtures on two or more floors that receive waste containing bubble bath or sudsy detergents.

Piping materials

Available above ground drainage and vent piping materials include the following:

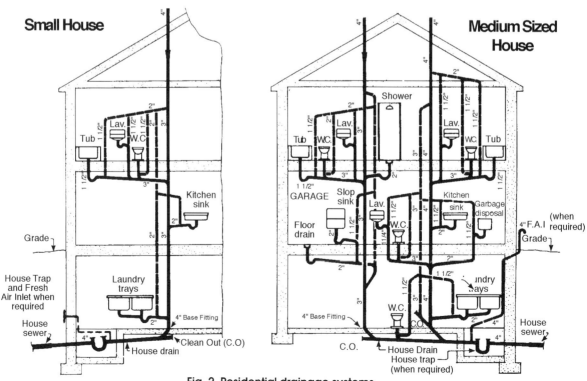

Fig. 2. Residential drainage systems

- Acrylonitrile butadiene styrene (ABS plastic pipe)

- Brass pipe

- Cast iron pipe

- Copper or copper alloy pipe

- Copper or copper alloy tubing (Type K, L, M, or DWV)

- Galvanized steel pipe

- Polyvinyl chloride (PVC plastic pipe type DWV)

Available underground building drainage and vent piping materials include the following:

- Acrylonitrile butadiene styrene (ABS plastic pipe)

- Cast iron pipe

- Concrete pipe

- Copper or copper alloy tubing (Type K or L)

- Polyvinyl chloride (PVC plastic pipe type DWV)

Sizing and ratings

Figs. 2 and 3 illustrate various types of plumbing details applicable to both residential and commercial buildings. Because of the wide variance in plumbing regulations, some of these diagrammatic details may be prohibited in certain localities; other details may indicate methods far in excess of mandatory requirements in other localities. All, however, reflect solutions to typical drainage problems by methods that generally constitute good plumbing practice.

Residential drainage systems

- The pipe sizes shown in Fig. 2 will meet every requirement usually encountered in residential work. A 3 in. (7.5 cm) main soil stack is adequate for residential use in the opinion of many authorities; a 4 in. (10 cm) main soil stack is mandatory, how-

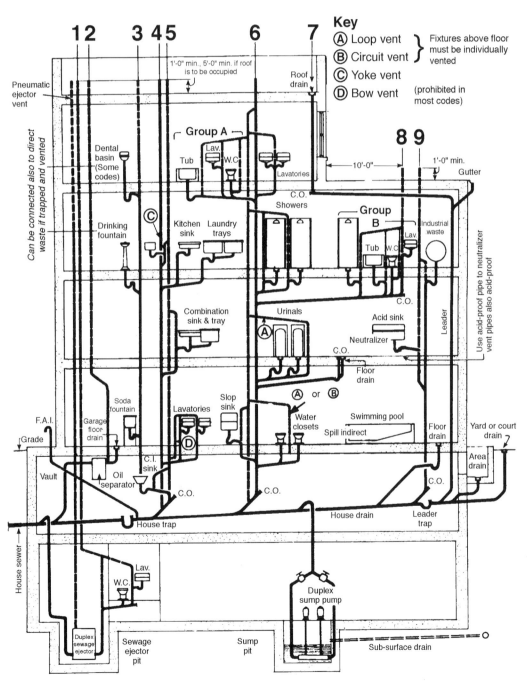

Fig. 3. Drainage system for commercial buildings

Table 1. Drainage fixture unit values for various plumbing fixtures (Source: BOCA 1990)

Type of fixture or group of fixtures	Drainage fixture unit value	Trap size (inches)
Automatic clothes washer standpipe — commercial	3	2
Automatic clothes washer standpipe — domestic	2	1 1/2
Bathroom group	6	—
Bathtub	2	1 1/2
Bidet	1	1 1/2
Combination sink and tray	2	1 1/2
Dental unit	1	1 1/4
Dishwasher	2	1 1/2
Drinking fountain	1/2	1 1/4
Emergency floor drains	0	2
Floor drains	2	2
Kitchen sink	2	1 1/2
Laundry tray	2	1 1/2
Lavoratory	1	1 1/4
Mop basin	2	2
Service sink	2	1 1/2
Shower (each head)	2	1 1/2
Sink	2	1 1/2
Urinal	4	2
Water closet, private	4	—
Water closet, public	6	—
Water closet, pneumatic assist, private or public installation	4[a]	

Note a. For the purpose of computing loads on building drains and sewers, water closets shall not be rated at a lower drainage fixture unit unless the lower values are confirmed by testing.

Table 2. Horizontal fixture branches and stacks (Source: BOCA 1990)

	Maximum number of fixture units			
		Stacks[b]		
Diameter of pipe (inches)	Total for a horizontal branch	Total discharge into one branch	Total for stack of three branch intervals or less	Total for stack greater than three branch intervals
1 1/2	3	2	4	8
2	6	6	10	24
2 1/2	12	9	20	42
3	20	20	48	72
4	160	90	240	500
5	360	200	540	1100
6	620	350	960	1900
8	1400	600	2200	3600
10	2500	1000	3800	5600
12	3900	1500	6000	8400
15	7000	Note c	Note c	Note c

Note a. Does not include branches of the building drain. Refer to Table P-603.2(1)

Note b. Stacks shall be sized and based on the total accumulated connected load at each story or branch interval. As the total accumulated connected load decreases.stacks are permitted to be reduced in size. Stack diameters shall not be reduced to less than one-half of the diameter of the largest stack size required.

Note c. Sizing load based on design criteria.

ever, in some localities. Main house drains should never be less than 4 in. (10 cm).

- If house sewers are connected to the septic tank of a private sewerage disposal system, no house trap or fresh air inlet is necessary. In many communities individual venting may be eliminated and a system of wet venting or combined waste and vent system can be utilized.

Commercial drainage systems

Fig. 3 shows a composite of drainage problems alsoencountered in a wide range of commercial and industrial work; the installations are not typical for any specific kind of building. As in the house sections, soil and waste lines are shown solid; vent lines are broken.

- Group A: Bathroom unit is rated for six fixture units, individually vented and connected by preferred methods to main soil and vent stacks.

- Group B: Bathroom unit is rated at seven fixture units, individually vented and connected by the preferred method to a horizontal soil branch.

- Loop Vent A and Circuit Vent B: Both are types of venting in which the branch drain is a "double duty" pipe carrying both air and discharge. The use of this pipe constitutes "wet venting," prohibited by some codes. It is generally not a desirable method of venting. If used, circuit or loop vents should not be connected to a group of more than eight fixtures in series. In a loop vent, a continuation of the branch runs up and over the fixtures to connect to the vent stack adjacent to the main soil. In a circuit vent, the connection is to a main vent stack opposite the main soil stack.

- Yoke Vent C: This connects the main soil and waste stacks, with the soil at the lower end of the yoke. The connection of the fixtures as at C adds greatly to the safe capacity of soil stacks. This type of connection can be made to bathroom units in residential as well as commercial buildings.

- Bow Vent D: This can be used for light discharge loads to avoid installation of an additional vent stack.

- Stacks 1 and 2: These indicate the need for separate venting of the sewage ejector and the oil separator from garage drains. The vent from a pneumatic sewage ejector should not be joined to any other pipe; sewage pumps do not require any special considerations.

- Stack 3: This is the vent from an indirect waste line discharging into a cast iron sink. Its fixtures must be trapped. If an indirect waste line is over 100 ft. (30 m) in developed length, it should be extended through the roof.

- Stacks 4, 5, and 6: The bents should be connected into these stacks at their lower ends, so that discharge will scour the connection and thus prevent fouling. Such a connection is specifically required for cast iron because of scaling.

- Stack 9: This applies to a special purpose type of installation. Corrosive wastes require acid proof pipe for waste, soil, and vent lines, for fittings, and for the house drain up to the base fitting of the next main soil stack.▶

Additional references

American Society of Mechanical Engineers, 345 East 47th Street, New York, NY 10017.

American Society of Plumbing Engineers, 3617 Thousand Oaks Blvd., Suite 210, Westlake, CA 91362.

American Society for Testing and Materials, 100 Barr Harbor Drive, West Conshohocken, PA 19428-2959.

Cast Iron Soil Pipe Institute, 5959 Shallowford Road., Suite 419, Chattanooga, TN 37421.

D2

SERVICES

Table 3. Minimum diameters and maximum length of individual, branch, and circuit vents for horizontal drainage branches (Source: BOCA 1990)

Diameter of[a] horizontal drainage branch (inches)	Slope of horizontal drainage branch (inches per foot)	Maximum developed length of vent (feet)[b] Diameter of vent (inches)									
		1 1/4	1 1/2	2	2 1/2	3	4	5	6	8	10
1 1/4	1/4	NL[b]									
	1/2	NL									
1 1/2	1/4	NL	NL								
	1/2	NL	NL								
2	1/8	NL	NL	NL							
	1/4	290	NL	NL							
	1/2	150	380	NL							
2 1/2	1/8	180	450	NL	NL						
	1/4	96	240	NL	NL						
	1/2	49	130	NL	NL						
3	1/8		190	NL	NL	NL					
	1/4		97	420	NL	NL					
	1/2		50	220	NL	NL					
4	1/8			190	NL	NL	NL				
	1/4			98	310	NL	NL				
	1/2			48	160	410	NL				
5	1/8				190	490	NL	NL			
	1/4				97	250	NL	NL			
	1/2				46	130	NL	NL			
6	1/8					190	NL	NL	NL		
	1/4					97	250	NL	NL		
	1/2					46	130	NL	NL		
8	1/8						190	NL	NL	NL	
	1/4						91	310	NL	NL	
	1/2						38	150	410	NL	
10	1/8							190	500	NL	NL
	1/4							85	240	NL	NL
	1/2							32	110	NL	NL
12	1/8								180	NL	NL

Note a. 1 foot = 304.8 mm; 1 inch per foot= 83.3 mm/n.
Note b. NL means no limit. Actual values in excess of 500 feet.

Table 4. Size and length of vent stacks and stack vents (Source: BOCA 1990)

Diameter of soil or waste stack (in.)	Total fixture units connected to stack (dfu)	Maximum developed length of vent (feet)[b] Diameter of vent (inches)									
		1 1/4	1 1/2	2	2 1/2	3	4	5	6	8	10
12											
1 1/4	2	30									
1 1/2	8	50	150								
2	12	30	75	200							
2	20	26	50	150							
2 1/2	42		30	100	300						
3	10		42	150	360	1040					
3	21		32	110	270	810					
3	53		27	94	230	680					
3	102		25	86	210	620					
4	43			35	85	250	980				
4	140			27	65	200	750				
4	320			23	55	170	640				
4	540			21	50	150	580				
5	190				28	82	320	990			
5	490				21	63	250	760			
5	940				18	53	210	670			
5	1400				16	49	190	590			
6	500					33	130	400	1000		
6	1100					26	100	310	780		
6	2000					22	84	260	660		
6	2900					20	77	240	600		
8	1800						31	95	240	940	
8	3400						24	73	190	720	
8	5600						20	62	160	610	
8	7600						18	56	140	560	
10	4000							31	78	310	960
10	7200							24	60	240	740
10	11000							20	51	200	630
10	15000							18	46	180	570
12	7300							31	120	380	940
12	13000							24	94	300	720
12	20000							20	79	250	610
12	26000							18	72	230	500
15	15000								40	130	310
15	25000								31	96	240
15	38000								26	81	200
15	50000								24	74	180

Note a. 1 foot = 304.8 mm.
Note b. The developed length shall be measured from the vent connection to the open air.

Table 5. Building drains and sewers (Source: BOCA 1990)

Diameter of pipe (inches)	Maximum number of fixture units connected to a portion of the building drain or the buildig sewer including branches of the building drain. Slope per foot[a]			
	1/16 inch	1/8 inch	1/4 inch	1/2 inch
1 1/4			1	1
1 1/2			3	3
2			21	26
2 1/2			24	31
3		36	42	50
4		180	216	250
5		390	480	575
6		700	840	1000
8	1400	1600	1920	2300
10	2500	2900	3500	4200
12	2900	4600	5600	6700
15	7000	8300	10000	12000

Note a. 1 inch per foot = 83.3

Table 6. Drainage fixture unit values for fixture drains or traps (Source: BOCA 1990)

Size (inches)	Drainage fixture unit value
1 1/4 or less	1
1 1/2	2
2	3
2 1/2	4
3	5
4	6

Table 7. Slope of horizontal drainage pipe (Source: BOCA 1990)

Size (inches)	Minimum slope (inch per foot)[a]
2 1/2 or less	1/4
3 to 6	1/8
8 to larger	1/16

Note a. 1 inch per foot = 83.3 mm/m.

D2 SERVICES

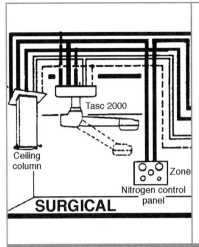

Tasc 2000

Ceiling column

Zone

Nitrogen control panel

SURGICAL

Special plumbing systems

Summary: The trend in modern hospitals and laboratories is toward central systems to supply oxygen, vacuum, nitrous oxide, and compressed air. With the use of the tables on the following pages, central systems for these special services can be properly designed.

Key words: compressed air, low-pressure alarm, nitrous oxide, oxygen, vacuum systems.

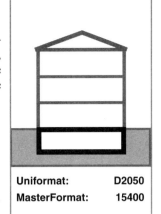

Uniformat:	D2050
MasterFormat:	15400

Oxygen

- Oxygen in medical facilities is primarily used for inhalation therapy and anesthesia. Continuous supply and immediate availability throughout the facility is essential.

- Oxygen contained in a cylinder is in liquid form. When released to atmospheric pressure it becomes a gas. Although the gas is not flammable, it is dangerous to handle because it supports combustion vigorously and can cause the slightest spark to erupt into an inferno.

- For methods of installing oxygen systems consult the National Fire Protection Association (NFPA) 56F Standard for Non-Flammable Medical Gas Systems.

- Great care should be exercised in handling oxygen under pressure with oils, greases, rubber, or other materials of organic nature. Regulations applicable to handling can be found in Compressed Gas Association (CGA) Pamphlet G-A Oxygen.

• Supply systems

- Oxygen systems may be fed from either a bulk supply or a cylinder manifold. Each should include both a normal service supply and an adequate reserve supply, which would become available automatically when the service supply is exhausted.

- Gas suppliers should be consulted on the type of storage most economical for a particular installation, considering the volume of gas to be used and the location of the installation. Bulk oxygen storage should not be located within 50' (15m) of any structure.

• Alarms

- A low pressure alarm should be installed where oxygen supply lines from a bulk storage or cylinder manifold enters the building. This alarm, signaling a loss of pressure in the supply line due to a leak, should be both audible and visual.

- A copper tubing header Type K or L with wrought or cast copper fittings should supply all oxygen risers and outlets. Solder should have a melting point of 1,000F.

• Multiple risers

- Each floor to be equipped for oxygen therapy should be served by more than one riser, so that if the supply to more than one riser is shut off, the entire floor will not be deprived of oxygen, and the patients can be moved to other rooms on the same floor for continuation of their oxygen therapy.

• Piping size

- Medical oxygen systems are typically designed to provide 50 psi at the outlet with a maximum pressure drop of 5 psi in the system. The size of the piping is usually determined by the length of the piping required from the supply to the furthest outlet. It should be noted, however, that the piping for a particular outlet closer to the supply could be sized on the basis of its own length, although generally this would not substantially reduce the overall cost of the system.

- Having determined the overall distance, and assuming a pressure drop of 2 psi, we can refer to Table 1 for a direct reading of the number of liters of oxygen that a given pipe can deliver per minute.

• Supply valves

Operating rooms, recovery rooms, and delivery rooms should all be supplied directly from the main, with a shutoff valve outside each room.

- The supplies for patient rooms must be zoned by valves, which should be located in boxes with break glass fronts, in order to eliminate the possibility of their being shut off by unauthorized persons. Valves can be either the ball valve type or the packless diaphragm type.

- Riser control valves and valves 1 in. (2.5 cm) or more in diameter must be specially packed in oxygen service and must be free of oil. All piping in the system must be washed with a solution of trisodium phosphate to remove all grease before oxygen is admitted into the system (Fig. 1).

Author: Arturo De La Vega

Credits: Drawing courtesy of Chemetron.

References: American National Standards Institute, 11 West 42nd Street, New York, NY 10036.

American Society of Mechanical Engineers, 345 East 47th Street, New York, NY 10017.

American Society of Plumbing Engineers, 3617 Thousand Oaks Blvd., Suite 210, Westlake, CA 91362.

BOCA. 1990. BOCA National Plumbing Code. Country Club Hills, IL: Building Officials and Code Administration.

Compressed Gas Association. *Pamphlet G-A Oxygen*. Arlington, VA: CGA.

NFPA. *56F Standard for Non-Flammable Medical Gas Systems*. Quincy, MA: National Fire Protection Association.

CHEMETRON MEDICAL GAS SYSTEM

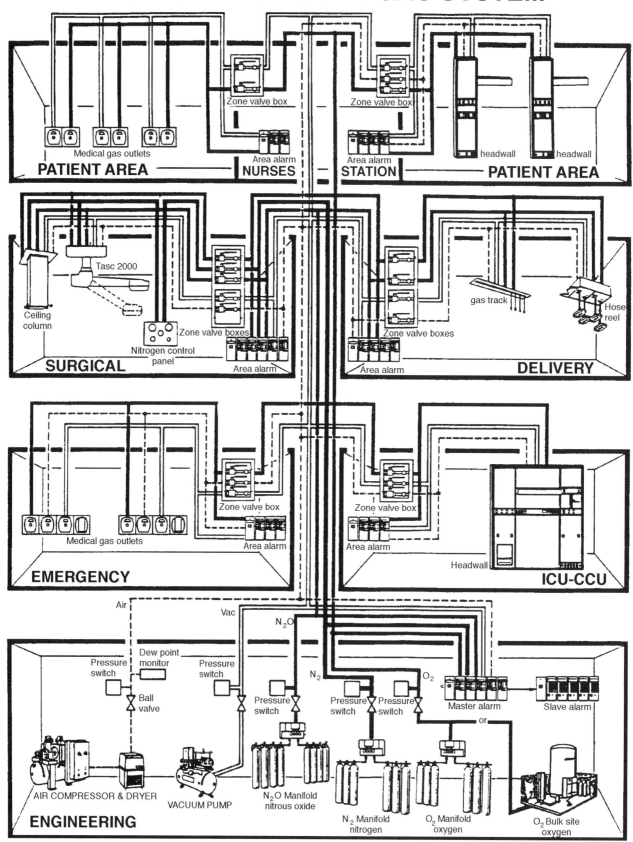

Fig. 1. Medical gas system

Table 1. Capacity of oxygen piping

Quantities listed are for pressure drops of 1 in. and 55.36 in. (or 2 psi) of water (at specific gravity 1.105). Assume 10 liters per minute per outlet. Deduct 10 per cent from listed quantities for friction loss due to valves and fittings. Diversity factor (percentage of simultaneous use) is 40 to 100 (see Table 11). Key: P = IPS threaded brass pipe; B = Type TP (threadless pipe) copper tubing; K = Type K or Type L copper tubing.

Pipe size, in. — reference columns: 55.36 | 1. Capacity, liters per minute.

Length of pipe, ft	Pressure drop, in. H_2O	3/8 P	3/8 B	3/8 K	1/2 P	1/2 B	1/2 K	3/4 P	3/4 B	3/4 K	1 P	1 B	1 K	1¼ P	1¼ B	1¼ K	1½ P	1½ B	1½ K	2 P	2 B	2 K	2½ P	2½ B	2½ K	3 P	3 B	3 K	4 P	4 B	4 K
50	0.9	177	230	105	310	445	205	640	840	505	1210	1580	1050	2300	3120	1750	3350	4200	2800	6400	7820	5700	10500	13000	9800						
55	1.0	165	212	100	290	420	193	610	800	480	1160	1490	980	2150	2850	1600	3200	3950	2650	6000	7400	5400	9800	12500	9100						
111	2.0	118	155	70	210	300	138	435	580	335	820	1050	700	1520	2080	1200	2250	2820	1900	4300	5400	3800	6900	8800	6500	11200	14400	10000			
166	3.0	98	125	58	170	245	112	352	470	276	670	870	580	1250	1700	980	1850	2350	1530	3500	4250	3100	5700	7200	5200	9000	11800	8300			
221	4.0	84	110	50	148	212	98	310	400	240	580	760	500	1100	1480	850	1600	2010	1320	3050	3720	2700	5000	6300	4650	7900	10000	7200			
277	5.0	75	98	45	133	192	89	275	360	212	515	680	450	980	1300	760	1440	1800	1180	2720	3350	2410	4200	5500	4125	7000	9100	6400			
332	6.0	68	89	41	122	172	80	252	330	196	490	620	405	900	1200	700	1320	1650	1080	2500	3050	2200	4050	5050	3750	6400	8100	5900			
388	7.0	63	83	38	112	160	75	235	305	182	440	580	375	840	1110	640	1220	1530	1010	2320	2820	2080	3710	4650	3500	6000	7600	5450			
443	8.0	60	78	35	103	150	70	220	285	170	415	540	350	780	1050	610	1140	1450	960	2150	2650	1920	3500	4400	3250	5500	7100	5100			
498	9.0	56	74	33	98	142	65	205	265	161	382	500	330	730	990	566	1080	1350	900	2030	2500	1850	3300	4080	3050	5200	6700	4800			
554	10	53	69	32	94	135	62	196	255	153	375	480	316	700	930	540	1020	1280	860	1910	2350	1725	3150	3900	2900	5000	6400	4600	9900	11800	9300
1107	20	38	50	28	68	96	44	138	182	108	265	340	225	500	670	380	740	920	540	1360	1650	1210	2220	2800	2100	3520	4500	3200	6950	8300	6500
1661	30	31	40	18	55	77	36	113	148	89	218	280	185	400	550	316	595	730	490	1120	1380	1000	1850	2300	1720	2900	3720	2650	5800	6800	5400

Table 2. Capacity of nitrous piping

Quantities listed are for pressure drops of 1 in. and 55.36 in. (or 2 psi) of water (at specific gravity 1.522). Assume 10 liters per minute per outlet. Deduct 10 per cent from listed quantities for friction loss due to valves and fittings. Diversity factor (percentage of simultaneous use) is 100. Key: P = IPS threaded brass pipe; B = Type TP copper tubing; K = Type K copper tubing.

Pipe size, in. — reference columns: 55.36 | 1. Capacity, liters per minute.

Length of pipe, ft	Pressure drop, in. H_2O	3/8 P	3/8 B	3/8 K	1/2 P	1/2 B	1/2 K	3/4 P	3/4 B	3/4 K	1 P	1 B	1 K	1¼ P	1¼ B	1¼ K	1½ P	1½ B	1½ K	2 P	2 B	2 K	2½ P	2½ B	2½ K	3 P	3 B	3 K	4 P	4 B	4 K
22	0.4	242	308	145	435	580	285	870	1150	680	1620	2180	1400	3050	4150	2420	4600	5900	3710	8200	10600	7600									
28	0.5	212	275	128	380	520	251	770	1020	600	1480	1920	1250	2720	3720	2120	4080	5300	3340	7400	9500	6700									
33	0.6	197	252	118	355	490	230	700	930	545	1320	1725	1140	2510	3400	1950	3710	4850	3050	6700	8600	6200									
39	0.7	182	230	108	327	445	210	650	860	500	1230	1600	1050	2320	3160	1820	3450	4500	2820	6210	8000	5600	10500	13000	9700						
44	0.8	170	218	100	302	417	200	608	810	470	1150	1520	970	2120	2920	1700	3260	4150	2650	5800	7400	5300	9800	12200	9100						
50	0.9	161	202	96	285	390	188	562	760	442	1090	1420	930	2050	2750	1600	3050	3900	2450	5420	7000	5000	9300	11400	8500						
55	1.0	151	195	91	270	375	176	550	725	420	1020	1350	883	1910	2600	1510	2860	3720	2320	5100	6700	4700	8800	10800	8000						
111	2.0	108	138	64	192	262	123	383	510	298	722	960	620	1350	1820	1060	2050	2600	1630	3620	4800	3320	6200	7800	5600	10100	12500	9100			
166	3.0	87	112	51	158	215	101	312	417	242	590	780	501	1120	1520	870	1630	2110	1350	2950	3800	2700	5000	6300	4650	8300	10200	7300			
221	4.0	75	97	45	135	185	89	271	355	210	510	662	435	960	1290	745	1450	1820	1160	2550	3300	2320	4320	5500	4000	7200	8800	6350			
277	5.0	68	87	40	122	165	79	243	318	188	450	600	388	860	1150	680	1280	1650	1050	2260	2950	2100	3850	4850	3520	6500	7900	5500			
332	6.0	61	79	37	110	151	77	220	290	171	418	550	355	780	1050	620	1160	1520	950	2100	2700	1900	3520	4450	3250	5900	7200	5200	11300	13500	10400
388	7.0	56	72	34	102	140	66	203	270	158	383	510	328	720	960	562	1070	1380	890	1910	2500	1760	3250	4100	3000	5420	6700	4800	10500	12500	9600

SERVICES

D2

Nitrous oxide

- All guidelines in reference to oxygen apply to a nitrous oxide installation with the exception of bulk storage. Because of the small quantities of gas involved, the system manifold for nitrous oxide can be located within the building in a fireproof room. Table 2 can be used for sizing nitrous oxide piping (Fig. 2).

Compressed air systems

- Compressed air for use in laboratories, nurseries, delivery rooms, dental rooms, plumbing shops, and for patient resuscitation must be oil free and cooled.

- The pumps for this system may be either rotary or reciprocating. If a reciprocating pump is used, an after cooler is required to reduce the temperature of the compressed gas. The units should be lubricated by carbon rings in order to eliminate all particles in the compressed gas.

- A receiver is also required in an compressed air installation, and the supply header from the receiver must be provided with an air filter and regulator. See Table 3 for pipe sizes and capacities (Fig. 3).

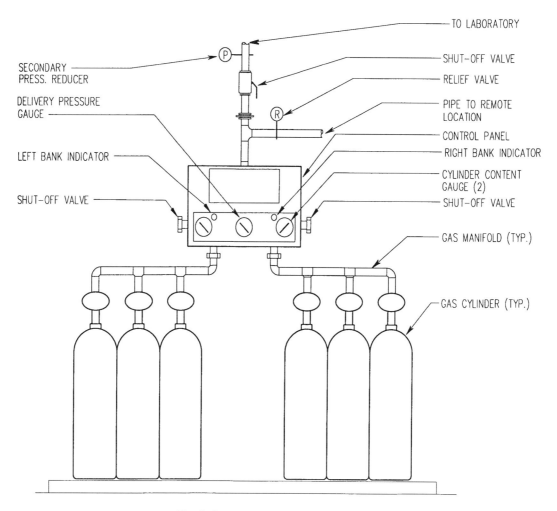

Fig. 2. Gas cylinder manifold detail

Table 3. Capacity of compressed air piping

Quantities are based on IPS steel pipe.

175	150	125	100	90	80	70	60	50	40	35	30	25	20	15	3/8	1/2	3/4	1	1¼	1½	2	2½	3	4	5	6
					Outlet gauge pressure, psi														Pipe size, in.							
															60	64	76	84	77	81	93	93	89	90	90	90
																Factor for Type K copper tubing in per cent of IPS steel pipe										
				Pressure loss, psi per 1000 ft of pipe																Capacity, cfm						
0.4	0.5	0.6	0.7	0.7	0.8	0.9	1	1.2	1.4	1.6	1.8	2.2	2.6	3.4	1.8	3.2	8.2	15	32	48	92	150	265	540	980	1600
0.8	1.0	1.1	1.4	1.5	1.6	1.8	2	2.4	2.9	3.2	3.6	4.3	5.2	6.7	2.5	4.5	11.5	21.5	45	67	130	210	375	770	1380	2300
1.2	1.4	1.7	2.0	2.2	2.4	2.7	3	3.6	4.3	4.8	5.5	6.5	7.8	10	3.1	5.5	14.0	26.5	55	82	160	260	460	940	1700	2800
1.6	1.9	2.2	2.7	2.9	3.2	3.5	4	4.8	5.7	6.4	7.3	8.6	10.4	13.4	3.5	6.3	16.0	30.5	64	95	185	300	530	1090	1950	3200
2.0	2.3	2.7	3.3	3.6	4.0	4.4	5	5.9	7.2	8	9.1	10.8	13	16.8	3.9	8.0	18.0	34	71	108	208	330	600	1200	2160	3600
4.0	4.6	5.4	6.6	7.1	7.9	8.8	10	11.8	14.3	16	18.2	21.5	26	34	5.5	10	25.5	48	100	150	290	470	840	1700	3100	5100
6.0	6.9	8.1	10	11	12	14	15	18	22	24	28	33	41	50	6.7	12	31	59	122	185	360	570	1020	2100	3700	6200
8	9.2	11	14	15	16	18	20	24	29	32	37	43	52	67	7.7	14	36	68	142	215	410	660	1180	2450	4300	7200
10	12	14	17	18	20	22	25	26	36	40	46	54	65	84	8.6	15.8	40	76	158	240	460	720	1320	2730	4420	8000
12	14	17	20	22	24	27	30	36	43	48	55	65	78	100	9.4	17.2	44	84	172	262	500	800	1450	3000	5300	8800
14	17	19	24	25	28	31	35	42	50	56	64	76	91	118	10	18.6	48	90	186	285	545	870	1570	3250	5700	9600
16	19	22	27	29	32	35	40	48	58	64	73	86	104	134	10.8	20	51	96	200	300	580	940	1700	3400	6100	10200
20	23	27	33	36	40	44	50	59	72	80	91	108	130	168	12	22	57	108	220	340	650	1050	1880	3850	6800	11500
24	28	33	40	43	48	53	60	71	86	96	110	129	156	201	13	24	62	118	245	375	720	1150	2050	4200	7500	12600
28	33	38	47	50	56	62	70	83	100	112	128	151	182	235	14	26	67	128	260	400	770	1230	2200	4500	8000	13600
32	37	44	53	57	64	71	80	95	115	128	146	175	208	268	15	28	72	137	280	430	820	1320	2350	4900	8600	14500
36	42	49	60	64	72	80	90	107	128	144	164	194	234	302	16	30	76	145	300	460	870	1400	2500	5200	9100	15500
40	46	54	66	71	79	88	100	118	144	160	182	215	260	340	17	31	80	150	310	480	910	1480	2600	5400	9600	16200

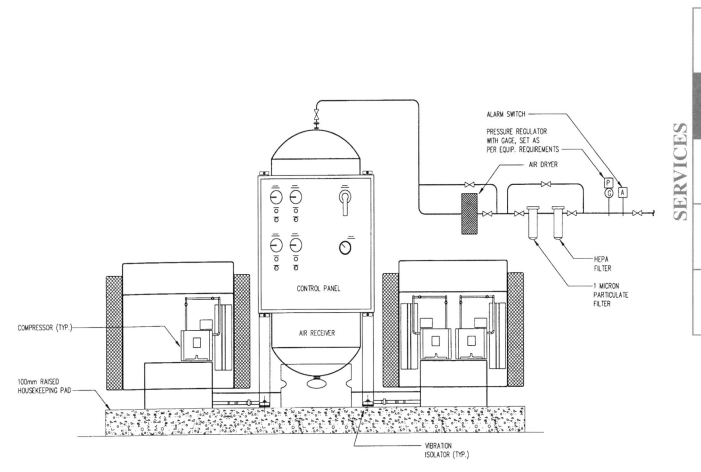

Fig. 3. Triplex air compressor detail

SERVICES   D2

Vacuum systems

-   Essentially, a vacuum system consists of a central vacuum pump with control equipment, distribution piping to points where suction may be required, and alarm and signaling equipment. A high vacuum is rarely required, since even a 15" (34cm) (mercury column) vacuum can damage skin tissue. It is quantity, not the pressure, that is most important (Fig. 4).

•   System sizing

-   In this system, sizing is determined by the pressure drop required and the length of the longest run (refer to Table 4). The vacuum pumps are sized for the peak draw; duplex pumps should be used to ensure a continuous source of supply.

-   If the units required become too large for one pump, then two thirds of the total capacity should be placed in each of two pumps.

-   The pumps evacuate a receiving tank to which the vacuum header is connected. The exhaust from the pumps should discharge to the outside air, and should be provided with a silencer and a filter.

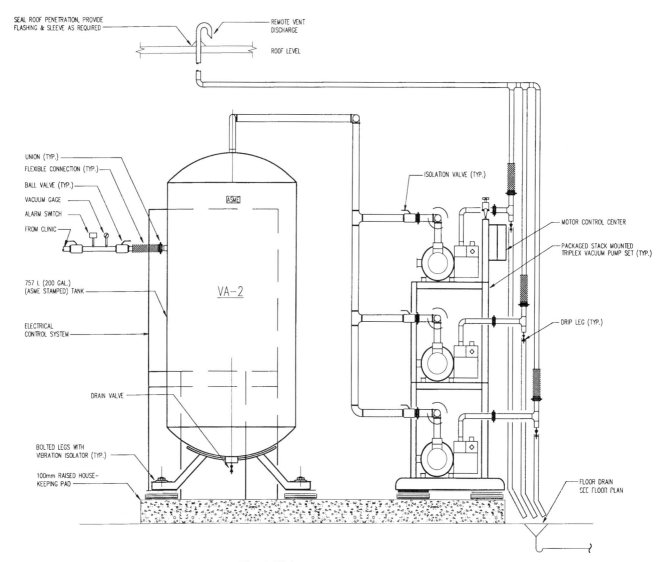

Fig. 4. Triplex vacuum pump detail

Table 4. Capacity of vacuum piping

gravity 1.00). Deduct 10 per cent from listed quantities for friction loss due to   copper tubing; K = Type K or Type L copper tubing.

Pipe size, in. — Capacity, cfm

Length of pipe, ft	3/8 P	3/8 B	3/8 K	1/2 P	1/2 B	1/2 K	3/4 P	3/4 B	3/4 K	1 P	1 B	1 K	1¼ P	1¼ B	1¼ K	1½ P	1½ B	1½ K	2 P	2 B	2 K	2½ P	2½ B	2½ K	3 P	3 B	3 K	4 P	4 B	4 K
40	8.6	11.2	5.3	15.8	22.0	10.3	31.6	42.3	24.6	60.8	80.0	51.6	113	153	88.3	166	216	140	308	391	283	516	641	483						
60	7.2	9.2	4.3	13.0	18.0	8.3	25.8	34.5	20.0	49.1	65.0	41.6	91.6	125	71.6	138	175	113	250	320	233	416	525	391						
80	6.2	7.8	3.7	11.3	15.3	7.2	22.5	30.0	17.5	44.1	55.8	36.3	80.0	108	61.6	118	153	98.3	216	278	200	366	450	338	600	733	533			
100	5.6	7.0	3.3	10.0	13.6	6.4	20.0	26.6	15.5	38.3	50.0	32.5	70.0	96.6	55.0	106	136	88.3	191	246	176	323	400	300	533	666	475			
120	5.0	6.6	3.0	9.2	12.6	5.8	18.3	24.1	14.1	35.0	45.8	29.1	65.0	88.3	50.8	96.6	123	80.0	176	225	161	291	366	276	491	608	433			
140	4.7	5.9	2.8	8.5	11.6	5.4	16.6	22.5	13.0	32.0	42.5	27.1	60.0	81.6	46.6	90.0	115	73.3	165	208	150	273	341	256	450	566	400	608	716	550
160	4.3	5.5	2.6	7.8	10.8	5.1	15.6	21.0	12.1	30.0	39.1	25.3	55.8	76.6	43.3	83.3	108	68.3	153	191	140	255	316	236	425	525	375	558	650	508
180	4.1	5.2	2.5	7.5	10.1	4.7	14.8	19.5	11.5	28.3	36.6	24.1	52.5	71.5	41.1	78.3	101	65.0	143	181	131	241	300	225	396	500	350	525	616	475
200	3.8	4.9	2.3	7.0	9.6	4.5	14.0	18.6	10.8	26.6	35.0	22.8	51.6	68.3	39.1	75.0	95.0	61.6	136	173	125	228	283	213	376	475	333	466	550	430
250	3.4	4.4	2.1	6.3	8.6	4.1	12.6	16.6	9.8	24.1	30.8	20.1	44.1	60.0	35.0	66.6	85.0	55.0	121	153	111	203	253	188	333	425	300	425	500	390
300	3.2	4.0	1.9	5.7	7.9	3.6	11.5	15.1	8.8	21.1	28.3	18.5	40.8	55.0	31.6	60.8	78.3	50.0	111	140	103	186	233	173	308	383	271	391	458	363
350	2.9	3.8	1.7	5.3	7.3	3.4	10.6	14.0	8.1	20.1	26.3	17.1	37.5	50.8	29.1	55.8	71.6	46.6	103	130	95.0	171	213	160	285	355	250	366	433	333
400	2.7	3.5	1.6	5.0	6.8	3.2	10.0	13.1	7.6	19.0	24.6	16.0	35.0	47.5	27.5	52.5	66.6	43.3	96.6	121	88.3	161	200	150	266	333	233	330	383	300
500	2.4	3.2	1.5	4.4	6.1	2.9	8.8	11.8	6.8	17.0	22.0	14.3	31.6	42.5	24.5	46.6	60.0	39.1	85.0	108	78.3	143	180	133	238	300	208	300	350	273
600	2.2	2.8	1.3	4.0	5.6	2.6	8.1	10.8	6.2	15.3	20.0	13.0	28.3	38.6	22.5	43.3	55.0	35.1	78.3	98.3	71.6	130	163	121	216	271	191			
700	2.0	2.6	1.2	3.7	5.1	2.4	7.5	9.9	5.7	14.1	18.5	12.0	26.3	35.8	20.8	40.0	50.8	32.8	73.3	91.6	66.6	120	150	113	200	250	178			
800	1.9	2.4	1.1	3.5	4.8	2.2	7.0	9.3	5.4	13.3	17.3	11.3	24.6	33.3	19.5	36.5	47.5	30.6	68.3	85.0	61.6	113	140	106	188	233	165			
1000	1.7	2.2	1.0	3.1	4.3	2.0	6.2	8.3	4.8	11.8	15.5	10.0	22.1	30.0	17.1	33.0	44.1	27.0	60.8	76.6	55.0	100	125	93.3	166	208	148			
1200	1.6	2.0	0.9	2.8	4.1	1.8	5.7	7.5	4.4	10.8	14.1	9.1	20.0	27.3	15.6	30.0	38.8	25.0	55.0	70.0	50.8	91.6	115	86.6	151	190	135			

Pressure drop, in. Hg: columns marked 2, 1

- Pump types

- Pumps may be either rotary vane or reciprocating. Care must be taken in the location and installation of reciprocating pumps, however, because they are noisy and require a large foundation to prevent vibration and movement. The receiving tank should be hot dipped galvanized steel, because condensation will form and collect in it.

- Switches

- Pressure switches for the motor starters should be mounted directly on the receiver, with only a wire running from the pressure switch to the starter, to ensure continuous vacuum supply.

Sizing examples

- Oxygen: Assume that a line is to supply 60 oxygen outlets, with a developed length of 250' from the source to the farthest outlet. The piping being used is Type K copper tubing, and the allowable pressure drop is 2 psi. The required capacity can be expressed as follows: 60 outlets times 10 liters per minute per outlet times 40 percent diversity, or 240 liters per minute. Referring to Table 9 we look opposite 277' under the column for 3/4" K and find 212 liters per minute, which is too small; under 1" K we find 450, which is ample even after deducting the percentage for fittings. Hence the line should be 1" in size. If screw pipe were to be used, we would select the appropriate column marked "P," and if Type TP copper tubing were to be used, we would select the column marked "B."

- Compressed air: Assume that there is an outlet pressure of 40 psi, 1,000' of pipe and an allowable pressure loss of 22 psi. In Table 3, in the column for 40 psi, we read down to 22, and then across, to find that a 1" black steel pipe of this length can supply 59 cfm, a 3" pipe can supply 1,020 cfm, and so forth. Knowing the quantity required, we can easily select the proper pipe size.

Piping materials

- Compressed air piping materials include the following:
- Copper tubing seamless ACR (type K or L)
- Brass pipe standard weight (Schedule 40)
- Vacuum piping materials include the following:
- Copper tubing (Type K or L)
- Brass pipe standard weight (Schedule 40)
- Oxygen and nitrous oxide piping materials include the following:
- Copper tubing seamless ACR (type K or L)
- Brass pipe standard weight (Schedule 40)
- Acid drainage and vent piping materials include the following:
- Borosilicate glass pipe
- High silicon iron pipe
- Polypropylene plastic pipe
- Polyethylene plastic pipe
- Ultrapure water (DI water) piping materials include the following:
- Polyvinylidene fluoride pipe (PVDF plastic pipe)
- Radioactive waste piping materials include the following:
- Stainless steel pipe (type 316)
- Natural gas piping materials include the following:
- Cast iron, wrought pipe
- Black steel pipe
- Galvanized steel pipe
- Copper pipe (Type K and L)

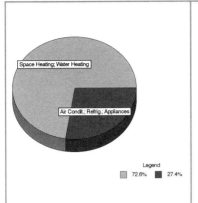

Fig. 1. Residential consumption of energy in the U. S.

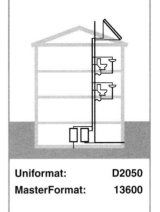

Solar domestic water heating

Summary: Domestic water heating is among the most feasible applications of solar technology. This article offers a rationale for using solar water heating systems for residences, discussion of system types, applications and installation considerations.

Key words: batch water heaters, domestic water heating, phase change, solar collectors, thermosyphon systems.

Uniformat:	D2050
MasterFormat:	13600

Introduction

Solar energy may be used to heat water for many applications, including domestic water for residential uses, water for swimming pools and spas; service water for commercial use, industrial process water, and water for agricultural uses.

Next to energy used for space heating, water heating at about 17% is the largest end use for energy in the typical home in the U. S. Fig. 1 shows energy for various end uses in the average U. S. home. Percentages given are developed by averaging the energy consumption patterns for a large number of homes, including apartments and single family detached houses. The percentages are in terms of primary energy usage, that is the amount of energy used to produce the energy consumed in the home. Approximately 30% of the fuel burned to produce electricity is available at a home for the various uses for that energy, the balance it used up it generating the electricity and getting it to the home. These are averages. The percentages for individual households can vary considerably. For instance, an efficient refrigerator/freezer will reduce the percentage for that end use to 2.5% or less. On the other hand, two members of a household that like to take 20 minutes showers daily, can increase the percentage of water heating to 25% or more of the total energy consumed.

A solar water heating system offers benefits to the system owner and to the electric power producer. While the installation cost of nearly all solar water heating equipment is more than that of conventional water heating equipment, the cumulative cost of owning and operating a solar water heating system is much less than that of conventional equipment. Fig. 2 indicates characteristic economic savings for an electric water heater and a solar water heater with an electric supplemental heater. Electricity was assumed to cost $.105/kw-hr. Hot water demand is calculated for a family of four. Returns on investment in a solar water heating system are comparable or better than returns on more traditional investments.

A solar water heating system will increase the amount of domestic hot water available to the system owner. This is particularly the case where an instantaneous heater has been used to heat water. Typically, an instantaneous heater, such as a tankless water heater in a boiler is unable to satisfy large volume hot water demands, such as for a shower or tub bath or when several fixtures are in use at one time. Within the solar tank is a large reservoir of water that has been preheated before it goes to the instantaneous heater. Since the water entering the instantaneous heater has been preheated the instantaneous heater does not have to increase the temperature of the water passing through nearly as much as if it were working alone, thus it is better able to meet large volume hot water demands.

The environmental benefits of solar water heating, while currently difficult to quantify in economic terms, are real. A solar water heating system will make a significant reduction if the amount of carbon dioxide discharged into the atmosphere compared to a fuel-fired water heating system. For instance, for every gallon of fuel oil that is burned about 20 lb. of carbon dioxide are released to the atmosphere as a product of combustion. Between 365 and 550 gallons per year of fuel oil is used to heat the water for a typical family of four in the U. S. Assuming an average use of 400 gallons per year, about 4 tons of carbon dioxide per year is released by that fuel-fired water heating system.

A typical solar water heating system will provide about 75% of the annual hot water requirement of a family of four. If a solar water heating system is used in conjunction with an oil-fired water heating system then only 1 - 1.5 tons of carbon dioxide is produced by the oil fired system. If the same amount of domestic water is heated by electricity, and the electricity is generated by burning oil then twice as much oil is needed to heat the same amount of domestic water because of the inefficiency of electric power generation and transmission. Thus twice as much carbon dioxide, 8 tons, is produced by burning the oil to generate the electricity to heat the water. If a solar water heating system were used in conjunction with the electric water heater then only 2 - 3 tons of carbon dioxide would be released per year.

Nearly all conventional water heating systems consume some type of non-renewable energy in the process of heating water. Non-renewable means that once that source of energy has been consumed there is no more on this planet. A solar water heating system uses a renewable source of energy to heat water. Thus, using solar energy for water heating consumes less of our planet's non-renewable sources of energy.

Suppliers of electric power also can benefit from solar water heating installations. Studies by electric utilities have shown that solar water heating systems have a significant potential for peak load reduction. Since the primary reason for new power plant construction in the United States is to meet peak loads, use of solar water heating systems can help to at least postpone the day when many utilities must invest in a new power plant.

Author: Everett M. Barber, Jr.

References: ASHRAE. 1995. *ASHRAE HVAC Applications Handbook.* Chapter 30. "Solar Energy Utilization." Atlanta, GA: American Society of Heating, Refrigeration and Air-Conditioning Engineers.

Additional references are listed at the end of this article.

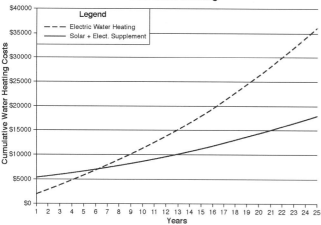

Fig. 2. Solar water heating with electric supplement vs. electric water heating

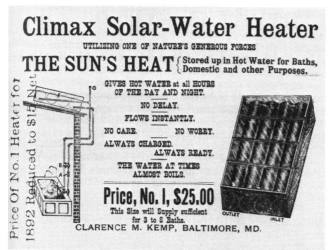

Fig. 3. Advertisement for the "Climax" water heater. 1892. First solar water heater commercially produced in the U. S. "Batch-type" glass-covered black-painted water tanks. (Butti and Perlin 1980).

Fig. 4. The "Day and Night" solar water heater, so named because the addition of an insulated "thermosyphon" tank inside the dwelling attic provided stored solar heated water for use at night. Seen here in a Pomona Valley, CA installation circa 1911. (Butti and Perlin 1980).

Solar electric and solar thermal collectors

Two fundamentally different types of solar collectors are in widespread use today: solar electric (often called photovoltaic) collectors and solar heat (often called "solar thermal") collectors. The former converts the sun's energy directly to electricity and is ideal for producing electricity. The latter converts the sun's energy directly to heat, and is thus ideal for water heating in the low temperature (below boiling) temperature range.

The typical solar electric (photovoltaic) collector is a flat plate type, usually within a glazed metal enclosure. When the sun's energy strikes the surface of the cell electrons flow from the cell, thus creating a flow of electricity. Each cell delivers about 4.5 volts in full sun. The photovoltaic cells are connected to one another in a series/ parallel arrangement so that the assembly will deliver somewhat more than 6 or 12 volts, direct current in full sun. The wattage produced by the collector depends on the number of photovoltaic cells that it contains. A common peak output range for solar electric collectors manufactured today is 55 to 120 watts. A solar electric collector weigh between 2.5 and 3.0 pounds per square foot. A well made collector should last at least 25 years.

The solar heat collector most commonly used for domestic water heating is also a flat plate collector. It consists of a glazed, metal enclosure. The enclosure frame is usually aluminum. The glazing is most often a tempered, low-iron content glass. Inside the enclosure is a metal absorber with integral flow passages, usually made of sheet metal. On the side of the absorber facing the glass is a black coating. The coating is either a black paint or a selective surface. The selective surface offers better heat retention than the black paint. The sun's heat is removed from a solar heat collector by a fluid flowing through the absorber. The fluid can be either a gas, such as air or a liquid, such as water. A layer of thermal insulation is used between the rear of the absorber and the rear of the enclosure. The collector is usually located outdoors, most often on a roof. A typical solar collector glazed with a single layer of glass weighs between 3 and 4 pounds per square foot. A well made solar collector should last 50 years.

There are other types of solar thermal collectors, with mirrors or heliostats that track the sun's movement. These are used for high temperature (above boiling) applications. As long as energy is needed in the form of low temperature heat <160F (71°C), then a solar heat collection system is superior to a solar electric system. If the need for energy is in the form of electricity, then a solar electric collector is preferred.

Factors for selecting a solar water heating system

A number of factors have a bearing on the type of solar water heating system for any given application. Some of the more significant of these factors are described below. Still farther on, Fig. 19, is a table which contains recommended systems for different applications.

- *Regularity of hot water demand.* When there is a daily demand for hot water that corresponds to the installed heat collection area, there is usually little chance that a solar water heating system will overheat. However, during the normal use of a dwelling, the hot water demand is rarely constant over the life of the dwelling. The occupants go away for weekends and vacations. Family size changes. Ideally the solar system should be capable of enduring periods of reduced or no hot water demand. Even if the original solar system owner knew how to prevent overheating, a new owner may not. The system chosen for a given installation should be capable of operating with a minimum of owner intervention over a range of hot water demands

Overheating will cause venting of water from open systems or loss of transport fluid from some types of closed systems. Both systems are described in more detail below. Water loss from open systems is an

SERVICES

D2

acceptable means of dealing with occasional overheating, as long as the water is discharged where it will cause no damage, such as onto the roof or into a drain. Some types of closed systems will loose their heat transport liquid when they overheat. Loss of liquid from a closed loop system is not desirable. If enough liquid is lost, the closed system will no longer collect heat and recharging the collection loop will be required.

- *Freeze protection:* If freezing weather occurs, even for a few weeks a year, then some means is necessary of protecting the collectors from damage caused by freezing. Ideally the means of freeze protection should be automatic`since an early frost may surprise a system owner. If water freezes in the absorber of most collectors, the absorber will be damaged by the expansion of the freezing water. In regions where freezing weather is of little or no concern, a simple solar system, usually one of the open systems, is preferrÖd.

- *Quality of water to be heated:* Water quality may dictate the type of solar system for a given application. If the water to be heated is "hard," that is, it contains a higher than normal percentage of dissolved carbonates; or if the water is acidic (pH<7.0), then it is very desirable to isolate the solar heat collection loop components from the water to be heated. For these applications some type of closed solar heat collection system is preferred because the closed system isolates the solar collection loop from the water to be heated.

- *Appearance of the system:* The style or form of the building on which the system is to be installed may dictate the type of solar water heating system to be used. Most passive solar water heating systems, which depend upon circulation due to a density difference between the collectors and storage, require that the collectors be located below the storage tank. On flat roofed buildings, it is relatively easy to place the collectors on the roof with the storage tank above them. But such an installation may be quite visible from the ground. The local zoning code or client's preference may preclude the visibility of this type of system. A ground mount may be a possible alternative in this case if the collectors will not be shaded. Alternatively, an active system may be preferred since its use permits the storage tank to be placed below the collectors. Passive and active systems are described in more detail below.

If the roof of a building is pitched, and one surface slopes toward the south (that is, the equatorial orientation in the Northern hemisphere), then it is usually possible to mount the solar collectors parallel to the roof. Mounted that way a collector resembles a large skylight. If the roof pitch or orientation is not what it should be for optimal solar heat collection, the roof ridge runs north-south, then solar collector tilt and/or orientation correction is required and a collector mounting frame must be used. (See discussion of collector orientation and tilt below).

- *Building structure:* The weight of the tank, or collectors plus tank must be considered in choosing a type of system and in deciding where to place the components. The weight of the collectors alone is generally not a deciding factor in where they can be placed since the collectors seldom weigh more than 4 pounds per square foot and that is well below the design snow load in most regions. The weight of the tank is a different matter. For example, an 80 gallon glass-lined tank, filled with water, weighs nearly 900 pounds. That weight, when applied to the normal tank footprint of a 26 - 28 in. diameter circle usually exceeds the (20 lb./sq. ft.) design dead load of most wood-frame floors. Even if the tank is placed on its side it represents a concentrated load that exceeds the design load of the typical wood-frame structure. If the tank is to be placed on a wood frame floor, or hung from roof rafters, the structure beneath it must be reinforced. The tank can be placed on a concrete floor with little risk of exceeding the design load.

Since both the storage tank and collectors of natural circulation systems and batch heaters must be placed on the roof their weight may

be sufficient cause to rule out the use of a natural circulation system. In such instances, the relatively light weight collectors used with some type of active system are preferred. The active system permits the collectors to be located on the roof and the much heavier tank to be located anywhere above or below the collectors.

From a structural point of view, the preferred location for the storage tank is on a ground level or basement floor slab where the structure is much more likely to be able to carry the load without reinforcement. Labor costs for tank installation and replacement are also lower when the tank is placed at or near grade level than when it is high in the building.

- *Water damage potential:* Virtually all tanks leak at some point in the life cycle. Some tanks used for residential water heating (regardless of fuel type) last no more than 7 to 12 years on average; others last 20 to 30 years. When the tanks leak they seem to have a perverse way of leaking when no one is around to discover and shut off the leak. It is not the 80 or 120 gallons of water in the tank that causes so much damage, but if continuously running, water from the well or city main will obvious cause the greatest damage.

The type of solar water heating system selected can determine the location of the hot water storage tank in the building. The collectors of most solar systems are placed on the roof of the building served to raise them above surrounding shade. In general, the passive systems require that the tank be located above the solar collectors. The active systems permit the tank to be located anywhere above or below the collectors.

If a passive system is used, the tank must be placed above the collectors for the system to function properly. If this system is to be installed in a warm climate, the tank can be placed outside without risk of freeze damage to the tank or connecting piping. In that case when the tank leaks, the water will usually run off the roof with little harm done. If the passive system is to be installed in a cold climate, then the tank should be located in a heated space. The heated space is preferred to reduce the heat loss from the tank and to minimize the risk of freezing the water lines serving the tank. The most convenient heated space is inside the dwelling. The placement of a tank high inside a building carries a significant risk of water leakage damage. The typical water tank overflow trays that are available for placement under hot water tanks have provided little protection from damage caused by ruptured tanks high in the dwelling. The tank leaks into the tray and the water runs off through the drain line unnoticed until the leak becomes a rupture and water spews out of the tank.

If a tank for a passive system must be placed inside the dwelling, in a heated space, that space must be easily accessible for inspection and tank replacement, and it should contains a water runoff barrier that channels leaking water outside. If the tank cannot to located in such a manner, then an active system used.

In cold climates, where it is desirable to place tanks and water-filled piping in heated spaces, experience has shown that placing a tank low in a building minimizes the damage that is caused when the tank leaks. This experience makes a strong argument for the use of some type of active system in a cold climate.

Solar thermal collection system types

There are a variety of solar heat collection and storage systems in use. Solar collectors were developed commercially over one hundred years ago in the United States and were common in warm climates in the twentieth century, such as in California and Florida (Figs. 3 and 4). The contemporary systems described below have had the benefit of at least twenty years of field experience. Some systems heat the domestic water directly in the collector. Others isolate the collector from the domestic water. Some require no electric power to operate, while others require electric power. Some are completely filled and others only

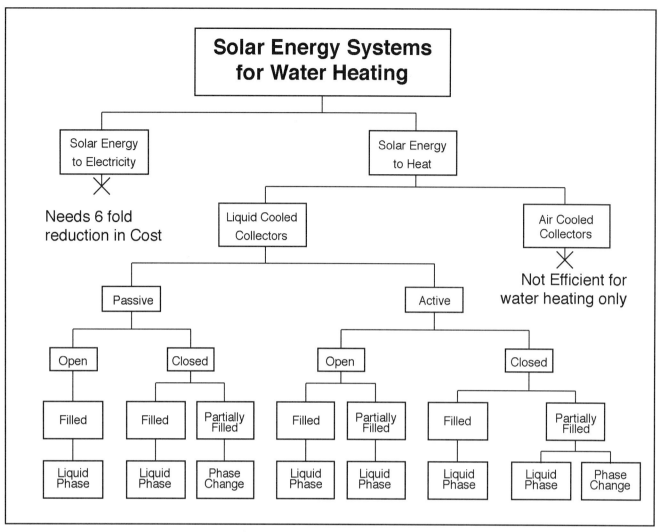

Fig. 5. Solar energy systems for water heating

partially filled. Some are better suited for freezing climates than others. The more significant of these different systems are described below. Fig. 5 provides an summary of different system types.

- *Air-cooled systems:* An air-cooled solar heat collection system uses air to transport heat from the solar collectors, through ducting, to a heat exchanger containing the domestic water to be heated. The movement of air through the collector may occur due to either passive or active means. There are some attractive features to air-cooled systems when they are used for space heating, or other functions such as drying. However, they are not efficient for water heating-only applications. If domestic water heating is incidental to the use of an air-cooled system that is primarily intended for space heating, then its use is acceptable.

- *Liquid-cooled systems:* For water heating, the liquid-cooled heat collection systems are preferred over air-cooled systems. A liquid-cooled solar heat collection system uses a liquid such as water to transport heat from the collectors through piping to the heat storage tank. The liquid-cooled collectors are more efficient than the air-cooled collectors for this application. If an active system is used, less energy is required to collect and transport heat from a liquid-cooled collector than from an air-cooled collector. The pipes of the liquid-cooled domestic water heating systems take up far less space than do the ducts of air-cooled systems. If an open system is used, the sun's heat is more efficiently transferred to the domestic water circulating through the collector than it is in an air-cooled system where the heat must first pass through an air/liquid heat exchanger to heat the domestic water. If a closed system is used, the sun's heat is more efficiently transferred from the collection loop liquid through a liquid/liquid heat exchanger to the domestic water than it is in an air cooled system where the heat must pass through an air/liquid heat exchanger to heat the domestic water.

- *Passive and active systems:* In addition to air-cooled and liquid cooled systems, solar systems are further divided into passive and active systems. There are a variety of subtypes of these, the more significant are described below.

- A *passive solar water heating system* is one that is capable of collecting and storing the sun's heat without the use of a motor driven fan or pump. Heat transport from collector to storage in these types of systems relies either on circulation due to density difference, or on circulation due to boiling and condensation.

- An *active solar water heating system* uses an external source of energy to power a motor driven fan or pump to force a fluid through the collectors, thereby removing the sun's heat and transporting that heat to storage. The fan or pump motor is usually turned on and off by a differential temperature thermostat. The power requirement of the pump motor is typically less than 3% of the total energy collected by the system. The pump motor may also be powered by a solar electric collector.

- *Open-loop and closed-loop systems:* Passive and active systems are further divided into open loop and closed loop systems. The term 'loop' refers to the flow path that permits a fluid to flow from heat storage, through the collector supply pipe, through the collectors, then back through the collector return pipe, to the heat storage tank. This circulation occurs when the collectors are warmer than the storage tank. The two systems each have merit for certain applications.

Open-loop systems
Fig. 6 illustrates one commonly used form of active open-loop system. When the collectors are warmer than the domestic water to be heated, the domestic water circulates between the storage tank and the absorber of the solar collector. The water moves through piping that connects the collectors to the storage tank. The water picks up the sun's heat as it passes through the collector. Circulation continues as long as the collectors are warmer than the storage tank. Over the period of the day the sun's heat is accumulated in the storage tank. In a passive open system, the sun's heat causes the circulation. In an active open system, a small pump moves the water through piping that connects the collector and the storage tank. The open system, passive or active, is preferred where the outside temperatures are not likely to drop below freezing.

Closed-loop systems
A closed-loop system includes a heat exchanger between the fluid circulated through the collectors and the domestic water in the storage tank. The heat exchanger permits the use of a low freezing point liquid in the collectors. The low freezing point liquid carries the sun's heat from the solar collectors to a heat exchanger. Fig. 7 illustrates one commonly used form of active closed-loop system in which the heat exchanger is located inside and near the bottom of a hot water storage tank. The sun's heat passes through the wall of the heat exchanger into the water in the tank. Closed-loop systems are somewhat less efficient than the open-loop systems because of the resistance to heat flow caused by the heat exchanger, but provide a very reliable means of freeze protection. The closed-loop system is also preferred where it is desirable to isolate the collectors from the potable water if the water quality is such that it will harm the collectors. Specific types of closed-loop and open-loop systems are described below.

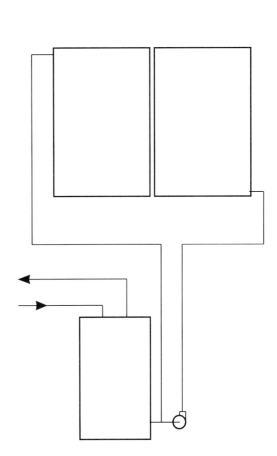

Fig. 6. Open system

SERVICES

D2

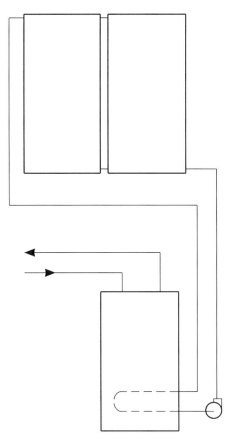

Fig. 7. Closed system

Liquid phase and phase-change systems

The vast majority of solar water heating systems in use today, passive and active, are systems in which the fluid circulating between the collectors and the storage tank remains in the liquid phase all of the time. Consequently the greatest amount of data and field experience has been gained with these systems. There are a limited number of closed-loop systems which allow the collection loop fluid to change phase from a liquid to a vapor as it circulates between collectors and storage. There are some potential advantages to these systems over the liquid-phase systems, however considerably less experience has been gained with these systems. All systems described below are liquid-phase systems unless indicated otherwise.

Built-up and unitary systems

Residential solar water heating systems may be classified into those that are assembled on-site and those that are pre-assembled before being delivered to the site. In the former instance, the collectors and tank arrive on-site as separate components. The collectors required to meet the hot water load are connected with piping to the hot water storage tank. The number of collectors and the size of the tank have been predetermined for the specific site. (See section below on system sizing.) The built-up system approach allows the installer the greatest flexibility in configuring a system to meet the expected hot water demand as well as to place the collectors and storage in the most desirable, respective locations. As noted above, the separation of collectors and storage is often desirable for structural and visual reasons as well as to minimize the risk of property damage.

Unitary systems have great merit in certain applications. Many residences have nearly the same hot water demand. In such cases it may be desirable to use one of the unitary solar hot water systems. The unitary systems include the collectors and storage as one assembly. The main advantage to this type of system is that the installation cost is usually much less than that of a built up system.

The unitary systems do have some limitations. Since the storage and collectors are integral parts of the package, they are visually much more bulky than the relatively thin flat plate collectors. This greater bulk may preclude their being used where they must be placed in a prominent location on a roof. Due to their weight, a crane is often required to place them on the roof. When they are in use, the unitary systems are also much heavier than flat plate collectors alone since they include a water storage tank. The combined weight when in use usually far exceeds the design load of the roof. The greater weight requires reinforcement of the roof structure if they are to be located on a wood-frame roof. Since the storage tank is located just above the collectors and water supply and return lines must run to and from the tank those lines are vulnerable to freeze damage. Thus, the unitary systems are largely limited to climates where there is little or no freezing weather.

Of the systems described below, only two are of the unitary type; the remainder are site-built systems.

In some systems the collection loop is filled with fluid at the time of installation and it remains filled as long as the system is in use. In others system the collection loop is filled only when the system is collecting heat, when it stops collecting heat the fluid may drain from the collection loop. In still other systems, the collection loop is never completely filled. The fully filled systems are generally simpler in operation and less expensive that the two other types. The partially filled systems, while generally more expensive than the fully filled systems, offer advantages in overheat protection and freeze protection. The advantages and disadvantages specific to each type of system are described below.

D2

SERVICES

Specific system types

Passive open loop systems

Where the climate and architecture permit, these systems are preferred for their economy, simplicity, and reliability. They can be used in climates where freezing weather occurs no more than two weeks per year. If they are used in climates where freezing occurs more often than that the risk of freeze damage to these systems increases significantly.

- *Integral collector-storage systems:* These are more commonly called batch heaters. They are the embodiment of the unitary system (Fig. 8). The batch heater is perhaps the oldest form of solar water heater, as indicated above in Fig. 3. Newer versions have been developed that are much more efficient than the earlier designs. The batch heater includes the collector and the storage tank in the same housing: The exterior surface of the tank wall is the solar heat absorber. Batch heaters are quite simple and usually easy to install. Just put them in the sun, add water, that is, connect a domestic water supply and return line, and they are ready to go. They are made relatively small so that two men can carry them to a roof without great difficulty. When they are filled with water they are considerably heavier than the more traditional flat plate collector. Because of their small size, two or more are needed to provide a majority of the hot water required by a U. S. family of four. They do not have as high a thermal efficiency as the thermosyphon systems described below, due to the heat loss from their cover. Since they do not have a large storage capacity they are generally installed as a supplement to an existing water heater. Further, due to the heat loss from the glazed cover, their effective use is limited to warmer climates.

- Overheat protection: The batch heaters should be installed with a pressure and temperature relief valve on the outlet piping from the batch heater. If the water in the heater becomes too hot during periods of low demand then hot water can be vented onto the roof through the relief valve.

- Freeze protection: While the large thermal mass of the storage container is usually sufficient to protect this type of heater at nighttime temperatures well below freezing, the water supply and return piping to and from the batch heaters have proven vulnerable to freezing at temperatures just slightly below freezing. A heat trace or some other positive means of freeze protection is needed to prevent damage to the piping. The heat trace is not a particularly reliable means of protection since it will not work when there is a power outage. Power outages often result from major winter storms. Alternatively, the batch heaters can be drained and bypassed during freezing weather. They are not recommended for use where more than two weeks of freezing temperatures occur per year.

- *Open-loop thermosyphon systems.* Unlike the batch heaters, the collectors and storage are separate components in this type of system. The separation permits the storage tank to be much better insulated than in the batch heater. Circulation of the sun's heat from collectors to storage occurs naturally due to a density difference between the fluid in the collectors and that in the storage tank. The density difference occurs when the sun warms the water in the collector. The warmed water is less dense than that in the storage tank. The less dense liquid in the collector rises and the cooler, more dense liquid in the storage tank falls to replace the rising warmer liquid. These systems are used in climates where freezing conditions occur infrequently or not at all. They are preferred where they can be used because they are simple, inexpensive and efficient compared to other types of solar water heating systems. The majority of the solar water heating systems used outside the U. S. are of the thermosyphon type.

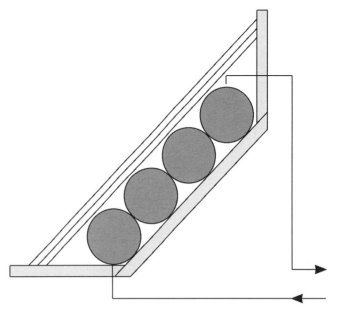

Fig. 8. Batch heater.

There are two frequently used variations of the thermosyphon system. In one form, the storage tank is horizontal; in the other, the storage tank is vertical.

- *Horizontal tank:* When the storage tank is placed above the collectors on the roof, as is the case with most passive systems, the lower profile of the horizontal tank is an important aesthetic advantage. The horizontal tank also distributes the weight of the tank over a larger area than the vertical tank thereby reducing somewhat the pounds per square foot roof loading. The horizontal tank also invites the manufacture of these system as a unitary system, or appliance, with one or two collectors below and a horizontal tank immediately above. This configuration offers the advantage of greater storage capacity than the batch heater described above. In addition, the tanks are available with an internal electric element, making them a self-contained water heating system. Use of this appliance often results in a significant savings in installation cost over a system that must be assembled on-site. In regions that receive a lot of sunshine, a unitary system consisting of two collectors and a tank are often adequate to meet the major portion of the expected hot water demand for a residence

There are some drawbacks to the horizontal tank, unitary systems. Because of the weight of this system when filled with water, reinforcement of the roof structure is often required. In regions that receive less sunshine than the southwestern U. S, multiple unitary systems are often required to meet the major portion of the hot water demand. A system assembled on site will offer more flexibility in system size.

- *Vertical tank:* The thermosyphon system which includes the vertical tank is usually installed as a built-up system and seldom as a unitary system. The vertical tank offers much better thermal stratification than the horizontal tank. This results in hotter water being available sooner and in a somewhat higher system efficiency. The built-up system has the advantage over the unitary system that the installer can determine the number of collectors and tank size required for a given application and then install and connect them accordingly. Because the collectors can be separated from the tank the installed system does not have the same bulk as the unitary system with horizontal tank.

Since the tank must be above the collectors, the vertical tank is potentially more prominent on the roof of a building than the horizontal tank. If the roof is flat and appearance is not a factor then the tank can be mounted on a frame directly above the collectors. If appearance is a concern and the building design permits, the vertical tank can be located in a cupola above the collectors. This artifice was used extensively in Florida during the 1920's and 1930's. The vertical tank represents a concentrated load, thus the surface that it sits on must often be structurally reinforced.

Figs. 9 & 10 illustrate the two types of natural circulation systems.

For the most effective operation of the natural circulation system, the bottom port on the storage tank should be about 12 - 18 in. (30 - 45 cm) higher than the high end of the collector. While natural circulation will occur with the tank somewhat lower than the collector, heat collection is less efficient and some of the collected heat will be lost at night due to reverse circulation when the collector cools. Check valves to prevent this reverse circulation may be used, but their long term reliability has been poor.

- *Overheat protection:* The thermosyphon systems should be installed with a pressure and temperature relief valve on the storage tank outlet piping. If the water in the heater becomes too hot during periods of clear sky and low demand then hot water can be vented onto the roof through the relief valve.

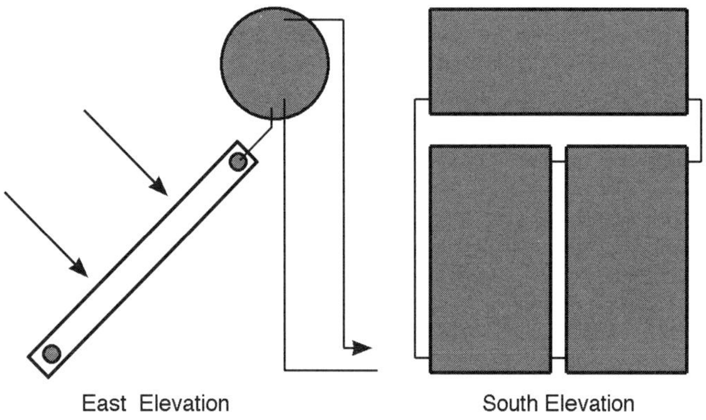

East Elevation   South Elevation

Fig. 9. Natural circulation system 1

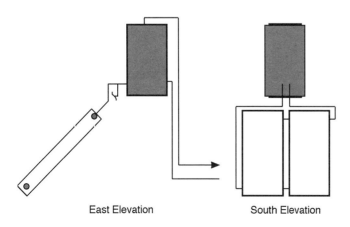

East Elevation   South Elevation

Fig. 10. Natural circulation system 2

SERVICES

D2

- *Freeze protection:* The collectors, as well as the water supply and return piping to and from the thermosyphon systems, have proven to be vulnerable to freeze damage in climates where freezing conditions occur for prolonged periods. An electric heat tape is installed behind the absorber of the collector of some of these systems. But the electric heat tape will not protect the absorbers during a power failure. The safest practice is to drain and bypass the thermosyphon heaters when freezing weather is expected.

Passive closed-loop systems

Passive closed loop systems may be used where freezing conditions occur, or in warm climates where the water quality is poor. As the term closed loop implies, a heat exchanger is used to separate some type of low freezing point fluid in the collection loop from the potable water in the storage tank. The heat exchanger causes these systems to be somewhat lower in efficiency than the passive open systems.

There are several types of passive closed loop systems. They all use some type of low freezing point liquid to transport heat from the collectors to the storage. One type operates like the thermosyphon system described above, relying on the density difference between the fluid in the collector and that in storage to cause circulation. The other type are the phase change systems which employ the force of boiling and condensing vapor to cause circulation.

- • *Closed-loop thermosyphon systems:* The storage tank and heat exchanger are located above the solar collectors (Fig. 11). Since this system, is used in climates where freezing occurs the storage tank and water supply and return piping must be located in a heated space. An antifreeze solution is used to transfer heat from the collectors to a heat exchanger inside or near the heat storage tank. The driving force that causes circulation in this passive system is not great thus the heat transfer rate across the heat exchanger in a passive system is not as good as in an active system. The diminished heat transfer results in a poorer efficiency for this type of system compared to that of a passive open loop system or active closed loop system. For effective use of this type of passive system the storage tank and heat exchanger should be located about 12 to 18 in. higher than the high end of the collector. This is done to minimize cooling of the tank at night due to reverse circulation.

- *Overheat protection:* The thermosyphon systems should be installed with a pressure and temperature relief valve on the storage tank outlet piping. If the water in the tank becomes too hot during periods of clear sky and low demand then hot water can be vented to the roof or a drain through the relief valve. If the water tank is empty on a sunny day the antifreeze charge will be lost through the collection loop relief valve.

- *Freeze protection:* The antifreeze protects the collectors and collector supply and return piping from freezing. Placing the tank in a heated space protects the water piping to and from the tank from freezing.

Phase-change systems

Few of the phase change systems have been in use as long as the liquid-phase systems. Thus, there has not been as much time to refine the phase-change systems through extensive field use. The phase change systems offer the promise of a solar heat collection and storage system that may be 25% more efficient that the liquid-phase systems. The solar heat collection loop in these systems is partially filled with a low boiling point, low freezing point liquid such as a refrigerant. Since those phase change systems that are truly passive don't rely on a differential thermostat to turn on a circulator they can begin heat collection as soon as the refrigerant in the collector begins to boil. The refrigerant vapor condenses in a heat exchanger inside the storage tank giving up the latent heat of vaporization to the water in the storage tank. In addition, the heat transfer in the absorber of the

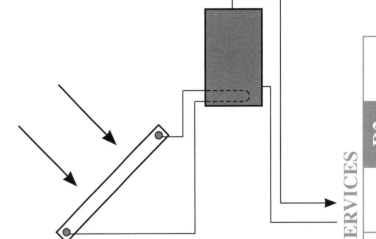

Fig. 11. Natural circulation closed loop

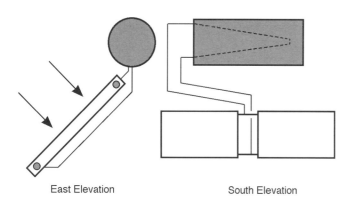

East Elevation   South Elevation

Fig.12. Phase change system 1

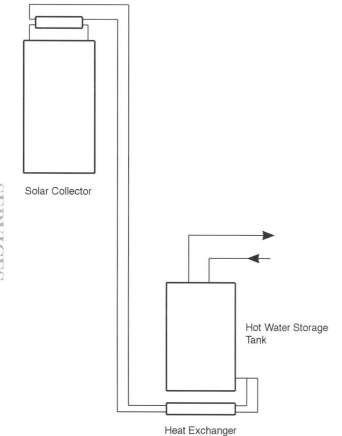

Solar Collector

Hot Water Storage
Tank

Heat Exchanger

Fig. 13. Phase change system 2

collector occurs at a higher rate than in a liquid-phase system because
the of the boiling that occurs as the sun heats the refrigerant above its
boiling point.

Unfortunately, these phase-change systems have not lived up to their
high expectations. They are more expensive to install than the liquid-
phase systems, in part because the installer must have the training and
tools of a refrigeration mechanic. If this were the only drawback the
higher cost would be worth the higher efficiency. The passive phase
change system requires that the storage tank be located above the
collectors in a heated space. If the heated space is above an occupied
part of a dwelling there is considerable potential for significant water
damage below when the tank leaks. Designing a heated enclosure for
the tank that would also shed water to the outside when the tank leaks
can certainly be done. However, that special enclosure further increases
the cost of the installation. Perhaps the most serious drawback to these
systems has been their poor resistance to overheating when the building they serve is unoccupied. The refrigerant develops high pressures
when there is no heat removal. Many of these systems have been found
some years after installation with their refrigerant charge lost. A technician skilled in charging refrigerant systems is required to recharge
them. It is rare that an refrigeration mechanic who is skilled in working on standard air conditioning and refrigeration equipment will work
on these system since they are unfamiliar with them.

Two variations of the phase change system are described below:

- *Phase change system 1:* In one form, the collectors are beneath
  the storage tank (Fig. 12). The collector loop is partially filled
  with a refrigerant. Piping connects the collectors to a heat exchanger inside the storage tank. When the sun warms the collectors, the refrigerant boils and the resulting vapor rises into the
  heat exchanger above, there it condenses, giving up its latent heat
  to the water in the tank. After it has condensed the refrigerant
  drains back into the collector. At night the collection loop is partially filled with refrigerant thus there can be no heat loss from the
  storage tank to the collectors due to reverse circulation because
  there is no liquid in the upper part of the system to carry heat
  away from the storage tank. The disadvantages to this system: it
  must be installed by a skilled technician; the storage tank must be
  located above the collectors.

- *Overheat protection:* This systems should be installed with a pressure and temperature relief valve on the storage tank outlet. If the
  water in the tank becomes too hot during periods of clear says and
  low hot water demand then hot water can be vented to the roof
  through the relief valve.

- *Freeze protection:* The refrigerant in the collector will not freeze
  at temperatures normally encountered in the U. S. Water piping to
  and from the storage tank should be protected from freeze damage.

- *Phase change system 2:* In another form of the phase change system, the collectors may be located above the storage tank which
  allows much greater flexibility when installing the system (Fig.
  13). This system employs the effect of an expanding vapor to force
  circulation between the collectors and a heat exchanger located
  nearby the storage tank. The system works in a similar manner to
  a percolator-type coffee maker. In a percolator, vapor bubbles
  formed at the bottom of the pot rise through a tube to the top of
  the pot. The bubbles entrain water between them as they rise
  thereby carrying water to the top of the pot, above the water surface, where it can pass through the coffee.

In this solar system, the heat collection loop is partially filled with a
mixture of alcohol and water. So that the system will begin 'percolat-
ing' well below the normal boiling point of water, the boiling point of
the mixture is lowered to about 75F (24°C) by drawing a vacuum in
the collection loop when the system is installed. While circulation is

forced by the vapor bubbles, the bubbles are formed by the sun's heat, hence the system is considered passive.

- *Overheat protection:* The only means of overheat protection is to cover the collectors when there will be no hot water demand during clear weather. If the collectors over heat the fluid charge and system vacuum is lost and the system will no longer collect heat until it is repaired. This has been a significant short coming of this system because experience has shown that system owners will the need to cover their collectors whenever they leave their home for more than a long weekend.

- *Freeze protection:* This system contains a mixture of alcohol and water. The mixture is chosen to have a sufficiently low freezing point that it will protect the collectors and piping from freeze damage.

Active open-loop systems

Systems that use an external source of energy, such as a motor driven pump, to force the circulation of a liquid between collectors and storage are considered active systems. While these systems are generally not as simple, efficient or inexpensive as passive, open-loop systems they can be used in a much greater range of applications than any of the passive open loop systems because the collectors and storage tank can be separated by considerable distances. The collectors can be installed above or below the storage tank. The pump motor can be powered by either line voltage (120 volts a/c) or by electricity from a photovoltaic array (usually 12 volts d/c).

- • *Basic open-loop system:* The solar heat collection loop of this system is filled with the domestic water that is to be heated (Fig. 14). The system is suitable for warm climates where there is little or no freezing weather. These systems are also used to a limited extent in cold climates for summer homes. At the end of the summer season, the collection loop and piping are drained, not to be refilled until the mid-spring. When the sun warms the collectors to a temperature of about 20F warmer than the storage tank a differential temperature control turns on the collection loop pump. The pump circulates water between the collectors and the storage tank, accumulating the sun's heat in the storage tank until the collectors cool to within about 5F of the storage tank temperature then the controller shuts off the circulator.

- *Overheat protection:* This type of system should be installed with a pressure and temperature relief valve on the solar collector outlet piping. If the water in the heat collection loop becomes too hot during periods of clear says and low hot water demand then hot water will be vented onto the roof through the relief valve.

- *Freeze protection:* Where freezing weather occurs for only a few weeks per year the collectors can be protected from freezing by recirculating the warm water from the hot water tank through the collectors. Through its sensor installed at the collector the differential thermostat can determine the temperature of the solar collectors. When the collector falls below a preset temperature, 50F (10°C) for example, then the controller turns on the circulator and sends water from the tank to warm the collectors. This is often referred to as a hot water recirculation system. Recirculation of the tank water becomes an expensive means of freeze protection where more than a few weeks of freezing weather occur per year, due to the heat lost from the tank. This type of system is also vulnerable to freeze damage in the event of a controller or circulator failure or power outage.

- • *Open-loop with automatic drain down:* This system operates like the basic open loop system described above during warm weather. However, it uses an automatic valve to drain the heat collection loop to protect the collectors from freeze damage and the storage tank from overheating. Thus during heat collection this system is filled, but during periods of low collector temperature or hot stor-

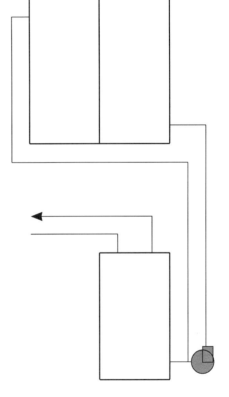

Fig. 14. Basic open system

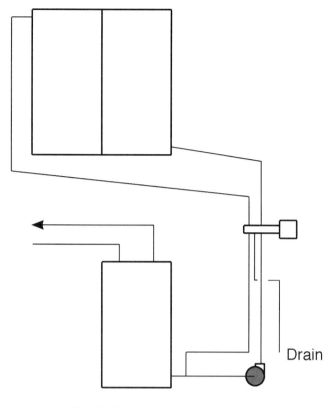

Fig. 15. Open loop drain down system

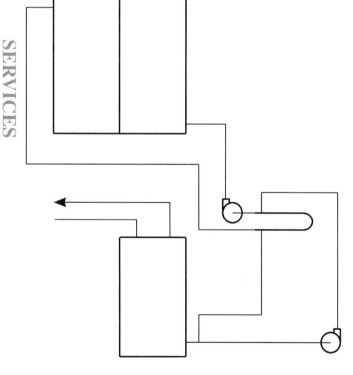

Fig. 16. Closed filled loop system with external heat exchanger (drain back)

age tank temperature the collection loop is empty (Fig. 15). The differential thermostat that normally turns the circulator on must have an added function that permits it to control the automatic valve. The water that drains from the collection loop is wasted to a drain. This is referred to as a drain-down system. The drain-down system should not be confused with the drain-back system described below. In the drain-down system, the water is wasted to a drain, while in the drain-back system the water returns to a reservoir to be used again when the collectors are warm.

- *Overheat protection:* The controller for the drain-down system protects the storage tank from overheating by positioning the drain-down valve to drain water from the solar heat collection loop when the storage tank temperature reaches a preset high limit, such as 160 or 180F (70 or 82°C).

- *Freeze protection:* The controller for the drain-down system protects the system from freeze damage by positioning the drain-down valve to drain water from the solar collection loop when one or more sensors at the collector indicate that the collector temperature has dropped below about 45F (7°C). While in theory these systems seem like a safe way to protect open systems from freeze damage in the coldest of climates, the reliability of this freeze protection means in cold climates has been extremely poor. For various reasons, the systems do not drain reliably. Sometimes they fail to drain because an air vent or vacuum breaker on the roof does not operate when it should. An additional drawback of the freeze protection feature is that on partially cloudy winter days they will drain and fill frequently. Since the collection loop is filled by water from the hot water tank there is often a net loss of temperature in the tank over the period of a winter day, not to mention the water lost down the drain. They are not recommended for use in climates where freezing weather occurs for more than a few weeks a year.

Active closed-loop systems
Closed-loop solar water heating systems are the most widely used type of system in climates where freezing weather occurs for more than a few weeks per year. They are also used in climates where freezing does not occur but where the water to be heated is heavily laden with minerals. They are not as efficient as the active open loop systems. However, due to refinements over the past twenty years, they are the most reliable type of active solar water heating systems available for cold climates.

Active closed-loop systems may be separated into those in which the solar heat collection loop is filled with the transport fluid, regardless of whether or not heat is being collected; and those in which the heat collection loop is filled when heat is being collected and empty or partially filled when heat is not being collected. Freeze protection and overheat protection means differ with these systems.

• *Closed filled loop with heat exchanger external to tank:* The sun's heat is carried by a low freezing point liquid from the solar collectors to a heat exchanger located external to but usually nearby a hot water storage tank (Fig. 16). A small circulator forces the liquid through a loop of piping that is run between collectors and heat exchanger. A second loop of piping connects the heat exchanger to the hot water storage tank. Another small circulator forces the water from the tank through the heat exchanger and back to the tank. The heat from the collectors passes from the low freezing point liquid, through the wall of the heat exchanger into the domestic water. A differential thermostat automatically turns on both circulators when the collector sensor is about 20F warmer than the storage tank. The circulators run until the collectors cool to about 5F above the storage tank temperature, then the thermostat shuts them off.

- *Overheat protection:* When there is no hot water demand for several clear summer days the heat collection loop will overheat. Overheat protection can be achieved in either of two ways. There are trade-offs with either choice. When a water based antifreeze solution is used as the low freezing point liquid then overheat protection is provided by manually switching on the circulator during the period of time that there will be no hot water demand. The circulator will then cause the system to waste the heat collected during the day to the night air. When the regular demand for hot water resumes then the differential thermostat is reset to automatic operation. Alternatively, a heat transport oil with a high boiling point can be used. An oil such as silicon can sit in the collectors and neither boil nor be damaged when there is no circulation on a clear day.

- *Freeze protection:* The solar collectors are usually placed outside, on a roof, for example. Since this is a filled system, the collectors and adjacent piping are always filled with the heat transport liquid, even when the system is not collecting heat .The antifreeze or heat transport oil protects the collectors and adjacent piping from freeze damage.

- *Closed filled loop - heat exchanger inside tank:* The sun's heat is carried by a non-toxic, low freezing point liquid from the solar collectors to a heat exchanger located inside and near the bottom of a hot water storage tank (Fig. 17). A small circulator forces the liquid to circulate between collectors and heat exchanger. The heat from the collectors passes through the wall of the heat exchanger into the water in the tank. A differential thermostat automatically turns on the circulator when the collector sensor is about 20F warmer than the storage tank. The circulator runs until the collectors cool to about 5F above the storage tank temperature, then the thermostat shuts off the circulator.

- *Overheat Protection:* When there is no hot water demand for several clear summer days the heat collection loop can overheat. Overheat protection may be achieved in either of two ways. There are trade-offs with either choice. When a water based non-toxic antifreeze solution is used as the low freezing point liquid, overheat protection is easily provided by manually switching on the circulator during the period of time that there will be no hot water demand. The circulator will then cause the system to waste the heat that was collected during the day to the night air. Alternatively, a heat transport oil with a high boiling point can be used. An oil such as silicon can sit in the collectors and neither boil nor be damaged when there is no circulation on a clear day.

- *Freeze Protection:* The solar collectors are usually placed outside, on a roof, for example. Since this is a filled system, the collectors and adjacent piping are always filled with the heat transport liquid, even when the system is not collecting heat .The non-toxic antifreeze or heat transport oil protects the collectors and adjacent piping from freeze damage.

- *Closed- partially filled loop - external heat exchanger system (drain back):* Closed-loop, drain back systems are particularly well suited to installations having a solar collector area that is too large for the hot water demand, or for use where there may be no hot water demand for weeks or months at a time. Drain back system are somewhat more expensive to install than the filled, closed loop systems.

When the system is not collecting heat from roof mounted solar collectors, the liquid used to transport heat from the solar collectors sits in a reservoir in a heated area of the building (Fig. 18). A differential thermostat controls one or two pumps in the heat collection piping loop and one in the domestic water piping loop. The thermostat turns

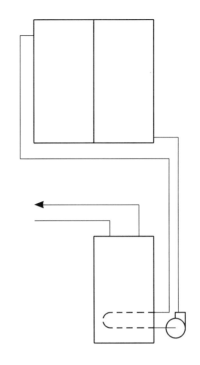

Fig. 17. Closed filled loop system with internal heat exchanger

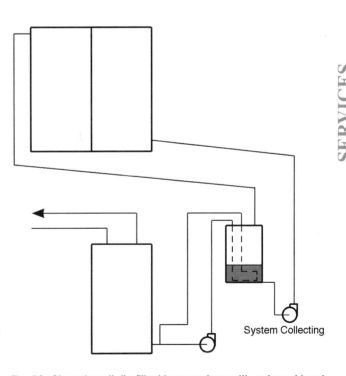

System Collecting

Fig. 18. Closed partially filled loop system with external heat exchanger (drain back)

SERVICES

D2

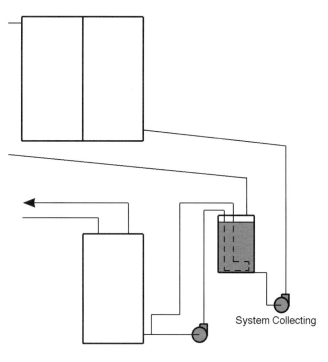

Fig. 19. Closed partially filled loop system with external heat exchanger (drain back)

the pumps on when the collectors become warmer than the hot water tank. The liquid in the reservoir is lifted by the pump(s) to the collectors. As it passes through the collectors the liquid removes the sun's heat. The heated liquid then returns to the reservoir. The liquid in the heat collection loop continues to circulate as long as the pump(s) run (Fig. 19). The pump in the domestic water loop moves water from the hot water tank through a heat exchanger in the drain-back reservoir where it is heated, and then back to the tank. When the collectors cool, the controller shuts the pump off and the liquid drains out of the collection loop into the reservoir. The wattage of the pumps for these systems can be three or four times that of the closed, filled loop systems. This is due to the collection loop pump(s) having to be powerful enough to lift the transport liquid to the top of the system and keep it circulating as long as there is heat to be collected. Because of the higher power requirement this system is not as amenable to use with photovoltaic powered circulators.

- *Overheat protection:* When there is no hot water demand for several clear summer days or longer, the collection loop of the drain-back system will not overheat. The storage sensor for the differential thermostat tells the controller when the hot water storage tank has reached a preset high temperature limit. At that point the controller shuts off the collection loop circulator(s) and the liquid drains from the collectors back into the reservoir. No additional heat is collected until the tank temperature drops below the preset temperature limit.

- *Freeze protection:* Since the heat collecting liquid drains back to the reservoir when the collectors are just slightly warmer than the storage tank, and the reservoir is in a heated space, there is little risk of freeze damage to the collectors and adjacent piping. Often the liquid is a non-toxic antifreeze, which further insures against freeze damage. The antifreeze has also been found to increase the longevity of the collection loop pump(s).

• *Closed- partially filled loop- internal heat exchanger system (drain back):* A slight variation of the drain-back system above is with a hot water storage tank with an internal heat exchange coil. Use of this type of tank obviates the heat exchanger in the drain-back tank as well as the water side circulator. There is a small saving in installed cost and in electricity use by eliminating the water side circulator, however the tank with the internal heat exchanger is more expensive than the plain glass lined water tank that would be used with the above version. In all other respects the two systems function in the same way.

Selecting the appropriate solar water heating system

Table 1 presents a summary of solar water heating system types appropriate for various applications. Where there is no expectation of freezing weather, then one of the open loop systems should be used because they are more efficient than closed loop systems.

• Where freezing weather is expected, then one of the closed loop systems will offer the greatest protection from freeze damage.

• Where there is no freezing weather and the architectural design permits, a passive unitary system such as a batch heater, or a natural circulation system is recommended. They are simple, reliable and efficient. However their use dictates that the storage be above the collectors which in many instances may not be acceptable.

• Where the storage must be located below the collectors then some type of active system is required.

• Where demand for hot water is expected to be intermittent, and the dwelling may be unoccupied for long periods then an active open loop drain down system or an active closed loop drain back system are preferred.

Table 1. Which solar system to use "Daily hot water demand" implies normal occupancy and a maximum period of two weeks in which there may be no hot water demand. "Irregular hot water demand" implies intermittent occupancy with periods on no hot water demand for weeks or months at a time. Closed systems should also be used where water quality is "hard" or low pH.

Which Solar Water Heating System to Use

		Where Storage may be above Collectors		Where storage must be Below Collector	
		Daily hw Demand	Irregular hw Demand	Daily hw Demand	Irregular hw Demand
Non-Freezing Climate	<50% Solar	Batch	Drain Down	Basic Open Loop	Drain-Down
	>50% Solar	Thermosyphon			
Freezing Infrequent	<50% Solar	Batch	Drain Down	Closed Loop Type 1 or 2	Drain Back
	>50% Solar	Thermosyphon			
Freezing Occurs	>50% Solar	Phase Change #1	NONE	Closed Loop Type 1 or 2	Drain Back

"Daily Hot Water Demand" implies normal occupancy, and no hot water demand for a maximum of several weeks per year.

"Irregular Hot Water Demand" implies no hot water demand for weeks or months at a time.
Closed systems should also be used where water quality is 'hard' or low pH.

Heat delivered monthly be a solar water heating system
Assuming a fairly uniform demand for hot water, the energy required to heat domestic water for a given residence varies little throughout the year. The only factor that can have a significant effect on the energy required is the temperature of the incoming water. If the water comes from a reservoir then the incoming water temperature may vary 25 to 30F between summer and winter. If the water comes from a deep well, the water temperature will be constant all year long. The energy consumed in heating domestic water can be significantly greater than the energy required. The energy consumed is determined by the efficiency of the appliance that is heating the water and by the standby losses.

The energy supplied by a given solar water heating system varies monthly with the availability of sunlight and outside air temperature. Fig. 20 illustrates the amount of energy supplied by a typical solar water heating system in relation to the energy required to heat water. The solar system used in the illustration supplies 70% of the annual energy required for water heating.

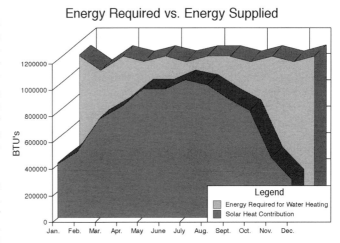

Fig. 20. Annual water heating profile

Improving the yield of a solar water heating system

There are a number of ways to increase the amount of heat that can be obtained from a solar system. Most involve changes which reduce the heat loss from the collector. The heat loss from a collector can be reduced by increasing the number of glazing layers; by using a selective coating on the absorber of the collector; by using an evacuated tube collector; by lowering the heat collection temperature; or by using a sun tracking collector. A few of the changes that improve efficiency involve system components other than the collector.

- *Collector cover glazing:* By adding layers of glazing to the cover of a solar collector the heat lost from the interior of the collector is reduced with each additional layer. There is a penalty to adding more layers of glazing: doing so reduces the amount of sunlight reaching the interior of the collector. In much of the southern part of the United States, particularly the Gulf Coast States and the warmer regions of the southwest, a single layer of glazing has proven to be adequate for solar collectors used to heat domestic water. The farther one travels toward the colder regions of the country the greater are the losses from the inside of the collector and thus the more desirable is some means of reducing those losses. One means is to use a second layer of glazing. A drawback to the use of two layers of glass glazing is the collectors are much heavier and thus more difficult to handle during installation than a single glazed collector. Sealed double glass units did not hold up well as a collector glazing material. The extreme temperature differential between inside the collector and outside was responsible for broken seals. While multiple plastic film glazing material lighten the weight of the collector and in some cases improve the transmittance through the cover, most do not last in the harsh environment of a solar collector glazing. In practice, a second layer of glazing is seldom used because of the significant efficiency improvement gained by using a selective coating (see below) on the absorber.

- *Absorber coating:* Perhaps the most common absorber coating is a flat black paint. In the warmer regions of the country the flat black coating is adequate for most domestic water heating applications. In the colder regions of the country, where heat loss from the collector is a greater concern, a selective coating on the absorber is preferred to adding a second layer of glazing to the collector enclosure. The selective coating significantly reduces the thermal radiation heat loss from the absorber while absorbing almost as much of the sun's heat as flat black paint. A good selective coating, such as black chrome, will absorb between 92 and 96% of the incident radiation and yet reradiate only 10 to 15% of the thermal radiation. For water heating systems that are to be installed in colder climates the selective coating is desirable.

- *Evacuated tube collectors:* Evacuated tube collectors are capable of collecting heat at higher temperatures than the non-evacuated flat plate collectors. Due to the vacuum surrounding the absorber of the collector, the heat loss from the absorber of an evacuated tube is much less than that from a flat plate. In warm, sunny regions of the country the evacuated tube collector is difficult to justify for domestic water heating applications in comparison to the flat plate collector. Due to the relatively low heat collection temperatures for domestic water heating the flat plate collectors are often more efficient than the evacuated tube collectors. Further, the evacuated tube collectors are much more expensive to install than the flat plates, on a per square foot basis. In colder regions, heat loss from the collector is more of a concern the evacuated tubular collectors have greater merit. At present costs, however the flat plate systems are able to produce adequate heat for domestic water heating at much less cost than the evacuated tube systems, even in the colder parts of the country.

- *Lowering the heat collection temperature:* The efficiency of a solar collector is determined by the amount of heat lost from the collector. For a given solar collector the larger the temperature difference between the fluid in the collector and the outside air the greater is the heat loss thus the lower the collector efficiency. Certain types of collectors are less sensitive to this temperature difference than others. Evacuated tube solar collectors, for example, are less sensitive to the temperature difference than non-evacuated collectors. Since the vast majority of solar collectors used for domestic water heating are non-evacuated the operating temperature of the collector is an important factor to consider. The heat collection temperature for a given collector area can be minimized by using a larger rather than smaller heat storage volume.

- *Suntracking solar systems:* Suntracking solar collectors follow the sun so they can use a mirror or linear lens to focus the sun's rays on the absorber of the collector. By so doing they are able to produce higher temperatures than flat plate collectors. In addition, since the absorber of the suntracking collector is much smaller than that of a flat plate collector of the same aperture area, the suntracking collectors are more efficient. Further, the suntracking collectors face the sun more hours of the day than fixed collectors, thus they can collect more heat. For industrial applications where high temperatures are often required, the tracking collectors have an advantage over flat plates. But high water temperatures are not required for domestic water heating, thus the tracking collector systems loose their advantage over flat plates, at least for this application. Further, the suntracking collectors do not collect at all during overcast conditions, while the flat plate collectors can deliver at least some heat to storage from the diffuse sunlight that makes its way through the clouds. The reliability of the sun tracking collector systems has been poor compared to that of the fixed flat plate collectors. For domestic water heating applications, the suntracking system is difficult to justify.

- *Proportional controller for active systems:* The vast majority of active systems use a differential thermostat that turns the collection loop circulator on and off. Typically these thermostats operate with a fixed differential to turn the circulator on when the collector sensor is 18 to 20F warmer than the storage sensor and then turn the circulator off when the collector sensor is about 5F warmer than the storage sensor. Ideally, heat would be removed from the collector when the collector is just slightly warmer than the storage tank, as in the case thermosyphon systems that begin to circulate when the liquid in the collector is slightly warmer than that in storage. A proportional differential thermostat will begin to power the circulator when the collector sensor is slightly warmer than the storage sensor, in this way the controller will cause the system to collect more heat. This is especially a benefit when the collectors heat and cool numerous times during the day as they would on a partly cloudy day. Only a few manufacturers made these controllers. They were more costly because they usually required a microprocessor to control the pulses of power supplied to the circulator. In recent years, the cost of microprocessors has dropped considerably thus the proportional differential controllers should be less expensive to manufacture. At present they are not available.

Installation considerations

- *Shade:* Solar collectors do not work well in shade! The shade from evergreens, from deciduous trees with or without their leaves, from an adjacent building, or even from another row of solar collectors can reduce the heat delivered by an array of solar collectors to an insignificant performance output. Limbs, branches and twigs of deciduous trees that have lost their leaves can cast as much as 40 - 60 percent of complete shade. If an array of collectors will be in shade during much of the heat collection period, the installation of the equipment will not be worthwhile. Ideally, solar collectors should have unobstructed exposure to the sun for about 6 hours

D2

SERVICES

per day. If the collector array faces south then there should be no shade between 9:00 am and 3:00 pm solar time.

- *Collector tilt and orientation:* These two factors have a bearing on the system performance. As a rule of thumb, collectors used for domestic water heating should be mounted at a tilt equal to the local latitude, the tilt measured from the horizontal. Varying the tilt by as much as 10 degrees either way does not have a great influence on the annual system performance. Tilting the collectors less than the optimum tends to increase heat collection during the summer and to decrease it during the winter. Too gentle a tilt may also cause overheating during the summer.

A steeper than optimum pitch increases winter heat collection, which is desirable because at that time of year the solar system provides the smallest portion of the total water heating load. But if the tilt is too steep, summer performance may suffer. Using a steeper than normal pitch is a way to reduce the tendency of a somewhat oversized array to overheat during the summer.

The collectors should be oriented approximately toward true south (or equatorial facing). The qualifying term "approximately" is used because orienting them 20 to 30 degrees off true south, either to east or west, does not have a significant reduced effect on annual heat collection.

- *Solar collector mounting:* While the collectors can be placed anywhere within a reasonable distance of the storage tank that they are heating, in most cases, the preferred location for them is on the roof of the building that they are serving. Side-wall and ground mounting are also used but to a lesser extent. The different considerations for collector mounting are discussed below.

- *Roof mounting:* While dormers, chimneys, skylight, cupolas, soil and waste vents, television satellite dishes, even air cooled condensing units have become an accepted part of present day roof vocabulary, roof mounted solar collectors have been slow to gain the same acceptance. The principal advantage to roof mounting is that when placed on the roof the collectors are higher than if they were on the ground, thus they are less likely to be shaded by nearby shade casting objects such as buildings or trees. In addition, many roofs are oriented and pitched properly for collector mounting, thus mounting costs on these roofs are usually less than in other locations. Even if the roof is flat or it does not offer the correct tilt or orientation, roof mounting of solar collectors is usually preferred if there are shade casting objects nearby. When the collectors are mounted on the roof, the piping between collectors and storage can often be run inside the building, which offers benefits of appearance and reduction in heat loss.

- *Collector mounting frame:* In many instances the roof is close enough to the desired tilt and orientation for the collectors that they can be mounted parallel to the roof. Mounted parallel to the roof the collectors often appear as a skylight thus their appearance is not objectionable. As noted above, the mounting hardware for a parallel mount is less expensive than for a mount which requires that the collectors be held at different tilt than the roof. If a properly pitched, equatorial facing roof is not available, or if the roof is flat or pitches to the east or west then a mounting frame is required to raise the collectors to the correct the tilt and orientation. Examples of different mounting schemes are shown below.

- *Collector mounting frame materials.* The preferred mounting frame material for long term durability and low maintenance is aluminum. Galvanized steel is suitable as long as the zinc coating is thick and not abraded or burned away during fabrication or assembly of the mounting frame. Ultimately galvanized steel will need to be painted to stop the spread of rust. Painted steel has not lasted long in as a collector mounting frame material without repainting every seven to ten years. Wood has proven to be a poor

choice for collector mounts because even pressure treated wood has not lasted much more than ten years. Wood mounts have often been the cause of roof leaks because wood rots first on the side against the roof surface where it cannot dry out quickly. Fasteners that are used to secure the collectors to the mounting frame and the mounting frame to the mounting surface should be either galvanized steel or stainless steel. Unprotected steel or even steel with thin zinc plating corrodes quickly.

- *Strength of collector mount:* The collector array, which includes the collector and the collector mount, should be able to withstand the force of expected design wind loads. In coastal regions, this wind load will usually be higher than for inland regions. ANSI/ASCE standard 7-95, section 6, covers design wind loads for buildings and other structures. The collector manufacturer should provide data on the wind load resistance of their product. The collector mounting frame manufacturer should provide that data on their products.

- *Appearance:* The collector array is usually the least obtrusive when it can be mounted parallel to the roof. Mounted in this way the collectors appear as skylights when viewed from the ground. Since skylights have become an accepted part of roof vocabulary the collectors that appear as such are little more obtrusive than large skylights. In order to achieve the "skylight look." the collector supply and return piping should turn and pass through the roof surface close to the collectors.

Where the collectors must be held at a different tilt from the roof, some type of support structure must be placed beneath the collectors. Such mounting may appear awkward when legs are used at each corner of each of the collectors. The appearance of such installations can be improved by partially hiding the collector support and piping behind the collectors. Held in this way, the collectors appear to 'float' above the roof from certain angles and their appearance is improved.

- *South sloping roof - parallel to roof mount:* As noted above the roof is often close enough to the desired tilt and orientation for the collectors that they can be mounted parallel to the roof (Fig. 21). If a south facing roof is not available or if the roof is flat or pitches to the east or west then a mounting frame is required to raise the collectors to the correct the tilt and orientation.

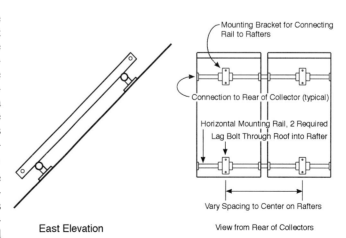

East Elevation

Mounting Bracket for Connecting Rail to Rafters

Connection to Rear of Collector (typical)

Horizontal Mounting Rail, 2 Required
Lag Bolt Through Roof into Rafter

Vary Spacing to Center on Rafters

View from Rear of Collectors

Fig. 21. Parallel to roof mount

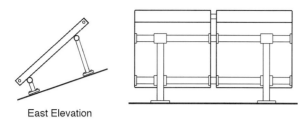

East Elevation

View from Rear - Parallel to Roof

Fig. 22. South sloping roof mount - tilt correction

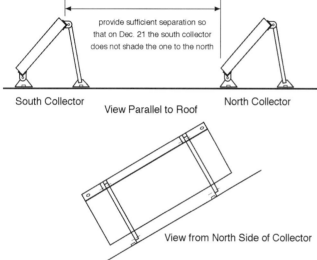

provide sufficient separation so that on Dec. 21 the south collector does not shade the one to the north

South Collector

View Parallel to Roof

North Collector

View from North Side of Collector

Fig. 23. East sloping roof mount

D2

SERVICES

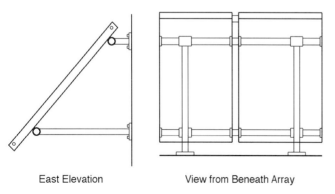

East Elevation

View from Beneath Array

Fig. 24. Side wall mounting

- *South sloping roof - tilt correction required:* Where the south (equatorial facing) sloping roof is too gently pitched then tilt correction is desirable to improve the year round heat collection. If the collectors are mounted parallel to a gently pitched roof the winter performance will suffer and the system will tend to overheat during the summer months (Fig. 22).

- *East or west sloping roof:* A house with a gabled roof ridge running north-south will usually have east and west facing roofs. Collectors can be mounted on the east of west facing roof if the collectors are oriented toward the south and tilted correctly for the latitude.

Collectors may be mounted on a frame on an east or west facing roof with their long axis inclined or they may be mounted with their long axis parallel to the roof. The former type of mounting will project higher above the roof than the latter, but the former will require less piping. The mounting shown in Fig. 23 is frequently used for east or west facing roofs. It is often called a saw tooth mount. Care should be taken when mounting the collectors in this fashion to prevent the southern most collector from shading the next one to the north during the winter months when the sun's altitude angle is the lowest of the year. A problem common to the saw tooth installation is the tendency of the collectors to become air bound. Where filled or closed- or open-loop type, systems are used an air vent should be installed on the collector outlet of each collector. Partially filled closed-loop systems are particularly prone to air blockage of one or more panels when installed in this manner.

- *South side wall mounting:* A side wall mount is preferred in those instances where no south (equatorial facing) sloping roof is available; or where the pipe runs from the roof to storage will be much longer than if the side wall location were used; or where the owner prefers not to have the collectors on the roof. If carefully placed, the collector array may also serve as an awning to shade south facing windows during summer time. The collectors may be mounted with the long axis of the collectors side by side, as in Fig. 24, or with the long axis of the collector parallel to the wall. If the former arrangement is used the collectors will project out from the wall more than if the latter is used. If the latter arrangement is used the collectors will be closer to the wall but more piping will be required.

- *Flat roof mounting:* The collectors may be mounted on a flat roof with the long axis of the collector inclined or with the long axis parallel to the roof. In the former arrangement they will project farther above the roof, but they will require less piping. If they are mounted with the long axis inclined then the mounting frame is the same as that shown below for ground mounting, the only difference being that the feet of the frame will be secured to roof structure rather than to railroad ties. If the roof membrane consists of multiple bituminous layer then pitch pockets should be used to seal around the feet of the mounting frame. If the roof membrane is an elastomeric material then the membrane may be extend above the foot of the mounting frame to seal around the mounting frame leg.

- *Ground mounting:* Ground mounting is preferred to roof mounting in a limited number of instances. If there is no south sloping roof surface available for the collectors or if the pitch of the south facing roof is too gentle for a parallel mount then a mounting frame that holds the collectors at the correct tilt is required. That frame can be placed on the ground as easily as it can be placed on an east or west facing roof or on a flat roof. As long as there is no shade from nearby trees or adjacent buildings then a ground mount may be used. If the collector array can be mounted on the ground close to or against the side of the building that it is serving then the piping runs may be much shorter that if the array were on the roof. Concerns about increased risk of collector cover breakage on ground mounted collectors have proven unfounded. Experience has shown that there is no greater likelihood of the glass cover breaking on a ground mounted solar collector than a roof mounted collector (Fig. 25).

Ground mounting becomes more costly than roof mounting when the collector array is more than a few feet from the building served because the supply and return piping must run under ground. Trenching and backfilling adds to the cost of the piping. In addition, underground piping requires pipe insulation that will function effectively and last for twenty years or more in a damp or even wet environment. Generally buried pipe insulation should be wrapped with a durable moisture seal. If the pipe insulation below ground becomes saturated, it will loose most of its insulating effect. If the piping must pass through a below grade wall, then the piping must be sealed carefully where it passes through the wall to prevent water penetration during periods of high water table or saturated ground.

- *Provisions for resurfacing the roof:* If the collectors are to be roof mounted, then in most cases they will have to be removed when the roof is resurfaced and then remounted when the resurfacing has been completed. If the solar water heating system is to be installed on an existing building and the roof is in imminent need of resurfacing, then that work should be done before the collector array is installed.

- *Pipe routing from roof mounted arrays:* When the collectors are roof mounted, the supply and return piping that runs between the collectors and the storage tank can either be routed through the roof and inside the building; or exterior to the roof, down the side wall and through the side wall close to the foundation. When the pipes pass through the roof membrane, they should be pass through a roof boot of the type that is used to seal around soil and waste vents. The flexible part of the boot should seal tightly to the pipe and not to the exterior of the pipe insulation. This is to prevent rain water from running between the pipe and the insulation to reach the interior of the house. Where the pipes are run along the roof surface they should be supported several inches off the roof to prevent the buildup of leaves and wind blown debris along the side of the insulated pipe. Pipe supports should be at least every 8 feet (2.4 m) apart, or as may be otherwise recommended for good practice. Vertical pipe runs inside or outside should be supported to carry the weight of the filled pipe and to prevent excessive wind movement of the piping.

- *Selection of a heat transport liquid:* From the standpoint of its ability to transport heat, water is better than any other liquid that is used in solar energy systems. Unfortunately water has the undesirable quality of freezing. When it freezes, it expands with great force. Until reliable, freeze resistant solar collectors are on the market, a liquid with a lower freezing point than water is needed for solar water heating systems installed in climates where freezing occurs.

The most commonly used antifreeze in solar water heating systems is an aqueous solution of propylene glycol, water and a buffering solution. It is non-toxic and quite compatible with the copper tubing which is used in the vast majority of solar water heating systems. Some of the better formulations of propylene glycol and water have been found to last more than 15 years under normal operating conditions. If the solar heat collection loop is composed of aluminum flow passages in the collectors and aluminum tubing between the collectors and the heat exchanger then propylene glycol based solution used in copper systems is not recommended. The propylene glycol antifreeze will offer freeze protection but it will not protect the aluminum from corrosion. The aluminum can be protected with the same fluid used to protect aluminum automobile radiators. It is an aqueous solution of ethylene glycol, water and a sacrificial corrosion inhibitors that pro-

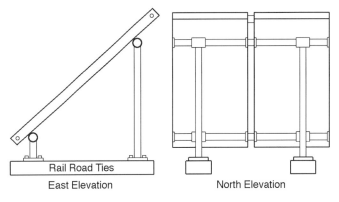

East Elevation   North Elevation

Fig. 25. Ground mounting

SERVICES

D2

tects the aluminum. While the solution is toxic, it effectively protects the aluminum from corrosion as long as it is replaced every 2 to 3 years. A mixture of methyl alcohol and water can be used instead of the glycols. A drawback to all the aqueous solutions is their tendency to build up pressure when they must remain for any length of time in the collector, on a clear hot day, under no flow conditions. Another relatively minor shortcoming of the aqueous solutions is that they are about 86 to 88% as effective a heat transport fluid as water. Their low freezing point makes this a acceptable penalty.

A few systems, such as some of the phase change systems, use low freezing point refrigerants to carry heat from the collectors. Heat transfer oils are also used to protect closed loop filled solar water heating systems from freezing. The two most commonly used oils in solar systems are silicon oil and Bray oil. They are non-toxic, non corrosive to the collectors and piping, and durable. One can expect them to last as long as the system. A particularly attractive feature of the oils is that they can remain in the collectors on sunny days with no circulation, without boiling. A major disadvantage to the oils is that they are only about 70% as effective a heat transport fluid as water. Where the expected use of the system indicates that overheating will frequently occur the use of one of the oils is preferred to the glycol solutions.

- *Heat exchanger selection:* Where closed systems are used, a heat exchanger is required to isolate the heat transport liquid in the heat collection loop from the potable domestic water. Where a non-toxic transport liquid is used a single wall heat exchanger has been found to provide acceptable separation of the non-potable liquid from the potable. In fact, there has not been a published incidence of contamination in this manner. Since the vast majority of closed loop solar water heating systems installed over the past 20 years use a non-toxic heat transport liquid, the single wall heat exchanger has demonstrated its reliability.

Where toxic heat transport liquids are used then a double wall, vented heat exchanger is recommended for separating the non-potable and potable liquids. If a leak develops in either of the two heat exchanger walls, the liquid will leak out through the vent rather than into the other liquid. Only a small percentage of the solar water heating systems installed required the use of a toxic antifreeze. Its use was required by one manufacturer of a collector with all aluminum tubing and liquid passages inside the collectors.

The type of heat exchanger that can be used when potable and non-potable liquids are in close proximity has traditionally been set by the local plumbing code. In general the plumbing codes require that, if one of the liquids is non-toxic a single wall heat exchanger may be used; but if one of the liquids is toxic then a double wall heat exchanger must be used. However, the local water provider's requirements can take precedence over the plumbing code. The U. S. Safe Drinking Water Act of 1986 made water providers responsible for the quality of the water that they provide up to the tap. Previously they were responsible up to the water meter. As a consequence of this change, the local water provider can require a double-wall heat exchanger to be used regardless of whether the heat transport liquid is toxic or non-toxic. If their requirements are not complied with, they will not supply water to the building.

- *Backflow preventers:* Where closed-loop systems are used, plumbing codes and water providers often require another from of insurance to protect the potable water source from contamination. The rationale for this added protection is as follows. If a heat exchanger were to leak a toxic substance into the potable water in a plumbing system and that system was served by a water main, then a loss of pressure in the main would draw some of the contaminated water back into the main. Such a pressure loss would occur if repairs were being made to the water main or water was

being pumped from the main to fight a fire. Once pressure was restored to the main the contaminated water could be supplied to many water users. Devices known as backflow preventers are used to prevent such contamination. There are two different types of backflow preventers that have been used with closed-loop solar water heating systems: a backflow preventer with an intermediate atmospheric break; and a "reduced pressure principle" backflow preventer. The former type should be acceptable in all cases, particularly where double wall vented heat exchangers are used. However, some water providers have required the latter. The latter is considerably more expensive than the former and requires periodic testing. Local requirements for backflow preventers should be determined before the solar water heating system is installed.

- *Piping materials for the collection loop:* Nearly all solar heat collectors made today that are used for domestic water heating are sold with either 7/8 in. O.D. or 1-1/8 in. O.D. copper tube size connections to the absorber. By soldering a copper coupling or threaded adapter to the absorber tube connection, several types of tubing or piping can be connected to the collector. The piping material chosen must be capable of enduring the occasional 2 to 3 minute-long high temperature surge that can come from a collector. During periods of no-flow, on a sunny day, the absorber of a solar collector with a selective coating can reach between 350 and 400F (177 and 205°C). The no-flow condition will occur on a sunny day during which the controller in a closed loop system had shut off the circulator because the temperature of the hot water tank had reached the high limit setting of the controller. The no-flow condition also occurs when the controller or circulator fails.

Experience has shown that the most suitable material for collector supply and return piping is copper tubing. As long as the pH of the heat transport fluid is 7 or higher, copper tubing is as durable a material as one can find. Copper supply and return tubing serving the collectors are easily soldered to the absorber. While brazing that connection to the absorber is overkill a low melting point solder should not be used either. A suitable solder is 95/5 tin/antimony which is commonly used for hydronic heating system installation.

Other piping materials that can be used are black steel pipe and the type of plastic tubing suitable for use in domestic hot water lines. Black steel can be connected to copper in a closed system, but it should not be connected to copper in an open system because it will be rapidly corroded by the copper. The material cost of black steel piping is less than that of copper tubing but the labor cost to install the black steel piping is much higher, thus copper tubing is used almost to the exclusion of black steel in domestic water heating applications. Polybutylene tubing can be used for collector supply and return lines but it should not connect directly to the collector because it will not withstand the high temperatures that occasionally come from the collector. A minimum 10 ft. length of copper should separate the polybutylene tubing from the absorber of the collector. In addition, horizontal runs of the polybutylene tubing should be supported continually or sags will develop which eventually will restrict or stop flow. Plastic piping suitable for use with domestic hot water, such as CPVC, can be used but it is and has been more costly than copper tubing. Attempts to use PVC piping are destined to failure, it melts, and serves only to impress the installer with how hot the collectors can become.

The majority of solar water heating systems for residential use require collector supply and return line sizes in the range of 1/2 to 3/4 in. nominal size. For small collector arrays of no more that 40 sq. ft., and pipe runs of no more than 50 ft. (round trip), the smaller size can be used. The larger size is adequate for most other applications.

- *Water piping exposed to freezing:* A safe assumption is that if pipes containing water are exposed to freezing conditions the water in the pipes will freeze, at some time over the life of the system, regardless of the precautions taken to prevent it from doing so. When water freezes it expands. The expansion will split the piping containing the frozen water. If the freeze damaged water line is high in the building the water that pours out through the split can cause considerable property damage to the spaces below. Particularly applicable here are water lines to and from open passive and open active systems. Insulation of the piping helps to reduce their vulnerability to freezing. The use of an electric heat trace provides an extra measure of protection from freezing. But weather can and does deteriorate exterior pipe insulation. And very cold weather often coincides with an electric power failure. Without electricity the heat trace will not protect the pipe. The water in the unprotected piping is very likely to freeze. The next thaw could result in water from a freeze damaged pipe pouring into the house below until the leak is discovered and shut off by the owner when he or she returns from vacation; or until the city main is empty, which ever comes first. Whenever possible, avoid running water piping through areas exposed to freezing conditions.

- *Protection from scalding:* The water in a solar heated tank can reach to 170 - 180F (77 - 82°C) especially during periods of clear skies and low hot water demand. First degree burns will be received by exposure to water slightly under 120F (49°C). Elderly people and small children are particularly vulnerable to this type of burn. Many plumbing codes require that a thermostatic mixing valve be installed in the hot water outlet of the solar tank. This valve will blend hot water from the tank with cold water to deliver nearly constant temperature water to the hot water supply mains. Even if the local plumbing code does not require this device it is recommended to prevent the risk of scalding.

- *Prevention of reverse circulation:* At night the collectors are usually much cooler than the storage tank. If permitted, the liquid in filled closed and open systems will circulate at night from the collectors to the storage tank thereby reducing the temperature of the storage tank. Temperature reductions of as much as 50F have been observed overnight. A check valve in the supply pipe to the collector array will prevent this unwanted heat loss.

System sizing

The solar system should be sized to meet the expected daily demand for hot water. The demand varies widely throughout the world. In the United States, the average person uses 20 gal. of hot water per day. In order to develop the energy efficiency labels that are applied to all conventional domestic water heating appliances the Department of Energy has estimated that the average U. S. family uses 64.3 gal/day of hot water.

The optimum solar collector area and storage capacity are determined by a number of variables which include not only the daily demand for hot water but also the climate, the cost of conventional forms of energy, the installed cost of the solar system, and the efficiency of the solar equipment.

Table 2 can be used for sizing a residential solar water heating system. A system selected from the table should provide between 50 - 75% of the annual hot water requirement for the number of hot water users and geographic regions shown. The sizes of the collectors and tanks are given in the standard U. S. size increments in which they are manufactured. Hot water consumption habits of specific individuals can have a pronounced effect on the actual solar fraction.

Table 2. Solar system sizing collector area (sq. ft.) / tank capacity (gal.) for typical U. S. climates

Hot water users/ system	Northeast /Northwest	Southeast	Midwest	Southwest
1-2	64/80	40/66	48/66	32/66
3-4	80/120	48/80	64/80	40/80
5-6	96/120	72/120	80/120	64/80
>6	120/160	80/120	96/120	72/120

Note: Standard U. S. collector sizes are: 3' x 8'; 4' x 8'; 4' x 10' = 24; 32; 40 sq. ft. respectively.

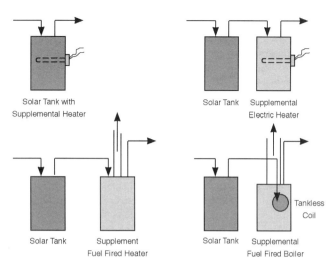

Fig. 26. Solar tank—supplemental heater arrangement

Fig. 27. Batch water heater with adjustable reflecting cover panel on an earth-covered home. New Canaan, CT. 1982.

Fig. 28. Solar heating for a pool house. Private Residence, CT. Architect: Charles W. Moore, FAIA. Solar design and engineering: Everett M. Barber, Jr. 1973.

As indicated in Table 2, the climate affects the ratio of collector area to storage volume for most types of systems. If the collector area is too large for the heat storage tank connected to it the system is more likely to overheat during the summer and to operate at a lower efficiency year round. In the Northeast U. S., the desirable ratio is in the range of 1.25 to 1.70 gal of water per square foot of collector. At the other extreme is the Southwest, where the ratio is in the range of 1.80 to 2.20 gallons per square foot of collector. Drain-down and drain-back types of solar systems with the proper controls are not restricted by the above ratios. When the storage tank in these systems reaches a preset high limit temperature the control causes the heat collection liquid to drain from the collectors thereby preventing the system from overheating.

A number of computer programs predict the system size required for a given hot water requirement in a given climate. Two of the better known programs are F-CHART, and SOL-COST. The former is available for use on microcomputers. The latter can only be used on mainframe computers. (Duffie & Beckman 1980).

Supplemental heating

A solar water heating system is almost always used with some type of supplemental heating equipment. The supplemental heater may be located inside the solar heat storage tank, such as an electric element in the upper part of the tank; or it may be a separate appliance such as a conventional electric, oil or gas fired water heater. In many localities, with a solar system properly sized for the load, the auxiliary heater can be shut off during the summer months.

The water heating installation should always be configured so the solar system preheats the water before it flows to the supplemental heater. If the system is installed so that water inside the solar tank or the water entering the tank has been heated by another source, then the contribution and resulting effectiveness of the solar system is obviously diminished.

Some typical system configurations are shown in Fig. 26.

Additional references

Butti, Ken and John Perlin. 1980. *Golden Thread: 2500 Years of Solar Architecture and Technology.* New York: Van Nostrand Reinhold. [out of print].

Duffie, John A.& Beckman, William A. 1980. *Solar Engineering of Thermal Processes.* New York: John A. Wiley & Sons.

Johnson, Russell K. 1987. "Solar/Electric Domestic Water Heating - Field Test, 1984-1987." Hartford, CT: Northeast Utilities Marketing Services Department.

Randolph, John and Robert P. Schubert. 1986. "Solar Hot Water Systems: Lessons from an Evaluation in Virginia." *Proceedings of Solar '96.* Asheville, NC. April 13-18, 1996. Boulder, CO: American Solar Energy Society.

ACSE. 1995. "ASCE Standard/ American Society of Civil Engineers. *Minimum Design Loads for Buildings and Other Structures.* ANSI/ ASCE 7-95. Washington, DC: American Society of Civil Engineers..

DOE/EIA. 1995. "Household Energy Consumption and Expenditures 1993." DOE/EIA-0321(93). October 1995. Washington, DC: Energy Information Administration.

FSEC. 1982. *Solar Water and Pool Heating, Design and Installation Manual.* FSEC-IN-21-82. Revised August 1992. Cocoa, FL: Florida Solar Energy Center.

D2

SERVICES

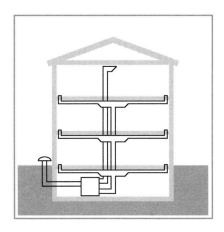

D   SERVICES

SERVICES

D3

Energy sources for houses

Summary: This article provides an overview of energy use in houses and the sources available to satisfy them. Selection criteria include availability, climate, cost, and environmental considerations. Choices are best made after first understanding how houses use energy in a specific location and what codes and standards may be applicable. Attention should then be given to other cost-effective conservation strategies.

Key words: Annual fuel utilization efficiency (AFUE), boilers, Btu, climate, cooling, degree days.

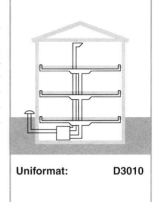

Uniformat: D3010

How Energy is Used in Houses

The pie chart (See Fig. 1 on next page) indicates how energy is used by average U.S. homes based upon Btu content. Obviously, averages can be misleading. For example, a house in a very hot climate would use a great deal of energy for cooling and very little for heating. In hot climates even the amount of energy used for water heating is reduced since water source temperatures (groundwater and reservoirs) are higher (approximately equal to the year-round ambient temperature).

Climate

Because heating accounts for most of residential energy use, selection of heating fuel type is primary. Demand for heating energy can be estimated by the "heating degree day" method. This method assumes that:

- a house needs to be heated whenever the outside air temperature falls below 65F.

- compares the average temperature for a given day to 65F.

For example, if the high temperature on a particular day is 30F, and the low temperature is 20F, the average temperature would be 25F, and a total of 40 heating degree days would accrue (65 - 25). When such a calculations are done for each day over the course of the heating season many thousands of heating degree days are totaled in most areas (see map in Fig. 2 on following page).

Conservation and Passive Solar Reduce Heating and Cooling Loads

Before deciding on the type of energy sources, attention should be given to reducing energy use. Energy (and building) codes generally stipulate:

- minimum insulation requirements (R-values)

- thermal conductance of windows (U-factors)

- equipment performance (AFUE)

However, these requirements should be considered as the minimum. Better construction will often save additional energy in a cost-effective manner.

To further maximize savings, designing to maximize the use of "free" solar heat should also be considered. In many areas, passive solar heating can provide a significant portion of a house's heating energy needs with the amount depending upon:

- insulation levels

- tightness of construction

- amount and type of south-facing windows

- inclusion of heat storage material ("thermal mass")

Savings also depend greatly upon local climate conditions. Assuming identical house design and construction, Table 1 indicates the percentage of heating energy saved (also the solar savings fraction or SSF) by passive solar heated houses by region and location including several Canadian cities.

These results are based upon the Load Collector Ratio (LCR) Method as put forth in the Passive Solar Design Handbook published by DOE (ASHRAE 1995). The comparative results listed are based on a reference design (low thermal mass, low-e south-facing windows, no night insulation) having a load collector ratio (LCR) of 40.

Note that, due to climatic variation, this particular reference design provides only about 9% of the annual heating energy needed in Binghamton, New York, whereas the same design can provide 44% of the annual heating energy needed in Albuquerque.

Author: William Bobenhausen.

References: Balcomb, J. D. 1987. *Passive Solar Heating Analysis* (and "Supplement One"). Atlanta, GA: American Society of Heating, Refrigerating and Air-Conditioning Engineers.

ASHRAE. 1995. *Passive Solar Design Handbook.* Atlanta, GA: American Society of Heating, Refrigerating and Air-Conditioning Engineers.

Bobenhausen, William. 1994. *Simplified Design of HVAC Systems.* New York: John Wiley & Sons.

Climatic Information: National Oceanic and Atmospheric Administration (NOAA), Asheville, NC.

Hinrichs, Roger A. 1996. *Energy, Its Use and The Environment.* Orlando, FL: Saunders College Publishing, a Harcourt Brace College Publisher.

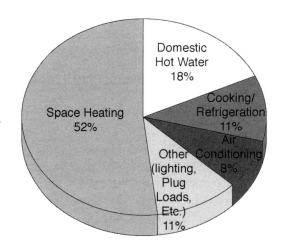

Fig. 1. How Energy is Used in American Houses on a Btu Basis, in percentage of Btus

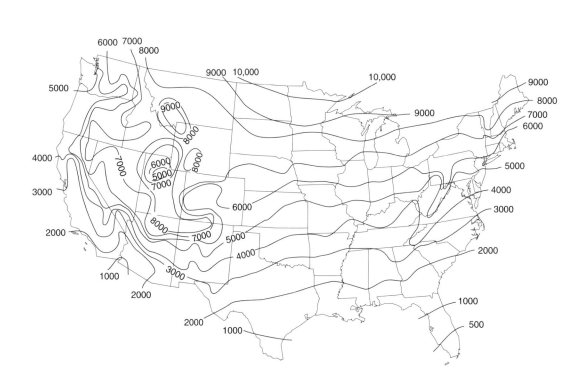

Fig. 2. Map of Heating Degree-Days (base 65) in the U.S.

Additional Energy Sources

As suggested by Table 1, the use of solar energy to provide a portion of a house's heating energy is a good option in many North American locations. However, most houses will still depend to a large extent on purchased heating fuel (Fig. 3).

Energy Sources for Space Heating

Natural Gas/Propane

Natural gas is now the heating fuel of choice for more than two-thirds of new houses. Moreover, since 1987 there have been more than 1 million heating system conversions from oil to gas across the U.S. Natural gas offers some distinct advantages:

- requires no storage space

- delivery is constant

- burns cleaner than other home heating fuels

- generally much less expensive than oil

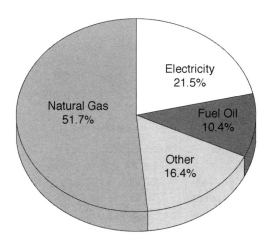

Fig. 3. Heating fuels used in american homes, by percentage. Source: U.S. Energy Information Administration, 1993

Table 1. Representative Annual Heating Energy Savings in Percent from Passive Solar Heating

NORTHEAST		NORTHCENTRAL	
Albany, NY	14%	Bismarck, ND	17%
Binghamton, NY	9%	Dodge City, KN	34%
Boston, MA	19%	Des Moines, IO	8%
Buffalo, NY	10%	Duluth, MN	11%
Caribou, ME	13%	Fargo, ND	14%
Concord, NH	15%	International Falls, MN	10%
Halifax, NS	18%	Kansas City, MO	25%
Hartford, CT	16%	Minneapolis, MN	15%
New York, NY	19%	North Omaha, NE	21%
Providence, RI	19%	Rapid City, SD	23%
Syracuse, NY	11%	St.Louis, MO	26%
Toronto, ON	18%		
		MOUNTAIN	
MIDDLE ATLANTIC		Billings, MT	23%
Baltimore, MD	24%	Casper, WY	29%
Newark, NJ	22%	Denver, CO	36%
Philadelphia, PA	22%	Eagle, CO	26%
Pittsburgh, PA	15%	Edmonton, AL	18%
Washington, DC	22%	Reno, NV	39%
Wilmington, DE	23%		
		NORTHWEST	
SOUTHEAST		Boise, ID	29%
Asheville, NC	31%	Portland, OR	25%
Louisville, KY	22%	Seattle, WA	24%
Roanoke, VA	29%	Vancouver, BC	24%
MIDWEST/GREAT LAKES		SOUTHWEST	
Chicago, IL	18%	Albuquerque, NM	44%
Cincinnati, OH	19%	Mt. Shasta, CA	30%
Cleveland, OH	14%	Prescott, AZ	45%
Detroit, MI	16%	Salt Lake City, UT	30%
Indianapolis, IN	18%		
Louisville, KY	22%		
Madison, WI	17%		

SERVICES

D3

Table 2. Purchased energy cost per million Btus

Energy Source	Efficiency	Dollars per Million Btu								
		5.00	7.50	10.00	12.50	15.00	20.00	30.00	40.00	50.00
		Dollar cost per hundred cubic feet (1 therm)								
Nat Gas	0.75	$ 0.38	$ 0.56	$ 0.75	$ 0.94	$ 1.13	$ 1.50	$ 2.25	$ 3.00	$ 3.75
	0.8	$ 0.40	$ 0.60	$ 0.80	$ 1.00	$ 1.20	$ 1.60	$ 2.40	$ 3.20	$ 4.00
	0.82	$ 0.41	$ 0.62	$ 0.82	$ 1.03	$ 1.23	$ 1.64	$ 2.46	$ 3.28	$ 4.10
	0.9	$ 0.45	$ 0.68	$ 0.90	$ 1.13	$ 1.35	$ 1.80	$ 2.70	$ 3.60	$ 4.50
		Dollar cost per gallon (93,000 Btu per gallon)								
Propane	0.75	$ 0.35	$ 0.52	$ 0.70	$ 0.87	$ 1.05	$ 1.40	$ 2.09	$ 2.79	$ 3.49
	0.8	$ 0.37	$ 0.56	$ 0.74	$ 0.93	$ 1.12	$ 1.49	$ 2.23	$ 2.98	$ 3.72
	0.82	$ 0.38	$ 0.57	$ 0.76	$ 0.95	$ 1.14	$ 1.53	$ 2.29	$ 3.05	$ 3.81
	0.9	$ 0.42	$ 0.63	$ 0.84	$ 1.05	$ 1.26	$ 1.67	$ 2.51	$ 3.35	$ 4.19
		Dollar cost per gallon (140,000 Btu per gallon)								
Oil	0.75	$ 0.53	$ 0.79	$ 1.05	$ 1.31	$ 1.58	$ 2.10	$ 3.15	$ 4.20	$ 5.25
	0.8	$ 0.56	$ 0.84	$ 1.12	$ 1.40	$ 1.68	$ 2.24	$ 3.36	$ 4.48	$ 5.60
	0.82	$ 0.57	$ 0.86	$ 1.15	$ 1.44	$ 1.72	$ 2.30	$ 3.44	$ 4.59	$ 5.74
	0.9	$ 0.63	$ 0.95	$ 1.26	$ 1.58	$ 1.89	$ 2.52	$ 3.78	$ 5.04	$ 6.30
		Dollar cost per cord (24 Million Btu per cord)								
Wood	0.6	72.00	108.00	144.00	180.00	216.00	288.00	432.00	576.00	720.00
		Cents per kilowatt hour								
Elec	100	1.71	2.56	3.41	4.27	5.12	6.83	10.24	13.65	17.07
		Cents per kilowatt hour								
Heat Pumps	1.5	2.56	3.84	5.12	6.40	7.68	10.24	15.36	20.48	25.60
(COP)	2	3.41	5.12	6.83	8.53	10.24	13.65	20.48	27.30	34.13
	2.5	4.27	6.40	8.53	10.67	12.80	17.07	25.60	34.13	42.66
	3	5.12	7.68	10.24	12.80	15.36	20.48	30.72	40.96	51.20
	3.5	5.97	8.96	11.95	14.93	17.92	23.89	35.84	47.78	59.73
	4	6.83	10.24	13.65	17.07	20.48	27.30	40.96	54.61	68.26

SERVICES

D3

Natural gas is purchased by the therm (100,000 Btu), the cubic foot (approximately 1030 Btu), or the CCF (100 cubic feet). As shown in Table 2, natural gas costing 80 cents a therm, and burned at an annual fuel utilization efficiency (AFUE) of 80% results in a delivered energy cost of $10 per million Btu. In rural locations where natural gas is not available, tanked propane can be used. However, propane comes at a higher cost and attention is needed to assure uninterrupted supply.

Electricity

Electric resistance heating has formidable advantages:

- it is quiet.

- at the house it is the cleanest of all the systems.

- eliminates the need for a heating unit, flue, large ducts or pipes.

- this results in a great reduction in installation cost.

- the ultimate in control when one thermostat is used per room .

The major disadvantage of electric resistance heating is its very high operating cost in most areas. For example, electricity costing 8 cents per kilowatt hour equates to a delivered energy cost of $23.44 per million Btu.

Electricity to power a heat pump in moderate climates (up to perhaps 4000 heating degree days) can be an attractive option because of the increased efficiency of operation (coefficient of performance or COP). Assuming a seasonal COP of 2.5, and a heating season electricity cost of 8 cents per kilowatt hour, equates to a delivered energy cost of $9.38 per million Btu. Noise can be a concern with heat pumps, since they do require an outdoor coil or unit packaged with a compressor.

Oil

Oil was once inexpensive and commonly chosen for home heating. This is no longer the case. Since the early 1970s, the price of oil has risen dramatically. Without a cost advantage, it is hard for oil to overcome these disadvantages:

- storage space requirements.

- delivery problems.

- a "dirty" fuel.

- environmental issues and regulations (underground tanks, *etc.*).

- additional maintenance.

For example, oil costing $1 a gallon, and burned at an 80% AFUE has a delivered energy cost of $8.93 per million Btu (see Table 2 and discussion below).

Other Fuels

The past few years have seen a remarkable resurgence in the use of wood for house heating and many of the new house designs are incorporating wood-burning equipment as a supplement to the normal heating equipment. Wood has these disadvantages:

- generates soot.

- requires a large storage area.

- Seasoned hardwoods must be burned to achieve any degree of efficiency.

- requires work and attention, but can be very economical if the wood is obtained for free.

Coal, once the most commonly used heating fuel, now has many distinct disadvantages for household use:

- it must be delivered.

- require a large storage area.

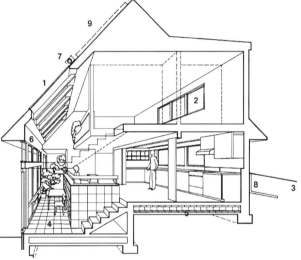

Fig. 4. Combination of passive solar, energy conservation and energy-efficient fuel system.

The design, built in various locations throughout North America, has been combined with electric, gas and oil fuel systems, in the latter case, utilizing the solar DHW as the auxiliary house heating system. Donald Watson, FAIA Architect.

1. skylight with movable shading cover.

2. dormer for cross ventilation.

3. earth berms on three sides.

4. tile floor and wall parapet for direct gain solar heat storage.

5. concrete masonry unit "heat storage" to provide solar heated   r a d i a t   floor.

6. insulating shades.

7. photovoltaic powered fan to recirculate indoor air during day l i g h t hours.

8. insulation outside of masonry foundation.

9. solar hot water system (DHW).

- ashes must be disposed.
- can burn dirty and even dangerously.

Energy Sources for Domestic Hot Water

Selecting an energy source for hot water is often pre-determined by how the house is heated. If a house is served by natural gas, then it is common to also have a natural gas domestic hot water heater. If gas is not available, then an electric water heater with a well insulated tank is the common choice. In warm climates, another option to consider is a heat pump hot water heater that extracts (and thus cools) heat from within the house to heat the water. Solar water heaters, use simple technology and are likely to continue as a viable option in the future.

Energy Sources for Mechanical Cooling

In many areas, the use of climate-sensitive design utilizing sun control, natural ventilation, landscaping, fans, and perhaps a few window units can eliminate the true "need" for central cooling. However, the "desire" for central cooling is ever increasing.

When houses are mechanically air conditioned (sensibly cooled), the primary energy source used by house-sized systems is electricity to drive a compressor. Very common is the coupling of a cooling coil with a warm air furnace and ducted distribution system. An option for houses in warm but dry climates are evaporative coolers ("swamp coolers") which use the "adiabatic" process to lower the dry-bulb temperature of house air while increasing the relative humidity.

Selection criteria

Climate

The colder the climate (as measured in heating degree days), the more important it is to select heating fuels that are relatively low in cost and to install high-efficiency heating system equipment.

Availability

Sometimes a regional issue affects choice. Availability will also be a function of a house's remoteness. For instance, houses in areas without natural gas pipelines must use another energy source such as propane.

Delivered Energy Cost

Table 2 provides the delivered energy cost for common energy sources. To use it all you need to know is the fuel type, its cost, and efficiency. Simple ratios can be used to modify the values shown. For example, oil costing $1 a gallon, and burned at an 80% AFUE has a delivered energy cost of $8.93 per million Btu. This value was quickly calculated by using the proper line and nearest value in the table ($1.12 a gallon equating to $10 per million Btu) and forming the ratio of $1/$1.12 X $10 = $8.93.

Reliability and Maintainability

Systems with few (if any) moving parts are most reliable, and require little maintenance. Electric resistance heat is such an energy source. Its use should be considered when permitted by code, in warm climates, and in areas with below-average electricity prices.

Other Factors

Central systems and packaged units provide automatic, thermostatic-controlled operation. Systems utilizing natural gas and electricity operate continuously and do not have to be monitored. Fuel choice has environmental impacts both at the house and upon society at large. For special applications, such as a weekend cottage, it may make sense to take advantage of the simplicity and dependability of electric resistance heat coupled with use of a wood stove. In all cases, combining climate design energy conservation and energy source/system, provides for optimal combinations that are most effective for long term vreliability and low energy/environmental impact.◗

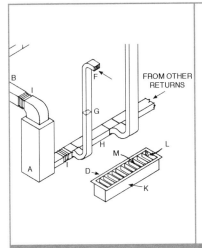

Heating and cooling of houses

Summary: A determination of heating and/or cooling system type must be made early in the design process for a house since the various types impact upon architectural needs differently. Most new houses use air systems for both heating and cooling and must provide space for distribution ducts. Hot water systems are more typically used in houses where only heating is provided and require relatively small pipes for distribution.

Key words: Baseboards, central cooling, electric resistance heat, geothermal heat pumps, heat pumps, warm air furnace.

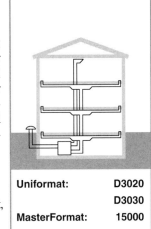

Uniformat:	D3020
	D3030
MasterFormat:	15000

System Selection

In the interest of energy efficiency and sustainability, the architect should begin with climate-sensitive design that takes advantage of passive solar heating and natural ventilation for cooling. Energy conservation measures (i.e, insulation thicknesses, types of windows, use of overhangs and other shading devices) should be evaluated to provide a house that can be naturally comfortable much of the time, without being overly dependent on energy-consuming mechanical systems. To the extent possible, conventional systems should be thought of as providing "supplemental" heating and cooling. The most common choices of supplemental heating and cooling systems include:

1. Heating with warm air using a furnace with ducted air supply for heat distribution. Most furnaces are fueled by natural gas or fuel oil (particularly in the Northeast). Propane is generally used for remote locations. The use of electric furnaces is limited to warm climates because of operational costs and code requirements. Systems with ducted air can also provide air conditioning when fitted with a cooling coil inside and condensing unit outside. The warm air furnace and cooling coil combination is the most common type of system now installed in new homes.

2. Heating by hot water using a boiler and terminal heaters (baseboard radiation). Such systems use small pipes usually 3/4" (2 cm) diameter for heat distribution at the house perimeter. If mechanical cooling is desired, individual window or through-the-wall units are typically used. These systems are generally installed in climates where the need for mechanically cooling is not overwhelming.

3. Electric resistance baseboard heat should be considered in warm climates where allowable by code and where electric charges are low. Cooling in houses with electric baseboard heating is normally provided by individual window or through-the-wall units.

4. In very hot climates it is common to have a central air conditioning system consisting of air handler and cooling coil (similar to a furnace), and ducted air supply system. The small amount of heat needed is normally provided by an electric resistance coil in the supply duct.

5. Heating and cooling can also be provided by a heat pump, either air-source or ground-source (see discussion on heat pumps below). When heat pumps are used in colder climates, back-up heat is normally needed to meet the heating load in the form of electric resistance heat or other means such as a hot water coil (heated by the domestic hot water heater). For this reason, and because of inefficient operation in cold climates, the use of heat pumps should be carefully considered in climates above about 4000 heating degree-days.

System Design

Following a decision about basic system category and fuel preference, there are options within each category. For a warm air system, type and location of the furnace are of prime importance. The distribution system can be one of many types, including a fully ducked installation, sub-slab perimeter duct, a trunk duct system in slab, etc. Several choices are offered in hot-water heating. Piping of the series-loop type or one-pipe circuits with special diverting fittings are possibilities. Terminal heating units can be convectors in cabinets or baseboard heaters. Electric resistance heating can utilize recessed wall units, electric baseboards, or radiant panels.

For residential installations, consulting engineer services are not always available. Designs can be made by an experienced architect, or sometimes by a heating and air conditioning contractor after consultation with the architect. However, the architect should be careful when using the services of a contractor, whose main goal is to provide a reliable, working system, not necessarily a properly sized or energy-efficient one. It is beyond the scope of this review to acquaint the designer with all the design choices available, the full design data needed to size components (ducts, pipes, fans and pumps), and the wide inventory of accessory components. Rather, the essence of system selections is given for the most common systems in modern practice.

Heating and Cooling by Air

Today's warm air furnace is part of a system that resembles a central station unit in large buildings. For basic warm air heating, the air (beginning with room return air) will travel a path similar to that shown in Fig. 1, and described as follows:

Author: William Bobenhausen

Credits: This article includes material from earlier editions of *Time-Saver Standards* by William J. McGuinness, McGuinness and Duncan, Consulting Engineers and August L. Hesselschwerdt, Jr., Professor of Mechanical Engineering, Massachusetts Institute of Technology.

References are listed at the end of this article.

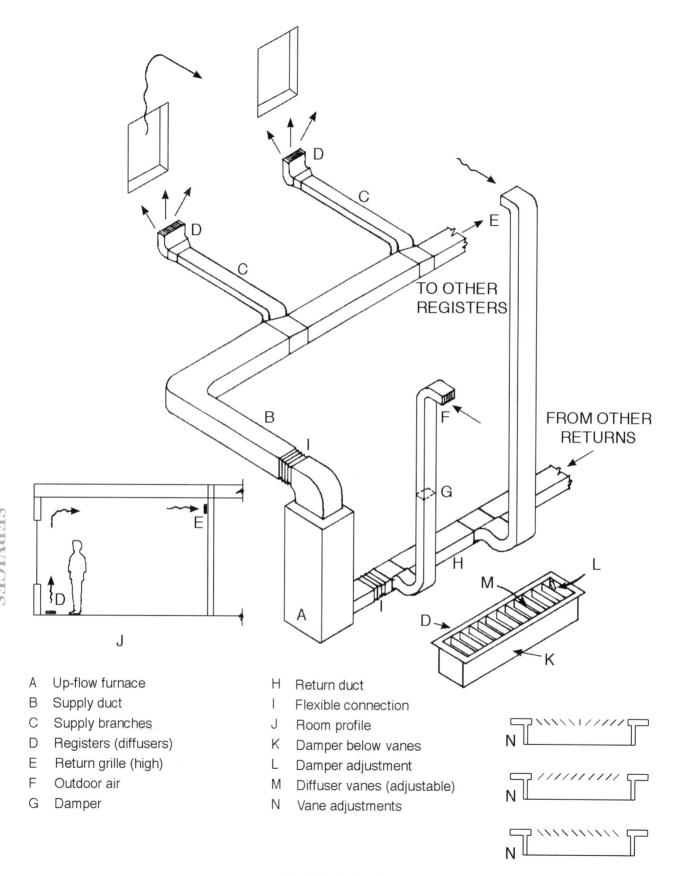

A	Up-flow furnace	H	Return duct
B	Supply duct	I	Flexible connection
C	Supply branches	J	Room profile
D	Registers (diffusers)	K	Damper below vanes
E	Return grille (high)	L	Damper adjustment
F	Outdoor air	M	Diffuser vanes (adjustable)
G	Damper	N	Vane adjustments

Fig. 1. Ducted system

SERVICES

D3

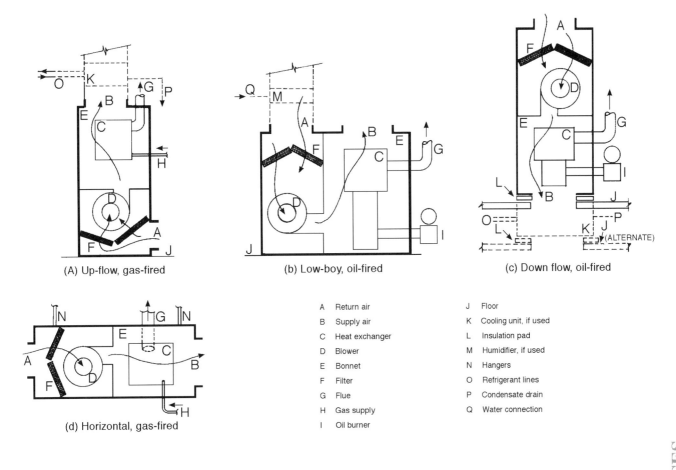

(A) Up-flow, gas-fired

(b) Low-boy, oil-fired

(c) Down flow, oil-fired

(d) Horizontal, gas-fired

A	Return air	J	Floor
B	Supply air	K	Cooling unit, if used
C	Heat exchanger	L	Insulation pad
D	Blower	M	Humidifier, if used
E	Bonnet	N	Hangers
F	Filter	O	Refrigerant lines
G	Flue	P	Condensate drain
H	Gas supply	Q	Water connection
I	Oil burner		

Fig. 2. Functional diagrams, typical warm air furnaces.

1. Return air after conditioning the room enters return grille(s) (Item E in Fig. 1), typically mounted high in heating only systems.

2. Return air is ducted to the furnace (H). Good practice includes an air inlet for outdoor air (F) feeding the return air supply. In houses with tight construction, such an air inlet may be required to maintain adequate indoor air quality.

3. After passing through a flexible duct connection (I) to minimize vibration noise, the return air passes over a filter (that needs periodic changing or cleaning) and enters the warm air furnace (A),in this case an up-flow model.

4. The furnace (A) contains either a burner and heat exchange chamber (in fossil fuel models), or a coil (in the case of electric furnaces). In any case the return air passes over a heated surface area and is warmed. A fan typically known as a "blower" propels the warmed air through the supply duct (B), joined again by a flexible

connection (I). In the case of combustion heating appliances, the combustion products must be vented (not shown).

5. The blower pushes warm air through the main supply duct (B) until individual supply branches (C) are encountered. Here the warm air is directed to registers (D) where the air is introduced into the room. Register details (D) include a damper to throttle air supply (K) including the adjustable lever (L). Vanes (N) also must be selected or adjusted to allow supply air to mix with the room air bcforc flowing to the return grilles (E).

Heating plant
Furnace types are shown in Fig. 2. Gas and oil firing are indicated at random because any of the models shown is available for either fuel. Electric central elements in the furnace may also supplant either fossil fuel for the heating phase of all-electric heating/cooling. The lowboy Fig. 2(b), is a traditional model that developed when basement headroom was limited and ductwork bulky. The upflow, type (a), is generally preferred.

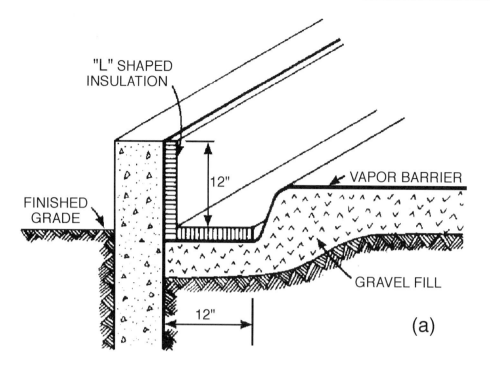

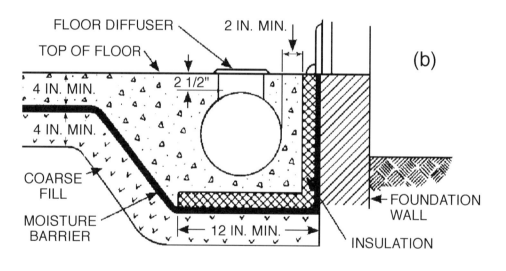

Fig. 3. Details at perimeter for below floor air distribution.

For subslab perimeter heating (loop perimeter air distribution system), the down-flow model (C) supplies air to feeder ducts either in a slab or crawl space.

For relatively small houses with no basements and with one living story an a concrete slab, a perimeter warm-air heating system is very effective. Partially radiant in its output through ducts that warm the slab, it has a fast response when heat is called for. Because of the partially radiant nature of this system, this method most often employs the principle of constant blower operation.

A vapor barrier and dry, well-drained earth are both important lest the heat be lost downward through fast-conducting wet soil or wet building components (Fig. 3a). Equally important is a 2 in. (5 cm) thickness of moisture-resistant rigid insulation placed as shown in Fig. 3b.

a) Dry earth needed below air ducts

b) Insulation to minimize loss of heat

In accordance with Federal law, conventional furnaces manufactured since 1992 must have a tested AFUE (Annual Fuel Utilization Efficiency) of at least 78%. Furnaces are typically available in the 78% to 84% range. These furnaces are known as "mid-efficiency" equipment and require a normal vent (chimney) to dispose of the hot (300F or above) combustion gases. High-efficiency furnaces with AFUE ratings of over 90% are also available. These units utilize additional heat exchange surface area to lower the combustion gases down to below 212F. The heated water vapor in the exhaust condenses, and gives back the approximately 1000 Btus per pound it took to produce it. Normally this heat goes up the chimney. With condensing appliances a chimney is not needed, just a small-diameter vent. Condens-

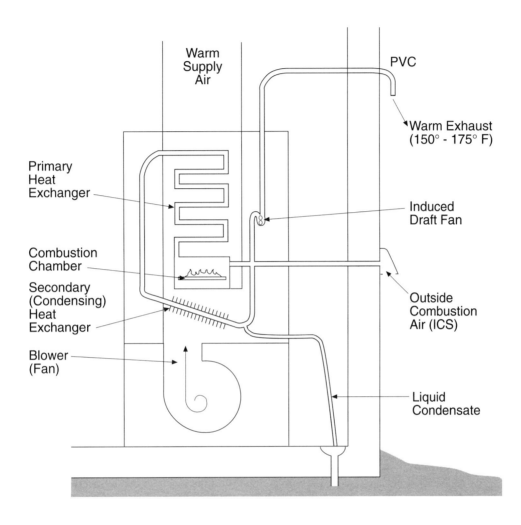

Fig. 4. Condensing warm air furnace for improved operational efficiency (AFUE). Note air intake for ICS (isolated combustion system).

ing furnaces cost more initially. However, they can be cost-effectively employed in very cold climates and as replacement equipment in houses with large heating loads (Fig.4) .

Older houses generally use the air in the space where they are installed for the combustion process. This practice can introduce potentially damaging chlorine-rich air (from laundry rooms) into the heat exchanger or even lead to incomplete combustion and the production of deadly carbon monoxide. Combustion air should be introduced directly from outside using an isolated combustion system (ICS) or "sealed combustion."

Easy access to all parts is essential for regular maintenance and repairs. Periodic cleaning or replacement of filters is important not only for cleanliness but to restore air flow that has been partially impeded by dust.

The Cooling Plant

More than 75% of new homes incorporate central air conditioning. However, in many areas, the use of climate-sensitive design utilizing sun control, natural ventilation, landscaping, and fans can eliminate this "need." Local mechanical cooling of one or more rooms in a house can also be accomplished by using individual window or through-the-wall units. A "ton" of air-conditioning capacity is the ability to remove 12,000 Btus per hour (Btu/h) of unwanted heat. Individual units are available that can remove from 3000 Btu/h (1/4 ton) to 18,000 Btu/h (1-1/2 tons).

The typical central air-conditioning system has components as shown in Fig. 5. The cooling coil (or "evaporator") is mounted in the ducted air stream, usually associated with the warm air furnace. Located nearby outside (within about 50 feet to minimize pipe friction losses;

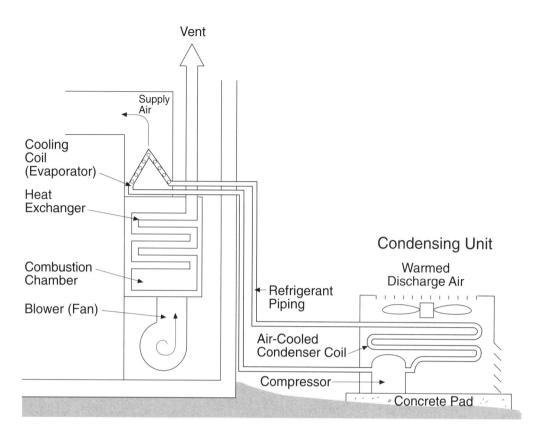

Fig. 5. Central air conditioning system

consult manufacturers' data) is the condensing unit containing the compressor and air-cooled condenser that rejects heat to the outside (See Fig. 5).

The term Energy Efficiency Ratio (EER) is used to measure the efficiency of refrigerators and window air-conditioning units. EER is the ratio of cooling capacity in Btus per hour divided by the electrical power input in watts at any given set of temperature rating conditions. EER values of 8.0 or more are typical.

More meaningful to overall performance and operational cost is the Seasonal Energy Efficiency Ratio (SEER) that reflects performance over the entire cooling season. Manufacturers must test their equipment in accordance with an ARI test method. Minimum SEER values of 10.0 are typical for split systems.

Ducts
Air conditioning includes heating, cooling, dehumidifying, humidifying or a combination. In an air system, the conditioned air is pushed through a system of ducts. These can be galvanized steel, aluminum, rigid fiberglass, or flexible mylar tubes. Ducts may be round, square, or rectangular. Excessive width-to-depth ratios of more than 3:1 should be avoided since they cause increased friction. Turns should be of generous radius to minimize friction. Joints between lengths of duct must be tight to minimize air leakage.

It is good practice to seal all junctions and transverse seams with metal surfaces rigid to prevent rattling. Metal ducts passing through unconditioned spaces (basements, garage, attic or crawl space) should be covered with 1-1/2 in. to 2 in. (3.7cm to 5cm) of insulation. If such ducts carry cool air through uncooled spaces a vapor barrier must be used on the exterior surface. Metal ducts in the vicinity of blowers are

sometimes' lined with acoustic material to reduce transmission of fan noise. The design size sets the dimensions of the inside of the lining. Rigid fiberglass ducts are effective for both thermal insulation and sound reduction.

Supply of warm air (cfm requirement)
The quantity of warm air needed to maintain comfortable conditions during the height of the winter depends upon the design heat loss for each room or space in the particular climatic location. The required warm air quantity that must be supplied in cubic feet per minute (cfm) is determined by the following equation:

$$cfm = \frac{Q_{tot}}{1.08 \times (T_s - T_i)}$$

where:

cfm   is the required supply air rate in cubic feet per minute needed by the room to maintain comfortable conditions during peak design periods

Q_{tot} is the total quantity of sensible heat needed by the space or zone being supplied, in Btu/h

1.08   is a constant used for heating design (based on the specific heat and density of air). Units are Btu.minute/deg. F.cubic foot.hour

T_s is the supply air temperature in degrees F

T_i is the inside design temperature for heating in degrees F

Preliminary Duct Sizing

Once the required air flow rate of a duct is known, the approximate duct size can also be determined for preliminary design purposes. For houses, the velocity of warm air at the beginning of the main supply duct is typically in the range of 750 to 1000 feet per minute (fpm).

As the air passes through the network of supply and branch ducts, and at the air outlet, friction is encountered that typically reduces the outlet velocity at the supply registers to 500 feet per minute or less. The area of supply ducts (in square inches) can be sized for preliminary design purposes by using the following equation:

$$A_{duct} = \frac{cfm \times 144}{V_{fpm}} \times FA$$

where:

A_{duct} is the required duct cross-sectional area in square inches

cfm   is the air flow rate in cubic feet per minute

144   is a conversion (144 square inches in 1 square foot)

Vfpm   is the air velocity in feet per minute

FA   is a friction allowance as follows: Use values of: 1.0 for round ducts; 1.10 for rectangular ducts where the depth to width ratio is up to 1:3 (recommended practice); 1.25 for thin rectangular ducts where the depth to width ratio is about 1:5.

Supply of Cool Air

The equation to determine the required quantity of cool air in cubic feet per minute (cfm) is determined by the following equation, which is very similar to the equation above for warm air:

$$cfm = \frac{Q_{tot}}{1.10 \times (T_i - T_s)}$$

Note that a slightly different air constant of 1.10 is used for cool air. The inside design temperature for cooling (T_i) is typically 78F to 80F. The supply air temperature (T_s) is typically about 55F.

Air Outlets and Returns

Supply air outlets deliver warm or cool air (known as primary air) to a room or space. This primary air induces some of the room air (known as "secondary air") to join in flow pattern that facilitates mixing. The quantity of secondary air induced by an air supply depends upon many factors (i.e., room geometry, outlet type, and cfm air flow). However, secondary air values of 10 to 20 times the amount of primary air are typical. Therefore, a supply air outlet which delivers 80 cfm of primary air will typically induce about 800 to 1600 cfm of secondary air to flow.

Warm air supply outlets are typically located in the floor below windows, although such placement is now less critical when high-performance low-e windows are used. Air distribution during the winter works well since the warm air is thrown up past windows to counter drafts from cold glass surfaces. The less dense warm air continues to rise and mixes with room air before flowing to returns typically located on interior partition walls (high locations are best).

For systems that provide both heating and cooling a low supply position is not optimum. During the cooling season, cool air will be denser than the room air and thus will stay low in the room and not mix well with the room air. In cooling climates, the solution is to use high wall outlets. For heating climates, the register and grille placement indicated in Fig. 1 is quite satisfactory.

For most flexibility, supply air outlets should have adjustable vanes or dampers to give the air a preferred direction. Return grilles typically need no directional air control. However, when more than one return air pickup position is called for, some designers feel that dampers at the grilles or in the branch ducts aid in system balancing.

Controls

Although it uses a relatively high amount of electricity, continuous operation of the blower at all times and in all seasons affords improved comfort, and improved indoor air quality (with proper filter maintenance). Assuming such a continuous air flow. the heating is activated when demanded by the thermostat, as does the operation of the cooling plant. A control in the bonnet of the furnace assures delivery of warm air at temperatures suitable for the rooms. Temperatures will be a little lower at the register than at the bonnet, which is usually about 140F.

Conventional furnace design typically affords two rates of air flow, one for heating and a higher one for cooling. The switch from heating air rate to cooling air rate is triggered by the thermostat when it is changed to a setting for cooling.

Heating by Hot Water

Heating by hot water is frequently an appropriate method in houses. Pipes are small and require little or no pitch. Heating elements, either convectors or baseboard, can be placed below windows or along exterior walls. Depending on the type of installation, adjustments of heat output in each room are possible, either by dampering the convected air flow at the heating unit, or by using thermostatic valves.

Boiler, tubing, and heating units are always completely water-filled. Air must be vented out, especially where it can accumulate at high points, Drains must permit emptying the system at all low points. Activated by an aquastat (which has a sensing element in the boiler-water), the fire (gas or oil) goes on whenever necessary to maintain the boiler at maximum design temperature at all times. Thus when the house thermostat calls for heat and turns on the circulating pump, there is minimal waiting time for heat to arrive. The typical temperature of circulating hot water is between about 180F and 200F. However, in some larger systems temperatures at or above 200F are used. Moreover, water will not boil even when exceeding 212F because the system is under greater than atmospheric pressure.

Prior to the energy crisis of 1973, it was common to oversize heating boilers so that they could double as a thermal source for heating domestic hot water. Such an approach is, however, very inefficient in the summer, and thus not allowed under many current energy codes.

Heating Plant and Accessories

In the closed system scheme there is very little loss of water. Water is added automatically whenever the pressure in the system drops below 12 psi. The street pressure in the cold-water main, often about 50 psi, will cause water to flow into the system. An expansion tank cushions the expansion of the system water with rises in temperature. An air purger and automatic vent isolate and expel any air bubbles trapped in the circulating hot water (see Fig. 6 on next page).

Circulation through the heating system is controlled by a small horse-power circulating pump and the flow control valve, which closes against gravity flow when the pump stops. The pressure relief valve,

SERVICES

D3

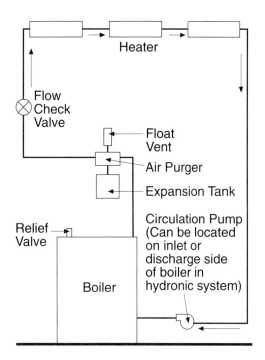

Fig 6. Basic components of a hot water heating system.

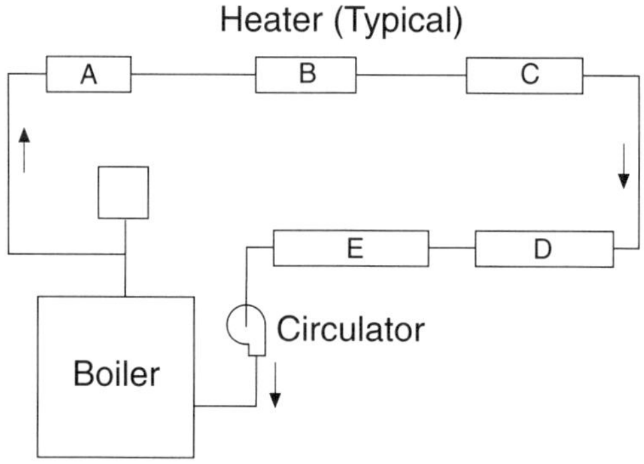

Fig. 7. Series loop piping arrangement.

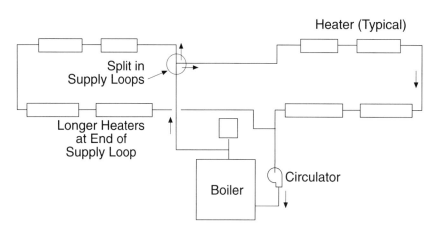

Fig. 8. Split series loop piping arrangement.

which operates only in an emergency, must always sense system pressure. There must be no valve between it and the boiler.

One-pipe systems

The simplest type of residential hot water heating system is a "series loop." Water travels from the boiler, goes through heaters (often baseboard radiation), and the temperature of the supply water decreases. Therefore, the size of heaters has to increase further down the line in order to provide the same heat output (heater E larger than heater D which is larger than heater C) (Fig. 7).

Most small residential hot water heating systems use 3/4 in. (2cm) piping that has a limitation of delivering about 45,000 Btu/h per circuit based upon a 20F temperature drop. Such an amount of heat loss is fairly small, and less than that of many houses. One easy remedy is use of a split series loop (Fig. 8).

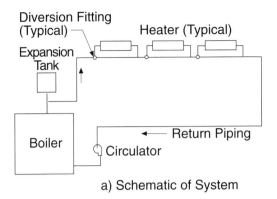

a) Schematic of System

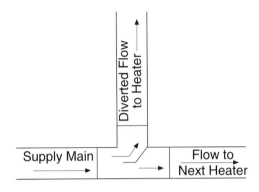

b) Detail of a Common Type of Diversion Fitting

Fig. 9. One-pipe "mono-flow" systems

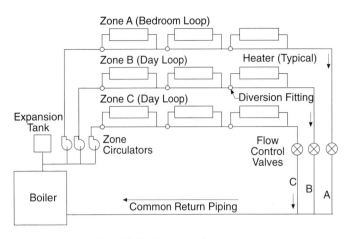

Fig. 10. Zoning of series loops

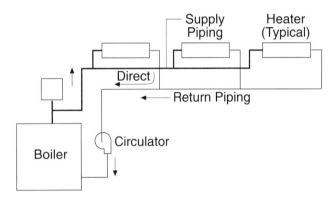

Fig. 11. Two-pipe direct return piping arrangement

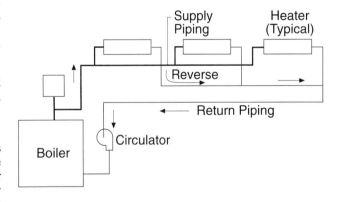

Fig. 12. Two-pipe reverse return piping

The biggest disadvantage of simple series loops is that individual temperature control of heaters is not possible. The simple remedy is to use a one-pipe "monoflow" type of system where the individual baseboard heaters are tapped off the water loop by special diversion fittings to facilitate flow (Fig. 9a & b).

In many houses, several series loops are run to provide for the zoned needs of a house (perhaps two "daytime loops" and one "bedroom loop") (Fig. 10).

Two-Pipe Systems
One-pipe systems are limited since the supply water temperature is increasingly lowered as more heaters are encountered. A separate pipe to return the water to the boiler after it has passed through a heater overcomes this problem. Two common piping arrangement are widely utilized: direct return and reverse return. The two-pipe direct return system saves on piping, but can be hard to balance on large systems (Fig. 11). Because the distance the water travels (and thus the amount of friction encountered) is different through each heater.

The simplest way to equalize pipe friction is to employ a two-pipe reverse return system where the length of travel through each heater is nearly identical. In larger commercial scale hot water heating systems balancing valves or orifice plates are used to equalize resistance.

SERVICES

D3

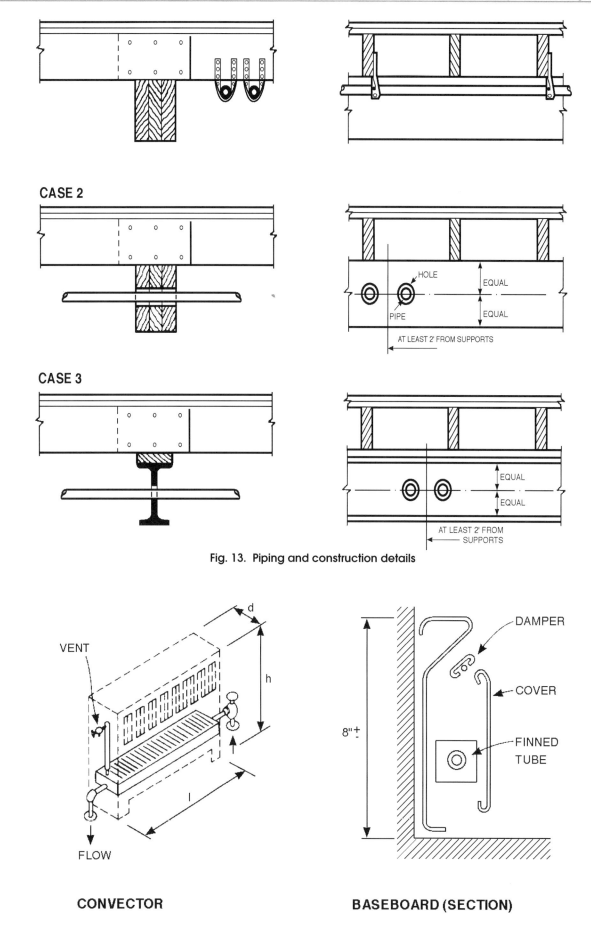

CASE 2

CASE 3

HOLE

EQUAL

EQUAL

PIPE

AT LEAST 2' FROM SUPPORTS

EQUAL

EQUAL

AT LEAST 2' FROM SUPPORTS

Fig. 13. Piping and construction details

VENT

d

h

l

FLOW

DAMPER

COVER

FINNED TUBE

8"±

CONVECTOR

BASEBOARD (SECTION)

Fig. 14. Terminal heating devices in hot water systems

SERVICES

D3

Piping and Construction Details

Copper tubing and "sweat fittings" are the most commonly used materials. Slope, once important to enhance gravity flow, is now unnecessary. A slight gradient for drainage is sometimes be used, but actually systems are seldom drained since houses are not often left unoccupied during freezing weather. Small amounts of residual water in level tubing can be "blown" out. Pipe insulation should be provided as required by the applicable energy code.

Expansion of pipe can be a problem, especially in large systems. Since copper expands considerably more than steel under the same temperature change, expansion fittings or loops are necessary on long straight runs. Copper tubing can be imbedded in concrete when necessary. The stresses set up by the restrained expansion can be taken by tubing and fittings.

Convectors and Baseboards

Heating elements of copper tubing with fins of copper or aluminum are the most commonly used. With regard to convectors (Fig. 14), the length width, and height of the convector and its cabinet also affect the output. There is a wide choice of size combinations in convectors. Manufacturer's literature and ratings should be consulted.

Baseboards are rated in Btu/h per linear foot for a given temperature with residential types not varying greatly. Table 1 is representative of typically available units, but the manufacturer's catalogs should be consulted.

Table 1. Typical residential baseboard radiation (output at 1 gpm water flow rate)

Average Water Temperature (degrees F)	Rated Output (Btu/h)
220	840
215	810
210	770
200	710
190	640
180	580
170	510
160	450

Example: Select a boiler and design the length of baseboard radiation needed for each room in the house shown (Fig. 15). The average water temperature in the baseboards will be 180F and the temperature drop will be 20F.

From Table 1, the approximate heat output per linear foot will be 580 Btu/h. Therefore, required baseboard heater lengths are computed as follows:

Space	Heat loss Btu/h	Computed Length (Feet)	Feet to Use
Living Room	12,000	20.7	21
BR 1	7,000	12.1	12
BR 2	5,200	8.9	9
Bath	1,800	3.1	3
Dining Room	2,700	4.7	5
Kitchen	4,000	6.9	7
Total	32,700		57

Tests and Maintenance

All piped systems containing fluids need to be tested. They should be put under a pressure in excess of contemplated operating pressure but well within the ultimate rating of the tube for a period of 24 hours or more. Aside from attention to the burner, hot-water systems need very little maintenance. It is important not to drain and refill the system periodically. After a short time the water, continuously circulated in

the tubing, becomes inert chemically and will not corrode metal. Added water always contains entrained air and corrosive compounds. The air that is thus brought in could also cause air binding in the vicinity of a clogged air vent.

Electric Heating Systems

Resistance Heat

While well-designed warm-air and hot-water heating systems are often comparable to each other in installation cost, both are more expensive to install than electric resistance heat. Another asset of electric heating is that every room can be a separately controlled zone; a thermostat at each wall switch can be set to control the temperature in that room.

The factor that precludes the wide-scale use of electric resistance heat is its cost. Moreover, due to its overall inefficiency (electrical generation and transmission losses) its use in new houses is not allowed by many codes. In warm climates where heating needs are very small and occasional, electric heat remains a viable option. However, like hot-water heating, electric resistance units are not suitable for controlling air circulation, humidity, and cooling, which must be provided separately.

Electric Heat Pumps

The high cost of electricity can be overcome to a degree by using heat pump technology. Heat pumps are units that use a compression refrigeration cycle to provide either heating or cooling of a house. The two commonly used types are "air-source" heat pumps (Fig. 15) and "geothermal" heat pumps (Fig 16). The source is where (either the air or ground) heat is extracted from in the winter. The source also acts as the "sink" into which heat is pumped during the summer.

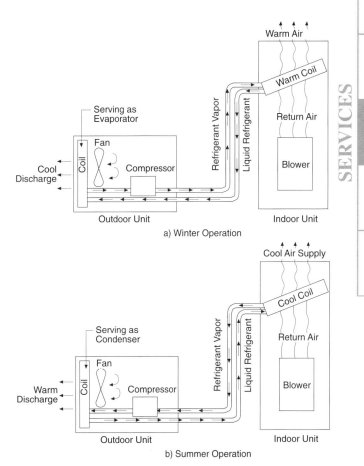

a) Winter Operation

b) Summer Operation

Fig. 15. Air-source heat pumps: indoor and outdoor units and their seasonal operation

Heat pump performance is measured by the ratio of energy output to work input (electricity into the compressor). This term is known as the coefficient of performance (COP). Heating season heat pump performance varies based upon the source temperature. Table 2 provides an example of typical air-to-air heat pump COPs at various outdoor air temperatures.

Table 2. Illustrative air-source heat pump COPs - heating mode - indoor temperature 70F

Outside Temp. (Degrees F)	COP
-13	1.05
-8	1.30
-3	1.55
2	1.80
7	2.00
12	2.20
17	2.40
22	2.60
27	2.75
32	2.90
37	3.00
42	3.10
47	3.15
52	3.20
57	3.25
62	3.30

Table 2 illustrates that at low temperatures the COP approaches 1.0, which equates to the same cost of operation as electric resistance heat. Electrical energy is also expended at low temperatures to defrost the cold coil outside that is functioning as the evaporator (of the refrigerant). More meaningful than an individual COP for a specific temperature is the overall heating season performance at various temperatures and including supplemental heat and cycling (on/off). The factor used to represent this is known as the Heating Seasonal Performance Factor (HSPF). Manufacturers must test and publish HSPF for their equipment in accordance with an ARI test method that assumes a climate with approximately 5800 heating degree days. Such a climate may also be thought of as the extreme limit to consider using air-to-air heat pumps. In colder climates, the COP will often be low and operational cost unacceptably high.◗

References

ASHRAE. 1993. *Handbook of Fundamentals*. Atlanta, GA: American Society of Heating, Refrigerating & Air-Conditioning Engineers.

Bobenhausen, William. 1994. *Simplified Design of HVAC Systems*. New York: John Wiley & Sons.

Bradshaw, Vaughn. 1995. *Building Control Systems*. New York: John Wiley & Sons.

HVAC Systems Applications. 1996. Vienna, VA: Sheet Metal and Air Conditioning Contractors National Association.

Monger, Samuel C. 1992. *HVAC Systems Operation, Maintenance, & Optimization*. Englewood Cliffs, NJ: Prentice Hall.

Rowe, William H. 1988. *HVAC Design Criteria, Options, Selections*. Kingston, MA: R.S. Means Company, Inc.

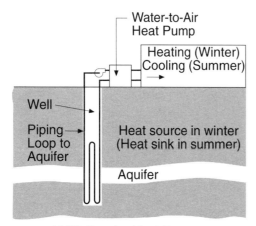

a) Ground-source Heat Pump

b) Well-water Heat Pump

Fig. 16. Types of geothermal heat pumps

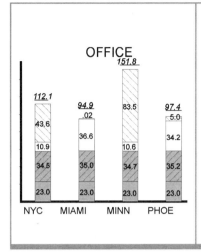

OFFICE

NYC 112.1 — 43.6 / 10.9 / 34.5 / 23.0

MIAMI 94.9 — .02 / 36.6 / 35.0 / 23.0

MINN 151.8 — 83.5 / 10.6 / 34.7 / 23.0

PHOE 97.4 — 5.0 / 34.2 / 35.2 / 23.0

Energy sources for commercial buildings

Summary: Most commercial building types use a large amount of electricity, which is usually relatively expensive to purchase, especially when high peak demand charges also exist. Opportunities to reduce operational costs are many, including conventional conservation strategies (e.g., careful glazing selection, insulation, high-efficiency HVAC equipment). Also to be considered is the use of daylight, ice storage, steam for heating and cooling (when available), and photovoltaics (when feasible).

Key words: balance point, energy demand, ground-coupling, ice storage, internal heat gains, peak demand, refrigerants.

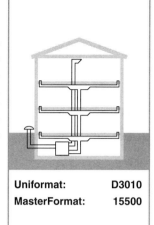

| Uniformat: | D3010 |
| MasterFormat: | 15500 |

How energy is used

While most of the energy used by a typical American house is in direct response to the climate with heating energy being the major energy source used in most areas, in other building types energy use will vary greatly depending upon many factors, including building type and schedule of operation.

Fig. 1 illustrates the approximate energy use of different building types in four distinct climates: New York (temperate), Miami (hot and humid), Minneapolis (cold), and Phoenix (hot and dry). In each case, "typically-built" (in general accordance with applicable codes and conventional practice) 10,000-square-foot buildings were modeled with a length to width aspect ratio of 1.5:1. The performance levels shown can generally be improved by 30% or more in a cost-effective fashion. Results are for "at the site" energy use and do not include the significant energy losses associated with production and transmission of electricity.

The comparative energy results suggest that an important energy source for most types of commercial buildings is electricity. This is because commercial buildings use so much of it for lighting, cooling, fans, office equipment, elevators, and pump motors. Moreover, electricity is almost always the most expensive energy form used in buildings (see Purchased energy cost per million Btus in "Energy sources for houses") even without giving consideration to peak demand charges.

The best decision to make regarding energy is to reduce loads and consumption first. Energy codes and standards such as ASHRAE 90.1 (Energy Efficient Design of New Buildings Except Low-Rise Residential Buildings) provide designers with the basic elements to achieve satisfactory levels of energy efficiency. They recommend:

- specific levels of insulation
- performance factors for glazing
- minimum equipment efficiency ratings

Optimized energy-conserving buildings use codes and standards as a "base case" starting point, and include other options to further reduce energy use cost-effectively. If these measures are evaluated early during design development, heating and cooling loads can be reduced substantially and smaller capacity, less-costly equipment installed.

Electrical peak demand

Utility companies must be able to satisfy the "demands" of their customer base for electricity year-round. These demands, however, often vary greatly, mostly due to climate. Most utilities are "summer peaking" due to the heavy use of mechanical cooling equipment. Some utilities have summer peaks 25% or more above their winter peaks. This leads to generation capacity needed during the summer but expensively idle for much of the year.

To recoup costs, utilities typically charge their commercial customers for their highest metered demand for electricity (in kilowatts or "KW") within blocks of time (usually 15 or 30 minutes). Peak electrical demand changes month-to-month, as illustrated below for a small office building in Minneapolis.

During the 1980s and early- to mid-1990s, utilities have sought to level their peak demand load profiles over the course of the year so that there is less cycling (turning on and off) of power plants, and more efficient and less costly generation of electricity. To help achieve this, dollar incentives (e.g., $X per compact fluorescent lamp, or $Y per ton of absorption cooling) have often been offered to commercial customers as part of a demand side management (DSM) program.

The future for electric utilities is now less clear. Impending legislation may deregulate segments of the electric supply industry and open up many new opportunities for both utilities and entrepreneurs alike. The era of "virtual utilities" is upon us where suppliers of electricity may not either actually generate or delivery it. Instead they purchase it from a generation company and distribute it through the established electrical grid for a fee.

Heating energy sources

Heat gains from building occupants, lights, and office equipment are significant in most commercial building types. As a result, many commercial building types do not need heat from their mechanical heating systems when occupied unless the outside air temperature is quite low, sometimes 30F or lower.

This temperature, at which the internal heat gains are no longer capable of maintaining comfortable conditions inside a building (Fig. 3), is known as the "heating balance point." While the mathematical aver-

Author: William Bobenhausen

References: Berger, Horst. *Light Structures, Structures of Light.* Boston: Birkhauser, 1996.

Lam, M. C. William. *Sunlighting as Formgiver for Architecture.* New York: Van Nostrand Reinhold, 1986.

Renewable Energy Information. National Renewable Energy Laboratory (NREL), Golden, CO.

Strong, Steven. *The Solar Electric House.* Emmaus, PA: Rodale Press, 1985.

SERVICES

D3

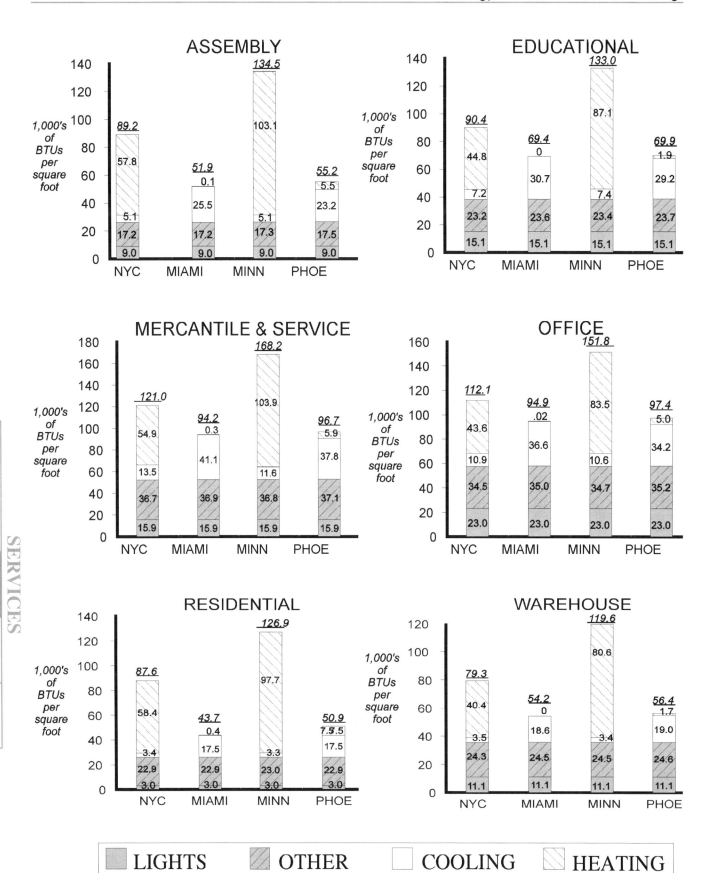

Fig. 1. Typical On-site Building Energy Use for Various Building Types in Four Representative Climates.

(All building types are two-stories in height, except warehouses [1 story] and residential [3 stories]) Note: These results were obtained through use of Version 1.0 of the ENERGY-10 Windows-based software developed by the National Renewable Energy Laboratory using all the default values that come prepackaged with the program. These defaults are based on "average" construction and operational practices, and the results are only intended for broad, comparative use.

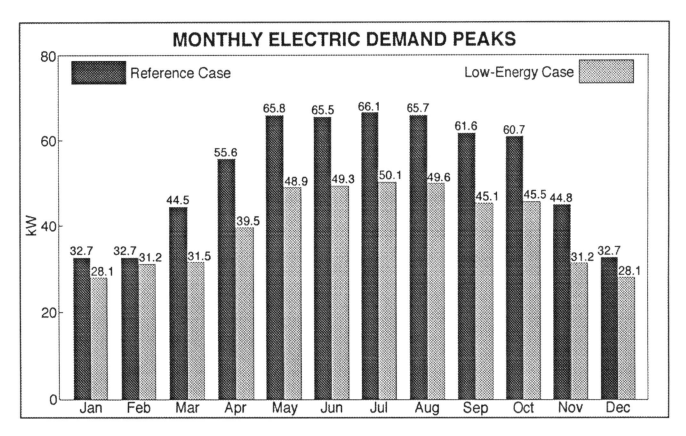

Fig. 2. Monthly electric demand peaks for a typical 10,000-square-foot office building in Minneapolis, MN (as modeled by ENERGY-10 software using all default values for typical construction)

age balance point for a building can be computed, a more realistic representation is depicted in Fig. 3 showing different balance points for the five principal thermal zones of a two-story building.

Two observations are critical here:

- the balance points are higher in the north zones since solar heat will not arrive through these windows during the heating season.
- the heating balance point for the second (top) floor is higher than the first floor because of heat loss through the roof.

In many commercial building types, the application of passive solar space heating is much more limited than in houses. This is because of:

- the high intensity of internal heat gains (as just discussed).
- objectionable glare from direct solar rays.
- the reduced number of hours that the building needs to be heated.

Still, the potential for solar heating design should be considered for every compatible building type (e.g., warehouses) or for parts of buildings (e.g., lobbies and circulation spaces).

Supplemental heat is needed in most climates on cold days and when buildings are unoccupied (typically with the temperature set back to 50F or 55F). Many of the basic systems and energy choices are similar to those available for houses, but with the following additional issues:

Natural gas
The natural gas pipeline system has a finite capacity. During very cold weather, natural gas suppliers may be unable to meet the complete demands of all their large customers. To address this issue, suppliers are beginning to sell "interruptible gas" at a very attractive rate

Second (Top) Floor

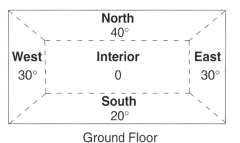

Ground Floor

Fig. 3. Representative heating balance points for a two-story office building

with the understanding that whenever the outdoor temperature reaches a certain level (perhaps 15F), commercial customers will switch to an alternate heating fuel (usually oil, with a reasonable supply stored in a tank awaiting such contingency). This requires a "dual-fuel" boiler or furnace.

Steam

A by-product of electricity generation is waste heat. Often (and in particular in the older cities) this heat is used to produce steam that is available for purchase. When purchased steam is used for heating, it generally comes into the building as steam and enters a heat exchanger (known as a converter) where it condenses and transfers the heat to hot water which is then circulated. Purchased steam can also be used for cooling (see below).

Ground-coupling

At a depth of about 20' (6m) the soil temperature remains relatively constant, about equal to the average annual outdoor air temperature in the area (*e.g.*, 52F in New York, 77F in Miami; see Fig. 4). Heat pump systems can make use of this earth temperature to efficient advantage in providing heating and cooling. Also known as "geothermal heat pumps," these systems have grown widely in popularity.

Cooling Energy

Compressor driven

Most building cooling equipment employs a vapor compression cycle powered by electricity. Two basic approaches are used:

- Direct expansion (DX) equipment directly cools the air that passes over the cooling coil (evaporator).

- Larger equipment produces chilled water, which is then piped to equipment (generally air handlers or perimeter fan-coil units).

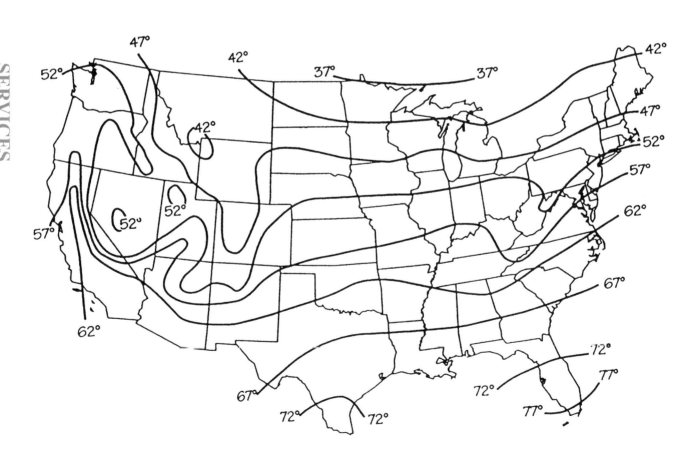

Fig. 4. Deep earth temperatures below the ground (20 ft. or more)

Also available is natural gas-powered compressor-driven DX equipment which is very well suited for areas with high electrical peak demand charges.

Refrigerants

Although technically not an energy source, refrigerants are vital to the operation of compressor-driven cooling equipment. The historically common refrigerants known as "freon" were actually chlorofluorocarbons (CFCs) now generally accepted as being damaging to earth's ozone layer. The US and most of the countries of the world have agreed (Montreal Protocol, 1987) to eliminate CFC production by 2000. Replacement refrigerants that either contain no chlorine, or are unstable so that they won't rise to the ozone layer have been and continue to be developed. Some of the replacements developed so far do not provide the same efficiency of cooling. Others may contribute to global warming, another potential atmospheric problem.

Absorption cooling

This cooling cycle uses various chambers to produce a cooling effect without a compressor. In one chamber, a salt solution absorbs water and in the process creates chilled water in another chamber. The salt solution must then be heated (often by purchased steam) to dry it out so that it can continue to function.

Ice storage

Chillers in large buildings are generally operated to satisfy cooling loads as they occur. This requires the installation of a large chiller that is only needed at the height of the summer.

Another approach is to produce a large amount of ice during overnight hours when "off-peak" electricity is available. When peaks occur during the day, the ice is melted to produce chilled water. On a larger scale a similar approach is being used in downtown Chicago where they have developed an ice-storage cooling district.

Renewable energy sources

Daylighting

Typically a third or more of the operational cost of most commercial building types is electricity for lighting. Across the country the majority of these buildings are one-story, thus the entire building floor area has the potential of being daylit by skylights or roof monitors.

For taller buildings, areas near the window wall within about 15' (4.5m) often receive daylight that can displace a significant portion of the artificial lighting energy in the area (see Fig. 5). To accomplish this, lighting fixtures need to be circuited in zones parallel to the window wall and equipped with sensors and automatic dimming controls.

The perimeter and interior courtyards serve to dramatically increase the percentage of floor area daylit and increase electrical lighting savings.

Daylighting is perhaps the most important design issue for commercial buildings, and can:

- enliven spaces.
- improve space enjoyment.
- improve productivity.
- save electrical energy by displacing artificial lights.
- reduce cooling loads.

Photovoltaics

Photovoltaic panels (also known as "solar cells") use a semiconductor material to create a flow of electrons when hit by sunlight. These panels are made of thin films of various materials including crystalline silicon, cadmium sulfide, gallium arsenide, and cadmium telluride.

Compact Building Form
Perimeter Area = 26%
Interior Area = 74%

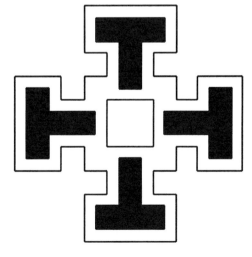

Extended Building Form
with Courtyard
Perimeter Area = 62%
Interior Area = 38%

Fig. 5. Daylighting potential for perimeter floor area (typically within 15 ft. of windows)

Continued research and competing technologies have led to great improvements in efficiency and reductions in manufacturing costs. More than 80 megawatts of photovoltaic modules were manufactured worldwide in 1995. An area of application for architects is the emerging use of solar cells as an integral part of the building envelope (particularly the roof).

Wind

Windpower continues to be used to pump water for farms and industrial purposes. The amount of energy produced by a wind turbine depends upon wind speed and the diameter of the rotor. Good sites for wind turbines should have average annual wind speeds of 12 miles per hour or greater.

Today, wind turbines have their greatest applications in large wind farms away from populated buildings. Wind farms consist of hundreds or even thousands of large machines, generating significant amounts of direct current electricity which is then converted to alternating current electricity by a "synchronous inverter" and fed into the grid. In 1996 approximately 3 billion kilowatt hours of electricity were produced by wind power in the U.S. Wind turbines are non-polluting.

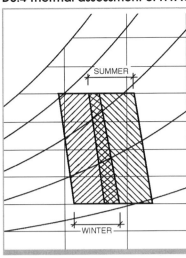

Thermal assessment of HVAC design

Summary: The physiology of human comfort is reviewed, from the point of view thermodynamic heat exchange with the environment, which is the basis of heating, ventilation and air-conditioning (HVAC) design principles. A method is described for assessing the thermal loads of non-residential buildings for preliminary design purposes.

Key words: building thermal loads, heat gains and losses, mean radiant temperature, psychrometric chart.

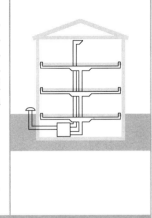

1 Thermal comfort

1.1 Human physiology

The human body is exceptionally versatile in its heat transfer capacity. We exchange heat with our environment through convection, conduction, radiation and evaporation. On average, convection accounts for 40% of total heat transferred, evaporation about 20%, radiation about 40% and conduction very little. Fig. 1 shows how dramatically this proportioning changes as a function of dry bulb temperature. The methods of heat transfer also change dramatically with varying metabolic rate. In addition to large variations in environment and metabolism, there is considerable variability among people. We are not alike "thermally" any more than we are alike otherwise.

Metabolic rate

Technically the metabolic rate is the rate at which the body metabolizes (converts) food into heat energy. For HVAC design considerations, however, we are most interested in the heat rejected from the body as a result of that metabolism. Numerous characteristics influence body metabolism such as age, health, body weight, and genetics. These characteristics tend to be specific to individuals. But because buildings are rarely designed for a specific individual, these characteristics have been averaged and typically relate varying metabolic rate to one dominant characteristic; physical activity. There is a convention used for metabolic rate. Table 1 shows the average metabolic rate (in terms of heat rejection) for various activities. The unit "met" is defined as 58.2 W/m^2 or 18.4 Btuh/ft^2. The average adult male has 21.7 ft^2 of surface area, thus one met unit results in 400 Btu per person.

Thermal stress

The body is continually modifying its metabolism and heat transfer with the environment to achieve comfort. While it is commonly assumed that thermal comfort is the absence of thermal stress, this is not the case. The following classical equation will help explain thermal stress:

$$M \neq R \neq C - E = \neq S \ (W/m^2)$$

where M is the net metabolic rate, R, C and E are radiation, convection and evaporative heat transfers respectively and S is storage in the body tissues. If S is zero, there is little thermal stress, thus if R, C and E negate M, there will be no residual heat (or cold) to store in body tissue. If the body is experiencing a cold environment and the net of R, C and E is greater than M, the metabolic rate can usually increase to achieve a balance and no thermal stress occurs. In extreme cold, if increasing metabolic rate cannot offset R, C and E, stress will occur and tissue temperature will store the difference (in this case becoming colder). Thermal comfort is not achieved. Even if the cold is not so extreme, an extraordinary increase in metabolism to achieve comfort will be seen as stress even though comfort is achieved.

With heat, however, the converse is not true. Metabolic rate cannot be reduced below about 0.8 mets. If R and C are both positive, increasing the perspiration rate is increasingly inefficient in heat transfer and comfort cannot be achieved. Body tissue temperatures begin to rise and thermal stress increases. Because extreme cold is infrequently experienced and the response is relatively simple and linear, we rarely associate thermal stress with cold environments. Thermal stress is almost always discussed as an overheating condition, i.e., "heat stress."

The body has a need to maintain "homeothermy," a constant deep body temperature. Shallow body and skin temperatures vary considerably from deep body temperature. Skin temperature at the extremities can be as low as 84.5F (12.5°C) and average skin temperature can vary from 88F to 92F (31°C to 33°C). Since this is the temperature at which heat transfer occurs, not 98.6F (37°C), HVAC system designers must be cognizant of this condition. For example; skin temperature drops considerably with age as a result of reduced capillary circulation at the skin surface. Because radiation heat exchange is a function of the fourth power of the two surfaces, radiant heating may be a

Authors: Richard Rittelmann, FAIA and John Holton, P.E., RA

References: ACCA (1986). *Manual J Load Calculation for Residential Winter and Summer Air-Conditioning.* Washington, DC: Air Conditioning Contractors of America.

ASHRAE. 1993. *ASHRAE Handbook of Fundamentals.* Atlanta, GA: American Society of Heating, Refrigerating and Air-Conditioning Engineers.

ASHRAE. 1989. *Standard 62-1989.* "Ventilation for Acceptable Indoor Air Quality." Atlanta, GA: American Society of Heating, Refrigerating and Air-Conditioning Engineers**.**

Egan, M. David. 1975. *Concepts in Thermal Comfort.* Englewood Cliffs, NJ: Prentice Hall.

Fanger, P. O. 1972. *Thermal Comfort.* New York: McGraw-Hill.

Olgyay, Victor. 1963. *Design with Climate: Bioclimatic Approach to Architectural Regionalism.* Princeton: Princeton University Press.

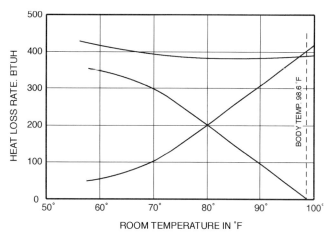

Fig. 1. Heat dissipated by a person at rest

much more effective heating technique for the elderly than raising the air temperature as is more commonly done.

The maintenance of human homeothermy is a function of two personal and four atmospheric parameters:

- metabolic rate
- clothing insulation
- air temperature
- radiant temperature of surroundings
- rate of air movement
- atmospheric humidity

In nonresidential indoor environments, it is never necessary to heat the human body (except in extreme cases of hypothermia). The principal objective of the architect and engineer in commercial building design is to create an environment to which the human body can comfortably reject heat. All too often this objective is forgotten.

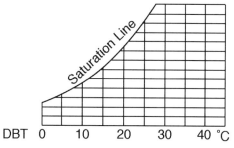

Fig. 3. Psychrometic chart indicating Dry Bulb temperature grid

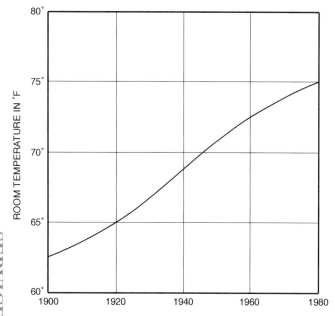

Fig. 2. Historic indoor design temperatures, compiled from Houghton & Yeglou (1923), ASHRAE and Kansas State (1950) and R. G. Nevins et. al. (1961).

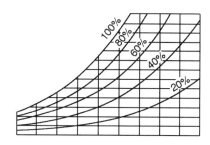

Fig. 4. Psychrometic chart indicating relative humidity (RH) curves

Table 1. Metabolic rates for various activities

Task	Metabolic rate (Met units)	W/m^2	Total Btuh/ person	Latent Heat Btuh/person	Sensible Heat Btuh/person
Reclining	0.8	46.6	320	140	180
Seated quietly	1.0	58.2	400	155	245
Sedentary activity (office, school)	1.2	69.8	480	220	260
Standing relaxed	1.2	69.8	480	240	240
Light activity (shopping, light work)	1.6	93.1	640	350	290
Walking	1.9	109	750	450	300
Medium activity (standing, shop work, domestic work)	2.0	116.5	800	480	320
Heavy activity (shop, garage work)	3.0	175	1200	800	400
Bowling	3.6	211	1450	870	580
Walking up stairs	11.0	640	4400	3000	1400

SERVICES

D3

1.2 Comfort measures

Air temperature

The most prevalent method of describing the thermal environment is dry bulb air temperature. This is not unexpected as air temperature is the single most influential characteristic of thermal comfort. We have traditionally expressed comfort in terms of dry bulb temperature as the basis for system control. Fig. 2 documents recommended dry bulb design temperatures over time. It can be seen that preferred design temperatures have increased significantly over time. It is important to note, however, that history notwithstanding, dry bulb temperature is inadequate to fully describe comfort conditions. The psychrometric chart is the classic graphical method to portray all of the variables of the air environment. Fig. 3 depicts a simplified psychrometric chart with only the grid for dry bulb temperature.

Relative humidity

Nearly as important as dry bulb temperature in determining comfort is the relative humidity. In its simplest term, humidity is an indication of the amount of moisture in the air. Relative humidity (RH) is the amount of moisture in the air relative to the total amount of moisture the air is capable of containing at that dry bulb temperature. While relative humidity is the most frequent indicator of moisture content for thermal comfort purposes, absolute humidity (a measure of the grains of moisture in a pound of air) is also frequently used in the calculation of latent heat removal or extraction. Relative humidity will determine the extent to which evaporation will be effective as a heat transfer technique. The higher the relative humidity, the less effective evaporation will be. Fig. 4 shows the way relative humidity is portrayed on a psychrometric chart. Fig. 5 shows the way that wet bulb temperature is portrayed on a psychrometric chart. Wet bulb temperature is simply an indication of the temperature at which condensation will occur for a given air sample. At this point, relative humidity is 100%.

Comfort envelope

The comfort "envelope" or area within the psychrometric chart within which most people are comfortable, has been developed in an attempt to relate dry bulb temperature with various conditions of relative humidity that define comfort under controlled laboratory conditions. It is important to note the laboratory conditions at published comfort zones appear to differ from the average persons perception of comfort. Fig. 6 shows the comfort zone boundaries defined in ASHRAE 1993, Chapter 6 "Psychrometrics." Fig. 7 shows the comfort zone described by Olgyay (1963) appropriate to outdoor conditions. The influence of wind speed for ventilative cooling and solar radiation for warming are included. These are not considered in the ASHRAE method.

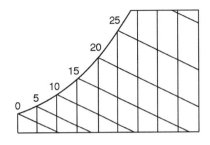

Fig. 5. Psychrometic chart indicating Wet Bulb temperature grid

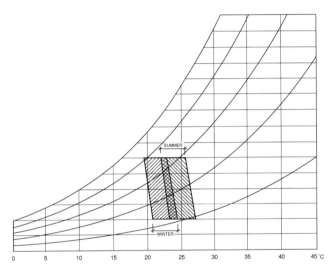

Fig. 6. Comfort zone defined by the ASHRAE Comfort Standard

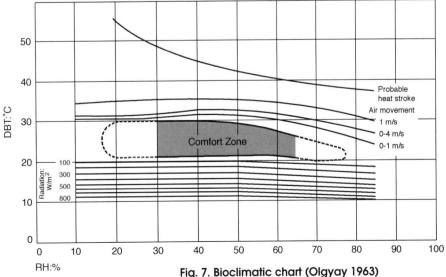

Fig. 7. Bioclimatic chart (Olgyay 1963)

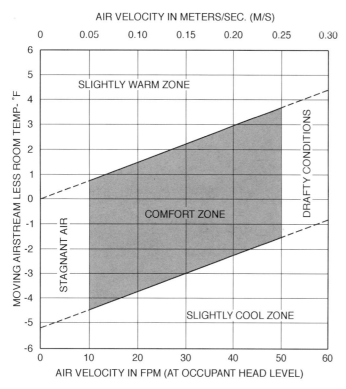

AIR VELOCITY IN METERS/SEC. (M/S)

Fig. 8. Comfort zone modified to consider air movement (after Egan 1975)

Table 2. Recommended Air Changes per Hour (ACH) for various spaces

Space	Air Changes Per Hour
Shops, machinery spaces industrial	8 to 12
Cafeterias, restaurants, hospital procedure rooms laboratories	10 to 20
Offices, hotel rooms, hospital rooms, libraries, retail shops	6 to 15
Churches, theaters, auditorium	12 to 20
Classrooms, conference rooms, kitchens, any smoking area	15 to 30

Air motion

Most treatises on comfort zones disregard air movement or at most, consider air movement negligible. This is not always useful. Air motion can contribute significantly to comfort. Fig. 8 shows how the consideration of air motion can change the comfort zone. Most system designs call for air velocities to be less than 50 ft/min. within the occupied zone. This ignores the positive benefits of air flow. Peoples' judgment of air velocities are:

50 ft/min.	unnoticed
50 - 100 ft/min.	pleasant
100 - 200 ft/min.	noticeable air movement
200 - 300 ft/min.	noticeable, drafty, unpleasant
300 ft/min. +	annoyingly drafty

These are relatively low velocities when its recalled that smoke from a cigarette in a still room rises at about 40 ft/min. Thus when the temperature of the moving air is quite near the conditions of the room, higher velocities are deemed pleasant. It should be remembered that a lack of air movement is frequently perceived as stagnant and uncomfortable. Air movement can be important in comfort cooling. Once air movement can be perceived (50 ft/min.), every 15 ft/min. increase is perceived as a one degree F drop in dry bulb temperature. This suggests that we should portray the comfort zone in a way that allows the influence of air movement to be seen.

Obviously, the exposed parts of the body are most sensitive to air movement. The head and neck areas are critical. If increased air movement is desirable, it is invariably first desired around the head. This fact is important when designing Personal Environmental Modules (PEMs) for office workers. When air movement is sensed by other portions of the body and not the head, the perception is almost invariably negative. Air movement detected on the ankles under a desk is rarely perceived as pleasant. Air directed straight at the face can also be unpleasant even if the velocities are reasonable due to the potential drying effect on the eyes. Air like light is usually best introduced from above and to the side. A good design guide is to introduce air from approximately the source of the light (assuming the lighting design was well considered).

There can be confusion among terms air movement, air changes, and ventilation. Air movement implies only that air is moving and nothing more. It may be the air in the room simply being moved by a ceiling fan. Air changes imply that the air in a space is being changed so many times in an hour. It is not necessarily "new air" or outside air. It may be completely recirculated. At any rate it has probably been heated, or cooled, depending on space conditions and, most likely, it is filtered. Table 2 gives some examples of air changes per hour (ACH) recommended for various types of spaces.

Table 3 indicates the recommended ventilation rate for replacement of building air with outside air. Recommended levels of ventilation in Cubic Feet per Minute (CFM) may be based on occupancy (CFM/person) area (CFM/sq. ft.), volume (CFM/cu. ft.), rooms (CFM/room) or some other indicator (such as CFM/toilet fixture, CFM/locker, or CFM/seat. ASHRAE/IES Standard 62-1989 is the principal reference on ventilation rates, and these standards have been made law by incorporation into building codes in most jurisdictions.

Mean radiant temperature

As noted, radiant exchange can be about 40% of the total heat dissipated from the body. It can be either an annoying or quite comfortable contribution to thermal comfort. The method of determining the likely result between these two extremes is to calculate the Mean Radiant Temperature (MRT). MRT is the average surface temperature of all the surfaces that the body can "see," weighted by the solid angle of each surface of a different temperature.

SERVICES

D3

Table 3. Typical ventilation rates

Application	Est. Max. Occupancy Per/1000 Ft^2	CFM/Person	CFM/Ft^2
Food Service			
Dining rooms	70	20	
Cafeteria	100	20	
Cocktail lounge	100	30	
Kitchen	20	30	
Auto Service			
Parking garages			1.5
Repair shops			1.5
Hotels, motels, dorm rooms			30 CFM/room
Lobbies	30	15	
Conference rooms	50	20	
Ballrooms	120	15	
Offices			
Office space	7	20	
Reception area	60	15	
Rest rooms	50	25	
Retail Stores			
Basement & street floors	30		0.30
Upper floors	20		0.20
Dressing rooms			0.20
Malls	20		0.20
Barber shop	25	15	
Beauty shop	25	25	
Supermartkets	8	15	
Pet shops			1.00
Sports & Amusement			
Spectator seating	150	15	
Hockey rinks			.50
Swimming pools			.50
Gymnasium	30	20	
Bowling alleys (seating area)	70	25	
Auditorium	150	15	
Stages, studios	70	15	
Education			
Classroom	50	15	
Laboratories	30	20	
Music rooms	50	15	
Libraries	20	15	
Health Care			
Hospital rooms	10	25	
Procedure rooms	20	15	
Opearting rooms	20	30	
Recovery - ICUs	20	15	

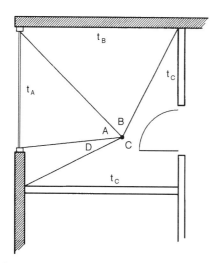

Fig. 9. Comfort zone modified to consider MRT (after Egan 1975)

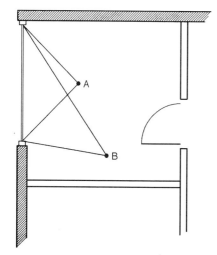

Fig. 10. MRT diagram of window radiant temperature calculation

$$\frac{\angle A \cdot t_A + \angle B \cdot t_B + \angle C \cdot t_C + \angle D \cdot t_D}{360}$$

In Fig. 9, the MRT would be:

For practical purposes, most interior surfaces can be considered at the same temperature. In very well insulated buildings, the inside surface of a solid outside wall is very nearly at room temperature. The problems with MRT are thus associated with large glazed surfaces. The governing criteria then become: glazing quality, window treatment, and distance to the glazing (Fig. 10).

Obviously a person in location A in Fig. 10 "sees" a much greater solid angle of lower temperature glass than a person in position B. If the glass is not well insulated and has no window treatment, the radiant loss can be excessive and the perception will be felt as a draft even though there is no air movement. The reverse situation could also occur on a warm summer day, particularly if the glass is sun struck and of the heat absorbing type.

A less obvious problem caused by excessive MRT can occur in large places of assembly. Where the entire volume of space is not cooled, hot air is allowed to stratify and the ceiling plane becomes quite warm. The ceiling will become a very large, low temperature radiator and, in extreme conditions, no amount of chilled air introduced at the occupied level can overcome the radiant gain and achieve comfort.

Fig. 11 relates the comfort zone to varying MRT's. It can be seen that increasing radiant exchange can achieve comfort at lower dry bulb air temperatures. This is why many people will describe the condition of greatest thermal comfort to be "cool, dry air and a warm sun." This set of conditions allows all of the body's heat exchange mechanism to work at minimum stress.

CLO units

All standards of comfort and comfort zones have been determined experimentally by asking the opinions of a significant number of people subjected to identical thermal conditions. In the earliest studies, it became apparent that the way subjects were clothed had a great bearing on their comfort. In the 1930's, researchers began to attempt to quantify clothing value to validate comfort studies. A common measurement unit, the CLO has been established for use in thermal comfort research. One CLO corresponds to the insulation value of a two piece business suit worn over a long sleeved shirt and cotton underwear. Table 4 shows the relative CLO values of common items of dress:

Interrelationship of thermal comfort factors

In addition to the dry bulb temperature and relative humidity, the other principal variables in determining thermal comfort are air movement, metabolic rate, Mean Radiant Temperature, and clothing as significant contributors. A review of these four influences offers some insight of their role in determining thermal comfort. Table 5 shows these interrelationships:

2   Building thermal loads

Building thermal loads are used for two purposes:

* peak design loads are used to size heating and cooling systems and to evaluate building envelope performance.

* typical loads and hourly load profiles for each hour of the year are used for annual energy use estimates.

Load calculation requires an understanding of building construction, material properties, occupant activity patterns, lighting, internal equipment, weather data, and current code requirements. For any but the simplest structure, good analytic engineering procedures are recom-

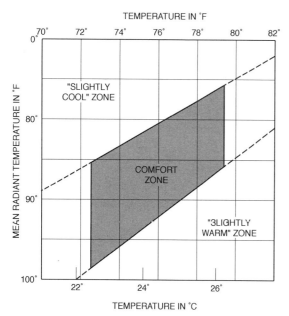

Fig. 11. Comfort zone modified to consider Mean Radiant Temperature (MRT) (after Egan 1975)

mended. There are a variety of such procedures available, ranging from simple but well tested manual analysis procedures for residential applications to sophisticated computer design programs capable of dealing with large buildings and complex systems. Many methods enable both peak system design and annual energy use calculations to be calculated, although some methods are stronger in one area than the other.

An appropriate level of thermal and HVAC engineering analysis must be applied to any building design project. Such analysis will likely use one of the computerized methods available. It is useful however to have a quick assessment for preliminary design purposes. The Approximate Design Load Assessment Method is described here. It provides a simplified, early assessment of the heating and cooling load characteristics of a building design, sufficiently facile to provide guidelines before a design schematic is formalized. It is based on widely used, code based performance factors and should give results that fall within 15%-20% of final design loads for typical buildings. Buildings of challenging thermal design character, large glass areas, large internal loads, and highly unusual geometry, will not be reasonably predictable using this method and must be evaluated using more sophisticated methods.

Tables 6 indicates the typical data required for the Approximate Design Load Assessment Method. Table 7 shows the calculations itemized according to heating or cooling. Each step is briefly described below. Tables 6 and 7 make reference to the accompanying nomographs (cited in the Tables as NG 1 - NG 9 (See end of this article).

Building type
The following are the classifications used in ASHRAE/IES Standard 90A-1980:

A1 Detached residential structures for 1 or 2 families

A2 All other residential structures 3 stories or less in height

B   All other buildings (including residential and greater than 3 stories height)

These following tables are for reference in completing the calculations:

    Table 8. Representative U values for walls.
    Table 9. Representative glazing shading coefficient.
    Table 10. Representative heat gain from office equipment.
    Table 11. Representative window shading.
    Table 12. Representative U values for windows.
    Table 13. Representative U values for doors.
    Table 14. Climatic conditions for the United States.
    Table 15. Outdoor air requirements for ventilation.
    Table 16. Recommended rate of heat gain from selected office
          equipment.
    Table 17. Representative unit lighting power.

Approximate Design Load
Assessment Method

HEATING LOAD CALCULATION

H1 Window/wall heat losses
This component combines the winter transmission losses through all components of the wall: windows, doors, opaque wall surfaces. Representative U values of walls are given in Table 8. Representative U values for windows are in Table 12 and for doors in Table 13. They are combined on an area-weighted basis as follows:

$$U_o = \frac{U_{wall} A_{wall} + U_{window} A_{window} + U_{door} A_{door}}{A_o}$$

Table 4. CLO units

Ensembles

Men: socks, briefs, shoes,	
short sleeved shirt, light trousers	0.57
undershirt, shirt, pullover, light trousers	1.00
undershirt, shirt, warm trousers & jacket	1.18
Women: underclothes, shoes,	
light dress	0.27
warm dress	0.73
warm blouse, slacks & sweater	1.20

Table 5. Interrelationship of thermal factors

Variable		*Temperature Compensation*	*Note*
Air movement	each ft/min above 30 ft/min	+1.0(F	max. 82(F
	each 0.005 m/s above 0.15 m/s	+0.6(C	max. 28(C
Activity	each met increase (max. 3 met)	-4.5(F -2.5(C	min. 59(F min. 15(C
Clothing	each 0.1 clo added	-1.0(F -0.6(C	
Radiation	each +1(F (+1(C) in MRT	-1.0(F -1.0(C	9. 0(F 5.0(F max. diff.

H2 Roof/skylight heat losses
This component combines the winter transmission losses through all components of the roof: skylights and opaque roof surfaces. Representative values of $U_{skylight}$ are given in Table 12. They are combined on an area weighted basis as follows:

$$U_o = \frac{U_{roof} A_{roof} + U_{skylight} A_{skylight}}{A_o}$$

H3 Infiltration heat losses
Infiltration is a complex and important load component. The range indicated, 0.25 - 0.75 air changes per hour, is reasonable for approximate estimating purposes. Air leakage around operable windows and doors is generally available in manufacturers literature and from ASHRAE Fundamentals Chapter 23. Leakage characteristics of other building components such as walls, are discussed in ASHRAE Fundamentals Chapter 23, "Infiltration and Ventilation," as is the importance of building height and stack effect leakage due to temperature and buoyancy effects.

H4 Slab losses
This component recognizes the conductive loss through a slab on grade. It would generally not be used for full depth basement floors.

H5 Below grade wall losses

These are not a large component of heat loss in commercial buildings.

COOLING LOAD CALCULATION

Cooling load calculations are considerably more complex than heating load calculations because time dependent solar and occupancy loads and latent loads (moisture removal) must be considered in addition to the basic thermal transmission loads. The Approximate Design Load Assessment Method presented here employs significant simplification to allow rapid approximate cooling load calculations to be made. More rigorous methods are referenced.

C1 Window/wall heat gains

This component combines the summer heat gains through all components of the wall: windows and opaque wall surfaces. The Overall Thermal Transfer Value (OTTV) combines load components on an area weighted basis as follows:

$$OTTV_w = [(U_{wall} \times A_{wall} \times TD_{eq}) +$$
$$(A_{fenestration} \times \text{Solar Factor} \times \text{Shading Coefficient}) +$$
$$(U_{fenestration} \times A_{fenestration} \times (T_s)]/A_o$$

This is a simplified method of combining the effects of several complex heat transfer processes. The $U_w A_w TD_{eq}$ component is an approach to accounting for the mass effects of wall construction. This is discussed in ASHRAE Fundamentals Chapter 26. The $A_f \times SF \times SC$ component introduces the solar load through glazing. This is frequently one of the largest cooling load components. Solar Heat Gain Factors vary with latitude, window orientation, time of year and time of day. Chapter 27 of ASHRAE Fundamentals, 1993 lists these values for the United States. Shading Coefficient (SC) the other key term in this component is a characteristic of the chosen glazing. SC offerings by manufacturers have increased greatly in recent years and it is now possible to achieve excellent solar control while still having good natural light and design control of glass color and reflectivity. Representative SC ranges for several basic types of glazing are presented in Table 9. The last term $U_f + A_f(T_s$ represents the conductive heat gain through the glass and utilizes the summer U values for fenestration which will vary slightly from winter values.

Another factor affecting the solar load through windows in a major way is window shading, both exterior and interior. For external shading devices, see "Solar Control" in Part I of this Volume and ASHRAE Fundamentals 1993, Chapter 27, "Fenestration." Venetian blinds, roller shades and drapery fabrics for shading are also described in Chapter 27. Table 11 describes representative types of window shading.

C2 Roof/skylight gains

This component combines the summer heat gains through all components of the roof: opaque surfaces and skylights. An OTTV for the roof of 8.5 Btu/h-sq. ft. is a representative maximum from ASHRAE/IES Standard 90A-1980. The $OTTV_r$ combines load components on an area weighted basis as follows:

$$OTTV_r = [U_r A_r TD_{eqr}) +$$
$$(A_{skylight} \times 138 \times \text{Shading Coefficient}) +$$
$$(U_{skylight} \times A_{skylight} \times \Delta T_s)]/A_o$$

This, again, is a simplified method of combining the effects of several complex heat transfer processes. The $U_r A_r TD_{eqr}$ component is an approach to accounting for the mass effects of roof construction. This is discussed in ASHRAE Fundamentals, 1993, Chapter 26. The $A_{skylight} \times 138 \times SC$ component introduces the solar load through skylights. Because skylights are more horizontal than windows they are less orientation influenced and a solar factor of 138 Btu/h-sq. ft. is used as a representative maximum value from ASHRAE/IES Standard 90A-1980. The last term, $U_s A_s \Delta T_s$ is the summer heat transmission through the skylights.

C3 Occupant heat gains

The value of 450 Btu/hr/person is a representative value for moderately active office work and includes both sensible and latent loads. Heat generation by humans can vary from 330 to 1800 Btu/hr. Table 1 provides information on rates of heat gain from occupants of conditioned spaces. Table 15 gives representative population densities for a number of building types.

C4 Heat gain from lights

Lighting load is a major part of the overall cooling load in many commercial buildings. Lighting systems are becoming more efficient and thus it is practical to achieve good lighting designs with modest Watt/sq. ft. energy levels. Table 17 presents a range of representative lighting power values for code complying installations.

C5 Heat gain from equipment

The major sources of equipment load are office equipment, food service equipment (including vending machines) and specialized equipment such as exercise rooms, medical and laboratory equipment, audio-visual equipment, and communications equipment. Generally, the approach to assessing the cooling load implications of this equipment is to evaluate at the design peak time, the following:

Heat Gain = Equipment Power Requirement x Use Factor x Allowance Factor

The Use Factor represents the percent of the equipment in use at the time of peak design compared to the total equipment installed, this is also known as the "Diversity Factor." The Allowance Factor accounts for the percent of the equipment load that will not be experienced by the cooling equipment. This may include some heat from ventilated light fixtures or latent loads from exhausted kitchen equipment. Table 10 gives representative Watts/sq. ft levels for several types of office occupancy and includes considerations of diversity. Table 16 presents information on the heat gain of various types of office equipment.

C6 Heat gain from ventilation

Ventilation can be another significant cooling load in buildings with the increased attention being given to indoor air quality (IAQ). It introduces two forms of cooling load, sensible, that is required to change the temperature and latent, that is required to remove moisture. Table 15 lists accepted ventilation requirements for various occupancies. The gains moisture content for latent removal is based on maintaining 50% RH indoors.

SERVICES

D3

Table 6. Approximate Design Load Assessment Method—data

DESIGN CONDITIONS

a) Project
b) Date   c) Location   d) Latitude
e) Winter Outside Design Temperature (ASHRAE 99%)   °F
f) Summer Outside Design Temperature (ASHRAE 2 1/2%)   °F
g) Summer Design Moisture Content (50% indoor RH)   grains
h) Annual Heating Degree Days, Base 65°F   HDD
i) Winter (T_W [72° - d]   °F
j) Summer (T_S [e - 74°F]   °F

BUILDING ENVELOPE PERFORMANCE REQUIREMENTS

k) Building Type
   [A-1, detached res. 1 or 2 family; A-2, all other res. 3 stories or less; B, all other bldg.]

l) Winter Wall U_O (use NG.1)
   [Fig. 1 using bldg. type (k) and HDD (h)]

m) Winter Roof U_O (use NG.2)
   [Fig. 2 using bldg. type (k) and HDD (h)]

n) Overall Thermal Transfer Value (OTTV) (use NG.3)
   [Fig. 3 using latitude (d)]

BUILDING AREAS AND VOLUME

o) Total area of above grade walls (including windows) A_w sq. ft.
p) Total area of roof (including skylights) A_r sq. ft.
q) Total area of slab-on-grade floor   sq. ft.
r) Total area of below grade walls   sq. ft.
s) Total gross building floor area   sq. ft.
t) Volume of conditioned space, V   sq. ft.

Notes:

Design conditions:

d. Latitude - select this value from Table 9 for the city nearest the project location or from any map showing the project location and latitude or from Fig. 1

e, f, g, h - Winter Outside Design Temperature, Summer Outside Design Temperature, Summer Design Moisture Content and Annual Heating Degree Days. Select these values from Table 9 for the city nearest the project location. Fig. 1 also gives degree day contours.

Building envelope performance requirements:

l.   Winter Wall U_O
Use NG.1 - Enter with Annual Heating Degree Days (h), proceed vertically to the line for construction classification (k), turn and read the winter U_O value from the vertical axis.

m.   Winter Roof U_O
Use NG.2 - Enter with Annual Heating Degree Days (h), proceed vertically to the line for construction classification (k), turn and read the winter U_O value from the vertical axis.

n.   Overall Thermal Transfer Value (OTTV)
Use NG.3 - Enter with latitude (d), proceed vertically to the line, turn and read the OTTV on the vertical axis.

Building Areas and Volumes:

Enter the data from the project being assessed.

SERVICES   **D3**

Table 7. Approximate Design Load Assessment Method—calculations

HEATING LOAD

H1	Window/Wall Losses: $U_o A (T_w = [l \cdot o \cdot i]$	Btu/hr (NG.4)	
H2	Roof/Skylight Losses: $U_o A (T_w = [m \cdot p \cdot i]$	Btu/hr (NG.5)	
H3	Infiltration Losses: $1.1 \cdot$ volume $\cdot$ ACH $\cdot 1/60 \cdot (T_w =$ $[1.1 \cdot t \cdot ACH \cdot 1/60 \cdot I]$	Btu/hr (NG.6)	
H4	Slab Floor Losses: A floor $\cdot$ 2 Btu/hr sf = $[q \cdot 2]$	Btu/hr	
H5	Below Grade Wall Losses: A wall $\cdot$ 4 Btu/hr sf = $[r \cdot 4]$	Btu/hr	
H6	Total Estimated Heat Loss $[H1 + H2 + H3 + H4 + H5]$	Btu/hr	

COOLING LOAD

C1	Window/Wall Gains: $A_w \cdot OTTV = [o \cdot n]$	Btu/hr (NG.3)	
C2	Roof/Skylight Gains: $A_r \cdot 8.5$ Btu/hr sf = $[p \cdot 8.5]$	Btu/hr	
C3	Occupant Heat Gains: no. of people $\cdot$ heat gain per person =	Btu/hr (NG.7)	
C4	Heat Gain from Lights: SF $\cdot$ W/SF $\cdot 3.4 = [s \cdot w/sf \cdot 3.4]$	Btu/hr	
C5	Heat Gain from Equipment: SF $\cdot$ W/SF $\cdot 3.4 = [s \cdot w/sf \cdot 3.4]$	Btu/hr	
C6	Heat Gain from Ventilation		
	Sensible: CFM $\cdot 1.1 \cdot (T_s = [CFM \cdot 1.1 \cdot j]$	Btu/hr (NG.8)	
	Latent: CFM $\cdot 0.68 \cdot Gr = [CFM \cdot 0.68 \cdot g]$	Btu/hr (NG.9)	
C7	Subtotal = Estimated Heat Gain $[C1 + C2 + C3 + C4 + C5 + C6]$	Btu/hr	
C8	Fan Motor Heat Allowance: 10% of cooling load = $[C7 \cdot 0.10]$	Btu/hr	
C9	Total = Estimated Heat Gain $[C7 + C8]$	Btu/hr	

Table 8. Representative U values for walls. Source: ASHRAE (1993) Chapter 22

	R Value	U Value
Wood Frame:		
gyp bd, 2 x 4, 16 in. OC, R-13 batts, R-4 ins sheathing, wood siding	14.8	0.067
gyp bd, 2 x 6, 24 in. OC, R-21 batts, 1/2 in. fiber bd sheathing, wood siding	17.6	0.057
Steel Frame:		
gyp bd, 2 x 4 steel studs, R-11 batts, gyp bd	6.61	0.15
Masonry:		
8 in. CMU w/poured Perlite ins	3.43	0.29

Source: ASHRAE Fundamentals, 1993, Chapter 22

Table 9. Representative glazing shading coefficient

Glazing	SC
Single Clear	.94
Double Clear	.81
Double Heat Absorbing	.55
Double "Low e" Combined With Tinted	.78 - .36
Double Reflective With Tinted	.54 - .15
Double with Suspended "Low e" Film with Tinted	.66 - .19

SERVICES

D3

Table 10. Representative heat gain from office equipment. Watts/gross sq. ft.

Automation Level	Heat Gain Watts/Gross FT^2
Non-Automated	0.5
Moderate use of PC-1/occupant	1.0
Intensive use of PC-1/occupant	1.5
PC's and CAD Equipment	2.0

Table 11. Representative window shading

Shading Method	Usual Application
Horizontal Shades in summer, may allow winter sun in	South side windows
Vertical Shades both winter and summer	East or west side
Egg Crate	Combined effect of horizontal and vertical shading
Movable Shading: Horizontal and Vertical optimum solar rejection or solar gain	Horizontal best on south, vertical best on east and west may be adjusted for
Interior Shading: Horizontal rr Vertical Blinds Translucent Opaque Shades, Curtains and Drapes	Rejects solar gain to the extent that visible radiation is reflected back out Or through glazing. Otherwise solar heat may be re-radiated back into the building. May provide some insulating value.

Table 12. Representative U values for windows. Source: ASHRAE (1993) Chapter 27

Glazing	Alum. no therm break	Frame		Sloped Skylight Alum. Fixed	Sloped Skylight Wood Fixed
		Alum. no therm break	Wood/ Vinyl		
Single 1/8 in.	1.3	1.07	0.94	1.92	1.47
Double	.81	.62	.51	1.29	0.84
Double e = .40	.74	.55	.45	1.23	0.78
Double e = .20	.70	.52	.42	1.19	0.74
Double e = .10	.67	.49	.40	1.17	0.72
Double e = .10 argon	.64	.46	.37	1.11	0.66
Triple e = .10 argon	.57	.40	.31	0.99	0.54
Triple e = .10 argon low e on two surfaces, ins. spacer	.53	.32	.23	0.94	0.44

*All values for operable windows (unless otherwise noted). All double glazing is 1/2 in., metal spacer, air fill, low-e on one surface (unless otherwise noted).

Source: ASHRAE Fundamentals, 1993, Chapter 27

Table 13. Representative U values for doors. Source: ASHRAE (1993) Chapter 22

	Door Alone	With Metal Storm
Wood Door		
Panel Door	0.54	0.36
Hollow Core Flush	0.46	0.32
Solid Core Flush	0.40	0.26
Steel Door		
Fiberglass or mineral wool core no thermal break	0.60	
Paper honeycomb core, no thermal break	0.56	
Polystyrene core, no thermal break	0.35	
Polyurethane core, no thermal break	0.29	
Polyurethane core, with thermal break	0.20	

Note: All doors 1 3/4 in. thick

Source: *ASHRAE Fundamentals*, 1993, Chapter 22

SERVICES

D3

Table 14. Climatic conditions for the United States - abstract. Source: ASHRAE (1993) Chapter 24; ACCA (1986)

State and station	Latitude °N	Annual heating degree-days	Winter Design dry-bulb 99%	Summer Design dry-bulb 2.5%	Grains moisture difference at 50% RH
AL Huntsville	35	3070	11	93	33
AK Anchorage	61	10864	-23	68	0
Barrow	71		-45	53	0
Fairbanks	65	1479	-51	78	0
Juneau	58	9075	-4	70	0
AZ Flagstaff	35	7152	-2	82	0
Phoenix	33	1765	31	107	0
AR Little Rock	35	3219	15	96	46
CA Los Angeles, AP	34	2061	41	80	13
Sacramento	39	2502	30	98	2
San Francisco CO	38	3001	38	71	0
Eureka	42		13	92	0
CO Denver	40	6283	-5	91	0
Grand Junction	39	5641	2	94	0
DC Washington	39	4224	14	91	36
FL Jacksonville	30	1239	29	94	49
Miami	26	214	44	90	56
Tampa	28	683	36	91	54
GA Atlanta	34	2961	17	92	34
HI Honolulu	21		62	86	38
ID Boise	44	5809	3	94	0
IL Chicago, O'Hare AP	42	6639	-8	89	38
IN Indianapolis	40	5699	-2	90	37
IA Des Moines	42	6588	-10	91	36
KA Wichita	38	4620	3	98	18
KY Lexington	38	4683	3	91	30
LA New Orleans	30	1385	29	92	58
ME Portland	44	7571	-6	84	29
MA Boston	42	5334	6	88	23
MI Detroit	42	6232	3	88	29
Sault Ste. Marie	46	9048	-12	81	23
MN Duluth	47	10000	-21	82	17
Minneapolis/St. Paul	45	8382	-16	89	33
MS Jackson	32	2239	21	95	40
MO St. Louis AP	39	4900	2	94	37
MT Billings	46	7049	-15	91	0
Missoula	47	8125	-13	88	0
NE Lincoln	41	5884	-5	95	28
NV Las Vegas	36	2709	25	106	0
Reno	40	6332	5	92	0
NH Concord	43	7383	-8	87	19
NM Albuquerque	35	4348	12	94	0
NY Albany	43	6875	-6	88	29
Buffalo	43	7062	2	85	22
NYC - Kennedy AP	41	5219	12	87	30
NC Raleigh/Durham	36	3393	16	92	40
ND Fargo	47	9226	-22	89	22
OH Cincinnati	39	4410	1	90	26
Cleveland	41	6351	1	88	29
OK Oklahoma City	35	3725	9	97	26
OR Medford	42	5008	19	94	0
Portland	46	4635	17	85	7
PA Philadelphia	40	5144	10	90	37
Pittsburgh AP	40	5987	1	86	26
SC Charleston	33	1794	25	92	58
Columbia	34	2484	20	95	35
SD Sioux Falls	44	7539	-15	91	24
TN Knoxville	36	3494	13	92	28
Memphis	35	3232	13	95	48
TX Amarillo	35	3985	6	95	40
Brownsville	26	600	35	93	51
Dallas	33	2363	18	100	27
El Paso	32	2700	20	98	0
Houston	30	1396	27	94	49
UT Salt Lake City	41	6052	3	95	0
VT Burlington	44	8269	-12	85	22
VA Norfolk	37	3421	20	91	48
Roanoke	37	4150	12	91	24
WA Seattle-Tacoma AP	47	5145	21	80	0
Spokane	48	6655	-6	90	0
WV Charleston	38	4476	7	90	31
WI Madison	43	7863	-11	88	35
WY Casper	43	7410	-11	90	0

Source: ASHRAE Fundamentals, 1993, Chapter 24, Acca, Manual J. 1986

SERVICES

D3

Table 15. Outdoor air requirements for ventilation

Application	Estimated Maximum* Occupancy P/1000 ft^2 or 100 m^2	cfm/ person	cfm/ft^2	Comments
Retail Stores, Sales Floors, and Show Room Floors				
Basement and street	30		0.30	
Upper floors	20		0.20	
Storage rooms	15		0.15	
Dressing rooms			0.20	
Malls and arcades	20		0.20	
Shipping and receiving	10		0.15	
Warehouses	5		0.05	
Smoking lounge	70	60		Normally supplied by transfer air, local mechanical exhaust; exhaust with no recirculation recomended.
Specialty Shops				
Barber	25	15		
Beauty	25	25		
Reducing salons	20	15		Ventilation to optimize plant growth may dictate requirements.
Florists	8	15		
Clothiers, furniture				
Hardware, drugs, fabric	8	15		
Supermarkets	8	15		
Pet shops			1.00	
Sports and Amusement				
Spectator areas	150	15		When internal combustion engines are operated for maintenance of playing surfaces, increased ventilation rates may be required.
Game rooms	70	25		
Ice arenas (playing areas)			0.50	
Swimming pools (pool and deck area)				Higher values may be required for humidity control.
Playing floors (gymnasium)	30	20		
Ballrooms and discos	100	25		
Bowling alleys (seating areas)	70	25		
Theaters				
Ticket booths	60	20		Special ventilation will be needed to eliminate special stage effects (*e.g.*, dry ice vapors, mists, *etc.*)
Lobbies	150	20		
Auditorium	150	15		
Stages, studios	70	15		
Transportation				
Waiting rooms	100	15		Ventilation within vehicles may require special considerations.
Platforms	100	15		
Vehicles	150	15		
Workrooms				
Meat processing	10	15		Spaces maintained at low temperatures (-10 °F to + 50 °F, or -23 °C to + 10 °C) are not covered by these requirements unless the occupancy is continuous. Ventilation from adjoining spaces is permissible. When the occupancy is intermittent, infiltration will normally exceed the ventilation requirement.
Photo studios	10	15		Installed equipment must incorporate positive exhaust and control (as required) of undesirable contaminants (toxic or otherwise).
Darkrooms	10		0.50	
Pharmacy	20	15		
Bank vaults	5	15		
Duplicating, printing			0.50	
Education				
Classroom	50	15		
Laboratories	30	20		Special contaminant control systems may be required for processes or functions including laboratory animal occupancy.
Training shop	30	20		
Music rooms	50	15		
Libraries	20	15		
Locker rooms			0.50	
Corridors			0.10	
Auditoriums	150	15		Normally supplied by transfer air.
Smoking lounges	70	60		Local mechanical exhaust with no recirculation recommended.

SERVICES

D3

Table 15. Outdoor air requirements for ventilation *(continued)*

Application	Estimated Maximum* Occupancy P/1000 ft² or 100 m²	cfm/ person	cfm/ft²	Comments
Hospitals, Nursing and Convalescent Homes				
Patient rooms	10	25		Special requirements or codes and pressure relationships may determine minimum ventilation rates and filter efficiency. Procedures generating contamination may require higher rates.
Medical procedure	20	15		
Operating rooms	20	30		
Recovery and ICU	20	15		
				Air shall not be recirculated into other spaces.
Autopsy rooms			0.50	
Physical Therapy	20	15		
Correctional Facilities				
Cells	20	20		
Dining halls	100	20		
Guard stations	40	15		
Dry Cleaners, Laundries				Dry-cleaning processes may require more air.
Commercial laundry	10	25		
Commercial dry cleaner	30	30		
Storage, pick up	30	35		
Coin-operated laundries	20	15		
Coin-operated dry cleaner	20	15		
Food and Beverage Service				
Dining rooms	70	20		
Cafeteria, fast food	100	20		
Bars, cocktail lounges	100	30		Supplemental smoke-removal equipment may be required.
Kitchens (cooking)	20	15		Makeup air for hood exhaust may require more ventilating air. The sum of the outdoor air and transfer air of acceptable quality from adjacent spaces shall be sufficient to provide an exhaust rate of not less than 1.5 cfm/ft² (7.5 L/s•m²)
Garages, Repair, Service Stations				
Enclosed parking garage			1.50	Distribution among people must consider worker locations and concentration of running engines; stands where engines are run must incorporate systems for positive engine exhaust withdrawal. Contaminant sensors may be used to control ventilation.
Auto repair rooms			1.50	
Hotels, Motels, Resorts, Dormitories			cfm/room	
Bedrooms				Independent of room size.
Living Rooms			30	
Baths			30	
			35	Installed capacity for intermittent use.
Lobbies				
Conference rooms	30	20		
Assembly rooms	120	15		
Dormitory sleeping areas	120	15		See also food and beverage services, merchandising, barber and beauty shops, garages
	20	15		
Gambling casinos	120	30		Supplementary smoke-removal equipment may be required
Offices				
Office space	7	20		Some office equipment may require local exhaust.
Reception areas	60	15		
Telecommunication centers and data entry areas	60	20		
Conference rooms	50	20		Supplementary smoke-removal equipment may be required.
Public Spaces			cfm/ft²	
Corridors and utilities			0.05	
Public restrooms, cfm/wc or cfm/urinal				Normally supplied by transfer air. Local mechanical exhaust with no recirculation recommended.
Locker and dressing rooms				
Smoking lounge	70		1.00	
				Normally supplied by transfer air.
Elevators			1.00	

*Net occupiable space.
Source: ASHRAE Standard 62 - 1989

Table 16. Recommended rate of heat gain from selected office equipment. Source: ASHRAE (1993) Chapter 26. For rates of heat gain from occupants of conditioned spaces, see Table 1.

Appliance	Size	Maximum Input Rating, Btu/h	Standby Input Rating, Btu/h	Recommended Rate Btu/h of Heat Gain,
Check processing workstation	12 pockets	16400	8410	8410
Computer devices				
Communication/ transmission		6140 to 15700	5600 to 9500	5600 to 9600
Disk drives/mass storage		3410 to 34100	3412 to 22420	3412 to 22420
Minicomputer		7500 to 15000	7500 to 15000	7500 to 15000
Optical reader		10240 to 20470	8000 to 17000	8000 to 17000
Plotters		256	128	214
Printers				
Letter quality	30 to 45 char/min	1200	600	1000
Line, high speed	5000 or more lines/min	4300 to 18100	2160 to 9040	2500 to 1300
Line, low speed	300 to 600 lines/min	1540	770	1280
Tape drives		4090 to 22200	3500 to 15000	3500 to 15000
Terminal		310 to 680	270 to 600	270 to 600
Copiers/Duplicators				
Blue print		3930 to 42700	1710 to 17100	3930 to 42700
Copiers (large)	30 to 67[a] copies/min	5800 to 22500	3070	5800 to 22500
Copiers (small)		1570 to 5800	1020 to 3070	1570 to 5800
Feeder	6 to 30[a] copies/min	100	—	100
Microfilm printer		1540	—	1540
Sorter/collator		200 to 2050	—	200 to 2050
Electronic equipment				
Cassette recorders/players		200	—	200
Receiver/tuner		340	—	340
Signal analyzer		90 to 2220	—	90 to 2220
Mailprocessing				
Folding machine		430	—	270
Inserting machine	3600 to 6800 pieces/h	2050 to 113001	—	1330 to 7340
Labeling machine	1500 to 30000 pieces/h	2050 to 22500	—	1330 to 14700
Postage meter		780	—	510
Vending machines				
Cigarette		250	51 to 85	250
Cold food/beverage		3920 to 6550	—	1960 to 3280
Hot beverage		5890	—	2940
Snack		820 to 940	—	820 to 940
Miscellaneous				
Barcode printer		1500	—	1260
Cash registers	200	—	160	
Coffee maker	10 cups	5120	—	3580 sensible
Microfiche reader		290	—	290
Microfilm reader		1770	—	1770
Microfilm reader/printer		3920	—	3920
Microwave oven	1 ft^3	2050	—	1360
Paper shredder		850 to 10240	—	680 to 8250
Water cooler	32 qt/h	2390	—	5970

[a] Input is not proportional to capacity.

Source: ASHRAE Fundamentals, 1993, Chapter 26

Table 17. Representative unit lighting power W/sq. ft. Source: ASHRAE/IES Standard 90.1 (1989)

Building Type Or Space Activity	0 to 2,000 ft^2	2,001 to ft^2	10,001 to 25,000 ft^2	25,0001 to 50,000 ft^2	50,001 to 250,000 ft^2	> 250,000 ft^2
Food Service						
Fast Food/Cafeteria	150	138	1.34	1.31	1.30	
Leisure Dining/Bar	2.20	1.91	1.71	1.56	1.46	1.40
Offices	1.90	1.81	1.72	1.65	1.57	1.50
Retail	3.30	3.08	2.83	2.50	2.28	2.10
Mall Concourse						
multi-store service	1.60	1.58	1.52	1.46	1.43	1.40
Service Establishment	2.70	2.37	2.08	1.92	1.80	1.70
Garages	0.30	0.28	0.24	0.22	0.21	0.20
Schools						
Preschool/elementary	1.80	1.80	1.72	1.65	1.57	1.50
Jr. High/High School	1.90	1.90	1.88	1.83	1.76	1.70
Technical/Vocational	2.40	2.33	2.17	2.01	1.84	1.70
Warehouse/Storage	0.80	0.66	0.56	0.48	0.43	0.40

Source: ASHRAE Standard 90.1 - 1989

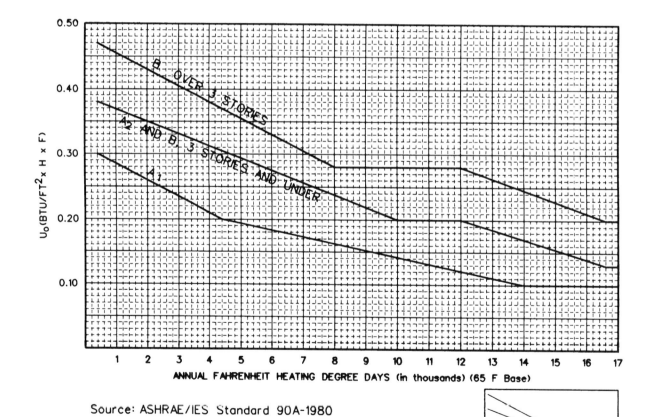

Source: ASHRAE/IES Standard 90A-1980

Nomograph 1

SERVICES

D3

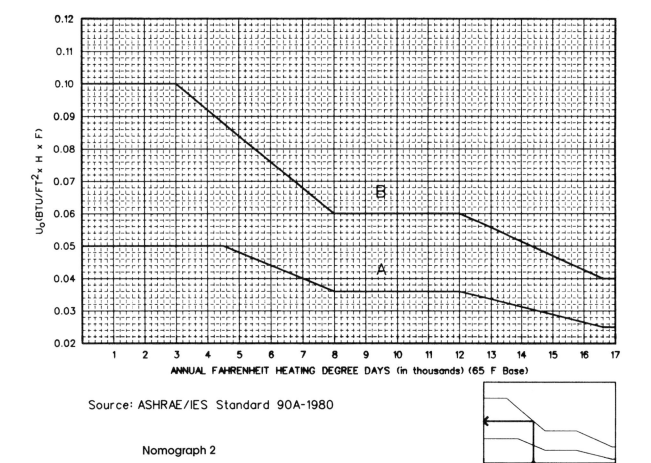

Source: ASHRAE/IES Standard 90A-1980

Nomograph 2

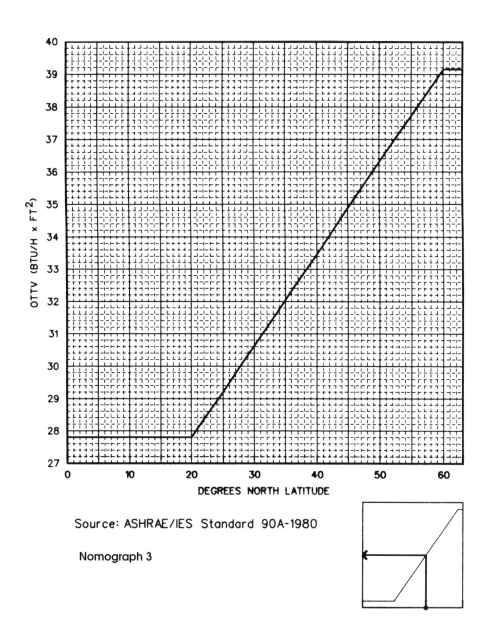

Source: ASHRAE/IES Standard 90A-1980

Nomograph 3

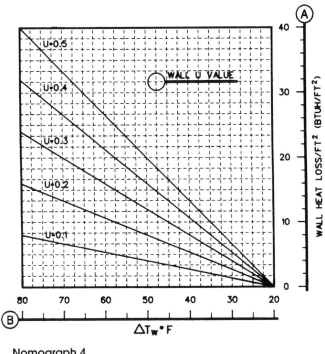
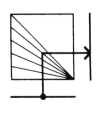

Nomograph 4

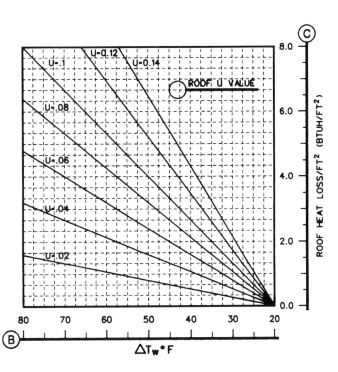
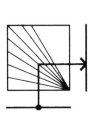

Nomograph 5

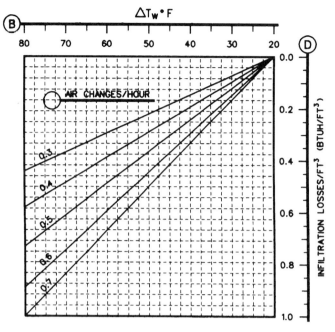

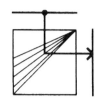

Nomograph 6

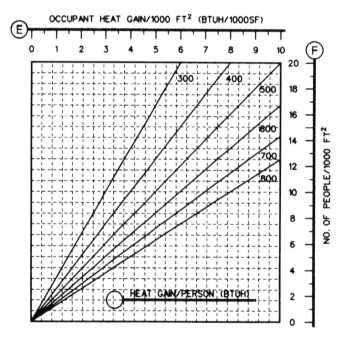

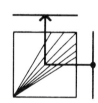

Nomograph 7

SERVICES

D3

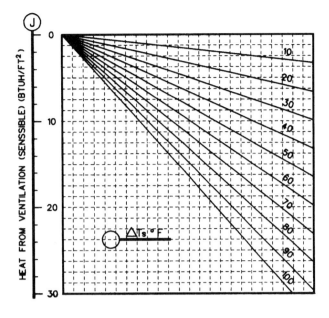

Nomograph 8

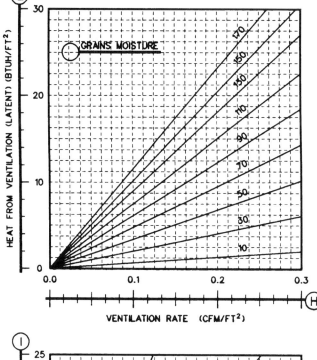

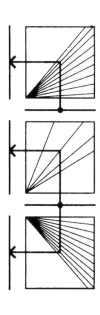

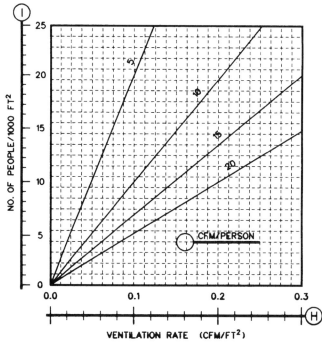

Nomograph 9

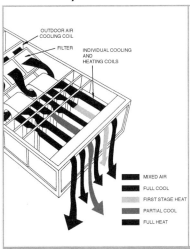

OUTDOOR AIR
COOLING COIL

FILTER

INDIVIDUAL COOLING
AND
HEATING COILS

MIXED AIR
FULL COOL
FIRST STAGE HEAT
PARTIAL COOL
FULL HEAT

HVAC systems for commercial buildings

Summary: Heating, Ventilating and Air-Conditioning (HVAC) systems provide the comfort and ventilation necessary for healthy and productive environments. This article reviews HVAC systems for commercial buildings and guidelines for preliminary system design and selection.

Key words: air-handling unit, boiler, chiller, condenser, cooling tower, diffuser, heat pump, ventilation.

Uniformat:	D3020
	D3030
MasterFormat:	15700

Outline of topics covered in this article

HVAC systems provide both the thermal comfort and ventilation necessary for healthy, productive environments. HVAC systems that are efficient, accessible for inspection, testing and balancing and economical to operate, are extremely important to the success of most building projects. The architect's understanding of HVAC design principles is essential for effective design and mechanical system integration. At the same time, technological innovation in HVAC systems and new information about the critical importance of energy efficiency and indoor air-quality requires continuous review of HVAC design practices.

From the architect's view, the type of HVAC system selected can significantly affect floor plan layouts. Mechanical equipment rooms and vertical distribution shafts typically occupy between 3% and 10% of the typical floor plan area, and an even greater percentage in highrise buildings with substantial mechanical cores. If not considered early in the design process, the number, size and location of ducts, air intake/exhaust louvers and rooftop equipment can also detract from the building aesthetics.

From the owner's view, the correct selection of the HVAC system can significantly affect project first costs as well as long-term operating and maintenance costs. The initial system cost (including the "hidden" cost of constructing mechanical equipment rooms and large duct shafts) can amount to a substantial percentage of total construction costs in modern fully serviced buildings (see, for example, the article on Building Economics in Part I of this Volume). Building users, on the other hand, are generally more affected by the long-term impacts of the system selection, annual utility bills, maintenance costs, and employee productivity.

The building owner's criteria for HVAC system selection can vary dramatically, from the speculative builder (low initial cost, marketability concerns, and "lost" rental income due to equipment and shaft space requirements) to the owner/user, who recognizes that poor HVAC system performance over the life of the building can adversely affect both operating and maintenance costs and the productivity of employees suffering from thermal discomfort or poor indoor air quality. Current research suggests that productivity improvements can be gained by providing occupants with more control over their personal

environments than that provided by the typical HVAC system (See "Flexible Infrastructure" in Chapter C1 of this Volume).

Building and office managers have a stake in the HVAC system to be installed in their building. In a survey conducted by the Building Owners and Managers Association (BOMA), close to 30% of the building managers surveyed cited "HVAC System" or "Indoor Air Quality" as their most critical management, operation, or design problem.

A pleasant, comfortable, healthy indoor environment can affect issues such as absenteeism, staff retention, and actual employee productivity. A simple calculation of the building occupant salaries over a ten year period, compared to the HVAC system construction costs, will usually reveal that a 1% decrease in productivity can cost more than 50 times the amortized construction costs, and 100 times the utility costs incurred by the system.

This article covers the HVAC design for commercial buildings in terms helpful to architects in preliminary design, including following topics:

1 Basic components of HVAC systems

2 Basic HVAC system types

3 HVAC systems for specific building applications

4 Space planning considerations

5 Equipment descriptions

1 Basic components of HVAC systems

The HVAC system is one of the most complex and least understood of all building service systems. This is partly due to the vast number of systems and options available, as well as a lack of standardization in terminology, equipment types, sizes, efficiencies, and compatibility among different manufacturers' lines of equipment. HVAC systems can be conceived as the "breathing system" that provides fresh air throughout a building, conditioned within proscribed temperature and humidity ranges, and that also removes and/or reconditions circulated air. Related to this are piping systems for heating and cooling and valves and dampers that control and modulate the system. Recently developed microchip electronic controls bring to the HVAC system a great deal of technological sophistication and capabilities,

Authors: Richard Rittelmann, FAIA, Paul Scanlon, P.E., Russ Sullivan, P.E., and Tim Beggs.

References: ASHRAE 1993. *ASHRAE Handbook of Fundamentals.* Atlanta, GA: American Society of Heating, Refrigerating and Air-Conditioning Engineers.

Bobenhausen, William. 1994. *Simplified Design of HVAC Systems.* New York: John Wiley and Sons.

Rowe, William H., III. 1994. *HVAC Design Criteria, Options, Selection.* Kingston, MA: R. S. Means Company.

including continuous monitoring and system balancing, such as with Energy Management Systems (EMS).

In HVAC system design, the coordination of components is critical, including the designation of different space occupancy requirements, and the designation of different heating/cooling zones as influenced by building orientation. Electronic controls engineering is a significant subspecialty of HVAC design, which must be carefully reviewed to conform with the architectural program and owner expectations during design, construction, building commissioning phases.

While HVAC systems tend to defy simple categorization, there are three basic components common to all HVAC equipment systems:

• generation equipment

• distribution system

• terminal equipment

• *Generation equipment*

Generation equipment produces the heat (steam or hot water boilers, warm air furnaces, and radiant panels) or cooling (chillers and cooling towers, and air-cooled compressors in packaged equipment). Packaged equipment (equipment which is self-contained, often all-electric) requires no central mechanical equipment; the source of heating and cooling is contained within each piece of HVAC equipment. While the type of generation equipment used does not identify the appropriate type of HVAC system to use in a given application, it can limit the choices available to the designer. For example, the Owner/Developer of a residential building project may dictate that the designer consider only packaged equipment to avoid the premium in first cost and on-site maintenance skills associated with central equipment such as boilers and chillers and provide a system where energy costs are directly charged to the occupant. The critical architectural decisions related to HVAC generation equipment are the location, size and service options of equipment rooms, which typically require both air intakes and exhausts, that must be separated for indoor air quality health and safety.

• *Distribution system*

The distribution system is the method by which cooling and heating energy is "moved" throughout the building (hot / chilled water piping systems, or ductwork that distributes warm or cool air around the building). For systems using packaged equipment, the distribution system is limited to a modest amount of ductwork (if any), limited by the capacity of the supply air fan provided as part of the packaged equipment. In larger central systems, the distribution system is powered by large central pumps and/or air handling units; these systems are almost unlimited in their capacity and can be quite complex, including both piping and ductwork which extends throughout the entire building. The critical architectural decisions in design of distribution system is coordination with all other structure and services to eliminate conflicts and to provide for effective and efficient distribution of air and water throughout the building. Most critical junctures in a distribution system have to be made accessible for testing and balancing.

• *Terminal equipment*

Terminal equipment include the devices which distribute conditioned air to the space (a diffuser is considered a terminal unit) and, in some cases, either a separate or integral device is used to control the local space temperature (the "temperature control device"). Both types of terminal equipment are usually located in close proximity to the occupant. In some systems, they are visible (as in the case of window air-conditioners or fan coil units, which act as both the terminal unit and temperature control device). In others systems, they are concealed above the ceiling(that is, a variable air volume box acts as the temperature control device which controls the amount of air discharged from a number of ceiling diffusers, the terminal units).

In a single zone system, there is no separate terminal control device; the local diffuser is the "terminal unit," and a single thermostat sends control signals straight to the distribution equipment to maintain the set-point temperature for the entire area served by the single zone system. Rather than having multiple zones served by one large air handling unit, multiple single zone air handlers are used to achieve multiple zones of temperature control within the building.

The terminal control device of the HVAC system is usually crucial in selecting the most appropriate HVAC system type; to a large extent, it dictates the degree of comfort which the system will be capable of providing. The type of terminal unit used, together with the number of thermostatic control zones desired, significantly affects both occupant satisfaction and the overall system capital cost and operating costs. Critical decisions related to terminal equipment is coordination with the architectural elements of the building interior.

2 Basic HVAC system types

The nomenclature used in the HVAC industry often relates to the size of the typical unit rather than the generic type of system; hence a single-zone self-contained unit might be referred to as a "through-wall air-conditioner" when discussing apartment buildings, a "unit ventilator" when discussing school buildings, or a "rooftop unit" when discussing a low-rise office building. Compounding this problem is the fact that a variety of heating and cooling energy sources are available for each type of equipment (that is, a unit ventilator isn't considered a "single-zone self-contained" unit unless it uses an air-source heat pump compressor to meet its heating and cooling requirements; if it relies on central hot water or chilled water from a central equipment room, it wouldn't be considered "self-contained").

To simplify understanding of the basic HVAC options, it's easiest to start by classifying all systems into one of two categories: self-contained or central systems.

2.1 Self-contained systems

Self-contained systems require no central equipment to perform their function. This basic system type could be described as "plug'n'play;" all system components (air circulating fan, refrigerant compressor / condenser / cooling coil, and heating coil) are contained within one box, which generally needs only to be plugged in to a source of electricity. As shown in Fig. 1, there are five different equipment configurations used for self-contained systems.

The most common heating options used in self-contained systems include electric resistance heating coils (sometimes called "strip heat") and air-source heat pumps (ASHP). ASHPs are two- to three-times more efficient than electric heating coils in mild weather, but still must rely on electric resistance heating coils when the outdoor air drops to about 25F (-4°C). Therefore, ASHPs are only 1.5 to 2.0 times more efficient than electric resistance heating coils on an annual basis in areas characterized by cold winters.

While many self-contained systems are all-electric, larger commercial rooftop applications may also use natural gas piped to each unit. Gas is used in these systems most frequently to provide a lower cost heating option (via direct gas-fired furnaces contained within the unit). A more recent product—the gas-fired desiccant air-conditioner—uses natural gas in its cooling cycle. Although these systems require a separately-piped fuel, they are still categorized as self-contained systems because they require no central equipment such as boilers, pumps, and chillers.

In most applications, each unit provides a single temperature control zone, so an individual unit is often provided for each space which has a different heating or cooling load. All self-contained units use air-cooled refrigeration equipment, so a portion of the unit must be exposed to the outdoor air. A "split system" unit is a variation of the self-contained unit, wherein the condensing section(part of the air-cooled refrigeration equipment) can be separated from the rest of the unit and be located 50 ft (15 m) or more away from the indoor unit.

A limitation of self-contained systems is that they are pre-engineered units, with limited sizes available. They are almost exclusively a commodity product designed to minimize material costs because their selection is normally price-based, and therefore tend to have relatively short expected service lives. Self-contained systems are also limited in the type of air filtration options available; normally, flat panel filters capable of screening out only the largest air-borne particles are provided.

In addition to low first cost, other advantages of self contained systems include minimal maintenance, full system quality control/testing at the factory, and reliance on many independent units so that failure of any one unit affects only a small portion of the building.

Self-contained systems for residential applications

The quality of self-contained systems can vary substantially. Smaller systems such as window units, through-wall units, and small split system units are considered "residential appliance" quality, with expected service lives of as low as 5 years and as high as 10 years. American Refrigeration Institute (ARI)-certified Package Terminal Air Conditioners (PTAC equipment) of the same size and type are manufactured to higher industry standards, and are considered commercial quality equipment with an expected service life closer to 15 years. Because these self-contained systems have limited capacities (1/2 to 3 tons) and must have access to outdoor air in order to reject heat from the conditioned space, their use is limited to conditioning small individual rooms at the building perimeter. Typical applications, therefore, include single-family homes, apartments, motels, hotels, and small, residential load type offices at the perimeter of commercial buildings. In multi-story buildings, the remote condensers of split system units are located either on grade or on the roof of the building.

Self-contained systems for commercial applications

Self-contained systems designed for larger commercial applications are often referred to as "unitary equipment" or "packaged" equip-

ment. Common equipment configurations include rooftop units, larger split system units, and floor-mounted indoor units (located at a perimeter wall). In areas characterized by mild climates and reasonably low electric costs, large through wall unit ventilators may be used in classroom applications.

Larger self-contained systems may include limited ductwork for distributing conditioned air over a relatively large area. Multiple single zone units are most commonly used to provide temperature control of the entire area served by each unit, but duct-mounted terminal control devices may also be used to provide additional zoning capabilities. For example, reheat coils or VAV boxes can be mounted at branch ducts and controlled by a local thermostat to give more localized control. These temperature control devices are described in the "central systems" section, since they are much more widely used in central, rather than self-contained, air handling systems. Self-contained rooftop multi-zone units are also available; a recent product introduced to the market uses multiple heating and cooling coils to provide multiple zones of temperature control (Fig. 2).

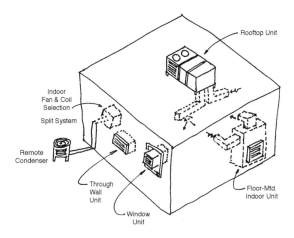

Fig. 1. Five configurations for self-contained systems

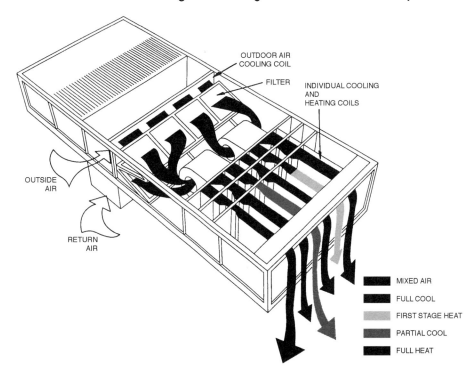

Fig. 2. Self-contained rooftop multi-zone unit (Source: Carrier Corporation)

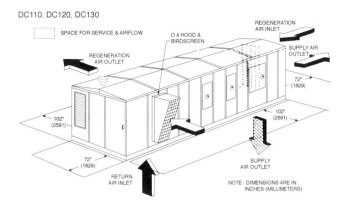

Fig. 3. Self-contained dessicant air conditioner (Source: Englehard/ICC)

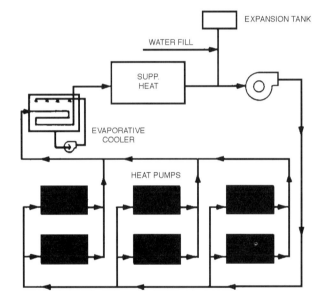

Fig. 4. Closed loop heat pump system

Heating options for each of these configurations include straight resistance electric heating coils or air source heat pumps. The most commonly used equipment capacities range from 5 tons to 25 tons refrigeration capacity, although much larger units are available for primarily industrial applications. Equipment quality can range from "light commercial" to "commercial," with an expected service life of 10 to 15 years.

Gas-fired desiccant air-conditioners (Fig. 3) are a relatively new product, and combine some of the ease-of-installation benefits of self-contained systems with the low operating costs more often associated with central systems. They are particularly applicable to areas characterized by high humidity and in buildings with high ventilation loads, since they have the capability to remove latent heat(from humid outdoor air) very efficiently.

The air-cooled equipment of commercial self-contained systems must be located at or near the outside of the building. Due to distance limitations of the refrigerant tubing, the use of these systems is limited to low-rise buildings. The capacity of the supply air fans provided with this type of equipment is also limited. Hence one of the most popular applications for self-contained systems is in the use of rooftop units serving a one-story structure, where multiple units, each serving up to 10,000 sq. ft. (929 m) of space, are easy to locate and require only minimum duct runs to the areas served. Table 1 summarizes the basic choices available in self-contained systems:

2.2 Central systems
Unlike systems using self-contained units, these systems require a central equipment space where boilers, chillers, cooling towers, pumps, and similar equipment are located and used to distribute the heating and/or cooling medium to remote terminal units. Central systems may be sub-classified into two types, based on the amount of central equipment required to support their operation:

Closed loop heat pump systems
Closed loop heat pump systems represent a special category of central systems. They employ water source heat pumps (WSHP) which require only a small heating source, a circulating pump, and a small evaporative cooler (Fig. 4). Each WSHP contains an air circulating fan, a water-cooled refrigerant compressor / condenser, and a DX heating and cooling coil.

Table 1. Basic choices for self-contained HVAC systems

Type of space	Equipment type	Typical unit cooling capacity range	Electric resistance	Air Source Heat Pump (ASHP)	Gas	Expected service life
Small [residential]	Window air-conditioner	1/2 to 3 ton	X	X		5 to 10 years
	Through-wall air-conditioner	1/2 to 5 tons	X	X		5 to 10 years
to	Unit ventilator					
	Commercial split system	3 to 5 tons	X	X		15 years
Large [commercial]	Rooftop unit	5 to 25 tons	X	X	X	15 years

Air source heat pumps reject heat to the ambient air (the heat sink) when operating in the cooling mode and extract heat from the air (the heat source) in the heating mode. In contrast, water source heat pumps use water from a closed loop piping system as both their heat source and heat sink. Each water source heat pump can operate in either the heating or cooling mode, as required to meet varying space loads. For this reason, they have an inherent heat reclaim capability. If one third of the heat pumps(that is, those located at perimeter zones of a commercial office building) serving a building operate in the heating mode while the remainder of the heat pumps(serving interior zones) operate in the cooling mode, no external source of supplemental heating or cooling would be required. The building is internally balanced.

The temperature in the piping loop needs to be maintained between 60F - 90F (15°C - 32°C) for the heat pumps to operate properly; if the loop temperature approaches 90F (32°C), an evaporative cooler is activated to decrease the loop temperature. If the water in the loop drops to 60F (15°C), supplemental heat is required. In conventional closed loop systems, a hot water boiler would perform this function. In the special case of an earth-coupled ground source heat pump (GSHP) system, a piping loop buried in the earth acts as both the source for supplemental heating and cooling.

Closed loop heat pump systems strike a balance between conventional central systems (energy-efficient, but expensive and requiring large central equipment rooms) and self-contained systems (low cost but limited capabilities and service life). Closed loop heat pump systems employing many small, or modular, WSHPs compete with residential self-contained systems in residential applications such as apartments, hotels, and dormitories. In these applications, wall-mounted console units replace the through-wall units of self-contained systems; they are also available as pre-piped, vertically-stacked closet units which offer improved aesthetics and quieter operation.

In modular WSHP systems using separately-ducted ventilation air, horizontal concealed units can also be located above the ceiling. Unlike air source heat pumps, they can be used in any space (interior rooms as well as perimeter rooms) and in any height building. Some small units require no more than a 12 in. (30 cm) ceiling cavity. Larger WSHPs also compete with commercial self-contained systems in larger commercial applications, and are available in both floor-mounted (Fig. 5) and rooftop units which can be ducted to serve limited areas—approximately 10,000 sq. ft. (929 sq. m) of space for the largest factory-built units commonly used.

Conventional central systems

Conventional central systems require a full complement of central equipment (boilers, chillers, cooling towers, and circulating pumps) and a distribution system (pipes and/or ducts). Conventional central systems are often described as one of three types:

- all-water systems

- all-air systems

- air-water systems

• **All-water systems**

All-water systems typically use small modular equipment, such as fan coil units or unit ventilators, to provide the local temperature control, In these systems, hot and chilled water piping systems are the primary distribution system. All-water systems offer more energy efficient operation than self-contained systems, but at a higher first cost. The use of chilled water and hot water coils offer closer control over temperature and relative humidity than do the DX refrigerant cooling coils and electric heating coils used in self-contained systems, but all-water terminal units also share the disadvantage of limited air filtration capabilities with self-contained terminal units. Another advantage over self-contained systems is that, like closed loop heat pump

systems, all-water systems can be used in any size and height building; they are not limited to exterior zones or low-rise structures.

Like watersource heat pumps, terminal units for all-water systems come in the same configurations: wall-mounted console units, vertically-stacked closet units, and horizontal ducted units designed to be concealed above the ceiling. Fig. 6 indicates a stacked unit fan coil unit placement commonly used in limited spaces.

Variations of all-water systems include two-pipe systems and four-pipe systems. While any system using chilled water coils requires a condensate drain line to carry off water which condenses on the cold coil and collects in the condensate drain pan, the condensate piping is not counted in the nomenclature which distinguishes two-pipe systems from four-pipe systems.

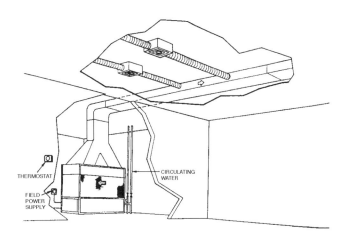

Fig. 5. Large ducted floor-mounted water source heat pump (Source: Carrier Corporation)

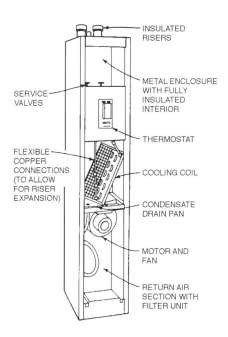

Fig. 6. Vertical "stacked" closed unit

The most common type of two-pipe system is the two-pipe change-over system, which employs a single heating/cooling coil in each terminal unit (typically called a fan coil unit) and a single set of distribution pipes. There is only one supply pipe and one return pipe, hence only hot water or chilled water can be made available to all the terminal units at any given time, and the building operator must change over the system from heating to cooling in the spring, and vice versa in the fall. This often creates comfort problems during swing seasons (spring and fall) such as a cold but sunny, clear day when the north side of a building requires heat and the side south requires cooling. For this reason, some two-pipe change-over systems are designed to include an electric resistance heating coil to provide partial heating capability for the changeover season; other systems are designed with full-size electric heating coils so either full heating or cooling is available at any time. These systems represent a compromise between the low cost of self-contained systems for residential applications such as hotels and the higher-cost of four-pipe systems.

Four-pipe systems use fan coil units which include two separate coils, a chilled water coil and a hot water coil. They also require two sets of supply/return pipes, one for hot water and one for chilled water. Four-pipe systems share the same advantages over competing systems as do two-pipe systems, but are capable of providing heating or cooling at any time at the first cost premium of an additional set of supply/return pipes and terminal coils. Four pipe systems are usually the most economical all-water system to operate.

- **All-air systems**

All-air systems employ large central air handling units, from which warm or cool air is distributed throughout the building primarily by duct distribution systems. Central all-air systems offer the most energy-efficient equipment options, and are the most flexible of any HVAC system; they can use a wide variety of terminal units to provide unlimited zoning capabilities, and factory-built air handlers can serve areas as large as 50,000 sq. ft. (4,650 sq. m) of conditioned space. The quality of construction of central system equipment can range from commercial to institutional grade, with institutional grade equipment service lives exceeding 25 years.

Each component of the central station air handling unit (AHU)—the fan, fan motor, cooling coil, heating coil, air filtration equipment, and humidification equipment—can be selected and sized *precisely* to meet the specific application needs, providing higher potential energy efficiency, comfort control, and indoor air quality. than can be accomplished with self-contained, closed loop heat pump, or all-water systems (Fig. 7).

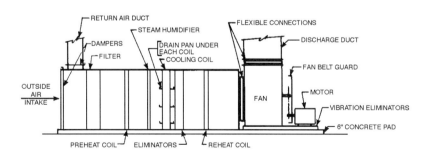

Fig. 7. Typical components of an air handling unit

SERVICES

D3

Central station air handling units are available as:

- off-the-shelf equipment which are pre-engineered and mass-produced in limited size ranges,

- modular components with the flexibility to select different sizes and configurations of each component, and

- custom units which are designed for a specific application and built up in the field.

All-air systems are usually described by two variables: the type of air handling unit provided, and the type of terminal control device used to control local zone comfort conditions. Hence a system might be described as "constant volume / reheat" or "variable volume / cooling-only." Central station air handling units are available as Constant Air Volume / Variable Air Temperature (CAV/VAT) units or Variable Air Volume / Constant Air Temperature (VAV/CAT) units.

CAV/VAT units (referred to simply as Constant Volume systems) supply a constant volume of air to the building; central heating and cooling coils vary the temperature of the air based on the building requirements (determined by local thermostats or sensors in the return air system, which indicate whether the spaces require heating or cooling). In a single zone application, this is all the control required. For some building applications with limited zoning requirements, this can be accomplished with multi-zone units, in which up to 12 sets of separate heating and cooling coils provide different temperature air to each zone.

Most central air handling systems are used to serve a large number of individual temperature control zones; therefore, the air provided by the central system must be cooled enough to meet the cooling load of the worst case zone of conditioned space; to provide local control for all the other zones, some form of reheat must be used. Hence an electric reheat coil or hot water reheat coil is used to reheat this central air—typically supplied around 55F (12°C)—as set by a local thermostat. While this system provides the best control of temperature and relative humidity, it is also very energy-inefficient to reheat the full volume of cool air supplied by the central air handler. For this reason, constant volume / reheat systems are restricted by energy codes and limited to special uses (such as hospital operating rooms and museums) which require such a high degree of control.

To overcome the inherent energy waste of constant volume / reheat systems, Variable Volume Air (VAV) systems were developed and became very popular in the 1970s. These systems include variable volume air handling units which are designed to conserve fan energy by varying the amount of central air to each zone, based on local zone requirements. Once a local control terminal (VAV box) throttles down the central air to the minimum required for ventilation and proper air circulation, reheat can be applied (at a minimum energy penalty) to the reduced volume of air to avoid overcooling the local space.

A wide range of terminal control devices, typically located above the ceiling of occupied spaces to provide local zone control, are available. To meet current energy codes, these devices must reduce the flow of central cool air to a minimum before any reheat is applied. The type of VAV box used is extremely important to the comfort conditions provided and the energy efficiency of the entire system; the types of VAV control devices available are:

- VAV cooling-only box

- VV / VT and VAV diffusers

- VAV / electric reheat coil

- VAV / hot water reheat coil

- VAV / fan-powered box, electric reheat

- VAV / fan-powered box, hot water reheat

- *VAV cooling-only box*
This is the simplest type of VAV terminal control device, consisting of dampers which regulate the flow of cool air based on a signal from the local thermostat. This is one of the more inexpensive control devices, often used to condition large interior zones of commercial office space (which typically require no heating during occupied periods). It can also be used to serve perimeter zones when either a separate heating system or VAV / reheat boxes are used to serve perimeter zones. Because this type of VAV box requires no reheat coil or piping connections, it is one of the most flexible to use. Changes to interior layouts may require only minor ducting and diffuser changes or, at the worst, changing out the VAV box with one of different capacity. VAV cooling only boxes range in capacity from approximately 200 CFM (e.g., 8x12x14 in.) to 3200 CFM (e.g., 18x65x54 in.).

- *VV / VT and VAV diffusers*
VV / VT (Variable Volume / Variable Temperature) systems rely on a complex controls and mechanical volume dampers at each individual supply air diffuser to provide zoning capabilities to small commercial systems. Both the supply air temperature delivered by the central air handler and the supply air volume at individual diffusers is varied to meet local space conditions; the control system must continuously "poll" thermostats to determine the appropriate mode of operation (heating or cooling) of the central air handler. VAV diffusers operate similarly to VAV / cooling-only boxes; each diffuser has its own mechanically-operated dampering system to control the volume of cool air discharged from the diffuser.

Both VV / VT systems and VAV diffusers rely heavily on sometimes intricate control systems and many mechanical devices, which usually have a shorter service life than the equipment they operate. Because of their limitations, they should be used to control only zones of very similar heating and cooling loads; otherwise, the system may revert to the heating mode because one or two perimeter zones require heating, even though the rest of the interior zones may be calling for cooling.

The central systems used in conjunction with these devices may or may not employ a variable speed fan; if not, all the energy efficiency benefits of "true VAV" systems are lost. VV / VT systems and VAV diffusers are generally successful when applied as a low-cost alternative, in smaller commercial buildings with many small zones (that is, many private offices in an interior area), where true VAV system costs are prohibitive.

- *VAV / electric reheat coil*
This VAV box is similar to a VAV cooling-only box, but has a small electric reheat coil attached to it. The reheat coil is not activated until the air volume is reduced to its minimum, and the electric coil must be matched to the minimum air flow to ensure adequate flow occurs across the coil. This is a flexible, low cost terminal control device, but using resistance electric heating coils involves a penalty in heating costs. Energy efficiency of the system is enhanced if a less costly heating fuel is used at the air handling unit, so the electric coil does not have to operate during overnight unoccupied periods. During the overnight heating period, the large central air handler must operate to heat the building, incurring a cost penalty in electricity usage compared to the use of fan-powered VAV boxes (described below).

VAV / electric reheat boxes also do not provide temperature control as closely as do VAV / hot water reheat boxes because the electric coil has a limited number of stages of heating (normally from one to three), whereas the hot water temperature / flow through a coil can be modulated to more closely match the heating need.

- *VAV / hot water reheat coil*
Similar in operation to the VAV / electric reheat coil, but more costly (due to additional hot water piping to each box). The main benefit of

using this VAV box is reduced heating costs compared to the VAV / electric reheat device. VAV-reheat boxes range in capacity from 200 CFM (e.g., 9x50x22 in.) to 5,000 CFM (20x60x80 in.).

• *VAV / fan-powered box, electric reheat*
This type of VAV box uses a small fan contained within the VAV box. Fan arrangements include:

- series fan / continuous operation arrangement

- parallel fan / intermittent operation

- series fan / continuous operation arrangement

The VAV box fan runs continuously, and provides the motive force to distribute the central air from the box to all associated diffusers. As the cooling load drops and the thermostat calls for heating, it reduces the volume of primary air (cold air from the central air handler) to the minimum required for ventilation while drawing warm return air from the ceiling plenum through the box. In this way it recovers heat from the ceiling plenum, and the reheat coil is activated only when the recovered heat is insufficient to heat the zone. While the use of recovered plenum heat does reduce the heating costs, these savings can be lost by the continuous use of the small (inefficient) fan, which adds heat to the primary cold air during operations in the cooling mode. Some analyses have shown this method of operation to actually use 4 to 5 times more energy than the parallel fan / intermittent operation arrangement described below.

This arrangement, although a true VAV application (providing efficient operation of the central air handling fan), actually provides a continuous volume of air to the occupied space. For this reason, it is sometimes used in conjunction with ice storage / cold air distribution systems which deliver colder air than the conventional 55F (12°C) supply air temperature; mixing the cold air with warm plenum air permits the use of conventional diffusers without creating the effect of "dumping" cold air on the occupants. It also helps to prevent condensate from forming on diffusers. This method of handling cold air distribution now competes with recently-introduced induction diffusers designed to obtain greater mixing of the supply air with room air before it enters the occupied zone.

- *Parallel fan / intermittent operation*
Parallel fan with intermittent operation: During the cooling cycle, the cool primary air volume is reduced as the cooling load decreases, until it reaches the minimum air volume required for ventilation. The VAV box is not activated until there is a call for heating. On the first call for heating, it draws 100% warm air from the ceiling plenum, making maximum use of the recovered heat. If the recovered heat from the ceiling plenum is insufficient to satisfy the thermostat, there will be a second call for heating. The reheat coil will then be activated.

The parallel fan is only sized to deliver the maximum amount of air required for heating, and therefore is much smaller than the fans designed for series / continuous operation. The parallel fan only runs during the heating cycle, when the heat given off by the inefficient motor provides useful work. For these reasons, the parallel fan / intermittent operation tends to be much more energy efficient than the series / continuous fan arrangement.

- *VAV / fan-powered box, hot water reheat*
This type of VAV box is the most energy efficient of all when used in the parallel fan / intermittent operation arrangement. Other than the opportunity to use a more efficient heating source from a central plant, its operation is similar to that described for the VAV / fan-powered box, electric reheat. Because it is more expensive and less flexible than other VAV boxes (due to the box fan and hot water piping), this VAV box is commonly used to condition perimeter zones which require more heat, and often are used for relatively fixed private office layouts. Less expensive, more flexible, cooling-only VAV boxes are then used to condition large interior spaces.

• **Air-water systems**
These systems include any type of air-water system which is combined with a separately-ducted ventilation air system, plus a unique system called the induction system. An induction system uses "primary air" from a high velocity central air handling system, which is ducted through a type of terminal unit which is specially designed to use the Venturi effect of the primary air stream to induce room air into the unit and across the heating / cooling coil. Hence it operates like a fan coil unit without requiring a local fan.

This type of system is found in to high-rise buildings where a minimum amount of ductwork is desirable). A good use is typified by building applications where modular units are desired for individual room control. Improved air quality and humidity control is provided since a central ventilation system air handler can be used to provide better outside air filtration, better control of relative humidity, and an opportunity to recover waste heat from building exhaust air streams). Primarily due to high maintenance costs, the constant volume induction system has fallen from favor and no new induction system has been installed since about 1985. It is still found, of course, in existing buildings. Table 2 summarizes the basic types of central systems currently available and their general characteristics:

Table 2. Basic central HVAC system types

Type of space	Equipment type	Electric resistance	Air Source Heat Pump (ASHP)	Water Source Heat Pump WSHP/GSHP	Steam/hot water water	Expected service life
Small [residential]	Modular fan coil units	X	X		X	20+ years
	Modular closed loop heat pumps			X		19 years
to	Unit ventilators & induction units	X	X	X	X	20+ years
Large [commercial]	Air handling units: Off-the-shelf Modular Custom	X	X	X	X	15 + years 15-20 years 25+ years

3   Overview of HVAC systems

Describing HVAC system types by category (as above) is a convenient method of explaining the nomenclature used by engineers and the engineering principles involved. However, the system selection process for any project begins with the application in mind. For this reason, the charts in this article were developed to provide an overview of the HVAC systems to be considered in different commercial building applications. Table 3 can be used to view all the HVAC systems commonly used in commercial building applications (densely-populated buildings with high internal air-conditioning loads due to people, lights, and office equipment).

3.1   Selecting the HVAC system

The following process can be used to efficiently select, or at least to shortlist, the final HVAC system options for a given building application:

1   Identify the range of HVAC system types that are appropriate for a given application from a master matrix of system types and building applications;

2   Shortlist the original set of generally applicable HVAC systems using a few key screening criteria which relate to a more specific building (high-rise vs. low-rise), owner criteria, or climatic consideration;

3   Once the number of potential HVAC systems is shortlisted to two or three, review the more detailed descriptions of each system's cost, equipment requirements, and performance characteristics to better understand their differences; either make the initial system selection at this point or

4   Review the final system shortlist with the Owner and engineering consultant to determine if more detailed analyses are required to select the best system, or to evaluate specific system options.

The matrices indicated in Tables 4 and 5 illustrate the basic HVAC system types (across the top of the chart) and basic building applications (left side of the chart) for residential and commercial building systems, respectively. Using this system selection matrix allows one to quickly narrow the potential system types to be evaluated further to three or four, simplifying the decision-making process.

Once a shortlist of potential system types is developed in this manner, further steps can be taken to reduce the final choices to perhaps one or two:

-   Rule out any system that does not fit with the basic category appropriate to the building application (that is, a speculative builder of apartment buildings might not want to consider any central system types; a university may rule out the use of self-contained systems due to a preference for central equipment rooms or the availability of campus-wide steam, hot water, or chilled water lines from a central plant).

-   Use the preliminary screening criteria noted in Table 6. Rule out any system type which is shown to be inappropriate for the given building application.

-   Review the detailed system selection criteria below and the HVAC system descriptions (on the following pages) for the remaining options to select the HVAC system most likely to meet the application's needs.

3.2   Summary of HVAC system selection criteria

•   *Site constraints and opportunities*

-   Climatic considerations: How do local weather factors affect annual utility costs, and how important are the annual energy costs to the client's business operation?

-   Ambient air quality: Does the general area air quality affect the degree of air filtration and treatment required? Do local condi-

tions affect the location of outdoor air intakes(that is, are there local pollution sources from street level traffic, or from the roofs of adjacent buildings?

-   Available utilities & costs: Which utilities are available (electricity, gas, district or central plant steam, hot water chilled water), and at what unit cost? Are their specific rate schedules available for all-electric systems? Are equipment rebates available from local utility providers for "preferred" equipment? Should the system be designed for flexibility in fuel choices, so that the least cost fuel can be switched based on periodic utility negotiations?

-   Visual sightlines: Will rooftop equipment be visible?

-   Building and site boundaries: Do current buildings abut sides of this building, or could they in the future?

•   *Owner / developer requirements*

-   First cost: How important is it relative to long-term operating costs? Should systems requiring large mech. equipment rooms, duct shafts, or increased ceiling heights be avoided?

-   Construction schedule: Is off-the-shelf packaged equipment required to avoid long lead times for equipment procurement?

-   Annual energy and utility costs: Are there economic criteria established for decision-making on any energy-related premiums in system first cost?

-   Capacity of building maintenance staff (number of staff and skill level): Will custodial staff be available to change air filters and clean condensate pans on many small modular terminal units, or should most maintenance be performed in a central equipment room by more skilled staff? Will the use of high pressure steam boilers require the presence of operating engineers around the clock?

-   Space considerations: If rental property, how much income is lost annually for lost rental space occupied by mechanical equipment and duct and pipe shafts?

-   Equipment location considerations: Should equipment locations at building perimeter and corner office space be avoided at all cost? Would this eliminate the use of self-contained or floor-by-floor indoor air handlers?

-   Durability: Will exposed equipment be vulnerable to vandalism or physical abuse?

-   Reliability: How important is redundant central equipment or multiple self-contained units?

-   Flexibility: How often are interior space layouts expected to change, and how much will it cost to make the required changes to the HVAC system? Is the churn rate high enough, or cubicle density requirements high enough, to warrant consideration of all-air, below-floor distribution plenums rather than conventional ceiling distribution systems?

-   Adaptability: How easily should the HVAC system be adaptable to a new space function; will the building be more marketable, now or in the future, with a more adaptable system?

•   *End user and occupant requirements*

-   Degree of temperature and humidity control: How precisely must indoor air temperature be controlled; is close control of relative humidity important?

-   Degree of air filtration required: Are low efficiency flat filters associated with self-contained and modular terminal units adequate, or is high efficiency filtration available with central all-air systems required?

-   Need to avoid cross-contamination between rooms: Should all-air systems using common return air plenums be ruled out?

Table 3. Overview of commercial (non-residential) HVAC system types

Legend:
- ■ = Not applicable or rarely used
- ● = Commonly Used
- ○ = Infrequently Used

HEATING SYSTEM OPTIONS — Heating System First Cost Premium: LOW → HIGH

Separate Systems:
- H.W. Radiant Panels @ Perimeter Ceiling
- H.W. Baseboard/Wall Convectors
- Elect. Radiant Panels @ Perimeter Ceiling
- Elect. Baseboard/Wall Convectors

In-Unit Options:
- Ground Source Heat Pump DX Coil
- Hot Water or Steam Heating Coil
- Watersource Heat Pump DX Heating Coil
- Air Source Heat Pump DX and Elect. Htg. Coil
- Direct Gas-Fired
- Elect. Heating Coil

TERMINAL CONTROL DEVICES for additional Temp. Control Zones — First Cost/Zone: LOW → HIGH
- VAV Box, Fan-Powered w/ H.W. Reheat Coil
- VAV Box, H.W. Reheat Coil
- VAV Box, Fan-Powered w/ Elect. Reheat Coil
- VAV Box, Electric Reheat Coil
- VAV Box (Cooling-Only)
- H.W. Reheat Coil
- Elect. Reheat Coil
- VVT & VAV Diffusers

NON-RESIDENTIAL HVAC SYSTEMS

Generic System Type	General Application Notes
SELF-CONTAINED — Unitary Ducted Air Conditioners	■ Often ALL-ELECTRIC; direct gas heat option avail.
DUCTED ALL-AIR SYSTEMS* [limited to low- and mid-rise bldgs. only] — Unitary Ducted Air Source Heat Pumps; Unitary Ducted Multizone AHU; Gas-Fired Dessicant Air-Conditioner	■ Multiple ROOFTOP UNITS = popular use; ■ Airside ECONOMIZER COOLING option avail.; ■ Largest units SERVE UP TO 10,000 SF AREA
CENTRAL DUCTED WATER LOOP HEAT PUMP SYSTEMS* — Central Water Source Heat Pump AHU; Central Ground Source Heat Pump AHU	
CENTRAL ALL-WATER SYSTEMS* (Small modular terminal units; may be referred to as "air-water system" if combined with central ducted ventilation air system) — 2-Pipe Modular Fan Coil Unit/Unit Vent.; Modular Closed Loop Heat Pump; 4-Pipe Modular Fan Coil Unit; 4-Pipe Modular Unit Ventilator	■ Most often used at bldg. perimeter; ■ VENTILATION thru-wall or centrally ducted; ■ NO airside ECONOMIZER COOLING avail.; ■ Largest units SERVE UP TO 1,000 SF AREA
CENTRAL ALL-AIR SYSTEMS — Central Station Multizone AHU; Central Station Constant Volume AHU; Central Station Variable Volume AHU	■ Most flexible systems, ECON. COOLING avail.; ■ Use is not limited by building size/height; ■ Largest units serve 40,000 SF AREA or more
CENTRAL AIR-WATER SYSTEMS — Air-Water Induction Unit	■ Limited to HIGH-RISES; 1500 SF AREA/unit

Cost / First Cost: LOW → HIGH

*** See Residential/Light Commercial systems chart for smaller, non-ducted system options.**

EQUIPMENT OPTIONS

HVAC System Type	Central Equipment	Mech. Equipment Locations
Unitary Air Conditioner AHU; Unitary Air Source Heat Pump AHU; Unitary Multizone AHU; Gas-Fired Dessicant Air-Conditioner	None	Self-Contained ROOFTOP Units, Indoor AHU's w/ Access to Outside Air, or Indoor AHU's with Remote Air-Cooled Condensers
Central Closed Loop Heat Pump(WSHP); Central Closed Loop Heat Pump(GSHP)	Boiler, Closed Ckt. Cooler, Pumps / Ground-Coupled Piping Loop	ROOFTOP Units or Indoor Units
2-Pipe Modular Fan Coil Unit; 2-Pipe Modular Unit Ventilator; 4-Pipe Modular Fan Coil Unit; 4-Pipe Modular Unit Ventilator	Boiler(s) / Air-Cooled Chiller(s) or Water-Cooled Chiller/Cooling Towers / Pumps(& AHU if separate vent. system used)	Central Mech. Eqpmt. Room, Rooftop Heat Rejection Equipment, and Local Terminal Eqpmt.
Central Station Multizone AHU; Central Station Constant Volume AHU; Central Station Variable Volume AHU	Boiler(s) & Chiller(s), Cooling Tower(s) & Pumps, Central AHU's	Central Mech. Eqpmt. Room & Rooftop Heat Rejection Equipment
Air-Water Induction Unit	Boiler(s),Chiller(s),Tower(s), Pumps, AHU's	Central M.E.R. & Rooftop Cooling Tower(s)

*** See Residential/Light Commercial systems chart for smaller, non-ducted system options.**

SERVICES / D3

Table 4. HVAC system selection matrix for heating-only applications

Legend:
- █ Not Applicable or rarely used
- ● Frequently used for application listed
- ○ Infrequently used for application listed

← ——————— Heating - Only Systems ——————— ——————— ——————— ——————— →

Application	Primary Building Function	Electric Baseboard	Warm Air Furnace	Infra-Red Heat	Radiant Electric	H.W. Baseboard or Convectors	Radiant H.W.
Residential	Single-Family Residence	●	●	█	○	●	●
	Low-Rise Multi-Family/Apartments	●	●	█	█	●	█
	Motels / Nursing Homes	█	○	█	○	█	○
	Dormitories	█	█	█	█	●	●
	Hotels	█	█	█	█	█	█
Light Commercial		█	█	█	█	█	█
	Country Club/Funeral Home	█	█	█	█	█	█
	Beauty/Barber Shops	█	█	█	█	█	█
	Small Retail Stores	█	█	█	█	█	█
	Department Stores	█	█	█	█	○	█
	Malls/Shopping Centers	█	█	█	█	█	█
	Restaurants	█	█	█	█	█	█
	Bowling Alleys	█	█	█	█	█	█
	Places of Worship	█	○	█	█	●	█
	Theatres	█	█	█	█	█	█
Commercial		█	█	█	█	█	█
	Auditoriums	█	█	█	█	█	█
	Class B Spec Office Building	█	█	█	█	█	█
	Class A Spec Office Building	█	█	█	█	█	█
	Corporate Office Building	█	█	█	█	█	█
	Radio/TV Studios	█	█	█	█	█	█
	Libraries (Standard)	█	█	█	█	█	█
	Libraries (Archival)/Museums	█	█	█	█	█	█
	Arenas/Exhibition Halls	█	█	█	█	█	█
	Service Garage	█	●	●	█	●	█
	Warehouse	█	●	●	█	●	█
Institutional		█	█	█	█	█	█
	Elementary Schools	█	█	█	█	●	█
	Secondary Schools	█	█	█	█	○	█
	Higher Education	█	█	█	█	█	█
	Laboratories	█	█	█	█	█	█
	Hospitals	█	█	█	█	█	█
Industrial		█	█	█	█	█	█
	Light Assembly/Fabrication	█	●	●	█	●	█

SERVICES

D3

Table 5. HVAC system selection matrix for combined heating/cooling applications

Legend:
▬ Not Applicable or rarely used
● Frequently used for application listed
○ Infrequently used for application listed

Application	Primary Building Function	Warm Air Furnace with Add-On A/C	Window & Thru-Wall A/C with Elect. Heat	2-Pipe Changeover Fan Coil Units & Unit Ventilators	Thru-Wall or Split-System Air-Source Heat Pumps & Unit Ventilators	Modular Water-Source Heat Pumps & Unit Ventilators	4-Pipe Fan Coil Unit & Unit Ventilators	Single Zone, Constant Air Volume	Single Zone, Constant Air Volume w/ Elect. Reheat	Single Zone V.A.V.	VAV Box w/ Elect. Reheat	Fan-Powered VAV w/ Elect. Reheat	Multizone, Constant Air Volume	Single Zone, Constant Air Volume w/ H.W. Reheat Coils	Cooling-Only VAV w/ Separate Perim. Heat	VAV w/ H.W. Reheat Coils	Fan-Powered VAV w/ H.W. Reheat Coils
Residential	Single-Family Residence	●	○		●	○											
	Low-Rise Multi-Family/Apartments	●	●	○	●	●											
	Motels / Nursing Homes	○	●	●	●	●											
	Dormitories			●	●	●	●										
	Hotels			●	●	●	●										
Light Commercial	Country Club/Funeral Home	●			●	○		●									
	Beauty/Barber Shops		●	●	●	●		●									
	Small Retail Stores	●		●	●	●	●	●									
	Department Stores					●	●	●		○					●		
	Malls/Shopping Centers	○	○	○	●	●	●	●		○							
	Restaurants			●	●	●	●	●	●	○	●	●	●		○	●	●
	Bowling Alleys				○	●		●		○	●	●	●	●	●	●	●
	Places of Worship			○	○			●	●	○	●	●	●				
	Theatres			○	○		●	●	●	○	○						
Commercial	Auditoriums						●	●	●		○						
	Class B Spec Office Building				●	●	○	○		○	●	●	●		●	●	●
	Class A Spec Office Building					●	●				●	●	●		●	●	●
	Corporate Office Building			●	●	●	●	○			●	●	●		●	●	●
	Radio/TV Studios											○					
	Libraries (Standard)					●	●	○			○	○	○		○	○	○
	Libraries (Archival)/Museums						●	○	●	●	○	○	○	●	○	○	○
	Arenas/Exhibition Halls												○				
	Service Garage																
	Warehouse																
Institutional	Elementary Schools		○	●	●	●	●	●			●	○			●	●	●
	Secondary Schools		○	●	●	●	●	●			●	○			●	●	●
	Higher Education			●	●	●	●	●				○			●	●	●
	Laboratories						●	●	●								
Industrial	Hospitals								●					●			
	Light Assembly/Fabrication																

- Number of separate temperature control zones required: What is the ratio of private spaces requiring individual thermostatic control compared to large open plan areas requiring only one temperature control zone per 1,000 SF or more of floor area? Should modular all-water terminal units be used in small perimeter spaces, with larger all-air VAV systems serving large interior cooling-only zones?

4   Space planning considerations

In this section, the critical planning and design considerations are reviewed for efficient layout of central mechanical equipment rooms and air handling equipment rooms ("fan rooms"). The space required to house HVAC equipment and associated pipe and duct shafts can amount to over 10 percent of the building floor area, depending upon the building application and type of HVAC system used. Heavy structural loads of central equipment will also effect the building's structural system design. The location of the mechanical equipment can impact both the building aesthetics and the acoustical environment in occupied areas. Due to such impacts, the spatial layout of the HVAC system needs to be programmed early in the design phase and coordinated with all other building elements.

Once the HVAC system has been selected, the first step in planning its layout is to identify the location and configuration of the central equipment. In large buildings using central systems, this often includes three types of equipment rooms:

- a central plant equipment space (usually one location in the building, housing central chillers, boilers and related equipment)

- a rooftop location for cooling towers, and

- equipment room(s) for large central air-handling units.

Central plant equipment rooms are often located at the top of a building to minimize the piping distance to connect the chillers to the rooftop cooling towers, and to minimize the length of expensive boiler flues which typically extend will above rooftop heights. Depending on the building application, the central plant equipment room may also be located on the lowest floor of the building, or the boilers and chillers may be located in two different locations.

The nomograph shown in Fig. 8 in conjunction with Table 7 provides a simple technique for approximating the sizes of the main air-conditioning system components, the space required to house them, and associated duct sizes.

4.1   System sizing nomograph: an example

The nomograph is used by entering with total building area on bar (A). To use and example:

- Consider a 300,000 sq. ft. office building. In Table 7, the data for an office building indicates a medium air conditioning load of 400 sq. ft. per ton and medium air quantity of .9 CFM/sq. ft.

  - Entering the nomograph with a building area of 300,000 sq. ft. and proceeding vertically up to (B), and the sloped line representing 400 sq. ft./ton on bar (C), the air conditioner size can be approximated as 750 tons.

  - Continuing horizontally to the right to the 45° turning line, we proceed vertically down to bar (D) and vertically up to bar (E). On bar (D) we read the mechanical equipment room volume as 45,000 cu. ft.

  - On bar (E), the cooling tower area would be read as 900 sq. ft.

  - Going back to bar (A) and proceeding vertically downward to (F) and turning to the 1 CFM/sq. ft. line, we read on bar (G) that the total air volume is 300,000 Cubic Feet per Minute (CFM).

- The above narrative on air handling equipment indicates that the largest commercially available units (not custom) are about 40,000 CFM. We know that this office building will require several air handlers. For design estimating purposes, assume we are designing a 10 story office building with 30,000 sq. ft. per floor and that we will have one 30,000 CFM air handler on each floor.

Table 6. Preliminary screening criteria

IF the building application:	THEN:
is not a hospital operating room, laboratory, museum, or other special use space requiring exceptionally close control of temperature, relative humidity, and/or space pressurization relationships	Rule out constant volume terminal reheat systems (current energy codes prohibit the use of this system type except for special use applications, unless the source of reheat is recovered heat).
considers building aesthetics to be crucial to commercial success	Rule out self-contained through-wall and window air-conditioners (which require many visible A/C system components penetrating exterior walls).
is greater than six stories high	Rule out self-contained rooftop, split systems, and multizone units (these system types typically don't have the capability to serve tall/large buildings due to inherent equipment limitations).
requires the use of economizer cooling ("free cooling" in winter) or maximum outside air capability for "purging" the building	Rule out all-water and air/water systems (which have little or no separately-ducted outside air capability).
requires simultaneous heating and cooling for different areas of the building at any time of the year	Rule out two pipe "change-over" fan coil unit systems OR provide supplemental electric heating coils designed to provide adequate heat for "in between" seasons.
is located in a climatic area characterized by high humidity at summer design conditions (hot/humid climates)	Rule out multizone systems (due to inherent system limitations in handling high humidity/high temperature conditions).

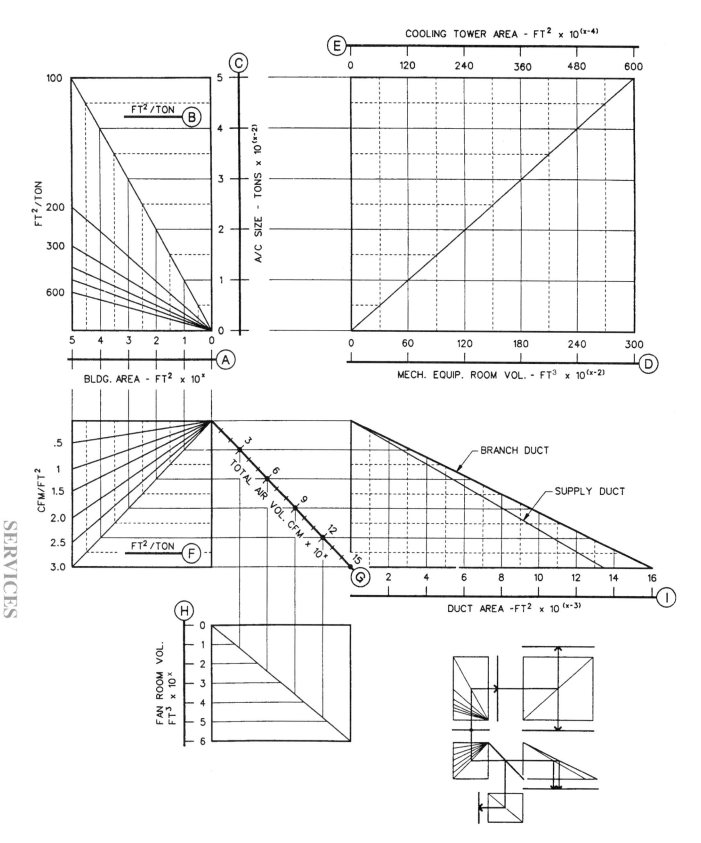

Fig. 8. Space and duct sizing nomograph

SERVICES

D3

Table 7. Air conditioning and air quantities for various building types

	Air Conditioning Load (SF/ton)			Air Quantities (CFM/SF)		
	Low	Medium	High	Low	Medium	High
Apartments, Hi Rise	500	425	350	0.8	1.0	1.3
Auditoriums, Churches, Theaters	400	300	150	1.0	1.8	2.5
Educational Facilities	400	300	200	0.8	1.2	1.8
Factories						
Light Manufacturing	350	250	150	1.2	1.6	2.0
Heaving Manufacturing	150	100	75	2.5	3.5	4.5
Hospitals						
Patient Rooms	350	250	180	.5	.75	.9
Public Areas	300	250	150	.8	1.0	1.1
Hotels, Motels, Dormitories	500	400	300	.9	1.2	1.4
Libraries & Museums	400	350	300	.9	1.0	1.1
Office Buildings	500	400	300	.7	.9	1.2
Residential						
Large, Single Family	800	600	400	.5	.7	1.0
Medium, Single Family	800	700	600	.5	.7	1.0
Shopping Centers						
Beauty & Barber Shops	300	250	200	.9	1.3	2.0
Department Stores	500	400	300	.9	1.4	2.0
Drug Stores	250	200	150	.7	1.0	1.3
Shoe Stores	400	300	200	.8	1.0	1.2
Malls	450	350	250	1.1	1.6	2.0

SERVICES

D3

- Enter bar (A) with 30,000 sq. ft.

- Bar (G) shows 30,000 CFM.

- Bar (H) shows 12,500 cu. ft. If we have a clear height of 12 ft. in the fan room, it would have a floor area of 1,041 sq. ft.

- Typical air handling unit data (e.g., Sweet's catalog manufacturer's literature) indicate, let us assume, an approximate unit size of 14x11x7.6 ft. This should fit comfortably within a room of 25 ft. x 40 ft. and have space for all associated ductwork and servicing. Proceeding from 3 on bar (G) horizontally to the branch duct and supply duct turning lines:

- We read on bar (I), a supply duct total area of 25 sq. ft.

- We read 33 sq. ft. of branch duct area.

- We now know we have a supply air duct of approximately 36 x 100 in., leaving the fan room before it begins to branch to smaller sizes to serve various areas of the floor. Note that the sum of the branch duct area is larger than the total supply duct area. This is dues to a lower air velocity being used in the branches.

- Remember that return air duct work with the same area as the branch ductwork will be required to for return air back to the fan room to complete the system ducting.

- Bear in mind that cooling towers can range in height from 12 ft. to over 40 ft. and should be located far away from building openings (such as windows and outside air intakes) to avoid the possibility of any carryover of moist, and possibly contaminated air back into occupied areas.

4.2   Central equipment room planning

Central equipment rooms housing boilers, chillers and large pumps should have between 12 - 16 ft. clear height available, from the finished floor to underside of structure, to allow for adequate clearance above the main equipment for accessories and large piping crossovers. Long narrow rooms—with an aspect ratio (width to length) of approximately 1:2—usually allow for the most flexible and efficient layout of equipment. The equipment room sizes given in the nomograph above should provide adequate space for typical equipment accessories, clearances around equipment for servicing and replacement, and "tube-pull" clearances. Equipment such as chillers and shell-and-tube heat exchangers require clear space equal to the length of the equipment in order to pull the heat exchange tubes for servicing. Often a "back-to-back" arrangement of equipment minimizes the total floor area required to accommodate such needs.

Care should be given to proper vibration isolation for large equipment, particularly rotating equipment, such as chillers and pumps. In addition to planning the location and configuration of equipment rooms, access to these rooms is an important consideration. Adequate equipment room doors and routes to freight elevators and/or the building exterior, should be planned such that the largest piece of equipment can be easily installed (and possibly removed in future).

4.3   Air-handling equipment planning

The number and location of central air handling unit equipment rooms (commonly called "fan rooms") are critical to a successful HVAC system, because they often occur in more than one location and tend to be closer to the occupied areas of a building. As noted above, the nomograph in Fig. 8 indicates an estimate of the CFM requirements for the building. Since the largest central fans typically used in commercial applications are approximately 40,000 CFM in capacity, dividing the building CFM by 40,000 yields the minimum number of air handlers required to serve the building. (If self-contained equipment, such as rooftop units, are to be used, a maximum size of 10,000 CFM per air handler should be used.)

Once the number of air handling units is determined, the next planning decision is how (or whether) they are to be grouped together in separate rooms. Generally speaking, the more "centered" or centrally located within the building, the more efficient and less costly will be the distribution systems. However, other planning considerations may dictate a more beneficial arrangement. The following discussion summarizes typical air-handling unity equipment room arrangement approaches:

- *"Scattered" or separated units*
In this approach, often used in low-rise buildings employing rooftop equipment, the air handlers are simply located as centrally as possible to the separate zones they serve (and are thus scattered throughout the building as a function of its separate zones). This arrangement results in the most efficient fan sizing and minimal duct sizes. Since the layout results in air handlers being located directly above occupied areas, noise and vibration isolation are critical factors.

- *"Central core" placement*
In "central core" placement, all air handling unit rooms are located together near the building core often on multiple floors in high-rise buildings. This arrangement, very common for large commercial buildings, tends to yield the most efficient equipment room layout and duct distribution layout if one air handler can serve and entire floor. However, horizontal or vertical ducting is required to admit and reject fresh outside air and to exhaust spent air.

- Air handling unit rooms placed in the central core can take advantage of other service elements such as elevator shafts and restrooms to buffer noise. Ideally, no equipment room wall should be located immediately adjacent to an occupied space and equipment rooms are best stacked vertically to minimize piping and air shaft space requirements. Also, in an ideal planning arrangement, at least two and preferable three sides of the equipment room are free of vertical obstructions so that supply and return ductwork can pass through them to serve the occupied areas.

- Because the floor-to-ceiling height is limited to the typical building floor height, the supply/return mains tend to be dimensioned "flatter" than desired for optimal air flow efficiency and noise control. This, coupled with tight space constraints and less than optimal fan ducting, often results in excessive fan noise and high velocity duct noise from the mains. For this reason, plans should place the exiting ducts to pass over low occupancy service spaces, such as closets and restrooms, and also to include a duct turn above these spaces to reduce duct transmitted noise.

- *"Perimeter" rooms*
Arranging the fan rooms at the building perimeter minimizes the ducting required for outside air and exhaust air, but can reduce the efficiency of the supply/return duct system, unless multiple units are required for each floor. Disadvantages to this configuration include the potential lost use of premium perimeter floor areas, the aesthetic impact of large air intake/exhaust louvers on the exterior, and proximity of potentially noisy equipment close to occupied areas of the building.

- *"Detached" rooms*
This arrangement moves the equipment room outside the main building, such as an adjacent protruding service shaft. While decreasing the efficiency of duct distribution, it sometimes allows for maximum space utilization and flexibility within the main floor plate of the building it serves.

4.4   System summaries

The descriptions that follow in tabular form (Tables 8 to 16) summarize the operating characteristics and key design considerations for the HVAC systems described above. These tables, listed here for reference, include:

SERVICES

D3

5 HVAC equipment descriptions

Boilers

Boilers are used to provide a building with steam or hot water for space heating, processes, and services. Steam is selected as the medium if required by the process needs, but hot water is more common for space heating because it is more flexible and offers better space temperature control. A boiler may be rated with a gross output in thousands of Btu per hour (MBH), boiler horsepower (33,475 Btu/hr = 1BHP), or pounds of steam per hour (970.3 Btu per pound). Fuels used include natural gas, oil, electricity, and coal. Outdoor air for combustion should be provided at the rate of approximately 12.5 CFM per BHP The net free area of direct openings in boiler rooms for combustion air should not be less than 1 square inch for every 4 MBH, or for every 2 MBH if the combustion air is ducted to the boiler. Boilers typically have turndown capability to reduce the boiler output in response to the load. Common turndown ratios are 4:1 and 10:1.

Boilers can be categorized by construction material. Cast iron boilers are built up in sections, and are expandable to add capacity. They are used in closed, low pressure heating systems. There are also several types of steel boilers. Among the steel firetube boilers are scotch marine and firebox types, which direct the flue gasses through tubes surrounded by water. Several varieties of watertube boilers, which direct water through tubes in the combustion gas chamber, are also used. Typical capacity ranges and other properties for a number of boiler types are shown in Table 17. Selection criteria are shown in Fig. 9.

General space requirements must allow ample room for service, which may include space to pull boiler tubes. As an example, firetube boilers, from 15 - 80 ft., have tube unit lengths of 8 - 27 ft., and widths of 4 - 10 ft. These units require an additional 5 - 23 ft. of space to pull tubes as necessary. The tube-pull space provided may be within the boiler room, or may extend through a doorway. The total weight associated with these boilers varies from 300 lb. per BHP (Boiler horsepower) at 15 BHP, to 110 lb. per BHP at 800 BHP. In general, boiler room heights should be 12 - 16 ft. For a given boiler system, multiple units should be considered. Matching total boiler capacity to a variable load requirement will provide backup capability if one boiler is out of service. Gross oversizing of boiler capacity should be avoided, because excessive cycling will compromise net efficiency.

Modular boilers are individual cast iron boilers which are installed in banks. Module capacities range from 9 to 57 BHP. Supply, return, and breeching systems are common to the entire bank of boilers, but the units are step-fired, using only the number of modules necessary to meet the load. Each module fires continuously or in long cycles, at its peak efficiency, and avoids the on-off cycling of single capacity boilers. This type of system can retain high efficiency through the heating season, and the entire assembly need not be shut down to repair a single unit. Also, the modules require less field assembly and at less than 30 in wide, are small enough to fit through standard door openings. Module lengths are approximately 3 in. per BHP, and heights before stacks are installed are less than 6 feet. Condensing boilers available today allow cooler return water temperatures, cooler stack temperatures, and higher efficiency than non-condensing boilers.

Cooling equipment

Cooling equipment is sized by ton of cooling capacity. A ton in refrigeration terms is equal to 12,000 Btu/hr, which corresponds to the hourly heat input required to melt one ton of ice in one day at 32F (0°C). Cooling equipment capacities range from less than one ton for small devices such as window air conditioners, to several thousand tons for the largest central plant equipment.

The vapor compression refrigeration cycle is the most common technology used in cooling equipment. In the basic process, a low temperature, low pressure refrigerant liquid is sent through an evaporator heat exchanger, where it absorbs heat (that is, from the heat load generated by the building) and evaporates into vapor form. A cooling effect is left in the building from which the heat was absorbed. The low temperature, low pressure refrigerant vapor is then mechanically compressed to raise its temperature and pressure. The high temperature, high pressure vapor is sent to a condenser heat exchanger, where it rejects the heat (to the outdoors) and condenses to a medium temperature, high pressure liquid. After flowing through an expansion device, the refrigerant again becomes a low temperature, low pressure liquid, and the cycle continues. The basic vapor compression cycle is illustrated in Fig. 10

The efficiency of cooling equipment is determined by the quantity of cooling generated for a given quantity of mechanical compressor energy used. There are several ways of expressing this. The Energy Efficient Ratio (EER) rating is used for residential equipment. It represents the cooling capacity in Btu/hr divided by the electrical input in watts. A seasonal energy efficiency ratio (SEER) is frequently used, which divides the total seasonal cooling Btu by the total watt-hours. Common SEER values range from 7 to 16. Coefficient of Performance (COP) is used for heat pumps and large equipment - up to a value of 7. COP is the EER divided by 3.412 Btu/watt. Chillers are often rated by kW/ton, with values ranging from .1 - 1.0.

In general, cooling equipment should not be oversized. Oversized cooling equipment compromises comfort (humidity) conditions, and short cycling leads to excessive equipment wear. When an oversized system short-cycles, the air is cooled but the cyclic behavior doesn't remove moisture adequately. The result can be a "cold and clammy" environment. If anything, a slight undersizing will allow improved comfort and operating conditions for a larger number of hours, if there are relatively few peak hours in the year.

Chillers

The primary piece of equipment in a central cooling system is the chiller. A chiller basically packages together those individual components necessary to support the vapor compression cycle and create a cooling effect (the evaporator, condenser, and compressor). These components may be contained in one piece of equipment, or separated with the evaporator inside, and the compressor / condenser outside. Chillers are usually classified by the type of compressor used to drive the refrigeration cycle. Several types of compressors are available, including centrifugal, reciprocating, rotary screw, and scroll.

Centrifugal chillers compress the refrigerant with a rotating impeller. Rated efficiencies are generally good, with values as low as .5 kW/ton, and COP's falling in the 4.2 - 6.0 range. When these units operate at less than 30% of full load, their efficiency drops off rapidly. Multistage compressors are available to increase part load efficiencies. Centrifugal chiller are available with capacities starting as low as 100 ton, but they are used primarily in large central plants, with capacities of 1,000 tons and more.

There are several types of compressors:

- Reciprocating (piston) compressors are common in the 3 to 50 ton range, where they are typically more efficient than centrifugal units. Reciprocating chillers use a proven technology, serve a wide variety of commercial applications, and generally have a lower initial cost than other chiller types. They have more individual parts than some other chiller types, and therefore require more maintenance. Reciprocating compressors produce more vibration than other machines. For this reason, care must be exercised in mounting, particularly if used on a rooftop.

- Rotating screw compressors operate with single or double interfitting rotors to compress the refrigerant. Screw compressors are rated as low as .57 kW/ton, and have superior part load characteristics. The COP of screw compressors is not reduced at higher

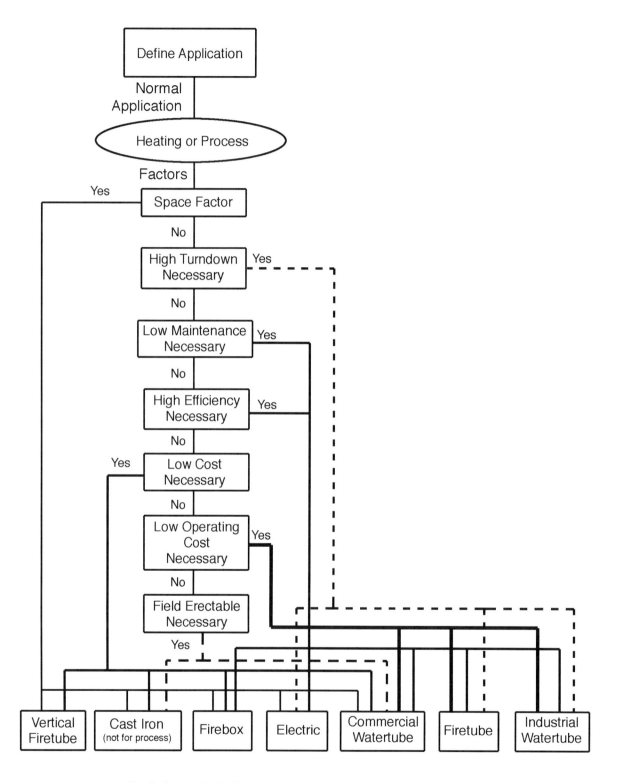

Fig. 9. General selection criteria for boilers (Source: Cleaver Brooks)

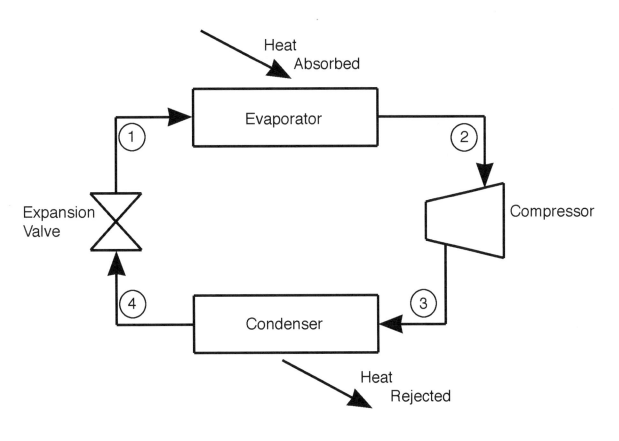

Refrigerant Conditions

①	Low T	Low P	Liquid
②	Low T	Low P	Vapor
③	High T	High P	Vapor
④	Med T	High P	Liquid

Fig. 10. Basic vapor compression cycle.

Table 8. Self-contained air conditioners and air-source heat pumps (window units, thru-wall units, and residential split-system units).

NOTE: This system <u>usually</u> used for perimeter space conditioning only, with separate all-air sytem serving large interior zones.

General building applications.	Small Residential/Light Commercial Rooms @ Exterior Wall, max. 6 stories.
System classification:	Self-Contained, All-Electric Equipment (Non-Ducted)
System type:	**Self-Contained Air-Conditioners & Air Source Heat Pumps(ASHP)**
Competing systems:	Modular WSHP's and GSHP's,
	2-Pipe and 4-Pipe Fan Coil Units

Common equipment configurations:	Window Unit Through-Wall Unit	Split System Unit
General System Characteristics		
Basic operating principle:	Constant Air Volume/Variable Air Temp.	Constant Air Volume/Variable Air Temp.
Equipment quality:	Residential "appliance" unless A.R.I. rated as PTAC (commercial)	Residential "appliance" unless A.R.I. rated as PTAC(commercial)
Cooling coil type:	DX refrigerant (R-22)	DX refrigerant (R-22)
Heating coil type:	Electric	Electric
Typical capacity limitations:	150 - 450 cfm, 1/2 to 2 tons cooling	300 to 2000 CFM, 1/2 to 5 tons cooling [Larger units avail. in comm. units]
Number of zones/unit:	One	One to two
Comfort Considerations		
Degree of temperature control:	Fair	Fair
RH control:	Fair	Fair
Air circulation:	Fair	Fair
Noise Levels:	Poor (compressor & fan in occupied room)	Fair (fan in occupied room)
Indoor Air Quality Considerations		
Continuous fresh air supply for recommended vent. rate:	Good	None
Air filtration capabilities:	Fair	Fair
Room pressurization capabilities:	Poor	Poor
Humidification capabilities:	None	None
Dehumidification capabilities:	Fair	Fair
IAQ maintenance issues:	Many filters to replace, cond.	Many filters to replace, cond.
IAQ maintenance issues:	pans to clean	pans to clean
Aesthetic Considerations		
In-room equipment:	Supply fan and compressor	Supply fan
Exterior wall penetrations:	Air-cooled condenser and Fresh air louvers	Refrigerant tubing penetrations
Rooftop and/or On-grade equipment:	None	Air-cooled condenser
Miscellaneous:	Coil condensate drains to exterior can stain wall surfaces	
First Cost Considerations		
System first cost:	Low	Low
Indoor equipment room space reqd.:	Minimum	Minimum
Interior pipe/duct shaft requirements:	None	None
Operating & Maintenance Cost Considerations		
Maintenance staff skill level required:	Low	Low
Maintenance hours/year required:	Low, but units easily damaged	Low
Expected service life:	10 years (15 yrs. if PTAC)	15 years
Airside economizer cooling option availability:	No	No
Energy efficiency of air-conditioning mode:	Good	Good
Energy efficiency of occupied period heating mode:	Poor	Poor
Energy efficiency during unoccupied period heating mode:	Poor	Poor
Optional energy-efficient equipment available:	ASHP heating	ASHP heating
Flexibility re: changes to space layouts:	Poor	Poor
Adaptability to changes in space function:	Poor	Poor

SERVICES

D3

Table 9. Self-contained single-zone (ducted) air conditioners (rooftop single zone units and large split-system units).

NOTE: This system limited to LOW-RISE Buildings due to refrigerant line limitations & supply fan limitations.

General building applications:	Light Commercial Buildings
System classification:	Unitary Ducted Single Zone Air-Conditioners & ASHP's
System type:	**Single Zone Self-Contained (Ducted) Air-Conditioners**
Competing systems:	Modular WSHP's and GSHP's, Central All-Air Systems
	2-Pipe and 4-Pipe Fan Coil Units

Common equipment configurations:	Rooftop Single Zone Units	Split System Unit
General System Characteristics		
Basic operating principle:	Constant Air Volume/Variable Air Temp.	Constant Air Volume/Variable Air Temp.
Equipment quality:	Light commercial grade	Light commercial grade
Cooling coil type:	DX refrigerant (R-22)	DX refrigerant (R-22)
Heating coil type:	Electric (or optional direct gas-fired heating)	Electric(or direct gas-fired heating)
Typical capacity range:	2,000 - 10,000 CFM, 5 to 25 tons cooling	2,000 - 10,000 CFM, 5 to 25 tons cooling
Standard Number of zones/unit:	One	One
Comfort Considerations		
Degree of temperature control:	Fair	Fair
RH control:	Fair	Fair
Air circulation:	Good	Good
Noise Levels:	Fair (good vibration control reqd.)	Fair (good vibration control reqd.)
Indoor Air Quality Considerations		
Ability to provide recommended fresh air rates on continuous basis:	Good	None
Air filtration capabilities:	Fair	Fair
Room pressurization capabilities:	Poor (air flow not continuous)	Poor (air flow not continuous)
Humidification capabilities:	None	None
Dehumidification capabilities:	Fair	Fair
IAQ maintenance issues:	Filter replacement, cond. pan cleaning	Filter replacement, cond. pan cleaning
Aesthetic Considerations		
In-room equipment:	None	None(fan above clg. or in adj. space)
Exterior wall penetrations:	None	None
	None	None
Rooftop and/or On-grade equipment:	Packaged fan/air-cooled condenser/compressor	Air-cooled condenser
Miscellaneous:		
First Cost Considerations		
System first cost:	Low	Low
Indoor equipment room space reqd.:	None	Foor-Mtd. or above-ceiling fan section
Outdoor equipment space reqd.:	Roof only	Roof or on-grade
Interior pipe/duct shaft requirements:	Min. (vert. duct shaft in multi-story buildings)	None(indoor unit typ. serves 1 floor)
Operating & Maintenance Cost Considerations		
Maintenance staff skill level required:	Low	Low
Maintenance hours/year required:	Low	Low
Expected service life:	15 years	15 years
Airside economizer cooling option availability:	Yes(optional, in units > 5 ton capacity only)	No(unless field-fabricated)
Energy efficiency of air-conditioning mode:	Good	Good
Energy efficiency of occupied period heating mode:	Poor(electric heat) to Good(direct gas-fired)	Poor(gas-fired option n/a)
Energy efficiency during unoccupied period heating mode:	Poor(electric heat) to Good(direct gas-fired)	Poor
Optional energy-efficient equipment available:	Air Source Heat Pump heating	Air Source Heat Pump heating
Flexibility re: changes to space layouts:	Good	Good
Adaptability to changes in space function:	Poor	Poor

Table 10. Self-contained ducted multi-zone air conditioners (rooftop units).

General building applications:	Light Commercial Buildings
System classification:	Self-Contained, All-Electric Equipment (Non-Ducted)
System type:	**Self-Contained Ducted Multizone Air-Conditioners**
Competing systems:	Central WSHP's, Central All-Air VAV Systems,
	Multiple Self-Contained Unitary Rooftop Systems

Common equipment configurations:	**Rooftop Unit**

General System Characteristics	
Basic operating principle:	Constant Air Volume/Variable Air Temp.
Equipment quality:	Light Commercial
Cooling coil type:	DX refrigerant (R-22)
Heating coil type:	Electric, Direct Gas-Fired Option
Typical capacity limitations:	6,000 - 12,000 CFM; 15 to 37 tons cooling
Number of zones/unit:	8 to 12

Comfort Considerations	
Degree of temperature control:	Fair
RH control:	Poor
Air circulation:	Good
Noise Levels:	Fair(good vibration isolation reqd.; unit close to occupied space)

Indoor Air Quality Considerations	
Ability to provide recommended fresh air rates on continuous basis:	Good
Air filtration capabilities:	Good
Room pressurization capabilities:	Fair
Humidification capabilities:	None
Dehumidification capabilities:	Poor
IAQ maintenance issues:	Filter replacement

Aesthetic Considerations	
In-room equipment:	None
Exterior wall penetrations:	None
Rooftop and/or On-grade equipment:	Air-cooled condenser, fan

First Cost Considerations	
System first cost:	Low
Indoor equipment room space reqd.:	None
Interior pipe/duct shaft requirements:	Minimum(vert. duct shafts, multi-story bldg.)

Operating & Maintenance Cost Considerations	
Maintenance staff skill level required:	Moderate
Maintenance hours/year required:	Low
Expected service life:	15 years
Airside economizer cooling option availability:	Yes (optional)
Energy efficiency of air-conditioning mode:	Fair
Energy efficiency of occupied period heating mode:	Poor(elect.) to Good(gas option)
Energy efficiency during unoccupied period heating mode:	Poor(elect.) to Good(gas option)
Optional energy-efficient equipment available:	Economizer cooling
Flexibility re: changes to space layouts:	Fair
Adaptability to changes in space function:	Poor

Table 11. Modular water source heat pumps (Closed loop heat pump systems with/without central ventilation air)

General building applications:	Commercial/Institutional/Industrial Buildings	
System classification:	Central System, All-Water & Air-Water	
System type:	**Modular Water Source Heat Pumps(WSHP's)**	
Competing systems:	2-Pipe Change-Over FCU's, 4-Pipe FCU's,	
	Window/Through-Wall Air-Conditioners & ASHP's.	
	Central All-Air Systems	

Common equipment configurations:	**Wall Console Units/Unit Ventilators & Vertically-Stacked Closet Units**	**Wall Consoles, Vert. Closet Units, or Above-Ceiling Concealed Units**
Ventilation air options:	**Local Fresh Air Inlets**	**Central Ducted Ventilation System**

General System Characteristics		
Basic operating principle:	Constant Air Volume/Variable Air Temp.	Constant Air Volume/Variable Air Temp.
Equipment quality:	Commercial grade	Commercial grade
Cooling coil type:	Water-Cooled DX (R-22)	Water-Cooled DX (R-22)
Heating coil type:	Water-Cooled DX (R-22)	Water-Cooled DX (R-22)
Typical capacity range, Console & Vert. Closet Units:	200 - 800 CFM, 1/2 to 2 tons cooling	200 - 800 CFM, 1/2 to 2 tons cooling
Horiz. Cocealed Units:	n/a	200 - 1600 CFM, 1/2 to 5 tons
Unit Ventilators:	750 - 1500 CFM, 2 to 4 tons cooling	n/a
Number of zones/unit:	One	One

Comfort Considerations		
Degree of temperature control:	Good	Good
RH control:	Fair	Fair
Air circulation:	Fair	Fair
Noise Levels:	Fair (console units) to Good (closet units)	Good (unit separated from room by ceiling or closet construction)

Indoor Air Quality Considerations		
Ability to provide recommended fresh air rates on continuous basis:	Fair	Very Good
Air filtration capabilities:	Fair	Fair
Room pressurization capabilities:	Poor	Poor
Humidification capabilities:	None	None
Dehumidification capabilities:	Fair	Fair
IAQ maintenance issues:	Many filters to replace, condensate pans to clean	Many filters to replace, condensate pans to clean

Aesthetic Considerations		
In-room equipment:	Console Unit(or in-closet)	Console Unit(or concealed/ in-closet)
Exterior wall penetrations:	Fresh air louvers	None
Rooftop and/or On-grade equipment:	Cooling tower	Cooling tower

First Cost Considerations		
System first cost:	Low	Moderate
Indoor equipment room space reqd.:	Moderate	Moderate
Outdoor equipment space reqd.:	Cooling Tower	Cooling Tower
Interior pipe/duct shaft requirements:	Minimum (S/R water pipes & condensate waste lines)	Low(S/R water pipes & condensate waste lines, vert. vent. ducts)

Operating & Maintenance Cost Considerations		
Maintenance staff skill level required:	Low	Low
Maintenance hours/year required:	Moderate	Moderate; ease of access to above-ceiling units very important.
Expected service life:	19 years	19 years
Airside economizer cooling option availability:	No	No
Energy efficiency of air-conditioning mode:	Good	Good
Energy efficiency of occupied period heating mode:	Good (heat reclaim from interior zones)	Good (heat reclaim from interior zones)
Energy efficiency during unoccupied period heating mode:	Good(improved w/ thermal storage)	Good(improved w/ thermal storage)
Optional energy-efficient equipment available:	Thermal water storage for recovered heat; GSHP loop or many boiler equipment selections available; variable speed pumping.	Thermal storage for recovered heat; GSHP loop or many boiler equipment selections available; variable speed pumping, ventilation heat recovery/dessicant cooling options.
Flexibility re: changes to space layouts:	Poor	Poor
Adaptability to changes in space function:	Poor	Poor

Table 12. Central ducted water source heat pumps (rooftop units, floor-mounted and horizontal indoor units)

General building applications:	Light Commercial Buildings	
System classification:	Central Air-Water System	
System type:	**Central Ducted Water Source Heat Pumps**	
Competing systems:	Central WSHP's, Central All-Air VAV Systems, Self-Contained Unitary Single Zone Systems	

Common equipment configurations:	**Rooftop Unit**	**Floor-Mounted Indoor Unit & Horiz. Indoor Units**
General System Characteristics		
Basic operating principle:	Constant Air Volume/Variable Air Temp.	Constant Air Volume/Variable Air Temp.
Equipment quality:	Commercial	Commercial
Cooling coil type:	Water-cooled DX	Water-cooled DX
Heating coil type:	Water-source DX	Water-source DX
Typical capacity limitations:	1,000 - 11,000 CFM; 3 to 25 tons cooling	300 - 4,000 CFM; 1 to 10 tons(Horiz. Unit) 340 - 9,000 CFM; 1 to 25 tons(Flr.-Mtd.)
Number of zones/unit:	One	One
Comfort Considerations		
Degree of temperature control:	Good	Good
RH control:	Good	Good
Air circulation:	Good	Good
Noise Levels:	Fair(good vibration isolation reqd.; unit close to occupied space)	Fair (vibration isolation reqd., init close to occupied space)
Indoor Air Quality Considerations		
Ability to provide recommended fresh air rates on continuous basis:	Good	Good
Air filtration capabilities:	Good	Good
Room pressurization capabilities:	Fair	Fair
Humidification capabilities:	Optional	Optional
Dehumidification capabilities:	Good	Good
IAQ maintenance issues:	Filter replacement	Filter Replacement, cond. pan cleaning
Aesthetic Considerations		
In-room equipment:	None	Fan, compressor
Exterior wall penetrations:	None	None
Rooftop and/or On-grade equipment:	Evap. cooler, air handler	Evap. cooler
First Cost Considerations		
System first cost:	Moderate	Moderate
Indoor equipment room space reqd.:	Small boiler, pump room	Small boiler, pump room
Outdoor equipment space reqd.:	None (roof only)	None (roof only)
Interior pipe/duct shaft requirements:	Minimum(vert. pipe shafts, multi-story bldg.)	Minimum(vert. pipe shafts, multi-story bldg.
Operating & Maintenance Cost Considerations		
Maintenance staff skill level required:	Low	Low
Maintenance hours/year required:	Low	Low
Expected service life:	20 years	20 years
Airside economizer cooling option availability:	Yes	Yes
Energy efficiency of air-conditioning mode:	Good	Good
Energy efficiency of occupied period heating mode:	Good (heat reclaim from interior spaces)	Good (heat reclaim from interior spaces)
Energy efficiency during unoccupied period heating mode:	Good (improved w/ thermal storage)	Good(improved w/ thermal storage)
Optional energy-efficient equipment available:	Thermal water storage	Thermal storage
Flexibility re: changes to space layouts:	Good	Good
Adaptability to changes in space function:	Poor	Poor

SERVICES

D3

Table 13. Two-pipe change-over systems (fan coil units and unit ventilators, with/without central ventilation air)

NOTE: This system is <u>sometimes</u> used for perimeter space conditioning only, with separate all-air system serving large interior zones.

General building applications:	Commercial institutional/industrial Buildings	
System classification:	Central System, All-Water & Air-Water	
System type:	**2-Pipe Change-Over Systems (Fan Coil Units & Unit Ventilators)**	
Competing systems:	Modular Piped WSHP's/GSHP's, 4-Pipe FCU's	
	Window/Through-Wall Air-Conditioners & ASHP's	

Common equipment configurations:	**Wall Console Units & Vertically-Stacked Closet Units(FCU only)**	**Wall Consoles; Vert. Closet Units & Above-Ceiling Concealed Units(FCU)**
Ventilation air options:	**Local Fresh Air Inlets**	**Central Ducted Ventilation System**
General System Characteristics		
Basic operating principle:	Constant Air Volume	Constant Air Volume
Equipment quality:	Commercial grade	Commercial grade
Cooling coil type:	Chilled water	Chilled water
Heating coil type:	Shares ch. wa. coil; supplemental elect. heating optional	Share ch. wa. coil; supplem. elect. heating optional
Typical capacity range, Console & Vert. Closet Units:	200 - 1200 CFM, 1/2 to 4 tons cooling	200 - 1200 CFM, 1/2 to 4 tons cooling
Horiz. Cocealed Units:	n/a	200 - 1600 CFM, 1/2 to 5 tons
Unit Ventilators:	750 - 1500 CFM, 2 to 4 tons cooling	n/a
Number of zones/unit:	One	One
Comfort Considerations		
Degree of temperature control:	Poor	Poor
RH control:	Fair	Fair
Air circulation:	Fair	Fair
Noise Levels:	Fair(w/ fan in room) to Good(unit fan separated from room by ceiling construction)	Good (fan separated from room by room by ceiling construction)
Indoor Air Quality Considerations		
Ability to provide recommended fresh air rates on continuous basis:	Fair	Very Good
Air filtration capabilities:	Fair	Fair
Room pressurization capabilities:	Poor	Poor
Humidification capabilities:	None	None
Dehumidification capabilities:	Fair	Fair
IAQ maintenance issues:	Many filters to replace,	Many filters to replace,
IAQ maintenance issues:	condensate pans to clean	condensate pans to clean
Aesthetic Considerations		
In-room equipment:	Wall Console Unit (or above-ceiling unit)	None exposed
Exterior wall penetrations:	Fresh air louvers	None
Rooftop and/or On-grade equipment:	Cooling tower	Cooling tower
First Cost Considerations		
System first cost:	Low	Moderate
Indoor equipment room space reqd.:	Moderate	Moderate
Interior pipe/duct shaft requirements:	Minimum (S/R water pipes & condensate waste lines)	Low(S/R water pipes & condensate waste lines, vert. vent. ducts)
Operating & Maintenance Cost Considerations		
Maintenance staff skill level required:	Low	Low
Maintenance hours/year required:	Moderate	Moderate; ease of service access to above-ceiling units very important.
Expected service life:	20 years	20 years
Airside economizer cooling option availability:	No	No
Energy efficiency of air-conditioning mode:	Good	Good
Energy efficiency of occupied period heating mode:	Good	Good
Energy efficiency during unoccupied period heating mode:	Good	Good
Optional energy-efficient equipment available:	Wide range of chiller, heat rejection, ice storage, boiler equipment selections available; variable speed pumping possible;	Wide range of chiller, ice storage, boiler equipment selections available; variable speed pumping possible; central ventilation heat recovery & dessicant cooling options.
Flexibility re: changes to space layouts:	Poor	Poor
Adaptability to changes in space function:	Poor	Poor

SERVICES

D3

Table 14. Four-pipe fan coil units and unit ventilators (with/without central ventilation air)

NOTE: This system is <u>sometimes</u> used for perimeter space conditioning only, with separate all-air system serving large interior zones.

General building applications:	Commercial/Institutional Buildings
System classification:	Central System, All-Water & Air-Water
System type:	**4-Pipe Fan Coil Units & Unit Ventilators**
Competing systems:	2-Pipe Change-Over FCU's, Modular Water Source Heat Pumps,
	Window/Through-Wall Air-Conditioners & ASHP's, and Central All-Air Systems

Common equipment configurations:	Wall Console Units/Unit Ventilators & Vertically-Stacked Closet Units	Wall Consoles, Vert. Closet Units, or Above-Ceiling Concealed Units
Ventilation air options:	Local Fresh Air Inlets	Central Ducted Ventilation System
General System Characteristics		
Basic operating principle:	Constant Air Volume/Variable Air Temp.	Constant Air Volume/Variable Air Temp.
Equipment quality:	Commercial grade	Commercial grade
Cooling coil type:	Chilled Water	Chilled Water
Heating coil type:	Hot Water or Steam	Hot Water or Steam
Typical capacity range, Console & Vert. Closet Units:	200 - 1200 CFM, 1/2 to 4 tons cooling	200 - 1200 CFM, 1/2 to 4 tons cooling
Horiz. Cocealed Units:	n/a	200 - 1600 CFM, 1/2 to 5 tons
Unit Ventilators:	750 - 1500 CFM, 2 to 4 tons cooling	n/a
Number of zones/unit:	One	One
Comfort Considerations		
Degree of temperature control:	Good	Good
RH control:	Fair	Fair
Air circulation:	Fair	Fair
Noise Levels:	Fair (console units) to Good (units in closet)	Good (unit separated from room by ceiling or closet construction)
Indoor Air Quality Considerations		
Ability to provide recommended fresh air rates on continuous basis:	Good	Very Good
Air filtration capabilities:	Fair	Fair
Room pressurization capabilities:	Poor	Poor
Humidification capabilities:	None	None
Dehumidification capabilities:	Fair	Fair
IAQ maintenance issues:	Many local filters to replace, condensate pans to clean	Many local filters to replace, condensate pans to clean
Aesthetic Considerations		
In-room equipment:	Console Unit(or in-closet)	Console Unit(or concealed/in-closet)
Exterior wall penetrations:	Fresh air louvers	None
Rooftop and/or On-grade equipment:	Cooling tower	Cooling tower
First Cost Considerations		
System first cost:	High	High
Indoor equipment room space reqd.:	Moderate	Moderate
Interior pipe/duct shaft requirements:	Minimum (S/R water pipes & condensate waste lines)	Low(S/R water pipes & condensate waste lines, vert. vent. ducts)
Operating & Maintenance Cost Considerations		
Maintenance staff skill level required:	Low	Low
Maintenance hours/year required:	Moderate	Moderate
Expected service life:	20 years	20 years
Airside economizer cooling option availability:	Unit Ventilator model only	No
Energy efficiency of air-conditioning mode:	Good	Good
Energy efficiency of occupied period heating mode:	Good	Good (heat reclaim from interior zones)
Energy efficiency during unoccupied period heating mode:	Good	Good(improved w/ thermal storage)
Optional energy-efficient equipment available:	Many chiller, heat rejection, ice storage options available; many boiler/heat source options available; var. speed pumping.	Many chiller, heat rejection, ice storage options available; many boiler/heat source equipment selections available; variable speed pumping, ventilation heat recovery/dessicant cooling options.
Flexibility re: changes to space layouts:	Poor	Poor
Adaptability to changes in space function:	Fair	Fair

SERVICES

D3

Table 15. Constant volume / reheat, central station air handling systems (with electric, hot water or steam reheat)

NOTE: These systems limited to hospital operating rooms, laboratories, museums requiring close temp./RH control unless reheat source is renewable/recovered heat.

General building applications:	Commercial/Institutional Buildings
System classification:	Central System, All Air
System type:	Constant Volume Reheat, Central Station Air Handling Units
Competing systems:	Central WSHP's, Central All-Air VAV Systems, Multiple Self-Contained Unitary Rooftop Systems

Common equipment configurations:	Electric Reheat	H.W. or Steam Reheat
General System Characteristics		
Basic operating principle:	Constant Air Volume/Variable Air Temp.	Constant Air Volume/Variable Air Temp.
Equipment quality:	Commercial to Institutional	Commercial to Institutional
Expected service life:	25 years	25 years
Cooling coil type:	Chilled Water	Chilled Water
Heating coil type:	Electric or Central Hot Water/Steam	Central Hot Water/Steam
Typical capacity limitations:	1,500 - 40,000 CFM	1,500 - 40,000 CFM
Number of zones/unit:	Unlimited	Unlimited
Comfort Considerations		
Degree of temperature control:	Very Good	Best
RH control:	Very Good	Best
Air circulation:	Very Good	Very Good
Noise Levels:	Very Good	Very Good
Indoor Air Quality Considerations		
Ability to provide recommended fresh air rates on continuous basis:	Best	Best
Air filtration capabilities:	Best	Best
Room pressurization capabilities:	Best	Best
Humidification capabilities:	Yes	Yes
Dehumidification capabilities:	Very Good	Very Good
IAQ maintenance issues:	Central M.E.R. maintenance	Central M.E.R. maintenance
Aesthetic Considerations		
In-room equipment:	None	None
Exterior wall penetrations:	Central M.E.R. only	Central M.E.R. only
Rooftop and/or On-grade equipment:	Central Cooling Tower or Air-Cooled Chiller	Central Cooling Tower or Air-Cooled Chiller
First Cost Considerations		
System first cost:	High	High
Indoor equipment room space reqd.:	High	High
Interior pipe/duct shaft requirements:	High	High
Operating & Maintenance Cost Considerations		
Maintenance staff skill level required:	High	High
Maintenance hours/year required:	Low	Low
Expected service life:	25 years+(10 years for elect. reheat coils)	25 years+
Airside economizer cooling option availability:	Yes	Yes
Energy efficiency of air-conditioning mode:	Poor(Reheat reqd.)	Poor(Reheat reqd.)
Energy efficiency of occupied period heating mode:	Poor(all-elect.)	Good(depending on central heating source)
Energy efficiency during unoccupied period heating mode:	Poor(all-elect.) to Good(central HW at AHU)	Good(depending on central heating source)
Optional energy-efficient equipment available:	Central plant equipment options	Central plant equipment options
Flexibility re: changes to space layouts:	Good	Good
Adaptability to changes in space function:	Good	Good

SERVICES

D3

Table 16. VAV central station air handling systems (with electric and hot water reheat VAV boxes)

NOTE: Energy efficiency of central VAV systems strongly dependent on type of VAV terminal device used.

General building applications:	Commercial/Institutional Buildings
System classification:	Central System, All Air
System type:	**V.A.V. Central Station Air Handling Units**
Competing systems:	Central WSHP's, Central Constant Volume Reheat Systems, Multiple Self-Contained Unitary Rooftop Systems

Common equipment configurations:	Electric Reheat V.A.V Boxes	H.W. Reheat V.A.V. Boxes
General System Characteristics		
Basic operating principle:	Variable Air Volume/Constant Air Temp.	Variable Air Volume/Constant Air Temp.
Equipment quality:	Commercial to Institutional	Commercial to Institutional
Cooling coil type:	Chilled Water	Chilled Water
Central AHU Heating coil type:	Electric or Central Hot Water/Steam	Central Hot Water/Steam
Typical capacity limitations:	1,500 - 40,000 CFM	1,500 - 40,000 CFM
Number of zones/unit:	Unlimited	Unlimited
Comfort Considerations		
Degree of temperature control:	Very Good	Best
RH control:	Very Good	Best
Air circulation:	Very Good	Very Good
Noise Levels:	Very Good	Very Good
Indoor Air Quality Considerations		
Ability to provide recommended fresh air rates on continuous basis:	Good	Good
Air filtration capabilities:	Best	Best
Room pressurization capabilities:	Very Good	Very Good
Humidification capabilities:	Yes	Yes
Dehumidification capabilities:	Yes	Yes
IAQ maintenance issues:	Central M.E.R. maintenance	Central M.E.R. maintenance
Aesthetic Considerations		
In-room equipment:	None	None
Exterior wall penetrations:	Central M.E.R. only	Central M.E.R. only
Rooftop and/or On-grade equipment:	Central Cooling Tower or Air-Cooled Chiller	Central Cooling Tower or Air-Cooled Chiller
First Cost Considerations		
System first cost:	High	High
Indoor equipment room space reqd.:	High	High
Interior pipe/duct shaft requirements:	High	High
Operating & Maintenance Cost Considerations		
Maintenance staff skill level required:	High	High
Maintenance hours/year required:	Low	Low
Expected service life:	25 years+(10 years for elect. reheat coils)	25 years+
Airside economizer cooling option availability:	Yes	Yes
Energy efficiency of air-conditioning mode:	Good	Very good
Energy efficiency of occupied period heating mode:	Good(all-elect.)	Good(depending on central heating source)
Energy efficiency during unoccupied period heating mode:	Poor(all-elect.) to Good(central HW at AHU	Good(depending on central heating source)
Optional energy-efficient equipment available:	Central plant equipment options	Central plant equipment options
Flexibility re: changes to space layouts:	Good	Good
Adaptability to changes in space function:	Good	Good

SERVICES

D3

Table 17. General characteristics of boilers

	Cast Iron	Membrane Watertube	Electric	Firebox	Firetube	Vertical Firetube
Typical Applications	Heating/ Process	Heating/ Process	Heating/ Process	Heating	Heating/ Process	Heating/ Process
Typical Sizes	To 200 hp	To 250 hp	To 300 hp	To 300 hp	To 800 hp	To 100 hp
Maintenance	Medium/ high	Medium	Medium/ high	Low	Low	Low
Floor Space Required	Low	Very low	Low	Medium	Medium/ high	Very low
Initial Cost	Medium	Low/ medium	High	Low	Medium/ high	Low
Efficiency	Low	Medium	High	Medium	High	Low/ medium
No. of Options Available	Low	Medium	Medium	Low/ medium	High	Low
Pressure Range	HW/LPS	HW/LPS HPS to 600 psig	HW/LPS HPS to 900 psig	HW/LPS	HW/LPS HPS to 300 psig	HW/LPS HPS to 150 psig
Comments	Field Erectable					

HW = Hot water
LPS = Low pressure steam
HPS = High pressure steam

SERVICES

D3

Table 18. General characteristics of chiller systems

	Centrifugal	Reciprocating	Screw	Absorption	Scroll
Capacity ranges, tons	50 - 10,000	3 - 400	20 - 1300	3 - 1700	1 - 50
Reliability/ maintenance	Good	Fair	Good - very good	Good	Good
Space requirements	Low	Low	Low	High	Low
Initial Cost	Medium	Low	Medium	High	Low
Noise/vibration	Low - medium	High	Medium	Very low	Low
Energy Costs	Good	Good	Very good	Good	Very good
Weight	Low	Low	Low	High	Low
Comments		Caution placing reciprocating equipment on the roof.	More efficient than centrifugal at less than 200 tons.	Use non ozone depleting refrigerants, i.e. water. Uses less space than electric chiller with separate boiler. Much lower kw/ton requirements.	

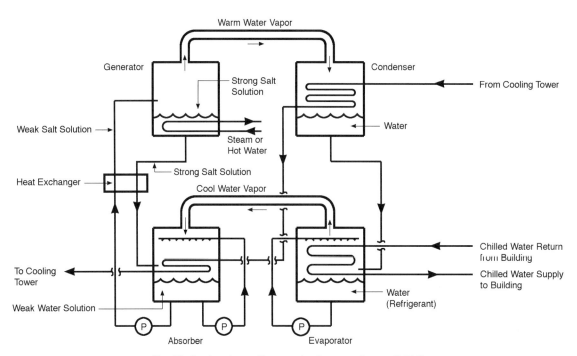

Fig. 11. Basic absorption cycle. Source: Rowe (1994)

condensor temperatures as much as other chillers. For this reason it is frequently selected for use as a heat recovery chiller.

- Scroll compressors generally have smaller capacities than many other types, and are becoming popular in some residential equipment. These units use two interfitting scroll members for compression. Chillers with scroll compressors are gradually taking over markets once dominated by reciprocating chillers. The scroll units have fewer parts and thus less maintenance concerns, have smoother, quieter operation, and can operate under dirtier conditions.

- Vapor compression chillers most often use electricity to drive the compressor. Gas engine driven chillers offer an alternative, with lower energy costs. However, space and weight requirements may increase, as well as the associated noise and vibration.

Absorption chillers use an absorption cycle rather than the vapor compression cycle to produce chilled water. The cycle, illustrated in Fig. 11, relies on the input of heat energy. The basic absorption cycle takes advantage of the affinity that a salt has for water. A lithium bromide salt solution acts as the absorbent, and water is the refrigerant. The cooling effect is created as the salt solution rapidly evaporates water from the low pressure evaporator section.

Absorption chillers are considered in applications where there is an existing low cost source of heat, often steam or waste heat. While their Coefficient of Performance (COP) ratings are quite low compared to vapor compression equipment (often .67 - 1.2 with kW/ton values as low as .1), the low cost heat input makes them attractive. Absorption chillers may also be direct-fired with natural gas, as in a combination chiller/boiler unit, where utility costs or rebates offer savings over electric units. In the case of the combination unit, less space is required than for a separate chiller and boiler, and simultaneous heating and cooling is available. In addition, a heating COP up to 1.8 is possible. Maintenance requirements for absorption machines have improved, but is still higher than vapor compression equipment. The advantage is that maintenance procedures are not as complex on absorption equipment.

Table 18 outlines many of the general characteristics of common chiller systems. This is a general outline, and many of the listed characteristics vary widely with chiller size, operating conditions, application, maintenance, number of units, and manufacturer. Generally for chiller equipment, space requirements range from .4 sq. ft./ton for large centrifugal units to 3 sq. ft./ton for smaller (100 ton) absorption units, usually with a 3 or 4:1 length to width ratio. Height requirements range from 10 ft. for 100 ton centrifugal units to 18 ft. for 1,000 ton 2-stage steam absorption units. Operating weights range from 40 to 160 pounds per ton of capacity. Absorption units typically are on the high end of the space and weight ranges, and often have more limitations in the size of opening for the individual sections that may be passed through for field erection. Heat recovery options are available with many chiller packages to use waste heat for purposes such as water heating. This option should be considered for buildings that require substantial hot water supply and space cooling simultaneously.

Heat rejection equipment
There are three common types of heat rejection equipment: air cooled, water cooled, and evaporative. The purpose of heat rejection equipment in a refrigeration system is to provide a heat transfer means to reject all the heat from the air conditioning system. This heat includes the heat absorbed by the evaporator from the space plus the heat of energy input into the compressor.

Air cooled, heat rejection equipment is typically used with refrigerant based air conditioning systems. Two variations of the air cooled heat rejection equipment are condensers and condensing units. An air cooled condenser has the refrigeration compressor located remotely. The condensing unit has the compressor included within the unit. This system typically contains centrifugal or propeller fans which draws air over aluminum fins with hot refrigerant running through copper tubing connected to the aluminum fins. Air cooled condensers and condensing units may be located indoors or outdoors and the discharge may be vertical or horizontal. The heat transfer in an air cooled condenser or condensing unit occurs in three phases: the super heating of the refrigerant; condensing of the refrigerant; and sub-cooling of the refrigerant. Air cooled heat rejection equipment typically has the lowest first cost installation.

Water cooled, heat rejection equipment is commonly used in four configurations: shell and tube, shell and coil, tube and tube, and braised plate. The type selected depends upon the capacity required, refrigerant used, temperature control required, and amount of water available. The water cooled condenser typically takes water from an external source to be superheat, condense, and subcool refrigerant. In most cases, the compressor is located remote from the water cooled condenser. Water cooled condensers typically have a higher cost and a higher maintenance cost associated with them. This cost, however, is offset by the higher efficiency of the water cooled types.

The last type of heat rejection equipment is the evaporative type. There are two major classifications in evaporative systems: the evaporative condenser used in refrigeration systems and the cooling tower used in water cooled systems. The evaporative condenser circulates refrigerant through a coil which is continuously wetted by outside recirculating water system. This allows the evaporative condenser to be the most efficient type of condenser system. A cooling tower is used for systems such as a water source heat pump system or chilled water system where water is used as the condenser source in lieu of refrigerant. In all cases where fans are used to assist in the heat rejection process, adequate space is required around the heat rejection equipment to allow proper air flow. If proper clearances cannot be maintained, considerable capacity reduction of the equipment will result. As a rule of thumb, free clearance at the air inlet should equal the length of the unit.

Diffusers, registers and grilles
There are three major types of air distribution outlets. The ceiling diffuser, linear slot diffuser and grilles and registers.

- The ceiling diffuser is the most common air outlet. Diffusers have either a radial or directional discharge which is parallel to the mounted surface. Some diffusers have adjustable vanes which allows discharge air to be directed. Diffusers come in a variety of shapes and sizes; round, rectangular, square, perforated face, louver face and modular type diffusers. Some typical applications for diffusers are spot heating or cooling, large capacity, mounting on exposed ductwork, horizontal distribution along a ceiling, and perimeter air distribution to handle the perimeter wall load in addition to the interior load.

- Linear slot outlets typically are a long narrow air supply device with an air distribution slot between 1/2 to 1 in. (12.7 to 25.4 mm) in length. Linear slot outlets are available with multiple slots and may be installed in continuous lengths to give the appearance of one long device (not all need to be active). Various types of linear supply outlets are available. These types are; linear bar, T-bar slot, linear slot and light diffuser. Some applications for linear slot outlets are high side wall installation with flow perpendicular to the mounting surface, high side wall installation with 15-30 degree upward or downward directional adjustability, perimeter ceiling installation, sill installations, and floor installations.

- A grille is a supply air outlet which consists of a frame enclosing a set of vanes which can be mounted vertically, horizontally, or in both directions. A grille combined with a volume control damper is called a register. Some types of grilles and registers are adjustable bar grilles, fixed bar grilles, security grilles, and variable area grilles. Applications for grilles and registers are high side wall and perimeter location in the sills, curbs, or floors. Grilles mounted in the ceiling and discharging down are unacceptable. Ceiling installation would require a special grille with curved vanes to discharge the air parallel to the mounting surface.

Fig. 12 is a sizing nomograph to approximate sizes and quantities of diffusers for various air quantities. For example, a room requiring 300 CFM (cubic feet per minute) of conditioned air could use one 12x12 louvered diffuser, one 10x10 in register or one 12 ft. long one slot linear diffuser. If multiple outlets are desired or required, read the appropriate sizes from the multiple outlet lines. For example, the same 300 CFM room could use four 6x6 louvered diffusers, four 6x6 registers, or one 4 ft. long 4 slot linear diffuser. For early planning purposes, the size and quantity of return outlets can also be approximated from this nomograph.

Pumps

The four most common types of centrifugal pumps are end suction, horizontal or vertical split case, in-line mounted, and vertical. The configuration of the pump shaft determines if the pump is a horizontal or vertical pump. Pumps are typically constructed of bronze or cast iron with the impeller made of steel, stainless steel, or bronze. Pumps may be arranged in a variety of configurations to provide the design flow and economical operation at partial flow or for system backup. These arrangements and control scenarios are as follows:

- multiple pumps in parallel

- one pump on, one pump on stand-by

- pumps with two speed motors

- primary and secondary pumping

- variable speed pumping

- distributed pumping

In-line pumps or circulator pumps are pipe-mounted, low pressure, low capacity pumps. In-line pumps are typically used in residential and small commercial applications. End suction pumps, either close coupled or frame-mounted, usually require a solid concrete pad for mounting. In addition, these pumps require a vibration isolation base to prevent vibration transmission to the floor. The coupling between the motor and the pump requires a guard. This pump takes up more room than the in-line circulator pump.

Horizontal or vertical split case pumps require mounting on a solid concrete pad with a vibration isolation base. This pump coupling requires a guard. The split case on this pump permits complete access to the impellers for maintenance. This pump is typically utilized in larger pumping systems over 1,000 GPM (Gallons Per Minute).

Vertical turbine pumps are a multiple stage pump that provides high pressure at normal flow rates. This unit typically has multiple impellers. Mounting requires a solid concrete pad above with a wet pit and accessibility to the pit for suction side maintenance.

Air handling equipment

There are two common types of air handling equipment: refrigerant type, which are considered air conditioning units, and chilled water type, which are called air handling units. An air conditioning unit is typically factory assembled with refrigerant type cooling and electric, steam, or hot water heating. These units are very basic in nature and do not have many options. Typical options are economizer or free cooling cycle, increased motor size, and upgrade DDC package controls.

Advantages of air conditioning units are fast delivery times and low installed cost. Disadvantages include higher operating costs, little or no control over indoor relative humidities, and higher maintenance costs. These units are also very inflexible relative to the type of filtration which can be provided.

Air handling units are usually a semi-custom type of air handling device which can be factory assembled, field assembled, or a combination of both. In the semi-custom variety, selection is made from a standard list of components to customize the air handling unit within set guidelines. The custom air handling unit will be constructed to any dimension, size, and configuration the designer chooses. Air handling units typically use chilled water or refrigerant as the cooling medium and electric, steam, or hot water as the heating medium. Disadvantages of this type of system are increased delivery time and a greater installed cost. Advantages of this type of system include complete flexibility with regard to size, configuration, fan size, and filtration types. These units typically have lower operating costs. In all cases, sufficient space is required around the air handling system to allow for proper maintenance. Access is required for regular maintenance: filter removal and replacement, fan and motor removal and replacement, coil pull in event of a coil failure, and access to belts and bearings.

Fans

Fans are available in a variety of impeller or wheel design and housing design. These variables effect the performance characteristics and applications for each individual type of fan. Refer to Table 19 for impeller or wheel information, performance characteristics, and applications.

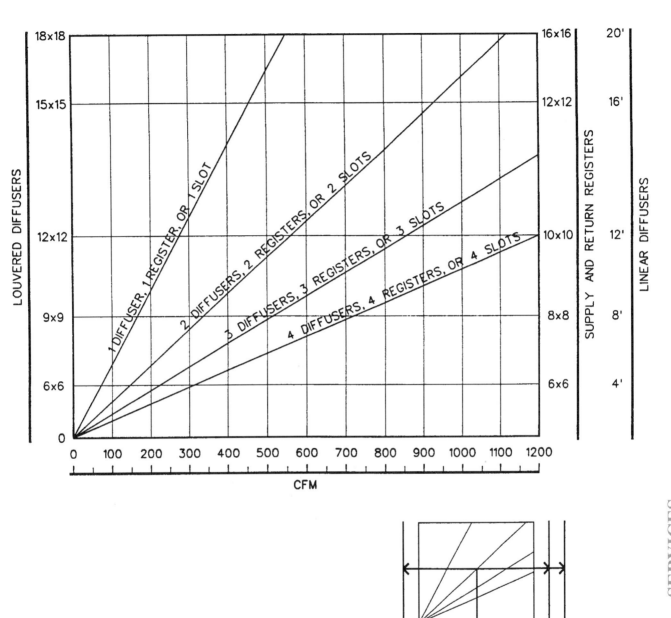

Fig. 12. Diffuser, register and grille sizing nomograph

Table 19. Fan performance characteristics.

	CENTRIFUGAL FANS			AXIAL			MISCELLANEOUS	
	Forward Curved	Backward Inclined	Air Foil	Vane Axial	Tube Axial	Propeller	Tube Centrifugal	Axial
Wheel Design	• Lowest efficiency of all centrifugals • Fan may overload if selected wrong	• Efficiency similar to air foil • Typically quieter than forward curved	• Highest efficiency of centrifugal fans • Highest speed of centrifugal fans	• Fan has good medium to high capacity and efficiency • Fan blades may be fixed or adjustable	• Less efficient than vane axial	• Low efficiency • Low pressure capabilities	• Performance similar to backward inclined • Lower efficiency than backward inclined	• Low pressure exhaust systems for factories and kitchens • Typical to a propeller fan
Housing Design	• Scroll design • Loose fit between wheel and inlet	• Scroll design • Maximum efficiency, close clearance between wheel and inlet	• Scroll design • Maximum efficiency, close clearance between wheel and inlet	• Cylindrical tube	• Cylindrical tube	• Cylindrical ring	• Cylindrical tube • Air discharges radially and turns 90° through guide vanes	• A propeller fan mounted in a structure • Air discharges from space between weatherhood
Performance	• High flow rate, low pressure • Discharge has air stream swirls	• High efficiencies with good pressure • Self-limiting toward free delivery	• High efficiencies with good pressure • Self-limiting toward free delivery	• High pressure with medium volume flow • Guide vanes correct circular motion in part by wheel	• High flow rate, medium pressure • Discharge has air stream swirls	• High flow rate, low pressure • Maximum efficiency reached near free delivery	• Performance similar to backward inclined	• Fans usually operate without ductwork • Pressure capabilities low with high volum
Applications	• Low pressure HVAC applications; residential furnaces and packaged air conditioners	• General heating, ventilating and air conditioning • Applies to larger systems with low to medium pressure • Industrial applications	• General heating, ventilating and air conditioning • Applies to larger systems with low to medium pressure • Industrial operations	• General HVAC systems, low to high pressure • Straight through air flow and compact installation • More compact than centrifugal fans	• Low and medium pressure ducted HVAC • Industrial applications	• Low pressure, high volume applications • Space ventilation through a wall without ductwork	• Low pressure, return air systems for HVAC • Straight through flow	• Low pressure exhaust systems General factory, kitchen, warehouse exhaust • Low first cost and low operating cost

SERVICES

D3

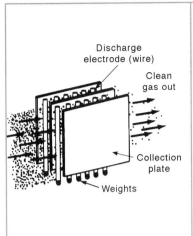

Discharge electrode (wire)

Clean gas out

Collection plate

Weights

Special HVAC equipment

Summary: This article reviews selected items, classified as "Special HVAC Equipment" in Uniformat D3070, including dust and fume collectors, air curtains, air purifiers, and paint spray ventilation systems.

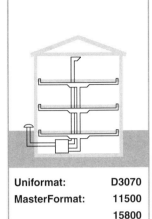

Uniformat:	**D3070**
MasterFormat:	**11500**
	15800

Key words: air filters, centrifugal collectors, chemical filters, curtain jet, industrial ventilation, pressurized air, scrubbers, spray booths.

Dust and fume collectors

Many industrial processes (milling, grinding, abrasive blasting, welding) use dust or fume collectors to improve the quality of the air discharged to the outdoors as well as to remove dust and fumes from the work area inside the plant. Fabric, wet or dry centrifugal collectors, or electrostatic precipitators may be used, depending on the application.

In industrial facilities, collectors are used in combination with an HVAC exhaust system to capture dust or fumes at their point of generation. This close-capture or local exhaust system consists of:

- a hood (plain, flanged, slotted, or canopy) to capture the dust or fumes where they are generated,

- flexible ductwork, and

- an exhaust fan that directs the dirty airstream towards the collector.

The typical capacity of dust or fume collectors are loadings of 0.003 grains per cubic foot and higher. Once the collector captures dust or fumes, the relatively dust- or fume-free air is then discharged from the exhaust stack to the outdoors or is recirculated to the room or process. During system design, the maximum pressure drop through the collector must be added to overall system pressure calculations.

Collectors are chosen to:

- comply with regulatory air emission standards and regulations.

- meet occupational exposure standards.

- prevent impacts to surrounding community (property damage, public nuisance or health hazard).

In some cases they are also chosen to:

- reclaim usable materials.

- permit recirculation of cleaned air to processes or work areas.

- eliminate highly visible (but relatively innocuous) exhaust plumes.

Generally, selection should favor the most efficient collector that can be installed at reasonable cost (capital cost plus operations and maintenance) while meeting prevailing air pollution regulations.

Factors to be considered include:

- the characteristics of the airstream (emission rate, temperature, water vapor, presence of corrosive chemicals).

- the type(s), particle size distribution, and concentrations of contaminants including chemical and physical properties.

- the degree of removal required to meet regulatory requirements or permit recirculation.

- fire safety and explosion control (need for explosion venting for combustible dusts).

- the disposal method.

- energy requirements.

Dust and fume collectors include:

- Fabric collectors.

- Wet collectors.

- Dry centrifugal collectors.

- Electrostatic precipitators.

Key features of fabric collectors:

- High efficiencies possible (>99%).

- Useful for small particles (<1 micron).

- Useful for dry collection.

- Sensitive to filter velocities.

- High temperature gases must be cooled.

- Affected by relative humidity.

Fabric collectors vary by:

- Type of fabric (woven or non-woven).

- Configuration (bags or tubes; envelopes (flat bags); pleated cartridges).

- Service (continuous, or intermittent (must be shut down during dust removal).

- Reconditioning (shaker, pulse-jet or reverse-air).

- Housing (single or multiple compartment).

Fabric collector operation: Dust particles are retained on fabric (by straining, impinging, intercepting, diffusing or electrostatically charging) and cleaned air passes through. The collected dust improves efficiency, increases resistance to air flow, and may change flowrate unless compensation is made. Generally, the mat is cleaned (by mechanical agitation or air motion) to keep the flowrate constant.

Key features of wet collectors (scrubbers):

- Suitable for high temperatures and wet gases (will cool and clean).

Author: Catherine Coombs, CIH, CSP

References: Topic references are listed within each section of this article.

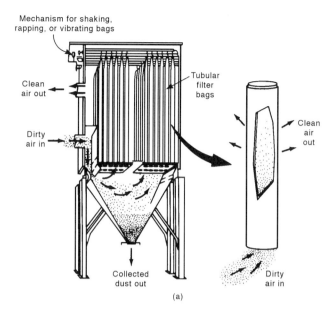

Fig. 1. Schematic of fabric collection

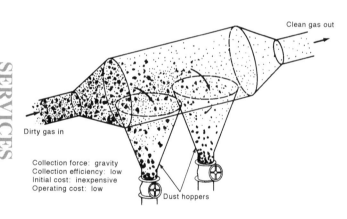

Fig. 2. Schematic of dry centrifugal collector (gravity separator).

- Can reduce explosion or fire hazard of combustible or explosive dust.

- Variable efficiency (<80%).

- May foster corrosion.

- Freeze protection will be necessary if collectors are outside in cold climates.

- Disposal may require pre-treatment of wastewater.

Types of wet collectors (scrubbers):

- chamber or spray tower.

- packed tower.

- wet centrifugal collector.

- wet dynamic precipitator.

- orifice type.

- Venturi type.

Wet collector operation: Dust particles impact on liquid droplets. Liquid droplets containing dust are then separated from the air stream by centrifugal force, impingement or impaction.

Key features of dry centrifugal collectors:

- simple to design and maintain.

- low to moderate pressure loss.

- temperature independent.

- low collection efficiency for small particles.

- substantial headroom is required for maintenance.

- sensitive to variable loadings and flowrates.

Types of dry centrifugal collectors:

- gravity separator.

- inertial separator.

- dynamic precipitator.

- cyclone collector.

- high efficiency centrifugal.

Dry centrifugal collector operation: Dust particles are separated from the airstream by centrifugal, inertial, or gravitational force.

Key features of electrostatic precipitators:

- high efficiency (>99%).

- low energy use (pressure drop usually less than 1 in. wg).

- nominal maintenance needs; few moving parts.

- high initial cost.

- The incoming gas stream may need to be pre-conditioned with a cooling tower in high voltage systems or with a wet scrubber, evaporative cooler or heat exchanger in low voltage systems to provide proper conditions for ionization.

- sensitive to variable loadings and flowrates.

Electrostatic precipitator operation: The airstream is ionized and then charging the dust particles, which migrate to a collecting plate of opposite polarity. The dust particles lose their charge and fall to a collecting plate where they are removed by washing, vibration, or gravity.

Types of electrostatic precipitators:

- Cottrell: single-stage or high voltage (ionization voltage of 40,000 to 70,000 volts DC).

- heavy-duty.

SERVICES

D3

- applications include utility boilers, large industrial boilers, cement kilns.

• Penny: two-stage or low voltage (ionization voltages of 11,000 to 14,000 volts DC).

- used in low concentration (less than 0.025 grains per cubic foot) operations.

- applications include plasticizer ovens, forge presses, die-casting machines, welding operations.

Improper selection of dust and fume collectors can result in system failure due to:

- high temperatures (searing fabric collectors).

- water vapor (plugging dry collectors).

- corrosive chemicals (damaging fabric or metal in collectors).

- presence of combustible dusts (organic or mineral dusts) creating explosion hazard.

References: dust and fume collectors

ASHRAE. 1993. *Handbook of Fundamentals*. Atlanta, GA: American Society of Heating, Refrigerating and Air Conditioning Engineers.

ASHRAE. 1995. *HVAC Applications*. "Chapter 24: Ventilation of the Industrial Environment" and "Chapter 26: Industrial Exhaust Systems." Atlanta, GA: American Society of Heating, Refrigerating and Air Conditioning Engineers.

Industrial Ventilation- A Manual of Recommended Practice. Lansing, MI: American Conference of Governmental Industrial Hygienists Committee on Industrial Ventilation. 1995.

NFPA 69. Standard on Explosion Prevention Systems. Quincy, MA: National Fire Protection Association.

NFPA 91. Standard for Exhaust Systems for Air Conveying of Materials. Quincy, MA: National Fire Protection Association.

NFPA 654. Standard for the Prevention of Fire and Dust Explosions from the Manufacturing, Processing and Handling of Combustible Particulate Solids. Quincy, MA: National Fire Protection Association.

ANSI Z9.2. Fundamentals Governing the Design and Operation of Local Exhaust Systems. New York: American National Standards Institute.

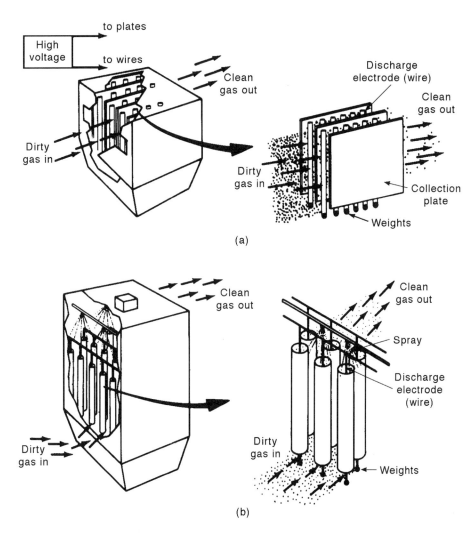

Fig. 3. Schematic of electrostatic precipitator.

Fig. 4. Air curtain installed over bay door on interior of loading dock. (Courtesy: Mars Air Door)

2 Air curtains

Air curtains are local ventilation devices that reduce airflow through building apertures and openings in process equipment (Fig. 4). They are used in place of flexible partitions such as plastic stripping, flapper doors, or canvas curtains, to create a barrier to air movement while permitting free passage of equipment and personnel through doorways and other openings. They thus reduce (although do not entirely prevent) the loss of conditioned (heated or refrigerated) air, and/or entry of humid/dry outdoor air at undesirable temperatures and/or entry of insects, dust, fumes, and odors. Typical applications are on exterior doors in warehouses, bus and air terminals, banks; and on freezer/cooler doors. Some air curtains generate an evenly distributed laminar air flow over an entryway (to create an "airlock"). Others, as in lobbies, establish a circular "curtain jet" pattern.

Air curtains are used to:

- deflect wind and reduce heat loss.

- promote the mixing of warm air to floor level and destratify room air.

- provide additional comfort in workspaces served directly by outdoor activities (such as loading docks).

- prevent loss of mechanical cooling (air conditioning).

Types of air curtains

- Heated (electric, steam, and hot water heated). ASHRAE recommends that heated models be used for doors smaller than 12 ft. x 12 ft. (4 m x 4 m), and for process apertures that are frequently

opened (more than five times or for longer than 40 minutes during an eight-hour shift), and that are located where design outdoor winter temperatures are 5F (-15°C) or lower.

- Unheated air at room temperature or outside temperature. Typical applications are in spaces with a heat surplus, a vertical temperature stratification, low air temperatures—less than 46F (7.8°C)—near the building aperture, or in mild climates.

- Laminar-flow: These generate an evenly-distributed barrier airstream over the entryway.

- Shutter-type: These direct air outward at an angle from 30 to 40 degrees; they may be double-sided or single-sided and projected upward or downward. Double-sided are often more effective. ASHRAE recommends upward projection when the gate width is greater than its height; additionally, upward projection provides more complete coverage of the lower part of the opening.

- Air curtains with a lobby: These function by directing air towards the outdoor airflow or at a small angle to it, forming a "curtain jet" which runs along the walls, slows down and makes a U-turn, reversing direction. For double-sided air curtains in this application, the length of the lobby should exceed 2.5 times its width, to prevent air from being forced outside. For shorter lobbies, air can be supplied by jet with a coerced angle of divergence.

- Combined air curtains: these are "double" air curtains, which can be used in very cold climates, for doors larger than 12 ft. x 12 ft. (4 m x 4 m), and for spaces with several doors. Examples of combined air curtains include those which supply unheated outdoor air at the entrance (or in the lobby), and another set which supplies heated air within the building.

Special options include:

- explosion-proof motors.

- adjustable louver damper controls to regulate air flowrates.

- adjustable air directional vanes to provide draft control.

- continuously running air curtains.

- intermittent air curtains that operate whenever the door is open or an activating temperature is reached.

Selection of an air curtain depends on:

- air flow requirements (standard, high velocity, or extra power).

- application (as barrier to insects, dust, and fumes; to contain heated or cooled building air; or use in freezers or coolers).

Design calculations are provided by ASHRAE for determination of the air velocity, airflow, and temperature supplied by the air curtain.

Limitations: Air curtains may malfunction if there are indrafts caused by negative pressurization of interior space. If other outside doors, windows or roof ventilator are open, a wind tunnel effect may result. Some air curtains create sufficient noise to generate complaints: decibel readings are available from manufacturers. Relying on air curtains to heat nearby workspaces may result in high energy consumption for these spaces.

References: Air curtains
ASHRAE 1995. *Applications Handbook*. "Chapter 24: Ventilation of the Industrial Environment." Atlanta, GA: American Society of Heating, Refrigerating and Air Conditioning Engineers.

3 Air purifiers

"Air purifiers" include gas-phase air filters that remove low levels of airborne gas- or vapor-phase contaminants as well as filters designed to remove low levels of dust in air in HVAC building systems. Chemical filters are typically disposable (or rechargeable) cartridges containing chemically-active material (adsorbent) that can be installed

SERVICES

D3

inside ventilation ducts to remove pollutants from the airstream. These filters may be located downstream of a respirable particulate filter (to protect them from dust) and/or upstream of air conditioning equipment (to protect them from humidity).

Gas-phase air filters include:

- activated carbon (adsorb organic solvents, ozone, sulfur dioxide, nitrogen oxide).

- activated alumina impregnated with potassium permanganate.

- acid-impregnated carbon (removes ammonia).

- base-impregnated activated carbon (removes corrosive acids, including hydrochloric and sulfuric acid).

- catalytic conversion (ozone converted to oxygen; nitrogen dioxide converted to nitrogen monoxide).

Granular activated carbon filters include:

- Type I: V-bank of large-mesh carbon trays.

- Type II: cartridge of pleated dry composite media with fine-mesh carbon.

- Type III: cell of pleated non-woven carbon-coated fabric.

The adsorption rate is variable and a function of:

- relative adsorptivity of multiple contaminants.

- temperature and relative humidity.

- air flow rate.

- adsorbent bed size.

- properties of the adsorbing medium.

Air filters (for particulates) differ by efficiency, dust holding capacity and pressure drop. They operate by:

- straining.

- impingement (often use adhesive coating).

- interception.

- diffusion.

- electrostatic forces.

Efficiency ratings can be misleading if reported by mass (may not trap smaller particles). Efficiency testing for air filters includes:

- ASHRAE Arrestance (measures filter's ability to remove coarse dust particles).

- ASHRAE Efficiency (measures ability of a filter to prevent staining or discoloration determined by light reflectance readings).

- DOP (0.3 micron particles of dioctylphthalate are drawn through a high efficiency particulate air (HEPA) filter; to be designated as a HEPA filter, filter must be at least 99.97% efficient).

References: Air purifiers

ASHRAE 1993. *Handbook of Fundamentals*. Atlanta, GA: American Society of Heating, Refrigerating and Air Conditioning Engineers.

ASHRAE Standard 62: Ventilation for Acceptable Indoor Air Quality. Atlanta, GA: American Society of Heating, Refrigerating and Air Conditioning Engineers.

ASHRAE 1995. *HVAC Applications*. "Chapter 41: Control of Gaseous Indoor Air Contaminants" Atlanta, GA: American Society of Heating, Refrigerating and Air Conditioning Engineers.

Committee on Industrial Ventilation. 1995. *Industrial Ventilation: A Manual of Recommended Practice*. Lansing, MI: American Conference of Governmental Industrial Hygienists.

4   Paint spray ventilation systems

Commercial spray painting is usually conducted inside prefabricated enclosed and ventilated spray booths, to ensure a good finish, to protect against fire and explosion hazards associated with flammable vapors and mists or combustible ingredients in the paints, and to prevent worker exposures (to harmful constituents of paint such as isocyanates in urethane paints). Spray booths are manufactured in a variety of forms including downdraft, semi-downdraft, crossdraft. Downdraft systems may include a waterwash of exhaust air, using scrubbers to reduce the amount of dust entering the exhaust and allow recovery of overspray finishing material. Options may include paint recycle/reclaim systems to reclaim overspray, reduce frequency of filter replacement, increase Volatile Organic Compounds (VOCs) and particulate removal efficiency, and reduce the amount of sludge generated.

The spray booth is typically a power-ventilated non-combustible (steel, concrete, or masonry) structure located inside a building, which functions as an enclosure-type hood. It is constructed to:

- enclose or accommodate a spray painting operation.

- confine and limit escape of "overspray" (paint droplets dispersed in air).

- draw air towards the exhaust system to provide safe and habitable conditions during spraying.

Operation:

- A fan moves supply air through a filter bank into the spray-painting booth.

- Air is moved out of the booth by an exhaust fan through filters to the exterior of the building.

- The mechanical system is operated during and after spraying operations to exhaust vapors from dry coated articles and drying finishing material residue.

- Each spray booth has an independent exhaust duct system.

- If more than one fan serves the booth, all fans are interconnected so that one fan cannot operate without all fans operating.

- Air exhausted during spray operations is generally not recirculated.

- Emissions are regulated by government environmental agencies.

Types of spray booths include those that differ by location of supply and exhaust:

- down-draft.

- semi-downdraft (or side-downdraft).

- crossdraft.

• *Down-draft*

- Filtered air enters from ceiling and is exhausted through filters that cover trenches under metal grating on floor, or through water scrubbers located beneath the metal grating in a water washing system.

• *Semi-downdraft* (or side-downdraft)

- Filtered air enters from ceiling and is exhausted through filters in the back of the booth.

• *Crossdraft*

- Filtered air enters in the front of the booth and is exhausted through filters in the back of the booth.

Dry type spray booths have:

- distribution or baffle plates to promote an even flow of air through the booth or reduce the overspray before it is pulled into the exhaust system,

SERVICES

D3

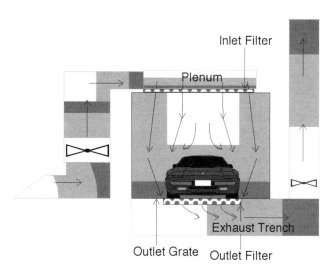

Fig. 5. Paint spray booth

SERVICES

D3

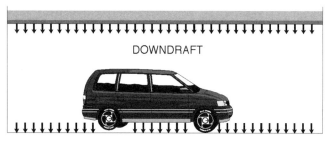

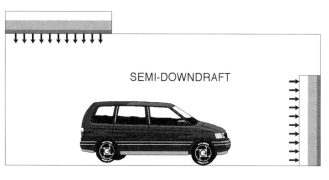

Fig. 6. Types of spray booths. Airflow indicated by arrows.

- dry media filters, either fixed or on rolls, to remove overspray from the exhaust airstream; and/or,

- powder collection systems that capture powder overspray.

Options:

- Paint recycle/reclaim systems can be used to:

- reclaim overspray.

- reduce the frequency of filter replacement.

- increase particulate and VOC removal efficiency.

- reduce the amount of sludge generated.

- The spray booth may include pneumatic lifts to aid operators. Booth may have a painting cycle and a curing cycle.

Ventilation requirements: NFPA recommends that vapor concentrations in the exhaust airstream be maintained below 25% of the lower flammable limit, requiring a sufficient flow and velocity of air through the booth.

Air velocities are to be increased to compensate for:

- high rates of spray application.

- operations where objects being coated are close to the open face or conveyor openings.

- operations where large objects are conveyed in and out of the booth at relatively high speeds.

Air velocities can be decreased for efficient application systems using heated materials, airless spray application apparatus, high volume/low pressure application equipment, electrostatic application equipment.▶

References: paint spray ventilation systems

Committee on Industrial Ventilation. 1995. *Industrial Ventilation: A Manual of Recommended Practice*. Cincinnati, OH: American Conference of Governmental Industrial Hygienists.

U.S. Department of Labor, Occupational Safety and Health Administration, Code of Federal Regulations, Title 29, Part 1910.107. *Spray Finishing Using Flammable and Combustible Materials*.

NFPA 1995. *NFPA 33, Standard for Spray Application Using Flammable and Combustible Materials*. Quincy, MA: National Fire Protection Association.

NFPA 1995. *NFPA 91, Standard for Blower and Exhaust Systems for Vapor Removal*. Quincy, MA: National Fire Protection Association.

NFPA 1994. *NFPA 101, Life Safety Code*. Quincy, MA: National Fire Protection Association.

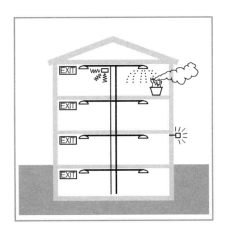

D SERVICES

SERVICES

D4

Fig. 1. Concept of the "fire triangle."

Fire safety design

Summary: Effective fire safety in buildings goes well beyond meeting codes. It requires a systemic and diligent approach on the part of the architect to fire prevention, protection from fire, and fire control in all aspects of building design, construction and use. This section reviews general principles and design issues of fire behavior, the influences buildings and contents on fire development and fire influences on building stability.

Key words: combustion control, emergency egress, fire prevention, fire spread, fire suppression, refuge areas.

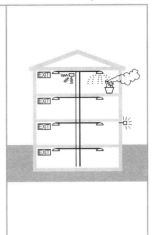

Principles of fire behavior

The "Fire Triangle:" This is a simplified model (Fig. 1) that describes fire in terms of its three essential elements; if one is absent or removed, combustion will not occur:

- Oxygen must be at least 16% of the atmosphere to sustain combustion. If oxygen is consumed by fire and drops below this level, combustion ceases.

- Fuel (solid, liquid, or gaseous) must be present in sufficient concentration to form combustible mixture with oxygen. Liquid and solid fuels must be pre-heated to temperatures at which they give off combustible gases. If the fuel supply is consumed, separated, or removed, combustion will cease.

- Heat must be sufficient to produce and ignite combustible gases; solid and liquid fuels must be pre-heated to distill these gases before they will ignite. Fuels kept or cooled below their ignition temperatures will not support combustion. A fire will also self-terminate if burning fuels do not produce adequate heat to ignite fire gases or distill new fire gases from liquid and solid fuels.

Stages of fire development: If left unattended, fires evolve through several predictable stages:

- Pre-burning occurs when fuel is exposed to the heat of an ignition source, leading to the distillation of combustible gases. Other than the original ignition source, no flame is visible and temperatures are not markedly elevated.

- Initial burning involves progress of a fire from the ignition of volatile fire gases to the production of sufficient heat to sustain the combustion process. At this point, flame height is approximately 10 in. (25 cm) and ceiling temperatures range from normal room temperature to 250F.

- Vigorous burning is the phase during which a fire advances from marginal self-sustained combustion to spreading across the fuel surface. Flame height is from 10 in. (25 cm) to 5 ft. (1.5 m) high, ceiling temperature from 250F to 600F. The fire begins to have an effect on the ignition of surrounding materials.

- Interactive burning occurs as fire makes the transition from full involvement of items and fuel packages to full involvement of whole rooms. Flame height is from 5 ft. (1.5m) to full contact with the ceiling and horizontally beyond; ceiling temperatures range from 600F to 1400F. The heat radiated by the burning of one fuel package speeds the combustion of another, causing an exponential growth in fire intensity.

- Remote burning occurs as fire makes the transition from involving entire rooms to rapidly consuming large sections of entire building. Horizontal flame spread at the ceiling would extend dozens of feet along open channels. Ambient temperatures would reach 1200F to 1500F.

Fire-safety design principles

General principles: Every fire is somewhat unique. Still, design professionals can do a great deal to enhance their background in fire safety by knowing useful generalizations concerning the requirements of fire-safe buildings. Consider the following:

- Fire safety planning should be based on knowledge of general fire behavior, fire behavior in buildings and building behavior under fire conditions.

- Structural fire resistance is a prerequisite to other considerations of occupant fire safety.

- Building contents, their selection and organization, must be recognized as a key influence on fire safety in buildings.

Author: Fred Malven, Ph.D.

References: American Society for Testing Materials. ASTM E119: *Standard Methods of Fire Tests of Building Construction and Materials.* Philadelphia, PA.

Egan, M. David. 1978. *Concepts in Building Firesafety.* New York: Wiley Interscience.

Lerup, Lars, David Cronrath and John Koh Chaing Liu. 1978. *Learning From Fire: A Fire Protection Primer for Architects.* NFPCA Grant #75008. Washington, DC: U. S. Government Printing Office.

National Fire Protection Association. *1989 NFPA 72E: Standard on Automatic Detectors.* Quincy, MA: NFPA.

_____ *NFPA 101: Life Safety Code.* 1994. Quincy, MA: NFPA.

_____ *NFPA 550: Fire Safety Concepts Tree.* 1986. Quincy, MA: NFPA.

Patterson, James. 1993. *Simplified Design for Building Fire Safety.* New York: John Wiley & Sons.

Solomon, R. 1991. "Automatic Sprinkler Systems." *Fire Protection Handbook*, 17th Edition. Quincy, MA: National Fire Protection Association.

SERVICES

D4

- Integrated fire protection should be a planning consideration in every building project.

- Redundant fire protection (*i.e.*, back-up provisions for key systems) should be part of an effective design.

- Worst case "possibilities" should parallel "probabilities" as planning tools in developing fire-safe designs.

Code compliance: This an indispensable part of effective fire-safety design. Building and life safety codes define the architect's minimum legal responsibilities for protecting building users from fire. Their provisions provide a useful framework for expanding the designer's general knowledge of general fire safety issues:

- Occupancy classification: The unique fire safety requirements of buildings based on the type of activity they accommodate.

- Configuration: The fire safety implications of buildings in context, including setback requirements, site access, *etc.*

- Egress and evacuation: Requirements for leaving all spaces and moving safely through the building.

- Exterior protection: From exterior fires, including adjacent buildings, wildlands, *etc.*

- Interior protection: Required to maintain structural stability.

- Internal separation: For various occupancies and functions.

- Mechanical requirements: To support fire prevention and control and to protect occupants and property.

Fire safety decision trees

These provide a valuable tool for defining and managing fire-safe design objectives. Two particularly useful conceptual models have been developed for use by architectural and design professionals. In general, both address three major fire safety goals (Fig. 2):

1   Prevent ignition of building materials and contents.
1.1   Regulate ignition sources.
1.2   Control fuel.
1.3   Control heat/fuel interaction.
1.4   Plan for occupant action.
2   Control fire development.
2.1   Detect fire.
2.2   Control combustion.
2.3   Suppress/extinguish fire.
2.4   Limit spread.
3   Protect the exposed building occupants.
3.1   Communicate emergency information.
3.2   Provide for emergency egress.
3.3   Defend in place.

1   Prevent ignition

1.1   Regulate ignition sources

The probability of fire ignition can be substantially reduced by regulating building features and contents that produce sufficient heat to ignite adjacent materials. Ignition sources that cannot be eliminated should be separated from possible fuels. Consider:

- Open flames and glowing combustion: fireplaces, pilot lights, industrial processes, smoldering cigarettes.

- Chemical heat: chemical reactions, oily rags, solvents, decomposition of organic materials,

- Resistance heating: electric space heaters and heating coils, overtaxed electrical wiring.

- Electrical arcing: electric shorts, poor electrical connections, poorly maintained equipment.

- Static electricity: excessive dryness, energized electrical equipment.

- Friction heating: faulty bearings or metal-to-metal contact between moving parts.

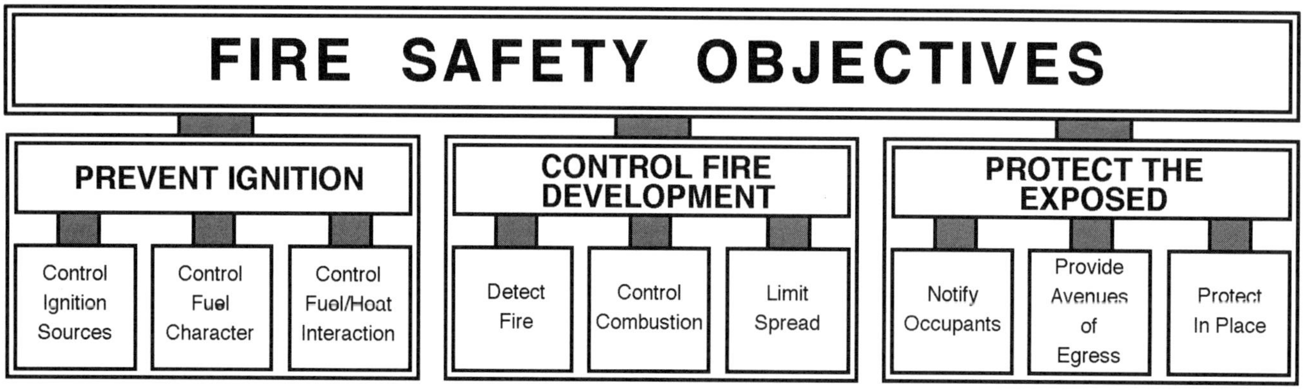

SERVICES

D4

FIRE SAFETY OBJECTIVES

PREVENT IGNITION			CONTROL FIRE DEVELOPMENT			PROTECT THE EXPOSED		
Control Ignition Sources	Control Fuel Character	Control Fuel/Heat Interaction	Detect Fire	Control Combustion	Limit Spread	Notify Occupants	Provide Avenues of Egress	Protect In Place

Fig. 2. Fire safety objectives.

1.2   Control fuel

The risk of fire ignition can be reduced by regulating selected fuel characteristics. Especially in routes of egress, areas of having high occupant loads, and other high risk areas, materials should be carefully selected with regard to:

- Volatility: the ease with which a material gives off flammable gases; many "flammable liquids," such as gasoline, give off flammable vapors at well below normal room temperatures.

- Ignition temperature: the temperature at which a material will ignite; the higher a material's ignition temperature the longer ignition will be delayed.

- Thermal inertia: the tendency for a fuel to absorb and disperse the heat of ignition, rather than allowing heat to saturate one area and ignite.

- Fuel orientation: the more of a material exposed to an ignition source, the more rapidly thermal inertia will be overcome and the material ignited.

- Surface to mass ratio: fuel surface exposed per unit of mass; more finely divided fuels expose more mass to heat, reach ignition temperatures more quickly, and burn more rapidly.

- Surface texture or roughness: increases the exposed area of a surface, increasing the amount of material progressing toward ignition at any one time.

1.3   Control heat/fuel interaction

Even in the presence of potential ignition sources and volatile fuels, ignition can be prevented by maintaining adequate separation between the two. Such planning should address the three primary means of heat transfer between areas:

- *Convection* is heat spread via a "fluid" (usually air). The buoyancy of heated air (its tendency to rise) is a major influence on fire spread. Spread is also influenced by pressure build-up in closed spaces and direct flame impingement on adjacent materials.

- *Conduction* is the transfer of heat along highly thermally conductive materials to fuel packages that are in contact with them.

- *Radiation* is heat transfer via electro-magnetic waves, along lines of sight, such as radio waves, sound, and light. If sight is blocked, heat is blocked.

Each of these three means should be considered in detail, as follows:

• *Heat transfer by convection*

Especially in the early stages of a fire, convection has a major influence on fire development. Heat rises and concentrates at the highest points in a space. Fuels located at these points are particularly subject to ignition. Openings and voids in walls, floors, and other barriers—particularly those located high in a space—are always likely avenues of heat and fire spread between areas:

- Open spaces: large rooms, undivided by walls.

- Circulation spaces: for movement of people, such as hallways, elevators, stairways, *etc.*

- Service voids: used to channel building services such as wiring, plumbing, heating, *etc.*

- Access features: doors, panels, hatches, *etc.*

- Functional features: windows, pass-throughs, conveyer openings, heating transfer grilles, *etc.*

- Decorative enclosures: for utilities, chimneys, defects, *etc.* to "clean up" appearance.

- Building defects: openings due to damage or aging, such as cracks and separation of barriers.

- Structural voids: naturally occurring spaces inside structural walls, floors, roofs, *etc.*:

   a. Chimney-like voids between wall studs.
   b. Long, trough-like spaces between floor joists.
   c. Wide-open attic or truss spaces.

• *Heat transfer by conduction*

Significant in that it may permit spread between areas. Even though there is no visible flame spread, conductive materials located high in the thermal column reach critical temperatures and contribute to fire spread earlier than those located lower. In general, conduction flame spread involves highly thermally conductive materials:

- Plumbing: pipes filled with water are not likely to conduct heat, but empty pipes can.

- Heating channels: metal ducts, flue pipes, and chimneys can be routes of conducted and convection heat spread.

- Service equipment: unrated metal enclosures that break up walls, such as hose or extinguisher cabinets, electrical panels, *etc.*

- Structural members: exposed I-beams, joists, and other structures running between areas.

- Conductive walls: sheet metal walls can spread heat quickly from one area to another. Masonry walls will initially absorb heat and cool a fire, but after continued exposure will begin to conduct it.

• *Fire spread by radiation*

Radiant fire spread occurs when unburned contents are visually exposed to flaming gases. Radiant heat transfer can occur through windows. The larger the window the more radiant heat can pass through it. Several building factors increase fire spread by radiation:

- Light, finely divided fuel: materials that expose the most fuel surface at one time produce the largest body of flaming gas and the most radiant heat.

- Concentrated fuel: the smaller the space in which a given quantity of fuel is loaded the more likely it is to give off its heat in a short period of time (Fig. 3).

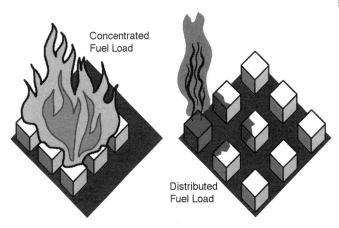

Concentrated Fuel Load

Distributed Fuel Load

Fig. 3. Types of fuel loads.

SERVICES

D4

Separation may take the form of physical barriers or spatial distance. Plan to separate fuel.

1.4 Plan for occupant action

Although occupant actions are not under design control, fire preventive behaviors can be encouraged by providing them with relevant information. Such actions might also include local officials and fire fighters.

- Building-use manuals can include guidelines for preventing ignition, making reference to possible ignition sources (*e.g.*, manufacturing equipment), probable fuel concentrations (*e.g.*, storage rooms, work areas), and possible ignition scenarios.

- In-house fire prevention checklists, addressing a variety of housekeeping and related fire safety issues, can be a standard document for distribution to clients.

- Anticipate unsafe behaviors: Parallel occupant fire prevention measures with focused safeguards in areas where complexity and human nature pose increased risks of fire ignition:

- Increase physical separation of fuel and ignition sources in such areas.

- Strengthen general security measures in areas where a threat of malicious or opportunistic fire-setting exists.

2 Control fire development

2.1 Detect fire

Automatic Fire Detection takes a variety of specialized forms and variations. The most common include:

- Heat detectors activate in the presence of hot smoke and gases.

- "Fixed temperature" types activate at preset temperatures.

- "Rate of rise" types detect unusually rapid temperature change.

- "Rate compensation" detectors combine characteristics of the two above.

- Smoke detectors activate in the presence of solid particles or droplets produced by a fire.

- "Ionization" types activate when smoke (especially when made up of small particles produced by fast, hot fires) causes a change in the electrical charge inside the detector.

- "Spot-type photoelectric" detectors activate when smoke (particularly large particles produced by smoldering fires) break up light internally.

- "Projected-beam photoelectric" detectors activate when smoke (particularly large particles) break an "electric eye."

- "Sampling" detectors collect and analyze smoke in a small, closed chamber.

- Supervised extinguishing systems, such as automatic sprinkler systems, incorporate detection as part of their operating systems. When the system is activated, an alarm also sounds.

- Flame detectors, especially useful where volatile fuels are present, detect infrared, ultraviolet, and other wavelengths of radiant energy produced by combustion.

Detector placement should be considered in the following locations:

- At required intervals stated in applicable codes and standards.

- Near anticipated hazards, to provide timely detection.

- Clear of nuisance sources (general cooking odors, dust sources, shower rooms, *etc.*) to minimize false alarms.

- At regular intervals throughout a space for even coverage.

- In accessible areas to facilitate testing and maintenance.

- Away from dead air pockets, where arrival and detection of fire products may be delayed.

Notification systems take a variety of forms:

- General alarm notification throughout a building is required for many types of occupancies.

- Zoned notification allows alerting of occupants in most affected areas of a large building first, to enable building evacuation on a priority basis.

- Presignal notification sounds an alert at a staffed station, giving staff time to investigate and correct situations before automatically sounding a general alarm.

Occupant detection and notification should include facilitation of occupant reporting with:

- Manual pull stations at intervals along exit routes.

- Emergency phones directly connected to alarm centers.

- Public phones, highly visible, outside exit routes.

2.2 Control combustion

Room geometry influences the upward and outward movement of fire through space, a pattern called "mushrooming." Heat rises until in encounters a horizontal barrier, then moves horizontally. Horizontal spread continues until the fire front can move upward along a new vertical path or strikes a vertical barrier and is forced downward by rising fire gases behind it. Several variables are important:

- Compartment height: The higher the ceiling, the more room air a plume of hot gases passes through before it contacts the building. High ceilings also provide more dilution of heat with fresh air and cool the fire gases before they reach the ceiling.

- Floor area: Ceiling height being equal, the room with the largest floor area distributes fire over the largest ceiling area (cooling it more quickly in the early stages), delaying its "mushrooming" down the walls to furnishings and contents on the floor.

- Volumetric configuration: Determines the route of heat and fire products within and along room boundaries. Flat ceilings tend to distribute heat equally in all directions; mono-pitched ceilings concentrate heat along their upper edge; pyramidal ceilings concentrate heat intensity at their peak, resulting in more rapid burn-through.

Fuel characteristics should be appropriately regulated with regard to fire spread, giving special attention to areas with increased probability of ignition, increased life hazard, special safety significance (egress routes, refuge areas, *etc.*) or to areas of particularly high value. Evaluate materials in terms of:

- Ignition temperature: the temperature at which a material will ignite; the higher a material's ignition temperature the longer ignition will be delayed.

- Flame spread: the speed with which fire spreads across a surface; review test results such as ASTM E-84 (Class A, 0-25 flame spread; Class B, 25-75; Class C, 75-250); the higher the flame spread rating, the more hazardous the material.

- Fuel contribution: the quantity of heat released by a material (in BTUs/pound) during combustion.

- Surface to mass ratio: affects probability and rate of combustion.

- Concentrated fuel "packages:" tight clusters or arrangements of fuel, focus their heat release on a small area when burned; concentrated fuel results in more rapid ignition of surrounding materials than uniformly distributed fuel.

- High placement of fuels: exposes them to higher temperatures near the ceiling, resulting in more rapid ignition.

SERVICES

D4

- "Chimney" configurations: placement of fuels near walls or other fuels to form vertical void spaces; heat rising through these "chimneys" radiates from one side to the other, causing more rapid pre-heating, air flow and burning.

- Vertical orientation of fuels: (drapery, tapestries, partitions) exposes upper surfaces to pre-heating by material burning below, resulting in exponentially rapid fire growth (Fig. 4).

2.3 Suppress/extinguish fire

Manual occupant suppression—the ability of occupants to put out a fire—early in a fire is the best chance of controlling active fires with the least threat to life and property. For this reason, buildings most often include provision for occupant-use extinguishing equipment, such as hose cabinets, manual suppression system activation, and various types of portable fire extinguishers:

- "Class A" rated extinguishers can be used on "ordinary combustibles," such as wood, paper, and natural fibers.

- "Class B" rated extinguishers can be used on flammable and combustible liquids.

- "Class C" rated extinguishers use non-conductive agents suitable for use around energized electricity.

- "Class D" rated extinguishers are for use on specific combustible metals such as magnesium and titanium.

Manual fire department suppression—the ability of trained fire fighters to control and extinguish a fire—can be aided through building design with a number of positive contributions to the response, capability and reliability of manual fire department suppression efforts:

- Early notification affords the best chance of effective fire department suppression, since fires develop exponentially over time. Rapid notification systems take several forms:

– Auxiliary alarm systems connect directly to the municipal fire department dispatch center.

– Central station systems route alarms through a private alarm office which relays them to the fire department.

– Proprietary systems are staffed by on-site employees who receive and relay alarm information to fire department.

- Site access can be improved by eliminating impediments to safe, efficient emergency operations:

– Hydrants that are highly visible and accessible

– Site features, including driveways, parking, pedestrian facilities, plantings and other landscaping, that provide unimpeded movement around the building.

– Key boxes, convenient alarm panels, and legible plan depiction to speed access to interior fire areas.

– Walk-through inspections with fire officials are helpful to firefighters and to building operators.

- Fire suppression support should be free of impediments to safe, efficient emergency operations:

– Standpipe systems inside fire resistive enclosures and easily accessible from major access points.

– Elevators that provide complete manual operation by emergency crews.

– Integrated building communications system (conventional radios are often ineffective in steel-frame and reinforced concrete buildings).

- Ventilation, the removal of smoke and hot fire gases, allows emergency crews to protect occupants, work under safer, more effi-

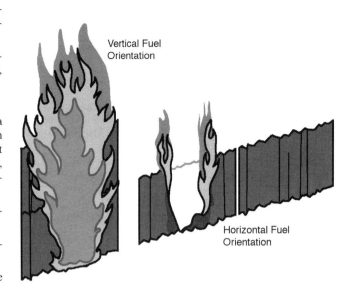

Fig. 4. Types of fuel orientation.

Vertical Fuel Orientation

Horizontal Fuel Orientation

SERVICES

D4

cient conditions, and isolate fire to smaller areas. Common building ventilation methods include:

– Rooftop gravity vents that exhaust heat directly outside.

– Engineered smoke-removal systems sometimes allow pressurization of fire floor(s) to prevent spread to uninvolved areas.

Automatic sprinkler suppression systems

These systems act immediately (even in unoccupied areas), exactly where they are needed, using a minimum of extinguishing agent. A well-designed and maintained automatic suppression system is faster, more efficient, and less likely to do additional damage than manual fire department suppression. All types of automatic sprinkler systems use prepiped waterways and regularly spaced sprinkler heads individually activated by fire contact. Sprinkler systems can be specialized in a variety of ways including large-drop systems for use in atrium and other high ceiling spaces, several quick-acting technologies, heads that are "hidden" from sight, *etc.* However, most installations are variations of the following general types:

– Wet pipe systems are fully charged with water under pressure. Activation of a head results in immediate flow.

– Dry pipe systems are commonly used in unheated buildings to avoid frozen water pipes. They are filled with compressed air to hold a "dry pipe valve" closed on the water supply. Activation of a head bleeds out the compressed air allowing water to fill the system.

– Preaction systems are much like dry pipe systems, but water is admitted into the system by activation of a fire detector, allowing staff a short time to take other action before the sprinkler system activates.

– Deluge systems activate all heads at once when a fire is detected. They are used to protect against large-scale flash fires.

Other automatic suppression systems rely on chemical extinguishing agents. Like sprinkler systems, they are fast-acting, focused, and produce relatively little additional property loss. They are generally used for special applications where water is not effective or poses unusual risk of property damage:

– Carbon dioxide systems extinguish fires by cooling and displacing oxygen, while leaving no residue.

– Inhibiting gas systems use an inert gas to chemically interrupt the combustion process. The lack of a chemical residue makes them popular for protecting computers and other electronic equipment.

– Dry chemical systems use chemical powder agents to halt combustion. They are most useful for protecting contained reservoirs of flammable liquids.

– Foam systems produce buoyant blankets of foam to float on flammable liquids, using cooling and smothering to extinguish fires.

Other suppression issues include:

• Water supply adequate to the size, occupancy, and hazard associated with a building. On-site holding tanks may be required in rural areas or municipal settings with substandard water systems.

• Adequate water pressure and volume may be a problem in areas with limited municipal water systems. Options include:

- Elevated water holding tank to boost pressure.

- On-site fire pump to maintain adequate water flow.

- Fire department connection to allow pumpers to supplement fixed equipment.

• In special cases, such as museums and archives with rare and precious artifact collections, the choice of fire suppression system, pipe lining and agent have to be selected to minimize or eliminate the possibility of damage to the collection due to sprinkler activa-

tion (*e.g.*, in areas or instances where the sprinkler system is activated by ultimately not affected by fire damage).

2.4　Limit spread

Compartmentation is a critical part of fire control. It involves the division of a building into separate fire areas, each separated from others by a perimeter of fire resistive "barriers." The commonly used test method for determining the fire resistance of an assembly (expressed as an hourly rating) is ASTM E119. In order to be an effective barrier, a floor, wall, or ceiling assembly must be:

- Physically complete: providing fire resistive assemblies to protect openings against the passage of flame, heat, or smoke.

- Thermally resistant: free of materials that conduct heat quickly from one area to another.

- Structurally stable: remaining physically sound under fire conditions.

• Physical completeness is generally ensured through the use of certified barrier (wall, floor, and ceiling) assemblies and details. Openings in barriers must be equipped with either self-closing devices that close them immediately after use, or automatic closers that close the assembly when fire is detected. Each piece of equipment inserted in a fire resistive barrier must be equipped with an individually rated assembly, of appropriate fire resistance, to close it off during a fire. In finalizing barrier details, attention should be given to specification of:

- Walls.

- Ceilings and floors.

- Separation of occupied and concealed spaces.

- Vertical barriers to spread between floors.

- Doors.

- HVAC equipment, such as ducts, transfer grilles, *etc.*

- Service openings, such as hose cabinets, access panels, and hatches.

- Lighting equipment.

- Poke-throughs for electrical, plumbing, and other utilities.

• Thermal resistance is important in barriers to ensure they do not spread heat to adjacent areas by conduction. Building codes specify minimum hourly fire-resistance requirements for barriers in various occupancies and minimum thickness requirements for various insulating materials to meet these requirements. Other details may be substituted upon documentation of certified fire resistance testing to the specified level.

• Inherent structural stability under fire conditions is partially dependent on a structural system's inherent performance under fire conditions. Factors effecting the strength include:

- Materials used and their unique fire resistive properties

- Alteration or changes in original properties or use.

- Physical condition: decay, rust, cracking, *etc.*

- Loading (static and anticipated dynamic loadings) and safety factor.

- Exposed surface area: the greater the exposed surface, the more rapid the effects of heat exposure.

- Height or span of structural components.

- Method(s) of connection.

• Structural fire protection is required. Despite their inherent resistance to fire, most structural systems need some sort of supplementary protection from fire. Common methods include (Fig. 5):

- Encasement of structural components inside close-fitting, fire re-

SERVICES

D4

sistive cladding (terra cotta blocks, concrete on wire lath, mineral and fiber boards, mineral wool bats and blankets, metal lath and plaster, gypsum blocks, gypsum wallboard).

- Coating of components with cementitious mixtures, intumescent mastics, fibrous sprays, and other topical insulating materials.

- Membrane protection, such as suspended ceilings, which separates structural components from fire exposure by distance.

3   Protect the exposed building occupants

3.1   Communicate emergency information

Notification of fire conditions is a key element of occupant fire safety. Notification should be taken seriously but not cause excessive alarm or panic. Messages should be concise, providing needed information without being overwhelming and foster confidence but not overconfidence in the fire protection systems present, *etc.* In designing systems, consider:

- Multiple sensory modes (sound, sight, touch) to accommodate various age groups, the sight and hearing impaired, *etc.*

- Redundancy, *e.g.*, using a combination of general alarm klaxons, flashing lights, and voice messages, to appeal to different levels of experience and comprehension.

Instruction concerning appropriate actions is a desirable supplement to alarm notification. Active systems such as auditory alarms, voice messages, *etc.*, can be reinforced by passive information modes such as signage, well-placed ambient lighting, and other features that reinforce correct fire-safety behaviors.

3.2   Provide for emergency egress

"Means of egress" consists of three separate and distinct parts or components:

- Exit access is the route from the point where people start to the point at which they reach the beginning of a protected exit. Exit access ends when occupants reach a protected exit.

- Exits are enclosed and protected passageways leading to the outside of the building. The most common enclosed exit is a stair shaft. There are also horizontal exit passageways, which have special fire resistive requirements exceeding those of corridors.

- Exit discharge is that section of the means of egress leading from the end of the exit to a "public way" (street, alley, sidewalk, *etc.*).

Planning for egress should include an effective system of building evacuation system should provide for:

- Adequate number and arrangement of exits, sufficient in capacity for the number of occupants, and configured so that no single failure shall result in unacceptable level of fire safety.

- Structural integrity sufficient to ensure safety during a fire while the occupants are exiting or in an area of refuge. Additional protection may be necessary for the safety of firefighting operations.

- Exit continuity to ensure that exits remain clearly visible, unobstructed, and unlocked. Occupants should normally be able to exit a building easily without any special knowledge, effort, keys, or tools.

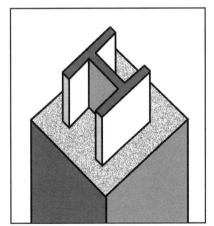

Encasement--
Concrete

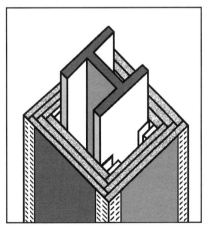

Encasement--
Gypsum Board

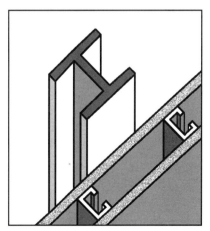

Membrane
Protection

Fig. 5. Types of fireproofing for a steel column.

- Adequate marking so that exits and routes of escape are clearly marked and unambiguous. Effective exit marking must be:

    a. Legible: visible from locations from which it might be viewed.

    b. Meaningful: accurately conveying the meaning and function of access point.

    c. Memorable: sufficiently distinctive to be remembered and found later, when emergency conditions may obscure its visibility.

- Adequate lighting that provides illumination appropriate to the safe use of the egress system, especially components such as stairs.

- Adequate redundancy, providing alternative exits so that at least two exits to be accessible from every area.

- Suitable enclosure of vertical openings to provide fire protection between building levels.

- Site-specific planning that moves beyond basic requirements to address unique issues of building size, shape, and occupancy. Large populations of mobility impaired occupants may require special accommodations such as wider, more numerous, and specially marked exits.

3.3   Defend in place

Refuge areas serve as an important alternative to egress systems. As buildings have gotten taller, the necessity of supplementing egress features with additional means of protecting occupants within buildings has become clear. However, regardless of building height or type, extreme conditions can develop wherein occupants are unable to avoid fire's threats by leaving. For this reason careful consideration should always be given to provisions for special refuge areas for protecting people in place. Attention should be given to:

- Refuge on each floor, as a supplement to conventional protection by evacuation.

- Quick and easy access, ideally along conventional egress routes.

- Proximity to exits enhances rescue via protected exit enclosures or subsequent occupant use of egress provisions.

- Structural integrity for protection from collapse.

- Communication provisions capable of keeping the occupants informed on the status of the emergency and for communicating problems that may develop.

- Life support, including protection from toxic gases, smoke and heat.

SERVICES

D4

Fire protection sprinkler systems

Summary: This article provides and overview of sprinkler system applications, including automatic sprinkler types, design criteria, modification in existing buildings, integrating systems with other building services, equipment and acceptance testing requirements.

Key words: deluge systems, dry-pipe system, preaction systems, spray pattern, sprinkler deflector, wet-pipe system.

Uniformat:	D4010
MasterFormat:	15300

An automatic sprinkler system is a system of pipes with automatic sprinklers placed at various intervals. The orifice of the automatic sprinkler is normally closed by a disk or cap held in place by a temperature-sensitive releasing element. Each sprinkler is automatically activated to discharge and distribute water on a fire in sufficient quantity to either control or extinguish it. The system shall also be provided with at least one automatic and reliable water supply source and provide an automatic alarm when activated. Selection considerations include:

- Automatic sprinkler systems are one of the most reliable methods available for controlling fires. Large areas, high-rise buildings, hazardous occupancies, high content value, and concentrations of large numbers of people in one area all tend to develop risk conditions that cannot be tolerated or accepted without automatic sprinkler protection.

- Sprinkler systems are effective for life safety because they warn of fire and at the same time apply water to the burning area during the very early stages of fire.

- Automatic sprinkler systems are required to be installed by building/fire codes and fire insurance companies. These requirements are usually based on occupancy type, construction, and size of building. Many governmental jurisdictions also have adopted local automatic sprinkler requirements.

Types of automatic sprinkler systems

- *Wet-pipe system*
  Automatic sprinklers are attached to a piping system that contains water under pressure at all times. When individual sprinklers are actuated, water flows through the sprinklers immediately. These types of systems are the most commonly found and can be installed in areas where the temperature will always be maintained above 40F (4°C).

- *Dry-Pipe system*
  Automatic sprinklers are attached to a piping system that normally contains air under pressure. When a sprinkler opens, air pressure is reduced to the point where water pressure on the supply side of a dry alarm valve forces open the valve. Water then flows into the system and out of any activated open sprinkler. These systems are

used in areas that cannot be heated. Dry-pipe systems can be used in conjunction with wet-pipe systems to protect areas such as attic or combustible concealed spaces or outside loading or covered storage areas. The dry-pipe alarm control valve must be kept within a heated enclosure and provided with an air compressor.

- *Preaction system*
  Automatic sprinklers are attached to a piping system in which there is air in the piping that may or may not be under pressure. When a fire occurs, a supplementary fire detection device in the protected area is actuated. A water control valve is then opened that permits water to flow into the piping system before a sprinkler is activated. When an individual sprinkler is activated by heat from the fire, water flows immediately from the sprinkler. The detection devices are designed with a sensitivity that will allow them to operate before a sprinkler fuses and activates. These systems are used in locations where accidental damage to the piping or sprinklers, on a wet- or dry-pipe system, could cause damage to facilities or equipment, such as computer centers.

- *Combined dry-pipe and preaction system*
  Automatic sprinklers are attached to a piping system that includes the features of both a dry-pipe and preaction system. The piping contains air under pressure. A supplementary heat detection device opens the water control valve and an air exhauster at the end of the feed main. The system then fills with water and operates like a wet-pipe system. If the heat detection system should fail, the system will still operate as a conventional dry-pipe system. This type of system has the same type of application as a standard preaction system. In addition, these systems are used for unheated piers. These systems have an economic advantage in the elimination of numerous dry-pipe valves that require regular maintenance.

- *Deluge system*
  In this type of system, all sprinklers are open at all times. When heat from a fire activates the fire detecting device, the deluge valve opens and water flows and discharges from all of the sprinkler heads in the piping. The area being protected is then deluged with water. This system is used primarily in special hazard situations where is it necessary to apply water over a large area to control a fast-developing fire. It is also used to apply foam for protection of flammable liquid hazards.

Author: Bruce W. Hisley

Credits: Photos courtesy of Firematic Sprinkler Devices, Inc.

References: NFPA. 1996. *NFPA Fire Protection Handbook.* 18th Edition. Quincy, MA: National Fire Protection Association. 1-800-344-3555.

Additional references are listed at the end of this article.

- *Special types*

  These systems depart from the normal types of systems in such areas as special water supplies and reduced pipe sizes. They are installed according to manufacturer's instructions in accordance with their listing by a testing laboratory. Examples include exterior exposure protection and circulating closed loop systems that are part of the building's heating system. These systems require very careful evaluation by qualified individuals to determine their suitability.

Benefits of sprinkler systems

- automatic sprinklers, properly installed and maintained, provide a highly effective safeguard against the loss of life and property from fire.

- the National Fire Protection Association (NFPA) has no record of a multiple death fire (a fire which kills three or more people) in a completely sprinklered building, where the system was operating properly, except in an explosion or flash fire.

- offer design flexibility, economic construction methods, and expanded choices of building materials.

- can be used to offset passive fire protection requirements such as fire resistance of building structural elements, compartmentalization, and fire rated exitways or corridors.

- building size may be increased in areas with a lesser degree of fire resistance rating. Some local jurisdictions have modified their local subdivision development requirements for residential type development where each type of residential unit is protected with a sprinkler system.

- offset deficiencies in existing buildings related to life safety requirements.

- improve life safety related to fire in residential buildings.

- reduce problem of access to the seat of a fire or of interference with visibility for firefighters due to smoke.

- generate less water damage than the water application of a hose stream by firefighters.

- sprinklers cool the smoke and make it possible for persons to remain in the area much longer than they could if the room were not sprinkled.

- savings from direct fire losses, business interruption caused by a fire, indirect business losses, and in fire insurance costs that make the expenditure for a sprinkler system a sound business investment.

Design criteria and requirements

- Considering the installation of a sprinkler system up front before the building is designed, whether the system is required or not, is essential in order to take full advantage of the effectiveness and economic variables that a sprinkler system can provide. This early up front planning and coordination with the sprinkler designer will provide maximum benefits in sprinkler area coverage and reduced installation costs.

- Sprinkler system design and installation is a special trade and should only be designed and installed by fully-qualified, experienced, and responsible parties.

- The sprinkler system must be provided with a water source of sufficient capacity to supply the number of sprinklers that will be opened during a fire. The water must have adequate pressure in order to be adequately distributed to the highest and farthest sprinkler on the system.

- The sprinkler system should be designed for installation throughout the building for complete protection to life and property. In some cases local adopted requirements may only require partial sprinkler installation for hazardous areas for limited protection.

- Outdoor hydrants, indoor hose standpipes, and hand hose connections also are frequently part of the sprinkler system.

- In older existing buildings some modifications may be needed to ensure effective sprinkler operation. These include:

- enclosing vertical openings to divide multi-story structures into separate fire areas

- removing unnecessary partitions that could interfere with sprinkler discharge

- removing needless sheathing and shelving

- checking combustible concealed areas, such as attic and areas between floor/ceiling, to see if they need sprinkler protection.

- Sprinkler systems in buildings subject to flooding require special attention to the following:

- location and piping arrangement so it will not be washed out or weaken supports

- location of control valves so that they will be accessible during high water

- location of alarm devices so that they will remain operable during high water

- location and arrangement of fire pumps and their power supply and controls to provide reasonable safeguards against interference.

- Earthquake bracing, where required, is necessary to keep the pipe network in place during seismic events.

- Planning for a sprinkler system is usually based upon four general areas:

- the sprinkler system itself

- type of construction

- hazard of occupancy

- water supply

Hazard classification

- A building's use is the primary consideration in designing a sprinkler system that is adequate to protect against hazards in the occupancy. These hazard classifications affect:

- spacing of sprinklers

- sprinkler discharge densities

- water supply requirements

- The three general classifications are:

- *light hazard:*

  Quantity and/or combustibility of materials is low and fires with relatively low rates of heat release are expected. Examples include apartments, churches, hotels, office buildings, and schools.

- *ordinary hazard:*

  Quantity and combustibility of contents is moderate, stock piles do not exceed 12 ft. (3.7 m), and fires with a moderate rate of heat release are expected. Examples include laundries, textile plants, printing plants, flour mills, and paper manufacturing and storage warehouses containing paper, furniture, and paint.

- *extra hazard:*

  Quantity and combustibility of contents is very high and flammable and combustible liquids, dust, lint, or other materials are present that can produce rapidly developing fires with high rates of heat release. Examples include rubber production, upholstering operations using plastic foams, and occupancies with large amounts of flammable liquids, varnish, and paint dipping.

- The three general hazard classifications serve as a good basic guide. It does not rule out the necessity of separately evaluating certain portions of an occupancy that may contain hazards more severe than the remainder of the building.

- In each of the three broad hazard classifications, the system may be designed according to hydraulic calculation requirements or using a set of predetermined pipe schedule tables. Hydraulically designed systems are preferable from a fire protection standpoint and are the most prevalent type of design being used today (see Fig. 1 for pipe schedule).

Installation specifications

- All sprinkler system equipment, devices, and materials are required to be listed (approved) by a testing laboratory. Both Factory Mutual Fire Insurance Company and Underwriter's Laboratories maintain testing facilities for testing and provide a listing or approved service.

- Before a sprinkler system is installed or remodeled, a detailed working plan is to be prepared. The plan identifies pertinent features of building construction and occupancy. The National Fire Protection Association (NFPA) Standard #13: Installation of Automatic Sprinkler Systems, is the primary standard for the installation of sprinkler systems and is quite precise on the data that must be shown on the plan. This plan is required to be submitted to the local authority having jurisdiction for review and approval before installation.

Integrating sprinklers with other building services and equipment

- The building designer needs to consider how the sprinkler system will be integrating into the design of the building. Examples:

- floor or roof structure elements required to support the pipe hanger.

- location of piping in ceiling spaces that will not be affected by the HVAC duct work.

- floor plan partition layout relating to sprinkler coverage.

- location of area for sprinkler control valve and heating, if required.

- piping installation that is aesthetically pleasing.

- architectural features that may obstruct the spray pattern or cause delayed activation, such as soffits, partitions, ducts, decorative ceilings, and light fixtures.

- Acceptance testing: NFPA Standard #13 requires that the installing contractor, in the presence of the building owner's representative and the local authority having jurisdiction, conduct system acceptance tests for major sprinkler system components. These tests are to be certified by the installing contractor in a format required by the standard. The following tests are required:

- before the underground water supply piping is connected to the inside riser, all new underground piping shall be thoroughly flushed to remove any obstructing materials that could impair the system.

- all new underground and above ground sprinkler piping shall be hydrostatically tested for strength and leakage—at not less than 200 psi for two hours or at 50 psi in excess of the maximum static pressure, when the pressure is in excess of 150 psi.

- an air pressure test of 40 psi for 24 hours is required for all above ground piping for a new dry-pipe type system.

- a main drain test is required with the control valves fully open to ensure that water will be safely and properly disposed.

- an inspector's test shall be conducted to determine that the automatic water flow alarms are operational.

- an operational test to determine satisfactory performance of the control valves is required for dry-pipe, preaction, and deluge type

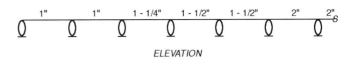

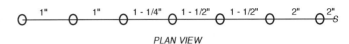

Fig. 1. Ordinary hazard pipe schedule (Source: NFSA Fire Sprinkler Plan Review Guide)

2 sprinklers fed by 1 in. (2.5 cm) pipe
2 + 1 = 3 sprinklers fed by 1-1/4 in. (3 cm) pipe
3 + 2 = 5 sprinklers fed by 1-1/2 in. (3.8 cm) pipe
5 + 2 = 7 sprinklers fed by 2 in. (5 cm) pipe (up to 10 allowable)

sprinkler systems. These tests shall be conducted in accordance with the valve manufacturer's specifications.

Water supply

Every sprinkler system must have at least one automatic water supply of adequate pressure, capacity, and reliability An automatic supply is one that is not dependent on any manual operation to supply water at the time of a fire. The rate of flow (capacity) and the duration (time) of that flow needs to be considered as part of an automatic supply.

- *Types of supplies*
  Sprinkler systems can be supplied from one or a combination of sources such as street mains, gravity/suction tanks, fire pumps, lakes, and wells. The most common source today is from a street main. A secondary supply may be necessary depending on the reliability of the primary supply; the value of the property, building area and height, construction type, occupancy, and outside exposures. NFPA Standard 13 requires at least one automatic reliable water supply source.

- *Connection to water works system*
  This is the preferred single or primary method of supply if the system is reliable and of adequate capacity and pressure. In determining adequacy, a determination of probable minimum pressures and flows available at peak domestic, or heavy demands must be considered.

- size and arrangement of the street mains are important.

- water mains less than 6 in. (15 cm) in diameter are usually inadequate.

- feeds from long dead-end mains are also undesirable.

- water meters, if required, should be of a type approved for fire service.

- flow and pressure tests under varying conditions are required to determine the amount of water available for fire protection.

- local government or water companies may require backflow prevention devices to protect the potable water supply that also supplies the sprinkler system. These devices can affect the available water supply and pressure.

- NFPA Standard 24: Private Fire Service Mains and Their Appurtenances, provides guidance for the installation of these devices.

- *Gravity tanks*
  These types of tanks provide an acceptable supply if of adequate

Fig. 2. Check valve

capacity and pressure that is provided by the available height of the water column in the tank. The capacity of the tank is determined by the sprinkler demand, hoselines, and duration of operation.

- *Suction tanks*
  These types of tanks require a fire pump to provide the necessary pressure to the sprinkler system. Suction tanks are now being used with the advent of the hydraulically designed sprinkler system.

- *Fire pumps*
  An automatic fire pump with a reliable power source and water supply is a desirable source of supply. Fire pumps:

- provide an advantage of having a water supply available at a higher pressure.

- can maintain higher pressures over a long period of time.

- can be powered by electric motors or diesel engines.

- are installed in accordance with NFPA Standard 20: Installation of Centrifugal Fire Pumps.

- *Pressure tanks*
  Have possible uses but an important limitation is the small volume of water than can be stored. Where an adequate volume of water is available but pressure is not sufficient, a pressure tank gives a good starting point for the first sprinklers to operate. Pressure tanks can be used in tall buildings where public water pressure is too low for effective supply to the highest sprinkler, until the fire department arrives to pump into the fire department connection.

- *Fire department connections*
  A connection that allows the fire department to pump water into the sprinkler system is an important secondary supply. These connections are a standard part of a sprinkler system. Fire department connections:

- shall be readily accessible at all times.

- shall be properly marked.

- shall be fitted with a check valve but not with a gate valve to prevent it from being inadvertently shut off (Fig. 2).

- can be designed to supply each sprinkler riser separately or connected to an outside yard system that would supply every riser.

Factors affecting water supply requirements
Establishing the water supply requirements for a sprinkler system requires good engineering judgment based on several factors relating to sprinkler control. Where conditions are favorable the fire should be controlled by the operation of only a small number of sprinklers. Factors that can affect the number of sprinklers that might open in a fire are:

- Initial water supply pressure: At higher pressures the discharge is greater. With greater discharge there is a better chance of fire control from fewer sprinklers.

- Obstructions to water patterns from sprinklers: Stock piled high, pallets, racks, and shelving can cause obstructions to water discharge, preventing fire control and in turn a greater chance that more sprinklers needing more water supply will be required.

- Ceiling height: Ceilings of unusual heights can produce drafts that will carry heat away from the sprinkler directly over the fire area, resulting in the delay in the application of water and the opening of sprinklers remote from the fire.

- Unprotected vertical openings: Sprinklers are designed on the assumption that fire will be controlled on the floor of fire origin. With unprotected openings, heat and fire may spread through the openings causing additional sprinklers to operate.

- Wet type versus dry type sprinklers: With the delay in exhausting the air pressure from a dry type system, more sprinklers will open in a dry type system than a wet type system.

- Floor-mounted and ceiling-mounted obstructions and concealed spaces: Beams, girders, light fixtures, and HVAC duct work can obstruct the water pattern, which in turn can cause additional sprinklers to operate to account for the obstruction.

- Floor obstructions such as office privacy partitions can also cause a problem.

- Concealed combustible spaces will also have an impact. When these concealed areas are not protected the sprinkler design area is doubled to account for the uncontrolled spread of fire in these areas.

Water supply requirements for sprinkler systems
The fire hazards represented by different building occupancies requires the establishment of guides to water supply for sprinkler systems. Water supply requirements will differ between a pipe schedule design and hydraulically calculated design.

- The total water supply required is determined by:

- occupancy hazard requirement for sprinkler.

- additional water for hose streams.

- if stored water is used, the total flow required must be multiplied by the duration of flow (time) to determine storage capacity.

- Pipe schedule design: Specifies the maximum number of sprinkler heads that can be installed on a pipeline of a given size for a specific hazard type (Table 1). With the development of newer sprinkler heads this type of design is very limited because of the special pressures and water capacity requirements of the newer sprinklers. NFPA Standard 13 now limits the use of this type of design for new buildings.

- Hydraulically calculated design: The pipe sizes are selected on a pressure-loss basis to provide a prescribed density in gallons per minute per square foot, with a reasonable degree of uniformity over a specified are. The selection of pipe sizes will depend on the water supply available. The stipulated design density and area of application (remote design area) will vary with each occupancy hazard. This is now the preferred method of sprinkler design (Fig.

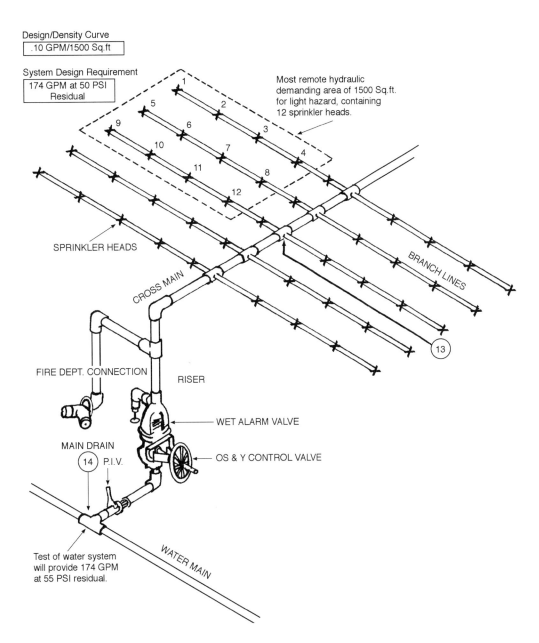

Design/Density Curve
.10 GPM/1500 Sq.ft

System Design Requirement
174 GPM at 50 PSI Residual

Most remote hydraulic demanding area of 1500 Sq.ft. for light hazard, containing 12 sprinkler heads.

SPRINKLER HEADS

BRANCH LINES

CROSS MAIN

FIRE DEPT. CONNECTION

RISER

WET ALARM VALVE

MAIN DRAIN

14 P.I.V.

OS & Y CONTROL VALVE

Test of water system will provide 174 GPM at 55 PSI residual.

WATER MAIN

Fig. 3. Example of hydraulically designed system for light hazard occupancy without hose stream demand

Table 1. Summary of NFPA Standard 13 Pipe Schedule Systems for Steel Pipe: Number of sprinklers fed by pipe size

Pipe size	Light Hazard	Ordinary Hazard
1"	2	2
1-1/4"	3	3
1-1/2"	5	5
2"	10	10
2-1/2"	30	20
3"	60	40
3-1/2"	100	65
4"	Maximum 52,000 sq. ft. floor area	100
5"	Maximum 52,000 sq. ft. floor area	160
6"	Maximum 52,000 sq. ft. floor area	275
8"	Maximum 52,000 sq. ft. floor area	Maximum 52,000 sq. ft. floor area

3). This type of design can address the newer various types of sprinklers that may require special pressures and water capacity.

Water supply for residential occupancies

With the development of the quick response residential sprinklers special water supply requirements have been developed for these types of systems.

- One- and two-family residences: These types of systems are installed in accordance with NFPA Standard 13D: Installation of Sprinkler Systems in One and Two Family Dwellings. Requirements for water supply are:

- minimum flow of 18 gpm (68 l/m) for a single residential sprinkler or 13 gpm (49 l/m) for each sprinkler with a minimum of two sprinklers operating.

- system shall have an automatic water supply.

- If supply is from a stored system it shall be able to provide a minimum flow for 10 minutes.

- system must be a wet-pipe type system using only residential type sprinklers.

- certain areas are exempt from complete coverage.

- Other residential occupancies up to four stories in height: These types of systems are installed in accordance with NFPA Standard 13R: Installation of Sprinkler Systems in Residential Occupancies up to Four Stories in Height. Requirements for water supply are:

- minimum flow of 18 gpm (68 l/m) for a single residential sprinkler or 13 gpm (49 l/m) for each sprinkler with a minimum of four sprinklers operating in the residential part of the occupancy.

- if supply is from a stored system it shall be able to provide a minimum flow for 30 minutes.

- system must be a wet-pipe type system using only residential type sprinklers protecting the residential areas.

Piping, valves, and fittings

Piping materials, valves, and fittings shall be tested and listed by a testing laboratory as being suitable for use in a sprinkler system. The Underwriter's Laboratory publishes a fire protection equipment directory that notes the different types of piping, valves, and fittings that have been tested and listed by manufacture and model types. The NFPA Standard 13 requires that piping valves and fittings be of a type that can withstand a working pressure of not less than 175 psi (1,208 kPa). Higher working pressures may be required in high-rise buildings or locations that are served by a fire pump, when the normal sprinkler system pressures exceed 175 psi (1,208 kPa).

Sprinkler piping

All pipe used in sprinkler systems shall be marked continuously along its length by the manufacturer to properly identify the type of pipe. Several different types of piping materials are approved for sprinkler systems which are:

- ferrous piping (welded and seamless);

- copper tube (drawn and seamless);

- non-metallic polybutylene and chlorinated polyvinyl chloride (CPVC).

- Ferrous piping can be either black steel, galvanized, or wrought steel pipe that are manufactures in various wall thickness. The most common for sprinkler systems being schedule 40, 30, and 10. NFPA Standard 13 notes minimum wall thickness for steel pipe depending on the method of joining the pipe.

- Non-metallic (plastic) piping is light-weight and has favorable hydraulic characteristics for water flow. Special installation re-

quirements are required as follows:

- restricted for use in light hazard occupancies only.

- limited to indoor wet-pipe systems.

- must be protected by a protective membrane.

- CPVC piping can be exposed when quick response or residential sprinklers are installed.

- strict adherence to manufacturers instructions for assembly is necessary.

Sprinkler system piping components

Sprinkler piping must be carefully planned and installed in accordance with NFPA Standard 13. A system consists of the following components:

- Branch lines: The pipelines in which the sprinklers are placed directly.

- Cross main: The pipe that directly supplies the branch lines.

- Feed main: The piping that supplies the cross main.

- Riser: The main supply to the system that feeds from the underground incoming piping from the water supply source.

- must be accessible and properly identified as to what area it is protecting.

- large buildings may have several separate risers supplying different parts of the building.

- the size of the riser will be determined hydraulically by calculating the maximum number of sprinklers expected to operate on one floor during a fire, or by the pipe schedule system that is determined by the maximum number of sprinkler heads supplied by the riser on one floor (Fig. 4).

Valves

Valves that control the water supply to the sprinkler system are the most important. It is critical to provide supervision of the control valves that will activate a signal on the premises or at a supervising office.

- Valves controlling connections to water supplies and supplying pipes to sprinklers: These types of valves must be of the listed indicating type. When water pressures exceed 175 psi (1,208 kPa) the valves shall be used in accordance with their pressure rating.

- Drain valves and test valves: Shall be of an approved type and provided with permanently marked identification signs.

- all systems shall be provided with a main drain valve and inspector test valve and connection.

- valves shall be readily accessible and provided with adequate discharge that can handle the drain discharge flow.

- Water flow alarm valves: Shall be listed for the service and designed to detect water flow from one sprinkler head within 5 minutes maximum after such flow begins (Fig. 5). Can be either mechanical or electrical in operation or both.

- Water flow detecting devices: These valves are determined by the type of sprinkler provided which are:

- wet-pipe system.

- dry-pipe system.

- preaction and deluge system.

- Check valves: Can be found in various parts of a sprinkler system. They must be:

- listed for fire protection service.

- installed within the system in the correct position in accordance with the designed water flow direction.

- Pressure reducing valves: Are found in systems or portions of systems where all components are not listed for pressures greater than 175 psi (1,208 kPa). These valves must be listed for fire sprinkler service.

Pipe fittings and attachments

- Pipe fittings: Shall be designed for use in sprinkler systems. Are installed by means of:

- screwed

- flanged

- mechanical joint

- brazed

- welded with specification given in the American Welding Society standard.

- flexible coupling

- Installation standards for joining non-metallic pipe are unique to the type of pipe used. The manufacturer's instructions are critical to ensure a correct installation.

- Pipe hangers: Are used to attach sprinkler piping to substantial structural elements of a building. The type of hangers necessary to meet various conditions of construction have been tested and listed by testing laboratories. The adequate support of sprinkler piping is an important consideration.

Corrosive conditions

Corrosive conditions call for the use of piping, fittings, valves, and hangers that are designed to resist the particular corrosive environment or for the application of a protective coating over the components.

- Water supply: For buildings that may contain corrosive properties, may require piping types that can resist the effects of the corrosion.

Sprinkler heads

- Operating principles: Under most conditions the discharge of water is restrained by a cap or valve held tightly against the orifice by a system of levers and links or other releasing devices pressing down on the cap. The operating elements can be:

- fusible link style: Operates when a metal alloy of a predetermined meeting point fuses (Fig. 6).
- bulb style: A frangible bulb, usually of glass, containing a liquid that does not completely fill the bulb. This small air bubble is then compressed by the expanding liquid and is absorbed by the liquid. Once the bulb disappears, the pressure rises and in turn shatters the glass bulb, releasing the valve cap (Fig. 7).
- other thermosensitive styles: bimetallic disc, fusible alloy pellets, and chemical pellets.

- Deflector design: The deflector is attached to the sprinkler frame and causes the water to be converted to a spray pattern to cover a specific area. The amount of water discharged is determined by:

- a flowing pressure of at least 7 psi (48 kPa), which is the minimum to develop a reasonable spray pattern and a sprinkler with a nominal 1/2 in. (13 mm) orifice will discharge 15 gpm (57 l/m).

- in order to have the minimum flowing pressure at sprinklers that are remote from the water supply source (riser) a water supply pressure in the range of 30 psi (207 kPa) to 100 psi (650 kPa) is required.

- Pendent deflector: Water is directed downward through the deflector.

- used below finished ceiling which conceals the sprinkler piping.

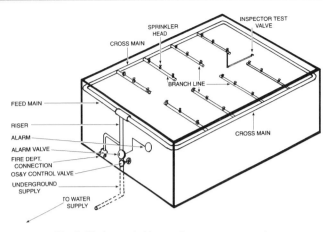

Fig.4. Major sprinkler system components

Fig. 5. Alarm valve

Fig. 6. Fusible link sprinkler

Fig. 7. Bulb style sprinkler

SERVICES

D4

Fig. 8. Sidewall horizontal deflector

- heads can be recessed in the ceiling, concealed by a cover plate, or mounted flush.

• Upright deflector: Water is directed upward through the deflector and then down onto the floor below.

- are used in buildings with no finished ceiling, such as warehouses and manufacturing plants.

- must be installed within 12 in. (30 cm) of the underside of the roof or floor decking.

- the design of the deflectors for pendent and upright sprinklers cause a solid stream of water from the orifice to break up to form an umbrella shaped spray. The pattern is roughly that of a half sphere filled with spray. Even water distribution is achieved by overlapping downward arcing coverage, by any two operating sprinklers located next to each other.

• Sidewall horizontal deflector: Water is directed horizontally through the deflectors to produce an arc of water that projects out from the sprinkler wall mounted position (Fig. 8).

- can only be used for light hazard occupancies such as hotels, dining rooms, offices, and residential occupancies.

- supply piping is in the walls and is used where piping would be objectionable.

- directional character of the discharge from the sidewall sprinkler makes them applicable to special protection design problems.

Temperature rating
Automatic sprinklers have various temperature ratings for application in areas that will have various maximum ceiling temperatures. NFPA Standard 13 notes the various maximum ceiling temperature that may be expected and the required sprinkler rating to be installed and also notes the different sprinkler temperature classifications and the color codes used for both fusible link and glass bulb type sprinklers.

• Generally, sprinklers of ordinary 135F (57°C) to 170F (77°C) temperature ratings should not be used in areas where the temperature would exceed 100F (38°C) to prevent premature operation. Areas that require special attention are:

- areas inside buildings exposed to direct sun rays such as skylights.

- blind attics without ventilation.

- under metal or tile roofs.

- near or above heating sources.

- within confined spaces where normal temperatures can be exceeded.

• In cases where extreme speed of operation is required because of the likelihood of a rapidly developing and spreading fire, the practice is to use a deluge system with open sprinklers. The system would be activated by a special fire detection system to open a deluge control valve and quickly allow water to enter the system and discharge through all the open sprinkler heads.

Area of coverage
The fundamental idea in locating and spacing sprinklers in a building is to make sure that there are no areas unprotected where a fire can start or spread. No areas should be left unprotected. NFPA Standard 13 notes areas where sprinklers are sometimes questioned. These include:

- stairways

- vertical shafts

- deep blind and combustible concealed spaces

- ducts

- basements

- subfloor spaces

- attics

- electrical equipment rooms

- small closets

- walk-in coolers

- spaces under decks

- tables

- canopies

- outdoor platforms

• Area and spacing limitations: The location of sprinklers on a branch line and the location of the lines in relation to each other determine the size of the area to be protected by a sprinkler. A definite maximum area of coverage is defined that is dependent upon the occupancy hazard and the type of ceiling or roof construction above the sprinkler. Those types being smooth ceiling, beam and girder, bar joist, wood joist, and wood truss. In general, area coverage of sprinklers are:

- 168 to 225 sq. ft. (15.6 to 21 sq. m) for light hazard.

- 130 sq. ft. (12 sq. m) for ordinary hazard.

- 100 sq. ft. (9.3 sq. m) for extra hazard.

- maximum spacing between any sprinklers cannot exceed 15 ft. (4.6 m) for light and ordinary hazard and 12 ft. (3.7 m) for extra hazard occupancies.

- the distance of a sprinkler to a wall is usually no more than half of the uniform spacing design being used.

- NFPA Standard 13 allows use of special sprinklers with greater areas of coverage when they have been tested and listed for the greater coverage. These types of sprinklers are referred to as "extended coverage" that will be addressed below.

• Design considerations: It is very important that the sprinkler designer be consulted as early as possible in planning for the piping installation. This planning can provide the following benefits for sprinkler placement:

- reduce the installation costs by taking advantage of the maximum spacing allowed for each sprinkler head for protection of individual rooms and areas, in turn reducing the number of heads required.

- plan individual room sizes around maximum coverage per sprinkler head.

SERVICES

D4

- plan for piping runs that will not be in conflict with other mechanical systems in the ceiling.

- placement of ceiling light fixtures where the will not interfere with sprinkler placement or discharge pattern.

- improve the aesthetics of sprinkler installation that blend with the building finishes.

- reduce architectural obstructions that would affect water discharge patterns and in turn eliminate the need for additional sprinkler heads.

Obstruction to water distribution

Certain limits of clearance have been established between sprinklers and structural members such as beams, girders, and truss to keep them from obstructing water discharge from sprinklers.

- obstruction can deflect the normal sprinkler discharge pattern and in turn reduce the area of protection for the sprinkler.

- NFPA Standard 13 is explicit in the limitation it places on distances between sprinklers and both vertical and horizontal obstructions near the sprinklers.

Types of automatic sprinklers

• *Recessed sprinkler:*
A type in which most of the body of the sprinkler is mounted in a recessed housing. The sprinkler is positioned in a pendent position (Fig. 9).

• *Flush sprinkler:*
Of a special design for pendent mounting within the ceiling. The design allows a minimum projection of the working parts below the ceiling without affecting the heat sensitivity or water distribution pattern.

• *Concealed sprinkler:*
A type whose entire body, including the operating mechanism is above its concealed cover plate. When a fire occurs, the cover plate drops, exposing the heat sensitive sprinkler element which in turn then operates (Fig. 10). Characteristics of these sprinklers:

- aesthetic in appearance because they do not protrude through decorated ceilings.

- cover plates are available in colors and patterns to match decorative ceiling assemblies.

• *Ornamental sprinkler:*
A sprinkler that has been decorated by attachment or by plating or enameling to give the desired surface finish. These types of sprinklers are for pendent installation.

• *Dry pendent and dry upright sprinkler:*
Used to provide protection in unheated areas, such as freezers, where the individual sprinklers are supplied from a wet type system outside of the unheated area. A seal is provided at the entrance of the dry sprinkler to prevent water from entering until the sprinkler fuses.

• *Sidewall sprinkler:*
Has components of standard sprinkler except for a special deflector which discharges the water toward one side in a pattern somewhat like one quarter of a sphere. Can only be used in light hazard occupancies. Can be mounted:

- in a vertical position along the junction between the ceiling and sidewall.

- in a horizontal position along the junction between the ceiling and sidewall.

• *Open sprinkler:*
A sprinkler that has had its valve cap and heat response element

Fig. 9. Recessed sprinkler

Fig. 10. Concealed sprinkler

SERVICES

D4

omitted and is used in deluge type systems.

- *Residential quick response sprinkler:*
  Specifically listed for use in residential occupancies. These are fast response sprinklers that have special low-mass fusible links or bulbs that make the time of temperature actuation much less than that of a sprinkler with a standard fusible link. For use in wet-pipe systems only, designed for pendent and horizontal sidewall position.

- *Intermediate level sprinkler:*
  Also referred to as in-rack sprinkler. These sprinklers are equipped with shields designed to protect the link assembly from spray of sprinklers mounted at higher levels. These heads are found in high rack storage arrangements.

- *Early suppression fast response (ESFR) sprinkler:*
  A fast-response sprinkler listed for its capability to provide fire suppression of specific high challenge fire hazards. The ESFR sprinklers can:

- achieve fire suppression quickly without opening more than one ring of sprinklers.

- optimize sprinkler performance by mounting a vigorous attack against a fire, regardless of its intensity or the degree of fire development when the first few sprinklers operate.

- be used in storage areas with high storage heights of highly combustible type storage.

- *Extended coverage (EC) sprinkler:*
  A sprinkler with special extended directional discharge patterns. The Underwriters Laboratories, Fire Protection Equipment Directory, notes that EC sidewall and pendent type sprinklers are designed to discharge water over an area having maximum dimensions indicated by the manufacturer in their individual listings. Extended coverage sprinklers:

- are designed for light hazard occupancies having smooth flat horizontal ceilings.

- deflector must be located from 4 in. (10 cm) to 6 in. (15 cm) below the ceiling.

- the maximum width and length dimensions are noted along with the minimum flow rate and pressure required in their individual listings.

Additional references

Byran, John C. *Automatic Sprinkler and Standpipe Systems.* Second Edition. Quincy, MA: National Fire Protection Association.

NFPA. *NFPA Fire Protection Handbook.* NFPA Standard 13: Installation of Automatic Sprinkler Systems. Quincy, MA: National Fire Protection Association

_____. NFPA Standard 13D: Installation of Sprinkler Systems in One and Two Family Dwellings. Quincy, MA: National Fire Protection Association

_____. NFPA Standard 13R: Installation of Sprinkler Systems in Residential Occupancies up to Four Stories in Height. Quincy, MA: National Fire Protection Association

_____. NFPA Standard 20: Installation of Fire Pumps. Quincy, MA: National Fire Protection Association

_____. NFPA Standard 22: Water Tanks for Private Fire Protection. Quincy, MA: National Fire Protection Association

SERVICES

D4

Standpipe systems

Summary: An overview is provided of standpipe systems, water supply requirements, flow rates and pressure, water supply, piping and valves, standpipe location, minimum sizes, pressure regulators; cabinets, hoses, and nozzles.

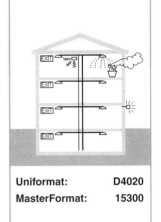

| Uniformat: | D4020 |
| MasterFormat: | 15300 |

Key words: fire department connection, fire hoses, indicating valves, water supply sources, zoned standpipe systems.

Standpipe systems provide a means for the manual application of water to fires in buildings. They are designed for large building areas and buildings over four stories. Standpipe systems are found in both horizontal and vertical design. Standpipe systems can be designed for use by occupants, although many fire departments prefer that standpipes be designed for fire department use without the attached hose for occupant use.

Classification of standpipes
The National Fire Protection Association document, NFPA 14: Installation of Standpipe and Hose Systems, classified standpipe systems as follows:

- Class I: System with 2-1/2 in. (6.4 cm) hose connections to supply water for use primarily by fire departments and those trained in handling heavy fire streams.

- Class II: System with 1-1/2 in. (3.8 cm) hose stations to supply water for use primarily by the building occupants or by the fire department during initial response.

- Class III: System with 1-1/2 in. (3.8 cm) hose stations for use by building occupants and 2-1/2 in. (6.4 cm) hose connection to supply a large volume of water for use by the fire department.

Water supply requirements
The water supply to a standpipe will vary with the design of the system. Acceptable water supply sources include connections to public or private water mains, pressure tanks, gravity tanks, and fire pumps. The typical sources of water of standpipe systems are similar to water sources for sprinkler systems.

- Minimum flow rates for Class I and Class III systems: For the hydraulically most remote standpipe, the minimum flow rate shall be:

- 500 gpm (32L/s)

- An additional flow rate of 250 gpm (16L/s) for each additional standpipe, with a total not to exceed 1,250 gpm (79L/s).

- For combined sprinkler/standpipe systems, a separate sprinkler demand shall not be required as long as the design demand can meet the sprinkler system requirements.

- Minimum flow rates for Class II systems: A minimum flow rate of 100 gpm for the hydraulically most remote standpipe hose connection.

- Minimum water supply: Automatic and semiautomatic standpipe systems shall be attached to a single approved water supply capable of supplying the system demand.

- Manual standpipe systems shall have an approved water supply accessible to a fire department pumper.

- For systems with two or more height zones in which portions of the second and higher zones cannot be supplied using the residual pressure by means of the fire department pumping into the fire department connection, an auxiliary means of supply shall be provided. This may be in the form of high level water storage with additional pumping equipment.

- Minimum Supply for Class I and Class III systems: Water supply sufficient to provide the system demand for at least 30 minutes.

- Minimum Supply for Class II systems: Water supply sufficient to provide the system demand for at least 30 minutes.

Minimum pressure requirements
Systems shall be designed so that the system demand can be supplied by both the attached water supply, where required, and the fire department connection as follows: minimum residual pressure of 100 psi for 2-1/2 (6.4 cm) hose connections and 65 psi for 1-1/2 in. (3.8 cm) hose connection.

Water supply sources
The typical source of water will be a direct connection to a public or private water main system. Pressures in these types of systems could be inadequate to overcome the loss of pressure because of the height of a high-rise building. There are several ways to make up for this pressure loss:

- *Fire Pumps*

- Pumps are the most common method used. With a fire pump and automatic starting controller the pump must be rated for the flow and pressure required.

Author: Bruce W. Hisley

Credits: Photos courtesy of Larsen's Manufacturing Company

References: Bryan, John L. *Automatic Sprinklers and Standpipe Systems.* 2nd Edition. Quincy, MA: National Fire Protection Association.

NFPA. 1996. *NFPA Fire Protection Handbook. 18th Edition.* Quincy, MA: National Fire Protection Association. 1-800-344-3555.

_____. NFPA 14: Installation of Standpipe and Hose Systems. Quincy, MA: National Fire Protection Association.

_____. NFPA 22: Water Tanks for Private Fire Protection. Quincy, MA: National Fire Protection Association.

- In a wet type standpipe normally filled with water, a water flow or pressure drop device will detect water flow when the standpipe is being used, thus starting the pump.

- Fire pumps are driven by either electric motors or diesel engines. Electric motor drivers may require a standby power generator.

- Manually controlled fire pumps can be used in combination with a pressure tank or gravity tank.

- Tanks may be located on a mechanical floor or on the roof.

- Tanks rely on gravity or compressed air to provide pressure, and they can add a considerable dead load to the structure.

- Manually operated fire pumps are used to fill tanks located on the upper levels.

- NFPA Standard 22: Water Tanks for Private Fire Protection, notes requirements for the installation and arrangement for these types of tanks.

- *Fire department connection*

  External connections into the standpipe systems are essential to provide adequate flows and pressures during their use by the fire department. A connection is required for each separate zone in the building. These connections should:

- be of a Siamese type with hose thread connections that match threads used by the local fire departments.

- be within 100 ft. (30 m) of a fire hydrant if available.

- may be mounted on the exterior of the building or along a sidewalk (remote).

Piping, fittings, and hangers

- *System materials*

- Steel pipe assembled with welded joints, screwed fittings, flanged fittings, rubber-gasketed fittings, or a combination of these are the most common materials used for standpipe systems.

- Ductile-iron pipe and copper tubing with brazed joints are also used.

- All piping shall be capable of withstanding the maximum pressures that can be developed in a system, but not less than 175 psi working pressure.

- *Minimum sizes of standpipes*

- For Class I and Class III systems the standpipe shall be at least 4 in. (10 cm).

- Standpipes that are part of a combined standpipe/sprinkler system shall be at least 6 in. (15 cm).

- In buildings with combined systems that have been hydraulically calculated, a 4 in. (10 cm) standpipe can be used.

- *Location and protection of piping*

- Dry-type standpipes shall not be concealed in building walls or built into pilasters.

- Standpipes and lateral piping supplied by standpipes shall be located in enclosed exit stairways or shall be protected by a degree of fire resistance equal to that required for enclosed stairways.

- In buildings protected by automatic sprinklers, the lateral piping to 2-1/2 in. (6.4 cm) hose connections is not required to be protected.

- Standpipes that are normally filled with water and pass through areas of the building that are not heated shall be protected by a reliable means to maintain the temperature of the water in the piping to at least 40F (4C).

- In corrosive conditions or piping exposed to the weather, corrosion-resistant type pipe or protective coatings shall be used.

- In areas subject to earthquakes the standpipe system shall be protected in accordance with NFPA Standard 13: Installation of Automatic Sprinkler Systems.

- *Standpipe piping support*

- Standpipes shall be supported by attachments connected directly to the standpipe.

- Standpipe supports shall be protected at the lowest level, at each alternate level above the lowest level, and at the top of the standpipe.

- Supports above the lowest level shall retain the pipe to prevent movement by the upward thrust where flangible fittings are used.

- Hanger supports shall be provided for horizontal piping runs.

- The components of hanger assemblies that directly attach to the pipe or to the building structure shall be listed.

- Hangers certified by a registered professional engineer can be used.

- *Pressure limitation*

- The maximum pressure at any point in a standpipe system cannot exceed 350 psi (2,416 kPa) at any time.

- When building heights with the combination of a fire pump operating produce pressures that exceed 350 psi (2,416 kPa), the standpipe system shall be divided into zones.

- *Standpipe fittings*

- Fittings are required to be rated to withstand either 175 psi (1,208 kPa) or maximum system pressure, whichever is greater.

- If pressures are to exceed 175 psi (1,208 kPa), extra-heavy fittings or fittings listed for greater pressures should be used for pressures up to 350 psi (2,416 kPa).

Valves

Several different types of valves may be used as components of standpipe systems that must be able to withstand the maximum pressures that can be developed within the system.

- *Indicating gate valves*

- installed at each permanent water source to allow isolation of any water source for servicing.

- should be provided at supply connections to allow each standpipe to be serviced independently without impairing the entire system.

- *Check valves*

- should be provided in each water source, to prevent backflow and in the piping connecting the fire department connection to the system.

- *Drain valves*

- Should be provided to allow individual standpipes, and the entire system, to be drained.

- Hose connection valves

- Shall be equipped with cap to protect hose threads.

- Shall be unobstructed and located not less than 3 ft. (90 cm) or more than 5 ft. (1.5 m) above the floor.

- Valves located in recessed cabinets shall have unobstructed access within the cabinet to allow for the removal of the cap, connection of hose, and openings of the valves (Fig. 1).

- When excessive pressures are expected at hose outlets, approved pressure regulating devices shall be provided to limit the pressure

SERVICES

D4

as follows: 1-1/2 in. (3.8 cm) hose connections where the residual (flowing pressure) at the outlet exceeds 100 psi (690 kPa) and where the static pressure at the hose connection exceeds 175 psi (1,208 kPa), an approved pressure regulating device shall be provided to limit static and residual pressure at the outlet to 100 psi for 1-1/2 in. (3.8 cm) hose connections and 175 psi (1,208 kPa) for 2-1/2 in. (6.4 cm) hose connections.

- Size of hose connection valves: For a Class I system 2-1/2 in. (6.4 cm); Class II 1-1/2 in. (3.8 cm); Class III 1-1/2 in. (3.8 cm) and 2-1/2 in. (6.4 cm) connections.

• *Hose connection locations*

For a Class I system with 2-1/2 in. (6.4 cm) hose connection:

- In every exit stairway at each intermediate landing between floors.

- Each side of the wall adjacent to exit openings in horizontal exits.

- In each passageway at the entrance from the building area into the passageway.

- In covered malls at entrances to each exit passage or exit corridor and at external or public entrances.

- At the highest landing of stairway with access to roof and roof where stairs do not access the roof.

- Additional hose connections are required in approved locations when the most remote part of a building floor is more than 150 ft. (46 m) travel distance from an exit stairway in an unsprinklered building and 200 ft. (61 m) travel distance in a sprinklered building.

For a Class II system with 1-1/2 in. (3.8 cm) hose connection:

- 1-1/2 in. (3.8 cm) hose connection located so that all portions of each floor are within 130 ft. (40 m) of a hose connection.

For a Class III system with 1-1/2 in. (3.8 cm) and 2-1/2 in. (6.4 cm) hose connections:

- Hose connections shall be provided as noted for both Class I and Class II systems.

Standpipe cabinets

Closets and cabinets are used to contain fire hose or other accessories, such as fire extinguishers, fire blankets, or fire axes. Cabinets should be of sufficient size to allow the installation of the necessary equipment at hose stations and to not interfere with the prompt use of the hose connection, the hoses, and other equipment.

• *Cabinet design*

Standpipe cabinets are only required when the local authority requires either a Class II or Class III type system. The cabinet should meet the following:

- Within the cabinet at least a 1 in. (2.5 cm) clearance is provided for the hose connection handle valve, with the valve in any position from fully open to fully closed.

- Cabinets shall be conspicuously identified and used only for fire equipment.

- Cabinets shall be labeled "fire hose for use by occupants" and with operating instructions.

- Cabinets shall have a front glass panel for easy identification.

- Where break glass-type protective covers for a latching device is provided, the device to break the glass shall be attached securely in the immediate area.

- Cabinets storing 1-1/2 in. (3.8 cm) hose must be designed to hold 100 ft. (30 m) of hose mounted in a listed rack or other approved storage facility (Fig. 2).

Fig. 1. Standpie valve in recessed cabinet

Fig. 2. Listed rack for fire hose

SERVICES

D4

- Cabinets with 1-1/2 in. (3.8 cm) hose, or 1-1/2 in. (3.8 cm) or 2-1/2 in. (6.4 cm) hose connections, shall be mounted so that the height of the hose connection will be between 3 ft. (.91 m) to 5 ft. (1.5 m) above the floor.

- When recessed cabinets are mounted within fire-resistive rated wall assemblies, the cabinets themselves must be listed for such use or protection provided behind the cabinets in order to maintain the required rating.

Standpipe hose

- Hose connections provided for use by the building occupants should be equipment with listed, lined, collapsible-type fire hose attached and ready to use.

- Each hose station with 1-1/2 in. (3.8 cm) hose should be equipped with a listed rack.

- The rack should be of the semiautomatic or "one-person" type, which allows the hose valve to be opened and the water automatically released as the last few feet of hose are pulled from the rack.

- Hose should be no more than 100 ft. (30 m) in length within a hose cabinet.

- Hose should be equipped with a 1-1/2 in. (3.8 cm) listed type nozzle, which can be an adjustable fog spray type, straight stream type, or a combination type (generally used).

Fire extinguishers and cabinets

Summary: An overview of fire extinguishers and mounting cabinets: Selecting the correct extinguisher, types of fires and hazard classification in buildings, extinguishers for different types of fires, identification, rating, approval, distribution, mounting requirements, and cabinet design.

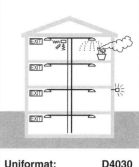

Key words: Class A, B, C, and D fires, extinguisher rating, hazard types.

| Uniformat: | D4030 |
| MasterFormat: | 10520 |

- *Extinguisher function*

- Fire extinguishers are the first line of defense against fires and should be installed regardless of the other fire control measures.

- Most fires start small, and may be extinguished easily if the proper type and amount of extinguishing agent is applied promptly.

- *Choosing an extinguisher*

  Selection should be based on the following criteria:

- nature of the fuels present

- who will operate the extinguisher

- the physical environment in which the extinguisher will be placed

- chemicals in the building that will react adversely with various extinguishing agents

- *Matching the extinguisher to the hazard*

  The most important item when selecting fire extinguishers is the nature of the area to be protected. Extinguishers are classified for use on one or more types of fires. *NFPA 10: Portable Fire Extinguishers*, classifies fires as:

- Class A: Ordinary building materials and contents use such as wood, paper, and clothing.

- Class B: Flammable or combustible liquids.

- Class C: Charged electrical equipment.

- Class D: Combustible metals.

In addition to the hazard, the fire loading (amount of combustibles contained) will also affect the degree of the hazard. There are three established types of hazards:

- *Light or low:*
  Few combustibles, and only small fires can be expected, such as offices, churches, school rooms, and assembly areas.

- *Ordinary or moderate:*
  Amount of combustibles are medium, such as mercantile, storage, and display areas.

- *Extra or high hazard:*
  Areas where a severe fire can be expected, such as woodworking, auto service areas, and storage areas with combustibles piled high.

It is not unusual to have multiple hazards within the same building, depending on what each area is to be used for (Table 1).

- *Extinguisher rating*

The rating number gives the relative effectiveness of the extinguisher and is found on the extinguisher approval labels.

- Example: An extinguisher rated 4-A, 20BC, designates that the unit should extinguish twice as much Class A fire as a 2A rated extinguisher, that it should extinguish considerably more Class B fire than a 1B rated extinguisher, and it is suitable for use on energized electrical equipment.

- No ratings are used for Class C fires, and the extinguisher should be selected based on the nature of the combustibles in the immediate area.

- Extinguishers for Class D fires have no rating but the extinguisher name plate will note what type of combustible metal it is suitable for.

- *Available personnel: ease of use*

- When selecting an extinguisher type, the ease of use should be given careful consideration.

- Standardizing an extinguisher is important so that potential users need only learn one set of instructions.

- Size and weight are important. The most common type of extinguisher weighs between 15 to 30 lb.

- *Physical environment*

- The area in which the extinguisher will be placed such as extreme temperatures, direct sunlight, weather, and corrosive fumes.

- Extinguishers located outdoors should be placed in cabinets, sheltered areas, or shielded with a protective cover.

- *Identification of extinguishers*
  Labeling of extinguisher type and location should include the following:

- The rating class and numeral of an extinguisher should be visible. Manufacturers are required to provide permanently attached markings that describe the type, rating, and operation on the front of the extinguisher.

SERVICES

D4

Author: Bruce W. Hisley

Credits: Photos courtesy of Larsen's Manufacturing Company

References: NFPA. 1996. *NFPA Fire Protection Handbook.* 18th Edition. Quincy, MA: National Fire Protection Association. 1-800-344-3555.

NFPA 1991. *NFPA Standard 10: Portable Fire Extinguishers.* Quincy, MA: NFPA.

- Wall- or column-mounted extinguishers should be marked by painting a red band above their location. The background on which it is mounted should also be marked.

- Extinguishers installed in recessed cabinets in the walls are difficult to find unless they are clearly marked.

• *Extinguisher approval*

- All types of fire extinguishers should be evaluated for construction, testing, and extinguishing rating.

- Underwriters Laboratories (U/L), and Factory Mutual Research Corporation (FMRC) have authorized manufacturers to affix a label to the extinguisher that notes they are either listed or approved.

• *Distribution of fire extinguishers*

- Extinguishers must be readily available. The travel distance to reach an extinguisher and return to the fire is critical. This distance is the actual route around partitions, through doorways, and aisles that a person must travel to reach the extinguisher.

- Extinguishers should be uniformly distributed, easily accessible, relatively free from blockage, and near normal paths of travel.

• *Extinguisher mounting*

- Most extinguishers are mounted on walls or columns by fastened hangers that support them adequately. In areas subject to physical damage they should be protected.

- Extinguishers with a gross weight not exceeding 40 lb. (18 kg) should be installed so that the top of the extinguisher is not more than 5 ft. (1.5 m) above the floor.

- Extinguishers with a gross weight greater than 40 lb. (18 kg) should be installed so that the top is no more than 42 in. (1.1 m) above the floor.

- The clearance between the bottom of the extinguisher and the floor cannot be less than 4 in. (10 cm).

• *Number of extinguishers required*
  NFPA Standard 10: Portable Fire Extinguishers, notes the minimum number and size of extinguishers required for each class of fire and hazard type based on floor area covered and travel distance.

- Class A Type Fires: The following applies (Table 2):

Table 1. Examples of fire extinguishers for different class fires

Examples	Class A Fire	Class B Fire	Class C Fire	Class D Fire
1. Multiple purpose dry	X	X	X	
2. Pressurized water	X			
3. Dry chemical		X	X	
4. Foam		X		
5. Carbon dioxide		X	X	
6. Special dry chemical				X

Table 2. Fire extinguisher size and placement for Class A Hazards

	Light (low) Hazard Occupancy	Ordinary (moderate) Hazard Occupancy	Extra (high) Hazard Occupancy
Minimum rated single extinguisher	2-A	2-A	4-A
Maximum floor area per unit of A	3,000 sq. ft.	1,500 sq. ft.	1,000 sq. ft
Maximum floor area for extinguisher	11,250 sq. ft.	11,250 sq. ft.	11,250 sq. ft.
Maximum travel distance to	75'	75'	75'

- Class B Fire Hazards: Contain two ratings; liquids 1/4 in. (6 mm) deep or less and other liquids deeper than 1/4 in. (6 mm). In areas where the liquid will not reach appreciable depth the following applies (Table 3):

- Class C Fire Hazards: The selection and number is based on the size of the electrical equipment, configuration, and the enclosure of units, which could effect the range of the extinguisher stream.

- Class D Fire Hazards: Agents are selected that are approved by the manufacturer for the combustible metal type present. The amount of agent is determined by the exposed surface area of the metal and the form of the metal. The maximum travel distance from the hazard to the extinguisher cannot exceed 75 ft. (23 m).

- *Extinguisher cabinets*
  When extinguishers are to be located within recessed wall cabinets, careful planning must be used to ensure that:

- They are located within the required travel distance for the hazard area to be protected.

- The number of extinguishers per maximum floor has been provided.

- They are located in uniform areas on each floor.

- They are easily accessible and identifiable.

- The required fire-resistive rating of the wall assembly is preserved when cabinets penetrate a fire-rated wall.

- *Cabinet design and location*

- Cabinet doors shall not be locked. In areas subject to vandalism, locked cabinets may be provided that include means of emergency access.

- Fire extinguishers in cabinets shall not be obstructed or obscured from view.

- Cabinet shall allow for the easy removal of the extinguisher.

- Extinguishers shall be placed in a manner such that the extinguisher operating instructions face outward (Fig. 1).

- Cabinets located outdoors are required to have ventilation.

- Cabinets may be designed to contain both standpipe hose connections, hose, and extinguisher (Fig. 2).

- Recessed cabinets on walls can be difficult to find unless clearly marked. In long corridors signs should be mounted perpendicular to the wall above the extinguisher cabinet.▶

Fig. 1. Extinguisher operating instructions should face outward from cabinet

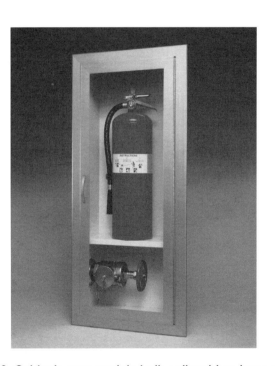

Fig. 2. Cabinets may contain both extinguisher, hose, and standpipe

SERVICES

D4

Table 3. Fire extinguisher size and placement for Class B Hazard excluding protection of deep layer flammable liquid tanks

Type of Hazard	Basic Minimum Extinguisher Rating	Maximum Travel Distance to Extinguishers
Low	5-B	30 ft. (9 m)
Low	10-B	50 ft. (15 m)
Moderate	10-B	30 ft. (9 m)
Moderate	20-B	50 ft. (15 m)
High	40-B	30 ft. (9 m)
High	80-B	50 ft. (15 m)

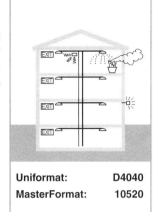

Special fire protection systems

Summary: An overview is provided of carbon dioxide and dry chemical fire extinguishing systems, life safety considerations, applications for halon systems, foam system guidelines, design and acceptance testing, and fire protection for grease ventilation and exhaust systems.

Key words: CO_2 systems, dry chemical extinguishing properties, foam expansion ratio, halogenated agent

Uniformat:	D4040
MasterFormat:	10520

The following special fire protection systems are described in this article:

- carbon dioxide (CO_2) systems
- dry chemical systems
- halon systems
- foam extinguishing systems
- grease exhaust hood fire protection systems

Carbon dioxide (CO_2) systems

CO_2 has been used for many years to extinguish flammable liquid fires, gas fires, and fires involving electrical equipment. CO_2 is non-combustible, does not react with most substances, and provides its own pressure for discharge from the storage container. Because it is a gas it can penetrate and spread to all parts of a fire area, will not conduct electricity, and leaves no residue after discharge.

- *Storage:*

CO_2 may be stored in high-pressure cylinders at normal temperatures or in low-pressure refrigerated containers designed to maintain a storage temperature of 0F (-18°C).

- *Static electricity:*

The dry ice particles produced during discharge can carry charges of static electricity. Static charges can build up on ungrounded discharge nozzles. In potentially explosive atmospheres all discharge nozzles must be grounded especially in playpipes used in hand hoseline systems.

- *Properties of CO_2*

- has a density of 1.5 times that of air.

- concentrations of 6% to 7% are considered the threshold level at which harmful effects become noticeable in human beings. Adequate safety precautions must be taken when designing the CO_2 system.

- is effective extinguishing agent primarily because it reduces the oxygen content of the atmosphere by dilution to a point where the atmosphere no longer will support combustion.

- *Life safety considerations:*

Total flooding systems should not be used in normally occupied spaces unless arrangements can be made to ensure evaluation before discharge.

- *Methods of application:*

- total flooding: CO_2 is discharged through nozzles to develop a uniform concentration in all parts of the enclosure. The amount of CO_2 required is based on the volume of the area and the concentration of CO_2 specified. The integrity of the enclosure is an important part of the total flooding system. All openings and ventilation systems must be closed to minimize leakage of the CO_2 after discharge (Fig. 1).

- local application: CO_2 is discharged directly on the burning surfaces through nozzles designed for this application. All areas that contain the combustible hazard are covered with nozzles, so located that they will extinguish all flames as quickly as possible. Local application of CO_2 can be used for fast fire knockdown (Fig. 2).

- *Hand hoselines:*

Hand hoselines are permanently connected by means of fixed piping to a fixed supply of CO_2. These types of systems are used for manual protection of small localized hazards. They may also be used to supplement a fixed system where the hazard is accessible for manual firefighting.

- *Components of CO_2 systems:*

The main components of a CO_2 system are:

- CO_2 supply
- discharge nozzles
- control valves
- piping
- operating devices
- fire detection equipment

- *CO_2 system design considerations:*

- quantity of stored CO_2

Author: Bruce W. Hisley

Credits: Illustrations courtesy of Kidde-Fenwal Protection Systems

References: NFPA. 1996. *NFPA Fire Protection Handbook*. 18th Edition. Quincy, MA: National Fire Protection Association. 1-800-344-3555.

Additional references are listed at the end of this article.

- method of actuation
- use of pre-discharge alarms
- ventilation shut down
- pressure venting

• *System control:*

- CO_2 systems for total flooding and local application should be designed to operate automatically.

- the detection device may be any of the listed or approved type that are actuated by heat, smoke, flame, flammable vapors, or other abnormal process conditions that could lead to a fire or explosion.

• *Acceptance testing:*
All new systems shall be inspected and tested to prove performance in accordance with design specifications.

Dry chemical systems

Dry chemical is a powder mixture that is used as a fire extinguishing agent for application by means of portable extinguishers, hand hoselines, or fixed systems. Regular or ordinary dry chemical are powders that are listed for use on Class B and C type fires. Multipurpose dry chemical refers to powders listed for use on Class A, B, and C type fires.

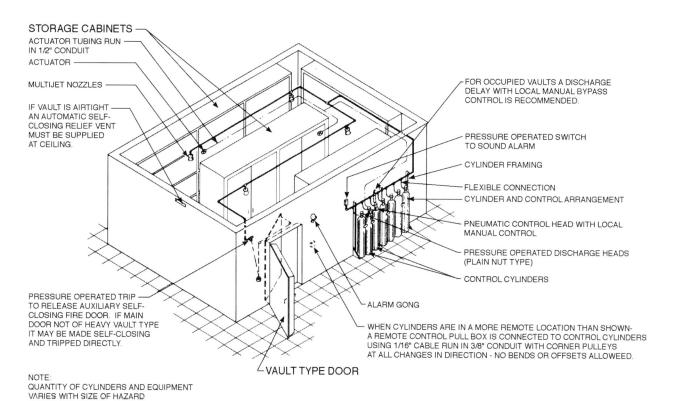

STORAGE CABINETS
ACTUATOR TUBING RUN IN 1/2" CONDUIT
ACTUATOR
MULTIJET NOZZLES
IF VAULT IS AIRTIGHT AN AUTOMATIC SELF-CLOSING RELIEF VENT MUST BE SUPPLIED AT CEILING.

FOR OCCUPIED VAULTS A DISCHARGE DELAY WITH LOCAL MANUAL BYPASS CONTROL IS RECOMMENDED.
PRESSURE OPERATED SWITCH TO SOUND ALARM
CYLINDER FRAMING
FLEXIBLE CONNECTION
CYLINDER AND CONTROL ARRANGEMENT
PNEUMATIC CONTROL HEAD WITH LOCAL MANUAL CONTROL
PRESSURE OPERATED DISCHARGE HEADS (PLAIN NUT TYPE)
CONTROL CYLINDERS

PRESSURE OPERATED TRIP TO RELEASE AUXILIARY SELF-CLOSING FIRE DOOR. IF MAIN DOOR NOT OF HEAVY VAULT TYPE IT MAY BE MADE SELF-CLOSING AND TRIPPED DIRECTLY.

ALARM GONG
WHEN CYLINDERS ARE IN A MORE REMOTE LOCATION THAN SHOWN- A REMOTE CONTROL PULL BOX IS CONNECTED TO CONTROL CYLINDERS USING 1/16" CABLE RUN IN 3/8" CONDUIT WITH CORNER PULLEYS AT ALL CHANGES IN DIRECTION - NO BENDS OR OFFSETS ALLOWEED.

VAULT TYPE DOOR

NOTE:
QUANTITY OF CYLINDERS AND EQUIPMENT VARIES WITH SIZE OF HAZARD
ALL EQUIPMENT IS APPROVED BY UNDERWRITERS AND FACTORY MUTUAL LABORATORIES
OPERATION OF ANY ACTUATOR RELEASES SYSTEM
ALL PIPE AND FITTINGS TO BE IN ACCORDANCE WITH DWG. L-5849
ALL DOORS AND OTHER OPENINGS TO REMAIN CLOSED FOR AT LEAST 60 MINUTES AFTER DISCHARGE OF SYSTEM

Fig. 1. Protection for record vault

SERVICES

D4

- *Applicxation:*

Dry chemical is efficient in extinguishing fires in flammable liquids and some types of electrical equipment that do not include telephone exchanges, and computer equipment rooms. Multipurpose dry chemical can be used on fires in ordinary combustible materials.

- *Extinguishing properties:*

When introduced directly to the fire areas, dry chemical causes the flame to go out almost at once. Smothering, cooling, radiation shielding, and chain-breaking reaction in the flame are the causes for extinguishment.

- *Uses for dry chemical systems:*

- systems are used where quick extinguishment is desired and where re-ignition sources are not present.

- they are used primarily for flammable liquid fire hazards, such as dip tanks, flammable liquid storage rooms, and areas where flammable liquid spills may occur.

- systems have been designed for kitchen range hoods, ducts, and range top hazards.

- systems can also be used on electrical equipment that contains flammable liquids such oil-filled transformers and oil-filled circuit breakers.

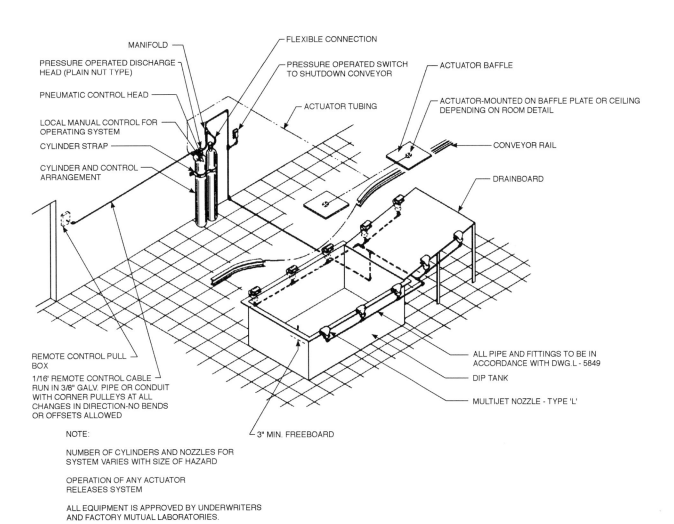

Fig. 2. Protection for dip tank and drainboard

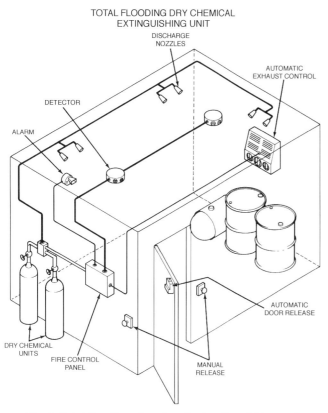

TOTAL FLOODING DRY CHEMICAL
EXTINGUISHING UNIT

DISCHARGE
NOZZLES

AUTOMATIC
EXHAUST CONTROL

DETECTOR

ALARM

AUTOMATIC
DOOR RELEASE

DRY CHEMICAL
UNITS

FIRE CONTROL
PANEL

MANUAL
RELEASE

Fig. 3. Total flooding dry chemical extinguishing unit

- *Methods of application:*

- fixed systems consist of a supply of dry chemical, an expellant gas, an actuating method, fixed piping, and nozzles through which the dry chemical can be discharged. Fixed systems are of two different types:

- total flooding: A predetermined amount of dry chemical is discharged through fixed piping and nozzles into an enclosed space of enclosure around a hazard. Can be used where the hazard is totally enclosed or when all openings can be automatically closed when the system is discharged (Fig. 3).

- local application: The nozzles are arranged to discharge directly into the fire. The principal use of local application systems is to protect open tanks of flammable liquids.

- hand hoseline systems consist of a supply of dry chemical and expellant gas with one or more hand hoselines to deliver the dry chemical to the fire. They are used to provide a quick knockdown and extinguishment of relatively large fires, such as gasoline loading racks, and aircraft hangars.

- *Design of dry chemical systems:*

Dry chemical systems are of two different types which are:

- engineered systems, in which individual calculations and design are needed to determine the flow rate, nozzle pressure, pipe size, quantity of dry chemical, and number, type, and placement of nozzles for the hazard protected.

- pre-engineered systems, in which the size of the system is predetermined by fire tests for specific sizes and types of hazards. This type of design is frequently used for kitchen range and hood fire protection (Fig. 4).

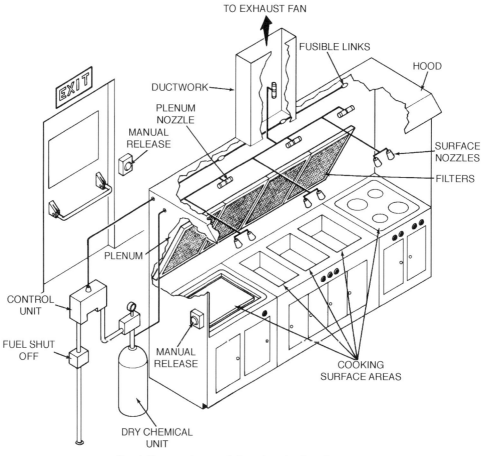

TO EXHAUST FAN

FUSIBLE LINKS

DUCTWORK

HOOD

PLENUM
NOZZLE

MANUAL
RELEASE

SURFACE
NOZZLES

FILTERS

PLENUM

CONTROL
UNIT

FUEL SHUT
OFF

MANUAL
RELEASE

COOKING
SURFACE AREAS

DRY CHEMICAL
UNIT

Fig. 4. Pre-engineered dry chemical system

- *System actuation:*

Initiated by automatic mechanisms that incorporate sensing devices, located in the hazard area and automatic, mechanical, or electrical releases that initiate the flow of dry chemical, actuate alarms, and shut down process equipment.

Halon systems

Halogenated extinguishing agents are hydrocarbons in which one or more hydrogen atoms have been replaced by atoms from the halogen series: fluorine, chlorine, bromine, or iodine. Halon 1301 systems are used to protect vital electrical facilities such as computer rooms and communications equipment.

- *Halon regulation:*

- halons have been identified as ozone-depletion agents. The Montreal protocol on substances that deplete the ozone layer requires a complete phase out of the production of halons by the year 2000, except to the extent necessary to satisfy essential uses for which no adequate alternatives are available.

- The U. S. Environmental Protection Agency has enacted further rules regulating these products' production, use, handling, and deposition. The user of this product should consult local authorities for their current regulations.

- *Application:*

Total flooding Halon 1301 systems are used primarily to protect hazards that are in enclosures, or equipment that in itself includes an enclosure to contain the agent. Some typical hazards are:

- electrical

- telecommunications

- flammable and combustible liquids

- gases

- *Extinguishing characteristic:*

The mechanism of halogenated agents is not clearly understood. However, a chemical reaction occurs that interferes with the combustion processes. This type of extinguishing action is referred to as a chain breakdown in the flaming process. In total flooding type systems the effectiveness of flammable liquids and vapor fires are quite dramatic.

- *Toxic and irritant effects:*

- human exposure to Halon 1301 in concentrations up to 7% by volume has had little noticeable effect on the subject.

- design concentration up to 10% in normally occupied areas and up to 15% in areas not normally occupied are allowed.

- decomposition of halon must be considered for life safety because of the effects of the breakdown of the product during extinguishment, that in turn produces relatively toxic by-products when the burning surface temperature is 900F (482°C) or higher.

- *Halon 1301 system components:*

- supply of agents

- means of releasing or propelling the agent from its container

- one or more discharge nozzles

- fire detection devices

- remote or local alarms

- piping network

- mechanical and electrical interlocks to close doors and shut down ventilation systems to the hazard area.

- *System design and types:*

The design requirements for Halon 1301 type systems are noted in NFPA 12A, Halon Fire Extinguishing Agent Systems. This standard classifies systems into two types which are:

- total flooding: These systems protect enclosures. A sufficient quantity of agent is discharged into the enclosure to provide a uniform fire extinguishing concentration throughout the entire enclosure,

- engineered system: Custom designed for a particular hazard. The pre-engineered type systems are determined by in advance and include the description of the systems approval and listing.

- local application: This type of system discharges the agent in a manner that the burning object is surrounded locally by a high concentration of agent to extinguish the fire. Examples of application are: printing presses, dip tanks, spray booths, and oil-filled electric transformers.

- *Acceptance testing:*

- testing and inspection of the completed entire system is required to ensure proper operation and design.

- such testing would include a nondestructive test of all system functions.

- full scale discharge tests should be avoided. Should a special need arise, a substitute test gas should be used.

Foam extinguishing systems

Firefighting foam is an aggregate of gas-filled bubbles from aqueous solutions of specially formulated concentrated liquid foaming agents. The foam solution floats on the burning liquid surface to exclude the air and cool at the same time in turn reducing and eliminating combustion. Foam is produced by mixing the concentrate solution with water in various concentrations. Foams are defined by their expansion ratio when mixed with water and air which are low expansion, medium expansion, and high expansion.

- *Uses and limitations:*

- Low expansion foam is used to extinguish burning flammable or combustible liquid spill or tank fires.

- Medium or high expansion foam may be used to fill enclosures such as basement rooms or confined space hazard areas. The foam acts to halt convection and access to air for combustion.

- Some foams have very low surface tension and penetration ability. Foams of this type are useful where Class A combustible materials are present.

- *Guidelines for foam systems:*

- the more gently the foam is applied, the more rapid the extinguishment and lower amount of agent required.

- successful use of foam is dependent upon the rate of application, which is the amount of volume of foam solution reaching the fuel surface.

- provide the minimum application rate found by tests to be the most practical in terms of speed of control and agent required.

- air foams are more stable when generated with water at ambient temperatures from 30F to 80F (0°C to 27°C).

- fixed foam makers should be located on the sides of, rather than directly over, the hazard.

- *Methods of generating foam:*

The generation of foam requires three different operations: the proportioning process, the generation phase, and the distribution method.

- nozzle eductor is the most simple in design and is widely used in portable foam-making nozzles. When foam is available in 5 gal (19 l) containers, the nozzle eductor drafts concentrate from the container through a pickup tube and mix with proper flow of water and air at the nozzle to produce foam.

- in line eductors, the proportioner educts or drafts the concentrate from a container or tank utilizing the operating pressure of the hose water stream.

- other types of generation using different fixed pipe systems consist of pumps, storage tanks, and proportioner eductors.

• *Types of low expansion foam systems:*

- fixed foam: piped from a central foam station, discharging through fixed delivery outlets to protect the hazard.

- semi-fixed system: the hazard is equipped with fixed discharge outlets connected to piping that terminates at a safe distance from the hazard. Foam making materials are transported to the scene after the fire starts and connected to the piping.

- mobile system: foam producing unit is mounted on wheels and is either self-propelled or towed by a vehicle. The unit can be connected to a water supply or can utilize a premixed foam solution. NFPA Standard 11C: Mobile Foam Apparatus, notes requirements for this type of system.

- portable system: foam producing equipment and materials are transported by hand.

• *Design:*
Low expansion foam systems should be designed in accordance with NFPA Standard 11, Low Expansion Foam.

• *Acceptance test:*
For low expansion foam systems tests should be completed by qualified personnel and should be conducted to determine that the system has been properly installed and functions as intended.

• *Types of medium and high expansion foam systems:*

- total flooding systems are designed to discharge into an enclosed space or enclosure around the hazard. Can be used where the required amount of fire extinguishing agent can be built up and maintained for the required period of time to ensure the control and extinguishment of fire.

- local application systems are designed to extinguish or control fires in flammable or combustible liquids, liquefied natural gas, and ordinary Class A combustibles, where the hazard is not totally enclosed. This type of system is suitable for flat surfaces such as confined spills, open tanks, drain boards, pits, and trenches.

- portable foam systems can be used to combat fires in all types of hazards where the other types of system could be used. This type of system is usually required to be transported to the designated hazard.

• *Design:*
Medium and high expansion foam systems should be installed in accordance with NFPA 11A, Medium and High Expansion Foam Systems.

• *Acceptance test:*
For low expansion foam systems tests should be completed by qualified personnel and should be conducted to determine that the system has been properly installed and functions as intended.

• *Other types of foam systems:*

- deluge foam–water sprinkler and foam-water spray systems, discharge water and foam from the same discharge devices. This type of system has all of the same characteristics of a sprinkler system with the exception of the added foam discharge and special discharge nozzles. The design requirements for this type of system are found in NFPA Standard 16: Installation of Deluge Foam-Water and Foam-Water Spray Systems.

- closed head foam-water sprinkler systems consist of closed heads that are installed on either a wet-pipe, dry-pipe, or preaction type sprinkler system. This type of system has all of the same characteristics of a sprinkler system with the exception of the added foam discharge and special automatic type foam/water sprinkler heads. The design requirements for this type of system are found in NFPA Standard 16A: Installation of Closed-Head Foam-Water Sprinkler Systems.

Grease exhaust hood fire protection systems

In restaurant, commercial, or institutional occupancies where cooking operations take place, the presence of grease deposits within the exhaust system are usually present. Also present are deep fat fryers that contain combustible frying oils and grills with grease deposits. Constant ignition sources can readily ignite grease, which in turn causes a rapidly spreading fire to extend throughout the exhaust system and also to the building interior. Automatic fire extinguishing systems have been designed and approved to protect this common hazard where cooking operations are performed (Fig. 5).

• *Common types of systems:*

- dry chemical systems (see above) are usually pre-engineered systems that must be installed in accordance with the manufacturer's instructions and within the limitations of their listing.

- wet chemical systems (see above) are systems that normally contain a solution of water and potassium, carbonate-based chemical, potassium acetate-based chemical, or a combination that forms an extinguishing agent. These systems are usually pre-engineered and must be installed in accordance with the manufacturer's listed installation instructions. This type of system is the most preferred choice today because of the minimum cleanup required after discharge.

- automatic sprinkler systems (see Fire Protection Sprinkler Systems article) can protect the cooking equipment and ventilation system.

- grease extractors are specially designed, automatic self-cleaning water wash systems that are installed within the hood plenum and exhaust ducts. These systems, when listed, can also provide automatic fire protection for the exhaust plenum and duct work. They may or may not be designed to also provide protection for the cooking equipment located under the exhaust hood.

• *Basic system design:*

- all pre-engineered systems must be installed in accordance with the manufacturer's listed instructions.

- system must protect the exhaust duct work, hood plenum, all surface areas of cooking appliances located below hood, and broilers if provided.

- system shall be actuated by both automatic detection and manual operation.

- fuel or power supply to protected cooking appliances, located under exhaust hood, shall shut off automatically when the systems actuate.

- manual actuation must be in a location away from the cooking area in a route to an exit.

- the ventilation fan control for run or shut off must be in accordance with the system manufacturer's requirements.

- the entire system shall discharge to all protected areas when actuated.

• *Acceptance testing:*
Dry and wet chemical systems should be tested by trained personnel as required by the manufacturer's listed installation requirements. The test should determine that the system has been properly installed and will function as intended.

Additional references

NFPA. 1991. *NFPA Fire Protection Handbook.* 17th Edition. NFPA Standard 11: Low-Expansion Foam. Quincy, MA: National Fire Protection Association. 1-800-344-3555.

SERVICES

D4

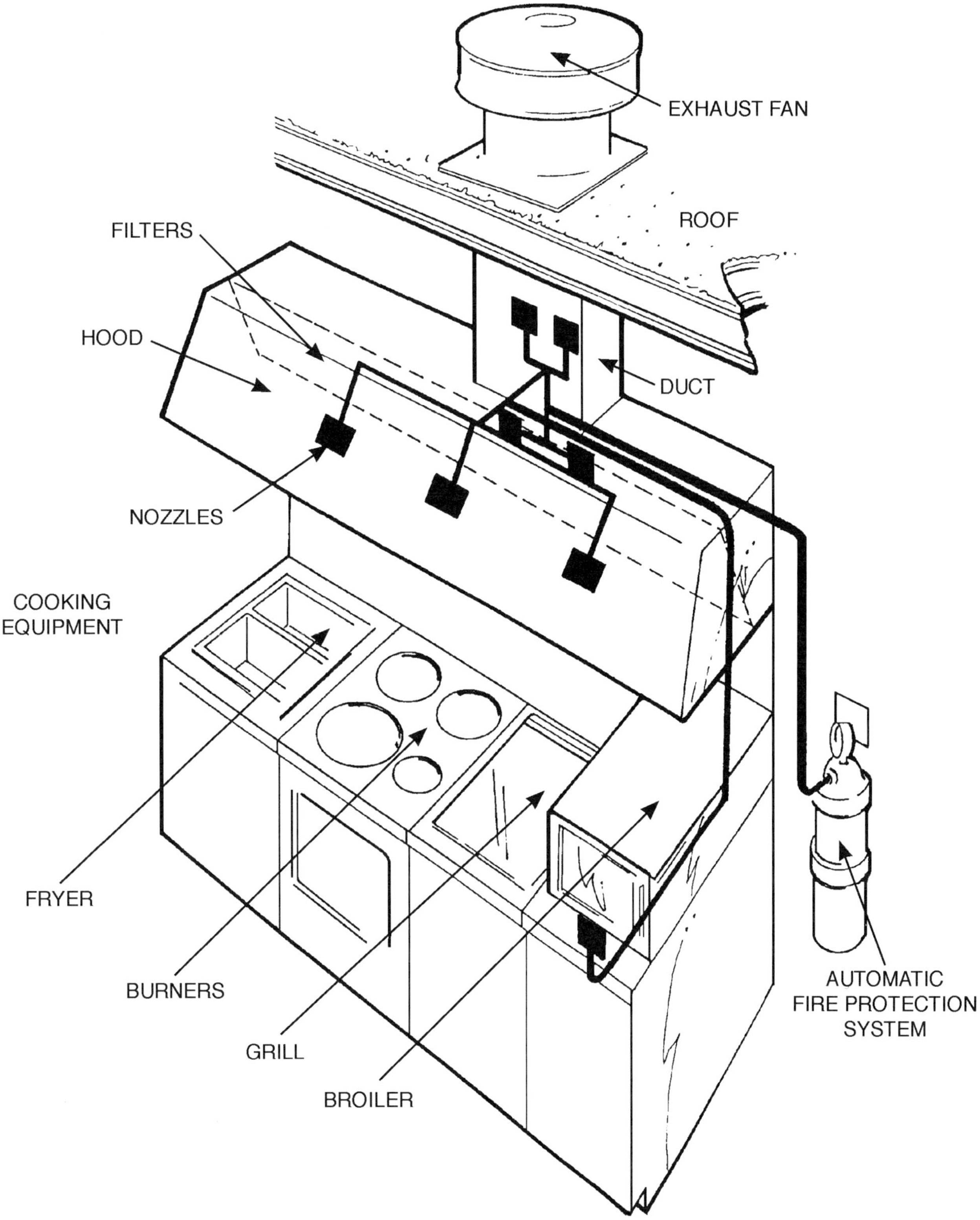

EXHAUST FAN

ROOF

FILTERS

HOOD

DUCT

NOZZLES

COOKING
EQUIPMENT

FRYER

BURNERS

GRILL

BROILER

AUTOMATIC
FIRE PROTECTION
SYSTEM

Fig. 5. Typical grease exhaust system

SERVICES

D4

_____. NFPA Standard 11A: Medium and High Expansion Foam Systems. Quincy, MA: NFPA.

_____. NFPA Standard 11C: Mobile Foam Apparatus. Quincy, MA: NFPA.

_____. NFPA Standard 12: Carbon Dioxide Extinguishing Systems. Quincy, MA: NFPA.

_____. NFPA Standard 12A: Halon 1301 Fire Extinguishing Systems. Quincy, MA: NFPA.

_____. NFPA Standard 13: Installation of Automatic Sprinkler Systems. Quincy, MA: NFPA.

_____. NFPA Standard 16: Deluge Foam-Water Sprinkler and Foam-Water Spray Systems. Quincy, MA: NFPA.

_____. NFPA Standard 16A: Installation of Closed Head Foam Water Sprinkler Systems. Quincy, MA: NFPA.

_____. NFPA Standard 17: Dry Chemical Extinguishing Systems. Quincy, MA: NFPA.

_____. NFPA Standard 96: Cooking Operations, Ventilation Controls, and Specific Listed Manufacturer's Installation Instruction. Quincy, MA: NFPA.

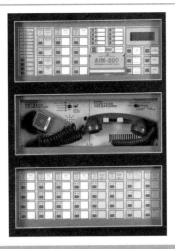

Fire alarm systems

Summary: A properly designed, code compliant fire alarm system is an essential part of the building's life safety system. It gives early warning and notification to occupants of a building as well as notification of an off-site central station to summon the fire department.

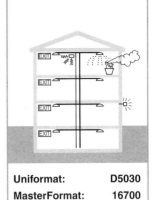

Key words: alarm verification, command center, multiplex systems, smoke detectors, storage batteries.

Uniformat:	D5030
MasterFormat:	16700

Function

The purpose of the fire alarm system is for the protection of life by automatically indicating the necessity for evacuation of the building or fire area, and the protection of property through the automatic notification of responsible persons and for the automatic activation of fire safety functions. Fire alarm systems include one or more of the following features:

- manual alarm signal initiation
- automatic alarm signal initiation
- activation of fire suppression systems
- activation of fire safety functions
- activation of alarm notification appliances
- monitoring of abnormal conditions in fire suppression systems
- emergency voice/alarm communications
- process monitoring supervisory systems
- activation of off-premise signals

Responsibilities

The design professionals are responsible for the design of a code compliant fire alarm system. It is very important to establish the local code requirements and their interpretation early on via review of the local building codes and meetings with the local code officials to review the design for code compliance. The first step is to review the local building codes to establish the required system for the project. Usually the code will direct readers to the National Fire Protection Association (NFPA), an international codes and standards organization that develops and publishes fire protection codes and standards (NFPA 1996).

Design Considerations

The height of the building will determine if the fire alarm system will have voice/alarm communication systems. Buildings over 75 ft. (23 m) in height are generally considered high-rise buildings and require devices such as firefighters telephones, warden stations, and voice notification and direction systems. In high-rise buildings, the code will direct the designer as to type of notification is required. In some jurisdictions, the alarm notification is on the floor of first alarm and on the floor above and below the floor of alarm initiation. When the Fire Department arrives at the building with such information, they can thus direct occupants on where to go for safety.

In a building less than 75 ft. (23 m) in height, the alarm notification will generally be for total evacuation of the building.

An example of some of the systems that would make-up a high rise fire alarm system are as follows:

- A stand-alone integrated, closed circuit, modified two-stage, electrically supervised manual and automatic fire alarm system using addressable, multiplexed technology (Fig. 1) and consisting of the following:

- A one-way emergency voice communication system and visual alarm system will be used to alert building occupants.

- A two-way fire department communication system will be installed for use by the Fire Department.

- Fire signals will be automatically transmitted to the Fire Department via approved central station.

- Elevator recall system.

- Interface with Building Management System for ventilation, pressurization and smoke exhaust systems.

- Interface with security system for automatic de-energization of electromagnetic locking devices.

- *Fire and smoke detection*

- Automatic sprinkler and standpipe water flow indicators.

- Area smoke detectors will be provided in all electrical and telecommunication equipment rooms and elevator machine rooms.

- Duct smoke detectors will be provided in recirculating air systems as required by code. In addition to activating alarm signals, activation of the smoke detectors will cause shut down of related fan systems.

- Smoke detectors will be provided in all elevator lobbies. Activation of this detector will initiate automatic elevator recall to the designated floor.

- Manual fire alarm stations will be located at entry to exit doors and exit stairs.

- *Fire Command Center*

Fire Command Center located on ground level in a location approved by the Fire Department, and consisting of:

Author: Walter Cooper

Credits: Illustrations are reproduced by permission of Notifier / Pittway Corporation.

References: NFPA. 1996. *NFPA 72 National Fire Alarm Code.* Quincy, MA: National Fire Protection Association.

SERVICES

D4

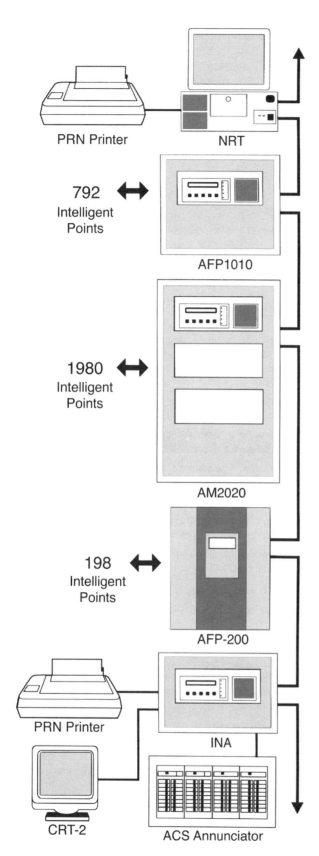

- emergency voice communication panel.

- Fire Department communication panel (Fig. 2).

- fire detection and alarm system annunciators.

- sprinklers and standpipe supervisory display panels.

- status indicators and controls for smoke control system.

- fire and sprinkler pump control and status indicator.

- emergency and stand-by power indicators and controls.

- special extinguishing system monitoring.

- elevator control panels with elevator positions and status indicators.

• *Activation.*

The activation of any manual or automatic alarm initiating device will automatically:

- transmit an alarm signal to the Fire Department via off-site central station monitoring service.

- sound an alert signal to all required selected locations via one-way voice communications system (Fig. 3).

- activate the pre-recorded message and evacuation signal to those areas where the evacuation signal is required to be sounded.

- activate strobe visual alarm system in all required locations.

- activate fire door release devices.

- initiate the elevator recall operation.

- stop operation of all escalators.

- provide signal indicating alarm type and location to the smoke management/control system for fan control.

Fig. 1. Integrated network fire alarm system

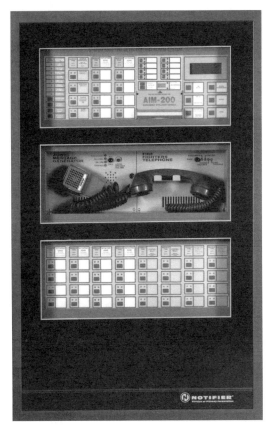

Fig. 2. Voice alarm multiplex system

Fig. 3. Voice-quality alarm speakers, with and without strobe

D SERVICES

SERVICES

D5

Electrical wiring systems

Summary: This article provides an overview of electrical wiring systems to guide the architect in initial planning decisions along with system selection criteria and references for electric distribution system design.

Key words: access floor, busway, cablebus, conduits, electric distribution, lighting track, raceway, underfloor duct.

Uniformat:	D5010
	D5020
MasterFormat:	16300

The major components of a building's electrical power system are illustrated in Figs. 1 and 2. The components can be described in three major categories:

- wiring, including conductors and raceways of all types.

- power-handling equipment, including transformers, switchboards, panelboards, large switches, and circuit breakers.

- control and utilization equipment, such as lighting, motors, controls, and wiring devices and receptibles.

The National Electric Code (NEC) of the National Fire Protection Association (NFPA) defines the fundamental safety measures that must be followed in the selection, construction, and installation of all electrical equipment. The code is used by inspectors, electrical designers, engineers, contractors, and the operating personnel charged with the responsibility for safe operation. Having been incorporated into OSHA (Occupational Safety and Health Act) and referenced in most building codes, it has, in effect, the force of law.

The Underwriters Laboratories (UL), Incorporated has been designated to assure a minimum standard of electrical safety for electrical equipment, to establish standards and to test and inspect electrical equipment. UL publishes lists of inspected and approved electrical equipment. These listings are universally accepted, and most building codes in the U.S. stipulate that only electrical materials bearing the Underwriters Laboratories (UL) label of approval will be accepted.

Electrical equipment ratings

All electrical equipment is rated for the normal service it is intended to perform. These ratings may be in voltage, current, duty, horsepower, kilowatts (kW), kilowatt Voltage-Ampheres (kVA), temperature, enclosure, and so on. The ratings that are specifically and characteristically electrical are those of voltage and current.

- *Voltage.* The voltage rating (V) of an item of electrical equipment is the maximum voltage that can safety be applied to the unit continuously. Frequently, but not always, it corresponds to the voltage applied in normal use. Thus, an ordinary wall electrical receptacle is rated at 250 V maximum, though in normal use only 120 V is applied to it. The rating is determined by the type and quantity of insulation used and the physical spacing between electrically energized parts.

- *Current.* The current rating of an item of electrical equipment is determined by the maximum operating temperature at which its components can operate properly and continuously. That rating in turn depends on the type of insulation used. Thus, although a motor is rated in horsepower (or kW where SI units are used), a transformer is rated in kVA and a cable is rated in amperes. The actual criterion on which all these ratings is based is maximum permissible operating temperature.

Interior wiring systems

To provide an overview of electric systems for architectural design purposes, it is helpful to survey the different types of interior wiring systems. The function of any wiring system is to conduct electricity from one point to another. When the primary purpose of the system is to distribute electrical energy, it is referred to as an electrical power system; when the purpose is to transmit information, it is referred to as an electrical signal or communications system.

Due to the nature of electricity, its distribution within a structure poses basically a single problem: how to construct a distribution system that will *safely* provide the energy required at the location required. The safety consideration is all-important, since even the smallest interior system is connected to the utility's powerful network and the potential for damage, injury, and fire is always present. The solution to this problem is to isolate the electrical conductors from the structure except at those specific points where electric contact is required, such as wall receptacles. This isolation is generally accomplished by insulating the conductors and placing them in closed raceways. The principal types of interior wiring systems in use today are exposed insulated cables, insulated cables in open raceways, and insulated conductors in closed raceways, each of which is described below.

- *Exposed insulated cables*
In this category would be included (using the NEC nomenclature) NM ("Romex") and AC ("BX"). Also included are other types where the cable construction itself provides the necessary electrical insulation and mechanical protection.

- *Insulated cables in open cable trays*
This system is specifically intended for industrial application and it relies upon both the cable and the tray for safety.

Author: Benjamin Stein

Credits: This article is adapted from Stein and Reynolds (1992) by permission of John Wiley & Sons and reviewed by Walter Cooper, whose contributions are gratefully acknowledged.

References: Stein, Benjamin and John S. Reynolds. 1992. *Mechanical and Electrical Equipment for Buildings.* Eighth Edition. John Wiley & Sons.

NFPA. 1996. *National Electric Code.* Quincy, MA: National Fire Protection Association.

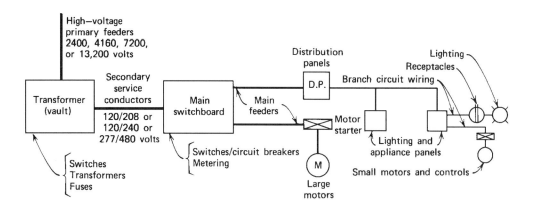

Fig. 1. Block diagram of an electrical system

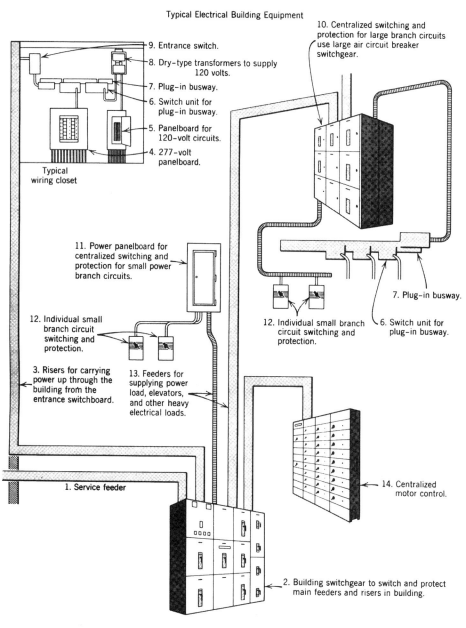

Fig. 2. Depiction of a basic electric system (courtesy of General Electric)

- *Insulated conductors in closed raceways*

This system is the most general type and is applicable to all types of facilities. It can be further subdivided into two major subcategories. In general, the raceway is installed first and the wiring pulled in later. The raceways themselves may be:

- buried in the structure, such as conduit the floor slab or under-floor duct.

- attached to the structure, such as in a surface raceway or above a suspended ceiling.

- part of the structure, as in a cellular concrete and cellular metal floor.

- *Combined conductor and enclosure*

This category is intended to describe all types of factory-prepared and factory-constructed integral assemblies of conductor and enclosure, including:

- flat cable intended for under-carpet installation,

- flat cable assemblies.

- lighting track,

- manufactured wiring systems.

- all types of busway, busduct and cable bus.

The discussion which follows details the components of the above systems and their application to electric wiring layout considerations.

Busway / busduct

A busway (busduct) is an assembly of copper or aluminum bars, in a rigid metallic housing. Its use is almost always the preferred economical choice in two instances:

- when it is necessary to carry large amounts of current (power), and

- when it is necessary to tap onto an electric power conductor at frequent intervals along its length.

The usual alternatives are to use several conductors in parallel or a single large conductor. Flat conductors (called busbars) are used for high-current-carrying application. The bars in a busduct, whether bare or insulated, are rigidly assembled by bolting them to insulating supports that are then connected to a stiff metal housing. A variety of fittings and joints are available to enable buswork to be installed with angles, bends, tap-offs, and curves (Fig. 3). The busduct is specified by material, number of buses (normally three or four, plus ground bus if required), current capacity, type, and voltage. In addition, maximum voltage drop is often specified. Thus, a typical brief description of a busduct would be:

- copper busduct, 4-wire, 1000 amp, low-impedance type, 600 V; or

- aluminum busduct, 3-wire, 2000 amp, plug-in type, 600 V,

- both with a maximum full-load voltage drop of 1.5% per 100 ft. (30 m) at 90% power factor.

Cablebus is similar to ventilated busduct, except that it uses insulated cables instead of busbars. These cables are rigidly mounted in an open space-frame. The advantage of this construction is that it carries the ampacity rating of its cables *in free air,* which is much higher than the conduit rating, thus giving a high amperes-per-dollar first-cost advantage. Its principal disadvantages are bulkiness and the difficulty in making tap-offs.

Light-duty busway, flat cable assemblies and lighting track

Special construction assemblies that act as light-duty (branch circuit) plug-in electrical feeders are widely used because of simplicity of installation and more important, the flexibility of use that derives from its plug-in mode of connection. Unlike the heavier plug-in busways,

they are specifically intended to directly feed utilization equipment or used as lighting equipment.

- *Light-duty plug-in busway.*

This construction, which may be used either for feeder or branch circuit wiring application, is covered by the NEC general article on busways, with restrictions when applied as branch circuit wiring. Their application is principally for direct connection of machine tools, light machinery and industrial lighting (with overcurrent protection as required by NEC).

- *Flat cable assemblies*

A specially designed cable consisting of two, three, or four conductors, No. 10 AWG is field installed in a rigidly mounted standard 1 5/8 in. (4.13 cm) square structural channel. Power tap devices, installed where required, puncture the insulation of one of the phase conductors and the neutral. Electrical connection is then made to the pigtail wires that extend from the tap devices. This connection can extend directly to the device or to an outlet box with a receptacle, which then acts as a disconnecting means for the electric device being served. Lights, small motors, unit heaters, and other single-phase, light-duty devices can be served without the necessity of "hard" (conduit and cable) wiring.

- *Lighting track*

This is a factory-assembled channel with conductors for one to four circuits *permanently* installed in the track. Power is taken from the track by special tap-off devices that contact the track's electrified conductors and carry the power to the attached lighting fixture.

Cable tray

This system, covered in NEC Article 318, is a continuous open support for approved cables. When used as a general wiring system the cables must be self-protected. The advantages of this system are free-air rated cables, easy installation and maintenance, and relatively low cost. The disadvantages are bulkiness and the required accessibility.

Raceways

The following describe the types and characteristics of closed wiring raceways:

- *Steel conduit*

The purpose of conduit is to:

- protect the enclosed wiring from mechanical injury and corrosion.

- provide a grounded metal enclosure for the wiring in order to avoid shock hazard.

- provide a system ground path.

- protect surroundings against fire hazard as a result of overheating or arcing of the enclosed conductors.

- support the conductors.

For these reasons, the NEC generally requires that all wiring be enclosed in a metallic raceway. Metal electrical conduits and associated fittings must be corrosion resistant. To this end, steel conduit is manufactured in several ways, among which are:

- heavy-wall steel conduit, also referred to simply as "rigid steel conduit."

- intermediate metal conduit, usually referred to as "IMC."

- electric metallic tubing, normally known as "EMT" or "thin-wall conduit."

- *Aluminum conduit*

The use of aluminum conduit has increased in recent years because of the weight advantage of aluminum, and a resulting economic advantage in labor cost savings. In addition, aluminum has better corrosion resistance in most atmospheres; it is nonmagnetic, giving lower volt-

SERVICES

D5

age drop; it is non-sparking; and, generally, it does not require painting. Its major drawback is its deleterious effect on many types of concrete, causing spalling and cracking of the concrete when embedded.

• *Flexible metal conduit*

This type of conduit construction—which consists of an empty spiral-wound interlocked armor raceway—is known to the trade as "Greenfield" and is covered in NEC Article 350. It is used principally for motor connections or other locations where vibration is present, where movement is encountered, or where physical obstructions make its use necessary. The acoustic and vibration isolation provided by flexible conduit is one of its most important applications. It should always be used in connections to motors, transformers, and ballasts. Flexible conduit material is either galvanized steel or aluminum.

• *Nonmetallic conduit*

A separate classification of rigid conduit (NEC Article 347) covers raceways that are formed from materials such as fiberglass, rigid polyvinyl chloride (PVC), and high density polyethylene. For use above ground, this conduit must be flame retardant, tough, and resistant to heat distortion, sunlight, and low-temperature effects. For use underground, the last two requirements are waived. A separate ground must be provided, since the ground provided by a metallic conduit is absent.

• *Surface metal raceways*

These raceways are covered in NEC Article 352. Surface metal raceways and multi-outlet assemblies may be utilized only in dry, nonhazardous, noncorrosive locations and may generally contain only wiring operating below 300 V. Such raceways are normally installed in exposed conditions and in places not subject to physical injury. The principal applications of surface metal raceways are:

- where the design or construction does not permit recessing, such as an exposed structure.

- where economy in construction weighs very heavily in favor of surface raceways and where expansion is anticipated.

- where outlets are required at frequent intervals, and where rewiring is required or anticipated.

- where access to equipment in the raceways is required or anticipated.

- in existing installations, to avoid extensive cutting and patching required to cover or hide a raceway.

• *Floor raceways*

The NEC recognizes three types of floor raceways:

- underfloor raceways

- cellular metal floor raceways

- cellular concrete floor raceways

All three types are applicable to all types of structures and none may be used in corrosive or hazardous areas. The fundamental difference between them is that underfloor raceways are added on to the structure, whereas cellular floor raceways are part of the structure itself—and therefore have a direct effect on the building's architectural design.

• *Underfloor raceways*

These raceways, which may be installed beneath or flush with the floor, are covered in NEC Article 354. Although relatively expensive since cast in place and thus likely to be either inadequate to enlargement or underutilized in other areas, they find their widest application in office spaces, since their use permits placement of power and signal outlets immediately under desks and other furniture. All underfloor duct systems use basically the same method of setting an outlet once an insert has been established. The inserts are either preset or afterset. Underfloor ducts may be cast into the structural slab in lieu of being in fill or topping, but the slab must be designed to accommodate them. The use of a fill or topping on the structural slab for underfloor duct has these advantages:

- Ducts can be run in any direction, without conflict to structural elements.

- Formwork and construction sequence are simplified.

- Finishing is simplified.

The disadvantages are:

- Additional concrete increases costs directly by increasing weight. This is particularly expensive in seismic designs.

- Height of building may be increased.

Underfloor duct systems are expensive. To justify their use, therefore, the building should meet these conditions:

- Open floor areas, with a requirement for outlets at locations removed from walls.

- Outlets from ceiling systems is unacceptable.

- Frequent rearrangement of furniture and other items requiring electrical and signal service.

• *Cellular metal floor raceway*

The underfloor duct system described above is most applicable to spaces with known furniture layouts and to rectilinear arrangements. Random arrangements, such as those found in office landscaping, require a fully accessible floor—if the floor is to be used for electrification. This may be provided by a cellular (metal) floor that is an integrated structural/electrical system. The floor can be fully or partially electrified. A floor designed with two or three electrified cells adjacent to several cells of structural floor, as shown in Fig. 3, will give sufficient coverage for all purposes. One of the many structural element designs available is depicted. The electrified cells can be arranged to feed lighting outlets in the floor below.

• *Precast cellular concrete floor raceways*

This structural concrete system is similar to a cellular metal floor in application. A cell is defined in NEC Article 358 as a "single, enclosed, tubular space in a floor made of precast cellular concrete slabs, the direction of the cell being parallel to the direction of the floor member." Feed for these cells is provided, as with metal cellular floor construction, by header ducts. Although header ducts are normally installed in concrete fill above the hollow core structural slab, a header arrangement with feed from the ceiling below is also entirely practical. Like the metallic cellular floor, the cells can be used for air distribution and even for piping, although these items are generally installed in a hung ceiling.

• *Full access floor*

Full access floor construction is applicable to spaces with very heavy cabling requirements, particularly if frequent recabling and reconnection is required. It provides for instant and complete access to an underfloor plenum. The approach was originally developed for data processing areas that have a requirement for large, fully accessible cable spaces. Construction alternatives include lightweight die-cast aluminum panels supported on a network of adjustable steel or aluminum pedestals that support floor panels from 18 in. sq. (46 sq. cm) to 3 ft. sq. (90 cm). The plenum depth is typically 12 in. (30 cm) to 24 in. (60 cm).

• *Under-carpet wiring system*

This system was originally developed as both an inexpensive alternative to an underfloor or cellular floor system and as a means for providing a flexible a flexible floor-level branch circuit wiring system. The system consists of a factory assemble flat cable (NEC type FCC),

SERVICES

D5

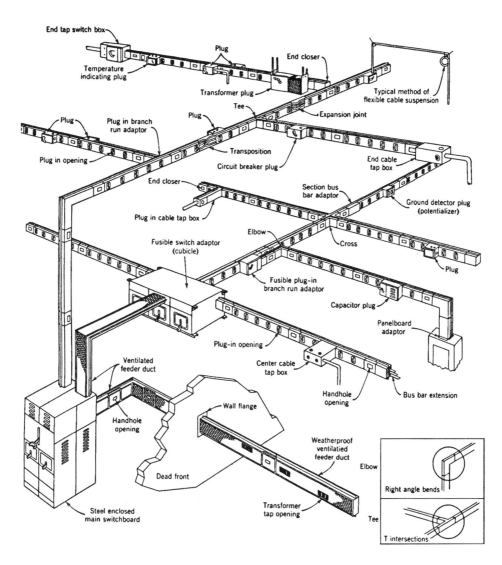

Fig. 3. Typical bus duct system (Courtesy: General Electric)

approved for installation only under carpet squares, along with accessories necessary for connection to 120-V outlets. Since the carpet can be removed in sections, the entire system can be repositioned to meet changing furniture layouts.

• *Ceiling raceway systems*

The need for electrical flexibility in facilities with limited budgets coupled with the high cost of underfloor electrical raceway systems encouraged the development of equivalent over-the-ceiling systems. These systems are actually more flexible than their under-floor counterparts, since they energize lighting as well as provide power and telephone facilities; furthermore, they permit very rapid changes in layouts at low cost. This last characteristic is particularly desirable in stores where frequent display changes necessitate corresponding electrical facility changes.

• *Ceiling raceways and modular wiring systems*

The need for electrical flexibility in facilities with limited budgets coupled with the high cost of underfloor electrical raceway systems encouraged the development of equivalent over-the-ceiling systems. These systems are more flexible than their underfloor counterparts, since they energize lighting as well as provide power and telephone facilities. They permit very rapid changes in layouts at low cost. Available systems vary among manufacturers but are essentially similar to underfloor systems. The standard method for extending ceiling level

wiring to floor- or desk-level signal and power outlets is by means of a vertical multisectional raceway fed from the top. These poles or posts are prewired with power wiring, contain several power outlets, a telephone connection and in some models data cable outlets or connectors, and are simply and easily installed at any desired location.

• *Boxes and cabinets*

In this category are included pull boxes, splice boxes, and outlet boxes. Splice boxes, as the name suggests, are placed in raceway runs at points where splices or taps must be made; the NEC prohibits having splices inside conduits. (Splices are permitted in wireways and troughs with removable covers.) Pull boxes are placed in conduit runs where it is necessary to interrupt the raceway for a wire pulling point. This depends on the pulling friction in the system. The size of pull boxes depends on the number and size of incoming conduits, the direction in which conduits leave, and whether or not splices will be made in the box. Minimum sizes based on the above data are specified in the NEC. When a box is equipped with a hinged door(s) and contains some equipment other than wiring, such as a terminal board, it is referred to as a cabinet. All boxes must be equipped with tightly fitting, removable covers.▮

SERVICES

D5

Communication and security systems

Summary: Possibly more than any other building service element, electronic systems have benefited from new technology developments and continue to do so, with electronic technology innovations, which involves close coordination of building design and electrical engineering specializations. This article provides the definitions and technical overview for preliminary design and coordination of communication and data systems and electronic security systems.

Key words: access control, card reader, communications spaces, equipment room, intrusion detection, optical fiber, security center, telephone system, telecommunications .

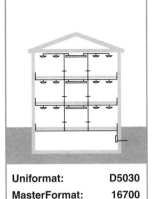

| Uniformat: | D5030 |
| MasterFormat: | 16700 |

Electronic innovations permit greatly increased capacity for communications, both within buildings and to external sites throughout the world, including visual (video) media and computer filing systems, and telephone/teleconferencing options, along with increased thoroughness and specificity in security systems in buildings.

The architect and engineer of a modern building must therefore be knowledgeable about these new technologies, and should provide for early planning and integration of electronic specialties into building and infrastructure planning. This article provides a description of the following electronic communication and security systems and components:

1 Communication spaces and pathways

2 Communications cabling systems

3 Voice and data communication systems

4 Electronic security systems

Acronyms and abbreviations
The following acronyms and abbreviations, useful in describing electronic communications and security systems, are referred to in this article:

ACD   Automatic Call Distribution
ATM   Asynchronous Transfer Mode
BICSI Building Industry Consulting Service International
CATV Cable TV
CCTV Closed circuit TV
CPU   Computer power unit
CTI   Computer-telephone integration
EIA   Electronic Industries Association
EPN   Expansion Port Network
HC   Horizontal cross connect
IC   Intermediate cross connect
IDF   Intermediate Distribution Facility
ISDN   Integrated Services Digital Network
LAN   Local area network
MATV Master antenna TV
MC   Main cross connect
MDF   Main Distribution Facility
MPD   Multiple Plastic Duct
NFPA   National Fire Protection Association
OFN   Optical Fiber (Nonconductive)
OFC   Optical Fiber (Conductive)

PTZ   Pan-tilt-zoom (camera lenses)
PCS   Personal communications system
PBX   Private branch exchange (communication)
PPN   Processing Port Network
STP   Shielded twisted pair (wiring)
TBB   Telecommunications Bonding Backbone
TGB   Telecommunications Grounding Busbar
TIA   Telecommunications Industry Association
UL   Underwriters Laboratories
UPS   Uninterruptible power system
VDT   Video display terminals
WAN   Wide area network

1   Communication spaces and pathways

A well-designed and coordinated infrastructure of communications spaces and pathways is an essential component of the modern commercial building. Recent standardization initiatives in the fields of voice and data networking, grounding systems, physical infrastructure, and cabling media have made it possible to define the basic layout of equipment spaces and cable pathways early in the building schematic design process.

The designer should therefore have a general understanding of the specific voice and data systems and network requirements to be accommodated for schematic design, leaving technical details for subsequent design development (Fig. 1). This approach provides the necessary features in the schematic design to accommodate complex information technology systems and to facilitate their detailing, design, installation, maintenance and long-term flexibility.

The dramatic impacts of electronic technology innovations and improvements in all communications systems is amply evident throughout modern society, and these in turn have raised the standard of communications technologies in modern buildings. Communications spaces and pathways, and their associated grounding systems, provide the physical infrastructure for voice, data, video, security, and control system cabling, network components and electronic equipment within a building, office park or campus environment.

Communications spaces always provide:

- physical protection and security for equipment.

- power and environmental facilities.

- provisions for cable interconnection and grounding.

- access to cables and equipment for modifications and maintenance.

Authors: Walter Cooper and Robert DeGrazio

References: Specific references are listed at the end of each topic section.

SERVICES

D5

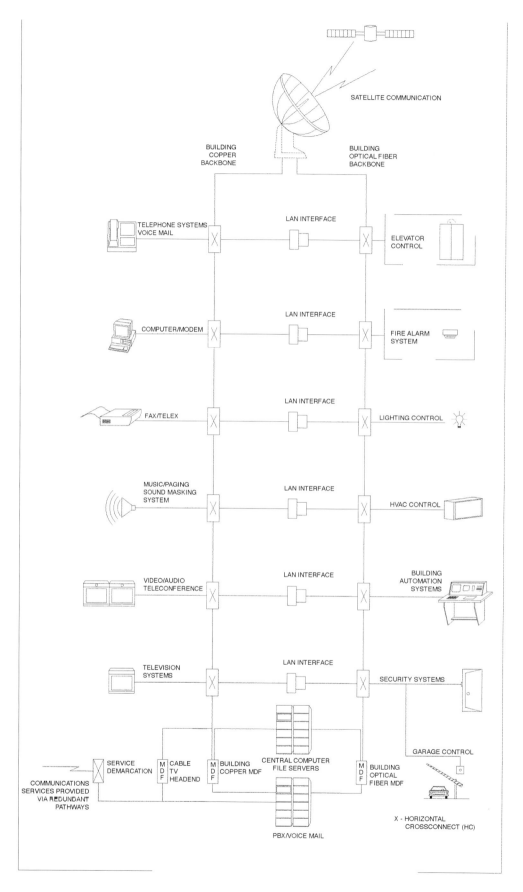

SERVICES

D5

Fig. 1. Electronic communication and security system options

In some cases, communications spaces also may provide:

- fire and smoke isolation.

- electromagnetic shielding.

- provisions for electrical and lightning protection of metallic circuits.

- backbone cable pathways (riser space) between floors.

- accommodations for operating personnel.

Cable pathways always provide:

- structured wire management and organization.

- access to cables for modification and maintenance.

In some cases, cable pathways may also provide:

- physical protection and security for cables.

- fire and smoke isolation.

- electromagnetic shielding.

Responsibilities: Base building (sometimes referred to as "backbone") communications spaces and pathways are the responsibility of the owner and are designed by the building architect and engineer team. In commercial buildings with rental spaces, the horizontal pathways and other communications spaces within tenant areas are typically the responsibility of the tenant or owner-occupant and are designed by the tenant architect-engineer team. The communications space and pathway designers and installation contractors must adhere to applicable EIA/TIA standards to ensure maximum utility, compatibility, and future flexibility of the building infrastructure system. In some cases (e.g., U.S. Federal Government projects), standards compliance is mandatory.

To visualize a complete communications infrastructure that must be accommodated within a building design, consider that the types of communications spaces are generally defined to include an entrance room (for utilities access), a telecommunications equipment room, and telecommunication closets.

- *Entrance room*

The entrance room is the transition point between outside cables and in-building cables. In individual buildings, this space is usually the demarcation point between the service provider's facilities and the owner's facilities. For increased security and reliability, there may be more than one entrance room per building. An entrance room:

- accommodates termination and interconnection points for incoming telecommunications cables, lightning protection for individual metallic conductors, and grounding for cable shields.

- provides space, access and a suitable environment for service provider's multiplexing and terminal equipment.

- *Telecommunications equipment room*

- provides space and a suitable environment for telecommunications and computer equipment serving all, or part of, a building or "campus" or group of buildings.

- may also contain the Main Distribution Facility (MDF) for building cabling and accommodation for operating and maintenance personnel.

- *Telecommunications closet*

The telecommunications closet is a smaller space, similar in function to a telecommunications equipment room, but typically serving a floor, or part of a floor, in a building, and:

- provides space, power and a suitable environment for electronic equipment such as Local Area Network (LAN) hubs and routers, backbone (riser) cable pathways, and Intermediate Distribution Facilities (IDF) for interconnections between backbone and horizontal cables.

- may also provide space for security, audio-visual, CATV (cable TV), building management, and other low voltage systems.

- Depending on the size of the floor plate, there may be more than one telecommunications closet per floor.

Design considerations for communications spaces

- *Communications entrance rooms*

Properly designed entrance rooms are:

- located on a lower building level within 50 ft. (15 m) of perimeter walls where cables enter building. (Entrance rooms may also be required near the building roof to accommodate cables and equipment associated with roof-top antennas).

- separated by at least 10 ft. (3 m) from sources of electromagnetic interference such as electric closets, switchrooms and mechanical spaces.

- separated from likely sources of flooding and excess humidity.

- provided with lighting and environmental conditions suitable for continuously operating electronic equipment (including emergency conditions).

- provided with maximum practical and usable wall space and provided with plywood and other suitable blocking for wall mounted equipment.

- provided with floor space for rack-mounted equipment and required service clearances.

- installed without windows and finished ceiling.

- fully accessible by service provider's maintenance personnel.

- require continuous operation and may require emergency power .

- Communications entrance rooms may be sized in accordance with Table 1.

- *Equipment rooms*

Equipment rooms (Fig. 2) are properly located in a secure area, centrally within building. In buildings with rental space, the size of equipment rooms should be based on flexibility to accommodate any future tenant program, in which case its outfitting is generally not part of the base building construction. Somewhat similar to the communication entrance room, although smaller, equipment rooms are:

- located at least 10 ft. (3 m) physical separation from sources of electromagnetic interference such as electric closets, switchrooms and mechanical spaces.

- located with suitable separation from likely sources of flooding and excess humidity.

- provided with lighting and environmental conditions suitable for continuously operating, computer-grade electronic equipment.

- without windows and possibly without finished ceilings.

- designed with maximize usable wall space and provided with plywood and or other blocking for wall mounted equipment.

- provided with floor space for rack-mounted equipment and required service clearances.

- may require an access floor, continuous operation and/or emergency power.

- *Telecommunications closets*

Telecommunication closets are located on each floor, vertically aligned within a core (vertical risers) accessway. The size of telecommunications closets, as a general rule, can be established as 50-100 sq. ft. per 10,000 usable sq. ft. (4.6-9.3 sq. m per 929 sq. m) of serviced floor area. Telecommunication closets are:

- located so that cabling distance to work locations is 295 ft. (90 m) or less.

Table 1. Guidelines for sizing Communications Entrance

Building Gross Floor Area (sq. ft.)	Entrance Room Approximate Size (LxW) (ft)
70,000	12x6
100,000	12x6
200,000	12x9
400,000	13x12
500,000	16x12
600,000	18x12
800,000	22x12
1,000,000	23x12

Table 2. Conduit provisions for entrance pathways

Building GFA (Gross Floor Area) sq. ft. (sq. m)	Minimum number of 4 in. (10 cm) conduits (including spares)*
70,000	1 + 1 spare
100,000	1 + 1 spare
200,000	2 + 1 spare
400,000	3 + 1 spare
500,000	4 + 1 spare
600,000	5 + 1 spare
800,000	5 + 1 spare
1,000,000	6 + 1 spare

* Note: conduits may be further subdivided using plastic innerduct.

SERVICES

D5

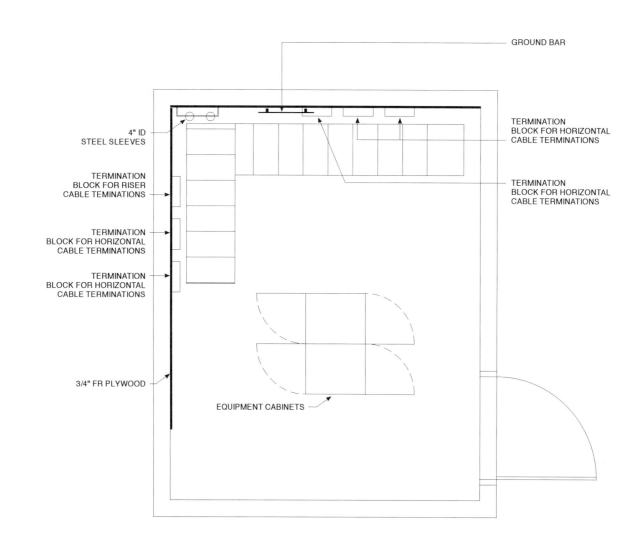

Fig. 2. Representative telecommunications equipment room plan

- floorplates greater than 10,000 sq. ft. (929 sq. m) may require more than one closet

- with a physical separation from sources of electromagnetic interference such as electric closets, switchrooms and mechanical spaces.

- separated from likely sources of flooding and excess humidity.

- provided with lighting and environmental conditions suitable for continuously operating electronic equipment.

- installed without omit ceilings and (typically) without finished floors.

- provided with vertically aligned sleeves or slots for riser cables.

- provided with suitable fire rating enclosure and/or fire protection.

- with maximize usable wall space and with plywood and or other blocking for wall mounted equipment.

- provided with floor space for rack-mounted equipment and required service clearances.

- if possible, provided with outward-opening doors to maximize usable floor and wall space.

- may require an access floor, and/or emergency power.

Types of communications cable pathways

Within the cabling system, the types of communication cable pathways include entrance pathways, building backbone pathways, and building horizontal cable pathways:

- *Entrance pathways*

Ductbank or cable trenches between the property line, service providers' point(s) of access, or central campus distribution point, and individual buildings. Provide space for service provider's incoming cables and/or campus backbone cables between buildings, and access (via manholes, handholes or vaults) for cable pulling, maintenance and additions. For added reliability and security, there may be more than one entrance pathway to a building or within a campus.

- *Building backbone pathways*

Horizontal cable tray, conduit, j-hook supports or delineated pathways in ceiling voids or under access floor which interconnect the entrance room(s), equipment room(s) and telecommunications closets. Vertical backbone pathways (risers) include sleeves or slots within vertically aligned telecommunications closets, conduit or ladder rack.

- *Building horizontal cable pathways*

The pathways between telecommunications closets and individual work station locations and can include horizontal cable tray, conduit, j-hook supports or delineated pathways in ceiling voids or under access floor. Trench headers and cells of cellular deck, and floor duct, surface-mounted raceways and raceways within modular furniture systems may also be used as horizontal pathways. Conduit stub ups, poke-through fittings, preset and afterset fittings and/or floor boxes complete the transition between horizontal pathway and the work station.

Design considerations for communications spaces

- *Entrance pathways*

- Properly rated cables may be direct buried in a cable trench or placed in a utility tunnel.

- Provided with at least 4 ft. (1.2 m) separation from power and other utilities in tunnels.

- Underground ductbanks are preferred for greater physical protection and cable pulling flexibility.

- Conduit or duct should be 4 in. (10 cm) inside diameter and may be PVC type A, B or C; Fiber Glass, Steel or Multiple Plastic Duct (MPD) construction.

- All underground bends should have a radius of 40 ft. (12.5 m) or greater.

- No more than two 90-degree bends are permitted between manholes/handholds.

- Provide a sufficient number of 4 in. (10 cm) ducts based on type and quantity of cable and at least one empty spare per ductbank.

- Slope the ductbank away from the building and provide steel sleeves at foundation wall penetrations.

- Consider providing redundant entrance pathways for increased reliability, security and/or capacity and flexibility.

- Size the entrance pathways to accommodate multiple services (voice/data, CATV) and multiple service providers, for which Table 2 can be used as a guide:

- *Backbone cable pathways*

- Provide sleeves or slots in vertically-aligned telecommunications closets for vertical backbone (riser) pathways.

- Interconnect telecommunications closets on the same floor with horizontal conduit or cable tray.

- Interconnect entrance rooms and telecommunications equipment rooms to telecommunications closets on the same floor using conduit or cable tray.

- Consider providing more than one riser per floor for increased reliability, security and/or capacity

- Extend backbone riser pathway to rooftop entrance room.

- Provide fire-stopping to maintain fire rating of all floors and walls penetrated by backbone pathways.

- Maintain a minimum bending radius of 40 in. (102 cm) in backbone pathways.

- Backbone conduit may have no more than two 90-degree bends between pull boxes or access points.

- Do not use pull boxes in lieu of conduit bends.

- Maintain at least a 1 ft. (30 cm) separation between backbone pathways and electrical cables.

- Cross electrical cables only at right angles

- Maintain at least 5 in. (13 cm) separation from fluorescent light fixtures.

- Avoid horizontal offsets in riser pathways.

- Consider using metal conduit or enclosed cable tray in air plenum spaces to preclude the need for plenum-rated cable (not applicable in all jurisdictions).

- Riser pathways can be sized using Table 3 as a guide.

- *Horizontal cable pathways*

- Provide pathways appropriate to the quantity of cable and necessity to provide the physical protection/radio frequency shielding.

- Maintain a bending radius at least 10 times the diameter of the largest cable to be accommodated.

- Horizontal conduit may have no more than two 90-degree bends between pull boxes or access points.

- Do not use pull boxes in lieu of conduit bends.

- Maintain at least 1 ft. (30 cm) separation between backbone pathways and electrical cables.

- Cross electrical cables only at right angles.

- Maintain at least 5 in. (13 cm) separation from fluorescent light fixtures.

Table 3. Conduit provisions for riser pathways

Total Floor Area (sq. ft.) Serviced by Riser	Minimum number of 4 in. (10 cm) sleeves (or equivalent slot area)
50,000	2 + 1 spare
100,000	3 + 1 spare
300,000	6 + 1 spare
500,000	10 + 1 spare
700,000	12 + 1 spare
800,000	13 + 1 spare
1,000,000	14 + 1 spare

- Avoid horizontal offsets in riser pathways.

- Consider using metal conduit or enclosed cable tray in air plenum spaces to preclude the need for plenum rated cable (not applicable in all jurisdictions).

- Use conduit to cross inaccessible ceiling areas

- Provide poke-through fittings, conduit stub-ups in walls, floor mounted boxes, or cellular floor aftersets to house outlet hardware and to terminate the horizontal pathways in the vicinity of each work station.

- Provide at least one voice and one data outlet or combined voice-data outlet fitting per 100 usable sq. ft. (9.29 sq. m) of typical office floor area.

- Refer to and comply with Americans with Disabilities Act (ADA) requirements concerning placement of, and access to, telecommunications outlets and devices.

Grounding system

An adequate telecommunications grounding is essential for the reliable and safe operation of current and future voice and data systems in buildings. Although telecommunications grounding and bonding systems are covered under separate standards, they are discussed together here because they are typically designed and constructed as an integral part of the spaces and pathways infrastructure and they physically interconnect major components of the spaces and pathways system. The telecommunications grounding and bonding system standard supplements, but does not replace or supersede, the requirements of NFPA 70 and other applicable electrical and safety codes.

- Provide a dedicated telecommunications bonding backbone (TBB) riser interconnecting the telecommunications closets, equipment rooms and service entry rooms.

- Provide a telecommunications grounding busbar (TGB) in telecommunications closets and equipment rooms.

- Bond each TGB to the TBB and to building structural steel (if present) and to the local electrical panelboard.

- Provide a telecommunications main grounding busbar (TMGB) in the telecommunications entrance room.

- Bond the TMGB to the TBB, building steel (if present), the local electrical panelboard and to the electrical service equipment grounding electrode conductor in the electrical entrance facility.

- Provide a telecommunications bonding backbone interconnecting bonding conductor (TBBIBC) to interconnect multiple TBBs at a minimum of every third floor in larger buildings

- The minimum conductor size for TBBs and TBBIBCs is No. 6 AWG. Much larger conductor sizes may be required in larger buildings

References: Communication spaces and pathways

BICSI. 1995. *Telecommunications Distribution Methods Manual.* Building Industry Consulting Service International, 10500 University Center Drive, Suite 100 Tampa, FL 33612.

Electronic Industries Association. 1990. *Commercial Building Standard for Telecommunications Pathways and Spaces.* ANSI/EIA/TIA-569. Washington, DC: Electronic Industries Association.

NFPA. 1995. *National Electrical Code.* National Fire Protection Association, Batterymarch Park, Quincy, MA 02269.

Telecommunications Industry Association. 1994. *Commercial Building Grounding and Bonding Requirements for Telecommunications.* ANSI/TIA/EIA-607. Washington, DC: Telecommunications Industry Association.

U.S. Department of Commerce. 1992. *Federal Building Standard for Telecommunications Pathways and Spaces.* Publication FIPS PUB 175. Springfield, VA: Federal Information Processing.

2 Communications cabling systems

Telecommunications service providers generally do not furnish cabling beyond the point of demarcation at the building entrance facility or project boundary. Provision of "backbone" and horizontal distribution cabling within the campus or building is the responsibility of the owner and/or tenant. Widely accepted standards for structured cabling and networks simplify the task of planning for and installing the cabling infrastructure as an integral part of the building design and construction process. In many cases (U.S. Federal Government projects, for example), compliance with structured cabling and infrastructure standards is mandatory for all renovation and new construction work.

Communications cabling systems provide the physical medium for the interconnection and transmission of voice, data, video, security, and control system information within a building, office park or campus environment. Communications cables are used for service entry (feeder) systems, campus backbone systems, building backbone and riser systems and building horizontal distribution systems, including distribution under access floors (Figs. 3 and 4). Comprehensive standards simplify the task of accommodating a wide range of services and applications using a single structured cabling infrastructure.

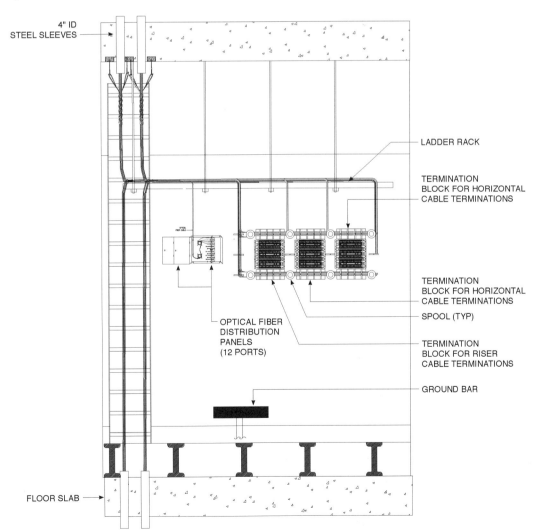

Fig. 3. Typical horisontal cable distribution under access floor.

Communications cabling systems always provide:

- capability for voice and low- to medium-speed data transmission.
- provisions for physical cable management, interconnection, and grounding.

In most cases, communications cabling systems also provide:

- transmission of high speed data for local and wide area networks.
- transmission of video and audio visual (including video teleconferencing) services.
- transmission of security, control and building management services.

Responsibilities: Service entry (feeder) cables are usually designed, installed, and owned by the telecommunications service provider(s) up to the building entrance facility or campus service demarcation point. Base building and campus backbone communications cabling systems are the responsibility of the owner and are designed by engineer or telecommunications designer. Horizontal dedicated backbone cabling within tenant spaces are typically the responsibility of the tenant or owner-occupant. It is imperative that cabling system designers and installation contractors adhere to applicable EIA/TIA standards to ensure maximum utility, compatibility, and future flexibility of the cabling system. In some cases (e.g., Federal Government projects), standards compliance is mandatory.

Types of communications cabling include:

- *High pair-count copper cable*

High pair-count copper cable is used as feeder cables to bring services into a campus or building and as horizontal backbone or riser cables within a building, and:

- accommodates voice, low speed data services and some types of high speed digital formats.
- may contain from 25 to several thousand individual twisted cable pairs, usually within an overall metallic shield.
- is being replaced by optical fiber in many backbone and riser applications, but is still widely used in buildings, especially for voice systems.
- UL classifications can include outdoor-only; riser, plenum and general location uses.

- *Unshielded twisted pair cable (UTP)*

Unshielded twisted pair cable (UTP) is used almost universally for horizontal distribution of voice and data services between horizontal cross-connect (HC) facilities in telecommunication closets and individual work station outlets and is:

- available in several performance classifications (Categories 3-5). Category 5 will support video and high speed local area networks.

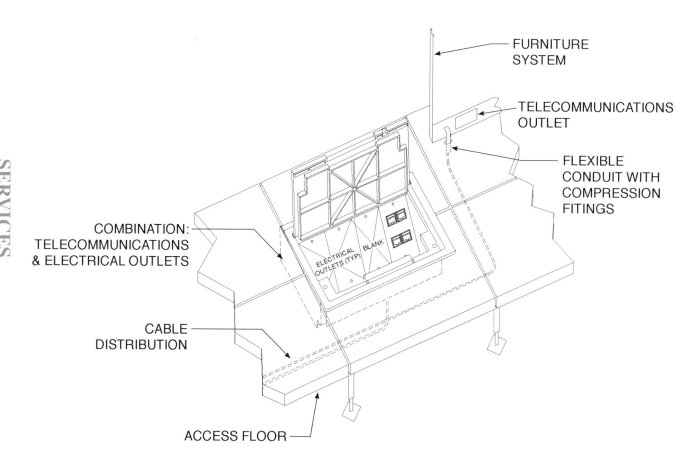

FURNITURE SYSTEM

TELECOMMUNICATIONS OUTLET

FLEXIBLE CONDUIT WITH COMPRESSION FITINGS

COMBINATION: TELECOMMUNICATIONS & ELECTRICAL OUTLETS

ELECTRICAL OUTLETS (TYP)   BLANK

CABLE DISTRIBUTION

ACCESS FLOOR

Fig. 4. Access panel to cable distribution in access floor.

SERVICES

D5

- normally contains four unshielded twisted copper pairs per cable.

- always terminated in modular type jack at the work station.

- UL classifications can include riser, plenum, general location, and under-carpet uses.

- under-carpet UTP is seldom used if conventional alternatives exist.

- Shielded-twisted pair cable (STP)

Shielded-twisted pair cable (STP) is used for medium to high speed data transmission and for some highly specialized systems, such as point-of-sale networks, and:

- does not support voice networks.

- is more difficult and costly to install than UTP.

- is seldom used in new installations.

- UL classifications can include outdoor-only; riser, plenum and general location uses.

- *Coaxial cable*

Coaxial cable was formally widely used for data terminals and local area networks, but has been almost universally replaced by UTP in these applications, and is:

- still used extensively for video distribution and closed circuit TV (CCTV).

- gradually being replaced by optical fiber and/or UTP for video as digital video standards evolve.

- UL classifications can include outdoor-only, riser, plenum, general location and under carpet uses.

- under carpet coaxial cable is seldom used of conventional alternatives exist.

- *Optical fiber cable*

Optical fiber cable is used mainly in outside plant, feeder and building horizontal and backbone applications as an economical and space-saving substitute for the larger high pair count copper cables, and:

- may also be used to connect work stations to horizontal cross-connects (HCs) in special circumstances, provides very high transmission capacity.

- is available in single mode and multi-mode versions.

- is not cost-justified for low speed/short distance applications.

- requires costly electro-optical interfaces to operate.

- UL classifications can include outdoor-only; general location, riser, and plenum uses.

UL classifications of communications cables
Permitted uses of copper cables and optical fiber cables are summarized in Tables 4 and 5 respectively.

Design considerations for communications cabling

- *Entrance (feeder) cables*

Entrance feeder cables are usually furnished and installed by the telecommunications service provider(s) and:

- terminate at the demarcation point in the building service entrance room.

- the building owner is usually responsible for providing the service entrance pathway (ductbank) for the feeder cables and the entrance room itself.

- may consist of high pair count copper or optical fiber, or both.

- Cable rated for outdoor use must be terminated and grounded within 50 ft. (15+ m) of the building entry point.

- Metallic cable pairs usually require high-voltage protective devices.

- All fiber and most copper feeder cables require electronic terminating equipment within the building.

- Copper and fiber entrance cables have bending radius restrictions ranging from 6 in. to 36 in. (15 cm to 90 cm).

Table 4. UL classification of communication cables

Marking*	Permitted use	Permitted substitutions
CMUC	Undercarpet	none
MPP	Plenums, risers & general locations	none
CMP	Plenums, risers & general locations	MPP
MPR	Risers & general locations only	MPP
CMR	Risers & general locations only	MPP, CMP, MPR
MPG, MP	General usage only	MPP, MPR
CMG, CM	General usage only	MPP, MPR, CMP, CMR
MPG, MP		

* Copper cables are marked with a two-letter designation: CM Communications Wires & Cables, MP Multipurpose Cables,
"P" suffix indicates Plenum usage, "R" suffix indicates Riser usage, "UC" suffix indicates Under Carpet usage

Table 5. UL classification of optical fiber cables

UL marking*	Permitted use	Permitted substitutions
OFNP	Plenums, risers & general locations	none
OFCP	Plenums, risers & general locations	OFNP
OFNR	Risers & general locations only	OFNP
OFCR	Risers & general locations only	OFNP, OFNR, OFCP
OFNG, OFN	General usage only	OFNP, OFNR
OFCG, OFC	General usage only	OFNP, OFNR, OFCP, OFNG,
OFN		

* Optical fiber cables are marked with a three-letter designation, OFN Optical Fiber (Nonconductive), OFC Optical Fiber (Conductive),
"P" suffix indicates Plenum usage, "R" suffix indicates Riser usage, "G" suffix indicates General Purpose usage

- For added reliability and security, there may be more than one set of entrance cables.

- A rough estimate of required entrance cable quantity is one pair per 100 usable sq. ft. (9.29 sq. m) of floor area.

• *Backbone cabling*

Backbone cabling is used to connect main cross-connects (MC), intermediate cross connects (IC) and horizontal cross-connects (HC) within a campus or building, and is:

- usually installed by the building or facility owner, not the service provider.

- may contain both horizontal an vertical (riser) elements.

- may include high pair count copper, UTP, STP, coaxial, and/or optical fiber.

- may require electronic terminating equipment at the MC, IC, and/ or HC.

- generally installed in dedicated raceway, cable tray, and/or riser shaft.

- must be terminated and grounded within 50 ft. (15.24 m) of building entry point.

• *Horizontal cabling*

Horizontal cabling is used to connect HCs (telecommunications closets) to individual work station locations, and is:

- usually furnished and installed by the tenant or system user.

- usually UTP, may also include STP, coaxial, or optical fiber.

- always installed in a "star configuration."

- usually direct homerun from the HC to each work station outlet.

- may also be distributed via "zone boxes" in open office plans.

- quantity required is at least two 4-pair UTP cables per work station outlet.

Material and installation standards

National and international committees proscribe minimum standards for commercial building cabling systems, which must be observed for proper system performance. The most critical requirements are to:

- use standards compliant materials and hardware.

- maintain standard topology and cross connect hierarchy.

- observe maximum cabling distances between cross connects.

- observe minimum cable bending radii.

- maintain pair geometry and twist rates in UTP and STP.

- provide physical separation from sources of electromagnetic interference

Cabling hierarchy

Cabling hierarchy is established by:

- one main cross-connect point (MC) per building or campus.

- one or more horizontal cross-connect points (HC) per floor of a building.

- one or more individual outlets per work area.

- intermediate cross-connect points (IC) may be provided between the MC and HCs.

- each cross connect element is star-connected to the subordinate elements.

- ICs and HCs may also be connected at the same level to facilitate ring-type networks.

- maximum cabling distances between hierarchical elements are shown in Table 6 and its accompanying Fig. 2.

Residential and light commercial cabling less restrictive codes and EIA/TIA standards apply to these installation (see appropriate references for more information).

References: communications cabling systems

BICSI. 1995. *Telecommunications Distribution Methods Manual.* Building Industry Consulting Service International, 10500 University Center Drive, Suite 100 Tampa, FL 33612; 1995.

EIA. 1991. *Residential and Light Commercial Telecommunications Wiring Standard.* ANSI/EIA/TIA-570. Washington, DC: Electronic Industries Association.

NFPA. 1996. *National Electrical Code.* Quincy, MA: National Fire Protection Association.

TIA. 1995. *Commercial Building Telecommunications Cabling Standard.* ANSI/TIA/EIA-568-A. Arlington, VA: Telecommunications Industry Association.

TIA. 1996. *Additional Horizontal Cabling Practices for Open Offices.* TIA-TSB 75. Arlington, VA: Telecommunications Industry Association.

U.S. Department of Commerce. 1992. *Federal Building Telecommunications Wiring Standard.* 1992. Publication FIPS PUB 174. Springfield, VA: Federal Information Processing Standards.

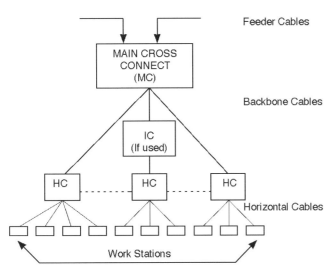

Fig. 5. Diagram of cabling hierarchy

Table 6. Cabling hierarchy and maximum distances indicated in ft. (m)

Medium	MC to HC	MC to IC	IC to HC	HC to Outlet
Single Mode Fiber	9840 (3000)	8200 (2500)	1640 (500)	295 (90)
Multi Mode Fiber	6560 (2000)	4820 (1500)	1640 (500)	295 (90)
UTP		2624 (800)	984 (300)	1640 (500)	295 (90)
STP		2624 (800)	984 (300)	1640 (500)	295 (90)

SERVICES

D5

3 Voice and data communication systems

Virtually all commercial and institutional buildings accommodate various voice, data, and (increasingly) video communications systems (Fig. 6). Telecommunications service providers generally do not furnish or install these systems, which are normally the responsibility of the building owner or tenant. All of these systems require spaces, pathways, cabling, and environmental support, which should be in-

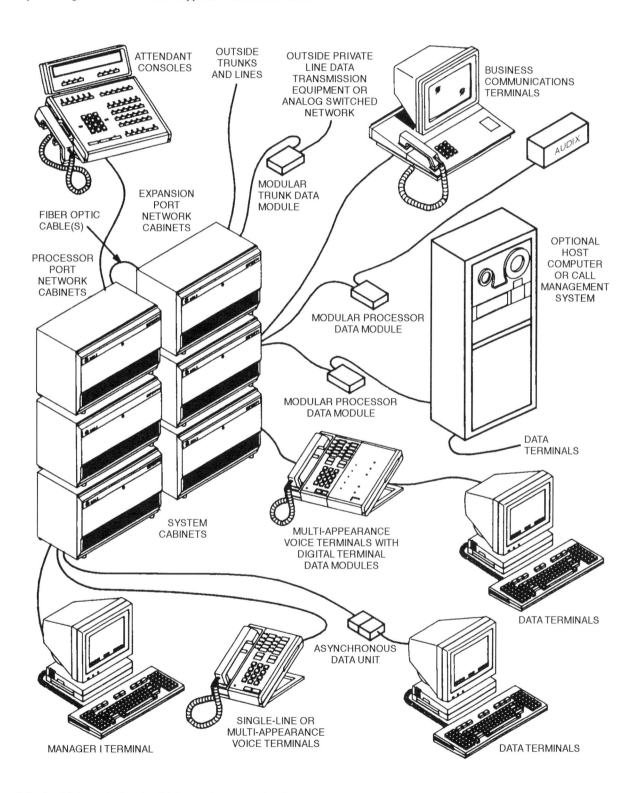

Fig. 6. Typical integrated voice/data and communication system with processing port network (PPN) and expansion port network (EPN).

cluded as an integral part of the building infrastructure design. There is increasing integration among voice, data, and video communications systems. This trend is expected to continue to the point where integrated, multifunction desktop terminals and multimedia networks will eventually support most voice, data, and video applications in the typical office environment.

Voice, data, and video communications systems provide the equipment, software and terminal devices (such as telephones, computer terminals and video displays) to transmit, process, administer, store and retrieve sound, image and computer data within a building, facility, or campus, or over wide areas.

Voice and data communications systems always provide the capability to connect two or more terminals for the purpose of exchanging information electronically.

Voice and data communications systems may also provide various degrees of information routing, processing, and storage and (increasingly) interconnection/integration of systems and media.

Responsibilities: Voice and data communications systems and equipment are usually owned and operated by the building tenant or owner-occupant. Telecommunications service providers typically do not provide equipment in conjunction with their voice and data network services, except under separate arrangements through equipment subsidiaries. Architects and engineers should design building communications spaces, pathways, and cabling systems to accommodate the tenant's communications equipment program. Construction schedules for new buildings and major renovations should reflect the need to have equipment spaces "room ready" well in advance of move-in to accommodate equipment installation, "burn-in," and testing.

Types of voice communications

Types of voice communications include:

- *Key telephone systems*

Key telephone systems are small telephone switching systems supporting from two to a few dozen telephones and providing basic telephone system features, including limited data switching. Common equipment:

- is usually a single wall-mounted cabinet.

- can be installed in a telecommunications closet or other convenient location.

- usually does not require any special environmental conditions beyond a normal office environment.

- may have a small internal or external battery back-up to retain memory and/or provide short term operation during power outages.

- Individual telephone sets are proprietary to the system and may require electrical power for operation.

- Virtually all key systems can connect directly to EIA standard building cabling systems.

- *Private branch exchanges (PBXs)*

Private branch exchanges (PBXs): support from a few to thousands of telephones within a building or campus and can provide a wide range of internal and external calling features. Larger systems have automatic call routing and accounting software and can be partitioned electronically among multiple departments or building tenants. Most have internal data switching capability up to at least 64 kilobits per second (kbs) and the ability to support Integrated Services Digital Network (ISDN) services from the public networks.

- Common equipment can range from a single wall mounted cabinet to multiple free-standing cabinets or equipment racks.

- Small PBXs have power and environmental requirements similar to key systems.

- Larger systems require a computer-like environment in a centralized equipment room.

- Components of large PBXs may also be distributed within a building or campus by placing individual cabinets in telecommunications closets or additional equipment rooms.

- Most large systems may be installed with or without raised access floor.

- Back-up power, if provided, may require a separate rectifier-battery system of self-contain interrupt power supply (UPS).

- Larger battery systems may require structural reinforcement and/or special ventilation systems.

- Since larger PBXs and centralized computer equipment have similar environmental and utility needs, it is often beneficial to locate them in the same (or adjacent) spaces.

- Most PBXs can support both industry standard analog telephone sets and proprietary digital/ISDN sets.

- Electronic sets must be powered locally or from the telecommunications closet.

- All modern PBXs can connect directly to EIA standard building cabling systems.

Table 7 provides approximate space and power requirements for typical PBX systems of various size ranges (actual products vary widely).

- *Central office telephone services*

Central office telephone services, available from telecommunications service providers under trademark names such as Centrex, eliminate the need for major PBX equipment installations in the customer's premises. The telecommunications switching and administration is provided at the central office using a central office switching machine that has been partitioned and programmed to function like an individual PBX.

- Individual circuits extend directly from the central office to each on premise telephone set.

- Using a telecommunications service provider eliminates the need for most (but not all) on-premise common equipment and environmental support.

- Space and environmental requirements for a typical large telecommunications service installation approximate those of a 100 line PBX.

- Industry standard analog telephone sets and proprietary digital/ISDN sets are typically available.

- Electronic sets may require dedicated power.

- Sets can connect directly to EIA standard building cabling systems.

- Central services may not be available in all localities.

- *Special purpose voice systems*

Special purpose voice systems include high capacity multi-line phone terminals ("turrets") for securities trading desks and (in the United States) for 911 emergency consoles. These systems use what are very specialized PBXs, characterized by very high capacity line switching equipment and station sets. Financial traders' turrets, for example, may accommodate up to several hundred direct lines on each set. 911 emergency consoles may integrate with computer networks and two way radio circuits. These systems require very specialized planning:

- Station sets are proprietary, require dedicated power, and may require special millwork.

- In most cases, these systems require special cabling to the desk; some use optical fiber.

SERVICES

D5

- Central equipment requirements vary. On a trading floor, for example, the approximate ratio of equipment rooms floor space to trading floor space that is served is approximately 1:4.

- Special voice systems almost always require back up power and continuous environmental support.

• *Ancillary voice systems*

Ancillary voice systems provide additional features and functions to standard key, PBX and telecommunications service providers' telephone systems. They may require additional equipment cabinets, integrated with, or connected to, the basic system. Ancillary voice systems include:

- voice mail and automatic call accounting systems.

- automatic call distribution (ACD) systems for customer service, reservation and telemarketing call centers.

- centralized dictation systems.

- voice recording equipment for police, hospital and trading floor systems.

- interfaces to computer systems and local area networks (LANs) for computer-telephone integration (CTI).

- conference bridges for high-end audio teleconferencing.

- hospitality systems for hotels may provide automated wake-up service, room environmental controls and room status/housekeeping tracking.

• *Intercommunication systems*

Intercommunication systems provide point-to-point or point-to-multipoint communications in conjunction with access control systems, trading floor positions, audio-visual facilities, sound and video studios, and similar applications. If hands-fee operation is needed, special equipment is usually required; otherwise conventional or electronic telephone sets may be programmed as interphones.

Types of data communications systems

Types of data communications systems include:

• *Terminal-host systems*

Terminal-host systems connect individual data terminals to large mini-computers or mainframes. These systems are becoming much less common in new installations and:

- may require the use of cluster controllers to connect groups of 16-32 terminals to the network.

- controllers are often placed in telecommunications closets.

- may use proprietary terminals or standard PCs with emulation cards.

- are often integrated with LANs in newer installations

- Virtually all systems can connect directly to (or be adapted to) EIA standard cabling systems.

- Systems required to be functional during power outages require backup power for the terminals, controllers, and mainframe and backup environmental support for the controllers and mainframes

• *Local area networks (LANs)*

Local area networks (LANs) are data communications systems of two or more (sometimes hundreds) of interconnected data devices, such as personal computers, printers and file servers operating within a limited geographic area (a department, a building or a campus). LANs and groups of LANs are becoming almost ubiquitous in the modern office and are rapidly increasing in capability and complexity (Fig. 7). Most LANs are peer-to-peer networks, meaning that all of the connected resources, such as computer programs. files, disk space, printers and wide area communications gateways, can be shared among the users. LANs vary widely in physical implementation. Typical characteristics include:

Table 7. Space and power requirements for PBX systems.

Number of Extensions	Approximate Equipment Room floor area (sq. ft.)	Approximate Connected Load (kW)	Average Demand Load (kW)
0-50	none (wall mount)	0.5 - 1.5	0.2 - 0.6
50-250	10 - 50	1.5 - 3.5	0.6 - 1.5
250-1,000	50 - 100	3.5 - 7.0	1.5 - 3.5
1,000-5,000	100 - 300	7.0 - 35.0	3.5 - 15.0
5,000-10,000	300 - 500	35.0 - 55.0	10.0 - 25.0

SERVICES

D5

- Desktop terminals are typically personal computers.

- Expensive resources, such as laser printers, are usually shared among several users.

- Individual PCs and other devices are connected to the LAN with a hub device, typically located in the telecommunications closet.

- File servers are also PCs and are located within a using department, telecommunications closet, or centralized equipment room.

- All modern LANs can connect directly to EIA standard cabling.

- UTP cabling is almost universally used for the horizontal wiring segment and can support all current LAN speeds up to 100 megabites per second (mbs).

- LAN backbone cabling is typically EIA standard optical fiber.

- Multiple LANs and LAN segments are interconnected with devices such as routers, bridges and switchers, which may be located in telecommunications closets or equipment rooms.

- Routers, bridges and switches present heat loads in telecommunications closets and equipment rooms and require adequate environmental support.

- Systems required to be functional during power outages require backup power at the terminals, hubs, routers, bridges, switches and file services and may require backup environmental support in telecommunications closets and equipment rooms.

- LANs frequently have backup power only for the file servers, due to the high cost of end-to-end backup support.

Fig. 7. LAN (Local Area Network) Workstation (Courtesy: Ergotron, Inc.)

- Most offices make provisions for one LAN terminal per desk.

- It is advisable to allow additional space and environmental support for printers and LAN devices in telecommunications closets and equipment rooms.

LAN power and environmental considerations

LAN components and other data communications devices present a significant power and heat load, which may be distributed throughout a building or facility. Initiatives such as the Environmental Protection Agency's Energy Star program have resulted in a new generation of products that dramatically reduce average energy consumption. In some cases (Federal Government projects, for example) the use of Energy Star products is mandatory. Table 8 provides approximate power requirements for typical system components comparing conventional and Energy Star compliant devices.

Types of LANs

Some of the most popular LANs include:

- Ethernet (currently the most widely used)

- Token Ring

- ARCnet

- Apple Talk

- FDDI

- TP-TMD

- Asychronous Transfer Mode (ATM)

• *Wide area networks (WANs)*

WANs are long distance voice and data networks extending beyond the limits of the individual building or campus. They may be part of the public network provided by local and long distance telecommunications service providers, dedicated sub-networks (virtual private networks) within the public networks, or they may be true private networks, owned and operated by the user. These networks are important to the building architect and engineer from the standpoint of required service entry facilities (including facilities for rooftop antennas) and equipment spaces for accessing these networks and connecting them to the building cabling backbone and internal voice and data networks, as discussed elsewhere in this chapter. Typical media for WANs include:

- copper cable

- optical fiber cable

- satellite earth stations

- microwave terminals

- mobile radio systems such as cellular

• *Integrated systems*

Many of the voice and data communications systems discussed herein have increasing degrees of integration. Telephones and computers are integrated into a single voice-data terminal in customer service facilities, reservation centers and similar installations. Data networks are becoming multifunctional and multimedia, with the ability to transmit, receive and display sound, graphics, and moving images. The newer LAN and WAN technologies such as Synchronous Optical Network (SONET) can handle voice, data, and video signals interchangeably and provide a true multimedia transport mechanism. This trend toward integration should continue to the point where distinctions among conventional voice, data, and video communications systems will disappear in favor of single networks of multifunction devices.

• *Wireless systems*

Most of the voice and data communications described herein are considered to be conventional wired systems. There is an increasing ca-

Table 8. Power requirements of LAN equipment. Conventional and U.S. EPA Energy Star products compared.

Type of Device	Typical Connected Load - Conventional Products (W)	Average Load - Energy Star Products (W)
Personal computer	200 - 500	30 or less
Computer monitor (CRT)	200 - 300	30 or less
Small printer, copier or Fax	750 - 850	15 or less
Large printer, copier or plotter	1,000 2,000	30 or less
High end color printer	3,000 - 5,000	45 or less
Router, switch, or file server	200 - 600	30 or less

pability to provide similar services within buildings using wireless (radio or infrared-based systems). These systems have utility in many applications requiring personal mobility or temporary installations, but they will probably not replace wired systems to any great extent due to their relatively higher cost, limited capacity, and susceptibility to interception and interference. Also, it is necessary to "wire for wireless" to accommodate the antennas and receiver-transmitter devices needed to make these systems work. While generic antenna wiring can be run throughout a building, it is almost always necessary to consult specific system vendors due to the proprietary nature of the systems. Some typical in-building wireless systems include:

- Wireless PBX: mobile telephones similar to the public cellular phones used outside buildings also known as personal communications systems (PCS).

- Wireless pagers: may be radio or infrared. Some can locate and identify users automatically.

- Two-way radios: "walkie-talkies" used by security and maintenance personnel.

- Wireless LANS take may forms, using radio and infrared; there is little standardization.

- Wireless modems: also called radio modems, are incorporated into laptop PCs for mobile computing and may also connect to a cellular phone.

• *Other data communications systems*
There are many types of special data combinations systems for automatic teller machines, point-of-sale devices, specialized systems for reservation, customer service and telemarketing centers (often integrated electronically with voice systems) control communications used for building management systems, telemetry and supervisory communications and data acquisition (SCADA). Many of these systems use standard LAN components and can be accommodated on EIA standard cabling systems. Consult manufacturers or suppliers for unique space and environmental requirements.

• *Video communications systems*
Video communications systems include closed circuit TV (CCTV), cable TV (CATV), master antenna TV (MATV), and video teleconferencing systems (video communications systems are discussed under a separate heading within this series of articles)

References: Voice and data communication systems
BISCI. 1995. *Communications Distribution Methods Manual.* Building Industry Consulting Service International, 10500 University Center Drive, Tampa, FL 33612

BISCI. 1995. *Local Area Network Design Manual.* Building Industry Consulting Service International, 10500 University Center Drive, Tampa, FL 33612.

NFPA. 1996. *National Electrical Code.* Quincy, MA: National Fire Protection Association.

TIA. 1995. *Commercial Building Telecommunications Cabling Standard.* ANSI/TIA/EIA-568-A. Arlington, VA: Telecommunications Industry Association.

TIA. 1996. *Additional Horizontal Cabling Practices for Open Offices.* TIA-TSB 75, Arlington, VA: Telecommunications Industry Association.

4   Electronic security systems

All modern buildings are candidates for electronic security systems which require planning and an understanding of its electronic infrastructure as part of architectural design and electrical systems. To en-

sure an appropriate and cost effective level of security in both the short and long term, architects need to be knowledgeable about the range of electronic security technologies and options that effect design. Security systems must also be responsive to codes and regulations, and appropriately interactive with other building systems. Finally, planning for security should be addressed early in the design process.

Electronic security systems provide monitoring and controls to enhance the safety of the employees, staff, and visitors who use a building and to protect property. Access control often extends beyond controlling who enters a building to monitoring when and where they do so. Electronic security systems augment, but do not replace, human security measures.

Electronic security systems provide controlled access within a facility, protection from damage and loss, and protection of information. In some cases, electronic security systems also provide alarm monitoring of critical building systems, fluid leak detection, vehicle access control, notification (also see "Fire Alarm Systems" in Chapter D4 of this Volume), and evidence for investigations.

Levels of security
Determining the level of required or desired degree of security helps to establish the appropriate level of cost and technology of electronic systems planning and installations.

• *Low level*
Simple physical barriers designed to obstruct and detect unauthorized activity, which may include electronic control of doors and locks, window bars and grates, timed or motion-detector lighting, and various intrusion detection systems.

• *Medium level*
In addition to low level measures, institute monitored electronic perimeters beyond the boundaries of the protected area, and various advanced intrusion detection systems.

• *High level*
In addition too low and medium levels, perimeter alarm system, CCTV system, access control system, and high security lighting.

Types of security technologies
Like other electronic systems for buildings, security technologies are constantly being developed. Current state-of-art security systems and technologies, discussed in turn below, include:

- Access control / card entry.
- Biometric Access Control technologies.
- Intrusion detection.
- Closed circuit television.

• *Access control / card entry*
The number and kind of electronic access control systems keeps growing. Over the past 10 to 15 years, card entry systems have become increasingly common.

- The card entry system is able to incorporate time zone access levels, time controlled events, report generation, capability of supporting multiple workstations, video display terminals (VDT) and printers.

- The most common card entry systems will support magnetic stripe readers, Wiegand effect readers, and proximity readers. Choices are augmented by alpha numeric key pad and chip readers.

- Once programmed, the system will be self supporting, except for adding and deleting cards, acknowledging alarms and generating reports.

Two basic card technologies are available:

- Magnetic stripe cards have the code located on a magnetic stripe on the back of the card,

- Wiegand cards have a unique card code sandwiched inside the card.

There are several choices for card readers: Swipe card readers have proven their reliability and flexibility (Fig. 8). Typically, swipe readers use standard credit card size cards, which can display a company's logo and incorporate a picture identification. Insertion readers have a higher incidence of mechanical stress with insertion readers, making for a short card life span and some risk that cards may break in the reader. Proximity card readers are more compact and have little change of damaging the card.

Alpha numeric key pads (requiring the user to enter a code) can stand alone at security points and can augment a card reader system to raise the level of security for a given space.

Chip reader technology utilizes a programmable chip permanently affixed to the access card; the reader sensor is a flat circle or plate.

• *Biometric Access Control technologies*
Biometric Access Control technologies are newer and constantly developing systems that directly measure physical characteristics of the individual. The main disadvantages of current state-of-art technologies, compared with conventional systems, are higher cost and a less desirable trade-off between speed and accuracy. They include fingerprint, hand geometry, eye retina scan, speech verification, signature verification, or thermogram technology.

• *Intrusion detection*
Intrusion Detection includes the many types of sensors and alarm systems now available. Infrared and microwave motion sensors can be ceiling- or wall-mounted (Fig. 9). Although such detectors are mostly used to detect intrusion in interior spaces, there are motion sensors available for exterior use. Related characteristics include:

- Glass break sensors are used to detect the shattering of glass.

- Magnetic alarm contacts are used to detect the opening of doors and windows.

- Duress alarm switches are used to notify security personnel of a crime situation or other emergency.

- Fence sensors designed to detect climbing or cutting.

- Buried line sensors can detect seismic activity, flooding or presence of ferrous metals.

• *Closed circuit television*
Closed Circuit Television (CCTV) has demonstrated its effectiveness as a security tool in all sorts of facilities, enabling multiple locations to be simultaneously monitored from a single security command center. CCTV console operators can direct a mobile security force to any area that requires assistance. CCTV recordings carry the additional value of aiding in the investigation and prosecution of crimes and disruptions that have occurred.

Design considerations for card entry systems

• *Typical locations for card entry*
Locations for card entry points can be established wherever limited access by designated personnel or other security checkpoints logically occur and may include: perimeter entrances, lobbies, vehicle entrances, data centers, telecommunications equipment rooms, service entry rooms, generator and uninterruptable power source (UPS) rooms, cash handling areas, document control rooms, laboratories, and passenger and freight elevators.

Fig. 8. Swipe card reader for building access (Courtesy: Von Duprin Co.)

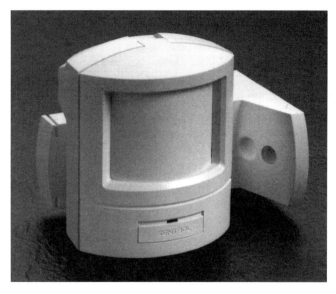

Fig. 9. Passive Infra-red intrusion detector for wall-mount. (Courtesy: Sentrol)

SERVICES

D5

- *Electrical locking devices*

Electrical locking devices, which control the hardware of doors, may include:

- electromagnetic locks for high security applications.

- electromechanical strikes for medium level security applications.

- electromechanical mortise locksets for medium to high security applications and wherever fail-safe mechanical latching is required by local code.

- electromechanical panic devices for perimeter emergency egress applications.

- coordination and compatibility with mechanical door hardware is required (also see "Exterior doors and hardware" in Chapter B2 of this Volume).

- *Card entry system power requirements*

- Typically, all field devices such as card readers, magnetic alarm contacts, electrical locking devices and request-to-exit devices require low voltage power, usually 24VDC. These devices are powered from security data gathering panels located in the security riser closets.

- Security data gathering panels and electrical lock power supplies typically require 120VAC power.

- Access control computer power unit (CPU) and workstations typically require 120VAC.

- All access control devices should be on emergency power source.

- CPU and data gathering panels must be powered by an uninterruptible power system (UPS).

- Power to all systems should be dedicated and unswitched.

- A good grounding system is required.

- *Card entry systems cabling requirements*

- All low voltage security cabling is typically telecommunications industry standard unshielded twisted pair copper (UTP).

- Data communication cabling between the data gathering panels and the CPU is UTP copper.

- In large buildings and campuses, backbone cabling may be optical fiber or the system may be integrated with a LAN.

- *Card entry system conduit requirements*

- Minimum conduit requirements should include conduit stub-ups and back boxes for all devices.

- Cabling must be installed in conduit where required by local code.

- High security applications may also require all security cabling in conduit.

- Cabling must be installed in conduit in all inaccessible areas.

- Exposed cabling should not be permitted.

- Cabling should be installed conduit where otherwise exposed exterior or other harsh environmental locations.

- *Card entry space requirements*

- Security riser closets typically require 64 sq. ft. (6 sq. m) of wall space for card entry equipment panels.

- May be contained in telecommunications closets.

- Security equipment rooms typically require 64 sq. ft. (6 sq. m) for card entry CPU and equipment.

- All security riser closets and equipment rooms must be physically secure, well lighted and ventilated.

- *Other card entry system design considerations*

- Compliance with ADA requirements for accessibility.

- Compliance with local building codes regarding means of egress.

- Coordination of electrical locking devices with mechanical door and hardware.

- Allocation of space for security equipment panels.

- Number of entry exit points that will require access control devices.

- Number of alarm points the access control system will process.

- Number of card holders.

- Peak use throughput capacity for each door.

- Flexibility and allocation for system expansion.

Design considerations for intrusion detection systems

- *External sensors*

Intrusion detection external sensors should be located where they are protected from accidental or intentional damage, and also accessible for routine maintenance. Their performance will be affected by:

- obscuring vegetation such as tall, grass movement of bushes and tree branches, and falling leaves.

- weather such as extreme heat and cold, lightning, wind snow accumulation, and fog.

- ambient conditions such as electromagnetic interference from underground service, overhead power lines and vibration from transportation vehicles.

- *Intrusion detection*

Location of internal intrusion sensors is critical to provide protection from accidental damage and from other local environmental conditions, such as:

- structural vibration.

- temperature fluctuations.

- direct exposure to sun light through windows.

- reflective finishes.

- sensor positioning with respect to furniture and partitions.

- accidental damage, such as from careless maintenance.

- nearness to radiant heating.

- nearness to mechanical diffusers.

- *Intrusion detection: magnetic alarm contacts*

- Flush mount devices are more secure and less obtrusive in appearance.

- Devices are typically mounted on the top of the door as far away from the hinge as possible.

- Doors and windows should be well fitting and not and have minimal vibration in wind conditions

- *Intrusion detection systems power requirements*

- Typically all sensors require low voltage power, usually 12 to 24VDC. These devices are powered from security data gathering panels located in the security riser closets or the alarm control communicator centrally located within the protected space.

- All intrusion detection device must be on emergency standby power source.

- Power to all systems should be dedicated and unswitched.

- A good grounding system is required.

- Typically, cabling for all security sensors is UTP copper.

- *Intrusion detection system conduit requirements*

- Minimum conduit requirements should include conduit stub-ups and back boxes for all devices.

- Cabling must be installed in conduit where required by local code.

- High security applications typically require all security cabling in conduit.

- Cabling must be installed in conduit in all inaccessible areas.

- Cabling should be installed in all locations where cable where the cabling would otherwise be exposed.

- Cabling should be installed in conduit where otherwise exposed to harsh environmental locations.

- Cabling should be installed in conduit in all exterior locations.

• *Closed Circuit Television (CCTV) lighting*

Municipal building codes in the U.S. typically require a minimum of 1 foot candle (10 lux) of illumination along exit/egress paths (note that higher levels are recommended at critical points such as stairs). These minima may seem to provide for sufficient light since most CCTV cameras can provide a fairly good amount of detail at 3 to 5 lux and even detect forms and motion in lighting levels as low as one lux. However, as an object moves away from a light source, illumination diminishes quickly. The illumination falls off with the square of the distance. The result is that if the illumination at a door is equal to 10 lux, an area 5 ft. (1.5 m) away from the door may be in near darkness at one lux or less, unless it is lit by a supplemental source.

- Accordingly, lighting along exit/egress pathways should be checked to provide sufficient illumination for all CCTV camera viewing angles and supplemented beyond the minimum standard.

- Infrared illumination enables cameras to produce high quality images in complete darkness.

• *CCTV cameras: number and location*

- Nonochrome (black and white) cameras provide higher resolution and better performance in low light applications.

- Color cameras, which may be considered to provide additional critical evidence of identification (e.g. color of clothing) require optimum lighting conditions and should be restricted to indoor applications only.

- Overt camera installations provide typical surveillance and act as a deterrent.

- Covert camera installations are designed to provide undercover surveillance. Their use may require legal notification (of building users) and be limited by local governance and law.

• *Camera housings*

- Interior rectangle housings are designed for surface mount wall and ceiling applications.

- Interior dome housings are designed for surface or recessed ceiling mount applications.

- Interior triangle housings are designed for ceiling and wall mount corner applications.

- Interior recessed housings are available for ceiling and wall mount applications.

- Exterior housings are available in rectangle, dome, and recessed configurations for wall, parapet, and pole mount applications.

• *CCTV monitor considerations*

- The following formula can be a guide to calculate monitor size and viewing distance: monitor size (in.) - 4 = monitor viewing distance (ft.). Example 9 in. - 4 = 5 ft.

- Maximum vertical viewing angle is approximately 30 degrees.

- Maximum horizontal viewing angle is approximately 45 degrees in either direction.

- Standard monitor security monitor sizes (measured diagonal in inches) are: 5, 9, 12, 17, 19, and 21 (in.).

• *CCTV power requirements*

- Cameras typically operate on either 24VAC or 120VAC provided at each camera or distributed from a central location.

- Monitors and switchers and recording equipment typically require 120VAC power.

- Power to all systems should be dedicated and unswitched.

- A good grounding system is required.

• *CCTV cabling requirements*

- Camera signals can be transmitted over coaxial, fiber optic, or unshielded twisted pair (UTP) cable.

- The most common camera signal cable in use currently is RG-59/U coaxial cable with a maximum cable distance between the camera and monitor of 1,000 ft. (305 m).

- Fiber optic cable can transmit camera signals over several miles.

- UTP copper cable will carry video signals up 1,200 ft. (365 m).

- Typically each camera will require cables one for power and for signal.

- PTZ (Pan-tilt-zoom) camera applications will require additional multi-conductor or fiber optic cables.

• *CCTV conduit requirements*

- Cabling must be installed in conduit where required by local code.

- High security applications typically require all security cabling in conduit.

- Cabling must be installed in conduit in all inaccessible areas.

- Cabling should be installed in all locations where cable where the cabling would otherwise be exposed.

- Cabling should be installed in conduit where otherwise exposed to harsh environmental locations.

- Cabling should be installed in conduit in all exterior locations.

• *CCTV space requirements*

- Security riser closets typically require 48 sq. ft. (4.5 sq. m) of wall space for CCTV equipment.

- Security equipment rooms typically require 75 sq. ft. (7 sq. m) of floor area for every 100 cameras.

- All security riser closets and equipment rooms must be physically secure, well lighted, and ventilated.

• *Other CCTV design considerations*

- Pan-tilt-zoom (PTZ) devices permit the remote control of CCTV cameras and zoom lenses.

- The CCTV system may require connection to emergency power sources,

- Number and location of monitoring consoles: switchers allow multiple cameras to be displayed on one or more monitors; time-lapse video cassette recorders are capable of condensing nearly 1,000 hours of continuous recording onto a single 120 minute VHS tape

- Distance between camera and monitor.

- Consider special environmental conditions for interior, exterior and hazardous locations.

- Staffing and number of console operators allocated for monitoring station.

SERVICES

D5

References: Electronic security systems

The key references for electronic security system design are applicable codes and standards, including:

- *Underwriters Laboratories (UL)*

UL 608   Burglar Resistant Vault Doors and Modular Panels
UL 609   Burglar Alarm Systems Local
UL 611   Burglar Alarm Systems Central Stations
UL 634   Standard for Connectors and Switches for Use with
            Burglar Alarm Systems
UL 636   Holdup Alarm Units and Systems
UL 639   Intrusion Detection Units
UL 681   Installation and Classification of Mercantile and
            Bank Burglar Alarm Systems
UL 972   Burglar Resistant Glazing Materials
UL 983   Surveillance Cameras
UL 1034   Burglary Resistant Electronic Locking Mechanism
UL 1037   Antitheft Alarms and Devices
UL 1076   Alarm System Units — Proprietary Burglar
UL 294   Access Control Systems

- *American Society for Testing Materials (ASTM)*

F12.10   Security Systems and Services
F12.40   Detection and Surveillance Systems and Services
F12.50   Locking Devices
F12.60   Controlled Access, Security Search and Screening

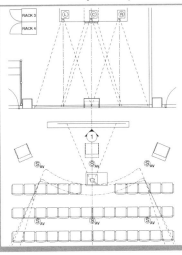

Electrical system specialties

Summary: Recent innovations in electronic systems for buildings include audiovisual and video conferencing systems and sound masking systems. This article provides an overview of the basic terminology and technology of these specialties for preliminary architectural design and coordination with electronic engineering specialists.

Key words: audiovisual facilities, electrical ground, fiber optics, speech privacy, sound masking, videoconferencing.

Uniformat:	D5040
MasterFormat:	11130
	16700

Continuing the discussion of electronic systems design presented in the prior article, the electronic specialties described in the article include:

1   Audiovisual facilities

2   Video distribution and video teleconferencing

3   Sound masking systems.

Acronyms and abbreviations

The following acronyms and abbreviations are useful in referring to the electronic system specialties described in this article.

AI   Articulation Index
ASTM American Society for Testing and Materials
ATM   Asynchronous Transfer Mode
AV   Audiovisual
CATV   Cable TV (originally, Community Antenna Television)
CCTV   Closed Circuit Television
dB   Decibels
EMT   Electrical metallic tubing
ISDN   Integrated Services Digital Network
LAN   Local Area Network
LCD   Liquid Crystal Display
MATV Master Antenna Television
NC   Noise Criteria
NEC   National Electric Code
NRC   Noise Reduction Coefficient
RF   Radio Frequency
RGB   Red, Green, Blue (used in video projector technology)
RT   Reverberation Time
RTA   Real Time Analyzer (used in acoustical measurement)
SPL   Sound Pressure Level
STC   Sound Transmission Class
TEF   Time-Energy-Frequency (used in acoustical measurement)
UL   Underwriters Laboratories
VDT   Video Display Terminal

1   Audiovisual facilities

An audiovisual facility is a specialized room that demands careful attention to space requirements for projection, audio, video, control, and computer equipment as well as to positioning and seating arrangements for presenters and meeting participants. Other elements of concern are environmental issues such as lighting, acoustics, and mechanical systems. It is important that these design issues are addressed at the initial stages of the design process. Establishing the appropriate

design criteria is essential not only to avoid expensive retrofitting, but to enable the AV facility to be used to its fullest potential. A successful facility may be realized only when adequate information regarding the user's needs is obtained, and by early design collaboration between the Architect, Engineers, and the AV designer.

An audiovisual facility provides the integration of different information technologies where presenters can interact with the systems for the purpose of presenting, training and lecturing. Audiovisual Facilities typically include:

-   front and/or rear projection screens.

-   projection equipment such as slide, video, and overhead transparency projectors.

-   audio systems for separate speech reinforcement and program sound amplification.

-   video system for playback of video tape, computer generated images, and CATV.

-   control system for remote control of AV equipment and the room environment.

-   computer system(s) for presentation applications.

Audiovisual facility space requirements

•   *Room size*

Proper room size is dependent upon the projected usage, that is, maximum number of participants to be accommodated, ceiling height, projected image size, provisions for front or rear projection, and whether flexible seating is desired to accommodate all options, that is, theater, classroom, U-shape, and so forth. When arranging the seating plan, it is critical to provide the required minimum distance between the front row of seating and the projection screen, which should be at least twice the height of the image to be projected. Also, the viewers seated closest to the screen should not need to rotate their eyes more than 30 degrees to see the top of the projected image (Fig. 1).

•   *Ceiling height*

The minimum ceiling height is predicated on the height of the projected image. The greater the distance to the most distant viewer, the greater the finished ceiling height must be. The sill height of the projection screen should be a minimum of 4 ft. (1.23 m) and if possible higher to avoid sightline conflict with the heads of seated persons. If the image is 6 ft. (1.8 m) high, the ceiling height must be at least 10 ft. (3 m), plus additional distance that may be required for framing and appearance details. If this clearance cannot be achieved, other options are:

Author: Andrew Prager

References: Specific references are listed at the end of each topic section.

SERVICES

D5

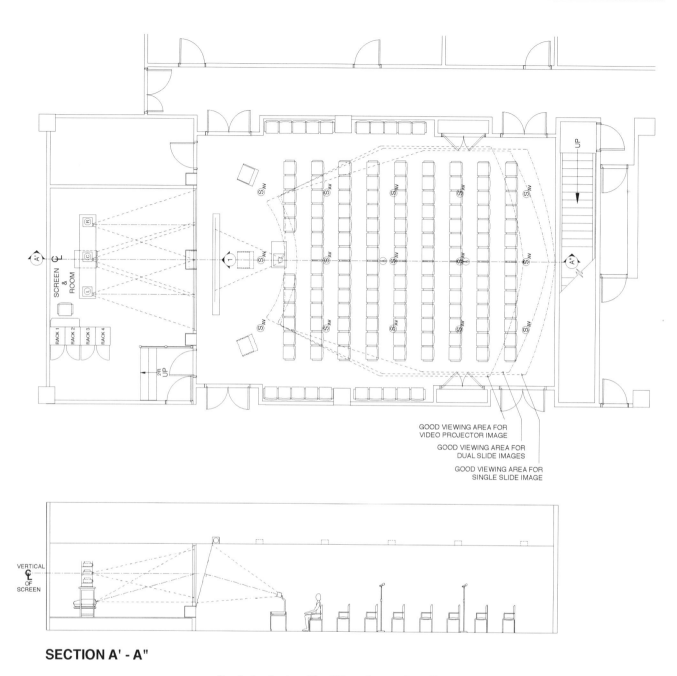

Fig. 1. Audiovisual facilities plan and section

Table 1. Typical aspect ratios of audiovisual images

Format	Aspect ratio - H:W
Video image	1:1.48
Slide image	1:1.33
Overhead transparency	1:1 (varies)
16mm film image	1:1.33

- sloping the ceiling up towards the screen wall (dependent on structural or mechanical conditions).

- utilizing tiered levels for fixed seating in an amphitheatre style (if the size of the room is adequate).

- limiting the seating arrangement to U-shape.

- rooms with staggered seating.

• *Projected image size*

The maximum distance from viewers in the last row to the projection screen should be eight times the height of the image for slides and six times the height of the image for (current technology) computer-generated images from a video projector (Fig. 2). The width of the image is determined by the aspect ratio of the format projected. Typical aspect ratios are indicated in Table 1.

Examples:

- If the furthest viewer is 36 ft. (11 m) from the projection screen, then the video image should be 6 ft. (1.8 m) high. Multiplying 6 ft. by the aspect ratio of 1:1.48 gives a projected image width of 8 ft. 10-1/2 in. Hence, the video projected image size is 6 ft. high x 8 ft. 10-1/2 in. wide (1.8 m high x 2.7 m wide).

- For slides, if the furthest viewer is 32 ft. (9.75 m) from the projection screen, divide 32 by 8 and the slide image is 4 ft. (1.22 m) high. 4 ft. multiplied by the aspect ratio of 1:1.33 equals 6 ft. Hence, the slide projected image is 4 ft. high x 6 ft. wide. (1.22 m high x 1.82 m wide).

Keep in mind that the projection of vertical slide images requires a screen size where the horizontal image size is equal to the vertical image size; therefore, the screen must accommodate an area of 6 x 6 ft. (1.82 x 1.82 m).

• *Rear projection vs. front projection*

There are advantages and disadvantages to each of these formats. Front projection is the most common. Advantages to front projection are that it doesn't necessarily require a separate room and provides the highest possible color fidelity. A disadvantage to front projection is that roll-down screens are not entirely rigid and can sway during a presentation, causing in and out of focus conditions.

Advantages to rear projection advantages include:

- allows ambient lighting levels to be higher for note taking, maintaining meeting participant alertness, and encouraging better eye contact with the presenter.

- people or objects crossing the screen do not cast shadows on the projected image.

- associated noise from equipment and operations personnel is isolated from the presentation space.

- ambient light spilling onto the front surface of the rear projection screen will not wash out a projected image to the same extent that it will on a front projection screen.

• *Rear projection room size*

A rear projection room must contain enough depth for projection throw distance to produce an image that is the correct size. Its basic plan and section is shown in Fig. 1. Two rules of thumb are:

- The rear projection room should be 1/3 the size of the usable conference room space, or

- The rear projection room should be three times the height of the required image size.

A more accurate method to determine rear projection room size uses formulas to determine throw distance based on focal length of the slide projector lenses (i.e., throw distance = image width x lens focal length/divided by 1.34), and manufacturer's specifications for video projectors (usually around 1.5 times the video image width).

In cases where the proper room depth is not possible, an alternative is to use mirrors that fold the optics of the projected beam to increase the length of the optical path, thus utilizing a minimum of space. The mirrors are made of high quality float glass, free from irregularities and impurities, and can be 1/4 in. or 3/8 in. (6.35 mm or 9.51 mm) thick depending on size. Mirrors should only be used as a last resort, due to inherent disadvantages such as vibration, cleaning maintenance, realignment requirements, and the general risk of damaging them.

Consideration should be given to providing the operator access behind the projection equipment—3 ft. (90 cm) is comfortable) for pro-

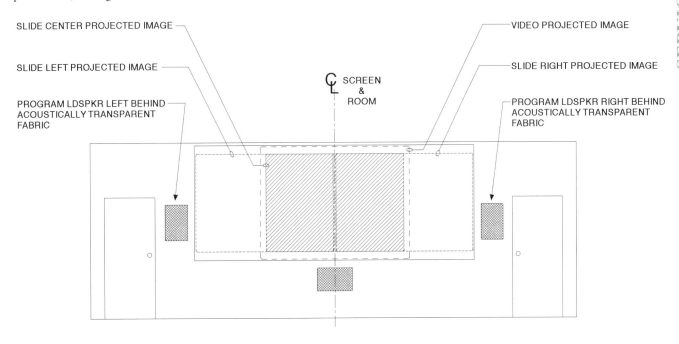

ELEVATION 1

Fig. 2. Elevation of teleconferencing facility projection wall and screen.

jector loading, slide-tray changing, and maintenance. Front operation is possible but not ideal. Slide projectors are usually table mounted with an adjustable slide projector stand or height extension base on a raised platform. This enables the horizontal center of the images to be coincident with the horizontal center of the screen.

A maximum three degree deviation between the centers of the slide projector lens and the screen is affordable before any noticeable keystoning or distortion occurs. Alternatives to rear projection rooms are a front projection cabinet or a front projection room in the back of the conference space, where only a 6 ft. (1.82 m) depth may be required.

Requirements for projection rooms

Space is required for equipment racks where the audio, video, control, and computer equipment reside. Additionally:

- Maintain a 3 ft. (90 cm) clearance behind equipment racks for installation and service.

- The footprint of a typical equipment rack is 22 in. (55 cm) wide by 26 in. (66 cm) deep and is 84 in. (2.13 m) high.

- There may be from two to four equipment racks, depending on the system's complexity.

- An operator's position may require a shelf 30 in. (76 cm) high x 12 in. (30 cm) deep and attached to one or several of the equipment racks.

- A raised access floor under equipment racks and projection support table is preferred for conduit routing of power and signal to feed equipment from below without unsightly cables exposed in the room.

- Railings shall be provided adjacent to riser steps for access flooring as required by applicable code.

- Omit windows or blackout windows with light-tight shades or cover over windows.

- Paint walls and ceiling slab or finished ceiling with a matte black, dark brown or charcoal gray to avoid unwanted reflection of light within the room.

- Do not use chrome finish for items such as railings, wall plates, light fixtures, and door accessories.

- Standard building florescent fixtures are suitable for maintenance lighting.

- For lighting during presentations, single or dual circuit track for track light fixtures that are low profile, 75 watts, a dark finish, and have a swivel function serve well.

- Glazing for a rear projection screen should be as recommended by the screen manufacturer.

- Frames are available from the screen manufacturer where glazing is installed in the factory and only blocking for the frame rough-in work is required before installation.

- Front projection rooms require a projection port utilizing float glass that is mounted with neoprene seals to provide acoustic isolation.

- The projection port shall be tilted 5 degrees from the vertical to deflect sound back towards the ceiling of the audience area.

Requirements for the conference room space

Rooms that have as one of their principal uses the proper setting for audiovisual presentation should provide for optimal technical display and control, but also recognize that such spaces are intended for comfortable human communication and ease of accommodation. The design and layout should therefore allow for different presentation styles, flexible seating, circulation within the space and entry/exiting that does not disrupt presentation. Also recognize that there are a wide variety of presentation formats, some involving many presenters at the front of the room, so that circulation space should permit different positions and movement of a presentation speaker or speakers. In addition to audiovisual presentation, critical technical requirements are related to lighting and acoustical control:

- Lighting should be zoned in such a way that front wall wash lighting fixtures can be dimmed to prevent light spill onto the screen during a presentation.

- A dimming control system can be utilized to preset and activate different scenes of lighting for different projection and conference modes.

- A sophisticated lighting system can be programmed with transitional scenes that can aid in the relief of eyestrain caused by the modulation from a dark projection mode to a bright presentation mode.

- Room finishes with hard acoustical properties such as sheetrock, wood, brick, concrete block, metal or aluminum, windows, and terrazzo floors cause reflections which can decrease the intelligibility of any sound, whether amplified or natural. Acoustically treated walls, ceilings, floors, and window coverings provide absorptive qualities that minimize reverberation and improve voice communication in the space; should include carpeting with underlayment, acoustical ceiling tile (with an NRC of .7 to .9), and medium weight drapes or curtains.

- Noise from mechanical systems should be minimized by low velocity air flow, supply registers with the appropriate acoustical rating (such as NC25 to NC28), and ducts lined with acoustical material.

- Noise from adjacent spaces can minimized with appropriate acoustical wall construction, door specifications, and glazing details for windows, front projection ports, and rear projection screens.

- Sound Transmission Class (STC) ratings for these items and ratings for NC and NRC should be specified by an acoustical consultant. Construction details, where appropriate, are also provided by the acoustician. (Also see the Part I article in this Volume, "Acoustics: theory and practice.")

Fixtures, furnishings and special mountings

Lecterns, built-in AV equipment, and special mounting supports are part of audiovisual facility design:

- Lecterns can either be stock items under the AV contract or custom designed millwork.

- AV equipment such as tape machines, video document camera, and computers can be built into walls, cabinets or credenzas for access by presenters.

- Special mounting supports will be required for ceiling-mounted video projectors and any TV monitors suspended from the ceiling.

Electrical infrastructure

Electrical power to audiovisual systems should be provided from a dedicated local circuit breaker panel, usually located in the projection room. Also note:

- Other utilities such as lighting, heavy motors, and convenience outlets (used for vacuum cleaners) should be not be fed from this panel.

- Where possible, three-wire dedicated or isolated ground plus hot and neutral should feed isolated ground receptacles in order to provide clean earth as the AC power safety ground; this grounding method complies with NEC Article 250.

- A grounding system for technical earthing should also be provided, to aid in preventing ground loops that are caused from dif-

SERVICES

D5

ferences in potential between the grounding of equipment where audio and/or video signal paths are connected.

- The frames of all equipment racks should be grounded via a grounding conductor from each rack, connected to a copper busbar, which is fed from the nearest cold water earth pipe, building steel with a low DC resistance to earth ground, or the isolated ground busbar within the circuit breaker panel.

- A raised access floor shall be grounded from the chassis of the circuit breaker panel, also to be considered as the building ground or conduit system ground.

- The conduit system for all low voltage cabling should be comprised of electrical metallic tubing (EMT) for physical protection and to prevent signal contamination.

- The conduits shall be bonded to the building's conduit ground system, as it will act as an additional shield to the cabling inside.

- Conduits are dedicated to specific signal levels to prevent crosstalk that can be induced from one signal level type cable to another.

- Conduits also should be separated by certain distances as a deterrent to crosstalk.

Signal characteristics and conduit separation requirements are indicated in Tables 2 and 3, respectively.

Audiovisual equipment

Projection systems such as slides, video and overhead transparency projectors are the most common equipment that establish the formats for large screen image viewing, including:

- Single image slides or dual side by side are most common.

- Slides can be front or rear projected. The horizontal centerline of the lens is the horizontal centerline of the projected image.

- Where it is not possible for centerlines to coincide, a maximum of 3 degrees deviation from the horizontal is permissible before any keystoning or distortion is detected.

- Video projectors can also project front or rear, and can be suspended from the ceiling or mounted in a floor cradle in a portable configuration.

- The horizontal centerline of the video projector lenses is at the top of the image when ceiling mounted and at the bottom of the image when projecting from the floor.

- The different types of video projectors (current technology) are: the three-gun (RGB) Schmidt optical system, the LCD light valve, and the LCD active matrix multi-media projector for smaller projection applications

- Overhead transparency projectors are generally used for front projection to enable the presenters to change their own transparencies.

- Another mode for using overhead projectors is in conjunction with an LCD projection panel fed from the VGA output of a computer to enable projection of computer generated images.

Audio systems

Audio systems required for audiovisual spaces may consist of two separate sound systems, one for speech reinforcement and one for amplification of program sound material.

- Speech reinforcement is accomplished through the use of microphones located at the lectern, head table, or even for the meeting participants in a larger space.

- Speech signals are mixed, processed, then amplified and delivered to flush mounted ceiling loudspeakers.

- Loudspeakers should be placed appropriately to provide even coverage with no "hot spots" or "holes" for the audience area.

- Uniform sound level throughout the audience area is measured with a pink noise signal, where 80 dBA is the target sound pressure level (SPL); with a tolerance of + or - 1.5 dBA.

- A formula to determine the distance between ceiling loudspeaker centers for even coverage based on 90-degree loudspeaker coverage pattern for speech, is the square root of 2, which is (1.4) x (ceiling height minus listener's ear level). Example: with a ceiling height of 10 ft. and with a seated ear level of 4 ft., the formula is 1.4 x (10 - 4), which equates to 1.4 x 6 = 8.4 ft. spacing, center to center, on a grid pattern. (The metric equivalent would read: 1.4 x 182 cm = 255 cm space, o.c.).

- Program sound material is defined as sound tracks from video tapes, computer programs, cable TV, and laser video disc, as well as audio cassette and compact disc.

- The loudspeaker system for program sound is stereo, whereby a loudspeaker is flush mounted on each side of the projection screen.

- Another option for loudspeaker placement when the screen size is too wide for adequate center coverage is below the screen.

- The ideal placement of the loudspeakers is at the listener's ear level: 4 ft. (1.21 m) seated and 5 ft.-10 in. (1.78 cm) standing; a compromise height of 6 ft. (1.83 cm) generally acceptable for both arrangements.

- If other room considerations dictate that the mounting requirement be higher, the loudspeakers may be tilted downwards.

- For more sophisticated applications, a surround sound program system will enable Dolby Pro-Logic or Dolby AC-3 encoded VCR tapes and laser video discs to be utilized.

Table 2. Signal characteristics

Signal	Level	Voltage	Sensitivity
Audio	Mic level	100mV to 500mV	Extremely sensitive
Audio	Line level	500mV to 5V	Mildly sensitive
Video	Baseband	500mV to 2V	Moderately sensitive
Video	Broadband	500mV to 2V	Moderately sensitive
Control	Digital	5V	Moderately sensitive
Control	Analog	24V	Moderately sensitive
Power	AC mains	120V/208V	none

Table 3. Conduit separation requirements

Sensitivity	Extreme	Moderate	Mild	None
Extreme	0"	3"	6"	12"
Moderate	3"	0"	3"	6"
Mild	6"	3"	0"	3"
None	12"	6"	3"	0"

SERVICES

D5

- Surround sound consists of front left, center, right loudspeakers as well as side left and right loudspeakers.

- Audio teleconferencing is available through the use of a digital telephone hybrid.

- Speech signals from the room are fed into the hybrid, sent over the telephone network to the remote caller's telephone; the remote signal is then fed in the other direction through the digital telephone hybrid and routed to the room's ceiling loudspeakers.

- Recording of these audio signals for training or archival purposes is also possible with a separately dedicated audio cassette recorder.

- If simultaneous interpretation is required, separate booths are dedicated for two interpreters for each language.

- The interpreter listens to the floor language with headphones and translates the signal simultaneously via microphone, while the signal is fed to a multi-channel wireless earphone system.

Video systems

Video systems are generally intended for playback and viewing of video material; although sometimes video recording or video teleconferencing is required. While equipment can be considered to be continually changing, current technology design considerations include:

- Sources that feed video projectors and monitors are typically video tape, computer generated images, video document camera, cable TV, internal RF distribution, laser disc, and baseband video signals via tie lines from another facility.

- The most widely used video tape format for audiovisual presentations is 1/2 in. (12.7 mm) VHS; others are 3/4 in. (19 mm) U-matic (almost obsolete) and 8mm (a popular consumer format).

- Slide-to-video units can be used to display slides via the video projector in place of a conventional slide projector. However, the currently available technology quality does not match the conventional method of showing slides.

- Video cameras can be set up in the room for the purpose of recording a presentation, meeting or preceding on to video tape, or for insertion into an RF video system, or broadcast to another meeting facility.

- Permanent video cameras can be remotely controlled from pan/tilt mechanisms all video sources are routed with their audio component via a video switcher that feeds distribution amplifiers, then the video projector, TV monitors, videocassette recorders, and external feeds.

- Video teleconferencing is achievable; however, additional special considerations for lighting, acoustics, interior finishes, seating arrangements and camera placement are recommended (see discussion below).

Control systems

Control systems enable remote control of various AV equipment and environmental functions. It is essential in planning the types and location of controls to consider the wide variety of presenter styles, including speakers who are unfamiliar with controls and/or otherwise preoccupied with their presentation content. Ease of use and communication with the control panel function and a variety of changes of speakers and formats within a presentation and conference area suggest a control panel that is accessible to both the speaker, but possible to one side, to permit fine-tuning adjustments of light, sound and image by a speaker assistant without interrupting the presenter. Related design considerations include:

- Control panels can be touch screen, illuminated push-button, hand held, wired or wireless and can be configured for flush mounting, consolette versions, or for equipment rack mounting.

- Control panels can be located at the lectern, the operator's control station at the equipment racks, in a flush mounted wall plate, or can be portable as in the case of the wireless hand-held or consolette.

- Virtually any combination or quantity of these panels can be utilized, depending on what is the best configuration for the room.

- The remote control of AV equipment typically operates the transport functions of any tape machine, such as an audio or video cassette recorder or player.

- Selection of volume control levels for speech, program, or audio teleconferencing may be remote.

- Slide projector system power is often accommodated on control panels.

- Audio teleconferencing controls are available to engage the telephone signal with the audio system.

- Audio sources to be heard and video sources to be displayed are control selectable.

- Projection screen raise/lower is a common remote control function.

- Environmental controls include the selection of different lighting scenes; drapes or curtains to open and close; movable walls or screen coverings that are motorized to open and close; controls interfaced with the mechanical system to enable remote control temperature settings for heating, air conditioning, and ventilation.

Audiovisual facilities installation

The overall design, its circulation and seating and its general environmental characteristics are the responsibility of the design team, including architecture, structure (if applicable), HVAC, lighting and acoustic configuration The design of the audiovisual systems by a professional AV Consultant should consist of drawings and specifications that are distributed to qualified AV Contractors for a competitive bidding process. The AV Contractor implements the design through fabrication, assembly, and wiring of the audiovisual systems.

Constant technological improvements are evident in audiovisual facility design, along with increasingly higher expectation of performance as users become more familiar with state-of-art and advanced audiovisual facilities design. Given the demanding nature of high performance installations, the following comments describe recommended practices for specialized audiovisual facilities:

- Even if the AV Contractors are not suppliers of the specified equipment, they should typically submit pricing as part of the base bid to allow bid returns to be compared as "apples-to-apples." This provides the Owner and design team with designated budget estimates.

- Bidders should be given an opportunity to offer alternatives of equipment by means of demonstrating to the AV Consultant, Architect, and Owner that there are advantages of technical performance, reliability, or cost savings. This provides for newly introduced technical developments.

- The successful bidder is required to submit shop drawings, perform pre-installation of equipment racks on their premises, then on-site installation of the equipment racks and wiring. This assures technical interface and coordination.

- After the installation is complete, the AV Contractor must perform proof-of-performance testing as specified by the AV Consultant. This provides documentation that the system is installed properly and performs to meet design specifications.

- The AV Consultant represents the interests of the Owner and the Architect by witnessing and participating in all final testing. This

SERVICES

D5

provides a clearly defined role and responsibility for coordination and quality assurance.

- As-built documentation consisting of completed systems drawings and operations manuals must be provided by the AV Contractor to the Owner. This record is essential for possible future adjustments and replacements.

- Training for the use and operation of the audiovisual systems is the responsibility of the AV Contractor, however, it is beneficial to the Owner for the AV Consultant to participate in the training process. This informs all parties in the case of future questions about system performance.

References: Audiovisual facilities

Ballou, Glen. 1990. *The New Audio Encyclopedia*. Indiana: Howard W. Sams & Co.

Davis, Don and Carolyn Davis. 1987. *Sound System Engineering*. 2nd edition. Indiana: Howard W. Sams & Co.

Wadsworth, Raymond H. 1983. *Basics for Audio and Visual Systems Design*. Indiana: Howard W. Sams & Co.

2   Video distribution and teleconferencing

As sophisticated AV installations become more common, it is important for design professionals to learn how these installations work and to be acquainted with the basic terminology used in AV design. The focus of the discussion in this section is on two widely used technologies, radio frequency (RF) video distribution and video teleconferencing. These systems can be integrated with one another, and together they carry certain design implications, both architectural and engineering, for overall facility design.

The term "audiovisual" (AV) may still invoke images of slides and overhead projectors, but today's sophisticated audiovisual installations are multimedia systems for information retrieval and display. In modern facilities with multiple meeting rooms (boardrooms, classrooms, computer training labs), a broad range of design and specification variables—cabling infrastructure, lighting, type and location of mechanical equipment, and furniture and finishes—may have a significant impact on an AV system's workability. In the past, the details of the AV design would be done in isolation from the project's architects, interior designers, and mechanical and electrical engineers. However, in an era of complex and highly interactive AV installations, that approach no longer suffices. Successful audiovisual system design depends upon close coordination among AV designers and other design professionals.

Radio frequency (RF) video distribution
Radio frequency (RF) video distribution—also known as broadband signal distribution—has the following characteristics:

- Currently the most common method for distributing video and audio signals.

- May be commonly called CATV (originally Community Antenna Television, now more commonly taken to mean cable TV) or MATV (Master Antenna Television), but these may only be program sources for the system as a whole.

- CATV (or Cable TV) was originally developed for communities that were located too deep in valleys between mountains to receive a signal from a nearby transmitter, these have evolved into fully wired systems.

- MATV refers to the reception and distribution of "off-air" signals throughout an office building or apartment building.

- Radio frequency (RF) distribution within a building allows network and cable TV stations to be combined with video program-

ming produced in-house, as well as programming from other in-house sources (VCRs, satellite feeds).

- For many applications, RF distribution is least costly and can provide the required versatility.

- Conventional RF distribution uses coaxial cable or twisted-pair cable with baluns; video may also be distributed via fiber-optic cable or through use of a LAN.

- Alternate methods of video and audio distribution, which are not RF signals, but instead use electro-optics and digital processing, include using fiber optics to transport baseband or encoded multichannel MPEG streams; transport technologies such as Asynchronous Transfer Mode (ATM) can provide a versatile protocol that allows multichannel MPEG transport over LANs (Local Area Networks).

- Each room using the system may have an outlet for use with portable monitor/ receivers, or might have built-in equipment, for viewing the distributed signal.

- In each of the rooms to which the system is linked, all of the system's channels can be accessed through an ordinary remote channel selector, with channel designations specific to the system: for example, channel 12 might always carry programming originating from a certain meeting room, while channel 21 might be designated for a local cable station, and channel 35 for use with a VCR.

- The available budget will play a role in determining the number of cable stations carried on an intrafacility system, because each cable station will require its own channel processor to convert the incoming signal (supplied by the local cable TV company) into a specific channel of the RF system; the greater the number of incoming channels, the greater the cost.

- A splitter/combiner takes all the separate RF sources and "squeezes" them into a single broadband signal that is distributed to the various RF outlets, or tap-offs, throughout a facility.
- The broadband signal will require greater amplification within the distribution line as the number of tap-offs increases.
- To allow for return channels, "subsplitting" can make the system bi-directional, which costs more, but provides flexibility, that is, reverse feeding a video camera to the head-end for distribution.

Baseband signals within the RF system

- Baseband refers to audio and video signals traveling separately through a system separate audio and video signals (from microphones and video cameras) of any programming produced on-site are combined by a device called a modulator, which converts them into a signal capable of being carried on the RF system.

- In a multi-purpose, multi-meeting-room facility, flexibility can be augmented by adding baseband tie-lines between the various meeting (or other) spaces and the central location housing the RF system's modulators (called the head-end).

- Signals from cameras and microphones may be patched into the modulators via in-room audio and video connection plates, to enable the use of these locations as in-house production sites for programming.

- Baseband tie-lines can also serve as a backup route for signals, in case of trouble with the broadband system or any of its components.

- Architects and engineers need to work closely with AV designers in mapping out areas in a facility that may be potentially used as additional production/reception sites, to ensure that the proper infrastructure is built in, and that design aspects (lighting and finishes) of these spaces are appropriate for such use.

Video teleconferencing

- *Space planning*

SERVICES

D5

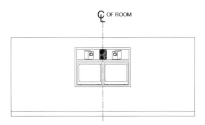

ELEVATION 1

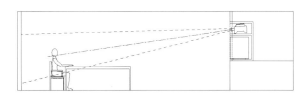

SECTION A' - A"

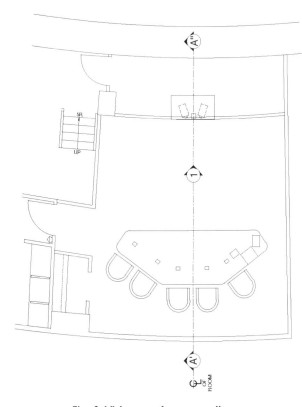

Fig. 3. Video conference suite

- Low-end, relatively inexpensive desktop video teleconferencing employs small, PC monitor-mounted cameras and can be run on ISDN voice/data lines.

- Fully equipped, dedicated video teleconferencing suites can, if desired, be interfaced with a facility's RF distribution system.

- Such suites are environments in which all design elements—lighting, mechanical systems, furniture, and finishes—are integrated, to foster conferees' comfort and to ensure high-quality transmission and reception of images.

- The layout of a video teleconferencing room usually includes two monitors at the front of the room, one small loudspeaker, and two cameras that are remotely controlled to pan, tilt, zoom, and focus (Fig. 3).

- The equipment is either integrated into the furniture, or housed in a "back of house" control room.

- Teleconferencing suites typically accommodate three to twelve people.

- At least two cameras will be needed when more than four conferees use the suite at a time, because their individual images on the TV screen might be too small for viewers to distinguish who is speaking; also, zooming and panning one camera can look awkward "on-air."

- *Lighting and HVAC*

- Color temperature of lighting must be correct for the cameras; the higher the color temperature, the more green the video camera sees.

- A good color temperature level for a video teleconferencing room is between 3200 and 3600 degrees Kelvin. For reference, daylight is 9500 Kelvin, fluorescent lighting is 2700 to 5000 Kelvin, and tungsten lights are around 2800.

- The light level for a video teleconference space is ideally 75 to 90 vertical foot candles at the desktop. For reference, typical light levels are: living room - 40 foot candles, kitchen - 75 foot candles, and television production studios - 100 to 120 foot candles.

- The mechanical system must provide sufficient cooling to offset the heat produced by the lights and equipment.

- *Acoustics*

- The mechanical system must be designed and situated so that its noise will be minimized and will not interfere with voice transmission.

- The teleconference room should not be located near areas that create noise, such as elevator machine rooms, or electrical closets with "humming" transformers and dimmers in a video teleconferencing space, the noise criteria (NC) rating should be 25 to 28. For reference, a typical office environment NC rating is 35 to 40; a broadcast television studio is specified at NC 25.

- The amount of sound that can penetrate a wall or door into an adjacent space is specified by its STC, or Sound Transmission Class.

- An STC of 55 for a teleconferencing space can be achieved by using double sheetrock walls with four-inch insulation between them.

- The acoustic tile used in the room's ceiling should have a noise reduction coefficient rating of 0.7. These coefficients range from 0.2 to 0.9, with the highest number being the most sound absorbent.

- RT ratings describe reverberation time, or how long it takes for sound to "decay" in a space; a very reflective room has a high RT60 rating. A video teleconference room should have an RT60 of no more than 500 ms (half a second).

- *Finishes, furnishings, and controls*

SERVICES

D5

- Wall finishes are important both for their acoustic and visual properties.

- The audiovisual consultant must coordinate with interior designers and lighting designers to make certain that all the suite's elements—including wall finishes, tabletop finishes, and backlighting—support the best possible transmission.

- The table for the conferees should ideally be trapezoidal or U-shaped, to allow for the greatest number of participants to be seated at a consistent distance from the cameras tabletop finishes should not be too dark, too light, or too reflective.

- Equipment on the table typically consists of low-profile surface-type microphones, and a touchscreen control panel.

- Voice-activated switching between cameras can be used, but can be triggered by coughs and sneezes.

- A sophisticated touchscreen control panel requires one of the conferees to operate it. (Fig. 4). Additionally, a camera dedicated for the purpose of transmitting documents and transparencies, a "document-viewing camera," can be positioned pointing straight down over the table.

- A custom light box may be built into the table to provide backlighting that will allow transparencies to be transmitted via the document viewing camera.

- Certain patterns and textures should be avoided in wall coverings and upholstery, as they can cause distracting *moiré* effects on-camera. Backlighting behind conferees—probably in the form of a wall-wash—will be needed to insure that the televised image will not appear too flat, as if the participants were painted on the wall.

- A VCR or other video player may be linked to the teleconferencing system, enabling all the conference participants at both ends of the video conference to view a videotape simultaneously.

- Video teleconferencing can be married to the RF distribution system of a multi-meeting-room facility through baseband tie-lines; people in the other rooms will be able to observe the teleconference, though they won't be able to participate.

Cabling and wiring

- In designing the signal infrastructure, it is preferable to separate different signal levels. Microphone-level signals should not be mixed with loudspeaker-level signals.

- Video and audio line-level signals should be separated to avoid the possibility of signal contamination or crosstalk.

- Specifying separate conduits for RF system cables and other video/audio cables can help prevent problems during a project's installation phase, when different contractors might be pulling cables through the same conduit.

- Conduits for power cables with high current need to be kept apart from audiovisual cable conduits to prevent the induction of a 60 Hz field caused by electromagnetic interference.

- Grounding must follow good engineering practices to minimize noise from interference and to adhere to electrical safety codes.

- If the system is grounded in too many places (creating ground loops) or the ground is not connected where it should be ("floating" ground), unwanted effects may be created, such as a "hum" in the audio signal and/or vertically rolling "hum-bars" in the video image.

- Careful collaboration between the AV consultant and electrical design professionals is essential to the system's performance. Refer to the discussion in the prior sections regarding quality control procedures in contracting and installation.

References: Video distribution and teleconferencing

Besinger, Charles. 1983. *The Video Guide.* 3rd edition. Indiana: Howard W. Sams & Co.

Cunningham, John. 1980. *Cable Television.* 2nd edition. Indiana: Howard W. Sams & Co.

Wadsworth, Raymond H. 1983. *Basics for Audio and Visual Systems Design.* Indiana: Howard W. Sams & Co.

3   Sound masking systems

Conversations and background noise can reduce work effectiveness through distraction and annoyance, disturbing the ability to concentrate and thus reduce productivity of any activity. Further, there is a psychological aspect of being overheard or of disturbing others that inhibits ones sense of privacy, particularly in open office plans. Or, alternatively, because an individual can't see the person in the adjacent space, he or she may have a false sense of privacy and feel comfortable talking more loudly than usual on the telephone or to a visitor.

Sound masking is a relatively new technology that is able to reduce the apparent level and effective intrusiveness of ambient speech and other noise, enhancing the perception of privacy in the work environment, which in turn improves the individual's capacity for focus and efficiency.

A sound masking system does not make a noisy space quiet. Rather, its function is to contribute to speech privacy by creating an acoustical background at a level that is regular and not disturbing, thus "drowning out erratic noises. The system is designed to provide a uniform and continuous level of background sound that contains all the frequency bands where human speech occurs. The sound masking system is functioning properly when it is not noticed, since the source of the sound is non-directional and concealed above the finished ceiling.

Sound masking systems are most frequently utilized in open office plan spaces, enclosed offices, hospitals, libraries, motels, and multi-tenant residences.

Characteristics of sound masking systems

The development of these systems dates from the 1960's when it was realized that the noise from HVAC supply registers, to some degree, actually served to improve speech privacy in offices.

- Up to a 40% improvement in speech privacy can be obtained with a sound masking system.

- Sound absorbing materials used on open office plan partitions (without the use of sound masking) will absorb some background noise, but not the frequencies of sound that characterize speech.

- Sound masking is not appropriate for all situations. There may be open office spaces where sound masking is not desirable, as in the case of a brokerage firm with a bullpen, where vocal interaction is essential to the work process.

Enclosing office spaces into separate cubicles does not necessarily guarantee adequate speech privacy, especially if wall partitions do not run as a continuously sealed separation from slab-to-slab. Voices outside the office may still be heard inside, and voices inside the office may be heard outside.

- Sound travels through air and thus through any cracks or voids in a partitioning system. If partitions extend from slab-to-slab, acoustical transmission can still occur if the walls are too thin, are not constructed with sound attenuation material, or if penetrations through the partition above the finished ceiling for electrical conduit, sprinkler pipes, or HVAC ducts are not properly sealed with acoustical caulking.

- Sound masking has proven to be very effective in enclosed offices where walls are constructed only to the finished ceiling level and/or are otherwise unable to be acoustically isolated.

- Intrusive speech signals are masked in enclosed offices with the same devices as are used in open office plans.

Sound masking system costs and planning

Sound masking should be planned during the initial stages of design. Although it is an element of construction that can't be seen, one should not neglect to consider the installation of sound masking as a benefit to overall space quality. Specifically:

- The proper sound masking "loudspeaker" devices should be installed during the construction period, when the ceiling is most accessible.

- If the sound masking system is in place from the start of the office operation, it will go unnoticed by office personnel, and thus be more effective. Installation after the opening of the office will require that the system be adjusted in small increments (for it to be introduced so as not to disrupt what people are used to); it will take time to have the system operating at full level.

- Installation cost is reasonable if part of other construction, with access to ceiling voids during new construction or renovation. To retrofit the system once the office is in operation, installers must access the ceiling after normal working hours, which could double the cost of installation, when priced as a separate item.

- The cost of sound masking is easily offset by the avoidance of the cost of extensive acoustical treatments. For example, sound masking is also much more cost-effective than slab-to-slab wall partitions.

- Wall partitions take up more floor space than open plan furniture, so utilization of a building floor plate is poorer with partitioning that is introduced for acoustical separation, compared to an open office with sound masking.

Recommendations for speech privacy

Sound masking is part of an integrated approach to a pleasant and productive acoustical environment. To assure a high degree of speech privacy, additional design provisions, along with sound masking, should include:

- Open office furniture with acoustical panels, as well as wall construction and absorbent ceiling material that allow the sound masking signal to penetrate below the ceiling plenum.

- Sound masking systems will not be effective in areas where there is no carpet, where there are no vertical partitions, or where partitions have excessive space at their bottom edges.

- If the ceiling is essentially "hard-surfaced," such as sheetrock, plaster, metal pan, wood or even painted acoustical tile, a masking system will be ineffective.

- For the purpose of absorption, open office plan partition panels and lay-in acoustic ceiling tile should have a high NRC (Noise Reduction Coefficient) of 0.7 to 0.9.

- "Hot spots" in the system may be caused by air return grilles in the ceiling. The best solution to this potential problem is to carefully coordinate the locations of the mechanical system grilles with the architect, interior designer and HVAC engineer early in the design phase, so their positions are effective for HVAC, but do not adversely affect the sound masking system's efficiency.

Articulation Index

Articulation Index is a measurement of the extent to which speech is articulate or clearly heard enough to be intelligible and is thus an inverse measure of speech privacy (Table 4). AI ratings range from AI 0.0 to AI 1.0. The higher the index number, the better the speech intelligibility from adjoining areas; thus, the higher the index number, the worse the speech privacy; for example, AI 0.0 indicates no speech intelligibility and AI 1.0 indicates good intelligibility, where everything can be heard.

Computer programs are used to provide simulation modeling to analyze the appropriateness and effectiveness of sound masking systems. With such specialized simulation modeling, the Articulation Index of an office plan can be predicted based on absorption of sound, density and type of office partitions and the presence of a properly adjusted sound masking system. Ideally, such analysis can occur in the design process before a space is fully designed and specified, in order to suggest design changes in partitioning, surfaces and other alternatives to achieve an optimum level of acoustical privacy.

Description of sound masking systems

Small sound masking systems have devices that are stand-alone, "plug-in" units.

- Systems that combine sound masking, background music, and paging can be installed with minimal additional cost.

- In many cases, a three-in-one sound system is not advisable, due to the diminished sound quality of the background music and paging with the use of sound masking loudspeaker devices.

- Typically, large-scale sound masking systems are used for open office plans. This type of sound system consists of a digital noise generator that feeds the masking sound, via audio distribution amplifiers, to zones of 1/3 octave equalizers, and then to power amplifiers which feed the sound masking loudspeaker devices, using a 70V distributed system (Fig. 5).

- The sound emanates upwards towards the slab from these devices and bounces or reflects off the slab to fill the plenum with sound.

- Sound masking loudspeaker devices are suspended by chains from the upper deck slab, or from structural members using beam clamps (Fig. 6)

- The sound penetrates the acoustical ceiling tiles of the occupied space in a uniform manner that avoids the "hot spots" that would occur with conventional ceiling loudspeaker devices that face down from the plane of the ceiling.

- It is a misnomer to call the sound masking signal "pink" or "white" noise; pink noise is properly defined as equal acoustic energy at all octaves; white noise is defined as acoustical energy with a 12dB per octave roll-off towards the lower octaves.

- In sound masking, the noise source is equalized to shape the sound to a particular curve that is best suited for sound masking and specifically intended to mask human speech, referred to as "NC-40 Contour." The NC-40 Contour consists of specific sound pressure levels at 1/3 octave frequencies between 200hz and 2Khz, below 200hz and above 2Khz, the curve provides a smooth natural roll-off (Table 5).

- The sound pressure level of the sound masking signal at 500 hz (the "0" reference frequency) must be 40dB, plus or minus 2.5dB, or the system will not perform optimally.

- An installation that does not have enough loudspeaker devices per area will have uneven coverage; this will be quite noticeable and distracting.

The success of the sound masking installation relies on the design, the installation, and the adjustment of the system with regard to equalization and level. These adjustments require a professional reading with a RTA (Real Time Analyzer) or TEF (Time-Energy-Frequency) instrument and a sound pressure level meter. Adjustments to the system are performed by the Audiovisual or Sound Contractor initially, then checked by the AV Consultant. Sound masking systems should be designed by a qualified AV consultant, acoustician, or electrical engineer and installed by an experienced electrical contractor and/or audiovisual or sound systems contractor.

SERVICES

D5

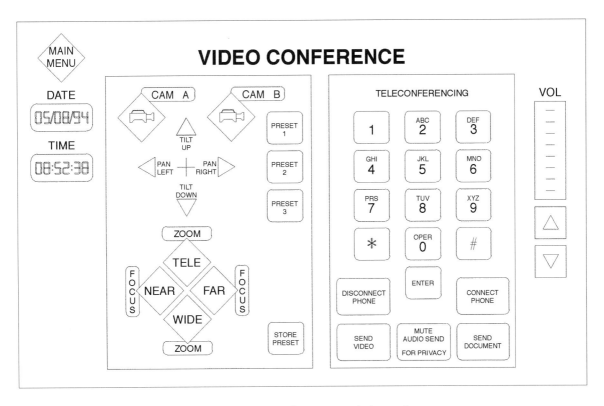

Fig. 4. Video conference control panel

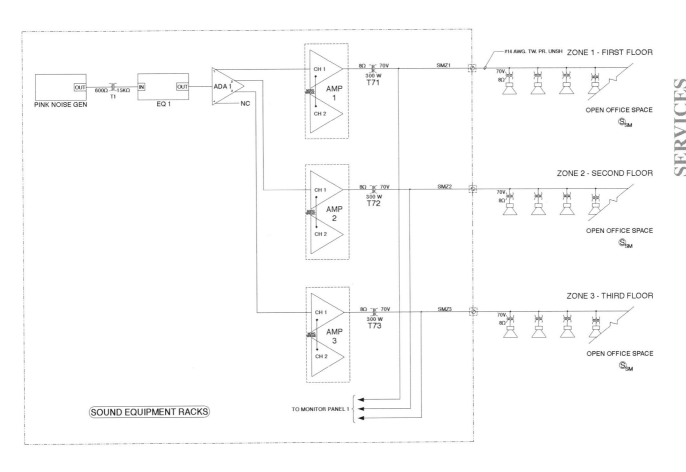

Fig. 5. Representative system layout of sound masking equipment

Table 4. Relationship between Articulation Index and degree of speech privacy

AI	Degree of Speech Privacy	% [1]
0.0		0
0.1	NORMAL	10
0.2		20
0.3		30
0.4	POOR	40
0.5		50
0.6		60
0.7		70
0.8	NONE	80
0.9		90
1.0		100

note [1] % = percent of words spoken that are intelligible

Table 5. NC-40 Contour equalization curve

Band - hz	Relative Level in dB - SPL
200	+4
250	+3
315	+2
400	+1
500	0
630	-1
800	-2
1000	-3
1250	-4
1600	-5
2000	-6

References: Sound masking systems

Associations and Manufacturers:

American Society for Testing and Materials (ASTM) Task Group E33.04C, Conshohocken, PA (610) 832-9598

Atlas/Soundolier, Fenton, MO (314) 349-3110

Dukane Corp., St. Charles, IL (630) 584-2300

Dynasound, Norcross, GA (800) 989-6275

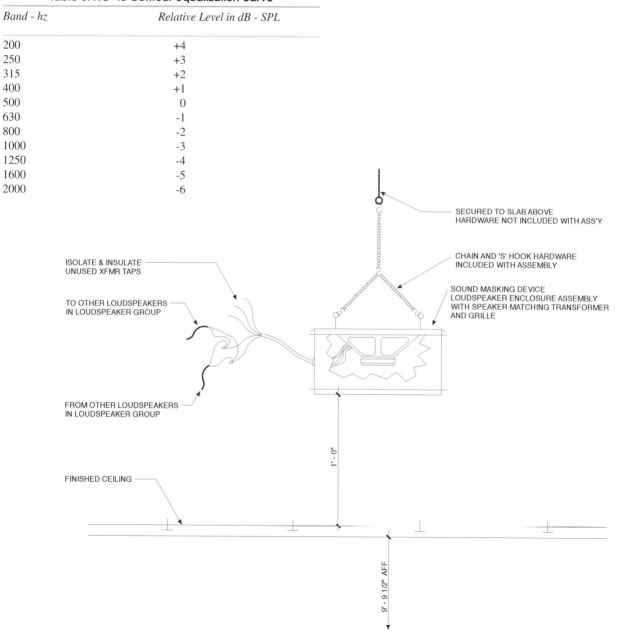

SECURED TO SLAB ABOVE
HARDWARE NOT INCLUDED WITH ASS'Y

CHAIN AND 'S' HOOK HARDWARE
INCLUDED WITH ASSEMBLY

SOUND MASKING DEVICE
LOUDSPEAKER ENCLOSURE ASSEMBLY
WITH SPEAKER MATCHING TRANSFORMER
AND GRILLE

ISOLATE & INSULATE
UNUSED XFMR TAPS

TO OTHER LOUDSPEAKERS
IN LOUDSPEAKER GROUP

FROM OTHER LOUDSPEAKERS
IN LOUDSPEAKER GROUP

FINISHED CEILING

1' - 0"

9' - 9 1/2" AFF

Fig. 6. Sound masking speaker installed within a suspended ceiling

SERVICES

D5

Lighting

Summary: This section presents information on the specification of lighting for architects, engineers and designers. General information on lighting is followed by application-specific information, including lighting for offices, schools, institutions and public facilities, and residences, and a checklist for lighting selection.

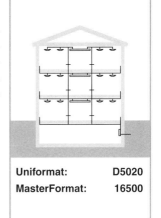

Key words: contrast ratio, electromagnetic spectrum, illumination, lighting design, luminaire, luminance, veiling reflections, visual performance.

Uniformat:	D5020
MasterFormat:	16500

This section presents information on the specification of lighting for architects, engineers and designers. It is based in part on information published by the Illuminating Engineering Society of North America (IESNA), of which IESNA (1993) is the principal reference for lighting designers and specifiers. Design and calculation data are presented. This section provides an overview and guide to published standards and recommended practices. In North America, IESNA is the principle source of technical information on lighting design and applications and works in close cooperation with the International Illumination Commission, or *Commission Internationale de l'Éclairage* (CIE), the worldwide body associated with the field of lighting.

1 Lighting fundamentals

For standardized definitions of lighting terminology, consult IESNA (1993) Ch. 34, "Glossary of Lighting Terminology."

Amperes (A): The unit of measure of electrical current.

Bulb: The glass enclosure of a lamp designed to contain inert gases, protect inner elements of the lamp and occasionally to determine distribution (diffuse or reflective).

Candlepower: The intensity of light from a source in a certain direction, and measured in candelas.

Coefficient of Utilization (CU): The ratio of illuminance to the lumens radiated for the light source.

Efficacy: The ratio of the approximate initial lumens produced by a light source divided by the necessary power to produce them (lumens per watt).

Footcandle (fc): A unit of illuminance measurement; the number of lumens that are incident on each square foot of work surface. 1 fc = 10.76 lux.

Illuminance: The light falling on a surface, measured in footcandles or lux.

Lamp: The mechanism which converts electricity into light by means of incandescent filament or gaseous discharge. Also used as the commonplace term for luminaires.

Lens: In a luminaire, an element which is used to alter or redirect light distribution using diffusion, refraction or filtration.

Light Loss Factor (LLF): The design factor that accounts for atmosphere dirt depreciation, normal degrading of lamp lumens over the life of the lamp, and other factors that add to the fact that less light is available over time.

Lumen (lm): A measure of total light-producing output of a source; the quantity of visible light emitted.

Luminaire: An assembly used to house one or more light sources (lamps), connect light and power sources and distribute light (also referred to as "light fixture").

Luminance: The emitted or reflected light from a surface in a particular direction, measured in candelas per square meter (cd/m^2). Formerly called photometric brightness.

Lux (lx): A unit of measurement used to gauge the illuminance falling on a surface; the number of lumens incident on each square meter of work surface. 1 lx = 0.093 footcandles.

Ohms: The unit of measure of resistance.

Visual acuity: A measure of the ability to distinguish fine details.

Volts (V): The unit of measure of electrical force.

Watts (W): The unit of measure of electric power; the power required to keep a current of 1 ampere flowing under the pressure of 1 volt.

Measurement of light

Light is visually perceived radiant energy, located between about 380 and 780 nanometers (nm; 1 nm = 10^{-9}) on the electromagnetic spectrum (Fig. 1). Light is only a small part of the entire electromagnetic spectrum which also includes x-rays, ultraviolet (UV) radiation, infrared (IR) radiation, and radio and television waves.

Electromagnetic radiation is measured in terms of its radiant power in Watts. However, not all visible wavelengths are evaluated equally by the human visual system. A given radiant power at 650 nm ("red" light) will not appear as bright as the same radiant power at 550 nm ("green" light). Furthermore, these relationships can change depending upon the overall ambient light level. Under typical indoor or daytime light levels, the visual system is most sensitive to a wavelength of 555 nm and sensitivity decreases for shorter or longer wavelengths. This is because photoreceptors in the retina, called *cones*, are used in daytime or *photopic* vision, and the cones are maximally sensitive to light at 555 nm (*cf.* Fig. 2, photopic or cone vision).

At very low levels, photoreceptors called rods are used for vision. This is called scotopic vision. Rods are maximally sensitive to light at

Author: John Bullough

Credits: Reviewers: Mark S. Rea, Lighting Research Center; Rita M. Harrold, Illuminating Engineering Society of North America.

References: IESNA. 1993. *Lighting Handbook: Reference and Application*, 8th edition. Rea, M.S., editor. New York: Illuminating Engineering Society of North America.

Additional references included at the end of this section.

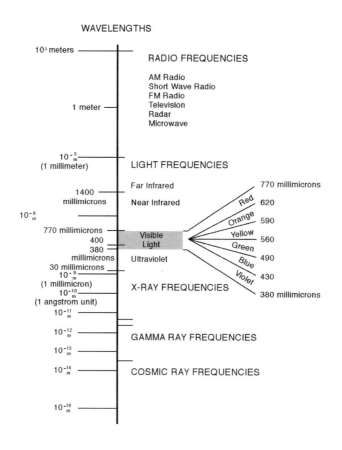

Fig. 1. The electromagnetic spectrum.

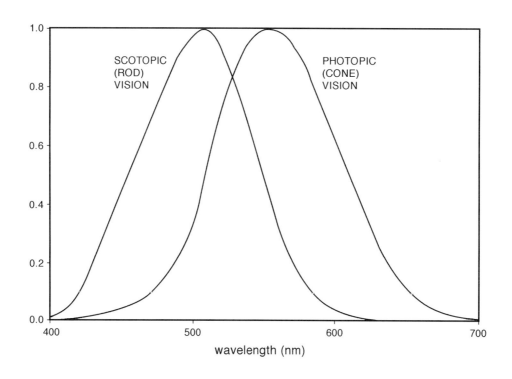

Fig. 2. The spectral sensitivity of cones (right) and rods (left).

507 nm (*cf.* Fig. 2, scotopic or rod vision). Scotopic vision is sometimes called nighttime vision, although most nighttime levels are actually in the range of levels called mesopic vision where the transition from cones to rods occurs and the maximal sensitivity will lie somewhere between 555 nm and 507 nm, depending upon the light level. At high mesopic light levels the maximum sensitivity will be closer to 555 nm and at low mesopic levels it will be near 507 nm.

Light is characterized in several different ways, as shown in Fig. 3. A point source with a uniform luminous intensity of 1 *candela* (cd) will produce a total of 4π, or about 12.56 lumens (lm). Furthermore, the luminous flux density, or illuminance, on the inner surface of the sphere will be 1 lm/ft^2 or 1 footcandle (fc) if the sphere radius is 1 ft., and will be 1 lm/m^2 or 1 lux (lx) if the sphere radius is 1 m. 1 fc is equal to 10.76 lx.

Light can also be measured in terms of luminance, which is the density of luminous intensity from a surface, in a particular direction. For many practical purposes, luminance is analogous to the perceived brightness of a surface. It is measured in cd/m^2.

The measures of light which are most commonly used by lighting specifiers and in recommendations of IESNA are *illuminance* and *luminance*. Portable meters for measuring illuminance and luminance in the built environment are available. Cf. Ch. 1 and 2 of IESNA (1993) "Light and Optics" and "Measurement of Light."

Color properties of lighting
Color properties of light sources are characterized in several ways. Two commonly used ways are the correlated color temperature and the color rendering index.

Correlated Color Temperature
The correlated color temperature (CCT) of a light source is a measure of its color appearance. It is based on the temperature in Kelvins (K) of a blackbody radiator that produces light of a certain color. Tungsten, used in incandescent lamp filaments, behaves much like a blackbody radiator. The temperature of a tungsten filament (about 2800 K in incandescent lamps) is equal to its CCT. CCTs of other lamp types are based on how close their color is to a blackbody radiator (or tungsten filament) of a certain temperature. At higher temperatures, a filament will become "bluer" in appearance. At lower temperatures, it will become "redder."

Color Rendering Index
The color rendering index (CRI) of a light source is a rating that is designed to correlate with a light source's ability to render several standard test colors. It has a maximum value of 100; a light source with a CRI approaching 100 will have good color rendering properties.

Optical Control
Light interacts with surfaces in several ways. It can be absorbed by some materials. Dark materials have a low reflectance and absorb more light than bright materials. It can be reflected by materials, such as a mirror or a painted wall. In the case of a mirror, the reflections are called *regular* or *specular* (Fig. 4); in the case of a wall, most of the reflected light is diffuse (Fig. 5). Light can be transmitted as through glass. Light can also be refracted. Fig. 6 shows how glass bends incident light rays. By using the optical properties of light, luminaires can use glass or clear plastic lenses to control the distribution of light through refraction, or can redirect light (through reflection) from elements such as parabolic or ellipsoidal reflectors.

The spectral (color) properties of materials affect the way they interact with light. For example, a red surface will reflect long visible wavelengths which are perceived as red light, and will absorb other wavelengths. A blue gel (filter) transmits short visible wavelengths which are perceived as blue light, and absorbs other wavelengths. (*Cf.* IESNA (1993) Ch. 1, "Light and Optics").

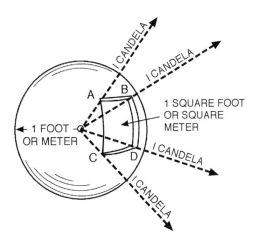

Fig. 3. Illustration of the relationship between intensity, luminous flux, and illuminance.

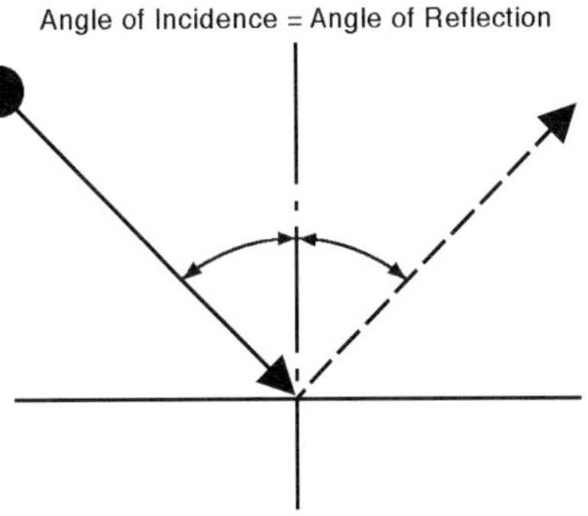

Angle of Incidence = Angle of Reflection

Fig. 4. Illustration of specular reflection.

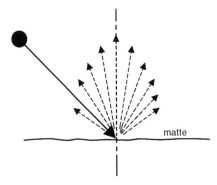

matte

Fig. 5. Illustration of diffuse reflection.

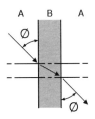

Density A:B = 1:2

Fig. 6. Refraction of a ray of light by glass.

Lighting and vision

Visual Performance

A primary purpose of lighting in the built environment is to aid vision. Owing to the concern for energy conservation, there has been a desire to provide enough light to allow people to safely and accurately perform visual tasks, without providing excessive lighting which could in fact waste electric energy. Thus, an understanding of visual tasks and the factors that affect visual performance can aid in providing the appropriate level of lighting for those tasks. Visual performance is affected by several factors. Those which are inherent in the task (largely independent of lighting) are discussed first:

- contrast
- size
- time

Contrast refers to the luminance difference between the critical detail of a task and its immediate background. A reading task such as black print on white paper has a very high contrast, approaching 1, while a sewing task involving white thread on white fabric will have a very low contrast, approaching 0. As the contrast of a task increases, performance will also increase (Rea 1986). However, once contrast is sufficiently high, further increases in contrast will have little effect on visual performance.

The *size* of the visual task is also important. A task with an infinitesimally small size will be invisible, with visibility increasing as size increases. As with contrast, once the size is sufficiently large, making it larger will not increase visual performance very much. For example, visual performance while reading 6-point type might be significantly better than visual performance reading 4-point type; but visual performance while reading 16-point type would only be marginally better than visual performance reading 14-point type.

The *time* a visual task is presented also affects visual performance. For visual tasks which are visible for only very brief periods of time (less than 0.1 sec), the intensity and time are traded off, such that a signal which appears for half the time of a second signal would need to be twice as intense to be as visible as the second signal. Many visual tasks for which lighting is specified, such as reading or drafting, appear for extended periods of time. For such tasks, time of presentation is not a factor.

For a visual task with a specific contrast, size and time of presentation, lighting directly affects an another factor which helps determine the overall visual performance. Unless a task is self-luminous, such as a Video Display Terminal (VDT) screen, the *task background luminance* is affected by the illuminance falling on the task surface and by the reflectance of the task. For example, a dark table top will have a much lower luminance than a white sheet of paper if both have the same illuminance falling on them, because the reflectance of the table top is much lower than that of paper. For diffuse (matte) surfaces, the luminance (L, in cd/m^2) of the surface can be estimated if the reflectance of the surface (r: ranging from 0 to 1) and the illuminance on the surface (E, in lx; multiply fc by 10.76 to obtain lx) are known according to the formula:

$$L = rE/\pi$$

The reflectance of a surface can be determined if its Munsell value (or lightness) is known. Table 1 lists the approximate equivalent reflectance for Munsell values from 0 to 10.

Task luminance affects the lowest contrast that can be detected. As the luminance is increased, the minimum contrast decreases so that contrasts which are invisible at low luminances may become visible at higher luminances. Similarly, *visual acuity* (ability to distinguish detail of the smallest objects that can be seen) improves with increas-

Table 1. Equivalent reflectances and Munsell values.

Munsell Value	Reflectance
0	0.00
1	0.01
2	0.03
3	0.06
4	0.12
5	1.19
6	0.29
7	0.42
8	0.58
9	0.77
1-	1.00

ing light levels. In addition, both speed and accuracy of visual processing improves with higher light levels.

Performance of a visual task improves with higher and higher light levels, although the rate of improvement decreases when the light level is high. This "plateau" effect is inherent to most visual tasks encountered in the work place or the home when objects in the field of view are well above the visual threshold (Rea 1986). For very fine, low contrast visual tasks, however, the light level will have a relatively larger impact on visual performance. Ch. 3 of IESNA (1993) "Vision and Perception" provides additional data about the interactions between lighting and vision.

In addition, the age of the occupant should be considered when planning the lighting in a space. The amount of light reaching the retina of a 50-year-old person is approximately 50% of that for a 20-year-old. As a result, lighting requirements for older persons differ from those of young people.

Veiling Reflections and Glare

Lighting also indirectly affects visual performance in several ways. When the task contains primarily specular (shiny) surfaces, such as a Video Display Terminal (VDT) or glossy magazine, light sources in some locations can cause veiling reflections that create a luminous veil over the visual task, reducing contrast and lowering visual performance. Note that for some tasks, especially some industrial inspection tasks, reflections can actually enhance one's ability to see, for example, scratches or chips in a metal plate (see *Industrial Lighting* below).

Bright sources of light such as bare lamps or windows, can also cause disability glare by creating scattered light within the eye. Such light acts to reduce the luminance contrast of the resulting retinal image inside the eye, and in essence, acts like a luminous veil. The scattered light may or may not cause discomfort. The lighting designer/specifier should consider the task-luminaire geometry in the space and take care to avoid veiling reflections and excessively bright luminaires and lamps, by using proper positioning and shielding.

Glare becomes more of a critical issue as people age due to scattered light in the lens of the eye. When very bright sources (or surfaces) exist within a space, they may cause discomfort glare, an annoying or painful sensation caused by the nonuniformity of lighting. Visual performance need not be impaired for discomfort glare to exist. The lighting designer/specifier can reduce discomfort glare in spaces by the following means:

- decreasing the luminance of the offending source of light.
- reducing the area or size of the offending source.

SERVICES

D5

- increasing the luminance of surfaces surrounding the offending source.

Ratings of discomfort glare can be calculated for specific lighting geometries. In the United States, *visual comfort probability* (VCP) is defined as the percentage of people who are likely to find a lighting system comfortable (that is, not creating discomfort glare). VCP itself is derived from the *discomfort glare rating* (DGR). The formulations for DGR and VCP are complex; see Ch. 9 of IESNA (1993), "Lighting Calculations."

IESNA recommends that to avoid discomfort glare, the VCP rating for any lighting system be no less than 70. In addition, maximum luminaire luminances at specific angles from the luminaire should not exceed the following values:

- 45° above nadir (the nadir is the point directly below the luminaire): 7710 cd/m^2

- 55° above nadir: 5500 cd/m^2

- 65° above nadir: 3860 cd/m^2

- 75° above nadir: 2570 cd/m^2

- 85° above nadir: 1695 cd/m^2

Lighting and psychology

In addition to its effects on vision, lighting can affect one's impressions of a space. Although visual performance will improve with increasing light levels, the light level can become excessive if people find spaces "too bright."

Spatial distributions of light are also important. Several researchers have investigated the *ratio of luminances* among the visual task, immediate surround (such as a desk top) and even the room surfaces which people preferred. These results have led to the recommendation of luminance ratios for various applications, such as offices, schools, industry and residences (see sections on specific applications).

Lighting can reinforce the intended mood of a room. Research has resulted in some approaches to lighting a space that tend to reinforce certain subjective impressions (Flynn 1977), including the following. Cf. IESNA (1993) Ch. 3, "Vision and Perception," and Ch. 10, "Lighting Design Process."

- *Visual clarity:* reinforced by bright, uniform lighting combined with high brightness of the walls.

- *Spaciousness:* reinforced by uniform (not necessarily bright) wall lighting.

- *Relaxation:* reinforced by non-uniform lighting and lower ceiling brightness.

- *Privacy/intimacy:* reinforced by non-uniform lighting (low levels around the occupants, higher levels further away).

- *Pleasantness/preference:* reinforced by non-uniform lighting with high wall brightness.

Lighting and biology

Lighting also affects people's biology (cf. IESNA 1993 Ch. 5, "Nonvisual Effects of Radiant Energy"). Direct visual exposure to very intense light sources—such as discharge arcs, filaments, and the sun—can damage the retina. Shielding of these sources by luminaire housings or other means is required to prevent retinal burns. Organizations such as the American Conference of Governmental Industrial Hygienists (ACGIH) publish recommendations for exposure limits to potentially hazardous light sources.

Other nonvisual effects of light which the lighting specifier should be aware of are its use in phototherapy for seasonal affective disorder (SAD) and hyperbilirubinemia (neonatal jaundice). Lighting also has important effects on circadian (day/night) rhythms, such as body temperature and hormone secretion cycles, and can impact, for example, the performance and mood of night shift workers (Boyce *et al.* 1996).

2   Light sources

Several types of light sources are commonly used in electric lighting systems. Consult Elenbaas (1972) or Ch. 6 of IESNA (1993), "Light Sources," for detailed technical information on electric light sources. The best type of light source for an application will depend several factors:

- light level needed.

- required lamp life.

- energy use (lamp efficacy).

- lumen maintenance (reduction in light output throughout lamp life).

- color rendering properties.

- optical control.

- restart characteristics.

- luminaire costs.

- operating costs.

- cost of auxiliary equipment (if needed).

Common light source types are compared according to several important characteristics in Table 2.

Incandescent Lamps

Incandescent lamps are available in many shapes and sizes (Fig. 7). Lamps are designated by a letter corresponding to the bulb shape and a number corresponding to the bulb diameter (in multiples of 1/8 in.). An A-19 lamp, therefore, designates a type "A" bulb (the typical household bulb shape) that is 19/8 or 2-3/8 in. (60 mm) in diameter.

Incandescent lamps have a filament (usually of tungsten) inside a glass envelope (or bulb). When a current is applied across the filament, it becomes so hot (around 2800 K) as to radiate light. Incandescent sources also generate significant heat (radiation in the infrared or IR region of the spectrum).

Incandescent lamps are often used in applications where color rendering is very important. They have a color rendering index (CRI) approaching 100. Typical incandescent lamps have luminous efficacies ranging from about 10 to 20 lm/W. Tungsten-halogen lamps, which are incandescent lamps with a halogen gas, are more efficient than standard incandescent lamps and have luminous efficacies ranging from 25 to 35 lm/W.

Reducing the voltage has the following effects on an incandescent lamp:

- reducing the lumens produced by the lamp (dimming).

- increasing lamp life.

- reducing the lamp efficacy (lm/W).

- decreasing the CCT (creating a "warmer" color).

It can be seen that light output and efficacy are reduced at lower voltages, while lamp life is significantly increased. This fact is sometimes used to extend the life of incandescent lamps in some applications, since the average operating life of most incandescent lamps is usually around 750 to 1000 hours.

Fluorescent Lamps

Fluorescent lamps are low-pressure gas discharge sources, where light is produced mainly by fluorescent powder coatings (phosphors) that are activated by UV energy generated by a mercury arc. Fluorescent lamps usually consist of glass tubes with electrodes at either end. The tubes contain mercury vapor at low pressure with a small amount

SERVICES

D5

Table 2. Common light source characteristics. (Compiled by R. M. Harrold)

Incandescent including properties/ specifications	tungsten halogen	Fluorescent	High - intensity discharge			
			Mercury - vapor (self - ballasted)	Metal halide	High pressure sodium (improved color)	Low pressure sodium
Wattages (lamp only)	15 - 1,500	15 - 219	40 - 1,000	175 - 1,000	70 - 1,000	60 - 180
Life (hours)	750 - 12,000	7,500 - 24,000	16,000 - 24,000	1500 - 15,000	24,000 (7500)	16,000
Efficacy, lumens per watt (lamp only)	15-25	55-100	50-60 (20 - 25)	80-100	75-140 (67 - 112)	Up to 180
Lumen maintenance	Fair to excellent	Fair to excellent	Very good (good)	Good	Excellent	Excellent
Color rendition	Excellent	Good to excellent	Poor to excellent	Very good	Fair (very good)	Poor
Light direction control	Very good to excellent	Fair	Very good	Very good	Very good	Fair
Source size	Compact	Extended	Compact	Compact	Compact	Extended
Relight time	Immediate	Immediate	3 - 10 minutes	10 - 20 minutes	Less than 1 minute	Immediate
Comparative fixture cost	Low—simple fixtures	Moderate	Higher than incandescent and fluorescent	Generally higher than mercury	High	High
Comparative operating cost	High—short life and low efficacy	Lower than incandescent	Lower than incandescent	Lower than mercury	Lowest of HID types	Low
Auxiliary equipment needed	Not needed	Needed— medium cost	Needed— high cost	Needed— high cost	Needed— high cost	Needed— high cost

SERVICES

D5

of an inert gas. The phosphors are applied to the inside of the glass tubes. When a current is applied to the electrodes, an arc forms which radiates some light, but radiates mostly UV energy. This UV energy excites the chemicals in the phosphors, which in turn emit light. Fluorescent lamps have a typical rated life of between 8,000 and 20,000 hours.

Fluorescent lamps require a ballast to operate. The ballast provides the starting and operating voltages and currents that keep the fluorescent lamp operating properly. Several types of ballast are available: magnetic ballasts which operate at standard ac current frequency (60 Hz in North America) and electronic ballasts which operate lamps at frequencies between 10,000 and 50,000 Hz. Fluorescent lamp efficacy is increased by more than 10% when electronic ballasts are used. Ballasts also exist which permit fluorescent lamps to be dimmed.

Fluorescent lamps come in many shapes and sizes (Fig. 8). The notation is similar to that for incandescent lamps: for example, a T-8 lamp is one with a "T" (tubular) shape that is 8/8 or 1 in. (25 mm) in diameter. They can also be tuned to produce different colors, depending upon the type and amount of phosphors they have. For most typical lighting applications, fluorescent lamps can be created with CCTs ranging from 2500 K to 6000 K.

The output of fluorescent lamps is dependent upon the ambient temperature and the operating position of the lamp. The temperatures within enclosed luminaires can become quite high in some conditions and the amount of light will be affected. Ventilated luminaires can be used to alleviate this problem somewhat.

Two main types of phosphors are used in fluorescent lamps. The first are the halophosphate types. These phosphors are used to create the "warm white" and "cool white" lamps. Note that 40-W 4 ft. (1220 mm) warm white and cool white T-12 lamps are being phased out of use in the U.S. to comply with federal energy legislation. Halophosphate coatings are still used on some energy-saving (34-W) lamps that comply with the energy legislation. CRI with halophosphate lamps tends to be between 50 and 60.

An increasingly used approach to fluorescent lamp phosphors is the triphosphor, or rare-earth phosphor system. Such lamps use three phosphors, each of which emits a narrow band of light in one of the primary color regions, mixed in various proportions to create different CCTs. Such lamps also tend to have very high CRIs (between 70 and 90).

Compact fluorescent lamps (CFLs) offer increased flexibility to lighting specifiers because their relatively small size means they can be substituted for incandescent lamps in some luminaires. Dedicated luminaires for CFLs also exist which take advantage of the better optical control that a compact source size allows. CFLs are designated by their shape and wattage: for example, a 13-W twin tube CFL will have the notation CFT13W (CFT indicates a compact fluorescent twin tube; 13W indicated the wattage). An 18-W quad (four) tube CFL will be designated CFQ18W.

Compared to incandescent lamps, fluorescent lamps are relatively diffuse, low-luminance sources. A T-8 fluorescent lamp has a surface luminance of around 10,000 cd/m²; a clear-bulb incandescent lamp filament can have a luminance exceeding 2,000,000 cd/m².

High-Intensity Discharge Lamps
High-intensity discharge (HID) lamps include mercury, metal halide (MH) and high-pressure sodium (HPS) lamps. Like incandescent lamps, they provide a relatively compact point of light; like fluorescent lamps, they are electric discharge lamps, tend to have long lives and require ballasts. Unlike both incandescent and fluorescent lamps, starting time for many HID lamps is on the order of several minutes.

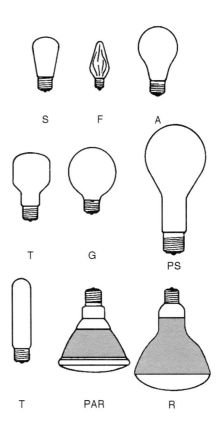

Fig. 7. Typical incandescent lamp shapes.

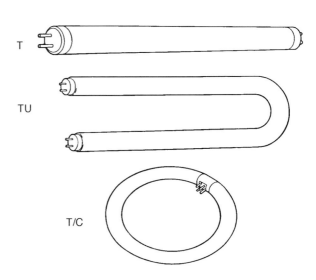

Fig. 8. Typical fluorescent lamp shapes.

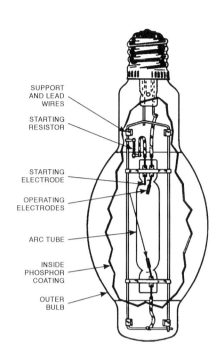

Fig. 9. Diagram of a mercury lamp; metal halide lamps have similar construction.

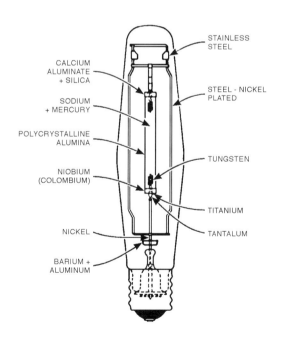

Fig. 10. Diagram of a high-pressure sodium lamp.

Mercury lamps: Light is produced in mercury lamps by applying a current through pressurized mercury vapor. Mercury lamps are constructed with two enclosures or envelopes (Fig. 9): an inner arc tube which contains the mercury arc, and an outer bulb which shields the arc tube from temperature fluctuations. The outer bulb also absorbs ultraviolet (UV) radiation produced by the arc and can be coated with phosphors similarly to fluorescent lamps. Mercury lamps have very long rated lives (16,000 to 24,000 hours).

Clear mercury lamps (with no phosphors) emit bluish-white light in several discrete wavelength bands from 405 to 579 nm. A deficiency of long wavelength energy results in poor color appearance of orange and red objects (which appear brown). Coated mercury lamps often use a phosphor which converts the UV radiation from the arc into long-wavelength visible light; this improves both the luminous efficacy and the CRI of the lamp. Typical mercury lamp efficacies are between 30 and 65 lm/W, and CRI ranges from 20 to 50.

Metal halide lamps: MH lamps are very similar in construction to mercury lamps, with the arc tube containing various metallic halide compounds in addition to mercury. These compounds emit light in different parts of the visible spectrum, and by using various mixtures of metallic halides, lamps with efficacies and CRIs much higher than mercury lamps are possible. Typical MH lamp efficacy ranges between 75 and 125 lm/W. CRI ranges from 60 to over 90, and CCT ranges from 3000 K (a warm white appearance) to over 6000 K (a very cool, bluish-white).

Compact MH lamps in relatively low wattages (70 to 150 W) exist which have a very high CRI (over 90) and can be used for accent display lighting. Many MH lamps are very sensitive to operating position with respect to color, efficacy and other operating characteristics. Some MH lamps are developed to be operated in a specific orientation.

High-pressure sodium lamps: HPS lamps produce light by applying a current to sodium vapor. Like mercury and MH lamps, HPS lamps have two envelopes (Fig. 10): an inner arc tube containing sodium and mercury, and an outer glass bulb to absorb UV energy and stabilize the temperature of the arc tube. Typical HPS lamp efficacies range between 45 and 150 lm/W, with rated lamp lives of about 24,000 hours.

HPS lamps radiate energy across the visible spectrum, although not uniformly. Light from standard HPS lamps is a golden-white color (CCT ranging from 1900 K to 2200 K) and color rendering is quite poor (CRI is 22). Improved color rendering HPS lamps can be created by increasing the sodium vapor pressure, which creates more long-wavelength energy and increases CRI to about 65 (while reducing efficacy and life), or by operating HPS lamps at higher frequencies (resulting in CCT between 2700 and 2800 K and CRI between 70 and 80).

Low-Pressure Sodium Lamps
In low-pressure sodium (LPS) lamps, light is generated by a current applied to sodium vapor at a lower pressure than that in an HPS lamp. The lamp shape is also different (more linear), since the arc itself is longer. These lamps emit a very narrow wavelength band of light near 589 nm and produce light that is yellow in appearance. Ballasts are required for operation of these lamps. They have fairly long rated lives (16,000 hours).

LPS lamps have very high efficacy, near 180 lm/W. Because they produce monochromatic light, color rendering is essentially nonexistent with these lamps (CRI of -44). LPS lamps are sometimes used for outdoor installations in the vicinity of observatories because it is relatively simple for the astronomical observers to filter out the narrow wavelength band emitted by LPS.

Other types of lamps
Although not discussed here, there are other types of light sources described in IESNA (1993) Ch. 6, "Light Sources:"

- electrodeless lamps: for compact sources with long rated lives

- compact-arc xenon and mercury lamps: for searchlights and projectors

- electroluminescent lamps: for instrument display panels or exit signs

- light-emitting diodes (LEDs): for display units or exit and emergency lighting

- carbon arc lamps: for projectors and spotlights

- gaslights: for historic lighting applications

Luminaires

A detailed treatment of luminaire types and design is presented in Ch. 7 of IESNA (1993), "Luminaires." This section briefly discusses several types of luminaires and some of their characteristics.

Interior luminaires
The CIE has developed several categories for interior luminaires:

- direct: providing 90-100% of its luminous output downward.

- semi-direct: providing 60-90% of its output downward.

- general diffuse: providing 40-60% of its output both downward and upward.

- direct-indirect: a general diffuse luminaire with little or no output at near-horizontal angles.

- semi-indirect: providing 60-90% of its output upward.

- indirect: providing 90-100% of its luminous output upward.

Luminaires can also be classified by their physical characteristics: recessed, ceiling-mounted, track-mounted, wall-mounted, suspended, architectural, and portable luminaires such as table lamps or plug-in torchieres (Figs. 11—17). It is important to consider that luminaires in buildings contribute to the heat produced in the building and can add to the cooling load (ASHRAE 1989). Proper integration of the lighting and HVAC systems will result in more economical building performance.

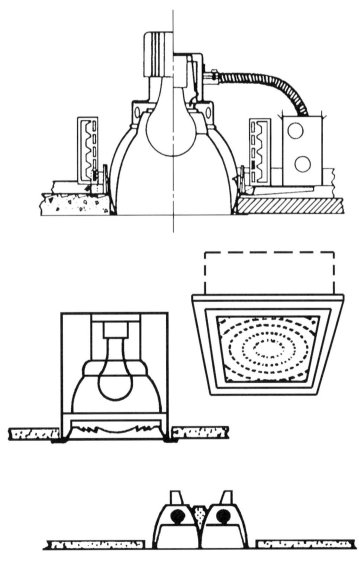

Fig. 11. Recessed luminaires.

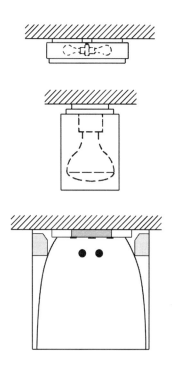

Fig. 12. Ceiling-mounted luminaires.

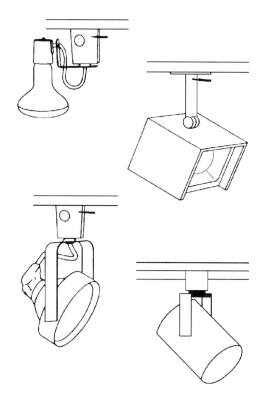

Fig. 13. Track-mounted luminaires.

SERVICES

D5

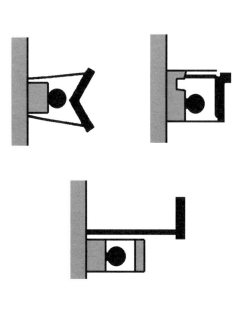

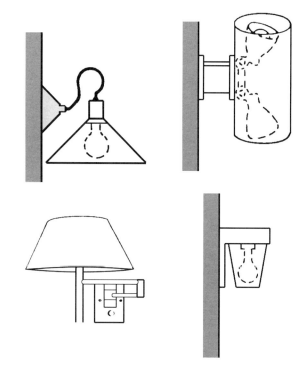

Fig. 14. Wall-mounted luminaires.

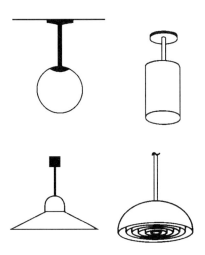

Fig. 15. Suspended luminaires.

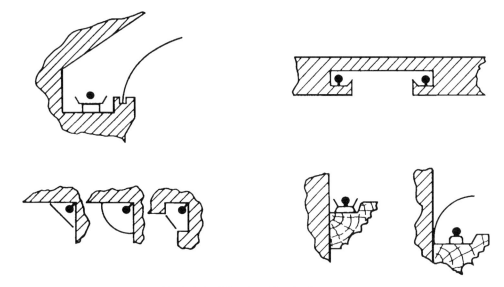

Fig. 16. Architectural luminaires.

Fig. 17. Portable luminaires.

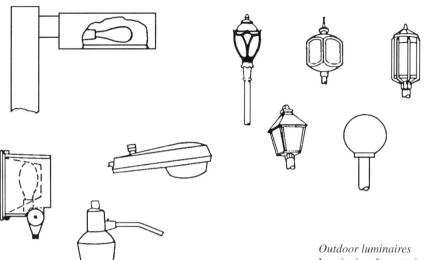

Fig. 18. Pole mounted luminaires.

Outdoor luminaires

Luminaires for exterior applications are classified by IESNA according to their intensity distribution and cutoff characteristics:

- Type I: narrow, symmetric distribution with maximum intensity at nadir (directly below the luminaire).

- Type II: wider distribution than Type I, maximum intensity 10°-20° from nadir.

- Type III: wide distribution, maximum intensity 25°-35° from nadir.

- Type IV: widest distribution.

- Type V: symmetrical distribution, circular illuminance pattern.

- Type VS or VQ: symmetrical distribution, square illuminance pattern.

Many outdoor luminaires use HID or LPS lamps. Outdoor fixtures include pole-mounted, surface-mounted, bollard-type, and landscape types (Figs. 18—21).

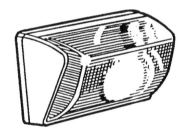

Fig. 19. Outdoor wall-mounted luminaire.

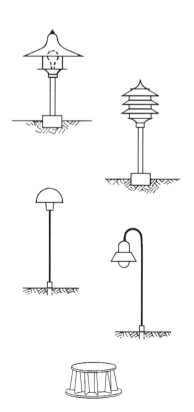

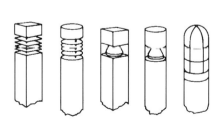

Fig. 20. Bollard luminaires.   **Fig. 21. Landscape luminaires.**

3   Lighting calculations

Ch. 9 "Lighting Calculations," and Ch. 12 "Basic Lighting Calculations" of IESNA (1993) describe principles and formulations that allow the designer/specifier to obtain information about the performance of a lighting installation. Two of the more useful methods that can be calculated by hand are briefly described here: the *inverse square cosine law* for calculating the illuminance at a point, and the *zonal cavity method* for estimating the average horizontal workplane illuminance in a space. Often, computer programs are required to perform more complex calculations.

Inverse Square Cosine Law

The illuminance E produced on any surface *A* centered at a point *P* is related to the luminous intensity *I* (in cd) of a light source or luminaire (in the direction of point *P*), the distance *D* between the source and the point *P*, and the angle x between the normal (or perpendicular) to the surface *A* and the direction along the distance *D* (Fig. 22). *E* can be calculated as:

$$E = (I \cos x)/D^2$$

This formula is called the inverse square cosine law. If *D* is measured in ft, then *E* is in fc; if *D* is measured in m, then *E* is in lx. Luminaire manufacturers publish luminous intensity (or candlepower) data at various angles from the luminaire which can be used to calculate the illuminance produced.

If the surface is diffuse (or matte), and the illuminance (*E*, in lx; 1 fc = 10.76 lx) and reflectance (r) of that surface is known, the luminance (*L*, in cd/m^2) of the surface can be estimated by the formula:

$$L = rE/\pi$$

One limitation of the inverse square cosine law is that the distance *D* should be greater than 5 times the greatest dimension of the light source or luminaire (the "five times" rule). Without this condition, calculations of illuminances can contain significant errors.

Zonal Cavity Method

The zonal cavity method is used to calculate the average maintained illuminance on the workplane in a room. Consult IESNA (1993) Ch. 9, "Lighting Calculations," for a detailed discussion of the calculation method and its limitations. The method as described here assumes a rectangular-shaped room, and that all walls have the same reflectance. It is also assumed that all room surfaces are diffuse (matte). Nondiffuse surfaces could result in different illuminances than would be calculated using this method.

Step 1: Determine room dimensions and reflectances. The length *l*, width *w*, ceiling reflectance r_c, wall reflectance r_w and floor reflectance r_f must be determined or estimated. Commonly used estimates for the reflectances are 0.8 for r_c, 0.5 for r_w and 0.2 for r_f if they are not known.

It is also necessary to calculate the height of the three "cavities" used in subsequent calculations, the ceiling cavity, the room cavity and the floor cavity (see Fig. 23). The ceiling cavity height h_{cc} is the vertical distance between the ceiling and the luminaires. If recessed or ceiling-mounted luminaires are used, then h_{cc} is 0. The room cavity height, h_{rc}, is the vertical distance between the luminaires and the workplane. A typical workplane height is 2.5 ft (0.75 m), which is a common height of desk and table tops. Finally, the floor cavity height h_{fc} is the vertical distance between the workplane and the floor. As a check, the height of the room is obtained by adding $h_{cc} + h_{rc} + h_{fc}$.

Step 2: Calculate the cavity ratios. The ceiling cavity ratio (CCR) and room cavity ratio (RCR) are determined next. They are both calculated by the same formula:

$$\text{cavity ratio} = 5h(l + w)/(lw)$$

In this formula, h is h_{cc} for the CCR, and h_{rc} for the RCR.

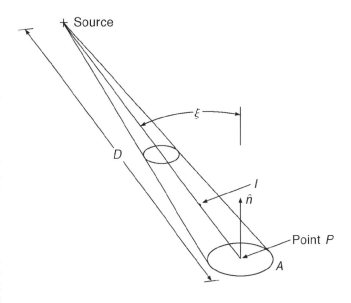

Fig. 22. Geometric arrangement for the inverse square cosine law. Adapted from IESNA Lighting Handbook (1993).

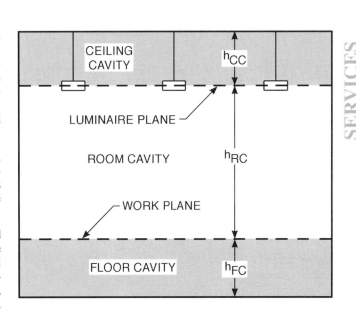

Fig. 23. Cavities used in the zonal cavity method.

Step 3: Determine the effective ceiling cavity reflectance. This value, r_{cc}, is determined by consulting Table 3 (the reflectance values in Table 3 are shown as two-digit numbers; for example, "64" means 0.64) and using the ceiling reflectance as the base reflectance, and the CCR as the cavity ratio. (See Table 3, *AP-19*)

Step 4: Determine the coefficient of utilization (CU). Most luminaire manufacturers produce CU tables which list the CU obtained with a specific RCR, r_{cc}, r_w and r_{fc} (the floor reflectance r_f can usually be substituted for r_{fc} with very little impact on the resulting calculations). As in Table 3, many CU tables list values as two-digit numbers which must be converted to decimal fractions. Table 4 shows CU tables for several luminaire types; these values should not be construed as typical. (See Table 4, *AP-20-24*)

Step 5: Determine the light loss factor (LLF). IESNA (1993) Ch. 9, "Lighting Calculations," describes the determination of light loss factors in detail. Steffy (1990) provides values which can be used for very rough estimations.

Recoverable light loss factors:

- lamp lumen depreciation factor: incandescent, 0.95; fluorescent, 0.9; HID, 0.65.

- luminaire dirt depreciation factor: 0.97 for most new commercial spaces.

- room surface depreciation factor: 0.97 for most new commercial spaces.

Nonrecoverable light loss factors:

- voltage factor: 1.0 for most commercial spaces.

- ballast factor: 0.93 for most ballasts.

- thermal factor: 0.95.

Nonrecoverable factors are those inherent in the lighting installation; recoverable factors include light losses that can be recovered (for example, by cleaning or relamping luminaires). All of the light loss factors should be multiplied together to obtain the total light loss factor LLF.

Step 6: Calculate the average maintained illuminance E. Combining the above factors, E can be determined by the following formula:

E = (number of luminaires) x (lamp lumens per luminaire) x CU x LLF / (room area)

When room dimensions are given in feet (ft), the calculated illuminance is in footcandles (fc); if dimensions are in meters (m), the illuminance is in lux (lx). If the required target illuminance is known, the formula above could be rearranged to determine the number of luminaires required to achieve that illuminance. When the luminaire layout for a room is determined, the spacing of those luminaires should be checked against the luminaire's spacing criterion (SC; formerly called spacing-to-mounting-height ratio or S/MH), which is published by most manufacturers. The SC gives the maximum spacing between luminaires, expressed as a ratio of the room cavity height h_{rc}. If the spacing exceeds the SC then the resulting illuminance distribution will not be uniform.

Illuminance selection procedure

This section briefly outlines IESNA illuminance selection procedure described in IESNA (1993), Ch. 11, "Illuminance Selection." Recommended illuminances are based on visual performance criteria. Selection of illuminance is only one of many design criteria that ought to be considered. Others include glare, color rendering, and flicker.

Step 1: Define the visual task. The visual task in question should be determined using the "Type of Activity" column in Table 5. IESNA

Table 5. Illuminance categories for several types of visual tasks. Adapted from IESNA Lighting Handbook (1993).

Type of Activity	Illuminance Category	Ranges of Illuminances Lux	Footcandles
Public spaces with dark surroundings	A	20 - 30 - 50	2 - 3 - 5
Simple orientation for short Temporary visits	B	50 - 75 - 100	5 - 7.5 - 10
Working spaces where visual tasks are only occasionally performed	C	100 - 150 - 200	10 - 15 - 20
Performance of visual tasks of high contrast or large size	D	200 - 300 - 500	20 - 30 - 40
Performance of visual tasks of low medium contrast or small size	E	500 - 750 - 1000	50 - 75 - 100
Performance of visual tasks of low contrast or very small size	F	1000 - 1500 - 2000	100 - 150 - 200
Performance of visual tasks of low contrast and very small size over a prolonged period	G	2000 - 3000 - 5000	200 - 300 - 500
Performance of very prolonged and exacting	H	5000 - 7500 - 10000	500 - 750 - 1000
Performance of very special visual tasks of extremely low contrast and small size	I	10000 - 15000 - 20000	1000 - 1500 - 2000

SERVICES

D5

(1993) also lists specific visual tasks for a wide range of activities. For example, one task might be reading 10-point printed type.

Step 2: Select the illuminance category. The illuminance category (letters A through I) associated with a task is given in Table 5. Continuing the example in Step 1, the reading task above is considered to be a "visual task of high contrast or large size," which means it has an illuminance category of D.

Step 3. Determine the illuminance range. Table 5 also gives illuminance ranges for each illuminance category. Categories A through C refer to general room illumination and categories D through I refer to illumination on the task. For example, the illuminance range for category D is 20-30-50 fc (or 200-300-500 lx).

Step 4. Establish the target illuminance. IESNA has developed a procedure for selecting the target illuminance from the illuminance range in Step 3; consult IESNA (1993). The target illuminance will depend upon three factors:

- Occupant age: Older people will require more light to see than younger people.

- Background reflectance: Tasks with dark surfaces will require more light than those with lighter surfaces.

- Importance of speed and accuracy: Critical tasks will require higher illuminance than leisure tasks, for example.

For example, if the factors above indicate older people, dark surfaces and important visual tasks, the highest illuminance in the range will likely be selected; if they indicate young people, light-colored surfaces and relatively unimportant tasks, the lowest illuminance in the range is likely to be appropriate.

Economic considerations
Economic concerns play a large role in the selection of a lighting system. Ch. 13 of IESNA (1993), "Lighting Economics," outlines procedures for performing life-cycle cost-benefit analysis (LCCBA), the economic analysis method recommended by IESNA. A technique called the simple payback method is described here which can act as a preliminary screening tool for assessing the economic viability of a lighting system in comparison with another system.

Simple Payback
Assume that a new lighting system entails an initial cost, I, and that this system will result in annual savings A. The payback period P, in years, is calculated as:

$$P = I/A$$

This method does not take into account the time value of money and is best used to evaluate short-lived projects where interest rates and inflation will be of little consequence. It can still be useful for more long-term projects; if such a project results in a very short payback period (such as 1 or 2 years) then it is likely to be profitable.

4 Energy management and lighting controls
About 20-25% of energy used in buildings is used for lighting. Since lighting contributes significantly to the cost of operating a building, energy management issues are of increasing importance. Ch. 30 ("Energy Management") of IESNA (1993) provides detailed consideration of this topic.

Energy management
Briefly, the elements of effective lighting energy management are:

- *Space design and utilization:* This includes the characteristics of the space that are often determined before considering the lighting system.

- *Daylighting:* The potential for effective use of daylighting should be considered early in the lighting design process.

- *Light sources:* The most efficient light sources that provide the required performance characteristics should be selected.

- *Luminaires:* As with light sources, efficient luminaires should be used; interactions with HVAC should also be considered.

- *Lighting controls:* Effective lighting control strategies should be implemented early in the design process.

- *Operation and maintenance:* A planned maintenance schedule can save energy and reduce long-term operating costs. See Barnhart *et al.* (1993) and Ch. 32 of IESNA (1993), "Lighting Maintenance."

Lighting controls
Common lighting control technologies include switching, dimming, and occupancy sensors. IESNA (1993) Ch. 31, "Lighting Controls," describes technologies and strategies for lighting control systems. Several general guidelines for implementing lighting controls are:

- Providing each room or work area with its own control switches (possibly including occupancy sensors).

- Work areas in open-plan spaces should be grouped and controlled together.

- Adjacent luminaires (or adjacent lamps within a luminaire) should be placed on separate circuits to allow multi-level lighting.

- In addition to multi-level lighting, consideration should be given to dimming.

- Lighting for specialized work areas requiring high illuminances should be placed on separate circuits from general ambient lighting.

- Luminaires along window walls should be controlled separately so that daylight can be utilized efficiently.

5 Lighting codes
This section cannot provide detailed information on lighting codes and regulations. Important U.S. federal codes of which the lighting specifier should be aware are:

- The 1990 Americans with Disabilities Act (ADA), PL101-336.

- The 1992 Energy Policy Act (EPACT), PL102-486.

According to EPACT regulations, for example, state energy codes for commercial buildings must meet or exceed the requirements set forth in Standard 90.1, *Energy Efficient Design of New Buildings Except New Low-Rise Residential Buildings* (ASHRAE/IESNA, 1989). See Ch. 14, "Codes and Standards," of IESNA (1993), or Davis and Meyers (1992) for more information on relevant codes and regulations.

Emergency and safety lighting

Emergency lighting
Emergency lighting is provided for safe egress from a building during fires or power failures. IESNA recommends that the initial minimum horizontal illuminance (on the floor) provided by emergency lighting for such conditions be at least 1 fc (10 lx) at the beginning of an emergency, and that the minimum maintained illuminance at every point along the path of egress be no less than 0.1 fc (1 lx). Higher illuminances in emergencies will likely result in faster and more confident passage through a space (Boyce 1991). Additionally, high illuminances are required for such spaces as hospitals, where lighting for life-support activities is critical.

Exit signs are required in all public buildings. The National Fire Protection Association (NFPA) Life Safety Code, NFPA 101 (1991), stipulates criteria for exit sign marking and placement. One requirement is that exit signs be no more than 100 ft. (30 m) apart along the path of egress.

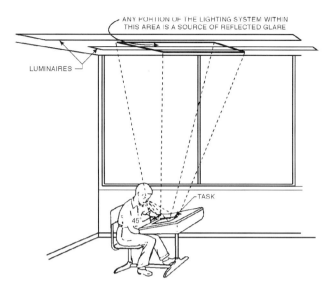

Fig. 24. Location of the "offending zone" or "glare zone" for a horizontal task such as reading at a desk.

Lighting for safety
At a minimum, the lighting in every space should be sufficient for safe working conditions, passage through a space and identification of potential obstructions. The recommended minimum illuminances required for spaces, depending upon the degree of potential hazard and the activity level of the space are as follows (IESNA 1993).

Non-hazardous areas:

- *Low activity level:* 0.5 fc (5.4 lx)

- *High activity level:* 1 fc (11 lx)

Hazardous areas:

- *Low activity level:* 2 fc (22 lx)

- *High activity level:* 5 fc (54 lx)

Changes in elevation, such as stairways or curbs, can be considered potentially hazardous areas and must be clearly illuminated and free of obstructing shadows. Note that conditions may often require higher illuminances than the minima listed above.

6   Lighting applications
Subsequent sections discuss lighting criteria for several common lighting applications: offices, schools, houses of worship, residences, industrial facilities, health care facilities, merchandising areas and exterior lighting. For detailed information on these and other applications not described here, consult IESNA (1993) and the appropriate IESNA recommended practices (see *Related References* below).

Office lighting
Specific recommendations for lighting in offices are given in "Office Lighting," Ch. 15 of IESNA (1993).

Luminance Ratios
IESNA recommends luminance ratios which should not be exceeded in the office worker's field of view. They are specified with the goal of minimizing disability glare. The ratios are:

- Between paper task and adjacent VDT screen: 3:1 or 1:3

- Between task and adjacent surroundings: 3:1 or 1:3

- Between task and remote (nonadjacent) surfaces: 10:1 or 1:10

It is important to remember that luminance is based on the illuminance on a surface and the reflectance of that surface.

Veiling Reflections
In the office, care should be taken to avoid a situation whereby light from luminaires causes veiling reflections on specular work surfaces (glossy reading materials or a VDT screen). Luminaires which provide high luminances within a task's "offending zone" or "glare zone" as shown in Figs. 24 and 25 should be avoided in such work spaces. Note that the location of the offending zone changes as the angle of the work plane changes from horizontal to vertical and might even be shielded by the worker in some conditions.

Offices with VDTs
Because reflected glare on VDT screens is a potential problem in spaces containing them, IESNA recommends a maximum horizontal illuminance of 50 fc (500 lx) in office spaces with VDTs. Luminaires in such spaces should not be too bright. Recommended luminances of luminaires at various angles, with a maximum luminance of 850 cd/m², are listed here for various viewing angles:

- 65° above nadir: 850 cd/m²

- 75° above nadir: 350 cd/m²

- 85° above nadir: 175 cd/m²

It is also recommended that for indirect lighting systems, the ceiling luminance does not exceed 850 cd/m². To reduce potential glare, visual comfort probability (VCP) ratings in spaces with VDTs should be no less than 80.

School lighting

Lighting recommendations for schools are given in Ch. 16, "Lighting for Educational Facilities" of IESNA (1993). Information on lighting for gymnasium and sports fields can be found in Ch. 23, "Sports and Recreational Areas" of the IESNA (1993). For information about lighting in auditoria and school stages, consult IESNA (1993) Ch. 21, "Theatre, Television and Photographic Lighting."

Daylighting and Glare Control in the Classroom

Illuminance recommendations for many visual tasks in schools are found in IESNA (1993). Care should be taken to provide sufficiently good color rendering in spaces such as art classrooms. In addition, many locations in the school use daylighting for illumination. Daylighting can:

- provide illumination for visual tasks.

- provide a relaxing distant focal point for the eyes.

- provide a psychologically pleasing view.

In addition, a glare-free and visually comfortable environment should be provided. In order to protect against glare from windows, the effective use of screens, overhangs, awnings, shades, blinds or drapes is required to meet the luminance ratio requirements described in Fig. 26.

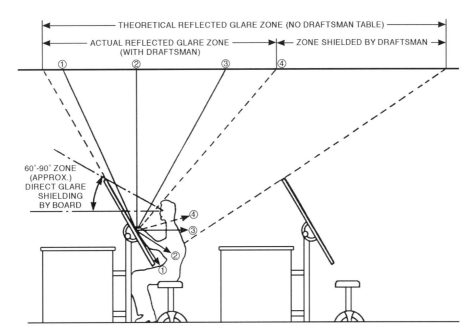

Fig. 25. Location of the "offending zone" or "glare zone" for a vertical or nearly vertical task, such as a drafting board or VDT.

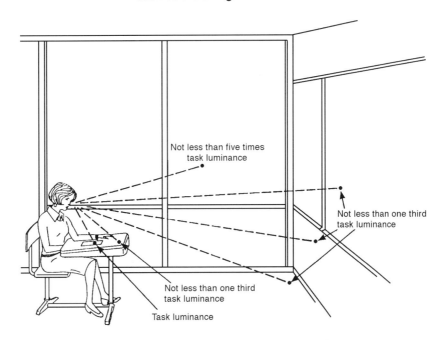

Fig. 26. Recommended luminance ratios in the classroom.

Luminaire selection and arrangement in the classroom should consider the following factors:

- flexible desk arrangements and use for other activities.
- placement of the blackboard.
- location of windows.
- room geometry.

Libraries

The book stack area in the library is one of the most challenging lighting problems, because sufficient vertical illuminances must be provided between rows of shelves to read titles on the spines of books. Rows of luminaires above the aisles can be used, or when aisle placement is not known, luminaires can be oriented perpendicular to the shelves (see Fig. 27). Refer to Ch. 17 of IESNA (1993), "Institution and Public Building Lighting."

Religious facilities

Proper lighting in houses of worship can enhance the religious experience of the worshippers occupying the space. Cf. IESNA (1993) Ch. 17, "Institution and Public Building Lighting."

Interior lighting

Interior lighting within the religious area serves four purposes which can be served by up to four separate components of the lighting system. These purposes are:

- light for reading.
- accent lighting focusing on the celebrant or on religious items.
- architectural lighting to highlight building features (ceiling or walls).
- celebration lighting (candles, lanterns and decorative elements).

For proper effect, illuminances for accent lighting (in the vertical plane) should be about 3 times the illuminance provided for reading; architectural lighting should be no more than 25% of that provided for reading. A preset control system with settings for various functions

(during readings, rituals, processions) can be effective in some worship facilities.

Exterior lighting

Lighting the facade of a house of worship can be an effective lighting technique. Consideration to the type of materials used will aid in selecting the proper light source. In addition, stained-glass windows, if available, can be illuminated from within the building to provide an attractive view to people passing by the building.

Residential lighting

Lighting in residences should reinforce the needs and desires of the occupant. The ability to easily and safely move about, the importance of considering the people within the space, flexibility, attractiveness and economical concerns are all important factors in residential lighting. Leslie and Conway (1993) offer a guide for energy efficient lighting techniques that can be applied to homes and residential applications.

Visual Activity Areas

Recommended illuminances for specific tasks in the home such as reading and kitchen tasks are found in IESNA (1993). Care should also be taken to provide sufficient uniformity for visual tasks by designing for the luminance ratios described in Table 6. Recall that for diffuse (matte) surfaces, if the illuminance on the surface and the reflectance are known, the luminance can be estimated. Recommended reflectances for common surfaces are given in Table 7.

Relaxation Areas

When relaxation is the primary consideration in the home, uniformity of illumination is not an important lighting criterion. Flexibility in the lighting, through localized lighting, dimming, or portable luminaires is important for relaxation in the home. Luminaire luminances should not exceed 1700 cd/m^2 in residences.

Industrial lighting

This section briefly describes some criteria for consideration when designing lighting installations for industrial facilities. For industry-specific lighting recommendations, consult Ch. 20 of IESNA (1993).

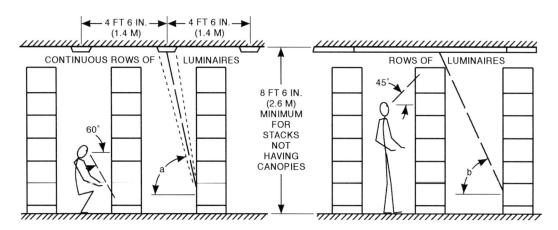

Fig. 27. Lighting for library stacks. Left, luminaires parallel with stacks. Right, luminaires at right angles to stacks provide better vertical illumination at lower shelves.

Luminance ratios
Providing visually effective and comfortable lighting is critical in industrial facilities. Recommended illuminances for industrial lighting are described in IESNA (1993). In addition, maximum luminance ratios for industrial tasks should not exceed those listed in Table 8.

Supplemental task lighting
Many industry-related visual tasks involve small details, low contrast and are usually three-dimensional in nature (and susceptible to shadows). Fig. 28 demonstrates several supplemental lighting strategies for industrial tasks.

Health care facilities
Hospitals and health care facilities are populated by populations with very different lighting requirements. Health care providers often require very high illuminances for their very critical tasks; and the psychological and emotional well-being of patients and visitors may require much lower levels and more relaxing approaches to lighting. See Ch. 17 of IESNA (1993) for a detailed discussion of lighting in these spaces.

Table 6. Recommended maximum luminance ratios for residences.

Between task and adjacent surroundings	1 to 1/10*
Between task and more remote darker surfaces	1 to 1/10
Between task and more remote lighter surfaces	1 to 10

* For special considerations (tasks of long duration and/or relatively high in luminance) no more than task and no less than 1/3 task.

Table 7. Recommended surface reflectances.

Ceiling	80 - 90
Walls	40 - 60
Furniture and equipment	25 - 45
Floor	20 - 40

Table 8. Recommended maximum luminance ratios for industrial areas.

	Environmental classification		
	A	*B*	*C*
1. Between tasks and adjacent darker surroundings	3 to 1	3 to 1	5 to 1
2. Between tasks and adjacent lighter surroundings	1 to 3	1 to 3	1 to 5
3. Between tasks and more remote darker surfaces	10 to 1	20 to 1	*
4. Between tasks and more remote lighter surfaces	1 to 10	1 to 20	*
5. Between luminaires (or windows, skylights, etc.) and surfaces adjacent to them	20 to 1	*	*
6. Anywhere within normal field of view	40 to 1	*	*

* Luminance ratio control not practical.
A—Interior areas where reflectances of entire space can be controlled in line with recommendations for optimum seeing conditions.
B—Areas where reflectances of immediate work area can be controlled, but control of remote surround is limited.
C—Areas (indoor and outdoor) where it is completely impractical to control reflectances and difficult to alter environmental conditions.

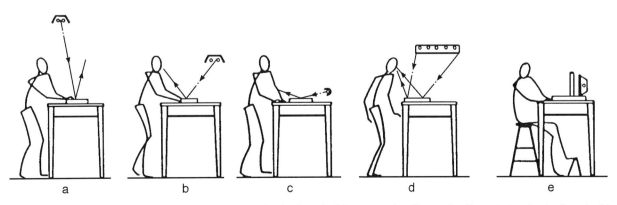

Fig. 28. Supplemental lighting for industrial tasks: a. luminaire located to prevent veiling reflections; b. luminaire located to cause veiling reflections; c. low-angle lighting to emphasize surface defects; d. large-area source is reflected toward the eye; e. transillumination from a diffuse source. Adapted from IESNA Lighting Handbook (1993).

Visual task lighting

Representative visual tasks and recommended illuminances for health care facilities are listed in IESNA (1993). Excellent color rendering ability is often critical and should be planned in the lighting. In the event of an emergency or power failure, sufficient emergency lighting should be provided, especially in critical care and surgical areas.

Lighting for the patient:

"Patient-friendly" lighting is important, especially in longer-term health care facilities. IESNA recommends the following approaches in lighting for patients:

- Use indirect lighting whenever possible.

- Provide uniform illumination on the floors.

- Provide sufficient illumination for visual tasks such as reading.

- Use high-color-rendering sources.

- Reinforce the physical environment to prevent confusion.

- Use patient-controlled lighting whenever possible.

- Use adjustable task lighting.

During nighttime, luminances in health care facilities should not exceed 70 cd/m^2 for extended periods or 200 cd/m^2 for short times. Patients with specific ailments or conditions, such as premature infants (Bullough and Rea 1996), may also have specific visual and lighting requirements which must be met in the health care facility.

Lighting for retail areas

Lighting for retail and merchandising areas is briefly discussed in this section. See IESNA (1993), Ch. 18, "Lighting for Merchandise Areas" for more detail.

Objectives of Retail Lighting

Lighting in the merchandising area must support three important objectives:

- To attract and guide the customer.

- To allow the customer to evaluate the merchandise.

- To complete the sale of the merchandise.

To meet these objectives, the architectural appearance of the store, methods for maintaining of lighting, and the type of store (a high-end boutique versus a wholesale discount outlet) must be considered.

Recommended illuminances for retail lighting

Table 9 lists recommended illuminances for retail areas, including the merchandise, circulation, sales and support areas. The recommendations are dependent in part upon the expected activity patterns within the store. Flexibility in lighting systems is often required, since displays of merchandise may be temporary and changed on a regular basis.

Outdoor Lighting

IESNA recommendations for outdoor lighting are described in IESNA (1993), Ch. 22 "Exterior Lighting," Ch. 24 "Roadway Lighting," and Ch. 33 "Emergency, Safety and Security Lighting." Further guidance to lighting specifiers can be found in *The Outdoor Lighting Pattern Book* (Leslie and Rodgers 1996).

Light pollution and trespass

Because of the increased nighttime use of electric lighting, proper shielding and control of lighting is essential to avoid light pollution and light trespass. Light pollution is caused by stray light from luminaires that is scattered by particles in the atmosphere at night. This scattered light creates a haze which can obscure views of the nighttime sky. Using well-shielded luminaires and avoiding light spilling over in facade or sign lighting can help alleviate light pollution.

Light trespass is unwanted or excessive light, usually in an area adjacent to an outdoor lighting installation. For example, a bright street light might shine, unwanted, into a window in one's house. Like light pollution, light trespass can be minimized by carefully surveying the site before the design phase, and by specifying luminaires with good optical control or shielding.

Outdoor lighting effects

Luminance ratios recommended by IESNA to achieve specific effects in the outdoor lighting design are as follows:

- 1 to 2: to blend in with surrounding areas.

- 1 to 3: to create soft accents.

- 1 to 5: to create accents.

- 1 to 10: to create strong accents.

Such ratios can be utilized, for example, to create a strong accent effect in the floodlighting of a building facade. Consideration should also be given to the color of the surface being illuminated. Red or yellow brickwork is best lighted by a "warm" (low CCT) source such as HPS or incandescent. Blue flowers are best lighted by a "cool" (high CCT) source such as mercury or MH.

Parking facilities

Recommended illuminances for open parking lots are as follows. Consult IESNA (1993) for additional information.

Low activity level:

- General parking and pedestrian areas: 0.2 fc (2 lx)

- Vehicle use areas: 0.5 fc (5 lx)

High activity level:

- General parking and pedestrian areas: 0.9 fc (10 lx)

- Vehicle use areas: 2 fc (22 lx)

Care should also be taken to provide sufficiently uniform lighting in parking areas.

Security lighting

Security lighting should increase the security of the people or property it surrounds. It has two main goals:

- To deter potential criminals from entering the area.

- To aid in visual searching by guards.

The recommended average illuminances for security lighting range from 0.5 to 2 fc (5 to 20 lx). The aim is to provide sufficient light to make potential intruders highly visible. Security lighting should also be arranged to limit a potential intruder's ability to see the secure area. Areas near entrances should be lighted to higher illuminances, about 10 fc (100 lx).

7   Lighting design and specification selection checklist

The following checklist summarizes lighting design guidelines discussed in this section. In all cases, the lighting design needs to be integrated with:

- The architectural intent, described as the aesthetic quality of a space and its architectural elements coordinated with how people are expected to perceive, understand and use a building with clarity, visual comfort and safety.

- The specific requirements and use of interior and exterior building spaces, which may range from high levels of light for specialized tasks to low levels of ambient lighting.

- Integration of electric lighting with daylighting. Consider specifing automated controls of electric light to allow dimming and switching to follow available daylighting levels.

SERVICES

D5

Table 9. Recommended illuminances for retail lighting. (From IESNA 1977).

Areas or tasks	Description	Type of activity area[1]	Foot-candles	Lux[2]
Circulation	Area not used for display or appraisal of merchandise or for sales transactions	High Medium Low	30 20 10	300 200 100
Merchandise[3] (including showcases & wall displays)	That plane area, horizontal to vertical, where merchandise is displayed and readily accessible for customer examination	High Medium Low	100 70 30	1000 700 300
Feature displays[3]	Single item or items requiring special highlight-ing to visually attract and set apart from the surround	High Medium Low	500 300 150	5000 3000 1500
Sales transactions area	The space needed for price veri-fication and re-cording of transaction	High Medium Low	70 70 70	700 700 700

[1] One store may encompass all three types within the building.

High activity area — Where merchandise displayed has readily recognizable usage. Evaluation and viewing time is rapid, and merchandise is shown to attract and stimulate the impluse buying decision.

Medium activity — Where merchandise is familiar in type or usage, but the customer may require time and/or help in evaluation of quality, usage, or for the decision to buy.

Low activity — Where merchandise is displayed that is purchased less frequently by the customer, who may be unfamiliar with the inherent quality, design, value or usage. Where assistance and time is necessary to reach a buying decision.

[2] Lux is an SI unit equal to 0.0929 footcandle.

[3] Lighting levels to be measured in the plane of the merchandise.

SERVICES

D5

- Directional wayfinding throughout a building including entry and visual orientation, transitions, changes of level, stairwells, and the entire passage of circulation including exterior spaces, parking and/or transport.

- Lighting controls, automatic or manual lighting dimmers and switches, located as a logical sequence of progression and use throughout a building.

- The need for vision and visibility under panic and in emergency conditions, achievable by both daylighting and emergency lighting design.

- Baffles, louvers, diffusers and other components of luminaires can be produced to offer creative opportunities of architectural illumination. Conversely, elements of architecture can be made part of a lighting design, such as ceiling or wall-scale louvers, reflectors and baffles.

The Visual Task

For task lighting, illumination and clarity of the visual task is of premiere importance:

- Provide adequate illumination at the plane of work, or upon the object, without excessive shadowing or veiling reflections and with adequate contrast. Consider light quality, source and direction as a function of visual task and task background.

- Ensure proper contrast of surround and background, not to exceed basic illumination ratios, but providing visual definition without excessive electric energy consumption.

- Selection of lamp should be based on lamp efficacy, lumen production, lumen maintenance and wattage, based on the life-cycle of the lamp and luminaire. Maintenance is critical to lighting efficacy. Provide easy access to luminaires for cleaning, maintenance and repair.

Distribution of Light.

Lighting design requires as much attention to both task area and function as luminaire specification. Distribution of light within the environment imparts the quality of illumination:

- The location of the light source should be chosen for surface brightness uniformity, for shadow and for lighting texture.

- Provide combinations of complimentary lighting for spatial distribution, continuity and interest. Variations of lighting levels can provide relief and variety between brightly illuminated required for task lighting and low-light areas appropriate for waiting areas, storage and relief spaces, *etc.*

- The suitability of distribution relies on the position of the lighting equipment within the environment. Side lighting can be more effective than toplighting for some tasks.

- Choose the light source for appropriate function: for precise beam concentration, for large area diffuse lighting, for wall wash, or for general horizontal illumination.

- Maximize diffuse-type high reflectance surfaces and diffuse transmission materials for general lighting. To increase general illumination from given sources, consider increasing lighting diffusion through translucent wall and interior partition materials.

- Choose surface finishes, type of distribution and angle of incidence to minimize veiling reflections. Light color surfaces significantly increase lighting levels. Matte finishes may reduce or eliminate veiling reflections.

- Minimize direct glare. This is important for safety in circulation spaces and at transition points. It is important for workplace comfort and productivity for all visual tasks, especially with VDT screens.

- Evaluating a design for lighting comfort requires careful design and specification coordination, and can be checked by:

- simulation (available through both CAD programs and physical modeling tests), —plan checks, reviewed with the user group to imagine and design for possible future uses and/or adaptations of a space.

- post-construction verification after initial occupancy, such as with mirrors placed at workstations to determine sources of unintended glare and/or veiling reflections.

Visual Interest.

Visual interest is a function of illumination quality, combining architectural surface treatment and luminaire design.

- Variable distribution, that is, multidirectional lighting, can be used to provide highlighting without veiling reflections.

- The distribution and incidence of light on a surface can be used to create certain perceptions or reveal qualities of the material.

- Use specular and spread reflection/transmission to reduce contrast.

Color of Lightt

Correct color of light may be essential:

- Select the light source with regard to requirements of work or process, psychological satisfaction, and coordination with daylight.

- Be particularly aware of color rendition for impact on environmental surfaces: color in decorations, on machines and equipment, and safety color considerations.

Energy Conservation

Operation, control and maintenance are a factor of illumination quality.

- Energy conservation is relative to lamp wattage and coverage as indicated by the following comparison: Given a particular height and distribution, a luminaire with a 46-W mercury lamp might illuminate 1000 ft^2 (100 m^2) of area to 1 fc (10 lx). Energy savings might be achieved by switching to a 28-W MH, 20-W HPS or 17-W LPS lamp without loss in illumination.

- High efficiency lighting (up-lighting mounted on partitions) can utilize a light painted ceiling as a light reflector (also effective for daylighting reflection strategies).

Appearance

Several guiding questions can be used to define the aesthetics of the luminaire. The eye is naturally drawn to highlights and bright areas. The design of lighting must be coordinated with illumination of surfaces and elements to provide clarity of space perception.

- How can the architecture of the environment be described? Style? Finishes? Purpose?

- What styles and finishes are compatible with the architecture?

- Is the luminaire to be perceived as subordinate to or a definable element with the environment? *E.g.*, recessed, shielded, on the periphery, or suspended or extended within the space as a visual element?

- Will the luminaire be independent of or integrated into other electrical, mechanical or architectural systems?

- Are the decorative properties of the luminaire appropriate when lighted? When unlighted?

- Does the luminaire enhance, maintain or subdue sound transfer?

- Are protective finishes necessary? Vandal resistant? Corrosion resistant? Impact resistant?

SERVICES

D5

Luminaire selection is greatly affected by component materials and their finishes. The decision to use a certain luminaire should be based on the following criteria:

- Illumination quality and efficiency: luminance, distribution, and color.

- Illuminating properties: transmission, reflection, absorption, and light stability.

- Maintenance properties: cleaning, handling, access, and durability.

- Safety: labeling, fire resistance, thermal properties, and power loading.

- Cost: first and operating cost (including cost of maintenance and replacement).

Luminaire selection should be weighted heavily as to the nature of its distribution:

- Is the light distribution to be subordinate to the environment, such as accent, perimeter, indirect, diffusing or shielded lighting?

- Is the light distribution to be prominent in the environment, such as direct concentrating or direct task lighting?

Maintenance
Incandescent lamps require certain special considerations, due to their conductive heating characteristics:

- Lamps should be properly matched to voltage and wattage specifications as both over-voltage operation and use of lamp wattage exceeding recommended levels can result in damage to the bulb seal, socket and wiring.

- Higher wattage lamps, compact lamps and reflectors may require certain types of glass or may limit lamp position in operation, based on the maximum safe operating temperature of the bulb glass.

- Gas-filled lamps must be protected from rain, snow, contact with cooler metallic pieces or other sources of great temperature variation in small areas. The resultant thermal shock is a cause of stress within the bulb resulting in breakage.

- Lamp base deterioration due to heat is reduced within the lamp by using mica or ceramic discs in the neck of the lamp to deflect convective radiation and shield the base when white and silver-bowl coatings are present. Deterioration is reduced outside the lamp by providing adequate ventilation to the lamp, yet minimizing the flow of cool air immediate to the neck and base of the lamp.

- Non-metallic housings are susceptible to charring or combustion when they are too close to the lamp components in a high-wattage luminaire, or when they are poorly ventilated.

- Lampholder materials should be appropriate for the intended use. Refer to UL ratings and manufacturer specifications. Examples include the limitations on porcelain sockets for spotlights (use only in recessed or totally enclosed luminaires), nickel-plated brass or other high-heat tolerant materials (little expansion) for tungsten-halogen and other high-wattage lamps.

Fluorescent lamp output is adversely affected by both extremes of high and low ambient temperatures:

- Low temperature operation may require glass jackets which retain lamp heat and special ballasts for lower temperature starting, below 50F (10°C).

- High temperature operation above 80F (27°C) often requires ventilation around the lamp.

- Ventilation should be limited to low velocities in order to optimize lamp output. High velocities typically reduce lamp efficacy

and shift the optimum ambient air temperature to about 90—100F (32°—38°C).

HID lamps rely on relatively precise arcs, which operate at high temperatures. Therefore, precautions are taken to insure proper operation:

- Over-voltage operation is detrimental to the arc tube. Voltage surges can also raise the arc temperature beyond the melting point of the tube.

- Selection of HID lamps should be made with respect to burning position. HID lamps are designated for base up, base down, horizontal or universal burning positions.

Ballasts should be mounted such that the internal vibration of the ballast is minimized:

- This vibration causes a humming noise which may be intensified when the ballast is in contact with luminaire components or structural material that can act as a resonator. Components which are not securely fastened in place will tend to produce additional noise.

- Consult manufacturer specifications for sound ratings.

Systems with dimmers require certain considerations:

- All such circuits should be grounded.

- Check lamp requirements for special ballast specifications.

- Cold-cathode fluorescent lamps should be operated at 20% of lamp load for dimming to 10% of light output.

- Constant wattage transformers cannot be used in dimmer circuits.

- Ensure that all dimming, ballast and lamp equipment is suitably matched.

Materials used for luminaire construction or placed adjacent to the luminaire should be resistant to light and heat degradation:

- Deformation due to thermal variation can cause seal and connection failure as well as create unsightly appearances.

- Some materials and finishes are susceptible to discoloration from ultraviolet, infrared and thermal radiation.

- Aging of materials can be accelerated in hot, dry environments. Some materials may become increasingly brittle or may experience breakdown in composition.

Luminaire design should facilitate easy maintenance (relamping and cleaning):

- Assembly should present a logical progression of parts, with connections and fastenings accessible for successive parts.

- Diffusers, louvers and baffles should be supported for easy removal without the use of a fixed or mechanical connection.

Although the visual components of a luminaire should be suited to the appearance of the overall environment, it is very important to use basic components in luminaire assemblies:

- The use of basic, or standard components creates flexibility of parts usage and relieves inventories in the maintenance department.

- Standards include wattage, lamp type, and lampholder/base type.

A major consideration for the selection of luminaires is its durability within the environment given a specific application:

- Vandal resistant housing and lens designs are recommended for any application which places the luminaire accessible to the public. Ground fault circuitry is required for damp locations in areas where the public comes in contact. Protection for restroom luminaires and ground-mounted floodlights are typical examples.

- Corrosion and chemical degradation must be evaluated.

- Applications, such as industrial lighting, where movement, vibration or impact occur should be fitted with luminaires which are designed to accommodate it.

8 Related references

ASHRAE. 1989. *ASHRAE Handbook: Fundamentals.* Atlanta, GA: American Society of Heating, Refrigerating and Air Conditioning Engineers.

ASHRAE/IESNA. 1989. Energy *Efficient Design of New Buildings Except New Low-Rise Residential Buildings,* Standard 90.1. Atlanta, GA: American Society of Heating, Refrigerating and Air Conditioning Engineers.

Barnhart, J. E., C. DiLouie and T. Madonia. 1993. *Lighten Up: A Training Textbook for Apprentice Lighting Technicians.* Princeton, NJ: International Association of Lighting Management Companies.

Boyce, P. R. 1991. *The Emergency Egress Roundtable.* Troy, NY: Rensselaer Polytechnic Institute, Lighting Research Center.

Boyce, P. R. et al. 1996. "The influence of a daylight-simulating skylight on the task performance and mood of night-shift workers." *Proceedings of the CIBSE National Lighting Conference.* Bath, London: Chartered Institution of Building Services Engineers.

Bullough, J. and M. S. Rea. 1996. "Lighting for neonatal intensive care units: Some critical information for design." *Lighting Research and Technology* 28(4):189-198. London: Chartered Institution of Building Services Engineers.

Davis, R. G. and S. A. Meyers. 1992. *Lighting Regulation in the United States.* Troy, NY: Rensselaer Polytechnic Institute, Lighting Research Center.

Elenbaas, W. 1972. *Light Sources.* New York: Crane, Russak and Co.

Flynn, J. E. 1977. "A study of subjective responses to low energy and nonuniform lighting systems." *Lighting Design and Application* 7(2):6-15. New York: IESNA.

IESNA Committee on Educational Facilities Lighting. 1998. *American National Standard Guide for Educational Facilities Lighting*, RP-3. New York: IESNA.

IESNA Committee on Health Care Facilities. 1991. *Lighting for Hospitals and Health Care Facilities,* RP-29. New York: IESNA.

IESNA Committee on Industrial Lighting. 1983. *American National Standard Practice for Industrial Lighting,* RP-7. New York: IESNA.

IESNA Committee on Lighting for Houses of Worship. 1991. *Lighting for Houses of Worship,* RP-25. New York: IESNA.

IESNA Committee on Residential Lighting. 1995. *Design Criteria for Lighting Interior Living Spaces*, RP-11. New York: IESNA.

IESNA Committee on Sports Lighting. 1988. *Current Recommended Practice for Sports Lighting*, RP-6. New York: IESNA.

IESNA Office Lighting Committee. 1993. *American National Standard for Office Lighting*, RP-1. New York: IESNA.

IESNA Roadway Lighting Committee. 1983. *American National Standard Practice for Roadway Lighting*, RP-8. New York: IESNA.

Leslie, R. P. and K. M. Conway. 1993. *The Lighting Pattern Book for Homes*. Troy, NY: Rensselaer Polytechnic Institute Lighting Research Center.

Leslie, R. P. and P. A. Rodgers. 1996. *The Outdoor Lighting Pattern Book*. New York: McGraw-Hill.

National Fire Protection Association (NFPA). 1991. *Life Safety Code,* NFPA 101. Quincy, MA: NFPA.

Rea, M. S. 1986. "Toward a model of visual performance: Foundations and data." Journal of the Illuminating Society. 15(2):41-57. New York: IESNA.

Steffy, G. R. 1990. *Architectural Lighting Design*. New York, NY: Van Nostrand Reinhold.

SERVICES

D5

Impact 2000 House. Boston Edison Company. Brookline, MA. 1984. Steven J. Strong, Consultant. Photo: Michael Lutch.

Solar electric systems for residences

Summary: This article provides an overview of solar electric (photovoltaic) systems. "Off-the-grid" and "grid-connected" systems are defined. The amount of energy consumed in a typical U.S. residence and the different end uses for that energy is given and compared to the amount of energy produced by an array of solar electric collectors. Means of reducing electric loads are described, along with aspects of installing and maintaining an off-the-grid solar electric system.

Key words: electricity inverter, off-the-grid, residential energy use, photovoltaics, solar electric system

Solar electric systems—also commonly referred to as photovoltaic systems—utilize photoelectric cells to convert the photons of the solar light spectrum directly into electricity. Solar electric cell technology has been developing since the early 1950s, in the first applications in the space industry, where solar cells have been used to power space satellites. Solar cells are now a common power source for portable appliances and battery chargers, evident in remote installations, including boating and road sign illumination. Applications for building energy supply has been explored since the early 1970s, including experimentation research applications, such as the University of Delaware Solar One House. An increasing improvement in solar electric cell technology and an increased awareness of the need to reduce fossil-fuel dependent means of producing power has resulted in the increased economic viability of solar electric installations. This article describes one of the primary applications for buildings, the design of off-the-grid solar electric systems for residences.

In this article, off-the-grid or utility independent systems are emphasized, in which case solar electric collectors provide electric energy for direct use and for an on-site battery storage system. Grid-connected systems for both residences and commercial buildings—which may or may not include an on-site battery storage system—are technically feasible and also may be economically attractive, but such systems require special arrangements with the local utility company, who must provide both safety provisions, interfacing equipment, and technical resources. While these needs are receiving the attention and cooperation of utility companies, in some cases mandated by local regulators and State legislation, off-the-grid systems can be installed without such interface requirements. Residences have a relatively manageable demand for electricity year-round, which also makes them reasonable candidates for photovoltaic systems.

A solar electric system offers a means to provide electric power for a residence that is not connected to the electric utility power grid. In many instances, the solar electric system is the only practical option for someone planning to live some distance from the electric power grid, because the cost of bringing in commercial power is prohibitive. In other instances, an owner may choose to be independent of the

utility infrastructure. The following article provides an overview for planning a residence that will not be connected to the electric utility grid. The article is intended to aid in the planning and design to accommodate the installation of a solar electric system.

When many people begin to investigate solar electric systems, they are often skeptical that an array of solar electric collectors can deliver more than a small fraction of the electrical energy. If the building owner is not interested in conservation measures including the possible substitution of other fuel-fired appliances for electric appliances, that skepticism is justified. If, however, one is willing to consider practical conservation measures and substitutions, it is possible to design or convert a residential scale installation so that it supplies the major portion of its energy from the sun.

Off-the-grid

The term "off-the-grid" is commonly used to refer to electric power installations that are not connected to the electric utility power lines that supply electricity to the vast majority of buildings in the United States. Electricity for off-the-grid installations must come from some other source than the public utility lines. For many years, the only source for these users was a fuel-fired generator, a small hydroelectric generator or a wind turbine. In recent years, however, thousands of houses have been built and powered with off-the-grid solar electric systems, also referred to as "stand alone" systems. Generally, off-the-grid residences are built some distance from the electric power lines, either due to inaccessibility or because the building site is less expensive than land served by electric power lines.

Grid-connected

The vast majority of residences in the U.S. are connected to electric power lines served by a public electric utility company, the primary advantage to this source of power being that the infrastructure already exists. For those planning a new residence, electricity from a public utility is, in most cases, readily available. It is usually the least first cost option. In most cases, there is no installation fee that a potential user must pay to connect to the power lines, unless they want the power lines run underground. In the case of either an existing or a new residence, the high first (installation) cost of a solar electric sys-

Author: Everett M. Barber, Jr.

References: Energy Information Administration. 1995. "Household Energy Consumption and Expenditures 1993." DOE/EIA-0321(93). Washington, DC: U.S. Department of Energy.

NREL. 1993. "Solar Radiation Data Manual." Pub. DE-AC02-83CH-10093. Golden, CO: National Renewable Energy Laboratory.

Sandia National Laboratories. 1987. "Stand-Alone Photovoltaic Systems: A Handbook of Recommended Design Practices." Document No. Sand87-7023. Albuquerque, NM: Sandia National Laboratories.

Scheller, William G. and Stephen J. Strong. 1991. *The Solar Electric House.* Still River, MA: Sustainability Press.

SERVICES

D5

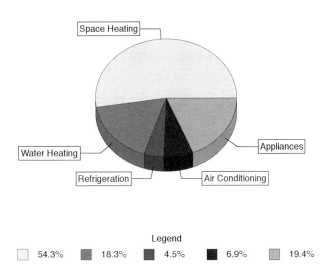

Legend

| 54.3% | 18.3% | 4.5% | 6.9% | 19.4% |

Fig. 1. Residential energy consumption in the United States (Energy Information Administration. 1995)

tem is difficult to justify if that justification is based solely on savings in electricity costs. There are more cost effective ways to reduce electricity costs. These include "reducing the electric energy load" by replacing inefficient electric appliances with those that are more efficient and/or replacing high demand electric appliances, such as refrigerators, with efficient fuel-fired appliances.

In some instances, other factors such as the need for total reliability and availability of power supply, may outweigh the high first cost of a solar-electric system for a grid connected home. In many locales, the supply of public utility power is sufficiently unreliable that many people have installed emergency fuel-fired generators to carry critical loads until the public utility power has been restored. If the utility power fails during a winter storm, damage can occur to a building that is without electricity. Where the public utility power outages are infrequent, a fuel fired generator is an adequate supplemental source of electricity. However, where public power outages occur several times a year for more than a day or two at a time, then a solar electric system is a viable alternative to a fuel-fired generator.

For anyone already connected to the public power lines and yet determined to have a solar electric system, a more practical solution than disconnecting from the grid is to install a "utility interactive" solar electric system. These are also known as "utility intertie systems." The solar panels supply electricity to the house when the sun is shining. If more electricity is supplied from the solar collectors than is being consumed in the house, then the system supplies electricity back to the power company. If more energy is being consumed in the house than is supplied by the solar panels then the utility company power makes up the difference. No batteries would be required with this system.

The utility interactive system concept has considerable appeal. A number of states have enacted legislation which requires electric utility companies to accept such systems. To date, a limited number of utility interactive installations have been completed. For utility companies, a number of safety issues have yet to be resolved to protect those working on the electric utility lines where utility interactive systems are used. Anyone planning for such a system should contact their local electric utility company to verify that they are ready for such a system.

Fig. 1 indicates the energy typically consumed for the various end uses in U.S. residences. The percentages are "end use," that is, consumption of energy delivered to the site. The percentages do not reflect the amount of energy required to generate electricity, which is often referred to as "primary energy consumption." The percentages are averages of many households. The particular profile for an individual household can vary considerably. For instance, an efficient refrigerator/freezer will reduce the percentage for that use to 2.5% of the total or less. On the other hand, if several members of a household each take 20 minutes showers daily, this can increase the percentage of water heating to 25% or more of the total energy consumed.

In the U.S., space heating is the single largest end use for energy in residences. Domestic water heating is next largest, after space heating. The two account for nearly 72% of the energy consumed in a typical house (averaged across all continental U.S. locations). In off-the-grid residences, because of the high energy consumption for space heating and water heating, these two energy end uses are best met with other forms of energy conservation and energy supply, passive solar combined with propane or a solar domestic water heater, for instance. It is not economically feasible to attempt to meet either of these end uses with a solar electric system.

Energy available from a solar electric collector:
To appreciate the importance in photovoltaic system design of "reducing load" or minimizing electricity consumption, it is helpful to

SERVICES

D5

know how much energy to expect from an array of solar electric collectors. Climate, latitude, collector tilt and collector orientation all affect the amount of energy produced by an array of solar electric collectors.

On a clear day at noon, the equivalent of about 1000 watts/sq. meter strikes a surface held perpendicular to the sun's rays. The exact amount of solar energy striking the earth varies with the time of year and the distance that the sun's rays must travel through earth's atmosphere. For calculation purposes, the 1.0 kW /sq. meter value, or ~1.0 kW per 10 sq. ft., is sufficiently accurate. This is equivalent to 3413 Btu/hr/10 sq. ft. A card table has a surface area of about 10 sq. ft.. A two slice electric toaster or a small, portable electric space heater releases about the same amount of heat when operating.

With current technologies, the amount of energy available from an array of collectors is a fraction of that available from the sun. An efficient solar electric collector can deliver between 12 to 15 % of the sun's energy at noon on a clear day. Thus, a solar electric collector can deliver about 120 watts/10 sq. ft. at noon on a clear day. Fig. 2 illustrates this point.

One widely used solar electric collector module measures 13 in. x 55 in.(33 cm x 140 cm) or 4.6 sq. ft. (5.1 sq. m); its rated output is about 55 watts at noon on a clear day. Two of these modules would have an area of slightly less than 10 sq. ft. (.9 sq. m)

The electricity from the solar electric collector module is available in either 6 volts direct current (dc) or 12 volts dc. Direct current is the same type of electrical current that comes from a battery. The 6 and 12 volt output values are nominal voltages. The collectors are designed to deliver somewhat more than the nominal voltage. In a 12 volt configuration, the design output voltage from the collector array is typically between 14 and 21 volts, depending upon the intended use of the collector. The output of the collector has to be higher than that of the battery it is charging in order to force a flow of current into the battery.

Usually more than one collector is required for most residential applications The collectors can be wired in either series or parallel configuration, as desired to increase voltage and or amperage. Fig. 3 shows for comparison the arrangements of typical flashlight batteries and solar panels in series and in parallel.

As noted, climate, latitude, collector tilt and orientation affect the amount of solar energy that reaches the solar collector. For generalized calculations, solar collector receives the most solar energy on an annual basis when it is mounted at a tilt angle which, when measured from the horizontal, is equal to the local latitude. This presumes that solar intensity at any particular site would approach this average, while in fact it varies as a function of daily and monthly sky conditions. The presumption of tilt angle equal to local latitude is nonetheless a good one for both solar electric and solar domestic water heating installations. In addition, like a solar thermal collection, the solar collector is mounted in an equatorial-facing orientation, that is oriented so that it receives the most irradiation for any fixed position.

In order to simplify the sizing of solar electric systems, the term "sun-hours" is used to expresses the effect of climate, latitude and tilt. For example, in Hartford, CT, for a collector tilt of about 42 deg. from the horizontal, the number of sun-hours/day ranges between 5.2 and 5.4 for the summer and between 2.7 and 4.1 for the winter. In contrast, Albuquerque, NM, with a collector tilt of 35 deg. from the horizontal, has 6.9 to 7.2 sun hours/day during the summer and 5.0 to 6.0 sun hours/day during the winter. Different tilts are used because the latitude is different for the two cities.

The sun-hour term is convenient for roughly approximating the output of a solar electric collector or an array of collectors. For example,

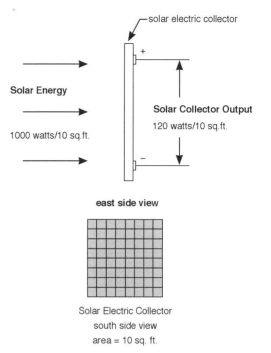

Solar Energy

1000 watts/10 sq.ft.

solar electric collector

Solar Collector Output

120 watts/10 sq.ft.

east side view

Solar Electric Collector
south side view
area = 10 sq. ft.

Fig. 2. Energy available from a solar electric collector

the output of one 55 watt solar electric collector on a clear day, between 11:30 AM and 12:30 PM is 55 watt-hours. If the collector is located in Hartford CT, then during an average summer day that solar collector will deliver 5.3 x 55 = 292 watt-hours. To give some familiar reference for these numbers: a 50 watt electric light bulb burning for 4 hours will consume 200 watt-hours of electricity. A 16 watt compact fluorescent light, which emits the same amount of light as the 50 watt incandescent light, will consume only 64 watt-hours in the same 4 hours of operation.

The simple approach to calculations given above is sufficient for rough estimates of the output of a solar electric system. One significant aspect of solar electric collector performance that this approach does not account for is the variation of photovoltaic cell performance with temperature. Typically, the output of a cell is rated at 77F (25°C). As the temperature of a cell decreases below this rated value, the output of the cell increases. Conversely, the higher the temperature of a cell, the lower is its output. Several computer programs are available to accurately account for the variation of cell output with temperature over the period of a year.

A computer based projection is shown in Table 1, indicating the monthly output of energy delivered by an array of 30-55 Watt solar electric collector modules. The array is located in Hartford, CT, it faces south and is tilted 40 deg. from the horizontal. The array monthly output voltage is 24 volts dc. The output of this array is shown in the right hand column.

Fig. 4 compares the electric energy supplied by the above solar electric system with the monthly energy profiles documented over two years by two representative dwellings located in the U.S. Northeast (parameters are indicated in the Fig. 4 caption). The energy profiles of the two reference dwellings are relevant because in both cases, the energy habits of the house occupants are documented, along side monitored energy consumption (information not always available for correlation when energy consumption alone is reported).

The designer of a solar electric system or home owner can create a similar plot of the energy consumption of any existing residence on the same graph. This may be done by reading the monthly kW-hr numbers on the electric bill and then marking those values as small crosses or dots on the chart. This allows a comparison of the electric energy consumption with the electric energy available from the solar electric system.

Current cost of a solar electric system
While cost comparisons are highly susceptible to local influences, the following provides a general guide. Currently (1997), typical U.S. costs for solar electric systems range from $10 to $20 per peak watt of solar electric collector output, installed. This price includes the collectors, charge controllers, batteries, inverters, cables, related equipment, installation labor, contractors overhead and profit. Thus, the above system which includes 30-55 watt solar electric collectors, would cost between $16,500 and $33,000 installed. When the cost of a solar electric system is viewed in light of the amount of energy available

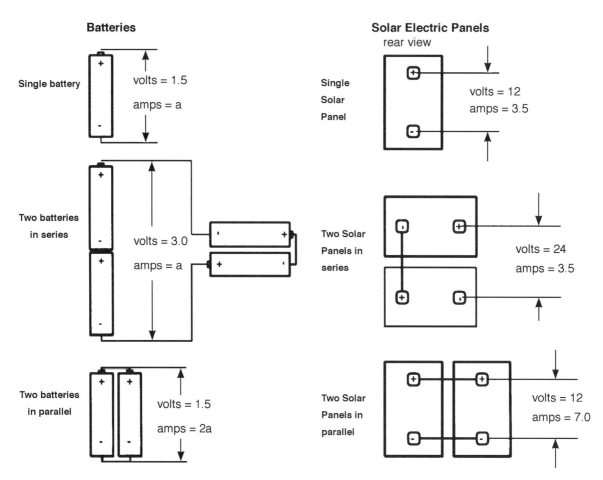

Fig. 3. Series and parallel connections - 2 Direct Current devices

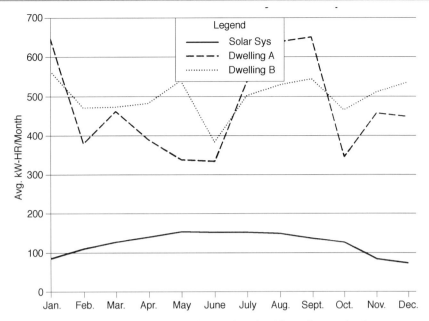

Fig. 4. Electrical demand vs. solar electric system output

Profiles of Dwellings A & B indicated in Fig. 4.

Monthly electrical energy consumption values for two dwellings in the U.S. Northeast are indicated in Fig. 4. One is a small, three bedroom house, the other is a large, old home. In neither dwelling is any particular attempt made to conserve energy. The kW-hr values given are two-year averages. The monthly cost of electricity for these residences may be determined by multiplying the monthly avg. kW-hr values by the current price of electricity.

Dwelling A is a 3800 sq. ft. single family detached residence. It is representative of an old home that has been attended to but not substantially weatherrized or modernized. Two people occupy this residence year round. There are periodic visits by relatives, by children who are still in school or who have left home and by friends of the family. The range is propane. A microwave oven is used frequently for cooking. The house is heated by a 60 year old oil-fired boiler; domestic hot water is heated in a coil in that boiler. Heat distribution to the house is by a forced hot water system and radiators. The house is not well insulated nor is the construction tight, thus heat loss from the house is high. There is no air conditioning, but a dehumidifier is run all summer in the basement. The clothes dryer uses electric resistance heat, about three dryer loads are run per week during most of the year. There is no separate freezer. The house uses a well pump for domestic water. The refrigerator is new and is an energy efficient type. There is an automatic dishwasher, the dry cycle is not used.

Dwelling B is a 1500 sq. ft. single family detached residence. Four adults occupy the house year-round, with frequent visits from family. The house was built in the 1930's. The house is heated by a natural gas fired furnace. Heat is distributed to the house by a forced air heating system. Domestic water heating, cooking and clothes drying are done with natural gas. There is no air conditioning. By present day standards the house is not well insulated. The refrigerator is not new. There is no separate freezer. The house uses city water for domestic water. There is an automatic dishwasher, the dry cycle is not used.

Monthly electric consumption values (two- year averages) for Dwellings A&B tabulated in Fig. 4

month	Avg. kW-Hrs Dwelling A	Avg. kW-Hrs Dwelling B
Jan.	380	566
Feb.	463	472
Mar.	390	474
Apr.	338	483
May	334	541.
June	536	384
July	638	502
Aug.	650	530
Sept.	346	545.
Oct.	458	466
Nov.	449	511
Dec.	650	536

Table 1. Computer projection of the monthly output of a solar electric system

month	daily dc amp-hours	Watt-hours/ avg. day	kW-hours/ avg. day	kW-hours/ month
Jan.	118.75	2850	2.85	85.5
Feb.	152.49	3659	3.66	110.1
Mar.	170.92	4102	4.10	127.1
Apr.	193.90	4654	4.65	139.5
May	205.75	4938	4.94	153.1
June	210.32	5048	5.05	151.5
July	210.46	5051	5.05	151.5
Aug.	199.70	4793	4.79	148.5
Sept.	189.37	4545	4.54	136.2
Oct.	170.32	4088	4.09	126.8
Nov.	116.96	2807	2.81	84.3
Dec.	98.65	2368	2.37	73.5

from that system, it should be clear to anyone who planning to live off the grid that "reducing load" is the most cost effective first step, rather than to "add capacity."

Minimizing electric power needs for an off-the-grid solar electric home

Fig. 4 makes clear the disparity between the energy delivered by a solar electric home and that required by a "typical" non-energy conserving residence. If a solar electric system is to be feasible, the electricity requirement of a typical single family dwelling must be reduced significantly.

There are a number of ways to reduce electric energy consumption in the average dwelling. One of the most significant is to use energy conservation, passive solar measures together with solar domestic water heating and/or a fuel-efficient heating plant, rather than using electricity for space heating and water heating. Fig. 5 is the same as Fig. 1, but with space heating and water heating grouped together.

Different measures required to cut electric power consumption are given below. They are grouped as follows:

- Substitute a fuel-fired appliance for an electric appliance.
- Eliminate high wattage loads.
- Use high efficiency electrical appliances.
- Schedule the use of certain heavy electric loads

- **Substitute fuel-fired appliances for those that use electricity**. Propane appliances are attractive for off-the-grid systems because they can replace many electric appliances, such as water heaters, ranges, and clothes dryers. In addition, unlike fuel oil burners, a propane burner requires no electricity to operate. Propane gas is recommended because in most cases natural gas is not available at the site of an off-the-grid house. Where natural gas is available then it can be substituted for propane since it is less expensive.:

- Use propane for cooking: Many people prefer gas to electricity for cooking because it is faster. For houses that are built some distance off the electric power grid, use of a wood fueled stove for cooking may be appropriate. These can be used for domestic water heating via a coil inside the stove and a tank located near the stove. The tank and stove coil are connected by piping. Water is heated by natural circulation between the stove and the tank. The stove can be a pleasant addition to a kitchen during the winter months but it can create an uncomfortably warm kitchen during the summer.

- Use propane for clothes drying, or use a clothes line.

- Use a solar domestic water heating system, with a propane-fired water heater as the supplemental source of hot water..

- Consider the use of a propane-fired refrigerator/freezer, or a propane/electric refrigerator such as the type used in recreational vehicles, rather than the standard electric refrigerator. The propane/electric refrigerator can be operated with electricity during the summer months when there is more sunlight to produce electricity from the solar system.

- Use a propane fired boiler for house heating, or use a dual fuel boiler that uses wood and propane rather than an oil fired boiler or oil-fired furnace. While No. 2 fuel oil is presently about 60% of the cost of propane per unit of heat delivered, older burners for No. 2 fuel oil draw more electric power than is desirable for a solar electric system. Some newer oil burners use as little as 1/5 of the electricity that older burners use. These may be worth considering due to the cost advantage of fuel oil over propane.

- Use hot water house heating rather that forced air house heating. The circulators for hot water heating use about 75% less power than the fans for forced warm air heating.

- For spa or hot tub heating, use a solar heating system or a propane heater rather than an electric heater.

- **Eliminate loads that use a lot of electricity**.
Certain amenities provided by high energy demand equipment and appliances are not practical with an off-the-grid, solar electric system. In some instances, an alternative approach to achieving the same benefit is available. The following energy-intensive uses may be precluded in order to make an off-the-grid solar electric system economically feasible:

- Central air conditioning: the compressor motor draws far too much power for too many hours a day to be used with a solar electric system. Even the compressor in a window mounted air conditioner draws 750 to 1500 watts when it runs. Since most off-the-grid houses are in the planning stage when the electric system is being planned the house can be designed to enhance natural ventilation. The use of window overhangs and attic exhaust fans or window fans will also help improve comfort in hot weather.

- Dehumidifiers: the compressor draws too much power over too many hours a day. Use window fans to ventilate high humidity areas such as basements.

- Any form of space heater that uses electric resistance heat. This includes portable space heaters and bathroom ceiling heaters.

- Central vacuum systems, they draw too much power. Since these appliances use power for relatively brief periods, perhaps an hour per week, the use of a central vacuum system could be scheduled for the time that the fuel fired electric generator is being operated.

- Swimming pools. The filter pump motor consumes too much electric power.

Typically they are run 6 to 8 hours per day.

- An electric heater for a spa or hot tub. Use a solar heater or propane fired heater to heat the hot tub. The filter motor and blower motor for the spa also use quite a bit of energy. If the spa or hot tub is considered essential, then operate the filter pump and blower motors when the supplemental generator is running.

- **Use high efficiency electrical appliances**
High efficiency electric appliances should be used where a fuel-fired appliance cannot substituted for them or where they cannot be eliminated.

- Use high efficiency lighting throughout the house and for outdoor lighting. Fluorescent lighting is preferable to incandescent lighting since it uses about 1/4 the energy of incandescent lighting. Several high lumen, low wattage lighting products are available for 120 v ac systems. Use timers for lights that don't need to remain on for long periods, outdoor, garage and basement lighting for example.

- If a propane fired refrigerator/freezer is not acceptable then use a high efficiency refrigerator/freezer, powered by electricity. While more than twice the cost of conventional refrigerators, current high efficiency models consume about 1/2 as much energy as an efficient refrigerator/freezer currently sold in appliance stores.

- Use water conserving toilets and shower heads. Low flush toilets and water conserving shower heads will minimize the amount of water that must be pumped by the well pump. The water conserving shower head will also reduce the amount of water that must be heated. If the house is connected to a municipal water source, which is unlikely for an off-the-grid house, then both of these measures are still useful because they will reduce water bills.

- If the house depends on a well for potable water, consider the use of a rain water cistern for storage of water for watering a garden, or lawn; or for washing a car. This will reduce the energy needed to run the well pump. Since over half the water used in the typical residence is used for toilet flushing, the cistern could be used for that purpose as well. The cistern would be fed by rain water run-off from the house and garage roofs.

- Insulate the house as well as possible in order to minimize the cost of heating the house as well as to minimize the wattage and the hours of operation of the heating water circulators used to heat the house. The number of circulators will depend upon the number of heating zones. R = 30 wall insulation and R = 40 roof/ceiling insulation are desirable objectives. Select tight windows and doors to minimize in-filtration losses.

- Use a microwave oven for incidental cooking. While a micro-wave oven may draw as much as 1200 to 1500 watts, the duration of operation is usually no longer than a few minutes.

• **Schedule the use of certain heavy electric loads**
Schedule the operation of certain appliances for the time of day or week when it is convenient to run the fuel fired generator. For ex-ample, numerous loads of clothes washing, operation of a central vacuum cleaner, and operation of power tools could be scheduled for a weekend day when the generator can be run to handle these loads as well as to recharge the batteries. Generally the generator will be run anyway for at least once per week for several hours to re-charge batteries.

Solar Electric System Schematic
Fig. 6 illustrates one conceptual arrangement for a solar electric system. Other configurations are used depending on the user's requirements.

Making up the deficit
In most off-the-grid residences, it is the norm that more energy is consumed in the house than is supplied by the solar system. Gener-ally, more supplemental energy is required during the winter months when there are less hours of sunlight than during the summer months. The deficit is usually made up with a fuel-fired generator. A typical residence will require a 5 to 7 kW generator. The generator will have to be run at least several times per month to exercise it, in accordance with manufacturer's requirements. If the generator is merely being exercised and it is not needed to charge batteries or carry heavy loads, then it need be run for no more than one hour at a time. If the batteries need to be charged and heavy loads are turned on, then the generator may need to be run for 4 to 5 hours at a time. During the winter the generator may need to be run as often as every 4-5 days to main-tain a good level of charge on the batteries. Allowing lead-acid batteries to remain in a deeply discharged state for several days at a time, awaiting the next sunny day, will shorten the life of the batteries considerably.

Living with a solar electric system
Expectations are an important aspect of living with any new technol-ogy. A solar electric system is no exception.

• Cellular phones are ideal for off-the-grid houses. A phone com-pany line may be just as costly to extend to a remote site as the electric utility company's lines.

• The battery bank should be located in an enclosed/heated space. The batteries will maintain their peak capacity if they can be main-tained between about 65F - 80F (18°C - 27°C). If the battery en-closure is ventilated then wet-cell, (flooded cell), batteries can be used. Wet-cell, lead acid batteries produce hydrogen gas when they are being charged, thus a ventilated enclosure is most desir-able. Ideally the battery enclosure should be mechanically venti-lated to prevent the 'stack effect' of the house from drawing bat-tery gases back into the house. While sealed batteries are pre-ferred where hydrogen release during charging cannot be toler-ated or where the batteries are unlikely to be maintained for months

Residential Consumption of Energy in U.S.

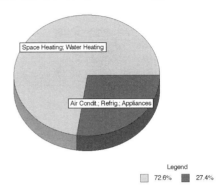

Fig. 5. Residential loads met with heat vs. loads met with electricity

at a time, they usually have a shorter life than the wet cell batteries. In addition, wet cell can tolerate higher rates of charging for extended periods than sealed batteries. The wet cell batteries do require the addition of water several times per year.

- Expect to run the supplemental electric generator more often during the months of December-to February, than during any other part of the year. This is due to the fewer hours of sunlight and to the increase in overcast sky conditions that usually occur during the winter months; and, in parts of the country where it is a concern, to snow cover on the solar collectors.

- The roof of a house is usually the preferred place to mount the solar collectors because in that location they are least likely to receive shade from surrounding trees. In addition, a roof is often a ready-made mounting surface for the collectors thereby eliminating the cost of a separate mounting structure. A draw-back to putting the panels on the roof is that access to them may be limited. After a snowfall the owner will either have to wait for the sun to melt the snow from the collectors before they can resume collecting, or a long handled broom will be needed to clear the snow from the collectors. If the collectors are on a ground-mount they are more accessible for snow removal.

- If the collectors are to be mounted on a house roof or on a ground-mount they should face in a southerly direction and have a tilt from the horizontal of 40 deg. or more. The southerly (equatorial facing) orientation can vary as much as 30 deg. east or west of

true south without significant loss of collected solar energy. The roof tilt can be less than 40 deg., but the lower tilt will result in the system collecting more energy during the summer than the winter. A higher tilt than 40 deg. increases the winter collection. Generally, a tilt that results in increased winter collection is preferred because there are fewer hours of sun during the winter. A higher tilt also helps the snow to side off during the winter. If the roof is not tilted at the optimum for the solar collectors then a collector mounting frame can be used to increase the collector tilt.

- When wiring the house the electrician should provide at least two ac panel (circuit breaker) boxes. The main panel will serve the heavy electrical loads that will be carried only by the fuel-fired generator. The second panel will carry the loads served by the solar electric system. See Fig 6.

- There are a number of reasons to use conventional (ac) appliances and wiring in the house. The fact that the wiring in the house will be conventional will simplify the electrical contractor's task. In addition, the consumer has a far greater selection of ac powered appliances than direct current (dc) powered appliances. The ac appliances are easily repairable and competitively priced. The wire sizes can be much smaller in the ac powered house than in the dc powered house. The dc wires must be large to reduce the resistance losses in them A disadvantage of the all-ac system is that the ac appliances are generally somewhat less efficient than the dc appliances, thus only the most energy conserving ac appliances

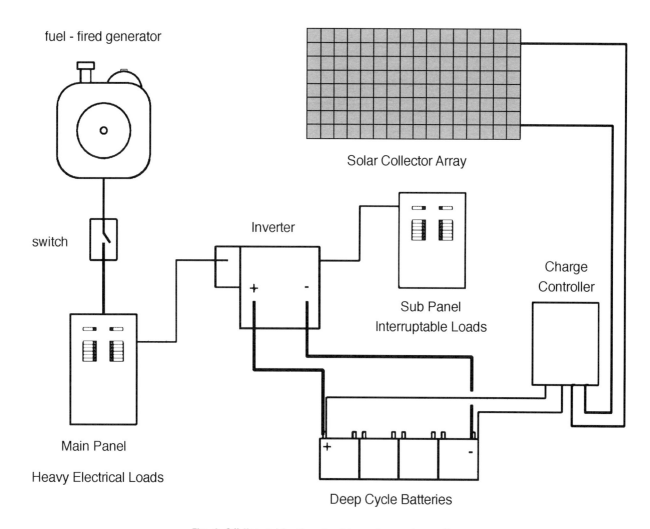

Fig. 6. Off-the-grid solar electric system schematic

should be purchased. Also, about 10% of the power stored in the batteries is lost in the inverter when it converts the dc produced by the batteries to ac required by the house.

- Battery Charging: The inverter (dc to ac device) used with the off-the-grid system is available with an integral, high quality, battery charger. This charger is used when the batteries are discharged and the solar array cannot keep up with the rate of discharge. A fuel fired generator can use this charger to recharge the battery bank when the battery charge level drops below the desired voltage. There is a clear savings in having the inverter and battery charger as one unit.

- There are several disadvantages to having the inverter with an integral battery charger. The batteries cannot supply power to the house when they are being charged by a battery charger that is integral with the inverter. Thus, there is a brief interruption in power to the normal loads while the power source is switched from battery/inverter mode to generator mode. The electrical system should be wired so the generator can supply power to certain house loads at the same time that it is charging the batteries. Once the batteries are charged then the system can be switched back to battery/inverter mode and the generator can be shut off or it can be used to serve high wattage loads. There is also a brief interruption in power supply when the inverter is switched on again. If there are any critical loads on the electrical system, such as a computer, then the computer should be plugged into an uninterruptible power supply so that 'rebooting' the computer is not required when the switching occurs.

- The rate at which the batteries can be recharged is limited by the capacity of the integral charger. More hours of generator operation are needed to charge the batteries with the integral charger than if a separate high capacity battery charger were used. If fast battery charging is desirable to minimize the hours of generator operation, or if it is really desirable to not interrupt the supply of electricity to certain circuits, then a separate, high capacity, battery charger should be used instead of the integral charger.

- Another advantage of a separate battery charger is, if the inverter with integral charger fails, an infrequent event, then the batteries cannot be charged by the fuel fired generator until the inverter has been repaired. They can still be charged by the solar array in this case.

- The batteries most commonly used with solar electric systems are the lead-acid, deep cycle type. The deep cycle designation means that they can be drawn down to some fraction of their total capacity, repeatedly, with little harm done to them. The type of battery used for starting automobiles is not appropriate for this application because several deep discharges will ruin that type of battery. Conversely, the deep cycle battery is not particularly suitable for automobile starting because it cannot provide the sudden burst of high amperage needed to crank an engine.

- Over the long term, the deep cycle batteries are affected by the number and depth of discharges. If they are discharged to no more than 80% of their total capacity, a 20% discharge, a good quality lead-acid battery may last 20 years. However, a more realistic depth of discharge for off-the-grid residences is to 50% of capacity. If the batteries are recharged within a day or so of a 50% deep discharge they may last 7 to 12 years. If they are repeatedly discharged to 20% of their total capacity, an 80% discharge, and not recharged within a day or two of that deep discharge then they may last only 2 or 3 years. Experience has shown that system owners tend to become less diligent in maintaining the battery charge level over the years of system operation.

- High quality deep cycle, lead-acid batteries are available that have a longer life than described above, but these are more costly than the batteries most commonly used with off-the-grid residences.

- Still better are the nickel-cadmium batteries. These can be discharged to almost 100% of their capacity for as much as 3000 cycles. The nickel-cadmium batteries cost as much as 10 times the cost of the lead acid batteries.

- Two inverters are desirable for off-the-grid systems. One is for all the expected loads except the well pump, and the other is for the well pump or similar high amperage load. A separate inverter is usually needed for the well pump because of the high in-rush current to the pump motor when the pump starts. Ideally the well pump motor should be 1/2 to 3/4 hp. A separate inverter will handle up to a one horsepower motor. If a larger pump motor is required then a larger inverter will be needed. The size of the well pump motor won't be known until the well has been drilled and its depth and yield determined. A second inverter may also be used as the reserve inverter in the unlikely event that the other inverter fails and must be repaired.

- If any electrical loads require 240 volt ac power then a 120/240 volt transformer will be needed to step up the 120 volt output of the inverter. The electrical service to a well pump motor. may well be 240 volt due to the long run between the panel box and the motor.

- Most dimmer switches will not work with the ac power produced by the ac inverter used with off-the-grid systems.

- Variable speed motors, such as those used in ceiling fans will buzz on ac power from the type of inverter used with off-the-grid systems. This causes no harm to the motor.

- AC transformers will have a somewhat louder hum with the ac produced by the inverter than they would with sine-wave ac (from the power company). The hum is only slightly audible in most cases. Some audio equipment will carry a 60hz hum which does not cause any harm to the equipment but it can be annoying to the listener. Some experimentation with different audio equipment will be required to find those makes that do not carry the noise.

- Battery powered AM band radios are preferred to the plug in type because of the radio frequency interference broadcast by the inverter. Keeping the radio 10 to 15 feet from the inverter helps diminish the noise picked up on the AM band.

- The are a number of small electrical loads in a typical dwelling that can significantly reduce the efficiency of an off-the-grid system. The effect of these loads is disproportionate to their actual wattage. Inverters for off-the-grid systems operate in the range of 85 to 95% efficiency for loads of 10% of rated capacity, or greater. But when they must serve very small loads the inverter efficiency falls considerably. Some of the small loads that are responsible for this power loss are: electric clocks, clocks in stoves, TV's, cordless phones, power cubes for devices such as phone answering machines and door bells; and electronic typewriters. These loads are sometimes referred to as 'ghost' or 'phantom' loads. They should either be eliminated or the solar system should be oversized to accommodate the loss of power due to those loads.

Resources

The designer or prospective owner of an off-the-grid home seeking the minimum compromise in comfort and convenience should consider the installation of a full sized solar electric system and fuel-fired generator for that home. The solar electric system should be sized to handle the majority of electric loads in the house for most of the year. The generator should be sized to handle battery charging during winter cloudy spells and to handle the heavy electric power loads which are often scheduled for weekends.

Anyone planning a vacation home or "week-end retreat" that will not be occupied full time will probably want a smaller solar electric system, one that is adequate for weekend use but which requires more frequent generator operation if the house is occupied daily as on vacations.

SERVICES

D5

The most basic solar electric system for a cabin would be a single solar panel, charge controller, battery and a 20 watt fluorescent light. This would provide several hours of light daily. Other energy needs would be provided with fuels such as wood or propane.

A solar electric system consultant should be retained to design and install the system. Electrical contractors, who are able to size and install the wiring for an alternating current system, are seldom familiar with direct current systems.

Some non-profit firms and solar equipment sales companies offer courses for people who are interested in learning to install their own solar electric system. In the past five or six years, frequent revisions have been made to the National Electric Code in an attempt to keep up with the rapidly developing solar electric industry and to provide for safe installation practices. As is the case with new technologies, local electrical inspectors may not be entirely familiar with solar electric system installation practices.

The references cite some of the increasing number of publications becoming available on the topic of solar electric systems. These provide background for anyone interested in this field. Sandia National Laboratories maintains a Photovoltaic Systems Assistance Center. They offer a variety of current publications dealing with the application of photovoltaic systems. They also offer an informative newsletter entitled "Highlights of Sandia's Photovoltaic Program."

SERVICES

D5

APPENDIX   III

Dimensions of the human figure

Dimensions and clearances provided in planning, building layout and furnishings often represent only minimum requirements for the average adult (Figs 1 and 2).

These dimensions and clearances should be increased to allow comfortable accommodation and improved safety for persons of larger than average stature. Designers of furniture and spaces where dimensioning must accommodate special conditions and/or universal design goals should investigate the range of anthropomorphic dimensions of the human figure (Fig. 3). See especially, Henry Dreyfuss Associates, *The Measure of Man and Woman: Human Factors in Design,* Whitney Library of Design, New York. 1993.

The height of tabletops shown in Fig. 2 is 29 in. (740 mm); some references recommend 30 in. (760 mm). A common metric standard is 750 mm. In each case, table and chair heights must coordinate.

Most references recommend a range of heights (adjustable) for workplace settings.

Dimensions of children

Children do not have the same physical proportions of adults, especially during early years, and their heights vary greatly. Their proportions may be approximated from Fig. 1 (bottom). Henry Dreyfuss Associates (*op cit.*) includes dimensions by age group and motor development.

Dimensions for maintenance access

Clearances for maintenance access are critical and are shown in Figs 4.

Dimensions for accessibility

Representative dimensions are indicated in Figs. 5 and 6.

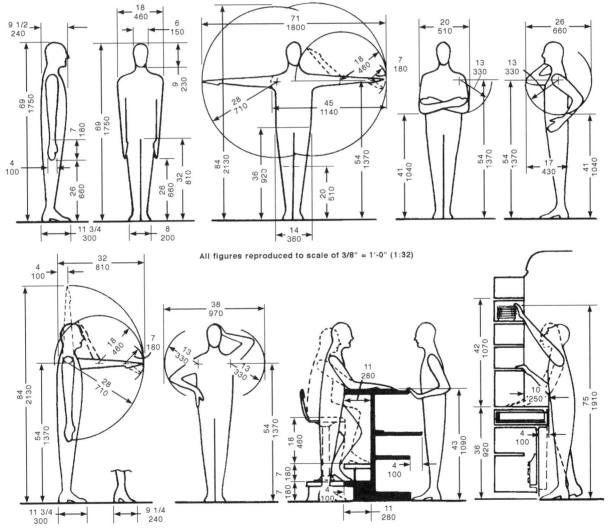

All figures reproduced to scale of 3/8" = 1'-0" (1:32)

Minimum dimensions and clearances

(Note: Upper figures are inches, lower figures are millimeters. Conversions are to nearest 10 mm.)

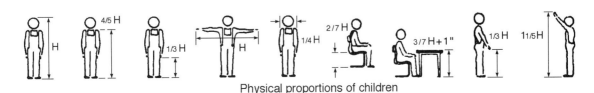

Physical proportions of children

Fig. 1. Minimum dimensions and clearances.

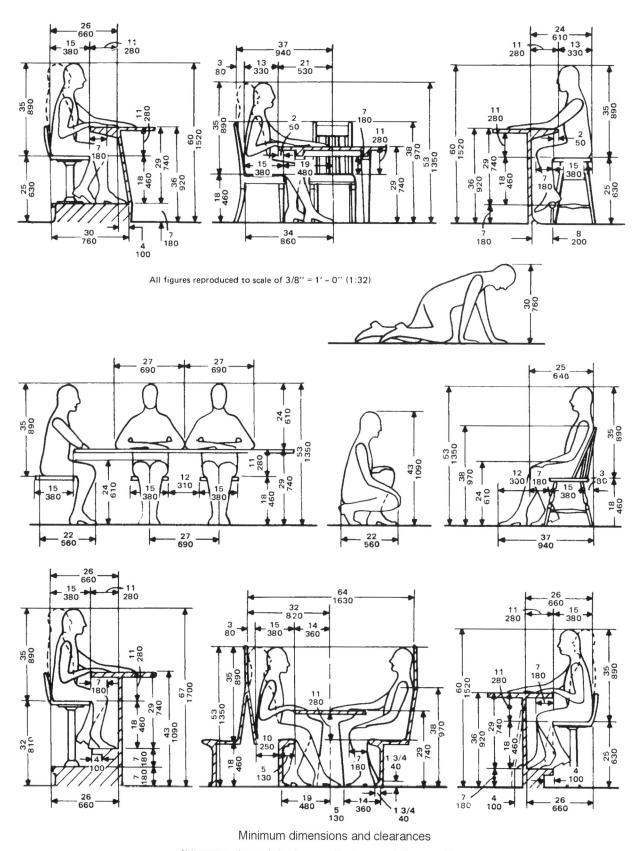

All figures reproduced to scale of 3/8" = 1' – 0" (1:32)

Minimum dimensions and clearances

Note: upper numbers are inches, lower are millimeters, converted to nearest 10 mm.

Fig.2. Minimum dimensions and clearances. Note: upper numers are inches, lower are millimeters, converted to nearest 10 mm.

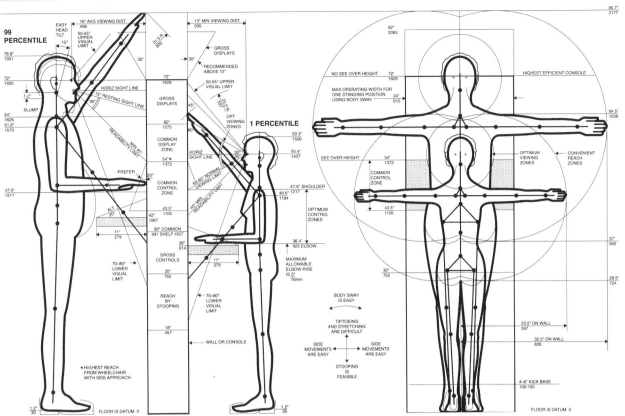

Fig. 3. Representative dimensions of standing human figure.

Reprinted by permission. Henry Dreyfuss Associates, *The Measure of Man and Woman: Human Factors in Design*, Whitney Library of Design, New York. 1993

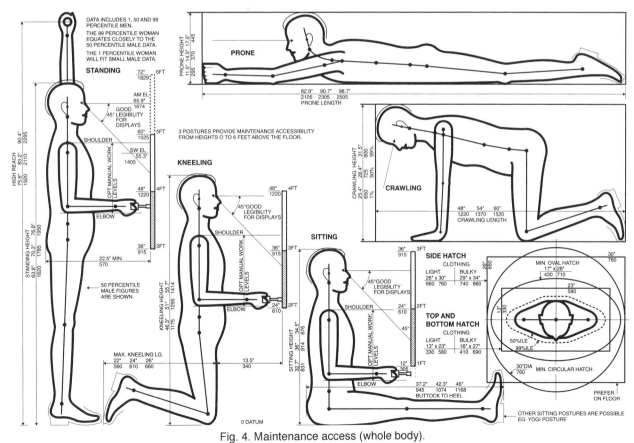

Fig. 4. Maintenance access (whole body).

Reprinted by permission. Henry Dreyfuss Associates, *The Measure of Man and Woman: Human Factors in Design*, Whitney Library of Design, New York. 1993

Fig. 3. Representative dimensions for maintenance access.

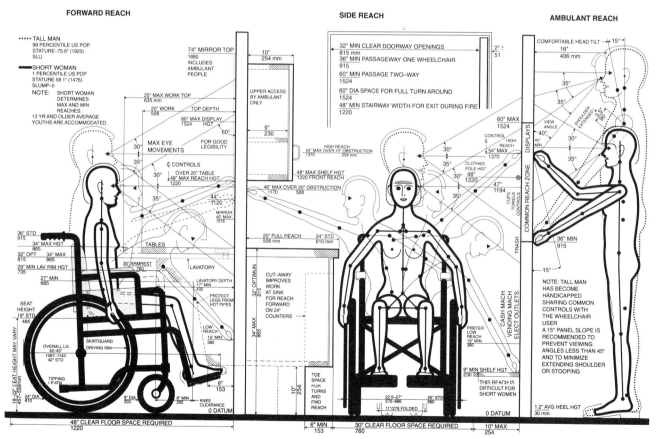

Reprinted by permission. Henry Dreyfuss Associates, *The Measure of Man and Woman: Human Factors in Design*, Whitney Library of Design, New York. 1993

Fig. 5. Reach factors for the differently abled.

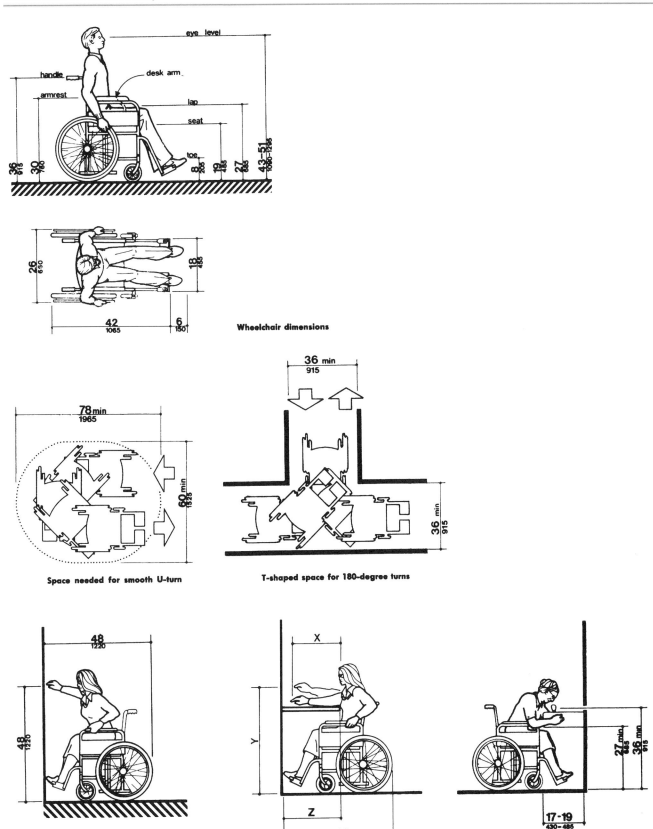

NOTE: X shall be ≤ 25 in (635 mm); Z shall be ⩾ X. When X < 20 in (510 mm), then Y shall be 48 in (1220 mm) maximum. When X is 20 to 25 in (510 to 635 mm), then Y shall be 44 in (1120 mm) maximum.

Fig. 6. Dimensions for accessibility

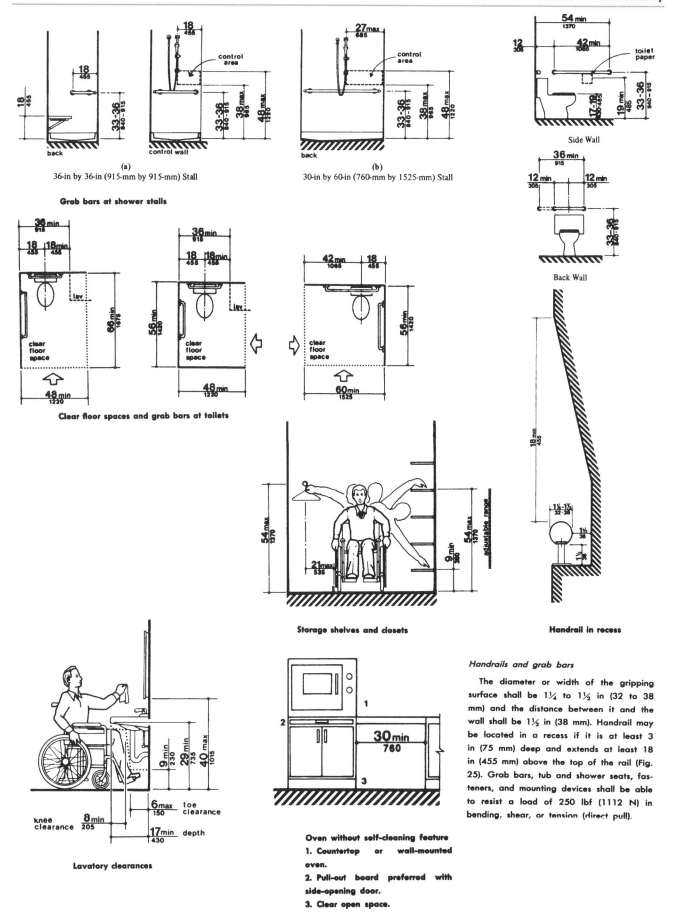

(a)
36-in by 36-in (915-mm by 915-mm) Stall

(b)
30-in by 60-in (760-mm by 1525-mm) Stall

Grab bars at shower stalls

Side Wall

Back Wall

Clear floor spaces and grab bars at toilets

Storage shelves and closets

Handrail in recess

Lavatory clearances

Oven without self-cleaning feature
1. Countertop or wall-mounted oven.
2. Pull-out board preferred with side-opening door.
3. Clear open space.

Handrails and grab bars

The diameter or width of the gripping surface shall be 1¼ to 1½ in (32 to 38 mm) and the distance between it and the wall shall be 1½ in (38 mm). Handrail may be located in a recess if it is at least 3 in (75 mm) deep and extends at least 18 in (455 mm) above the top of the rail (Fig. 25). Grab bars, tub and shower seats, fasteners, and mounting devices shall be able to resist a load of 250 lbf (1112 N) in bending, shear, or tension (direct pull).

Fig. 7. Handrails and grab bars

The following tables supplement Figures and Tables given in B2.2 "Thermal Insulation"

Table 4. Thermal resistances of plane air spaces[a,e]

(Reproduced by permission from *ASHRAE Handbook of Fundamentals*, 1977.)

All resistance values expressed in (hour)(square foot)(degree Fahrenheit temperature difference) per Btu

Values apply only to air spaces of uniform thickness bounded by plane, smooth, parallel surfaces with no leakage of air to or from the space.
Thermal resistance values for multiple air spaces must be based on careful estimates of mean temperature differences for each air space.

Position of Air Space	Direction of Heat Flow	Mean Temp[b] (F)	Temp Diff[b,d] (deg F)	0.5-in. Air Space[a] Value of E[b,c]					0.75-in. Air Space[a] Value of E[b,c]				
				0.03	0.05	0.2	0.5	0.82	0.03	0.05	0.2	0.5	0.82
Horiz.	Up	90	10	2.13	2.03	1.51	0.99	0.73	2.34	2.22	1.61	1.04	0.75
		50	30	1.62	1.57	1.29	0.96	0.75	1.71	1.66	1.35	0.99	0.77
		50	10	2.13	2.05	1.60	1.11	0.84	2.30	2.21	1.70	1.16	0.87
		0	20	1.73	1.70	1.45	1.12	0.91	1.83	1.79	1.52	1.16	0.93
		0	10	2.10	2.04	1.70	1.27	1.00	2.23	2.16	1.78	1.31	1.02
		-50	20	1.69	1.66	1.49	1.23	1.04	1.77	1.74	1.55	1.27	1.07
		-50	10	2.04	2.00	1.75	1.40	1.16	2.16	2.11	1.84	1.46	1.20
45° Slope	Up	90	10	2.44	2.31	1.65	1.06	0.76	2.96	2.78	1.88	1.15	0.81
		50	30	2.06	1.98	1.56	1.10	0.83	1.99	1.92	1.52	1.08	0.82
		50	10	2.55	2.44	1.83	1.22	0.90	2.90	2.75	2.00	1.29	0.94
		0	20	2.20	2.14	1.76	1.30	1.02	2.13	2.07	1.72	1.28	1.00
		0	10	2.63	2.54	2.03	1.44	1.10	2.72	2.62	2.08	1.47	1.12
		-50	20	2.08	2.04	1.78	1.42	1.17	2.05	2.01	1.76	1.41	1.16
		-50	10	2.62	2.56	2.17	1.66	1.33	2.53	2.47	2.10	1.62	1.30
Vertical	Horiz.	90	10	2.47	2.34	1.67	1.06	0.77	3.50	3.24	2.08	1.22	0.84
		50	30	2.57	2.46	1.84	1.23	0.90	2.91	2.77	2.01	1.30	0.94
		50	10	2.66	2.54	1.88	1.24	0.91	3.70	3.46	2.35	1.43	1.01
		0	20	2.82	2.72	2.14	1.50	1.13	3.14	3.02	2.32	1.58	1.18
		0	10	2.93	2.82	2.20	1.53	1.15	3.77	3.59	2.64	1.73	1.26
		-50	20	2.90	2.82	2.35	1.76	1.39	2.90	2.83	2.36	1.77	1.39
		-50	10	3.20	3.10	2.54	1.87	1.46	3.72	3.60	2.87	2.04	1.56
45° Slope	Down[d]	90	10	2.48	2.34	1.67	1.06	0.77	3.53	3.27	2.10	1.22	0.84
		50	30	2.64	2.52	1.87	1.24	0.91	3.43	3.23	2.24	1.39	0.99
		50	10	2.67	2.55	1.89	1.25	0.92	3.81	3.57	2.40	1.45	1.02
		0	20	2.91	2.80	2.19	1.52	1.15	3.75	3.57	2.63	1.72	1.26
		0	10	2.94	2.83	2.21	1.53	1.15	4.12	3.91	2.81	1.80	1.30
		-50	20	3.16	3.07	2.52	1.86	1.45	3.78	3.65	2.90	2.05	1.57
		-50	10	3.26	3.16	2.58	1.89	1.47	4.35	4.18	3.22	2.21	1.66
Horiz.	Down[d]	90	10	2.48	2.34	1.67	1.06	0.77	3.55	3.29	2.10	1.22	0.85
		50	30	2.66	2.54	1.88	1.24	0.91	3.77	3.52	2.38	1.44	1.02
		50	10	2.67	2.55	1.89	1.25	0.92	3.84	3.59	2.41	1.45	1.02
		0	20	2.94	2.83	2.20	1.53	1.15	4.18	3.96	2.83	1.81	1.30
		0	10	2.96	2.85	2.22	1.53	1.16	4.25	4.02	2.87	1.82	1.31
		-50	20	3.25	3.15	2.58	1.89	1.47	4.60	4.41	3.36	2.28	1.69
		-50	10	3.28	3.18	2.60	1.90	1.47	4.71	4.51	3.42	2.30	1.71

Position of Air Space	Direction of Heat Flow	Mean Temp (F)	Temp Diff (deg F)	1.5-in. Air Space[a]					3.5-in. Air Space[a]				
				0.03	0.05	0.2	0.5	0.82	0.03	0.05	0.2	0.5	0.82
Horiz	Up	90	10	2.55	2.41	1.71	1.08	0.77	2.84	2.66	1.83	1.13	0.80
		50	30	1.87	1.81	1.45	1.04	0.80	2.09	2.01	1.58	1.10	0.84
		50	10	2.50	2.40	1.81	1.21	0.89	2.80	2.66	1.95	1.28	0.93
		0	20	2.01	1.95	1.63	1.23	0.97	2.25	2.18	1.79	1.32	1.03
		0	10	2.43	2.35	1.90	1.38	1.06	2.71	2.62	2.07	1.47	1.12
		-50	20	1.94	1.91	1.68	1.36	1.13	2.19	2.14	1.86	1.47	1.20
		-50	10	2.37	2.31	1.99	1.55	1.26	2.65	2.58	2.18	1.67	1.33
45° Slope	Up	90	10	2.92	2.73	1.86	1.14	0.80	3.18	2.96	1.97	1.18	0.82
		50	30	2.14	2.06	1.61	1.12	0.84	2.26	2.17	1.67	1.15	0.86
		50	10	2.88	2.74	1.99	1.29	0.94	3.12	2.95	2.10	1.34	0.96
		0	20	2.30	2.23	1.82	1.34	1.04	2.42	2.35	1.90	1.38	1.06
		0	10	2.79	2.69	2.12	1.49	1.13	2.98	2.87	2.23	1.54	1.16
		-50	20	2.22	2.17	1.88	1.49	1.21	2.34	2.29	1.97	1.54	1.25
		-50	10	2.71	2.64	2.23	1.69	1.35	2.87	2.79	2.33	1.75	1.39
Vertical	Horiz.	90	10	3.99	3.66	2.25	1.27	0.87	3.69	3.40	2.15	1.24	0.85
		50	30	2.58	2.46	1.84	1.23	0.90	2.67	2.55	1.89	1.25	0.91
		50	10	3.79	3.55	2.39	1.45	1.02	3.63	3.40	2.32	1.42	1.01
		0	20	2.76	2.66	2.10	1.48	1.12	2.88	2.78	2.17	1.51	1.14
		0	10	3.51	3.35	2.51	1.67	1.23	3.49	3.33	2.50	1.67	1.23
		-50	20	2.64	2.58	2.18	1.66	1.33	2.82	2.75	2.30	1.73	1.37
		-50	10	3.31	3.21	2.62	1.91	1.48	3.40	3.30	2.67	1.94	1.50
45° Slope	Down[d]	90	10	5.07	4.55	2.56	1.36	0.91	4.81	4.33	2.49	1.34	0.90
		50	30	3.58	3.36	2.31	1.42	1.00	3.51	3.30	2.28	1.40	1.00
		50	10	5.10	4.66	2.85	1.60	1.09	4.74	4.36	2.73	1.57	1.08
		0	20	3.85	3.66	2.68	1.74	1.27	3.81	3.63	2.66	1.74	1.27
		0	10	4.92	4.62	3.16	1.94	1.37	4.59	4.32	3.02	1.88	1.34
		-50	20	3.62	3.50	2.80	2.01	1.54	3.77	3.64	2.90	2.05	1.57
		-50	10	4.67	4.47	3.40	2.29	1.70	4.50	4.32	3.31	2.25	1.68
Horiz.	Down[d]	90	10	6.09	5.35	2.79	1.43	0.94	10.07	8.19	3.41	1.57	1.00
		50	30	6.27	5.63	3.18	1.70	1.14	9.60	8.17	3.86	1.88	1.22
		50	10	6.61	5.90	3.27	1.73	1.15	11.15	9.27	4.09	1.93	1.24
		0	20	7.03	6.43	3.91	2.19	1.49	10.90	9.52	4.87	2.47	1.62
		0	10	7.31	6.66	4.00	2.22	1.51	11.97	10.32	5.08	2.52	1.64
		-50	20	7.73	7.20	4.77	2.85	1.99	11.64	10.49	6.02	3.25	2.18
		-50	10	8.09	7.52	4.91	2.89	2.01	12.98	11.56	6.36	3.34	2.22

[a] Credit for an air space resistance value cannot be taken more than once and only for the boundary conditions established.

[b] Interpolation is permissible for other values of mean temperature, temperature differences, and effective emittance E. Interpolation and moderate extrapolation for air spaces greater than 3.5 in. are also permissible.

[c] Effective emittance of the space E is given by $1/E = 1/e_1 + 1/e_2 - 1$, where e_1 and e_2 are the emittances of the surfaces of the air space (See section B of Table 3.)

[d] Resistances of horizontal spaces with heat flow downward are substantially independent of temperature difference.

[e] Thermal resistance values were determined from the relation $R = 1/C$, where $C = h_c + Eh_r$, h_c is the conduction-convection coefficient, Eh_r is the radiation coefficient $\cong 0.00686E [(460 + t_m)/100]^3$, and t_m is the mean temperature of the air space. For interpretation from Table 4 to air space thicknesses less than 0.5 in. (as in insulating window glass), assume $h_c = 0.795 (1 + 0.0016)$ and compute R-values from the above relations for an air space thickness of 0.2 in.

Table 5. Thermal properties of typical building and insulating materials—(design values)[a]

These coefficients are expressed in Btuh-ft² (deg F difference in temperature between the air on the two sides),
and are based on an outside wind velocity of 15 mph

These constants are expressed in Btu per (hour) (square foot) (degree Fahrenheit temperature difference). Conductivities *(k)* are per inch thickness, and conductances *(C)* are for thickness or construction stated, not per inch thickness. All values are for a mean temperature of 75°F, except as noted by an asterisk (*) which have been reported at 45°F.

Description	Density (lb/ft³)	Conductivity (k)	Conductance (C)	Resistance[b] (R) Per inch thickness (1/k)	Resistance[b] (R) For thickness listed (1/C)	Specific Heat, Btu/(lb) (deg F)	Resistance[b] (R) (m · K) W	Resistance[b] (R) (m² · K) W
BUILDING BOARD								
Boards, Panels, Subflooring, Sheathing								
Woodboard Panel Products								
Asbestos-cement board	120	4.0	—	0.25	—	0.24	1.73	
Asbestos-cement board . . . 0.125 in.	120	—	33.00	—	0.03			0.005
Asbestos-cement board . . . 0.25 in.	120	—	16.50	—	0.06			0.01
Gypsum or plaster board . . . 0.375 in.	50	—	3.10	—	0.32	0.26		0.06
Gypsum or plaster board . . . 0.5 in.	50	—	2.22	—	0.45			0.08
Gypsum or plaster board . . . 0.625 in.	50	—	1.78	—	0.56			0.10
Plywood (Douglas Fir)	34	0.80	—	1.25	—	0.29	8.66	
Plywood (Douglas Fir) . . . 0.25 in.	34	—	3.20	—	0.31			0.05
Plywood (Douglas Fir) . . . 0.375 in.	34	—	2.13	—	0.47			0.08
Plywood (Douglas Fir) . . . 0.5 in.	34	—	1.60	—	0.62			0.11
Plywood (Douglas Fir) . . . 0.625 in.	34	—	1.29	—	0.77			0.19
Plywood or wood panels . . . 0.75 in.	34	—	1.07	—	0.93	0.29		0.16
Vegetable Fiber Board								
Sheathing, regular density . . . 0.5 in.	18	—	0.76	—	1.32	0.31		0.23
. . . 0.78125 in.	18	—	0.49	—	2.06			0.36
Sheathing intermediate density . . . 0.5 in.	22	—	0.82	—	1.22	0.31		0.21
Nail-base sheathing . . . 0.5 in.	25	—	0.88	—	1.14	0.31		0.20
Shingle backer . . . 0.375 in.	18	—	1.06	—	0.94	0.31		0.17
Shingle backer . . . 0.3125 in.	18	—	1.28	—	0.78			0.14
Sound deadening board . . . 0.5 in.	15	—	0.74	—	1.35	0.30		0.24
Tile and lay-in panels, plain or acoustic	18	0.40	—	2.50	—	0.14	17.33	
. . . 0.5 in.	18	—	0.80	—	1.25			0.22
. . . 0.75 in.	18	—	0.53	—	1.89			0.33
Laminated paperboard	30	0.50	—	2.00	—	0.33	13.86	
Homogeneous board from repulped paper	30	0.50	—	2.00	—	0.28	13.86	
Hardboard								
Medium density	50	0.73	—	1.37	—	0.31	9.49	
High density, service temp. service underlay	55	0.82	—	1.22	—	0.32	8.46	
High density, std. tempered	63	1.00	—	1.00	—	0.32	6.93	
Particleboard								
Low density	37	0.54	—	1.85	—	0.31	12.82	
Medium density	50	0.94	—	1.06	—	0.31	7.35	
High density	62.5	1.18	—	0.85	—	0.31	5.89	
Underlayment . . . 0.625 in.	40	—	1.22	—	0.82	0.29		0.14
Wood subfloor . . . 0.75 in.		—	1.06	—	0.94	0.33		0.17
BUILDING MEMBRANE								
Vapor-permeable felt	—	—	16.70	—	0.06			0.01
Vapor-seal, 2 layers of mopped 15-lb felt	—	—	8.35	—	0.12			0.02
Vapor-seal, plastic film	—	—	—	—	Negl.			
FINISH FLOORING MATERIALS								
Carpet and fibrous pad	—	—	0.48	—	2.08	0.34		0.37
Carpet and rubber pad	—	—	0.81	—	1.23	0.33		0.22
Cork tile . . . 0.125 in.	—	—	3.60	—	0.28	0.48		0.05
Terrazzo . . . 1 in.	—	—	12.50	—	0.08	0.19		0.01
Tile—asphalt, linoleum, vinyl, rubber	—	—	20.00	—	0.05	0.30		0.01
vinyl asbestos						0.24		
ceramic						0.19		
Wood, hardwood finish . . . 0.75 in.			1.47		0.68			0.12
INSULATING MATERIALS								
Blanket and Batt								
Mineral Fiber, fibrous form processed from rock, slag, or glass								
approx.[c] 2–2.75 in.	0.3–2.0	—	0.143	—	7[d]	0.17–0.23		1.23
approx.[c] 3–3.5 in.	0.3–2.0	—	0.091	—	11[d]			1.94
approx.[c] 5.50–6.5	0.3–2.0	—	0.053	—	19[d]			3.35
approx.[c] 6–7 in.	0.3–2.0		0.045		22[d]			3.87
approx.[d] 8.5 in.	0.3–2.0		0.033		30[d]			5.28

Notes are located at the end of the table.

Table 5 *(cont.).* **Thermal properties of typical building and insulating materials—(design values)**[a]

Description	Customary Unit						SI Unit	
	Density (lb/ft³)	Conductivity (k)	Conductance (C)	Resistance[b](R)		Specific Heat, Btu/(lb)(deg F)	Resistance[b] (R)	
				Per inch thickness (1/k)	For thickness listed (1/C)		(m·K) / W	(m²·K) / W
BOARD AND SLABS								
Cellular glass	8.5	0.38	—	2.63	—	0.24	18.23	
Glass fiber, organic bonded	4–9	0.25	—	4.00	—	0.23	27.72	
Expanded rubber (rigid)	4.5	0.22	—	4.55	—	0.40	31.53	
Expanded polystyrene extruded								
Cut cell surface	1.8	0.25	—	4.00	—	0.29	27.72	
Expanded polystyrene extruded								
Smooth skin surface	2.2	0.20	—	5.00	—	0.29	34.65	
Expanded polystyrene extruded								
Smooth skin surface	3.5	0.19	—	5.26	—		36.45	
Expanded polystyrene, molded beads	1.0	0.28	—	3.57	—	0.29	24.74	
Expanded polyurethane[f] (R-11 exp.)	1.5	0.16	—	6.25	—	0.38	43.82	
(Thickness 1 in. or greater)	2.5							
Mineral fiber with resin binder	15	0.29	—	3.45	—	0.17	23.91	
Mineral fiberboard, wet felted								
Core or roof insulation	16–17	0.34	—	2.94	—		20.38	
Acoustical tile	18	0.35	—	2.86	—	0.19	19.82	
Acoustical tile	21	0.37	—	2.70	—		18.71	
Mineral fiberboard, wet molded								
Acoustical tile[g]	23	0.42	—	2.38	—	0.14	16.49	
Wood or cane fiberboard								
Acoustical tile[g] . . . . 0.5 in.	—	—	0.80	—	1.25	0.31		0.22
Acoustical tile[g] . . . . 0.75 in.	—	—	0.53	—	1.89			0.33
Interior finish (plank, tile)	15	0.35	—	2.86	—	0.32	19.82	
Wood shredded (cemented in								
preformed slabs)	22	0.60	—	1.67	—	0.31	11.57	
LOOSE FILL								
Cellulosic insulation (milled paper or								
wood pulp)	2.3–3.2	0.27–0.32	—	3.13–3.70	—	0.33	21.69–25.64	
Sawdust or shavings	8.0–15.0	0.45	—	2.22	—	0.33	15.39	
Wood fiber, softwoods	2.0–3.5	0.30	—	3.33	—	0.33	23.08	
Perlite, expanded	5.0–8.0	0.37	—	2.70	—	0.26	18.71	
Mineral fiber (rock, slag or glass)								
approx.[e] 3.75–5 in.	0.6–2.0	—	—		11	0.17		1.94
approx.[e] 6.5–8.75 in.	0.6–2.0	—	—		19			3.35
approx.[e] 7.5–10 in.	0.6–2.0	—	—		22			3.87
approx.[e] 10.25–13.75 in.	0.6–2.0	—			30			5.28
Vermiculite, exfoliated	7.0–8.2	0.47	—	2.13	—	3.20	14.76	
	4.0–6.0	0.44	—	2.27	—		15.73	
ROOF INSULATION[h]								
Preformed, for use above deck								
Different roof insulations are available in different			0.72		1.39		—	0.24
thicknesses to provide the design C values listed.[h]			to		to			to
Consult individual manufacturers for actual			0.12		8.33		—	1.47
thickness of their material.								
MASONRY MATERIALS								
CONCRETES								
Cement mortar	116	5.0	—	0.20	—		1.39	
Gypsum-fiber concrete 87.5% gypsum,								
12.5% wood chips	51	1.66	—	0.60	—	0.21	4.16	
Lightweight aggregates including ex-	120	5.2	—	0.19	—		1.32	
panded shale, clay or slate; expanded	100	3.6	—	0.28	—		1.94	
slags; cinders; pumice; vermiculite;	80	2.5	—	0.40	—		2.77	
also cellular concretes	60	1.7	—	0.59	—		4.09	
	40	1.15	—	0.86	—		5.96	
	30	0.90	—	1.11	—		7.69	
	20	0.70		1.43			9.91	
Perlite, expanded	40	0.93		1.08			7.48	
	30	0.71		1.41			9.77	
	20	0.50		2.00		0.32	13.86	
Sand and gravel or stone aggregate								
(oven dried)	140	9.0	—	0.11		0.22	0.76	
Sand and gravel or stone aggregate								
(not dried)	140	12.0	—	0.08			0.55	
Stucco	116	5.0	—	0.20			1.39	
MASONRY UNITS								
Brick, common[i]	120	5.0	—	0.20	—	0.19	1.39	
Brick, face[i]	130	9.0	—	0.11	—		0.76	

Table 5 (cont.). Thermal properties of typical building and insulating materials—(design values)[a]

Description	Density (lb/ft³)	Conductivity (k)	Conductance (C)	Resistance[b] (R) Per inch thickness (1/k)	Resistance[b] (R) For thickness listed (1/C)	Specific Heat, Btu/(lb) (deg F)	SI Unit Resistance[b] (R) (m·K) W	SI Unit Resistance[b] (R) (m²·K) W
Clay tile, hollow:								
1 cell deep .... 3 in.	—	—	1.25	—	0.80	0.21		0.14
1 cell deep .... 4 in.	—	—	0.90	—	1.11			0.20
2 cells deep .... 6 in.	—	—	0.66	—	1.52			0.27
2 cells deep .... 8 in.	—	—	0.54	—	1.85			0.33
2 cells deep .... 10 in.	—	—	0.45	—	2.22			0.39
3 cells deep .... 12 in.	—	—	0.40	—	2.50			0.44
Concrete blocks, three oval core:								
Sand and gravel aggregate .... 4 in.	—	—	1.40	—	0.71	0.22		0.13
.... 8 in.	—	—	0.90	—	1.11			0.20
.... 12 in.	—	—	0.78	—	1.28			0.23
Cinder aggregate .... 3 in.	—	—	1.16	—	0.86	0.21		0.15
.... 4 in.	—	—	0.90	—	1.11			0.20
.... 8 in.	—	—	0.58	—	1.72			0.30
.... 12 in.	—	—	0.53	—	1.89			0.33
Lightweight aggregate .... 3 in.	—	—	0.79	—	1.27	0.21		0.22
(expanded shale, clay, slate .... 4 in.	—	—	0.67	—	1.50			0.26
or slag; pumice)....................... 8 in.	—	—	0.50	—	2.00			0.35
.... 12 in.	—	—	0.44	—	2.27			0.40
Concrete blocks, rectangular core.*ʲ								
Sand and gravel aggregate								
2 core, 8 in. 36 lb.ᵏ* .ː.	—	—	0.96	—	1.04	0.22		0.18
Same with filled coresʲ*	—	—	0.52	—	1.93	0.22		0.34
Lightweight aggregate (expanded shale, clay, slate or slag, pumice):								
3 core, 6 in. 19 lb.ᵏ*	—	—	0.61	—	1.65	0.21		0.29
Same with filled coresˡ*	—	—	0.33	—	2.99			0.53
2 core, 8 in. 24 lb.ᵏ*	—	—	0.46	—	2.18			0.38
Same with filled coresˡ*	—	—	0.20	—	5.03			0.89
3 core, 12 in. 38 lb.ᵏ*	—	—	0.40	—	2.48			0.44
Same with filled coresˡ*	—	—	0.17	—	5.82			1.02
Stone, lime or sand....................	—	12.50	—	0.08	—	0.19	0.55	
Gypsum partition tile:								
3 × 12 × 30 in. solid	—	—	0.79	—	1.26	0.19		0.22
3 × 12 × 30 in. 4-cell	—	—	0.74	—	1.35			0.24
4 × 12 × 30 in. 3-cell	—	—	0.60	—	1.67			0.29

PLASTERING MATERIALS

Description	Density (lb/ft³)	Conductivity (k)	Conductance (C)	Resistance[b] (R) Per inch thickness (1/k)	Resistance[b] (R) For thickness listed (1/C)	Specific Heat, Btu/(lb) (deg F)	SI Unit Resistance[b] (R) (m·K) W	SI Unit Resistance[b] (R) (m²·K) W
Cement plaster, sand aggregate	116	5.0	—	0.20	—	0.20	1.39	
Sand aggregate .... 0.375 in.	—	—	13.3	—	0.08	0.20		0.01
Sand aggregate .... 0.75 in.	—	—	6.66	—	0.15	0.20		0.03
Gypsum plaster:								
Lightweight aggregate.................... 0.5 in.	45	—	3.12	—	0.32			0.06
Lightweight aggregate .... 0.625 in.	45	—	2.67	—	0.39			0.07
Lightweight agg. on metal lath .... 0.75 in.	—	—	2.13	—	0.47			0.08
Perlite aggregate........................	45	1.5	—	0.67	—	0.32	4.64	
Sand aggregate.........................	105	5.6	—	0.18	—	0.20	1.25	
Sand aggregate................... 0.5 in.	105	—	11.10	—	0.09	—		0.02
Sand aggregate................. 0.625 in.	105	—	9.10	—	0.11			0.02
Sand aggregate on metal lath........ 0.75 in.	—	—	7.70	—	0.13			0.02
Vermiculite aggregate	45	1.7	—	0.59	—		4.09	

ROOFING

Description	Density (lb/ft³)	Conductivity (k)	Conductance (C)	Resistance[b] (R) Per inch thickness (1/k)	Resistance[b] (R) For thickness listed (1/C)	Specific Heat, Btu/(lb) (deg F)	SI Unit Resistance[b] (R) (m·K) W	SI Unit Resistance[b] (R) (m²·K) W
Asbestos-cement shingles.....................	120	—	4.76	—	0.21	0.24		0.04
Asphalt roll roofing	70	—	6.50	—	0.15	0.36		0.03
Asphalt shingles	70	—	2.27	—	0.44	0.30		0.08
Built-up roofing .... 0.375 in.	70	—	3.00	—	0.33	0.35		0.06
Slate............................... 0.5 in.	—	—	20.00	—	0.05	0.30		0.01
Wood shingles, plain and plastic film faced	—	—	1.06	—	0.94	0.31		0.17

SIDING MATERIALS (On Flat Surface)

Shingles

Description	Density (lb/ft³)	Conductivity (k)	Conductance (C)	Resistance[b] (R) Per inch thickness (1/k)	Resistance[b] (R) For thickness listed (1/C)	Specific Heat, Btu/(lb) (deg F)	SI Unit Resistance[b] (R) (m·K) W	SI Unit Resistance[b] (R) (m²·K) W
Asbestos-cement........................	120	—	4.75	—	0.21			0.04
Wood, 16 in., 7.5 exposure...................	—	—	1.15	—	0.87	0.31		0.15
Wood, double, 16-in., 12-in. exposure	—	—	0.84	—	1.19	0.28		0.21
Wood, plus insul. backer board, 0.3125 in........	—	—	0.71	—	1.40	0.31		0.25
Siding								
Asbestos-cement, 0.25 in., lapped..............	—	—	4.76	—	0.21	0.24		0.04
Asphalt roll siding	—	—	6.50	—	0.15	0.35		0.03
Asphalt insulating siding (0.5 in. bed.)	—	—	0.69	—	1.46	0.35		0.26
Hardboard siding, 0.4375 in..............	40	1.49	—	0.67	—	0.28	4.65	
Wood, drop, 1 × 8 in...................	—	—	1.27	—	0.79	0.28		0.14

Table 5 *(cont.)*. Thermal properties of typical building and insulating materials—(design values)[a]

Description	Density (lb/ft³)	Conduc-tivity (k)	Conduc-tance (C)	Resistance[b] (R) Per inch thickness (1/k)	Resistance[b] (R) For thick-ness listed (1/C)	Specific Heat, Btu/(lb) (deg F)	SI Unit Resistance[b] (R) (m·K) W	SI Unit Resistance[b] (R) (m²·K) W
Wood, bevel, 0.5 × 8 in., lapped	—	—	1.23	—	0.81	0.28		0.14
Wood, bevel, 0.75 × 10 in., lapped	—	—	0.95	—	1.05	0.28		0.18
Wood, plywood, 0.375 in., lapped	—	—	1.59	—	0.59	0.29		0.10
Aluminum or Steel[m], over sheathing Hollow-backed	—	—	1.61	—	0.61	0.29		0.11
Insulating-board backed nominal 0.375 in.	—	—	0.55	—	1.82	0.32		0.32
Insulating-board backed nominal 0.375 in., foil backed			0.34		2.96			0.52
Architectural glass	—	—	10.00	—	0.10	0.20		0.02
WOODS								
Maple, oak, and similar hardwoods	45	1.10	—	0.91	—	0.30	6.31	
Fir, pine, and similar softwoods	32	0.80	—	1.25	—	0.33	8.66	
Fir, pine, and similar softwoods ...0.75 in.	32	—	1.06	—	0.94	0.33		0.17
......1.5 in.		—	0.53	—	1.89			0.33
......2.5 in.		—	0.32	—	3.12			0.60
......3.5 in.		—	0.23	—	4.35			0.75

Notes for Table 5

[a] Representative values for dry materials were selected by ASHRAE Technical Committee on Insulation and Moisture Barriers. They are intended as design (not specification) values for materials in normal use. For properties of a particular product, use the value supplied by the manufacturer or by unbiased tests.

[b] Resistance values are the reciprocals of C before rounding off C to two decimal places.

[c] Also see Insulating Materials, Board.

[d] Does not include paper backing and facing, if any. Where insulation forms a boundary (reflective or otherwise) of an air space, see Tables 3 and 4 for the insulating value of air space for the appropriate effective emittance and temperature conditions of the space.

[e] Conductivity varies with fiber diameter. Insulation is produced in different densities; therefore, there is a wide variation in thickness for the same R-value among manufacturers. No effort should be made to relate any specific R-value to any specific thickness. Commercial thicknesses generally available range from 2 to 8.5.

[f] Values are for aged board stock. Conductivity increases slowly with time as air permeates the cells.

[g] Insulating values of acoustical tile vary, depending on density of the board and on type, size, and depth of perforations.

[h] The U. S. Department of Commerce, *Simplified Practice Recommendation for Thermal Conductance Factors for Preformed Above-Deck Roof Insulation*, No. R 257-55, recognizes the specification of roof insulation on the basis of the C-values shown. Roof insulation is made in thicknesses to meet these values.

[i] Face brick and common brick do not always have these specific densities. When density is different from that shown, there will be a change in thermal conductivity.

[j] Data on rectangular core concrete blocks differ from the above data on oval core blocks, due to core configuration, different mean temperatures, and possibly differences in unit weights. Weight data on the oval core blocks tested are not available.

[k] Weights of units approximately 7.625 in. high and 15.75 in. long. These weights are given as a means of describing the blocks tested, but conductance values are all for 1 ft² of area.

[l] Vermiculite, perlite, or mineral wool insulation. Where insulation is used, vapor barriers or other precautions must be considered to keep insulation dry.

[m] Values for metal siding applied over flat surfaces vary widely, depending on amount of ventilation of air space beneath the siding; whether air space is reflective or nonreflective; and on thickness, type, and application of insulating backing-board used. Values given are averages for use as design guides, and were obtained from several guarded hotbox tests (ASTM C236) or calibrated hotbox (BSS 77) on hollow-backed types and types made using backing-boards of wood fiber, foamed plastic, and glass fiber. Departures of ±50% or more from the values given may occur.

Table 6A. Coefficients of transmission (U) of frame walls*

(Reproduced by permission from *ASHRAE Handbook of Fundamentals*, 1977)
These coefficients are expressed in Btuh-ft² (deg F difference in temperature between the air on the two sides),
and are based on an outside wind velocity of 15 mph

Replace Air Space with 3.5-in. R-11 Blanket Insulation (New Item 4)

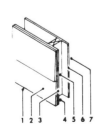

Construction	1 Resistance (R) Between Framing	1 At Framing	2 Resistance (R) Between Framing	2 At Framing
1. Outside surface (15 mph wind)	0.17	0.17	0.17	0.17
2. Siding, wood, 0.5 in.× 8 in. lapped (average)	0.81	0.81	0.81	0.81
3. Sheathing, 0.5-in. asphalt impregnated	1.32	1.32	1.32	1.32
4. Nonreflective air space, 3.5 in. (50 F mean; 10 deg F temperature difference)	1.01	—	11.00	—
5. Nominal 2-in. × 4-in. wood stud	—	4.38	—	4.38
6. Gypsum wallboard, 0.5 in.	0.45	0.45	0.45	0.45
7. Inside surface (still air)	0.68	0.68	0.68	0.68
Total Thermal Resistance (R)	R_i=4.44	R_s=7.81	R_i=14.43	R_s=7.81

Construction No. 1: $U_i = 1/4.44 = 0.225$; $U_s = 1/7.81 = 0.128$. With 20% framing (typical of 2-in. × 4-in. studs @ 16-in. o.c.), $U_{av} = 0.8(0.225) + 0.2(0.128) = 0.206$ (See Eq 9)

Construction No. 2: $U_i = 1/14.43 = 0.069$; $U_s = 0.128$. With framing unchanged, $U_{av} = 0.8(0.069) + 0.2(0.128) = 0.081$

* See text section on overall coefficients for basis of calculations.

Table 6B. Coefficients of transmission *(U)* of solid masonry walls*
(Reproduced by permission from *ASHRAE Handbook of Fundamentals,* 1977)
Coefficients are expressed in Btuh·ft² (deg F difference in temperature between the air on the two sides), and are based on an outside wind velocity of 15 mph

Replace Furring Strips and Air Space with 1-in. Extruded Polystyrene (New Item 4)

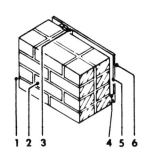

Construction	1 Resistance *(R)*		2
	Between Furring	At Furring	
1. Outside surface (15 mph wind)	0.17	0.17	0.17
2. Common brick, 8 in.	1.60	1.60	1.60
3. Nominal 1-in. ×3-in. vertical furring	—	0.94	—
4. Nonreflective air space, 0.75 in. (50 F mean; 10 deg F temperature difference)	1.01	—	5.00
5. Gypsum wallboard, 0.5 in.	0.45	0.45	0.45
6. Inside surface (still air)	0.68	0.68	0.68
Total Thermal Resistance (R)	R_i = 3.91	R_s = 3.84	R_i = 7.90 = R_s

Construction No. 1: U_i= 1/3.91=0.256; U_s=1/3.84=0.260. With 20% framing (typical of 1-in. × 3-in. vertical furring on masonry @ 16-in. o.c.) U_{av} = 0.8 (0.256) + 0.2 (0.260) = 0.257
Construction No. 2: $U_i = U_s = U_{av}$ = 1/7.90 = 0.127

* See text section on overall coefficients for basis of calculations.

Table 6C. Coefficients of transmission *(U)* of frame partitions or interior walls*
(Reproduced by permission from *ASHRAE Handbook of Fundamentals,* 1977)
Coefficients are expressed in Btuh·ft² (deg F difference in temperature between the air on the two sides),
and are based on still air (no wind) conditions on both sides

Replace Air Space with 3.5-in. R-11 Blanket Insulation (New Item 3)

Construction	1 Resistance (R)		2	
	Between Framing	At Framing	Between Framing	At Framing
1. Inside surface (still air)	0.68	0.68	0.68	0.68
2. Gypsum wallboard, 0.5 in.	0.45	0.45	0.45	0.45
3. Nonreflective air space, 3.5 in. (50 F mean; 10 deg F temperature difference)	1.01	—	11.00	—
4. Nominal 2-in. × 4-in. wood stud	—	4.38	—	4.38
5. Gypsum wallboard, 0.5 in.	0.45	0.45	0.45	0.45
6. Inside surface (still air)	0.68	0.68	0.68	0.68
Total Thermal Resistance (R)	R_i = 3.27	R_s = 6.64	R_i = 13.26	R_s = 6.64

Construction No. 1: U_i = 1/3.27 = 0.306; U_s = 1/6.64 = 0.151. With 10% framing (typical of 2-in. × 4-in. studs @ 24-in. o.c.), U_{av} = 0.9 (0.306) + 0.1 (0.151) = 0.290
Construction No. 2: U_i = 1/13.26 = 0.075, U_s = 1/6.64 = 0.151. With framing unchanged, U_{av} = 0.9(0.075) + 0.1(0.151) = 0.083

* See text section on overall coefficients for basis of calculations.

Table 6D. Coefficients of transmission *(U)* of masonry walls*
(Reproduced by permission from *ASHRAE Handbook of Fundamentals,* 1977)
Coefficients are expressed in Btuh·ft² (deg F difference in temperature between the air on the two sides),
and are based on an outside wind velocity of 15 mph

Replace Cinder Aggregate Block with 6-in. Light-weight Aggregate Block with Cores Filled (New Item 4)

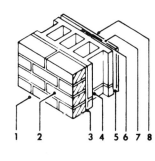

Construction	1 Resistance (R)		2	
	Between Furring	At Furring	Between Furring	At Furring
1. Outside surface (15 mph wind)	0.17	0.17	0.17	0.17
2. Face brick, 4 in.	0.44	0.44	0.44	0.44
3. Cement mortar, 0.5 in.	0.10	0.10	0.10	0.10
4. Concrete block, cinder aggregate, 8 in.	1.72	1.72	2.99	2.99
5. Reflective air space, 0.75 in. (50 F mean; 30 deg F temperature difference)	2.77	—	2.77	—
6. Nominal 1-in. × 3-in. vertical furring	—	0.94	—	0.94
7. Gypsum wallboard, 0.5 in., foil backed	0.45	0.45	0.45	0.45
8. Inside surface (still air)	0.68	0.68	0.68	0.68
Total Thermal Resistance (R)	R_i = 6.33	R_s = 4.50	R_i = 7.60	R_s = 5.77

Construction No. 1: U_i = 1/6.33 = 0.158; U_s = 1/4.50 = 0.222. With 20% framing (typical of 1-in. × 3-in. vertical furring on masonry @ 16-in. o.c.), U_{av} = 0.8 (0.158) + 0.2 (0.222) = 0.171
Construction No. 2: U_i = 1/7.60 = 0.132, U_s = 1/5.77 = 0.173. With framing unchanged, U_{av} = 0.8(0.132) + 0.2(0.173) = 1.40

* See text section on overall coefficients for basis of calculations.

Table 6E. Coefficients of transmission (U) of masonry cavity walls*
(Reproduced by permission from *ASHRAE Handbook of Fundamentals*, 1977)
Coefficients are expressed in Btuh·ft² (deg F difference in temperature between the air on the two sides), and are based on an outside
wind velocity of 15 mph

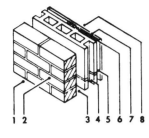

Replace Furring Strips and Gypsum Wallboard with 0.625-in. Plaster (Sand Aggregate) Applied Directly to Concrete Block-Fill 2.5-in. Air Space with Vermiculite Insulation (New Items 3 and 7.

Construction	1 Resistance (R)		2
	Between Furring	At Furring	
1. Outside surface (15 mph wind)	0.17	0.17	0.17
2. Common brick, 8 in.	0.80	0.80	0.80
3. Nonreflective air space, 2.5 in. (30 F mean; 10 deg F temperature difference)	1.10*	1.10†	5.32‡
4. Concrete block, stone aggregate, 4 in.	0.71	0.71	0.71
5. Nonreflective air space 0.75 in. (50 F mean; 10 deg F temperature difference)	1.01	—	—
6. Nominal 1-in. × 3-in. vertical furring	—	0.94	—
7. Gypsum wallboard, 0.5 in.	0.45	0.45	0.11
8. Inside surface (still air)	0.68	0.68	0.68
Total Thermal Resistance (R)	R_i = 4.92	R_s = 4.85	$R_i = R_s$ = 7.79

Construction No. 1: U_i = 1/4.92 = 0.203; U_s = 1/4.85 = 0.206. With 20% framing (typical of 1-in. × 3-in. vertical furring on masonry @16-in. o.c.), U_{av} = 0.8(0.203) + 0.2(0.206) = 0.204
Construction No. 2: $U_i = U_s = U_{av}$ = 1.79 = 0.128

* See text section on overall coefficients for basis of calculations.
† Interpolated value from Table 4.
‡ Calculated value from Table 5.

Table 6F. Coefficients of transmission (U) of masonry partitions*
(Reproduced by permission from *ASHRAE Handbook of Fundamentals*, 1977)
Coefficients are expressed in Btuh·ft² (deg F difference in temperature between the air on the two sides),
and are based on still air (no wind) conditions on both sides

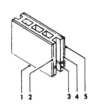

Replace Concrete Block with 4-in. Gypsum Tile (New Item 3) Construction	1	2
1. Inside surface (still air)	0.68	0.68
2. Plaster, lightweight aggregate, 0.625 in.	0.39	0.39
3. Concrete block, cinder aggregate, 4 in.	1.11	1.67
4. Plaster, lightweight aggregate, 0.625 in.	0.39	0.39
5. Inside surface (still air)	0.68	0.68
Total Thermal Resistance(R)	3.25	3.81

Construction No. 1: *U* = 1/3.25 = 0.308
Construction No. 2: *U* = 1/3.81 = 0.262

* See text section on overall coefficients for basis of calculations.

Table 6G. Coefficients of Transmission (U) of frame construction ceilings and floors*
(Reproduced by permission from *ASHRAE Handbook of Fundamentals*, 1977)
Coefficients are expressed in Btuh·ft² (deg F difference between the air on the two sides), and are
based on still air (no wind) on both sides

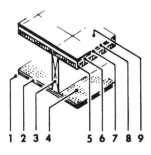

Assume Unheated Attic Space above Heated Room with Heat Flow Up—Remove Tile, Felt, Plywood, Subfloor and Air Space—Replace with R-19 Blanket Insulation (New Item 4)

Construction (Heat Flow Up)	1 Resistance (R)		2	
	Between Floor Joists	At Floor Joist	Between Floor Joists	At Floor Joists
1. Bottom surface (still air)	0.61	0.61	0.61	0.61
2. Metal lath and lightweight aggregate, plaster, 0.75 in.	0.47	0.47	0.47	0.47
3. Nominal 2-in. × 8-in. floor joist	—	9.06	—	9.06
4. Nonreflective airspace, 7.25-in.	0.93†	—	19.00	—
5. Wood subfloor, 0.75 in.	0.94	0.94	—	—
6. Plywood, 0.625 in.	0.78	0.78	—	—
7. Felt building membrane	0.06	0.06	—	—
8. Resilient tile	0.05	0.05	—	—
9. Top surface (still air)	0.61	0.61	0.61	0.61
Total Thermal Resistance (R)	R_i= 4.45	R_s = 12.58	R_i = 20.69	R_s=10.75

Construction No. 1 U_i= 1/4.45 = 0.225; U_s = 1/12.58 = 0.079. With 10% framing (typical of 2-in. joists @ 16-in. o.c.), U_{av} = 0.9 (0.225) + 0.1 (0.079)= 0.210
Construction No. 2 U_i = 1/20.69 = 0.048; U_s = 1/10.75 = 0.093. With framing unchanged, U_{av} = 0.9 (0.048) + 0.1 (0.093) = 0.053

* See text section on overall coefficients for basis of calculations.
† Use largest air space (3.5 in.) value shown in Table 4.

Table 6H. Coefficients of transmission (U) of flat masonry roofs with built-up roofing, with and without suspended ceilings*† (winter conditions, upward flow)

(Reproduced by permission from *ASHRAE Handbook of Fundamentals,* 1977)
These coefficients are expressed in Btuh·ft² (deg F difference in temperature between the air on the two sides), and are based upon an outside wind velocity of 15 mph

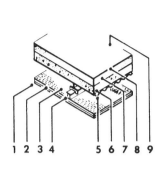

Add Rigid Roof Deck Insulation, $C = 0.24$ ($R = 1/C$) (New Item 7) Construction (Heat Flow Up)	1	2
1. Inside surface (still air)	0.61	0.61
1. Metal lath and lightweight aggregate plaster, 0.75 in.	0.47	0.47
3. Nonreflective air space, greater than 3.5 in. (50 F mean; 10 deg F temperature difference)	0.93‡	0.93‡
4. Metal ceiling suspension system with metal hanger rods	0§	0§
5. Corrugated metal deck	0	0
6. Concrete slab, lightweight aggregate, 2 in.	2.22	2.22
7. Rigid roof deck insulation (none)	—	4.17
8. Built-up roofing, 0.375 in.	0.33	0.33
9. Outside surface (15 mph wind)	0.17	0.17
Total Thermal Resistance (R)	4.73	8.90

Construction No. 1: $U_{av} = 1/4.73 = 0.211$
Construction No. 2: $U_{av} = 1/8.90 = 0.112$

* See text section on overall coefficients for basis of calculations.
† To adjust *U*-values for the effect of added insulation between framing members, see Table 7 or 8.
‡ Use largest air space (3.5 in.) value shown in Table 4.
§ Area of hanger rods is negligible in relation to ceiling area.

Table 6I. Coefficients of transmission (U) of wood construction flat roofs and ceilings* (winter conditions, upward flow)

(Reproduced by permission from *ASHRAE Handbook of Fundamentals,* 1977)
Coefficients are expressed in Btuh·ft² (deg F difference in temperature between the air on the two sides), and are based upon an outside wind velocity of 15 mph

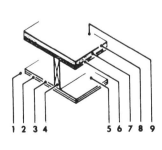

Replace Roof Deck Insulation and 7.25-in. Air Space with 6-in. R-19 Blanket Insulation and 1.25-in. Air Space (New Items 5 and 7)	1		2	
	Resistance (R)			
Construction (Heat Flow Up)	Between Joists	At Joists	Between Joists	At Joists
1. Inside surface (still air)	0.61	0.61	0.61	0.61
2. Acoustical tile, fiberboard, glued, 0.5 in.	1.25	1.25	1.25	1.25
3. Gypsum wallboard, 0.5 in.	0.45	0.45	0.45	0.45
4. Nominal 2-in. × 8-in. ceiling joists	—	9.06	—	9.06
5. Nonreflective air space, 7.25 in. (50 F mean; 10 deg F temperature difference)	0.93†	—	1.05‡	—
6. Plywood deck, 0.625 in.	0.78	0.78	0.78	0.78
7. Rigid roof deck insulation, c = 0.72, ($R = 1/C$)	1.39	1.39	19.00	—
8. Built-up roof	0.33	0.33	0.33	0.33
9. Outside surface (15 mph wind)	0.17	0.17	0.17	0.17
Total Thermal Resistance (R)	R_i=5.91	R_s=14.04	R_i=23.64	R_s=12.65

Construction No. 1 $U_i = 1/5.91 = 0.169$; $U_s = 1/14.04 = 0.071$. With 10% framing (typical of 2-in. joists @ 16-in. o.c.), $U_{av} = 0.9 (0.169) + 0.1 (0.071) = 0.159$
Construction No. 2 $U_i = 1/23.64 = 0.042$; $U_s = 1/12.65 = 0.079$. With framing unchanged, $U_{av} = 0.9 (0.042) + 0.1 (0.079) = 0.046$

* See text section on overall coefficients for basis of calculations.
† Use largest air space (3.5 in.) value shown in Table 4.
‡ Interpolated value (0°F mean; 10°F temperature difference).

Table 6J. Coefficients of transmission (U) of metal construction flat roofs and ceilings*
(winter conditions, upward flow)
(Reproduced by permission from *ASHRAE Handbook of Fundamentals,* 1977)
Coefficients are expressed in Btuh·ft² (deg F difference in temperature between the air on the two sides),
and are based on upon outside wind velocity of 15 mph

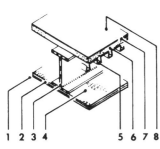

Replace Rigid Roof Deck Insulation ($C = 0.24$) and Sand Aggregate Plaster with Rigid Roof Deck Insulation, $C = 0.36$ and Lightweight Aggregate Plaster (New Items 2 and 6)		
Construction (Heat Flow Up)	1	2
1. Inside surface (still air)	0.61	0.61
2. Metal lath and sand aggregate plaster, 0.75 in.	0.13	0.47
3. Structural beam	0.00†	0.00†
4. Nonreflective air space (50 F mean; 10 deg F temperature difference)	0.93‡	0.93‡
5. Metal deck	0.00†	0.00†
6. Rigid roof deck insulation, $C = 0.24 (R = 1/c)$	4.17	2.78
7. Built-up roofing, 0.375 in.	0.33	0.33
8. Outside surface (15 mph wind)	0.17	0.17
Total Thermal Resistance (R)	6.34	5.29

Construction No. 1: $U = 1/6.34 = 0.158$
Construction No. 2: $U = 1/5.29 = 0.189$

* See text section on overall coefficients for basis of calculations.

† If structural beams and metal deck are to be considered, the technique shown in ASHRAE Handbook may be used to estimate total R. Full-scale testing of a suitable portion of the construction is, however, preferable.

‡ Use largest air space (3.5 in.) value shown in Table 4.

Table 6K. Coefficients of transmission (U) of pitched roofs* †
(Reproduced by permission from *ASHRAE Handbook of Fundamentals,* 1977)
Coefficients are expressed in Btuh·ft² (deg F difference in temperature between the air on the two sides), and are based on an outside wind velocity of 15 mph for heat flow upward and 7.5 mph for heat flow downward

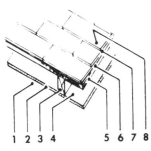

Find U_{av} for same Construction 2 with Heat Flow Down (Summer Conditions)				
	1		2	
Construction 1 (Heat Flow Up) (Reflective Air Space)	Between Rafters	At Rafters	Between Rafters	At Rafters
1. Inside surface (still air)	0.62	0.62	0.76	0.76
2. Gypsum wallboard 0.5 in., foil backed	0.45	0.45	0.45	0.45
3. Nominal 2-in. × 4-in. ceiling rafter	—	4.38	—	4.38
4. 45 deg slope reflective air space, 3.5 in. (50 F mean, 30 deg F temperature difference)	2.17	—	4.33	—
5. Plywood sheathing, 0.625 in.	0.78	0.78	0.78	0.78
6. Felt building membrane	0.06	0.06	0.06	0.06
7. Asphalt shingle roofing	0.44	0.44	0.44	0.44
8. Outside surface (15 mph wind)	0.17	0.17	0.25§	0.25§
Total Thermal Resistance (R)	R_i=4.69	R_s=6.90	R_i=7.07	R_s=7.12

Construction No. 1: $U_i = 1/4.69 = 0.213$; $U_s = 1/6.90 = 0.145$. With 10% framing (typical of 2-in. rafters @16-in. o.c.), $U_{av} = 0.9 (0.213) + 0.1 (0.145) = 0.206$
Construction No. 2: $U_i = 1/7.07 = 0.141$; $U_s = 1/7.12 = 0.140$. With framing unchanged, $U_{av} = 0.9 (0.141) + 0.1 (0.140) = 0.141$

Find U_{av} for same Construction 2 with Heat Flow Down (Summer Conditions)				
	3		4	
Construction 1 (Heat Flow Up) (Non-Reflective Air Space)	Between Rafters	At Rafters	Between Rafters	At Rafters
1. Inside surface (still air)	0.62	0.62	0.76	0.76
2. Gypsum wallboard, 0.5 in.	0.45	0.45	0.45	0.45
3. Nominal 2-in. × 4-in. ceiling rafter	—	4.38	—	4.38
4. 45 deg slope, nonreflective air space, 3.5 in. (50 F mean; 10 deg F temperature difference)	0.96	—	0.90‡	—
5. Plywood sheathing, 0.625 in.	0.78	0.78	0.78	0.78
6. Felt building membrane	0.06	0.06	0.06	0.06
7. Asphalt shingle roofing	0.44	0.44	0.44	0.44
8. Outside surface (15-mph wind)	0.17	0.17	0.25§	0.25§
Total Thermal Resistance (R)	R_i=3.48	R_s=6.90	R_i=3.64	R_s=7.12

Construction No. 3: $U_i = 1/3.48 = 0.287$; $U_s = 1/6.90 = 0.145$. With 10% framing typical of 2-in. rafters @ 16-in. o.c.), $U_{av} = 0.9 (0.287) + 0.1 (0.145) = 0.273$
Construction No. 4: $U_i = 1/3.64 = 0.275$; $U_s = 1/7.12 = 0.140$. With framing unchanged, $U_{av} = 0.9 (0.275) + 0.1 (0.140) = 0.262$

* See text section on overall coefficients for basis of calculations.   ‡ Air space value at 90°F mean, 10°F temperature difference.
† Pitch of roof—45 deg.   § 7.5-mph wind.

Table 7A. Determination of U-value resulting from addition of insulation to the total area[e] of any given building section

(*Reproduced by permission from ASHRAE Handbook of Fundamentals, 1977.*)

Given Building Section Property[a,b]		Added R[c,d,e]						
		R=4	R=6	R=8	R=12	R=16	R=20	R=24
U	R	U	U	U	U	U	U	U
1.00	1.00	0.20	0.14	0.11	0.08	0.06	0.05	0.04
0.90	1.11	0.20	0.14	0.11	0.08	0.06	0.05	0.04
0.80	1.25	0.19	0.14	0.11	0.08	0.06	0.05	0.04
0.70	1.43	0.19	0.13	0.11	0.07	0.06	0.05	0.04
0.60	1.67	0.19	0.13	0.10	0.07	0.06	0.05	0.04
0.50	2.00	0.18	0.13	0.10	0.07	0.06	0.05	0.04
0.40	2.50	0.16	0.12	0.10	0.07	0.05	0.05	0.04
0.30	3.33	0.14	0.11	0.09	0.07	0.05	0.04	0.04
0.20	5.00	0.11	0.09	0.08	0.06	0.05	0.04	0.03
0.10	10.00	0.06	0.06	0.06	0.05	0.04	0.04	0.03
0.08	12.50	0.06	0.06	0.05	0.04	0.04	0.03	0.03

[a] *For U- or R-values not shown in the table, interpolate as necessary.*
[b] *Enter column 1 with U or R of the design building section.*
[c] *Under appropriate column heading for Added R, find U-value of resulting design section.*
[d] *If the insulation occupies a previously considered air space, an adjustment must be made in the given building section R-value.*
[e] *If insulation is applied between framing members use equation given on sheet 4 to determine average U-value.*

Table 7B. Determination of U-value resulting from addition of insulation to uninsulated building sections

(*Reproduced by permission from ASHRAE Handbook of Fundamentals, 1977.*)

U Value of Roof without Roof-Deck Insulation[a]	Conductance C of Roof-Deck Insulation					
	0.12	0.15	0.19	0.24	0.36	0.72
	U	U	U	U	U	U
0.10	0.05	0.06	0.07	0.07	0.08	0.09
0.15	0.07	0.08	0.08	0.09	0.11	0.12
0.20	0.08	0.09	0.10	0.11	0.13	0.16
0.25	0.08	0.09	0.11	0.12	0.15	0.19
0.30	0.09	0.10	0.12	0.13	0.16	0.21
0.35	0.09	0.10	0.12	0.14	0.18	0.24
0.40	0.09	0.11	0.13	0.15	0.19	0.26
0.50	0.10	0.12	0.14	0.16	0.21	0.29
0.60	0.10	0.12	0.14	0.17	0.22	0.33
0.70	0.10	0.12	0.15	0.18	0.24	0.35

[a] *Interpolation or mild extrapolation may be used.*

Note: for U-values for solid wood doors and for glass windows, doors; also see Tables 3 and 4 in section on Heating, Ventilating, and Air Conditioning.

Table 8. Effective resistance of ventilated attics[a] (summer condition)

(*Reproduced by permission from ASHRAE Handbook of Fundamentals, 1977.*)

PART A. NONREFLECTIVE SURFACES

Ventilation Air temp., F	Sol-air[d] temp., F	No Ventilation	Natural Ventilation		Power Ventilation[e]					
					Ventilation rate, cfm/sq ft					
		0	0.1[b]		0.5		1.0		1.5	
					1/U Ceiling resistance, R[c]					
		10	10	20	10	20	10	20	10	20
80	120	1.9	1.9	2.8	3.4	6.3	9.3	9.6	16	11	20
	140	1.9	1.9	2.8	3.5	6.5	10	9.8	17	12	21
	160	1.9	1.9	2.8	3.6	6.7	11	10	18	13	22
90	120	1.9	1.9	2.5	2.8	4.6	6.7	6.1	10	6.9	13
	140	1.9	1.9	2.6	3.1	5.2	7.9	7.6	12	8.6	15
	160	1.9	1.9	2.7	3.4	5.8	9.0	8.5	14	10	17
100	120	1.9	1.9	2.2	2.3	3.3	4.4	4.0	6.0	4.1	6.9
	140	1.9	1.9	2.4	2.7	4.2	6.1	5.8	8.7	6.5	10
	160	1.9	1.9	2.6	3.2	5.0	7.6	7.2	11	8.3	13

PART B. REFLECTIVE SURFACES[f]

80	120	6.5	6.5	8.1	8.8	13	17	17	25	19	30
	140	6.5	6.5	8.2	9.0	14	18	18	26	20	31
	160	6.5	6.5	8.3	9.2	15	18	19	27	21	32
90	120	6.5	6.5	7.5	8.0	10	13	12	17	13	19
	140	6.5	6.5	7.7	8.3	12	15	14	20	16	22
	160	6.5	6.5	7.9	8.6	13	16	16	22	18	25
100	120	6.5	6.5	7.0	7.4	8.0	10	8.5	12	8.8	13
	140	6.5	6.5	7.3	7.8	10	12	11	15	12	16
	160	6.5	6.5	7.6	8.2	11	14	13	18	15	20

[a] *The term effective resistance is used when there is attic ventilation. A value for no ventilation is also included. The effective resistance of the attic may be added to the resistance (1/U) of the ceiling (Table 6G) to obtain the effective resistance of the combination based on sol-air (see section on HVAC) and room temperature. These values apply to wood frame construction with a roof deck and roofing having a conductance of 1.0 Btu/(hr·ft2·°F)*
[b] *When attic ventilation meets the requirements of Table 2 in section on Condensation Control, 0.1 cfm/ft2 may be assumed as the natural summer ventilation rate for design purposes.*
[c] *Resistance is one (hr·ft2·°F)/Btu. Determine ceiling resistance from Tables 6G and 7A and adjust for framing. Do not add the effect of a reflective surface facing the attic to the ceiling resistance from Table 6G, as it is accounted for in Table 8, Part B.*
[d] *Roof surface temperature rather than sol-air temperature may be used if 0.25 is subtracted from the attic resistance shown.*
[e] *Based on air discharging outward from attic.*
[f] *Surfaces with effective emissivity E of 0.05 between ceiling joists facing the attic space.*

Table 3

Per Cent Base* Reflectance	80								70								60								30								20								10							
Per Cent Wall Reflectance	80	70	60	50	40	30	20	10	80	70	60	50	40	30	20	10	80	70	60	50	40	30	20	10	80	70	60	50	40	30	20	10	80	70	60	50	40	30	20	10	80	70	60	50	40	30	20	10
Cavity Ratio																																																	
0.2	78	78	77	77	76	76	75	74	69	68	68	67	67	66	66	65	59	59	59	58	57	56	56	55	31	30	30	29	29	28	28	28	20	20	20	20	20	19	19	19	11	11	10	10	10	10	09	09
0.4	77	76	75	74	73	72	71	70	68	67	66	65	64	63	62	61	59	59	58	57	55	54	53	52	31	30	30	29	28	28	27	26	21	20	20	20	19	19	18	18	11	11	11	10	10	10	09	09
0.6	76	75	73	71	70	68	66	65	67	65	64	63	61	59	58	57	58	57	56	55	53	51	51	50	31	30	29	28	27	26	26	25	21	21	20	19	19	18	18	17	13	12	11	11	10	10	09	08
0.8	75	73	71	69	67	65	63	61	66	64	62	60	58	56	55	53	57	56	55	54	51	48	47	46	31	30	29	28	26	25	25	23	22	21	20	19	19	17	16	16	14	13	12	11	10	10	09	08
1.0	74	72	69	67	65	62	60	57	65	62	60	58	55	53	52	50	57	55	53	51	48	45	44	43	32	30	29	27	25	24	23	22	23	22	20	19	18	16	15	15	14	13	12	11	11	10	09	08
1.2	73	70	67	64	61	58	55	53	64	61	59	57	54	50	48	46	56	54	51	49	46	44	42	40	32	30	28	27	25	23	22	21	23	22	20	19	17	16	15	14	15	14	13	12	11	10	09	07
1.4	72	68	65	62	59	55	53	50	63	60	58	55	51	47	45	44	56	53	49	47	44	41	39	38	32	30	28	26	24	22	21	19	24	22	20	18	17	16	15	13	16	14	13	12	11	10	09	07
1.6	71	67	63	60	57	53	50	47	62	59	56	53	47	45	43	41	55	52	48	45	42	39	37	35	33	29	27	25	23	22	20	18	24	22	20	18	17	15	13	13	17	15	14	12	11	09	08	07
1.8	70	66	62	58	54	50	47	44	61	58	54	51	46	42	40	38	55	51	47	44	40	37	35	33	33	29	27	25	23	21	19	17	25	23	20	18	17	14	12	12	17	15	14	13	11	09	08	06
2.0	69	64	60	56	52	48	45	41	60	56	52	49	45	40	38	36	54	50	46	43	39	35	33	31	33	29	26	24	22	20	18	16	25	23	20	18	16	13	11	11	18	16	14	13	11	09	08	06
2.2	68	63	58	54	49	45	42	38	60	55	51	48	43	38	36	34	53	49	45	42	37	34	31	29	32	29	26	24	22	19	17	15	25	23	20	18	16	14	12	10	19	16	14	13	11	09	07	06
2.4	67	61	56	52	47	43	40	36	60	54	50	46	41	37	35	32	53	48	44	41	36	32	30	27	32	29	26	24	22	19	16	14	26	23	20	18	16	14	12	10	19	17	15	13	11	09	07	06
2.6	66	60	55	50	45	41	38	34	59	54	49	45	40	35	33	30	53	48	43	39	35	31	28	26	32	29	25	23	21	18	16	14	26	23	20	18	16	14	11	09	20	17	15	13	11	09	07	06
2.8	65	59	53	48	43	39	36	32	59	53	48	43	38	33	30	28	53	47	43	38	34	29	27	24	33	29	25	23	20	17	15	13	27	23	20	18	15	13	11	09	20	18	16	13	11	09	07	05
3.0	65	58	52	47	42	37	34	30	58	52	47	42	37	32	29	27	52	46	42	37	32	28	25	23	33	29	25	22	20	17	15	12	27	23	20	17	15	13	11	09	21	18	16	13	11	09	07	05
3.2	65	57	51	45	40	35	33	28	58	51	46	40	36	31	28	25	51	45	41	36	31	27	23	22	33	29	25	22	19	16	14	12	27	23	20	17	15	12	11	09	21	18	16	13	11	09	07	05
3.4	64	56	49	44	39	34	32	27	57	50	45	39	35	29	27	24	51	45	40	35	30	26	23	20	33	29	24	22	19	16	14	11	27	23	20	17	15	12	10	08	22	18	16	13	11	09	07	05
3.6	63	54	48	43	38	32	30	25	56	49	44	38	33	28	25	22	50	44	39	34	29	25	22	19	33	29	24	21	18	15	13	10	27	23	20	17	15	12	10	08	22	19	16	13	11	09	06	04
3.8	62	53	47	41	36	31	28	24	56	49	43	37	32	27	24	21	50	43	38	33	29	24	21	19	33	28	24	21	18	15	13	10	28	23	20	17	15	12	10	07	23	19	17	14	11	09	06	04
4.0	61	53	46	40	35	30	26	22	55	48	42	36	31	26	23	20	49	42	37	32	28	23	20	18	33	28	24	21	18	14	12	09	28	23	20	17	14	11	09	07	23	20	17	14	11	09	06	04
4.2	60	52	45	39	34	29	25	21	55	47	41	35	30	25	22	19	49	42	37	32	27	22	19	17	33	28	24	20	17	14	12	09	28	23	20	17	14	11	09	07	24	20	17	14	11	09	06	04
4.4	60	51	44	38	33	28	24	20	54	46	40	34	29	24	21	18	49	42	36	31	27	22	19	16	33	28	23	20	17	14	11	09	28	23	20	17	14	11	09	07	24	20	17	14	11	08	06	04
4.6	59	50	43	37	32	27	23	19	53	45	39	33	28	24	21	17	49	41	35	30	26	21	18	16	33	28	23	20	17	13	10	08	29	24	20	17	14	11	09	07	25	20	17	13	11	08	06	04
4.8	58	49	42	36	31	26	22	18	53	45	38	32	27	23	20	16	48	41	34	29	25	20	16	15	33	28	23	19	16	13	10	08	29	24	20	16	13	10	08	06	25	20	17	13	11	08	06	04
5.0	58	48	41	35	30	25	21	18	52	44	36	31	26	22	19	16	48	40	34	28	24	20	17	14	33	28	23	19	16	13	10	08	29	24	20	16	13	10	08	06	25	20	17	14	11	08	06	04
6.0	55	44	38	31	27	22	19	15	51	41	35	28	24	19	16	13	45	37	31	25	21	17	14	11	33	27	23	18	15	11	09	06	30	24	20	16	13	10	08	05	26	21	18	14	11	08	06	03
7.0	53	41	35	28	24	19	16	12	48	38	32	26	22	17	14	11	43	35	30	24	20	15	12	09	33	26	22	17	14	10	08	05	30	24	20	15	12	09	07	04	27	21	17	13	11	08	06	03
8.0	50	38	32	25	21	17	14	11	46	35	29	23	19	15	13	10	42	33	28	22	18	14	11	08	33	26	21	16	13	09	07	04	30	23	19	15	12	08	06	03	27	21	17	13	10	07	05	03
9.0	49	36	30	23	19	15	13	10	45	33	27	21	18	14	12	09	40	31	26	20	16	12	10	07	32	25	20	15	12	08	07	04	29	23	19	14	11	08	06	03	28	21	17	13	10	07	05	02
10.0	46	33	27	21	18	14	11	08	43	31	25	19	16	12	10	08	39	29	24	18	15	11	09	07	32	24	19	14	11	08	06	03	29	22	18	13	10	07	05	03	28	21	17	12	10	07	05	02

* Ceiling, floor, or floor of cavity.

Table 4. (page 1)

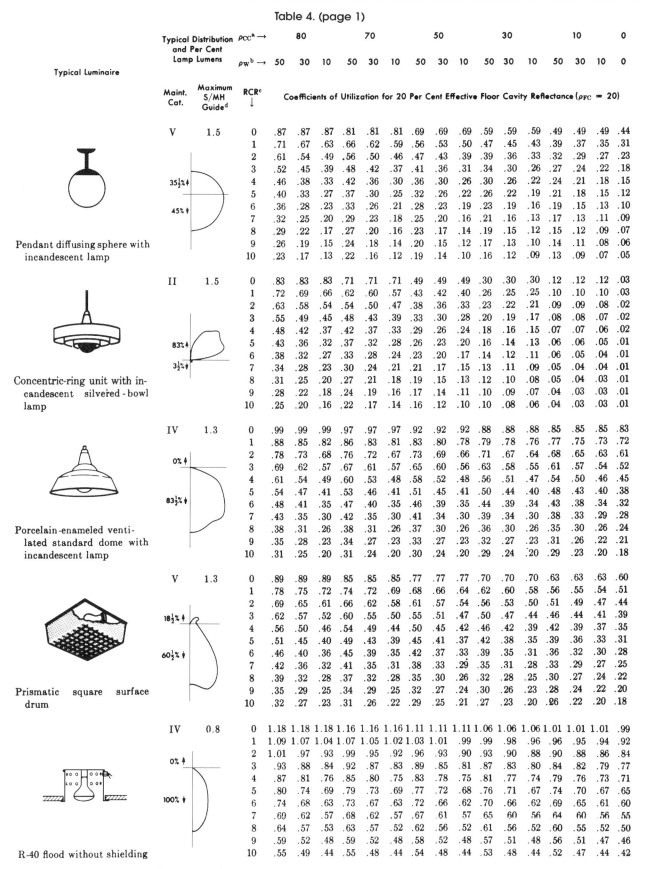

Typical Luminaire	Maint. Cat.	Maximum S/MH Guide[d]	RCR[c]	ρ_{CC}[a] → 80 pw[b] → 50	30	10	70 / 50	30	10	50 / 50	30	10	30 / 50	30	10	10 / 50	30	10	0 / 0
Pendant diffusing sphere with incandescent lamp	V	1.5	0	.87	.87	.87	.81	.81	.81	.69	.69	.69	.59	.59	.59	.49	.49	.49	.44
			1	.71	.67	.63	.66	.62	.59	.56	.53	.50	.47	.45	.43	.39	.37	.35	.31
			2	.61	.54	.49	.56	.50	.46	.47	.43	.39	.39	.36	.33	.32	.29	.27	.23
			3	.52	.45	.39	.48	.42	.37	.41	.36	.31	.34	.30	.26	.27	.24	.22	.18
			4	.46	.38	.33	.42	.36	.30	.36	.30	.26	.30	.26	.22	.24	.21	.18	.15
			5	.40	.33	.27	.37	.30	.25	.32	.26	.22	.26	.22	.19	.21	.18	.15	.12
			6	.36	.28	.23	.33	.26	.21	.28	.23	.19	.23	.19	.16	.19	.15	.13	.10
			7	.32	.25	.20	.29	.23	.18	.25	.20	.16	.21	.16	.13	.17	.13	.11	.09
			8	.29	.22	.17	.27	.20	.16	.23	.17	.14	.19	.15	.12	.15	.12	.09	.07
			9	.26	.19	.15	.24	.18	.14	.20	.15	.12	.17	.13	.10	.14	.11	.08	.06
			10	.23	.17	.13	.22	.16	.12	.19	.14	.10	.16	.12	.09	.13	.09	.07	.05
Concentric-ring unit with incandescent silvered-bowl lamp	II	1.5	0	.83	.83	.83	.71	.71	.71	.49	.49	.49	.30	.30	.30	.12	.12	.12	.03
			1	.72	.69	.66	.62	.60	.57	.43	.42	.40	.26	.25	.25	.10	.10	.10	.03
			2	.63	.58	.54	.54	.50	.47	.38	.36	.33	.23	.22	.21	.09	.09	.08	.02
			3	.55	.49	.45	.48	.43	.39	.33	.30	.28	.20	.19	.17	.08	.08	.07	.02
			4	.48	.42	.37	.42	.37	.33	.29	.26	.24	.18	.16	.15	.07	.07	.06	.02
			5	.43	.36	.32	.37	.32	.28	.26	.23	.20	.16	.14	.13	.06	.06	.05	.01
			6	.38	.32	.27	.33	.28	.24	.23	.20	.17	.14	.12	.11	.06	.05	.04	.01
			7	.34	.28	.23	.30	.24	.21	.21	.17	.15	.13	.11	.09	.05	.04	.04	.01
			8	.31	.25	.20	.27	.21	.18	.19	.15	.13	.12	.10	.08	.05	.04	.03	.01
			9	.28	.22	.18	.24	.19	.16	.17	.14	.11	.10	.09	.07	.04	.03	.03	.01
			10	.25	.20	.16	.22	.17	.14	.16	.12	.10	.10	.08	.06	.04	.03	.03	.01
Porcelain-enameled ventilated standard dome with incandescent lamp	IV	1.3	0	.99	.99	.99	.97	.97	.97	.92	.92	.92	.88	.88	.88	.85	.85	.85	.83
			1	.88	.85	.82	.86	.83	.81	.83	.80	.78	.79	.78	.76	.77	.75	.73	.72
			2	.78	.73	.68	.76	.72	.67	.73	.69	.66	.71	.67	.64	.68	.65	.63	.61
			3	.69	.62	.57	.67	.61	.57	.65	.60	.56	.63	.58	.55	.61	.57	.54	.52
			4	.61	.54	.49	.60	.53	.48	.58	.52	.48	.56	.51	.47	.54	.50	.46	.45
			5	.54	.47	.41	.53	.46	.41	.51	.45	.41	.50	.44	.40	.48	.43	.40	.38
			6	.48	.41	.35	.47	.40	.35	.46	.39	.35	.44	.39	.34	.43	.38	.34	.32
			7	.43	.35	.30	.42	.35	.30	.41	.34	.30	.39	.34	.30	.38	.33	.29	.28
			8	.38	.31	.26	.38	.31	.26	.37	.30	.26	.36	.30	.26	.35	.30	.26	.24
			9	.35	.28	.23	.34	.27	.23	.33	.27	.23	.32	.27	.23	.31	.26	.22	.21
			10	.31	.25	.20	.31	.24	.20	.30	.24	.20	.29	.24	.20	.29	.23	.20	.18
Prismatic square surface drum	V	1.3	0	.89	.89	.89	.85	.85	.85	.77	.77	.77	.70	.70	.70	.63	.63	.63	.60
			1	.78	.75	.72	.74	.72	.69	.68	.66	.64	.62	.60	.58	.56	.55	.54	.51
			2	.69	.65	.61	.66	.62	.58	.61	.57	.54	.56	.53	.50	.51	.49	.47	.44
			3	.62	.57	.52	.60	.55	.50	.55	.51	.47	.50	.47	.44	.46	.44	.41	.39
			4	.56	.50	.46	.54	.49	.44	.50	.45	.42	.46	.42	.39	.42	.39	.37	.35
			5	.51	.45	.40	.49	.43	.39	.45	.41	.37	.42	.38	.35	.39	.36	.33	.31
			6	.46	.40	.36	.45	.39	.35	.42	.37	.33	.39	.35	.31	.36	.32	.30	.28
			7	.42	.36	.32	.41	.35	.31	.38	.33	.29	.35	.31	.28	.33	.29	.27	.25
			8	.39	.32	.28	.37	.32	.28	.35	.30	.26	.32	.28	.25	.30	.27	.24	.22
			9	.35	.29	.25	.34	.29	.25	.32	.27	.24	.30	.26	.23	.28	.24	.22	.20
			10	.32	.27	.23	.31	.26	.22	.29	.25	.21	.27	.23	.20	.26	.22	.20	.18
R-40 flood without shielding	IV	0.8	0	1.18	1.18	1.18	1.16	1.16	1.16	1.11	1.11	1.11	1.06	1.06	1.06	1.01	1.01	1.01	.99
			1	1.09	1.07	1.04	1.07	1.05	1.02	1.03	1.01	.99	.99	.98	.96	.96	.95	.94	.92
			2	1.01	.97	.93	.99	.95	.92	.96	.93	.90	.93	.90	.88	.90	.88	.86	.84
			3	.93	.88	.84	.92	.87	.83	.89	.85	.81	.87	.83	.80	.84	.82	.79	.77
			4	.87	.81	.76	.85	.80	.75	.83	.78	.75	.81	.77	.74	.79	.76	.73	.71
			5	.80	.74	.69	.79	.73	.69	.77	.72	.68	.76	.71	.67	.74	.70	.67	.65
			6	.74	.68	.63	.73	.67	.63	.72	.66	.62	.70	.66	.62	.69	.65	.61	.60
			7	.60	.62	.57	.68	.62	.57	.67	.61	.57	.65	.60	.56	.64	.60	.56	.55
			8	.64	.57	.53	.63	.57	.52	.62	.56	.52	.61	.56	.52	.60	.55	.52	.50
			9	.59	.52	.48	.59	.52	.48	.58	.52	.48	.57	.51	.48	.56	.51	.47	.46
			10	.55	.49	.44	.55	.48	.44	.54	.48	.44	.53	.48	.44	.52	.47	.44	.42

Coefficients of Utilization for 20 Per Cent Effective Floor Cavity Reflectance ($\rho_{FC} = 20$)

[a] ρ_{CC} = per cent effective ceiling cavity reflectance.
[b] ρ_W = per cent wall reflectance.
[c] RCR = Room Cavity Ratio.
[d] Maximum S/MH guide—ratio of maximum luminaire spacing to mounting or ceiling height above work-plane.

Table 4. (page 2)

Typical Luminaire	Maint. Cat.	Maximum S/MH Guide[d]	RCR[c] ↓	80			70			50			30			10		0
ρcc[a] → / ρw[b] →				50	30	10	50	30	10	50	30	10	50	30	10	50	30	10	0
				Coefficients of Utilization for 20 Per Cent Effective Floor Cavity Reflectance (ρFC = 20)														
R-40 flood with specular anodized reflector skirt; 45° cutoff (0% ↑ 85% ↓)	IV	0.7	0	1.00	1.00	1.00	.98	.98	.98	.94	.94	.94	.90	.90	.90	.86	.86	.86	.84
			1	.96	.94	.92	.94	.92	.91	.90	.89	.88	.87	.86	.85	.84	.84	.83	.82
			2	.91	.88	.86	.90	.87	.85	.87	.85	.83	.84	.83	.82	.82	.81	.80	.79
			3	.87	.84	.81	.86	.83	.81	.84	.81	.79	.82	.80	.78	.80	.78	.77	.76
			4	.83	.80	.77	.82	.79	.77	.81	.78	.76	.79	.77	.75	.78	.76	.74	.73
			5	.79	.76	.73	.79	.75	.73	.77	.74	.72	.76	.73	.71	.75	.73	.71	.70
			6	.76	.73	.70	.76	.72	.70	.75	.72	.69	.74	.71	.69	.73	.70	.68	.67
			7	.73	.69	.66	.73	.69	.66	.72	.68	.66	.71	.68	.66	.70	.67	.65	.64
			8	.70	.66	.63	.70	.66	.63	.69	.65	.63	.68	.65	.63	.67	.65	.63	.62
			9	.67	.63	.60	.67	.63	.60	.66	.62	.60	.65	.62	.60	.65	.62	.60	.59
			10	.64	.60	.58	.64	.60	.58	.63	.60	.58	.63	.60	.57	.62	.59	.57	.56
Reflector downlight with baffles and inside frosted lamp (0% ↑ 44½% ↓)	IV	0.7	0	.53	.53	.53	.52	.52	.52	.49	.49	.49	.47	.47	.47	.45	.45	.45	.44
			1	.51	.50	.49	.50	.49	.48	.48	.47	.47	.46	.46	.45	.45	.44	.44	.43
			2	.48	.47	.46	.48	.46	.45	.46	.45	.44	.45	.44	.44	.44	.43	.43	.42
			3	.47	.45	.44	.46	.45	.43	.45	.44	.43	.44	.43	.42	.43	.42	.41	.41
			4	.45	.43	.42	.44	.43	.42	.43	.42	.41	.43	.41	.41	.42	.41	.40	.40
			5	.43	.41	.40	.43	.41	.40	.42	.40	.39	.41	.40	.39	.41	.40	.39	.38
			6	.42	.40	.39	.41	.40	.38	.41	.39	.38	.40	.39	.38	.40	.39	.38	.37
			7	.40	.38	.37	.40	.38	.37	.39	.38	.37	.39	.38	.37	.38	.37	.36	.36
			8	.39	.37	.36	.38	.37	.36	.38	.37	.35	.38	.36	.35	.37	.36	.35	.35
			9	.37	.36	.34	.37	.35	.34	.37	.35	.34	.36	.35	.34	.36	.35	.34	.33
			10	.36	.34	.33	.36	.34	.33	.36	.34	.33	.35	.34	.33	.35	.34	.33	.32
Wide-distribution unit with lens plate and inside frost lamp (0% ↑ 53½% ↓)	V	1.4	0	.63	.63	.63	.62	.62	.62	.59	.59	.59	.56	.56	.56	.54	.54	.54	.53
			1	.58	.56	.54	.57	.55	.54	.54	.53	.52	.52	.51	.50	.50	.50	.49	.48
			2	.53	.50	.48	.52	.49	.47	.50	.48	.46	.48	.47	.45	.47	.45	.44	.43
			3	.48	.45	.42	.47	.44	.42	.46	.43	.41	.44	.42	.40	.43	.41	.40	.39
			4	.44	.40	.37	.43	.40	.37	.42	.39	.37	.41	.38	.36	.40	.38	.36	.35
			5	.40	.36	.33	.39	.36	.33	.38	.35	.33	.37	.35	.32	.36	.34	.32	.31
			6	.36	.32	.30	.36	.32	.29	.35	.32	.29	.34	.31	.29	.33	.31	.29	.28
			7	.33	.29	.26	.33	.29	.26	.32	.28	.26	.31	.28	.26	.30	.28	.26	.25
			8	.30	.26	.23	.30	.26	.23	.29	.26	.23	.28	.25	.23	.28	.25	.23	.22
			9	.27	.23	.21	.27	.23	.21	.26	.23	.21	.26	.23	.20	.25	.22	.20	.19
			10	.25	.21	.18	.25	.21	.18	.24	.21	.18	.24	.20	.18	.23	.20	.18	.17
Recessed unit with dropped diffusing glass (1½% ↑ 50½% ↓)	V	1.3	0	.61	.61	.61	.60	.60	.60	.57	.57	.57	.54	.54	.54	.51	.51	.51	.50
			1	.53	.51	.48	.52	.50	.47	.49	.47	.46	.47	.45	.44	.45	.44	.42	.41
			2	.46	.42	.39	.45	.42	.39	.43	.40	.38	.41	.39	.37	.39	.37	.35	.34
			3	.40	.36	.33	.40	.35	.32	.38	.34	.31	.36	.33	.31	.35	.32	.30	.29
			4	.36	.31	.28	.35	.31	.28	.34	.30	.27	.32	.29	.26	.31	.28	.26	.25
			5	.32	.27	.24	.31	.27	.24	.30	.26	.23	.29	.25	.23	.28	.25	.22	.21
			6	.29	.24	.20	.28	.24	.20	.27	.23	.20	.26	.22	.20	.25	.22	.19	.18
			7	.26	.21	.18	.25	.21	.18	.24	.20	.17	.23	.20	.17	.22	.19	.17	.16
			8	.23	.19	.16	.23	.18	.15	.22	.18	.15	.21	.18	.15	.20	.17	.15	.14
			9	.21	.17	.14	.21	.16	.14	.20	.16	.13	.19	.16	.13	.19	.15	.13	.12
			10	.19	.15	.12	.19	.15	.12	.18	.14	.12	.18	.14	.12	.17	.14	.12	.11
Intermediate-distribution ventilated reflector with clear HID lamp (1% ↑ 76% ↓)	III	1.0	0	.91	.91	.91	.89	.89	.89	.84	.84	.84	.81	.81	.81	.77	.77	.77	.75
			1	.84	.81	.79	.82	.80	.78	.79	.77	.76	.76	.74	.73	.73	.72	.71	.69
			2	.77	.73	.70	.76	.72	.70	.73	.70	.68	.70	.68	.66	.68	.66	.65	.63
			3	.71	.66	.63	.69	.65	.62	.67	.64	.61	.65	.62	.60	.63	.61	.59	.57
			4	.65	.60	.56	.64	.59	.56	.62	.58	.55	.60	.57	.54	.59	.56	.54	.52
			5	.59	.54	.50	.59	.54	.50	.57	.53	.50	.56	.52	.49	.54	.51	.48	.47
			6	.54	.49	.45	.54	.49	.45	.52	.48	.45	.51	.47	.44	.50	.47	.44	.42
			7	.50	.44	.40	.49	.44	.40	.48	.43	.40	.47	.43	.39	.46	.42	.39	.38
			8	.45	.40	.36	.45	.40	.36	.44	.39	.36	.43	.39	.35	.42	.38	.35	.34
			9	.41	.36	.32	.41	.36	.32	.40	.35	.32	.39	.35	.32	.38	.35	.32	.30
			10	.38	.33	.29	.37	.32	.29	.37	.32	.29	.36	.32	.29	.35	.31	.28	.27

[a] ρcc = per cent effective ceiling cavity reflectance.
[b] ρw = per cent wall reflectance.
[c] RCR = Room Cavity Ratio.
[d] Maximum S/MH guide—ratio of maximum luminaire spacing to mounting or ceiling height above work-plane.

Table 4. (page 3)

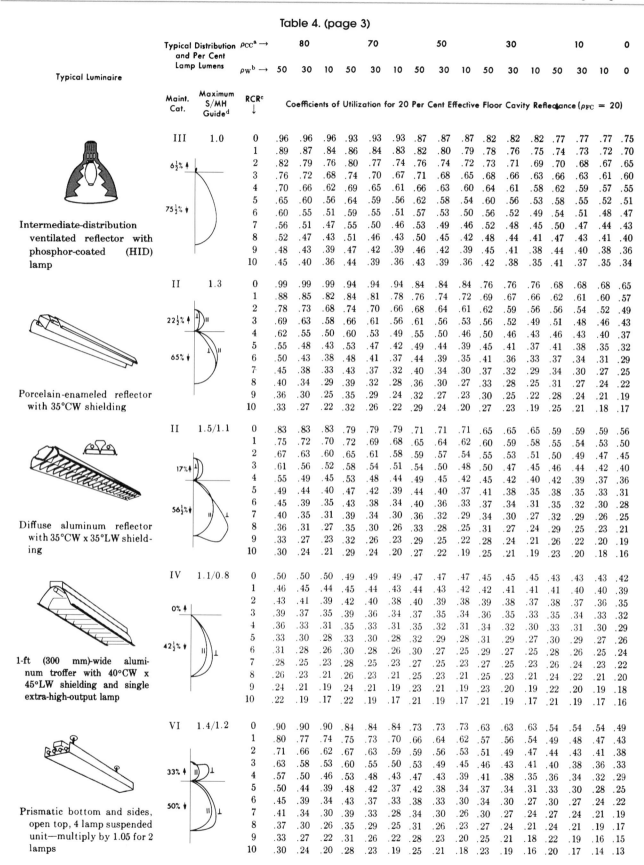

Typical Luminaire	Maint. Cat.	Maximum S/MH Guide[d]	RCR[c] ↓	ρcc[a]→ 80			70			50			30			10			0
				ρw[b]→ 50	30	10	50	30	10	50	30	10	50	30	10	50	30	10	0
Intermediate-distribution ventilated reflector with phosphor-coated (HID) lamp	III	1.0	0	.96	.96	.96	.93	.93	.93	.87	.87	.87	.82	.82	.82	.77	.77	.77	.75
			1	.89	.87	.84	.86	.84	.83	.82	.80	.79	.78	.76	.75	.74	.73	.72	.70
			2	.82	.79	.76	.80	.77	.74	.76	.74	.72	.73	.71	.69	.70	.68	.67	.65
			3	.76	.72	.68	.74	.70	.67	.71	.68	.65	.68	.66	.63	.66	.63	.61	.60
			4	.70	.66	.62	.69	.65	.61	.66	.63	.60	.64	.61	.58	.62	.59	.57	.55
			5	.65	.60	.56	.64	.59	.56	.62	.58	.54	.60	.56	.53	.58	.55	.52	.51
			6	.60	.55	.51	.59	.55	.51	.57	.53	.50	.56	.52	.49	.54	.51	.48	.47
			7	.56	.51	.47	.55	.50	.46	.53	.49	.46	.52	.48	.45	.50	.47	.44	.43
			8	.52	.47	.43	.51	.46	.43	.50	.45	.42	.48	.44	.41	.47	.43	.41	.40
			9	.48	.43	.39	.47	.42	.39	.46	.42	.39	.45	.41	.38	.44	.40	.38	.36
			10	.45	.40	.36	.44	.39	.36	.43	.39	.36	.42	.38	.35	.41	.37	.35	.34
Porcelain-enameled reflector with 35°CW shielding	II	1.3	0	.99	.99	.99	.94	.94	.94	.84	.84	.84	.76	.76	.76	.68	.68	.68	.65
			1	.88	.85	.82	.84	.81	.78	.76	.74	.72	.69	.67	.66	.62	.61	.60	.57
			2	.78	.73	.68	.74	.70	.66	.68	.64	.61	.62	.59	.56	.56	.54	.52	.49
			3	.69	.63	.58	.66	.61	.56	.61	.56	.53	.56	.52	.49	.51	.48	.46	.43
			4	.62	.55	.50	.60	.53	.49	.55	.50	.46	.50	.46	.43	.46	.43	.40	.37
			5	.55	.48	.43	.53	.47	.42	.49	.44	.39	.45	.41	.37	.41	.38	.35	.32
			6	.50	.43	.38	.48	.41	.37	.44	.39	.35	.41	.36	.33	.37	.34	.31	.29
			7	.45	.38	.33	.43	.37	.32	.40	.34	.30	.37	.32	.29	.34	.30	.27	.25
			8	.40	.34	.29	.39	.32	.28	.36	.30	.27	.33	.28	.25	.31	.27	.24	.22
			9	.36	.30	.25	.35	.29	.24	.32	.27	.23	.30	.25	.22	.28	.24	.21	.19
			10	.33	.27	.22	.32	.26	.22	.29	.24	.20	.27	.23	.19	.25	.21	.18	.17
Diffuse aluminum reflector with 35°CW x 35°LW shielding	II	1.5/1.1	0	.83	.83	.83	.79	.79	.79	.71	.71	.71	.65	.65	.65	.59	.59	.59	.56
			1	.75	.72	.70	.72	.69	.68	.65	.64	.62	.60	.59	.58	.55	.54	.53	.50
			2	.67	.63	.60	.65	.61	.58	.59	.57	.54	.55	.53	.51	.50	.49	.47	.45
			3	.61	.56	.52	.58	.54	.51	.54	.50	.48	.50	.47	.45	.46	.44	.42	.40
			4	.55	.49	.45	.53	.48	.44	.49	.45	.42	.45	.42	.40	.42	.39	.37	.36
			5	.49	.44	.40	.47	.42	.39	.44	.40	.37	.41	.38	.35	.38	.35	.33	.31
			6	.45	.39	.35	.43	.38	.34	.40	.36	.33	.37	.34	.31	.35	.32	.30	.28
			7	.40	.35	.31	.39	.34	.30	.36	.32	.29	.34	.30	.27	.32	.29	.26	.25
			8	.36	.31	.27	.35	.30	.26	.33	.28	.25	.31	.27	.24	.29	.25	.23	.21
			9	.33	.27	.23	.32	.26	.23	.29	.25	.22	.28	.24	.21	.26	.22	.20	.19
			10	.30	.24	.21	.29	.24	.20	.27	.22	.19	.25	.21	.19	.23	.20	.18	.16
1-ft (300 mm)-wide aluminum troffer with 40°CW x 45°LW shielding and single extra-high-output lamp	IV	1.1/0.8	0	.50	.50	.50	.49	.49	.49	.47	.47	.47	.45	.45	.45	.43	.43	.43	.42
			1	.46	.45	.44	.45	.44	.43	.44	.43	.42	.42	.41	.41	.41	.40	.40	.39
			2	.43	.41	.39	.42	.40	.38	.40	.39	.38	.39	.38	.37	.38	.37	.36	.35
			3	.39	.37	.35	.39	.36	.34	.37	.35	.34	.36	.35	.33	.35	.34	.33	.32
			4	.36	.33	.31	.35	.33	.31	.35	.32	.31	.34	.32	.30	.33	.31	.30	.29
			5	.33	.30	.28	.33	.30	.28	.32	.29	.28	.31	.29	.27	.30	.29	.27	.26
			6	.31	.28	.26	.30	.28	.26	.30	.27	.25	.29	.27	.25	.28	.26	.25	.24
			7	.28	.25	.23	.28	.25	.23	.27	.25	.23	.27	.25	.23	.26	.24	.23	.22
			8	.26	.23	.21	.26	.23	.21	.25	.23	.21	.25	.23	.21	.24	.22	.21	.20
			9	.24	.21	.19	.24	.21	.19	.23	.21	.19	.23	.20	.19	.22	.20	.19	.18
			10	.22	.19	.17	.22	.19	.17	.21	.19	.17	.21	.19	.17	.21	.19	.17	.16
Prismatic bottom and sides, open top, 4 lamp suspended unit—multiply by 1.05 for 2 lamps	VI	1.4/1.2	0	.90	.90	.90	.84	.84	.84	.73	.73	.73	.63	.63	.63	.54	.54	.54	.49
			1	.80	.77	.74	.75	.73	.70	.66	.64	.62	.57	.56	.54	.49	.48	.47	.43
			2	.71	.66	.62	.67	.63	.59	.59	.56	.53	.51	.49	.47	.44	.43	.41	.38
			3	.63	.58	.53	.60	.55	.50	.53	.49	.45	.46	.43	.41	.40	.38	.36	.33
			4	.57	.50	.46	.53	.48	.43	.47	.43	.39	.41	.38	.35	.36	.34	.32	.29
			5	.50	.44	.39	.48	.42	.37	.42	.38	.34	.37	.34	.31	.33	.30	.28	.25
			6	.45	.39	.34	.43	.37	.33	.38	.33	.30	.34	.30	.27	.30	.27	.24	.22
			7	.41	.34	.30	.39	.33	.28	.34	.30	.26	.30	.27	.24	.27	.24	.21	.19
			8	.37	.30	.26	.35	.29	.25	.31	.26	.23	.27	.24	.21	.24	.21	.19	.17
			9	.33	.27	.22	.31	.26	.22	.28	.23	.20	.25	.21	.18	.22	.19	.16	.15
			10	.30	.24	.20	.28	.23	.19	.25	.21	.18	.23	.19	.16	.20	.17	.14	.13

Coefficients of Utilization for 20 Per Cent Effective Floor Cavity Reflectance (ρFC = 20)

[a] ρcc = per cent effective ceiling cavity reflectance.
[b] ρw = per cent wall reflectance.
[c] RCR = Room Cavity Ratio.
[d] Maximum S/MH guide--ratio of maximum luminaire spacing to mounting or ceiling height above work-plane.

Table 4. (page 4)

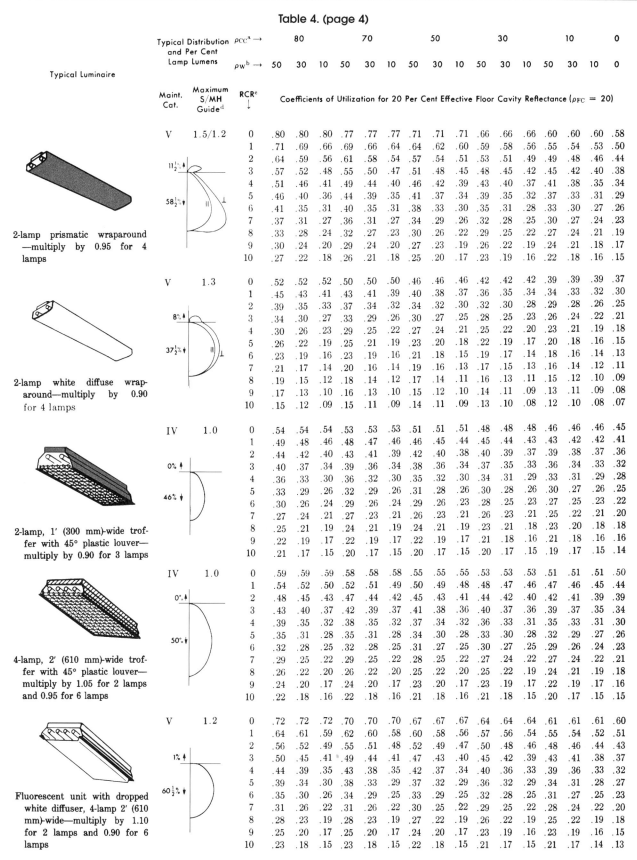

	Typical Luminaire	Maint. Cat.	Maximum S/MH Guide[d]	RCR[c]	ρ_{CC}[a] → 80			70			50			30			10			0
				ρ_W[b] →	50	30	10	50	30	10	50	30	10	50	30	10	50	30	10	0
					— Coefficients of Utilization for 20 Per Cent Effective Floor Cavity Reflectance ($\rho_{FC} = 20$)															
2-lamp prismatic wraparound—multiply by 0.95 for 4 lamps		V	1.5/1.2	0	.80	.80	.80	.77	.77	.77	.71	.71	.71	.66	.66	.66	.60	.60	.60	.58
				1	.71	.69	.66	.69	.66	.64	.64	.62	.60	.59	.58	.56	.55	.54	.53	.50
				2	.64	.59	.56	.61	.58	.54	.57	.54	.51	.53	.51	.49	.49	.48	.46	.44
				3	.57	.52	.48	.55	.50	.47	.51	.48	.45	.48	.45	.42	.45	.42	.40	.38
				4	.51	.46	.41	.49	.44	.40	.46	.42	.39	.43	.40	.37	.41	.38	.35	.34
				5	.46	.40	.36	.44	.39	.35	.41	.37	.34	.39	.35	.32	.37	.33	.31	.29
				6	.41	.35	.31	.40	.35	.31	.38	.33	.30	.35	.31	.28	.33	.30	.27	.26
				7	.37	.31	.27	.36	.31	.27	.34	.29	.26	.32	.28	.25	.30	.27	.24	.23
				8	.33	.28	.24	.32	.27	.23	.30	.26	.22	.29	.25	.22	.27	.24	.21	.19
				9	.30	.24	.20	.29	.24	.20	.27	.23	.19	.26	.22	.19	.24	.21	.18	.17
				10	.27	.22	.18	.26	.21	.18	.25	.20	.17	.23	.19	.16	.22	.18	.16	.15
2-lamp white diffuse wraparound—multiply by 0.90 for 4 lamps		V	1.3	0	.52	.52	.52	.50	.50	.50	.46	.46	.46	.42	.42	.42	.39	.39	.39	.37
				1	.45	.43	.41	.43	.41	.39	.40	.38	.37	.36	.35	.34	.34	.33	.32	.30
				2	.39	.35	.33	.37	.34	.32	.34	.32	.30	.32	.30	.28	.29	.28	.26	.25
				3	.34	.30	.27	.33	.29	.26	.30	.27	.25	.28	.25	.23	.26	.24	.22	.21
				4	.30	.26	.23	.29	.25	.22	.27	.24	.21	.25	.22	.20	.23	.21	.19	.18
				5	.26	.22	.19	.25	.21	.19	.23	.20	.18	.22	.19	.17	.20	.18	.16	.15
				6	.23	.19	.16	.23	.19	.16	.21	.18	.15	.19	.17	.14	.18	.16	.14	.13
				7	.21	.17	.14	.20	.16	.14	.19	.16	.13	.17	.15	.13	.16	.14	.12	.11
				8	.19	.15	.12	.18	.14	.12	.17	.14	.11	.16	.13	.11	.15	.12	.10	.09
				9	.17	.13	.10	.16	.13	.10	.15	.12	.10	.14	.11	.09	.13	.11	.09	.08
				10	.15	.12	.09	.15	.11	.09	.14	.11	.09	.13	.10	.08	.12	.10	.08	.07
2-lamp, 1' (300 mm)-wide troffer with 45° plastic louver—multiply by 0.90 for 3 lamps		IV	1.0	0	.54	.54	.54	.53	.53	.53	.51	.51	.51	.48	.48	.48	.46	.46	.46	.45
				1	.49	.48	.46	.48	.47	.46	.46	.45	.44	.45	.44	.43	.43	.42	.42	.41
				2	.44	.42	.40	.43	.41	.39	.42	.40	.38	.40	.39	.37	.39	.38	.37	.36
				3	.40	.37	.34	.39	.36	.34	.38	.36	.34	.37	.35	.33	.36	.34	.33	.32
				4	.36	.33	.30	.36	.32	.30	.35	.32	.30	.34	.31	.29	.33	.31	.29	.28
				5	.33	.29	.26	.32	.29	.26	.31	.28	.26	.30	.28	.26	.30	.27	.26	.25
				6	.30	.26	.24	.29	.26	.24	.29	.26	.23	.28	.25	.23	.27	.25	.23	.22
				7	.27	.24	.21	.27	.23	.21	.26	.23	.21	.26	.23	.21	.25	.22	.21	.20
				8	.25	.21	.19	.24	.21	.19	.24	.21	.19	.23	.21	.18	.23	.20	.18	.18
				9	.22	.19	.17	.22	.19	.17	.22	.19	.17	.21	.18	.16	.21	.18	.16	.16
				10	.21	.17	.15	.20	.17	.15	.20	.17	.15	.20	.17	.15	.19	.17	.15	.14
4-lamp, 2' (610 mm)-wide troffer with 45° plastic louver—multiply by 1.05 for 2 lamps and 0.95 for 6 lamps		IV	1.0	0	.59	.59	.59	.58	.58	.58	.55	.55	.55	.53	.53	.53	.51	.51	.51	.50
				1	.54	.52	.50	.52	.51	.49	.50	.49	.48	.48	.47	.46	.47	.46	.45	.44
				2	.48	.45	.43	.47	.44	.42	.45	.43	.41	.44	.42	.40	.42	.41	.39	.39
				3	.43	.40	.37	.42	.39	.37	.41	.38	.36	.40	.37	.36	.39	.37	.35	.34
				4	.39	.35	.32	.38	.35	.32	.37	.34	.32	.36	.33	.31	.35	.33	.31	.30
				5	.35	.31	.28	.35	.31	.28	.34	.30	.28	.33	.30	.28	.32	.29	.27	.26
				6	.32	.28	.25	.32	.28	.25	.31	.27	.25	.30	.27	.25	.29	.26	.24	.23
				7	.29	.25	.22	.29	.25	.22	.28	.25	.22	.27	.24	.22	.27	.24	.22	.21
				8	.26	.22	.20	.26	.22	.20	.25	.22	.20	.25	.22	.19	.24	.21	.19	.18
				9	.24	.20	.17	.24	.20	.17	.23	.20	.17	.23	.19	.17	.22	.19	.17	.16
				10	.22	.18	.16	.22	.18	.16	.21	.18	.16	.21	.18	.15	.20	.17	.15	.15
Fluorescent unit with dropped white diffuser, 4-lamp 2' (610 mm)-wide—multiply by 1.10 for 2 lamps and 0.90 for 6 lamps		V	1.2	0	.72	.72	.72	.70	.70	.70	.67	.67	.67	.64	.64	.64	.61	.61	.61	.60
				1	.64	.61	.59	.62	.60	.58	.60	.58	.56	.57	.56	.54	.55	.54	.52	.51
				2	.56	.52	.49	.55	.51	.48	.52	.49	.47	.50	.48	.46	.48	.46	.44	.43
				3	.50	.45	.41	.49	.44	.41	.47	.43	.40	.45	.42	.39	.43	.41	.38	.37
				4	.44	.39	.35	.43	.38	.35	.42	.37	.34	.40	.36	.33	.39	.36	.33	.32
				5	.39	.34	.30	.38	.33	.29	.37	.32	.29	.36	.32	.29	.34	.31	.28	.27
				6	.35	.30	.26	.34	.29	.25	.33	.29	.25	.32	.28	.25	.31	.27	.25	.23
				7	.31	.26	.22	.31	.26	.22	.30	.25	.22	.29	.25	.22	.28	.24	.22	.20
				8	.28	.23	.19	.28	.23	.19	.27	.22	.19	.26	.22	.19	.25	.22	.19	.18
				9	.25	.20	.17	.25	.20	.17	.24	.20	.17	.23	.19	.16	.23	.19	.16	.15
				10	.23	.18	.15	.23	.18	.15	.22	.18	.15	.21	.17	.15	.21	.17	.14	.13

[a] ρ_{CC} = per cent effective ceiling cavity reflectance.
[b] ρ_W = per cent wall reflectance.
[c] RCR = Room Cavity Ratio.
[d] Maximum S/MH guide—ratio of maximum luminaire spacing to mounting or ceiling height above work-plane.

Table 4. (page 5)

Typical Distribution and Per Cent Lamp Lumens ρcc[a] →		80			70			50			30			10			0
Typical Luminaire	ρw[b] →	50	30	10	50	30	10	50	30	10	50	30	10	50	30	10	0

Maint. Cat.	Maximum S/MH Guide[d]	RCR[c] ↓	Coefficients of Utilization for 20 Per Cent Effective Floor Cavity Reflectance (ρFC = 20)															
V	1.4/1.2	0	.73	.73	.73	.72	.72	.72	.68	.68	.68	.66	.66	.66	.63	.63	.63	.62
		1	.66	.64	.62	.65	.63	.61	.62	.60	.59	.60	.58	.57	.57	.56	.55	.54
		2	.59	.55	.52	.58	.54	.52	.56	.53	.50	.54	.51	.49	.52	.50	.48	.47
		3	.53	.48	.45	.52	.48	.44	.50	.46	.44	.48	.45	.43	.47	.44	.42	.41
		4	.47	.42	.39	.46	.42	.38	.45	.41	.38	.43	.40	.37	.42	.39	.37	.36
		5	.42	.37	.33	.41	.37	.33	.40	.36	.33	.39	.35	.32	.38	.35	.32	.31
		6	.38	.33	.29	.37	.32	.29	.36	.32	.29	.35	.31	.28	.34	.31	.28	.27
		7	.34	.29	.25	.33	.29	.25	.33	.28	.25	.32	.28	.25	.31	.27	.25	.23
		8	.30	.25	.22	.30	.25	.22	.29	.25	.22	.28	.24	.21	.28	.24	.21	.20
		9	.27	.22	.19	.27	.22	.19	.26	.22	.19	.25	.21	.19	.25	.21	.18	.17
		10	.25	.20	.17	.24	.20	.16	.24	.19	.16	.23	.19	.16	.23	.19	.16	.15

Fluorescent unit with flat prismatic lens, 4 lamp 2' (610 mm)-wide—multiply by 1.10 for 2 lamp

		80			70			50									
	1	.42	.40	.39	.36	.35	.33	.25	.24	.23							
	2	.37	.34	.32	.32	.29	.27	.22	.20	.19							
	3	.32	.29	.26	.28	.25	.23	.19	.17	.16							
	4	.29	.25	.22	.25	.22	.19	.17	.15	.13							
	5	.25	.21	.18	.22	.19	.16	.15	.13	.11							
	6	.23	.19	.16	.20	.16	.14	.14	.12	.10							
	7	.20	.17	.14	.17	.14	.12	.12	.10	.09							
	8	.18	.15	.12	.16	.13	.10	.11	.09	.08							
	9	.17	.13	.10	.15	.11	.09	.10	.08	.07							
	10	.15	.12	.09	.13	.10	.08	.09	.07	.06							

Coves are not recommended for lighting areas having low reflectances.

Single-row fluorescent lamp cove without reflector, mult. by 0.93 for 2 rows and by 0.85 for 3 rows.

		70			50						
ρCC from below ~65%	1	.60	.58	.56	.58	.56	.54				
	2	.53	.49	.45	.51	.47	.43				
	3	.47	.42	.37	.45	.41	.36				
	4	.41	.36	.32	.39	.35	.31				
	5	.37	.31	.27	.35	.30	.26				
	6	.33	.27	.23	.31	.26	.23				
	7	.29	.24	.20	.28	.23	.20				
	8	.26	.21	.18	.25	.20	.17				
	9	.23	.19	.15	.23	.18	.15				
	10	.21	.17	.13	.21	.16	.13				

Diffusing plastic or glass

(1) Ceiling efficiency ~60%; diffuser transmittance ~50%; diffuser reflectance ~40%. Cavity with minimum obstructions and painted with 80% reflectance paint—use ρc = 70.

(2) For lower reflectance paint or obstructions—use ρc = 50.

		70			50			30		
ρCC from below ~60%	1	.71	.68	.66	.67	.66	.65	.65	.64	.62
	2	.63	.60	.57	.61	.58	.55	.59	.56	.54
	3	.57	.53	.49	.55	.52	.48	.54	.50	.47
	4	.52	.47	.43	.50	.45	.42	.48	.44	.42
	5	.46	.41	.37	.44	.40	.37	.43	.40	.36
	6	.42	.37	.33	.41	.36	.32	.40	.35	.32
	7	.38	.32	.29	.37	.31	.28	.36	.31	.28
	8	.34	.28	.25	.33	.28	.25	.32	.28	.25
	9	.30	.25	.22	.30	.25	.21	.29	.25	.21
	10	.27	.23	.19	.27	.22	.19	.26	.22	.19

Prismatic plastic or glass.

1) Ceiling efficiency ~67%; prismatic transmittance ~72%; prismatic reflectance ~18%. Cavity with minimum obstructions and painted with 80% reflectance paint—use ρc = 70.

2) For lower reflectance paint or obstructions—use ρc = 50.

		50			10		
ρCC from below ~45%	1	.51	.49	.48	.47	.46	.45
	2	.46	.44	.42	.43	.42	.40
	3	.42	.39	.37	.39	.38	.36
	4	.38	.35	.33	.36	.34	.32
	5	.35	.32	.29	.33	.31	.29
	6	.32	.29	.26	.30	.28	.26
	7	.29	.26	.23	.28	.25	.23
	8	.27	.23	.21	.26	.23	.21
	9	.24	.21	.19	.24	.21	.19
	10	.22	.19	.17	.22	.19	.17

Louvered ceiling.

Ceiling efficiency ~50%; 45° shielding opaque louvers of 80% reflectance. Cavity with minimum obstructions and painted with 80% reflectance paint—use ρc = 50.

[a] ρcc = per cent effective ceiling cavity reflectance.

[b] ρw = per cent wall reflectance.

[c] RCR = Room Cavity Ratio.

[d] Maximum S/MH guide—ratio of maximum luminaire spacing to mounting or ceiling height above work-plane.

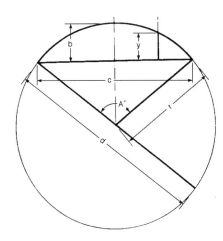

Functions of π with Logarithmic Equivalents

$\pi = 3.14159265, \quad \log = 0.4971499$

$\dfrac{1}{\pi} = 0.3183099, \quad \log = \overline{1}.5028501$

$\pi^2 = 9.8696044, \quad \log = 0.9942997$

$\dfrac{1}{\pi^2} = 0.1013212, \quad \log = \overline{1}.0057003$

$\sqrt{\pi} = 1.7724539, \quad \log = 0.2485749$

$\sqrt{\dfrac{1}{\pi}} = 0.5641896, \quad \log = \overline{1}.7514251$

$\dfrac{\pi}{180} = 0.0174533, \quad \log = \overline{2}.2418774$

$\dfrac{180}{\pi} = 57.2957795, \quad \log = 1.7581226$

Circumference $= C$
$= d\,\pi = d \times 3.1416$
$= 2\,\pi\,r = 2 \times r \times 3.1416$

Diameter $= d$
$= C \div 3.1416$
$= C \times 0.31831$

Diameter of Circle, having circumference equal to periphery of square
$= $ side of square $\times 1.27324$

Side of Square, having periphery equal to circumference of circle
$= \dfrac{d\pi}{4} = d \times 0.7854$

Diameter of Circle, circumscribed about square
$= $ side of square $\times 1.41421$

Side of Square, inscribed in circle
$= d \times 0.70711$

Arc, $\quad a = \dfrac{\pi\,r\,A°}{180} = 0.017453\ r\,A°$

Angle, $A° = \dfrac{180°\,a}{\pi\,r} = 57.29578\ \dfrac{a}{r}$

Radius, $r = \dfrac{4\,b^2 + c^2}{8\,b}$

Diameter, $d = \dfrac{4\,b^2 + c^2}{4\,b}$

Chord, $c = 2\sqrt{2\,b\,r - b^2} = 2\,r\,\sin\dfrac{A°}{2}$

Rise, Trigonometric Calculations
$b = \dfrac{c}{2}\,\tan\dfrac{A°}{4} = 2\,r\,\sin^2\dfrac{A°}{4}$

Rise, Algebraic Calculations
$b = r + y - \sqrt{r^2 - x^2}$
$b = r - \tfrac{1}{2}\sqrt{4\,r^2 - c^2}$
$x = \sqrt{r^2 - (r + y - b)^2}$
$y = b - r + \sqrt{r^2 - x^2}$

TABLE 1—AREAS OF CIRCLES IN SQUARE FEET—Diameter in Feet and Inches

Feet	Inches											
	0	1	2	3	4	5	6	7	8	9	10	11
0	.0000	.0055	.0218	.0491	.0873	.1364	.1963	.2673	.3491	.4418	.5454	.6600
1	.7854	.9218	1.069	1.227	1.396	1.576	1.767	1.969	2.182	2.405	2.640	2.885
2	3.142	3.409	3.687	3.976	4.276	4.587	4.909	5.241	5.585	5.940	6.305	6.681
3	7.069	7.467	7.876	8.296	8.727	9.168	9.621	10.08	10.56	11.04	11.54	12.05
4	12.57	13.10	13.64	14.19	14.75	15.32	15.90	16.50	17.10	17.72	18.35	18.99
5	19.63	20.29	20.97	21.65	22.34	23.04	23.76	24.48	25.22	25.97	26.73	27.49
6	28.27	29.07	29.87	30.68	31.50	32.34	33.18	34.04	34.91	35.78	36.67	37.57
7	38.48	39.41	40.34	41.28	42.24	43.20	44.18	45.17	46.16	47.17	48.19	49.22
8	50.27	51.32	52.38	53.46	54.54	55.64	56.75	57.86	58.99	60.13	61.28	62.44
9	63.62	64.80	66.00	67.20	68.42	69.64	70.88	72.13	73.39	74.66	75.94	77.24
10	78.54	79.85	81.18	82.52	83.86	85.22	86.59	87.97	89.36	90.76	92.18	93.60
11	95.03	96.48	97.93	99.40	100.9	102.4	103.9	105.4	106.9	108.4	110.0	111.5
12	113.1	114.7	116.3	117.9	119.5	121.1	122.7	124.4	126.0	127.7	129.4	131.0
13	132.7	134.4	136.2	137.9	139.6	141.4	143.1	144.9	146.7	148.5	150.3	152.1
14	153.9	155.8	157.6	159.5	161.4	163.2	165.1	167.0	168.9	170.9	172.8	174.8

If given diameter is not found in this table, reduce diameter to feet and decimals of a foot by aid of the following auxiliary table, and then find area from Table 4.

TABLE 2—Conversion from Inches and Fractions of an Inch to Decimals of a Foot

Inches	1	2	3	4	5	6	7	8	9	10	11
Feet........	.0833	.1667	.2500	.3333	.4167	.5000	.5833	.6667	.7500	.8333	.9167
Inches......	⅛	¼	⅜	½	⅝	¾	⅞				
Feet........	.0104	.0208	.0313	.0417	.0521	.0625	.0729				

Example. 5 ft. 7⅜ in. = 5.0 + 0.5833 + 0.0313 = 5.6146 ft.

NOTE 1

HOW TO FIND CIRCUMFERENCES (from Table 3)
This table gives the product of π times any number D from 1 to 10; that is, it is a table of multiples of π. ($D =$ diameter.) Moving the decimal point one place in column D is equivalent to moving it one place in the body of the table.

Circumference $= \pi \times$ diam. $= 3.141593 \times$ diam.

Conversely,

Diameter $= \dfrac{1}{\pi} \times$ circumf. $= 0.31831 \times$ circumf.

Examples:

Diameter given; Circumference sought:
Diameter $= 3.57$ feet. Find 3.5 in left hand column, read right to column 7 and find 11.22 feet $=$ circumference.

Circumference given; Diameter sought:
Circumference $= 20.17$ feet. Find 20.17 in body of table, read left and find 6.4, note 20.17 is in column 2, which add $= 6.4 + .02 = 6.42 =$ diameter.

NOTE 2

HOW TO FIND AREAS (from Table 4)
Moving the decimal point one place in column D is equivalent to moving it two places in the body of the table. ($D =$ diameter.)

Area of circle $= \dfrac{\pi}{4} \times (\text{diam.}^2) = 0.785398 \times (\text{diam.}^2)$

Conversely,

Diam. $= \sqrt{\dfrac{4}{\pi}} \times \sqrt{\text{area}} = 1.128379 \times \sqrt{\text{area}}$

Examples:

Diameter given; Area sought:
Diameter $= 12.3$ feet. Move decimal one point left $= 1.23$. Find 1.2 in left column, read right to column 3, find area of 1.23 $= 1.188$. Move decimal two points right $= 118.8$ sq. ft. $=$ area.

Area given; Diameter sought:
Area $= 4927$ sq. in. Move decimal two points left $= 49.27$. Find 49.27. Read left and find 7.9. Note 49.27 is in column 2, which add $= 7.9 + .02 = 7.92$. Move decimal one point right $= 79.2$ inches $=$ diameter.

Editor's note: Section 2 of the Appendix of the Seventh Edition includes classic articles and references from prior editions of Time-Saver Standards on Mathematics, considered p(art of architectural knowledge since the writings of Cicero, Vitruvius and Alberti.

TABLE 3—CIRCUMFERENCES BY HUNDREDTHS. SEE NOTE 1

D	0	1	2	3	4	5	6	7	8	9
1.0	3.142	3.173	3.204	3.236	3.267	3.299	3.330	3.362	3.393	3.424
.1	3.456	3.487	3.519	3.550	3.581	3.613	3.644	3.676	3.707	3.738
.2	3.770	3.801	3.833	3.864	3.896	3.927	3.958	3.990	4.021	4.053
.3	4.084	4.115	4.147	4.178	4.210	4.241	4.273	4.304	4.335	4.367
.4	4.398	4.430	4.461	4.492	4.524	4.555	5.587	4.618	4.650	4.681
1.5	4.712	4.744	4.775	4.807	4.838	4.869	4.901	4.932	4.964	4.995
.6	5.027	5.058	5.089	5.121	5.152	5.184	5.215	5.246	5.278	5.309
.7	5.341	5.372	5.404	5.435	5.466	5.498	5.529	5.561	5.592	5.623
.8	5.655	5.686	5.718	5.749	5.781	5.812	5.843	5.875	5.906	5.938
.9	5.969	6.000	6.032	6.063	6.095	6.126	6.158	6.189	6.220	6.252
2.0	6.283	6.315	6.346	6.377	6.409	6.440	6.472	6.503	6.535	6.566
.1	6.597	6.629	6.600	6.692	6.723	6.754	6.786	6.817	6.849	6.880
.2	6.912	6.943	6.974	7.006	7.037	7.069	7.100	7.131	7.163	7.194
.3	7.226	7.257	7.288	7.320	7.351	7.383	7.414	7.446	7.477	7.508
.4	7.540	7.571	7.603	7.634	7.665	7.697	7.728	7.760	7.791	7.823
2.5	7.854	7.885	7.917	7.948	7.980	8.011	8.042	8.074	8.105	8.137
.6	8.168	8.200	8.231	8.262	8.294	8.325	8.357	8.388	8.419	8.451
.7	8.482	8.514	8.545	8.577	8.608	8.639	8.671	8.702	8.734	8.765
.8	8.796	8.828	8.859	8.891	8.922	8.954	8.985	9.016	9.048	9.079
.9	9.111	9.142	9.173	9.205	9.236	9.268	9.299	9.331	9.362	9.393
3.0	9.425	9.456	9.488	9.519	9.550	9.582	9.613	9.645	9.676	9.708
.1	9.739	9.770	9.802	9.833	9.865	9.896	9.927	9.959	9.990	10.022
.2	10.05	10.08	10.12	10.15	10.18	10.21	10.24	10.27	10.30	10.34
.3	10.37	10.40	10.43	10.46	14.49	10.52	10.56	10.59	10.62	10.65
.4	10.68	10.71	10.74	10.78	10.81	10.84	10.87	10.90	10.93	10.96
3.5	11.00	11.03	11.06	11.09	11.12	11.15	11.18	11.22	11.25	11.28
.6	11.31	11.34	11.37	11.40	11.44	11.47	11.50	11.53	11.56	11.59
.7	11.62	11.66	11.69	11.72	11.75	11.78	11.81	11.84	11.88	11.91
.8	11.94	11.97	12.00	12.03	12.06	12.10	12.13	12.16	12.19	12.22
.9	12.25	12.28	12.32	12.35	12.38	12.41	12.44	12.47	12.50	12.53
4.0	12.57	12.60	12.63	12.66	12.69	12.72	12.75	12.79	12.82	12.85
.1	12.88	12.91	12.94	12.97	13.01	13.04	13.07	13.10	13.13	13.16
.2	13.19	13.23	13.26	13.29	13.32	13.35	13.38	13.41	13.45	13.48
.3	13.51	13.54	13.57	13.60	13.63	13.67	13.70	13.73	13.76	13.79
.4	13.82	13.85	13.89	13.92	13.95	13.98	14.01	14.04	14.07	14.11
4.5	14.14	14.17	14.20	14.23	14.26	14.29	14.33	14.36	14.39	14.42
.6	14.45	14.48	14.51	14.44	14.58	14.61	14.64	14.67	14.70	14.73
.7	14.77	14.80	14.83	14.86	14.89	14.92	14.95	14.99	15.02	15.05
.8	15.08	15.11	15.14	15.17	15.21	15.24	15.27	15.30	15.33	15.36
.9	15.39	15.43	15.46	15.49	15.52	15.52	15.58	15.61	15.65	15.68
5.0	15.71	15.74	15.77	15.80	15.83	15.87	15.90	15.93	15.96	15.99
.1	16.02	16.05	16.08	16.12	16.15	16.18	16.21	16.24	16.27	16.30
.2	16.34	16.37	16.40	16.43	16.46	16.49	16.52	16.56	16.59	16.62
.3	16.65	16.68	16.71	16.74	16.78	16.81	16.84	16.87	16.90	16.93
.4	16.96	17.00	17.03	17.06	17.09	17.12	17.15	17.18	17.22	17.25
5.5	17.28	17.31	17.34	17.37	17.40	17.44	17.47	17.50	17.53	17.56
.6	17.59	17.62	17.66	17.69	17.72	17.75	17.78	17.81	17.84	17.88
.7	17.91	17.94	17.97	18.00	18.03	18.06	18.10	18.13	18.16	18.19
.8	18.22	18.25	18.28	18.32	18.35	18.38	18.41	18.44	18.47	18.50
.9	18.54	18.57	18.60	18.63	18.66	18.69	18.72	18.76	18.79	18.82
6.0	18.85	18.88	18.91	18.94	18.98	19.01	19.04	19.07	19.10	19.13
.1	19.16	19.20	19.23	19.26	19.29	19.32	19.35	19.38	19.42	19.45
.2	19.48	19.51	19.54	19.57	19.60	19.63	19.67	19.70	19.73	19.76
.3	19.79	19.82	19.85	19.89	19.92	19.95	19.98	20.01	20.04	20.07
.4	20.11	20.14	20.17	20.20	20.23	20.26	20.29	20.33	20.36	20.39
6.5	20.42	20.45	20.48	20.51	20.55	20.58	20.61	20.64	20.67	20.70
.6	20.73	20.77	20.80	20.83	20.86	20.89	20.92	20.95	20.99	21.02
.7	21.05	21.08	21.11	21.14	21.17	21.21	21.24	21.27	21.30	21.33
.8	21.36	21.39	21.43	21.46	21.49	21.52	21.55	21.58	21.61	21.65
.9	21.68	21.71	21.74	21.77	21.80	21.83	21.87	21.90	21.93	21.96
7.0	21.99	22.02	22.05	22.09	22.12	22.15	22.18	22.21	22.24	22.27
.1	22.31	22.34	22.37	22.40	22.43	22.46	22.49	22.53	22.56	22.59
.2	22.62	22.65	22.68	22.71	22.75	22.78	22.81	22.84	22.87	22.90
.3	22.93	22.97	23.00	23.03	23.06	23.09	23.12	23.15	23.18	23.22
.4	23.25	23.28	23.31	23.34	23.37	23.40	23.44	23.47	23.50	23.53
7.5	23.56	23.59	23.62	23.66	23.69	23.72	23.75	23.78	23.81	23.84
.6	23.88	23.91	23.94	23.97	24.00	24.03	24.06	24.10	24.13	24.16
.7	24.19	24.22	24.25	24.28	24.32	24.35	24.38	24.41	24.44	24.47
.8	24.50	24.54	24.57	24.60	24.63	24.66	24.69	24.72	24.76	24.79
.9	24.82	24.85	24.88	24.91	24.94	24.98	25.01	25.04	25.07	25.10
8.0	25.13	25.16	25.20	25.23	25.26	25.29	25.32	25.35	25.38	25.42
.1	25.45	25.48	25.51	24.54	25.57	25.60	25.64	25.67	25.70	25.73
.2	25.76	25.79	25.82	25.86	25.89	25.92	25.95	25.98	26.01	26.04
.3	26.08	26.11	26.14	26.17	26.20	26.23	26.26	26.30	26.33	26.36
.4	26.39	26.42	26.45	26.48	26.52	26.55	26.58	26.61	26.64	26.67
8.5	26.70	26.73	26.77	26.80	26.83	26.86	26.89	26.92	26.95	26.99
.6	27.02	27.05	27.08	27.11	27.14	27.17	27.21	27.24	27.27	27.30
.7	27.33	27.36	27.39	27.43	27.46	27.49	27.52	27.55	27.58	27.61
.8	27.65	27.68	27.71	27.74	27.77	27.80	27.83	27.87	27.90	27.93
.9	27.96	27.99	28.02	28.05	28.09	28.12	28.15	28.18	28.21	28.24
9.0	28.27	28.31	28.34	28.37	28.40	28.43	28.46	28.49	28.53	28.56
.1	28.59	28.62	28.65	28.68	28.71	28.75	28.78	28.81	28.84	28.87
.2	28.90	28.93	28.97	29.00	29.03	29.06	29.09	29.12	29.15	29.19
.3	29.22	29.25	29.28	29.31	29.34	29.37	29.41	29.44	29.47	29.50
.4	29.53	29.56	29.59	29.63	29.66	29.69	29.72	29.75	29.78	29.81
9.5	29.85	29.88	29.91	29.94	29.97	30.00	30.03	30.07	30.10	30.13
.6	30.16	30.19	30.22	30.25	30.28	30.32	30.35	30.38	30.41	30.44
.7	30.47	30.50	30.54	30.57	30.60	30.63	30.66	30.69	30.72	30.76
.8	30.79	30.82	30.85	30.88	30.91	30.94	30.98	31.01	31.04	31.07
.9	31.10	31.13	31.16	31.20	31.23	31.26	31.29	31.32	31.35	31.38

TABLE 4—AREAS BY HUNDREDTHS. SEE NOTE 2

D	0	1	2	3	4	5	6	7	8	9
1.0	0.785	0.801	0.817	0.833	0.849	0.866	0.882	0.899	0.916	0.933
.1	0.950	0.968	0.985	1.003	1.021	1.039	1.057	1.075	1.094	1.112
.2	1.131	1.150	1.169	1.188	1.208	1.227	1.247	1.267	1.287	1.307
.3	1.327	1.348	1.368	1.389	1.410	1.431	1.453	1.474	1.496	1.517
.4	1.539	1.561	1.584	1.606	1.629	1.651	1.674	1.697	1.720	1.744
1.5	1.767	1.791	1.815	1.839	1.863	1.887	1.911	1.936	1.961	1.986
.6	2.011	2.036	2.061	2.087	2.112	2.138	2.164	2.190	2.217	2.243
.7	2.270	2.297	2.324	2.351	2.378	2.405	2.433	2.461	2.488	2.516
.8	2.545	2.573	2.602	2.630	2.659	2.688	2.717	2.746	2.776	2.806
.9	2.835	2.865	2.895	2.926	2.956	2.986	3.017	3.048	3.079	3.110
2.0	3.142	3.173	3.205	3.237	3.269	3.301	3.333	3.365	3.398	3.431
.1	3.464	3.497	3.530	3.563	3.597	3.631	3.664	3.698	3.733	3.767
.2	3.801	3.836	3.871	3.906	3.941	3.976	4.011	4.047	4.083	4.119
.3	4.155	4.191	4.227	4.264	4.301	4.337	4.374	4.412	4.449	4.486
.4	4.524	4.562	4.600	4.638	4.676	4.714	4.753	4.792	4.831	4.870
2.5	4.909	4.948	4.988	5.027	5.067	5.107	5.147	5.187	5.228	5.269
.6	5.309	5.350	5.391	5.433	5.474	5.515	5.557	5.599	5.641	5.683
.7	5.726	5.768	5.811	5.853	5.896	5.940	5.983	6.026	6.070	6.114
.8	6.158	6.202	6.246	6.290	6.335	6.379	6.424	6.469	6.514	6.560
.9	6.605	6.651	6.697	6.743	6.789	6.835	6.881	6.928	6.975	7.022
3.0	7.069	7.116	7.163	7.211	7.258	7.306	7.354	7.402	7.451	7.499
.1	7.548	7.596	7.645	7.694	7.744	7.793	7.843	7.892	7.942	7.992
.2	8.042	8.093	8.143	8.194	8.245	8.296	8.347	8.398	8.450	8.501
.3	8.553	8.605	8.657	8.709	8.762	8.814	8.867	8.920	8.973	9.026
.4	9.079	9.133	9.186	9.240	9.294	9.348	9.402	9.457	9.511	9.566
3.5	9.621	9.676	9.731	9.787	9.842	9.898	9.954	10.01	10.07	10.12
.6	10.18	10.24	10.29	10.35	10.41	10.46	10.52	10.58	10.64	10.69
.7	10.75	10.81	10.87	10.93	10.99	11.04	11.10	11.16	11.22	11.28
.8	11.34	11.40	11.46	11.52	11.58	11.64	11.70	11.76	11.82	11.88
.9	11.95	12.01	12.07	12.13	12.19	12.25	12.32	12.38	12.44	12.50
4.0	12.57	12.63	12.69	12.76	12.82	12.88	12.95	13.01	13.07	13.14
.1	13.20	13.27	13.33	13.40	13.46	13.53	13.59	13.66	13.72	13.79
.2	13.85	13.92	13.99	14.05	14.12	14.19	14.25	14.32	14.39	14.45
.3	14.52	14.59	14.66	14.73	14.79	14.86	14.93	15.00	15.07	15.14
.4	15.21	15.27	15.34	15.41	15.48	15.55	15.62	15.69	15.76	15.83
4.5	15.90	15.98	16.05	16.12	16.19	16.26	16.33	16.40	16.47	16.55
.6	16.62	16.69	16.76	16.84	16.91	16.98	17.06	17.13	17.20	17.28
.7	17.35	17.42	17.50	17.57	17.65	17.72	17.80	17.87	17.95	18.02
.8	18.10	18.17	18.25	18.32	18.40	18.47	18.55	18.63	18.70	18.78
.9	18.86	18.93	19.01	19.09	19.17	19.24	19.32	19.40	19.48	19.56
5.0	19.63	19.71	19.79	19.87	19.95	20.03	20.11	20.19	20.27	20.35
.1	20.43	20.51	20.59	20.67	20.75	20.83	20.91	20.99	21.07	21.16
.2	21.24	21.32	21.40	21.48	21.57	21.65	21.73	21.81	21.90	21.98
.3	22.06	22.15	22.23	22.31	22.40	22.48	22.56	22.65	22.73	22.82
.4	22.90	22.99	23.07	23.16	23.24	23.33	23.41	23.50	23.59	23.67
5.5	23.76	23.84	23.93	24.02	24.11	24.19	24.28	24.37	24.45	24.54
.6	24.63	24.72	24.81	24.89	24.98	25.07	25.16	25.25	25.34	25.43
.7	25.52	25.61	25.70	25.79	25.88	25.97	26.06	26.15	26.24	26.33
.8	26.42	26.51	26.60	26.69	26.79	26.88	26.97	27.06	27.15	27.25
.9	27.34	27.43	27.53	27.62	27.71	27.81	27.90	27.99	28.09	28.18
6.0	28.27	28.37	28.46	28.56	28.65	28.75	28.84	28.94	29.03	29.13
.1	29.22	29.32	29.42	29.51	29.61	29.71	29.80	29.90	30.00	30.09
.2	30.19	30.29	30.39	30.48	30.58	30.68	30.78	30.88	30.97	31.07
.3	31.17	31.27	31.37	31.47	31.57	31.67	31.77	31.87	31.97	32.07
.4	32.17	32.27	32.37	32.47	32.57	32.67	32.78	32.88	32.98	33.08
6.5	33.18	33.29	33.39	33.49	33.59	33.70	33.80	33.90	34.00	34.11
.6	34.21	34.32	34.42	34.52	34.63	34.73	34.84	34.94	35.05	35.15
.7	35.26	35.36	35.47	35.57	35.68	35.78	35.89	36.00	36.10	36.21
.8	36.32	36.42	36.53	36.64	36.75	36.85	36.96	37.07	37.18	37.28
.9	37.39	37.50	37.61	37.72	37.83	37.94	38.05	38.16	38.26	38.37
7.0	38.48	38.59	38.70	38.82	38.93	39.04	39.15	39.26	39.37	39.48
.1	39.59	39.70	39.82	39.93	40.04	40.15	40.26	40.38	40.49	40.60
.2	40.72	40.83	40.94	41.06	41.17	41.28	41.40	41.51	41.62	41.74
.3	41.85	41.97	42.08	42.20	42.31	42.43	42.54	42.66	42.78	42.89
.4	43.01	43.12	43.24	43.36	43.47	43.59	43.71	43.83	43.94	44.06
7.5	44.18	44.30	44.41	44.53	44.65	44.77	44.89	45.01	45.13	45.25
.6	45.36	45.48	45.60	45.72	45.84	45.96	46.08	46.20	46.32	46.45
.7	46.57	46.69	46.81	46.93	47.05	47.17	47.29	47.42	47.54	47.66
.8	47.78	47.91	48.03	48.15	48.27	48.40	48.52	48.65	48.77	48.89
.9	49.02	49.14	49.27	49.39	49.51	49.64	49.76	49.89	50.01	50.14
8.0	50.27	50.39	50.52	50.64	50.77	50.90	51.02	51.15	51.28	51.40
.1	51.53	51.66	51.78	51.91	52.04	52.17	52.30	52.42	52.55	52.68
.2	52.81	52.94	53.07	53.20	53.33	53.46	53.59	53.72	53.85	53.98
.3	54.11	54.24	54.37	54.50	54.63	54.76	54.89	55.02	55.15	55.29
.4	55.42	55.55	55.68	55.81	55.95	56.08	56.21	56.35	56.48	56.61
8.5	56.75	56.88	57.01	57.15	57.28	57.41	57.55	57.68	57.82	57.95
.6	58.09	58.22	58.36	58.49	58.63	58.77	58.90	59.04	59.17	59.31
.7	59.45	59.58	59.72	59.86	59.99	60.13	60.27	60.41	60.55	60.68
.8	60.82	60.96	61.10	61.24	61.38	61.51	61.65	61.79	61.93	62.07
.9	62.21	62.35	62.49	62.63	62.77	62.91	63.05	63.19	63.33	63.48
9.0	63.62	63.76	63.90	64.04	64.18	64.33	64.47	64.61	64.75	64.90
.1	65.04	65.18	65.33	65.47	65.61	65.76	65.90	66.04	66.19	66.33
.2	66.48	66.62	66.77	66.91	67.06	67.20	67.35	67.49	67.64	67.78
.3	67.93	68.08	68.22	68.37	68.51	68.66	68.81	68.96	69.10	69.25
.4	69.40	69.55	69.69	69.84	69.99	70.14	70.29	70.44	70.58	70.73
9.5	70.88	71.03	71.18	71.33	71.48	71.63	71.78	71.93	72.08	72.23
.6	72.38	72.53	72.68	72.84	72.99	73.14	73.29	73.44	73.59	73.75
.7	73.90	74.05	74.20	74.36	74.51	74.66	74.82	74.97	75.12	75.28
.8	75.43	75.58	75.74	75.89	76.05	76.20	76.36	76.51	76.67	76.82
.9	76.98	77.13	77.29	77.44	77.60	77.76	77.91	78.07	78.23	78.38

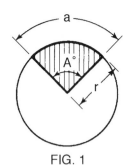

FIG. 1

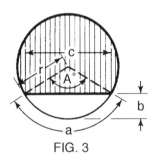

FIG. 2

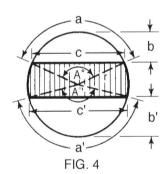

FIG. 3

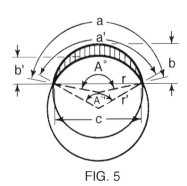

FIG. 4

FIG. 5

Nomenclature—

$A° = $ Angle in degrees $= \dfrac{180° \ a}{\pi \ r}$

$a = $ Arc $= 0.017453 \ r \ A°$

$b = $ Rise $= 2 \ r \ \sin^2 \dfrac{A°}{4}$

$c = $ Chord $= 2 \ r \ \sin \dfrac{A°}{2}$

$d = $ Diameter $= 2 \ r = \dfrac{4 \ b^2 + c^2}{4 \ b}$

$\pi = 3.1416$

$r = $ Radius $= \dfrac{d}{2} = \dfrac{4 \ b^2 + c^2}{8 \ b}$

$S = $ Area $= \dfrac{\pi \ d^2}{4} = 0.7854 \ d^2$

AREA OF CIRCULAR SECTOR—Figure 1

$$\text{Area} = \frac{a \ r}{2} = \frac{S \ A°}{360}$$

AREA OF CIRCULAR SEGMENT—Figure 2
(Less than half circle)

$$\text{Area} = \frac{a \ r - c \ (r - b)}{2} = \frac{S A°}{360} - \frac{c \ (r - b)}{2}$$

AREA OF CIRCULAR SEGMENT—Figure 3
(Greater than half circle)

$$\text{Area} = S - \left[\frac{a \ r - c \ (r - b)}{2} \right] = S - \left[\frac{S \ A°}{360} - \frac{c \ (r - b)}{2} \right]$$

AREA OF CIRCULAR ZONE—Figure 4

$$\text{Area} = S - \left[\frac{a \ r - c \ (r - b)}{2} + \frac{a^1 \ r - c^1 \ (r - b^1)}{2} \right]$$

$$= S - \left[\frac{S \ A°}{360} - \frac{c \ (r - b)}{2} + \frac{S A^{°1}}{360} - \frac{c^1 \ (r - b^1)}{2} \right]$$

AREA OF CIRCULAR LUNE—Figure 5

$$\text{Area} = \left[\frac{a \ r - c \ (r - b)}{2} \right] - \left[\frac{a^1 \ r^1 - c \ (r^1 - b^1)}{2} \right]$$

$$= \left[\frac{S A°}{360} - \frac{c(r - b)}{2} \right] - \left[\frac{S^1 A^{°1}}{360} - \frac{c \ (r^1 - b^1)}{2} \right]$$

AREA OF CIRCULAR SEGMENT—From Table 5
(Using Rise and Chord)

Area $= c \times b \times$ coefficient.

Example: chord, $c = 3.52$; rise, $b = 1.49$

$\dfrac{b}{c} = \dfrac{1.49}{3.52} = 0.4233$

coefficient of $0.4233 = 0.7542$

$3.52 \times 1.49 \times 0.7542 = 3.9556 = $ area of segment

AREA OF CIRCULAR SEGMENT—From Table 6
(Using Rise and Diameter)

Area $= d^2 \times$ coefficient

Example: diameter, $d = 5\frac{3}{32}$; rise, $b = 2\frac{7}{16}$

$5\frac{3}{32} = 5.09375$; $2\frac{7}{16} = 2.4375$

$\dfrac{b}{d} = \dfrac{2.4375}{5.09375} = 0.478528$

Interpolation:

Coefficient for $0.479 = 0.371705$

$\phantom{\text{Coefficient for }} 0.478 = 0.370706$

$\phantom{\text{Coefficient for }}\overline{.001} = \overline{0.000999}$

$.478528$
$.478000$
$\overline{.000528}$ $\times$ $\dfrac{528}{0.000527}$

Coefficient $+ 0.370706$
for $0.478528 = \overline{0.371233}$

$5.09375 \times 5.09375 \times 0.371233 = 9.6321 = $ area of segment

AREAS OF CIRCULAR SEGMENTS

Table 5. For ratios of rise and chord

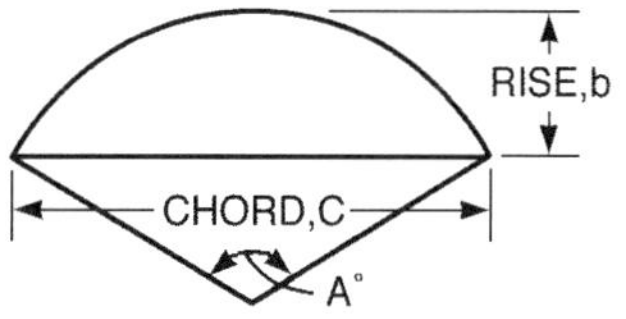

Area = C x b x Coefficient

A°	Coeff.-cient	b/C	A°	Coeff.-cient	b/C	A°	Coeffi-cient	b/C	A°	Coeffi-cient	b/C
1	.6667	.0022	16	.6674	.0350	31	.6691	.0681	46	.6722	.1017
2	.6667	.0044	17	.6674	.0372	32	.6693	.0703	47	.6724	.1040
3	.6667	.0066	18	.6675	.0394	33	.6694	.0725	48	.6727	.1063
4	.6667	.0087	19	.6676	.0416	34	.6696	.0747	49	.6729	.1086
5	.6667	.0109	20	.6677	.0437	35	.6698	.0770	50	.6732	.1109
6	.6667	.0131				36	.6700	.0792			
7	.6668	.0153	21	.6678	.0459	37	.6702	.0814	51	.6734	.1131
8	.6668	.0175	22	.6679	.0481	38	.6704	.0837	52	.6737	.1154
9	.6669	.0197	23	.6680	.0504	39	.6706	.0859	53	.6740	.1177
10	.6670	.0218	24	.6681	.0526	40	.6708	.0882	54	.6743	.1200
			25	.6682	.0548				55	.6746	.1224
11	.6670	.0240	26	.6684	.0570	41	.6710	.0904	56	.6749	.1247
12	.6671	.0262	27	.6685	.0592	42	.6712	.0927	57	.6752	.1270
13	.6672	.0284	28	.6687	.0614	43	.6714	.0949	58	.6755	.1293
14	.6672	.0306	29	.6688	.0636	44	.6717	.0972	59	.6758	.1316
15	.6673	.0328	30	.6690	.0658	45	.6719	.0995	60	.6761	.1340

A°	Coeffi-cient	b/C	A°	Coeffi-cient	b/C	A°	Coeffi cient	b/C	A°	Coeffi-cient	b/C
61	.6764	.1363	91	.6895	.2097	121	.7100	.2916	151	.7408	.3871
62	.6768	.1387	92	.6901	.2122	122	.7109	.2945	152	.7421	.3906
63	.6771	.1410	93	.6906	.2148	123	.7117	.2975	153	.7434	.3942
64	.6775	.1434	94	.6912	.2174	124	.7126	.3004	154	.7447	.3977
65	.6779	.1457	95	.6918	.2200	125	.7134	.3034	155	.7460	.4013
66	.6782	.1481	96	.6924	.2226	126	.7143	.3064	156	.7473	.4049
67	.6786	.1505	97	.6930	.2252	127	.7152	.3094	157	.7486	.4085
68	.6790	.1529	98	.6936	.2279	128	.7161	.3124	158	.7500	.4122
69	.6794	.1553	99	.6942	.2305	129	.7170	.3155	159	.7514	.4159
70	.6797	.1577	100	.6948	.2332	130	.7180	.3185	160	.7528	.4196
71	.6801	.1601	101	.6954	.2358	131	.7189	.3216	161	.7542	.4233
72	.6805	.1625	102	.6961	.2385	132	.7199	.3247	162	.7557	.4270
73	.6809	.1649	103	.6967	.2412	133	.7209	.3278	163	.7571	.4308
74	.6814	.1673	104	.6974	.2439	134	.7219	.3309	164	.7586	.4346
75	.6818	.1697	105	.6980	.2466	135	.7229	.3341	165	.7601	.4385
76	.6822	.1722	106	.6987	.2493	136	.7239	.3373	166	.7616	.4424
77	.6826	.1746	107	.6994	.2520	137	.7249	.3404	167	.7632	.4463
78	.6831	.1771	108	.7001	.2548	138	.7260	.3436	168	.7648	.4502
79	.6835	.1795	109	.7008	.2575	139	.7270	.3469	169	.7664	.4542
80	.6840	.1820	110	.7015	.2603	140	.7281	.3501	170	.7680	.4582
81	.6844	.1845	111	.7022	.2631	141	.7292	.3534	171	.7696	.4622
82	.6849	.1869	112	.7030	.2659	142	.7303	.3567	172	.7712	.4663
83	.6854	.1894	113	.7037	.2687	143	.7314	.3600	173	.7729	.4704
84	.6859	.1919	114	.7045	.2715	144	.7325	.3633	174	.7746	.4745
85	.6854	.1944	115	.7052	.2743	145	.7336	.3666	175	.7763	.4787
86	.6869	.1970	116	.7060	.2772	146	.7348	.3700	176	.7781	.4828
87	.6874	.1995	117	.7068	.2800	147	.7360	.3734	177	.7799	.4871
88	.6879	.2020	118	.7076	.2829	148	.7372	.3768	178	.7817	.4914
89	.6884	.2046	119	.7084	.2858	149	.7384	.3802	179	.7835	.4957
90	.6890	.2071	120	.7092	.2887	150	.7396	.3837	180	.7854	.5000

AREAS OF CIRCULAR SEGMENTS

Table 6. For ratios of rise and diameter

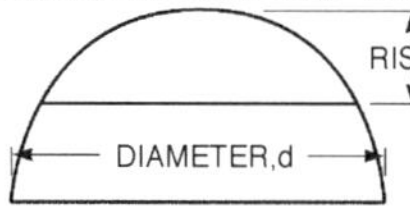

Area = d^2 x Coefficient

b/d	Coeffi-cient	b/d	Coeffi-cient	b/d	Coeffi-cient	b/d	Coeffi-cient	b/d	Coeffi-cient
.001	.000042	.046	.012971	.091	.035586	.136	.064074	.181	.096904
.002	.000119	.047	.013393	.092	.036162	.137	.064761	.182	.097675
.003	.000219	.048	.013818	.093	.036742	.138	.065449	.183	.098447
.004	.000337	.049	.014248	.094	.037324	.139	.066140	.184	.099221
.005	.000471	.050	.014681	.095	.037909	.140	.066833	.185	.099997
.006	.000619			.096	.038497			.186	.100774
.007	.000779	.051	.015119	.097	.039087	.141	.067528	.187	.101553
.008	.000952	.052	.015561	.098	.039681	.142	.068225	.188	.102334
.009	.001135	.053	.016008	.099	.040277	.143	.068924	.189	.103116
.010	.001329	.054	.016458	.100	.040875	.144	.069626	.190	.103900
		.055	.016912			.145	.070329		
.011	.001533	.056	.017369	.101	.041477	.146	.071034	.191	.104686
.012	.001746	.057	.017831	.102	.042081	.147	.071741	.192	.105472
.013	.001969	.058	.018297	.103	.042687	.148	.072450	.193	.106261
.014	.002159	.059	.018766	.104	.043296	.149	.073162	.194	.107051
.015	.002438	.060	.019239	.105	.043908	.150	.073875	.195	.107843
.016	.002685			.106	.044523			.196	.108636
.017	.002940	.061	.019716	.107	.045140	.151	.074590	.197	.109431
.018	.003202	.062	.020197	.108	.045759	.152	.075307	.198	.110227
.019	.003472	.063	.020681	.109	.046381	.153	.076026	.199	.111025
.020	.003749	.064	.021168	.110	.047006	.154	.076747	.200	.111824
		.065	.021660			.155	.077470		
.021	.004032	.066	.022155	.111	.047633	.156	.078194	.201	.112625
.022	.004322	.067	.022653	.112	.048262	.157	.078921	.202	.113427
.023	.004619	.068	.023155	.113	.048894	.158	.079650	.203	.114231
.024	.004922	.069	.023660	.114	.049529	.159	.080380	.204	.115036
.025	.005231	.070	.024168	.115	.050165	.160	.081112	.205	.115842
.026	.005546			.116	.050805			.206	.116651
.027	.005867	.071	.024680	.117	.051446	.161	.081847	.207	.117460
.028	.006194	.072	.025196	.118	.052090	.162	.082582	.208	.118271
.029	.006527	.073	.025714	.119	.052737	.163	.083320	.209	.119084
.030	.006866	.074	.026236	.120	.053385	.164	.084060	.210	.119898
		.075	.026761			.165	.084801		
.031	.007209	.076	.027290	.121	.054037	.166	.085545	.211	.120713
.032	.007559	.077	.027821	.122	.054690	.167	.086290	.212	.121530
.033	.007913	.078	.028356	.123	.055346	.168	.087037	.213	.122348
.034	.008273	.079	.028894	.124	.056004	.169	.087785	.214	.123167
.035	.008638	.080	.029435	.125	.056664	.170	.088536	.215	.123988
.036	.009008			.126	.057327			.216	.124811
.037	.009383	.081	.029979	.127	.057991	.171	.089288	.217	.125634
.038	.009764	.082	.030526	.128	.058658	.172	.090042	.218	.126459
.039	.010148	.083	.031077	.129	.059328	.173	.090797	.219	.127286
.040	.010538	.084	.031630	.130	.059999	.174	.091555	.220	.128114
		.085	.032186			.175	.092314		
.041	.010932	.086	.032746	.131	.060673	.176	.093074	.221	.128943
.042	.011331	.087	.033308	.132	.061349	.177	.093837	.222	.129773
.043	.011734	.088	.033873	.133	.062027	.178	.094601	.223	.130605
.044	.012142	.089	.034441	.134	.062707	.179	.095367	.224	.131438
.045	.012555	.090	.035012	.135	.063389	.180	.096135	.225	.132273

b/d	Coeffi-cient	b/d	Coeffi-cient	b/d	Coeffi-cient	b/d	Coeffi-cient	b/d	Coeffi-cient
.226	.133109	.281	.180918	.336	.231689	.391	.284569	.446	.338804
.227	.133946	.282	.181818	.337	.232634	.392	.285545	.447	.339799
.228	.134784	.283	.182718	.338	.233580	.393	.286521	.448	.340793
.229	.135624	.284	.183619	.339	.234526	.394	.287499	.449	.341788
.230	.136465	.285	.184522	.340	.235473	.395	.288476	.450	.342783
		.286	.185425			.396	.289454		
.231	.137307	.287	.186329	.341	.236421	.397	.290432	.451	.343778
.232	.138151	.288	.187235	.342	.237369	.398	.291411	.452	.344773
.233	.138996	.289	.188141	.343	.238319	.399	.292390	.453	.345768
.234	.139842	.290	.189048	.344	.239268	.400	.293370	.454	.346764
.235	.140689			.345	.240219			.455	.347760
.236	.141538	.291	.189956	.346	.241170	.401	.294350	.456	.348756
.237	.142388	.292	.190865	.347	.242122	.402	.295330	.457	.349752
.238	.143239	.293	.191774	.348	.243074	.403	.296311	.458	.350749
.239	.144091	.294	.192685	.349	.244027	.404	.297292	.459	.351745
.240	.144945	.295	.193597	.350	.244980	.405	.298274	.460	.352742
		.296	.194501			.406	.299256		
.241	.145800	.297	.195423	.351	.245935	.407	.300238	.461	.353739
.242	.146656	.298	.196337	.352	.246890	.408	.301221	.462	.354736
.243	.147513	.299	.197252	.353	.247845	.409	.302204	.463	.355733
.244	.148371	.300	.198168	.354	.248801	.410	.303187	.464	.356730
.245	.149231			.355	.249758			.465	.357728
.246	.150091	.301	.199085	.356	.250715	.411	.304171	.466	.358725
.247	.150953	.302	.200003	.357	.251673	.412	.305156	.467	.359723
.248	.151816	.303	.200922	.358	.252632	.413	.306140	.468	.360721
.249	.152681	.304	.201841	.359	.253591	.414	.307125	.469	.361719
.250	.153546	.305	.202762	.360	.254551	.415	.308110	.470	.362717
		.306	.203683			.416	.309096		
.251	.154413	.307	.204605	.361	.255511	.417	.310082	.471	.363715
.252	.155281	.308	.205528	.362	.256472	.418	.311068	.472	.364714
.253	.156149	.309	.206452	.363	.257433	.419	.312055	.473	.365712
.254	.157019	.310	.207376	.364	.258395	.420	.313042	.474	.366711
.255	.157891			.365	.259358			.475	.367710
.256	.158763	.311	.208302	.366	.260321	.421	.314029	.476	.368708
.257	159636	.312	.209228	.367	.261285	.422	.315017	.477	.369707
.258	.160511	.313	.210155	.368	.262249	.423	.316005	.478	.370706
.259	.161386	.314	.211083	.369	.263214	.424	.316993	.479	.371705
.260	.162263	.315	.212011	.370	.264179	.425	.317981	.480	.372704
		.316	.212941			.426	.318970		
.261	.163141	.317	.213871	.371	.265145	.427	.319959	.481	.373704
.262	.164020	.318	.214802	.372	.266111	.428	.320949	.482	.374703
.263	.164900	.319	.215734	.373	.267078	.429	.321938	.483	.375702
.264	.165781	.320	.216666	.374	.268046	.430	.322928	.484	.376702
.265	.166663			.375	.269014			.485	.377701
.266	.167546	.321	.217600	.376	.269982	.431	.323919	.486	.378701
.267	.168431	.322	.218534	.377	.270951	.432	.324909	.487	.379701
.268	.169316	.323	.219469	.378	.271921	.433	.325900	.488	.380700
.269	.170202	.324	.220404	.379	.272891	.434	.326891	.489	.381700
.270	.171090	.325	.221341	.380	.273861	.435	.327883	.490	.382700
		.326	.222278			.436	.328874		
.271	.171978	.327	.223216	.381	.274832	.437	.329866	.491	.383700
.272	.172868	.328	.224154	.382	.275804	.438	.330858	.492	.384699
.273	.173758	.329	.225094	.383	.276776	.439	.331851	.493	.385699
.274	.174650	.330	.226034	.384	.277748	.440	.332843	.494	.386699
.275	.175542			.385	.278721			.495	.387699
.276	.176436	.331	.226974	.386	.279695	.441	.333836	.496	.388699
.277	.177330	.332	.227916	.387	.280669	.442	.334829	.497	.389699
.278	.178226	.333	.228858	.388	.281643	.443	.335823	.498	.390699
.279	.179122	.334	.229801	.389	.282618	.444	.336816	.499	.391699
.280	.180020	.335	.230745	.390	.283593	.445	.337810	.500	.392699

FORM		METHOD OF FINDING AREAS
TRIANGLE		Base × ½ perpendicular height. $\sqrt{s(s-a)(s-b)(s-c)}$, **s** = ½ sum of the three sides **a, b, c**.
TRAPEZIUM		Sum of area of the two triangles
TRAPEZOID		½ sum of parallel sides × perpendicular height.
PARALLELOGRAM		Base × perpendicular height.
REG. POLYGON		½ sum of sides × inside radius.
CIRCLE		$\pi r^2 = 0.78540 \times$ diam^2. $= 0.07958 \times$ circumference^2
SECTOR OF A CIRCLE		$\frac{\pi r^2 A°}{360} = 0.0087266 \; r^2 A°$, = arc × ½ radius
SEGMENT OF A CIRCLE		$\frac{r^2}{2} \left(\frac{\pi A°}{180} - \sin A° \right)$
CIRCLE of same area as a square		Diameter = side × 1.12838
SQUARE of same area as a circle		Side = diameter × 0.88623
ELLIPSE		Long diameter × short diameter × 0.78540
PARABOLA		Base × ⅔ perpendicular height.
IRREGULAR PLANE SURFACE		Divide any plane surface **A, B, C, D**, along a line **a - b** into an even number, **n**, of parallel and sufficiently small strips **d**, whose ordinates are $h_1, h_2, h_3, h_4, h_5, \ldots h_{n-1}, h_n, h_{n+1}$, and considering contours between three ordinates as parabolic curves, then for section **A B C D**, Area $= \frac{d}{3} \left[h_1 + h_{n+1} + 4 (h_2 + h_4 + h_6 \ldots + h_n) + 2 (h_3 + h_5 + h_7 \ldots + h_{n-1}) \right]$ or, approximately, Area = sum of ordinates × width **d**.

METHOD OF FINDING SURFACES AND VOLUMES OF SOLIDS

SHAPE	FORMULAE	SHAPE	FORMULAE

S = lateral or convex surface   **V** = volume

Parallelopiped

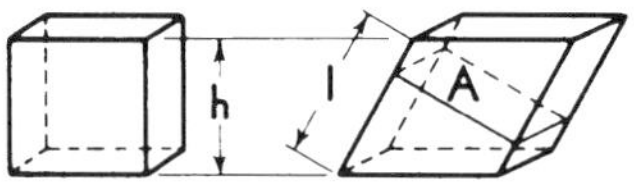

S = perimeter, **P**, perp. to sides × lat. length **l** :   **Pl** :
V = area of base, **B**, × perpendicular height, **h** :   **Bh**.
V = area of section, **A**, perp. to sides, × lat. length **l** :   **Al**.

Prism right, or oblique, regular or irregular

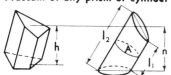

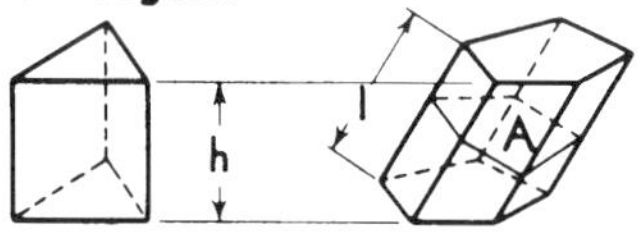

S = perimeter, **P**, perp. to sides × lat. length **l** :   **Pl** :
V = area of base, **B**, × perpendicular height, **h** :   **Bh**.
V = area of section, **A**, perp. to sides, × lat. length **l** :   **Al**.

Cylinder, right or oblique, circular or elliptic etc.

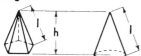

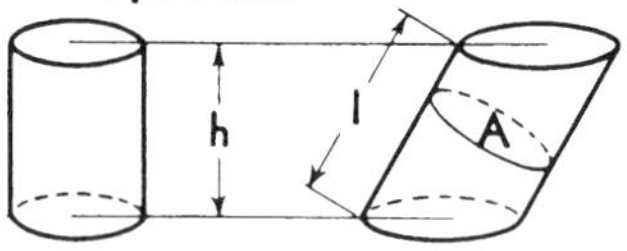

S = perimeter of base, **P**, × perp. height, **h**: **Ph**. S_l=perimeter, P_l, perp, × lat. length, **l** : $P_l l$.
V = area of base, **B**, × perp. height, **h**: **Bh**. V=area of section, **A**, perp. to sides × lat. length **l**: **Al**.

Frustum of any prism or cylinder

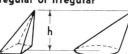

V = area of base, **B**, × perpendicular distance **h**, from base to centre of gravity of opposite face: **Bh**.
for cylinder, ½ **A** (l_1 + l_2)

Pyramid or Cone, right and regular

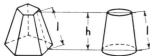

S = perimeter of base, **P**, × ½ slant height **l** : ½ **Pl**.
V = area of base, **B** × ⅓ perpendicular ht., **h** : ⅓ **Bh**.

Pyramid or Cone, right or oblique, regular or irregular

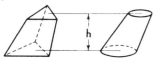

V = area of base, **B**, × ⅓ perp. height, **h** : ⅓ **Bh**.
V = ⅓ vol. of prism or cylinder of same base & perp. height.
V = ½ vol. of hemisphere of same base and perp. height.

Frustum of pyramid or cone, right and regular, parallel ends

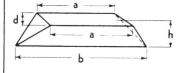

S = (sum of perimeter of base, **P**, and top, **p**) × ½ slant height **l** : ½ **l** (**P**+**p**).
V = (sum of areas of base, **B**, and top, **b**+sq. root of their products) × ⅓ perp. height, **h** : ⅓ h (**B**+**b**+√**B b**)

Frustum of any pyramid or cone, parallel ends

V = (sum of areas of base, **B**, and top, **b**,+sq. root of their products) × ⅓ perpendicular height, **h** : ⅓ h (**B**+**b**+√**B b**).

Wedge, parallelogram face

V = ⅙ (sum of three edges, **a b a**, × perpendicular height, **h**, × perpendicular width, **d**) : ⅙ d h (2 **a**+**b**)

Sphere   **S** = lateral or convex surface   **V** = volume

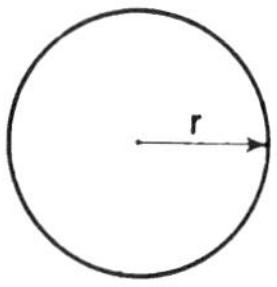

$S = 4\pi r^2 = \pi d^2 = 3.14159265\ d^2$.
$V = \frac{4}{3}\pi r^3 = \frac{1}{6}\pi d^3 = 0.52359878\ d^3$.

Spherical Sector

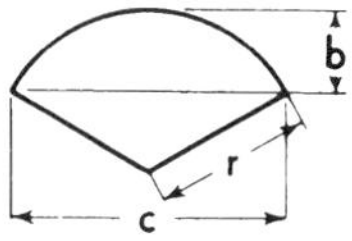

$S = \frac{1}{2}\pi r\ (4b + c)$.
$V = \frac{2}{3}\pi r^2 b$.

Spherical Segment

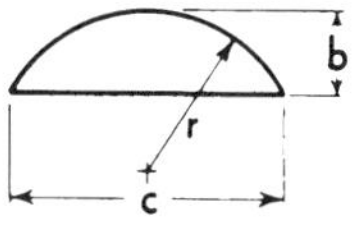

$S = 2\pi rb = \frac{1}{4}\pi\ (4b^2 + c^2)$.
$V = \frac{1}{3}\pi b^2\ (3r - b) = \frac{1}{24}\pi b\ (3c^2 + 4b^2)$.

Spherical Zone

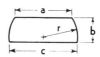

$S = 2\pi rb$.
$V = \frac{1}{24}\pi b\ (3a^2 + 3c^2 + 4b^2)$.

Circular Ring

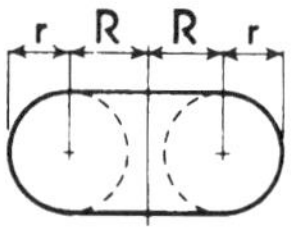

$S = 4\pi^2 Rr$.
$V = 2\pi^2 Rr^2$.

Ungula of right, regular cylinder
1. Base = segment, bab.   2. Base = half circle

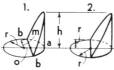

S = (2rm − o × arc, bab) $\frac{h}{r-o}$.   **S** = 2 r h.
V = (⅔ m³ − o × area, bab) $\frac{h}{r-o}$. $V = \frac{2}{3} r^2 h$.

1. Base = segment, cac.   2. Base = circle

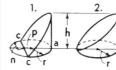

S = (2 rn + p × arc, cac) $\frac{h}{r+p}$.   **S** = π r h.
V = (⅔ n³ + p × area, cac) $\frac{h}{r+p}$. $V = \frac{1}{2} r^2 \pi h$.

Ellipsoid

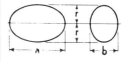

$V = \frac{1}{3}\pi rab$.

Paraboloid

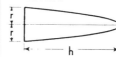

$V = \frac{1}{2}\pi r^2 h$.
Ratio of corresponding volume of a Cone, Paraboloid, Sphere & Cylinder of equal height: ⅓, ½, ⅔, 1.

RIGHT-ANGLED TRIANGLES

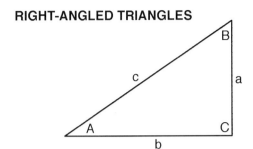

OBLIQUE-ANGLED TRIANGLES

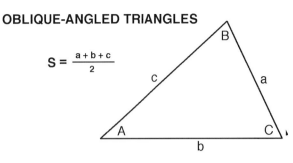

$$S = \frac{a+b+c}{2}$$

Given	Sought	Formulae
a, c	A, B, b	$\sin A = \dfrac{a}{c}$, $\qquad \cos B = \dfrac{a}{c}$, $\qquad b = \sqrt{c^2 - a^2}$
	Area	$Area = \dfrac{a}{2}\sqrt{c^2 - a^2}$
a, b	A, B, c	$\tan A = \dfrac{a}{b}$, $\qquad \tan B = \dfrac{b}{a}$, $\qquad c = \sqrt{a^2 + b^2}$
	Area	$Area = \dfrac{a\,b}{2}$
A, a	B, b, c	$B = 90^\circ - A$, $\qquad b = a\cot A$, $\qquad c = \dfrac{a}{\sin A}$
	Area	$Area = \dfrac{a^2 \cot A}{2}$
A, b	B, a, c	$B = 90^\circ - A$, $\qquad a = b\tan A$, $\qquad c = \dfrac{b}{\cos A}$
	Area	$Area = \dfrac{b^2 \tan A}{2}$
A, c	B, a, b	$B = 90^\circ - A$, $\qquad a = c\sin A$, $\qquad b = c\cos A$
	Area	$Area = \dfrac{c^2 \sin A \cos A}{2} \;\; or \;\; \dfrac{c^2 \sin 2A}{4}$

Given	Sought	Formulae
a, b, c	A	$\sin \tfrac12 A = \sqrt{\dfrac{(s-b)(s-c)}{bc}}$, $\cos \tfrac12 A = \sqrt{\dfrac{s(s-a)}{bc}}$, $\tan \tfrac12 A = \sqrt{\dfrac{(s-b)(s-c)}{s(s-a)}}$
	B	$\sin \tfrac12 B = \sqrt{\dfrac{(s-a)(s-c)}{ac}}$, $\cos \tfrac12 B = \sqrt{\dfrac{s(s-b)}{ac}}$, $\tan \tfrac12 B = \sqrt{\dfrac{(s-a)(s-c)}{s(s-b)}}$
	C	$\sin \tfrac12 C = \sqrt{\dfrac{(s-a)(s-b)}{ab}}$, $\cos \tfrac12 C = \sqrt{\dfrac{s(s-c)}{ab}}$, $\tan \tfrac12 C = \sqrt{\dfrac{(s-a)(s-b)}{s(s-c)}}$
	Area	$Area = \sqrt{s(s-a)(s-b)(s-c)}$
a, A, B	b, c	$b = \dfrac{a\sin B}{\sin A}$ $\qquad c = \dfrac{a\sin C}{\sin A} = \dfrac{a\sin(A+B)}{\sin A}$
	Area	$Area = \tfrac12\,a\,b\sin C = \dfrac{a^2 \sin B \sin C}{2\sin A}$
a, b, A	B	$\sin B = \dfrac{b\sin A}{a}$
	c	$c = \dfrac{a\sin C}{\sin A} = \dfrac{b\sin C}{\sin B} = \sqrt{a^2 + b^2 - 2ab\cos C}$
	Area	$Area = \tfrac12\,a\,b\sin C$
a, b, C	A	$\tan A = \dfrac{a\sin C}{b - a\cos C}$, $\qquad \tan \tfrac12(A-B) = \dfrac{a-b}{a+b}\cot \tfrac12 C$
	c	$c = \sqrt{a^2 + b^2 - 2ab\cos C} = \dfrac{a\sin C}{\sin A}$
	Area	$Area = \tfrac12 ab\sin C$

$$a^2 = b^2 + c^2 - 2bc\cos A, \quad b^2 = a^2 + c^2 - 2ac\cos B, \quad c^2 = a^2 + b^2 - 2ab\cos C$$

Degrees	SINES							Cosines
	0′	10′	20′	30′	40′	50′	60′	
0	0.00000	0.00291	0.00582	0.00873	0.01164	0.01454	0.01745	89
1	0.01745	0.02036	0.02327	0.02618	0.02908	0.03199	0.03490	88
2	0.03490	0.03781	0.04071	0.04362	0.04653	0.04943	0.05234	87
3	0.05234	0.05524	0.05814	0.06105	0.06395	0.06685	0.06976	86
4	0.06976	0.07266	0.07556	0.07846	0.08136	0.08426	0.08716	85
5	0.08716	0.09005	0.09295	0.09585	0.09874	0.10164	0.10453	84
6	0.10453	0.10742	0.11031	0.11320	0.11609	0.11898	0.12187	83
7	0.12187	0.12476	0.12764	0.13053	0.13341	0.13629	0.13917	82
8	0.13917	0.14205	0.14493	0.14781	0.15069	0.15356	0.15643	81
9	0.15643	0.15931	0.16218	0.16505	0.16792	0.17078	0.17365	80
10	0.17365	0.17651	0.17937	0.18224	0.18509	0.18795	0.19081	79
11	0.19081	0.19366	0.19652	0.19937	0.20222	0.20507	0.20791	78
12	0.20791	0.21076	0.21360	0.21644	0.21928	0.22212	0.22495	77
13	0.22495	0.22778	0.23062	0.23345	0.23627	0.23910	0.24192	76
14	0.24192	0.24474	0.24756	0.25038	0.25320	0.25601	0.25882	75
15	0.25882	0.26163	0.26443	0.26724	0.27004	0.27284	0.27564	74
16	0.27564	0.27843	0.28123	0.28402	0.28680	0.28959	0.29237	73
17	0.29237	0.29515	0.29793	0.30071	0.30348	0.30625	0.30902	72
18	0.30902	0.31178	0.31454	0.31730	0.32006	0.32282	0.32557	71
19	0.32557	0.32832	0.33106	0.33381	0.33655	0.33929	0.34202	70
20	0.34202	0.34475	0.34748	0.35021	0.35293	0.35565	0.35837	69
21	0.35837	0.36108	0.36379	0.36650	0.36921	0.37191	0.37461	68
22	0.37461	0.37730	0.37999	0.38268	0.38537	0.38805	0.39073	67
23	0.39073	0.39341	0.39608	0.39875	0.40142	0.40408	0.40674	66
24	0.40674	0.40939	0.41204	0.41469	0.41734	0.41998	0.42262	65
25	0.42262	0.42525	0.42788	0.43051	0.43313	0.43575	0.43837	64
26	0.43837	0.44098	0.44359	0.44620	0.44880	0.45140	0.45399	63
27	0.45399	0.45658	0.45917	0.46175	0.46433	0.46690	0.46947	62
28	0.46947	0.47204	0.47460	0.47716	0.47971	0.48226	0.48481	61
29	0.48481	0.48735	0.48989	0.49242	0.49495	0.49748	0.50000	60
30	0.50000	0.50252	0.50503	0.50754	0.51004	0.51254	0.51504	59
31	0.51504	0.51753	0.52002	0.52250	0.52498	0.52745	0.52992	58
32	0.52992	0.53238	0.53484	0.53730	0.53975	0.54220	0.54464	57
33	0.54464	0.54708	0.54951	0.55194	0.55436	0.55678	0.55919	56
34	0.55919	0.56160	0.56401	0.56641	0.56880	0.57119	0.57358	55
35	0.57358	0.57596	0.57833	0.58070	0.58307	0.58543	0.58779	54
36	0.58779	0.59014	0.59248	0.59482	0.59716	0.59949	0.60182	53
37	0.60182	0.60414	0.60645	0.60876	0.61107	0.61337	0.61566	52
38	0.61566	0.61795	0.62024	0.62251	0.62479	0.62706	0.62932	51
39	0.62932	0.63158	0.63383	0.63608	0.63832	0.64056	0.64279	50
40	0.64279	0.64501	0.64723	0.64945	0.65166	0.65386	0.65606	49
41	0.65606	0.65825	0.66044	0.66262	0.66480	0.66697	0.66913	48
42	0.66913	0.67129	0.67344	0.67559	0.67773	0.67987	0.68200	47
43	0.68200	0.68412	0.68624	0.68835	0.69046	0.69256	0.69466	46
44	0.69466	0.69675	0.69883	0.70091	0.70298	0.70505	0.70711	45
	60′	50′	40′	30′	20′	10′	0′	
Sines			COSINES					Degrees

Degrees	COSINES							Sines
	0′	10′	20′	30′	40′	50′	60′	
0	1.00000	1.00000	0.99998	0.99996	0.99993	0.99989	0.99985	89
1	0.99985	0.99979	0.99973	0.99966	0.99958	0.99949	0.99939	88
2	0.99939	0.99929	0.99917	0.99905	0.99892	0.99878	0.99863	87
3	0.99863	0.99847	0.99831	0.99813	0.99795	0.99776	0.99756	86
4	0.99756	0.99736	0.99714	0.99692	0.99668	0.99644	0.99619	85
5	0.99619	0.99594	0.99567	0.99540	0.99511	0.99482	0.99452	84
6	0.99452	0.99421	0.99390	0.99357	0.99324	0.99290	0.99255	83
7	0.99255	0.99219	0.99182	0.99144	0.99106	0.99067	0.99027	82
8	0.99027	0.98986	0.98944	0.98902	0.98858	0.98814	0.98769	81
9	0.98769	0.98723	0.98676	0.98629	0.98580	0.98531	0.98481	80
10	0.98481	0.98430	0.98378	0.98325	0.98272	0.98218	0.98163	79
11	0.98163	0.98107	0.98050	0.97992	0.97934	0.97875	0.97815	78
12	0.97815	0.97754	0.97692	0.97630	0.97566	0.97502	0.97437	77
13	0.97437	0.97371	0.97304	0.97237	0.97169	0.97100	0.97030	76
14	0.97030	0.96959	0.96887	0.96815	0.96742	0.96667	0.96593	75
15	0.96593	0.96517	0.96440	0.96363	0.96285	0.96206	0.96126	74
16	0.96126	0.96046	0.95964	0.95882	0.95799	0.95715	0.95630	73
17	0.95630	0.95545	0.95459	0.95372	0.95284	0.95195	0.95106	72
18	0.95106	0.95015	0.94924	0.94832	0.94740	0.94646	0.94552	71
19	0.94552	0.94457	0.94361	0.94264	0.94167	0.94068	0.93969	70
20	0.93969	0.93869	0.93769	0.93667	0.93565	0.93462	0.93358	69
21	0.93358	0.93253	0.93148	0.93042	0.92935	0.92827	0.92718	68
22	0.92718	0.92609	0.92499	0.92388	0.92276	0.92164	0.92050	67
23	0.92050	0.91936	0.91822	0.91706	0.91590	0.91472	0.91355	66
24	0.91355	0.91236	0.91116	0.90996	0.90875	0.90753	0.90631	65
25	0.90631	0.90507	0.90383	0.90259	0.90133	0.90007	0.89879	64
26	0.89879	0.89752	0.89623	0.89493	0.89363	0.89232	0.89101	63
27	0.89101	0.88968	0.88835	0.88701	0.88566	0.88431	0.88295	62
28	0.88295	0.88158	0.88020	0.87882	0.87743	0.87603	0.87462	61
29	0.87462	0.87321	0.87178	0.87036	0.86892	0.86748	0.86603	60
30	0.86603	0.86457	0.86310	0.86163	0.86015	0.85866	0.85717	59
31	0.85717	0.85567	0.85416	0.85264	0.85112	0.84959	0.84805	58
32	0.84805	0.84650	0.84495	0.84339	0.84182	0.84025	0.83867	57
33	0.83867	0.83708	0.83549	0.83389	0.83228	0.83066	0.82904	56
34	0.82904	0.82741	0.82577	0.82413	0.82248	0.82082	0.81915	55
35	0.81915	0.81748	0.81580	0.81412	0.81242	0.81072	0.80902	54
36	0.80902	0.80730	0.80558	0.80386	0.80212	0.80038	0.79864	53
37	0.79864	0.79688	0.79512	0.79335	0.79158	0.78980	0.78801	52
38	0.78801	0.78622	0.78442	0.78261	0.78079	0.77897	0.77715	51
39	0.77715	0.77531	0.77347	0.77162	0.76977	0.76791	0.76604	50
40	0.76604	0.76417	0.76229	0.76041	0.75851	0.75661	0.75471	49
41	0.75471	0.75280	0.75088	0.74896	0.74703	0.74509	0.74314	48
42	0.74314	0.74120	0.73924	0.73728	0.73531	0.73333	0.73135	47
43	0.73135	0.72937	0.72737	0.72537	0.72337	0.72136	0.71934	46
44	0.71934	0.71732	0.71529	0.71325	0.71121	0.70916	0.70711	45
	60′	50′	40′	30′	20′	10′	0′	
Cosines			SINES					Degrees

Degrees	TANGENTS 0′	10′	20′	30′	40′	50′	60′	Cotangents
0	0.00000	0.00291	0.00582	0.00873	0.01164	0.01455	0.01746	89
1	0.01746	0.02036	0.02328	0.02619	0.02910	0.03201	0.03492	88
2	0.03492	0.03783	0.04075	0.04366	0.04658	0.04949	0.05241	87
3	0.05241	0.05533	0.05824	0.06116	0.06408	0.06700	0.06993	86
4	0.06993	0.07285	0.07578	0.07870	0.08163	0.08456	0.08749	85
5	0.08749	0.09042	0.09335	0.09629	0.09923	0.10216	0.10510	84
6	0.10510	0.10805	0.11099	0.11394	0.11688	0.11983	0.12278	83
7	0.12278	0.12574	0.12869	0.13165	0.13461	0.13758	0.14054	82
8	0.14054	0.14351	0.14648	0.14945	0.15243	0.15540	0.15838	81
9	0.15838	0.16137	0.16435	0.16734	0.17033	0.17333	0.17633	80
10	0.17633	0.17933	0.18233	0.18534	0.18835	0.19136	0.19438	79
11	0.19438	0.19740	0.20042	0.20345	0.20648	0.20952	0.21256	78
12	0.21256	0.21560	0.21864	0.22169	0.22475	0.22781	0.23087	77
13	0.23087	0.23393	0.23700	0.24008	0.24316	0.24624	0.24933	76
14	0.24933	0.25242	0.25552	0.25862	0.26172	0.26483	0.26795	75
15	0.26795	0.27107	0.27419	0.27732	0.28046	0.28360	0.28675	74
16	0.28675	0.28990	0.29305	0.29621	0.29938	0.30255	0.30573	73
17	0.30573	0.30891	0.31210	0.31530	0.31850	0.32171	0.32492	72
18	0.32492	0.32814	0.33136	0.33460	0.33783	0.34108	0.34433	71
19	0.34433	0.34758	0.35085	0.35412	0.35740	0.36068	0.36397	70
20	0.36397	0.36727	0.37057	0.37388	0.37720	0.38053	0.38386	69
21	0.38386	0.38721	0.39055	0.39391	0.39727	0.40065	0.40403	68
22	0.40403	0.40741	0.41081	0.41421	0.41763	0.42105	0.42447	67
23	0.42447	0.42791	0.43136	0.43481	0.43828	0.44175	0.44523	66
24	0.44523	0.44872	0.45222	0.45573	0.45924	0.46277	0.46631	65
25	0.46631	0.46985	0.47341	0.47698	0.48055	0.48414	0.48773	64
26	0.48773	0.49134	0.49495	0.49858	0.50222	0.50587	0.50953	63
27	0.50953	0.51320	0.51688	0.52057	0.52427	0.52798	0.53171	62
28	0.53171	0.53545	0.53920	0.54296	0.54674	0.55051	0.55431	61
29	0.55431	0.55812	0.56194	0.56577	0.56962	0.57348	0.57735	60
30	0.57735	0.58124	0.58513	0.58905	0.59297	0.59691	0.60086	59
31	0.60086	0.60483	0.60881	0.61280	0.61681	0.62083	0.62487	58
32	0.62487	0.62892	0.63299	0.63707	0.64117	0.64528	0.64941	57
33	0.64941	0.65355	0.65771	0.66189	0.66608	0.67028	0.67451	56
34	0.67451	0.67875	0.68301	0.68728	0.69157	0.69588	0.70021	55
35	0.70021	0.70455	0.70891	0.71329	0.71769	0.72211	0.72654	54
36	0.72654	0.73100	0.73547	0.73996	0.74447	0.74900	0.75355	53
37	0.75355	0.75812	0.76272	0.76733	0.77196	0.77661	0.78129	52
38	0.78129	0.78598	0.79070	0.79544	0.80020	0.80498	0.80978	51
39	0.80978	0.81461	0.81946	0.82434	0.82923	0.83415	0.83910	50
40	0.83910	0.84407	0.84906	0.85408	0.85912	0.86419	0.86929	49
41	0.86929	0.87441	0.87955	0.88473	0.88992	0.89515	0.90040	48
42	0.90040	0.90569	0.91099	0.91633	0.92170	0.92709	0.93252	47
43	0.93252	0.93797	0.94345	0.94896	0.95451	0.96008	0.96569	46
44	0.96569	0.97133	0.97700	0.98270	0.98843	0.99420	1.00000	45
Tangents	COTANGENTS 60′	50′	40′	30′	20′	10′	0′	Degrees

Degrees	COTANGENTS 0′	10′	20′	30′	40′	50′	60′	Tangents
0	∞	343.77371	171.88540	114.58865	85.93979	68.75009	57.28996	89
1	57.28996	49.10388	42.96408	38.18846	34.36777	31.24158	28.63625	88
2	28.63625	26.43160	24.54176	22.90377	21.47040	20.20555	19.08114	87
3	19.08114	18.07498	17.16934	16.34986	15.60478	14.92442	14.30067	86
4	14.30067	13.72674	13.19688	12.70621	12.25051	11.82617	11.43005	85
5	11.43005	11.05943	10.71191	10.38540	10.07803	9.78817	9.51436	84
6	9.51436	9.25530	9.00983	8.77689	8.55555	8.34496	8.14435	83
7	8.14435	7.95302	7.77035	7.59575	7.42871	7.26873	7.11537	82
8	7.11537	6.96823	6.82694	6.69116	6.56055	6.43484	6.31375	81
9	6.31375	6.19703	6.08444	5.97576	5.87080	5.76937	5.67128	80
10	5.67128	5.57638	5.48451	5.39552	5.30928	5.22566	5.14455	79
11	5.14455	5.06584	4.98940	4.91516	4.84300	4.77286	4.70463	78
12	4.70463	4.63825	4.57363	4.51071	4.44942	4.38969	4.33148	77
13	4.33148	4.27471	4.21933	4.16530	4.11256	4.06107	4.01078	76
14	4.01078	3.96165	3.91364	3.86671	3.82083	3.77595	3.73205	75
15	3.73205	3.68909	3.64705	3.60588	3.56557	3.52609	3.48741	74
16	3.48741	3.44951	3.41236	3.37594	3.34023	3.30521	3.27085	73
17	3.27085	3.23714	3.20406	3.17159	3.13972	3.10842	3.07768	72
18	3.07768	3.04749	3.01783	2.98869	2.96004	2.93189	2.90421	71
19	2.90421	2.87700	2.85023	2.82391	2.79802	2.77254	2.74748	70
20	2.74748	2.72281	2.69853	2.67462	2.65109	2.62791	2.60509	69
21	2.60509	2.58261	2.56046	2.53865	2.51715	2.49597	2.47509	68
22	2.47509	2.45451	2.43422	2.41421	2.39449	2.37504	2.35585	67
23	2.35585	2.33693	2.31826	2.29984	2.28167	2.26374	2.24604	66
24	2.24604	2.22857	2.21132	2.19430	2.17749	2.16090	2.14451	65
25	2.14451	2.12832	2.11233	2.09654	2.08094	2.06553	2.05030	64
26	2.05030	2.03526	2.02039	2.00569	1.99116	1.97680	1.96261	63
27	1.96261	1.94858	1.93470	1.92098	1.90741	1.89400	1.88073	62
28	1.88073	1.86760	1.85462	1.84177	1.82907	1.81649	1.80405	61
29	1.80405	1.79174	1.77955	1.76749	1.75556	1.74375	1.73205	60
30	1.73205	1.72047	1.70901	1.69766	1.68643	1.67530	1.66428	59
31	1.66428	1.65337	1.64256	1.63185	1.62125	1.61074	1.60033	58
32	1.60033	1.59002	1.57981	1.56969	1.55966	1.54972	1.53987	57
33	1.53987	1.53010	1.52043	1.51084	1.50133	1.49190	1.48256	56
34	1.48256	1.47330	1.46411	1.45501	1.44598	1.43703	1.42815	55
35	1.42815	1.41934	1.41061	1.40195	1.39336	1.38484	1.37638	54
36	1.37638	1.36800	1.35968	1.35142	1.34323	1.33511	1.32704	53
37	1.32704	1.31904	1.31110	1.30323	1.29541	1.28764	1.27994	52
38	1.27994	1.27230	1.26471	1.25717	1.24969	1.24227	1.23490	51
39	1.23490	1.22758	1.22031	1.21310	1.20593	1.19882	1.19175	50
40	1.19175	1.18474	1.17777	1.17085	1.16398	1.15715	1.15037	49
41	1.15037	1.14363	1.13694	1.13029	1.12369	1.11713	1.11061	48
42	1.11061	1.10414	1.09770	1.09131	1.08496	1.07864	1.07237	47
43	1.07237	1.06613	1.05994	1.05378	1.04766	1.04158	1.03553	46
44	1.03553	1.02952	1.02355	1.01761	1.01170	1.00583	1.00000	45
Cotangents	TANGENTS 60′	50′	40′	30′	20′	10′	0	Degrees

Degrees	SECANTS 0′	10′	20′	30′	40′	50′	60′	Cosecants
0	1.00000	1.00000	1.00002	1.00004	1.00007	1.00011	1.00015	89
1	1.00015	1.00021	1.00027	1.00034	1.00042	1.00051	1.00061	88
2	1.00061	1.00072	1.00083	1.00095	1.00108	1.00122	1.00137	87
3	1.00137	1.00153	1.00169	1.00187	1.00205	1.00224	1.00244	86
4	1.00244	1.00265	1.00287	1.00309	1.00333	1.00357	1.00382	85
5	1.00382	1.00408	1.00435	1.00463	1.00491	1.00521	1.00551	84
6	1.00551	1.00582	1.00614	1.00647	1.00681	1.00715	1.00751	83
7	1.00751	1.00787	1.00825	1.00863	1.00902	1.00942	1.00983	82
8	1.00983	1.01024	1.01067	1.01111	1.01155	1.01200	1.01247	81
9	1.01247	1.01294	1.01342	1.01391	1.01440	1.01491	1.01543	80
10	1.01543	1.01595	1.01649	1.01703	1.01758	1.01815	1.01872	79
11	1.01872	1.01930	1.01989	1.02049	1.02110	1.02171	1.02234	78
12	1.02234	1.02298	1.02362	1.02428	1.02494	1.02562	1.02630	77
13	1.02630	1.02700	1.02770	1.02842	1.02914	1.02987	1.03061	76
14	1.03061	1.03137	1.03213	1.03290	1.03368	0.03447	1.03528	75
15	1.03528	1.03609	1.03691	1.03774	1.03858	1.03944	1.04030	74
16	1.04030	1.04117	1.04206	1.04295	1.04385	1.04477	1.04569	73
17	1.04569	1.04663	1.04757	1.04853	1.04950	1.05047	1.05146	72
18	1.05146	1.05246	1.05347	1.05449	1.05552	1.05657	1.05762	71
19	1.05762	1.05869	1.05976	1.06085	1.06195	1.06306	1.06418	70
20	1.06418	1.06531	1.06645	1.06761	1.06878	1.06995	1.07115	69
21	1.07115	1.07235	1.07356	1.07479	1.07602	1.07727	1.07853	68
22	1.07853	1.07981	1.08109	1.08239	1.08370	1.08503	1.08636	67
23	1.08636	1.08771	1.08907	1.09044	1.09183	1.09323	1.09464	66
24	1.09464	1.09606	1.09750	1.09895	1.10041	1.10189	1.10338	65
25	1.10338	1.10488	1.10640	1.10793	1.10947	1.11103	1.11260	64
26	1.11260	1.11419	1.11579	1.11740	1.11903	1.12067	1.12233	63
27	1.12233	1.12400	1.12568	1.12738	1.12910	1.13083	1.13257	62
28	1.13257	1.13433	1.13610	1.13789	1.13970	1.14152	1.14335	61
29	1.14335	1.14521	1.14707	1.14896	1.15085	1.15277	1.15470	60
30	1.15470	1.15665	1.15861	1.16059	1.16259	1.16460	1.16663	59
31	1.16663	1.16868	1.17075	1.17283	1.17493	1.17704	1.17918	58
32	1.17918	1.18133	1.18350	1.18569	1.18790	1.19012	1.19236	57
33	1.19236	1.19463	1.19691	1.19920	1.20152	1.20386	1.20622	56
34	1.20622	1.20859	1.21099	1.21341	1.21584	1.21830	1.22077	55
35	1.22077	1.22327	1.22579	1.22833	1.23089	1.23347	1.23607	54
36	1.23607	1.23869	1.24134	1.24400	1.24669	1.24940	1.25214	53
37	1.25214	1.25489	1.25767	1.26047	1.26330	1.26615	1.26902	52
38	1.26902	1.27191	1.27483	1.27778	1.28075	1.28374	1.28676	51
39	1.28676	1.28980	1.29287	1.29597	1.29909	1.30223	1.30541	50
40	1.30541	1.30861	1.31183	1.31509	1.31837	1.32168	1.32501	49
41	1.32501	1.32838	1.33177	1.33519	1.33864	1.34212	1.34563	48
42	1.34563	1.34917	1.35274	1.35634	1.35997	1.36363	1.36733	47
43	1.36733	1.37105	1.37481	1.37860	1.38242	1.38628	1.39016	46
44	1.39016	1.39409	1.39804	1.40203	1.40606	1.41012	1.41421	45
Secants	COSECANTS 60′	50′	40′	30′	20′	10′	0′	Degrees

Degrees	COSECANTS 0′	10′	20′	30′	40′	50′	60′	Secants
0	∞	343.77516	171.88831	114.59301	85.94561	68.75736	57.29869	89
1	57.29869	49.11406	42.97571	38.20155	34.38232	31.25758	28.65371	88
2	28.65371	26.45051	24.56212	22.92559	21.49368	20.23028	19.10732	87
3	19.10732	18.10262	17.19843	16.38041	15.63679	14.95788	14.33559	86
4	14.33559	13.76312	13.23472	12.74550	12.29125	11.86837	11.47371	85
5	11.47371	11.10455	10.75849	10.43343	10.12752	9.83912	9.56677	84
6	9.56677	9.30917	9.06515	8.83367	8.61379	8.40466	8.20551	83
7	8.20551	8.01565	7.83443	7.66130	7.49571	7.33719	7.18530	82
8	7.18530	7.03962	6.89979	6.76547	6.63633	6.51208	6.39245	81
9	6.39245	6.27719	6.16607	6.05886	5.95536	5.85539	5.75877	80
10	5.75877	5.66533	5.57493	5.48740	5.40263	5.32049	5.24084	79
11	5.24084	5.16359	5.08863	5.01585	4.94517	4.87649	4.80973	78
12	4.80973	4.74482	4.68167	4.62023	4.56041	4.50216	4.44541	77
13	4.44541	4.39012	4.33622	4.28366	4.23239	4.18238	4.13357	76
14	4.13357	4.08591	4.03938	3.99393	3.94952	3.90613	3.86370	75
15	3.86370	3.82223	3.78166	3.74198	3.70315	3.66515	3.62796	74
16	3.62796	3.59154	3.55587	3.52094	3.48671	3.45317	3.42030	73
17	3.42030	3.38808	3.35649	3.32551	3.29512	3.26531	3.23607	72
18	3.23607	3.20737	3.17920	3.15155	3.12440	3.09774	3.07155	71
19	3.07155	3.04584	3.02057	2.99574	2.97135	2.94737	2.92380	70
20	2.92380	2.90063	2.87785	2.85545	2.83342	2.81175	2.79043	69
21	2.79043	2.76945	2.74881	2.72850	2.70851	2.68884	2.66947	68
22	2.66947	2.65040	2.63162	2.61313	2.59491	2.57698	2.55930	67
23	2.55930	2.54190	2.52474	2.50784	2.49119	2.47477	2.45859	66
24	2.45859	2.44264	2.42692	2.41142	2.39614	2.38107	2.36620	65
25	2.36620	2.35154	2.33708	2.32282	2.30875	2.29487	2.28117	64
26	2.28117	2.26766	2.25432	2.24116	2.22817	2.21535	2.20269	63
27	2.20269	2.19019	2.17786	2.16568	2.15366	2.14178	2.13005	62
28	2.13005	2.11847	2.10704	2.09574	2.08458	2.07356	2.06267	61
29	2.06267	2.05191	2.04128	2.03077	2.02039	2.01014	2.00000	60
30	2.00000	1.98998	1.98008	1.97029	1.96062	1.95106	1.94160	59
31	1.94160	1.93226	1.92302	1.91388	1.90485	1.89591	1.88709	58
32	1.88709	1.87834	1.86970	1.86116	1.85271	1.84435	1.83608	57
33	1.83608	1.82790	1.81981	1.81180	1.80388	1.79604	1.78829	56
34	1.78829	1.78062	1.77303	1.76552	1.75808	1.75073	1.74345	55
35	1.74345	1.73624	1.72911	1.72205	1.71506	1.70815	1.70130	54
36	1.70130	1.69452	1.68782	1.68117	1.67460	1.66809	1.66164	53
37	1.66164	1.65526	1.64894	1.64268	1.63648	1.63035	1.62427	52
38	1.62427	1.61825	1.61229	1.60639	1.60054	1.59475	1.58902	51
39	1.58902	1.58333	1.57771	1.57213	1.56661	1.56114	1.55572	50
40	1.55572	1.55036	1.54504	1.53977	1.53455	1.52938	1.52425	49
41	1.52425	1.51918	1.51415	1.50916	1.50422	1.49933	1.49448	48
42	1.49448	1.48967	1.48491	1.48019	1.47551	1.47087	1.46628	47
43	1.46628	1.46173	1.45721	1.45274	1.44831	1.44391	1.43956	46
44	1.43956	1.43524	1.43096	1.42672	1.42251	1.41835	1.41421	45
Cosecants	SECANTS 60′	50′	40′	30′	20′	10′	0′	Degrees

By WILLIAM BLACKWELL

Geometry in architecture, sometimes boldly expressed and sometimes artfully concealed, is a part of the common core of knowledge and understanding which the architect uses to enclose space for human needs—one of his instruments, one of the tools, to be used in organizing and planning and decorating and integrating spaces so they can be built and understood and used. This study of some of the formal, basic series of geometric shapes which the architect uses, or may use, takes as its structure the unchanging relationship between the area and the perimeter of each shape.

Some shapes enclose an area with more or less perimeter than others, and this is a characteristic of the shape which can easily be expressed mathematically.

For example, the area enclosed by each unit of perimeter of a square is equal to the length of a side divided by four. The larger the square, the greater will be the area enclosed per unit of perimeter—the area/perimeter value. The same thing is true of a circle where the area enclosed per unit of circumference is equal to the diameter divided by four; and so the larger the circle, the greater will be the area/perimeter value. It is true also of any other shape that the larger it is the larger will be the area/perimeter value.

Because of this scale effect, because the area/perimeter value of all shapes changes with size in the same way, they have always the same relationship one to the other with respect to their area enclosure properties. For any given area then, the area/perimeter value of one shape can be expressed relative to the area/perimeter value of another shape.

Because a circle encloses a given area with less perimeter than any other closed shape, its area/perimeter value will always be greater —and so it is used here to express the relative area enclosure properties of other plane shapes. The area/perimeter value of a square, for instance, will always be 88.6 per cent of the area/perimeter value of a circle with the same area. This value is the area/perimeter factor, a comparison of the area enclosure properties of a square to those of a circle. Similar values can be found for other shapes, regular or irregular, by using the equation:

$$A_f = \frac{2\sqrt{\pi a}}{p} \times 100 \text{ or } \frac{354.5\sqrt{A}}{p}$$

Once the area/perimeter factor has been found for a shape, the process can be reversed and the area/perimeter factor used to find the actual area or perimeter of a shape if one or the other is known, providing a useful numerical relationship between the two similar to the 'k' and 'f' factors sometimes employed in handbooks to simplify calculations.

If the area is known, the perimeter can be found using the equation in this way:

$$p = \frac{2\sqrt{\pi A}}{A_f / 100} \text{ or } \frac{354.5\sqrt{A}}{A_f}$$

If the perimeter is known, the area can be found by the equation:

$$A = \frac{1}{4\pi}\left[\frac{A_f}{100} \times p\right]^2 \text{ or } .0796\left[\frac{A_f}{100} \times p\right]^2$$

For circles, squares or rectangles finding the area or perimeter isn't a very serious problem but in the case of many sided polygons, ellipses or irregular shapes, the area/perimeter factor can be useful.

The reciprocal of the area/perimeter factor can also be used to express the difference in the area enclosure properties of a shape and a circle. A square has a perimeter/area value of 1.128 (100/88.6) compared to a circle of 1, which is to say that a square has 12.8 per cent more perimeter than a circle with the same area.

It might be emphasized, too, that although the area/perimeter factor is independent of "the scale effect" and is an unchanging factor regardless of the size of the shape, it is nonetheless an expression of the relative area enclosure properties of shapes for a given area. A large square might have an actual area/perimeter value twice that of a small circle. The usefulness of the factor lies then only in comparing the area enclosure properties of shapes for a given area.

The chart below illustrates the relative area enclosure properties of four related series of geometric shapes. They are arranged from bottom to top according to their area/perimeter factors, from 0 to 100 per cent, and from left to right according to the number of sides in the shape, from one to infinity.

In outline form and starting with the square are also shown some rectangles of different proportion to illustrate the change that occurs in the area enclosure properties of rectangles as the length-to-width ratio changes.

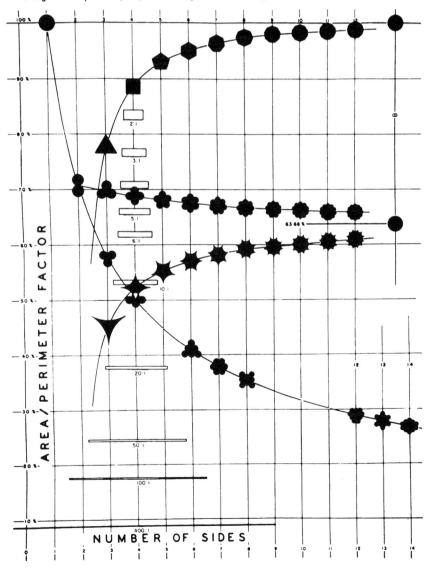

The shapes on the chart all have the same area, so the difference in apparent size, as between one shape and another, can be seen.

The Regular Polygons

First of the four series of shapes shown in black on the chart is the regular straight-sided polygon series—the triangle, square, pentagon, etc. It begins, theoretically, with a straight line. Having two sides, a perimeter equal to twice its length but zero area, a straight line has an area/perimeter factor of 0 per cent. The first solid equilateral shape is the equilateral triangle (77.7 per cent), then a square (88.6 per cent), the five-sided pentagon (93 per cent) and so on—gradually approaching a circle (100 per cent) as the number of sides increases to infinity. Area/perimeter factors for some of the polygons in this series are given in the table below. The latter shapes in this series are extremely compact, with polygons of 13 sides or more having area/perimeter factors within 1 per cent of the area/perimeter factor of a circle.

In a limited sense, area/perimeter factors are a kind of efficiency factor, reflecting the degree of proximity of a shape to the area enclosure properties of a circle—as for instance, when a circular structure is divided into a number of straight sides for ease of fabrication.

Concave-Convex Series:

Under the regular polygons are two complementary series of shapes, seldom used, but still familiar to architects as the shapes of brightly colored rose windows and vertically lined, fluted columns. These are the concave and convex aspects of the straight-sided polygons. Actually, which is which depends on whether the point of view is from the outside or the inside but the upper curve, the "rose" shapes, are taken to be the convex series and the lower curve, the "fluted" shapes, the concave.

Of the shapes in these two series, the most interesting is the three-sided concave shape formed by the interior arcs of three mutually tangent circles. It might be called a "triarc." This shape has an area/perimeter factor of 45.2 per cent, the lowest of the regular geometric shapes. Although actually having the same area, it appears larger than any other shape on the chart. The circle and the "triarc" represent two extremes in area enclosure—the one with minimum and the other with maximum perimeter for a given area in a regular shape. Because of this difference (a 55 per cent difference in area/perimeter factors) and because of their opposite curvature, the two together form a very strong contrast in shape.

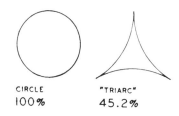

CIRCLE
100%

"TRIARC"
45.2%

As the number of arcs in the circumference of both the concave and convex shapes increases, they converge on what appears to be a circle. Theoretically, it is a circle with its circumference made up of a very large number of very small arcs. With the area of each shape the same as it is on the chart, the arcs in the circumference become smaller as more are added. Finally, they are no longer apparent—the shape appears to be a circle. The actual circumference, greatly enlarged, would appear to be a line of semi-circles, like a series of arches, turned outward for the convex shapes, inward for the concave:

Because of the small arcs, the circumference is 1.57 times longer than the circumference would be without them. The area/perimeter factor of the shape then is 1:1.57 or 63.66 per cent.

The Area/Perimeter Factor For Any Number of Separate Identical Shapes:

Beginning with one circle at the upper left-hand corner of the chart is a curve showing the area/perimeter factor for various groups containing different numbers of circles. The groups shown were arrived at by starting with one, two or three circles at the center and proceeding outward, adding circles in the vacant pockets of each concentric ring. The same number of circles might, however, have been arranged in any other manner or even randomly placed and still have the same area/perimeter factor. Providing they all are of the same size, only the number of circles considered determines the area/perimeter factor.

The area/perimeter factor of any number of separate circles of the same size is equal to the area/perimeter factor of one circle (100 per cent) divided by the square root of the number of circles considered. And, it happens that this is true of other shapes: the area/perimeter factor of any number of separate, identical shapes taken as a whole is equal to the area/perimeter factor of one of the shapes divided by the square root of the number of shapes. One square has an area/perimeter factor of 88.6 per cent; nine squares, 29.5 per cent (88.6/3). A single leaf on a tree might have an area/perimeter factor of say 50 per cent, but if all the leaves are counted they would as a whole have an area/perimeter factor of very nearly zero.

The curve showing the area/perimeter factor for groups containing a different number of circles, then, illustrates what happens to the area/perimeter factor of any shape when it is divided into a number of separate identical shapes.

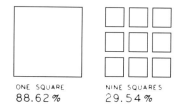

ONE SQUARE
88.62%

NINE SQUARES
29.54%

Instead of being arranged in their more compact form as they are on the chart, the same number of circles might have been arranged in a ring, adjacent to one another and equidistant from the center, as illustrated on the next page.

Lines between the centers (or the points of tangency) of adjacent circles form the regular straight-sided polygon series—the pentagon

REGULAR POLYGON SERIES:			
No. of Sides	Area/Perimeter Factor	No. of Sides	Area/Perimeter Factor
3	77.756%	20	99.587
4	88.623	24	99.714
5	92.995	25	99.736
6	95.231	27	99.774
8	97.368	30	99.817
9	97.931	32	99.839
10	98.330	36	99.872
12	98.846	40	99.897
15	99.264	45	99.920
16	99.354	48	99.929
18	99.490	50	99.934

in the illustration. The exterior perimeter of the whole form is the convex aspect of the polygon and the interior perimeter of the circles the concave. The circles themselves, the regular polygon and its concave and convex aspects make up the four series of shapes shown in black on the chart.

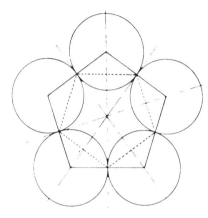

Rectangles:

In outline form, and starting with the square in the regular polygon series are some rectangles, the shapes most frequently used by architects because of the ease with which they accommodate most needs for enclosed space. The area/perimeter factor of a rectangle is determined simply by the length-to-width ratio, the proportion. A square (1:1) has the highest factor, 88.6 per cent, and the farther the rectangle deviates from the square in proportion, the lower will be its area/perimeter factor. As the length becomes very great with respect to the width, the "width" disappears, leaving a straight line with an area/perimeter factor of 0 per cent. It is possible then for a rectangle, depending on its proportion, to have any area/perimeter factor from 0 to 88.6 per cent.

The greatest difference in the area/perimeter factors of two closed shapes is, of course, 100 per cent—reached between a straight line and a circle and approached between a circle and a very long rectangle. There is one example of this contrast, used architecturally to a softer degree, in the chapel Saarinen designed for M.I.T. Here one enters the dimly-lighted, circular brick chapel through a lightly enclosed rectangular passageway. Between the high area/perimeter factor of the circle and the lower factor of the rectangular entry, there is a difference of about 25 per cent. Looking at the chart and the range of shapes normally used architecturally, this is a very considerable difference.

Room shapes, for instance, are normally nearly square in plan, with length-to-width ratios from 1:1 to about 1½:1; seldom greater than 2:1. The difference in the area/perimeter

factor of a square room and one with a relatively high length-to-width ratio of 2:1 is only about 5 per cent.

Building shapes, especially low buildings, cover virtually the whole range of rectangles, from squares to the mile-long production line enclosures of the Second World War. "L" and "T" and other arrangements are equivalent to relatively long rectangles. Because they have lower area/perimeter factors (more perimeter) they have also a higher degree of light and openness and flexibility in the arrangement and rearrangement of the internal spaces than the more compact shapes.

On the other hand, economy of exterior perimeter is an important consideration in almost every building, too, because of material and labor saving, maintenance costs, and reduction in heating and cooling loads. It is particularly important in multistory buildings where the outside wall surface is very large compared to the roof area. These buildings tend to have more compact shapes, with the perimeter reduced just to the point where if it were reduced further the spaces within would be adversely affected. To give one example, the glass-enclosed rectangles of Lever House have a length-to-width ratio of about 3:1 and an area/perimeter factor of 77.5 per cent. A square plan (88.6 per cent) might have been more economical in terms of the perimeter but would not have the same degree of light and openness and planning flexibility (and interest, too) that the rectangular shape has with some additional perimeter.

As a matter of interest, the "golden section" (1.62:1) has an area/perimeter factor of 86.12 per cent, 2½ per cent less than a square. The area/perimeter factor for other rectangles can be found by using the equation

$$A_f = \frac{\sqrt{\pi l/w}}{1 + l/w} \times 100$$

or taken directly from the curve below.

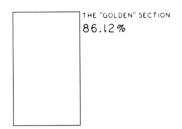

THE "GOLDEN" SECTION
86.12%

Ellipses:

On the same graph with the rectangle curve is another curve showing the area/perimeter factor for ellipses of different proportion. In the same manner as the rectangles, ellipses have lower and lower area/perimeter factors the further they deviate from a circle in proportion. It happens that for proportions less than about 5.75:1 ellipses have higher area/perimeter factors than rectangles of the same proportion but for proportions greater than 5.75:1 rectangles have the higher factors. With a length-to-width ratio of 5.75:1, both have an area/perimeter factor of 62.98 per cent.

When the major and minor axis of an ellipse are known, the area can be found using the equation, πab. The circumference can then be found by taking the approximate area/perimeter factor from the curve and using the basic equation:

$$p = \frac{2\sqrt{\pi A}}{A_f/100}$$

This will be as accurate as the area/perimeter factor can be read from the curve, plotted from tabulated values of elliptic integrals.

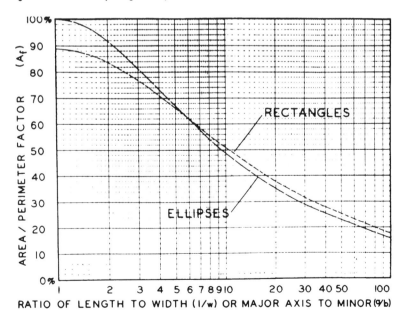

By SEYMOUR HOWARD, *Architect*
Associate Professor, Pratt Institute

The forms most suitable for the solution of many structural problems require facility in drawing and using curves. Many good designs have never been carried out because information has not been readily available on curve characteristics and methods for laying them out. These and subsequent sheets will provide such information, not only on the familiar curves, but also on curves used for geodesic lines on surfaces and for thin shells.

Simple, direct methods exist for drawing some curves. Most, however, require the setting of points by calculation or by geometrical construction. Great care must be taken in connecting the points to obtain a "fair" curve.

A fair curve is one in which there are no local undesired irregularities. The easiest way to judge fairness is to look along the curve as nearly as possible in the plane of the curve.

When a large number of similar curves must be drawn it is economical to use special machines.

Plastic or wooden templates are available in many types for joining points in a smooth curve. Sets of railroad curves are arcs of circles of varying radii and different arc lengths. Copenhagen ship curves are based on the most usual curves found in hull design. Small circle and ellipse templates are often an aid in drafting. Parabolic templates would be a great help for making structural analysis drawings. The usual French curves can be manipulated to join points by smooth curves, but they must be used carefully when they do not fit the curve exactly.

For drawing curves which do not lend themselves to simple mathematical analysis, the best method is to use wood splines or battens, held in position by lead weights called ducks.

It is not always necessary or desirable that a curve be one for which a simple equation can be written. The curves which determine the shape of a ship's hull, for example, are developed by eye on the basis of experiment and past experience.

Curves developed purely by drawing should be drawn on a material unaffected by changes in temperature or humidity, or the temperature and humidity should be kept constant in the drawing room. Marble slabs are sometimes used. If paper must be used, check points or grid lines can be marked for subsequent verification.

Such curves can be reproduced by measuring offsets from a baseline or preferably from the nearest gridline. Once a table of offsets has been made the curve can be redrawn easily at any time and at any scale.

Remarks on Curves Included

Each curve on the following sheets is accurately drawn, and its most characteristic relationships are shown. In architectural design and layout, direct geometrical methods of constructing the curve and finding tangents, etc. are the most useful and are shown where possible. For use in checking points and for engineering calculations the formulas may be more useful.

The *standard form* of the equation of a curve is one based on rectangular Cartesian coördinates in which the y ordinates are given as a function of the x intercepts. It is the form most often used in the building field.

The *parametric* equation is also based on rectangular coördinates but both the y ordinates and the x intercepts are expressed in terms of a third variable. (Such as x = a cos t; y = b sin t.)

The *polar equation* of a curve gives points as measured along a line from a central point or pole. The distance from the pole is expressed as a function of the angle between the base line and the line along which the distance is measured. Curves such as spirals are best given in this form.

In field layout the polar equation can be used to find points on a curve by chaining out from a centrally located transit, measuring off angles from a base line.

Tangents and normals to a curve at various points are necessary in order to work out neatly the intersections of straight lines or curves with the particular curve under consideration. The tangent and normal at any point on a curved structure such as an arch or a shell also give the directions along which forces should be resolved in order to analyze their effect on the structure most easily.

If the centers of curvature for all points on a curve are plotted, a new curve will be generated called the *evolute*, which is useful in visualizing the curvature of the curve. In engineering analysis the curvature of a deflection curve is the link by which deflection and bending moment (and therefore shear and loading) can be related.

From the evolute the original curve can be generated as indicated in Fig. 2.

Lengths of curves are given where convenient expressions exist. For practical drafting room use the length can be found most quickly by measuring along the curve with a strip of paper. By ticking off points as this is done the work can be done accurately and can be checked. For other purposes, such as determining lengths of cables for cutting, the exact formulas must be used, with allowance for stretch due to loading and temperature.

The *moment* of *inertia* of a curve

can be useful for long-barrel thin-shell structures in which the cross section of the shell (basically only a curved line) corresponds to the cross section of a beam.

The *areas* under certain curves and their centroids or centers of gravity are given and can be used for calculating the cubages and surfaces of parts of a building. They may also be useful in calculation of deflection (the moment-area method).

Conic Sections

Curves formed by the intersection of a plane with a right circular cone are all of the class called *conic sections*. The relationship between the plane, the cone and the conic section can be seen by the construction in Fig. 1.

A right circular cone is shown with vertex at V, cut by the plane of a conic. The plane is tangent at F to a sphere which lies wholly inside of the cone and which is tangent to the cone along a circle (like a latitude circle on the earth). The center of this tangent circle is at M; the center of the sphere is at C. The centerline of the cone lies on the line VNMC, in

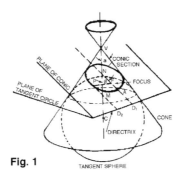

Fig. 1

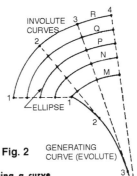

Fig. 2 GENERATING CURVE (EVOLUTE)

Right: The use of an evolute curve in generating a curve such as an ellipse, and curves parallel to it, can be visualized by imagining a flexible, elastic ruler starting at point 1 on curve R and lying along the evolute curve. As it springs away from the evolute, its straight portion would be 2-2, 3-3, 4-4, etc. In this sketch only curve P is a true ellipse; other curves are parallel

Left: Basic relationships of a conic section. See also Sheet 19

which N is the intersection of the centerline or axis of the conic section with the centerline of the cone.

In all conic sections (ellipse, parabola, hyperbola) the focus is the point of tangency between the plane of the conic and the tangent sphere; and the directrix is the line of intersection of the plane of the conic with the plane of the tangent circle.

If α is the angle which the axis of the cone makes with the side of the cone and ϕ is the angle which the

plane of the conic makes with the axis of the cone.

$$\frac{PF}{PD_2} = \frac{\cos \phi}{\cos \alpha}$$

This is called the eccentricity of the conic.

Note that the same shape of curve can be generated on cones of different slope (α) by varying the angle of the plane of the conic (ϕ). For the same shape of curve only $\frac{\cos \phi}{\cos \alpha}$ must have the same value.

PARABOLA

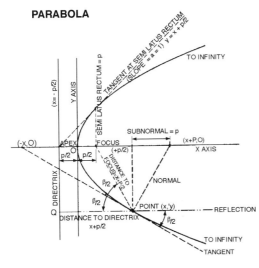

Definition:

$$\frac{\text{Distance from any point to focus}}{\text{Distance from point to directrix}} = \frac{PF}{PQ} = 1 = \text{eccentricity (e)}$$

Equation (standard form): $y^2 = 2px$

Note from characteristics of tangent, that a line from the focus (a ray of light, for example) to any point on the parabola will be reflected parallel to the axis of the parabola

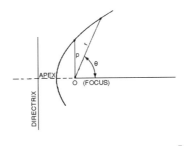

Equation (polar form, pole at focus): $r = \dfrac{p}{1 - \cos \phi}$

METHODS OF DRAWING A PARABOLA

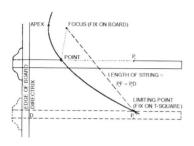

STRING METHOD

Above: attach a string (length equal to distance from limiting point on parabola to the focus) to the edge of the T-square and to the focus; hold string taut against T-square with a pencil and slide T-square.

Below: the parabola also can be constructed by knowing the heights of ordinates expressed as a ratio of the apex height (in this sketch 100.0). All parabolas have the same shape, differing only in scale. These relations hold true no matter what the ratio of height to width, provided the apex is included.

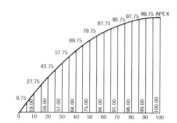

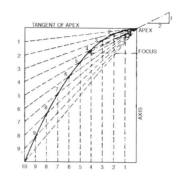

PARALLELOGRAM METHOD

To draw a parabola knowing apex, axis and one point: divide distance from point to axis in any number of equal parts; divide distance from point to the tangent through the apex into the same number of parts; draw lines parallel to the axis through points in the first line; draw lines from points in second line to apex; intersections of corresponding lines are points on the curve. To find focus, draw line through apex with slope = 1/2; from intersection with parabola drop perpendicular to axis

LENGTHS OF ARCS

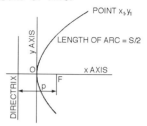

POINT x_1, y_1

LENGTH OF ARC = S/2

Length of arc from origin to point x_1, y_1

$$\frac{S}{2} = \frac{y_1}{2p} \sqrt{y_1^2 + p^2}$$

$$+ \frac{p}{2} \log_e \left[\frac{y_1 + \sqrt{y_1^2 + p^2}}{p} \right]$$

LENGTH OF ARC = S

Length of parabola

Let $\frac{H}{L} = n$

Exact formula:

$$S = 2L \left\{ \sqrt{n^2 + \frac{1}{16}} + \frac{1}{16n} \left[\log_e \left(n + \sqrt{n^2 + \frac{1}{16}} \right) + \log_e 4 \right] \right\}$$

Approximate formula:

$$S = L \left(1 + \frac{8}{3} n^2 \right),$$ sufficiently accurate for construction purposes up to $n = 1/8$

CENTERS OF CURVATURE

Radius of curvature: $R = \dfrac{(p + 2x)^{3/2}}{\sqrt{p}}$

Equation of evolute: $y^2 = \dfrac{8}{27p} (x - p)^3$ (curve of centers of curvature)

To find center of curvature C_4 for a point P_4, draw a line through P_4 parallel to x axis; set off $P_4Q_4 = 2P_4F$ and draw perpendicular through Q_4; draw normal P_4N_4 to P_4 by setting off subnormal $M_4N_4 = p$, and extend to meet perpendicular from Q_4 at C_4.

Radius of curvature at apex, $P_1C_1 = p$; ($P_1F = p/2 = FC_1$) Center of curvature can also be found by same procedure as shown for ellipse and hyperbola: P_4N_4; N_4Q; QC_4 (see Evolute of Ellipse, Sheet 5).

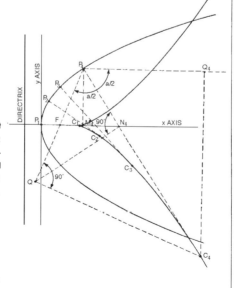

AREAS AND CENTROIDS

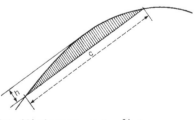

Area (A) of any segment = ⅔ ch

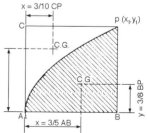

x = 3/10 CP

C.G.

C.G.

y = 3/8 BP

x = 3/5 AB

Area of half segment (APB) = 2/3 AB × BP

Area of spandrel (ACP) = 1/3 AC × CP

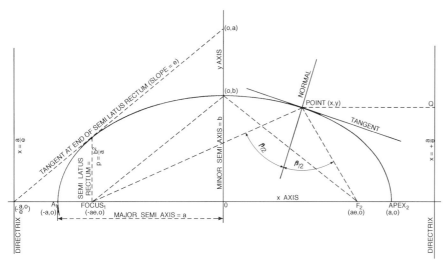

Note from characteristics of tangent (see diagram) that a line from a focus (a ray, for example) will be reflected by the ellipse and will pass through the other focus.

STANDARD FORM

$$\frac{x^2}{a^2} + \frac{y^2}{b^2} = 1 \qquad \text{(b always less than a, except for circle when a = b)}$$

Definition I: $\dfrac{\text{Distance of Any Point to Focus}}{\text{Distance of Point to Directrix}} = \dfrac{PF}{PQ} = \text{Constant} = \text{Eccentricity (e)} = \sqrt{1 - \dfrac{b^2}{a^2}} = \text{Less Than 1}$

Definition II: Distance of Any Point to Focus₁ + Distance from Point to Focus₂ = $PF_1 + PF_2$ = Constant = 2a

See Sheet 20 for Conjugate Diameters, Sheet 34 for Parallelogram Method.

To Draw: (String Method) Find foci by swinging arc = a from end of minor semi axis; insert pins at foci and at end of minor semi axis; tie string around three pins; replace pin on minor axis by pencil; slide pencil against string, keeping string taut. The larger the ellipse, the better this method is (smallest practical size, major axis = 12 in (305 mm). It can easily be used for full size layout. For smaller ellipses, use method based on parametric equation.

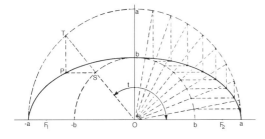

PARAMETRIC FORM

$$x = a \cos t$$
$$y = b \sin t$$

To Draw: Draw one circle with radius = a and one with radius = b, centers at O; from O draw any straight line, intersecting circle of radius b at S and circle of radius a at T; draw line through S parallel to x axis and a line through T parallel to y axis; the intersection of these lines is a point on the ellipse. Angle t is called the eccentric angle of point P (see Sheet 37).

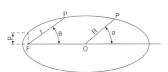

For the circle these equations become

$$r = R = a = b$$

POLAR FORM

Pole at focus: $r = \dfrac{P}{1 - e \cos \theta}$

Pole at intersection of axes:

$$R^2 = \frac{a^2 b^2}{a^2 \sin^2 \phi + b^2 \cos^2 \phi}.$$

$$P = \frac{b^2}{a} \text{ (semi-latus rectum)}$$

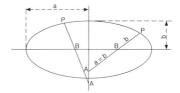

TRAMMEL METHOD

Make a stick (or piece of paper) of length PA = a; mark off PB = b, slide point A along minor axis and point B along major axis, point P will describe ellipse

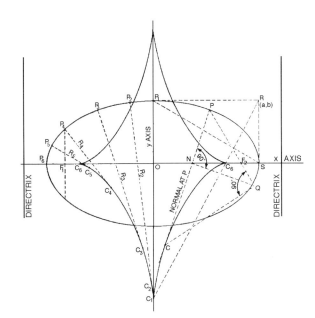

EVOLUTE OF ELLIPSE

The evolute can be used to visualize the curvature of the ellipse and to aid in constructing a curve parallel to the ellipse. (For example the intrados and extrados of an arch of uniform thickness whose centerline is an ellipse.) Such curves, called parallels to the ellipse, are not ellipses.

To find center of curvature for any point P: draw normal through P; from intersection N with major axis, erect perpendicular intersecting PF_2 extended at Q; from Q erect perpendicular to PQ intersecting normal PN extended at C. C is center of curvature, CP is radius of curvature.

Radius of Curvature

$$R = a^2 b^2 \left(\frac{x^2}{a^4} + \frac{y^2}{b^4} \right)^{3/2} \text{ for any point x, y on the ellipse}$$

To find points C_1 and C_6 on the evolute (see right hand half of curve): from point R drop perpendicular to line P_1 S; this cuts major axis at C_6, minor axis extended at C_1.

$$\text{Radius } C_6 P_6 = \frac{b^2}{a} = p \qquad \text{Radius } C_1 P_1 = \frac{a^2}{b}$$

Equation of Evolute (Standard form)

$$a^{2/3}x^{2/3} + b^{2/3} y^{2/3} = (a^2 - b^2)^{2/3}$$

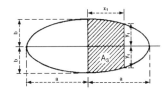

LENGTH OF ELLIPSE

Total Length

$$L = \pi \left[a+b \right] \left[1 + \tfrac{1}{4} \left(\frac{a-b}{a+b} \right)^2 + \frac{1}{64} \left(\frac{a-b}{a+b} \right)^4 + \frac{1}{256} \left(\frac{a-b}{a+b} \right)^6 + \cdots \right]$$

For lengths of arcs of ellipse, see the following publications: Smithsonian Mathematical Formulas and Tables of Elliptic Functions (Smithsonian Publ. No. 2672) Smithsonian Elliptic Functions Tables (Smithsonian Publication No. 3863).

AREAS

Total area bounded by ellipse $= A = \pi a b$

Area of segment bounded by ellipse, axis and line x = x_1 (as shaded) $A_s = x_1 y_1 + ab \arcsin \frac{x_1}{a}$

Note that these equations hold true for a circle, when $a = b = r$ and the eccentricity is zero.

ORDINATES of Quadrant of Circle. To find corresponding ordinates of quadrant of an ellipse, multiply each ordinate as figured for circle by the ratio $\frac{b}{a}$. This process is called a *dilatation.*

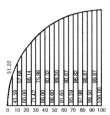

CENTROIDAL AXIS

For an arc of a circle the distance of the centroidal axis (normal to the central radius) from the center of the circle is:

$$Y = \frac{R \sin \alpha}{\alpha} \quad (\alpha \text{ in radians})$$

The "moment of inertia" of this arc about the centroid =

$$I = R^3 \left[\alpha + \tfrac{1}{2} \sin 2\alpha - \frac{2 \sin^2 \alpha}{\alpha} \right]$$

α in radians

Unfortunately there is no simple equation for finding the centroidal axis for an arc of an ellipse.

CENTROID

("Center of Gravity") of quadrant bounded by ellipse and two semi axes $\left(\text{Area} = \dfrac{\pi a b}{4} \right)$

$$x_0 = \frac{4}{3\pi} a = 0.4244 a$$

$$y_0 = \frac{4}{3\pi} b = 0.4244 b$$

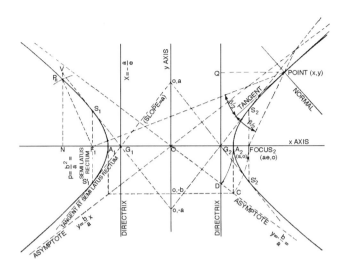

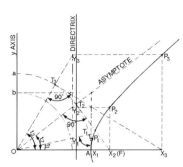

STANDARD FORM

$$\frac{x^2}{a^2} - \frac{y^2}{b^2} = 1 \quad \text{Asymptotes (tangents at infinity)} \begin{cases} \dfrac{x}{a} - \dfrac{y}{b} = 0 \\[2mm] \dfrac{x}{a} + \dfrac{y}{b} = 0 \end{cases}$$

Note that b may be greater than a; in that case the curve is flatter. When a = b, asymptotes are at right angles to each other (called a rectangular hyperbola).

Definition I: $\dfrac{\text{Distance of any Point to Focus}}{\text{Distance of Point to Directrix}} =$

$$\frac{PF}{PQ} = \text{Constant} = \text{Eccentricity (e)} = \sqrt{1 + \frac{b^2}{a}} = \text{Greater Than 1}$$

Definition II: Distance of Any Point to Focus₁ — Distance of Point to Focus₂ = $PF_1 -$
$PF_2 = \text{Constant} = 2a$

To Draw: Given a and b, draw asymptotes. Apex is at a or − a on x axis. Find directrix by swinging arc = Oa to intersect asymptote at D (see lower right quadrant). Find focus by swinging arc OC to intersect x axis at F ($OC = \sqrt{a^2 + b^2} = ae$). Erect perpendicular through F. From points O, a and O, − a, draw lines through G_1 and G_2 and intersecting perpendiculars through F_1 and F_2 at S_1, S'_1, S_2, S'_2. To find any point on hyperbola (P_n, upper left quadrant), erect perpendicular at N to intersect $G_1 S_1$ at V. From F_1 swing an arc = NV to intersect NV at P_n. See also Sheet 33 for other methods.

PARAMETRIC FORM

$$x = a \sec t = \frac{a}{\cos t}$$

$$y = b \tan t$$

(only one quadrant shown)

To Draw: Draw circles with radii = a and = b, centers O. From O draw any line, intersecting circle of radius a at T. From T erect perpendicular (tangent to circle) intersecting x axis at X. From intersection of circle of radius b with x axis, erect perpendicular intersecting OT at Y. Through Y draw line parallel to x axis, which will intersect a line parallel to y axis drawn through X at P. P is a point on the hyperbola.

Note that tangent to circle of radius a at intersection with asymptote passes through focus.

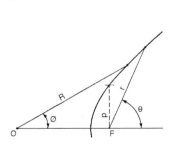

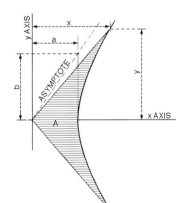

POLAR FORM

Pole at focus

$$r = \frac{P}{1 - e \cos \theta}$$

Pole at center O

$$R^2 = \frac{a^2 b^2}{b^2 \cos^2 \phi - a^2 \sin^2 \phi}$$

AREA

$$A = ab \log_e \left(\frac{x}{a} + \frac{y}{b} \right) \qquad = ab \sinh^{-1} \frac{y}{b}$$

$$= ab \cosh^{-1} \frac{x}{a} \qquad = ab \tanh^{-1} \frac{ay}{bx}$$

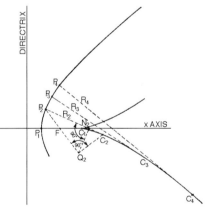

EVOLUTE OF HYPERBOLA

(For part of one quadrant)

Radius of Curvature

$$R = a^2 b^2 \left(\frac{x^2}{a^4} + \frac{y^2}{b^4} \right)^{3/2} \quad \text{For any point}$$

x, y on the hyperbola.

At apex (P_1), Radius $C_1 P_1 = \dfrac{b^2}{a} = p$

Equation of Evolute

Standard form: $a^{2/3} x^{2/3} + b^{2/3} y^{2/3} = (a^2 + b^2)^{2/3}$

Center of curvature of hyperbola can be found by same procedure as shown for ellipse.

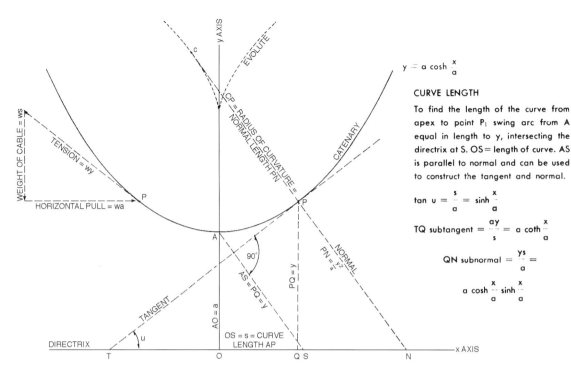

$$y = a \cosh \frac{x}{a}$$

CURVE LENGTH

To find the length of the curve from apex to point P_1 swing arc from A equal in length to y, intersecting the directrix at S. OS = length of curve. AS is parallel to normal and can be used to construct the tangent and normal.

$$\tan u = \frac{s}{a} = \sinh \frac{x}{a}$$

$$TQ \text{ subtangent} = \frac{ay}{s} = a \coth \frac{x}{a}$$

$$QN \text{ subnormal} = \frac{ys}{a} =$$

$$a \cosh \frac{x}{a} \sinh \frac{x}{a}$$

DEFINITION

The catenary is the curve described by a perfectly flexible cord of uniform weight, hanging freely between two supports. All catenaries have the same shape and differ only in scale (size). The measure of this scale is the parameter "a," which is the distance from the apex to the directrix.

The relationship between the tension at any point in the cable and the horizontal and vertical components is shown above. w = weight of cable per unit of length.

Upside down, the catenary is also the curve of the pressure line of an arch of uniform cross section, loaded only by its own weight.

When the catenary is reversed, what is tension in the cable becomes compression in the arch.

METHODS OF DRAWING: THE CATENARY AS THE ROULETTE OF A PARABOLA

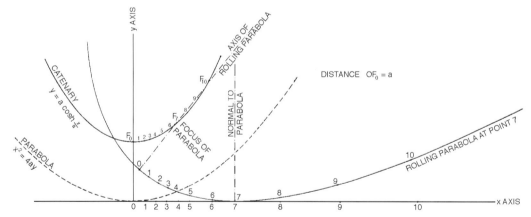

The catenary may be drawn by calculating points for the equation $y = a \cosh \frac{x}{a}$ and joining points, or it can be generated directly by rolling a parabola along the directrix. In either case the parameter "a," must be determined. As this is a trial and error procedure, the values of a in terms of SAG/SPAN ratios have been calculated and can be found directly from the graph on sheet 9. Having determined "a," the catenary can be drawn directly by first drawing a parabola with a parameter of 4a (2p in the notation on parabolas, Sheet 2–3), shown here as the parabola $x^2 = 4ay$. The parabola is then rolled along the x axis as shown above and its focus will describe the desired catenary.

This is known as a roulette curve (cycloids are the most well known roulettes). The only practical difficulty consists in preventing the rolling curve from slipping as it is rolled. The curve which is to be rolled (in this case the parabola) should be drawn on a piece of tracing paper. Make a hole in the paper at the point whose locus is sought (in this case the focus). Draw the curve (in this case the x axis) along which the curve is to be rolled on another piece of paper. Mark points along the length of the parabola and draw normal (and/or tangent) at each point. Mark points at the same distances measured along the straight line and draw normal at each point. Roll the parabola along the straight line, matching points and lining up normals (and/or tangents) at each point. Mark through the hole the corresponding point of the roulette (in this case the catenary).

PROBLEMS OF THE CATENARY FALL INTO THREE GENERAL CASES

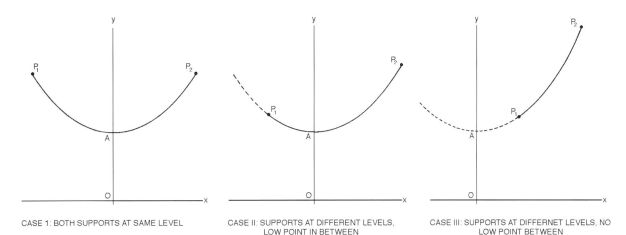

CASE 1: BOTH SUPPORTS AT SAME LEVEL

CASE II: SUPPORTS AT DIFFERENT LEVELS, LOW POINT IN BETWEEN

CASE III: SUPPORTS AT DIFFERNET LEVELS, NO LOW POINT BETWEEN

1. If locations of P_1, P_2 and A are known, the SAG/SPAN ratio can be calculated and the parameter "a" found from curve on sheet 9.

2. If only the locations of P_1 and P_2 are known, some additional information must be available. This may be:

a. The length of the curve between P_1 and P_2. With this it is possible to find "a" by trial and error graphically, remembering that the shape of the catenary is fixed and that the problem is one of scale. Over a catenary curve which has been accurately drawn,

establish points P_1 and P_2 to some scale. The angle between the line which joins them and the y or x axis will be fixed. Measure the distance from P_1 to P_2 along the curve to this same scale. If this distance is less than the given distance, the points P_1 and P_2 must be moved higher (keeping their relative positions the same). (If greater, the points must be slid down the curve.) The correct scale for the new position must be worked out, the length along the curve measured according to the new curve and so on. When the scale is correct, measure the distance from A to O

using this scale, and you will have the correct "a." This procedure can also be done algebraically, solving $S = a \sinh \dfrac{x}{a}$ by trial and error for each of the two distances P_1 A and P_2 A.

b. The tension in the cable and the weight per unit of length. Since $y = \dfrac{\text{tension}}{\text{unit weight}}$, the distance from P_1 or P_2 to the x axis can be found, and by adjusting the scale and drawing over an accurate curve, the apex A can be found and the parameter "a" calculated.

NOTES

TABLES OF HYPERBOLIC FUNCTIONS CAN BE FOUND:

1. "Smithsonian Mathematical Tables: Hyperbolic Functions," Pub. No. 1871, Gov. Printing Office, 1909, gives values to 5 decimal places
        for x = 0.0001 to x = 0.1000
        for x = 0.001 to x = 3.000
   and for x = 3.00   to x = 6.00

2. "Tables of Circular and Hyperbolic Sines and Cosines for Radian Arguments," published as a WPA project, New York, 1939, gives values to 9 decimal places
        for x = 0.0001 to x = 1.9999
   and for x = 2.0   to x = 10.00

CATENARY AS ROULETTE OF PARABOLA

The demonstration of the catenary as the roulette of a parabola was first made by James Clerk Maxwell, "Theory of Rolling Curves," Transactions Royal Soc. Edin., Vol. XVI, Part 5 (1849), republished in "Scientific Papers of James Clerk Maxwell," edited by W. D. Niven, Dover Pub., New York, 1952.

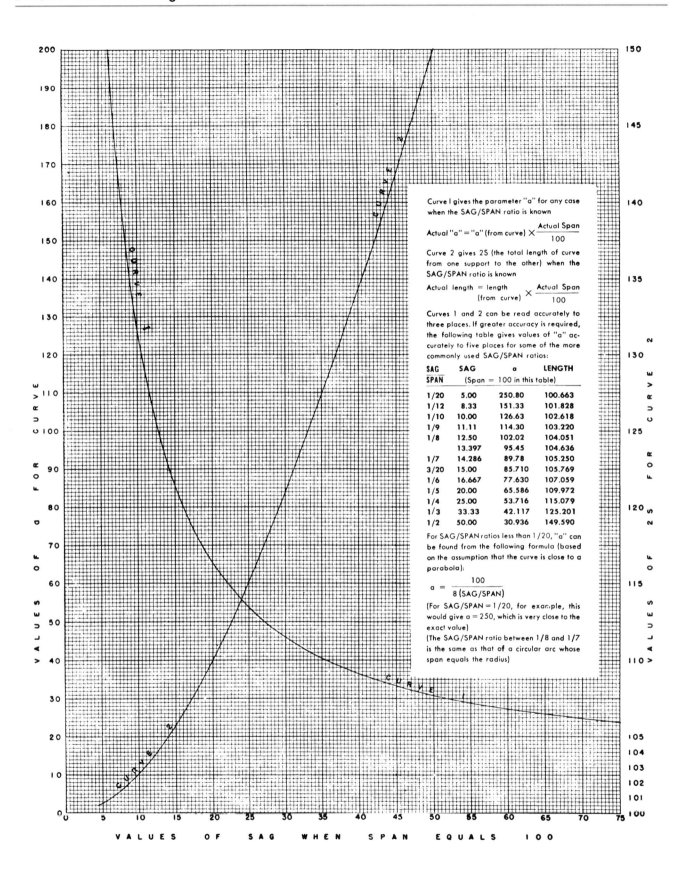

Curve I gives the parameter "a" for any case when the SAG/SPAN ratio is known

Actual "a" = "a" (from curve) × $\dfrac{\text{Actual Span}}{100}$

Curve 2 gives 2S (the total length of curve from one support to the other) when the SAG/SPAN ratio is known

Actual length = length (from curve) × $\dfrac{\text{Actual Span}}{100}$

Curves 1 and 2 can be read accurately to three places. If greater accuracy is required, the following table gives values of "a" accurately to five places for some of the more commonly used SAG/SPAN ratios:

$\dfrac{\text{SAG}}{\text{SPAN}}$	SAG (Span = 100 in this table)	a	LENGTH
1/20	5.00	250.80	100.663
1/12	8.33	151.33	101.828
1/10	10.00	126.63	102.618
1/9	11.11	114.30	103.220
1/8	12.50	102.02	104.051
	13.397	95.45	104.636
1/7	14.286	89.78	105.250
3/20	15.00	85.710	105.769
1/6	16.667	77.630	107.059
1/5	20.00	65.586	109.972
1/4	25.00	53.716	115.079
1/3	33.33	42.117	125.201
1/2	50.00	30.936	149.590

For SAG/SPAN ratios less than 1/20, "a" can be found from the following formula (based on the assumption that the curve is close to a parabola):

$$a = \frac{100}{8\,(\text{SAG}/\text{SPAN})}$$

(For SAG/SPAN = 1/20, for example, this would give a = 250, which is very close to the exact value)
(The SAG/SPAN ratio between 1/8 and 1/7 is the same as that of a circular arc whose span equals the radius)

VALUES OF a FOR CURVE I

VALUES OF 2S FOR CURVE 2

VALUES OF SAG WHEN SPAN EQUALS 100

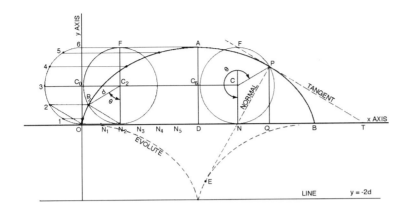

DEFINITION

The locus of a point P on the circumference of a circle which rolls along a straight line without slipping is called a cycloid. It has been used as a cross section of concrete shells.

PARAMETRIC EQUATION (most convenient)

$$x = a\,(\theta - \sin\theta)$$
$$y = a\,(1 - \cos\theta)$$ (θ in radians)

STANDARD FORM

$$x = a\,\arccos\left(\frac{a-y}{a}\right) - \sqrt{2\,ay - y^2}$$

METHODS OF DRAWING

1. Draw directly as a roulette (see definition, sheet 7) by rolling a circle of radius "a" along x axis. Take care that circle does not slip.

2. On y axis draw generating circle, radius = a, center at C_0 ($C_0O = a$). Divide half circumference into whole number of arcs (here 6). On x axis lay off the lengths of these arcs ON_1, N_1N_2, N_2N_3, etc., by measuring directly or by measuring $OD = \pi a$ and dividing into same number of parts. Draw a horizontal line through C and project points N_1, N_2, etc.

up to find successive positions of center of circle. At each center draw the radius vector, where θ is the corresponding multiple of

$$\frac{180}{\text{number of arcs}} \quad (C_2P_2 = a, \theta_2 = 2 \times \frac{180}{6} = 60°$$

for example). P_2 also lies on a horizontal line through point 2 on the generating circle as shown in initial position.

3. Proceed as directed in method 2, as far as measuring arc lengths along x axis. Then through points 1, 2, 3, etc. on circle in initial

position, draw horizontal lines. Measure on each line the corresponding length of arc and the corresponding point on the cycloid will be found. (For example, to find P_2, measure 2, $P_2 = ON_2$.)

4. Proceed as directed in method 2, as far as measuring arc lengths along x axis. To find P_2 shown, describe arc of radius 0, 2 from center N_2 and intersect horizontal line drawn through 2. Note that P_2N_2 is the normal to point P_2 and is half the length of the radius of curvature at P_2.

TANGENT to any point P passes through F at top of generating circle in corresponding position. Subtangent $QT = a\,\dfrac{(1 - \cos\theta)^2}{\sin\theta}$

NORMAL to any point P passes through N at bottom of generating circle. Normal $PN = \sqrt{2\,ay}$. Subnormal $QN = a\sin\theta$.

LENGTH OF CURVE for one arch = 8a. Centroid of this length is $\dfrac{4a}{3}$ above x axis.

LENGTH OF AN ARC of curve $AP = 2 \times PF$ (length of arc $BP = 4a - 2\,PF$)

AREA UNDER ONE ARCH = $3\pi a^2$. Centroid of this area is $\dfrac{5a}{6}$ above x axis.

RADIUS OF CURVATURE = EP = twice length of normal $PN = 2\sqrt{2\,ay}$.

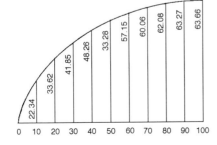

ORDINATES OF A CYCLOID expressed in terms of a half length of 100.

$$x = \frac{100}{\pi}\,(\theta - \sin\theta)$$

$$y = \frac{100}{\pi}\,(1 - \cos\theta)$$

$$\frac{100}{\pi} = 31.831$$

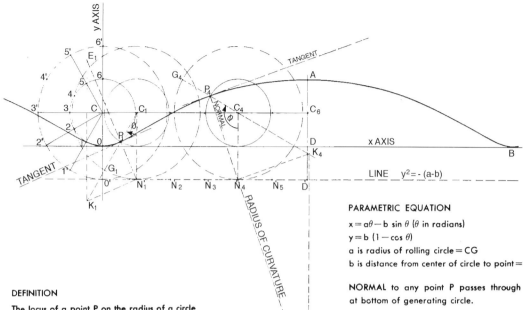

DEFINITION

The locus of a point P on the radius of a circle which rolls along a straight line without slipping is called a trochoid. If P lies inside the circle it is a prolate trochoid shown here. If outside, a curtate trochoid. The curtate trochoid curve has little possibility of use in the building field. The prolate trochoid has potentialities as a section for corrugated concrete shells (see Structural Forms—Reinforced Concrete). It is also used (upside down from position shown) as the curve of ocean waves for ship analysis, with a height (DA) equal to 20 times length (OB) and a length equal to length of ship.

METHODS OF DRAWING

The same methods as described for drawing a cycloid may be used. Note that the distance OB on the x axis is equal to $2\pi a$ and the height AD = 2b. Lengths of arcs must be measured on the circumference of the outer circle, heights from the inner circle.

PARAMETRIC EQUATION

$x = a\theta - b \sin \theta$ (θ in radians)
$y = b (1 - \cos \theta)$
a is radius of rolling circle = CG
b is distance from center of circle to point = CP

NORMAL to any point P passes through N′ at bottom of generating circle.

TANGENT is found as perpendicular to normal at P

RADIUS OF CURVATURE = PE. Point E is found as follows. Erect perpendicular to normal at N′. Extend radius line PC to intersect perpendicular at K. Draw vertical line through K to intersect PN′ extended at E. E is center of curvature and PE is radius of curvature.

Equation:

$$PE = R = \frac{[a^2 - 2ab \cos \theta + b^2]^{3/2}}{2a^2 - ab(\cos \theta + 2) + b^2}$$

At point 0, $\theta = 0$ and

$$R = \frac{(a - b)^3}{2a^2 - 3ab + b^2}$$

At point A, $\theta = 180° = \pi$ and

$$R = \frac{(a + b)^3}{2a^2 - ab + b^2}$$

EVOLUTE for the prolate trochoid is in two parts, one on each side of the curve. The normal which makes the smallest angle with the x axis passes through the point of contra-flexure and is asymptotic to each portion of the evolute.

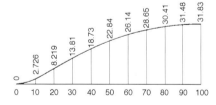

ORDINATES FOR A TROCHOID in which a = 2b, expressed in terms of a half-length of 100. This might be used as the cross-section of a shell roof.

$$x = \frac{50}{\pi} (2\theta - \sin \theta)$$

$$y = \frac{50}{\pi} (1 - \cos \theta)$$

$$\left[\frac{50}{\pi} = 15.915\right]$$

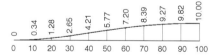

ORDINATES FOR A TROCHOID whose height is $\frac{1}{20}$ of its length, expressed in terms of a half-length of 100. This is the standard ocean wave, but upside down, i.e. the "0" ordinate is the crest, the "10" ordinate the hollow of the wave.

$$x = 5\left(\frac{20}{\pi} \theta - \sin \theta\right) \qquad \left[\frac{20}{\pi} = 6.366\right]$$

$$y = 5 (1 - \cos \theta)$$

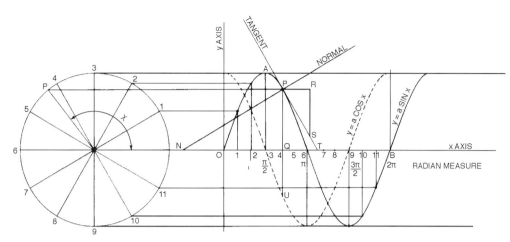

DEFINITION

The Sine Curve represents the vertical projection of a point P, moving with uniform velocity on the circumference of a circle, plotted against angular displacement. If a is the radius of the circle and b is the angular velocity of the point P on its circumference, and t is time; then x = bt and y = a cos bt. The amplitude = a and the period = 2π or 360° = OB.

In building work this curve has been used as the centerline of the cross section of corrugated concrete shells (see Structural Forms—Reinforced Concrete). It is also the elevation of a so-called spiral (helical) stair. And it is the projection of geodesic lines on a cylinder, such as plan projections of lamella arches.

EQUATION

$y = a \sin x$

METHODS OF DRAWING

1. Draw the generating circle with radius a and divide circumference into a whole number of parts (here 12). Lay off the distance OB on the x axis and divide into the same number of parts. Erect a perpendicular at each point of division of the x axis. Draw horizontal lines through the corresponding points on the circumference of the circle and the intersections will be points on the curve. Note that distance OB = 2π radians and that 57°18' = one radian. To find the point at which x = 1 radian, divide OB into 2π or 6.283 parts and locate 1 cn this scale.

2. Calculate and plot points using table of sines.

TANGENT

The slope of the tangent at any point = a cos x. The curve y = a cos x has been drawn and has exactly the same shape but is displaced π/2 radians or 90° to the left. To draw the tangent at P, draw a horizontal line through P and measure PR = 1 radian. Draw a vertical line through P intersecting x axis at Q and extend to intersect cosine curve at U. Draw a vertical line RS through R of length RS = QU. The line PS is tangent to the sine curve at P, and can be extended to cut x axis at T.

NORMAL is drawn as perpendicular to tangent.

AREA under one arch (from origin to π or 180°) = 2a. Centroid of this area is $\frac{\pi a}{8}$ above x axis.

RADIUS OF CURVATURE $R = \frac{(1 + a^2 \cos^2 x)^{3/2}}{a \sin x}$. At apex A, $R = \frac{1}{a}$

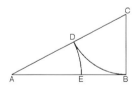

GOLDEN SECTION

Used by Greek artists and architects and often revived in theories of proportion. Basis of Modular of Le Corbusier, using 2 m 26 (or 7 ft 5 in.) or 1 m 13 (or 3 ft 8½ in.) as starting points for his two series. If a line AB is divided so that $\frac{AB}{AE} = \frac{AE}{EB}$ it is in golden section. Or if g is ratio such that AE = gEB,

$g^2 = g + 1$ or $g - \frac{1}{g} = 1$ and $g = \frac{\sqrt{5} + 1}{2} = 1.6180$

To find graphically, erect perpendicular $CB = \frac{AB}{2}$ and swing arc CD = CB. Then swing arc AD to cut AB at E.

The angle which the diagonal of a rectangle whose sides are in the ratio g:1 makes with the short side = arc tan 1.618 = 58° 17'.

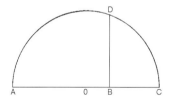

GEOMETRICAL MEAN

General case of which golden section is a particular case. To find distance BD which is geometrical mean or mean proportional between AB and BC, divide AC in half at O and with O as center and radius equal to AO = OC, draw semicircle. Draw perpendicular at B to intersect circle at D

Then $BD^2 = AB \times BC$ or $\frac{AB}{BD} = \frac{BD}{BC}$

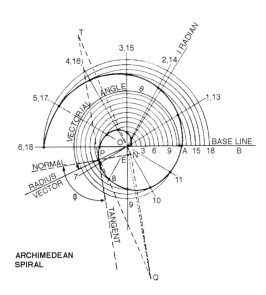

ARCHIMEDEAN
SPIRAL

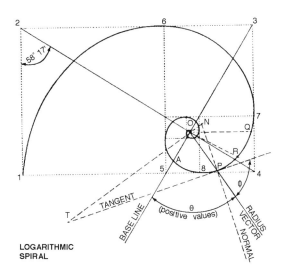

LOGARITHMIC
SPIRAL

ARCHIMEDEAN SPIRAL

The locus of a point P which moves with uniform linear velocity along a line OP as OP revolves with uniform angular velocity about O is called a Spiral of Archimedes.

EQUATION:

$r = a\theta$ (θ in radians)

METHOD OF DRAWING (only positive values of θ are shown) Draw baseline OB. Measure off OA = $2\pi a$. Divide OA into whole number of parts (here 12). Through O draw radial lines at equal spaces corresponding to the same number of parts (here $\frac{360}{12} = 30°$ or $\frac{2\pi}{12} = \frac{\pi}{6}$ radians). With O as center, draw arcs of circles with radii = O1, O2, O3 etc. Where each radius intersects corresponding radial line is a point on the spiral. Note that successive values of r are in arithmetical progression. To measure a, draw radial line at 1 radian (57° 18'), where r = a.

NORMAL

Through O draw ON = a perpendicular to radius vector OP. PN is normal. TANGENT is drawn at right angles to normal at P. Note that the angle Φ between radius vector and tangent is the angle whose tangent = $\frac{r}{a}$ and that this angle is constantly increasing as θ increases.

RADIUS OF CURVATURE

Through N draw NQ parallel to tangent.

Through P draw PQ at right angles to radius vector. Line OQ cuts PN at E. E is center of curvature to spiral at P. Radius of curvature

$$R = \frac{(r^2 + a^2)^{\frac{3}{2}}}{r^2 + 2a^2}$$

LENGTH OF ARC = OP

$$\frac{a}{2}\left[\theta\sqrt{1+\theta^2} + \log_e\left(\theta + \sqrt{1+\theta^2}\right)\right]$$

LOGARITHMIC (EQUIANGULAR) SPIRAL

The curve that cuts the radius vector at a constant angle Φ is called an Equiangular Spiral. If successive values of the vectorial angle θ are in arithmetical progression, the corresponding values of the radius vector are in geometric progression.

EQUATION

$r = ae^{m\theta}$ or $\log_e \frac{r}{a} = m\theta$

$m = \cotan \Phi$ and $a = r = OA$ (when $\theta = 0°$)

METHODS OF DRAWING

In general, draw radial lines from pole O for equal increments of θ, calculate corresponding values of r and measure on each radial line. If r is calculated for large increments of θ and the points plotted, intermediate points can be found as follows: If OP and OQ are any two radii and if OR is a radius bisecting angle POQ, then OR is the mean proportional between OQ and OP (see sheet 12 for drawing method).

NORMAL

Through O draw ON = rm = r cot Φ perpendicular to radius vector OP. PN is normal. TANGENT is drawn at right angles to normal at P and intersects ON extended at T.

RADIUS OF CURVATURE

$R = PN = r\sqrt{1 + m^2} = r\ \text{cosec}\ \Phi$.

Center of curvature is at N. Evolute is an identical spiral whose axis is inclined

$$\left[\frac{\pi}{2} - \frac{\log_e m}{m}\right]$$ to axis of given spiral.

LENGTH OF SPIRAL from O to p = $r \sec \Phi = PT$

AREA swept by radius (from r = O to r = OP) = $\frac{r^2}{4m}$ = ½ triangle OPT

The golden section spiral shown here is one whose radius vectors, separated by 90°, are in the golden section ratio. It is extensively discussed in theories of proportion. It can be drawn geometrically, without calculation. Here the rectangle 1234 is shown whose sides are in the golden section ratio. If a square (here 1265) is cut off, a similar rectangle (3456) is left, turned through 90°. This process can be continued indefinitely. Note the value of the diagonals in drawing the rectangles correctly. The diagonals cross at right angles at the pole O and are the axes of the equiangular spiral for which $\Phi - 73°$ (approx.) The corners of the squares (1, 6, 7, 8 etc.) are points on the spiral. The spiral crosses outside of the rectangle at these points.

ANALYTIC DESCRIPTION

Surfaces and skew curves can be described by a greater variety of analytical systems than curves which exist in only one plane. In architectural and related work we do not need all of these and will limit the descriptions to three types: 1. Triaxial Cartesian coordinates (a point is fixed by its projected distance on x, y and z axes); 2. Cylindrical coordinates (a point is fixed by a plane normal to a z axis and by its radius vector from a pole on this axis); and 3. Spherical coordinates (the familiar latitude and longitude or meridian lines). The purposes in analyzing a surface are:

a) to be able to recreate the surface;
b) to know its area and the volume enclosed;
c) to discover the stresses acting in the surface;
d) to discover the manner in which the surface will reflect light, heat, sound.

METHODS OF STUDY

Models are the best, and should be made as large as practicable. Wire and string can be used; sheet materials (cardboard, plastic) can be bent into the shape of developable surfaces, or can be cut to represent planes cutting the surface and put together like an egg-crate. Soft white pine can be carved in the solid and its surface studied. A solution of soap and glycerine* can be used to make minimal surfaces or membranes between wire boundary curves. From the models the surfaces can be transferred to paper, showing the traces of the surface as it is cut by a system of planes. Once drawn, the best method of construction in the field can be worked out. Usually a table of offsets should be prepared.

SKEW CURVE

A **skew curve** (also called a space curve or a twisted curve) is one which does not lie entirely in one plane. (See dwg.) The tangent line at any point defines the direction of the curve at that point. The normals to the tangent define the normal plane. The osculating

*Soap solution recommended: Dissolve 10 grams of dry sodium oleate in 500 grams of distilled water. Mix 15 cubic parts of this solution with 11 cubic parts of glycerine. Alternatively, buy a prepared solution.

plane makes a right angle with the normal plane, contains the tangent and is the plane in which the curve most closely lies at the given point. The curve will pass through the osculating plane at a regular or ordinary point. The principal normal is the intersection of the osculating and normal planes. The radius of curvature (R) is found on this principal normal. The ratio $\frac{1}{R}$ is called the first curvature. The third orthogonal line of reference at the point is called the binormal and its plane the rectifying plane. The angular rate of change of the binormal as a point moves along the curve is called the torsion or second curvature.

SURFACES

At any regular (i.e. not singular) point on a surface there will exist a **tangent plane**. If **the surface is cut by any variable plane, the** tangent to the curve of intersection at the given point will always lie in this tangent **plane. For a cup-shaped region of a surface** this tangent plane will be entirely on one side of the surface; for a saddle-shaped region it will cut the surface. (See dwg.)

At right angles to the tangent plane an infinity of normal planes can be drawn. Each of these cuts the surface in a curve called a normal section; each of these sections has a radius of curvature at the given point. One of these radii will have a minimum value R_1 and another a maximum R_2. The normal planes in which these two radii lie are called **the principal normal planes** and they are at right angles to each other. The tangents to the principal normal sections are called **the principal directions. For a cup-shaped** region of a surface the centers of both radii **will lie on the same side of the surface, (See** dwg.), and will have the same sign. Such a point is called an elliptic point and the curvature of the surface is called positive. For a saddle-shaped region the center of one radius will lie on one side, and the center of the other on the opposite side of the surface; and the radii will have opposite signs. Such a point is called a hyperbolic point and the curvature is called negative. Parabolic points also exist; at these the maximum radius of curvature is infinite.

On a surface can be traced a **line of curvature**, which lies along one of the principal directions of each of a sequence of points.

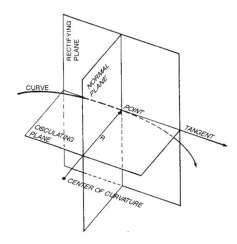

SKEW CURVE

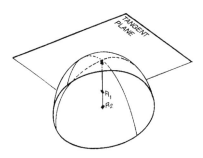

SURFACE OF POSITIVE CURVATURE

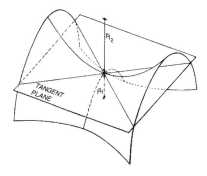

SURFACE OF NEGATIVE CURVATURE

Through each point there will regularly be two such lines of curvature, which are at right angles to each other. On any surface of revolution the lines of curvature are the meridians (intersection with the surface of a plane containing the axis) and the circles of latitude. On any developable surface the rulings constitute one family of lines of curvature.

The **mean (or average) curvature** of a surface at a given point is the arithmetic mean of the two principal curvatures: $\frac{1}{2}\left(\frac{1}{R_1} + \frac{1}{R_2}\right)$. It is always zero for a minimal surface.

The **Gaussian curvature** (also called the total curvature) of a surface at a given point is the product of the two principal curvatures: $\frac{1}{R_1 R_2}$. It is positive at elliptic (cup-shaped) points, negative at hyperbolic (saddle-shaped) points, and zero at parabolic points. When a surface is bent, its Gaussian curvature does not change. This fact can be used to determine whether one surface can be formed or developed into another.

The **Dupin indicatrix** at a point is found by plotting, on the tangent plane, in the direction of every normal section, a distance from the point equal to the square root of the radius of curvature corresponding to that section. The indicatrix is always a conic section (including the degenerate conics). At an **elliptic point** (cup-shaped or synclastic region) the Dupin indicatrix is an ellipse. When both radii of curvature are equal, the ellipse becomes a circle and the point is called an **umbilic**. The umbilics are therefore singular points and have no principal directions. At a **hyperbolic point** the indicatrix is a hyperbola for all the radii of curvature on one side of the surface and the conjugate hyperbola for all the radii on the other side. The asymptotes of the hyperbolas give the **asymptotic directions**. The **asymptotic lines** consist of the family of curves which follow the asymptotic directions for every hyperbolic point and form a net over a negative surface. At a **parabolic point** one of the radii of curvature usually becomes infinite (and the corresponding curvature vanishes) and the Dupin indicatrix becomes a pair of straight lines.

On a surface on which some regions are negative, some positive, the locus of points separating the two regions traces a curve called the **parabolic curve** of the surface.

A **ruled surface** is generated by a straight line (called a generator of the surface) which moves continuously in some predetermined manner with respect to a curve or curves (called the directrix) and/or a point.

A **developable surface** is always a ruled surface, and the tangent plane to the surface at any point as the point moves along a given ruling lies in one plane throughout the length of the ruling. Cones and cylinders are typical. In general any surface generated by the tangents to a skew curve is a developable surface (called the tangential developable of the curve.) The Gaussian curvature of a developable surface is everywhere zero (as is that of a plane) and all its points are parabolic.

For all **other ruled surfaces** (which are not developable) the tangent plane at any point as the point moves along a given ruling turns through two right angles as it moves from infinity at one end to infinity at the other. The point at which the tangent has moved through only one right angle is called the **center point**. The locus of center points for the surface is called the **line of striction**.

Doubly ruled surfaces have two distinct families of rulings or straight lines on them. Only two such surfaces exist: the hyperbolic paraboloid and the hyperboloid of one sheet. The rulings are the asymptotic lines of the surfaces. The Gaussian curvature is everywhere negative and all the points are hyperbolic.

A **conoid** is generated by a straight line which, remaining parallel to a given plane, moves along a straight line (which is not parallel to the plane) and along some other geometrical figure. The hyperbolic paraboloid is thus a conoid as are the helicoids. The surface commonly referred to as a conoid in construction is Pluecker's conoid or cylindroid, generated by a straight line which moves along a straight line and an ellipse (or circle).

A **surface of revolution** is generated by rotating a curve about an axis. Typical are: the right circular cone and cylinder; the spheroids; the paraboloid of revolution; the hyperboloids of revolution, of one sheet and of two sheets; the unduloids (generated by rotating the roulette of any conic curve.) The two centers of curvature at any point on a surface of revolution are: 1) In the meridian plane, the center of curvature of the curve whose rotation generates the surface; and 2) The intersection with the axis of revolution of the line normal to the surface.

A **geodesic curve** is the shortest distance, measured on the surface, between two points on the surface. For any developable surface it can be found by drawing a straight line on the surface when developed out onto a plane and then bending the plane back onto the surface. Through any point on a surface there exists in general an infinite number of geodesic curves, going out from it in every direction and joining it to every other point on the surface. On a sphere all the geodesics are great circles. On a cylinder all the geodesics are helices (including meridian lines which are helices of infinite pitch and latitude circles which are helices of zero pitch). On a surface of revolution all the meridians are geodesics, but the other geodesics cannot be found so simply. The circles of latitude are generally not geodesics.

A **minimal surface** is the surface of smallest area among all the surfaces bounded by a given closed curve or curves. It is created automatically by the membrane formed when a wire model of the boundary curve(s) is dipped into a soap solution. Except for the plane, a minimal surface is saddle-shaped (anticlastic) at all points; all points are therefore hyperbolic. The Gaussian curvature is everywhere negative. The mean curvature vanishes for every point; i.e.

$$\frac{1}{2}\left(\frac{1}{R_1} + \frac{1}{R_2}\right) = 0.$$

In other words the least radii of curvature at any point are equal in magnitude and on opposite sides of the surface. The Dupin indicatrix for every point is an equilateral hyperbola and the asymptotic lines form an orthogonal net over the entire surface.

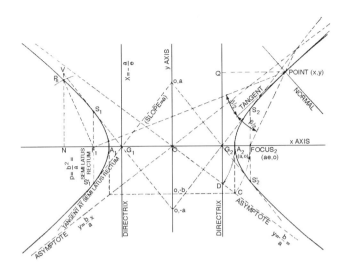

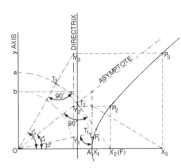

STANDARD FORM

$$\frac{x^2}{a^2} - \frac{y^2}{b^2} = 1$$ Asymptotes (tangents at infinity) $\begin{cases} \dfrac{x}{a} - \dfrac{y}{b} = 0 \\[2mm] \dfrac{x}{a} + \dfrac{y}{b} = 0 \end{cases}$

Note that b may be greater than a; in that case the curve is flatter. When a = b, asymptotes are at right angles to each other (called a rectangular hyperbola).

Definition I: Distance of any Point to Focus / Distance of Point to Directrix =

$$\frac{PF}{PQ} = \text{Constant} = \text{Eccentricity (e)} = \sqrt{1 + \frac{b^2}{a}} = \text{Greater Than 1}$$

Definition II: Distance of Any Point to Focus$_1$ — Distance of Point to Focus$_2$ = PF$_1$ — PF$_2$ = Constant = 2a

To Draw: Given a and b, draw asymptotes. Apex is at a or — a on x axis. Find directrix by swinging arc = Oa to intersect asymptote at D (see lower right quadrant). Find focus by swinging arc OC to intersect x axis at F (OC = $\sqrt{a^2 + b^2}$ = ae). Erect perpendicular through F. From points O, a and O, — a, draw lines through G$_1$ and G$_2$ and intersecting perpendiculars through F$_1$ and F$_2$ at S$_1$, S$'_1$, S$_2$, S$'_2$. To find any point on hyperbola (P$_n$, upper left quadrant), erect perpendicular at N to intersect G$_1$ S$_1$ at V. From F$_1$ swing an arc = NV to intersect NV at P$_n$. See also Sheet 33 for other methods.

PARAMETRIC FORM

$$x = a \sec t = \frac{a}{\cos t}$$

$$y = b \tan t$$
(only one quadrant shown)

To Draw: Draw circles with radii = a and = b, centers O. From O draw any line, intersecting circle of radius a at T. From T erect perpendicular (tangent to circle) intersecting x axis at X. From intersection of circle of radius b with x axis, erect perpendicular intersecting OT at Y. Through Y draw line parallel to x axis, which will intersect a line parallel to y axis drawn through X at P. P is a point on the hyperbola.

Note that tangent to circle of radius a at intersection with asymptote passes through focus.

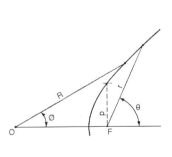

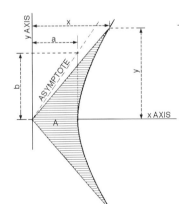

POLAR FORM

Pole at focus

$$r = \frac{P}{1 - e \cos \theta}$$

Pole at center O

$$R^2 = \frac{a^2 b^2}{b^2 \cos^2 \phi - a^2 \sin^2 \phi}$$

AREA

$$A = ab \log_e \left(\frac{x}{a} + \frac{y}{b} \right)$$

$$= ab \cosh^{-1} \frac{x}{a}$$

$$= ab \sinh^{-1} \frac{y}{b}$$

$$= ab \tanh^{-1} \frac{ay}{bx}$$

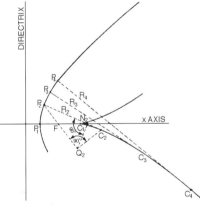

EVOLUTE OF HYPERBOLA

(For part of one quadrant)

Radius of Curvature

$$R = a^2 b^2 \left(\frac{x^2}{a^4} + \frac{y^2}{b^4} \right)^{3/2}$$ For any point

x, y on the hyperbola.

At apex (P$_1$), Radius C$_1$ P$_1$ = $\dfrac{b^2}{a}$ = p

Equation of Evolute

Standard form: $a^{2/3} x^{2/3} + b^{2/3} y^{2/3} = (a^2 + b^2)^{2/3}$

Center of curvature of hyperbola can be found by same procedure as shown for ellipse.

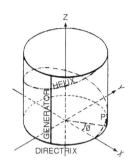

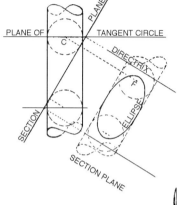

A cylinder is generated by a straight line element (the generator or generatrix) which moves along a plane curve (the directrix) parallel to an axis which is not in the plane of the curve. When the axis makes a right angle with the plane of the curve, the surface is called a right cylinder. For design purposes we can always arrange the cylinder to be right.

Any curve can be used for the directrix. If a conic is used, the cylinders are quadric surfaces and all sections are also conics. Only quadric cylinders are shown here, but other forms such as a catenary cylinder may be preferable for structural reasons.

The right circular cylinder is the surface
$$x^2 + y^2 = r^2; \; z = z$$
or, in cylindrical coordinates: $r = r, \; z = z$
$$x = r \cos \Theta; \; y = r \sin \Theta; \; z = z$$
[The elliptical cylinder, not shown, would have similar equations derived from those of the ellipse, (see sheet 4 on curves).]

The geodesics on the right circular cylinder are all circular helices and the most useful form of their equation is:
$$x = r \cos \Theta; \; y = r \sin \Theta; \; z = k \Theta$$

where $k = \dfrac{2\pi r}{h}$ and h = pitch of helix or distance traveled in one revolution. The angle Θ which the helix makes with any generating element = arc tan $\dfrac{2\pi r}{h}$. Length of geodesic $= z/\cos \Theta$ and for one revolution $= \sqrt{(2\pi r)^2 + h^2}$

The projection of the circular helix on the *xz* or *yz* planes (i.e. "side elevation") is always a sine curve (see sheet 12 on curves).

The lamellas or elements of a lamella roof (**see sheet 41, Structural Design—Wood**) trace helices on the surface of a cylindrical roof. The drawing of the parabolic cylinder explains this.

Any **section of a circular cylinder** is an ellipse. The foci of the ellipse are the projections on the section plane of the centers of the spheres tangent to the cylinder and to the plane. They are also the points of tangency of these spheres and the section plane. The directrix of the ellipse is the intersection of the section plane with the plane of the circle of tangency of the sphere.

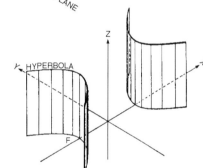

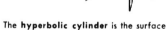

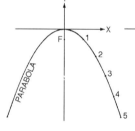

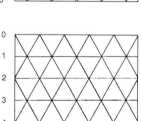

The **hyperbolic cylinder** is the surface
$$\frac{x^2}{a^2} - \frac{y^2}{b^2} = 1; \; z = z$$

All sections are conics and are most easily drawn by projecting a few points and using Pascal's method.

The **parabolic cylinder** (coordinates as shown) is the surface
$$x^2 = -2py; \; z = z$$
Sections are all conics and are drawn as

described for the hyperbolic cylinder.

The parabolic cylinder is shown in orthogonal projection with lines of equal arc length drawn on the surface. To find the geodesics, the developed surface is drawn showing these same lines. Then any system of straight lines drawn on this developed surface is a system of geodesics. They can then be projected back on the *yz* plane.

This method of drawing geodesics can be used for any developable surface. In the case of cylinders the geodesics are all helices or portions of helices. (See sheet 18 for possible regular patterns.)

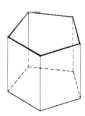

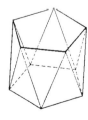

Prisms or anti-prisms offer convenient approximations to cylinders or may be chosen for their own shape. Any regular polygon can be used for the two bases; for the anti-prisms the two bases are twisted so that the vertices of one are above the mid points of the sides of the other.

(For areas, surfaces and volumes of cylinders, prisms, and anti-prisms see Mathematics—Areas and Solids.)

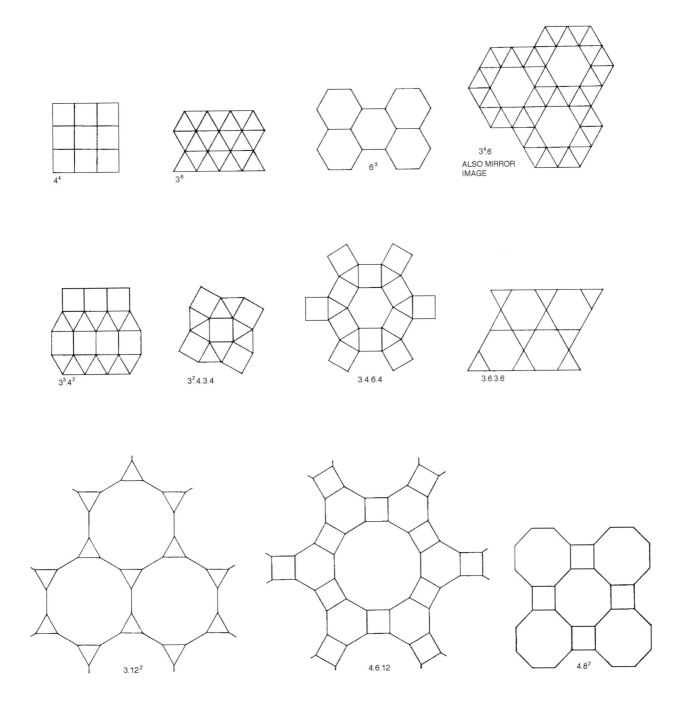

4⁴   3⁶   6³

3⁴.6
ALSO MIRROR
IMAGE

3³.4²   3².4.3.4   3.4.6.4   3.6.3.6

3.12²   4.6.12   4.8²

REGULAR AND SEMI-REGULAR PATTERNS

The division of a plane into regular polygons is often necessary for structural or decorative reasons. There are only three regular tessellations (patterns) in which all the polygons are identical. There are only eight semi-regular tessellations in which all the polygons are regular but not identical; all the sides are of equal length. One of the semi-regular tessellations has two forms which are mirror-images of each other. All vertices are congruent. The notation is based on the vertex figure of each tessellation. The polygons are listed by the number of sides as they are found in sequence around a vertex. These tessellations are related not only to the plane but to every surface which is developable and which can therefore be drawn without distortion on a plane. The sides of the polygons will, of course, all be geodesics. Not every tessellation can be used for every surface; it will be necessary to experiment to find which will fit and which will be most suited to the structural or esthetic purpose. Any polygon used structurally must be held rigid, either by division into triangles or by provision of a continuous membrane.

If every point on a plane curve is joined by a straight line to a point not in the plane of the curve, a cone is generated. Each straight line is called an element (or generator) of the cone; the curve is called the directrix. Since there is an infinity of possible plane curves, there is an infinity of possible cones. Every cone is a developable surface.

It helps in constructing a cone to know that every section of the surface is a curve of the same general type or degree as the directrix curve. All sections parallel to the plane of the directrix curve are curves which are parallel to the directrix curve (i.e. they are of the same shape, but larger or smaller.)

This fact is of value in drawing perspectives, since perspective projection consists essentially in drawing sections of a cone. Every second degree curve (conic section) drawn in perspective will therefore be a second degree curve. And every third degree curve will be some third degree curve; every transcendental curve (trig. functions, etc.) will be a transcendental curve.

The second degree or quadric cone is the one most used. Such a cone will be generated by using an ellipse, parabola or hyperbola as the directrix. These do not constitute different cones, in the way different cylinders are generated (see Sheet 17) but all generate cones of the general type:

$$\frac{x^2}{a^2} + \frac{y^2}{b^2} = \frac{z^2}{c^2}$$

Or, where $k = \tan \alpha = \frac{a}{c}$ and

$l = \tan \beta = \frac{b}{c}$

$$\frac{x^2}{k^2} + \frac{y^2}{l^2} = z^2$$

See drawing of the general elliptic cone on Sheet 20.

All sections of this cone parallel to a tangent plane of the cone are parabolas; all sections which cut only one nappe or sheet (surface on one side of the vertex) are ellipses,

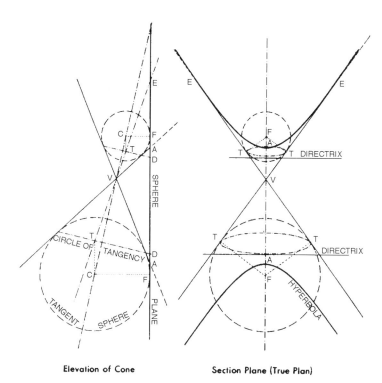

Elevation of Cone   Section Plane (True Plan)

Section of a Right Circular Cone By a Plane Which Cuts Both Nappes

(See also Sheet 20 for text)

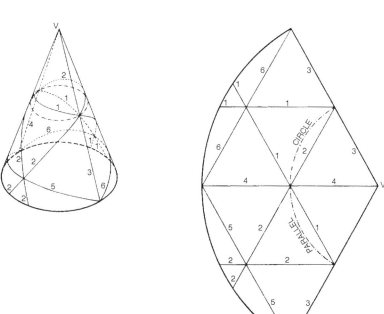

Isometric Projection of a Right Circular Cone and Its Development, Showing Geodesics

(See also Sheets 20, 21 for text)

the circle being a special case; and all sections which cut both nappes are hyperbolas.

It often happens that a pair of conjugate diameters of an ellipse are known, but not the major and minor axes. In the figure below (which shows the same ellipse as used for the generator of the general elliptic cone shown) the conjugate diameters Q_1CQ_2 and P_1CP_2 are known along the isometric axes. (Q_1CQ_2 and P_1CP_2 are defined as conjugate diameters if the tangents at Q_1 and Q_2 are parallel to P_1CP_2 and if the tangents at P_1 and P_2 are parallel to Q_1CQ_2.)

To find the major and minor axes, draw P_1A perpendicular to CQ_1. Make $P_1B_1 = P_1B_2 = CQ_1$ The line bisecting the angle B_1CB_2 is the major axis D_1CD_2. The minor axis is the line E_1CE_2 at right angles. Then find F, the midpoint of CB_2. Join P_1 to F, cutting CD at G and CE at H. The distance P_1G equals the semi-minor axis CE and P_1H equals the semi-major axis CD.

In the case of the isometric projection of a circle, the conjugate diameters are the 30 degree axes and the major and minor axes are along vertical and horizontal lines. Knowing P on the 30 degree axis, the line corresponding to PF can be drawn directly at 45 degrees.

The cone most often used, because it is the simplest, is the right circular cone, in which the directrix is a circle and the vertex is on the straight line which is perpendicular to the plane of the circle and which passes through the center of the circle. The equations of the right circular cone simplify from those of the elliptic cone to:

$$x^2 + y^2 = k^2z^2$$

and, in cylindrical coordinates:

$$r = kz$$

and in spherical coordinates, where ϕ is the co-latitude:

$$\phi = \text{constant} = \alpha.$$

The properties of the sections of the right circular cone are discussed on Sheet 2 of this series and also are the same as mentioned above under the general elliptic cone. In order to show clearly how the foci and directrices of the conic sections can be found geometrically, the diagram on Sheet 19 has been drawn showing a plane which cuts both nappes; the section is therefore an hyperbola. (The ellipses and parabolas are found in a similar fashion. See also the similar construction for the section of a cylinder, which gives an ellipse, on Sheet 17.)

Draw the two spheres which are tangent to the cone and to the section plane. Find the intersection of the plane of the circle of tangency with the section plane. This line is the directrix of the hyperbola. The point of tangency of the sphere with the section plane is the focus. It is also the projection of the center of the sphere. With the directrices and the foci established, follow one of the procedures of Sheet 6 for drawing the hyperbola.

Note that the traces of the sides of the cone as projected can be located by drawing on the elevation a line through the center of the sphere parallel to the section plane. The point T where this intersects the circle of tangency is a point on the trace. The line joining this point to the vertex is the edge desired. The point E is the intersection of this edge with the section plane.

The most useful way to draw a right circular cone so that it can be drawn in any projection, including perspective, is to utilize spheres which are tangent to the inside of the surface of the cone. The spheres are circles in any projection and the cone is always tangent.

To develop the surface of a right circular cone, draw an arc of a circle with the vertex as center and an element (straight line on the side) as radius. Measure off on this arc a length equal to circumference of the base circle. Join end points to vertex. (See drawing, Sheet 19.)

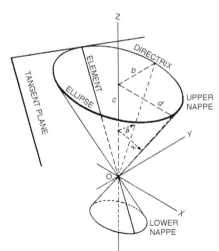

GENERAL ELLIPTIC CONE (ISOMETRIC PROJECTION)

(See also text on Sheet 19)

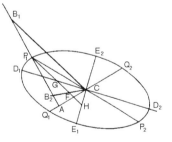

CONJUGATE DIAMETERS OF AN ELLIPSE

General definition of Conjugate Diameters (true for all conic sections): A and B are conjugate diameters if both are lines through the center and if B bisects all the chords parallel to A, and if A bisects all the chords parallel to B.

Geodesics can always be found by drawing straight lines on this developed surface when flat. One triangular net of geodesics which might be used structurally is shown. The development, of course, gives the true area of any portion of the surface.

The lines of curvature on a right circular cone are the straight elements (or meridians), lines 3 and 4 on the drawing on Sheet 19, and the parallel (or latitude) circles, only one of which is shown here as a dot-dash line.

Note that the parallel circles are not geodesics, although the elements are. The parallel circles show as arcs on the development.

The conical helix (not shown) is the space curve which lies on the surface of the right circular cone and which makes a constant angle with each parallel or latitude circle. Its plan projection is a logarithmic spiral (see Sheet 13). It is not a geodesic line.

To develop any arbitrary conical surface (see drawing): Given the plan and elevaton, divide the length of the directrix curve into any convenient number of parts by a series of points, here 16. Draw the straight line elements joining each of these points to the vertex. Starting with number one, find the true length of each element, by setting V'V as the true height of the vertex and V'1 as the true plan projection. The hypotenuse V.1 is the true length. For the development, from the vertex draw a line V1; then swing an arc of length V2 from V, and from 1 swing an arc of the true arc length 1.2; where these intersect is the developed position of 2. Continue in this way until all the elements are drawn. Then draw a smooth curve through all the numbered points. It will be noted that the accuracy of this method depends on the number of elements used, since the chord lengths are used as arc lengths in the development.

The elements are also lines of curvature; the other lines of curvature are found by drawing arcs on the development with the vertex as center. One such line is shown here as a dotted line. These can then be transferred to the plan and elevations or other projections. These lines of curvature are helpful when using rolls to bend a flat plate into a cone; the axes of the rollers can be inclined, and the lines of curvature which are at right angles to the elements must form closed curves.

Pyramids are surfaces generated by joining every point on a polygon to a point not in the plane of the polygon. They may be used to approximate cones or for their own sake.

For areas and volumes of pyramids and cones see Mathematics— Areas and Solids.

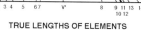

ELEVATION

TRUE LENGTHS OF ELEMENTS

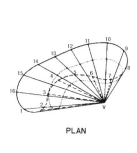

PLAN

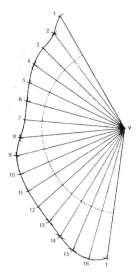

DEVELOPMENT

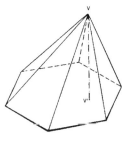

AN OBLIQUE REGULAR HEXAGONAL PYRAMID

DEFINITION

Every point on the sphere is equidistant from a fixed point called the center. It is the only surface for which this is true. It is also the surface of revolution generated by the rotation of a circle about a diameter. Every section of a sphere is a circle. When the section plane contains the center, the circle is called a great circle or geodesic and has the same radius as the sphere; otherwise the section will be a "little circle" and may have any radius less than that of the sphere and more than zero. Longitude circles (or meridians) on the earth are all great circles; and latitude circles except the equator are little circles.

Every point on a sphere is an umbilical point; i.e. there is no principal direction and no line of curvature (see Sheets 14 and 15). Every geodesic line is a portion of a great circle. The mean curvature is everywhere constant and positive (equaling 1/R); the sphere is the only closed surface (without a boundary) for which this is true. The Gaussian curvature is also everywhere constant and positive (equaling $1/R^2$); and again it is the only closed surface for which this is true.

Of all closed surfaces the sphere contains the maximum possible volume for a given amount of surface.

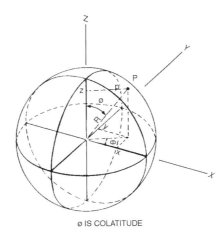

ø IS COLATITUDE

Equations:

In rectangular coordinates:
$$x^2 + y^2 + z^2 = R^2$$

In cylindrical coordinates:
$$z^2 = R^2 - \rho^2$$
$$[\text{where } x = \rho \cos ()$$
$$\text{and } y = \rho \sin ()]$$

In spherical coordinates:
$$r = R$$
$$[\text{where } x = R \sin \phi \cos ()$$
$$y = R \sin \phi \sin ()$$
$$z = R \cos \phi]$$

The area of the sphere $= 4\pi R^2 =$ lateral area of circumscribed cylinder.

The volume enclosed $= \dfrac{4}{3}\pi R^3 = \dfrac{2}{3}$ volume of circumscribed cylinder.

A lune (sometimes called a gore) is the surface between two great circles passing through the same pair of poles. A spherical wedge is the volume between the planes of these two great circles and the lune.

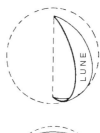

A zone is the surface between any two parallel section planes. The volume is called a segment and equals
$$\frac{1}{6}\pi h (3\rho_1^2 + 3\rho_2^2 + h^2)$$

where h = distance between two planes and ρ_1 and ρ_2 are radii of section circles. Area = $hR2\pi$

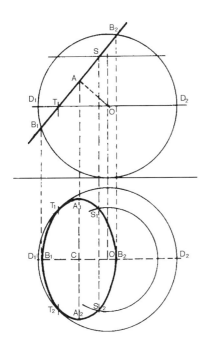

To draw the plan projection of the section of a sphere by any plane normal to the elevation, given the elevation: (Unless the section plane is parallel to that of the plane, the section will be projected as an ellipse.)

1. Draw AO normal to B_1B_2. Draw D_1OD_2 parallel to the plan.

2. Draw the plan below. Project B_1 and B_2 onto D_1OD_2 in the plan. The line joining B_1B_2 is the minor axis. Project A as a line normal to D_1OD_2 on the plan. This lies on the major axis and in plan $A_1C = CA_2 =$

true radius of the little circle, which can be measured as AB from the elevation.

3. With these two axes given, an ellipse can now be drawn by any of the methods shown on Sheet 4. T_1 and T_2 are the points of tangency of the ellipse with the plan. If desired, other points such as S_1 and S_2 can be found by drawing a line through S on the elevation parallel to the plan. The length of this line is the diameter of the little circle through S. Draw this circle on the plan and project S down to S_1 and S_2.

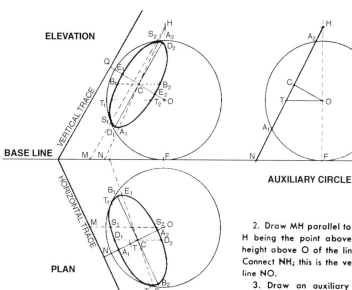

ELEVATION

AUXILIARY CIRCLE

PLAN

To draw the plan and elevation projections of the section of a sphere cut by any plane, given the horizontal and vertical traces of the plane on the plan and elevation. (The Base Line is the plane of the plan as seen in elevation and the plane of the elevation as seen in plan.)

1. On the plan, draw ON normal to the horizontal trace. This line represents a plane cutting the sphere in a great circle and cutting the section plane in a straight line. Draw OM parallel to the elevation plane. Project N and M up to the Base Line.

2. Draw MH parallel to the vertical trace, H being the point above O. H is the true height above O of the line NO in the plan. Connect NH; this is the vertical trace of the line NO.

3. Draw an auxiliary circle in line with the elevation. This is to be the true elevation of the plane through NO; the section plane appearing as the line NH. Set FH = FH and NF = true plan length = NO measured on the plan. Join NH: this cuts the circle at A_1 and A_2. Draw OC normal to A_1A_2. C is the center of the little circle which is the required section of the sphere, and is the center of the ellipses in plan and elevation which are the projections of this little circle.

4. Project C back onto NH on the elevation and the plan. The axes of the ellipse in plan lie along NO and a line through C parallel to the horizontal trace. The axes

of the ellipse in elevation lie along CQ, normal to the vertical trace and a line through C parallel to the vertical trace.

5. From the auxiliary circle, project A_1 and A_2 onto NH in elevation. These are points on the ellipse in elevation. Project them down to the plan; they are the ends of the minor axis of the ellipse in plan. Draw a line through C parallel to the horizontal trace and measure $CB_1 = CB_2$, equal to the diameter of the little circle, which can be measured from the auxiliary circle as A_1C. B_1 and B_2 are the ends of the major axis of the ellipse in plan. The ellipse can be completed by any convenient method (see Sheet 4). To verify the points of tangency T_1 and T_2, draw OT on the auxiliary circle. Transfer the distance OT onto the plan and draw T_1TT_2 parallel to the horizontal trace.

6. From the plan ellipse the elevation ellipse can be drawn. On the plan, draw a line through C parallel to the Base Line, cutting the plan ellipse at D_1 and D_2. This is the plan projection of the major axis of the ellipse in elevation. Draw a line through C in the elevation, parallel to the vertical trace and project D_1 and D_2 up onto it. These are the ends of the major axis. The length $CD_1 = CD_2$ (in elevation) = CB_1 = CB_2 (in plan) and is equal to the true diameter of the little circle. This is the plan projection of the minor axis of the ellipse in elevation. Project E_1 and E_2 up to the elevation; these are the ends of the minor axis. Draw the ellipse. The points of tangency S_1 and S_2 can be checked by projecting S_1 and S_2 on OM up from the plan to the elevation.

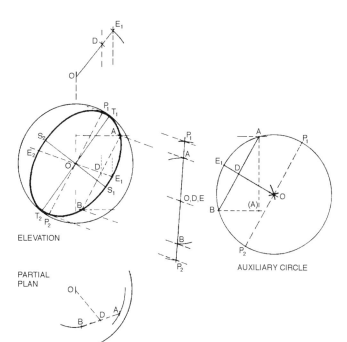

ELEVATION

PARTIAL PLAN

AUXILIARY CIRCLE

Given any two points, A and B, on the elevation of a sphere, to draw the projection of the geodesic (arc of great circle) through them. (This projection will be typically an ellipse.)

1. Draw the chord AB on the elevation. Join the center O to the midpoint D of the chord AB. Draw a line through O parallel to AB. These two lines through O lie on perpendicular diameters of the great circle and therefore lie on conjugate diameters of the ellipse.

2. Draw part of the plan below, showing the portions of the arcs of the little circles on which A and B lie. Project down A and B.

3. From the elevation project horizontal lines through A and B. On one of these lines measure B (A) equal to the true plan length AB. Erect a perpendicular on (A) to A. The hypotenuse of this right triangle is the true length of the chord AB. Draw the circle, of the same radius as the sphere, through A and B. Draw the diameter EDO normal to the chord AB and draw the diameter P_1OP_2 at right angles. (This auxiliary circle is the true plan or elevation of the great circle and gives the true angular length of the geodesic AEB.)

4. With proportional dividers or by measuring along oblique lines, as shown here, find the projected points P_1, P_2 and E on the elevation.

5. OP_1 and OE on the elevation are now conjugate semi-diameters of the ellipse. Use method of Sheet 20 to find the major axis T_1OT_2 and the minor axis S_1OS_2 and draw the ellipse. T_1 and T_2 are of course the points of tangency between the circle and the ellipse, the length of the major axis always being the diameter of the circle.

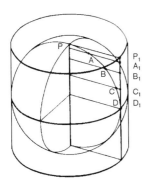

MAPPINGS OF THE SPHERE

Since the sphere cannot be developed onto a plane, many methods of studying it in various projections or mappings have been devised. The construction of spherical domes, particularly the newly developed "geodesic dome," is facilitated by understanding some of these.

A. Cylindrical projection

This is an "area-preserving" mapping of the sphere onto a cylinder. Each point on the sphere is projected onto the circumscribed cylinder along the normals to the cylinder. The area (zone) on the sphere cut off by any two parallel planes, normal to the axis of the cylinder, will be equal to the corresponding area cut off on the cylinder.

The great circles which have the axis of the cylinder as a diameter (i.e. longitude lines) become straight lines; the latitude circles are mapped as straight lines. All geodesics except the longitude lines and the equator are mapped as curves. The whole sphere is mapped onto a plane rectangular area, $2\pi R$ wide and $2R$ high.

B. Mercator's Projection

Like the cylindrical projection, this shows all meridian and latitude lines as straight lines, forming an orthogonal network. The longitude lines are equally spaced, proportionately to the degree of longitude; the latitude lines are spaced further and further apart as the latitude angle increases. On the map $x = R\Theta$; $y = R \log_e (\sec \psi + \tan \psi)$ where Θ is longitude and ψ latitude. This projection was developed for navigation: to map rhumb lines or loxodromes as straight lines. The rhumb line is a curve on the sphere which cuts all meridians at the same angle; it is the path taken by a ship whose course is fixed on a constant bearing with respect to true north. The whole sphere is mapped on a plane strip $2\pi R$ wide and of infinite height (although it is only the last fraction of a latitude degree which goes to infinity). Angles are preserved. The only geodesics which become straight lines are the longitude lines and the equator.

C. Stereographic projection

All points on the sphere are projected onto a plane which is tangent to the sphere, by rays from the pole which is diametrically opposite the point of tangency. All circles, geodesics and little circles, on the sphere are preserved as circles on the mapping. The arc of a geodesic is shown here as a dotted line. The radii of the projected circles are generally not the same as the circles on the sphere; the geodesics which pass through the pole are mapped as straight lines (which can be considered as circles whose radii are infinite). The angles between lines on the sphere are preserved on the mapping. Areas and distances are increasingly distorted as the mapping goes outward. However, the ratios of distances in any small area are approximately correct, and the stereographic projection can therefore be called a "conformal" mapping. The whole sphere is mapped onto the whole infinite plane once.

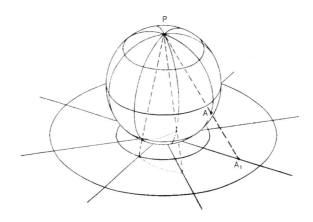

D. Central projection (sometimes called gnomonic projection)

If a sphere is projected from its center onto a tangent plane, all geodesics become straight lines. A geodesic is shown here as a dotted line. Such a projection is called a geodesic map, because all the geodesics on one surface, i.e. the sphere, are geodesics on the other, i.e. the plane. Angles are not preserved, nor are areas. The whole sphere is mapped twice onto the infinite plane; in other words each half of the sphere covers the plane once.

Both stereographic and central projections may be useful in studying geodesic domes. The plane of projection can be moved about at will to show different portions with a minimum of distortion.

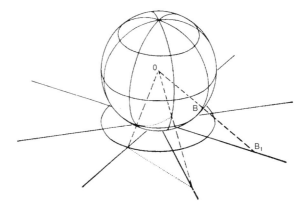

Since the sphere is curved in two directions and cannot be developed, many methods have been used to build domes of this shape. These may be grouped under the headings of radial domes and geodesic domes.

1. Radial Domes. This is the most commonly used method and is based on the image of latitude and longitude circles. Curved ribs are built along the longitude circles, radiating from the top, with without transverse ribs on the latitude lines. The lune or gore spaces between the ribs are filled with thinner vaulting or paneling. If the lune (see Sheet 22) is thought of as the unit, this method is adaptable for prefabrication; domes have been built with a minimum of formwork by first erecting two diametrically opposite lunes, forming an arch against which the others can be constructed. The only difficulty is to join the many ribs which converge at the top; this is solved by introducing a compression ring. The ring may be closed or open.

If the radial dome is constructed as a triangulated network, with one side of each triangle lying on a latitude line, this system has the inconvenience of presenting ever diminishing triangles as the latitude circles become smaller toward the top. The lamella dome is built on this principle, with the latitude ribs replaced by a membrane or by simple struts.

Essentially similar is the method of building by zones (see Sheet 22), particularly adapted to small vaults. All the stones in one zone can be cut alike, but those in the next higher zone must be different. If the blocks follow along some kind of a helical line, as in an igloo, every block would have to be different to make an accurate sphere.

2. Geodesic Domes. The so-called spherical geodesic dome consists of a network of framing members which make a more or less uniform pattern over the whole surface, particularly the truncated icosahedron and the snub dodecahedron. (See drawings of polyhedra, Sheet 26.) It could be built with curved members which would lie along geodesic curves and thus be a portion of a true sphere, but is usually built as a polyhedron with straight members which form the chords of geodesic arcs. The perimeter of the dome at the bottom usually presents an irregular, ragged line.

If one attempts to cover a sphere with such a network, certain basic principles must be observed. Since the triangle is the simplest polygon and also the only one which is rigid in itself, the network will usually consist of triangles. These form larger configurations, depending on how many triangles meet at a point or vertex.

If six equilateral triangles meet on a plane surface, they form a regular hexagon. This is impossible on a sphere because the sum of the angles must be less than 360° around the vertex. On the sphere, therefore, all the members cannot be of the same length and the hexagons formed cannot be regular. Even if the pattern is made up of irregular hexagons, no matter how distorted, it is impossible to cover a complete sphere with them. A minimum of 12 pentagons must be introduced in order to satisfy Euler's formula.

Euler's formula states that, in any convex polyhedron, the number of faces (F), the number of vertices (V) and the number of edges (E) are related:

$$F + V - 2 = E$$

This formula can be used to check a dome which is not a complete sphere by considering the open bottom as a single face or non-plane polygon, the number of whose sides equals the number of members along the perimeter of the framework of the dome.

The basic possibilities and limitations of this type of framework are given by studying all the regular and semi-regular polyhedra and their duals, remembering that polygonal faces can be subdivided. Their number is quite limited.

There are only five regular polyhedra, all of whose edges are the same length and all of whose faces are regular, identical polygons. Called the Platonic polyhedra, they can have a sphere inscribed within them touching each face in its center, or have a sphere circumscribed about them, passing through each vertex. These points of tangency or vertices are the only regular systems of points which are equidistant from each other on the surface of a sphere.

There are the 13 semi-regular polyhedra, called Archimedean. All edges are the same length and every face is a regular polygon, but all the faces are not identical. The

vertices are all congruent (identical) but not regular (the angles between pairs of edges are not all the same). These polyhedra can have a sphere circumscribed about them, passing through each vertex. Prisms and anti-prisms (see sheet 17 for drawings) also meet these conditions if the top and bottom polygons are regular and if the sides are squares in the case of the prisms and equilateral triangles in the case of the anti-prisms.

There are also the 13 duals of the Archimedean polyhedra. A polyhedron P_2 is the dual of polyhedron P_1 if the faces of P_2 correspond to the vertices of P_1. Thus, the octahedron is the dual of the cube, the icosahedron is the dual of the dodecahedron. The number of vertices and the number of faces are interchanged; the number of edges remains constant. The vertices of the Archimedean duals do not fall on a sphere, but a sphere tangent to every face at its center can be inscribed within each dual. Every face is identical but is not a regular polygon. Every vertex is regular but all vertices are not identical. (The duals of the prisms are called dipyramids, made of two pyramids placed base to base. The faces are all isosceles triangles. The duals of the antiprisms are called trapezohedra. The faces are kites, or quadrilaterals with adjacent pairs of sides of equal length.)

In order to keep strut lengths as short as possible and avoid buckling, and in order to provide complete triangulation for rigidity, the polygons forming the polyhedra can be subdivided into triangles, and all triangles can be further subdivided. If the members thus added are the same length as the others, the added vertex will not be on the sphere; if the added vertex is held on the sphere, the added members will have to be of a different length. Continuous membranes, plane or warped, may also be used to provide rigidity.

See Sheets 26 and 27 following for diagrams and schedules of the polyhedra. The index number lists the number of faces of the polygons meeting at a vertex (see sheet 18 for similar index numbering system). For the Archimedean duals the index number of the corresponding semi-regular polygon is used with the prefix V.

Drawings of the Polyhedra, shown in plan, with some of each and number of faces, vertices, and edges of each. (Cube not shown)

TETRAHEDRON

F	V	E
4	4	6

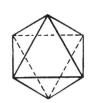

OCTAHEDRON

F	V	E
8	6	12

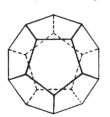

DODECAHEDRON

F	V	E
12	20	30

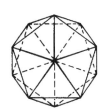

ICOSAHEDRON

F	V	E
20	12	30

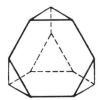

TRUNCATED TETRAHEDRON

F_3	F_4	V	E
4	4	12	18

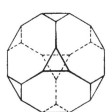

TRUNCATED CUBE

F_3	F_8	V	E
8	6	24	36

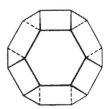

TRUNCATED OCTAHEDRON

F_4	F_6	V	E
6	8	24	36

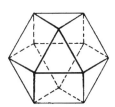

CUBOCTAHEDRON

F_3	F_4	V	E
8	6	12	24

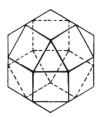

RHOMBICUBOCTAHEDRON

F_3	F_4	V	E
8	18	24	48

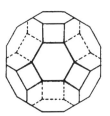

TRUNCATED CUBOCTAHEDRON

F_4	F_6	F_8	V	E
12	8	6	48	72

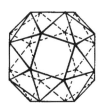

SNUB CUBE

F_3	F_4	V	E
32	6	24	60

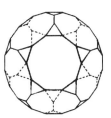

TRUNCATED DODECAHEDRON

F_3	F_{10}	V	E
20	12	60	90

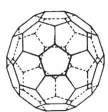

TRUNCATED ICOSAHEDRON

F_5	F_6	V	E
12	20	60	90

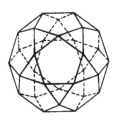

ICOSIDODECAHEDRON

F_3	F_5	V	E
20	12	30	60

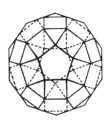

RHOMBICOSIDODECAHEDRON

F_3	F_4	F_5	V	E
20	30	12	60	120

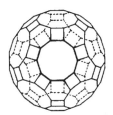

TRUNCATED ICOSIDODECAHEDRON

F_4	F_6	F_{10}	V	E
30	20	12	120	180

SNUB DODECAHEDRON

F_3	F_5	V	E
80	12	60	150

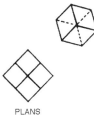

PLANS

PROJECTION

RHOMBIC DODECAHEDRON

F	V	E
12	14	24

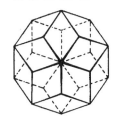

RHOMBIC TRIACONTAHEDRON

F	V	I
30	32	60

Notes:
1. Only two of the Archimedean duals are shown. The rhombic dodecahedron is drawn in an oblique or axonometric projection, as well as in two plan views. Note it is a cube (shown in fine dotted line) with a square pyramid added to each face. The others can be drawn from the corresponding Archimedean polyhedron: (a) Draw plan with vertex in center; (b) Draw on plan the perpendicular bisector of each edge which meets at vertex; (c) Extend all bisectors until they intersect; they form irregular polygonal face of the dual.
2. For making models, polygons can be drawn on a flat sheet, with some edges of each polygon in common with adjacent polygons, making a continuous strip called a net.

INDEX NO.	DUALS OF SEMI-REGULAR POLYHEDRA	E/r	DIHEDRAL ANGLE	FACE ANGLES	R/r
V.3.6²	Triakis Tetrahedron	3.127 / 1.876	129° 32'	112° 53' / 33° 33½'	1.2222
V.3.8²	Triakis Octahedron	2.083 / 1.219	147° 21'	117° 14' / 31° 23'	1.0858
V.4.6²	Tetrakis Hexahedron	1.491	143° 8'	83° 37' / 48° 11½'	1.1111
V.(3.4)²	Rhombic Dodecahedron (Octahedric Granatohedron)	1.118 / 1.225	120°	109° 28' / 70° 32'	1.3333
V.3.4³	Trapezoidal Icositetrahedron	0.887 / 0.686	138° 7'	115° 16' / 81° 34½'	1.1464
V.4.6.8	Hexakis Octahedron	1.070 / 0.878 / 0.656	155° 5'	87° 12' / 55° 1½' / 37° 46½'	1.0488
V.3⁴.4	Pentagonal Icositetrahedron (Two Enantiomorphs)	0.727 / 0.513	136° 20'	114° 48½' / 80° 46'	1.1602
V.3.10²	Triakis Icosahedron	1.254 / 0.728	160° 36'	119° 3' / 30° 28½'	1.0302
V.5.6²	Pentakis Dodecahedron	0.780 / 0.692	156° 43'	68° 36' / 55° 42'	1.0425
V.(3.5)²	Rhombic Triacontahedron (Icosahedric Granatohedron)	0.727	144°	116° 34' / 63° 26'	1.1056
V.3.4.5.4	Trapezoidal Hexecontahedron	0.584 / 0.379	154° 8'	118° 16' / 86° 59' / 67° 46'	1.0530
V.4.6.10	Hexakis Icosahedron	0.689 / 0.586 / 0.373	164° 54'	89° 0' / 58° 14' / 32° 46'	1.0174
V.3⁵	Pentagonal Hexecontahedron (Two Enantiomorphs)	0.500 / 0.286	153° 10'	118° 8' / 67° 28'	1.0574

NOTES:

e = length of edge of regular and semi-regular polyhedra. θ = angle subtended by edge at center (for regular and semi-regular polyhedra). R = Radius of circumscribed sphere (regular + semi-regular polyhedra). r = radius of inscribed sphere (regular polyhedra and duals of semi-regular polyhedra). E = length of edges of duals of semi-regular polyhedra. R/r: This ratio, when given for the Archimedean duals, is the ratio of the radius of the circumscribed sphere of the corresponding Archimedean polyhedron to the radius of the sphere inscribed within the dual. Enantiomorph means form of opposite hand (in drawing, change broken lines to solid and solid lines to broken). There are only five possible ways of filling up three dimensional spaces with only one type of regular or Archimedean polyhedra and their duals = cubes; triangular prisms; hexagonal prisms; truncated octahedra; rhombic dodecahedra. There are three additional ways, using more than one type = tetrahedra + octahedra; tetrahedra + truncated tetrahedra; octahedra = cuboctahedra.

INDEX NO.	REGULAR POLYHEDRA	e/R	DIHEDRAL ANGLE	θ	R/r
3³	Tetrahedron	1.633	70° 32'	109° 28'	3.00
4³	Cube	1.155	90°	70° 32'	1.732
3⁴	Octahedron	1.414	109° 28'	90°	1.732
5³	Dodecahedron	0.714	116° 34'	41° 49'	1.258
3⁵	Icosahedron	1.051	138° 11'	63° 26'	1.258

INDEX NO.	SEMI-REGULAR POLYHEDRA	e/R	DIHEDRAL ANGLES		θ
			Faces	Angles	
3.6²	Truncated Tetrahedron	0.853	6-6 / 6-3	70° 32' / 109° 28'	50° 28'
3.8²	Truncated Cube	0.562	8-8 / 8-3	90° / 125° 16'	32° 39'
4.6²	Truncated Octahedron (Tetrakaidecahedron)	0.6325	6-4 / 6-6	125° 16' / 109° 28'	36° 52'
(3.4)²	Cuboctahedron	1.00		125° 16'	60°
3.4³	Rhombicuboctahedron	0.715	4-4 / 3-4	135° / 144° 44'	41° 53'
4.6.8	Truncated Cuboctahedron	0.431	8-4 / 8-6 / 6-4	135° / 125° 16' / 144° 44'	24° 55'
3⁴.4	Snub Cube (Two Enantiomorphs)	0.744	4-3 / 3-3	142° 59' / 153° 14'	43° 40'
3.10²	Truncated Dodecahedron	0.337	10-10 / 10-3	116° 34' / 142° 37'	19° 24'
5.6²	Truncated Icosahedron	0.4035	6-6 / 6-5	138° 11' / 142° 37'	23° 17'
(3.5)²	Icosidodecahedron (Triacontagon)	0.618		142° 37'	36°
3.4.5.4	Rhombicosidodecahedron	0.448	5-4 / 3-4	148° 17' / 159° 6'	25° 52'
4.6.10	Truncated Icosidodecahedron	0.263	10-4 / 10-6 / 6-4	148° 17' / 142° 37' / 159° 6'	15° 6'
3⁴.5	Snub Dodecahedron (Two Enantiomorphs)	0.464	5-3 / 3-3	152° 56' / 164° 10'	26° 50'

References: Cundy and Rollett, Mathematical Models (Oxford, 1951); Matila C. Ghyka, Esthetique des Proportions (Gallimard, 1927).

The most perfect development of the geodesic dome has been made by R. Buckminster Fuller. Combining the tetrahedron and the sphere, it is derived from his concept of "energetic geometry." Of all regular convex polyhedra the tetrahedron encloses the minimum of space with the maximum of surface, and is the stiffest form against external and tangential pressures. The sphere encloses the maximum of space with a minimum of surface and is the strongest form against internal or radial pressures.

In the Fuller dome a space-frame, built up of elongated tetrahedra, is given the overall shape of a sphere. The basic unit is rhombus or diamond shaped in plan, triangular in elevation.

The unit may be built of struts or, in the type being manufactured by the Kaiser Aluminum Co., of a bent sheet, stiffened by edge flanges and with one strut across the short axis.

The tetrahedral units are combined to form a complete framework by joining six units together. Assuming the diagonal members to be fastened already to the short axis and long axis members, a six-way fastener is required at the vertices of the short axes. As the units are combined to cover the whole sphere, there will be a minimum of 12 cases where five instead of six units come together. (See sheet 25 for explanation.)

The framework is dimensioned so that

TETRAHEDRON UNITS

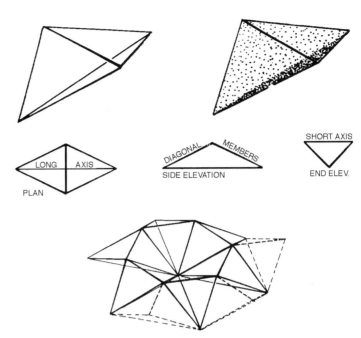

The structures designed according to the information in this article are covered by United States Patent No. 2,682,235 and Canadian Patent No. 512,422 granted to R. Buckminster Fuller. They include any building framework designed with an overall pattern of three-way great circle gridding.

all the long axis vertices of the tetrahedra lie on a sphere. The struts forming the long axes thus lie along chords of geodesic arcs. The other struts are placed to lie outside the surface of the sphere and are dimensioned to give the depth of frame considered necessary for stiffness. (In the aluminum dome manufactured by Kaiser this depth is 12 in (305 mm) and is used for their standard dome with a sphere radius of 80 ft (24.4 m). See Sheet 35 of Structural Design—Steel.)

The method of subdividing the surface of the sphere to find the correct position of these long axis vertices is as follows:

1. Divide the surface of the sphere into 20 equilateral spherical triangles. Graphically this can most easily be done by starting with icosahedron (see Sheets 26 and 27) and joining the vertices by geodesic arcs instead of by straight lines. All the angles of the equilateral triangle are 72°; the sides are 63° 26' 5.47" or 1.107147 radians. This is a spherical icosahedron and is the maximum number of equilateral triangles into which a sphere can be divided. Usually only five of these equilateral triangles would be used, making a dome that is one-quarter of a sphere, with a $\frac{rise}{span}$ ratio of about $\frac{1}{3}$. The method of division can be carried out

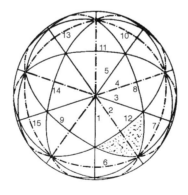

PLAN

Plan of opposite side is identical, but rotated through 36°

Shaded area is typical spherical isosceles triangle, as analyzed on the following page and as shown on Sheet 9 of Structural Forms—Steel.

over the whole surface of a sphere, however, and will be described in this way.

2. Draw the medians of each of these triangles, dividing each side in half. This is the same as extending the sides of all triangles to form 15 complete great cir-

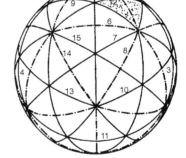

ELEVATION

Elevation from other side is identical, but turned upside down

cles. These lines will be the only complete symmetrically spaced, great circles on the sphere, no matter how much further it is subdivided. (In the diagrams the icosahedral division is shown with a dot-dash line, the medians and other subdivisions with a full line.)

3. The medians divide each equilateral triangle into six identical spherical right triangles, with the angles 90°, 60° and 36.° On the complete sphere there are 6 x 20 or 120 of these right triangles.

4. Pair off the 120 right triangles into 60 isosceles triangles. The apex angle is 72°, the two base angles are each 60°.

6. The minimum number of divisions or the smallest "frequency" is 2. For $\nu = 2$, the only arc projected is the altitude of the isosceles triangle itself. The lengths of the long axes of the tetrahedra or diamonds (marked as I and II) are the lengths of the sides of the triangle. The dimensions are given on sheet 30. In the plan of the basic isosceles triangle we now have three "half" diamonds, the other halves being provided by the neighboring triangles (shown here dashed). The diagonal struts

7. For a "frequency" of 4 ($\nu = 4$), the base is divided into four equal arcs. Three arcs at 90° to the base are projected into the triangle from the points of division; and two additional arcs are projected at 60° to the base from the second or center point of division. All calculations can be performed on the basis of the formulas for spherical right triangles (see Sheet 39 for the list of these formulas). These 60° lines divide the large isosceles triangle into four smaller, non-identical isosceles triangles of three sizes. The sides of

8. For a "frequency" of 6 ($\nu = 6$), the base is divided into six equal arcs. Five arcs at 90° to the base are projected into the triangle from the points of division; and two additional arcs are projected at 60° to the base from both the second and fourth points of division. These 60° lines divide the basic isosceles triangle into nine smaller isosceles triangles of five sizes. The sides of these triangles are the long axis diagonals of the tetrahedra or diamonds. They are marked I, II, III, IV, V and VI; the lengths are tabulated below.

The lengths of the two equal sides are 37° 22' 38.5" (0.652358 radians); the length of the base 41° 48' 37.1" (0.729727658 radians). The altitude is 31° 43' 2.7" (0.553574 radians) or half the side of the original equilateral triangle.

5. The 60 identical spherical isosceles triangles are further subdivided by using the

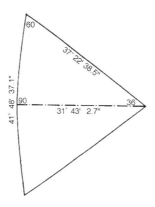

and the short axis struts are above or outside of the sphere. There are a total

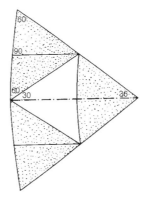

these triangles are the long axis diagonals of the tetrahedra or diamonds. They are marked I, II, III and IV and the lengths are tabulated on Sheet 30. We now have four types of diamond and a total of three

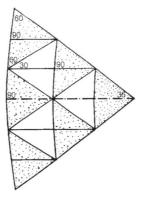

We now have six types of diamonds and a total of nine complete and nine half diamonds in the plan of the basis isosceles

base as the measuring line. The base is divided into any even number of equal arcs, called the "frequency" and referred to by the Greek letter nu ν. From each point of division a great circle arc is projected out at 90° to the base across the triangle until it intersects the other side. The simplest cases in order are:

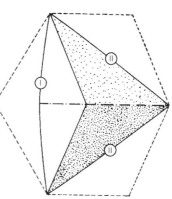

of 3/2 x 60 = 90 diamonds for a complete sphere.

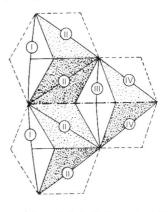

complete and six half diamonds within the plan of the basic isosceles triangle. Thus there are 6 x 60 = 360 diamonds in the complete sphere.

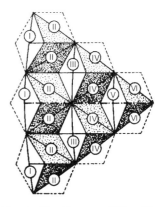

triangle. Thus there are 13½ x 60 = 810 diamonds on the complete sphere.

9. This procedure can be continued without limit. In every case:

a) The number of smaller isosceles triangles into which the basic isosceles triangle is divided is $\left(\dfrac{\nu}{2}\right)^2$.

b) The number of types of tetrahedra or diamonds is equal to the frequency number ν (number of divisions of the base).

c) The number of tetrahedra or diamonds in one of the basic isosceles triangles is $\dfrac{3}{2}\left(\dfrac{\nu}{2}\right)^2$. Since there are 60 basic isosceles triangles, the number of tetrahedra to a complete sphere is $90\left(\dfrac{\nu}{2}\right)^2$.

The following table gives the lengths of the long axes of the tetrahedra for different frequencies. The lengths are measured as geodesic arcs along the surface of the sphere.

Frequency ν or number of divisions of base	2	4	6	8	10	12
Number of types of tetrahedra	2	4	6	8	10	12
Number of tetrahedra to complete sphere $90\left(\dfrac{\nu}{2}\right)^2$	90	360	810	1440	2250	3240
I	41° 48′ 37.12″ 0.729728	20° 54′ 18.56″ 0.364864	13° 56′ 12.4″ 0.243243	10° 27′ 9.3″ 0.182432	8° 21′ 43.4″ 0.145946	6° 58′ 6.2″ 0.121621
II	37° 22′ 38.5″ 0.652358	20° 15′ 8.4″ 0.353470	13° 44′ 11.4″ 0.239747	10° 22′ 1.4″ 0.180939	8° 19′ 4.8″ 0.145176	6° 56′ 34.2″ 0.121175
III		19° 56′ 1″ 0.347908	13° 37′ 59.2″ 0.237943	10° 19′ 17.8″ 0.180146	8° 17′ 39.4″ 0.144762	6° 55′ 43.9″ 0.120932
IV		17° 7′ 30.1″ 0.298888	12° 39′ 33.5″ 0.220947	9° 53′ 7″ 0.172531	8° 3′ 51.7″ 0.140750	6° 47′ 37.2″ 0.118572
V			12° 51′ 22.8″ 0.224385	9° 58′ 0.5″ 0.173954	8° 6′ 17.4″ 0.141456	6° 48′ 59.6″ 0.118971
VI			10° 58′ 53.6″ 0.191664	9° 3′ 23.8″ 0.158068	7° 36′ 18.5″ 0.132735	6° 30′ 57″ 0.113723
VII				9° 27′ 51.9″ 0.165185	7° 49′ 23.5″ 0.136540	6° 38′ 40.3″ 0.115969
VIII				8° 4′ 6.3″ 0.140820	7° 0′ 58″ 0.122454	6° 8′ 36.5″ 0.107224
IX					7° 28′ 57.6″ 0.130597	6° 25′ 41.4″ 0.112193
X					6° 22′ 25.5″ 0.111243	5° 42′ 54.6″ 0.099748
XI						6° 11′ 11″ 0.107973
XII						5° 15′ 59″ 0.091916

LENGTHS OF LONG AXIS DIAGONALS IN DEGREES AND RADIANS
To convert to linear measure, multiply length in radians by radius of sphere

The hyperbolic paraboloid, a quadric surface, is shown here in isometric and orthogonal projection. It is a doubly curved surface and therefore not developable. However, since it is ruled surface, it can easily be formed or molded in a framework of straight members.

It can be generated in two ways:

1. A generating parabola (AOA in diagrams) is moved along another directrix parabola (BOB) in such a way that the successive positions of the plane of AOA are always parallel and the successive positions of the line AA are always parallel.

2. As a ruled surface: Given two straight lines (here 5′5′ and 5 5) lying in a horizontal plane, two vertical planes containing these straight lines. Move one of these lines, say 5′5′, called the generator, along the other (5 5), called the directrix, in such a way that its successive positions are always skew but always parallel to its initial position. Thus no plane can contain any two positions of the line 5′5′. These successive positions are the straight lines of one family, sometimes called a regulus. The other family is found by sliding the other straight line 5 5 along the line 5′5′.

The equation, with axes as shown.

$$\frac{x^2}{a} - \frac{y^2}{b^2} = \frac{z}{c}$$

(See below for the equations referred to the asymptotes as axes.)

All sections containing the z axis are parabolas. As such a section is rotated about the z axis, from one principal plane (the xz) to the other (the yz), the parabolas become wider and wider, but all with their centers of curvature above the xy plane, until at the sections containing 5 5 or 5′5′, the parabola becomes a straight line; as rotation continues, the parabolas have their centers of curvature below the xy plane, and become narrower until the section plane reaches the yz plane. All sections parallel to any given plane containing the z axis are identical parabolas (or a straight line).

Every section parallel to the xy plane is a hyperbola. The lines 5′5′ and 5 5 are the asymptotes of all of these hyperbolas. Every section above the xy plane will be a hyperbola with its axis parallel to the x axis; every section below the xy plane has its axis parallel to the y axis. The hyperbolas at the same distance above and below the xy plane (i.e. when z = +d or −d) are conjugate. On the xy plane the hyperbola becomes the pair of straight lines 5′5′ and 5 5.

Every section which is not parallel to a plane containing the z axis is also a hyperbola (or a straight line). There are no elliptical or circular sections.

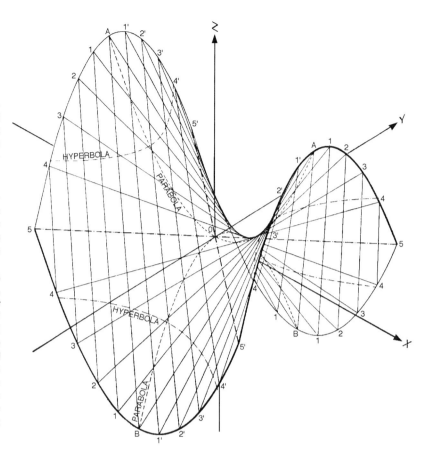

ISOMETRIC PROJECTION

X Z-PLANE

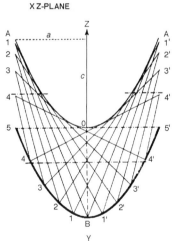

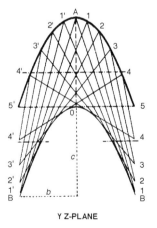

Y Z-PLANE

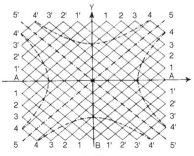

PLAN

Every contour or visible edge in axonometric or orthogonal projection is a parabola.

A plane can be passed through any two straight lines of different families or reguli; no plane can be passed through two straight lines of the same family. Through any point on the surface pass only two straight lines, one from each family. The tangent plane at that point is defined by these two straight lines.

Note that the plan projection consists of two families of parallel lines, forming a network of identical rhombuses. When $a = b$, the rhombus becomes a square. Note also that, although the angle between two straight lines of different families is constant in plan, it varies on the surface. (Therefore the hyperbolic paraboloid cannot be a minimal surface, since two such straight lines are the asymptotic lines at the point. On a minimal surface asymptotic lines must meet everywhere at right angles.) The lines of curvature bisect the angles between the straight lines on the surface.

TO DRAW: Given the rectangular plan with the parabolas 5'A5, 5A5', 5'B5 and 5B5' as the sides, divide each side into the same number of spaces (here 10) and draw the diagonal straight lines connecting corresponding points. These are the plan projections of the straight line generators of the surface. See Sheet 31.

The numbered points can be used to construct the parabolas, in elevation, in isometric or other projection, following the method of Sheet 31. These points are equidistant from the xz or yz planes; they are not equidistant along the true length of the parabolas.

Draw the elevations (projections on the xz and yz planes) by establishing the height c of A above the xy plane and the equal height c of B below the xy plane. Join the corresponding points on the parabolas with straight lines. With the numbering system shown, for example, each point such as 2 is joined by two straight lines to the two nearest points also numbered 2, the point such as 2' is joined to the nearest points numbered 2'. These straight lines will generate the surface.

In elevation the straight lines are tangents to the contour parabola AOA; this parabola is identical to the parabola 5B5'. In axonometric projection (here an isometric) the contour is also always a parabola, which can be drawn from the straight line tangents.

Warped Parallelogram

Axonometric projection

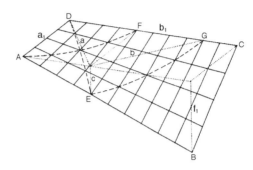

Plan

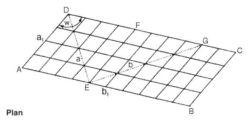

The hyperbolic paraboloid as a warped parallelogram. A surface which is a parallelogram in plan can be set so that three corners (here A, C and D) are all in one plane (here horizontal), and the fourth corner (B) is not in the plane (here lowered). Divide the sides into equal spaces and join the pairs of opposite sides by straight lines. The surface will be a portion of a hyperbolic paraboloid.

Comparing this with the diagrams on Sheet 31, the lines AD and DC correspond to the lines 05 and 05'. The parabola DE corresponds to the parabola OB. The parabolas AF and EG correspond to the parabola AOA as it slides down OB; and their tangents are horizontal at the intersections with DE.

In writing the equation, the edges AD (length a_1) and DC (length b_1) are usually taken as axes, with the angle w between them. The equation is

$$k \, x_1 \, y_1 \, \sin w = z \quad \text{Where}$$

$$k = \frac{f}{a_1 b_1 \sin w}$$

Note that, since $c = \frac{a_1}{b_1} f_1$,

$$k = \frac{c}{a_1^2 \sin w}$$

This therefore corresponds to the equation $x_1 y_1 = a_1^2 \frac{z}{c}$ (see below). The area of the plan projection of the parallelogram is $a_1 b_1 \sin w$.

When the edges of the parallelogram, corresponding to the principal asymptotes of the hyperbolic paraboloid, are taken as the axes, care must be used to compare the constants used in the two types of equation. The difference is basically the same as that between the equation of a hyperbola referred to its center line and that referred to its asymptotes. (When $z = c$, the section of the hyperbolic paraboloid is the hyperbola whose parameters are a and b.)

For the hyperbola, the two cases are:

1. The equilateral hyperbola (corresponding to rectangular hyperbolic paraboloid). In standard form, referred to x and y axes:

$$x^2 - y^2 = a^2 \text{ or } \frac{x^2}{a^2} - \frac{y^2}{a^2} = 1$$

Axes rotated through $45°$ to x_1 and y_1:

$$x_1 y_1 = a_1^2,$$

where

$$a_1 = \frac{a}{\sqrt{2}}$$

2. The general hyperbola. In standard form, referred to x and y axes:

$$\frac{x^2}{a^2} - \frac{y^2}{b^2} = 1$$

Axes changed from rectangular to oblique and rotated to x_1 and y_1

$$x_1 y_1 = a_1^2$$

where

$$a_1 = \sqrt{\frac{a^2 + b^2}{2}}$$

Or, if w = angle between x_1 and y_1,

$$x_1 y_1 \sin w = \frac{ab}{2}$$

All equations referred to the asymptotes as axes can be checked by the fact that the area of the parallelogram made by the x_1 and y_1, coordinates of any point on a hyperbola is constant. This is shown shaded on the diagrams.

The values of the functions of the angle w are:

$$\tan \frac{w}{2} = \frac{b}{a} \qquad \tan w = \frac{2ab}{a^2 - b^2}$$

$$\sin \frac{w}{2} = \frac{b}{\sqrt{a^2 + b^2}} \qquad \sin w = \frac{2ab}{a^2 + b^2}$$

$$\cos \frac{w}{2} = \frac{a}{\sqrt{a^2 + b^2}} \qquad \cos w = \frac{a^2 - b^2}{a^2 + b^2}$$

The drawing of hyperbolas may be simplified by using one of these two methods instead of those shown on Sheet 6.

1. Secant or chord method. Given the two asymptotes as shown and any point P_1 (which may be the apex). Draw any secant line through P_1, cutting the asymptotes at A and B. Measure BP_2 equal to AP_1. P_2 is a point on the hyperbola. This process can be continued, using more lines through P_1 or through P_2.

2. Parallelogram method. Given the apex A_1 and the apex A_2 and one point P. Draw the axis through $A_1 A_2$. Draw PN perpendicular to the axis. Draw PB parallel to the axes and of length A_2N. Divide PB into any number of equal spaces (here four); divide PN into the same number of equal spaces. From A_1, draw lines to the points on PN; from A_2, draw lines to the points on PB. The intersections of corresponding lines are points on the hyperbola. (This is basically the same method as that shown on Sheet 3 for drawing the parabola.)

TWO CASES FOR HYPERBOLA

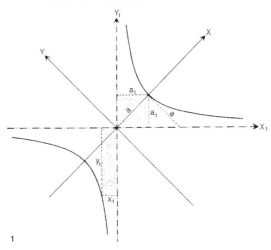

1

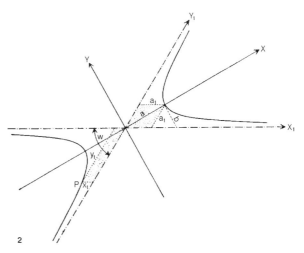

2

DRAWING OF HYPERBOLAS

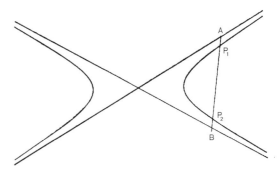

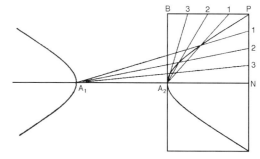

The ellipsoid, shown here in isometric projection, is one of the quadric surfaces and is generated by rotating a variable ellipse about an axis. It has three principal sections, shown here as the sections by the xy, xz and yz planes.

Its equation:

$$\frac{x^2}{a^2} + \frac{y^2}{b^2} + \frac{z^2}{c^2} = 1$$

where $a = OA$ in the diagram,
$b = OB$
$c = OC$

Every section is an ellipse (or a circle; for the circular sections, see construction right). When $b = a$, the ellipsoid becomes the surface of revolution called an oblate spheroid (Dutch cheese shape); when $b = c$, it is a prolate spheroid (watermelon shape), also a surface of revolution. When $a = b = c$, it is, of course, a sphere. The volume is $\frac{4}{3} \pi\, a\, b\, c$. There is no simple formula for the area.

To draw in projection, first draw the projections of the ellipses on the three principal planes. The axes will be conjugate diameters (see Sheet 20) and the ellipses can be constructed from them. Then, second, draw the ellipse which is the projected or contour edge of the ellipsoid; (a) find its points of tangency T_1 and T_2 with the ellipse on the xy plane by simply drawing any two parallel chords (see separate diagram below giving general method of finding points of tangency); (b) construct the auxiliary ellipse (one quarter of which is shown) which is the section of the ellipsoid by the vertical plane through the z axis normal to the plane of projection; draw a chord DD normal to the plane of projection, find M the midpoint, draw OM extended to V_1; this is the point on the contour ellipse corresponding to the vertical plane through the z axis; (c) project V_1 back onto the isometric projection and mark V_2 at the same distance on the opposite side of O; (d) V_1V_2 and T_1T_2 are conjugate diameters of the contour ellipse; use method of Sheet 20 or parallelogram method to complete ellipse; (e) check points of tangency between contour ellipse and ellipse of xz plane by drawing a chord parallel to the y axis, finding its midpoint and extending to cut the ellipse at the point of tangency; repeat procedure for ellipse of yz plane, using a chord parallel to x axis.

Parallelogram method of drawing ellipse. This is often easier than other methods, particularly in projections. Given two diameters D_1D_2 and D_3D_4, draw the surrounding parallelogram. Divide one of the sides into any number of equal spaces; divide the intersecting diameter into the same number of equal spaces. From D_2 draw rays through

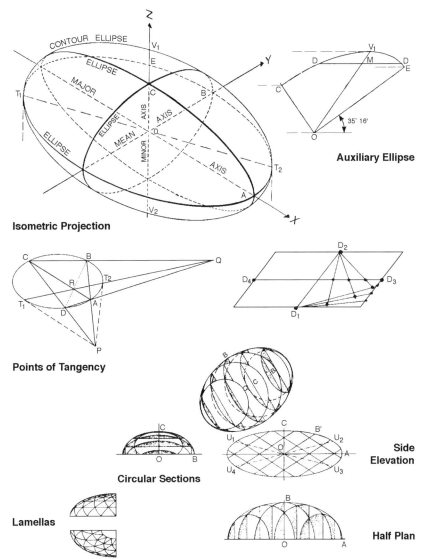

Isometric Projection

Auxiliary Ellipse

Points of Tangency

Circular Sections

Lamellas

Side Elevation

Half Plan

the points on the diameter; from D_1 draw rays through the points on the side. The points of intersection of the rays lie on the ellipse. The same construction can be used with any two conjugate diameters. (This is basically the same construction as shown on Sheet 3 for the parabola; in the case of the parabola, D_2 is at infinity and the rays from it through the points on the chord D_3D_4 are all parallel).

To find the points of tangency between an ellipse and the tangents to it drawn from any external point: From P draw any two lines cutting the ellipse at A B C D. Draw CB and DA extended to meet at Q. Draw the diagonals of the quadrilateral ABCD, intersecting at R. Draw QR, cutting the ellipse at T_1 and T_2, which are the required points of tangency. When P is at infinity, AB and CD become parallel chords and the line QR bisects both of them.

Construction of Ellipsoid: Lamellas. Ellipsoids have been built as domes on the

lamella principle, using a radial distribution of points of intersection of the lamellas along latitude lines, similar to the lamella construction of a spherical dome. This means that every lamella in a half ellipse is different; there is no repetition along a given latitude line such as there is on a sphere.

Circular Sections. Another method, which might simplify construction, is based on the fact that on every ellipsoid there are two families of parallel circles which are sections of the ellipsoid. Looking at the isometric drawing of the ellipsoid, imagine the plane yz rotated about the mean axis. The minor semi-axis of the ellipse which is OC in the vertical position will increase continuously until the plane is coincident with the xy plane, when this semi-axis will become equal to OA. Somewhere between these two values, this semi-axis will have the value equal to OB and the section would therefore be a circle.

Given an ellipsoid, to find the two families of circles which are its sections.

Draw the side elevation of the ellipsoid, showing an ellipse with semi-axes OA and OC. Swing an arc OB of length equal to half the mean axis to intersect the ellipse at B'. All the circular sections of one family will be parallel to this radius vector; the other family will be symmetrical, making the same angle with the base on the opposite side of the minor axis.

On the side elevation the lines U_1OU_2 and U_3OU_4 are the conjugate diameters of the two principal circular sections (shown here as straight lines passing through O). Each bisects every chord of the family. The four points U are the umbilical points of the ellipsoid.

Lines of curvature on the ellipsoid are the traces of the intersection of the ellipsoid with the hyperboloids of one and two sheets which are confocal with the ellipsoid. At the umbilical points the curvature is the same for all normal sections. A drawing can be found in Hilbert "Geometry and The Imagination," p. 189.

The principal sections of the ellipsoid are lines of curvature and are also the only closed geodesic curves on the ellipsoid. All other geodesics are not closed curves and are very difficult to work out in detail. Every geodesic passing through one umbilical point passes through the umbilical point diametrically opposite, but not symmetrically. One set of geodesic curves is shown in Hilbert on p. 223.

Elliptic Paraboloid

The elliptic paraboloid, shown here in isometric projection, is one of the quadric surfaces and is generated by rotating a variable parabola about an axis.

Its equation (with the axis as shown)

$$\frac{x^2}{a^2} + \frac{y^2}{b^2} = \frac{c-z}{c}$$

The sections of the surface by any plane parallel to the z axis is a parabola. The two principal sections are the xz and yz planes. All other sections are ellipses. The section by the xy plane is an ellipse with semi-major axis equal to the constant a (OA in the diagram) and semi-minor axis equal to constant b (OB in the diagram). This ellipse is drawn here as the bottom of the paraboloid, although the surface actually continues to infinity. When a equals b, it is a paraboloid of revolution, and its equation may also be written in cylindrical coordinates as:

$$\frac{r^2}{a^2} = \frac{c-z}{c}$$

Volume $= \frac{1}{2}$ (area of base) (altitude)

To draw in projection, first draw the projections of the paraboloids on the xz and yz planes. These will also be parabolas in projection. Second, draw the projection of the ellipse on the xy plane. Third, on z axis, measure CW equal to OC. W is the vertex of an elliptic cone which is tangent to the paraboloid at every point around the ellipse in the xy plane. Fourth, draw tangents WT_1 and WT_2 to the ellipse (see method of finding exact points of tangency above), and draw T_1T_2. Fifth, find M the midpoint of T_1T_2, which will be on the vertical line OW, and find V the midpoint of MW. Sixth, with MV as vertical axis and T_1MT_2 as base, draw a parabola. This is the parabola which is the contour or visible edge of the paraboloid in projection. To check the point of tangency between the contour parabola and the parabola in the xz plane, draw a chord of the xz parabola

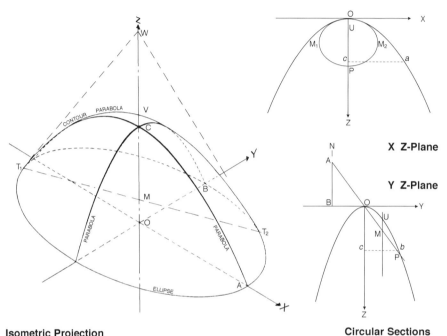

Isometric Projection

Circular Sections

X Z-Plane

Y Z-Plane

parallel to the y axis; find the midpoint of the chord and draw a line parallel to the z axis through it; the point where this line cuts the parabola is the required point of tangency. The point of tangency between the contour parabola and the parabola in the yz plane is found in the same way, using a chord parallel to the x axis.

All sections parallel to a plane containing the z axis are identical parabolas; i.e. they are all the same size. All sections normal to a plane containing the z axis are ellipses of the same proportions; i.e. the major axis is always equal to $\frac{a}{b}$ times the minor axis.

To find the circular sections: On every elliptic paraboloid there are two families of parallel circles which are sections of the surface (this is similar to the general ellipsoid, see sheet 34. Given the elliptic paraboloid $\frac{x^2}{a^2} + \frac{y^2}{b^2} = \frac{z}{c}$, draw the

projections on the yz and xz planes as shown. Draw OB of length b along the y axis and draw BN at right angles at B. Swing an arc OA of length a to intersect BN at A. Draw AO extended to cut the parabola at P. OP is the trace of one of the circular sections. It is shown in projection, as an ellipse, on the xz plane.

The planes of all the other circular sections of this family will be parallel to OP. The other family is symmetrical on the opposite side of the z axis.

To find the umbilical point U, find M the midpoint of OP. Draw a line through M parallel to the z axis. This line is the conjugate diameter (i.e. passes through the mid-points) of all the chords parallel to OP. It cuts the parabola at U. Every elliptic paraboloid has only two umbilical points. In the case of the paraboloid of revolution, the two families of circular sections coincide (as parallels of "latitude") and the two umbilici coincide at the vertex O.

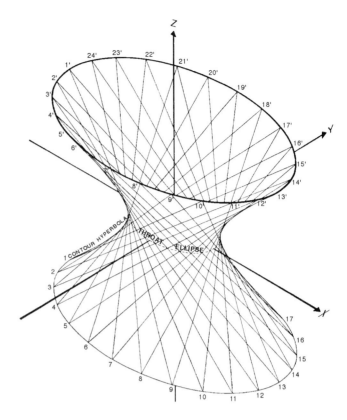

ISOMETRIC PROJECTION

Another quadric surface, the hyperboloid of one sheet (or of one nappe) is shown here in isometric and orthogonal projections. It is one of the only two possible doubly ruled curved surfaces; the other is the hyperbolic paraboloid. It is easily constructed from straight members. It can be generated in several ways:

1. As a ruled surface: A straight line (such as 3'12) is moved so that it touches at all times three given, non-intersecting straight lines (such as 3'18, 4'19 and 5'20), no two of which are in the same plane and which are not all parallel to any one plane. The three given straight lines are all members of one family or regulus; the successive position of the line 3' 12 generate the other family (such as 4' 13, 5' 14, 6' 15, etc.).

2. By the rotation of a variable hyperbola about its conjugate axis (here the z axis), with its apex always in contact with an ellipse (the throat ellipse) which is in a plane normal to this axis. When the throat ellipse is a circle, the hyperbola does not vary and the surface is a hyperboloid of revolution of one sheet.

3. By the translation of a variable (but always similar) ellipse with its plane always normal to a straight line through its center (here the z axis) and with the extremities of its axes on two fixed hyperbolas (here the sections of the xz and yz planes) whose planes are perpendicular and whose conjugate axis is this straight line.

The equation (axes as shown): $\dfrac{x^2}{a^2} + \dfrac{y^2}{b^2} - \dfrac{z^2}{c^2} = 1$

(The equation of the asymptotic cone, shown here in section as a dotted line, is $\dfrac{x^2}{a^2} + \dfrac{y^2}{b^2} - \dfrac{z^2}{c^2} = 0$)

All sections containing the z axis are hyperbolas. The xz and yz hyperbolas are principal sections. All sections parallel to any given plane containing the z axis are hyperbolas whose asymptotes are the projections on this section plane of the parallel section of the asymptotic cone containing the z axis. Such vertical sections which cut the throat ellipse will have the axes of the hyperbolas in the xy plane; **sections which do not, will have their axes parallel to the z axis.** The vertical section which is tangent to the throat ellipse will consist of the pair of straight lines passing through the point of tangency. (The dotted lines shown on the xz and yz planes are projections of these.) Portions of the hyperboloid as cut off by two parallel planes, both parallel to the z axis, have been used for shell roofs, such as the Hippodrome at Madrid by Torroja.

All sections parallel to the xy plane are similar ellipses.

All other sections are conics, including circles, ellipses, parabolas and hyperbolas. Circular sections are shown on Sheet 38. The contour edge of the "inside" will be an ellipse, of the "outside" a hyperbola.

The nature of such curves can be determined for each case by a simple test (see diagram). Given a curve such as ACB. Draw the chord AB and the tangents AO and BO. Find the midpoint M of AB. Draw OM, cutting the curve at C. If C lies at the midpoint of OM (such as C_2) the curve is a parabola; if C is closer to M (such as C_1) it is an ellipse; if closer to O (such as C_3) a hyperbola.

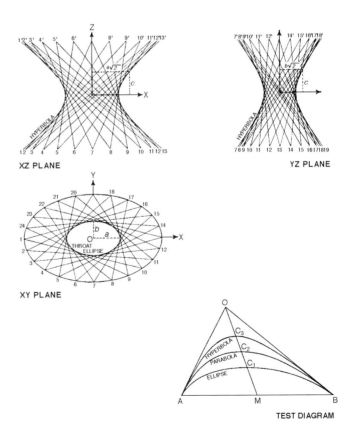

XZ PLANE

YZ PLANE

XY PLANE

TEST DIAGRAM

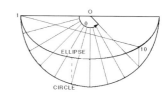

As in the case of the hyperbolic paraboloid, two straight lines, and only two, one from each family, pass through every point on the surface. These two define the tangent plane at that point.

The hyperboloid of one sheet is not a minimal surface. The minimal surface connecting two circular sections (corresponding to the top and bottom ellipses shown in drawing of the hyperboloid) is a catenoid; the edges which are hyperbolas for the hyperboloid are catenaries for the catenoid.

To Draw:

Given the two principal hyperbolas, draw them on the xz and yz planes. Draw the plan, showing the upper (and lower) and throat ellipses. In plan, from a point (such as 1') on the upper ellipse, draw the two tangents to the throat ellipse. These are the plan projections of the two straight lines, one from each family, passing through point 1'.

To find the angular distance (in plan) between this point 1' and the two points where the straight lines touch the lower

ellipse (here numbered 10 and 16) we use the eccentric angle of points on the ellipse. See diagram, where θ is the eccentric angle, in this case 135°. Dividing this into a convenient number of parts, here 9, we find the corresponding points on the ellipse whose eccentric angles all have a constant difference, (here 15°). It is then easy to draw the rulings on the surface, in elevation or projection.

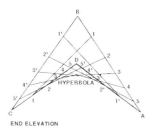

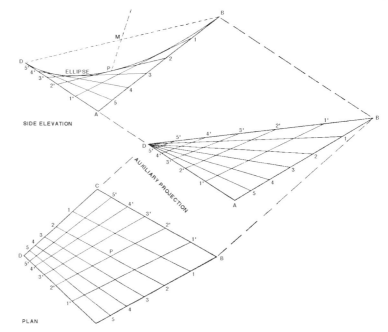

The hyperboloid of one sheet as a warped quadrilateral

Given the quadrilateral in space ABCD, shown in plan, side and end elevations, to draw a hyperboloid of one sheet passing through these four lines and one point P. P has been chosen here on the plane of symmetry passing through BD and the midpoint of AC and also on a line between this midpoint and the midpoint M of BD, closer to M.

Draw the auxiliary projection which makes DC appear as a point, locate P and draw DP extended to intersect AB at 2. Project this point 2 back onto side elevation and plan. Draw 2'P 2' symmetrically on the plan, project the points 2' back onto the side elevation and onto the auxiliary projection. (If this is done correctly, the line 2' P 2 on the side elevation will be found to be parallel to BD).

On the auxiliary projection we now have three skew lines (CD, 2'P 2' and AB) of one family (N') and line AD and CB of the other family (N). To find other lines of N family, draw rays through D on the auxiliary projection to intersect lines 2'2' and AB at various points. Project these points back onto the side elevation and plan. The rulings on the surface can now be drawn and the end elevation completed.

The contour edge DPB in elevation must here be an ellipse, while the contour in end elevation is a hyperbola. Note that if P were chosen as closer to the midpoint of AC than to M, **the contour edge DPB of the**

side elevation would become a hyperbola and the contour edge of the end variation would become an ellipse.

The warped quadrilateral as a hyperbolic paraboloid

If P is chosen at the midpoint between the midpoint of AC and M, the surface would be a hyperbolic paraboloid. This would be evident on the auxiliary projection, where all the lines of the N' family

(5'5, 4'4', etc.) would be found to be parallel (satisfying one condition for the hyperbolic paraboloid). Also the points in plan would be found to be evenly spaced along each side. In this case the Z axis of the hyperbolic paraboloid would be parallel to the line PM; the xy plane can be found from the rulings which would appear normal to the line PM in side elevation.

SUMMARY OF SYSTEMS OF DOUBLE RULINGS

Given, in Space;	Two Families of Rulings Will Generate;
Two Parabolas or three Straight lines, non-intersecting but parallel to one plane	a Hyperbolic Paraboloid
Two Circles or two Ellipses or one Hyperbola and one Ellipse or three general Straight Lines	a Hyperboloid of One Sheet
Two Hyperbolas or one Hyperbola and one Parabola or two Straight Lines, non-intersecting or a general Quadrilateral	a Hyperbolic Paraboloid or a Hyperboloid of One Sheet

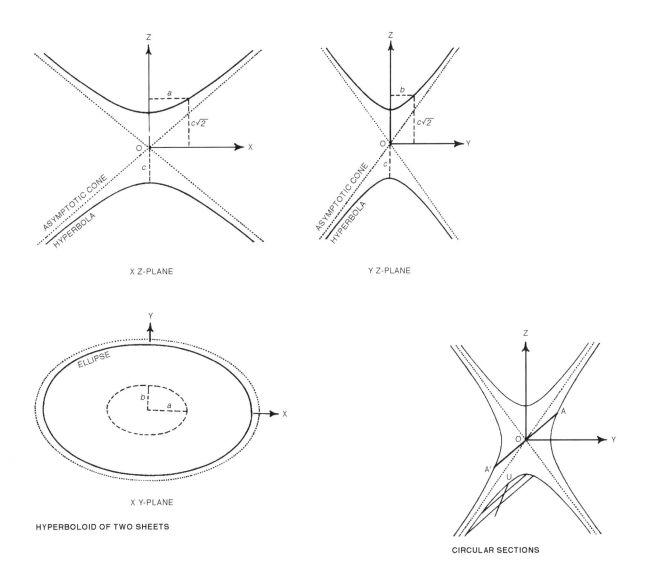

X Z-PLANE

Y Z-PLANE

X Y-PLANE

HYPERBOLOID OF TWO SHEETS

CIRCULAR SECTIONS

One of the nine quadric surfaces, the hyperboloid of two sheets (or two nappes) is shown here in orthogonal projections. It consists of two cup-shaped surfaces facing each other across the xy plane, each extending into infinity on its own side. The curvature is always positive and there are no straight lines on the surface.

The equation: $\dfrac{z^2}{c^2} - \dfrac{x^2}{a^2} - \dfrac{y^2}{b^2} = 1$

All sections parallel to the xy plane are similar ellipses (except for the region between $z = c$ and $z = -c$). All sections parallel to any given plane containing the z axis are hyperbolas whose asymptotes are the projection on this section plane of the parallel section of the asymptotic cone containing the z axis. All other sections are also conics, in general of the same type as corresponding sections of the asymptotic cone.

Circular Sections of the Elliptic Cone and of the Hyperboloids of One and Two Sheets

As for the ellipsoid and the elliptic paraboloid, there exist circular sections of these three surfaces. (See sheet 34 on the ellipsoid for more discussion.)

To find the circular sections, we make use of the hyperboloid of one sheet. The equations of the three surfaces are as given above in describing each type.

Draw the section by the yz plane, showing all three surfaces. The section of the asymptotic cone is drawn as a dotted line, the other two by solid lines. Note that the z axis is the axis of the cone and of the hyperboloid of two sheets, but is the conjugate axis of the hyperbola which is the section of the hyperboloid of one sheet.

From O swing an arc of length equal to a, intersecting the hyperboloid of one sheet at A and A'. This line is in the plane of a circular section of the hyperboloid of one sheet. All planes parallel to this will cut all three surfaces in circles. There is also a symmetrical system of planes making the same angle with the xy plane, but tilted from upper left to lower right.

There are no umbilics on the cone or the hyperboloid of one sheet.

To find the umbilics on the hyperboloid of two sheets, draw on the yz section any two chords parallel to the plane of circular sections (as shown), to find their midpoints, join them by a line which cuts the hyperbola at U. The other three umbilics are symmetrically arranged about O.

In order to calculate in detail any spherical dome or any astronomical information, such as sun angles and insolation, we must use the formulas of spherical trigonometry.

SPHERICAL TRIANGLE

In the diagram, ABC is a spherical triangle. The letters A, B, and C refer to the *angles* at the vertices (measured in degrees or radians). Angle A, for example, is the angle between the tangents to the sides b and c at the vertex. Angle A is also the dihedral angle between the plane containing the side b and the center O and the plane containing the side c and the center O. The letters a, b, and c refer to the three *sides* and are measured in degrees or radians. Each side is a portion or arc of a great circle, and its length is sometimes referred to as the central angle. The side b, for example, is the angle AOC. Both OA and OC are radii of the sphere.

Unlike plane triangles, the *sum of the angles* is not the same for all spherical triangles. It is always greater than 180° and less than 540°:

$$180° \text{ (or } \pi) < \Sigma (A + B + C) < 540° (3\pi)$$

The amount by which the sum of the angles **exceeds 180°** (or π) is called the *spherical excess*:

$$E = \Sigma (A + B + C) - 180° \text{ (or } \pi)$$

E can be used to find the area of a spherical triangle:

$$\frac{\text{Area of spherical triangle}}{\text{Area of sphere } [4\pi P^2]} = \frac{E°}{720°}$$
$$= \frac{E \text{ (in radians)}}{4\pi}$$

Thus,

Area of spherical triangle $= E_{\text{(radians)}} R^2$

A *steradian* is the solid angle subtended by the portion of a sphere whose area $= R^2$. (The area of a spherical polygon can be found in the same manner. If N is the number of sides of the polygon, the spherical excess

$$E° = \Sigma (A + B + C + D \ldots + X_N)$$
$$- (N-2) 180°$$

E° can be substituted in the formula given above for the spherical triangle.) The sum of the sides is always less than 360°:

$$\Sigma (a + b + c) < 360° \text{ (or } 2\pi)$$

The sides and the angles are related by the following formulas:

Law of cosines:

cos a = cos b cos c + sin b sin c cos A
cos b = cos a cos c + sin a sin c cos B
cos c = cos a cos b + sin a sin b cos C
cos A = - cos B cos C + sin B sin C cos a
cos B = - cos A cos C + sin A sin C cos b
cos C = - cos A cos B + sin A sin B cos c

Law of sines:

$$\frac{\sin A}{\sin a} = \frac{\sin B}{\sin b} = \frac{\sin C}{\sin c}$$

Haversine formula:

hav a = hav (b - c) + sin b sin c hav A
hav b = hav (a - c) + sin a sin c hav B
hav c = hav (a - b) + sin a sin b hav C

The haversine of any angle θ is defined as

$$\text{hav } \theta = \frac{1 - \cos \theta}{2}$$

Haversine is an abbreviation for half versed sine.

Half-angle formula:

$$\tan \frac{A}{2} = \frac{f}{\sin (s - a)}$$
$$\tan \frac{B}{2} = \frac{f}{\sin (s - b)}$$
$$\tan \frac{C}{2} = \frac{f}{\sin (s - c)}$$

in which

$$s = \frac{a + b + c}{2}$$

and

$$f = \sqrt{\frac{\sin (s - a) \sin (s - b) \sin (s - c)}{\sin s}}$$

Half-side formula:

$$\tan \frac{a}{2} = F \cos (S - A)$$
$$\tan \frac{b}{2} = F \cos (S - B)$$
$$\tan \frac{c}{2} = F \cos (S - C)$$

in which

$$S = \frac{A + B + C}{2}$$

and

$$F = \sqrt{\frac{- \cos S}{\cos (S - A) \cos (S - B) \cos (S - C)}}$$

The significance of f and F in the half-angle and half-side formulas is found in the inscribed and circumscribed circles of the spherical triangle: the tangent of the radius of the inscribed circle $= f$; the tangent of the radius of the circumscribed circle $= F$. These radii are arcs of great circles and are measured from their respective centers, which are the poles of the corresponding circles. The inscribed and circumscribed circles are always little circles.

SPHERICAL RIGHT TRIANGLE

If one (or more) of the angles of a spherical triangle is a right angle, the triangle is a spherical right triangle. The diagram shows two spherical right triangles: ABC and $a_2 b_2 c_2$, with C equal to a right angle.

SHERICAL TRIANGLE

SPHERICAL RIGHT TRIANGLE

The formulas can be simplified as follows:

sin a = sin A sin c
sin b = sin B sin c
sin a = cot B tan b
sin b = cot A tan a
cos c = cos a cos b
cos c = cot A cot B
cos A = sin B cos a
cos B = sin A cos b
cos A = tan b cot c
cos B = tan a cot c

If B is also a right angle, then b and c are both right angles and A = a. Conversely, if b = c = 90°, then B = C = 90° and A = a; if A = B = C = 90°, then a = b = c = 90°, and conversely.

REFERENCES FOR COMPLETE SERIES

1. *Practical Geometry* by David Allen Low, Longmans Green, 1912.

2. *Mechanical Engineers' Handbook* by Lionel S. Marks — section "Mathematics" by E. V. Huntington (McGraw Hill, 1941).

3. *The Mathematics of Engineering* by Ralph E. Root (Bailliere, Tindall and Cox, 1927).

4. *Elements of the Differential and Integral Calculus* by Granville, Smith and Longley (Ginn 1941).

5. *Geometry and the Imagination* by D. Hilbert and S. Cohn-Vossen (Chelsea, 1952).

6. *Mathematical Models* by H. Martyn Cundy and A. R. Rollett (Oxford 1951).

7. *The Geometry of Repeating Design* by A. Day Bradley (Columbia, 1933).

8. *Elementary Crystallography* by M. J. Buerger (Wiley, 1956).

9. *Engineering Graphics* by John T. Rule and Earle F. Watts (McGraw-Hill, 1951).

10. *Technical Descriptive Geometry* by B. Leighton Williams (McGraw-Hill, 1957).

11. *What is Mathematics?* by Richard Courant and Herbert Robbins (Oxford, 1941).

12. *Solid Analytical Geometry and Determinants* by Arnold Dresden (Wiley, 1930).

By STERLING M. PALM, Architect

The handling of curved and double curved surfaces has long been commonplace in the shipbuilding, automotive and airplane industries. Although such surfaces have not appeared so frequently in architectural design, they are becoming more and more apparent in contemporary design. It is not the intent of the present discussion to go into the method of such surface delineation, but a brief statement of the basic principle provides a good starting point.

A curved surface, to be a smooth surface, without humps or depressions, must be so formed that a section through the surface will be projected as a "smooth" regular curve in that plane. A curve to be "smooth" must be such that the rate of curvature, or radius, at any point does not change too rapidly with respect to the rate of curvature at any adjacent point. All conics meet this requirement and, in general, any curve that is pleasing to the eye will usually be found to be a "conic" of some type, or a combination of conics. Thus a review of the characteristics of the conics is essential to the study of surfaces.

The study of these curves also provides a valuable tool for the delineation of curves of any type and has a number of practical applications in architectural or engineering work.

A "conic" may be defined as any curve formed by the intersection of a plane with a right circular cone. Referring to Fig. 1, it is evident that an infinite variety of curves is possible, dependent on the slope of the sides of the cone, the slope of the cutting plane, and the relation between the cutting plane and the axis of the cone.

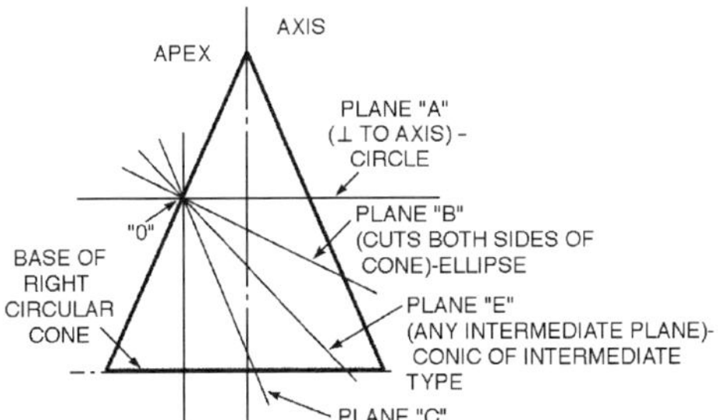

All of the conics described by planes A to D in Fig. 1 are familiar curves, susceptible of simple mathematical description and analysis.

Although the mathematics of the conics forms an interesting study, no space will be devoted to it here. We are primarily interested in an understanding of the conditions differentiating one curve from another, and in a practical application of the principles involved. Fortunately these principles are extremely simple and entirely general in nature. To anyone familiar with the procedure it should no longer be necessary to refer to a handbook to refresh one's memory as to the method of constructing a parabola or hyperbola; for these, together with an ellipse or even a circle, can all be constructed by the same simple process.

In the latter part of this discussion I will, for the benefit of those interested, develop a proof of the method about to be described. However, for those who just wish something for ready reference, it will only be necessary to follow the procedure outlined in Figs. 3 to 7 inclusive. Fig. 2 is introductory, but shows clearly the entire procedure necessary for the determination of any one point on the curve, developed to greater length in Fig. 3.

It can be shown that every conic or second-degree curve can be determined, given any one of the following five sets of conditions:

Case I. One point and two point-slopes (direction of tangent).

Case II. Three points and one point-slope.

Case III. Five points.

Case IV. Two points and a point-slope-curvature.

Case V. A point-slope and a point-slope-curvature.

Cases IV and V will not be discussed as their treatment would require more space than warranted. Fig. 5 illustrates the method of determining a sixth point on a conic given five points (Case III). In practice it generally will be found that one or two tangents are known, together with one or two points of tangency and with an additional point or points on the curve available, so that Cases I and II above will

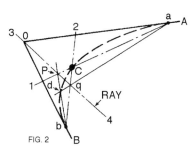

FIG. 2

be found to be those most generally useful. These cases are illustrated in Figs. 3 and 4.

Referring to Fig. 2, we have two tangents, OA and OB, with two points of tangency, a and b. Point a on the tangent OA and point b on the tangent OB constitute two point-slopes. These are, in themselves, insufficient to determine a curve. If, however, we are given an additional point, such as point c, it will be seen that we have the previously listed first set of conditions, namely, "one point and two point-slopes."

In order to find any other point on the curve the procedure is as follows: Draw a line through a and c prolonged to intersect OB at 1, and a line through b and c prolonged to intersect OA at 2. Now through O draw any line, 3 4, known as a "ray," or in later reference, a "Pascal line." Designate as p the intersection of this ray with line a–1 and as q the intersection of the ray with line b–2. Draw lines through a and q and through b and p. These lines extended will intersect in a point, d, which is the point sought lying on the curve. Additional points on the curve are found by repeating the above process, after which the points are connected with a smooth curve by means of a french curve, ship curve or spline.

Fig. 3 illustrates merely an expansion of the above principle so as to determine a number of points on the curve. Fig. 4 illustrates the application of the method by the second set of conditions, namely three points (P, 4 and B) and one point-slope (point of tangency T on the tangent X).

It will at times be found necessary to draw a tangent to a given curve at a given point. Figs. 6 and 7 illustrate the application of the foregoing principle, in reverse, in determining such tangents.

AXIS

APEX

PLANE "A"
(⊥ TO AXIS) –
CIRCLE

PLANE "B"
(CUTS BOTH SIDES OF
CONE)-ELLIPSE

"O"

BASE OF
RIGHT
CIRCULAR
CONE

PLANE "E"
(ANY INTERMEDIATE PLANE)-
CONIC OF INTERMEDIATE
TYPE

PLANE "C"
(PARALLEL TO ELEMENT OF CONE)-
PARABOLA

PLANE "0" (PARALLEL TO AXIS)-
HYPERBOLA

FIG. 1

Fig 3 TO CONSTRUCT A SECOND-DEGREE CURVE THROUGH A CONTROL POINT D AND TANGENT TO LINES OA AND OB AT POINTS A AND B:

1. Draw line BE through D and line AF through D
2. Divide DF into any number of spaces, e.g. four. This gives points G_1, G_2, and G_3.
3. Draw BG_1, BG_2, and BG_3.
4. Draw OG_1, OG_2, and OG_3, intersecting BE at H_1, H_2, and H_3.
5. From A, draw AH_1, AH_2, and AH_3, extended to intersect BG_1, BG_2, and BG_3, respectively, at points P_1, P_2, and P_3, which are points on required curve.
6. Additional points P_4, P_5, and P_6 are found likewise.
7. Curve fitted to these points is the required curve.

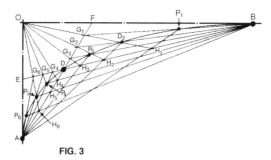

FIG. 3

Fig 4 TO CONSTRUCT A SECOND-DEGREE CURVE TANGENT TO LINE XY AT POINT T, GIVEN THREE OTHER POINTS ON THE CURVE, P, A, AND B:

1. Draw lines BT and PA extended to intersect at point 1.
2. Draw lines PB and TA intersecting at point 2
3. Draw a line through points 1 and 2, extending to intersect tangent XY at point O
4. Draw line OP, which will be tangent to the required curve.
5. Having two tangents, OT and OP, two points of tangency, T and P, and a control point, A or B (whichever is more convenient), proceed as in Fig. 3 to find additional points on the curve

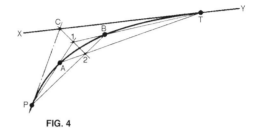

FIG. 4

Fig 5 TO FIND A SIXTH POINT WHEN FIVE POINTS (1 2 3 4 AND 5) ARE GIVEN

1. Draw lines 1–3 and 2–4, calling intersection point o
2. Draw lines 2–5 and 1–5
3. Draw any "ray" AB, through point o, cutting line 2–5 at p and line 1–5 at q
4. Draw lines through 3 and p and through 4 and q, intersecting at point 6, which will be an additional point on the curve
5. Repeat procedure with different rays to find other points.

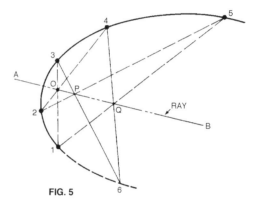

FIG. 5

Fig 6 TO CONSTRUCT A TANGENT:

(Given second-degree curve OB, tangent to CO and CB at points O and B, respectively, tangent to be constructed at any point, P.)

1. Select any two points, M and N, on curve OB.
2. Draw PN and BM, intersecting at point D.
3. Draw PS and BN extended to intersect PS at point E.
4. Draw a line through intersections D and E, extending it to intersect tangent BC at point R
5. Draw a line through P and R, which will be required tangent.

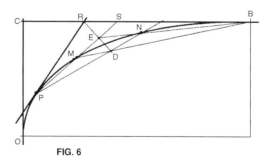

FIG. 6

Fig 7. TO CONSTRUCT A TANGENT:

(Given, second-degree curve HJ; tangents to be constructed at any two points, P and T.)

1. Select any three points, A, B, and C, located conveniently between points P and T.
2. From P, draw lines PA, PB, and PC.
3. From point T, draw TA, TB, and TC.
4. Extend PA and TC to intersect at E.
5. Extend TB to intersect PE at G.
6. Call intersection of lines TA and PC, point D, and intersection of lines TA and PB, point F.
7. Draw lines DE and FG, extended to intersect at R.
8. Lines RP and RT are required tangents at points P and T.

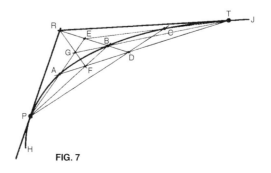

FIG. 7

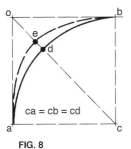

FIG. 8

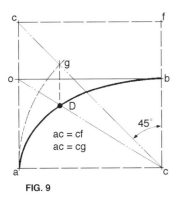

FIG. 9

Referring again to Fig. 2, it should be noted that the point *c*, which was selected somewhat at random in this case, is of particular importance, in that, with two point-slopes *oa* and *ob* given, the character of the curve will vary considerably depending on the location of the point *c*, known as the "control" or "shoulder" point. The extent to which the control or shoulder point influences the shape of the conic is illustrated in Fig. 8, in which, with two equal tangents, *ob* = *oa*, the control point *d* is so taken that *cd* = *cb* = *ca*. The resulting curve in this case will be, as expected, an arc of a circle.

If point *e* were to be used as a control point, the resulting curve would be a parabola or other conic, depending on the exact location of point *e*.

In Fig. 9, the control point *D* is determined by projecting down to diagonal *oc* from the intersection of circular arc *ag* with diagonal *ec*. With *D* as a control point, tangents *ob* and *oa* and points of tangency *b* and *a*, a quarter ellipse would be anticipated.

Following the procedure previously outlined and using the conditions stated, it will be found that an accurate ellipse will result.

A parabola, hyperbola or other conic will be determined similarly when there is given, in addition to the point-slopes, a control point which is known to lie on the curve in question. Mathematically, the slope of the tangents can be determined once the equation of the parabola or hyperbola is known. In a great number of cases however the tangents will be given, so that it will be possible to construct these curves without recourse to mathematics.

PRACTICAL APPLICATIONS

There are many practical applications of the foregoing principles, among which might be included the following examples. In all, it should be noted that the process consists of determining two points of tangency on their respective tangents (*i.e.*, two point-slopes) together with a control point. Following this, the method outlined in Figs. 2 and 3 is followed to determine points along the curve.

Possibly one of the most useful applications consists of transforming a curve, carefully determined by freehand methods, into a definite geometric figure which can be duplicated, enlarged or otherwise utilized. Such a curve thus becomes definitely tied down. Fig. 10 might represent a profile, a section of a surface or possibly a roadway.

The usual method of duplicating this curve would be to determine, by trial, a series of radii describing sections of the curve, or possibly a system of offsets from a traverse line might be established. Both of these methods or others of a similar nature are tedious, inaccurate, and crude as compared to the simple and direct method of conics. This principle, as applied to the case at hand, would consist of splitting the curve up into convenient sections, such as *ab*, *bc* and *cd* of Fig. 10. Tangents would then be determined at points *a*, *b*,

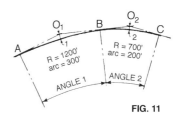

FIG. 11

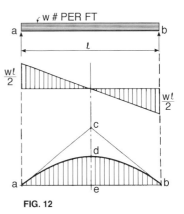

FIG. 12

c and *d* and control points in each section, such as k_1, k_2, and k_3. The curve is now definitely tied down and can be reproduced exactly. Some points on the curve should be checked by the method described in Fig. 3, and if discrepancies appear it will undoubtedly be apparent that the freehand curve was not smooth at the point in question.

A similar application is illustrated in Fig. 11, which represents a street line consisting of two circular arcs *AB* and *BC* of radii such that the centers are inaccessible or off the drawing. The arc lengths being given, the central angles, *1* and *2*, can easily be determined and consequently the tangents for both sections can be plotted. The distances $O_1 1$ and $O_2 2$ may then be computed, being in each case equal to *R* times exsec of half the angle. We would then have established for each section the two tangents and control point, after which points on the curve would be determined as previously described.

Fig. 12 illustrates the application of the principle to the construction of a moment diagram, such as might be required for use in the design of a plate girder. The bending moment curve for the portion of a beam subject to uniform loading can be described as a portion of a parabola. Inasmuch as the shear diagram gives the slope of the parabola representing the moment diagram at any point along the span, the slope at the two supports *a* and *b* are each equal to

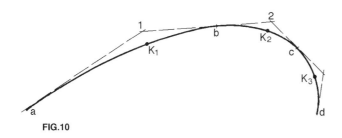

FIG.10

one-half of wl. The ordinate ce is thus equal to wl^2 divided by 4, while the ordinate de is half of this or wl^2 divided by 8. With w and l given, it is necessary only to plot, at some convenient scale, the two tangents ac and bc and the ordinate de locating the control point d, after which additional points on the curve are determined, as before. This method will, in a great number of cases, be found considerably simpler than the usual method of determining points by figuring moments at various points along the span.

Always bearing in mind that the two tangents and a control point fix definitely the shape of the curve, the principle outlined can be put to use in solving problems such as the intersection of surfaces of all types, vaulting and vault ribs, graphs and diagrams, or in fact any problem involving curves or curved surfaces. The examples just given have all fallen under the previously cited Case I, involving two tangents and a control point. It will be found in practice that these conditions are usually present or can be established. Where this is not possible it will only then be necessary to fall back upon one of the other applications, Cases II and III as illustrated in Figs. 4 and 5 respectively.

BASIC THEORY

It will possibly be of interest to some readers to follow the development of the relationship upon which the foregoing is based. This relationship, known as the "Pascal Theorem," is diagrammed in Fig. 13, and may be stated as follows: "If the extremities of any hexagram inscribed in a conic are numbered in consecutive order 1 to 6 as shown in the sketch, the intersection of the opposite pairs of sides *1–3* and *2–4*, *4–6* and *1–5*, and intersection of the diagonals *2–5* and *3–6* will always lie in a straight line, known as a 'Pascal line'." Thus the intersections o, p and q lie on a "Pascal line" ab.

A "hexagram" may be briefly described as a six-pointed star, and in Fig. 13 is clearly visible as such when the sides *3–5* and *2–6* (dotted) are drawn. The term "hexagram" is, however, possible of much broader application: the figure need not be regular in shape, nor is the curve in which the hexagram is inscribed limited, except in one respect — it must be a conic.

In Fig. 14, the same relationship is again indicated, the nomenclature of Fig. 13 being retained; the hexagram in this case being irregular in form and inscribed in an ellipse. In both Figs. 13 and 14, lines *1–3* and *2–4* intersect at o, lines *1–5* and *4–6* intersect at q and lines *2–5* and *3–6* intersect at p. From the "Pascal theorem" above stated, points o, p and q will always lie in a straight line known as a Pascal line.

Earlier in this article we stated as Case III the condition that five points on a conic curve were sufficient to determine the curve, or stated otherwise: five points on a conic are sufficient to establish a sixth point, also on the conic. A comparison of Fig. 14 with Fig. 5 will show that the procedure outlined in Fig. 5 is derived directly from the relationship shown in Fig. 14, the only difference being that in Fig. 5, with five points given, the Pascal line passed through the point o at random determines the two other intersection points p and q, which immediately determine the location of the sixth point as shown.

It will be observed that as the position of the fifth point varies the sixth will also vary, but the ensuing curve will be the same. Referring again to Fig. 5 it will be noticed that if point *3* is moved, but always remains between points *2* and *4*, the intersection o will lie on the inside of the curve. If point *3* is moved, however, until it lies between points *1* and *2* the intersection of lines *2–4* and *1–3* will lie outside the curve. If now we assume that point *2* is rotated clockwise until it coincides with point *4*, and point *3* is rotated counterclockwise until it coincides with point *1*, indicating the combined points *2–4* and *1–3*, as in Fig. 15, it will be seen that the lines joining points *1* and *3* and points *2* and *4* must be tangents to the curve at the combined points *1–3* and *2–4* respectively. As before, the intersection of these two lines will be indicated as point o.

It was previously indicated that the fifth point was not restricted as to position as long as it remained on the conic. Assume point *5*, in Fig. 15, to be intermediate between the combined points *1–3* and *2–4*. With this arrangement we would now have established the first set of conditions mentioned earlier: "One point and two point-slopes."

Proceeding as in Fig. 5, we draw

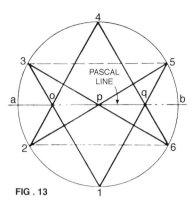

FIG . 13

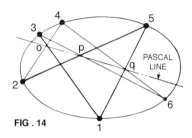

FIG . 14

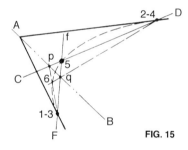

FIG. 15

lines CD through points *2* and *5* and EF through points *1* and *5*. If we then pass a Pascal line AB at random through point A and call the intersection of this line with line CD (or *2–5*) the point p as before, and also the intersection with line EF (or *1–5*) the point q, we will then have retained the same relationship of lines and points in both cases. Continuing as in Fig. 5, we will draw lines through points *3* and p and through *4* and q intersecting at point *6*, which is the point sought. If we now compare Fig. 15 with Fig. 2, it will be seen that the procedure is the same as previously outlined.

Also, since the procedure followed in Figs. 5 and 15 was identical it is apparent that the method is general as to Cases I and III. A study of Fig. 4 will show that the procedure in Case II is likewise similar.

Summary: Modular coordination originated in the United States during the 1920s and 1930s and provided an all-inclusive basis to "pre-coordinate" dimensions of structural components, building materials, and installed equipment, founded on standard grids. It achieves dimensional compatibility between building dimensions, spans, or spaces and the sizes of components and equipment, and offers an industry-wide system of coordinated sizes and methods for drafting, construction documents, and a discipline for design and construction clarity.

Key words: Building systems, dimensional tolerances, drafting, grid, modular coordination, unit dimension.

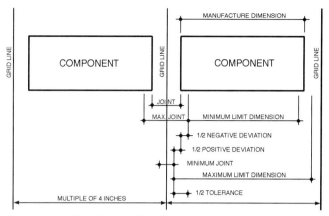

Fig. 1. Basis for sizing a component

Modular Coordination

Modular coordination originated in the United States during the 1920s and 1930s, widely credited to the pioneering work of the American industrialist Albert Farwell Bemis (1870-1936), who outlined principles for dimensional coordination based on a cubical modular of design using a 4-inch module as fundamental "unit 1." The concept provided a basis to "pre-coordinate" the dimensions of structural components, building materials, and installed equipment, founded on "modular lines" and standard grids with 4-inch intervals to reference building plans and details. Bemis's ideas also gave impetus to the notion of prefabrication, which removes assembly from the building site to the factory where better quality control and volume production became possible.

In 1974, responsibility for the development of standards on dimensional coordination was undertaken by the American Society for Testing and Materials (ASTM) to continue the work in both U.S. customary (foot-inch) units and metric (SI) units. ANSI/ASTM "Standard for Dimensional Coordination of Rectilinear Building Parts and Systems" proposed assigning the symbol U for "unit dimension" to the 100-mm module in metric units and the 4-inch module in customary units. While this simplifies "modular" choices, their actual dimensions differ in metric and nonmetric units, due to the 1.6 percent difference between 4 inches [101.6 mm] and 100 mm. Examples that follow have been chosen to reflect traditional U.S. practices.

Objectives of Modular Coordination

The aim of modular coordination is to achieve dimensional compatibility between building dimensions, spans, or spaces and the sizes of components and equipment, by using modular dimensions. This reduces the need for "special" sizes, minimizes field cutting, and simplifies drafting and in cost- and quantities estimating.

The basis of the modular dimensioning and sizing is to indicate dimensions from joint-center line to joint-center line, using multiples of the standard module of 4 inches (or 100 mm). Therefore, the modular size of a component is an "ideal size" which takes into account half a joint width all round the actual size, which is smaller. The joint "width"

is computed to also allow for manufacturing deviations and installation clearances so that there is neither a need for cutting materials on site nor for excessive clearances to be filled or covered over.

Fig. 1 (above) shows the basic sizing of a component and the concepts of minimum and maximum acceptable joint width to accommodate deviations in manufacturing. Different components have different joint width requirements, but for all modular products, one-half the minimum joint width at any change of material is intended to allow adequate clearances for installation. The joint-center line to joint-center line principle is illustrated for a modular masonry unit in Fig. 2, also indicating how the actual size of a modular component is determined—in this case the joint width is 3/8 inches. The method of combining modular components is illustrated in Fig. 3, showing a door frame assembly located within different materials. The outside dimensions of the frame assembly are important, not the size of the door itself. This dimensioning method applies to all modular components, assemblies of components, building parts (elements or systems), and dimensions of building spaces.

Coordinating planes and lines

Modular coordination uses a three-dimensional (orthogonal) "grid" in which the lines are one module apart, as indicated in Fig. 4. The modular grid is a three-dimensional system of horizontal and vertical reference planes, one module apart.

Various conventions have been used to designate the coordinates, so that any point on the grid can be referenced in relation to a datum, or zero datum point. A numerical shorthand, adopted by ANSI, for the location of reference planes, lines, and points in relation to a zero datum point is shown in Fig. 5. All coordinate planes parallel to a datum plane are identified by the same number following the decimal point as that which identifies the datum plane in the particular direction. That is, all coordinate planes parallel to 0.1 are identified by the suffix 0.1; planes parallel to 0.2 by suffix .2; and planes parallel to 0.3 by the suffix 0.3. The distance from the datum plane, in multiples of the basic module, is indicated by the number in front of the decimal

Authors: Hans J. Milton, FRAIA and Byron Bloomfield, AIA

References: ANSI A62.8-1971. 1971. *American Standard Numerical Designation of Modular Grid Coordinates.* New York: American National Standards Institute.

ANSI/ASTM E-577-85 (Reapproved 1994). *Standard Guide for Dimensional Coordination of Rectilinear Building Parts and Systems.* Philadelphia, PA: American Society for Testing and Materials.

Bemis, Albert F. and John Burchard. 1936. "The Evolving House." *Vol. III: Rational Design.* Cambridge, MA: The Technology Press.

National Bureau of Standards. 1980. NBS Special Publication 595. *International and National Standard on Dimensional Coordination, Modular Coordination, Tolerances and Joints in Building .* Washington, DC: U.S. Superintendent of Documents.

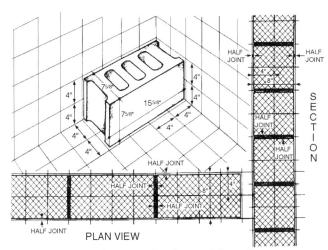

Fig. 2. Example of a modular unit

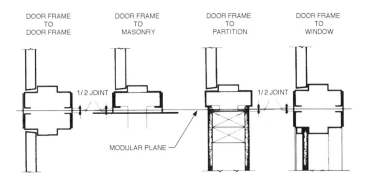

Fig. 3. Combining modular components

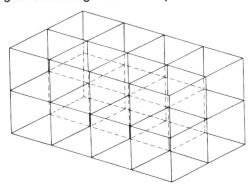

Fig. 4. The modular space grid

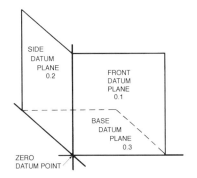

Fig. 5 Position of the coordinate datum planes and their numerical designation

point. For example, coordinate plane 2.1 is parallel to datum plane 0.1 at a distance of two basic modules. The designation 24.2 indicates a coordinate parallel to datum coordinate 0.2 at a distance of 24 basic modules. Suffix numbers (positive numbers) are used as follows:

- In the 0.1 series, from the front datum plane toward the back.
- In the 0.2 series, from the side datum plane on the left toward the right.
- In the 0.3 series, from the base datum plane upward.

For any locations in opposite directions from the zero datum, negative suffix numbers are used. However, with an appropriate choice of zero datum point, this would be rare. A graphic representation of the coordinate numbering system is shown in Fig. 6.

The referencing of building parts and components by coordinates is useful in plan layout, detailing, and in computer applications. When noting the position of a component, its relation to the 0.1 coordinate series is noted first, the 0.2 series next, and the 0.3 series last. When all three dimensions are specified, the coordinate series need not be shown, since the sequence does so automatically. Thus, a notation 34-38, 8-16, and 21-24 indicates that a component lies between 34.1 and 38. 1, between 8.2 and 16.2, and between 21.3 and 24.3. The notation 34/8/21 (to designate the coordinate datum point) and the notation 4M/8M/3M (to designate component size) would have conveyed the same information. The datum point for a component is established at its lower left-front corner as placed in the building. In the change to metric modular dimensions, this method has the advantage that the numerical designations can be converted directly to millimeters by adding two zeros. For example, a datum point 34/8/21 is located 3400 mm toward the back of the zero datum.

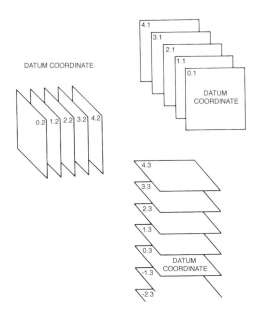

Fig. 6. Numerical designation of coordinates

Application to Building Systems

Coordination in the horizontal plane of a building plan can be related to the surfaces of structural elements, called boundary lines, or to the center lines of structural elements, called axial lines. The establishment of modular dimensioning reduces the variety of multiples of the basic module used in a project. For large spans or spaces, a larger module called the "systems module" (SM) been established as equal to 60 modules (1 SM = 60M = 20 feet in customary units, and l SM = 60M = 6000 mm in metric units). Preferred coordinating dimensions for the horizontal plane and building components are therefore 30M, 20M, 15M, 12M, lOM, 0M, 5M, 4M, 3M, and 2M, all being subunits of 60M.

Coordination in the vertical plane of a building can be related to datum reference lines at the floor plane, ceiling plane, or roof plane. In addition, window and door head and window sill lines form an intermediate datum plane in many buildings. Fig. 7 shows the application of preferred vertical dimensions. The list of preferred dimensions in the Fig. 7 caption provides both series, with values common to both ANSI and ISO standards italicized.

Where structural or economic factors prevent adherence to coordinated dimensions, a second preference would be to select a whole multiple of the basic module. Where this is not possible, the designer handles the nonconforming dimensions as an uncoordinated zone. For example, in a single-story building without suspended ceiling, it may not be practical for the horizontal structure thickness of the roof to be a coordinated dimension. In such an instance, the choice is between a preferred dimension for the story height (A) or the ceiling height (B).

On-site Tolerances

For practical on-site layout, the accuracy in positioning elements and coordinates is dependent upon measuring instruments and practices. The range of tolerances indicated in Table 1 can be used for reference in accuracy calculations.

Modular drafting

Modular drafting techniques have been developed for use by the architectural draftsperson as well as the manufacturer. The three basic conventions of modular drafting include the grid, the arrowhead, and the dot (Fig. 8). The grids provide imaginary reference planes extending through the structure in a three-dimensional aggregate fashion, 4 inches on center in all directions. When drafting, the architect actually draws certain grid lines on large-scale drawings to provide key dimensional reference planes (or "controlling planes"), such as the location of foundation lines, floor lines, and door or window heads and jambs. A larger multiple of the 4-inch module, called a multimodule, may be used as a planning grid and shown on certain plans. The arrowhead is used for all dimensions that originate or terminate on a modular grid line. In the U.S., a solid arrow has been commonly used, while an open arrow is used in international practice. Dots are used on all dimensions that are off the grid and nonmodular.

The use of standardized drafting conventions in dimensioning all plans, elevations, and details reduces the need for fractional dimensions and corresponding errors in the addition or subtraction of dimensions involving such fractions. Construction drawings are simpler to prepare and simpler to use, resulting in savings during all subsequent phases. Also worth noting:

• If only dots were used on a drawing, it would not differ from any "premodular" architectural drawing.

• The fewer dots and the greater the number of arrowheads indicates greater simplicity of the construction and fewer joining problems. If only arrowheads were shown, the construction drawing would exemplify drafting clarity and the construction clarity and simplicity.

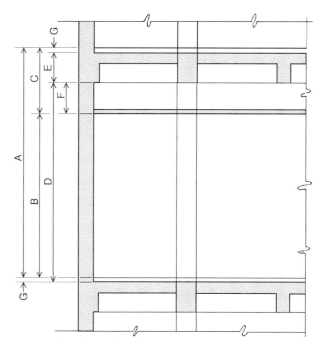

Fig. 7. Application of preferred dimensions

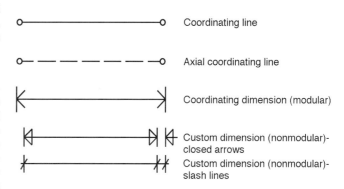

Fig. 8. Modular drafting conventions

Table 1. Range of tolerances for on-site layout of coordinates

Spacing of coordinates	Acceptable tolerance
1M to 20M	+ 3/64 in. (1 mm)
	- 0
Over 20M to 60M (1 5M)	+ 5/64 in, (2 mm)
	- 0
Over 3 SM (180M)	+ $\sqrt{\text{no. of SMs}} \times 1/8$ in. (3 mm)
	-0

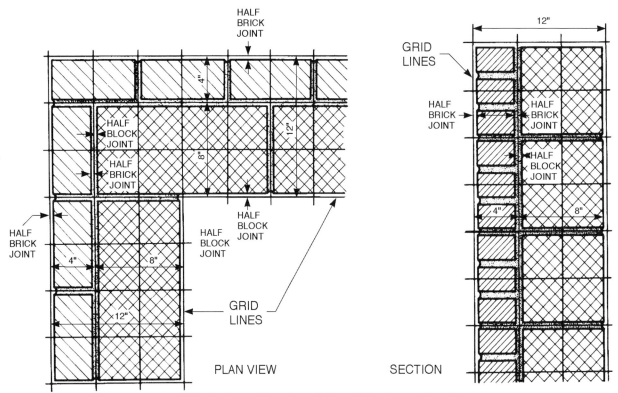

Fig. 9. Expression of modular grid in plan and section

Consider, for example, the use of modular dimensioning in the assembly of units to comprise a building element in masonry construction. Fig. 9 shows the relative positions of the masonry units to grid lines in plan and section. The actual units would not, of course, appear in the final plan, nor would the grid lines. Arrowheads identify the locations of the grid planes. The final plan expression is shown in Figs. 10 and further illustrates the use of the modular drafting conventions: By inspection, dots and arrows reveal that column center lines are not on grid planes, although the distances between columns are indeed multiples of 4 inches. Jointing conditions around the windows (Fig. 11) can be defined later, along with selection and specification of windows. All that remains is to correlate plan and detail by indicating on the plan the location of the same reference grid lines used in the large detail.

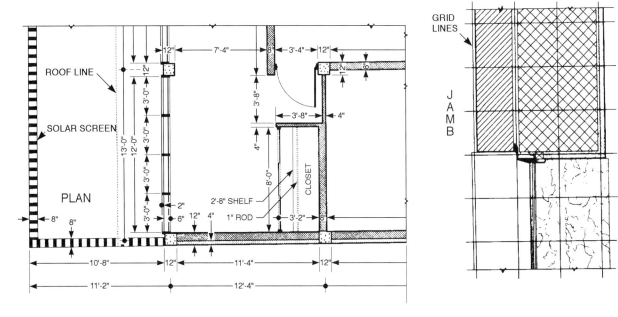

Fig. 10. Dimensioned masonry plan   **Fig. 11. Modular window detail**

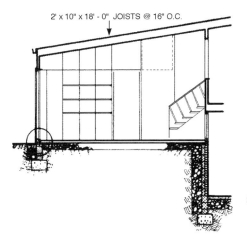

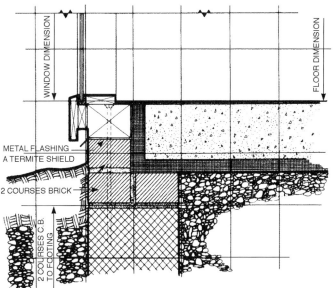

Fig. 12 shows the evolution of a large-scale detail from its relationship in cross section. To start the detail study, the intersection of floor grid plane and principal foundation grid plane is marked off. From this point, it is possible to relate, reading downward, the floor-slab thickness, insulation, gravel fill, and top of footing. From the outside foundation grid plane, reading inward, the foundation thickness and sill-width dimensions are then established. Although optional, the complete 4-inch grid is shown on the construction-drawing detail.

Fig. 12. Section and detail of frame building

The brick-veneer construction plan shown in Fig. 13 illustrates choices available in delineating modular construction. In general, wood-frame construction is most efficiently planned when the stud framing members are centered between grid lines. Then both sheathing and interior finish materials can be efficiently installed in multiples of 4 inches. In masonry veneer, the 10-inch total wall thickness requires further consideration of the best location of grid lines. Either studs or the masonry may be centered between grid lines. Construction efficiency would not necessarily be affected by either choice; the overall masonry, gypsum board, and sheathing dimensions would still remain multiples of 4 inches. However, drawings are simplified by making the outside reference planes conform to the masonry placement and using center line notations for all wood-frame interior partitions, shown in the Fig. 13 details.

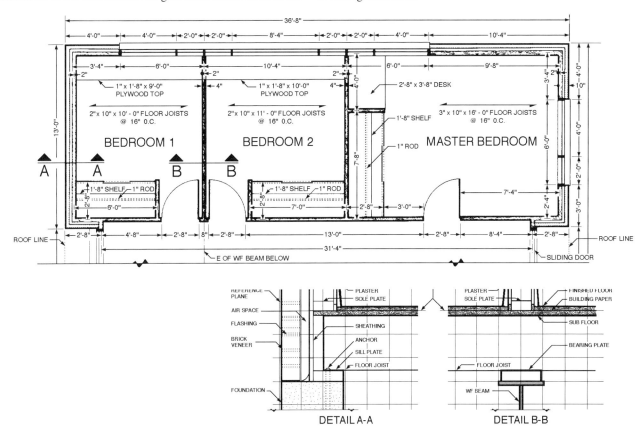

Fig. 13. Plan and details of brick-veneer construction

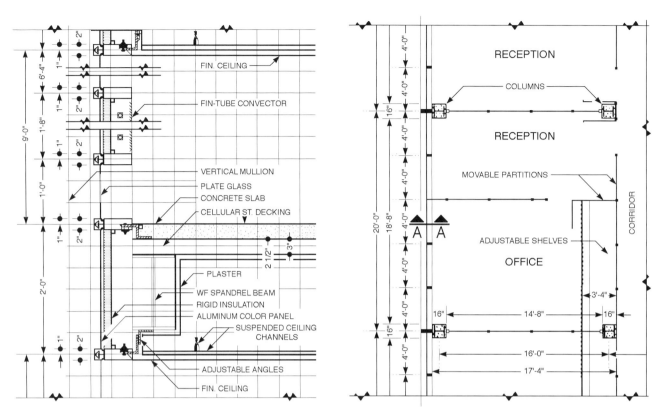

Fig. 14. Plan and detail of modular curtain wall

Panelized construction

Modular coordination is a dimensional reference system that encourages simplified construction details and takes advantage of the dimensional uniformity of modular building materials and components. Panelized construction based on modular dimensioning offers simpler dimensional relationships than other types of construction. Modular drafting is appropriate for panelized construction because it permits easy and continuous checking for the most efficient use of standard production items. For illustration purposes, Fig. 14 includes the complete modular grid. All sash-extrusion sizes are shown, although in actual applications, the principal grids plus a typical mullion size would be adequate.

Design and construction drawing process

The above overview indicates that both designing and preparation of drawings on a modular basis follow conventional methods; the important difference is the helpful discipline of a 4-inch grid. The small size of the grid and the possibility of integrating nonmodular-sized items accommodate any plan and elevation variations.

By way of summary, planning for modular dimensioning generally follows five steps:

• Preparation of preliminary drawings based on modular dimensioning
• Selection of overall dimensions
• Identification of significant details
• Development of modular details
• Cross-referencing of details on working drawings.

Preliminary modular dimensioning is developed during schematic design, best illustrated as a discipline of design organization as well as of construction. Grid placement should be carefully studied at this point. The 4-inch grid may be used, but more often a large layout module is employed, using some multiple, e.g., a 4-foot module. Overall dimensions for the entire structure, wall lengths, opening widths and heights, partition locations, etc. should all be planned to the extent possible in multiples of 4 inches to ensure agreement of plans with grid and to eliminate unnecessary details.

Significant details should be identified for development into working drawings; duplications should be avoided. Similar sills, heads, jambs, and other details that fall on corresponding grid openings need only be shown once. Modular details are then selected and/or individually developed. Modular architectural plans are most successful if the structural drawings are also modular. Simplified checking results when all shop drawings are submitted on the basis of modular dimensioning and reference points. Contractors in the United States are generally familiar with the modular dimensioning system and its use in construction layout. Notes on the dimensioning conventions can be noted as appropriate on cover sheet and/or individual sheets issued to separate subcontractors.▶

U. S. customary units

Measures of weight

Weights
(The grain is the same in all systems)

Avoirdupois weight

16 drams	= 437.5 grains	= 1 ounce
16 ounces	= 7000 grains	= 1 pound
100 pounds		= 1 cental
2000 pounds		= 1 short ton
2240 pounds		= 1 long ton
1 std. lime bbl., small		= 180 lb. net
1 std. lime bbl., large		= 280 lb. net

Also (in Great Britain)

14 pounds		= 1 stone
2 stone	= 28 lb.	= 1 quarter
4 quarters	= 112 lb.	= 1 hundred-weight (cwt.)
20 hundred weight		= 1 long ton

Linear measure

Measures of length

12 inches		= 1 foot
3 feet		= 1 yard
5-1/2 yards	= 16-1/2 feet	= 1 rod, pole or perch
40 poles	= 220 yards	= 1 furlong
8 furlongs	= 1760 yards	
	= 5280 feet	= 1 mile
3 miles		= 1 league
4 inches		= 1 hand
9 inches		= 1 span

Nautical units

6080.20 feet	= 1 nautical mile
6 feet	= 1 fathom
120 fathoms	= 1 cable length
1 nautical mile per hr.	= 1 knot

Volumetric measure

Measures of volume

1728 cubic inches	= 1 cubic foot
27 cubic feet	= 1 cubic yard
1 cord of wood	= 128 cu. ft.
1 perch of masonry	= 16-1/2 to 25 cu. ft.

Liquid or fluid measure

4 gills	= 1 pint
2 pints	= 1 quart
4 quarts	= 1 gallon
7,4805 gallons	= 1 cubic foot

There is no standard liquid barrel. By trade custom, 1 bbl. of petroleum oil, unrefined = 42 gal.

Troy Weight

24 grains		= 1 pennyweight (dwt.)
20 pennyweights	= 480 grains	= 1 ounce
12 ounces	= 5760 grains	= 1 pound

1 Assay Ton = 29,167 milligrams, or as many milligrams as there are troy ounces in a ton of 2000 lb. *avoirdupois.* Consequently, the number of milligrams of precious metal yielded by an assay ton of ore gives directly the number of troy ounces that would be obtained from a ton of 2000 lb. avoirdupois.

Apothecaries' Weight

20 grains		= 1 scruple
3 scruples	= 60 grains	= 1 dram
8 drams		= 1 ounce
12 ounces	= 5760 grains	= 1 pound

Surveyor's or Gunter's Measure

7.92 inches		= 1 link
100 links	= 66 ft. = 4 rods	= 1 chain
80 chains		= 1 mile
33 1/3 inches		= 1 vara (Texas)

Measures of area

144 square inches	= 1 square foot
9 square feet	= 1 square yard
30-1/4 square yards	= 1 square rod, pole or perch

160 square rods		
	= 10 square chains	
	= 43,560 sq. ft.	= 1 acre
	= 5645 sq. *vara* (Texas)	
	= 4 roods	

640 acres = 1 square mile = 1 section of U. S. Govt. surveyed land

Dry measure

2 pints	= 1 quart
8 quarts	= 1 peck
4 pecks	= 1 bushel

1 std. bbl. for fruits and vegetables quarts, struck measure. = 7056 cu. in. or 105 dry

Board measure

1 board foot	= 144 cu. in	= volume of board 1 ft. sq. and 1 in. thick.

To calculate the number of board feet in a log = $[1/4 \, (d - 4)]^2 L$, where d = diameter of log in inches (usually taken inside the bark at small end), and L = length of log in feet. The 4 in. deducted are an allowance for slab. This rule is variously known as the Doyle, Conn. River, St. Croix, Thurber, Moore and Beeman, and the Scribner rule.

LENGTH EQUIVALENTS

	Inches	Feet	Yards	Chains	Miles	Millimeters	Meters	Kilometers
Inches	1	0.083 33	0.027 78	0.001 263	1.578×10^{-5}	25.4	0.0254	2.54×10^{-5}
Feet	12	1	0.3333	0.015 15	1.894×10^{-4}	304.8	0.3048	3.048×10^{-4}
Yards	36	3	1	0.045 45	5.682×10^{-4}	914.4	0.9144	9.144×10^{-4}
Chains	792	66	22	1	0.0125	20 116.8	20.1168	0.020 117
Miles	63 360	5280	1760	80	1	1 609 344	1609.344	1.609 344
Millimeters	0.039 37	0.003 281	0.001 094	4.971×10^{-5}	6.214×10^{-7}	1	0.001	0.000 001
Meters	39.3701	3.280 8	1.0936	0.049 710	6.214×10^{-4}	1000	1	0.001
Kilometers	39 370	3280.84	1093.61	49.7097	0.621 37	1 000 000	1000	1

AREA EQUIVALENTS

	Square inches	Square feet	Square yards	Square rods	Square Chains	Acres	Square miles	Square meters	Hectares*
Square inches	1	0.006 944	7.716×10^{-4}	2.834×10^{-6}	——	——	——	6.452×10^{-4}	——
Square feet	144	1	0.1111	0.003 673	2.296×10^{-4}	2.296×10^{-5}	3.587×10^{-8}	0.092 903	9.290×10^{-6}
Square yards	1296	9	1	0.033 058	0.002 066	2.066×10^{-4}	3.228×10^{-7}	0.836 127	8.361×10^{-5}
Square rods	39 204	272.25	30.25	1	0.0625	0.006 25	9.766×10^{-6}	25.2929	0.002 529
Square chains	627 264	4356	484	16	1	0.1	1.562×10^{-4}	404.6856	0.040 469
Acres	6 272 640	43 560	4840	160	10	1	0.001 562	4046.856	0.404 686
Square miles	——	27 878 400	3 097 600	102 400	6400	640	1	2 589 988	258.9988
Square meters	1550.00	10.7639	1.1960	0.039 537	0.002 471	2.471×10^{-4}	3.861×10^{-7}	1	0.0001
Hectares*	——	107 639	11 959.9	395.3686	24.7105	2.4711	0.003 861	10 000	1

* 1 hectare = 10 000 square meters (m²) = 0.01 square kilometer (km²)

VOLUME AND CAPACITY EQUIVALENTS

	Cubic inches	Cubic feet	Cubic yards	U.S. Fluid ounces	U.S. Quart (liquid)	U.S. Gallon (liquid)	U.S. Gallon (dry)	Liter	Cubic meter
Cubic inches	1	5.787×10^{-4}	2.143×10^{-5}	0.554 113	0.017 316	0.004 239	0.003 720	0.016 387	1.639×10^{-5}
Cubic feet	1728	1	0.037 037	957.506	29.922	7.4805	6.4285	28.3168	0.028 317
Cubic yards	46 656	27	1	25 852.7	807.896	201.974	173.57	764.555	0.764 555
U.S. Fl. oz.	1.8047	0.001 044	3.868×10^{-5}	1	0.031 25	0.007 812	0.006 714	0.029 574	2.957×10^{-5}
U.S. Quart (liq)	57.75	0.033 42	0.001 238	32	1	0.25	0.214 84	0.946 352	9.464×10^{-4}
U.S. Gallon (liq)	231	0.133 68	0.004 951	128	4	1	0.859 37	3.785 412	0.003 785
U.S. Gallon (dry)	268.8	0.1556	0.005 761	148.95	4.6546	1.1636	1	4.404 884	0.004 404
U.S. Bushel	2150.4	1.244 46	0.046 091	1191.57	37.237	9.3092	8	35.2391	0.035 239
Liter	61.024	0.035 31	0.001 308	33.814	1.0567	0.264 17	0.227 02	1	0.001
Cubic meter	61 024	35.3147	1.307 95	33 814	1056.67	264.172	227.021	1000	1

MASS (WEIGHT) EQUIVALENTS

	Grains	Ounces [Avoirdup.]	Ounces [Troy]	Pounds [Avoirdup.]	Pounds [Troy]	Short tons [2000 lb]	Long tons [2240 lb]	Kilograms	Metric tons
Grains	1	0.002 286	0.002 083	1.429×10^{-4}	1.736×10^{-4}	7.143×10^{-8}	6.378×10^{-8}	6.378×10^{-5}	6.480×10^{-8}
Ounces [Avoirdupois]	437.5	1	1.097 14	0.0625	0.075 95	3.125×10^{-5}	2.790×10^{-5}	0.028 35	2.835×10^{-5}
Ounces [Troy]	480	0.911 458	1	0.068 57	0.083 33	3.429×10^{-5}	3.061×10^{-5}	0.031 10	3.110×10^{-5}
Pounds (lb) [Avoirdupois]	7000	16	14.5833	1	1.215 28	0.0005	4.464×10^{-4}	0.453 59	4.546×10^{-4}
Pounds [Troy]	5760	13.1674	12	0.822 86	1	4.114×10^{-4}	3.673×10^{-4}	0.373 24	3.732×10^{-4}
Short Tons [2000 lb]	14 000 000	32 000	29 166.7	2000	2430.55	1	0.892 86	907.185	0.907 18
Long Tons [2240 lb]	15 680 000	35 840	32 666.7	2240	2722.22	1.12	1	1016.05	1.016 05
Kilograms	15 432.4	35.274	32.151	2.2046	2.6792	0.001 102	9.842×10^{-4}	1	0.001
Metric tons	15 432 358	35 273.96	32 150.8	2204.623	2679.23	1.102 311	0.984 207	1000	1

DECIMAL EQUIVALENTS OF FRACTIONS OF AN INCH

$\frac{1}{64}'' = 0.015\ 625$	$\frac{17}{64}'' = 0.265\ 625$	$\frac{33}{64}'' = 0.515\ 625$	$\frac{49}{64}'' = 0.765\ 625$
$\frac{1}{32}'' = 0.031\ 25$	$\frac{9}{32}'' = 0.281\ 25$	$\frac{17}{32}'' = 0.531\ 25$	$\frac{25}{32}'' = 0.781\ 25$
$\frac{3}{64}'' = 0.046\ 875$	$\frac{19}{64}'' = 0.396\ 875$	$\frac{35}{64}'' = 0.546\ 875$	$\frac{51}{64}'' = 0.796\ 875$
$\frac{1}{16}'' = 0.062\ 5$	$\frac{5}{16}'' = 0.312\ 5$	$\frac{9}{16}'' = 0.562\ 5$	$\frac{13}{16}'' = 0.812\ 5$
$\frac{5}{64}'' = 0.078\ 125$	$\frac{21}{64}'' = 0.328\ 125$	$\frac{37}{64}'' = 0.578\ 125$	$\frac{53}{64}'' = 0.828\ 125$
$\frac{3}{32}'' = 0.093\ 75$	$\frac{11}{32}'' = 0.343\ 75$	$\frac{19}{32}'' = 0.593\ 75$	$\frac{27}{32}'' = 0.843\ 75$
$\frac{7}{64}'' = 0.109\ 375$	$\frac{23}{64}'' = 0.359\ 375$	$\frac{39}{64}'' = 0.609\ 375$	$\frac{55}{64}'' = 0.859\ 375$
$\frac{1}{8}'' = 0.125$	$\frac{3}{8}'' = 0.375$	$\frac{5}{8}'' = 0.625$	$\frac{7}{8}'' = 0.875$
$\frac{9}{64}'' = 0.140\ 625$	$\frac{25}{64}'' = 0.390\ 625$	$\frac{41}{64}'' = 0.640\ 625$	$\frac{57}{64}'' = 0.890\ 625$
$\frac{5}{32}'' = 0.156\ 25$	$\frac{13}{32}'' = 0.406\ 25$	$\frac{21}{32}'' = 0.656\ 25$	$\frac{29}{32}'' = 0.906\ 25$
$\frac{11}{64}'' = 0.171\ 875$	$\frac{27}{64}'' = 0.421\ 875$	$\frac{43}{64}'' = 0.671\ 875$	$\frac{59}{64}'' = 0.921\ 875$
$\frac{3}{16}'' = 0.187\ 5$	$\frac{7}{16}'' = 0.437\ 5$	$\frac{11}{16}'' = 0.687\ 5$	$\frac{15}{16}'' = 0.937\ 5$
$\frac{13}{64}'' = 0.203\ 125$	$\frac{29}{64}'' = 0.453\ 125$	$\frac{45}{64}'' = 0.703\ 125$	$\frac{61}{64}'' = 0.953\ 125$
$\frac{7}{32}'' = 0.218\ 75$	$\frac{15}{32}'' = 0.468\ 75$	$\frac{23}{32}'' = 0.718\ 75$	$\frac{31}{32}'' = 0.968\ 75$
$\frac{15}{64}'' = 0.234\ 375$	$\frac{31}{64}'' = 0.484\ 375$	$\frac{47}{64}'' = 0.734\ 375$	$\frac{63}{64}'' = 0.984\ 375$
$\frac{1}{4}'' = 0.250$	$\frac{1}{2}'' = 0.500$	$\frac{3}{4}'' = 0.750$	$1'' = 1.000$

CONVERSION OF INCHES AND COMMON FRACTIONS TO DECIMALS OF A FOOT

Conversions have been given to six decimal places. Boldface values are exact. Factors may be rounded to the appropriate degree of precision required, for example, to three decimal places.

Common fractions	0	1"	2"	3"	4"	5"	6"	7"	8"	9"	10"	11"
								Inches				
0	—	0.083 333	0.166 667	**0.250**	0.333 333	0.416 667	**0.500**	0.583 333	0.666 667	**0.750**	0.833 333	0.916 667
1/16"	0.005 208	0.088 542	**0.171 875**	0.255 208	0.338 542	**0.421 875**	0.505 208	0.588 542	**0.671 875**	0.755 208	0.838 542	**0.921 875**
1/8"	0.010 417	**0.093 75**	0.177 083	0.260 417	**0.343 75**	0.427 083	0.510 417	**0.593 75**	0.677 083	0.760 412	**0.843 75**	0.927 083
3/16"	**0.015 625**	0.098 958	0.182 292	**0.265 625**	0.348 958	0.432 292	**0.515 625**	0.598 958	0.682 292	**0.765 625**	0.848 958	0.932 292
1/4"	0.020 833	0.104 167	**0.187 5**	0.270 833	0.354 167	**0.437 5**	0.520 833	0.604 167	**0.687 5**	0.770 833	0.854 167	**0.937 5**
5/16"	0.026 042	**0.109 375**	0.192 708	0.276 042	**0.359 375**	0.442 708	0.526 042	**0.609 375**	0.692 708	0.776 042	**0.859 375**	0.942 708
3/8"	**0.031 25**	0.114 583	0.197 917	**0.281 25**	0.364 583	0.447 917	**0.531 25**	0.614 583	0.697 917	**0.781 25**	0.864 583	0.947 917
7/16"	0.036 458	0.119 792	**0.203 125**	0.286 458	0.369 792	**0.453 125**	0.536 458	0.619 792	**0.703 125**	0.786 458	0.869 792	**0.953 125**
1/2"	0.041 667	**0.125**	0.208 333	0.291 667	**0.375**	0.458 333	0.541 667	**0.625**	0.708 333	0.791 667	**0.875**	0.958 333
9/16"	**0.046 875**	0.130 208	0.213 542	**0.296 875**	0.380 208	0.463 542	**0.546 875**	0.630 208	0.713 542	**0.796 875**	0.880 208	0.963 542
5/8"	0.052 083	0.135 417	**0.218 75**	0.302 083	0.385 417	**0.468 75**	0.552 083	0.635 417	**0.718 75**	0.802 083	0.885 417	**0.968 75**
11/16"	0.057 292	**0.140 625**	0.223 958	0.307 292	**0.390 625**	0.473 958	0.557 292	**0.640 625**	0.723 958	0.807 292	**0.890 625**	0.973 958
3/4"	**0.0625**	0.145 833	0.229 167	**0.312 5**	0.395 833	0.479 167	**0.562 5**	0.645 833	0.729 167	**0.812 5**	0.895 833	0.979 167
13/16"	0.067 708	0.151 042	**0.234 375**	0.317 708	0.401 042	**0.484 375**	0.567 708	0.651 042	**0.734 375**	0.817 708	0.901 042	**0.984 375**
7/8"	0.072 917	**0.156 25**	0.239 583	0.322 917	**0.406 25**	0.489 583	0.572 917	**0.656 25**	0.739 583	0.822 917	**0.906 25**	0.989 583
15/16"	**0.078 125**	0.161 458	0.244 792	**0.328 125**	0.411 458	0.494 792	**0.578 125**	0.661 458	0.744 792	**0.828 125**	0.911 458	0.994 792

Summary: The SI system (after *Le Système International d'Unites*) is the internationally adopted standard of measurement, based on the meter-kilogram-second-ampere system of fundamental units, modifying the prior European metric unit system and replacing the Unites States customary measurement systems. This introduction provides a brief overview.

Key words: metrics, metrification, customary measurement units, SI units.

What is SI metric?

SI metric is the name given to the new measurement system being adopted on a worldwide basis. It differs somewhat from the long-standing European metric system. SI stands for Le Système International d'Unites, a name generated by the thirty six nations meeting at the 11th General Conference on Weights and Measures (CGPM) in 1960. SI is a coherent means of measurement based on the meter-kilogram-second-ampere system of fundamental units. Conversions within the system are never necessary (e.g., as in the customary system, ounces to pounds and inches to feet, etc.).

How new is the Metric System to the United States?

Developed at the time of the French Revolution, the metric system spread throughout Europe during the Napoleonic era. It was promoted in the United States first by Thomas Jefferson and subsequently by John Quincy Adams. In 1866, Congress made the metric system a legal system of units for U.S. use. In 1875 the United States and sixteen other nations formed the General Conference on Weights and Measures (CGPM). The United States has been active in the periodic meetings of this group. In 1893, an Executive Order made the meter and the kilogram fundamental standards from which the pound and the yard would henceforth be derived. In 1960 the CGPM established the SI system and has subsequently modified it in several meetings.

Who is coordinating the conversion to SI Metric in the United States?

The Omnibus Trade and Competitiveness Act of 1988 and its amendments declared the metric system as the preferred system of measurement in the United States and required its use in all federal activities to the extent feasible. Federal agencies formed the Construction Metrification Council within the National Institute of Building Sciences (NIBS) in Washington, DC. The Council is responsible for coordinating activities and distributing information and metric resources (NIBS 1991).

What are some rules of "grammar"?

- Double prefixes should never be used; *e.g.*, use Gm (gigameter), not Mkm (megakilometer).

- Base units are not capitalized unless in writing a symbol derived from a proper name; *e.g.*, 12 meters or 12m, 60 newtons or 60N.

- Plurals are writen normally except for quantities less than 1. In such cases the "s" is deleted; *e.g.*, 2.6 meters and 0.6 meter.

- Prefix symbols are not capitalized except for M (mega), G (giga), and T(tera). This avoids confusion with m (meter), g (gram), and t (metric ton). One metric ton (t) is equal to one megagram (Mg).

- Periods are not used after symbols except at the end of a sentence. Commas should not be used to clarify groups of digits; instead, use spaced groups of three on each side of the decimal point.

Table 1

What are the principal units used in structures which will be of concern to the architect?

Name	Symbol	Use
Meter	m	Site plan dimensions, building plans
Millimeter	mm	Building plans and details
Square millimeters	mm^2	Small areas
Square meters	m^3	Large areas
Hectare	ha	Very large areas (1 hectare equals 10^4 m
Cubic millimeters	mm^3	Small volumes
Cubic meters	m^3	Large volumes
Section modulus	mm^3	Property of cross section
Moment of inertia	mm^4	Property of cross section
Kilogram	kg	Mass of all building materials
Newton	N	Force (all structural computations)
Pascal	Pa	Stress or pressure (all structural computations; one pascal equals one newton per square meter)
Mass density	kg/ m^3	Density of materials
Degree Celsius	°C	Temperature measurement

Table 2

Multiplication factors	Prefix	Symbol
10^{12}	tera	T
10^9	giga (jiga)	G
10^6	mega	M
10^3	kilo	k
10^2	hecto	h
10^1	deka	da
10^{-1}	deci	d
10^{-2}	centi	c
10^{-3}	milli	m
10^{-6}	micro	m
10^{-9}	nano (nano)	n
10^{-12}	pico (peco)	p
10^{-13}	femto	f
10^{-18}	atto	a

frequently used by architects

To be consistent and avoid confusion, prefixes should change in steps of 10^3; therefore, these four should be avoided if at all possible.

Author: R. E. Shaeffer

Credits: Introduction reproduced from R.E. Shaeffer, *Building Structures: Elementary analysis and design.* Englewood Cliffs, NJ: Prentice-Hall. 1980. by permission of the author. ASTM Standard (following pages) reproduced by permission American Society for Testing and Materials.

References: ASTM. 1994. *ASTM E621—Standard Practice for the Use of Metric (SI) Units in Building Design and Construction.* Philadelphia: American Society for Testing and Materials.

NIBS. 1991. *Metric Guide for Federal Construction.* Washington, DC: National Institute of Buidling Sciences.

832 604.789 06 not 832,604.78906
20 800 not 20,800

Exception: The space is optional in groups of four digits; e.g.,

1486 or 1 486
0.3248 or 0.324 8

- Division is indicated by a slash; e.g., a certain steel beam has a mass of 100 kg/m.

- Multiplication is indicated by a dot placed at mid-height of the letters; e.g., a certain moment or torque might be given as 100kN·m.

- Decimals (not dual units) should be used; e.g., for the length of one side of a building lot, state 118.6 m rather than 118 m, 600 mm.

- All dimensions on a given drawing should have the same units.

What is the major change from the customary system to SI for structural design?

In the SI metric system of units, a clear distinction is made between mass and force. The customary system treated mass and force as if they both had force units; i.e. it would be eritten that a beam weighed 100 lb. per foot and that the force in a truss member was 1800 lb. It was correct to use pounds for force but not for weight (mass). In the former European metric system, it was said that the beam weighed 149 kg per meter and that the force is a truss member was 818 kg of force (kgf). It was correct to use kilograms for weight (mass) but not for force.

F is equal to MA   F is not equal to M

SI units do not confuse the two terms. One can "weigh" items such as cubic meters of concrete by establishing the mass in kilograms, but force is expressed in newtons. Pressure (stress) is in newtons per square meter (pascals).

A commonly used illustration to explain the difference between force and mass is to look at what happens in different fields of gravity. Assume that you are holding a 1-kg mass in the palm of your hand. On earth, the kg would exert a force of 9.8 N downward on your hand. (This would vary slightly, depending upon whether you were located at sea level or on top of Mt. Everest.) At Tranquility Base on our moon, it would push with a force of 1.6 N, and on the surface of Jupiter one would feel a force of 24.1 N!

For engineering purposes on earth, we can multiply loads (if given in kg) by 9.8 to get the number of newtons of force for which to design.

How will the new units modify design drawings?

Conceptually, the square meter is the new unit of plan area replacing the square foot. Length measurements may be in meters or millimeters, except that it is desirable to express all the measurements on a single drawing in the same units. (Among other advantages, this obviates the need for placing m or mm as a suffix to each dimension.) The millimeter is preferred for all detail, section, and plan drawings up through the scale of 1:200. On plans, this results in small numbers for wall thickness and large numbers for room dimensions, but eliminates the need for fractions. Even on details, the millimeter is small enough so that, with few exceptions, fractions can be avoided.

The basic building modules recommended are 100 mm and 300 mm. The 300-mm dimension is very close to 12 inches and will be an easy concept to adopt. At the same time, it is much more flexible that the foot, in that it is evenly divisible by 2, 3, 4 ,5, 6, 10, 15, 20, 25, 30, 50, 60, 100, and 150.

Tables of conversion factors commonly available. However, the more one uses conversion factors, the longer it will take to "think" in metric. In any event, one must keep the desired level of accuracy in mind when making conversions.

For example, working with a reinforced concrete beam 12 x 20 inches in cross section and converting its area in square inches to millimeters squared (The dimensions imply an accuracy of plus or minus 1 square inch, or about 0.4%): Following the table below, one could convert to metric by multiplying 240 by 6.451 600 E+02 to get an area of 154 838 mm^2. To use this quantity would be deceiving in terms of accuracy because it is subject to the same ±0.4% tolerance level, or in this case about 600 mm^2. In other words, the area could range from approximately 154 200 to about 155 400. Expressing the converted area as simply 155 000 mm^2 would be much more consistent.

Table 3

Commonly Used Scales

Customary	Nearest convenient ratio	Metric equivalent
1/16" = 1'- 0"	1:200	5 mm = 1m
1/8" = 1'- 0"	1:100	10 mm = 1m
1/4" = 1'- 0"	1:50	20 mm = 1m
1/2" = 1'- 0"	1:20	50 mm = 1m
3/4" = 1'- 0"	1:10	100 mm = 1m
1-1/2" = 1'- 0"	1:10	100 mm = 1m
3" = 1'- 0"	1:5	200 mm = 1m
1" = 20'	1:200	5 mm = 1m
1" = 50'	1:500	2mm = 1m

Table 4

A few conversion factors that may prove useful in structural analysis are presented below.

To convert from	to		Multiply by
inches	mm		2.540 000 E+01
feet	m		3.048 000 E-01
in.^{2}	mm^2		6.451 600 E+02
ft^2	m^2		9.290 304 E-02
in.^{3}	mm^3		1.638 706 E+04
ft^3	m^3		2.831 685 E-02
in.^{4}	mm^4		4.162 314 E+05
°F	°C		$t°C = (t°F - 32)/1.8$
lb (mass) per foot	kg/m		1.488 163 E+00
lb. (force) per foot	N/m		1.459 390 E+01
strain/°F (thermal expansion)	strain/°C		1.800 000 E+00
lb (force)	N		4.448 222 E+00
kip (force)	kN		4.448 222 E+00
lb-ft	(movement)N·m		1.355 818 E+00
kip-ft (movement)	k N·m		1.355 818 E+00
psi (stress)	kPa		6.894 757 E+00
ksi (stress)	Mpa		6.894 757 E+00
psf (uniform load)	kN/m^2		4.788 026 E-02

ASTM Designation: E 621 – 94

AMERICAN SOCIETY FOR TESTING AND MATERIALS
1916 Race St. Philadelphia, Pa 19103
Reprinted from the Annual Book of ASTM Standards. Copyright ASTM
If not listed in the current combined index, will appear in the next edition.

Standard Practice for the Use of Metric (SI) Units in Building Design and Construction[1] (Committee E-6 Supplement to E 380)

This standard is issued under the fixed designation E 621; the number immediately following the designation indicates the year of original adoption or, in the case of revision, the year of last revision. A number in parentheses indicates the year of last reapproval. A superscript epsilon (ε) indicates an editorial change since the last revision or reapproval.

This practice has been approved for use by agencies of the Department of Defense. Consult the DoD Index of Specifications and Standards for the specific year of issue which has been adopted by the Department of Defense.

INTRODUCTION

The International System of Units (SI) was developed by the General Conference on Weights and Measures (CGPM), which is an international treaty organization. The abbreviation SI, derived from the French "Système International d'Unités," is used in all languages.

SI is a rational, coherent, international, and preferred measurement system which is derived from earlier decimal metric systems but supersedes all of them.

The use of the metric system in the United States was legalized by an Act of Congress in 1866, but was not made obligatory.

The *Meric Conversion Act of 1975*, as amended by the *Omnibus Trade and Competitiveness Act of 1988*, established the modernized metric system (SI) as the preferred system of measurement in the United States and required that, to the extent feasible, it be used in all federal procurement, grants, and business-related activities. Executive Order 12770 of July 25, 1991, *Metric Usage in Federal Government Programs*, mandated that federal agencies prepare metric transition plans, add metric units to their publications, and work with other governmental, trade, professional, and private sector metric organizations on metric implementation.

In the building design and construction community the application of SI units, together with preferred numerical values, will simplify and speed up calculations and facilitate all measurement intensive activity.

This document has been prepared to provide a single, comprehensive, and authoritative standard for SI units to be used in building design, product manufacture, and construction applications.

---

[1] This practice is under the jurisdiction of ASTM Committee E-6 on Performance of Buildings, and is the direct responsibility of Subcommittee E06.62 on Coordination of Dimensions for Building Materials and Systems.

Current edition approved Nov. 15, 1994. Published February 1995. Originally published as E 621 – 78. Last previous edition E 621 – 84 (1991)ε1.

ASTM E 621

1. Scope

1.1 This standard outlines a selection of SI units, with multiples and submultiples, for general use in building design and construction.

1.2 In addition, rules and recommendations are given for the presentation of SI units and symbols, and for numerical values shown in conjunction with SI.

1.3 A selection of conversion factors appropriate for use within the construction community is given in Appendix X1.

1.4 The SI units included in this document comply with and augment the ASTM Standard for Metric Practice E 380 – 82 and are generally consistent with International Standards Organization (ISO) 1000 – 1981 SI Units and Recommendations for the Use of Their Multiples and Certain Other Units, and the ISO/31 Series of Standards, Quantities, and Units of SI.

2. Terminology

2.1 *Definitions:*

2.1.1 *SI*—The International System of Units (abbreviation for "le Système International d'Unités) as defined by the General Conference on Weights and Measures (CGPM)—based upon seven base units, two supplementary units, and derived units, which together form a coherent system.

2.1.2 *quantity*—measurable attribute of a physical phenomenon. There are base units for seven quantities and supplementary units for two quantities upon which units for *all* other quantities are founded.

2.1.3 *unit*—reference value of a given quantity as defined by CGPM Resolution or ISO Standards. There is *only one* unit for each quantity in SI.

2.1.4 *coherent unit system*—system in which relations between units contain as numerical factor only the number "one" or "unity," because all derived units have a unity relationship to the constituent base and supplementary units.

2.1.5 *numerical value of a quantity*—magnitude of a quantity expressed by the product of a number and the unit in which the quantity is measured.

3. The Concept of SI

3.1 The International System of Units (SI) was developed to provide a universal, coherent, and preferred system of measurement for world-wide use and appropriate to the needs of modern science and technology.

3.2 The principal features of SI are:

3.2.1 There is only one recognized unit for each physical quantity.

3.2.2 The system is fully coherent; this means that all units in the system relate to each other on a unity (one-to-one) basis.

3.2.3 A set of internationally agreed prefixes can be attached to units to form preferred multiples and submultiples of 10 raised to a power that is a multiple of 3. This provides for convenient numerical values when the magnitude of a quantity is stated.

3.2.4 Units and their prefixes are represented by a set of standardized and internationally recognized symbols.

3.3 Because of their practical significance, the use of additional non-SI units in conjunction with SI is permitted for some quantities.

3.4 SI units, permissible non-SI units, and prefixes are discussed in Sections 4, 5, and 6.

3.5 The diagram below shows graphically the types of units within SI or associated with SI:

4. SI Units

4.1 The International System of Units (SI) has three classes of units:

4.1.1 Base units for independent quantities,

4.1.2 Supplementary units for plane angle and solid angle, and

4.1.3 Derived units.

4.2 The seven base units and two supplementary units are unique units which, except for the kilogram (Note 1), are defined in terms of reproducible phenomena.

NOTE 1—The primary standard for mass is the international prototype kilogram maintained under specified conditions at the International Bureau of Weights and Measures (BIPM) near Paris in France.

E 621

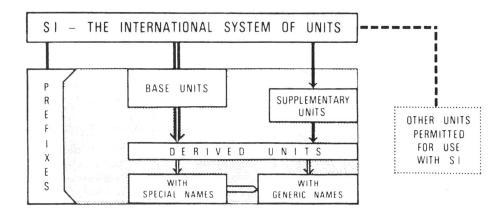

4.3 Derived units can all be defined in terms of their derivation from base and supplementary units. They are listed in two categories:

4.3.1 Derived units with *special* names and symbols, and

4.3.2 Derived units with *generic* or complex names.

4.4 A chart, indicating diagrammatically the relationship between the base units, supplementary units, and derived units that have been given special names, is shown in Appendix X2.

4.5 Table 1 contains base, supplementary, and derived units of significance in design and construction, listing:

4.5.1 Quantity,

4.5.2 Unit name,

4.5.3 Unit symbol,

4.5.4 Unit formula,

4.5.5 Unit derivation (in terms of base and supplementary units), and

4.5.6 Remarks.

5. Non-SI Units for Use with SI

5.1 There is an additional group of acceptable, but non-coherent traditional units retained in association with SI, because of their practical significance in general applications.

5.2 Non-SI units of significance to design and construction are shown in Table 2, under two categories:

5.2.1 Units for general use, and

5.2.2 Units for limited application only.

5.3 Appendix X3 shows a group of superseded metric units not recommended for use with SI in design and construction applications.

6. SI Unit Prefixes

6.1 SI is based on the decimal system of multiples and submultiples, and therefore the use of common fractions is minimized. Multiples are formed by attaching standard prefixes to SI units.

6.2 Preferred multiples range in geometric steps of 1000 (10^3) up to 10^{18}; submultiples range in geometric steps of 1/1000 (10^{-3}) down to 10^{-18}.

6.3 *Preferred Multiples and Submultiples*—The preferred prefixes shown in Table 3 are relevant in design and construction. Prefixes outside the range 10^{-6} (micro) to 10^6 (mega) will occur only in rare instances.

6.4 *Other Multiples for Limited Application*—SI includes a number of additional historically used multiples and submultiples, shown in Table 4, but these should be avoided as far as possible.

7. Rules and Recommendations for the Use of SI

7.1 Two tables of rules and recommendations have been prepared to facilitate the correct application of SI units and symbols and the correct presentation of units, symbols, and numerical values shown in conjunction with units and symbols.

7.2 Table 5 gives "Rules and Recommendations for the Presentation of SI Units and Symbols."

7.3 Table 6 gives guidance on "Presentation of Numerical Values with SI."

7.4 The tables provide a convenient reference guide for the editorial checking of metric documents to ensure that the presentation of data is in line with accepted practice.

8. SI Units for Use in Design and Construction

8.1 Correct selection of units for use in building design calculations and in documentation is essential to minimize errors and to optimize the coordination between the various sectors and groups within the construction community.

8.2 Tables 7 to 13 list SI units, and other units acceptable with SI as recommended, for use in building design and construction related activities. Where appropriate, working ranges are indicated for selected units, and typical examples of their field(s) of application provided. In addition, explanatory remarks are provided to briefly deal with special considerations.

8.3 The following subdivision has been adopted:

Table 7	Space and Time: Geometry, Kinematics, and Periodic Phenomena
Table 8	Mechanics: Statics and Dynamics
Table 9	Heat, Thermal Effects, Heat Transfer
Table 10	Moisture Movement
Table 11	Electricity and Magnetism
Table 12	Lighting
Table 13	Acoustics

8.4 *Preferred Range of Values*—The use of an appropriate unit or multiple of a unit depends upon the context in which it is used.

8.4.1 In printed or typed material it is preferable to use numbers between 1 and 1000, wherever possible, by selecting an appropriate prefix. For example: 725 m is preferred to 0.725 km or 725 000 mm.

E 621

TABLE 1 Units in the International System—SI

Unit Group Quantity	Unit Name	Symbol	Formula	Unit Derivation	Remarks
Base Units:					
Length	metre	m			
Mass	kilogram	kg			
Time	second	s			
Electric current	ampere	A			Already in common use
Thermodynamic temperature	kelvin	K			The customary unit for temperature is the degree Celsius (°C).
Amount of substance	mole	mol			The "mol" has no application in construction.
Luminous intensity	candela	cd			Already in common use
Supplementary Units:					
Plane angle	radian	rad			Already in common use
Solid angle	steradian	sr			Already in common use
Derived Units with Special Names:					
Frequency (of a periodic phenomenon)	hertz	Hz	l/s	s^{-1}	The hertz replaces "cycle per second."
Force	newton	N	$kg \cdot m/s^2$	$m \cdot kg \cdot s^{-2}$	
Pressure, stress, elastic modulus	pascal	Pa	N/m^2	$m^{-1} \cdot kg \cdot s^{-2}$	
Energy, work, quantity of heat	joule	J	$N \cdot m$	$m^2 \cdot kg \cdot s^{-2}$	
Power, radiant flux	watt	W	J/s	$m^2 \cdot kg \cdot s^{-3}$	Already in common use
Quantity of electricity, electric charge	coulomb	C	$A \cdot s$	$s \cdot A$	Already in common use
Electric potential, potential difference, **electromotive force**	volt	V	J/C or W/A	$m^2 \cdot kg \cdot s^{-3} \cdot A^{-1}$	Already in common use
Electric capacitance	farad	F	C/V	$m^{-2} \cdot kg^{-1} \cdot s^4 \cdot A^2$	Already in common use
Electric resistance	ohm	Ω	V/A	$m^2 \cdot kg \cdot s^{-3} \cdot A^{-2}$	Already in common use
Electric conductance	siemens	S	A/V or l/Ω	$m^{-2} \cdot kg^{-1} \cdot s^3 \cdot A^2$	The 'siemens' was formerly referred to as "mho."
Magnetic flux	weber	Wb	$V \cdot s$	$m^2 \cdot kg \cdot s^{-2} \cdot A^{-1}$	Already in common use
Magnetic flux density	tesla	T	Wb/m^2	$kg \cdot s^{-2} \cdot A^{-1}$	Already in common use
Electric inductance	henry	H	Wb/A	$m^2 \cdot kg \cdot s^{-2} \cdot A^{-2}$	Already in common use
Celsius temperature	degree Celsius	°C	K		See 9.7
Luminous flux	lumen	lm	$cd \cdot sr$	$cd \cdot sr$	Already in common use
Illuminance	lux	lx	lm/m^2	$m^{-2} \cdot cd \cdot sr$	
Activity (of a radionuclide)	becquerel	Bq	l/s	s^{-1}	No application in construction.
Absorbed dose	gray	Gy	J/kg	$m^2 \cdot s^{-2}$ (*)	(*) kg is canceled out. No application in construction.
Derived Units with Generic Names:					
a. Units Expressed in Terms of One Base Unit:					
Area	square metre	m^2		m^2	
Volume, capacity	cubic metre	m^3		m^3	(1 m^3 = 1000 L)
Section modulus	metre to third power		m^3	m^3	
Second moment of area	metre to fourth power		m^4	m^4	
Curvature	reciprocal (of) metre		l/m	m^{-1}	
Rotational frequency	reciprocal (of) second		l/s	s^{-1}	Revolution per second (r/s) is used in specifications for rotating machinery.
Coefficient of linear ther-**mal expansion**	reciprocal (of) kelvin		l/K	K^{-1}	
b. Units Expressed in Terms of Two or More Base Units:					
Linear velocity	metre per second		m/s	$m \cdot s^{-1}$	
Linear acceleration	metre per second squared		m/s^2	$m \cdot s^{-2}$	
Kinematic viscosity	square metre per second		m^2/s	$m^2 \cdot s^{-1}$	
Volume rate of flow	cubic metre per second		m^3/s	$m^3 \cdot s^{-1}$	
Specific volume	cubic metre per kilogram		m^3/kg	$m^3 \cdot kg^{-1}$	
Mass per unit length	kilogram per metre		kg/m	$m^{-1} \cdot kg$	
Mass per unit area	kilogram per square metre		kg/m^2	$m^{-2} \cdot kg$	
Density (mass per unit volume)	kilogram per cubic metre		kg/m^3	$m^{-3} \cdot kg$	In this SI form, mass density is conveniently 1000 times specific gravity.
Moment of inertia	kilogram metre squared		$kg \cdot m^2$	$m^2 \cdot kg$	
Mass flow rate	kilogram per second		kg/s	$kg \cdot s^{-1}$	
Momentum	kilogram metre per second		$kg \cdot m/s$	$m \cdot kg \cdot s^{-1}$	
Angular momentum	kilogram metre squared per second		$kg \cdot m^2/s$	$m^2 \cdot kg \cdot s^{-1}$	

🜀 E 621

TABLE 1 *Continued*

Unit Group	Quantity	Unit Name	Symbol	Formula	Unit Derivation	Remarks
Magnetic field strength		ampere per metre	A/m	$m^{-1} \cdot A$	
Current density		ampere per square metre	A/m^2	$m^{-2} \cdot A$	
Luminance		candela per square metre	cd/m^2	$m^{-2} \cdot cd$	

c. Units Expressed in Terms of Base Units and/or Derived Units with Special Names:

Moment of force, torque		newton metre	N·m	$^2 \cdot kg \cdot s^{-2}$	
Flexural rigidity		newton square metre	N·m^2	$m^3 \cdot kg \cdot s^{-2}$	
Force per unit length, surface tension		newton per metre	N/m	$kg \cdot s^{-2}$ (1)	(1) m is canceled out
Dynamic viscosity		pascal second	Pa·s	$m^{-1} \cdot kg \cdot s^{-1}$	
Impact ductility		joule per square metre	J/m^2	$kg \cdot s^{-2}$ (2)	(2) m^2 is canceled out
Combustion heat (per unit volume)		joule per cubic metre	J/m^3	$m^{-1} \cdot kg \cdot s^{-2}$	
Combustion heat (per unit mass), specific energy, specific latent heat		joule per kilogram	J/kg	$m^2 \cdot s^{-2}$ (3)	(3) kg is canceled out
Heat capacity, entropy		joule per kelvin	J/K	$m^2 \cdot kg \cdot s^{-2} \cdot K^{-1}$	
Specific heat capacity, specific entropy		joule per kilogram kelvin	J/(kg·K)	$m^2 \cdot s^{-2} \cdot K^{-1}$ (4)	(4) kg is canceled out
Heat flux density, irradiance, sound intensity		watt per square metre	W/m^2	$kg \cdot s^{-3}$ (5)	(5) m^2 is canceled out
Thermal conductivity		watt per metre kelvin	W/(m·K)	$m \cdot kg \cdot s^{-3} \cdot K^{-1}$	(6) m^2 is canceled out
Thermal conductance		watt per square metre kelvin	W/(m^2·K)	$kg \cdot s^{-3} \cdot K^{-1}$ (6)	
Thermal resistance		square metre kelvin per watt	K·m^2/W	$kg^{-1} \cdot s^3 \cdot K$ (7)	(7) m^2 is canceled out
Electric field strength		volt per metre	V/m	$m \cdot kg \cdot s^{-3} \cdot A^{-1}$	
Electric flux density		coulomb per square metre	C/m^2	$m^{-2} \cdot s \cdot A$	
Electric charge density		coulomb per cubic metre	C/m^3	$m^{-3} \cdot s \cdot A$	
Electric permittivity		farad per metre	F/m	$m^{-3} \cdot kg^{-1} \cdot s^4 \cdot A^2$	
Electric permeability		henry per metre	H/m	$m \cdot kg \cdot s^{-2} \cdot A^{-2}$	
Electric resistivity		ohm metre	Ω·m	$m^3 \cdot kg \cdot s^{-3} \cdot A^{-2}$	
Electric conductivity		siemens per metre	S/m	$m^{-3} \cdot kg^{-1} \cdot s^3 \cdot A^2$	
Light exposure		lux second	lx·s	$m^{-2} \cdot s \cdot cd \cdot sr$	
Luminous efficacy		lumen per watt	lm/W	$m^{-2} \cdot kg^{-1} \cdot s^3 \cdot cd \cdot sr$	

d. Units Expressed in Terms of Supplementary Units and Base and/or Derived Units:

Angular velocity		radian per second	rad/s	$s^{-1} \cdot rad$	
Angular acceleration		radian per second squared	rad/s^2	$m^{-2} \cdot rad$	
Radiant intensity		watt per steradian	W/sr	$m^2 \cdot kg \cdot s^{-3} \cdot sr^{-1}$	
Radiance		watt per square metre steradian	W/(m^2·sr)	$kg \cdot s^{-3} \cdot sr^{-1}$ (8)	(8) m^2 is canceled out

8.4.2 If the numerical quantity is part of a group of numbers in a different range, select the prefix that most adequately covers the range, without unduly large or small numbers. For example: If 725 m is part of a group of numbers shown in kilometres, show it as 0.725 km.

8.4.3 Although physical data generally should be presented in the most condensed form possible, by using appropriate prefixes, it will be advantageous in calculations to use exponential notation, instead of prefixes, for example: 900 mm^2 = 0.9×10^{-3} m^2; 36 MPa = 36×10^6 Pa = 36×10^6 N/m^2.

8.4.4 In drawings it will be of advantage to show one measurement unit throughout, so that numerical values can be represented by numbers only, and the unit symbol can be deleted. For example, in a drawing on which all dimensions are shown in millimetres, 5-digit numbers (indicating millimetres) are quite acceptable.

9. Special Considerations in the Use of SI Units in Building Design and Construction

9.1 *Linear Measurement (Length):*

9.1.1 The preferred units for measurement of length in building design, construction, and production are the millimetre (mm) and the metre (m).

9.1.2 In special applications, the kilometre (km) is used for the measurement of long distances, and the micrometre (μm) is used for precision measurements.

9.1.3 The centimetre (cm) is to be avoided in all building design and construction applications.

9.1.4 The reasons for the deletion of the centimetre are:

9.1.4.1 The centimetre is not consistent with the preferred use of multiples that represent ternary powers of 10.

9.1.4.2 The order of magnitude between millimetre and centimetre is only 10, and the use of both units would lead to confusion.

9.1.4.3 The millimetre (mm) provides integers within

ASTM E 621

TABLE 2   Other Units Whose Use Is Permitted with SI

Quantity	Unit Name	Symbol	Relationship to SI Unit	Remarks
Units for General Use:				
Volume	litre[A]	L	$1 L = 0.001 m^3 = 10^6 mm^3$	The litre may only be used with the SI prefix "milli."
Mass	metric ton[B]	t	$1 t = 1000 kg = (1 Mg)$	
Time	minute	min	$1 min = 60 s$	See also Section 9.6.
	hour	h	$1 h = 3600 s = (60 min)$	
	day (mean solar)	d	$1 d = 86 400 s = (24 h)$	
	year (calendar)	a	$1 a = 31 536 000 s$ $= (365 d)$	
Plane angle	degree (of arc)	°	$1° = 0.017 453 rad$ $= 17.453 mrad$	$1° = (\pi/180) rad$
Velocity	kilometre per hour	km/h	$1 km/h = 0.278 m/s$	$1 m/s = 3.6 km/h$
Units Accepted for Limited Application Only:				
Area	hectare	ha	$1 ha = 10 000 m^2$	For use in land measurement.
Energy	kilowatthour	kWh	$1 kWh = 3.6 MJ$	For measurement of electrical energy consumption only.
Speed of rotation	revolution per minute	r/min	$1 r/min =$	To measure rotational speed in slow-moving equipment only.

[A] The international symbol for "litre" is the lowercase "l", which can be easily confused with the numeral "1." Several English-speaking countries have adopted the script "ℓ" as symbol for "litre" in order to avoid any misinterpretation. The symbol "L" (capital ell) has been adopted for United States use to prevent confusion.
[B] The international name for "metric ton" is "tonne." The metric ton is equal to the "megagram" (Mg).

TABLE 3   Preferred Multiples and Submultiples

Multiplication Factor			Prefix		Pronunciation
			Name	Symbol	
10^{12}	or	1 000 000 000 000	tera	T	as in *terrace*
10^9	or	1 000 000 000	giga	G	jig'a
10^6	or	1 000 000	mega	M	as in *megaphone*
10^3	or	1 000	kilo	k	kill'oh
10^{-3}	or	0.001	milli	m	as in *military*
10^{-6}	or	0.000 001	micro	μ	as in *microphone*
10^{-9}	or	0.000 000 001	nano	n	nan'oh
10^{-12}	or	0.000 000 000 001	pico	p	peek'oh

appropriate tolerances for all building dimensions and nearly all building product dimensions, so that decimal fractions are almost entirely eliminated from documents. In contrast, acceptance of the centimetre would inevitably lead to extensive use of decimal fractions, which is undesirable.

9.1.5 On drawings, unit symbols may be deleted if the following rules are applied:

9.1.5.1 The drawing is designated "all dimensions shown in millimetres unless otherwise noted" or "all dimensions shown in metres unless otherwise noted."

9.1.5.2 Whole numbers always indicate millimetres, for example, 3600; 300; 25.

(*1*) Any length up to 328 ft can be shown by a simple 5-digit number, for example, 327 ft 10¹¹/₁₆ in. = 99 941 mm.

(*2*) Similarly, any length up to 32 ft 9 in. can be shown by a 4-digit number; any length up to 3 ft 3⁵/₁₆ in. can be shown by a 3-digit number.

TABLE 4   Other Multiples for Limited Application

Multiplication Factor	Prefix Name	Prefix Symbol	Pronunciation
10^2 or 100	hecto	h	heck'toe
10^1 or 10	deka	da	deck'a
10^{-1} or 0.1	deci	d	as in *decimal*
10^{-2} or 0.01	centi	c	as in *sentiment*

(*3*) Decimalized expressions taken to three places always indicate metres, for example, 3.600; 0.300; 0.025.

9.1.6 The use of millimetres and metres, as recommended, saves both space and time in drawing, typing, and computer applications, and it also improves clarity in drawings with a lot of dimensions.

9.1.7 *Survey Measurement*—The change to SI units will also eliminate the discrepancies between "international" foot and "U.S. survey" foot, "international" mile and "U.S. survey" mile (the survey mile is approximately 3 mm longer), and corresponding derived units for area measurement.

NOTE 2—Since 1893, the U. S. basis of length measurement has been derived from metric standards. In 1959, the definition of the length of the "foot" was changed from 1200/3937 m to 0.3048 m exactly, which resulted in the new value being shorter by two parts in a million.

At the same time it was decided that any data derived from and published as a result of geodetic surveys within the United States would remain with the old standard.

Thus all land measurements in U. S. customary units are based upon the "U. S. survey foot" which relates to the metre by the old standard (1200/3937 = 0.304 800 6 m).

9.2 *Area:*

9.2.1 The preferred unit for area measurement is the square metre (m²). Very large areas can be expressed in square kilometres km²), and small areas will be expressed in

E 621

square millimetres (mm^2), or in square metres using exponential notation (for example, 10^{-6} m^2).

9.2.2 The hectare (ha) is used for land and water measurement *only*. (1 ha = $(100 \text{ m})^2$ = 10 000 m^2 = 10^4 m^2 = 10^{-2} km^2).

9.2.3 The square centimetre (cm^2) is to be avoided to minimize confusion. Any measurement given in square centimetres should be converted to square millimetres or square metres. (1 cm^2 = 100 mm^2 = 10^{-4} m^2).

9.2.4 At times, it will be more appropriate to indicate the surface or cross-sectional area of building products by linear dimensions, for example, 40 by 90 mm; 300 by 600. It is preferred practice to indicate the width dimension first and height second.

9.3 *Volume and Fluid Capacity:*

9.3.1 The preferred unit for measurement of volume in construction and for large storage tank capacities is the cubic metre (m^3).

9.3.2 The preferred units for measurement of fluid capacity (liquid volume) are the litre (L) and the millilitre (mL).

9.3.3 By international definition, the litre is equal to one thousandth of a cubic metre or one cubic decimetre (dm^3). (1 L = 10^{-3} m^3); (1 L = 1 dm^3); (1 m^3 = 1000 L).

TABLE 5   Rules and Recommendations for the Presentation of SI Units and Symbols

	Typical Examples	Remarks
A. *General*		
1. All unit names should either be denoted by correct symbols or be written in full. In the interest of simplification and to reduce the amount of writing, use unit symbols rather than fully written forms.	USE: J/kg *or* joule per kilogram	NOT: joule per kg NOT: J/kilogram
2. DO NOT USE mixtures of names and symbols.		
B. *Symbols for Unit Quantities and Prefixes*		
1. SI symbols are internationally agreed and there is only *one* symbol for each unit. Multiples and submultiples are formed by using the unit symbol and attaching a prefix symbol in front of it.	m, kg, s, A, cd, K, L	See also B.5–B.7
2. All unit symbols are shown in upright letters, and can be produced by a normal typewriter keyboard with the exceptions of the symbols for the SI unit "ohm" and the prefix "micro" which are represented by Greek letters "Ω" and "μ" respectively.		EXCEPTIONS: Ω, μ
3. Unit symbols are NEVER followed by a period (full stop) except at the end of a sentence.	60 kg/m	NOT: 60 kg./m.
4. Unit symbols are normally written in lowercase, except for unit names derived from a proper name, in which case the initial is capitalized. Some units have symbols consisting of two letters from a proper name, of which *only* the first letter is capitalized. (The symbol for the unit name "ohm" is the capital Greek letter Ω.)	m, kg, s, mol, cd, etc. A, K, N, J, W, V, etc. Pa, Hz, Wb, etc.	EXCEPTION: L
5. Prefixes for magnitudes from 10^6 to 10^{18} have capital upright letter symbols.	M, G, T, etc.	See also C.1
6. Prefixes for magnitudes from 10^{-18} through to 10^3 have lowercase upright letter symbols. (The symbol for 10^{-6} or micro is the lowercase Greek letter μ.)	p, n, μ, m, k, etc.	See also C.1
7. Prefix symbols are directly attached to the unit symbol, *without a space* between them.	mm, kW, MN, etc.	NOT: m m, k W, M N
8. DO NOT USE compound prefixes to form a multiple or submultiple of a unit (for example, USE nanometre, DO NOT USE micromillimetre *or* millimicrometre).	nm	NOT: μmm or mμm
9. In the case of the base unit kilogram, prefixes are attached to the "gram" (for example, milligram, NOT microkilogram).	mg	NOT: μkg
10. USE ONLY ONE PREFIX when forming a multiple or a submultiple of a compound unit.	km/s; mV/m	NOT: mm/μs; μV/mm EXCEPTION: MJ/kg NOT kJ/g
11. Any prefix should appear only in the numerator and never in the denominator with the exception of the base unit kg.	MN/m	NOT: kN/mm
C. *Areas of Possible Confusion Requiring Special Care*		
1. The symbols for SI units and the conventions that govern their use shall be followed. A number of prefix and unit symbols use the same letter, but in different form. EXERCISE CARE to present the correct symbol for each unit and prefix.	g (gram); G (giga) k (kilo); K (kelvin) m (milli); M (mega) m (metre) n (nano); N (newton)	*OTHERS:* c (centi); C (coulomb) °C (degree Celsius) s (second); S (siemens) t (metric ton); T (tera) T (tesla)
2. All prefix and unit symbols retain their prescribed form regardless of the surrounding typography. In printouts from limited character sets (telex, computer printers) special considerations apply to symbols for mega, micro, ohm, and siemens. Where confusion is likely to arise, WRITE UNITS IN FULL.		

E 621

TABLE 5 *Continued*

	Typical Examples	Remarks
D. *Unit Names Written Out in Full*		
1. Unit names, including prefixes, are treated as common names and are *not capitalized*, except at the beginning of sentences or in titles. (The only exception is "Celsius" in "degree Celsius," where degree is considered as the unit name and is shown in lowercase, while Celsius represents an adjective and is capitalized.)	metre, newton, etc.	NOT: Metre, Newton EXCEPTION: degree Celsius
2. Where a prefix is attached to an SI unit to form a multiple or submultiple, the combination is written as one word. (There are three cases where the final vowel of the prefix is omitted in the combination: megohm, kilohm, and hectare.)	millimetre; kilowatt	NOT: milli-metre NOT: kilo watt
3. Where a compound unit is formed by multiplication of two units, the use of a space between units is preferred, but a hyphen is acceptable and in some situations more appropriate, to avoid any risk of misinterpretation.	newton metre *or* newton-metre	NOT: newtonmetre
4. Where a compound unit is formed by division of two units, this is expressed by inserting "per" between the numerator and the denominator.	metre per second joule per kelvin	NOT: metre/second NOT: joule/kelvin
5. Where the numerical value of a unit is written in full, the unit should also be **written in full**.	seven metres	NOT: seven m
E. *Plurals*		
1. Units written in full are subject to the normal rules of grammar. For any unit with a numerical value greater than one (1), an "s" is added to the written unit to denote the plural.	1.2 metres; 2.3 newtons; 33.2 kilograms	BUT: 0.8 metre
2. The following units have the same plural as singular when written out in full: hertz, lux, siemens.	350 kilohertz 12.5 lux	
3. Symbols NEVER change in the plural.	2.3 N; 33.2 kg	NOT: 2.3 Ns; 33.2 kgs
F. *Compound Unit Symobols—Products and Quotients*		
1. The product of two units is indicated by a dot placed at mid-height between the unit symbols.	kN·m; Pa·s	NOT: kNm; Pas NOT: kN m; Pa s
2. To express a derived unit formed by division, any one of the following methods **may be used:**		
a. a solidus (slash, /)	kg/m^3; W/(m·K)	See also F.3 and F.5
b. a horizontal line between numerator and denominator	$\frac{kg}{m^3}$, $\frac{W}{m \cdot K}$	
c. a negative index (or negative power)	kg·m^{-3}; W·m^{-1}·K^{-1}	
3. *Only one* solidus may be used in any combination.	m/s^2; m·kg/(s^3·A)	NOT: m/s/s NOT: m·kg/s^3/A
4. DO NOT USE the abbreviation "p" for "per" in the expression of a division.	km/h	NOT: kph *or* k.p.h.
5. Where the denominator is a product, this should be shown in parentheses.	W/(m^2·K)	

9.3.4 Because the cubic metre contains one billion (10^9) cubic millimetres, the cubic decimetre (dm^3) and the cubic centimetre (cm^3) may find limited application, particularly as they represent preferred steps of 1000 in volume measurement. It is suggested that any such cases be converted to preferred units for volume measurement as shown in Table 13.

9.4 *Geometrical Cross-Sectional Properties:*

9.4.1 The expression of geometrical cross-sectional properties of structural sections involves raising the unit of length to the third, fourth, or sixth power. Values can be shown either in mm^3, mm^4, or mm^6 with exponential notation, or in m^3, m^4, or m^6, with exponential notation.

9.4.2 The following are appropriate measurement units:

9.4.2.1 Modulus of section:
$$\text{mm}^3 \text{ or } \text{m}^3 \ (1 \text{ mm}^3 = 10^{-9} \text{ m}^3);$$

9.4.2.2 Second moment of area or torsional constant:
$$\text{mm}^4 \text{ or } \text{m}^4 \ (1 \text{ mm}^4 = 10^{-12} \text{ m}^4);$$

9.4.2.3 Warping constant:

mm^6 or m^6 (1 mm^6 = 10^{-18} m^6).

9.4.3 The cross-sectional properties of a wide-flange beam, 460 mm deep with 82 kg/m mass per unit length, could be expressed as follows:

9.4.3.1 Plastic modulus, Z_x
$$= 1.835 \times 10^6 \text{ mm}^3 \text{ or } 1.835 \times 10^{-3} \text{ m}^3;$$

9.4.3.2 Second moment of area, I_{x-x}
$$= 0.371 \times 10^9 \text{ mm}^4 \text{ or } 0.371 \times 10^{-3} \text{ m}^4;$$

9.4.3.3 Torsional constant, J
$$= 0.691 \times 10^6 \text{ mm}^4 \text{ or } 0.691 \times 10^{-6} \text{ m}^4;$$

9.4.3.4 Warping constant, C_w
$$= 0.924 \times 10^{12} \text{ mm}^6 \text{ or } 0.924 \times 10^{-6} \text{ m}^6.$$

9.5 *Plane Angle:*

9.5.1 While the SI unit for plane angle, the radian (rad), should be used in calculations for reasons of its coherence, the customary units of angular measure, degree (°), minute ('), and second (") of arc are likely to continue to be used in many applications in cartography and surveying.

E 621

9.5.2 The degree (°), with parts denoted by decimals (as in 27.25°), is likely to be utilized in engineering and in construction.

9.6 *Time Interval:*

9.6.1 In general applications, the day (d), hour (h), and minute (min) are permitted non-SI alternatives to the SI base unit for time, the second.

9.6.2 It is recommended that the minute (min) be avoided as far as possible to minimize the variety of units in which time is a dimension.

9.6.3 For instance, *flow rates* should be expressed in cubic metres per second, litres per second, or cubic metres per hour, rather than in cubic metres per minute or litres per minute. For example:

TABLE 6 Presentation of Numerical Values with SI

	Typical Examples	Remarks
A. *Decimal Marker*		
1. Whereas most European countries use the comma on the line as the decimal marker and this practice is advocated by ISO, a special exception is made for documents in the English language which have traditionally used the point (dot) on the line, or period, as decimal marker.		See also under G.
2. The recommended decimal marker for use in the United States is the point on the line (period), and the comma should not be used.	9.9; 15.375	NOT: 9,9; 15,375
3. *Always* show a zero before the decimal point for all numbers smaller than 1.0 (one).	0.1; 0.725	NOT: .1; .725
B. *Spacing*		
1. *Always* leave a gap between the numerical value associated with a symbol and the symbol, of at least half a space in width.	900 MHz; 200 mg; 10⁶ mm² or 10⁶ mm²	NOT: 900MHz; 200mg NOT: 10⁶mm²
In the case of the symbol for the "degree Celsius" this space is optional, but the degree symbol must always be attached to C.	20°C or 20 °C	NOT: 20° C
2. In non-SI expressions of plane angle (°, ', "), DO NOT LEAVE A SPACE between the numerical value and the symbol.	27°30' (of arc)	NOT: 27 ° 30 '
3. *Always* leave a space on each side of signs for multiplication, division, addition, and subtraction	100 mm × 100 mm; 36 MPa + 8 MPa	NOT: 100 mm×100 mm NOT: 36 MPa+8 MPa
C. *Fractions*		
1. *Avoid* common fractions in connection with SI units.	WRITE: 0.5 kPa	NOT: ½ kPa
2. *Always* use decimal notation to express fractions of any number larger than 1.0 (one).	1.5; 16.375	NOT: 1-½; 16-⅜
3. While the most common fractions such as half, third, quarter, and fifth will remain in speech, *always* show decimal notation in written, typed, or printed material.	0.5; 0.33; 0.25; 0.2	NOT: ½; ⅓; ¼; ⅕
D. *Powers of Units and Exponential Notation*		
1. When writing unit names with a modifier "squared" or "cubed," the following rules should be applied:		
a. In the case of area and volume, the modifier is written before the unit name as "square" and "cubic."	cubic metre; square millimetre	NOT: metre cubed; millimetre squared
b. In all other cases, the modifier is shown after the unit name as "squared," "cubed," "to the fourth power," etc.	metre per second squared	NOT: metre per square second; (or "metre per second per second")
c. The abbreviations "sq." for "square," and "cu." for "cubic" should *not* be used.		NOT: sq. millimetre NOT: cu. metre
2. For unit symbols with modifiers (such as square, cubic, fourth power, etc.) *always* show the superscript immediately after the symbol.	m²; mm³; s⁴	NOT: m ²; mm ³; s ⁴
3. Show the superscript as a reduced size numeral raised half a line space. Where a typewriter without superscript numerals is used, the full size numeral should be raised half a line space, provided that this does not encroach on print in the line above.	mm³, m/s²	PERMITTED: mm3, m/s2
4. Where an exponent is attached to a prefixed symbol, it indicates that that multiple (or submultiple) is raised to the power expressed by the exponent.	$1 \text{ mm}^3 = (10^{-3} \text{ m})^3 = 10^{-9} \text{ m}^3$ $1 \text{ km}^2 = (10^3 \text{ m})^2 = 10^6 \text{ m}^2$	NOT: $1 \text{ mm}^3 = 10^{-3} \text{ m}^3$

E 621

TABLE 6 *Continued*

	Typical Examples	Remarks
E. *Ratios*		
1. Do not mix units in expressing a ratio of like unit quantities.	0.01 m/m 0.03 m²/m²	NOT: 10 mm/m NOT: 30 000 mm²/m²
2. Wherever possible, use a non-quantitative expression (ratio or percentage) to indicate measurement of slopes, deflections, etc.		PREFERRED: 1:100; 0.01; 1 % 1:33; 0.03; 3 %
F. *Range*		
1. The choice of the appropriate prefix to indicate a multiple or submultiple of an SI unit is governed by convenience to obtain numerical values within a practical range and to eliminate nonsignificant digits.		
2. In preference, use prefixes representing ternary powers of 10 (10 raised to a power which is a multiple of 3).	milli, kilo, mega	AVOID: centi, deci, deka, hecto
3. Select prefixes so that the numerical value or values occur in a common range between 0.1 and 1000.	120 kN 3.94 mm 14.5 MPa	INSTEAD OF: 120 000 N 0.003 94 m 14 500 kPa
4. Compatibility with the general range must be a consideration; for example, if all dimensions on a drawing are shown in millimetres (mm), a range from 1 to 99 999 (a maximum of five numerals) would be acceptable to avoid **mixing of units.**		NOTE: Drawings should show "All dimensions shown in millimetres unless otherwise noted".
G. *Presentation and Tabulation of Numbers*		
1. In numbers with many digits it has been common practice in the United States to separate digits into groups of three by means of commas. This practice must *not* be used with SI, to avoid confusion. It is recommended international practice to arrange digits in long numbers in groups of three from the decimal marker, with a gap of not less than half a space, and not more than a full space, separating **each group.**	54 375.260 55 54 375.260 55	NOT: 54,375.260,55 NOT: 54375.26055
2. For individual numbers with four digits before (or after) the decimal marker this space is not necessary.	4500; 0.0355	
3. In all tabulations of numbers with five or more digits before or after the decimal marker or both, group digits into groups of three: For example, 12.5255; 5735; 98 300; 0.425 75	12.525 5 5 735 98 300 0.425 75 ————— 104 047.951 25	
H. *Use of Unprefixed Units in Calculations*		
Errors in calculations involving compound units can be minimized if all prefixed units are reverted back to coherent base or derived units, with numerical values expressed in powers-of-ten notation.	PREFERRED: 136 kJ = 136 × 10³ J 20 MPa = 20 × 10⁶ Pa 1.5 t (Mg) = 1.5 × 10³ kg	ALSO ACCEPTABLE: (or 1.36 × 10⁵ J) (or 2 × 10⁷ Pa)

$1 \text{ m}^3/\text{s} = 1000 \text{ L/s}$ (DO NOT USE 60 m³/min)
$1 \text{ L/s} = 3.6 \text{ m}^3/\text{h}$ (DO NOT USE 60 L/min)
$1 \text{ m}^3/\text{h} = 1000 \text{ L/h}$ (DO NOT USE 16.67 L/min)

9.6.4 Because of its variability, the month should not be used to indicate a time dimension, unless a specific calendar month is referred to.

9.6.5 Where the calendar year (symbol "a") is used as a measurement for time interval, it represents 365 days or 31 536 000 s.

9.7 *Temperature and Temperature Interval:*

9.7.1 The SI base unit of (thermodynamic) temperature is the kelvin (K), and this unit is used for expressing both thermodynamic temperature and temperature interval.

9.7.2 Wide use is also made of the degree Celsius (°C) for the expression of ambient temperature levels in Celsius temperature and temperature intervals.

9.7.3 The temperature interval of one degree Celsius equals exactly one kelvin. For this reason, the degree Celsius (°C) may be used instead of the kelvin in calculations involving temperature interval.

9.7.4 A temperature expressed in degrees Celsius is equal to the temperature expressed in kelvins less 273.15. There are no negative (minus) temperature values in the kelvin scale.

9.7.5 The degree Celsius (°C) for Celsius temperature has been included in the table of derived SI units with special names approved by CIPM in 1976.

E 621

9.8 *Mass, Weight, and Force:*

9.8.1 A significant feature of SI is the use of explicit and distinctly separate units for "mass" and for "force."

9.8.2 The SI base unit *kilogram* (kg) denotes the *base unit of mass* (the unit quantity of matter of an object which is constant and independent of gravitational attraction).

TABLE 7   Space and Time: Geometry, Kinematics, and Periodic Phenomena

Quantity (and SI Unit Symbol)	Preferred Units (Symbols)	Other Acceptable Units	Unit Name	Typical Applications	Remarks
Length (m)	m		metre	*Architecture and General Engineering:* Levels, overall dimensions, spans, column heights, etc., in engineering computations *Estimating and Specification:* Trenches, curbs, fences, lumber lengths, pipes and conduits; lengths of building materials generally *Land Surveying:* Boundary and cadastral surveys; survey plans; heights, geodetic surveys, contours *Hydraulic Engineering:* Pipe and channel lengths; depth of storage tanks or reservoirs; height of potentiometric head, hydraulic head, piezometric head	Use metres on all drawings with scale ratios between 1:200 and 1:2000. Where required for purposes of accuracy, show dimensions to three decimal places.
	mm		millimetre	*Architecture and General Engineering:* Spans, dimensions in buildings, dimensions of buildings products; depth and width of sections; displacement, settlement, deflection, elongation; slump of concrete, size of aggregate; radius of gyration, eccentricity; detailed dimensions generally; rainfall *Estimating and Specification:* Lumber cross sections; thicknesses, diameters, sheet metal gages, fasteners; all other building product dimensions *Hydraulic Engineering:* Pipe diameters; radii of ground water wells; height of capillary rise; precipitation, evaporation	Use millimetres on drawings with scale ratios between 1:1 and 1:200. Avoid the use of centimetres (cm). Where "cm" is shown in documents, such as for snow depth, body dimensions, or carpet sizes, etc., convert to "mm" or "m".
	km		kilometre	Distances for transportation purposes geographical or statistical applications in surveying; long pipes and channels	
	μm		micrometre	Thickness of coatings (paint, galvanizing etc.), thin sheet materials, size of fine aggregate	
Area (m^2)	m^2		square metre	*General Applications:* Small land areas; area of cross section of earthworks, channels and larger pipes; surface area of tanks and small reservoirs; areas in general *Estimating and Specification:* Site clearing; floor areas; paving, masonry construction, roofing, wall and floor finishes, plastering, paintwork, glass areas, membranes, lining materials, insulation, reinforcing mesh, formwork; areas of all building components	($1\ m^2 = 10^6\ mm^2$) Replaces sq. ft.; sq. yd., and square. Specify masonry construction by wall area × wall thickness.
	mm^2		square millimetre	Area of cross section for structural and other sections, bars, pipes, rolled and pressed shapes, etc.	Avoid the use of cm^2 (square centimetre) by conversion to mm^2. ($1\ cm^2 = 10^2\ mm^2$ $= 100\ mm^2$)
	km^2		square kilometre	Large catchment areas or land areas	
		ha	hectare	Land areas; irrigation areas; areas on boundary and other survey plans	($1\ ha = (10^2\ m)^2$ $= 10^4\ m^2$ $= 10\ 000\ m^2$
Volume, Capacity (m^3)	m^3		cubic metre	*General Applications:* Volume, capacity (large quantities); volume of earthworks, excavation, filling, waste removal; concrete, sand, all bulk materials supplied by volume and large quantities of timber *Hydraulic Engineering:* Water distribution, irrigation, diversions, sewage, storage capacity, underground basins	$1\ m^3 = 1000\ L$ As far as possible, use the cubic metre as the preferred unit of volume for engineering purposes.

E 621

TABLE 7 *Continued*

Quantity (and SI Unit Symbol)	Preferred Units (Symbols)	Other Acceptable Units	Unit Name	Typical Applications	Remarks
	mm^3		cubic millimetre	Volume, capacity (small quantities)	
		L	litre	Volume of fluids and containers for fluids; liquid materials, domestic water supply, consumption; volume/capacity of full tanks	The litre and its multiples or sub-multiples may be used for domestic and industrial supplies of liquids $1 L = 1 dm^3$
		mL	millilitre	Volume of fluids and containers for fluids (limited application only)	See Section 9.3
Modulus of Section (m^3)	mm^3		millimetre to third power	Geometric properties of structural sections, such as plastic section modulus, elastic section modulus, etc.	See Section 9.4
	m^3		metre to third power		
Second Moment of Area (m^4)	mm^4		millimetre to fourth power	Geometric properties of structural sections: moment of inertia of a section, torsional constant of cross section	See Section 9.4
	m^4		metre to fourth power		
Plane Angle (rad)	rad mrad		radian milliradian	Generally used in calculations only to preserve coherence *General Applications:*	Slopes and gradients may be expressed as a ratio or as a percentage: $26.57° = 1:2$
		(—°)	degree (of arc)	Angular measurement in construction generally; angle of rotation, torsion, shear resistance, friction, internal friction, etc. (decimalized degrees) *Land Surveying:*	$= 50\%$ $= 0.4637$ rad
				Bearings shown on boundary and cadastral survey plans; geodetic surveying	$(1$ rad $= 57.2958°)$ See Section 9.5
Time, Time Interval, Duration (s)	s		second	Time used in test methods; all calculations involving derived units with a time component, in order to preserve coherence	Avoid the use of minute (min) as far as possible
		h d a	hour day year (annum)	Time used in test methods, all calculations involving labor time, plant hire, maintenance periods, etc.	$(1$ h $= 3600$ s$)$ $(1$ d $= 86\ 400$ s$)$ $= 86.4$ ks$)$
Frequency (Hz)	Hz		hertz	Frequency of sound, vibration, shock	$(1$ Hz $= I/s = s^{-1})$ Replaces cycle per second (c/s or cps) See also Table 11.
	kHz MHz		kilohertz megahertz		
Rotational Frequency, Speed of Rotation (s^{-1})		r/s	revolution per second	Widely used in the specification of rotational speed of machinery Use r/min *only* for slow-moving equipment.	$(1$ r/s $= 2\ \pi$ rad/s$)$
Velocity, Speed (m/s)	m/s		metre per second	Calculations involving rectilinear motion, velocity and speed in general; wind velocity; velocity of fluids; pipe flow velocity	$(1$ m/s $= 3.6$ km/h$)$
		km/h	kilometre per hour	Wind speed; speed used in transportation; speed limits	
		mm/h	millimetre per hour	Rainfall intensity	
Angular Velocity **(rad/s)**	rad/s		radian per second	Calculation involving rotational motion	
Linear Acceleration (m/s^2)	m/s^2		metre per second squared	Kinematics and calculation of dynamic forces	Recommended value of acceleration of gravity for use in U.S.: $g_{us} = 9.8$ m/s^2
Volume Rate of Flow (m^3/s)	m^3/s	$m^3 n$	cubic metre per second cubic metre per hour	Volumetric flow in general; flow in pipes, ducts, channels, rivers, irrigation spray demand	$(1$ m^3/s $= 1000$ L/s$)$
		m^3/d	cubic metre per day		
		L/s	litre per second	Volumetric flow of fluids only	
		L/d	litre per day		

9.8.3 The derived SI unit *newton* (N) denotes the *absolute derived unit of force* (mass times acceleration: kg·m/s^2).

9.8.4 The general use of the term "weight" should be avoided in technical practice for the following reasons:

9.8.4.1 Considerable confusion exists because the term "weight" has been used to mean either "mass" or "force of gravity."

9.8.4.2 In commercial and everyday use, the term "weight" has nearly always meant mass.

⟨ASTM⟩ E 621

9.8.4.3 In technical use, the term "weight" has often been applied to mean "force of gravity," a *particular force*, related solely to gravitational acceleration, which varies on the surface of the earth.

9.8.4.4 Where quantities are shown as "weight" it is important to establish whether "mass" or "force" is intended, and to use the appropriate SI units, that is, kilogram for "mass" and newton for "force."

9.8.5 As serviceable as customary gravitational systems may seem in the area of "statics," the absolute and more universally useful concepts of the clear SI distinction between "mass" and "force" will become increasingly significant as engineering and construction become more and more involved in "dynamic" considerations.

9.8.6 In dynamic calculations, the value of a mass in kilograms (kg) is used directly with the appropriate acceleration to determine force, the applicable equation being $F = ma$. The frequently used equation $W = mg$, in which W is

considered to equal "weight" should be superseded (see 9.8.4) by $F_g = mg$, in which F_g is the force of gravity.

9.8.7 For engineering design purposes, in United States locations the recommended value to be used for acceleration of gravity is: $g = 9.8$ m/s^2. (The standard international value is 9.806 65.)

9.8.8 The use of the factor 9.8 (m/s^2) is recommended for g because:

9.8.8.1 It provides adequate accuracy in nearly all instances,

9.8.8.2 It gives fewer decimal places than the use of 9.81 or 9.806 65 which was advocated in Britain, and

9.8.8.3 It provides a different number in the product than would be obtained with the use of a factor of 10 (advocated by some), which can be easily overlooked and cause errors.

9.8.9 The newton extends through to derived quantities for pressure and stress, energy, work and quantity of heat, power, and many of the electrical units.

TABLE 8   Mechanics: Statics and Dynamics

Quantity (and SI Unit Symbol)	Preferred Units (Symbols)	Other Acceptable Units	Unit Name	Typical Applications	Remarks
Mass (kg)	kg		kilogram	Mass of materials in general, mass of structural elements and machinery	USE kilograms (kg) in calculations and specifications
	g		gram	Mass of samples of material for testing	Masses greater than 10^4 kg (10 000 kg) may be conveniently expressed in metric tons (t):
		t	metric ton	Mass of large quantities of materials, such as structural steel, reinforcement, aggregates, concrete, etc.; ratings of lifting equipment	1 t = 10^3 kg = 1 Mg = 1000 kg
Mass per Unit Length (kg/m)	kg/m		kilogram per metre	Mass per unit length of sections, bars, and similar items of uniform cross section	Also known as "linear density"
		g/m	gram per metre	Mass per unit length of wire and similar material of uniform cross section	
Mass per Unit Area (kg/m^2)	kg/m^2		kilogram per square metre	Mass per unit area of slabs, plates, and similar items of uniform thickness or depth; rating for load-carrying capacities on floors (display on notices only)*	*DO NOT USE in stress calculations
		g/m^2	gram per square metre	Mass per unit area of thin sheet materials, coatings, etc.	
Mass Density, Concentration (kg/m^3)	kg/m^3		kilogram per cubic metre	Density of materials in general; mass per unit volume of materials in a concrete mix; evaluation of masses of structures and materials	Also known as "mass per unit volume"
		g/m^3	gram per cubic metre	Mass per unit volume (concentration) in pollution control	
		μg/m^3	microgram per cubic metre		
Momentum (kg·m/s)	kg·m/s		kilogram metre per second	Used in applied mechanics; evaluation of impact and dynamic forces	
Moment of Inertia (kg·m^2)	kg·m^2		kilogram square metre	Rotational dynamics. Evaluation of the restraining forces required for propellers, windmills, etc.	See also Section 9.10.5
Mass per Unit Time (kg/s)	kg/s		kilogram per second	Rate of transport of material on conveyors and other materials handling equipment	1 kg/s = 3.6 t/h
		t/h	metric ton per hour		
Force (N)	N		newton	Unit of force for use in calculations	1 N = 1 kg·m/s^2
	kN		kilonewton	Forces in structural elements, such as columns, piles, ties, pre-stressing tendons, etc.; concentrated forces; axial forces; reactions; shear force; gravitational force	See also Section 9.8
Force per Unit Length (N/m)	N/m		newton per metre	Unit for use in calculations	
	kN/m		kilonewton per metre	Transverse force per unit length on a beam, column, etc.; force distribution in a linear direction	

E 621

TABLE 8 *Continued*

Quantity (and SI Unit Symbol)	Preferred Units (Symbols)	Other Acceptable Units	Unit Name	Typical Applications	Remarks
Moment of Force, Torsional or Bending Moment, Torque ($N \cdot m$)	$N \cdot m$ $kN \cdot m$ $MN \cdot m$		newton metre kilonewton metre meganewton metre	Bending moments (in structural sections), torsional moment; overturning moment; tightening tension for high-strength bolts; torque in engine drive shafts, axles, etc.	See also Sections 9.10.4 and 9.10.5
Pressure, Stress, Modulus of Elasticity (Pa)	Pa		pascal	Unit for use in calculations; low differential pressure in fluids; duct pressure in air conditioning, heating, and ventilating systems	($1 Pa = 1 N/m^2$)
	kPa		kilopascal	Uniformly distributed pressure (loads) on floors; soil bearing pressure; wind pressure (loads), snow loads, dead and live loads; pressure in fluids; fluid flow resistance in closed systems; differential pressure in high-pressure ventilation systems	Where wind pressure, snow loads, dead and live loads are shown in kN/m^2, CHANGE units to kPa
	MPa		megapascal	Modulus of elasticity; stress (ultimate, proof, yield, permissible, calculated, etc.) in structural materials; concrete and steel strength grades	$1 MPa = 1 MN/m^2$ $= 1 N/mm^2$
	GPa μPa		gigapascal micropascal	Modulus of elasticity in high-strength materials Sound pressure ($20 \mu Pa$ is the reference quantity for sound pressure level)	
Compressibility (Pa^{-1})	1/Pa		reciprocal (of) pascal	Settlement analysis, coefficient of compressibility, bulk compressibility	($1/Pa = 1 m^2/N$)
	1/kPa		reciprocal (of) kilopascal		
Dynamic Viscosity ($Pa \cdot s$)	$Pa \cdot s$ $mPa \cdot s$		pascal second millipascal second	Shear stresses in fluids	($1 Pa \cdot s = 1 N \cdot s/m^2$) The centipoise (cP) = $10^{-3} Pa \cdot s$ WILL NOT BE USED
Kinematic Viscosity (m^2/s)	m^2/s		square metre per second		The centistokes (cSt) = $10^{-6} m^2/s$ WILL NOT BE USED
	mm^2/s		square millimetre per second	Computation of Reynold's number, settlement analysis (coefficient of consolidation)	$1 cSt = 1 mm^2/s$
Work, Energy (J)	J kJ MJ		joule kilojoule megajoule	Energy absorbed in impact testing of materials; energy in general; calculations involving mechanical and electrical energy	
		kWh	kilowatthour	Electrical energy applications only	$1 kWh = 3.6 MJ$
Impact Strength (J/m^2)	J/m^2		joule per square metre	Impact strength; impact ductility	
	kJ/m^2		kilojoule per square metre		
Power (W)	W kW		watt kilowatt	Power in general (mechanical, electrical, thermal); input/output rating, etc., of motors, engines, heating and ventilating plant, and other equipment in general	
	MW		megawatt	Power input/output rating, etc., of heavy power plant	
	pW		picowatt	Sound power level (1 pW is the reference quantity for sound power level)	

9.8.10 The unit kilogram-force (kgf) is inconsistent with SI, and is in the process of being dropped and replaced by the newton in traditionally metric countries. The kilogram-force (kgf) should *not* be used in the United States.

9.9 *Pressure, Stress, and Elastic Modulus:*

9.9.1 The SI unit for both pressure and stress (force per unit area) is the pascal (Pa). It replaces a large number of customary units and also supersedes a few traditional but non-SI metric units.

9.9.2 While it may be useful in some applications to read out test results in N/mm^2 (which is identical with MN/m^2), or in kN/m^2, it is preferable and recommended always to show calculations and results in MPa or kPa.

9.9.3 The non-SI units, the "bar" (which equals 100 kPa or 0.1 MPa) and the "millibar" (which equals 100 Pa or 0.1 kPa) should *not* be used.

9.10 *Energy, Work, and Quantity of Heat:*

9.10.1 The SI unit of energy, work, and quantity of heat is the joule (J), which is equal to a newton metre ($N \cdot m$) and a watt second ($W \cdot s$).

9.10.2 The joule provides one coherent unit to supersede a large number of traditional units: Btu, therm, calorie, kilocalorie, foot pound-force, etc.

9.10.3 For many years, and since long before the joule was named, the kilowatthour (kWh) (Note 3) has been used extensively as the unit of energy in electrical energy consumption. Most existing electricity meters show kWh, and recalibration in megajoules (MJ) would be needlessly costly. For this reason, the kWh will be permitted as an alternative unit in electrical applications, but should not be introduced in new areas.

⟨ASTM⟩ E 621

NOTE 3—The accepted symbol in the United States is "kWh," but the correct SI symbol would be kW·h.

9.10.4 The joule should *never* be used for torque for which the widely designated unit is newton metre (N·m).

9.10.5 For dimensional consistency in rotational dynamics, torque should be expressed as newton metre per radian (N·m/rad), and moment of inertia as kilogram square metre per radian squared (kg·m^2/rad^2).

9.11 *Power and Heat Flow Rate:*

9.11.1 The SI unit for power and heat flow rate is the watt (W), which is already in world-wide use as the general unit for electrical power.

9.11.2 The watt, and its multiples, will now replace a number of traditional units of power and heat flow rate:

9.11.2.1 For general power: the horsepower (electric, boiler) and the foot pound-force per hour (or minute or second)

9.11.2.2 For heat flow rate: the Btu per hour and the calorie (or kilocalorie) per minute (or second); the ton of refrigeration

9.12 *Moisture Movement in Buildings:*

9.12.1 Moisture vapor movement through materials and constructions is expressed by the quantities vapor permeance and vapor permeability. The word vapor should always be used to distinguish the quantities from permeance and permeability, which are used in the electro-magnetic field and have different meanings.

9.12.2 The traditional unit "perm" represents a specification of performance, the lower the "perm" value, the greater the retardation of moisture movement. The "metric perm" (g/(24 h·m^2·mmHg)) is a non-SI unit and should not be used.

9.12.3 Resistance to moisture movement is expressed by the quantities vapor resistance and vapor resistivity. Vapor resistances are additive so that the higher the vapor-resistance value, the better the resistance to moisture movement.

9.13 *Electrical Units:*

9.13.1 There are no changes in units used in electrical engineering, except

TABLE 9 Heat, Thermal Effects, Heat Transfer

Quantity (and SI Unit Symbol)	Preferred Units (Symbols)	Other Acceptable Units	Unit Name	Typical Applications	Remarks
Temperature Value (K)	K		kelvin	Expression of thermodynamic temperature; calculations involving units of temperature	($t°C = T_K - 273.15$)
		°C	degree Celsius	Common temperature scale for use in meteorology and general applications; ambient temperature values	Temperature values will normally be measured in °C (degrees Celsius)
Temperature Interval (K)	K		kelvin	Heat transfer calculations; temperature intervals in test methods, etc.	(1 K = 1°C) The use of K (kelvin) in compound units is recommended
		°C	degree Celsius		
Coefficient of Linear Thermal Expansion (1/K)	1/K	1/°C	reciprocal (of) kelvin	Expansion of materials subject to a change in temperature (generally expressed as a ratio per kelvin or degree Celsius)	
			reciprocal (of) degree Celsius		
Heat, Quantity of Heat (J)	J		joule	Thermal energy calculations. Enthalpy, latent heat, sensible heat	
	kJ		kilojoule		
	MJ		megajoule		
Specific Energy, Specific Latent Heat; Combustion Heat (mass basis) (J/kg)	J/kg		joule per kilogram	Heat of transition; heat and energy contained in materials; combustion heat per unit mass; calorific value of fuels (mass basis); specific sensible heat, specific latent heat in psychrometric calculations	
	kJ/kg		kilojoule per kilogram		
	MJ/kg		megajoule per kilogram		
Energy Density, Combustion Heat (volume basis) (J/m^3)	J/m^3		joule per cubic metre	Combustion heat per unit volume	
	kJ/m^3		kilojoule per cubic metre		(1 kJ/m^3 = 1 J/L)
	MJ/m^3		megajoule per cubic metre	Calorific value of fuels (volume basis)	(1 MJ/m^3 = 1 kJ/L)
Heat Capacity, Entropy (J/K)	J/K		joule per kelvin	Thermal behavior of materials, heat transmission calculations, entropy	
	kJ/K		kilojoule per kelvin		
Specific Heat Capacity, Specific Entropy (J/(kg·K))	J/(kg·K)		joule per kilogram kelvin	Thermal behavior of materials, heat transmission calculations	
	kJ/(kg·K)		kilojoule per kilogram kelvin		
Heat Flow Rate (W)	W		watt	Heat flow through walls, windows, etc.; heat demand	(1 W = 1 J/s)
	kW		kilowatt		

⬡ E 621

TABLE 9 *Continued*

Quantity (and SI Unit Symbol)	Preferred Units (Symbols)	Other Acceptable Units	Unit Name	Typical Applications	Remarks
Power Density, Heat Flux, Density, Irradiance **(W/m²)**	W/m² \ kW/m²		watt per square metre \ kilowatt per square metre	Density of power or heat flow through building walls and other heat transfer surfaces; heat transmission calculations	
Heat Release Rate (W/m³)	W/m³ \ kW/m³		watt per cubic metre \ kilowatt per cubic metre	Rate of heat release per unit volume over time (for gases and liquids)	$1 \text{ W/m}^3 = 1 \text{ J/(m}^3 \cdot \text{s})$
Thermal Conductivity (W/(m·K))	W/(m·K)	W/(m·°C)	watt per metre kelvin \ watt per metre degree Celsius	Estimation of thermal behavior of homogeneous materials and systems; heat transmission calculations	$1 \text{ W/(m} \cdot \text{K)} =$ \ $1 \text{ W/(m} \cdot \text{°C)} =$ \ $1 \text{ W.m/(m}^2 \cdot \text{K)}$
				Thermal conductivity of structural and building materials in fire-resistance testing, insulation, etc.	("k" value)
Thermal Conductance (W/(m²·K))	W/(m²·K) \ \ \ kW/(m²·K)	W/(m²·°C) \ \ \ kW/(m²·°C)	watt per square metre kelvin \ watt per square metre degree Celsius \ kilowatt per square metre kelvin \ kilowatt per square metre degree Celsius	Heat transfer calculations for buildings, building components and equipment. Transmittance of construction elements; calculation of coefficients of heat transfer	("U" value) \ In ISO 31/IV this quantity is called *coefficient of heat transfer*
Thermal Resistivity ((m·K)/W)	(m·K)/W	(m·°C)/W	metre kelvin per watt \ metre degree Celsius per watt	Heat transmission calculations for materials and building elements (Reciprocal of thermal conductivity)	
Thermal-Resistance ((m²·K)/W)	(m²·K)/W	(m²·°C)/W	square metre kelvin per watt \ square metre degree Celsius per watt	Heat transmission calculations; rating of thermal insulating materials (thermal resistances are additive)	("R" value) \ In ISO 31/IV this quantity is called thermal insulance and the quantity thermal resistance has the unit K/W

9.13.1.1 The renaming of the unit of conductance to siemens (S) from "mho."

9.13.1.2 The use of the SI unit for frequency, hertz (Hz), instead of cycles per second (cps).

9.14 *Lighting Units:*

9.14.1 The SI unit for luminous intensity, candela (cd), and for luminous flux, lumen (lm), are already in common use.

9.14.2 The candela (cd) directly replaces the former units "candle" and "candlepower."

9.14.3 Illuminance will be expressed in the SI unit lux (lx), which is equal to the lumen per square metre (lm/m²), and replaces lumen per square foot and footcandle.

9.14.4 Luminance will be expressed in candela per square metre (cd/m²), which replaces candela per square foot, footlambert, and lambert.

9.15 *Dimensionless Quantitites*—Dimensionless quantities, or ratios, such as relative humidity, specific gravity, decibel (dB), pH, parts per million, etc., remain unchanged when converting to SI.

9.16 *Constants for Use in Building Design Calculations*—Table 14 shows a selection of internationally agreed values and empirical constants for use in design calculations, taken to no more than six significant figures.

10. Conversion and Rounding

10.1 Rules for conversion and rounding are not covered by this standard. They are given in Section 4 of ASTM E 380, Standard for Metric Practice.

10.2 Conversion factors for the conversion of the principal quantities in building design and construction are given in Appendix X1. A more detailed list of conversion factors, to six places of decimals and in exponential notation for ready adaptation in computer readout and electronic data transmission, is given in Appendix X3, Conversion Factors of ASTM E 380.

10.3 In the conversion of data, the need for precision is determined by the legal requirements or by any requirement for the interchangeability of parts. To obtain a more convenient numerical expression, it will often be preferable to round an "exact conversion" within tolerances of the original value. This is termed a "soft conversion." The change to a new and non-interchangeable value based on preferred or convenient numbers is termed a "hard conversion" and generally involves a physical change in size or properties.

10.4 Guidance on preferred numbers and number series is contained in international standards ISO 3, ISO 17, and ISO 497, as well as in ANSI Z17.1. The selection of preferred metric values for design and construction is also discussed in NBS Technical Note 990.

E 621

TABLE 10 Moisture Movement

Quantity (and SI Unit Symbol)	Preferred Units (Symbols)	Other Acceptable Units	Unit Name	Typical Applications	Remarks
Mass (of Moisture Vapor) (kg)	mg µg ng		milligram microgram nanogram	Measurement of quantity of moisture vapor	
Vapor Pressure (Pa)	Pa		pascal	Measurement of vapor pressure, vapor pressure difference, vapor pressure drop	Do not use millibar (mbar) or millimetre of mercury (mmHg)
Vapor Permeance $(kg/(Pa \cdot s \cdot m^2))$	$\mu g/(Pa \cdot s \cdot m^2)$ $ng/(Pa \cdot s \cdot m^2)$		microgram per pascal second square metre nanogram per pascal second square metre	Transmission of moisture vapor through building elements (roofs, walls, floors); surface coefficient of vapor transfer in still or moving air	In some countries, the SI unit $kg/(N \cdot s)$ is used for this quantity, with m^2 cancelled out. Vapor permeance is the reciprocal of vapor resistance
Vapor Permeability $(kg/(Pa \cdot s \cdot m))$	$\mu g/(Pa \cdot s \cdot m)$ $ng/(Pa \cdot s \cdot m)$		microgram per pascal second metre nanogram per pascal second metre	Transmission of moisture vapor through a specified thickness of a homogeneous material or construction	The unit has been reduced from $kg \cdot m/(Pa \cdot s \cdot m^2)$. In some countries $kg \cdot m/(N \cdot s)$ is used. Vapor permeability is the reciprocal of vapor resistivity
Vapor Resistance $(Pa \cdot s \cdot m^2/kg)$	$MPa \cdot s \cdot m^2/kg$ $GPa \cdot s \cdot m^2/kg$		megapascal second square metre per kilogram gigapascal second square metre per kilogram	Resistance to moisture vapor transmission by building elements; surface vapor resistance in still or moving air	
Vapor Resistivity $(Pa \cdot s \cdot m/kg)$	$MPa \cdot s \cdot m/kg$ $GPa \cdot s \cdot m/kg$		megapascal second metre per kilogram gigapascal second metre per kilogram	Resistivity to moisture vapor transmission by a specified thickness of a homogeneous material or construction	Vapor resistivities are additive

E 621

TABLE 11 Electricity and Magnetism

Quantity (and SI Unit Symbol)	Preferred Units (Symbols)	Other Acceptable Units	Unit Name	Typical Applications	Remarks
Frequency (Hz)	Hz kHz MHz		hertz kilohertz megahertz	Frequencies of electromagnetic waves; power frequency for electric motors; radio frequencies	1 Hz = 1/s = s⁻¹ Replaces cycle per second (c/s or cps) See also Table 7
Electric Current (A)	A kA mA μA		ampere kiloampere milliampere microampere	Maintenance rating of an electrical installation. Leakage current	
Magnetomotive Force, **Magnetic Potential Difference** (A)				Used in the calculations involved in magnetic circuits	
Magnetic Field Strength, Magnetization (A/m)	A/m kA/m		ampere per metre kiloampere per metre	Magnetic field strength is used in calculation of magnetic circuitry such as transformers, magnetic amplifiers, and general cores.	(1 kA/m = 1 A/mm)
Current Density (A/m²)	A/m² kA/m²	A/mm²	ampere per square metre kiloampere per square metre ampere per square millimetre	Design of cross-sectional area of electrical conductor	(1 A/mm² = 1 MA/m²)
Electric Charge, Quantity of Electricity (C)	C kC μC nC pC		coulomb kilocoulomb microcoulomb nanocoulomb picocoulomb	The voltage on a unit with capacitive-type characteristics may be related to the amount of charge present (for example, electrostatic precipitators). Storage battery capacities	1 C = 1 A·s DO NOT USE ampere hour: 1 A·h = 3.6 kC
Electric Potential, Potential Difference, Electromotive Force (V)	V MV kV mV μV		volt megavolt kilovolt millivolt microvolt		1 V = 1 W/A
Electric Field Strength (V/m)	V/m MV/m kV/m mV/m μV/m		volt per metre megavolt per metre kilovolt per metre millivolt per metre microvolt per metre	The electric field strength gives the potential gradient at points in space. This may be used to calculate or test electrical parameters such as dielectric strength.	
Active Power (W)	W GW MW kW mW μW		watt gigawatt megawatt kilowatt milliwatt microwatt	The useful power of an electrical circuit is expressed in watts (W). (The apparent power in an electrical circuit is expressed in volt-amperes (V·A).)	1 W = 1 V·A
Capacitance (F)	F mF μF nF pF		farad millifarad microfarad nanofarad picofarad	Electronic components. Electrical design and performance calculators	1 F = 1 C/V

E 621

TABLE 11 *Continued*

Quantity (and SI Unit Symbol)	Preferred Units (Symbols)	Other Acceptable Units	Unit Name	Typical Applications	Remarks
Resistance (Ω)	Ω $G\Omega$ $M\Omega$ $k\Omega$ $m\Omega$		ohm gigaohm megohm kilohm milliohm	The design of electrical devices with resistance, such as motors, generators, heaters, electrical distribution systems, etc.	$1\ \Omega = 1\ V/A$
Conductance, Admittance, Susceptance (S)	S MS kS mS μS		siemens megasiemens kilosiemens millisiemens microsiemens		The siemens (S) was formerly known as "mho"
Resistivity ($\Omega \cdot m$)	$\Omega \cdot m$ $G\Omega \cdot m$ $M\Omega \cdot m$ $k\Omega \cdot m$ $m\Omega \cdot m$ $\mu\Omega \cdot m$ $n\Omega \cdot m$		ohm metre gigaohm metre megohm metre kilohm metre milliohm metre microohm metre nanoohm metre		
(Electrical) Conductivity (S/m)	S/m MS/m kS/m μS/m		siemens per metre megasiemens per metre kilosiemens per metre microsiemens per metre	A parameter for measuring water quality	
Magnetic Flux, Flux of Magnetic Induction (Wb)	mWb		milliweber	Used in the calculations involved in magnetic circuits	$1\ Wb = 1\ V \cdot s$
Magnetic Flux Density, Magnetic Induction (T)	T mT μT nT		tesla millitesla microtesla nanotesla	Used in the calculations involved in magnetic circuits	$1\ T = 1\ Wb/m^2$
Magnetic Vector Potential (Wb/m^2)	kWb/m^2		kiloweber per square metre	Used in the calculations involved in magnetic circuits	
Self-Inductance, Mutual Inductance, Permeance (H)	H mH μH nH pH		henry millihenry microhenry nanohenry picohenry	Used in analysis and calculations involving transformers	$1\ H = 1\ Wb/A$
Reluctance (1/H)	1/H		reciprocal of henry	Design of motors and generators	
Permeability (H/m)	H/m μH/m nH/m		henry per metre microhenry per metre nanohenry per metre	Permeability gives the relationship between the magnetic flux density and the magnetic fluid strength.	

E 621

TABLE 12 Lighting

Quantity (and SI Unit Symbol)	Preferred Units (Symbols)	Other Acceptable Units	Unit Name	Typical Applications	Remarks
Luminous Intensity (cd)	cd		candela		
Solid Angle (sr)	sr		steradian		
Luminous Flux (lm)	lm klm		lumen kilolumen	Luminous flux of light sources, lamps and light bulbs	1 lm = 1 cd·sr Already in general use
Quantity of Light (lm·s)	lm·s	lm·h	lumen second lumen hour		1 lm·h = 3600 lm/s
Luminance (cd/m²)	cd/m² kcd/m²	cd/mm²	candela per square metre kilocandela per square metre candela per square millimetre	Assessment of surface brightness; luminance of light sources, lamps and light bulbs; calculation of glare in lighting layouts	Replaces stilb (1 sb = 10⁴ cd/m²) and apostilb (1 apostilb = cd/πm²)
Illuminance (lx)	lx klx		lux kilolux	Luminous flux per unit area is used in determination of illumination levels and design/evaluation of interior lighting layouts. (Outdoor daylight illumination on a horizontal plane ranges up to 100 klx.)	a) Formerly referred to as illumination 1 lx = 1 lm/m² b) Replaces phot (1 ph = 10⁴ lx) c) Luminous exitance is described in lm/m²
Light Exposure (lx·s)	lx·s klx·s		lux second kilolux second		
Luminous Efficacy (lm/W)	lm/W		lumen per watt	Rating of luminous efficacy of artificial light sources	

E 621

TABLE 13   Acoustics

Quantity (and SI Unit Symbol)	Preferred Units (Symbols)	Other Acceptable Units	Unit Name	Typical Applications	Remarks
Wavelength (m)	m mm		metre millimetre	Definition of sound wave pitch	
Area of Absorptive Surface (m²)	m²		square metre	Surface areas in the calculation of room absorption	Absorptive properties of buildings and building materials have also been expressed in the non-SI unit "metric sabin"
Period, Periodic Time (s)	s ms		second millisecond	Measurement of time, reverberation time, and duration of sound	
Frequency (Hz)	Hz kHz		hertz kilohertz	Frequency bands or ranges in acoustical calculations and measurements; frequency of vibrations	$1\ Hz = 1/s = s^{-1}$ Replaces cycle per second (c/s or cps)
Sound Pressure (Pa)	Pa mPa		pascal millipascal	Measurement of instantaneous or peak sound pressure, normally expressed in root-mean-square (rms) values. The standard reference value for sound pressure is 20 μPa. Sound pressure levels are generally shown in the non-dimensional logarithmic unit decibel (dB) signifying the ratio of actual pressure to reference pressure.	Do NOT USE dyne (1 dyn = 10 μPa)
	μPa		micropascal	Sound pressure level $L_p = $ $20 \log_{10} \dfrac{\text{actual pressure (Pa)}}{20 \times 10^{-6}\ \text{(Pa)}}$	
Sound Power, Sound Energy Flux (W)	W mW μW		watt milliwatt microwatt	Measurement of sound power and rate of flow of sound energy. The standard reference value for sound power is 1 pW (10^{-12}W).	
	pW		picowatt	Sound power level, $L = $ $10 \log_{10} \dfrac{\text{actual pressure (W)}}{20 \times 10^{-12}\ \text{(W)}}$	
Sound Energy Density (J/m³)	J/m³		joule per cubic metre	Measurement of mean sound energy density	
Sound Intensity (W/m²)	W/m²		watt per square metre	Measurement of sound intensity	The standard reference value for sound intensity is 1 pW/m² (10^{-12}W/m^2)
	pW/m²		picowatt per square metre	Sound intensity level $L_i = $ $10 \log_{10} \dfrac{\text{actual intensity (W/m}^2)}{10^{-12}\ \text{(W/m}^2)}$	
Specific Acoustic Impedance (Pa·s/m)	Pa·s/m		pascal second per metre	Sound impedance measurement	$(1\ Pa\cdot s/m = 1\ N\cdot s/m^3)$
Acoustic Impedance, Acoustic Resistance (Pa·s/m³)	Pa·s/m³		pascal second per cubic metre	Sound impedance measurement	

TABLE 14   Units for Volume and Fluid Capacity and Their Relationships

Preferred Units			Relationships
All Volumes	Fluid Volume Only	Limited Application	
m³			1 m³ = 1000 L = 1000 dm³
	L	dm³	1 L = 1 dm³ = 10⁻³ m³ = 1000 mL 10⁶ mm³
	mL	cm³	1 mL = 1 cm³ = 10⁻⁶ m³ 10³ mm³
mm³			1 mm³ = 10⁻⁹ m³

TABLE 15   Constants for Use in Building Design Calculations

Name	Symbol	Value	Unit
Standard atmosphere pressure (international value)	P_0	101.325	kPa
Absolute (zero) temperature	T	0.0 (−273.15)	K (°C)
Velocity of sound in air (P_0, 20°C, 50 % relative humidity)	M	344	m/s
Specific volume of perfect gas at STP	V_0	22.414	m³/kmol (L/mol)
Characteristic gas constant for air	R_a	287.045	J/(kg·K)
Characteristic gas constant for water vapor	R_v	461.52	J/(kg·K)

⟨ASTM⟩ E 621

APPENDIXES

X1. CONVERSION FACTORS FOR THE MOST COMMON UNITS USED IN BUILDING DESIGN AND CONSTRUCTION

X1.1 Where appropriate, conversion factors are taken to six significant figures. Underlined values denote exact conversions.

Metric to Customary			Customary to Metric		
LENGTH					
1 km	= 0.621 371	mile (international)	1 mile (international)	= 1.609 344	km
1 m	= 49.7096	chain	1 chain (survey unit)	= 20.1168	m
	= 1.093 61	yd	1 yd	= 0.9144	m
	= 3.280 84	ft	1 ft	= 0.3048	m
1 mm	= 0.039 370 1	in		= 304.8	mm
			1 in	= 25.4	mm
			(1 U.S. survey foot	= 0.304 800 6	m)*

* Section 9.1.7 deals with U.S. survey measurement.

AREA					
1 km²	= 0.386 101	mile² (U.S. survey)	1 mile² (U.S. survey)	= 2.590 00	km²
1 ha	= 2.471 04	acre (U.S. survey)	1 acre (U.S. survey)	= 0.404 687	ha
1 m²	= 1.195 99	yd²		= 4046.87	m²
	= 10.7639	ft²	1 yd²	= 0.836 127	m²
1 mm²	= 0.001 550	in²	1 ft²	= 0.092 903	m²
			1 in²	= 645.16	mm²

VOLUME, MODULUS OF SECTION					
1 m³	= 0.810 708 × 10⁻³	acre feet (U.S. survey)	1 acre ft (U.S. survey)	= 1233.49	m³
	= 1.307 95	yd³	1 yd³	= 0.764 555	m³
	= 35.3147	ft³	100 board ft	= 0.235 974	m³
	= 423.776	board ft	1 ft³	= 0.028 316 8	m³
1 mm³	= 61.0237 × 10⁻⁶	in³		= 28.3168	L (dm³)
			1 in³	= 16 387.1	mm³
				= 16.3871	mL (cm³)

(FLUID) CAPACITY					
1 L	= 0.035 314 7	ft³	1 gal (U.S. liquid)**	= 3.785 41	L
	= 0.264 172	gal (U.S.)	1 qt (U.S. liquid)	= 946.353	mL
	= 1.056 69	qt (U.S.)	1 pt (U.S. liquid)	= 473.177	mL
1 mL	= 0.061 023 7	in³	1 fl oz (U.S.)	= 29.5735	mL
	0.033 814	fl oz (U.S.)			

** 1 gal (U.K.) approx. 1.2 gal (U.S.)

SECOND MOMENT OF AREA					
1 mm⁴	= 2.402 51 × 10⁻⁶	in⁴	1 in⁴	= 416 231	mm⁴
				= 0.416 231 × 10⁻⁶	m⁴

PLANE ANGLE					
1 rad	= 57° 17′ 45″	(degree)	1° (degree)	= 0.017 453 3	rad
	= 57.2958°	(degree)		= 17.4533	mrad
	= 3437.75′	(minute)	1′ (minute)	= 290.888	μrad
	= 206 265″	(second)	1″ (second)	= 4.848 14	μrad

VELOCITY, SPEED					
1 m/s	= 3.280 84	ft/s	1 ft/s	= 0.3048	m/s
	= 2.236 94	mile/h	1 mile/h	= 1.609 344	km/h
1 km/h	= 0.621 371	mile/h		= 0.447 04	m/s

ACCELERATION					
1 m/s²	= 3.280 84	ft/s²	1 ft/s²	= 0.3048	m/s²

VOLUME RATE OF FLOW					
1 m³/s	= 35.3147	ft³/s	1 ft³/s	= 0.028 316 8	m³/s
	= 22.8245	million gal/d	1 ft³/min	= 0.471 947	L/s
	= 0.810 709 × 10⁻³	acre ft/s	1 gal/min	= 0.063 090 2	L/s
1 L/s	= 2.118 88	ft³/min	1 gal/h	= 1.051 50	mL/s
	= 15.8503	gal/min	1 million gal/d	= 43.8126	L/s
	= 951.022	gal/h	1 acre ft/s	= 1233.49	m³/s

TEMPERATURE INTERVAL					
1°C	= 1 K = 1.8°F		1°F	= 0.555 556	°C or K
				= 5/9°C = 5/9 K	

ⒶⓢⓉⓂ E 621

Metric to Customary			Customary to Metric	

EQUIVALENT TEMPERATURE VALUE ($t_C = T_K - 273.15$)

	$= 5/9\,(t_F - 32)$		t_F	$= 9/5\,t_C + 32$	
t_C					

MASS

1 kg	= 2.204 62	lb (avoirdupois)	1 ton (short)***	= 0.907 185	metric ton
	= 35.2740	oz (avoirdupois)		= 907.185	kg
1 metric ton	= 1.102 31	ton (short, 2000 lb)	1 lb	= 0.453 592	kg
	= 2204.62	lb	1 oz	= 28.3495	g
1 g	= 0.035 274	oz	1 pennyweight	= 1.555 17	g
	= 0.643 015	pennyweight		= 1016.05	kg)

*** (1 long ton (2240 lb)

MASS PER UNIT LENGTH

1 kg/m	= 0.671 969	lb/ft	1 lb/ft	= 1.488 16	kg/m
1 g/m	= 3.547 99	lb/mile	1 lb/mile	= 0.281 849	g/m

MASS PER UNIT AREA

1 kg/m^2	= 0.204 816	lb/ft^2	1 lb/ft^2	= 4.882 43	kg/m^2
1 g/m^2	= 0.029 494	oz/yd^2	1 oz/yd^2	= 33.9057	g/m^2
	= 3.277 06 × 10^{-3}	oz/ft^2	1 oz/ft^2	= 305.152	g/m^2

DENSITY (MASS PER UNIT VOLUME)

1 kg/m^3	= 0.062 428	lb/ft^3	1 lb/ft^3	= 16.0185	kg/m^3
	= 1.685 56	lb/yd^3	1 lb/yd^3	= 0.593 276	kg/m^3
1 t/m^3	= 0.842 778	ton/yd^3	1 ton/yd^3	= 1.186 55	t/m^3

MOMENT OF INERTIA

1 kg·m^2	= 23.7304	lb·ft^2	1 lb·ft^2	= 0.042 140 1	kg·m^2
	= 3417.17	lb·in^2	1 lb·in^2	= 292.640	kg·mm^2

MASS PER UNIT TIME

1 kg/s	= 2.204 62	lb/s	1 lb/s	= 0.453 592	kg/s
1 t/h	= 0.984 207	ton/h	1 ton/h	= 1.016 05	t/h

FORCE

1 MN	= 112.404	tonf (ton-force)	1 tonf (ton-force)	= 8.896 44	kN
1 kN	= 0.112 404	tonf	1 kip (1000 lbf)	= 4.448 22	kN
	= 224.809	lbf (pound-force)	1 lbf (pound-force)	= 4.448 22	N
1 N	= 0.224 809	lbf			

MOMENT OF FORCE, TORQUE

1 N·m	= 0.737 562	lbf·ft	1 lbf·ft	= 1.355 82	N·m
	= 8.850 75	lbf·in	1 lbf·in	= 0.112 985	N·m
1 kN·m	= 0.368 781	tonf·ft	1 tonf·ft	= 2.711 64	kN·m
	= 0.737 562	kip·ft	1 kip·ft	= 1.355 82	kN·m

FORCE PER UNIT LENGTH

1 N/m	= 0.068 521 8	lbf/ft	1 lbf/ft	= 14.5939	N/m
1 kN/m	= 0.034 260 9	tonf/ft	1 lbf/in	= 175.127	N/m
			1 tonf/ft	= 29.1878	kN/m

PRESSURE, STRESS, MODULUS OF ELASTICITY (FORCE PER UNIT AREA)
(1 Pa = 1 N/m^2)

1 MPa	= 0.072 518 8	tonf/in^2	1 tonf/in^2	= 13.7895	MPa
	= 10.4427	tonf/ft^2	1 tonf/ft^2	= 95.7605	kPa
	= 145.038	lbf/in^2	1 kip/in^2	= 6.894 76	MPa
1 kPa	= 20.8854	lbf/ft^2	1 lbf/in^2	= 6.894 76	kPa
			1 lbf/ft^2	= 47.8803	Pa

WORK, ENERGY, HEAT (1 J = 1 N·m = 1 W·s)

1 MJ	= 0.277 778	kWh	1 kWh	= 3.6	MJ
1 kJ	= 0.947 817	Btu	1 Btu (Int. Table)	= 1.055 06	kJ
1 J	= 0.737 562	ft·lbf	1 ft·lbf	= 1055.06	J
				= 1.355 82	J

POWER, HEAT FLOW RATE

1 kW	= 1.341 02	hp (horsepower)	1 hp (550 ft·lbf/s)	= 0.745 700	kW
1 W	= 3.412 14	Btu/h	1 Btu/h	= 745.700	W
	= 0.737 562	ft·lbf/s	1 ft·lbf/s	= 0.293 071	W
				= 1.355 82	W

HEAT FLUX DENSITY

1 W/m^2	= 0.316 998	Btu/(ft^2·h)	1 Btu/(ft^2·h)	= 3.154 59	W/m^2

COEFFICIENT OF HEAT TRANSFER

1 W/(m^2·K)	= 0.176 110	Btu/(ft^2·h·°F)	1 Btu/(ft^2·h·°F)	= 5.678 26	W/(m^2·K)

⚙ E 621

| Metric to Customary | | | | Customary to Metric | |

THERMAL CONDUCTIVITY

| 1 W/(m·K) | = 0.577 789 | Btu/(ft·h·°F) | 1 Btu/(ft·h·°F) | = 1.730 73 | W/(m·K) |

CALORIFIC VALUE (MASS AND VOLUME BASIS)

1 kJ/kg					
(1 J/g)	= 0.429 923	Btu/lb	1 Btu/lb	= 2.326	kJ/kg (J/g)
1 kJ/m³	= 0.026 839 2	Btu/ft³	1 Btu/ft³	= 37.2589	kJ/m³

THERMAL CAPACITY (MASS AND VOLUME BASIS)

| 1 kJ/(kg·K) | = 0.238 846 | Btu/(lb·°F) | 1 Btu/(lb·°F) | = 4.1868 | kJ/(kg·K) |
| 1 kJ/(m³·K) | = 0.014 910 7 | Btu/(ft³·°F) | 1 Btu/(ft³·°F) | = 67.0661 | kJ/(m³·K) |

MOISTURE (VAPOR) MOVEMENT

| 1 μg/(Pa·s·m²) | = 17.4057 | perm (23°C) | 1 perm (23°C) | = 57.4525 | ng/(Pa·s·m²) |
| 1 ng/(Pa·s·m) | = 0.685 26 | perm-in (23°C) | 1 perm/in. (23°C) | = 1.459 29 | ng/(Pa·s·m) |

ILLUMINANCE

| 1 lx (lux) | = 0.092 903 | lm/ft² (footcandle) | 1 lm/ft² (footcandle) | = 10.7639 | lx (lux) |

LUMINANCE

1 cd/m²	= 0.092 903	cd/ft²	1 cd/ft²	= 10.7639	cd/m²
	= 0.291 864	footlambert	1 footlambert	= 3.426 26	cd/m²
1 kcd/m²	= 0.314 159	lambert	1 lambert	= 3.183 01	kcd/m²

X2. SUPERSEDED METRIC UNITS NOT RECOMMENDED FOR USE WITH SI

X2.1 It is strongly recommended that the traditional and "cgs" metric (non-SI) units listed below be *avoided* in building design or construction applications. Any data showing these units should be converted to the appropriate SI units that **supersede** them.

Unit Name	Symbol	Value in SI Units		
dyne	dyn	10^{-5}	N	(or 10 μN)
bar	bar	10^{5}	Pa	(or 100 kPa)
erg	erg	10^{-7}	J	(or 100 nJ)
poise	P	10^{-1}	Pa·s	(or 100 mPa·s)
stokes	St	10^{-4}	m²/s	(or 100 mm²/s)
gauss	Gs,(G)	10^{-4}	T	(or 100 μT)
maxwell	Mx	10^{-8}	Wb	(or 10 nWb)
stilb	sb	10^{4}	cd/m²	(or 10 kcd/m²)
phot	ph	10^{4}	lx	(or 10 klx)
kilogram-force	kgf	9.806 65	N	
calorie (int.)	cal	4.1868	J	
kilocalorie (int.)	kcal	4.1868	kJ	
langley	ly	4.184	kJ/m³	
torr	torr	133.322	Pa	
oersted	Oe	79.5775	A/m	

X3. SI UNITS AND RELATIONSHIPS CHART

X3.1 The SI Units and Relationships Chart (Fig. X3.1) emphasizes four categories of SI units, their unit symbols, and their relationships:

X3.1.1 **Base units,**

X3.1.2 Supplementary units,

X3.1.3 Derived units expressed in terms of base units, and

X3.1.4 Derived units with special names.

X3.2 Arrows indicate the derivation of all derived units with special names:

X3.2.1 Solid lines represent a relationship in which the derived unit is a product of the constituent units (J = N·m; Wb = V·s).

X3.2.2 Broken lines represent a relationship in which the derived unit is a quotient of the constituent unit (Hz = 1/s; S = 1/Ω).

X3.2.3 Solid and broken lines indicate a relationship involving both a product and a quotient (Pa = N/m²; W = J/s; Ω = V/A).

X3.2.4 The degree Celsius (°C) is shown as a derived unit, related directly to the kelvin (K) with the temperature interval 1°C = 1 K, and the temperature value $t_C = T_K - 273.15$.

INDEX

READER RESPONSE FORM

READER RESPONSE FORM

Please help the editors of *Time-Saver Standards: Architectural Design Data* improve this book. Your response will guide the selection of articles and features of the 8th edition, now in preparation.

Please mail, FAX or e-mail your comments, along with a copy of this form.
Editors, *Time-Saver Standards: Architectural Design Data*
54 Larkspur Drive
Trumbull, CT 06611
FX (203) 268-9248
e-mail: lakesideDJ@aol.com

Indicate by a circle your rating of those articles that you have read:

I found the article to be:

Individual articles:	Very valuable		Average		Not valuable	Comment
Preface	5	4	3	2	1	
Introduction	5	4	3	2	1	

Part I: Architectural fundamentals

1	Universal design and accessible design	5	4	3	2	1	
2	Architecture and regulation	5	4	3	2	1	
3	Bioclimatic design	5	4	3	2	1	
4	Solar control	5	4	3	2	1	
5	Daylighting design	5	4	3	2	1	
6	Natural ventilation	5	4	3	2	1	
7	Indoor air quality	5	4	3	2	1	
8	Acoustics: theory and applications	5	4	3	2	1	
9	History of building and urban technologies	5	4	3	2	1	
10	Construction materials technology	5	4	3	2	1	
11	Intelligent building systems	5	4	3	2	1	
12	Design of atriums for people and plants	5	4	3	2	1	
13	Building economics	5	4	3	2	1	
14	Estimating and design cost analysis	5	4	3	2	1	
15	Environmental life cycle assessment	5	4	3	2	1	
16	Construction waste management	5	4	3	2	1	
17	Construction specifications	5	4	3	2	1	
18	Design-Build delivery system	5	4	3	2	1	
19	Building commissioning: a guide	5	4	3	2	1	
20	Building performance evaluation	5	4	3	2	1	
21	Monitoring building performance	5	4	3	2	1	

Part II: Design data

A   SUBSTRUCTURE
A1   Foundations and basement construction

A1-1	Soils and foundation types	5	4	3	2	1	
A1-2	Retaining walls	5	4	3	2	1	
A1-3	Subsurface moisture protection	5	4	3	2	1	
A1-4	Residential foundation design	5	4	3	2	1	
A1-5	Termite control	5	4	3	2	1	*(continued)*

Indicate by a circle your rating of those articles that you have read:

I found the article to be:

Individual articles:	Very valuable		Average		Not valuable	Comment
B SHELL						
B1 Superstructure						
B1-1 An overview of structures	5	4	3	2	1	
B1-2 Design loads	5	4	3	2	1	
B1-3 Structural design-wood	5	4	3	2	1	
B1-4 Structural design-steel	5	4	3	2	1	
B1-5 Structural design-concrete	5	4	3	2	1	
B1-6 Structural design - masonry	5	4	3	2	1	
B1-7 Earthquake resistant design	5	4	3	2	1	
B1-8 Tension fabric structures	5	4	3	2	1	
B2 Exterior closure						
B2-1 Exterior wall systems: an overview	5	4	3	2	1	
B2-2 Thermal Insulation	5	4	3	2	1	
B2-3 Building movement	5	4	3	2	1	
B2-4 Corrosion of metals	5	4	3	2	1	
B2-5 Moisture control	5	4	3	2	1	
B2-6 Watertight exterior walls	5	4	3	2	1	
B2-7 Exterior doors and hardware	5	4	3	2	1	
B2-8 Residential windows	5	4	3	2	1	
B3 Roofing						
B3-1 Roofing systems	5	4	3	2	1	
B3-2 Gutters and downspouts	5	4	3	2	1	
B3-3 Roof openings and accessories	5	4	3	2	1	
B3-4 Radiant barrier systems	5	4	3	2	1	
C INTERIORS						
C1 Interior constructions						
C1-1 Suspended ceiling systems	5	4	3	2	1	
C1-2 Interior partitions and panels	5	4	3	2	1	
C1-3 Interior doors and hardware	5	4	3	2	1	
C1-4 Flexible infrastructure	5	4	3	2	1	
C2 Staircases						
C2-1 Stair design checklist	5	4	3	2	1	
C2-2 Stair design to reduce injuries	5	4	3	2	1	
C2-3 Stair dimensioning	5	4	3	2	1	
C3 Interior finishes						
C1-1 Wall and ceiling finishes	5	4	3	2	1	
C1-2 Flooring	5	4	3	2	1	
D SERVICES						
D1 Conveying Systems						
D1-1 Escalators and elevators	5	4	3	2	1	
D2 Plumbing						
D2-1 Plumbing systems	5	4	3	2	1	
D2-2 Sanitary waste systems	5	4	3	2	1	
D2-3 Special plumbing systems	5	4	3	2	1	
D2-4 Solar domestic water heating	5	4	3	2	1	*(continued)*

Indicate by a circle your rating of those articles that you have read:

I found the article to be:

Individual articles:	Very valuable		Average		Not valuable	Comment

D3   HVAC

D3-1 Energy sources for houses	5	4	3	2	1	
D3-2 Heating and cooling of houses	5	4	3	2	1	
D3-3 Energy sources commercial buildings	5	4	3	2	1	
D3-4 Thermal assessment HVAC design	5	4	3	2	1	
D3-5 HVAC systems commercial buildings	5	4	3	2	1	
D3-6 Special HVAC equipment	5	4	3	2	1	

D4   Fire Protection

D4-1 Fire safety design	5	4	3	2	1	
D4-2 Fire protection sprinkler systems	5	4	3	2	1	
D4-3 Standpipe systems	5	4	3	2	1	
D4-4 Fire extinguishers and cabinets	5	4	3	2	1	
D4-5 Special fire protection systems	5	4	3	2	1	
D4-6 Fire alarm systems	5	4	3	2	1	

D5   Electrical

D5-1 Electrical wiring systems	5	4	3	2	1	
D5-2 Communication/security systems	5	4	3	2	1	
D5-3 Electrical system specialties	5	4	3	2	1	
D5-4 Lighting	5	4	3	2	1	
D5-5 Solar electric systems for residences	5	4	3	2	1	

Appendices:

Tables and reference data

• Dimensions of the human figure	5	4	3	2	1	
• Dimensions for accessibility	5	4	3	2	1	
• Insulation values	5	4	3	2	1	
• Lighting tables	5	4	3	2	1	

Mathematics

• Properties of the circle	5	4	3	2	1	
• Area-Perimeter ratios	5	4	3	2	1	
• Useful curves and curved surfaces	5	4	3	2	1	
• Drawing accurate curves	5	4	3	2	1	
• Modular coordination	5	4	3	2	1	

Units of measurement and metrification

• Units of measurement	5	4	3	2	1	
• Introduction to SI metric system	5	4	3	2	1	
• Metrication	5	4	3	2	1	

Your overall evaluation of *Time-Saver Standards: Architectural Design Data (7th edition)*

5   4   3   2   1

Please add your suggestions and recommendations (use additional sheets as necessary)
The editors will acknowledge all signed evaluations, accompanied with your return address.

Your name_____   **Address:**_____